METRIC HANDBOOK

- Significantly updated in reference to the latest construction standards and evolving building types
- Many chapters revised including housing, transport, offices, libraries and hotels
- New chapter on flood-aware design
- Sustainable design integrated into chapters throughout
- Over 100,000 copies sold to successive generations of architects and designers – this book belongs in every design studio and architecture school library

The *Metric Handbook* is the major handbook of planning and design information for architects and architecture students. Covering basic design data for all the major building types, it is the ideal starting point for any project. For each building type, the book gives the basic design requirements and all the principal dimensional data, and succinct guidance on how to use the information and what regulations the designer needs to be aware of.

As well as building types, the *Metric Handbook* deals with specific aspects of design such as materials, acoustics and lighting, and general design data on human dimensions and space requirements. The *Metric Handbook* provides an invaluable resource for solving everyday design and planning problems.

Pamela Buxton is a freelance architecture and design journalist. She has contributed to many national newspapers, consumer magazines and trade publications, including the architecture publications *Building Design* and *RIBA Journal.*

METRIC HANDBOOK
Planning and Design Data

Fifth Edition

Edited by Pamela Buxton

Routledge
Taylor & Francis Group

LONDON AND NEW YORK

First edition published 1968
by Architectural Press

Second edition published 1999
by Architectural Press

Third edition published 2007
by Architectural Press

Fourth edition published 2012
by Architectural Press

Fifth edition published 2015
by Routledge
2 Park Square, Milton Park, Abingdon, Oxon OX14 4RN

and by Routledge
711 Third Avenue, New York, NY 10017

Routledge is an imprint of the Taylor & Francis Group, an informa business

British Library Cataloguing-in-Publication Data
A catalogue record for this book is available from the British Library

Library of Congress Cataloging-in-Publication Data
Metric handbook: planning and design data/ [edited by] Pamela Buxton.—Fifth edition.
pages cm
Rev. ed. of: Metric handbook/ [edited by] David Littlefield, 2012.
Includes bibliographical references and index.
TH2031.M48 2015
720—dc23
2014012510

ISBN: 978-0-415-72542-2 (pbk)
ISBN: 978-1-315-75933-3 (ebk)

Typeset in Times New Roman
by Swales & Willis Ltd, Exeter, Devon, UK

MIX
Paper from
responsible sources
FSC   FSC® C013056
www.fsc.org

Printed and bound in Great Britain by
TJ International Ltd, Padstow, Cornwall

Contents

Preface
Acknowledgements

DESIGN BASICS

1 **Design information and dimensional coordination**
Terry Nichols with David King

2 **People and space**
Updated by Professor Norman Wienand

3 **People and movement**
Updated by Professor Norman Wienand

4 **Access and inclusion**
Neil Smith and David Dropkin

5 **Capital and whole life costs of buildings**
David Holmes, Chris Bicknell and John Davies

ESSENTIALS

6 **Structure**
David Adler and Norman Seward
Revised by Andrew Peters

7 **Materials**
Arthur Lyons with AHR Architects

8 **Thermal environment**
Phil Jones

9 **Light**
Joe Lynes

10 **Sound**
Chris Steel

11 **Fire**
Beryl Menzies

12 **Flood-aware design**
Robert Barker and Richard Coutts

13 **Crime prevention design**
Nick Hughes

BUILDING TYPES

14 **Agricultural buildings**
John Weller, Rod Sheard, Frank Bradbeer and others

15 **Auditoria**
Ian Appleton and Stefanie Fischer

16 **Civic buildings**
Updated by David Selby (town halls) and
Martin Sutcliffe and Neil Sansum of BDP (law courts)

17 **Community centres**
Jim Tanner

18 **Emergency services**
Including Fire stations by Michael Bowman

19 **Hospitals**
David Clarke

20 **Hotels**
Fred Lawson

21 **Houses and flats**
John Chapman

22 **Homes for older people**
Ian Smith (updated by David Littlefield)

23 **Student housing and housing for young people**
Liz Pride

24 **Industrial facilities**
Jolyon Drury and Ian Brebner

25 **Industrial storage buildings**
Jolyon Drury, updated with advice from Stephen
George & Partners

26 **Laboratories**
Catherine Nikolaou and Neville Surti

27 **Libraries**
Brian Edwards with Ayub Khan

28 **Masterplanning and landscaping**
David Simister with Guy Walters, with contributions
by Sarah Burgess, Hugh Barton and Marcus Grant

29 **Museums, art galleries and temporary**
exhibition spaces
Geoffrey Mathews

30 **Offices**
Frank Duffy with Jack Pringle, Angela Mullarkey and
Richard Finnamore of Pringle Brandon Perkins+Will

31 **Payment and counselling offices**
Richard Napier

32 **Places of worship**
Leslie Fairweather, Ian Brewerton, Atba Al-Samarraie,
David Adler and Derek Kemp. Revised by Maurice Walton

33 **Primary health care**
Geoffrey Purves

34 **Restaurants and foodservice facilities**
Fred Lawson

35 **Retail shops and stores**
Fred Lawson

36 **Schools**
Anthony Langan

37 **Security and counter-terrorism**
Mark Whyte and Chris Johnson

38   Sports facilities: indoor and outdoor
Philip Johnson and Tom Jones

39   Streets and spaces for people and vehicles
Updated by Ben Hamilton-Baillie (introduction, shared space and place-making) and Sustrans (cycling routes and parking)

40   Studios for sound and vision
David Binns

41   Transport terminals and interchanges
Airports updated by Andrew Perez with additional contributions by Richard Chapman. Railways by Declan McCafferty

42   Tropical design
Patricia Tutt

43   Universities
Mike Hart and Rod McAllister

Appendix A – SI system

Appendix B – Conversion factors and tables

Index

Preface

Welcome to the fifth edition of *Metric Handbook*. As well as updating and rewriting more than a quarter of the chapters, this latest edition has a new structure to enable the reader to navigate more easily through the volume. Chapters are grouped into design basics, universal themes and then building types, the latter arranged alphabetically. We hope this will provide a more reader-friendly way to access the vast array of information within this resource.

As society changes, building design must adapt to suit changing behaviours and needs. Nowhere is this more clear than in the design of the office, which has undergone a revolution since the development of computer technology and in particular wireless, mobile working. Our new Offices chapter, written by Frank Duffy with Pringle Brandon Perkins + Will, reflects these changes and gives architects the information they need to rise to the challenge of designing the new workplace.

We have also extensively updated chapters on other fast-evolving building types such as libraries, transport terminals, schools, housing and civic architecture, and also reflected changing attitudes to street design in our chapter on Streets and Spaces for People and Vehicles. Basic information on space requirements for people and movement through buildings has been extensively overhauled in Chapters 2 and 3 respectively, and the Materials section has been updated. But perhaps one of the most significant additions to this edition of *Metric Handbook* is the new chapter on Flood-aware Design, introduced in response to the increased risk of flooding as a result of climate change.

But while much of the content has changed, the ambition of the *Metric Handbook* remains the same. By bringing together best practice and regulatory requirements from sizes to volumes, materials to standards, this book gives readers a thorough grounding and an essential headstart when tackling a new building type.

Pamela Buxton
December 2014

Acknowledgements

This fifth edition of Metric Handbook is greatly indebted to the time and efforts of its many contributors in updating and writing anew the large number of updated chapters within this new edition. Their generosity and expertise is much appreciated.

Thanks too are due to commissioning editors Fran Ford and Jennifer Schmidt at Routledge, and also to their editorial, design and production colleagues who all played such important roles in the Herculean task of updating such a substantial volume.

1 Design information and dimensional coordination

Terry Nichols with David King

Terry Nichols, Director, ELE and David King, HOK London, Director for Project Delivery

KEY POINT:
- *For clear understanding the conventions must be followed*

Contents

1 Design information standards
2 Metric annotation
3 Drawings
4 Drawing content
5 Dimensional coordination
6 Reprographics and paper sizes
7 Ordnance survey maps
8 References
9 Case study

1 DESIGN INFORMATION STANDARDS

1.1 Production methods

Several methods for the production and sharing of project information are available to the AEC industry. Though some firms continue to use traditional manual drafting techniques, many have adopted 2D CAD systems and an increasing number have progressed onto 3D parametric object-based design systems and Building Information Modelling. Whichever of these methods is selected, the adoption of standards is important for clarity in communication between the members of the design team. This section summarises standards as they relate to visual output whether that be on paper or screen display.

1.2 Traditional drafting

In traditional drafting, paper is the main information exchange mechanism. Though individual drawing styles can be accommodated, it is only by the inclusion of standard drawing conventions and symbols that the content can be correctly interpreted.

1.3 2D CAD systems

2D CAD tools provide easier ways of editing and copying drawing content. Information sharing can be achieved by the transfer of drawing files and this has led to improved levels of collaboration between members of the design team. In some cases the data transfer is supported by web-based collaboration services. For this data exchange to be effective, standards have been introduced for file naming conventions, drawing layering structures. When different CAD systems are employed, translation processes are also needed to overcome any system incompatibilities.

The AEC (UK) CAD Standards Initiative was formed in 2000 to improve the process of design information production, management and data exchange. The initiative addressed CAD layering conventions as the primary concern for users of design data. As design needs and technology have developed, the scope has expanded to cover other aspects of design data production and information exchange. The AEC (UK) CAD Standard Basic Layer Code was released in 2001, with an Advanced Code released in 2002.

1.4 3D parametric object based systems

The introduction of 3D parametric object-based modelling systems offers further advantages in terms of the automatic co-ordination of 3D views, plans, sections, elevations and component schedules, the ability to carry out clash detection plus structural and environmental analysis.

1.5 BIM

Building Information Modelling (BIM) involves more than the adoption of a 2D CAD or 3D object based tool. It is founded on the development of a Common Data Environment for sharing information between the members of the design, manufacturing and construction teams. The technicalities involved are set out in BS 29481-1:2010 *Building information modelling. Information delivery manual – methodology and format.* Typically many different software applications will access and interrogate the common data set to generate information that is appropriate for a specific purpose. Ultimately the aim is for a fully integrated set of data incorporating 4D (construction timing) and 5D (costing) elements plus any other data necessary for the life-cycle management of the facility. These features are becoming increasingly important as a part of the drive for Integrated Project Delivery (IPD).

With the increased use of computer methods for electronic transfer and the combining of models from different members of the design team, the use of common standards is essential. For BIM much of the work on standards originated with organisations such as BuildingSmart who have developed and promoted the adoption of Industry Foundation Class (IFC). This open system is designed to enable interoperability between different proprietary systems. It is registered as the international standard ISO 16739.

The AEC (UK) BIM Standards build on the guidelines defined by world-wide standards initiatives, including BS1192:2007, the US National BIM Standard (NBIMS) and existing, proven internal company procedures. It is aimed at providing a base starting point for a unified BIM standard that can easily be adopted 'as is' or developed and adapted for implementation within projects that have specific requirements for the structuring of their BIM data. In 2011 the UK government published its Building Information Modelling (BIM) Working Party Strategy and announced the intention to require collaborative 3D BIM (with all project and asset information, documentation and data being electronic) on its projects by 2016. The standard recommended for non-graphical information is COBie: Construction Operations Building information exchange. This was developed by a number of US public agencies to improve the handover process to building owner-operators. A growing number of software packages now support the import and export of data in this format.

2 METRIC ANNOTATION

2.1 Units

The main units should be used as shown in Table I.

Table I Summary of symbols and notation

Quantity	Description	Correct unit symbol	Acceptable alternatives	Incorrect use	Notes
Numerical values		0.1 0.01 0.001		.1 .01 .001	When the value is *less* than unity, the decimal point should be preceded by zero
Length	metre millimetre	m mm		m. M meter m.m. mm. MM M.M. milli-metre	
Area	square metre	m²	sqm	m.sq sm sq.m sqm.	
Volume	cubic metre cubic millimetre litre (liquid volume)	m³ mm³ 1, ltr	cu m cumm	cu.m m.cu cu.mm. mm.cub. mm.cu. l. lit	Preferably write *litre* in full to avoid 'l' being taken for figure 'one'
Mass (weight)	tonne kilogram gram	t kg g		ton Kg kG kg. kilogramme g. G.	Preferably write *tonne* in full to avoid being mistaken for imperial ton
Force	newton	N		N. n	Note that when used in written text, the unit of newton is spelled out in full and begins with a lower-case letter 'n'. When used as unit symbol, in calculation or in a formula it is then expressed as capital letter 'N'

On a drawing, either metres or millimetres should be used: these units should not be mixed. If this rule is followed, ambiguity is avoided – it is not possible to confuse which units are intended. Common practice is to use mm without a decimal, so 2 m is shown simply as 2000.

2.2 Decimal marker
The decimal marker (full stop) on the baseline is the standard decimal point in the UK; but the marker at the halfway position is also acceptable. It should be noted that Continental practice is to use the comma on the baseline. The appropriate number of decimal places should be chosen depending on the circumstances in which the resulting value is to be used.

2.3 Thousand marker
To avoid confusion with the Continental decimal marker, no thousand marker should be used. Where legibility needs to be improved a space can be left in large groups of digits at every thousand point. Where there are only four digits, a space between the first digit and the others is not desirable (e.g. 15000, 1500). (However, the comma is used in currency, e.g. £115,000.)

2.4 Notation
As a rule the sizes of components should be expressed in consistent and not mixed units, e.g. 1500 mm × 600 mm × 25 mm thick and not 1.5 m × 600 mm × 25 mm thick. However, for long thin components such as timbers, it is preferable to mix the units, e.g. 100 mm × 75 mm × 10 m long.

It is important to distinguish clearly between the metric tonne and the imperial ton. The tonne is equivalent to 2204.6 lb while the ton is equal to 2240 lb – a difference of 1.6 per cent.

The interval of temperature should be referred to as degree Celsius (°C) and not as centigrade. The word centigrade is used by the Continental metric countries as a measure of plane angle and equals 1/10000th part of a right angle.

Examples

Correct use	Incorrect use
33m	3cm 3mm
10.100m	10m 100mm*
50.750kg	50kg 750g

Note. Some metric values are expressed differently in certain countries. The value of 10.100m, for example, could mean ten thousand one hundred metres and not ten metres one hundred millimetres, as in the UK.

3 DRAWINGS
3.1 Information required
Table II indicates the typical drawings required during the design phases of a project. The work stage summary is taken from the RIBA Outline Plan of Work 2007 (amended November 2008). This organises the process of managing and designing projects into a number of key work stages. The sequence or content of these stages may vary and/or overlap dependent on the procurement method selected – and the RIBA Outline Plan of Work provides guidance on their applicability to the principal procurement routes.

3.2 Graphic techniques
Graphic techniques should follow the recommendations in BS EN ISO 9431, and in particular:

(a) line thickness should be not less than 0.25 mm on drawings to be reproduced without reduction, or to be microfilmed;
(b) if different line thicknesses are used, each thickness should be at least twice the next thinner line;
(c) the space between lines should be not less than 0.7 mm;
(d) inclined lines should be at an angle of 15 or a multiple of 15;
(e) lettering (including numbers) should have a capital height of:
   (1) not less than 2.5 mm for drawings as in (a) above;
   (2) not less than 3.5 mm for drawings as in (b) above.

While these guidelines originally refer to manual drafting the same principles should ensure clarity when applied to plotted output from 2D CAD and 3D modelling systems.

3.3 Drawing scales
The internationally agreed and recommended range of scales for use in the construction industry is given in Table III.

Where two or more scales are used on the same sheet, these should be clearly indicated.

3.4 Traditional types of drawings
Types of drawings at the most suitable scales are shown in Figures 1.1 to 1.7. Note that in Figures 1.5 and 1.6 alternative dimensional units are shown for comparison. The method of expressing dimensions as shown in the shaded drawings is not recommended. 2D CAD systems provide the capability for creating similar output but with the advantage of being able to edit, copy and rescale portions of the drawing set.

Table II RIBA work stages – outline plan of work (design phase)

Work stage	Information required	Typical drawings
C: Concept design *(previously called Outline Proposals)*	Prepare concept design, including outline proposals for structure and building systems, outline specifications and preliminary cost plan. *Submit for outline planning if required.*	*Drawings will typically illustrate the outline proposals for each building element. This may include diagrammatic analyses of requirements, use of site, functional and circulation criteria, massing, construction and environmental strategies; the design sufficiently developed for the client to approve as a basis for proceeding to Stage D.*
D: Design development *(previously called Detailed Proposals, and often still referred to as 'Scheme Design')*	Develop concept design with fully coordinated structural and services systems; update outline specification and cost plan. *Submit detailed planning application as required.*	*Drawings will typically illustrate the design for each building element and the size and character of the project in sufficient detail for the client to agree planning and spatial arrangements, elevational treatment, environmental systems, buildability, materials and internal/external appearance. Drawings should be at a scale suitable for planning application, and the design sufficiently developed for the client to approve as a basis for proceeding to Stage E.*
E: Technical design *(previously called Final Proposals, and before that 'Detail Design')*	Prepare technical design(s) and specifications, sufficient to complete the co-ordination of all project components and elements; *information for statutory approvals/ construction safety.*	*Drawings will typically illustrate the finalised proposals for each building element and the details of all principal construction materials, components, junctions, interfaces, interior and exterior finishes. Drawings should be at a scale suitable for building regulations application. This stage essentially completes the design phase, except for those elements subject to design development by specialist sub-contractors in later stages.*
F: Production information	**F1** Prepare production information in sufficient detail for tenders to be obtained; with performance specifications where appropriate. *Apply for statutory approvals.* **F2** Prepare further information for construction as required under building contract. Review buildability and construction safety.	*The RIBA Outline Plan of Work includes diagrams illustrating different sequences for the completion of tender information (F1) and construction information (F2) for various procurement methods.*

Table III Preferred scales

Use	Scale
Maps	1:1000000 1:500000 1:200000 1:100000
Town surveys	1:50000 1:20000 1:10000 1:5000 1:2500 1:2000 1:1250 1:1000
Location drawings Site plan	1:500 1:200
General location	1:200 1:100 1:50
Ranges	1:100 1:50 1:20
Component drawings Assembly	1:20 1:10 1:5
Details	1:10 1:5 1:1

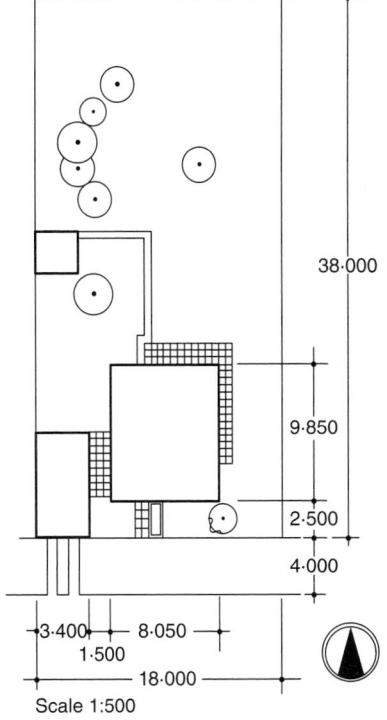

1.2 *Site plan*

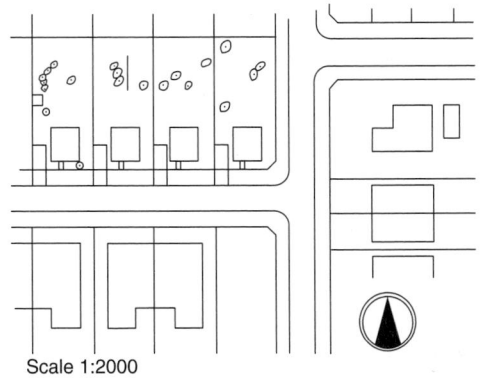

Scale 1:2000

1.1 *Layout plan (note that the Ordnance Survey continue to use the 1:2500 scale)*

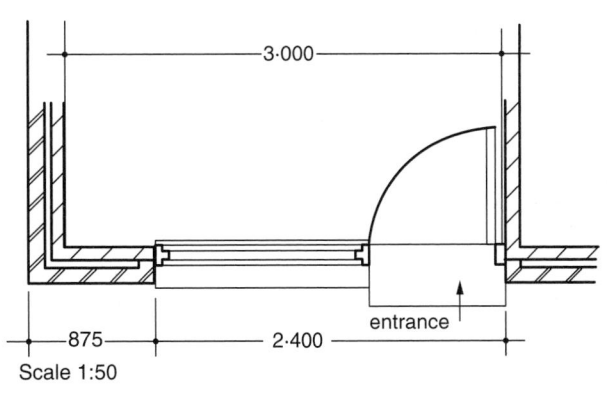

Scale 1:50

1.3 *Location drawing*

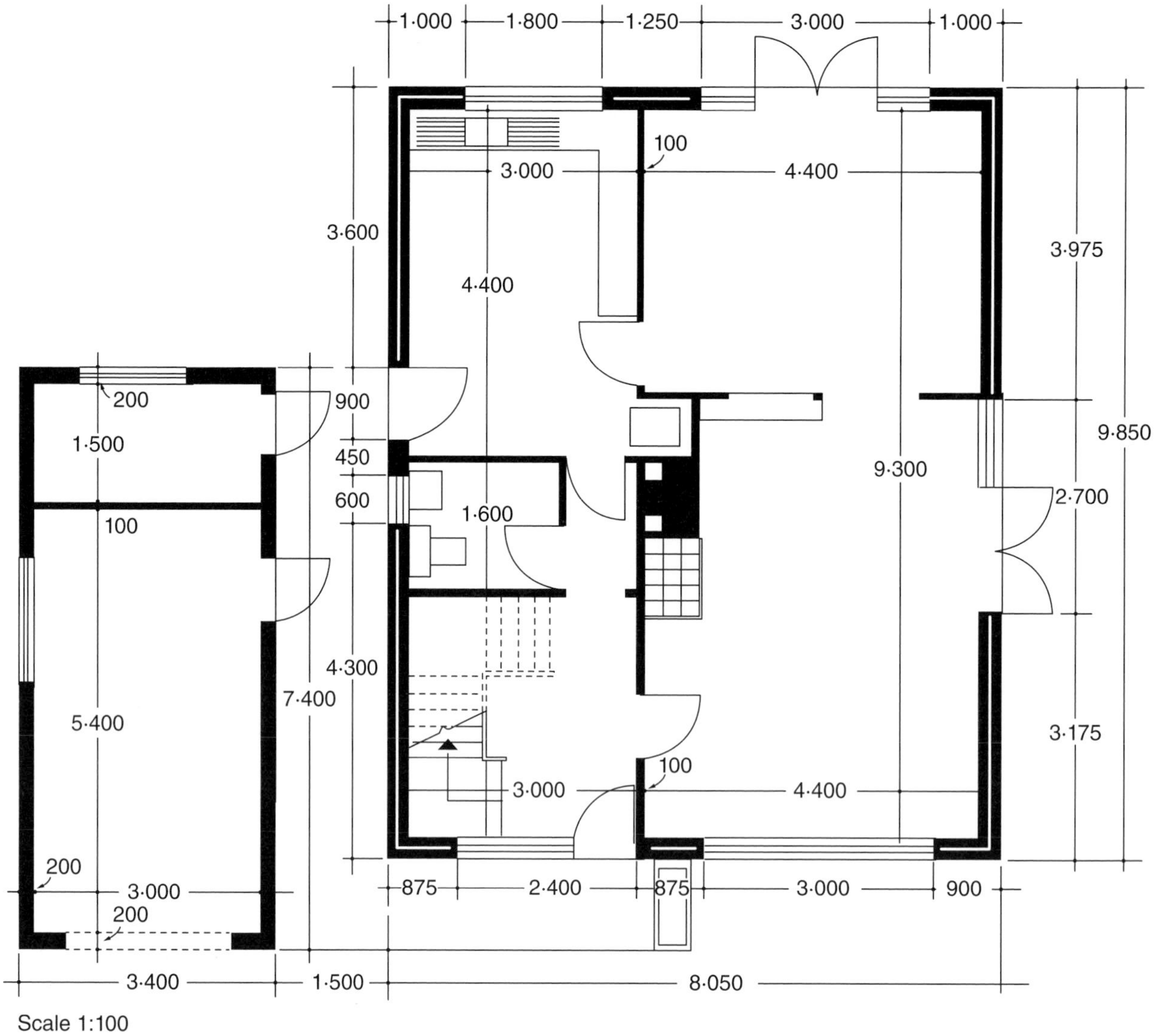

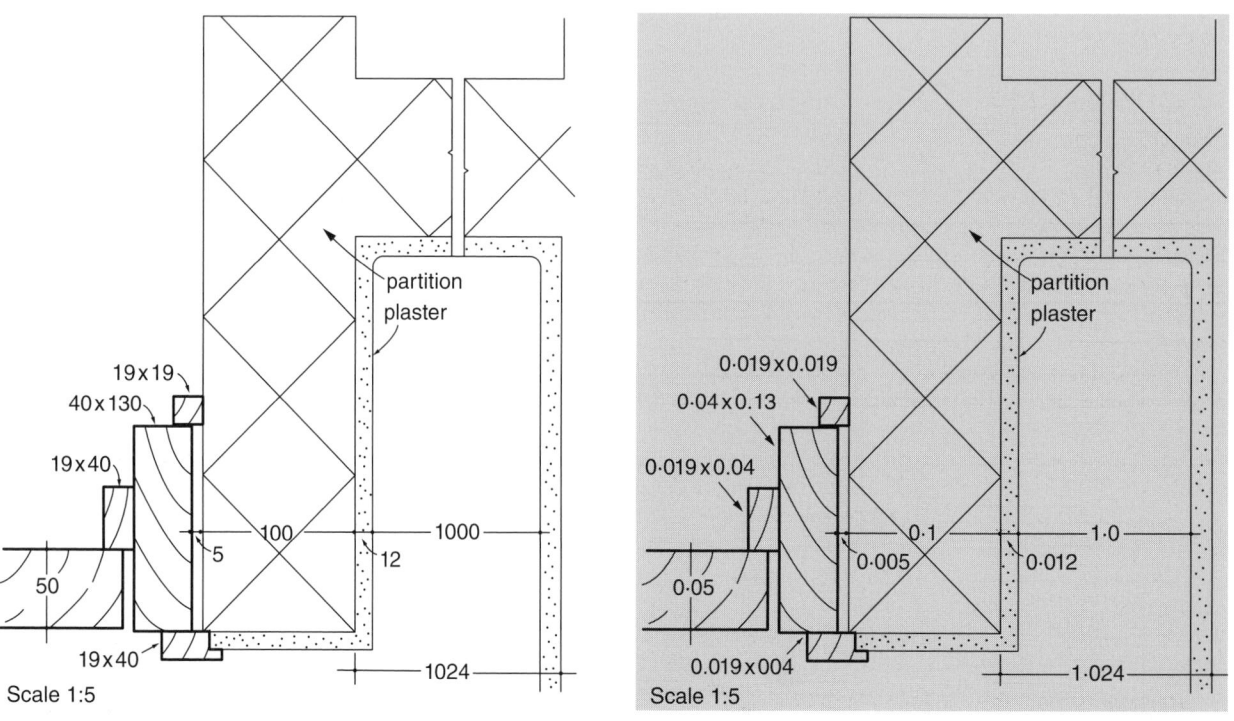

Scale 1:100

1.4 *Location drawing (sketch plan)*

1.5 *Assembly detail drawing (shaded version not recommended)*

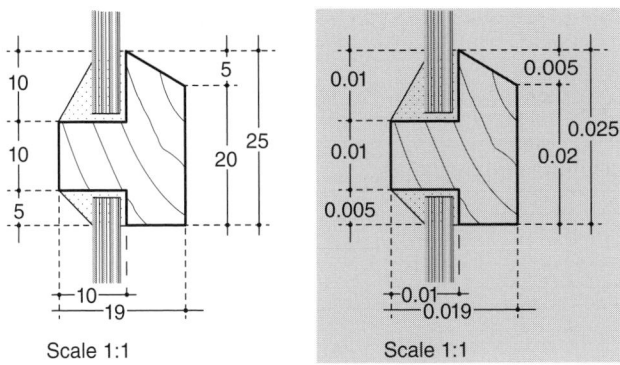

1.6 *Full size detail (shaded version not recommended)*

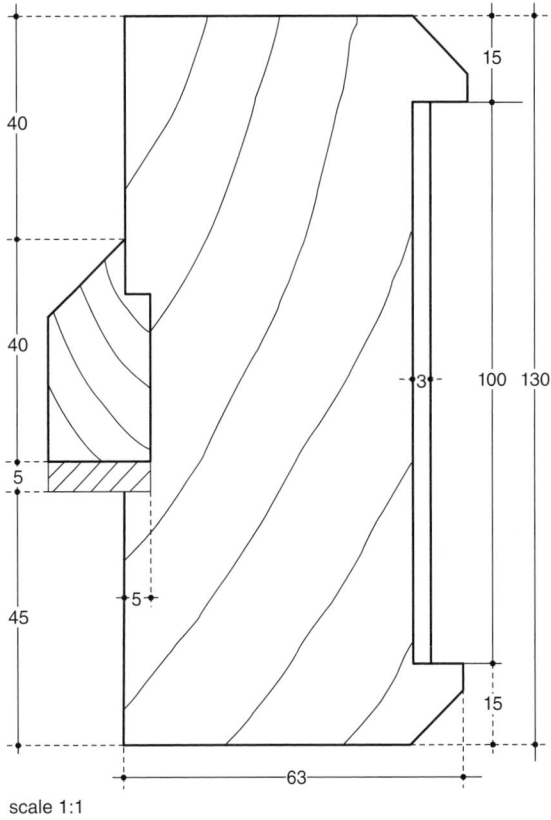

scale 1:1

1.7 *Full size detail*

3.5 Drawings from 3D systems and BIM

Similar 2D building plans, sections, and elevations can be created using a 3D modelling system. Being derived from a single model these have the added benefit of being automatically coordinated. The scale, location and cut planes of any particular view can be adjusted dynamically making the production of a drawing set extremely flexible. Of course, not everything needs to be modelled in 3D and it is common practice to include conventional 2D details within the drawing set. Using callouts, these can be cross-referenced to their location on the model. Overall this approach simplifies management of the drawing set helping to ensure that the information provided remains consistent.

A typical system will allow for the project model to commence with simple massing diagrams and evolve to fully detailed construction drawings. In particular the concept of the single data model allows for additional software to be employed for specific applications such as:

1   Providing photo-realistic perspective still images and animated views of the project.
2   Studying environmental planning issues such as sun paths, daylighting, acoustics and escape simulations.
3   Checking for clashes between structure, components and services. This may be carried out visually and in certain instances automatically at an early stage in the project to help avoid costly mistakes occurring on-site.
4   Using the data as a basis for component manufacture.

The case study at the end of this chapter illustrates some of the practical benefits of this approach.

4 DRAWING CONTENT

4.1 Standard elements

In manual drafting, repeated standard elements and symbols are often introduced in the form of printed transfers. In 2D CAD, blocks are used for this purpose and can be scaled. With 3D CAD, parametric objects are employed for almost all of the drawing content and can be created to automatically generate different representations of elements and components that show a level of detail relevant to the chosen scale of a view.

BS 8541-2 provides guidance and recommendations for 2D symbols and other graphic conventions for use on drawings for the construction industry. The symbols covered by this BS are restricted to the architectural and land registry symbols as the base for architecture drawing, modelling and planning activities. The more specific symbols for mechanical, electrical and plumbing along with the structural steel sections and welding are deferred to those institutes that have a greater understanding of the needs of their members in a fast changing world. BSRIA has a large symbol library for the MEP and Building Services engineers and the Institution of Engineering and Technology (IET) covers both electronic and electrical symbols.

The BS stresses that:

The amount of detail in a simplified representation should be limited to the essential attributes of the object.
A geometric shape should not be used if its meaning is not determined by context and experience.
Over-complexity of building elements components and symbols should be avoided by one of the following methods:

(a) omitting unnecessary information (for example, if all the items in a project are of the same type);
(b) annotating differences between one item and another;
(c) referring differences to a schedule or other document.

4.2 Conventions

BS 1153 specifies certain traditional symbols for use on drawings. A selection of these are shown in Figure 1.8.

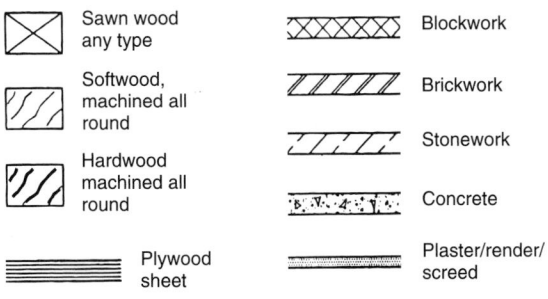

1.8 *Conventional shadings for various materials in section*

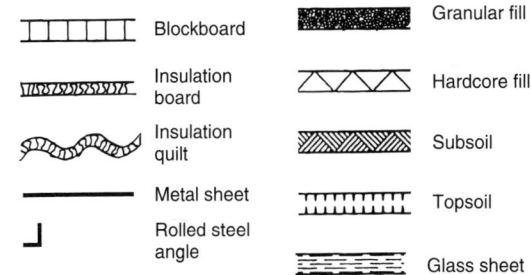

4.3 Symbol representations

In object modelling systems, the representation of a symbol may be created so that it changes automatically depending on the scale of the output. BS 8541-2 includes a comprehensive set of tables showing standards for typical symbols, elements and components.

Item	Symbol	Simplified representation	Representation
Interlocking concrete block paving			
Fence		(to scale)	(to scale)
Gas meter and shut-off valve	Gas	Gas meter	Gas meter

4.4 Levels on plan section and elevation

The standards shown are from BS 8541-2.

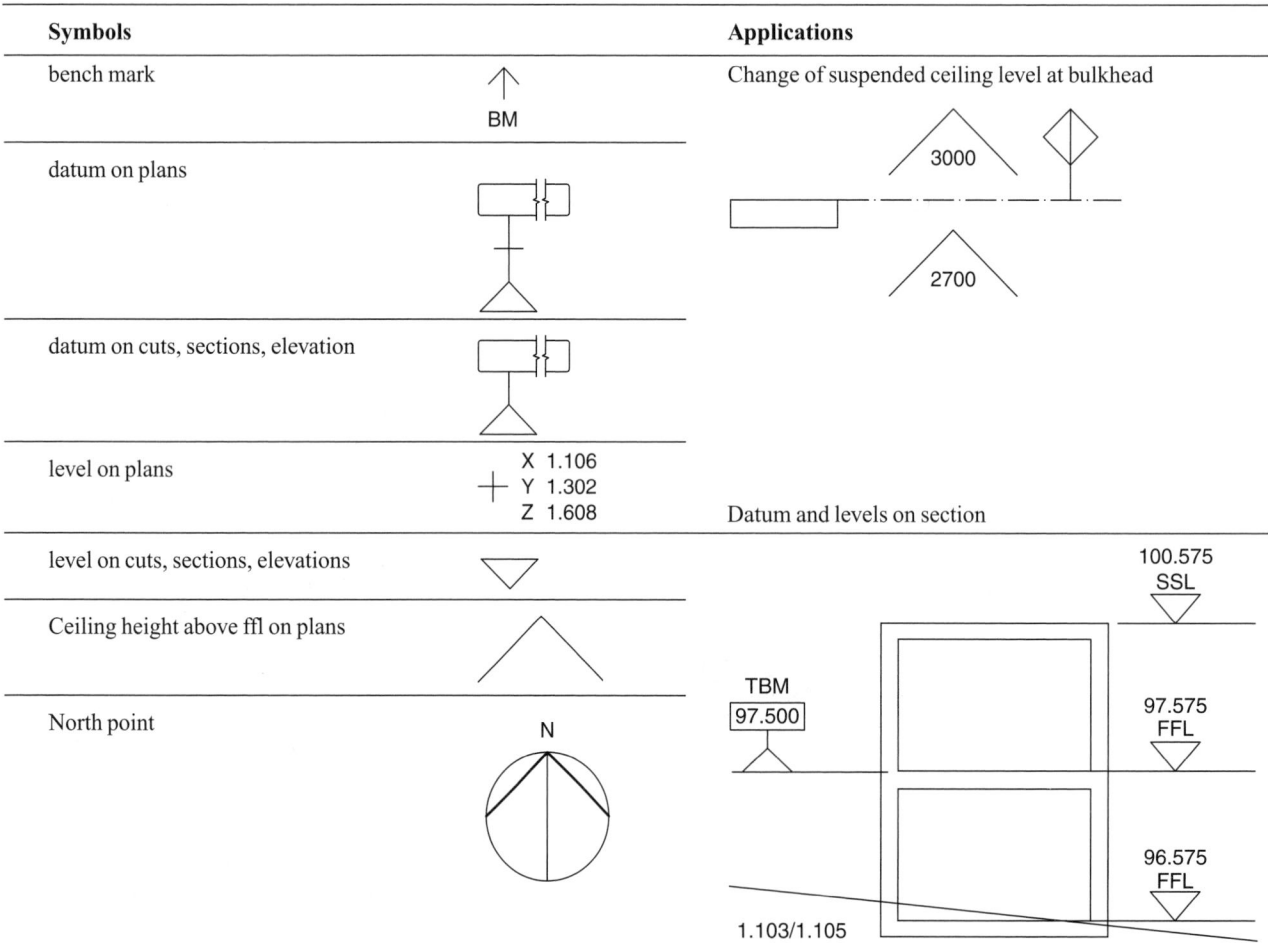

Symbols		Applications
bench mark	BM	Change of suspended ceiling level at bulkhead
datum on plans		
datum on cuts, sections, elevation		
level on plans	X 1.106 Y 1.302 Z 1.608	Datum and levels on section
level on cuts, sections, elevations		
Ceiling height above ffl on plans		
North point	N	

4.5 Scales and representations of elements

The level of detail shown to represent a building element varies depending on the representative scale: if the detail is too complex it may not be possible to reproduce clearly on the plotted output. In 3D modelling systems this process may be automated.

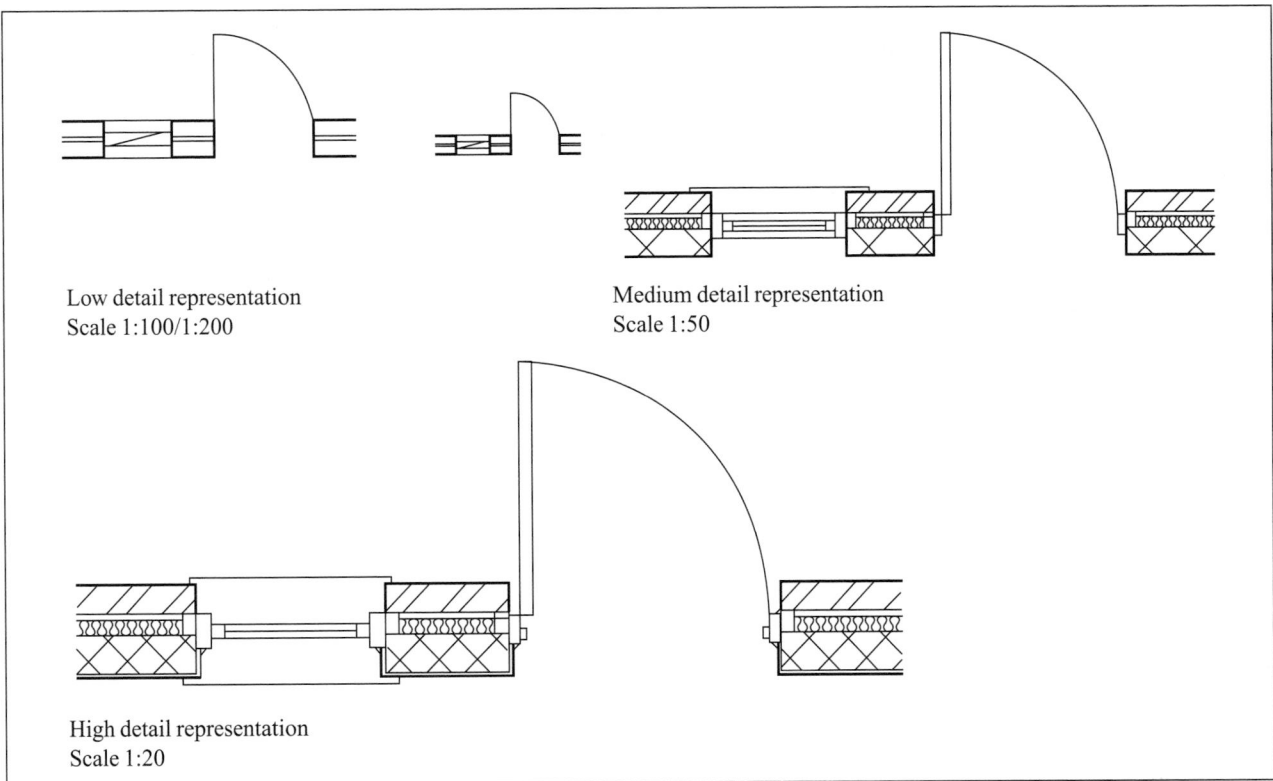

Low detail representation
Scale 1:100/1:200

Medium detail representation
Scale 1:50

High detail representation
Scale 1:20

4.6 Graded components

With 3D modelling systems it is possible to replace an object with another showing more detail as the design progresses. To facilitate this, the AEC BIM Standards recommend that all components created, or otherwise obtained should be graded, named and stored accordingly in the project structure as follows.

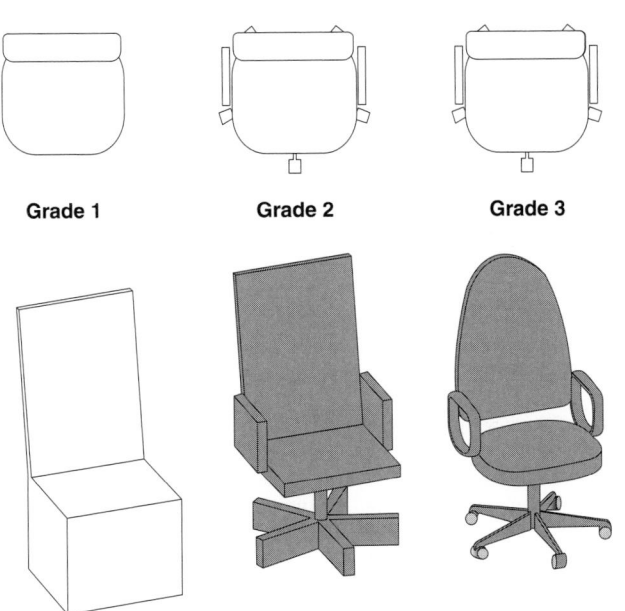

Grade 1   **Grade 2**   **Grade 3**

Component Grade 1 – Concept

- Simple place-holder with absolute minimum level detail to be identifiable, e.g. as any type of chair.
- Superficial dimensional representation.
- Generic in terms of manufacturer information and technical data.

Component Grade 2 – Defined

- Contains all relevant meta-data and technical information, and is sufficiently modelled to identify type of chair and component materials.
- Typically contains level of 2D detail suitable for the 'Preferred' scale.
- Sufficient for most projects.

Component Grade 3 – Rendered

- Identical to the Grade 2 version if scheduled or interrogated by annotation. Differs only in 3D representation.
- Used only when a 3D view at a sufficient scale deems the detail necessary due to the object's proximity to the camera.

In addition to the grading, a component may make use of Low, Medium and High levels of detail to control its graphical representation in relation to the chosen scale as indicated in Section 4.3.

5 DIMENSIONAL COORDINATION

5.1 General

Current building practice involves the assembly of many factory-made components: in some cases the whole project consists of such components slotted together like a child's construction kit. Dimensional coordination (DC) is essential to ensure the success of the system, and consists of a range of dimensions relating to the sizing of building components and assemblies, and to the buildings incorporating them. DC enables the coordination of the many parts that go to make up the total construction which are supplied from widely separated sources. At an international level, 100 mm is accepted as the basic module (often referred to by the letter 'M').

Dimensional coordination relies on establishment of rectangular three-dimensional grids of basic modules into which components can be introduced in an interrelated pattern of sizes, Figure 1.9. The

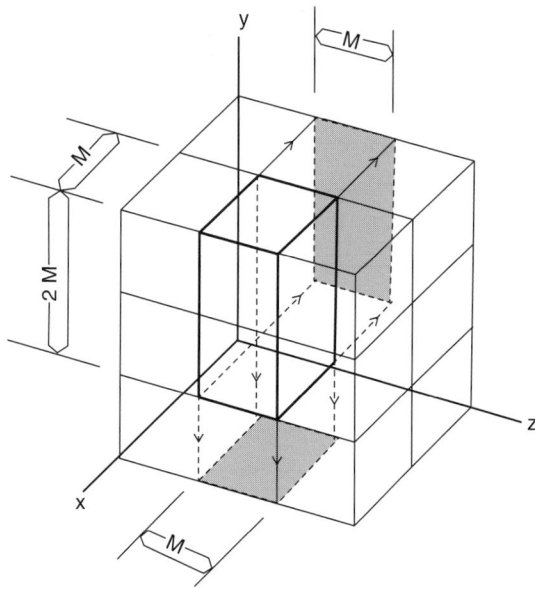

1.9 *Three-dimensional grid of basic modules*

modular grid network delineates the space into which each component fits. The most important factor of dimensional coordination is that the component must always be undersized in relation to the space grid into which it has to fit (but not to too great an extent).

In the engineering world the piston and cylinder principle establishes the size relationship between dimensional space grid and component, Figure 1.10. The size of the cylinder must allow for the right degree of accuracy and tolerance to enable the piston to move up and down.

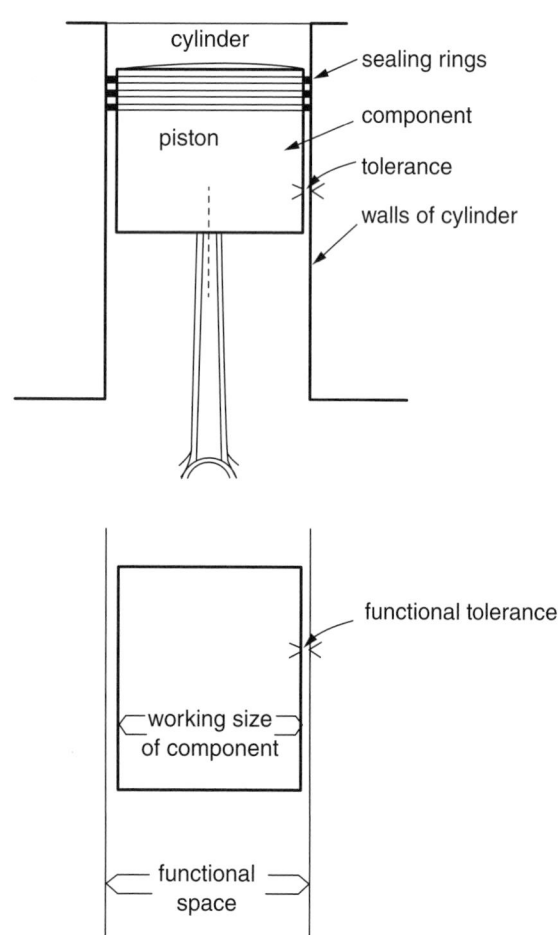

1.10 *The piston and cylinder principle*

The degree of inaccuracy to be allowed for in the building process is related to the economics of jointing. Adequate space must be allowed for size of component plus joint. Transgressing the rules of locating components within the allotted space contained by grid lines will cause considerable difficulty in site assembly.

The basic arrangement of components within the grid layout shows them fitting into the spaces allocated to them: dimensionally they are coordinated, thus allowing the designer maximum use of standard components, Figure 1.11.

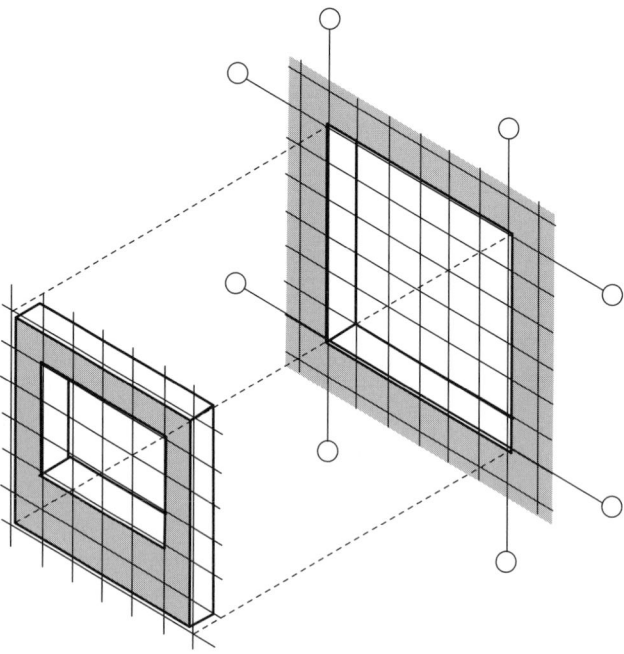

1.11 *Fitting a component into a dimensionally coordinated grid*

Advantages to designers may include:

- reduction in design labour
- reduced production of working drawings by the use of standard details
- choice of interrelated standard components at the various price levels.

5.2 Basic aims of DC
The basic aims of DC (as defined in BS 4011:1966) were:

- to obtain maximum economy in the production of components
- to reduce the manufacture of non-standard units
- to avoid wasteful cutting on-site.

Potential advantages to manufacturers include:

- more effective use of labour in producing standard lines
- reduction in the stocking, invoicing and other operations connected with numerous differently sized products. there should also be advantages to contractors, not only through better design of components for fit but also through increasing familiarity with standard components.

BS 4011 was superseded by BS 6750:1986.

5.3 Basic elements of DC

Preference for size
The preferred increments are:

- First preference (multimodule) multiples of 300 mm
- Second preference (basic module) multiples of 100 mm
- Third preference (submodule) multiples of 50 mm up to 300 mm
- Fourth preference (submodule) multiples of 25 mm up to 300 mm.

Reference systems
Grid and line: the DC reference system identifies controlling dimensions by the use of a grid on plans and a series of horizontal lines on elevations and sections. The terminology is precise:

- Controlling dimensions lie between key reference planes (e.g. floor-to-floor height). They provide a framework within which to design and to which components and assemblies may be related.
- Key reference planes define the boundaries of controlling zones or structural axes.
- Controlling lines on a drawing represent a key reference plane.
- Axial controlling lines are shown on drawings by a chain dotted line with a circle at the end, in which the grid reference is given.
- Face controlling lines are shown by a continuous line with a circle at the end in which the grid reference is given.
- Zones between vertical or horizontal reference planes provide spaces for one or more components which do not necessarily fill the space. Provided that use of associated components is not inhibited, a building component (or group of components) may extend beyond the zone boundary, as may trims and finishes.

5.4 Drawings
The representation of the dimensional coordination framework should be consistent on all drawings. On general location drawings a grid representing 300 mm (or a multiple of 300 mm) may be used. Assembly details may use grids of 300 or 100 mm.

Reference lines
Reference lines or grids should be thin, to distinguish them from other, particularly constructional, lines.

Dimension lines
Different types of dimensions should be distinguished by the type of arrowhead, Figure 1.12.

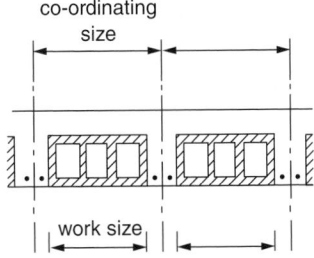

1.12 *Coordinating and work sizes*

Running dimensions should be set off from a datum, Figure 1.13.

1.13 *Running dimensions. The symbol at the datum should be as shown. An arrowhead is sometimes used, but is not the preferred alternative*

Assembly details
Assembly details should show components in their context, that is, in relation to the adjoining element, with details of the joint.

5.5 Locating components by grid

Types of grid
The structural grid of axial controlling lines, Figure 1.14, is established physically by the contractor on-site; it serves as the main reference in construction. It is subject to setting-out deviations which affect the spaces required for assemblies of components; but this should have been allowed for in the design stage. A planning grid of face controlling lines, Figure 1.15, locates non-structural elements.

- A neutral zone is a zone that does not conform to the recommended dimensions given in Table IV.

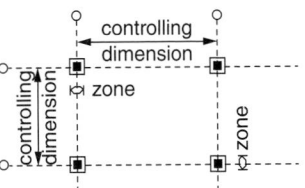

1.14 *Axial control*

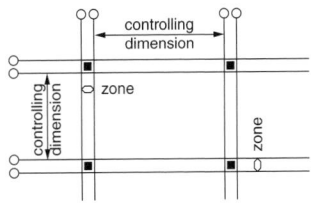

1.15 *Facial control*

Table IV Sizing of zones and heights

Range (mm)	Multiples of size (mm)
Horizontal controlling dimensions	
Widths of zones for columns and loadbearing walls	
100 to 600	300 (first preference)
	100 (second preference)
Spacing of zones for columns and loadbearing walls	
From 900[1]	300
Vertical controlling dimensions	
Floor to ceiling heights	
2300[2] to 3000	100
3000 to 6600	300
over 6600	600
Heights of zones for floors and roofs	
100 to 600[3]	100
over 600	300
Floor to floor (and roof) heights	
2700[4] to 8400	300
over 8400	600
Changes in level	
300 to 2400	300
above 2400	600

[1] Housing may use 800
[2] Farm buildings may use 1500 and 1800
Domestic garages may use 2100
Housing may use 2350
[3] Housing may use 250
[4] Housing may use 2600

Relation between structural and planning grids
Structural and planning grids may coincide but do not necessarily do so. The controlling dimensions for spacing structural elements on plan on axial lines are in multiples of 300 mm (Table IV). If a 300 mm square grid is used then axial controlling lines will coincide with the grid, Figure 1.16, but if the grid is a multiple of 300 mm then the controlling lines will be offset from the axial grid by 300 mm or by a multiple of 300 mm, Figure 1.17.

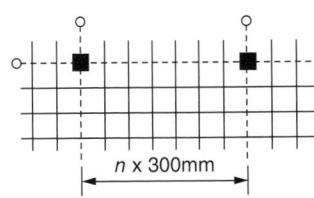

1.16 *Uninterrupted grid*

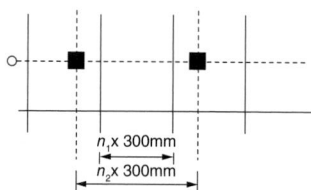

1.17 *Controlling lines offset from grid*

Relating zones to a 300 mm grid
If widths of structural zones are multiples of 300 mm, the grid is continuous, Figure 1.18. If the zone is not a multiple of 300 mm, however, the grid is interrupted by the dimension of that zone, Figure 1.19. This is referred to as a neutral zone.

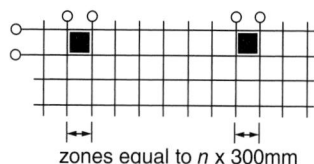

1.18 *Continuous grid*

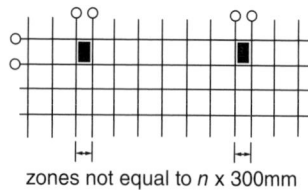

1.19 *Interrupted grid and neutral zones (tartan)*

Key reference planes
Key reference planes, Figure 1.20, should generally occur at:

- finished floor level
- finished suspended ceiling level
- finished wall surface.

Sizes of zones indicated by key reference planes should be selected from Table IV. Where controlling or reference lines bound floor or roof soffits, deflection should be allowed for in the zone.

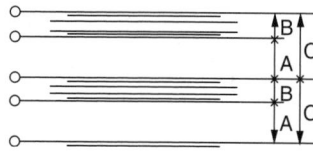

1.20 *Vertical control: A being floor-to-ceiling height controlling dimension; B floor and roof zone; C floor-to-floor and floor-to-roof controlling dimension*

5.6 Size of components

Coordinating and work sizes
Controlling dimensions are coordinating sizes:

- Coordinating sizes, **1.12**, make allowance for fitting and jointing. They represent the overlaid grid which does not usually coincide with actual junction lines on the face of the building. They are indicated by open arrowheads.
- Work sizes are the specified manufactured sizes (within permissible deviations). They are indicated by closed arrowheads.

Tolerance and fit
Joint sizes are critical. There are graphical aids (see References) to help reconcile all the factors affecting tolerance, such as

- expansion and contraction
- variability in manufactured size
- satisfactory joint clearance range
- variations in setting out dimensions, adjacent components, etc.
- number of components in an assembly
- variations in interpretation of work size from a given coordinating size.

Degree of accuracy
Designers should identify where fit is critical and where not, or they must assess:

- where standard sizes are appropriate and readily available
- if some components can be made to order without a significant cost penalty
- whether cutting is acceptable (and the effect on performance)
- the likely order of assembly.

5.7 Boundary conditions
Some assembly and support conditions may necessitate variations in elements to allow for:

- an extended floor slab beyond the clear span to gain a bearing on a wall
- reduction in size to permit the application of a finish
- an increased height of positioning to allow for building directly off the floor slab or extending through a suspended ceiling to reach the soffit of the floor slab.

These allowances (termed 'boundary conditions') should be in multiples of 25 mm. They may be uneconomic to produce, limiting the applications of the product to which they apply.

6 REPROGRAPHICS AND PAPER SIZES

6.1 Paper
Traditionally paper was the main means of information transfer. The use of CAD and BIM systems coupled with various forms of electronic transfer now means that team collaboration can be supported by using interactive screen displays. But for many purposes paper is still the preferred medium and the International A-series of paper sizes is used for all plotted drawings and printed material.

6.2 Sizes in the A-series
The A range is derived from a rectangle AO of area 1 m² with sides x and y such that x:y = 1:√2 (i.e. x = 841 mm; y = 1189 mm). The other sizes in the series are derived downwards by progressively halving the size above across its larger dimension. The proportions of the sizes remain constant, Figure 1.21.

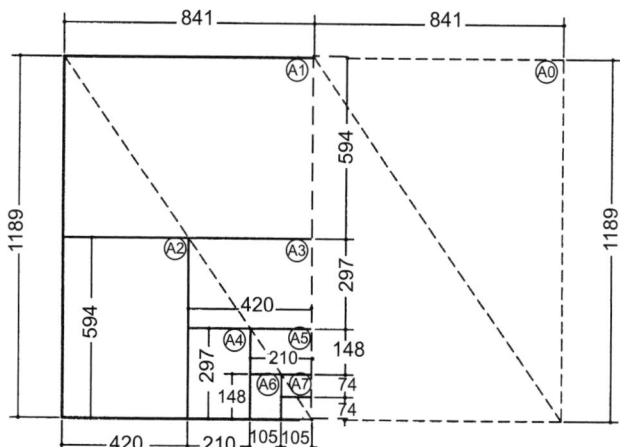

1.21 *A-sizes retain the same proportion (1:√2), each size being half the size above folding A1 size*

6.3 Trimmed sizes and tolerances

The A formats are trimmed sizes and therefore exact; stubs of tear-off books, index tabs, etc. are always additional to the A dimensions. Printers purchase their paper in sizes allowing for the following tolerances of the trimmed sizes:

- For dimensions up to and including 150 mm, þ1.5 mm
- For dimensions greater than 150 mm up to and including 600 mm, þ2 mm
- For dimensions greater than 600 mm, þ3 mm. Recommended methods of folding the larger A-sized prints are given in Figure 1.22.

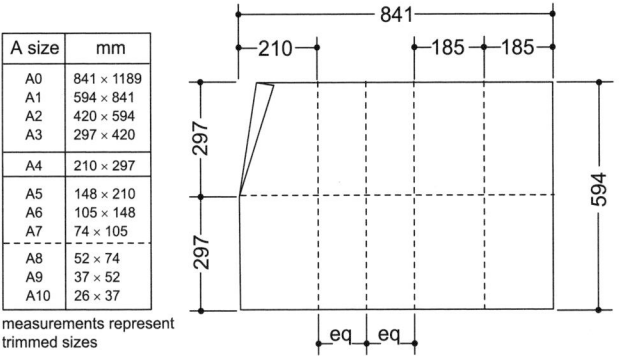

A size	mm
A0	841 × 1189
A1	594 × 841
A2	420 × 594
A3	297 × 420
A4	210 × 297
A5	148 × 210
A6	105 × 148
A7	74 × 105
A8	52 × 74
A9	37 × 52
A10	26 × 37

measurements represent trimmed sizes

folding A1 size

1.22 *A-series of paper sizes*

7 ORDNANCE SURVEY MAPS

7.1 Scales

Ordnance Survey maps are available to the following scales: 1:50000, 1:25000, 1:10000, 1:2500 and 1:1250. However, computer methods of storage and retrieval mean that maps can be reproduced to any desired scale. Architects and surveyors inevitably need to refer back to old maps and plans from time to time. These may have been drawn to almost any scale, but the common scales to which OS maps were drawn were as follows: 1 inch to the mile (1:63360), 6 inches to the mile (1:10560), 88 feet to the inch (1:1056).

7.2 Bench marks and levels

Points used for measuring and marking levels are known as *bench marks*. On a particular site a temporary *bench mark* (TBM) may be established, to which all other levels on that site are referred. The level value allocated to the TBM may be to Ordnance Datum; more commonly it is given an arbitrary value. This value should be large enough not to require any negative levels (including levels of drains, etc.), as these can lead to errors. All levels in and around buildings are recommended to be given to three decimal places, although BS 1192 permits two decimal places for landscape work.

The heights of Ordnance Survey bench marks are given in Bench Mark Lists obtainable from Ordnance Survey Headquarters, Adanac Drive, Southampton, SO16 0AS. Modern OS maps to the larger scales include Ordnance Bench Marks related to Newlyn Datum. Older maps may have levels to Liverpool Datum; levels on maps other than of Great Britain will be related to other datums. Where known, the datum and date of levelling should be stated. OS maps include contours. On the 1:10000 series the contour interval is 10 metres in the more mountainous areas and 5 metres in the remainder of the country.

8 REFERENCES

AEC (UK) BIM Standard – Version 1.0 November 2009, free download from http://www.aec-uk.org

BS 6750: 1986 Modular co-ordination in building. International Organisation for Standardisation

BS 8541–2: 2011 Library objects for engineering and construction – Part 2 Recommended 2D symbols of building elements for use in building information modelling

BS 5606: 1990 Guide to accuracy in building

BS EN ISO 9431: 1999 Construction drawings. Spaces for drawing and for text, and title blocks on drawing sheets

BS 1192: 2007 Collaborative production of architectural, engineering and construction information. Code of practice

BIP-2207: 2010 Building Information Management: A Standard Framework and Guide to BS 1192, Mervyn Richards

BS 29481-1: 2010 Building information modelling. Information delivery manual – Methodology and format

Government Construction Strategy: Cabinet Office: June 2011

A report for the Government Construction Client Group, Building Information Modelling (BIM) Working Party Strategy Paper: Department of Business, Innovation and Skills: July 2011

ISO 2776: 1974 Modular co-ordination – co-ordinating sizes for door-sets – external and internal general

ISO 6512: 1982 Modular coordination – Storey heights and room heights

ISO 1040: 1983 Modular co-ordination – multimodules for horizontal co-ordinating dimensions

ISO 1006: 1983 Modular co-ordination – basic module

ISO 1791: 1983 Modular co-ordination – vocabulary

ISO 2848: 1984 Modular co-ordination – principles and rules

ISO/TR 8390: 1984: Modular coordination – application of horizontal multimodule

ISO 16739: Industry Foundation Classes for AEC/FM data sharing

RIBA Outline Plan of Work 2007 (UPDATED): Including Corrigenda Issued January 2009 – available as a free download from http://www.ribabookshops.com

9 CASE STUDY – USING BUILDING INFORMATION MODELLING FOR PROJECT DELIVERY

Project: 5 Churchill Place, London
Client: Canary Wharf Group Plc
Architects: HOK International Ltd
Structural Engineer: WSP
Services Engineer: HMP
Contractor: Canary Wharf Contractors Ltd

1 *5 Churchill Place, London, completed 2008*

Situated at the eastern gateway to Canary Wharf, the site presented a particular challenge built partially over water, comprising a complex series of irregular existing ramps, platforms and marine decks between ground and dock level. The design concept developed by HOK used Building Information Modelling (BIM) in a collaborative manner with the design team, creating a single project environment to promote full coordination as early as possible in the design process.

The result is a structurally complex office building with a floor area of 28,000 m² net, spread over 14 storeys with a three-level basement, clad in alternating clear glass and granite panels. The distinctive elevations draw inspiration from optical art so that, as the observer's vantage point moves, the character and materials of the building change. Depending on the perspective view, the dominant building material appears to be glass, granite or metal.

Glass on the northern elevation maximizes natural light with minimal solar gain. Stainless steel edges catch light and sun reflections. With high emphasis on sustainability, the building was specifically designed to achieve a BRE Environmental Assessment Method (BREEAM) rating of excellent, and the computability of the design data was an essential part of ensuring this was achieved. Environmental data and projected performance criteria were continually evaluated in relation to the complex structural geometry.

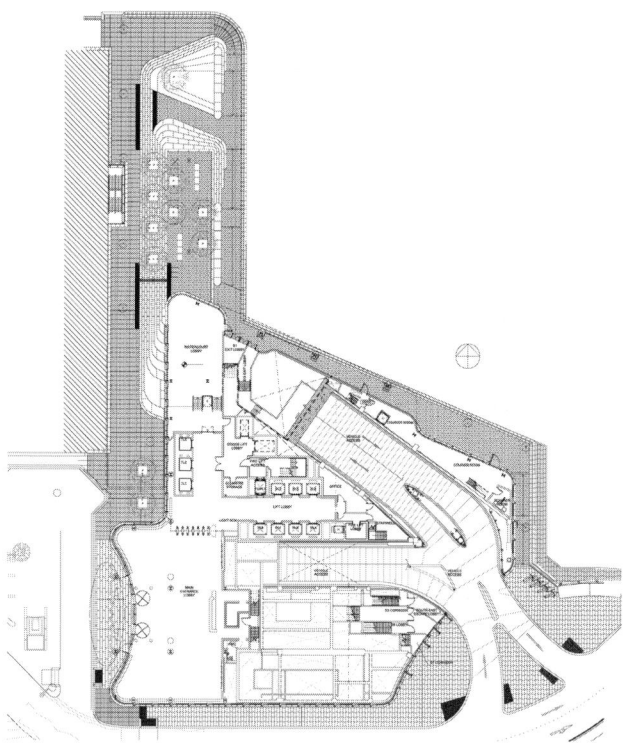

3 *Floor plans, and other key drawings such as sections, can be extracted from the BIM model rather than created independently*

model. This ensures that the drawing deliverables are at all times coordinated and up to date. If a change is made in one part of the model all the associated views of the model are automatically updated.

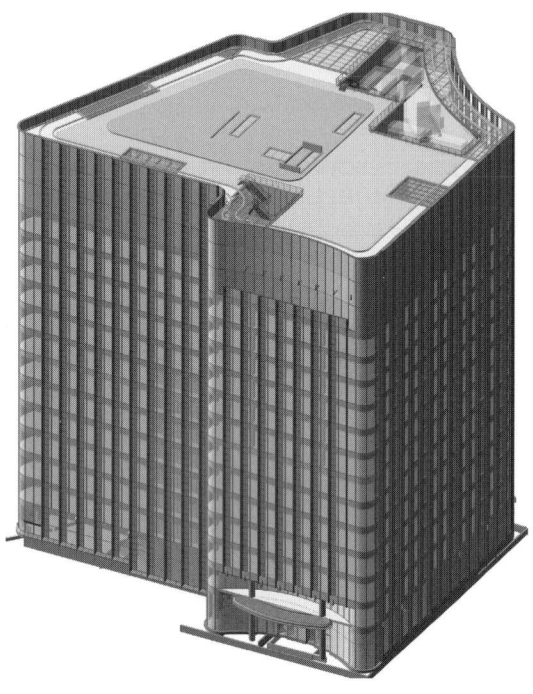

2 *Building model as a complete volume*

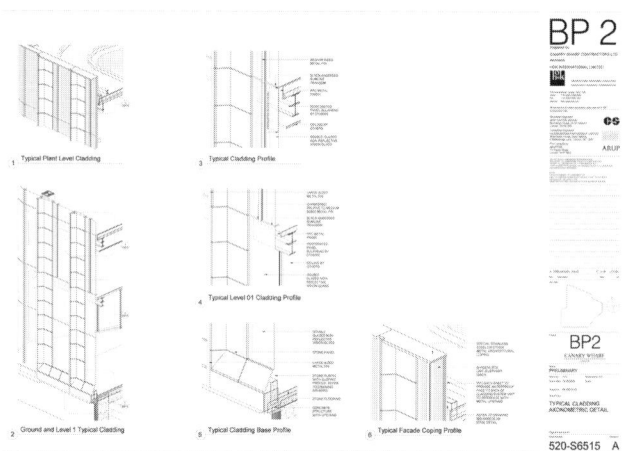

4 *Typical isometric facade. Architect and structural engineer exchanged models and data to improve cooperation and create efficient workflows*

Using a BIM process and integrated software solutions were key factors in helping the design team to deliver the project, while at the same time demonstrating the commitment to building SMART; wherein Integrated Practice, Information Modelling and Sustainability are combined to deliver the best solution for the client. BIM provided the design platform for concept design, design development and detail design – and the same model was used to generate photographic quality visual renderings to illustrate the design for the stakeholders.

The project design team adapted quickly to this new way of working; an eight person team working together in close proximity on the architectural design model. This approach encouraged better communication, a greater understanding of what the team members where working on and how this complex building would be assembled.

The BIM software is essentially a database design solution, and one of the major benefits of this software is that all general arrangements – floor plans, sections and elevations – are extractions from the overall

All the details produced for this project were coordinated callout views from the virtual building model; these views were then placed on drawing sheets. Working with the model as a background gave the detailer an accurate profile of which elements need to be enhanced with additional linework, drafting components, dimension and keynotes which are anchored into the model. 3D isometric views were also used to help interrogate more complex details and assemblies.

HOK and WSP, the structural engineers, regularly shared their respective building models: the architectural model being used as background information for the structural concrete, steelwork and analysis model, which in turn was linked back into the architectural model to illustrate the structural engineer's design. The sharing of model data and the ease of interoperability led to improved workflow coordination.

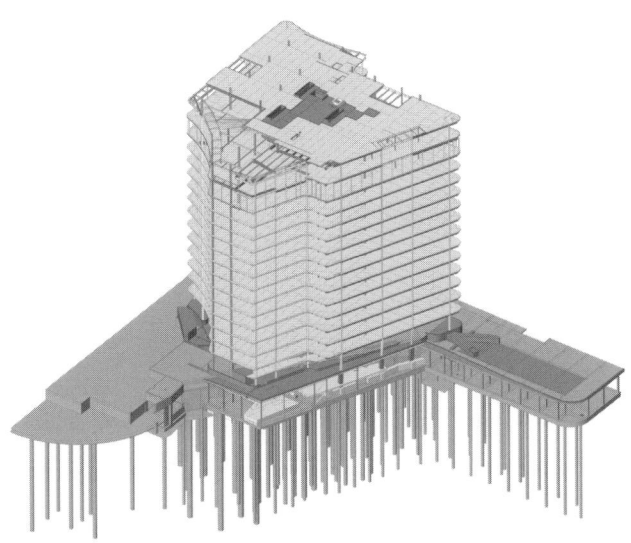

The client recognised the benefits of this collaborative approach to design and delivery, and actively encouraged the use of the BIM approach by the project team. The client was also keen to explore the value that BIM could obtain from the supply chain.

The structural model was further developed by the steelwork contractor for fabrication. This more complex 3D steelwork fabrication model was then used by the design team in a clash detection check. All the principal MEP elements were modelled in 3D, together with all of the major plant areas and risers – ensuring detail coordination.

The design team worked in an integrated manner with the contractor and the specialist trade contractors, the client knew what was possible and what they wanted from BIM, and all parties bought into the process, the key trade contractors being involved in development and review of the design with the construction manager actively managing the review process.

5 *Structural model. This complex 3D model, used by the steelwork contractor for fabrication, was also used by the design team for clash detection and detail coordination*

2 People and space

Updated by Professor Norman Wienand

Professor Norman Wienand is head of department for the Natural and Built Environment at Sheffield Hallam University

KEY POINTS:
- *Certain dimensions are crucial to individual use and health*
- *Satisfying the average situation is unlikely to help the majority*
- *Each case must be carefully considered with all classes of users, particularly people with different abilities, in mind*

Contents
1 Introduction
2 Anthropometrics
3 Ergonomics
4 Sanitary facilities
5 Domestic space standards
6 Bibliography

1 INTRODUCTION

1.1 Universal design

As a general aim, this chapter should be viewed primarily as a starting point in the design process, as a guide to the principles and conventions that govern how particular building types are planned to suit their eventual occupants. A primary and guiding principle adopted throughout is the concept of universal (or inclusive) design.

> Universal Design refers to the design and composition of an environment so that it can be accessed, understood and used to the greatest extent possible by all people, regardless of their age, size, ability or disability.
>
> Disability Discrimination Act, 2005

The benefits of adopting this position include the production of designs that aim to exclude no one from enjoying the end results. This also has the potential to future proof the building for adaptation later. However this inclusive approach can have some considerable associated problems. For instance, the section on *Anthropometrics* will illustrate that simply identifying the broad range of physical size for users can be problematic, as is the design of appropriate *Ergonomic* living environments when bespoke solutions are not always possible but may also exclude many other users. Universal design is therefore often a compromised solution but the guiding principle ensures that it is the best possible fit under any particular circumstances.

1.2 Specialist guides

In recent years, specialist and readily accessible design guides have been produced by bodies such as the RIBA or the Centre for Excellence in Universal Design, Dublin. As these guides interpret and clarify legislative requirements in a highly comprehensible manner, reference is made to each of these guides by pointing to them as sources of further detailed information and particularly how that information is developed.

This chapter is therefore an introduction to the principles of anthropometrics and ergonomics, the setting up of basic sanitary and domestic spaces standards, but premised on the notion that this information is the preface to further research and design review.

2 ANTHROPOMETRICS

2.1 Size and variation

The human form comes in many different shapes and sizes and designing to accommodate people in whatever capacity requires a working knowledge of the interaction between designed objects or spaces and the ultimate users. Much of this knowledge can be intuitive because we all have experience of our own. However this knowledge can also be limiting as it is not just about proportion, scale or ease of movement; there are health and safety issues involved as well as designing for inclusion and equality in access. Anthropometrics is concerned with the size and variations of the human body and when combined with ergonomics, the allied study of the interaction of humans and the designed world, we have two entire scientific disciplines devoted to the subject. This section aims to introduce only the basic concepts involved and will point to reference sources for further information.

2.2 Primary data

Much of the primary anthropometrical data comes from a collection of various different studies conducted over the last twenty years and can be surprisingly inaccurate when used in isolation. Understanding the value of anthropometric data therefore also needs an understanding of the basic statistical tools that allow us to make good use of the data. Firstly, we have to recognise that there is no standard human shape type; average height people can be thin, fat, young or old. Average heights can vary between ages, sexes, and different ethnic and national backgrounds. For example, the Dutch are Europe's tallest people and a study of Polish industrial workers suggests that they are Europe's shortest.

The primary data collected on individual population proportions is usually presented as a frequency distribution curve, Figure 2.1. Also known as a bell curve because of its shape, it represents a cross section of the distribution of data for any particular dimension

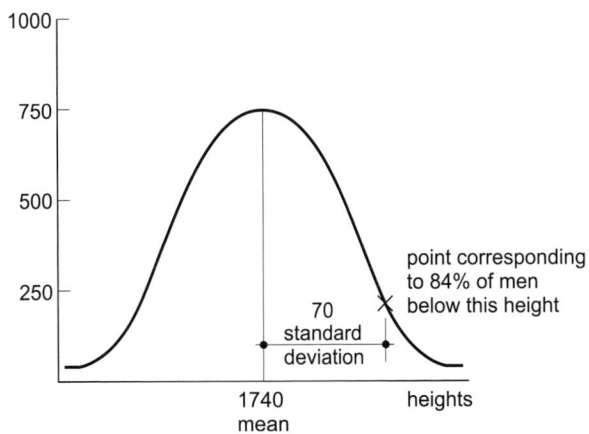

Figure 2.1 *Normal distribution 'bell' curve. The y-axis plots the numbers of men (in this example) in a group who are the height given on the x-axis (within certain limits). In a normal distribution the average, the mean and the median are all equal*

across a particular population. So using height for an example, the curve will indicate that at one end the number of short people starts from roughly zero and builds to the peak where the largest numbers are, representing the average (or mean) in most cases and then decreasing as the number of taller people also diminishes towards the highest end in a symmetrical pattern.

2.3 Percentiles

This bell curve allows us to derive some very useful information commonly referred to as the percentiles. Statistically, we can use this symmetrical curve to illustrate that if we split the curve at the mid point we will have 50 per cent of the population measured falling on one side of the divide and 50 per cent on the other. This midway point is called the 50th percentile or abbreviated to 50th %ile. At either end we can also split the curve, removing the lowest and the highest 5 per cent. By doing this we end up with a range of sizes that excludes the top and bottom 5 per cent, giving us the range that will accommodate 90 per cent of a particular population. These ends are known as the 5th %ile and the 95th %ile respectively.

This is very useful information when designing something for large populations where accommodating the top or bottom 5 per cent can prove unnecessarily difficult or expensive. The size of seats on a train, for instance, allows more passengers to be carried if seat sizes are limited to the 95th %ile. However, using the 95th %ile would be wholly inappropriate if designing a fire escape that would prevent 5 per cent of the population from getting out. Where the population size is fairly consistently variable such as in the UK, the 5%ile and 95%iles will accommodate 90 per cent of the population and are used for most design solutions where safety is not an issue. In other countries, the USA in particular where there are discrete pockets in the population that may have a larger number within the outer 5 per cent ranges, the 1%ile and 99%iles are more commonly used incorporating 98 per cent of the population.

2.4 Standard deviation

In order to move between percentiles we have to manipulate the data concerned provided we have two basic pieces of information. The mean in most cases is represented by the peak of the curve, but we have not yet considered the width of the 'bell'. Essentially the wider the base of the curve, the more variable are the values and this spread is called the standard deviation (SD). For example, the bell curve for the height of all women in a population compared to the population of women high jumpers would be expected to be flatter as the average height would be lower and the spread wider as the number of female high jumpers is likely to be constrained to a smaller group of tall women. The mean and the SD allow us to calculate the other percentiles using the formula:

$$X_p = m + zSD$$

where: X_p is the value you are looking for
p represents the percentile in question
SD is the standard deviation
z is a constant for selected percentiles found in Table I.
m is the mean value or 50th %ile.

So, calculating the 99th %ile for British adult women with an average height of 1620 mm and a SD of 61 (found in Table II), we see that for $p = 99$, $z = 2.33$. Therefore the 99th %ile for women's height is: 1620 + 2.33 x 61 = 1762 mm.

To include women high jumpers, we may need to go to the 99.999th %ile where $z = 4.26$ so the 99th %ile for women's height is: 1620 + 4.26 x 61 = 1880 mm.

2.5 Extracting information from the tables

Anthropometric data comes in a standard form for any particular population, normally based on two postures, standing and sitting, with 36 measurements in total. There is a standard format for taking

Table I Percentile z values
Selected p and z values for the normal distribution curve

Percentile (p)	z value
0.001	−4.26
0.01	−3.72
0.1	−3.09
1	−2.33
2.5	−1.96
5	−1.64
10	−1.28
25	−0.67
50	0.00
99.999	4.26
99.99	3.72
99.9	3.09
99	2.33
97.5	1.96
95	1.64
90	1.28
75	0.67
50	0.00

these measurement as well such as standing against an upright surface and keeping the parts of the ear in line with parts of the eye to keep the head in a standardised position. This defined positioning needs to be accounted for when using the data to design for different postures, a reclining chair for instance.

2.6 Standing and sitting dimensions

The particular dimensions are numbered to correspond to the information in the anthropometric tables. The number of different anthropometric tables provided here has been limited to British adults up to 65 years old (Table II), British adults over 65 (Table III) and two for British children aged 11 years to accommodate those in primary education (Table IV) and those aged 18 years to accommodate those in secondary education (Table V). Those over 65 tend to shrink slightly with age and, more significantly, the body tends to be less flexible in adapting to dimensionally unfavourable situations.

It is important to recognise that these data refer to naked sizes so extra needs to be added to account for clothing. Clothing and particularly shoe heights can vary according to the situation but as a general rule it is accepted that for most situations it is appropriate to add a specific, although different, amount to all dimensions for men and women. Specific situations will have to be calculated individually such as areas where tool belts may be worn, extra thick clothing may be required or fashion may dictate extra high heels for periods.

- Add 25 mm to all dimensions for men.
- Add 45 mm to all dimensions for women.

Clearance is the extra space needed to accommodate people comfortably or safely. Where health and safety concerns dictate clearances, advice should be sought elsewhere. However, there are some general rules that can be applied for personal space requirements. These space standards assume face-to-face interaction with other people and place a radius around individuals depending on the following social interactions:

- Intimate up to 450 mm.
- Personal 450 to 1200 mm.
- Social 1200 to 3600 mm.
- Public over 3600 mm.

These standards are often broken however, as air travel or the London Underground at rush hour will clearly demonstrate. It is also worth noting that intruding into this personal space is more acceptable if it is not on the facing side.

Table II British adult dimensions up to 65 years old

This table provides anthropometric data for adults aged 19 to 65, corresponding to the numbered measurements in Figure 2.2. For other percentiles, use the SD and 50th %ile values and the method shown in Section 2.4.

DIMENSIONS	Men				Women			
	5th %ile	50th %ile	95th %ile	SD	5th %ile	50th %ile	95th %ile	SD
STANDING								
1 Stature	1640	1760	1880	73	1520	1620	1720	61
2 Eye height	1530	1650	1770	72	1415	1515	1615	60
3 Shoulder height	1330	1445	1555	69	1225	1320	1410	57
4 Elbow height	1020	1105	1195	54	940	1015	1090	45
5 Hip height	850	935	1020	52	745	815	885	43
6 Knuckle height	695	765	835	42	665	725	785	35
7 Fingertip height	595	665	730	40	565	630	690	38
SITTING								
8 Sitting height	855	915	980	37	800	855	915	35
9 Sitting eye height	740	795	855	36	690	745	800	33
10 Sitting shoulder height	545	600	655	33	510	560	610	31
11 Sitting elbow height	195	245	300	32	180	230	275	28
12 Thigh – thickness	130	160	185	16	120	150	175	16
13 Thigh – outer length	545	595	650	32	520	565	615	29
14 Thigh – inner length	445	500	555	34	430	475	525	29
15 Knee height	495	550	605	33	460	500	545	26
16 Under thigh height	400	445	495	30	355	400	445	27
17 Shoulder breadth a)	415	465	510	29	355	395	435	24
18 Shoulder breadth b)	370	405	440	21	330	360	390	18
19 Hip width	300	350	400	31	300	350	400	29
20 Chest depth	185	225	270	26	190	235	275	26
21 Abdominal depth	195	240	280	26	185	220	260	22
22 Elbow – shoulder length	335	370	405	21	305	330	360	17
23 Elbow – fingertip length	445	480	515	22	400	430	465	19
24 Arm – shoulder to fingertip	730	790	850	37	660	710	760	32
25 Arm – shoulder to grip	615	670	730	34	560	605	650	29
APPENDAGES								
26 Head length	185	195	210	8	170	180	190	7
27 Head breadth	145	155	165	7	135	145	155	5
28 Hand length	175	190	210	10	160	175	190	9
29 Hand breadth	80	90	95	5	70	75	85	4
30 Foot length	245	270	290	15	220	240	260	12
31 Foot breadth	90	100	110	7	80	90	100	5
REACH								
32 Span	1670	1815	1955	86	1500	1615	1730	70
33 Elbow span	875	955	1035	49	785	855	925	42
34 Vertical grip reach – standing	1950	2085	2220	83	1805	1915	2030	70
35 Vertical grip reach – sitting	1155	1260	1360	63	1070	1155	1245	52
36 Forward grip reach	730	790	845	36	655	705	755	31

(Source: Pheasant & Haslegrave, 2006, p. 245, table 10.2)

Tabel III British adult dimensions over 65 years old

This table provides anthropometric data for adults aged over 65, corresponding to the numbered measurements in Figure 2.2. For other percentiles, use the SD and 50th %ile values and the method shown in Section 2.4.

DIMENSIONS	Men				Women			
	5th %ile	50th %ile	95th %ile	SD	5th %ile	50th %ile	95th %ile	SD
STANDING								
1 Stature	1575	1685	1790	66	1475	1570	1670	60
2 Eye height	1470	1575	1685	65	1375	1475	1570	59
3 Shoulder height	1280	1380	1480	62	1190	1280	1375	56
4 Elbow height	975	1055	1135	49	910	985	1055	44
5 Hip height	820	895	975	47	740	810	875	42
6 Knuckle height	670	730	795	38	645	705	760	35
7 Fingertip height	575	635	695	36	550	610	670	37
SITTING								
8 Sitting height	815	875	930	36	750	815	885	41
9 Sitting eye height	705	760	815	34	645	710	770	38
10 Sitting shoulder height	520	570	625	32	475	535	590	36
11 Sitting elbow height	175	220	270	29	165	210	260	28
12 Thigh – thickness	125	150	175	15	115	145	170	16
13 Thigh – outer length	530	580	625	29	520	565	615	29
14 Thigh – inner length	430	485	535	31	430	480	525	29
15 Knee height	480	525	575	30	455	500	540	26
16 Under thigh height	385	425	470	27	355	395	440	26
17 Shoulder breadth a)	400	445	485	26	345	385	425	23
18 Shoulder breadth b)	350	375	405	17	320	350	380	17
19 Hip width	305	350	395	28	310	370	430	37
20 Chest depth	225	260	290	20	220	265	305	26
21 Abdominal depth	245	300	355	33	225	270	320	30
22 Elbow – shoulder length	320	350	385	19	295	320	350	17
23 Elbow – fingertip length	425	460	490	20	390	420	450	19
24 Arm – shoulder to fingertip	700	755	810	34	640	690	740	31
25 Arm – shoulder to grip	595	645	695	30	540	590	635	28
APPENDAGES								
26 Head length	175	190	200	7	165	175	185	7
27 Head breadth	140	150	160	6	130	140	150	5
28 Hand length	170	185	200	9	155	170	185	9
29 Hand breadth	75	85	90	5	65	75	80	4
30 Foot length	235	255	280	13	210	230	250	12
31 Foot breadth	85	95	105	6	80	85	95	5
REACH								
32 Span	1605	1735	1860	78	1460	1570	1685	68
33 Elbow span	840	915	985	44	760	830	900	41
34 Vertical grip reach – standing	1840	1965	2090	75	1725	1835	1950	68
35 Vertical grip reach – sitting	1110	1205	1295	57	1040	1125	1210	52
36 Forward grip reach	700	755	805	32	640	685	735	30

(Source: Pheasant & Haslegrave, 2006, p. 248, table 10.5)

Table IV British children dimensions aged 11 years old

This table provides anthropometric data to be used for primary school children, corresponding to the numbered measurements in Figure 2.2. For other percentiles, use the SD and 50th %ile values and the method shown in Section 2.4.

		Boys				Girls			
DIMENSIONS		5th %ile	50th %ile	95th %ile	SD	5th %ile	50th %ile	95th %ile	SD
STANDING									
1	Stature	1325	1430	1535	65	1310	1440	1570	79
2	Eye height	1215	1315	1415	62	1195	1325	1455	78
3	Shoulder height	1060	1160	1260	60	1050	1165	1280	69
4	Elbow height	795	890	985	57	800	890	980	56
5	Hip height	685	765	845	50	670	750	830	48
6	Knuckle height	560	620	680	35	575	645	715	42
7	Fingertip height	460	520	575	35	475	545	615	42
SITTING									
8	Sitting height	685	740	795	34	680	745	810	41
9	Sitting eye height	575	620	665	28	570	635	700	39
10	Sitting shoulder height	425	470	515	26	415	470	525	33
11	Sitting elbow height	160	200	240	24	155	200	245	26
12	Thigh – thickness	100	120	140	11	100	125	150	16
13	Thigh – outer length	435	480	525	28	430	490	550	37
14	Thigh – inner length	345	395	445	30	365	410	455	26
15	Knee height	420	460	500	25	405	455	505	30
16	Under thigh height	330	375	420	26	335	375	415	24
17	Shoulder breadth a)	300	345	390	26	285	340	395	34
18	Shoulder breadth b)	280	315	350	21	280	315	350	21
19	Hip width	220	265	310	27	225	280	335	34
20	Chest depth	130	170	210	24	115	175	240	38
21	Abdominal depth	150	190	230	23	145	195	245	29
22	Elbow – shoulder length	270	300	325	16	265	300	330	20
23	Elbow – fingertip length	350	385	420	22	340	385	430	28
24	Arm – shoulder to fingertip	560	630	700	43	555	630	705	46
25	Arm – shoulder to grip	460	530	600	43	455	530	605	46
APPENDAGES									
26	Head length	170	185	200	8	155	170	185	8
27	Head breadth	135	145	155	5	125	135	145	5
28	Hand length	140	155	170	10	135	155	175	11
29	Hand breadth	60	70	80	5	60	70	80	5
30	Foot length	205	225	245	13	195	220	245	14
31	Foot breadth	75	85	95	7	75	85	95	7
REACH									
32	Span	1310	1440	1570	78	1270	1415	1560	87
33	Elbow span	685	760	830	44	660	750	835	53
34	Vertical grip reach – standing	1575	1740	1905	100	1575	1760	1945	111
35	Vertical grip reach – sitting	895	990	1080	56	900	990	1085	56
36	Forward grip reach	535	595	655	37	530	600	670	42

(Source: Pheasant & Haslegrave, 2006, p. 272, table 10.31)

Table V British children dimensions aged 18 years old

This table provides anthropometric data to be used for secondary school children, corresponding to the numbered measurements in Figure 2.2. For other percentiles, use the SD and 50th %ile values and the method shown in Section 2.4.

		Boys				Girls			
DIMENSIONS		5th %ile	50th %ile	95th %ile	SD	5th %ile	50th %ile	95th %ile	SD
STANDING									
1	Stature	1660	1760	1860	60	1530	1620	1710	56
2	Eye height	1555	1650	1745	59	1430	1520	1610	55
3	Shoulder height	1355	1445	1535	54	1235	1320	1405	52
4	Elbow height	1010	1105	1175	44	940	1010	1080	42
5	Hip height	865	935	1005	43	755	820	885	40
6	Knuckle height	705	765	825	35	670	725	780	32
7	Fingertip height	585	640	700	35	560	610	665	32
SITTING									
8	Sitting height	860	915	970	32	800	855	910	32
9	Sitting eye height	745	800	855	32	695	745	795	30
10	Sitting shoulder height	550	600	650	30	515	560	605	28
11	Sitting elbow height	200	245	290	26	185	230	275	26
12	Thigh – thickness	135	160	185	15	120	145	170	14
13	Thigh – outer length	545	590	635	26	515	560	605	28
14	Thigh – inner length	450	500	550	29	435	480	525	27
15	Knee height	505	550	595	26	455	500	545	26
16	Under thigh height	405	445	485	25	365	405	445	25
17	Shoulder breadth a)	415	455	495	23	360	395	430	21
18	Shoulder breadth b)	365	395	425	17	335	360	385	16
19	Hip width	300	340	380	25	300	345	390	27
20	Chest depth	190	225	260	21	195	235	275	24
21	Abdominal depth	205	240	275	21	185	220	255	20
22	Elbow – shoulder length	340	370	395	17	310	335	360	16
23	Elbow – fingertip length	450	480	510	18	395	425	455	17
24	Arm – shoulder to fingertip	740	790	840	31	660	710	760	29
25	Arm – shoulder to grip	615	665	715	31	550	595	645	29
APPENDAGES									
26	Head length	185	200	215	8	170	180	190	7
27	Head breadth	145	155	165	5	135	145	155	5
28	Hand length	175	190	205	8	160	175	190	8
29	Hand breadth	85	90	95	4	70	75	80	4
30	Foot length	250	270	290	12	220	240	260	11
31	Foot breadth	90	100	110	5	80	90	100	5
REACH									
32	Span	1695	1810	1925	71	1520	1620	1720	62
33	Elbow span	890	955	1020	40	795	855	920	38
34	Vertical grip reach – standing	2045	2150	2255	65	1830	1970	2110	85
35	Vertical grip reach – sitting	1170	1250	1335	52	1065	1150	1235	52
36	Forward grip reach	675	740	805	41	610	670	730	37

(Source: Pheasant & Haslegrave, 2006, p. 279, table 10.38)

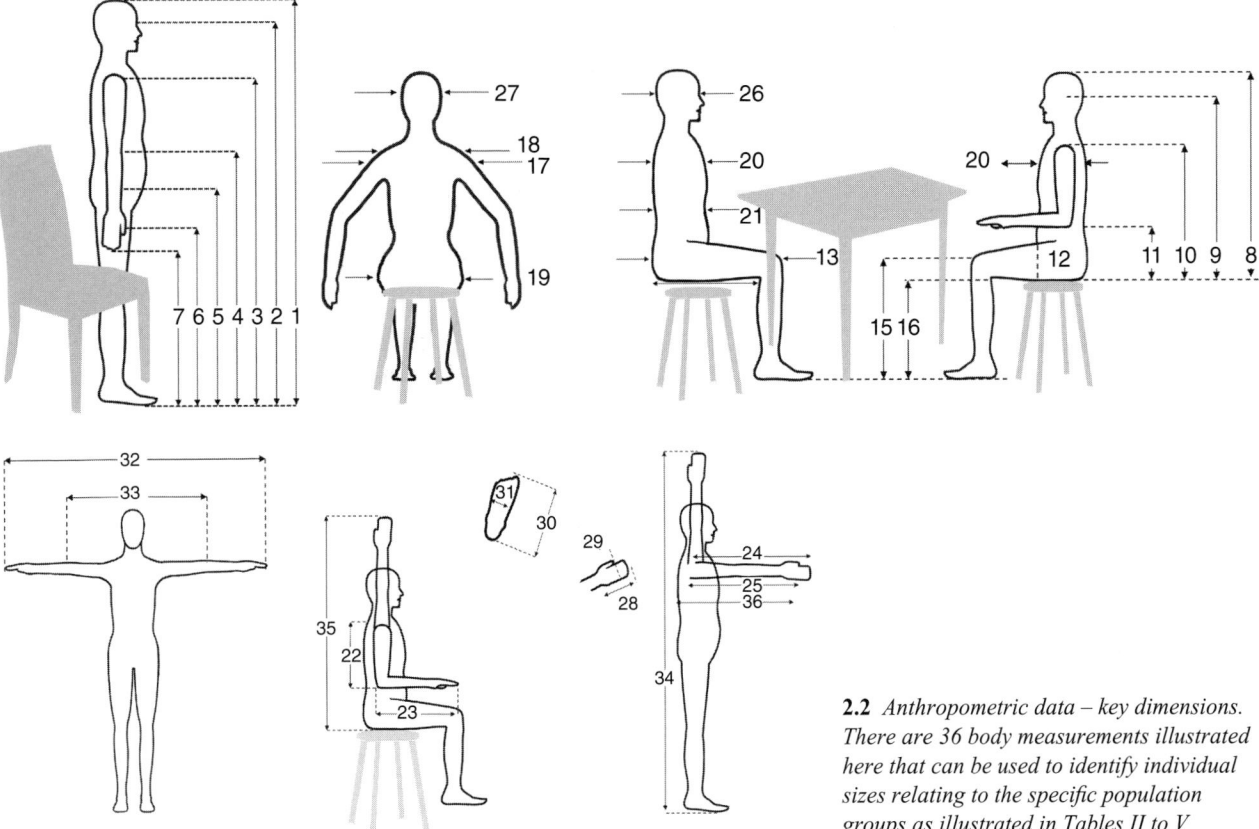

2.2 *Anthropometric data – key dimensions. There are 36 body measurements illustrated here that can be used to identify individual sizes relating to the specific population groups as illustrated in Tables II to V*

3 ERGONOMICS

3.1 Introduction

Ergonomics is strictly the science of work including the people, the methods and the tools they use, but it also includes the places they work in and significantly also the psychological aspects of that environment (Pheasant & Haslegrave 2006). For the purposes of ergonomic design however we can limit ourselves to the collection of data that with appropriate referencing permit satisfactory, although conventional, design solutions focused on the user. The term conventional design is used here to differentiate it from the equally important (if not more so) universal design referred to in the introduction.

True ergonomic design aims to *fit the job to the worker and the product to the user*, including equal reference to criteria such as efficiency, ease of use, comfort, health & safety and quality of working life (Pheasant & Haslegrave 2006). Here we limit ourselves to some practical data for use in conventional domestic and non-domestic building design. This data is broken down into two main areas:

- Personal working spaces – heights and reach when sitting or standing.
- Maintenance and access – openings and space requirements.

3.2 Personal working spaces

Sitting at work
Given the variation in human dimensions, it follows that the spaces humans require will also vary and can be planned for by using the statistical tools provided. In addition however, there are also strict regulatory requirements governing the design and manufacture of most work related furniture. The design of an office desk for example could be subject to requirements coming under the jurisdiction of:

- International Standards (ISO)
- European Standards (EN)
- British Standards (BS)
- British Health & Safety (HSE).

The sizes required for computer workstations are therefore tightly controlled as well as following ergonomic principles. Figure 2.3 illustrates the sizes required for desks to accommodate computers and associated chairs. These dimensions are simplified however

as the actual requirements are understandably complicated. For instance, the height of a desk should be suitable for everyone who may need to use it. A height of 740 mm can accommodate 95 per cent of the population whereas a height adjustable desk (from 660 mm to 900 mm) can accommodate almost everyone.

Standing at work and home
Common practice for work surface heights suggests:

- For delicate tasks – from 50–100 mm above elbow height.
- For manipulative tasks needing some force – from 50–100 mm below elbow.
- For heavy work – from 100–300 mm below elbow height.

With the great variety of human sizes and the variety of tasks usually associated with work surfaces, standardised work surface heights are by definition compromised solutions. However specialist tasks can be accommodated and surface heights designed around those tasks.

Kitchen heights
Domestic kitchen worktops are included here as functional working areas because they illustrate both the basic design requirements and the compromises necessary to accommodate standard population

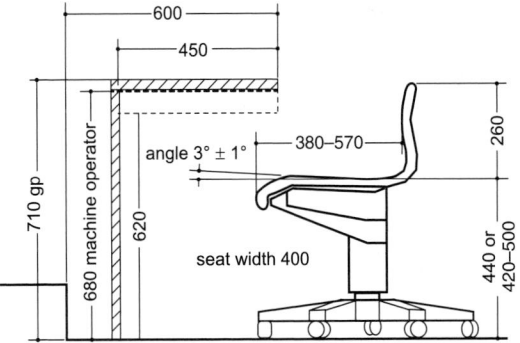

2.3 *Sitting worktop – useful working dimensions for deskspace or computer workstations but more detailed information should be sought for specialist or specific tasks*

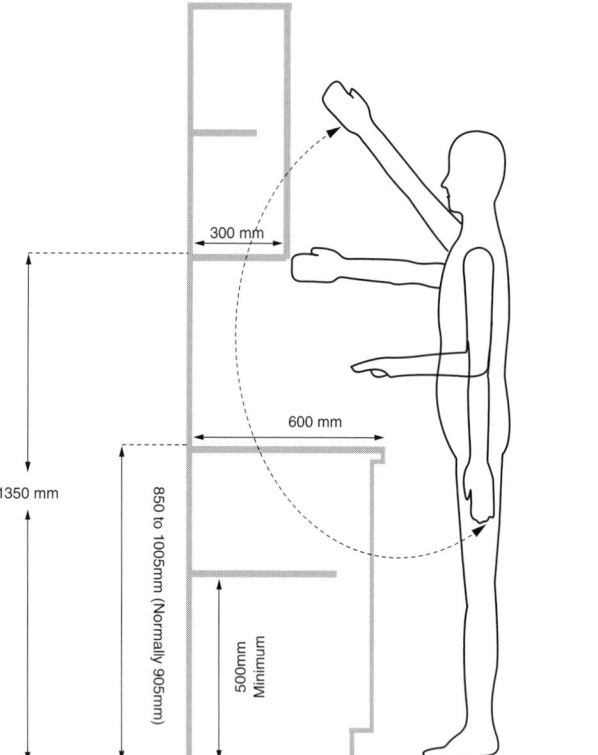

2.4 *Sitting worktop – useful working dimensions for kitchens or similar spaces but more detailed information should be sought for specialist or specific tasks*

variations. Although Figure 2.4 illustrates the normal heights for kitchen units the story behind these figures makes useful reading.

As with the common practice heights above, research (Pheasant & Haslegrave 2006) suggests that there are also three 'working heights' for kitchen design. But the weighted conclusions pointed to the ideal height as being 100 mm below elbow height. For the 50%ile for British adults this provides a figure of 905 mm for women and 990 mm for men. However the range from the 5%ile women to the 95%ile men goes from 830 to 1005 mm. The dimensions recommended here assume that the data will be used to design for a wide range of the British population but aimed specifically to accommodate 95 per cent of the elderly whose strength, reach etc., is most likely to be limited. For more specific populations where heights can be individualised as in specific workplaces, please refer to specialist literature e.g. British Health & Safety (HSE).

Accessing storage at work and home.
The ideal layout of storage space and its accessibility bears a strong relationship to the weights involved, the frequency of use and the range of people involved. Here again we turn to the domestic kitchen to detail recommendations for storage zones. The heaviest and certainly the most dangerous items to be used and stored are dishes and pots lifted into and out of ovens. Research (Noble 1982) suggests that 300 mm deep and 1400 mm high (reduced to 1350 mm when reaching over an obstruction) shelves can be used by 95 per cent of the elderly population. As this group are more likely to have difficulty in kneeling and bending, deep shelves should be kept above 500 mm. It is worth noting here that the optimal storage height is also the most advantageous worktop height, resulting in maximum demand for space in this zone.

3.3 Maintenance, access and openings
Buildings need constant maintenance, whether it is the services that are located within the building or the building fabric itself. These are not publically accessible spaces and, as there is a requirement to provide a safe working environment, also fall within relevant Health & Safety legislation (the list is extensive but can be accessed at www.hse.gov.uk). As the access required is also very

task specific, it is well beyond the scope of this work to go into any detail, particularly as it could legitimately be restricted to certain people, i.e. those who are sufficiently able and agile. Some general and basic dimensions are provided in Figures 2.5 to 2.10.

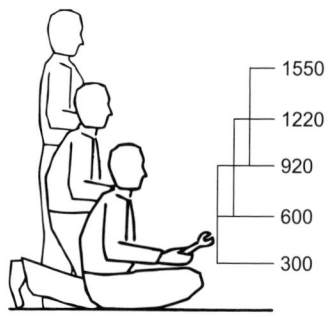

2.5 *Body clearance: maintenance reach levels*

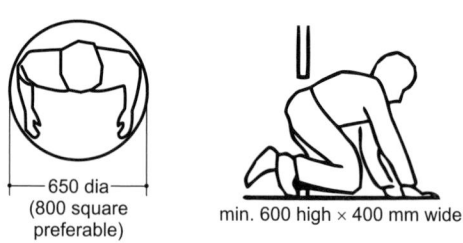

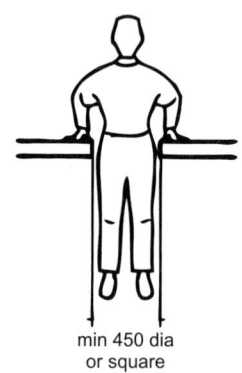

2.6 *Service accesses*

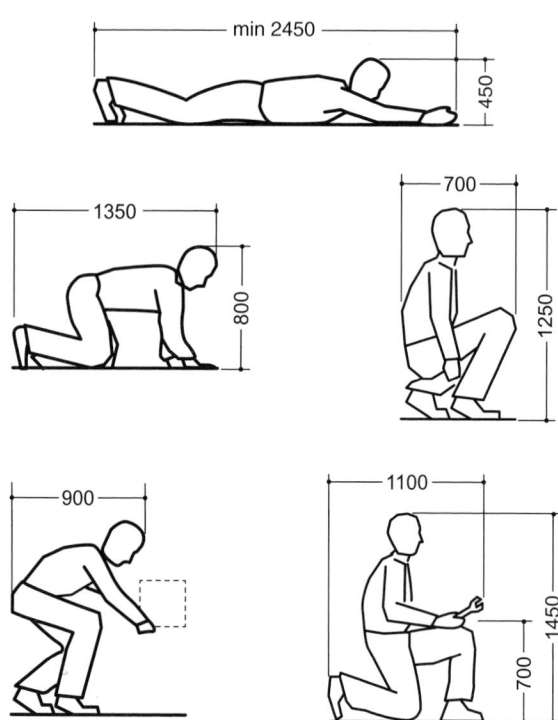

2.7 *Body clearances*

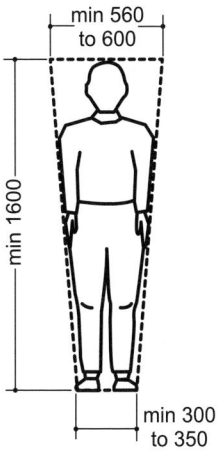

2.8 *Service access: catwalk*

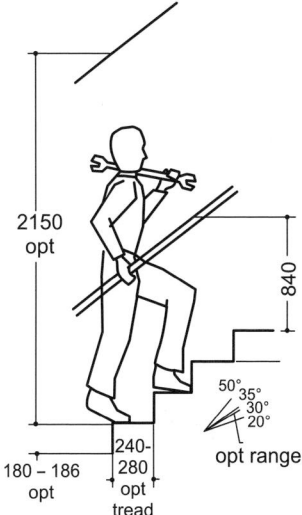

2.9 *Service access: stairs*

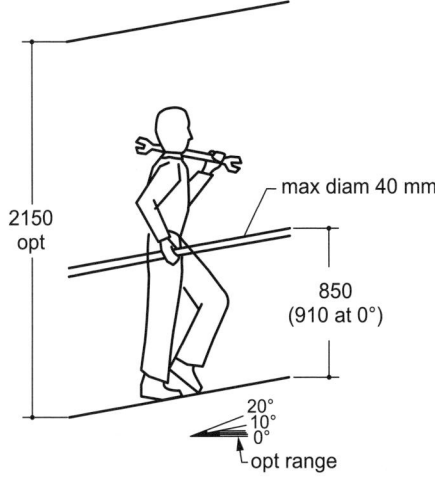

2.10 *Service access: ramps*

4 SANITARY PROVISION

4.1 Inclusivity

The space requirements for sanitary facilities should be designed to accommodate the needs of all a building's users as those users could include adults and children of all ages, sizes and abilities. Be they independent, accompanied, or assisted, it is assumed that a universal (or inclusive) design approach will be adopted to ensure that the facilities can be accessed and used by that diverse population.

The extent of the provision in a particular building will depend on its type and size, the occupancy, patterns of use and gender ratio. It is recognised that females take longer to use toilet facilities than males so the gender ratio should be taken into account, recognising that the ratio may change over time. To illustrate this the British Toilet Association recommends that the required number of female cubicles should equal *twice* the number of male cubicles and urinals added together.

The added value of an inclusive design approach that addresses the needs of one group can have benefits for many others as well. Level access facilities designed for wheelchair users are also helpful for people with sticks, crutches, frames, push-chairs, luggage or other mobility aids, larger compartments likewise and clear signage can help those with reading difficulties or whose first language is not English, as well as the poorly sighted. Wheelchair-accessible compartments can also be preferable for those using assistance dogs, those with dwarfism, parents with small children, those accompanied by carers, anyone with luggage and many more.

It is estimated that about 20 per cent of the adult population in the UK (around 11.7 million people) are covered by the disability legislation, there are around 5,000 working assistance dogs and around half a million people use a wheelchair all or part of the time. In addition there are 3.3 million families with children under the age of five (*Housing Design Standards, Evidence Summary*, 2010).

4.2 Design aspects

Provision of sanitary facilities

In the provision of sanitary facilities compromise is always probably necessary because of the large gap between what is desirable and what is possible. Therefore minimum requirements provide the starting point for particular building types and circumstances. Good design practice would use these as minima but with the aim of inclusive design solutions always uppermost. The overall scale of the provision will depend on:

- The size and particular nature of the building as well as the people being catered for. This is an aspect that should be considered very early in the design process and should involve consultation with a wide range of interested parties from users to regulatory authorities. For particular building types, suggested gender ratios are given in Table VI.

Table VI Gender ratios

The figures given here are based on predicted ratios and can be used to provide an initial assessment of the balance of sanitary facilities required.

Building type	Predicted ratio
Assembly buildings	50% male and 50% female
Swimming pools	50% male and 50% female
Cafes, nightclubs, restaurants	50% male and 50% female
Theatres and concert halls	50% male and 50% female
Public houses	**75% male and 25% female**
Shopping centres	**35% male and 65% female**

(Source, p 14, table 5.1, *Building for Everyone: A Universal Design Approach, Sanitary facilities 5,* Centre for Excellence in Universal Design, Dublin, 2012)

- Access routes and convenience in relation to other key facilities within a building. Routes to toilets should be as short as possible. In large public buildings, the horizontal travel distance to the nearest toilet facilities should not exceed 40 m. In schools, this is reduced to 25 m. In addition, a clearly identified, fully accessible unisex toilet should be provided on each floor of a building with a lift. If no lift is available accessible toilet facilities should provided at the entrance level. The sanitary requirements for schools are given in Table VII.

Table VII Sanitary requirements in schools

Type of school	Sanitary item	Number	Notes
special	wc urinal	1 per 10 pupils	*Not more than 2/3 of boys' appliances to be urinals*
	washbasin	1 per WC or urinal	*Every WC or urinal to be close to a washbasin*
	shower	1 per 10 pupils	*Where provided*
nursery	WC	1 per 10 pupils, not less than 4	
	washbasin	1 per WC or urinal	
	sink, bath or shower	1 per 40 pupils	
primary	wc and urinal	1 per 10 pupils under 5 years	*Not more than 2/3 of boys' appliances to be urinals*
		1 per 15 pupils over 5 years	
	washbasin	1 per WC or urinal	*Every WC or urinal to be close to a washbasin*
	shower	1 per 10 pupils	*Where provided*
secondary	boys' WC and urinal	1 per 20 pupils	*Not more than 2/3 of boys' appliances to be urinals*
	girls' WC	1 per 20 pupils	
	washbasin	1 per WC or urinal where there are up to 3 appliances	*Every WC or urinal to be close to a washbasin*
		2 per 3 WCs or urinals where there are more than 3 appliances	
	shower	1 per 10 pupils	*Easy access for all places where physical education takes place*
boarding school (residential)	boys' WC and urinal	1 per 5 boarders, 2/3 to be urinals	*These provisions are in addition to those sanitary items shown above in this table, unless they are close to living and sleeping areas*
	girls' WC	1 per 5 boarders	
	washbasin	1 per 3 boarders	
	bath and shower	1 per 10 boarders, minimum 25% to be baths	

(Source, Armitage Shanks, *Schools Solutions . . . what works and why, an informative guide to school washroom requirements*, 2007)

- Likely use patterns such as those in a concert arena or cinema having a much greater demand during the intervals. The number in this case should serve the maximum number of people likely to make use of the facilities at these times. The sanitary requirements for some public assembly settings are given in Tables VIII to Table X.

Table VIII Sanitary requirements in cinemas, theatres etc.

Sanitary item	Males	Females
WC	In single-screen cinemas, theatres, concert halls and similar premises without licensed bars:	In single-screen cinemas, theatres, concert halls and similar premises without licensed bars:
	1 for up to 250 males plus 1 for every additional 500 (or part of 500) males.	2 for up to 40 females 3 for 41 to 70 females 4 for 71 to 100 females plus 1 for every additional 40 (or part of 40) females.
Urinal	In single-screen cinemas, theatres, concert halls and similar premises without licensed bars:	
	2 for up to 100 males plus 1 for every additional 80 (or part of 80) males.	
Wash Basins	1 per WC plus 1 per 5 (or part of 5) urinals.	1, plus 1 per 2 (or part of 2) WCs.
Cleaners' Sink	Adequate provision should be made for cleaning facilities including at least one cleaners' sink.	

(Source: the Food Team, Environmental Health, Canterbury City Council, n.d.)

Table IX Sanitary requirements in cafes & restaurants etc.

Sanitary item	Male customers	Female customers
WC	1 per 100 up to 400 males plus 1 for every additional 250 (or part of 250) males	2 per 50 up to 200 females plus 1 for every additional 100 (or part of 100) females
Urinal	1 per 50 males	
Wash Basins	1 per WC and plus 1 per 5 (or part of 5) urinals.	1 per WC
Cleaners' Sink	Adequate provision should be made for cleaning facilities including at least one cleaners' sink.	

(Source: the Food Team, Environmental Health, Canterbury City Council, n.d.)

Table X Sanitary requirements in hotels & guest houses

Type of accommodation	Sanitary facilities	Number	Notes
Hotel with en-suite accommodation	En-suite	1 per residential guest bedroom	*Containing: bath/shower, WC and wash basin*
	Staff bathroom	1 per 9 residential staff	*Containing: bath/shower, WC and wash basin*
	Bucket/cleaners' sink	1 per 30 bedrooms	*At least 1 on every floor*
Hotels and guest houses without en-suite accommodation	WC	1 per 9 guests	
	Wash basin	1 per bedroom	
	Bathroom	1 per 9 guests	*Containing: bath/shower, wash basin and additional WC*
	Bucket/cleaner's sink	1 per floor	
Tourist Hostels	WC	1 per 9 guests	
	Wash basin	1 per bedroom or 1 for every 9 guests in a dormitory	*Containing: bath/shower, washbasin and additional WC*
	Bathroom	1 per 9 guests	
	Bucket/cleaner's sink	1 per floor	

(Source: the Food Team, Environmental Health, Canterbury City Council, n.d.)

Layouts for sanitary facilities – accessible facilities

There are clear minimum size requirements for accessible sanitary facilities as outlined in Part M of the Building Regulations where recommended layouts and positions of individual appliances are also covered. In addition, the *Good Loo Design Guide* (2004) and the Volume 5 (Sanitary Facilities) (2012) from the Centre for Excellence in Universal Design are exceptionally good design guides in this area, covering the principles in depth. Figures 2.11 to 2.17 outline the requirements for accessible sanitary accommodation. Figures 2.11 to 2.16 contain public sector information licensed under the Open Government License v2.0.

Compartments and cubicles

To provide the requisite numbers of sanitary facilities within a defined space envelope there is still the need to provide some that do not meet the accessibility standards. WC *compartments* (fully enclosed) and WC *cubicles* (partitions only) need to ensure privacy. The doors are traditionally a problem area as inward opening doors require more space and outward opening doors compromise the safety of others outside of the cubicle. The space requirements and possible layouts for single WC layouts with both opening styles are illustrated in Figures 2.18 to 2.22.

Hand washing facilities are also a requirement and can be provided within each compartment/cubicle, although efficient space use would normally place them in an adjoining space if possible. The space requirements and possible layouts for single WC layouts with washbasins and both opening door styles are illustrated in Figures 2.23 to 2.29.

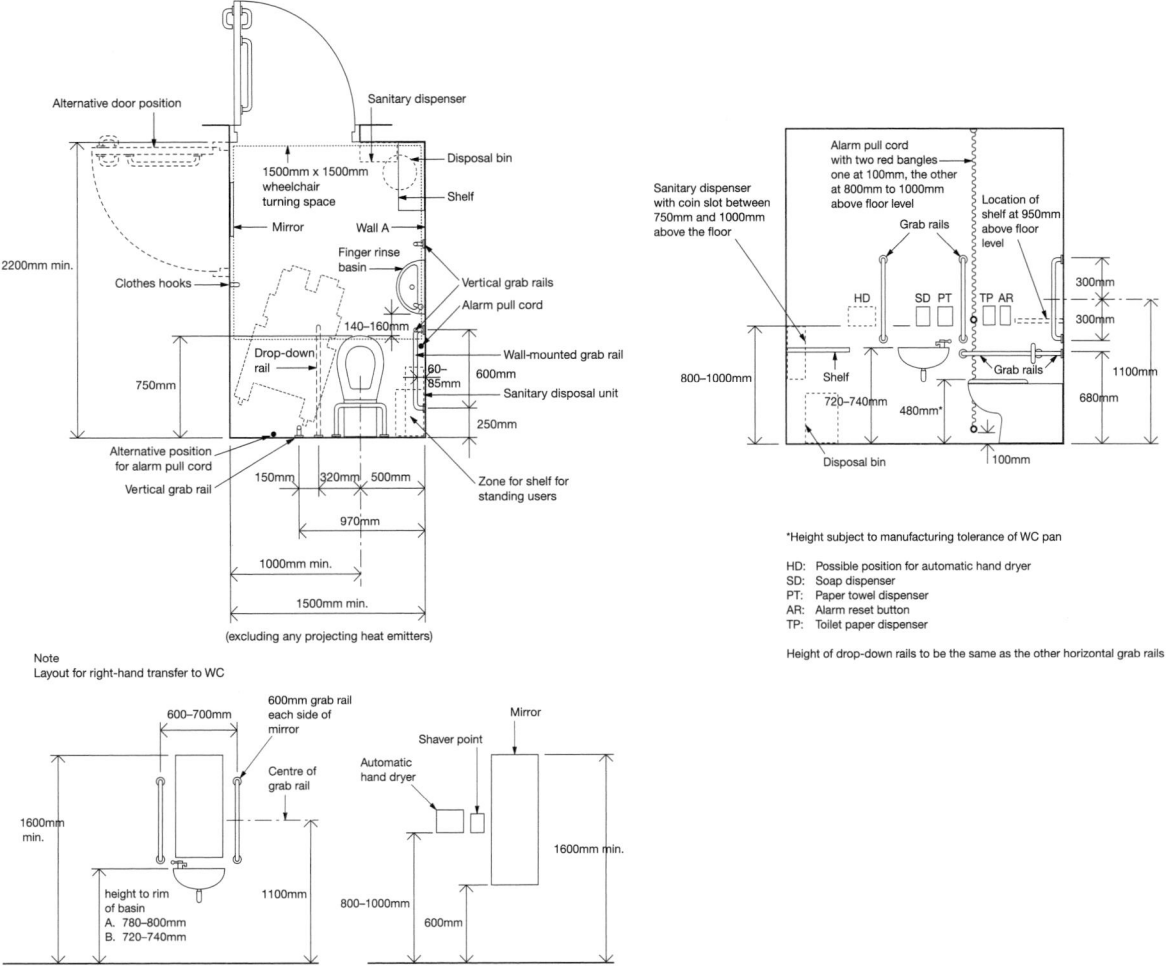

2.11 *Unisex wheelchair-accessible toilet (Source: Building Regulation Part M Diagrams 18, 19, 20)*

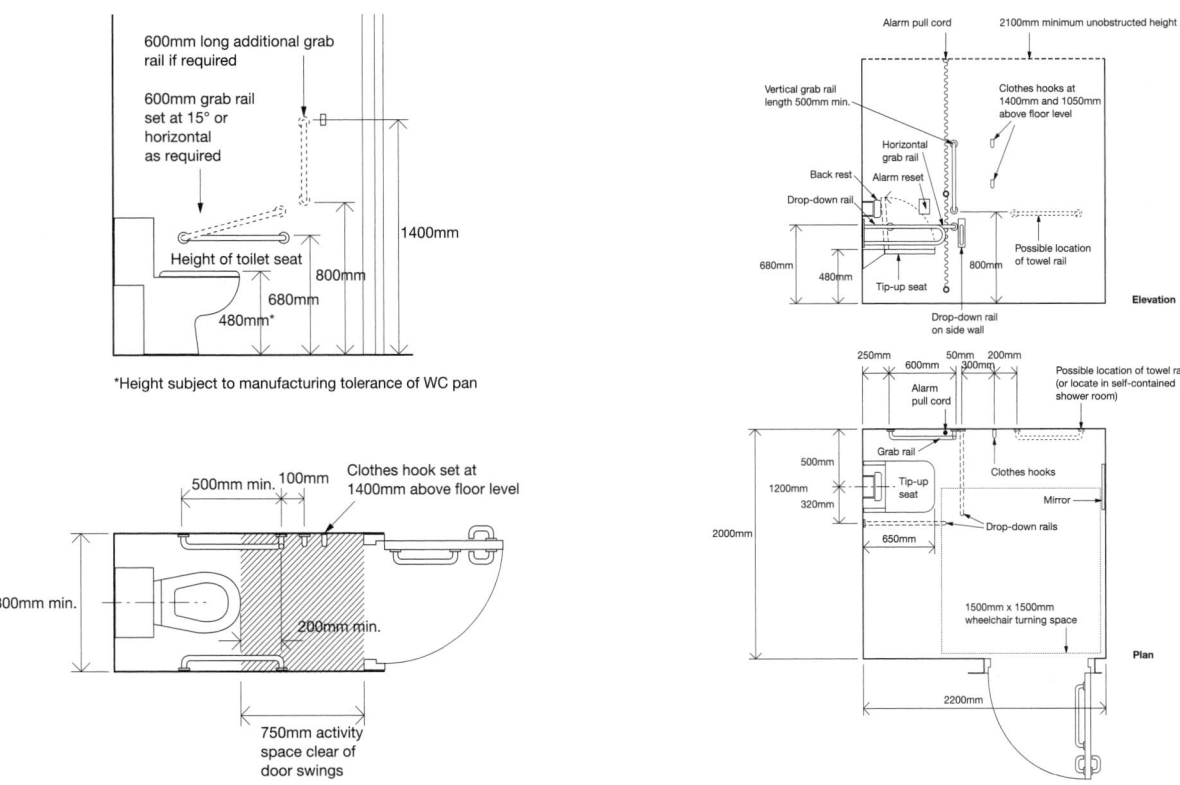

2.12 *Accessible toilet cubicle (Source: Building Regulation Part M Diagram 21)*

2.13 *Accessible self-contained changing room (Source: Building Regulation Part M Diagram 22)*

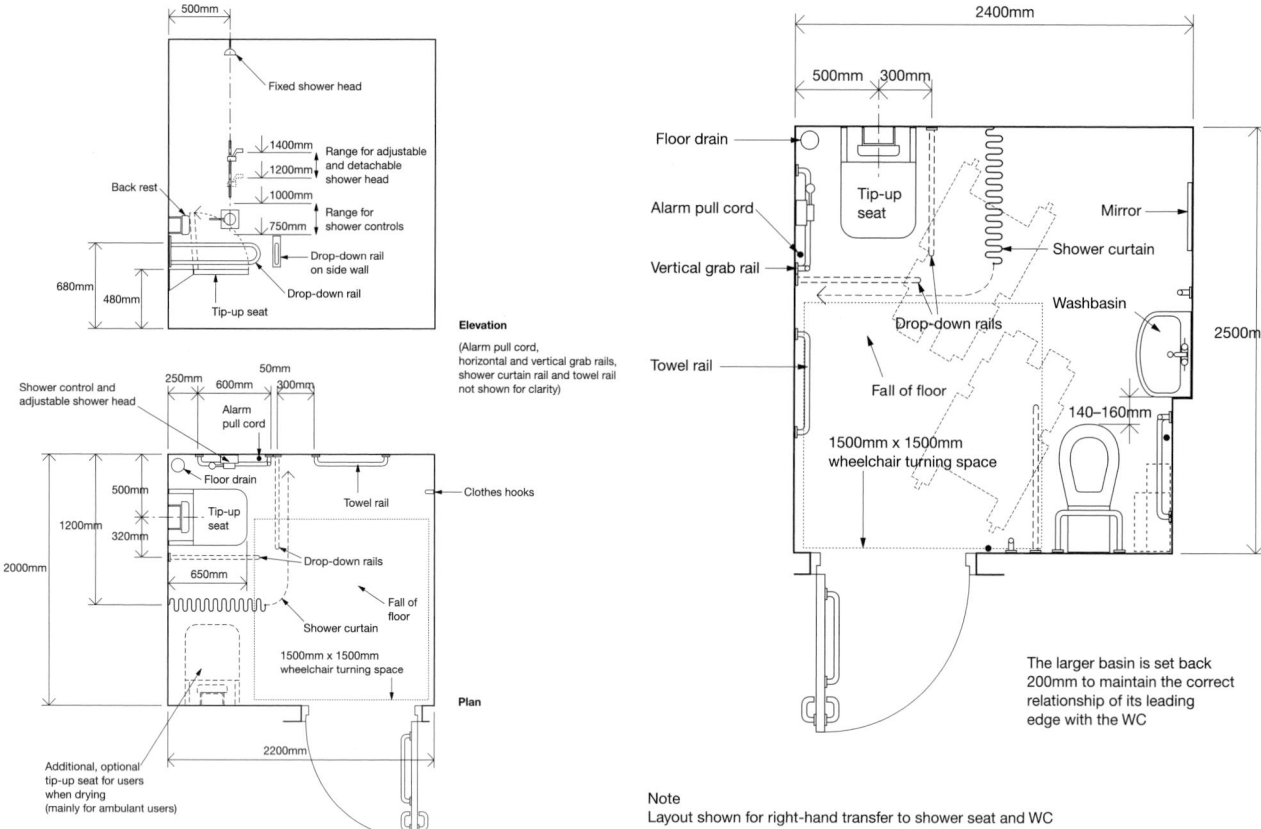

2.14 *Accessible self-contained changing room with shower (Source: Building Regulation Part M Diagram 23)*

2.15 *Accessible self-contained changing room with toilet & shower (Source: Building Regulation Part M Diagram 24)*

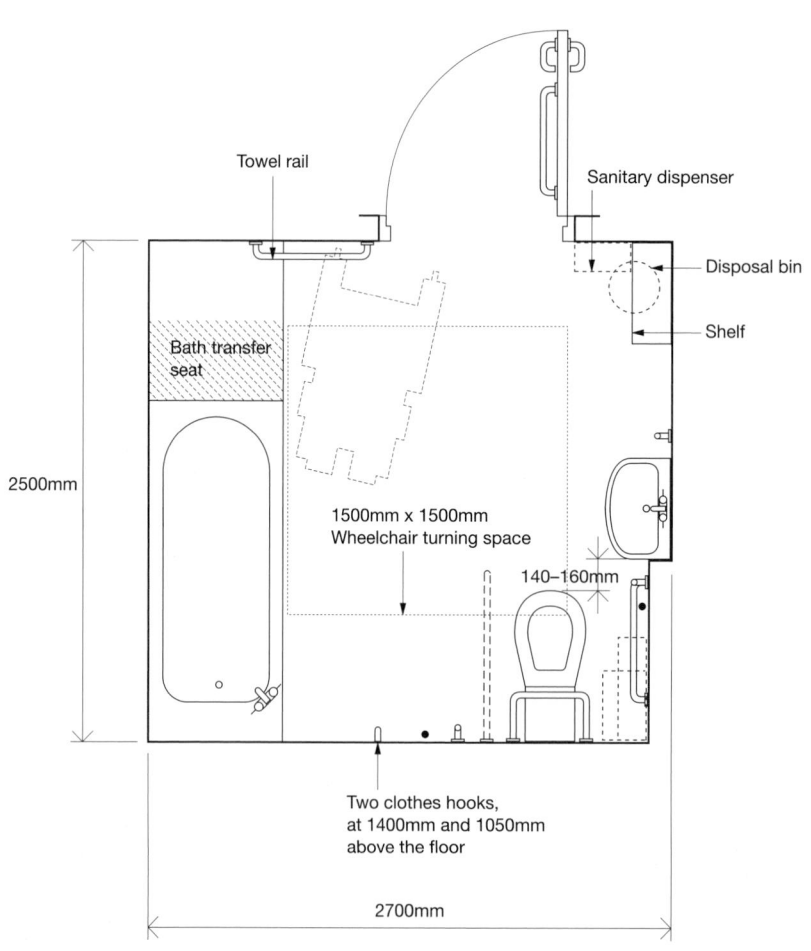

2.16 *Accessible self-contained changing room with bath (Source: Building Regulation Part M Diagram 25)*

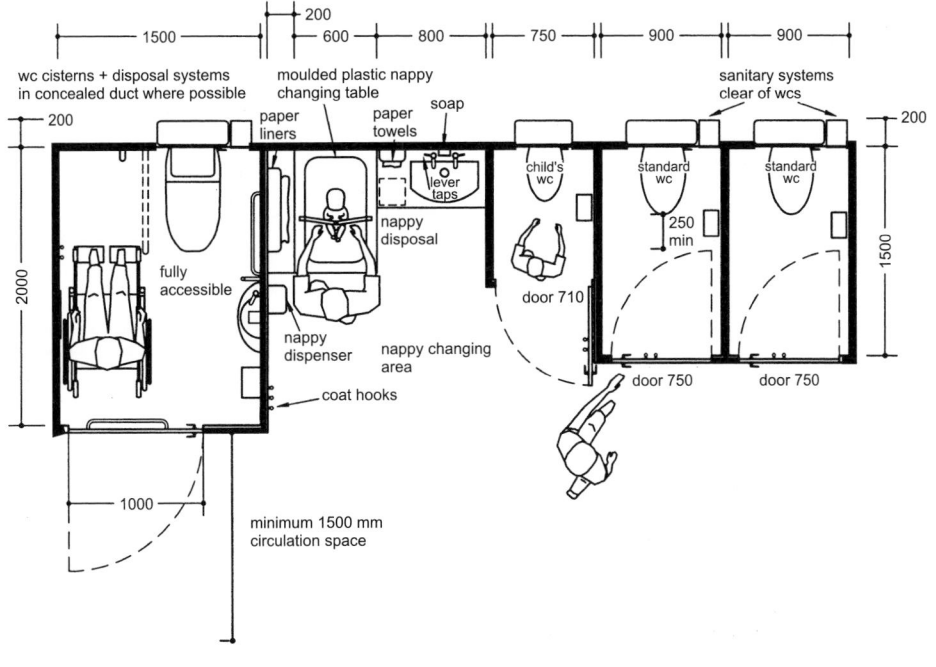

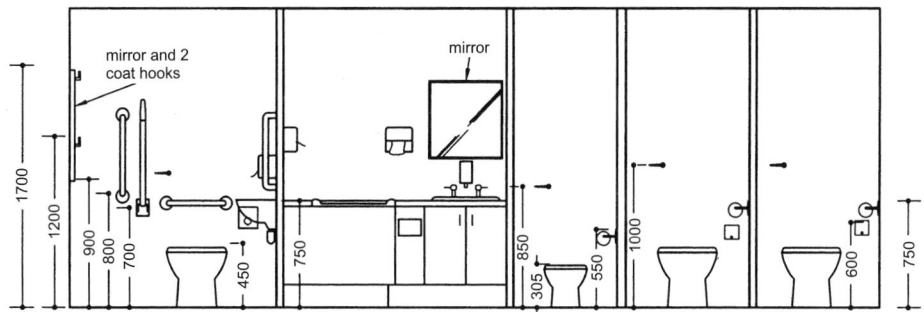

2.17 *A possible layout including baby changing facilities*

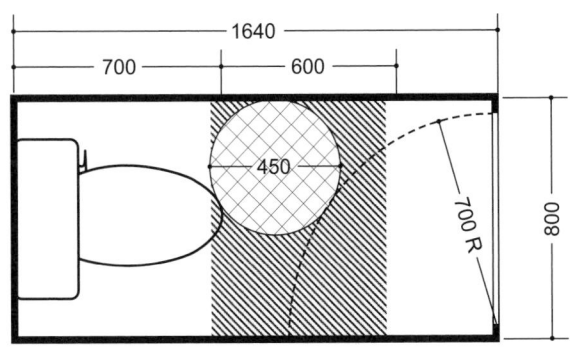

2.18 *WC cubicle, inward-opening door, no sanitary bin zone*

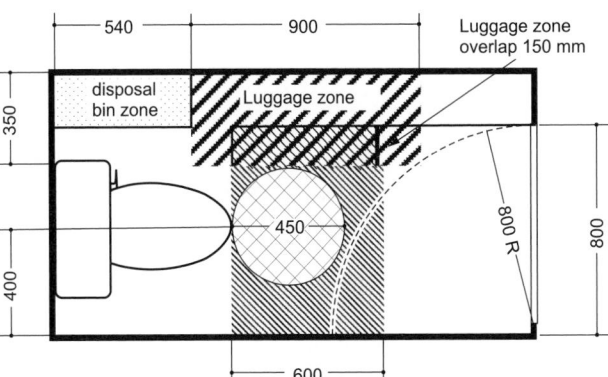

2.20 *Public WC cubicle, inward-opening door*

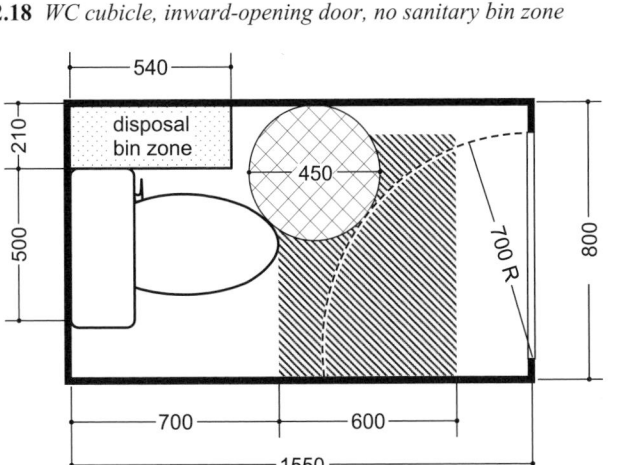

2.19 *WC cubicle, inward-opening door, sanitary bin zone*

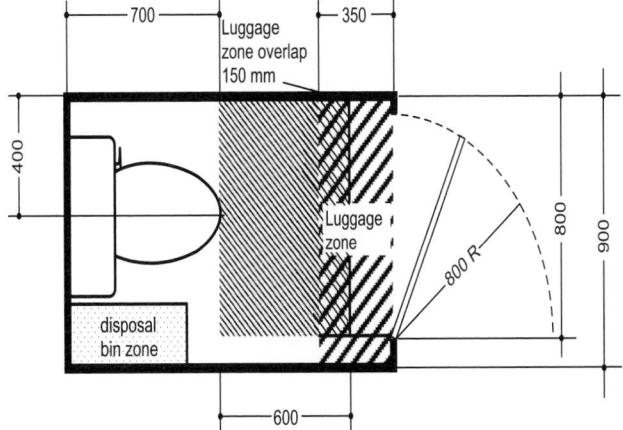

2.21 *Public WC cubicle, outward-opening door*

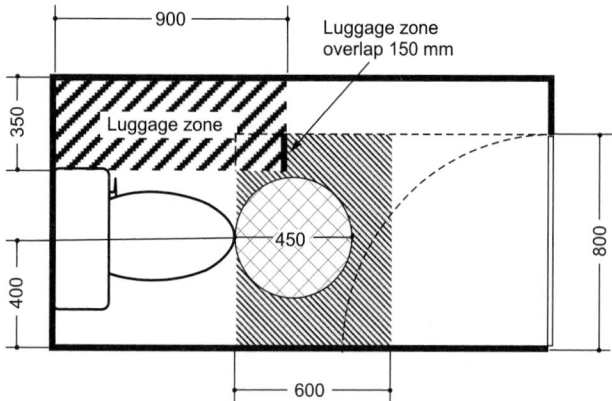

2.22 *Alternative public WC cubicle, inward-opening door, no sanitary bin*

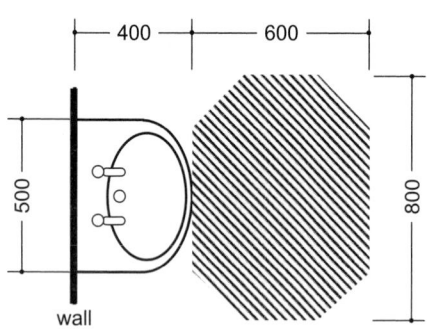

2.23 *Hand-rinse basin and activity space*

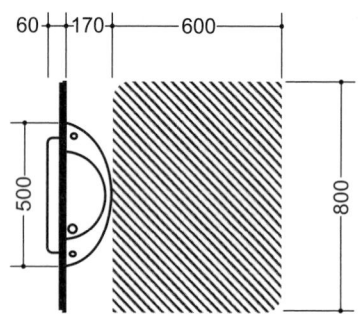

2.24 *Recessed hand-rinse basin and activity space*

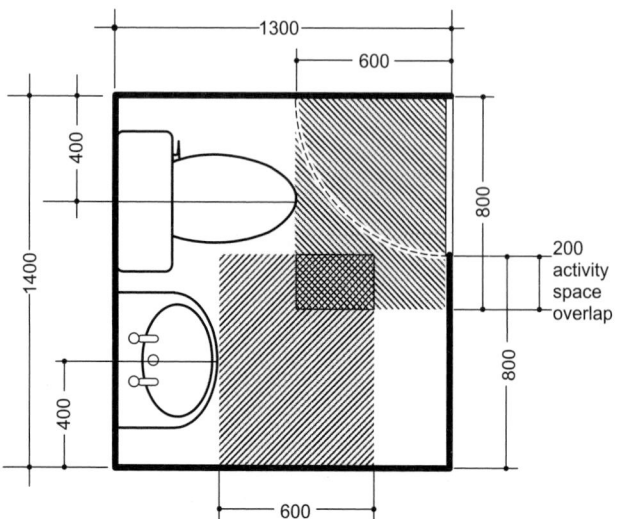

2.25 *WC and washbasin compartment, appliances on same wall*

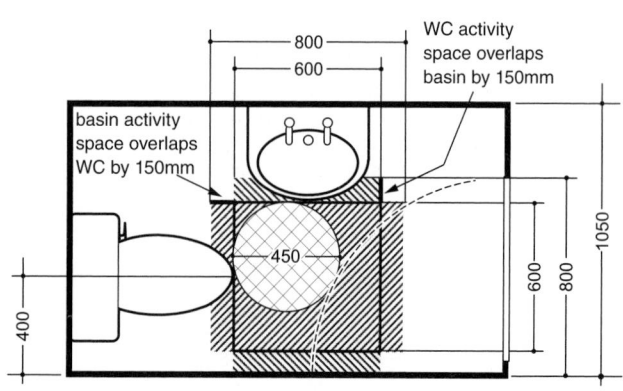

2.26 *WC and washbasin compartment, inward-opening door, appliances on adjacent walls*

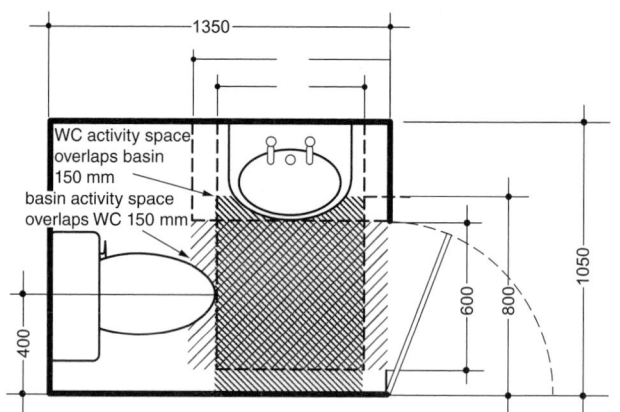

2.27 *WC and washbasin cubicle, outward-opening door, appliances on adjacent walls*

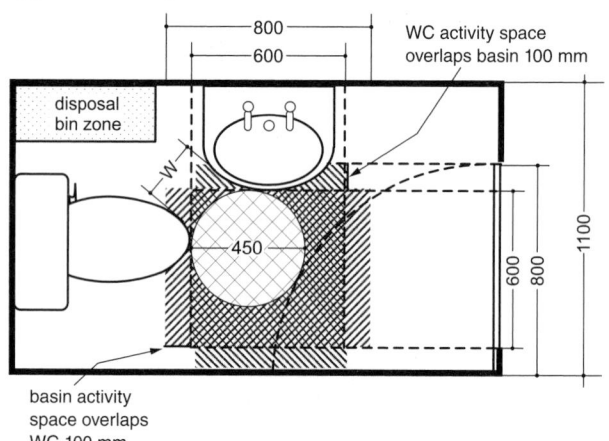

2.28 *WC and washbasin cubicle, sanitary bin zone, appliances on adjacent walls*

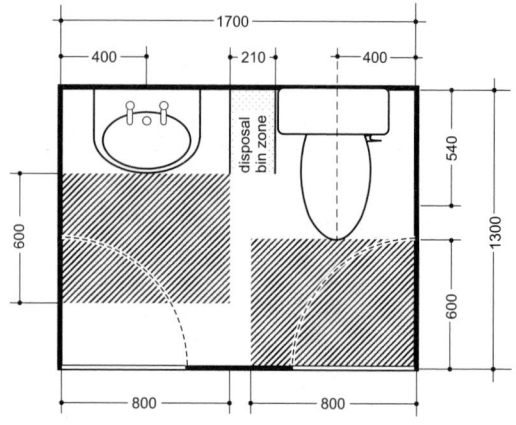

2.29 *WC and washbasin cubicle, sanitary bin zone, appliances on same wall 785 mm to 800 mm for most other situations*

Communal sanitary spaces

The communal provision of hand washing facilities is the more common and space efficient solution and the space requirements for both individual basins and larger groups are illustrated in Figures 2.30 to 2.33. Fixing heights vary from 700 mm as ideal for smaller children, 760 mm in hospitals and 785 mm to 800 mm for most other situations.

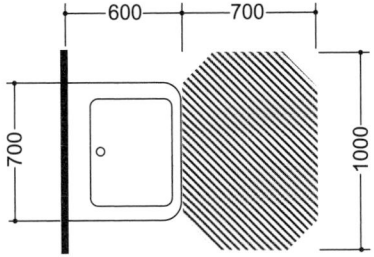

2.30 *Domestic washbasin and activity spaces*

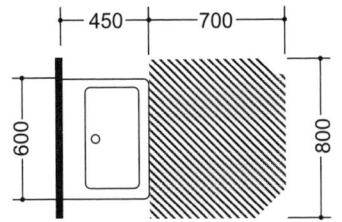

2.31 *Non-domestic washbasin and activity space*

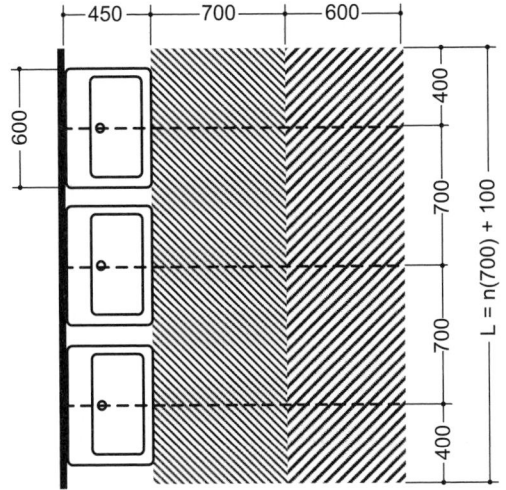

2.32 *Range of non-domestic washbasins, activity and circulation spaces*

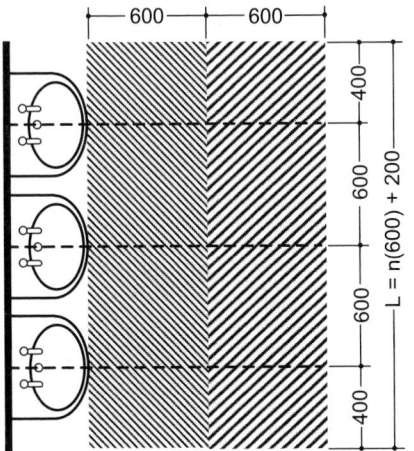

2.33 *Range of hand-rinse basins (non-recessed), activity and circulation spaces*

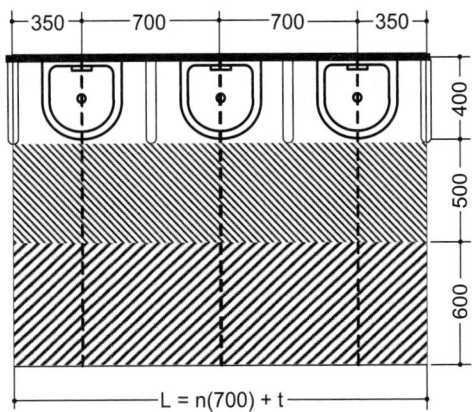

2.34 *Range of urinals, activity and circulation spaces*

Individual urinals (for male use only) are also commonly provided as groups, ranged along rows in a communal fashion. Normally fixed with the leading edge 610 m above floor level with one at 510 mm for small boys. The space requirements are illustrated in Figure 2.34.

Hand drying facilities are generally expected to be provided in close association with the washbasins (up to two washbasins per dryer) and if electrically powered to also have a towel type backup. Heights of 800 mm to 1200 mm are recommended to cover a wider range of people. Positioning within the communal space should avoid doors and obstructions whilst also taking into account traffic flows, aiming to be positioned en route from the washbasins to the exit.

5 DOMESTIC SPACE STANDARDS

There is evidence that space standards are related to health and well-being and although not part of UK national planning frameworks, space standards do currently exist in some district and local planning guidance. These include the Lifetime Homes standard that aims to ensure that new dwellings can adapt to the needs of their occupants, particularly as they change in later life and The Mayor of London's *London Housing Design Guide* (2010).

6 BIBLIOGRAPHY

Armitage Shanks (2008) *Schools Solutions . . . what works and why, an informative guide to school washroom requirements*.

British Toilet Association. Available at: www.britloos.co.uk, accessed 7 June 2014.

Building for Everyone: A Universal Design Approach, Sanitary Facilities 5, Centre for Excellence in Universal Design at the National Disability Authority, Ireland, 2012. Available at: www.universaldesign.ie/buildingforeveryone, accessed 7 June 2014.

The Building Regulations, Approved Document Part M 2010. HMSO.

Disability Discrimination Act, 2005, The Stationery Office.

Food Team – Canterbury City Council (n.d.) *Provision of toilets in commercial premises open to the public*. Available at: https://www.canterbury.gov.uk/media/253481/sanitaryaccommodation.pdf, accessed 7 June 2014.

Goodman, C. (2011) *Lifetime Homes Design Guide*. IHS BRE.

Good Loo Design Guide (2004) RIBA Enterprises.

Henry Dreyfous Associates (2002) *The Measure of Man and Woman: Human Factors in Design*. Rev. edn. John Wiley & Son.

Mayor of London (2010) *Housing Design Standards, Evidence Summary*. GLA.

Mayor of London (2010) *London Housing Design Guide*. London Development Agency.

Noble, J. (1982) *Activity and Spaces: Dimensional Data for Housing Design*. Architectural Press.

Pheasant, S. and Haslegrave, C. (2006) *Bodyspace, Anthropometry, Ergonomics and the Design of Work*, 3rd edn. Taylor & Francis.

3 People and movement

Updated by Professor Norman Wienand

Professor Norman Wienand is head of department for the Natural and Built Environment at Sheffield Hallam University

KEY POINTS:
- *Buildings are generally static but people need to move around them in many different ways*
- *Circulation strategies must be carefully considered with all classes of users, particularly people with different abilities, in mind*
- *Mechanical movement of people in buildings is highly effective but due to the high cost, must be expertly designed to achieve the requisite operating efficiency*

Contents
1. Introduction
2. Access to buildings
3. Horizontal movement within buildings
4. Vertical movement within buildings
5. Mechanical movement around buildings

1 INTRODUCTION

The aim here is to ensure that the design process is founded on the principle that all people – regardless of age, gender or ability – should be able to gain access to buildings and once inside, they should be able to use the building whether it is a home, a place of work or even if just visiting. This means that people moving about that building – its very lifeblood – should be carefully considered in the earliest stages of the design process. It therefore recognises that the overall strategy may need to include plans for access to the building and also horizontal circulation as well as vertical movement between storeys, whether mechanical or human-powered.

This chapter provides some basic design information. But it must not be used to bypass the fundamental principle that a design team should include expert input on the very complicated matter of circulation and the physical constraints, psychological aspects and long-term sustainability of the building. To illustrate this point, lift shafts in particular (a significant structural element) can be designed and arranged to serve the required population needs as part of an overall circulation strategy in the very early stages of the design process.

Figures 3.1 to 3.6, 3.8–3.13, 3.16 contain public sector information licensed under the Open Government Licence v2.0.

2 ACCESS TO BUILDINGS

2.1 Background

All people should be able to reach the main entrance of the building from the site boundary or designated car parking provision in a way that is suitable and safe. Essential aspects of the design process therefore are the slope involved, the width of access and the materials used in construction. In particular, access routes should be designed so that people can travel along them safely 'without excessive effort and without the risk of tripping or falling' (according to Part M of the Building Regulations). They should also be wide enough to accommodate people moving in different directions.

2.2 Ramps and gradients

A ramp is essentially a sloping pathway, used where a difference in levels exists between the site access point and the main building entrance. There are some clear design requirements (Figure 3.1). First among these is the concept that a slope is not a comfortable place to be for many people, particularly those with impaired mobility because of gravity pulling them down the slope. Level approaches and landings are therefore essential to allow people to stop and take breath if necessary. The length of slope between landings and the steepness (gradient) are also crucial. In addition, any design solution should recognise that some ambulant disabled people find ramps particularly difficult and prefer a stepped access.

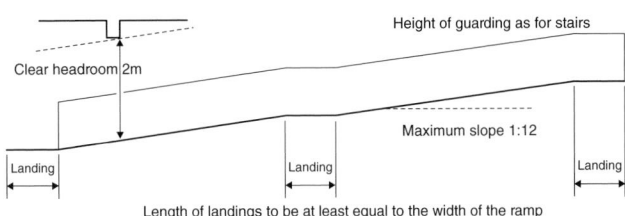

3.1 *Ramp design – essential elements are the slope, length and defined landing areas for resting (Source: Building Regulation Part K1 1.10)*

Slope gradients are normally defined in terms of their height to distance ratio. A 1:20 slope is therefore one where for every 1 metre achieved vertically, 20 metres has also been travelled horizontally. This ratio can also be expressed as a percentage where a 1:20 slope equals a 5 per cent change in height for any particular distance travelled. It can also be viewed as an angle of slope where 1:20 equals 2.86°.

For reference, a 1:1 slope (100 per cent), equal to 45°, illustrates that expressions of slope can be counterintuitive.

In designing ramps, it is usual to use the terms 'going' for the horizontal distance travelled and 'rise' for the vertical distance (terms also used in staircase design). Because of the potential difficulties outlined above, ramp gradients and lengths are strictly controlled. Part M of the Building Regulations states that no ramp should have 'a going more than 10 m or a rise more than 500 mm' between level landings. This equates to a 1:20 gradient, although slightly steeper slopes are allowed if the distance travelled is less; for a maximum going of 5 m, a gradient of 1:15 is allowed and at 2 m going it rises to 1:12. Figure 3.2 illustrates the relationship of ramp going and rise and can be used to interpolate for dimensions between the three examples.

2.3 Ramp design
- **Width:** Ramps should be a minimum of 1.8 m wide to allow people and wheelchairs to pass freely. This can be reduced to 1.5 m provided passing spaces (1.8 m) are provided (reduced to 0.9 m for domestic situations).
- **Landings:** Ramps should have level landings. These are defined as 1:60 maximum slope along their length and 1:40 slope cross-fall to allow water drainage. They should be at least 1.2 m long at the foot and head of the ramp with intermediate landings of 1.5 m. Where it is not possible to see the full length of the ramp, 1.8 m square passing space landings should be provided (reduced to 1.2 m for domestic situations).
- **Handrails:** Handrails should be provided on both sides of a ramp (see section **4.3**).
- **Kerbs:** A 100 mm minimum high kerb should be provided on any open side of a ramp and be clearly visible.
- **Surfaces:** All surfaces should be slip resistant especially when wet, and landings should be clearly noticeable and visually contrasting.

2.4 Stairs

The design of a staircase or a stepped access involves the combination of gradient and the idea of a standard footfall – the step itself. For more complex staircase design, the three-dimensional aspect becomes important where the flight of stairs has to repeat itself above the original, following on from one storey to another so that maintaining sufficient headroom is a primary concern.

2.5 Step design

One major advantage of steps over ramps is that while ramps offer a sloping surface that can be difficult for many, steps essentially offer a level landing at each step. It is worth noting that a single step rise is not recommended under most circumstances.

As with ramp design, steps have a going and a rise, but in this case it exists for each individual step as well as the overall flight. Traditionally, where space was short, steps were designed with a 'nosing' (Figure 3.3) which for any particular going, allowed a larger space for the footfall. The going is measured from the nosing to nosing but the footfall is in effect the going plus the nosing. For many ambulant disabled or poor sighted people the nosing can present a real hazard as it can catch the toe of the foot when going forward. Poorly sighted people may understandably wish to push their foot to the back of each step to ensure that they are totally secure.

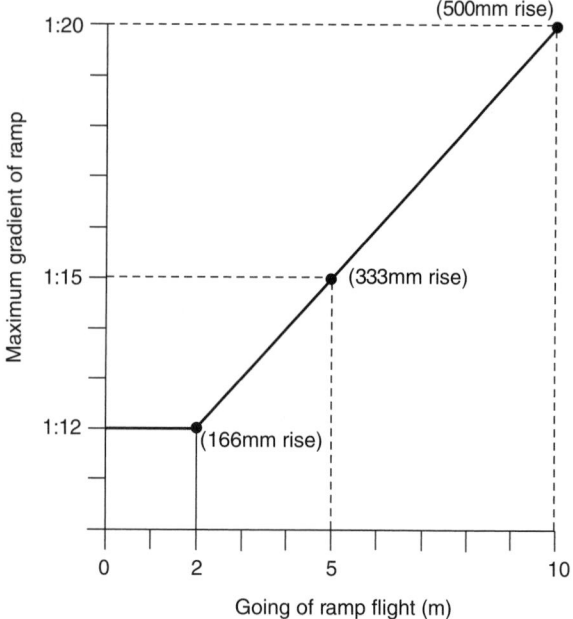

3.2 *Slope design – various permutations can be obtained from this diagram across the permissible range (Source: Building Regulation Part K1 2.1)*

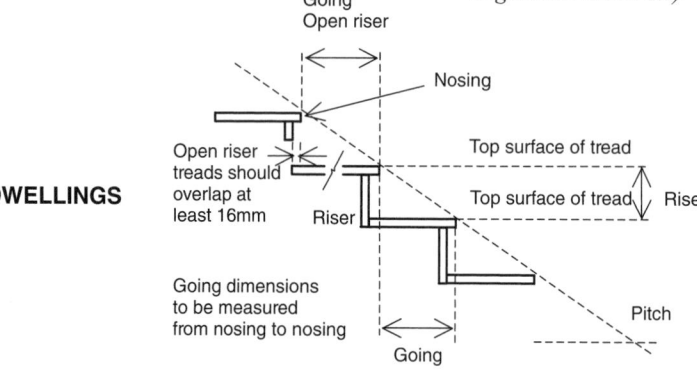

Note: Two examples of tread profiles have been shown together for illustrative purposes only

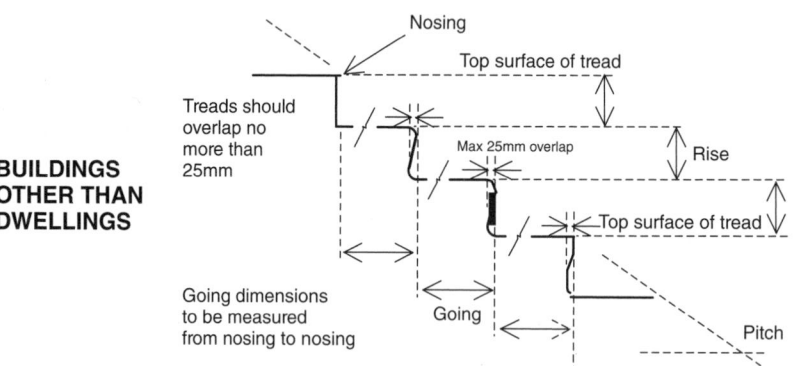

Note: Four examples of tread profiles have been shown together for illustrative purposes only

3.3 *Step design – essential elements are the rise, the going and the pitch. See section 4.2 for more on pitch calculation (Source: Building Regulation Part K1 1.1)*

2.6 External stepped access design

- **Width:** Access stairs should be no less than 1.2 m wide (reduced to 0.9 m for domestic situations).
- **Treads**: Treads should be consistent throughout the flight with a rise of between 150 mm and 170 mm and with a going of between 280 mm and 450 mm (reduced to between 75 mm and 150 mm rise with a minimum going of 280 mm in domestic situations). There should be no open risers.

- **Landings:** Access stairs should have landings provided not less than 1.2 m wide, for every 12 risers for a going of less than 350 mm or 18 risers if the going is more than 350 mm (total of 1.8 m rise in domestic situations). There should be at least a 1.2 m level approach at the foot and head of the stair with intermediate landings also of 1.2 m (reduced to 0.9 m for domestic situations).
- **Handrails:** Handrails should be provided on both sides (see Figure 3.4). In the case of stair access that is wider than the minimum, additional

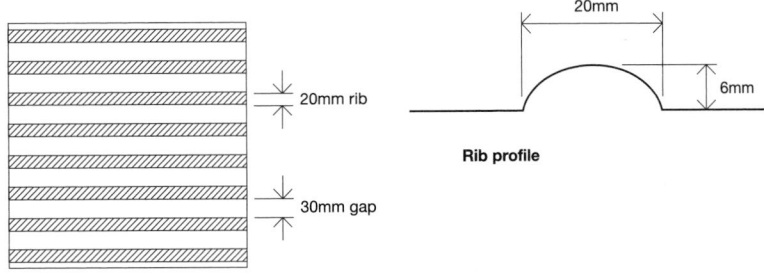

'Corduroy' hazard warning surface (with 8mm ribs)

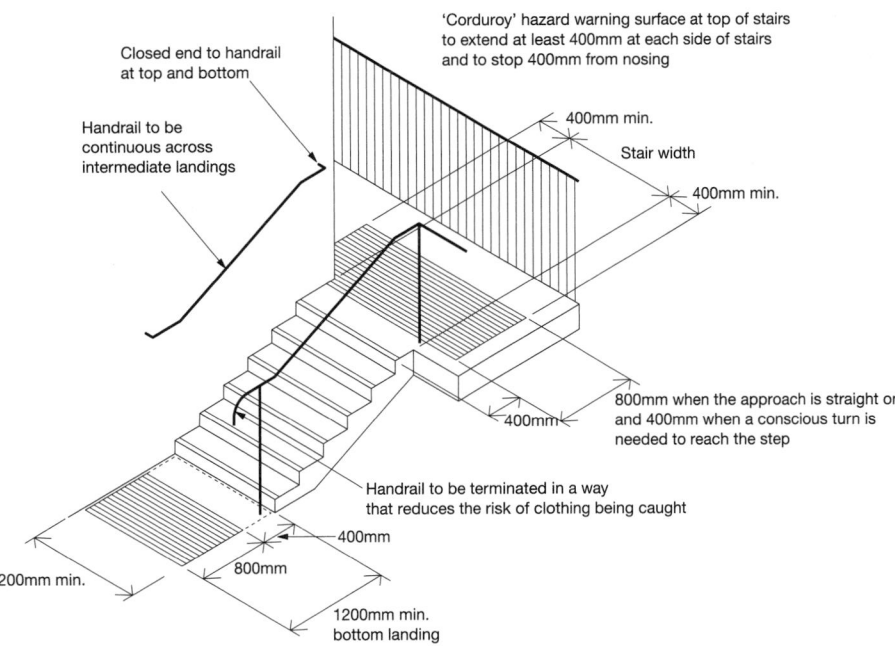

3.4 *Stepped access design – essential elements are the surfaces, landings and handrails (Source: Building Regulation Part M Diagram 4)*

handrails are required along the centre line to ensure that the effective width of access is not less than 1.0 m, or more than 1.8 m wide.

- **Surfaces:** External stepped access routes need to have warning surfaces provided. These are commonly termed a corduroy hazard warning strip and provide a clearly identifiable change in surface condition that warns of an approaching change in level. A 55 mm wide visually contrasting material is also required on both the tread and riser of each step.

2.7 Access doors

Unless designing main (or alternative access) entrance doors it is important to consider all potential users. Wheelchair users will have certain requirements, as will the poorly sighted or those with limited strength. For example, a manually operated self-closing door set with sufficient power to close against normal wind speeds will probably be beyond the strength capacity of most wheelchair users or those with limited strength.

Specifically, this limit is exceeded when 'the opening force at leading edge of the door is not more than 30N at the leading edge from 0° (the door in the closed position) to 30° open, and not more than 22.5N at the leading edge from 30° to 60° of the opening cycle' (from Building Regulations Part M 2.17 paragraph a). Revolving doors are not considered accessible because of the difficulties they create for a whole host of potential users.

Preferences:

- Glazed doors allow people to see potential obstacles and others approaching, but must also be made visually noticeable for the poorly sighted.
- Powered sliding doors do not waste the space associated with the arc of a door swing, and automatic opening sliding doors do not require access to a manual opening device.

- An opening and closing system operated by remote sensors requires no contact with the door.

2.8 Door width

To take account of different door styles and support systems, the 'effective clear width' is referred to as it states the total width of opening available that is devoid of any obstructions caused by such items as door handles, hinges or limited turning capacity. Unpowered access doors should also have a minimum of 300 mm extra unobstructed space alongside the operating latch to allow for wheelchair approach.

Figure 3.5 provides the minimum effective door widths as defined by Part M of the Building Regulations.

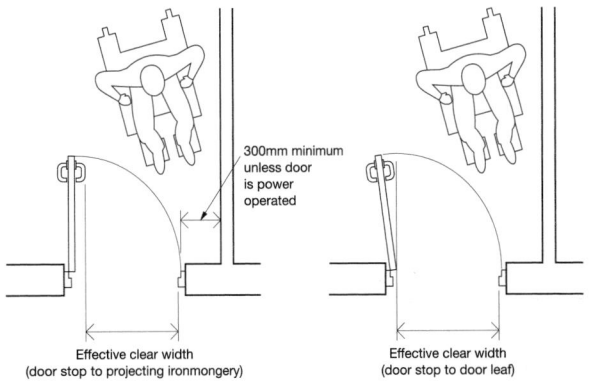

3.5 *Effective door width – wheelchair users need more space to access the opening controls (Source: Building Regulation Part M Diagram 9)*

3 HORIZONTAL MOVEMENT WITHIN BUILDINGS

3.1 Entrance lobbies

Providing a lobby space at the entrance to a building makes sense in many ways. Environmentally, it can limit uncontrolled air movement, reducing heat loss and draughts. It can also provide a space to shed rainwater to avoid the associated slip hazard further in the building, and it can also provide transitional lighting levels.

3.2 Entrance lobby design

- **Size:** The lobby should be large enough to allow a wheelchair user (accompanied) or a parent with a pushchair to negotiate the doors at either end, clear of the opening arc of the other door, see Figure 3.6. For a lobby length, this means adding 1570 mm to the space created by the arcs. For width, it is the effective clear door width plus 300 mm to allow wheelchair access to the operating system.
- **Surfaces:** Floor surfaces to lobbies should be level without changes in surface that may constitute a trip hazard. They should also assist in the removal of rainwater but without impeding the movement of pushchairs and wheelchairs. Coir matting, for example, is not suitable.

3.3 Corridors

The provision of corridors within buildings will aim to satisfy many different requirements. To satisfy inclusive design principles, minimum sizes and surface material conditions should be expected for general horizontal movement around a building. For other, non-standard access, a more ergonomic approach can be employed.

3.4 Inclusive corridor design

- **Width:** The corridor should be large enough to allow wheelchair users (accompanied) or a parent with a pushchair to move freely. Localised narrowing is acceptable provided the basic principle is not compromised. A minimum unobstructed width of 1200 mm is required with 1800 mm square passing places at intervals.
- **Surfaces:** Floor surfaces to corridors should be level (see Figure 3.2) with a non-slip surface without patterns that may be mistaken for stairs. There should be sufficient contrast between the floor, wall and ceiling to assist people with visual impairment, together with good lighting levels.

For non-standard corridor widths Figure 3.7a–e gives some indication of what can be used.

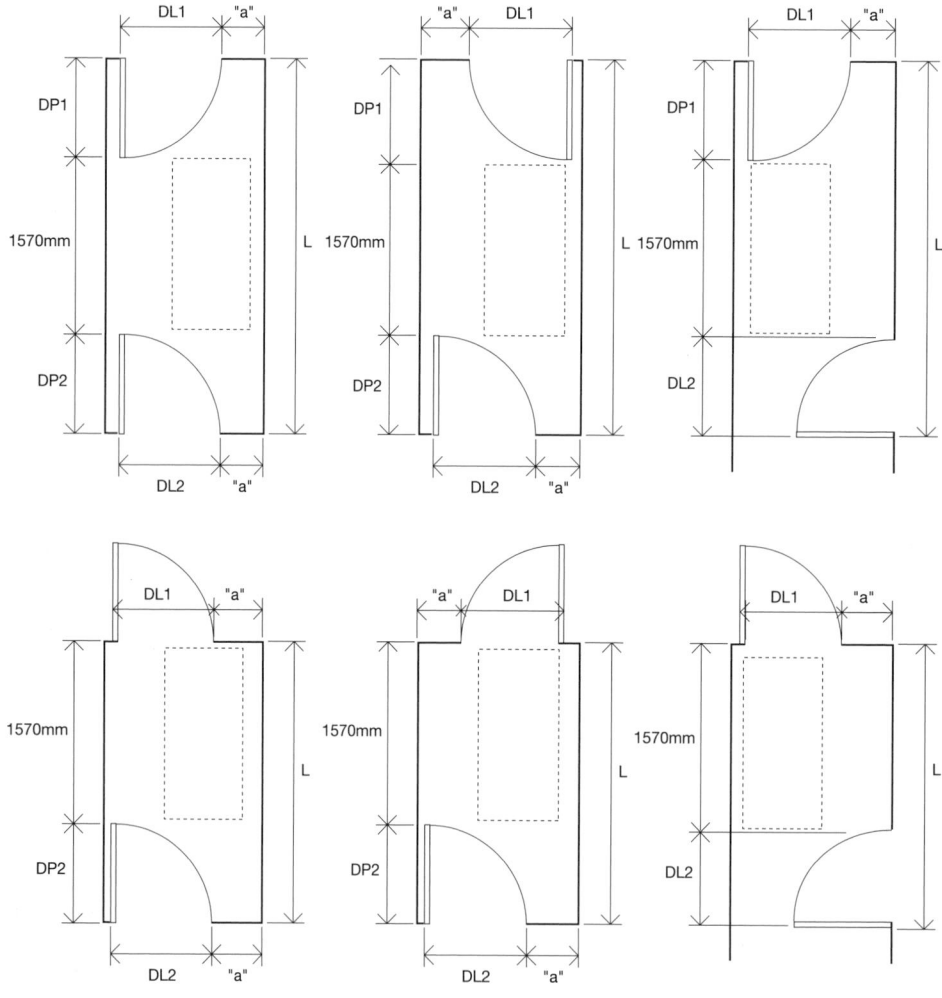

DL1 and DL2 = door leaf dimensions of the doors to the lobby
DP1 and DP2 = door projection into the lobby (normally door leaf size)
L = minimum length of lobby, or length up to door leaf for side entry lobby
"a" = at least 300mm wheelchair access space (can be increased to reduce L)
1570mm = length of occupied wheelchair with a companion pushing (or a large scooter)

NB: For every 100mm increase above 300mm in the dimension "a" (which gives a greater overlap of the wheelchair footprint over the door swing), there can be a corresponding reduction of 100mm in the dimension L, up to a maximum of 600mm reduction.

3.6 *Lobby design with single doors – essential element is adequate space to manoeuvre (Source: Building Regulation Part K1 1.10)*

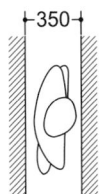

3.7a *Edging width: suitable for short distances or occasional use*

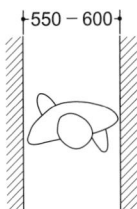

3.7b *One person width (750 clearance would give comfort for various postures)*

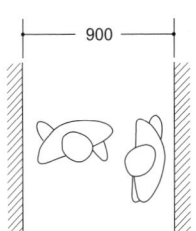

3.7c *Normally used by one person, but occasional passing required*

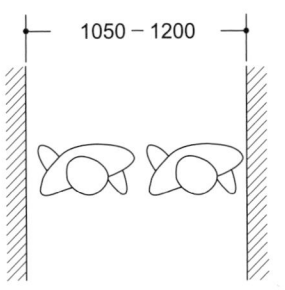

3.7d *Two people use in same direction*

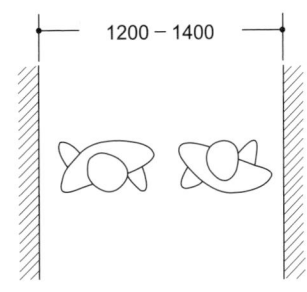

3.7e *Two people passing*

3.5 Corridor widths

Corridor handling capacity (C$_c$) in people per minute can be calculated using:

$$C_c = 60 \, v \, D \, W$$

where: v is the average pedestrian speed (m/s)
D is the average pedestrian density (people per m^2)
W is the corridor width (m)

Free flow design: D = 0.3 people per m^2 and v = 1.0 to 1.3 m/s

Full flow design: D = 1.4 people per m^2 and v = 0.6 to 0.8 m/s

Note: People tend to wander about in corridors

4 VERTICAL MOVEMENT WITHIN BUILDINGS

4.1 Internal stairs
Internal stairs come in three basic forms:

- private stairs as would be found in domestic situations
- utility stairs that cover escape and maintenance requirements
- general access stairs that cover most of the remaining circumstances.

A fourth version includes certain assembly buildings such as sports stadia, theatres or cinemas where the access stairs form part of the slant of the floor where seating is designed to maximise sightlines for spectators. In these cases, the stairs need to follow those inclines so the resulting designs are very project specific. However, there are specific Building Regulations covering these instances and reference should be made to Part K1, Section 1.4 for further information and guidance.

4.2 Stair pitch
In the case of private stairs, the maximum pitch is 42°. The pitch or angle of the stair is not designated as a gradient as in the case of ramps, but as an angle derived from an arithmetic computation of the rise and going.
From basic trigonometry:

*Tangent Function: tan (θ) = **Opposite/Adjacent***

where θ is the angle we require, *opposite* is the rise and *adjacent*, the going, we can derive:

Stair pitch (θ) = tan^{-1} (rise/going)

Or, using a specific example, where the rise is 170 mm and the going is 250 mm:

tan^{-1} (170/250) = 34.2°

A simpler rule of thumb for normal stairs (based on the approximate adult stride on a stair) suggests that the going plus twice the rise should fall between 550 mm and 700 mm:

Going + (2 × rise) = 550 mm to 700 mm

Or, using the same example where the rise is 170 mm and the going is 250 mm:

250 + (2 × 170) = 590 mm

For the maximum and minimum rise and goings, refer to Table I but it is also worth noting that for schools, the recommended rise is 150 mm with a going of 280 mm.

Table I Rise and going
The range of permissible design dimensions for common stairs.

	Rise (mm)		Going (mm)	
	Minimum	Maximum	Minimum	Maximum
Private stairs	150	220	220	300
Utility stairs	150	190	250	400
General access stairs	150	170	250	400

Source: Part K

Under certain limited domestic circumstances, an alternating stair can be used (Figure 3.8). In order to save space and increase the pitch to well over the standard 42°, these stairs maintain the minimum going of 220 mm and the maximum rise of 220 mm but only for each individual footfall. These stairs require people to walk up taking each step alternatively, so someone who may have to negotiate one step at a time for both feet would have to zigzag up the stair. Equally, turning around halfway up can be problematic, requiring both feet on one step to avoid encountering a double rise going down.

4.3 Internal stair design
- **Width:** Stairs should not be less than 1.2 m wide. (There is no minimum in domestic situations but 850 mm is suggested with 600 mm when the stair is serving only one room.)
- **Treads:** Treads should be consistent throughout the flight with a rise and going as shown in Table I. There should be no open risers (except in domestic situations where they are constructed

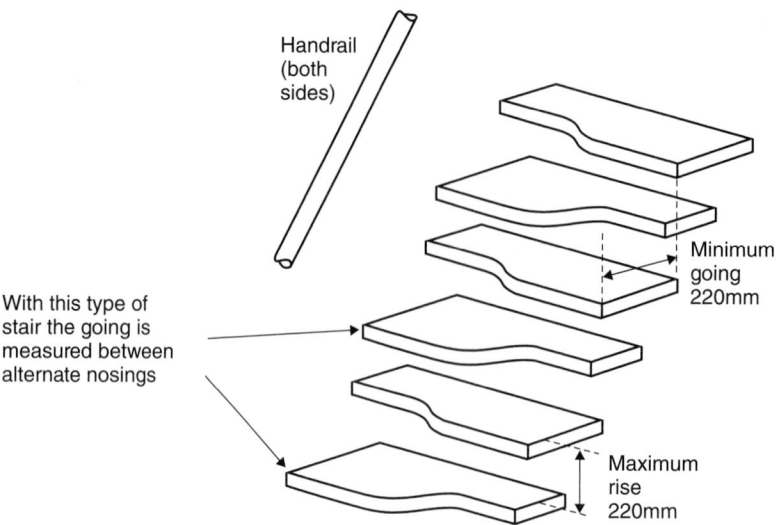

3.8 *Alternating stair tread layout (Source: Building Regulation K1 1.10)*

with a minimum 16 mm overhang and a 100 mm diameter sphere cannot pass through the risers). For tapered treads, the standard design principles should still be adhered to but with the going measured at the middle of the stair, subject to a minimum 50 mm tread at the narrow end (Figure 3.9).

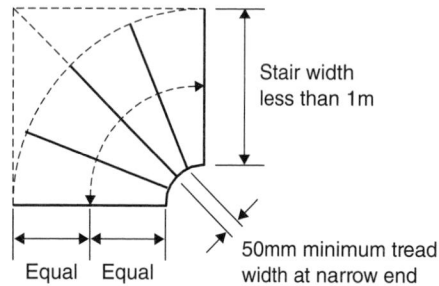

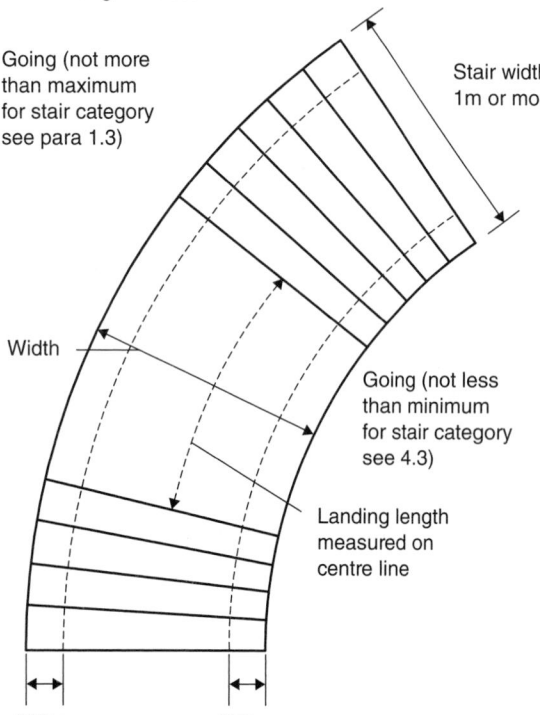

Measure going at centre of tread; measure from curved stair line, even when tread is in rectangular closure

3.9 *Curved staircase and tapering treads – essential elements are the going and the minimum tread size (Source: Building Regulation Part K1 1.9)*

- **Landings:** Stairs should have landings provided not less than 1.2 m long, for every 16 risers in the case of a utility stair and for every 12 risers for general access stairs (Figure 3.10). There should be at least a 1.2 m level approach at the foot and head of the stair with intermediate landings also of 1.2 m (reduced to the stair width with 400 mm unobstructed by door openings for domestic situations).
- **Handrails:** Handrails should be provided on both sides (see Figure 3.3). In the case of general access stairs that are wider than the minimum, additional handrails are required to ensure that the effective width of access is not less than 1.0 m or more than 2.0 m wide.
- **Headroom:** A minimum of 2000 mm clear headroom should be provided at all landings and access points as well as above the pitch line, measured at the outer limit of each going (Figure 3.11).

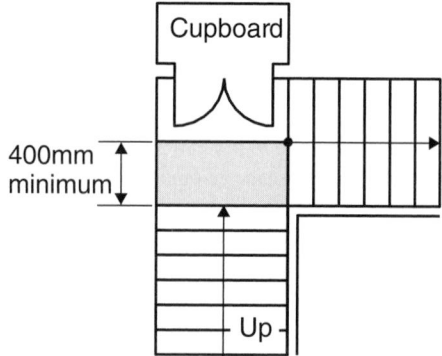

3.10 *Staircase landings (Source: Building Regulation Part K1 1.7)*

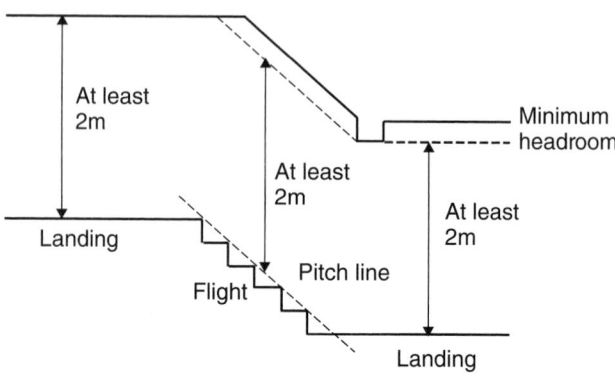

3.11 *Staircase headroom – essential elements are the points at which it is measured (Source: Building Regulation Part K1 1.3)*

4.4 Staircase handling capacity

Staircase handling capacity (C_s) in people per minute can be calculated using:

$$C_s = 0.83\,(60\,v\,D\,W)$$

where: v is the average pedestrian speed (m/s)

D is the average pedestrian density (people per m²)

W is the corridor width (m)

Free flow design: D = 0.6 people per m² and v = 0.6 to 0.8 m/s

Full flow design: D = 2.0 people per m² and v = 0.6 to 0.8 m/s

---

Note: People tend to walk in an orderly fashion on stairs.

4.5 Handrails

The design of handrails needs to take account of the principle that all people, regardless of age, gender or ability should be able to use them. They could in certain circumstances provide a physical aid to assist ambulant disabled in hauling themselves upward and therefore be subject to significant loading. They should also provide a distinctive visual contrast to assist in location.

In most circumstances, handrails should be fixed between 900 mm and 1100 mm above the floor or pitch line (see Figure 3.12) and subject to the design requirements set out in Figure 3.13.

4.6 Guarding

Handrails and stair guarding serve distinctly different purposes although they can also be combined into one element. Where handrails, usually wall mounted, are used to assist in negotiating stairs as a handhold, stair guarding is there to prevent people falling over an exposed edge of the stair; banisters serve both purposes.

In the case of staircase design, guarding should be provided to the same height requirements as the associated handrails when there is a drop of more than 600 mm.

Building Regulation Part K1 requires that in buildings that will be used by children under five, additional conditions come into force. Inclusive design principles suggest that this should include all buildings where children under five may visit, thereby including almost all buildings.

These additional yet very sensible requirements suggest that guarding should be designed to accomplish the following:

- Prevent children being held fast by the guarding.
- Ensure that a 100 mm sphere cannot pass through any openings in the guarding.
- Prevent children from readily being able to climb the guarding.

5 MECHANICAL MOVEMENT WITHIN BUILDINGS

5.1 Introduction

Mechanical devices for moving people around buildings are now essential aspects of all large building design and they involve significant energy demands and safety backups for when energy supplies are restricted. Before reliable and safe systems were produced, the effective height of buildings was restricted to the number of storeys individuals would be happy to walk up. It is worth noting that mechanical systems are often found to be a compromise between moving small number of people very quickly (with a low overall population movement) and moving large numbers of people more slowly (with high overall population movement).

5.2 Escalators

Escalators are essentially moving staircases but where the people on them are expected to remain standing on one step whilst the step itself moves. For this reason, the rise and going are not governed by the same criteria as normal stairs. It is also why climbing a static escalator is more difficult than conventional stairs.

- Escalators typically operate at speeds of 0.5 m/s to 0.65 m/s (0.75 m/s in London Underground).
- Escalators are normally constructed at 30° incline.
- People walk up stairs typically at 0.5 m/s.
- Depending on the design (speeds and width), escalators can move more than 10 000 people per hour.

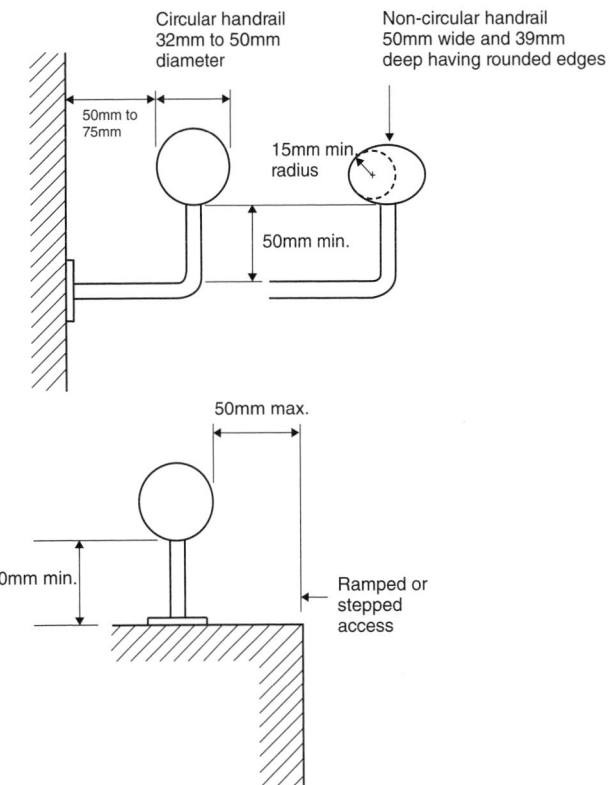

3.13 *Handrail design – essential elements are those related to grip and structural integrity (Source: Building Regulation Part K1 1.13)*

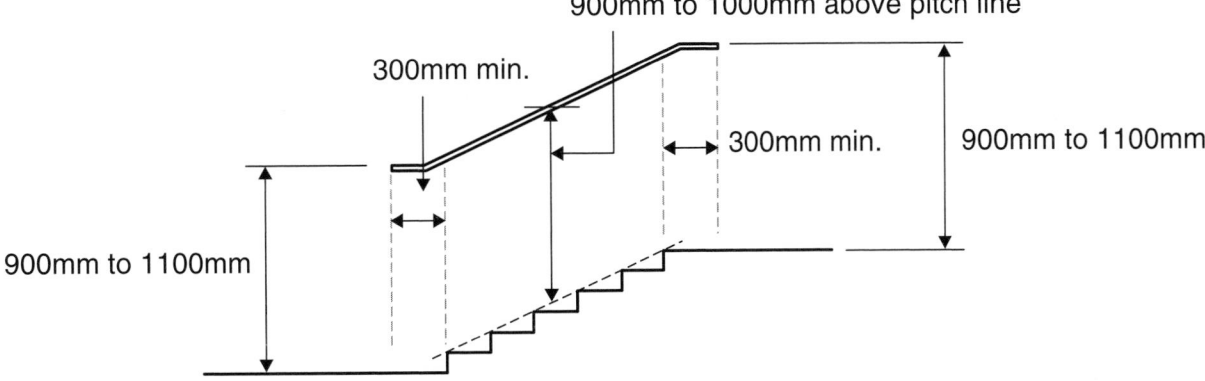

3.12 *Handrail positioning – essential elements are the dimensions and structural integrity (Source: Building Regulation Part K1 1.12)*

The standard shape of an escalator is provided by a steel truss that supplies the framework to support the moving staircase between storeys (see Figure 3.14). The individual steps in an escalator are roughly triangular in section and connected to two different guiding tracks that loop around the system and govern the relative position of each step as well as the movement. One track is the driving mechanism (chain) where the leading edge of the step is connected on each side and the step is essentially pulled around the loop in this way. The lower edge simply follows with two wheels located in a guiding track. This follows the main drive chain but by altering the relative position of the track to the drive chain, the position of each step is changed. By altering the space between the two loops, the steps are kept horizontal throughout the journey and as the pitch flattens at the top and bottom, they fold onto each other. This process is assisted by a series of grooves where each step fits together with the next in a tongue and groove alignment.

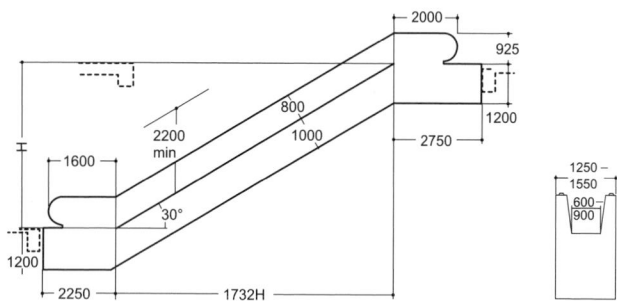

3.14 *Dimensions of 30° escalator, elevation and section*

The movement of an escalator is powered by an electric motor housed within the truss and geared to move the drive chain and the handrail as required keeping it aligned with the steps. The handrail is simply a synthetic rubber conveyer belt looped around a similar path but off set from the main step drive mechanism.

Design and construction considerations:

- Clear access areas should be provided equal to twice the escalator tread width in length and the escalator tread width plus 100 mm either side in overall width.
- Minimum clear headroom of 2130 mm (measured vertically from the pitch line) should be maintained across the whole of the system.
- The handrail should have 100 mm clearance horizontally and 25 mm clearance vertically from any adjacent surfaces.

- All connecting floor surfaces should be continuous with any abrupt change in level limited to a maximum of 6 mm.

(Source: Kone's Escalators and Autowalks Planning Guide, page 49, Section 6.2 parts A to D)

Escalator handling capacity (C_e) in people per minute can be calculated using:

$$C_e = 60\,(V\,k\,s)$$

where: V is the speed along the incline (m/s)

k is the average density of people (people per step)

s is the number of steps per metre (m) e.g. for a 400 mm step rise, $s = 2.5$

Step density is theoretically related to escalator width where:

600 mm wide $k = 1.0$
800 mm wide $k = 1.5$
1000 mm wide $k = 2.0$

People tend not to fill escalator stairs to capacity, so use half these values.

An example from Table II indicates a 1000 mm wide step at 0.50 m/s will carry 150 people per minute, in reality this should be assumed to be 75 people per minute or 4500 people per hour.

Table II Escalator design

Essential elements to consider are the step size, the speed and the degree of occupancy on each step.

Speed	1000mm Step width People per minute		800mm Step width People per minute		600mm Step width People per minute	
	Theory	Practice	Theory	Practice	Theory	Practice
0.50 m/s	150	75	113	57	75	38
0.65 m/s	195	98	146	73	98	49
0.75 m/s	225	113	169	85	113	57

(Source: Barney, 2003, p. 13, Table 1.8)

5.3 Moving walkways

Moving walkways (or a mechanised passenger conveyor system) can be assumed to have the same design and performance characteristics as escalators, moving similar amounts of people and subject to similar speed and operating mechanics (Figure 3.15). They generally come in two forms. The pallet variety is simply a flat escalator with individual

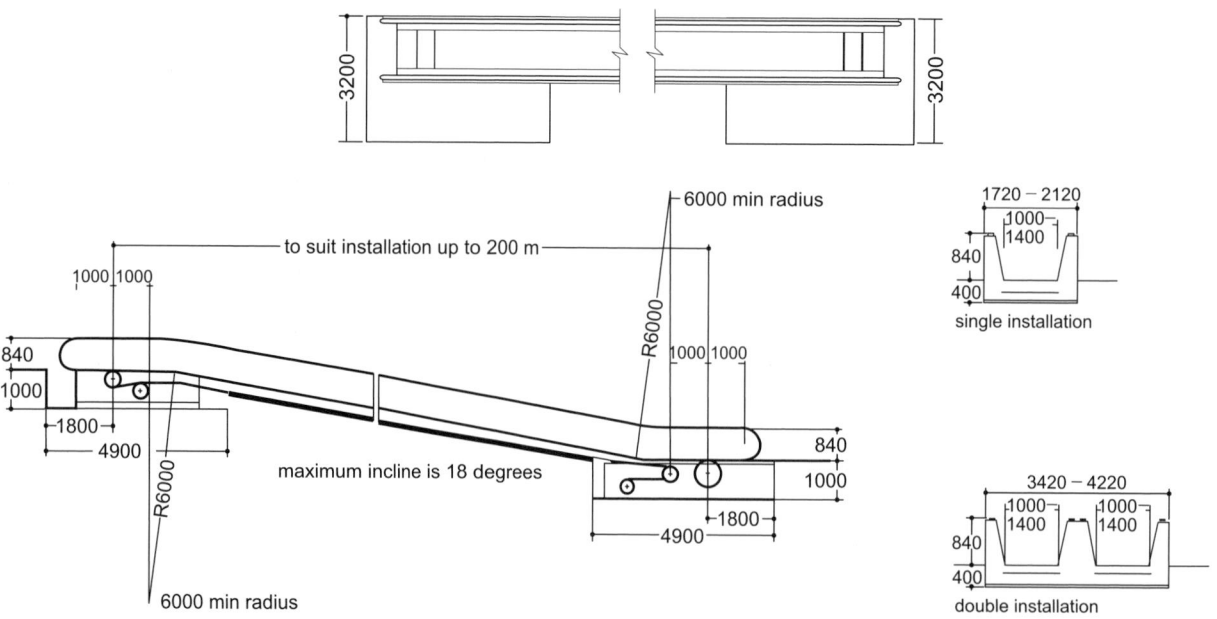

3.15 *A one-speed mechanised passenger conveyor system, may be flat, or up to 12° for prams, shopping trolleys, etc., or up to 15° for special installations. Other systems available permit 'valley' and 'hill' longitudinal profiles; also surface laying of conveyor on drive motor on existing floors. Capacity of system shown is 7200 persons per hour. Systems are available up to 8000 pph. Speed range is 0.45–0.6 m/s. Tread widths, 1000–1400 mm*

steps (pallets) running horizontally (or inclined as required). These do have a potential advantage due to the interconnection provided by extended grooves between each step, allowing the speed to be varied over the journey. The grooves close up at lower embarking and disembarking speeds but increase during the middle higher speed portion of the journey. The second form has a continuous conveyor belt constructed of metal belts or rubber walkways running over rollers.

5.4 Lifts

In most circumstances, a passenger lift is the most suitable method of vertical transportation within buildings. Because of their reliance on a power source they should always also have a fire protected stair access provided as well. They also come in a wide range of sizes from a simple two storey hydraulic lift to the sophisticated operating systems needed in 100 storey skyscrapers. A lift car size of 2000 mm wide by 1400 mm deep will provide adequate space for any wheelchair and a number of other users although Figure 3.16 illustrates the minimum size required.

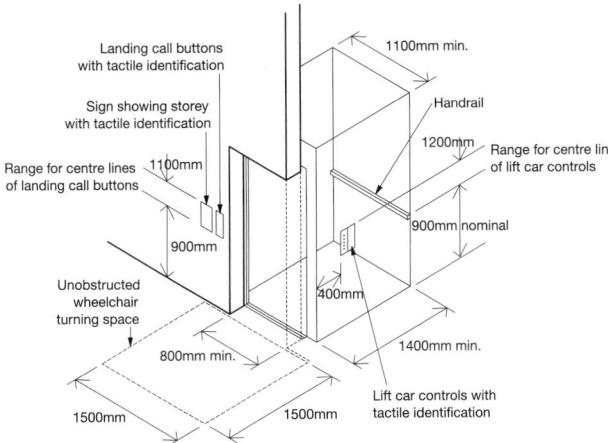

3.16 *Lift design – key minimum dimensions (Source: Building Regulation Part M Diagram 11)*

A well-designed passenger lift provision will include most, if not all, of the inclusive design principles. However in certain refurbishment situations, a full scale lift provision is not possible and in those cases, specific wheelchair platform stairlift or lifting platform may be suitable. Wheelchair platform stairlifts differ from lifting platforms in that they take a single wheelchair up a flight of stairs by means of a mechanical rail and traction device. Lifting platforms by contrast raise a platform that can accommodate a wheelchair plus attendant or partially sighted people over a certain vertical distance. These can be relatively short distances such as negotiating a change in level or more fully enclosed journeys between storeys.

5.5 Wheelchair platform stairlifts and lifting platforms

Where a platform stairlift is installed, the minimum stair widths need to be increased to accommodate the extra width required by the stairlift (Figure 3.17). They also require a platform of 800 mm wide and 1250 mm deep and are limited to a speed of 0.15 m/s. In addition, they should also have controls that restrict usage to those in need and authorised to do so. These controls should include a 'continuous pressure' control device where if the pressure is released, the lift comes to a halt.

5.6 Lifting platforms

Lifting platforms, like stairlifts, are not replacements for a good passenger lift service and therefore are also not ideal. Both require the continuous pressure control device which can be too strenuous for some users to maintain. Lifting platforms have the same speed restriction and minimum platform size for single wheelchair users. In addition, however, they are also restricted to a 2000 mm travel if they are not enclosed. Where they are enclosed, the minimum

dimensions increase to 900 mm wide and 1400 mm deep and if the wheelchair user has an attendant, to 1100 mm wide and 1400 mm deep.

5.7 Hydraulic lifts

These lifts appear the same as any other standard lift design in that the most apparent aspect, the lift car, would not be any different. The difference lies in the driving mechanism (Figure 3.18). Hydraulic lifts use a hydraulic ram to move the lift car between storeys and because it consists of a piston that is forced upwards by a fluid pumping system (usually oil) they are limited to the structural and height restrictions of the piston. Some use a hole in the ground to house the piston when fully descended, others use telescopic pistons. The mechanism is relatively simple in that an electrically operated pump forces the fluid from a reservoir into the piston to ascend and a valve allows and controls the returning oil when descending. Even if the reservoir were to fail, the action of having to force the oil back through the system means that hydraulic lifts would return to ground level fairly slowly and therefore also safely.

In action, as the ascending lift car approaches the correct floor, a control system gradually reduces the pumping speed. At each floor, with the pump off, the oil in the cylinder cannot flow back through the pump, and with the valve closed the car is supported by the full piston. To descend, the control system opens the valve so that the oil in the cylinder can return to the reservoir. It is the weight of the car and contents that push down on the piston driving the oil back into the reservoir. To stop the car at a lower floor, the control system simply closes the valve.

Although a very safe mechanism, hydraulic lifts are limited in scope because of the length of pistons required and also because they are relatively energy intensive when compared with the alternative traction system. In raising a lift car and its contents, a hydraulic system has to produce all of the required power via the pump to overcome the force of gravity for the full weight of the lift car and load. In a traction system, the weight of the lift car is balanced by a counterweight so that moving only the difference in weights requires power.

5.8 Traction lifts

The most common design for lifts is the traction variety where the lift car is raised and lowered by steel wire ropes attached to the car and looped around a **sheave**. In effect a pulley, the sheave has grooves around the edge, designed and shaped to grip the ropes so that a rotating sheave moves the ropes simply because of the friction between the two. In higher speed lifts, the ropes are wrapped around the sheave twice to provide extra friction. A traction lift therefore works by an electric motor turning the sheave directly (or via a gearing system), either one way or another to ascend or descend.

The great advantage of traction lifts is that the ropes are also connected to a counterweight on the other side of the sheave. The counterweight is normally designed to balance the lift car at 40 per cent capacity, considered to be the average load in use. When loaded equally like this, the sheave motor has little work to do in moving the lift up or down. In addition to guide rails in the lift shaft, traction lifts usually locate the sheave, motor and control system in a machine room above the lift shaft, adding to the overall height required as well as the overall structural loading on the building (Figure 3.19).

The safety of traction systems depends on two fundamental principles. Firstly, the fear that a rope may snap or become disconnected is overcome by using multiple ropes, typically four to eight wound steel wire ropes where each rope individually can support the lift car. Secondly, they will also use a braking system. Physical braking systems typically use a governor and sprung flyweights that activate when the lift is travelling too fast and then through linkages bring the braking system into operation. Electromagnetic braking systems keep the brakes open in normal operation so that a loss of power would trigger them. They can also be used as part

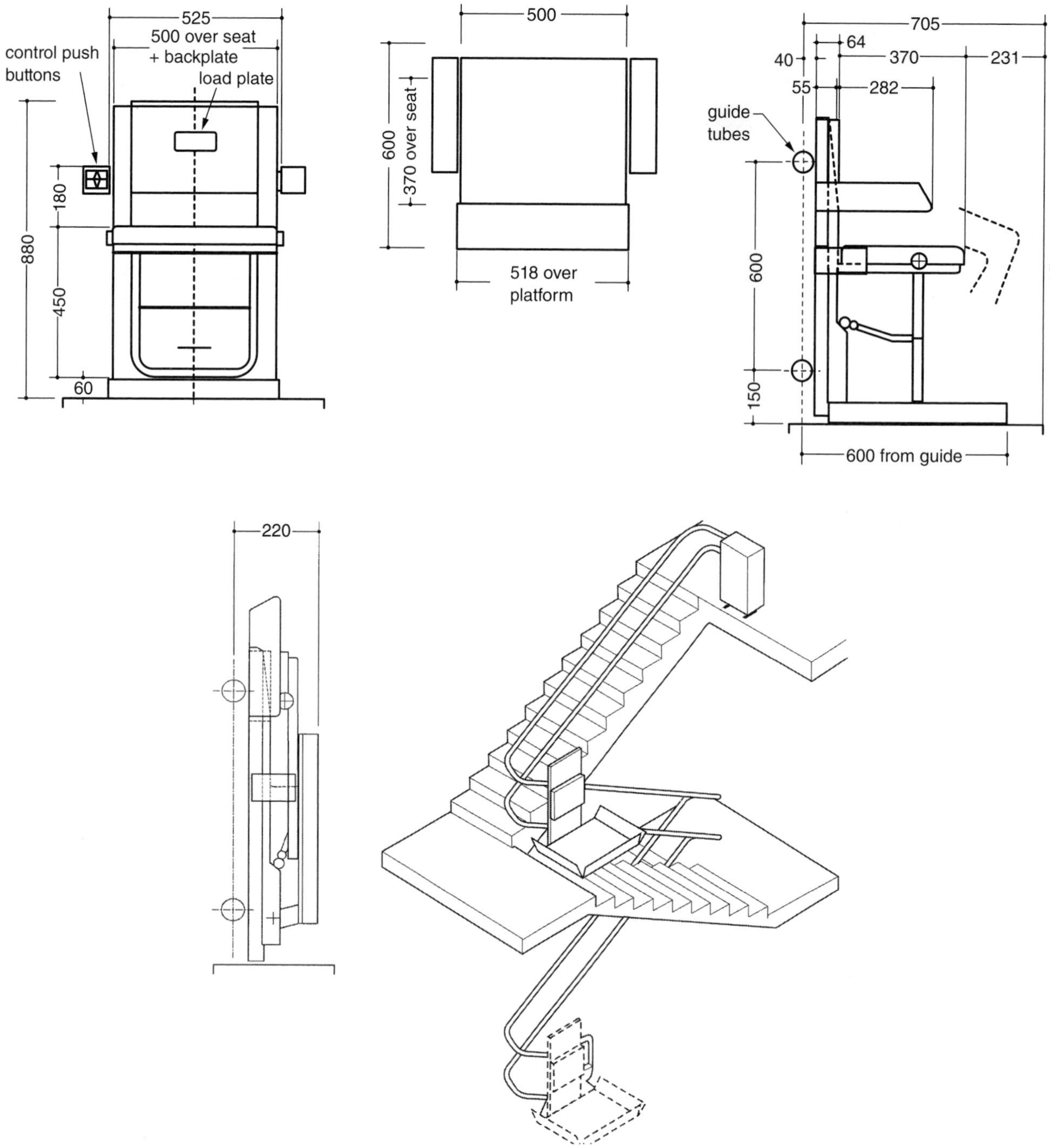

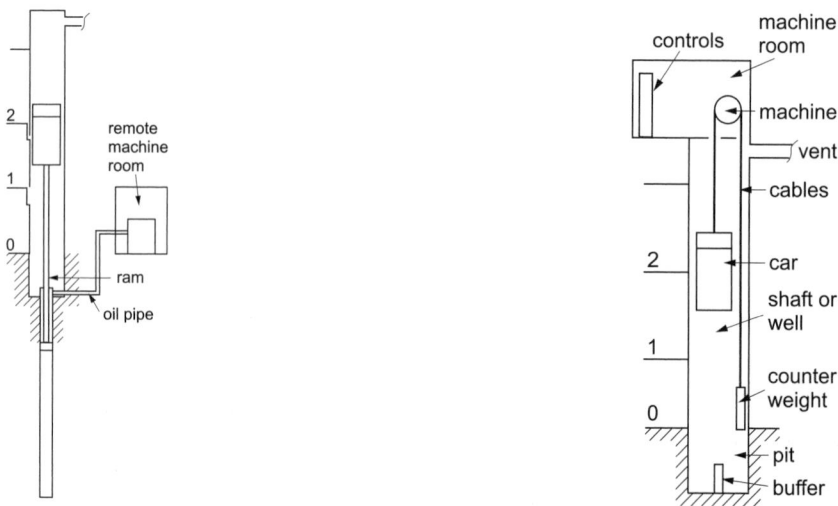

3.17 *Details of stair lift for wheelchair, or for seated passenger. (Courtesy of Gimson Stairlifts Ltd)*

3.18 *Schematic diagram of a direct-acting hydraulic lift with remote machine room*

3.19 *Schematic diagram of a conventional electric traction lift with high-level machine room*

of the control system at each stop. In addition to overrun braking protection at the top and bottom of shafts, a heavy-duty piston shock absorber system at the bottom will cushion a runaway car's landing.

- Gearless traction lifts – the industry standard – typically operate at speeds in excess of 2.5 m/s.
- Geared traction lifts – more efficient – typically operated at speeds between 1.75 and 2.5 m/s (Otis 2011).

5.9 Design of lift systems
The design of lift systems is a complicated and in most instances, a specialist operation. This is because of the very many parameters involved including such things as the number of lifts available, the populations being served, usage patterns (peak flows), number of storeys being served and also the quality of the service required, to name just a few. Specialist design services will include evaluation of 'round trip times', passenger demands, limitations and assumptions around peak traffic flows as well as car size, number and location, clearly well beyond the scope of this chapter. Yet there is some basic information that is useful and can form the basis of ongoing design work.

5.10 Handling capacity of lifts
It is important to recognise that lifts provide a different service to that of stairs and escalators discussed previously. Where escalators can carry large amounts of people relatively slowly, lifts carry much smaller amounts much more quickly.

- A previous example showed a relatively small 1000 mm wide escalator at 0.50 m/s carrying 75 people per minute or 4500 people per hour.
- The most efficient group of 8 lifts serving 14 floors at full 21 person capacity can only handle 50 people per minute or 3000 people per hour.
- Take that down to 3 lifts in 8 storeys at 10 person capacity and the figure reduces to 16 people per minute or 960 people per hour.

5.11 Location and number of cars
The most efficient design layout for lift lobbies is in a cul-de-sac layout as indicated in Figures 3.20 and 3.21 as it provides the shortest distance from any waiting position; it also provides the best view of all lifts in operation and, most importantly, it avoids obstruction by passers-by.

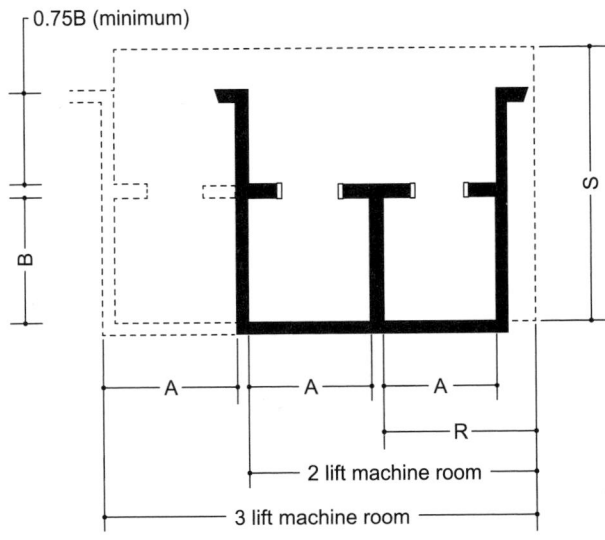

3.20 *Plan of recessed lobby and machine room for multi-lift installation – dimensions refer to the values in Table IV*

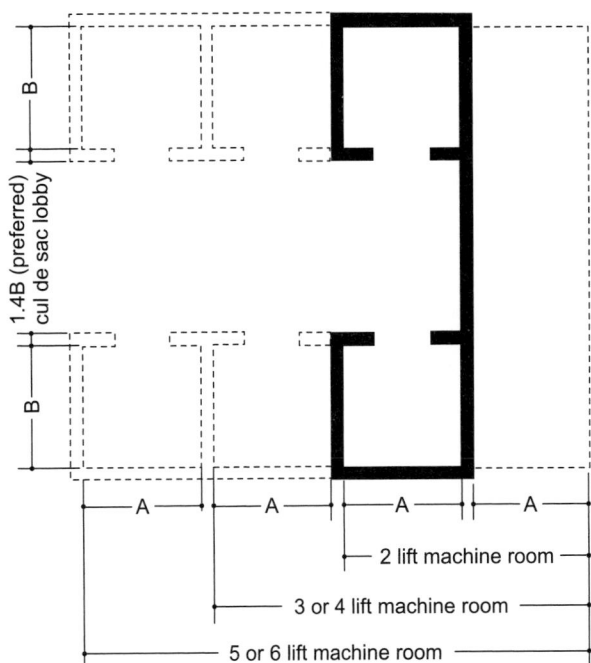

3.21 *Plan of cul-de-sac lobby and machine room – dimensions refer to the values in Table IV*

Lift cars are rated by their load capacity in kilograms and the number of people they can carry. The load capacity is defined in EN81(1998) and must not be exceeded but people capacity ratings can be misleading and experience has found that in reality, the figure should be adjusted for variations in people size, luggage etc. A further reduction comes from statistical analysis of passenger behaviour suggesting that a 20 per cent reduction should be applied to get the true capacity of individual cars.

In very tall buildings, where the number of lift cars becomes very large to serve all storeys from the access point, 'sky lobbies' provide an intermediate access point where a specific lift will only take people to this point for further distribution at higher 'local' levels.

Table III Lift car requirements

Effective lift system design is a specialist design function but some basic assumptions can be made relating to the number of cars to the number of storeys and populations served.

Number of storeys served	Number of lifts in group	Approximate population served per storey
4	1 to 2	60 to 200
5	1 to 2	30 to 200
6	2 to 3	50 to 200
7	2 to 4	70 to 210
8	2 to 5	50 to 210
9	3 to 6	75 to 200
10	3 to 6	60 to 160
11	3 to 6	50 to 170
12	3 to 6	50 to 145
13	3 to 6	45 to 125
14	3 to 6	40 to 110
15	4 to 6	50 to 100
16	4 to 6	45 to 90
17	4 to 6	40 to 80
18	4 to 6	40 to 70

Table III provides a range of information on the number of lift cars required to serve various storeys for a typical office building with associated population numbers per floor.

Table IV provides information on design capacity, rated capacity, car size and the required structural size requirements for two different lift traffic systems.

Table IV Lift specification

Effective lift system design is a specialist design function but some basic assumptions can be made relating to car size, shaft dimensions and traffic flows.

	Car size C × D	Shaft size A × B	Machine room S × R	Load rating (Kg)	Rated Capacity (people)	Design Capacity (people)
Light traffic				320	4	3.6
	1100 × 950	1800 × 1600	3200 × 2500	400	5	
				450	6	5.0
	1100 × 1400	1800 × 2100	3700 × 2500	630	8	6.3
	1350 × 1400	1900 × 2300	3700 × 2500	800	10	7.6
	1100 × 2100	1800 × 2600	4200 × 2500	1000	13	9.1
General purpose lifts	1600 × 1400	2400 × 2300	4900 × 3200	1000	13	9.1
	1950 × 1400	2600 × 2300	4900 × 3200	1250	16	
				1275	16	11.0
	1950 × 1750	2600 × 2600	5500 × 3200	1600	21	13.5
	1600 × 2400	2400 × 3000	5800 × 3200	1800	24	14.9
	1500 × 2700	2400 × 3300	5800 × 3200	2000	26	16.0
	1800 × 2700	2700 × 3300	5800 × 3500	2500	33	19.0

Note: machine room sizes are for traction lifts, the size is considerably reduced for hydraulic lifts.

6 BIBLIOGRAPHY

Barney, G. (2003) *Elevator Traffic Handbook*. Taylor & Francis.

Kone: Escalators and Autowalks Planning Guide, 2010. (http://cdn.kone.com/www.kone.us/Images/kone-escalator-autowalk-planning-guide.pdf?v= 1)

Otis: About lifts, 2011 (http://www.otis.com/site/gb/pages/About Elevators.aspx?menuID=2)

Straksch, G. and Caporale, R. (2010) *The Vertical Transportation Handbook*. 4th edn. John Wiley & Sons.

4 Access and inclusion

Neil Smith and David Dropkin

Senior Access Consultants, Buro Happold Ltd, London

KEY POINTS:
- *Consider the needs of all disabled people not just wheelchair users, who form a small percentage of such a diverse group of people*
- *At some times in their lives, people may require the same provision that is made for disabled people; flexibility is all important*

Contents

1 Inclusive design
2 People
3 Mobility equipment
4 Reach
5 Walking distances
6 Toilets

1 INCLUSIVE DESIGN

1.1 Design principles

Good design reflects the diverse nature of people and does not impose barriers of any kind. Designing inclusively guarantees accessibility to all, including disabled people, older people and families with small children.

'The Principles of Inclusive Design' (CABE) encourage high quality, inclusive design in the built environment. Incorporating these principles ensures projects are:

- Inclusive – everyone uses safely, easily and with dignity
- Responsive – takes account of what people say they need and want
- Flexible – allows different people to use in different ways
- Convenient – everyone uses without too much effort or separation
- Accommodating – for all, regardless of age, gender, mobility, ethnicity or circumstances
- Welcoming – no disabling barriers that might exclude some people
- Realistic – recognising that one solution may not work for all and offering additional solutions as required.

1.2 Design process

In order to deliver inclusive environments, the principles of inclusive design must be integrated into the design process from first principles. Making environments easy to use for everyone requires consideration other than just physical factors. These include signage/way-finding, lighting, visual contrast, controls and door furniture, and materials.

Inclusive design relates as much to the design process as to the final product, bonding user-experience with professional expertise and management practice. The process extends from inception, through the planning process, detailed design, construction to occupation, management and operation.

The goal of creating aesthetic and functional environments that can be used equally by everyone, irrespective of age, gender, faith or disability, requires a creative and inclusive design process working towards accommodating a diverse range of users.

Following the minimum provisions of the building regulations or best practice guidance alone will not deliver inclusive projects. For this, the involvement of design team, client and community are required.

2 PEOPLE

2.1 Disabled people

The UK's Disability Discrimination Act 1995 (DDA) defines a person as having a disability if they have a physical or mental impairment, which has a substantial and long-term adverse effect on their ability to carry out normal day-to-day activities. It is estimated that approximately 20 per cent of the UK population (over 10 million people) may have rights under the DDA.

While the spatial needs of wheelchair users and people with mobility impairments are important in terms of designing the physical environment, it is also necessary to understand the barriers experienced by people with learning difficulties and mental illness, visual impairments and hearing impairments as well as conditions such as HIV, cancer, heart disease or diabetes.

2.2 Benefits

In general, designing to provide access, whether physical or intellectual, will yield results that benefit the community at large. Many aspects of an inclusively designed environment will be helpful to all or most disabled people (and many others as well). In order to deliver the whole, it is useful to understand the diverse and complex nature of disability, recognising that degrees of disability vary greatly as do the combinative effect of multiple impairments.

2.3 Statistics

Some key statistics relating to disability are:

- Some 70 per cent of disabled people in the UK have reduced or limited mobility. They represent 14 per cent of the overall population.
- Wheelchair users account for only 0.85 per cent of the general population.
- About 2 million people in the UK (approximately 4 per cent of the UK population) define themselves as having a sight problem or seeing difficulty.
- There are over 8 million deaf or hard of hearing people in the UK (14.5 per cent of the population).
- There are 700,000 in the UK who are severely or profoundly deaf
- 14 per cent of the UK population have difficulty on reaching, stretching or have reduced dexterity.
- 5.6 million people have difficulty with physical coordination.
- 3.9 million people in the UK have difficulty learning and understanding.
- 700 000 people have difficulties in perceiving risk.

2.4 Older people

The number of older people in the population is increasing. Many of them have or will have an impairment of some kind. Over the next 30 years, while the overall population is expected to rise by less than 7 per cent, the proportion of the population over 65 will increase by approximately 40 per cent, doubling the number of people over 65. In addition, the proportion of the population over 80 is expected to treble.

There is a correlation between age and disability. Approximately 5 million people over the age of 65 have a longstanding illness and more than half the population over 75 has some kind of disability. Two-thirds of disabled people are over pension age.

People also tend to shrink slightly with age. More significantly, the body tends to be less flexible in regard to adapting to dimensionally unfavourable situations. Older people tend to have more than one impairment. It is, therefore, more important that design allows for older people.

Table I gives dimensions for people between the ages of 65 and 80.

Table I Dimensions for British people aged 65–80

	Men percentiles			Women percentiles		
	5th	50th	95th	5th	50th	95th
Standing						
1 Stature	1575	1685	1790	1475	1570	1670
2 Eye height	1470	1575	1685	1375	1475	1570
3 Shoulder height	1280	1380	1480	1190	1280	1375
4 Elbow height	975	895	975	740	810	875
5 Hand (knuckle) height	670	730	795	645	705	760
6 Reach upwards	1840	1965	2090	1725	1835	1950
Sitting						
7 Height above seat level	815	875	930	750	815	885
8 Eye height above seat level	705	760	815	645	710	770
9 Shoulder height above seat level	520	570	625	475	535	590
10 Length from elbow to fingertip	425	460	490	390	420	450
11 Elbow above seat level	175	220	270	165	210	260
12 Thigh clearance	125	150	175	115	145	170
13 Top of knees, height above floor	480	525	575	455	500	540
14 Popliteal height	385	425	470	355	395	440
15 Front of abdomen to front of knees	210	280	350	325	295	365
16 Buttock–popliteal length	430	485	535	430	480	525
17 Rear of buttocks to front of knees	530	580	625	520	565	615
19 Seat width	305	350	395	310	370	430
Sitting and standing						
20 Forward grip reach	700	755	805	640	685	735
21 Fingertip span	1605	1735	1860	1460	1570	1685
23 Shoulder width	400	445	485	345	385	380

Table II Statures (or equivalents) for Britons in various age groups

	Percentiles		
	5th	50th	95th
New-born infants	465	500	535
Infants less than 6 months old	510	600	690
Infants 6 months to 1 year old	655	715	775
Infants 1 year to 18 months	690	745	800
Infants 18 months to 2 years	780	840	900

	Boys/men percentiles			Girls/women percentiles		
	5th	50th	95th	5th	50th	95th
Children, 2 years old	850	930	1010	825	890	955
Children, 3 years old	910	990	1070	895	970	1045
Children, 4 years old	975	1050	1125	965	1050	1135
Children, 5 years old	1025	1110	1195	1015	1100	1185
Children, 6 years old	1070	1170	1270	1070	1160	1250
Children, 7 years old	1140	1230	1320	1125	1220	1315
Children, 8 years old	1180	1280	1380	1185	1280	1375
Children, 9 years old	1225	1330	1435	1220	1330	1440
Children, 10 years old	1290	1390	1490	1270	1390	1510
Children, 11 years old	1325	1430	1535	1310	1440	1570
Children, 12 years old	1360	1490	1620	1370	1500	1630
Children, 13 years old	1400	1550	1700	1430	1550	1670
Children, 14 years old	1480	1630	1780	1480	1590	1700
15 years old	1555	1690	1825	1510	1610	1710
16 years old	1620	1730	1840	1520	1620	1720
17 years old	1640	1750	1860	1520	1620	1720
18 years old	1660	1760	1860	1530	1620	1710
Aged 19–25	1640	1760	1880	1520	1620	1720
Aged 19–45	1635	1745	1860	1515	1615	1715
Aged 19–65	1625	1740	1855	1505	1610	1710
Aged 45–65	1610	1720	1830	1495	1595	1695
Aged 65–85	1575	1685	1790	1475	1570	1670
Elderly people	1515	1640	1765	1400	1515	

2.5 Children and adolescents

Statures (or equivalents) for various ages in Britain are given in Table II (Statures (or equivalents) for Britons in various age groups).

Where facilities are to be used solely by small children, specific heights should be adjusted to meet their requirements. There are approximately 3.3 million families in the UK with children under 5. Design in general should also consider the needs of children, for example, when providing family facilities or sinks at lower heights in toilets.

It is also worth noting that approximately 7 per cent of children in the UK are disabled (around 770 000). Disabled children and young people currently face multiple barriers, making it more difficult for them to achieve their potential, to achieve the outcomes their peers expect and to succeed in education.

Disabled parents and carers should be considered at all stages of the design process.

2.6 Large people

Obesity also needs to be considered. The prevalence of obesity in children aged under 11 increased from 9.9 per cent in 1995 to 13.7 per cent in 2003. This trend is expected to continue. Since the 1980s, the prevalence of obesity in adults has trebled. Well over half of all adults in the UK are either overweight or obese, almost 24 million adults.

Pregnant women, like large people, can be disadvantaged by the design of the environment. Long routes and stairs can be very tiring, narrow seats, doors and small toilet cubicles are other common barriers.

In certain buildings such as football stadia, deliberately narrow doorways are used to ensure control over entry. In these cases, and also where turnstiles are used, additional provision for large people should be made.

Where there is fixed seating, for example, in a theatre, there should be a number of easily accessed amenity seats, which may have increased legroom, have removable arms or fold-down arms and may include a space for an assistance dog.

3 MOBILITY EQUIPMENT

3.1 Key dimensions

Wheelchair users need quite a lot of space to move comfortably and safely; people who walk with two sticks may require a wider circulatory route than someone using a wheelchair. It is worth noting that a double pushchair may be wider than an occupied electric wheelchair.

3.2 Wheelchairs users

The range of wheelchair dimensions is considerable, particularly given the overall length and width that an occupied wheelchair may extend to. The figures given for the width of a wheelchair user do not usually make allowance for their elbows and hands. The ISO standard for wheelchairs (ISO 7193) notes that to propel a wheelchair manually a clearance of not less than 50 mm, preferably 100 mm, on both sides is required.

At the present time, the maximum length a conventional wheelchair user with leg supports or an electric scooter is likely to occupy is 1600 mm. Conventionally seated wheelchair users do not usually occupy a length of more than approximately 1250 mm. However, if a wheelchair user has a companion then the combined length of the space they occupy will be typically 1375 mm – design guidance allows for 1570 mm.

The average height of wheelchair users is 1080 mm but can range as high as 1535 mm. The average height of a scooter user is approximately 1170 mm but can range as high as a maximum of 1500 mm.

In designing for wheelchair users, the critical dimensions are:

- eye height, around 120–130 mm below seated height, giving a 5th–95th per cent range for wheelchair users from 960 to 1250 mm (1080–1315 mm for scooter users)
- knee height, 500–690 mm
- seat height, 460–490 mm
- ankle height, manual wheelchair users, 175–300 mm; electric wheelchair users, 380–520 mm
- height to bottom of foot support, 60–150 mm.

The ground clearance offered by typical scooters currently on the market can vary from 80 to 125 mm. The climbing capacity of typical scooters on the market also varies depending on the motor power and battery charge; however, most vary between 10° and 20°.

3.3 Wheelchair-user dimensions
These dimensions exclude the wheelchair user and only consider length and width, Figure 4.1. Dimensions in Table III are given for occupied and unoccupied wheelchairs over a range of wheelchair types including scooters.

3.4 Pushchair dimensions
The length and width dimensions of child pushchairs are very much variable. There is not, as is the case with manual wheelchairs, a standard model for informing design criteria. Table IV gives common dimensions.

3.5 Turning spaces
Mobility aid vehicles clearly need adequate space to turn around and this will need to be considered in particular along circulation routes and in queue systems, Tables V and VI.

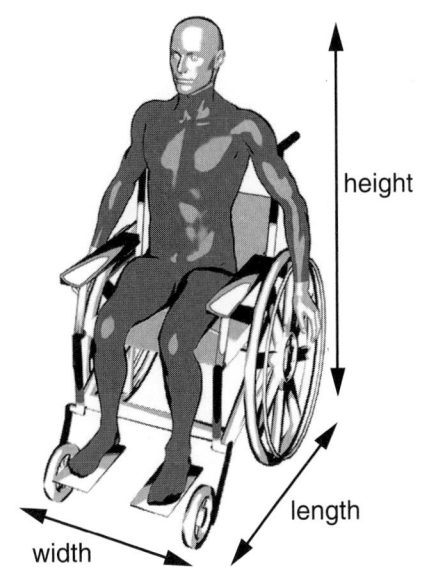

4.1 *Wheelchair dimensions*

Table III Wheelchair dimensions

Chair type (excluding children)	Occupied		Unoccupied	
	Length (mm)	Width (mm)	Length (mm)	Width (mm)
Manual wheelchair	850–1250	560–800	700–1200	560–750
Attendant propelled	1200–1570	560–700	800–1350	550–660
Electric wheelchair	860–1520	560–800	700–1400	560–750
Electric scooter	1170–1600	630–700	1170–1500	620–640

Table IV Pushchair dimensions

Single buggy	Double buggy	Single Pushchair	Double Pushchair	Double Pushchair
900 mm 840 mm 435 mm	900 mm 840 mm 740 mm	900 mm 560 mm 1060 mm	900 mm 950 mm 860 mm	900 mm 560 mm 1210 mm
Length = 840 mm Width = 435 mm	Length = 840 mm Width = 740 mm	Length = 1060 mm Width = 560 mm	Length = 860 mm Width = 950 mm	Length = 1210 mm Width = 560 mm

Table V Space required for users of self-propelled wheelchairs to turn through 90° (Figure 4.2)

Chair type	Space required	
	Length (mm)	Width (mm)
Manual wheelchair	1345*	1450*
Attendant propelled	1200–1800	1500–1800
Electric wheelchair	1600*	1625*
Electric scooter	1400–2500	1300–2500

*90% of users.

Table VI Space required for users of self-propelled wheelchairs to turn through 180° (Figure 4.3)

Chair type	Space required	
	Length (mm)	Width (mm)
Manual wheelchair	1950*	1500*
Attendant propelled	1600–2000	1500–1800
Electric wheelchair	2275*	1625*
Electric scooter	2000–2800	1300–2200

*90% of users

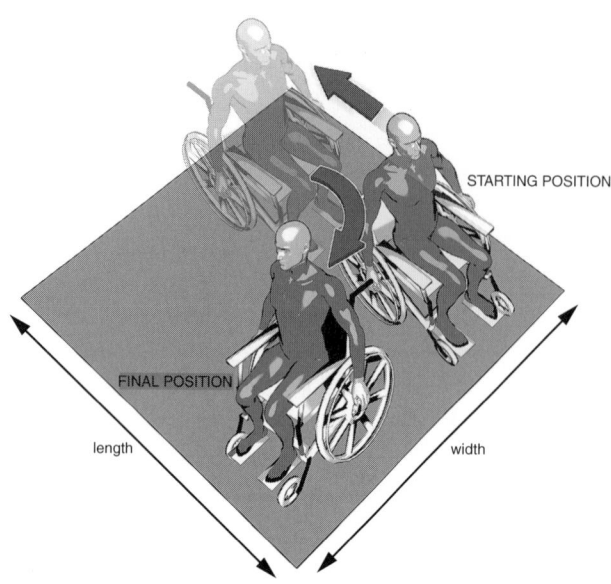

4.2 *Wheelchair users performing a 90° turn*

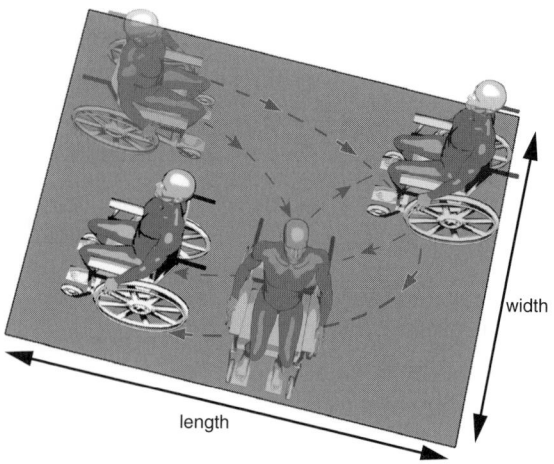

4.3 *Wheelchair users performing a 180° turn*

3.6 Considerations for people that use a stick, cane or crutches

It is important to consider people with a visual impairment that use a cane, Figure 4.4, or people with a mobility impairment that may prefer to walk using crutches, Figures 4.5 and 4.6.

Most people who use crutches use them for a short time following an accident, and will be inexpert in their use. Users fall into two broad groups: those who have some use of both legs and feet, and those who have use of only one leg. Those who can use only one leg require a handhold wherever there are steps, even at a single step at a building threshold.

3.7 Space provision for assistance dogs

Assistance dogs include guide dogs and hearing dogs. While people primarily with sensory impairments have an assistance dog, people with mobility impairments and wheelchair users may also have an assistance dog. Inclusive Mobility identifies that people with assistance dogs require a clear unobstructed width of at least 1100 mm.

4 REACH

4.1 Range

The distance and angle that an individual can reach is dependent on their size, agility, dexterity and whether they are seated or standing.

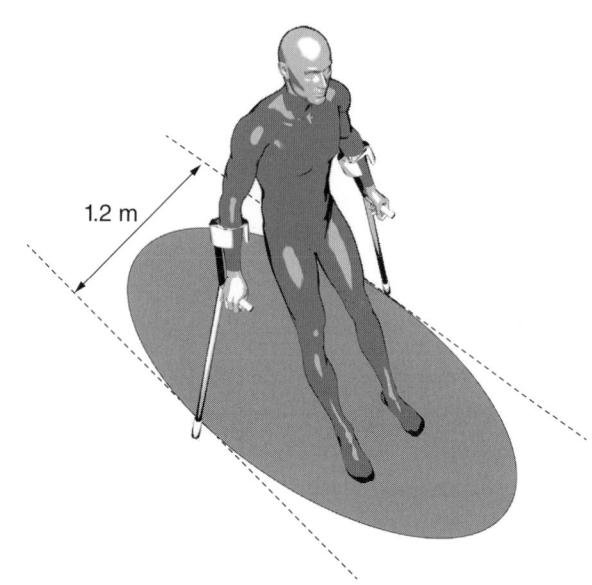

4.5 *Person on crutches*

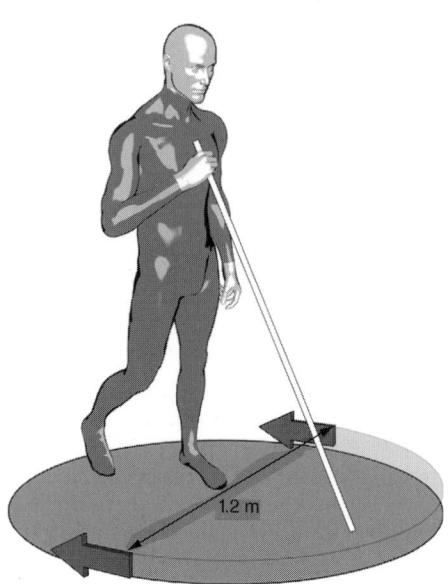

4.4 *Blind person with cane*

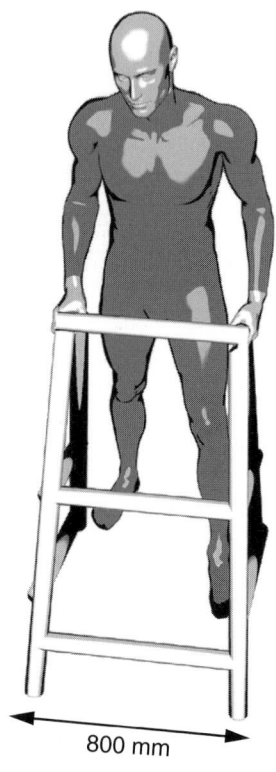

4.6 *Person with a walking frame*

Table VII Reach ranges

Person	Access	Reach angle	Height (H)		Depth (D)	
			Comfortable	Extended	Comfortable	Extended
Wheelchair user	Front	+70	1000	1150	90	120
		Horizontal* (750)	–	–	180	230
		–24	650	650	120	200
	Side	+70	1060	1170	100	135
		Horizontal** (750)	–	–	220	310
		–24	665	630	165	230
Ambulant disabled	Front	+70	1500	1625	200	250
		Horizontal (850)	–	–	280	400
		–24	750	700	180	310

* With suitable knee recess provided.

**With suitable knee recess provided.

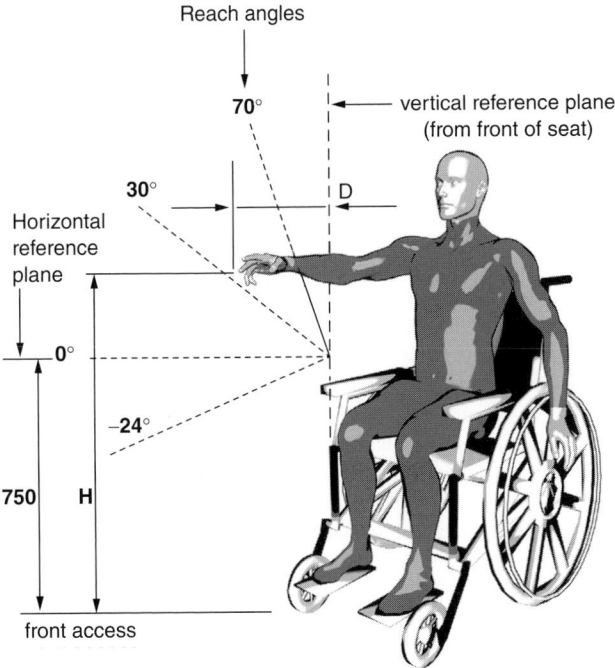

4.7 *Front access*

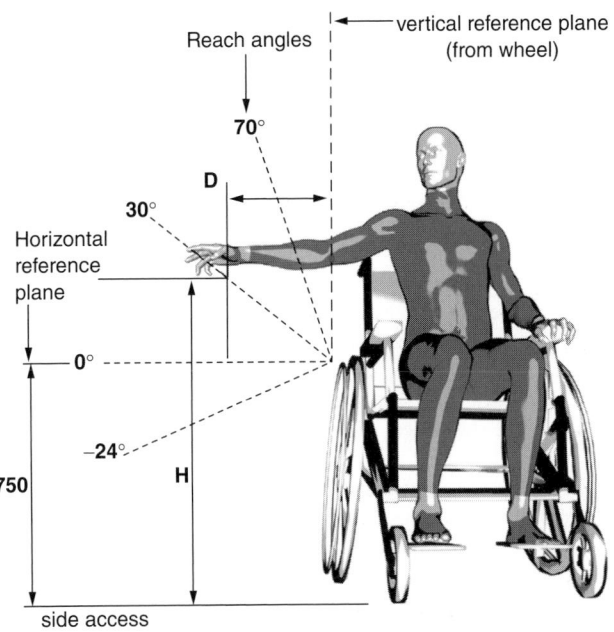

4.8 *Side access*

The ability of a seated person, for example, in a wheelchair to reach, forward, sideways, upwards or downwards is different than someone standing.

Reach distance forms an arc, based on shoulder level. Reach range can be described as easy or comfortable (reach without much movement of the torso) or maximum or extended (just possible with movement of the torso). Research carried out for the preparation of BS 8300:2001 gives figures for comfortable and extended reach ranges, see Table VII and Figures 4.7 and 4.8.

5 WALKING DISTANCES

5.1 Mobility ranges
Walking distances were researched in some detail in the late 1980s. US regulations, for example, note that on distances over 100 feet (30 m) disabled people are apt to rest frequently. These regulations suggest that to estimate travel times over longer distances, allowance should be made for 2 minutes rest time every 30 m.

Research based on a follow-up study to the London Area Travel Survey found that of disabled people who were able to walk, approximately 30 per cent could manage no more than 50 m without stopping or severe discomfort. A further 20 per cent could only manage between 50 and 200 m.

Mobility ranges vary enormously between individuals with age and disability, while factors such as weather, topography (gradients) and obstacles can also affect mobility ranges.

In pedestrian schemes, travel distances should not exceed:

- 50 m on unprotected routes
- 100 m on covered routes
- 200 m on completely enclosed routes.

Where gradients exist travel distances should be reduced. Conversely, the provision of seating and resting places can extend the distance people can traverse. The recommended maximum distance on level ground between resting places should be no more than 50 m.

5.2 Changes in level
Any gradient less than 1:60 can be considered level. Changes in level cause problems for many people, particularly people with mobility or visual impairments. Even a single step can prevent access for someone with a mobility impairment and can present a trip hazard for all people.

Where changes in level cannot be avoided, slopes or ramps should be designed in a user-friendly manner, although it should be noted that ramps are not always the ideal solution and can take up a great deal of space.

Table VIII Maximum ramp length between landings

Gradient	Length of ramp between level landings (m)
1:20	10
1:19	9
1:18	8
1:17	7
1:16	6
1:15	5
1:14	4
1:13	3
1:12	2

Slopes or ramps provide access for people who use wheels, such as wheelchair users or parents with pushchairs. However, some people may find it easier to negotiate a flight of steps than a ramp and for them, the presence of handrails for support is essential. Where a change in level no greater than 300 mm, a ramp may be acceptable as the only means of access, avoiding the need for steps. Otherwise, steps would also be required.

Where ramps are provided, they should be no steeper than 1:12 but preferably 1:20. Table VIII indicates the maximum length of a ramp before level landings are required.

It should be noted that if the level change exceeds 2 m, then the ramps become very difficult to use for many people including wheelchair users. There should be an alternative means of access for wheelchair users, such as a lift. (Details of lifts are given in Chapter 3.)

Many people find long flights of stairs difficult to use; therefore, the maximum recommended number of steps should be 12 in a flight. If there are successive flights, it is important there are resting places, at least 1200 mm long (preferably 1800 mm) across the full width of the stair. There should be an unobstructed landing space at the top and bottom of a flight of stairs to avoid any collision.

The design of suitable stairs will be dependent on a variety of factors such as location (external or internal), building type, floor-to-floor levels and other dimension constraints as well as whether they are fire escape stairs. As a rule of thumb, a comfortable step will have a rise of between 150 and 170 mm with a going between 280 and 425 mm deep, with a preference for a minimum of 300 mm.

Stair risers should be closed. Steps without projecting nosings remove a potential trip hazard. If necessary, the projection of a step nosing over the tread should be a maximum of 25 mm. All nosings should be made apparent on both the riser and tread, which will assist people ascending and descending the stair.

Stairs and steps should have a minimum clear width between handrails of 1000 mm. A handrail should be provided on both sides of the stair to allow people a choice as some people may only have strength on one side of their body.

If the width of stairway is greater than 1800 mm there should be central/additional handrails to give people extra support. The channels themselves should not be less than 1000 mm between handrails. This precludes the design of stairs between 1800 and 2000 mm in width.

6 TOILETS

6.1 Provision

Without adequate toilets many people, especially disabled people, are limited in their ability to go out to work, to shop and so forth. The majority of disabled people do not require the use of unisex wheelchair accessible WCs.

It is important that all toilet facilities are accessible, catering for a wide range of people, including older people and children. Therefore, things such as door opening pressures, range of heights of sinks and urinals, easy to use door furniture and tap design are key design factors in making all toilets useable.

Another consideration is that women may require to use toilets more frequently than men and on average take longer than men (this is particularly true during menstruation or during and after pregnancy). The British Toilet Association recommends that twice the number of male cubicles plus number of male urinals is the appropriate number of cubicles for women.

6.2 Children's toilets

Children are often not considered in the design of toilets. Many children can be deterred from independent use of toilet facilities by poor design and specification. It should also be possible in developments that are likely to have many children using them, for example, leisure facilities, to provide separate children's toilets. These could be provided with associated family facilities, such as nappy-changing facilities. Nappy-changing facilities must never be situated in accessible toilets. It is important that separate wheelchair accessible nappy-changing areas are provided.

There are approximately 1.6 million people who have continence problems. Up to 4 million people, mainly men, are affected by 'shy bladder syndrome' (avoidant paruresis) and therefore the layout of toilets should provide 'line of sight' privacy, an adequate number of cubicles and privacy screens.

6.3 Adult-changing facilities

In larger developments, consideration should also be given to adult-changing facilities. Some people, including people with profound and multiple disabilities, need to be laid flat to be changed within WC accommodation. If adult-changing facilities are not provided, people may have to change a person on the floor. This is undignified, unhygienic and involves heavy lifting by others, such as carers or personal assistants, which could cause serious back injuries.

5 Capital and whole life costs of buildings

David Holmes, Chris Bicknell and John Davies

Davis Langdon, an AECOM Company

KEY POINT:
- Clear communication with clients from the beginning of the project is vital
- Changes made later in the project are more difficult and more costly to implement than those made at an earlier stage
- Maintenance and operational costs of a building dwarf the construction costs
- Whole life costing is a valuable tool to enhance decision making, but can be heavily influenced by decisions on time-span and discounted cash flow

Contents
1 Introduction
2 Why are construction costs so important?
3 Procurement
4 New rules of measurement and cost estimating
5 Whole life costs
6 Conclusion

1 INTRODUCTION

This chapter examines the relationship between cost and value in construction projects, and discusses why architects should pay particular attention to their client's budgetary constraints. We also describe the degree of risk which clients accept when undertaking construction projects, and the steps which designers can take to mitigate these risks. In describing the estimating and cost planning process, we explain the discipline of the cost planning process, and the importance of the achievement of an appropriate level of fixity of design and specification at the conclusion of each RIBA project stage. We also describe the information that is available to cost consultants in preparing estimates at different project stages, and the degree of certainty that can be attached to these estimates.

The expenditure on design and construction can have significant leverage relative to the costs of occupation. For example, appropriate investment in design and construction could potentially have a significant and valuable impact on the productivity of building occupiers. With many buildings procured by the public sector on the basis of design, build and operate arrangements such as LIFT, used for primary healthcare, whole life costing is being taken far more seriously today than hitherto. Furthermore, with the growing significance of the sustainability agenda, concerned with managing energy consumption, carbon emissions and other environmental impacts, opportunities to invest to save energy and to mitigate environmental impacts are taken increasingly seriously.

2 WHY ARE CONSTRUCTION COSTS SO IMPORTANT?

2.1 Cost planning

Cost planning is a key due diligence step in preparing for a construction project. Cost planning informs the client and the project team how much a proposed project is likely to cost. Additionally, cost planning will tell when the expected expenses will most likely occur, a cash flow programme. This information is critical for obtaining project financing and for determining whether a project can be affordable.

Very few clients have the luxury of an unlimited budget, and even with generous funding, all clients will want to make sure that the proposed design solution represents the best way of meeting their purpose and that their investment makes the best use of their resources. Financial discipline on a project does not mean that budgets have to be unrealistically tight. However, it does mean that the client's investment should be managed responsibly by the project team to focus on elements which relate specifically to the client's value criteria. Typical value criteria influencing projects are discussed below.

2.2 The value agenda

For many buildings, particularly those constructed for commercial markets, the client's principal measure of worth is the building's exchange value, typically measured by rental or sales revenue. Exchange value is used by clients in investment appraisals to determine whether projects are financially viable. In effect, exchange value determines the 'bottom line' of most schemes. Exchange value is generally defined by third parties and, particularly in commercial property markets, it is often difficult to secure a premium valuation for innovation. As a result, clients may have surprisingly little room for manoeuvre in setting their construction budgets. Exchange value issues can affect public sector projects too. Many public sector clients operate internal marketplaces where facilities are bought – using the volume of demand to establish the size and quality of the building that can be afforded.

Value is of course not just about financial considerations and there are many other ways in which buildings are able to contribute benefits to their owners, occupiers and neighbours. Some of the sources of these are listed below:

- *Operational value.* The benefits generated through the occupation and use of the building, which might include greater staff productivity, or improved educational outcomes associated with a new school.
- *Social value.* The broader benefits to society of a development, which might include local residents feeling more secure in their neighbourhood following the completion of an urban realm improvement project.
- *Brand value.* Messages communicated by a building derived from its design, and which reflect positively on the occupier. The DEFRA building at Alnwick is a good example of this benefit; a flagship development designed to achieve exemplary standards of sustainability and environmental performance.
- *Civic/esteem value.* The contribution that a development can make to a neighbourhood in terms of physical improvement to the quality of the building fabric, public realm and so on, this benefit is secured by all users of the neighbourhood. The reflected prestige that neighbouring buildings can secure from proximity to a high quality development, be it Tate Modern or a major redevelopment scheme such as Kings Cross in London, can be secured by owners and occupiers of neighbouring buildings and may reflect in an increase in the exchange value of the neighbouring buildings.

Whilst not all of these sources of value have an immediate financial dimension, all require a focused and disciplined approach by the design team to concentrate effort and investment on aspects of the design which maximise the client's, end users' and wider community benefits, without compromising the fundamental financial viability of the project.

2.3 Risk and value management

Risk and value management should be carried out throughout a project lifecycle, with early involvement of the entire integrated project team to minimise/manage risks. Risk management ensures that risks are identified as early in the project life cycle as possible and their potential impacts are understood and allowed for, and where possible their impacts minimised. The main emphasis is to identify the risks, analyse them and then ensure that they are effectively managed in order to minimise negative consequences and maximise opportunities. Rigorous follow up of identified risk mitigation actions and regular updates of the Risk Register are essential if the full benefits of Risk Management are to be realised.

The project team create a Risk Register and assign a RAG traffic light system to each risk (Table I). Obviously Red risks need actioning immediately. Rigorous follow up of identified risk mitigation actions and regular updates of the Risk Register are essential if the full benefits of Risk Management are to be realised (Figure 5.1).

Table I Risk matrix of probability and impact

Risk description		Probability		
		Low	Medium	High
Impact	Low	Green	Green	Amber
	Medium	Green	Amber	Red
	High	Amber	Red	Red

5.1 *Risk management circle*

High Impact and High Probability risks will need addressing immediately and the project team need to ensure that the risk is owned by someone in the team – which could be the client. All need to agree what measures are required to ensure a successful outcome. Value management is about adding or enhancing value and not solely about cutting cost, although this may be a by-product. The principles and techniques of value management aim to provide the required quality at optimum whole-life cost during the process of developing a project.

3 PROCUREMENT

3.1 Strategy

Selection of the procurement strategy and contract selection is one of the most important decisions facing the client. It has been estimated that the optimum strategy can influence the overall project cost by between 10–15%.

Source: Treasury guidance to Government Departments

The primary consideration in the procurement of construction projects is the need to obtain best value for money in the whole life of the service or facility. The design and operation of the facility should maximise the delivery of effective services; this is most likely to be achieved through integration of the design, construction, operation and ongoing maintenance. Some compromises will almost certainly have to be made to achieve an optimum balance of risk, benefit and funding for a particular project.

3.2 Influencing factors

- Project objectives – example, to provide office space for 1,000 people to deliver the client services.
- Constraints – such as budget and funding; the timeframe in which the project has to be delivered.
- Cultural factors – such as considerations about the workspace environment that will best support the way people work.
- Risks – such as late completion of the facility; innovative use of materials; carbon reduction strategies.
- The client's capabilities to manage a project of this type.
- The length of operational service required from the facility.

3.3 Procurement routes and associated risk

Critical issues:

- Relationship between design and construction
- Allocation of design risk (time, cost, quality)
- Allocation of construction risk (time, cost, quality)
- Status of design at point of committing to construction
- Incidence of change
- The project brief.

3.4 Design and build

- Design team employed by client to develop brief.
- Project design progressed to suitable stage prior to tender.
- Employer's requirements issued to main contractors who submit their contractor's proposals, lump sum tender and agreed programme.
- Main contractor has an obligation to deliver the project as defined within the contractor's proposals to the cost and programme agreed within the returned tender.
- Contractor retains responsibility for the design and design development.

3.5 Traditional lump sum

- Design team employed by client to develop brief.
- Project design completed prior to tender.
- Main contractor submits a lump sum tender and agreed programme.
- Main contractor has responsibility to deliver the project as specified to the cost and programme agreed at tender stage.
- Client retains responsibility of sufficiency of design.

3.6 Construction management

- Fundamentally different approach to the two previous routes – no main contractor is appointed.
- The brief is developed by a design team appointed by the client who are responsible for developing the design.
- A construction manager is appointed by the client as a fee earning consultant to programme, coordinate and manage the design and construction activities executed by the trade contractors.
- Trade contractors are employed directly by the client.

Figure 5.2 is looking at financial risk and who owns it for the most common procurement options. Management of risk is an ongoing process throughout the life of the project, as risks will be constantly changing. Risk management plans should be in place to deal quickly and effectively with risks if they arise. It is important to work as an integrated project team from the earliest

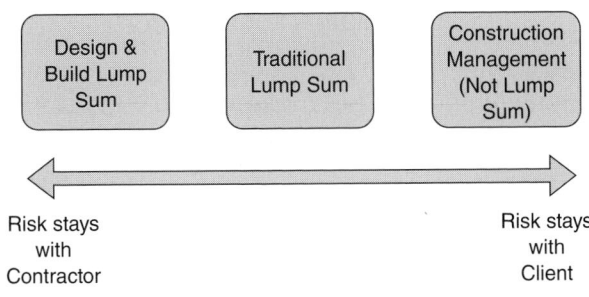

5.2 *Procurement routes*

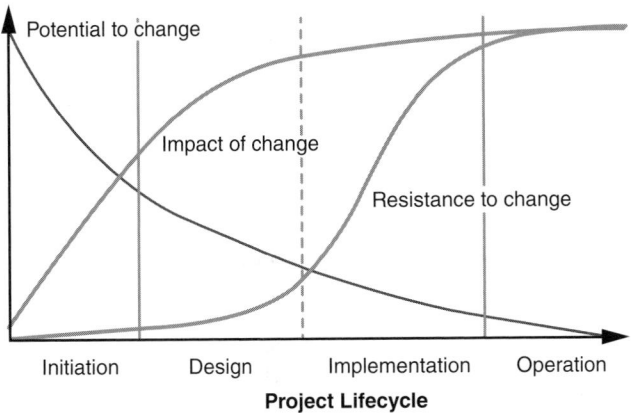

5.3 *Relationship between programme and change*

possible stages on an open book basis to identify risks throughout the team's supply chains.

3.7 Design stages
As a client's brief and concept designs are developed, a greater degree of fixity in terms of the design solution and predicted costs can be provided by the project team. This process is discussed in more detail in the section focused on cost planning. However the design develops and cost certainty increases, so does the cost of changing the design, and the client and project team's resistance to change. This relationship is illustrated in Figure 5.3 and emphasises why it is so important to stick to the discipline of progressive sign-off at the end of each design stage.

As a project progresses to the appointment of contractors, the client's overall financial commitment becomes better defined. More risk can also be transferred to third parties if the client so wishes. Whilst under most procurement routes the client is required to accept risks associated with design performance, they will generally seek to transfer commercial and construction risks to the contractor through some form of a fixed-price, lump sum contract. Quite clearly, if the design information upon which the client obtains a contractual commitment is not complete, is ambiguous or is not fully coordinated then, not only will the client retain outstanding design risk, but will also find that the basis of his commercial risk transfer to the contractor is weakened.

Evidence from Construction Key Performance Indicators, published by the BIS, indicates the scale of this potential problem, showing that fewer than 80 per cent of projects are completed with +/– 10 per cent of their original tender sum. Moreover, only around 50 per cent of projects are completed within +/– 5 per cent of the tender sum. Whilst some of this cost variation may reflect client changes, or problems on site, it is likely that some of these increases will have resulted from the consequences of continuing design development.

In order to mitigate the client's risk it is incumbent upon the team to ensure that the design is completed to the appropriate level of detail and fixity required by the procurement route. To do

otherwise risks rendering some of the effort expended in design development and cost planning abortive.

3.8 Order of cost estimating and elemental cost planning
For which of you, intending to build a tower, sit not down first, and count the cost, whether he have sufficient to finish it? Lest happily, after he has laid the foundation, and is not able to finish it, all the onlookers begin to mock him, saying, 'This man began to build, and was not able to finish'.

St Luke (Ch. 14)

It is often said that the first cost received by the client is the cost that is always remembered, so it is important that the entire project team clearly understand each other's requirements and that estimates submitted to the client include all relevant heads of cost.

4 NEW RULES OF MEASUREMENT AND COST ESTIMATING
4.1 Rules
The Standard Method of Measurement (SMM) has provided quantity surveyors with rules of measurement for building works since 1922. These rules enabled quantity surveyors to measure building work items for inclusion in bills of quantities which, in turn, are used for the purpose of obtaining a tender price for a building project in a consistent way. The SMM does not provide specific guidance on the measurement of building works for the purpose of producing cost estimates or cost plans.

In May 2009 the New Rules of Measurement (NRM) Order of cost estimating and elemental cost planning were introduced by the RICS. The NRM have been written to provide a standard set of measurement rules that are understandable by all those involved in a construction project, including the employer, thereby aiding communication between the project/design team and the employer. In addition, the NRM should assist the quantity surveyor/cost manager in providing effective and accurate cost advice to the employer and the rest of the project/design team.

4.2 Order of cost estimate
The purpose of an *order of cost estimate* is to establish if the proposed building project is affordable and, if affordable, to establish a realistic *cost limit* for the building project. The *cost limit* is the maximum expenditure that the *employer* is prepared to make in relation to the completed building project, which will be managed by the project team (i.e. authorised budget).

Order of cost estimates are produced as an intrinsic part of RIBA Work Stages A: Appraisal and B: Design Brief, or OGC Gateways 1 (Business Justification) and 2 (Delivery Strategy). There are comprehensive guidelines within the NRM and readers are recommended to read the relevant sections of the NRM where more detailed explanations and examples can be found.

At this early stage, in order for the estimate to be representative of the proposed design solution, the key variables that a designer needs to have developed to an appropriate degree of certainty are:

- The floor areas upon which the estimate is based
- Proposed elevations
- The implied level of specification.

Table II sets out feasibility cost information for a range of building types, illustrating the range of costs that can relate to a particular building function.

The variation in costs illustrated in Table II is driven by a wide range of factors and they are not minimum and maximum costs. They only give an indication of typical costs received.

Table II Sample of a typical order of cost estimating rates

Office buildings	Construction cost (£/m² gifa)
Offices for letting	
low rise, air conditioned, high quality speculative	1,125 to 1,375
medium rise, air conditioned, high quality speculative, 8–20 storeys	1,475 to 1,825
medium rise, air conditioned, city fringe, deep plan speculative office towers	1,750 to 2,150
Offices for owner occupation	
low rise, air conditioned	1,225 to 1,475
medium rise, air conditioned	1,575 to 1,925
high rise, air conditioned	1,875 to 2,300
Offices, prestige	
high rise, air conditioned, iconic speculative towers	2,700 to 3,300
Housing	
Private developments	
Single detached houses	890 to 1,380
Houses two or three storey	780 to 1,930
High-quality apartments in residential tower – Inner London	2,290 to 2,500
High-quality multi-storey apartments – Inner London	1,770 to 2,030
Mid market apartments in residential tower – Outer London	1,770 to 2,140
Affordable apartments in mixed tenure development – Inner London	
three-to-four storey villa – Inner London	1,230 to 1,460
multi-storey	1,410 to 1,560

The building costs set out in Table II should be applied to the gross internal floor area of a building. The rates are current at third quarter 2011 based on an outer London location, they include preliminaries and contractor's overheads and profit but do not include demolitions, external works and services, loose furniture and equipment or specialist installations. Professional fees and VAT are also excluded.
(Source: Spon's Architects' and Builders' Price Book, 2011, Taylor & Francis)

The scope of sources of additional costs which are not related to the floor areas of the building, including external works, fittings and furniture and loose equipment.

Rates will need to be updated to current estimate base date by the amount of inflation occurring from the base date of the cost data to the current estimate base date. The percentage addition can be calculated using published indices (i.e. tender price indices (TPI)) or derived from in-house sources of indices.

Main contractor's preliminaries, overheads and profit need to be added to the cost of building works. Generally this is a percentage addition ascertained from previous benchmarked studies. The accuracy associated with feasibility estimates of this nature is probably no better than +/– 20–25 per cent. However, most clients require a single point estimate, even at the earliest stage of a project, and the architect and cost consultant must agree an appropriate allowance for design development and other unknowns, balancing requirements for early cost certainty alongside the need for competitive, value for money solutions appropriate to the client's needs.

4.3 Wall to floor ratio
One common measure of efficiency is the wall to floor ratio for the building. Figure 5.4 shows the ratio can effect the cost of a tall office tower.

If you simply pick an average price from the rate range in Table II then it may not reflect the true building complexity. A wall to floor ratio of 0.40 is a relatively simple box. The addition of recesses, returns, increased floor to floor heights to that box can add a significant cost to the building. This is particular relevant in tall towers, where the external façade represents a significant proportion of the overall building cost. Similarly a higher than assumed specification can add significant cost to the project.

In the UK cost plans are typically organised into 'building elements'. Consistently defined elements, such as substructure, frame,

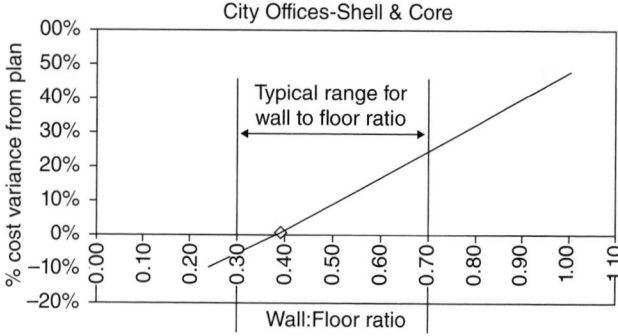

5.4 *Example of a wall to floor ratio. Source: Davis Langdon*

external walls, are widely used by cost consultants when preparing cost plans. They enable the costs of buildings or individual elements to be benchmarked with data from other similar schemes. As the design becomes increasingly detailed, budgets are set for each element providing further discipline for the project team as the design develops. According to client preference, and depending upon the procurement route adopted, some estimates may also be organised in accordance with trade-based packages. The definition of the content of packages varies from project to project. For projects procured either on the basis of construction management or two-stage tenders, estimates prepared in a packages format provide a direct link between the documentation necessary to procure the package, and the management of its costs.

4.4 Formal cost planning stages
The NRM schedules a number of formal cost planning stages (Figure 5.5), which are comparable with the RIBA Design and Pre-Construction Work Stages and OGC Gateways 3A (Design Brief and Concept Approval) and 3B (Detailed Design Approval) for a building project. The employer is required to 'approve' the cost plan on completion of each RIBA Work Stage before authorising commencement of the next RIBA Work Stage.

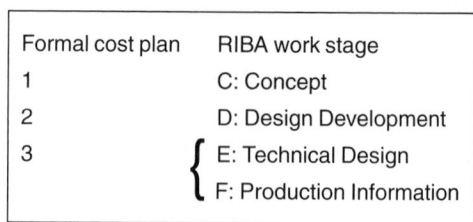

5.5 *Formal cost planning stages*

Formal Cost Plan 1 is prepared at a point where the scope of work is fully defined and key criteria are specified but no detailed design has begun. Formal Cost Plan 1 will provide the frame of reference for Formal Cost Plan 2. Likewise, Formal Cost Plan 2 will provide the frame of reference for Formal Cost Plan 3. Neither Formal Cost Plans 2 or 3 involve the preparation of a completely new elemental cost plan; they are progressions of the previous cost plans, which are developed through the cost checking of price significant components and cost targets as more design information and further information about the site becomes available.

The cost targets within each formal cost plan approved by the employer will be used as the baseline for future cost comparisons. Each subsequent cost plan will require reconciliation with the preceding cost plan and explanations relating to changes made. In view of this, it is essential that records of any transfers made to or from the risk allowances and any adjustments made to cost targets are maintained, so that explanations concerning changes can be provided to both the employer and the project team.

Cost consultants recognise that the design process is not linear, and in many instances the cost plan will include allowances based

Table III Sample cost planning rates

External walls – brick and block cavity walling

Item	Unit	Range £
Cavity wall; block outer skin; 50 mm insulation; lightweight block inner skin; outer block rendered	m²	61.00–79.00
Extra for		
Architectural masonry outer block	m²	1.50–1.950
75 mm thick cavity insulation	m²	4.60–5.90
Cavity wall; facing brick outer skin; 50 mm thick insulation; plasterboard on stud inner skin; emulsion paint	m²	83.00–110.00
machine made facings; PC £350.00/1000		
hand made facings; PC £475.00/1000	m²	98.00–125.00
Cavity wall; facing brick outer skin; 50 mm thick insulation; with plaster on		
lightweight block inner skin; emulsion		
machine made facings; PC £350.00/1000	m²	86.00–110.00
hand made facings; PC £475.00/1000	m²	105.00–140.00
Add or deduct for		
each variation of £100.00/1000 in PC value	m²	0.90–1.20
Extra for		
heavyweight block inner skin	m²	1.50–1.95
insulating block inner skin	m²	3.70–4.80
75 mm thick cavity insulation	m²	4.60–5.90
100 mm thick cavity insulation	m²	5.80–7.50

The estimating rates set out above should be applied to the quantity of the work itself, calculated using approximate quantities. The rates are current at third quarter 2011 based on an outer London location, include for all labour, materials, plant and incidental items. The rates also include for the contractor's overhead and profit. Preliminaries, professional fees and VAT are excluded.
(Source: Spon's Architects' and Builders' Price Book, 2011, Taylor & Francis)

upon informed assumptions as to what the designer's eventual solution will be. Working together effectively, an architect and cost consultant can ensure that the cost plan provides appropriate allowances for the realisation of the design, whilst at the same time delivering a cost effective and functional solution. Where the designer does not engage actively in the cost planning process, there is a risk that a cost consultant will make inappropriate allowances for incomplete work, potentially creating unnecessary constraints for future design development.

Table III sets out examples of cost planning rates used in a typical stage D plan. The rates are presented as a range to account for variations in specification, quantity and working method. A higher rate might apply for discontinuous work for example. In the cost plan itself, a single rate will be used, which the cost manager feels reflects the complexity and specification of the project.

Cost planning items at this stage are headline descriptions of the work and their selection and pricing should follow the principles of the *pareto rule*, where 80 per cent of the value of the work is captured by 20 per cent of the measurable items. Cost planning rates such as these include all costs associated with materials, labour, interfaces and detailing, together with specialist contractors and main contractor's overheads and profit. Many of these rates are obtained by 'market testing' with indicative costs obtained from contractors. Architects sometimes undertake elements of market testing themselves. If an architect does undertake such market testing exercises, then in presenting the results to the design team and client they should ensure that all costs necessary to complete the work have been included, and proper allowance has been made for the cost implications of the procurement route adopted.

At stage D, the cost plan is intended to provide a greater degree of accuracy. For this to be achieved, the design needs to have reached a corresponding degree of certainty and detail so that quantities can be relied upon, sources of complexity recognised and the cost implications of the proposed specification can be properly assessed.

In preparing cost plans, cost consultants obtain information from a wide range of sources which will include:

- Prices of similar work undertaken on previously completed projects.
- Quotations obtained from suppliers and specialist contractors.

- Cost information published by third parties, including price books, journal articles and so on.

In order to normalise this diverse range of information for location, price inflation etc., cost consultants apply a range of adjustment factors derived from the statistical analysis of large project datasets, undertaken by bodies such as the Building Cost Information Service (BCIS) or large practices who have their own in-house research teams.

When presenting estimates, to the client, the cost consultant and design team make some important decisions with regard to costs that are included and excluded from an estimate. Heads of costs which are typically excluded from a cost plan, but might need to be reinstated or included elsewhere in the client's budget include:

- Site acquisition costs
- Professional and statutory fees
- Furniture, fittings and equipment
- Costs related to planning agreements (sections 106 and 278)
- Contributions to major infrastructure projects
- The client's own project management, finance and insurance costs
- Overall project contingencies
- Value Added Tax
- Local authority and statutory authority charges for road closures etc.
- Costs of services diversions and off-site services reinforcement.

Clearly the list of exclusions for any particular project could be very extensive. The intention of presenting them in the cost plan is to make it clear that the client may potentially be exposed to these additional costs and that allowances have to be made somewhere within the overall project budget.

The cost plan is generally submitted as part of the RIBA stage design report. It is a detailed document, which requires a considerable amount of time and effort to prepare. It also provides a valuable resource for the project team to monitor the development of the design. In order for it to be an effective control document, the cost plan must provide an accurate reflection of the quantum and specification of the design at the conclusion of the design stage. This means that whilst designers can continue to develop detailed design solutions ahead of the completion of a stage, they should freeze the key parameters of their design sufficiently early for the cost plan to be produced with some certainty. Whilst technology such as CAD-based measurement has sped up the production process, proper allowance still has to be made in the programme for the compilation of the cost plan based on relatively firm information.

Other considerations which may be made at this time include:

- Capital allowances for provision of tax relief on items such as plant and machinery, industrial building allowance, hotel building allowance
- Land remediation allowances
- Grants.

It is recommended that specialist advice is sought to maximise the availability and magnitude of capital allowances.

4.5 Option studies

Throughout the design process, architects and engineers need to examine alternative design solutions, be it structural options, different air conditioning systems or alternative floor finishes. The cost consultant can contribute to the selection of preferred solution through the preparation of a option study, taking into account the full cost implications of each choice, which might include effects on the costs of other building elements, overall project duration and so on. Increasingly, option studies are prepared on the basis of whole life costs, taking into account the operational dimensions of specification as well as short-term considerations based on capital cost, programme and procurement.

4.6 Cost checking

Once the Formal Cost Plan 3 is agreed, and the client approves substantial investment in the preparation of production information, then the focus of the cost consultant should shift from projecting what the cost of the scheme should be, to ensuring that the design, as it develops, remains within the set budget. In these circumstances, the cost consultant will produce detailed estimates of specific elements or trade packages, which will confirm whether or not the architect's scheme can be delivered within the disciplines of allowances stated in the Cost Plan.

5 WHOLE LIFE COSTS

5.1 Lifetime

Buildings are long lived assets, and often have quite high operational costs, related to heating, ventilation and lighting, repair, maintenance and so on. Research undertake by CeBe (Constructing Excellence in the Built Environment) referred to in the introduction has identified that the cost of maintenance over a building's lifetime can equate to 3 times the original construction cost. Furthermore the costs of the operation, including the salaries of occupants equate to 35 times the build cost.

What these findings illustrate is that the lifetime costs of running and occupying a building dwarf the initial design and build costs, so if the design can be changed to reduce operating costs or enhance staff productivity, the client may agree to invest additional capital costs to find these improvements.

Given these opportunities, it is surprising that whole life costing has not been adopted more widely, but with the sustainability agenda very high up on many clients' agendas, designers can be expected in the future to demonstrate a greater appreciation of long term performance issues of their building designs.

Before getting into detail and having briefly touched on the sustainability agenda, it is important to clarify the distinction between life cycle costs and life cycle analysis (LCA). The former is concerned with calculating the costs associated with the operation and occupation of an asset, and is the subject of this chapter. By contrast, life cycle analysis is concerned with the full range of environmental impacts of a building, covering embodied impacts, construction and operational effects, together with those associated with asset disposal. As well as greenhouse gases, the scope of LCA will include impacts on landfill, water, biodiversity and so on.

The whole life cost agenda is potentially a very powerful tool for designers to create the case for investment in design which promotes greater productivity, flexibility, durability or longer operational life. However, as with all forms of analysis, the whole life cost assessment needs to be prepared in a way which meets the client's objectives and which provides an accurate representation of future performance. The problems affecting the take-up of whole life cost analysis include difficulties in obtaining unambiguous and corroborated performance and durability data, together with widespread confusion surrounding the use of discounted cashflows.

5.2 Considerations

Without getting into the detail of the production of whole life cost estimates, architects should be aware of the following considerations:

- The purpose of the assessment, as whole life cost studies are typically produced for three purposes:
  - An estimate of the operational cost of an asset. In this instance, the whole life cost study should cover all potential sources of cost associated with the occupation of a building. These cost centres might include energy, cleaning, insurances, maintenance and so on. Total operating cost assessments such as these are typically used by clients to confirm that they will be able to afford to run and maintain their assets.
  - Capital asset replacement. Whole life costs studies which focus solely on modelling the operational life of durable assets such as mechanical systems; roof finishes etc., that require replacement during the life of the building, enabling the client to plan for long term maintenance obligations.
  - Option comparisons. Option studies can be prepared to identify preferred options on the basis of long term performance. The approach could be used to select alternatives that have either different energy use, maintenance or replacement profiles such as window systems, floor finishes, air conditioning options. In an extreme case the choice between a leased building or a self-financed scheme could be supported. Option studies involve the comparison of alternatives which might have different life spans, replacement cycles, income or expenditure profiles. As a result, in many instances comparison can only be undertaken using *discounted cash flow techniques*. The use of discounting enables cash flows which occur in different time frames to be totalled and compared on a like for like basis, enabling a best value option to be selected on the basis of *net present cost/value*.

5.3 Life cycle factors

When reviewing the results of option studies based on life cycle cost methodologies, the architect should ensure that the following aspects of the study have been properly taken into account:

- Discount rate, the selection of the discount rate should take into account the client's requirements. In the case of the public sector discount rates are published by the Treasury, and in the private sector, discount rates generally reflect the client's cost of finance or expectations for rates of return. As it can have such an impact on the end result, the discount rate must always be confirmed by the client.
- That costs for all options have been consistently calculated. Where appropriate both cost and income streams associated with each option should be considered. For example, all cleaning and maintenance costs should be included in a floor finishes assessment together with some revenues associated with the disposal of high value, long-life assets such as stone finishes.

WINDOW WHOLE LIFE COSTS – WORKED EXAMPLE

	Life expectancy	Capital Cost of Installation £/m²	Annual cost of Maintenance £/m²	Redecorations interval (years)	cost (£/m²)	PERIODIC COSTS replace gaskets/beads interval (years)	cost (£/m²)	Repair sills/frames interval (years)	cost (£/m²)
PC Aluminium	55	£320.00	£3.00	5 after 25	£24.00	15	£22.00	n/a	£0.00
Painted Softwood	30	£300.00	£2.50	5	£12.00	15	£25.00	5 after 20	£15.00

Year	Discount Factor	Powder Coated Aluminium Installation £/100m²	R&M £/100m²	Periodic Redecs £/100m²	Periodic Replacement £/100m²	Periodic Repairs £/100m²	Periodic Total £/100m²	Painted Softwood Installation £/100m²	R&M £/100m²	Periodic Redecs £/100m²	Periodic Replacement £/100m²	Periodic Repairs £/100m²	Periodic Total £/100m²
0	1.000	32,000						30,000					
5	0.681		204						170	816.70			816.70
10	0.463		139						116	555.83			555.83
15	0.315		95		693.53		693.53		79	378.29	788		1166.39
20	0.215		64						54	257.46		322	579.28
25	0.146		44	350.44			350.44		37	175.22		219	394.25
30	0.099		30	238.51	219		457.14	3,876	25				
35	0.068		20	162.32			162.32		17	81.16			81.16
40	0.046		14	110.47			110.47		12	55.24			55.24
45	0.031		9	75.19	68.92		144.11		8	37.59	78		115.91
50	0.021		6						5	25.59		32	57.57
TOTAL £/100m²		32,000.00	3,670.05	936.93	981.08	0.00	1918.02	33,875.72	3,058.37	2,383.08	866.42	572.83	3822.33
NET PRESENT COST £/m²							£375.88						£407.56

5.6 *Whole life cost comparison. Source: Davis Langdon*

- Presentation. The presentation of a whole life cost study based on discounted cash flow should make it clear that the reported cost does not reflect what the client or end user will actually pay. Furthermore, if the net present cost differential between two or more options is relatively small, the team should ensure that other criteria, such as the initial capital expenditure, are considered in the selection of the preferred option.
- Accuracy. The report should clearly state how accurate and reliable the source information upon which it is based is.

Figure 5.6 is a simple worked example of a whole life cost based option study examining the capital and maintenance costs of softwood and aluminium windows over an extended period of 50 years. The comparison illustrate that the aluminium windows, installed at a £20/m² cost premium have a lower life time costs.

Features of the example that are worth noting include:

- Total cost. This example is based on a discounted cashflow and the results are presented as a 'Net Present Cost'. This is the cost of all expenditure over the 50 year period, discounted to the present day at a rate of 8 per cent per annum.
- Effects of discounting. The costs of all future work are discounted to comparison on a like for like basis. This has the effect of reducing the significance and cost of future expenditure. The higher the discount rate, the lower the value of future expenditure. On this basis, high discount rates favour projects with lower initial capital costs. The effects of the discount factor can be seen in the declining cost of repair and maintenance over the study period. Even by year 5, at a discount rate of 8 per cent, the present day cost of £300 is discounted to £204.

- Inclusion of relevant costs only. Other operational costs that would be the same for the two options, cleaning for example, are excluded from the study.
- The importance of the length of the study period. In the worked example, the requirement to replace timber windows at 30 years is the key driver behind the differences in Net Present Cost. If the duration of the study were limited to 25 years, painted softwood would emerge the preferred option.

6 CONCLUSION

Clients will judge the success of their capital projects by many criteria, and there is no doubt that the imagination shown by the design team in delivering a carefully targeted solution to their client's requirements, together with a commitment to achieving a good level of finished quality will be very high on most clients' agendas. Delivery on budget is also usually a high priority, and unlike other aspects of project delivery is easy to monitor and measure. Design teams need to work closely with their cost consultants to make sure that budgets are appropriate, and that design solutions directly address aspects of the client's brief which deliver greatest value.

Techniques such as whole life costing and value management can be used by the cost consultant and design team to help to identify design solutions which best meet the client's requirements.

By collaborating closely from the earlier stages of a project to establish an appropriate capital cost budget, and by maintaining the discipline of working within the budget set by the client and project team, the design team will give itself the best opportunity of delivering a project which meets the design team's expectations, the client's requirements and provides all parties with an appropriate financial reward.

6 Structure

David Adler, Norman Seward and Andrew Peters

This chapter, originally written by David Adler and Norman Seward, was revised by Andrew Peters in 2011. Andrew Peters is a senior lecturer in the Department of Planning and Architecture at the University of the West of England and an architect in practice

KEY POINTS:
- *Current Codes of Practice require experts for the analysis and design of the specific type of structure and material*
- *Simplified approximate analysis and design methods as well as even simpler 'rules of thumb' do exist, but should not replace a rigorous final approach*

Contents
1 Introduction
2 Basic structural theory
3 Structural materials
4 Masonry
5 Timber
6 Reinforced concrete
7 Structural steelwork and other metals
8 Glass
9 Other materials
10 Foundations
11 Thumb-nail structures
12 Bibliography

1 INTRODUCTION

1.1 Scope
Structural engineering ensures that the loads of the building and its contents are transmitted safely and economically to the ground, allowing for considerations of function, aesthetics, internal and external environment and incorporating restraints imposed by other members of the building team, legislation, etc.

Structural engineering requires the use of mathematics to determine the forces in the framing elements of a structure (structural analysis). Sizing of these elements is then carried out based on interpretation of guidance provided in Codes of Practice relevant to the material being used (structural design). A competent structural engineer will have suitable training and be experienced in the required analysis and design techniques. Innovative and non-standard structures may require special consideration with the use of model testing to confirm analytical assumptions and member sizing.

1.2 Complexity
In recent years, mathematical methods prescribed in new Codes of Practice, particularly the Eurocodes, have become more complex, making the use of computer programs essential.

1.3 Philosophy
The treatment of the subject in this chapter is necessarily brief. It will be even less comprehensive than in previous editions, but will still try to give the architect something of a feel for structure, and help him or her in discussions with a structural engineer. And this is the key. An understanding of the numbers involved is not as important as an appreciation of the structural 'philosophy'. A grasp of how the structure is 'working' will enable the architect to have a meaningful conversation with a structural engineer. It should always be remembered that structure will have a definable impact on a design and if the wish is to keep control of that design even a basic level of involvement with the engineer will be beneficial. Because of the complexity of the methods now used, Local Authorities are increasingly insisting on the submission of calculations prepared by a Chartered Engineer from the recognized qualifying bodies, the Institution of Structural Engineers and the Institution of Civil Engineers who are entitled to use the designations CEng MIStructE or CEng MICE, respectively.

1.4 Key factors
There are three important factors in structural analysis and design:

- accurate assessment of the behaviour of the structural form;
- accurate identification and calculation of all the forces acting;
- full knowledge of the properties of the structural materials.

An outline of the methods used is given below.

2 BASIC STRUCTURAL THEORY

2.1 Introduction
This section will summarise basic structural concepts and the terms that might be met in dealing with structural matters. Examination in greater depth may be found in the references given at the end of the chapter.

2.2 Limit state
Current techniques in the majority of structural engineering Codes of Practice are based on the concept of limit state design. Traditionally, design involved calculating the maximum stress and deflection in a member under working load. That stress was compared with the stress in that material known, through experiment, to lead to failure. Safe design included a margin, called the *factor of safety*, between the working and failure stress values. This traditional method was generally referred to as *permissible stress* design.

It is however important to anticipate how the form of the structure will behave under increasing load as factors other than excessive stress can cause building failure. These are known as *limit states* and must all be considered for satisfactory design. Apart from collapsing completely (*limit state of collapse or ultimate limit state*), a building may crack locally so badly as to let in the weather, it may deflect until the users feel unsafe (*limit state of deflection or serviceability limit state*). The task of the structural designer is to ensure that none of the possible limit states is ever reached.

In the case of the ultimate limit state, this is done by making sure that ultimate material stresses are not exceeded under critical ultimate load combinations. Ultimate stresses are derived by dividing the material failure stress by a prescribed material safety factor and ultimate loads are calculated by multiplying the loads (see Section 2.3) by prescribed load factors. Both material and load factors are listed in the Codes of Practice relevant to the material being used.

The serviceability limit states of cracking and deflection are checked using working loads rather than ultimate loads, as the actual crack width and deflection in service is of interest.

2.3 Loads
In Section 2.2, reference was made to loads. A load is an example of a force, and the term is usually used to describe those outside forces that

act on a building structure. In Eurocodes, all loads and factors producing stress or deflection are called actions. Actions are of four types:

- Dead loads: from the weight of the structure itself and that of other fixed parts of the building such as cladding, finishes, partitions, etc.
- Imposed loads: from the weight of people, furniture and of materials stored in the building.
- Dynamic loads: these are of many origins. The most common dynamic load on a building is that caused by wind, which can produce horizontal and vertical pressures and suctions. Other dynamic loads are produced by moving machinery such as overhead cranes in large workshops and by earthquakes. For the purposes of design, dynamic loads were often transformed into approximate equivalent static loadings. The widespread availability of sophisticated analytical software now allows more accurate dynamic analysis to be carried out.
- The fourth type of action is one that is not produced by an outside force, but by internal factors such as thermal expansion.

2.4 Force units

Forces, including loads, are measured in Newtons (N). One Newton is the force required to give a mass of 1 kg an acceleration of 1 m/s^2. A tip to remember is that a Newton is about the weight of an apple. Most forces in structural engineering are expressed in kN (kilonewtons). Table I gives conversions from and to SI, MT and FPS (Imperial) units for loadings of all types.

2.5 Mass and weight

Confusion often arises between the terms *mass* and *weight*. Outside nuclear physics, the *mass* of an object is a fixed quantity which is a basic property of that object. Its *weight* will depend on the mass, but also on the value of the gravitational effect on the object. This is not a constant, but can vary, not only in extra-terrestrial conditions

Table I Various conversions for loadings

Point loads

1 N = 0.102 kgf = 0.225 lbf
1 kN =101.972 kgf = 224.81 lbf = 0.1004 tonf
1 MN = 101.972 tf = 224.81 kipf = 100.36 tonf
1 kgf = 9.807 N = 2.205 lbf
1 tf = 9.807 kN = 2.205 kipf = 0.9842 tonf
1 lbf = 4.448 N = 0.4536 kgf
1 kipf = 4.448 kN = 453.59 kgf = 0.4536 tf
1 tonf = 9.964 kN = 1.016 tf

Linearly distributed loads

1 N/m = 0.0685 lbf/ft = 0.206lbf/yd
1 kN/m = 68.5 lbf/ft = 0.0306 tonf/ft
1 kgf/m = 9.807 N/m = 0.672 lbf/ft = 2.016 lbf/yd
1 tf/m = 9.807 kN/m = 0.672 kipf/ft = 2.016 kipf/yd = 0.3 tonf/ft = 0.9 tonf/yd
1 lbf/ft = 14.59 N/m =1.488 kgf/m
1 kipf/ft = 14.58 kN/m =1.488 tf/m
1 ton/ft = 32.69 kN/m = 3.33 tf/m
1 tonf/yd = 10.90 kN/m = 1.11 tf/m

Superficially distributed loads

1 N/m^2 = 0.0209lb/ft^2
1 kN/m^2 = 20.89 lb/ft^2
1 MN/m^2 = 9.324 tonf/ft^2
1 kgf/m^2 = 9.80665 N/m^2 = 0.2048lbf/ft^2 =1.843lbf/yd^2
1 tf/m^2 = 9.80665 kN/m^2 = 0.2048 kipf/ft^2 = 0.0914 tonf/ft^2 = 0.823 tonf/yd^2
1 lb/ft^2 = 47.88 N/m^2 = 4.88 kgf/m^2
1 kipf/ft^2 = 47.88 kN/m^2 = 4.88 tf/m^2
1 tonf/ft^2 = 107.25 kN/m^2 =10.93 tf/m^2
1 tonf/yd^2 = 11.92 kN/m^2 = 1.215 tf/m^2

Densities

1 N/m^3 = 0.00637 lbf/ft^3
1 kN/m^3 = 6.37lbf/ft^3
1 MN/m^3 = 2.844 tonf/ft^3
1 kg/m^3 = 0.0624lb/ft^3 (mass density)
1 t/m^3 = 62.4lb/ft^3
1 lb/ft^3 = 16.02 kg/m^3 1 lbf/ft^3 =157 N/m^3
1 ton/ft^3 = 35.88 t/m^3 1 ton/ft^3 = 351.9 kN/m^3
1 ton/yd^3 = 1.33 t/m^3

Table II Densities of bulk materials

	kg/m^3	kN/m^3
Aggregates		
Coarse		
Normal weight, e.g. natural aggregates	1600	15.7
Fine		
Normal weight, e.g. sand	1760	17.3
Bricks (common burnt clay)		
Stacked	1602–1920	15.7–18.8
Cement		
Bags	1281	12.6
Concrete, plain		
Aerated	480–1600	
brick aggregate	1840–2160	
Clinker	1440	14.1
stone ballast	2240	22.0
natural aggregates	2307	
Concrete, reinforced 2% steel	2420	23.7
Glass		
Plate	2787	27.3
Gypsum		
Plaster	737	7.2
Metals:		
Aluminium cast	2771	27.2
Iron		
Cast	7208	70.7
Wrought	7689	75.4
Lead:		
cast or rolled	11 325	111.1
Stone		
Bath	2082	20.4
masonry, dressed	2403	23.6
Granite	2643	25.9
Marble	2595–2835	25.4–27.8
Slate:		
Welsh	2803	27.5
Timbers:		
Ash (Canadian)	737	7.2
Balsawood	112	1.1
Beech	769	6.9
Birch	641	6.3
Cedar, western red	384	3.8
Deal, yellow	432	4.2
Ebony	1185–1330	11.6–13.1
Elm		
English	577	5.6
Fir:		
Douglas	529	5.2
Silver	481	4.7
Hemlock, western	497	4.9
Iroko	657	6.4
Larch	593	5.8
Mahogany: (African)	561	5.5
Maple	737	7.2
Oak: English	801–881	7.8–8.6
Pine: New Zealand	609	6.0
Plywood	481–641	4.7–6.3
Plastic bonded	721–1442	7.0–14.2
Resin bonded	721–1362	7.0–13.4
Poplar	449	4.4
Spruce Canadian	465	4.6
Sycamore	609	6.0
Teak, Burma or African	657	6.4
Walnut	657	6.4
Whitewood	465	4.6
Water	1001	9.8

but even very slightly on different places on earth. However, for all practical purposes the acceleration of gravity is taken as 9.81 m/s^2, so that the weight of a kilogram mass is 9.81 N. This figure is invariably rounded up to 10 for ease of computation.

2.6 Loading assessment

Perhaps, the most important calculation the structural engineer carries out relates to the accurate assessment of loading. Table II shows the loads of various materials which may comprise the

Table III Superficial masses of materials in kg/m³ and weights in N/m². This is based on figures in BS 648:1964, and should be taken as approximate

	kg/m²	N/m²
Aluminium sheet		
Corrugated (BS 2855) (including 20% added weight for laps 'as laid') 0.71 mm	2.9	28
Battens		
Slating and tiling, 40 × 20 mm softwood 100 mm gauge	3.4	33
Blockwork, walling (per 25 mm thickness)		
Clay		
Hollow	25.5	250
Concrete		
Stone aggregate		
Cellular	40.0	392
Hollow	34.2	335
Solid	53.8	528
Lightweight aggregate		
Cellular	28.3	278
Hollow	25.5	250
Solid	31.7	311
Aerated		
Based on 560 kg/m³	14.4	141
Based on 800 kg/m³	19.2	188
100 mm thick	52.4	514
115 mm thick	56.9	558
Brickwork (all per 25 mm thick)		
Clay		
Solid		
Low density	50.0	490
Medium density	53.8	528
High density	58.2	571
Perforated		
Low density, 25% voids	38.0	373
Low density, 15% voids	42.3	415
Medium density, 25% voids	39.9	391
Medium density, 15% voids	46.2	453
High density, 25% voids	44.2	433
High density, 15% voids	48.0	471
Concrete	57.7	566
Flagstones		
Concrete 50 mm thick	115	1130
Natural stone 50 mm thick	56	549
Floors		
Hollow concrete units (including any concrete topping necessary for constructional purposes)		
100 mm	168	1650
150 mm	217	2130
200 mm	285	2800
Glass		
Float 6 mm	16.7	164
Gypsum panels and partitions		
Dry partition		
65 mm thick	26.5	260
Lathing		
Wood	6.3	62
Lead sheet (BS 1178)		
0.118 in (3.0mm)	34.2	335
Plaster		
Gypsum		
Two coat, 12 mm thick		
Normal sanded undercoat and neat finishing	20.8	204
One coat, 5 mm thick, neat gypsum	6.7	66
Lime (non-hydraulic and hydraulic) 12 mm thick	23.1	227
Lightweight		
Vermiculite aggregate, two coat, ditto	10.5	103
Plasterboard, gypsum		
Solid core		
9.5 mm	8.3	81
12 mm	10.6	104
18 mm	16.1	158
Plywood		
Per mm thick	0.6 ± 0.1	6 + 1
Rendering		
Portland cement: sand (1:3) 12 mm thick	27.7	272
Screeding		
Portland cement: sand (1:3) 12 mm thick	27.7	272

	kg/m²	N/m²
Slate		
Welsh		
Thin	24.4	239
Thick	48.8	479
Steel		
Mild, sheet Corrugated (1 mm)	15.6	153
Stonework, natural		
Note: For cramps add 80 kg/m³ (5lb/ft³)		
Limestone		
Light, e.g. Bathstone		
100 mm thick	206.6	2026
Medium, e.g. Portland stone		
100 mm thick	225.9	2215
Heavy, e.g. marble		
20 mm thick	53.7	527
Sandstone		
Light, e.g. Woolton		
100 mm thick	221.1	2168
Medium, e.g. Darley Dale		
100 mm thick	230.7	2262
Heavy, e.g. Mansfield Red		
100 mm thick	240.3	2357
Granite		
Light, e.g. Peterhead		
50 mm thick	129.7	1272
Medium, e.g. Cornish		
50 mm thick	134.5	1319
Heavy, e.g. Guernsey		
50 mm thick	144.2	1414
Thatching		
Reed (including battens) 300 mm thick	41.5	407
Tiling, roof		
Clay		
Plain Machine made, 100 mm gauge	63.5	623
Concrete		
Stone aggregate		
Plain		
75 mm gauge	92.8	910
100 mm gauge	68.4	671
115 mm gauge	61.0	598
Interlocking (single lap)	48.8 ± 7.3	479± 72

fabric of a building that may be included in the dead load computation. It also gives the densities of materials that may be stored within it: part of the imposed loads. The figures are given both in the usual mass density form: kg/m³, and also in the more convenient weight density kN/m³. Some loadings are more conveniently calculated from superficial or linear unit weights, and a few are given in Table III. For a comprehensive list of weights of building materials, reference should be made to BS648 *Schedule of weights of building materials*.

Table IV indicates minimum imposed loads that should be allowed for in designing buildings for various purposes. These figures are intended to allow for the people in the building, and the kind of material normally stored. However, these loads sometimes need to be checked against the figures in Tables II and III for more unusual circumstances.

2.7 Structural elements
For convenience of design, large structures are broken up into elements. These are of different types according to the function they perform in the building. Before describing each type, it will be necessary to explore the forces that are found internally in the materials of the structure.

2.8 Stress and strain
If a bar of uniform cross-section has an outward force applied at each end, Figure 6.1, it will stretch slightly. This stretch is called the strain in the bar, and is defined as the extension divided by the original length.

Table IV Typical minimum imposed floor loads extracted from BS 6399 – 1 Loading for buildings: Code of practice for dead and imposed loads

Type of activity/or occupancy for part of the building or structure	Examples of specific use		Uniformly distributed load (kN/m²)	Concentrated load (kN)
A Domestic and residential activities (also see category C)	All usages within self-contained single family dwelling units. Communal areas (including kitchens) in blocks of flats with limited use (see note 1) (for communal areas in other blocks of flats see C3 and below)		1.5	1.4
	Bedrooms and dormitories except those in single family dwelling units and hotels and motels		1.5	1.8
	Bedrooms in hotels and motels Hospital wards Toilet areas		2.0	1.8
	Communal kitchens except in flats covered by note 1		3.0	4.5
	Balconies	Single family dwelling units and communal areas in blocks of flats with limited use (see note 1)	1.5	1.4
		Guest houses, residential clubs and communal areas in blocks of flats except as covered by note 1	Same as rooms to which they give access but with a minimum of 3.0	1.5/m run concentrated at the outer edge
		Hotels and motels	Same as rooms to which they give access but with a minimum of 4.0	1.5/m run concentrated at the outer edge
B Offices and work areas not covered elsewhere	Operating theatres, X-ray rooms, utility rooms		2.0	4.5
	Work rooms (light industrial) without storage		2.5	1.8
	Offices for general use		2.5	2.7
	Kitchens, laundries, laboratories		3.0	4.5
	Rooms with mainframe computers or similar equipment		3.5	4.5
	Factories, workshops and similar buildings (general industrial)		5.0	4.5
	Balconies		Same as rooms to which they give access but with a minimum of 4.0	1.5/m run concentrated at the outer edge
C Areas where people may congregate	Public, institutional and communal dining rooms and lounges, cafes and restaurants (see note 2)		2.0	2.7
C1 Areas with tables	Reading rooms with no book storage		2.5	4.5
	Classrooms		3.0	2.7
C2 Areas with fixed seats	Assembly areas with fixed seating (see note 3)		4.0	3.6
	Places of worship		3.0	2.7
C3 Areas without obstacles for moving people	Corridors, hallways, aisles, stairs, landings, etc. in institutional type buildings (not subject to crowds or wheeled vehicles), hostels, guest houses, residential clubs, and communal areas in blocks of flats not covered by note 1. (For communal areas in blocks of flats covered by note 1, see A.)	Corridors, hallways, aisles, etc. (traffic foot only)	3.0	4.5
		Stairs and landings (foot traffic only)	3.0	4.0
	Corridors, hallways, aisles, stairs, landings, etc. in all other buildings including hotels and motels and institutional buildings	Corridors, hallways, aisles, etc. (foot traffic only)	4.0	4.5
		Corridors, hallways, aisles, etc. subject to wheeled vehicles, trolleys, etc.	5.0	4.5
		Stairs and landings (foot traffic only)	4.0	4.0
	Balconies (except as specified in A)		Same as rooms to which they give access but with a minimum of 4.0	1.5/m run concentrated at the outer edge
C4 Areas with possible physical activities (see clause 9)	Dance halls and studios, gymnasia, stages		5.0	3.6
C5 Areas susceptible to overcrowding (see clause 9)	Assembly areas without fixed seating, concert halls, bars, places of worship and grandstands		5.0	3.6
	Stages in public assembly areas		7.5	4.5
D Shopping areas	Shop floors for the sale and display of merchandise		4.0	3.6
E Warehousing and storage areas. Areas subject to accumulation of goods. Areas for equipment and plant	General areas for static equipment not specified elsewhere (institutional and public buildings)		2.0	4.5
	Reading rooms with book storage, e.g. libraries		4.0	4.5
	General storage other than those specified		2.4 for each metre of storage height	7.0
	File rooms, filing and storage space (offices)		5.0	4.5
	Stack rooms (books)		2.4 for each metre in storage height but with a minimum of 6.5	7.0
	Dense mobile stacking (books) on mobile trolleys, in public and institutional buildings		4.8 for each metre of storage height but with a minimum of 9.6	7.0
	Plant rooms, boiler rooms, fan rooms, etc. including weight of machinery		7.5	4.5
F	Parking for cars, light vans, etc. not exceeding 2500 kg gross mass, including garages, driveways and ramps		2.5	9.0

Note 1. Communal areas in blocks of flats with limited use refers to blocks of flats not more than three storeys in height and with not more than four self-contained single family dwelling units per floor accessible from one staircase.
Note 2. Where these same areas may be subjected to loads due to physical activities or overcrowding, e.g. a hotel dining room used as a dance floor, imposed loads should be based on occupancy C4 or C5 as appropriate. Reference should also be made to clause 9.
Note 3. Fixed seating is seating where its removal and the use of the space for other purposes is improbable.

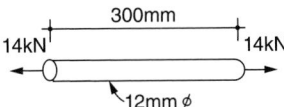

6.1 *A bar of uniform cross-section under a tensile force*

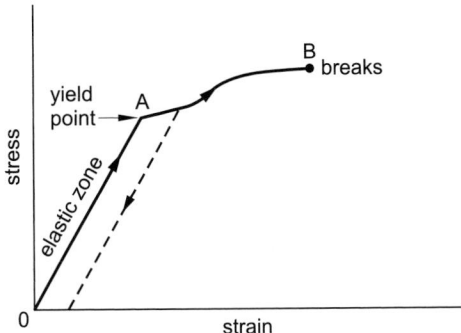

6.2 *Stress–strain diagram for steel showing the yield point where Hooke's Law (stress is proportional to strain) no longer operates. Dotted line shows deformation caused when stress is reduced after the yield point, material does not return to its original form*

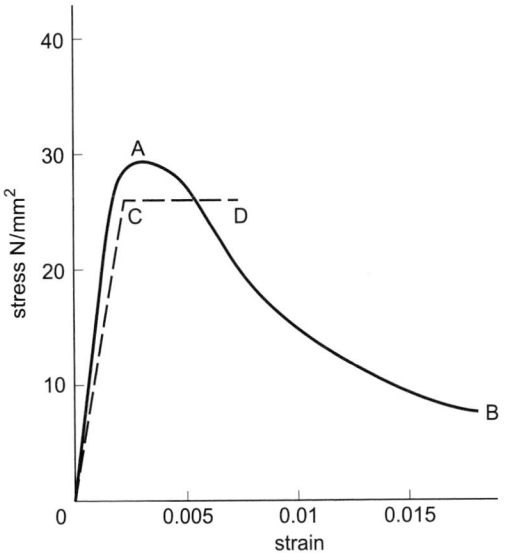

6.3 *Stress–strain diagram for a typical concrete*

The *stress* on this bar is the force on the cross-section divided by its area. The relationship between the strain and the stress is an important factor in structural engineering. Figure 6.2 shows a graph of this relationship for steel. The length OA is a straight line and is called the *elastic zone*. In the *elastic zone*, the ratio of stress to strain is a constant called *Young's Modulus*. At A, there is a sudden change called the *yield point*. *Hooke's Law*, which says that stress and strain are proportionate, only applies in the elastic zone. Beyond this point along the curve AB there is no constant relationship between the stress and the strain. In fact, even if there is no increase in stress, the strain can increase over time until the bar breaks at B. This length of curve is known as the *plastic zone*.

In Figure 6.3, OAB shows the actual stress/strain relationship for a typical concrete. This, for many practical purposes, can be substituted by OCD. OC is the elastic and CD the plastic zone.

2.9 Units of stress

The basic SI unit of stress is the N/m^2 (which is also called the Pascal, Pa), but this is too small a unit for practical purposes. The correct form for the normal unit is the mega Pascal, MPa or mega Newton MN/m^2 but this is expressed by engineers in units of N/mm^2.

2.10 Tension members

If the stress in a member tends to lengthen it, it is said to be in *tension*. Elements in tension are called *ties*. In many ways, this is the simplest kind of stress. Some materials, steel members in particular are ideal for resisting it. Cables, wires and chains can be used to carry tension. Materials such as stone, cast iron and unreinforced concrete have little or no resistance to tension.

2.11 Compression members

If the stress in a member tends to shorten it, it is in *compression*. Elements in compression are called *struts, columns, piers or stanchions*. The term used depends on their location and the material of which they are made.

Most materials other than cables, wires and chains can be used to carry compression. However, there is an instability phenomenon that occurs in compression members called *buckling*. For some members, particularly those that are slender in comparison with their length, increase in compressive load will cause bending until failure occurs in tension on one side. It is this buckling effect that can be the cause of the collapse of slender towers and high walls of masonry construction.

2.12 Pin-jointed frames

Some structures are designed and constructed of members that act as struts and ties. Analysis methods assume that the members are pin jointed at their ends, which allows only the development of compressive or tensile forces in each member. A roof truss is typical of this type, the general term for which is *pin-jointed frame*. In practice, very few such structures are actually physically pin-jointed (although some have been built), but the use of flexible bolted connector plates adequately approximates the theoretical assumption of a pin at member ends.

2.13 Bending

Unlike struts and ties which transmit only compressive and tensile forces along their length, beam members support loads by bending action. Internal forces known as bending moments are developed within the beam allowing it to support loads acting at right angles to its length. An example of beam action is that of a lintel spanning an opening and carrying the applied loads from floor and walls above safely around the opening.

Bending is the phenomenon by which a single member of significant depth develops both compression and tension across its section. Consider the case of a beam supported at each end with a load in the centre of the span, the deflected shape is a downward sag resulting in maximum compression in the top layers of the beam, and maximum tension in the bottom layers. Somewhere in the middle of the beam will be layer with no stress at all. This layer is known as the *neutral axis*, Figure 6.4. The externally applied bending moment is resisted by an internal moment in the beam which is a function of the product of the compressive and tensile forces and the distance between their lines of action.

2.14 Materials in bending

Since the internal moment of resistance of a beam depends upon the development of both compressive and tensile forces, only materials that are strong in both compression and tension are generally suitable

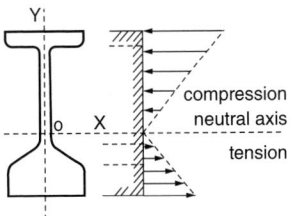

6.4 *Structural member under pure bending*

Table V Comparison of material properties

Property	Masonry (clay brickwork)	Reinforced concrete (with 4% reinforcement)	Steel (mild steel)	Wood (whitewood)	Glass reinforced plastic (polyester)	Annealed glass	Fabric (polyester yarn with pvc coating)
Type of material	Ceramic	Cementitious with metal	Metal	Natural Composite	Synthetic Composite	Glass	Polymer
Weight (p) kN/mm³	22	24	78	4.5	18	25	14
Tensile strength (σ_{TS}) N/mm²	1	18	400	75	250	5000 but fracture governed	1000
Compressive strength (σ_c) N/mm²	15	45	400	25	150	1000 but complimentary tensile strength will govern	none
Coefficient of thermal expansion (α) × 10⁻⁶/°C	6	12	12	4	14	7.7–8.8	. . .

for beams. Steel and timber are good examples of such materials. Stone, being weak in tension, makes poor bending members. The ancient Greeks had to construct buildings with closely spaced columns, as stone lintels would not span very far. Only when the arch had been invented could the spans be increased, because the arch is wholly in compression. Cast iron is weak in tension, although not as weak as stone. The bottom flanges of cast iron beams were often larger than the top flanges to allow for this inequality in strength. Concrete is also poor under tensile force, so steel is used in the tension zone (which is usually at the bottom, except for cantilevered and continuous beams – see below), to reinforce concrete beams.

2.15 Beams
Beams can be categorised as follows:

- *Simply supported*. The beam ends are assumed to be completely free to move rotationally resulting in zero moment at each end. In addition, one end is assumed to be supported on a roller bearing allowing freedom of movement in the direction of the beam length resulting in zero horizontal reaction at the roller bearing end. If the loading is uniformly distributed along the length of the beam then the bending moment will be a maximum at midspan. This type of beam is known as statically determinate as the support reactions and bending moments can be calculated using the basic equations of equilibrium.
- *Cantilever*. This beam type is supported only at one end where it is fixed in both position and rotationally. The bending moment will be zero at the free end and a maximum at the support causing tension in the top of the beam.
- *Encastré or fixed end*. This beam is built-in at both ends. This type of beam is statically indeterminate as the values of the bending moments are not calculable by normal statistical methods. These values actually depend on a number of imponderables, such as how much fixity exists at each support. Maximum moments will occur in encastré beams either at midspan or at one, other or both ends, depending upon the disposition of the loads.
- *Continuous*. A beam on several supports is known as a continuous beam. Generally, the maximum moments occur over the supports. Tension in the beam section over the supports occurs at the top but occurs at the bottom at midspan. Continuous concrete beams have to be reinforced accordingly.
- *Lintels*. Beams that are supported on brickwork, such as lintels over doorways and windows, are not considered structurally encastré, and are normally designed as simply supported.

2.16 Bending moments
In order to design a beam, an engineer first calculates the bending moments at critical sections generated by the worst case loading combination. Maximum internal stresses are then computed at those sections. For anything other than the simplest structure, this can be a time-consuming and complicated matter. For a large number of the simpler cases, the moment at midspan of an assumed simply supported beam will suffice to give a safe answer, if not

perhaps the most economical. Table V gives maximum bending moments and deflections for the common cases likely to be met.

2.17 Bending stresses
Once the bending moment M is known, the stress f at any layer at distance y from the neutral axis can be found from elastic or plastic theory relationships. The choice of elastic or plastic design theory is dictated by the code of practice for the material being considered.

For elastic design, the relationship is:

$$\frac{M}{y} = \frac{f}{l}$$

The stress in the extreme fibre of a beam therefore depends on the *second moment of area* (I) of the cross-section, proportional to the cube of the depth of the section. Suffice it to say that the larger the depth of the section, the smaller will be the maximum stress. It is therefore beneficial to choose cross-section shapes that have large I-values for the given area of material. For this reason, the most common shape of cross-section for a steel beam is an I, a greater distance between the flanges results in a reduction of material for the required second moment of area.

There is a limit to this, however. Since the top flange is in compression, if it becomes too slender it can buckle. This is particularly significant in the design of steelwork and is the reason that beams have to be checked for lateral torsional buckling when the compression flange is not fully restrained.

2.18 Shear
In addition to internal forces generated by bending moments, most beam cross-sections will also have to carry a force in the plane of the section, called a *shear force*. Generally, the shear will be greatest at the supports of a beam, and least at midspan.

In the case of an I-section, the shear force acts mainly within the web connecting together the two flanges that are in compression and tension. If the web becomes too slender it can buckle under the influence of the shear force.

2.19 Deflection
Since the top of a loaded beam is in compression, it must reduce in length; the bottom, in tension, must stretch. This will lead to the beam taking up a curved form: in the case of a simply supported beam with vertical loading, it will sag. Excessive sagging is not only unsightly, but also may cause damage to finishes such as plaster ceilings, or cause load to be transferred onto partitions that are not designed to carry such load. Formulae are published in many texts giving the deflections of various kinds of beams under different loads.

3 STRUCTURAL MATERIALS
3.1 Behaviour
The third major factor in structural design is an adequate knowledge of the behaviour of the materials used. The basic palette of materials consists of masonry (stone, brick and block), timber, steel

and reinforced concrete. Design in new materials such as plastics, fabric and glass are becoming more widespread.

4 MASONRY

4.1 Use

Masonry is the general term used for loadbearing construction in brick, block and stone; these are materials of interest to architects. Since they and the mortar that is used to fill the gaps between their elements are all weak in tension, such construction is normally used to carry only simple compressive forces in vertical elements such as walls and piers, sometimes in arches. Masonry can also be used to resist lateral loads from soil and water pressures in retaining walls and wind loads when used in loadbearing masonry or when used as a cladding to a framed building structure. Masonry can be reinforced with steel bars and/or mesh to increase its tensile resistance and hence overall strength.

4.2 Design

Design of masonry should be carried out in accordance with *BS5268 – 1 Code of practice for the use of masonry. Structural use of unreinforced masonry*, a limit state code based upon plastic design theory. The Eurocode for masonry, BS EN 1996-3:2006, *Eurocode 6; Design of masonry structures. Simplified calculation methods for unreinforced masonry structures* will replace BS5628 on its withdrawal.

The Institution of Structural Engineers *Manual for the design of plain masonry in building structures* (the Red Book) offers design guidance for simple structural masonry.

4.3 Vertical loadbearing elements

A *wall* is a vertical load-carrying element whose length in plan is at least four times its width, otherwise it is a *column*. A *pier* is a column integral with a wall. References to walls apply also to columns and piers unless stated otherwise.

The load-carrying capacity of a wall depends on:

- the crushing strength of the masonry unit;
- the composition of the mortar;
- the size and shape of the masonry unit;
- the height of the wall relative to its width – its slenderness ratio;
- the eccentricity of the loading.

Figures 6.5 and 6.6 give information on typical masonry designs. Although popular in the past, masonry is rarely used for floors nowadays. However, vaults and domed roofs continue to be built in traditional types of buildings such as churches.

5 TIMBER

5.1 Structure of timber

Timber is probably the oldest building material used. Wood is composed of hollow tubular fibres of cellulose impregnated with the resin lignin, packed closely together not unlike a bundle of drinking straws. The result is that the material is strong in the longitudinal direction – in tension and compression – but weak along the interface between the fibres.

5.2 Advantages of timber

Consequently, timber has the supreme virtue of 'toughness'. It usually gives a forewarning of imminent failure, as the weakness between the fibres inhibits the progress of transverse cracks. Even when failure has occurred, there is often enough residual strength to carry a substantial load. Its principal drawbacks are susceptibility to insect and fungal attack and vulnerability to fire. Biological resistance can be fortified by treatment and a constant charring rate allows fire resistance to be designed in by over sizing members for the required period.

Timber is one of that minority of materials that is almost equally strong in tension and compression. This strength is such that buckling of the compression flange of bending members is rarely a problem. Rectangular sections are easily formed and used for this purpose. Timber is easily worked by hand and machine tools and it is simple to connect with other members, both other timber members and those of steel, masonry and concrete. However, even moderately stressed connections require plenty of room to accommodate the required number of fixings and usually this is the defining factor in sizing timber elements. For instance, on a simple dining table the section of the legs is not related to its need to withstand the compressive forces due to vertical downward forces but more to do with how the leg is fixed to the table top or sub-frame.

5.3 Design

Advances in the technology of timber started in the railway era when it was used for elaborate viaducts and bridges. These were generally constructed by trial and error, calculation methods being developed later. In recent years, these methods of calculation have been taken to the point where it has become an extremely specialised field. The use of the current Codes of Practice by nonspecialists is not recommended. In complicated timber structures, the sizes of the members tend to depend more on the design of the connections than on the internal stresses.

Design of timber should be carried out in accordance with BS 5268-2:2002 *Structural use of timber. Code of practice for*

Element	Horizontal and vertical section	Typical heights (h) (m)	h/d between lateral supports	Critical factors for sizing	Remarks
Masonry column		1–4	15–20	Buckling and crushing ($h/d>6$) Crushing ($h/d<6$) Bending	h is vertical distance between lateral supports and d is thickness of column
Masonry wall		1–5	18–22	Buckling and crushing ($h/d>6$) Crushing ($h/d<6$) Bending	h is vertical distance between horizontal lateral supports; wall may also have vertical lateral supports
Reinforced and prestressed masonry columns and walls		2–7	20–35	Bending	h is vertical distance between horizontal lateral supports; wall may also have vertical lateral supports

6.5 *Masonry – vertical support elements*

Element	Section	Typical heights (H) (m)	Typical H/d	Remarks
Reinforced masonry retaining wall		1–6	10–15	Wall made of reinforced hollow blocks or units with reinforced concrete pockets w about $H/2$–$2H/3$
Masonry rubble in baskets (gabions)		1–3	1–2	Rubble masonry gabion walls usually more economic than thick mass concrete retaining wall

Plan/on element	Vertical section	Formulae for preliminary sizing only – elastic theory	Remarks
Single wall		$\dfrac{h}{t} < 20$	Formula valid when lateral movement is prevented at top and bottom of wall, at right angles to wall; such restraint usually provided by floor and roof construction Wall has greater bending strength in the horizontal direction so that vertical supports would be preferred to horizontal supports Walls fail by crushing if $h/t < 10$ or by buckling and crushing if $h/t > 10$
Column		$\dfrac{h}{t}$ and $\dfrac{2h}{w} < 20$ $p < \dfrac{t.w.u}{5}$ where u is ultimate compressive strength of small masonry sample $\dfrac{h}{t_{cf}} < 20$	Column illustrated given lateral restraint at top in one direction only and effective height of column in that direction taken as actual height; effective height in direction at right angles taken as twice actual height Columns fail by crushing if slenderness ratio, $h_{cf}/t < 10$ where h_{cf} is unfactored value of load applied near centre of column t_1 and t_2 are thicknesses of leaves of cavity wall which are tied together Wall illustrated has vertical load from floor taken by inner leaf only
Cavity wall		where t_{cf} is greater of t_1, t_2 or $2/3\,(t_1 + t_2)$	
Single wall with piers or intersecting walls		$\dfrac{L}{t} < 20$ $\dfrac{2.5c}{t} < 20$	Vertical piers or intersecting walls used to restrain walls as alternative to horizontal supports at top and bottom of wall. Dimension c is distance of outhang from last vertical support d is depth of pier of intersecting wall which should be greater than 500 mm

6.6 *Masonry elements carrying gravity loads*

permissible stress design, materials and workmanship, a permissible stress design code based upon elastic design theory. The Eurocode for timber, BS EN 1995-1-1:2004, *Eurocode 5. Design of timber structures. General. Common rules and rules for buildings* will replace BS5268 on its withdrawal.

5.4 Timber sources and grades
Timber can be home-produced or imported from many places. There is a degree of standardisation, but the designer can encounter a wide variation in qualities. The structural properties of some common types are given later in Figure 6.10, and Tables VI and VII.

5.5 Large timber sections
Because of the shape and composition of the tree trunks from which timber comes, it is difficult to directly produce the larger

size sections often required for modern construction, particularly for beams. For such larger sections, smaller timbers are glued together to form *laminated beams*, Figure 6.7. These are extremely useful for many purposes, and manufacturers produce handbooks giving comprehensive data for their use.

5.6 Timber frame
Over 80 per cent of the world's housing is composed of timber frame and it is becoming more common in the UK. Figures 6.8, 6.9 and 6.10 give information relating to vertical support in timber and on frame and wall systems.

5.7 Roof trusses
The average UK architect meets timber in two common places: roof trusses and floor joists. Nowadays, most trusses are of the

Table VI Maximum permissible spans for rafter members shown in Figure 6.11 (ref BS 5268-3 Table B2)

Strength class of timber[b]	Finished size[c]	Pitch								
		15°	17½°	20°	22½°	25°	27½°	30°	32½°	35°
	mm	m	m	m	m	m	m	m	m	m
C16	35 × 72	5.06	5.17½	5.34	5.49	5.63	5.77	5.91	6.06	6.21
	35 × 97	6.35	6.53	6.70	6.87	7.05	7.22	7.40	7.57	7.75
	35 × 120	7.55	7.75	7.94	8.15	8.36	8.54	8.74	8.94	9.14
	35 × 145	8.83	9.07	9.29	9.53	9.74	9.97	10.21	10.43	10.67
	38 × 72	5.25	5.40	5.54	5.68	5.82	5.97	6.11	6.26	6.41
	38 × 89	6.16	6.33	6.50	6.66	6.83	7.00	7.16	7.33	7.50
	38 × 114	7.48	7.53	7.87	8.07	8.28	8.47	8.67	8.81	9.07
	38 × 140	8.73	8.98	9.25	9.49	9.71	9.95	10.18	10.41	10.65
	47 × 72	5.83	5.98	6.12	6.26	6.41	6.56	6.70	6.85	7.00
	47 × 97	7.32	7.50	7.69	7.88	8.06	8.25	8.44	8.63	8.81
	47 × 120	8.51	8.73	8.96	9.19	9.41	9.64	9.87	10.10	10.32
	47 × 145	9.63	9.90	10.16	10.43	10.71	10.99	11.25	11.53	11.79
C22	35 × 72	5.60	5.76	5.92	6.09	6.25	6.41	6.57	6.74	6.90
	35 × 97	7.03	7.23	7.42	7.62	7.82	8.02	8.22	8.41	8.61
	35 × 120	8.35	8.58	8.80	9.03	9.26	9.48	9.71	9.93	10.15
	35 × 145	9.76	10.04	10.29	10.56	10.80	11.00	11.00	11.00	11.00
	47 × 72	6.46	6.63	6.79	6.95	7.12	7.29	7.45	7.62	7.78
	47 × 97	8.10	8.31	8.53	8.74	8.95	9.16	9.38	9.59	9.80
	47 × 120	9.41	9.67	9.93	10.19	10.45	10.70	10.96	11.22	11.47
	47 × 145	10.65	10.96	11.26	11.57	11.88	12.00	12.00	12.00	12.00
	35 × 72	5.96	6.12	6.30	6.46	6.63	6.80	6.96	7.13	7.25
	35 × 97	7.50	7.71	7.92	8.12	8.33	8.54	8.74	8.94	9.00
	35 × 120	8.71	8.95	9.20	9.42	9.66	9.89	10.12	10.15	10.15
	35 × 145	10.25	10.54	10.80	11.00	11.00	11.00	11.00	11.00	11.00
C24	38 × 72	6.19	6.34	6.51	6.66	6.83	6.99	7.14	7.30	7.43
	38 × 89	7.27	7.46	7.65	7.83	8.02	8.21	8.39	8.57	8.74
	38 × 114	8.66	8.90	9.14	9.36	9.59	9.82	10.06	10.15	10.21
	38 × 140	10.16	10.45	10.72	10.99	11.25	11.25	11.25	11.25	11.25
	47 × 72	6.87	7.01	7.14	7.28	7.42	7.55	7.69	7.82	7.96
	47 × 97	8.64	8.81	8.99	9.17	9.35	9.52	9.70	9.87	10.05
	47 × 120	9.81	10.07	10.32	10.58	10.83	11.10	11.34	11.60	11.85
	47 × 145	11.10	11.41	11.73	12.00	12.00	12.00	12.00	12.00	12.00

[a]These maximum permissible spans are suitable for trussed rafters fabricated and used in accordance with the conditions given in Annex B.
[b]Subject to the visual grading criteria in 5.1.2.
[c]Measured at a moisture content of 20% and subject to the manufacturing tolerance in 5.1.3.

Table VII Maximum permissible spans for ceiling ties (ref BS 5268-3 Table)

Strength class of timber[b]	Finished size[c]	Pitch								
		15°	17½°	20°	22½°	25°	27½°	30°	32½°	35°
	mm	m	m	m	m	m	m	m	m	m
	35 × 72	3.70	3.97	4.24	4.50	4.77	5.02	5.29	5.55	5.82
	35 × 97	5.13	5.51	5.90	6.28	6.65	7.03	7.41	7.78	8.15
	35 × 120	6.29	6.79	7.29	7.78	8.24	8.72	9.20	9.69	10.14
	35 × 145	7.36	8.04	8.71	9.38	10.05	10.73	11.00	11.00	11.00
C16	38 × 72	3.85	4.14	4.42	4.69	4.97	5.24	5.52	5.79	6.07
	38 × 89	4.84	5.20	5.56	5.89	6.27	6.63	6.98	7.33	7.68
	38 × 114	6.15	6.64	7.13	7.60	8.07	8.55	9.02	9.49	9.95
	38 × 140	7.27	7.94	8.59	9.25	9.91	10.57	11.23	11.25	11.25
	47 × 72	4.31	4.63	4.95	5.26	5.58	5.89	6.20	6.51	6.82
	47 × 97	5.81	5.26	6.70	7.14	7.57	8.01	8.45	8.88	9.31
	47 × 120	6.91	7.50	8.09	8.67	9.25	9.82	10.37	10.94	11.50
	47 × 145	7.77	8.59	9.33	10.11	10.88	11.66	12.00	12.00	12.00

[a]These maximum permissible spans are suitable for trussed rafters fabricated and used in accordance with the conditions given in Annex B.
[b]Subject to the visual grading criteria in 5.1.2.
[c]Measured at a moisture content of 20% and subject to the manufacturing tolerance in 5.1.3.

gang-nail type supplied to order for the required conditions. The manufacturer will supply calculations based on the Code of Practice for submission to the local building inspector.

5.8 Floor joists

For the design of floor joists Table VIII gives a guide to maximum spans of joists for timber of strength class C16, based on the TRADA publication 'Span tables for solid timber members in floors, ceilings and roofs (excluding trussed rafter roofs) for dwellings' alternatively, calculations should be prepared for final design by a qualified engineer in accordance with BS 5268.

6 REINFORCED CONCRETE

6.1 Composition

Reinforced concrete is one of the most prolific and versatile structural materials available to the designer. It is composed of two distinct materials: concrete and reinforcement, each of which can

Table VIII Permissible clear spans for domestic floor joists (m) (Ref TRADA Technology Design Aid DA 1/2004)

Table 6 Permissible clear spans for domestic floor joists Imposed load not exceeding 1.5 kN/m²
Strength Class C 16   Service class 1 or 2

Size of joist		Dead load (kN/m²) excluding self-weight of joist								
		Not more than 0.25			More than 0.25 but not more than 0.50			More than 0.50 but not more than 1.25		
Breadth (mm)	Depth (mm)	Spacing of joists (mm)								
		400	450	600	400	450	600	400	450	600
		Maximum clear span (m)								
38	97	1.84	1.70	1.31	1.73	1.56	1.22	1.43	1.31	1.04
38	120	2.45	2.34	1.88	2.33	2.17	1.72	1.91	1.76	1.42
38	145	2.96	2.84	2.49	2.83	2.69	2.30	2.43	2.26	1.84
38	170	3.46	3.33	2.89	3.30	3.12	2.70	2.82	2.66	2.28
38	195	3.96	3.78	3.28	3.75	3.54	3.07	3.21	3.03	2.62
38	220	4.46	4.23	3.67	4.20	3.96	3.44	3.59	3.39	2.93
44	97	1.97	1.86	1.50	1.87	1.77	1.39	1.59	1.46	1.17
44	120	2.58	2.47	2.14	2.46	2.36	1.94	2.12	1.95	1.58
44	145	3.11	2.99	2.68	2.97	2.85	2.51	2.62	2.47	2.05
44	170	3.63	3.49	3.11	3.48	3.34	2.91	3.03	2.86	2.48
44	195	4.16	4.00	3.53	3.98	3.81	3.30	3.45	3.25	2.82
44	220	4.68	4.51	3.95	4.48	4.26	3.70	3.86	3.64	3.16
47	97	2.03	1.92	1.59	1.93	1.82	1.47	1.67	1.53	1.23
47	120	2.63	2.53	2.26	2.52	2.42	2.05	2.22	2.05	1.66
47	145	3.17	3.05	2.77	3.04	2.92	2.59	2.70	2.55	2.15
47	170	3.71	3.57	3.21	3.55	3.42	3.00	3.14	2.96	2.56
47	195	4.25	4.09	3.64	4.07	3.91	3.41	3.56	3.36	2.91
47	220	4.75	4.61	4.08	4.58	4.39	3.82	3.99	3.76	3.26
50	97	2.10	1.98	1.68	1.98	1.88	1.56	1.75	1.61	1.29
50	120	2.69	2.58	2.33	2.57	2.47	2.15	2.29	2.14	1.74
50	145	3.24	3.12	2.83	3.10	2.98	2.67	2.78	2.63	2.24
50	170	3.79	3.65	3.31	3.63	3.49	3.10	3.23	3.05	2.64
50	195	4.34	4.17	3.76	4.15	3.99	3.52	3.67	3.47	3.01
50	220	4.82	4.69	4.20	4.67	4.50	3.94	4.11	3.88	3.36
63	97	2.33	2.21	1.93	2.20	2.09	1.83	1.94	1.85	1.54
63	120	2.90	2.79	2.54	2.78	2.67	2.42	2.50	2.40	2.05
63	145	3.60	3.36	3.06	3.35	3.22	2.92	3.01	2.89	2.56
63	170	4.09	3.93	3.58	3.91	3.77	3.42	3.52	3.39	2.97
63	195	4.67	4.50	4.10	4.48	4.31	3.92	4.03	3.88	3.37
63	220	5.10	4.96	4.61	4.94	4.80	4.41	4.54	4.34	3.77
75	120	3.07	2.96	2.69	2.94	2.83	2.57	2.65	2.54	2.29
75	145	3.70	3.56	3.24	3.54	3.41	3.10	3.19	3.07	2.78
75	170	4.32	4.16	3.79	4.14	3.99	3.63	3.73	3.59	3.23
75	195	4.87	4.73	4.34	4.72	4.56	4.15	4.27	4.11	3.67
75	220	5.32	5.17	4.82	5.15	5.01	4.67	4.77	4.63	4.11
ALS/CLS										
38	140	2.86	2.74	2.41	2.73	2.60	2.18	2.34	2.16	1.76
38	184	3.74	3.58	3.11	3.56	3.36	2.91	3.04	2.87	2.48
38	235	4.73	4.50	3.91	4.45	4.21	3.66	3.82	3.60	3.12
89	184	4.86	4.73	4.33	4.71	4.55	4.15	4.27	4.11	3.73
89	235	4.80	5.65	5.28	5.63	5.47	5.11	5.22	5.07	4.72
		See clause 4.1.4								

be varied in strength, disposition and quantity to fulfil almost any requirement.

The concrete component is itself an amalgam of at least three constituents: aggregate, cement and water. These are mixed together into a homogeneous mass, placed in formwork and left for the chemical and physical changes to occur that result in a hard and durable material. The strength and durability will depend on the quality and quantity of each of the constituents, and whether any additives have been introduced to the wet mix. Onsite mixing of concrete for structural purposes is only carried out for larger jobs which merit the setting up of a batching plant. Concrete mixed offsite at the premises of the ready-mix supplier is a quality controlled product, designed to meet the requirements of the specifier. An indication of early concrete strength can be assessed by 7 or 14 day tests, but the specified strength can only be checked by crushing cubes of hardened concrete at 28 days. Cylinder tests are specified for strength comparison of mixes designed in accordance with Eurocodes. The crushing test will not necessarily indicate that sufficient cement has been included to fulfil the requirement for long-term durability. Sometimes additives are included in the mix to promote workability, early strength, frost resistance, etc. Deterioration in the material due to some of these factors may not become evident for some years, but may then be disastrous. For properties of various types of concrete, see Chapter 7 Section 5.

6.2 Specification
Provided a clear specification is prepared and concrete placement is checked by site staff, the concrete should fulfil its function

Table IX Span to depth ratios for preliminary design

Beams	
Simply supported beams	20
Continuous beams	25
Cantilever beams	10
Slabs	
Slabs spanning in one direction, simply supported	30
Slabs spanning in one direction, continuous	35
Slabs spanning in two directions, simply supported	35
Slabs spanning in two directions, continuous	40
Cantilever slabs	12

indefinitely. This specification should be in accordance with BS 8500-1 *Complementary British Standard to BS EN 206-1. Method of specifying and guidance for the specifier* and BS EN 2006 – 2. *Complementary British Standard to BS EN 206-1. Specification for constituent materials and concrete,* which cover not only strength requirements but also minimum cement content, aggregate size, cement type and other relevant aspects.

6.3 Design
Design of reinforced concrete should be carried out in accordance with BS 8110-1:1997 *Structural use of concrete. Code of practice for design and construction,* the limit state code for the structural use of concrete in buildings and structures. The Eurocode for concrete BS EN 1992-1-1: 2004 *Eurocode 2. Design of concrete structures. General rules and rules for buildings* will replace BS8110 on its withdrawal. A succinct guide to the requirements of BS 8100

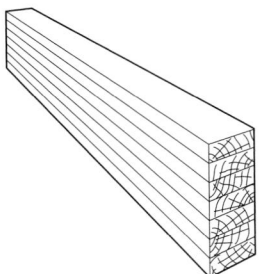

6.7 A laminated timber beam

can be found in the *Manual for the Design of Reinforced Concrete Building Structures* (the Green Book), prepared by the Institution of Structural Engineers.

6.4 Reinforcement

Reinforcement is generally steel rods, although other materials such as glass fibres and steel fibres have been tried in cladding units and steel and polypropylene fibres are now commonly used for crack control in floor slabs on ground. The reinforcing bars may be smooth round mild steel, in which case the bars are referred to as R25, etc. the letter R indicating mild steel and the numbers indicating the diameter in millimetres.

The other type of bar reinforcement is a high-yield bar referred to as T25, etc. In this case, the letter indicates hot rolled or cold worked high-yield steel and the numbers refer to the plain bar diameter of equivalent cross-sectional area. The actual bar size will be about 10% greater than this due to the deformation.

6.5 Mesh reinforcement

For many structural elements, such as slabs and walls, it is convenient to use reinforcement in the form of a pre-welded mesh consisting of bars in both directions. Care should be taken in specifying the correct mesh as they have different areas of bars in each direction depending upon their designation letter. An 'A' square mesh has the same area of bars in each direction. A 'B' structural mesh has larger bars in the main direction and the area of bars in the cross direction satisfies the minimum area of secondary reinforcement requirement of BS 8110. It is important therefore to ensure that a structural mesh is oriented correctly, as indicated on the reinforcement drawing in order that structural strength is not compromised. A 'C' long mesh is similar to a 'B' mesh except that the area of cross wires does not meet the requirements of BS 8110. These meshes are generally used for reinforcing slabs on ground.

6.6 Reinforcement position

Concrete is strong in compression, but weak in tension and reinforcement is used to compensate for this weakness. Adequate

Element	Horizontal and vertical section	Typical heights (h) (m)	h/d between lateral supports	Critical factors for sizing	Remarks
Glued laminated timber column		2–4	15–30	Splitting and crushing ($h/d < 15$) Crushing and buckling ($h/d > 15$)	Ratio $w/d \approx 2$–3 Multi-storey columns may require lower h/d ratios than those given.
Stud frame wall panel		2–4	20–35	Crushing and buckling Thickness of insulation required	Studs usually at about 400mm centres with plywood or other sheeting nailed to it.
Solid timber column		2–4	15–30	Warping or distortion of timber	Multi-storey columns may require lower h/d ratios than those given

6.8 Wood – vertical support elements

Element	Section and plan	Typical depths (d) (mm)	Typical spans (L) (m)	Typical L/d	Critical factors for sizing/remarks
Particle boards		12–30	0.3–0.6	24	Strength Creep deflection
Plywood floor decking		12–30	0.3–0.9	30–40	Deflection Point loads Strength
Softwood floor boards		16–25	0.6–0.8	25–35	Deflection Strength
Joists with floor board – Softwood – Hardwood		200–300 100–250	2–6 2–7	12–20 22–28	Deflection Spacing of joists is about 450–600 mm
Glued laminated timber beam		180–1400	5–12	14–18	Deflection Ratio d/b about 3–5 to prevent instability of unrestrained section.

6.9 Wood – floors

Element	Section and elevation	Typical depths (d) (mm)	Typical spans (L) (m)	Typical L/d	Critical factors for sizing/remarks
Roof planks		25–75	2–6	45–60	Deflection Planks assumed to be simply supported
Plywood floor decking		10–20	0.3–1.2	50–70	Deflection Decking assumed to be continuous
Stressed skin plywood roof panels		100–450	3–7	30–35	Deflection Panel assumed to be simply supported Dimension *a* is about 300–500 mm
Joists with roof deck – Softwood – Hardwood		100–225 100–250	2–6 3–8	20–25 30–35	Deflection Joists assumed to be simply supported and spaced at 600 mm
Roof purlins – Softwood – Hardwood		150–300 200–400	2–5 3–8	10–14 15–20	Available length and depth of wood Bending strength Purlin assumed to be vertical, simply supported and carrying about 2 m width of roof
Glued laminated timber beam with roof deck		180–1400	4–30	15–20	Deflection Beams assumed to be simply supported with spacing L/3–L/5 Ratio *d/b* about 5–8
Trussed rafter without purlins		1200–2000	6–10	4–6	Strength of joints Bending in rafter Assumed spacing 600mm

6.10 *Wood – roofs, beam and deck*

reinforcement must therefore be placed wherever any tension is likely to occur. Simply spanning beams are reinforced near the bottom, with most reinforcement at midspan. Shear forces also produce tensile stresses – links or stirrups are used to reinforce the concrete against the effects of these stresses. Sometimes the compressive strength of the concrete is insufficient for the loading. In this case, reinforcing bars can be used to help take the compression as well. Such use for reinforcement is expensive and is only used when increasing the size of the beam is not possible.

In cantilever beams, the tension occurs near the top. These beams have their heaviest reinforcement at the top, with most near the support.

6.7 Effective depth
The effective depth of a beam is the distance from the top (or compression flange) to the centroid of area of the tensile steel reinforcement. It is indicated by the symbol d.

6.8 Minimum reinforcement
Stresses arise in concrete not only from the applied loads but also from a variety of other causes. For example, when concrete dries and sets it tends to shrink slightly. If it cannot move, it will tend to crack. Similar cracking will occur if movement induced by thermal expansion and contraction is inhibited. Consequently, to reduce the tendency to form large cracks, a modicum of reinforcement is used throughout, allowing the formation of a multitude of fine cracks which are invisible to the naked eye.

6.9 Deflection
In addition to limiting the stresses below the ultimate values, reinforced concrete must possess sufficient stiffness to prevent deflection or deformation which might impair the strength or efficiency of the structure, or produce unsightly cracks in finishes or partitions.

6.10 Concrete cover to reinforcement
In all cases, there must be sufficient concrete cover to reinforcement. This is:

- To preserve it from corrosion
- To ensure an adequate bond with the concrete
- To ensure sufficient protection in case of fire.

Tables A.6, A.10, A.12 and A.13 of BS 8500-1 give limiting values for the nominal cover of concrete made with normal weight aggregates. In no case should the cover be less than the nominal maximum aggregate size, or, for the main reinforcement, the bar size.

7 STRUCTURAL STEELWORK AND OTHER METALS

7.1 Metals
Steel is by far the metal most widely used for building structures, but other materials are used in ancillary elements.

7.2 Design
Design of steelwork should be carried out in accordance with BS 5950-1:2000 *Structural use of steelwork in building. Code of practice for design. Rolled and welded section*, a limit state code based upon plastic theory. Eurocode 3 BS EN 1993-1-1:2005. *Design of steel structures. General rules and rules for buildings*, should be used after the withdrawal of BS 5950.

A book of tables published by the Steel Construction Institute, (the blue book) gives dimensions and section properties of currently manufactured steel sections. Tables X–XIII show the dimensions for universal beams, columns and joists. This book also contains capacity tables which may be used to quickly determine the suitability of a particular section for preliminary design. More rigorous calculations to BS 5950 are generally required for final design. The *Manual for the design of steelwork building structures* issued by the Institution of Structural Engineers provides guidance for design.

7.3 Grades of steel
Steel for structural purposes is available in the United Kingdom in three grades increasing in strength: S275, which corresponds to the previous description of 'mild steel', S355 and S460.

8 GLASS

8.1 Use
Glass is being used to create spectacular structures in modern architecture and it can be incorporated as a structural material in a number of ways.

8.2 Design
The structural use of glass requires an understanding of the behaviour of both the structure and the material. The inherent brittle nature of glass dictates consideration of the nature and consequences of any failure modes.

The choice of international standards for the design of edge supported glass panels is wide-ranging, but BS 6262-1:2005, *Glazing for buildings. General methodology for the selection of glazing*, is the current British Standard.

8.3 Types of glass
A number of processes are used to produce the main glass types used in structures.

Annealed float glass is made by melting the ingredients (silicon, soda ash and recycled broken glass) together. The molten glass is then poured onto a float bath of molten tin where it undergoes controlled cooling after which it is further cooled in an annealing oven. The resulting product exhibits elastic properties, but suffers brittle fracture under impact, bending and thermal loading. Typical properties of annealed glass are shown in Table V.

Toughened glass is produced by heating and then rapidly cooling annealed glass. This results in a glass core which is in tension, sandwiched between surface layers which are in compression. Toughened glass therefore has an ability to sustain higher stresses than annealed glass. Toughened glass is prone to sudden shattering due to nickel sulphide inclusions. Such failure will also be instigated if the compressive surface layers are breached by scratching.

Table X Properties of steel and aluminium

Property	Prestressing strand	High strength low-alloy steel	Structural carbon steel	Cold formed steel	Casting steel	Wrought iron	Grey cast iron	Wrought aluminium Alloy
Carbon content %	0.60–0.90	0.10–0.28	0.10–0.25	0.20–0.25	0.15–0.50	0.05	2.50–4.50	...
Weight kN/m^3	77	77	77	77	77	75	71	27
Tensile strength N/mm^2	1200–1800	400–700	400–560	280–600	400–600	300–350 (in line of rolling)	150–350	200–550
Yield stress or 0.2% proof stress N/mm^2 – stress at or near which permanent deformation starts	1100–1700	340–480	240–300	200–500	200–400	180–200 (in line of rolling)		120–500
Elastic modulus kN/mm^2	165	210	210	210	210	190	210	70
Elongating % – ductility	4	15	15–25	12–25	15–20	8–25	2	8–20
Weldability	Not suitable for welding	Good with right alloys	Good if low-carbon steel	Generally good	Moderate	Generally poor	Poor	Good if right alloys
Coefficient of thermal expansion × 10^{-6}/°C	12	12	12	12	12	12	12	24
Temperature at which metal has 50% of room temperature strength °C	350–500	500	500	500	500	500	can crack at high temperature	190
Corrosion resistance of untreated metal	Poor	Moderate to good	Poor	Poor to moderate	Moderate	Good	Good	Very good

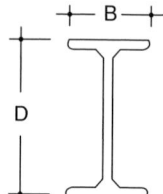

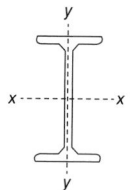

Table XI Universal beams

Dimensions

Section Designation	Mass per Metre D Kg/m	Depth of Section D mm	Width of Section B mm	Thickness Web t mm	Thickness Flange T mm	Root Radius r mm	Depth between Fillets d mm	Ratios for Local Buckling Flange b/T	Ratios for Local Buckling Web d/t	Dimensions for Detailing End Clearance C mm	Dimensions for Detailing Notch N mm	Dimensions for Detailing Notch n mm	Surface Area Per Metre m²	Surface Area Per Tonne m²
305×165×54	54.0	310.4	166.9	7.9	13.7	8.9	265.2	6.09	33.6	6	90	24	1.26	23.3
305×165×46	46.1	306.6	165.7	6.7	11.8	8.9	265.2	7.02	39.6	5	90	22	1.25	27.1
305×165×40	40.3	303.4	165.0	6.0	10.2	8.9	265.2	8.09	44.2	5	90	20	1.24	30.8
305×127×48	48.1	311.0	125.3	9.0	14.0	8.9	265.2	4.47	29.5	7	70	24	1.09	22.7
305×127×42	41.9	307.2	124.3	8.0	12.1	8.9	265.2	5.14	33.1	6	70	22	1.08	25.8
305×127×37	37.0	304.4	123.4	7.1	10.7	8.9	265.2	5.77	37.4	6	70	20	1.07	29.0
305×102×33	32.8	312.7	102.4	6.6	10.8	7.6	275.9	4.74	41.8	5	58	20	1.01	30.8
305×102×28	28.2	308.7	101.8	6.0	8.8	7.6	275.9	5.78	46.0	5	58	18	1.00	35.4
305×102×25	24.8	305.1	101.6	5.8	7.0	7.6	275.9	7.26	47.6	5	58	16	0.992	40.0
254×146×43	43.0	259.6	147.3	7.2	12.7	7.6	219.0	5.80	30.4	6	82	22	1.08	25.1
254×146×37	37.0	256.0	146.4	6.3	10.9	7.6	219.0	6.72	34.8	5	82	20	1.07	29.0
254×146×31	31.1	251.4	146.1	6.0	8.6	7.6	219.0	8.49	36.5	5	82	18	1.06	34.2
254×102×28	28.3	260.4	102.2	6.3	10.0	7.6	225.2	5.11	35.7	5	58	18	0.904	31.9
254×102×25	25.2	257.2	101.9	6.0	8.4	7.6	225.2	6.07	37.5	5	58	16	0.897	35.6
254×102×22	22.0	254.0	101.6	5.7	6.8	7.6	225.2	7.47	39.5	5	58	16	0.890	40.5
203×133×30	30.0	206.8	133.9	6.4	9.6	7.6	172.4	6.97	26.9	5	74	18	0.923	30.8
203×133×25	25.1	203.2	133.2	5.7	7.8	7.6	172.4	8.54	30.2	5	74	16	0.915	36.4
203×102×23	23.1	203.2	101.8	5.4	9.3	7.6	169.4	5.47	31.4	5	60	18	0.790	34.2
178×102×19	19.0	177.8	101.2	4.8	7.9	7.6	146.8	6.41	30.6	4	60	16	0.738	38.8
152×89×16	16.0	152.4	88.7	4.5	7.7	7.6	121.8	5.76	27.1	4	54	16	0.638	39.8
127×76×13	13.0	127.0	76.0	4.0	7.6	7.6	96.6	5.00	24.1	4	46	16	0.537	41.3

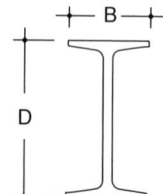

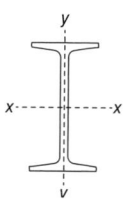

Table XII Joists

Dimensions

Section Designation	Mass per Metre D Kg/m	Depth of Section D mm	Width of Section B mm	Thickness Web t mm	Thickness Flange T mm	Root Radius r mm	Depth between Fillets d mm	Ratios for Local Buckling Flange b/T	Ratios for Local Buckling Web d/t	Dimensions for Detailing End Clearance C mm	Dimensions for Detailing Notch N mm	Dimensions for Detailing Notch n mm	Surface Area Per Metre m²	Surface Area Per Tonne m²
254×203×82 #	82.0	254.0	10.2	19.9	19.6	19.6	9.7	166.6	5.11	16.3	7	104	44	14.8
254×114×37 ¥	37.2	254.0	7.6	12.8	12.4	12.4	6.1	199.3	4.46	26.2	6	60	28	24.2
203×152×52 #	52.3	203.2	8.9	16.5	15.5	15.5	7.6	133.2	4.62	15.0	6	78	36	17.8
152×127×37 #	37.3	152.4	10.4	13.2	13.5	13.5	6.6	94.3	4.81	9.07	7	66	30	19.8
127×114×29 #	29.3	127.0	10.2	11.5	9.9	9.9	4.8	79.5	4.97	7.79	7	60	24	22.0
127×114×27 #	26.9	127.0	7.4	11.4	9.9	9.9	5.0	79.5	5.01	10.7	6	60	24	24.2
127×76×16 ¥	16.5	127.0	5.6	9.6	9.4	9.4	4.6	86.5	3.97	15.4	5	42	22	31.0
114×114×27 ¥	27.1	114.3	9.5	10.7	14.2	14.2	3.2	60.8	5.34	6.40	7	60	28	22.8
102×102×23 #	23.0	101.6	9.5	10.3	11.1	11.1	3.2	55.2	4.93	5.81	7	54	24	23.9
102×44×7 #	7.5	101.6	4.3	6.1	6.9	6.9	3.3	74.6	3.65	17.3	4	28	14	46.6
89×89×19 #	19.5	88.9	9.5	9.9	11.1	11.1	3.2	44.2	4.49	4.65	7	46	24	24.4
76×76×15 ¥	15.0	76.2	8.9	8.4	9.4	9.4	4.6	38.1	4.76	4.28	6	42	20	27.9
76×76×13 #	12.8	76.2	5.1	8.4	9.4	9.4	4.6	38.1	4.54	7.47	5	42	20	32.1

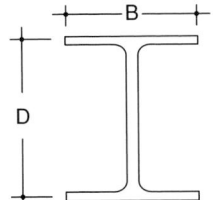

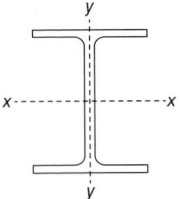

Table XIII Universal columns

Dimensions

| Section Designation | Mass per Metre D Kg/m | Depth of Section D mm | Width of Section B mm | Thickness | | Root Radius r mm | Depth between Fillets d mm | Ratios for Local Buckling | | Dimensions for Detailing | | | Surface Area | |
				Web t mm	Flange T mm			Flange b/T	Web d/t	End Clearance C mm	Notch N mm	n mm	Per Metre m²	Per Tonne m²
254×254×167	167.1	289.1	265.2	19.2	31.7	12.7	200.3	4.18	10.4	12	134	46	1.58	9.45
254×254×132	132.0	276.3	261.3	15.3	25.3	12.7	200.3	5.16	13.1	10	134	38	1.55	11.7
254×254×107	107.1	266.7	258.8	12.8	20.5	12.7	200.3	6.31	15.6	8	134	34	1.52	14.2
254×254×89	88.9	260.3	256.3	10.3	17.3	12.7	200.3	7.41	19.4	7	134	30	1.50	16.9
254×254×73	73.1	254.1	254.6	8.6	14.2	12.7	200.3	8.96	23.3	6	134	28	1.49	20.4
203×203×86	86.1	222.2	209.1	12.7	20.5	10.2	160.8	5.10	12.7	8	110	32	1.24	14.4
203×203×71	71.0	215.8	206.4	10.0	17.3	10.2	160.8	5.97	16.1	7	110	28	1.22	17.2
203×203×60	60.0	209.6	205.8	9.4	14.2	10.2	160.8	7.25	17.1	7	110	26	1.21	20.1
203×203×52	52.0	206.2	204.3	7.9	12.5	10.2	160.8	8.17	20.4	6	110	24	1.20	23.0
203×203×46	46.1	203.2	203.6	7.2	11.0	10.2	160.8	9.25	22.3	6	110	22	1.19	25.8
152×152×37	37.0	161.8	154.4	8.0	11.5	7.6	123.6	6.71	15.5	6	84	20	0.912	24.7
152×152×30	30.0	157.6	152.9	6.5	9.4	7.6	123.6	8.13	19.0	5	84	18	0.901	30.0
152×152×23	23.0	152.4	152.2	5.8	6.8	7.6	123.6	11.2	21.3	5	84	16	0.889	38.7

Laminated glass is produced by bonding two layers of glass with a layer of acrylic resin. The resulting material does not shard on impact but remains intact, minimising the risk of injury on failure.

9 OTHER MATERIALS

9.1 Fabric
Plastics are used in the manufacture of many structural fabrics which are finding increasing uses. See Chapter 7, Section 7.12.

10 FOUNDATIONS

10.1 Nature
The purpose of a foundation is to transmit the dead and live loads from a building structure to the ground. The nature of the foundation will depend on:

- the characteristics of the soil;
- the magnitude of the loads from the structure;
- the nature of the loads from the structure.

In the majority of buildings, the loads transmitted to the ground will arrive either as point loads down columns or line loads down walls. For the type of building with which these notes deal, the magnitudes of these loads will not be so great as to significantly affect the choice of foundation system.

10.2 Soil
This will basically depend on the strength of the soil to carry the load. The term 'soil' in this context means not vegetable material suitable for growing crops (topsoil), but the material forming the surface of the earth to a depth of about 100 m, which is not so hard as to be classified as a 'rock'.

The technology of the physical properties of soil is called soil mechanics. It is not appropriate to deal in depth with this subject, but some simple principles are useful to appreciate the design of foundations.

10.3 Bearing pressure
The bearing pressure that can be carried by the soil is the additional load that can be carried on a unit area. A soil stratum at a depth of, say, 3 m is already carrying the weight of that 3 m (overburden) of soil. In fact, the bearing capacity of many soils increases substantially with depth. This is because a common mode of failure under excessive load is sideways spillage of the soil, often accompanied by upward heave of the material around the area of application. Obviously this is much less likely where the load is carried at some depth.

Since the bearing capacity represents the additional load the soil can carry, the greater the depth, the smaller proportion of the total (or gross) pressure this will form. In fact, it is even possible to produce zero or negative net pressure by removing the overburden, and replacing it with something weighing much less, for example a hollow box. This is the principle by which loads can be carried on soft marshy soil; the analogy is that of a boat floating on water. In many cases, the architect will be told what the bearing capacity of the soil is at normal foundation depth – about 1 m.

10.4 Pad and strip foundations
These are the types of foundation most commonly met by architects, and their design should only require the use of an engineer if there are complications. Care should however be taken in soft soils where settlement rather than bearing capacity is the critical criterion. See Figures 6.11 and 6.12 for examples.

10.5 Other foundation types
It is frequently found that the loads of the building are so large, or the bearing capacity of the soil is so poor, that suitable pad or strip foundations will be either very deep, or required to be so large that adjoining bases impinge on one another. The two common solutions to this problem are:

- Raft foundations, Figure 6.13, where the bases are combined together to form one large base. The raft has to be so reinforced to cater for the stresses induced by inequalities of loading and bearing capacity
- Piles, Figure 6.14, which are devices for carrying loads down to deeper levels than would otherwise be practical.

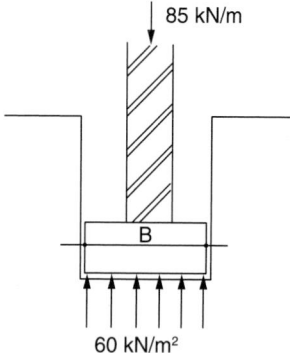

6.11 *Width of a strip foundation, section (Example 1)*

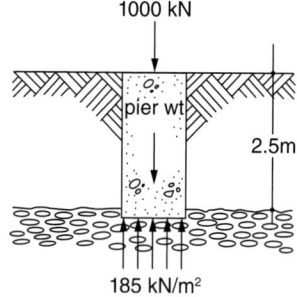

6.12 *Concrete pier of gravel layer (Example 2)*

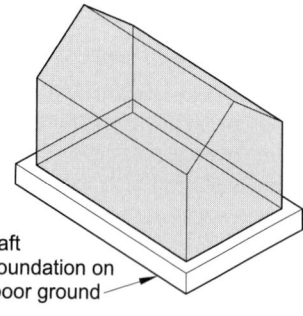

6.13 *Raft foundation as used on poor ground*

Raft foundations are beyond the scope of this section; however, useful guidance on raft design is given in the Structural Foundation Designers Manual (see Bibliography).

10.6 End-bearing piles

Piles can be divided into those that carry their loads into the soil mainly by end bearing, Figure 6.15 and those that act by virtue of the shaft friction at the interface between the pile length and the soil, Figure 6.16. End-bearing piles normally sit on rock or gravel strata with high bearing capacities. They may consist of a precast concrete shaft, driven into place with a large mechanical hammer. Alternatively, a hollow shell is driven and afterwards filled with wet concrete to form the pile. In either of these cases, the amount of penetration achieved at each hammer blow is an indication of the load carrying capacity of the pile. A design method for simple end-bearing piles in the shape of the short-bored variety sometimes used in housing is illustrated in Figure 6.17.

10.7 Skin-friction piles

Skin-friction piles, mostly appropriate for cohesive soils such as clays, are usually bored, Figure 6.16. In this method, a circular hole is excavated in the ground by a large auger or other methods. If

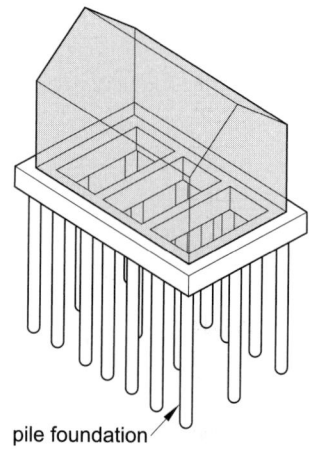

6.14 *Alternative pile foundation*

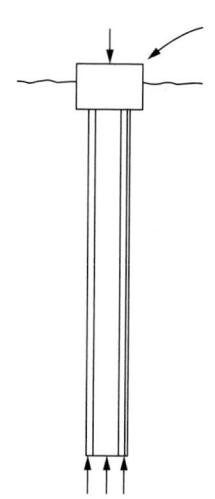

6.15 *End-bearing pile*

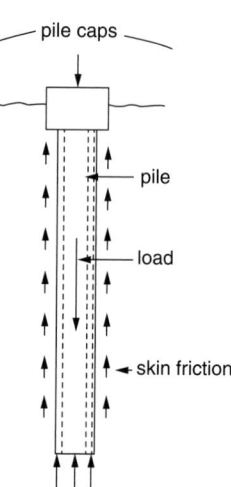

6.16 *Friction pile*

necessary, the sides of the hole are temporarily sleeved. When the necessary depth has been reached, reinforcement is lowered into the hole and concrete is poured in. Some method of compacting the concrete is employed, so that all cavities in the ground are properly filled. The sleeve is withdrawn as the concrete goes in, to ensure intimate contact between pile and soil.

The capacity of this type of pile is not self-evident as in the case of driven piles. Calculation is used to determine the length of pile required, based on the shear strength of the clay at various depths below the ground. Parameters for soil properties are gained by carrying out a site investigation prior to the design.

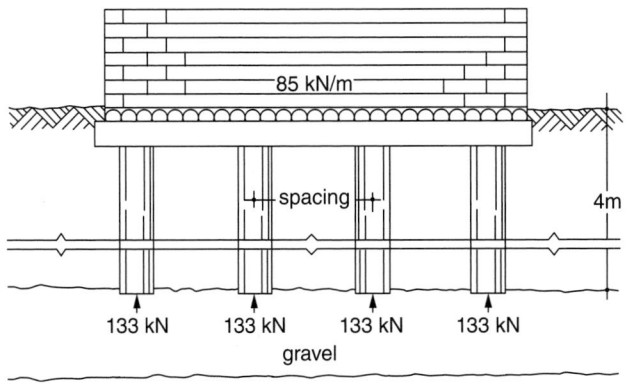

6.17 *Short-bored piles (Example 3)*

While the calculations themselves are not particularly difficult, the subject is one where engineering judgment is required in their interpretation. It is recommended that this type of pile should be designed by the specialist piling contractor and checked by the consulting engineer, with adequate supervision and testing on site to ensure that the pile is suitable for the design loads.

10.8 Pile testing
In both driven and bored piles, it is usual to carry out one or more tests on the actual piles on each contract. On very large contracts, additional piles are tested to failure, but normally one of the working piles is loaded to 1.5 times the working load to prove the efficacy of the design. These maintained load static tests are expensive and time consuming, requiring the use of large concrete blocks (kentledge) or the installation of tension piles against which a jacking load can be applied to the test pile. Other, more rapid methods of testing by measuring the dynamic response of the pile to a

hammer strike at the pile head can be employed, but engineering judgement is required to determine the correct regime and method/methods of test required.

10.9 Under-reamed piles
There is a third type of pile which is a bored end-bearing pile. The shaft is augured in the usual way, but when the required depth has been reached a special tool is used to enlarge the base to a bell-shape, Figure 6.18. These piles are substantial in size, and remote inspection of the base must be carried out to check the integrity of the soil on which the load will rest. It is not often possible to test this type of pile using static methods due to the magnitude of the loads carried.

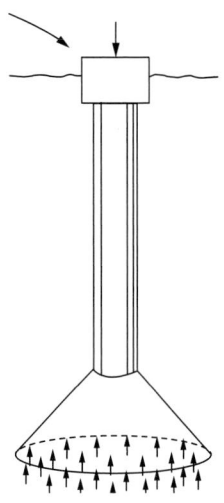

6.18 *Under-reamed pile*

11 THUMB-NAIL STRUCTURES: WHAT ARCHITECTS NEED TO CONSIDER

11.1 Dead loads

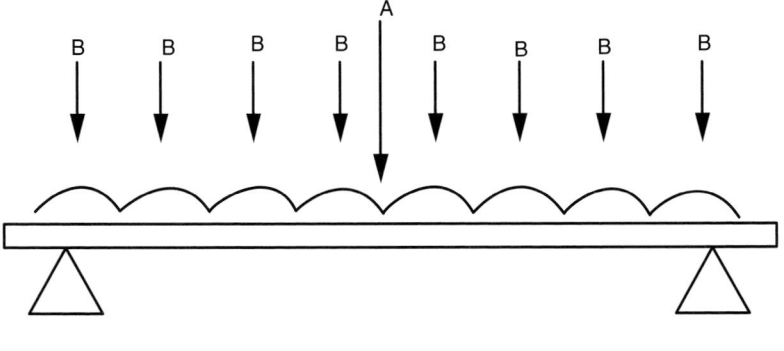

A = a POINT LOAD e.g. a piece of furniture, machinery or even a person, where a force is concentrated in a small area.
B = a UNIFORMLY DISTRIBUTED LOAD e.g. books in a library, cars in a car park etc., where a force is distributed over a wider area.

In reality most loads imposed upon a structural member are a combination of both POINT LOAD and UDL

11.2 Deflection

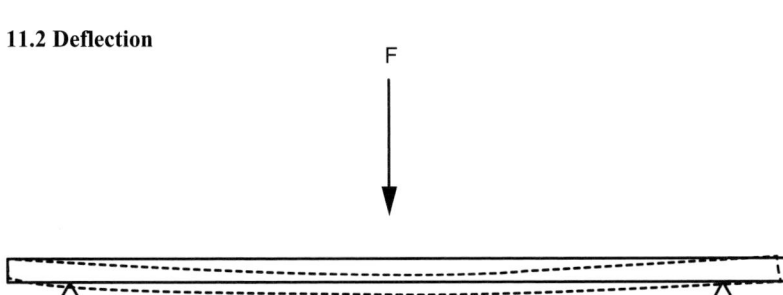

When a force is applied [F] the beam will be in BENDING and will DEFLECT

It is the size of this DEFLECTION that architects need to be aware of:

SERVICEABILITY
Will the DEFLECTION be so great that items of furniture move or users will feel unsteady?

LOAD TRANSFER
Will the DEFLECTION be so great that loads intended to be taken by the framing member (i.e. beam or floor plank) are transferred to infill panels?

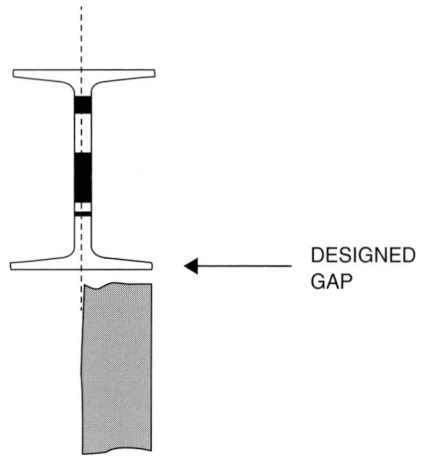

DESIGNED
GAP

The infill blockwork is built up to within 10–15 mm of the u/s of the steel beam depending on the designed DEFLECTION. The gap will be filled with a compressible compound

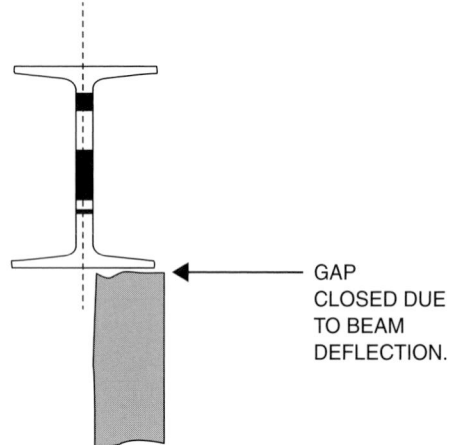

GAP
CLOSED DUE
TO BEAM
DEFLECTION.

The MOVEMENT JOINT must be greater than the designed deflection in the beam

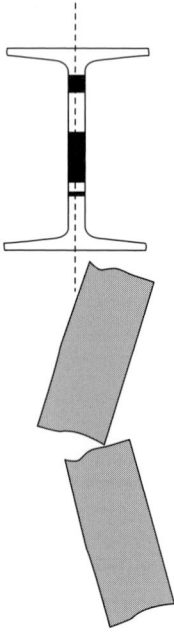

If the DEFLECTED beam comes into contact with an infill panel or blockwork the latter may BUCKLE as it will not have been designed to take the loading

11.3 Cantilever

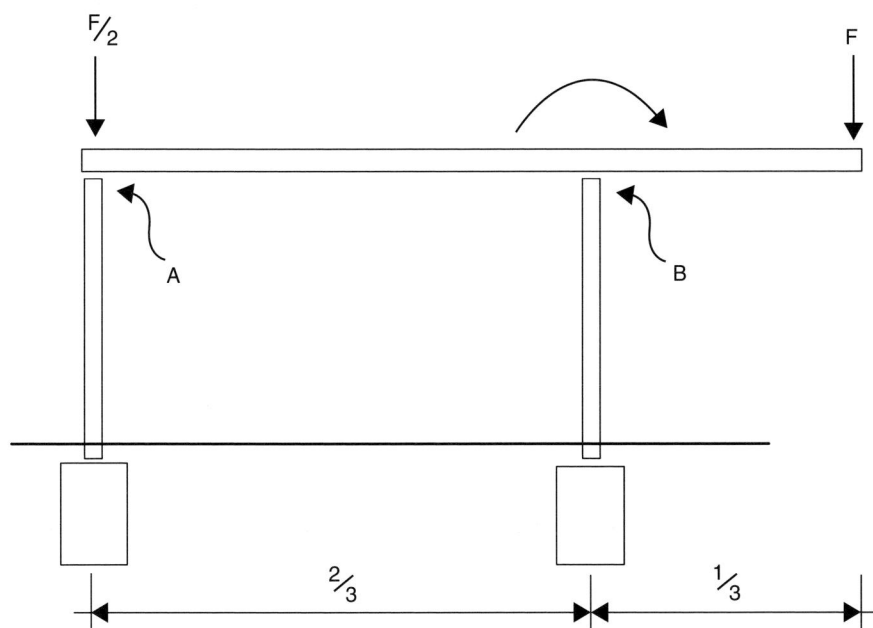

The diagram illustrates a very simple CANTILEVER arrangement achieved by balancing loads alone. This is an unlikely scenario.

More likely is that there will be a PIN or MOMENT connection at A & B

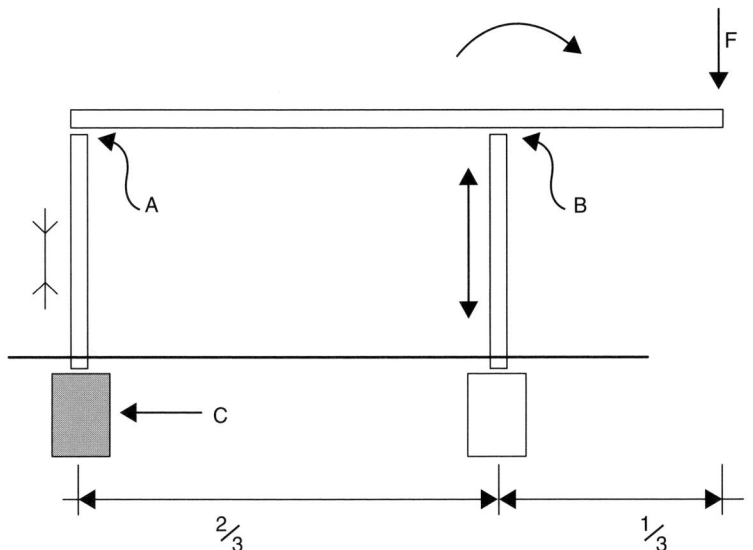

The beam will be in ROTATION about B. The column below B will be in COM-PRESSION and the column below A will be in TENSION. Being in tension it will require RESTRAINT – some means of keeping it from pulling out of the ground. This may take the form of a heavy or deep (or both) foundation at C.

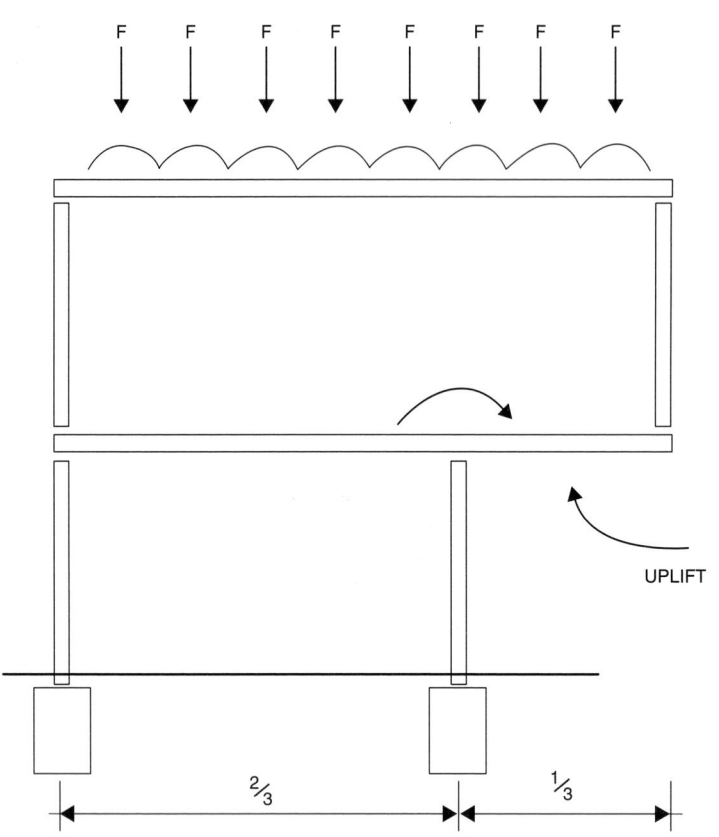

In reality the forces will be far more complex than those indicated but the rule-of-thumb for a CANTILEVER of 2/3 BACKSPAN and 1/3 cantilever remains

UPLIFT (due to wind) needs to be addressed as much as other forces

11.4 Bracing, racking and tri-angulation

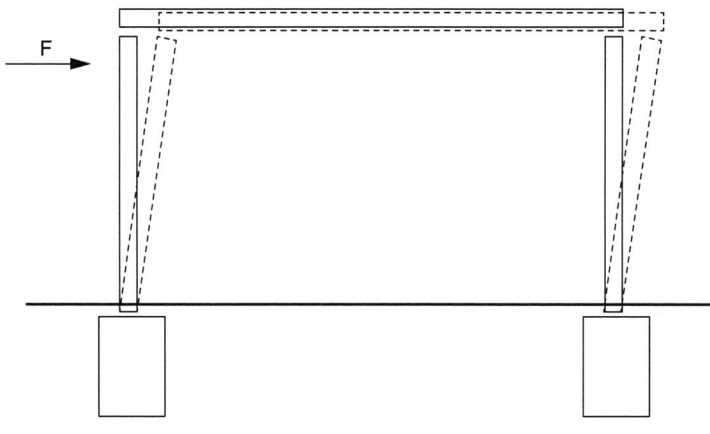

A LATERAL force (e.g. wind) imposed upon a structure will induced RACKING unless precautions are taken to mitigate this.

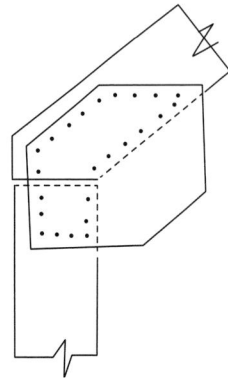

One method of achieving this to provide sufficiently robust MOMENT connections where the major structural members come together. A PORTAL frame used in many warehouses and other industrial buildings is an example of this.

Another method (other design parameters considered) to BRACE the frame is by introducing an element that will TRIANGULATE the structure. This element may be acting in COMPRESSION or TENSION (or both).

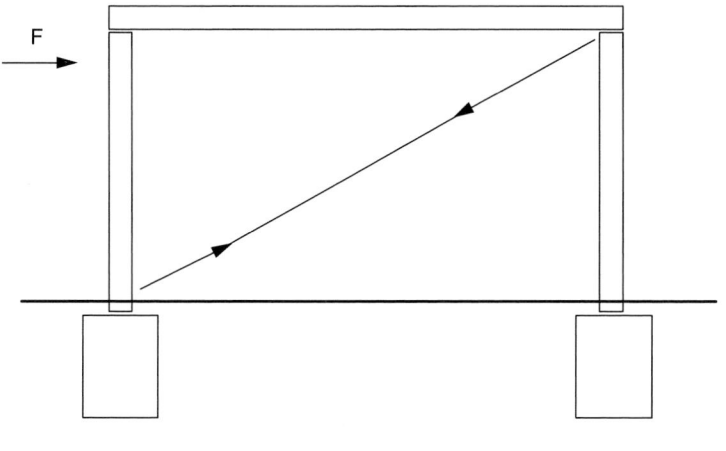

Member in TENSION (may therefore be a wire or cable – a TIE)

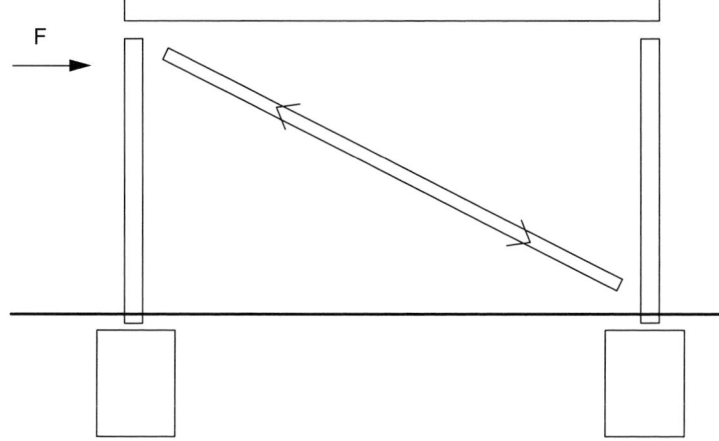

Member in COMPRESSION (member would need to be substantial and able to resist compressive forces – a STRUT). Note that a lateral force exerted from the right side of the frame would put the diagonal member into TENSION. A single strut can be designed to resist both TENSION and COMPRESSION.

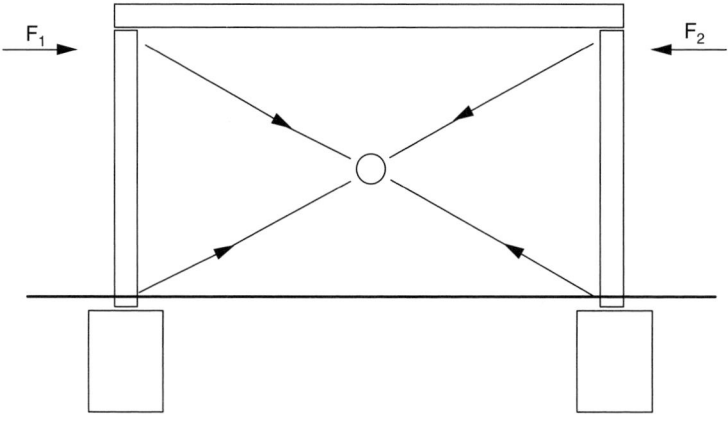

Unpredictable lateral forces (and that is most of them) need to be addressed by designing elements that resist both compression and tension. This can be achieved by using 1 strut or alternatively 2 ties – the latter is often preferred for aesthetic reasons.

Another means available to resist RACKING is the use of board or sheet material, such as plywood or OSB. In addition the newer sheathing materials provide adequate bracing as well as acting as a breathable moisture barrier.

11.5 Arching

The ARCH is an ancient method of spanning and its use has enabled our ancestors to span far greater distances than would have been achievable using stone or timber lintels.

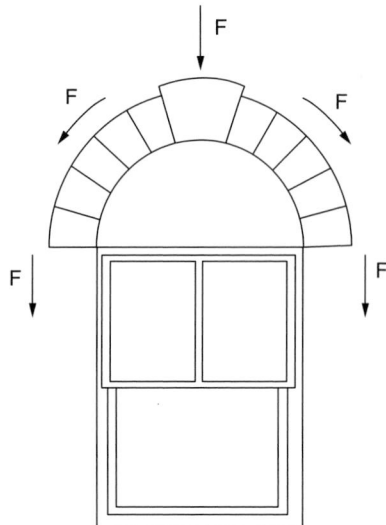

The early 'Roman' arch, semi-circular in shape resolves its forces vertically where the arch 'springs'. The lack of a horizontal component means that very thick walls or buttressing is not so important in ensuring the arch does not collapse.

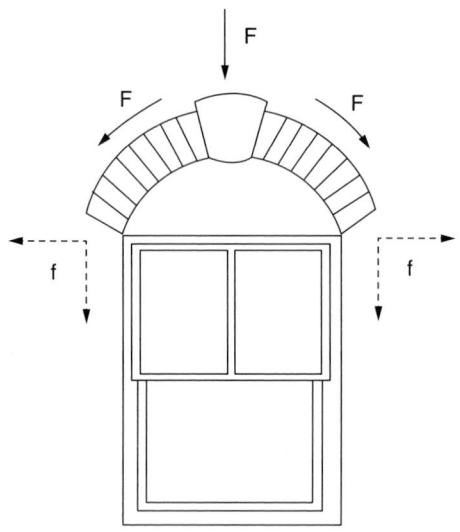

The later 'GOTHIC' arch, pointed at the top and not resolving its forces vertically at the spring point requires something, usually the mass of the wall or additional buttresses and piers to resist the horizontal forces.

11.6 Buckling

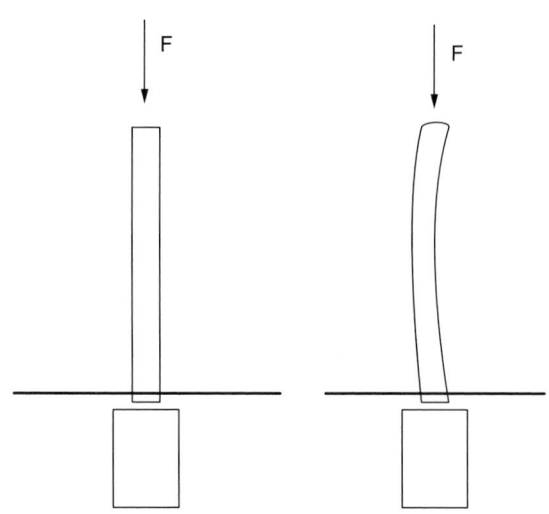

It is evident that as F increases, BUCKLING is likely to occur. In theory a perfectly vertical force acting through a perfectly vertical column along the central axis would result in a compressive force. In practice construction is less than perfect.

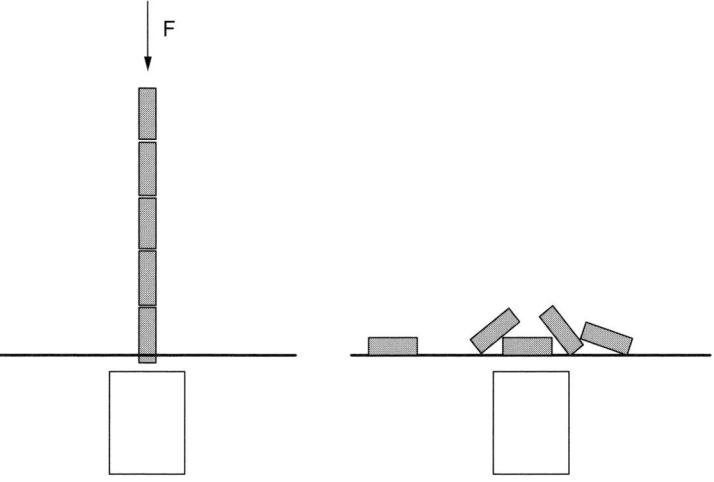

In a column buckling will tend to cause deflection, in block-work or brickwork the result can be collapse.

11.7 Increasing the effective span

We know that the effective span of a beam can be extended by increasing the value of the Y-axis. However, this can be achieved by a number of methods.

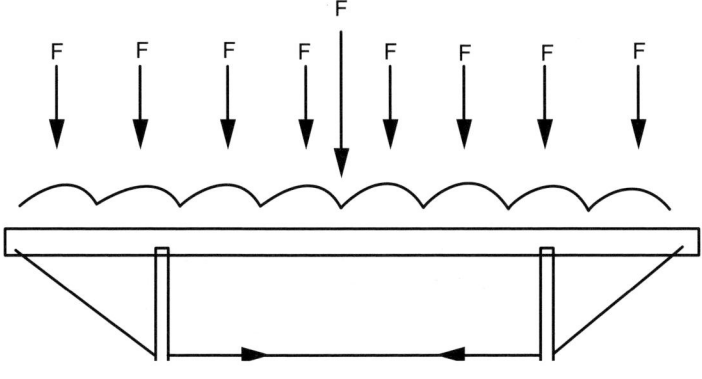

A bow-string truss is a system of tension members held away from the main member. The lower horizontal tension member effectively deepens the beam.

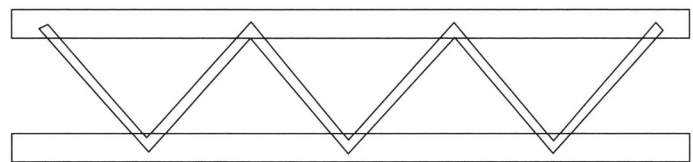

The same is true for a truss where the top and bottom flanges are separated by angled struts.

11.8 Roofing

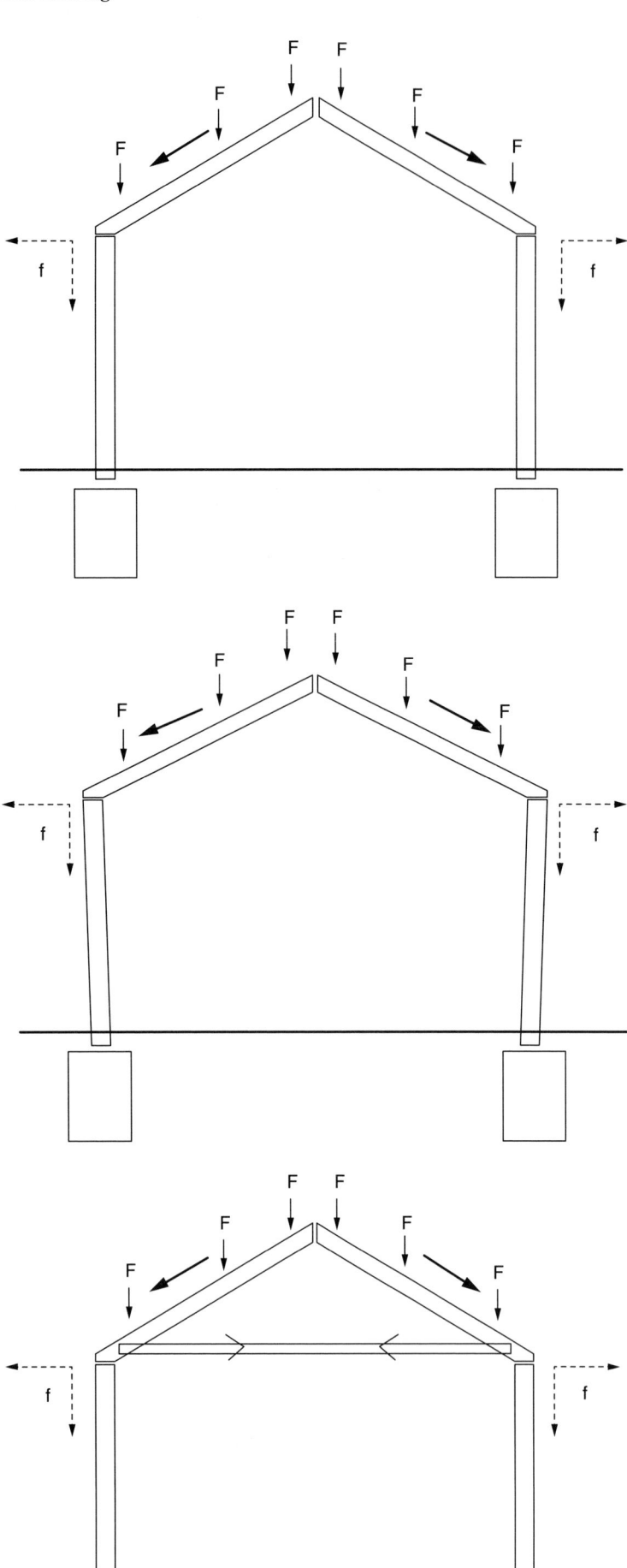

The members of a simple pitched roof arrangement resolve their DEAD and LIVE load forces along the line of the pitch. In practice this single force is resolved into vertical and horizontal components.

It can be seen that the horizontal component forces the vertical supporting members (they may be columns, they may be walls) outwards allowing the roof to collapse downward. The eaves being pushed outward is a sign of this.

One way of avoiding this is to tie across the rafters either with timber (working as a tension and compression member) or with wire (tension only).

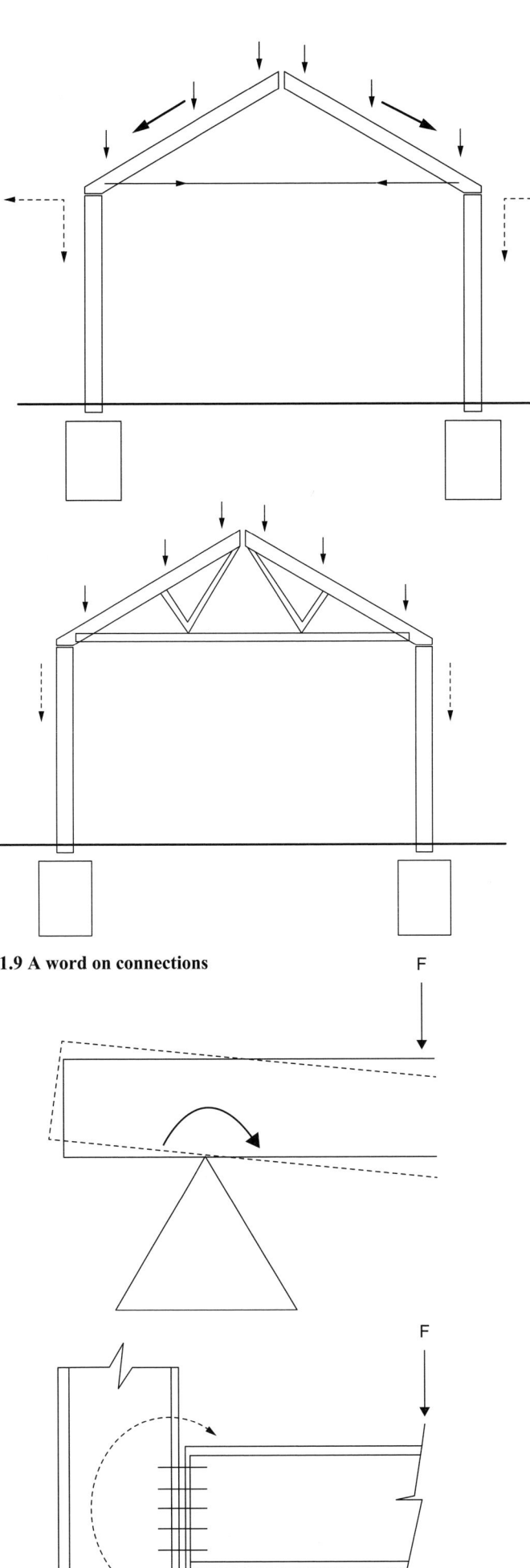

A steel TIE is sometimes used in situations where a heavy timber member may not be aesthetically appropriate.

The common roof truss, used by volume house builders is a lightweight and efficient way of designing a domestic scale roof structure. However, the potential of using the roof space is lost.

11.9 A word on connections

F

PIN JOINT

As the beam deflects due to the imposed loads it is free to ROTATE about the support.

MOMENT JOINT

In reality most connections are either bolted or welded (steel), bolted or nailed (timber) or cast (in situ concrete).

F

11.10 Typical sections

For various constructional and aesthetic reasons the architect often favours a steel section that the engineer is less keen on. The channel section is commonly suggested for a number of reasons although the engineer will point out that because of its eccentric profile it is far less efficient than the RHS or I section.

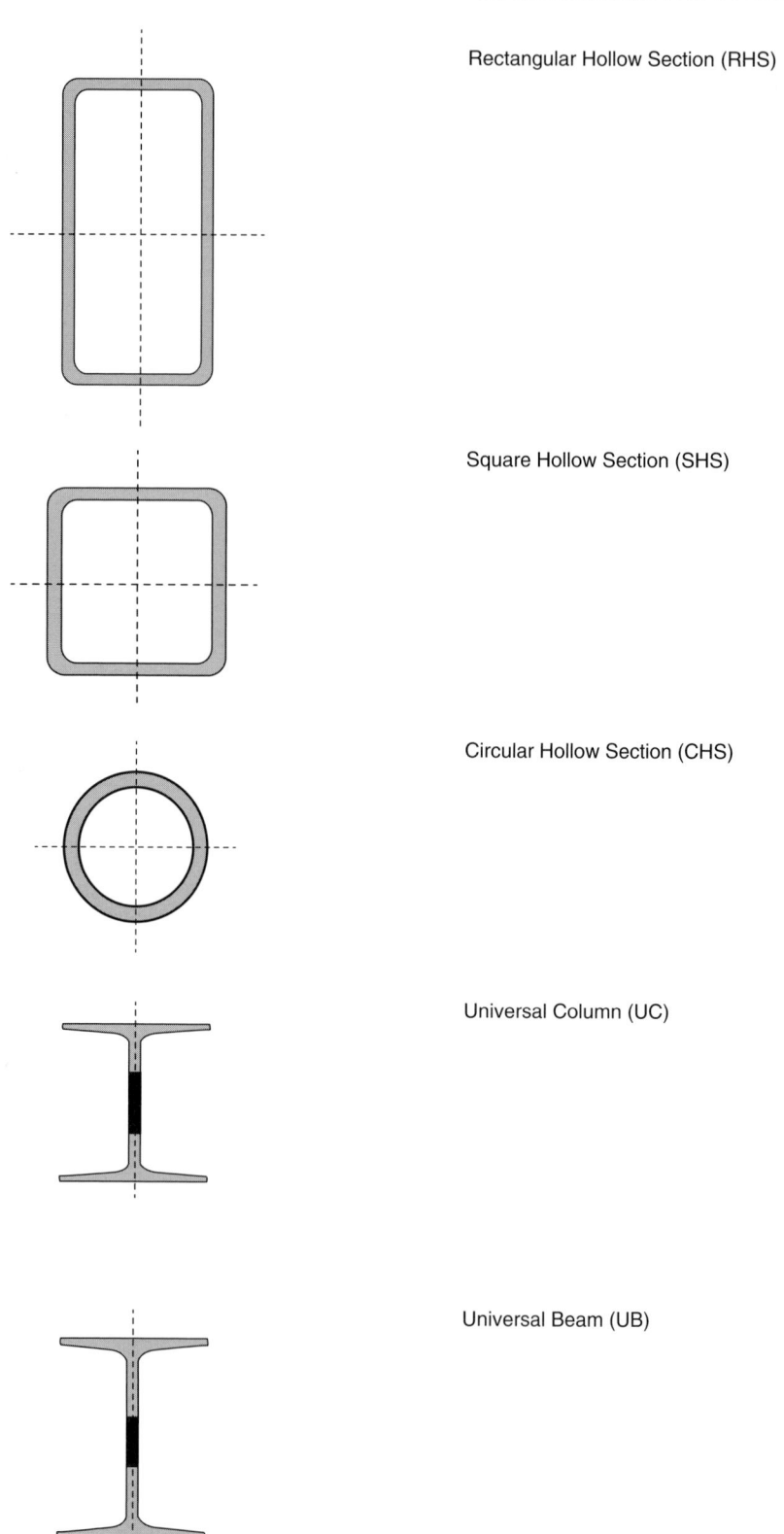

Rectangular Hollow Section (RHS)

Square Hollow Section (SHS)

Circular Hollow Section (CHS)

Universal Column (UC)

Universal Beam (UB)

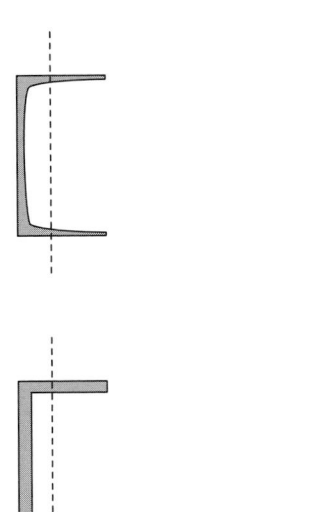

Channel

Parallel Flange Channel (PFC)

12 BIBLIOGRAPHY

12.1 General

Hodgkinson, A (ed.) 1974. *AJ Handbook of Building Structure*, London, Architectural Press

Orton, A. 1988. *The Way We Build Now*, London, E & F N Spon

Gauld, B. J. B. 1995. *Structures for Architects*, Longman Scientific & Technical

Building Regulations, *Approved Document A, 2004. Structure*

Institution of Structural Engineers, 1987. *Aims of structural design*

Institution of Structural Engineers, 1989. *Stability of buildings*

Institution of Structural Engineers, 1989. *The achievement of structural adequacy in buildings*

12.2 Loading

BS 648: 1964. *Schedule of weights of building materials*

BS 6399-1:1996. *Loading for buildings. Code of practice for dead and imposed loads*

BS 6399-2:1997. *Loading for buildings. Code of practice for wind loads*

BS 6399-3:1988. *Loading for buildings. Code of practice for imposed roof loads*

12.3 Masonry

BS 5628-1:1992. *Code of practice for use of masonry. Structural use of unreinforced masonry*

BS 5628-3:2005. *Code of practice for the use of masonry. Materials and components, design and workmanship*

Institution of Structural Engineers, 2005. *Manual for the design of plain masonry in building structures*

12.4 Timber

BS 5268-2:2002. *Structural use of timber. Code of practice for permissible stress design, materials and workmanship*

BS 5268-3:2006. *Structural use of timber. Code of practice for trussed rafter roofs*

Ozelton, E. C., Baird, J. A. 2006. *Timber designers' manual*, London, Blackwell

12.5 Concrete

BS EN 206-1:2000. *Concrete. Specification, performance, production and conformity*

BS 8500-1:2006. *Concrete. Complementary British Standard to BS EN 206-1. Method of specifying and guidance for the specifier*

BS 8500-2:2002. *Concrete. Complementary British Standard to BS EN 206-1. Specification for constituent materials and concrete*

BS 8110-1:1997. *Structural use of concrete. Code of practice for design and construction*

The Institutions of Civil and of Structural Engineers, 1985. *Manual for the design of reinforced building structures*

The Institution of Structural Engineers, 1991. *Recommendations for the permissible stress design of reinforced concrete building structures*

Reynolds, C. E., Steedman, J. C. (1988) *Reinforced concrete designer's handbook*, (10th ed) London, Spon Press

12.6 Steel

BS 5950-1:2000, *Structural use of steelwork in building. Code of practice for design of cold formed thin gauge sections*

The Institutions of Civil and of Structural Engineers, 2002. *Manual for the design of steelwork building structures*

Davison, B., Owens, G. W. 1992. *Steel designers' manual* (6th ed) London, Blackwell

12.7 Glass

The Institution of Structural Engineers, 1999. *Structural use of glass in buildings*

12.8 Foundations

BS 8004:1986. *Code of practice for foundations*

Curtin, W. G., Shaw, G., Parkinson, G., Golding, J., Seward, N. 2006. *Structural Foundation Designers' Manual*, London, Blackwell

7 Materials

Arthur Lyons with AHR Architects (formerly Aedas)

Dr Arthur Lyons authors texts on building materials and architecture. He was formerly head of quality, principal lecturer and teacher fellow in the Leicester School of Architecture, Faculty of Art, Design and Humanities, De Montfort University, Leicester. He is currently an honorary visiting researcher to the University. AHR Architects is an interdisciplinary design and building consultancy.

KEY POINT:

- *Standards and specifications are constantly changing; always refer to current regulations and manufacturers' details*

Contents

1 Introduction
2 Steel
3 Timber
4 Bricks and blocks
5 Concrete (cement)
6 Aluminium
7 Roofing and cladding
8 Glass
9 Ceramic materials
10 Stone and cast stone
11 Plastics
12 Glass-fibre reinforced plastics, concrete and gypsum
13 Plaster and board materials
14 Insulation materials
15 Sealants, gaskets and adhesives
16 Paints, wood stains and varnishes
17 Commodities
18 Bibliography
19 Acknowledgements

1 INTRODUCTION

The majority of construction materials are supplied to metric dimensions; however, a few materials still retain their imperial designations. Where appropriate, the listings are taken from British and European Standards or trade organisations and will therefore not necessarily correspond to the full ranges offered by individual suppliers. Inevitably, changes in published Standards and Building Regulations will occur, affecting availability of particular products. Specifiers are, therefore, always advised to check current availability and delivery times.

2 STEEL

2.1 General

BS 6722: 1986 defines the recommended dimensions for ferrous and non-ferrous metal wires, bars and flat products. These preferred dimensions are listed in Tables I and II.

2.2 Steel sheet, plate and bars

Steel sheet: Cold reduced mild steel sheet is produced with standard thickness ranging from 0.5 to 3.2 mm (Table III). Hot rolled sheet

Table I Recommended thicknesses (mm) for ferrous and non-ferrous metal bars and flat products (BS 6722: 1986)

0.10, *0.11*, 0.12, *0.14*, 0.16, *0.18*, 0.20, *0.22*, 0.25, *0.28*, 0.30, *0.35*, 0.40, *0.45*, 0.50, *0.55*, 0.60, *0.70*, 0.80, *0.90*, 1.0, *1.1*, 1.2, *1.4*, 1.6, *1.8*, 2.0, *2.2*, 2.5, *2.8*, 3.0, *3.5*, 4.0, *4.5*, 5.0, *5.5*, 6.0, *7.0*, 8.0, *9.0*, 10.0, *11.0*, 12.0, *14.0*, 16.0, *18.0*, 20.0, *22.0*, 25.0, *28.0*, 30.0, *35.0*, 40.0, *45.0*, 50.0, *55.0*, 60.0, *70.0*, 80.0, *90.0*, 100.0, *110.0*, 120.0, *140.0*, 160.0, *180.0*, 200.0, *220.0*, 250.0, *280.0*, 300.0

Note: First preference ordinary type, second preference italics.

Table II Recommended widths and lengths (mm) for ferrous and non-ferrous metal flat products (BS 6722: 1986)

400, 500, 600, 800, 1000, 1200, 1250, 1500, 2000, 2500, 3000, 4000, 5000, 6000, 8000, 10000.

($<$ 3 mm) and plate ($\geq$3 mm) is produced with a range from 1.6 to 150 mm (Table IV). Standard dimensions are given in the tables.

Steel bars – flats, rounds, squares and hexagons: The standard sizes for flats, rounds and squares are given in Tables V–VII, respectively.

The standard BS EN 10061: 2003 gives the preferred dimensions for hot rolled hexagon bars (Table VIII); however, standard stock is in the range 7–75 mm.

Table III Cold reduced steel sheet

Thickness (mm)	0.5	0.6	0.7	0.8	1.0	1.2	1.6	2.0	2.5	3.0	3.2
Mass (kg/m²)	3.93	4.71	5.50	6.28	7.85	9.42	12.56	15.70	19.63	23.55	25.12

Note: Standard range from Tata Steel.
Standard sheet sizes are 2000 × 1000, 2500 × 1250 and 3000 × 1500 mm and coil widths 750–2000 mm.

Table IV Hot rolled steel sheet and plate

Thickness (mm)	1.6	2.0	2.5	3.0	4.0	5.0	6.0	8.0	10.0	12.5	15
Mass (kg/m²)	12.6	15.7	19.6	23.6	31.4	39.6	47	63	79	98	118
Thickness (mm)	20	22	25	30	32	35	40	45	50	55	60
Mass (kg/m²)	157	173	196	236	252	275	314	353	393	432	471
Thickness (mm)	65	70	75	80	85	90	95	100	120	130	150
Mass (kg/m²)	510	550	589	628	667	707	746	785	942	1021	1178

Note: Standard range from Tata Steel.
Typical size range for plate – Width: 1000–3000 mm, Length: 2000–9000 mm.

2.3 Structural steel sections

Most steel sections of British origin are still based on the old imperial sizes although sized in metric dimensions and billed in kilograms or tonnes. Tables IX–XI summarise the standard dimensions, but it should be noted these are quoted as nominal sizes and that exact dimensions should be verified from manufacturers' data.

Tolerances on nominal dimensions for joists and channels are given in BS 4-1: 2005, and for I and H sections in BS EN 10034: 1993. Some structural steel sections, listed in Table XII, are made in metric co-ordinated sizes.

Structural steel hollow sections: Structural hollow sections may be hot finished or cold formed. Hot finished structural steel hollow sections are manufactured in either 275 or 355 MPa minimum yield strength steel (e.g. S275J2H or S355J2H respectively) to BS EN 10210-1: 2006. Cold formed sections, produced in both 235 and 355 MPa minimum yield strength steel, are limited to thicknesses of 8 and 16 mm, respectively. Hot finished hollow structural steel is available as square, rectangular, circular and oval sections. Cold

Table V Hot rolled flats

Width (mm)	Thickness (mm)																	
	3	4	5	6	8	10	12	15	20	25	30	35	40	45	50	60	65	75
10	×																	
12	×																	
13	×	×	×	×														
15	×	×	×															
16	×	×	×		×	×												
20	×	×	×	×	×	×	×											
22	×		×			×												
25	×	×	×	×	×	×	×	×	×									
30	×	×	×	×	×	×	×	×	×	×								
35	×	×	×	×	×	×	×	×										
40	×	×	×	×	×	×	×	×	×	×	×							
45	×	×	×	×	×	×	×	×	×	×	×							
50	×	×	×	×	×	×	×	×	×	×	×			×				
55		×	×	×	×	×	×	×	×	×	×							
60	×	×	×	×	×	×	×	×	×	×	×	×	×					
65	×	×	×	×	×	×	×	×	×	×	×	×	×	×	×			
70	×		×	×	×	×	×	×	×	×	×		×		×			
75	×	×	×	×	×	×	×	×	×	×	×		×		×	×	×	
80	×	×	×	×	×	×	×	×	×	×	×	×	×	×	×	×	×	
90	×	×	×	×	×	×	×	×	×	×	×	×	×	×	×			
100	×	×	×	×	×	×	×	×	×	×	×	×	×	×	×	×	×	×
110	×		×	×	×	×	×	×	×	×	×		×	×	×			
120			×	×	×	×	×	×	×	×	×							
130	×	×	×	×	×	×	×	×	×	×	×			×	×	×		×
140				×	×	×	×	×	×	×	×							
150	×	×	×	×	×	×	×	×	×	×	×			×	×	×	×	×
160				×		×	×	×	×	×								
180			×	×	×	×	×	×	×	×	×			×		×		
200		×		×	×	×	×	×	×	×	×			×	×	×		×
220			×	×	×	×	×	×	×	×	×			×		×		
250				×	×	×	×	×	×	×	×			×	×	×		
275				×	×	×	×											
300				×	×	×	×	×	×	×	×			×	×	×	×	
350						×	×	×	×	×	×			×				
375							×	×	×	×	×			×				
400						×	×	×	×	×	×			×				
450							×	×	×	×								
500						×	×	×	×	×	×							

Note: Stock range from Tata Steel.
Tolerances on dimensions and shape for flat steel bars are given in BS EN 10058: 2003.

Table VI Rounds

Diameter (mm)	Mass/length (kg/m)	Diameter (mm)	Mass/length (kg/m)	Diameter (mm)	Mass/length (kg/m)
6	0.22	70	30.20	165	168.0
8	0.39	75	34.70	170	178.0
10	0.62	80	38.50	180	200.0
12	0.89	85	44.50	185	211.0
13	1.04	90	49.90	190	223.0
15	1.39	95	55.60	195	234.0
16	1.58	100	61.70	200	247.0
20	2.47	105	68.00	210	272.0
22	2.98	110	74.60	220	298.0
25	3.85	115	81.50	230	326.0
30	5.55	120	88.00	240	356.0
32	6.31	125	96.30	250	385.0
35	7.55	130	104.0	260	417.0
40	9.86	135	112.0	270	448.0
45	12.50	140	121.0	275	466.0
50	15.41	145	130.0	280	483.0
55	18.63	150	139.0	300	555.0
60	22.20	155	148.0	305	573.0
65	26.00	160	158.0		

Note: Stock range from Tata Steel.
Tolerances on dimensions and shape for round steel bars are given in BS EN 10060: 2003.

Table VII Squares

Side length	Mass/length (kg/m)
8.0	0.50
10.0	0.79
12.0	1.13
15.0	1.77
16.0	2.01
20.0	3.14
25.0	4.91
30.0	7.07
35.0	9.62
40.0	12.6
45.0	15.9
50.0	19.6
60.0	28.3
65.0	33.2
75.0	44.2

Note: Stock range from Tata Steel.
Tolerances on dimensions and shape for square steel bars are given in BS EN 10059: 2003.

formed hollow structural steel is available as square, rectangular and circular sections.

The standard BS EN 10210-2: 2006 covers hot finished sections to the following maximum sizes: circular – outside diameter 2500 mm, square – outside dimensions 800 × 800 mm, rectangular – outside dimensions 750 × 500 mm and oval – outside dimensions 500 × 250 mm, although not all section sizes available are fully described in the standard.

2.4 Steel alloys

Weather-resistant steel: Weather-resistant steels (BS 7668: 2004 and BS EN 10025-5: 2004) are structural steels alloyed with a small proportion of copper, which together with other alloying constituents has the effect of making the natural rust adhere tenaciously to the surface to prevent further loss by spalling. The design

Table VIII Hexagons (BS EN 10061: 2003)

Width across flats (mm)	Mass/length (kg/m)	Width across flats (mm)	Mass/length (kg/m)
13	1.15	37.5	9.56
14	1.33	39.5	10.6
15	1.53	42.5	12.3
16	1.74	47.5	15.3
17	1.96	52	18.4
18	2.20	57	22.1
19	2.46	62	26.1
20.5	2.86	67	30.5
22.5	3.44	72	35.2
23.5	3.75	78	41.4
25.5	4.42	83	46.8
28.5	5.52	88	52.6
31.5	6.75	93	58.8
33.5	7.63	98	65.3
35.5	8.56	103	72.1

Note: Preferred dimensions to BS EN 10061: 2003.
Tolerances on dimensions and shape for hexagon steel bars are given in BS EN 10061: 2003.

Table IX British Standard structural steel sections to BS4: Part 1: 2005
Universal beams (BS4: Part 1: 2005)

Nominal dimensions (mm)	Standard mass per unit length (kg/m)
1016 × 305	*487, 437, 393, 349, 314, 272, 249, 222*
914 × 419	388, 343
914 × 305	289, 253, 224, 201
838 × 292	226, 194, 176
762 × 267	197, 173, 147, 134
686 × 254	170, 152, 140, 125
610 × 305	238, 179, 149
610 × 229	140, 125, 113, 101
610 × 178	*100, 92, 82*
533 × 312	*272, 219, 182, 150*
533 × 210	138, 122, 109, 101, 92, 82
533 × 165	*85, 74, 66*
457 × 191	*161, 133, 106,* 98, 89, 82, 74, 67
457 × 152	82, 74, 67, 60, 52
406 × 178	*85,* 74, 67, 60, 54
406 × 140	53, 46, 39
356 × 171	67, 57, 51, 45
356 × 127	39, 33
305 × 165	54, 46, 40
305 × 127	48, 42, 37
305 × 102	33, 28, 25
254 × 146	43, 37, 31
254 × 102	28, 25, 22
203 × 133	30, 25
203 × 102	23
178 × 102	19
152 × 89	16
127 × 76	13

Note: Dimensions in italics are Tata Steel production in addition to the standard range of BS4–1: 2005 sections.

Universal columns (BS4: Part 1: 2005)

Nominal dimensions (mm)	Standard mass per unit length (kg/m)
356 × 406	634, 551, 467, 393, 340, 287, 235
356 × 368	202, 177, 153, 129
305 × 305	283, 240, 198, 158, 137, 118, 97
254 × 254	167, 132, 107, 89, 73
203 × 203	*127, 113, 100,* 86, 71, 60, 52, 46
152 × 152	*51, 44,* 37, 30, 23

Note: Dimensions in italics are Tata Steel production in addition to the standard range of BS4–1: 2005 sections.

Joists with taper flanges (BS4: Part 1: 2005)

Nominal dimensions (mm)	Standard mass per unit length (kg/m)
254 × 203	82
254 × 114	37
203 × 152	52
152 × 127	37
127 × 114	29, 27
127 × 76	16
114 × 114	27
102 × 102	23
102 × 44	7
89 × 89	19
76 × 76	15, 13

Table IX (continued)
Universal bearing piles (BS4: Part 1: 2005)

Nominal dimensions (mm)	Standard mass per unit length (kg/m)
356 × 368	174, 152, 133, 109
305 × 305	223, 186, 149, 126, 110, 95, 88, 79
254 × 254	85, 71, 63
203 × 203	54, 45

Note: Tolerances on dimensions and shape for structural steel I and H sections are given in BS EN 10034: 1993 and for taper flange I sections in BS 10024: 1995.

Table X Structural hollow sections
Hot finished circular hollow sections (BS EN 10210–2: 2006)

Nominal external diameter (mm)	Thickness (mm)
1219	*25, 20, 16, 14.2, 12.5, 10*
1168	*25, 20, 16, 14.2, 12.5, 10*
1067	*30, 25, 20, 16, 14.2, 12.5, 10*
1016	*30, 25, 20, 16, 14.2, 12.5, 10, 8*
914	*30, 25, 20, 16, 14.2, 12.5, 10, 8*
813	*30, 25, 20, 16, 14.2, 12.5, 10*
762	*50, 40, 30, 25, 20, 16, 14.2, 12.5, 10, 8, 6.3*
711	*60, 50, 40, 30, 25, 20, 16, 14.2, 12.5, 10, 8, 6.3*
1219	*25, 20, 16, 14.2, 12.5, 10*
1168	*25, 20, 16, 14.2, 12.5, 10*
1067	*30, 25, 20, 16, 14.2, 12.5, 10*
1016	*30, 25, 20, 16, 14.2, 12.5, 10, 8*
914	*30, 25, 20, 16, 14.2, 12.5, 10, 8*
813	*30, 25, 20, 16, 14.2, 12.5, 10*
762	*50, 40, 30, 25, 20, 16, 14.2, 12.5, 10, 8, 6.3*
711	*60, 50, 40, 30, 25, 20, 16, 14.2, 12.5, 10, 8, 6.3*
610	*50, 40, 30, 25, 20, 16, 14.2, 12.5, 10, 8, 6.3*
508	*50, 40, 36, 30, 25, 20,* **16,** *14.2,* **12.5, 10,** *8, 6.3*
457	*40, 30, 25, 20,* **16,** *14.2,* **12.5, 10, 8,** *6.3*
406.4	*40, 30, 25, 20,* **16,** *14.2,* **12.5, 10, 8,** 6.3
355.6	*25, 20, 16, 14.2, 12.5, 10, 8, 6.3*
323.9	*25, 20,* **16,** *14.2,* **12.5, 10, 8, 6.3,** *5.0*
273	*25, 20,* **16,** *14.2,* **12.5, 10, 8, 6.3,** *5.0*
244.5	*25, 20,* **16,** *14.2, 12.5, 10, 8, 6.3, 5.0*
219.1	*20,* 16, *14.2,* **12.5, 10, 8, 6.3, 5.0**
193.7	*16, 14.2,* 12.5, **10, 8, 6.3, 5.0**
177.8	*12.5, 10, 8, 6.3, 5.0*
168.3	12.5, **10, 8, 6.3, 5.0,** *4.0*
139.7	12.5, **10, 8, 6.3, 5.0,** *4.0*
114.3	*10, 8,* **6.3, 5.0,** *4.0,* **3.6, 3.2**
101.6	*10, 8, 6.3, 5.0, 4.0, 3.2*
88.9	6.3, **5.0, 4.0, 3.2**
76.1	**5.0,** 4.0, **3.2,** *2.9, 2.6*
60.3	**5.0,** 4.0, 3.2, *2.6*
48.3	**5.0,** 4.0, 3.2, 2.6
42.4	5.0, 4.0, 3.2, 2.6
33.7	4.0, 3.2, 2.6
26.9	*3.2, 2.6, 2.3*
21.3	*3.2, 2.6, 2.3*

Note: Not all listed sizes are readily available.
Standard Tata Steel hot finished circular hollow sections are in bold, non-regular production sizes are in normal type. Other dimensions quoted in BS EN 10210–2: 2006 are in italics.
Cold formed circular hollow sections (BS EN 10219-2: 2006) are manufactured with dimensions ranging from 26.9 × 2 mm to 508 × 16 mm.

Hot finished square hollow sections (BS EN 10210–2: 2006)

Nominal side dimensions (mm)	Thickness (mm)
400 × 400	*20,* **16,** *14.2,* **12.5, 10**
350 × 350	**16,** *14.2,* **12.5, 10, 8.0**
300 × 300	**16,** *14.2,* **12.5, 10, 8.0,** 6.3
260 × 260	*16, 14.2, 12.5, 10, 8.0, 6.3*
250 × 250	**16,** *14.2,* **12.5, 10, 8.0, 6.3**
220 × 220	*16, 14.2, 12.5, 10, 8.0, 6.3*
200 × 200	**16,** *14.2,* **12.5, 10, 8.0, 6.3, 5.0**
180 × 180	**16,** *14.2,* **12.5, 10, 8.0, 6.3,** *5.0*
160 × 160	*16, 14.2,* **12.5, 10, 8.0, 6.3, 5.0**
150 × 150	*16, 14.2,* **12.5, 10, 8.0, 6.3, 5.0**
140 × 140	**12.5, 10, 8.0, 6.3, 5.0**
120 × 120	**12.5, 10, 8.0, 6.3, 5.0**
100 × 100	**10, 8, 6.3, 5.0, 4.0**
90 × 90	**8.0, 6.3, 5.0, 4.0,** 3.6
80 × 80	**8.0, 6.3, 5.0, 4.0,** 3.6, *3.2,* **3.0**
70 × 70	8.0, 6.3, **5.0,** 4.0, *3.6,* 3.2
60 × 60	8.0, **6.3, 5.0,** 4.0, 3.2, **3.0,** *2.6*
50 × 50	**6.3, 5.0,** 4.0, **3.2,** 3.0, *2.6*
40 × 40	**5.0,** 4.0, 3.2, 3.0, *2.6*

Note: Not all listed sizes are readily available.
Standard Tata Steel hot finished square hollow sections are in bold, non-regular production sizes are in normal type. Other dimensions quoted in BS EN 10210–2: 2006 are in italics.
Cold formed square hollow sections (BS EN 10219-2: 2006) are manufactured with dimensions ranging from 25 × 25 × 2 mm to 300 × 300 × 12.5 mm.

Table X (continued)

Hot finished rectangular hollow sections (BS EN 10210–2: 2006)

Nominal external dimensions (mm)	Thickness (mm)
500 × 300	*20*, **16**, *14.2*, 12.5, **10**, 8.0
500 × 200	16, 12.5, 10, 8.0
450 × 250	**16**, 14.2, **12.5, 10, 8.0**
400 × 200	**16**, 14.2, **12.5, 10, 8.0**
350 × 250	*16, 14.2, 12.5, 10, 8.0, 6.3*
350 × 150	16, 12.5, 10, 8.0
300 × 200	**16**, *14.2*, **12.5, 10, 8.0,** 6.3
300 × 100	12.5, **10, 8.0**
260 × 180	*16, 14.2, 12.5, 10, 8.0, 6.3*
250 × 150	**16**, *14.2*, **12.5, 10, 8.0, 6.3, 5.0**
200 × 150	**10, 8.0**
200 × 120	12.5, **10, 8.0,** 6.3, 5.0
200 × 100	*16*, **12.5, 10, 8.0,** 6.3, **5.0**
180 × 100	*12.5, 10, 8.0, 6.3, 5.0, 4.0*
160 × 80	*12.5,* **10, 8.0, 6.3, 5.0,** *4.0*
150 × 100	12.5, **10, 8.0,** 6.3, **5.0,** *4.0*
140 × 80	*10, 8.0, 6.3, 5.0, 4.0*
120 × 80	**10, 8.0, 6.3, 5.0,** *4.0*
120 × 60	*10,* **8.0, 6.3, 5.0,** *4.0,* 3.6
100 × 60	**8.0, 6.3, 5.0,** *4.0,* 3.6, *3.2*
100 × 50	10, **8.0, 6.3, 5.0,** *4.0,* 3.2, **3.0**
90 × 50	*8.0,* 6.3, **5.0,** *4.0,* 3.6, *3.2*
80 × 40	8.0, 6.3, **5.0,** *4.0,* 3.2
60 × 40	*6.3,* 5.0, 4.0, *3.6,* 3.2, 3.0, 2.6
50 × 30	*5.0, 4.0, 3.2, 2.6*

Note: Not all listed sizes are readily available.
Standard Tata Steel hot finished rectangular hollow sections are in bold, non-regular production sizes are in normal type. Other dimensions quoted in BS EN 10210–2: 2006 are in italics.
Cold formed rectangular hollow sections (BS EN 10219-2: 2006) are manufactured with dimensions ranging from 40 × 20 × 2 mm to 400 × 200 × 12.5 mm.

Hot finished oval hollow sections (BS EN 10210–2: 2006)

Nominal external dimensions (mm)	Thickness (mm)
500 × 250	**16, 12.5, 10**
480 × 240	*14, 12, 10*
400 × 200	**16**, *14,* **12.5,** *12,* **10, 8**
320 × 160	*14, 12, 10, 8.0*
300 × 150	**16, 12.5, 10, 8**
250 × 125	**12.5,** *12,* **10, 8, 6.3,** *6.0*
220 × 110	*10, 8, 6.0*
200 × 100	**12.5, 10, 8,** *6.3,* **6.0, 5.0**
180 × 90	*10, 8, 6.0*
150 × 75	*10, 8,* 6.3, **6.0, 5.0,** *4.0*
120 × 60	*8, 6.0, 5.0, 4.0, 3.2*

Note: Not all listed sizes are readily available.

Tata Steel hot finished oval hollow sections are in bold type. Other dimensions quoted in BS EN 10210–2: 2006 are in italics.

Table XI Channels and angles
Equal angles (BS EN 10056–1: 1999)

Nominal dimensions (mm)	Thickness (mm)
200 × 200	**24, 20, 18, 16**
150 × 150	**18, 15, 12, 10**
120 × 120	**15, 12, 10, 8**
100 × 100	**15, 12, 10, 8**
90 × 90	**12, 10, 8, 7, 6**
80 × 80	**10, 9, 8, 7, 6**
75 × 75	**10, 9, 8, 7, 6**
70 × 70	**10, 9, 8, 7, 6, 5**
65 × 65	9, 7, 6
60 × 60	**10, 9, 8, 7, 6, 5, 4**
55 × 55	**6**
50 × 50	**8, 6,** 7, **5,** 4, **3**
45 × 45	8, 7, **6, 5, 4.5,** 4, 3
40 × 40	**6, 5, 4, 3**
35 × 35	5, 4, 3.5
30 × 30	**5,** 4, **3**
25 × 25	**5,** 4, **3**
20 × 20	5, 4, 3

Note: Standard Tata Steel stock dimensions are in bold, non-regular production sizes are in normal type.
The standard BS EN 10056–1: 1999 refers to a wider range up to 250 × 250 mm.
Tolerances on dimensions and shape for equal leg angles are given in BS EN 10056–2: 1993.

Unequal angles (BS EN 10056–1: 1999)

Nominal dimensions (mm)	Thickness (mm)
200 × 150	**18, 15, 12**
200 × 100	**15, 12, 10**
150 × 90	**15, 12, 10**
150 × 75	**15, 12, 10**
130 × 65	10, 8
125 × 75	**12, 10, 8**

Table XI (continued)
Unequal angles (BS EN 10056–1: 1999)

Nominal dimensions (mm)	Thickness (mm)
120 × 80	12, 10, 8
100 × 75	**12, 10,** 9, **8**
100 × 65	**10,** 9, **8,** 7
100 × 50	10, 8, **6**
90 × 70	8
90 × 65	8, 6
80 × 65	10, 8, 6
80 × 60	**8, 7, 6**
80 × 40	8, 6
75 × 55	9. 7, 5
75 × 50	**10, 8,** 7, 6, 5
70 × 50	6
65 × 50	**8,** 7, **6, 5**
60 × 40	**7, 6, 5**
60 × 30	**6, 5**
50 × 40	**5**
50 × 30	5
45 × 30	5, 4
40 × 25	**4**
40 × 20	4, 3
30 × 20	4, 3

Note: Standard Tata Steel stock dimensions are in bold, non-regular production sizes are in normal type.
Tolerances on dimensions and shape for unequal leg angles are given in BS EN 10056–2: 1993.

Parallel flange channels

Nominal dimensions (mm)	Standard mass per unit length (kg/m)
430 × 100	64
380 × 100	54
300 × 100	46
300 × 90	41
260 × 90	35
260 × 75	28
230 × 90	32
230 × 75	26
200 × 90	30
200 × 75	23
180 × 90	26
180 × 75	20
150 × 90	24
150 × 75	18
125 × 65	15
100 × 50	10

Note: Standard Tata Steel stock dimensions.
Tolerances on dimensions, mass and shape for hot rolled steel channels are given in BS EN 10279: 2000.

Tapered flange channels

Nominal dimensions (mm)	Standard mass per unit length (kg/m)
76 × 38	6.7

Note: Standard Tata Steel stock dimensions. A range of dimensions from 140 × 60 × 7 mm to 40 × 20 × 5 mm are also available.

Tolerances on dimensions, mass and shape for hot rolled steel channels are given in BS EN 10279: 2000.

Table XII Metric structural sections
Beams with parallel flanges (Euronorm 19–57)

Nominal dimensions (mm)	Standard mass per unit length (kg/m)
750 × 265	222, 210, 196, 185, 173, 160, 147, 137
600 × 225	184, 154, 144, 122, 108
550 × 210	159, 134, 123, 106, 92
500 × 200	129, 111, 107, 91, 79
450 × 190	104, 95, 92, 78, 67
400 × 180	84, 82, 76, 66, 57
360 × 170	70, 66, 57, 50
330 × 160	60, 57, 49, 43
300 × 150	52, 49, 42, 37
270 × 135	44, 42, 36, 31
240 × 120	37, 34, 31, 26
220 × 110	32, 29, 26, 22
200 × 100	27, 25, 22, 18
180 × 90	22, 21, 19, 15
160 × 80	18, 16, 13
140 × 75	14, 13, 11
120 × 65	10, 8.7
100 × 55	8.1, 6.9

Note: Dimensions and properties to Euronorm 19-57/DIN 1025. Tolerances to EN 10034: 1993.

Table XII (continued)
Parallel wide flange beams (Euronorm 53–62)

Nominal dimensions (mm)	Standard mass per unit length (kg/m)
1000 × 300	349, 314, 272, 222
900 × 300	333, 291, 252, 198
800 × 300	317, 262, 224, 172
700 × 300	301, 241, 204, 166, 150
650 × 300	293, 225, 190, 138
600 × 300	285, 212, 178, 175, 151, 137, 129
550 × 300	278, 199, 166, 120
500 × 300	270, 187, 155, 107
450 × 300	263, 171, 140, 124, 100
400 × 300	256, 155, 125, 107, 92
360 × 300	250, 142, 112, 84
340 × 300	248, 134, 105, 79
320 × 300	245, 127, 98, 74
300 × 300	238, 117, 88, 70
280 × 280	189, 103, 76, 61
260 × 260	172, 93, 68, 54
240 × 240	157, 83, 60, 47
220 × 220	117, 72, 51, 40
200 × 200	103, 61, 42, 35
180 × 180	89, 51, 36, 29
160 × 160	76, 43, 30, 24
140 × 140	52, 34, 25, 18
120 × 120	52, 27, 20, 15
100 × 100	41, 20, 17, 12

Note: Dimensions and properties to Euronorm 19-57/DIN 1025. Tolerances to EN 10034: 1993.

detailing of weathering steel (Cor-Ten®) must ensure that rainwater run-off does not cause staining to adjacent materials, particularly concrete and glass, during the first few years of exposure to rain. Also detailing should ensure no entrapment of pockets of water or damp debris to prevent continuing corrosion at these locations. Weather-resistant steel has been used for exposed structures in buildings, bridges and as a cladding material.

Stainless steel: Stainless steels are a range of alloys containing at least 10.5 per cent chromium. The corrosion resistance of the material is due to the natural passive film of chromium oxide, which is naturally regenerated if the surface is scratched. The grades of stainless steel for construction are listed in Table XIII (BS EN 10088-1: 2005). Stainless steel is available in hollow and standard sections for structural use and in sheet form for cladding, roofing and trim.

2.5 Coated steels

The range of metal-coated steels includes traditional hot-dip galvanized steel, aluminium–zinc alloy-coated and terne-coated steels. The durability of zinc-coated steel is dependent on the thickness of the coating and the environment, also the avoidance of contact with other metals particularly copper, and the alkalis in wet mortar and plaster. In addition to hot-dip galvanizing, a zinc coating may be applied by molten metal spraying, sherardizing or electrolytically. Aluminium–zinc alloy coatings are more durable than the equivalent thickness of pure zinc. The standard alloys contain 5 per cent (ZA) and 55 per cent (AZ) aluminium in zinc respectively. A further alloy containing 1.6 per cent silicon is durable without further protection in non-aggressive environments. Terne, an alloy of lead

Table XIII Stainless steel grades for different environmental conditions (BS EN 10088–1: 2005)

Type	Metallic alloying components (%)	Number	Suitable environments
Austenitic	Chromium/nickel 18–10	1.4301	Rural and clean urban
	Chromium/nickel/molybdenum 17–12–2	1.4401	Industrial and marine
Ferritic	Chromium 17	1.4406	Interior
Duplex	Chromium/nickel/molybdenum 22–5–3	1.4462	Severe industrial and marine

and tin, hot-dipped onto either steel or stainless steel, produces a durable cladding and roofing material. Tin coated stainless steel, manufactured by electrodeposition, is also used for roofing where an appearance similar to lead is required, but without the associated risk of lead theft.

The predominant organic coatings to steel are polyvinyl chloride plastisol (PVC[P]), polyvinylidene fluoride (PVDF) and polyurethane on zinc–aluminium alloy or zinc-coated steel. PVC[P] has a leather grain finish, PVDF has a smooth finish with good colour stability and polyurethane offers colour and metallic gloss finishes. The products are available in a wide range of colours for use in roofing, cladding and interior finishes. Other organic finishes include polyester incorporating acrylic beads and patterned or textured polyvinyl chloride (PVC) film.

2.6 Steel reinforcement for concrete

For details of sizes of steel reinforcement, refer to Chapter 6, Structure.

Concrete should be specified to BS EN 206: 2013, and steel reinforcement to BS 4449: 2005 + A2: 2009 (bar/coil and decoiled steel), BS 4482: 2005 (steel wire) and BS 4483: 2005 (steel fabric). The Standard BS 4482: 2005 refers to 250 MPa yield strength plain bars and the higher grade steel, 500 MPa, for plain, ribbed and indented bars. The Standard BS 4449: 2005 specifies high yield steel (500 MPa) with three levels of ductility, for ribbed bars. Austenitic stainless steel may be used for concrete reinforcement where failure due to corrosion is a potential risk. Stainless steels suitable for reinforcement are specified in BS 6744: 2001 + A2: 2009.

3 TIMBER

3.1 General

For the supply of both softwoods and hardwoods, independent global certification schemes operated by the Forest Stewardship Council (FSC) and Programme for the Endorsement of Forest Certification (PEFC) ensure sustainable forest management and a verifiable chain of custody.

Timber used in building is either softwood or hardwood, depending on species; each may be supplied sawn or finished.

Sizes are usually quoted 'ex', meaning the sawn size. Structural timber is classified into strength classes (Table XIV) to BS EN 338: 2009 (and pr EN 338: 2013) for both softwoods and hardwoods.

Table XIV Relationship between strength classes and physical properties for structural softwoods and hardwoods (BS EN 338: 2009, incorporating pending pr EN 338: 2013)

Softwood species											
Strength class	C14	C16	C18	C20	C22	C24	C27	C30	C35	C40	C45	C50
Bending strength (MPa)	14	16	18	20	22	24	27	30	35	40	45	50
Mean density (kg/m³)	350	370	380	390	410	420	430	460	470	480	490	520

Hardwood species													
Strength class	D18	D24	D27	D30	D35	D40	D45	D50	D55	D60	D65	D70	D75	D80
Bending strength (MPa)	18	24	27	30	35	40	45	50	55	60	65	70	75	80
Mean density (kg/m³)	570	580	610	640	650	660	700	740	790	840	960	1080	1080	1080

Note: C refers to coniferous softwoods and D refers to deciduous hardwoods.
Timber conforming to C45 and C50 may not be readily available.

3.2 Softwood

Target cross-sectional sizes for sawn softwood based on imperial and metric units (Tables XV and XVI respectively) have been agreed within the European Union (BS EN 1313-1: 2010), but with provision for additional complementary sizes for twelve of the individual member states. The complementary preferred cross-sectional sizes for the UK and Ireland are included in Table XVII. Permitted tolerances on structural timber to BS EN 336: 2013 are given in Table XVIII.

Joinery timber requires a high level of finish and straightness, and is classified into seven quality classes (BS EN 942: 2007) according to the number and size of visible natural defects, particularly knots.

A wide range of standard softwood profiles are available. Tongue-and-groove boarding to BS 1297: 1987 is to thicknesses of 16, 19, 21 and 28 mm with standard widths of 65, 90, 113 and 137 mm.

Table XV Common target cross-sectional sizes based on imperial measure (BS EN 1313–1: 2010)

Thickness (mm)	Width (mm)						
	75	100	125	150	175	200	225
38		X	X	X			
50		X	X	X	X	X	X
63		X	X	X	X		
75					X	X	X
100						X	

Table XVI Common target cross-sectional sizes based on metric measure (BS EN 1313–1: 2010)

Thickness (mm)	Width (mm)							
	80	100	120	140	160	180	200	220
50	X	X	X	X	X	X	X	X
60		X	X	X	X	X		
80		X	X	X	X	X	X	
100	X	X	X	X	X		X	
120	X	X	X			X	X	X
140	X	X		X			X	
160	X	X	X			X		X

Table XVII Complementary preferred target cross-sectional sizes in United Kingdom (UK) and Ireland (IR) (BS EN 1313–1: 2010)

Thickness (mm)	Width (mm)											
	75	100	115	125	138	150	175	200	225	250	275	300
35	IR	IR	IR	IR		IR	IR	IR	IR		IR	
38	UK		UK		UK		UK	UK	UK	UK	UK	UK
44	IR	IR	IR	IR		IR	IR	IR				
47	UK	UK		UK		UK	UK	UK	UK	UK		UK
50	UK									UK		UK
	IR											
63	IR							UK	UK			
								IR	IR			
75		UK		UK						UK	UK	UK
		IR		IR							IR	
100						UK			UK	UK	UK	UK
150						UK	UK					UK
250										UK		
300												UK

Note: The Standard BS EN 1313–1: 2010 also gives complementary preferred target cross-sectional sizes for Austria, Switzerland, Germany, Finland, France, Italy, Netherlands, Norway, Sweden and Poland.

Table XVIII Permitted deviations of cross-sectional sizes of structural timber (BS EN 336: 2013)

Maximum deviations from target sizes	Tolerance class T1	Tolerance class T2
Thicknesses and widths ≤ 100 mm	−1 to + 3 mm	−1 to + 1 mm
Thicknesses and widths >100 and ≤ 300 mm	−2 to + 4 mm	−1.5 to + 1.5 mm
Thicknesses and widths >300 mm	−3 to + 5 mm	−2.0 to + 2.0 mm

Note: Permitted deviations of cross-sectional sizes for general sawn softwood timber to BS EN 1313–1: 2010 correspond to the data for Tolerance class T1.

Regularly available softwood species and their origin include Douglas Fir (N. America and UK), Western Hemlock (N. America), European Larch (Europe), Parana Pine (S. America), Corsican Pine (Europe), Pitch Pine (Southern USA), Radiata Pine (S. Africa, S. America and New Zealand), Scots Pine (UK and Europe), Southern Pine (Southern USA), Yellow Pine (N. America), Spruce (Canada), Sitka Spruce (N. America and UK), Western Red Cedar (N. America) and European Whitewood (Europe and Russia).

3.3 Hardwood

Hardwood is normally supplied in planks of specified thickness but arbitrary width and length, depending on species and thickness. The preferred dimensions including complementary thicknesses are given in Table XIX. Maximum reductions for planing are listed in Table XX.

Table XIX Standard sizes of sawn hardwood (BS EN1313–2: 1999)

Preferred thicknesses EU (mm)	20	27	32	40	50	60	65	70	80	100
Complementary thicknesses UK (mm)	19	26		38	52		63	75		

Preferred widths

EU 10 mm intervals for widths between 50 mm and 90 mm,
20 mm intervals for widths of 100 mm or more.

Preferred lengths

EU 100 mm intervals for lengths between 2.0 m and 6.0 m,
50 mm intervals for lengths less than 1.0 m.

Table XX Maximum reductions from sawn sizes of hardwoods by planing two opposed faces (BS EN1313–2: 1999)

Typical application	Reduction from sawn sizes of width or thickness (mm)				
	15 to 25	26 to 50	51 to 100	101 to 150	151 to 300
Flooring, matchings, interlocked boarding and planed all round	5	6	7	7	7
Trim	6	7	8	9	10
Joinery and cabinet work	7	9	10	12	14

Regularly available hardwood species and their origin include American Ash (USA), European Ash (Europe), Beech (Europe), American Birch (N. America), European Birch (Europe and UK), Iroko (W. Africa), Jelutong (Malaysia), Keruing (S.E. Asia), Mahogany (Africa), American Mahogany (Central and S. America), Maple (N. America), Meranti/Red Lauan (Malaysia), Meranti/ White Lauan (S.E. Asia), American Red Oak (N. America), American White Oak (N. America), Obeche (W. Africa), Sapele (W. Africa), Teak (Burma, Indonesia and Thailand) and Utile (Africa). Predominant UK production includes oak, sweet chestnut, ash, beech and sycamore.

3.4 Strength classes

Timber for structural purposes is machine or visually graded into an appropriate strength class. The machine strength classes, which relate directly to bending strength, range from C14 to C50 for softwood species (coniferous), and D18 to D80 for hardwood species (deciduous). The characteristic physical properties of timber in the various strength classes are listed in BS EN 338: 2009 and pending pr EN 338: 2013.

3.5 Use classes

Timber and all timber products are, to a greater or lesser degree affected by moisture. The environmental conditions in which wood and wood products are used, are therefore categorised into five use classes by BS EN 335: 2013 as in Table XXI.

3.6 Timber products

The wide range of products manufactured from wood includes laminated timber, cross-laminated timber (CLT), laminated veneer

Table XXI Use classes for wood and wood-based products (BS EN 335: 2013)

Use Class	General service situation for wood or wood-based products
Class 1	Inside a construction and not exposed to weather or wetting.
Class 2	Under cover and not exposed to weather but where occasional but not persistent wetting may occur.
Class 3	
3.1	Above ground and exposed to weather, but will not remain wet for long periods. Water will not accumulate.
3.2	Above ground and exposed to weather, and will remain wet for long periods. Water may accumulate.
Class 4	Direct contact with ground and/or fresh water.
Class 5	Permanently or regularly submerged in salt water.

lumber (LVL), plywood, particleboard, fibreboard and modified wood.

Laminated timber: Laminated timber sections, Figure 7.1, can be manufactured to any transportable size, typically 30 m although spans of over 50 m are possible. Strength-graded timber sections, continuously glued with resin adhesive and the use of scarf or finger jointing within the laminates ensure a uniform structural product. Sections may be joined on site by finger jointing (BS EN14080: 2013). Units are classified to the appropriate overall strength class GL24, 28, 32 or 36 to BS EN 1194: 1999. Standard stock straight sections range typically between 35 mm and 200 mm in thickness and between 90 mm and 630 mm in depth although larger standard sections are available from some suppliers. Arches, cranked beams, portal frames and other geometrical forms are made to design specification.

Laminated veneer lumber: LVL is manufactured by laminating timber strands with polyurethane resin followed by heat or microwave curing under pressure. It can be produced in sheets or billets up to 26 m long and subsequently machined as solid timber. It is frequently used in I-section joists for roof and floor construction. The three grades appropriate to different environmental conditions (BS EN 14279: 2004 + A1: 2009) are listed in Table XXII. The requirements for structural LVL are detailed in BS EN 14374: 2004.

Cross-laminated timber: CLT (X-LAM) is similar to conventional plywood except that the laminates are thicker. Panel

7.1 *Laminated timber: Bodegas Protos, Spain. Architect: Rogers Stirk Harbour+Partners*

thicknesses are generally between 50 mm and 300 mm, although 500 mm can be produced. Stock panel sizes are up to 15 × 4.8 m, but the standard production limit is 24 m (subject to transportation limits). Panels manufactured from spruce, larch or pine are classified by surface quality which is either planed or sanded (BS EN 13017-1: 2001), Table XXIII.

Plywood: Plywood is classified (BS EN 313-1: 1996) according to its construction and properties including durability, strength and surface condition. Bonding properties and biological durability for Use Classes 1–3 (dry, humid and exterior conditions) are specified in BS EN 636: 2012. Softwood plywood (predominantly pine and spruce) is imported from North America and Scandinavia. Temperate hardwood products are imported from Finland (birch) and Germany (beech), while tropical hardwood sheets are imported from Indonesia, Malaysia, South America and Africa. The standard sheet sizes are 1220 mm × 2440, 3050 and 3660 mm but larger sizes to 3660 × 3050 mm are available especially for concrete formwork. Thicknesses range typically from 4 to 30 mm.

Particleboards: Particleboards are manufactured from particles of wood, flax or hemp and a binder. Wood particleboard (BS EN 309: 2005) and cement-bonded particle board (BS EN 634-2: 2007) are bonded with resin and cement binder, respectively.

Oriented strand board (OSB) is manufactured from larger wood flakes and binder to BS EN 300: 2006.

The standard sizes of wood particleboard (chipboard) are 2440 × 1220, 2750 × 1220, 3050 × 1220 and 3660 × 1220 mm, with the common thicknesses within the range 12–38 mm. Two generic manufacturing processes are used for the production of wood particleboard giving products with different properties. The pressed product is stronger, whereas the extruded board (BS EN 14755: 2005) may be solid or with void spaces. Standard grades of wood particleboard are hygroscopic and respond to changes in humidity, but humid-resistant grades are tolerant to occasional wetting. Grades of wood particleboard and extruded particleboard are listed in Tables XXIV and XXV.

Cement-bonded particle board has good resistance to fire, water, fungal attack and frost. The Standard (BS EN 634-2: 2007) specifies only one grade as in Table XXVI. Board sizes are typically 1200 × 2400, 2660 or 3050 mm with standard thickness of 12 and 18 mm, although sheets up to 40 mm thickness are manufactured.

Table XXII Grades of laminated veneer lumber (BS EN 14279: 2004)

Type	Exposure class	Exposure	Purpose/loading
LVL/1	class 1	dry	load-bearing
LVL/2	class 2	humid	load-bearing
LVL/3	class 3	exterior conditions (with appropriate finish)	load-bearing

Note: Dry, humid and exterior Service Classes are defined in BS EN 1995–1–1: 2004 + A2: 2014.

Table XXIII Surface quality classification of cross-laminated timber (BS EN 13017–1: 2001)

Class	Grade	Typical use
Class C	Standard	Non-visible
Class AB	Interior grade	Residential visible
Class BC	Interior grade	Industrial visible

Table XXIV Grades of wood particleboard (BS EN 312: 2010)

Type	Exposure	Colour coding		Purpose/loading
P1	Dry	White, white	blue	General purpose
P2	Dry	White	blue	Interior fitments
P3	Humid	White	green	Non-load-bearing
P4	Dry	Yellow, yellow	blue	Load-bearing
P5	Humid	Yellow, yellow	green	Load-bearing
P6	Dry	Yellow	blue	Heavy-duty load-bearing
P7	Humid	Yellow	green	Heavy-duty load-bearing

Table XXV   Grades of extruded wood particleboard (BS EN 14755: 2005)

Grade	Description
ES	Extruded Solid: Board with a minimum density of 550kg/m³
ET	Extruded Tube: Board with a minimum solid density of 550kg/m³
ESL	Extruded Solid Light: Board with a density of less than 550kg/m³
ETL	Extruded Tube Light: Board with a solid density of less than 550kg/m³

Note: Grades ET and ETL must have at least 5 mm of material over the void spaces.

Table XXVI   Grade of cement-bonded particleboard (BS EN 634–2: 2007)

Exposure	Colour coding		Purpose/loading
Dry, humid and exterior	White, white	brown	Non-load-bearing

Note: Within the one grade there are two Technical Classes 1 and 2 which relate only to the modulus of elasticity in bending.

Table XXVII   Grades of oriented strand board (OSB) (BS EN 300: 2006)

Grade	Exposure	Colour coding		Purpose/loading
OSB/1	Dry	White	blue	General purpose Interior fitments
OSB/2	Dry	Yellow, yellow	blue	Load-bearing
OSB/3	Humid	Yellow, yellow	green	Load-bearing
OSB/4	Humid	Yellow	green	Heavy duty load-bearing

Note: Boards of grades OSB/3 and OSB/4 are suitable for Use Classes 1 and 2 to BS EN 335: 2013.

OSB is graded (Table XXVII) to its anticipated loading and environmental conditions (BS EN 300: 2006). It is available in sheet thicknesses from 6 to 38 mm, although the standard range is from 9 to 18 mm.

Fibreboards: Fibreboards (BS EN 622-1: 2003) are manufactured from wood or other plant fibres, and generally are bonded under pressure using the natural adhesive properties and felting of the fibres. In the case of medium density fibreboard (MDF) a resin bonding agent is used. Essentially, differing degrees of compression give rise to the product range, although some products are impregnated with additives. Tables XXVIII–XXXI give the grades of MDF (BS EN 622-5: 2009), hardboard (BS EN 622-2: 2004), mediumboard (BS EN 622-3: 2004) and softboard (BS EN 622-4: 2009), respectively.

Modified wood: Wood may be modified either by heat treatment or by chemical reagents. Thermal modification (DD CEN/TS 15679: 2007) involves the heating of usually pine or spruce, but also certain hardwoods, to between 180°C and 240°C within an inert atmosphere The durability is significantly increased, but with

Table XXVIII   Grades of medium density fibreboard (MDF) (BS EN 622–5: 2009)

Grade	Exposure	Colour coding		Purpose / loading
MDF	Dry	White, white	blue	General purpose Interior fitments
MDF.H	Humid	White, white	green	General purpose
MDF.LA	Dry	Yellow, yellow	blue	Load-bearing
MDF.HLS	Humid	Yellow, yellow	green	Load-bearing (Instantaneous or short-term loading only)
L–MDF	Dry			
L–MDF.H	Humid			
UL1–MDF	Dry			Insulating panels with limited stiffening function
UL2–MDF	Dry			Insulating panels with a stiffening function
MDFRWH	Underlay conditions			Rigid underlays in roofs and walls. [Instantaneous (e.g. wind) or short-term loading (e.g. snow) only]

Note: Prefix L refers to light, Prefix UL refers to ultra-light and RW refers to roof and walls.

Table XXIX   Grades of hardboard (BS EN 622–2: 2004)

Grade	Exposure	Colour coding		Purpose/loading
HB	Dry	White, white	blue	General purpose
HB.H	Humid	White, white	green	General purpose
HB.E	Exterior	White, white	brown	General purpose
HB.LA	Dry	Yellow, yellow	blue	Load-bearing
HB.LA1	Humid	Yellow, yellow	green	Load-bearing
HB.LA2	Humid	Yellow	green	Heavy-duty load-bearing

Table XXX   Grades of mediumboard (BS EN 622–3:2004)

Grade	Exposure	Colour coding		Purpose/loading
MBL	Dry	White, white	blue	General purpose
MBH	Dry	White, white	blue	General purpose
MBL.H	Humid	White, white	green	General purpose
MBH.H	Humid	White, white	green	General purpose
MBL.E	Exterior	White, white	brown	General purpose
MBH.E	Exterior	White, white	brown	General purpose
MBH.LA1	Dry	Yellow, yellow	blue	Load-bearing
MBH.LA2	Dry	Yellow	blue	Heavy-duty load-bearing
MBH.HLS1	Humid	Yellow, yellow	green	Load-bearing
MBH.HLS2	Humid	Yellow	green	Heavy-duty load-bearing

Note: MBL refers to low density medium board and MBH refers to high density medium board.

Table XXXI   Grades of softboard (BS EN 622–4: 2009)

Grade	Exposure	Colour coding		Purpose / loading
SB	Dry	White, white	blue	General purpose
SB.H	Humid	White, white	green	General purpose
SB.E	Exterior	White, white	brown	General purpose
SB.LS	Dry	Yellow, yellow	blue	Load-bearing (Instantaneous or short-term loading only)
SB.HLS	Humid	Yellow, yellow	green	Load-bearing (Instantaneous or short-term loading only)

Table XXXII   Classes of thermally modified timber

Classes	Typical uses
Softwoods	
Class D (212°C)	Garden structures, external cladding, exterior doors, window frames, decking, internal floors and internal decoration
Class S (190°C)	Construction materials, structural components, garden furniture, interior floors, exterior doors and window frames
Hardwoods	
Class D (212°C)	Garden furniture, patio floors, interior floors and interior decoration
Class S (190°C)	Construction materials, mouldings, furniture, interior floors and interior decoration

some reduction in strength. Thermally modified timber classes are listed in Table XXXII. Chemical modification involves the acetylation (Accoya®) or furfurylation (Kebony®) of the timber leading to a Class 1 durable material, without changes to the physical properties of the material.

4 BRICKS AND BLOCKS

4.1 Bricks

The standard work size for UK clay bricks is 215 × 102.5 × 65 mm (coordinating size 225 × 112.5 × 75 mm). However, larger units up to 490 mm in length offer variations in bonding and enhanced horizontal effects. Clay bricks are supplied in a wide variety of face colours, textures (including glazed), frost resistance/active soluble salt content (Table XXXIII) and other properties. Most UK bricks are defined by the National Annex to BS EN 771-1: 2011 as High Density masonry units. The National Annex refers to the standard UK brick size, also to the two grades of Engineering/DPC bricks common within the UK (Table XXXIV). The standard BS EN 771-1: 2011 lists the wide-ranging specifications required for clay

Table XXXIII Freeze/thaw resistance and active soluble salt content limits for clay bricks (High Density units) (BS EN 771–1: 2011)

Durability designation	Freeze/thaw resistance
F2	Masonry subjected to severe exposure
F1	Masonry exposed to moderate exposure
F0	Masonry subjected to passive exposure
	Active soluble salt content
S2	Sodium/potassium 0.06%. magnesium 0.03%
S1	Sodium/potassium 0.17%. magnesium 0.08%
S0	No requirement

Table XXXIV Properties of clay engineering bricks (High Density [HD] units) (National Annex to BS EN 771–1: 2011)

	Clay engineering bricks	
Performance characteristics	Class A	Class B
Compressive strength (MPa)	125	75
Water absorption (% by mass) and also	4.5	7.0
when used as DPC units	(and DPC 1)	(and DPC 2)
Freeze/thaw resistance category	F2	F2
Active soluble salt content category	S2	S2

Note: For HD DPC bricks water absorption not compressive strength is the defining limitation. DPC 1 refers to damp-proof courses for buildings and DPC 2 for external works.

bricks. Only imported calcium silicate bricks (BS EN 771-2: 2011) are available. The UK standard sizes for concrete bricks are covered by the National Annex to BS EN 771-3: 2011 (Table XXXV). Brick manufacturers usually offer specials from within the British Standard range (BS 4729: 2005).

An extensive range of fired clay blocks of low and high density other than bricks is illustrated in BS EN 771-1: 2011, but not all are readily available from UK suppliers.

4.2 Blocks

The standard BS EN 771-3: 2011 does not limit the sizes of dense and lightweight concrete blocks (masonry units), but it does refer to a fairly restricted range listed in Table XXXVI. In addition the Standard BS 6073-2: 2008 lists work sizes for aggregate coursing units and aircrete blocks (Table XXXVII). Additional sizes for floors and foundations are available, although each manufacturer produces a restricted range.

Table XXXV Standard work sizes for concrete bricks (National Annex to BS EN 771–3: 2011)

Length (mm)	Width (mm)	Height (mm)
215	103	65
290	90	90
190	90	90
190	90	65

Table XXXVI Common work sizes of concrete blocks (BS EN 771–3: 2011)

	Width (mm)									
Length (mm)	75	90	100	140	150	190	200	215	225	Height (mm)
390		*	*	*		*	*			190
440	*	*	*	*	*	*	*	*	*	215

Note: Asterisk indicates common size to BS EN 771-3: 2011. Other widths may be available but manufacturers do not normally produce the complete range.

Masonry unit sizes are recorded as length, width and height in that order to BS EN 771-3: 2011. Tolerances on block sizes for concrete and autoclaved aerated concrete blocks are given in Tables XXXVIII and XXXIX respectively.

5 CONCRETE

5.1 Cement

Cements are classified according to their main constituents, such as Portland cement or blast furnace cement. The standard BS EN 197-1: 2011 lists five main types of cement:

Table XXXVII Typical work sizes of aggregate coursing and aircrete blocks (BS 6073–2: 2008)

	Length (mm)	Width (mm)	Height (mm)
Aggregate coursing blocks			
	190	90	65
	190	90	90
	215	100	65
	290	90	90
	440	90	65
	440	100	65
	440	90	140
	440	100	140
Aircrete standard blocks			
	440	50–350	215
	610	50–350	215
	620	50–350	215
Aircrete coursing blocks			
	215	90–150	65
	215	90–150	70

Note: Other heights of aircrete blocks are available for foundations and for thin layer mortar construction.

CEM I	Portland cement
CEM II	Portland-composite cement
CEM III	Blast furnace cement
CEM IV	Pozzolanic cement
CEM V	Composite cement

Within these five main types a wide range of additional constituents including silica fume, natural or industrial pozzolanas, calcareous or siliceous fly ash and burnt shale may be incorporated. The full range of permitted compositions and strength classes are listed in the standard BS EN 197-1: 2011.

Appropriate properties of aggregates for concrete are listed in the standard BS EN 12620: 2013.

5.2 Concrete

The five methods for the specification of concrete mixes are described in BS 8500-1: 2006 + A1: 2012 and BS EN 206: 2013:

Designated concrete
Designed concrete
Prescribed concrete
Standardised prescribed concrete
Proprietary concrete

Table XXXVIII Limit of tolerance on block sizes (BS EN 771–3: 2011)

Dimensions	Tolerance category			
	D1 (mm)	D2 (mm)	D3 (mm)	D4 (mm)
Length	+3	+1	+1	+1
	−5	−3	−3	−3
Width	+3	+1	+1	+1
	−5	−3	−3	−3
Height	+3	+2	+1.5	+1
	−5	−2	−1.5	−1

Note: BS 6073-2: 2008 states that tolerance categories D3 and D4 are intended for use with thin-layer mortar joint systems. Therefore, most units used within the UK conform to tolerance categories D1 and D2.

Table XXXIX Limit of tolerance on autoclaved aerated concrete block sizes (BS EN 771 4: 2011)

Dimensions	Standard mortar joints (mm)	Thin layer mortar joints TLMA (mm)	Thin layer mortar joints TLMB (mm)
Length	+3 to −5	±3	±1.5
Height	+3 to −5	±2	±1.0
Width	±3	±2	±1.5
Flatness of bed faces	No requirement	No requirement	≤1.0
Plane parallelism of bed faces	No requirement	No requirement	≤1.0

For routine applications designated concrete is usually appropriate. The purchaser correctly specifies the proposed use and the mix designation, and the producer fulfils the normal performance criteria. In designed concrete the purchaser takes more responsibility for the mix by specifying a complete set of performance criteria. For prescribed concrete the purchaser specifies all materials including any admixtures by weight. Standardised prescribed concretes are a set of five standard mixes for routine applications as in housing. Proprietary concrete must fulfil the appropriate performance criteria but the composition is to the producer's choice.

5.3 Reinforced concrete
Reinforced concrete is described in Chapter 6, Structure.

5.4 Concrete components
Paving flags: Concrete paving flags are manufactured to the requirements of BS EN 1339: 2003. The standard does not specify preferred dimensions, except a maximum length of 1m. UK flags, however, are traditionally supplied in the dimensions given in Table XL. Tactile flags are used in the pedestrian pavement adjacent to pedestrian crossings to indicate their presence to people who are visually impaired.

The standard (BS EN 1339: 2003) refers to four classes of flag related to ranges of strength and durability. Class 1 flags are appropriate for light domestic use (gardens/drives), Class 3 flags are suitable for normal public areas, but Class 4 are required for very heavy pedestrian and vehicular use. Class 1 products are not resistant to freeze/thaw effects, but Class 3 flags are resistant to repeated freezing and thawing and the regular use of de-icing salts.

Roofing tiles: Concrete plain roofing tiles may normally be used on pitches down to 30° or 35°. Some concrete interlocking tiles may be used down to a 12.5° or 15° pitch, subject to manufacturer's specification. Concrete slates are manufactured with either deep or shallow profiles to emulate thin or rustic natural slate.

Precast concrete panels: Precast concrete panels, Figure 7.2, may be cast vertically or horizontally, although the latter is more common. Horizontally cast units may be manufactured face up or face down according to the surface finish required. Moulds may be of plywood, plastics or steel and indirect finishes, e.g. bush hammering, can be applied. Appropriate reinforcements and/or facings of stone or brick may be incorporated into the moulds.

6 ALUMINIUM

6.1 General
Wrought aluminium and its alloys are designated by the letters European Norm Wrought Aluminium (EN AW) followed by a

Table XL   Typical sizes and types of paving flags

Paving flag designation	Nominal size (mm)	Work size (mm)	Thickness (mm)
A	600 × 450	598 × 448	50 or 63
B	600 × 600	598 × 598	50 or 63
C	600 × 750	598 × 748	50 or 63
D	600 × 900	598 × 898	50 or 63
E	450 × 450	448 × 448	50 or 70
F	400 × 400	398 × 398	50 or 65
G	300 × 300	298 × 298	50 or 60

unique four digit coding to BS EN 573-1: 2004. The standard BS EN 573-3: 2013 details the chemical composition and form of the products. Table XLI gives examples of the standard construction alloys. Aluminium may also be cast into components. Aluminium is used for a wide range of non-structural products, Figure 7.3. The range of aluminium finishes includes anodizing, texturing, metallic (zinc) and plastic (polyester or PVC) coatings.

6.2 Aluminium bars and flats
Aluminium bars are made to the dimensional requirements of BS 6722: 1986 (see Tables I and II, Section 2.1). Stock sizes for round section typically range from 3 to 200 mm diameter, for square section from 3 to 180 mm side and for flat sections from 3 to 70 mm × 10 to 250 mm depending upon the manufacturer.

6.3 Aluminium structural sections
Table XLII based on BS 1161: 1977 gives the sizes of standard I, T and channel sections.

Table XLI   Aluminium alloys in construction

Code number	Composition	Typical application
EN AW-1080A	99.8% pure	Flashings
EN AW-1050A	99.5% pure	Flashings
EN AW-1200	99% pure	Fully supported sheet roofing, insulating foils
EN AW-3103	Manganese alloy	Profiled roofing and cladding
EN AW-5083SP	Superplastic alloy Magnesium/manganese alloy	Rainscreen cladding
EN AW-6061	Magnesium/silicon/copper alloy	Tubular structural forms
EN AW-6063	Magnesium/silicon alloy	Extruded sections – curtain walling, windows and doors
EN AW-6082	Structural aluminium Magnesium/manganese/silicon alloy	Load-bearing structures

Note: A more comprehensive list is quoted in BS EN 1999–1–1: 2007 + A1:2009.

7.2 *Pre-cast concrete cladding panels: Hilton Hotel, Liverpool. Architect: AHR Architects*

7.3 *Perforated aluminium ceiling panels: North Satellite Concourse, Hong Kong International Airport. Architect: AHR Architects*

Table XLII Aluminium alloy structural sections (BS 1161: 1977)

Equal angles

	Thickness (mm)	Mass/length (kg/m)
120 × 120	10	6.47
	7	4.68
100 × 100	8	4.31
	6	3.34
80 × 80	6	2.59
	5	2.23
60 × 60	5	1.62
	3.5	1.17
50 × 50	4	1.08
	3	0.84
40 × 40	3	0.65
30 × 30	2.5	0.40

Unequal angles

Nominal size (mm)	Thickness (mm)	Mass/length (kg/m)
140 × 105	11	7.26
	8.5	5.83
120 × 90	10	5.65
	7	4.11
100 × 75	8	3.77
	6	2.94
80 × 60	6	2.26
	5	1.96
60 × 45	5	1.41
	3.5	1.03
50 × 38	4	0.95
	3	0.74

Channels

Nominal size (mm)	Thickness (mm)		Mass/length (kg/m)
	Web	Flange	
240 × 100	9	13	12.5
200 × 80	8	12	9.19
180 × 75	8	11	8.06
160 × 70	7	10	6.58
140 × 60	7	10	5.66
120 × 50	6	9	4.19
100 × 40	6	8	3.20
80 × 35	5	7	2.29
60 × 30	5	6	1.69

Table XLII (continued)

I-sections

Nominal size (mm)	Thickness (mm)		Mass/length (kg/m)
	Web	Flange	
160 × 80	7	11	7.64
140 × 70	7	10	6.33
120 × 60	6	9	4.77
100 × 50	6	8	3.72
80 × 40	5	7	2.54
60 × 30	4	6	1.59

Tees

Nominal size (mm)	Thickness (mm)	Mass/length (kg/m)
90 × 120	10	5.68
75 × 100	8	3.79
60 × 80	6	2.27
45 × 60	5	1.42
38 × 50	4	0.95

7 ROOFING AND CLADDING

7.1 General

The choice of roofing materials is related to a combination of cost, durability and particularly aesthetics. Many roofing materials such as asphalt are available only in neutral colours, but single-layer PVC, for example, is available in a range of colours. Metal roofing systems give visual articulation, and the choice of the particular metal or coated metal determines both the initial and weathered finish. In all cases careful detailing enhances the period to first maintenance.

Sheet metal for roofing and cladding is covered in the standards BS EN 14782: 2006 and BS EN 14783: 2013 for self-supporting and fully supported sheet metal, respectively. The standards list minimum thicknesses for aluminium, steel, stainless steel, zinc and copper, also lead for fully supported systems. However, it is noted that European Union member states may require thicknesses greater than those described. The standard BS 8747: 2007 relates to reinforced bitumen membranes for roofing and traditional mastic asphalt is covered by BS 6925: 1988.

7.2 Steel

The standard BS EN 508-1: 2014 details typical profiles for self-supporting sheet and tile steel roofing. The minimum thickness for the finished coated steel is 2.4 ± 0.2 mm.

The standard BS EN 505: 2013 gives information on fully supported steel roofing for which the minimum sheet thickness is 0.6 mm. The metallic and organic coatings listed in these standards are described in Section 2.5 Coated Steels.

7.3 Stainless steel

Stainless steel as a sheet roofing material is covered by BS EN 508-3: 2008 for the self-supporting material and by BS EN 502: 2013 for the fully supported product. The standard BS EN 508-3: 2008 gives examples of sheet and tile profiles also organic coatings including polyvinylchloride (plastisol), polyvinylidene fluoride, polyurethane and polyesters. The standard BS EN 502: 2013 lists the equivalent data for fully supported roofing systems.

Table XLIII gives the most commonly used grades of stainless steel sheeting with and without organic coatings. The appropriate grade and finish depends upon the local environment and durability requirements.

7.4 Aluminium

The Code of Practice for aluminium sheet roof and wall covering, CP143 Part 15: 1973, is still current. Sheeting comes to site in coils, and is passed continuously through a machine to form standing seams in-situ. This long strip system removes the necessity to form joints transverse to the standing seams up to a maximum of 7 m. The standard thickness for long strip aluminium roofing is 0.8 mm and the recommended maximum width of 450 mm produces standing seams at 375 mm centres. A minimum fall of $1.5°$ is recommended. The standard BS EN 507: 2000 gives the specification for fully supported sheet aluminium roofing and the standard factory applied organic coatings including polyesters, acrylics, alkyds, polyurethanes and polyvinylidene fluoride.

Self-supporting aluminium sheet is described in BS EN 508-2: 2008, which gives examples of profiles for sheet and tile units also the standard organic coatings.

7.5 Copper

The standard grade of copper for fully supported and self-supported roofing is Cu-DHP (C106) (phosphorus deoxidized non-arsenical copper) to BS EN 1172: 2011. Sheet copper is available in a range of thicknesses from 0.4 to 1.0 mm (up to 3.0 mm for curtain walling) with 0.6 and 0.7 mm the standard thicknesses for roofing. Sheet widths range from 500 to 1000 mm with 600 mm standard for roofing. The standard BS EN 504: 2000 gives the specification for fully supported sheet copper roofing.

The two methods of copper roofing available are traditional, Figure 7.4, and long-strip. Fully annealed copper strip is normally used in traditional roofing as detailed in Table XLIV. For long-strip roofing, 1/8 to 1/4 hard temper copper strip is required to prevent buckling with thermal movement. Typical long strip dimensions are listed in Table XLV. Copper sheet is also used for tiles, Figure 7.5.

Table XLIII   Stainless steel self supported and fully supported sheet

Steel grade	Steel designation	
	Steel name	Steel number
Ferritic with organic coating	X6Cr13	1.4000
Ferritic with or without organic coating	X6Cr17	1.4016
	X6CrMo17–1	1.4113
	X3CrTi17	1.4510
	X2CrMoTi18–2	1.4521
Austenitic with or without organic coating	X5CrNi18–10	1.4301
Austenitic/molybdenum with or without organic coating	X5CrNiMo17–12–2	1.4401

Note: X is carbon content, Cr Chromium, Ni Nickel, Mo Molybdenum and Ti Titanium.

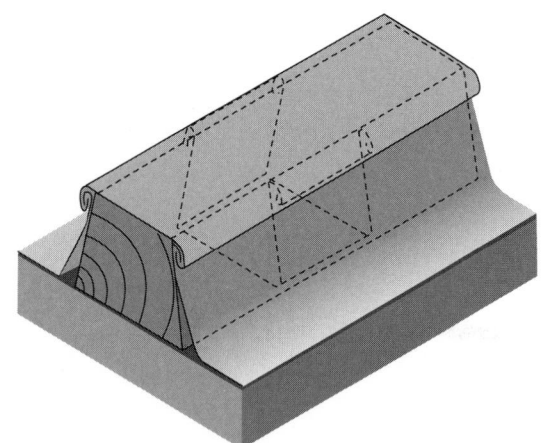

7.4 *Traditional batten roll copper roofing (courtesy of Copper in Architecture)*

7.5 *Copper tiles (courtesy of Aurubis)*

Table XLIV   Standard thicknesses and sizes of copper sheet for traditional roofing

Sheet thickness (mm)	Standard width of sheet to form bay (mm)	Bay width with standing seam (mm)	Bay width with batten roll (mm)	Length of each sheet (m)	Mass (kg/m²)
0.60	600	525	500	1.8	5.4
0.70	750	675	650	1.8	6.3

Note: The maximum sheet length is 2.0 m.

The standard BS EN 506: 2008 describes the use of Cu-DHP copper for self-supporting profiled sheet and tile roofing systems.

Prepatinised copper is available if the immediate effect of green colouration is required, alternatively a gold-coloured copper/aluminium/zinc alloy may be used if the copper colour is to be retained externally.

Copper alloys have good antimicrobial properties at room temperature and normal humidity. Alloys high in copper content (e.g. phosphor bronze and brass) can control bacteria such as MRSA and E.*coli* and are therefore beneficial for use in touch surface applications for hospitals and other public locations.

Direct contact between copper and aluminium, steel or zinc should be avoided to prevent bi-metallic corrosion in the presence of moisture. Lead, stainless steel and brass are normally unaffected. Rainwater run off from exposed bitumen and cedar wood can cause corrosion.

7.6 Lead

The sizes of milled lead sheet and strip are specified in BS EN 12588: 2006, and summarised in Table XLVI. The traditional UK lead codes are not referenced in the European Standard; however, the current Code of Practice for fully supported lead sheet roof and wall coverings, BS 6915: 2001, does refer to lead codes in addition to metric thicknesses. Sand-cast lead is manufactured for conservation work. Patination oil can be applied to new lead work to prevent the production of unsightly white lead carbonate staining. Typical lead roof details are shown in Figure 7.6.

Table XLV Recommended widths of copper strip for the long strip system

Width of strip (mm)	400	450	500	600	670
Standing seam centres (mm)	325	375	425	525	595

Note: Using 0.6 or 0.7 mm copper strip at ¼ or ½ hard temper with a fixed zone of 1.5 m within a maximum 10 m length.

Table XLVI Milled lead sheet and strip sizes (BS EN 12588: 2006 and BS 6915: 2001)

Lead code	Thickness (mm)	Average weight (kg/m²) (based on larger thicknesses)	Colour coding
3	1.25 or 1.32	14.97	Green
	1.50 or 1.59	18.03	Yellow
4	1.75 or 1.80	20.41	Blue
5	2.00 or 2.24	25.40	Red
6	2.50 or 2.65	30.06	Black
7	3.00 or 3.15	35.72	White
8	3.50 or 3.55	40.26	Orange

Note: The 1.50 mm (1.59 mm) thickness sheet does not appear in the standard BS 6915: 2001, and has no equivalent Code number. Code 3 lead sheet is not suitable for roofing, cladding and gutters.

Whilst lead is not prone to bi-metallic corrosion in most non-marine building applications, the use of a building paper underlay is appropriate on hardwood roofs (particularly oak) and bitumen painting of the lead for contact with cedar shingles, hardwood cills and new concrete or mortar is advised.

7.7 Zinc

Zinc is covered by BS EN 988: 1997. The standard thicknesses are 0.6, 0.65, 0.7, 0.8 and 1.0 mm (Table XLVII). Preferred lengths are 2.0 and 3.0 m, in a range of widths from 100 to 1000 mm. Pure zinc sheet roofing is no longer used, as it had a lifetime of approximately 40 years in urban conditions (CP 143-5: 1964). However, zinc-copper-titanium alloy is the standard product and may be used directly or coated. Factory induced patina is grey or black, but mineral pigments rolled into the surface and coated with a protective film produce subtle red, blue, green or brown preweathered finishes. Lacquered finishes include green, blue, red, brown, grey and gold. The minimum thickness to BS EN 501: 1994 for fully supported roofing is 0.6 mm. Either traditional or long-strip roofing may be used with titanium zinc. A

Table XLVII Zinc-copper-titanium alloy standard sheet thicknesses (BS EN 988: 1997)

Nominal thickness (mm)	Approximate mass (kg/m²)
0.60	4.3
0.65	4.7
0.70	5.0
0.80	5.8
1.00	7.2

minimum fall of 3° is recommended. Where bays are longer than 3 m, a fixed zone and sliding clips will be required to accommodate thermal movement.

The standard BS EN 506: 2008 describes the use of zinc-copper-titanium alloy for self-supporting sheet and tile profile roofing systems. Organic coatings including polyvinyl chloride (plastisol), polyvinylidene fluoride, polyesters and acrylic are listed.

7.8 Titanium

Titanium sheet (0.3–0.4 mm) may be used as roofing or cladding. The 99 per cent pure material used for construction work has a density (4510 kg/m³) intermediate between that of steel and aluminium and a low coefficient of expansion (8.9 ×10⁻⁶ °C). The natural oxide film can be thickened by anodising to a range of colours between blue and cream, or a textured finish may be applied.

7.9 Reinforced bitumen membranes for roofing

The standard BS 8747: 2007 is a guide to the selection and specification of reinforced bitumen roofing membranes. It describes the standard types of glass-fibre and polyester based reinforced bitumen roofing membranes, also the high performance polymer-modified bitumen membranes manufactured with atactic polypropylene (APP) or styrene–butadiene–styrene (SBS).

The measurable tensile class S and resistance to puncture class P are categorised in Table XLVIII. The standard describes SNPN combinations appropriate to specified standard constructions.

The Annex to BS 8747: 2007 describes the under slating/tiling sheets and perforated venting layers as listed in Table XLVIII with reference to the superseded standard BS 747: 2000.

Table XLVIII Reinforced bitumen membranes to BS 8747: 2007

Description	Type (former BS 747 designation)	Colour code	Tensile class S	Puncture class P	SNPN classification
Glass fibre – fine granule surface	3B	Red	S1	P1	S1P1
Glass fibre – mineral surface	3E	Red	S1	P1	S1P1
Polyester – fine granule underlay	5U	Blue	S2	P3	S2P3
Polyester – fine granule surface	5B/180	Blue	S4	P4	S4P4
Polyester – fine granule surface	5B/250	Blue	S5	P5	S5P5

Note: The puncture class P is derived from a combination of resistance to impact (subclass D) and resistance to static loading (subclass L).

BS 747: 2000 has been superseded and was withdrawn in 2007, but the former designations are referenced in BS 8747: 2007.

Type 1F membranes are underlays for discontinuous roofs.

Type 3G is not classified to BS 8747 as it is a venting layer and not waterproof.

Type 4A membranes are underlays for mastic asphalt.

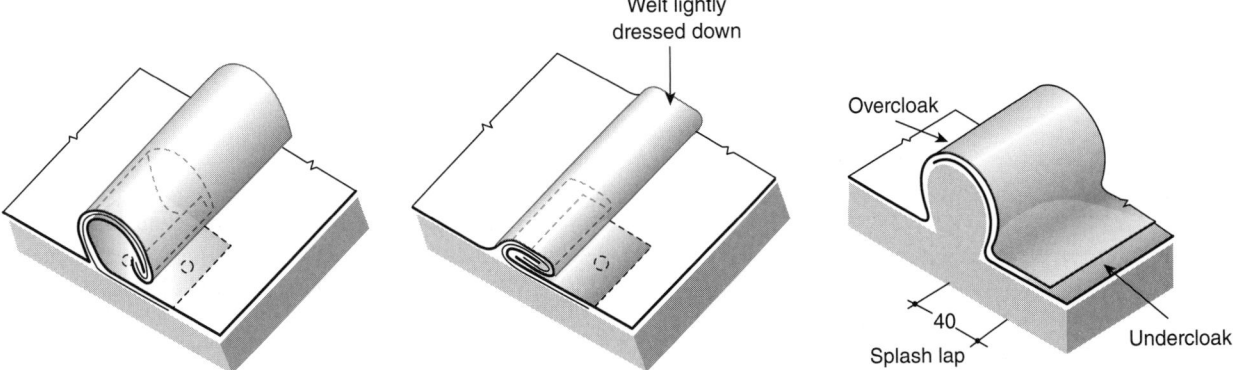

7.6 *Traditional lead roofing – hollow roll and welt joins wood-cored, (diagrams taken from Rolled Lead Sheet: The Complete Manual published by the Lead Sheet Association.*

Table XLIX Mastic asphalt grades (BS 6925: 1988)

Type	Composition
BS 988B	100% bitumen
BS 988T25	75% bitumen, 25% lake asphalt
BS 988T50	50% bitumen, 50% lake asphalt
Specified by manufacturers	Polymer-modified grades

The characteristics of bitumen roofing membranes are described in BS EN 13707: 2013 and BS 8217: 2005 is the current Code of Practice.

7.10 Mastic asphalt roofing

Mastic asphalt for roofing (also flooring and damp-proofing) is specified in BS 6925: 1988, to the grades listed in Table XLIX. Polymer modified mastic asphalts containing SBS are more durable with enhanced flexibility. BS 8218: 1998 is the current Code of Practice for mastic asphalt roofing.

7.11 Single-ply roofing systems

Single-ply roofing systems are described in the standard BS EN 13956: 2012. They usually consist of a continuous membrane between 1 and 3 mm thick covering any form of flat or pitched roof with limited access. The membrane material is typically a thermoplastic, elastomeric or a modified bitumen system which may be glass-fibre or polyester reinforced. Joints between sheets are either heat or solvent welded or sealed with adhesives. The waterproofing sheet may be fixed to the substructure by mechanical fastening, full or partial adhesive bonding or by ballasting to prevent wind uplift, Figure 7.7. Mechanically fixed sheets require the fastenings to be covered by a further layer of waterproofing material, usually at the joints between sheets. Many membranes are backed with a polyester fleece to smooth out any discontinuities in the substructure and where appropriate to assist adhesive bonding. Certain materials are available in a variety of colours or have mineral finishes.

Within the range of thermoplastic systems PVC, flexible polyolefin (FPO), flexible polypropylene alloy (FPA), vinyl ethylene terpolymer (VET), chlorinated polythene (CPE), chlorosulphonated polyethylene (CSM) and polyisobutylene (PIB) are standard products. While ethylene propylene diene monomer (EPDM) and SBS or APP modified bitumen are the standard elastomeric and bitumen-based products, respectively. The modified bitumen products are usually up to 5 mm in thickness.

Mechanically fastened

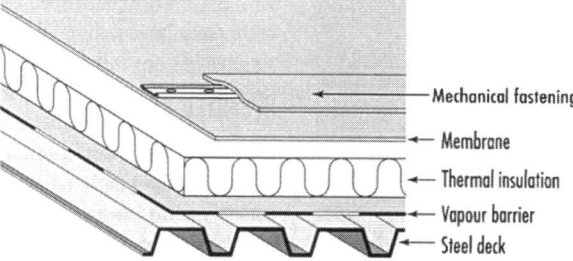

Gravel ballasted

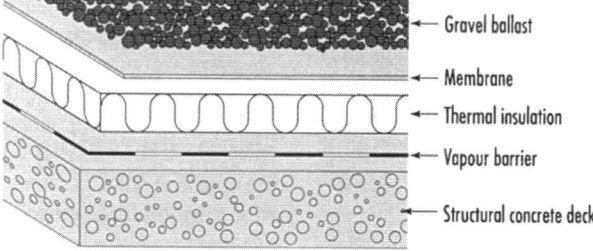

7.7 *Typical single-ply roofing system – mechanically fastened and gravel ballasted*

7.12 Tensile fabric structures

The two alternative materials for tensile roof structures are PVC-coated polyester fabric and PTFE-coated woven glass fibre. PVC-coated polyester is available in a variety of colours and has an anticipated lifespan of approximately 10–15 years, although this can be increased by the application of fluoropolymer lacquers to the exposed weathering surface. The more expensive white PTFE-coated glass fibre material is self-cleaning and non-combustible with an anticipated lifespan of 25+ years. A range of standard design canopies and shelters are commercially available as alternatives to bespoke designs.

7.13 Green roofs

Green roofs are defined as either extensive or intensive according to the type of planting and the associated loading. Extensive roofs are not designed for general access, but are planted with low maintenance, drought and frost tolerant species such as sedums, herbs and grasses. Only occasional access will be required for weeding and the filling of any bare patches. Intensive roofs, which support recreational activity with hard and soft landscaping, require depths of soil typically between 200 and 300 mm, and for large trees up to 1500 mm, giving additional structural loading. Intensive green roofs with access require appropriate health and safety edge protection. Biodiverse or wildlife roofs replicate particular species habitats, which may have been lost from the building site and may incorporate areas of gravel, stones or decaying timber as well as traditional planting. A typical green roof will require a multi-layer system, Figure 7.8 to support the planting and to ensure secure waterproofing of the substructure. Green roofs have the advantage of significantly reducing rapid rainwater run-off as a Sustainable Drainage System (SuDS), whilst enhancing air quality and giving improved thermal and acoustic insulation to the roof.

8 GLASS

8.1 General

The selection of glazing for buildings is highly complex due to the wide variety of design requirements that need full consideration. A suitable methodology to ensure appropriate attention to all significant factors is described in the British Standard BS 6262-1: 2005. The additional parts of the standard BS 6262 give more detailed information on the following aspects of glazing for buildings.

BS 6262	Glazing for buildings:
BS 6262-1: 2005	General methodology for the selection of glazing.
BS 6262-2: 2005	Code of practice for energy, light and sound.
BS 6262-3: 2005	Code of practice for fire, security and wind loading.
BS 6262-4: 2005	Code of practice for safety related to human impact.
BS 6262-6: 2005	Code of practice for special applications. (This relates mainly to structural fixings)
BS 6262-7: 2005	Code of practice for the provision of information.

The key design requirements from BS 6262-1: 2005 are listed in Table L together with additional commentary. Types of glass fulfilling the functions are listed in Table LI.

Current Building Regulations with a focus on Dwelling (DER) and Building Emission Rates (BER) for energy conservation make the use of solar control and energy efficient glazing systems virtually mandatory in most new building situations. The Building Regulations Part L1A and Part L2A 2010 (2013 edition) give concurrent notional specifications for new dwellings and new buildings other than dwellings, respectively. The notional criteria for new dwellings (including the Target Fabric Energy Efficiency

Table L Design requirements for glazing in buildings (BS 6262–1: 2005)

Design requirements	Additional considerations
Natural Lighting	View in and out by day and night. Size and shape of glazing, aesthetic considerations. Appropriate natural and artificial task and amenity lighting levels. Legislative requirements. Glare from sun, sky, reflections/diffraction. Privacy – embossed, etched, sandblasted, and coloured glass; variable transmission glass. Clear white glass.
Thermal considerations	Energy balance of solar gains versus heat losses. Dwelling Emission Rate. Dwelling Fabric Energy Efficiency. Building Emission Rate. Building Regulations – Part L. Double/triple glazing, low emissivity glass, inert gas fill, Window Energy Ratings and Door Set Energy Ratings, U-values. Solar control glass – body tinted/reflective coated, glazing orientation. Active and static shading devices. Intelligent glass. Condensation.
Sound	Acoustic control from inside/outside. Low, middle and high frequency band sounds. Glass thickness, laminated glass of differing thicknesses with inter-layers, double glazing spacing with sound absorbing material, sealed systems.
Safety	Location of glass – impact damage, barriers, manifestation (BS 6262–4: 2005). Toughened glass, heat-strengthened glass, laminated glass, applied plastic films. Radiation protection. Antibacterial glass.
Security	Protection of persons and property. Vandalism, use of firearms and explosives. Laminated glazing resistant to manual attack, one-way observation glass, alarm glass, glass blocks.
Fire	Classification – integrity (E)/insulation (I)/radiation (W). Regulations. Georgian wired glass, toughened, laminated glass. Non-insulating, insulating, partially insulating glass.
Durability	Verify durability of glass or plastics glazing sheet materials.
Wind loading	Determine wind pressure (BS EN 1991-1-4: 2005 + A1: 2010).
Maintenance	Access, ease and cost of replacement, self-cleaning glass.

Note: In addition glass may be used as a structural material. Applications include walkways, stairs and all-glass structures constructed with laminated toughened glass joined with metal fixings or clear high-modulus structural adhesives.

(TFEE) rate) approximate to the Code for Sustainable Homes Code Level 3, but there is no direct relationship. For replacement windows in existing dwellings, a Window Energy Rating (WER) at band C is the norm, but many manufacturers are targeting A+, A and B rated units. In addition, health and safety legislation and regulation requires the use of safety glasses in many locations.

9 CERAMIC MATERIALS

9.1 General
The wide selection of ceramic building products arises from the diverse range of natural and blended clays. Clay bricks are described in Section 4.1.

9.2 Roof tiles
Ceramic roof tiles are manufactured from finely screened clay, to produce the traditional red, brown or buff finish, or sanded to increase the product range including brindles and blue. Plain clay tiles, including fishtail, club, arrowhead and beavertail features are normally hung to a minimum pitch of 30° or 35°. Alternatives include interlocking plain tiles, pantiles and Roman tiles with plain, sanded or glazed finish, suitable for lower pitches to individual manufacturers' specification, Figure 7.9. Specific flat clay interlocking tiles are compatible with photovoltaic tiles of the same profile. Standard accessories include hip, valley, verge and ridge tiles also vents and finials.

The types, tolerances and physical properties of clay roofing tiles are defined in BS EN 1304: 2013. The current Code of Practice for slating and tiling is BS 5534: 2014.

9.3 Floor and wall tiles
Tiles for floors and walls, manufactured by dry-pressing or extrusion, are classified in BS EN 14411: 2012. The standard refers to both glazed and unglazed tiles. Key physical properties include water absorption, breaking strength, durability and abrasion resistance. The Codes of Practice for wall and floor tiling under various conditions are the Parts 1–5 of the British Standard BS 5385.

Floor tiles, Figure 7.10, are manufactured from a range of clays, typically fired to high temperatures (e.g. 1130°C) to ensure sufficient vitrification to give a highly durable and water-resistant product. Water absorption of Group 1 tiles to BS EN 14411: 2012 is less than 3 per cent. Group 2 tiles have a water absorption range between 3 per cent and 10 per cent, and for Group 3 tiles the range is over 10 per cent. Where high slip resistance is required a studded profile or carborundum grit may be incorporated into the surface. Floor tiles are graded Class 0 (least) to Class 5 (greatest) according to their resistance to abrasion. Wide ranges of stock sizes are produced by individual manufacturers.

Wall tiles are generally manufactured from earthenware clay to which talc or limestone has been added to ensure a white product when fired. Glaze may be added before a single firing or after an initial biscuit stage before a second firing. Adhesives for tiles are classified in BS EN 12004: 2007 + A1: 2012 and grouts in BS EN 13888: 2009. Wide ranges of square and rectangular sizes are currently available.

9.4 Ceramic components
Sanitary ware is manufactured from vitreous china which limits water penetration through any cracks or damage to the glaze to a maximum of 0.5 per cent. For large units such as WCs and basins, a controlled drying out period of the moist clay is required before firing to prevent cracking. Glaze containing metallic oxides for colouration is applied to all visually exposed areas before firing.

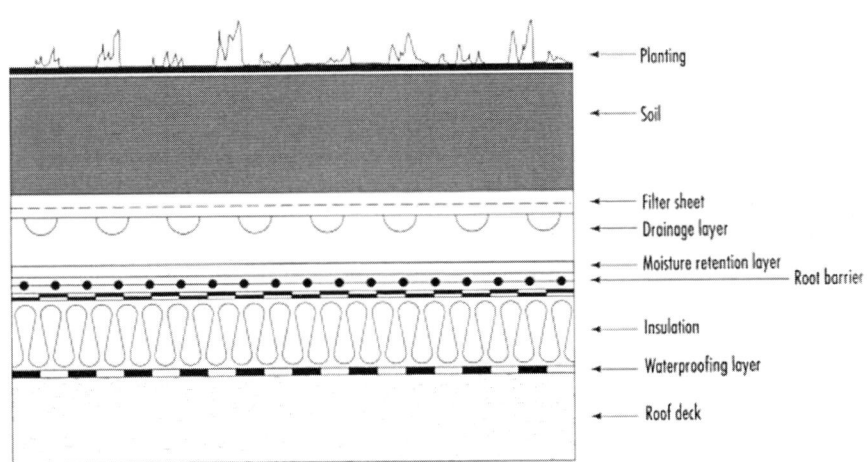

7.8 *Typical green roof system*

Table LI Types of glass and glazing

It should be noted that glass fulfils many functions concurrently, and the following table should only be used as general guidance on specific key glazing functions.

Function / Type	Description
LIGHTING AND VISUAL LINK	
Float glass	Standard annealed glass product (Type A breakage with sharp edges)
	(Typical maximum size 9000 × 3200 mm - larger units subject to transportation)
White glass	Reduced level of iron oxide impurities giving high light transmission, virtually colourless
	(Typical maximum size 6000 × 3210 mm)
Privacy	
Embossed / texture	Range of decorative patterns with differing levels of privacy (obscuration factors)
	(Typical maximum sizes 2160 × 1650 mm and 2140 × 1320 mm)
Screen printed	White or coloured ceramic frit printed and fused onto clear or tinted float glass
	(Typical maximum size 2800 × 1400 mm)
Etched/sand blasted	Range of acid etched or sand blasted designs on clear or tinted glass
	Bespoke designs (Typical maximum size 3210 × 2400 mm)
Translucent finish	Diffusing frosted standard or white float glass
	(Typical maximum size 3210 × 2400 mm)
Electro-optic glass	Changes by electrical switching from transparent to translucent (liquid crystal film interlayer)
Coloured glass	Through coloured glass, bevels and laminated plastic films
	Standard and bespoke designs
THERMAL CONSIDERATIONS	
Solar Control	
Coated glass	Off-line metal or metal oxide sputter coatings (neutral, silver, blue, green, grey) (maximum control)
	On-line pyrolytic coating (clear, neutral, silver, grey, bronze, blue/green) (medium control)
	(Typical maximum sizes 6000 × 3210 mm and 5180 × 3300 mm)
Body-tinted glass	Body-tinted glass (green, bronze, blue, grey) (lower control)
	(Typical maximum sizes 6000 × 3210 mm and 5180 × 3300 mm)
Laminated glass	Tinted plastic interlayers
Blinds	Insulating glass units with integral blinds operated by hand or mechanical control
Thermal Insulation	
Multiple glazing	Double/triple glazing systems with inert gas fill (90% argon – standard)
	(Typical maximum size 6000 × 3210 mm)
Low emissivity glass	Soft off-line ultra-low emissivity coating (ε_n 0.04)
	Pyrolytic low emissivity hard coating on clear and tinted glass (ε_n 0.15)
SOUND	
Noise control	Laminated glass with 0.8 mm PVB (polyvinyl butyral) interlayer
	Sealed units with differing thicknesses of glass or large spacing and acoustic insulation around perimeter
SAFETY	
Toughened	Five times stronger than annealed glass – safety glass
	(Type C breakage into relatively harmless granules)
	(Typical maximum sizes 4200 × 2000 mm and 4500 × 2440 mm)
Heat soaked toughened glass	Reduces the risk of spontaneous breakage of toughened glass due to nickel sulphide inclusions
Heat-strengthened	Half the strength of toughened glass and breaks into pieces like annealed glass
	Not a safety glass
	(Often used in laminated glass.)
	(Type A breakage with sharp edges)
Laminated	Laminated glass gives protection from injury in case of breakage
	PVB interlayer for flat glass – resin interlayer for curved laminates
	(Type B breakage – cracks but the fragments hold together)

Table LI Continued

Function / Type	Description
Plastic film	A range of thin plastic films to change the optical and/or thermal properties of glass
	Thick structural plastic interlayer – 1.52 or 2.28 mm
	(Appropriate plastics film coverage to annealed glass can give a Type B breakage as in laminated glass)
SECURITY	
Laminated	Accident/vandalism/resistant to manual attack/bullet or explosion resistant depending upon number and thickness of glass laminates (PVB layers 0.4 or 0.8 mm)
	(Type B breakage – cracks but the fragments hold together)
One-way vision	Requires low level of lighting on the observer's side (7:1 lighting ratio required)
FIRE PROTECTION	**E = Integrity, I = Insulation, W = Radiation**
Non-insulating wired glass	Wired glass – polished or cast giving 30 or 60 min integrity only (E30 to E60)
	(Up to 120 min in specialist steel frames)
	(Type B breakage – cracks but the fragments hold together) Heavier grade of wire to meet BS 6206: 1981 impact test (Typical maximum sizes 3300 × 1980 (polished), 3353 × 1829 (cast))
Integrity	Restricts flame and hot gases only. (E30) – (E60) E120 in specialist steel frames
Integrity and insulation	Laminated with interlayers. 30, 60, 90, 120, 180 min insulation (in appropriate frame system)
	(EI 30, EI 60 single glazing and up to EI 180 in double glazing units)
	(Intumescent or gel interlayers)
Integrity with some radiation protection	Laminated with interlayers
	Reduced heat radiation
	EW 30 to EW 60 giving 30 or 60 minutes integrity with some radiation protection
MAINTENANCE	
Self-cleaning	Hydrophilic and photocatalytic on-line coating spreads water and oxidises dirt on the surface
	Clear and blue available
SPECIAL APPLICATIONS	
Spandrel glass	Range of colours and screen print designs
	Annealed, toughened or laminated
Curved glass	CIP (cast in place) if required laminated
	Also double glazing units
Mirror glass	Mirror (Typical maximum sizes 3210 × 2000 mm)
Anti-reflective glass	Coated on both faces. Appropriate for shop fronts etc.
Radiation protection	X-ray and gamma ray protection
	Lead rich glass – amber colour
	Lead and barium glass – neutral colour
GLASS SYSTEMS	
	Double and triple glazed systems. Fixings to BS 6262–6: 2005 – bolts, sealant, fins or tension wires
	High efficiency 90% argon fill double glazing units up to U = 1.1 W/m²K
	Triple glazing units up to U = 0.8 W/m²K, or U = 0.5 W/m²K with two low-e coatings and two argon fills
	Maximum efficiency with krypton fill and warm edge spacer systems

Solar factor: The fraction of the incident solar radiation directly transmitted by the glass, including heat absorbed by the glass and re-emitted to the interior.

Shading coefficient: The ratio of the solar factor of a glass relative to that of 3 mm clear float glass.

Light reflectance: The fraction of the incident light that is reflected by the glass.

U-value: The measure of heat loss through the component or unit, measured in W/m²K.

Weighted noise reduction: A single figure rating for the sound insulation of building elements.

Combinations of functions e.g. self-cleaning and patterned glass are available.

The descriptions of breakages are in accordance with BS EN 12600: 2002.

Critical locations for safety glass are illustrated in BS 6262–4: 2005.

Where there is a risk of human impact on glass in buildings, its manifestation is required in the form of lines, patterns or logos between 850 and 1000 mm also between 1400 and 1600 mm above floor level (BS 6262–4: 2005).

Maximum sheet sizes are not necessarily safe sizes.

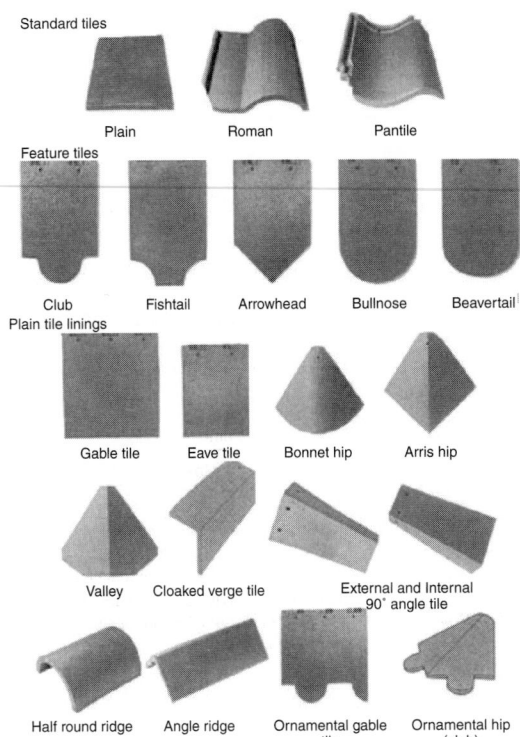

7.9 *Standard and feature roof tiles*

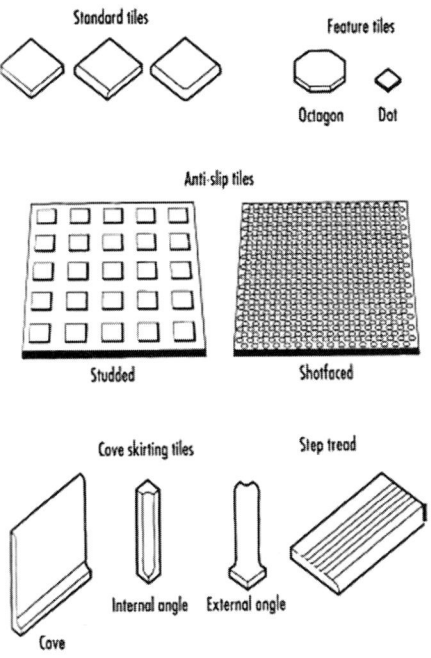

7.10 *Floor tiles*

The quality of vitreous china sanitary appliances is categorised in BS 3402: 1969. The specifications for vitrified clay pipes, typically manufactured from salt glazed earthenware, are Parts 1–7 of BS EN 295.

9.5 Terracotta

The russet colour of terracotta is associated with the presence of iron oxide within the clay. Terracotta is used for traditional features, particularly decorative wall blocks, ridge tiles and roofing finials. In addition it is manufactured into durable rainscreen cladding units for fixing into proprietary façade systems. Faience, which is glazed terracotta, is a highly durable material, but it can be chipped on impact.

10 STONE AND CAST STONE

10.1 General

Natural stone may be classified as igneous (e.g. granite), metamorphic (e.g. slate, marble and quartzite) or sedimentary (e.g. sandstone and limestone). Cast stone (BS EN 771–5: 2011) is often manufactured to emulate the natural materials. Igneous stones, such as granite and basalt, are the most durable materials, whereas the softer sandstones and limestones are more workable for shaping to the required form, particularly when directly extracted from the quarry. Low grade slate delaminates and marble can be affected by acid environments. Sedimentary stone should be laid correctly according to the natural bedding planes, Figure 7.11, and may be tooled to a variety of finishes, Figure 7.12.

Thin section natural stone (6 mm) may be bonded to lightweight backing materials as an alternative to traditional heavyweight cladding attached with durable fixings, Figure 7.13. The detailed classification of stones and stone-working terminology is listed in BS EN 12670: 2002. The Code of Practice for the design and installation of natural stone cladding and lining is BS 8298 Parts 1–4: 2010. The technical specifications for stone masonry units and slabs for cladding are BS EN 771 Part 6: 2011 and BS EN 1469: 2004 (pr EN 1469: 2012) respectively. The specification for cast stone is BS 1217: 2008. Traditional stone walling is illustrated in Figure 7.14.

10.2 Granite

Most granites are hard and dense and are therefore highly durable building materials, impermeable to water and resistant to impact damage. Colours from within the UK range from red through pink and grey to virtually black. Imported colours also include blue,

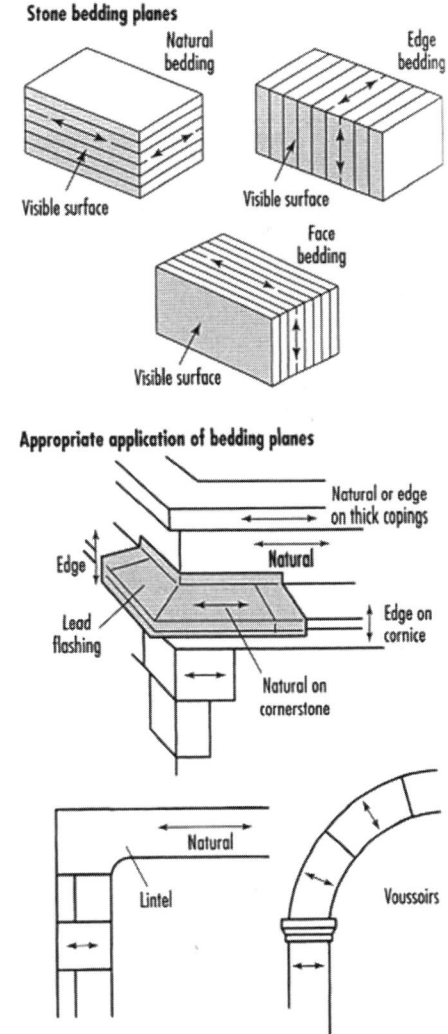

7.11 *Natural stone bedding planes*

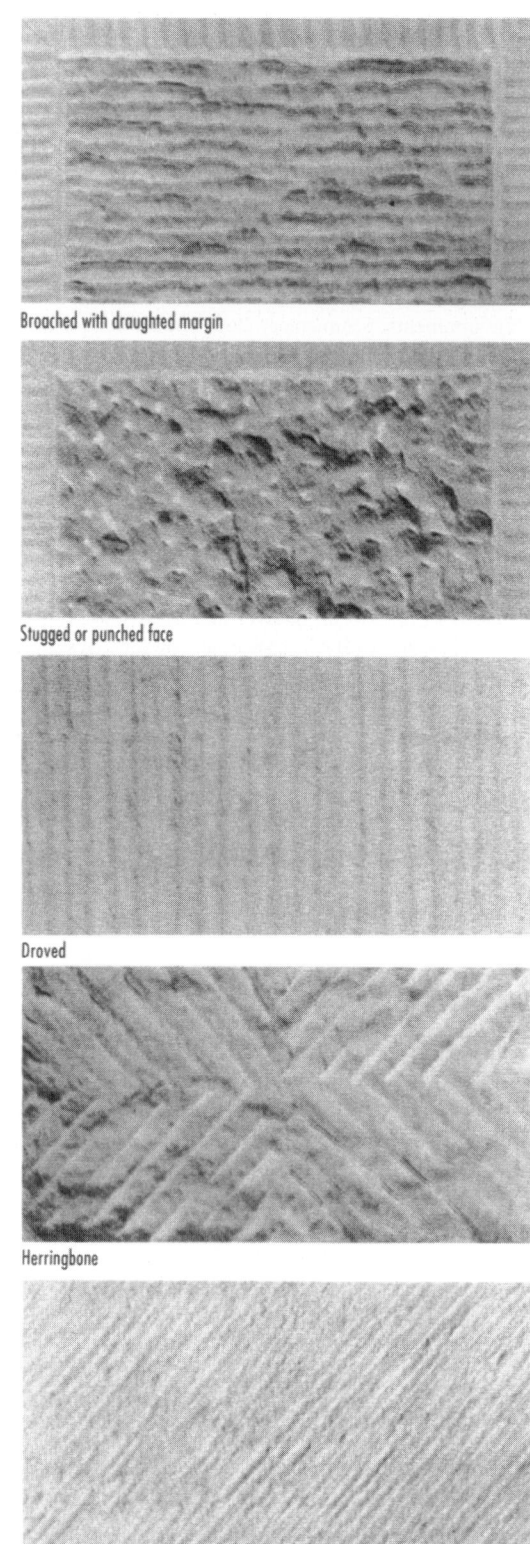

Broached with draughted margin

Stugged or punched face

Droved

Herringbone

Bats

7.12 *Tooled stone finishes*

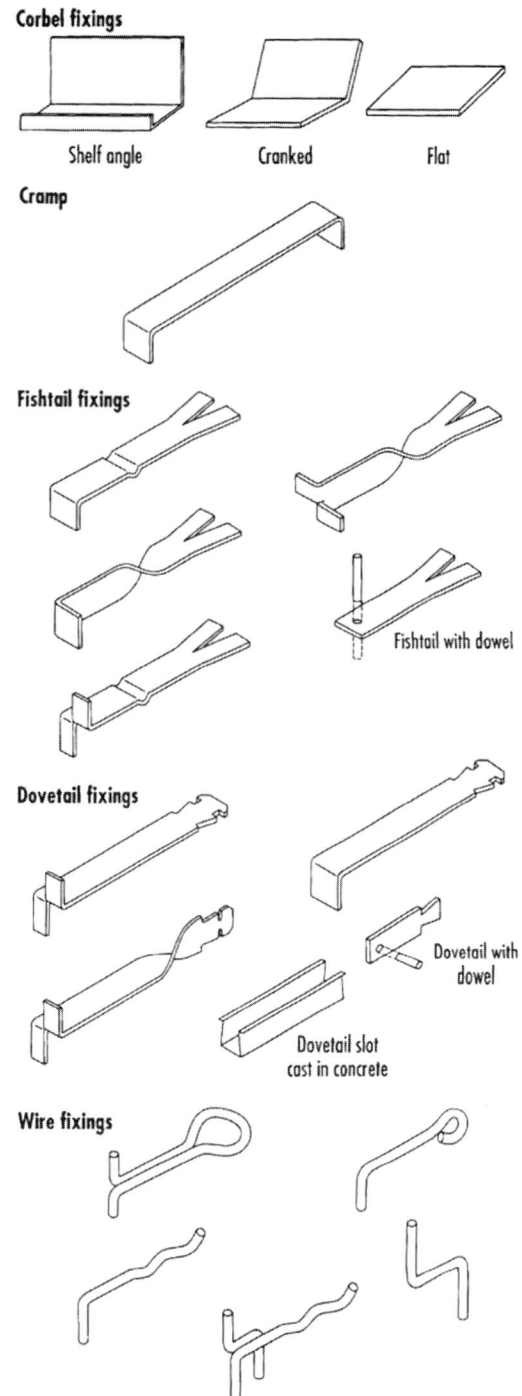

Corbel fixings

Shelf angle   Cranked   Flat

Cramp

Fishtail fixings

Fishtail with dowel

Dovetail fixings

Dovetail with dowel

Dovetail slot cast in concrete

Wire fixings

7.13 *Typical fixings for stone cladding*

green, yellow and brown. The range of finishes include flamed, picked, fine tooled, honed and polished. For maximum colour and crystalline sparkle a highly polished finish is required. The high cost material is frequently used as a cladding (40 mm externally, 20 mm internally) or cast directly onto concrete structural units.

10.3 Slate

Roofing slates range in thickness between 4 mm and 10 mm according to their origin. Roofing slates are traditionally riven, although a range of textured to polished finishes are optional for larger components such as flooring, sills and cladding. Colours from within

the UK include blue, blue/grey, silver/grey, green and plum red. Slates are imported from Spain, China, Canada, France, Ireland, Brazil and India. The minimum pitch for slate roofing under sheltered conditions is 20°, or 22.5° in exposed situations, and fixings must be copper or aluminium. Recycled slates are generally available for conservation work.

10.4 Marble

Marble is metamorphosed limestone in which the calcium carbonate has been recrystallised forming the characteristic veined patterns. Pure calcite is white, but colours arise from the impurities in the original limestone. The range of colours available within Europe includes red, pink, violet, brown, green, beige, cream, grey and black. Marble is used for external and internal cladding, flooring and tiling.

Roughly squared split faced random rubble

Polygonal random rubble

Sawn bedded pitched face random walling

Sawn bedded pitched face coursed walling

7.14 *Traditional stone walling*

10.5 Quartzite
Quartzite is metamorphosed sandstone which, as a hardwearing material, is frequently used for flooring. Most quartzite is imported from Norway, Italy, Brazil and Ireland where it is available in white, grey, grey-green, blue-grey, yellow and ochre colours.

10.6 Sandstone
Sandstone is formed by the natural cementing together of sand particles by calcium carbonate, silica, iron oxide or dolomite, giving calcareous, siliceous, ferruginous or dolomitic sandstones respectively. Sandstones may be coarse or fine in texture and range in colour from white, buff and grey through to brown and red. They are generally frost resistant. Finishes include sawn, split-faced and various tooled surfaces. Apart from UK supplies, sandstones are imported from Spain and Italy. Sandstone cladding is normally 75–100 mm thick, and must be fixed with non-ferrous cramps and corbels.

10.7 Limestone
Limestones consist mainly of calcium carbonate arising from recrystallised calcite or accumulations of fossilised shells. Oölitic limestones are formed by the crystallisation of concentric layers of calcium carbonate, producing spheroidal grains or oöliths. English limestones are off-white, cream, grey and blue, but additional colours are imported from France, Ireland and Portugal. Externally limestones must not be mixed with or located above sandstones as this may cause rapid deterioration of the sandstone.

10.8 Cast stone
The appearance of natural stones, such as Bath, Cotswold, Portland and York, can be recreated from concrete manufactured with appropriate stone dust and cement. Either a dry or wet casting system is used. Where standard steel reinforcement is incorporated it requires 40 mm cover from visual faces unless galvanised. Corrosion-resistant non-ferrous materials require a minimum 10 mm cover. Many architectural components such as classical columns and balustrades are standard items, but custom-made products can be cast to designers' specifications.

10.9 Gabions
Gabions are wire cages filled with crushed stone, Figure 7.15. The cages are usually constructed from heavy gauge woven or welded steel mesh which may be coated for protection or in stainless steel. Most sizes are based on the metre module. The standard use is for earth-retaining civil engineering applications.

7.15 *Natural stone filled gabions: Small Animals Hospital, Glasgow. Architect: Archial (photograph: Andrew Lee)*

11 PLASTICS

11.1 General
The plastics used in the construction industry are generally low-density non-load-bearing materials. Unlike metals, they are not subject to corrosion, but they may be degraded by the action of direct sunlight, with a corresponding reduction in mechanical strength. Many plastics are flammable unless treated; the majority emit noxious fumes in fires. Typical reaction to fire is cited in Table LII. The family of plastics used in construction is shown in Figure 7.16. Table LIII lists their typical uses in building.

PVC (polyvinyl chloride) accounts for 40 per cent of the plastics used within construction, predominantly in pipes, but also in cladding, electrical cable insulation, windows, doors and flooring applications. Foamed plastics for thermal and acoustic insulation are formulated either as open or closed-cell materials, the latter being resistant to the passage of air and water.

Whilst some materials such as rubber and cellulose derivatives are based on natural products, the majority of plastics are produced from petrochemical products.

11.2 Thermoplastics
Thermoplastics soften on heating and reset on cooling. The process is reversible and generally can be repeated without significant degradation of the material. Polyethylene (polythene) is available with a range of physical properties as listed in Table LIV. Polyvinyl chloride (PVC), the most widely used plastic material, is available in the unplasticised form (PVC-U) and the plasticised product (PVC). Chlorinated polyvinyl chloride (CPVC) has a higher softening point than the standard PVC material. Extruded cellular unplasticised polyvinyl chloride (PVC-UE) is used in the manufacture of components of uniform section, such as cladding and fascias. The full range and typical construction uses of thermoplastics are listed in Table LIII.

11.3 Thermosetting plastics
Thermosetting plastics have a three-dimensional cross-linked molecular structure. This prevents the material melting when

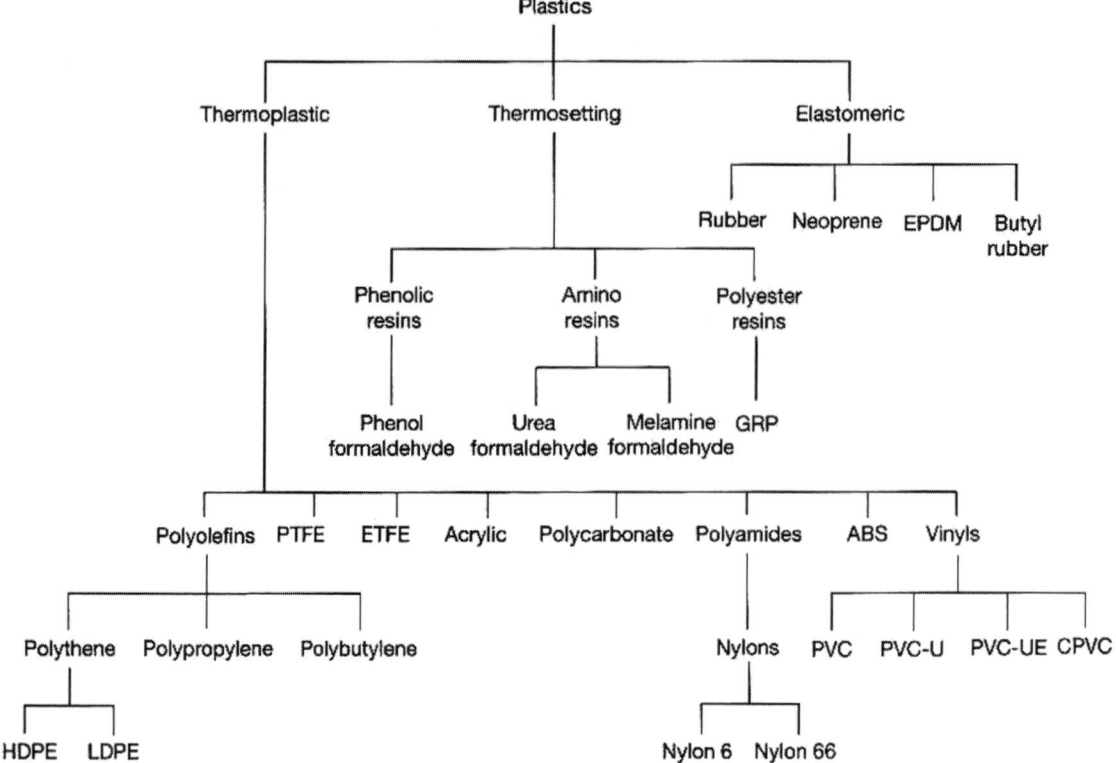

7.16 *Plastics used in construction*

heated. Thermoset components are usually produced from partially polymerised powder, or by mixing two components, such as a resin and hardener, immediately prior to forming. The cross-linked structure of thermosetting polymers gives rise to good heat-resistant properties. The materials are generally resistant to ignition, but will burn within a fire. Typical uses are listed in Table LIII.

11.4 Elastomers

Elastomers are long-chain polymers in which the natural zigzag molecular chains are free to straighten and relax when stretched and released. The degree of elasticity depends upon the extensibility of the helical molecules and the degree of cross-linking between the adjacent chains. Rubber is based on the natural latex product, whereas neoprene and other copolymers are petrochemical

products. Standard elastomers and their typical uses in construction are listed in Table LIII.

11.5 Composite plastics

Composite plastics include glass-fibre reinforced polyester which is described in Section 12.2.

Wood plastic composites formed from polyethylene, polypropylene or PVC, blended with natural fibre products including wood chips, hemp or sisal, are durable materials. They have the significant advantage of incorporating recycled materials or waste by-products from other processes. These materials are described in BRE Digest 480: 2004 and relevant characteristics are listed in the publication DD CEN/TS 15534-2: 2007. Wood plastic composites are used for products such as cladding (EN 15534 Part 5: 2014), external decking (EN 15534 Part 4: 2014), fencing and garden furniture, where durability is advantageous.

12 GLASS-FIBRE REINFORCED PLASTICS, CONCRETE (CEMENT) AND GYPSUM

12.1 General

Composites such as the glass-fibre reinforced materials GRP (glass-fibre reinforced polyester), GRC (glass-fibre reinforced cement) and GRG (glass-fibre reinforced gypsum) rely on the advantageous combination of the disparate physical properties associated with the individual component materials.

12.2 Glass-fibre reinforced plastics

The majority of glass-fibre reinforced plastics are manufactured from polyester resin, although other thermosetting resins may be used. For most purposes the glass fibres are in the form of continuous rovings or chopped strand; however, the highest strength products are obtained with aligned fibres or woven glass-fibre fabrics. The proportion of glass fibres ranges from 20 per cent to 80 per cent, depending upon the strength required. Higher strength materials can be achieved using carbon or polyaramid fibres. The traditional laying-up process is used for the manufacture of most components. The mould is coated with release agent and then the gel coat applied, followed by the required thickness of GRP, which may incorporate reinforcements and fixing devices.

Table LII Behaviour of common building plastics in fire

Material	Behaviour in fire
Thermoplastics	
Polyethylene, polypropylene	Melts and burns readily
Polyvinyl chloride	Melts, does not burn easily, but emits smoke, carbon monoxide and hydrogen chloride
PTFE/ETFE	Does not burn, but at high temperatures evolves toxic fumes
Polymethyl methacrylate	Melts and burns rapidly, producing burning droplets
Polystyrene	Melts and burns readily producing black smoke and burning droplets (BS 6203: 2003 – Expanded polystyrene)
ABS copolymer	Burns readily
Polyurethane	The foam burns readily producing highly toxic fumes including cyanides and isocyanates
Thermosetting plastics	
Phenol formaldehyde, melamine formaldehyde, urea formaldehyde	Resistant to ignition, but produces noxious fumes including ammonia
Glass-fibre reinforced polyester (GRP)	Burns producing smoke, but flame-retardant grades are available
Elastomers	
Rubber	Burns readily producing black smoke and sulphur dioxide
Neoprene	Better fire resistance than natural rubber

Table LIII Typical uses of plastics in construction

Material	Examples of plastics in construction
Thermoplastics	
Polyethylene	
Low density (LD)	DPC, DPM, vapour checks, roof sarking
High density (HD)	Cold water tanks, cold water plumbing
Cross-linked (PEX)	Hot and cold water plumbing
Polypropylene (PP)	Pipework and fittings, cold water plumbing, drainage systems, water tanks, WC cisterns, DPCs, fibres in fibre-reinforced concrete
(BS EN ISO 1873–1: 1995)	
Polybutylene (PB)	Hot and cold water pipework and fittings
(BS EN ISO 8986–1: 2009)	
Polyvinyl chloride	
Unplasticised (PVC-U)	Rainwater goods, drainage systems, cold water, underground services, window and door frames, conservatories, garage doors, translucent roofing sheets, cold water tanks
Extruded unplasticised (PVC-UE)	Claddings, barge boards, soffits, fascias, window boards
(BS 7619: 2010)	
Plasticised (PVC)	Tile and sheet floor coverings, single-ply roofing, cable insulation, electrical trunking systems, sarking, tensile membrane structures, glazing to flexible doors, door seals, handrail coatings, vinyl-film finishes to timber products
Chlorinated (CPVC)	Hot and cold water systems
ETFE	Inflated systems for translucent wall and roof membranes
(BS EN ISO 12086–1: 2006)	
PTFE	Sealing tape for plumbing, tensile membrane structures, low-friction movement joints
(BS EN ISO 12086–1: 2006)	
Polymethyl methacrylate	Baths, shower trays, kitchen sinks, glazing, roof lights, luminaires
(BS EN ISO 8257–1: 2006)	
Polycarbonate	Vandal-resistant glazing, spa baths, kitchen sinks
(BS EN ISO 7391–1: 2006)	
Polystyrene	Bath and shower panels, decorative expanded polystyrene tiles
ABS copolymer	Pipes and fittings, rainwater goods, drainage systems, shower trays
Nylons	Electrical conduit and trunking, low-friction components – hinges, brush strips for sealing doors and windows, carpet tiles and carpets, shower curtains
Thermosetting plastics	
Phenol formaldehyde	Decorative laminates
Melamine formaldehyde	Laminates for working surfaces and doors, moulded electrical components, WC seats
Urea formaldehyde	Decorative laminates
Glass-fibre reinforced polyester (GRP)	Cladding and roofing panels, simulated cast iron rainwater goods, cold water tanks, spa baths, garage doors, decorative tiles and panels
Elastomers	
Rubber	Flooring, door seals, anti-vibration bearings
Neoprene	Glazing seals, gaskets
EPDM	Glazing seals, gaskets, single-ply roofing systems
Butyl rubber	Sheet liners to water features and land-fill sites
Nitrile rubber	Tile and sheet flooring

Table LIV Grades of polyethylene

Grades of polyethylene		Density (kg/m³)
LLDPE	Linear low-density polyethylene	900–939
VLDPE	Very low-density polyethylene	880–915
LDPE	Low-density polyethylene	916–925
MDPE	Medium-density polyethylene	926–940
HDPE	High-density polyethylene	941–970
HMWPE	High molecular weight polyethylene	947–950
UHMWPE	Ultra-high molecular weight polyethylene	930–935
PEX	Cross-linked polyethylene	926–970

12.3 Glass-fibre reinforced concrete (cement)

Glass-fibre reinforced concrete is produced from a mixture of alkali-resistant glass fibres, Portland cement, sand and water. Typically 5 per cent by weight of 25–40 mm glass fibres are used within the cement matrix. Most GRC units are manufactured by spraying the cement slurry to the required thickness within an appropriate mould, although extrusion and injection moulding techniques are also possible for small components. GRC is a durable material with high impact strength and low permeability to moisture. It is frequently used for lightweight cladding and soffit panels. Guidance on factory quality control is given in BS EN 1169: 1999.

12.4 Glass-fibre reinforced gypsum

Glass-fibre reinforced gypsum with typically 5 per cent of standard E-glass fibres, has enhanced impact strength and fire resistance compared to standard gypsum plaster boards. Standard GRG boards are available in a range of thicknesses between 5 mm and 15 mm. The material is easily worked and can be curved on site. GRG boards offer good fire protection to steelwork, when up to 120 minutes' fire protection can be achieved using a double layer of 30 mm boards with staggered joints and appropriate fixings.

13 PLASTER AND BOARD MATERIALS

13.1 General

The majority of plaster types used within construction are based on retarded hemi-hydrate gypsum. This is manufactured by heating rock gypsum to between 130°C and 170°C. Keratin is the standard retarding agent which is added to adjust the setting time to between 1.5 and 2 hours. Other additives and admixtures include fillers, fibres, lime, lightweight aggregates, pigments and plasticisers.

13.2 Gypsum plaster

Undercoat and one-coat plasters are blended with anhydrous gypsum, limestone, clay and sand to produce the required water-retention properties and setting time. Lime is incorporated in finish-coat plaster to accelerate the set. Lightweight aggregates are commonly expanded perlite and exfoliated vermiculite. On smooth surfaces or low suction backgrounds an initial bonding coat is required. Typical applications for walls are 11 mm for undercoats with a finish coat of 2 mm or a single 13 mm coat.

The types of gypsum binders and plasters are categorised in BS EN 13279-1: 2008, Table LV.

13.3 Plasterboard

Plasterboard consists of a gypsum core bonded to strong paper liners. The finish surface may be either tapered or square edged. A plaster skim is usually applied as a finish. Standard board sizes are 900 mm and 1200 mm wide and 9.5, 12.5, 15 or 19 mm thick. Nail fixings should be driven straight in leaving a shallow depression.

Table LV Types of gypsum binders and plasters (BS EN 13279–1: 2008)

Notation	Designation
A	Gypsum binder for further processing
A1	Gypsum binder for direct use
A2	Gypsum binder for direct use on site
A3	Gypsum binder for further processing
B	Gypsum plaster
B1	Gypsum building plaster
B2	Gypsum-based building plaster (minimum 50% gypsum)
B3	Gypsum-lime building plaster (>5% lime)
B4	Lightweight gypsum building plaster (inorganic or organic aggregates)
B5	Lightweight gypsum-based building plaster
B6	Lightweight gypsum-lime building plaster
B7	Enhanced surface hardness gypsum plaster
C	Gypsum plaster for special purposes
C1	Gypsum plaster for fibrous reinforcement
C2	Gypsum mortar
C3	Acoustic plaster
C4	Thermal insulation plaster
C5	Fire protection plaster
C6	Thin-coat plaster, finishing product
C7	Finishing product

Table LVI Types of plasterboard (BS EN 520: 2004 + A1: 2009)

Type	Designation
A	Gypsum plasterboard with a face suitable for a gypsum finish coat or decoration
H	Gypsum plasterboard with a reduced water absorption rate
E	Gypsum sheathing board for external walls but not permanently exposed to weather conditions
F	Gypsum plasterboard with improved core adhesion at high temperatures
P	Gypsum baseboard to receive gypsum plaster
D	Gypsum plasterboard with controlled density
R	Gypsum plasterboard with enhanced strength
I	Gypsum plasterboard with enhanced surface hardness

Types of plasterboard are listed in BS EN 520: 2004 + A1: 2009, Table LVI. These include a range of products with a high density core for sound insulation, enhanced moisture resistance, increased fire protection and greater impact resistance.

The types of natural fibre reinforced gypsum boards are listed in BS EN 15283: 2008 + A1: 2009, Table LVII.

Composite thermal/acoustic plasterboard panels are categorised in BS EN 13950: 2014 and prefabricated cellular paperboard core panels are defined in BS EN 13915: 2007.

13.4 Accessories for plastering

Angle and stop beads are manufactured from galvanised or stainless steel and aluminium as perforated strip or expanded metal. Beads for internal plastering are described in BS EN 13658-1: 2005. Angle beads for plasterboard are defined in BS EN 14353: 2007 + A1: 2010. Self-adhesive 50 mm or 100 mm glass fibre tape is normally used across joints between plasterboards and in standard plastering.

13.5 Special plasters

Special plasters include renovating plaster for use following the successful installation of damp-proofing and X-ray plaster containing barium sulphate for use in medical environments. Fibrous plaster (BS EN 13815: 2006 and BS EN 15319: 2007) is used for casting ornate plasterwork. Projection plaster is sprayed onto the background as a ribbon from a mechanical plastering machine; it then coalesces for trowelling to a smooth finish.

13.6 Calcium silicate boards

Calcium silicate boards are manufactured from silica with lime and/or cement, usually incorporating additional fillers and fibres to produce the required density. Calcium silicate boards are durable and non-combustible with good chemical and impact resistance. Standard thicknesses are 6, 9 and 12 mm, although thicknesses

Table LVII Types of fibre-reinforced gypsum boards (BS EN 15283: 2008 + A1: 2009)

Type	Designation
GM	Gypsum board with mat reinforcement
GM-H1, GM-H2	Gypsum board with mat reinforcement and reduced water absorption rate
GM-I	Gypsum board with mat reinforcement and enhanced surface hardness
GM-R	Gypsum board with mat reinforcement and enhanced strength
GM-F	Gypsum board with mat reinforcement and improved core cohesion at high temperatures
GF	Gypsum fibre board
GF-H	Gypsum fibre board with reduced water absorption rate
GF-W1, GF-W2	Gypsum fibre board with reduced surface water absorption rate
GF-D	Gypsum fibre board with enhanced density
GF-I	Gypsum fibre board with enhanced surface hardness
GF-R1, GF-R2	Gypsum fibre board with enhanced strength

up to 100 mm incorporating vermiculite are manufactured for fire protection lightweight boards. Appropriate products achieve 240 minutes' fire resistance.

14 INSULATION MATERIALS

14.1 General

Thermal and sound insulating materials may be categorised variously according to their use in construction, physical forms or material of origin. Generally the key forms of materials are:

Structural insulation materials
Rigid and semi-rigid sheets and slabs
Loose fill, blankets, rolls and applied finishes
Multi-layer thermo-reflective products

Table LVIII gives typical thermal conductivity values for a range of building materials.

14.2 Inorganic insulation materials

Foamed concrete: Foamed concrete with an air content of 30–80 per cent is fire and frost-resistant. It does however, exhibit a higher drying shrinkage than dense concrete. It is used for insulation under floors and on flat roofs where it can be laid to an appropriate fall.

Lightweight aggregate concrete: Lightweight concrete materials offer a wide range of insulating and load-bearing properties. Typical aggregates include expanded perlite, exfoliated vermiculite, expanded polystyrene, foamed blast furnace slag, expanded clay and pulverised fuel ash. The range of thermal properties is listed in Table LVIII.

Wood wool slabs: Wood wool slabs manufactured from long wood shavings and Portland or magnesite cement are non-combustible and resistant to rot. They combine load-bearing and insulating properties, and are typically used for roof decking. For longer spans up to 3 m, units with steel edge channel reinforcement are available. Composite slabs of rigid polystyrene or mineral wool between wood wool layers offer high levels of thermal insulation. The standard BS EN 13168: 2012 gives the specification for wood wool (WW) insulation products.

Mineral wool: Mineral wool is manufactured from blended volcanic rock which is melted and spun into fibres. The material is available as loose fill, blanket, batts, semi-rigid or rigid slabs, ceiling and dense boards, according to the degree of compression during manufacture. Mineral wool is non-combustible and resistant to decay. Typical uses include loft, cavity wall and frame insulation. In addition to thermal insulation, mineral wool absorbent quilts are effective at reducing sound transmission within plasterboard separating walls. The standard BS EN 13162: 2012 gives the specification for mineral wool (MW) insulation products.

Glass wool: Glass wool is made by spinning glass into fibres by the Crown process, similar to that for mineral wool fibres. The material is available as loose fill, rolls, semi and rigid batts and compression-resistant slabs. Laminates with plasterboard and PVC

Table LVIII Typical thermal conductivity values for building materials

Material	Thermal conductivity (W/mK)
Aerogel	0.013
Phenolic foam	0.018–0.031
Polyurethane foam (rigid)	0.019-0.023
Foil-faced foam	0.021
Polyisocyanurate foam	0.023–0.025
Sprayed polyurethane foam	0.024
Extruded polystyrene	0.029
Expanded PVC	0.030
Mineral wool	0.031–0.039
Glass wool	0.031–0.040
Expanded polystyrene	0.033–0.040
Cellulose (recycled paper)	0.035–0.040
Sheep's wool	0.037–0.039
Rigid foamed glass	0.037-0.055
Flax	0.038
Urea formaldehyde foam	0.038
Hemp wool	0.040
Corkboard	0.042
Coconut fibre board	0.045
Perlite board	0.045–0.050
Fibre insulation board	0.050
Straw bales	0.060
Exfoliated vermiculite	0.062
Thatch	0.072
Wood wool slabs	0.077
Medium-density fibreboard (MDF)	0.10
Foamed concrete (low density)	0.10
Lightweight to dense concrete	0.10–1.7
Compressed straw slabs	0.10
Softwood	0.13
Orientated strand board (OSB)	0.13
Hardboard	0.13
Particleboard/plywood	0.14
Gypsum plasterboard	0.19
Bituminous roofing sheet	0.19
Cement bonded particleboard	0.23
Unfired clay blocks	0.24
Calcium silicate boards	0.29
GRC – lightweight	0.21–0.5
GRC – standard density	0.5–1.0
Mastic asphalt	0.5
Calcium silicate brickwork	0.67–1.24
Clay brickwork	0.65–1.95
Glass sheet	1.05

Notes: Individual manufacturers' products may differ from these typical figures. Additional data is available in BS 5250: 2011, BS EN 12524: 2000 and BS EN ISO 10456: 2007.

Table LIX Standard grades of polystyrene (BS EN 13163: 2012)

Grade (BS 3837)	Type (BS EN 13163)	Description	Typical density (kg/m³)	Thermal conductivity (W/mK)
SD	EPS 70	Standard duty	15	0.038
HD	EPS 100	High duty	20	0.036
EHD	EPS 150	Extra high duty	25	0.035
UHD	EPS 200	Ultra high duty	30	0.034

Note: BS EN 13163: 2012 lists the range of types from EPS 30 to EPS 500.

are also manufactured. The standard BS EN 13162: 2012 gives the specification for glass wool insulation products.

Cellular glass: Cellular or foamed glass is manufactured from a mixture of crushed glass and carbon powder. The black material is durable, non-combustible and water resistant due to its closed-cell structure. The material is used for insulation in roof-top car parks and green roofs where high compressive strength is required due to the loading. The standard BS EN 13167: 2012 gives the specification for cellular glass (CG) insulation products.

Exfoliated vermiculite: Exfoliated vermiculite is manufactured by heating the natural micaceous material, causing it to expand to a product with approximately 90 per cent air by volume. The non-combustible material is used as loose fill, sprayed fire protection to exposed structural steelwork and in fire-stop seals. The standards BS EN 14317-1: 2004 and BS EN 14317-2: 2007 give the specification for exfoliated vermiculite (EV) insulation products before and after installation respectively.

Expanded perlite: Expanded perlite is manufactured by heating natural volcanic rock minerals. It is used as loose or bonded in-situ insulation for roofs, ceilings, walls and floors. Additionally it is available as preformed boards. The non-combustible material (EPB) is described in the standard BS EN 13169: 2012. It is also specified in BS EN 14316 Part 1: 2004 and Part 2: 2007 for before and after installation respectively.

14.3 Organic insulation materials

Cork: Cork is harvested from the cork oak on a 9- or 10-year cycle. For the production of insulating boards, the natural cork granules are expanded then formed under heat and pressure into blocks, bonded by the natural resin within the cork. Cork products are unaffected by the application of hot bitumen in flat roofing systems. The standard BS EN 13170: 2012 gives the specification for expanded cork (ICB) insulation products.

Wood fibre board: Wood fibre products are manufactured from a slurry of wood fibres which is compressed, causing the fibres to felt together. A bonding agent may be added. The degree of compression dictates the final density and insulating properties of the product. The product is available as roll, batts or semi-rigid slabs and boards. The standard BS EN 13171: 2012 gives the specification for wood fibre (WF) insulation products.

Expanded polystyrene: Expanded polystyrene is a closed-cell product unaffected by water, but readily dissolved by organic solvents. It is combustible producing noxious black fumes. Polystyrene beads may be used as loose fill. Four grades of polystyrene boards are listed in Table LIX. Polystyrene boards must be protected with heat-resisting insulation when hot bitumen is to be applied. Although a closed-cell material, polystyrene boards are good sound absorbers for use within building voids. Grey expanded polystyrene, incorporating graphite, has enhanced thermal insulating properties. The standard BS EN 13163: 2012 gives the specification for expanded polystyrene (EPS) insulation products.

Extruded polystyrene: Extruded polystyrene is normally produced by a vacuum process. It is slightly stronger in compression than expanded polystyrene, but has a lower thermal conductivity. Its closed cell structure, is highly resistant to water absorption, so the material is frequently used below concrete slabs and on inverted roofs, as well as for standard cavity wall and pitched roof insulation. Laminates with flooring grade particleboard and with plasterboard are available. The standard BS EN 13164: 2012 gives the specification for extruded polystyrene (XPS) insulation products.

Polyurethane foam: Rigid polyurethane foam is a closed-cell foam, blown mainly by carbon dioxide but also with pentane. Polyurethane foam is a combustible material producing smoke and noxious fumes, but a flame-resistant material is available. The material is thermally stable and can be used under hot bitumen, and good durability permits its use for inverted roofs. Polyurethane foam is frequently used in composite panels due to its good adherence to profile metal sheeting and other materials. Flexible polyurethane foam is an open-cell material offering good noise absorbing properties. The standards BS EN 13165: 2012 and BS EN 14315: 2013 give the specification for rigid polyurethane foam (PUR) insulation products.

Polyisocyanurate foam: Polyisocyanurate foam used for wall and floor insulation is combustible, but is more resistant to fire than polyurethane foam and can be treated to achieve a fire-resistant rating. The material tends to be rather brittle and friable. The standard BS EN 14315: 2013 gives the specification for in-situ polyisocyanurate foam (PIR).

Phenolic foam: Phenolic foams are used as alternatives to polyurethane and polyisocyanurate foams where a self-extinguishing low smoke emission material is required. Phenolic foams are closed-cell materials which are stable up to 120°C. The standard BS EN 13166: 2012 gives the specification for products of phenolic foam (PF).

Expanded PVC: Expanded PVC is produced as open, partially open and closed-cell foams, which are self-extinguishing in fire. The low density open-cell material has good sound absorbing qualities. Expanded PVC is typically used in sandwich panels and wall linings.

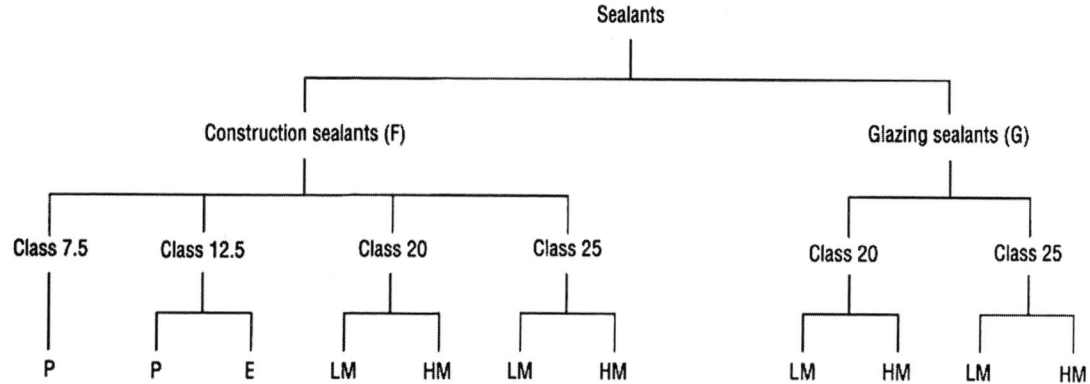

Notes: F refers to facade, G to glazing.
Class number indicates the movement accommodation as a percentage.
P refers to plastic, E to elastic, LM to low modulus and HM to high modulus.

7.17 *Classification of sealants in construction*

Sheep's wool: Sheep's wool, as a renewable resource insulation material, is available in batts ranging from 50 mm to 100 mm thick. It is a hygroscopic material reversibly absorbing and releasing water vapour which has a stabilising effect on the internal temperature of the building. It is normally sprayed with borax as a fire retardant and insect repellent.

Cellulose: Cellulose insulation is manufactured from shredded waste paper. It is treated with borax as a flame retardant and insect repellent. Cellulose insulation may be used in floors and ventilated lofts. For other cavities the material is dry injected filling the void spaces. The material is hygroscopic. The standard BS EN 15101 Parts 1 and 2: 2013 gives the specification for loose fill cellulose insulation (LFCI).

14.4 Multi-layer thermo-reflective materials

Thermo-reflective insulating products consist of multi-layers of aluminium foil, non-woven fibrous wadding and thin cellular plastics. The aluminium foil may be plain or reinforced. The material acts by reducing conduction, convection and radiation. High levels of insulation can be achieved in relatively thin quilts which may be loose laid or fixed.

15 SEALANTS, GASKETS AND ADHESIVES

15.1 General

Although used in relatively small quantities compared with the load-bearing construction materials, sealants, gaskets and adhesives play a significant role in the perceived success or failure of buildings. A combination of correct detailing and appropriate use of these materials is necessary to prevent the need for expensive remedial work. Selections of typical uses are listed as examples.

15.2 Sealants

Sealants are classified as either for glazing or construction, Figure 7.17.

The standards BS 6213: 2000 + A1: 2010 and BS EN ISO 11600: 2003 +A1: 2011 relate to the definitions and specification of sealants in construction joints. Sealants are generally classified according to their movement accommodation as either plastic or elastic. Elastic sealants may be of low or high modulus. Sealants must be matched to the appropriate application. Typical joint design and sealant systems are illustrated in Figures 7.18 and 7.19, respectively.

Plastic sealants: Plastic materials include butyl, acrylic, polymer/bitumen sealants also oil-based mastics and linseed oil putty. Butyl sealants have a rubbery texture and are mainly used in small joints, preferably protected from direct sunlight. Acrylic sealants are typically used around windows for new and remedial work.

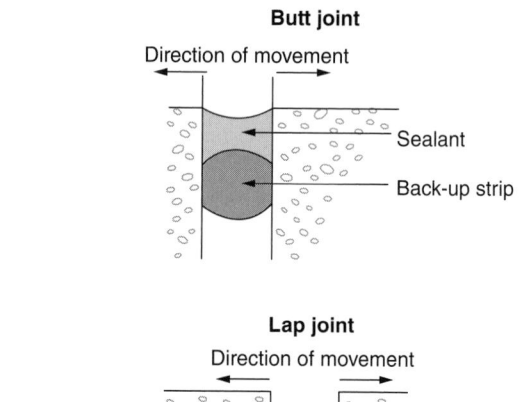

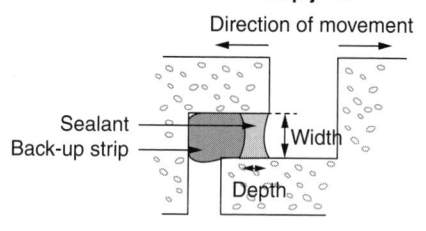

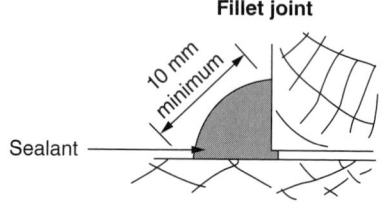

7.18 *Butt, lap and fillet joints*

Solvent-based bitumen sealants are frequently used in gutters and flashings. Hot poured bitumen is used in asphalt and concrete movement joints.

Elastoplastic sealants: Polysulphide sealants are available as one- or two-component systems. The one-component systems cure slowly by absorption of moisture from the air. They are suitable for joints up to 25 mm. The two-component systems cure within 24–48 hours and are generally used for wider structural movement joints in masonry and precast panel systems.

Elastic sealants: Elastic sealants include polyurethane, silicone and epoxy materials. Polyurethane sealants are available as one- and two-component systems and are typically used in glazing, curtain walling, cladding panels and floors. Silicone sealants are available as high- and low-modulus systems. The high-modulus material is typically used in glazing, curtain walls, tiling and around sanitary ware. The low-modulus systems are used around

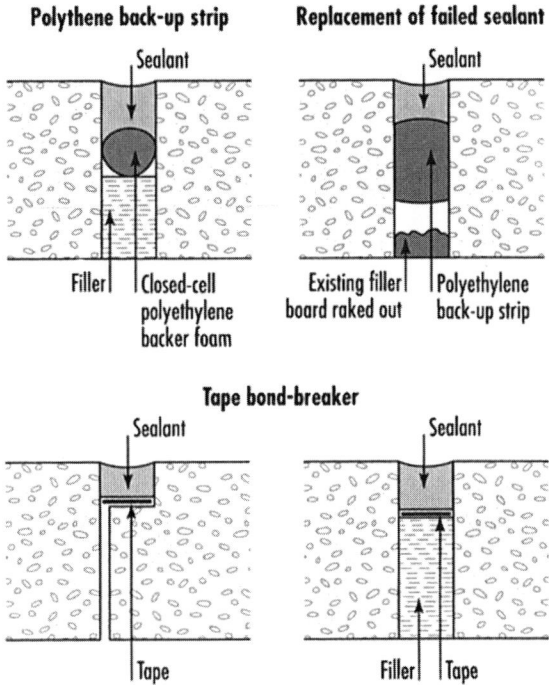

7.19 *Typical sealant systems*

PVC-U and aluminium glazing systems and for cladding. Epoxy sealants are used in stress-relieving joints where larger movements in compression than tension are anticipated, for example in floor joints and tiling in swimming pools.

15.3 Gaskets
Gaskets, Figure 7.20, are lengths of flexible components of various profiles which may be solid or hollow and manufactured from either cellular or non-cellular materials. Typical applications include the weather sealing of precast concrete cladding units and façade systems. The standard materials are neoprene, EPDM and silicone

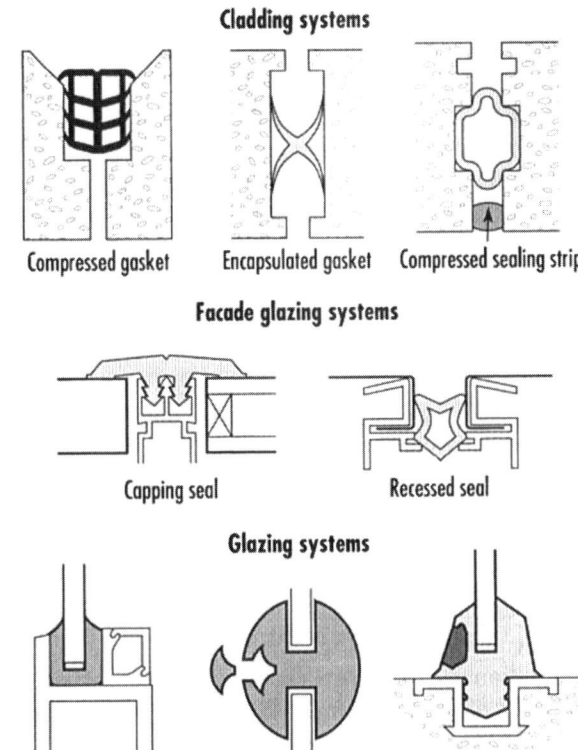

7.20 *Typical gaskets for cladding and glazing systems*

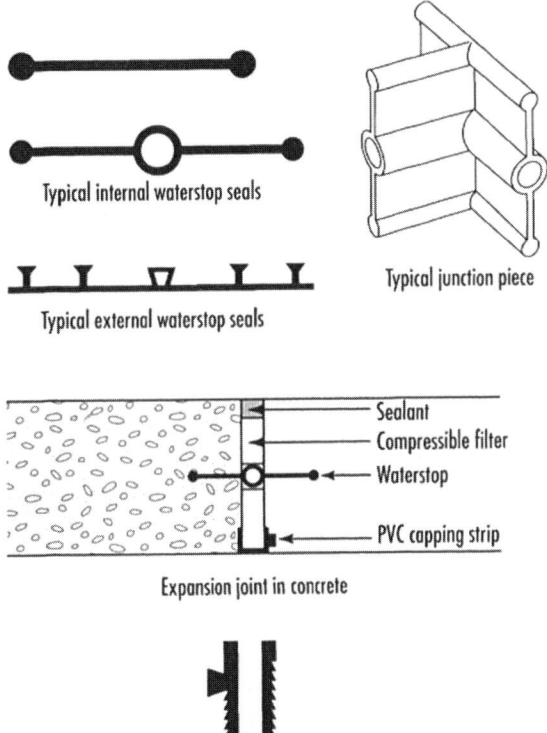

7.21 *Concrete waterstop seals*

Table LX Classification of tile adhesives by composition and properties (BS EN 12004: 2007 + A1: 2012)

Classification	Composition and properties
Type	
Type C	Cementitious adhesive – hydraulic binding resin
Type D	Dispersion adhesive – aqueous organic polymer resin
Type R	Reaction resin adhesive – one or two component synthetic resin
Class	
Class 1	Normal adhesive
Class 2	Improved adhesive
Class F	Fast setting adhesive
Class T	Reduced slip adhesive
Class S1	Deformable adhesive
Class S2	Highly deformable adhesive

rubbers. Within cladding systems, gaskets may be compressed or encapsulated. In glazing systems, gaskets are either encapsulated or fixed with a zipper component. Waterstop seals manufactured from rubber or PVC are used in concrete construction joints, Figure 7.21.

15.4 Adhesives
Tile adhesives: The standard BS EN 12004: 2007 + A1: 2012 classifies ceramic tile adhesives into three types: cementitious (C), dispersion (D) and reaction resin (R) also sub-classes as listed in Table LX.

The majority of ceramic floor tile adhesives are cement based. Grouting can be coloured as required. Thin-bed epoxy based adhesives are more water and chemical resistant and may be used where repeated spillage is anticipated.

Wall tile adhesives are usually polyvinyl acetate (PVA), acrylic or cement-based compositions. The acrylic-based adhesives are more resistant to water than the PVA materials, and therefore appropriate for domestic showers, etc. The water resistant cement-based products are useable both internally and externally. Polymer-modified cement-based adhesives are appropriate for fixing marble, granite and slate up to 15 mm in thickness.

Vinyl floor tile and wood block adhesives are generally rubber/bitumen, rubber/resin or modified bitumen emulsions.

Wood adhesives: The majority of wood adhesives are based on polyvinyl acetate (PVA). Water-resistant PVA adhesives which partially cross-link on curing are suitable for external use but not for immersion in water. Structural thermosetting wood adhesives are mainly two-component systems based on phenolic or amino-plastic resins. Their Service Class conditions are specified in the standard BS EN 301: 2013.

Epoxy resin adhesives: Epoxy resins are two-component thermosetting adhesives which produce high strength durable bonding. Epoxy resins may be used both internally and externally for fixing metals, ceramics, glass, timber, rigid plastics and concrete.

Cyanoacrylate adhesives: Cyanoacrylate resins are single-component adhesives which bond components held in contact. Curing is quickly activated by surface moisture. The bonding is resistant to chemical attack but does not offer high impact resilience.

Hot-melt adhesives: Hot-melt adhesives for application by glue gun are usually based on the thermoplastic copolymer ethyl vinyl acetate (EVA). Formulations are available for joining materials to either rigid or flexible substrates. Similar adhesives are used in iron-on plastic and wood edging veneer.

Gap-filling adhesives: Gun-grade gap filling adhesives are normally rubber/synthetic rubber resins with filler reinforcement. Both solvent-borne and solvent-free systems are available. Typical uses include fixing timber and timber products to plaster and masonry.

Plastic pipe adhesives: Solvent-based vinyl resins are used for bonding PVC-U and ABS pipes and fittings. The adhesive is applied to both components which are then united and slightly rotated to ensure a full seal.

Bitumen-based adhesives: Bitumen-based adhesives for bonding bituminous sheet roofing may be applied hot or from solvent or emulsion based formulations. Products require even spreading to eliminate air pockets which could cause delamination.

16 PAINTS, WOOD STAINS AND VARNISHES

16.1 Paints
The Code of Practice BS 6150: 2006 + A1: 2014 gives a detailed description of paint systems and their appropriate applications to the full range of building materials. The Code includes the preparation of surfaces, selection of paints systems and maintenance. Paints and varnishes specific to exterior wood are described in BS EN 927-1: 2013, and classified for masonry and concrete in BS EN 1062-1: 2004, for steel in BS EN 12944-5: 2007 and for internal surfaces BS EN 13300: 2001.

Colours can be specified according to several systems. The British Standards BS 5252: 1976 (237 colours) and BS 4800: 2011 (122 colours) define colours and colour for building purposes respectively. However colour may also be specified by other systems including: the *RAL® Classic System* (213 colours), the *Natural Colour System®* (1950 colours), the *Colour Palette®* notation or *Pantone®*. Some colour systems permit a conversion to RGB computer or CMYK printing colours. Visual comparison of paint colours based on observation and controlled illumination conditions is specified in BS EN ISO 3668: 2001.

Paint systems generally incorporate a primer, offering protection and good adherence to the substrate, an undercoat, usually an alkyd resin or acrylic emulsion providing cover, and a finishing coat providing a durable decorative surface. Finishing coats may be gloss, silk or matt finish. The majority of paints are increasingly becoming water-borne in response to environmental considerations.

16.2 Special paints
Special paints include light-reflecting, heat-resisting, intumescent, flame-retardant, water-repellent, multi-colour, masonry, anti-graffiti and fungicide products. Acrylated rubber paints are resistant to chemical attack; micaceous iron oxide paints have good resistance to moisture on iron and steelwork and epoxy paints are resistant to abrasions, oils and dilute aqueous chemicals. Anti-microbial coatings incorporating silver ions can reduce bacteria levels within medical environments.

16.3 Natural wood finishes
Natural wood finishes include wood stains, varnishes and oils. Wood stain microporous coatings for exterior use usually require a basecoat preservative, followed by a low-, medium- or high-build finish. Generally for sawn timber deeply penetrating systems are appropriate, whereas for smooth planed timber a medium- or high-build system offers the best protection from weathering. Whilst some solvent-based systems are available, many are now water-based to reduce VOC emissions.

Most varnishes are based on modified alkyd resins either as solvent- or water-based systems. Polyurethane finishes may be matt, satin or gloss. The solvent-based polyurethane systems generally give a harder and more durable coating. Most varnishes for external use incorporate screening agents to reduce the degradation effects of ultra-violet light.

Finishes such as teak and tung oil are used mainly for internal applications where the visual effect of the wood grain is to be featured. Certain formulations, high in solids giving a micro-porous UV-resistant finish, are however, suitable for external applications.

17 COMMODITIES

17.1 Windows
The typical range of window and doorset types (BS 644: 2012) is illustrated in Figure 7.22. BS 6375 Parts 1–3: 2009 gives guidance on the performance, selection and specification of windows and doors. The Code of Practice for the installation of windows and external doorsets is BS 8213-4: 2007. The European terminology for windows and doors is referenced in BS EN 12519: 2004. Most standard windows are based on increments of 150 mm in height. A standard range of timber window sizes is listed in Table LXI.

Table LXI Standard timber frame window sizes

Standard window heights (mm)						
450	600	750	900	1200	1350	1500

Standard window widths (mm)						
488	630	915	1200	1342	1770	2339

Note: Imperial sizes are also available from some manufacturers.

The following standards relate to windows constructed from the standard materials: Timber (BS 644: 2012), Aluminium alloy (BS 4873: 2009), Steel (BS 6510: 2010) and PVC-U (BS 7412: 2007). Timber and aluminium composite windows are referenced in BS 644: 2012. The safety aspects of cleaning windows are specified in the Code of Practice BS 8213-1: 2004. Where required by the Building Regulations Part B 2006 (incorporating amendments 2010 and 2013), fire egress windows must be provided with a clear opening of greater than 0.33 m^2 and minimum clear dimensions of 450 mm (e.g. 450 × 735 mm). The bottom of the openable area must not be more than 1100 mm above the floor. These windows must not be restricted or lockable with removable keys. Aspects of domestic window security are covered by PAS 24: 2012 and BS 8220-1:2000.

Safety considerations (BS 6180: 2011) dictate that any opening window less than 800 mm from the floor should be protected to 800 mm by a barrier or restricted to less than 100 mm opening. It is a requirement (BS 6262-4: 2005) that all glazing less than 800 mm above floor (or ground level) should be of safety glass. Large openings up to 1100 mm above floor level should be guarded to that level when there is a drop outside of more than 600 mm (BS 8213-1: 2004).

Window Energy Ratings (WERs) are an established measure of window energy efficiency. A formula combines the elements of solar heat transmittance, *U*-value and air infiltration to produce an overall rating on the A+ to G scale, with A+ the most energy efficient for the whole window unit. Standard building practice

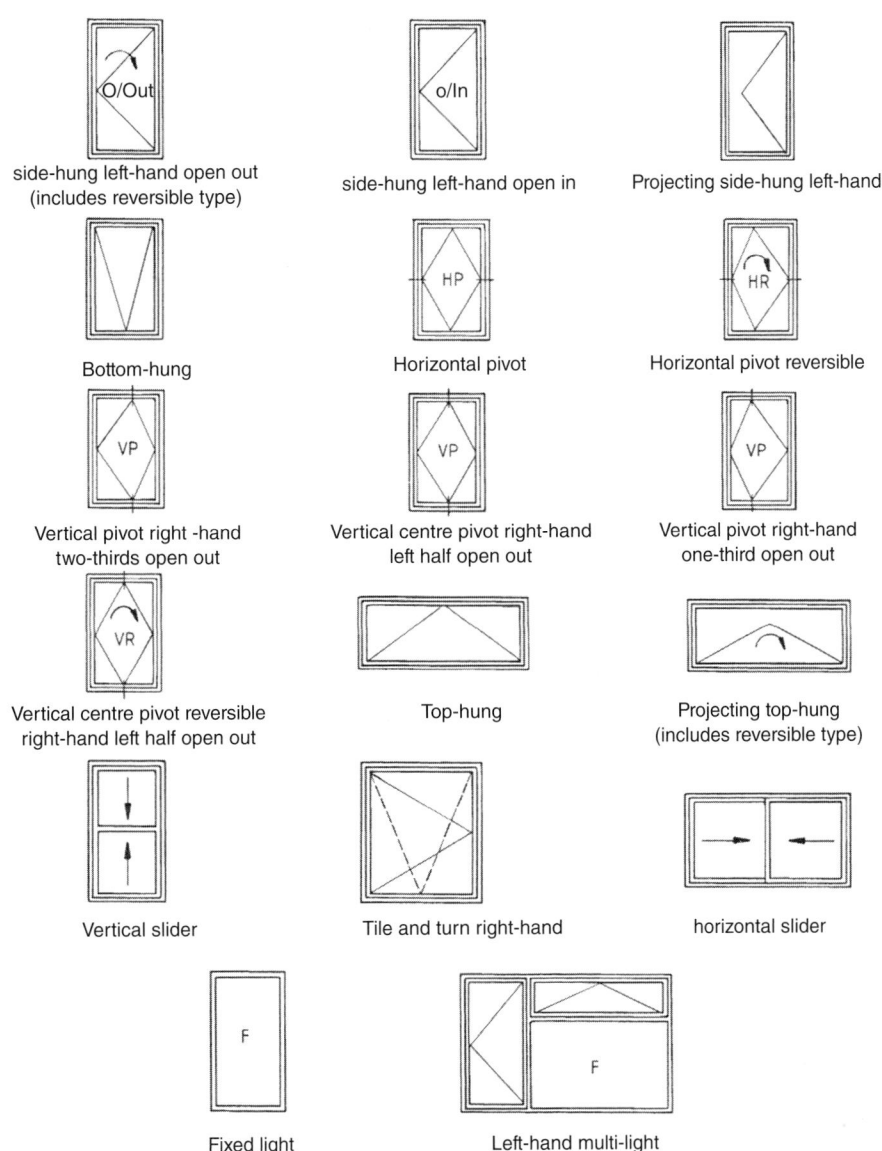

7.22 *Standard timber window and doorsets – British Standard BS 644: 2012 (permission to reproduce extracts from: BS 644: 2012 Timber windows and doorsets. Fully furnished factory assembled windows and doorsets of various types. Specification is granted by the British Standards Institute.)*

effectively requires windows with a minimum rating of C, but many manufacturers are producing windows that are A+, A or B rated and increasingly these will be demanded.

17.2 Doors
The majority of UK doors are manufactured to imperial dimensions but the imperial sizes are also quoted in metric units. Standard imperial sizes for internal doors are 1981 mm × 457, 533, 610, 686, 762, 838, and 864 mm. The metric sizes for internal doors are 2040 mm × 526, 626, 726, 826 and 926 mm. Standard thicknesses are 35 and 40 mm.

Fire doors, typically 35, 44 or 54 mm thick, are rated either to BS 476-22: 1987 (e.g. FD 30) or to the European Standard BS EN 13501-2: 2007 + A1: 2009 (e.g. E30) for integrity in minutes. The ratings are normally subject to the use of appropriate frames with intumescent strips and any fire-resistant glazing being factory-fitted. In certain locations the Building Regulations Part E, related to the passage of sound, require minimum sound reduction criteria, and these can be achieved by the used of appropriately sealed doorsets.

The standard imperial sizes for external inward opening doors are 1981 mm × 686, 762, 813, 838 and 914 mm. The corresponding frame sizes are 2081 mm × 783, 859, 910, 935 and 1011 mm. Additionally a taller 2032 mm × 813 mm door is standard, matched to a 2132 mm × 910 mm frame.

The standard metric size for external doors is 2000 mm × 807 mm with a frame size of 2100 mm × 900 mm with a sill or 2053 mm × 900 mm without a sill. The larger 2040 mm × 826 mm metric doors require a 2140 mm × 920 mm frame with a sill or 2093 mm × 920 mm without a sill.

The Building Regulations Part M 2004 (incorporating 2010 and 2013 amendments) requires a wheelchair access into buildings, preferably level but with any threshold no higher than 15 mm and any upstands over 5 mm chamfered or rounded. Normally the minimum effective clear entrance width required is 800 mm in new buildings, but 1000 mm in buildings used by the general public. Visibility zones are required in doors or side panels between 500 mm and 1500 mm from floor level. The height for door controls to be used by people in wheelchairs should be between 750 and 1000 mm from the floor.

Door Set Energy Ratings (DSERs) range from A to G, depending on U-value and air leakage. The scheme covers all external pedestrian doors. F and G ratings are normally appropriate only for listed buildings and architecturally sensitive locations.

17.3 Curtain walling

Curtain walling can be used within commercial buildings or domestic properties where a large visual glazed area is required; this is advantageous because of the natural light it provides. If treated sensitively large glazed areas of façades can be aesthetically pleasing and create a contemporary, open-air look both inside and outside the building.

Curtain walling is loosely defined in the standards (BS EN 13830: 2003 + pr EN 13830: 2013) as an external vertical building enclosure produced by elements mainly of timber, metal or plastic. This standard applies to curtain walling consisting of vertical and horizontal members, connected together and anchored to the supporting structure of the building and in-filled to form a lightweight space enclosing continuous skin, which does not take on any load-bearing characteristics of the building structure. The standard applies to curtain walling ranging from a vertical position to 15° from the vertical. It can include elements of sloping glazing contained within the curtain wall.

Curtain walling embraces many different forms of construction but generally comprises one of the following:

- Stick construction – light carrier framework of site assembled components supporting prefabricated opaque and/or translucent infill panels.
- Unitised construction – pre-assembled interlinking storey height or multi-storey height modules, complete with infill panels.
- Spandrel construction – pre-assembled interlinking part-storey height modules, complete with infill panels.

The standard specifies characteristics of curtain walling and provides technical information on the varying performance requirements which apply throughout Europe, the test criteria and sequence of testing to which the product is subjected, in order to demonstrate conformity. Reference is also made to other European standards which relate to products incorporated into curtain walling. Curtain walling is not a product which can be completed in all respects within a manufacturing area, but is a series of components and/or prefabricated units which only become a finished product when assembled together on site. This standard is applicable to the whole of the curtain walling, including the flashings, closures and copings.

Curtain walling should be sufficiently rigid to resist wind loads (BS EN 13116: 2001), sustain its own weight and transfer associated loads to the building structure. It must be resistant to impact (BS EN 14019: 2004), the transfer of heat/cold and sound, and be air (BS EN 12152: 2002) and water tight (BS EN 12154: 2000). It must be designed to be fire resistant, prevent the transmission of fire or smoke through voids and react to fire within prescribed limits. These and other factors, such as durability, water vapour permeability, equipotentiality (bonding to electrical earth), seismic shock resistance, thermal shock resistance, building thermal movement and resistance to live horizontal loads, must be proven by testing and calculation methods defined in the standards.

18 BIBLIOGRAPHY

18.1 Steel

Technical information:

Steel Construction Institute, *Steel Designers' Manual*, 7th edition, Wiley-Blackwell, 2012.

Tata Steel, 2012: Stock range and specifications.

Tata Steel, 2013: Tata Steel sections interactive 'Blue Book' London.

BS 4-1 Structural steel sections: Part 1: 2005 Specification for hot-rolled sections.

BS ISO 404: 2013 Steel and steel products. General technical delivery requirements.

BS 3692: 2001 ISO metric precision hexagon bolts, screws and nuts. Specification.

BS 4449: 2005 Steel for the reinforcement of concrete. Weldable reinforcing steel. Bar, coil and decoiled product. Specification.

BS 4482: 2005 Steel wire for the reinforcement of concrete products. Specification.

BS 4483: 2005 Steel fabric for the reinforcement of concrete products. Specification.

BS 6722: 1986 Recommendations for dimensions of metallic materials.

BS 6744: 2009 Stainless steel bars for the reinforcement of and use in concrete.

BS 7668: 2004 Weldable structural steels. Hot finished structural hollow sections in weather-resistant steels. Specification.

BS EN 206 Concrete: Part 1: 2000 Concrete. Specification, performance, production and conformity.

BS EN 10020: 2000 Definition and classification of grades of steel.

BS EN 10024: 1995 Hot rolled taper flange I sections. Tolerances on shape and dimensions.

BS EN 10025 Hot rolled products of structural steels:

   Part 1: 2004 General technical delivery conditions.
   Part 2: 2004 Technical delivery conditions for non-alloy structural steels.
   Part 5: 2004 Technical delivery conditions for structural steels with improved atmospheric corrosion resistance.

BS EN 10029: 2010 Hot rolled steel plates 3mm thick or above. Tolerances on dimensions and shape.

BS EN 10034: 1993 Structural steel I and H sections. Tolerances on shape and dimensions.

BS EN 10048: 1997 Hot rolled narrow steel strip. Tolerances on dimensions and shape.

BS EN 10051: 2010 Continuously hot-rolled strip and plate/sheet cut from wide strip of non-alloy and alloy steels. Tolerances on dimensions and shape.

BS EN 10052: 1994 Vocabulary of heat treatment terms for ferrous products.

BS EN 10056 Structural steel equal and unequal leg angles:

   Part 1: 1999 Dimensions.
   Part 2: 1993 Tolerances on shape and dimensions.

BS EN 10058: 2003 Hot rolled flat steel bars for general purposes. Dimensions and tolerances on shape and dimensions.

BS EN 10059: 2003 Hot rolled square steel bars for general purposes. Dimensions and tolerances on shape and dimensions.

BS EN 10060: 2003 Hot rolled round steel bars for general purposes. Dimensions and tolerances on shape and dimensions.

BS EN 10061: 2003 Hot rolled hexagon steel bars for general purposes. Dimensions and tolerances on shape and dimensions.

BS EN 10079: 2007 Definitions of steel products.

BS EN 10088 Stainless steels: Part 1: 2005 List of stainless steels.

BS EN 10130: 2006 Cold rolled low carbon steel flat products for cold forming, technical delivery conditions.

BS EN 10131: 2006 Cold rolled uncoated and zinc or zinc-nickel electrolytically coated low carbon and high yield strength steel flat products for cold forming. Tolerances on dimensions and shape.

BS EN 10149: Hot rolled flat products made of high yield strength steels for cold forming:

   Part 1: 2013 General technical delivery conditions.
   Part 2: 2013 Technical delivery conditions for thermomechanically rolled steels.
   Part 3: 2013 Technical delivery conditions for normalized rolled steels.

BS EN 10210 Hot finished structural hollow sections of non-alloy and fine grain steels:

Part 1: 2006 Technical delivery conditions.
Part 2: 2006 Tolerances, dimensions and sectional properties.

BS EN 10219 Cold formed welded structural hollow sections of non-alloy and fine grain steels:

Part 1: 2006 Technical delivery conditions.
Part 2: 2006 Tolerances, dimensions and sectional properties.

BS EN 10220: 2002 Seamless and welded steel tubes. Dimensions and masses per unit length.
BS EN 10279: 2000 Hot rolled steel channels. Tolerances on shape, dimension and mass.

18.2 Timber

Technical information:
TRADA Technology Ltd.
BS 1297: 1987 Specification for tongued and grooved softwood flooring.
BS EN 300: 2006 Oriented Strand Boards (OSB). Definitions, classification and specifications.
BS EN 309: 2005 Particleboards. Definition and classification.
BS EN 312: 2010 Particleboards. Specifications.
BS EN 313 Plywood. Classification and terminology:

Part 1: 1996 Classification.
Part 2: 2000 Terminology.

BS EN 335: 2013 Durability of wood and wood-based products. Use classes, definitions, applications to solid wood and wood-based products.
BS EN 336: 2013 Structural timber. Sizes, permitted deviations.
BS EN 338: 2009 Structural timber. Strength classes.
BS EN 387: 2001 Glued laminated timber. Large finger joints. Performance requirements.
BS EN 622 Fibreboards. Specifications:

Part 1: 2003 General requirements.
Part 2: 2004 Requirements for hardboards.
Part 3: 2004 Requirements for mediumboards.
Part 4: 2009 Requirements for softboards.
Part 5: 2009 Requirements for dry process boards (MDF).

BS EN 634 Cement-bonded particleboards. Specifications:

Part 1: 1995 General requirements.
Part 2: 2007 Requirements for OPC bonded particleboards for use in dry, humid and external conditions.

BS EN 636: 2012 Plywood. Specifications.
BS EN 942: 2007 Timber in joinery. General requirements.
BS EN 1194: 1999 Timber structures. Glued laminated timber. Strength classes.
BS EN 1309 Round and sawn timber. Method of measurement of dimensions:

Part 1: 1997 Sawn timber.
Part 2: 2006 Round timber.

BS EN 1313 Round and sawn timber. Permitted deviations and preferred sizes:

Part 1: 2010 Softwood sawn timber.
Part 2: 1999 Hardwood sawn timber.

BS EN 1315: 2010 Dimensional classification of round timber.
BS EN 1995–1–1: 2004 Eurocode 5. Design of timber structures. General. Common rules and rules for buildings.

BS EN 13017 Solid wood panels. Classification by surface appearance:

Part 1: 2001 Softwood.
Part 2: 2001 Hardwood.

BS EN 14279: 2004 Laminated veneer lumber (LVL). Definitions, classification and specifications.
BS EN 14374: 2004 Timber structures. Structural laminated veneer lumber. Requirements.
BS EN 14755: 2005 Extruded particleboards. Specifications.
DD CEN/TS 1099: 2007 Plywood. Biological durability. Guidance for the assessment of plywood for use in different class uses.
DD CEN/TS 12872: 2007 Wood-based panels. Guidance on the use of load-bearing boards in floors, walls and roofs.
DD CEN/TS 15679: 2007 Thermal modified timber. Definitions and characteristics.

18.3 Bricks and blocks

BS 4729: 2005 Clay and calcium silicate bricks of special shapes and sizes. Recommendations.
BS 6073-2: 2008 Precast concrete masonry units. Guide for specifying precast concrete masonry units.
BS EN 771 Specification for masonry units:

Part 1: 2011 Clay masonry units.
Part 2: 2011 Calcium silicate masonry units.
Part 3: 2011 Aggregate concrete masonry units (dense and light-weight aggregates).
Part 4: 2011 Autoclaved aerated concrete masonry units.
Part 5: 2011 Manufactured stone masonry units.

18.4 Concrete

Technical information:
British Cement Association.
Concrete Society.
Mineral Products Association.
BS 4449: 2005 Steel for the reinforcement of concrete.
BS 4482: 2005 Steel for the reinforcement of concrete products. Specification.
BS 4483: 2005 Steel fabric for the reinforcement of concrete. Specification.
BS 8000 Workmanship on building sites: Part 2: 1990 Code of practice for concrete work.
BS 8500 Concrete. Complementary British Standard to BS EN 206–1: Part 1: 2006 + A1: 2012 Method of specifying and guidance to the specifier.
BS EN 197 Cement: Part 1: 2011 Composition specifications and conformity criteria for common cements.
BS EN 206: 2013 Concrete Part 1: 2000 Specification, performance, production and conformity.
BS EN 413 Masonry cement: Part 1: 2011 Composition, specifications and conformity criteria.
BS EN 934 Admixtures for concrete, mortar and grout: Part 1: 2008 Common requirements.
BS EN 1339: 2003 Concrete paving flags. Requirements and test methods.
BS EN 10080: 2005 Steel for the reinforcement of concrete. Weldable reinforcing steel. General.
BS EN 12620: 2013 Aggregates for concrete.
BS EN 13055 Lightweight aggregates: Part 1: 2002 Lightweight aggregates for concrete, mortar and grout.
BS EN 13263 Silica fume for concrete: Part 1: 2005 Definitions, requirements and conformity.
BS EN 14216: 2004 Cement. Compositions, specifications and conformity criteria for very low heat special cements.
BS EN 15167 Ground granulated blast furnace slag for use in concrete, mortar and grout: Part 1: 2006 Definitions, specifications and conformity criteria.

18.5 Aluminium

BS 1161: 1977 Specification for aluminium alloy sections for structural purposes.

BS EN 485 Aluminium and aluminium alloys. Sheet, strip and plate:

  Part 1: 2008 Technical conditions for inspection and delivery.
  Part 2: 2013 Mechanical properties.
  Part 3: 2003 Tolerances on dimensions and form for hot-rolled products.

BS EN 573 Aluminium and aluminium alloys:

  Part 1: 2004 Numeral designation system.
  Part 3: 2013 Chemical composition and form of products.

BS EN 754 Aluminium and aluminium alloys. Extruded rod/bar, tube and profiles:

  Part 1: 2008 Cold drawn rod, bar and tube. Technical conditions.
  Part 2: 2013 Cold drawn rod, bar and tube. Mechanical properties.
  Part 3: 2008 Round bars, tolerances on dimension and form.
  Part 4: 2008 Square bars, tolerances on dimension and form.
  Part 5: 2008 Rectangular bars, tolerances on dimension and form.
  Part 6: 2008 Hexagonal bars, tolerances on dimension and form.
  Part 7: 2008 Seamless tubes, tolerances on dimension and form.

BS EN 755 Aluminium and aluminium alloys. Extruded rod/bar, tube and profiles:

  Part 1: 2008 Technical conditions for inspection and delivery.
  Part 2: 2013 Mechanical properties.
  Part 3: 2008 Round bars, tolerances on dimension and form.
  Part 4: 2008 Square bars, tolerances on dimension and form.
  Part 5: 2008 Rectangular bars, tolerances on dimension and form.
  Part 6: 2008 Hexagonal bars, tolerances on dimension and form.
  Part 7: 2008 Seamless tubes, tolerances on dimension and form.
  Part 9: 2008 Profiles, tolerances on dimension and form.

BS EN 1999-1-1:2007 + A2: 2013 Design of aluminium structures. General structural rules.

18.6 Roofing and cladding

BS 4842: 1984 Liquid organic coatings for application to aluminium extrusions, sheet and preformed sections for external architectural purposes.

BS 4868: 1972 Specification for profiled aluminium sheet for building.

BS 6229: 2003 Flat roofs with continuously supported coverings. Code of practice.

BS 6915: 2001 + A1: 2014 Design and construction of fully supported lead sheet roof and wall coverings. Code of practice.

BS 6925: 1988 Specification for mastic asphalt for building and civil engineering.

BS 8217: 2005 Reinforced bitumen membranes for roofing. Code of practice.

BS 8218: 1998 Code of practice for mastic asphalt roofing.

BS 8747: 2007 Reinforced bitumen membranes for roofing. Guide to selection and specification.

BS EN 501: 1994 Roofing products from metal sheet. Specification for fully supported roofing products of zinc sheet.

BS EN 502: 2013 Roofing products from metal sheet. Specification for fully supported products of stainless steel sheet.

BS EN 504: 2000 Roofing products from metal sheet. Specification for fully supported roofing products of copper sheet.

BS EN 505: 2013 Roofing products from sheet metal. Specification for fully supported roofing products of sheet steel.

BS EN 506: 2008 Roofing products from metal sheet. Specification for self-supporting products of copper or zinc sheet.

BS EN 507: 2000 Roofing products from metal sheet. Specification for fully supported products of aluminium sheet.

BS EN 508 Roofing products from metal sheet. Specification for self-supporting products of steel, aluminium or stainless steel sheet:

  Part 1: 2014 Steel.
  Part 2: 2008 Aluminium.
  Part 3: 2008 Stainless steel.

BS EN 988: 1997 Zinc and zinc alloys. Specification for flat rolled products for building.

BS EN 1172: 2011 Copper and copper alloys. Sheet and strip for building purposes.

BS EN 1179: 2003 Zinc and zinc alloys. Primary zinc.

BS EN ISO 9445 Continuously cold-rolled stainless steel. Tolerances on dimensions and form:

  Part 1: 2010 Narrow strip and cut lengths.
  Part 2: 2010 Wide strip and plate/sheet.

BS EN 10140: 2006 Cold rolled narrow steel strip. Tolerances on dimensions and shape.

BS EN 12588: 2006 Lead and lead alloys. Rolled lead sheet for building purposes.

BS EN 13108-6: 2006 Bituminous mixtures. Material specifications. Mastic asphalt.

BS EN 13707: 2013 Flexible sheets for waterproofing. Reinforced bitumen sheets for waterproofing. Definitions and characteristics.

BS EN 13859-1: 2014 Flexible sheets for waterproofing. Definitions and characteristics of underlays. Underlays for discontinuous roofing.

BS EN 13956: 2012 Flexible sheet for waterproofing. Plastic and rubber sheets for roof waterproofing. Definitions and characteristics.

BS EN 14782: 2006 Self-supporting metal sheet for roofing, external cladding and internal lining. Product specification and requirements.

BS EN 14783: 2013 Fully supported metal sheet and strip for roofing, external cladding and internal lining. Product specification and requirements.

BS EN 14964: 2006 Rigid underlays for discontinuous roofing. Definitions and characteristics.

CP 143 Code of practice. Sheet roof and wall coverings:

  Part 5: 1964 Zinc.
  Part 12: 1970 Copper. Metric units.
  Part 15: 1973 Aluminium. Metric units.

18.7 Glass

Technical information:

Pilkington Building Products (www.pilkington.com)

Saint-Gobain Glass, (uk.saint-gobain-glass.com)

BS 6180: 2011 Barriers in and about buildings. Code of practice.

BS 6206: 1981 Specification for impact performance requirements for flat safety glass and safety plastics for use in buildings.

BS 6262 Glazing for buildings:

    Part 1: 2005 General methodology for the selection of glazing.
    Part 2: 2005 Code of practice for energy, light and sound.
    Part 3: 2005 Code of practice for fire, security and wind loading.
    Part 4: 2005 Code of practice for safety related to human impact.
    Part 6: 2005 Code of practice for special applications.
    Part 7: 2005 Code of practice for the provision of information.

BS EN 1991-1-4: 2005 Eurocode action on structures. General actions.

BS EN ISO 12543 Glass in building. Laminated glass and laminated safety glass:

    Part 1: 2011 Definitions and descriptions of component parts.
    Part 2: 2011 Laminated safety glass.
    Part 3: 2011 Laminated glass.

BS EN 12600: 2002 Glass in building. Pendulum test. Impact test method and classification for flat glass.

BS EN 13022 Glass in building. Structural sealant glazing:

    Part 1: 2014 Glass products for structural sealant glazing systems.
    Part 2: 2014 Assembly rules.

BS EN 13363 Solar protection devices combined with glazing. Calculation of solar and light transmittance:

    Part 1: 2003 Simplified method.
    Part 2: 2005 Detailed calculation method.

18.7 Ceramic materials

BS 3402: 1969 Specification for quality of vitreous china sanitary appliances.

BS 5385 Parts 1-5 2006 – 2009 Wall and floor tiling.

BS 5534: 2014 Code of practice for slating and tiling (including shingles).

BS EN 295: 2012 – 2013 Vitrified clay pipes and fittings for drains and sewers.

BS EN 1304: 2013 Clay roofing tiles and fittings. Product definitions and specifications.

BS EN 12004: 2007 Adhesives for tiles. Requirements, evaluation of conformity, classification and designation.

BS EN 13888: 2009 Grout for tiles. Requirements, evaluation of conformity, classification and designation.

BS EN 14411: 2012 Ceramic tiles. Definitions, classification, characteristics, evaluation of conformity and marking.

18.8 Stone and cast stone

BS 1217: 2008 Cast stone. Specification.

BS 8298: Code of practice for design and installation of natural stone cladding and lining:

    Part 1: 2010 General.
    Part 2: 2010 Traditional handset external cladding.
    Part 3: 2010 Stone-faced pre-cast concrete cladding systems.
    Part 4: 2010 Rainscreen and stone on metal frame cladding systems.
    Part 5: pending Internal linings.

BS EN 771 Specification for masonry units:

    Part 5: 2011 Manufactured stone masonry units.
    Part 6: 2011 Natural stone masonry units.

BS EN 1469: 2004 Natural stone products. Slabs for cladding. Requirements.

BS EN 12670: 2002 Natural stone. Terminology.

18.9 Plastics

BS 743: 1970 Specification for materials for damp-proof courses.

BS 3012: 1970 Specification for low and intermediate density polythene sheet for general purposes.

BS 3757: 1978 Specification for rigid PVC sheet.

BS 4901: 1976 Specification for plastics colours for building purposes.

BS 5955-8: 2001 Plastics pipework (thermoplastics materials).

BS 6203: 2003 Guide to the fire characteristics of expanded polystyrene materials.

BS 6398: 1983 Specification for bitumen damp-proof courses for masonry.

BS 6515: 1984 Specification for polyethylene damp-proof courses for masonry.

BS 7619: 2010 Extruded cellular unplasticized white PVC (PVCUE) profiles. Specification.

BS 8215: 1991 Code of practice for design and installation of damp-proof courses in masonry construction.

BS EN 1013: 2012 Light transmitting single skin profiled plastic sheets for internal and external roofs, walls and ceilings. Requirements and test methods.

BS EN ISO 1873 Plastics. Polypropylene (PP) moulding and extrusion materials: Part 1: 1995 Designation system and basis for specifications.

BS EN ISO 7391 Plastics. Polycarbonate (PC) moulding and extrusion materials: Part 1: 2006 Designation system and basis for specifications.

BS EN ISO 8257 Plastics. Polymethyl methacrylate (PMMA) moulding and extrusion materials: Part 1: 2006 Designation system and basis for specifications.

BS EN ISO 8986 Plastics. Polybutene-1 (PB-1) moulding and extrusion materials: Part 1: 2009 Designation system and basis for specifications.

BS EN ISO 11542 Plastics. Ultra high molecular weight polyethylene (PE-UHMW) moulding and extrusion materials: Part 1: 2001 Designation system and basis for specifications.

BS EN ISO 12086 Plastics. Fluoropolymer dispersions and moulding and extrusion materials: Part 1: 2006 Designation system and basis for specifications.

BS EN 14909: 2012 Flexible sheets for waterproofing. Plastic and rubber damp-proof courses. Definitions and characteristics.

BS EN 15347: 2007 Plastics. Recycled plastics. Characterisation of plastics waste.

DD CEN/TS 15534 Parts 2: 2007 Wood-plastics composites (WPC).

BS EN 15534 Parts 1, 4 and 5: 2012 Composites made from cellulose-based materials and thermoplastics.

18.10 Glass-fibre reinforced plastics, concrete (cement) and gypsum

BRE Digest 480: 2004 Wood plastic composites and plastic lumber.

BS EN 492: 2012 Fibre-cement slates and fittings. Product specification.

BS EN 494: 2012 Fibre-cement profiled sheets and fittings. Product specification.

BS EN 1013: 2012 Light transmitting single skin profiled sheets for internal and external roofs, walls and ceilings.

BS EN 1169: 1999 Precast concrete products. General rules for factory production control of glass-fibre reinforced cement.

BS EN 12467: 2012 Fibre-cement flat sheets. Product specification and test methods.

BS EN 15422: 2008 Precast concrete products. Specification of glass fibres for reinforcement of mortars and concretes.

18.11 Plaster and board materials

Technical information:

British Gypsum: The White Book. 2009 (updated 2011) www.british-gypsum.com/literature/white-book

British Gypsum: The Fire Book, 2011 www.british-gypsum.com/literature/fire-book

BS EN 520: 2004 Gypsum plasterboards. Definitions, requirements and test methods.

BS EN 13279-1: 2008 Gypsum binders and gypsum plasters. Definitions and requirements.

BS EN 13658-1: 2014 Metal lath and beads. Definitions, requirements and test methods. Internal plastering.

BS EN 13815: 2006 Fibrous gypsum plaster casts. Definitions, requirements and test methods.

BS EN 13915: 2007 Prefabricated gypsum plasterboard panels with a cellular paperboard core.

BS EN 13950: 2005 Gypsum plasterboard thermal / acoustic insulation composite panels.

BS EN 14353: 2007 Metal beads and feature profiles for use with gypsum plasterboards.

BS EN 15283 Gypsum boards with fibrous reinforcement:

> Part 1: 2008 Gypsum boards with mat reinforcement.
> Part 2: 2008 Gypsum fibre boards.

BS EN 15319: 2007 General principles of design of fibrous (gypsum) plaster works.

18.12 Insulation materials

BS 3837–1: 2004 Expanded polystyrene boards. Boards and blocks manufactured from expandable beads.

BS 5250: 2011 Code of practice for control of condensation in buildings.

BS EN ISO 10456: 2007 Building materials and products. Hygrothermal properties.

BS EN 12524: 2000 Building materials and products. Hygrothermal. properties. Tabulated design values.

BS EN 13162: 2012 Thermal insulation products for buildings. Factory made mineral wool (MW) products. Specification.

BS EN 13163: 2012 Thermal insulation products for buildings. Factory made products of expanded polystyrene (EPS). Specification.

BS EN 13164: 2012 Thermal insulation products for buildings. Factory made products of extruded polystyrene foam (XPS). Specification.

BS EN 13165: 2012 Thermal insulation products for buildings. Factory made rigid polyurethane foam (PUR) products. Specification.

BS EN 13166: 2012 Thermal insulation products for buildings. Factory made products of phenolic foam (PF). Specification.

BS EN 13167: 2012 Thermal insulation products for buildings. Factory made cellular glass (CG) products. Specification.

BS EN 13168: 2012 Thermal insulation products for buildings. Factory made wood wool (WW) products. Specification.

BS EN 13169: 2012 Thermal insulation products for buildings. Factory made products of expanded perlite (EPB). Specification.

BS EN 13170: 2012 Thermal insulation products for buildings. Factory made products of expanded cork (ICB). Specification.

BS EN 13171: 2012 Thermal insulation products for buildings. Factory made wood fibre (WF) products. Specification.

BS EN 13499: 2003 Thermal insulation products for buildings. External thermal insulation composite systems (ETICS).

BS EN 14063-1: 2004 Thermal insulation products for buildings. In-situ formed expanded clay lightweight aggregate products. Specification for loose-fill products before installation.

BS EN 14315 Thermal insulation products for building. In-situ formed sprayed rigid polyurethane (PUR) and polyisocyanurate (PIR) foam products:

> Part 1: 2013 Specification for the rigid foam spray system before installation.
> Part 2: 2013 Specification for the installed insulation products.

BS EN 14316 Thermal insulation products for buildings. In-situ thermal insulation formed from expanded perlite (EP) products:

> Part 1: 2004 Specification for bonded and loose-fill products before installation.
> Part 2: 2007 Specification for the installed products.

BS EN 14317 Thermal insulation products for buildings. In-situ thermal insulation formed from exfoliated vermiculite (EV):

> Part 1: 2004 Specification for bonded and loose-fill products before installation.
> Part 2: 2007 Specification for the installed products.

BS EN 15101 Thermal insulation products for building. In-situ formed loose fill cellulose (LFCI) products:

> Part 1: 2013 Specification for the products before installation.
> Part 2: 2013 Specification for the installed products.

18.13 Sealants, gaskets and adhesives

BS 6213: 2000 Selection of construction sealants. Guide.

BS EN 301: 2013 Adhesives, phenolic and aminoplastic for load-bearing timber structures.

BS EN ISO 11600: 2003 Building construction jointing products. Classification and requirements for sealants.

BS EN ISO 12004: 2007 Adhesives for tiles. Requirements, evaluation of conformity, classification and designation.

18.14 Paints, wood stains and varnishes

BS 4800: 2011 Schedule of paint colours for building purposes.

BS 5252: 1976 Framework for colour co-ordination for building purposes.

BS 6150: 2006 Painting of buildings. Code of practice.

BS EN 927-1: 2013 Paints and varnishes. Coating materials and coating systems for exterior wood. Classification and selection.

BS EN 1062-1: 2004 Paints and varnishes. Coating materials and coating systems for exterior masonry and concrete. Classification.

BS EN ISO 3668: 2001 Paints and varnishes. Visual comparison of the colour of paints.

BS EN ISO 12944-5: 2007 Paints and varnishes. Corrosion protection of steel structures by protective paint systems. Protective paint systems.

BS EN 13300: 2001 Paints and varnishes. Water-borne coating materials and coating systems for interior walls and ceilings. Classification.

18.15 Commodities; windows, doors and curtain walling

Windows and doors

Technical information:

Jeld-Wen Windows, patio doors, and external doorsets, 2012, www.jeld-wen.co.uk

Jeld-Wen Internal, external doors, patio doors and external doorsets, 2013, www.jeld-wen.co.uk

BS 459: 1988 Specification for matchboarded wooden door leaves for external use.

BS 476–22: 1987 Fire tests on building materials and structures. Fire resistance of non-loadbearing elements of construction.

BS 644: 2012 Timber windows. Fully finished factory-assembled windows and doorsets of various types. Specification.

BS 1245: 2012 Pedestrian doorsets and door frames made from steel sheet. Specification.

BS 4787-1: 1980 Internal and external doorsets, door leaves and frames. Specification for dimensional requirements.

BS 4873: 2009 Aluminium windows and doorsets. Specification.

BS 6180: 2011 Barriers in and about buildings. Code of practice.

BS 6262–4: 2005 Glazing for buildings. Code of practice for safety related to human impact.

BS 6375 Performance of windows and doors:

Part 1: 2009 Classification for weathertightness and guidance on selection and specification.

Part 2 2009 Classification for operation and strength characteristics and guidance on selection and specification.

Part 3: 2009 Classification for additional performance characteristics and guidance on selection and specification.

BS 6510: 2010 Steel-framed windows and glazed doors.

BS 7412: 2007 Specification for windows and doorsets made from unplasticized polyvinyl chloride (PVC-U) extruded hollow profiles.

BS 8213 Windows, doors and rooflights:

Part 1: 2004 Design for safety in use and during cleaning of windows. Code of practice.

Part 4: 2007 Code of practice for the survey and installation of windows and external doorsets.

BS 8220–1: 2000 Guide for security of buildings against crime. Dwellings.

BS EN 1529: 2000 Door leaves. Height, width, thickness and squareness. Tolerance classes.

BS EN 12519: 2004 Windows and pedestrian doors. Terminology.

BS EN 13501-2: 2007 Fire classification of construction products and building elements.

BS EN 14220: 2006 Timber and wood-based materials in external windows, external door leaves and external doorframes. Requirements and specifications.

BS EN 14221: 2006 Timber and wood-based materials in internal windows, internal door leaves and internal doorframes. Requirements and specifications.

BS EN 14351-1: 2006 Windows and doors. Product standard, performance characteristics.

PAS 24: 2012 Enhanced security performance requirements for doorsets and windows in the UK.

Curtain walling

BS EN ISO 140 Acoustics. Measurement of sound insulation in buildings and of building elements.

BS EN ISO 717 Acoustics. Rating of sound insulation in buildings:
Part 1: 2013 Airborne sound insulation.

BS EN 1991 Eurocode 1: Actions on structures: Part 1-1: 2002 General actions. Densities, self-weight, imposed loads for buildings.

BS EN 12152: 2002 Curtain walling. Air permeability. Performance requirements and classification.

BS EN 12153: 2000 Curtain walling. Air permeability. Test method.

BS EN 12154: 2000 Curtain walling. Watertightness. Performance requirements and classification.

BS EN 12155: 2000 Curtain walling. Watertightness. Laboratory test under static pressure.

BS EN 12179: 2000 Curtain walling. Resistance to wind load. Test method.

BS EN 12600: 2002 Glass in building. Pendulum test. Impact test method and classification for flat glass.

BS EN 13116: 2001 Curtain walling. Resistance to wind load. Performance requirements.

BS EN 13119: 2007 Curtain walling. Terminology.

BS EN 13501 Fire classification of construction products and building elements:

Part 1: 2007 Classification using test data from reaction to fire tests.

Part 2: 2007 Classification using data from fire resistance tests, excluding ventilation services.

BS EN 13830: 2003 Curtain walling. Product standard.

BS EN 13947: 2006 Thermal performances of curtain walling. Calculation of thermal transmittance. Simplified method.

BS EN 14019: 2004 Curtain walling. Impact resistance. Performance requirements.

19 ACKNOWLEDGEMENTS

Permission to reproduce extracts from BS 644: 2012 Timber windows and doorsets. Fully furnished factory assembled windows and doorsets of various types. Specification, is granted by BSI. British Standards can be obtained in PDF or hard copy formats from the BSI online shop: www.bsigroup.com/Shop or by contacting BSI Customer Services for hardcopies only: Tel: +44 (0)20 8996 9001, Email: cservices@bsigroup.com.

Images of buildings were supplied by AHR Architects.

Component images and drawings are reproduced with permission from *Materials for Architects and Builders*, Arthur Lyons, 5th edition, Routledge, 2014.

Support and access to technical information through De Montfort University Library and the Leicester School of Architecture is gratefully acknowledged.

8 Thermal environment

Phil Jones

Professor Phil Jones occupies the chair in Architectural Science at the University of Wales, Cardiff

KEY POINTS:
- Safety and comfort for the inhabitants are the main considerations for an internal environment
- The efficient use of energy and reduction in greenhouse gas emissions come a close second

Contents
1 Introduction
2 Heat transfer mechanisms
3 Thermal comfort
4 Site and climate
5 Building fabric
6 Condensation
7 Infiltration and ventilation
8 Heating and cooling systems
9 Prediction and measurement

1 INTRODUCTION

1.1 Thermal design

Thermal design is concerned with the heat transfer processes that take place within a building, and between the building and its surroundings and the external climate, Figure 8.1. It is primarily concerned with providing comfort and shelter for the building's occupants and contents. Thermal design therefore includes consideration of the

- climate
- building form and fabric
- building environmental services
- occupants and processes contained within the building.

It is also concerned with the energy used to provide heating, cooling and ventilation of buildings, and the local and global impact of energy use, especially in relation to carbon dioxide emissions. The thermal design should be integrated with the visual and acoustic aspects of the design in order to achieve an overall satisfactory environmental solution.

1.2 Three stages to thermal design

Stage 1: Internal environmental conditions for occupants or processes

The prime aim is to create spaces that are comfortable, healthy and productive for their occupants, Figure 8.2. People will spend typically 90 per cent of their time indoors. The environments people live and work in must promote a good quality of life. Thermal conditions should be within acceptable comfort limits and the indoor air quality should be free from any harmful pollutants. Buildings must also provide appropriate thermal conditions for their contents, processes and for maintaining the building fabric itself. The required environmental conditions of all spaces should be clearly defined at the initial design stage in relation to the activities and contents of the space.

Stage 2: Climate modification through the building envelope

Buildings can be designed to interact with the external environment in order to benefit from the natural energy of the sun and wind, Figure 8.3. The envelope of the building can be used to 'filter' or 'modify' the external climate to provide internal comfort conditions for much of the year without the use of fuel. The heat from the sun can be used to heat spaces in winter or to drive air movement for ventilation and cooling through

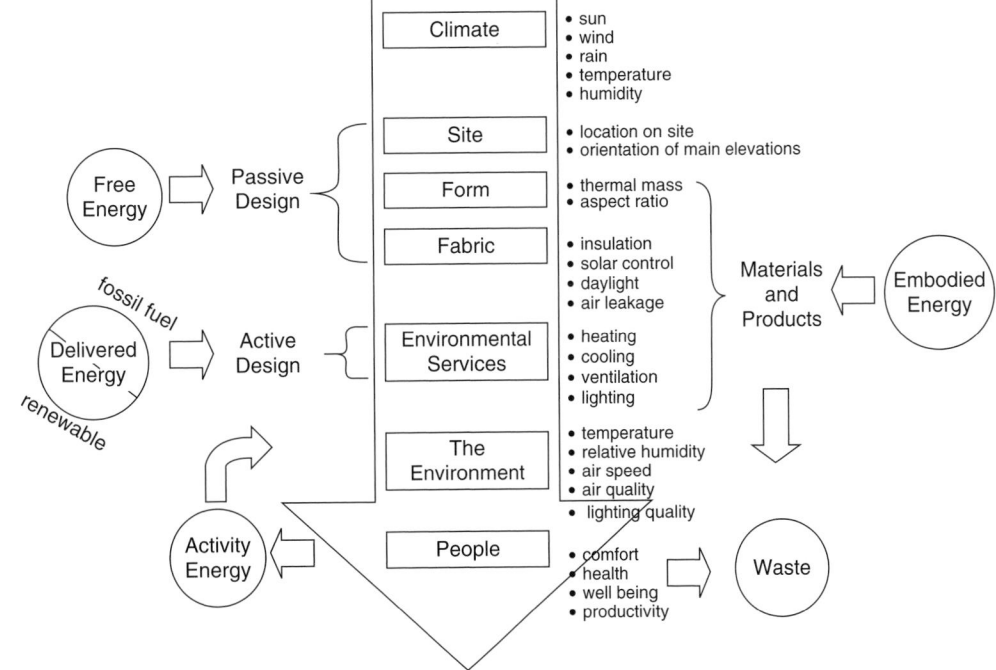

8.1 *Thermal design to achieve comfort for a given climatic condition. Passive design is related to building form and fabric. Active design is related to mechanical services, energy use and environmental impact. The environmental conditions must be suitable for the health and comfort of the occupants. There are a number of energy inputs associated with a building's construction and operation*

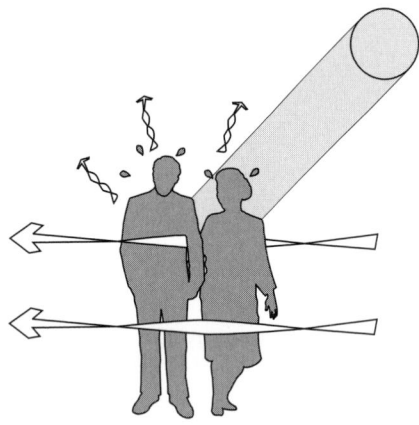

8.2 *Thermal comfort is influenced by air temperature, air movement, relative humidity and the surrounding radiant environment*

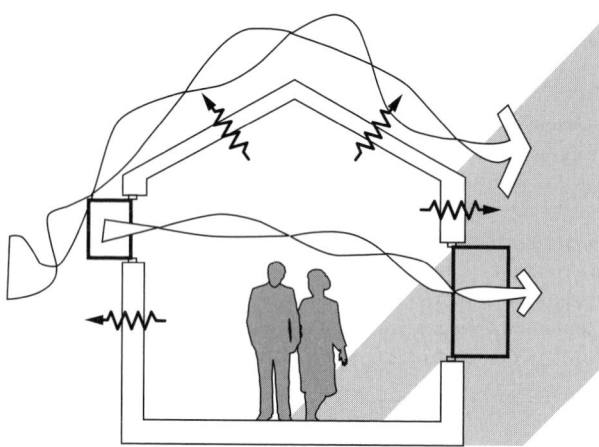

8.3 *Climatic modification can be achieved through manipulation of a building's form and construction usually referred to as Passive Design*

buoyancy forces. The building form and fabric can be used to control solar gains in summer to avoid overheating. The wind can also be used to provide ventilation and cooling. The fabric of the building can be used to insulate against heat loss or gain, and using thermal mass to stabilise the internal environment against extremes of temperatures (hot or cold). The form, mass, orientation and construction of the building need to be designed in response to the climate and specific location. This process is often termed 'passive design'.

Stage 3: Mechanical services
If a building is designed to respond positively to the climate then its dependence on mechanical services to heat, cool and ventilate spaces can be minimised, Figure 8.4. However, there are few climates in the world where mechanical systems can be eliminated altogether. In temperate climates such as the UK a heating system will still generally be required during the winter period, and some buildings require mechanical cooling in summer. In hot climates, mechanical cooling is often needed, sometimes the whole year round, for example, for commercial buildings. These services should be provided in an energy-efficient way in order to minimise energy use from fossil fuels, and to reduce the impact that buildings have on polluting the environment. Low and zero carbon sources of energy should be considered, such as renewable energy sources, including wind power, photovoltaics, solar thermal, biomass, combined heat and power (CHP) and ground source heat pumps. The mechanical systems and their controls should be designed to be able to respond to the specific needs of the occupants and be simple to use. Systems should be commissioned and

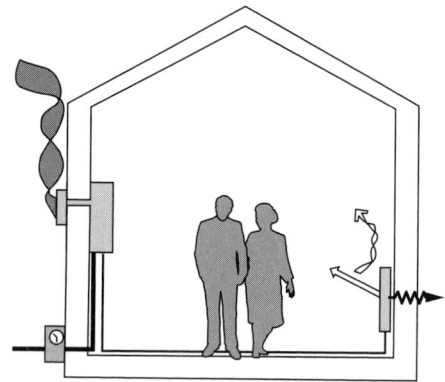

8.4 *Mechanical services should be designed to minimise energy use and environmental impact*

recalibrated against any change of use throughout the lifetime of the building.

It is important to adopt a holistic integrative approach to thermal design incorporating an appropriate blend of architectural (passive design) and engineering (active design) solutions.

1.3 Energy inputs
Thermal design is closely associated with energy use and carbon dioxide emissions. However, of all the energy inputs to a building, Figure 8.1, it is only the energy from fossil fuel sources that have associated carbon dioxide emissions. There will be free energy from the sun, wind and external temperatures that can be used to heat, cool, light and ventilate the building. This passive design approach uses the building's envelope, form and glazing to optimise the benefits from external environmental conditions.

The delivered energy is that used to provide electricity and heat to the environmental systems. This has traditionally been supplied from electricity and gas grid systems and involves the use of fossil fuels either to generate electricity or to produce heat. The aim of sustainable design is to replace fossil fuel sources of delivered energy with renewable and low and zero carbon energy supply systems.

The embodied energy is that associated with processed materials and products used during a building's construction and fit-out. This includes the process energy to acquire natural resources and to produce the materials and components, and the transport energy associated with their production and delivery to site. As the delivered energy is reduced through a more energy efficient design, the embodied energy becomes of increasing significance. In some low carbon buildings the embodied energy is equal to the lifetime delivered energy. The embodied energy is closely linked with the life-cycle and environmental costs of raw materials and material manufacture, lifetime durability and end of use disposal. In sourcing a building material or component the embodied energy is a major factor in determining its sustainability. The use of local materials is favoured as transportation energy costs are reduced. In general terms the more highly processed a material is, the higher its embodied energy. The highest embodied energy is found in metals (steel requires 75,000 kWh/m³), compared to building timber (typically 1500kWh/m³) or those made from salvaged materials or local natural materials, which can require virtually no energy. It is also preferable to use reclaimed materials, or materials with a high recycled content such as metals although the process of recycling adds to their embodied energy. Sustainable design should encourage construction systems which use fewer materials. Some construction types are inherently more wasteful than others. Standardisation, the use of less packaging and using more locally sourced off-site construction methods should be encouraged. Transportation of materials also plays a significant role in embodied energy calculations, especially

Table I Embodied energy of common building materials

Materials	Embodied energy (MJ/Kg)	Embodied carbon (KgC/Kg)
Bricks		
General	3	0.060
Limestone	0.85	–
Cement		
General	4.6+/–2	0.226
Portland cement, wet kiln	5.9	0.248
Portland cement, semi-wet kiln	4.6	0.226
Portland cement, dry kiln	3.3	0.196
Portland cement, semi-dry kiln	3.5	0.202
Fibre cement	10.9	0.575
Mortar (1:3 cement: sand mix)	1.4	0.058
Mortar (1:4)	1.21	0.048
Mortar (1:0.5:4.5 cement: lime: sand mix)	1.37	0.053
Mortar (1:1:6 cement: lime: sand mix)	1.18	0.044
Mortar (1:2:9 cement: lime: sand mix)	1.09	0.039
Soil-cement	0.85	0.038
Concrete		
General 1:2:4 as used in construction of buildings under three storeys	0.95	0.035
Precast concrete, cement: sand: aggregate		
1:1:2	1.39	0.057
1:1.5:3	1.11	0.043
1:2.5:5	0.84	0.030
1:3:6	0.77	0.026
1:4:8	0.69	0.022
Autoclaved aerated blocks (AACs)	3.5	0.076–0.102
Fibre-reinforced	7.75	0.123
Road and pavement	1.24	0.035
Road example	2.85MJ/m²	51KgC/m²
Wood-wool reinforced	2.08	–
Glass		
General	15	0.232
Fiberglass (Glasswool)	18	0.417
Toughened	23.5	0.346
Steel		
General, 'typical' (42.3% recycled content)	24.4	0.482
General, primary	35.3	0.749
General, secondary	9.5	0.117
Bar & rod, 'typical' (42.3% recycled content)	24.6	0.466
Bar & rod, primary	36.4	0.730
Bar & rod, secondary	8.8	0.114
Engineering steel, secondary	13.1	0.185
Galvanised sheet, primary	39	0.768
Pipe, primary	34.4	0.736
Plate, primary	48.4	0.869
Section, 'typical' (42.3% recycled content)	25.4	0.485
Section, primary	36.8	0.757
Section, secondary	10	0.120
Sheet, primary	31.5	0.684
Wire	36	0.771
Stainless	56.7	1.676
Timber		
General	8.5	0.125
Glue laminated timber	12	–
Hardboard	16	0.234
MDF	11	0.161
Particle board	9.5	0.139
Plywood	15	0.221
Sawn hardwood	7.8	0.128
Sawn softwood	7.4	0.123
Veneer particleboard (furniture)	23	0.338

Source: G. P. Hammond and C. I. Jones (2008) Embodied energy and carbon in construction materials. In *Proceedings of the ICE – Energy*, 161/2: 87–98.

where buildings are remotely located. Typically the embodied energy of a house might be between 500 and 1000kWh/m², whilst delivered energy for a house built to current standards might be less than 50kWh/m²/year. Table I gives values of embodied energy in units of Mj/Kg, which can be converted to kWh/m³ by multiplying by (material density/3.6). Values of embodied energy for a specific material can vary depending on the process assumed in their production, including any recycled material.

The activity energy is that derived from the use of the building. This is generally in the form of heat emitted from the

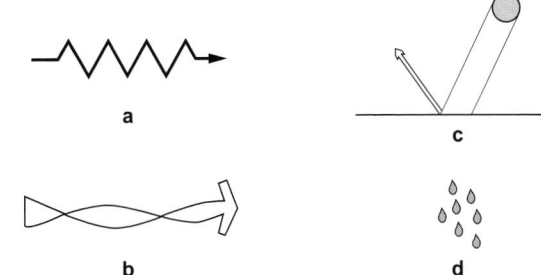

8.5 *Heat is transferred by: a Conduction; b Convection; c Radiation; d Evaporation*

processes of cooking, lighting, the use of small power, and the heat generated by the occupants themselves and the specific processes that occur in buildings. All these can provide a useful heat gain to the building in the winter, but can give rise to overheating in the summer and for some building types even in winter. In many countries, the energy use associated with occupant activities is increasing, through more consumer electrically powered goods. Typical internal energy loads are presented later in Table XXXV.

2 HEAT TRANSFER MECHANISMS

2.1 Introduction

There are four types of heat transfer that relate to thermal environmental design, Figure 8.5. These are conduction, convection, radiation and evaporation. They are described below with examples of how they relate to building thermodynamics.

Heat is a form of energy, measured in joules (J). The rate of energy use is termed power which is measured in watts (W), where:

$$1W = 1J/s \ (1kW = 1000J/s)$$

Another unit of energy is the kilowatt-hour (kWh), where:

$$1kWh = 3600J \ (or \ 3.6MJ)$$

and the therm (which is equal to 100,000 British thermal units (BTU) and is approximately the energy equivalent of burning 100 cubic feet of natural gas) where:

$$1 \ therm = 29.3 \ kWh$$

2.2 Conduction

Conduction normally applies to heat transfer through solids. It is the transfer of heat from molecule to molecule from relatively warm to cool regions. The rate of heat transfer through a solid is dependent on its thermal conductivity, or k-value. The k-value is loosely related to the density of the material, Figure 8.6 (see Table II). High-density materials generally have high k-values – they are termed 'good conductors' of heat (e.g. high-density concrete and metals). Low-density materials have low k-values – they are termed 'good thermal insulators' (e.g. mineral fibre batts and low-density concrete blocks). The thermal resistance of a given thickness of material in a construction is calculated by dividing its thickness by its k-value:

$$R = x/k \tag{1}$$

where R = thermal resistance (m²K/W)
  x = thickness (m)
  k = thermal conductivity (W/m-K)

Materials with a high thermal resistance provide good thermal insulation.

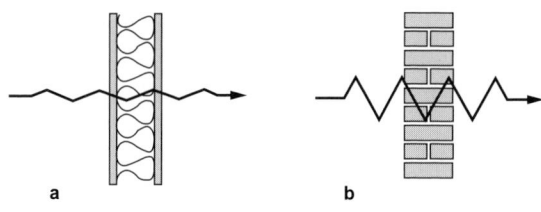

a   b

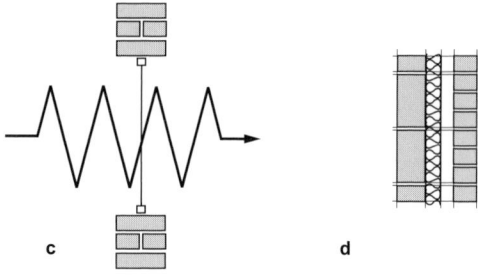

c   d

8.6 *Comparison of thermal conduction properties of different constructions. a Mineral wool has a low density (25kg/m³) and is a good thermal insulator (k = 0.035 W/m-K). b Bricks have a relatively high density (1700kg/m³) and is a fairly poor insulator (k = 0.84 W/m-K). c Glazing has a relatively high density (1700kg/m³) and a poor insulator (k = 1.05 W/m-K). d Walls need to have structural and weatherproofing properties as well as thermal insulation properties. Most wall constructions are therefore composed of a number of layers, the resistances of which can be added to give an appropriate overall thermal resistance of the wall*

Table II Thermal conductivity and density of common building materials

Material	Density (kg/m³)	Thermal conductivity (W/m.K)
Walls		
Brickwork (outer leaf)	1700	0.84
Brickwork (inner leaf)	1700	0.62
Cast concrete (heavyweight)	2000	1.70
Cast concrete (lightweight)	620	0.20
Concrete block (heavyweight, 300mm)	2240	1.31
Concrete block (mediumweight, 300mm)	1940	0.83
Concrete block (lightweight, 300mm)	1800	0.73
Concrete block (insulating)	470	0.11
Cement mortar	1860	0.72
Fibre board (preformed)	240	0.042
Plasterboard	950	0.16
Timber	720	0.14
Glass (solid)	2500	1.05
Surface finishes		
Rendering (moisture content 8%)	1330	0.79
Plaster (dense)	1200	0.52
Plaster (lightweight)	720	0.23
Calcium silicate brick	2000	1.50
Roofs		
Aerated concrete slab	500	0.16
Asphalt (roofing, mastic)	2230	1.15
Roofing felt layer	960	0.19
Screed	1200	0.41
Stone chippings	1800	0.96
Tile	1900	0.84
Wood wool slab	500	0.10
Floors		
Cast concrete (dense, reinforced)	2000	1.30
Screed	2100	0.41
Timber flooring	720	0.14
Insulation		
Expanded polystyrene slab	23	0.035
Glass wool quilt	12	0.040
Glass wool board	25	0.035
Phenolic foam board	30	0.040
Polyurethane board	24	0.023
Paper (cellulose)	43	0.042
Straw board	310	0.05

Source: CIBSE Guide A: Environmental Design, 2006.

The resistivity, *r*, of a material is the inverse of its conductivity *k*, that is,

$$r = 1/k$$

Example 1

What is the thermal resistance of a wall comprising 102.5mm brick, 200mm mineral wool slab insulation, 100mm lightweight concrete block?

Material	Thickness (m)	k-value (W/m/K)	Resistance (m² K/W)
Brick	0.1025	0.84	0.12
Insulation	0.20	0.035	5.71
Block (insulating)	0.10	0.11	0.91
Total thermal resistance	–	–	6.74

Notes:
1) Values for conductivity are from Table II.
2) The thermal resistance of each layer is calculated according to formula 1:R = x/k.
3) The main contribution to the total thermal resistance is from the mineral wool slab insulation.
4) Thermal resistance will be used later in the calculation of *U*-values (in Section 5).

2.3 Convection

Convection takes place in a fluid such as air or water. Once heated the fluid becomes less dense and more buoyant. Fluids are normally heated by conduction from a warm surface such as the electric element in a hot water cylinder, or the hot surface of a panel heater. A cold surface will conduct heat from the adjacent fluid, thereby cooling the fluid. This will make the fluid more dense and cause the fluid to become less buoyant, for example, causing a down-draught from the internal surface of a cold window. For a typical room, the relatively warm and cool surfaces set up a series of interacting convective flow patterns. The convection of air in a room is an integral part of most heating and cooling systems.

In the example, Figure 8.7, heat is conducted from the air to the cooler surface of the glazing, causing a downdraught. Heat is conducted to the air from the warmer surface of the panel heater, causing an updraught. Although panel heaters are usually called radiators they mainly provide heat (typically 60–70 per cent) through convection. The formula for convective heat transfer from a surface to air is:

$$Q_c = h_c x\ (t_a - t_s) \tag{2}$$

where Q_c = convective heat transfer (W)
h_c = convective heat transfer coefficient (Wm⁻²K⁻¹)
t_a = air temperature (°C)
t_s = surface temperature (°C)

Heat flow upwards from a horizontal surface: $h_c = 4.3 Wm^{-2}K^{-1}$
Heat flow downwards from a horizontal surface: $h_c = 1.5\ Wm^{-2}K^{-1}$
Heat flow from a vertical surface: $h_c = 3.0 Wm^{-2}K^{-1}$
Note: Values of h_c are at room temperature (21°C).

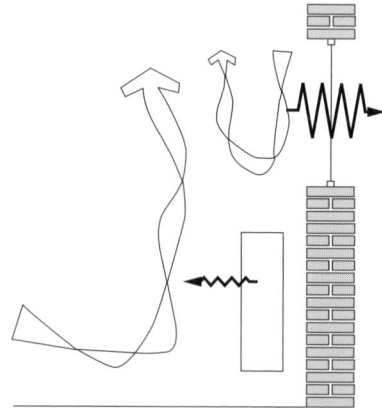

8.7 *Typical convection patterns generated by relatively warm (panel heater) and cool (glazing)*

2.4 Radiation

Radiation is the transfer of heat between two surfaces without heating the air between them. Solar heat travels by radiation from the sun to the earth through the vacuum of space. Radiant heat is in the infrared part of the electromagnetic spectrum (which includes X-rays, ultraviolet, visible light, infrared, microwaves and radio waves – which differ from each other by their wavelength and frequency). The sun emits radiation with wavelengths between 0.29 and 3.0 mm, which includes the visible spectrum (0.38 and 0.78 mm), Figure 8.8. The hotter the emitting body, the shorter the wavelength. Infrared radiation below a wavelength of 3.0 mm (or 3000 nm) is termed short-wave; above this it is termed long-wave. The sun therefore emits most of its heat energy as short-wave radiation, while lower-temperature surfaces, such as buildings, tend to emit only long-wave radiation.

Glass is relatively transparent to short-wave radiation while opaque to long-wave radiation. This is the principle of the 'greenhouse effect', Figure 8.9, which is important in 'passive solar design'. The short-wave radiation from the sun passes through glass and warms up the internal surfaces, which in turn emit long-wave radiation which is 'trapped' within the space. The only heat loss therefore takes place by conduction through the glass. A similar effect takes place in the atmosphere which gives rise to global warming. The 'greenhouse gases' (including carbon dioxide and methane) act like the glass in the greenhouse in letting through the short-wave solar radiation but blocking the longer wave radiation re-emitted by the earth's surface.

Solar radiation incident on solid walls will heat up the external wall surface, Figure 8.10. This heat is conducted through the wall where it will result in a rise in the internal surface temperature. The internal surface will then radiate long-wave radiation in proportion to its surface temperature and emissivity (see Section 2.6). Normal glazing, however, is mostly transparent to 'short-wave' solar radiation and radiative heat is transmitted directly through the glass, Figure 8.11. Some glass types are designed to be more absorbing in order to reduce the direct solar transmission (see also Sections 5.6 to 5.13).

2.5 The Stefan-Boltzmann law

The amount of radiation emitted by a surface is related to its temperature and emissivity according to the Stefan-Boltzmann law:

$$Q_r = (5.673 \times 10^{-8}) \times E \times T^4 \qquad (3)$$

where Q_r = radiation emitted by the surface
E = surface emissivity
T = surface temperature (°C)
5.673×10^{-8} = Stefan-Boltzmann constant (W/m² K⁴)

2.6 Emissivity and absorptance

The emissivity of a surface is the amount of radiation emitted by the surface compared to that radiated by a matt black surface (a 'black body') at the same temperature. The best emitters are matt dark surfaces and the worst are silvered surfaces (although they are good reflectors of radiation). The emissivity of a surface varies between 0 and 1, with most common building materials, such as bricks and plaster, having an emissivity of about 0.85 to 0.95. The absorptivity is the amount of radiation absorbed by a surface compared to that absorbed by a black body. For low-temperature surfaces, values for absorptivity and emissivity are presented in Table III.

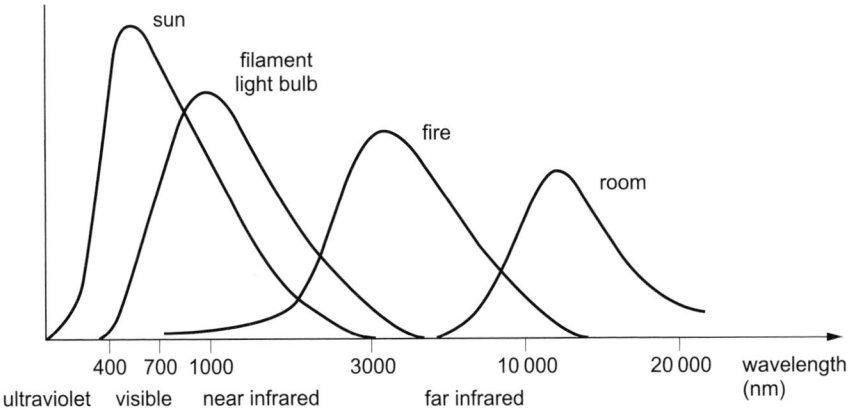

8.8 Spectrum of long-wave (low-temperature) and short-wave (solar) radiation; Vertical axis is not to scale

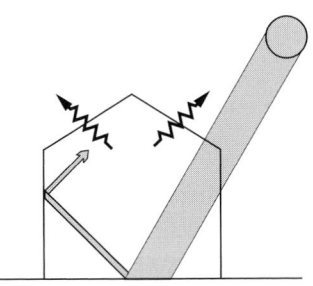

8.9 *Heat transfer process in a greenhouse, which forms the basis of passive solar design*

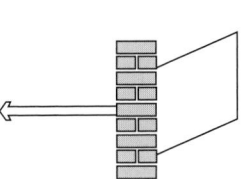

8.10 *Solar radiation incident on a solid wall of passive solar design*

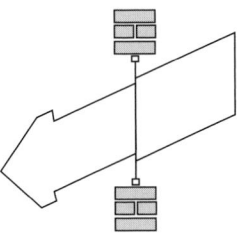

8.11 *Radiation transmission through glass*

Table III Surface emissivities/absorptivities

Finish	Absorptivity	Emissivity
Aluminium, dull/rough polished	0.40–0.65	0.18–0.30
Aluminium, polished	0.10–0.40	0.03–0.06
Asbestos cement, old	0.83	0.95–0.96
Asbestos cement, new	0.61	0.95–0.96
Brick, dark	0.63–0.89	0.85–0.95
Brick, light	0.36–0.62	0.85–0.95
Galvanised iron, new	0.64–0.66	0.22–0.28
Galvanised iron, old	0.89–0.92	0.89
Glass (normal)	–	0.88
Glass (hemispherical)	–	0.84
Limestone	0.33–0.53	0.90–0.93
Marble	0.44–0.592	0.90–0.93
Paint (zinc)	0.30	0.95
Wood, oak	–	0.89–0.90

Source: CIBSE Guide A: Environmental Design, 2006.

2.7 Evaporation

Evaporation takes place when a liquid such as water changes state to a vapour. A vapour is a mixture of gases which exerts a vapour pressure. The water molecules that escape from the liquid tend to have a higher energy content than those left behind and so the average energy content of the liquid is reduced, and therefore its temperature is also reduced. In order for evaporation to take place, the vapour pressure of water (in the form of droplets or a wetted surface) must be greater than the partial pressure of the water vapour in the surrounding atmosphere. The lower the relative humidity of the air, the greater the evaporation that will take place. The evaporation rate can be calculated as follows:

$$W = (8.3 \times 10^{-4})\, h_c/135 \times (p_{va} - p_s) \tag{4}$$

Where W = rate of evaporation from the surface
   h_c = convective heat transfer coefficient
   p_{va} = vapour pressure in air
   p_s = saturation vapour pressure at surface temperature.

Evaporation produces local cooling on wetted surfaces. This can be used to advantage in hot countries where roof ponds, cooled by evaporation, can be used to cool the roof construction. The tradition in some hot dry countries is to simply spray the floors of courtyards with water to cool the floor surface. Air passed over wetted surfaces is cooled and its moisture content is raised. The rate of evaporation increases with increased liquid temperature, reduced vapour pressure of the surrounding atmosphere, or increased air movement across the wetted surface.

Condensation is the reverse of evaporation and takes place when air comes into contact with a relatively cold surface. The air adjacent to the cold surface is cooled and becomes saturated and the vapour condenses into a liquid forming droplets on the surface (condensation is dealt with in more detail in Section 6).

2.8 Thermal capacity

The thermal capacity of a material is a measure of its ability to store heat from the surrounding air and surfaces. Generally, the more dense a material, the greater its capacity to store heat (Table IV). Therefore, high-density materials, such as concrete, will store more heat than low-density materials, such as mineral wool. The thermal capacity of a material can be calculated from the formula:

$$\begin{array}{ll} \text{Thermal capacity} = \text{volume (m}^3) \times \text{density (kg/m}^3) \\ \quad\text{(J/kgK)} \qquad\qquad\quad \times \text{specific heat (J/kg:K)} \end{array} \tag{5}$$

Dense masonry materials typically have 100 times the thermal capacity of lightweight insulating materials (Table IV).

Table IV Density, specific heat and thermal capacity of common materials

Material	Density (kg/m³)	Specific heat (J/kg.K)	Thermal capacity (J/K.m³)
Granite	2880	840	2419×10^3
Brick	1700	800	1360×10^3
Concrete (dense)	2240	840	1882×10^3
Concrete (light)	620	840	521×10^3
Mineral fibre	12	710	9×10^3
Polystyrene board	23	1470	34×10^3

Source: CIBSE Guide A: Environmental Design, 2006.

2.9 Thermal capacity and thermal response

Lightweight buildings will respond quickly to heat gains, Figure 8.12, from either internal sources (people, lights, machines) or external sources (solar radiation, high external air temperatures). They have a relatively low thermal capacity. The internal air will therefore warm up quickly as the mass of the building will have a relatively low capacity to absorb internal heat. They will also cool down quickly when the heat source is turned off, as there is little residual heat in the construction to retain air temperatures. They are more likely to overheat during warm weather and be cool during colder weather. They therefore require a more responsive heating/cooling system, and are more suited to intermittent occupancy.

Heavyweight buildings are slower to respond to changes of temperature, Figure 8.12, and therefore have the potential to maintain a more stable internal environment. Buildings constructed of heavyweight materials will have a high thermal capacity. They will be slow to heat up as the mass of the

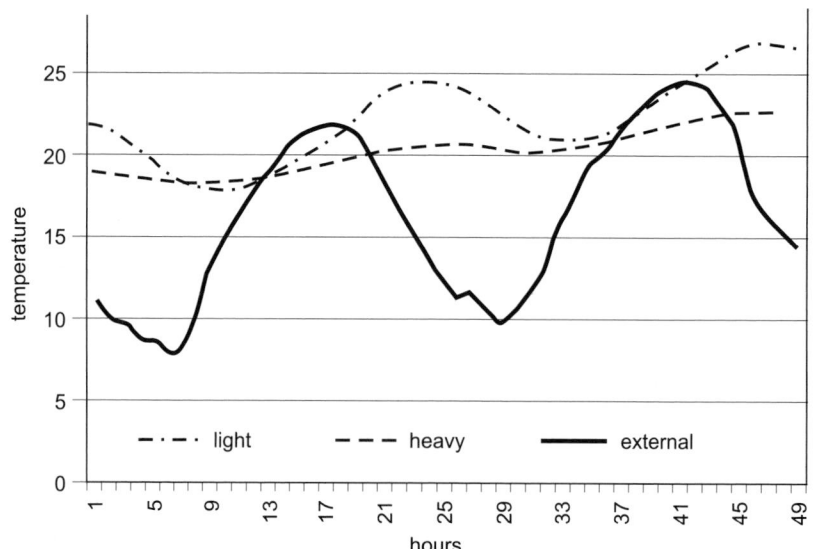

8.12 *Thermal responses of lightweight and heavyweight buildings against external temperature over a two-day period*

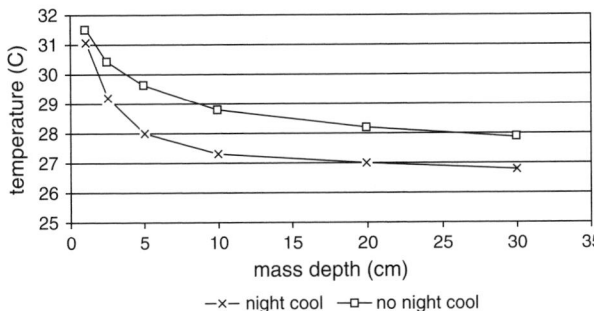

8.13 *Typical reduction in peak temperatures with increasing thermal mass thickness without night cooling (night time infiltration 0.1 ac/h; daytime ventilation 1 ac/h), and with night cooling(nighttime ventilation 5.0 ac/h; daytime ventilation 1 ac/h)*

Table V Metabolic heat generation for different activities at 20°C in MET and in watts (W) for sensible (S) and latent (L) heat loss

Activity	MET	S(W)	L(W)
Seated at rest (theatre, hotel, lounge)	1.1	90	25
Light work (office, dwelling, school)	1.3	100	40
Standing activity (shopping, laboratory)	1.5	110	50
Standing activity (shop assistant, domestic)	2.2	130	105
Medium activity (factory, garage work)	2.5	140	125
Heavy work (factory)	4.2	190	250

Source: CIBSE Guide A: Environmental Design, 2006.

Table VI Clothing resistance in CLO and thermal resistance

	CLO	Thermal resistance (m²K/W)
Nude	0	0
Light summer clothes	0.5	0.08
Light working ensemble	0.7	0.11
Winter indoor	1.0	0.16
Heavy business suit	1.5	0.23

Source: CIBSE Guide A: Environmental Design, 2006.

building will absorb heat from the space. However, they will also be slow to cool down and are able to retain relatively high internal air temperatures between heating periods. Heavyweight buildings can maintain relatively cooler internal environments in warmer weather by absorbing peaks in heat gains. Typical cooling effects may be up to 3° to 5°C reduction, Figure 8.13, in internal air temperature peaks due to thermal mass effects. In addition, the mean radiant temperature will be lower due to the lower surface temperatures. The use of chilled surface cooling is discussed also in Section 8.3.

The thermal mass effect is related to the exposed surface area of material and its thickness and heat capacity. Surface area is relatively more important than thickness of material. For example, for absorbing short-term (diurnal) peaks in heat gain, the thickness of the thermal mass layer needs only be about 5 to 10 cm, Figure 8.13.

3 THERMAL COMFORT

3.1 Introduction
The body produces heat through metabolic activities and exchanges heat with its surroundings by conduction, convection and radiation (typically 75 per cent), and evaporation (typically 25 per cent). Thermal comfort is achieved when there is a balance between metabolic heat production and heat loss. It is mainly dependent on the thermal environmental conditions and the activity and clothing of the person in that environment.

3.2 Metabolic activity
The human body produces metabolic heat as a result of its muscular and digestive processes. It has to maintain a constant core temperature of 37°C. If the core body temperature is reduced by more than about 1°C hypothermia sets in; if it increases by more than about 1°C the person may suffer a heat stroke. The body must therefore lose the metabolic heat it generates in a controlled way. Clothing is one way of controlling heat loss. There are also physiological control mechanisms; for example, shivering when cold increases metabolic activity; the formation of 'goose-pimples' increases the body's surface resistance to heat loss; sweating when warm increases heat loss by evaporation. The heat generated by metabolic activity is measured in units of MET (1 MET = 58.2 W/m² of body surface area; the average surface area of an adult is 1.8 m²). Typical values of MET for different activities are given in Table V.

3.3 Clothing
Clothing provides insulation against body heat loss. The insulation of clothing is measured in units of CLO (1 CLO = 0.155 m²K/W; the units are those of thermal resistance). Values of CLO for typical clothing ensembles are given in Table VI.

3.4 Air temperature
Air temperature is often taken as the main design parameter for thermal comfort. The CIBSE recommended range for internal air temperature is between 19 and 23°C in winter and not exceeding 27°C in summer. The air temperature gradient between head and feet is also important for comfort; the temperature at feet should generally not be less than 4°C below that at head.

3.5 Radiant temperature
Radiant temperature is a measure of the temperature of the surrounding surfaces, together with any direct radiant gains from high temperature sources (such as the sun). The mean radiant temperature is the area-weighted average of all the surface temperatures in a room. If the surfaces in a space are at different temperatures then the perceived radiant temperature in a space will be affected by the position of the person in relation to the various surfaces, with the closer or larger surface areas contributing more to the overall radiant temperature. Comfort can be affected by radiant asymmetry, and people are especially sensitive to warm ceilings (a 10°C radiant asymmetry from a warm ceiling can give rise to 20 per cent comfort dissatisfaction). The vector radiant temperature is a measure of the maximum difference in a room between the radiant temperatures from opposite directions.

3.6 Relative humidity
Relative humidity (RH) of a space will affect the rate of evaporation from the skin. The RH is a percentage measure of the amount of vapour in the air compared to the total amount of vapour the air can hold at that temperature. When temperatures are within the comfort range (19–23°C) the RH has little effect on comfort as long as it is within the range 40–70 per cent. At high air temperatures (approaching average skin temperature of 34°C) evaporation heat loss is important to maintain comfort. Wet bulb temperature is a measure of the temperature of a space using a wetted thermometer. A 'dry bulb' temperature sensor will exchange heat with the surrounding air by convection. A wet bulb thermometer loses additional heat by evaporation and can be used in combination with a dry bulb, to obtain a measure of RH by referring to the psychrometric chart, Figure 8.14. An example of the use of this is shown in Figure 8.15, where a dry bulb temperature (dbt) of 19°C and a wet bulb temperature (wbt) of 14°C indicates a relative humidity (RH) of 60 per cent.

3.7 Air speed
Air speed is a measure of the movement of air in a space. People begin to perceive air movement at about 0.15 m/s. Air speeds greater than 0.2 m/s can produce a 20 per cent and greater comfort dissatisfaction due to perceived draught. For most naturally ventilated spaces the air speed will be less than 0.15 m/s, away from

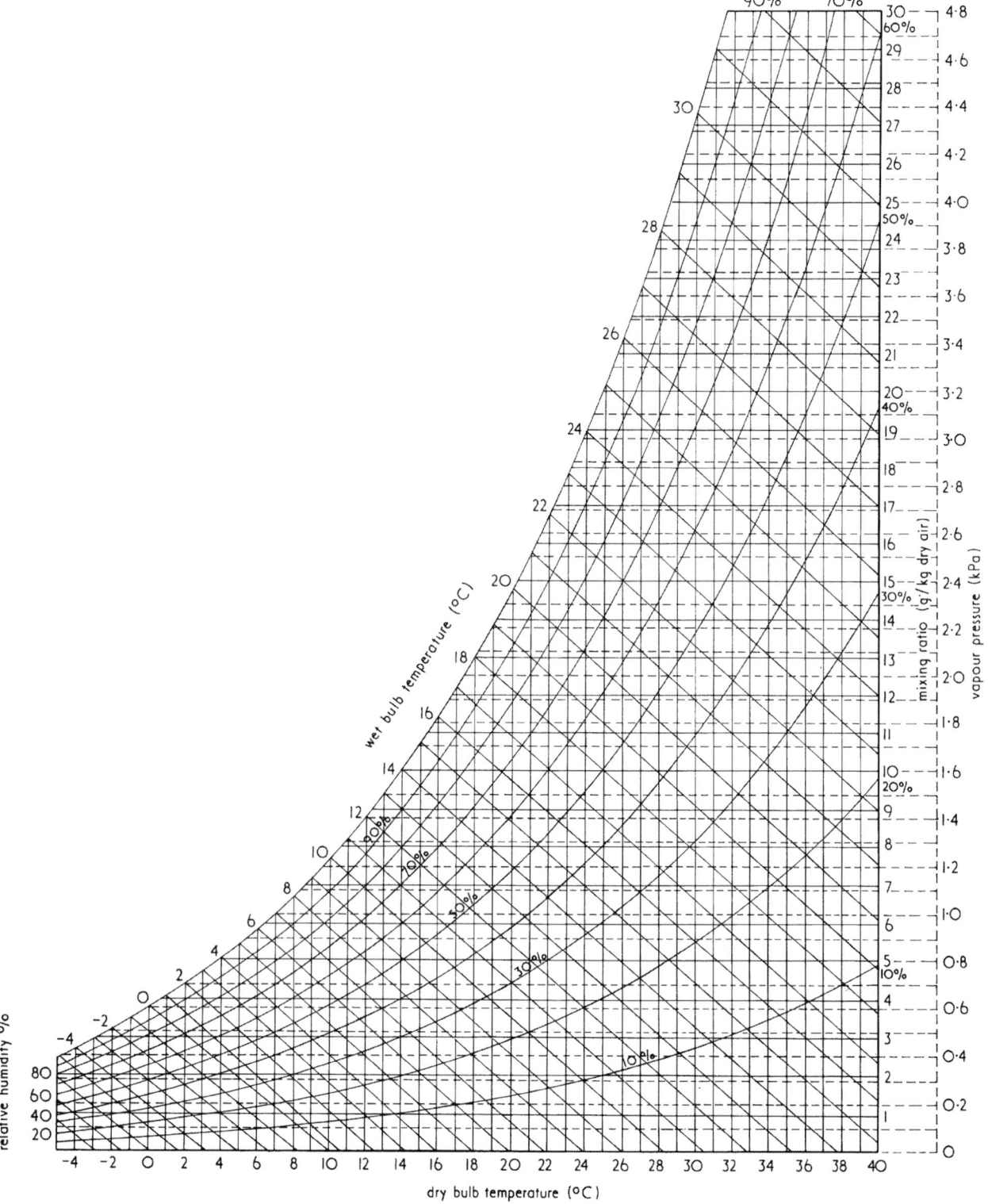

8.14 *Psychrometric chart (from figures in CIBSE Guide). This relates dry bulb temperature, wet bulb temperature and moisture content to relative humidity (RH)*

the influence of open windows and in the absence of major down-draughts from cold internal surfaces. For mechanically ventilated spaces, the air speed is generally greater than 0.15 m/s and could be greater than 0.2 m/s in areas close to air supply devices or where supply air jets are deflected by downstand beams or other geometric features of the space, and such speeds should be avoided. It is possible to counter draught discomfort to a certain extent by increasing air temperatures, as indicated in Figure 8.16.

3.8 Thermal comfort: compensation and adaption

The perception of thermal comfort is a function of the combination of the physical environment (air and radiant temperature, air

movement and relative humidity) and the activity and clothing level of the person. To some extent the environmental factors are compensatory. For example, during cool conditions, an increase in air movement can be compensated for by an increase in air temperature, while in warm conditions, an increase in relative humidity can be compensated for by an increase in air movement. People can also adapt their clothing levels, activity levels and posture in response to the prevailing thermal conditions. In this way they are varying either their rate of metabolic heat production or their rate of body heat loss. Thermal indices use combinations of the comfort parameters in a compensatory way to provide a single measure of thermal comfort.

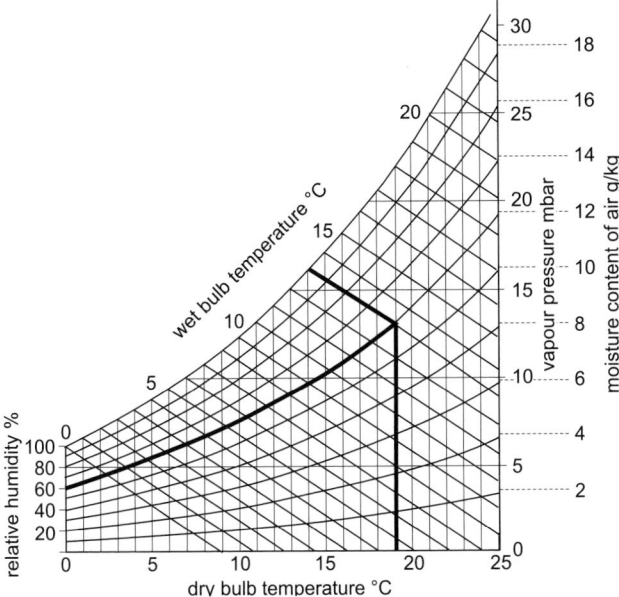

8.15 *A psychrometric chart showing that a dry bulb temperature of 19°C and a wet bulb temperature of WC relates to an RH of 60%*

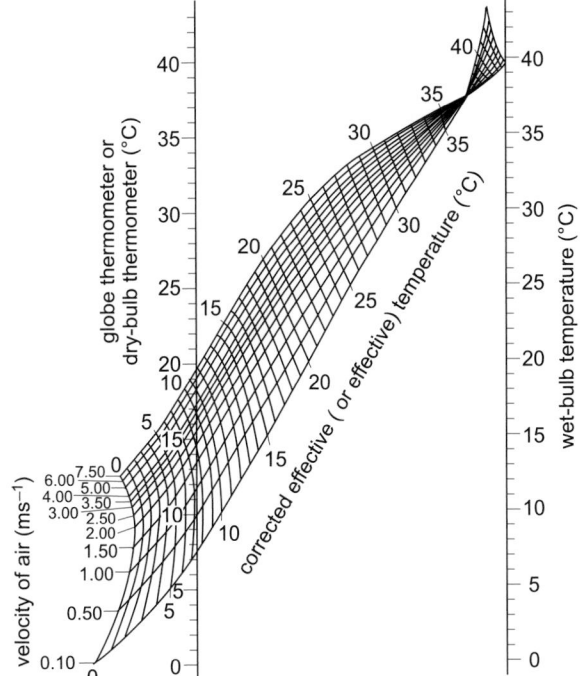

8.17 *Nomogram for estimating corrected effective temperature (CET)*

Hot	+3
Warm	+2
Slightly warm	+1
Neutral	0
Slightly cool	−1
Cool	−2
Cold	−3

The PMV can be calculated from *Fanger's comfort equation* which combines air temperature, mean radiant temperature, RH and air speed together with estimates of activity and clothing levels. The *percentage people dissatisfied (PPD)* provides a measure of the percentage of people who will complain of thermal discomfort in relation to the PMV. This is shown graphically in Figure 8.18 and can be calculated from:

$$PPD = 100 - 95 \exp(10.03353\ PMV^4 - 0.2179\ PMV^2) \qquad (7)$$

The implication of PPD is that there is no condition where every one will experience optimum comfort conditions. It predicts that for a typical occupied work place, there will always be 5 per cent of people who will report discomfort.

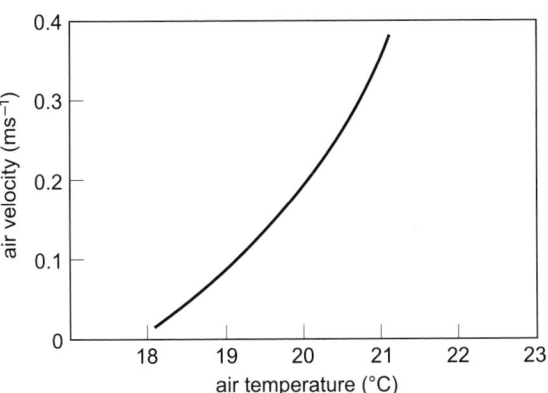

8.16 *The interaction of air temperature and air movement on perceived comfort*

The *resultant temperature*, sometimes called *globe temperature*, can be used to give a more representative measure of comfort than air temperature alone. It is a combination of air temperature and mean radiant temperature, in a proportion comparable to that of the body's heat loss. At low air speeds (<0.1 m/s) the following relationship can be applied:

$$t_{res} = 0.5\ t_{mrt} + 0.5\ t_a \qquad (6)$$

where t_{res} = resultant temperature (°C)
t_{mrt} = mean radiant temperature (°C)
t_a = air temperature (°C)

The resultant temperature can be measured at the centre of a black globe of 100 mm diameter (although globes between 25 and 150 mm will give acceptable results).

The *corrected effective temperature (CET)* relates globe temperature, wet bulb temperature and air speed. It is equivalent to the thermal sensation in a standard environment with still, saturated air for the same clothing and activity. CET can be represented in nomogram form as shown in Figure 8.17.

3.9 PMV and PPD

The *predicted mean vote (PMV)* is a measure of the average response from a large group of people voting on the scale below:

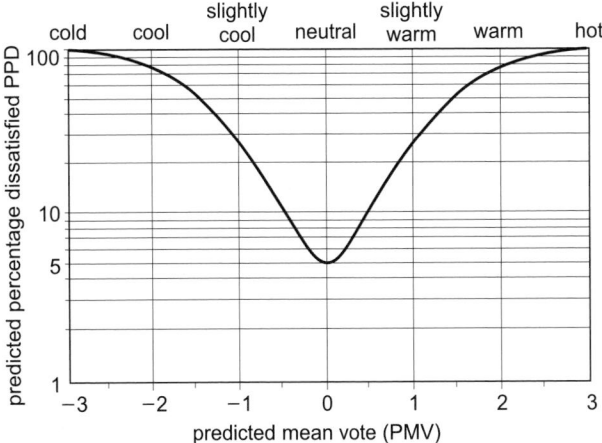

8.18 *PPD as a function of PMV*

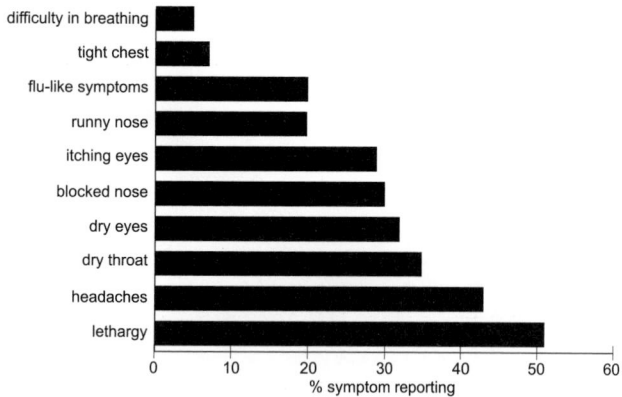

8.19 *Sample percentage sick building syndrome symptom reporting for air conditioned offices*

Table VII Air and infiltration rates for building types

Type of building	Air t_{ei} (°C)	Air infiltration allowance (h^{-1})
Art galleries and museums	19–21	1
Assembly and lecture halls	22–23	0.5
Airport terminals:		
Baggage reclaim	12–19	
Check-in areas	18–20	
Customs areas	12–19	
Departure lounges	19–21	
Banking halls	19–21	1–1.5
Bars	20–22	1
Canteens and dining rooms	22–24	1
Churches and chapels	19–21	0.5–1
Computer rooms	19–21	
Conference/board rooms	22–23	
Dining and banqueting halls		0.5
Exhibition halls	9–21	0.5
Factories:		
Sedentary work	19–21	
Light work	16–19	
Heavy work	11–14	
Up to 300m³ volume		1.5–2.5
300m³ to 3000m³		0.75–1.5
3000m³ to 10,000m³		0.5–1.0
Over 10,000m³		0.25–0.75
Fire stations, ambulance stations:		
Watch rooms	22–23	0.5–1
Recreation rooms	20–22	0.5–1
Gymnasia		0.75
Flats, residences and hostels:		
Living rooms	20–23	1
Bedrooms	17–19	0.5
Bed-sitting rooms		1
Bathrooms	26–27	2
Toilets	19–21	1.5
Service rooms		0.5
Hall/Stairs/Landing	19–24	1.5
Kitchen	17–19	
Public rooms		1
Hospitals:		
Wards and patient area	22–24	2
Circulation spaces	19–24	1
Consulting/treatment rooms	22–24	
Nurses stations	19–22	1
Operating theatres	17–19	0.5
Waiting rooms		1
Storerooms		0.5
Hotels:		
Bathrooms	26–27	1
Bedrooms	19–21	1
Public rooms		1
Corridors		1.5
Foyers		1.5
Laboratories		1
Law courts	19–21	1
Libraries:		
Reading rooms	22–23	0.5–0.7
Stack rooms	19–21	0.5
Store rooms	15	0.25
Offices:		
General	21–23	1
Executive	21–23	
Open plan	21–23	
Private		1
Storerooms		0.5
Police cells	19–21	5
Railway/coach stations		
Concourse (no seats)	12–19	
Ticket office	18–20	
Waiting room	21–22	

Table VII (continued)

Type of building	Air t_{ei} (°C)	Air infiltration allowance (h^{-1})
Restaurants and cafes	22–24	1
Schools and colleges:		
Classrooms	19–21	2
Lecture rooms	19–21	1
Studios	19–21	1
Retail buildings:		
Shopping malls	19–24	
Small shops, department stores	19–21	
Supermarkets	19–21	
Sports pavilions:		
Dressing rooms	22–24	1
Hall	13–16	
Squash courts	10–12	
Swimming pools:		
Changing rooms	23–24	0.5
Pool hall	23–26	0.5
Television studios	19–21	
Warehouses:		
Working and packing spaces		0.5
Storage space		0.2

The values quoted for rates of air infiltration in this table should not be used for the design of mechanical ventilation, air conditioning or warm air heating systems.

3.10 Sick building syndrome (SBS)

This is a term used to describe a set of commonly occurring symptoms that affect people at their place of work, usually in office-type environments, and which disappear soon after they leave work. These symptoms include dry eyes, watery eyes, blocked nose, runny nose, headaches, lethargy, tight chest and difficulty with breathing. A typical percentage of symptom reporting for air-conditioned offices is shown in Figure 8.19. *The personal symptom index (PSI) is often used as a measure of the average number of symptoms per person for a whole office or zone.*

Workers who report high levels of symptoms also often report problems associated with thermal comfort, and in general perceive the air quality as stale, dry and warm. Studies have indicated that air-conditioned buildings appear to have a higher level of complaint of SBS than naturally ventilated buildings. Possible reasons for this include cost cuts in their design, difficulties and complexities in their maintenance and operation, problems associated with hygiene and cleanliness (especially the air-distribution ductwork) and low ventilation effectiveness due to short-circuiting between supply and extract. Workers with a higher risk of symptoms are those in open-plan offices more than those in cellular ones, clerical workers more than managerial, women more than men, those in public sector buildings more than private, those in air-conditioned offices more than naturally ventilated ones, and those buildings where there is poor maintenance and poor operation of controls.

3.11 Ventilation and indoor air quality

Ventilation is required to maintain good air quality for health and comfort. Tables VII and VIII give recommended values for internal temperatures, infiltration rates and ventilation rates. The outside air requirement for occupants is generally taken as 10l/s/person. Ventilation is considered in more detail in Section 7.

Table VIII Ventilation rates for various types of building

Building use	Air supply rate
Public and commercial buildings	8L/Person
Hotel bathrooms	12L/Person
Hospital operating theatres	650 to 1000m³/s
Toilets	>5 air change per hour
Changing rooms	10 air change per hour
Squash courts	4 air change per hour
Ice rinks	3 air change per hour
Swimming pool halls	1.5L/m² (of wet area)
Bedrooms and living rooms in dwellings	0.4 to 1 air change per hour
Kitchens in dwellings	60L/s
Bathrooms in dwellings	15L/s

Source: CIBSE Guide B: Heating, Ventilating, Air Conditioning and Refrigeration, 2005.

4 SITE AND CLIMATE

4.1 Introduction

The site and climatic conditions have a major impact on the thermal design of a building, and should be considered during the early stages of design. Also, the building will modify the existing climate of the site to create a specific microclimate surrounding itself and affecting the microclimate of existing neighboring buildings. Climate data is available for many parts of the world, often as hourly values compiled into a standard *Test Reference Year (TRY)* format. The climate conditions that relate directly to thermal design include:

- solar radiation, sun path and cloud cover;
- wind speed and direction;
- air temperature;
- relative humidity;
- rainfall and driving rain index.

4.2 Solar radiation and sun path

Solar radiation impacts on the building in three forms, Figure 8.20:

- direct radiation, from the position of the sun in the sky;
- diffuse radiation, from the whole of the visible sky;
- reflected radiation *(albedo)* from adjacent surfaces.

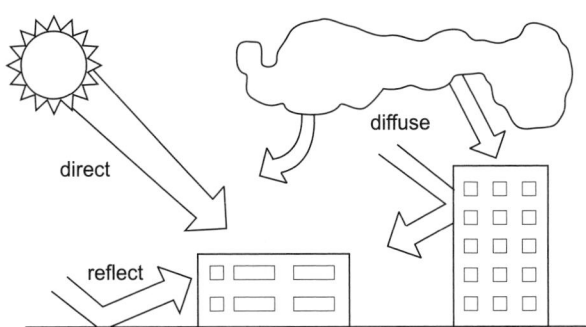

8.20 *Direct, diffuse and reflected solar radiation*

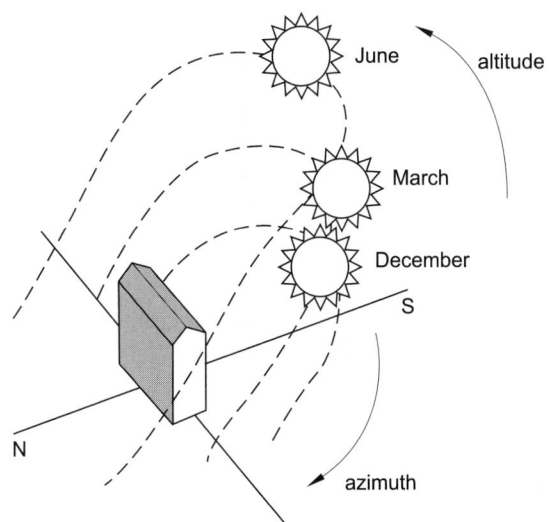

8.21 *Sun angles indicating azimuth and altitude*

All three components will vary according to time of day, time of year and cloud cover, and how much sky is seen by the building depending on natural and man-made obstructions. The solar path can be determined from the altitude and azimuth angles of the sun as in Figure 8.21. Typical values of solar radiation are given in Tables IX and X, and the effect of sun angle and overshadowing in Figure 8.22. The annual variation of possible hours of daily sunshine for the UK is presented in Figure 8.23.

Table IX Solar altitude, and direct and diffuse solar radiation (cloudy and clear sky) at mid-day for South-east England

Month	Altitude	Direct Normal (W/m²)	Diffused (W/m²) Cloudy	Clear
June	64	900	310	100
July/May	60	895	295	100
August/April	52	865	255	95
September/March	40	815	195	85
October/February	2	700	140	75
November/January	20	620	90	60
December	17	560	75	50

Table X Daily mean solar irradiances (W/m²) on vertical and horizontal surface, diffused for cloudy/clear sky condition

	S	SE/SW	E/W	NE/NW	N	H	DF
June	105	135	140	85	35	295	120/50
July/May	110	140	135	75	20	270	110/45
August/April	150	150	115	45	5	215	90/40
September/March	175	145	80	20	0	140	60/30
October/February	165	120	50	5	0	80	35/20
November/January	125	90	25	0	0	35	20/15
December	100	70	20	0	0	25	15/10

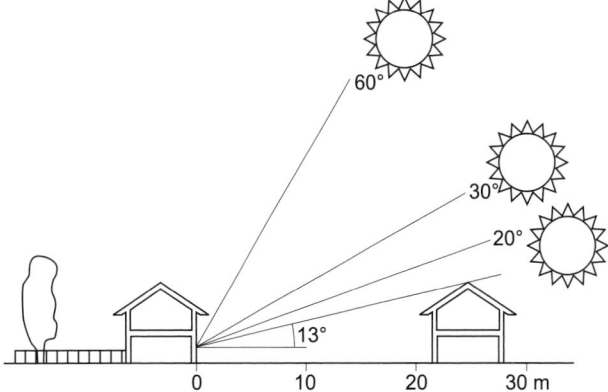

8.22 *Sun angle and overshadowing*

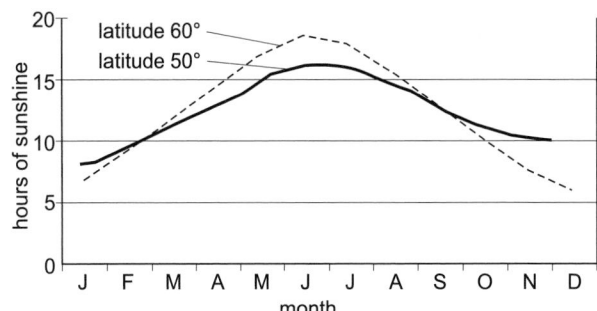

8.23 *The annual variation of possible hours of sunshine for the UK. Northern regions receive more hours in summertime*

The largest component of solar radiation is the direct radiation, but the reflected radiation can be significant where there are hard light-coloured reflective surfaces adjacent to the building, either from the built form itself or from existing buildings and landscaping. Table XI contains data on reflected radiation for different surfaces (the solar absorption of a surface is: 1 – reflectance).

Cloud cover is measured in octal on a scale of 0 to 8, with 0 being completely cloudless and 8 completely overcast. The diffuse radiation component will be higher for an overcast sky as shown in Table IX. Cloudiness (C) is a measure of the proportion of cloud in the sky. C is zero for a clear sky and 1 for an overcast sky.

4.3 External air temperature

The external air temperature will affect the rate of transmission and convective heat loss from a building. It will typically vary over a

Table XI Reflected radiation for different surfaces

Surface	Reflectance (R)
Glass	0.10
Concrete, light grey	0.25—0.40
Brick, fletton	0.30
Brick, white gault	0.70
Timber panelling, oak	0.25
Plaster, pink	0.65
White emulsion paint on plain plaster surface	0.80
White emulsion paint on no-fines concrete	0.60
White emulsion paint on wood wool slab	0.50
White asbestos cement; Portland cement, smooth	0.40
Portland cement, rough	0.25
Cement screed	0.45
PVC tile, cream/brown/dark brown	0.45/0.25/0.10
Paper, white	0.80
Stainless steel	0.35
Asphalt	0.15
Uncultivated field	0.26
Bare soil	0.17
Grass	0.25
Water	0.05–0.22
Snow (fresh)	0.80–0.90
Snow (old)	0.45–0.70

Source: CIBSI Lighting Guide LG10:1999.

24-hour period (the diurnal variation) and over a year (seasonal variation). It will also vary with location. Table XII presents the average monthly external air temperature for different locations within the UK. Figure 8.24 shows the typical diurnal temperature variations for southern England.

4.4 Sol-air temperature

When solar energy is absorbed by an external wall it has the same effect, in relation to heat loss, as a rise in external air temperature. The sol-air temperature is the external air temperature which, in the absence of solar radiation, would give rise to the same heat transfer through the wall as takes place with the actual combination of external temperature and incident solar radiation:

$$t_{sa} = (\alpha I_s + \varepsilon I_l)\, R_{so} + t_{ao} \tag{8}$$

where t_{sa} = sol-air temperature
t_{ao} = external air temperature
α = solar absorptance
ε = long-wave emissivity
R_{so} = external surface resistance
I_s = solar irradiance (W/m²)
I_1 = long-wave radiation loss (W/m²)
= 93–79 C (horizontal surfaces)
= 21–17 C (vertical surfaces)
C = cloudiness (see para 4.2)

4.5 External relative humidity

The external RH will vary with external air temperature and moisture content of the air. During periods of warmer weather, the RH may be relatively low due to the higher external air temperatures, although at night it will rise as the air temperature falls, Figure 8.25. During cold weather the external RH can rise typically to over 90 per cent. Figure 8.26 presents seasonal average RH values for the UK.

4.6 Rainfall and driving rain index

Rainfall can affect thermal performance. If an external surface is wet then it will lose heat by evaporation and this will reduce the external surface temperature, sometimes to below air temperature, increasing heat loss. Wind-driven rain ('driving rain') can penetrate some constructions, causing a reduction in thermal resistance. In areas of high incidence of driving rain, care must be taken to select constructions that provide protection against rain penetration.

4.7 Wind

The impact of wind on a building has two main consequences for thermal design. It affects the convective heat loss at the external

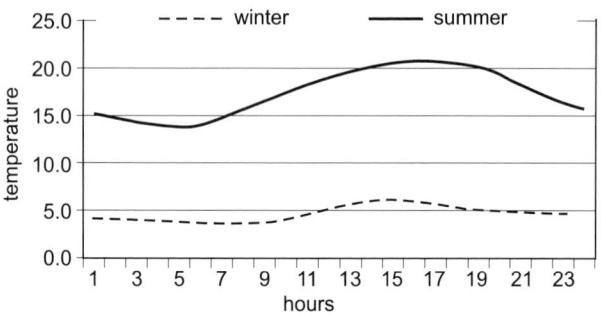

8.24 *Diurnal UK variations for winter (January) and summer (June) for south-east England*

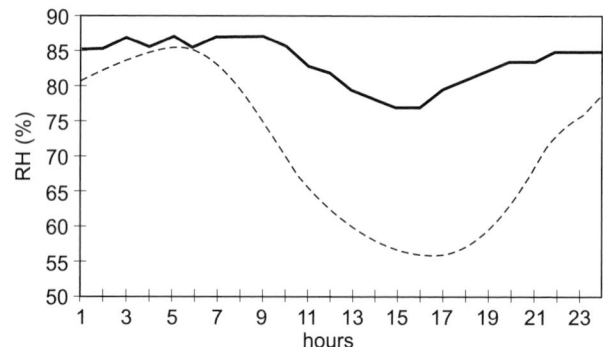

8.25 *Diurnal RH variation for January (solid) and June (dotted)*

Table XII UK average daily temperature

	J	F	M	A	M	J	J	A	S	O	N	D	Annual
Belfast													
Max.	8.3	10.8	11.3	15.3	18.9	19.5	23.4	23.6	19.5	15.6	11.7	12.9	15.9
Min.	−2.2	−1.7	0.4	2.8	2.6	4.6	8.1	9.0	7.1	2.0	0.6	−0.2	2.8
Ave.	4.0	4.1	6.0	7.9	10.8	12.7	14.9	14.6	11.9	9.7	6.6	5.2	9.0
Glasgow													
Max.	11.0	11.1	12.6	13.4	16.2	21.0	22.2	24.4	20.4	18.4	14.2	11.5	16.4
Min.	−2.3	−4.8	−3.6	−1.7	0.5	3.5	6.4	7.0	4.2	−1.0	−2.9	−3.2	0.2
Ave.	4.8	3.7	6.0	6.5	9.8	13.3	14.8	14.3	12.3	9.9	5.1	5.5	8.8
London													
Max.	10.1	9.7	13.1	13.7	19.7	23.5	30.3	25.6	20.7	17.3	17.1	13.7	17.9
Min.	−1.3	−2.2	1.4	0.0	3.5	6.2	10.3	9.4	7.5	1.4	2.6	−1.1	3.1
Ave.	5.3	3.4	8.0	8.1	11.2	15.8	19.7	16.9	13.1	9.9	10.4	6.7	10.7
Cardiff													
Max.	13.9	14.7	14.9	14.3	22.7	23.5	22.6	26.8	23.1	18.4	15.1	12.2	18.5
Min.	2.5	1.7	4.1	3.3	6.2	9.3	10.6	11.6	9.4	4.9	1.6	−1.1	5.3
Ave.	7.5	9.1	10.1	9.4	15.6	15.7	16.9	17.4	15.6	12.2	8.1	7.5	12.1

Source: Energy Plus Weather Data.

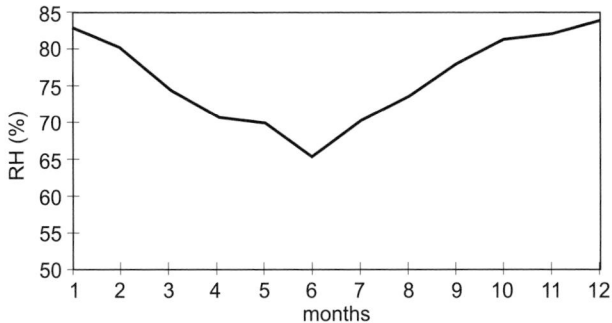

8.26 *Seasonal average daily RH values for the UK*

surfaces, as well as the ventilation and infiltration rate and the associated heat loss.

4.8 Wind speed and direction

Wind speed is measured in m/s or sometimes in knots where 1 knot equals 0.4 m/s. Wind direction is usually measured at eight points of the compass or, when required in more detail, in degrees clockwise from south. The wind speed and direction can be represented by a *wind rose*, Figure 8.27, which indicates the relative frequency and speed of wind from different directions.

It is often useful to know the average temperatures associated with each wind direction, Figure 8.28. For example, for a specific location, the main prevailing wind may have relatively warmer temperatures, whereas a less frequent wind direction might have cold temperatures and give rise to greater problems.

Wind speed increases with height due to the frictional drag of the ground. The profile of variation with height is called the *boundary layer,* and it will vary from town to open country locations, as shown in Figure 8.29, and according to the relationship:

$$v/v_r = kH^a \qquad (9)$$

where v = mean wind speed (m/s) at height H (m)
v_r = mean wind speed (m/s) at height 10 m
values of k and a from Table XIII

4.9 Dynamic and static wind pressures

The static pressure (P_s) of the air is the pressure in the free-flowing air stream (as shown on the isobars of a weather map). Differences in static pressure arise from global thermal effects and cause windflow. The dynamic pressure (P_d) is the pressure exerted when the wind comes into contact with an object such as a building, Figure 8.30. The total or stagnation pressure (P_t) is the sum of the static and dynamic pressures $(P_t = P_s + P_d)$. In most cases P_s can be ignored in thermal design as it is usual to deal with pressure differences across a building, i.e. the difference in P_d. The dynamic wind

Table XIII   Values of coefficients for formula (9)

Terrain	k	a
Open, flat country	0.68	0.17
Country with scattered wind breaks	0.52	0.19
Urban	0.35	0.22
City	0.21	0.24

Source: CIBSE Guide A: Environmental Design, 2006.

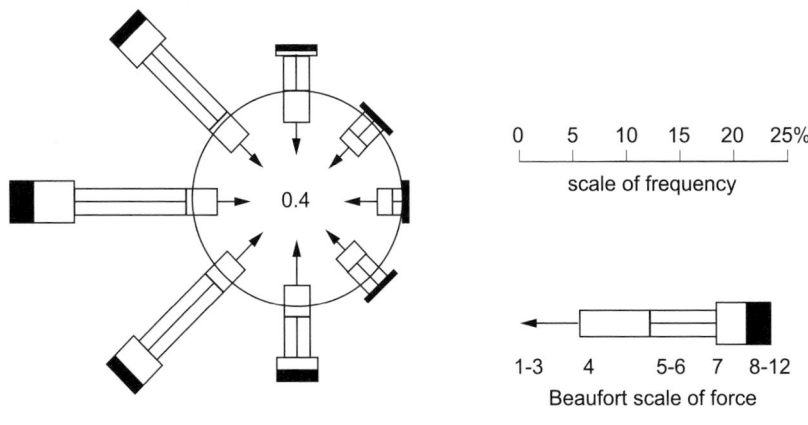

8.27 *Standard wind rose*

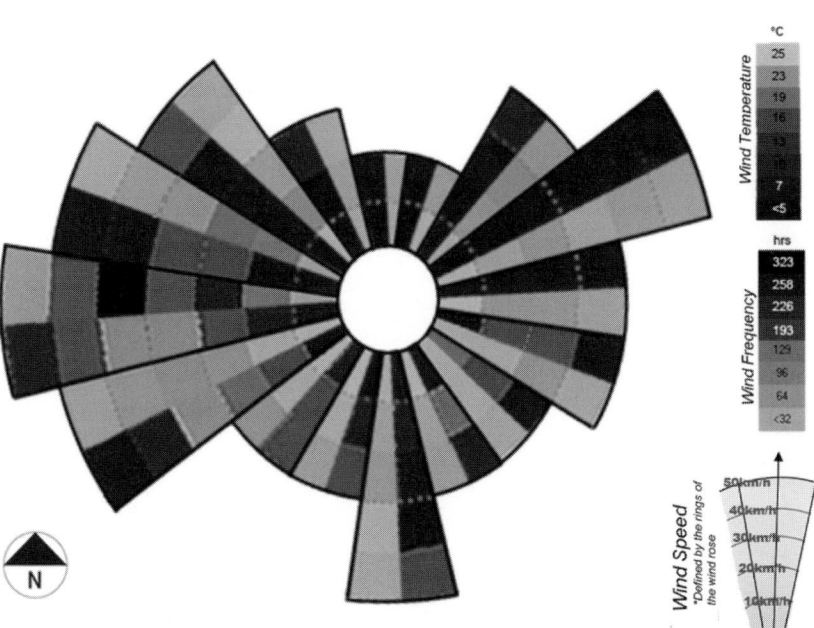

8.28 *Wind rose with temperature*

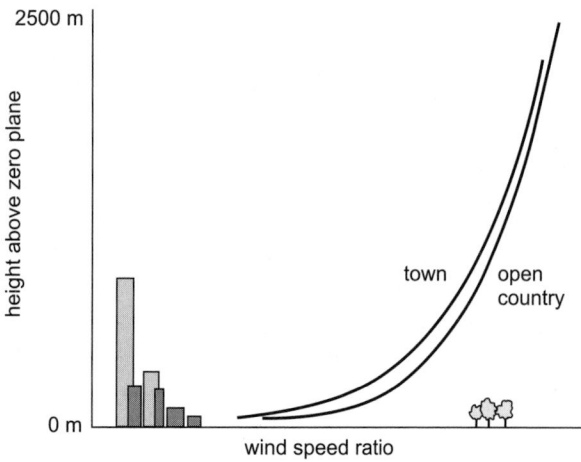

8.29 *Boundary layer wind profile*

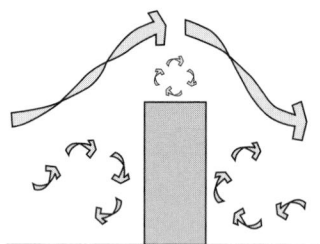

8.30 *Wind pressure over a building envelope*

pressure is related to the air density (ρ) and the square of the wind speed (*v*) ($P_d = 0.5 . ρ . v^2$ (Pa)).

4.10 Pressure coefficients

The impact of wind on the building form generally creates areas of positive pressure on the windward side of a building and negative pressure on the leeward and sides of the building. The pressure coefficient is the relative pressure at a specific location on the building and it can be used to calculate the actual dynamic pressure for a given wind speed and air density.

$$P_d = C_p \times 0.5 \, ρv^2 \text{ (Pa)} \qquad (10)$$

where ρ = density of the air (kg/m)
  v = wind speed (m/s) at a reference height, *h* (m)
  C_p = pressure coefficient measured with reference to the wind speed at the height *h*.

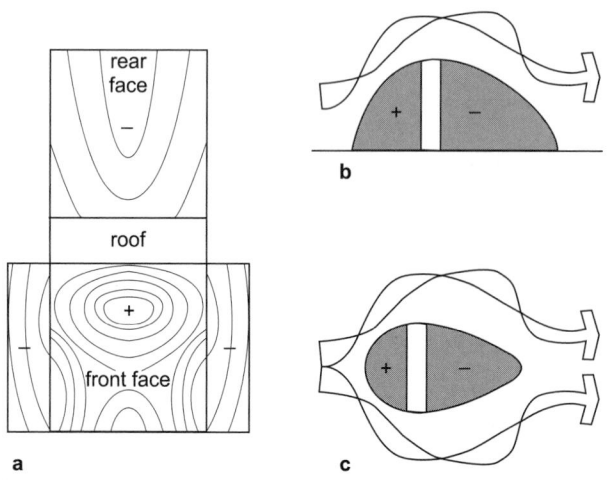

8.31 *Pressure coefficients can be manipulated by the form of the building: a Pressure distribution; b Section; c Plan*

The pressure coefficients are dependent on general building form, as shown in the example in Figure 8.31. A scale model of the building can be placed in a wind tunnel to predict C_{ps}. Building form is the main determinant of pressure distribution for a given wind direction. Openings should then be located to produce the required 'cross-ventilation' from pattern, Figure 8.32.

4.11 External sheltered areas

There are 'rules of thumb' which can be applied to estimate the impact of wind on buildings, in relation to creating external sheltered areas (e.g. courtyards). These are shown in Figure 8.33. The figures show that distances between buildings should be less than about 3.5 times the building height, in order to create shelter from the prevailing wind.

Barriers can be used to reduce wind speed and create external sheltered areas. Porous barriers are often more suitable than 'hard' barriers as they reduce wind speed and do not induce counter wind flow areas as shown in Figure 8.34. High wind conditions can be created by downdraughts from tall buildings (as in Figure 8.30), wind 'canyons' or acceleration around corners Figure 8.35.

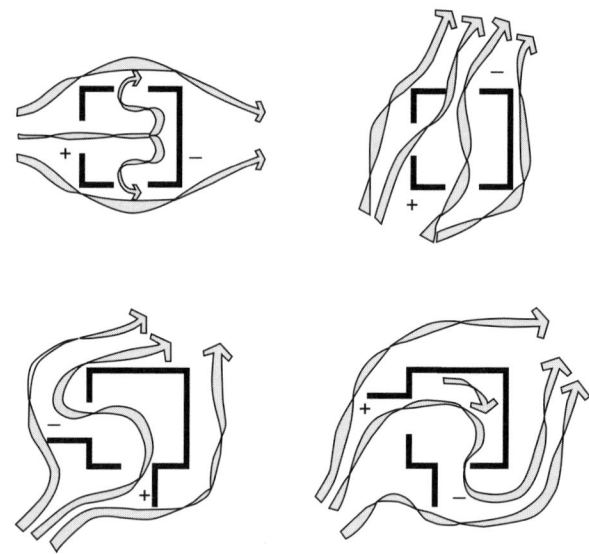

8.32 *Typical wind flow pattern around a high-rise building*

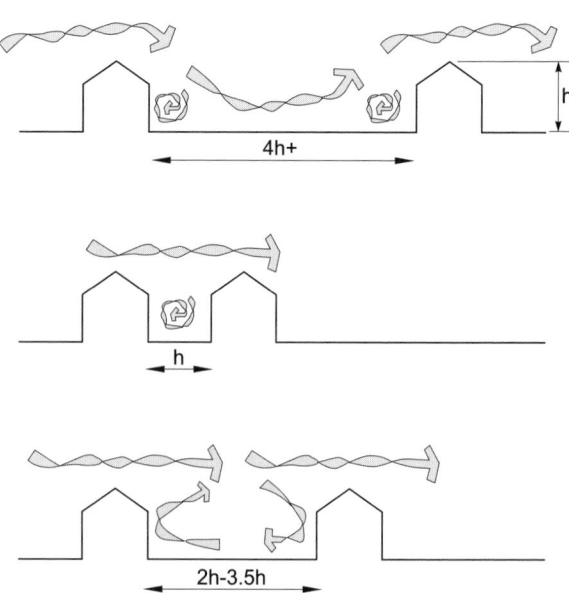

8.33 *Building spacing and provision of sheltered external spaces*

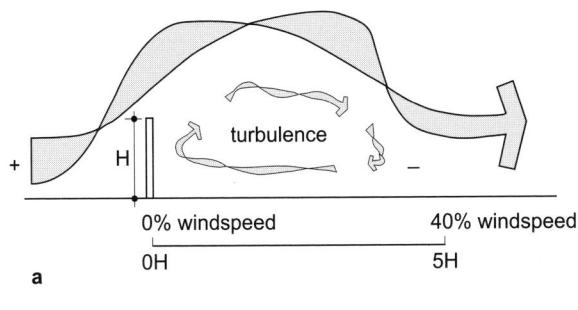

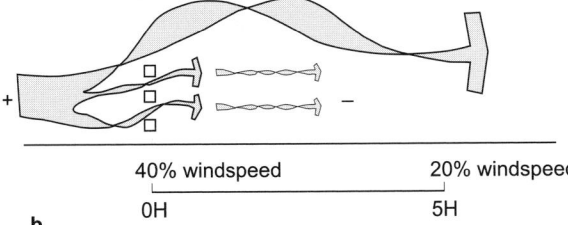

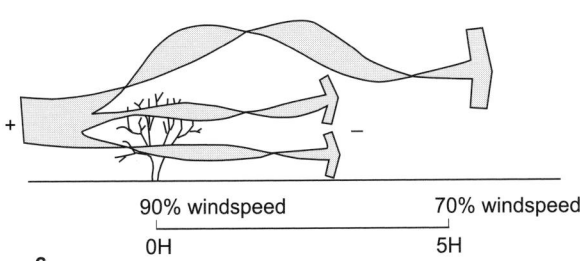

a
0% windspeed   40% windspeed
OH   5H

b
40% windspeed   20% windspeed
OH   5H

c
90% windspeed   70% windspeed
OH   5H

8.34 *Barriers and their effect on wind flow: a Dense barrier; b Medium barrier; c Loose barrier*

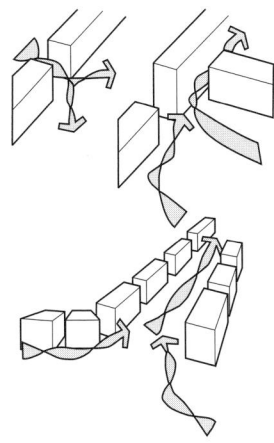

8.35 *Localised high wind speeds can be caused by 'canyon' effects and acceleration around corners*

4.12 Site analysis

An overall site analysis should identify the prevailing wind, the seasonal sun paths, and existing shelter and obstructions, well as other aspects, such as noise sources and views, as in Figure 8.36.

4.13 Global warming

It is now generally accepted that there will be global warming based on the past emission of greenhouse gases. The current predicted average temperature rise due to global warming for the UK is around 2°C by the middle of this century, and between 3 and 6°C by the end of the century. By 2080 degree days are predicted to fall by about between 25 to 40 per cent from north UK down to London respectively, and since the early 1980s until now there has already been a 10 per cent reduction. Buildings should therefore be designed to respond to future weather data rather than historical data and there is now future weather data available through CIBSE. The thermal design will likely be affected by increases in

8.36 *Example of environmental site analysis*

temperature and increases in extreme events of wind and rain. In some countries there may be untypical cooler periods, for example in the hotter places where heating was not required there may be the need in future, while in more temperate climates cooling may become more an issue. The predicted increase in summer temperatures in temperate climates might lead to the adoption of a heavyweight construction with ventilation night cooling or ground cooling. There should be more attention to shading and microclimate design to reduce heat gains. There is therefore the need to adopt an adaptive approach to design to allow for future climate change, as well as a mitigating approach to reduce carbon dioxide emissions in order to reduce climate change.

5 BUILDING FABRIC

5.1 U-values

The U-value of the wall, roof or floor element of a building can be used to provide an estimate of its heat loss (or gain). The U-values of typical construction types are given in Table XIV. The U-value of a wall construction can be calculated using the following procedure:

1 Calculate the resistance of the individual layers of the construction (see Section 2 and refer to *k*-values in Table I).

$$R_{1,2,3...} = x/k \qquad (11)$$

where $R_{1,2,3...}$ = thermal resistance of element 1, 2, 3 . . . (m²K/W)
x = thickness (m)
k = thermal conductivity (W/mK)

Select the appropriate values for the internal and external surface resistances $(R_s i$ and $R_{se})$ by referring to Tables XV and XVI.

2 Select the appropriate resistance of any air cavities (R_{cav}) by referring to the standard Table XVII.

3 Calculate the total thermal resistance (R_{total}) of the wall using the following formula:

$$R_{total} = R_1 + R_2 + R_3 + \ldots + R_{si} + R_{se} + R_{cav} \qquad (12)$$

4 Calculate the U-value, that is, the conductance, of the wall using the following formula:

$$\text{U-value} = 1/R_{total} \qquad (13)$$

The heat loss (Q_f) associated with an element of the construction of area (A) and with a temperature difference (D_T) across it can be estimated as follows:

$$Q_f = U \times A \times D_T \qquad (14)$$

Table XIV U-values of typical construction types

Type	2010 Building Regulation		2013 Projected Targets	
Masonry walls	**U = 0.28W/m²/K** *(from left to right)* Brickwork (102.5mm, k = 0.77W/mk) Glass wool (90mm, k = 0.035W/mk) Blockwork (100mm, k = 0.11W/mk Plaster (6mm, k = 0.16W/mk)		**U = 0.15W/m²/K** *(from left to right)* Brickwork (102.5mm,k = 0.77W/mk) Glass wool (210mm, k = 0.035W/mk) Blockwork (100mm, k = 0.11W/mk Plaster (6mm, k = 0.16W/mk)	
Masonry walls with cavity	**U = 0.28W/m²/K** Brickwork (102.5mm, k = 0.77W/mk) Cavity (50mm) Polyurethane (60mm, k = 0.029W/mk) Blockwork (100mm, k = 0.11W/mk Plaster (6mm, k = 0.16W/mk)		**U = 0.15W/m²/K** Brickwork (102.5mm, k = 0.77W/mk) Cavity (50mm) Polyurethane (125mm, k = 0.029W/mk) Blockwork (100mm, k = 0.11W/mk Plaster (6mm, k = 0.16W/mk)	
Timber frame walls	**U = 0.28W/m²/K** Brickwork (102.5mm, k = 0.77W/mk) Cavity (50mm) Mineral wool (140mm, k = 0.035 W/mk) Blockwork (100mm, k=0.11W/mk) Plaster (6mm, k=0.16W/mk)		**U = 0.15W/m²/K** Brickwork (102.5mm, k = 0.77W/mk) Cavity (50mm) Mineral wool outside of frame (90mm, k = 0.035) Mineral wool (140mm, k = 0.035) Blockwork (100mm, k = 0.11W/mk) Plaster (6mm, k = 0.16W/mk)	
Composite steel panel walls	**U = 0.28W/m²/K** Composite panel (80mm) Steel structure		**U = 0.15W/m²/K** Composite panel (125mm) Steel structure	
Timber truss roof	**U = 0.20W/m²/K** *(from top down)* Roof slats (12.5mm, k = 0.84W/mk) Timber rafter Mineral wool insulation above rafters (75mm, k = 0.035 W/mk) Mineral wool insulation between rafters (125mm, k = 0.035 W/mk)		**U = 0.13W/m²/K** *(from top down)* Roof slats (12.5mm, k = 0.84W/mk) Timber rafter Mineral wool insulation above rafters (125mm, k = 0.035 W/mk) Mineral wool insulation between rafters (200mm, k = 0.035 W/mk)	

Table XV Internal surface resistance, R_{si}

Building element	Direction of heat flow	Surface resistance (m²K/W)
Walls	Horizontal	0.13
Ceiling or roofs (flat or pitched), floor	Upward	0.10
Ceiling or floors	Downward	0.17

Source: CIBSE Guide A: Environmental Design, 2006.

Table XVI External surface resistance, R_{se}

		Surface resistance (m²K/W)		
Building element	Direction of heat flow	BS NE ISO 6946 (normal design value)	Sheltered	Exposed
Wells	Horizontal	0.04	0.06	0.02
Roofs	Upward	0.04	0.06	0.02
Floors	Downward	0.04	0.06	0.02

Source: CIBSE Guide A: Environmental Design, 2006.

Table XVII Values of surface and airspace resistance (m²K/W)

Structure	External surface resistance	BS NE ISO 6946 (normal design value)	Airspace resistance
External walls	0.04	0.13	0.18
Party walls and internal partitions	0.13	0.13	0.18
Floors			
Pitched	0.04	0.10	0.16
Flat	0.04	0.10	0.16
Ground floors	0.04	0.17	0.21
Internal floors/ceilings	0.13	0.13	0.18

Example 2

U-value calculation

Calculate the U-value of the insulated cavity wall construction shown in 8.37 for a normal exposure site. Estimate the rate of heat loss through 10 m² of the fabric for a 20°C temperature difference across the wall.

The Resistance is calculated in Table XVIII, giving a total resistance of 3.57 m²K/W.

Hence U-value = 1/3.57 = 0.28 W/m²K

and heat loss $Q_t = 0.28 \times 10 \times 20 = 56$ W

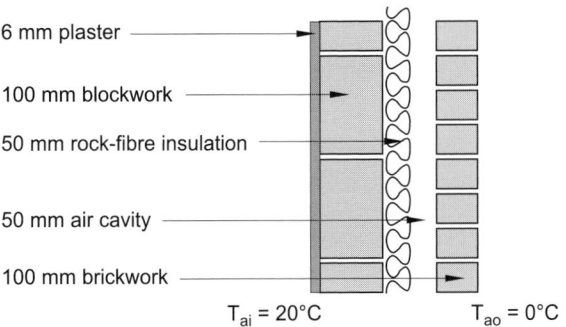

8.37 *Construction of wall in Example 2*

Table XVIII Calculation for Example 2

	Thickness (m)	K-value (W/mK)	Resistance (m²K/W)
Rsi	–	–	0.13
Plaster	0.006	0.16	0.08
Blockwork	0.10	0.11	0.91
Cavity Insulation	0.06	0.029	2.10
Airgap	0.50	–	0.18
Brickwork	0.1025	0.84	0.12
Rse	–	–	0.04
Total	–	–	3.57

5.2 Thermal insulation

A high standard of thermal insulation in buildings in a temperate climate such as in the UK has the following benefits:

1 It reduces the rate of heat loss, and therefore buildings use less energy to maintain comfortable internal thermal conditions. This also means that people are more able to afford to heat their buildings to comfortable conditions, and

2 It raises internal surface temperatures and therefore reduces the risk of surface condensation.

5.3 Types of insulation

Most thermal insulating materials have k-values of 0.03–0.04 W/mK. The most common types are:

- Mineral fibre – this can be glass fibre or rock fibre and is available in lower-density roll form or higher-density batt form. The roll form is usually used to insulate roofs, while the batt form is often used in walls where, because of its greater rigidity, it is more appropriate to vertical fixing. Mineral fibre insulation forms a good attachment to the inner skin of the construction, leaving no air gap. It is often used in wall and roof industrial cladding type constructions. Mineral fibre may also be in a loose form that can be 'blown' into a cavity, to 'cavity fill' an existing or new construction (see below).

- Rigid board – this is usually made from foamed plastic or foamed glass. k-values are typically 0.037 W/m-K. It can be gas filled to give lower k-values, although boards which use ozone-depleting gases should be avoided. If rigid board insulation is used, it is essential to achieve a good attachment to the inner skin of the construction in order to avoid airflow between the inner skin and the insulation layer, which will detract from its U-value performance. The cavity should be kept clean and mortar 'snobs' and other sources of blockage on the inner skin should be eliminated before the insulation is fixed. Rigid board insulation is often used in composite 'factory made' cladding system constructions, where it is installed between two layers of metal sheeting.

- Blown insulation cavity fill, including mineral or cellulose fibres or plastic granules. Insulation is blown into the cavity after completion of construction. Care is needed in installing blown insulation in order to avoid any voids in the insulation in areas where the insulation has difficulty in penetrating, for example, blocked areas of the cavity. This method of cavity insulation has the advantage that it can be applied to existing constructions. Recycled paper insulation, for example, produced from 100 per cent recycled newspaper, has very low embodied energy compared to most other insulation materials. It has a k-value of 0.035 W/m-K.

- Low-density concrete blocks. Blocks with densities down to 480kg/m³ give thermal insulation with k-values of 0.11 W/mK. Such blocks are normally 210 mm in thickness and are used for the inner skin of a construction; this may be an infill panel or a loadbearing wall. They contribute to the thermal insulation of cavity construction, especially when the cavity needs to be left empty for weather resistance in exposed locations. Lightweight blockwork requires sufficient expansion joints to avoid cracking.

5.4 Thermal bridging

Thermal bridging takes place through the details of a construction that have relatively low thermal resistance to heat flow; they have a high U-value in comparison with the rest of the construction. Common areas of thermal bridging are around windows, doors and structural elements. Heat will flow from high to low temperatures by conduction along the path of 'least thermal resistance'. In the case of jambs, sills, lintels and floor edges, the least resistance path will generally be along the highly conductive materials such as metal and dense concrete. Heat loss at thermal bridges can be reduced by adding insulation and thermal breaks, and ensuring that the insulation is continuous over the building envelope. If thermal bridging occurs it will result in increased heat loss and increased risk of condensation.

There are two types of thermal bridging, non-repeating and repeating. The heat loss through solid ground floors is a specific case of a non-repeating thermal bridge where heat will follow the three-dimensional line of least thermal resistance as shown in Figure 8.38. Where there are structural elements such as timber joists in ceilings, these are repeating thermal bridges, Figure 8.39.

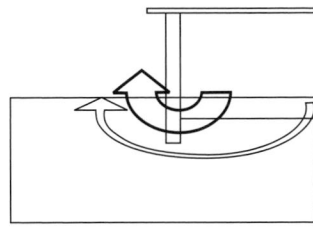

8.38 *The edge losses are dominant in floor heat loss*

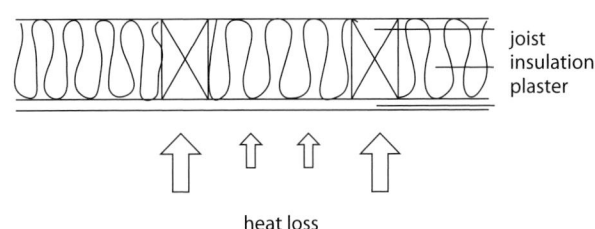

8.39 *Increase in heat loss through repeating thermal bridging due to structural elements*

The heat loss due to repeating thermal bridging can be included in a standard U-value calculation using the 'combined method'. The heat loss at a non-repeating thermal bridge can be estimated from its thermal transmittance, or psi (ψ) value. This is defined as the rate of heat flow per degree temperature difference per unit length of a thermal bridge, measured in W/mK. ψ values can be obtained from measurement or from detailed calculations. If the ψ value is known (Table XIX): the heat loss $_{(HTB)}$ through a thermal bridge can be estimated using,

$$H_{TB} = 1 \times \psi$$

where l = length of the thermal bridge in meters.

Table XIX Common ψ values

Junction detail in external wall	Default ψ value (W/mK)
Steel lintel with perforated steel base plate	0.50
Other lintels (including other metal lintels)	0.30
Sill	0.04
Jamb	0.05
Ground floor	0.16
Intermediate floor within a dwelling	0.07
Eaves (insulation at ceiling level)	0.06
Corner (normal)	0.09
Corner (inverted)	−0.09

Source: SAP 2009.

This must then be added to the elemental heat loss for the wall, roof, or floor.

5.5 Installation of insulation
The following guidelines should be followed when designing an insulated construction.

Insulation should always be located on the 'warm and dry side' of a ventilated cavity (unless informed otherwise, it is usual to assume that all cavities are ventilated). If a cavity or air gap is ventilated on the warm side of the insulation this could provide a 'short circuit' for heat loss as indicated in Figure 8.40.

Avoid air infiltration through or around the insulation material as indicated in Figure 8.41. This will result in short-circuiting of heat loss. Ensure continuity of insulation at design details, e.g. eaves and floor junctions.

- Ensure that there is a vapour barrier on the warm side of the insulation to guard against condensation, and degrading of the insulation properties through dampness.
- Avoid compression of low-density insulation when installed in a construction.

5.6 Glazing
Glass is the main material used for glazing. It is available in a wide range of configurations with different thermal properties.

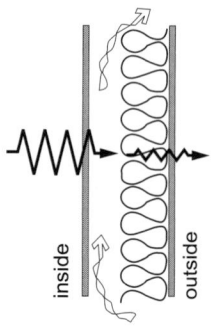

8.40 *Insulation should not be placed on the cold side of a ventilated cavity as its insulation value will be considerably reduced*

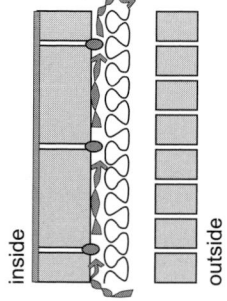

8.41 *Mortar snobs may distance the insulation from the inner skin introducing airflow on the warm side of the insulation and short-circuiting the heat flow through convective losses*

5.7 Thermal performance of glass
Glass is transparent to short-wave infrared radiation and opaque to long-wave radiation (see Section 2.4). It is also a good conductor of heat. Although glass transmits the short-wave infrared part of the solar radiation spectrum, it will also reflect and absorb a proportion of the radiation as shown in Figure 8.42, the amount of which will vary with solar angle of incidence.

5.8 U-Value of glass
The main thermal resistance for a single layer of glass can be attributed to the surface resistances. The glass material itself has practically no thermal resistance.

Example 3
Calculate the U-value of a single layer of glass

Internal surface resistance is 0.13

External surface resistance is 0.04

For a *k*-value of glass of 1.05 and thickness of 6 mm the resistance can be calculated:

$$R = 0.13 + 0.006/1.05 + 0.04$$

Total resistance (R) = 0.1757 m²K/W

U-value is 1/R = 5.7 W/m²K

Adding layers of glass will improve the insulating properties of glazing due to the resistance of the trapped layer of air (or another gas). The thermal resistance of an air- or gas-filled cavity increases in proportion to its width up to about 20 mm and remains constant up to 60 mm, after which it decreases slightly. Increasing the layers of glass will reduce the solar transmittance by about 80 per cent per layer for standard glass. The glazing frame can provide a thermal bridge, which will increase the overall U-value of the glazing system (Table XX).

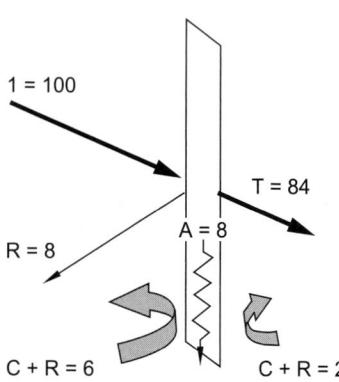

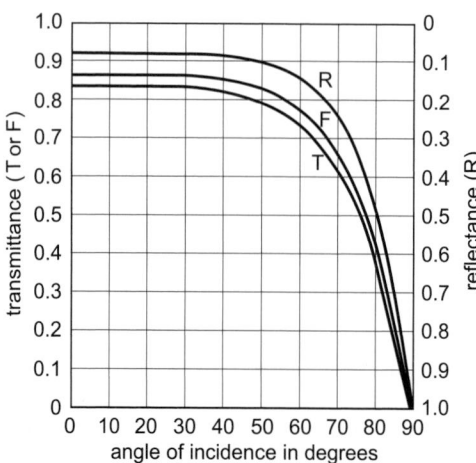

8.42 *Transmitted, reflected, absorbed and re-emitted solar radiation as a percentage of incident value for 4 mm single glazing, and graph indicating variation of solar transmittance with angle of incidence:*

Incident (I) =100%, Reflected (R) = 8%, Transmitted (T) = 84%, Absorbed (A) =8%
Convected and radiated inside (C +R) =2%
Convected and radiated outside (C + R) = 6%

Table XX   Typical U-value and G-value for vertical glazing systems

Glazing systems	Glass pane U-value (W/m²K)	Window U-value with PVC frames (W/m²K)	G-value
Single glazing	5.75	4.80	0.85
Double glazing, air filled	2.76	3.30	0.76
Double glazing, low-e, air filled	1.45–1.85	1.80–2.70	0.63–0.72
Double glazing, low-e, argon filled	1.21–1.65	1.70–2.60	0.63–0.72
Triple glazing, low-e, air filled	–	1.40–2.0	0.57–0.64
Triple glazing, low-e, argon filled	–	1.30–1.90	0.57–0.64

Source: U-values are from: CIBSE Guide A: Environmental Design, 2006; and G-values are from SAP 2009, total solar energy transmittance for glazing.

5.9 Low-emissivity glass

A coating of metal oxide can be applied to a glass surface to reduce its emissivity. This will reduce its long-wave radiation loss, which will reduce the overall transmission loss by about 30 per cent. The low-emissivity coating is usually applied to the inside surface of the inner pane of a double-glazed unit.

5.10 G-value of glazing

The g-value of a glazing system is a measure of the total solar gains to a space, which includes the direct 'short wave' transmitted gains through the glass and the secondary gains through the heated internal glass surface due to absorption of solar gains within the glazing system, Figure 8.43. The direct gains themselves will be absorbed by internal surfaces the subsequent rise in surface temperature will result in convective and radiant gains to the space. The transmission of solar radiation through windows can be reduced by different glazing treatment or the use of blinds or solar shading. Blinds can be incorporated within a layered glazing system to provide additional solar control, Figure 8.44. Internal blinds convert short-wave radiant heat gains to convective and long-wave radiant heat gains. Blinds located externally or between layers of glass are

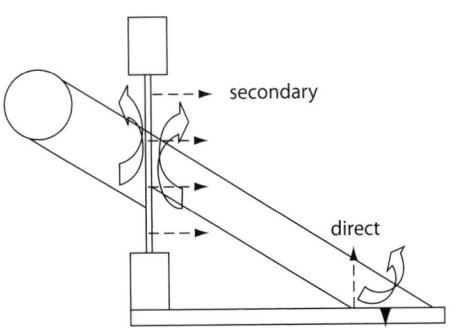

8.43 *Comparison of heat gains through external and internal shading. Typically there could be solar gain of 12% for external white louvres, and 46% for internal white louvres*

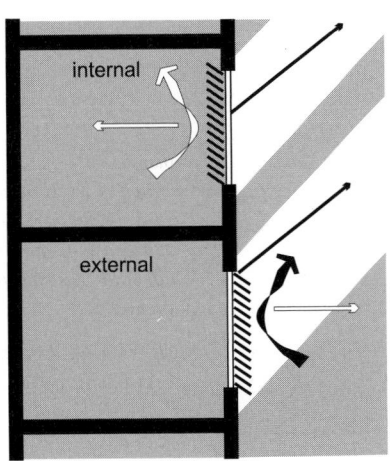

8.44 *Direct and secondary solar heat gains through a glazing system*

more effective in reducing solar heat gains. In some cases it may be necessary to ventilate the cavity which contains the blinds, otherwise the solar heat gains 'trapped' within the glazing system may give rise to secondary heat gains through the heated internal glass surface. As a rule of thumb the internal glass surface temperature should be no more than 5°C above the internal air temperature in order to avoid excess secondary heat gains and thermal discomfort near the glazing zone.

5.11 Layered glazing systems

In recent years there has been an increase in layered glazing systems in buildings allowing large areas of glazing to maximise daylight and for architectural aesthetics, while provided good thermal insulation and solar control. Solar control is often achieved by a combination on glazing treatment and blinds, resulting in G-values below 0.15 (Table XXI).

Table XXI   Solar control system

Single glazing	Double glazing	Triple glazing
G-value ~ 0.80	G-value ~ 0.60	G-value ~ 0.50
Double skin façade with external blind	Double skin façade with interpane blind	Double skin façade with internal blind
G-value ~ 0.12–0.57	G-value ~ 0.28–0.61	G-value ~ 0.44–0.66

Note:
The example G-values of double skin façade with blind are based on the G-value of double skin façade is 0.75 with the slat angles range from 20°to 70°.
The G-value of the double glazing system (when without the roller blind) is 0.75
Source: Mylona, A. 2007. Modelling the thermal performance of complex glazing systems. Welsh School of Architecture, Cardiff University.

There are a range of options for blinds. Louvre type 'venetian' blinds can be controlled in terms of their opening angle and this will affect their G-value as well as where they are positioned within the glazing system. Material 'roller' blinds can reflect, absorb and transmit solar radiation according to their colour and materiality. In some cases external blinds are made of diffuse glass which reflects sunlight whilst allowing daylight to enter.

5.12 Matrix glazing systems

Matrix glazing systems are designed to make maximum use of daylight, while at the same time controlling solar heat gain. They usually consist of a reflective matrix located between two layers of glass. The blades of the reflector are angled to respond to the particular orientation of the glass and the requirement for accepting or rejecting the solar heat gains, Figure 8.45.

5.13 Transparent insulation material (TIM)

This can be applied to the face of an opaque south-facing facade to provide insulation while at the same time allowing the passage of solar gains to the solid wall behind, Figure 8.46. It can also be installed between two layers of glass where light but not view is required.

6 CONDENSATION

6.1 Introduction

Condensation occurs when moist air meets a relatively cool surface. Water condenses out of the air and is deposited on the cool

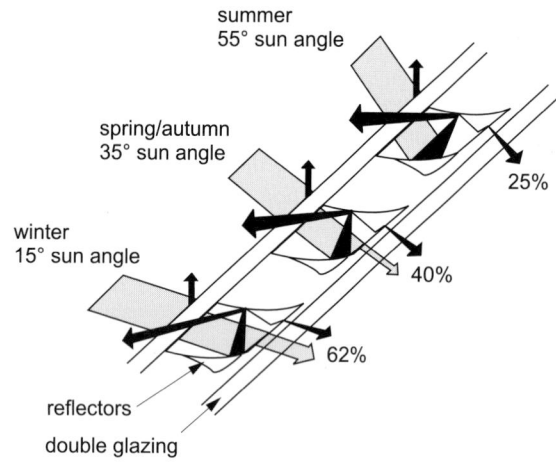

8.45 *Matrix glazing system*

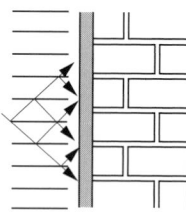

8.46 *Transparent insulation material (TIM)*

surface. It can result in dampness, surface mould growth and deterioration of the building fabric.

6.2 Terminology
- The amount of water vapour that the air can contain is limited and when this limit is reached the air is said to be *saturated*.
- The saturation point varies with temperature. The higher the air temperature, the greater the amount of water vapour it can contain.
- Water vapour is a gas, and in a mixture of gases such as air, the water vapour contributes to the total vapour pressure exerted by the air.
- The ratio of the vapour pressure in any mixture of water vapour and air to the vapour pressure of saturated air at the same temperature is the *relative humidity* (RH).
- If air is cooled it will eventually reach saturation point, that is, 100 per cent RH, and any further cooling will cause the vapour to condense. The temperature at which condensation occurs is called the *dewpoint* temperature.

6.3 Surface condensation
When air with a relatively high RH comes into contact with a cold surface condensation can take place. The risk of surface condensation depends on:

- Air and surface temperature
- Moisture content of the air

6.4 Mould growth
Surface condensation can cause mould growth. Mould spores can germinate at RHs above 80 per cent. If the RH is generally greater than 70 per cent for long periods mould will spread.

6.5 Estimating surface temperature
The following formula can be used to estimate the surface temperature:

Temperature drop between the air and the surface
$$= \Delta T \times U \times R_{si} \qquad (15)$$
where ΔT = inside/outside air temperature difference
U = wall U-value
R_{si} = internal surface resistance

Example 4
What is the internal surface temperature of single glazing (U-value – 5.8W/m²K), if the internal air temperature is 20°C and the external air temperature is 0°C? The internal surface resistance is 0.123 mK/W.

$$D_T = 20 \ U = 5.8 \ R_{si} = 0.123$$

Temperature drop (air to wall surface) = 20 × 5.8 × 0.123
= 13.9°C

Therefore the internal surface temperature = 20 – 13.9 = 6.1°C

6.6 Surface temperature and U-value
The internal surface temperature is affected by the U-value of the construction element, Figure 8.47. The higher the U-value, the lower the internal surface temperature for a given heat input to the space. Thermal bridging constitutes a localised increase in U-value which will result in a lower surface temperature. High U-value elements at risk include single glazing and thermal bridging.

6.7 Moisture content of the air
Moisture is contained in the external air and this is added to by various building use activities (Table XXII). The main moisture sources are:

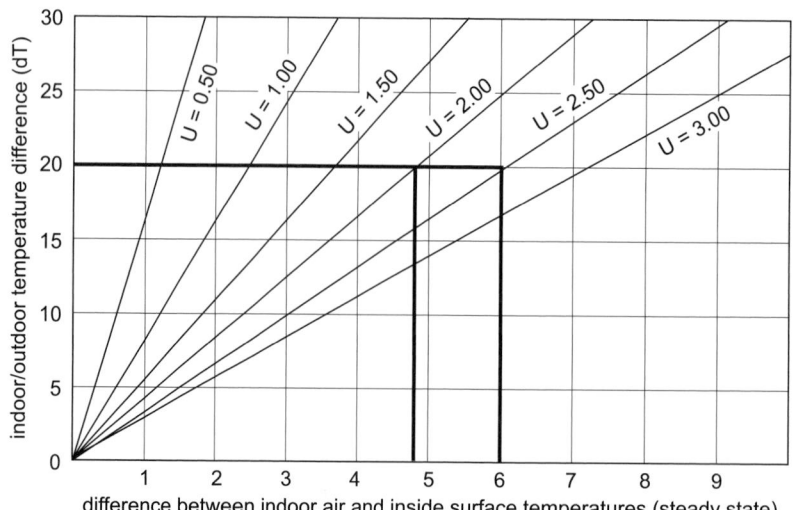

8.47 *Internal air-to-surface temperature versus inside/outside temperature difference for different U-values*

Table XXII Moisture addition to internal air

Room type	kg/kg dry air
Dwelling	0.0034
Offices shops, classrooms	0.0017
Catering	0.0068

External air: external air enters the building through ventilation. Its RH will depend on its moisture content and temperature. For example, on a typical winter's day external air at 90 per cent RH and 5°C will contain about 5 g/kg (dry air) of water vapour. Saturated air at 0°C will contain 3.8 g/kg. These values can be obtained from the psychrometric chart, Figure 8.14; see Section 3.6.

Drying out: building materials contain moisture (Table XXIII). A building could take a year to dry out after construction. A new house might contain 4000 litres of water which will be released during the drying-out period.

Table XXIII Moisture content of materials

Material	Water content	
	Protected	Exposed
Brick (fired clay)	1% by volume	5% by volume
Brick (calcium silicate)	1% by volume	5% by volume
Dense aggregate concrete	3% by volume	5% by volume
Blast furnace slag concrete	3% by weight	5% by volume
Pumice aggregate concrete	3% by weight	5% by volume
Other lightweight aggregate concrete	3% by weight	5% by volume
Autoclaved aerated concrete	3% by weight	5% by volume

Source: CIBSE Guide A: Environmental Design, 2006.

Occupants: moisture is produced as a result of occupants' activities (Table XXIV). On average, 3.4 g/kg of moisture is added to the air by internal activities in a house.

6.8 Causes of surface condensation

Minimising the risk of surface condensation requires a balanced approach to heating, ventilation and insulation, together with minimising moisture production:

Heating: inadequate heating can result in low air temperatures and higher levels of RH. It also means colder surface temperatures. Intermittent heating can result in the fabric and surface temperatures significantly cooler than the air temperature (during warm-up). Warm moist air coming into contact with cool surfaces can then result in condensation. Partial heating of a house can result in warm, moist air convecting to cooler rooms with cooler surfaces. Surface areas shielded from heating (e.g. behind wardrobes) will be more at risk.

Ventilation: low ventilation rates will result in a build-up of moisture in the air causing higher levels of RH. Too much ventilation could give rise to lower internal air temperatures which will again increase the RH, and also reduce surface temperatures. Ventilation should therefore be balanced as illustrated in Figure 8.48.

Table XXIV Moisture emission rates within houses

Source	Moisture produced
Combustion in room heater/cookers without flues	
Paraffin	0.1 kg/h/kW
Natural gas	0.16 kg/h/kW
Butane	0.12 kg/h/kW
Propane	0.13 kg/h/kW
Household activities	
Cooking (3 meals)	0.9–3.0 kg/day
Dish washing (3 meals)	0.15–0.45 kg/day
Clothes washing	0.5–1.8 kg/day
Cloth drying (indoors)	2–5 kg/day
Baths/showers	0.2–0.5 kg/person/day
Floor washing	0.5–1.0 kg/day
Indoor plants	0.02–0.05 kg/day
Perspiration and respiration of building occupants	0.04–0.06 kg/day

Source: CIBSE Guide A: Environmental Design, 2006.

6.9 Estimating risk of surface condensation

The risk of surface condensation can be estimated if the RH and air and surface temperatures are known.

Example 5

Predict the risk of surface condensation using the psychrometric chart Figure 8.49.

- The outdoor dry-bulb air temperature is 0°C and contains 3.8 g/kg of moisture, which gives an RH of 100% (point A).

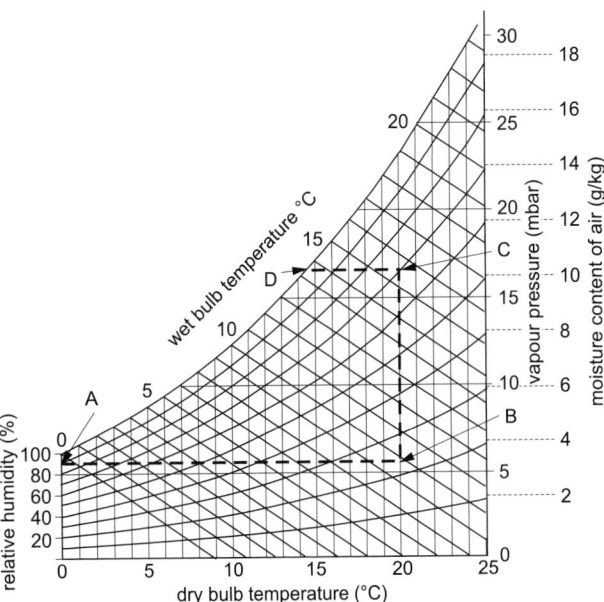

8.49 *Illustration to Example 5: predicting the risk of surface condensation using a psychrometric chart*

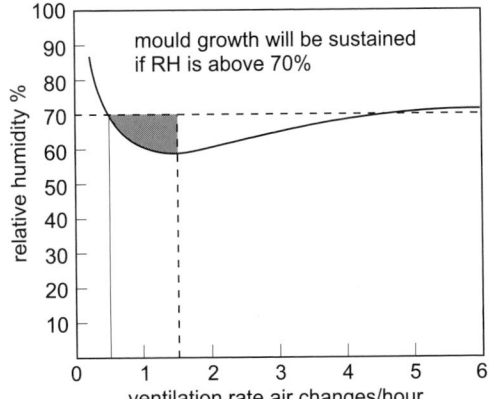

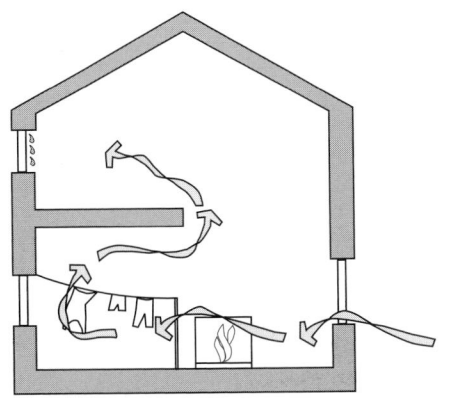

8.48 *Ventilation rate versus RH, indicating that low and high rates can give rise to higher RHs*

- On entering the building the air warms to 20°C. If its moisture content remains the same, its RH will reduce to 27% (point B).
- Internal activities are assumed to generate additional moisture of 7 g/kg, increasing the RH to 70% (point C).
- The dewpoint temperature for air at 70% RH is 15°C (point D).

This means that condensation will occur if the air comes into contact with a surface at a temperature of 15°C or less.

Referring to the graph in Figure 8.47 for an internal/external air temperature difference of 20°C, surface condensation will occur if the U-value is greater than 2 W/m²K, in which case the internal surface temperature will be 15°C, i.e. 5°C less than the air temperature.

6.10 Interstitial condensation

Condensation can occur within a construction. The dewpoint temperature profile of a wall can be predicted. If the actual temperature at any point within the construction falls below the dewpoint temperature then there is a risk of interstitial condensation taking place, as shown in Figure 8.50.

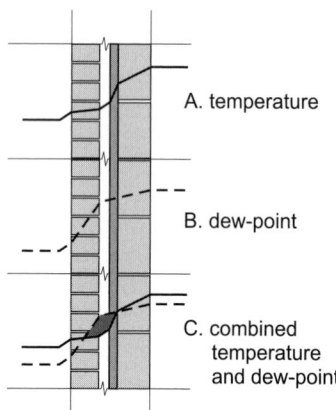

8.50 *Set of three diagrammatic representations of:*

A Temperature profile through wall,
B Dewpoint temperature profile, and
C Overlap of these two profiles indicating area of interstitial condensation risk

6.11 Vapour resistance

A material will resist the passage of vapour depending on its vapour resistivity or vapour resistance (Tables XXV and XXVI) (analogous to thermal resistivity). The vapour resistance of a given thickness of material within a construction is:

$$V_r = x \times v_r \qquad (16)$$

where v_r = vapour resistivity (Ns/kg-m)
  x = thickness of material (m)
  V_r = vapour resistance (Ns/kg)

6.12 Vapour pressure

The vapour pressure can be estimated from the moisture content using a psychrometric chart. The dewpoint temperature for a given vapour pressure will be the dry bulb temperature at 100% RH. The drop in vapour pressure across a given thickness of material in a construction is:

$$dV_p = (V_r/V_K) \times dV_p \qquad (17)$$

where dV_p = drop in vapour pressure across a given thickness of material (kPa)
  V_r = vapour resistance of material (Ns/kg)
  V_r = vapour resistance of construction (Ns/kg)
  dV_p = vapour drop across construction (kPa)

Table XXV K-value and vapour resistivity and resistances

Material	K-value (W/m·K)	Vapour resistivity (MNs/g)
Brickwork (heavyweight)	0.84	45–70
Concrete (blocks, lightweight)	0.66	15–150
Render	1.3	100
Plaster (cement based)	0.72	75–205
Wood (pine)	0.12	45–1850
Plywood	0.12	150–2000
Fibreboard	0.042	150–375
Hardboard	0.14	230–1000
Plasterboard	0.16	30–60
Compressed strawboard	0.1	45–70
Wood-wool slab	0.11	15–40
Expanded polystyrene	0.035	100–750
Glass wool	0.04	5–7
Phenolic (closed cell)	0.04	150–750

Source: CIBSE Guide A: Environmental Design, 2006.

Table XXVI Vapour resistance of membranes

Membranes	Vapour resistance (MNs/g)
Average gloss paint	40–200
Polythene sheet	110–120
Aluminium foil	4000

Source: CIBSE Guide A: Environmental Design, 2006.

ΔT = 20.0 °C

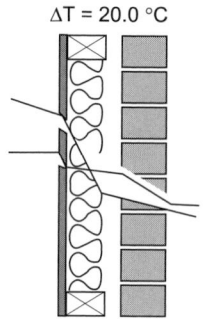

8.51 *Construction of wall in Example 6*

Example 6
Calculate the dewpoint temperature and actual temperature across a construction, Figure 8.51.

1 Calculate thermal resistance of each layer.
2 Calculate temperature drop across each layer: $\Delta t = \Delta T \times U \times R_s$
3 Plot temperature profile.
4 Calculate vapour resistance for each layer from formula (16).
5 Calculate vapour pressure drop across each layer from formula (17).
6 Calculate vapour pressure at the interface of each layer.
7 Look up dewpoint temperature on psychrometric chart, Figure 8.14.
8 Plot dewpoint temperature profile.
9 Check crossover for condensation risk.

The calculation and results are shown in Table XXVII.

7 INFILTRATION AND VENTILATION

7.1 Ventilation

Ventilation is the process of supplying and removing air by natural or mechanical means to and from a space. It is a combination of infiltration and purpose ventilation. Purpose ventilation can be either natural (opening windows), or mechanical (turning on a fan), or a combination of each. Ventilation rate is measured in air changes per hour (ac/h), m³/s or litres per second per person (1/s/p). Typical ventilation rates are in Table XXVIII and more detailed rates can be found in Tables VII and VIII.

7.2 Air infiltration

Air infiltration is the term used to describe the fortuitous leakage of air through a building due to imperfections in the structure, such as:

Table XXVII Calculation for Example 6

The values between the main columns are the temperatures (°C) at the interfaces of the materials.

	Temp.	Inside surface		Plaster-board		Insulation		Cavity		Brick		Outside surface	Temp.
Thickness				0.15		0.05		0.05		0.1			
Thermal resistance		0.12		0.9		2.5		0.18		0.12		0.055	2.1
Temperature drop		0.78		0.59		16.31		1.17		0.78		0.36	
Temperature	**20.0**		**19.2**		**18.6**		**2.3**		**1.2**		**0.4**		**0.0**
Vapour resistance ($X \times V_r$)				7.9		2.8				6.3			
Vapour pressure crop				0.3		0.1				0.25			
Vapour pressure						1.0		0.9		0.9			0.65
Dewpoint temperature	**10.7**				**7.0**		**6.0**		**6.0**				**0.8**

Table XXVIII Typical ventilation rates

Building type	l/s/person
Domestic:	
Habitable rooms	0.4–1.0
Kitchens	60
Bathrooms	15
Offices	10
Schools	10
Bars	10

Source: CIBSE Guide A: Environmental Design, 2006.

- cracks around doors, windows, infill panels;
- service entries, pipes, ducts, flues, ventilators;
- through porous constructions, bricks, blocks, mortar joints.

7.3 Natural ventilation
Natural ventilation is the movement of outdoor air into a space through intentionally provided openings, such as windows, doors and non-powered ventilators. This is in addition to the ventilation due to air infiltration. In many cases, for much of the year infiltration alone will provide sufficient outdoor air to ventilate the building. However, it is uncontrollable, and if excessive, it can incur a high-energy penalty and/or make the building difficult to heat (or cool) to comfort levels.

7.4 Mechanical ventilation
Mechanical ventilation is the movement of air by mechanical means to and/or from a space. It can be localised using individual wall or roof fans, or centralised with ducted distribution. It is controllable and can, for example, incorporate a heat-recovery system to extract heat from exhaust air and use it to pre-heat supply air.

7.5 Build tight, ventilate right!
Infiltration is present in both naturally ventilated and mechanically ventilated spaces. It is considered 'best practice' to reduce the infiltration as much as possible by sealing measures, and then to depend on controllable natural or mechanical means to provide the main ventilation.

7.6 Ventilation effectiveness and efficiency
The term *ventilation effectiveness* is used to describe the fraction of fresh air delivered to the space that reaches the occupied zone. It should ideally be 100 per cent. However, if air 'short-circuits' between supply and extract points then it could be greatly reduced, down to as low as 50 per cent, Figure 8.52.

The term *ventilation efficiency* is used to describe the ability of a ventilation system to exhaust the pollutants generated within the space. For a specific pollutant, it is the mean concentration level of the pollutant throughout the space in relation to its concentration at the point of extract. The ventilation efficiency at a single location is the ratio of pollutant concentration at that location in the space to its concentration at the point of extract.

$$\text{Ventilation efficiency } E = (C_e - C_s)/(C_o - C_s) \quad (18)$$

where E = ventilation effectiveness
C_e = concentration of pollutant in extract
C_s = concentration of pollutant in supply
C_o = concentration of pollutant at occupant location

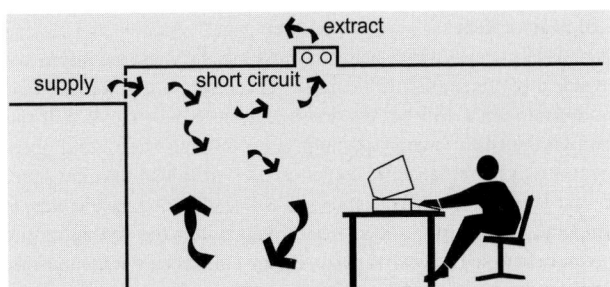

8.52 *Short-circuiting of air between supply and extract reduces ventilation effectiveness and efficiency*

If there is a significant level of the pollutant in the supply air then this should be subtracted from the internal and exhaust concentration levels.

7.7 Metabolic carbon dioxide as an indicator of air quality
Metabolic carbon dioxide is often used as an indicator of air quality. For naturally ventilated spaces in winter when windows are closed, the carbon dioxide level may rise to typically 1500 ppm for offices, and 2500 ppm for school classrooms. For mechanically ventilated buildings the carbon dioxide level should not rise above 1000 ppm and will generally be less than 800 ppm. Metabolic carbon dioxide can also be used to estimate ventilation efficiency using formula (18).

7.8 Ventilation heat loss
The air supplied to a space has to be heated in winter and sometimes cooled in summer. In a mechanical ventilation system, this is achieved by pre-heating or cooling the air before it is delivered to the space. For natural ventilation it is usually achieved by incoming fresh air mixing with air already in the space and then this mixture is heated by the heating system, for example by contact with 'radiator' surfaces. The air that is exhausted from the space, through natural or mechanical means, contains heat energy. For a mechanical ventilation system this heat is sometimes recovered through a heat exchanger – otherwise it is wasted. The ventilation component of heat loss can be a significant and sometimes major proportion of the total building heat loss. It can also be very variable, especially in naturally ventilated buildings, as it depends on external wind velocity and air temperature.

The heat lost or gained through ventilation can be estimated from:

$$Q_v = V_a \times \text{volume} \times \Delta T \times C\rho/3600 \quad (19)$$

or

$$Q_v = V_l \times \text{number of people} \times \Delta T \times C\rho/1000 \quad (20)$$

where Q_v = heat loss or gain in watts
V_a = ventilation rate in air changes per hour (ac/h)
V_l = ventilation rate in litres per second per person (l/s/p)
C_ρ = volumetric heat capacity of air = 1200 Jm–3K^{-1}
ΔT = internal/external air temperature difference (°C).

An increase in internal/external temperature difference causes an increase in ventilation rate and an increase in heat loss or gain.

When designing a heating system the ventilation rate used to calculate the design heat loss should correspond to a design ventilation rate. However, when estimating seasonal energy performance the ventilation rate will be the average ventilation rate over a heating season.

7.9 Natural ventilation design
Natural ventilation through leakage and purpose ventilation is a result of two processes, termed *stack effect* and *wind effect*.

7.10 Stack effect
Stack effect occurs when there is a difference between the inside and outside air temperature. If the inside air temperature is warmer than the outside air it will be less dense and more buoyant. It will rise through the space escaping at high level through cracks and openings. It will be replaced by cooler, denser air drawn into the space at low level. Stack effect increases with increasing inside/outside temperature difference and increasing height between the higher and lower openings. The neutral plane, Figure 8.53, occurs at the location between the high and low openings at which the internal pressure will be the same as the external pressure (in the absence of wind). Above the neutral plane, the air pressure will be positive relative to the neutral plane and air will exhaust. Below the neutral plane the air pressure will be negative and external air will be drawn into the space. The pressure difference due to stack is estimated from:

$$P_s = -\rho \times T \times g \times h \times (1/T_e - 1/T_i) \qquad (21)$$

where P_s = pressure difference in pascals (Pa)
ρ = density of air at temperature T
g = acceleration due to gravity = 9.8 m/s²
h = height between openings (m)
T_i = inside temperature in kelvins, and
T_e = external temperature in kelvins.

7.11 Wind effect
Wind effect ventilation, sometimes referred to as *cross-ventilation*, is caused by the pressure differences on openings across a space due to the impact of wind on the external building envelope, Figure 8.54. Pressure differences will vary, depending on wind speed and direction and location of the openings in the envelope. The pressure at any point on a building envelope can be calculated for a given

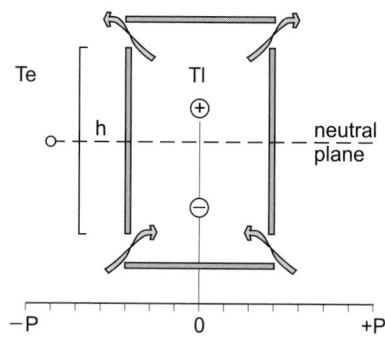

8.53 *Pressure gradient due to stack effect, indicating the location of the neutral plane*

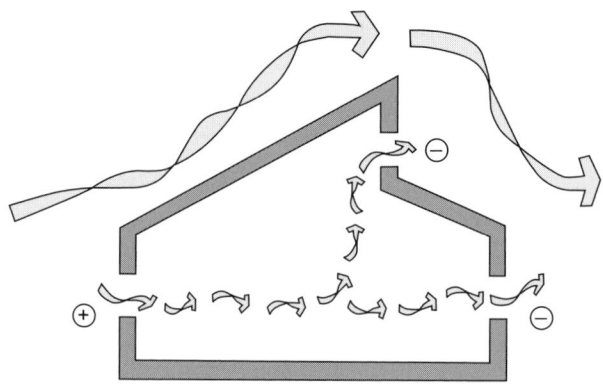

8.54 *Wind driven cross-ventilation*

wind speed and direction if the pressure coefficient at the point is known (see Section 4.10). Pressure coefficients are usually derived from wind tunnel tests. The pressure difference across a building due to wind can be estimated from:

$$P = 0.5\rho v^2 (Cp_1 - Cp_2) \qquad (22)$$

where P_w = pressure difference across the building (Pa)
Cp_1 and Cp_2 = pressure coefficients across the building in relation to the wind speed (v) and air density (ρ).

7.12 Natural ventilation strategies
Figure 8.55 presents a range of natural ventilation strategies with depths limits for single-sided and cross-ventilated spaces.

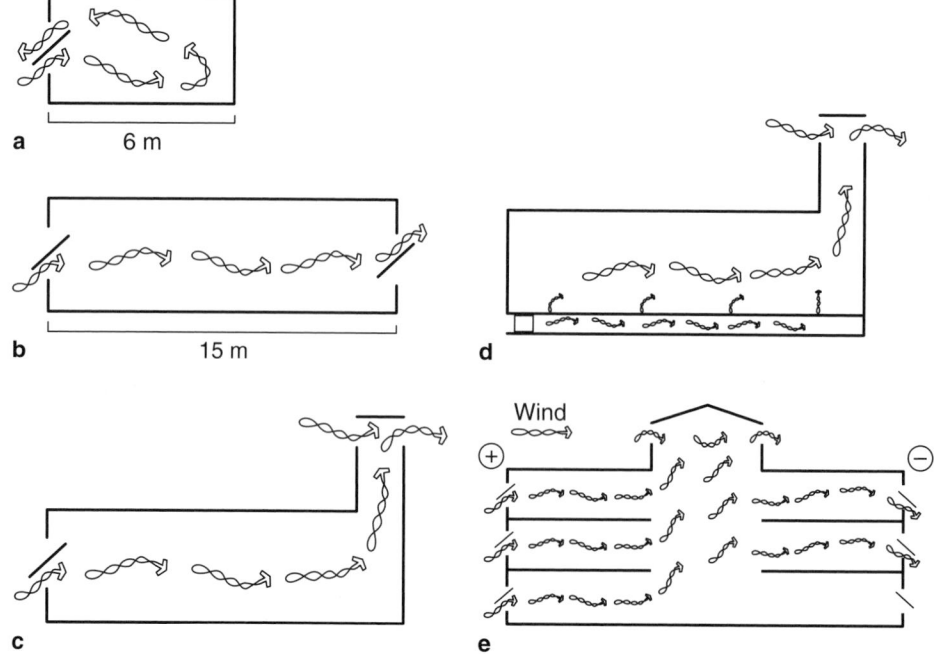

8.55 *Natural ventilation strategies: a Single-sided; b Cross-ventilation; c Cross-ventilation with chimney; d Cross-ventilation with underfloor supply; e Atrium: stack and wind effects*

8.56 *Passive stack ventilation (PSV) can be used instead of mechanical ventilation for local extract, for example in kitchens and bathrooms*

Figure 8.56 illustrates *passive stack ventilation (PSV)* used in domestic buildings.

8 HEATING AND COOLING SYSTEMS

8.1 Introduction
The purpose of heating systems is to maintain internal air and radiant temperatures within the comfort zone. During the 'heating season' a building will lose heat through the fabric and through air infiltration and ventilation. However, a building will also gain heat from internal sources (cooking, electric power and people) and from external solar heat gains through areas of glazing. A heating system is required to make up the difference between the heat gains and the heat losses. If a building is well insulated, has a low air infiltration rate and controlled ventilation then during the heating season, after some initial 'warm up' period, it can be heated some times entirely from the incidental heat gains. A heating system should be sized and controlled such that it can provide the appropriate amount of heat input when needed in an efficient and effective way.

8.2 Types of heating systems
There are direct and indirect heating systems. Direct systems are located in the space, and include solid fuel fires, gas fires, direct electric panel heaters and electric storage heaters. For industrial applications there are high-temperature gas-fired radiant tubes and plaques. The main types of indirect systems are wet central heating systems, Figure 8.57, and ducted warm air systems, Figure 8.58. There are also low-temperature 'surface' heating systems such as under-floor heating, and ceiling and wall systems, where heat is input to the building's internal surface or mass.

8.3 Heat distribution
Heat can be distributed in water or in air. As water has a higher specific heat capacity than air, it requires smaller pipes in comparison to air ducts for the same heat transfer (Table XXIX). Water distribution can be 'gravity' feed or pressurised. An open system will require a header tank, whereas a pressurised system is sealed and requires a pressurisation unit. Pressurised systems can be used to carry water at temperatures higher than 100°C, and are some times used for commercial and industrial systems.

8.4 Heat emitters
Surface panel or tube heaters emit heat by a mixture of convection and radiation. The balance changes with surface temperature and finish. For low-temperature emitters the heat output is mainly convection, whereas for high-temperature emitters the radiant component of heat output increases (see Table XXX). In some cases the convective heat component may not be useful, as for overhead industrial localised heating systems. Some emitters, for example

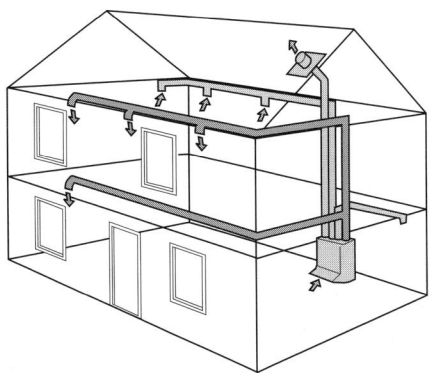

8.58 *Domestic mechanically ventilated heat recovery system with extract in kitchen and bathroom and supply in living spaces, with heat recovery in cooker hood*

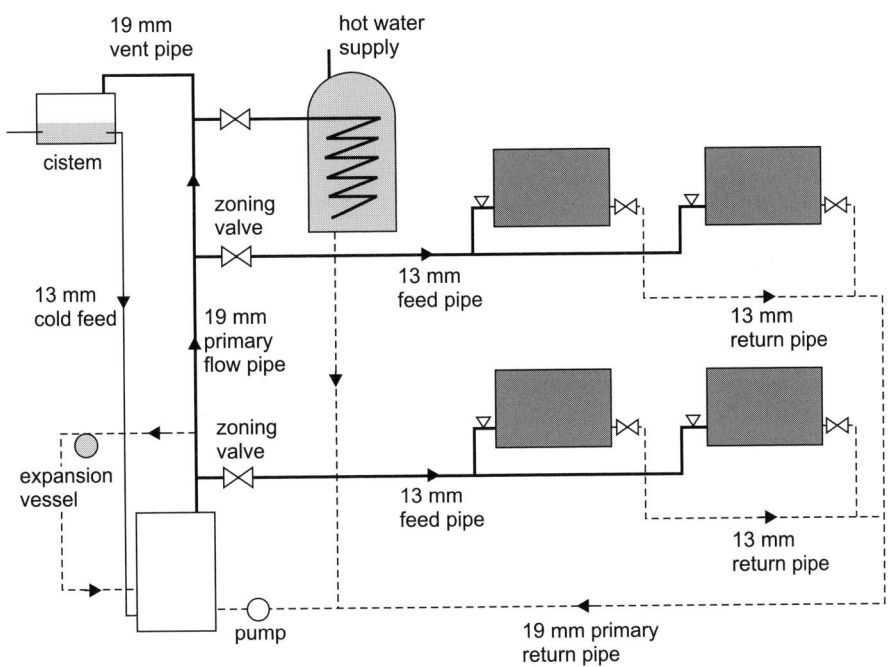

8.57 *Domestic two-pipe wet central heating system with flow and return to each radiator. The system can either be pressurised using an expansion vessel (dotted circuit); or gravity feed, in which case it requires a header tank located above the top radiator*

Table XXIX Water is more efficient than air in transferring heat because it has a higher volumetric specific heat capacity

Specific heat capacity	Specific heat capacity (kJ/Kg·K)	Volumetric specific heat capacity (kJ/m³·K)
Water	4.2	4150
Air	1.01	1.2

Table XXX Radiant and convective output from heated surfaces, based on heating surface emissivity of 0.9

Type	Surface temperature (°C)	Direction of heat flow	Heat output (W/m²) Convective	Radiant
Underfloor heating	24	Up	18	27
Low temperature radiators	40	Vertical	75	114
Domestic radiators	70	Vertical	255	330
Medium pressure hot water panels	110	Down	178	727
		Vertical	558	727
Gas-fired radiant tubes*	150		1709	1078
	300		4414	4367
	500		8627	15184

*Gas radiant tubes are usually mounted at a high level and operate between 150 and 500°C. The convective component is generally lost to the high level; the radiant component is based on a floor level temperature of 18°C.

electric storage heaters, use a combination of heated surface plus forced convection.

8.5 Boilers

Boilers convert fuel to heat. In doing so they produce products of combustion which must be flued. The boiler efficiency (see Table XXXI) is a measure of the conversion of the energy in the fuel (its calorific value) to the useful heat extracted. Condensing boilers are also able to recover latent heat from the flue gases and therefore have a higher efficiency. Boiler efficiency is usually reduced at part-load operation. In larger buildings, modular boilers allow maximum efficiency with sequencing a number of smaller boilers instead of a few large ones so that the majority operate at full-load. Combination boilers allow for direct heating of domestic hot water, thus avoiding the need for storage and reducing the standing heat losses.

Table XXXI Boiler efficiencies

System	Seasonal efficiency %
Condensing boilers:	
Under-floor, or warm water system	90 or greater
Standard size radiators, variable temperature circuit (weather compensation)	87
Standard fixed temperature emitters (83/72°C flow/ return)*	85
Non-condensing boilers:	
Modern high-efficiency non-condensing boilers	80–82
Good modern boiler design closely matched to demand	75
Typical good existing boiler	70
Typical existing oversized boiler (atmospheric. cast-iron sectional)	45–70

*Not permitted by current Building Regulations
Source: CIBSE Guide F, Energy Efficiency in Buildings, 2004.

8.6 Distribution losses

There will be heat loss associated with the distribution system. Pipes and ducts should be well insulated (Table XXXII). There will also be standing 'case' heat losses associated with the boiler, which may be considered useful (although it is uncontrolled) if they contribute to space heating.

Table XXXII Heat losses from pipes and ducts

		Heat loss (W/m)	
	Fluid temperature (T!)	Un-insulated	With 25 mm insulation
15 mm dia pipe	50	32	6
15 mm dia pipe	70	62	11
500 mm dia duct	40	333	47

8.7 Building 'design heat loss'

Fabric and ventilation heat loss has been explained in Sections 5 and 6. The *design heat loss* of a building is its heating demand for a given external air temperature, which will vary for different parts of the UK. It can be estimated as follows:

Fabric heat loss rate: Q_f (W/°C)
Ventilation heat loss rate: Q_v (W/°C)
Total heat loss rate: $Q = Q_f + Q_v$ (W/°C)
Design internal air temperature: T_i (°C)
Design external air temperature: T_e (°C)

$$\text{Design heat loss} = Q \times (T_i - Te)\ (W) \qquad (23)$$

8.8 Seasonal energy use

The seasonal energy use can be calculated from the design heat loss, but using some form of seasonal temperature instead of a design temperature. Also, an allowance has to be made for system efficiency and incidental heat gains. The seasonal temperature can be in the form of a heating season average temperature or *degree days* (Table XXXIII). If average temperature is used, then some account of seasonal heat gains are required. Degree days already assume some level of useful heat gains in relation to a *base temperature*, which is the temperature below which heating is required. The standard base temperature is 15.5°C, which takes account of typical internal heat gains.

8.9 Heat gains

There will be heat gains from internal activities and solar effects (Table XXXIV). For domestic buildings, the internal gains can be estimated depending whether the household has high, medium or low activities (Table XXXV). Not all the internal gains will usefully supplement the heating. Some may cause overheating and some may occur where or when they are not required.

Table XXXIII Seasonal energy design temperatures

Region	Seasonal Average Temperature Tsa (°C)	Annual Degree Days
Thames Valley	7.5	2033
South Eastern	6.7	2255
Southern	7.8	2224
South Western	8.3	1858
Seven Valley	7.2	1835
Midland	6.7	2425
West Pennines	6.7	2228
North Western	6.4	2388
North Eastern	5.9	2483
East Pennines	6.6	2370
East Anglia	6.7	2307
Borders	6.1	2254
West Scotland	5.8	2494
East Scotland	6.0	2577
North-east Scotland	5.5	2668
Wales	7.2	2161
Northern Ireland	6.4	2360

Source: CIBSE Guide A: Environmental Design, 2006.

Table XXXIV Solar heat gains

	Single glazing			Double glazing		
	S	SE/SW	E/W	S	SE/SW	E/W
J	14	12	6	12	10	5
F	19	16	11	16	13	9
M	35	31	23	30	26	19
A	35	34	30	29	29	26
M	42	44	42	35	37	35
J	41	45	46	35	38	39
J	39	43	42	33	36	35
A	40	41	37	34	34	31
S	39	36	29	33	30	24
O	31	27	18	26	22	15
N	19	16	9	16	13	7
D	14	12	5	12	10	4

Table XXXV   Domestic internal heat gains

Heat source	Total heat gain (kWh/day)	
	Low	High
Occupants	4.02	5.46
Lighting	2.17	2.50
Cooker	2.89	4.25
Refrigerator	1.44	1.44
Television	0.45	0.54
Hot water	3.70	4.70
TOTAL	14.67	18.89

8.10 Environmental temperature

It is more accurate in cases where the radiant temperature is significantly different from air temperature to calculate the heat transfer to the internal surface of a wall using the *environmental temperature* which combines air temperature and mean radiant temperature:

$$t_{ei} = 2/3\ t_{mrt} + 1/3\ t_{ai} \tag{24}$$

where t_{ei} = environment temperature
t_{mrt} = mean radiant temperature, and
t_{ai} = air temperature.

Figure 8.59 illustrates the use of resultant temperature (formula (6)), environment temperature (formula (24)) and sol-air temperature (formula (8)).

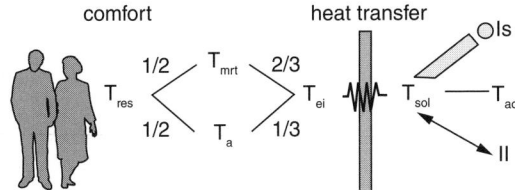

8.59 *Resultant temperature, environmental temperature and sol-air temperature*

This may also apply to cooling where a low radiant component of the environment temperature may improve comfort because it is more comfortable to exchange heat by radiation to surrounding (cooler) surfaces than by convection to the surrounding air.

8.11 Seasonal energy use (E)

To calculate the seasonal energy use for space heating:

(i)   Using average temperature:

$$E = (Q_f + Q_v) \times (T - T_a)$$
$$\times \text{ number of hours} - \text{seasonal heat gains}) \times eff \tag{25}$$

where E = the seasonal energy use (W)
Q_f = fabric heat loss <2
Q_v = ventilation heat loss
T_i = average internal temperature
T_{sa} = seasonal average temperature (Table XXXIII)
eff = efficiency of heating system.

(ii)   Using degree days:

$$E = (Q_f + Q_v) \times \text{degree days} \times 24 \times eff \tag{26}$$

8.12 Carbon dioxide emissions

Table XXXVI gives the carbon dioxide emissions associated with fuel use.

Table XXXVI   Carbon dioxide emission factors for UK in 2010

Fuel	Carbon emission per unit of delivered energy (kgCO$_2$/kWh)
Natural gas	0.206
Liquid petroleum gas (LPG)	0.251
Gas oil/ burning oil	0.290
Coal	0.382
Electricity	0.591

Source: SAP 2009.

Example 7

Calculation of seasonal heating, fuel use and carbon dioxide emission from a modern detached house located in Cardiff, and heated by a gas condensing boiler.

Fabric heat loss

Element	Area (m²)	U-value (W/m²/°C)	Heat loss (W/°C)	
Walls	115	0.23	26.45	Table XIV
Roof	35	0.19	6.65	Table XIII
Floor	35	0.25	8.75	
Windows	30	2.00	60.0	Table XX
Total			102.0	

Ventilation heat loss   Formula (19)

Air change rate (/h)	Volume (m³)	Heat loss (W/°C)	
0.75	210	52.5	Table XXIII
Total heat loss		155	

Seasonal heat loss (October–May)   Formula (25)

External temperature	7	Table XXXIII
Internal temperature	17	
Hours of use	5760	
Seasonal heat loss (kWh/year)	8910.7	

Heat gains

Windows	Area (m²)	Unit gains (kWh/m²)	Total gains (kWh)	
Solar gains				Table XXXIV
South	10	190	1900	
North	5	0	0	
East	5	110	550	
West	10	110	1100	
Total			3550	
Internal gains				Table XXXV
People	4	370	1480	
Hot water			450	
Electrical			1100	
Cooking			950	
Total			3980	
Total heat gains (kWh/year)			7530	
Assume 50% of the gains contribute to useful heating			3765	
Heating system load (kWh/year)			5145.7	Formula (25)
Heating system efficiency (%)			88	Table XXXI
Heating system fuel use (gas) (kWh/year)			5847	
Carbon dioxide emission associated with heating fuel use (kg/year)			1111	Table XXXVI

8.13 Mechanical ventilation

Mechanical ventilation may be required in buildings as an alternative or in addition to natural ventilation. Specific applications include:

- Deep plan spaces which cannot be ventilated from the side by natural means.
- Spaces with a high occupancy or high heat gain.
- Spaces with high source levels of pollution, including industrial processes and moisture in kitchens and bathrooms.
- Where the external air quality may be poor and so the external air needs to be filtered or taken in at high level.
- Where high ventilation rates are required in winter, mechanical ventilation (with pre-heated air) can be used without incurring cold draughts.

8.14 Mechanical extract

Local mechanical extract can be used to exhaust pollutants at source (e.g. in kitchens, bathrooms and toilets; and locally for industrial processes such as solder baths and welding booths).

8.15 Mechanical supply systems

Mechanical supply systems can be used in situations where a positive flow needs to be established between a space and its surroundings. Examples are:

- in a house or apartment to maintain a minimum ventilation rate and reduce condensation risk;
- mechanical induction systems where high-velocity warm air is supplied to a space, and extract is through natural leakage;
- mechanical supply to an office and extract naturally, perhaps through an atrium or chimney/tower.

8.16 Balanced supply and exhaust

Mechanical ventilation systems in larger buildings usually have a balanced supply and extract, Figure 8.60. This allows:

- control of higher ventilation rates;
- heating and/or cooling of incoming air;
- filtration of incoming air;
- humidity control of air;
- heat recovery from exhaust to supply air.

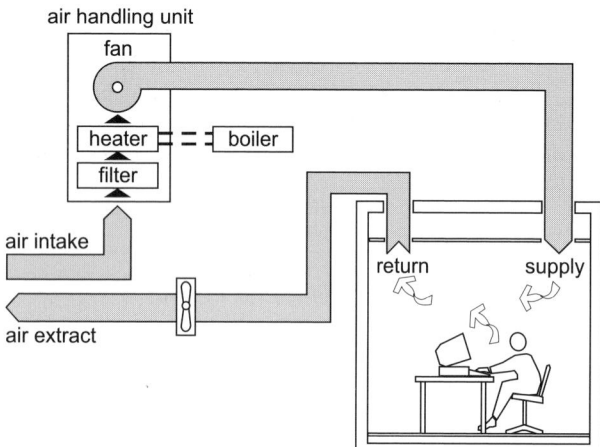

8.60 *Components of one type of balanced supply and extract mechanical ventilation system*

8.17 Air supply rates

If the air supply is for ventilation, then the volume flow rate can be estimated from the number of occupants in the space. This will be typically 10 litres/second/person for normal environments, that is, average levels of pollution. If air is required as the sole source of heating then the volume flow rate can be estimated from the following formulae:

$$\text{Volume flow rate} = \text{design heat loss}/((T_{su} - T_{ex}) \times C_p) \quad (27)$$

where T_{su} = supply air temperature
T_{ex} = extract air temperature, and
C_p = volumetric specific heat of air

In modern 'low energy' buildings, including dwellings, the rate of air supply for ventilation is similar to that required to meet the design heat loss. Therefore warm air systems incorporating heat recovery can prove an appropriate option for a combined heating and ventilation system.

Example 8

Calculate the volume flow rate of air to ventilate a 1000 m office space, height of 2.5 m, occupied by 100 people (each requiring 8 l/s/person). If the design heat loss of the space is 15 kW, what is the volume flow rate required to (assume at room temperature) heat the space if the supply air temperature is 30°C and the extract is 23°C?

$$\text{Ventilation volume flow rate} = (100 \times 8)/1000$$
$$= 0.8 \text{m}^3/\text{s}$$
$$= 0.8 \times 3600/2500$$
$$= 1.12 \text{ac/h}$$

$$\text{Heating volume flow rate} = 15000/((30 - 23) \times 1200)$$
$$= 1.8 \text{m}^2/\text{s}$$
$$= 1.8 \times 3600/2500$$
$$= 2.6 \text{ac/h}$$

8.18 Air distribution

For a mechanical ventilation system air is distributed from an air handling unit (AHU) to the space through a system of ducts, Figure 8.61. The cross-section area of the AHU and ducts depends on the air speed for a given volume flow rate, and can be calculated from:

$$csa = \text{volume flow rate/air speed} \quad (28)$$

where *csa* is the cross-sectional area in m².

The velocity through the AHV would typically be 2m/s. The velocity through the main riser ducts may vary from 3 m/s (low velocity) to 7 m/s (medium velocity).

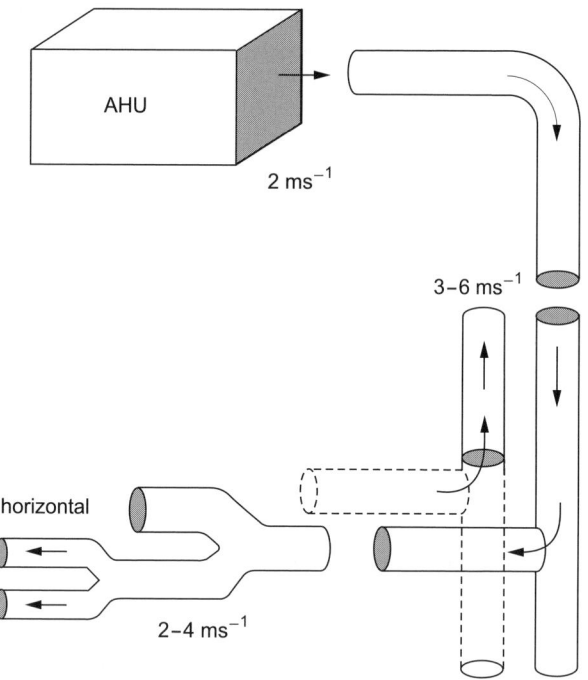

8.61 *Ducted air distribution system indicating typical flow velocities*

8.19 Fan power

The fan power required to supply the air through the ducted system depends on the volume flow rate and the pressure drop in the system, which are related to the air speed. For an energy-efficient mechanical ventilation system with low duct velocity, the *specific fan power* could be less than 2 kW/m³ of air supply.

8.20 Heat-recovery systems

An advantage of mechanical ventilation is that it can use heat recovery. This can be applied at all scales of building from domestic to large-scale commercial. It is especially appropriate for achieving energy efficiency in full fresh-air systems. Heat recovery is only worthwhile if the recovered heat is useful and is greater than the energy used due to the increase in fan power from the increased pressure drop of the heat-recovery equipment. Table XXXVII lists

Table XXXVII Heat-recovery systems and typical efficiencies

Heat-recovery system	Efficiency (%)
Recuperator	50 to 80 (sensitive)
Run-around coil	50 (sensitive)
Thermal wheel	65 to 90 (sensitive)
Heat pipe	50 to 60 (sensitive)
Regenerator	85 to 95 (sensitive)

Source: CIBSE Guide B, Heating, Ventilating, Air Conditioning and Refrigeration 2005.

the efficiency ranges of heat-recovery systems. Heat-recovery systems should have a by-pass option to reduce fan power when heat recovery is not needed.

8.21 Air cooling systems
Some buildings require cooling in addition to what can be achieved from ventilation alone. Such buildings may have a high internal heat gain, where mechanical ventilation will not provide sufficient cooling, especially during warm weather. The building itself may be located in a hot climate, where air-conditioning with cooling and humidity control is necessary. Cooling of air is achieved by passing the air over cooling coils in the AHU.

8.22 Heat gains
The main reason for mechanical cooling is in response to heat gains from people, office machinery, lighting, solar gains and high external air temperatures. Solar gains have been discussed in Section 4.2. Internal gains from lighting and machines can be high (Table XXXVIII), but they are often overestimated, which can result in over-capacity of the system design. Wherever possible, internal heat gains should be minimised by specifying low energy lighting and other electrical equipment.

8.23 Room air delivery
Chilled air can be delivered to the space, either in a mixing mode or a displacement mode.

8.24 Mixing mode of air delivery
The air supplied to the space is typically about 14°C at the design cooling load. The air is jetted into the space such that it mixes with air already in the space by entrainment and when the air enters the occupied zone it is at the appropriate temperature, speed and RH

Table XXXVIII Internal heat gains for a typical office

Factor		Heat gains (W/m²)				
Density (/person/m²)		4	8	12	16	20
Sensible heat gain	People	20	10	6.7	5	4
	Equipment	25	20	15	12	10
	Lighting	12	12	12	12	12
Latent heat gain		15	7.5	5	4	3

Source: CIBSE Guide A: Environmental Design, 2006.

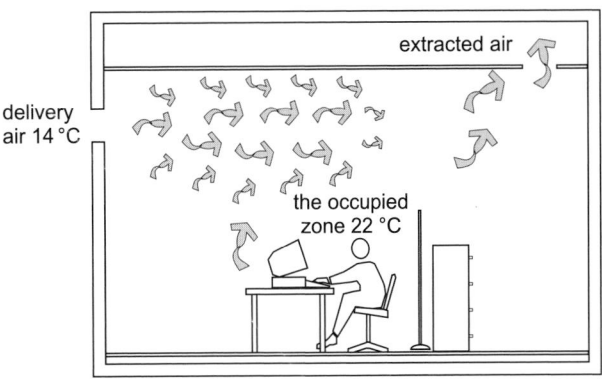

8.62 *Mixing mode of air delivery*

for comfort, Figure 8.62. Air may be supplied from the perimeter, the ceiling or even the floor.

8.25 Coanda effect
Ceiling systems often rely on the *coanda effect,* Figure 8.63a, to ensure that the cool supply air remains at high level ('sticks' to the ceiling) until it is mixed. The coanda effect does not work at low jet velocities and the jet becomes 'unstuck' and can cause cold air 'dumping', Figure 8.63b.

8.26 Displacement air delivery
Air is supplied to the space at a low velocity such that it displaces the air already in the space towards the ceiling extract, Figure 8.64. Air is usually supplied at the floor or through low-level diffusers. However, some floor systems, that use *swirl* diffusers, are assumed to be displacement but are really mixing systems. The temperature of the air supply for these systems is usually above 18°C to avoid draughts.

8.27 Air supply
The temperature and volume flow rate of the supply air will often determine the type of system used. Displacement systems should have air delivery temperatures greater than 18°C or they are likely to cause cool draughts. So if low-temperature supply is needed to deal with a high heat load, then mixing systems are usually more suitable. Figure 8.65 shows the relationship between air supply temperature, volume flow and internal heat gains.

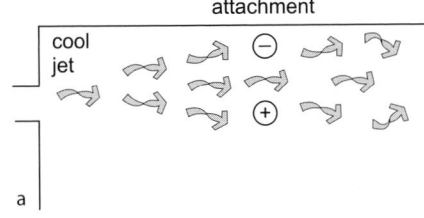

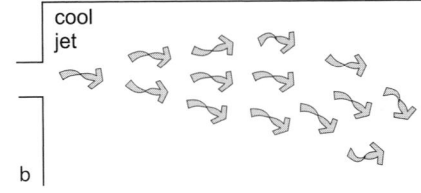

8.63 *Coanda effect*

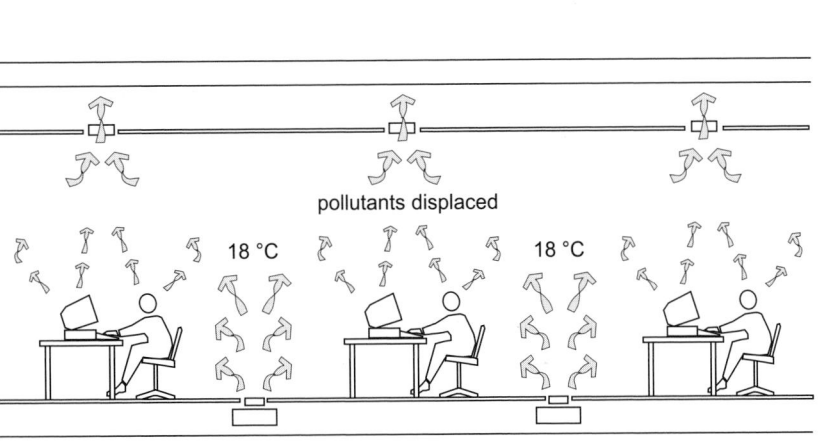

8.64 *Air displacement system*

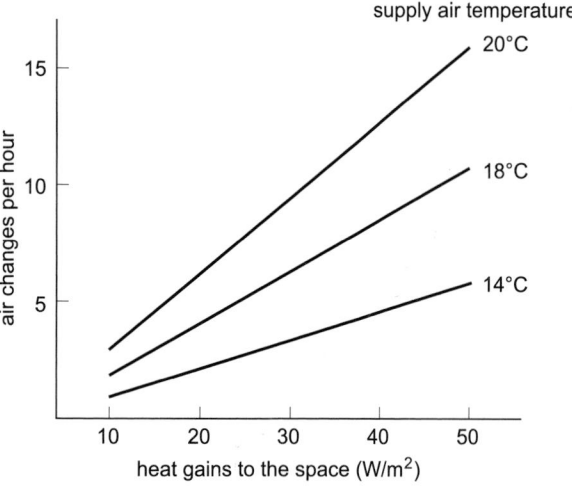

8.65 *Relation between volume flow, supply air temperature and cooling load*

8.28 Central air-conditioning systems

Figure 8.66 illustrates a typical central air-conditioning system layout. Such systems may supply air with a variable air volume (VAV) or a constant air volume (CAV).

8.29 Variable air volume (VAV)

In this system the volume of air is controlled in response to the cooling load. As the cooling load is reduced the volume of air is also reduced until a minimum air supply is reached, after which the supply air temperature is increased.

8.30 Constant air volume (CAV)

With this the air is supplied at a constant volume and the temperature of the air is varied in response to the space cooling or heating load.

8.31 Localised systems

These are usually either fan coil units or heat pump units. They can be located around the perimeter of a space or in the ceiling void,

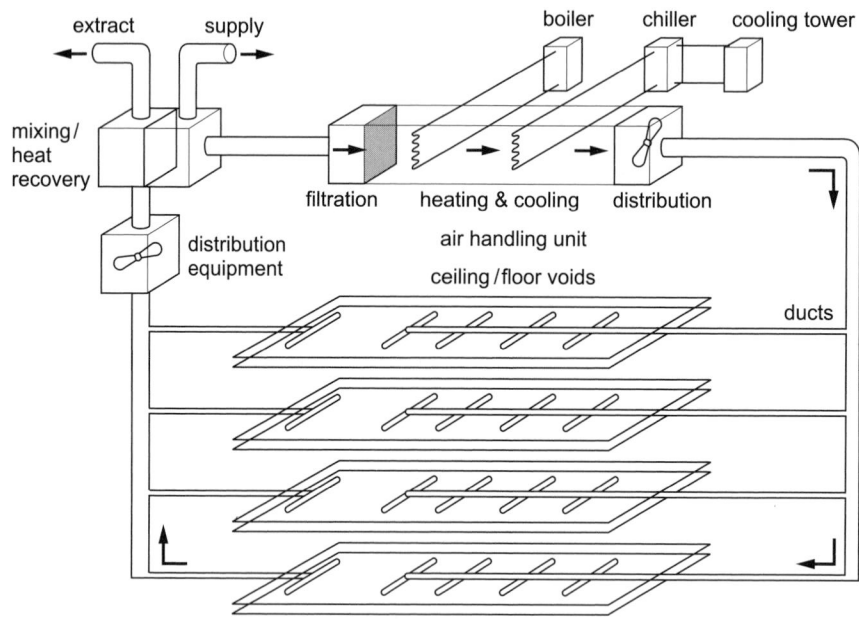

8.66 *Layout of a central air conditioning system*

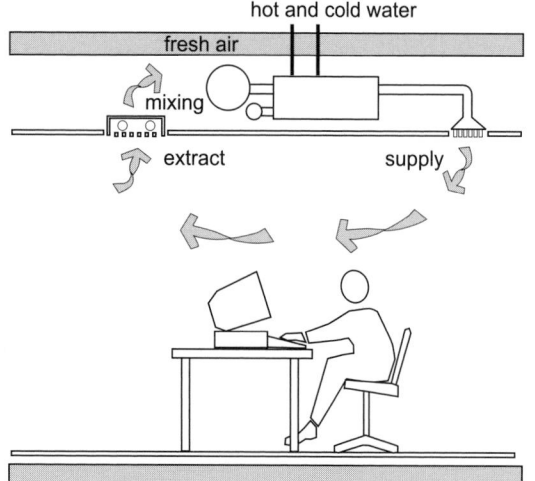

8.67 *Ceiling fan coil system*

Figure 8.67. A space may have multiple units, or one unit may supply a single floor. They usually take air from the space and heat or cool it as demanded. Ventilation air can either be supplied directly to the unit from outside or be ducted separately from a central unit

which only supplies ventilation air requirements and not heating and cooling requirements. Fan coil units are served by hot and cold water systems that supply the main heating and cooling load.

8.32 Chilled surface cooling systems

Passive cooling is achieved by means of introducing chilled surfaces in a room, which could be naturally chilled, for example using night ventilation, or actively chilled, by water or air, Figure 8.68. These surfaces absorb heat from the air in the space by convection/conduction and radiative heat exchange from warmer surfaces, including people. Chilled surface cooling devices can be in the form of fins, panels or beams. Sometimes the whole surface is cooled or heated, for example through passing water or air through the concrete floor slab and exposing the slab soffit to the room. In cooling mode, surface temperatures vary from typically 17°C for panels or beams to 20°C for chilled ceilings, with respective cooling loads of typically 70(+)W/m² down to 30 W/m². To avoid the risk of condensate forming on the chilled surfaces in situations of high relative humidity, sensors can be incorporated into the design to raise the surface temperatures. Alternatively, if mechanical ventilation is used the ventilation air can be dehumidified at the AHU. Air leakage through the facade should be minimised to avoid uncontrolled moist air entering the space. Chilled surface cooling systems can be combined with displacement ventilation, Figure 8.69.

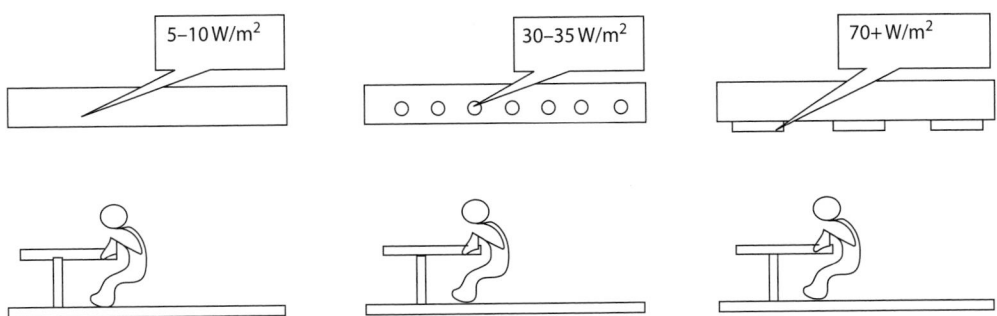

8.68 *Chilled surface cooling systems and their approximate cooling capacities*

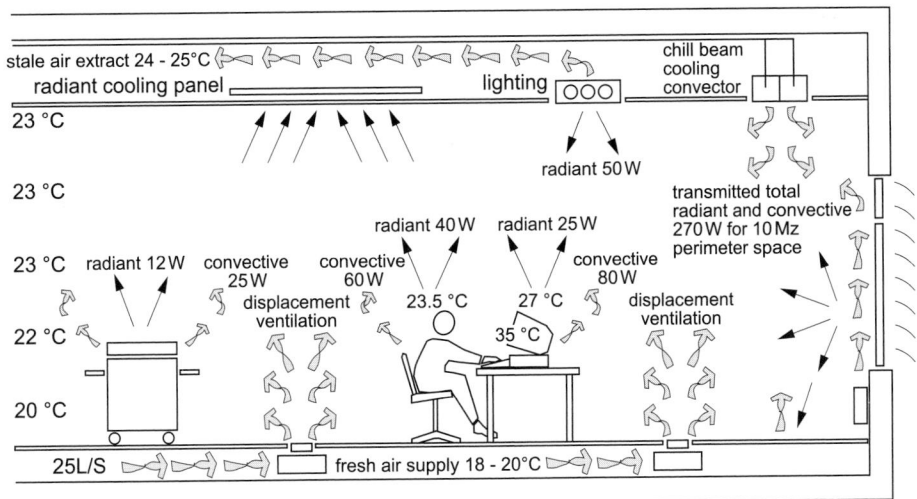

8.69 *Passive cooling systems (chilled beams or panels) can be combined with displacement*

8.33 Refrigeration

Cooling systems require some form of refrigeration equipment in order to extract heat from the cooling fluid that flows in the cooling coils in the air handling unit, or in the passive cooling system. A standard heat pump circuit is shown in Figure 8.70 and an absorption circuit in Figure 8.71. This can be used to cool or reversed to provide heating. The COP is a measure of the heat or coolth divided by the energy used to operate the heat pump.

8.34 Ground and air source heat pumps

Ground and air source heat pumps can provide a low carbon solution for heating and cooling. They are particularly suitable for providing heated or chilled water for surface heating and cooling systems. Ground source heat pumps have the advantage of working to a ground temperature of about 11°C, which enables them to retain a relatively high COP, whereas air source heat pumps work to an external temperature, which can be relatively low in winter and high in summer, reducing their operating COP considerably. However air source heat pumps, although potentially noisy, are relatively easy and low cost to install. Ground source heat pumps may have be vertical or horizontal heat exchanger (Figure 8.72).

8.35 Ground cooling

Ground cooling can be used for an air based ventilation cooling system by passing the supply air through pipes buried in the ground. The ground temperature at depths of 2 m or more remains fairly constant throughout the year. The amount of cooling obtained depends on the volume supply rate and the exposed contact surface area of the pipes. Alternatively air may be passed through a labyrinth of tunnels which have a high thermal mass in order to pre-cool it. In any system the heat absorbed by the mass must be extracted through night ventilation or natural seasonal effects. During the heating season the supply air may also be pre-heated through

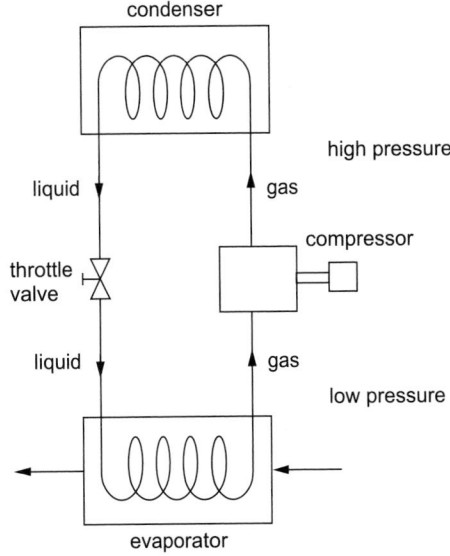

8.70 *Diagrammatic heat pump circuit. The refrigerant is in a liquid state as it enters the evaporator where it absorbs heat and changes state to gas. It is compressed to a hot gas and enters the condenser where it gives out heat and returns to liquid state. In reverse operation it can be used to cool*

the same system, when the external air temperature is lower than the ground or labyrinth surface temperature.

8.36 Hybrid systems

Hybrid, or mixed-mode, systems combine mechanical and natural ventilation in either a spatial or a seasonal mix. Seasonal hybrid buildings may be naturally ventilated in summer and mechanically

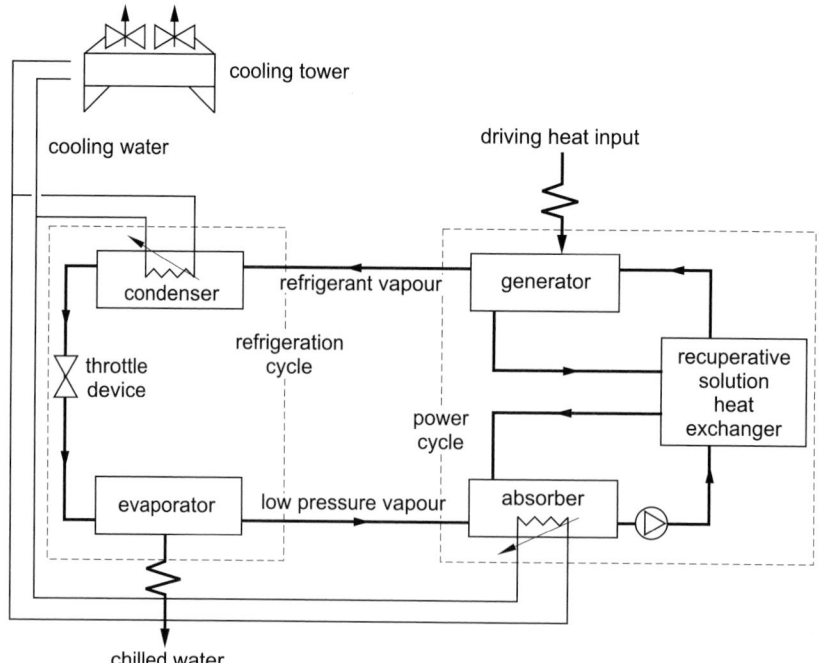

8.71 *Schematic diagram of an absorption cooling system. Refrigerant vaporised in the generator passes to the condenser where it rejects heat and condenses. Its pressure (and temperature) is then reduced by a throttling device before it enters the evaporator, here it absorbs heat from the chilled water circuit and becomes a low-pressure vapour. It then returns to the absorber*

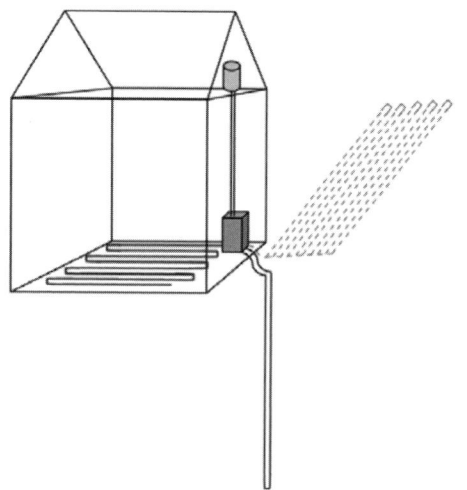

8.72 *Ground source heat pump*

ventilated in winter. Spatial hybrid buildings may have spaces that are both naturally ventilated (say, at the perimeter) and mechanically ventilated (say, in the depth of space).

8.37 Space for services

The space requirements for the location of mechanical services and their distribution systems can be considerable: typically 2–15 per cent depending on building type, and must be considered early in the design process (Table XXXIX).

8.38 Passive Haus

Towards the end of the 1980s and early 1990s the concept of Passive Haus was developed in Germany, with its standards for

Table XXXIX **Typical space requirements for different systems for an office building as a percentage of total floor space**

	Natural ventilation	Mechanical ventilation	Air conditioning
AHUs	–	2	4
Boiler	1.5	1.5	1.5
Chiller	–	–	2
Total	1.5	3.5	7.5

total energy demand for space heating and cooling to be less than 15 kWh/m²/annum of floor area, and a total primary energy use for all appliances, domestic hot water and space heating and cooling of less than 120 kWh/m²/annum. To achieve this performance standard, heating is normally combined with ventilation using a mechanical ventilation heat recovery system, where typically, heated fresh air is supplied to the main living spaces and air is extracted from kitchen and bathroom spaces. Passive Haus walls are super insulated with U-values of 0.10 to 0.15 W/(m².K) and triple glazing with U-values, typically 0.85 to 0.70 W/(m².K). For some houses air is passed through underground pipes to pre-heat (or pre-cool) the intake air for the ventilation system. Passive Haus method can typically cost up to 15 per cent more, although costs can potentially be reduced if a holistic approach is used.

8.39 Low carbon design

Low carbon design of buildings can be divided into four stages, Figure 8.73. These stages need to be closely linked through a holistic approach to ensure that cost savings in reducing heating and cooling equipment, can contribute to increased costs, for example, for renewable energy systems. A life-time costing or life-time carbon approach can also encourage investment in aspects of low carbon design that will be realised in future reduced running costs and security of energy supply. The asset value of a low carbon building should also ensure that it does not depreciate in value and it will be relatively easy to sell or let in future.

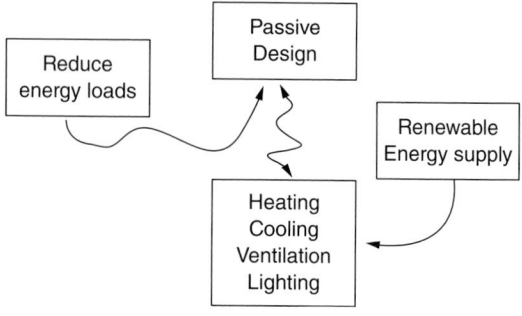

8.73 *Schematic diagram of low carbon design using a holistic approach*

The stages outlined in 8.73 are as follows:

1 *Reduce energy demand associated with activities*. This includes reducing the electricity load associated with lighting, small power and other electrical equipment. This will benefit in two ways. Firstly the electricity used will be directly reduced, and secondly, the heat associated with the use of electrical equipment will be reduced thereby reducing any potential cooling needs. Of course the incidental heat gains associated with equipment will be reduced from the point of providing useful heat to the space, but in a low carbon building this is not always useful and uncontrolled in relation to heating needs. The ventilation load should also be minimised by reducing any internal sources of air pollution and separately ventilating any specific sources of activity requiring additional ventilation.

2 *Passive design*. To adopt a passive design approach to reduce the energy demand associated with heating, ventilation, air conditioning and lighting. This maximises the use of the climate (Section 1.2), through solar control, use of natural daylight, thermal mass effects and natural ventilation (where appropriate). The design should be sensitive to the orientation and form of the building, its construction and distribution of glazing with shading or glazing treatment, ventilation opening and devices and use of materials. The Passive Haus standard is a useful target, although this will require mechanical ventilation with heat recovery and very high standards of thermal insulation and minimising thermal bridging. In future, reducing the embodied energy associated with construction materials and building services equipment will need to be considered, as the embodied energy becomes comparable to the operating energy over the building lifetime.

3 *Efficient environmental services*. Once the energy demand has been reduced through 1 and 2 above, the provision of heating and cooling etc. becomes simpler and more efficient. The current trend for low carbon buildings is to use surface heating and cooling, Figure 8.68, often in combination with mechanical ventilation systems, which can incorporate heat recovery and some element of heating and cooling. It is advisable to decouple the ventilation from heating and cooling, such that any air supply system is primarily designed for ventilation and the main component of heating or cooling delivered is through the surface system (heated or cooled floor, ceiling, panels, etc.). The control of environmental services should be simple and responsive to people's needs. In general, over-complicated controls quickly go out of calibration, especially with change of use, and are often illegible to the people who operate the building.

4 *Renewable energy systems*. The final stage in low carbon design is to provide the energy needed for heating, cooling, ventilation and lighting from low or zero carbon systems, such as solar PV, solar thermal, wind, biomass, hydro, heat-pumps and CHP. Once the energy demand of the building is reduced the amount of energy supply is also reduced, so making building or community integrated renewables more achievable. The thermal energy from heat pumps and solar systems is also more appropriate to the reduced temperatures required for heating low carbon buildings. Higher water temperature for cooling, say chilled ceilings, can increase the operating COP of heat pumps.

The above stages bring together many of the topics discussed in this chapter. In many ways reducing energy loads and the passive design aspect (1 and 2) are well understood by designers. What is less understood is how to provide appropriate environmental services and renewable energy systems, as part of an integrated approach to low carbon design.

8.40 Zero carbon buildings
Zero carbon buildings combine a reduced energy demand for heating, cooling, ventilation, lighting, cooking and electrical appliance load, with the use of renewable energy sources, such as solar thermal, solar PV, wind and biomass. An optimum balance of demand reduction and renewable energy supply is needed and this may differ for different building types and location. This definition of zero carbon only addresses the operating energy of the building. Other definitions might include the use of renewable energy through the lifetime of the building to offset the embodied energy incorporated in the building construction, or even to offset some lifestyle energy uses, such as transport, food and consumer goods. All definitions of zero carbon buildings imply:

- Energy demand reduction through reduced internal loads and passive design.
- Renewable energy systems, building integrated or community based.
- Energy storage either through local or grid systems (e.g. 2-way flows).

9 PREDICTION AND MEASUREMENT

9.1 Technique
There are a number of prediction and measurement techniques now available that the designer can use to help achieve a good thermal design. Prediction techniques can be used during the design to inform the design process. Measurement techniques can be applied after construction, during the 'hand-over' period, in order to check the thermal design performance. Some of the more common techniques are introduced below.

9.2 Building energy models
Computational dynamic building energy models can be used to predict the time-varying thermal performance of a building. They are able to predict the dynamic performance of a building and can account for the thermal capacity of the structure as well as time-varying response to internal heat gains and solar radiation, Figure 8.74. They will predict on a regular time interval (usually hourly) the following parameters:

- Internal air temperature
- Internal surface temperatures (including those from chilled surface cooling systems)
- Temperatures and heat flows within constructions (e.g. in relation to thermal mass effects)
- Internal relative humidity
- Energy used for space heating or cooling
- Temperature profiles through the construction (including glazed facades).

These values can be predicted for each space in the building over any time period (e.g. day, week, year). The models require the following input data:

- Meteorological data: temperature, solar, wind. This is available in standard *test reference year (TRY)* format for various sites.
- Construction data: k-values, density, specific heat capacity, and dimensions for materials used.
- Building geometry: areas and locations of walls, floors, etc.
- Occupancy patterns: hours of use, energy use, activities.
- Heating, ventilating and cooling operation: times of use, system and control details.

9.3 Ventilation and airflow models
Network models
Network or *zonal* models can be used to calculate the flow of air between one or more zones in a building and between the spaces and outside. They are computer based and calculate the flows between pressure nodes both within and outside the building. Their main advantage is that they can be used to calculate inter-zone

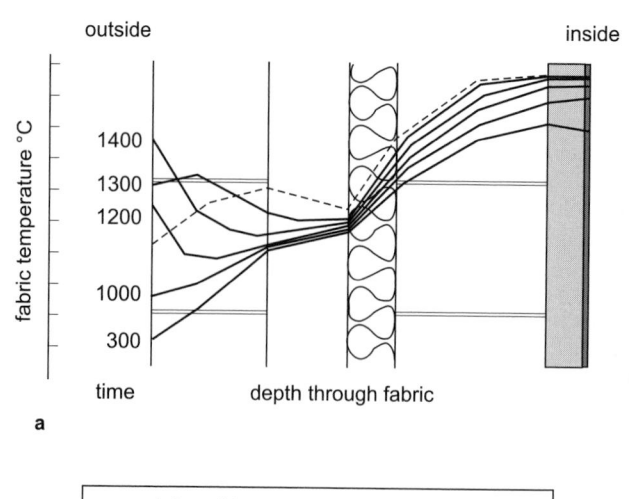

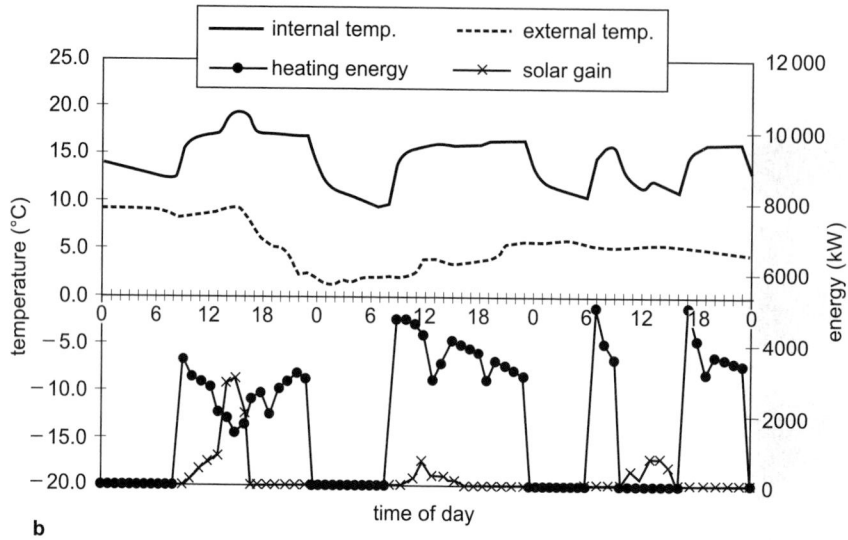

8.74 *Example of the results of the building energy model HTB2: a Predicting the temperature profile through a wall over time; b Forecasting the internal air temperature and energy use as they vary with external temperature and solar gain over a three-day period*

flows and therefore air change rates, ventilation heat transfer and the transfer of contaminants. They can be used to study new building forms, can handle a wide range of opening and crack types and can predict the interaction of buoyancy and wind-driven effects.

Computational fluid dynamics (CFD) models
CFD can be used to predict the internal airflow and heat distribution, driven by the combination of the external forces of wind and stack and the internal forces from buoyancy (warm or cold

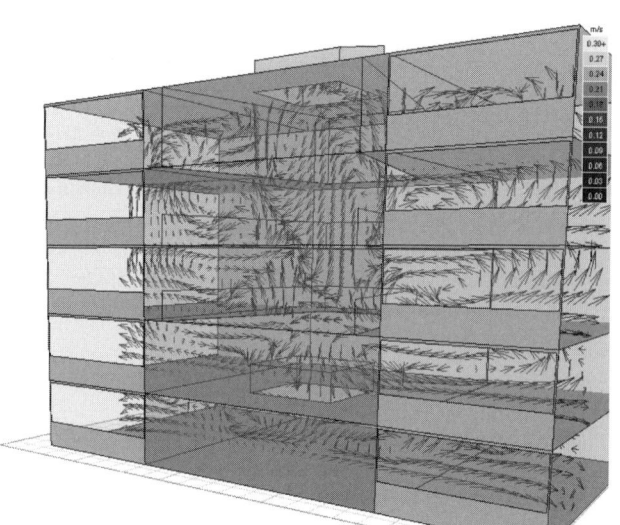

8.75 *Example of the use of computational fluid dynamics (CFD) to predict air movement in an atrium*

surfaces) and momentum (airjets) sources, Figure 8.75. It can also be used to predict the ventilation rate and the dispersal of a pollutant through the space or smoke movement in the event of a fire. CFD can be used to predict the external wind flow around a building and the resulting pressure field from which the pressure coefficients (C_p) can be calculated. It is therefore an extremely versatile and useful technique in the field of ventilation and air quality prediction. It is, however, highly complex and requires a high level of skill and understanding of ventilation design, building physics and computational numerical techniques in order to obtain credible solutions. However, models are becoming easier to use by the non-specialist and the need to use such models in ventilation design will eventually result in their widespread use.

Wind tunnel modelling
A physical model of a building and its surroundings can be constructed and placed in a wind tunnel, Figure 8.76, where it is subjected to a controlled wind flow. Pressure sensor taps can be installed at various points on the building envelope, corresponding to ventilation openings. The pressure at each opening can be measured. This can then be related to the free wind pressure, at a point of known height above the surface, in order to obtain the C_p value as described in Section 4.

9.4 Thermographic surveys
All objects emit heat energy (i.e. infrared radiation), the amount being dependent on the surface temperature and its emissivity.
Thermography is the term used to describe the process of making this heat energy visible and capable of interpretation. An infrared camera can be used to scan the surfaces of a

8.76 *Boundary layer wind tunnel and model at the Welsh School of Architecture used for measuring Cps*

building and produce a 'live' heat energy picture that can be viewed. The picture appears in colour or greyscale. The differences in colour or tones of grey correspond to differences in surface temperature across the surface being viewed. Surface temperature differences of the order of 0.5°C can be identified. Areas of defective or missing insulation can be detected by identifying locally warm (viewed from the outside) or cool (viewed from the inside) surface areas. Generally images taken from the inside, compared to those taken from the outside, can exhibit greater temperature variations due to their relative higher internal surface thermal resistance, and therefore be of higher resolution. If there is air leakage into a building it can produce a locally cooled area on the internal surface which can be detected by the camera. If there is air leakage to the outside this can produce a locally heated area. Figure 8.77 presents some examples of thermographic images.

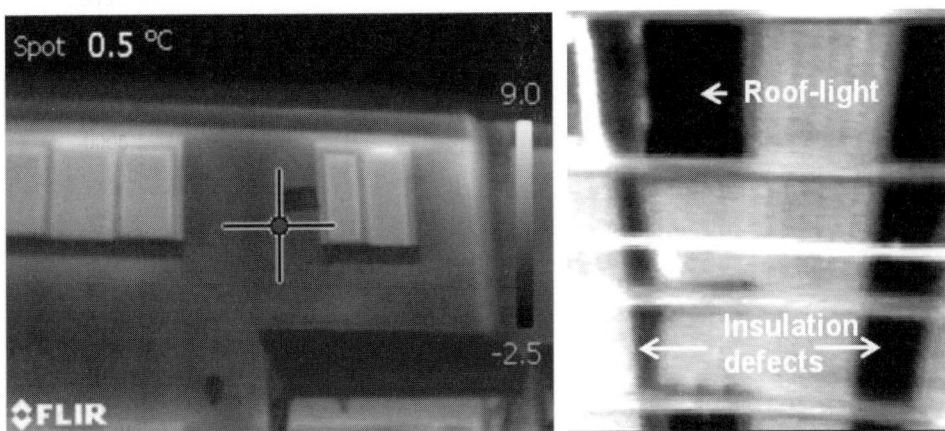

8.77 *Examples of thermographic images from outside (left) and inside (right)*

9.5 U-value measurement

The U-value of a construction can be estimated from measurements of internal and external surface temperature and heat flux. These measurements need to be carried out over a period of time to minimise the effects of thermal capacity. For lightweight cladding constructions an estimate of the U-value can be achieved in about eight hours. In heavyweight masonry construction a period of a week to ten days may be needed. Measurements should be carried out on a north-facing wall or roof to avoid interference from solar gains.

9.6 Air leakage measurements

These offer a means of assessing the airtightness of different buildings by comparison with values. The air leakage of a building can be measured by pressurising or depressurising the building using a fan measuring the volume flow of air needed to maintain a fixed pressure difference between inside and outside.

Table XL Air leakage standards, for 50Pa Internal/external pressure difference of 50Pa

	$m^3/h/m^2$ @50Pa
Domestic	7
Commercial	
Natural ventilation	10
Air conditioning	5
Industrial	15

Source: BSRIA.

Air leakage rate standards are normally specified either for whole buildings (in air changes per hour) or in normalised form relating to envelope area (m^3s^{-1} per m^2 of envelope area). Table XL presents typical design air leakage values.

9 Light

Joe Lynes

Joe Lynes is a lighting consultant

KEY POINTS:
- *Daylight and sunlight for energy conservation*
- *Energy-efficient electric lighting*
- *Lighting in the Building Regulations*

Contents

1 A passive solar resource
2 Daylight indoors
3 Window design
4 Electric lighting – energy efficiency
5 Lighting controls
6 Sizing an overall lighting installation
7 Display lighting
8 Visual display terminals
9 Glossary
10 Bibliography

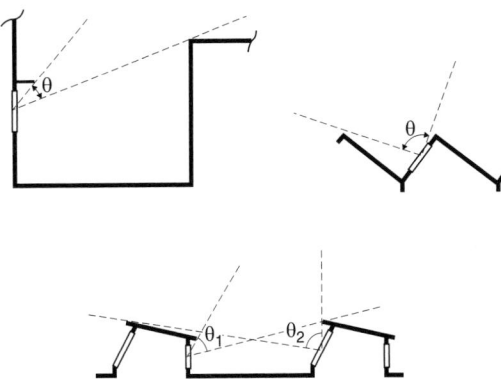

9.1 *θ is the angle subtended at the window by the visible sky*

INTRODUCTION

Recent advances in software and computer graphics mean that electric lighting design is increasingly computer-based, and handled by specialist consultants. Architects should note fresh demands of Building Regulations in this field. They should be aware of continuous gains in lamp efficacy, especially in connection with LED lamps (light emitting diodes). They should also appreciate how the choice of luminaires can affect the character of a lit interior.

Window design largely remains in architectural hands. Natural lighting has important implications for site layout and massing, and for energy conservation. Sunlight is increasingly important; solar geometry is the key to harnessing sunlight. Daylight factors remain significant, average values now replacing traditional minimum requirements. Switches and lighting controls, encouraged by Building Regulations, give extra scope for energy savings when thoughtfully applied.

1 A PASSIVE SOLAR RESOURCE

1.1 Siting and orientation

Thermal applications of solar energy have long been recognised. The potential of sunlight, direct and diffused, in saving electrical energy by reducing the demand for artificial lighting, is less obvious. Here early decisions on siting and orientation may be more effective than later decisions on fenestration. Detailed guidance on the strategy of daylighting is contained in Littlefair (2011).

High-rise buildings should ideally be sited to the north, and low-rise or low-density buildings to the south of a new development, taking care not to overshadow existing buildings. Full advantage should be taken of south-facing slopes. Terraced housing should run east-to-west, so that one wall can face south. Detached or semi-detached dwellings can be on north-south link roads. Courtyards should ideally be open to the southern half of the sky. Garages and parking spaces should preferably face north. The pitch of north-facing roofs should be shallow to minimise overshadowing.

1.2 Site planning criteria

The skylight illumination reaching any point depends largely on how much sky is visible from the point in question. The amount of light striking a window (and hence entering a room) on a densely overcast day is roughly proportional to the angle θ, Figure 9.1, i.e. to the effective angle in degrees subtended in a vertical plane by the sky visible from the centre of the window.

The BRE Report 'Site layout planning for daylight and sunlight' (Littlefair, 2011) expresses the daylight reaching a vertical wall or window, on a densely overcast day, in terms of the *vertical sky component* SC_v. This is the direct *illuminance* (lux) on the vertical surface, expressed as a percentage of the simultaneous horizontal illuminance under an unobstructed overcast sky. An unobstructed vertical surface would have a vertical sky component of 39 per cent.

An additional check on the penetration of skylight is provided by the *no-sky line*, Figure 9.2. This is the 'line' (actually a surface in three-dimensional space) which divides a room into two parts: one part is exposed to a view of the sky, the other part receives no direct daylight at all. The latter zone is disadvantaged with regard to both view and natural lighting.

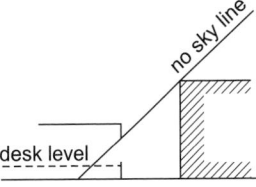

9.2 *No sky is directly visible from indoors to the left of the no-sky line*

The recommendations in the BRE Report are summarised below in Sections 1.3 to 1.8 and in Table I.

1.3 New developments – skylight potential

Two alternative checks are recommended to ensure that surrounding obstructions do not unduly detract from the natural lighting in a room. First, from a standard reference height 2 m above ground level, check whether any visible obstruction projects above the 25° horizontal roofline limit, Figure 9.3. Odd trees may be ignored. If the 25° line is substantially clear of obstruction then a target

Table I BRE criteria and planning aids

Criterion	Where	Standard	Indicator	Short cut	Count
Skylight potential	New-build	Within 4m of SC$_v$ 27%	Skylight indicator, **39.4**	Clear above 25°	54 crosses
Skylight potential	Existing window	SC$_v$ at window at least 27%	V Skylight indicator, **39.4**	Clear above 25°	54 crosses
Skylight potential	Boundary	Within 4m of SC$_v$ 17%	Skylight indicator, **39.4**	Clear above 34 43°	crosses
Sunlight potential	New-build	1 principal wall within 90° of due south. Within 4m of exposure to 25% of probable sunlight hours, including at least 5% in winter 6 months	Sunlight availability indicator, **39.5**	25 and 5 dots	
Sunlight potential	Existing window	25% of probable sunlight hours, including at least 5% in winter 6 months	Sunlight availability indicator, **39.5**	Clear above 25 and 25°	5 dots
Sunlight potential	Open space	Not more than 40% totally shaded at equinoxes	Sun-on-ground indicator, **39.6**	% area shaded	
Planning for sunlight			Sunpath indicator, **39.7**		

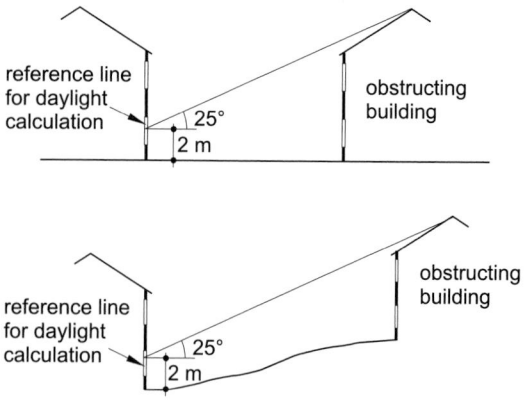

9.3 *The 25° criterion*

1.4 New developments – sunlight potential

Incident sunlight is expressed in terms of *probable sunlight hours*. These are the total number of hours per year when the sun would, under typical cloud conditions, shine directly onto a given point.

In a new dwelling, and in any other new buildings in which sunlight would be desirable, two recommendations for incident sunlight should both be met:

(a) One principal window wall should face within 90° of due south, and

(b) Along this window wall, every point on the standard 2 m reference line should be within 4 m (measured sideways) of a point exposed to at least one quarter of the annual probable hours of sunlight on an open site. These hours of exposure should include at least 5 per cent of probable hours of sunlight in the six winter months between 21 September and 21 March.

The BRE Report contains *sunlight availability indicators*, Figure 9.5, for three latitudes: 51.5°N (London), 53.5°N (Manchester) and 56°N (Glasgow). These can be used for estimating hours of *probable sunlight* on an obstructed site.

vertical sky component of at least 27 per cent should be achieved. If this first check fails, the obstruction may still be narrow enough to allow adequate daylight around its sides. To check this, it is necessary to ensure that every point on the façade, along the standard 2 m reference line, is within 4 m (measured sideways) of a point which does have a vertical sky component of 27 per cent or more. The BRE Report contains a *skylight indicator*, Figure 9.4, for estimating vertical sky components on an obstructed site.

1.5 Existing buildings – skylight protection

If any part of a new building or extension, seen from the lowest window of an existing building, projects above the 25° horizontal reference limit, Figure 9.3, then two further tests must be applied:

(a) The *vertical sky component* at the centre of each existing main window must be not less than 27 per cent, and not less than 0.8 times its previous value, and

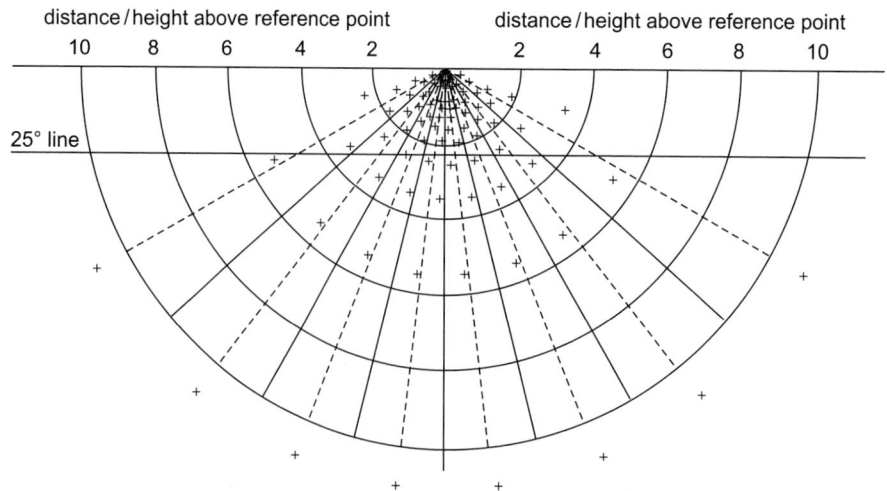

9.4 *Skylight indicator (with kind permission of BRE)*

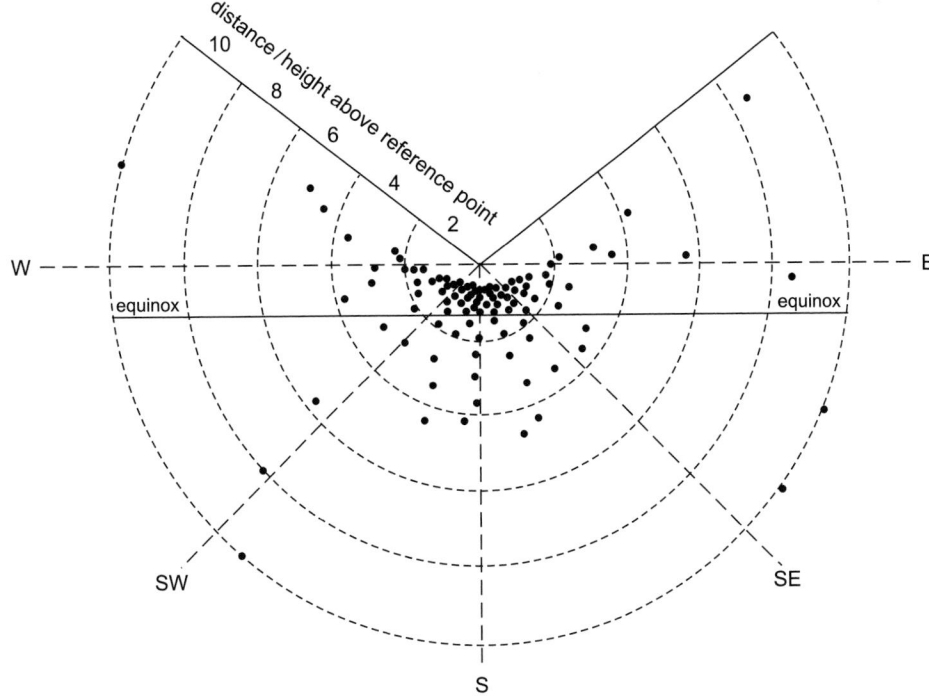

9.5 *Sunlight availability indicator for latitude 53.5° N. The annual total of unobstructed hours of probable sunlight would be 1392 hours (with kind permission of BRE)*

(b) The area of the *working plane* within the *no-sky line*, 9.2, must not be less than 0.8 times its previous value.

The BRE *skylight indicator*, Figure 9.4, is designed for checking vertical sky components.

In some cases, legal rights to light may supplement the BRE recommendations. A right to light may be gained either by legal agreement or if a window has received the light without interruption for 20 years or more. Infringement of a right to light is judged by comparing *sky factor* contours indoors before and after the infringement.

1.6 Existing buildings – sunlight protection
If an existing living room has a main window facing within 90° of due south, one of two alternative conditions should be met: either

(a) No part of a new building, seen from the centre of the window and projected onto a vertical plane perpendicular to the window wall, is more than 25° above the horizon, or
(b) The point at the centre of the window, on the indoor plane of the window wall, must be exposed to at least a quarter of annual *probable sunlight hours*, including at least 5 per cent of annual probable sunlight hours in the six winter months between 21 September and 21 March, and not less than 0.8 times its previous sunlight hours in either period. The BRE *sunlight availability indicators*, Figure 9.5, are used to check compliance.

1.7 Adjoining development land
For a building to be a 'good neighbour', it should stand well back from the plot boundary to avoid unduly restricting well-daylit development on adjoining properties. A neighbouring site will have acceptable daylight protection if, along each common boundary line, one of the following alternative criteria is met: either

(a) No new building, seen from a point 2 m above ground level and projected onto a vertical plane perpendicular to the boundary, is more than 43° above the horizon, or
(b) Every point 2 m above the boundary line should lie within 4 m (measured along the boundary) of a point which has a *vertical sky component* (facing the new obstruction) of 17 per cent or more.

Note: There is no protection for sunlight (or view), as distinct from skylight, along boundaries.

1.8 BRE site planning aids
The Building Research Establishment has issued a number of indicators to assist designers in meeting their site planning recommendations:

- Skylight indicator, Figure 9.4;
- Sunlight availability indicator, Figure 9.5;
- Sun-on-ground indicator, Figure 9.6;
- Sunpath indicator, Figure 9.7.

Table I summarises the BRE criteria, indicating which planning aid is applicable to each criterion.

1.9 Solar geometry
The sun's apparent position in the sky is specified in terms of two angular coordinates:

- the *altitude* γ in degrees above the horizon;
- the *azimuth* α in degrees clockwise in plan, measured from due north.

These coordinates are given by the equations:

$$\gamma = \arcsin\,(sin\varphi\;sin\delta - cos\varphi\;cos\,\delta\;cos\;15t) \qquad \text{equation (1)}$$
$$\alpha = \arccos\,[(sin\;\varphi - sin\delta\;sin\gamma)/(cos\varphi\;cos\gamma)] \qquad \text{equation (2)}$$

where φ = geographical latitude of site (positive in the northern hemisphere)
δ = *solar declination*, Table II (north is positive, south negative)
t = hours since midnight (note that the term *15t* is in degrees, not in radians)

the *altitude* of the sun at noon is $(90° - (\varphi - \delta))$.

1.10 Sunlight – the use of models
A simple block model is adequate for most studies of solar penetration and for the choice of solar protection. It can be illuminated by a small lamp located as far from the model as possible to ensure near-parallel 'sunlight'. Better still, in conjunction with the matchbox sundial, one can use the real sun outdoors as a light source. The relative positions of source and model

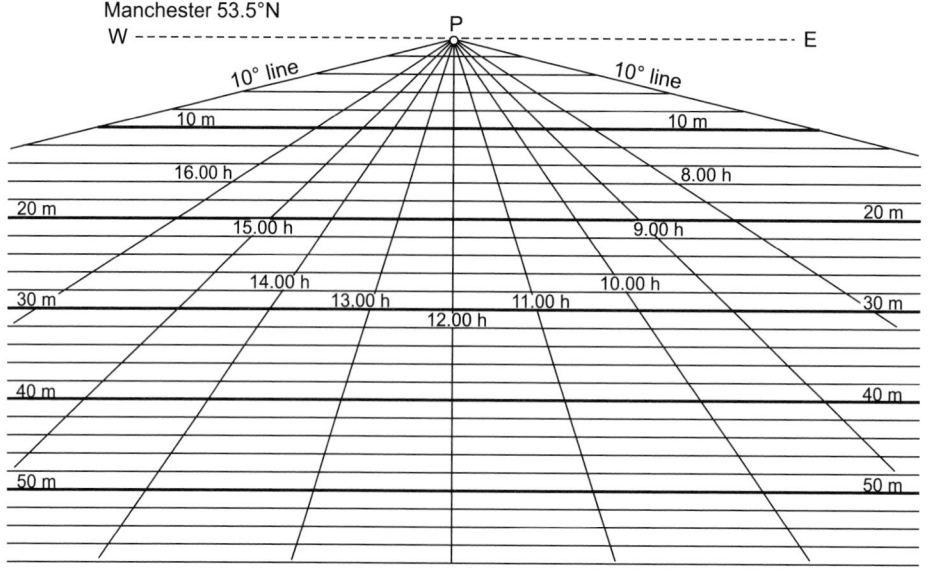

9.6 *Sun on ground indicator for 21 March, latitude 53.5° N (with kind permission of BRE)*

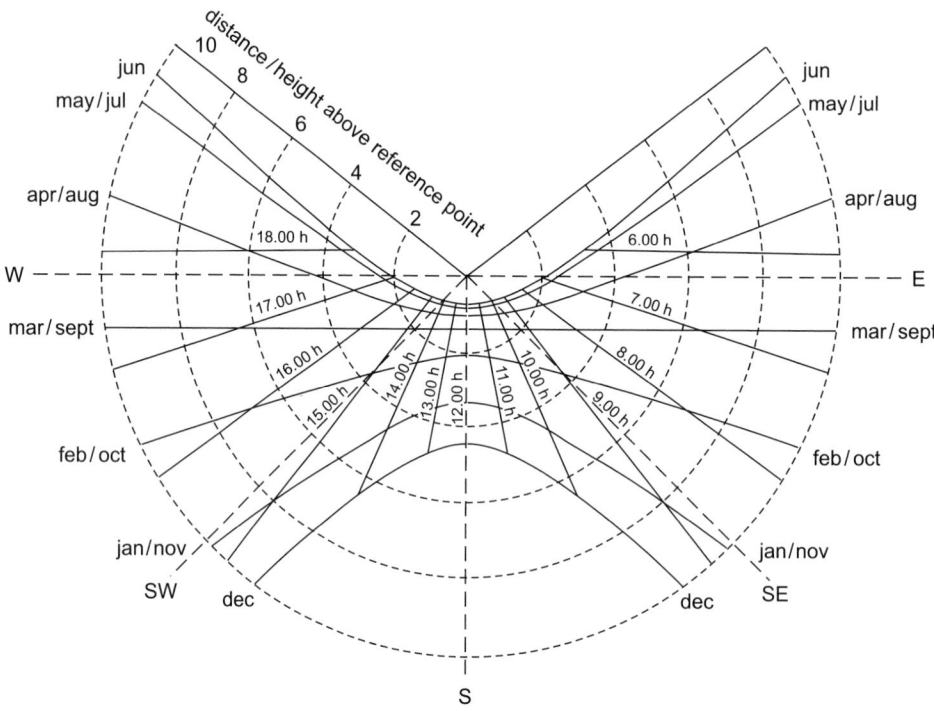

9.7 *Sunpath indicator for latitude 53.5 N (with kind permission of BRE)*

are so arranged that the direction of the incident light will replicate the direction of the sun's rays at the time and season under
investigation.

One way of bringing the correct angles of sunlight to bear on the
model is to mount it on a *heliodon,* Figure 9.8. A simple turntable
carries a platform which is tilted so as to be parallel to the earth's
surface at the relevant latitude, ground at the north pole being
taken as horizontal. The artificial sun is moved above or below
this horizontal datum plane, depending on the season/*declination*;
it may slide up and down a vertical scale, Figure 9.9, whose sol-
stice-to-solstice height subtends 46.6° at the centre of the tilted heliodon platform. The centre of the vertical scale should be level with
the platform. The earth's daily rotation is simulated by spinning
the tilted platform so that the movement of shadows throughout a
chosen day can be observed.

Table II Solar declinations

Dates	Solar declination
22 June	23.4°N (Summer solstice)
21 May/24 July	20°N
26 April/28 August	10°N
21 March/23 September	0° (Equinox)
23 February/20 October	10°S
21 January/22 November	20°S
22 December	23.4°S (winter solstice)

The matchbox sundial, Figure 9.10, has been described as the
poor person's heliodon. It comprises a stick (the 'gnomon') standing in a folded tray which fits inside a matchbox. A grid of lines on
the tray traces the position of the shadow of the tip of the gnomon at

different hours and seasons. The seven monthly shadow orbits correspond to the dates and *solar declinations* shown in Table II. The matchbox sundial illustrated is suitable only for latitude 53.5°N. To use it elsewhere, tilt it about an east-west axis through an angle equal to the difference in latitude, shadows being shorter as you approach the equator.

Align the north point on the sundial with the north point of the model. Shine a distant lamp on the sundial, casting the shadow of the gnomon at the month and time of day under consideration. The pattern of sunlight and shadow should be correct on the model. Ideally this is a three-person activity. The first person – the tallest! – holds the lamp as far from the model as possible. The second watches the sundial and directs the first accordingly. The third takes photographs – always from due north in the northern hemisphere,

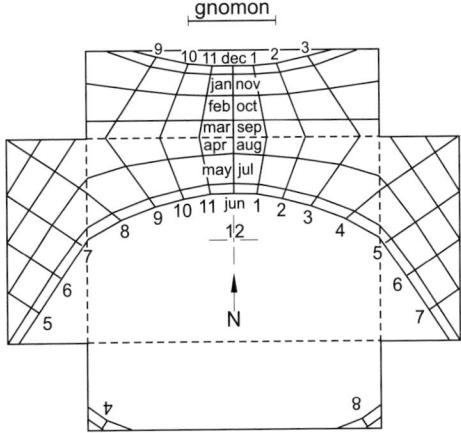

9.10 *Matchbox sundial for latitude 53.5° N*

otherwise a shadow of the photographer, camera and tripod will appear in the photograph. Remember to include in each photograph a card to show the time and date under investigation. Otherwise you may not be sure afterwards which photograph is which!

The alternative 'aviator method' avoids the need for colleagues, and for plunging your environment into darkness, but there are no photographs to show for it. This approach depends on the fact that the sun never 'sees' a shadow. Solar shadows are cast only on surfaces hidden from direct sunlight. Place a matchbox sundial, correctly orientated, beside a model. Align your eye with the tip of the gnomon, and with the chosen time and date marks. Those parts of the model which you can see from that position will be sunlit at the chosen time. Those parts which are concealed will be in shadow. The aviator method also works with a heliodon if you place your eye in the position of the 'sun'.

Model studies are useful for three types of sunlight investigation:

1 Seeing how far direct sunlight can penetrate inside a modelled room, and how effectively it is controlled by sunbreaks.
2 Seeing how adjacent buildings intercept each other's sunlight.
3 Judging the quality of sunlight illumination received indoors after reflection from the ground and from nearby sunlit buildings; this is more applicable to dry tropical areas than to the UK.

2 DAYLIGHT INDOORS

2.1 Daylight factors

Daylight design in the UK has traditionally been based on the convention of a Standard Overcast Sky for three reasons:

(a) Prudence: if the natural lighting is sufficient on an overcast day it is likely to be more than adequate when the sun shines.
(b) Convenience: a densely overcast sky looks the same whichever direction (in plan) one faces – north, south, east or west. The effect of orientation vanishes from the calculation but not, one hopes, from the designer's awareness!
(c) Given the overall brightness profile of a Standard Overcast Sky, the *illuminance* at any given point indoors must be directly proportional to the simultaneous outdoor illuminance under the unobstructed overcast sky vault, whether the sky itself is bright or dull.

The constant ratio of indoor to unobstructed outdoor illuminance is usually expressed as a percentage, and is referred to as the *daylight factor*. Thus the daylight factor at a given point may be defined as the *illuminance* (lux) at that point, expressed as a percentage of the simultaneous horizontal illuminance under an unobstructed overcast sky.

Until recently it was customary to specify natural lighting levels in terms of the minimum daylight factor in a given interior. This

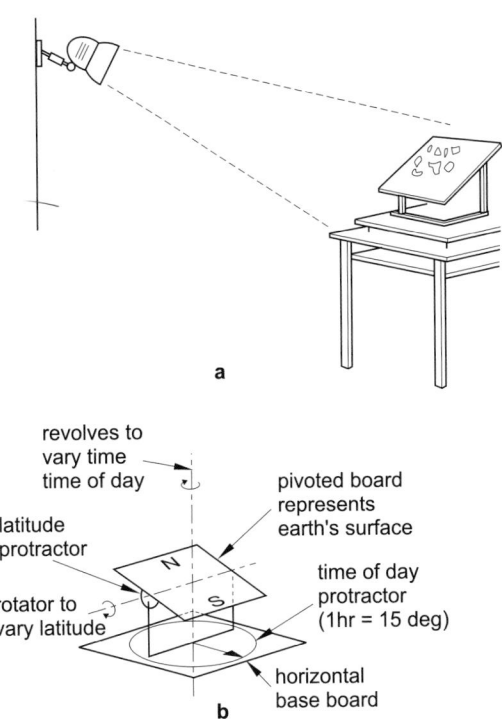

9.8 *The heliodon: a In use; b Explanatory diagram*

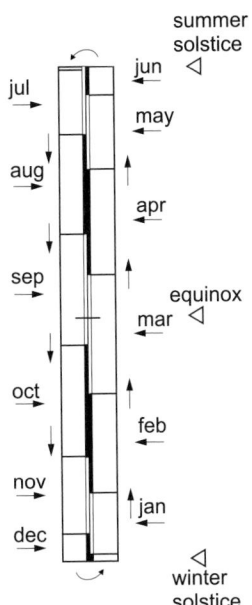

9.9 *Graduated season scale for heliodon. A lamp slides up and down this scale to simulate the sun's position month by month*

involved a painstaking calculation at the end of which there was little assurance that people's impression of daylit spaces would actually correlate with the minimum daylight factors. The current trend is to express the natural lighting of a room in terms of the average (as distinct from the minimum) daylight factor. This requires only a back-of-the-envelope calculation (see Section 2.3), and yields, for each room, a single figure which characterises the daylight level.

Limitations of the average daylight factor must not be overlooked. In a medium-sized room we can usually form a unitary impression of the natural lighting: we sum it up as 'bright', 'adequate', 'dim', etc., as the case may be. But in a deeper side-lit space our impression is more complex; one end of a room may look bright, the other end dim by comparison. To interpret an average daylight factor with discernment we need to know at what point the concept will break down.

Broadly speaking, a side-lit room is too deep – or the natural lighting unbalanced – when either the *no-sky line,* Figure 9.2, cuts off a substantial area of the *working plane,* and/or

when $l/w + l/h > 2 / (1 - R_b)$ 　　　　　equation (3)

where 　　l = depth of room from window to back wall
　　　　w = width of room measured across the window wall
　　　　h = height of window head above floor
　　　　R_b = area-weighted average *reflectance* in back half of room

Unless the average daylight factor has been ruled out by one of the above considerations, it may be quoted with confidence to characterise the daylit appearance of a room. Thus an average daylight factor greater than 5 per cent will generally give the impression of generous natural lighting (except, of course, on a dull day or in the evening); an average below 2 per cent would be judged gloomy, and electric lighting would be switched on as soon as an occupant entered the room.

2.2 The use of models in daylight prediction

Scale model rooms have often been used for the prediction of daylight factors. The basic laws of illumination (the additivity, inverse square and cosine laws acting together) dictate that daylight factors in a perfectly scaled model must agree with those in the full-scale building. Unfortunately immediate application of this principle is fraught with pitfalls for the unwary.

Architectural models commissioned for other purposes are unlikely to be suitable. Joints and corners must be perfectly light-tight. Walls must be opaque: balsa and white card are out. Surface colours, and especially *reflectances,* must be correctly simulated. Glass *transmittance* must also be correct or, failing that, must be offset by applying a correction factor to the end result. Outdoor obstructions must be properly scaled, at least with regard to their angular subtense, and also finished appropriately. Finally the measured daylight factor must be adjusted to take account of dirt on the glass and on room surfaces, and to allow for any curtains or glazing bars, and for absorption of light by furniture and other impediments.

In principle the daylight factor inside a model can be obtained by measuring the indoor illuminance at some chosen position with a lightmeter, and expressing it as a percentage of the illuminance on the roof of the model. This assumes that the roof of the model is exposed to the whole sky vault. It assumes too that the sky is densely overcast; this requirement follows from the definition of a *daylight factor.*

The necessity of waiting for overcast conditions to occur unaccompanied by rain, snow or gusty winds has led, logically enough, to the development of artificial skies, providing a Standard Overcast brightness profile at the flick of a switch. These too have their pitfalls. Mirror-box skies produce multiple reflections of the model above horizon level. Those too small to accommodate a model inside will be unsuitable for testing rooflights. Sky domes will suffer from parallax and horizon errors unless the 'sky' is very large compared with the model under test.

Since most of the potential errors would cause daylight measurements in models to be overestimated, one can anticipate that, unless exceptional precautions are taken, daylight factors measured in a model will considerably exceed those in the real building. This need not discourage the use of models. However one may wonder why a designer would bother with daylight factors when he or she can judge and fine-tune the daylit appearance of his or her model by eye. The best advice must be to formulate in advance the questions – they may be qualitative rather than numerical – which the model study is designed to answer. Analysis of these key questions may well reveal that specific daylight factors are unimportant, and that more may be learned by studying a model under real sky conditions, facing alternately towards and away from the sun, than by leaving the overcast sky convention to dictate a programme of expensive measurements which may turn out to be irrelevant.

2.3 Calculating the average daylight factor

The average *daylight factor df* is given by the following equation:

$$df = (T \times W \times \theta \times M) / [A(1 - R^2)] \text{ per cent} \qquad \text{equation (4)}$$

where 　　T = *transmittance* of glazing material (clear single glazing = 0.82; clear double glazing = 0.70)
　　　　W = net area of glazing material
　　　　θ = vertical angle of sky seen from centre of window, Figure 9.1
　　　　M = maintenance factor, Table III
　　　　A = total area of interior surfaces: floor + ceiling + walls, including windows
　　　　R = area-weighted average *reflectance* of interior surfaces

2.4 Shaping a window

Increasingly the prime function of a window is as much to provide a view as to illuminate the interior. In principle the analysis of view presents no great problem. A straight line can be drawn from the eye of an occupant to an object of regard outside the building. If the straight line passes through a window opening, in both plan and section, then the object will be visible; if not it may be necessary to alter the shape or position of the window. In practice, occupants move around, and the indoor end of the straight line moves with them; a good view from the back of a room will be harder to achieve than a view from just inside the window. The choice of desirable objects of regard is usually easier in reality than in theory; but it is a choice that needs to be made consciously and deliberately if the window is to be optimised.

The skyline plays a key role. Ideally the view of the skyline should not be interrupted by the window head. Should this be impracticable, some direct view of the sky remains desirable, if only to reveal the clarity or cloudiness of the local weather.

But the need for a view interacts with other aspects of the environment. A direct view of the sky can be a source of discomfort ('glare'), especially when the patch of sky is close to the direction of the sun. On the other hand, the daylight factor at the back of a room depends largely on the amount of sky directly visible, see Section 1.2. Thus there is a potential conflict between the imperatives of view, comfort and uniform daylighting. This conflict can be resolved only by prioritising. The relative importance of the three factors will largely determine the right shape and position for each window.

3 WINDOW DESIGN

3.1 A sequence for window design

We return to equation (4) for the average daylight factor, in Section 2.3. Inspection of the expression suggests a natural sequence for window design decisions.

Stage 1

The first item to be fixed in the equation is the angle θ defined by the position of exterior obstructions. This depends mainly on the

Table III Maintenance factors for natural lighting (Tregenza, Stewart and Sharples, 1999)

| | | Slope of glazing | | | | | |
| | | Vertical | | Inclined | | Horizontal | |
Room function	Exposure	Rural/ suburban	Urban	Rural/ suburban	Urban	Rural/ suburban	Urban
Residential	**Driving rain exposure**	0.98	0.95	0.94	0.88	0.88	0.76
Private rooms and communal areas, few occupants, good maintenance, no smoking.	**Normal exposure**	0.96	0.92	0.92	0.84	0.88	0.76
	Heavy snow exposure	0.96	0.92	0.88	0.76	0.84	0.68
	Sheltered by overhang	0.88	0.76				
Commercial, educational	**Driving rain exposure**	0.98	0.95	0.94	0.85	0.88	0.70
Rooms used by groups of people, areas with office equipment or with some smoking	**Normal exposure**	0.96	0.90	0.92	0.80	0.88	0.70
	Heavy snow exposure	0.96	0.90	0.88	0.70	0.84	0.60
	Sheltered by overhang	0.88	0.70				
Polluted and heavily used interiors	**Driving rain exposure**	0.92	0.90	0.76	0.70	0.52	0.40
Swimming pools, gymnasia, heavy industry or heavy smoking	**Normal exposure**	0.84	0.80	0.68	0.60	0.52	0.40
	Heavy snow exposure	0.84	0.80	0.53	0.40	0.36	0.20
	Sheltered by overhang	0.52	0.40				

spacing and massing of surrounding buildings. The block layout is effectively fixed quite early in the design process, well before fenestration has been thought about. Access, prospect, privacy, site utilisation and microclimate are some of the formative factors at this stage. Because these will act as constraints on the daylight factor, the determination of the angle θ is identified as the first stage in window design. Some relevant criteria and design aids were listed in Table I.

Stage 2
A side-lit room may be too deep to be satisfactorily daylit. This outcome was discussed in Section 2.1. It occurs when the *no sky line* seriously encroaches on the *working plane*, or when equation (3) indicates that the natural lighting at the back of the room will look unacceptably dim.

If the room is indeed too deep for stand-alone natural lighting, the average daylight factor will not be a useful design criterion. Instead the windows should be optimised mainly for view and for thermal performance and, if daylight linked controls, as in Section 5.2, are contemplated, for the dimming and extinction of the row of luminaires closest to the window wall. Unless the room survives the two tests in Stage 2 the designer should proceed straight to Stage 4, omitting Stage 3 of this window design sequence.

Stage 3
The window area W is estimated by inverting equation (4):

$$W = df \times A(1 - R^2)/(T \times \theta \times M)$$

At this point there is the familiar conflict between visual and thermal considerations. The average daylight factor *df* is proportional to the window area *W*, but so is the winter heat loss through the windows, and so (other things being equal) is the daily mean solar heat gain. Passive solar design, harnessing both daylight and solar gain, may optimise by reducing heat loss through the glazing. Other approaches to design must face and resolve a three-way conflict:

daylight versus heat loss and summer heat gain. It is important to resolve these pressures on the window area at this stage, before proceeding to Stage 4 which is concerned with optimising window shape and position for each window.

Stage 4
By this stage either the window area is established and the average daylight factor settled in Stage 3, or the room has been identified in Stage 2 as too deep for stand-alone natural lighting. In either case the shape and position of the windows have yet to be finalised, but the completion of the design is obviously simplified by the prior decisions in Stages 2 and 3.

The competing claims of view, visual comfort and daylight uniformity were reviewed in Section 2.4 above. They centred on the visibility of the skyline. The avoidance of glare required as little visible sky as possible. A good view implied a good sight of the skyline itself but no additional access to the sky. Uniform daylighting mandated as much sky as possible visible from the depths of the room. The conflict must be resolved, in Stage 4 as in Stage 3, by identifying and balancing the relevant priorities.

Also in Stage 4 the possible advantages of multilateral fenestration may merit review. Windows in more than one wall may improve the natural lighting in two respects: by increasing the area of sky seen from the worst-lit parts of the room, and by reducing the brightness contrast between the sky and the window walls. In a naturally ventilated building they will also promote cross-ventilation, mitigating summertime overheating.

Applicability
Obviously the above idealised sequence is remote from the reality of window design. The results of applying it slavishly window-by-window would be a chaotic elevation, maybe unbuildable. A formal design sequence should provide a safety-net for architects in trouble. They can retrace their steps and recognise false turns if need be. The key to good natural lighting design is to identify significant crunch points: What is the most important or the most

Table IV Circuit efficacies

Lamps	Circuit efficacy (lumens per watt)
Filament lamps	
60 W general lighting service (GLS)	10 lm/W
150 W linear halogen	15 lm/W
T8 fluorescent tubes	
58 W triphosphor with conventional ballast	77 lm/W
58 W triphosphor with high-frequency ballast	98 lm/W
58 W multiphosphor with conventional ballast	54 lm/W
58 W multiphosphor with high-frequency ballast	68 lm/W
Compact fluorescent	
18 W four-limb, high-frequency	60 lm/W
Metal halide	
400 W MBI-T	85 lm/W
70 W CDM	100 lm/W
High-pressure sodium	
250 W SON-T	102 lm/W
250 W SONDL-T (improved colour)	82 lm/W
100 W "White" SDW-T	42 lm/W
"White" Light-emitting diodes (LED)	
1100 lumens	53 lm/W
2000 lumens	56 lm/W

demanding room on a given facade? Design its windows properly. Repeat variants of the solution up and down the elevation. Then the windows will do their job, both as external visual elements and as components of the interior environment.

4 ELECTRIC LIGHTING – ENERGY EFFICIENCY

4.1 Lamp efficacy

The *efficacy* of an electric lamp is defined as its *luminous flux (lumens)* divided by the electric power consumed (watts). Efficacy is expressed in lumens per watt (lm/W). Lamp manufacturers specify the lumen output of a lamp as that of a clean lamp once its output is reasonably stable. For fluorescent and other discharge lamps this condition is said to be reached after 100 hours of normal running.

Note that lamp manufacturers normally express lamp efficacy as lumens per lamp watt, whereas Part L of the Building Regulations specifies lumens per circuit watt including power consumed by control gear. Some representative *circuit efficacies* are listed in Table IV.

4.2 Luminaires

The term *luminaire* covers a lighting fitting complete with control gear and suspension where applicable. The *light output ratio* (LOR) of a luminaire is the proportion of *luminous flux (lumens)* from the lamps which emerges from the luminaire. The LOR for a bare lamp would be 1.00. Other things being equal, a luminaire having a high LOR is more efficient than one with a lower LOR. Typical values are listed in Table V.

Table V Light output ratios for typical luminaires

Luminaire	Light output ratio (LOR)
Bare lamp	1.0
Open reflector	0.8
Pendent or surface-mounted diffuser	0.65
Louvered luminaire	0.6
Recessed diffuser	0.5

The *luminaire efficacy* is the *luminous flux* output from the luminaire, divided by the electric power consumed, including losses in control gear. Luminaire efficacy, like *lamp efficacy*, is measured in lumens per watt (lm/W).

$$\text{Luminaire efficacy} = \text{lamp efficacy} \times \text{LOR}$$

The *flux fraction ratio* (FFR) of a luminaire is the ratio of the flux (*lumens*) emerging in directions above the level of the luminaire, to the flux directed below the level of the luminaire. For a downlight the FFR is zero; for an uplighter, infinity.

With an FFR greater than 0.8, the ceiling may be more brightly lit than the working plane. With an FFR less than 0.1, the ceiling may look dark; so low-FFR luminaires work best when the ceiling, floor and table top all have a reasonably high *reflectance*. The FFR has a significant effect on the character of the lit environment. See Table VI.

Table VI Effects of luminaire light distribution on the atmosphere in a room

Flux fraction ratio FFR	Spread of downward light		
	light Tight	Medium	Widespread
0 to 0.1	Concentration on task in hand.	Dark ceiling may look oppressive.	Danger of glare?
0.1 to 0 8	Well-mannered, formal.	Safe, characterless?	Welcoming, expansive.
Over 0.8	Dignified.	Safe, relaxing.	Relaxing.

4.3 Building regulations – dwellings

In new dwellings, and in existing dwellings where major refurbishment is undertaken, at least 75 per cent of luminaires in regularly used rooms (i.e. other than cupboards, wardrobes and storage spaces) must use lamps with a *circuit efficacy* greater than 45 lumens per watt, and emitting over 400 lumens. Filament lamps fall well short of the circuit efficacy requirement.

Any fixed lighting must satisfy one or other of the following sets of requirements:
Either

> lamp wattage must not exceed 100 lamp-watts per fitting, and must be automatically extinguished if the area becomes unoccupied, or when daylight is adequate;

or alternatively

> *Lamp efficacy* must be greater than 45 lumens per circuit watt, luminaires must be controllable manually, and automatically extinguished when daylight is adequate.

4.4 Building regulations: non-domestic buildings

The following requirements apply to general lighting in offices, industrial or storage spaces, classrooms, seminar rooms and conference rooms. They apply to new buildings and to buildings where substantial refurbishment is undertaken.

The average initial *luminaire efficacy* must be not less than 55 luminaire lumens per circuit watt. The circuit wattage for each luminaire may be multiplied by the control factors in Table VII. To derive the average luminaire efficacy, divide the total luminaire output (lumens) by the total circuit wattage adjusted by control factors.

In other spaces the average initial *lamp efficacy* should be at least 55 lamp lumens per circuit watt; for display lighting, at least 22 lumens per circuit watt.

Electric lighting energy consumption must be metered separately from other electrical supplies, either by kWh meters in dedicated lighting circuits or in the lighting controls of a lighting or building management system, or by automatically logging energy consumed by the lighting.

Lighting controls should be tailored to the nature and use of each space.

Table VII Luminaire control factors

Output control	Control factor
(a) Photocell switching or dimming control in a daylit space. (A daylit space is an area within 6 m of a window wall at least 20 per cent glazed, or below rooflights with a glazing area at least 10 per cent of floor area).	0.9
(b) Occupancy detection. Lighting extinguished automatically when occupants leave, subject to safety considerations. Lighting switched on manually by occupants,	0.9
(c) (a) and (b) together.	0.85
(d) None of the above	1.00

5 LIGHTING CONTROLS

Five families of electric lighting controls may be distinguished as follows.

5.1 Constant illuminance control

Dimmable high-frequency fluorescent *luminaires* can be linked to indoor photocells set to sustain a fixed target *illuminance*. Otherwise a clean installation of new lamps would provide a substantially higher illuminance, missing an opportunity for energy savings. As time passes the controls will gradually pass additional power to the lamps, to compensate for light losses due to dirt and deterioration. When the lamps are fully loaded the time is overdue to alert the maintenance staff to clean the luminaires. This system has an additional advantage when the room changes from one use to another which permits a lower task illuminance: the setting can be adjusted to maintain the reduced lighting level.

5.2 Daylight linking

One or more rows of luminaires along a window wall may be linked to either interior or exterior photocells which monitor day light levels and adjust the electric lighting accordingly, preferably by top-up (dimming) rather than by automatic daylight-linked on-off switching The latter may be resented by occupants unless they understand and fully accept the purpose and value of the provision. Note that high-intensity discharge lamps, and most compact fluorescent lamps, are unsuitable for dimming. Control zones should be parallel to the main windows. Daylight linking can be combined with the occupancy detection system, Section 5.5.

5.3 Manual switching

Manual switches should be close to the luminaires they control. A bank of unlabelled switches invites indiscriminate switching. As a rule of thumb, the number of switches in a space should be not less than the square root of the number of luminaires. Thus twelve luminaires would require at least four switches. Options include low-voltage switching, pull-cords and remote 'wireless' switches such as ultrasonic or infrared; or a telephone signal to an energy-management system.

Manual switching is particularly suitable for a cellular office or consulting room, or for work stations which are occupied only intermittently.

5.4 Time switching

Electric lighting is switched off automatically at a control panel at the same time each day, perhaps to coincide with work breaks, e.g. at midday. It is better to switch half the lights at first, the rest 10 minutes later. A manual override then permits users to relight the lamps they still need. This system shares the responsibility for energy saving with the occupants, whose understanding and cooperation should be assured in advance.

There are several alternative methods for implementing a synchronised or staggered switch-off:

- low-voltage wiring to a relay in each lighting circuit
- a mains-borne signalling system
- a one-second interruption of the mains supply to each luminaire, causing latching relays to switch off.

In each case pull-switch or other manual overrides should be provided, for occupants to switch lamps straight back on if needed.

Time switching is particularly suitable for a hotel lounge, a restaurant, a shop, a corridor or an atrium.

5.5 Occupancy-linked switching

The aim of occupancy-linked lighting controls (presence detectors) is to operate the lighting when, but only when, somebody is there to make use of it. Some units beep or flash a warning signal just before lights are turned off, so that an undetected occupant can wave an arm and avoid being left in the dark. Fluorescent lamps require a time delay before switching off, as repeated switching shortens lamp life. Occupancy-linked discharge lamps with long restrike times should be supplemented by separate background lighting.

Occupancy detectors are suited to daylit spaces, and may be combined with daylight sensors, Section 5.2. Presence detectors can double as part of a security system. At night or at weekends they can activate an alarm instead of working the lights. They can also assist security patrols at night.

Occupancy detectors may be triggered by air movement, by a flapping curtain, or by events in a corridor outside the monitored space. Ultrasonic detectors seem more prone than passive infrared detectors to these extraneous stimuli. The sensitivity of some units can be adjusted to minimise such failings, at the price of their effective surveillance area. But the best arrangement is always to insist on manual-on/automatic-off occupancy controls with a manual override.

The best applications are where occupancy is infrequent or unpredictable, e.g. private offices, conference rooms, lecture rooms, toilets, warehouse storage aisles, photocopy rooms, and bookcase lighting in libraries.

6 SIZING AN OVERALL LIGHTING INSTALLATION

The sizing of overall lighting installations for working interiors and for floodlighting is nowadays left to computers. However the choice of target lighting levels remains in the hands of the specifier. The Building Regulations do not mandate target lighting levels. Wise choices may offer opportunities for appreciable savings in energy and in costs. Table VIII lists some recommendations from the Lighting Code of the Society of Light and Lighting (SLL), part of the Chartered Institution of Building Services Engineers. In many cases, especially in residential or public areas, a critical visual task is hard to identify and the *illuminance* should be chosen to provide the right atmosphere for getting together or for relaxing. Especially where this is the case, listed values of standard maintained illuminance should be treated as a point of departure, not as a target. If a designer seeks a subdued atmosphere a lower value would be right; if a livelier ambience is envisaged, a higher illuminance would be justified.

Table VIII Standard maintained illuminance recommendations

Location	Illuminance
Walkways Corridors	50 lux (can range from 5 to 100 lux)
Machine and turbine halls	100 lux (can range from 20 to 200 lux)
Classrooms	200 lux
General offices	300 lux (500 lux for adult education)
Technical drawing	200 to 500 lux
CAD work stations	750 lux 500 lux
General inspection and precision assembly	200 to 1000 lux
Minute assembly	2000 lux

7 DISPLAY LIGHTING

The effectiveness of display lighting depends as much on the skill of the person responsible for aiming it as on the good intentions of the specifier. The latter would be well advised to consider who is likely to take responsibility for the lighting once his or her back is turned. It may well be a caretaker, a shop assistant or a clerk of works, with no training in display lighting techniques. If so, any track lighting is likely to become poorly positioned and wrongly aimed. Fixed lighting, perhaps above egg-crate louvers, may well be preferable. The following notes relate mainly to track lighting, but the same principles apply to fixed lighting.

In a space where visitors are free to move around it is virtually impossible to light vertical surfaces without shining light straight into somebody's eyes. To remedy this, start from the principal entrance and plan a route through the exhibits. Run lighting track across, not along, this route. Arrange spotlights to shine over the shoulders of visitors following the preferred route. At each point along the route, make sure that the next stopping point is attractively lit, to encourage circulation in the right direction. Visitors moving the opposite way will face darker surfaces and will have to brave the dazzle of spotlights planned for their more accommodating brethren. They may take the hint.

Track lighting should preferably be 2.5 to 3 m high. Lower mounting would invite glare, tampering, discomfort from heat radiated from the lamps, and the shadows of visitors thrown on exhibits. Higher mounting would make aiming more difficult, and spotlights might remain unadjusted month after month.

Effective display lighting depends as much on darkness as on illumination. Objects will stand out only if they look significantly brighter than their surroundings. Brightness has two aspects:

- *Illuminance:* to appear noticeably brighter the illuminance on a surface should be at least three times the background illuminance; to stand out strongly would require a ratio of 10:1 or more.
- *Reflectance:* if an object has a lower reflectance than its background it will respond much less to an increase in illuminance; spotlighting may well be inappropriate, or the profile of the beam may need careful trimming to the profile of the target.

The overall pattern of light and shade deserves careful consideration. To pick out a single focus of attention is simple and always effective. To highlight two objects risks an impression of disunity. To spotlight more than three requires skill and invites confusion. Aim for a simple and clear hierarchy of illuminance.

The lighting of paintings, notice-boards, chalk-boards, etc. must meet two constraints:

- It must not produce shiny reflections, which reduce legibility
- It must provide reasonably even illumination over the target surface.

In Figure 9.11, the closest distance from which an observer can comfortably regard the picture as a whole is equal to the length of the picture's corner-to-corner diagonal. This fixes the distance D, which shows the best position for a luminaire. If it were mounted closer to the target surface, the foot of the target would look dimly lit compared with the top. If it were further back, a visitor would see shiny reflections.

In conclusion, the Golden Rule for successful spotlighting is 'Light the objects, not the people'. The positioning of luminaires should be constrained as much by the need to avoid glare and distraction as by the need to reveal an illuminated object.

8 VISUAL DISPLAY TERMINALS

The front surface of a visual display terminal (VDT) acts as a partial mirror. Screen visibility is impaired when shiny reflections

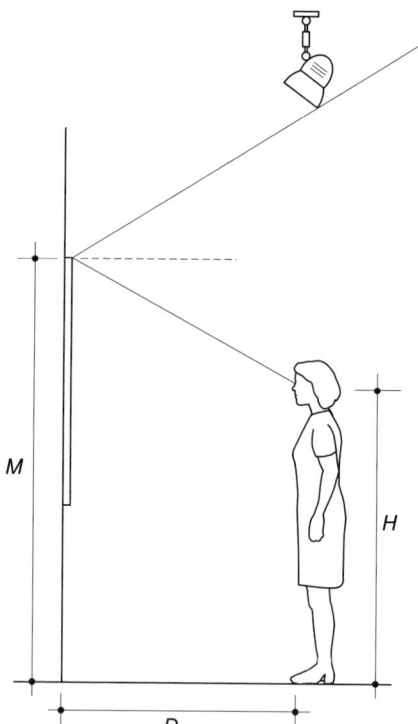

9.11 *The geometry of picture lighting. M = height of top of tallest picture frame, H = eye level of short adult, say 1.5 m.*

approach or exceed the brightness of the luminous pixels. Side windows present a double problem. If operators face a window they may be distracted because the outside scene is brighter than the VDT. If their backs are to the window they will pick up its reflection in the VDT screen. The face of the VDT should ideally be at right angles to the face of the window. If there are windows on two adjacent walls this remedy may fail, and solid partitions might be considered.

In a private office the choice of luminaire is seldom critical; a ceiling-mounted fitting would not normally be reflected in the display screen. In an open-plan office the choice is more restricted.

If the height of the ceiling is greater than 2.5m, uplighters containing metal halide or high-pressure sodium lamps, possibly integrated into the office furniture, should be suitable. If the ceiling height exceeds 3.5m, one might consider *direct-indirect lighting,* suspended uplighters or column-mounted uplighters.

For ceiling heights below 2.5 m the best solution is a modular VDT luminaire providing a suitable illuminance (perhaps 2–300 lux) on the desk, with restricted light sideways to reflect in the screen. This combination of low *flux fraction ratio* and lateral constraint can result in an unsympathetic luminous environment, see Table VI. Consider wall hangings or pictures, perhaps with wall-washers, to brighten up the walls.

9 GLOSSARY

Altitude

An angle in a vertical plane, measured upward in degrees from the horizontal. The solar altitude is the altitude of the sun above the horizon.

Azimuth

An angle in plan, also called the bearing. The solar azimuth is usually measured from due north.

Circuit efficacy

The *luminous flux (lumens)* emitted by a lamp or *luminaire,* divided by the *circuit wattage.* See also *lamp efficacy* and *luminaire efficacy.*

Circuit wattage
The power consumed by the lamps in an electric lighting system, by their control gear, and by associated equipment for power factor correction.

Daylight factor
Equal to the *illuminance* (lux) at a point indoors, expressed as a percentage of the simultaneous horizontal illuminance under an unobstructed overcast sky outside, see Section 2.1.

Direct-indirect lighting
Provided by a luminaire designed to combine the lighting characteristics of an uplighter and a downlight. It provides upward and downward illumination, sometimes in variable proportions, but little or no light sideways.

Efficacy
Luminous flux output (lumens), divided by the electric power consumed (watts). See also *lamp efficacy* and *luminaire efficacy*.

Flux
See *luminous flux*.

Flux fraction ratio
Equal to the upward *luminous flux* from a *luminaire*, divided by the downward flux.

Heliodon
Figures 9.8, 9.9. A physical simulation of the changing geometrical relation between the earth and the sun. The heliodon incorporates seasonal and hourly changes. A model of a building is mounted on a rotating platform whose tilt from the vertical corresponds to the geographical latitude of the building's location.

Illuminance (E)
The degree of concentration of light, in *lumens* per square meter (lux), striking a surface. Illuminance is measured by a special light-meter – an illumination photometer; photographic lightmeters are unsuitable.

Lamp efficacy
The *efficacy* of an electric lamp, i.e. the *luminous flux (lumens)* emitted by an electric lamp, divided by the wattage consumed by the lamp. It is known as the *lamp circuit efficacy* if power consumed by the electric circuit is included.

Light output ratio (LOR)
The *luminous flux (lumens)* emitted by a *luminaire*, expressed as a fraction of the flux emitted by the lamp(s) inside the luminaire. The LOR is sometimes known as the 'luminaire efficiency'.

Lumen
See *luminous flux*.

Luminaire
A lighting fitting complete with control gear and suspension where applicable. In North America but not usually in the UK the term includes associated lamps.

Luminaire efficacy
The *efficacy* of a luminaire, i.e. the *luminous flux (lumens)* emitted by a *luminaire*, divided by the wattage consumed by the lamp(s) in the luminaire. It is known as the luminaire circuit efficacy if power consumed by the electric circuit is included.

Luminous flux (φ)
The rate in lumens at which light energy is emitted from a source or received by a surface. For a given illuminance E lux, the flux striking a surface will be proportional to the area A (m²):

$$\varphi = E \times A \text{ lumens}$$

equation (5)

Hence 1 lux = 1 lumen per square metre.

Lux
See *illuminance*.

Maintenance factor (MF)
The ratio of the *illuminance (lux)* of a lighting system, or, in the case of natural lighting, the *daylight factor*, after a given interval, expressed as a fraction of the illuminance or daylight factor when the same installation was clean and newly commissioned. See Table III for maintenance factors for natural lighting.

No-sky line
The dividing line, Figure 9.2, in a room between the area which is exposed to a direct view of the sky, and the area which receives no direct daylight at all.

Probable sunlight hours
The long-term average number of hours per year when direct sunlight is visible from a given point. Long-term weather conditions are taken into account.

Reflectance (R)
The proportion of incident light which a surface reflects. A perfectly white surface would have a reflectance of 1.00, a perfectly black surface would have zero reflectance. Table IX gives some values for typical surfaces.

Sky factor
The horizontal *illuminance* (lux) at a given point due to light received directly through an unglazed window opening from a sky of uniform brightness, expressed as a percentage of the horizontal illuminance under an unobstructed vault of the same sky. See Section 1.5. Zero *reflectance* is ascribed to interior and exterior surfaces.

Table IX Reflectance of some familiar surfaces

Surface	Reflectance
White emulsion paint on plaster	0.80
Pink plaster	0.65
Cork tiles	0.20
Red quarry tiles	0.10
Black chalkboard	0.05
Painted surfaces, (with BS 4800 colour code)	
White 00 E 55	0.85
Light grey 00 A 01	0.68
Mid grey 00 A 05	0.45
Dark grey 10 A 11	0.14
Black 00 E 53	0.05

Skylight indicator
Figure 9.4, for checking the daylight potential of new buildings and daylight protection for existing buildings. It provides an estimate of *the vertical sky component* on a built-up site. The centre of the semi-circular indicator corresponds to the position in plan of the reference point. Its base should run along the plane of the window wall. Radial distances correspond to the ratio (distance of obstruction on plan)/(height of obstruction above *reference* point). Each little cross stands for a vertical sky component of 0.5 per cent. Count how many crosses fall within the outline of the sky. Divide by 2. The answer equals the vertical sky component, expressed as a percentage.

Solar declination
At any moment the sun is precisely overhead at some point on the earth's surface. The latitude of this point depends on the season,

and is known as the solar declination. Some values of solar declination are shown in Table II.

Sunlight availability indicator

Figure 9.5, for checking sunlight protection for existing buildings and sunlight potential for new buildings. It provides a measure of the *probable sunlight hours* on a built-up site. The centre of the indicator corresponds to the position in plan of the reference point. Radial distances correspond to the ratio (distance of obstruction on plan) / (height of obstruction above reference point). Align the south-point of the indicator with the south-point of the site plan. Each of the 100 dots on the indicator stands for 1 per cent of the annual probable hours of sunlight. Choose the indicator whose stated latitude (51.5°, 53.5° or 56°) is closest to the geographical latitude of the site. If a dot is closer to the centre than any obstruction in that direction, then sunlight from that dot is unobstructed (unless, of course, it comes from behind the facade). Count the unobstructed dots. The total is the percentage of probable sunlight hours. Littlefair (2011) recommends an annual exposure to at least 25 unobstructed dots, including at least five from beyond the equinox line.

Sun-on-ground indicator

Figure 9.6, designed for site planning, and shows the length and direction of shadows at the equinox. The Building Research Establishment has issued indicators for the following latitudes – 51.5°, 53.5° and 56° – each at scales of 1:100, 1:200, 1:500 and 1:1250. Place the point P of the indicator over a reference point at ground level on plan. Line the south point of the indicator with the south point on the plan. Parallel east-west lines on the indicator show the heights of obstructions which would just intercept direct sunlight at the time indicated. Hence one can estimate the hours of potential sunlight reaching any point on the ground at the equinox. Sunlight less than 10° above the horizon is ignored.

Sunpath indicator

Figure 9.7, for checking times and seasons when direct sunlight strikes a given reference point on a built-up site. It is aligned and scaled in the same way as the *sunlight availability indicator*. Choose the indicator whose stated latitude (51.5°, 53.5° or 56°) is closest to the geographical latitude of the site. If a point on one of the sunpath lines is closer to the centre than any obstruction in that direction, then the sunlight at that moment is unobstructed (unless, of course, it comes from behind the facade).

Transmittance (T)

The proportion of *luminous flux* in lumens striking the upper surface of a transparent or translucent sheet which emerges from the lower surface. The transmittance of clear window glass is taken as 0.82; double glazing 0.70.

Note: These values refer to diffuse incidence; figures from glass manufacturers usually refer to normal incidence, and are correspondingly higher.

Vertical sky component (SCv)

The *illuminance* in lux on a vertical element at a point due to direct light from the overcast sky vault, expressed as a percentage of the simultaneous horizontal illuminance under the whole unobstructed sky vault.

Working plane

The flat plane on which the visual task is located. In a corridor this would be at floor level. In a shop, at counter height. In an office 0.7 m, a factory or kitchen 0.85 m above floor level. Unless otherwise stated the working plane is assumed to be horizontal.

10 BIBLIOGRAPHY

Daylighting

British Standards Institution (1992) BS 8206: Part 2: 1992 *Code of practice for daylighting*, BSI.

Littlefair, P. J. (1988) Information Paper IP 15/88: *Average daylight factor: a simple basis for daylight design*, Building Research Establishment.

Littlefair, P. J. (2011) Report BR209: *Site layout planning for daylight and sunlight: a guide to good practice*, Building Research Establishment.

Society of Light and Lighting (1999) *Lighting Guide No. 10: Daylighting and Window Design*, CIBSE (under revision).

Tregenza, P. R., Stewart, L. and Sharples, S. (1999) Reduction of glazing transmittance by atmospheric pollutants, *Lighting Research and Technology*, 31(4): 135–138.

Electric lighting

Code for Lighting (2009) Chartered Institution of Building Services Engineers (CIBSE)/Society of Light and Lighting.

Lighting Guide No. 7: Office Lighting (2005) Chartered Institution of Building Services Engineers (CIBSE)/Society of Light and Lighting.

10 Sound

Chris Steel

Robin Mackenzie Partnership/Edinburgh Napier University

KEY POINTS:
- More detailed performance requirements available to the designer
- Performance criteria have been broadened and minimum standards raised
- Regulatory control in many areas is now proved through completion testing placing more emphasis on good design

Contents

1 Introduction
2 Fundamentals of acoustics
3 Reducing sound transmission from external sources
4 Reducing sound transmission through layout and design
5 Reducing sound transmission through a structure
6 Permissible noise levels within a building
7 Sound insulation performance parameters
8 Sound insulation performance criteria
9 Specifying airborne and impact insulation from laboratory test data
10 Reverberation criteria
11 General guidance on the acoustics of performance spaces
12 Bibliography

1 INTRODUCTION

There are three main areas for consideration when designing buildings for good acoustics:

1 The control of sound break-in from external noise sources; most commonly from transportation, industrial and/or commercial (pubs, clubs, etc.) activities.
2 The control of sound transmission through a building; most commonly from building users (voices, TV, stereo, footfall, living activities) but can also include control of sound from building services (fixed plant, ventilation systems).
3 The acoustic quality of a room; most commonly the level of reverberation (echo) in a room.

The consideration of acoustic design during the early stages of a project can substantially reduce the potential for costly remedial works. Equally important is the correct use of the most appropriate design parameters and criteria. This chapter aims to provide a base upon which the designer, architect or specifier can start to identify the most suitable design parameters and criteria for each of the three areas outlined above.

2 FUNDAMENTALS OF ACOUSTICS

The following section gives a narrative explanation of sound, sound transmission and sound control. More mathematical explanations of these processes can be found in the building acoustic text books listed in the bibliography.

2.1 Creating sound

Imagine a tuning fork. When the fork is struck the prongs vibrate. As the prongs vibrate the air particles around the prongs are pushed away. These air particles in turn push the air particles next to them and so on thereby creating a wave motion through the air. This *forced wave* through the air is what our senses interpret as sound in the inner ear (Figure 10.1).

In all instances we will have a source (e.g. the tuning fork), a path (the air) and a receiver (normally a person) (Figure 10.2).

2.2 Sound transmission

Forced particle motion forms wave patterns and so allows sound to carry through the air. This wave motion allows noise to diffract, propagate and curve like any other wave motion which is why sound can be heard round corners or through small gaps in a structure. We can reduce the effects of sound by reducing the noise at source, altering the sound transmission path or by changing the acoustics of the room where the listener is located.

The first option, reducing noise at source, is normally not a consideration for most noises affecting a building as they normally emanate from sources outwith the designer's control (motorway traffic, the activities of a neighbour etc.). The exception to this would be from noise sources associated with the design of the building (fixed plant, services, ventilation). Here the selection of suitable equipment and plant will reduce the likelihood of noise complaint.

The second option, altering the sound transmission path, is the most readily used method of reducing sound from a source. This can be seen in the use of heavy double glazed windows to reduce road traffic noise or the specification of a twin stud partition instead of a single stud partition within buildings. By varying and altering

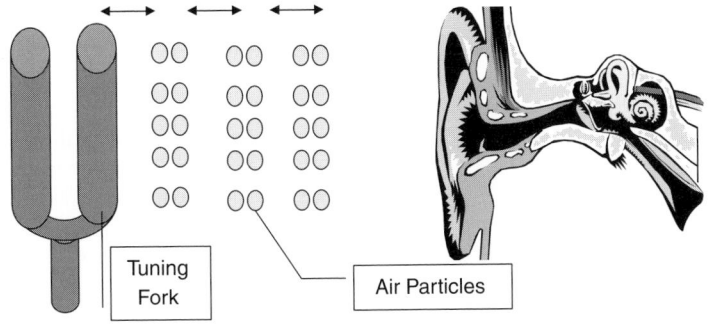

10.1 *How sound is created*

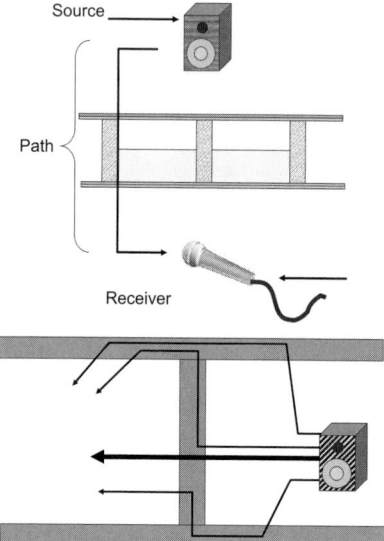

Source – Path - Receiver

Source

Path

Receiver

10.2 *Source–path–receiver*

Table I Absorption coefficients

	Frequency					
	125	250	500	1000	2000	4000
Smooth unpainted concrete	0.01	0.01	0.02	0.02	0.02	0.05
Plaster on solid wall	0.04	0.05	0.06	0.08	0.04	0.06
Plasterboard on frame 100 mm cavity	0.08	0.11	0.05	0.03	0.02	0.03
Plasterboard on frame, 100 mm cavity with mineral wool	0.30	0.12	0.08	0.06	0.06	0.05
6 mm glass	0.10	0.06	0.04	0.03	0.02	0.02
Double glazing, 2–3 mm glass, 10 mm air gap	0.15	0.05	0.03	0.03	0.02	0.02
22 mm chipboard, 50 mm cavity filled with mineral wool	0.12	0.04	0.06	0.05	0.05	0.05
Acoustic timber wall paneling	0.18	0.34	0.42	0.59	0.83	0.68
Plaster on lath, deep air space	0.20	0.15	0.10	0.05	0.05	0.05
Curtains hung in folds against solid wall	0.05	0.15	0.35	0.40	0.50	0.50
Raised computer floor, steel-faced 45 mm chipboard 800 mm above concrete floor, no carpet	0.08	0.07	0.06	0.07	0.08	0.08
Wooden floor on joists	0.15	0.11	0.10	0.07	0.06	0.07
Linoleum or vinyl stuck to concrete	0.02	0.02	0.03	0.04	0.04	0.05
5mm needle-felt stuck to concrete	0.01	0.02	0.05	0.15	0.30	0.40
Medium pile carpet on sponge rubber underlay	0.50	0.10	0.30	0.50	0.65	0.70
Solid timber door	0.14	0.10	0.06	0.08	0.10	0.10
50mm mineral wool (96 kg/m³) behind 25% open area perforated steel.	0.20	0.35	0.65	0.85	0.90	0.80
Plaster decorative panels, ceilings	0.20	0.22	0.18	0.15	0.15	0.16
Seating, slightly upholstered, unoccupied	0.07	0.12	0.26	0.42	0.50	0.55
Empty plastic or metal chairs (per chair) in m² units	0.07	0.00	0.14	0.00	0.14	0.14
Fully upholstered seats (per item) in m²	0.12	0.00	0.28	0.00	0.32	0.37
Water surface, e.g. swimming pool	0.01	0.01	0.01	0.01	0.02	0.02

the materials and properties of a façade, floor or wall we can alter the sound path and alter the way that sound is transmitted.

The third option is to alter the acoustics of the space or room in which the receiver is situated. While this will have a limited effect on the annoyance of noise from external sources, more importantly it does have the effect of altering the acoustic environment within a room. This is equally important when considering things such as speech intelligibility or suitable listening environments.

2.3 Reverberation time

Acoustic absorption occurs when sound comes into contact with an acoustically porous material. In a bedroom the carpet, curtains, bed and bedding are all acoustically absorbent and so have the effect of reducing the reverberation time (echo) within a space. This can make the room sound quieter than a 'live' room or a room with lots of hard reflective surfaces, such as the bathroom. Hard smooth surfaces within a room will increase the reverberation time (echo) within a space. The size or volume of a space will also have an effect on the reverberation time.

We can measure this effect in a room by creating an interrupted sound (a sudden bang or burst of noise) and measuring the time it takes this noise level to fall by 60 dB. Alternatively if we know the properties of the room (its volume, the area of each surface in the room and its absorption coefficient) we can calculate the reverberation time in a room using the Sabine formula.

$$T = \frac{0.16}{S\acute{a} + x\text{V}}$$

where   T = Reverberation Time (seconds)
        V = room volume in m³
        Sá = total surface absorption in m²
        x is the coefficient related to the sound attenuation of air

Total surface absorption is calculated by adding together the separate areas of absorption.

$$S\acute{a} = S_1\acute{a}_1 + S_1\acute{a}_1 + S_2\acute{a}_2 + S_3\acute{a}_3 + ... + S_5\acute{a}_5$$

where S_1 is the area in m² and d_1 is the absorption coefficient of the material.

Table I lists the expected absorption coefficient of some common materials. These values can be used in the Sabine formula to help calculate the reverberation time within a room. By altering the selection of ceiling and wall finishes the most advantageous reverberation time can be calculated long before a room is ever built or the materials selected for use.

The acoustic absorption characteristics detail can also be rated into different classifications in line with the guidance given in BS EN ISO 11654:1997, *Acoustics – Sound Absorbers for Use in Buildings – Rating of Sound Absorption*. This allows the designer to specify a classification of material rather being forced into giving a prescriptive specification.

Figure 10.3 details the absorption classifications that are normally associated with absorbent materials specified in the UK. They run from Class A materials (those with the highest levels of acoustic absorption) to Class E materials (those with the lowest levels of acoustic absorption).

Classification of a material against the absorption coefficient graph shown in Figure 10.3 may not be suitable for all material types, e.g. panel absorber will tend to perform better at particular frequencies. This means that while a panel absorber can provide good average levels of absorption it may be limited across the frequency band. Therefore BSEN ISO 11654 also allows for the average absorption coefficient of a material to be used as a method of defining its absorption classification. This is detailed in Table II where $\acute{a}_w$ is the average acoustic absorption of the material.

By detailing appropriate materials we can achieve a required reverberation time (T) within a room. For this reason the

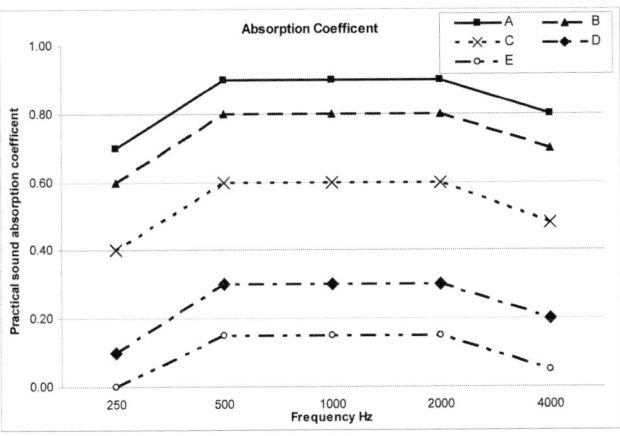

10.3 *BS EN ISO 11654 absorption classifications*

Table III Likely external ambient noise levels

Source	A weighted sound pressure level L_{Aeq} (dB)
Urban area close to motorway	70–90
20m from the edge of a busy motorway (110km/h)	78
Urban area close to main road	65–75
20m from the edge of a busy main road (50km/h)	68
Suburban area remote from main road	55–65
On a road parallel to a busy main road and screened by buildings for traffic	58
Parkland within a large town or city	55–60
Secluded country location	35–45

reverberation time of a room is normally used as the performance criteria when designing rooms for good speech intelligibility or suitable listening environments.

The reverberation time (T) of a room is normally specified for the space when unoccupied. It is important to note that for rooms with volumes greater than 200 m³ the use of the Sabine formula becomes less reliable. It is therefore always preferable to seek professional advice when detailing or designing for good room acoustics in large or complex spaces. However there is no reason why the designer cannot provide a performance criterion for the reverberation time within a room.

3 REDUCING SOUND TRANSMISSION FROM EXTERNAL SOURCES

In the UK the level of noise at which disturbance from particular noise sources is likely to occur within a dwelling can be found in planning documents such as Planning Policy Guideline 24 (England) or Planning and Noise 1 (Scotland). In addition to the planning guidelines there are other guidance documents that can be used when assessing noise within non-domestic builds. In all instances we are concerned with the level of noise break in from external sources which are outwith the control of the building owner or occupier.

Such documents set the maximum noise level (L_{Aeq}) that can be measured within a room when unoccupied or not in use.

L_{Aeq}: The L_{Aeq} level is effectively the average measured noise level over a defined period of time ($L_{Aeq\ 16hours}$, $L_{Aeq\ 8hours}$, etc). The 'A' in the L_{Aeq} parameter means that the noise level has been weighted so that it is akin to the subjective noise level that the average person would hear.

For most transportation sources it is suggested that external average noise level of $L_{Aeq(16hour)}$ 55 dB during the daytime and $L_{Aeq(8hour)}$ 45dB during the night time are set as target levels, however, as can be seen from Table III these levels are likely to be below the normal noise level in many urban and suburban areas.

Table II BS EN ISO 11654 Absorption classifications for average absorptions values

Sound absorption	Class $\acute{\alpha}_w$
A	0.90, 0.95, 1.00
B	0.80, 0.85
C	0.60, 0.65, 0.70, 0.75
D	0.30, 0.35, 0.40, 0.45, 0.50, 0.55
E	0.25, 0.20, 0.15
Not classified	0.10, 0.05, 0.00

L_{Amax}: In addition to the average noise level the other parameters that may need to be controlled would be the maximum noise level (L_{Amax}) or the highest single noise event, such as would be associated with a sudden increase in noise such as a train passing by.

L_{A90}: For some noise sources, such as industrial noise affecting a dwelling, it is common to attempt to control noise in line with the background noise level (L_{A90}). This is the underlying noise level or the average noise level which is exceeded for 90 per cent of the measurement period. This allows for noise to be assessed against the quiet periods or lulls in average noise levels to ensure that a disturbance is not created, i.e. the periods between vehicles passing by a dwelling will result in quiet passages of time where the noise under consideration (industrial noise) may not be masked by other events (road traffic noise) and so cause a disturbance.

3.1 Control of external noise levels

The permissible level of noise outside a building can differ greatly depending on the nature of the development or even the policy of the local authority. As a starting point guidance issued by the World Health Organisation suggests external free-field levels of below $L_{Aeq\ (16hrs)}$ 50–55 dB as being suitable to avoid serious disturbance or annoyance during the daytime with more recent European guidance suggesting maximum external free-field levels outside a dwelling of $L_{Aeq\ (8hours)}$ 40 dB as being suitable to avoid noise disturbance at night. However in many instances (city centre, some urban and suburban areas) a different approach may be suitable.

Table IV defines some of the standard noise criteria applied in a range of cases. External noise is normally considered an issue for residential properties but can be a requirement for outdoor workspaces or education spaces. It should be noted that the requirements of different local authorities can differ greatly and so consultation with Planning and Environmental Health should always be sought when designing for the control of external noise levels, particularly for dwellings.

Noise from entertainment sources (bars, clubs, pubs) is not normally required to be controlled outside the nearest residential property as in most cases noise from these sources is associated with night time use and sleep disturbance within a property. Control levels for such noise will again differ from one local authority to another and so they should always be consulted either when building dwellings next to an entertainment source or when introducing a new source of entertainment noise.

3.2 Distance attenuation

The more distant a building is from a noise source the quieter the level of noise from the source will be within the building. This will depend upon whether the noise source is considered as a *point source*, such as individual items of fixed plant or as *a line source*, such as noise from a railway line or motorway. If a house were located 20 m from a railway line or a road this would be considered a line source and so the level of noise would reduce by 13 dB. If the house were 20 m from a point source (a lawn mower or aeroplane)

Table IV Suitable external noise levels

Noise source and receiver description	Method of control	Performance criteria Maximum noise level at the receptor
New **Industrial noise** affecting existing residential properties or existing industrial affecting new residential	Noise levels should be controlled in relation to the pre-existing background noise level L_{A90} dB	−10 dB below the background = positive indication that complaints are unlikely Around +5 dB higher than the background level = Moderate likelihood of disturbance + 10 dB higher than the background level = likelihood of complaint significant
New **office development plant noise** affecting existing residential properties	Noise levels should be controlled in relation to the pre-existing background noise level L_{A90} dB	−5 dB below the background −10 dB below the background if noise source is tonal.
Construction noise affecting existing residential and commercial activities	Noise levels should be controlled to a maximum ambient level and operating times on site are restricted	$\geq L_{Aeq}$ 75 dB 8am–6pm Mon–Friday 8am–12am Saturday Restricted activity at other times
Road, rail, affecting new residential developments	Noise levels should be controlled for private amenity spaces (e.g. rear gardens, balconies)	$\geq L_{Aeq}$ 55 dB 7am–11pm $\geq L_{Aeq}$ 45 dB 11pm–7am
Airport noise, affecting new residential developments	Noise levels should be controlled for private amenity spaces (e.g. rear gardens, balconies)	$\geq L_{Aeq}$ 57 dB 7am–11pm $\geq L_{Aeq}$ 48 dB 11pm–7am

*For rail noise sources it is also expected that during the night time period maximum individual noise events should not *regularly* exceed $_{LAmax}$ 82 dB.

the level would be reduced by 26 dB relative to the measured noise level at the source.

As a general rule of thumb the difference between line source and point source attenuation is:

- −3 dB reduction in noise level for each doubling of distance from a line source
- −6 dB reduction in noise level for each doubling of distance from a point source

3.3 Acoustic barriers

Noise can be further reduced by the construction of an acoustic barrier. An acoustic barrier can be as simple as a close boarded fence or earth bund. By breaking the direct line of sight between a noise source and the receiver (a person or a building) we reduce the level of sound because we are increasing the distance the sound has to travel between source and receiver (i.e. the sound has to go over the top of the barrier).

The level of attenuation for an acoustic barrier will be dependent on the following factors.

- The height of the barrier: the higher the barrier the greater its expected performance.
- The type of noise source: barriers are more effective for stationary noise sources such as fixed plant than for a moving source such as vehicles.
- The height of the noise source: the higher the source the higher the barrier will have to be to break the line of sight.
- The height of the receiver: the higher the receiver is the higher the barrier will have to be to break the line of sight.
- The distance between the source and the barrier: it is always preferable to place the barrier as close to the source as possible.
- Where this cannot be achieved the next best option is to position the barrier as close to the receiver as possible.
- The worst position for a barrier is half way between the source and the receiver.
- The mass of the barrier: generally the minimum surface mass of any acoustic barrier should not be less than 5 kg/m².

The calculation of the attenuation offered by an acoustic barrier can be complicated but a good rule of thumb is to assume a 5 dB reduction for a partial barrier effect and 10 dB for a full barrier effect (see Table V). For example a 2 m barrier is likely to provide 10 dB reduction from road traffic at ground floor level and 5 dB reduction at first floor level.

Table V Basic sound reduction levels from acoustic barriers

Full barrier (full break in line of sight from source to receiver)	−10dB
Partial barrier (partial break in line of sight from source to receiver)	−5dB

Higher levels of acoustic insulation can be provided by acoustic barriers, however to achieve this they normally have to be significantly higher. If a reduction of more than 10 dB from an external noise source is required then it is likely that a barrier with an effective height greater than 2 m would be required.

3.4 Angle of view

The orientation of a building or a noise sensitive room away from a noise source can also reduce the level of noise disturbance experienced. Where a room directly overlooks a noise source (road, railway line etc.) the design is entirely dependent upon the distance from the source or the inclusion of an acoustic barrier for attenuation. If the room is angled away from the source then there is an expected reduction in noise due to the angle of view between the receiver and the source. Table VI outlines the expected reductions in sound levels at 500 Hz and 1000 Hz dependent on the angle of view from source to receiver.

3.5 Façade attenuation

The final method for reducing noise within a building from external sources is through the specification of the building envelope.

If we take the glazing element to be the dictating factor in the acoustic insulation of a façade it can be used as the means by which façade insulation can be specified.

It is commonly accepted that for some noise sources (commercial noise and industrial noise) internal noise levels within an affected building should be calculated in relation to an open window. In many other instances (transportation noise in particular) the assessment of internal noise levels can be calculated with closed windows. A wide range of acoustic performance data is published by most glazing manufacturers and will normally detail frequency performance levels along with average or single figure values. When assessing the acoustic performance of a glazing unit it is best to base any assessment on the R_{TRA} criteria. This is the reduction (R) in noise level provided by the glazing unit when adjusted for a traffic noise spectrum (TRA). Table VII details the expected insulation values for some typical glazing specifications. In addition it shows expected levels of reduction (D_w) from open windows dependent on the source noise.

Table VI Angle of view correction

| Building orientation | Sound attenuation (dB) | |
	500 Hz	1000 Hz
0°	0	0
45°	1	1
90°	6	6
135°	15	17
180°	17	19

Table VII Insulation values for open and closed glazing units

Open windows – expected D_w for windows with a free open area of 0.05 m²	D_w dBA
Road traffic noise	12–18
Railway noise	12–18
Aircraft noise	14–19
Amplified music	15–20

Closed windows – expected R_{TRA} dB insulation values for typical glazing types	
Glazing type	R_{TRA} **dB**
4 mm float glass/12 mm cavity/4 mm float glass	25
6 mm float glass/12 mm cavity/6 mm float glass	26
6 mm float glass/12 mm cavity/6.4 laminate glass	27
10 mm float glass/12 mm cavity/4 mm float glass	29
6 mm float glass/12 cavity/7 float glass	31
10 mm float glass /12 mm cavity/6 mm float glass	32
6 mm float glass/12 cavity/11 mm float glass	33
10 mm float glass/12 cavity/6.4 mm laminate glass	34

4 REDUCING SOUND TRANSMISSION THROUGH LAYOUT AND DESIGN

Consideration of the layout of a building interior can either enhance or reduce its suitability in controlling noise. It is generally good practice to locate noise sensitive activities away from noisy activities. An example of this process in action can be seen in the design of the traditional Glasgow tenement flat popular at the turn of the century. While not perfect it is clear that the design has taken cognisance of the limitations of the building fabric, the expected use of each space and the number of occupants within the flat. Of equal importance is the understanding that the occupants of such flats would be living compatible lifestyles, a luxury not often afforded to modern designers.

Quiet and noisy areas between dwellings are grouped together with bedrooms in one flat backing onto bedrooms in the other (Figure 10.4). The parlour and kitchen locations are next to the mass 600mm masonry wall where acoustic insulation would be better. Habitable spaces are located away from the stairwell by cupboards and double entrance lobbies helping to further reduce stairwell noise. The party wall between the bedrooms (denoted by the grey line) is a relatively poor single brick wall but it was considered that this would be acceptable because it separates two quiet spaces where the occupants live compatible lifestyles.

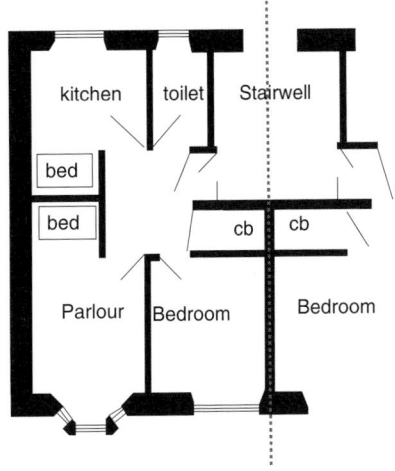

10.4 *Traditional tenement flat layout Glasgow circa 1890*

The following should be considered in order to reduce noise issues from building users:

- Avoid placing noise sensitive activities next to rooms with higher levels of noise.
- Avoid detailing services (such as SVP or HVAC) through noise sensitive spaces
- Avoid placing rooms with heavy service demands or high activity above quiet rooms (e.g. kitchens above sleeping areas).
- Locate external bin areas away from noise sensitive rooms.
- Avoid locating lift shafts in areas where they directly back onto noise sensitive rooms.
- Place plant rooms and building services in as remote a location as practical from a noise sensitive area.
- Fire doors in communal corridors should be located away from the entrance doors to dwellings or noise sensitive rooms.
- Try to avoid locating rooms with high occupancy rates at the end of corridors where there are noise sensitive rooms along the corridor in order to reduce possible disturbance from foot traffic in a corridor.

5 REDUCING SOUND TRANSMISSION THROUGH A STRUCTURE

Sound transmission through a structure is the passage of the sound pressure wave from the air, into the structure, through the structure and then out the other side. Low frequency noise pushes the whole structure causing the sound pressure wave to be transmitted by the surface of the wall or floor. As we move up the frequency range the wavelength of the sound gets shorter and so instead of being able to force the whole partition into motion the sound finds paths through the structure. Finally sound will also find ways of transmitting through small gaps or voids within the structure or through weaker flanking elements such as adjoining walls or service runs.

There are six key factors in the reduction of sound through a building structure. By taking cognisance of these six issues when specifying a partition, be it a floor, wall, roof or external cladding element, it can be possible to determine which construction type is likely to provide the best performance.

5.1 Stiffness of a structure

The stiffness of a partition affects how it will transmit sound particularly at low frequencies and also some higher frequencies. Materials will naturally resist any force against them such as a sound wave and the greater the stiffness or rigidity the better a material will be at reducing the transmission of low frequency sound.

Cast in-situ concrete decks can provide a very high level of acoustic insulation between floors despite the apparently slim section of concrete slab. The profiles, while adding mass to the structure, also act as stiffeners to the floor structure. Increased dwangs or noggins in a timber floor help improve the stiffness of a floor. Similarly timber floors with heavy deafening or pugging also help to improve stiffness in the floor as well as mass.

5.2 Isolation of a structure

Separating (or isolating) the different elements of a structure can break the sound transmission paths like a break in a circuit board. Isolation also reduces forced transmission by creating large cavities between surfaces. Finally the more materials sound has to transmit through the more energy is lost.

Isolation is particularly important for the acoustic insulation of floors against impact sound. Impact resistant mats, isolated floor battens and floating floor systems all help to isolate a structure from impact sound. They will also have an effect on the transmission of airborne sound as will twin stud or twin leaf wall systems, or independent ceiling or wall lining systems.

5.3 Mass of a structure

The more mass a material or structure has the more difficulty the sound pressure wave has in forcing it into vibration. For most materials mass is the defining factor in acoustic performance. For every doubling of mass in a structure or material we should see a 6 dB improvement in acoustic insulation. However this will only be noticed at the mass controlled frequencies. This normally occurs at the mid range of frequencies.

The reason why some single leaf brick walls can provide similar levels of acoustic insulation to a metal or timber stud partition with multiple linings is the substitution of isolation (i.e. the isolation of the two plasterboard layers by the frame) for increased mass (the inherent mass of the brick or block work).

5.4 Absorption within a structure

By adding absorbent materials to the cavities within a partition we can increase the amount of sound that is absorbed within the cavity and so reduce the amount of sound that can be transmitted. This is normally achieved by adding acoustically porous materials such as mineral fibre quilt. The inclusion of such materials can improve the acoustic insulation of a partition by between 3 and 6 dB.

5.5 Flanking sound affecting a structure

Sound always takes the path of least resistance. Flanking sound transmission relates to noise which is transmitted into an adjoining room or space but which does not come directly through the separating partition. It is possible for there to be at least 12 possible flanking transmission paths between two rooms separated by a simple wall construction (flank via the walls, floor and ceiling).

Flanking transmission can be a particular problem with masonry supported timber floors where there is a strong structural connection between flats due to continuous masonry walls running up through a building (Figure 10.5).

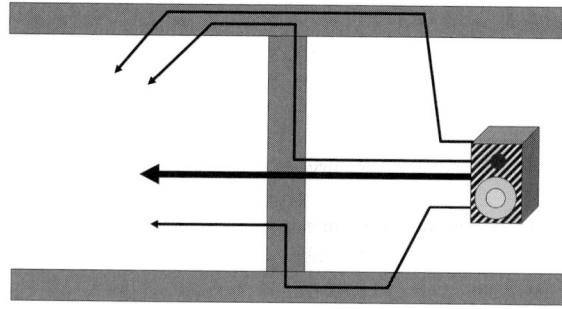

10.5 *Flanking paths through a separating wall*

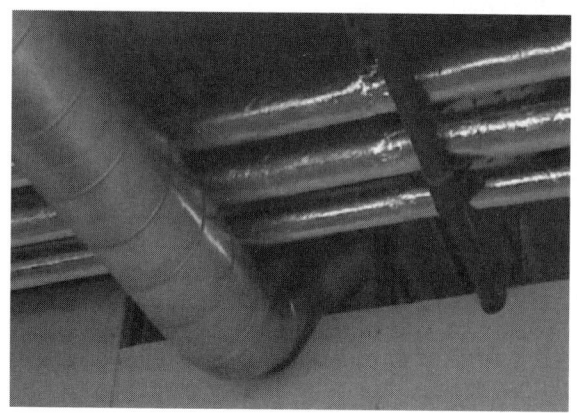

10.6 *Service penetration at wall head where no detailing has been issued to site*

5.6 Completeness of a structure

Without a complete structure sound can leak through any gaps or holes in the same way that water would leak through the cracks in a dam. In addition to gaps or holes in constructions incompleteness of a structure or weaknesses in a structure will also have a similar effect. In some instances this can be a result of poor workmanship (badly finished joints) but it can equally be attributed to poor detailing (e.g. wall head details or detailing of service penetrations, Figure 10.6).

6 PERMISSIBLE NOISE LEVELS WITHIN A BUILDING

It often falls to the lead designer on a project to outline suitable performance parameters and criteria for permissible noise levels within a building. The required levels will depend upon the client's requirement, the expected use of the building and the types of room within a building. Defining the most suitable parameter to use is the first task of any design process. There are two main performance parameters that should normally be applied: the Ambient Noise (L_{Aeq}), outlined in Section 3, and/or the Noise Rating (NR) parameter. In addition the maximum noise level (L_{Amax}), outlined in Section 3, is often applied.

6.1 Noise rating curves

NR is the noise rating curve. This is applied to noises which may cause disturbance but which emanate from a steady noise source or a tonal noise source (e.g. fixed plant and equipment). The NR criterion sets a maximum noise limit for each frequency band rather than setting a maximum average noise level as is the case with the L_{Aeq} parameter. Most noise sources are made up of noise across a range of frequencies. Deep or rumbling noises represent low frequency noise while sharp or piercing noises represent higher frequency noise. Fixed noise sources such as plant and machinery are known for having high levels of noise at a particular frequency and so it is important to have a performance parameter that can set a maximum level at each frequency band. If an average noise level were set, such as the L_{Aeq} criterion, then it could be possible for noise from say a fan to meet an L_{Aeq} criterion but still be perceived as disturbing. This is because it would have a high level of noise at one particular frequency but a lower level of noise at other frequencies which would have a great effect on the average noise level. Figure 10.7 details the NR curves.

6.2 Guidance on performance criteria by room type

Table VIII details suitable ambient noise levels and suitable NR levels for a range of building types and room types. The guidance given in the table is an amalgamation of current performance criteria from the most relevant guidance documents (Building Bulletin 93, HTM08-01, BS8233, CSDG2007, BCO Specification Guide 2009 BREEAM).

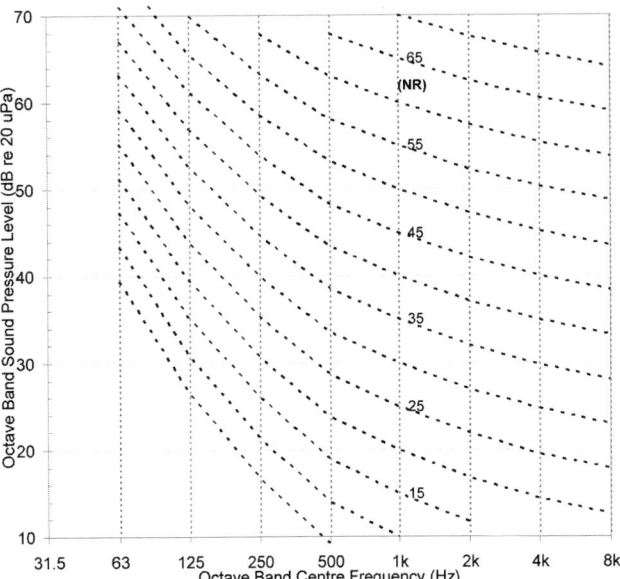

10.7 *Noise rating curves*

Table VIII Suitable maximum ambient noise levels and NR levels

Type of building/room	Maximum L_{Aeq} dB*	Maximum NR
School		
Nursery school playrooms	35	30
Nursery school quiet rooms	35	30
Primary school; classrooms, class bases, general teaching areas, small group rooms	35	30
Secondary school; classrooms, general teaching areas, seminar rooms, tutorial rooms, language laboratories	35	30
Open-plan teaching area	40	35
Open-plan resource area	40	35
Music classroom	35	30
Small practice/group room	35	30
Ensemble room	30	25
Performance/recital room	30	25
Recording studio	30	25
Control room for recording	35	30
Small lecture room (<50 people)	35	30
Large lecture room (>50 people)	30	25
Classroom designed specifically for use by hearing impaired students (including speech therapy rooms,	30	25
Study room (individual study, withdrawal, remedial work, teacher preparation)	35	30
Libraries – quiet study areas	35	25
Libraries – resource areas	40	35
Science laboratories	40	35
Drama studios	30	25
Design & Technology – resistance materials, CAMCAD Areas	40	35
Design & Technology – electronics/control, textiles, food, graphics, design/resource areas	40	35
Art rooms	40	35
Assembly halls, multi-purpose halls (drama, PE, audio/visual presentations, assembly, occasional music)	35	30
Audio-visual, video conference rooms	35	30
Atria, circulation spaces used by students	45	40
Indoor sports hall	40	35
Dance studio	40	35
Gymnasium	40	35
Swimming pool	50	45
Interviewing/counseling rooms, medical rooms	35	30
Dining rooms	45	40
Kitchens	50	45
Office, staff rooms	40	35
Corridors, stairwells	45	40

Type of building/room	Maximum L_{Aeq} dB*	Maximum NR
Coat and changing areas	45	40
Toilets	50	45
Hospital		30
Single bed/on-call room	40 Day / 35 Night	
Children & older people (single bed)	40 Day / 35 Night	30
Children & older people (multi-bed)	45 Day / 35 Night	30
Consulting room	40	35
Examination room	40	35
Treatment room	40	35
Counseling/bereavement room	40	35
Interview room	40	35
Operating theatre suite	40	40 (50 Laminar flow)
Nurseries	40 Day / 35 Night	30
Birthing room	45	40
Laboratories	45	40
Dirty utility/sluice	55	40
Clean utility	55	40
Speech and language therapy	30	25
Snoezelen/multi-sensory room	30	25
Multi-faith/chapel	40	35
Corridor (no door)	55	40
Atrium	55	40
Dining	50	40
Public/staff toilets (non cubicles)	55	45
En suite toilets (non cubicles)	45	40
Waiting (large > 20 people)	50	40
Waiting (small ≤ 20 people)	50	40
Main kitchen	55	50 (55 at extract hood)
Ward kitchen, pantry	50	40
Storeroom	n/a	n/a
Rest room	45 Day / 35 Night	30
Locker/changing room	55	40
Large training/seminar (>35m²)	35	30
Small training/seminar (≤ 35m²)	40	35
Lecture theatre	35	30
Library/archiving room	40	35
Single-person office	40	35
Multi-person office (2–4 people)	40	40
Open-plan office (≥ 5 people)	45	40
Boardroom	35	30
Large meeting room (> 35m²)	35	30
Small meeting room (≤ 35m²)	40	35

(continued)

Table VIII (continued)

Type of building/room	Maximum L_{Aeq} dB*	Maximum NR
Offices**		
Cellular office	40	35
Speculative offices	43	38
Open plan office	45	40
Entrance lobbies	45	40
Circulation spaces	45	40
Toilets	50	45
Loading bays	60	55
Underground parking	60	55
Drafting rooms	≤45–55	≤40–50
Staff room	≤35–45	≤30–40
Meeting room	≤35–40	≤30–35
Executive office	≤35–40	≤30–35
Industrial		
Heavy engineering	≤70–80	≤55–75
Light engineering	≤65–75	≤45–65
Warehouses	≤65–75	≤45–65
Commercial laboratories	≤45–55	≤40–50
Garages	≤65–75	≤45–65
Loading bays	≤60–75	≤55–60
Workshops	≤50–60	≤60–70
Canteen	≤50–55	≤45–50
Commercial		
Hotel bedrooms	≤30–35	≤20–25
Department store	≤50–55	≤35–45
Retail unit	≤50–55	≤35–45
Underground parking	≤60–70	≤55–65
Café	≤50–55	≤35–45
Commercial kitchens/laundries	≤ 55–65	≤ 40–50
Restaurant	≤40–55	≤35–40
Reception rooms	≤35–40	≤30–35
Public house	≤40–45	≤35–40
Night club	≤40–45	≤35–40
Ball room	≤35–40	≤30–35
Banquet hall	≤35–40	≤30–35
Cinema	≤30–35	≤30–35
Commercial recording studio	≤20–25	≤15–20
Civic & Amenity		
Library	≤40–50	≤35–45
Museum	≤40–50	≤35–45
Church/religious (serious liturgical music)	30	20
Church/religious (small)	35	25
Court rooms (with public address)	40	35
Court rooms (no public address)	30	25
Magistrates/judge retiring, judges chambers	40	35
Interview rooms	40	35
Committee rooms	40	35
Custody areas	45	40
Video conferencing	30	25
Concert halls	≤25–30	≤20–25
Theatre	≤25–30	≤20–25
Toilets	≤45–50	≤40–45
Washrooms	≤45–50	≤40–45
Control centres	L_{A90} between 30–35	≤25–30
Public baths/swimming pools	≤50–55	≤45–50
Domestic		
Living rooms	≤30–40	≤25–35
Bedrooms	≤30–35	≤20–25

*BB101 allows for a +5dB increase to the ambient noise levels where natural ventilation is part of the design with the exclusion of designed for the hearing impaired.

**a +5dB increase in ambient levels can be allowed in naturally ventilated office buildings

6.3 Maximum or impulsive noise levels

The control of sudden noise events is also worthy of consideration in building design. This is normally described by the parameter L_{Amax}, the A-weighted maximum noise level recorded during a measurement period although the $L_{A1,30min}$ parameter is used for schools. These parameters should be considered when assessing noise sources which may include a sudden increase in noise levels or individual high noise events. Examples of this would be train pass-bys or bangs and knocks from industrial sources. These parameters are not normally used in isolation but in conjunction with the L_{Aeq} or even the NR criteria. It is generally only reasonable to enforce maximum parameters in situations where sudden noise events occur regularly and during the night time periods (11pm to 7am) although there are some exceptions. 'Regularly' is normally taken to mean more than twice in any single hour. Table IX defines some appropriate L_{Amax} and $L_{A1,30min}$ performance criteria to avoid disturbance.

Table IX Suitable internal $_{LAmax}$ levels

Type of building/room	$L_{Amax(f)}$ dB
Bedroom	45 (night time)
Teaching spaces with a maximum ambient noise level of L_{Aeq} 35dB (see Table VII)	55dB ($L_{A1,30min}$)
Single person ward, multi-bed ward	45 (night time)
Operating theatres	50 (day and night)
Open plan/speculative offices	55dB (60dB when naturally ventilated)
Cellular offices	50dB (55dB when naturally ventilated)

7 SOUND INSULATION PERFORMANCE PARAMETERS

Detailing the correct performance parameter for separating partitions has become a more complex task since the advent of new guidance documents such as Approved Document E, Building Bulletin 93 and Health Technical Memorandum 08–01. This is because different terms are used to define acoustic insulation. For example airborne laboratory tests on a sample partition are normally defined as the R_w value (the weighted sound reduction) while testing on site in Scotland the $D_{nT,w}$ term is used (difference in transmitted sound) and in England and Wales the $D_{nT,w} + C_{tr}$ term is used (the difference in transmitted sound adjusted using a C traffic noise weighted adaptation term).

It is also important to know whether airborne sound insulation or impact sound has been measured. As a general rule any parameter which starts with 'D' or 'R' ($D_{nT,w}$, R_w, D_w etc.) will be an airborne sound test while any parameter which starts with an 'L' ($L'_{nT,w}$, L_{nw}, ΔL_w) will be an impact sound test.

Note: Simply stating a dB requirement for the acoustic insulation of a partition is inadequate as it does not describe the method by which the partition is to be assessed and can lead to substantial differences in actual performance (e.g. the difference in on site performance between specifying a partition with a D_{nTw} of 50 dB compared to a partition with a $D_{nT,w} + C_{tr}$ of 50 dB can be more than 10 dB). Therefore it is necessary to state the performance parameter ($D_{nT,w}$ R'_w, etc.) as well as the performance criteria (45 dB, 50 dB etc). The most commonly used parameters are listed in Table X outlining what they mean and where they are used.

8 SOUND INSULATION PERFORMANCE CRITERIA

The level of insulation required is set as a performance criterion and stated in dB. For example if we were to be undertaking sound

Table X Sound insulation performance parameters

Building type	Regulations/guidance used	Performance parameter
Residential	England and Wales – A.D.E	Airborne – $D_{nT,w} + C_{tr}$
		Impact – $L'_{nT,w}$
	Scotland – Section 5	Airborne – $D_{nT,w}$
		Impact – $L'_{nT,w}$
	Northern Ireland – Technical	Airborne – $D_{nT,w}$
	Booklet G	Impact – $L'_{nT,w}$
	Eire – Technical Document E	Airborne – $D_{nT,w}$
		Impact – $L'_{nT,w}$
Schools	BB93 (new version)	Airborne – $D_{nT,(Tmf,max)\,w}$
		Impact – $L'_{nT,(Tmf,max)\,w}$

The $T_{mf,max}$ adjustment used in the schools document emphasises the importance of controlling of reverberation

Hospitals	HTM 08-01	Airborne $D_{nT,w}$
		Impact $L'_{nT,w}$
Offices	British Council for Offices	Airborne D nT,w
		Impact
	BS8233/BREEAM	Airborne D_w
		Impact

The D_w is a simple measurement of the difference between the source and receiving room values when measured on site. Acoustic insulation is not often considered when designing office accommodation; however it can be a real issue particularly in areas where confidentiality is important.

Hotels/care	England and Wales	Airborne $D_{nT,w} + C_{tr}$
Homes/student accommodation	ADE	Impact $L'_{nT,w}$
	Scotland	Airborne $D_{nT,w}$
	S8233	Impact $L'_{nT,w}$
	Ad Hoc Hotel Chain	D_w
		Various mainly $D_{nT,w}$

Hotels, care homes and student accommodations in England and Wales and Scotland are covered under the building regulations. Most hotel chains also apply their own performance parameter either in line with previous experience of what is suitable or what is used in the hotel chains home country e.g. French hotel chains tend to use the $R'_w + C$ parameter.

Cinema	UK	$D_{nT,w}$
	Ad hoc cinema operators	+ a minimum performance at 100Hz.
	levels	

The performance for cinema walls usually requires very high levels of insulation across the frequency range. A minimum performance criterion is also normally given for one of the low frequency bands; usually 100Hz.

Civic amenity	UK Ad Hoc	Airborne D_w
	Courts Standards and Design Guidance 2007	Impact $L'_{nT,w}$
Manufacture	UK – BS EN ISO 140 Lab	Airborne R_w
Data	Test	Impact ΔL_w

The R_w value relates to the laboratory performance of a partition. The ΔL_w value is the test of an impact isolation material on a standard concrete floor in a laboratory. It is the improvement over the base construction when overlaid with the isolation material.

Enhanced	Robust Details	Airborne $D_{nTw} + C_{tr}$
Performance	BREEAM	Impact $L'_{nT,w}$
Criteria	Code for Sustainable Homes	
	Ecohomes	

Used primarily in residential or residential type buildings (e.g. student accommodation). Code and Ecohomes still expect testing to use the C_{tr} adjustment even when tested outside England & Wales.

---

insulation testing in England and Wales we know that the performance parameter is $D_{nT'w+Ctr}$ (as shown previously in Table IX) but if we were testing in Northern Ireland the performance parameter is $D_{nT,w}$. As these parameters determine the way in which the result is calculated the resultant dB level is likely to be different, i.e. if we test a blockwork wall and calculate the insulation value using the $D_{nT,w+Ctr}$ parameter we may get a dB level of 45 but if it were calculated using the $D_{nT,w}$ parameter we may get a dB level of 52dB.

Because of the different ways that airborne and impact sound measurements are conducted there is a difference in how we determine what is a good result for airborne sound insulation than for impact sound insulation; in short:

- Airborne sound insulation values are always set as *minimum* performance levels.
- Impact sound insulation values are always set as *maximum* performance levels.

Therefore *for airborne sound insulation the higher the result the better* while *for impact sound insulation the lower the result the better*.

8.1 Residential performance criteria

Table XI details the performance criteria for the British Isles. It is generally the case that the regulations for England and Wales are adopted in the Channel Islands and the Isle of Man.

Guidance for internal partitions is only relevant for the regulations in England and Wales and Scotland.

Regulations for Northern Ireland show a previous test evidence method whereby test data from lab reports or other site reports can be submitted as evidence that a structure is suitable.

8.2 Acoustic lining systems performance

When selecting suitable acoustic lining systems, such as Bonded Resilient Coverings, Floating Floor Treatments (batten, cradle or deck overlay systems) or Resilient Ceiling Bar systems in domestic

Table XI Sound insulation requirements for dwellings

Type of Building Room	Walls Mean Value	Walls Individual Value	Floors Mean Value	Floors Individual Value
England & Wales Approved Document E 2003 Amended 2004 – Performance standards for separating walls, floors and stairs that have a separating function [*]				
Dwelling houses and flats – Purpose Built	N/A	$D_{nT,w} + C_{tr} \geq 45dB$	N/A	$D_{nT,w} + C_{tr} \geq 45dB$ $L'_{nT,w} \leq 62dB$
Dwelling houses and flats – Formed by a material change of use	N/A	$D_{nT,w} + C_{tr} \geq 43dB$	N/A	$D_{nT,w} + C_{tr} \geq 45dB$ $L'_{nT,w} \leq 64dB$
Rooms for Residential Purpose	N/A	$D_{nT,w} + C_{tr} \geq 43dB$	N/A	$D_{nT,w} + C_{tr} \geq 45dB$ $L'_{nT,w} \leq 64dB$
England & Wales Approved Document E 2003 Amended 2004 – Laboratory Values for new internal walls and floors within dwelling houses, flats and rooms for residential purpose				
Purpose built or formed by a material change of use	N/A	$R_w \geq 40dB$[#]	N/A	$R_w \geq 40dB$[#]
Scotland Section 5 Noise 2010 Performance standards for separating walls and floors and stairs that have a separating function, Dwelling houses, flats and residential purpose				
New build	N/A	$D_{nT,w} \geq 56dB$	N/A	$D_{nT,w} \geq 56dB$ $L_{nT,w} \leq 56dB$
Refurbishment	N/A	$D_{nT,w} \geq 53dB$	N/A	$D_{nT,w} \geq 53dB$ $L_{nT,w} \leq 58dB$
Scotland Section 5 Noise 2010 Laboratory Values for new internal walls and floors within dwelling houses, flats and rooms for residential purpose				
Purpose built or formed by a material change of use	N/A	$R_w \geq 43dB$[#]	N/A	$R_w \geq 43dB$[#]
Northern Ireland Technical Booklet G/G1 1990/1994 Performance standards for separating walls and floors and stairs that have a separating function, Dwelling houses, flats and residential purpose				
New Build	$D_{nT,w} \geq 53dB$	$D_{nT,w} \geq 49dB$	$D_{nT,w} \geq 52dB$ $L_{nT,w} \leq 61dB$	$D_{nT,w} \geq 48dB$ $L_{nT,w} \leq 65dB$
Conversion Previous Test Evidence Method (Site Data option)	N/A	$D_{nT,w} \geq 49dB$	N/A	$D_{nT,w} \geq 48dB$ $L_{nT,w} \leq 65dB$
Conversion Previous Test Evidence Method (Lab Data option)	N/A	R_w 53dB	N/A	
Eire Technical Guidance Document E 1997 Performance standards for separating walls and floors and stairs that have a separating function, Dwelling houses, flats and residential purpose				
New Build & Change of use/ Conversions Tests in at least 4 Pairs of rooms	$D_{nT,w} \geq 53dB$	$D_{nT,w} \geq 49dB$	$D_{nT,w} \geq 52dB$ $L_{nT,w} \leq 61dB$	$D_{nT,w} \geq 48dB$ $L_{nT,w} \leq 65dB$
New Build & Change of use/ Conversions Tests in at least 8 Pairs of rooms	$D_{nT,w} \geq 52dB$	$D_{nT,w} \geq 49dB$	$D_{nT,w} \geq 51dB$ $L_{nT,w} \leq 62dB$	$D_{nT,w} \geq 48dB$ $L_{nT,w} \leq 65dB$

[*]The requirements of ADE can also be met by adopting the Robust Details Scheme
[#]Internal partition requirements in ADE are only for partitions which separate rooms for sleeping purposes from other rooms and so exclude walls between bedrooms and circulation spaces, and bedrooms to their own en-suite. In Section 5 the requirement applies to any partition which forms a room for sleeping purposes with the exception of en-suites attached to the bedroom.

buildings manufacturers should prove that their systems can meet minimum standards based on laboratory data.

In this instance the ΔL_w or ΔR_w parameters are used. This is the level of improvement a system has achieved when tested on a base timber or concrete floor under laboratory conditions. Regardless of whether it is an impact (ΔL_w) or airborne (ΔR_w) result the Δ character means that the higher the value the better the performance. The minimum requirement for each lining system is listed below:

- Bonded Resilient Coverings on concrete floors – ΔL_w 17dB
- Floating Floor Treatments on concrete floors – ΔR_w 5dB; ΔL_w 22dB
- Floating Floor Treatments on timber floors – ΔR_w 17dB; ΔR_w+Ctr 13dB; ΔL_w 16dB
- Resilient Ceiling Bars on timber floors – ΔR_w 16dB; ΔR_w+Ctr 14dB; ΔL_w 16dB

8.3 Enhanced performance criteria (domestic)

Many new housing developments are built under the BREEAM Ecohomes or Code for Sustainable Homes (CforSH) credit system.

CforSH supersedes Ecohomes, however it is still widely used in some parts of the UK (e.g. Scotland). In order to gain credits it is necessary to provide a higher level of acoustic insulation than that outlined in the building regulations. Regardless of where in the UK a dwelling is constructed the airborne performance parameter outlined for England and Wales is always applied ($D_{nT,w}$ +C_{tr}).

For the Code for Sustainable Homes credits are dependent upon 10 per cent of the site being tested and performance levels which exceed the basic pass rate as detailed in Table XII.

Ecohomes credits are dependent upon the level of testing undertaken and the improvement over the basic requirements of Approved Document E. To gain more than two credits the minimum required

Table XII Code for sustainable homes – credit system

Credits	Improvement on Approved Document E Levels (dB)	
	Airborne $D_{nT,w}$ + C_{tr}	Impact L'
1	+3	–3
3	+5	5
4	+8	8

rate of testing is increased. The amount of testing required is also affected by the number of plots on site and the number of different dwelling types (flats, houses).

Table XIII details the required testing and improvement over the minimum requirement needed to gain the relevant credits. It should be noted that the volume of testing requirements under the Ecohomes systems is substantial in comparison to the requirements under CforSH.

Under both the CforSH and the Ecohomes scheme it is possible to gain credit points without testing on site if the Robust Details scheme is adopted and the relevant constructions are used. In order to gain multiple credits the correct Robust Detail partition must be specified. Details of the number of credits that can be achieved for each partition type can be found on the Robust Details website (www.robustdetails.com).

In Scotland, Section 7 applies a gold, silver and bronze rating scheme. A 4 dB improvement beyond the standard achieves gold, a 2 dB improvement beyond the standard achieves silver and meeting the standard achieves the bronze rating.

8.4 Performance standards for dwellings in other countries
Table XIV details the performance criteria set in other countries for sound insulation in dwellings as of May 2004 taken from COST TU0901 and *Architectural Acoustics* (Cavanaugh et al., 2010).

8.5 School performance criteria
The guidance offered in this section is based on the performance criteria set out in Building Bulletin 93. Table XV details the $D_{nT(Tmf,max),w}$ airborne sound insulation requirements for school developments.

Table XVI details the impact sound insulation requirements for schools. The impact requirement for each room listed in Table XV would be for the floor above the room in question so that the room is protected from impact sound to the prescribed level.

Table XIII Summary HEA2 credit requirement of Ecohomes 2006

No. credits	Approximate no. tests required	Sound insulation performance
1	~ 50% plots	As ADE
2	~ 50% plots+ 2	As ADE
3	~ 50% plots + 2	3 dB improvement over ADE
4	~ 50% plots + 2	5 dB improvement over ADE

8.6 School performance criteria – corridor/circulation space walls
For schools it is accepted that the level of sound insulation for corridor walls separating rooms from circulation spaces which have doors or glazing in them would not be testable on site. Therefore a performance criterion based on laboratory performance should be set. This means that laboratory test data can be used as evidence that a partition specification is suitable for use.

For all rooms to circulation spaces except music rooms the minimum requirement would be R_w 40dB for the wall and R_w 30dB for the door set. For music rooms to circulation spaces the minimum requirement would be R_w 45dB for the wall and R_w 35dB for the door.

8.7 Hospital performance criteria
The guidance offered in this section is based on the performance criteria set out in Health Technical Memorandum 08-01.

Impact sound insulation – Guidance for impact insulation given in HTM08-01 is limited and recommends that the aim should be to avoid locating heavy traffic areas above sensitive spaces such as wards.

The performance requirement set is a maximum $L'_{nT,w}$ of 65dB.

Airborne sound insulation – Table XVII details the D_{ntw} airborne sound insulation requirements for hospital developments.

Locating rooms adjacent to one another which will result in a partition which requires a $D_{nT,w}$ of 57dB should be avoided.

Table XIV Domestic sound insulation requirements in other countries (May 2004)

Country	Airborne performance parameter	Multi-storey house (dB)	Terraced house (dB)	Impact performance requirement	Multi-storey house (dB)	Terraced house (dB)
Austria	$D_{nT,w}$	≥ 55	≥ 60	$L'_{nT,w}$	≤ 48	≤ 46
Australia	$D_{nT,w}+C_{tr}$	≥ 45	≥ 45	$L'_{nT,w}+C_I$	≤ 62	–
Belgium	$D_{nT,w}$	≥ 54	≥58	$L'_{nT,w}$	≤ 58	≤ 50
Czech	R'_w	≥ 52	≥ 57	L'_{nw}	≤ 58	≤ 53
Denmark	R'_w	≥ 52	≥ 55	L'_{nw}	≤ 58	≤ 53
Estonia	R'_w	≥ 55	≥ 55	L'_{nw}	≤ 53	≤ 53
Finland	R'_w	≥ 55	≥ 55	L'_{nw}	≤ 53	≤ 53
France	$D_{nT,w}+C$	≥ 53	≥ 53	$L'_{nT,w}$	≤ 58	≤ 58
Germany	R'_w	≥ 53	≥ 57	L_{nw}	≤ 53	≤ 48
Hungary	R'_w	≥ 52	≥ 57	L'_{nw}	≤ 55	≤47
Iceland	R'_w	≥ 52	≥ 55	L'_{nw}	≤58	≤ 53
Italy	R'_w	≥ 50	≥ 50	L'_{nw}	≤ 63	≤ 63
Latvia	R'_w	≥ 54	≥ 54	L'_{nw}	≤ 54	≤ 54
Lithuania	$D_{nT,w}$ or R'_w	≥ 55	≥ 55	L'_{nw}	≤ 53	≤ 53
Netherlands	I_{luk}	≥ 0	≥ 0	I_{co}	≤+5	≤+5
New Zealand	STC	≥ 55	≥ 55	IIC	≤ 55	–
Norway	R'_w	≥ 55	≥ 55	L'_{nw}	≤ 53	≤ 53
Poland	R'_w+C	≥ 50	≥ 52	L'_{nw}	≤ 58	≤ 53
Portugal	$D_{n,w}$	≥ 50	50	L'_{nw}	≤ 60	≤ 60
Russia	I_b	≥ 50	–	I_y	≤ 67	–
Slovakia	R'_w	≥ 52	≥ 52	L'_{nw}	≤ 58	≤ 58
Slovenia	R'_w	≥ 52	≥ 52	L'_{nw}	≤ 58	≤ 58
Spain	$D_{nT,w}+C_{100-5000}$	≥ 50	≥50	$L'_{nT,w}$	≤ 65	≤ 65
Sweden	$R'_w+C_{50-3150}$	≥ 53	≥ 53	$L'_{nw}+C_{50-3150}$	≤ 56	≤ 56
Switzerland	$D_{nT,w}+C$	≥ 54	≥ 54	$L'_{nT,w}+C_I$	≤ 50	≤ 50
USA*	STC	≥ 48–55+	≥ 48–55+	IIC	≤ 55–48+	–

*USA guidance for federal housing, state guidance may differ.
+performance requirement dependent on grade of existing background level (Grade 1 [34–50dBA] =1 STC55 ICC48; Grade 2 [40–45dBA] STC52 IIC 52; Grade 3 [55dBA] STC48 IIC 55)

Table XV Airborne $D_{nT(Tmf,max),w}$ sound insulation requirements for schools (BB93)

	Toilets	Coat and changing areas	Corridors, stairwells	Office, staff rooms	Kitchens	Dining rooms	Interviewing/counselling rooms, medical rooms	Swimming pool	Gymnasium	Dance studio	Indoor sports hall	Atria, circulation spaces used by students	Audio-visual, video conference rooms	Assembly halls, multi-purpose halls (drama, PE,audio/visual presentations, assembly, occasional music)	Art rooms	Design & Technology - Electronics/control, textiles, food, graphics, design/resource areas	Design & Technology - resistance materials, CAMCAD areas	Drama studios	Science laboratories	Libraries - resource areas	Libraries - quiet study areas	Study room (individual study, withdrawal, remedial work, teacher preparation)	Classroom designed specifically for use by hearing impaired students (including speech therapy rooms)	Large lecture room (>50 people)	Small lecture room (<50 people)	Control room for recording	Recording studio	Performance/recital room	Ensemble room	Small practice/group room	Music classroom	Open-plan Resource area	Open-plan Teaching area	Secondary school: classrooms, general teaching areas, seminar rooms tutorial rooms, language laboratories	Primary school: classrooms, class bases, general teaching areas, small group	Nursery school quiet rooms	Nursery school playrooms
Nursery school playrooms	45	55	55	50	55	55	55	55	55	55	55	50	55	55	50	50	55	55	50	50	55	55	55	55	55	55	55	55	55	55	55	50	50	55	55	55	55
Nursery school quiet rooms	45	55	55	45	55	55	40	55	55	55	55	45	45	55	45	45	55	55	45	45	40	40	45	45	55	55	55	55	55	55	55	45	45	45	45	40	
P school; classrooms, classbases, gen teach areas, small group	45	45	55	45	55	55	45	55	55	55	55	45	45	55	45	45	55	55	45	45	45	45	50	50	45	55	55	55	55	55	55	45	45	45	45		
S school; class, gen teach areas, seminar/tutorial, language lab	45	55	55	45	55	55	45	55	55	55	55	45	45	55	45	45	55	55	45	45	45	45	50	50	45	55	55	55	55	55	55	45	45	45			
Open-plan Teaching area	40	50	50	40	50	50	45	50	50	50	50	40	45	50	40	40	50	50	40	40	45	45	50	50	45	50	55	55	55	55	55	40	40				
Open-plan Resource area	40	50	50	40	50	50	45	50	50	50	50	40	45	50	40	40	50	50	40	40	45	45	50	50	45	50	55	55	55	55	55	40					
Music classroom	55	55	55	55	55	55	55	55	55	55	55	55	55	55	55	55	55	60	55	55	55	55	60	60	55	55	60	60	60	55	55						
Small practice/group room	55	55	55	55	55	55	55	55	55	55	55	55	55	55	55	55	55	60	55	55	55	55	60	60	55	55	60	60	60	55							
Ensemble room	55	55	55	55	55	55	55	55	55	55	55	55	55	55	55	55	55	60	55	55	55	55	60	60	55	55	60	60	60								
Performance/recital room	55	55	55	55	55	55	55	55	55	55	55	55	55	55	55	55	55	60	60	55	55	55	60	60	55	55	60	60									
Recording studio	55	55	55	55	55	55	55	55	55	55	55	55	55	55	55	55	55	60	60	55	55	55	60	60	55	55	60										
Control room for recording	45	55	55	50	55	55	55	55	55	55	55	50	55	55	50	50	55	55	50	50	55	55	55	55	55	55											
Small lecture room (<50 people)	45	55	55	45	55	55	45	55	55	55	55	45	45	55	45	45	55	55	45	45	45	45	50	50	45												
Large lecture room (>50 people)	50	55	55	50	55	55	45	55	55	55	55	50	50	55	50	50	55	55	50	50	45	45	50	50													
Classroom designed specifically for use by hearing impaired students (including speech	50	55	55	50	55	55	45	55	55	55	55	50	50	55	50	50	55	55	50	50	45	45	50														
Study room (individual study, withdrawal, remedial work, teacher preparation)	45	55	55	45	55	55	40	55	55	55	55	45	45	55	45	45	55	55	45	45	40	40															
Libraries - quiet study areas	45	55	55	45	55	55	40	55	55	55	55	45	45	55	45	45	55	55	45	45	40																
Libraries - resource areas	40	50	50	40	50	50	45	50	50	50	50	40	45	50	40	40	50	50	40	40																	
Science laboratories	40	50	50	40	50	50	45	50	50	50	50	40	45	50	40	40	50	50	40																		
Drama studios	50	55	55	50	55	55	55	55	55	55	55	50	55	55	50	50	55	55																			
Design & Technology - resistance materials, CAMCAD areas	45	45	45	50	45	45	55	45	50	50	50	50	55	55	50	50	45																				
Design & Technology - Electronics/control, textiles, food, graphics, design/resource	40	50	50	40	50	50	45	50	50	50	50	40	45	50	40	40																					
Art rooms	40	50	50	40	50	50	45	50	50	50	50	40	45	50	40																						
Assembly halls, multi-purpose halls (drama, PE,audio/visual presentations, assembly)	45	55	55	50	55	55	55	55	55	55	55	50	55	55																							
Audio-visual, video conference rooms	45	55	55	45	55	55	45	55	55	55	55	45	45																								
Atria, circulation spaces used by students	40	50	50	40	50	50	45	50	50	50	50	40																									
Indoor sports hall	45	50	50	50	50	50	55	50	50	50	50																										
Dance studio	45	50	50	50	50	50	55	50	50	50																											
Gymnasium	45	50	50	50	50	50	55	50	50																												
Swimming pool	45	45	45	50	45	45	55	45																													
Interviewing/counselling rooms, medical rooms	45	55	55	45	55	55	40																														
Dining rooms	45	45	45	50	45	45																															
Kitchens	45	45	45	50	45																																
Office, staff rooms	40	50	50	40																																	
Corridors, stairwells	45	45	45																																		
Coat and changing areas	45	45																																			
Toilets	35																																				

Table XVI Performance standards for impact sound insulation of school floors (BB93)

Type of room	Maximum impact sound pressure level $L'_{nT(Tmf,max),w}$ (dB)
Nursery school playrooms	
Science laboratories	
Design & Technology resistance material CAMCAD areas	
Atria, circulation spaces for students	
Indoor sports halls	
Gymnasium	65
Swimming pool	
Dining rooms; kitchens	
Offices. staff rooms	
Corridors, stairwells	
Coats and changing areas	
Toilets	
Nursery school quiet rooms	
Primary school, classrooms, class bases, general teaching areas, small groups	
Secondary school, classrooms, general teaching areas, seminar rooms, tutorial rooms, language laboratories	
Open plan teaching areas	
Open plan resource areas	
Small lecture rooms (fewer than 50 people)	
Study room (individual study, withdrawal, remedial work, teacher preparation)	60
Libraries	
Design & Technology electronic/control, textiles, food, graphics, design/resource areas	
Art room	
Assembly halls, multi-purpose halls (drama. PH. audio/visual presentations, assembly, occasional music)	
Audio-visual, video conference rooms	
Dance studio	
Interview/counselling rooms, medical rooms	
Music: music classroom, small practice/group room, ensemble room, performance/recital room, recording studio, control room for recording.	
Large lecture room (more than 50)	55
Classrooms designed specifically for use by hearing impaired students (including speech therapy rooms)	
Drama studios	

Note: Where it is not possible to meet the minimum acoustic absorption requirements (set out in section 10) then the level of insulation for the partitions in these areas should be increased by 3dB.

8.8 Hospital performance criteria – corridor/circulation space walls

The level of sound insulation for corridor walls separating rooms from circulation spaces which have doors or glazing in them would not be testable on site. Therefore a performance criterion based on laboratory performance should be set. Laboratory test data can be used as evidence that a partition specification is suitable for use. For all rooms to circulation spaces the minimum requirement would be R_w 40–45dB for the wall and R_w 30–35dB for the door set respectively.

8.9 Performance criteria for civic buildings

Guidance for many civic buildings will be ad hoc; however guidance is available in the Courts Standards and Design Guide 2007 (CSDG) document which outlines reasonable performance specifications for airborne and impact sound insulation. Table XVIII details the airborne insulation requirements while Table XIX details the impact requirements.

8.10 Performance criteria for other building types

Sound insulation in other building types is often not considered as an area of concern however in many cases sound transmission in offices, cinemas and other building types is important. Table XX outlines good practice for airborne sound insulation in a variety of building types. Performance standards given for office accommodation are taken from the BCO Specification Guide 2009.

8.11 Broadcasting

The guidance requirements for commercial recording studios and television broadcast studios are considered a highly specialised area and should be considered the remit of an acoustic consultant or specialist design consultant. Further guidance can be found in BBC Engineering's 'Guide to Acoustic Practice'.

9 SPECIFYING AIRBORNE AND IMPACT INSULATION FROM LABORATORY TEST DATA

9.1 Laboratory to site

It can often be difficult to find site performance data for a partition and so a designer may have to rely on test data gathered from laboratory testing. In most instances airborne and impact sound insulation is measured in a suppressed flanking laboratory. This type of laboratory reduces the effects of the other sound paths between the two test rooms (see Section 5.5) so that only the performance of the specimen partition is tested.

In order to assess if the laboratory performance of a partition is good enough to be used on site it is necessary to adjust the laboratory result. The level of adjustment required is partly based on the performance parameter that is used on site ($D_{nT,w}$, $D_{nT,w} + C_{tr}$ etc.) and the anticipated effects of flanking. For these estimations to be meaningful it is assumed that the partition specification used on site is identical to that tested in the laboratory and that a high level of workmanship has been undertaken on site.

9.2 Domestic performance conversions

The following rules of thumb are normally applied when converting site performance requirements to laboratory performance levels;

Site $D_{nT,w}$ = Lab R_w +5dB for masonry partitions
Site $D_{nT,w}$ = Lab R_w +7dB for light weight partitions
Site $D_{nT,w}+C_{tr}$ = Lab R_w +C_{tr} + 10dB for masonry partitions
Site $D_{nT,w}+C_{tr}$ = Lab R_w +C_{tr} + 15dB for lightweight partitions

9.3 Hospital performance conversions

For hospitals the HTM08-01 document suggests that additional care be taken when specifying partitions with relevance to room volume.

Figure 10.8 shows the relationship between on site performance ($D_{nT,w}$) and laboratory performance (R_w) in relationship to the room width. The minimum that should be added is taken to be +5dB for heavy constructions and +7dB for light constructions; however as the room width reduces, the level of insulation that a wall would have to provide under laboratory conditions increases in order to provide the required level of insulation on site.

9.4 School performance conversions

For schools projects the use of the $D_{nT(Tmf,max),w}$ parameter has broadly similar properties to the $D_{nT,w}$ parameter discussed in Sections 9.2 and 9.3. Note the use of the $T_{mf,max}$ parameter. This is a set maximum reverberation time to be used in the calculation of the result. If the correct reverberation time within a room is not achieved it will have an effect on the overall sound insulation performance of the partition.

While it is suitable to use the rules of thumb outlined in Section 9.2 (+5 and +7dB added to the R_w value depending upon the partition type) this will only be credible if the correct reverberation time in the receiving room is also achieved (see Section 10).

Table XVII $D_{nT,w}$ Airborne sound insulation requirements for hospitals (HTM08-01)

Room Types	Single bed/on-call room	multi-bed room	Children & older people (single bed)	Children & older people (multi-bed)	Consulting room	Examination room	Treatment room	Counseling/bereavement room	interview room	Operating theatre suite	Nurseries	Birthing room	Laboratories	Dirty utility/sluice	Clean utility	Speech and language therapy	Snoezelen/multi-sensory room	Multi-faith/chapel	Corridor (no door)	Atrium	Dining	Toilets (non cubicles)	Waiting (large > 20 people)	Waiting (small ≤ 20 people)	Toilets (non cubicles)	Main kitchen	Ward kitchen, pantry	Storeroom	Rest room	Locker/changing room	Large training/seminar (>35m2)	Small training/seminar(≤ 35m2)	Lecture theatre	Library/archiving room	Single-person office	Multi-person office (2-4 people)	Open-plan office (≥ 5 people)	Boardroom	Large meeting room (> 35m2)	Small meeting room (≤ 35m2)
Single bed/on-call room	47																																							
multi-bed room	47	37																																						
Children & older people (single bed)	47	47	47																																					
Children & older people (multi-bed)	47	42	47	42																																				
Consulting room	47	47	47	47	47																																			
Examination room	47	47	47	47	47	47																																		
Treatment room	47	47	47	47	47	47	47																																	
Counseling/bereavement room	47	47	47	47	47	47	47	47																																
interview room	47	47	47	47	47	47	47	47	47																															
Operating theatre suite	47	42	52	47	47	47	47	52	47	47																														
Nurseries	52	52	52	52	52	52	52	52	52	57*	52																													
Birthing room	52	52	52	52	52	52	52	52	52	57*	52	52																												
Laboratories	47	37	47	42	47	47	47	47	47	42	52	52	37																											
Dirty utility/sluice	47	42	42	42	47	47	47	47	47	47	47	47	42	n/a																										
Clean utility	47	37	42	37	47	47	47	47	47	42	47	47	37	n/a	n/a																									
Speech and language therapy	47	47	52	47	47	47	47	52	47	52	57*	57*	47	47	47	52																								
Snoezelen/multi-sensory room	47	47	52	47	47	47	47	52	47	52	57*	57*	47	47	47	52	52																							
Multi-faith/chapel	47	47	52	47	47	47	47	52	47	52	57*	57*	47	47	42	52	52	52																						
Corridor (no door)	47	37	42	37	47	47	47	47	47	42	47	47	37	n/a	n/a	47	47	42	n/a																					
Atrium	47	42	42	42	47	47	47	47	47	47	47	47	42	n/a	n/a	47	47	47	n/a	n/a																				
Dining	47	42	42	42	47	47	47	47	47	47	47	47	42	n/a	n/a	47	47	47	n/a	n/a	n/a																			
Toilets (non cubicles)	47	37	42	37	47	47	47	47	47	42	47	47	37	37	37	47	47	42	37	37	37	37																		
Waiting (large > 20 people)	47	42	42	42	47	47	47	47	47	47	47	47	42	n/a	n/a	47	47	47	n/a	n/a	n/a	37	n/a																	
Waiting (small ≤ 20 people)	47	37	42	37	47	47	47	47	47	42	47	47	37	n/a	n/a	47	47	42	n/a	n/a	n/a	37	n/a	n/a																
Toilets (non cubicles)	47	37	42	37	47	47	47	47	47	42	47	47	37	37	37	47	47	42	37	37	37	37	37	37	37															
Main kitchen	52	52	52	52	52	52	52	52	52	57*	52	52	52	47	47	47	57*	57*	47	47	47	47	47	47	47	47														
Ward kitchen, pantry	47	37	42	37	47	47	47	47	47	42	47	47	37	n/a	n/a	47	47	42	n/a	n/a	n/a	37	n/a	n/a	37	47	n/a													
Storeroom	47	37	42	37	47	47	47	47	47	42	47	47	37	n/a	n/a	47	47	42	n/a	n/a	n/a	37	n/a	n/a	37	47	n/a	n/a												
Rest room	47	42	47	42	47	47	47	47	47	47	52	52	42	42	37	47	47	47	37	42	42	37	42	37	37	52	37	37	42											
Locker/changing room	47	37	42	37	47	47	47	47	47	42	47	47	37	37	37	47	47	42	37	37	37	37	37	37	37	47	37	37	37	37										
Large training/seminar (>35m2)	47	47	47	47	47	47	47	47	47	52	52	52	47	42	42	47	52	52	42	42	42	42	42	42	42	52	42	42	47	42	47									
Small training/seminar (≤ 35m2)	47	42	47	42	47	47	47	47	47	47	52	52	42	42	42	47	47	47	42	42	42	42	42	42	42	52	42	42	42	42	47	42								
Lecture theatre	47	47	52	47	47	47	47	52	47	52	57*	57*	47	47	42	52	52	52	42	47	47	42	47	42	42	57*	42	42	47	42	52	47	52							
Library/archiving room	47	42	52	47	47	47	47	52	47	47	57*	57*	42	47	37	52	52	52	42	47	47	42	47	42	42	57*	42	37	47	42	52	47	52	37						
Single-person office	47	42	47	42	47	47	47	47	47	47	52	52	42	42	42	47	47	47	42	42	42	42	42	42	42	52	42	42	42	42	47	42	47	47	42					
Multi-person office (2-4 people)	47	37	47	42	47	47	47	47	47	42	52	52	37	42	37	47	47	47	37	42	42	37	42	37	37	52	37	37	42	37	47	42	47	42	42	37				
Open-plan office (≥5 people)	47	37	47	42	47	47	47	47	47	42	52	52	37	42	n/a	47	47	47	n/a	42	42	37	42	n/a	37	52	n/a	n/a	42	37	47	42	47	42	42	37	n/a			
Boardroom	47	47	47	47	47	47	47	47	47	52	52	52	47	47	47	47	52	52	47	47	47	47	47	47	47	52	47	47	47	47	47	47	52	52	47	47	47	47		
Large meeting room (> 35m2)	47	47	47	47	47	47	47	47	47	52	52	52	47	42	42	47	52	52	42	42	42	42	42	42	42	52	42	42	47	42	47	47	52	52	47	47	47	47	47	
Small meeting room (<35m2)	47	42	47	42	47	47	47	47	47	47	52	52	42	42	42	47	47	47	42	42	42	42	42	42	42	52	42	42	42	42	47	42	47	47	42	42	42	47	47	42

Table XVIII $D_{nT,w}$ Airborne sound insulation requirements for court houses (CSDG 2007)

	Toilets	Witness Waiting Room	Defendants Holding Area	Cells	Public Areas	Restricted Circulation Areas	Advocates' Rooms	Assembly Areas	Offices	Multi-purpose Rooms	Waiting Areas	Usher Rooms	Jury Rooms	Conference Rooms	Consultation Rooms	Committee Rooms	Interview Rooms	Magistrates' & Judges' Retiring Chambers	Courtroom
Courtroom	53	53	53	53	53	53	53	53	53	53	53	53	53	53	53	53	53	53	53
Magistrates' & Judges' Retiring Chambers	50	50	50	55	50	48	50	50	50	50	50	50	55	50	50	50	50	50	
Interview Rooms	42	50	50	55	35	42	50	42	42	42	43	45	55	42	42	42	42		
Committee Rooms	42	50	50	55	42	42	45	42	42	42	42	45	55	42	42	42			
Consultation Rooms	42	50	50	55	35	42	45	42	42	42	42	45	60	42	42				
Conference Rooms	42	50	50	55	35	42	45	42	42	42	42	45	55	42					
Jury Rooms	55	55	55	55	50	50	55	50	55	55	50	45	53						
Usher Rooms	42	50	50	50	35	50	45	53	40	40	35	42							
Waiting Areas	42	50	50	55	35	42	45	35	35	35	42								
Multi-purpose Rooms	42	50	50	55	35	50	45	35	42	42									
Offices	42	50	50	55	35	50	50	35	42										
Assembly Areas	42	50	50	55	45	50	48	42											
Advocates' Rooms	42	50	50	55	45	50	50												
Restricted Circulation Areas	50	50	50	55	45	50													
Public Areas	42	50	50	55	50														
Cells	55	55	55	48															
Defendants Holding Area	42	50	50																
Witness Waiting Room	42	50																	
Toilets	42																		

Table XIX Performance standards for impact sound insulation of court buildings (CSDG 2007)

Room type	Maximum impact sound pressure level $L'_{nT,w}$ (dB)
Courtrooms/critical areas	50
Private offices/ conference	55
Public/non-critical areas	60

Table XX Sound insulation performance guidance for a variety of building types

Type of building/room	Airborne sound (dB)	Impact sound (dB)
Offices		
General office – general office (fitted out to Cat A Standard)	$D_{nT,w} \geq 48$dB	N/A
Private offices/meeting room to another space	$D_{nT,w} \geq 50$dB	$L'_{nT,w} \leq 65$dB
Commercial	$D_{nT,w} \geq 65$dB	
Cinema to cinema	(plus minimum D_{nT} of 35dB at 63Hz)B	N/A
Cinema to foyer/bar	$D_{nT,w} \geq 55$dB	N/A
Cinema to corridors/concourse (where doors are present)	$R_w \geq 71$dB	N/A
Cinema to corridors/concourse (where no doors are present)	$D_{nT,w} \geq 55$dB	N/A
Cinema to projection room	$D_{nT,w} \geq 55$dB	N/A
Retail/commercial to dwelling	As outlined for separating partition in relevant building regulations*	

*It is normal for additional acoustic insulation to be required in such situations and is usually detailed during the planning phase.

9.5 Perception of sound insulation values

Table XXI details the perceived relationship between the level of sound insulation offered by a partition and how speech would be perceived in the adjoining room.

10 REVERBERATION CRITERIA

Two performance parameters are normally set when considering reverberation time in a room. Either the room must not exceed a maximum reverberation time or a minimum area of acoustically absorbent material should be specified within the room. For the second parameter described it is also normal to dictate the minimum level of absorption offered by the material.

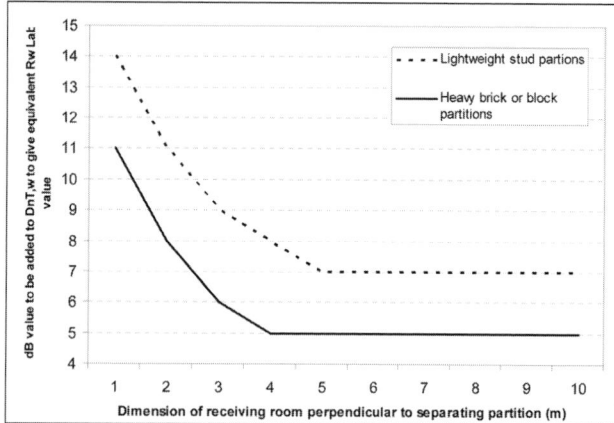

10.8 HTM08-01 Converting site performance requirements to laboratory performance requirements

Table XXI Perceived relationship between sound insulation values and speech

Description	DnT,w
Talk at a normal level can be heard and followed in the room next door	30
Talk at a normal level can be heard and partly distinguished in the room next door	35
Talk at a normal level can be heard but words cannot be distinguished in the room next door	40
Talk at a normal level cannot be heard in the room next door	45
Loud speech can be heard through the wall but words cannot be distinguished	50
Loud speech cannot be heard through the wall	55
Loud shouting can be heard through the wall, but words cannot be distinguished	60
	Wood Focus Oy

Table XXII Suitable maximum reverberation times

Type of building/room	Maximum reverberation time (second
School	
Nursery school playrooms	0.6
Nursery school quiet rooms	0.6
Primary school; classrooms, class bases, general teaching areas, small group rooms	0.6
Secondary school; classrooms, general teaching areas, seminar	
Rooms, tutorial rooms, language laboratories	0.8
Open-plan teaching area	0.8
Open-plan resource area	1.0
Music classroom	1.0
Small practice/group room	0.8
Ensemble room	0.6–1.2
Performance/recital room	1.0–1.5
Recording studio	0.6–1.2
Control room for recording	0.5
Small lecture room (<50 people)	0.8
Large lecture room (>50 people)	1.0
Classroom designed specifically for use by hearing impaired students (including speech therapy rooms)	0.4
Study room (individual study, withdrawal, remedial work, teacher preparation)	0.8
Libraries – quiet study areas	1.0
Libraries – resource areas	1.0
Science laboratories	0.8
Drama studios	1.0

Table XXII (continued)

Design & Technology – resistance materials, CAMCAD areas	0.8
Design & Technology – electronics/control, textiles, food, graphics, design/resource areas	0.8
Art rooms	0.8
Assembly halls, multi-purpose halls (drama, PE, audio/visual presentations, assembly, occasional music)	0.8–1.2
Audio-visual, video conference rooms	0.8
Atria, circulation spaces used by students	1.5
Indoor sports hall	1.5
Dance studio	1.2
Gymnasium	1.5
Swimming pool	2.0
Interviewing/counselling rooms, medical rooms	0.8
Dining rooms	1.0
Kitchens	1.5
Office, staff rooms	1.0
Corridors, stairwells	See Note
Coat and changing areas	1.5
Toilets	1.5
Offices	
Cellular office	1.0
Staff room	1.0
Meeting room	0.6
Executive office	0.6
Open plan office	0.8
Industrial	
Workshops	0.8
Canteen	1.0
Civic & Amenity	
Library	0.6
Court rooms (up to 500m³) with 50% room occupancy	<0.6 @ 125Hz-2kHz (+ 0.1sec)
Court rooms (over 500m³) with 50% room occupancy	1.0 @ 125Hz-2kHz (± 0.2sec)
Magistrates/judge retiring, judges' chambers	0.6
Control centres	0.4–0.75
Interview rooms (for recording)	0.3
Toilets	1.5
Public sports halls/games halls	2.0
Public gymnasium	2.0
Washrooms	1.5
Public baths/swimming pools	2.0
Domestic	
Living rooms	0.8
Bedrooms	0.6

Note: Corridors and stairwells can provide suitable reverberation time levels by applying a Class B absorbent ceiling to all areas.

10.1 Reverberation times

The reverberation time (RT), given in seconds, is normal consider as the average reverberation time for the frequency bands 500Hz, 1000Hz and 2000Hz. Table XXII details the required maximum reverberation times for a range of rooms. Instances where an alternative frequency range should be used are noted in the table.

10.2 Optimum reverberation times in performance spaces

For performance spaces, including churches, the optimum reverberation time will differ dependent upon the type of performance (speech, music), the type of building and the volume of the space. Figure 10.9 gives guidance values for reverberation times in some common performance spaces (Cavanaugh et al., 2010; BS 8233; Ballou, 2005).

These guidance levels show the optimum reverberation time dependent on room volume at the 500Hz frequency band width. Achieving these reverberation times will be dependent on specialist acoustic design. General guidance on this subject is given in Section 11.

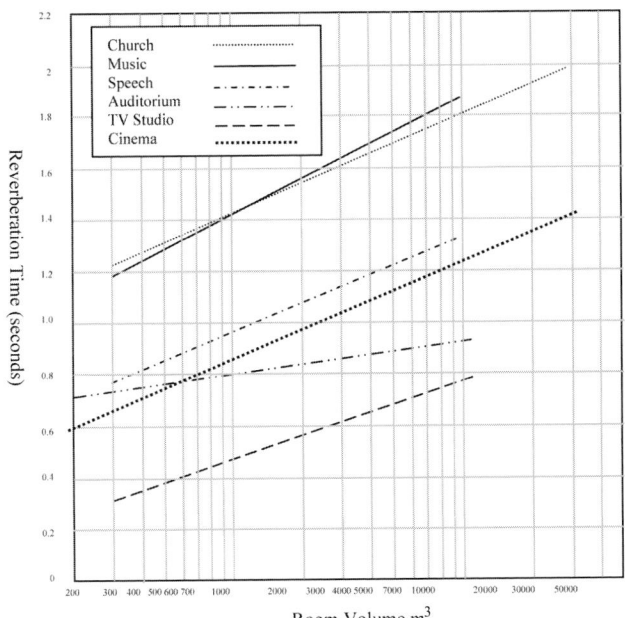

10.9 *Reverberation vs volume criteria in performance spaces (500Hz)*

Table XXIII Recommended absorption requirements

Type of building/room	Recommendations for achieving suitable reverberation times in a space based on absorbent areas in a room
Schools (BB3)	
Entrance halls, corridors, hallways	Cover an area equal to or greater than the floor area with a Class C absorber
	Cover an area equal to or greater than the total stair tread, intermediate landings and top landing (excluding ground floor area) with a Class D absorber
Stairwells, stair enclosures	OR
	Cover 50% of the calculated area with a Class C absorber
Hospitals (HTM08–01)	
All rooms excluding unimportant rooms (e.g. storerooms) where cleaning, infection-control, patient-safety, clinical and maintenance requirements allow.	Cover an area equal to or greater than 80% of the floor areas with a Class C absorber
Rooms requiring optimum acoustic conditions (e.g. lecture theatres)	Specialist advice should be sought
Large areas such as Atria	Specification should be agreed on a case by case basis (see options in Table XXII)
Common areas in domestic developments (ADE)	
Entrance halls, corridors, hallways	Cover an area equal to or greater than the floor area with a Class C absorber
	Cover an area equal to or greater than the total stair tread, intermediate landings and top landing (excluding ground floor area) with a Class D absorber
Stairwells, stair enclosures	OR
	Cover 50% of the calculated area with a Class C absorber

10.3 Minimum area of absorption

The other performance parameter commonly used is to define the minimum area of absorption required for a space and to define the absorption classification of the material. This is used in hospital developments or in circulation spaces (e.g. in schools or stairwells in domestic developments).

The absorption classification of a material is defined in BS EN ISO 11654 at each frequency as the $\acute{\alpha}_s$ and as a single figure value as the $\acute{\alpha}_w$. From this the classification of a material is rated from A–E, Class A absorbent material being the highest classification with the most absorption and Class E materials being the lowest classification with the least absorption. Table XXIII details the likely absorbent classification and area requirement for particular room types.

11 GENERAL GUIDANCE ON THE ACOUSTICS OF PERFORMANCE SPACES

When designing performance spaces such as auditoria, theatres etc. it is always advised that a specialist in building acoustics is involved. However there are some basic guidance rules that the non-specialist designer should be aware of to allow them to begin the initial design.

- Halls for music performance required a minimum of 8m³ per audience member.
- Halls for theatres or cinemas require a minimum of 4m³ per audience member.
- Rectangular shaped halls with high ceilings are normally preferable, fan shaped halls normally provide poor acoustics for musical performances.
- Domes and barrel vaults can cause focusing and should be avoided or treated with additional absorption.
- Acoustic scattering treatments are recommended for side walls. Side-wall diffusion will increase the musical clarity
- A proscenium stage enclosure will benefit the balance and ensemble of orchestrations.
- Large overhangs or balconies will reduce the quality of sound reaching those seated below. The depth of an overhang should not exceed the height between the floor and the underside of the overhang.
- Shallow pitched roofs can cause flutter effects.

- Seating should be arranged to allow for a clear line of sight to the performance space for acoustic as well as visual reasons. This should help to ensure the same acoustics at each seat.
- Steeply raked seating should be avoided particularly for musical performance spaces.
- The walls, floor and ceiling around the performance space should preferably be acoustically reflective. Acoustic absorption in this area should be avoided.
- For music performance spaces the acoustic absorption provided by unoccupied seating should be as similar as possible to when the seats are occupied. Upholstered seating is best. Where tip-up seating is used it is preferable to upholster the underside of the seat.
- Background noise levels should be kept to a minimum. The acoustic performance of the building envelope is important when designing in noisy (city centre) areas.
- Plant and machinery should be as quiet as possible.
- See Figure 10.9 for advice on suitable Reverberation Times versus room volumes.
  - Concert Halls 8–12 m³ per occupant
  - Opera Halls 4–6 m³ per occupant
  - Theatres 2.5–4 m³ per occupant
  - Churches 6–14 m³ per occupant
  - Lecture Rooms 3–6 m³ per occupant

12 BIBLIOGRAPHY

BS5228 *Code of practice for noise control on construct and open sites*

BS8233 *Code of Practice for sound insulation and noise reduction for buildings*

BS EN ISO 140 *Acoustics – Measurement of sound insulation in buildings and of building elements*

BS EN ISO 1996 *Acoustics – Description and measurement of environmental noise*

BS EN ISO 717 *Methods for rating sound insulation in buildings and of building elements*

BS EN ISO 11654 *Sound absorbers for use in buildings – Rating of sound absorption*

BS4142 *Method for rating industrial noise affecting mixed residential and industrial areas*

BS EN ISO 11064-6 *Ergonomic Design of Control Centres* Planning Advice Note 56 Planning and Noise The Scottish Office, HMSO

Planning Policy Guidance 24 Department of the Environment, HMSO

Approved Document E Resistance to the Passage of Sound, Department of the Environment and the Welsh Office, The Building Regulations 2003 – HMSO London

Building Standards (Scotland) *Regulations Section 5 2010* as amended HMSO London

DOE Northern Ireland *Technical Booklet G/G1* 1990 HMSO

Technical Document E Department of the Environment Heritage and Local Government, The Stationery Office (Eire) 1997

Calculation of Road Traffic Noise Department of the Environment 1988

Noise Insulation Regulations HMSO 1975

Railway Noise and the Insulation of Dwellings Department of Transport, HMSO 1991

Courts Standards and Design Guidance 2007 HMSO

Ecohomes BREEAM BRE Press

Wood Focus, Oy 2005

Woods Practical Guide to Noise Control 5th Edition, Courier International Ltd

Code for Sustainable Homes BREEAM BRE Press

Guide to Acoustic Practice BBC Engineering, BBC

Building Bulletin 93 – Acoustic Design of Schools Department for Education and Skills, HMSO 2003

Health Technical Memorandum 08-01 Acoustics, Department of Health, HMSO 2008

Guide to Specification, British Council for Offices, BCO 2009

Sound Control for Homes, BRE/CIRIA BRE Press 1993

The Development and Production of a Guide for Noise Control from Laminate and Wooden Flooring, T. Waters-Fuller et al. Main Report. February 2005

Department of the Environment, Digest, Information Papers, Building Research Establishment, Garston

Robust Standard Details, Robust Details Ltd

Housing and Sound Insulation, Improving Existing Attached Dwellings and Designing for Conversions, SBSA, Historic Scotland, Communities Scotland

Engineering Noise Control, Hansen and Bies, Taylor & Francis 2009

Sound Insulation, Carl Hopkins Butterworth-Heinemann 2007

Architectural Acoustics: Principles and Practice, William J. Cavanaugh et al., John Wiley & Sons 2010

Handbook for Sound Engineering, Glen M Ballou, Focus Press 2005

Open/closed Window Research: Sound Insulation through Ventilated Domestic Windows, Tim Waters-Fuller et al., BPC Napier, DEFRA 2006

Neighbour Noise: Control of noise from laminate and wooden flooring. T. Waters-Fuller et al. Noise Nuisance Section, Environment Division, Scottish Executive 2006

The Building Regulations 2000 – amendment of the building regulations to allow robust standard details to be used as an alternative to pre-completion testing. R. S. Smith et al., Public Consultation Document. Office of the Deputy Prime Minister. August, 2003.

Guidelines for Community Noise, Brigitta Berglund et al., World Health Organisation 1999

Night Noise Guidelines for Europe, Charlotte Hurtley et al., World Health Organisation 2009Table XVII $D_{nT,w}$ Airborne sound insulation requirements for hospitals (HTM08-01)

11 Fire

Beryl Menzies

CI/Sfb (K)

Beryl Menzies is a consultant in fire safety

KEY POINTS:
- *Consider from first principles how a fire can start*
- *Then how can it grow?*
- *Will it threaten life, property or both?*
- *How can it be fought?*
- *How will people escape?*
- *Only after considering all these points, refer to regulations*

Contents
1 Introduction
2 Components of fire
3 Principles of fire protection
4 Means of escape
5 Materials
6 Fire protection appliances and installations
7 Statutory requirements
8 Bibliography

1 INTRODUCTION

When designing a building with fire safety in mind, particularly ease of escape, it is important not to forget the needs also for usability and security. If the fire measures are seen to be too onerous (for example, a multiplicity of fire doors) they will be circumvented (propped open) and their purpose will be frustrated. Fire escape doors are often weak points when it comes to unauthorised ingress, particularly in places of public assembly.

2 COMPONENTS OF FIRE

2.1 Combustion
Fire is combustion producing heat and light. Combustion will occur and continue if three factors are present: oxygen, heat and fuel. These are generally referred to as the combustion triangle, Figure 11.1.

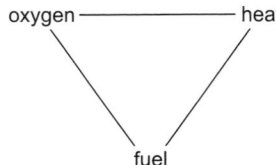

11.1 *Triangle of fire*

2.2 Extinguishing
Fire can be extinguished by removing one corner of the combustion triangle:

- Starve or limit the fuel by removing it.
- Smother by limiting or stopping the further supply of oxygen.
- Cool by dissipating the heat faster than it is generated.

2.3 Source
A source of heat comes into contact with a combustible material (the fuel) which ignites and supports combustion while oxygen is present. The heat sources within a building are many – cooking, smoking, heating equipment, overheating/faulty equipment (particularly electrical).

2.4 Fuel
Three kinds of fuel have been identified:

- tinder, material ignitable by a match which will continue to burn after its removal;
- kindling, material which will ignite and burn if associated with sufficient tinder, but in which a match will not produce a continuing fire;
- bulk fuel, which needs kindling to cause to burn.

2.5 Flammability
The fuel may be present in the building structure, fittings and/or contents and can be in the form of solids, liquids or gases. Most organic materials will burn. Certain materials spontaneously combust and care is required in their storage, e.g. linseed oil, certain chemicals, grains. Certain industrial processes involving high levels of dust, e.g. printing, flour mills, can result in flash fires. Specialist advice should be sought in respect of these matters.

2.6 Risk
The initial source of heat cannot ignite most bulk fuels unless the fire is able to follow the tinder-kindling chain. Of course, this does not apply when the bulk fuel is itself highly combustible; but it does apply to elements of building construction and to many stored materials.

This leads to the point that fire risks in most buildings can be greatly reduced if measures are taken to avoid build-ups of tinder. Dust, waste paper, sawdust, rags, etc. are materials which will act as tinder; so will a number of man-made organic materials which are now coming under stricter control.

2.7 Smoke
This is formed when organic materials decompose by heat giving off tarry and sooty decomposed materials. It is likely that most smoke will be generated by the building contents.

2.8 Heat
This can be transmitted in three forms:

- Conduction – heat energy is passed from one molecule to the next. The conductivity of a material (which varies with the material) may affect the fire resistance of a component or structure. A steel member in contact with combustible materials may transfer the heat generating a fire or damage away from the original source.
- Radiation – heat is transmitted in straight lines without any contact between the radiating material and the target which may absorb or reflect the heat. The intensity reduces inversely as the square of the distance from the source of radiation. Combustible materials placed in close proximity to a radiant fire will ignite.

- Convection – only occurs in liquids and gases. The heated combustion gases become buoyant and rise through voids and shafts with the potential of causing ignition in other areas of a building.

3 PRINCIPLES OF FIRE PROTECTION

Note: specific recommendations relating to periods of fire resistance for specific uses, structural elements etc. are given in various codes only some of which are referred to here.

3.1 Potential problems

- Unrestricted growth and spread of a fire within a building that will cause extensive damage and may result in its collapse.
- Rapid spread of fire across surfaces within the building, ignition of adjacent fuels, means of escape prejudiced.
- Spread of fire, smoke and hot gases in a building through ducts, voids and shafts affecting the means of escape, access for firefighters and causing extensive damage to decorations and property.
- Spread of fire to adjacent buildings affecting life safety and property.
- Loss of contents, disruption of work, loss of trade/production.

3.2 Restriction

The aim of fire precautions within a building is to inhibit the growth and to restrict the spread of any fire. The influencing factors are:

- the size of building – area, height, volume;
- the layout and configuration within the building;
- the uses accommodated, and the requirements of the occupants;
- the construction materials, linings and claddings;
- the type of construction;
- the services installed;
- the furniture.

3.3 Precautions

The precautions are:

- protection of loadbearing structure to prevent untimely collapse, limitation of combustibility of key structural elements;
- adequate and appropriate provisions for means of escape;
- access for firefighters up to and through the building to reach the seat of the fire and promptly extinguish it;
- compartmentation and separation to restrict spread of fire, maintenance of these by protection of openings, fire stopping and cavity barriers within concealed spaces;
- safe installation and maintenance of services, heat-producing equipment and user equipment;
- separation of different uses to protect, for example, a risk to sleepers from commercial uses;
- enclosure of high risks with fire-resisting construction to protect adjacent areas;
- active fire-extinguishing installations to detect and/or contain fire in its early stages and restrict its spread and growth;
- limitation of flame spread by selective use of materials;
- fire-resisting external walls and/or space separation to prevent spread of fire to adjacent properties, protection of openings in external walls, limited flame spread across external walls and roofs, use of insulation with limited combustibility to restrict ignition and spread;
- the provision of natural or mechanical ventilation, smoke extraction and/or smoke control measures to facilitate means of escape and firefighting;
- management training and procedures for evacuation, maintenance of fire precautions, risk analysis, management policy.

3.4 Growth and spread

An analysis of the growth and spread of fire is explained in detail and substantiated by Malhotra in BRE publication BR 96 *Fire Safety in Buildings.*

3.5 Fire load and ignitability

The majority of a fire load within a building will be its contents, over which a designer may have no influence. Some types of occupancies have controls relating to the ignitability of furniture (domestic and assembly buildings under licensing legislation, hospitals and prisons under government directives), see Table I. Electricity, often cited as the cause of fires, while not itself a risk presents a potential hazard when brought into contact with combustible material; all new electrical installations should be installed in accordance with the current edition of the regulations of the Institution of Electrical Engineers and existing installations periodically examined and tested for potential risks.

3.6 Smoke

The limitation of smoke spread is considered mainly as an aspect of safe means of escape. Specific limitations of smoke production are not, to date, generally specified. There is no generally accepted test related to smoke emission. The production of toxic gases which accompanies all fires would be very difficult to specify.

3.7 Combustibility

While it would be possible to construct a totally non-combustible building, it is not practical and not required by legislation; although some codes do relate means of escape to a classification based on the 'combustibility' of a building. Non-combustible materials should be used where hazardous conditions are anticipated or there is a need to maintain the integrity of a structure for the maximum time, e.g. a compartment wall or floor, or an escape stair in a high building.

3.8 Fire resistance

The need for a degree of fire resistance within a structure may be dictated by Building Regulations (Table II), insurance or damage-limitation requirements. The prevention of untimely collapse allows evacuation, containment of a fire and therefore protection of adjacent areas, and access for firefighters. This is essential in high-rise buildings. Factors relating to the need for fire resistance are building height and size, occupancy and anticipated fire severity. While a specific period of fire resistance may be specified and an element constructed accordingly, it should not be assumed that the period will be attained; it may be longer or shorter due to, among other factors, interaction with other elements or non-maintenance, or more severe fire conditions than those anticipated in the test.

Guidance is also available in BS 5950 Structural use of steelwork in building. Part 8 Code of practice for fire resistant design.

3.9 Fire compartments

These are formed around areas of different uses or hazards, or to divide an area into a size in which it is considered a fire could be contained and dealt with by firefighters, and thereby protecting adjacent areas. The addition of automatic active measures such as sprinklers to contain and control the growth of a fire allows larger compartments or, in some cases, their omission. If the only consideration is life safety, it can be argued that if all persons can safely escape there is no need for compartmentation, and the potential exists for reduced fire resistance. This principle is often adopted in low-rise or single-storey buildings. However, in the case of high-rise or buildings with phased or staged evacuation, compartmentation is an essential part of the safety package. Flats and maisonettes are constructed such that every unit is a compartment; in the event of a fire it is only necessary initially to evacuate the unit on fire.

Effective compartmentation requires attention to detail. Openings, including those for ventilation and services, must be protected; where shafts perforate compartment floors 'protected shafts' should be detailed, see Table III.

3.10 Recommendations

Compartments within residential, institutional and health buildings require careful consideration as they form an essential part of the scheme for means of escape. All floors should be compartment floors. It is recommended that compartments do not exceed 2000 m² in multi-storey hospitals and 3000 m² in single-storey hospitals.

Table I Classification of purpose groups (from Approved Document B, Table DI)

Title	Group	Purpose for which the building or compartment of a building is intended to be used
Residential (dwellings)	1(a)*	Flat or maisonette.
	1(b)**	Dwellinghouse which contains a habitable storey with a floor level which is more than 4.5 m above ground level.
	1(c)**	Dwellinghouse which does not contain a habitable storey with a floor level which is more than 4.5 m above ground level
Residential (Institutional)	2(a)	Hospital, home, school or other similar establishment used as living accommodation for, or for the treatment, care or maintenance of persons suffering from disabilities due to illness or old age or other physical or mental incapacity, or under the age of 5 years, or place of lawful detention, where such persons sleep on the premises.
(Other)	2(b)	Hotel, boarding house, residential college, hall of residence, hostel, and any other residential purpose not described above.
Office	3	Offices or premises used for the purpose of administration, clerical work (including writing, book keeping, sorting papers, filing, typing, duplicating, machine calculating, drawing and the editorial preparation of matter for publication, police and fire and rescue work), handling money (including banking and building society work), and communications (including postal, telegraph and radio communications) or radio, television, film, audio or video recording, or performance (not open to the public) and their control.
Shop and Commercial	4	Shops or premises used for a retail trade or business (including the sale to members of the public of food or drink for immediate consumption and retail by auction, self-selection and over-the-counter wholesale trading, the business of lending books or periodicals for gain and the business of a barber or hairdresser and the rental of storage space to the public) and premises to which the public is invited to deliver or collect goods in connection with their hire repair or other treatment, or (except in the case of repair of motor vehicles) where they themselves may carry out such repairs or other treatments.
Assembly and Recreation	5	Place of assembly, entertainment or recreation; including bingo halls, broadcasting, recording and film studios open to the public, casinos, dance halls; entertainment-conference, exhibition and leisure centres; funfairs and amusement arcades; museums and art galleries; non-residential clubs, theatres, cinemas and concert halls; educational establishments, dancing schools, gymnasia, swimming pool buildings, riding schools, skating rinks, sports pavilions, sports stadia; law courts; churches and other buildings of worship, crematoria; libraries open to the public, nonresidential day centres, clinics, health centres and surgeries; passenger stations and termini for air, rail, road or sea travel; public toilets; zoos and menageries.
Industrial	6	Factories and other premises used for manufacturing, altering, repairing, cleaning, washing, breaking-up, adapting or processing any article; generating power or slaughtering livestock
Storage and other non-residential†	7(a)	Place for the storage or deposit of goods or materials [other than described under 7(b)] and any building not within any of the purpose groups 1 to 6.
	7(b)	Car parks designed to admit and accommodate only cars, motorcycles and passenger or light goods vehicles weighing no more than 2500 kg gross.

*Includes live/work units that meet the provisions of paragraph 2.52 of Volume 2 of Approved Document B.

**Includes any surgeries, consulting rooms, offices or other accommodation, not exceeding 50 m² in total, forming part of a dwelling and used by an occupant of the dwelling in a professional or business capacity.

†A detached garage not more than 40 m² in area is included in purpose group 1(c); as is a detached open carport of not more than 40 m², or a detached building which consists of a garage and open carport where neither the garage nor open carport exceeds 40 m² in area.

Table II Minimum periods of fire resistance

Purpose group of building	Minimum periods of fire resistance (minutes) in a:					
	Basement storey(S) including floor over			Ground or upper storey		
	Depth (m) of a lowest basement			Height (m) of top floor above ground, in a building or separated part of a building		
	More than 10	Not more than 10	Not more than 5	Not more than 18	Not more than 30	More than 30
1 Residential:						
a. Block of flats						
– not sprinklered	90	60	30*	60**†	90**	Not permitted
– sprinklered	90	60	30*	60**†	90**	120**
b. Institutional	90	60	30*	60	90	120#
c. Other residential	90	60	30*	60	90	120#
2 Office:						
– not sprinklered	90	60	30*	60	90	Not permitted
– sprinklered(2)	60	60	30*	30*	60	120#
3 Shop and commercial:						
– not sprinklered	90	60	60	60	90	Not permitted
– sprinklered	60	60	30*	60	60	120#
4 Assembly and recreation:						
– not sprinklered	90	60	60	60	90	Not permitted
– sprinklered	60	60	30*	60	60	120#
5 Industrial:						
– not sprinklered	120	90	60	90	120	Not permitted
– sprinklered(1)	90	60	30*	60	90	120#
6 Storage and other non-residential:						
a. any building or part not described elsewhere:						
not sprinklered	120	90	60	90	120	Not permitted
sprinklered(2)	90	60	30*	60	90	120#
b. car park for light vehicles:						
i. open sided car park(3)	Not applicable	Not applicable	15* +	15* +(4)	15* +(4)	60
ii. any other car park	90	60	30*	60	90	120#

Single storey buildings are subject to the periods under the heading 'not more than 5'. If they have basements, the basement storeys are subject to the period appropriate to their depth.

SThe floor over a basement (or if there is more than 1 basement, the floor over the topmost basement) should meet the provisions for the ground and upper storeys if that period is higher.

*Increased to a minimum of 60 minutes for compartment walls separating buildings.

**Reduced to 30 minutes for any floor within a flat with more than one storey, but not if the floor contributes to the support of the building.

#Reduced to 90 minutes for elements not forming part of the structural frame.

+Increased to 30 minutes for elements protecting the means of escape.

†Refer to paragraph 7.9 regarding the acceptability of 30 minutes in flat conversions.

Notes:
1. Refer to Table A1 for the specific provisions of test.
2. 'Sprinklered' means that the building is fitted throughout with an automatic sprinkler system in accordance with paragraph 0.16.
3. The car park should comply with the relevant provisions in the guidance on requirement B3, Section 11.
4. For the purposes of meeting the Building Regulations, the following types of steel elements are deemed to have satisfied the minimum period of fire resistance of 15 minutes when tested to the European test method:

(i) Beams supporting concrete floors maximum Hp/A = 230 m⁻¹ operating under full design load.
(ii) Free standing columns, maximum Hp/A =180 m⁻¹ operating under full design load.
(iii) Wind bracing and struts, maximum Hp/A ~ 210 m⁻¹ operating under full design load.
Guidance is also available in BS 5950 Structural use of steelwork in building. Part 8 Code of practice for fire resistant design.

Table III Maximum dimensions of multi-storey non-residential buildings and compartments (from Approved Document B, Table 12)

Purpose group of building or part	Height of floor of top storey above ground level (m)	Floor area of any one storey in the building or any one storey in a compartment (m²)	
		In multi-storey buildings	In single-storey buildings
Office	No limit	No limit	No limit
Assembly and recreation			
Shop and commercial:			
a. Shops – not sprinklered	No limit	2000	2000
Shops – sprinklered[1]	No limit	4000	No limit
b. Elsewhere – not sprinklered	No limit	2000	No limit
Elsewhere – sprinklered[1]	No limit	4000	No limit
Industrial[2]			
Not sprinklered	Not more than 18	7000	No limit
	More than 18	2000[3]	N/A
Sprinklered[1]	Not more than 18	14,000	No limit
	More than 18	4000[3]	N/A

	Height of floor of top storey above ground level (m)	Maximum compartment volume m³		Maximum floor area (m²)	Maximum height (m)[4]
		Multi-storey buildings	Single-storey buildings		
Storage[2] and other non-residential:					
a. Car park for light vehicles	No limit	No limit	No limit	No limit	
b. Any other building or part:					
Not sprinklered	Not more than 18	20,000	20,000	18	
	More than 18	4000[3]	N/A	N/A	
Sprinklered[1]	Not more than 18	40,000	No limit	No limit	
	More than 18	8000[3]			

Notes

[1] 'Sprinklered' means that the building is fitted throughout with an automatic sprinkler in accordance with paragraph 0.16.

[2] There may be additional limitations on floor area and/or sprinkler provisions in certain industrial and storage uses under other legislation, for example in respect of storage of LPG and certain chemicals.

[3] This reduced limit applies only to storeys that are more than 18 m above ground level. Below this height the higher limit applies.

[4] Compartment height is measured from finished floor level to underside of roof or ceiling.

In non-residential buildings floors over and generally within basements and any floor at a height of 30 m above ground level should be constructed as compartment floors.

3.11 Growth

To limit the growth of fire within the main structural elements is generally relatively easy provided that they do not contain large voids. The addition of linings and claddings can facilitate the rapid spread of fire beyond its area of origin. Flame can spread quickly in all directions and fixings are important. It has been found by experiment that the better the material is as an insulator, the greater the likelihood that flame spread will be more rapid and further.

3.12 Surface spread of flame

This is generally tested in accordance with BS 476 Part 7 1971, the results being classified 1 to 4 (Class 1 being very good, Class 4 very poor) on the basis of flame spread from the point of ignition. Class 0 is a classification defined for the purposes of recommendations under the building regulations (not a British Standard). Current codes vary in their recommendations but generally all escape routes and circulation spaces should have Class 0, all other areas other than small rooms Class 1.

3.13 Ventilation

Ventilation to release heat and control and/or dispel smoke from a fire will allow easier and rapid access by fire fighters to extinguish a fire. Its relationship to means of escape is outlined elsewhere.

Ventilation can be natural or mechanical. The latter is preferable as it is controllable, can be activated automatically and, when designed correctly, not influenced by wind, internal layout and configurations, outside temperature or stack effect. It does, however, add considerable cost, as it is necessary to safeguard its operation by using fans tolerant of high temperatures, protected wiring, fire and smoke dampers, automatic detection, secondary power supplies and monitoring. It may require sophisticated computerised controls.

3.14 Mechanical extraction systems

Opinions vary on the design of mechanical smoke extract systems, and the need or otherwise to incorporate fail-safe measures. It is necessary to determine if the system is for smoke extraction or smoke control. There is no generally accepted comprehensive code for mechanical smoke control systems; specialist advice should be sought.

3.15 Natural ventilation

Natural ventilation by the provision of open, openable or breakable vents is usually intended for operation by firefighters who will take into consideration aspects of wind etc. Openings should aggregate not less than 5 per cent of a total floor area within basements and areas of high or special risk, and 2.5 per cent above ground. If vents are not accessible, they should be permanent, open automatically or open by remote control.

3.16 Smoke reservoirs

The use of natural ventilation in large open areas such as single-storey factories, auditoria, exhibition halls and the like will necessitate the formation of smoke reservoirs to restrict the spread of smoke. See BRE publications Digest 260, *Smoke control in buildings: design principles* and BR 186 *Design principles for smoke ventilation in enclosed shopping centres.*

3.17 Access

Specific access for firefighters will allow their prompt action. Access is required up to, into and through a building. Various dimensional information is given in Table IV but it should be

Table IV Fire service vehicle access to buildings not fitted with fire mains (from Approved Document B, Table 19)

Total floor area of building (m²)	Height of floor of top storey above ground	Provide vehicle access to:	Type of appliance
up to 2000	up to 11	see paragraph 16.2	pump
	over 11	15% of perimeter	high reach
2000–8000	up to 11	15% of perimeter	pump
	over 11	50% of perimeter	high reach
8000–16,000	up to 11	50% of perimeter	pump
	over 11	50% of perimeter	high reach
16,000–24,000	up to 11	75% of perimeter	pump
	over 11	75% of perimeter	high reach
over 24,000	up to 11	100% of perimeter	pump
	over 11	100% of perimeter	high reach

remembered that fire equipment is not standardised; it is also constantly changing, giving many variations in sizes and weights.

If a building is provided with a fire main, access is required to within 18 m of the inlet to a dry riser or the access to a firefighting shaft containing a wet riser. The setdown point should be within sight of the dry riser inlet or shaft access.

No appliances should have to reverse more than 20 m. Dead-end roads should be provided with hammerhead turning spaces if longer than this, see Tables IV, V and VI and Figures 11.2 to 11.5.

3.18 Firefighting shafts

Access into the building should be provided via a firefighting shaft. In the cases of all buildings and those with deep basements this should incorporate a firefighting lift to transport equipment and personnel at speed. In all cases it should include a staircase 1.1 m in width between walls or balustrades, ventilated or pressurised, entered from the floor areas via a lobby, both of which are separated from the remainder of the building by 2-hour fire-resisting construction. BS 5588 Part 5 details the technical

Table V Typical vehicle access route specification (from Approved Document B, Table 20)

Appliance type	Minimum width of road between kerbs (m)	Minimum width of gateways (m)	Minimum turning circle between kerbs (m)	Minimum turning circle between walls (m)	Minimum clearance height (m)	Minimum carrying capacity (tonnes)
Pump	3.7	3.1	16.8	19.2	3.7	12.5
High Reach	3.7	3.1	26.0	29.0	4.0	17.0

Notes:
(1) Fire appliances are not standardised. Some fire services have appliances of greater weight or different size. In consultation with the Fire Authority, Building Control Authorities and Approved Inspectors may adopt other dimensions in such circumstances.
(2) Because the weight of high-reach appliances is distributed over a number of axles, it is considered that their infrequent use of a carriageway or route designed to 12.5 tonnes should not cause damage. It would therefore be reasonable to design the roadbase to 12.5 tonnes, although structures such as bridges should have the full 17 tonnes capacity.

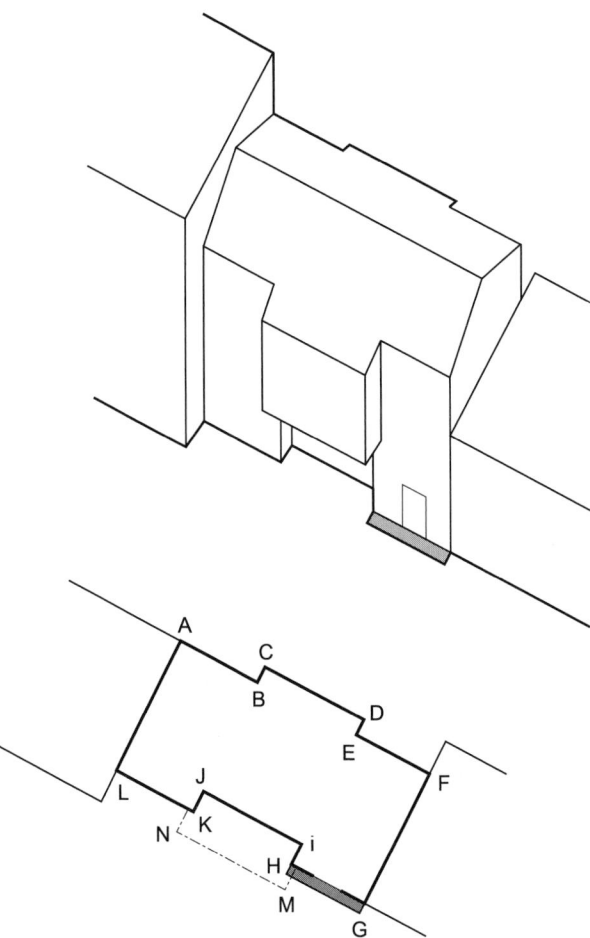

11.2 *Example of building footprint and perimeter. The building is AFGL where walls AL and FG are shared with other buildings. The footprint is the maximum aggregate plan perimeter found by the vertical projection of any overhanging storey onto a ground storey: i.e. ABCDEFGHMNKL. The perimeter for the purposes of the table is the sum of the lengths of the two external walls taking account of the footprint, i.e. (A to B to C to D to E to F) + (G to H to M to N to K to L). If the dimensions of the building require vehicular access by the table, the shaded area illustrates a possible example of 15% of the perimeter. Note that there should be a door into the building in this length. If the building has no walls common with other buildings, the lengths AL and FG would be included in the perimeter. From Approved Document Part B 2006*

Table VI Dimensions required for fire appliances (see Figure 11.3)

Dimension	Description	Type of appliance	
		Turntable ladder	Hydraulic platform
A	Maximum distance of near edge of hardstanding from building	4.9m	2.0 m
B	Minimum width of hardstanding	5.0m	5.5 m
C	Minimum distance of further edge of hardstanding from building	10.0m	7.5 m
D	Minimum width of unobstructed space for swing of appliance platform	NA	2.2m

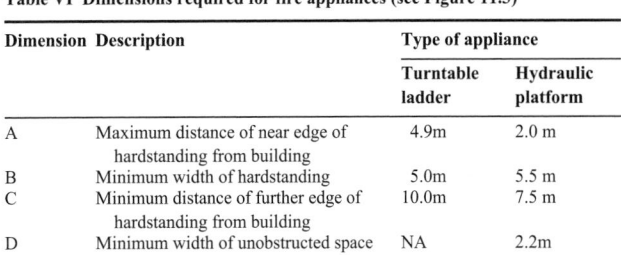

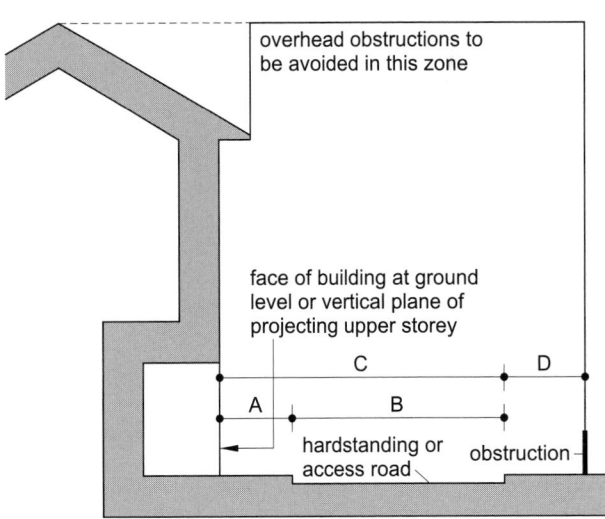

11.3 *Relationship between building and hardstanding or access roads for high-reach fire appliances. For key, see Table VI. From Approved Document Part B 2006*

and dimensional specification for a firefighting shaft. The criteria for the provision and number of shafts in any particular building are set out in that part of the BS 5888 series relating to the specific use or within Building Regulations. A firefighting lift can be one normally used for passengers; it should not be one used as a goods lift, see Figures 11.6 and 11.7.

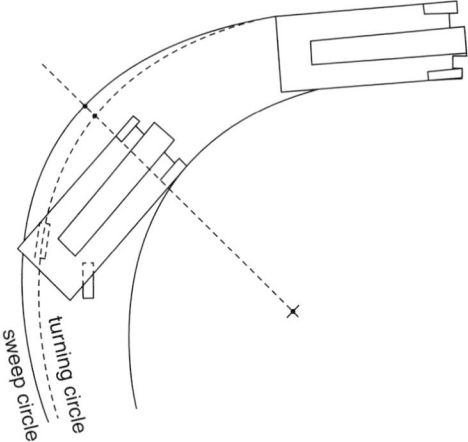

11.4 *A pumping appliance (drawing not to scale) Max length 8.5 m, max height 3.3 m, max width 2.3 m, max weight 13.21 ts, on front axle 5.5 ts, on rear axle 6.1 ts, max wheelbase 3.81 m, rear wheel track 2 m, ground clearance 229 mm, roadway width required 3.66m, turning circle 16.75 m, sweep circle 18.3 m*

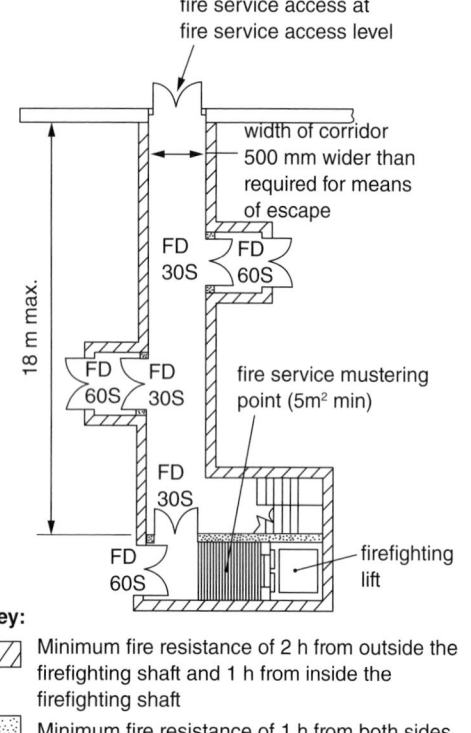

Key:

| | Minimum fire resistance of 2 h from outside the firefighting shaft and 1 h from inside the firefighting shaft |
| | Minimum fire resistance of 1 h from both sides |

11.6 *Typical firefighting shaft layout at fire service access level, access via a corridor*

3.19 Spread

The spread of fire to adjacent buildings can be prevented by:

- clear space
- fire-resisting walls
- external walls of limited combustibility and limited surface spread of flame, and/or
- roof coverings resistant to penetration of fire.

If precautions are taken within a building to limit a fire's growth and spread, it can be assumed that its effects on an adjacent building are reduced. Openings in an external wall or walls having no fire resistance present weaknesses to an adjoining building by radiation and convection. If property protection in addition to life safety is a consideration, then all buildings should be considered as being of equal risk.

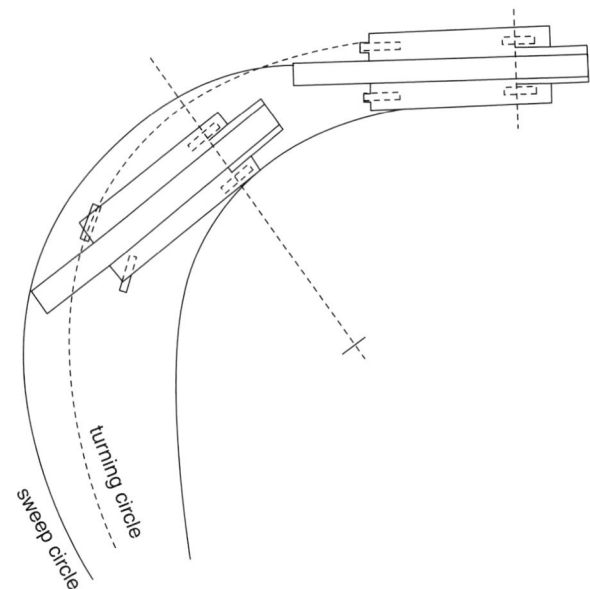

11.5 *A hydraulic platform and turntable ladders (drawing not to scale) max length 10 m, max height 3.5 m, max width 2.5 m, max width with jacks out 4.4 m, laden weight 16.25 t, av. weight front axle 6 t, av. weight rear axle 10 t, max wheelbase 5.33 m, rear wheel track 2 m, min ground clearance 229 mm, road width required 6m, turning circle 21.5m, sweep circle 24.5 m. The overhang of the booms on the headrest do not exceed 1.83 m from foremost part of the vehicle. Turntable ladders and hydraulic platforms ('cherry-pickers') are fitted with four ground jacks as stabilisers, for which the working load is normally less than 7.5 t*

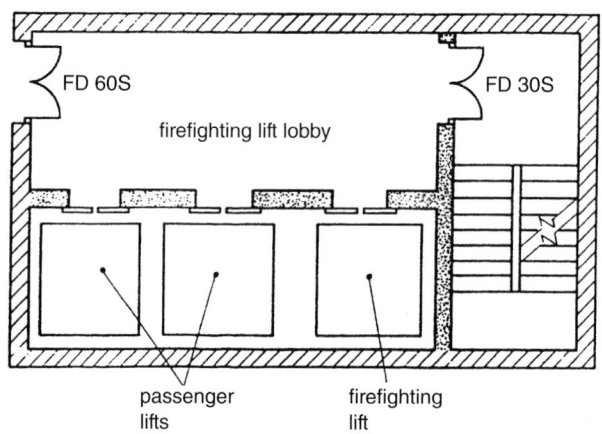

11.7 *Passenger lifts within the firefighting shaft. Firefighting lobbies should have a clear floor area of not less than 5 m². The clear floor area should not exceed 20 m² for lobbies serving up to four lifts, or 5 m² per lift for lobbies serving more. All principal dimensions should be not less than 1.5 m and should not exceed 8 m in lobbies serving up to four lifts, or 2 m per lift in lobbies serving more*

If life safety is the only factor, then residential, assembly and recreational uses are at greater risk from external fire sources and warrant additional safeguards. It is generally assumed that only one compartment is involved in a fire and as such the risk emanates only from its external enclosures.

3.20 Protection

Methods generally used for determining the necessary degrees of protection are based on acceptable percentages of 'unprotected areas' (openings, non-fire-resisting walls, combustible claddings and insulation) having regard to heat radiation exposure from a

Table VII Unprotected areas for small residential buildings. See Figure 11.8 (from Approved Document B, Vol 1, Diagram 22)

Minimum distance (A) between side of building and relevant boundary (m)	Maximum total area of unprotected areas (m²)
1	5.6
2	12
3	18
4	24
5	30
6	no limit

Table VIII Permitted unprotected areas in small buildings or compartments (from Approved Document B, Table 15)

Minimum distance between side of building and relevant boundary (m)

Purpose groups Residential, Office, Assembly and Recreation	Shop and Commercial Industrial, storage and other Non-residential	Maximum total percentage of unprotected area (%)
(1)	(2)	(3)
n.a	1	4
1.0	2	8
2.5	5	20
5.0	10	40
7.5	15	60
10.0	20	80
12.5	25	100

Notes:
n.a. 1/4 not applicable.
(1) intermediate values may be obtained by interpolation.
(2) For buildings which are fitted throughout with an automatic sprinkler system, meeting the relevant recommendations of BS 5306 Part 2, the values in columns (1) and (2) may be halved, subject to a minimum distance of 1 m being maintained.
(3) In the case of open-sided car parks in purpose group 7(b) the distances set out in column (1) may be used instead of those in column (2).

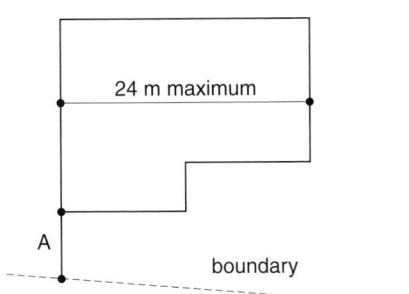

11.8 *Permitted unprotected areas in small residential buildings*

known use. The basis of the necessary calculations is set out in BRE document BRE 187 *External fire spread: building separation and boundary distances*; Approved Document B makes

recommendations in relation to small buildings or compartments, both residential in Table VII and Figure 11.8 and non-residential in Table VIII.

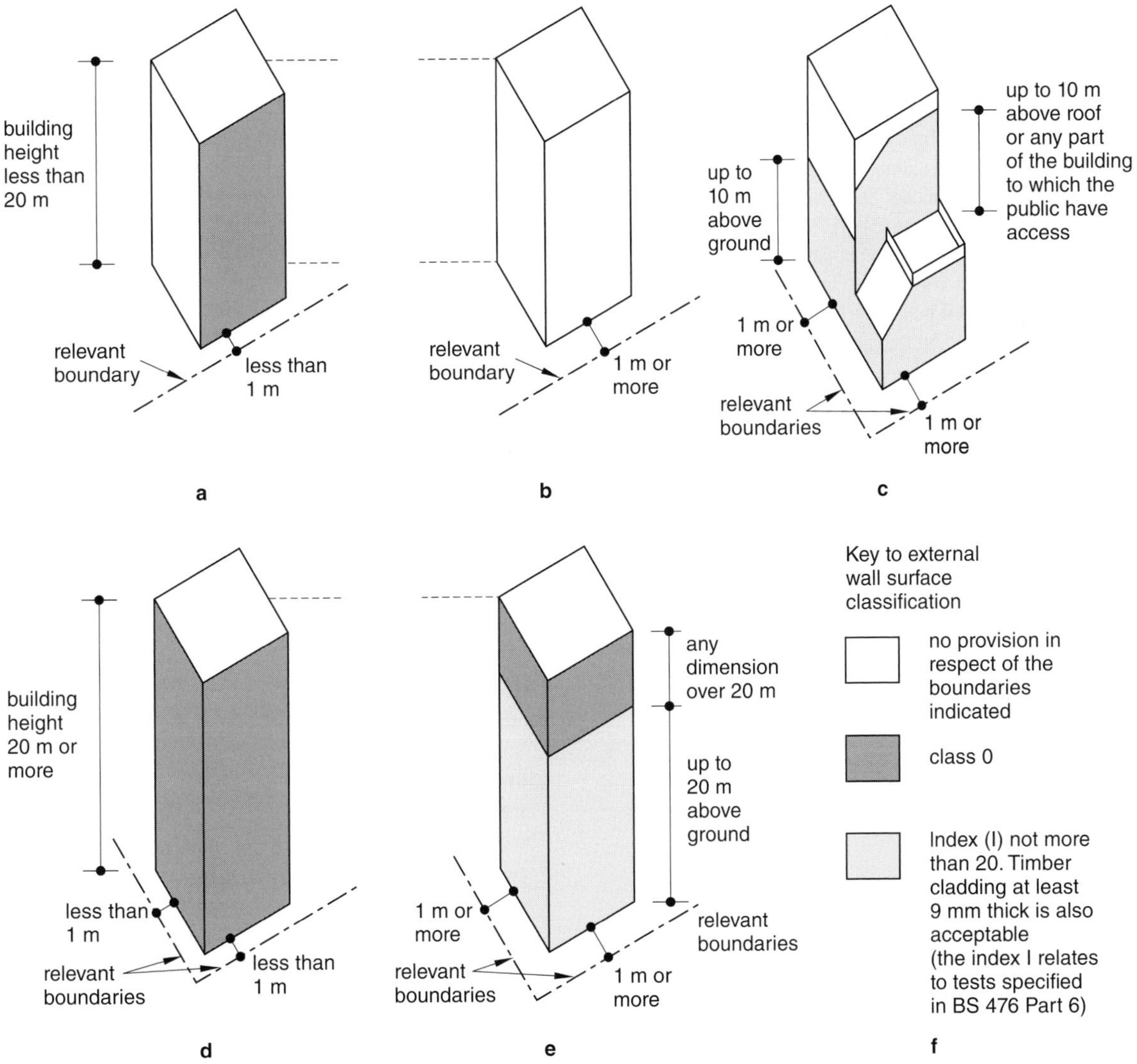

11.9 *Provisions for external surfaces of walls. a Any building. b Any building other than as shown in c. c Assembly or recreational building of more than one storey. d Any building. e Any building. f Key to external wall surface classification*

3.21 Cladding

Combustible claddings and insulation present a risk, especially in tall buildings. While claddings and their supports are not always required to be fire-resisting, insulation at a height exceeding 15 m is recommended to be of limited combustibility, Figure 11.9.

Table IX Limitations on roof coverings* (from Approved Document B, Table 16)

Designation† of covering of roof or part of roof		Minimum distance from any point on relevant boundary			
National class	European class	Less than 6 m	At least 6 m	At least 12 m	At least 20 m
AA, AB or AC	BROOF(t4)	•	•	•	•
BA, BB or BC	CROOF(t4)	○	•	•	•
CA, CB or CC	DROOF(t4)	○	•[(1)(2)]	•[(1)]	•
AD, BD or CD	EROOF(t4)	○	•[(1)(2)]	•[(1)]	•[(1)]
DA, DB, DC or DD	FROOF(t4)	○	○	○	•[(1)(2)]

Notes:

*See paragraph 14.8 for limitations on glass; paragraph 14.9 for limitations on thatch and wood shingles; and paragraphs 14.6 and 14.7 and Tables 18 and 19 for limitations on plastic rooflights.

†The designation of external roof surfaces is explained in Appendix A. (See Table A5, for notional designations of roof coverings.)

Separation distances do not apply to the boundary between roofs of a pair of semidetached houses (see 14.5) and to enclosed/covered walkways. However, see Diagram 30 if the roof passes over the top of a compartment wall. Polycarbonate and PVC rooflights which achieve a Class 1 rating by test, see paragraph 15.7, may be regarded as having an AA designation.

Openable polycarbonate and PVC rooflights which achieve a Class 1 (National class) or Class C-s3, d2 (European class) rating by test, see paragraph 10.7, may be regarded as having an AA (National class) designation or BROOF(t4) (European class) classification.

• Acceptable.

   ○   Not acceptable.

[1]Not acceptable on any of the following buildings:

  a. Houses in terraces of three or more houses.

  b. Industrial, storage or other non-residential Purpose Group buildings of any size.

  c. Any other buildings with a cubic capacity of more than 1500 m³.

[2]Acceptable on buildings not listed in Note 1, if part of the roof is no more than 3 m² in area and is at least 1500 mm from any similar part, with the roof between the parts covered with a material of limited combustibility.

3.22 Roof coverings

Roof coverings (not structures) in close proximity to boundaries should have limited flame spread and penetration to fire. The performance of coverings is designated by reference to BS 476 Part 3 which classifies the results on the flame spread and time taken to penetrate: AA being the best (specimen not penetrated within one hour, no spread of flame), DD the worst (penetrated in preliminary flame test, extensive and continuing spread of flame). The addition of a suffix 'x' denotes one or more of dripping from the underside, mechanical failure, development of holes. Approved Document B sets out specific classification recommendations relating to distances from the boundary, see Table IX together with recommendation for plastic rooflights, Figure 11.10 and Table X.

11.10 *Limitations on spacing and size of plastic rooflights having a Class 3 or TP(b) lower surface: see Table IX. Note: the surrounding roof covering should be of limited combustibility for at least 3 m*

4 MEANS OF ESCAPE

4.1 General

There are numerous codes and guides relating to means of escape from various uses, some of which, as they have evolved, have overlapped and derived different recommendations for the same matters.

Occasionally, they include matters outside those of life safety. Generally, means of escape is the provision of safe routes for persons to travel from any point in a building to a place of safety.

4.2 Fire engineering

At the time of writing, various aspects of fire safety, particularly the basis on which adopted standards and practices are founded, are under review. However, there is nothing to stop an alternative, innovative or unorthodox approach to means of escape being adopted. Fire-engineering solutions may be used where the established practices are unsuitable; methods such as smoke control and automatic detection and suppression can be used to evolve a package of safety measures for a specific user and building design requirements. It should be noted that a change in specific user may require a reassessment of the fire safety provisions.

4.3 Tailored solutions

Whatever method is adopted, the means of escape must be tailored to the individual occupancy and building. Where a project is speculative a judgement must be made as to the necessary provisions for means of escape: to assume the worst case may not be feasible, although it will result in a level of provision acceptable for the majority of occupancies. In the case of designs such as atria, persons should be at no greater risk than those in a nonatrium building.

4.4 Basic principles

The aim is to make provision such that escape can take place unaided. The occupants of some buildings, however, will not be able to achieve this. There are certain basic principles and provisions accepted as necessary for the provision of minimum means of escape. These are:

- Exits and escape routes of adequate number and width within a reasonable distance of all points in the building
- An alternative means of escape (in the majority of cases)
- Protected escape routes where necessary
- Lighting and directional signage
- Readily openable exit doors
- Smoke control to safeguard escape routes
- Separation of high or special risks

Table X Plastics rooflights: limitations on use and boundary distance (from Approved Document B)

Minimum classification on lower surface	Space which rooflight can serve	Minimum distance from any point on relevant boundary to rooflight with an external designation of:	
		AD BD CD (National class) or $E_{ROOF}(t4)$ (European class) CA CB CC or $D_{ROOF}(t4)$ (European class)	DA DB DC DD (National class) or $F_{ROOF}(t4)$ (European class)
Class 3	a. Balcony, verandah, carport, covered way or loading bay, which has at least one longer side wholly or permanently open b. Detached swimming pool c. Conservatory, garage or outbuilding, with a maximum floor area of 40m²	6m	20m
	d. Circulation space (except a protected stairway) e. Room	6m	20m

		Minimum distance from any point on relevant boundary to rooflight with an external surface classification of:	
		TP(a)	TP(b)
1. TP(a) rigid 2. TP(b)	Any space except a protected stairway a. Balcony, verandah, carport, covered way or loading bay, which has at least one longer side wholly or permanently open b. Detached swimming pool c. Conservatory, garage or outbuilding, with a maximum floor area of 40m²	6m Not applicable	Not applicable 6m
	d. Circulation space (except a protected stairway) e. Room	Not applicable	6m

- Access for fire brigade to attack the seat of a fire swiftly for protection of life
- Audible/visual warning of fire and active measures
- First aid fire appliances
- Instruction of action to be taken in the event of a fire and evacuation procedure.

The last three items are additional to structural provision for means of escape. However, some procedures for evacuation and the life safety systems associated with certain designs of building, e.g. atria and shopping malls, and certain uses, e.g. hospitals, necessitate the utilisation of active measures to provide effective means of escape-pressurisation/depressurisation of escape routes to control smoke, automatic detection by heat and smoke detectors, etc.

4.5 Flats and maisonettes
The concept for escape from flats and maisonettes differs from that of other uses. This is based on the high standard of compartmentation

and separation recommended in Approved Documents Part B, in particular B3 *Internal Fire Spread (structure)*. Major factors are difficulties in alerting the population of the block to a fire (fire alarms in this situation being a potential source of acute nuisance), and also in ensuring that everyone in fact is evacuated.

4.6 Containment
Each residential unit is a separate fire compartment, and it is considered only necessary initially to evacuate the unit on fire. Consequently the necessary width of escape exits and routes may be minimalised. The spread of fire and smoke is controlled under the principles of smoke containment. As it has been shown that most fires are containable within the room of origin, the current edition of BS 5588 Part 1 (*Code of practice for residential buildings*) and Approved Document B have reduced the recommendations relating to fire separation within the unit from those previously given. The travel distance, any alternative means of escape and the layout dictate the level of internal protection necessary, which influences the common area protection, see Figures 11.11 to 11.35.

Key:

⟩ Entrance to dwelling

◀ Alternative exit from dwelling

— 30 min fire-resisting construction

⌐ Self-closing FD 20 fire door

AOV Automatically opening vent (1.5 m² minimum)
OV   Openable vent for fire service use
▬▭ Fire-resisting construction up to height of 1.1 m above deck level
∇   Self-closing FD 20S fire door
⟍   Self-closing FD 30S fire door

11.11 *Key to following drawings 11.12 to 11.35*

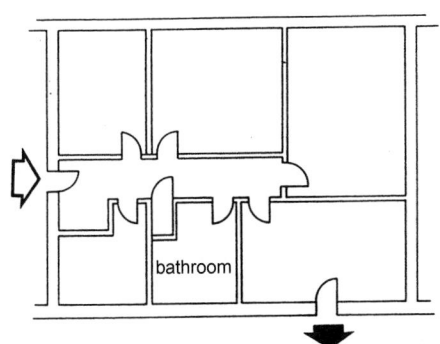

11.12 *Flat with alternative exit and where all habitable rooms have direct access to an entrance hall*

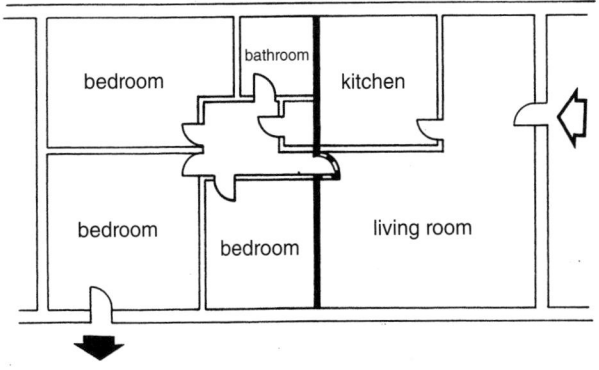

11.13 *Flat with alternative exit and where all habitable rooms do not have direct access to an entrance hall. The fire-resisting partition separates living and sleeping accommodation*

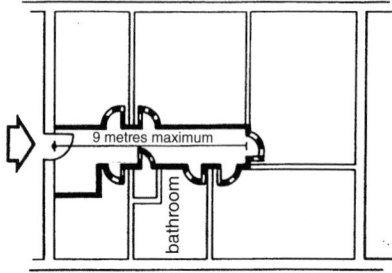

11.14 *Flat with a protected entrance hall and restricted travel distance. If the partitions between bathroom and adjacent rooms have 30 minutes fire resistance, then the partition between it and the entrance hall need not be fire-resisting and its door need not be a fire door. The cupboard door need not be self-closing*

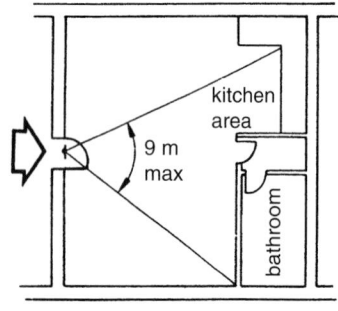

11.15 *Open-plan flat (bed-sitter) with restricted travel distance*

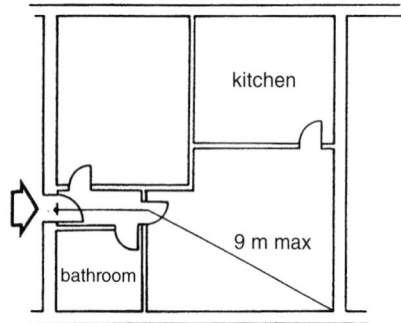

11.16 *Flat with separate habitable rooms and restricted travel distance*

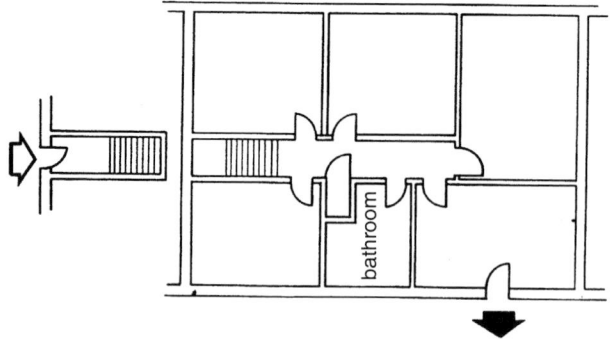

11.17 *Flat entered from above or below with an alternative exit and where all habitable rooms have direct access to an entrance hall*

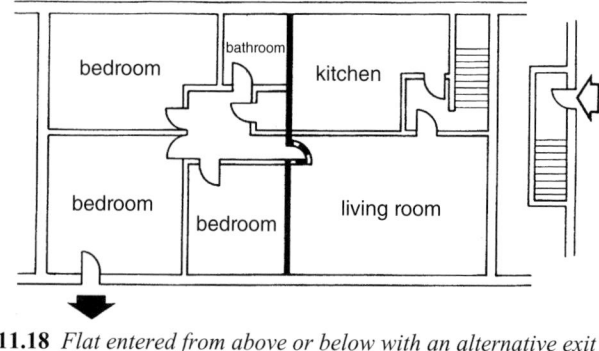

11.18 *Flat entered from above or below with an alternative exit and where all habitable rooms do not have direct access to an entrance hall. The fire-resisting partition separates living and sleeping accommodation*

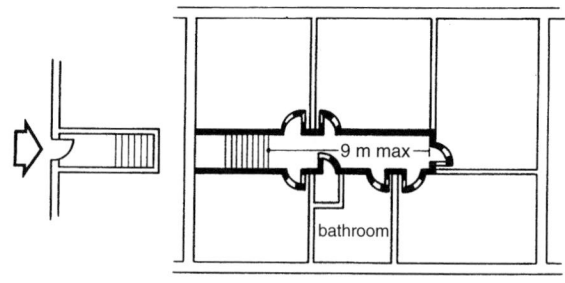

11.19 *Flat entered from below with a protected entrance and restricted travel distance. If the partitions between bathroom and adjacent rooms have 30 minutes fire resistance, then the partition between it and the entrance hall need not be fire-resisting and its door need not be a fire door. The cupboard door need not be self-closing*

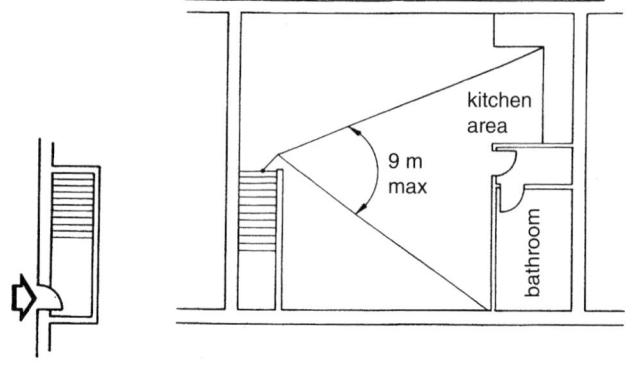

11.20 *Open-plan flat (bed-sitter) entered from below with a restricted travel distance*

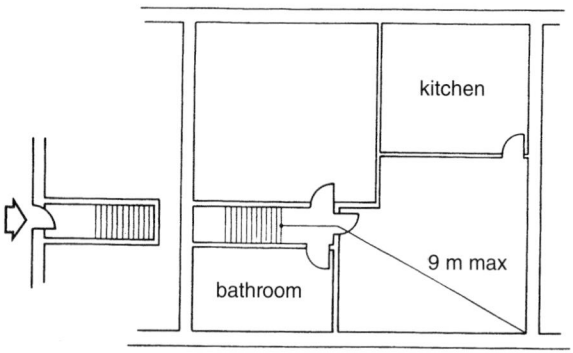

11.21 *Flat with separate habitable rooms entered from below with a restricted travel distance*

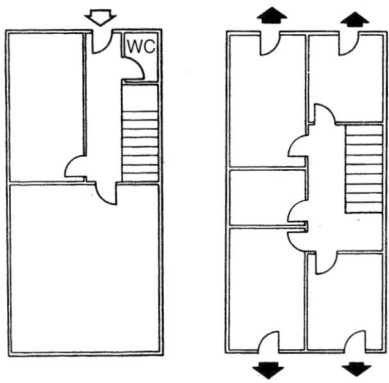

11.22 *Maisonette with alternative exits from each room not on the entrance floor level*

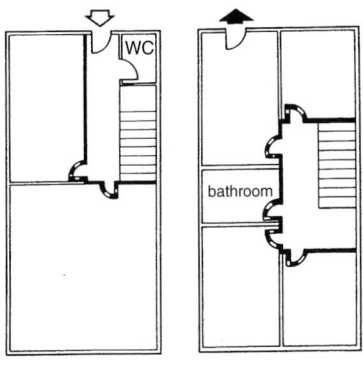

11.23 *Maisonette with protected entrance floor and landing. If the partitions between bathroom and adjacent rooms have 30 minutes fire resistance, then the partition between it and the entrance hall need not be fire-resisting and its door need not be a fire door*

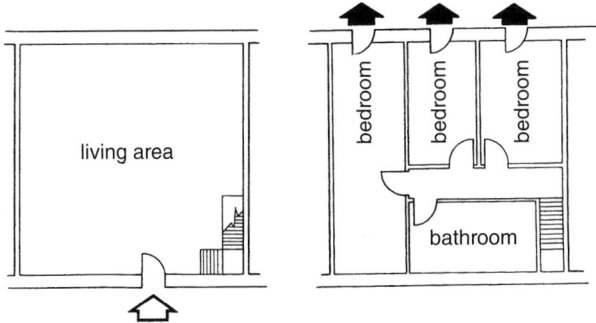

11.24 *Open-plan maisonette*

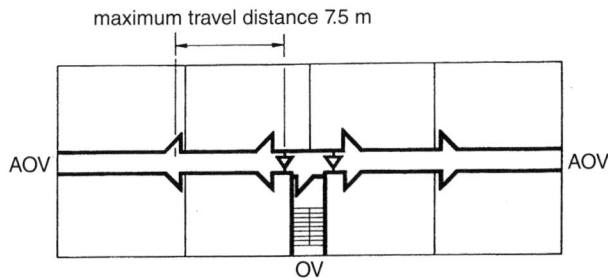

11.25 *Common escape routes in single stair buildings more than 11 m high with corridor access dwellings. Where all dwellings on a storey have independent alternative means of escape, the maximum travel distance may be increased to 30 m. Where a firefighting lift is required, it should be sited not more than 7.5 m from the door to the stair. The openable vents (OVs) to the stairway may be replaced by an openable vent over the stair*

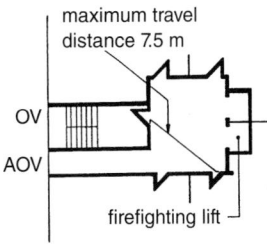

11.26 *Common escape routes in single stair tower blocks more than 11 in high, with the stair adjacent to an external wall. See riders to Figure 11.25*

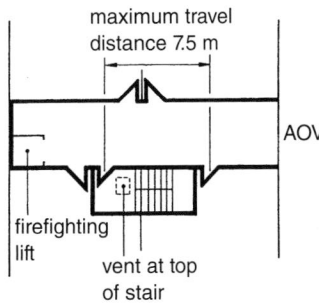

11.27 *Common escape routes in single stair tower blocks more than 11 m high with internal stair. See riders to Figure 11.25*

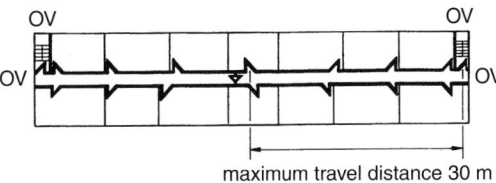

11.28 *Common escape routes in multi-stair buildings with corridor access dwellings and no dead-ends*

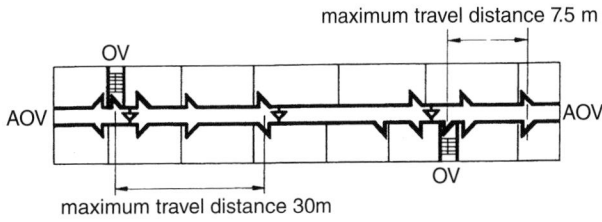

11.29 *Common escape routes in multi-stair buildings with corridor access dwellings and with dead-ends. The central fire door may be omitted where the maximum travel distance does not exceed 15m*

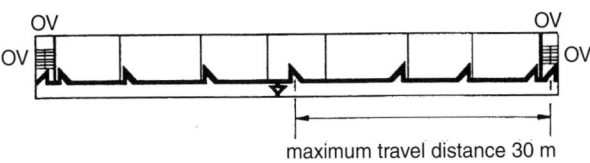

11.30 *Common escape routes in multi-stair buildings with corridor access dwellings on one side only*

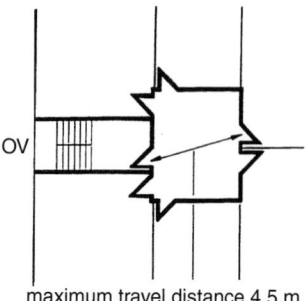

maximum travel distance 4.5 m

11.31 *Common escape routes in small single-stair buildings*

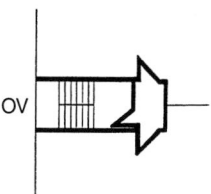

11.32 *Common escape routes in small single-stair buildings with not more than two dwellings per storey. The door between the stair and lobby should be free from security fastenings. Where the dwellings have protected entrance halls, the separation between the stair and the dwelling entrance doors is not necessary*

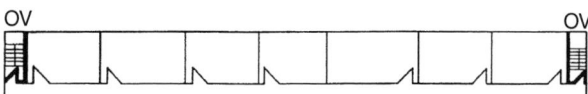

11.33 *Common escape routes in balcony/deck approach multi-stair buildings*

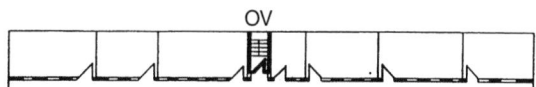

11.34 *Common escape routes in balcony/deck approach single-stair buildings*

11.35 *Common escape routes in balcony/deck approach single-stair buildings with an alternative exit from each dwelling. One of the external enclosures A or B must be fire resisting*

4.7 Offices and shops

Parts 2 and 3 of BS 5588 (*Fire precautions in the design, construction and use of buildings*) deal with offices and shops respectively.

4.8 Number of exits and escape routes

In order to determine the number of exits from a room or storey, their occupancy must be established. This may be known, or it can be assessed by the use of recognised space factors for specific uses. These are only indicators and can be varied. These numbers will also affect the width of escape routes. In existing buildings

Table XI Floor space factors[1] (from Approved Document B, Volume 2, Table C1)

	Type of accommodation[2][3]	Floor space factor m²/person
1	Standing spectator areas, bar areas (within 2 m of serving point) similar refreshment areas	0.3
2	Amusement arcade, assembly hall (including a general purpose place of assembly), bingo hall, club, crush hall, dance floor or hall, venue for pop concert and similar events and bar areas without fixed seating	0.5
3	Concourse, queuing area or shopping mall[4][5]	0.7
4	Committee room, common room, conference room, dining room, licensed betting office (public area), lounge or bar (other than in 1 above), meeting room, reading room, restaurant, staff room or waiting room[6]	1.0
5	Exhibition hall or studio (film, radio, television, recording)	1.5
6	Skating rink	2.0
7	Shop sales area[7]	2.0
8	Art gallery, dormitory, factory production area, museum or workshop	5.0
9	Office	6.0
10	Shop sales area[8]	7.0
11	Kitchen or library	7.0
12	Bedroom or study-bedroom	8.0
13	Bed-sitting room, billiards or snooker room or hall	10.0
14	Storage and warehousing	30.0
15	Car park	Two persons per parking space

Notes:

[1] As an alternative to using the values in the table, the floor space factor may be determined by reference to actual data taken from similar premises. Where appropriate, the data should reflect the average occupant density at a peak trading time of year.

[2] Where accommodation is not directly covered by the descriptions given, a reasonable value based on a similar use may be selected.

[3] Where any part of the building is to be used for more than one type of accommodation, the most onerous factor(s) should be applied. Where the building contains different types of accommodation, the occupancy of each different area should be calculated using the relevant space factor.

[4] Refer to section 4 of BS 5588-10:1991 Code of practice for shopping complexes for detailed guidance on the calculation of occupancy in common public areas in shopping complexes.

[5] For detailed guidance on appropriate floor space factors for concourses in sports grounds refer to 'Concourses' published by the Football Licensing Authority (ISBN: 0 95462 932 9).

[6] Alternatively the occupant capacity may be taken as the number of fixed seats provided, if the occupants will normally be seated.

[7] Shops excluding those under item 10, but including – supermarkets and department stores (main sales areas), shops for personal services such as hairdressing and shops for the delivery or collection of goods for cleaning, repair or other treatment or for members of the public themselves carrying out such cleaning, repair or other treatment.

[8] Shops (excluding those in covered shopping complexes but including department stores) trading predominantly in furniture, floor coverings, cycles, prams, large domestic appliances or other bulky goods, or trading on a wholesale self-selection basis (cash and carry).

Table XII Floor space factors for assembly buildings (from BS 5588: Part 6, Table 3)

	Description of floor space	Floor space per person (m²)
1	Individual seating	0.4 to 0.5
2	Bench seating	0.3[1]
3	Dance area	0.5
4	Ice rinks	1.2
5	Restaurants and similar table and chair arrangements around a dance area	1.1 to 1.5
6	Bars without seating and similar refreshment areas	0.3
7	Standing spectator areas	0.3
8	Exhibition	1.5[2]
9	Bowling alley, billiard or snooker hall	9.5
10	Museum/art gallery	5.0
11	Studio (radio, television, film, recording)	1.4

[1] If the number and length of benches is known, a factor of 450 mm per person should be used.

[2] Alternatively, a factor of 0.4 m² may be used over the gross area of gangways and other clear circulation space between stalls and stands.

Note. These floor space factors are for guidance only and should not be taken as the only acceptable densities. Where the number of seats is known this should be used in preference to the floor space factors.

the width of doors, stairways, passages etc., if not to be altered, will dictate the numbers of people that can be accommodated, see Tables XI, XII and XIII:

$$\text{Occupancy} = \frac{\text{Area of room or storey (m}^2)}{\text{Floor space per person (m}^2)}$$

Table XIII Capacities of exits in shopping complexes other than from malls (from BS 5588 Part 10, Table 3)

Maximum number of persons	Width (mm)
50	800
110	900
220	1100
240	1200
260	1300
280	1400
300	1500
320	1600
340	1700
360	1800

1. Other values of width for a maximum number of persons greater than 220 may be obtained by linear interpolation or extrapolation.

2. For the purposes of this table, the width of a doorway is that of the leaf or leaves, and the width of a passage is between the sides at shoulder level (that is about 1.5 m above finished floor level).

Table XIV Widths of escape routes and exits (from Approved Document B, Table 4)

Maximum number of persons	Minimum width mm
50	750
110	850
220	1050
more than 220	5 per person

4.9 Occupancy

Once the occupancy factor for an area is known the number of exits must equate to the necessary total width of escape required, although a minimum number of exits is specified within Approved Document B and Part 6 of BS 5588 (assembly buildings). Not less than two exits should be provided, except in the case of an occupancy of less than 50, or a small storey with a limited travel distance ('dead end').

4.10 Capacities

The capacities of exits are given in various tables. Most recommendations equate to approximately 40 persons passing through a unit width of 500 mm in 2 1/2 minutes. While not all exits need be of equal width, they should be evenly distributed to provide alternatives. Where there are two or more exits, it is assumed that fire may affect one of them, therefore the largest exit should be discounted. Hence the total number of exits = calculated number +1, see Table XIV.

4.11 Travel distances

Alternatively, the number of exits may be determined by recommended travel distances, i.e. the actual distance to be travelled to the nearest exit, having regard to obstructions such as partitions. The distances currently recommended are historical, based on experience and accepted practice. They are not sacrosanct, but should be shorter rather than longer. Extension of travel distances may be justified where compensatory factors such as smoke control systems or early warning of fire is provided. Only one exit need be within the travel distance, alternatives may be at any distance, see Tables XV to XVIII.

4.12 Alternative means of escape

A person should be able in most circumstances to turn their back on a fire and walk to an alternative exit. If escape is in one direction only, an exit or alternative escape route should be near enough for people to reach it before being affected by heat and smoke. The Scottish Building Regulations and the Home Office Guide for

Table XV Limitations on travel distance (from Approved Document B, Volume 2, Table 2)

Purpose group	Use of the premises or part of the premises		Maximum travel distance[1] where travel is possible in:	
			One direction only (m) M	More than one direction (m)
2(a)	Institutional		9	18
2(b)	Other residential:			
	a. in bedrooms[2]		9	18
	b. in bedroom corridors		9	35
	c. elsewhere		18	35
3	Office		18	45
4	Shop and commercial[3]		18[4]	45
5	Assembly and recreation:			
	a. buildings primarily for disabled people		9	18
	b. areas with seating in rows		15	32
	c. elsewhere		18	45
6	Industrial[5]	Normal Hazard	25	45
		Higher Hazard	12	25
7	Storage and other non-residential[5]	Normal Hazard	25	45
		Higher Hazard	12	25
2–7	Place of special fire hazard[6]		9[7]	18[7]
2–7	Plant room or rooftop plant:			
	a. distance within the room		9	35
	b. escape route not in open air (overall travel distance)		18	45
	c. escape route in open air (overall travel distance)		60	100

Notes:

[1]The dimensions in the Table are travel distances. If the internal layout of partitions, fittings, etc. is not known when plans are deposited, direct distances may be used for assessment. The direct distance is taken as 2/3rds of the travel distance.

[2]Maximum part of travel distance within the room. (This limit applies within the bedroom (and any associated dressing room, bathroom or sitting room, etc.) and is measured to the door to the protected corridor serving the room or suite. Sub-item (b) applies from that point along the bedroom corridor to a storey exit.)

[3]Maximum travel distances within shopping malls are given in BS 5588: Part 10. Guidance on associated smoke control measures is given in a BRE report *Design methodologies for smoke and heat exhaust ventilation* (BR 368).

[4]BS 5588: Part 10 applies more restrictive provisions to units with only one exit in covered shopping complexes.

[5]In industrial and storage buildings the appropriate travel distance depends on the level of fire hazard associated with the processes and materials being used. Higher hazard includes manufacturing, processing or storage of significant amounts of hazardous goods or materials, including: any compressed, liquefied or dissolved gas, any substance which becomes dangerous by interaction with either air or water, any liquid substance with a flash point below 65°C including whisky or other spirituous liquor, any corrosive substance, any oxidising agent, any substance liable to spontaneous combustion, any substance that changes or decomposes readily giving out heat when doing so, any combustible solid substance with a flash point less than 120° C, any substance likely to spread fire by flowing from one part of a building to another.

[6]Places of special fire hazard are listed in the definitions in Appendix E to Approved Document B.

[7]Maximum part of travel distance within the room/area. Travel distance outside the room/area to comply with the limits for the purpose group of the building or part.

Table XVI Maximum travel distances in assembly buildings (from BS 5588: Part 6, Table 2)

Available direction of escape	Areas with seating in rows (m)	Open floor areas (m)
(a) In one direction only	15	18
(b) In more than one direction	32[1]	45[2]

[1] This may include up to 15 m in one direction only.

[2] This may include up to 18 m in one direction only.

Table XVII Maximum travel distances in shopping malls (from BS 5588: Part 10, Table 1)

Available direction of escape	Uncovered malls (m)	Covered malls (m)
(a) In one direction		
(1) malls at ground level	25	9
(2) malls not at ground level	9	9
(b) In more than direction		
(1) malls at ground level	not limited	45
(2) malls not at ground level	45	45

Table XVIII Maximum travel distances in shopping complexes other than in malls (from BS 5588: Part 10, Table 2)

	Maximum part of travel distance within room or area		Maximum travel distance to nearest storey exit	
Accommodation	Escape in one direction only (m)	Escape in more than one direction (m)	Escape in one direction only (m)	Escape in more than one direction (m)
Accommodation other than the following list	18	45[1]	18	45[1]
Engineering services installation rooms				
Boiler rooms	9	18	18	45[1]
Fuel storage spaces				
Transformer, battery and switchgear rooms				
Rooms housing a fixed internal combustion engine				

Notes:
[1] This may include up to 18 m with escape in one direction only.

premises requiring a fire certificate recommend that the angle of divergence should be not less than 45° plus 2 1/2° for every metre travelled in one direction, see Figures 11.36, 11.37 and 11.38.

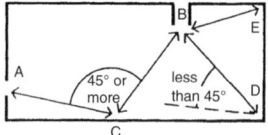

11.36 *Alternative escape routes are available from C because angle ACB is at least 45°, so that either CA or CB should be less than the maximum travel distance given in Table XV. Alternative routes are not available from D because angle ADB is less than 45°, so that DB should not exceed the distance for travel in one direction. There is also no alternative route from E. From Approved Document Part B, Volume 2, Diagram 11*

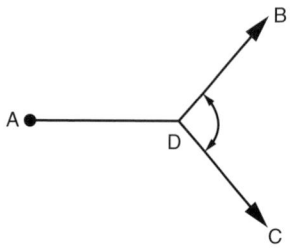

11.37 *Alternative escape routes in principle, A being the point of origin and D the point of divergence of alternative routes. Angle BDC = 45° + 2 1/2° for each metre travelled from A to D*

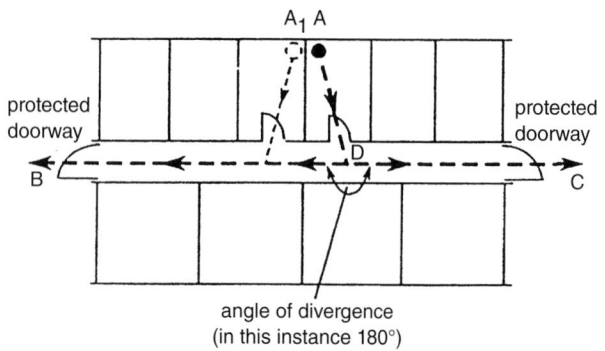

11.38 *Alternative escape routes in practice*

4.13 Width of escape routes and exits

An escape route should be as wide or wider than an exit leading to it, and should be of uniform width. The width of a final exit should equate to the route or routes it serves. This may comprise the total number of persons descending a stair plus a ground-storey population plus those ascending from a basement.

4.14 Measuring width

Unfortunately to date there is no agreed method of measuring width. In addition to means of escape, access for the disabled may be a consideration with specific details for projection of handrails. The variations should be accommodated by measuring an absolute clear width with no allowances for the projection of handrails, door thickness, etc., except door furniture with a maximum intrusion of 100 mm. The safe and rapid use of a stair is dependent on all persons being within reach of a handrail, therefore no staircase should exceed 1.4 m in width unless additional central handrails are provided.

4.15 Evacuation

The capacity and therefore the width of a stair differ from that of a horizontal escape route being influenced by the rate of descent and the standing position on the stairs. The width necessary is also influenced by the type of evacuation – total or phased – the stair having to accommodate only the population of a phase in the latter instance.

Total evacuation: on the raising of the alarm the total population moves to evacuate the whole of the building in a single phase.

Phased evacuation: on the discovery of a fire the alarm is given in the following manner. The fire floor and the floor above are given the signal to evacuate immediately, all other floors are given the alert signal to stand by to evacuate. If the fire is extinguished no further evacuation is necessary; if not, the next two floors immediately above the initial phase are evacuated; and so progressively in separate phases of two floors up the building to the top. Evacuation then proceeds down the building, starting with the floors nearest the fire, until it is complete or the fire extinguished. As the population of only two floors are evacuated at a time, the stair width dimensions can be decreased.

4.16 Additional measures

As people remain in the building during the fire-phased evacuation, it can take place only if additional protective measures are incorporated:

- All compartment floors with openings through them protected to maintain compartmentation.
- All stairs protected by lobbies or corridors of fire-resisting construction.
- A fire alarm system incorporating a personal address system operated from a central control point from where occupants can be instructed and orderly evacuation directed.
- An automatic sprinkler installation (although this may not be necessary in a low-rise building with, say, three phases of evacuation which would be complete within 30 minutes).

4.17 Phased evacuation

Phased evacuation is not generally accepted for any basements, assembly, hotel, recreational and similar buildings, and, to date, the majority of shops. However, in the case of mixed user and large complexes total evacuation may not be necessary or prudent and enforcing authorities should be consulted at an early stage.

4.18 Stairs

Where two or more stairs are provided, it is reasonable to assume that one will not be available for use due to fire or smoke unless a sufficiently high degree of protection is afforded. If a stair is approached through a lobby, or protected by a pressure-differential smoke control system, it can be assumed that it will be available. Where such protection is not provided, a stair should be discounted (number of stairs required = calculated number plus 1). Each stair should be discounted in turn, to ensure that the capacity of the remaining stairs in total is adequate, see Tables XIX and XX.

Table XIX Minimum widths of escape stairs (from Approved Document B, Table 6)

Situation of stair	Maximum number of people served[1]	Minimum stair width (mm)
1a. In an institutional building (unless the stair will only be used by staff)	150	1000[2]
1b. In an assembly building and serving an area used for assembly purposes (unless the area is less than 100 m²)	220	1100
1c. In any other building and serving an area with an occupancy of more than 50	Over 220	See Approved Document
2. Any stair not described above	50	800[3]

Notes

[1]Assessed as likely to use the stair in a fire emergency.

[2]BS 5588-5 recommends that firefighting stairs should be at least 1100 mm wide.

[3]In order to comply with the guidance in the Approved Document to Part M on minimum widths for areas accessible to disabled people, this may need to be increased to 1000 mm.

Table XX Capacity of a stair for basements and for total evacuation of the building (from: Approved Document B, Table 7; also BS 5588: Part 6, Table 5)

No. of floors served	Maximum number of persons served by a stair of width:								
	1000 mm	1100 mm	1200 mm	1300 mm	1400 mm	1500 mm	1600 mm	1700 mm	1800 mm
1	150	220	240	260	280	300	320	340	360
2	190	260	285	310	335	360	385	410	435
3	230	300	330	360	390	420	450	480	510
4	270	340	375	410	445	480	515	550	585
5	310	380	420	460	500	540	580	620	660
6	350	420	465	510	555	600	645	690	735
7	390	460	510	560	610	660	710	760	810
8	430	500	555	610	665	720	775	830	885
9	470	540	600	660	720	780	840	900	960
10	510	580	645	710	775	840	905	970	1035

Notes:

The capacity of stairs serving more than 10 storeys may be obtained by using the formula in para **419**.

This table can also apply to part of a building.

4.19 Stair design

Stair design should accord with Approved Document K or BS 5395, *Stairs, ladders and walkways*, see Figures 11.39, 11.40 and 11.41, and Table XXI.

For buildings over 10 storeys Approved Document B recommends the use of the following formula to assess the capacity of stairs:

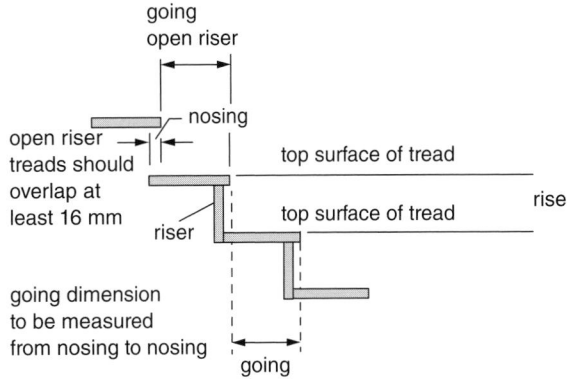

11.39 *Measuring rise and going on staircases*

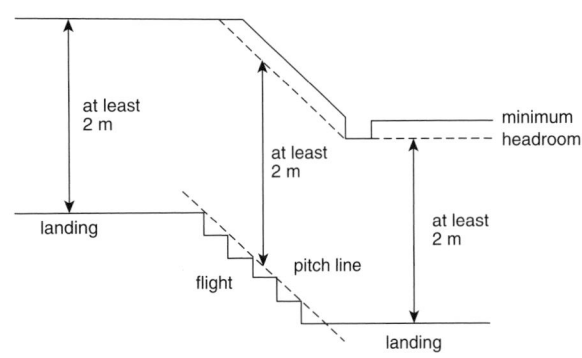

11.40 *Measuring headroom on staircases*

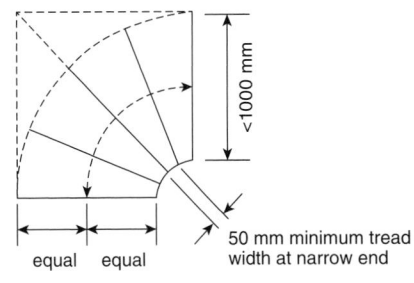

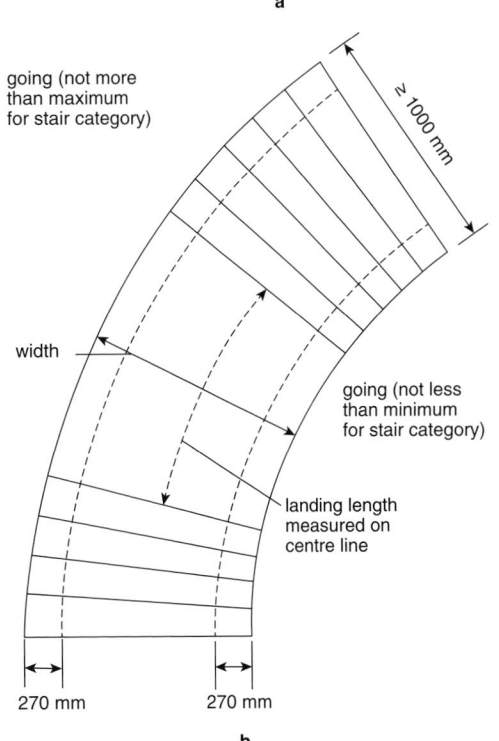

11.41 *Measuring tapered treads. a Stair width less than 1 m. b Stair width equal to or greater than 1 m*

Table XXI Rise and going (from Approved Document K, Table 1)

	Maximum rise (mm)	Minimum going (mm)
1 Private stair	220‡	220*
2 Institutional and assembly stair	180‡	280†
3 Other stair	190‡	250

*The maximum pitch for a private stair is 42°.

†If the area of a floor of the building is less than 100 m², the going may be reduced to 250 mm.

‡For maximum rise for stairs providing the means of access for disabled people reference should be made to Approved Document M: Access and facilities for disabled people.

$$P = 200w + 50(w-0.3)(n-1)$$

where

P is the number of people that can be accommodated

w is the width of the stair in metres

n is the number of storeys in the building

Where phased evacuation is envisaged, the minimum widths in Table XXII may be adopted.

Table XXII Minimum aggregate width of stairs designed for phased evacuation (from Approved Document B, Table 38)

Maximum number of people in any storey	Stair width[1] (mm)
100	1000
120	1100
130	1200
140	1300
150	1400
160	1500
170	1600
180	1700
190	1800

[1]Stairs with a rise of more than 30m should not be wider than 1400 mm unless provided with a central handrail (see para 4.6). As an alternative to using this table, provided that the minimum width of a stair is at least 1000 mm, the width may be calculated from: [(P × 10) – 100 mm] where P = the number of people on the most heavily occupied storey.

Small buildings occupied by a limited number of persons and satisfying the criteria for travel distance and a single exit can have a single stairway, see Tables XXIII and XXIV.

Table XXIII Maximum permitted distances of travel in small shops (from BS 5588: Part 2, Table 6)

	Maximum travel distance (m)	Maximum direct distance (m)
Ground storey with a single exit	27	18
Basement or first storey with a single stairway	18	12
Storey with more than one exit/stairway	45	30

*See footnote to 9.2.3 in BS 5588.

Table XXIV Capacity of a stairway for an office building permitted to be served by a single stairway (from BS 5588: Part 3, Table 6)

Maximum number of persons per storey	Width of stairway (mm)
50	900
more than 50	1100

4.20 Population

The recommended widths assume a uniform distribution of population. If any floor within a building has a higher population, e.g. a conference room or restaurant, extra or wider stairs necessary to accommodate the increased population should extend down to the final exit.

4.21 Independent escape

Separate stairs should be provided for use by residential or assembly occupancies independent of any other use. Where a totally independent escape can be provided from these higher risk uses, e.g. using an access deck or walkway, it is reasonable that some stairs may be shared.

4.22 External stairs

The use of external stairs should be avoided if possible, due to the psychological effect of using unfamiliar external stairs at high levels and the effects of bad weather. The width and design of external stairs is the same as for internal ones. External stairs are not considered suitable for use by the general public, nor for hospital or similar uses. They should only be used as an alternative escape unless they are the only stair, see Figure 11.42.

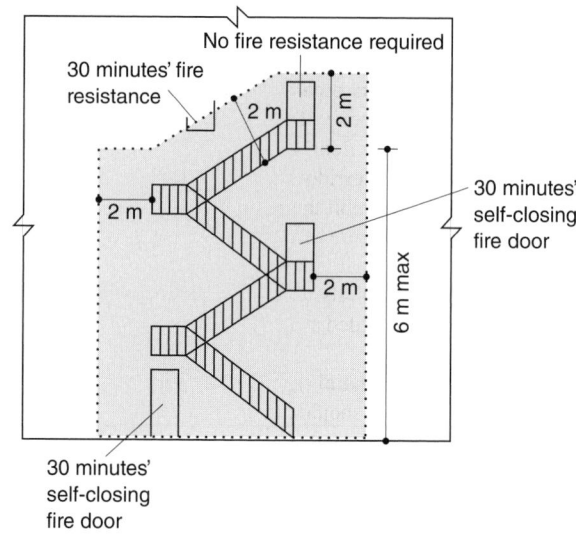

11.42 *Enclosure of escape stairs and ramps, not drawn to scale. The shaded area should have not less than 30 minutes fire resistance*

An external escape route should be protected against the accumulation of ice and snow. This may be in the form of an enclosure, partial shielding or trace heating

4.23 Escape routes

Recommendations related to means of escape are generally based on a 30-minute period of fire resistance. Higher periods may result by reason of the need to maintain compartmentation or provide firefighting shafts.

Escape stairs, other than external, should be enclosed by fire-resisting construction to protect against the effects of smoke, heat and fire, and to retard the progress of fire and smoke affecting escape routes. Escape routes should lead to final exits.

4.24 Lobbies or corridors

Additionally, lobbies or corridors of fire-resisting construction should be provided to give additional protection to stairs in the following positions:

- between a floor area and stair in all buildings over 20 m in height at all levels;
- between a stair and a basement storey as the stair is at greater risk from heat and smoke;
- between a stair and an enclosed car park;

- between a stair and a higher risk area, e.g. a boiler room;
- between a stair and a floor area in a single-storey building other than a small shop (see BS 5588 Part 2) to protect the stair from smoke;
- in assembly buildings to protect the public and performers – where an opening occurs in a proscenium wall, and between stage and dressing-room corridors;
- where phased evacuation is used;
- where a stair is not discounted.

4.25 Enclosure
Escape routes do not necessarily have to be enclosed; in some situations this would create great problems – open-plan offices, exhibition halls, warehouses, factories.

4.26 Dead-end corridors
Where a corridor dead-end situation exists, the escape route must be protected against fire, heat and smoke by fire-resisting construction, as it may be necessary to pass the room on fire to reach the exit, see Figure 11.43.

4.27 Corridors
Where a corridor connects escape routes, it should be protected against the ingress of smoke. To be effective, the construction should be from structural floor to structural floor or imperforate suspended ceiling. The corridors should also be subdivided by cross-corridor doors to inhibit the progress of smoke. These doors do not necessarily require fire resistance. Their purpose is to make it possible to take an alternative means of escape, not to subdivide the corridor at given intervals. Corridors exceeding 12 m should be subdivided (not subdivided at 12 m intervals), see Figure 11.44.

4.28 Lighting and directional signage
General artificial lighting should be provided for persons to move about a building effectively and safely.

4.29 Emergency lighting
This should be provided in those areas necessary for escape purposes in case the artificial lighting fails. It may be a maintained system (continuously illuminated in conjunction with the general lighting) or be non-maintained, only coming into operation on the failure of the general lighting. Maintained systems are usually provided in areas with large numbers of the public unfamiliar with their surroundings, and where darkened situations may be common.

Escape lighting should be provided in:

- areas occupied or used by the public
- windowless accommodation
- escape routes, including internal corridors without borrowed light
- basements

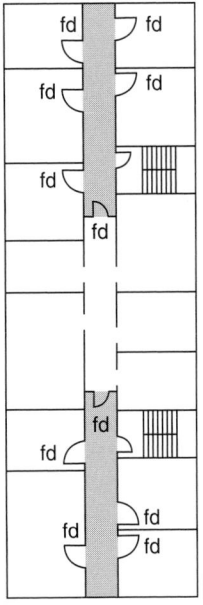

11.43 *Dead-end corridors continued past stairway*

- areas used outside normal daylight hours
- rooms containing essential equipment.

4.30 Signs
These are required to indicate the way to exits, and the exits themselves. Preferred colours, sizes, typeface and graphics are set out in BS 5499. The criterion is that signs should be distinguishable against their background and surroundings and be of a size that can be read at the required distance. If the use of the building warrants it, the signs may have to be in more than one language. Signs should also be provided to indicate fire doors, and those that should be kept locked shut. In public assembly areas, signs are usually internally illuminated; elsewhere it is normally sufficient for escape lights to be positioned so as to illuminate a sign.

4.31 Fastenings
Fastenings on exit doors should allow exit without the use of a key or other device. Unless careful consideration is given to fastenings security may be undermined. The degree of security required will depend on the use of the building and user requirements. Access into a building is not required for escape purposes: re-entry into a floor area is neither necessary nor desirable. Fastenings that prevent a person entering a floor area from a staircase are acceptable. This is often a necessity to prevent theft in offices, factories and hotels and the like. The use of electronic fastenings and the use of card systems or similar to gain entry are acceptable provided that on the raising of the

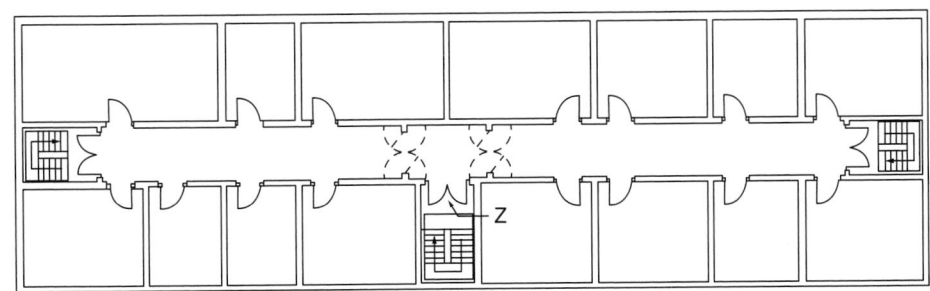

11.44 *Corridors connecting alternative exits. Doors to central stairway should be at position Z, doors may also be required across the corridors*

fire alarm or failure of the electrical system all locks 'fail-safe' in the unlocked position. However, consideration should also be given to the possibility of criminals setting off a false fire alarm in order to circumvent security arrangements.

Panic bolts and latches are most suitable where there are large numbers of persons. Turnbuckle locks with lever handles are commonly used where no public is involved. These may not be suitable in some institutional buildings, or places used predominantly by the elderly or disabled who may find a small turnbuckle difficult to operate; appropriate door ironmongery should be fitted in these circumstances.

4.32 Smoke control

If a smoke control system is for life safety purposes, it is essential that its initiation is automatic on the detection of smoke; and if mechanical, that it remains operational at all times by the use of duplicate equipment and secondary power supplies etc. Specialist advice should be sought regarding the type, design and installation of a life safety system.

The measures required to protect a means of escape from the effects of smoke will depend on the escape scheme adopted. Where escape is over a reasonable travel distance, the enclosure of the routes by partitions constructed to resist smoke, i.e. to maintain their integrity, should be adequate. Some smoke will enter escape routes, but should not reach a level to make their use untenable in the time it takes to reach an exit.

As described earlier, the addition of lobbies will retard the entry of smoke. Ventilating the lobbies will further dilute the smoke and hopefully direct it away from the escape route. It is also possible to protect escape routes from the ingress of smoke by the use of pressure differentials to retard the movement of smoke whereby fans, ducts and vents are used to create different pressures between the fire and protected area (pressurisation or depressurisation). Any such system should be designed and installed with the recommendations of BS 5588 Part 4.

4.33 Mechanical ventilation

These systems should not adversely affect a means of escape by perforation of enclosures without adequate protection, or by directing smoke into escape routes. Systems should have regard to BS 5720 and BS 5588 Part 9.

4.34 Ancillary accommodation

Service areas such as boiler and switch rooms should include provision in accordance with Tables XXV and XXVI.

4.35 Escape for people with disabilities

Escape for disabled people should be provided from all buildings to which they have access. BS 5588 Part 8 gives guidance on means of escape for them. Buildings designed particularly for use by persons with disabilities will require specific additional facilities and protection to escape routes depending on the disability. In any case,

Table XXV Maximum permitted part of travel distance in certain areas of ancillary accommodation (from BS 5588: Part 3, Table 8)

Areas of ancillary accommodation	Cross-reference	Maximum part of travel distance within the room (m)	
		For escape in one direction only, or in directions less than 45° apart that are not separated by fire-resisting construction	For escape in more than one direction in directions 45° or more apart, or in directions less than 45° apart but separated by fire-resisting construction
1 Higher fire risk areas other than items 2, 3, 4 and 5	11.6		
2 Transformer and switchgear rooms	12.2		
3 Boiler rooms	14.6.2	6	12
4 Some fuel storage spaces	14.7		
5 Room housing a fixed internal combustion engine	14.8		

Table XXVI Structural fire protection of areas of ancillary accommodation (from BS 5588: Part 3, Table 9)

Area of ancillary accommodation	Cross-reference	Structural fire protection: the area of ancillary accommodation should be separated from other parts of the building by:
1 Storage area not greater than 450 m² (see notes 1 and 2)	18	Robust construction having a minimum standard of fire resistance of 30 min (see note 3)
2 Repair and maintenance workshops and reprographic rooms (see note 1)	20	
3 Kitchens (separately or in conjunction with an associated restaurant/canteen)	21	
4 Transformer, switchgear and battery rooms, for low voltage or extra low voltage equipment	12.2	
5 Loading bays	18	
6 Storage areas greater than 450 m² (see notes 1 and 2)	18	
7 Service installation rooms other than those covered by items 4 and 10 to 14 inclusive		Robust construction having a minimum standard of fire resistance of 60 min (see note 3)
8 Car parks within or adjoining an office building and not greater than 450 m² in area	19	
9 Car parks within or adjoining an office building and greater than 450 m² in area	19	
10 Boiler rooms (see note 4)	14.6	Robust construction having a minimum standard of fire resistance equivalent to that required of the elements of construction of the building and in no case less than 60 min (see note 3)
11 Fuel storage spaces (see notes 4 and 5)	14.7	
12 Transformer and switchgear rooms for equipment above low voltage	12.2	
13 Rooms housing fixed internal combustion engines	14.8	
14 Any higher fire risk area other than items 10 to 13	11.6	

Notes

[1] Not higher fire risk areas.

[2] Other than refuse storage.

[3] Any openings in the required construction should be protected by doors having a similar standard of fire resistance.

[4] Other than oil fired boiler installations and oil storage.

[5] Other than liquefied petroleum gas storage.

controlled escape by effective management is vital and assistance should be available.

The Building Regulations require access for disabled persons to the majority of buildings; therefore a number of factors to facilitate their escape will exist – additional width escape routes to accommodate wheelchairs, position and height of guarding on stairs and ramps. Also, in some cases lifts, if adequately protected, may be used by them in the event of fire. It may be necessary to construct protected refuges adjacent to lifts and stairs for those in wheelchairs and with limited mobility to await the use of a lift or assistance to evacuate the building.

When assessing escape arrangements for disabled people it is important not to consider only those that are in wheelchairs. Among others, blind people need help to find the exits, and deaf people require audible warnings to be duplicated by visual ones.

4.36 Fire safety management
This is the prevention and control of a fire, and the maintenance of the fire safety facilities. The understanding and maintenance of these is essential, particularly in a large or complex building; therefore the occupier/management should have comprehension of the safety measures incorporated into the design of the building. This means that the designer must supply all relevant information in a fire safety manual. Details should include:

- the basis on which the means of escape was planned;
- the type of management structure and staff responsibilities envisaged;
- operational details of mechanical and electrical systems;
- record drawings of active and passive protection measures.

5 MATERIALS
5.1 General
The materials forming a building should be chosen having regard to the safety of the structure and occupants. The adequacy of their resistance or their ability to sustain load for any particular period may necessitate their protection to prevent the premature failure of the structure by collapse or failure of loadbearing capacity. Additional resistance may be achieved by protective coverings, casings or membranes.

5.2 Form of construction
Fire resistance relates to the form of construction, not the material, and is stated in terms of performance in relation to British Standards methods of test:

- loadbearing capacity (resistance to collapse);
- integrity (resistance to fire penetration);
- insulation (resistance to transfer of excessive heat).

5.3 Loadbearing capacity
The criterion *loadbearing capacity* has replaced stability. In line with international practice, under BS 476 Part 22, non-loadbearing elements are assessed only for integrity and insulation. Loadbearing elements are tested in accordance with Part 21. BS 476 Part 8 is still often referred to, although superseded in 1987 by Parts 20, 21, 22 and 23. When tested specifications are used, the construction must replicate that tested in total. Consideration of products or systems having an Agrément Certificate issued by the British Board of Agrément or a product complying with a European Technical Approval (refer to the EEC Construction Products Directive) may be of use.

5.4 Ease
Regard should be given to the ease of acquiring the required fire protection, ease of construction, and durability. Although the last

is not required under the Building Regulations, a material should be 'fit for the purpose'. There are several terms used in Approved Document B issued in support of the Building Regulations specifically relevant to materials and their choice.

5.5 Flame spread
Restriction of the spread of flame across the surface of a material is an important factor of fire safety, as it affects fire growth and spread, and means of escape. The surface spread is referred to in terms of class classification in accordance with BS 476 Part 7 1971 and reference to Class 0. Flame spread can be reduced by the application of chemicals in the form of a surface application or pressure impregnation. In the latter case mechanical damage to the surface exposing a substratum will not be detrimental to the material. Materials chosen for low spread of flame properties may later be compromised by inappropriate painting.

5.6 Steel
Exposed steel can lose strength very quickly when exposed to fire, buckling and collapsing in as little as 10 to 15 minutes. The actual temperature at which it starts to lose strength depends on the type of steel, whether it is in tension or compression, and its restraint if any. Encasing the steel insulates it against temperature rise. Protection can be in the form of concrete, fire-retardant boards, fibrous sprayed or intumescent coatings, or suspended ceilings. Water cooling has been used to protect columns.

5.7 Aluminium
Some forms fail structurally at quite low temperatures but it has good properties for flame spread.

5.8 Concrete
This loses its crushing strength in fire, see Table XXVII. The heat of the fire also affects the strength of steel reinforcement. Adequate concrete cover is essential, and may require the addition of mesh reinforcement to restrict spalling; this is caused by the reinforcement expanding with heating.

5.9 Clay masonry, brickwork
As a form of ceramic clay performs well at high temperatures albeit some expansion may take place. Any steel in clay can expand causing failure and should be protected.

5.10 Timber
This performs better than steel in a fire. It is a low conductor of heat; it progressively chars, protecting itself with a charcoal layer. The charring rate can be assessed, and the ability of the residual timber to sustain the required loads calculated – see BS 5268 Part 4 Section 4.1 *Method of calculating fire resistance of timber members*. Timber studwork with plasterboard can easily achieve 30 minutes' fire resistance, one hour with additional protection. Existing timber floors can be upgraded to improve their fire resistance by the addition of soffit protection and insulation – see BRE Digest 208, *Increasing the fire resistance of existing timber floors*.

5.11 Asbestos
This is no longer used in its basic form for health reasons.

Table XXVII Behaviour of concrete in fire

Temperature (°C)	Permanent loss of compressive strength as demonstrated by crushing test
250	5%
600	64%
1200 and above	collapse

Table XXVIII Provisions for fire doors (from Approved Document B, Table B1)

Position of door	Minimum fire resistance of door in terms of integrity (minutes) when tested to BS 476-22[1]	Minimum fire resistance of door in terms of integrity (minutes) when tested to the relevant European standard[3]
1 In a compartment wall separating buildings	As for the wall in which the door is fitted, but a minimum of 60	As for the wall in which the door is fitted, but a minimum of 60
2 In a compartment wall:		
a. If it separates a flat from a space in common use;	FD 30S[2]	E30 Sa[2]
b. Enclosing a protected shaft forming a stairway situated wholly or partly above the adjoining ground in a building used for Flats, Other Residential, Assembly and Recreation, or Office purposes;	FD 30S[2]	E30 Sa[2]
c. enclosing a protected shaft forming a stairway not described in (b) above;	Half the period of fire resistance of the wall in which it is fitted, but 30 minimum and with suffix S[2]	Half the period of fire resistance of the wall in which it is fitted, but 30 minimum and with suffix Sa[2]
d. enclosing a protected shaft forming a lift or service shaft;	Half the period of fire resistance of the wall in which it is fitted, but 30 minimum	Half the period of fire resistance of the wall in which it is fitted, but 30 minimum
e. not described in (a), (b), (c) or (d) above.	As for the wall it is fitted in, but add S (2) if the door is used for progressive horizontal evacuation under the guidance to B1	As for the wall it is fitted in, but add Sa[2] if the door is used for progressive horizontal evacuation under the guidance to B1
3 In a compartment floor	As for the floor in which it is fitted	As for the floor in which it is fitted
4 Forming part of the enclosures of:		
a. a protected stairway (except as described in item 9); or	FD 30S[2]	E30 Sa[2]
b. a lift shaft (see paragraph 5.42b); which does not form a protected shaft in 2(b), (c) or (d) above.	FD 30	E30
5 Forming part of the enclosure of:		
a. a protected lobby approach (or protected corridor) to a stairway;	FD 30S[2]	E30 Sa[2]
b. any other protected corridor; or	FD 20S[2]	E20 Sa[2]
c. a protected lobby approach to a lift shaft (see paragraph 5.42)	FD 30S[2]	E30 Sa[2]
6 Affording access to an external escape route	FD 30	E30
7 Sub-dividing:		
a. corridors connecting alternative exits;	FD 20S[2]	E20 Sa[2]
b. dead-end portions of corridors from the remainder of the corridor	FD 20S[2]	E20 Sa[2]
8 Any door within a cavity barrier	FD 30	E30
9 Any door forming part of the enclosure to a protected entrance hall or protected landing in a flat;	FD 20	E20
10 Any door forming part of the enclosure		
a. to a place of special fire risk	FD 30	E30
b. to ancillary accommodation in care homes (see paragraph 3.50)	FD30	E30

Notes:

[1]To BS 476-22 (or BS 476-8 subject to paragraph 5 in Appendix A).

[2]Unless pressurization techniques complying with BS EN 12101-6:2005 Smoke and heat control systems – Part 6: Specification for pressure differential systems – Kits are used, these doors should also either:

(a) have a leakage rate not exceeding 3 m³/m/hour (head and jambs only) when tested at 25 Pa under BS 476 *Fire tests on building materials and structures,* Section 31.1 *Methods for measuring smoke penetration through doorsets and shutter assemblies, Method of measurement under ambient temperature conditions; or*

(b) meet the additional classification requirement of Sa when tested to BS EN 1634-3:2001 *Fire resistance tests for door and shutter assemblies,* Part 3 – *Smoke control doors.*

[3] The National classifications do not automatically equate with the equivalent classifications in the European column, therefore products cannot typically assume a European class unless they have been tested accordingly.

5.12 Protective board, plasterboard, mineral fibre boards

This is used to protect structural members and form fire-resisting enclosures on suitable frames. Some forms of construction and systems can achieve in excess of 2 hours' fire resistance when constructed correctly. Care is necessary when cutting for services, etc. to maintain the fire resistance. There are many proprietary systems utilising protective boards on timber and metal frames.

5.13 Glass

Plain glass (also depending on whether it is toughened or laminated) offers negligible fire resistance. Wired glass can achieve a 1 hour standard of fire resistance in terms of integrity but with little insulation. Recent developments have resulted in plain glass giving 15 minutes' insulation. Insulating fire-resisting glazing can achieve in excess of 2 hours; the size of glazing panels may be restricted.

5.14 Plastics

Thermosetting harden when heated and thermoplastic soften on heating. Plastics often fall from their supports, making an assessment of their action in fire difficult under test conditions. The material may not burn, but can drip flaming droplets and spread fire. See Approved Document B regarding the acceptable use of thermoplastic materials for ceilings, rooflights and lighting diffusers.

5.15 Doors and shutters

These can be wooden, glass, metal or composite, see Table XXVIII. Some can achieve a fire resistance in excess of 4 hours. They are tested with regard to their integrity and insulation; most do not require insulation. Shutters are generally held open and close on the actuation of a fusible link, or automatically following detection of heat or smoke. Doors are designated according to their performance in minutes in terms of their integrity. Doors forming part of a protected enclosure (stair, lobby or corridor) for means of escape should have not less than a 30-minute standard of fire resistance. Additionally these doors should be able to resist the passage of smoke at ambient temperatures; these are generally denoted by the suffix 'S', i.e. FD30S.

Most door sets require the addition of an intumescent strip to attain a 30-minute standard of fire resistance. The seal intumesces at high temperature swelling to seal any imperfections of fit or gaps and thereby protecting the edges of the door to maintain its integrity. The ambient temperature seal, which may be in the form of a brush, retards the passage of smoke around the door when the fire is at a lower temperature but possibly producing large quantities of smoke. Various codes require 'S' doors in different situations. To be effective for means of escape doors must be self-closing. Where a door is in constant use it may be acceptable to use a hold-open device (usually electromagnetic) to avoid it being wedged open or damaged.

5.16 Materials for fire stopping and cavity barriers

These must effectively close a concealed cavity, and stop spread of fire and smoke around a service or element, by sealing an imperfection of fit. The material must be capable of sustaining movement, including expansion, be adequately fixed and, in the case of barriers, have fire resistance. Materials include intumescent mastics, fire-protective boards, cement mortar, gypsum plaster and glass fibre; there are numerous proprietary systems.

5.17 Intumescent coatings

These are formed of differing materials with varying characteristics and foam on exposure to heat to form a protective coating. They can be used to improve fire resistance and reduce surface spread of flame. If adopted the following points should be considered:

- The intumescent system must be compatible with the material to be protected.
- The system must suit site conditions by virtue of the necessary mode of application, and in accordance with that tested and achieving the required standard. This includes atmospheric conditions.
- Not all are suitable in areas of high humidity.
- Protection against mechanical damage may be necessary.
- The possible damage of the protection by secondary fixings, follow-on trades or water damage.

6 FIRE PROTECTION APPLIANCES AND INSTALLATIONS

6.1 General

Fire protection appliances and installations are increasingly forming a part of an overall fire protection system. Active extinguishing systems are often installed to compensate for inadequate structural protection, or to facilitate an innovative concept or design which would be hampered by protective construction or division by fire walls.

6.2 Systems

The following brief descriptions give an indication of some of the appliances and systems available and their application. The adoption of any particular system requires careful consideration – the nature of the risk, effectiveness of protection, reliability, ease of maintenance. Specialist advice should be sought. Reference should be made to the relevant British Standards – see Section 9. Although the use of a foreign system or component is not prohibited, the prior agreement and approval of any enforcing authority, insurer or water undertaker should be obtained.

6.3 Hand fire appliances: extinguishers, fire buckets, fire blankets

These are first aid appliance for use by general public. The extinguishing medium of hand-held extinguishers varies to suit the risk; they are colour coded for quick reference.

6.4 Hose reels

These are first aid appliance for use by occupants and firefighters, connected to a pressurised water supply.

6.5 Automatic sprinklers

These provide an automatically released water spray above a fire to contain its growth and inhibit its spread. There are various types and systems for specific areas, applications and risk categories. It should be noted that some systems are meant for property protection only, and that special provisions relate to life safety. Certain situations are not considered suitable for protection by sprinklers because of the potential water damage (art galleries, museums, historical libraries), the risk of accidental discharge or the unsuitability of water as the extinguishing medium for certain processes and materials. There may also be a need to provide large volumes for on-site water storage.

6.6 Water drenchers

A curtain of water, usually to protect the outside of a building or the safety curtain of a theatre.

6.7 Water spray projector systems

For fires involving oils or similar flammable liquids.

6.8 Hydrant systems (sometimes known as mains)

This is a rising main to deliver water for firefighting onto the floor of a building via landing valves. A wet rising main is a pipe permanently charged with water and is generally installed in buildings above 60 m in height, beyond the pumping capabilities of a fire service pumping appliance; it requires water storage. A dry riser is a pipe charged by a fire service pump at ground/access level; it can be at any height but is generally provided in a building over 18 m. Any horizontal section should not exceed 12 m in length unless the delivery of the required rate of water at each outlet can be proven hydraulically. Falling or dropping mains deliver water to low levels. Private hydrants are provided within the curtilage of a site where statutory hydrants are too distant or where the risk is such as to require large volumes of water immediately.

6.9 Foam installations

These are of limited application, generally for the extinction of flammable liquid fires. They may require space for on-site foam-making equipment. There are various forms; specialist advice will be needed. A foam inlet is a fixed pipe through which foam can be pumped to protect rooms containing oil fuel, oil fired boilers etc.

6.10 Gaseous and vaporising liquid installations

These can be:

Carbon dioxide to protect an enclosed area acting in the main by dilution of the atmosphere. Not suitable for all fires. Satisfactory for electrical, computer and telephone equipment, flammable liquids, some chemicals, libraries, archives, art stores, diesel engines and textiles.

Vaporising liquids (halogenated hydrocarbons). Because of the stated detrimental effects of halon on the atmosphere alternatives are being developed; the Building Research Establishment should be consulted for information on acceptable alternatives.

Dry powder installations are suitable for use on flammable liquid and metal fires. Clearance after use is a problem.

6.11 Automatic detectors

Note that their effectiveness is dependent upon the correct selection and siting – see the various Building Research Establishment reports.

Smoke detectors detect the presence of smoke by optical (obscuration) or ionisation methods and raise an alarm. Ionisation detectors are sensitive in the early stages of a fire when smoke particles are small, most suitable in a controlled environment such as a computer suite. Optical detectors react to the visible products of combustion and are the most effective.

Heat detectors detect heat at a pre-selected temperature or on a rapid rise in temperature. Use where smoke may be present as part of process or function but regard should be had to normal temperature of area where sited.

Radiation and ultraviolet detectors respond to distinctive flame flicker. Suitable for large open areas and can detect certain chemical fires.

Laser beam detectors: rising hot air affects laser beam being projected onto receiver by obscuration or movement. Suitable for covering large open areas but note that the receiver may be subject to building movement; beware of false alarms from falling objects or birds.

6.12 Fire alarms manual and automatic (as defined in BS 5839 Part 1)
The system must be carefully chosen to meet specific needs – property or life safety; special needs of those with impaired hearing or sight; public entertainment application (possibly muted alarms) or a specific evacuation procedure (two stage/phase evacuation).

6.13 System type
A manual system (gongs, handbells, etc.) is only to be used in exceptional cases for very small buildings or specific areas. An automatic system in which an alarm of fire can be initiated automatically by the breaking of a call point or by a detector is the more common form. The complexity of the evacuation may require a message relayed via a public address system, initial alarms and alert signals, or the provision of fire telephones. Modern systems can be highly technical, incorporating computers and other data-processing equipment; specialist advice should be obtained at an early stage in any design.

7 STATUTORY REQUIREMENTS

7.1 Legislation
The statutory requirements to provide fire precautions almost without exception relate to life safety and the diminution of fire, although in consequence a degree of property protection is achieved. Some counties and most major conurbations have local Acts or bylaws in relation to access for firefighting. Many large towns and cities have provisions relating to 'large' buildings. At the time of writing the legislation relating to fire is under major review, with a view to rationalisation and streamlining aimed at deregulation. This will involve the repeal of many Acts and Regulations where the Building Regulations have a similar requirement, and extension of existing fire safety legislation to encompass uses such as public entertainment currently dealt with under numerous statutes. A list of national legislation relating to fire is contained in Section 8.

7.2 Regional variations
The Building Regulations (England and Wales) are substantive; the Scottish Building Regulations are currently prescriptive (but are under review); the Building Regulations (Northern Ireland) are currently prescriptive.

7.3 Adoption
The fire safety aspect of the Regulations in England and Wales (Part B) applies to all buildings other than certain prisons. While there is an Approved Document of technical standards to Part B there is no obligation to adopt its recommendations. Provided that the substantive requirement is fulfilled any solution acceptable to the enforcing authority (or Approved Inspector) may be used. If a recognised code is used it is only necessary for the purposes of fulfilling the statutory requirement to adopt the recommendations pertaining to the requirement. However, care should be exercised, as any one recommendation may be reliant on the adoption of another. Section 9 details current codes and guides.

7.4 Requirements
The requirements for fire safety under the Building Regulations of England and Wales are as follows.

B1: Means of escape.
The building shall be designed and constructed so that there are means of escape in case of fire from the building to a place of safety outside the building capable of being safely and effectively used at all material times.

B2: Internal fire spread (linings)
(1) To inhibit the spread of fire within the building the internal linings shall

    (a)   resist the spread of flame over their surfaces; and

    (b)   have, if ignited, a rate of heat release which is reasonable in the circumstances

(2) In this paragraph 'internal linings' means the materials lining any partition, wall, ceiling or other internal structure.

B3: Internal fire spread (structure)
(1) The building shall be designed and constructed so that, in the event of fire, its stability will be maintained for a reasonable period.
(2) A wall common to two or more buildings shall be designed and constructed so that it resists the spread of fire between those buildings. For the purposes of this subparagraph a house in a terrace and a semi-detached house are each to be treated as a separate building.
(3) To inhibit the spread of fire within the building, it shall be subdivided with fire-resisting construction to an extent appropriate to the size and intended use of the building.
(4) The building shall be designed and constructed so that the unseen spread of fire and smoke within concealed spaces in its structure and fabric is inhibited.

B4: External fire spread
(1) The external walls of the building shall resist the spread of fire over the walls and from one building to another, having regard to the height, use and position of the building.
(2) The roof of the building shall resist the spread of fire over the roof and from one building to another, having regard to the use and position of the building.

B5: Access and facilities for the fire service
(1) The building shall be designed and constructed so as to provide facilities to assist firefighter in the protection of life.
(2) Provision shall be made within the site of the building to enable fire appliances to gain access to the building.

7.5 Application
B2, B3(1), (2) and (4), B4 and B5 apply to all buildings; certain prisons are exempt from the other requirements.

7.6 Advice
The Building Regulations relate to a building under construction, certain changes of use, and certain extensions and alterations. Once occupied the Fire Precautions Act may be applicable. To avoid any potential conflict, the Department of the Environment and the Home Office have issued an advice document to enforcing authorities on how the required consultation process should take place. The document, *Building Regulation and Fire Safety Procedural Guidance*, also provides a guide for an applicant through the approval procedure outlining the aims and varying responsibilities of the authorities concerned.

7.7 Statutory bar
Section 13 of the Fire Precautions Act 1971 imposes a 'statutory bar' on a Fire Authority preventing them making the issue of a fire certificate conditional on works to the means of escape approved under the Building Regulations, provided that such matters were shown on deposited plans, and circumstances have not changed.

If such matters did not have to be shown the statutory bar does not apply.

8 BIBLIOGRAPHY

Building Regulations
Approved Document B (Fire safety). Volume 1: Dwellinghouses (2006 Edition).
Approved Document B (Fire safety). Volume 2: Buildings other than dwellinghouses (2006 Edition)
(These documents are available for purchase, but can be downloaded free of charge from the UK Government's Planning Portal website.)

British Standards
BS 476: Fire tests on building materials and structures
BS 5306: Fire extinguishing installations and equipment on premises
    Part 2: Specification for sprinkler systems
    Part 3: Code of practice for selection, installation and maintenance of portable fire extinguishers
BS 5446: Components for automatic fire alarm systems for residential premises
    Part 1: Specification for self-contained smoke alarms and point type smoke detectors
BS 5449: Fire safety signs, notices and graphic symbols
BS 5588: Fire Precautions in the design, construction and use of buildings
    Part 1: Code of practice for residential buildings
    Part 5: Access and facilities for firefighting
    Part 6: Code of practice for places of assembly
    Part 7: Code of practice for the incorporation of atria in buildings
    Part 8: Code of practice for means of escape for disabled people
    Part 9: Code of practice for ventilation and air conditioning ductwork
    Part 10: Code of practice for shopping complexes
    Part 11: Code of practice for shops, offices, industrial, storage and other similar buildings
    Part 12: Managing fire safety
BS 5839: Fire detection and alarm systems for buildings
BS 5867: Specification for fabrics for curtains and drapes
BS 7974: Application of fire safety engineering principles to the design of buildings, Code of practice
BS 8214: Code of practice for fire door assemblies with nonmetallic leaves
BS 9251: Sprinkler systems for residential and domestic occupancies, Code of practice
BS 9990: Code of practice for non-automatic fire fighting systems in buildings

Codes of Practice
Code of Practice – hardware for timber fire and escape doors, Association of Building Hardware Manufacturers
Crown Fire Standards, Property Advisers to the Civil Estate
DD 9999: Code of practice for fire safety in the design, construction and management of buildings
Department for Education and Employment, Constructional Standards for Schools
Guide to Safety at Sports Grounds
BRE Information Paper 8/82: Increasing the fire resistance of existing timber doors
BRE Digest 208: Increasing the fire resistance of existing timber floors
NHS Estates Fire Codes, Firecode
Safety signs and signals, The Health and Safety Regulations 1996, Guidance on Regulations
Technical Standards for Places of Entertainment (District Surveyors Association and The Association of British Theatre Technicians)
The Workplace (Health, Safety and Welfare) Regulations 1992, Approved Code of Practice and Guidance
Housing Health and Safety Rating System Operating Guidance, 2006
Fire safety in adult placements: a code of practice (Department of Health)
LPC Rules for Automatic Sprinkler Installations, incorporating BS EN 12845, Fire Protection Association, 2009

Books
Andrew H Buchanan. *Structural Design for Fire Safety*. John Wiley and Sons Ltd, 2001.
Simon Ham. *Legislation Maze: Fire*. RIBA Publishing, 2007.
Peter Muir. *The New Fire Safety Legislation*. RICS Books, 2007.
J. A. Purkiss. *Fire Safety Engineering; Design of Structures*, 2006.

12 Flood-aware design

Robert Barker and Richard Coutts

Robert Barker and Richard Coutts are directors of Baca Architects

DISCLAIMER

The information contained in this chapter is an introduction to flood risk only. The authors take no responsibility for the subsequent use of this information, nor for any errors or omissions it may contain. Professional advice should always be sought when considering any development, particularly where flood risk may be present.

KEY POINTS:

- *Urbanisation and changing weather patterns are increasing the frequency of flooding*
- *Flooding cannot always be prevented, so designing developments that work with and make space for water is becoming increasingly important*
- *The optimum solution to reducing and managing flood risk may require a combination of different design measures*
- *All development should seek to include sustainable drainage*

Contents

1 Introduction
2 Understanding flooding
3 Planning for flood risk
4 Reducing flood risk
5 Case study
6 Bibliography

1 INTRODUCTION

Flooding is a natural part of the weather cycle. Many people live in areas of high flood risk such as river systems, deltas and coasts, drawn by fertile land and waterway transport links. But throughout the world, flooding has had a devastating impact, at times destroying whole cities and communities.

As global warming influences the natural water cycle, a paradigm shift in our approach to the design of new and existing settlements is required. Coastal communities are increasingly threatened by rising sea levels and stormier weather, whilst inland towns and homes suffer from more intense rainstorms with worse and more frequent flooding.

As a result, the number of people at risk of flooding is rising, particularly in urban areas, where population rises, increased hard surfaces and changing weather patterns exacerbate the problem. According to the Environment Agency in 2014, over 5.5 million, or one in six, properties are at risk of flooding from all types of floods across England and Wales.

However, by better understanding the nature of flood-risk, cities and buildings can be better designed to manage and reduce the risk to people and property.

2 UNDERSTANDING FLOODING

2.1 Flood risk

Natural disasters appear to be occurring with both greater frequency and intensity around the globe. In part, this is a result of more people living in high-risk areas, particularly through urbanisation and unplanned development.

Floods are typically caused by:

- extreme weather events such as rainstorms, hurricanes or tsunamis, or variation such as rapid snow melt;
- man-made activities such as structural failure of man-made facilities such as dams or embankment.

Flood risk is commonly considered a combination of probability (likelihood of exposure to flooding) and consequence (the vulnerability of the receptor to being flooded). This is the likelihood of a flood occurring in any given year and the impact of that flood.

Reducing flood risk requires consideration of both factors. For instance, it is possible to reduce the probability of flooding by installing defences, but increase the consequence of a flood by building more homes behind the defences. However, if the homes are designed to be flood resilient then the consequence of them flooding is low and the overall risk reduced. Equally, it is possible to increase the probability of flooding by removing defences but reduce the consequence by relocating occupants and changing to natural wetlands.

2.2 Probability

The probability of flooding is described as the annual percentage probability of a flood occurring, such as 5 per cent. This is also described as 1 in 20 years, but this can be misleading as a 5 per cent probability flood could occur 3 years in a row and then not again for 60 years.

The probability of a flood also reflects the magnitude. A 1 per cent (1 in 100 year) flood will be bigger than a 5 per cent (1 in 20 year) flood; that is why it is less likely to occur. However, climate change is affecting the magnitude of floods and confusing this method of understanding. In the future, a 5 per cent probability flood could be more extensive, perhaps equivalent to a current 2 per cent flood.

2.3 Consequence

The consequences of flooding are usually measured in terms of the impact of flooding on the people or things that were flooded, the receptors. It is typically measured in terms of loss of life and financial costs, from both direct and indirect causes. The main consideration for the built environment is the vulnerability of the receptors. A hospital is likely to be considered to be more vulnerable than an office or workshop, due to the nature of its occupants and equally its role in society.

2.4 Sources of flooding

Flooding can occur from various sources, as outlined in guidance such as Technical Guidance to the National Planning Policy Framework:

- **River (fluvial)** flooding when excess water bursts the riverbanks, Figure 12.1. This occurs when the run off following a large rainstorm overwhelms the capacity of the river or artificial channel. The land around the river that is flooded is known as the flood plain and can extend for hundreds of metres, sometimes miles. This is the most common and well-known type of flooding.

12.1 *River flooding, Marlow 2014*

- **Coastal flooding** when sea-water is driven on to the land by storms, tsunamis and high tides. This occurs when seismic activity causes tidal waves or when meteorological events, such as hurricanes or storms, combine with strong winds and low pressure to cause sea levels to rise above expected peak levels. If these storm surges overwhelm or breach the sea defences they can have devastating consequences, particularly for communities in low-lying areas.
- **Pluvial, overland and sewer flooding** when drains are overwhelmed leading to rain ponding and flowing over the land, Figure 12.2. This occurs when excessive rain cannot be absorbed in the ground, and runs off hard (or water-logged) surfaces too quickly for the drains to discharge it. It is becoming more prevalent in urban areas, where green space has been paved over and where drainage systems are old and insufficient for the population. Sewer flooding

occurs when too much rainwater enters the sewers causing the drains to become surcharged and spill over the land.
- **Groundwater flooding** when the below ground water rises above the surface of the ground. This typically occurs in winter months or in the rainy season and flooding can last for several months until the water level subsides in the summer months or dry season.
- **Failure of artificial systems** such as a dam failure, a burst water main or an embankment collapsing. If a collapse or breach occurs then this can result in fast flowing water, in unexpected locations, catching people unaware.

2.5 Climate change impacts

Climate change is likely to result in rising sea levels, more intense rainstorms and monsoons, higher peak wind speeds, stormier seas,

12.2 *Sewer flooding (source: Environment Agency)*

higher waves and wetter winters. Today's extreme events could start to become the normal events, and tomorrow's extreme events could be far more extreme than we are prepared for. Sea level rise will put low-lying coastal communities at greater threat from storms. Intense rainstorms could regularly overwhelm our drains and sewers. Heat waves and drought could put undue stress on buildings and landscapes, and it could leave occupiers short of water.

The current consensus, according to the IPCC is that sea levels will rise by less than 1 m by the end of the century. However, it will not stop rising in 2100.

These changes create a challenge for planners, engineers and designers, demanding a paradigm shift in our approach to new and existing settlements.

3 PLANNING FOR FLOOD RISK

3.1 Guiding principles

Flood risk is one of the most well-recognised constraints to planning, typically indicated through flood zones. However, the status quo has been challenged by both changing weather patterns and through changing technology. Changing weather patterns are changing the extent of the flood zones. Changing technology is finding solutions to overcome the challenges of flooding, water shortage and other issues.

Strict policies on development restriction within the floodplain are advisable. This is not to say that the floodplain must only have the one use but that the use should be compatible with its primary function to provide space for rivers to expand and flow during times of flood. Once this is understood, and integrated into land use planning, there is an opportunity to use the floodplain productively as part of good town planning. For instance, when preserved as parkland it can provide amenity space for high-density development away from the floodplain, transport corridors, urban heat island reduction, buffers to storms and habitat.

There are different approaches to planning in flood risk areas in different countries around the world but many follow these principles:

- Assess the risk from flooding.
- Avoid building in areas at risk of flooding.
- If this is not possible, then identify less vulnerable uses that are compatible with the level of flood risk.
- Design the development to be resilient to flooding (see Section 4.5) without increasing flood risk.
- Ensure, where possible, that there is a means to evacuate to safety/higher ground.

Following these principles may result in a mixture of uses that matches different levels of flood risk, often with public space along higher risk areas such as riverbanks and coastal areas.

3.2 Location

Like spatial planning, designing for flood risk is developed at different scales from a national and regional level through to city planning. Detailed planning is developed from a neighbourhood level down to a building/plot level.

Understanding the location within a river or water catchment, particularly in combination with an understanding of the topography can help with preliminary assessment of flood risk and the appropriate solutions. For instance in low-lying areas flooding can be extensive and long lasting and the water may take a long time to drain away after a flood. In hilly areas the onset of flooding can be rapid and unexpected.

Typically, the upper catchment of a river is set within hillier land and often (though not always) the lower catchment of a river is within low-lying land along the coast. Though there are examples of low-lying upper catchments and of mountainous lower catchments the characteristics described above are more common.

3.3 Flood zones

Flood zones are used to indicate areas of high to low flood risk, typically based upon probability of flooding. The Environment Agency publishes online maps indicating the Flood Zones in England and Wales. These flood zones indicate the areas that could be at risk of flooding from rivers or the sea but ignoring the presence of defences. The maps also indicate flood defences and the areas that benefit from them. The Scottish Environment Protection Agency (SEPA) and the Rivers Agency in co-operation with the Department of the Environment (DOE) publish similar maps for Scotland and Northern Ireland respectively.

In England, the Flood Zones are defined as follows:

- Flood Zone 1 is considered low probability and is defined as areas with less than 0.1 per cent (1 in 1000) annual chance of flooding from rivers or the sea.
- Flood Zone 2 is considered medium probability and is defined as areas with between a 1 per cent and 0.1 per cent (1 in 100 to 1 in 1000) annual chance of river flooding and between a 0.5 per cent and 0.1 per cent (1 in 200 to 1 in 1000) annual chance of flooding from the sea.
- Flood Zone 3 is considered high probability and is defined as an area with a greater than 1 per cent (1 in 100) annual chance of river flooding and a greater than 0.5 per cent (1 in 200) annual chance of flooding from the sea.
- Flood Zone 3b is also considered high probability. This zone includes areas where water must flow or be stored in times of flood. It is often (but not explicitly) considered to be land that has a greater than 5 per cent (1 in 20) annual chance of river flooding.

The area of land that would be affected by the 1 per cent (1 in 100) annual chance of flooding is used in many countries to define the floodplain. The 1 in 100 flood level is sometimes referred to as the design flood level on the basis that floor levels should be set above this level.

The Environment Agency also publishes interactive online maps should typically indicating the probability of flooding taking into account defences for various flood sources. For rivers, seas and surface water these are indicated as very low to high probability. The area of high probability is that with a greater than 3.3 per cent (1 in 30) chance and is similar to the extent of Flood Zone 3b, which is 5 per cent (1 in 20).

Therefore as a simple reference, the areas of high probability give some indication of the highest risk areas. However, it is very important that a site specific Flood Risk Assessment (FRA) taking into account all sources of flooding and local characteristics including topography is undertaken to determine risk to any given site.

None of these maps indicate how deep the floodwater can be or how fast it will flow but give a good idea of the likelihood an area may flood and importantly, the need to find out more information. A common sense approach to considering flood risk is to look at the topography of a site. Water follows the path of least resistance so it will typically channel in low valleys and pond in depressions. If a site is located on a hill it is not always safe to assume that it is not at risk of flooding as it could be within a local channel or depression.

A site specific Flood Risk Assessment (FRA) can provide a more detailed assessment of the hazard, to include depth and velocity of water as well as the character of the area whether it is urban or rural.

3.4 Planning policy

The English planning policy (National Planning Policy Framework (NPPF) 2012) sets out the need to apply a sequential test with regards to flood risk when considering sites for development. This test is carried out by local government, to determine if development can be located on sites with a 'very low' probability of flooding (Flood Zone 1). If there are not suitable sites for development or if there are other benefits of developing sites in flood risk areas, then sites in Flood Zones 2 and 3 can be considered for development so long as it can be demonstrated that development:

- provides wider sustainability benefits (such as enhancing a deprived area of a town or cleaning up contaminated land);
- will be safe for its users over the lifetime of the development (taking into consideration the effects of climate change), and it will not result in an increase in flood risk elsewhere, and ideally reduce flood risk overall.

Both the 'sequential test' and the second test, which is referred to as the 'exception test', provide a good principle to follow for all development in the UK and beyond.

Key considerations for planning individual development sites to reduce the risk from flooding are:

- planning the site to locate the most vulnerable uses in the lowest risk areas;
- provide safe access and escape routes.

Even where flood defences are provided it is also important to consider residual risk of flooding should defences be breached or overtopped.

3.5 Use and vulnerability

The English planning policy identifies vulnerability according to five categories, with the aim to protect the most vulnerable users and to ensure that key infrastructure that is required to help during floods is protected:

1. Less vulnerable – which includes shops, offices, warehouses.
2. More vulnerable – which includes dwellings and residential institutions, hospitals.
3. Highly vulnerable – basement flats, caravans and mobile homes, police, fire and ambulance stations and telecoms centres which would be needed during a flood.
4. Water compatible – includes flood defences, marinas, water based recreation.
5. Essential infrastructure – including essential transport links, primary electricity sub-stations and water treatment works.

The first three categories of less to more vulnerable uses are most relevant to architects and designers.

A more complete list of uses is given in the National Planning Policy Framework (NPPF) technical guidance. This document also provides a table to determine which of the vulnerability classifications are appropriate in which flood zone and in which flood zones development should not be permitted (see Table I).

4 REDUCING FLOOD RISK

4.1 Introduction

Planning by means of zoning according to high to low levels of risk is only a first step. Flooding may vary in depth, velocity and hazard even within one area. Different building technologies and uses may be more adapted to one flood hazard than another:

- Areas with low flood depths may be managed by variations in land levels to raise some areas above flood levels for say housing, compensated for by lowering other areas which may only be used for gardens.
- For areas potentially affected by deeper floodwaters, buildings may need to be elevated high above the ground or designed to float with the rising water.
- For areas with substantial flood risk, the solution may be for regional flood storage areas and wetlands to be provided.

Measures to reduce flood risk can be structural or non-structural:

- Structural measures include flood defences (soft and hard), building resilience, drainage systems including Sustainable Urban Drainage Systems (SuDS), temporary barriers.
- Non-structural measures include early warning systems, flood forecasting, land use planning, insurance, evacuation and recovery plans.

Table I Appropriate uses according to flood risk (based upon NPPF/PPS25) indicating which are required to pass the exception test in England

Use	Very low flood risk	Low flood risk	Medium flood risk	High flood risk
Less vulnerable uses • Shops and restaurants • Offices • Industry and warehouses • Agriculture and forestry • Water and sewage treatment	Yes	Yes	Yes	No
More vulnerable • Residential houses and flats • Residential institutions, hostels and prisons • Hospitals, health centres • Hotels, bars and nightclubs • Holiday lets or short let caravans	Yes	Yes	Maybe[1]	No
Highly vulnerable • Basement flats • Caravans and mobile homes for permanent residence • Police, fire and ambulance stations • Telecoms centres needed during a flood	Yes	Maybe[2]	No	No
Water compatible • Flood defences • Docks, marinas and ship building • Water based recreation • Amenity open space • Outdoor sports and recreation grounds	Yes	Yes	Yes	Yes
Essential infrastructure • Essential transport links • Primary electricity sub-stations • Sewage and water treatment works	Yes	Yes	Maybe[2]	Maybe[2]

1 Cells indicated as Maybe correspond to uses which are required to pass the exception test in England. The general principle is to direct highly vulnerable uses towards lower flood risk areas.
2 For all sites in Flood Zones 2 or 3, or for sites with over 10 units proposed or with an area of over 1 hectare it is essential to carry out a site specific Flood Risk Assessment (FRA).

For most architects, planners and engineers, it is the structural measures which will be most relevant. Measures are discussed in more detail in the *Cities and Flooding* guide by the World Bank (GFDRR and World Bank 2012).

Different measures are appropriate at different scales. These are introduced below.

4.2 Planning and sustainability

Where flood risk exists on a site it should be seen as a design driver to lead to safe and responsible planning. There are opportunities to use areas at risk of flooding for beneficial functions to the development and the wider area. For instance, it is possible to use flood storage areas for recreation, helping to contribute to the amenity provision for a development. They may also be used for wildlife, increasing habitat and biodiversity. In some circumstances, flood storage areas can be used for renewable energy technology such as wind power, hydro electric, solar farms and tidal turbines. This is well illustrated by the Long-term Initiatives for Flood-risk Environments (LifE) approach (www.lifeproject.info) to development, in which flood risk is managed through the creation of parks, gardens, public squares and wetlands all designed to form an integral part of new sustainable development. This approach, which was developed with funding from Defra as part of the making space for water programme, is illustrated in Figure 12.3.

Examples of a new village blue/green along the River Wandle in Hackbridge, Figure 12.4, and a tidal flood storage lagoon, Figure 12.5, along the River Arun in Littlehampton show how making space for water to store flood water could enhance the public realm with generous public spaces, recreation areas (on land and water), wildlife walks and new habitat, as well as providing space for renewable power generation through Ground Source Heat Pump Arrays, and Wind and Tidal Turbines respectively.

4.3 Designing buildings for flood risk

There are a number of building design improvements that can be used to reduce the effects of flooding. Different approaches can be implemented, depending on whether they are added to an existing building or constructed as part of a new building.

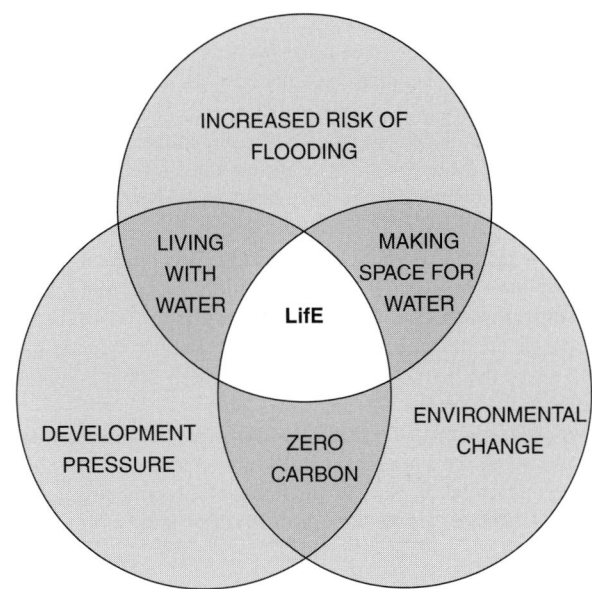

12.3 *LifE is an integrated design approach in which measures to make space for water also help reduce carbon emissions through sustainable (Zero Carbon, Passivhaus and Code Level 6) development*

There are four main approaches to tackling flood risk at a building level, Figure 12.6:

- Avoidance
- Resistance
- Resilience
- Floating

A coherent flood resilient masterplan may consist of a combination of the above building types, organised around urban landscape that uses soft and hard landscape that accumulatively mitigate flood risk across the site.

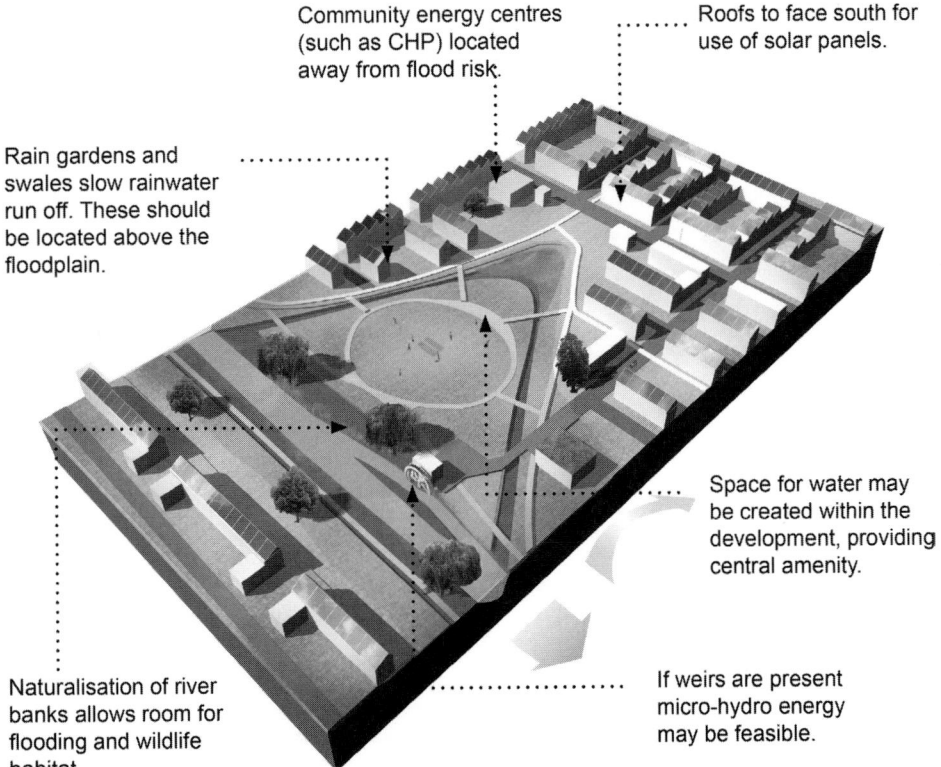

Community energy centres (such as CHP) located away from flood risk.

Roofs to face south for use of solar panels.

Rain gardens and swales slow rainwater run off. These should be located above the floodplain.

Space for water may be created within the development, providing central amenity.

Naturalisation of river banks allows room for flooding and wildlife habitat.

If weirs are present micro-hydro energy may be feasible.

12.4 *The 'village blue/green' provides a flexible informal recreation area, with landscaped hollow designed to regularly accommodate floodwater and slow the flow downstream (source: Baca Architects)*

4.4 Flood avoidance

Flood avoidance is the most usual building design measure with many examples of buildings on stilts or raised ground throughout the world.

For flood avoidance to be effective, the ground floor level of the building must be set above the design flood level, including an allowance for climate change and tolerance (freeboard).

- For residential units the floor level is typically required to be set above the 1 per cent (1 in 100) flood level + 300 mm (climate change allowance) + 300 mm (freeboard).
- For commercial units, the floor level is typically required to be set above the 5 per cent (1 in 20) flood level + 300 mm (climate change allowance) + 300 mm (freeboard).
- For residential car parking, the flood level is typically required to be set above the 1 per cent (1 in 100) flood level.
- For commercial car parking, the flood level is typically required to be set above the 5 per cent (1 in 20) flood level.

Though land raising may seem an obvious solution to reducing flood risk it is often not possible as raising the land would result in increasing the flood risk elsewhere. Where land raising is to be considered, the loss of flood storage would normally need to be compensated for by an area of excavation at the same level as the area of raising for it to be effective – this is referred to as level for level compensation. In areas with limited land level variation it is unlikely to be feasible.

Working with the natural topography of a site it may be possible to reduce the flood risk to areas by increasing the land level whilst compensating for the loss of flood storage by reducing levels elsewhere, see case study, Section 5.

Buildings may be elevated on stilts, columns or walls to raise the floor levels above the potential flood level. Buildings elevated on stilts or columns help to preserve space for floodwater where building raised on walls may still require compensation for loss of flood plain, unless there are adequate openings in the walls to allow water to pass through. An elevated building can result in

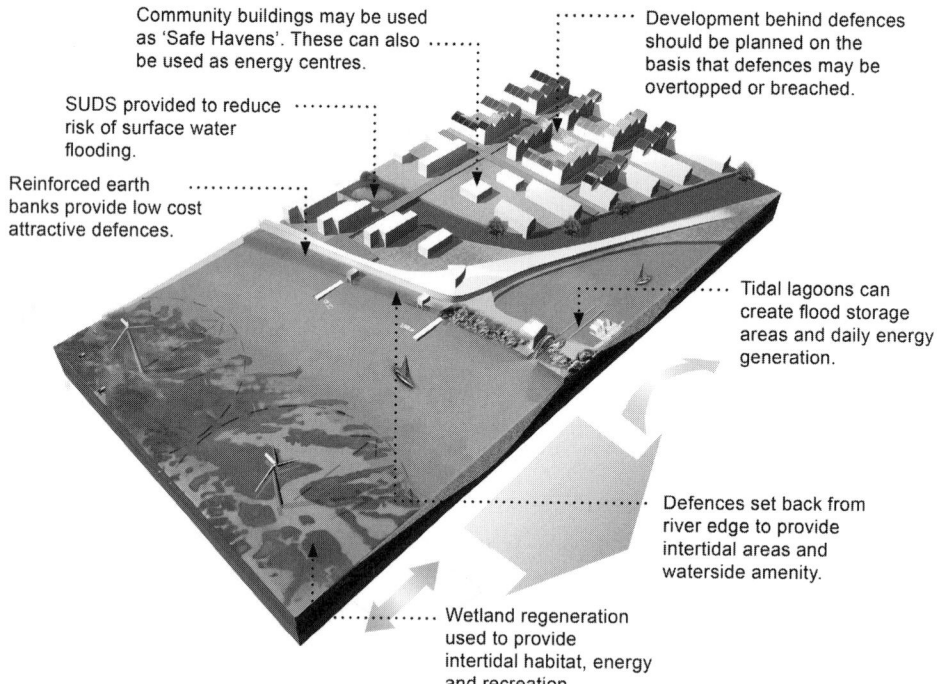

12.5 *Land at risk of flooding, could be elevated above future flood levels on spoil from the excavation of a new, 'tidal lagoon', flood storage area and wetlands (source: Baca Architects)*

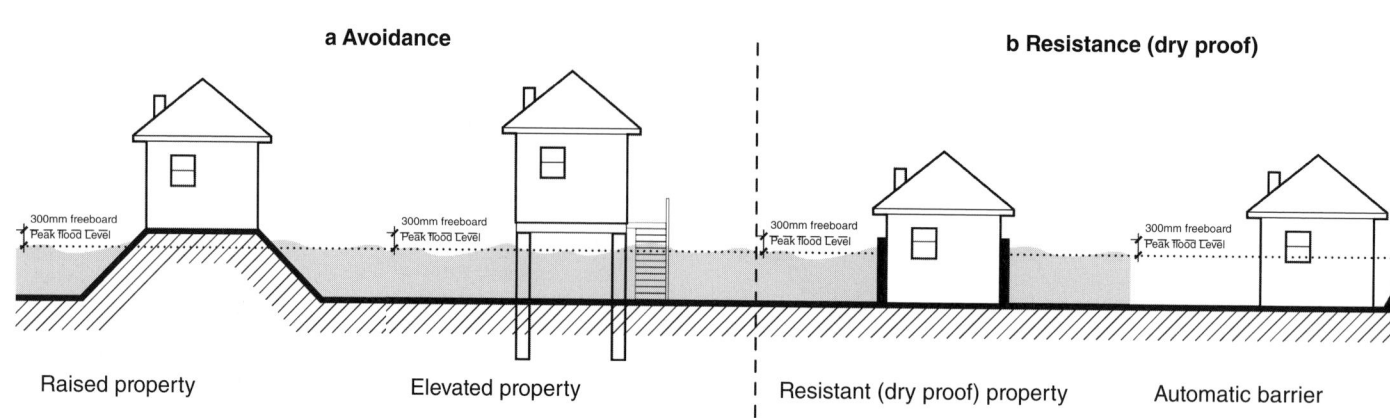

12.6 *Different building measures to manage flood risk (© Baca Architects)*

floor levels being set well above the ground level, requiring raised or stepped access routes, which may be at odds with level access for disabled users. It may also result in a disconnection between the floor and ground level, reducing natural surveillance of streets.

4.5 Flood resistance/dry proofing

Flood resistance and resilience measures are not normally acceptable for new buildings other than to manage residual flood risk (Figure 12.7). This is because it is safer to avoid flood risk rather than relying on flood defences to keep water out or allowing floodwater into a building that carries obvious health risks.

Flood resistance measures include flood defences, flood barriers, door guards and back flow drains with the purpose of preventing water from entering the property – hence keeping it dry.

Typically flood resistance measures are only effective for short duration shallow flooding (below 300 mm in depth or below 600 mm in depth depending on structural assessment). Tests have shown that floodwater may still infiltrate different building constructions designed to resist flooding though the duration of resistance may vary. There are examples of buildings designed to withstand greater depths of flooding, but these require heavy-duty water resisting construction such as tanking, waterproof concrete and steel flood doors.

For most cases it should be assumed that flood resistance measures will only be effective where predicted flood levels are no more than 300 mm above the surrounding ground level.

A flood proofing matrix is shown in Table II.

4.6 Flood resilience/wet proofing

Flood resilience measures or wet proofing involves constructing a building in such a way that although floodwater may enter the building, its impact is minimised, the structural integrity is maintained, and the time to clean up and use is minimised (Figure 12.8). It relies on using building materials that can survive being waterlogged without requiring repair or replacement according to the Communities and Local Government guidance *Improving the flood performance of new buildings*. Flood resilience measures are typically used where flood depths are greater than 600 mm.

12.7 *A new building at the BRE Innovation Park will show how different building techniques may be used to keep water out (resistance) as well as cope if water enters into the building (resilience)*

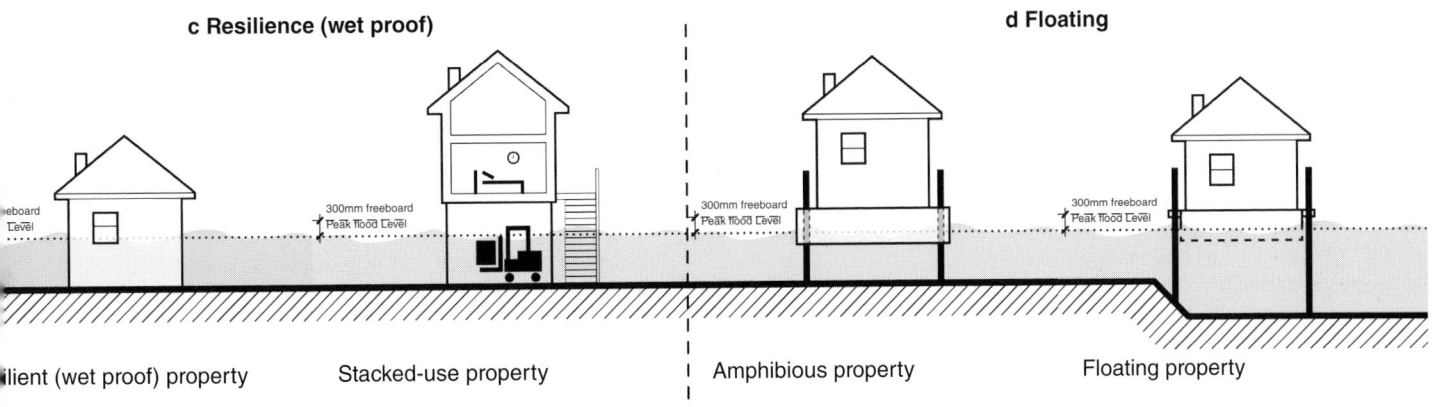

Table II Application of flood proofing measures, based on flood depth, velocity and construction types

Flood Proofing Matrix		Elevation on foundation walls	Elevation on Piers	Elevation on posts or columns	Elevation on piles	Relocation	Walls and levees	Flood walls and levees with closures	Dry flood proofing/ resistance	Wet flood proofing/ resilience
Flood Characteristics										
Depth	Shallow (<1m)*	✓	✓	✓	✓	✓	✓	✓	✓*	✓
	Moderate (1-2m)*	✓	✓	✓	✓	✓	✓	✓	×	✓
	Deep (>2m)*	✓	✓	✓	✓	✓	×	×	×	×
Velocity	Slow (<1m/s)	✓	✓	✓	✓	✓	✓	✓	✓	✓
	Moderate (1-2m/s)	✓	✓	✓	✓	✓	✓	✓	×	×
	Fast (>2m/s)	×	×	✓	✓	✓	×	×	×	×
Subject to rapid/flash flooding		×	✓	✓	✓	✓	✓	×	×	×
Subject to ice and debris flow		×	✓	✓	✓	✓	✓	×	×	×
Site Characteristics										
Location	Coastal floodplain	×	✓	✓	✓	✓	✓	×	×	×
	Riverine floodplain	✓	✓	✓	✓	✓	✓	✓	✓	✓
Soil type	Permeable	✓	✓	✓	✓	✓	×	×	×	✓
	Impermeable	✓	✓	✓	✓	✓	✓	✓	✓	✓
Building Characteristics										
Foundation	Slab	✓	✓	✓	✓	✓	✓	✓	✓	✓
	Sub-floor void	✓	✓	✓	✓	✓	✓	✓	✓	✓
	Basement**	✓	×	×	×	✓	✓	✓	×	×
Construction	Concrete/masonry	✓	✓	✓	×	✓	✓	✓	✓	✓
	Wood/other	✓	✓	✓	×	✓	✓	✓	×	×
Condition	Excellent to good	✓	✓	✓	✓	✓	✓	✓	✓	✓
	Fair to poor	×	×	×	×	×	✓	✓	×	×

*Note: that the levels within this international guidance differ from that of English National Guidance (advice should always be sought from an expert)
(Source: GFDRR and World Bank 2012, adapted from USACE)

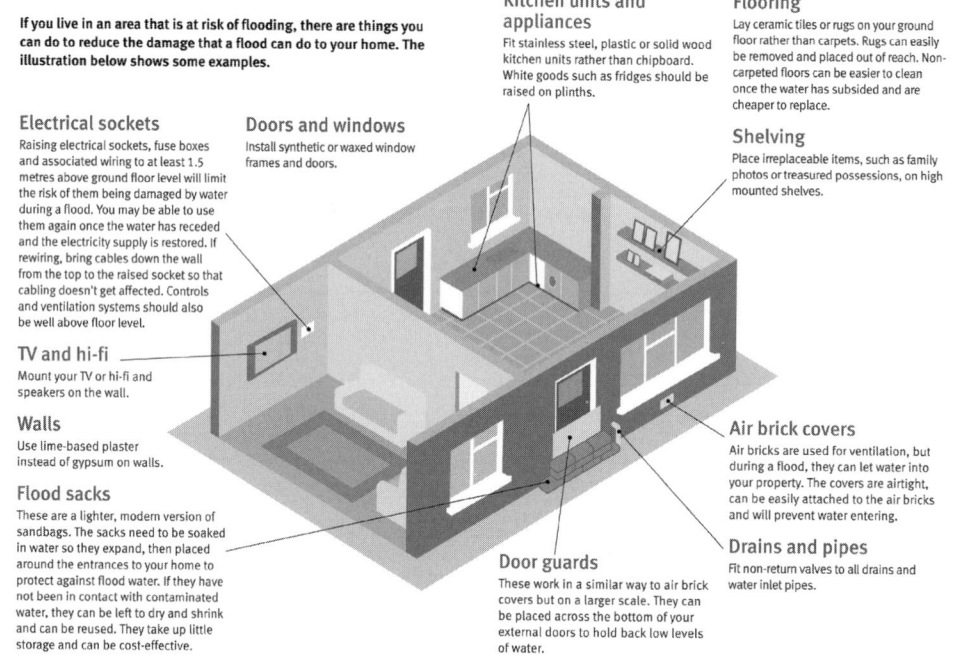

If you live in an area that is at risk of flooding, there are things you can do to reduce the damage that a flood can do to your home. The illustration below shows some examples.

Electrical sockets
Raising electrical sockets, fuse boxes and associated wiring to at least 1.5 metres above ground floor level will limit the risk of them being damaged by water during a flood. You may be able to use them again once the water has receded and the electricity supply is restored. If rewiring, bring cables down the wall from the top to the raised socket so that cabling doesn't get affected. Controls and ventilation systems should also be well above floor level.

TV and hi-fi
Mount your TV or hi-fi and speakers on the wall.

Walls
Use lime-based plaster instead of gypsum on walls.

Flood sacks
These are a lighter, modern version of sandbags. The sacks need to be soaked in water so they expand, then placed around the entrances to your home to protect against flood water. If they have not been in contact with contaminated water, they can be left to dry and shrink and can be reused. They take up little storage and can be cost-effective.

Doors and windows
Install synthetic or waxed window frames and doors.

Kitchen units and appliances
Fit stainless steel, plastic or solid wood kitchen units rather than chipboard. White goods such as fridges should be raised on plinths.

Flooring
Lay ceramic tiles or rugs on your ground floor rather than carpets. Rugs can easily be removed and placed out of reach. Non-carpeted floors can be easier to clean once the water has subsided and are cheaper to replace.

Shelving
Place irreplaceable items, such as family photos or treasured possessions, on high mounted shelves.

Air brick covers
Air bricks are used for ventilation, but during a flood, they can let water into your property. The covers are airtight, can be easily attached to the air bricks and will prevent water entering.

Drains and pipes
Fit non-return valves to all drains and water inlet pipes.

Door guards
These work in a similar way to air brick covers but on a larger scale. They can be placed across the bottom of your external doors to hold back low levels of water.

12.8 *Flood resilience measures (source: Environment Agency)*

Water resistance, impermeability, drying ability, rot avoidance, mould resistance and replacement are all key considerations for materials to provide resilience.

Resilience measures include:

- raise susceptible infrastructure above flood level (such as electric sockets and supply);
- non-return valves (fitted to drains);
- secure drainage (such as sealed drain covers and concrete man holes to prevent pollution and floatation);
- impervious/wash down materials (such as tiled floors, plastic doors, rendered masonry walls);
- solid core materials, (such as use of solid kitchen units instead of chipboard, or solid wall construction below potential flood levels);
- replaceable materials (such as horizontally fitting plasterboard where just the lowest boards can be replaced).

The purpose of these measures is to reduce the susceptibility of the building fabric to being inundated by water and if they are flooded to improve the ability to recover from inundation. Buildings need time to dry out thoroughly after being inundated to avoid the risk of mould, permanent damage and rot. This may be difficult with materials that form part of a composite structure and therefore solid materials or construction such as partitions may be preferable below flood levels.

In addition to the flood depth, the velocity of floodwater and the potential for it to carry debris should be considered as high velocity flows and debris impact have the potential to cause scour and structural damage to foundations and superstructure.

4.7 Floating or amphibious structures

Floating or amphibious structures are unlikely to be an option for managing flood risk in most cases due to the need to site the building in water, which is often a high flood risk area, incompatible with the vulnerability of the use.

- source controls/interception devices (such as green roofs and rain water harvesting);
- infiltration devices (such as permeable paving);
- retention and detention devices (such as ponds, below ground storm tanks);
- conveyance devices (used to transfer water);
- constructed wetlands.

The aim of source controls, such as green roofs or water butts, is to intercept and slow the run off rate of water before it reaches the ground and other drainage devices.

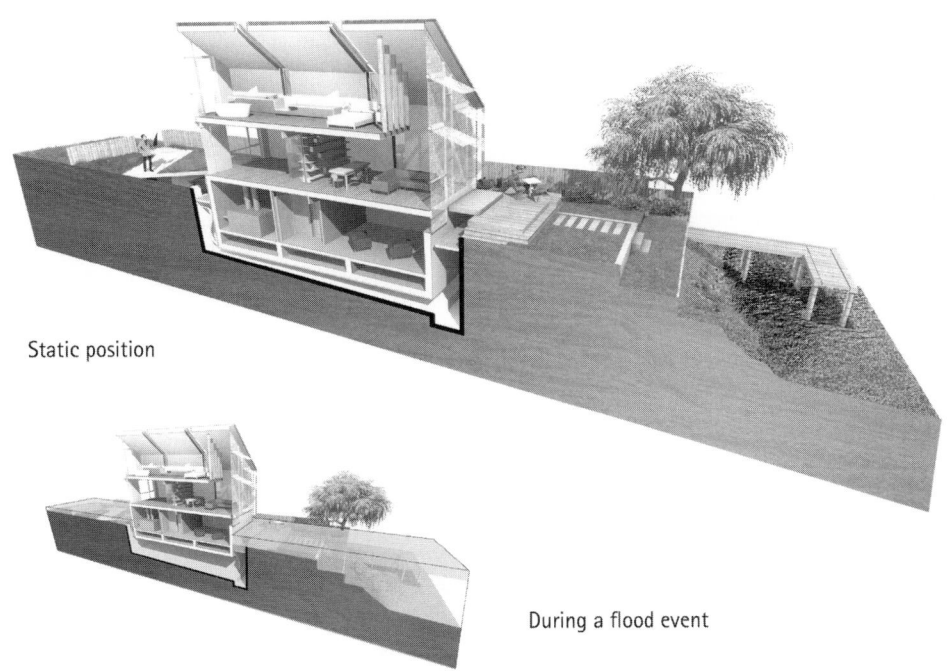

Static position

During a flood event

12.9 *Amphibious house design (source: © Baca Architects)*

A floating building is, typically, a lightweight structure, which rests on a buoyant base or foundation designed to rise and fall with the level of the water. The benefit of this form of construction is that it can be designed to cope with significant flood depths and can respond to variable flood levels, beneficial where there may be uncertainty in predictions.

An amphibious structure, Figure 12.9, is a floating building set on or within the ground. It can rest on the ground, only floating when the water level rises. These types of construction require careful assessment, design and engineering to provide sufficient resistance to flood flows, debris and manage services.

4.8 Safe access and egress

With all of these building types it is important to provide safe access and egress in the event of a flood. This is particularly relevant for emergency vehicles, which are likely to be called upon during times of flood, and it is a key planning requirement.

Safe access and egress is not required to be dry but it is required to be safe. The Defra document *Flood Risk Assessment Guidance for New Development* (Defra 2005) identifies conditions for creating safe access and egress into developments.

4.9 Sustainable Drainage Systems (SuDS)

In addition to flood resilience measures, it is also important to mitigate flood risk through drainage control. Sustainable Drainage Systems provide the means to manage rainwater run off so that it emulates natural drainage systems. The various devices can be summarised as:

The aim of infiltration devices, such as permeable paving and underground soakaways, is to facilitate infiltration of rainwater into the ground. A soakaway is typically a stone filled circular chamber, shallow linear trenches or perforate pipes depending on the depth of the groundwater and permeability of the ground.

Permeable paving may be used in parking areas or paths to allow infiltration into the ground or into below ground detention tanks.

It is important that pollution control measures are used to intercept contaminants from vehicles or other sources, before they have the potential to pollute groundwater. Filter strips may be used between parking areas to control run-off (Figure 12.10).

Retention and detention devices are storm water storage facilities such as ponds or below ground cellular storage devices, which detain water during a storm before releasing via a controlled outflow. They need to be designed to remain (predominantly) dry at other times to provide effective storage during a storm.

Conveyance devices, such as swales and filter strips, are channels (typically landscaped) that transfer water from one device into another such as the run-off from a roof into an infiltration pond.

Constructed wetlands, such as ponds and lakes, are neighbourhood and regional control measures that emulate the natural benefits of wetlands and are usually the last device in larger SuD systems.

Vegetated SuDS devices (such as green roofs, walls and planted swales) can also provide environmental benefits, such as cooling through evapotranspiration, habitat and visual enhancement. SuDS can enhance masterplanning through increasing the opportunity for landscaping, greater provision of amenity and better place making.

12.10 *A filter strip can be introduced between parking bays to manage run-off (© Baca Architects)*

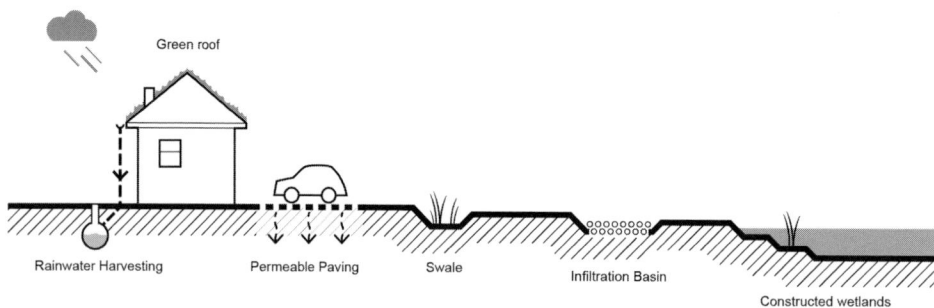

12.11 *Sustainable drainage options (© Baca Architects)*

A sustainable drainage system typically comprises a range of these devices, which in combination help to detain run-off and release it slowly into watercourses or to ground, Figure 12.11.

SuDS can include below ground drainage as well as above ground drainage solutions. In contaminated areas or in areas with poor SuDS, options often rely on storage rather than infiltration.

Water Sensitive Urban Design (WSUD) is a term that was established in Australia to describe the integration of water cycle management within the planning and urban realm. Components of this are similar to those used in sustainable drainage but expand water management beyond drainage. Good design and planning should integrate water management and at all levels of development.

There is much guidance on sustainable drainage systems available from CIRIA and from many technical suppliers. To determine the type and scale of system required it is important to carry out ground investigations to understand the type of soil and geology. It is also important to undertake drainage calculations to determine the storage required and run off rates.

5 CASE STUDY – DEAL GROUND
Design: Baca Architects

5.1 Context
The Deal Ground site is located on the eastern outskirts of Norwich, and on the western boundary of the Norfolk Broads. The site lies within 1000 m of the Railway Station and about a mile to the Cathedral in the city centre but is cut off from this route by the River Wensum. The site is bordered by both the River Wensum and the River Yare.

The site was previously used for storage, manufacture and most recently light industry and is therefore considered to be brownfield land. The site also contained an unmanaged County Wildlife Site - Carrow Abbey Marsh.

Baca Architects (working with a team of experts) were commissioned by Serruys Property to develop a masterplan for the redevelopment of the site that simultaneously managed flood risk.

5.2 Understanding flood risk
The main source of flood risk is from the rivers, Figure 12.12. They are tidally influenced at the site, but flood flows are dominated by fluvial effects. Surface water run-off from rainfall must also be considered. Due to the topography, this is limited to rainfall on the site and not run off from adjacent sites.

Environment Agency Flood Zone Maps indicated that the site lies within Flood Zone 2 and 3. A site specific Flood Risk Assessment was carried out. This involved on the ground topographical studies combined with LiDAR data where it was difficult to determine the land levels. 2D flood modeling was used to determine flood flow paths, water levels, duration, flood depths and velocities across the site.

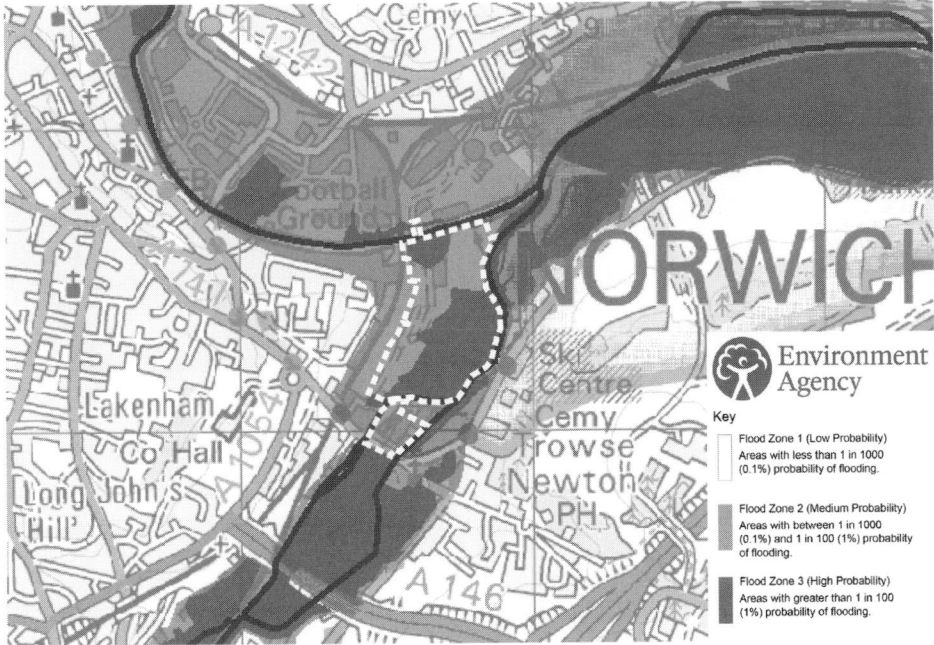

12.12 *Flood zones (source: Environment Agency)*

This indicated that:

- An area to the west of the site lies within Flood Zone 1.
- Approximately 37 per cent of the site lies within Flood Zone 2.
- Approximately 30 per cent of the site lies within Flood Zone 3a.
- Approximately 30 per cent of the site lies within Flood Zone 3b.

These flood zones were agreed with the Environment Agency and used to inform the choice of development.

5.3 Planning for flood risk (use and vulnerability)

A masterplan that 'worked with water' was conceived, Figure 12.13, in which the marsh would be extended between development on higher ground, allowing flood water to flow around and (in some cases) under the buildings.

Development was located in the areas of least risk – Flood Zone 2, with some development located in an area of Flood Zone 3a. The County Wildlife Site is located in Flood Zone 3b therefore there was no development proposed in these locations.

The residential use proposed would be considered appropriate in Flood Zone 2 but would be required to pass the Exception Test where located in Flood Zone 3a. The restaurants and shops proposed in areas of Flood Zone 3a would be considered appropriate. Because the site is subject to flood risk it required a detailed FRA to demonstrate that the development would be safe over its lifetime and not increase risk elsewhere.

The redevelopment of the site would provide a number of sustainability benefits to Norwich and the area, which meant that if the flood risk could be managed over the lifetime of the development without increasing risk elsewhere it would be appropriate to redevelop. These benefits include:

- improved transport infrastructure, through the provision of a new cycle route, part of the Sustrans, national cycle network, two new bridges and improved public transport;
- environmental gains through habitat generation;
- management and enhancement of the County Wildlife Site, with better access;
- increased flood storage;
- provision of housing, including affordable housing;
- access to a further redevelopment site;
- an exemplar development, sympathetic to and enhancing the surroundings.

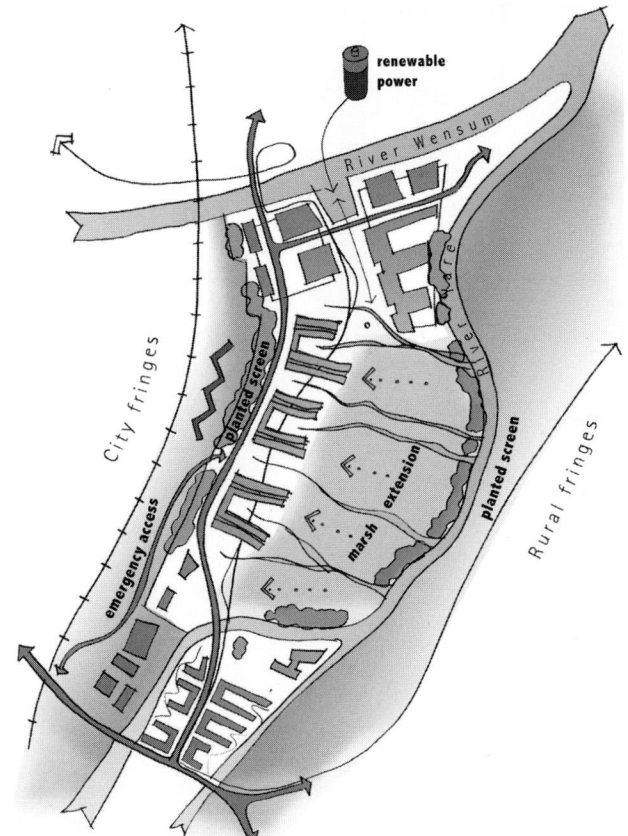

Concept Plan

12.13 *Concept plan (© Baca Architects)*

5.4 Reducing flood risk

Because flood flows overland were found to be slow the critical concern was ensuring that the development was located above the peak flood levels.

The flood levels were not the same across the site, and the Environment Agency provided design flood levels generally based

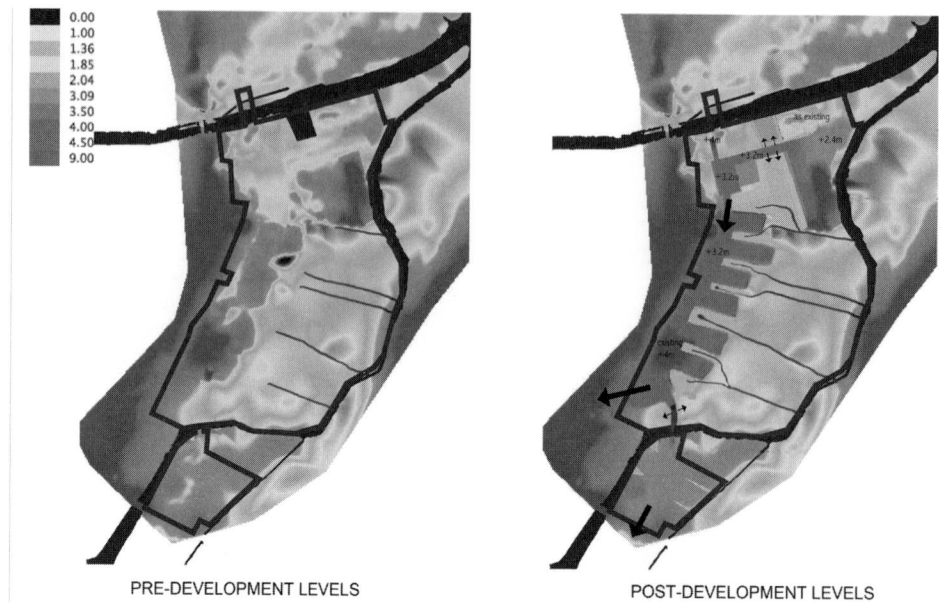

12.14 *Land level changes following development (source: Baca Architects & JBA Consulting)*

12.15 *Flood flows across the site during 1 in 1000 event (source: JBA consulting)*

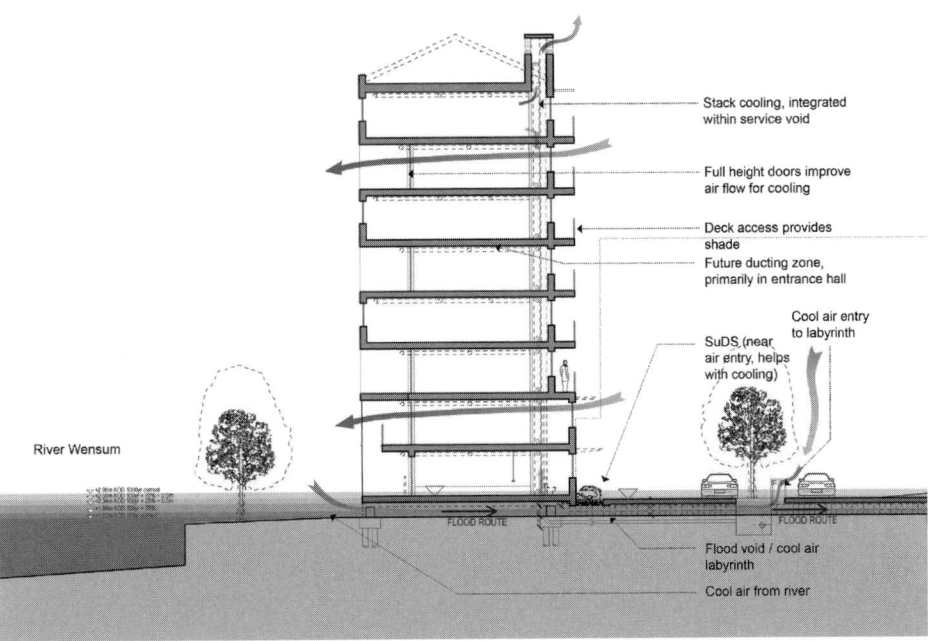

Stack cooling, integrated
within service void

Full height doors improve
air flow for cooling

Deck access provides
shade

Future ducting zone,
primarily in entrance hall

Cool air entry
to labyrinth

SuDS (near
air entry, helps
with cooling)

River Wensum

FLOOD ROUTE

FLOOD ROUTE

Flood void / cool air
labyrinth

Cool air from river

12.16 *Flood voids used for stack cooling (source: Baca Architects)*

upon the highest flood levels. Based on this guidance, the flood levels were as follows:

- 0.1% (1 in 1000) 3.09 m AOD
- 1% (1 in 100) + climate change 2.04 m AOD
- 1% (1 in 100) 1.85 m AOD
- 5% (1 in 20) 1.36 m AOD (for the May Gurney & middle of the Deal Ground), 1.24 m AOD (for the north of the Deal Ground).

The Environment Agency required the ground floor of the 'more vulnerable' residential uses to be located 300 mm above the 1 per cent (1 in 100) flood level including allowing for climate change, and the floors of the 'less vulnerable' commercial uses to be located 300 mm above the 5 per cent (1 in 20) flood level including allowing for climate change.

5.5 Design approach
The entire development adopts a non-defensive approach to flood risk management – meaning that there are no defences.

A combination of design measures has been used to create a comprehensive and an integrated flood risk management plan. These include:

- land raising, particularly below access roads;
- this is compensated by excavation of areas of corresponding height, increasing the overall flood storage, Figure 12.14;
- elevated building construction, raised on stilts, to the north of the site;
- flood resilient construction, elsewhere to cope with the risk of a flood exceeding the 1 in 100 + climate change level;
- sustainable drainage systems;
- safe access and escape through raised routes;
- flood warning and evacuation plan.

These measures have been integrated into the design, such that additional flood storage areas double as shared gardens, and local play areas. They have been designed between development areas to provide landscape features and separation between units. Two dimensional flood modeling was used to test the impact of the development on surrounding flood levels and to refine the scheme. Modeling during a theoretical 1 in 1000 probability flood, Figure 12.15 shows areas where the flood water passes beneath the buildings in flood voids.

The buildings and car parking along the River Wensum waterfront were all elevated without raising land levels to maintain the flood storage. In the following Climate Adaptive Neighbourhoods research carried out for the Technology Strategy Board, the cooling capacity of using the void beneath the buildings, Figure 12.16, to manage increased temperatures was calculated. In combination with a heavy building construction (also beneficial in providing flood resilience) and shading devices was found to tackle the overheating risk for future climate predictions up to 2080.

Infiltration systems would have been inappropriate because of the superficial geology on the site, high water table and previous uses on parts of the site. The system developed, Figure 12.17, combined the following:

- green roofs to apartment blocks;
- cellular storage below pedestrian streets;
- a 'rain square' detention basin;
- filter strips along road edges and parking areas to intercept run off;
- swales to channel water into drainage ditches;
- constructed wetlands in the form of extensions to the ditch system in the marsh.

This provides a robust system through the underground storage facilities combined with the environmental benefits of planted systems. An open storage facility within the proposed 'rain square', creates a demonstration of sustainable drainage systems in operation and educational facility, Figure 12.18.

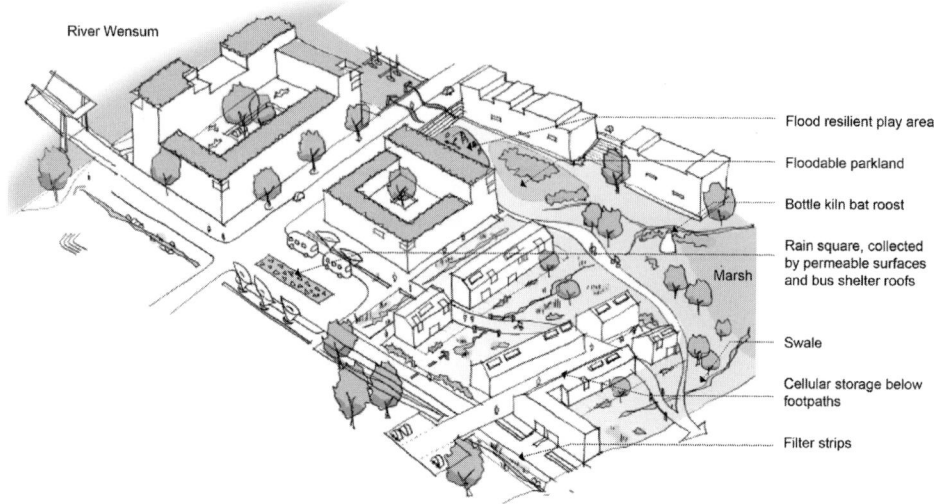

River Wensum

Flood resilient play area

Floodable parkland

Bottle kiln bat roost

Rain square, collected
by permeable surfaces
and bus shelter roofs

Marsh

Swale

Cellular storage below
footpaths

Filter strips

12.17 *Sustainable Drainage System (SuDS)*

12.18 *Development located around an extension of the marsh (source: Atelier Pro)*

6 BIBLIOGRAPHY

Baca Architects with BRE for Defra (2009) *LifE handbook Long-Term Initiatives for Flood-Risk Environments,* IHS BRE Press.

Baca Architects with BRE for Defra (2009) *LifE project*, IHS BRE Press.

Barker, R. (2011) *Water strategies*, RIBA Sustainability Hub.

Barker, R. and Coutts, R. (2015) *Aquatecture*, RIBA Publishing.

Defra (2005) *Flood risk assessment guidance for new development*, Defra.

GFDRR and World Bank (2012) *Cities and Flooding: A Guide to Integrated Flood Risk Management for the 21st Century and A Summary for Policy Makers*, GFDRR and World Bank.

Improving the flood performance of new buildings, Department for Communities and Local Government, London, 2007

Planning Policy Statement 25: Development and Flood Risk – Practice Guide, Department for Communities and Local Government, London, 2009

Woods Ballard, B. (2007) *SuDS manual*, Ciria.

Websites

Environment Agency's e-learning programme http://www.ioutsidedesign.co.uk

RIBA Designing for flood risk www.architecture.com

Susdrain www.susdrain.org

13 Crime prevention design

Nick Hughes

Nick Hughes is a Crime Prevention Design Advisor at Avon and Somerset Police

KEY POINTS:

- *Designing out crime is not an exact science; rather, it involves weighing up factors designed to minimise opportunities for criminals*
- *Consider Victim (or target), Offender and Location*
- *Designers of buildings should ask themselves: 'If I were to break into this building, how would I do it?'*

Contents

1 Introduction
2 Legislation and primary planning policy
3 Secured by Design
4 The principles of Crime Prevention Through Environmental Design (CPTED)
5 Access and movement
6 Surveillance
7 Layout and land use
8 Defensible space
9 Management
10 Parking
11 CCTV
12 Planting
13 Lighting
14 Security hardware
15 Planning companion guides and supporting documents

1 INTRODUCTION

CPTED is not an exact science; it is more a series of considerations that need to be weighed up in order to come up with a design that minimises the opportunity for criminals. CPTED can work on all levels from an individual property to a whole town or city. Whilst there is no definitive 'right answer', it is easy to spot the 'wrong answers' where CPTED has not been considered.

The 'Problem Analysis Triangle' explains why crime occurs. At the three apexes of the triangle are 'Victim (or target), Offender and Location.' It is the coincidence of these three in time and space that allows for a crime to take place. By working on the location, crime can be reduced even if there is still an offender and target present, such as a laptop by an open window. For example, a well-designed development with well-used and defined access routes, together with good surveillance from the houses opposite and the use of defensible space outside of the open window, might mean the offender feels s/he was less likely to get away with stealing the laptop.

Good CPTED has been proven to reduce the incidence of burglary, robbery and other crimes as well as anti-social behaviour (ASB). A 'Secured by Design' refurbishment of an affordable housing scheme in Glasgow resulted in a 75 per cent reduction in burglary (figures from Strathclyde Police). ASB manifests itself in many ways such as graffiti, fly tipping, drug taking, (underage) alcohol consumption and dog fouling. Good CPTED can reduce ASB and crime significantly, working as the antithesis of the 'Broken Windows Theory' (Wilson and Kelling), which can then lead to the increased legitimate usage of an area; this in turn increases surveillance and can create a sense of pride in an area and a stronger community spirit. This 'upward spiral' can continue, with safety and increased legitimate usage both positively influencing each other.

Conversely, poor design can create an environment in which those who commit crime and ASB feel at home. Legitimate users are then less likely to use the area and ASB and crime become the accepted norm, which in turn can lead to a downward spiral in which the seriousness of incidents can increase and go unchallenged by the local community.

Central to good CPTED is the early involvement of the local Crime Prevention Design Advisor (CPDA). CPDA is the more recent term for an Architectural Liaison Officer (ALO) but the difference is purely semantic. The local CPDA will have access to the local crime statistics and can speak to police colleagues to ascertain the specific problems in a given area. The introduction of various websites has made these statistics more accessible for the public but designers should not underestimate the advantage of having access to the knowledge possessed by local police officers. The term 'site-specific' is seldom more important than in the realm of CPTED. While good CPTED should be used regardless of the area, the level of security deemed necessary will vary greatly. Heights of fences, the location of parking provision and the required security ratings of locks and other hardware will all vary with location.

Sociological factors have a massive impact on crime rates and safety in a given area. What may be deemed necessary in terms of security will change with the demographics of the location; the level of required security depends on the likelihood of a crime happening in a given area.

In the world of policing, CPTED and crime reduction are closely related. Crime reduction has traditionally been split into 10 principles and there is overlap between these and the principles of CPTED. Indeed, one of the 10 principles is 'Environmental Design' – this essentially means CPTED. The most important distinction between the two is that CPTED is pro-active whereas crime reduction is reactive. Prevention is better than cure and a consideration at design stage of the themes to be discussed in this chapter can obviate retro-fit measures such as alley-gates, razor wire and the overreliance on CCTV. Having anticipated the potential crimes and ASB that may occur in and around a development, good CPTED makes the built environment less conducive for crime.

It used to be thought that by making the commission of offences harder in a certain location, crime, especially burglary, would be displaced to neighbouring areas. Research has disproved this assumption and there can even be a 'diffusion of benefits' (manifested as a reduction in burglary) to neighbouring areas. Research also shows that burglars tend to operate within a certain radius of their home and, when presented with less opportunity locally due to good CPTED, are not always willing to travel further afield to commit crime.

Good CPTED can make developments more sustainable. Taking the definition from *Our Common Future* (1987), sustainable development is 'development that meets the needs of the present without compromising the ability of future generations to meet their own needs'. By reducing the opportunity for crime, CPTED aims to create safe and secure environments where, other factors allowing, residents can enjoy living and where community spirit can flourish.

2 LEGISLATION AND PRIMARY PLANNING POLICY

- Circular 5/94 made crime reduction a material consideration in planning.
- Section 17 of the Crime and Disorder Act 1998 states: 'Without prejudice to any other obligation imposed upon it, it shall be the duty of each authority to which the section applies to exercise its various functions with due regard to the likely effect of the exercise of those functions on, and the need to do all it reasonably can to prevent, crime and disorder in its area.' The Local Authority, Police Authority and Fire Authority are included under this.
- Planning Policy Statement 1 (2005) states that design policies should ensure that developments, 'create safe and accessible environments where crime and disorder or fear of crime does not undermine quality of life or community cohesion'.
- Planning Policy Statement 3 states that the shared vision of the local planning authorities should develop design policies aimed at 'Creating places, streets and spaces which meet the needs of people, are visually attractive, safe, accessible, functional, inclusive, have their own distinctive identity and maintain and improve local character'.
- Planning Policy Statement 4 states: 'Local planning authorities should manage the evening and night-time economy in centres, taking account of and complementing the local authority's Statement of Licensing Policy and the promotion of the licensing objectives under the Licensing Act 2003. Policies should: set out the number and scale of leisure developments they wish to encourage taking account of their potential impact, including the cumulative impact, on the character and function of the centre, anti-social behaviour and crime, including considering security issues raised by crowded places, and the amenities of nearby residents.'

3 SECURED BY DESIGN

The term Secured by Design (SBD) is owned by the Association of Chief Police Officers (ACPO) and is the corporate title for a group of national police projects focusing on the design and security for new and refurbished homes, commercial premises and car parks as well as the acknowledgement of quality security products and crime prevention projects. It contains two key elements:

- Part 1 – Layout and design
- Part 2 – Physical security

The local CPDA administers the developments that apply and ultimately decides if developments have reached the required standard. Developers can apply for compliance with both parts or just with Part 2. Early involvement of the local CPDA is vital and officers should be consulted at all stages from initial design through to handover to the end user.

4 THE PRINCIPLES OF CPTED

The principles overlap and it is difficult to neatly categorise all considerations. Other CPDAs may choose to put the principles into different categories although there is a general consensus over the themes and considerations outlined here. This is why the principles should all be considered together when designing a development.

5 ACCESS AND MOVEMENT

'Safer Places' defines the ideal as 'places with well-defined routes, spaces and entrances that provide for convenient movement without compromising safety'. The word 'permeability' is used to define the ease with which someone may move through an area, whether on foot or in a vehicle. The number of roads/paths and the ways in which they interconnect are at the heart of this issue. Due to the factors mentioned below, cul-de-sacs can prove to be very safe places to live providing that there is only one way in and out, and there are no paths or alleys leading out of the end. Cul-de-sacs with large numbers of houses or networks of cul-de-sacs leading off each other also work to counteract the inherent safety of the design.

Considerations in this topic are:

- Are all of the routes necessary? To and from where does it provide access, and is this access needed? The higher the number of routes, the fewer the average number of users for each route. A large part of personal safety is avoiding quiet routes so increasing the number of footpaths will inevitably result in some of them being underused and therefore potentially less safe. A balance needs to be struck between the need for easy movement and over-permeability. An excess of routes means that a criminal has a variety of escape routes and can come and go to the scene of a crime easily without passing the same house more than once. As the criminal does not want to be spotted or to arouse suspicion, the anonymity afforded by a large choice of exits suits their needs.
- Do the access routes divide users of different types? Having footpaths alongside roads rather than separated from them allows for more passive surveillance of the path by road users, thus (in theory) making them safer.
- Has access to the back of the property been minimised? The majority of burglaries involve entry from the rear, therefore public access should be restricted. Different research quotes the percentage of burglaries that involve rear access as anywhere from 55 to 80 per cent. The proliferation of alley-gating schemes across the country has been necessary due to the large number of older estate designs that incorporated rear lanes, often for coal delivery. Many of these lanes and alleys are not used by the residents but instead provide burglars with secluded and unobserved access to the rear of houses.
- Are the footpaths designed with safety in mind? Where they are not adjacent to roads, paths should be wide, straight and well over-looked. They should ideally be at least 3 m wide with a 2 m verge or mown strip on either side. There should be no possible hiding places, therefore trees or shrubs should be set well back from the path. Subways and underpasses should be avoided where possible. If this is not possible, they should be as short and wide as possible, well lit, with chamfered entrances.
- How legible and easy to navigate are the routes? Locals and visitors should be able to find their way easily. Signs should be clear and the routes should be easy to understand.

6 SURVEILLANCE

Surveillance can be split into two categories: formal and informal. Formal surveillance means a person or system is specifically there to keep watch on an area. A CCTV system or a security guard would be an example of this. Informal, or 'natural', surveillance is that which occurs as people go about their everyday business. People have not been asked or employed to keep watch but they oversee nearby people and places merely by their presence.

Sociological factors play a large role. The principle of safety through surveillance relies on the assumption that it acts as a deterrent because people who witness a crime may intervene or call the police. In reality, people may choose to turn a blind eye; just because a place is well populated does not necessarily make it safe. A crowded street with lots of people in close proximity may be the ideal environment for a pick-pocket, for example. Surveillance should therefore be seen as a vital part in the overall design rather than as a panacea.

The main considerations here are:

- Do blank walls face the public realm? All aspects of buildings fronting the public realm should have windows. A commonly used term for this is 'active frontages'. Windows are the obvious ways to offer the chance for surveillance and even if it is unlikely that someone may be looking out, a window may deter a criminal as there is at least a chance he may be seen. In order to generate the maximum amount of surveillance, thought should be given to the use of the room containing the window. The chance of seeing something from a bed/bathroom is lower than from a sitting room or kitchen. Frosted glass would also indicate that the room is likely to be a bathroom and therefore being observed is less likely.

- Is parking overlooked? Surveillance over parking is crucial unless the car park is secure with good access control. The issues with parking are discussed in their own section.
- Does planting reduce surveillance? Trees and bushes can block lines of sight (for CCTV cameras as well as for people) and can also provide hiding places. Careful thought should be given to the location of planting and to the maximum growth heights. What may start as a low shrub may grow into a large barrier to surveillance and a climbing aid for criminals. Some trees have high canopies that allow clear lines of sight underneath. Canopy heights should be no lower than 2 metres from the ground. Together with the use of shrubs with a maximum growth height of 1 metre, such trees still allow for a window of surveillance between 1 and 2 metres.
- How will it look in the dark? Lighting must also be considered when discussing surveillance. If the designer wants an area to be visible 24/7, then it must be lit to an appropriate standard.

7 LAYOUT AND LAND USE

Building type and usage, together with the nature of the boundaries between them and how they interact with each other and with the intervening spaces, are all vital considerations in good CPTED. The land uses and spaces within a development should all be considered together rather than fitting in the 'less important' (often meaning less profitable) features in the remaining space regardless of their suitability, as is often done with playgrounds or public open space.

Consider:

- How compatible are neighbouring uses? Consider whether segregating or mixing land use would be beneficial. There are pros and cons to each choice and consideration of local context is therefore important. Segregating uses might mean that traffic and noise associated with businesses do not disturb residents; but this may mean that there would be no local residents to act as a deterrent to commercial burglars overnight.
- Has the impact of possible 'crime generators' been considered? Crime generators comprise built environment elements that can act to increase crime. Out-of-scale facilities such as large shopping centres can have a detrimental effect on the local area. The increased traffic and daytime population of these areas can bring associated crime problems which work against the fostering of a local community spirit. 'Honey pots' are another potential crime generator. These are facilities such as pubs, takeaways or convenience stores that encourage people to congregate and loiter in an area, thus potentially causing ASB and disturbance to local residents. Care should be taken when deciding where to position such places within a development so as to minimise disruption while maximising legitimate usage. Consider grouping them together to minimise the proliferation of negative impacts.
- How many faces of a building front the public realm? The number of such faces should be minimised to improve security and reduce access. For residential properties, it is generally safer to have gardens flanked by other gardens, with just the front of the property facing the public realm. Side access should be gated as close to the building line as possible.
- What boundary treatment option has been chosen? Using the 'onion peeling' principle of crime reduction, intruders should be stopped as far from the interior of the building as possible. Rather than letting people have access to the shell of the building itself, stopping them at the boundary is preferable. The standard height of boundaries to the rear and side of residential properties is 1.8 metres; local crime statistics may suggest higher boundaries are required. Gates should be the same height as the boundary to either side. There are many options for boundary treatments:

o Wooden fencing is cheap but can be flimsy and lack longevity. If using featherboard fencing, ensure that the horizontal rails are on the inside to avoid creating a makeshift ladder for intruders. The addition of a trellis to the top of fencing adds height and acts as deterrent as it breaks noisily if climbed. Thorny plants trained along a trellis are a further deterrent.
o Walls are sturdy but can attract graffiti. Consider using coping stones or angled bricks on the top to deny handholds to those trying to climb in. Low walls at the front of houses may be used as seats so consider angled bricks or another topping to prevent this.
o Hedges can be cheap and attractive but may require maintenance and could potentially be breached using secateurs. Some thorny varieties can provide excellent protection.
o Railings and metal fences allow surveillance and can be very strong but can look too imposing or institutional. Weldmesh or expanded metal fencing is generally considered to be a preferable option to 'pallisade' style fencing.

8 DEFENSIBLE SPACE

This term, coined by Oscar Newman, is a fundamental concept of CPTED. Defensible space describes the area over which one feels a sense of ownership or responsibility, whether individual or collective. At the micro scale, this may be a back garden. At the macro scale this may be a park that is part of the identity of a city of which the city's inhabitants are proud. The theory is that if an individual or group has (or feel they have) ownership and responsibility for an area, then someone who does not share this (perceived) ownership stands out and is less welcome – especially if misbehaving. People feel the right to challenge others who do not belong in their defensible space.

By clearly defining space and giving it a use and ownership, those who own it are more likely to take care of it, especially if that group is small.

Front gardens are an example of defensible space. There is an implied permission to access the front door to deliver a letter but no right-minded person would argue that they had the right to sit therein to eat their lunch. Contrast this with houses that front directly on to the pavement. Members of the public have a free right of access right up to the building line and the resident could not legitimately ask pedestrians to move.

Blocks of flats have traditionally had undefined areas of public space between them, over which residents have no control. Demarcating that space and assigning it to different blocks would be a way of improving control in the hope that residents would take care of it if they felt it was theirs. Whilst this does not always happen in practice, it is usually an improvement on any indistinct space that existed previously. Linking back to the idea of anonymity mentioned in the section on Access and Movement, criminals are more likely to be denied anonymity and to feel that they stand out in an area with clear ownership over which someone obviously takes pride.

The boundaries to such space need not be high and may comprise merely a line of low plants or a change of texture/colour of the pavement or road. A sign may suffice or a high fence may be needed. The main principle is that it becomes clear to the outsider that this space is not for free roaming.

Points to consider are:

- Is there a buffer between the private and public realm?
- Is the intended use for each area clear, such as a car park, playground, garden etc.?

- Are the boundaries between the different areas clear? Could anyone reasonably claim they thought they were in a fully public area when they were not?
- How many people 'own' or have shared responsibility for a space? The higher the number, the lower the sense of individual responsibility felt by each member of the group (in theory).
- Has the appropriate boundary been chosen? Does it need to be visually permeable or would a solid wall or fence be better? How high should it be? Could the boundary be symbolic rather than a physical barrier?
- Have local people been consulted and involved in the design of areas for their use? Consultation can help to foster a feeling of ownership among users; this approach has had particular success for youth facilities. Community murals are another example of where involving local people in a project can help to engender pride in the result. Murals are often left relatively graffiti-free in comparison to nearby blank walls.

9 MANAGEMENT

Good CPTED should ensure that a new development will deter criminal activity. If, however, no thought is given to ongoing maintenance and management then design work may go to waste as the area deteriorates over time. Linking back to the 'broken windows theory', quickly addressing minor issues can prevent them becoming serious as it sends out a clear message as to what will be tolerated in the area. In order to be sustainable, ongoing management must be considered. Points to consider are:

- If management is needed, who will pay for it? Will a residents' committee or management company be needed?
- What quality are the materials, products and finishes? Consider how long everything should last. Using cheaper products may eventually lead to problems.
- Will plants need maintenance such as cutting and watering? Is there access for maintenance vehicles.
- Will roads be adopted? If not, then there are many issues to consider such as lighting, road repairs, refuse collection etc.
- Are there sufficient bins to minimise littering, thus preventing excessive street cleaning?

10 PARKING

The best CPTED option is to accept parking as part of the design challenge and to make appropriate allowance for the safe and secure parking of vehicles. Individual integral garages tend to be the safest, followed by 'in-curtilage' parking (i.e. on a drive/parking space on the residential plot), on-street parking visible from the house, followed by remote car parks. In the case of the last option, gated parking courts can vastly increase the security. It should be borne in mind, however, that if people park in a rear court, they tend to enter the house from the rear for convenience; this often means rear garden gates are left unlocked and the back of house becomes used as the front.

Convenience plays a big role in people's decision of where to park; few people want to walk far to their car. This can clearly be seen at work in many newer estates where parking courts are ignored in favour of 'fly parking' in front of houses on roads not designed to accommodate it. Consider:

- What type of parking (on-street, parking court etc.) should you select? A mixture of types may work best and will depend on many things including topography, the likely occupant and proximity of local services.
- Is the parking option safe and convenient? If it is not both of these things then many will choose not to use it.
- Are the spaces allocated or not? Research by Jenks and Noble (1996) indicates that more spaces are needed if a high number of them are allocated.

- If not parked in garages, can residents' cars be seen from houses? Trees and shrubs can hinder surveillance. Car ports are often a 'worst of both worlds' option; they do not allow for surveillance yet are not secure and can act as impromptu shelters.
- Is the car park lit to appropriate standards (BS 5489 and BS EN 13201)? Lighting helps with surveillance and makes people using the car park feel safer.
- Is the car park easy to navigate with separate spaces for vehicles and pedestrians? Clear signage and different ground colours can be useful in this regard.
- If the car park is underground, could it be a target for terrorism? Counter-terrorism security advisors (CTSAs, contactable through the local constabulary) can advise on these issues. Vehicle borne explosive devices are even more lethal if detonated beneath a building rather than outside it. The use of the building above (e.g. as government offices) or the potential for large numbers of casualties (e.g. under a shopping centre or stadium) may indicate a higher vulnerability and necessitate 'hostile vehicle mitigation' or mean that an underground car park is not suitable.
- Is CCTV necessary?

11 CCTV

Per capita, there are more CCTV cameras in the UK than in any other country in the world. As the UK is not the safest country in the world, it follows that CCTV is not the answer to all problems of security. It does have an important part to play in improving security but should not be relied on in isolation. The single most important question is 'Why is the system there?' If designers cannot answer this question, they should ask why CCTV is being installed. An 'Operational Requirement' should be the starting point for a new system. Many systems provide images of poor quality and of no use for investigating crime. Many also do not comply with the Data Protection Act. CCTV may act as a deterrent but to be effective in this regard, someone should be watching the pictures live and be in a position to call the police. A well-designed system considered at design stage can be an excellent crime reduction tool.

Consider the following:

- Will images be monitored or will they merely be looked at retrospectively if something occurs?
- Are fixed cameras sufficient or are 'pan, tilt, zoom (PTZ)' cameras needed? PTZ cameras would be more suited to a monitored system, enabling an operator to track a person/vehicle.
- How many frames per second (FPS) will each camera record? Twenty-five FPS is broadcast standard. The higher the number, the smoother the image transition and the lower chance of missing something. All of the images need to be stored and the higher the frame rate, the more storage is required. Multiply the frame rate by the number of cameras by the amount of time the images are stored for (usually 31 days) and data storage requirements quickly mount.
- How close-up does the image need to be? 'Identification quality' images used to secure convictions usually require the person to fill the frame. This means that only a small field of view is covered by the camera. If the purpose of the camera is merely to see if someone is present in a part of a site, then a much larger field of view will suffice. Designers must know what they want from each camera.
- Does the camera need to function in all light conditions?
- Can images be exported easily, e.g. to a disc for police after an incident?

12 PLANTING

Planting can hinder or help a CPDA. Again, this should be part of the design process rather than considered as an after-thought. Consider:

- Will the plant block surveillance, street light or a CCTV camera? Remember: maximum 1 metre growth height for shrubs and minimum 2 metre canopy height for trees.
- Is the species suitable for the location? What size and shape will it be when fully grown?
- Will it act as a climbing aid? Expensive fences can be made redundant by running them alongside an easily climbable tree.
- Will the plant offer a hiding place?
- Will the plant require ongoing maintenance and who will pay for this?
- Can thorny plants be used to enhance security, especially around boundaries? Species such as berberis, pyracantha and brambles all help deter intruders.
- Can shrubs be used to help create buffer zones? Low planting against a wall helps keep people a certain distance away so could prevent access for graffiti. It could also reduce access to a vulnerable ground floor window.
- Can planting be used as a means of marking out (defensible) space? A line of low shrubs may stop people cutting across the corner of an unfenced front garden.

13 LIGHTING

The CPDA can provide some advice but a qualified lighting engineer will be needed for developments of any significant size. Good lighting has been proven to reduce the fear of crime but has a less proven effect on actual crime. Reducing fear of crime can, however, lead to increased legitimate use of an area, which can in turn make the area safer. Lighting facilitates surveillance and can be essential for CCTV and road safety.

Footpaths should be lit to the same standard as the adjacent road so that pedestrians are not in shadow. Uniformity is vital and lighting schemes should achieve an even spread of light so as to avoid pooling and shadowing, unless there is a specific reason not to. To work out the uniformity, divide the average lux into the minimum lux and express this as a percentage; 25 per cent is the minimum; 40 per cent and above is the usual aim. Lighting should be in accordance with BS EN 13201 and guidance on lighting design is given in BS 5489.

Points to consider are:

- Why is lighting needed? If the area or building gets no use during the hours of darkness then what is the use in lighting it? It may just facilitate criminal activity. If no one can overlook the area, no increased surveillance is facilitated by the lighting.
- Has light pollution been minimised? The light should be trained to where it is needed and prevented from spilling. 'Security' lights activated by PIR sensors can irritate neighbours and dazzle road users.
- How will the light be activated? Some turn on automatically in low lights, whereas others are activated using a switch or a PIR sensor. Energy efficient lights illuminated all night are the preferred security option over PIR-activated types and are usually cheaper to run than bright lights that turn on and off in reaction to movement.
- What type of 'bulb' will be used? High pressure sodium, metal halide and LEDs are all options. The 'colour' of the light is important. Clear daylight is represented as 100 on the colour rendering index and allows for excellent differentiation between colours. Low pressure sodium on the other hand gives a very orange light under which many colours appear similar.

- What housing will be used and at what height? Bollard lighting can be vulnerable to vandalism, can be a reversing hazard and can fail to illuminate the faces of anyone approaching; it therefore becomes difficult to judge if people appear friendly or not.

14 SECURITY HARDWARE

The 'Secured by Design' scheme goes into great detail on this topic. The 'New Homes 2010' document is the guide used by CPDAs. Much hard CPTED work can be negated by fitting inferior hardware. Doors, windows, gates, fences and the locks and bolts used to secure them are essential elements of a development. Compliance with Part 2 of SBD is all about using the right hardware and this alone can hugely reduce the risk of burglary.

If additional security is needed such as roller shutters, then it is easier and cheaper to design this in at the start rather than installing them later. Other design features may assist the burglar in bypassing hardware. Walls, porches, flat roofs etc. may facilitate access to first floor windows that are more likely to be left open or unlocked. Designers should imagine how they would break into the building they are designing.

15 PLANNING COMPANION GUIDES AND SUPPORTING DOCUMENTS

Below is a list of reference material. This list draws from the introduction to the booklet *The Compendium of Crime Prevention and Reduction in the Planning System* compiled by Thames Valley Police (http://www.thamesvalley.police.uk/compendium-intro.pdf). The compendium is an excellent guide and index to the advice on CPTED contained within the listed documents:

Better Places to Live by Design A Companion Guide to PPG3, Commission for Architecture and the Built Environment, 2001.
By Design Urban Design in the Planning System: Towards Better Practice, Department of the Environment, Transport and the Regions, 2000
Urban Design Compendium. By Llewelyn Davies Yeang in association with Alan Baxter and Associates, and published by English Parterships in 2000, updated 2013 by the HCA with studio|REAL.
Safer Places – The Planning System and Crime Prevention, Department for Communities and Local Government, 2004
Design and access statements (CABE). Available from: http://webarchive.nationalarchives.gov.uk/
Manual for Streets, Department for Transport, 2007
Car Parking – What Works Where? Homes and Communities Agency, 2006
The Code for Sustainable Homes, Department for Communities and Local Government, 2007
Secured by Design New Homes, ACPO Secured by Design, 2010.
The above list is reproduced with kind permission from Thames Valley Police.

References

Noble, J. and Jenks, M. (1996) Parking; Demand and Provision in Private Sector Housing Development. School of Architecture, Oxford Brookes University.
For more information on Wilson and Kelling's 'Broken Window Theory', see, for example, http://www.theatlantic.com/magazine/archive/1982/03/broken-windows/304465/?single_page=true.
More information on Oscar Newman and defensible space can be found at http://www.defensiblespace.com/start.htm.

14 Agricultural buildings

John Weller, Rod Sheard, Frank Bradbeer and others

CI/SfB: 26, 565

KEY POINTS:

- *Farming is an industry subject to continual change*
- *Animal welfare and concern about pollution is leading to legis-lative constraints, both domestic and European*

Contents

1 Introduction
2 Farm animals
3 Farm machinery
4 Dairy cattle housing
5 Beef cattle and calf housing
6 Sheep housing
7 Pig housing
8 Poultry housing
9 Crop storage and effluent produced
10 Equestrian design
11 Building legislation
12 Bibliography

1 INTRODUCTION

1.1 The agricultural economy

Agriculture in the UK and also in the rest of Europe (particularly in the West) is becoming big business. Small farms and small farm-ers are becoming increasingly rare; marginal land is coming out of production. Owners of hitherto agricultural land are seeking other revenue-earning uses such as golf courses.

1.2 Planning

Buildings, irrespective of the enterprise, should be planned in terms of their functions for storage, processing or production. Food, like other industrial processes, should be designed for materials handling and flow-line production. Superimposing linear buildings within or over traditional courtyard forms is both a visual and a tactical problem.

Stock housing produces effluents. Farm waste management is an essential part of the building design and increasingly subject to statutory control. Wastes should normally be recycled, provided that this is done safely.

1.3 Building functions

Depending on managerial philosophy, building functions may be specialist, semi-specialist or flexible in their form. Farmers tend to equate flexibility with general-purpose layouts and with low capital investments; this can be a false equation. The loss of quality con-trol, often difficult to evaluate, makes most 'cheap umbrellas' poor performers for specific end products.

The demand for flexibility reflects two factors – lack of confi-dence in stable markets and the rapidity of technical change. UK food production is essentially controlled by EU policy (via CAP, the Common Agricultural Policy), which aims at market stabil-ity. Technical change is liable to continue, although expansion of power demand may become more selective.

1.4 Stock housing and storage requirements

In simple terms, most storage requirements are those of contain-ers: cylinders, bins and bunkers. Wide-span portals are suitable for some layouts for cattle, bulk storage and general farm machin-ery. Compact and insulated 'boxes' of low profile are best for calves, pigs or poultry. They may include total or partial envi-ronmental control. In contrast, 'kennels' are cheaply framed, semi-open, mono-pitch structures suitable for some cattle and pig layouts.

1.5 Construction and procurement

Most buildings are partially or wholly prefabricated, or are pur-chased under package deals. Standard frames can be obtained 'off the shelf' and infilled by 'self-build'.

Performance specifications are rare. Overall costs are lower than for most buildings of similar type, partly due to lower stand-ards being demanded (see BS 5502, *Buildings and Structures for Agriculture*, in its many parts).

1.6 Lifespan of buildings

Most pre-1960 buildings are inefficient for modern production and many traditional buildings are redundant. A few are suitable for casual storage, administration, isolation units or spare boxes. The issue of redundancy is not easy to resolve. Some historic barns have been dismantled and relocated. Tourism, recreation and craft work are all encouraged in rural areas. A tenth of all farms have some tourist income. In upland areas, it may be the principal source of income. Farm planning should allow for alternative uses for buildings and land.

The normal economic life for farm buildings is ten years, though some are depreciated over five. This is a major design constraint. Some estates may permit a longer term of 20–60 years, especially for 'umbrella' enclosures. Grants are available for all except plas-tic, cheap tents and for factory farms (i.e. without supporting land). EU grants are more generous but require carefully prepared devel-opment proposals.

The moving, alteration or demolition of historic farm build-ings may be subject to listed building legislation. Some unlisted structures are also subject to listed building consent because they are curtilage structures to a listed farmhouse or manor house: the demolition of an unlisted but curtilage building usually requires listed building consent even if their alteration and repair does not.

1.7 Appearance

Farm building appearance, especially since many are exempt from control and since most are cheap compared to other building types, is a contentious issue. Simple forms, good colour, defined planes and coordinated fittings such as vent pipes and flues, combined with careful siting and landscaping, make buildings acceptable. However, large roof surfaces are likely to conflict with vernacular buildings and can, near rising land, become dominant. Component design is often poor and unrelated to the basic structure. Surrounds to buildings, including yards, tanks, fences, etc., are often more unsightly than the buildings.

1.8 Criteria

Farm management in relation to resources of land area and terrain, climate, soil, capital, etc. is such that every farm building problem is different, despite prefabrication, package deals and BS 5502. In many enterprises, it is difficult to establish a good design brief.

The basic layout, Figure 14.1, shows the relationships between the elements of the farm and the main service road. Figure 14.2 shows a typical farm.

2 FARM ANIMALS

Average sizes and weights of animals are shown in Figure 14.3. Width of animal given is normal trough space allowed (i.e. about two-thirds of overall width). Length given is normal standing (not fully extended).

3 FARM MACHINERY

Average sizes and weights of tractors and other machinery are given in Figure 14.4.

4 DAIRY CATTLE HOUSING

Table I gives dimensions for cattle housing; examples suitable for a 120-cattle unit are shown in Figures 14.5 and 14.6. A typical cubicle house is 27 m wide × 55 m long plus 10 m turn area at one end plus a 4 m road. A 'kennel' has the same basic dimensions but the roof is lower and is held by the cubicle division and the passage is not completely roofed, as Figure 14.7. Various systems of milking parlour are shown in Figure 14.8. Rotary parlours are now considered obsolete, and the current favourite is the herringbone, Figure 14.9.

5 BEEF CATTLE AND CALF HOUSING

Straw-covered and slatted yards for beef cattle are shown in Figures 14.10 and 14.11. A calf house illustrated in Figures 14.12 and 14.13 is a 'general-purpose' straw-covered yard for cattle (700 mm/head for manger for adults, 500 mm for yearlings).

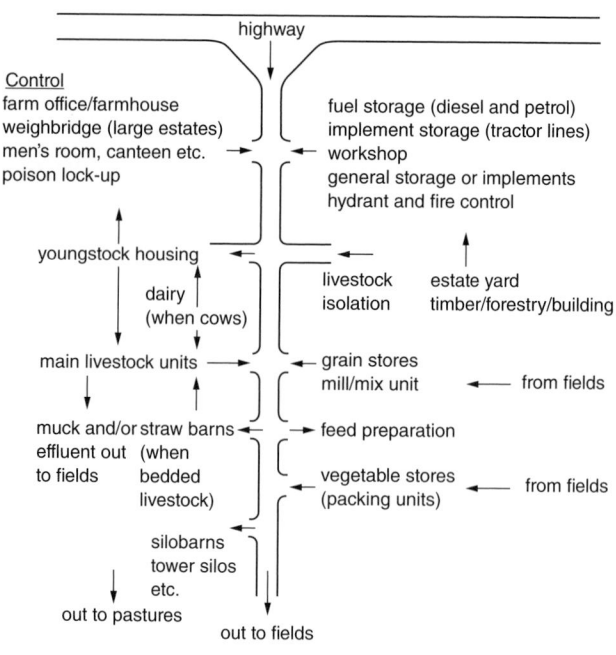

14.1 *Basic layout, mixed arable and stock farm. Although the arrangement shown has been stylised, in fact farms are usually linear to the main service road*

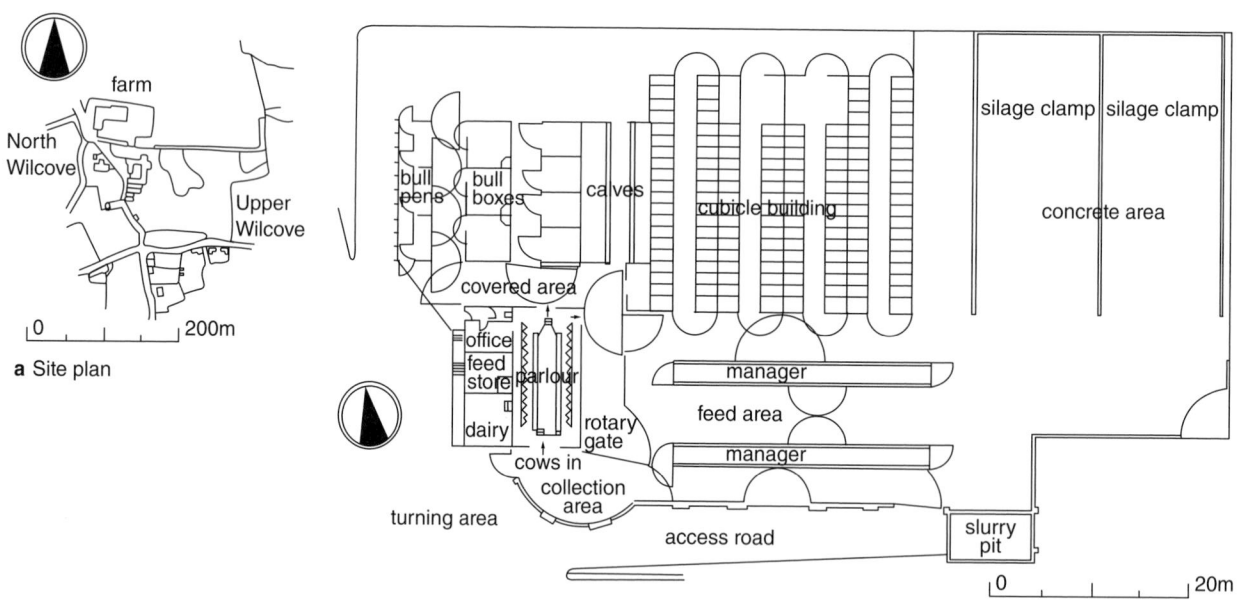

14.2 *Typical farm: Wilcove*

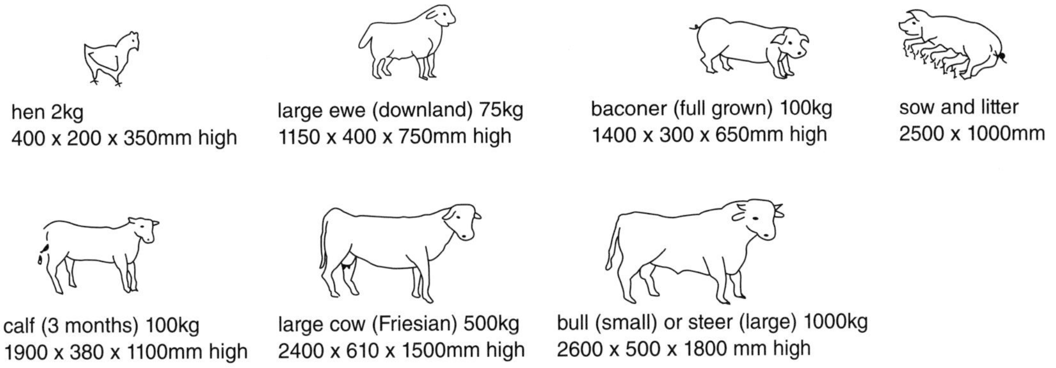

hen 2kg
400 x 200 x 350mm high

large ewe (downland) 75kg
1150 x 400 x 750mm high

baconer (full grown) 100kg
1400 x 300 x 650mm high

sow and litter
2500 x 1000mm

calf (3 months) 100kg
1900 x 380 x 1100mm high

large cow (Friesian) 500kg
2400 x 610 x 1500mm high

bull (small) or steer (large) 1000kg
2600 x 500 x 1800 mm high

14.3 *Farm animals: average size and weights*

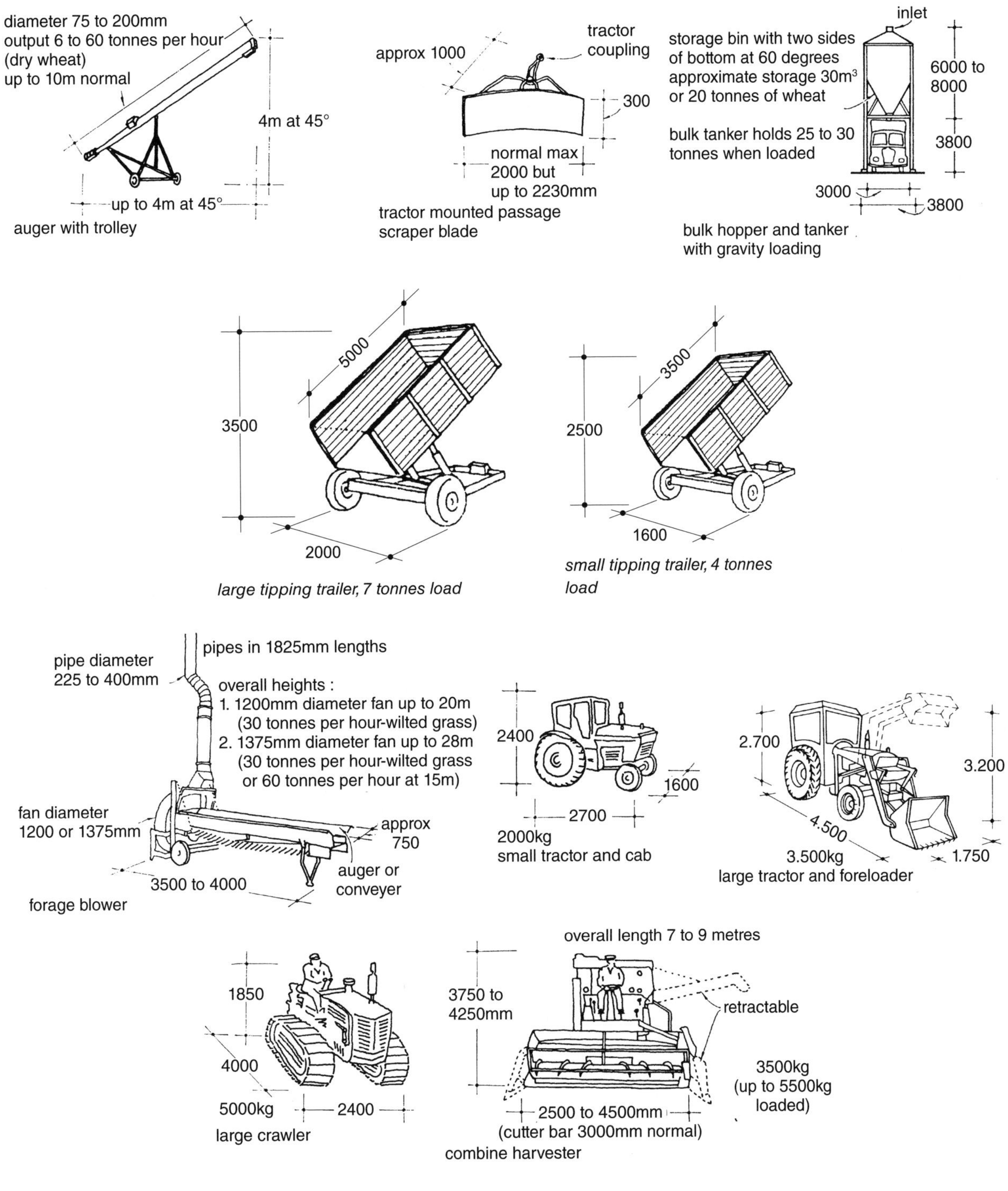

diameter 75 to 200mm
output 6 to 60 tonnes per hour
(dry wheat)
up to 10m normal

4m at 45°

up to 4m at 45°

auger with trolley

approx 1000

tractor
coupling

300

normal max
2000 but
up to 2230mm

tractor mounted passage
scraper blade

inlet

storage bin with two sides
of bottom at 60 degrees
approximate storage 30m³
or 20 tonnes of wheat

bulk tanker holds 25 to 30
tonnes when loaded

6000 to
8000

3800

3000

3800

bulk hopper and tanker
with gravity loading

5000

3500

2000

large tipping trailer, 7 tonnes load

3500

2500

1600

*small tipping trailer, 4 tonnes
load*

pipe diameter
225 to 400mm

pipes in 1825mm lengths

overall heights :
1. 1200mm diameter fan up to 20m
   (30 tonnes per hour-wilted grass)
2. 1375mm diameter fan up to 28m
   (30 tonnes per hour-wilted grass
   or 60 tonnes per hour at 15m)

fan diameter
1200 or 1375mm

approx
750

auger or
conveyer

3500 to 4000

forage blower

2400

1600

2700

2000kg
small tractor and cab

2.700

3.200

4.500

3.500kg

1.750

large tractor and foreloader

1850

4000

5000kg

2400

large crawler

overall length 7 to 9 metres

3750 to
4250mm

retractable

3500kg
(up to 5500kg
loaded)

2500 to 4500mm
(cutter bar 3000mm normal)

combine harvester

14.4 Farm machinery: average weights and sizes

Table I Dimensions of cattle housing

	Dimensions of cubicles (m)					Dimensions of cowsheds (m)			
Mass of cow (kg)	Length including kerb	Length behind trough	Minimum clear width between partitions	Length of standing without trough	Length of standing behind 0.75 to 0.9 wide trough	Clear width between stall divisions of a two-cow standing	Gangway width	Minimum width of feed passage (if any)	Longitudinal fall along gangway and dung channel
350–500	2.00	1.45	1.00	2.00	1.45	2.00	Single range: 2.0	0.9	1%
500–600	2.15	1.60	1.10	2.15	1.60	2.15			
600–650	2.30	1.80	1.15	2.30	1.80	2.40	Double range: 3.0		
650–700	2.30	1.80	1.15						
700–800	2.50	2.00	1.20						

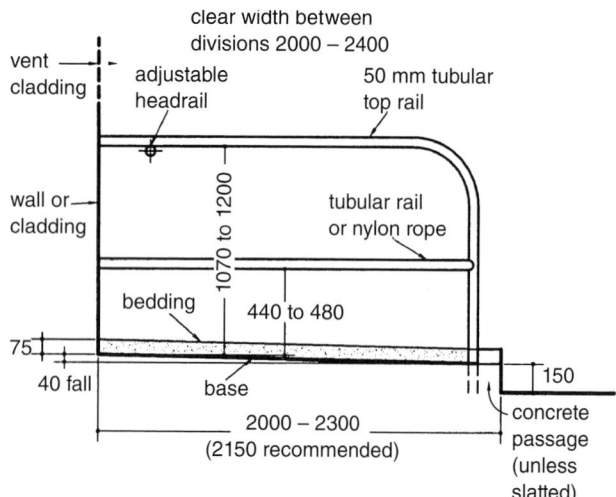

14.5 *Section showing cubicle division: dimensions for Friesian cows*

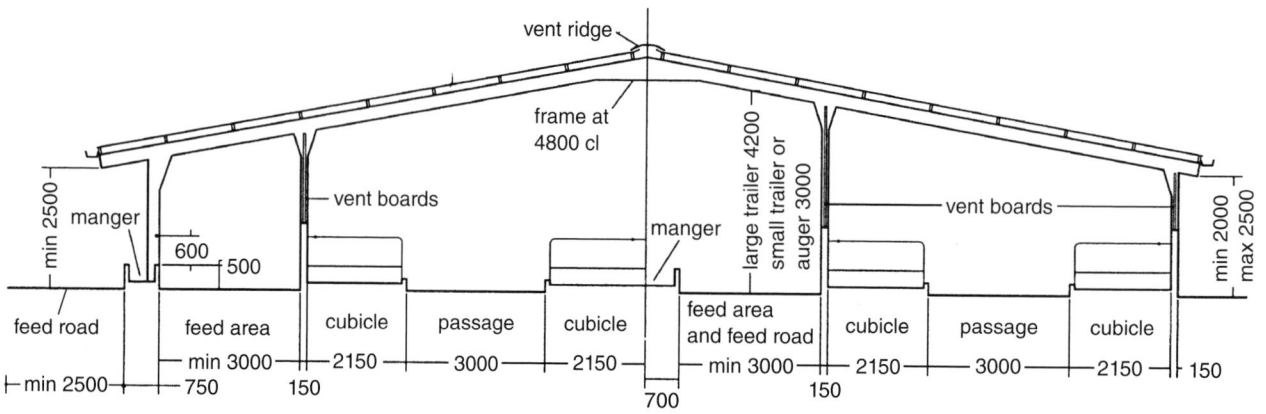

14.6 *Alternative sections of cubicle house showing perimeter feeding to left of centreline, centre feeding to right*

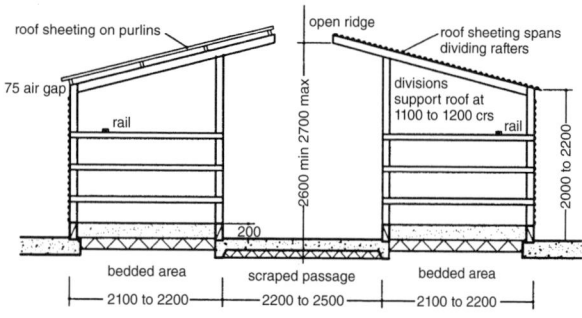

14.7 *Section through kennel for beef or dairy cattle*

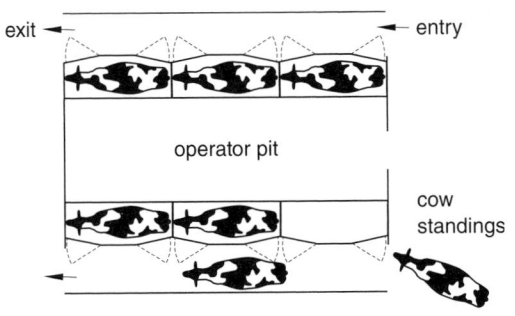

a *abreast*

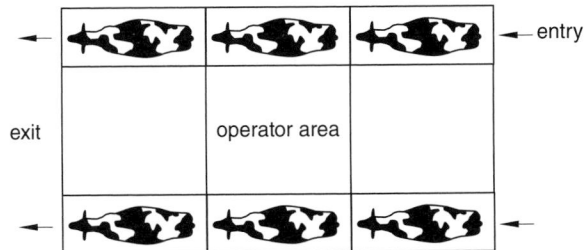

b *tandem*

c *chute*

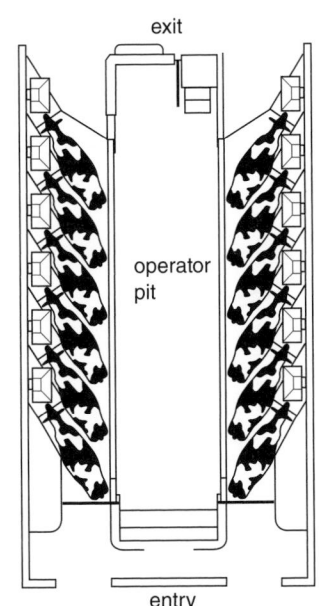

d *herringbone*

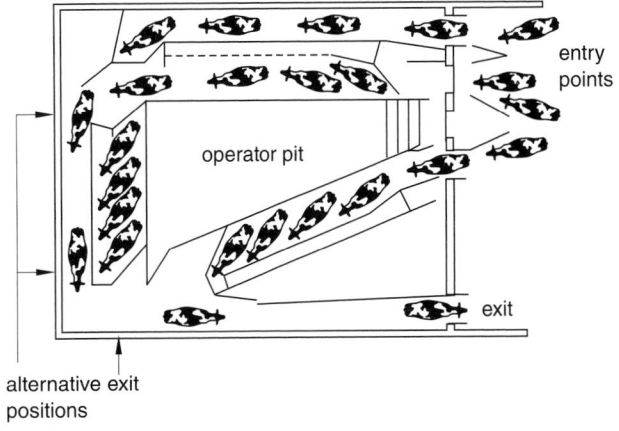

e *trigon*

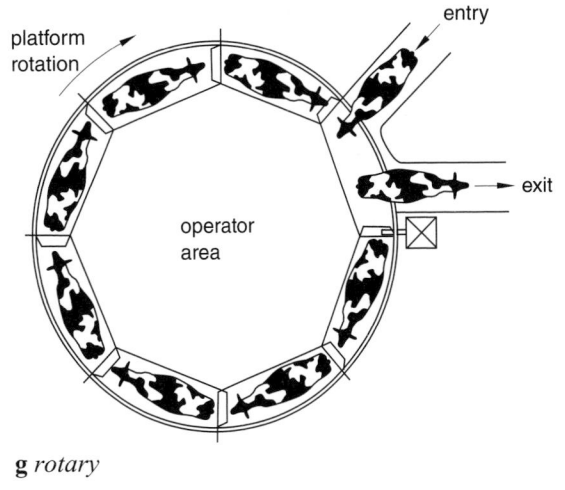

f *polygon*

g *rotary*

14.8 *Milking parlour systems*

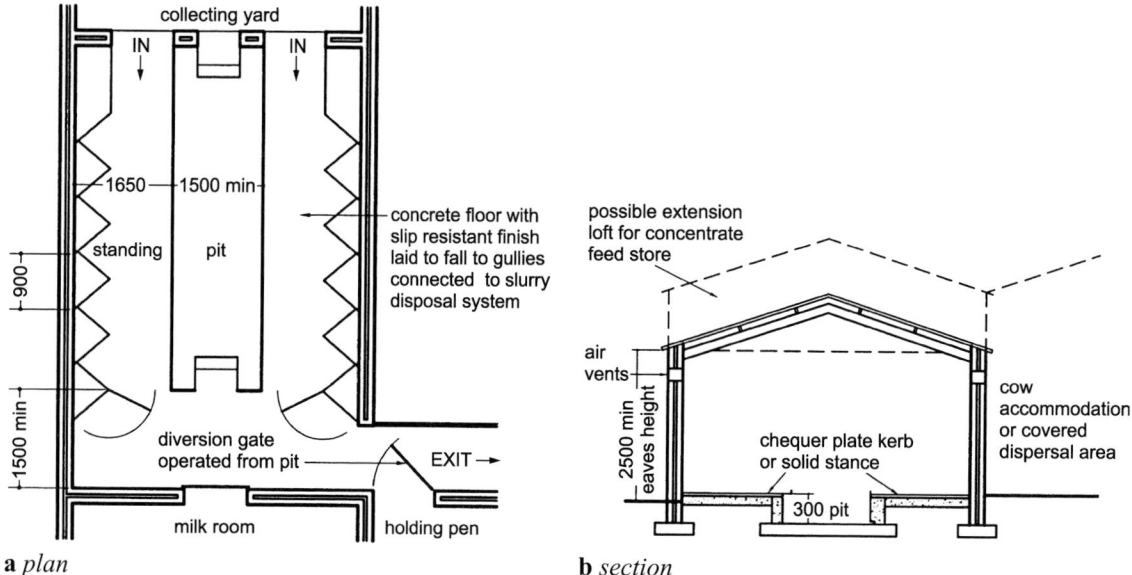

14.9 *Herringbone system milking parlour*

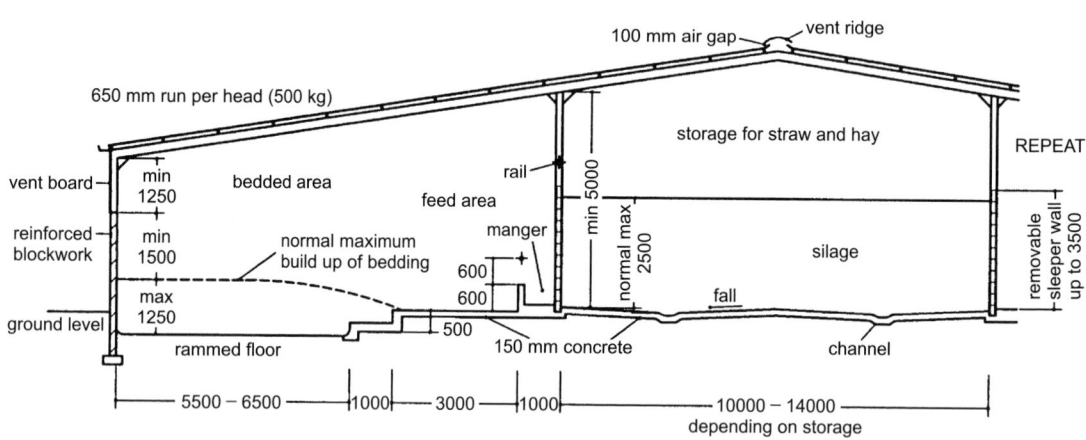

14.10 *Section through straw-covered yard for beef cattle with easy feeding*

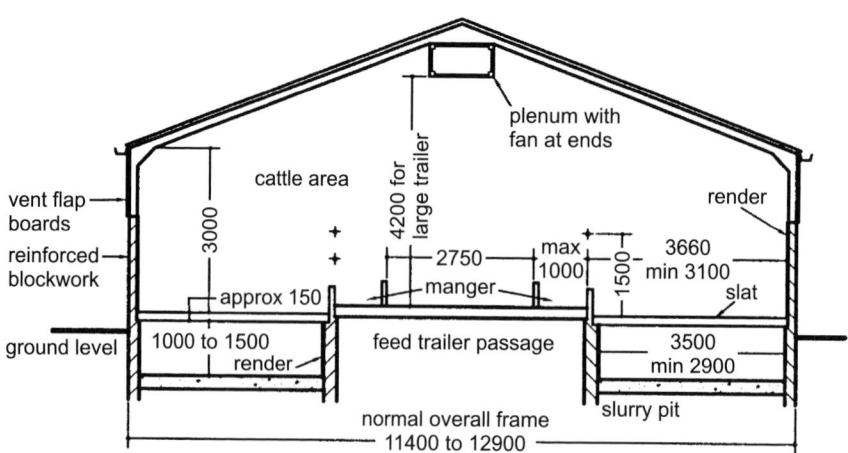

14.11 *Section through slatted yard for beef using self-unloading trailers. Note: fully slatted yards are not approved by Brambell Committee*

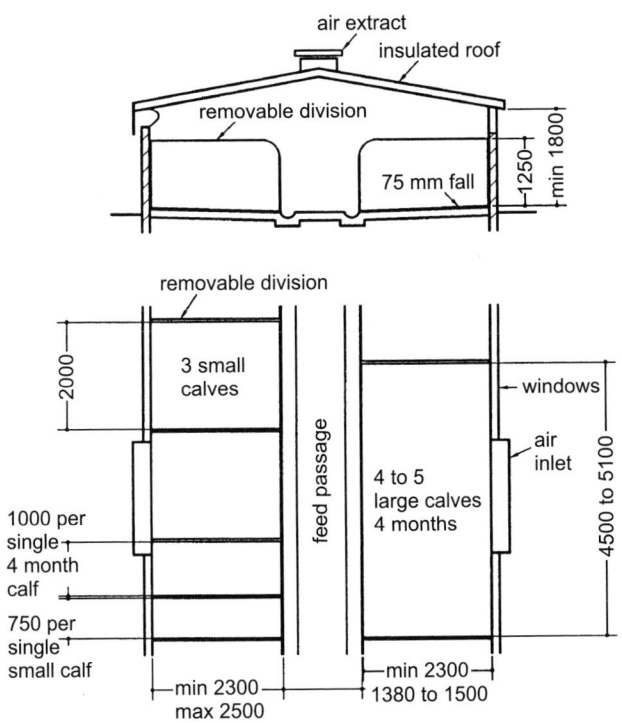

14.12 *Plan and section of calf house*

6 SHEEP HOUSING

Required dimensions are given in Table II. A section through sheep housing is shown in Figure 14.14. A dipping tank suitable for large breeds is shown in Figure 14.15.

7 PIG HOUSING

Table III covers the dimensional requirements. Three types of fattening house are shown in Figures 14.16–14.18, and two types of farrowing house in Figures 14.19 and 14.20.

8 POULTRY HOUSING

Dimensions are given in Table IV. Rearing, fattening and egg houses are shown in Figures 14.21–14.25 and a pole barn for fattening turkeys in Figure 14.26.

9 CROP STORAGE AND EFFLUENT PRODUCED

Some typical feed and produce stores are shown in Figures 14.27–14.34. Table V indicates the scope of manure likely to be produced.

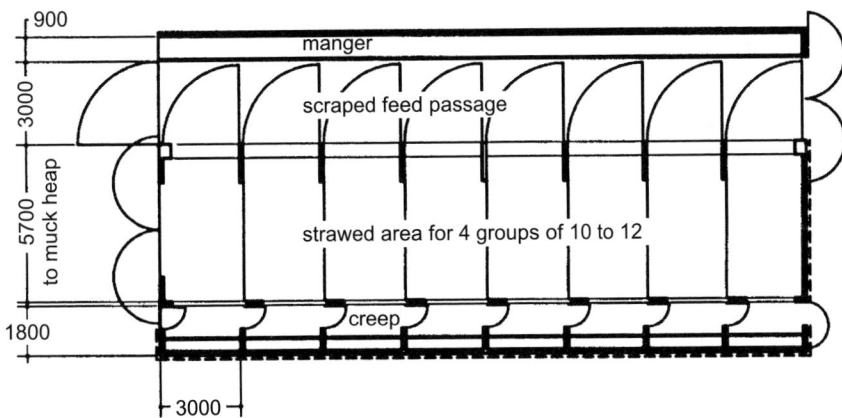

14.13 *Plan of general purpose straw-covered yard for cattle*

Table II Sheep housing

| Type of sheep | Age or mass | Area per animal (m²) | | Length of trough (mm) depending on feeding system | | |
		Perforated floor	Solid floor with straw	Compounds/ concentrates	Ad lib hay/silage	Big bale silage, self-feed
Pregnant ewes	45–60 kg	0.8	1.0	400	175	100
	60–75 kg	0.9	1.2	460	200	150
	75–90 kg	1.1	1.4	500	225	150
Ewes with lambs	Individually penned	–	2.2			
	Groups, 45 kg ewe	1.0	1.3	420	175	100
	Groups, 68 kg ewe	1.4	1.7	460	200	150
	Groups, 90 kg ewe	1.7	1.8	500	225	150
Lambs	Individually penned	–	2.1			
	Group housed	–	1.5			
	Creep area at 2 weeks	–	0.15			
	Creep area at 4 weeks	–	0.4			
Hoggs	20–30 kg	0.5	0.7	300	125	100
	30–40 kg	0.6	0.8	350	150	100
	40–50 kg	0.8	0.9	400	175	100

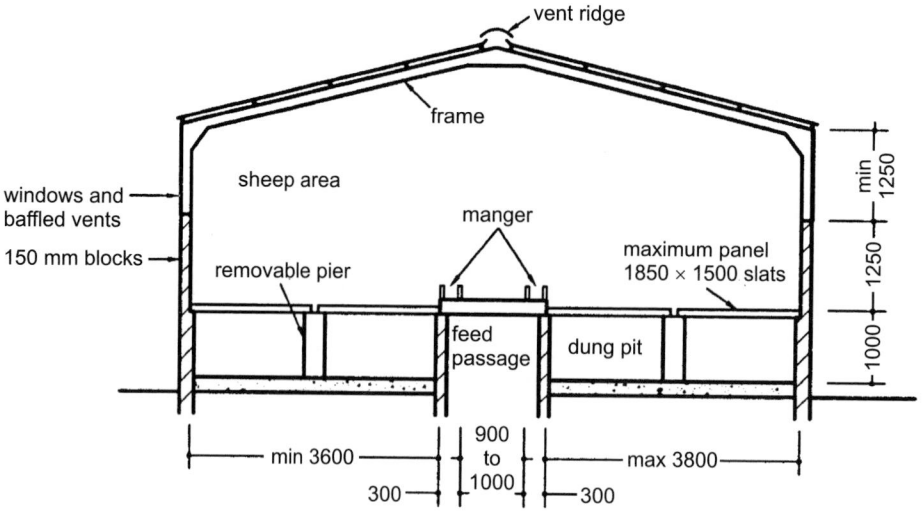

14.14 *Sheep housing, manger run per head: fattening lamb 300 mm ewe and lamb 400 mm yearling 500 mm*

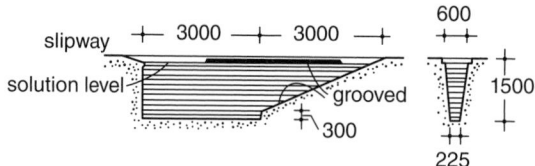

14.15 *Sections through dipping tank for large breed ewes. Allow 2.25 litres of solution per head*

Table III Pig housing: dimensions required for 10 animals

Typical age (days)	Mass (kg)	Type	Lying area (m²)	Min dung area (m²)	Total (m²)	Trough length (mm)	Lying pan depth (mm)
0	1.5	Piglets			1.3/litter	500	
20	5	Early weaners			1.75/litter	500	
35	9	Weaners	0.7	0.3	1.0	600	1170
65	20	Weaners	1.5	0.6	2.1	1750	860
115	50	Porkers	3.5	1.0	4.5	2250	1560
140	70	Cutters	4.6	1.6	6.2	2750	1280
160	85	Baconers	5.5	2.0	7.5	3000	1840
185	110	Heavy hogs	6.7	2.3	9.0	4000	1680
210	140	Overweight	8.5	3.0	11.5	5000	1700
–		Dry sows	15.0	5.0	20.0		3000
–	–	In-pig sows	15.0	5.0	20.0		3000
–	–	Boar		8.0/boar	500/boar		

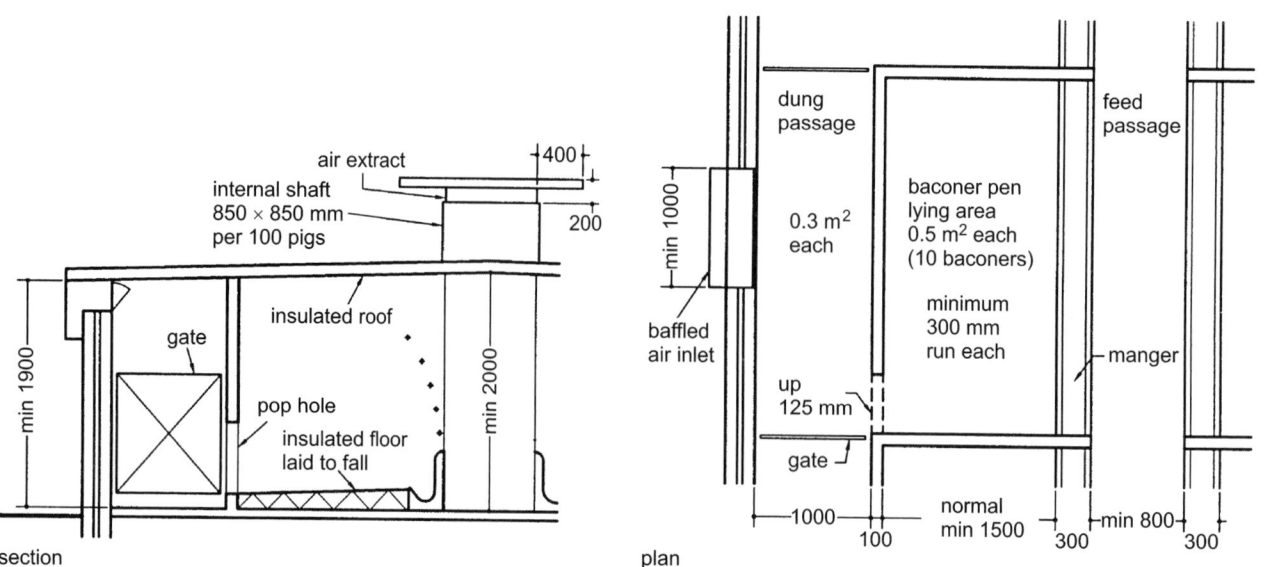

14.16 *Plan and section of fattening house with side dung passage*

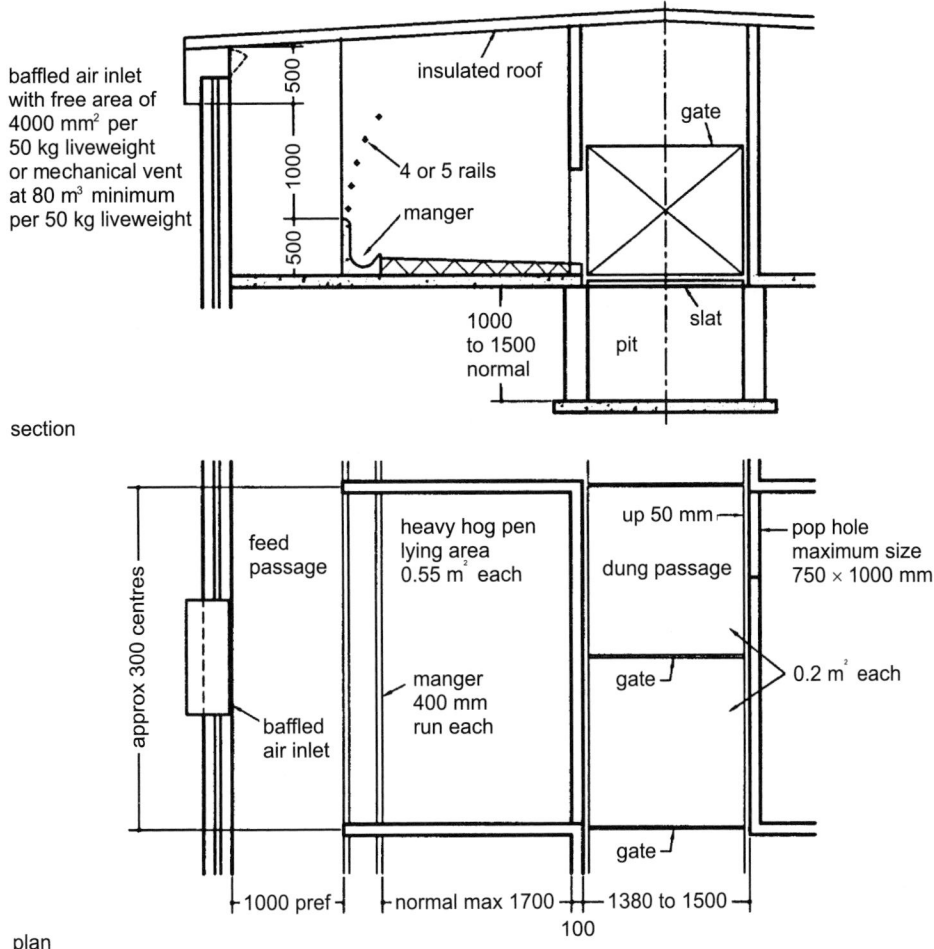

14.17 *Plan and section of fattening house with centre slatted dung passage*

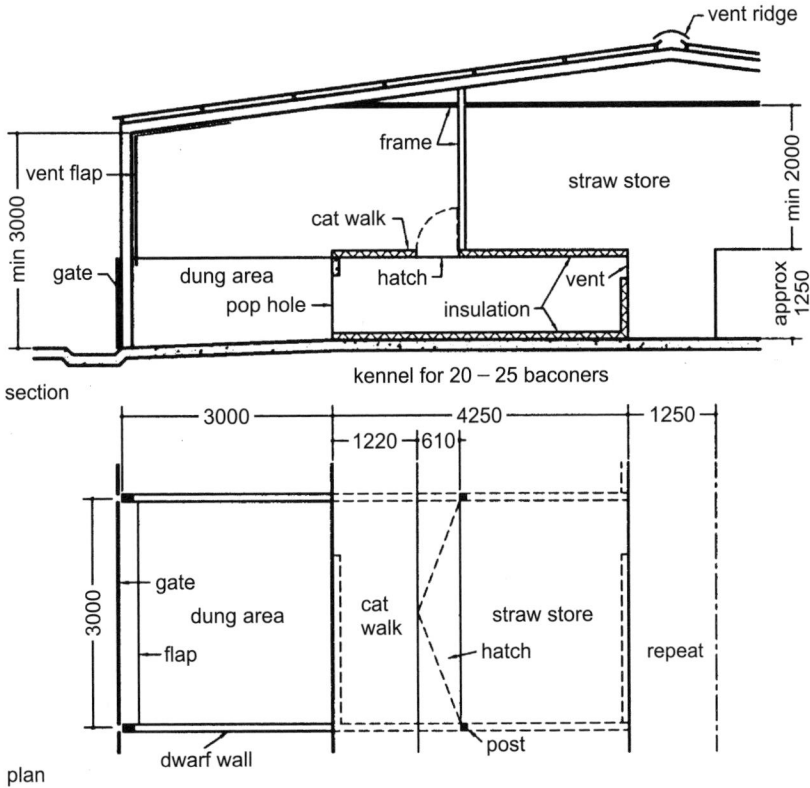

14.18 *Plan and section of fattening house with straw-covered system and floor feeding*

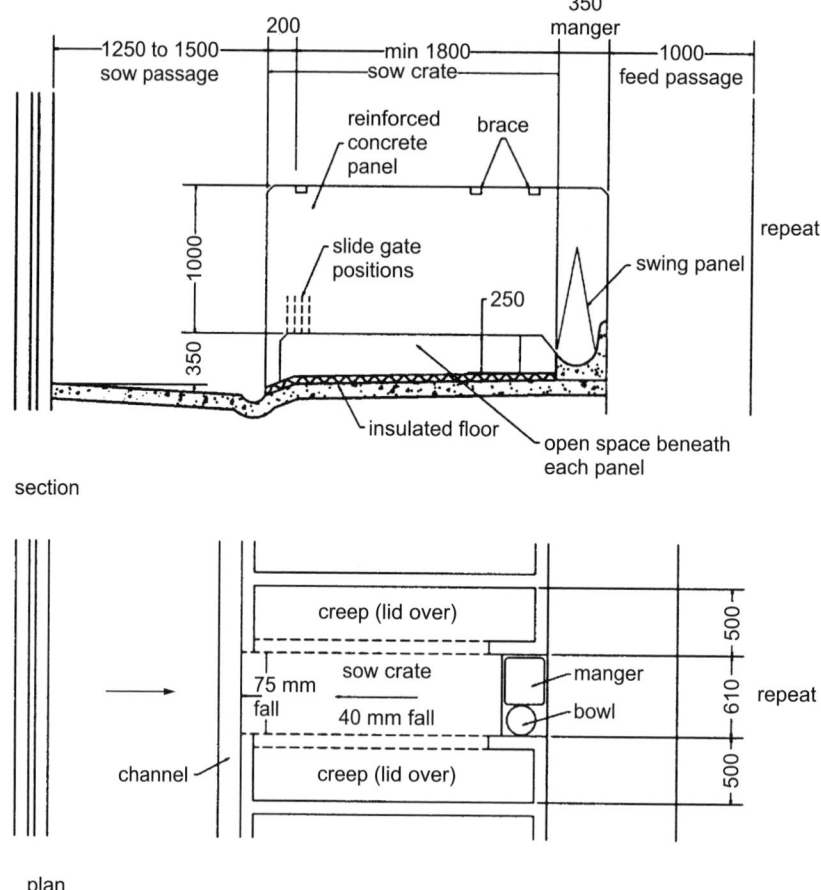

14.19 *Plan and section of permanent crate farrowing house*

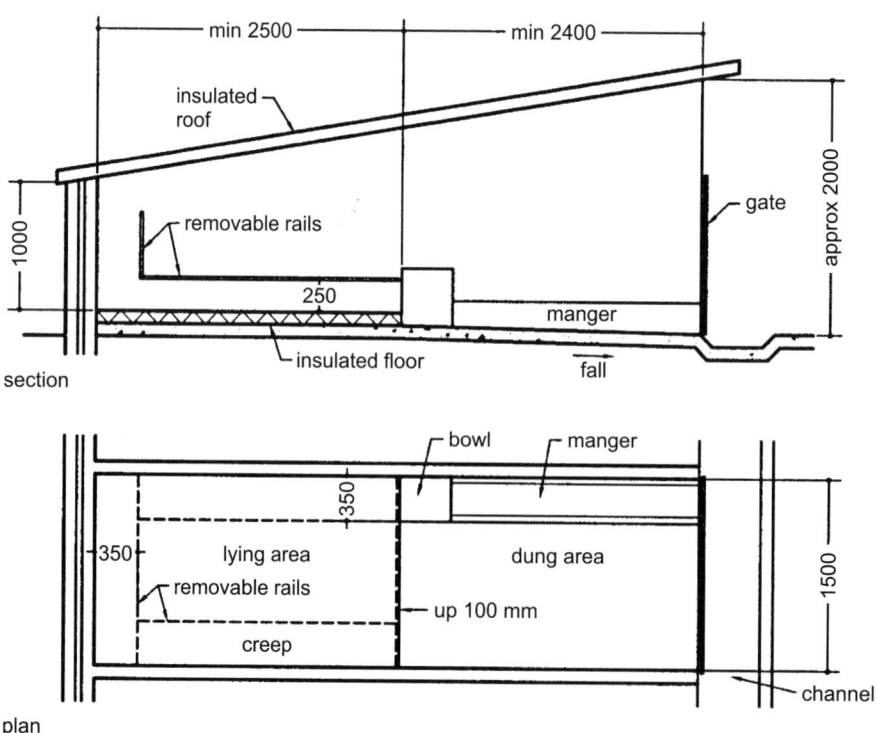

14.20 *Plan and section of Soleri open front farrowing house*

Table IV Poultry housing

System	Species/cage numbers	0–4 weeks	4–8 weeks	9–16 weeks
Battery or tier brooder and cooling cage	One hen in cage	0.1	0.1	0.1–0.43
	Two hens in cage	0.075	0.09	0.1–0.43
	Three hens in cage	0.055	0.09	0.1–0.43
	Four hens in cage	0.043	0.09	0.1–0.43
Floor rearing on litter	Layers	0.025	0.09	0.18–0.28
	Broilers		0.09	
	Turkeys	0.09	0.14	0.37–0.46
Part wire or slatted floor rearing	0.015	0.09	0.09–0.14	
	Ducks	0.09	Free range	
Trough length (mm)	Birds in cages	100		
	Layers	30	40	60
	Broilers	30	50	75
	Turkeys	36	73	73
	Ducks	55	122	Free range

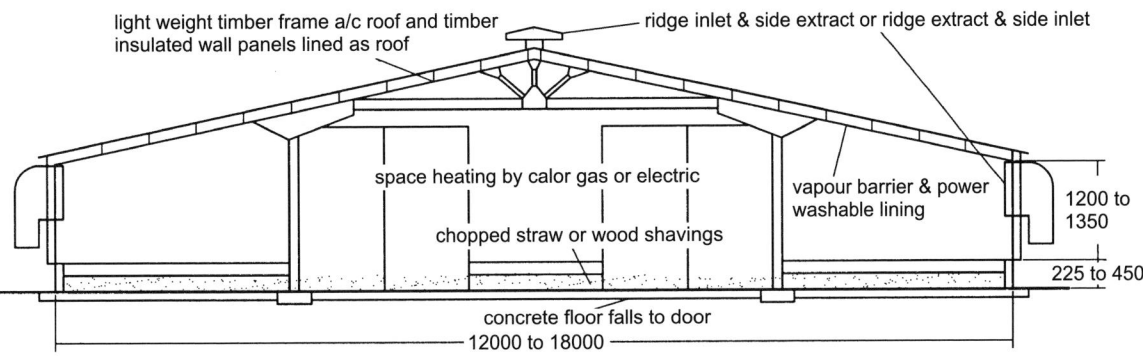

14.21 *Section through poultry broiler and rearing house. Roof insulated with minimum 25 mm rigid polyurethane or equivalent. Stocking density 10 birds/m², RH 60%, temperature 30°C*

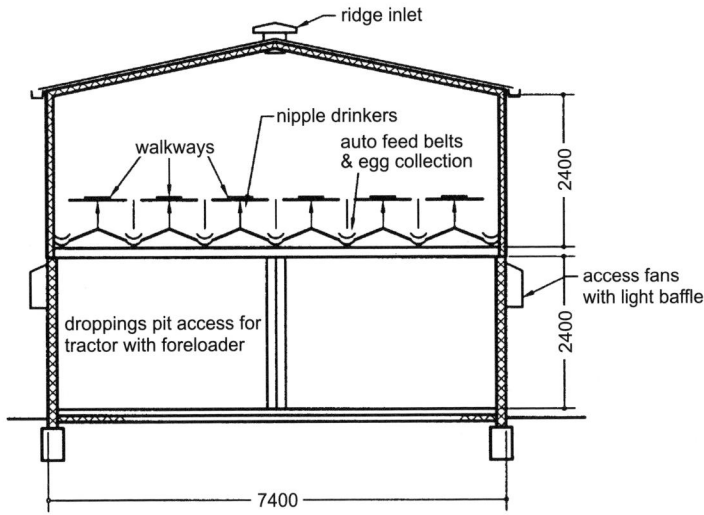

14.22 *Section through flat deck deep pit battery house. Roof insulated with minimum 25 mm rigid polyurethane or equivalent. Stocking at 100 mm trough per bird in multibird cages for light hybrids, 125 mm for heavier birds. RH 60%, temperature 20–25°C. If falls to 12° does not harm output but increases food conversion ratio*

Table V Average production of effluent

		Production per head per week					
		Mass (kg)	Output (l)	Volume (m³)	Total solids (kg)	BOD (kg)	BOD population equivalent
Man	Adult	75	10	0.01	0.57	0.41	1.0
Cow	Dairy	450	250	0.25	21.20	4.20	10.2
Cow	Large dairy	550	380	0.38	32.22	6.13	14.8
Calf	3-month	100	200	0.20	19.05	2.54	6.2
Pig	Porker	50	38	0.04	3.00	1.20	2.0
Pig	Baconer	95	51	0.05	3.50	1.40	3.4
Pig	Wet-fed	95	100	0.10	3.50	1.40	3.4
Pig	Farrow sow	110	75	0.08	3.60	1.45	3.6
Poultry	Adult layer	2.25	3.75	0.005	1.27	0.09	0.13
Sheep	Adult ewe	75	35	0.04	3.81	0.70	1.7
Silage	30% dry matter	Tonne	3.20	0.001	–	–	–
Silage	20% dry matter	Tonne	37.00	0.04	–	–	–

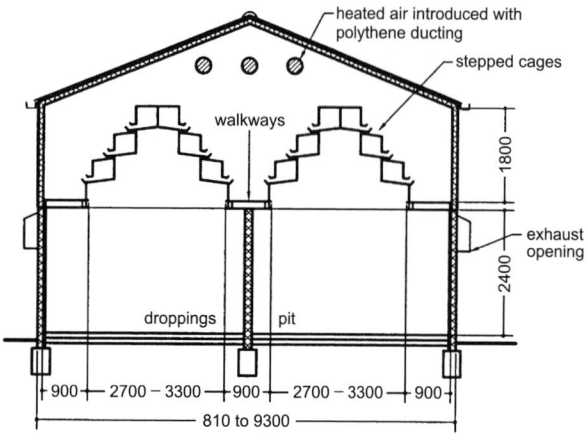

14.23 *Section through California cage deep pit battery house. Roof insulated with minimum 25 mm rigid polyurethane or equivalent*

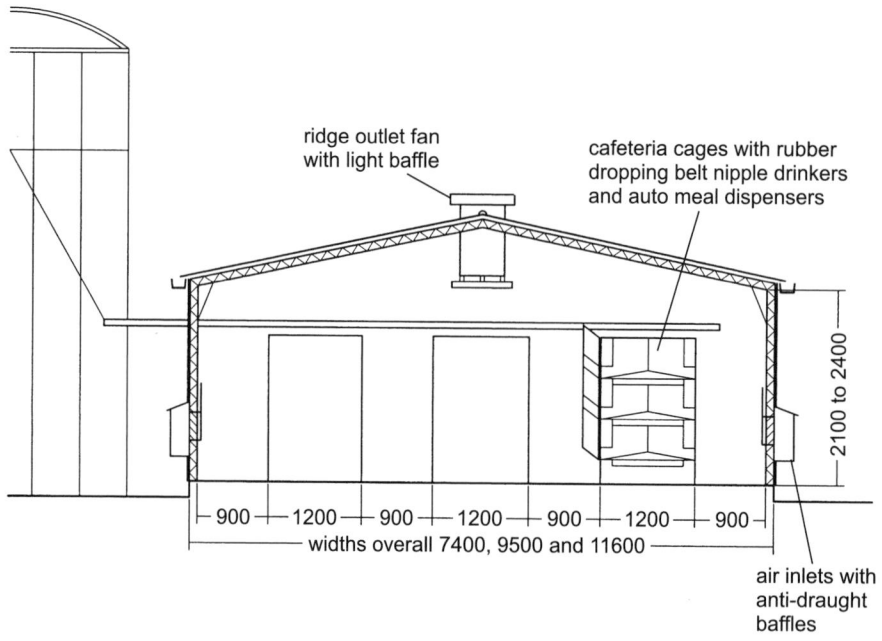

14.24 *Section through cafeteria cage battery house*

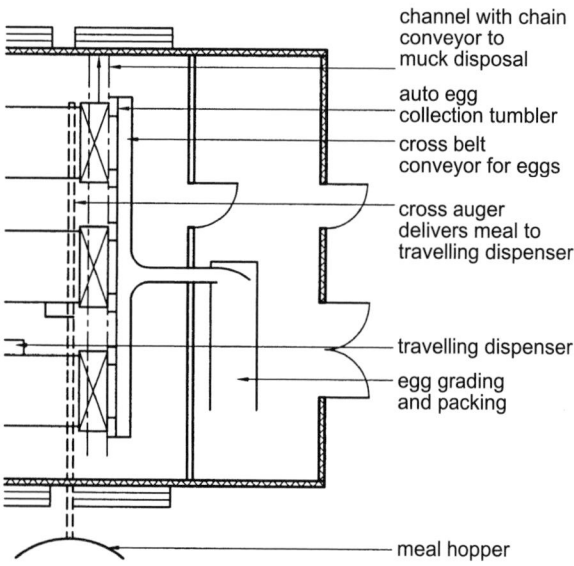

14.25 *Plan of end of cafeteria cage battery house showing gear*

10 EQUESTRIAN DESIGN

10.1 Horse riding today

Facilities for keeping horses are mainly constructed for recreational riding, equestrian sport and breeding purposes. The use of horses for commercial haulage is unusual nowadays, and together with police or military facilities there is likely to be a specific brief.

10.2 Planning elements in private stables

Private stables range from a stable for one horse to large complexes to accommodate a thousand horses or more, complete with full health and training facilities. The principal elements remain the same, Figure 14.35, and are based on the physical and psychological requirements of the horses.

1 Boxes
- Loose boxes
- *Sick box/boxes (50 per cent larger)
- *Utility box/boxes

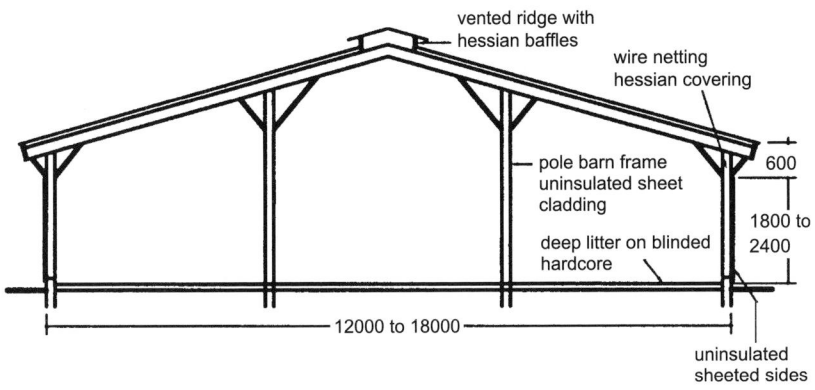

14.26 *Section through pole barn for fattening turkeys. Stocking density 30 kg/m2*

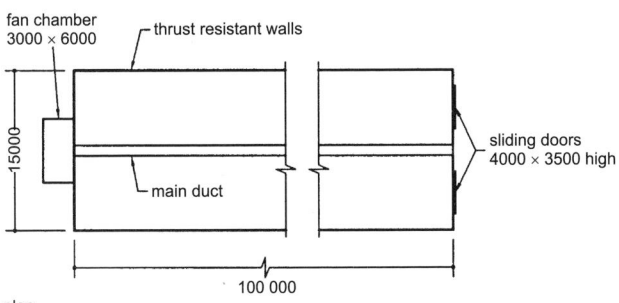

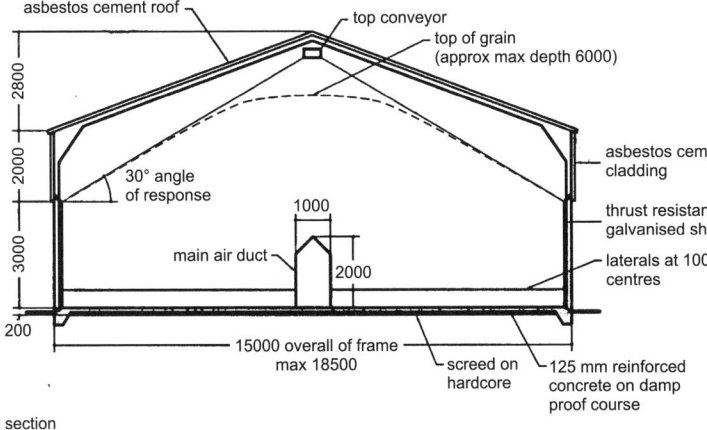

14.27 *Tower silo for wilted grass with 40–50% dry matter. Wet grass is stored in towers of 6 m diameter × under 12 m height*

14.28 *Plan and section of storage for food grain, showing lateral system for 1200 tonnes storage*

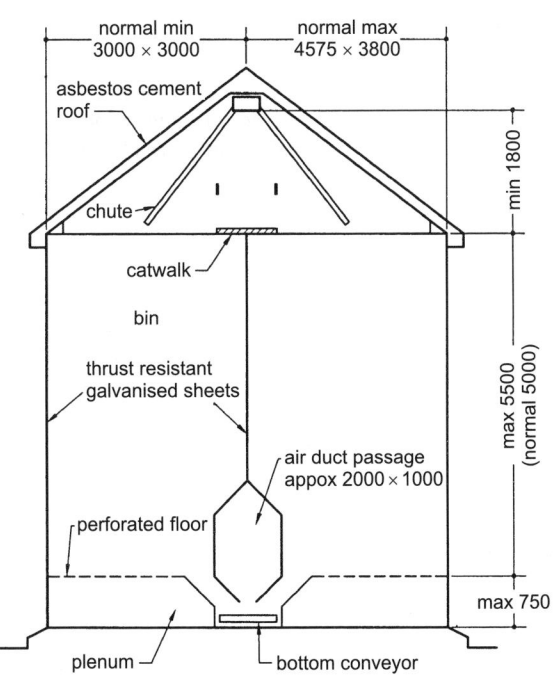

14.29 *Grain drying and storage: section through a nest of bins (square or rectangular) with roof. A bin 4.575 × 3.8 × 5m holds 60 tonnes of wheat*

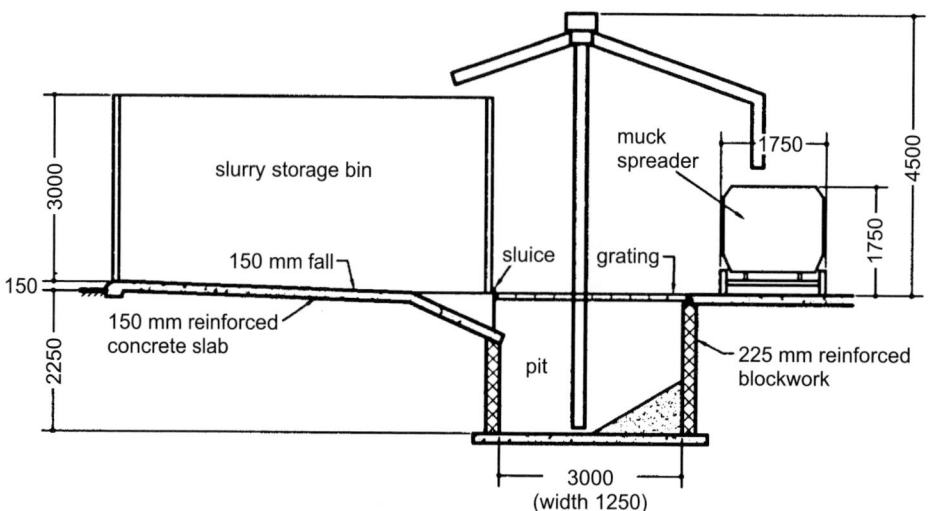

14.30 *Section through above-ground slurry storage*

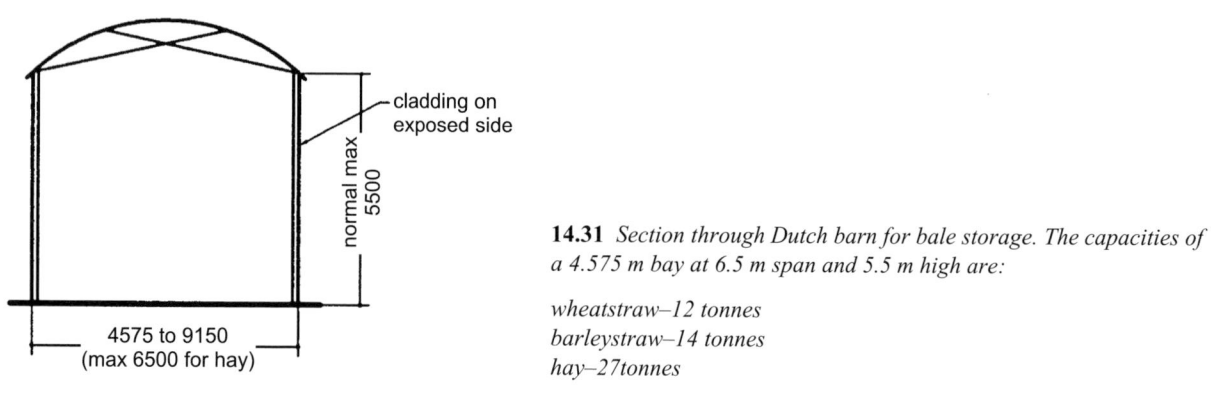

14.31 *Section through Dutch barn for bale storage. The capacities of a 4.575 m bay at 6.5 m span and 5.5 m high are:*

wheatstraw–12 tonnes
barleystraw–14 tonnes
hay–27tonnes

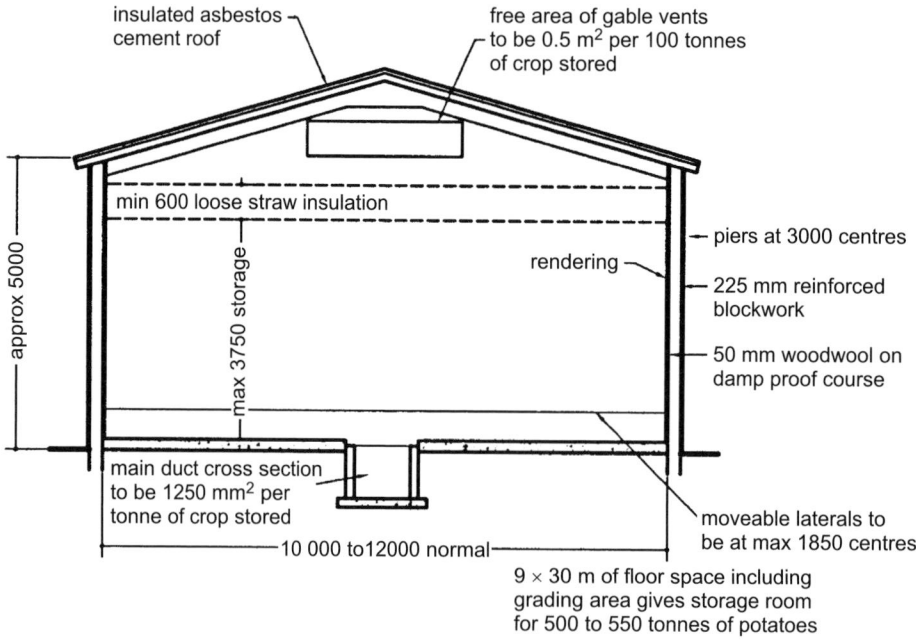

14.32 *Section through floor storage for potatoes. 9 × 30 m of floor space stores 500–550 tonnes. Movable laterals maximum 1.85m centres. Free area of gable vents 0.5m²/100 tonnes stored, main duct cross-section 1250 mm²/tonne*

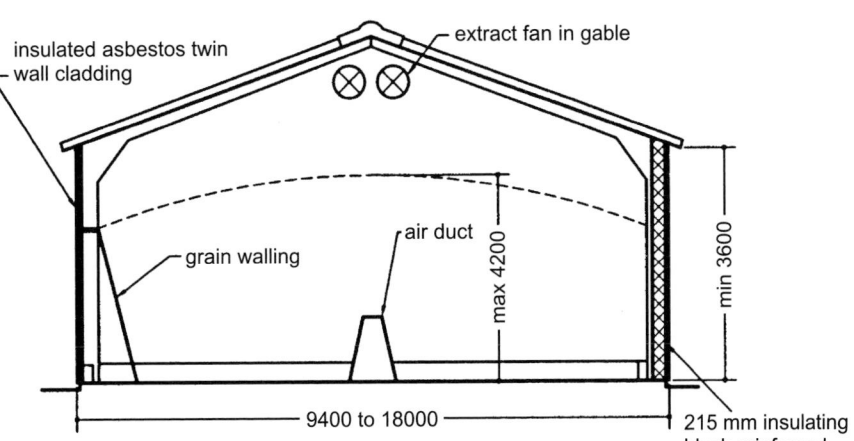

14.33 *Section through radial flow bins in a barn for grain drying and storage. The air duct delivers 400m³/h.t to dry and 100m³/h.t to store. Air temperature above 0°C, RH 75%*

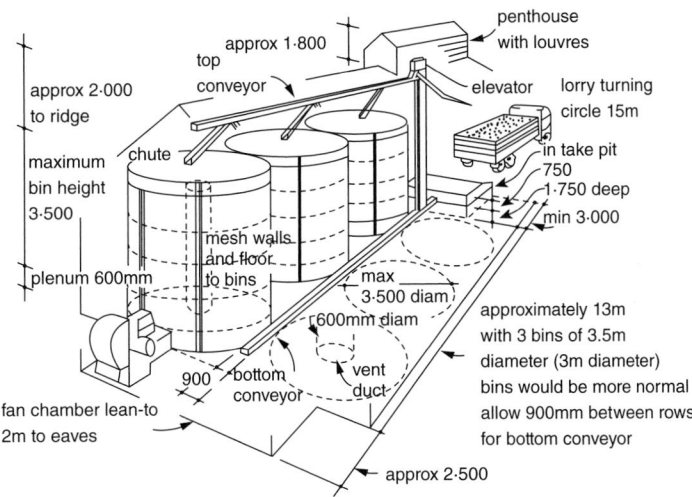

14.34 *Onion store*

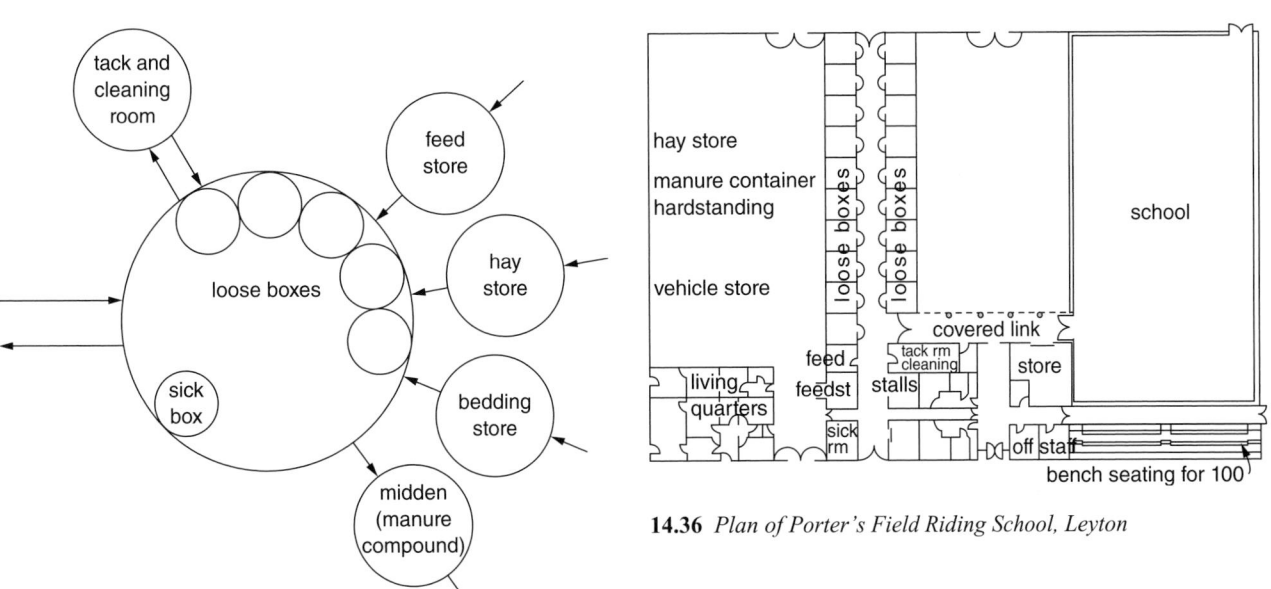

14.35 *Relationships between elements of the plan*

14.36 *Plan of Porter's Field Riding School, Leyton*

Table VI Common breeds of horses and ponies, with heights in hands and equivalent metric measure, Figure 14.37
(1 hand = 4 inches, 12.2 hands = 12 hands + 2 inches)

Breed	Height in hands	Height in mm	Breed	Height in hands	Height in mm
Horses			**Ponies**		
Cleveland bay	16	1625	Connemara	14.2	1475
Clydesdale	16	1625	Dartmoor	12	1220
Morgan	14–15	1420–1525	Exmoor	12.2	1270
Percheron	16–16.3	1625–1700	Fell	13.1	1345
Shire	17	1725	Highland	12.2–14.2	1270–1475
Suffolk	16	1625	New Forest	14.2	1475
Tennessee Walker	15.2	1575	Shetland	39–42 inches	990–1065*
Thoroughbred	16	1625	Welsh	12	1220

*Shetland ponies are always described in inches.

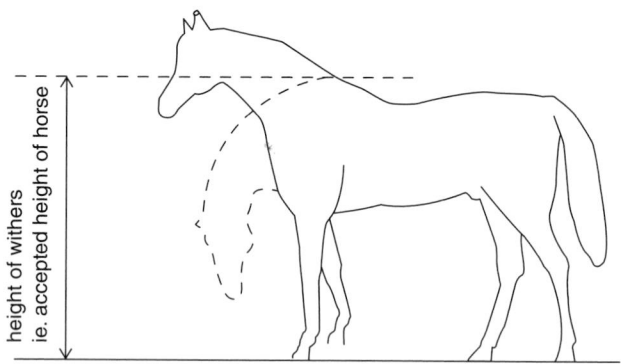

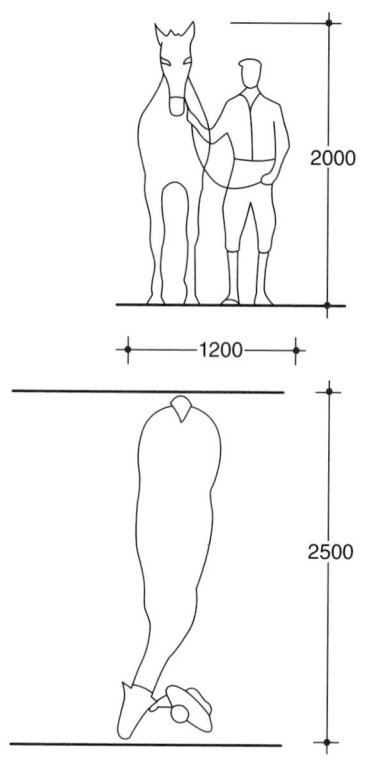

14.37 *Measurement of the height of a horse at the withers. Traditionally the height was measured in hands (4 inches), but a hand is equivalent to a decimeter (100 mm) within the limits of accuracy attainable. Table VI gives the heights of a number of breeds of horses and ponies*

Table VII Typical dimensions of horse or pony and rider, Figure 14.39

Dimension	Thoroughbred	New Forest pony	Welsh pony
A	1600	1450	1200
B	550	500	415
C	900	815	675
D	1620	1470	1215
E*	2450	2225	1840
F	1625	1475	1220

*Assuming that the rider is in proportion to the horse or pony

14.38 *The led horse. a Front view. b Plan*

2 Stores
- Feed
- Hay
- Bedding
- Equipment (wheelbarrows, mowers, etc.)

3 Housekeeping
- Tack room
- *Cleaning room
- *Drying room
- Staff lavatories/showers
- *Staff rest room
- *Office
- *Vet room

4 External facilities
- Midden
- *Washdown area
- Trailer parking
- Staff parking
- *Carriage store

5 Health/exercise
- Sand roll
- Lungeing yard
- Treadmill
- Weighing machine/weigh bridge
- Equine pool

*In many cases, the accommodation will not require these items because of their small-scale activities.
   A typical plan is shown in Figure 14.36.

10.3 Dimensional criteria
Dimensionally standardised criteria may be applied:

- The size of the horse, with and without rider, Figures 14.37–14.39, Tables VI and VII.
- Stabling and care of the horse, Figures 14.40–14.43.

   Section
   Plan
   Tack rooms, Figure 14.44.

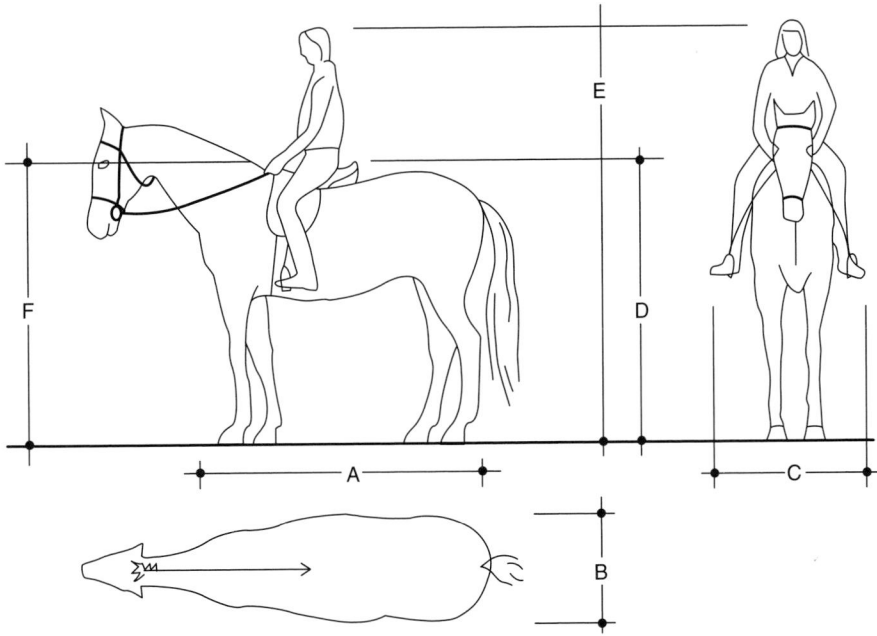

14.39 *Dimensions of the horse and rider, see Table VII*

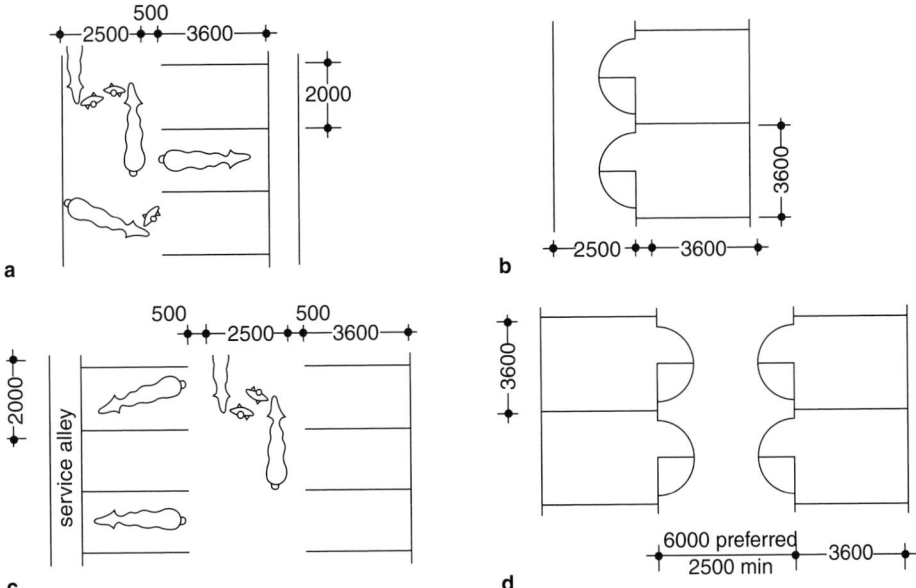

14.40 *Arrangements of stables. a Stalls on one side. b Loose boxes on one side. c Stalls on both sides. d Loose boxes on both sides: doors should not be directly opposite one another*

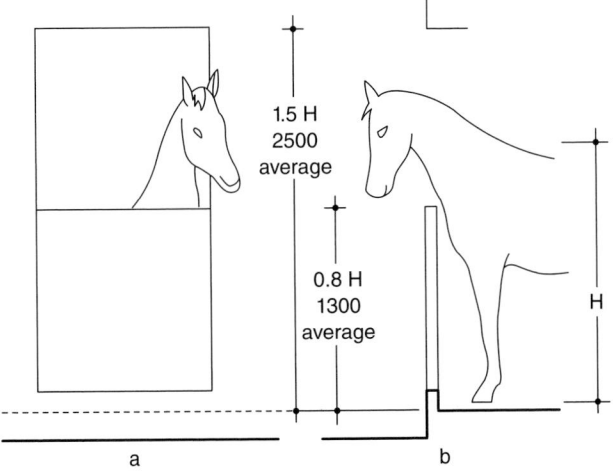

14.41 *The stable door. It is essential for the horse's mental wellbeing for it to see out – horses are inclined to be very inquisitive! H is the height at the withers (see 14.37). a Front view. b Section*

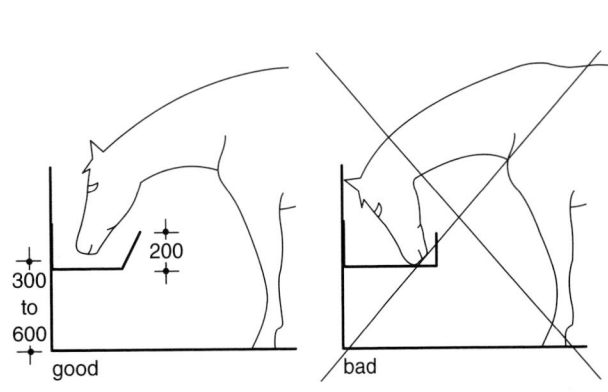

14.42 *Height of the manger*

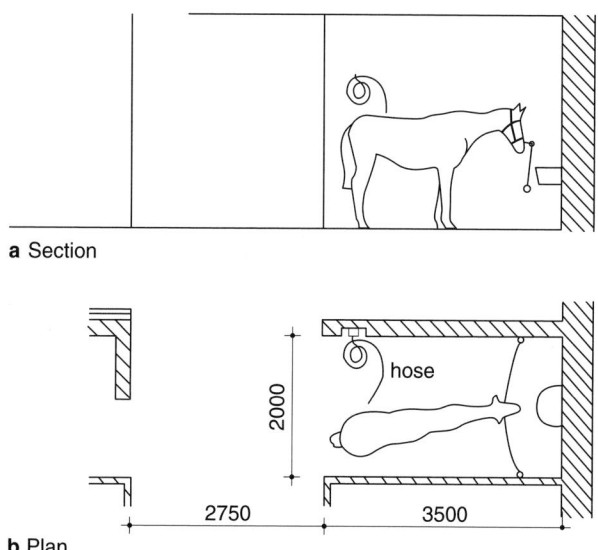

a Section

b Plan

14.43 *Veterinary box 'Stallapotheke'*

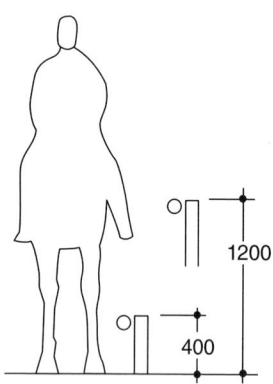

14.45 *Rails for the outside school*

- Schooling, Figure 14.45 and 14.46
- The dressage arena, Figure 14.47
- Polo, Figure 14.48
- Transportation, Figures 14.49–14.51

10.4 Stabling and environmental conditions
The principal requirements can be identified as follows:

1 Dryness and warmth
2 Adequate ventilation without draughts
3 Adequate supply of water and good drainage
4 Good daylight and good artificial light.

Siting

- On well-drained ground.
- Avoid the tops of hills and hollows.
- Protected from severe prevailing winds.
- Avoid sites hemmed in without free circulation of air.

Temperature
The stable should moderate extremes of exterior conditions. Therefore a degree of air circulation is helpful and adequate ventilation essential. However, care should be taken to avoid draughts.

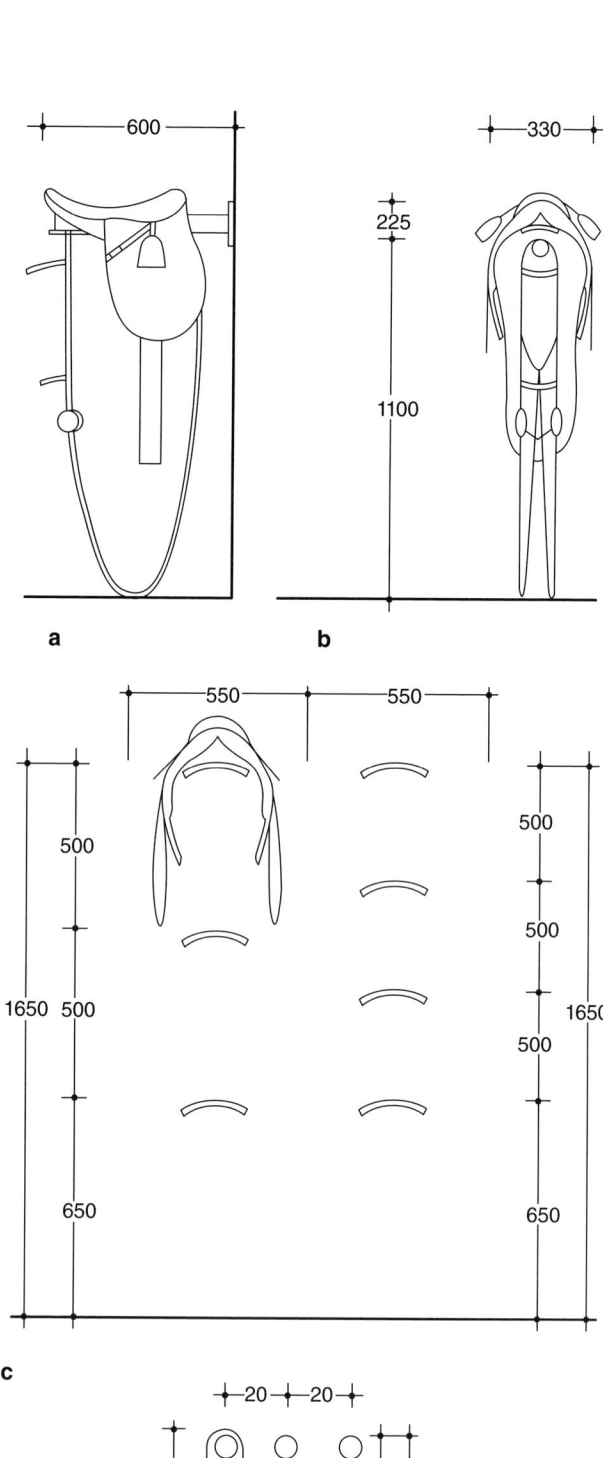

a

b

c

d

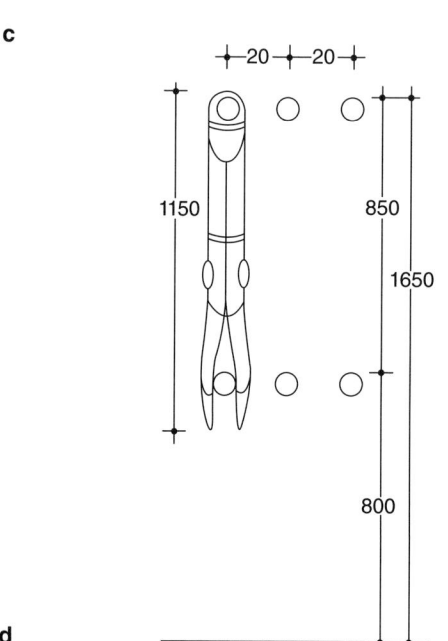

14.44 *Tack rooms. a Saddles and bridles together, side view. b Saddles and bridles, front view. c Saddles only. d Bridles only, when kept separate*

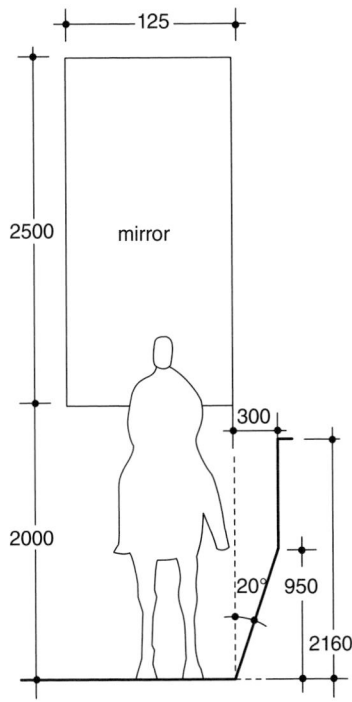

14.46 *Indoor school: batten to walls and arrangement of mirror tilted to give self-vision*

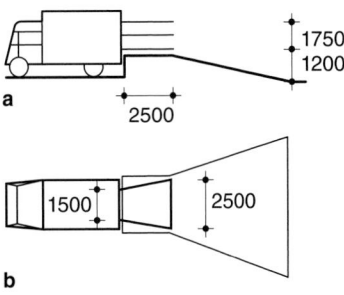

14.49 *Ramp for loading horses into horse-boxes or trailers. a Section. b Plan*

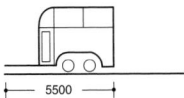

14.50 *Large trailer*

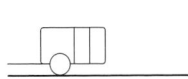

14.51 *Small trailer*

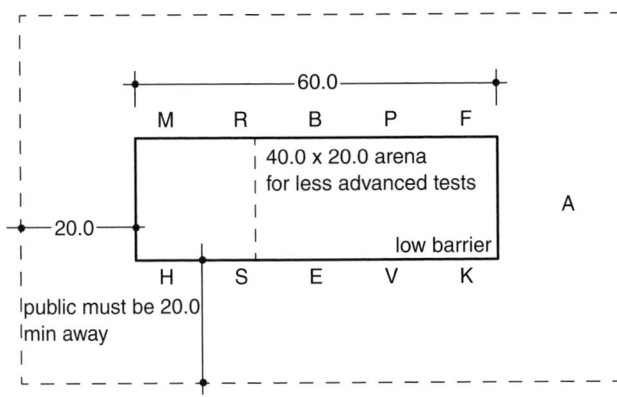

14.47 *Dressage arena*

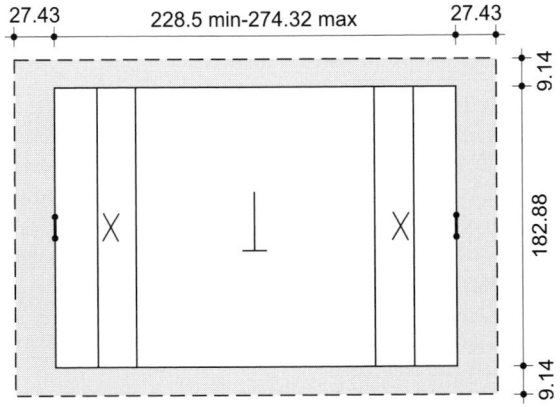

14.48 *Polo*

Size
Unless a particularly small breed is kept the standard dimensions should be adhered to.

Noise
Sudden noise may startle horses and disrupt sleep during the night, therefore relationship to public roads or urban developments requires careful consideration.

10.5 Detailed stabling design

Floor
The floor should be impervious to moisture, hard wearing, nonslip, easily cleaned and protect the horse from any ground moisture. Selection of floor finish can vary from dense concrete, granolithic concrete or engineering brick-laid herringbone pattern to proprietary rubber mats and seamless rubber flooring.

Walls
The walls should be smooth for cleanliness and, wherever possible, free from projections. It is preferable that masonry walls are protected up to at least 120 mm by stout timber or plywood panelling on battens. Masonry should be painted white or a light shade to encourage cleanliness. Horses are gregarious animals and therefore it is normal for the partitions to be solid up to 1200–1500 mm and have a metal grille up to 2100 mm above floor level.

Ceilings
The ceiling should not be less than 3050 mm high and care should be exercised in the choice of materials to avoid the build-up of condensation.

Fire resistance
In large installations, the fire resistance of the structure and the location of fire separation barriers should be carefully considered bearing in mind the difficulty of evacuating frightened horses and the often rural location.

Doors and windows
Doors to loose boxes should be positioned to one side of the box to allow the horse to keep clear of the draught when the upper half is left open. Doors to two adjoining boxes should not be placed next to each other. The door should open back to 180° and any exposed edges be protected with a galvanised steel capping to avoid 'crib biting'. There should be no sharp arisses and a minimum clear width of 1200 mm. Windows should, where possible, be fitted at high level. Any low-level windows should have Georgian wired glass and a steel protective grille.

Fittings
Usually, these will consist of a manger, drinking water receptacle and two tie rings. The exact position of these items will depend to some extent on the management of the stables, and to whether automatic replenishment is incorporated. Tie rings are generally fixed between 1525 and 1800 mm in order to avoid a horse dropping a leg over the tie.

Services
An exterior quality plug socket will be required (one per six stalls maximum) for portable equipment. This should be sited outside the stall. Artificial lighting should provide illumination to both sides of the horse switched from outside the stalls.

Drainage
The floor should be laid to a fall of between 1:80 and 1:60 to a gulley outside the stall or loose box. Channels may be formed to enhance drainage. Good housekeeping is the key to drainage and all gullies should be equipped with a removable perforated bucket to collect bedding and feed that may wash down the gulley.

Midden
The midden must be arranged so that effluent does not run away into groundwater. There should be a gulley and an adjacent water supply to enable regular periodic cleaning. For hygiene reasons, it should be sited away from the stables.

11 BUILDING LEGISLATION

Town and Country Planning Act 1990
General Development Order 1988 amended and extended 1991
   Many farm buildings and developments are no longer classed as permitted development under planning law. Details of all schemes have to be sent to the local planning authority together with a fee. The authority will rule in each case whether further information needs to be submitted for formal planning approval before work can commence.
   Particular developments normally requiring formal planning approval include:

- buildings for non-agricultural purposes;
- dwelling houses;
- conversions of farm buildings to commercial or industrial or residential use;
- buildings not designed for agriculture, e.g. containers, lorry bodies, etc.
- buildings exceeding 465 m² – in any 2-year period within 90 m – includes yards and slurry lagoons;
- buildings 12 m and over in height;
- buildings 3 m and over in height within 3 km of an airfield;
- buildings within 25 m from the metalled part of a classified road;
- livestock buildings within 400 m of a 'protected building';
- caravan sites for which special rules apply;
- holiday cottages;
- recreational pursuits of a recurring nature, e.g. adventure games, canoeing, hang-gliding, windsurfing, water skiing, need consent if exceeding 28 days per year;

- farm shops: permission is needed for shops if produce is not derived from the farm involved and for new buildings to be used as shops. Particular care is required over access, parking and advertising signs.

The Building Regulations 2000
Many agricultural building are exempt from the Building Regulations 2000 – but not all. The following extract from the Regulations details the buildings that are exempt – all others are subject to Building Control and details must be submitted to the Local Authority before work commences.

   Schedule 3 – Exempt Buildings and Works
   Regulation 9 – Greenhouses and Agricultural Buildings

1 A building used as a greenhouse unless the main purpose is for retail packing or exhibiting.
2 a   A building used for agriculture which is:

   i.   Sited at a distance not less than one and a half times its own height from any building containing sleeping accommodation, and
   ii. Provided with an exit which may be used in the case of fire which is not more than 30 m from any point within the building (unless the main purpose for which the building is used is for retailing, packing and exhibiting).

   b   In this paragraph, 'agriculture' includes horticulture, fruit growing, seed growing, dairy farming, fish farming and the breeding and keeping of livestock (including any creature kept for the production of food, wool, skins or fur or for the purpose of farming the land).

Other relevant legislation
   The Environmental Assessment Regulations, 1988
   Health and Safety at Work Act, etc., 1974
   Control of Substances Hazardous to Health Regulations, 1988 (COSHH)
   Electricity at Work Regulation, 1989
   The Noise at Work Regulations, 1989
   The Food Safety Act, 1990
   The Food Hygiene (HQ) Regulation, 1990
   Code of Practice for the Control of Salmonella
   The Environmental Protection Act, 1990
   The Code of Good Agricultural Practice for the Protection of Air
   Control of Pollution Act 1974 – Water Act 1989
   The Control of Pollution (Silage, Slurry and Agricultural Fuel Oil) Regulations, 1991
   The Code of Good Agricultural Practice for the Protection of Water July, 1991
   The Welfare of Livestock Regulations
   The Building Standards (Scotland) Regulations, 1988

12 BIBLIOGRAPHY
BS 5502 Code of practice for the design of buildings and structures for agriculture.
   Published in separate parts as follows:

   Part 0: 1992 Introduction
   Part 11: 2005 Guide to regulations and sources of information
   Part 20: 1990 Code of practice for general design considerations
   Part 21: 1990 Code of practice for the selection and use of construction materials
   Part 22: 2003 Code of practice for design, construction and loading
   Part 23: 2004 Code of practice for fire precautions
   Part 25: 1991 Code of practice for design and installation of services and facilities
   Part 30: 1992 Code of practice for control of infestation

Part 32: 1990 Guide to noise attenuation

Part 33: 1991 Guide to the control of odour pollution

Part 40: 2005 Code of practice for the design and construction of cattle buildings

Part 41: 1990 Code of practice for design and construction of sheep buildings and pens

Part 42: 1990 Code of practice for design and construction of pig buildings

Part 43: 1990 Code of practice for design and construction of poultry buildings

Part 49: 1990 Code of practice for design and construction of milking premises

Part 50: 1993 Code of practice for design, construction and use of storage tanks and reception pits for livestock slurry

Part 51: 1991 Code of practice for design and construction of slatted, perforated and mesh floors for livestock

Part 52: 1991 Code of practice for design of alarm systems and emergency ventilation for livestock housing

Part 60: 1992 Code of practice for design and construction of buildings for mushrooms

Part 65: 1992 Code of practice for design and construction of crop processing buildings

Part 66: 1992 Code of practice for design and construction of chitting houses

Part 70: 1991 Code of practice for design and construction of ventilated on floor stores for combinable crops

Part 71: 1992 Code of practice for design and construction of ventilated stores for potatoes and onions

Part 72: 1992 Code of practice for design and construction of controlled environment stores for vegetables, fruit and flowers

Part 74: 1991 Code of practice for design and construction of bins and silos for combinable crops

Part 75: 1993 Code of practice for the design and construction of forage stores

Part 80: 1990 Code of practice for design and construction of workshops, maintenance and inspection facilities

Part 81: 1989 Code of practice for design and construction of chemical stores

Part 82: 1997 Code of practice for design of amenity buildings

15 Auditoria

Ian Appleton and Stefanie Fischer

CI/SfB 52

*Ian Appleton is a partner in The Appleton Partnership. Stefanie Fischer, who contributed
the section on cinema design with input from Ron Inglis of Mayfield Arts and Media, and
Richard Boyd, technical director, BFI Southbank, is a principal of Burrell, Foley Fischer LLP*

KEY POINTS:
- *Each member of an audience should clearly see a performance, screen or speaker, as well as clearly hearing speech, music or sounds*
- *Auditorium design must consider audience comfort, fire safety, acoustic quality, sound insulation, sound systems, lighting, receptive atmosphere and access to technical equipment*
- *Stage and audio-visual technologies are constantly evolving*

Contents
1 Introduction
2 Seating
3 Auditorium design
4 Theatre
5 Studio theatres
6 Concert hall
7 Conference halls
8 Cinemas
9 Multi-purpose auditoria
10 Support facilities
11 Facilities for people with a disability
12 Legislation

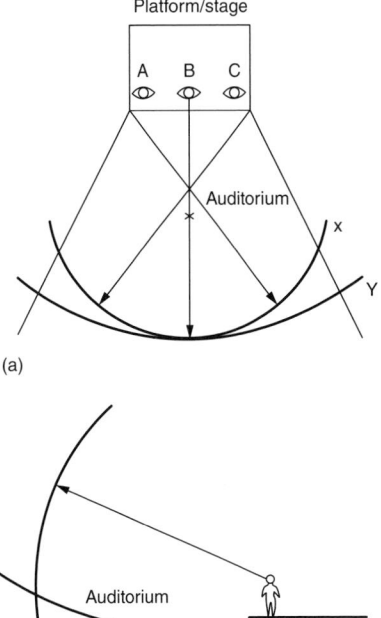

15.1 *Visual and aural limitations: a Plan: for a performer at centre stage B there is an arc Y beyond which visual and aural perceptions are impaired. However, for performers nearer the sides of the stage at A and C produce more restrictive curves X. b Section: Similarly, visual and aural limits in section also set an arc centred on the performer*

1 INTRODUCTION

The three-dimensional volume of an auditorium is conditioned by the need for all members of the audience to be able to see the whole of the platform or stage; and to hear the actor, singer, musician or speaker, Figure 15.1. Seating density, floor rake and seating layout are partly determined by this, partly to give the audience an appropriate level of comfort and essentially to ensure a means of escape in an emergency, such as a fire, within the time required by safety considerations and by legislation.

2 SEATING

2.1 Design of the auditorium seat

The aim is to provide an appropriate standard of comfort. The range of human body dimensions is wide; while in most auditoria a single size of seat is provided, Figure 15.2 and Table I. Tolerance levels vary: young people can tolerate simple seating found less comfortable by older people. Those attending concerts of classical music seem to expect more comfort than those watching drama. Seats are generally designed for the average person expected to use it; this varies according to age and nationality. Minor variation is achieved by the upholstery and adjustment of the back and seat pan material when the seat is occupied: otherwise the seat selection is a common size within the whole, or part of, the auditorium layout. The best able to be achieved is in the order of 90 per cent of the audience within an acceptable range of comfort.

2.2 Working dimensions

Seat width: the minimum dimension as stipulated by legislation is 500 mm with arms and 450 mm without. For seats with arms a width of 525 mm is the least for reasonable comfort.

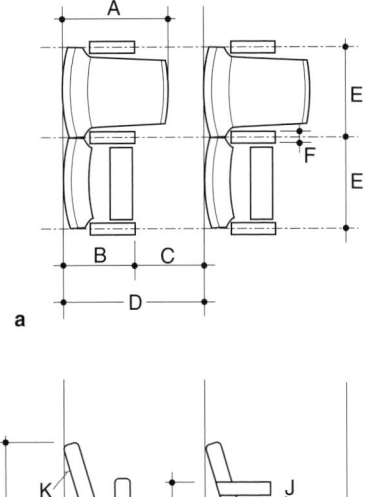

15.2 *Auditorium seating: definitions of terms and dimensional information (to be read in conjunction with Table I): a Plan. b Section*

Table I Dimensions of auditorium seats

Dimension	Description	Minimum	Maximum	Drawn as
A	Overall seat depth	600 mm	720 mm	650 mm
B	Tipped seat depth (same as length of arm)	425	500	450
C	Seatway (unobstructed vertical space between rows)	305		400
D	Back-to-back seat spacing	760		850
E	Seat width for seats with arms	500	750	525
	Seat width for seats without arms	450		
F	Armrest width	50		50
G	Seat height	430	450	440
H	Armrest height	600		600
I	Seatback height	800	850	800
J	Seat inclination from horizontal	7°	9°	7°
K	Back inclination from vertical	15°	20°	15°

Seat height: 430–450 mm.

Seat inclination: an angle to the horizontal of 7–9°.

Back height: 800–850 mm above floor level (may be increased for acoustic reasons).

Back inclination: angle to the vertical of 15–20°.

Seat depth: 600–720 mm for seat and back depth overall, reducing to 425–500 mm when the seat is tipped. The seat depth varies and depends on thickness of upholstery and backing and if the rear of the seat contains the air-conditioning. For a modest seat with arms, the dimensions can be as low as 520 mm deep, 340 mm when tipped. The ability of the seat to tip, activated silently by weight when not occupied, allows a clearway (which is a critical dimension) to pass along a row while limiting row to row distance. Where space is severely limited such as in studio theatres, an especially slim seat, Figure 15.3 can be used.

Arm rests: 50 mm minimum width, with the length coinciding with the tipped seat to avoid obstructing the clearway; the height about 600 mm above floor level; the upper surface may be sloped or not.

2.3 Supports

The permanent fixing of a seat can be:

- side supports shared by adjacent seats, Figure 15.4;
- a pedestal or single vertical support, Figure 15.5;
- cantilevered brackets fixed to riser (if of sufficient height) and shared by adjacent seats, Figure 15.6;
- a bar supporting a group of seats with leg or bracket support, Figure 15.7.

2.4 Other factors

Acoustics: upholstery to satisfy the acoustic requirements, usually the level of absorbency when unoccupied, especially the case with music, Figure 15.8.

   Ventilation and heating: for air supply or extract under a seat, allow space in floor or riser to receive grille, Figure 15.9.

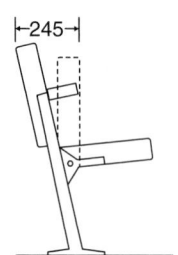

15.3 *A slim 'studio theatre' seat for use when space is limited*

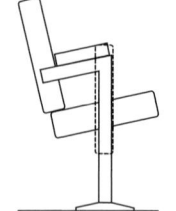

15.4a *Tip-up seat*

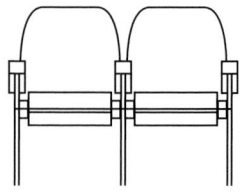

15.4b *Fixed seating with side support off floor or tread*

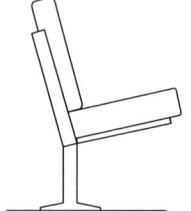

15.5a *Fixed continuous upholstered bench seating*

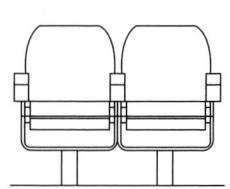

15.5b *Fixed seating with pedestal support off floor or tread*

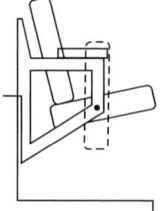

15.6 *Fixed seating with cantilevered support off high riser without overlap of riser*

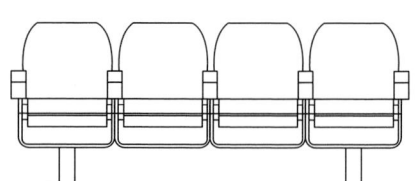

15.7 *Fixed seating with bar support off floor or tread*

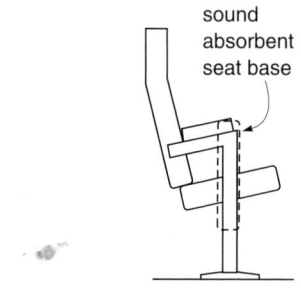

sound absorbent seat base

15.8 *Acoustic control seating (for when unoccupied)*

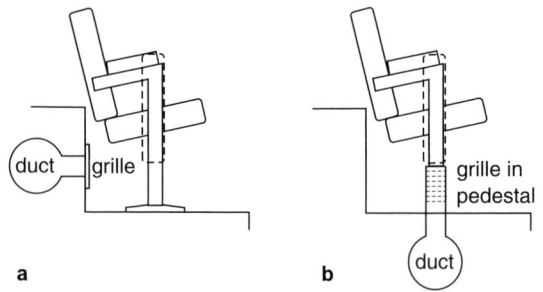

15.9 *a Ventilation grille below seat in riser or floor. b Ventilation grille incorporated into pedestal*

Upholstery: thickness of padding should provide comfort and avoid fatigue, but not encourage excessive relaxation; material of padding and finish must satisfy fire regulations.

2.5 Writing surface

Conference use may require a writing surface for note-taking. The writing surface may be:

- a tablet fixed to each seat, Figure 15.10;
- a removable tablet;
- a tablet pivoted to slide away vertically, Figure 15.11;
- a writing shelf on the back of the row in front, which can be fixed in position, hinged or retractable, Figure 15.12;
- a fixed table with loose seat;
- a fixed table with fixed pivoting or sliding seat, Figure 15.13.

Table seating has the advantage that delegates can pass behind the row of seats, and assistants can sit behind the delegates.

In a theatre or concert hall where there is occasional conference use every other row of seats can be used with temporary tables, Figure 15.14.

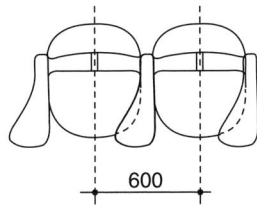

15.10 *Fixed tablet arm*

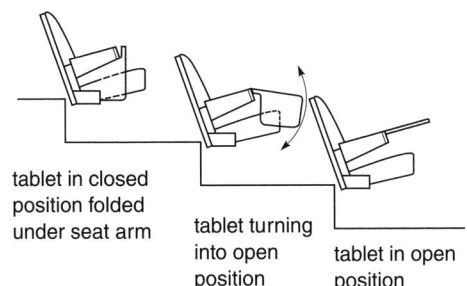

15.11 *Folded writing tablet under seat arm*

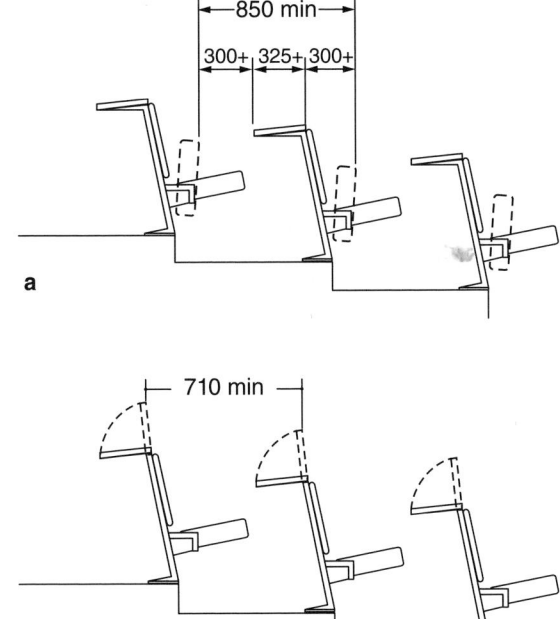

15.12 *a Fixed writing surface and tip-up seat. b Fixed seat and tip-up writing surface*

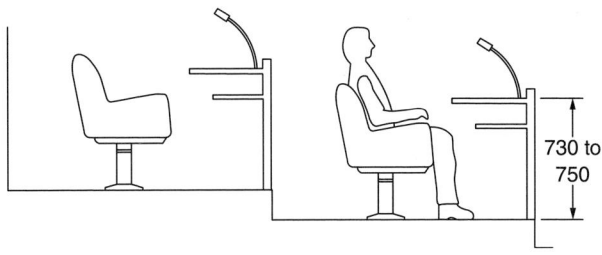

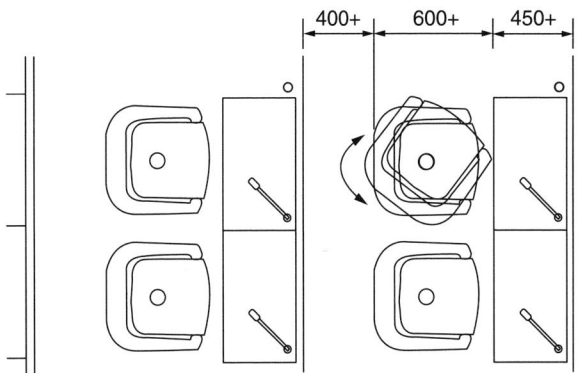

15.13 *Fixed writing surface, individual pivoting seats, section and plan*

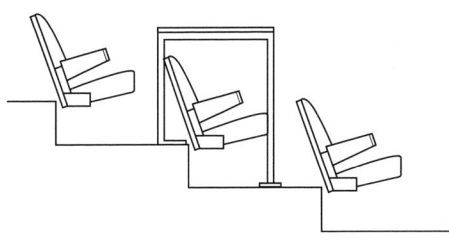

15.14 *Table added to every other row of fixed seating in theatre or concert hall for occasional conference use*

2.6 Wired services

These may be required for conference use. They can be incorporated into the arm of the seat, Figure 15.15 or into the rear of the seat or table in front. Further details will be found in Section 7.4.

For music, drama and cinema there may be provision for earphones for people with hearing impairment, or this facility may be provided by an induction loop.

15.15 *Controls and microphone in seat arm*

3 AUDITORIUM DESIGN

3.1 Audience requirements

As stated above, every member of the audience should be able to see and hear clearly whatever is happening on every part of the stage or platform. This is an ideal rarely (if ever) totally attainable in practice. However, a clear view for everyone of the main part of the stage or platform is normally achievable in modern auditoria. Where an existing building is undergoing renovation, further compromises may well be necessary for some seats.

The greater the encirclement of the audience of platform or stage, more people can be accommodated within the aural and visual limitations up to 180° encirclement. With a full encirclement, the distance from platform or stage should be restricted to six rows.

3.2 Visual limitations

Visual limitations determine the maximum distance from platform or stage at which the audience is able to appreciate the performance and for the performers or speaker to command an audience. This distance varies according to function type and the scale of the performance:

- For drama it is essential to discern facial expression, and the maximum distance should be 20 m measured from the setting line of a proscenium stage or geometric centre of an open stage.
- For opera and musicals discerning facial expressions is less critical and the distance can be 30 m.
- For dance the audience needs to appreciate the whole body of dancers and facial expression: the distance should not exceed 20 m.
- For full symphonic concerts acoustic conditions predominate.
- For chamber concerts acoustic conditions also predominate but visual definition assists achieving an intimate setting.
- For conference speaker and lecturer there are two scales: discerning facial expression, restricted by 20 m; larger scale where facial expression is not regarded as critical.
- For slide, video, television, overhead projector and other projections, visual limitations are determined by their respective technologies.

3.3 Aural limitations

This refers to the distances across which speech, singing and music can be clearly heard without the need for amplification, and beyond which they cannot. For drama, opera and classical music amplification is deprecated; but it is acceptable for variety and pantomime and essential for rock music.

For amplified sound the auditorium requires a dead acoustic with no reflected sound from the platform or stage and limited or no reverberation; loudspeakers are positioned to provide full and even coverage of the audience.

The volume and quality of the unamplified sound is dependent on the volume, shape, size and internal finishes of the auditorium, and on its resultant reverberation time. It is therefore not possible to lay down limits as for visual appreciation. Even experts in acoustics find that their predictions are not always borne out in practice, although they should be consulted and their advice followed wherever possible. It has been found feasible to improve the acoustic of existing auditoria, for example, the famous 'flying saucers' in the hitherto notorious Royal Albert Hall.

3.4 Levels in the auditorium

With a single level only, the pitch of the rake requires particular attention to achieve a sense of enclosure. The Greek amphitheatre is the exemplar.

Seating capacity within aural and visual limitations can be increased by the addition of one or more balconies within the overall permissible volume of the auditorium. Similarly, boxes, side galleries and loges can be added to the side walls, especially in the case of the proscenium format.

3.5 Number of seats in a row

With traditional seating the maximum number is 22 if there are gangways at both ends of the row, and 11 for gangway at one end. Thus in all but the smallest auditorium the gangways divide the seating into blocks.

Rows with more than 22 seats are permitted if the audience is not thereby imperilled. The term 'continental seating' is used for rows of seats with an increased back-to-back dimension extending the width of the auditorium with exits at both ends. This arrangement is usually only appropriate to proscenium stage, platform or cinema.

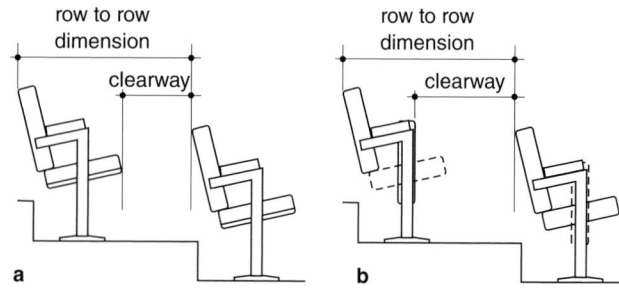

15.16 *a Row to row dimension and clearway with fixed seating. b Row to row dimension and clearway with tipped-up seating*

3.6 Row-to-row spacing

Spacing is controlled by the clearway between the leading edge of the seat (in an upright position, if tippable) and the rear of the back of the seat in front, Figure 15.16. For traditional seating the minimum clearway for people to pass along the row is 300 mm and this dimension increases with the number of seats in a row. For continental seating the clearway is not less than 400 mm and not more than 500 mm. Legislation also dictates the minimum row-to-row dimension at 760 mm: this is usually not adequate and the minimum should be 850 mm for traditional seating.

3.7 Gangways

As gangways are essential escape routes, their widths are determined by the number of seats served. The minimum is 1100 mm. They can be ramped up to 10 per cent, but only 8.5 per cent if likely to be used by people in wheelchairs. If the seating rake is steeper, gangways must have steps extending the full width and these must have consistent treads and risers in each run. This means that the row-to-row spacing and row rise should be compatible with a convenient gangway tread and riser; and this in turn means that the shallow curve produced by sightline calculations should be adjusted to a straight line.

3.8 Seating geometry

Seating is usually laid out in straight or curved rows focused towards the platform or stage. Further forms are the angled row, straight row with curved change of direction and straight rows within emphasised blocks of seats, Figures 15.17 and 15.18.

3.9 Seating density

Seats with arms and tippable seat can occupy a space as small as 500 mm wide (less for seats without arms) with a row-to-row dimension of 760 mm; but can be as large as 750 mm wide by 1400 mm, Figure 15.19. The area per seat therefore varies between 0.38 m^2 and 3.05 m^2. Increased dimensions reduces seating capacity. Minimum dimensions as laid down by legislation offer a low standard of comfort and should not be taken as a norm, but the social cohesion of the audience may be lost if the standards are too high.

In conference halls where writing space is required, lower densities are inevitable, Figure 15.20.

3.10 Sightlines for a seated audience

For every member of the audience to have an uninterrupted view of the platform or stage over the heads in front and clear of overhangs the section and plan of the auditorium need to conform to certain limitations set by vertical and horizontal sightlines.

Vertical sightlines, Figure 15.21, may be calculated by establishing:

P   Lowest and nearest point of sight on the platform or stage for the audience to see clearly.

HD Horizontal distance between the eyes of the seated members of the audience, which relates to the row spacing and can vary from 760 mm to 1150 mm and more.

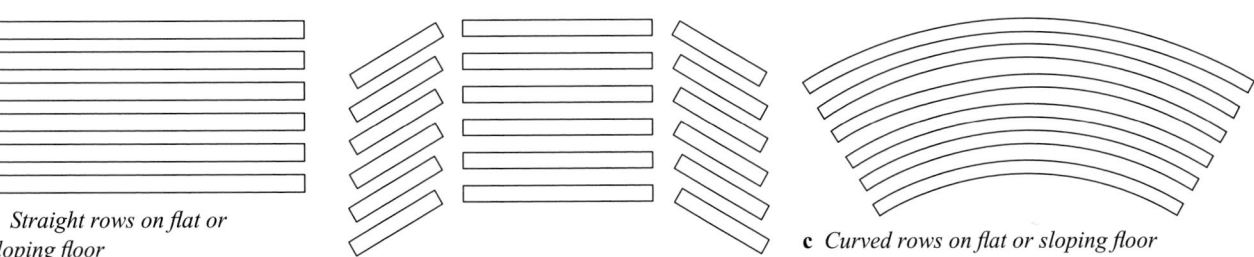

a *Straight rows on flat or sloping floor*

b *Straight rows with separate angled side blocks on flat or sloping floor*

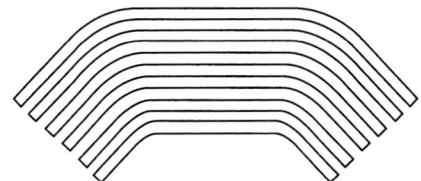

c *Curved rows on flat or sloping floor*

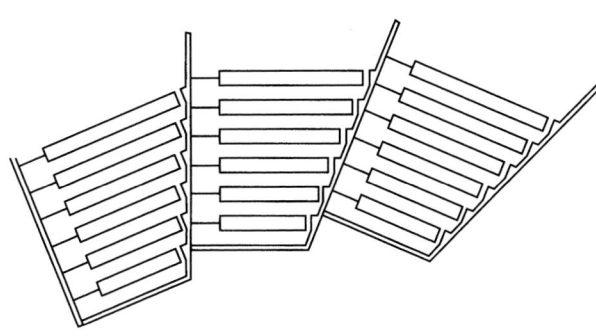

d *Straight and angled rows on flat or sloping floor*

e *As d but with curves at change of angle*

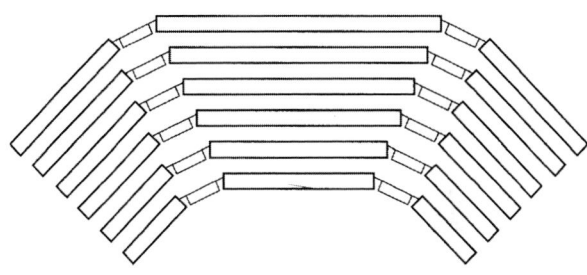

f *Separated stepped blocks focused on stage*

g *Straight stepped rows and separated angled side blocks*

15.17 *Alternative auditorim seating arrangements*

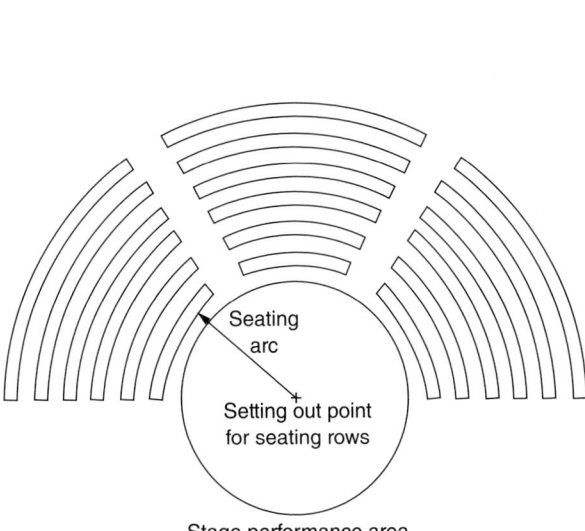

a *Open stage and theatre-in-the-round layouts*

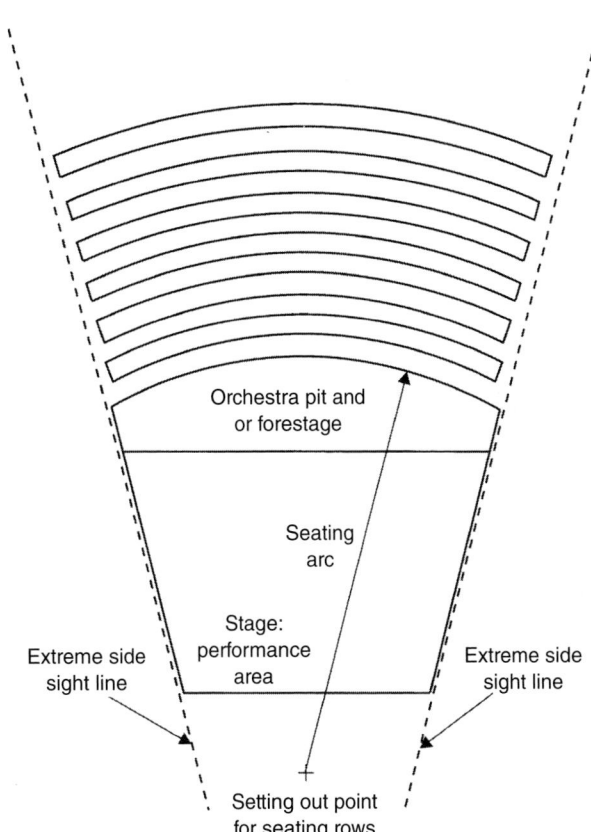

b *Proscenium layout*

15.18 *Setting-out of auditorium seating rows*

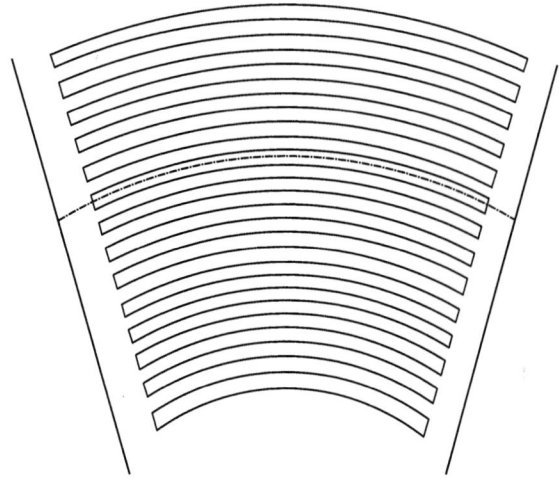

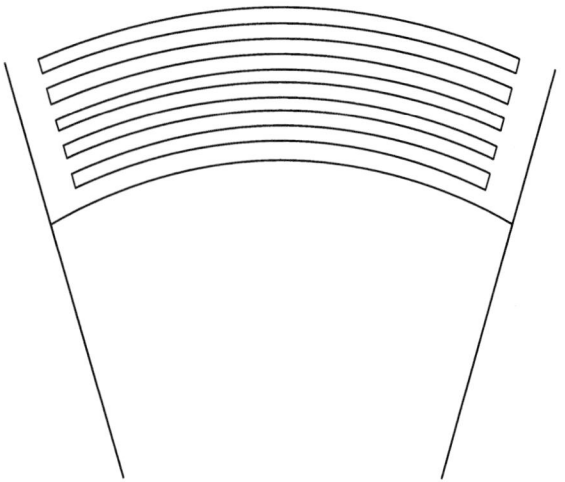

Setting out point
for seating rows

Stalls: lowest level of seating

c *Proscenium and end stage layout 1: stalls*

Setting out point
for seating rows

Balconies: upper seating levels

d *Proscenium and end stage layout 1: balcony*

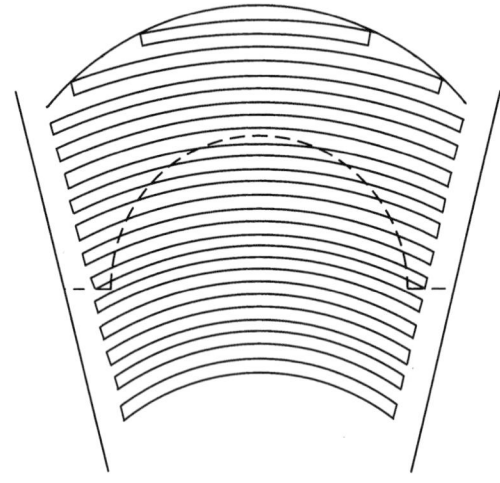

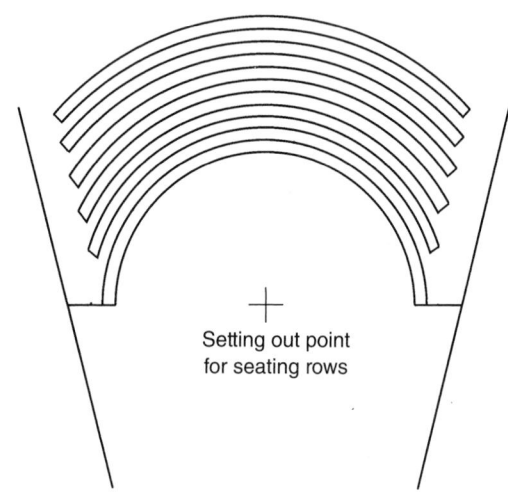

Setting out point
for seating rows

Stall: lowest level of seating

e *Proscenium and end stage layout 2: stalls*

Setting out point
for seating rows

Balconies: upper seating levels

f *Proscenium and end stage layout 2: balcony*

15.18 *Setting-out of auditorium seating rows (contd.)*

EH Average eye height at 1120 mm above the theoretical floor level: the actual eye point will depend on seat dimensions.

E Distance from the centre of the eye to the top of the head, taken as 100 mm as a minimum dimension for the calculations of sightlines. For assurance that there is a clear view over the heads of those in the row in front this dimension should be a least 125 mm.

D Front row of seats: the distance from point P to the edge of the average member of the audience in the front row. The relationship is shown in Figure 15.21.

The longitudinal section is a parabolic stepped floor as a theoretical rake produced by the sightline calculation. This gives every member of the audience similar viewing conditions. This may be reduced to a single angle or series of angles.

When applied as described the rake will also be steep. This is satisfactory for a single tier of seating with no balconies and is especially appropriate for open-stage formats. If a balcony or balconies are introduced, the rake of the lower bank of seats can be reduced, assuming vision to be every other row allowing for point P being seen between heads in the row in front. The vertical distance between point from eye to top of the head for calculation purposes can be reduced to 65 mm if seats are staggered. This is particularly applicable with the design of a large auditorium where, within the visual and aural limitations, the aim is to maximise the seating capacity. This implies a balance between sightlines, height of

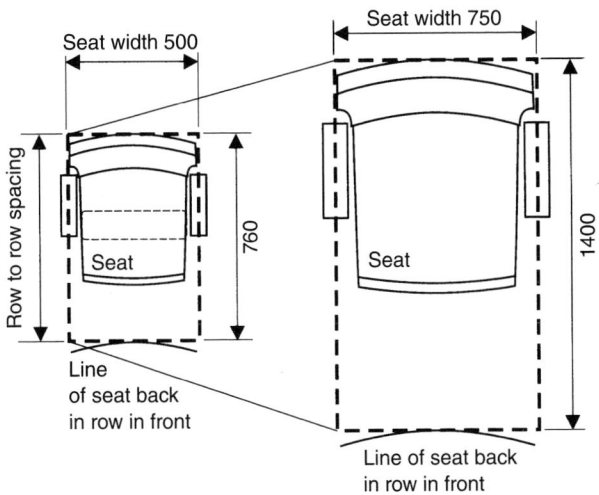

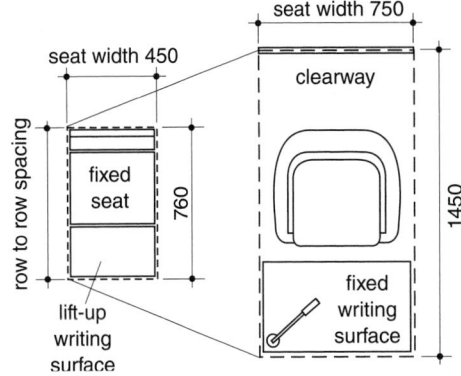

15.20 *Seating density in conference halls, from 0.34 m² to 1.09m² per person*

15.19 *Seating density, from 0.38m² to 1.05m² per person*

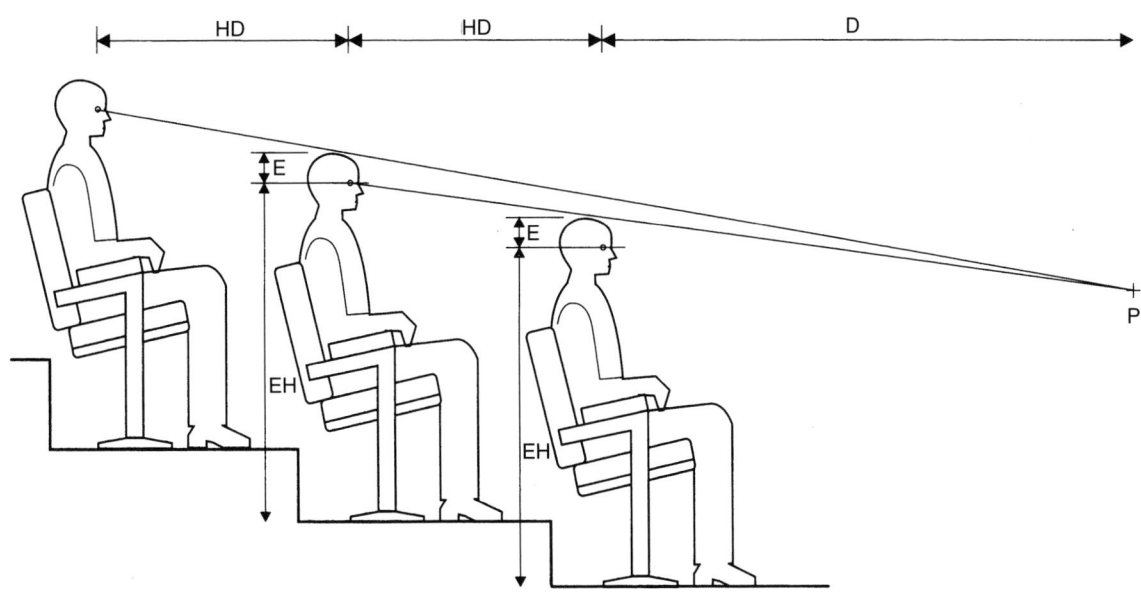

15.21 *Graphic representation of vertical sightlines, P lowest and nearest point on stage clearly visible by audience, HD horizontal distance between eyes in successive audience rows, EH average audience eye height above floor, E height between eye and top of head, D distance from eye of person in front row to P*

auditorium and seating capacity. Reducing the accumulative height of the lower level of seating allows more height for balconies.

With the smaller auditorium, especially with the audience partially or wholly surrounding the stage and a limited number of rows of seats, an increased height of the rake to the seating encourages a sense of enclosure of the stage, while providing good sightlines. Figure 15.22 shows how the eye position relates to the seat and the stepped floor.

Cross-gangways
With *cross-gangways* the line of the auditorium rake must continue so that the audience can see the performance area above the gangway as below. With stepped rows there requires a handrail to the upper side of the gangway and, if a steep rake, a handrail to the lower side. See Figure 15.23.

Horizontal sightlines
Given a particular size and shape of the platform or stage, horizontal sightlines limit the width of the seating area in the auditorium. This is more critical with the proscenium stage and with film, video and slide projection.

Without head movement, the arc to view the whole platform or stage on plan is 40° from the eye, Figure 15.24. Debatable is an

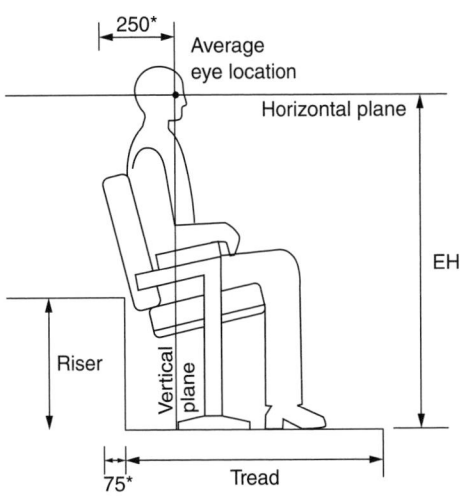

15.22 *Position of eye in relation to seat and stepped floor. Dimensions vary according to upholstery thickness, and inclinations of both seat and back. Working dimensions are starred**

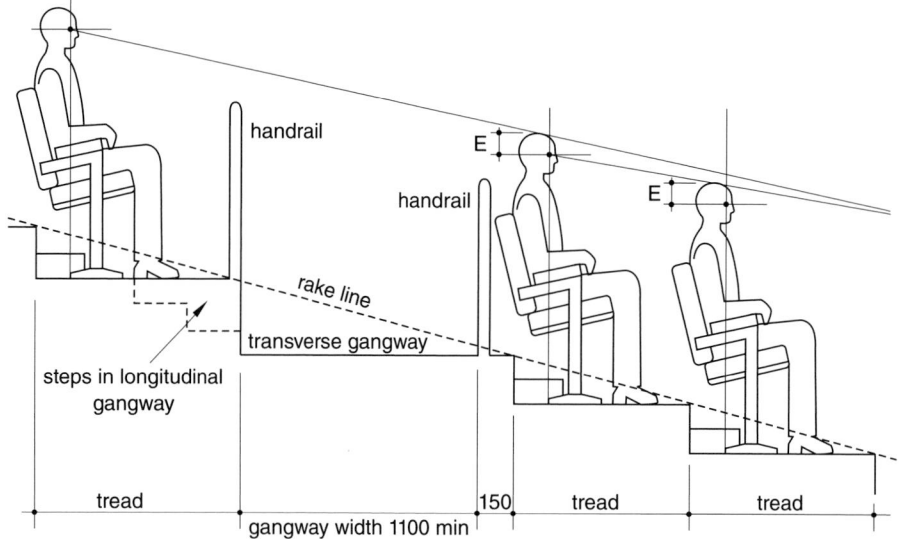

15.23 *Sightlines at transverse gangway; the angle of the rake line is constant*

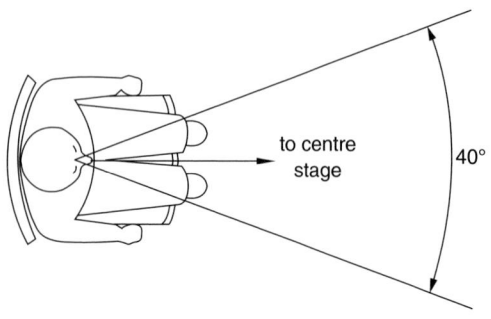

15.24 *The angle of horizontal vision for a stationary head is 40°*

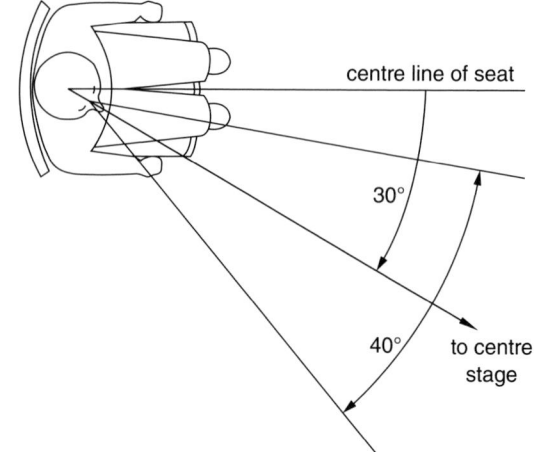

15.25a *The maximum comfortable amount the head can be turned from the seat centreline is 30°*

acceptable head movement, where the seat is focused away from the platform or stage, such as with side galleries requiring the head to be turned by the member of the audience, Figure 15.25.

The horizontal sightline of the performer may also need consideration, Figure 15.26.

3.11 Wheelchair location

Regulations require a minimum of six places for wheelchair users, or 1/100th of the audience capacity, whichever is the greater. Their location as discrete areas can be at the rear, front, side or within the seating, Figure 15.27. Wheelchairs can be centrally positioned by forming a bay off a cross-gangway.

A wheelchair user should be able to sit with a party of friends not in wheelchairs, Figure 15.28. Sightlines from the wheelchair should be checked, as should the sightlines of those audience members behind. Some wheelchair users can transfer into auditorium seats.

3.12 Means of escape

The aim is for all in the auditorium to be able to escape to a place of safety within a set period of time. The escape route is from the seat, along the clearway and gangway, and through exit doors immediately, or through an enclosed corridor, to the place of safety.

Travel distance

The maximum travel distance from seat to exit within the auditorium is determined by the need to evacuate from each level of the auditorium within 2½ minutes. For traditional seating the maximum travel distance is 18 m measured from the gangway, for continental seating 15 m from any seat.

Exits

From each level of the auditorium two separate exits must be provided for the first 500 seats with an additional exit for each further

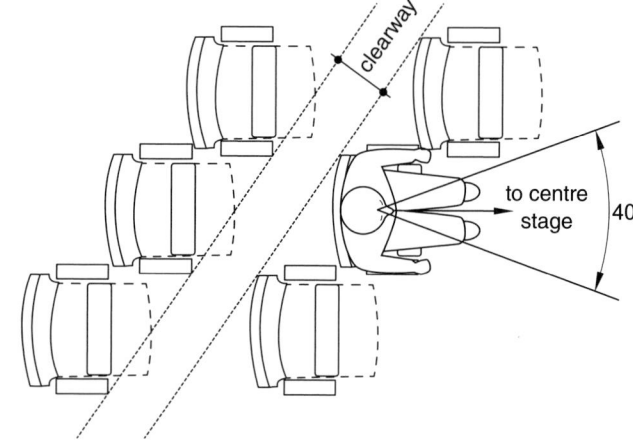

15.25b *Where the head angle would exceed 30°, the seats may be angled within the row*

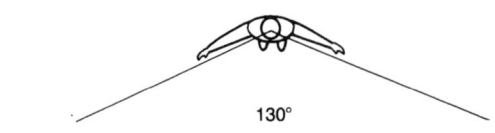

15.26 *Horizontal sightlines of the performer*

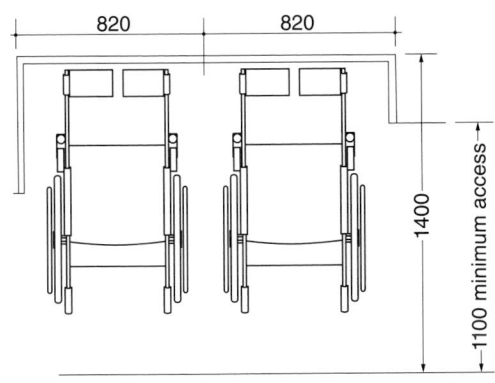

15.27 *Designated wheelchair area, required dimensions*

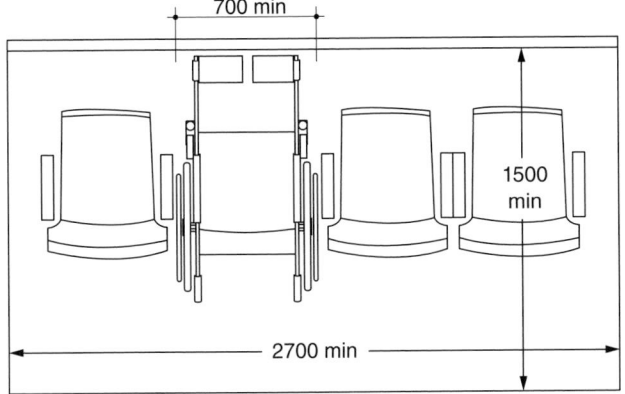

15.28 *Plan of a box designed for a wheelchair plus loose chairs*

Table II Total exit widths required by legislation

Numbers of people	Minimum total exit width (m)
up to 200	2.2
201–300	2.4
301–400	2.8
401–500	3.2
501–750	4.8
751–1000	6.4
1001–2000	14.4
2001–3000	20.8

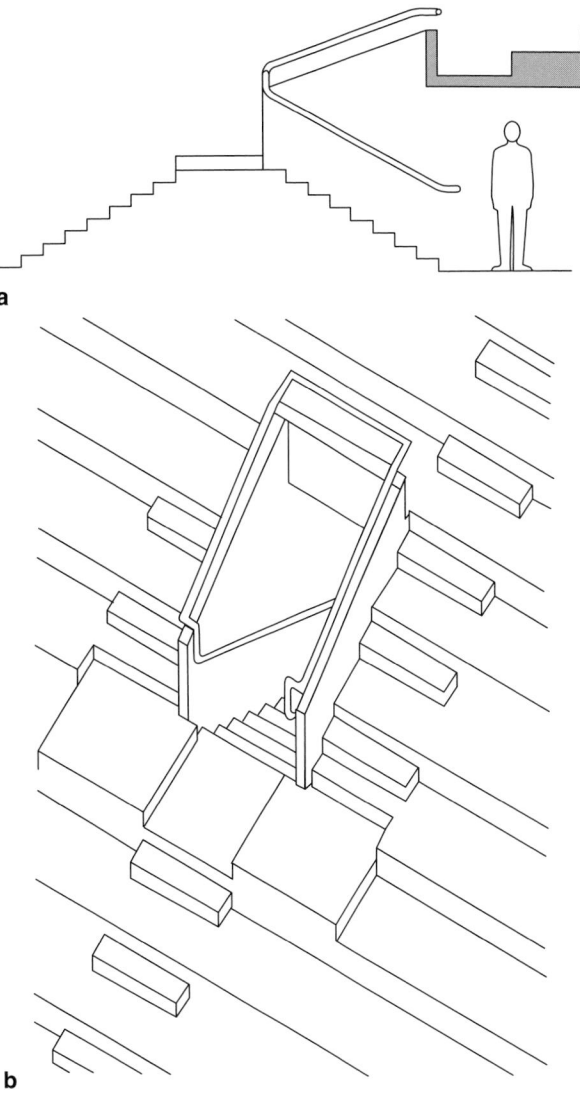

15.29 *Audience vomitory: a public entrance to and exit from the auditorium through a seating block as distinct from through the side or rear walls: a Section. b Axonometric view*

250 seats. Table II gives the minimum total of exit widths required by legislation. Each exit from the auditorium must lead directly to a place of safety.

Exit routes
The route must be a consistent width the same as the exit. There must be no bottlenecks and all doors within the route must open in the direction of escape. Routes within the building should have fire-resistant enclosures. There are special requirements for all doors opening onto fire escape routes.

Stairs
Staircase flights should have at least two risers and not more than 16. All treads should be 275 mm and risers 180 mm.

Ramps
Wheelchair users should be provided with flat or ramped escape routes which may be separate from other routes. Ramps should not be longer than 4.5 m or steeper than 8.5 per cent.

3.13 Circulation
While gangway lengths and widths are calculated as part of the fire escape route, they also provide the circulation through the auditorium, with possible additional gangways from the audience entry points to individual rows and seats.

3.14 Entry points
The audience can enter the auditorium from the foyer at the rear, at the sides of the seating or from vomitories within the seating banks, Figure 15.29; and the entry points need to connect directly with the gangways. There should be a threshold space at the entry points for ticket check, programme sales and for members of the audience to orientate themselves.

Sometimes, particularly in theatre-in-the-round, performers make their entrances from within the audience area, Figure 15.30.

3.15 Handrails
Balcony handrails, Figure 15.31, are specified by legislation covering height, width and structure: they must also not interfere with sightlines.

Handrails will also be required to stepped gangways:

- adjacent to enclosing wall;
- if there is a drop at the side.

They are also needed:

- at landings;
- at the rear of rostra;
- where there is a drop of more than 600 mm.

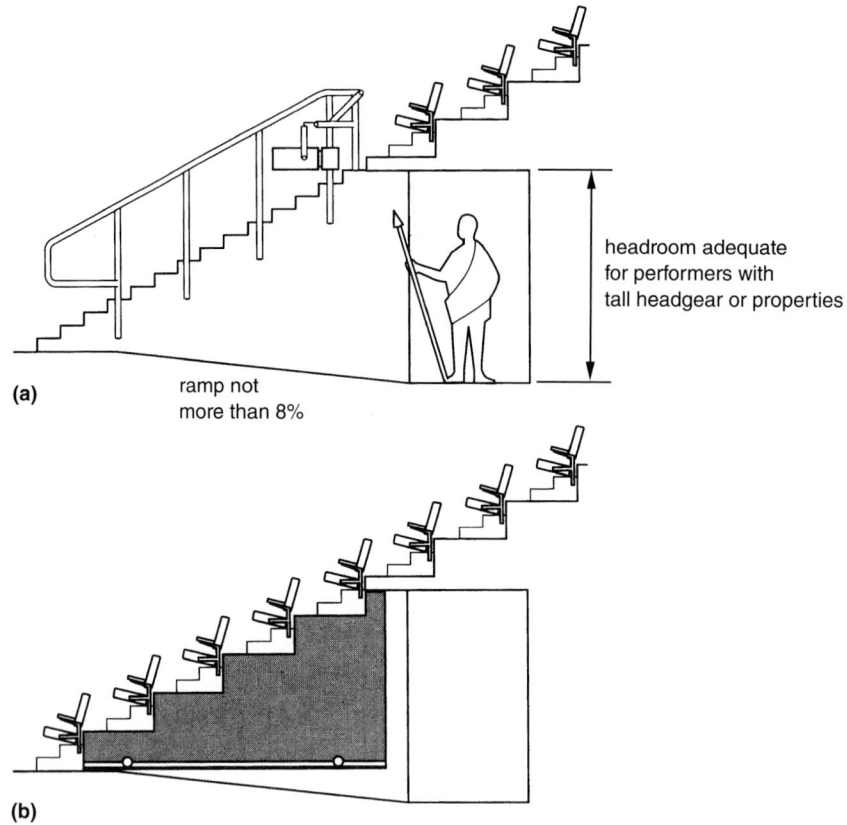

(a) ramp not more than 8%

headroom adequate
for performers with
tall headgear or properties

(b)

15.30 *Performers' vomitory: access to the stage through a block of seating, usually in an open stage or theatre-in-the round format. a Section. b Section showing removable seating in place when vomitory not required*

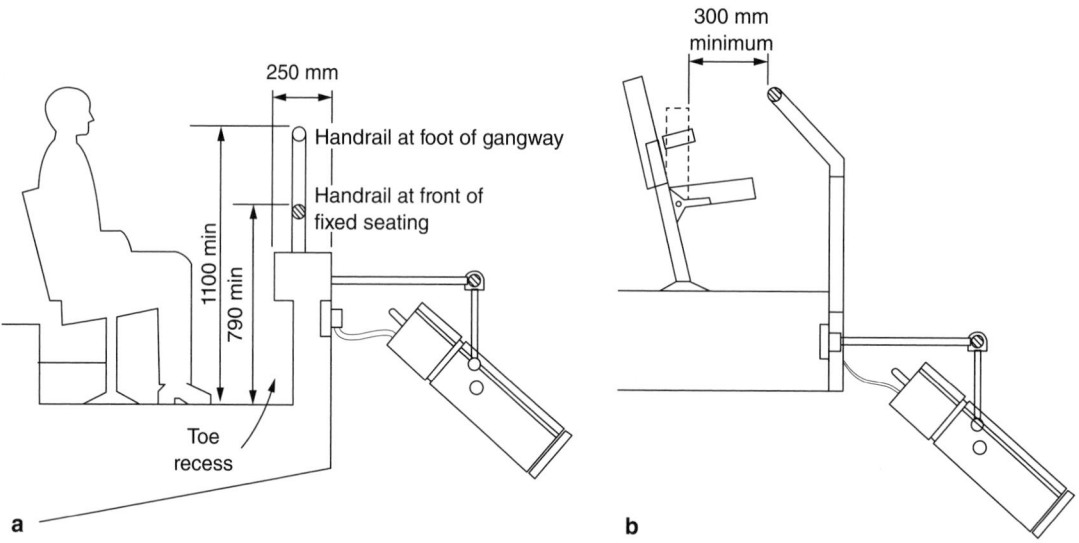

a   b

15.31 *The minimum balcony handrail height (BH) is set by legislation at 790 mm in front of fixed seating and 1100 mm at the ends of gangways. Balcony fronts are used to support performance lighting and need socket outlets connected to stage lighting controls: a Traditional balcony front incorporating shelf below handrail and adequate legroom. b Simpler front for side galleries with minimum clearway allowing the audience to lean on the handrail. This front is removable as part of a flexible auditorium*

Where the rake of a gangway is above 25° the ends of the rows should have a loop rail, Figure 15.32.

Rails are usually 900 mm above pitch line and 1200 mm above landings, with infill panels that are solid or have no gap greater than 100 mm.

3.16 Floors
The floor of the auditorium is an acoustic factor in the success of an auditorium. Some venues now dispense with carpets as plain wooden floorboards offer a better acoustic for orchestral music.

Consideration should be given as to whether the auditorium floor should be flexible to account for acoustic variability.

3.17 Latecomers
A waiting area at the rear of the auditorium either within the auditorium or in a separate enclosed space with viewing panel and tannoyed sound, or elsewhere with a closed-circuit television facility.

3.18 Attendants
Legislation dictates a number of attendants present at public events, each requiring a seat in the auditorium.

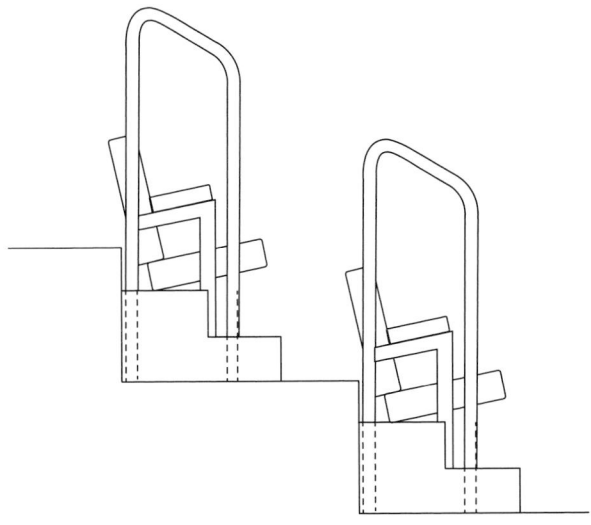

15.32 *Loop guardrail at the end of a row where the rake is steep*

3.19 Adaptation

Relevant for multi-purpose auditoria where different formats or uses are combined or part of the raked seating will require to be moved. This can be achieved by forming structure off a flat floor, and methods include:

- Bleacher seating, Figure 15.33: telescopic structure with tippable upholstered seating with backs, able to be retracted into the depth of a single and highest row; rows are straight and the extended structure is a simple rectangular block, which places a discipline on the seating layout.
- Rostra, Figure 15.34: complete raked units with either permanent or removable seats, on wheels or air palettes for ease of movement into storage areas when not in use.
- Sectional rostra, Figure 15.35: a set of boxes able to be built up to form raked units with removable seats; storage requirements less than complete rostra.
- Kit of parts, Figure 15.36: scaffolding or equivalent set of components able to form raked levels to receive seating; the most

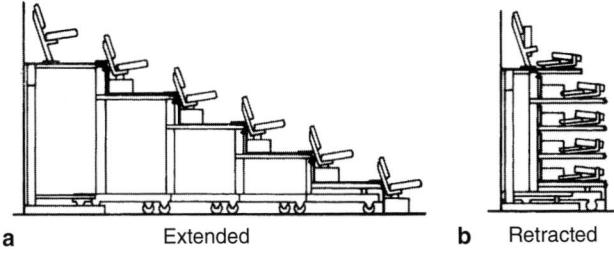

15.33 *a Bleacher seating: one of a number of proprietary systems of permanently installed retractable systems. The length of seating in a single unit is limited to 6 m. For tip-up seats with arms the minimum riser height is 250 mm. b Bleacher seating retracted*

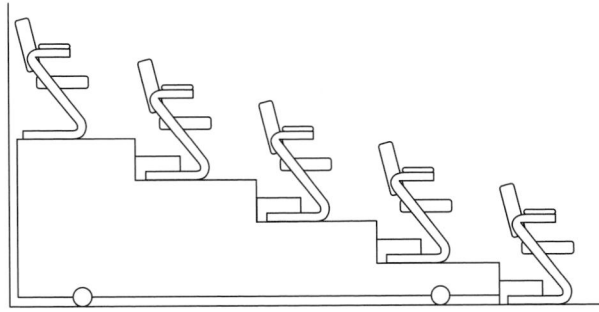

15.34 *Large units on brakable casters or air cushions*

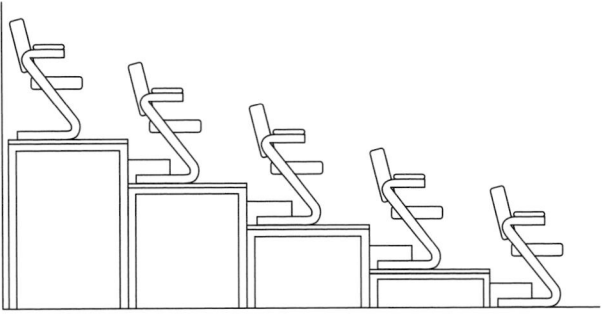

15.35 *Rostra: a set of metal or timber units built up to form a stepped floor on a flat base. Seats are secured onto floor or riser. Each rostrum unit collapsible for storage*

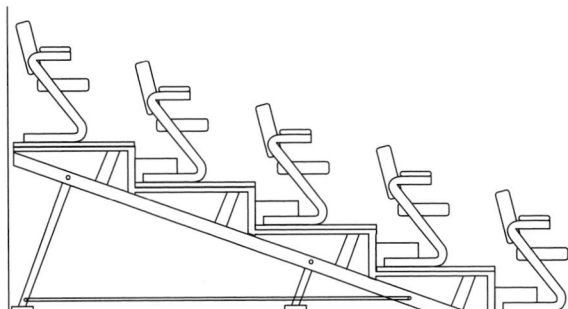

15.36 *Proprietary scaffolding-type system*

flexible system, efficient storage requirements, but labour intensive.

- Hydraulic lifts, Figure 15.37: mechanical method of raising sections of the flat floor to form a rake floor to receive seating.
- Loose seats, Figure 15.38, secured in position when required for performances, can be used with functions requiring a flat floor.

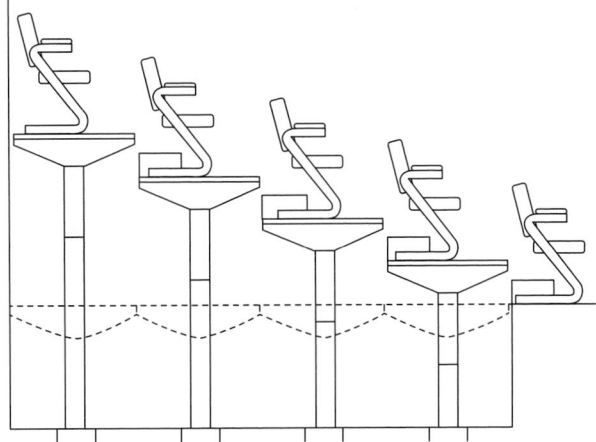

15.37 *Floor sections that can be raised and lowered hydraulically*

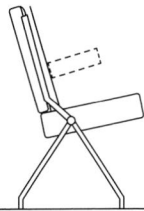

15.38 *Loose seating, capable of removal. May or may not have arms, and be stackable. Needs to be firmly fixed down when in public use*

Following a number of failures of such flexible spectator facilities, legislation has been tightened up and official inspections are often necessary whenever seating arrangements are changed. This means that it is not usually possible to stage a series of different events within a short space of time.

3.20 Sound insulation from outside noise sources

The standards are expressed as Noise Rating (NR). To achieve the appropriate rating auditorium design may require:

- isolation of the auditorium structurally;
- sound locks to all doors at point of entry;
- services acoustically sealed;
- noise reduction to air conditioning/heating/ventilation system.

3.21 Air conditioning, heating and ventilation

The design depends on the internal standards required in the auditorium, the thermal insulation of the enclosure and on the external climatic conditions. Ventilation needs to provide fresh air at a rate of change to achieve comfort conditions: rates are set down by legislation and include a proportion of recycled conditioned air which vary locally. A common condition is a minimum air supply per occupant of 8 litres per second, 75 per cent of outside air and 25 per cent recirculated.

Extract ductwork can be at ceiling level and under balconies with supply below the seating.

Plant should be remote from auditorium to avoid noise transmission.

3.22 Lighting

There are six different requirements for auditorium lighting.

Performance lighting

For theatre, opera and dance performance lighting is an integral part of the staging of productions, with lighting positions not only on the stage but also within the auditorium at ceiling level, on side and rear walls and balcony fronts. Further details are given in Section 4.11.

For classical music and serious jazz sufficient lighting for the performers to see their music and the conductor (if any), and for them to be seen by the audience is usually all that is required. Similar lighting is required for the platform at conferences.

Pop music requires as complex lighting as for drama and opera – perhaps even exceeding that with elaborate effects.

House lighting before and after performance and during intervals

Illumination is needed to enable the audience to move around, find their seats and read programmes; decorative lighting to emphasis architectural features. This form of lighting will also be required during conferences.

House lighting during performance

For cinema lighting is only for exit signs and escape routes. For the latter, small lights just above floor level have advantages in not obscuring the screen and being most effective in smoke-logged conditions.

For theatre a slightly higher level of illumination may be used, particularly if the performance demands a contrast with a time of almost total darkness. For classical music it is now usual to have sufficient lighting for near-normal vision and following scores.

Pop music may nowadays require house lighting as sophisticated as performance lighting, with strobe and laser facilities.

Certain lighting is required during performances to ensure safety in emergency, particularly the statutory exit signs. Other lighting may be required to come on automatically in emergency situations; this may work off a separate protected supply. Alternatively, each item can incorporate a battery and be programmed to come on when a failure in the mains supply is detected.

House lighting at other times

It should not be forgotten that the seating area will also require a working level of lighting for cleaning, maintenance and probably during rehearsals and auditions.

Front-of-house lighting

Escape routes have to be adequately lit at all times, during performances as well as before and after. Foyers, bars and ticket offices require careful lighting design to enhance their attraction.

Backstage lighting

Corridors are escape routes for the performers and service staff, and must be kept illuminated whenever the building is occupied. Dressing rooms and workshops will have normal lighting for such facilities, and may be fitted with proximity detectors to ensure that lights are not left on when the rooms are unoccupied.

3.23 Fire protection

Fire precautions should be discussed with the local fire authority and with fire insurers. Means of escape have already been covered in Section 3.12. However, it is important to consider four other factors.

Preventing fires occurring
- Non-combustibility of materials including finishes and seating.
- Protection of electrical circuits.
- Care with lighting.
- Separation of hazardous processes such as scene-painting.

Detecting them early when they do occur
- Smoke and heat detectors backstage, in auditorium and all voids.
- Alarms connected to the automatic detector system and central indicator panel, and possibly direct link to local fire station. These should be visual (flashing light) in auditorium and not audible.

Preventing them spreading
- Enclosing walls and floors to be fire-resistant.
- Self-closing firedoors to openings.
- Either a safety curtain to the stage area or special on-stage precautions.

Facilitating extinguishing
- Hose-reels.
- Portable extinguishers.
- Automatic sprinkler systems backstage (not allowed over seating areas).

3.24 Ceiling zone

Functional requirements cover:
- Acoustics: profiled reflector panels and possible adjustable diffusers. For non-amplified music, reflectors also over concert platform.
- Lighting: bridges for access and support for auditorium lighting, working lights and emergency lighting as well as performance lighting.
- Ventilation: air ducts and plenums, diffusers, noise attenuation and monitoring equipment, supporting hangers and means of access for servicing.
- Production requirements: for operas, dance musicals and drama, a grid and pulley suspension for suspending scenery over forestage, including access by technicians.
- Fire control: detection system in voids and fire dampers in ducts.
- Structure: support for roof, ducts, lighting bridges, etc.

4 THEATRE

4.1 Range

Theatre covers productions of drama, opera, ballet, musicals, variety and pantomime, 15.39.

4.2 Types

Theatre structures are enormously varied and much alteration work is done in theatres during their working lives. This work usually includes upgrading or modernising the stage equipment, and improving the seating quality. The reasons are market driven: equipping to take larger or more complex productions, enabling more productions within a given time and labour-saving measures. Front-of-house improvements are made to attract greater attendance through increased facilities and comfort.

Theatres and studio spaces, which for these purposes also include 'fringe' venues formed out of existing buildings, also see themselves as fitting into a particular bracket, for example small, medium or large scale. These categories are determined by a sliding scale involving seating capacity, size of stage, backstage accommodation and even geographical location. The intended scale of use should be apparent in any brief, or should be clarified. It will need to be reflected in the design proposals.

Medium-scale theatres would normally be considered as those with perhaps less than 1000-seat capacity, without a significant array of stage machinery, but provided with proper fly suspension systems and orchestra pit facilities suitable for taking smaller productions with cast not normally exceeding 20–25 individuals.

4.3 The proscenium

For most opera, dance and musicals, the formats are restricted to the proscenium and end stage. The proscenium form is a conventional arrangement placing the audience facing the stage, viewing the performance through an architectural opening. Scenery on the stage can be developed as a major design element. The traditional position is for the orchestra to be located in a pit between audience and stage, with the conductor in a pivotable location controlling orchestra and singers. The auditorium formats, Figure 15.40, include the horseshoe, fan with or without balconies, and courtyard. The latter consists of shallow balconies of no more than three rows around three sides of the auditorium. The end stage is similar to the proscenium format but without the architectural opening, placing audience and performance in the same space and suitable for small-scale productions.

For drama there is a wider range of formats: the initial distinction is between the proscenium format and open stage forms.

The proscenium format is outlined above. There are five variations of open stage formats, Figure 15.41:

- End stage
- Fan-shaped
- Thrust stage
- Theatre-in-the-round
- Transverse stage.

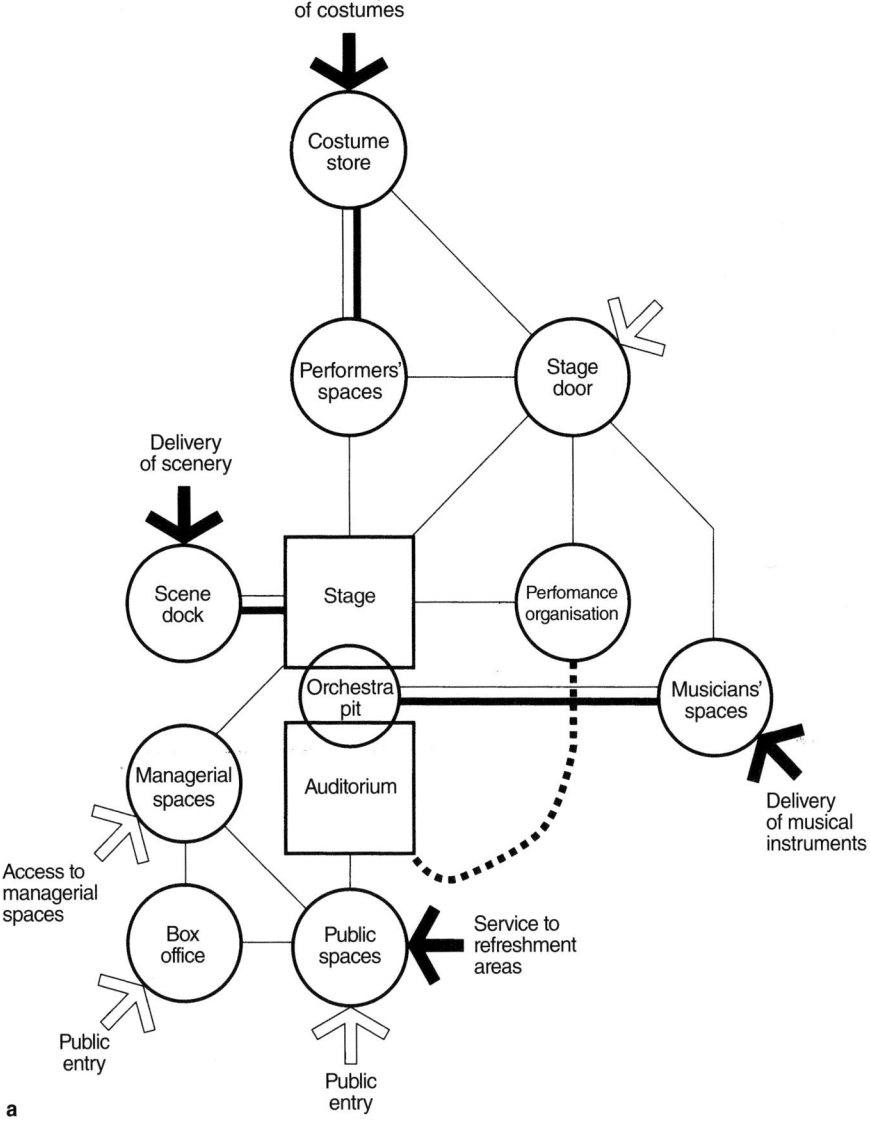

15.39 *Relationship diagrams for buildings for opera, musicals, dance and drama. If for drama only, the orchestra pit and musicians spaces may not be required: a Where the building serves only touring companies or with a resident company whose production facilities are elsewhere. b Where production facilities are needed*

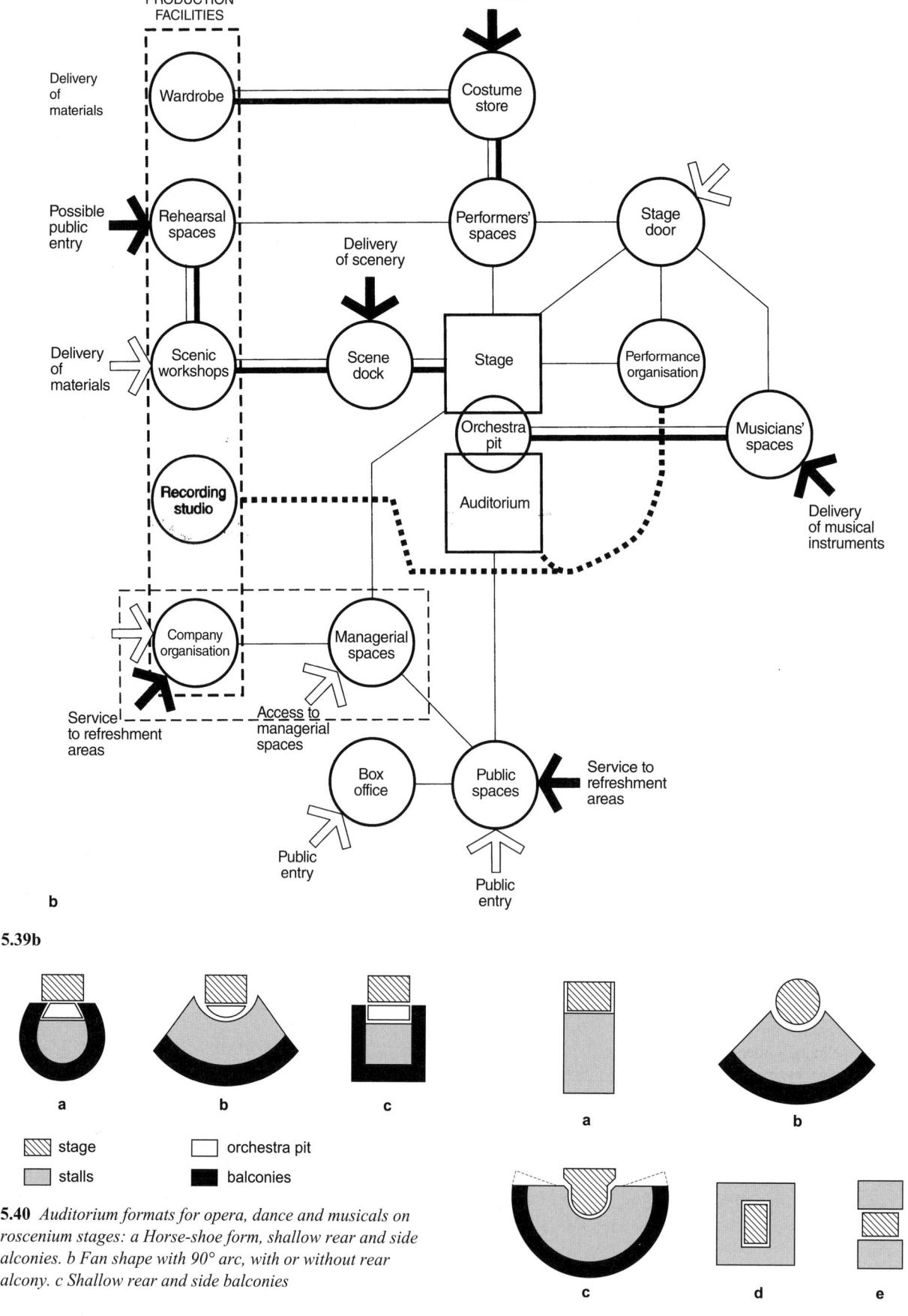

b

15.39b

□ stage   □ orchestra pit
▨ stalls   ■ balconies

15.40 *Auditorium formats for opera, dance and musicals on proscenium stages: a Horse-shoe form, shallow rear and side balconies. b Fan shape with 90° arc, with or without rear balcony. c Shallow rear and side balconies*

The viewing criteria in the auditorium will depend on the performance volume on stage, 15.42.

4.4 Stage

Stage refers to the main performance area and its associated fly-tower, side and rear stages and orchestra pit if these are provided.

15.41 *Auditorium formats for drama on open stages: a End stage. b Fan shape, 90° arc with or without rear balcony. c Thrust stage, 180° + arc, with or without rear balcony. d Theatre-in-the-round. e Transverse: audience on sides of stage*

The stage floor is a vital part of the working system. It is essential that access can be made to the underside of the stage floor, and that

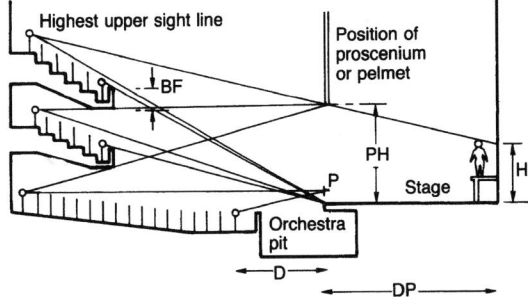

15.42a *Vertical sightlines for proscenium stage*

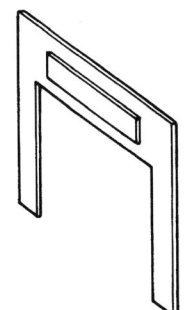

15.42b *Subtitle panel over proscenium opening: needs to be visible to whole audience. These are increasingly essential for opera, and when drama is performed in a language foreign to most of the audience*

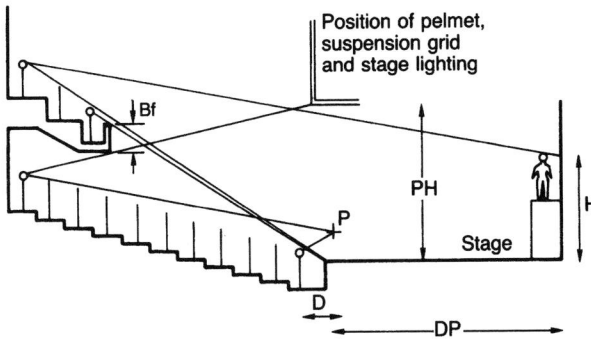

15.42c *Vertical sightlines for open stage*

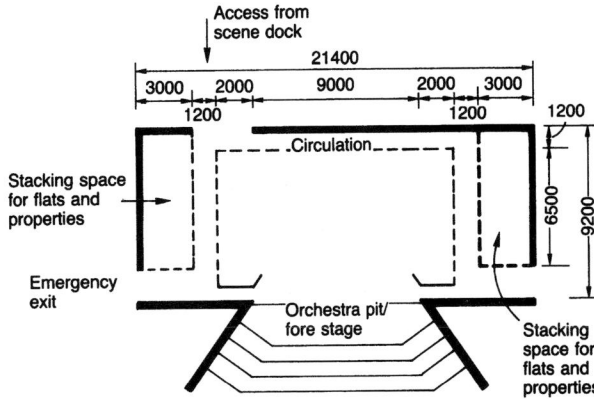

15.43 *Stage layout and dimensions for a medium-size theatre without flytower*

Table III Widths of proscenium opening in metres for various types of performance

	Small scale	Medium scale	Large scale
Drama	8	10	10
Opera	12	15	20
Dance	10	12	15
Musical	10	12	15
All-purpose	12	15	20

Side and rear stages

Sizes should relate to the size of the performance area. These areas may need to hold sets as on the performance area, with circulation all round. The clear height required is to be the highest scenery plus 1 m.

Stage basement

The space under the stage should be fully accessible with a minimum headroom of 4.5 m.

Safety curtain

In the case of fire on the stage it must be separated from the auditorium, with the proscenium opening being closed off by a safety curtain. The normal form is a rigid curtain suspended immediately behind the proscenium opening and dropping on the stage from the flytower, Figure 15.44. The fire seal must continue below stage level.

Examples of existing fly-tower stages are shown in Figures 15.45–15.48.

4.7 Stage machinery

Large dedicated buildings such as opera houses require an amount of stage machinery to be installed:

Bridges are long lifts which span the width of the proscenium opening, giving a rise and fall facility over the main acting area. They are driven by screw jacks, scissors, chain or hydraulic systems.

Revolving stages require to be set into the stage floor to provide a flush fit surface, but this can sometimes be organised to coincide with the system of lifts and bridges.

Wagon stages are large pallets capable of taking an entire set which may be moved into place behind the proscenium fully built, thereby saving labour during the performance period. If wagon stages are used, sound separation shuttering needs to be provided around the stage area to shut off the off-stage areas where work is going on to the wagon stages. Depending on the flying configuration, up to three wagon stage positions (left, right and upstage) may be involved in an immediate off stage situation. It is also possible to mount revolves in wagon stages. Much larger installations have in fact extended the wagon principle so that they are used as a system of gigantic palletised storage to store up to a dozen or more sets fully erected in large spaces below the stage, provision being made to have them lowered below the stage surface.

it be constructed of such material that screws, nails etc. can be used with relative ease.

4.5 Proscenium stage without flytower

For the smaller auditorium without a flytower, suspension of scenery, curtains, pelmets, borders and lighting barrels above the stage, Figure 15.43, is necessary. Lines can be fitted to pulleys hung on a grid, with flying from a side gallery above the stage, or from the stage level. Side stages are required for stacking spaces for flats, properties and rostra, as well as circulation routes within the stage.

4.6 Proscenium stage with flytower

The dimensions and shape of the performance area are determined by the recommended proscenium opening as in Table III. A wider opening can be reduced by screens or curtains, so that an all-purpose stage should be sized for opera. Ideally, the depth of the performance area front to rear should be equal to the proscenium opening.

Raised stage

The height of the stage can be between 600 mm and 1100 mm with a straight, angled or curved front edge. The floor to the performance area, in part or total, may be a series of traps, that is modular sections usually 1200 mm square which can be removed selectively.

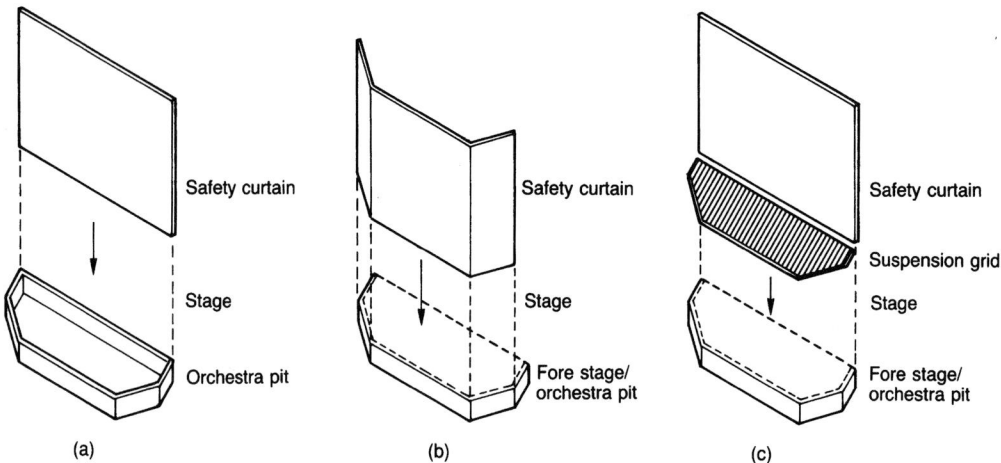

15.44 *Safety curtains, essential for a proscenium stage: a Simple flat design. b Cranked design for when orchestra pit is covered to make a forestage. c Flat design where scenery and properties on forestage are fully incombustible*

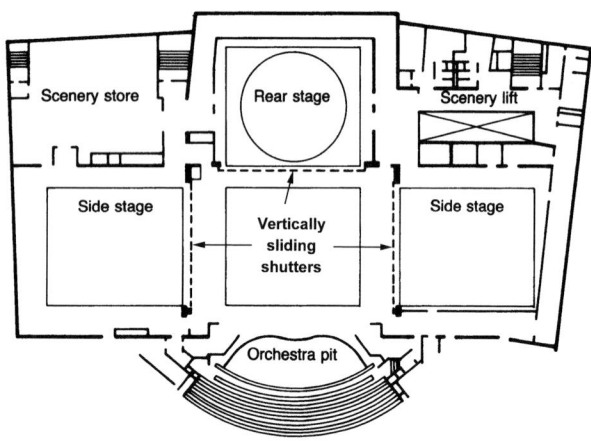

15.45 *Opera House, Essen: stage layout for a proscenium stage with a flytower for opera and dance*

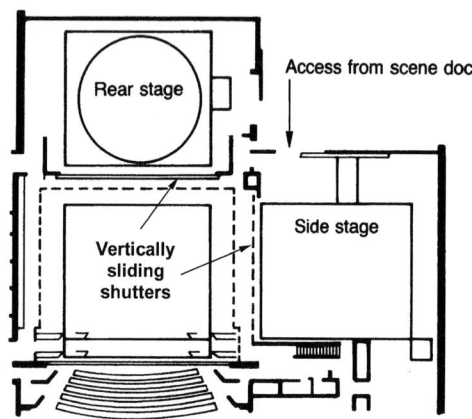

15.47 *Lyttleton Theatre, Royal National Theatre, London: proscenium stage with flytower for drama*

4.8 Flytower

Where there is a space dedicated for use as a stage, then it is essential to provide this with means of suspension overhead. This suspension is to be used for both scenic and lighting instruments.

The grid above the stage from where the suspensions come should provide clear walking space above for personnel to move about over the floor area. The received wisdom is to place the pulleys supporting the suspension bridge at the high point with the walking grid space below it. The key to overhead suspension is the load and the frequency of suspension points. Multi-use, intensively used venues will have bars suspended every 200 mm with load capacity up

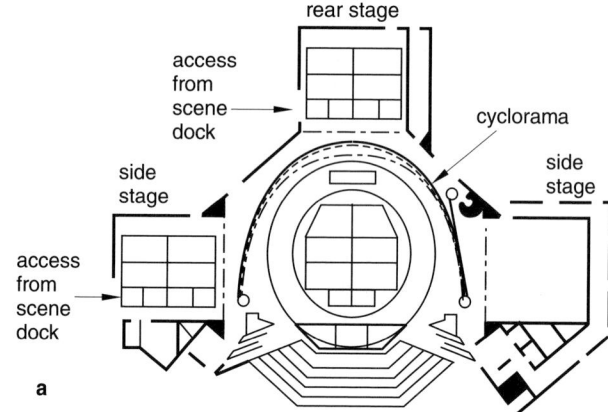

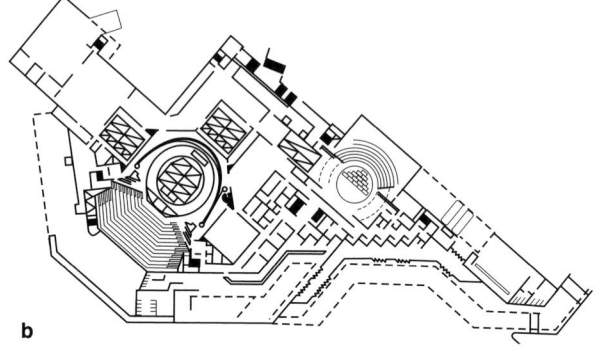

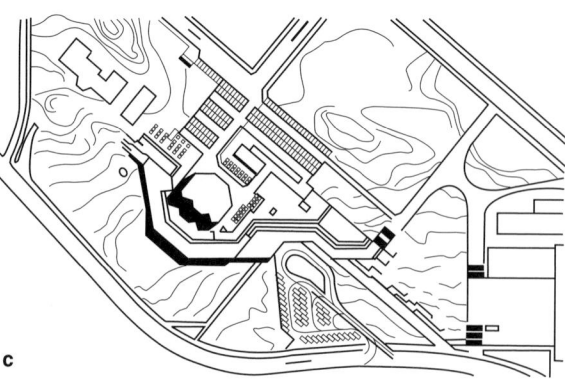

15.46 *Civic Theatre, Helsinki: a proscenium stage with flytower for drama and dance: a Stage layout. b Plan at entrance level. c Site plan*

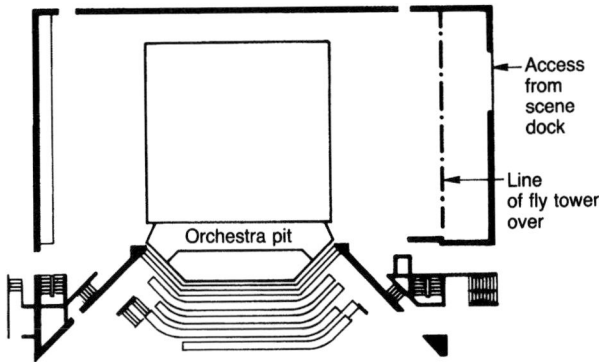

15.48 *Theatre Royal, Plymouth: stage for touring opera, dance, musicals, drama and concerts*

to 500 kgf per bar. Less intensively used installations may have bars 300 mm apart and, depending on the nature of the performance to be given, the load capacity may come down to 350 kgf per bar.

It is essential that the means of suspension can be lowered to the floor. Depending on the frequency of usage, this suspension system can either be winched, or in smaller installations be operated using rope hand lines. In the theatre, all items suspended overhead are 'flown'. The space above the stage is referred to as the 'flys'. The greater the height over the stage is usually considered the better, offering greater flexibility for designers both of scenic and lighting disciplines. Where the scenic suspension system is raised considerably above the stage it can then be described as a flytower.

Conventionally the clear height of the flytower was 2½ times the proscenium height. Nowadays greater heights are usually demanded, with a minimum of 2½ times the proscenium height to the underside of the grid and a clear 2 m above the grid.

There are different means of suspension: the main ones are counterweight and hydraulic systems.

Counterweight systems

A 'cradle' laden with weights travels up and down special places vertically either side of the stage. There are two types:

• Single-purchase counterweights where the travel distance is equal to the height of the grid above the stage, Figure 15.49: a continuous vertical wall running higher than the grid is required for the guides.
• Double-purchase counterweights where the distance travelled by the counterweights is halved in relation to the distance of the suspension, Figure 15.50. This allows the operation to occur from a gallery above the stage level: an extra loading gallery is necessary between the flying gallery and grid.

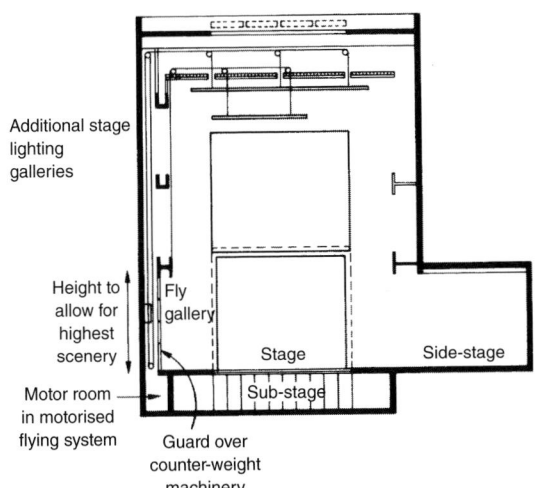

15.49 *Section through flytower showing single-purchase flying system permitting only one side stage*

Hydraulic systems

These obviate the need for space for the cradles by containing the entire system at the very highest point in the building, opening up the possibility of side stages on either side.

It is important to locate flyfloors either side of the flytower to provide horizontal access above the nominal height of the scenery.

This is used by technicians to locate and control horizontal movement of vertically suspended components. If the building is likely to have dedicated usage by a single-occupancy user, then certain suspension positions may be dedicated for lighting systems, in which case a special provision may be made for horizontal access by personnel to reach these positions as well as their raise and lower facility. It will also be possible to feed the necessary electrical supply from directly above the position in a self-monitoring system which caters for the vertical movement. Figure 15.51 shows a flytower stage with a rear stage.

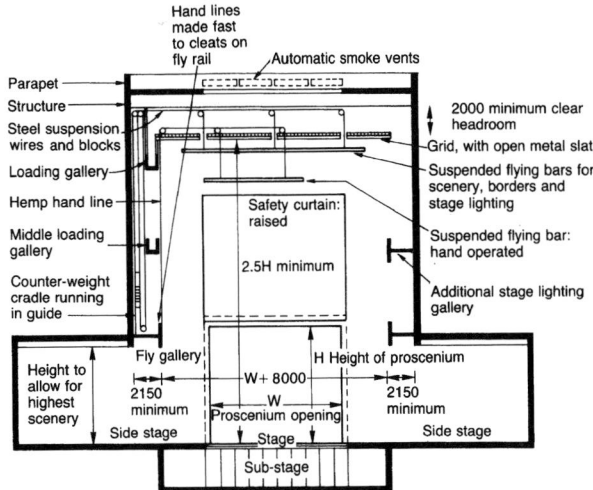

15.50 *Section showing double-purchase flying system and side stages*

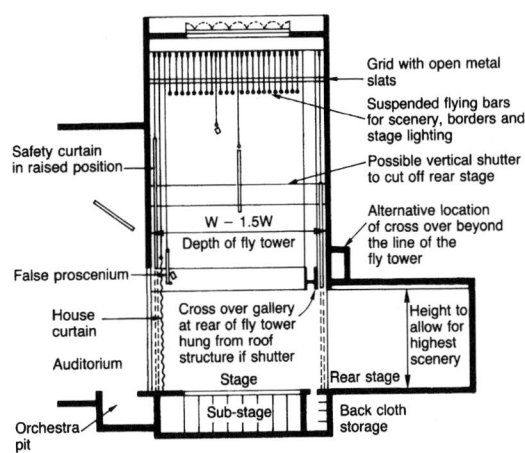

15.51 *Cross-section showing rear stage*

An automatic smoke vent is required at the top of the flytower: regulations require the cross-sectional area of the vent to be a particular proportion of the stage – usually 10 per cent.

4.9 Orchestra pit

A limiting factor is for the conductor to be seen both by the singers and dancers on the stage, and by the musicians in the pit. The audience needs a balance of performance from stage and orchestra.

Allow 3.3 m² average per player, 5 m² for the piano, 10 m² for tympani and percussion, and 4 m² for the conductor. The conductor's eye level must not be lower than stage level when seated on a high stool. To minimise the gulf between stage and audience, the pit can extend under the stage front for a distance no greater than 2 m.

For opera, the pit requires to hold a maximum of 100 musicians, 60 for musicals, 60–90 for dance. The numbers can be less with touring companies. The pit should be horizontally reducible, with the floor level vertically adjustable.

Where there is a multi-use facility orchestra lifts, Figure 15.52, are common. These can provide:

- a fore stage when elevated;
- two or three extra rows of seating when level with the auditorium floor;
- the orchestra pit when in the down position.

4.10 Open-stage formats

End stage

For dance and opera, the minimum performance area is 10 m × 10 m, for drama 10 m × 8 m. Modest side stages with masking are

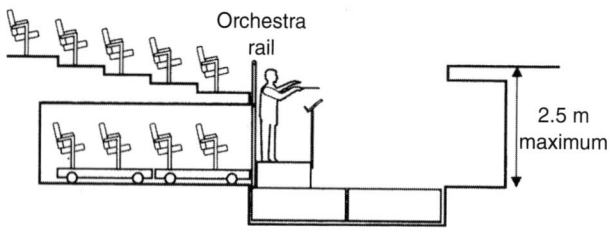

a Lift in lowest position with seat waggons in store under fixed seating

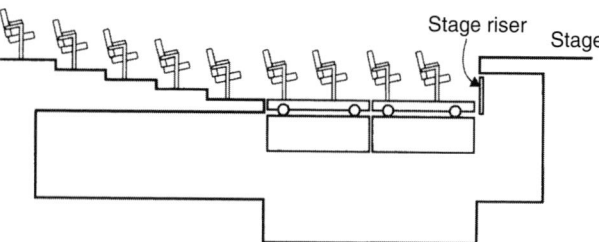

b Lift partially raised for maximum additional seating

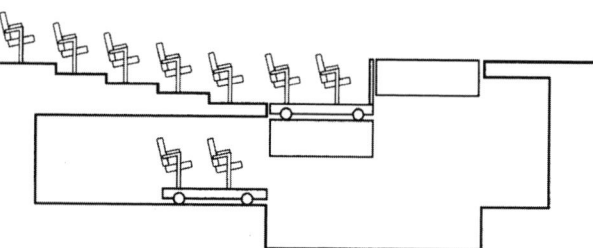

c Half lift raised for seating and half fully raised for stage extension

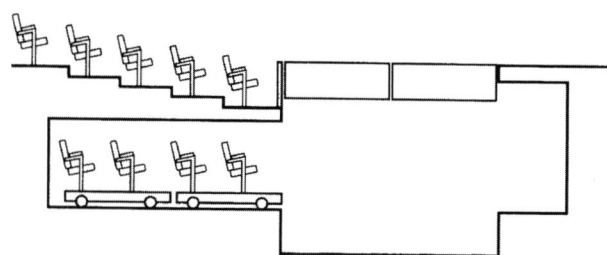

d Lift fully raised for maximum stage size

15.52 *Orchestra pit lifts*

necessary for the storage of scenery as well as performers' entrances. Orchestra pit can be formed between stage and auditorium.

90° fan

Dimensions vary, based on a circle or faceted circle, with diameters ranging from 8 to 11 m, Figure 15.53.

Thrust stage

The performance area as a peninsula projecting from rear setting, Figure 15.54.

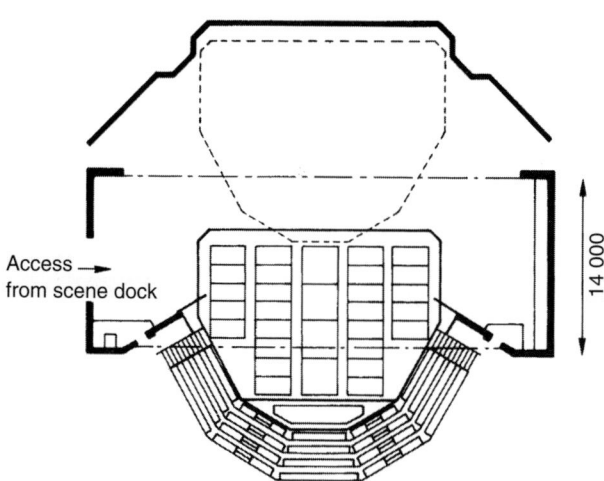

15.53 *West Yorkshire Playhouse, Leeds: plan of a stage where the audience encircles it by 90°. This theatre has a single-purchase flying system and a retractable wagon stage*

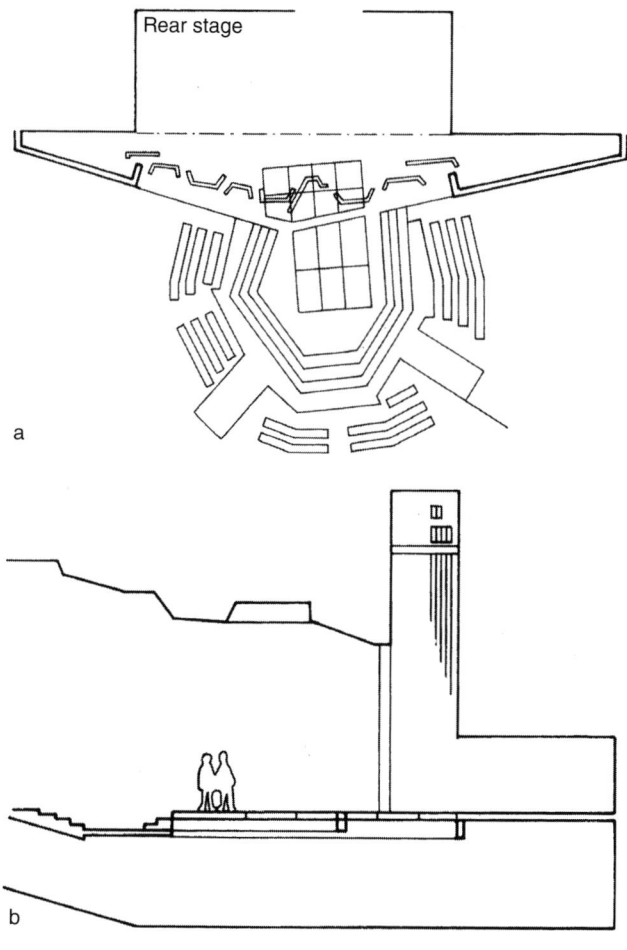

15.54 *Tyrone Guthrie Theatre, Minneapolis: thrust stage with steps at the edge permitting performers to access from various parts of the auditorium. The stage has traps, a rear stage and a backcloth flying system: a Plan. b Section*

Theatre-in the-round

The performance area can be circular, square, polygon, rectangular or elliptical, Figure 15.55. The performers' entry can be combined or separate from the public access.

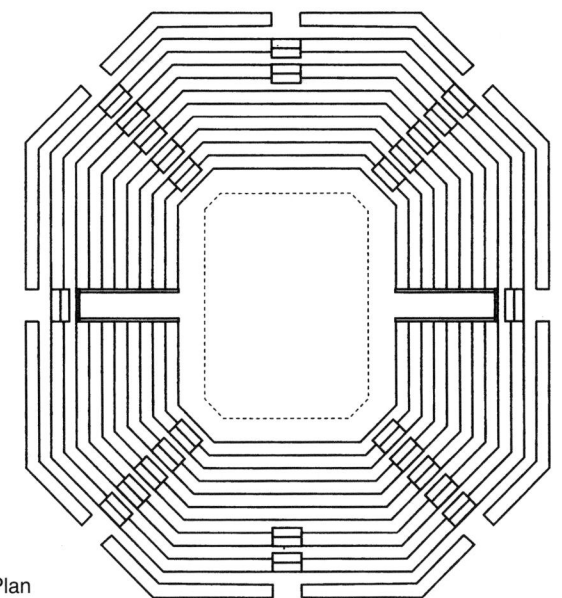

Plan

15.55 *Theatre-in-the-round with a rectangular performance area and performers entering at stage level from vomitories. The audience enters from rear of seating*

The stage is usually not raised, but can be 300–750 mm with 600 mm a favourite dimension. The minimum clear height over the stage including scenery suspension grid and stage lighting is 6.5 m. The whole or part of the performance area can receive traps as previously described, with one 'grave' trap 1200 × 2400 mm as a minimum. If there are traps a basement will be needed with access for the performers and minimum ceiling height of 4.4 m.

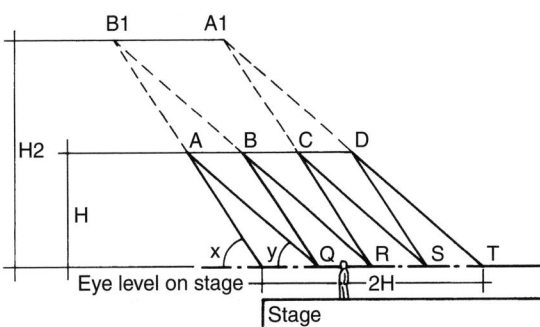

15.56 *Method of locating theoretical positions of spotlights. Spots at A will light a performer at stage edge at 55° in section, about 45° to 50° after crossing, but as the performer moves in from the edge the angle decreases. At Q it is only 40° in section, about 35° after crossing and this is the minimum. Another lighting position B must be provided to cover the area Q to R within the same range of angles, and then C and D to light areas R to S and S to T*

4.11 Auditorium lighting positions

There are three main factors governing these positions.

Ease of access is dependent upon the intended use of the auditorium. For intensively used auditoria, staff will require almost daily access to the instruments and this should be provided in such a way that they are not required to use loose ladders in order to carry out their functions. The access needs to be to the rear of the instrument with ample room for the staff to reach around the instrument to the front and also sufficient free space for the instrument to be readily demountable should repair be required.

Location. Over a third of the total number of instruments in a modern rig are likely to be located in the auditorium area (front of house), Figure 15.56. The desired angle is normally between 42° and 44° at an angle to a horizontal plane emanating at the stage front. Lanterns are required at a high angle either side as well as across the main front area of the stage. Depending on auditorium design, lanterns are either housed on bridges which cross the auditorium, Figure 15.57 or are

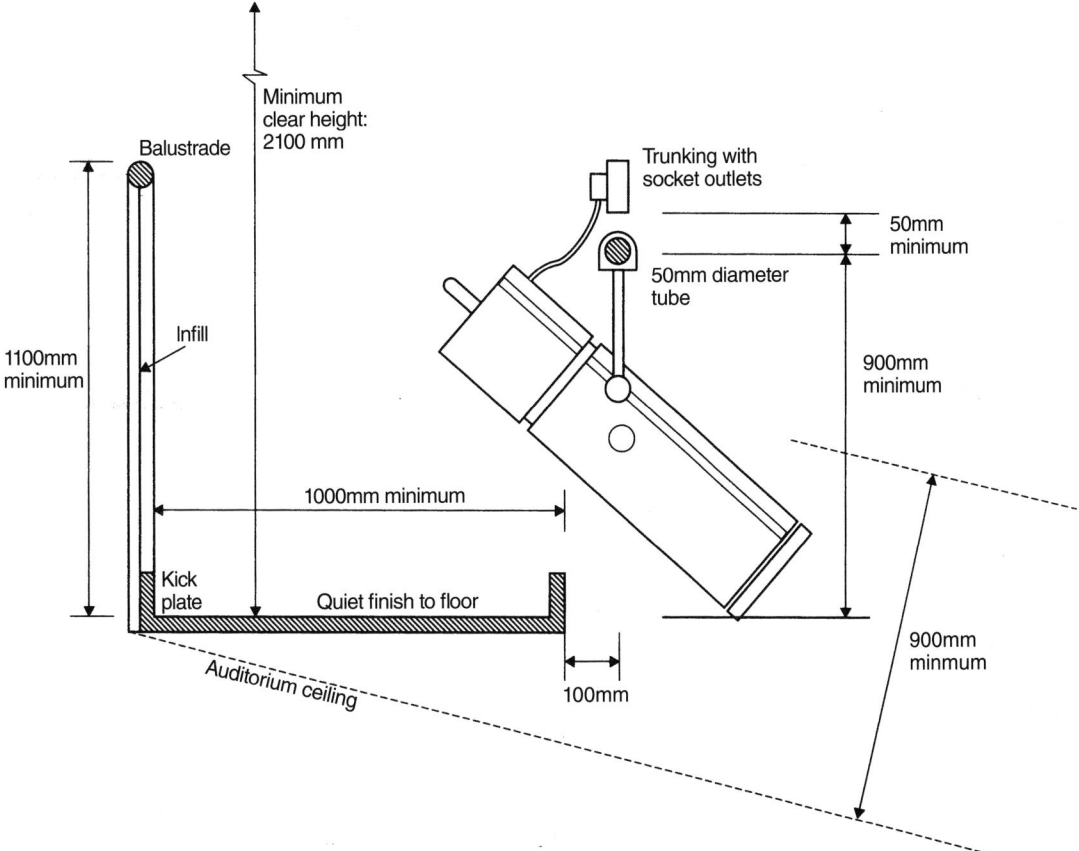

15.57 *Auditorium lighting bridge at ceiling level*

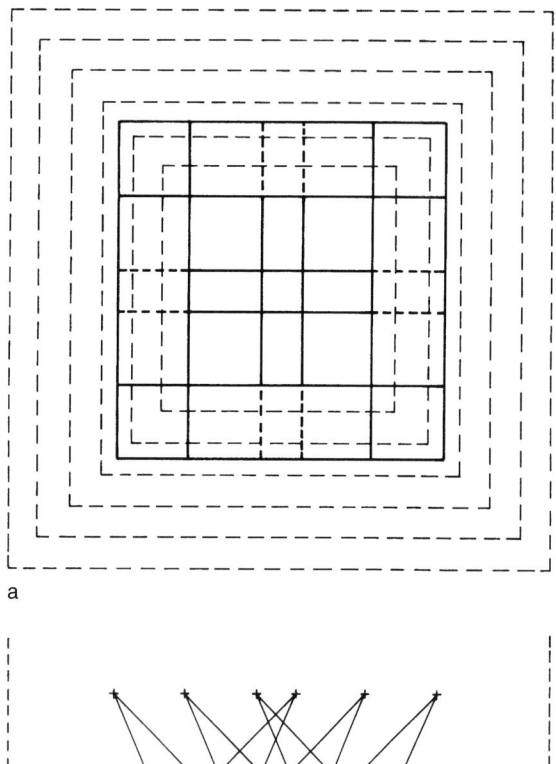

a

b

15.58 *On thrust and theatre-in-the-round stages virtually all the lighting comes from overhead to avoid glare in the eyes of the audience: a Plan. b Section*

attached to the auditorium structure itself. Provision for instruments on the auditorium side of the proscenium arch in a vertical plane is also recommended. Lighting design for theatre-in-the-round is particularly complex, Figure 15.58.

Integrity of design. Many people consider lanterns and their relevant bulky cabling and paraphernalia to be unsightly in the context of formal auditorium design and therefore steps need to be taken to provide housings for the instruments such that they are not normally in the view of the majority of the audience. However, auditoria which carry a 'high tech' design ethic will find it just as acceptable to place lanterns in exposed positions, provided they are sympathetically arranged as they then become part of the design integrity. When considering lighting positions, account must be taken of the lanterns themselves intruding into the audience's line of sight, as well as providing a safe means of suspension.

Follow spots

These are an integral part of much musical, ballet and operatic work. An operator directs a movable beam of light onto one or more performers during the course of the performance, Figure 15.59. Depending on the intended usage of the building, the provision of specific chambers at least 2m square for this work should be located behind or over seating. The angle of the position to the stage should be around 45° or more, because the whole point of follow spotting is to isolate what is being lit in this way.

A pair of instruments located in a high central position allows the individual operators easy contact, especially if they are separated by glass from the auditorium area. Provision should be considered for two further spotlight positions, either side of the auditorium, at a similarly high angle.

It must be noted that the position should be so that the lantern can reach most of the main acting area of the stage. Sometimes the lanterns are situated within the auditorium on specially constructed

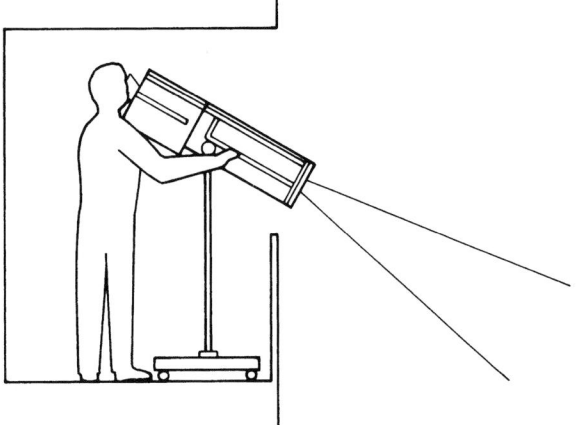

15.59 *Follow spot, minimum size for equipment and operator 1.5 m × 2 m*

platforms at the expense of a number of seats. Provision has to be made for barricading the follow spot position from the audience.

Follow spots as instruments are becoming increasingly powerful and correspondingly larger. Some are more than 2 m in length. Therefore, the overall size of the proposed auditorium will be a factor in determining the size of the follow spot situation. Its position should allow for the instrument, the instrument to swing, and the operator to stand either behind or beside the instrument while this activity is going on. A place for the operator to sit and a local means of isolating the instrument should also be catered for.

4.12 Spaces associated with the audience area

Lighting control room

This is a room centrally at the rear of the auditorium fully enclosed and sound-proofed with an observation window and space for the lighting control console and for the operator who needs to sit by the console and view the performance through the observation window which has an unrestricted view of the stage, Figure 15.60. There should also be space for an assistant, a worktop for plans and scripts. A minimum size would be 3 m wide, 4.5 m deep and 4.4 m high.

Dimmer rooms

Space is required for the dimmer racks which are the direct means of control for all of the stage lighting instruments. The racks also contain the individual fusing for each stage lighting circuit. Mains cabling runs from the dimmer room to all outlets of the stage lighting installation, and also to the house lights, but the connection between the dimmer racks and the lighting control itself is not a mains voltage line.

The dimmer room should be placed so that quick access may be achieved either from the lighting control position or from the stage area. The dimmer room will also normally contain the mains isolation for the stage lighting system. In large installations which have a three-phase supply, each single-phase installation should be physically separated.

Sound control room

An open enclosure in a representative position within the auditorium. The operator requires an interrupted view of the performance area as well as being able to hear the performance. The room contains a control desk, equipment racks, monitor loudspeakers and worktop for scripts. The minimum size is 3 m wide, 4.4 m deep and 4.4 m high.

Auditorium sound-mixing position

This is for the mixing of amplified sound from the stage by an operator who requires to hear the same sound as the audience. The area requires to be flat, set within the seating area: minimum area of 2 m × 2 m, with mixer pad sound control desk and protective barrier.

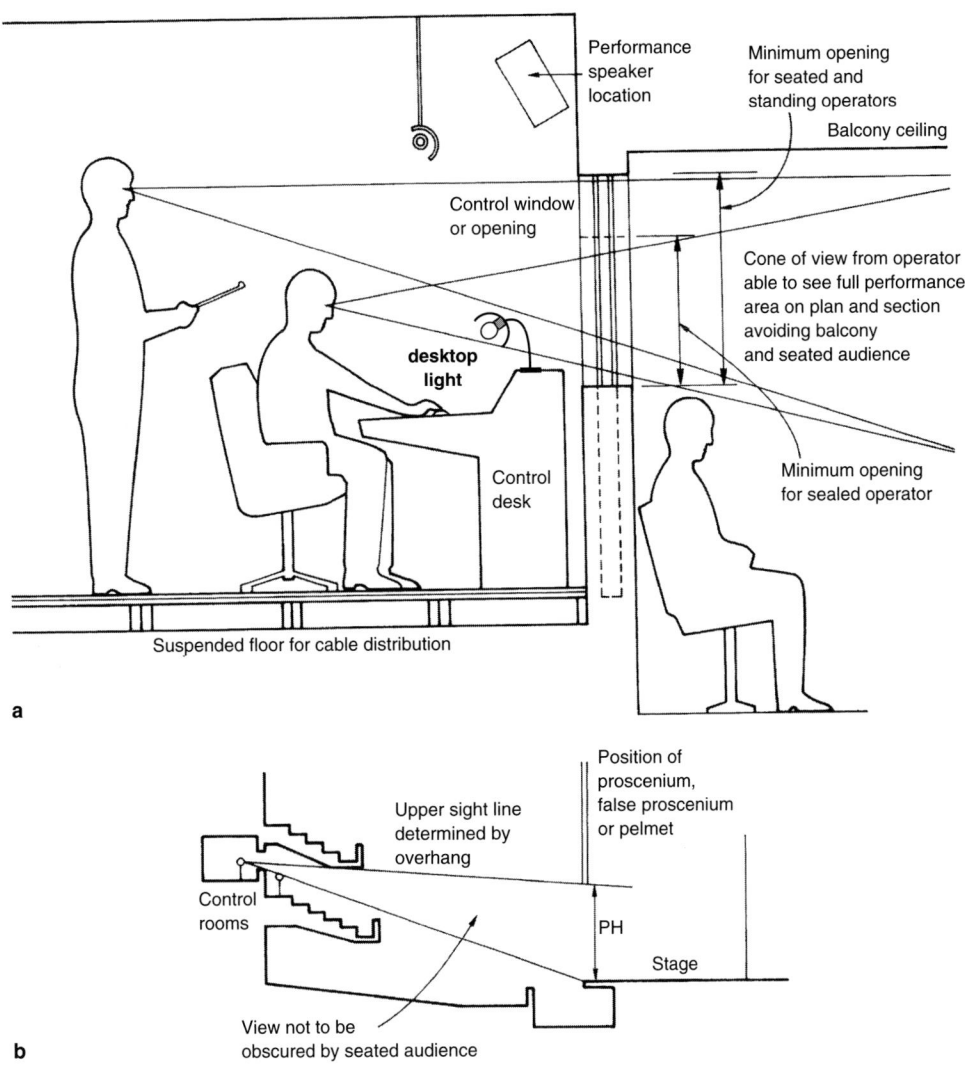

15.60 *Control room with direct view of the stage: a Section. b Vertical sightlines*

TV, radio and recording control room
This is a separate soundproof control room, with observation window and clear view of the stage. It will accommodate announcers, and staff for balancing and directing transmissions and recording. A minimum area of 2 m × 2 m, but should be larger.

Observation room
Those associated with production may need to check activities on the stage from a room at the rear of the auditorium, with a clear view of the stage through an observation window, minimum area, 2 m × 2 m.

4.13 Stage-related spaces

Quick change
Separate rooms immediately off the stage, each with two make-up positions and hanging rails.

Properties room
This is a store room, opening directly off a side stage for properties for use during a performance. It requires a sink with hot and cold running water.

Scene dock
At the same level as the stage for storage of scenery.

Loading bay
For the delivery of scenery and properties into the scene dock. Allow for more than one pantechnicon to reverse.

Scenery
A repair and maintenance area at the side of the stage to maintain scenery and properties in use on the stage.

Piano store
For a grand piano when not in use. A separate room kept at a temperature similar to stage conditions; minimum area 4.5 m × 3.5 m.

Lighting equipment
Requires direct access off the side stage for chandeliers, hand properties, etc.

Sound equipment
Storage and maintenance space for such items as microphones, speakers, stands and so on.

Stage manager
Located stage left (facing the audience). Control equipment includes public address, safety curtain and/or drencher release, flytower vent release, and communication with lighting and sound technicians, fly gallery, conductor, etc. as well as cueing performers.

4.14 Spaces for actors, singers and dancers

Dressing rooms
Arrangements are illustrated in Figures 15.61 to 15.69 covering single shared and communal occupancy rooms.

Green room with kitchen and servery: 3.4 m² per occupant.
Laundry for repair and maintenance of costumes, 20 m² minimum.
Costume store, including skips and rails
Costume delivery.
Specialist make-up room: 10 m² minimum per person.
Pre-performance practice room(s) (singers): 15 m² minimum.
Pre-performance dance studio (dancers): 1000 m² minimum.

Physiotherapy room (dancers): 15 m² minimum.
Wig store and hairdresser's room: 5–10 m².
Waiting area for visitors and dressers.
Offices: children's supervisor, company manager, touring manager, etc. 10 m² minimum per office.
Toilets.
Performers' assembly areas: at points of entry to stage.

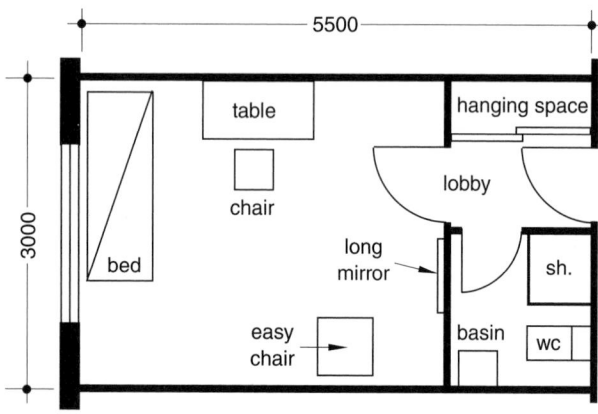

15.61 *Single dressing room: a Elevation. b Plan. Dimension marked • is minimum; a greater length is desirable to allow space for flowers, etc*

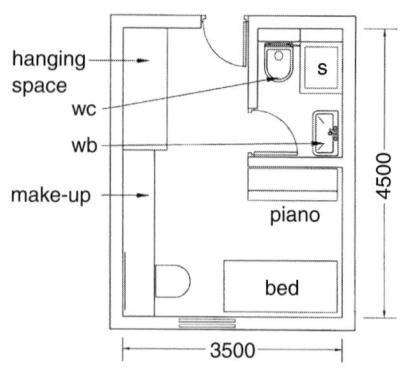

15.64 *Single dressing room with piano, area 15.7m²*

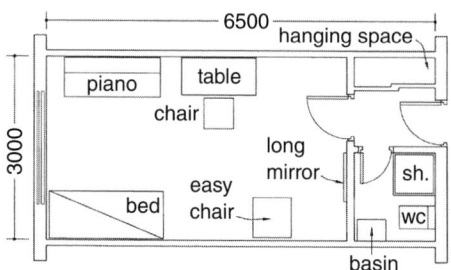

15.65 *Single dressing room with piano and en-suite WC and shower*

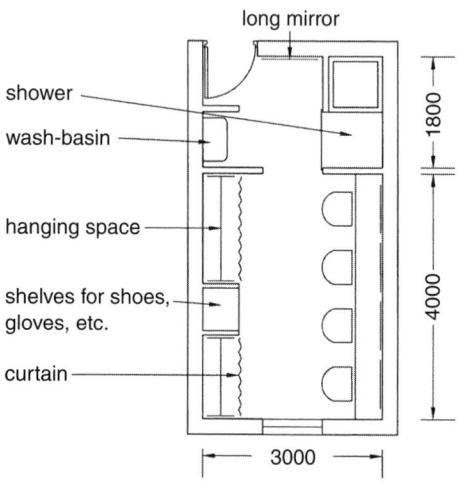

15.66 *Dressing room for four, area 17.4m²*

4.15 Spaces for musicians
- Changing rooms: at least two rooms.
- Musical instruments store: large instruments and their cases.
- Pre-performance practice room(s).
- Musicians' common room: 3.4 m² per occupant.
- Conductor's room.
- Offices: orchestra manager, tour manager, etc.
- Musicians' assembly area: at point of entry to orchestra pit.

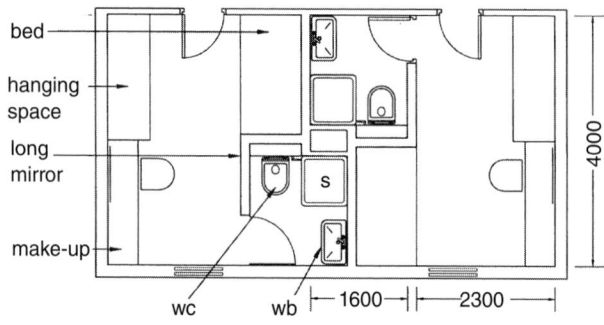

15.62 *Single dressing room with en-suite WC and shower*

15.63 *A pair of single dressing rooms each 14.4 m²*

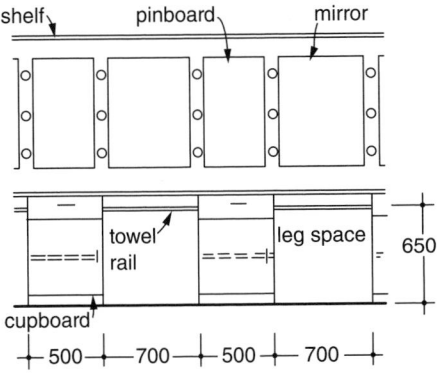

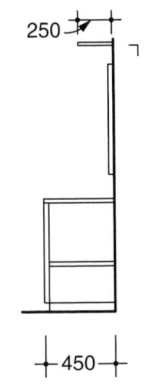

b Section

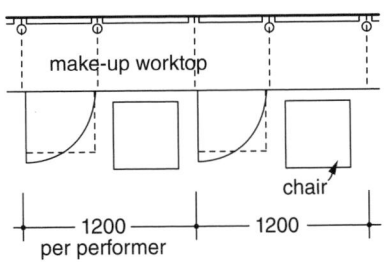

lighting is according to
preference or cost;
that shown is only a
diagrammatic
representation

c Plan

15.67 *a–c Shared dressing room*

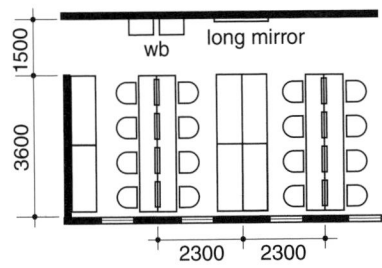

15.68 *Communal dressing room, area of each bay 8.3 m²*

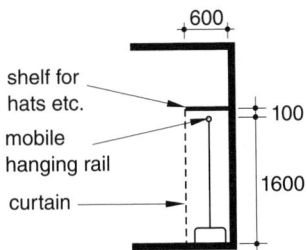

15.69 *Section through hanging space*

5 STUDIO THEATRES

5.1 Introduction
Studio theatres, by definition, do not contain moving stage machinery. They usually have some form of mobile or movable seating either to provide for different layouts or to clear the space for other uses at different times.

There are a number of well-developed, flexible seating systems offering great variety and compliance with normal seating regulations, with a foldaway and mobile facility. However, bleacher seating systems demand a dedicated space into which the seating can be concertinaed when not in use. There is a significant point load factor under the supporting wheels. Bleacher seating arrangements do not offer flexible layout possibilities.

5.2 Access
Studio theatres should have different access points, allowing for seating and performer flexibility. A passage around allows performers to access any entrance. In all cases it is assumed that audience circulation and amenities are located adjacent to designated exits which should have immediate access to further doors on the outer side of the passage leading to the regulatory place of safety. Provision for drapes to be hung and moved around the walls offers the potential for varying the acoustic as well as the colour of the space. Either the walls or the drapes should be black.

Height is a key factor.

5.3 Lighting grid
One of the great selling points for the studio theatre is the speed and ease with which one can move from one production to another. Frequently this is serviced by having a grid made up of 50 mm OD tubing over the whole space from which lighting instruments can be hung in any location. It is doubly advantageous if this can be organised in such a way that there are walk gantries with lighting tubes either side, allowing the personnel to effect all the lighting changes without the use of access equipment and ladders, thereby allowing for completely different functions to be carried out at floor level simultaneously. If the gantry is not possible then it is essential that all of the lighting grid can be accessed from below by a mobile access system. From a desirable lighting point of view, the head of the instrument should not be less than 4 m above the nominal floor level.

6 CONCERT HALL

6.1 Introduction
A relationship diagram for a concert hall is shown in Figure 15.70. For orchestral and choral classical music in concert hall or recital room there are three broad categories of relationships between audience and platform, Figure 15.71:

- Audience focused towards the orchestra and choir on the platform, with or without choir stalls, in a single direction, Figure 15.71a;
- Audience on three sides semi-surrounding the platform, Figure 15.71b;
- Audience surrounding the platform, Figure 15.71c.

Types of single-direction relationship include the rectangular box as in the diagrams shown, variations on the rectangular box and the fan-shaped auditorium, Figure 15.72. The rectangular box is a simple well-established form. It allows full cross-reflection of audience, is central to the platform and receives a good sound balance. The fan-shaped auditorium is a particular variation on the rectangular box but suffers from the lack of side- and cross-reflection. Other shapes, Figure 15.73, include the coffin and elliptical.

6.2 Viewing conditions
For vertical sightlines see Figure 15.74.

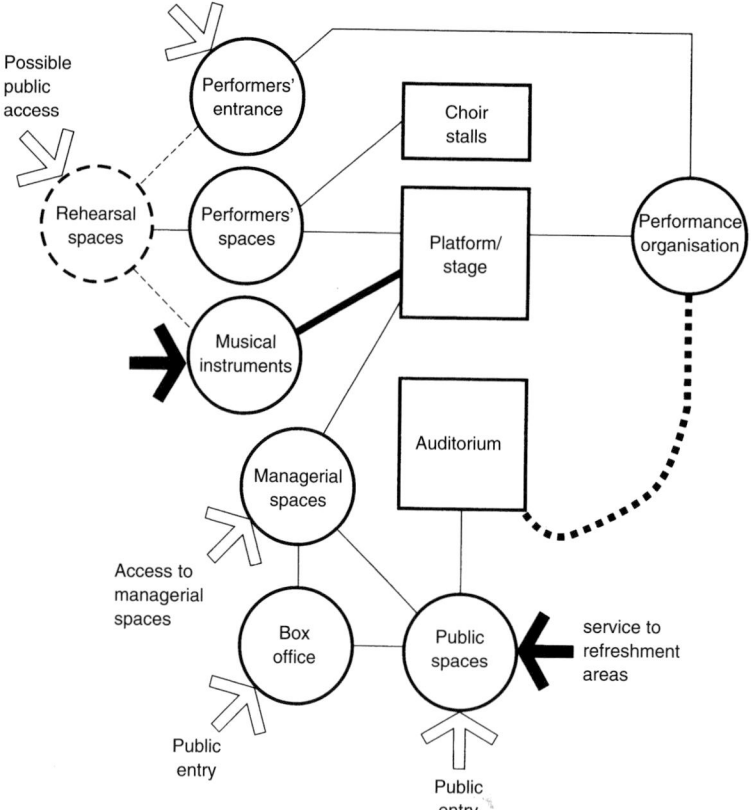

15.70 *Relationship diagram for buildings for orchestral and choral classical music with choir stalls, and for jazz and pop/rock music without choir stalls*

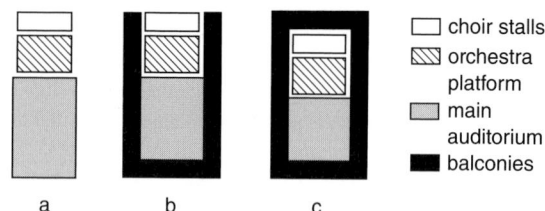

15.71 *Relationships between audience and platform in various rectangular formats: a Single direction. b Audience partially surrounding the platform. c Audience surrounding the platform. With or without rear and side balconies*

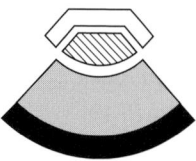

15.72 *90° fan shape, with or without rear and side balconies, in single direction relationship*

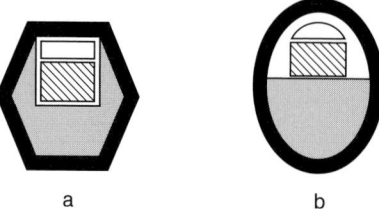

15.73 *Orchestral and choral music formats for audience surrounding the platform. With or without rear and side balconies: a Coffin. b Elliptical*

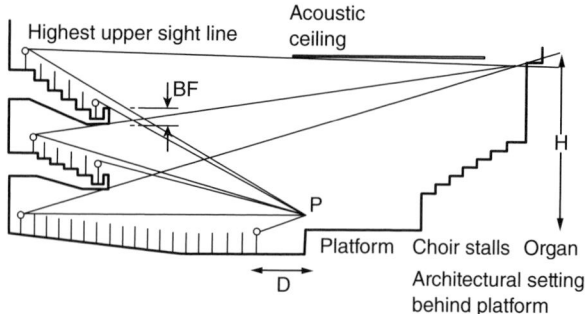

15.74 *Vertical sightlines through auditorium with concert platform. These need to include choir stalls, architectural setting behind the platform as well as the conductor, soloists and orchestra. However, acoustic requirements of direct and reflected sound may override sightline parameters*

6.3 Platform design

The music components include orchestra platform, choir stalls and organ, Figure 15.75.

Platform design relates to orchestra size:

- Symphony orchestra and choir
- Symphony orchestra, 80–120 musicians
- Chamber orchestra, 40–50 musicians
- Small ensemble

For a chamber orchestra, the platform can be 6 m deep, 9 m wide and 900 mm high, for a full orchestra an area of 12 m × 12 m, with a platform height of 1000 mm. Various configurations are shown in Figure 15.76 and a section in Figure 15.77.

6.4 Areas for individual musicians

- Violin players and small wind instruments 1000 × 600 mm; the horns and bassoons, 1000 × 800 mm.

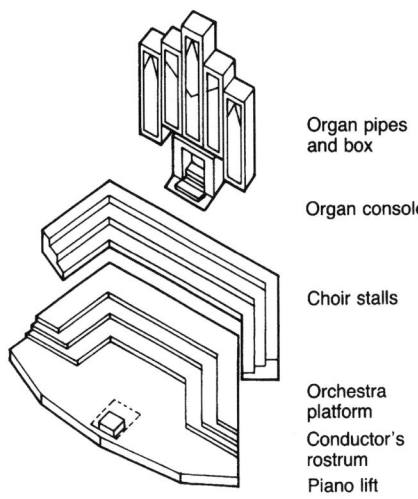

Organ pipes
and box

Organ console

Choir stalls

Orchestra
platform

Conductor's
rostrum

Piano lift

15.75 *Components of the platform for classical music*

- 1200 mm tiers for string and wind players, including cellos and double base.
- Tiers up to 2 m for percussion or concert grand piano: 2.75 m × 1.6 m.
- Choir: 0.38 m² minimum per singer in choir stalls with seats. The longitudinal section can be flat and stepped transversely, rising from the conductor's rostrum.

6.5 Associated spaces
- Lighting and control room
- Dimmers
- Television and radio transmission and recording control room
- Follow spot
- Observation room.

See also Section 6.8.

6.6 Platform-related spaces
- Piano store
- Storage of musical instruments

- Delivery of musical instruments
- Access for deliveries
- Parking provision for touring vans
- Offices
- Technicians' changing
- Electrical workshop
- Electrical store.

6.7 Performers' spaces
- Changing rooms: not more than 20 people per room, 3.5 m² each
- Single rooms, 15.62, 19 m²
- Single room with piano, 15.65, 23.5 m²
- Single room with space for auditions 40 m²
- Shared rooms 2 m² per occupant.

6.8 Associated spaces
- Conductor's green room
- Pre-performance practice room(s)
- Orchestra assembly area
- Choir assembly area
- Musicians' common room
- Orchestra manager's office
- Other offices (e.g. tour manager)
- Toilets.

7 CONFERENCE HALLS
7.1 Relationships
Figure 15.78 shows the relationships between the parts of a conference suite.

7.2 Formats
Formats depend on use:

- Traditional lecture theatre formats with the audience focused towards a platform on which is provision for a speaker or speakers, possibly served by a range of audio-visual aids, Figure 15.79. The speaker is the controlling point with audience in a receptive role. Slide, film and video projection limit the extent of encirclement of the platform.
- Participation by each member of the audience which suggests the debating formats of semi-circle, *U*-shape and circle, controlled

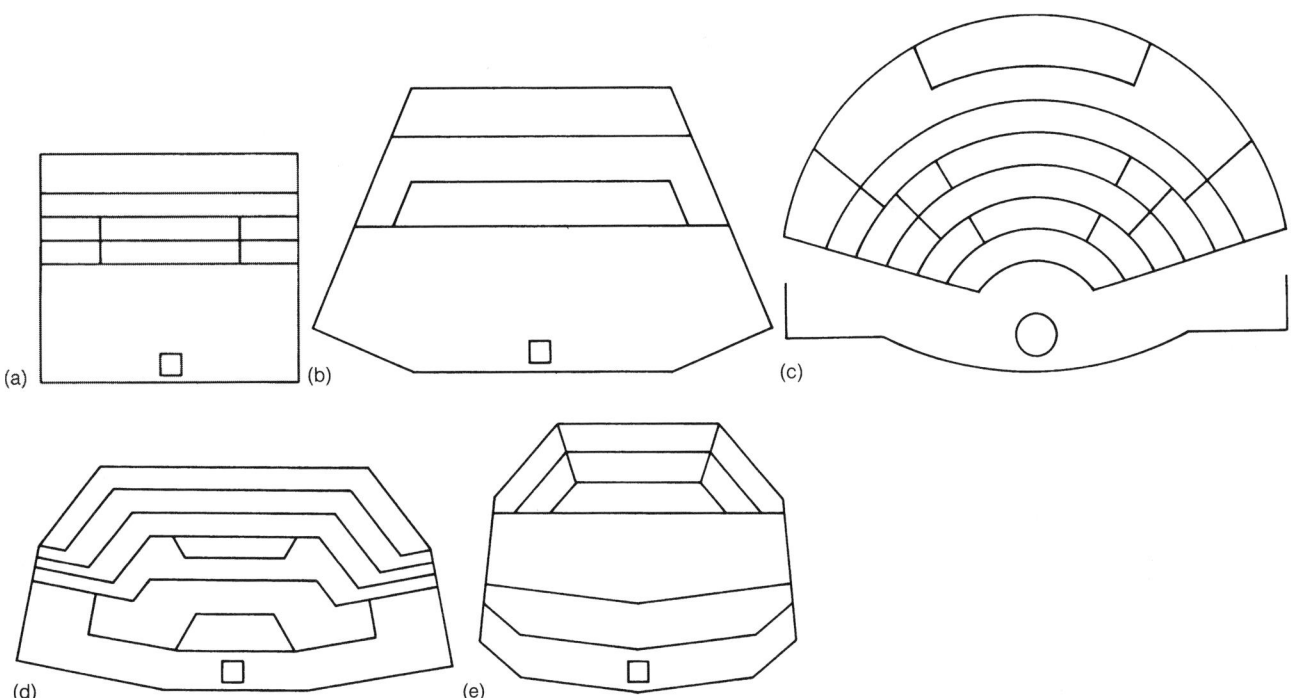

15.76 *Platform designs, each on multi-levels: a Rectangular. b Trapezoidal. c Semi-circular. d Wide shallow plan. e Design for a small orchestra*

15.77 *Section through an orchestra platform showing piano store and lift*

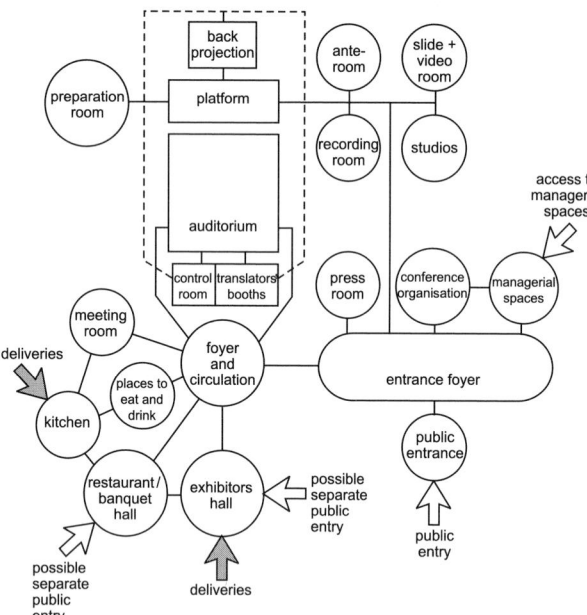

15.78 *Relationship diagram for conference hall*

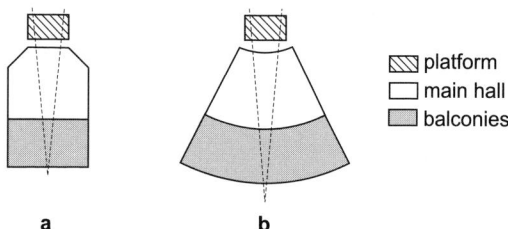

15.79 *Conference hall formats for lectures requiring projection facilities: a Rectangular with or without rear balcony. b 60° fan with or without rear balcony*

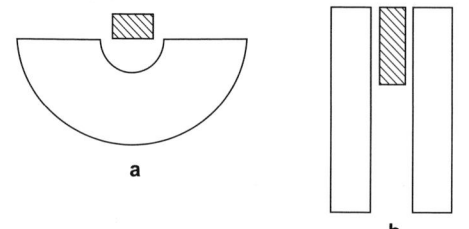

15.80 *Conference hall formats for debating: a Fan with 180° arc (US Senate). b Audience in two facing banks (House of Commons)*

by a chairperson, with little or no audio-visual aids, Figure 15.80. The need for equal distribution and viewing of all delegates' facial expressions implies a single row only. However, it is possible to have up to six rows where delegates can still be aware of the spoken contribution of each.

The plan shape of the conference hall can be:

* Rectangular
* Fan-shaped, with angles of 135°, 90° or 60°. The last is best for screening
* Hexagonal
* Circular
* Oval, or
* Coffin.

7.3 Functional requirements
With the lecture format the functional requirements include:

* The audience needs to see and hear the speaker, chairperson and panel of speakers in the various positions on the platform.
* They need a clear view of screens, chalkboard and other visual displays: each has its own physical requirement.
* Acoustic clarity of sound listening to speaker and to reproduced sound.
* Adequate presentation and viewing of any demonstrations.

With the debating format:

* Awareness of the whole audience by every member
* The audience able to hear all speakers and chairperson
* A clear view of the chairperson.

An example of a facility used only for lecturing is shown in Figure 15.81.

7.4 Audience facilities
Seating design for conference use is covered earlier in this chapter in Section 2.5. In fully equipped conference halls each person in the audience may be provided with:

* voting buttons: yes, no and abstain
* simultaneous translation headphones
* headphones for the hard of hearing
* small individual light.

The following is normally provided to be shared by two adjacent participants:

* microphone controlled by the chairperson from the platform
* button for 'request-to-speak'.

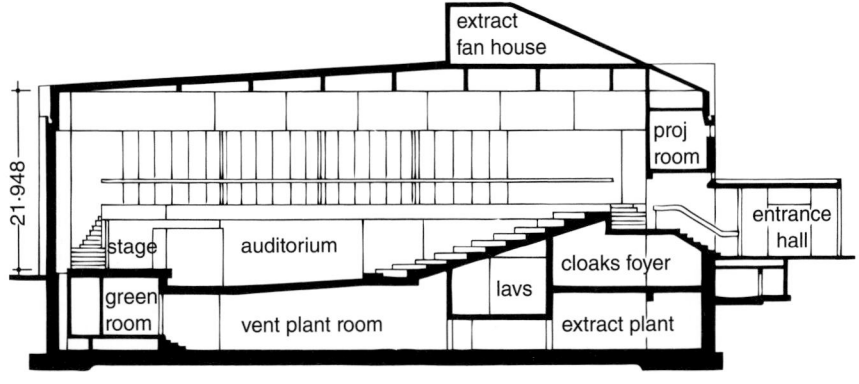

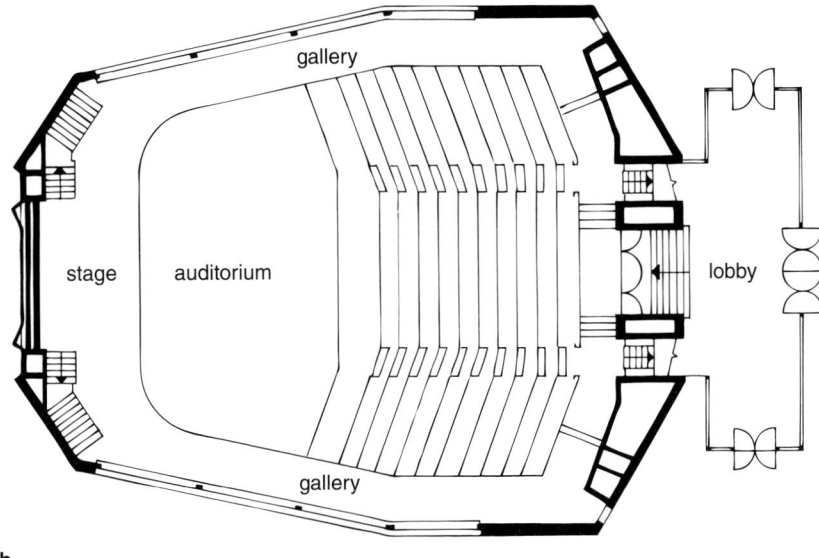

15.81 *Lady Mitchell Hall, Cambridge. A large lecture theatre for 450 students. Architects: Casson, Conder and Partners: a Longitudinal section. b Plan of auditorium*

7.5 Platform

Height depends on hall capacity and sightlines:

- 300 mm up to 150 seating capacity
- 600 mm 150–300
- 750 mm over 300.

Steps are required from the auditorium to provide ease of access for speakers onto the platform at ends of gangways and front rows. Ramps may also be needed for wheelchair users.

Size and shape depends on extent of audio-visual aids, lectern, demonstration table, panel table and other equipment as well as sightlines and size and shape of auditorium.

The platform may need to accommodate only a single speaker at one time, with no (or limited) audio-visual aids as the least provision, Figure 15.82. In other cases it will require to allow for scientific demonstrations, a panel of speakers with or without a lectern, or major presentations as with commercial, political and institutional organisations. For major political conferences there can be as many as fifty people to accommodate on the platform.

The setting about the platform can be an architectural setting common to all types of presentations or a shell in which complete new settings can be constructed for each conference.

7.6 Lectern

This is the normal position for the speaker. The lectern, Figure 15.83, should have:

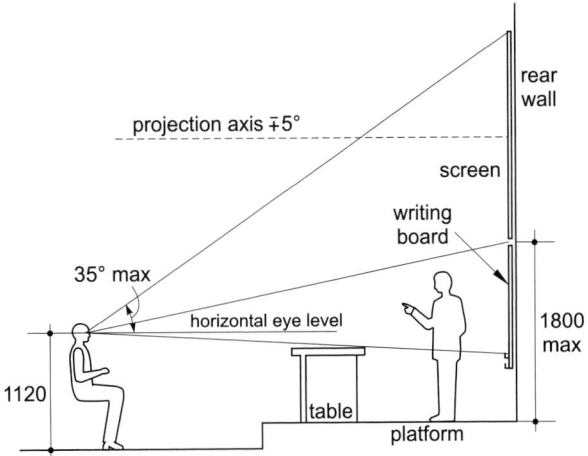

15.82 *Section through lecture theatre showing platform and front wall arrangements*

- a top sloping at 15° large enough for two A4 sheets;
- an adjustable screened light to illuminate script;
- a mounted microphone with switch;
- a jack point for lapel microphone;
- a microphone connection to simultaneous interpretation and/or recording systems;
- a level surface for pencils and glass of water and jug;
- controls for dimming house lights;

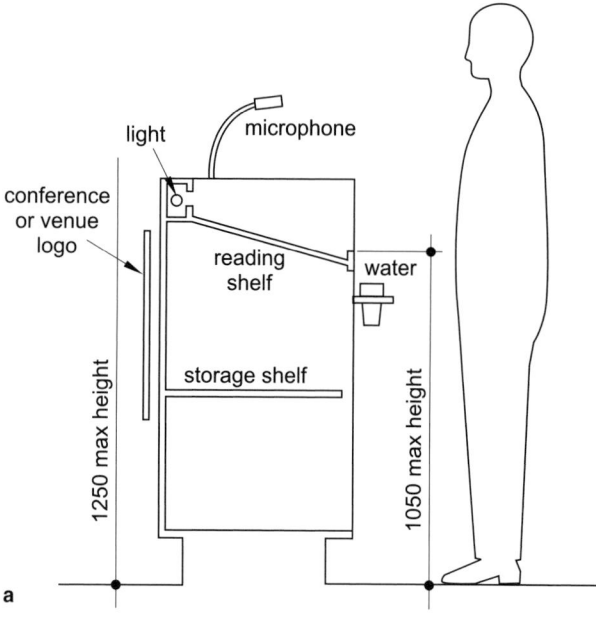

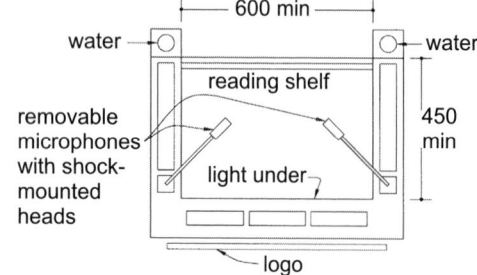

15.83 *Lectern: a Section. b Plan*

- controls for remote operation of projectors and screens;
- a manual or motorised raise and lower device for lectern stand;
- a hand-operated light pointer;
- a teleprompter screen (autocue);
- a clock;
- remote cueing;
- possibly red, yellow and green lights visible to both speaker and audience to indicate time available to speaker;
- a shelf below the top for brief-case, demonstration items, etc.
- for presentations using laptop images to be operated by a speaker, horizontal table 900 mm high, adjacent to the lectern, would be necessary.

7.7 Other platform facilities

The chairperson may introduce speakers from the lectern or a separate position elsewhere on the platform, with or without a lectern. It is usual for the chairperson to remain in a prominent position on the platform during speaking, questions and discussion, unless slides or films are shown on a screen behind their seat. Anyone on the platform in that case will move to a reserve seat in the body of the hall.

Control panel
It is common to have a separate panel operable by the chairperson. Alternatively, it could be duplicated at the lectern. This panel might incorporate:

- a buzzer to the projection room;
- a telephone link to the projection room;
- remote operation to black out windows (if any);
- house lights dimmer;
- separate lighting over platform;
- a teaching board light.

For the chairperson only:

- control for red, yellow and green lights on lectern;
- clock and/or timer;
- panel showing 'request-to-speak' indicators;
- on/off control for individual audience microphones;
- voting numbers display (see Section 7.4);
- control of large audience voting number panel.

Demonstration bench
A 'laboratory' fully serviced bench on the platform for the scientific demonstrations, with the supply of electricity, gas, water and drainage. The bench should be able to be wheeled off the platform if it is to be used for non-demonstration presentations, with plug-in services: the bench can be stored in the adjacent side preparation room.

Panel table
For discussion and presentations by a panel of speakers and a chairperson, a long table, parallel to the front edge of the platform, is a recognised format, with a chair and microphone for each panellist, and possibly simultaneous translation earphones. The table should be at least 750 mm deep, allowing 1 m length for each person. The name and details of each panellist may be mounted on the front edge of the table or on a stand in front of each. The lectern may or may not be used.

Rear and side walls of platform
Either a permanent enclosure with all or some of the following (see further details see Section 7.9ff):

- chalkboards
- projection screens
- space for conference name, logo and setting
- clock
- fixed lectern, overhead projector, table
- fixed or mobile demonstration table.

Curtains, masking, sliding panels may be incorporated to cut off sections of side and rear walls when not in use. Alternatively, there may be a shell with rear and side walls and equipment constructed for a particular conference: similar to theatre open stage with suspension over platform for setting and lighting.

An easily visible place is needed for a person to stand to translate the speaker's words into sign language.

7.8 Translators' booths

Conferences with international audiences will probably require simultaneous interpretation by translators in booths of those speaking in various languages.

Booths need to be located at the rear or perhaps the side of the auditorium with an unobstructed view by the translator of the speaker, chairperson, projection screens and chalkboards as well as any visual display, Figure 15.84. The booths are soundproofed, with the translator listening to the speech on headphones.

Booths should be located side by side with acoustic isolation and small connecting windows. They should open off a corridor giving discreet but secure access from the public areas. Booth interior should have absorbent material to walls, floor and ceiling, in dark matt colours.

Each booth needs to be able to accommodate two or three seated persons, minimum size 6.5 m wide and 6.4 m deep. The soundproof observation window can be full width of the booth, 800 mm high, and may be inclined to avoid acoustic reflections on either side. The translators need a clear working surface 500 mm wide in front of the window for scripts, notes, microphone, channel-selection buttons, indicator lights, etc.

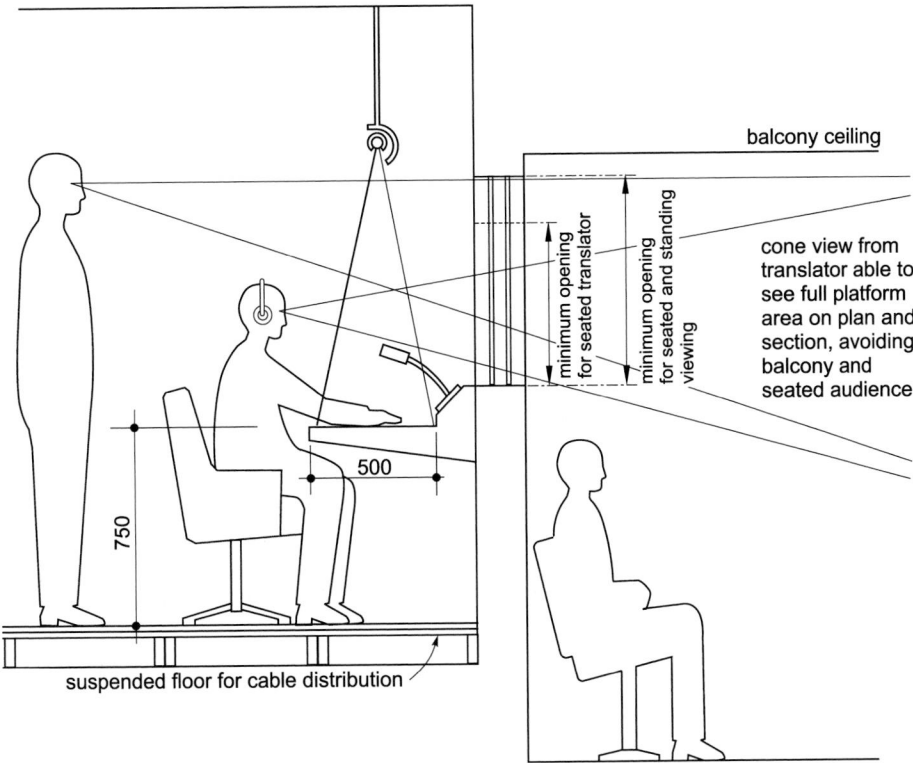

15.84 *Section through translators' booth at rear of auditorium*

Translators' ancillary rooms
A common room for translators should be located near the booths. This should have easy chairs, tables, telephones, cloakroom and toilets.

Simultaneous translation systems in the auditorium
Available methods are:

- Induction loop: magnetic field transmission generated by a conductor looped around auditorium. Conference delegates have portable receivers.
- Infra-red: modulated light signals radiated from a number of sources. Delegates have portable receivers.
- Hard-wired: cable within underfloor trunking connected to panels in arm rest or back of each seat for heavily used conference facilities.

7.9 Audiovisual facilities

Writing boards
Conventional chalkboards are now uncommon as they have now been superseded by overhead projectors for which material can be pre-prepared. Where they are used they would be a black or white chalkboard, fixed to a rear wall or moveable. The audience viewing angle is critical to avoid glare and reflections. The visibility tends to be restricted to twelve rows. Chalk and pen channel to be incorporated, with a ledge for an eraser.

Boards can slide vertically or horizontally to increase writing surface within a restricted space, Figure 15.85, or they can revolve vertically or horizontally, if made of a rubber or plastic material.

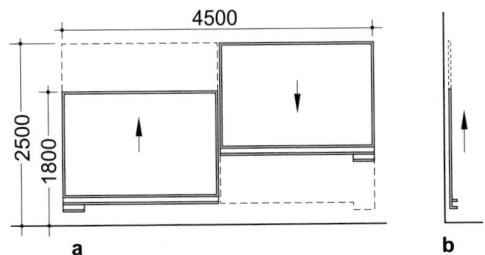

15.85 *Writing boards: vertically sliding: a Elevation. b Section*

The extent of chalkboard may be nominal, 1 m × 3.5 m for limited use by a speaker, or, in the case of the presentation of complex and mathematical formulae, a board extending the full width of the platform.

Small conference rooms are often equipped with whiteboards which are written or drawn on using special felt-tipped pens. These are permanently mounted on a wall, and have a ledge beneath for the pens and the eraser.

Flipcharts
Commonly used in small conferences and seminars, particularly in debating format. A1 size portrait orientation on a board 750 × 900 mm on a loose easel with ledge at 900 mm above platform. A storage space for this and for the pens etc. is useful. Sometimes they are fixed to a rear wall; good visibility is restricted to twelve rows.

Overhead projector
Figure 15.86 shows a projector on a stand. The image surface is 250 × 250 mm for writing on or for prepared images. A surface beside the projector is needed for the prepared acetate sheets and pens. The lecturer can be standing or seated. The projector may be located at a lower level in front of the platform to assist sightlines from the front auditorium rows to see the screen over the projector and speaker.

The screen needed to receive the image should be tipped forward to an angle of 20–25° to the vertical to avoid 'keystone' distortion, Figure 15.87; the distance from the projector to the screen equals the screen width. Such screens are available that can be swung or rolled away when the main projection screen is used.

Projection room
A projection room, Figure 15.88, may or may not be needed. Its advantages are that:

- The operator and operations will not disturb the audience.
- Noise is reduced or eliminated.
- The equipment and the media are more secure from interference and theft.
- It is easier to lift the projection beam over the heads of the audience.

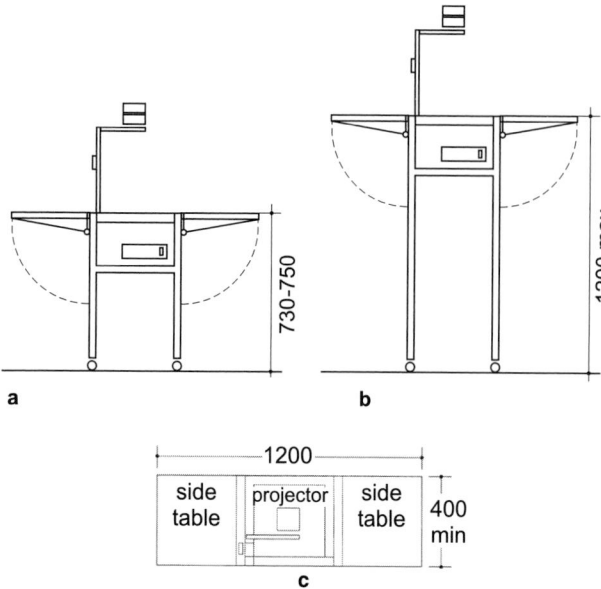

15.86 *Overhead projector: a Elevation of a projector on a table for a seated speaker. b Elevation of a projector on a table for a standing speaker. c Plan of either*

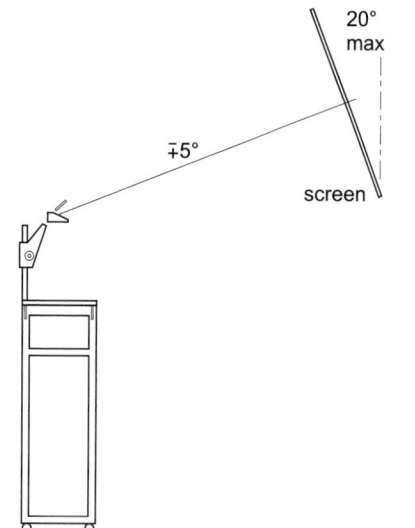

15.87 *Overhead projector screen: tilting helps to avoid the keystone effect*

The equipment needs to be grouped near the axis of the screen(s). It is more convenient for it to be on loose mobile stands, and the beam should be above the heads of a standing audience. Each port should be provided with a separate black-out shutter. The room should have separate extract ventilation and should open off a ventilated lobby.

Lighting control room
This is a limited requirement for conferences, but lighting control could be incorporated into a projection room at the rear of the auditorium, minimum size 2 m × 3.5 m. In some cases a dimmer room may be needed (see Section 4.10).

Sound control room
In this case an open room preferably at rear of the auditorium adjacent to the lighting control room, minimum size 2 m × 3.5 m. Here the amplified sound from one or more speakers can be mixed and balanced. The sound control desk may alternatively be situated within the auditorium.

Screens
Increasingly, back-projection screens are being used. In this case the projection room will be behind the platform rather than behind

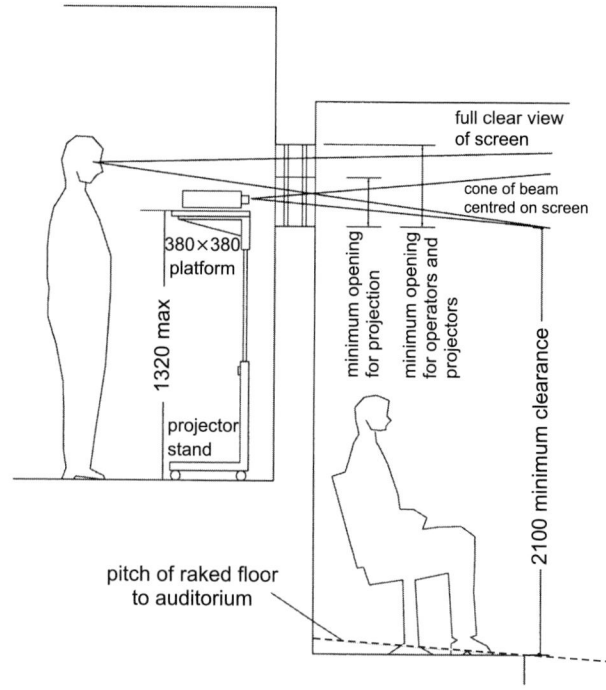

15.88 *Section through projection room at rear of auditorium (projecting slides)*

the audience. Back projection for video, film and slide requires wide-angle lenses but allows more freedom for speaker. Where conventional screens are used, they will be mounted above the heads of seated people on the platform. If multiple slide projection is to be used, a wide-screen format is necessary. Sometimes the side screens are angled up to 60°; this tends to limit seating positions with good visibility. Where wide flat screens are used curtains should be provided to reduce the width of these for film and video projection.

Slide projection
One, two and maybe more projected images from 35 mm slides, Figures 15.89–15.91, able to be used individually or simultaneously;

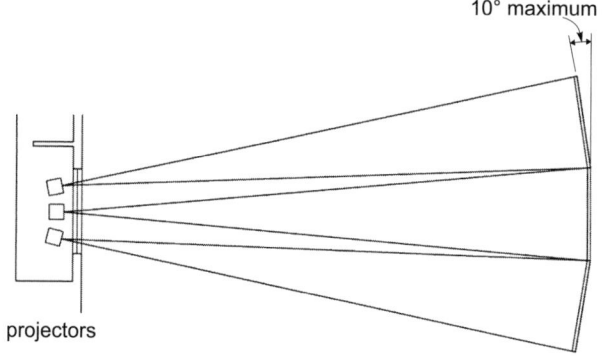

15.89 *Slide projection: multi-screen presentation*

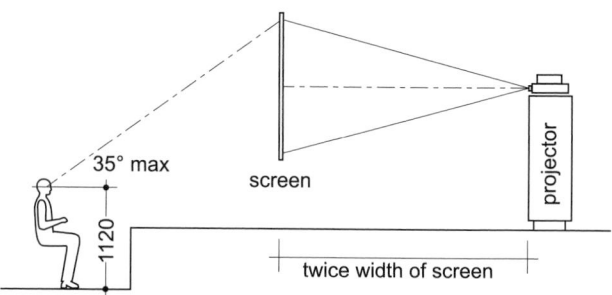

15.90 *Back projection for slides and 16 mm film*

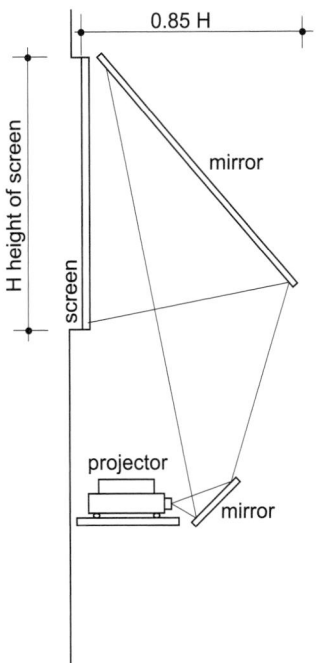

15.91 *Back projection of slides using mirrors*

the usual type of projector is the carousel. High-intensity projectors allow some light in auditorium for note taking. Screen areas for projecting slides should be square, as slides may be in portrait or landscape format. For three-screen projection the side screens are sometimes angled as much as 30° from the centre screen.

Video, DVD, data and other projection
Projectors are now usually mounted at high level in the auditorium, Figure 15.92, on stands or behind the screen. Close-range projectors can produce pictures up to 3 m high; they should be 3.5 to 3.6 times the picture width from the screen. DVDs, for example, may be loaded in a projection room, or from some position on the platform.

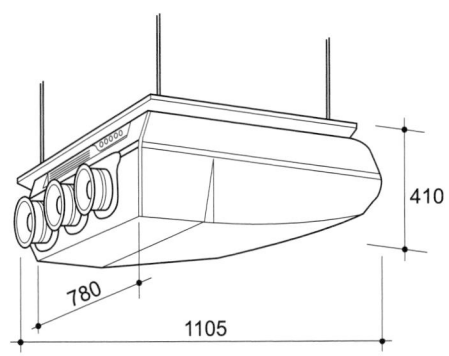

15.92 *Video projector mounted at high level in auditorium*

For a large screen a long-range projector is used producing a picture up to 7.5 m high. It should be housed in a projection room, with room for control and back-up equipment consisting of racks for VCR equipment, monitor screens, off-air times and ancillary control unit.

For small conference and seminar rooms, conventional TV sets can be used, Figure 15.93. Sometimes a number of these each serving a section of the audience are suspended at high level in a larger conference facility, but this is a somewhat primitive arrangement.

Film projection
Where films are used they are rarely greater than 35 mm and are usually 16 mm: 8 mm is now uncommon as video has taken its place. Films can be projected from a position within the seating

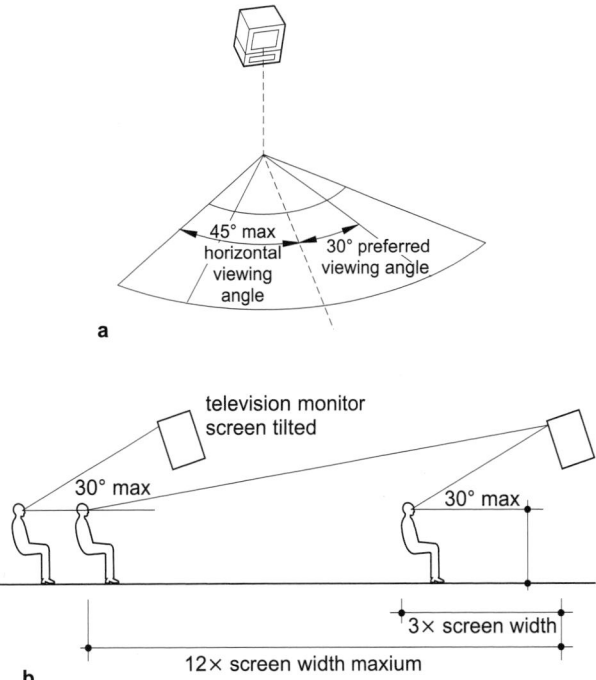

15.93 *Television viewing: a Horizontal angles. b Vertical angles*

area, but care must be taken that the beam is not interrupted by standing or sitting members of the audience. It is preferable to use a projection room where the beam can be at a higher level, although here the video projector must be avoided (more details in Section 8.2).

Television and film cameras
Conferences are frequently televised and recorded. Speakers and demonstrations are often projected oversize on screens both within the main conference hall and in overflow venues. Cameras are usually mobile, but require suitable floor surfaces.

A room may be required for recording and editing purposes, but this may not need direct vision of the conference, and could in fact be a remote studio.

Voting panel
This is a panel indicating electronically the numbers voting by pressing buttons at each seat, mounted above the platform and controlled by the chairperson.

7.10 Platform: associated spaces
- Ante-room: reception and waiting areas for conference chairperson and speakers, with lounge, changing facilities and toilets; sound and light lobby onto platform; access for guests from public areas.
- Preparation room: preparation of scientific and other demonstrations in room immediately off the platform.
- Slide and video room: viewing room for speakers, to sort and check slides, inspect videos and films, check overhead projector material.
- Studios: television, film and still photography preparation.
- Recording room: separate facility with tape-recording equipment linked to the auditorium and platform amplification system for the recording of the conference proceedings.

7.11 Conference organisation offices
- Offices with desks and chairs
- General office, with desks and chairs, fax machines, telephones, photocopier, computers, typewriters, intercom, translations, secretarial work.

7.12 Press room
- General room: desks and chairs, telephones, fax machines, computers
- Television and radio interview rooms.

Table IV Film type and application

Type	Projection	Application	Quality	Light source/screen size
35 mm	Usually permanent installation. Portable versions possible.	Multiplex, independent and specialist cinemas, arts centres, high quality lecture halls, TV	Excellent – a world standard for commercial cinema	Usually high pressure Xenon lamps. 1 Kw–7 Kw lamps. Older projectors may use carbon arc lamphouses. Long throw and large screen sizes require higher power lamps
70 mm	Usually permanent installation. Equipment will also project 35 mm	Mainly specialised cinemas and venues	Excellent – normally used for prestigious films	High pressure Xenon lamps
2 K and 4 K High definition digital cinema (D-Cinema)[1]	Usually permanent installation occupying similar space to 35 mm projectors. Smaller semi-portable projectors available for small/ mid-size auditoria	Multiplex, independent and specialist cinemas, arts centres, high quality lecture halls, TV	Excellent – rivals or exceeds 35 mm film quality	High pressure Xenon lamps. Certain models require high levels of ventilation. 1 Kw–12Kw lamps
3D D-Cinema	As above	As above	Excellent	As above but with increased demands on lamp power and ventilation
1 K and 1.3 K High definition digital cinema (E-Cinema)	Portable or semi-portable projectors offering a lower quality image	Specialist cinemas, arts centres, lecture halls.	Very good – this standard is widely used by cinemas in Asia and South America. It is not considered acceptable for major Hollywood films.	Lamps usually rated below 1 Kw, consequently ventilation requirements are modest.
LCD/Data projectors	Portable projectors	Film clubs, lecture halls, conferences, business meetings	Varies from poor to satisfactory. Not acceptable for public cinema applications	Lamps usually rated below 1 Kw.

Note: [1]2 K and 4 K refer to the number of horizontal pixels produced by the digital projector (2048 and 4096 respectively). 2 K projectors are considered to be the minimum quality standard for feature films by the major Hollywood studios.

8 CINEMAS

8.1 Types of film and method of projection

Cinema projection is traditionally film based but is increasingly being supplemented or completely replaced by high definition digital projection technologies. Film projection in cinemas normally uses 35 mm film but can also use 70 mm (mainly for larger cinemas with wide screens) or 16 mm (generally for smaller or specialised cinemas). Large formats such as IMAX use special film projection systems to produce very wide and tall screen images. Digital projection systems are capable of replicating a similar range of screen formats to film projection at comparable or superior quality levels. Both film and digital projection systems can be adapted to produce 3D images. The various film and digital projection types are shown in Table IV.

8.2 Methods of projection

There are three methods of film projection:

• Direct projection from the rear of the auditorium onto the screen. The most common method by far.
• Indirect projection, where the film projection requires one or more mirrors. This method is used where lack of space or structural difficulties make direct projection difficult to achieve. Mirror projection requires a powerful light source and the screen cannot be wider than 9 m.
• Rear projection. Not possible with curved screen, but may be applicable for the smaller auditorium. For this method the picture needs to be reversed, for which mirrors are an economic solution.

8.3 Auditorium design

Functional requirements include:

• Every member of the audience requires an unobstructed view of the whole picture area on the screen, without visual and physical discomfort and picture distortion.
• Picture sharpness and luminance need to be uniform and satisfactory, and sound reproduction needs to be distortion free.
• Integration of seating for members of the audience with mobility disabilities.

8.4 Viewing conditions

Viewing criteria are shown in plan, Figure 15.94, and section, Figure 15.95. The size and shape of the screen must be related to the shape and rake of the auditorium floor. Seating rake is less critical than for concert halls and theatres as the screen can be elevated and sound comes from overhead speakers.

Seating arrangements

Few new auditoria are designed with galleries or balconies (unless the auditorium is required for other forms of performance). Steeply tiered stadia seating offers an opportunity for good sightlines onto a large screen relative to audience numbers.

In small auditoria, stadia seating may be arranged in a single tier in order to optimise seating capacity. In order to provide a choice of seating for members of the audience with mobility disabilities access should be provided for wheelchair users to the front and rear row.

In larger auditoria, access may be provided onto a cross aisle with steeply tiered stadia seating to the rear of the cross aisle and a gentle rake to the front rows. A choice of seating position for members of the audience with mobility disabilities can be on the cross aisle or in the front row.

Seating types

To meet expectations of comfort, seat centres are generally at least 550 mm. Seat tier widths are governed by expectations of comfort, choice of seat type and statutory requirements for minimum clear seatways.

The design of modern multiplexes has established an expectation in cinema-going audiences that seat tiers should be at least 1100 mm wide. This is wide enough to accommodate most comfortable models of cinema seats. With tip-up seats 1000 mm can be acceptable. Accommodating comfortable fixed cinema seats or small sofa style seats may require increases in the width of the tiers to 1200 mm.

To accommodate 'premium' armchair or sofa style seats offering extra comfort, seat tiers of up to 1500 mm wide may be required. A requirement to accommodate cup holders, bottle holders or small tables will influence the choice of seat, seat centres and seat tier widths.

In multi-use auditoria with a flat floor regularly used for cinema screenings, retractable seating systems with straight and curved rows and comfortable cinema style seats are available.

Aisle arrangements

The maximum number of seats permitted in a row is not only governed by viewing criteria but statutory requirements. The aisle arrangement and clear seatway are critical factors. The maximum

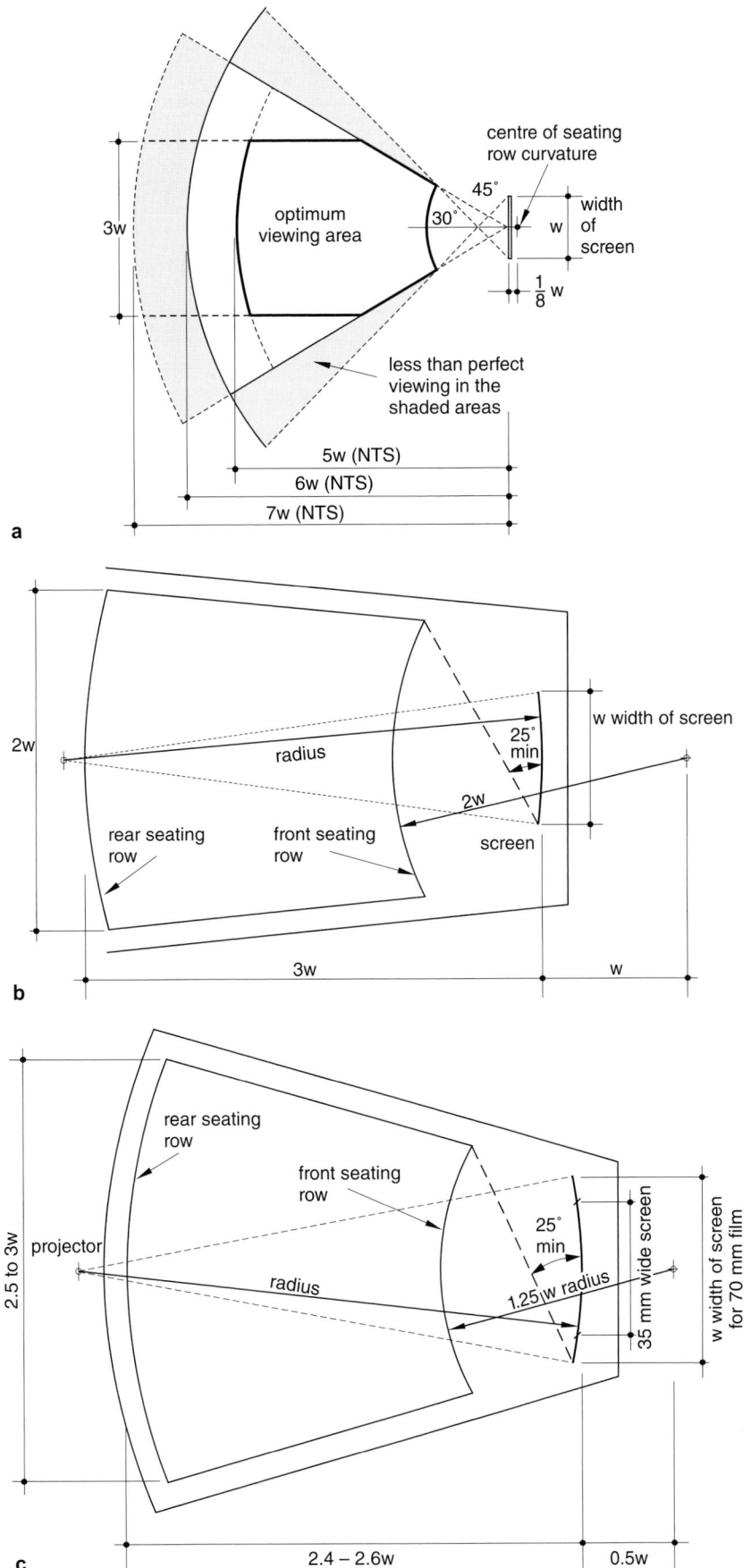

15.94 *Projection criteria for various formats: a 16mm film. b 35mm film. c 70mm film*

number of seats permitted in a row with a single aisle is 12, irrespective of the seatway width.

A single centre aisle is not favoured as it occupies seat positions with the best viewing conditions, as well as splitting the audience.

An off set single aisle provides a more cohesive seating arrangement for the audience as a whole and provides an opportunity to accommodate seats for couples in the shorter row. The provision of two side aisles enables the numbers in a single row to be increased.

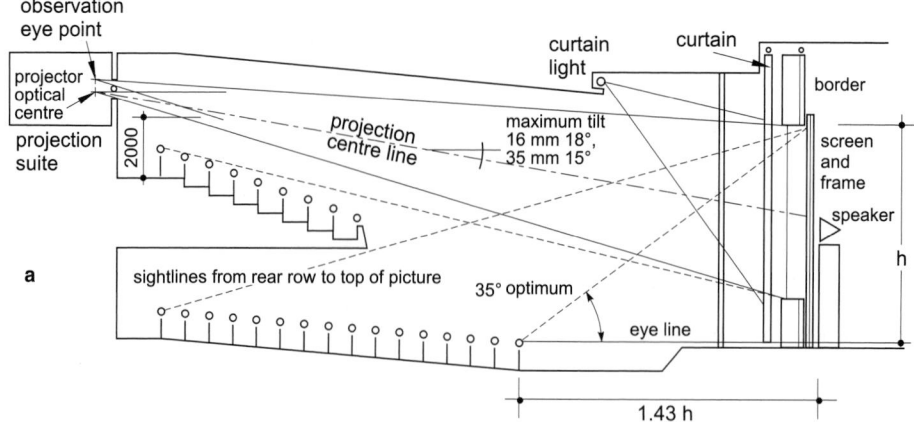

15.95a *Vertical sightlines: a 16 mm and 35 mm*

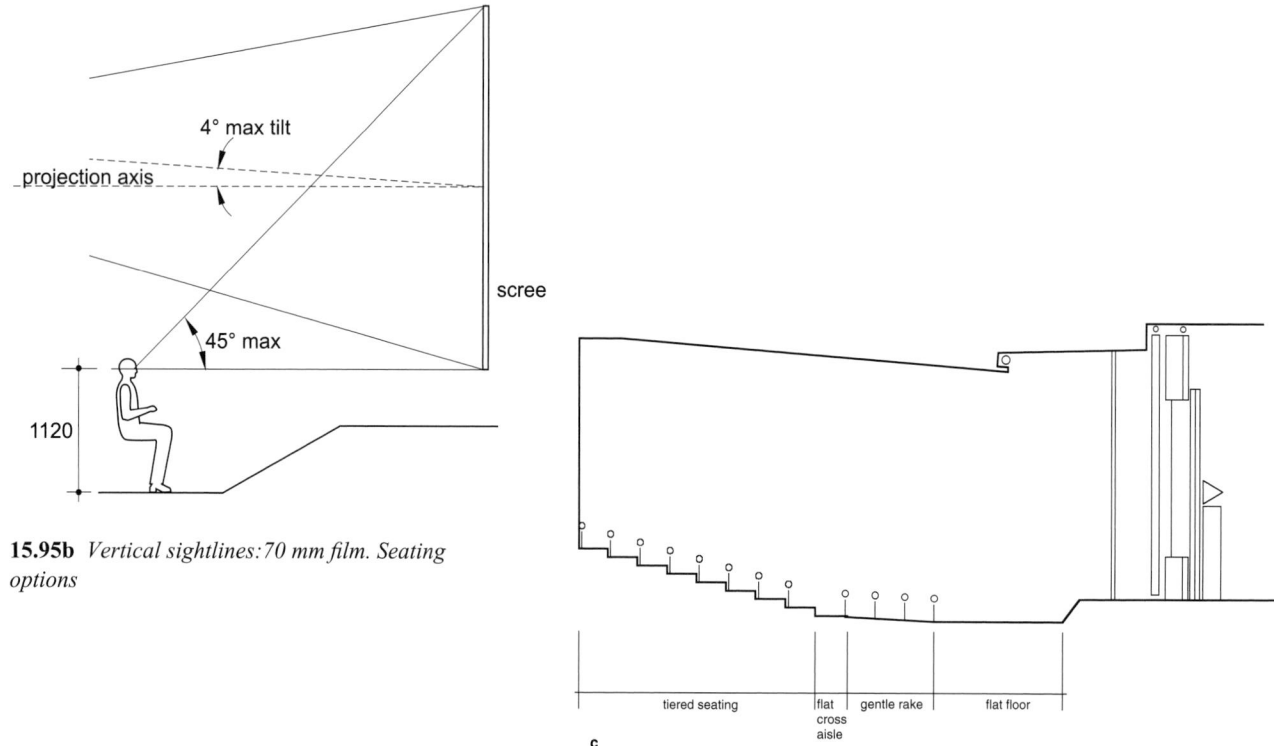

15.95b *Vertical sightlines:70 mm film. Seating options*

15.95c *Vertical sightlines: tiered seating*

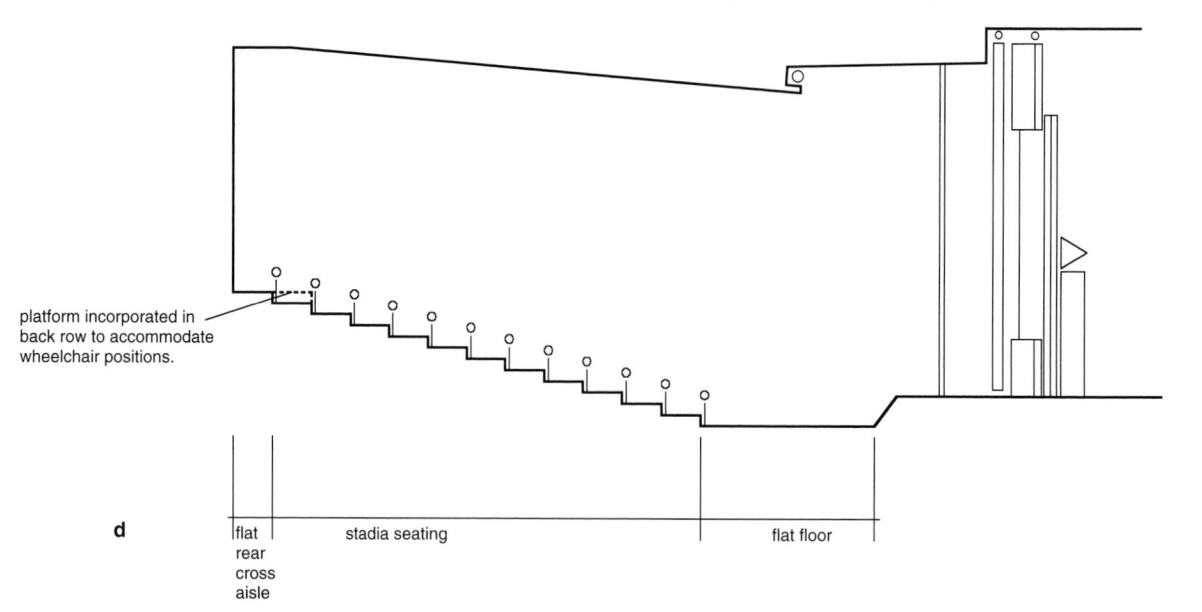

15.95d *Vertical sightlines: stadia seating*

It is good practice to avoid entrances at the screen end of the cinema, so as to avoid disturbance by latecomers.

8.5 Acoustics for films

The sound track is an integral part of the audience experience and the quality of sound reproduction has vastly improved. Cinemas are now equipped with stereophonic sound systems which require acoustically dead auditoria; the ideal is a zero reverberation time. Hence all finishes – floor, walls, ceiling and seats – need to be sound absorbent. Side walls should not be parallel, and a fan shape is preferred. The auditorium should be structurally and enclosure-wise insulated from external noise. A suitable ambient noise standard for cinemas is NR30 to NR35. The volume per occupant should be at least 1.25 m^3 for large cinemas and 5 m^3 per person for small auditoria.

8.6 Access

The design of the auditoria should optimise the experience of going to the cinema for all members of the audience.

Mobility disabilities

A choice of position for wheelchair users should be provided, integrated within the main body of seating. Suitable positions on a level surface may include the front row, cross aisle or back row. It should be possible for a wheelchair user to sit next to a companion, whether another wheelchair user or not.

Visual impairment

Space should be provided for a guide dog at the end of a row. Facilities for screening films with audio description run off a CD for 35 mm film with professionally produced audio description synchronised with the film. Audience members pick up head sets from the box office which run off one of the channels on the infra red system. Digital Cinema servers have additional channels which provide audio descriptions.

Low level lighting on stepped or raking aisles, with the light source located out of the line of vision of the screen is an aid to all members of the audience.

Aural impairment

Facilities may include inductive loops and/or infra-red systems. Ideally both systems should be installed to cater for different types of hearing impaired user. A system of superimposing a subtitle (soft title) by use of the video projecting onto a projected 35 mm image is also available for the profoundly deaf. This system is incorporated into a single digital cinema projector.

8.7 Lighting

The different types of lighting which need to be provided within a cinema auditorium are:

- *House lights*. These are the decorative lights which set the ambience of the auditorium when the audience enters and are gradually dimmed before the screening.
- *Curtain lights*. These highlight the screen curtains/screen surface prior to the screening and often have coloured gels.
- *Primary lighting*. These are mains powered and provide a low level of lighting during screenings, equivalent to the level of lighting provided by the secondary emergency lighting in the event of mains failure. It is essential that they are no brighter than required to meet statutory requirements in order to avoid distractions during screenings.
- *Secondary (emergency) lighting*. These are powered by a central battery or local battery packs and provide a low level of illumination in the event of mains failure.
- *Illuminated emergency exit signs*. These are dual fed, that is mains powered and powered by a central battery or local battery packs and remain illuminated during screenings and in the event of mains failure and an emergency. It is bad practice to locate exits and hence illuminated emergency exit signs within

the same plane or in close proximity to the screen. Illuminated exit signs should be selected to minimise disturbance through light spillage during screenings.

- *Cleaners' lights*. House lights that are energy efficient may double up as cleaners' lights. Alternatively separate cleaners' lights are installed. These need to be controllable from the projection room and the ushers' position in the event of an emergency (other than mains failure) for example a medical emergency. Regard needs to be given to lamp life and ease of changing the bulbs when considering the location and specification of all light fittings within a cinema auditorium.
- *Speakers' lights*. In auditoria used for awards ceremonies and panel discussions before or after screenings or for conference use, speakers' lights should be provided.

8.8 Interiors

It is good practice to avoid light colours and reflective surfaces within a cinema auditorium, to avoid distraction during screening.

It is good practice for the lighting design and colour scheme on the approaches to the auditorium to assist members of the audience adjust to lighting levels within the auditorium.

8.9 Screens

Shape

Film and digital projectors may be required to project material in a variety of width-to-height ratios. Typical ratios for commercial cinemas are 1:1.66, 1:1.85 and 1:2.39. Specialist cinemas and lecture halls may require ratios as low as 1:1.33 (described as 4:3 in video terminology) for archive, independent or television material. High definition television normally uses a 1:1.78 ratio (16:9 for video).

Size

The largest 35 mm screens will usually be less than 18 m in width. 2 K digital cinema projectors can now illuminate a picture size in excess of 25 m.

Curvature

For uniform focus a large screen should be curved to keep its surface equidistant from the centre of the lens.

Luminance

Screens may have a matt white surface or a special high reflectivity surface which is particularly suitable for larger screens where the luminance needs to be enhanced. Some 3D projection systems require a high reflectivity silver surface although these are unsatisfactory for conventional 2D projection.

Position

The centre of screen should be on the central axis of the auditorium seating

Masking

Mechanically adjustable black masking to the sides and top of the screen is normally provided to contain the picture surface and obtain maximum apparent brightness. The masking is usually wool serge on metal rails, and the gear should be fixed at floor level for ease of maintenance. Movement is remotely controlled from the projection room.

Unmasked screens

Unmasked screens are used in many multiplex cinemas and some specialised cinemas. They are most suitable when used with digital projection systems which can produce a 'clean' picture edge.

Construction

Screen material is either PVC or metallised fabric, held by cord lacing to hooks on a metal lattice frame. Generally cinema screens are perforated to allow high quality sound reproduction from the speakers positioned behind the screen. Different sized perforations are available. Digital cinema projection and small auditoria usually require smaller size perforations. Unperforated screens may be used in specific circumstances such as lecture halls.

Temporary screens

In some multi-use auditoria screens may require to be easily and conveniently removed. A flat screen up to 6 m wide can be incorporated into a proscenium stage of a theatre form either housed, when rolled, in the stage or flown in the flytower. Curved screens could be flown, but take up much valuable space in the flytower; or they could be stored at the rear of the stage if fitted with rollers or castors for ease of movement.

Speaker installation

The speakers need to be located behind the screen, firmly fixed to the platform or screen frame. One speaker is needed for monophonic sound; for multi-channel and stereophonic sound from 35 mm film, three speaker units are necessary: one centrally placed and the others equidistant from it to the left and right. 70 mm sound production requires five symmetrically placed about the horizontal axis of the central speaker.

A sub-woofer low-frequency speaker is usually located centrally behind the cinema screen. Surround sound systems are widely used in cinemas and require a number of small or mid-size wall-mounted units on the left, right and rear auditorium walls.

Platform

The back of the screen frame, including the speaker, needs to be covered with heavy felt to absorb sound. Alternatively the entire wall surface behind the screen and speaker frame can be covered with black tissue faced insulation. The screen is set over a platform with a forestage, carpeted with black carpet to prevent reflection of sound and light. The forestage edge can be vertical, splayed or stepped. Some theatres now build baffle walls behind the screen which incorporate the theatre stage loudspeakers.

Stage for speakers

In cinemas used for speeches or panel discussions before or after screenings, awards ceremonies or occasional lecture or conferences it should be possible for all audience members to have a clear view of the speakers' panels' faces.

Usually this will require the provision of a raised stage in front of the screen, although with steeply tiered stadia seating this may not be necessary.

AV and IT provision at the speakers' position, linked back to the projection room, needs to be considered. It is also useful to incorporate within the design of the cinemas a reasonable sized pipe such as a drain pipe so that A/V lines can be added on an ongoing basis from the projection box to behind the screen area.

Access to the stage for speakers or panel members with mobility disabilities needs to be considered.

8.10 Projection suite

A projection suite provides space for all the image projection and sound reproduction equipment in a cinema. Contemporary cinema design aims for a single projection suite to cover all the auditoria. Most cinemas provide automated systems which allow complete performance to be screened with minimal staff input. Specialised cinemas and lecture halls rely less on automated systems.

Digital cinema systems remove the need for film preparation and storage equipment and film transport systems therefore may require smaller projection suites.

Projection suites should be secure from access by the general public.

Digital projection

Digital cinema projectors have approximately the same footprint as 35 mm projection. 2 K and 4 K projectors can achieve image widths up of 25 m.

A single projector can be used for 3D projection, but has to produce approximately twice the light output as used for 2D projection. This could, in larger auditoria, reduce the standard picture size; two projectors can be used to increase the luminance in the largest theatres. To achieve 3D in 4 K projection two projectors will be required. Some 3D equipment is fitted to the lens on 2 K projectors and requires approximately 500 mm from the projection lens to the porthole glass for installation and removal.

There are two types of 3D glasses in use, the disposable and reusable. It should be taken into account that glasses should be easy to distribute and to collect. The reusable glasses are expensive and security issues should be taken into account. Facilities will be required to wash, dry and store the glasses.

A standard digital projection system is comprised of the following:

* A projection head, lamphouse and rectifier. These are usually housed together in a single module.
* Digital cinema film server and storage system can be rack mounted with the theatre's sound processor and amplification system or in some cases under the projector's lamphouse. The film server will require an ADSL or IDSN connection to download security keys for diagnostic tests.
* In some theatres there may be a requirement to play alternative content, which includes/definition any image that is not high and digital cinema. This may comprise of corporate PowerPoint presentations, live concerts, DVDs, Playstation type gaming or other video formats.

Additional equipment may include:

* Multimedia playback box, digital to analogue sound interface, audio delay, DVD playback, satellite dish and transcoder for live events and downloading digital cinema content, space for HD disc player/VR playback, monitor.

Digital cinema projectors require venting at approximately 600/650 cfm. Projection boxes should be cooled to approximately 21°C.

9 MULTI-PURPOSE AUDITORIA

9.1 Requirements

Multi-purpose auditoria refers to an approach where compatible activities are combined within one volume. An example, Figure 15.96, covers a single form with a modest level of flexibility while combining opera, dance, musicals and drama, as well as concerts, conference and film shows. This is a multi-purpose proscenium stage with flytower and a flexible proscenium zone; the seating in the auditorium can remain constant.

9.2 Physical restraints

Problems can arise in combining different types of production in a single auditorium. Required volumes and reverberation times differ for speech and for music. To adjust the volume, arrangements to lower the auditorium ceiling can be incorporated into the design. Temporary alterations to the surface treatment of walls and ceilings can alter reverberation times, as can electronic 'assisted resonance'.

10 SUPPORT FACILITIES

10.1 Entrance doors and lobbies

These require:

* Ease of access from car parking and public transport
* Canopy: to provide shelter at entrance
* Provision for posters and other information
* Draught lobby
* Automatic sliding doors

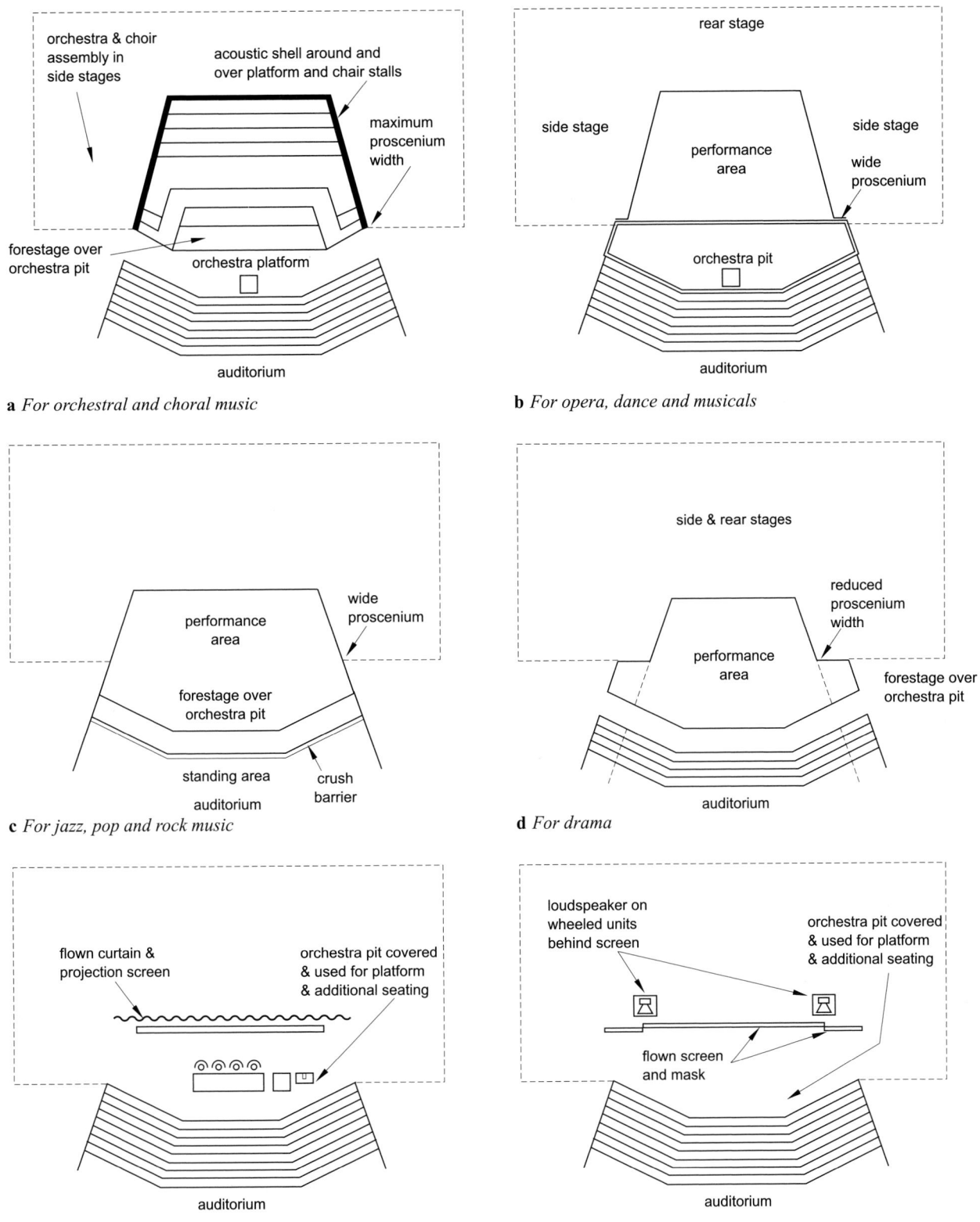

a *For orchestral and choral music*

b *For opera, dance and musicals*

c *For jazz, pop and rock music*

d *For drama*

e *For conferences*

f *For cinema*

15.96 *Multi-use stage with flytower and flexible proscenium usable in the following ways*

10.2 Entrance foyer

Box office, Figure 15.97 (in theatre, concert hall, cinema): counter for the sale of tickets; computer ticket dispenser

Registration (conference hall): counter or table

Reception and information: counter

Cloakroom (not usual in cinema): attended or unattended

Creche: at least 6.5 m² per child

First-aid room: bed, washhand basin

Toilets: see Chapter 2

Foyer and circulation: table, chairs, display stands

Performance area: within foyer or separate area

Space and display for exhibitions: see Chapter 29

Auditorium lobbies: barriers to sound and light at entry points into the auditorium; the level of lighting should assist adaptation to and from dark auditorium and the brighter foyer lighting, as with a cinema.

10.3 Places to eat and drink

- Coffee bar
- Licensed bar

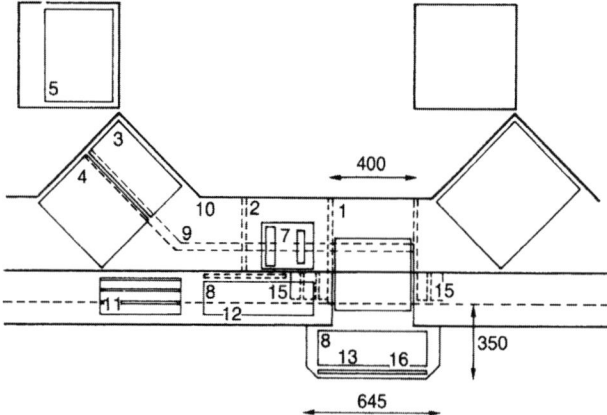

a *Plan*

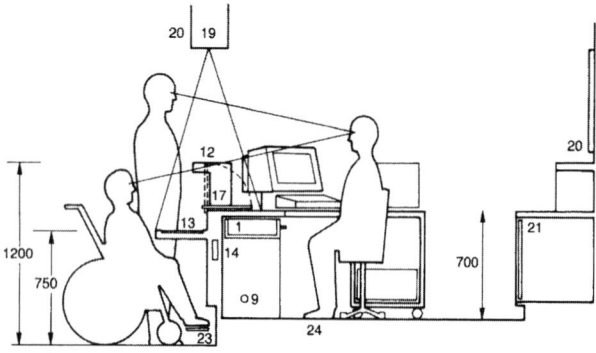

b *Section*

15.97 *Box office. KEY: 1 stationery drawer, 2 till drawer, 3 keyboard, 4 VDU, 5 mobile ticket printer, 7 telephone, 8 seating layout plans, 9 footrest, 10 writing space, 11 leaflets, 12 upper customer counter, 13 lower customer counter, 14 cable trunking, 15 pigeon holes for tickets and messages to be collected, 16 cheque writing upstand, 17 counter flap, 19 counter lighting, 20 display, 21 storage, 24 raised floor*

- Cafeteria
- Restaurant
- Banquet room
- Private room
- Associated spaces: bar store, cellar, kitchen, storage, staff rooms, manager's offices, delivery, refuse.

See Chapter 34.

10.4 Sales
- Shops and merchandise outlets: display cases, shelving; office, storage, security; see Chapter 35.
- Kiosk and other food outlets: display cases, shelving, microwave oven, stockroom (confectionery, drinks, etc.) with possible refrigerator; security.

10.5 Meeting rooms
Break-out rooms, sponsors' rooms; equipped for receptions, and small group lectures, discussions and workshops.

10.6 VIP rooms
Reception rooms for distinguished visitors; lounge and toilets.

10.7 Exhibition hall
Displays including trade exhibitions; storage, deliveries, possible separate public entrance, see Chapter 29.

10.8 Art gallery
Permanent and/or temporary exhibitions, see Chapter 29.

10.9 Office services
Conference halls: access by delegates to fax machines, telephones, photocopiers, translators, secretarial work, see Chapter 30.

10.10 Outdoor areas
Gathering area at front doors; associated with foyer and places to eat and drink as external terraces; store for outdoor furniture; landscaping.

10.11 Signage
- External: name of venue, current and future events.
- Internal: direction signs to the various public attractions.

10.12 Managerial spaces
Administrative offices
- Offices: functions may include policy, house management, accounts, personnel, marketing, press and publicity, development and community programmes, clerical work; see Chapter 30.
- Associated spaces may include boardroom, storage, strong room, office services and equipment, entrance and reception, toilets.

Box office: room for postal and telephone bookings, storage of sales records and accounts; access to changing, relaxation and toilet facilities.
Men's and women's staff rest rooms: lockers, lounge chairs, refreshments and toilets.
Sales and trays store: refrigerator for ice cream, shelves for confectionery, programmes, documents and other items for sale or distribution; storage of sales trays; table; washhand basin; located directly off the public areas.
Maintenance workshop, office and store: for the maintenance of the building fabric, equipment, emergency services, external works.
Cleaners' stores: central storage of materials and equipment; cupboards with sink, cleaning materials and equipment throughout building.
Security control room: surveillance monitors, fire-detection systems, alarms, service monitors, paging systems, locking devices.
Refuse: external provision for dust-bins, well ventilated and easily cleaned.
Catering facilities: the scale of the operation may justify the inclusion of catering facilities for all staff.

10.13 Production spaces
For those opera, dance, musical and drama companies which initiate their own productions, the following spaces are required:

- Offices for the functions of artistic policy, direction, production development, instruction, design, production organisation, business management, development programmes and clerical work.
- Associated spaces may include boardroom, library, music room, audition room, working conference room, model-making facilities, dark room, general storage, office services, refreshment areas, toilets, entrance and reception.

10.14 Rehearsal spaces
A relationship diagram for a rehearsal suite is shown in Figure 15.98.

- Rehearsal room or rehearsal studio able to accommodate largest performing area on the stage plus 2 m on three sides and 3 m on one long side as a minimum.
- Practice studios for individual or small group practice, for example for dancers, Figure 15.99.
- Associated spaces may include lounge, changing rooms, toilets, storage of equipment.

10.15 Scenery workshops
The substantial facilities required where the manufacture and maintenance of scenery is involved is well illustrated in Figure 15.100.

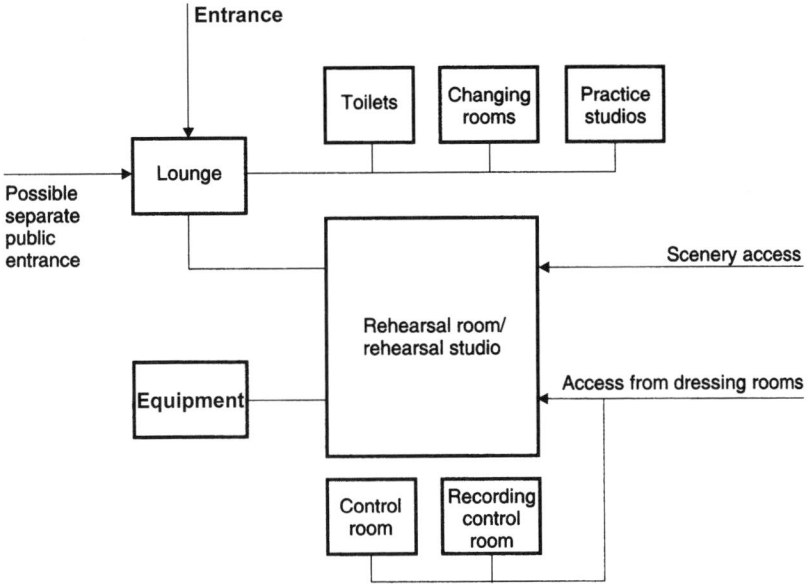

15.98 *Relationship diagram for a rehearsal room or studio*

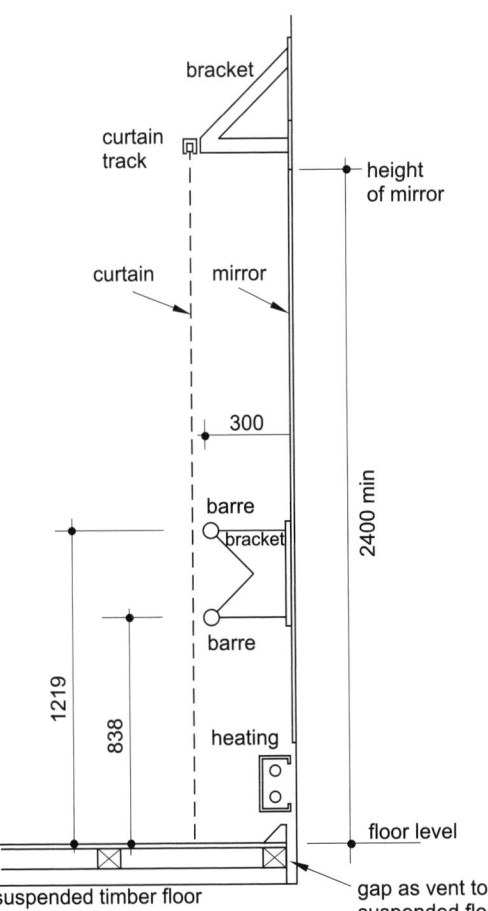

15.99 *Section through wall barres in rehearsal studio for dance practice*

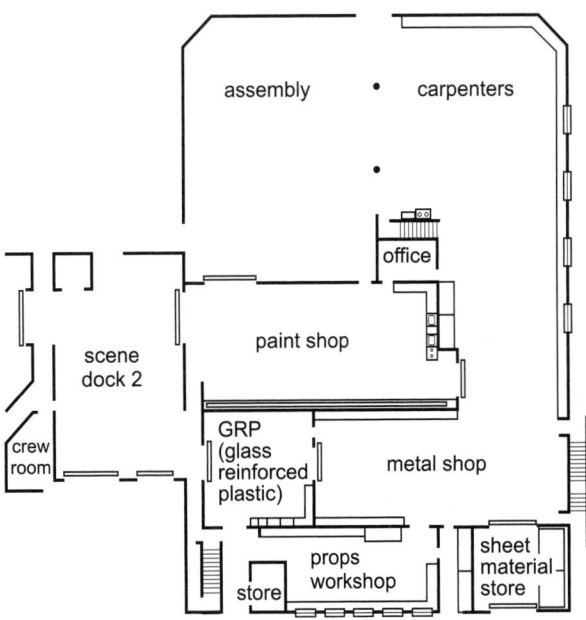

15.100 *Plan of workshops in the West Yorkshire Playhouse, Leeds*

Offices: for head of carpentry workshop, head of paint shop, and head of property department.

Carpentry workshop: for the construction of scenery; power-operated tools (such as woodworking machine, mortise, circular and bandsaws and lathes); benches for carpentry, assembly and canvassing; storage of raw materials such as timber, sheet materials, rolls of materials, nails and screws and so on, including polystyrene sheets which may require a separate fire-resistant enclosure

Paint shop: for the painting of scenery, the method of painting backcloths and flats (flat on the floor, on mobile frame or fixed frame and gantry), and three-dimensional pieces: the extent of benches for mixing paints and other preparation and cleaning brushes; storage requirements for raw materials such as paints and fire-proofing, and equipment such as brushes and spray equipment. Paints may require to be stored in a fire-proof enclosure.

Metalwork shop: the use of metal in the preparation of scenery; provision for welding, cutting and fabricating metalwork items; benches, welding screens and bending machinery; storage of raw materials such as sheets, tubes and bars, bolts, nuts and screws.

Trial assembly area: area for the erection of a trial assembly of the set under construction, the size of the performing area of the stage.

Property department: worktops and storage of raw materials. Two separate workshops may be required: one for polystyrene and fibre-glass work with associated fire-resistant requirements and extraction of toxic gases, the other for work with other materials.

Delivery and storage of raw materials to the carpentry workshop, paint shop, metalwork shop and property department, including unloading bay and parking of delivery vans and lorries.

Storage of scenery and properties for re-use.

10.16 Layout of workshops

A level floor is required through unloading bays, workshops, scenery store and stage, giving a clear, broad passage of movement of scenery onto the stage. Where a change of level is unavoidable a lift will be inevitable but is not recommended. If touring companies are anticipated, passage from the unloading bay to the stage should be direct without interfering with the workshops.

The paint frame and backcloth storage should be placed so that the rolled backcloths can be moved horizontally into position under the flytower or grid with the painted surface facing the audience. The large doors or roller shutters required for the movement of scenery should not also be used for people. The minimum dimensions of the openings should be determined by the maximum size of scenery expected.

The carpentry shop should be isolated from the paint shop to avoid noise and sawdust penetration, and both areas should be acoustically insulated from the stage. Scenery storage located between workshops and stage acts as a sound barrier.

10.17 Wardrobe

Space is required for:

- making and fitting of performers' costumes;
- making and fitting associated items such as wigs;
- storing, repairing and cleaning costumes;
- making millinery and accessories;
- dyeing cloth and spraying materials;
- storing rolls of cloth and pattern paper;
- storing small items such as sewing materials, dyestuffs;
- delivery of raw materials including unloading bay and parking of delivery vans;
- office for costume supervisor.

Performers require easy access to the wardrobe for fitting costumes, while the distribution of finished costumes for, and their cleaning during, a production suggests a location close to the dressing rooms.

10.18 Recording studio

For sound effects and music. An isolated space, with control room. Associated areas may include a library of tapes and discs, entry lounge and lobby. Further details may be found in Chapter 40.

10.19 Common facilities

Provision for resting, changing, refreshment, toilets and showers.

10.20 Transport

Van or vans for the collections and delivery of goods, with parking spaces within the curtilage of the site.

11 FACILITIES FOR PEOPLE WITH A DISABILITY

Access:

- Dedicated car parking spaces at public and staff entrances.
- Drop-off points at entrances.
- Wheelchair users use main entrance.
- External and internal ramped access, handrails and lifts comply with Building Regulations.
- Unrestricted access to all levels and non-public areas (it may not be feasible to provide access for people in wheelchairs to access such areas as the grid over a stage, or lighting walkways over an auditorium).
- Dedicated wheelchair spaces in auditorium seating areas.
- Accessible toilets complying with Building Regulations.
- Box office reception desk and information counter with accessible height and width.

Facilities for people with sensory impairment:

- Induction loop system or infra-red hearing provision in auditorium.
- Induction loop system in box office, reception desk and information counter.
- Visual fire alarm system.
- Braille/large print/tactile signs.
- Audio description provision.
- Facilities for guide dogs.

12 LEGISLATION

Local authorities have a responsibility for licensing places of public entertainment. It is essential that contact be made with the appropriate local authority before plans are too far advanced. Before taking any decision they would normally consult the fire authority and the Health and Safety Executive as well as their own safety officer.

The areas of particular concern will be inflammability of materials, seating layout, emergency lighting levels, escape routes, signage and building services. Reference BS5499 and BS5588.

16 Civic buildings

David Selby, Martin Sutcliffe and Neil Sansum

CI/SfB: 314, 317, 372, 373, 374

Updated with David Selby (town halls) and Martin Sutcliffe and Neil Sansum of BDP (law courts)

David Selby is a senior partner at Hopkins Architects. Martin Sutcliffe is chairman and Neil Sansum is an architect director at BDP Bristol.

KEY POINTS:

- *Flexibility is needed to accommodate likely future change*
- *Value-for-money is a major design criterion*
- *The need for security while ensuring full access to those entitled is an increasing design challenge*

Contents

1 Town halls
2 Law courts
3 References

1 TOWN HALLS

1.1 Introduction

The concept of the town hall as a local civic and community focus has a continuing importance for communities. Local authorities are however significantly reviewing their modus operandi and the physical needs of their buildings.

A developing direction in the design of town halls is towards a flexible, modern facility that delivers high quality services to the public. Local authorities are consolidating their property portfolios in order to achieve greater efficiencies operationally and in terms of building stock. The name civic centre is considered as a more appropriate description or title, and even more fashionable expressions such as 'The Hub' or 'The Cube' have been adopted where the association with an outdated concept of local authority administration is no longer desired.

Although many of the key spatial requirements are similar to the traditional town hall model the emphasis has changed from the corridors of power to a building that provides services and facilities for the community, see Figure 16.1. The nature of the spaces has arguably become more demanding in terms of flexibility and therefore more generic rather than bespoke to a location.

Although local authorities may have different requirements, the new town hall or civic centre is likely to require the following principal components:

- members' accommodation
- council chamber
- community hall
- committee rooms and meeting rooms
- offices
- reception
- customer services
- library
- events spaces.

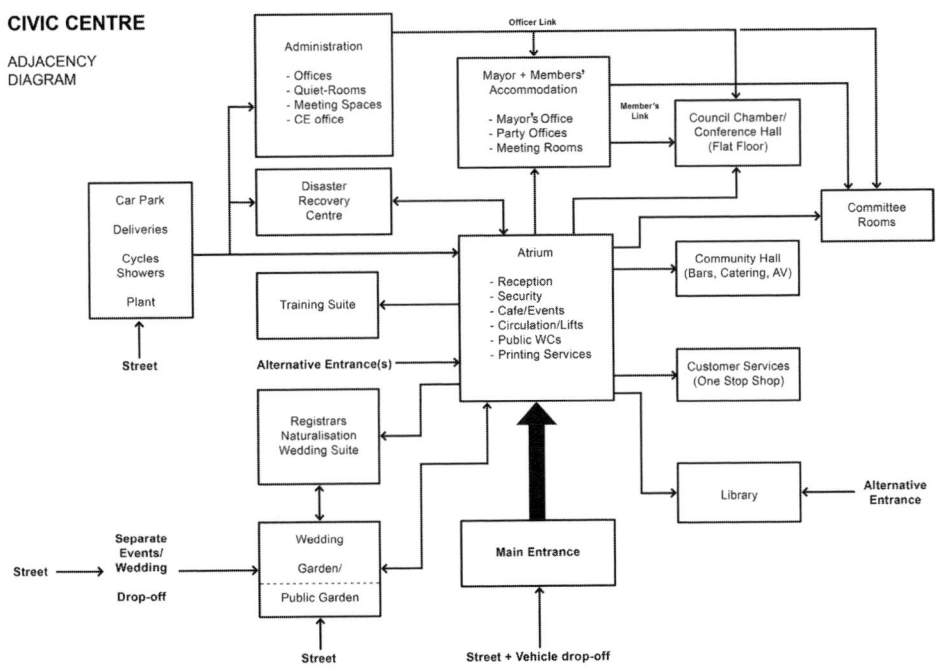

16.1 *Relationship diagram for civic centre functions (Hopkins Architects)*

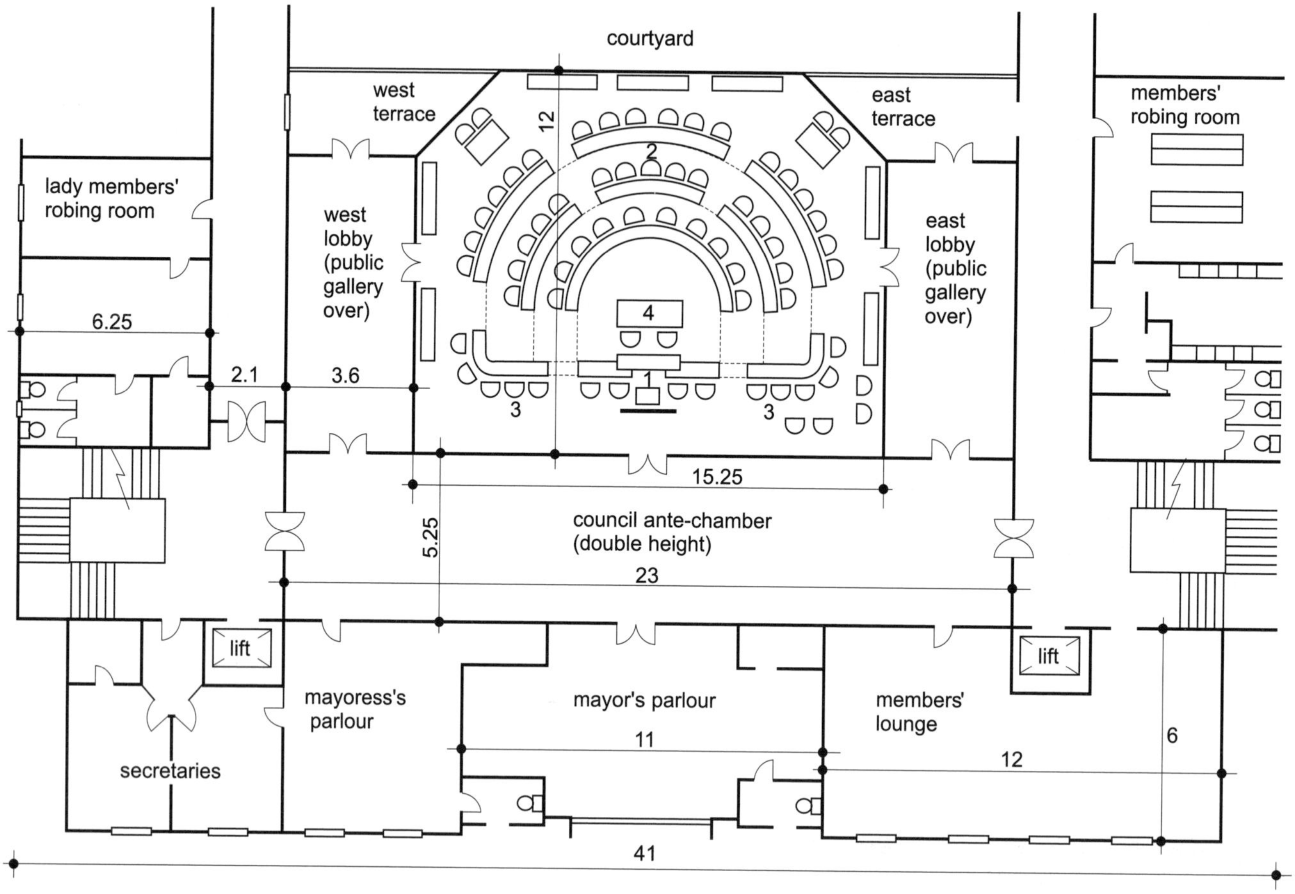

courtyard
west terrace
east terrace
members' robing room
lady members' robing room
west lobby (public gallery over)
east lobby (public gallery over)
12
2
4
1
3
3
6.25
2.1
3.6
15.25
5.25
council ante-chamber (double height)
23
lift
lift
mayoress's parlour
mayor's parlour
members' lounge
secretaries
11
12
6
41

16.2 *Hammersmith Town Hall's Council Chamber suite is an example of a triple-tiered horseshoe configuration*

5
2
3
1

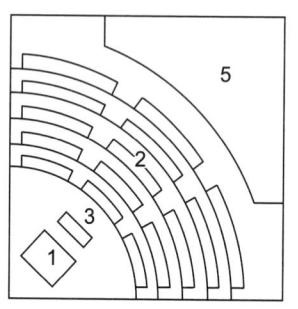

a *Approximately 300 seats in a five-tiered quadrant*

5
2
3
4
1
4

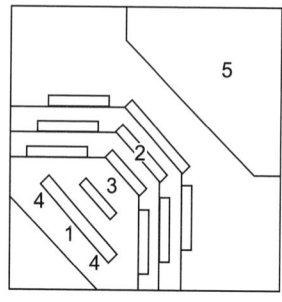

b *Approximately 60 seats in a three-tiered quadrant*

5
5
2
2
3
1

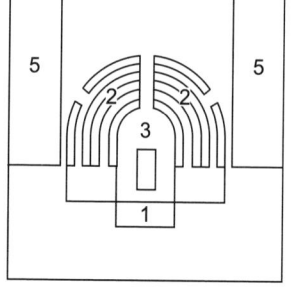

c *Approximately 30 seats in a two-tiered horseshoe*

5
2
3
1

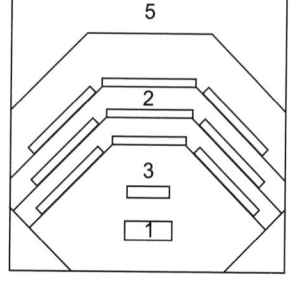

d *Approximately 100 seats in a three-tiered segment*

5
2
3
4
4

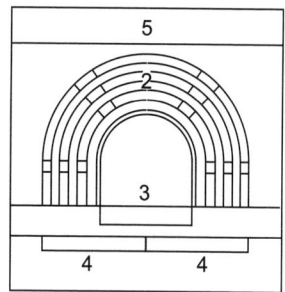

e *Approximately 60 seats in a three-tiered horseshoe*

5
Tiered
seating rows
in new
gallery
2
3
1

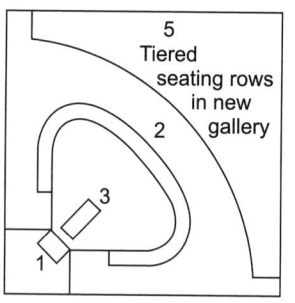

f *Approximately 30 seats a level*

16.3 *Council chamber, various layout types (1= mayor, 2 = ordinary members, 3 = officers, 4 = committee clerks, 5 = press and public)*

1.2 Members' accommodation

Traditionally, the town hall was a place where the facilities accorded to the decision-making role of elected councillors were celebrated by a very high quality of traditional finishes setting those areas above others in terms of importance and status.

More recently, however, where members' facilities are provided in new accommodation the standard of finishes and furniture is required to match that of the council's offices or administration areas in order that members are not seen to have a higher standard of finishes or be enjoying lavish benefits associated with their elected position. Instead, members' offices are modern, flexible and deliberately non-specific to party colours.

1.2 Council chamber

The function of the council chamber as a space for council meetings continues and is likely to continue as long as the current format for local democracy exists. Their traditional forms are mostly segmental or horseshoe, see Figures 16.2 and 16.3.

Council meetings are held on a monthly basis and may be supplemented by youth parliament and other quasi-democratic meetings or presentations. For the remainder of the year the chamber is available for other potential uses, most of which would not require the tiered seating (see Figure 16.4) and public galleries so common in historic town halls but rather favouring a flat-floored space with flexible furniture, which can then be used for various functions or conferences that can be a source of potential revenue to the council.

The character of the civic chamber as a traditional oak-paneled room with all the allusions of grandeur attributed to outdated civic notions is not something that is prized by forward-looking councils. However, allusion to the civic nature of the room can be accommodated by a modern system of paneling utilised also for its acoustic performance. This space may be renamed. At Brent, for example, the civic chamber and its associated meeting and committee rooms are known as Conference Hall and Board Rooms.

1.3 Civic suite

In support of the civic functions of the council, meeting spaces and committee rooms are required in proximity to the civic chamber. These are to provide spaces serviced with audio-visual and catering for the needs of the council in conducting its business through committees. When not required for this use they can be let for community/private/corporate use.

1.4 Committee rooms

Local government business is conducted principally through numerous committees and sub-committees. Meeting rooms of various sizes are required; these (including the council chamber) are often available for letting by outside organisations, producing useful additional revenue for the council. For this reason, if for no other, they should be well designed and fitted out.

1.5 Community hall

A central feature of the community function of the town hall/civic centre is the community hall. This is a space essentially for the use of the community but also for corporate events. It might accommodate large-scale weddings, concerts, pantomimes, plays, dances and banquets.

1.6 Offices

These can account for the bulk of accommodation within the town hall/civic centre as local authorities consolidate resources and departments in order to better deliver public services 'under one roof'. This breaks down the traditional 'silo' thinking of separate departments to encourage integrated delivery.

Administration areas within local authorities are now recognised as being as demanding as commercial office requirements (see Chapter 30). Smart desking and new ways of working are becoming accepted

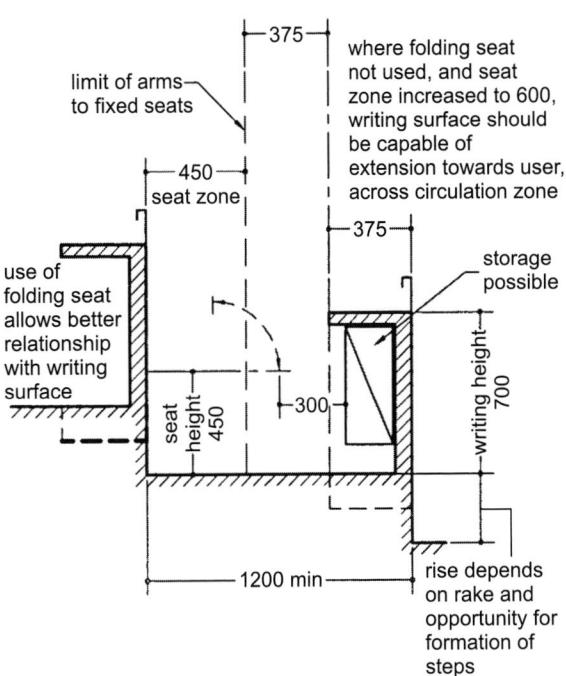

a *Section through fixed seating at 600 to 750 mm centres. Number of seats in a row limited to avoid disturbance*

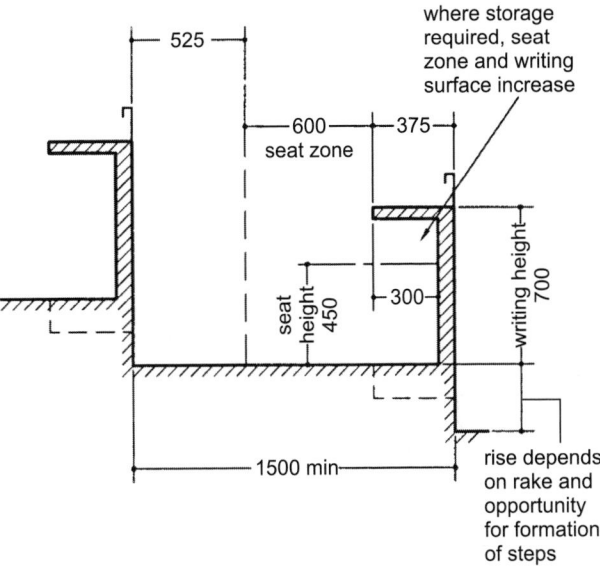

b *Section through moveable seating at 750 to 900 mm centres*

16.4 *Council chamber seating*

and have benefits in terms of space utilisation and efficiency. A ratio of 10 employees per 8 or even 7 desks is not unusual.

Flexible open plan areas with fixed island desking are punctuated with quiet rooms, breakout spaces, staff storage lockers, business support units for printing, re-cycling, storage and wet support areas for tea points.

1.7 Public reception and information

A large entrance or atrium space is required for the public to arrive and orientate. People will be met by 'meeters and greeters', who will answer any immediate questions and give directions to departments as appropriate. A large reception desk is required with space for several receptionists, some potentially in wheelchairs, who will receive the public, provide information or coordinate meetings.

1.8 Customer services

Also known in some local authorities as a 'one-stop shop', this is a large space consisting of a seating/waiting area, queuing system

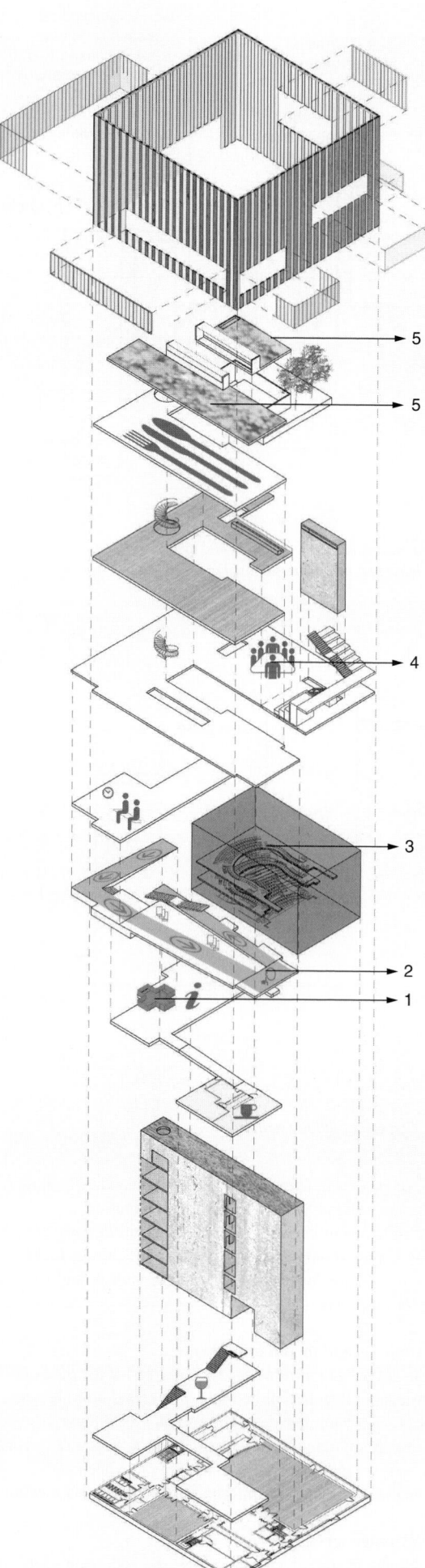

16.5 *Axonometric of the CUBE civic centre in Corby, designed by Hawkins Brown. Key: 1 entrance foyer information desk; 2 library ramp; 3 theatre auditorium; 4 Council chamber; 5 roof terrace and restaurant*

and large number of desks manned by council staff to answer queries and provide information to the public on all matters (planning, building control, council tax, education, social services, leisure). Additionally, a series of rooms for confidential consultations are required with alternative staff exits if necessary for security and escape reasons.

1.9 Cash facility

The need for cash transactions is diminishing as more and more are dealt with online. Dedicated cashier stations are generally no longer required.

1.10 Library

Public libraries (Chapter 27) are often incorporated into town halls/civic centres in order to benefit from the proximity with other services and facilities (Figure 16.5).

The nature of the public library has changed to more of an internet café and indeed many have informal seating and a café facility. Books are displayed face-on rather than end-on and study tables with Wi-Fi are mixed in. Children's book areas are linked and not separated.

1.11 Events spaces

With a growing emphasis on mixing up civic and community functions, the scope for impromptu or even scheduled performance events in visible areas within the town hall suggests that reception and circulation spaces can double-function as 'given' or 'found' spaces for such uses thereby animating the potentially otherwise institutional character of this area.

1.12 Case study – Brent Civic Centre

Introduction

London Borough of Brent commissioned Hopkins Architects to design a multi-purpose civic centre on a site close to Wembley Stadium. The aim was to house civic, public and administrative facilities within one building including office space for 2000 staff. It was also conceived as a new community hub for the public to meet within the newly landscaped Arena Square. There is also a wedding garden for guests attending wedding parties in the community hall.

Size

Brent Civic Centre totals 39,683 sq m. Of this, 14,154 sq m is public/civic space, 18,073 sq m administrative, and 7,456 sq m basement.

Layout

The building's spaces are arranged around a 31 m high, naturally lit foyer and atrium (Figure 16.6). This houses a large public amphitheatre and wide civic steps as well as the circular civic drum containing a multi-purpose, a library (1211 sq m), customer services centre (768 sq m) and 26 m diameter community hall (1177 sq m) (Figure 16.7).

The chamber (284 sq m), on level three, can be reconfigured to suit a variety of civic and public uses (Figure 16.8 a, b, c). There is also an atrium foyer and civic hall lobby (473 sq m) and committee rooms (407 sq m).

Two glazed office wings provide open-plan and flexible administrative space to the rear of the site, included at a ratio of 7 seats to every 10 staff to reflect anticipated occupancy levels.

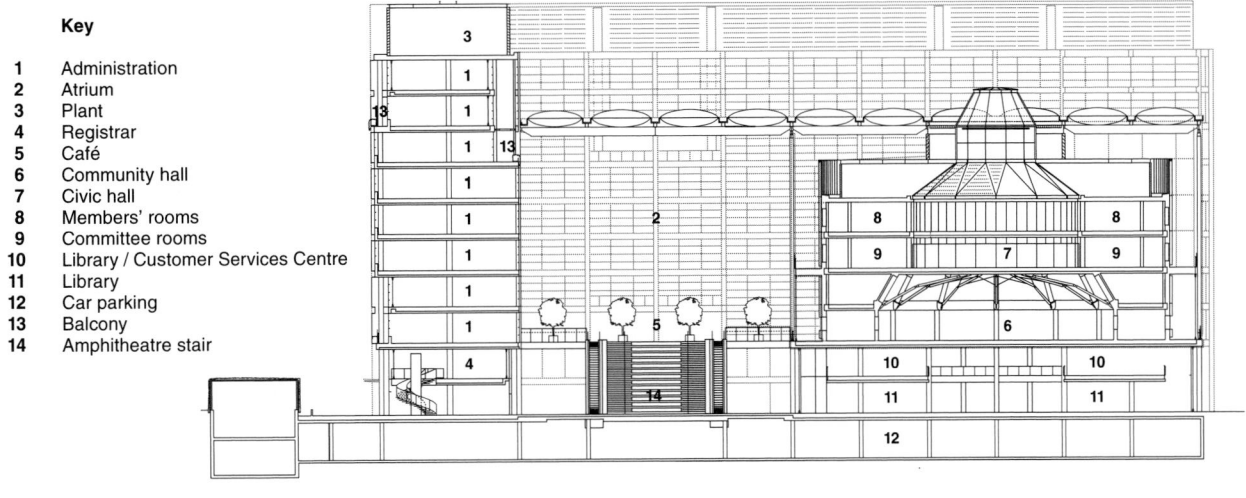

Key

1	Administration
2	Atrium
3	Plant
4	Registrar
5	Café
6	Community hall
7	Civic hall
8	Members' rooms
9	Committee rooms
10	Library / Customer Services Centre
11	Library
12	Car parking
13	Balcony
14	Amphitheatre stair

0 ⊢———⊣ 10m

HOPKINS ARCHITECTS I BRENT CIVIC CENTRE
long section looking north

16.6 *Section looking north of Brent Civic Centre in north London, designed by Hopkins Architects*

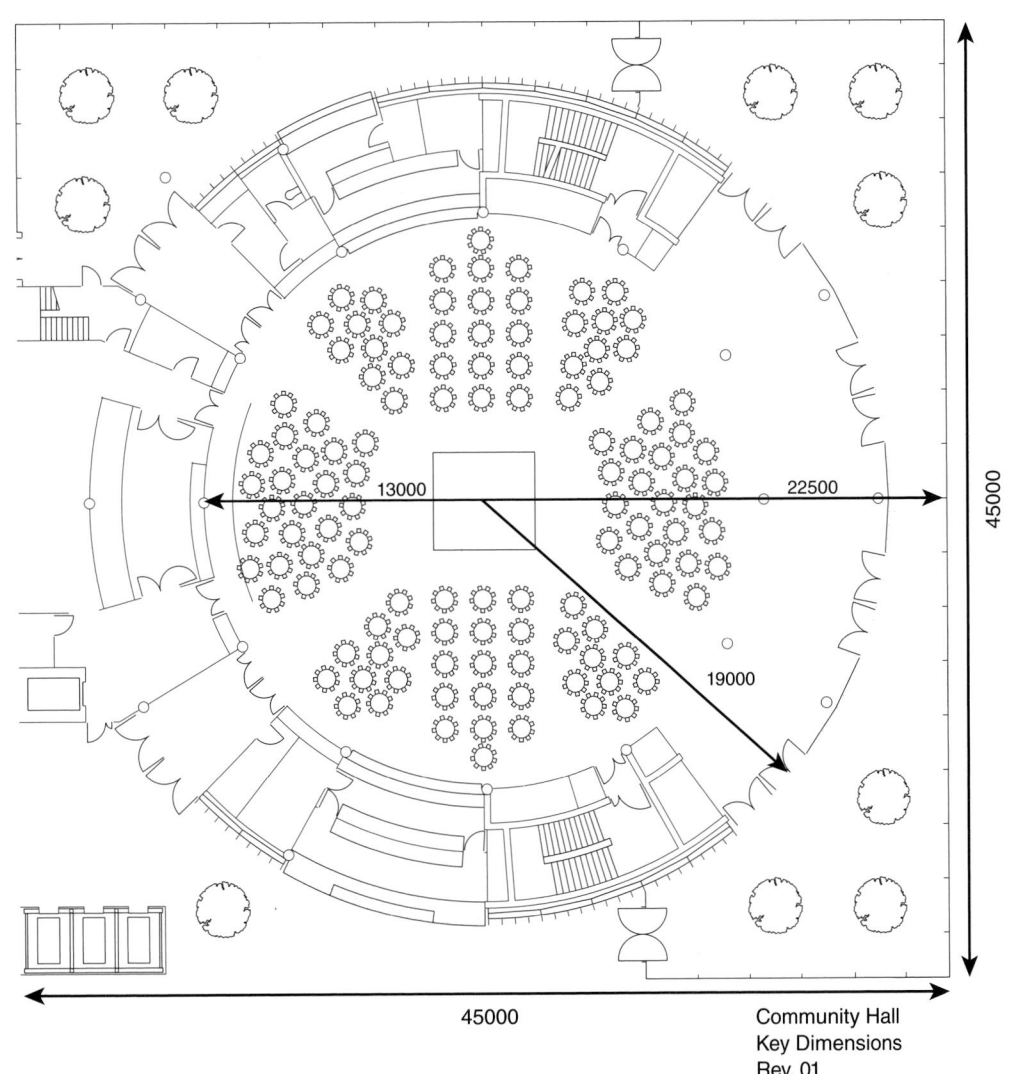

Community Hall
Key Dimensions
Rev. 01

16.7 *Community hall, designed to be configured for a variety of uses including boxing matches, as shown here*

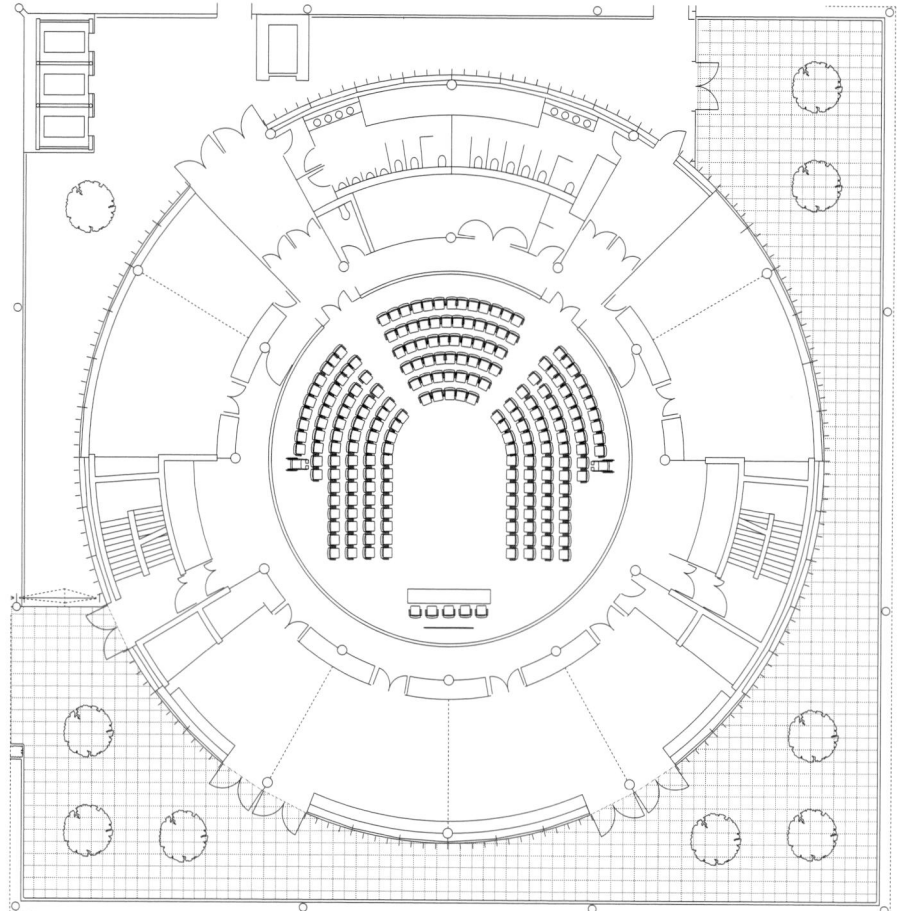

16.8a

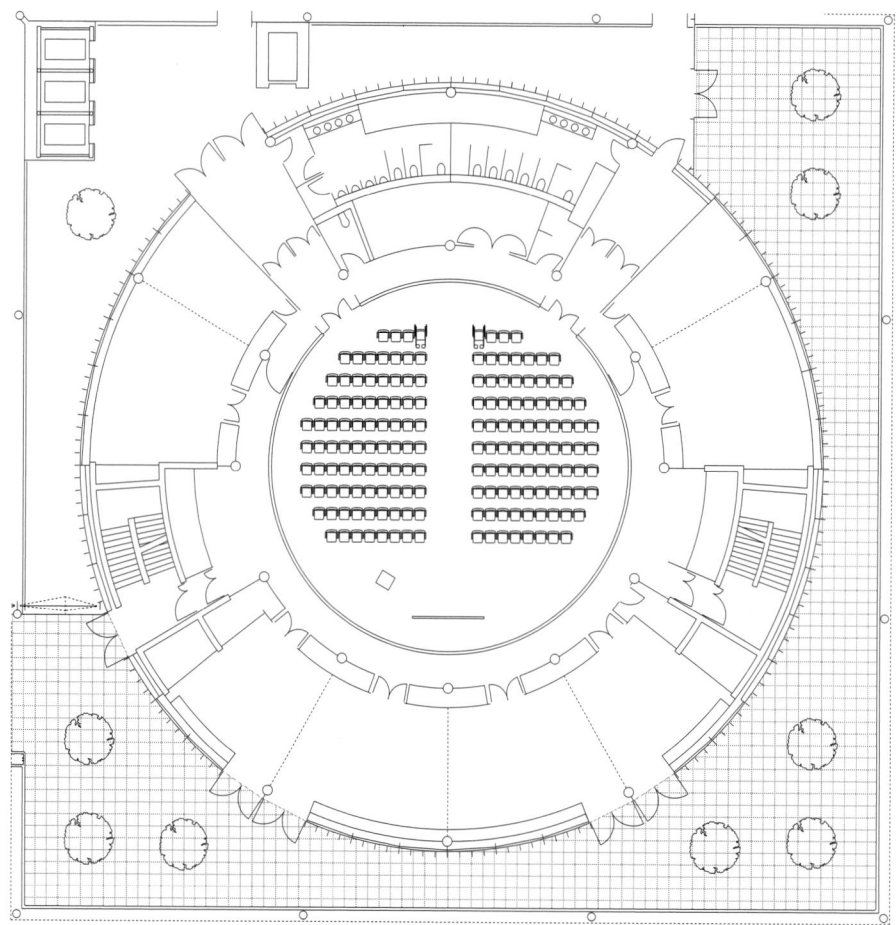

16.8b

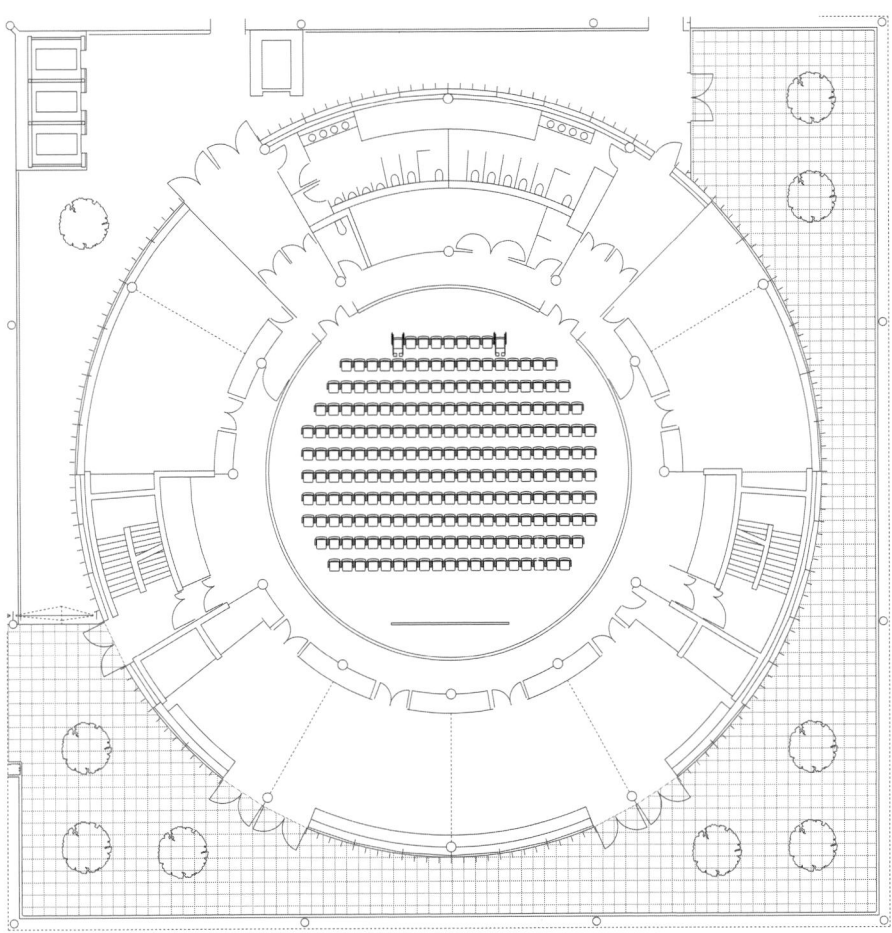

16.8a–c *Brent Civic Centre civic chamber, shown configured for, a, council meetings; b, conference use; c, as a cinema*

Building performance

Brent Civic Centre has a BREEAM 'Outstanding' rating and was the first of its building type to have achieved this. As such, it attained a 33 per cent reduction in carbon emissions due to a combination of solar shading, natural ventilation, high-performance façade, and combined cooling, heating and power.

2 LAW COURTS

2.1 Background

The judicial system of England and Wales is in direct line of descent from that established by William I nearly a thousand years ago, subsequently modified by Magna Carta and many other reforms. Courthouses are the visible manifestation of one of the most fundamental sets of principles upon which our society is based.

How this is to be expressed in architectural terms is the particular challenge facing the designer of a courthouse. He or she will have to consider the contextual and environmental constraints that apply to any urban structure, especially those on prominent sites in town centres. Planning problems posed by the specific requirements for a courthouse must also be addressed, such as the four segregated circulation routes (for judge, jury, defendant in custody and public), the servicing of the many and varied spaces within a complex layout and the need for flexibility to accommodate future developments in information technology. Although courtrooms built 200 years ago are still able to cope, the law is constantly evolving and both the courtrooms and the ancillaries need to be receptive to inevitable change.

2.2 Court system

HMCS (Her Majesty's Court Service) has existed in various forms for over 900 years. Following the Courts Act 1971 it was given the task of running a new system covering all courts above the level of Magistrates' Courts. It is directly responsible for:

- the Court of Appeal
- the Royal Courts of Justice
- the High Court
- the Crown Court
- the County Court.

The Crown Court is a national court which sits at different centres. Practically all its work is concerned with cases committed for trial or sentence from the Magistrates' Courts, or appeals against their decisions. Cases for trial are heard before a judge and jury. Centres are classified as first, second or third tier according to the nature and complexity of the court business.

Magistrates' courts were traditionally local courts but are increasingly organised regionally. Some are part of larger combined courts such as Newport Law Court, which combines County and Magistrates Courts (Figure 16.9).

2.3 The courtroom

The Crown Court sits in a courtroom, the design of which will always be subject to the continuous adjustments dictated by changes in attitudes to child witnesses, the need to protect witnesses and jurors from possible intimidation and developments in technology.

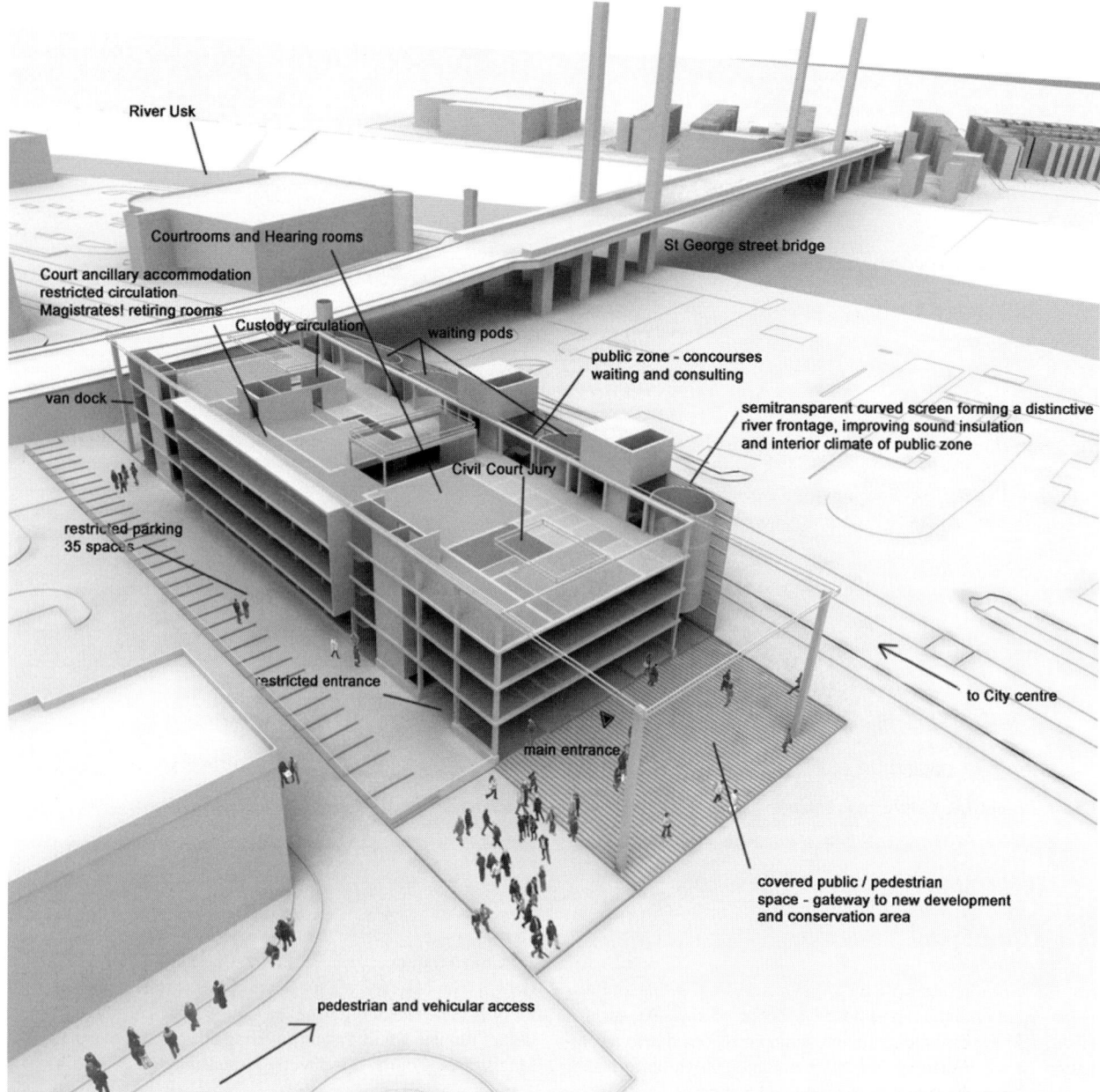

16.9 *Newport Law Court, in South Wales, designed by Feilden + Mawson, with clear delineation of public, court and court ancillary zones. Gross internal area: 9100m²*

The courtroom is the primary workspace and focal point in a courthouse, which is developed around it. It is the only place where all parties in a case are likely to meet. Of paramount importance is the need to segregate judge, jury, defendant and others in the courtroom and within the courthouse. Segregated circulation routes are provided so that the judge, jury and defendants (if in custody) make their way to the courtroom without meeting each other or any other users such as members of the public.

The exception is the magistrates court in which there is no jury, so therefore no need to provide space for jury seating or circulation (see case study in Section 2.15).

In all other courts, dedicated entrances are provided for:

- judge
- jury
- defendants in custody
- public, witnesses and defendants on bail.

Some prosecution witnesses have to be protected from intimidation; a separate secure waiting room for them is often situated with its entrance off the vestibule provided between the public entrance and the courtroom itself. An alternative arrangement has a separate access from the secure waiting area into the courtroom adjacent to the witness box.

The public enter the court behind or to the side of the public seating at the rear of the courtroom; neither public nor witnesses pass areas dedicated to other participants (e.g. jury or defendants in custody) on entering or leaving the courtroom.

2.4 Relationships within the courtroom

Courtroom layout incorporates specific and well-defined relationships between the various participants by means of carefully arranged sightlines, distances and levels. There are four main elements in Crown Court cases:

- judge
- jury

- witness
- counsel (barristers and solicitors).

Defendants do not take part except as witnesses. Each element must be closely related, and be able to see and hear each other clearly at all times without mechanical or electrical aids, and without excessive turning from side to side. The basic positioning of the occupants is shown in Figure 16.10.

The theory behind these relationships can be summarised as follows:

- *The judge or magistrate.* Presides over the courtroom, should be able to observe the whole of it, to see clearly the principal participants as well as the defendant in the dock and, when called, the antecedents and probation officers. The judge or magistrates' bench is always elevated, usually by 450 mm (Figure 16.11).
- *The court clerk.* Administers the case and needs to keep a watching eye over the court. He or she often advises the judge and should be able to stand up and speak to the judge without being overheard.
- *The exhibit table.* This is in front of the counsel benches for the display of exhibits put forward for evidence.
- *Counsel.* These are barristers and solicitors who represent the defendant or prosecution. They need to be able to see the jury, judge and witness to whom they address their remarks. The

barrister at each end of the front bench should be able to keep every jury member and the witness on the stand within about a 90° angle to obviate too much turning to ensure that the judge, the other main party, shall have at least a part face view. The counsel benches are wide enough to hold the large, and numerous, documents and books that are often in use.

- *The defendant.* The defendant is assumed to be innocent until proved guilty and current practice is to reduce any prison-like appearance of the dock by lowering the barriers enclosing it as much as possible compatible with security. Defendants sit in separate fixed seats and if they are thought to be a security risk may sit in an enclosed glazed cubicle within the court. The dock is controlled by a dock officer and situated at the back of the courtroom.
- *The jury.* This comprises twelve members of the public whose duty it is to reach a verdict based on the evidence presented. The jury sits opposite the witness stand and must be able to see the defendant in the dock, as well as the judge and counsel. Jurors must have a writing surface and a place to put documents.
- *The witness.* The witness waits outside the courtroom and when called gives evidence from the witness stand near to the judge's bench. They stand facing the jury who must be able to observe his or her face. The witness is questioned by the barristers and occasionally by the judge. If the judge directs that a witness should be retained, he or she can wait seated within the courtroom.

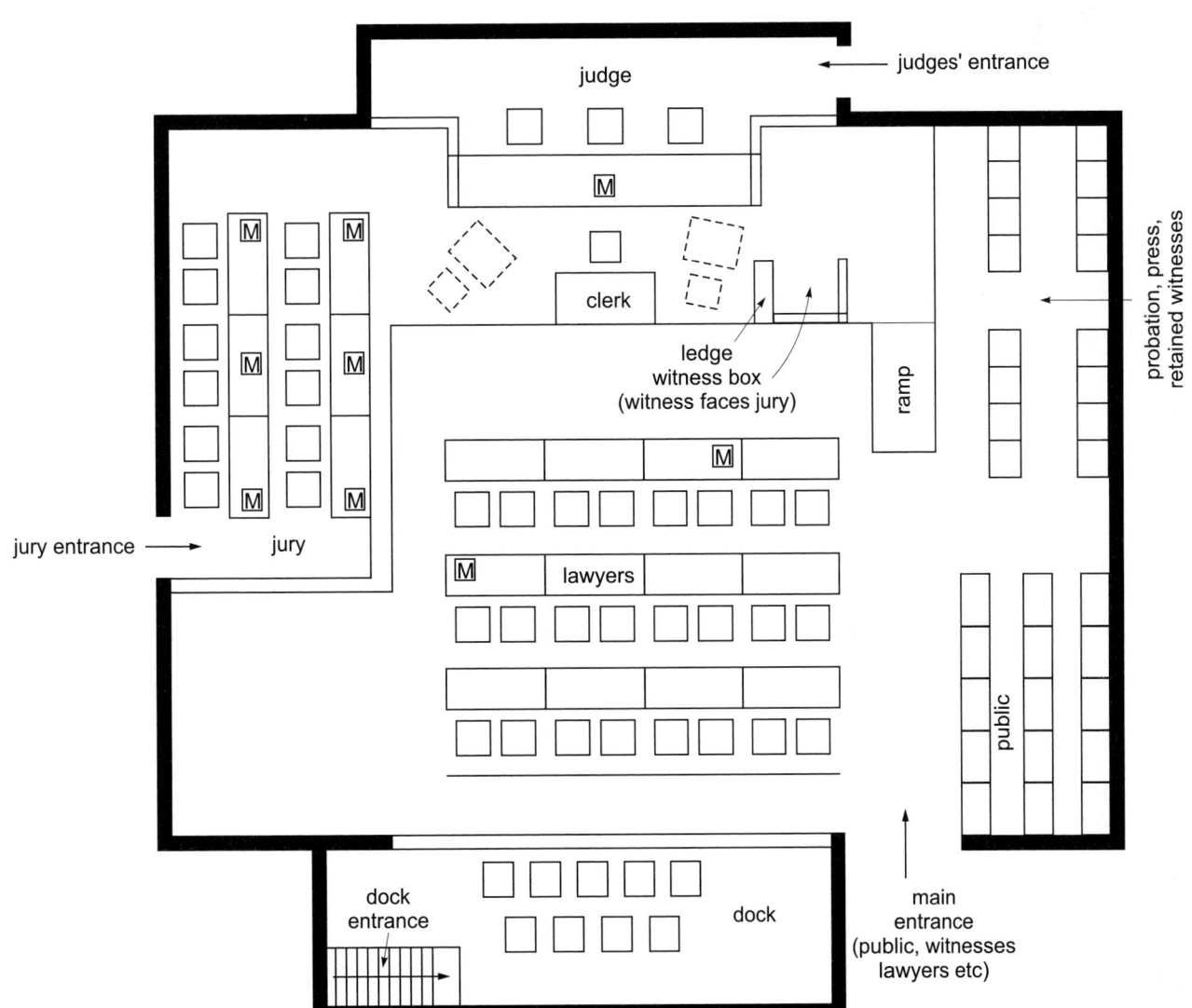

16.10 *Standard Crown Courtroom*

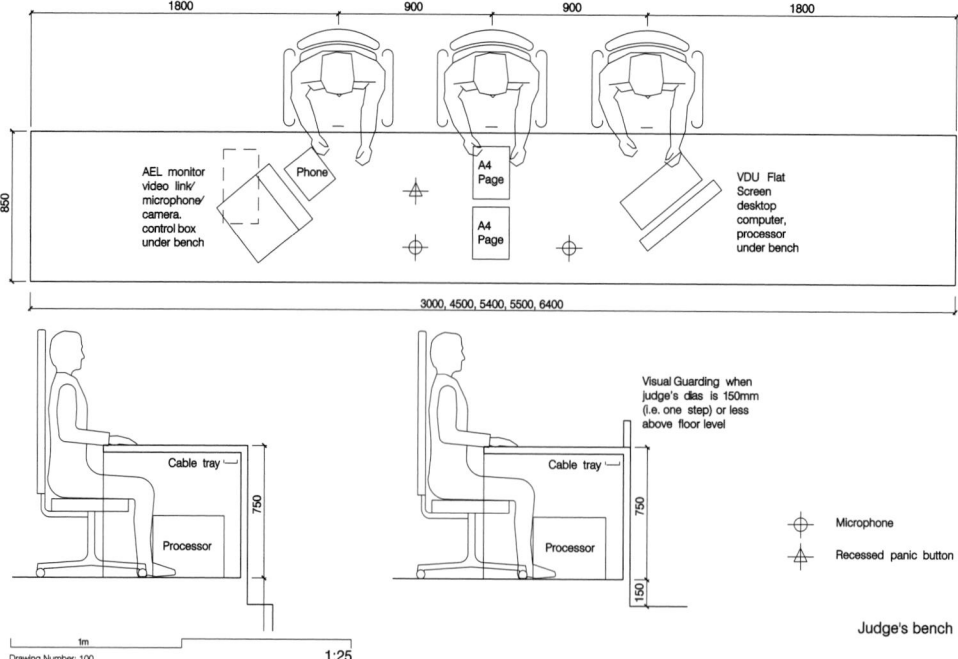

16.11 *Judge's Bench. Source: Court Standards Design Guide, Ministry of Justice*

- *The shorthand writer*. This official keeps a transcript of the trial and consequently must be able to see and hear everyone who speaks.
- *Probation and antecedents officers*. These give evidence from their seats after the jury has reached a verdict. This evidence is used to assist the judge in passing sentence.
- *The press*. These are not party to the proceedings, but they should be able to see the participants.
- *The public*. These are in court to see that 'justice is done'. They are placed at the near end of the courtroom and have a general view of the proceedings, but with the minimum possible direct eye contact with the jury to reduce the risk of intimidation. A public gallery over the jurors is the most effective method of eliminating possible intimidation; but access to such a gallery and the increase in height of the courtroom has to be considered. The glass screen between the public and the dock is partially obscured to prevent members of the public from seeing the defendant(s) (and vice versa) while seated.

2.5 The courtroom environment

The design of Crown Court rooms should reflect the quiet dignity of the law rather than its power. A fully accessible (Figures 16.12, 16.13), well-detailed, comfortable and quiet courtroom with efficient and simply managed ventilation, lighting and acoustics is the ideal.

- **Youth court** – Magistrates' courts often contain a court appropriate for juveniles, where magistrates and defendants and legal teams can sit around the same table. These courts should have their own circulation routes which can be kept separate to that of any other courts operational that day in the building.
- **Ventilation** – Well-balanced environmental conditions within the courtroom are essential to the smooth running of the court. They keep the participants comfortable and interested, and avoid distractions. The current trend, supported by most users, is for natural ventilation with openable windows. This will subject the courtroom to wider temperature fluctuations; but this can be minimised by integrated automatic control systems.

  Mechanical assistance (or in extreme cases full air conditioning) will be necessary where there would be unacceptable

noise intrusion; or where the courtroom cannot have the height to induce air flow by the natural stack effect. It is normally more economical and energy-efficient to have separate air handling units for each courtroom, managed by time switches and occupancy sensors.

- **Lighting** – Daylight is provided if possible; but direct sunlight must be controlled and security risks avoided. The controlled use of daylight alone improves environmental comfort, but when it becomes for any reason insufficient, artificial lighting will be required. A combination of uplighters and downlighters reduces glare and contrast, and enhances the character of the courtroom. Lighting levels and colour should ensure correct colour rendering, and that all participants, exhibits and written evidence can be clearly seen without strain or dazzle.
- **Acoustics** – The acoustics and noise levels should ensure that the proceedings can be heard in all parts of the courtroom while avoiding distraction and annoyance from movement by the public, press or others. There may be a need for reflective or absorbent surface treatment to walls and ceilings.
- **Communications** – The courtroom should accommodate data connections and telephones for the legal teams and judiciary, with cabling concealed within a raised floor. Screens to show testimony from witnesses outside the courtroom should also be incorporated.

2.6 Functional relationships outside the courtroom

Courthouse accommodation is divided into areas, each with its own self-contained circulation. Movement between areas is limited and restricted. Even those who need to move freely can only enter certain restricted areas by passing through manned control points or other secure doors. The relationship and pattern of movement between the elements is shown in the functional relationship diagram in Figure 16.14.

2.7 Judiciary

The judiciary (judges, recorders, etc.) arrive at the court building and enter through a manned or otherwise restricted entry directly into their own secure area of the building. This contains the judges' retiring rooms and all areas devoted to judicial use.

The only other users of this area in 'working hours' are the staff, i.e. ushers, court clerks, security staff and invitees, i.e.

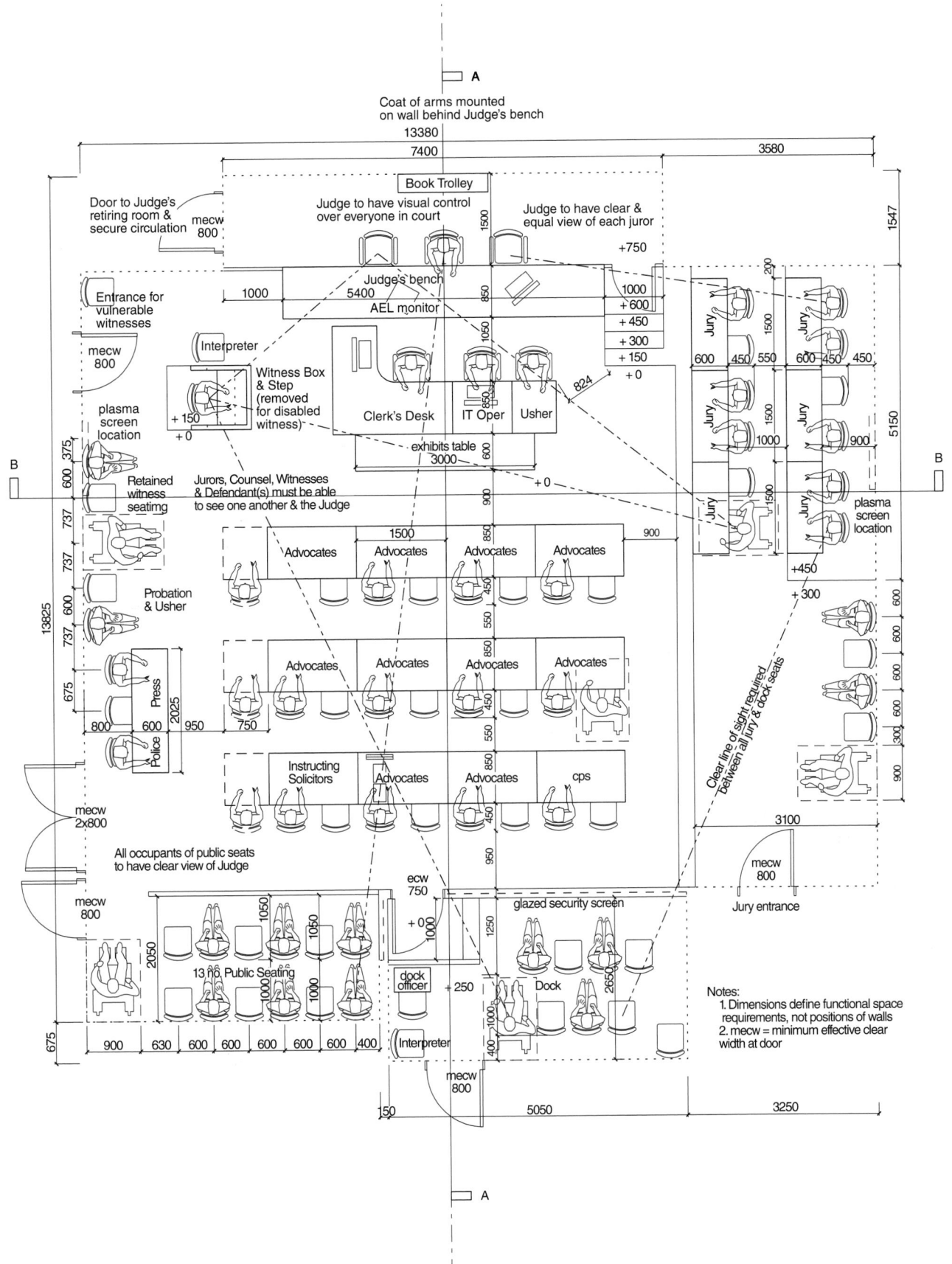

16.12 *DDA compliant standard criminal court, 14.4m x 13.5m, 172m². Source: Court Standards Design Guide, Ministry of Justice*

legal representatives, guests and some members of the public invited to a judge's room. Invitees will always be escorted, and access for all will be either via the judges' entrance into court or through staff areas. Each entrance will be via a self-locking, secure door.

2.8 Jurors

Persons, the number depending on the number and size of trials programmed, are summoned to the court building. They enter through the main public areas until they reach the reception area to the jury assembly suite where they are booked in.

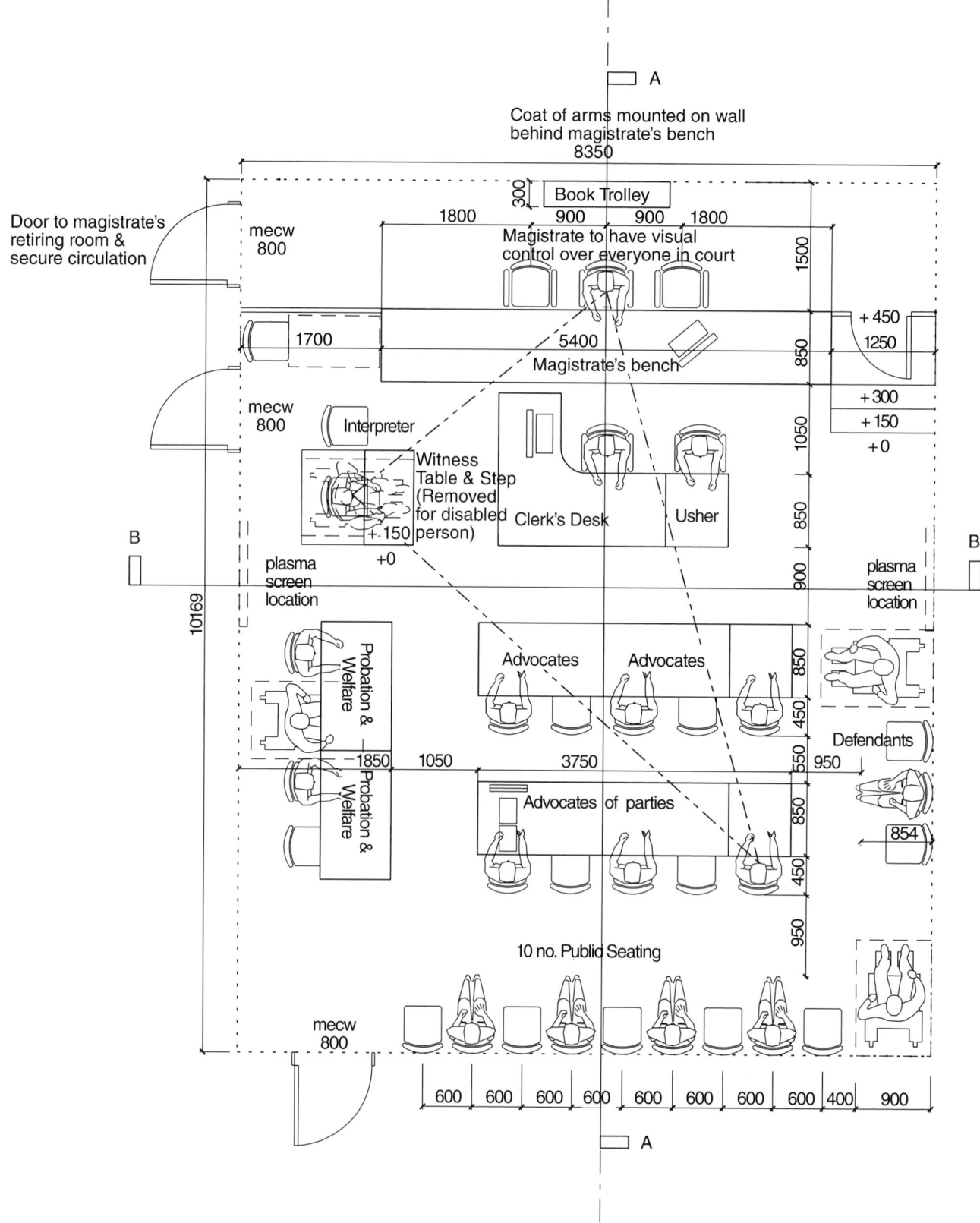

16.13 *DDA compliant standard criminal court, 10.2m x 8.4m, 84.9m². Source: Court Standards Design Guide, Ministry of Justice*

They then wait in the lounge or dining area where refreshments are available until called upon to form a jury panel. The period of waiting is variable and can be all day. Highest usage is before courts sit, and during lunch periods.

Egress from the assembly area, other than back past reception, is into jury-restricted circulation, which leads to court and jury retiring rooms. These should be adjacent or close to related court rooms, and all capable of supervision by one jury bailiff.

Once jurors have entered the jury assembly suite they remain there, in court or in the jury retiring room, until sent home at the end of the day, or on dismissal.

2.9 Defendants

The custody area (see Chapter 18, 3.5) is a self-contained compartment within the court building designated for the temporary use of prison governors in the discharge of their duties to the court to

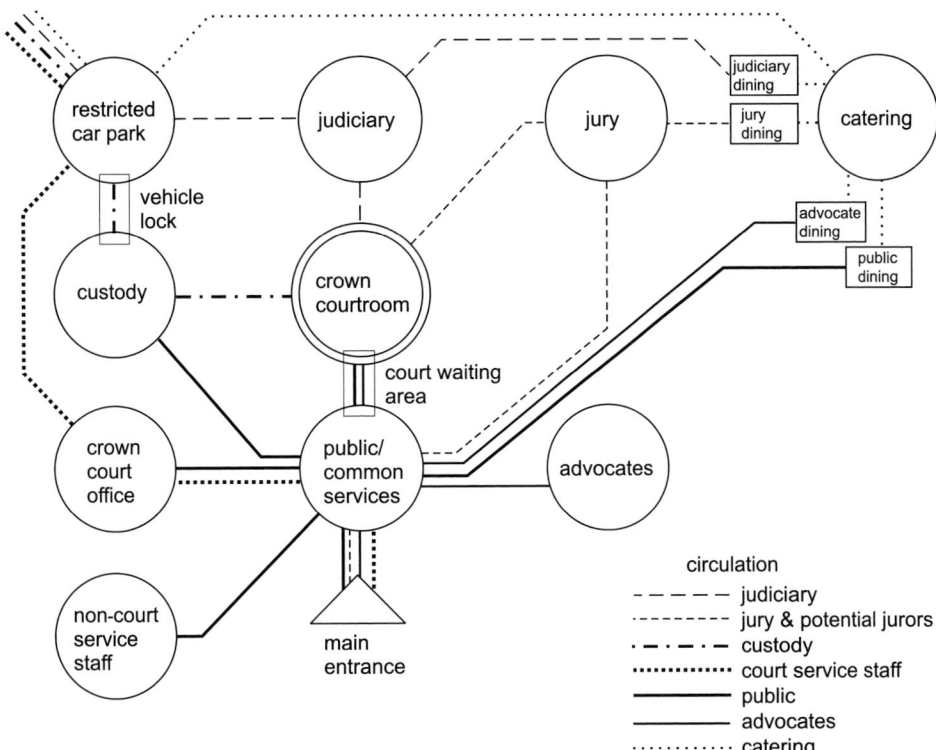

16.14 *Functional relationship diagram for a courthouse*

produce and retain prisoners in custody. It consists of the following principal parts, each separate from its neighbour and all non-custody uses:

- the custody core;
- the vehicle entrance;
- the visitors' entrance;
- the courtroom entrance;
- three independent secure connecting routes from custody core to vehicle dock; courtroom entrance; and visitors' entrance.

While courts are sitting, the custody area is staffed and administered by prison officers. A principal or senior officer is in charge, supported by number of officers according to the number of courts and the level of risk. Some officers have fixed duties, for instance dock officer and cells officer, but the remainder are on escort duties.

Custody areas are designed and constructed to contain defendants, and to produce them to the court. Containment requires the meticulous and consistent application of passive security measures. Confinement and attendance at court for defendants is stressful, and this is compounded by natural frustration and anxiety. The designer must:

- give careful attention to all aspects of the design from the overall plan and its approaches, down to fixtures, fittings, fixings, finishes, alarms and communications.
- devise a layout that will achieve maximum control, make the best use of staff resources and maintain an acceptable level of safety and security.
- use the building fabric and the facilities within it to provide a secure envelope.
- deny the public direct view or contact with defendants while they are inside the custody area, except during authorised visits.

2.10 Public
The public areas with their associated circulation form the central core or axis from which most non-judicial functions of the court building radiate.

Except for the judiciary and specified car park users, all users enter the building by the main entrance door where space and facilities for security checks are provided. The arrival concourse contains the information/enquiry point and the Cause List display, both of which should be clearly seen on entering.

Public circulation then leads to court waiting areas. These may be combined with associated circulation to form concourses off which are located the courtrooms and consultation/waiting rooms. Waiting areas should be visually interesting, preferably with external views. All furniture should be fixed.

Public circulation also gives access to private and semi-private accommodation occupied by Court Service (CS) staff, non-CS staff, the Probation Service, custody visits and to refreshment facilities. Access must also be available to the Crown Court Office counters. Direct access from the arrivals concourse to the jury assembly area is desirable.

2.11 Advocates
Advocates enter the court building by the main entrance, reaching their suite via the public circulation. This is the area reserved for solicitors and barristers preparing for court, combining lounge/study/retiring room for relaxation and quiet study in comfortable conditions, and for assembly, discussion, robing, etc. The lounge and robing room should if possible be contiguous otherwise direct access should be provided.

The suite has easy access to courtrooms via the public concourse where advocates meet clients, and to the advocates' dining room. The advocates' clerks' room is closely related and shares the same private 'advocates' circulation.

2.12 Crown Court office
The Crown Court office is occupied by executive and administrative staff engaged in the general administration of Crown Court business.

The general office counter must be conveniently located to allow easy access for the public and for the legal profession; payment of expenses to jurors and witnesses may be made here.

There should be separate circulation to other staff areas and for direct access to the judges restricted circulation by ushers. Within

16.15 *North Somerset Courthouse*

the Crown Court offices, accommodation is provided for some more specialised groups:

- court clerks who are responsible for business in specific court-rooms and who spend part of their day in court;
- ushers who spend part of their time in court and also attending to judge and/or jury but will also do minor clerical work;
- listing staff who are responsible for the planning and programming of the court timetable (lists of cases).

2.13 Non-courts service users

Non-courts service users includes police, Crown Prosecution Service, Probation Service and shorthand writers, concerned with the running of the court.

The police area consists of two sections:

- *The Police Liaison Unit.* This is the suite of offices for police staff attached to the courts and providing antecedents, etc. Included is a room where police witnesses can assemble and change if necessary.
- *The Police Law and Order Unit.* This suite of offices is for police who maintain security or 'Law and Order' in the building.

The Crown Prosecution Service is responsible for the prosecution of defendants in court. It needs an office for law clerks to perform casework arising during the progress of the case, and to consult with members of the legal profession and witnesses.

The Probation Service, as attached to a Crown Court, will be active where persons have been made subjects of probation orders or inquiry reports at court, although they may do some paperwork on other cases. The probation suite is a separate individual unit and, where night reporting facilities are required, must be able to operate in isolation while full security to the remainder of the court building is maintained.

Shorthand writers are usually hired directly or via a service firm to take notes and transcribe court proceedings.

2.14 Catering

Catering within Crown Courts involves self-service facilities for advocates, jurors, public and court staff, together with waitress service from a sideboard or servery for the judiciary. The catering area should be sited on one floor with easy access for all court users, maximising usage and minimising operating costs. Multilevel catering areas should be avoided as less convenient and more expensive to operate.

2.15 Case study – North Somerset Courthouse, Worle, Weston-super-Mare

Architect: BDP

Introduction

A new courthouse was required as part of a rationalisation of magistrate courts in North Somerset. BDP's brief was to provide five courtrooms and associated facilities in a building that embodied the gravitas of the British legal system. Alongside the court building are offices for Avon and Somerset Area Probation Office. The project was procured as part of the Avon & Somerset Courts PFI Project for HM Courts Service.

Site

The greenfield site was an edge-of-town location close to low-rise housing and a supermarket.

Design

The courthouse is organised as an L-shaped orthogonal block containing the courtrooms behind a softer, curved form containing the court halls. This sweeps around the front of the building to create a butterfly shape to give a strong visual identity (Figure 16.15).

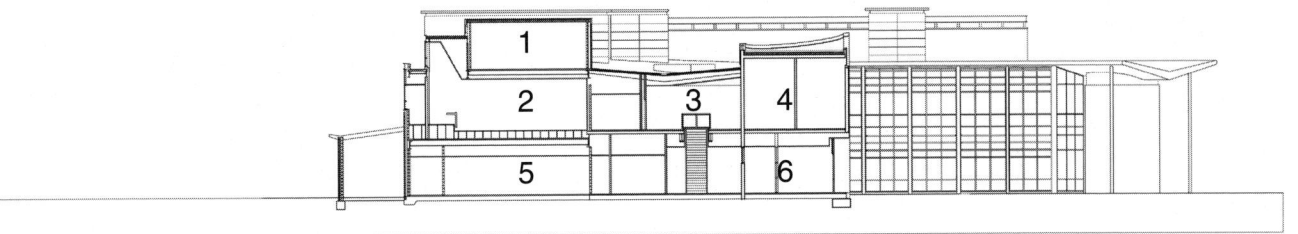

16.16 *Section of North Somerset Courthouse. Key: 1, Plant; 2, Court; 3, Courthall; 4, Café; 5, Custody Suite; 6, Entrance*

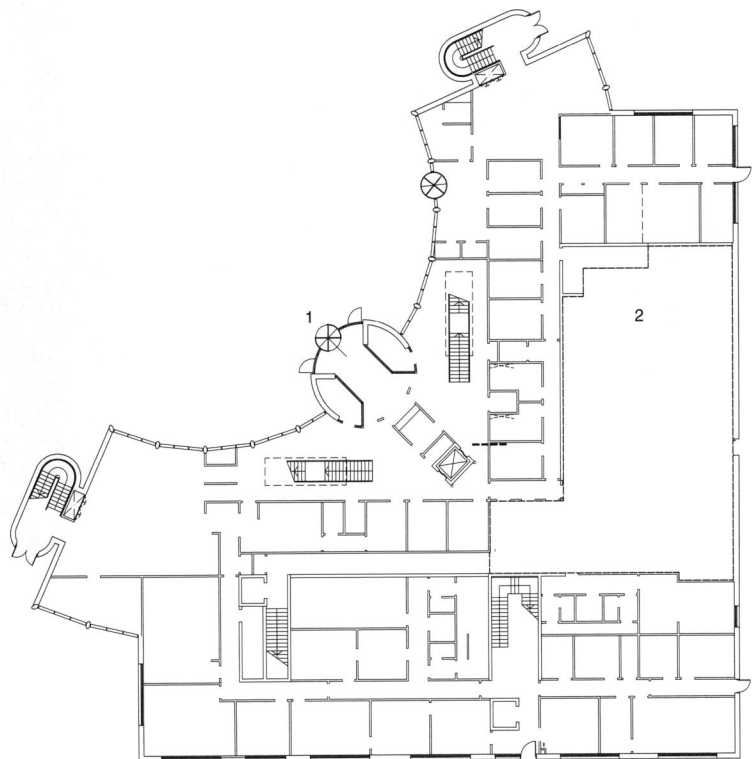

16.17a *Plans of North Somerset Courthouse. Key: 1, Entrance; 2, Custody suite; 3, Courtrooms; 4, Magistrates' quarters; 5, Courthalls*

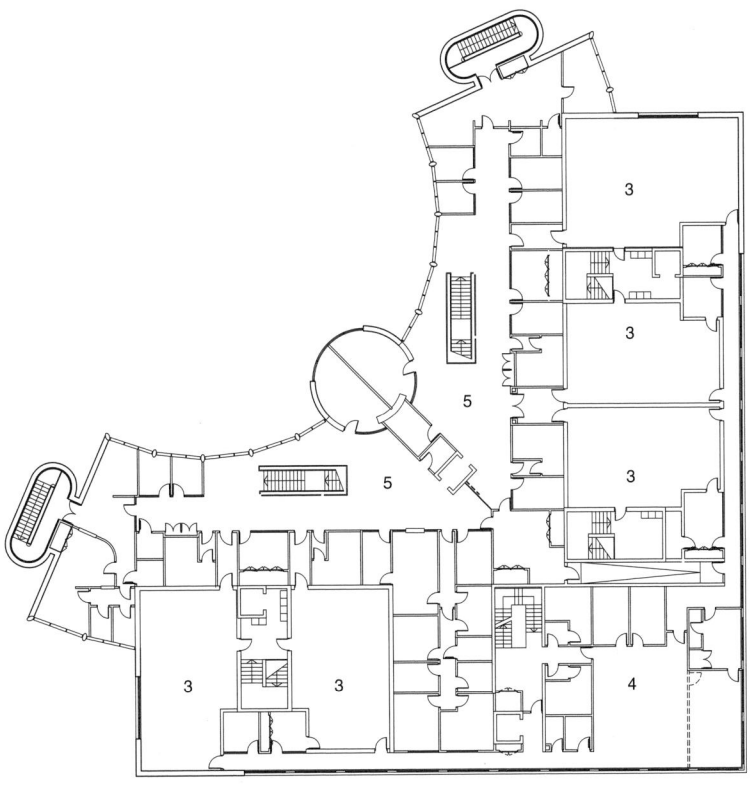

16.17b

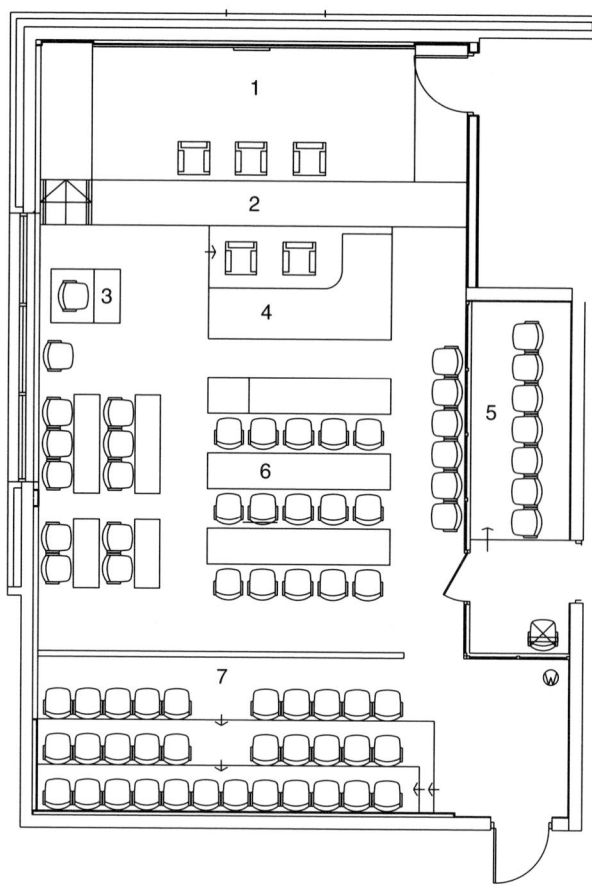

16.18 *Typical courtroom A: Key: 1, Magistrates; 2, Magistrates' bench; 3, Witness box; 4, Clerk's Bench; 5, Dock; 6, Lawyers; 7, Public gallery*

The courtrooms are located on the first floor with the custody suite on the ground floor. The core challenge was achieving the separation of circulation needed for members of the public, the judiciary, and the defendants.

At Worle, the public circulation and waiting area is positioned to the front of the building served by two staircases. The custody suite contains male, female and juvenile cells and associated legal and officers' facilities, control room, van dock and assembly area. This suite is served by dedicated stair and lift cores to the courtrooms, one to every two courts.

A number of small interview rooms are positioned off the first floor public waiting area as well as toilets and a kitchen. Seating is robust and fixed and toilets have low-level lighting to deter intravenous drug use. A separate staircase and waiting area is provided to segregate accommodation for youth and children's court cases.

Five courts are positioned to the rear of the building on either side of the central magistrates' and courts staff area. They range from approximately 80–100 sq m each. Of these, Court 1 has full height security glazing to the dock while Courts 2, 3, 4 have half height, non-secure screens. Court 5, as a family court, has neither.

The magistrates' bench is raised 450 mm at the rear to provide security and authority, with separate access for judiciary. The room is timber-paneled to provide a warmer, less intimidating atmosphere. Two courts at the corners have side windows to let in natural light. In the others, clerestory windows are incorporated into a double-height space above the magistrate's bench.

3 REFERENCES
Ministry of Justice (2010) *Court standards and design guide.*

17 Community centres

Jim Tanner

CI/SfB 532

Jim Tanner is a partner of Tanner and Partners

KEY POINTS:
- There is a need for a community facility in most areas
- Existing centres are often inadequate

Contents
1 Introduction
2 Planning and design
3 Elements of the plan
4 Bibliography

1 INTRODUCTION

1.1 Briefing
By their nature community buildings must serve a variety of functions among which are:

- meetings
- child care (crèche, day nursery, pre-school playgroup)
- children's activities (scouts, guides)
- concerts and plays
- dances
- parties and receptions
- exhibitions
- sporting and leisure activities
- adult education.

The client, such as a church or a local authority, may have its own specific requirements; but the financial viability of community facilities usually depends on letting them out to other organisations. At the briefing and planning stage it is wise to consider activities which could or should be accommodated.

1.2 Space requirement and arrangement
The following points should be borne in mind:

- Meetings can range from committee meetings of half a dozen people to public meetings with an audience of a couple of hundred. If this range is anticipated then accommodation should include one or two smaller meeting rooms as well as the main hall.
- Child care and children's activities invariably require storage for furniture and equipment. If Scouts use the facilities on a regular basis, for example, they are likely to need permanent storage for camping equipment, such as tents and poles, and cooking as well as games equipment.
- Some indoor sporting activities such as badminton, require generous space provision. See Chapter 38. These are likely to dictate the dimensions of the hall.

2 PLANNING AND DESIGN

2.1 Relationships
The principal plan elements and their relationship to each other illustrated in Figures 17.1, 17.2 and 17.3 are typical examples of the type.

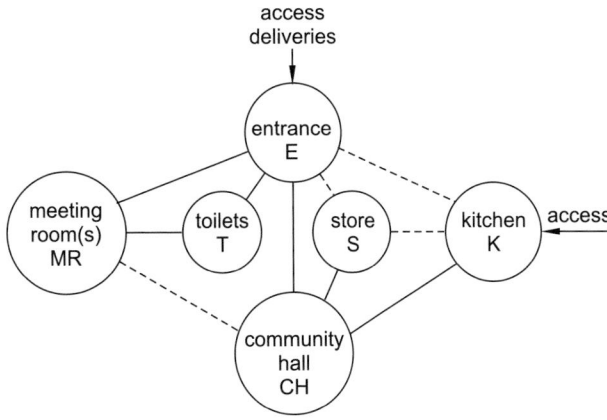

17.1 *Elements of the plan of a community centre*

2.2 Space requirements
Table I gives recommended floor areas for various functions and activities.

2.3 Design
Community centres are multi-purpose buildings. Needs and priorities will often conflict; the skill of the designer in consultation with the client, statutory authorities and specialists must be exercised so that a balance is struck. All the following factors should be considered.

2.4 Structure and construction
Most new-build self-contained community centres are domestic in scale. The most economic forms of construction are those used in domestic building: solid ground floors, masonry load-bearing walls and lightweight flat roofs or framed pitched roofs. Alternative forms of construction are only occasionally justified: for a difficult site or when only a short-life building is required. In the latter case, it is worth considering proprietary off-the-peg buildings. The appearance of such a building is not always aesthetically pleasing, but there are exceptions. Where the community facilities are to be accommodated in a larger building also used for other purposes, structure and construction will be determined by the wider considerations.

2.5 Materials and finishes
For self-contained community centres it is worthwhile designing for minimum maintenance, as upkeep funds are always limited. Choice of finishes should be influenced by the following considerations.

Nature of use may dictate forms of construction and finish which are non-standard. For example, when regular provision for dancing (particularly classical ballet) or indoor sport such as badminton or gymnastics is required, the floor should provide some resilience and specialist advice should be sought.

Durability: Some uses, particularly sporting activities, can be exceptionally hard on surface finishes. The main hall may

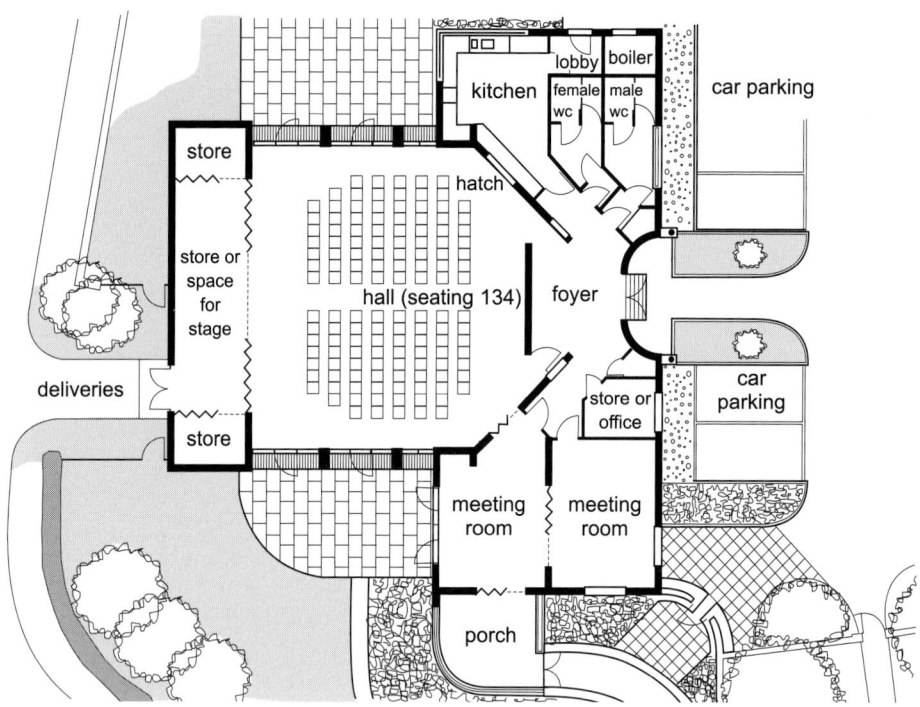

17.2 *Church centre for St James's Church, Finchampstead. Architects: Nye, Saunders & Partners*

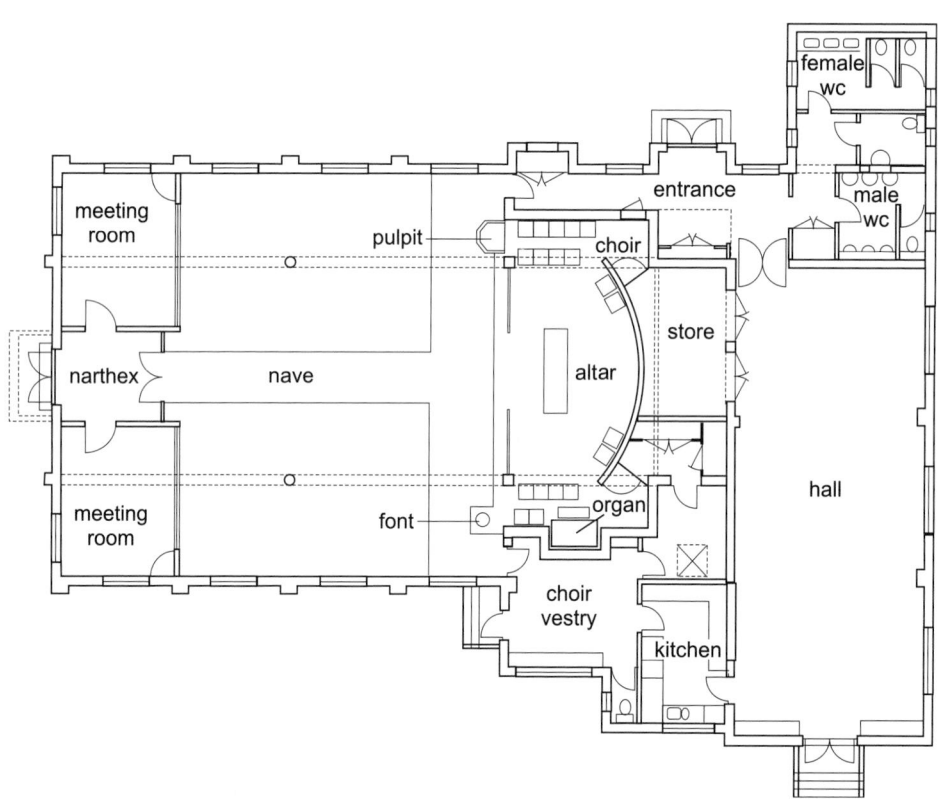

17.3 *Community centre for St Francis Church, Westborough: an example of an addition to an existing building. Architects: Nye, Saunders & Partners*

need to be equipped with retractable bleacher seating as used in sports centres and educational buildings. Pulling out and stacking back such seating creates localised loading and wear. Resilient floors are particularly vulnerable. The manufacturers of the seating and of the floor finishes should be consulted at an early stage.

Safety: Users of a community centre range from small children to elderly and disabled people. Finishes should be chosen with a view to safety, all floors, ramps and steps should be non-slip. Projections, sharp corners and angles should be avoided.

Cleaning: Community facilities get heavy use and limited operating budgets. The building should be easy to clean.

Table I Minimum floor areas for various activities

Function	Area per person (m²)	
Main hall:		
Closely seated audience	0.46 (based on movable seats, usually armless, 450 mm centre to centre; with fixed seating 500 mm centre to centre will increase to 0.6 m²)	
Dances	0.55 to 0.9	
Dining	0.9 to 1.1	
Crèche, day nursery or	0-2 years	3.75
pre-school playgroup	2-3	3
	3-5	2.5
Children 5–8 years (out of school and holiday schemes, open access projects)	2.5	
Meeting rooms	2.25	up to 4 people
	2	6 people
	1.55	8–12 people
	1.25	20 people

2.6 Means of escape

Care in planning and signposting the means of escape in case of fire is especially important because:

- the users, such as audiences at occasional concerts and meetings will not be familiar with the building layout.
- small children are likely to be present in a crèche or day care centre.
- elderly and disabled people may use the centre.
- facilities for leisure or educational purposes may be used by people with learning difficulties.

Early consultation with the local fire authority is essential.

2.7 Licensing

A licence will be required for certain uses and these invariably have conditions attached.

2.8 Noise

A community centre is more likely to generate than to suffer from high noise levels. They are commonly used at night and at the weekend, and are often situated within residential communities. They must therefore be designed to avoid nuisance. Where uses take place simultaneously, sound separation will be necessary between a noisy activity such as a dance and one requiring relative quiet such as a lecture.

The basic principles of acoustic design should be applied:

- orientation, e.g. location of entrances, exits and windows relative to adjoining buildings;
- layout;
- shape of rooms;
- double glazing, only viable in association with mechanical ventilation;
- sound-absorbent finishes, balanced with requirements of durability and cleanability;
- landscaping, including trees, to contain external noise.

Unless unavoidable, noise-producing spaces should not be located alongside quiet spaces. Absorbent surfaces may have to be concentrated at ceiling level or provided by means of drapes and wall hangings. Management can also play a significant part in controlling noise and this should be discussed with the client at an early stage.

2.9 Security

Community centres are more than usually vulnerable to break-ins and vandalism as they do not have resident caretakers or 24-hour

surveillance, are not continuously occupied, are visited by a large number of people, contain expensive equipment and are isolated from other buildings. Requirements for security can conflict with those of means of escape, so it is important to consult with experts and local authorities.

2.10 Child care

Table II is a checklist of design considerations where creches, day nurseries or playgroups use the facility.

Table II Requirements for child care

Item	Comment
Child care: (crèche, day nursery, playgroup)	
Regulation	Child care for children in their early years (generally defined as under 8) usually comes within the Children Act 1989 (see Section 3) and local authorities are responsible for approving and registering facilities. Many of these authorities provide published requirements and guidance on standards
Staffing ratios	0–2 year olds 1:3
	2–3 year olds 1:4
	3–5 year olds 1:8
	(minimum staff 2)
Outdoor play	A safe area with easy access from the building is a usual requirement
Catering	The Pre-school Playgroups Association recommends that children and adults should sit together during meals and consequently separate dining accommodation for staff is not required

2.11 Disabled people

There are statutory regulations relating to access for disabled people. These apply not only to those using wheelchairs but also include people with visual and auditory impairments and those using other types of walking aids. All these have difficulties with steps and changes of direction, and the design of entrances, circulation spaces and toilets should take this into account.

2.12 Legislation

This is constantly changing. Table III gives some current examples but is not exhaustive. The local authority will advise on the latest requirements. It is particularly important to ensure full conformity if the public are going to be charged for admission.

Table III Legislation

Legislation	Comment
Licensing Act 2003	Legislation requires that a licence is obtained for premises which are to be used, regularly or occasionally for the following purposes:
	• Public music or public music and dancing
	• Public performance of plays
	• Cinematograph exhibitions to which the public are admitted on payment
	• Cinematograph exhibitions for children who are members of a cinema club
	• Indoor sports entertainment
	Statutory requirements must be satisfied in terms of means of escape in case of fire and other safety considerations. Administered by the local authority
The Children Act 1989	Covers requirements for premises used by children in, for instance, day nurseries, playgroups, crèches, out-of-school clubs, holiday play schemes, adventure playgrounds and open-access projects. Administered by the local authority

3 ELEMENTS OF THE PLAN

3.1 Entrance

This should be large enough to accommodate an influx of people, such as prior to a meeting or concert. Signposting should be clear as many will be unfamiliar with the building. Unless there is a separate goods entrance, it should allow for bulk delivery of food and drink, display material and equipment. Consider the arrangement of the doors, the durability of surfaces and easy accesses to both the kitchen and the hall.

3.2 Hall
For sports purposes refer to Chapter 18. A rectangular shape is likely to be suitable for a wider range of uses than a square or any other shape. If black-out is required, pay special attention to size and location of windows; mechanical ventilation may be needed.

3.3 Meeting rooms
If more than one, make them different sizes. Alternatively, have one space that can be divided using sliding folding doors, although some of these do not provide adequate sound insulation. At least one meeting room should have direct access to the hall.

3.4 Toilets
Separate toilets will be needed for men, women and disabled people. There may also be a need for smaller toilets for little children. Unisex baby-changing facilities should be provided. If considerable sports usage is expected, showers will be necessary for each sex.

3.5 Kitchen
There should be little need for more than a domestic kitchen. If catered functions are expected, provide space for setting out and final preparations.

3.6 Storage
A separate store should be provided for each main use:

- kitchen
- sports
- seating and other furniture
- crèche/kindergarten
- Scouts.

The kitchen store should be directly accessible from the kitchen, the others from the hall. Storage space should be as generous as space and budget will allow.

3.7 Furniture
Refer to trade catalogues, and seek specialist advice.

4 BIBLIOGRAPHY
PPA Guidelines, published by the Pre-School Playgroups Association

18 Emergency services

Michael Bowman

Including fire stations by Michael Bowman MA (Cantab) Dip. Arch. Dip. Cons (AA) RIBA

Michael Bowman is the senior design manager for the London Fire Brigade

KEY POINTS:
- *Many of these functions are tightly controlled by regulation*
- *The need for security against attacks from people both inside and outside while ensuring full access to those entitled makes design increasingly difficult*
- *Each Fire and Rescue Authority will have a detailed brief for the design of new fire stations including retained fire stations*
- *Fire stations are unique buildings and are 'Sui Generis' in planning terms. Their location will be determined by the attendance times that the fire and rescue service is required to meet within their 'fire ground'. Noise and lighting nuisance may need to be mitigated either by the design of the site or by management of these activities*

Contents
1 Fire stations
2 Ambulance stations
3 Police stations
4 References

1 FIRE STATIONS

1.1 Introduction

Fire stations must accommodate firefighting appliances and their crew to enable them to efficiently carry out their duties as set by the national, regional and metropolitan authorities that manage the fire and rescue services.

Each Fire and Rescue Authority will have a detailed brief for the design of new fire stations including retained fire stations. Full time firefighters typically work a 48 hour shift system over 8 days. Retained firefighters work a Retained Duty System and may have full time employment outside the fire service. The Retained Duty System requires the firefighters to live and work close to the fire station they serve. Full time firefighters operate a duty system of four watches of equal numbers identified by colours which work in sequence – RED, BLUE, GREEN and WHITE. Each 24 hours consists of a day duty and a night duty to cover the whole period. Each watch works 2 consecutive day duties, rests the next day and then works 2 consecutive night duties. The watch then has 4 days off duty. There are 'stand easy' intervals throughout the watch periods. The following is a guide for the design of a full time community fire station.

1.2 Planning

Fire stations are unique buildings and are 'Sui Generis' in planning terms. Their location will be determined by the attendance times that the fire and rescue service are required to meet within their 'fire ground'. The activities of training and appliances turning out to answer emergency calls can cause nuisance to neighbours by noise, vibration and external lighting. This nuisance may need to be mitigated either by the design of the site or by management of these activities.

Radio and wireless communication is a vital part of the service's infrastructure and there must be good reception at the site. If the station is close to residential properties care must be taken that the position of the drill tower does not interfere with residents' TV reception.

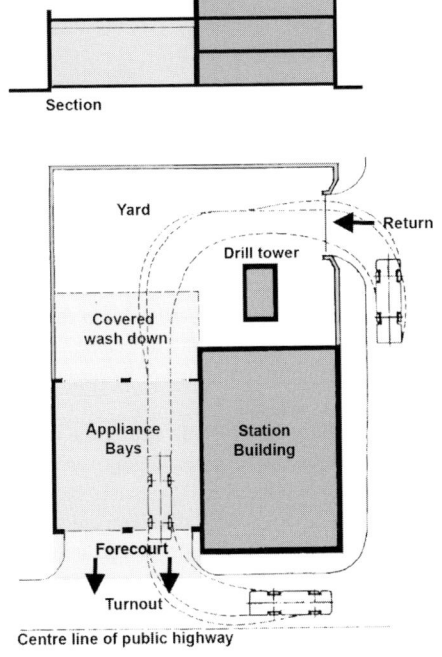
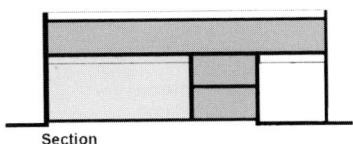
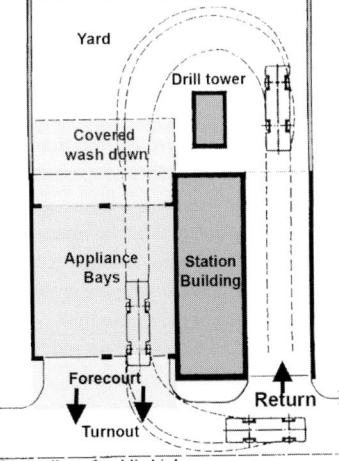

18.1 *Site layout for 2 bay fire station*

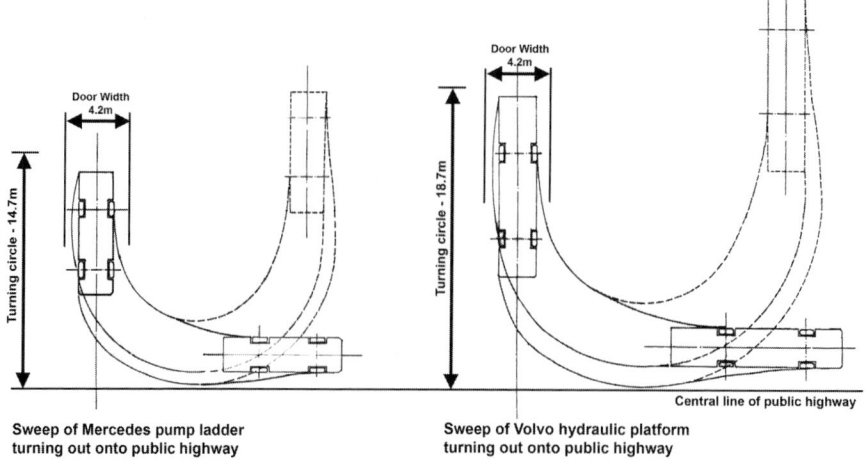

Sweep of Mercedes pump ladder
turning out onto public highway

Sweep of Volvo hydraulic platform
turning out onto public highway

18.2 *Appliance turnout*

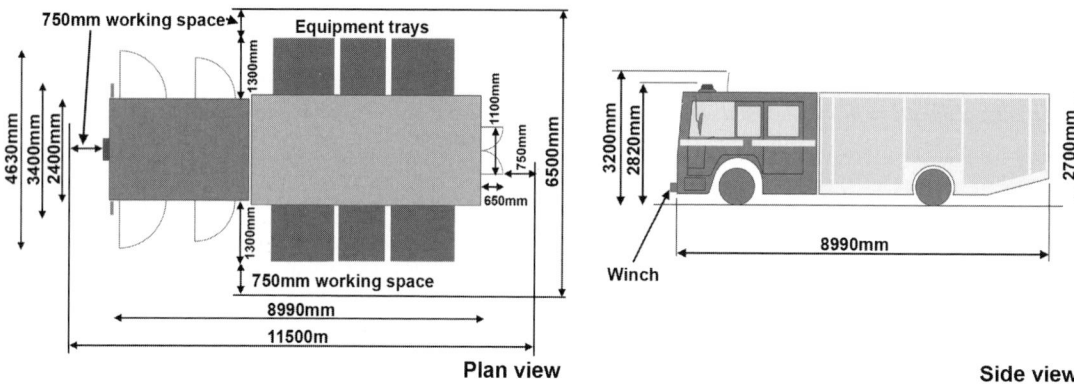

18.3 *Fire rescue unit (Mercedes)*

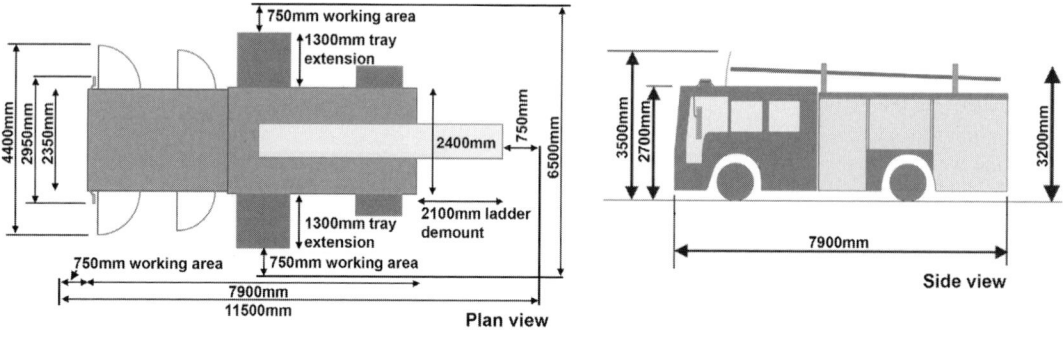

18.4 *Pump ladder (Mercedes)*

1.3 Egress/turnout

In an emergency the primary consideration is to get the fire fighting appliance onto the road quickly. A workable vehicular circulation pattern is therefore fundamental to the success of the station design, Figure 18.1. The turnout route of each appliance should not be interrupted by other traffic or returning appliances and maximum visibility is required. Appliances must be able to turn out without crossing the crown of the road. A forecourt will normally be necessary to achieve this.

A forecourt of 9 m depth will allow appliances to pull clear of the bay doors and turn out onto the highway without crossing the crown of the road. With this depth of forecourt a clear sightline to the edges of the site should be possible from a line 5 m back from the pavement. On restricted sites the forecourt may have to be reduced in depth or even omitted altogether. The vehicle turning circles illustrated in Figure 18.2 indicate the critical space requirements.

1.4 Ingress/return

The returning appliances should be able to navigate a clear sweeping approach from the return access to the covered wash down area, stopping on the centre line of its respective appliance bay.

1.5 Appliances and their appliance bays

Fire and Rescue Services deploy various appliances which undertake specific tasks. Such appliances include urban search and rescue units, water tanker and bulk foam units, command support and incident response units. The fire rescue unit (Figure 18.3) is an important strategic appliance. The most common appliances are pumps, pump ladders (Figure 18.4) and aerial ladder platforms (Figure 18.5). As well as accommodating the turnout and return sweep of these vehicles the appliance bays must allow sufficient working space for their maintenance and re-equipment. Some appliances have equipment trays that extend up to 1300 mm from the sides of the vehicles.

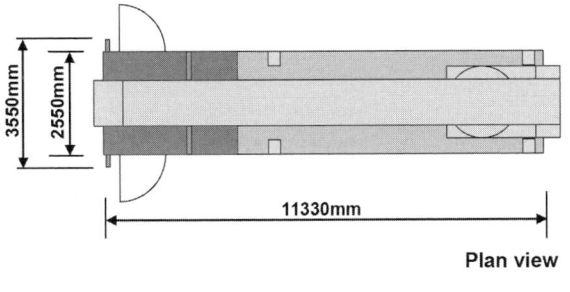

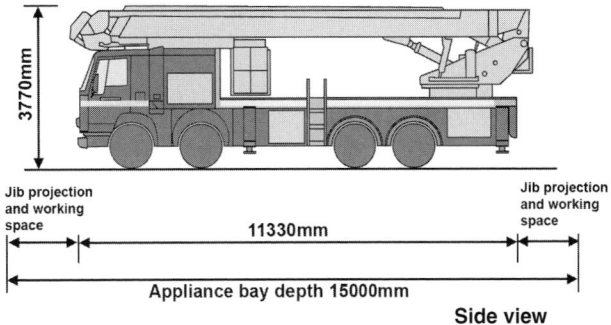

Plan view

Side view

18.5 *Aerial ladder platform (Volvo)*

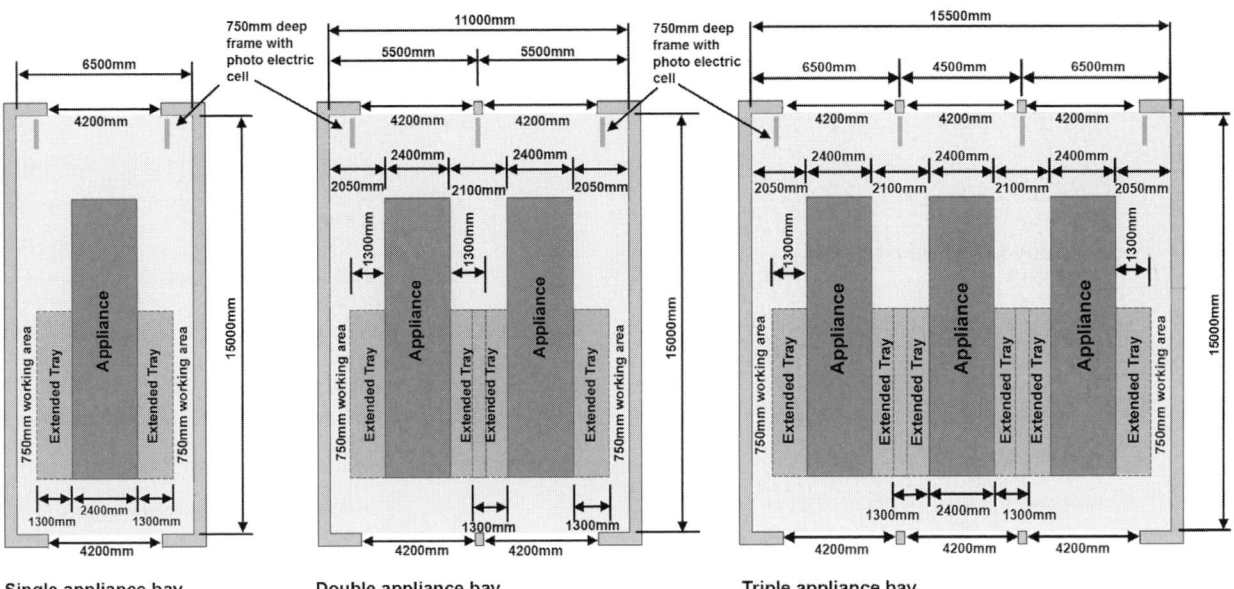

Single appliance bay   Double appliance bay   Triple appliance bay

18.6 *Appliance bay dimensions*

A single appliance bay 15 m deep and 6.5 m wide will accommodate any appliance that the Fire and Rescue Services currently deploy. Multiple appliance bays need a width of 5.5 m as the appliances can share the working space between them. Doors should give a clear width of 4.2 m and a clear height of 4.2 m. Doors are operated on electric controls with photo electric cells and close automatically after the appliance has left (Figure 18.6).

1.6 The station building

Rooms and areas of a community fire station can be grouped into six main categories:

A: Operational – rooms and spaces that are essential to the operational readiness and performance of the service.
B: Training – spaces that contribute to the firefighters' skill and professionalism acquired through regular training.
C: Control and administration – accommodation for the station's communications, administrative duties, incident records and public advisory duties.
D: Amenity – accommodation for ancillary support activities.
E: Services – provision for engineering plant and controls.
F: Community engagement – rooms where emergency services can meet with residents and businesses and advise on fire risk, smoke detectors, extinguishers etc. Local communities can also use this facility for local community purposes.

Table I gives recommended areas for 2, 3 and 4 bay stations.

Security is vital as the station will be unmanned when all firefighters are attending calls. All external doors and all doors off

appliance bays should be able to be locked. The community facilities must be separate from the rest of the station and be accessible without compromising the station's security. The station office should oversee the appliance bays, the reception area and the forecourt.

All finishes, fixtures and fittings must be robust, easy to clean and be easily maintained. Figure 18.7 shows the necessary relationships for the rooms detailed in Table I.

Other rooms may be accommodated within a fire station building depending on the Fire and Rescue Service's strategic planning. Such rooms include: fire safety office, borough manager's office, fire investigation offices etc.

Firefighters will descend to the appliance bays either via a staircase or the pole house. Pole drops are always of one storey only. For descents of more than one storey the pole house will discharge onto a landing and the firefighter will then enter a second pole drop for a further storey. A diagram of a typical pole house is shown in Figure 18.8.

1.7 Training facilities

Firefighters will acquire their skills at specialist training centres. The maintaining and improvement of existing skills is carried out at the fire station, space permitting. The yard should be able to accommodate a deep lift pit (underground water tank) and a road traffic collision (RTC) area of at least 30 m² for training purposes. The configuration of the training tower will depend on the local requirements. Standard training towers are typically 5–6 storeys high. A three storey training tower with training roof is a suitable alternative where planning constraints limit the height of buildings.

Training lectures are given in the lecture room and the gym provides for maintaining physical fitness. The training tower

Table I Accommodation schedule for 2, 3 and 4 bay fire stations

Accommodation		Area (m²)			Notes
		2 Bay*	3 Bay**	4 Bay***	*max. watch strength 15
					**max. watch strength 21
					***max. watch strength 23
A	**OPERATIONAL**				
A1	Appliance Bays	165	233	300	
A2	Covered Wash Down	99	140	180	9m deep across all bays
A3	Slide Poles	7	7	7	Extra drops needed if more than 2 storeys
A4	Fire Gear (Uniform) Store	32	40	42	4 peg spaces per watch strength
A5	Operational Equipment Store	12	12	12	Close to appliance bays
A6	Operational Equipment Cleaning	8	8	8	Close to appliance bays
A7	Drying Room	10	10	10	Close to appliance bays
A8	Breathing Apparatus (BA) Room	15	15	15	Close to appliance bays
A9	Forecourt	–	–	–	Provides easy turnout on to highway
A10	Personal Protective Equipment (PPE) Store	6	6	6	For gas tight suits etc.
A11	Dry Cleaning Store	2	2	2	For collection/delivery of uniforms
A12	Specialist Equipment Store	20	20	20	For kit bags with specialist gear
A13	Drying Room for personal items	4	4	4	May be combined with A7
A14	Toilet (Men)	2	2	2	For firefighters in fire gear
A15	Toilet (Women)	2	2	2	For firefighters in fire gear
B	**TRAINING**				
B1	Yard	–	–	–	For training and return access. Should include a road traffic collision (RTC) area.
B2	Deep Lift Pit	–	–	–	Below ground water tank for training
B3	Drill Tower and Training Roof	–	–	–	Height and configuration dictated by training regime
B4	Fuel Storage/Pump	–	–	–	Not required at all stations
C	**CONTROL AND ADMINISTRATION**				
C1	Station office	30	36	42	Oversees reception and appliance bays. Includes call out equipment
C2	Reception/waiting	12	12	12	
C3	Station Manager's Office	15	15	15	
C4	Watch Manager's Room	15	15	15	
D	**AMENITY**				
D1	Fire fighters' Lockers and Changing Area	56	80	88	Area split into rooms to accommodate up to 6 watch members
D2	Shower Rooms	5no. × 4m² = 20m²	7no. × 4m² = 28m²	8no. × 4m² = 32m²	Each room has shower, wc and whb
D3	Firefighters' Rest Area	84	120	138	Area split into rooms to accommodate up to 6 watch members
D4	Lecture/TV room	45	60	65	
D5	Lecture Storage	10	10	10	
D6	Quiet Study Room	10	10	10	
D7	Gymnasium	35	42	42	
D8	Kitchen	30	30	30	
D9	Dining Area	35	45	50	
D10	Cleaner's Store	2	2	2	
D11	Consumables Store	2	2	2	
D12	First Aid Room	15	15	15	
E	**SERVICES**				
E1	Electrical Intake and distribution	3	3	3	
E2	Standby Generator	12	12	12	
E3	Plant Room	15	15	15	May be larger depending on servicing strategy
E4	Bins/recycling	4	4	4	May be larger depending on recycling regime
E5	Gas meter	–	–	–	On ground floor
E6	Comms. room	15	15	15	
E7	Water meter	–	–	–	On ground floor
F	**COMMUNITY ENGAGEMENT**				
F1	Meeting Room	45	45	45	Must be accessible without public having to access operational areas of the fire station
F2	Kitchenette	6	6	6	
F3	Accessible wc	4	4	4	
F4	Toilet (men)	2	2	2	
F5	Toilet (women)	2	2	2	
F6	Meeting Room Store	5	5	5	
Total		**913**	**1136**	**1291**	
Total including 30% circulation (excepting bays and wash down)		**1108**	**1365**	**1534**	Main circulation routes should be a minimum of 1500mm wide

illustrated in Figure 18.9 allows a 135 (13.5 m) ladder to be pitched to the third floor opening. The upper storeys allow training scenarios for Aerial Ladder Platforms.

1.8 Staffing

The fire station is staffed by the station manager and the watch members. Each watch comprises a watch manager and the crews for each of the appliances. As there are four watches there must be four sets of fire gear and four lockers per watch member. The watch strength will depend on the types of appliances deployed at the station. The watch strengths given in the accommodation schedule above assume the following deployment scenarios:

- bay station – pump ladder and fire rescue unit – watch strength 15.
- bay station – pump ladder, pump and fire rescue unit – watch strength 21.
- bay station – pump ladder, pump, fire rescue unit and an aerial ladder platform – watch strength 23.

1.9 Working practices

For the relationship of spaces in and around a fire station to succeed they must address the working practices of the firefighters. The

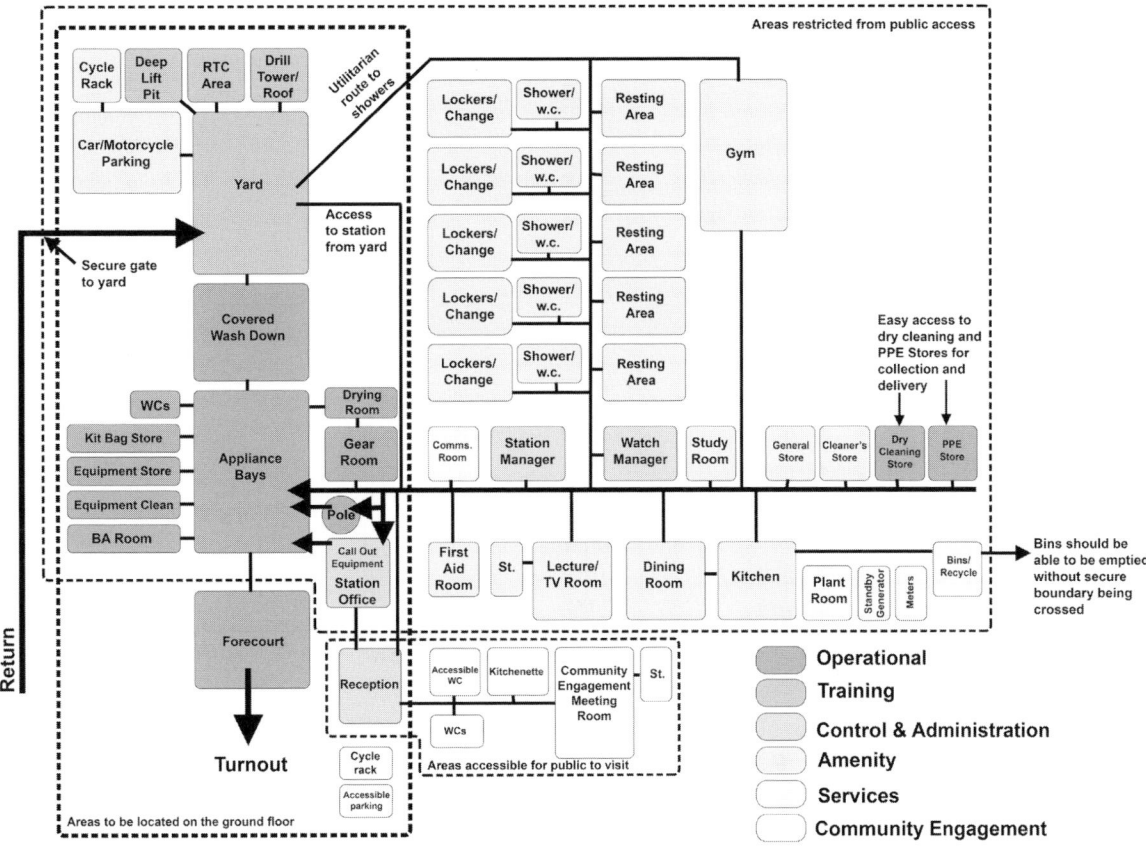

18.7 *Relationship diagram (with thanks to Building Design Partnership)*

practices can be grouped into seven routines which can be divided into wet-dirty and clean-dry (Table II).

The mobilisation procedure demands that the firefighters move at speed through the building to the appliance bays. It is essential that circulation routes are generously sized to permit this movement to be undertaken safely. In particular junctions must be eased so that they do not become collision points. Main circulation paths should have a minimum width of 1500 mm and be well illuminated.

Routine a – mobilisation

The mobilisation of a crew originates from a central mobilising control centre. The system is fully computerised so that when a 999 call reveals an identifiable address the computer flags up the risk and recommends to the control officer the location of the resources that shall be mobilised to meet the predetermined attendance (PDA) requirements. If there are no overriding circumstances the mobilisation signal is sent.

A central control computer is aware of the operational status of every front line appliance. Each appliance is equipped with a mobile data pack which informs the control centre of its operational status indicated in Table III.

The command to mobilise is received by equipment located either in the station office or a watch room and simultaneously the mobilisation bells sound throughout the station. The firefighters proceed to the appliance bay as quickly as possible while the duty firefighter attends the call out equipment. He then operates the appropriate coloured dispatch lights which tell the assembled crew which appliances are to attend the incident. The crews not dispatched assume their normal duties about the station.

On return from an incident the appliance proceeds to the external covered wash down area where equipment in need of cleaning, repair or replacement is attended to. The appliance is then moved into its ready position in the appliance bay. The firefighters then attend to

their own needs and should be able to gain access to their lockers and shower facilities without passing through clean/dry accommodation.

Routine b – training and drill

On station training is a combination of external physical activity and lectures and private study. Training is carried out in duty time and can be interrupted by a call out. The location of these spaces therefore must not hinder a crew's ability to achieve normal call out requirements. Training is carried out by every watch and entails the practice of those skills already acquired and also to check that operational equipment is in full working order.

Routine c – cleaning and maintenance of operational equipment

Station personnel are responsible for the working performance of the many items of operational equipment in their care. They must ensure that such items receive the required standard of cleaning and periodic maintenance. This work is carried out in the breathing apparatus room, operational equipment cleaning room and the operational equipment store (work bench area). All these rooms require easy access from the appliance bays.

Routine d – administration

Administrative duties for a Fire and Rescue Service will include logging incident reports and managing operational policy notes, records, training and personnel issues. Each watch will have a staff member attached to administrative duties. These duties are carried out within the station office. Confidential matters will be dealt with by the station manager or watch manager within their private rooms.

Routine e – public interface

A community fire station needs to be designed to create an environment for firefighters to engage effectively with the local community and to provide facilities able to be used by the community and

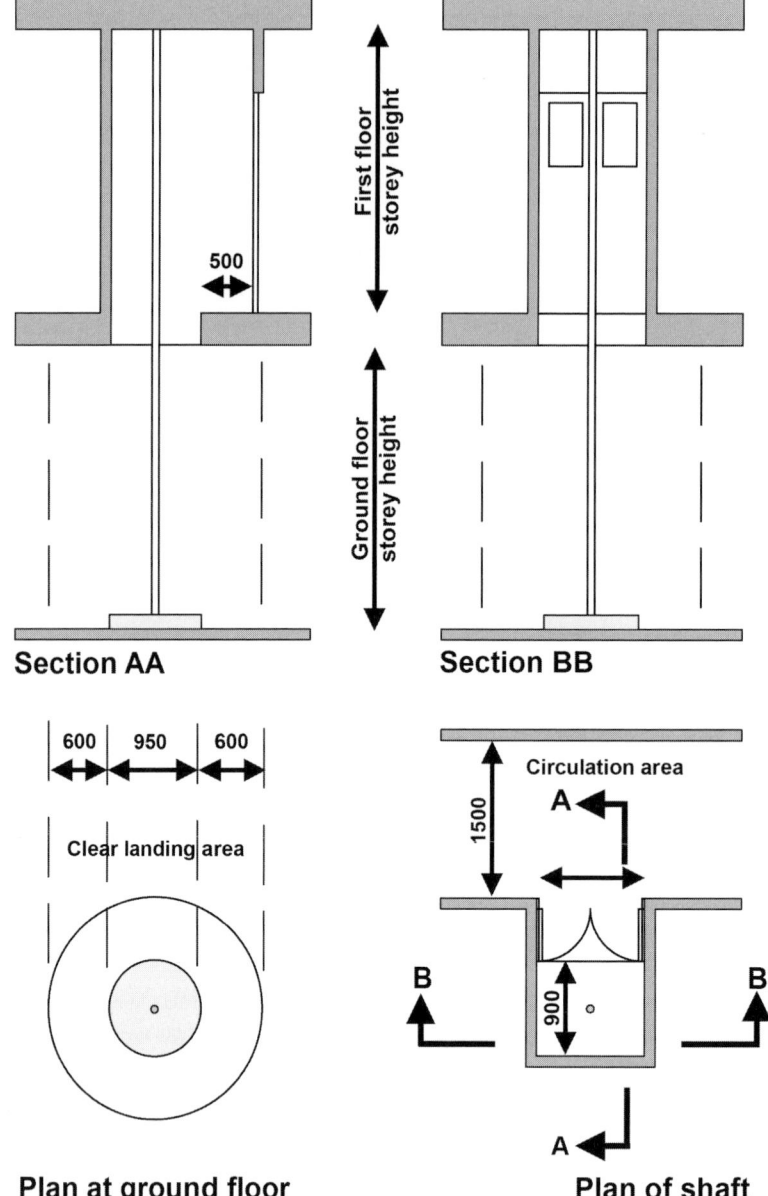

18.8 *Pole house layout*

which are accessible and welcoming. Members of the public visit fire stations for many different reasons. Visitors and events include:

- open days
- organised school visits
- local commerce
- local politicians
- local community groups
- charity organisers
- fire safety – education
- fire safety – legislative
- sports organisations.

Visiting members of the public are met at reception and escorted to their appointment. Visitors' names are entered into the station's day book. The public should not be allowed unaccompanied access around the station. Rooms to which the public will require access from the reception area are normally limited to the community engagement facilities.

Routine f – stand easy/recreation
The inclusion of a fully equipped gymnasium at fire stations provides the firefighter with the means to achieve and maintain the high level of fitness that their job demands. Television viewing is provided in the lecture room. Rest areas can be used during 'stand easy' periods.

Routine g – arrival for duty
On arrival for duty firefighters go to the locker rooms and change into their basic operational uniform. At the same time there will be firefighters preparing to come off duty using the locker rooms and showers. Firefighters will then proceed to the fire gear room to collect their individual fire gear; helmet, boots, uniform etc., and proceed to the appliance bay. Their fire gear is placed at the side of or on to the appliance. At watch changeover there is a roll call in the appliance bays where firefighters receive briefing and deployment instructions from the watch manager. Following the roll call all equipment is examined, checked and restored. Firefighters then go to the dining area for a short break before taking up their normal working routines or those allocated at roll call.

1.10 Special training facilities
Specialist training facilities may be attached to the fire station or have their own site. A typical local training centre for Breathing

Table II Working practices and spatial types

Routine	Routine type
a Mobilisation – call out	Wet–dirty
b Training and drill	Wet–dirty
c Cleaning and maintenance	Wet–dirty
d Administration	Clean–dry
e Public Interface	Clean–dry
f 'Stand easy'	Clean–dry
g Arrival for duty	Clean–dry

Table III Status hierarchy

STATUS 1	Readiness
STATUS 2	Proceeding to incident
STATUS 3	Attending at incident
STATUS 4	Mobile from incident
STATUS 1	Return to station/readiness
STATUS 0	Crew/appliance is incapable of further operational duty (injury etc.)

Table IV Accommodation schedule for local training venue

Accommodation	Area (m²)	Notes
Reception area	12	
Trainers' office	25	3 workstations
Lecture room	50	
Lecture room store	10	
Dining area	45	
Kitchenette	8	
Fire gear store	20	30 peg spaces for operational clothing
Drying room	15	30 rack spaces for operational clothing
Locker area (men)	20	20 locker spaces
Locker area (women)	20	20 locker spaces
Trainers' lockers (men)	10	10 locker spaces
Trainers' lockers (women)	10	10 locker spaces
Shower rooms (unisex)	$10 \times 4m^2 = 28$	Each room has shower, wc and whb
Breathing apparatus (BA) Chamber	200	Provides multiple scenarios for BA training. Rooms can be filled with smoke and be heated to high temperature. Specialist facilities will provide Real Fire Training scenarios.
BA control room	10	Controls smoke, temperature and any 'real fire' in the chamber. Also monitors trainers and trainees within the chamber.
BA maintenance room	55	Classroom for training in the maintenance of BA equipment.
BA storage room	20	For storage of BA cylinders
External areas	–	Area must accommodate drills for 2 to 4 pumping appliances, drill tower/training roof, deep lift pit and road traffic collision area.
Total	558	
Total including 30% circulation	725	

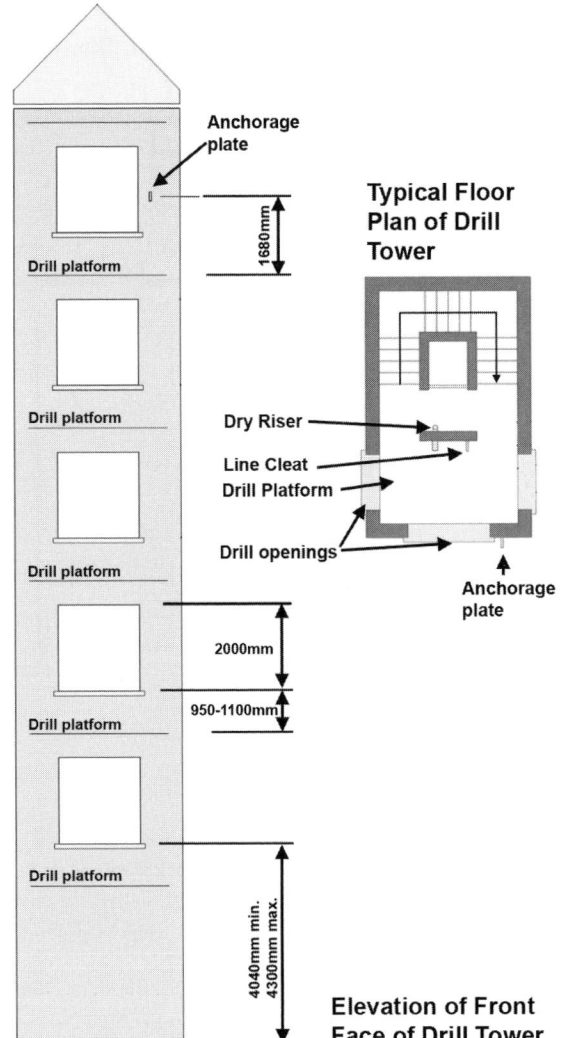

18.9 *Training tower*

Apparatus and real fire training may comprise the accommodation shown in Table IV.

If the local training centre shares its site with an operational fire station some of the above accommodation may be omitted and the station's facilities be shared with the local training centre.

1.11 Further Information
The Department for Communities and Local Government (CLG) publish advice in their *Design Guide Achieving Design Quality in Fire and Rescue Service Buildings*. This is available for downloading from the CLG website (www.gov.uk/government/organisations/department-for-communities-and-local-government).

2 AMBULANCE STATIONS
2.1 Introduction
Ambulance stations are either control stations or their satellites. The control stations contain larger store areas and a divisional office, and may have dining, recreation and activity areas. On-site sleeping accommodation is no longer required. Satellite stations have from two to six ambulances and deal only with accident and emergency calls. They do not require dining or recreation facilities, as off-duty time is spent off the premises, but a rest room will be needed for waiting and relaxing between calls.

Because drugs may be stored on the premises all doors need to be lock controlled.

Like the police, more and more control equipment such as faxes, trackers and radios are in the ambulance, permitting greater use of these facilities with no need to return to base. However, to provide adequate hospital cover, ambulances are stationed there for half-hour periods.

2.2 Function
Apart from accidents and emergencies, the larger stations also cover:

- patient transfer
- hospital to hospital
- home to hospital for consultancy
- taxi service.

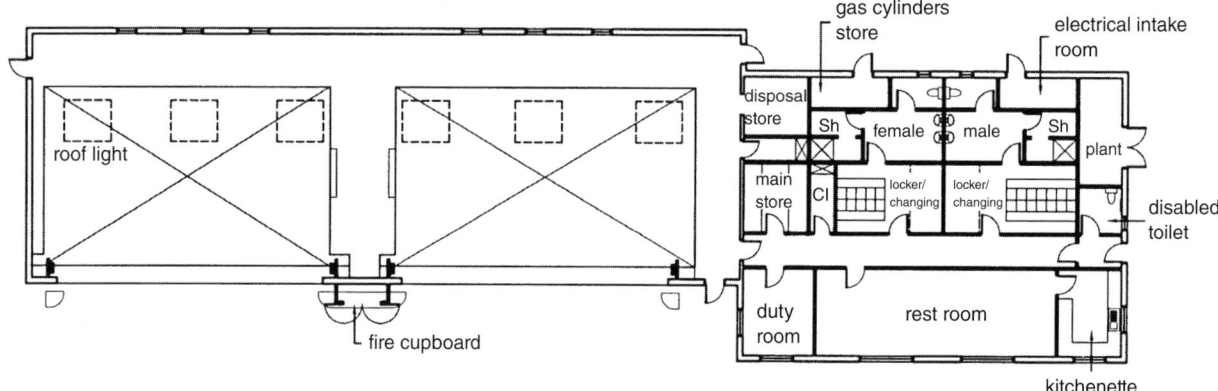

18.10 *Layout of an ambulance station with six vehicles*

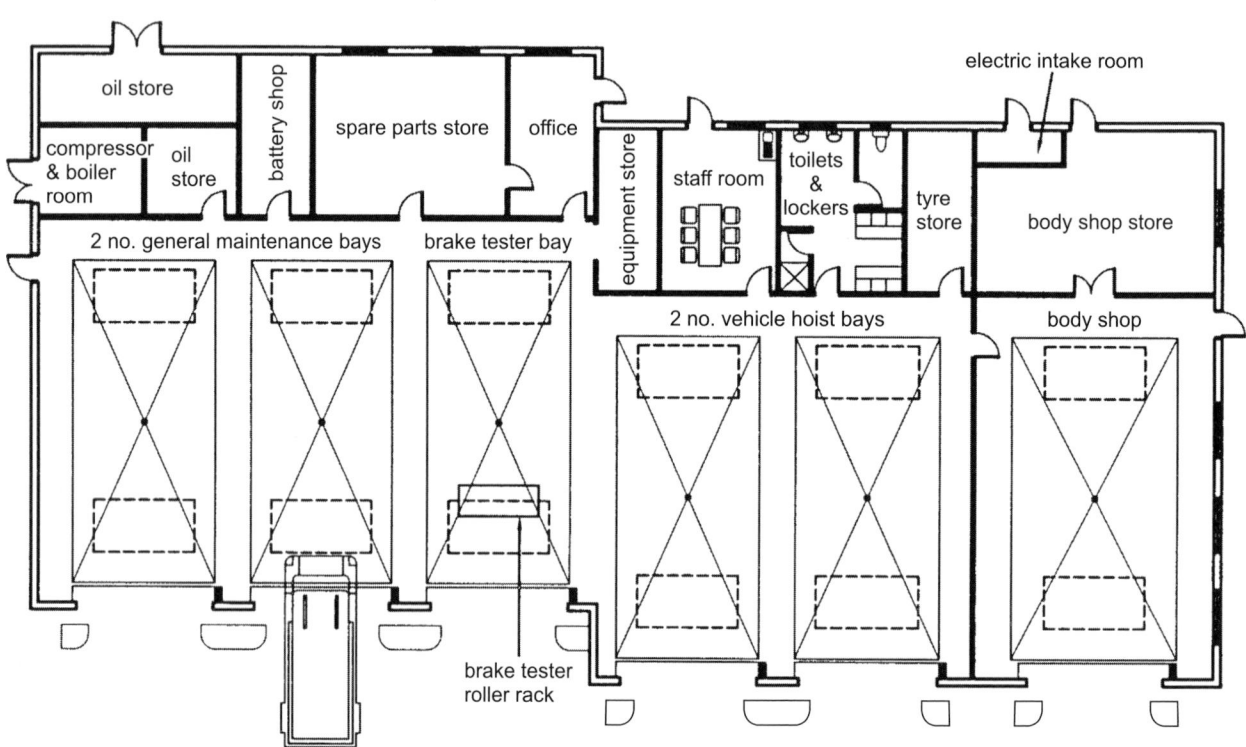

18.11 *Layout of a workshop for servicing ambulance vehicles*

2.3 Organisation
Regions are split into about four divisions with a central control. Each division normally consists of about six larger stations and twelve satellites, varying according to population density. All accident and emergency calls are received at central control.

2.4 Provision for vehicles
In small stations with less than seven ambulances, vehicles will be reversed onto their parking bays. The station will have an easy-to-open individual exit door to each bay (Figure 18.10). Larger stations use echelon parking with in-and-out access. There must be sufficient space behind the parked ambulance to permit easy removal of equipment.

Large stations require a fuel loading bay, but not the smaller stations. The current trend is towards using petrol rather than diesel,

for smoother running and fewer fumes. A vehicle wash-down is required for each station.

2.5 Vehicle workshops
Vehicle maintenance is carried out in separate workshop buildings (Figure 18.11), covering at least six stations. It does not need to be on the same site as an ambulance station.

A workshop normally caters for up to six vehicles at a time, so front access only is required. Larger workshops are designed for echelon parking with a through-access system. All workshops will be capable of carrying out day-to-day maintenance and repairs, including the equivalent of MOT testing, standard servicing and body repairs. They are not expected to replace engines or crankshafts or do heavy repairs. Finishes must be robust and durable and floor surfaces non-slip.

2.6 Duty rooms
Duty rooms should be close to the garage, have adequate wall space for maps and natural lighting and ventilation. Staff in the rest room must be able to see what is happening in the duty room, so it should be adjacent with a glazed screen between.

2.7 Lockers and changing facilities
Lockers and changing facilities are linked to showers and toilets. In the smaller stations unisex toilets and showers are acceptable. Elsewhere they should be designed to facilitate adjustment when the male/female ratio changes.

2.8 Toilets for disabled users
A toilet for wheelchair users and other disabled people is needed although the ambulance operatives themselves need to be fully able-bodied.

2.9 Stores
The main store needs to be a secure facility close to the garage. It will accommodate the following in a single area or in separate stores:

- linen such as blankets, sheets, pillowcases and towels;
- medical supplies such as first-aid dressings, bandages and splints;
- paramedic equipment such as defibrilators and resuscitators;
- spare items to replace equipment normally stored in the ambulance;
- trolleys, stretchers, etc. belonging to de-kitted vehicles;
- expendable items and documents, log books and files.

A separate store within the main store is required for drugs. This is separately lockable and alarmed to the duty room.

Blankets should be kept well ventilated and heated.

Dirty blankets, linen and contaminated clothes are temporarily kept in containers in a disposal store until they can be sent to a laundry. This disposal store should be near the ambulance parking, but away from clean stores and other clean areas. The same place can also be used for storing general refuse awaiting removal. Medical materials including used needles must be in separate containers for special disposal.

The gas store holds entonox and oxygen in small cylinders for use by paramedics. This store must be warm and well ventilated with easy access to the ambulances.

2.10 Laundries
Some regions still require a small blanket laundry in the larger stations. However, due to health and safety legislation, with stringent regulations relating to temperature controls, cleanliness and hygiene, there is a strong move towards using contract cleaning companies instead.

3 POLICE STATIONS
3.1 Introduction
The police aim to foster public goodwill; their buildings should be as pleasing and friendly to the visitor as possible compatible with essential security requirements.

The Home Office has produced most detailed and comprehensive guides covering legislative requirements, cost and design. New stations should be based on the Home Office *Police Buildings Design Guide* (2010), modified to suit the individual local requirements.

3.2 Organisation
Over the last few years there has been radical change in organisation. Some forces still maintain divisions and subdivisions; others have gone over to regions and areas. Some police forces collaborate with others to provide support services for their joint use. Regional crime squads come under this heading.

Because so much of the work has become extremely technical and specialised, many of the specialities are accommodated away from the custody and public departments.

The different levels of the organisation require different building types:

1 Headquarters buildings with control extending over a force area;
2 Divisional HQs;
3 sub-Divisional HQs, which may be located separately or may be combined.

Headquarters buildings and police stations are all based on the same principles, and only vary according to need. A facility like a custody suite or communications centre is located in the most suitable place regardless of the rank of the building.

3.3 Siting
Stations should be near public transport, readily available both to the local inhabitants and easily found by strangers. They no longer need to be near magistrates' courts. However, when they are, they should be totally separate with no shared facilities.

In busy shopping centres and high streets, police posts with direct communications to their headquarters are proving popular with both police and public, who provide information there that might never be otherwise obtained. The authorities are even considering having police posts in supermarkets.

3.4 Design of the station
The zoning diagram (Figure 18.12) is a guide to circulation.

The public area must be designed with an awareness of the dangers posed by explosives and people with weapons. It should still try to maintain a pleasing and welcoming atmosphere. It must be easily accessible from the police area. Access and toilet accommodation for disabled people is essential.

The reception counter should be located to permit officer-on-duty supervision of the building entrance. A security screen between counter area and waiting is desirable in some circumstances, so that only a limited number can enter at a time. This provides both privacy and security. Where there is no screen a privacy booth in or on the counter is desirable.

Waiting areas are provided with seating and notice boards for posters on road safety and crime prevention, etc.

The public interview area is entered off the waiting area. Interview rooms should be large enough to take several people at a time and are fitted with taping equipment.

The victim examination suite should be adjacent to the public entrance and is for interviewing and medical examination of assault, child molestation or rape victims. It must be pleasantly designed in order to reduce stress (Figure 18.13).

Found property
This is an area accessible only to the police for storing unclaimed stolen property and items handed in by the public or found by the police. No live animals are kept there, although some stations do have special facilities for animals.

People seeking lost property enquire for it at the reception counter, so this should have easy access to the found property store. Its size will depend on local requirements. Some forces use warehouses due to the very large quantities that are collected. Where no large store or warehouse is available, bulky items such as bicycles are usually stored in out-buildings.

Assembly room, lockers, changing and drying rooms
They should be located close to the police entrance. Showers and toilets should be adjacent to the lockers and to the drying areas which should be operational in summer as well as winter.

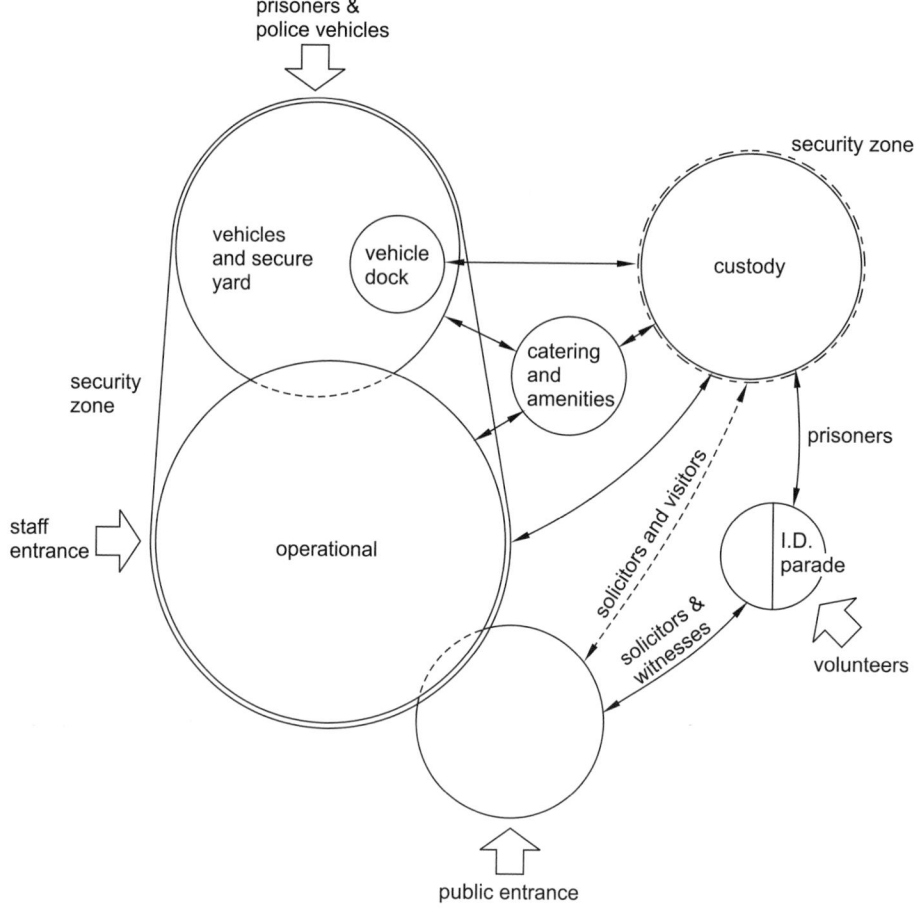

18.12 *Relationship and zoning diagram for a large police station*

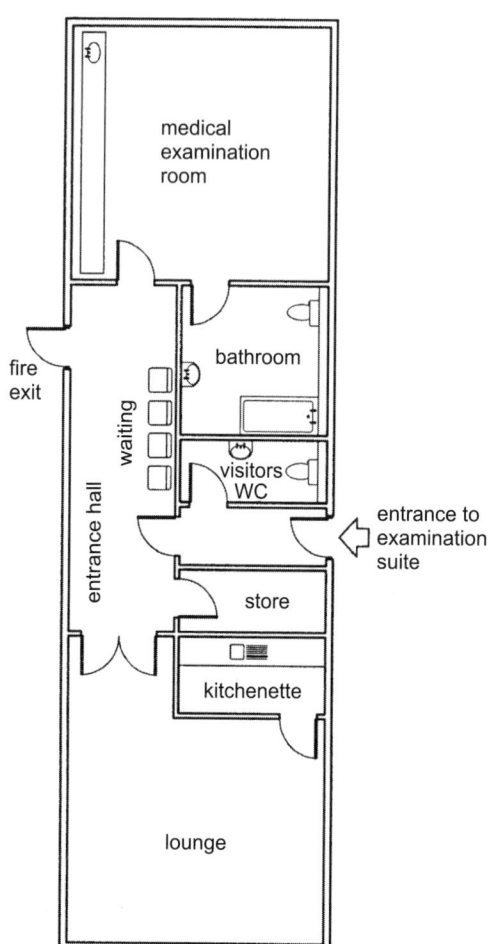

18.13 *Plan of a victim examination suite*

Report writing room
These should be adjacent to the assembly room. Booths and acoustic treatment are advisable.

Communications and control are central to the police function. Workload is extremely heavy and the working environment should be designed to mitigate stress (Figure 18.14). The control room deals with force or area-wide facilities including VHP radio, and has direct access to police resource information and criminal records. Communications rooms are principally used for message transfer and receipt of information.

The location and design of the central control room should be such as to frustrate any deliberate attempt to dislocate its vitally important functions by physical or electronic attack. Its vehicular access must ensure an uninterrupted road in an emergency; but no parking should be allowed within 15 m of its perimeter.

Major incident room
A force will on occasions need to work on serious crimes requiring extensive investigation, civil emergencies or major incidents. Accommodation with easy communication connections will be required for temporary use by CID, traffic or uniformed branches; when not so required, it will be designated for an alternative function such as a gymnasium.

Criminal justice office
This is for documentation of cases to be brought before the courts.

Criminal Investigation Department (CID)
In some cases CID would have their own unit separate from the police station.

Operational group provides office accommodation for:

- beat patrols
- uniformed section
- operational control
- general administration.

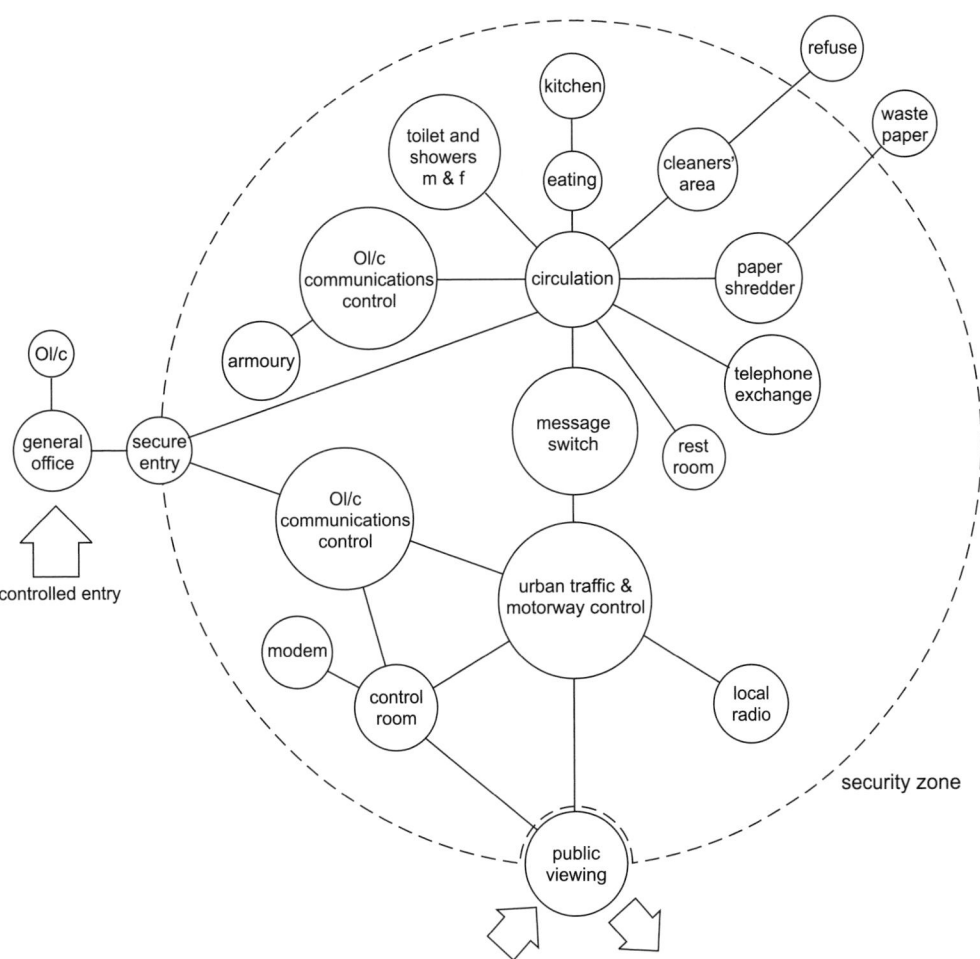

18.14 *Relationship diagram of a Control Room suite*

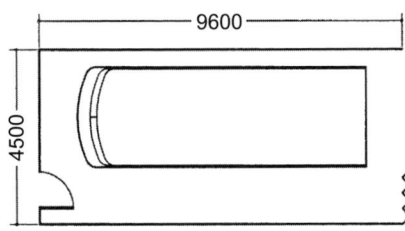

18.15 *Plan of a prisoner transport vehicle dock*

Administration covers general administration as opposed to operational dependent administration and activities.

Traffic includes accommodation for motor patrols, traffic wardens, garages and workshops.

Garages and workshops may be on the same site as the station, or be a separate unit with attached accommodation for motor patrols depending on the size of the area and the number of vehicles. It is preferable not to have this unit in a busy city centre where it would add to congestion, and also hinder police cars quickly reaching the scene of an incident. If the police area includes motorways the unit should be sited near an access point, or even within a motorway service area.

The police car is becoming more 'high tech', with built-in computers in addition to two-way radios. It is becoming an office in its own right, so that there is less need for the occupants to report in person to a police station.

Prisoners' vehicle dock
This must be provided away from the main police vehicle yard, totally secure and adjacent to the prisoners' entrance to the building (Figure 18.15). Figure 18.16 gives data for the prisoner transport vehicle.

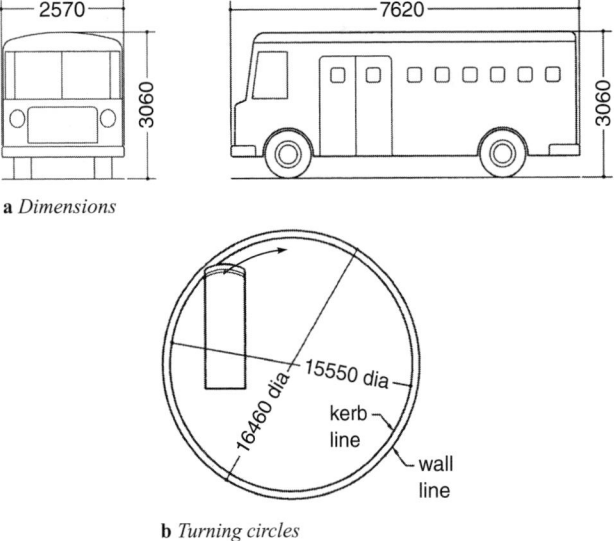

a *Dimensions*

b *Turning circles*

18.16 *A vehicle for transporting prisoners*

Identification parade facility
This has to be carefully sited outside the custody area but linked to it by a secure access route. Witnesses should be rigidly segregated from each other, and from all members of the parade before, during and after the parade; there must be no possibility of physical contact at any time, or visual contact except during the parade itself (Figure 18.17). Toilet facilities should be available for witnesses and volunteers.

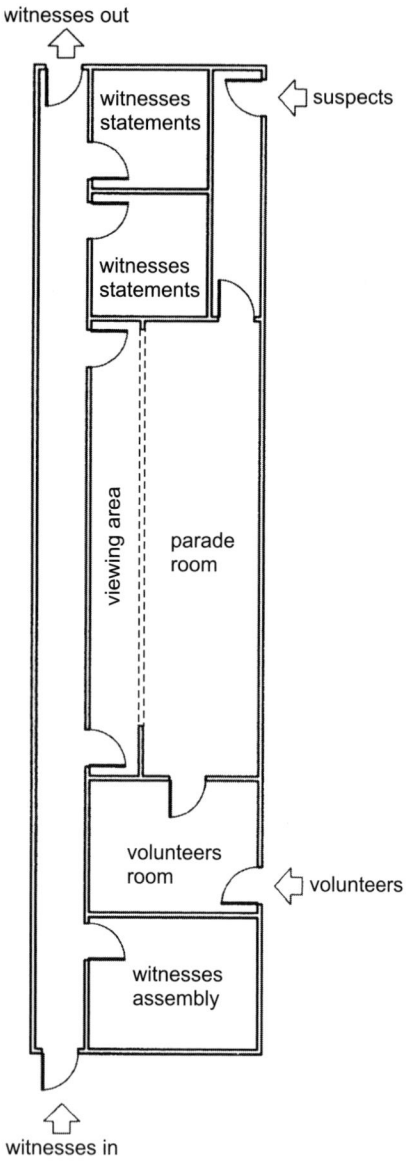

witnesses out

witnesses statements

⇦ suspects

witnesses statements

viewing area

parade room

volunteers room

⇦ volunteers

witnesses assembly

witnesses in

18.17 *Plan of an identity parade suite*

Messing and recreation
Catering is usually provided by self-help appliances such as frozen packaged food with grills or microwave ovens and hot/cold drink dispensers. In large stations there may be a canteen, but 24-hour operation is easier to control through packaged meals.

Toilets
Lavatory accommodation is related to size of station and disposition of rooms. Separate provision is made for:

- male sergeants, constables and civilian staff;
- female sergeants, constables and civilian staff;
- senior officers;
- chief constables and assistant chief constables have en-suite facilities;
- visitors, usually located at the public entrance;
- disabled people, also close to the public entrance;
- cell accommodation.

Blast proofing is now mandatory for all police stations; no car parking should be positioned within 15 m of the buildings, 10 m for operational vehicles.

Mechanical ventilation and cooling is provided for information and communications accommodation without natural ventilation.

Emergency electrical supply is essential throughout, not only for power failure but also in the event of fire. In large stations it will be necessary to ensure continuity of supply to the custody suite, radios, computers, teleprinters and communication service equipment, and must have 'direct on-line automatic start'.

An uninterrupted power supply (UPS) will be required for computer areas.

3.5 Custody suite
This includes detention rooms, charge desk(s) and ancillary accommodation (Figures 18.18 and 18.19). The police have to be alert to the possibility of someone in custody attempting suicide. Care needs to be taken to avoid this eventuality particularly in the design of the cells (see Section 3.6).

The custody area should be securely separated from other parts of the building. It should be located on a single level to avoid moving prisoners up and down stairs which should be avoided at all costs. Where minor changes in level are unavoidable internally or externally, ramps should be used.

Corridors and cells for female prisoners should be segregated from those for male prisoners. Each should have separate access to the exercise yard. Detention rooms for juveniles should also be separate from adult areas.

Catering
Prisoners and police within the custody area need to be fed. However, a kitchenette within the custody area is undesirable as it would divert the custody officer from essential tasks and also be a fire risk. The self-catering facility in the amenity area is also unacceptable as it would take officers away from the custody area. There is little alternative, therefore, to a staffed kitchen immediately outside the custody area preparing food in compliance with food hygiene regulations and providing the meals close to the users. If there is a canteen which is fully staffed for 24 hours, this may be used.

Detention suite
This is a facility where the WC is outside the cell (Figure 18.20), where additional washing facilities can be securely provided.

WCs
The compartment should have a stable-type hinged door, not a sliding one, with an observation aperture. The cistern should be outside the compartment with secured access and a protected flushing pipe. The flushing device should be outside the reach of a prisoner attempting suicide by drowning, and should not be a chain or project from the wall. There should be no projecting toilet roll holder, exposed overflow pipe, bracket, service pipe or stopcock. Fittings should not be able to be broken or extracted to make tools or weapons.

Washing facilities
Basins should not be inside cells. They should be supported on metal stands, not cantilever brackets, and provided with captive plugs without chains. Towel holders are not used as the towels could be used to facilitate suicide, and the holder would provide points to which a ligature could be attached. Facilities for female prisoners must be properly screened. For use inside cells, prisoners are provided with disinfectant/cologne-impregnated washpads as on aircraft.

Cell corridor
The entrance should be fitted with an iron gate. The corridor should have alarm pushes for the custody officer's use if attacked. There should be no exposed pipes, valves, electric cables or conduit, and any thermometer should be outside the reach of a passing prisoner.

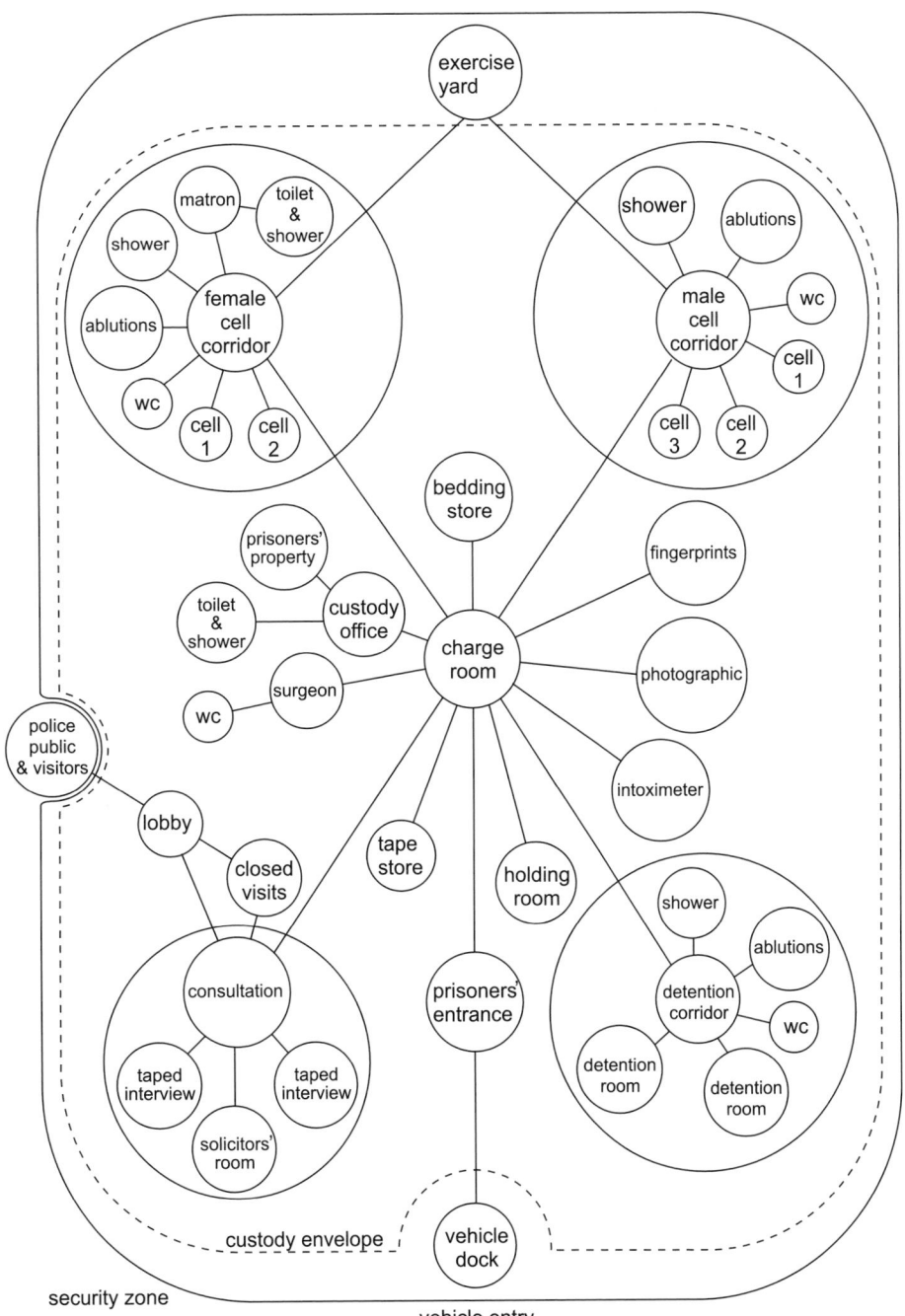

18.18 *Relationship and zoning diagram for a custody suite*

Exercise yard

The walls should be high enough to prevent a prisoner escaping, at least 3.6 m. There should be no ledges or other features which enable a prisoner to climb. However, where for any reason the height and detailing of the walls are deemed insufficient to prevent escape, a top cover may be used. There should be no doors or windows opening into the yard which might enable a prisoner to reach the top cover, nor any unlockable inspection chamber covers or gully gratings which could be lifted. Rainwater and soil pipes should be flaunched up in cement mortar to obviate handholds.

3.6 Cell design

The Police Design Guides are explicit in their requirements reflected in a typical design, as shown in Figure 18.21.

Windows

Cell windows which are unguarded and with openable panes should not overlook roads or other public areas. Windows overlooking exercise yards should be both guarded and screened to prevent observation. Windows to ancillary accommodation within the cell suite such as blanket store, property store, cell corridor, gaoler's room, toilets, etc. should all be guarded. The glazing should be of toughened opaque glass fitted flush to the wall with no protrusions to facilitate injury or suicide, or ledges facilitating escape and attacks on officers. The thickness of the glass increases with larger panes. Glass should not be replaced for ventilation purposes with, for example, perforated zinc.

Ceilings

Most suspended ceilings can be easily broken, giving access to other parts of the building and possibly providing improvised tools or weapons.

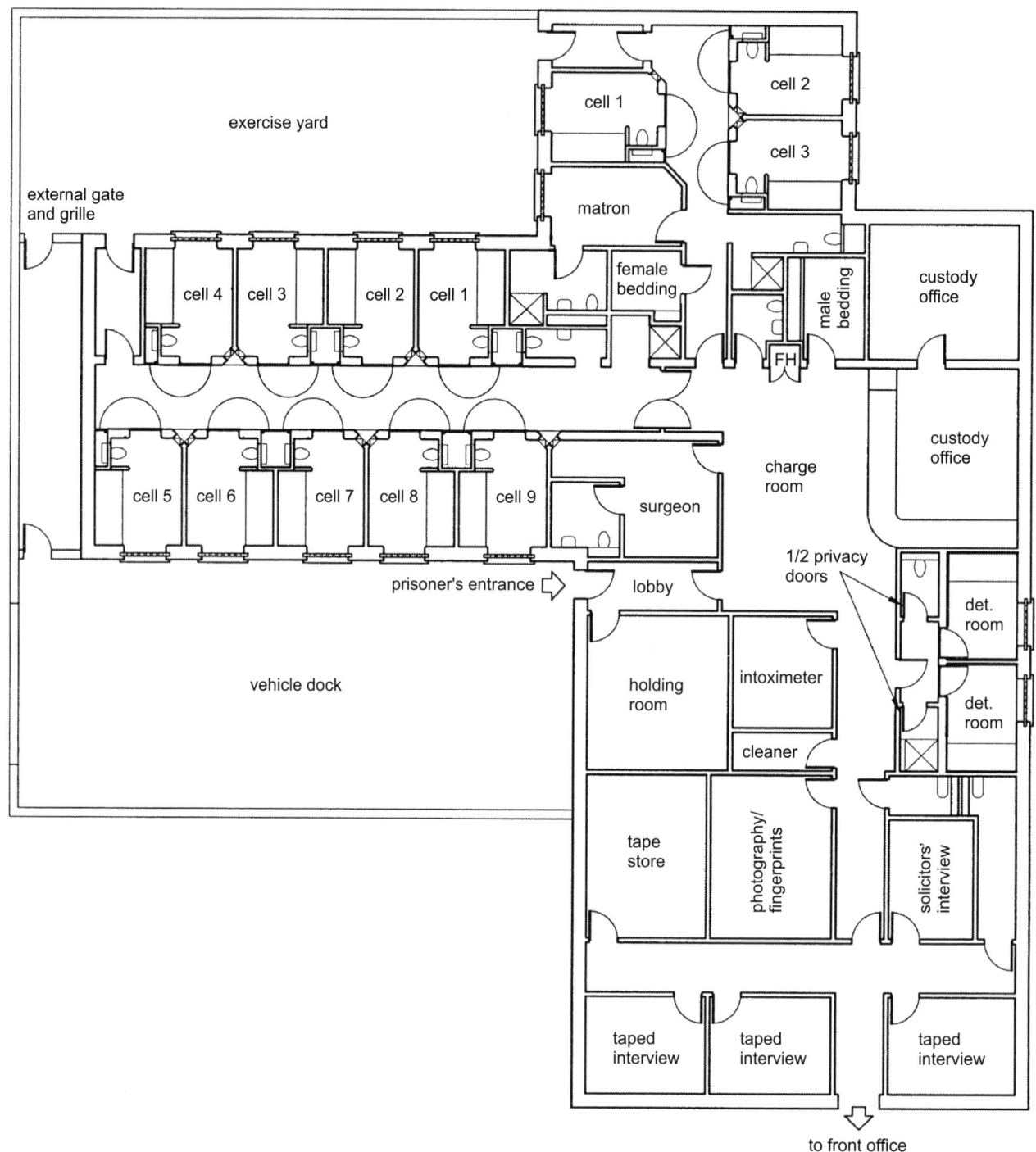

18.19 *Plan of a custody suite (for security reasons this is based on the design principles, but is not an actual example)*

Doors
All doors should be prisoner-proof and flush.

Cell furniture
These should not be of timber or able to be prised loose to make a tool or a weapon.

Ventilation
Casings to trunking should be secure against breakage and use by prisoners to facilitate suicide. Grilles under cell benches should be securely fixed using non-withdrawable screws. High-level airvents with perforations should not be larger than 4.7 mm diameter, of a material that will break under load and fitted flush with the wall surface.

Lighting
Cell light fittings should be fitted flush with the ceiling with unwithdrawable screws. They should have twin lamp holders and plastic lenses. Electrical supplies should not be exposed and the switches should be outside the cell with cover plates that cannot be removed to gain access to live parts.

Heating
Electric radiant heaters with exposed wiring should not be used to heat cells, neither should exposed hot water radiators. There should be no protrusions of any kind to which a ligature could be attached.

Cell call system
This should comprise a press button within the cell fitted flush with the wall operating a bell and indicator light externally. It should be

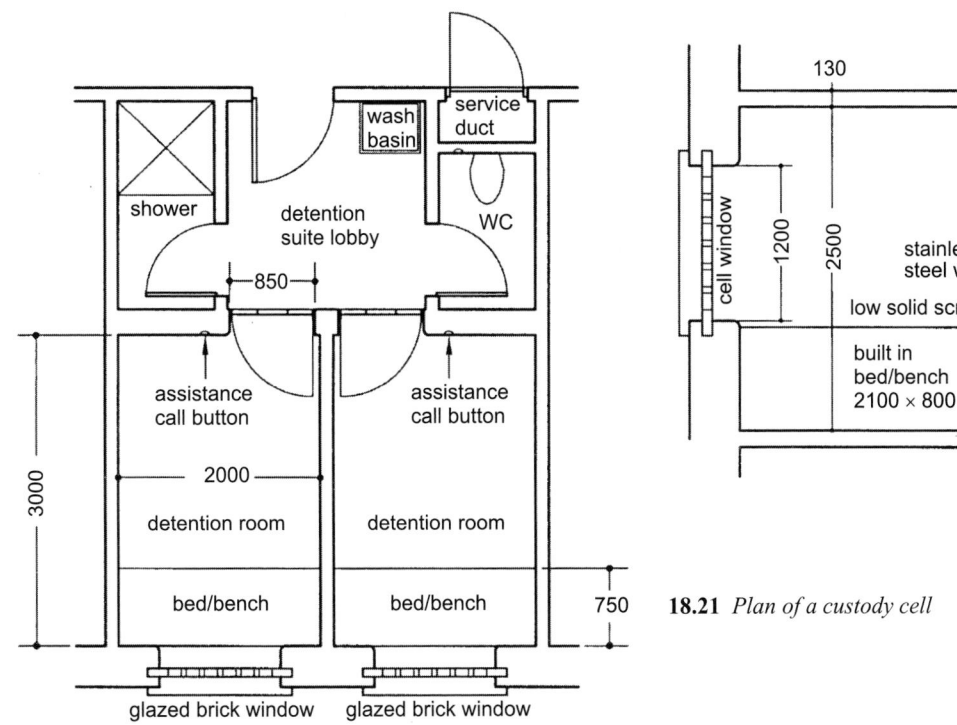

18.20 *Plan of a detention suite*

18.21 *Plan of a custody cell*

on a separate circuit from the lighting, and the indicator light board should be under constant observation by the officer-in-charge.

Maintenance
Damaged cells should be withdrawn from use.

4 BIBLIOGRAPHY
Department for Communities and Local Government CLG (2007) *Achieving Design Quality in Fire and Rescue Service Building*.
Home Office *Police Buildings Design Guide* (2010).
Nadel, B. (2004) *Building Security: Handbook for Architectural Planning and Design*. McGraw Hill.
NHS Estates, *Health Building Note 44.***a** *Dimensions*
b *Turning circles*

19 Hospitals

David Clarke

David Clarke is an architect with a background in hospital design. Formerly of Nightingale Associates, he now runs his own consultancy, Clearwell Healthcare Planning Ltd

CI/SfB: 41

KEY POINTS:

- *Health services are trying to move closer to the patient*
- *More work is being undertaken in the primary sector*
- *Shorter stays in hospital are the norm*

Contents

1 Introduction
2 Services delivery
3 Facilities design
4 Healthcare provision – activities
5 Support services – outsourcing
6 Publications and guidance

1 INTRODUCTION

1.1 General

The provision of health services, and therefore the design of hospitals and other health facilities, has long been a politically charged issue which is subject to frequent policy change; the agendas and administrative structures which govern the provision of healthcare in the UK obviously impact on the design of the health estate, but this is a subject which is far too vast and changeable to set in detail here. The broad principles of hospital design, and notions of best practice, described below were accurate at the time of publication.

A healthcare building includes a large number of functions and activities across a range of healthcare provision services and non-healthcare support services such as laundries, kitchens, supplies and disposal services and estates maintenance facilities. These were previously collectively known as departments. We would like to avoid the use of this term as it has its history in an inflexible organisational structure. This is reflected in a building based on historic concepts of standard sized, standard types of healthcare buildings (Figure 19.1). District General Hospitals, Teaching Hospitals, Community Hospitals are examples of these stereotypes. The terminology will continue in use for some time but this chapter aims to separate out activities and the physical requirements for these activities. In some cases, these will be rooms, in others suites. Each could be applied in the context of a larger or smaller facility.

The almost universal use of market tested subcontracting of some services has also changed the key drivers in the design of elements such as catering facilities which are now largely briefed and designed in detail by the partner organisation responsible for the provision of the service. Some elements straddle clinical and non-clinical support services such as pathology services; this particular service is subject to a Department of Health mandate for the provision of central services supporting a number of different healthcare facilities in an area. Similarly sterilising services, known as centralised facilities, pathology and equipment sterilisation (CSSD) or HSDU are now considered under the heading of decontamination and are subject to a similar strategic approach by the Department of Health. This is also a separate area which will not be covered in detail by this chapter. Other facilities such as pharmacy services are heavily influenced by technology, in this case robotic dispensing, and a categoric template is determined in conjunction with providers of such equipment.

2 SERVICES DELIVERY

2.1 Drivers of change

In the search for ways of containing health service costs, health care delivery through the hierarchy of the organisation and the corresponding hierarchy of building types is also being reappraised. The aspirations of an extensive assessment of patient needs and wishes were the subject of a Department of Health review entitled *Your Health, Your Care, Your Say* (2006); this extended the momentum towards providing services which are devolved from the expensive acute sector out towards primary care organisations, community services and even into the home.

Similarly, the length of patient stay in hospital is being reduced; patients are being required earlier than before to recover at home, where they need additional community support; and many basic diagnostic and treatment procedures are being tested in the primary care setting. One consequence for the acute hospital is that patients who remain are, on average, more dependent and the procedures, on average, more sophisticated and complex.

2.2 The hospital and the patient

Management concern for patients' response to the hospital service and environment encompasses such diverse issues as first impressions, signposting, waiting times in out-patient and accident departments and relationship with the ward nurse. It has recently been extended to reassessment of the basic relationships between treatment departments and the in-patient areas they serve. The idea of a hospital organised so as to ameliorate some of the more distressing aspects of patient stay – being shunted around the hospital, waiting in strange departments, disorientation and lack of a sense of place which is their own – found expression in the 1980s–1990s as a 'patient-focused hospital', often renamed in the UK as a 'patient centred hospital'.

The principle which relied on the decentralisation of diagnostic services towards, principally, ward areas to reduce the amount patients needed to travel around the hospital also required a degree of multi-skilling which resulted in only limited implementation. Some physiotherapy, which had previously been centralized, moved to ward areas and bed areas but this was carried out by roving members of the physiotherapy team. The result has been a substantial increase in the required size of a bed bay to accommodate these activities, see Table I. Bed bay areas have also increased as the impact of lifting patients, use of hoists and more demand for the safety of nursing staff have come forward as priorities.

2.3 Information technology

The implementation of information technology has not had the substantial impact on the design of the building that had been anticipated. The dramatic reductions in the size of computer equipment, almost universal use of flat-screen displays and the relatively slow implementation of Patient Records systems and its evolution to the use of hand held pads rather than conventional computers has not generated significant effects. Medical records are still kept in paper form and the most appropriate future provision is for such areas to be located and able to adapt to future alternative uses.

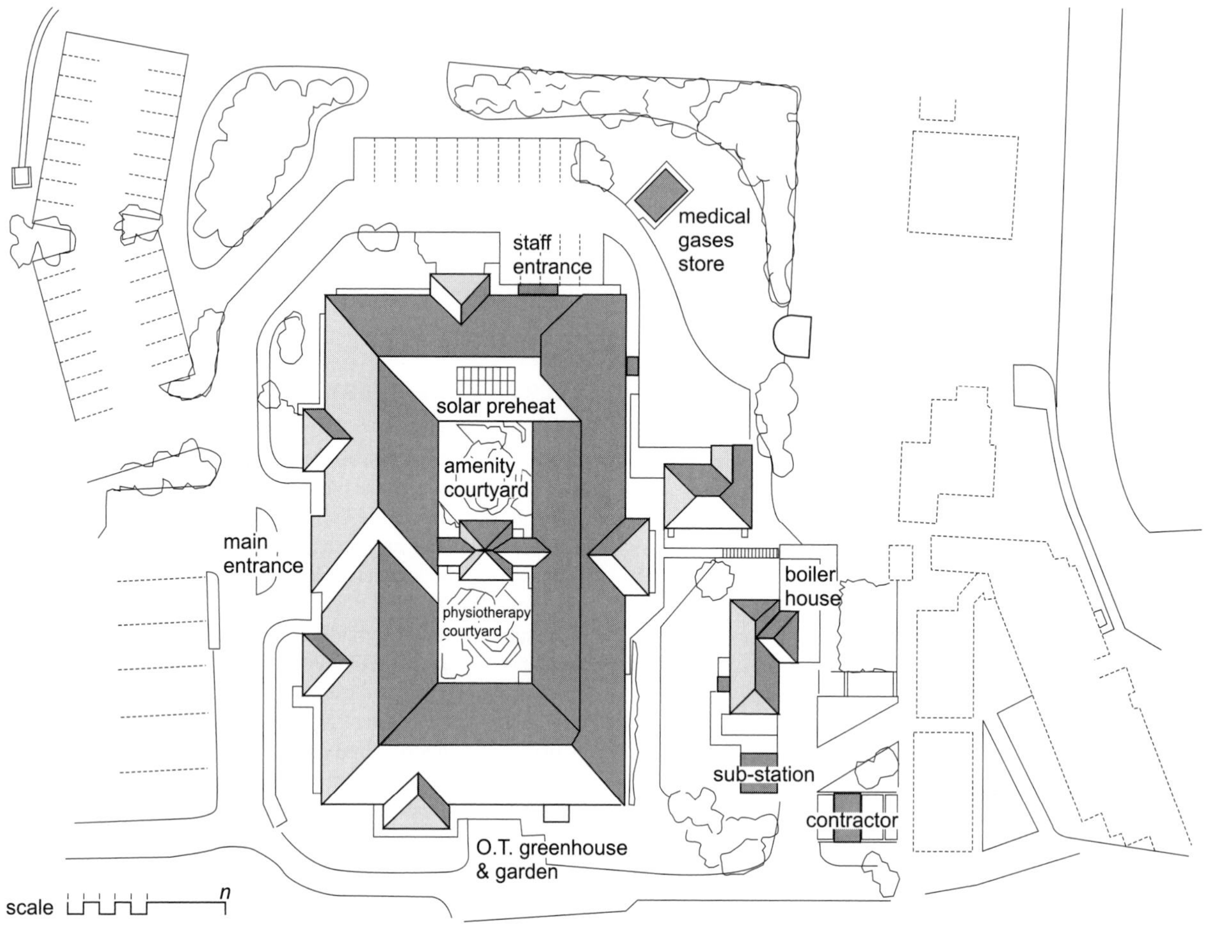

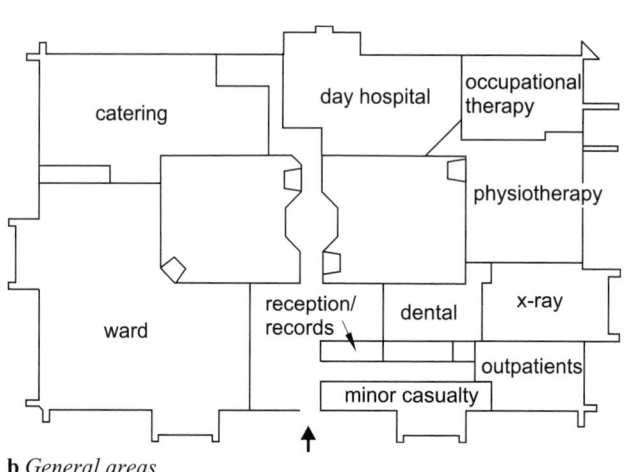

scale

a *Site plan*

b *General areas*

19.1 *Community Hospital in Mold. Clwyd Architect: William H. Simpson, Chief Architect, WHCSA*

3 FACILITIES DESIGN

3.1 Design drivers for the patients' experience

The Patients Charter, first published in 1991, set out objectives for the health service based on identified reasonable expectations of patients. These included timescales for delivery of services and importantly issues related to privacy and dignity that should be afforded to patients, particularly during a hospital stay.

It is now paramount, although often not achievable in older hospital premises, that toilet facilities are immediately available to patients, not only in single bedrooms but in multi-bed bays if provided. It is not acceptable for patients to walk through or be seen by patients of the opposite sex in order to visit bathroom areas.

An example of a four-bed bay with ensuite accommodation has been developed by Nightingale Associates to suite a number of issues related to multi-bed ward design (Figure 19.2).

Single bedrooms have advantages for privacy, dignity, confidentiality and safety. However, surveys have identified that by no means all patients wish to be in a single bedroom. A four-bed ward generates not only a small community with opportunities for companionship, but also a support structure in the event of a patient

Table I Hospitals, typical room dimensions

Suggested areas for clinical and clinical support rooms with dimensions

	Room type	Width	Length	Area	Notes	Areas where used
1.01	Consult/Exam Two Side access	4.3	3.9	16.6		
1.02	Consult/Exam Single Side access	3.8	3.9	14.6		
1.03	Interview Room	3.3	3.3	10.6		
1.04	Treatment Room	4.2	4.0	16.8		
1.05	Venepuncture Room	2.7	3.0	8.1		
1.06	Patient Recovery (2 patients)	5.0	4.4	21.8		
1.07	Near Patient Testing Room	3.0	2.4	7.2		
1.08	Clean Supply Room	3.6	4.2	14.9		
1.09	Clean Utility Room	3.5	4.2	14.7		
1.10	Dirty Utility (Outpatients)	2.8	3.0	8.4		
1.11	Dirty Utility (Inpatient)	2.9	4.2	12.2		
1.12	Cleaners' Room	2.3	3.0	6.9	Dependent on FM provider	
1.13	Disposal Hold			10.0	Dependent on FM provider	
1.14	Relatives' Overnight Stay	3.7	3.7	13.7	Access to ensuite required	
1.15	Pantry/Refreshment Area	2.9	2.4	6.8		
1.16	Staff Rest Room	4.3	8.4	35.7		
1.17	Mini Kitchen (within Staff Rest)	2.2	0.6	1.3 0.0	Requires adjacent handwash	
2.01	Ambulant WC	1.1	1.7	1.8	Assumes concealed cistern not included in dimensions	Only areas for staff
2.02	Semi-Ambulant WC	1.2	1.8	2.1	Assumes concealed cistern not included in dimensions	All patient access ambulant WCs
2.03	Independent Wheelchair Accessible WC	2.0	1.9	3.8	Equivalent to Disabled WCs in public areas	
2.04	Assisted WC	2.8	2.7	7.6	Allows access for 2 assistants	
2.05	Standard Shower Room	2.3	1.1	2.5	Only suitable for ambulant	
2.06	Semi-ambulant shower room incl. WC	2.6	2.5	6.5		
2.07	Wheelchair Access Shower	2.6	2.0	5.2	Independent wheelchair user, no WC	
2.08	Assisted Shower & WC	2.3	3.1	7.1		
2.09	Ensuite full access WC/Shower	2.3	2.1	4.8	Assumes overhead hoist and door + folding door access	
2.10	Semi-ambulant accessible bathroom	2.3	2.7	6.1	Also possible with bidet at 2.4 × 3.1	
2.11	Independent Wheelchair Accessible Bathroom	2.7	3.3	8.9		
2.12	Assisted Bathroom Side Access	2.4	4.9	11.8	Assumes largest hi-lo bath Min. 1.7 × 4.65 m	
2.13	Assisted Bathroom End Access	2.9	5.1	14.6	Assumes largest hi-lo bath Min. 2.9 × 4.83 m	
2.14	Nappy Change	1.7	2.6	4.4		
2.15	Child Change	3.3	3.3	10.7		
2.16	Changing Room – Standard	1.1	1.8	2.0		
2.17	Changing Room – Wheelchair	2.2	2.0	4.4		

requiring assistance while being unable to use the nurse call system. A provision of single rooms is essential for those who either prefer that ward type or for whom it is a clinical necessity. Where multi-bedrooms are provided interview rooms are required for confidential discussions between the clinical staff and the patient. This will be disruptive to the doctors' ward round but of importance to the wellbeing of the patient.

The drive towards 100 per cent single rooms is laudable but not universally agreed upon as an objective. Current good practice is inclined to the provision of 75 per cent single rooms with four-bed bays providing the balance.

High-quality architecture and internal environment is demonstrated not only to enhance the experience of patients, staff and visitors but also to reduce the recuperation time required by patients. There is clear evidence, for example, in intensive care environments, that daylight and external views improve recovery times.

3.2 Design agendas

Hospital design is also the subject of a variety of centrally driven design guides and 'agendas' via organisations such as the Commission for Architecture and the Built Environment (CABE), the Building Research Establishment (BRE) and the Construction Industry Council (CIC).

Two significant initiatives that have emerged over recent years are the 'AEDET' design toolkit and the 'NEAT' environmental assessment procedure.

AEDET ('achieving excellence design evaluation toolkit', now known as 'AEDET Evolution') evaluates a design by posing a series of clear, non-technical statements which encompass the three areas

of Impact, Build Quality and Functionality. Each area is assessed across a range of specific criteria:

- 'Impact'
  ○ Character and innovation
  ○ Form and materials
  ○ Staff and patient environment
  ○ Urban and social regeneration

- 'Build quality'
  ○ Performance
  ○ Engineering
  ○ Construction

- 'Functionality'
  ○ Use
  ○ Access
  ○ Space

The idea is that if all three areas provide added value, the combined result will be excellence.

A further tool, ASPECT (standing for 'a staff and patient environment calibration tool'), provides extra assessment processes which can supplement AEDET. Details of both tools can be found on the Department of Health's online portal http://design.dh. gov.uk.

The NHS Environmental Assessment Tool (NEAT) is a self-assessment procedure, based on 'yes' or 'no' answers, that helps to assess the negative impact healthcare facilities may have on the environment. NEAT can be applied to any type of NHS healthcare

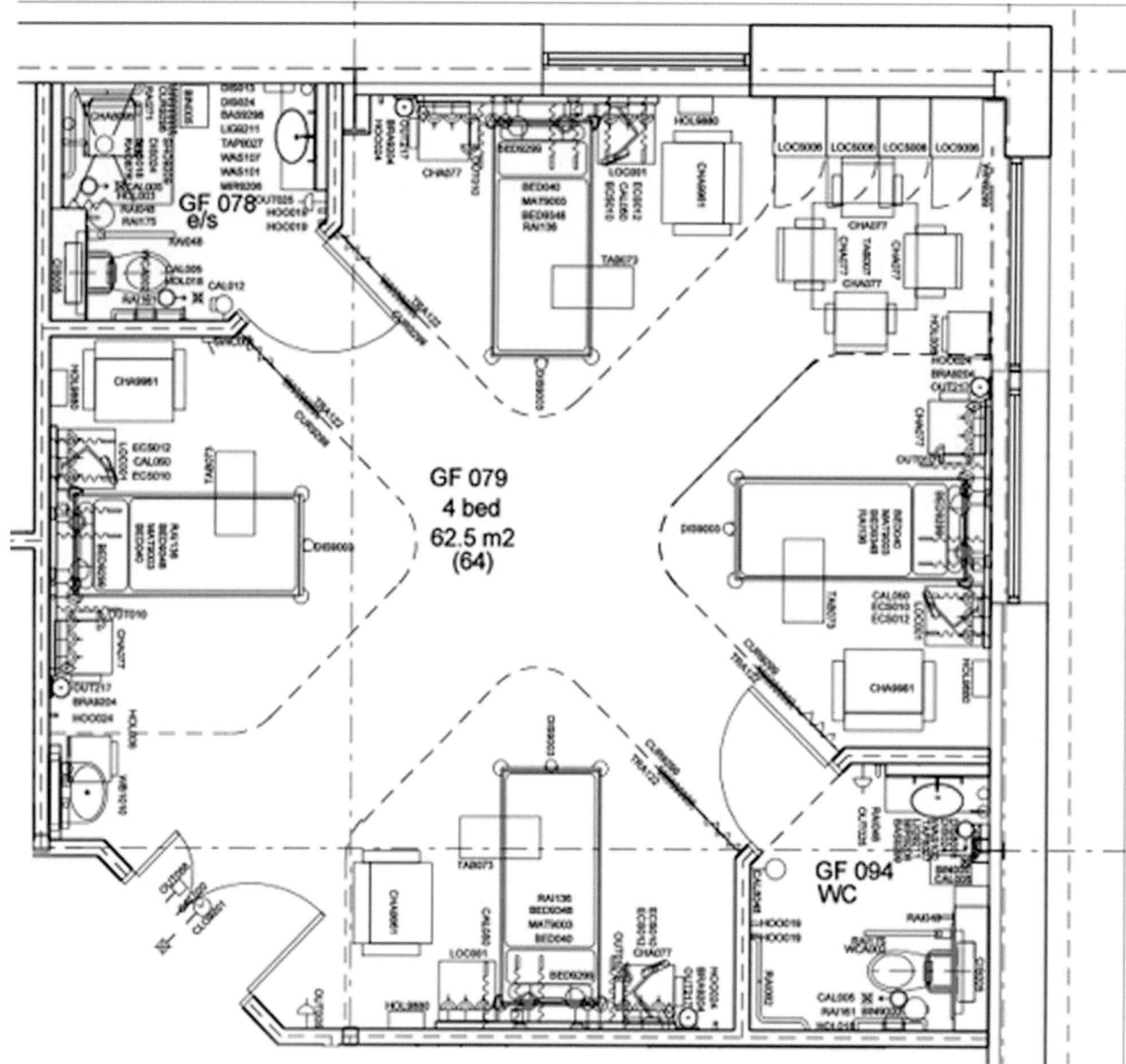

19.2 *The four-bed 'New Nightingale Ward', designed by Nightingale Associates*

facility. The Excel-based system issues a numerical score along the following lines:

- below 25 per cent fail
- over 25 per cent pass
- over 40 per cent good
- over 55 per cent very good
- over 70 per cent excellent.

NEAT requires all new buildings achieve a rating of Excellent; refurbished buildings should achieve a rating of Very Good. NEAT covers 10 areas:

- Management
- Energy
- Transport
- Water
- Materials
- Landuse and ecology
- Pollution
- Internal environment
- Social factors
- Operational waste.

The toolkit can be downloaded from DH websites.

3.3 Functional relationships in healthcare buildings

The discussions of individual clinical areas below includes reference to adjacencies appropriate for efficient usage of space and minimising unnecessary travel by patients and staff (Figure 19.3).

Logical adjacencies also ease the understanding of the building by patients, visitors and staff who are unfamiliar with the layout. Clear signposting, or way-finding, is obviously essential but the principle that 'people do not read signs' should not be dismissed. Table II illustrates some of the relationships between major activity spaces and their associated activities.

3.4 Future proofing – designing for change – growth and shrinkage

The delivery of healthcare services and the consequent healthcare estate configurations will continue to change. As more acute services are delivered closer to home, or at home, different building types will appear. Increased partnerships with the private sector will develop alongside partnerships with leisure, commerce and retail delivering healthcare closer to the places people spend their days.

While the concept of flexibility has for many years been a criterion of judgement about the quality of a healthcare building design, it is now recognised that flexibility, and its consequent cost penalties, should be considered more in the context of adaptability. The continued use of steel and concrete frames for the primary structure in major healthcare buildings provides the greatest

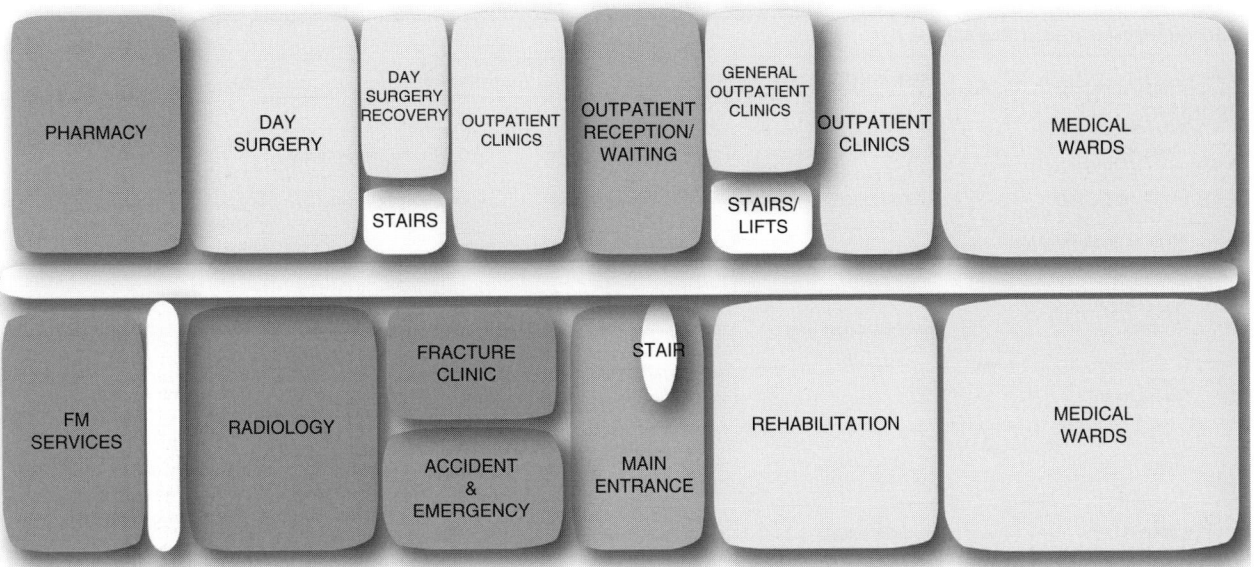

19.3 *Relationship diagram of Darent Valley Hospital in Dartford Kent, an early PFI hospital designed by Paulley Nightingale Architects and completed in 2002*

Table II Hospital department relationship in an acute hospital

Department relationships in an acute hospital

Activities		Access requirements	Location	Relationship	Notes
In-patient services					
1	Adult acute wards		Level not important	Surgical beds to theatres	
2	Children's wards	To outdoor play area	Preferably ground floor	Theatre Includes parents overnight stay	
3	Geriatric wards		Preferably ground floor	Geriatric day hospital Rehabilitation	
4	Intensive therapy unit		Level not important	Accident dept; theatres	
5	Maternity dept			Antenatal clinic in OPD	
5.1	Wards			Delivery suite	
5.2	Delivery suite	Ambulance access may be required for dept as a whole	Level not important	Wards, theatres SCBU	Area includes dept. admin, etc.
5.3	Special care baby unit			Delivery suite	
6	Psychiatric dept	External access	Self-contained units may need private internal access		
6.1	Wards				
6.2	Day hospital				
7	Isolation ward	Private external access for infected cases	Level not important, but see 'access'	Children's dept	
Diagnosis and treatment					
8	Operating dept		Level not important	Surgical beds; accident dept	Special ventilation needs include refrigeration
9	X-ray dept		Usually ground floor	Accident dept; fracture clinic	Special ceiling heights and heavy equipment
10	Radiotherapy		Level not important	X-ray dept	
11	Pathology dept	External supply access may be required	Level not important but see 'access'	Radio isotopes, outpatient dept	Special attention to ventilation of noxious fumes
12	Mortuary and postmortem	Private external access for undertakers' vehicles	Level not important, but see 'access'	Morbid anatomy Section of pathology	Special attention to ventilation of postmortem area
13	Rehabilitation	Ambulance access	Ground floor	Medical and geriatric beds	Includes physiotherapy gymnasium (extra height), hydrotherapy pool (special engineering requirements) and occupational therapy
14	Accident and emergency	Ambulance access for emergency cases	Usually ground floor – see 'access'	Direct access to X-ray dept, fracture clinic, main theatres, intensive therapy unit	Relationships assume no separate X-ray or theatres in accident department
15	Out-patient department including fracture clinic, antenatal, dental, clinical measurement, ears, nose and throat, eyes, children's outpatients and comprehensive assessment	Pedestrian and ambulance access for large numbers, approx. 300–400 morning and afternoon	Main reception and waiting area usually ground floor but parts may be on other levels	Fracture clinic to accident dept, convenient access to pharmacy, good access to medical records dept-often adjacent	
16	Elderly day hospital	Ambulance access, access to outdoor area	Usually ground floor – see 'access'	Elderly wards, rehabilitation dept	
17	Adult day ward		Level not important	Theatres, X-ray, pathology	Includes additional space for 'sitting' cases

(continued)

Table II (continued)

Department relationships in an acute hospital

Activities		Access requirements	Location	Relationship	Notes
Support services					
18	Paramedical:				
18.1	Pharmacy	External supply, access may be required	Usually ground floor – see 'access'	OPD. hospital supply routes	
18.2	Sterile supply dept	External supply access	Usually ground floor – see 'access'	Hospital supply routes, operating dept	Special ventilation needs – wild heat problems
18.3	Medical illustration		Level not important		Often using digital images anywhere in the hospital
18.4	Anaesthetics dept		Level not important	Theatres, intensive therapy	
19	Non-clinical:				
19.1	Kitchens	External supply access	May be ground floor (for supply access) above ground (nearer to bed areas)	Hospital supply routes and bed areas served – dining room servery	
19.2	Dining room		Level not important but see 'kitchens'	Access from kitchen to servery, good staff access from whole hospital	
19.3	Stores	Supplies vehicle	Usually in services area, ground floor	Hospital supply routes	Special height may be needed for mechanical handling, increased use of 'Just in Time' provisions
19.4	Laundry	Supplies vehicle	Ground floor, service area	Hospital supply routes	
19.5	Boilerhouse – fuel storage	Fuel delivery vehicles	Usually ground floor in services area but may be elsewhere (e.g. rooftop) depending on choice of fuel	Work and transport dept	
19.6	Works – transport dept	Vehicle parking	Usually ground door in services area	Boiler house	
19.7	Administration		Level not important (tel. exchange ground floor)		Includes telephone exchange Purely administration functions could be off site
19.8	Main entrance accommodation	External access for inpatients, visitors, perhaps out-patients and staff	Usually ground floor – see 'access'	In-patient reception area or medical records main hospital horizontal and vertical communication routes	Also includes facilities such as bank, shops, etc.
19.9	Medical records		Level not important, Ground floor suits ground floor – see 'relationships'	Hospital communication routes	Only short term 'live' records on site, 24 h call up for others
20	Staff:				
20.1	Education centre		Level not important		
20.2	Non-resident staff changing		On route between staff entrance and departments served, level not important	Hospital supply route for clean and dirty linen	
20.3	Occupational health service	Level not important			May be in OPD complex
21	Miscellaneous: This will include car parking, garages, medical gas installation, recreational buildings				

level of adaptability although within these two principles there are significant variations which, in themselves, increase or decrease adaptability. Hospitals are very intensive in their requirements for penetrable floor slabs, walls tend to follow column lines and it must be recognised that the least penetrable locations in a floor are likely to be around columns and along the line of major structural beams. The introduction of penetrable zones in these areas will substantially improve the ease with which future adaptations can be made.

Expansion zones at the perimeter of buildings must be considered, with the capability of major circulation routes extending beyond the envelope without significant disruption. Expansion also occurs within the building for particular activities. Some specialties can be reasonably predicted as likely to expand, radiology and day surgery for example. Some can be predicted as likely to reduce, medical records for example. Some are likely to be relocated, CSSD being an example. Placing facilities likely to expand alongside those that will contract enables an inbuilt flexibility which can minimise the effect of disruption in the future.

Services may also contract. As more activity moves out of an acute hospital environment, they may not be replaced by an increase in the remaining acute services. The capability for both expansion and contraction is required to be demonstrated at business case stage and considered as part of the Strategic Outline Case.

3.5 Fire design

Healthcare buildings have to comply with requirements for fire safety and means of escape: those for hospitals are set out in Firecode published by the Department of Health. This guidance is covered by the Documents HTM 05-01, HTM 05-02 and HTM 05-03 in various sections. This guidance is deemed to satisfy Building Regulation Part B requirements. The major change is in the responsibility of the NHS client in England to prepare a Fire Safety Policy in response to HTM 05-01 Managing Healthcare Fire to inform the design process. The requirements for Scotland and Wales may differ, the 05-01 process is also not mandatory for Foundation Trusts. Some of the requirements influence overall form and will be dealt with here; others affect internal organisation and will be dealt with below.

Relationship of departments by fire characteristics
The risk to human life is greatest in those areas where patients are confined to bed and especially where they would be incapable, in the event of a fire, of moving to a place of safety without assistance. Those areas are termed normal dependency or very high dependency departments.

Departments posing the fire threat are those such as supply zones, fuel stores and other materials stores containing large quantities of flammable materials and those in which ignition is more likely such as kitchens, laundries, laboratories and boiler houses, referred to as

Hazard Departments. The principle to be followed is that independent departments should not be placed adjacent to or above Hazard Departments unless protected by a 60 min barrier; auto suppression in the Hazard Department is required in some instances. Very High Dependency departments, such as ITU, Operating Theatres or Special Care Baby Units should not be located adjacent, vertically or horizontally to Hazard Departments. These requirements are noted in Table 1 in Section 3 of HTM 05-02.

Hospital Streets
The Hospital Street, a primary circulation route between areas of the hospital, can form a major fire-fighting platform. It also provides an alternative to an adjacent department for the purposes of progressive horizontal evacuation. Hospital Streets have particular requirements of maximum travel distances defined within Firecode. It is not necessary to provide a designated Hospital Street but a central circulation spine would naturally fall into this category.

Where a Hospital Street is designated, and in major units it has significant advantages for fire design and fire fighting, particular rules apply. The street must have a minimum width between handrails of 3 m. On the ground floor it must have at least two final exits no more than 180m apart. On upper levels a minimum of two staircases are required at a maximum distance of 60 m apart. The distance from a department entrance to a staircase should be no more than 30 m. This is not an exhaustive list of requirements, reference to HTM 05-02 paras 5.40–5.45 should be made.

Compartmentation
Compartmentation of a large building into areas of limited size, divided by fire-resisting partitions, allows escape away from the fire source into a nearby place of relative safety in the initial stages of the fire. In a hospital, it is essential that this movement is horizontal. Lifts cannot generally be used in a fire and staircase evacuation of physically dependent patients takes far too long to be a practical means of escape in this first stage.

The primary compartment is by floor, each floor being a 60 min fire compartment unless the building is above 30 m or nine stories in height in which case it is 90 min.

On each floor, the compartments are limited to 2000 m² in area and a minimum of three for each floor, one of which may be the Hospital Street, are required to satisfy the above conditions.

In practice, it is unusual to have a compartment as large as this. The requirements of section 5 for compartmentation by department boundaries will generally generate compartments of about 1000 m² as a maximum.

If a compartment is larger than 750 m², or which provides access to more than 30 patients, there is a requirement to sub-compartment the area. In general, more compartments should be provided on each floor, particular attention should be made to vulnerable patient groups such as the elderly and those with limited mobility such as orthopaedic patients. Further compartmentation is necessary in Very High Dependancy departments such as operating theatres and other critical care areas.

Sprinklers are not normally used in hospital buildings but in central urban areas may be required. Firecode includes requirements for both circumstances.

In a single storey construction, the maximum compartment area is 3000 m² although similar departmental rules apply as noted above.

Travel distances and escape routes
There is a limitation on maximum travel distance within a compartment and sub-compartments. Within a compartment the maximum distance is 60 m, within a sub-compartment 30 m. There is also a limit on travel distance to a major escape route. The escape route is a protected, smoke-free path leading to an unenclosed space at ground level and the main Hospital Street is commonly designed to satisfy these criteria. A general rule is that a compartment should

have an exit to either two adjacent departments or one department and a Hospital Street.

It should be noted that most areas of a hospital are occupied by trained staff for substantial parts of the day and in some cases 24 hours. Unoccupied rooms such as stores and rooms which have a hazardous function, such as kitchens, or contain flammable materials represent the greatest fire risk and are designated as Fire Hazard Rooms. These rooms are required to maintain 30 min fire integrity and insulation.

3.6 Control of infection
The control of infection is a vital part of healthcare provision, and measures include behavioural and procedural ones (including the frequent washing of hands, use of alcohol gel and access restrictions) to design tactics (everything that is designed will have to be cleaned – all surfaces should be accessible to cleaning teams).

It should be recognised that infection by different pathogens can be minimised by different methods. Alcohol gel, for example, can work against MRSA but not C. Difficile which requires meticulous hand washing. The design of the environment cannot in itself eliminate the risk of infection but the strategic placement of hand wash basins and alcohol gel dispensers can enable good management by encouraging good practice.

Horizontal surfaces which are difficult to clean represent a hazard, radiused skirtings and the elimination of inaccessible areas, behind WCs for example, assist a cleaning regime in being effective.

The presence of highly infectious and dangerous pathogens such as MRSA and C. Difficile is a constant concern for medical staff and patients, and the situation regarding these bacteria is very changeable. Designers should be mindful of the dangers these bacteria pose and should take advice from medical and infection control experts at all stages of the design process.

4 HEALTHCARE PROVISION – ACTIVITIES
4.1 Emergency care
The provision of facilities for emergency care has evolved to enable cost-effective provision to be provided as quickly as possible. Greater emphasis is placed on paramedic services by response teams to emergency calls and on the provision of facilities for minor injuries. Minor Injury Units (MIU) are providing services from approximately 8.00am–11.00pm for patients not requiring the full scope of emergency care. This requires a degree of 'self-diagnosis' and has yet to achieve its full potential in efficiency savings.

Emergency care is increasingly being associated with other elements of critical care such as intensive therapy and operating theatres as a management unit and the overall facility is now under the umbrella of critical care. Emergency care has an obvious requirement for ground-floor access; operating theatres, being highly dependent on mechanical ventilation provisions tend to be on an upper floor. Dedicated vertical circulation is therefore important between the Accident & Emergency (A&E) and operating theatres. An alternative would be the provision of an interstitial plant floor. The Intensive Therapy Unit (ITU) would usually be co-located with the operating theatres and would share this vertical access from the A&E (Figures 19.4 and 19.5).

Specialist A&E facilities for cardiac care may be provided.

Because of the urgent nature of a high proportion of accident cases, the relationship with supporting departments is crucial. In particular, there should be direct access – by separate entrance if necessary – to the X-ray department for speedy diagnosis; alternatively separate X-ray facilities can be provided within A&E. Circulation of patients on beds or trolleys means that dimensions for these items are critical (Figures 19.6 and 19.7).

If X-ray facilities are not integral to the A&E facility a means of providing 24 hour access to a limited section of the X-ray department will be required.

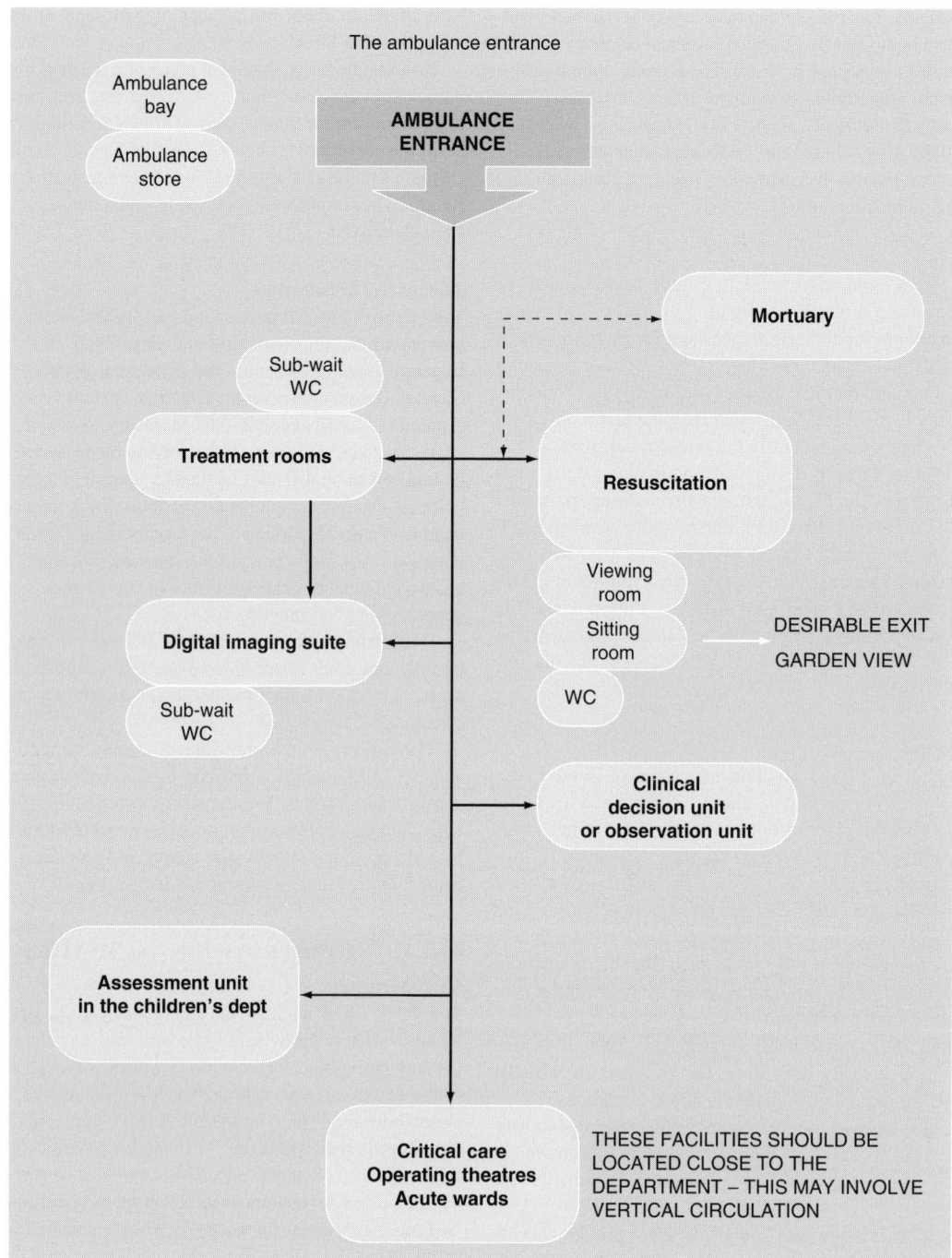

The ambulance entrance

Ambulance bay

Ambulance store

AMBULANCE ENTRANCE

Mortuary

Sub-wait WC

Treatment rooms

Resuscitation

Viewing room

Sitting room

DESIRABLE EXIT

GARDEN VIEW

Digital imaging suite

WC

Sub-wait WC

Clinical decision unit or observation unit

Assessment unit in the children's dept

Critical care Operating theatres Acute wards

THESE FACILITIES SHOULD BE LOCATED CLOSE TO THE DEPARTMENT – THIS MAY INVOLVE VERTICAL CIRCULATION

19.4 *Diagram showing the relationships between spaces in a hospital emergency facility for patients arriving by ambulance. Source: Health Building Note 22*

Close proximity is also required to the fracture clinic because of the weight of traffic.

As direct access as possible should be provided from the A&E department to the operating department although its location has to respect the overriding needs of surgical wards and the ITU.

Out-patients should have access to the OPD directly through the main entrance. The OPD has the largest single daily requirement for provision of patients' records but whether this dictates a close relationship with the medical records department depends on the organisation and form of the records themselves.

There will be considerable traffic from the OPD to the X-ray department and to the fracture clinic (which is usually shared with the A&E department). Until recently, a large proportion of out-patients called in at the pharmacy with their prescriptions but patients are now encouraged to use external community pharmacies and the location of the hospital department is not so critical, although it should be reasonably easy to find.

4.2 Invasive medicine

An operating department consists of one or more operating suites together with common ancillary accommodation such as changing and rest rooms, reception, transfer and recovery areas. An operating suite includes the operating theatre with its own anaesthetic room, preparation room (for instrument trolleys), disposal room, scrub-up and gowning area and an exit area which may be part of the circulation space (Figure 19.9). An operating theatre is the room in which surgical operations and some diagnostic procedures are carried out.

Infection control is one of the key criteria in operating department design and this is one of the few departments requiring air conditioning that includes humidity control. To assist infection control, four access zones are defined: operative zone (theatre and preparation room); restricted zone for those related to activities in the operative zone who need to be gowned (scrub-up, anaesthesia and utility rooms); limited access zone for those who need to

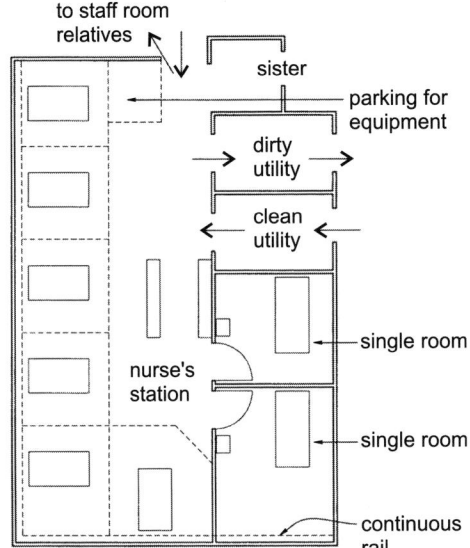

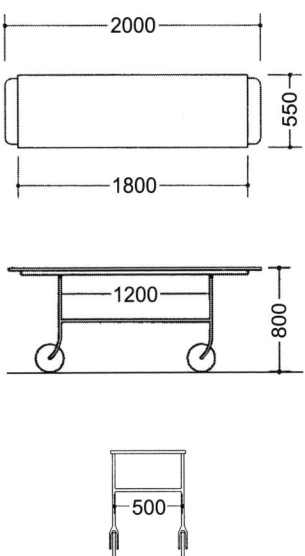

19.5 *Intensive therapy unit (ITU). Cubicle curtains are not used but movable screens may be. The location of the bed within the space varies with needs of patient, staff and equipment*

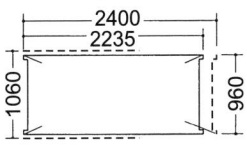

a *Plan*

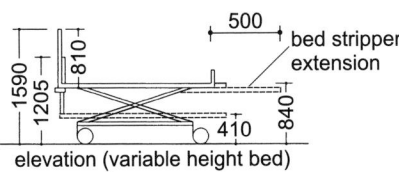

b *Elevation of the variable height bed*

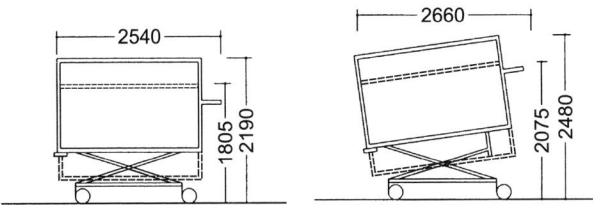

c *Elevations of the variable height bed with balkan beam*

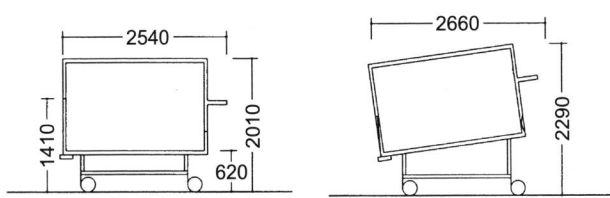

d *Elevations of fixed height bed with balkan beam*

19.6 *King's Fund bed; critical dimensions given. These are likely to occur frequently and/or importantly. They may be increased by the various accessories which are available*

19.7 *Hospital trolley*

enter areas adjacent to the above (recovery, mobile X-ray store, darkroom, staff rest, cleaner); and general access zone to which anyone is admitted (staff changing, porters' base, transfer area, stores).

Separate 'clean' and 'dirty' corridors are no longer required for infection control reasons, although the four major components of traffic (patients, staff, supplies and disposal) may be segregated, in a number of possible combinations, into two corridors – on either side of the theatre – for reasons of good workflow.

There are strong economic arguments for centralising operating facilities in one department, located on the same floor as the surgical beds and in particular paediatric surgical beds should be on the same floor located as close as is feasible.

The ITU should be immediately adjacent with direct access which does not require usage of the main hospital circulation routes.

The journey from the A&E area should be as direct as possible although it may not be feasible for them to occur on the same floor.

4.3 Diagnostic imaging

Also known as radiology, this is usually taken to refer to the use of X-rays for diagnostic imaging; when used for treatment, the term radiotherapy is used (Figure 19.10).

In addition to the conventional techniques for imaging bone structures, supplemented in the case of soft organs by the use of radio-opaque materials such as barium, an X-ray Department will now generally accommodate a computerised tomography (CT) scanner which builds up three-dimensional images and a unit for magnetic resonance imaging (MRI).

CT and MRI have a significantly increased purpose in the rapid diagnosis of tumours and are used in increasing numbers by emergency services, particularly associated with head injuries and for cardiac patients. Although MRI does not use X-ray radiation, very particular design requirements are needed for the MRI examination rooms because of the magnetic field generated by the magnet. The influence of the magnet extends beyond the examination room to an extent dependent on the power of the magnet and the amount of shielding built into the enclosure. All materials within the examination room need to be non-ferrous and MRI compatible. CT does use X-ray radiation and, since it uses 'slices' to build up a three-dimensional image a CT investigation will result in a far higher dose of radiation for the patient than a conventional X-ray; for this reason, it is used as sparingly as possible on one patient.

Of even greater impact in terms of throughput – and still growing – is imaging by ultrasound, which is simpler (not needing the

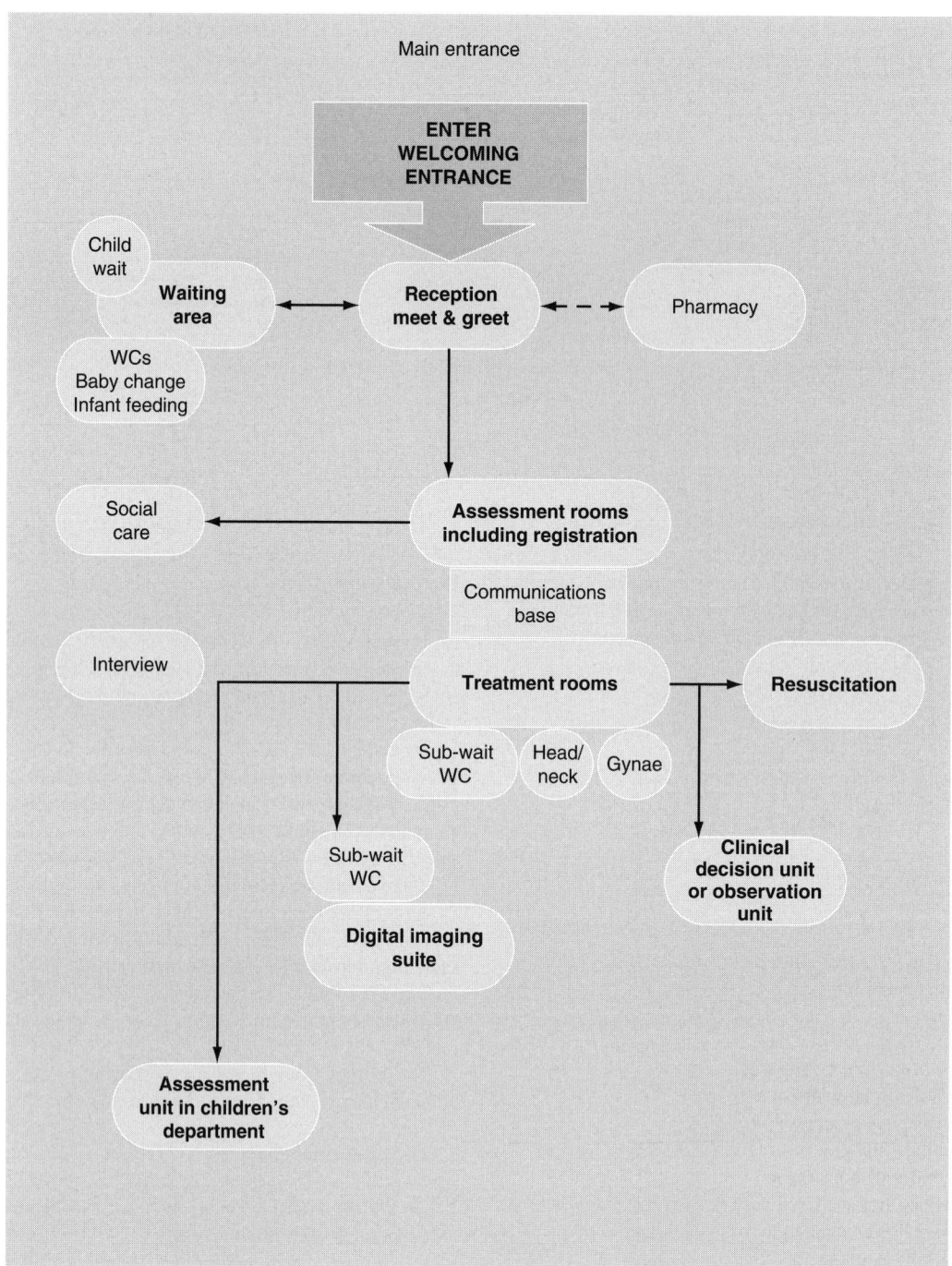

Main entrance

ENTER
WELCOMING
ENTRANCE

Child
wait

Waiting
area

Reception
meet & greet

Pharmacy

WCs
Baby change
Infant feeding

Social
care

Assessment rooms
including registration

Communications
base

Interview

Treatment rooms

Resuscitation

Sub-wait
WC

Head/
neck

Gynae

Sub-wait
WC

Clinical
decision unit
or observation
unit

Digital imaging
suite

Assessment
unit in children's
department

19.8 *Relationship diagram, illustrating the emergency-related spaces for patients arriving by public or private transport. Source: Health Building Note 22*

protective measures demanded of X-rays), cheaper, faster and not requiring as much space.

Each of these services requires its own reception, waiting and changing areas. The X-ray services may in addition be grouped into, for example, specialised rooms, general-purpose rooms and barium rooms although the X-ray reception desk would probably be common to all. Where there are a large range of possible investigations departments are sometimes split into 'fast-flow' and 'slow-flow' areas depending on the throughput level of the area. The increased use of Picture Archiving and Communication Systems (PACS) has resulted in a reduced need for film processing and storage within the Imaging area, reporting can similarly be carried out in locations remote from the radiology facility, away from the hospital, or in a different country. This facility greatly enhances the possibility of using remote expertise to quickly arrive at a diagnosis which would not otherwise be achievable. The introduction of PACS has also had an impact on the take up of a more

'paperless' hospital environment although the full development of patient records available across the healthcare community remains fraught with technical, ethical and confidentiality issues.

The department should be located next to the A&E and near the OPD with as direct an access as possible for in-patients. (Satellite departments in, for example, the AED are not generally cost-effective.) The layout should allow access to some diagnostic rooms outside working hours without opening the whole department (Figures 19.11 and 19.12).

4.4 Inpatient nursing care

The ward concept
Beds for in-patients in hospitals are grouped, for effective management, into wards of anything from 20 to 36 beds, under the charge of a sister or charge nurse who is supported by a team of qualified nurses, student nurses and aides. This team has to ensure that

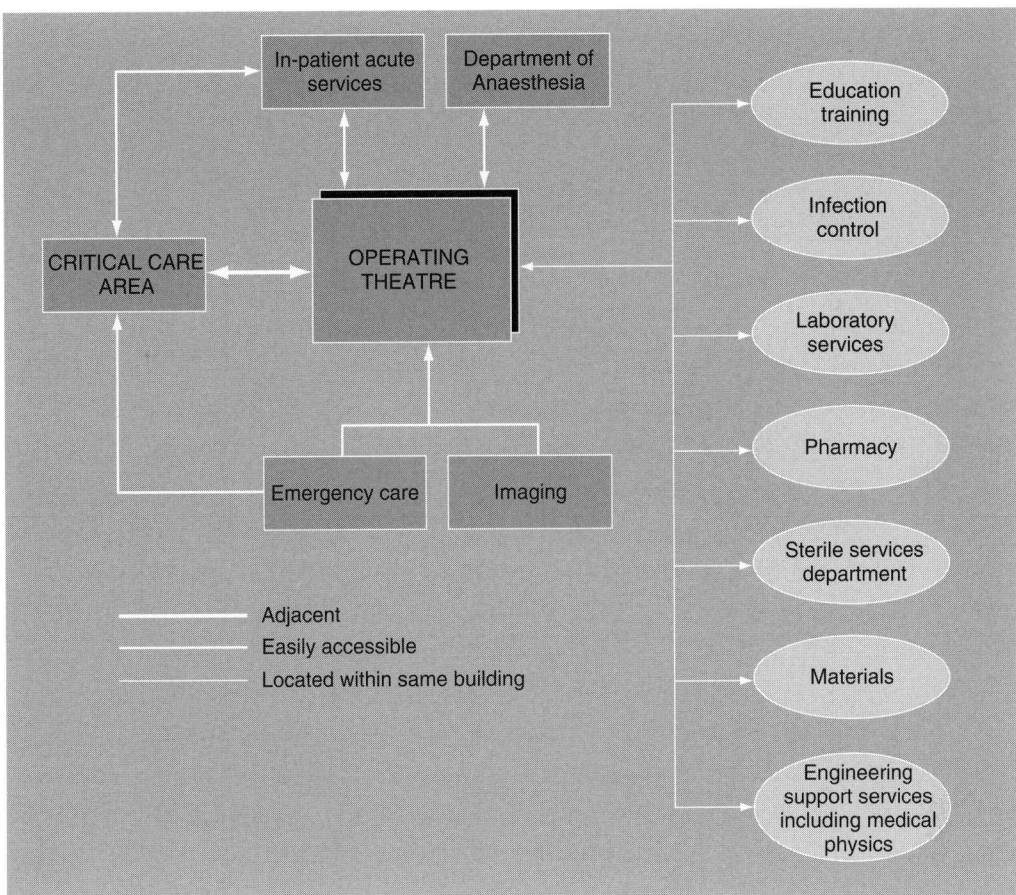

19.9 *Diagram illustrating the relationships between an operating theatre and other hospital services. Source: Health Building Note 26 volume 1*

patients are monitored, fed, allowed to sleep and use toilet facilities, kept clean, treated if required and encouraged to move around (Figure 19.13).

Patients will be taken from the ward to other departments for more complex diagnostic testing and treatment. Doctors will visit ward patients at least daily and other staff will come to administer treatment such as physiotherapy.

The ward will be supplied with food, linen, pharmaceuticals and sterile goods and will hold equipment such as wheelchairs, drip stands and walking frames. Used returns and refuse in various categories will be collected on a regular basis.

Two factors have come to radically influence the design of inpatient hospital wards in recent years.

Firstly, the recognition that, although beds may be grouped in clusters of 20–30 the nurses' responsibility is allocated to a smaller number of patients, normally around 12. Thus, the historically centralised staff base has been replaced by a number of smaller bases, each allocated to a nursing unit of around 12 beds. These contain the necessary facilities for managing the allocated group of patients but the clerical component of the ward administration is centralised to a facility for the Ward Clerk, usually at the entrance to the ward to allow monitoring of visitors to the ward area. A group of these clusters, containing up to 60 beds, provides a manageable unit for the provision of facilities management services such as catering and cleaning.

The second and more significant debate revolves around the provision of single bedrooms and multi-bed bays. Previous use of six-bed bays, heavily utilised by Best Buy and Nucleus together with other standard template designs, is no longer acceptable. More significantly strong arguments have been made about the use of 100 per cent single bedrooms. Clearly, the capital cost is higher but the counter arguments around control of cross infection, ability to isolate Hospital Aquired Infection (HAI) patients, reductions

in medication errors, more dignified and quieter patient environments, more confidential discussions between patients and clinicians, all combine towards a strong case for 100 per cent single rooms. Ideally, each room should have a similar plan, i.e. not being a pair of handed rooms.

There are arguments against single room provision. Companionship in a strange and stressful environment is a benefit to many. Patients within a multi-bed ward also support each other when necessary, summoning staff, for example. The debate will continue but experience in Europe, particularly Denmark, indicates that such provision is a tangible, and provable in terms of Evidence-Based Design, factor in the elimination of HAI.

With so much claim on ground-floor locations, wards tend to be on upper floors unless, like geriatric and children's wards, they have a particular need for access to outside space.

Wards occupy about half the total area of a hospital so it is not possible for all wards to be adjacent to the most relevant departments. For surgical wards, location on the same floor is generally considered satisfactory on the grounds that horizontal travel is more predictable than vertical travel by lift. This is particularly pertinent to paediatric wards where lift travel following surgery is considered a high risk.

Wards cater for many types of patient such as surgical, medical, paediatric (children), elderly, intensive therapy but it is important that a common general pattern be adopted as far as possible so that changes of use can be made without disruption. High-dependency provisions including Intensive Care have such specific requirements that they cannot generally be provided within an acute ward design. Paediatric wards also have particular requirements such as overnight accommodation in the bed area for carers and are generally subject to specific design solutions.

Architects should refer to Health Building Note 4 for further details on ward design.

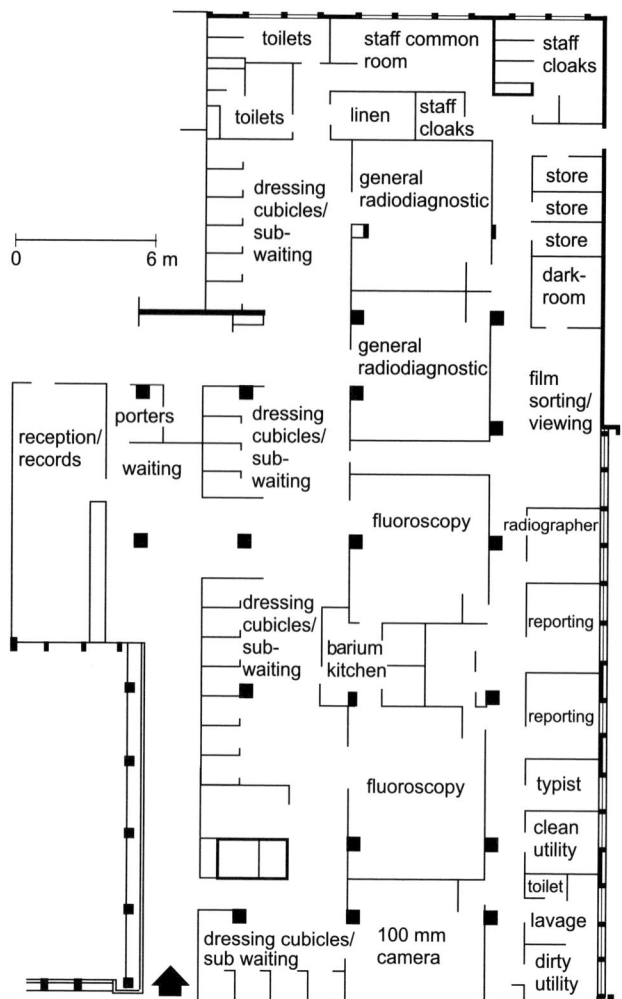

19.10 *X-ray Department at King Edward Memorial Hospital, Ealing. This illustration depicts a film approach to taking and developing X-rays. Digital techniques (known as Picture Archive and Communication, PAC, facilties) are more flexible*

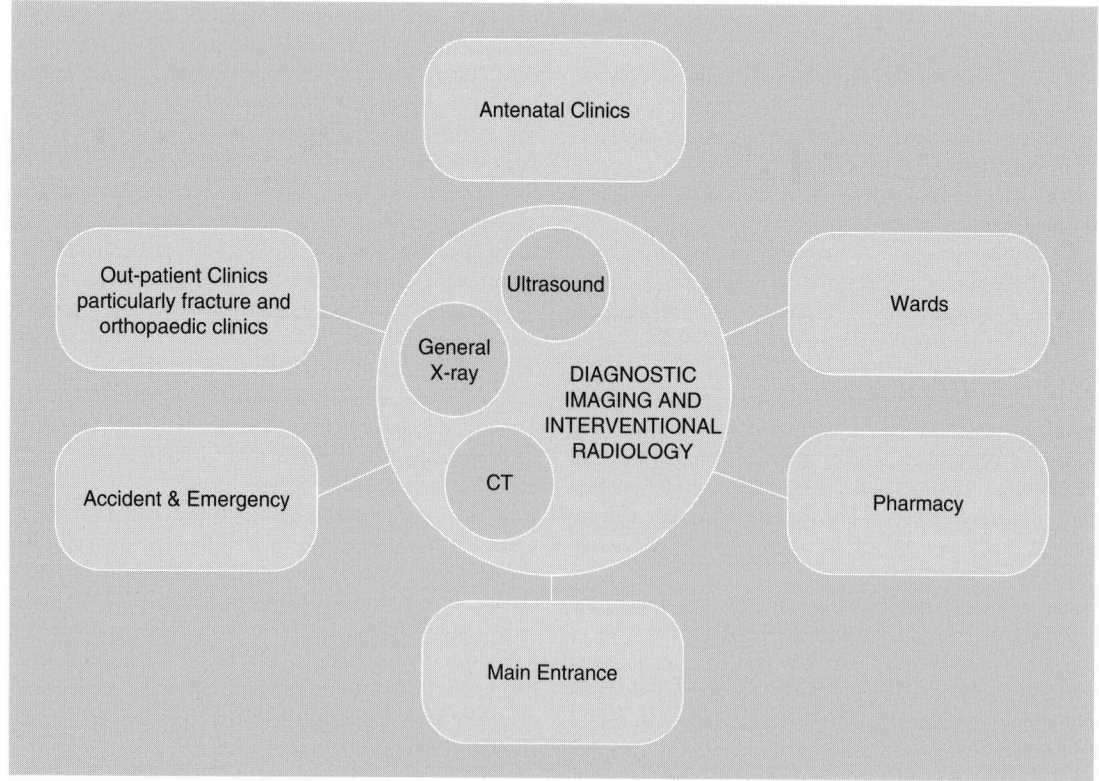

19.11 *Diagram showing relationships between diagnostic imaging departments and other hospital units. Source: Health Building Note 6*

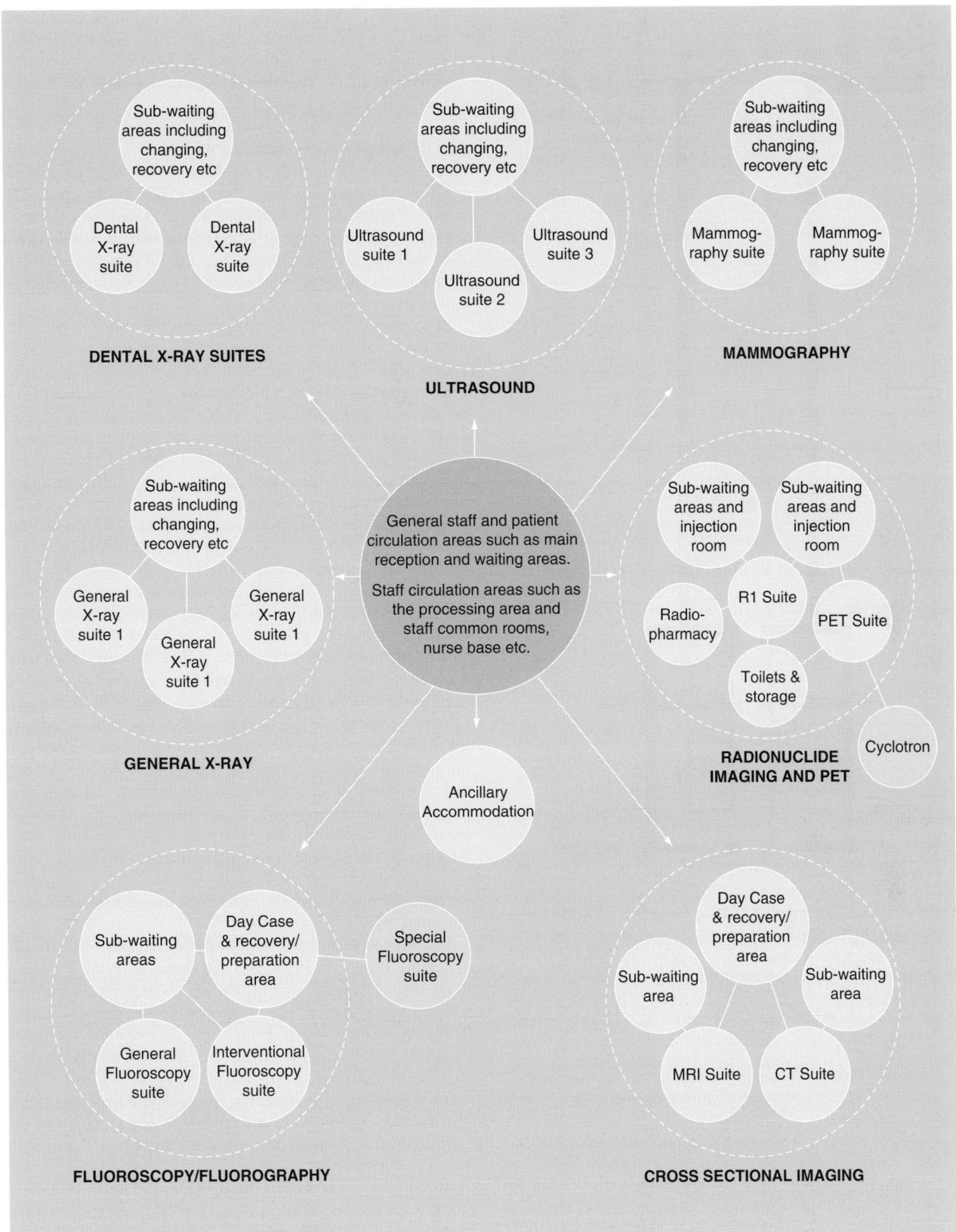

19.12 *Diagram showing relationships between different imaging areas within a hospital. Source: Health Building Note 6*

Ward types

- *Adult acute wards* accommodate general medical or general surgical patients. Although a ward generally will accommodate either one or the other (for doctors' convenience and efficiency of location) there is no significant difference in their facility needs and the ward is standard in its area provision and layout. Between half and three-quarters of a hospital's beds are to be found in these wards. Stroke rehabilitation wards would also generally follow the pattern of a general acute ward. Cardiac

wards can generally be of a similar format to a general acute ward although the provision of telemetry to monitor vital signs to a central location provides for greater flexibility in the use of single bedrooms (Figure 19.14).

- *Children's wards* vary from adult acute wards in the greater areas devoted to day/play space and the need for access to an outside play area, the provision of education facilities and, of course, the specially designed fittings and furniture. Separate provision for adolescents is an important consideration as educational and recreational provisions are not compatible with

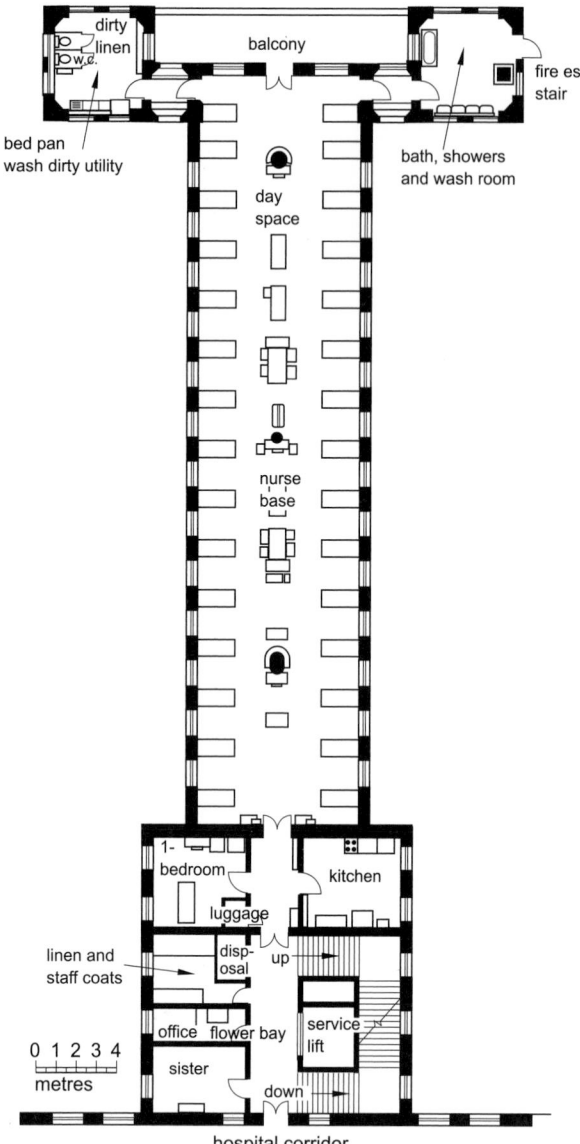

19.13 *Nightingale ward in St Thomas' Hospital. Although the traditional Nightingale Wards provided excellent observation for nurses and some reassurance for patients, lack of privacy (and perhaps dignity) and increased disturbance was felt to be compromised*

lower age ranges. Provision for separate accommodation for males and females becomes significantly more important for this age range.

- *Wards for elderly people* again have more day space than adult acute wards because these patients spend longer in hospital and are ambulant for more of the time. Providing dignity and separation of sexes can be preserved, accommodation for elderly patients may benefit from a limited provision of multi-bed accommodation.

- *The intensive therapy and high dependency* units hold seriously ill patients, often transferred direct from the operating theatre. Significantly more space is required around the bed for monitoring and other equipment. Bed centres of 4.5 m are required for Intensive Care compared to 3.3 m in acute care. No day space is required, and the bed areas are designed primarily for efficient nursing. Because of the high staff/patient ratio, the size of the ward is usually limited to about 20 patients and a more usual provision at a district hospital (i.e. serving a population of 300 000) is between 10 and 12 bed spaces. The Planetree Foundation in the USA have devoted particular effort

to providing critical care facilities which enable the patient to be nursed in a highly technical clinical environment but providing accommodation for relatives and carers to be in close contact without compromising care or hygiene requirements. Refer to Griffin Hospital, Derby, CT.

4.5 Outpatient services including pharmacy

The function of the OPD is to diagnose and treat home-based patients and if necessary admit them as in-patients. It is one of the largest departments in the hospital and is visited by the greatest number of patients daily. It is, therefore, best accessed directly from the main hospital entrance. Separate OPD facilities for children may be considered in the context of a hospital wide policy for children's services.

The patients' first point of contact is the main OP reception desk from which they are directed to the sub-waiting area serving the suite of consulting rooms in which their clinic is being held (Figure 19.15). The building block of the department is the consulting/examination suite which can be a number of combined Consult/Examination (C/E) rooms or some combination of consulting rooms and examination rooms. Combined C/E rooms are generally described as single or two sided, depending on the provision of permanent access to one or both sides of the couch. Typically single sided access requires 14.5 m² and two sided 16.5 m². The side to the right of the patient is prioritised for the staff.

In the combined C/E room, the doctor will both consult with the patient and examine the patient on a couch; while the patient is dressing, the doctor may move to an adjoining C/E room to deal with another patient and the rooms should, therefore, have interconnecting doors. Issues of confidentiality between rooms need to be carefully considered in these circumstances as without intrusive acoustic protection privacy will be compromised. In the consulting room + examination rooms arrangement, the patient moves to the separate room, undresses and waits for the doctor. The normal provision is an examination room either side of a consulting room. Because of the greater flexibility of space the C/E room provision is considered to have better utilisation. In a clinic where there is rapid throughput, a consultant, registrar and house officer may occupy a string of six or seven combined C/E rooms; where the throughput is slower (e.g. psychiatry), each doctor will occupy one room only.

To provide such flexibility, strings of at least 6 rooms, and preferably 12, are required. This can, however, make it difficult to provide an external view for the sub-waiting area, a provision valued more highly in Scottish guidance. The potential further flexibility of these rooms being used, or converted for use as treatment facilities, suggests that this consideration be made at an early design stage, in particular, the room size and ventilation requirements. All consulting rooms should have an external wall location with natural ventilation and consideration of privacy needs to be made when overlooking may occur, in particular across a courtyard.

A move towards Rapid Diagnostic and Treatment Centres (RDTC) has resulted in the increased provision of facilities where the concept of a 'one stop shop' means that in some cases diagnosis and treatment can occur within the same visit. All diagnostic tools are provided within the facility and although the patient visit lasts longer, up to 5 h, consultation, diagnostic procedures and treatment in one visit substantially improves that patient experience.

Orthopaedic and fracture clinics are often provided as part of the A&E department since many of their patients are receiving follow-up treatment resulting from injuries and some accommodation, like the plaster room, can be used in common.

Centralised pharmacy services, which may include manufacturing and preparation of intravenous fluids, are making increased use of robotic dispensing, particularly for outpatients and ward boxes. It is less necessary for the pharmacy to be located adjacent to the

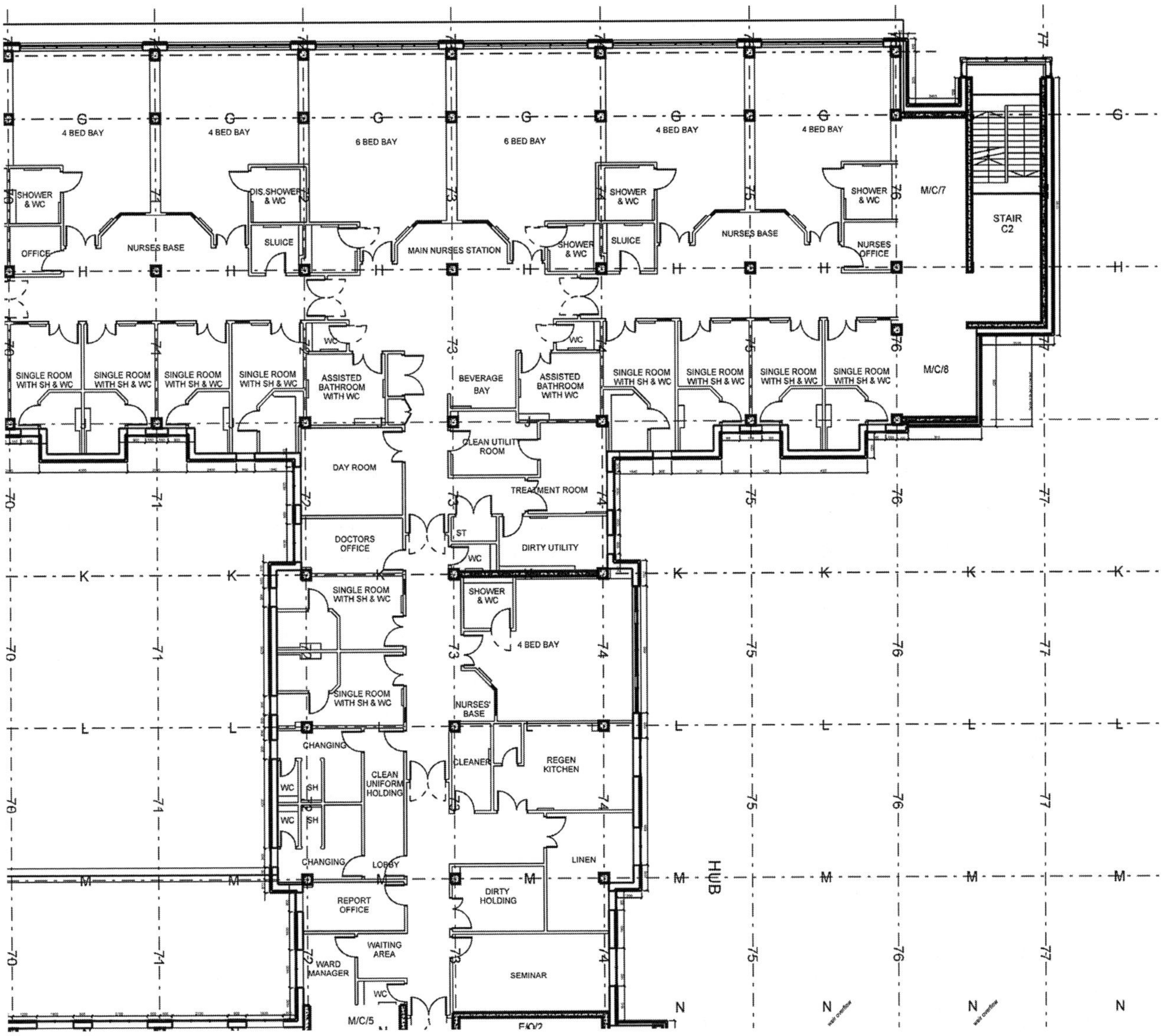

19.14 *General acute ward at The University Hospital of Coventry and Warwickshire. This could be split down the middle as the wards are a matching unit. Architects Nightingale Associates*

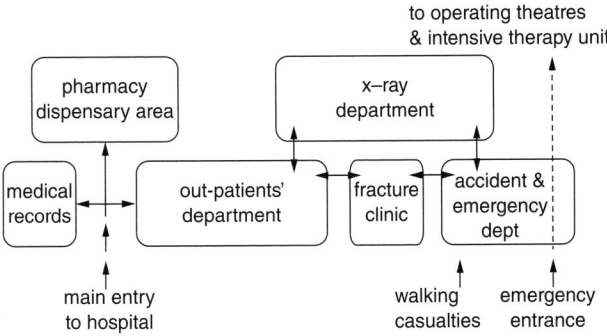

19.15 *Relationship diagram of out-patient and accident cluster*

outpatient service although the provision of a dispensing facility close to the main access point for outpatients is necessary. See Figures 19.16–19.20

4.6 Day patient services including ISTCs

Improvements in anaesthetic techniques and the vastly increased use of 'keyhole surgery' endoscopy and laparoscopy together with laser surgery have enabled routine invasive and ophthalmic procedures to be carried out in one day meaning that a patient does not require an overnight stay.

Day surgery operating theatres are generally designed and equipped to a similar level as inpatient theatres and often include an ultra clean hood, a ceiling mounted enclosure which provides a highly effective low-velocity hepa filtered environment, sometimes to the extent that surgical staff wear full body ventilated suits. Such provisions were previously exclusive to orthopaedic surgery and are still critical to this specialty but are in more general usage.

Day surgery theatres may be provided within the main operating department; however, the principle of day surgery facilities is to separate the elective (i.e. planned) service from the disruption caused by emergency admissions and procedures. Although potentially less efficient in theatre usage, day surgery theatres are often located adjacent to the outpatients department providing a centralised service for all non-inpatient clinical interventions. Such facilities are known as Ambulatory Care Centres.

Pressures on waiting lists have generated an increased scope for partnership between the NHS and the private sector. One such instance is the Independent Sector Treatment Centre (ISTC). These facilities, including staff, are provided by the private sector and the private sector partner is contracted to provide a prescribed service level over a prescribed period in a contract which transfers the estate related risks to the private sector. There are a number of ISTCs currently in operation.

Increasingly minimally invasive surgery (keyhole surgery) is likely to be used in the future, and as the trend towards moving

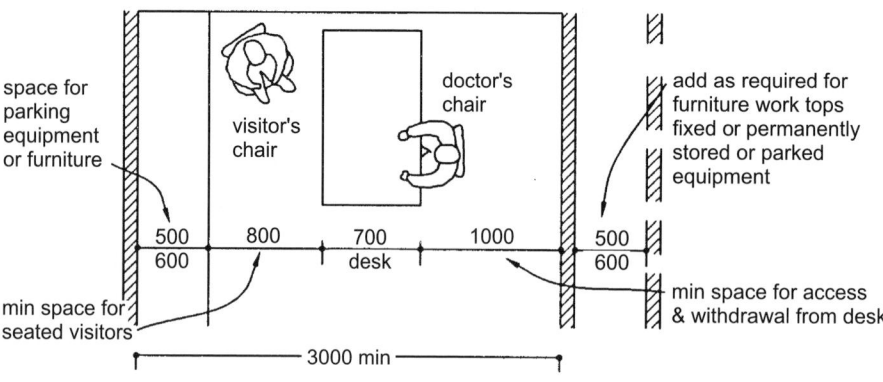

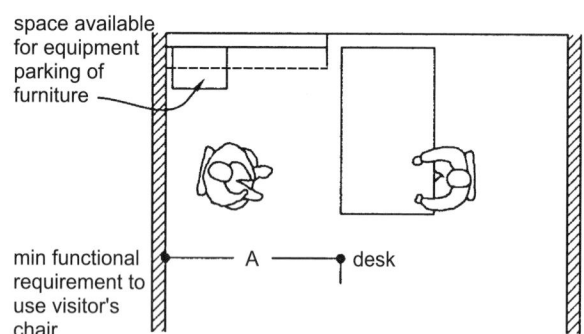

19.16 *Space requirements for room width in consulting areas Dimension A:*

- *minimum 1200 mm, psychologically unsatisfactory. The space in front of the desk should be larger than that behind*
- *preferred minimum 1300 mm giving more flexibility in arrangement and use of the space in front of the desk, and psychologically more acceptable*
- *1400 mm is the minimum permitting movement past a seated visitor*
- *1500 mm will permit passage behind a seated visitor*

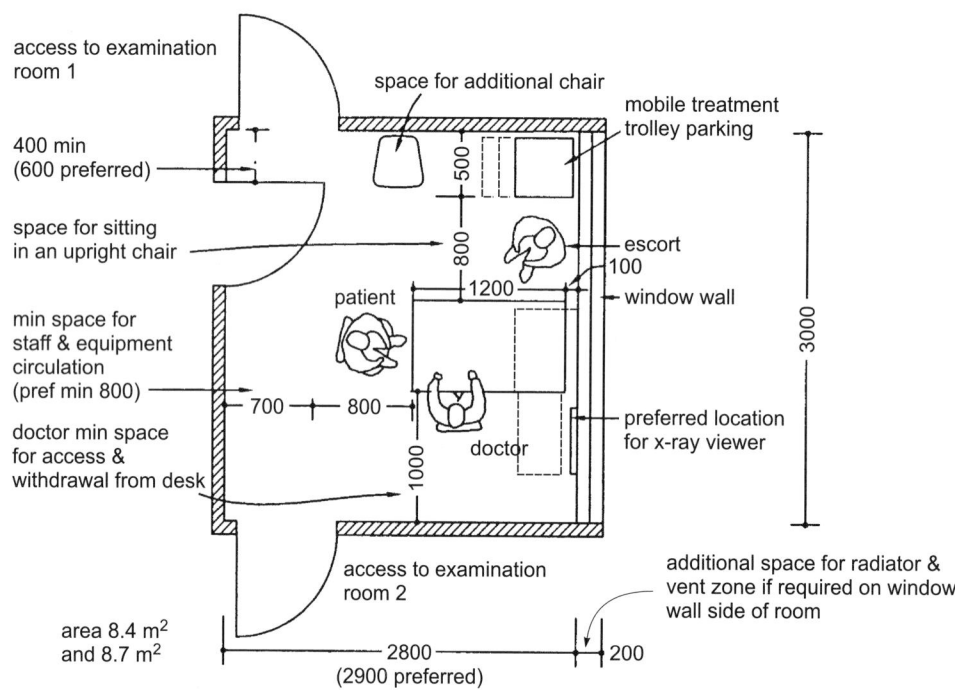

19.17 *Separate consulting room*

care closer to the patients' home continues will move into locations further removed from acute hospital sites.

4.7 Rehabilitation services

To encourage an integrated approach to patient treatment, the rehabilitation department encompasses a number of therapies:

- *Physiotherapy*: Dealing with problems of mobility and function using natural approaches such as movement and manual therapy, supported by electrotherapy, cryotherapy and hydrotherapy.
- *Occupational therapy*: Improving patients' function and minimising handicaps through the holistic use of selected activities,

environment and equipment adaptation so that they can achieve independence in daily living and regain competence in work and leisure.

- *Speech therapy*: Dealing with communication problems, either individually or in groups, if necessary by introducing alternative methods of communication; family members may be involved and family counselling plays an important part.

In addition, accommodation is needed for consultant medical staff.

Patients may be disabled: the department may need its own entrance if it is remote from the main entrance and must be near to car parking.

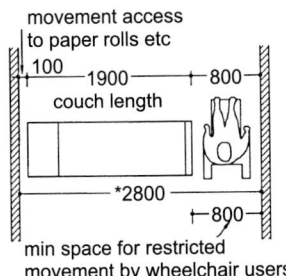

a *Access at foot end of couch for wheelchair movement.*
*2800 mm is also the preferred minimum dimension room length when standing workspace at foot or head ends of couch is required

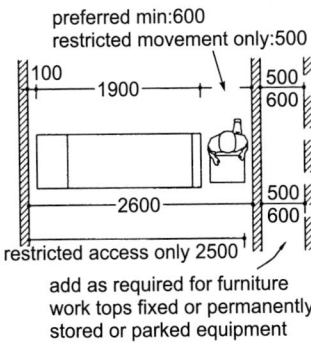

b *Where wheelchair movement at foot end not required*

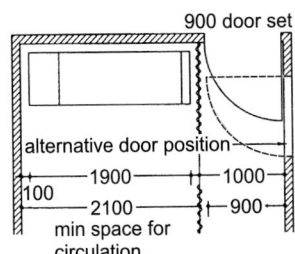

c *No access across foot end of couch*

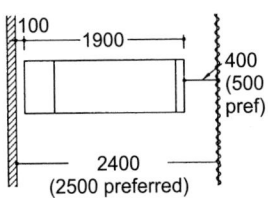

d *Minimum for restricted sideways access within curtained area*

19.18 *Space requirements for room lengths in examination area*

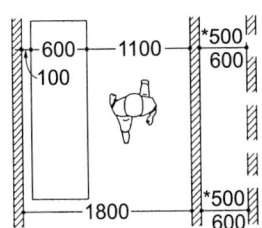

a *Access to one side of couch only. 1100 mm is the minimum space for an ambulant patient changing*

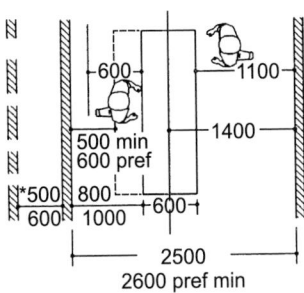

c *Access to both sides of couch*

600 mm is the essential unobstructed space for access and examination
1100 mm is the space at the side of the couch for changing 1400 mm is the space at the side of the couch for wheelchair access
800 mm to 1000 mm is the clear workspace at the side of the bed or couch for examination and treatment, preferred minimum 900 mm
*add as required for furniture, workshop or equipment, which may be fixed, permanently stored or parked.

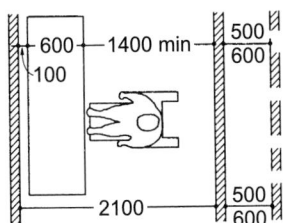

b *Access to one side of couch only. 1400mm is the minimum space for a wheelchair patient changing*

19.19 *Space requirements for room width in examination areas*

In some instances, staff from the unit may require regular visits to outlying areas to provide services at home or in local health-care facilities. This may include the transport of equipment and the co-location of parking facilities for these peripatetic activities should be considered and discussed with planning authorities.

There are no strong internal relationships except between hydrotherapy and physiotherapy and between the central waiting space and all treatment areas. This generally means a close association with the Out-patients department or Ambulatory care unit described above.

4.8 Children's services

The needs of children are best met by having them together in children's units, nursed by staff with the relevant qualifications. Accommodation is required for out-patient facilities; comprehensive assessment and care (for the investigation, treatment and diagnosis of children who fail to develop physically or mentally); in-patient facilities in 20-bed wards; and a day care unit.

The out-patient unit and assessment accommodation should be on one floor, either at ground level or served by a convenient lift, near to

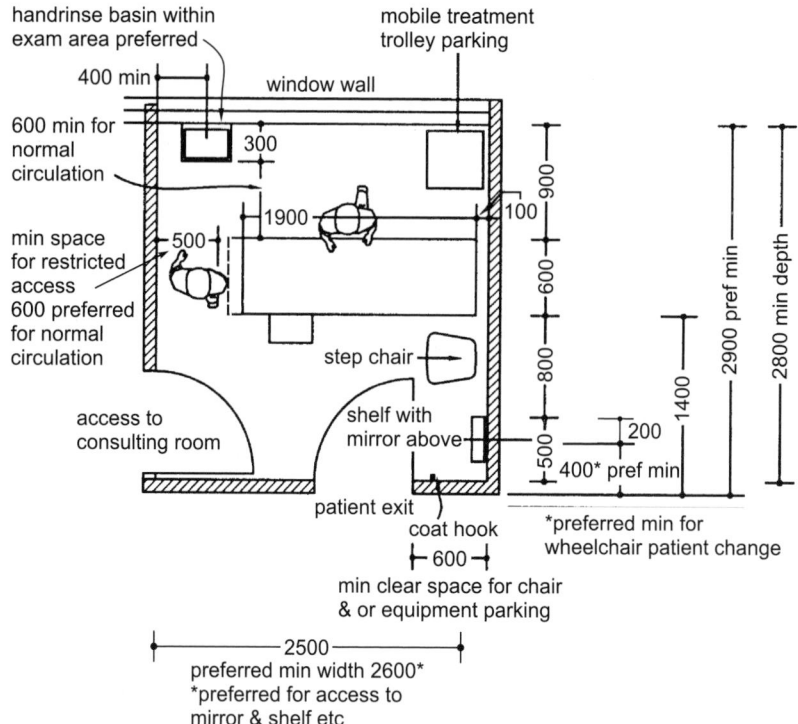

19.20 *Separate examination room: area 7 m² and 7.6 m²*

public transport and car parking. The out-patient unit should be near the plaster room and fracture clinic and could adjoin the main OPD.

In the children's ward, the need for observation is greater than in an adult's, but the need for privacy is less and more partitions can be glazed at both high and low level. All bedrooms should consider the need for a parent to stay with a child. Play space is required and space for teaching and physiotherapy; this should include outside areas, although these may double with other functions such as eating.

Avoiding an institutional atmosphere in the design is important in adult wards but even more so in children's: a light and sunny atmosphere should be the aim. Graphics and themes should be developed to stimulate, enable an understanding of the areas of the unit without the assumption of reading ability, and enable children to associate themselves with a particular area and become more comfortable with their environment. The Evelina Childrens Hospital at St Thomas' Hospital by Hopkins Architects and RKW is a good example of the development of the brief and the accommodation in consultation with children.

The accommodation generally will need to provide for infants, toddlers, school-age children and adolescents: the design should as far as possible take account of their varying needs.

4.9 Older people's services

More 'acute' elderly patients – those undergoing assessment or rehabilitation – are in most respects satisfied by the design for adult acute wards.

The development of Hospital Trusts and the separation of services into acute and mental health provided by separate Trusts has inevitably resulted in the dislocation of the services, often to different sites. It should be recognised, however, that elderly patients often have mental health difficulties alongside medical episodes. The reverse is also the case that mental health patients have medical demands in addition to mental health problems and facilities for the management of these issues should be considered as a component part of the accommodation.

Longer stay elderly wards, including those for the mentally infirm, should be more like home than hospital and include a higher variety of room types to accommodate different preferences, and more day space. More storage space is required for storing patients' belongings, including suitcases, mobility aids, continence aids, etc.

4.10 Maternity services

Policies concerning maternity care can vary widely and client policy towards the whole maternity process should be established at the outset. Co-location of Womens' services, and the co-location of Womens' and Childrens' services should be considered.

Nearly all births take place in hospital but current trends are towards increasing antenatal testing and, on that basis, prioritising cases so that low-risk ones can be delivered in the community (at home or in a community hospital) while higher-risk cases are dealt with in the hospital where operating theatres and other back-up facilities are closer to hand.

A strengthened community care service, with midwives accommodated in community clinics or local health care resource centres, could deal with most of the antenatal care process and minimise the need for visits to the hospital antenatal clinic. Such buildings would incorporate spaces for antenatal exercise classes and mother and baby clinics.

A number of philosophies concerning delivery may be encountered. Traditionally, the woman would be admitted direct to the delivery room or, if admitted early, to an antenatal ward. During labour, she would move to a separate delivery room – perhaps in a suite, central to all the maternity wards and near to the neonatal unit for the nursing of small or ill babies – for delivery of the baby, then returned to a postnatal ward which would be designed to allow rest following birth and to allow the mother to get to know her baby.

An alternative, used routinely in the USA, is the 'complete stay room' (or LDRP room – labour, delivery, recovery and postpartum) in which the whole process is enacted and which may include accommodation for the mother's partner. The provision of a birthing pool is another option with implications for the structure and infection control issues.

Within this range, there are many possible scenarios, each with its own implications for ward facilities (such as day rooms and sanitary provision) and for provision for abnormal delivery.

Occupancy of maternity wards is variable, throughout the year and with population changes. In principle, they should, therefore, be planned for easy conversion to adult acute use, although this might be difficult with some options such as the complete stay room. In the postnatal ward, the baby will be nursed in a cot alongside the mother, although nursery accommodation should also be provided to enable the mother to get some much needed rest on occasions.

The out-patient suite will incorporate a suite of consulting/examination rooms and supporting facilities; waiting areas which can double as space for classes and clinics; and a diagnostic ultrasound room with associated changing and waiting areas.

The design approach in all maternity accommodation should centre around the fact that the pregnant woman is not sick but undergoing a natural function: there is no strong reason for the environment to be particularly clinical in appearance. Concealing obvious clinical elements such as medical gas outlets behind removable folding panels greatly reduces the clinical appearance.

4.11 Mental health services
The scope of facilities for mentally ill people on the hospital site is subject to local initiative. It is, however, likely to include accommodation for the assessment and short-term treatment of adults, including the elderly, who are acutely mentally ill: this group of patients is most likely to need the support of diagnostic services and access to general acute facilities. They also gain from sharing catering, supply and disposal services.

The primary elements in the department will be the wards of 15 beds for adult patients and 20 beds for elderly patients and the day hospital which includes consulting, treatment and social areas together with occupational therapy. Very few adults will remain in the wards during the day but if ward and day hospital are intended to share day, dining, sitting and recreation facilities, experience has shown that full integration is required for this to work successfully.

The department should ideally be integrated into the hospital so as to facilitate communication but be independent enough to have its own (not too clinical) environment, although comments above under older people's services should be noted. Its configuration is unlikely to match that of other wards and evening activities may be disturbing to other in-patient departments. One solution is to plan it as a satellite with its own entrance, perhaps linked to the main hospital and possibly sharing some accommodation with an adjacent rehabilitation department. Although there are exceptions a ground-floor location with good access to safe, secure and observable external spaces is a high priority.

Within wards, the current recommendation of Building Note 35 is for 100 per cent single rooms. This caused some concern related to staffing levels and observation when introduced but has generally been accepted as the norm and has not shown substantial increases in staffing requirements. The wards should consider the needs of patients with varying levels of dementia. Functional and organic dementia provoke very different responses by patients to their environment, however it is still standard practice to nurse both groups of patients in the same ward area. For this reason, all wards should consider patients' needs for wandering, continuous walking, often on a circular, racetrack type route, and a variety of environments which provide either stimulation or a calming effect. Clinical discussions and handover between shifts, because confidential, tend to take place in the sister's office which, therefore, needs to be larger.

Psychiatric out-patient clinics are generally held in the main OPD. Many patients never enter the psychiatric department but others may attend the day hospital from one to three days a week, undertaking various types of occupational therapy and group therapy. They are also given a mid-day meal in two sittings. These activities can be accommodated in a number of rooms with comfortable sitting space for 10–20 people. Electro-convulsive therapy (ECT) may need to be accommodated: it requires treatment and recovery rooms but they would only be in use for perhaps 4 h a week and should be usable for other purposes.

Environmental design generally, particularly of the interior, is of even more importance in this department than elsewhere. Providing a non-institutional appearance, domestic scale and a 'sense of place' should be high priorities. Soft floor coverings may be appropriate for some non-wet areas but the need for cleaning after 'accidents' has resulted in a preference for a hard but non-institutional surface, hardwood floors are particularly successful; divan beds and careful choice of soft furnishings are crucial in creating a suitable atmosphere. Sound attenuation is needed for all rooms used for confidential interviewing; noisy areas (e.g. music room, workshop) should be located to reduce nuisance.

4.12 The Hi-tech specialties
A number of Hi-tech specialties are being introduced, some more quickly than others. These are dependent on specialist design and not within the scope of this chapter.

Robotically Assisted Surgery almost exclusively uses the 'Da Vinci Surgical System' – however, the costs associated with this technique are immense and it is not anticipated to be in general use for more than a very limited number of specialties.

Imaging, particularly interventional radiology, open MRI, which is less claustrophobic for the patient, and the co-location of MRI and Cardiac Catheterisation are developing activities which will see an increase in the shorter term.

Some subjects, such as 'Barn' theatres where a number of operating tables, with ultra clean hoods are located in the same room, have had a small impact on service delivery. Space savings are achievable though not considerable and the opportunity for surgeons to work across more than one table without leaving a sterile area has advantages.

5 SUPPORT SERVICES – OUTSOURCING
The following services are either now outsourced facilities (i.e. provided externally by third parties) or require little direct architectural input:

- sterile services/decontamination;
- pathology – hot, cold, automation;
- catering;
- linen service;
- supplies and disposal/clinical waste management;
- health records (policy debates regarding the retention of paper records or transfer to a digital database are ongoing).

6 PUBLICATIONS AND GUIDANCE
The Department of Health and previously NHS Estates have over years produced much valuable reference and guidance material. However, the very extensive scope of this material, the changing methods of service delivery and technological advances have meant that keeping the publications up to date is a task that has not been universally successful. Two key components of the guidance, Health Building Notes (HBNs) and Health Technical Memoranda (HTMs) are fundamental.

Both HTMs and HBNs have been contained within briefs for new hospitals either as mandatory or advisory documents. Such usage is unfortunate as although parts of the documents can reasonably be considered as mandatory, those related to infection control for example, it is rare for a whole document to be relevant. This has led to a demand for derogations and a loss of the spirit of most of the material which is intended to be for guidance and modification to suit particular circumstances.

It is, however, essential to have access to these documents in order to engage in informed dialogue during the design process. The documents are available online to the NHS only via the Department of Health Knowledge and Information Portal (KIP) but only available outside the NHS via third party construction industry information suppliers.

It is essential to discuss the relevance and status of the guidance with the Department of Health at the time of design.

20 Hotels

Fred Lawson

CI/SfB: 85

Fred Lawson is a hotel expert and the author of many books on hotels and tourism.

KEY POINTS:
- *Competitive industry with high capital and operating costs*
- *Standards dictated by market demands and location*
- *Increasingly dominated by chain operators and branding*
- *Design must ensure efficient operation and value for money*
- *Ancillary facilities may be a major generator of business*

Contents
1 Introduction
2 General considerations
3 Guestrooms and suites
4 Public areas
5 Back of house facilities
6 Case studies
7 Bibliography

1 INTRODUCTION

1.1 The hotel industry

Hotels serve the needs of travellers, tourists, business visitors and others seeking temporary accommodation and other services. Essential requirements are clean, quiet and comfortable bedrooms together with good services that usually include meals. Ancillary facilities for business users and/or leisure attractions often influence choice although the costs involved and value for money are primary considerations.

Prior to the design stage many of the key requirements will have already been decided such as the location, number and types of rooms and the extent of facilities to be provided. Preliminary estimates of costs and revenues form part of the feasibility analysis for the investment. Design briefs are normally provided by developers, including hotel companies who may be involved in managing the property.

The trend is towards multiple chain operating groups specialising in hotel management. These offer a wide range of services including professionally trained staff, established confidence in the standards provided and the advantages of scale in their advertising and reservation systems. Chain hotels may be company owned but are frequently financed by separate investors and then operated by the hotel company under contract or through a franchise.

Hotels are seen as a business investment rather than property investment. The specific design requirements generally make future conversion to other uses difficult and expensive. High grade hotels typically offer a choice of suites as well as standard rooms and often extend their hotel services to apartments in associated developments such as in condominiums. Aparthotels are designed with apartments, instead of individual bedrooms.

1.2 Hotel classification

Standards of services and facilities in hotels vary widely from luxury to basic. Hotel groups distinguish the types of hotels they operate by branding with specific names and design features. Tourism authorities in most countries use symbols (stars, crowns, etc.) to classify hotels and other types of tourist accommodation. Some commercial agencies and travel publications also grade their members by prices and services offered.

Hotels are primarily categorised by their location (e.g. city, suburban, resort, country, airport, motel) and also by the main markets they serve (e.g. business travellers, convention groups, holiday seekers, motorists). Typical categories cover:

- 5* Luxury: exclusive named hotels in exotic destinations and prime city locations.
- 4* High class: with extensive facilities for business users and high spend tourists.
- 3* Mid-grade: full service traditional hotels, independent or company managed.
- 2* Budget: standard branded designs with some services for motorists and tourists.
- 1* Basic: economy brands designed with minimal space and limited facilities.

Grading also takes account of the extent of services offered. Staff requirements in a full service hotel are substantial with payroll absorbing up to one-third of the turnover. Designs must ensure maximum working efficiency and provide adequate employee facilities including controlled entry, separate changing rooms, lockers, toilets, restroom, canteen, security, personnel offices and – often – some living accommodation. Ratios of employees to guestrooms range from 0.2–0.3 budget, 0.5–0.6 mid-grade, 0.8–1.0 high grade, to 1.5 luxury standard.

Demands for value and convenience have led to increases in standardised chains' budget hotels (e.g. motels, inns) sited with highway service stations or around towns and near attractions. Some brands are designed to provide basic facilities operated with a minimum of staff.

1.3 Other tourist accommodation

Internet tourism services provide choice from a wide range of alternatives including domestic properties (e.g. B&B, guest houses), traditional inns and vacation use of university and college accommodation. Tourists, particularly families, increasingly choose self-catering facilities in new or converted properties and resort areas with alternative choice of eating places nearby.

Resort complexes are developed as self-contained tourist destinations complete with extensive leisure facilities and supporting services on site. Most are designed as seaside, marina, ski, spa, golf or forest-based holiday village resorts. Tourist resorts may be operated by a commercial company, or co-ownership management. In the latter, accommodation is based on apartments, lodges and other properties for sale on individual, time-share or condominium arrangements.

2 GENERAL CONSIDERATIONS

2.1 Sites and surroundings

The location and site largely dictate the design and relationship of the different parts of a hotel:

- Resorts – views of the attractions (e.g. sea, lake, park, spectacular scenery) provide marketing and higher value revenue benefits. This should be maximised for guestrooms and public areas such as restaurants. Interesting site activities (e.g. marina, golf course, swimming pool) and exotic landscaping also influence the layout.

- City centre developments – these are determined mainly by site constraints and planning considerations. High site costs may lead to high value frontages being used for shops and malls; penthouse floors as luxury serviced apartments or suites. Invariably, development costs are increased by the need for underground parking and basement services, including goods entry and docking. Multiple floors of guestrooms require extensive guest and service lifts as well as complex technical systems. The need for ancillary facilities such as convention/function halls can occupy a large part of the site area.
- Key city sites – these allow for high rise statement buildings which, themselves, attract attention. They may be designed entirely as a hotel or for multiple users with specific floors allocated for hotel accommodation and services. The latter requires more complex separate arrangements for guest reception and transportation as well as for goods services. Tower buildings require large structural core areas housing vertical services (lifts, stairs, ducts, service rooms, etc.) and the ratio of perimeter rooms per floor area is limited.
- Suburban sites – here site and construction costs are lower and allow greater flexibility in site layout and building design. There are savings in foundation and structural costs, technical services are often simplified and lift systems may be rationalised. These include hotels sited within or near airports on the outskirts of towns, or in locations which attract a mixed market of tourists, local functions and business travellers.
- Roadside and stopover places – these cater for motorists and other travellers and are invariably chain operated budget designs, with standardised rooms and minimal facilities for meals. Typical buildings are modular with prefabricated technical services, one or two storeys in height. Optimum sites are associated with other motorway services along highways, at main junctions and near attractions along tourist routes.

2.2 Access and site development

In the preliminary design stage, consideration must be given to:

- Restrictions, including planning, property rights and other legal limitations, which may limit plot ratio and height of building.
- Access routes to separate guests from goods delivery/services and employee entries.
- Site planning for parking requirements and potential future extensions.
- The main entrance must be prominent, appropriate for the style and grade of hotel. In urban hotels, secondary access from the car park must lead directly to the reception lobby. A separate entrance and reception may be required for large convention/function groups.

Car parking space depends on the location, patterns of use, transport modes and availability of public parking/taxi services. Motor and airport hotels typically provide 1.1 spaces/room, city centre hotels about 0.3 spaces/room plus 0.2 spaces/convention or function seat. Resort hotels may require only 0.2 spaces/room plus coach parking.

Provisions must also be made for separate staff parking.

2.3 Spatial and functional relationships

The functional requirements of a full-service hotel can be grouped into three distinct but linked areas: public, guest room and back of house/administrative (Figure 20.1).

2.4 Public areas

For guests and usually open to non-residents, public rooms include lounges, restaurants, bars, meeting rooms, ballrooms and other rooms catering for functions. Other facilities, such as fitness rooms, spas and leisure pools, may also allow for local club membership. Typical requirements include:

- large span spacious areas, to accommodate planned numbers of users and allow changes in layout and design to suit different requirements.
- situated at or near ground floor level to allow easy access, control and emergency exit.
- external views required for restaurants. Speciality restaurants and bars may be sited at roof-top level in tall buildings with dedicated lift access and services. In lobbies and convention/function halls an impressive, spacious interior design is important. Natural light is an advantage in lounges and break-out foyers.
- support areas (e.g. foyers, equipment stores, food service facilities, staff access) must be sited adjacent or easily accessible with effective screening to avoid disturbance in use.

2.5 Guestrooms

Bedrooms and suites for resident guests are located to benefit from views and designed to minimise noise and disturbance. Residential accommodation is the largest generator of net revenue and typically occupies some 70–75 per cent of the built area in full service hotels, see Table I.

Design features include:

- repetitive modular construction of rooms adjacent to vertical ducts enclosing pipes, cables and other technical services;
- careful planning of stairs, lifts and corridors to facilitate easy circulation and access for guests;
- guest circulations via the main reception area while staff have direct access from back-of-house areas (e.g. house keeping, laundry, kitchens, maintenance, stores);
- specific requirements apply for disabled access, fire escapes, security, safety and noise reduction.

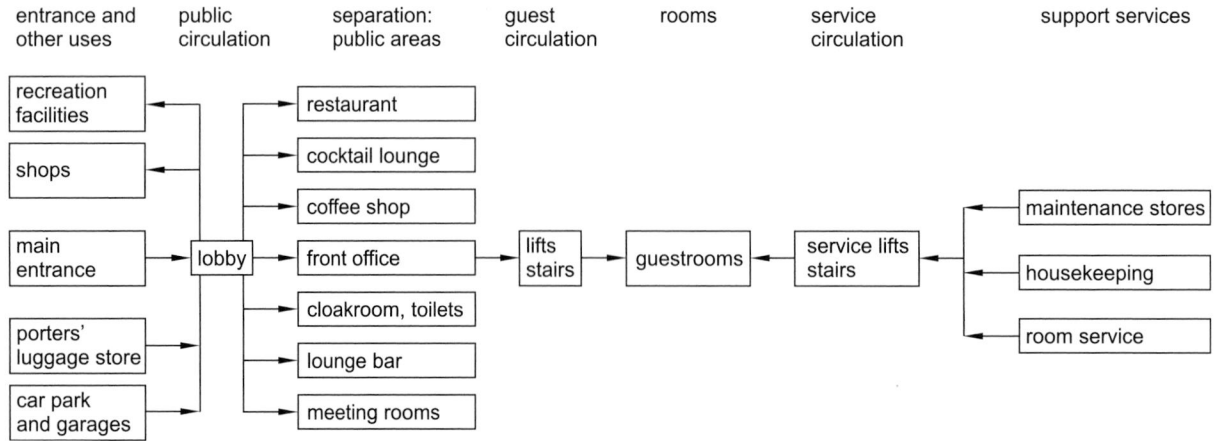

20.1 *Circulation and relationship diagram*

Table I Residential area ratios

Grade	Basic	Budget	Mid-grade	High-grade	Luxury
Room area (net)[a]	17.5	21.7	25.2	30.0 (+5%)	36.0 (+5%)
Gross factor[b]	0.25	0.25	0.3	0.4	0.4
Gross residential area[c]	22	27	33	44	53
Public & support areas[d]	5.5	8	12	18	22
Residential % of total	80%	77%	73%	71%	71%

(a) Median areas (m²) for European hotels. 5% suites included for higher grade hotels. American hotels tend to use larger rooms
(b) Depends on building format. Higher grade includes part use of single loaded corridors.
(c) Figures rounded
(d) Increased to 22 for high grade hotels in developing countries and for hotels with extensive convention or casino facilities

2.6 Back of house and administration areas

These accommodate the technical and operational installations including staff facilities and workrooms. They are located in the least valuable areas with vehicle access for goods delivery and waste/recycling removal, maintenance and emergency services. Facilities include:

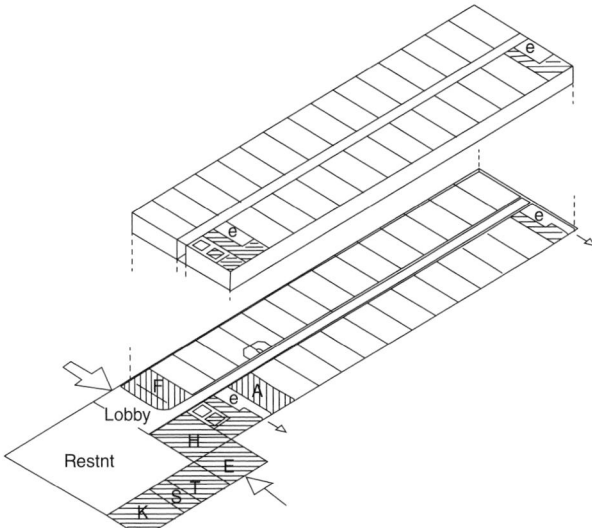

20.2a *Basic or budget hotel with restaurant illustrating the service arrangements (shaded). Guest rooms are generally in two storeys*

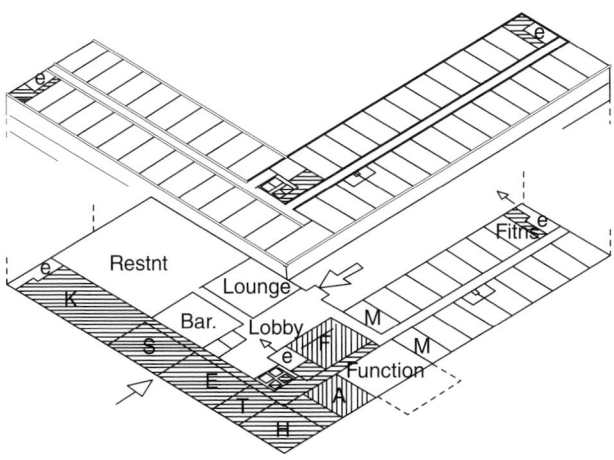

20.2b *Typical midgrade suburban and motor hotels, providing a wider range of public and function/meeting rooms with extended service areas. Residential areas are two or more storeys high and may be arranged as a square around a central lawn or enclosed atrium accommodating the restaurant bar areas.*

20.2 *Examples of three typical hotel types*

- Basements in large hotels and high value sites. Lift motor housing and ventilation/air-conditioning plant sited in screened roof top locations.
- Separate areas for loading docks, waste containment, control, storage rooms, engineering, housekeeping, laundries, employees, and main food storage and production.
- Internal service access (separate from guest areas) to guestrooms, and from service areas to public rooms (restaurants, bars, function rooms, furniture/equipment stores).
- Separate facilities for hotel administration are required. Offices for duty management are located near the reception lobby with access to the reception desk.

2.7 Circulation and signage

Routes to be taken by guests, non-residents and staff must be carefully planned to facilitate easy movement and control (Figure 20.2a–c). This also indicates the optimum locations for support facilities and the services required. All routes must be kept clear of obstruction and be wide enough to avoid congestion, particularly in areas where people congregate (e.g. reception desk, foyers, lift lobbies, luggage handling, service areas). Signs are required for directions and information, including evacuation routes. Graphic design must be an integral part of interior design and be co-ordinated throughout. Approved symbols must be used and all signs must be sited within normal viewing patterns.

2.8 Corridors and staircases

Corridors, stairs, ducts and room service lobbies add to net room areas, increasing the built areas and costs. Circulation in public

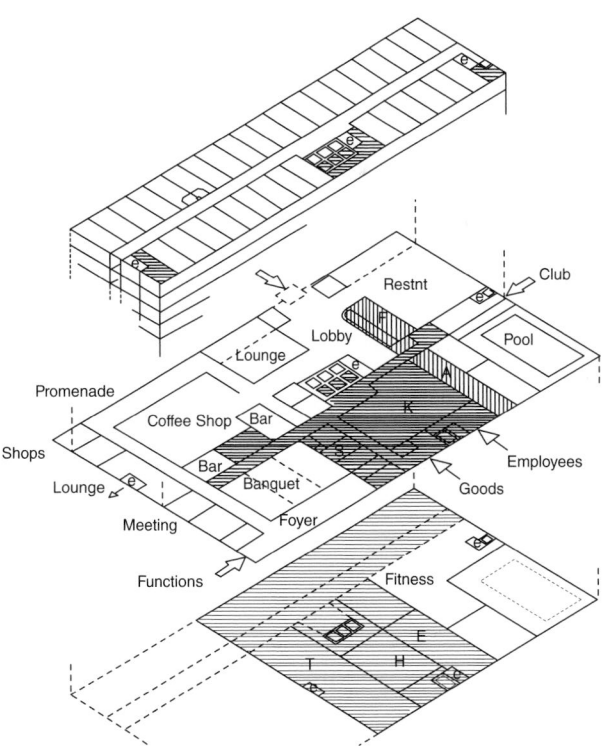

20.2c *Simplified diagram of public, residential and services areas (shaded) of a high grade multi-storey hotel.*

Key: A, administration and security offices; e, fire escape stairs and exits; E, employee entrance control, changing areas, toilets, canteen/restroom, Personnel offices; F, front desk and office; H, Housekeeping and general storage areas; K, primary kitchen and storage areas with access to finishing kitchens serving individual food and beverage outlets; S, storage for function room furniture and equipment; T, Technical plant and equipment

spaces should, wherever possible, be through areas of other use such as the lobby, lounges or shopping malls.

In residential floors, economic considerations (gross factors, corridor lengths) generally require bedrooms to be sited on both sides of the corridor. Typical gross factors are central 'double loaded' corridors 20–30 per cent, and 'single loaded' corridors and tower buildings up to 35–45 per cent.

Corridor and staircase design is dictated by fire regulations and codes. The main stairs should be prominently located beside the lift bank to allow easy alternative use and evacuation.

Secondary stairs must be provided at or near the end of each corridor and within the maximum travel distances allowed.

For corridors with sprinkler systems allowing two alternative means of escape this distance is usually 60 m although 90 m may be permitted. For one route of escape (suites and rooms beyond the end staircase) this is reduced to 9 m. Automatic self-closure smoke doors must be provided midway along the corridor. All exits must be clearly indicated, protected by smoke doors or ventilation control, meet fire resistance standards and lead to safe evacuation areas. (See Section 2.16 Fire safety.)

2.9 Lifts

Lift installations are generally required for guestroom floors above the second storey. The lift entry for guests must be visible from the reception desk and monitored by cameras on each floor. Guest lifts must be set back from corridors, have wide opening doors for easy access, good lighting and ventilation and have durable surfaces to resist damage by baggage. Floor leveling at landings is important.

Lift shafts must meet requirements for structural stability, fire resistance of shafts and doors, smoke venting and control. Machine rooms housing motors, pulleys, controls and hoisting beam are normally located above the shaft. All lifts must have safety mechanisms and efficient control systems, including emergency power, lighting and lifting gear together with fire over-ride controls with return to lobby or exit floor.

Performance requirements for large high-grade hotels:

- Carrying capacities – maximum number of passengers to be carried at peak times based on business pattern, and guestroom population.
- Waiting times – depend on round trip time and numbers of lifts installed but a good service for high standard hotels is around 25–30 seconds in peak use.
- Inter-connected collective controls – advanced signaling on landings are necessary in tall hotel buildings. In large hotels, banks of lifts are grouped in facing rows of no more than four with adequate space for assembly (3.5 m wide for guestroom lifts).
- Specialist installations – include basement car park lifts with fire safety provisions, direct lifts to leisure facilities and transparent lifts in atriums. High rise buildings may require fire protected enclosures with separate power supply and controls for fire fighting access.

2.10 Service lifts

- Separate provision of service lifts is needed for housekeeping and room services.
- Typically in the ratio of 1:2, 2:3 or 3:4 guest lifts depending on standards.
- Lifts open on to service lobbies and pantries on each floor and are commonly grouped back to back with the guest lift shaft.
- Service lifts extend down to the back-of-house areas and are designed for practical use transporting staff, trolleys, supplies and equipment.
- At least one must be large enough to take furniture such as a bed or, in emergency, a stretcher requiring direct transfer to ambulance.
- Large hotels may require a heavy duty lift for goods/equipment transfer from loading docks, including convention exhibits.

2.11 Environment

The internal environment must be attractive, engender confidence in the operation and leave a favourable impression. Each area will need to meet specified needs of space and facilities to achieve the design objectives within its allocated budget. In general, interiors and fittings must be safe, resist damage and be easy to repair or replace. Domestic furniture and furnishings are usually not suitable or sufficiently robust for hotel use.

2.12 Lighting

Lighting should assist in providing an appropriate environment, differentiate spaces, and illuminate signs and hazards.

- Light sources and controls are selected to serve particular requirements ranging from external flood lighting, to highlighting interior features and work areas such as reception desks, service counters and bars.
- Energy conservation in lighting, air-conditioning and power consumption is important in controlling utility costs. Provisions include zoned area regulation, guestroom electricity control with entry card, central energy recovery and recycling.
- Hotels must ensure that there is adequate provision of emergency lighting for safety and basic essential services. In high grade hotels, installed generators have capacity to meet all requirements. Automatic switchover is required.

2.13 Noise control

Hotels may necessarily be located in areas of high ambient noise such as highway and street traffic, airports and urban surroundings. Many hotel activities and equipment also generate noise externally (e.g. car parks, loading docks, generators and rooftop plant).

Internal work areas, plant rooms and other noise generating environments are largely grouped together in the back-of-house areas which can be separated or insulated from those used by residents and visitors.

Adequate standards of insulation are essential for rooms sensitive to noise intrusion particularly for the residential guestrooms at night. Sound insulation performance criteria for maximum ambient noise levels in rooms are usually based on Noise Rating (NR) curves covering a range of frequencies, for example:

- guest bedrooms: NR25 broadly an ambient level of 30–35 decibels;
- conference halls: NR25 with acoustic design to limit reverberation for clarity;
- smaller meeting rooms: NR30 including partitioned areas;
- restaurants: NR50 with noise/light screening from kitchens.

Construction of bedroom blocks is usually based on floor slabs with structural cross-walls which also provide a large mass and high density for good sound insulation and fire resistance. Acoustic treatment of flanking paths (e.g. bathroom ducts, ceiling voids, interconnecting doors) is necessary. Double glazing is usually required in busy urban areas with increased width/insulated spacing facing noisy highways. Insulation performance of various construction elements are expressed as Sound Transmission Class (STC) Ratings.

Provision must also be made for reduction of noise transmission through air-conditioning, plumbing and other installed systems as well as impact noise from lift movements. Measures include confinement of machine generated noise, reduction of vibration, design of distribution networks and sealing of ducts and voids.

Disturbance in bedrooms may also arise from internal sources. The design must minimise impact noise with resilient/absorbent floor-covering (carpets) as well as quiet door closures, locking systems, and moveable fittings. In adjacent rooms, noise generating areas such as bathrooms are grouped back to back and similar considerations determine the layout for quiet zones.

Public areas involve other considerations. Ballrooms and convention halls cater for large assemblies of visitors and alternative uses ranging from noise sensitive conferences and functions (speeches) to noisy entertainment. Noise control measures involve the location of public rooms away from residential areas and provision of foyers and service pantries as intermediary areas together with insulation requirements for the sensitive areas.

2.14 Safety
Providing accommodation for transient travellers and tourists who are unfamiliar with the layout and equipment, hotels need to have particular regard to their safety and security. Safety for employees and their work areas must also be considered.

Requirements are governed by statutory legislation, insurance conditions, hotel grading and operating standards. Safety features in all aspects of planning, design, operation and maintenance and the provisions for fire egress have a major influence on the arrangement of rooms and circulations.

2.15 Design checklists
For details of general requirements see Chapter 3 People and Movement and Chapter 11 Fire. Hotel design requires particular attention to the following.

Guest and visitor areas:

- Circulation: changes in floor level, positioning of signs, space for assembly.
- Stairs: maximum 16 steps between landings and minimum 3, non-slip with distinct edges, appropriate handrails.
- Door swings: landing areas, viewing panels, visibility of glass doors.
- Windows: glass specifications, method of cleaning, risk of accidental opening (locking/sealing), vertigo (sill height below 1120 mm).
- Balconies: safety/entry risks, structural stability, wind turbulence, drainage.

Service and work areas:

- Space: for work, equipment use, circulation.
- Ergonomics: (dimensions, shelf heights).
- Equipment protection: machinery, hot surfaces, flames (fire control), electrical safety.
- Environment: lighting (levels, shadowing), ventilation (temperatures, humidity, fumes).
- Fire: high risk areas, fire control, evacuation.
- First aid: locations, treatment facilities.
- Maintenance: requirements, accessibility, drainage

2.16 Fire safety
Protection and means of escape in event of fire imposes specific requirements in hotels. This is due to the large numbers of people who are sleeping in separate rooms, and are unfamiliar with the building and warning systems and need to be alerted and evacuated. Also, many guests may be elderly or very young, disabled, tired or inebriated. There may be large numbers of visitors attending functions or conventions, creating crowd control problems. In addition, staff are on duty intermittently, in different departments with few at night.

Requirements are:

- Fire loadings are high due to furnishings. Many areas present high fire risks (e.g. kitchens, stores, workshops, basement car parks).
- Minimum fire resistance periods for escape stairs are normally 1 hour, increasing to 2 hours for heights over 30 m. Basements require special provisions. Combustible material and surface flame spread ratings are controlled in escape routes.
- Sprinkler systems with fire mode ventilation switching, and alarm, smoke door and lift activation are commonly used in large hotels. Fire alarm, indication panel and hydrant systems must be installed together with portable and CO_2 extinguishers (for electrical equipment) in specific areas.

- Access for fire fighting vehicles, appliances, ambulances and other emergency services
- Tall buildings may require the provision of a fire fighting lift with independent power, external access and protected enclosure.

(See Chapter 11 Fire for details).

2.17 Security
Security is an important consideration for guests in unfamiliar surroundings, for confidential meetings and large group events as well as for control of loss and damage of hotel property. In operational terms security in hotels must be effective without becoming obtrusive or unduly restrictive.

By the nature of their business, hotels involve high investment costs in property and furnishings. They must be open to a wide spectrum of transient residents and visitors, many bringing valuable items. A high ratio of hotel employees are temporary with a high turnover rate and many services are contracted out. Theft, deliberate damage and vandalism are not uncommon.

Security measures include:

- Prevention of theft: construction (doors, walls, windows, access points), CCTV monitoring and sensor indicator systems, control of entry/exit through fire-escape and service doors, surveillance of car-parks, grounds, all hotel entrances.
- Control of entry: electronic card locking systems for residents and for staff (with restricted area access and master control). Staff and goods entrances through personnel and security controlled areas.
- Separation: residential lifts and stairs in view of reception desk. Planned and monitored circulations for restaurants, meeting/function rooms and support areas, service circulations separated from those for guests.
- Baggage: handling and checking controlled, baggage/lost property rooms isolated and have explosion relief.
- Administration: location and design of security offices. Banks of monitor screens and recording equipment, lockable secure interview room, direct lines to police, fire, ambulance and other emergency services.
- Hotel management: integrated computer systems of guest information, billing, accountancy, purchasing and stock records, employee and personnel details, maintenance, equipment and property records and contracts.

2.18 Hygiene
Hotels must maintain high hygiene standards to meet public health legislation and their reputation. This covers most areas, particularly design of food services, rubbish storage, water supplies, sanitation and air-conditioning including cooling towers.

2.19 Communication systems and services
The multiple functions involved in hotel operations call for highly sophisticated systems of telecommunications. Hotel management, finance, personnel, property operations, marketing, ordering and stock control, guest services and other requirements are increasingly computerised with automatic controls and customised software.

The rapid changes in equipment, installed networks and services have many implications in planning hotel buildings as well as for interior design, for example:

- High speed, large capacity external telecommunication network connections, receivers and booster equipment where required.
- Automatic back up installations, including power generators and information storage.
- Changes in requirements and mode of operation affecting design of reception desks and other departmental services.
- Extensive installation of sensing, monitoring and automatic response integrated computer systems for control of building engineering services, security, fire safety and other networks.

- Provision of secure computer rooms with independent air-conditioning, work areas and associated equipment.
- Ensuring adequate access and space for maintenance and future changes in terminal equipment, cable conduits and ducts.
- Specialist design of cable networks including safe separation of different voltages, colour coding, access and detailed records.

Design of computer installations depends on the size, sophistication and complexity of hotel services ranging from fully integrated computerised systems in large high standard hotels to interfaced standalone systems and wi-fi supporting the required number of terminals.

2.19 Building engineering services

Requirements for technical and engineering installations vary with location, size construction and sophistication of the hotel. Guestrooms call for service ducts, conduits and tunnels to enclose pipe work and cables connected to each room. Zoned distribution networks are required for lighting, power, central ventilation and air-conditioning systems.

Site planning includes arrangements for foul and surface water drainage, utility connections, and requirements such as transformers. Most engineering services plant is located in back of house areas including basements. Ventilation and air cooling plant and other machinery is often located at rooftop level. High rise and complex buildings often require intermediary transfer/technical services floors. In all cases, space, access and facilities must be provided for maintenance as well as for future changes including additional requirements and replacement.

3 GUESTROOMS AND SUITES

3.1 Commercial criteria

Guestrooms take up between 65 per cent (luxury) and 85 per cent (budget) of the total built area of a modern hotel. The income from rooms is invariably the largest source of hotel revenue and makes the greatest contribution to gross profits.

Requirements for guestrooms are largely dictated by market analysis of the potential users including:

- Main markets: demand for single, double, twin and family rooms. Work areas for business guests.
- Fluctuation: weekend, seasonal, etc. changes. Furniture and equipment. Adaptability.
- Quality and grade: standards of sophistication, size and room services. Suites.
- Lengths of stay: size and layout of rooms, amount of furniture and storage space.

Room dimensions are critical. A reduction or increase in room area is multiplied by the number of rooms involved. However, rooms which are too small are often visually restrictive or crowded, inflexible, difficult to service and liable to increase in damage.

3.2 Standardisation

There are a number of generic block form hotel types ranging from linear to circular, Figure 20.3a-f.

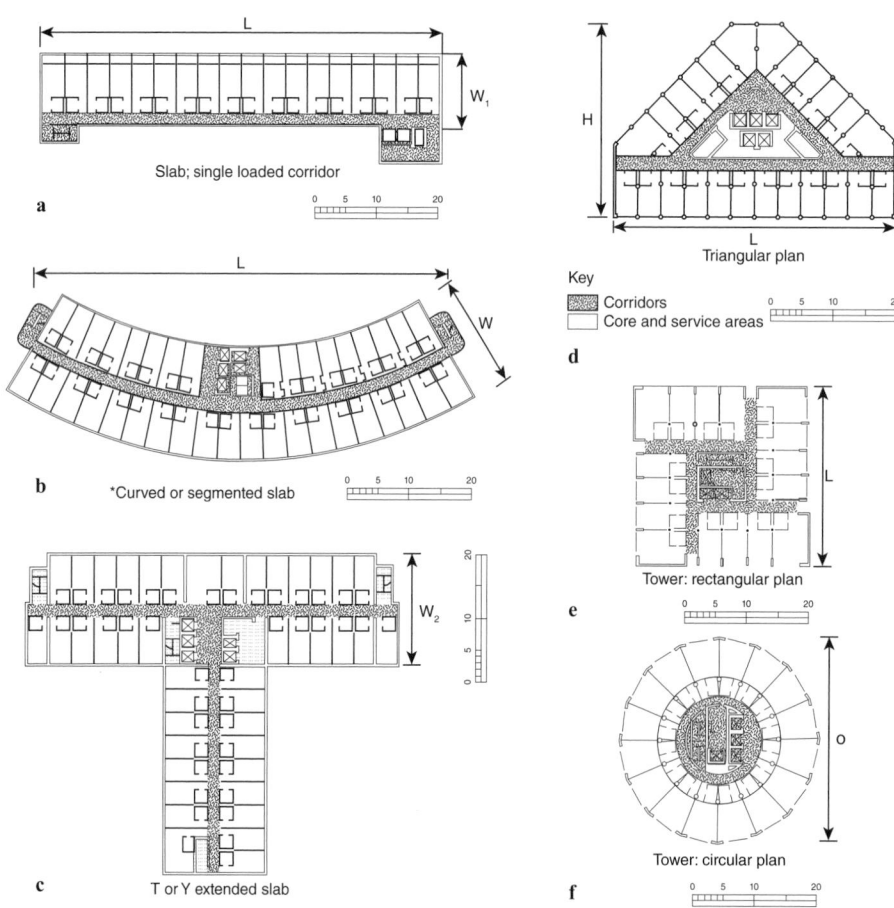

20.3a-f *Guest room floor plans*

The configuration of guest room floors is largely determined by the site, orientation, support requirements of lower floors and lift arrangements. Slab construction is based on extended linear blocks which may be (a) single or double loaded, rectangular or (b) curved, or (c) T configurations or extended as an atrium round public spaces. Tower configurations include (d) triangular, (e) rectangular or (f) circular arrangements of rooms around a central structural core of lifts, stairs ducts and service rooms.

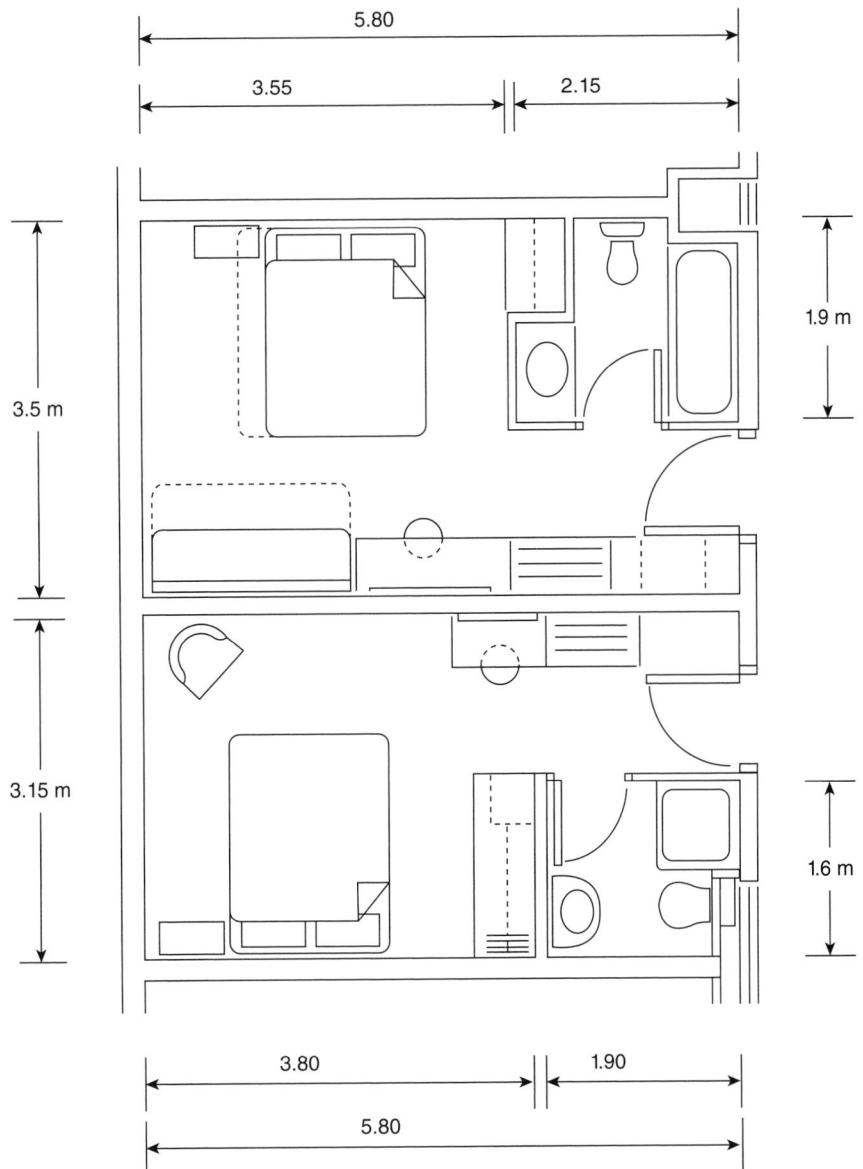

20.4 *Reduced dimensions for economy hotels*

In multi-storey hotel buildings, repetitive modules from floor to floor are essential for structural design and location of service ducts. Hotel guest rooms are predominantly the same size and designed using similar furniture with options for internal arrangement. Standardisation of requirements is important for:

- cost and time savings in construction, prefabrication;
- uniform quality and pricing, particularly in brand design;
- efficiency in organising routines in housekeeping services;
- economy in bulk purchasing of equipment, furniture and furnishings;
- rationalisation of maintenance work and replacements.

3.3 Room dimensions
Standard room widths are based on bed length of 2000 mm with wall furniture widths of 600 mm and circulation/activity space of 1000 mm adding to 3.65 m. For economy, this can be reduced to 3.5 m or increased to give a more spacious impression. Construction modules (to wall centres) add 200–230 mm.

It is important to ensure the most efficient use of room dimensions. Increase in width reduces the number of rooms or increases the length of corridors adding to gross areas and costs. Structural modules are invariably based on pairs of rooms sharing a common services duct.

Room lengths are generally more variable although these may be dictated by site or structural restrictions. Bathroom dimensions are dictated by the number and spacing of fitments.

Net room areas vary with locations, land costs, standards and brand designs, Figures 20.4, 20.5, 20.6, 20.7, 20.8.

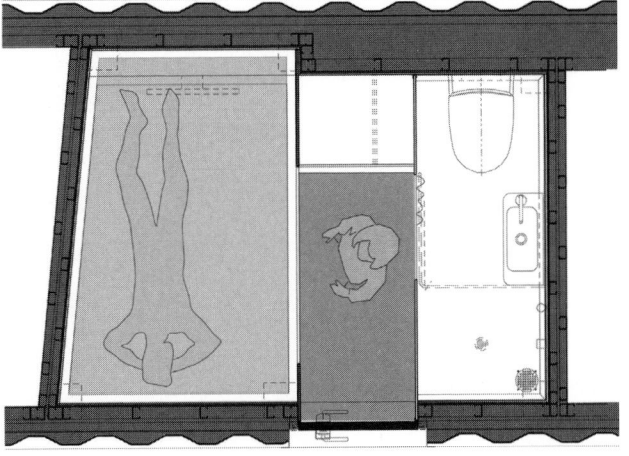

20.5 *Concept for a 2000mm x 2760mm bedroom in a converted shipping container (The Manser Practice)*

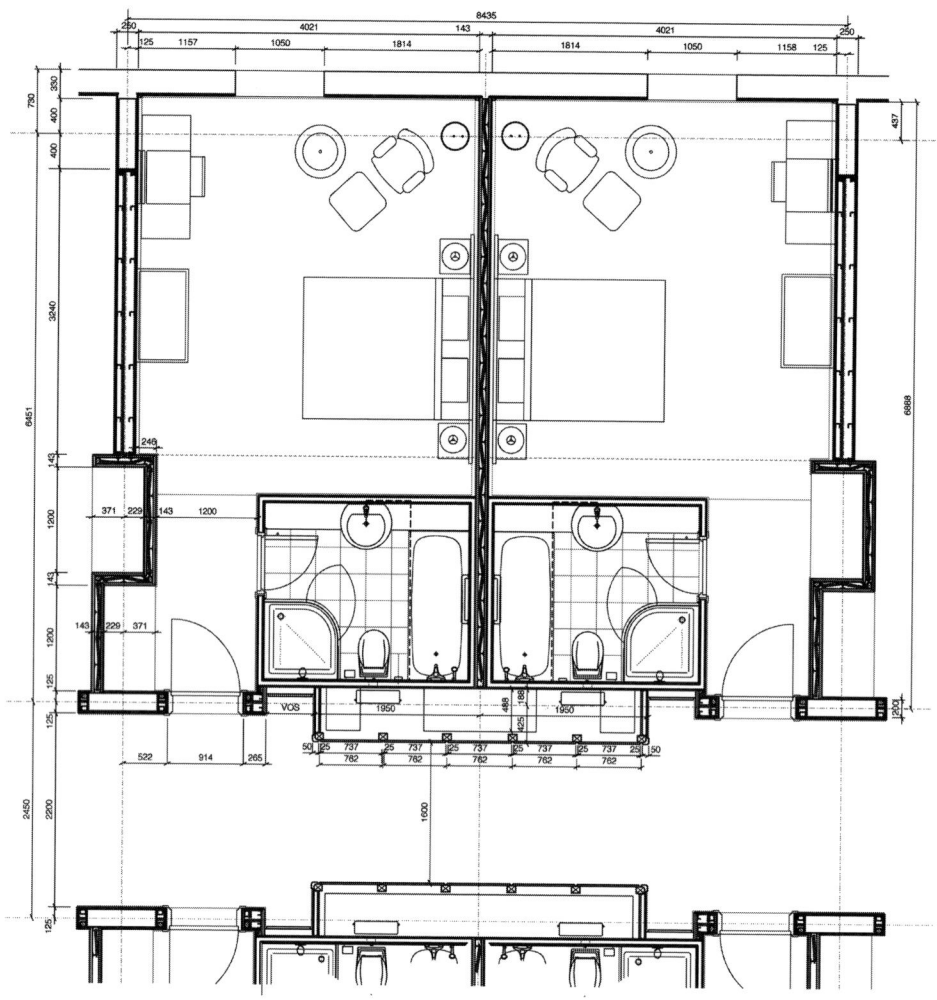

20.6 *Standard 28 sq m room designed for Gatwick Hilton (The Manser Practice)*

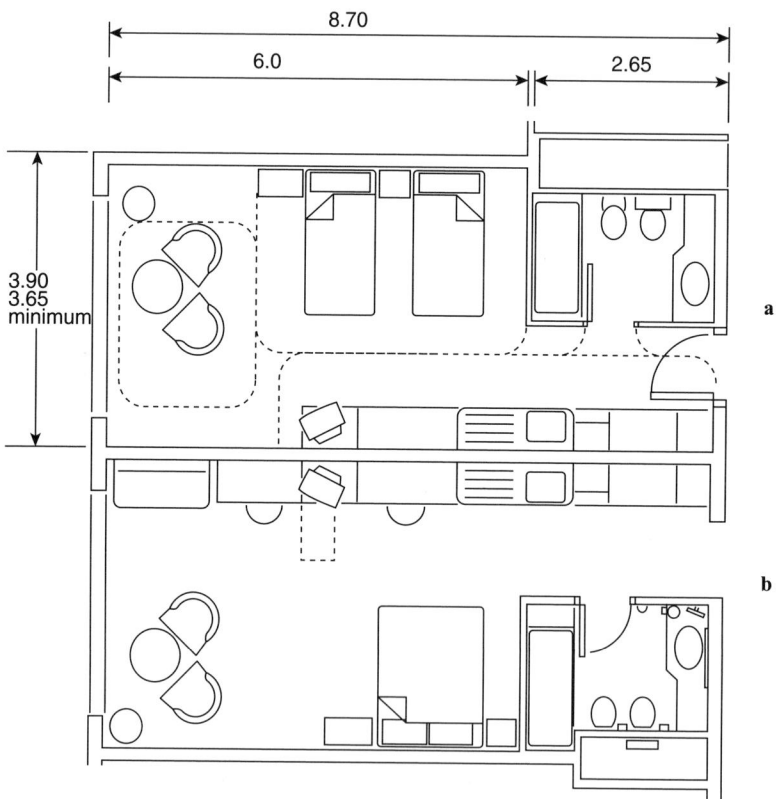

20.7 *Room layouts for a high grade hotel showing functional zones in a twin bedded room and an alternative double bed room with working area for business guests*

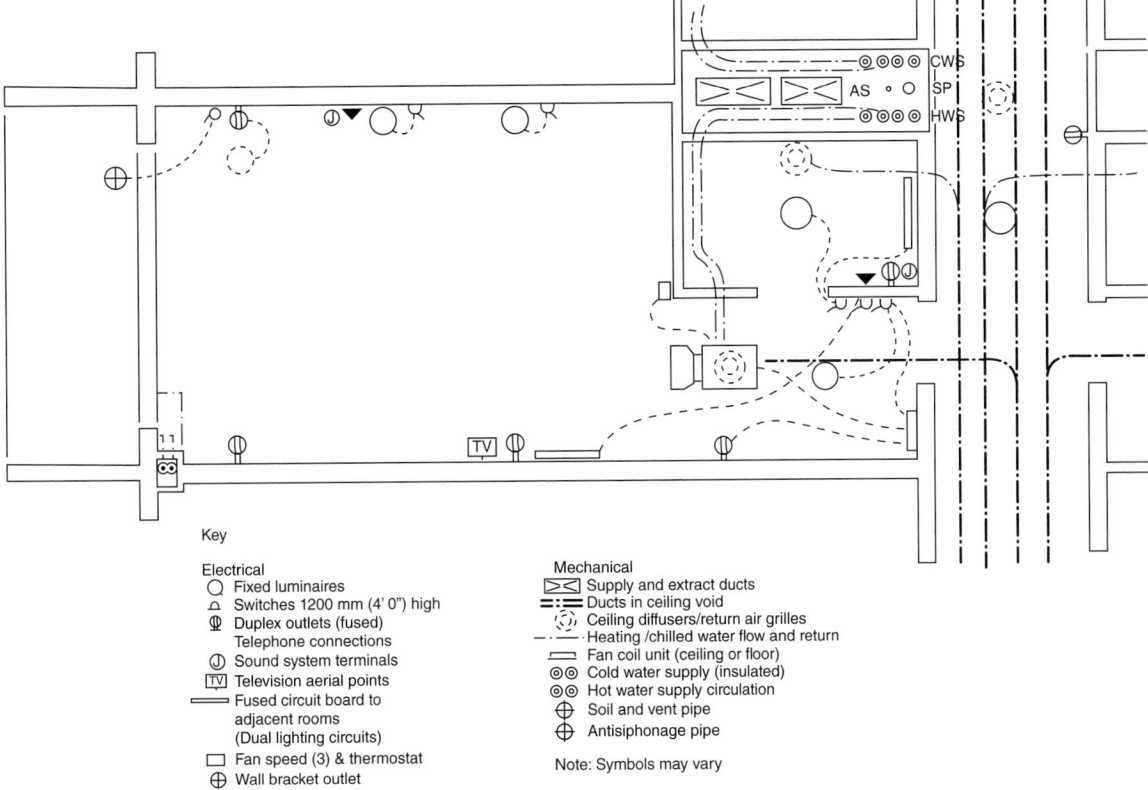

Key

Electrical
○ Fixed luminaires
△ Switches 1200 mm (4' 0") high
℗ Duplex outlets (fused)
   Telephone connections
Ⓙ Sound system terminals
TV Television aerial points
▭ Fused circuit board to
   adjacent rooms
   (Dual lighting circuits)
▢ Fan speed (3) & thermostat
⊕ Wall bracket outlet

Mechanical
▷◁ Supply and extract ducts
═╪═ Ducts in ceiling void
⦂⦂⦂ Ceiling diffusers/return air grilles
—·—·— Heating /chilled water flow and return
▭ Fan coil unit (ceiling or floor)
◎◎ Cold water supply (insulated)
◎◎ Hot water supply circulation
⊕ Soil and vent pipe
⊕ Antisiphonage pipe

Note: Symbols may vary

20.8 *Technical installations in a high grade hotel guestroom*

Table II Typical room sizes

Typical standard	Area m²	Bedroom + bathroom and lobby
Basic (1*)	18	Shower or shared facilities
Budget (2*)	20–22	Variable use including families
Midgrade (3*)	25–27	Standard provisions. Twin rooms
High grade (4*)	27–30	Business and high spend users
Luxury (5*)	34–36	Individual designs. Variable layouts

(Note: Basic rooms adaptable for family use)

Table II gives typical sizes. In general, rooms are designed for double occupancy allowing flexibility in use.

3.4 Functional zones

Room interiors are planned to provide zoned areas for various functions with adequate space for furniture, convenient use and cleaning. Zoning indicates optimum positions for controls, switches, lighting/power connections, fittings and other installations required for planning engineering and technical services:

- lounge/work: near windows, views, daylight, moveable furniture;
- sleeping: quiet areas away from windows, beds screened from entrance;
- bedside: controls, lighting, telephone, easy access;
- dressing: good lighting, mirror, table, drawers, chair/stool, multiple use;
- luggage: convenient position/design, durable, damage protection, secure safes;
- storage: near entrance, wardrobe/shelves, visible interiors, supplementary lighting;
- circulation: width (luggage), dual use of space.

3.5 Variations in rooms

To rationalise circulation, guest rooms in multi-storey hotels are invariably grouped in linear blocks arranged to meet site, structure and statutory – particularly fire escape – requirements.

Housekeeping efficiency is also a consideration in grouping numbers of rooms.

Variations in room sizes and suites are best located on the top floors, at junctions of blocks and in specifically designed areas.

Most standard suites occupy two modules. Connecting double doors (sound proofed, dual locks) between adjacent guestrooms provide for occasional family and special needs.

Balconies and terraces give rise to problems of safety, wind damage, drainage and security. They are normally limited to resort locations, Figures 20.9, 20.10.

By their nature, aparthotel rooms require additional space, Figure 20.11.

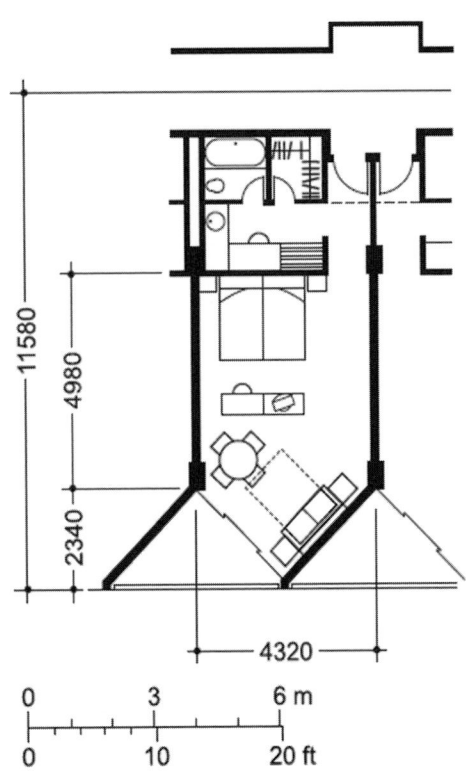

20.9 *Bedroom in a saw-tooth façade hotel*

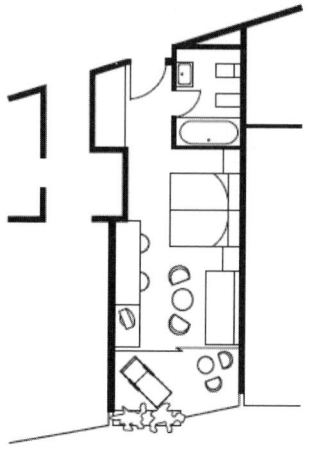

20.10 *Bedroom with small terrace*

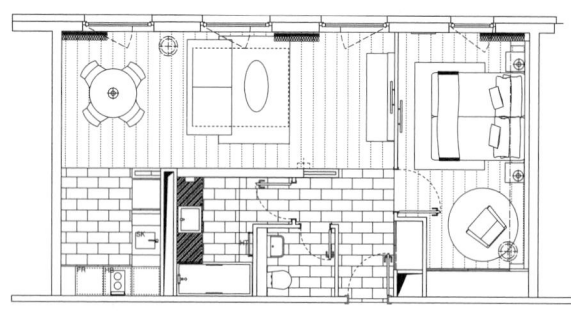

20.11a *One-bed apart hotel suite (Source: Citadines Frankfurt by Buckley Gray Yeoman for PBMG Projekt-und-Baumangement gesellschaft mbH and The Ascott Limited)*

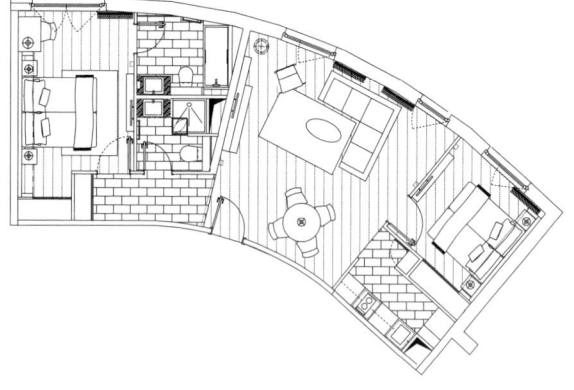

20.11b *Two-bed apart hotel suite (Source: Citadines Frankfurt by Buckley Gray Yeoman for PBMG Projekt-und-Baumangement gesellschaft mbH and The Ascott Limited)*

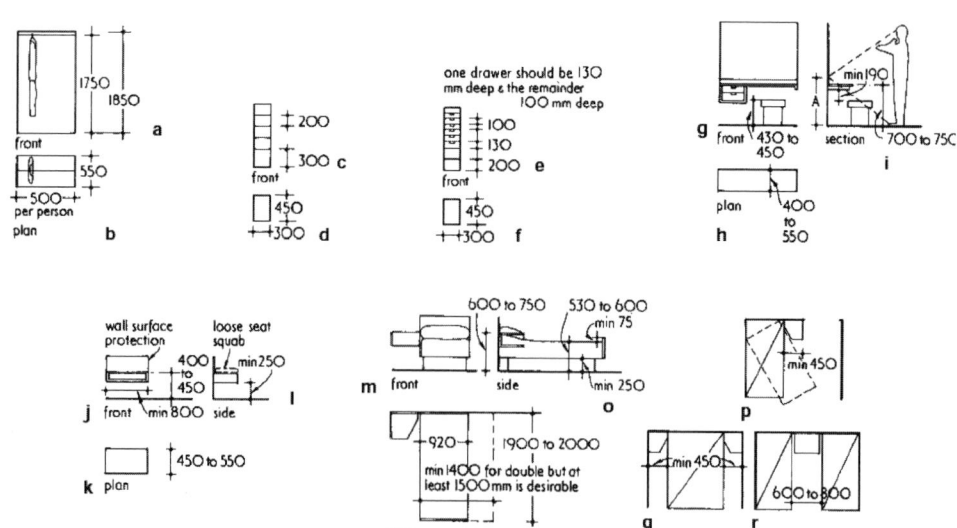

20.12 *Space requirements for hotel bedroom furniture. Note: the dimensions for wardrobe, shelf and drawer units are minimum clear internal dimensions. a Wardrobe front – per person; b Wardrobe plan; c Shelf unit front; d Shelf unit plan; e Drawer unit front; f Drawer unit plan; g Dressing/writing table front; h Dressing/writing table plan; i Dressing/writing table section. Dimension A must not exceed half eye height to achieve full-length view. For combined dressing and writing use the minimum table top area is 0.6m²; j Luggage rack front; k Luggage rack plan; l Luggage rack side; m Bedside table and single bed front; n Bedside table and single bed plan; o Bedside table and single bed side; p Bedside table for single bed; q Bedside tables for a double bed; r Bedside table for twin beds*

3.6 Furniture and furnishings

Room and bed occupancies (bednights) in hotels are perishable. They require high turnovers, intense use and efficient house-keeping to maximise revenues. Furniture, furnishings and interiors must be practical, robust and resistant to damage whilst meeting standards expected by the guests, Figures 20.12, 20.13, 20.14.

This calls for detailed specifications to meet quality and performance requirements.

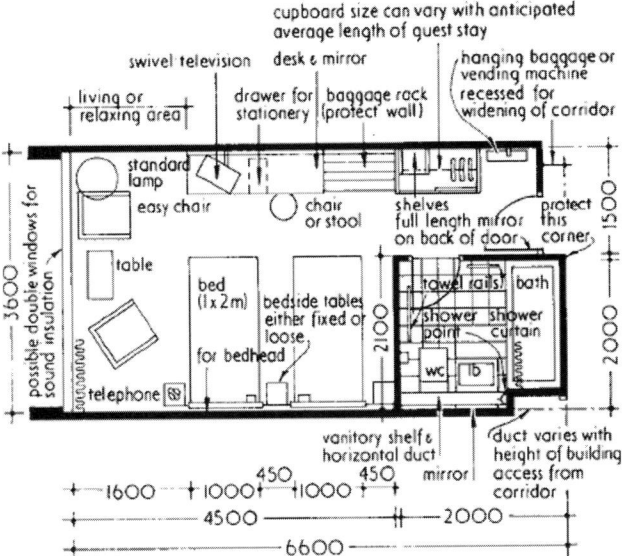

20.13 *Twin-bedded room with clothes storage and dressing table along party wall. Size varies according to site constraints and standard of accommodation*

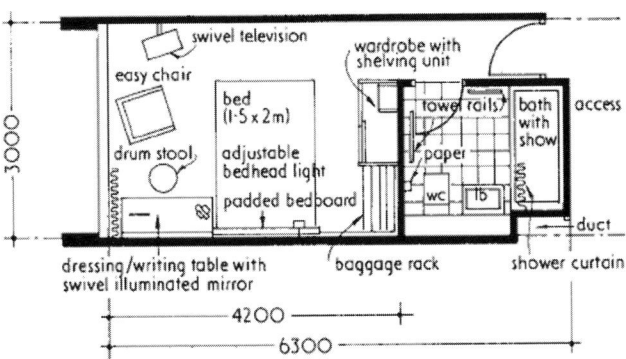

20.14 *Layout for single bedroom. Note double bed for use as double room is required*

Particular considerations include:

- Surfaces: resistant to breakage/damage by scraping, burns, stains and cosmetics etc. Vulnerable areas protected (dressing tables, luggage racks, walls, entrances).
- Support: firm anchorage in walls for cantilevered furniture and fittings.
- Framework: strong, rigid joints and construction. Ergonomic design standard units.
- Fittings: durable design, simple, easy use, quiet movement.
- Floor covering: carpets should be easy clean, durable, retain appearance, camouflage markings.
- Chairs, fabrics: complementary to design scheme, fire retarded, curtain closure.
- Beds: comfort, durability, retention of shape, edge reinforcement, quietness, standard dimensions, wall-fixed bedhead, cantilevered side cabinets, lamps.
- Bed linen, towels hard wearing, quality standards, duvet/blanket/pillow options/storage.

3.7 Bathroom location and design

Bathrooms are invariably located internally, back-to-back, enabling adjacent rooms to be serviced through a shared duct. This requires mechanical ventilation (in lowered ceiling void over the lobby) but allows savings in pipework and drainage, maintenance access, and efficient use of space and outside walls. Air extraction is automatically activated by the bathroom light switch (outside the door).

Exceptionally, luxury bathrooms (spa resorts) or economy shower rooms may be on an external wall. Bathrooms sited between guestrooms increase corridor lengths, built areas and drainage but may be suitable in low rise motels and building conversions.

Bathroom dimensions are dictated by number and arrangement of fitments, particularly baths:

- Typical fitments: 1500 mm bath, with grab bars, shower spray, retractable clothes line and curtain/screen; wc and washbasin. High grade hotels use 1700 mm bath, twin basins set in vanitory surrounds, wc and bidet. Luxury units include separate dressing rooms and shower.
- Requirements: acoustic ceiling; non-slip, drained flooring; tiled walls; mirror over washbasin; screened moisture-proof lighting; electrical safety provisions; mixer valve; thermostatic control of hot water; warmed air inflow/extraction; electric shaver point, shelf space; towel racks; toilet paper holder; coat hanger; toiletry tray; tissue dispenser; lidded waste bin. High grade hotels provide a telephone in the bathroom and music relay.

3.8 Rooms for guests with disabilities

As a rule, 1–2 per cent of guestrooms should be equipped for disabled use. Rooms for the ambulant disabled are generally on the ground floor for fire escape with easy access from the car park. Design requirements for access and room layouts must be consulted:

- Corridor width: Minimum of 915 mm with door openings 815 mm minimum with wider lobbies.
- Bathrooms: larger than standard with central turning space (1.52 m). Basin tops (860 mm high) with knee space. Toilet seat height (430 mm) Mirrors extended down. Grab bars fitted on head wall and sides of toilet and bath with easy access.
- Bedrooms: standard 3.65 m wide rooms can be adapted (with furniture changes), e.g. lower switches (1.2 m), increased space between beds, knee space below dressing tables, low window cill height (610 mm) where practicable.

4 PUBLIC AREAS

4.1 Hotel entrance and reception lobby

The main entrance and lobby must be prominent, spacious, appropriate to the style and grade of hotel. Design considerations:

- Mode of transport: parking, taxis, vehicle turn round, drop off facility, shelter.
- Identification: illumination, corporate styling, signage, assistance.
- Doorway: type, mechanism, width, safety, fire exit, security, transitional temperature/draught control, disabled use.
- Services: porter/luggage store.

4.2 Lobbies

The lobby is the hub of hotel operations and is important in creating the desired impression. It provides access to all the hotel facilities and about half the space is taken up by circulation.

The trend is for lobbies to be social spaces with cafes, workstations, wi-fi etc. and less dominated by the front desk.

Lobby facilities include the front desk, lounge seating, retail space, toilets, cloakrooms, information/assistance and other services. Typical areas, based on the number of guestrooms, are 0.3 m²/room – budget hotels, 0.5 m²/room – motor and airport hotels, 1.0 m²/room – resort and city centre hotels.

The front desk is traditionally the main focus of activity and must be set back at least 1.25 m from circulation increasing to

6 m or more for large convention hotels. Counters are typically designed with a convenient counter height for the guest and lower working height behind.

Counter lengths are planned around 1.5–1.8 m wide designed workstations fitted with angled video display screens and keyboards. Functions such as registration, checkout and guest information are generally adaptable for open desk arrangement. Increasingly reservation services provide for automatic check-in and in room facilities can be used for check out payment reducing the peak demands on the desk. Desk lengths vary with size and grade of hotel e.g. 3 m – 50 rooms, 4.5 m – 100/150 rooms, 6.0 m – 200/300 rooms. Some hotels use individual podium stations instead of a continuous counter.

The desk has direct access to the front office including cashier and front office manager.

Locations for other administration services (security, telephone exchange and management offices) are more flexible.

In larger hotels, separate counters are usually provided for information, (concierge), assistance and group reception. A separate area for convention registration and assistance may be required.

4.3 Food and beverage services
Food services involve high investment and operating costs, short design life cycles (5-7 years) and rationalisation of restaurant seating and food preparation to ensure efficient use.

- Basic/budget: limited breakfast service or use of commercial restaurant operated independently.
- Midgrade/full service: single restaurant with adjacent bar and lounge. Seating capacity depends on location, types of guests, lengths of stay and local demand. Kitchen design for set or cyclical menus. Meeting/function room(s) may be provided for groups/parties/weddings.
- High grade: room service of meals provided with service pantries on guest floors. Most large high grade hotels offer a multiple choice of restaurants, including main, coffee shop/brasserie, ethnic cuisines and speciality themed designs. The largest is adapted for breakfast (mainly self service). Food production is centralised with zoned areas for storage, preparation and cooking. Direct access is required to individual finishing areas designed to serve each restaurant, Figure 20.15.

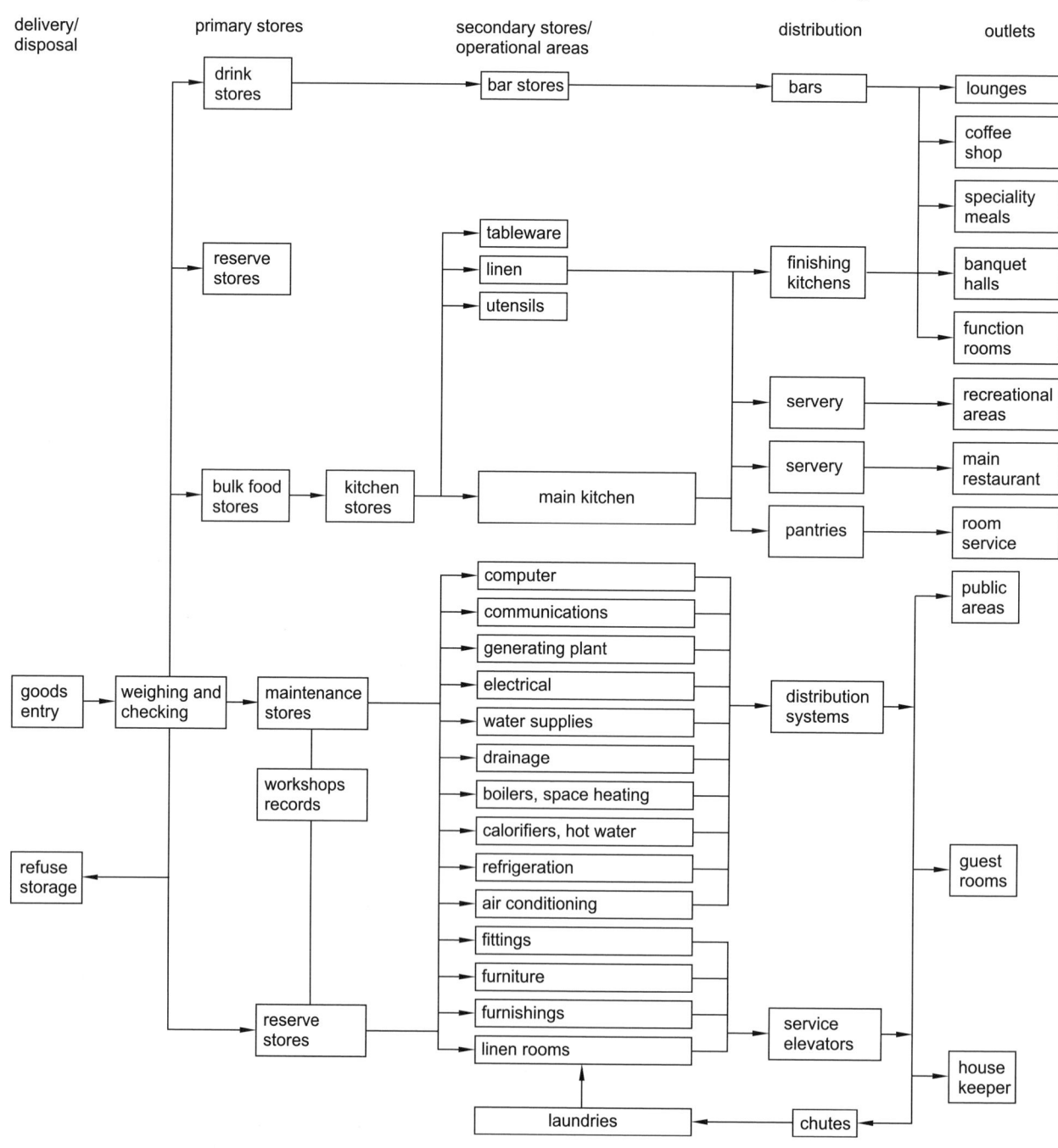

20.15 *Relationship diagram for technical and catering services*

Typically, a sophisticated cocktail lounge and bar is located near the main restaurants and a general bar/lounge to provide a focus for relaxation. Refreshments are also served in the lobby lounge and some luxury hotels provide a café style tea room for daytime visitors.

Typical areas required per seats are given in Table III.

4.4 Conference/convention/function facilities

High grade hotels invariably offer extensive meeting/conference/function rooms and banquet halls, Figure 20.16. Rapid food service for large numbers requires specially fitted pantries with purpose designed systems and equipment. These are located adjacent to the function rooms with direct service access from the main kitchen. Noise and light screening is important.

High capacity halls for convention/banquet/exhibition use are limited to major catchment areas (large towns/cities and resorts). Good access to large car parks and truck facilities is necessary.

Table III Food service areas in m² according to numbers of seats

	Area per seat (m²)	Notes
Food services		
A-la-carte restaurant	2.0 to 2.4	Fine dining and ethnic speciality restaurants
Brasserie/coffee shop	1.6 to 1.8	Limited menu. Including counter
Lounge and bar	1.2 to 1.4	Including counter. 50% seated
Functions, banquet style	1.2	
Functions, conference style	1.6	
Foyer to banquet hall	0.3	Cloakrooms, toilets, add 20%
Staff canteens	1.1 to 1.2	Based on numbers per shift
Service facilities		
Main kitchen	0.7 to 0.9	Includes main preparation areas
Coffee shop kitchen	0.3 to 0.5	Including dishwashing
Food, liquor and china storage	0.2	Cold stores, etc.
Banquet kitchen	0.24	Or 20% of banquet room
Banquet storage	0.05	Or 8% of banquet room

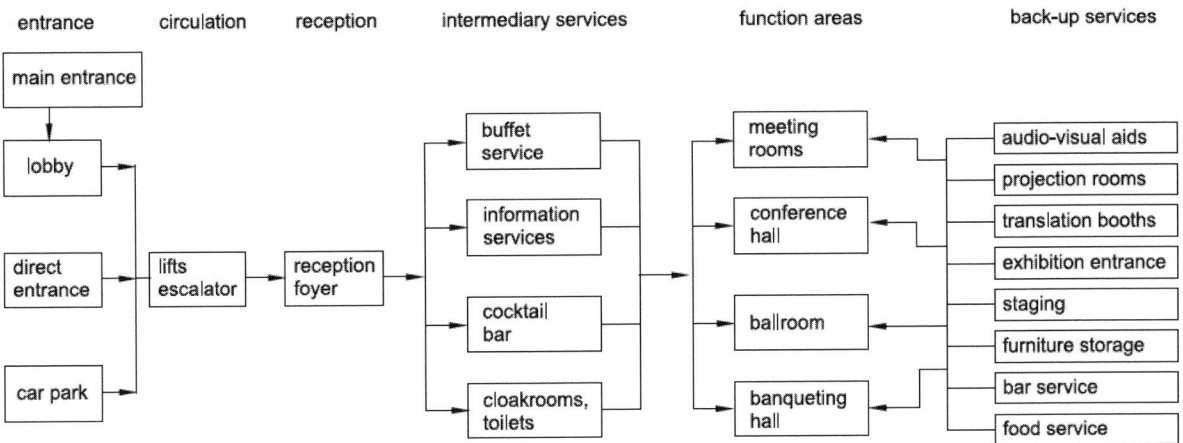

20.16 *Relationship diagram for public functions*

Convention demand is mainly seasonal requiring adaptation for multiple use. Essential requirements include:

- Specific entrances for visitors, furniture and display equipment. Services must be provided together with planned and controlled circulations.
- Design requires large spans, high ceilings, division partitions and foyer/anteroom facilities for each area.
- Engineering: installations include individual controlled/zoned air-conditioning systems, sophisticated communication and audio-video installations, lighting and power controls and numerous technical services connections for alternative layouts.
- Screened access to food service lobbies and furniture storage. Purpose-designed furniture and carrier systems.

Table IV Areas for various spaces

Function	Area
Circulation and reception	
General allowance	Gross factors: 25–35% added to room areas
Lobby areas	2-star 0.6 m² per room to 4-star 1.0 m² per room
Cloakrooms	
Fixed rows of hooks	0.1 m² per user including staff circulation and space around counter
Hooks plus seats or lockers	0.2 to 0.3 m² per user
Health and fitness clubs	
Swimming pool	15.0 × 7.0 × 1.4 m plus 2 m surround plus changing rooms
Gymnasium	15 m² for a small fitness room to 65 m² for a large complex
Public assemblies	
Conferences (theatre style)	0.6 to 1.0 m² per person plus stage, plus translation booth or 1.0 to 1.2 m² overall
Dances	0.6 to 0.9 m² per person plus band space up to 12 m² for a 6-piece band

4.5 Leisure and other facilities

Most business and resort hotels provide leisure facilities for guests. Depending on grade and location, this may range from a basic exercise room to a fully equipped leisure centre with pool(s), sauna, and fitness rooms. Typical areas for these various spaces are given in Table IV.

In town centre locations leisure facilities are commonly located in basements. Costs of provision and operation are high and local club membership is common to increase usage.

Casino hotels specialising in gaming typically require large purpose-designed halls allowing zoned areas for various users with strict supervision and security measures. Public rooms are elaborate and large numbers of guestrooms usually required.

Resort hotels are planned to maximise the benefit of the area attractions with direct access to the golf course, beach, ski-lift system or marina. In each case the hotel facilities are designed to complement the tourist experience, Figure 20.17.

5 BACK OF HOUSE FACILITIES

5.1 General

Central support areas in hotels typically take up 12–14 per cent (high standard) to 7–8 per cent (budget) of the total built space. Requirements depend on the availability of offsite services. Most of the laundry, maintenance, and refurbishing requirements are contracted out saving space and labour. Hotel facility management requires planned maintenance and life cycle replacements which can be specified and organised in advance:

- Services – general checklist.
- Loading docks – vehicle (dimensions), rubbish storage, protection/screening, recycling facilities (separation/compression/chilling), delivery/security office.

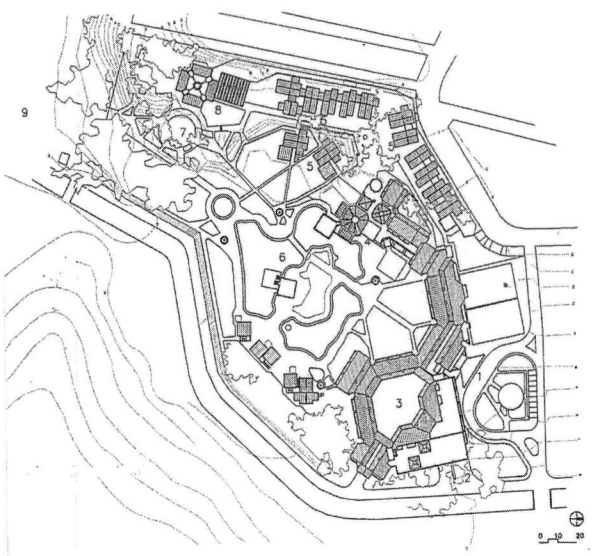

20.17 *Arum Hotel, Side, Turkey. The 22,750m² hotel provides 196 guestrooms in tiers of interlinked blocks, most facing landscaped pools and the beach. Includes restaurants and cafes as well as outdoor and indoor leisure facilities. Architect: Professor Cengis Eren*

Key: 1 Main entrance, 2 Service entrance, 3 Guestrooms, 4 Indoor pool, fitness centre, Turkish baths, 5 Apartments, 6 Swimming pool, 7 Childrens' pool and play area, 8 Café, 9 Beach

- Storage – furniture/equipment/general. Food stores (frozen/chilled/dry goods/vegetables), access to service areas, transportation.
- Plant/technical – water supplies (circulations), heating/chilling (combined power) electric (switchgear/generators) workshops/offices.

- Housekeeping – laundry/sorting/storage/supervision, other stores, service lifts/control.
- Employees – entry control, personnel rooms, changing facilities/lockers, canteens/restrooms.

6 CASE STUDIES

6.1 Travelodge, Southwark, London
Architect: Dexter Moren Associates

Introduction
This 202 bedroom hotel is for budget hotel brand Travelodge and is situated close to Tate Modern at Bankside just south of the Thames in central London. See Figures 20.18–20.22.

Site and restrictions
The 0.14ha Union Street site is on the main pedestrian route from Southwark Station to the Tate Modern and backs onto rail viaducts. It is close to the landmark Palestra building.

Solution
At street level the 6105 sq m building features a tall glazed ground floor designed as sub-divisible commercial outlets. Internally, the spaces are conceived as a 'donut' form around a central courtyard and accommodate 202 bedrooms, a bar and 60-seater restaurant facilities. Bedrooms range from 15 sq m to 21 sq m.

The building incorporates two very different elevational languages relating directly to the surrounding context, the Palestra building in particular. This has been achieved by using silver metal-clad modules with blue vertical trims in a staggered rhythm. The rear elevations fronting rail viaducts have been designed as robust brick facades with regimented windows framed with blue metal hoods.

'Our sector is based on efficiency and maximising returns, a philosophy that DMA embraces, reflected in the fact that in some instances DMA have "found" up to 15 per cent extra bedrooms within the same envelope produced by their competitors,' says Travelodge development manager Rob Ryan.

KEY
1. Reception
2. Staff Room
3. Office
4. Guestroom
5. Accessible Guestroom
6. Kitchen
7. Bar
8. Restaurant
9. Linen Room

20.18 *Travelodge Southwark first floor plan showing reception area, restaurant and bar surrounded by perimeter guestrooms*

GAMBIA STREET

UNION STREET

20.19 *Travelodge Southwark third floor plan with rooms arranged around a central light well*

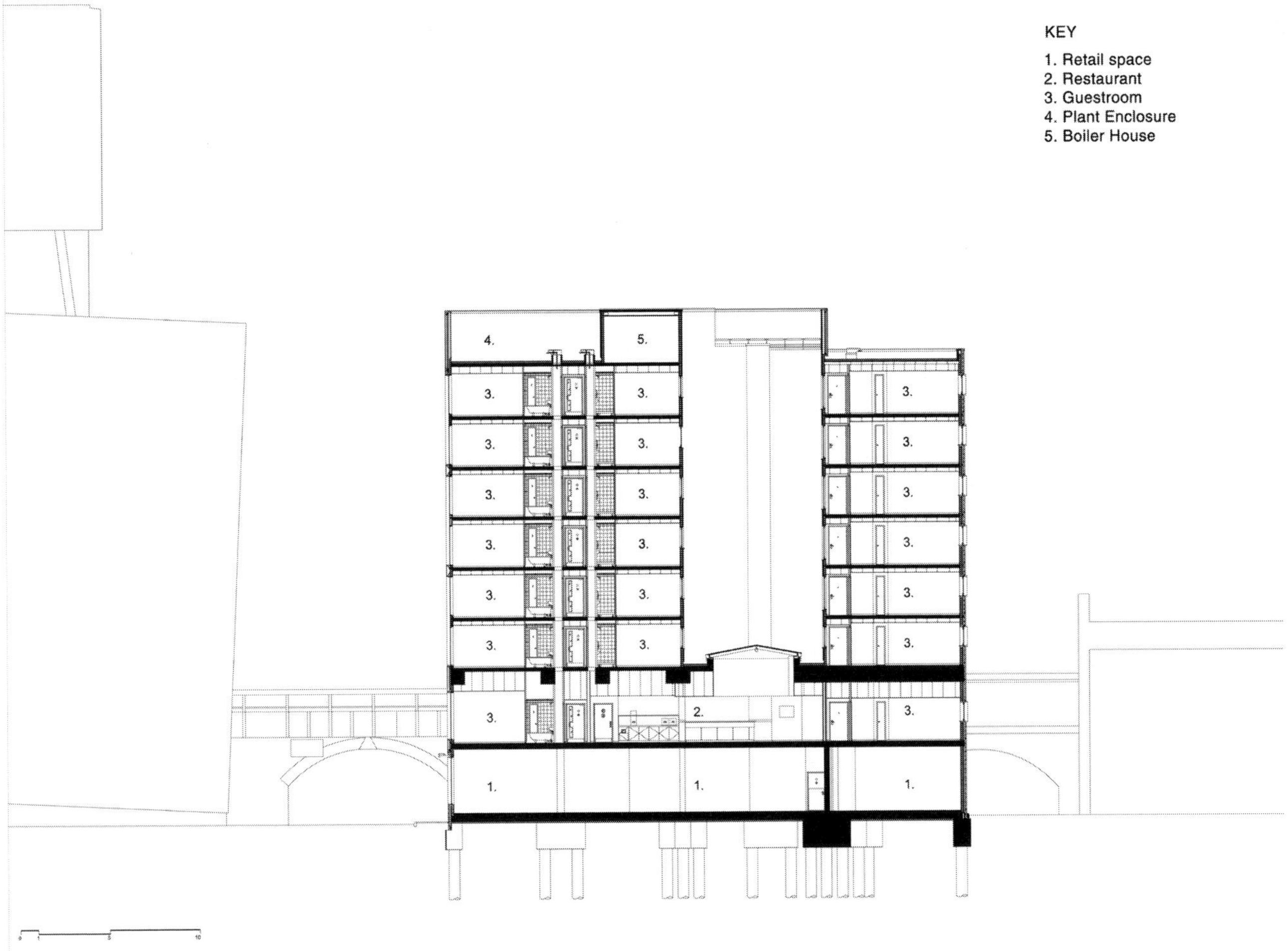

20.20 *Section through Travelodge Southwark*

20.22 *External view of Travelodge Southwark*

20.21 *Overhead image of individual room at Travelodge Southwark*

6.2 InterContinental, Westminster, London
Architect: Dexter Moren Associates

Introduction
This 18,416 m² redevelopment provided a new 256-bedroom hotel for the luxury hotel chain InterContinental in London's Westminster. See Figures 20.23–20.25.

The site
The project is a reworking of Queen Anne's Chambers, a nineteenth-century former hospital turned government office building.

Solution
The challenge was achieving a modern and coherent design within the constraints of the property's disjointed historic structure. This required major architectural interventions including the creation of a new porte cochère leading guests into an atrium reception featuring a triangular glass skylight.

Across the lower ground floor structural modifications and 2 m of excavation were required to accommodate conference facilities and a 24 hour gym for hotel guests. In addition, DMA installed eight new lifts within 2 new lift cores and incorporated a grand elliptical feature staircase to the lower ground floor. Much of the original facade was restored and retained.

On the ground floor, public spaces have been designed as a series of rooms that transition seamlessly into one another (Figure 20.23). The ground floor comprises reception, concierge, lobby lounge and Emmeline's lounge. At the heart of the hotel is a smokehouse and pub with its own entrance.

The hotel incorporates 256 new rooms including 30 studios, 14 one-bedroom suites, and a rooftop penthouse. These are arranged around four distinct wings and spread over six floors (Figures 20.24–20.25). Rooms are an average of 30 m², excluding suites and executive rooms.

The hotel interior space planning design was completed by Dexter Moren Associates and IDS with interior finishes by RPW.

20.23 *InterContinental, Westminster, ground floor. Key: 1, Driveway; 2, Reception; 3, Store; 4, Hotel offices; 5, Tea lounge; 6, Wintergarden/ lounge; 7, Restaurant; 8, Private dining room; 9, Bar; 10, Kitchen; 11, BOH corridor; 12, WC; 13, Delivery/service bay*

20.24 *InterContinental Westminster, bedroom floor. Key: 1, Guestroom: Suite; 2, Guestroom: King; 3, Guestroom: Accessible; 4, Guestroom: Twin; 5, Guestroom: Premium standard; 6, Guestroom: Duplex; 7, Lightwell; 8, BOH; 9, Linen room*

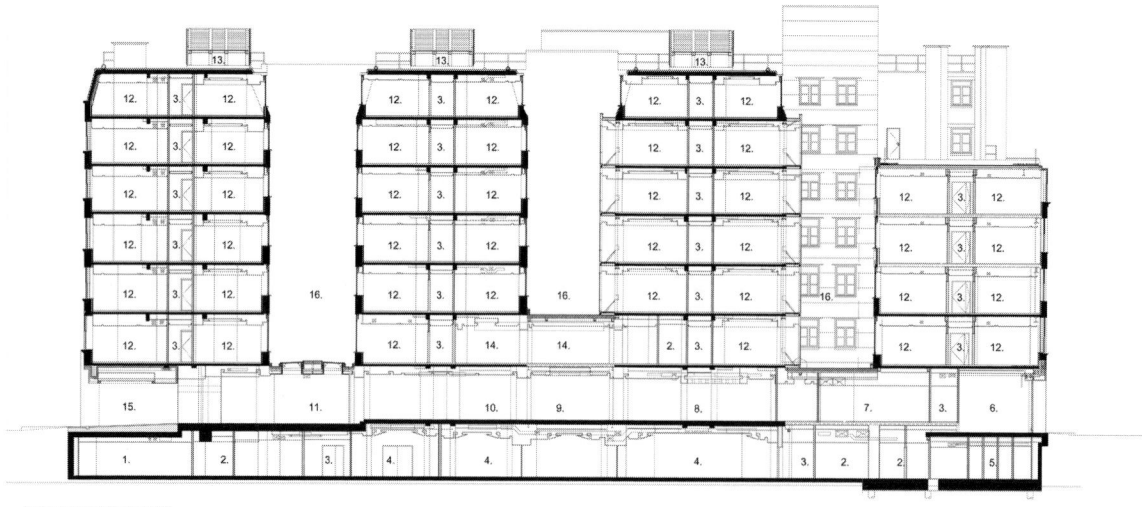

20.25 *InterContinental Westminster, Section. Key: 1, Hotel offices; 2, Store; 3, Corridor; 4, Meeting room; 5, WC; 6 Service Bay; 7, Kitchen; 8, Restaurant; 9, Lounge; 10, Tea Lounge; 11 Reception/lobby; 12 Guestroom; 13, Plant; 14, Executive Lounge; 15, Driveway/Entrance; 16, Lightwell*

7 BIBLIOGRAPHY

Architect & Designer Series, *Hotel Specification International*, Purple Media Solutions. (www.hotelspeconline.com)

Manuel Baud-Bovy, Fred Lawson. *Tourism and Recreation: Handbook of Planning and Design*, Architectural Press, Elsevier, 1998

Fred Lawson, *Congress, Convention & Exhibition Facilities: Design, Planning and Management*, Architectural Press, Elsevier, 2000 (Requirements, design of centres, hotels, examples)

Fred Lawson, *Hotels and Resorts: Planning, Design and Refurbishment*, Architectural Press (Elsevier), 1995 (Planning criteria, master plans, examples)

Richard Penner, Lawrence Adams, Stephanie K.A Robson, *Hotel Design, Planning and Development*, Routledge, 2012

World Tourism Organisation, UNWTO, (www.unwto.org) (Reports on tourism statistics, sustainability, trends)

21 Houses and flats

John Chapman

CI/SfB: 81

John Chapman is a director at PRP Architects LLP, with contributions by Kathy Watkins, architect and standards auditor at PRP Architects LLP. PRP specialises in residential design and was on the advisory panel for the government's recent Housing Standards Review.

KEY POINTS:

- *Housing standards in England are currently (2014) under review by the Department for Communities and Local Government (DCLG). It is likely that a number of significant changes will be introduced in the coming years, both to planning policy and Building Regulations*
- *Housing space standards in the UK are considered to be amongst the lowest in Europe*
- *Low space standards lead to dissatisfaction particularly for public sector (social) housing which tends to be more fully occupied*
- *Accommodation has to be tailored to numbers and characteristics of expected residents*

Contents

1 Introduction
2 Published standards
3 Design data
4 Single-family houses
5 Purpose-built flats
6 House conversions
7 Accommodation for single people
8 Estate regeneration
9 Case study
10 References

1 INTRODUCTION

1.1 Housing standards

Successive governments have made attempts to influence or impose standards in housing over the last century. The Tudor Walters Report of 1918 and the Dudley Report in 1944 reflected the 'homes fit for heroes' feeling of post-war social optimism.

In 1961 the report 'Homes for Today and Tomorrow' was published by the Parker Morris Committee of the Ministry of Housing and Local Government (MHLG). The standards in this report, which subsequently became widely known as Parker Morris Standards, were imposed as mandatory on local authority housing in 1967 and were converted to metric in 1968. They were not adhered to by the private sector and ceased to be mandatory in 1981.

In 2013, the government began the Housing Standards Review, a fundamental review of housing regulations and standards in collaboration with various industry bodies and experts. As this edition went to press, the review was expected to result in a new national housing space standard to apply cross-tenure, with optional requirements for age-friendly and wheelchair housing to be incorporated into Building Regulations, and the withdrawal of several current standards including the Code for Sustainable Homes and Building for Life.

1.2 Public and private sector housing

In Britain, as in many other countries, housing is divided into privately and publicly funded sectors. Early in the twentieth century, the new local authorities (LAs) increasingly took over the provision of social housing from charitable foundations (such as the Peabody, William Sutton and Guinness Trusts).

The growth of municipal housing became such that in some urban boroughs most of the housing was in their ownership. This has been reversed in recent years by a number of government measures: right-to-buy, restriction of LA expenditure and by the growth (or birth) of charitable Housing Associations (HAs) and other Registered Providers (RPs), funded and subsidised through the Housing Corporation – now known as the Homes and Communities Agency. There is now an accelerating trend for local authorities to transfer some, or even all, of their housing stock to HAs, or other Registered Providers.

While historically the privately funded sector used to be geared to the provision of housing for rent, it now almost exclusively provides for purchase through mortgages, mainly from banks and building societies. With the volatility of interest rates, the level of affordable payments is crucial for most of its customers. There is therefore a tendency for standards in the 'spec housing' market to be cut to the minimum and private developers have a long tradition of resisting space standards imposed other than by the market.

There has, until recently, been a steady demand for small 'starter homes' – both flats and houses – at affordable prices. This reflects the demographic changes over the last century. Household sizes have fallen dramatically, but the numbers of independent households have grown rapidly, partly due to the steady growth of failed marriages and partnerships. Later, some of these initially small households, as occupants have more money, and perhaps a family, are able to sell and buy somewhere bigger. This may be a large, older house, or it may be one of the superior-quality, speculative houses that some developers are building at, or even above, social housing standards. It is uncertain whether the demand for starter homes will continue. In some cases they have been found difficult to sell when the original owners have required more space. Even people living on their own are beginning to demand more generous accommodation.

The public sector is very different. Tenants of social housing have less choice in their dwellings. Also, once the household is accommodated, their ability to move home is limited. Often the only opportunity is likely to be a mutual swap with another household. Clearly this does not happen very often, so the tenant is likely to be in his or her flat or house for a long time. Recent government changes to benefits – widely referred to as 'the bedroom tax' – are intended to encourage residents to move out of under-occupied properties. However the LA housing department, HA or RP is unlikely to have a larger, or smaller, dwelling becoming available for a requested transfer at the right time and in the right place. This is the argument for ensuring, especially in the publicly funded sector, that reasonable standards are maintained.

People must have the room to settle satisfactorily into what is likely to be their long-term home. Post-Parker Morris standards, the Housing Corporation (HC) did not lay down space standards, preferring to leave these to the experience and judgment of HAs or RPs, and to their architects. Instead, during the 1980s and 1990s the HC funded HA schemes according to its Total Cost Indicators (TCI), which laid down cost allowances based upon gross internal area in 5 m^2 increment bands. These bands were related to probable occupancies, but they were also very broad and approximate, so that the bands varied from well below to well above PM dwelling sizes.

Table I   Comparison of dwelling sizes

Comparison of internal areas, including storage

Standard		Parker Morris[1] min area (m²)	HQI's[2] target area (m²)	London Plan min area (m²)	Lifetime Homes[4] min area (m²)*	Wheelchair[4] min area (m²)*	Wheelchair[5] min area (m²)*	Wheelchair[6] min area (m²)
Single	1b2p	47.5–48.5	45–50	50	50	60	65	55–60
storey	2b3p	60.0–61.0	57–67	61	55	66	75	70–75
dwelling	2b4p	71.5–73.5	67–75	70	75	86	85	75–80
	3b4p			74			100	80–85
	3b5p	80.0–82.5	75–85	86	85	95	110	90–95
	3b6p	88.5–90.0		95			115	95–100
	4b5p			90			116	
	4b6p		85–95	99	105	110	125	100–105
Two	2b4p	76.5–79.0	67–75	83	75	86	100	80–85
storey	3b4p			87			110	85–90
dwelling	3b5p	86.5–89.5	82–85	96	85	95	120	100–105
	3b6p	97.0					125	100–105
	4b5p			100			125	
	4b6p		95–100	107	105	110	130	105–110
	7p	114.5	108–115		111			
Three	3b5p	98.5	85–95	102				
storey	3b6p	102.5						
dwelling	4b5p			106				
	4b6p		100–105	113				
	7p +	118.5	add 10m² per person					

[1]Parker Morris (1961) (mandatory for publicly funded housing from 1967 to 1981)
[2]p27, Housing Quality Indicators v4 (May 2007 updated April 2008) published by the Housing Corporation (now the Homes and Communities Agency)
[3]p87, The London Plan (2011) published by the GLA
[4]p18, Habinteg Housing Association Design Guide (2003)
[5]p3, Wheelchair homes design guidelines published by the South East London housing partnership. It should be noted that the requirements in this document are more onerous than those of the WHDG
[6]Northern Ireland Department for Social Development
*Areas are the probable minimum. There are no mandatory minimum areas for these types of housing in England.

TCIs were replaced as a means of funding social housing by the Scheme Development Standards (SDS). These were in turn replaced by the Design and Quality Standards (D&QS), first introduced by the Housing Corporation in 2007 (see Section 2.3).

Following the formation of the Homes and Communities Agency (HCA) in 2008 by a merger of the Housing Corporation and English Partnerships, the National Affordable Housing Programme continues to operate according to the HCA Design and Quality Standards (see 2.3), accompanied by the Housing Quality Indicators (HQI) version 4 (updated April 2008), as inherited from the Housing Corporation.

1.3 Housing for different users

A significant proportion of the population is disabled in some way. While many people with disabilities are able to cope in normal dwellings, others, such as those in wheelchairs, require substantial modifications to enable them to live satisfactorily. Housing to special-needs standards is now being built, both for mobility and more onerous wheelchair use. Housing not specifically designed for people with disabilities is known as general needs housing. Part M of the Building Regulations, first introduced in 1999, extended the requirements for disabled access to all new dwellings, although the requirements do not go as far as those for wheelchair-using residents.

1.4 Parker Morris standards

For the reasons given above, it is important that public-sector housing, at least, is not allowed to slip below the standards that came to be accepted as reasonable during the period when Parker Morris ruled by statute. Research into housing built to PM standards has shown that, while there may be much wrong with other aspects of estate design, such as the confused and insecure arrangement of external spaces, there is usually a good level of satisfaction with the internal layout and space standards. Conversely, where public sector housing has been designed to lower than PM standards, or where PM housing has been over-occupied, the tenants have responded by consistently expressing dissatisfaction.

This edition of *Metric Handbook* therefore continues to include the minimum unit areas of the Parker Morris standards against which to benchmark and compare various other later standards as set out in Table I and in Table II. It should be emphasised that Parker Morris did not lay down minimum areas for rooms. The report simply stated that the dwelling had to be furnishable with a specified amount of furniture which had to be shown on the plans.

It also required reasonable storage space, which has proved to be a popular and successful feature of Parker Morris housing.

1.5 Room area standards

In the publicly funded housing sector an additional set of space standards came to be widely accepted for the minimum sizes of individual rooms. These are quite commonly but erroneously referred to as 'Parker Morris'. As stated above, the PM committee went out of their way to avoid being prescriptive about individual rooms. The origin of these figures is understood to have been the Greater London Council (GLC), which funded many HA projects in the capital in the 1970s and early 1980s. They were particularly applied to refurbishment or rehabilitation projects, to which Parker Morris standards were never mandatorily applied.

After the demise of Parker Morris standards as statutory minimum, these room sizes were still widely adopted as reasonable, minimum, design standards for social housing. Many HAs still include them in their briefing documents to architects, and these are set out in Table II. Some London boroughs included these minimum room areas in the standards sections of their Unitary Development Plans, published in the early 1990s, as minimum which had to be achieved in any housing schemes, public or private, for which planning approval was sought.

2 PUBLISHED STANDARDS

2.1 Building Regulations (England & Wales)

The Building Regulations, which apply to all tenures of housing across England and Wales (including London), are generally clear and easy to understand. All parts of the Building Regulations, now including Approved Document M (Access to and use of buildings), apply to housing. (See Table III.)

The extension of Approved Document M to cover dwellings from October 1999 was an important development. It came about following a gradual change in thinking in recent years that all housing should be accessible to people in wheelchairs, not least to permit them to visit friends and relations. This should also permit people to remain in their homes well into old age or infirmity, instead of having to move to more accessible special accommodation. As such, significant requirements now apply to, for example, provision of downstairs toilets and level front door access, and minimum corridor and door widths. (See Table IV.)

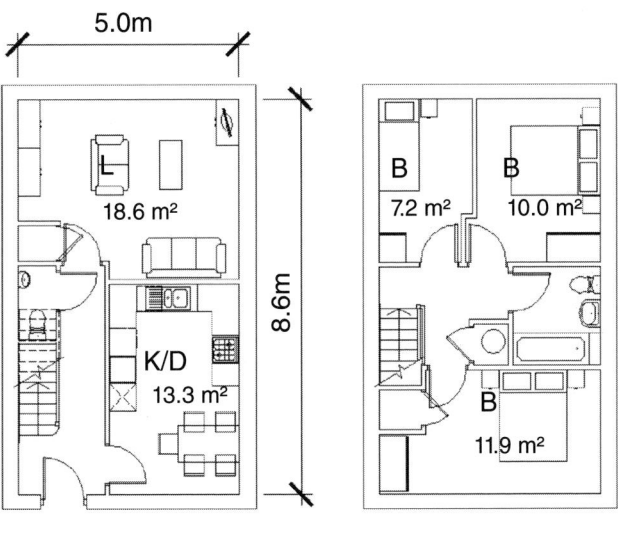

a *Private for sale 85.0m²*

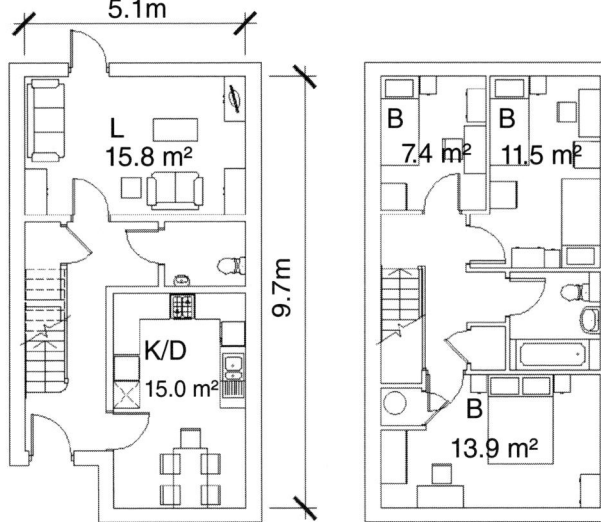

b *Design Quality Standards and Lifetime Homes Standard compliant 96.5m²*

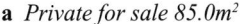

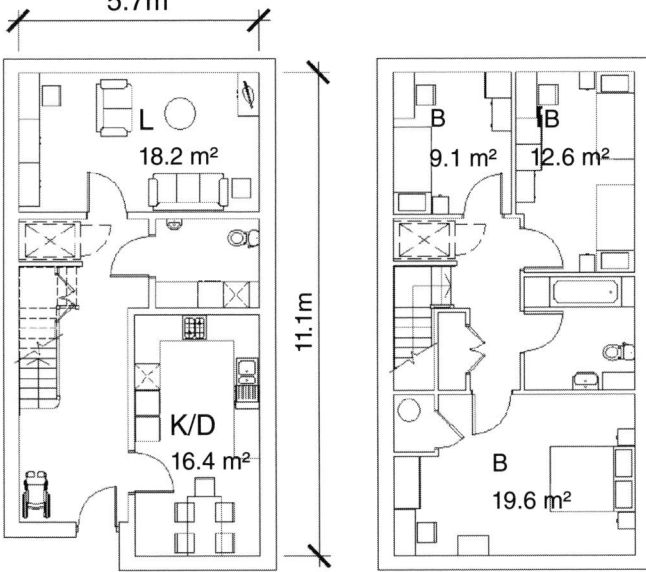

c *Wheelchair Housing Design Guide compliant 124.5m²*

21.1 *Examples of three-bedroom, five person, two storey terrace houses to meet different standards. Architects: PRP Architects.*

Approved Document L was revised in 2013 and came into effect in 2014. This requires all new housing to achieve that equivalent of Code for Sustainable Homes Level 4.

All Approved Documents are available online via the Planning Portal.

The main parts affecting the planning of housing are set out in Table III.2.2

2.2 National Planning Policy Framework (NPPF)

The legal framework for planning decisions requires planning applications to be determined in accordance with the development plan unless material considerations indicate otherwise. The development plan will consist of the local plan for the relevant local authority (together with the London Plan in the case of London Boroughs) with more detailed guidance often produced as Supplementary Planning Documents (SPD).

Policies in local plans or guidance in SPDs often include detailed design standards for housing and can relate to external amenity, privacy, overlooking, sustainability, car parking etc. They can also cover such areas as defining appropriate housing density, external design and, in some cases, minimum room sizes. Although there is no minimum density prescribed in the NPPF, local authorities often use density as a tool in assessing the acceptability of a

Table II Comparison of 'Parker Morris' derived standards with current London housing standards

Parker Morris room sizes, minimum and recommended (area in m²)

Number of residents	1	2	3	4	5	6	7
Living room in a dwelling with dining kitchen	11 (11)	12 (12)	13 (13)	14 (14)	15 (15)	16 (16)	17 (17)
Living room in a dwelling with galley kitchen	13 (13)	14 (14)	16 (15)	17 (16)	19 (17.5)	20 (18.5)	21 (19.5)
Dining kitchen	8 (8)	9 (9)	10 (10)	11 (11)	12 (12)	13 (13)	14 (14)
Galley kitchen	5.5 (5.5)	6.5 (5.5)	6.5 (5.5)	7 (7)	8 (7)	8 (7)	9 (9)
Main bedroom (double)	9 (8)	12 (11)	12 (11)	12 (11)	12 (11)	12 (11)	12 (11)
Other double bedrooms				12 (11)	12 (11)	12 (11)	12 (11)
Single bedroom		9 (8)*	8 (6.5)	8 (6.5)	8 (6.5)	8 (6.5)	8 (6.5)

*a flat for two single people should have two single bedrooms of recommended 9m², minimum 8m² each
Minimum sizes (given in brackets)

Current London room sizes and widths (applicable to all housing in London)

Number of residents	1	2	3	4	5	6	7
Living/kitchen/dining *recommended width*		23	25	27	29	31	
		2.8	2.8	3.2	3.2	3.2	
Main bedroom (double) recommended width 2.75m		12 (11.5)*	12 (11.5)*	12 (11.5)*	12 (11.5)*	12 (11.5)*	
Other double bedrooms recommended width 2.75m				12 (11.5)*	12 (11.5)*	12 (11.5)*	
Single bedroom			8 (7.5)*	8 (7.5)*	8 (7.5)*	8 (7.5)*	
Bathroom**		4.4	4.4	4.4	4.4	4.4	
WC**		2.4	2.4	2.4	2.4	2.4	

*Recommended figures for all tenures, minimum sizes are acceptable for publically funded housing
**Figures are applicable to funded housing only

Table III Building Regulations 2000 (England and Wales) applying to dwellings

Approved Document		Last revision	Applies to housing	Relevant to planning of housing
A	Structure	2004 edition (*incorporating 2004, 2010 and 2013 amendments*)	*	
B Vols 1 & 2	Fire Safety (means of escape, etc.)	2006 edition (*incorporating 2010 and 2013 amendments*)	*	*
C	Site preparation (resistance to moisture)	2004 edition (*incorporating 2010 and 2013 amendments*)	*	
D	Toxic substances (cavity insulation)	1992 edition (*incorporating 2002 and 2010 amendments*)	*	
E	Resistance to passage of sound	2010 edition*	*	*
F	Ventilation	2010 edition*	*	*
G	Sanitation, hot water safety and water efficiency	2010 edition*	*	*
H	Drainage and waste disposal	2002 edition*	*	*
J	Combustion appliances and fuel storage systems	2010 edition*	*	*
K	Protection from falling, collision and impact	2013 edition	*	*
L1A	Conservation of fuel and power (new dwellings)	2013 edition	*	*
L1B	Conservation of fuel and power* (existing dwellings)	2010 edition* (*incorporating 2010 and 2011 amendments*)	*	*
L2A	Conservation of fuel and power (new non-dwellings)	2013 edition		
L2B	Conservation of fuel and power (existing buildings other than dwellings)	2010 edition* (*incorporating 2010 and 2011 amendments*)		
M	Access to and use of buildings	2004 edition (*incorporating 2010 and 2013 editions*)	*	*
P	Electrical safety – dwellings	2013 edition	*	
	Regulation 7 – Material and workmanship	2013 edition	*	

* to be read in conjunction with 2013 amendments

proposal. Planning densities are normally expressed in dwellings per hectare (or acre) or habitable rooms per hectare (or acre). The definition of habitable rooms is normally taken to be all living rooms, bedrooms and dining kitchens (the latter commonly only if more than 13 m²). Densities for new housing commonly vary from around 150 habitable rooms per hectare (60 habitable rooms per acre) to 250 habitable rooms per hectare (100 habitable rooms per acre), see Figures 21.2 and 21.3 for illustrations of layouts at these densities. Different planning authorities have widely differing minimum dimension requirements, Figure 21.4. Some authorities allow higher densities for non-family housing, or for areas close to urban centres or good transport links.

Material considerations can cover broad and far reaching issues. Particular regard should be given to the effect of the proposal on the site's surrounding context, its bulk, scale and massing in the streetscene as well as the proposal's effect on privacy, outlook and loss of daylight/sunlight. Other important material

Table IV Summary of key requirements for accessible general needs housing from Building Regulations Approved Document M, 2004 edition.

Sections 6 to 10 apply to new dwellings

Section 6 – Means of access to and into the dwelling
This section covers level, ramped or stepped approach.

- Level approach should be no steeper than 1:20
- Ramped approach is allowed if the plot gradient exceeds 1:20, but not 1:15
- Ramps must be a minimum of 900 mm wide
- Ramp flights no longer than 10 m at 1:15, or 5 m at 1:12
- Top and bottom landings a minimum of 1.2 m length
- Stepped approach is allowed if the plot gradient exceeds 1:15
- Steps must be a minimum of 900 mm wide
- Rise of flight between landings must not exceed 1.8 m
- Top and bottom landings a minimum of 900 mm
- Suitable tread nosing profiles, and uniform rise of between 75 mm and 150 mm
- Going (tread) of steps no less than 280 mm
- Handrail to one side of steps with three or more risers, extending 300 mm at top and bottom
- Thresholds should be accessible
- In exceptional circumstances (a stepped approach) a stepped threshold of a maximum 150 mm rise
- External entrance door minimum clear opening 775 mm

Section 7 – Circulation within the entrance storey of the dwelling
This section covers internal corridor and door widths.

- Corridors should be minimum width 900 mm to 1200 mm, depending on door widths
- Corridors can be a minimum of 750 mm opposite obstruction such as radiator, for no longer than 2 m
- Door clear opening widths should be minimum as follows:

  750 mm at end of 900 mm wide corridor
  750 mm off 1200 mm wide corridor when approach not head-on
  775 mm off 1050 mm wide corridor when approach not head-on
  800 mm off 900 mm wide corridor when approach not head-on

- In exceptional circumstances (severely sloping plots) steps are allowed within the entrance storey. Such steps should be a minimum of 900 mm wide, with handrails to both sides

Section 8 – Accessible switches and socket outlets in the dwelling
This section gives heights for fittings to assist people whose reach is restricted.

- Switches and sockets in habitable rooms should be between 450 mm and 1200 mm height above floor level

Section 9 (and AD Part K) – Passenger lifts and common stairs in blocks of flats
This section gives requirements on lift dimensions, and on stair dimensions in blocks which do not have lifts.
Requirements for passenger lifts:

- 400 kg minimum load capacity
- 1.5 m × 1.5 m landings in front of entrances
- Lift door clear opening 800 mm
- Car minimum width 900 mm and minimum length 1250 mm
- Controls between 900 mm and 1200 mm above floor level

Requirements for common stairs in blocks of flats without a lift:-

- Contrasting brightness step nosings
- Suitable step nosing profiles (illustrated in the Approved Document)
- Step maximum rise 170 mm; maximum going (tread) 250 mm
- Non open risers
- Continuous handrail on both sides of flights of more than 2 steps, extending 300 mm onto landings

Section 10 – WC provision in the entrance storey of the dwelling
This section requires a WC on the entrance floor of any dwelling, and gives dimensional guidance.

- If there is a habitable room on the entrance floor, there should be a WC on that floor
- WC door should open outward, and opening should overlap WC pan by 250 mm
- Door widths should observe the measurements described in Section 7 (with clear opening widths in accordance with Table 4 of the Approved Document)
- In a front access WC, compartment should be 1000 mm wide (or minimum 900 mm wide)
- In an oblique access WC, compartment should be 900 mm wide (or minimum 850 mm wide)
- Transfer space 750 mm deep should be provided in front of WC

considerations include the contents of the NPPF as well as a proposal's effect on the existing situation, e.g. flood risk, ecology and energy footprint.

Car-parking requirements vary considerably between planning authorities. Inner city authorities may require only one space per house and less for a flat, but suburban areas may demand two or more spaces per house. Visitors' spaces need to be added at 10 to

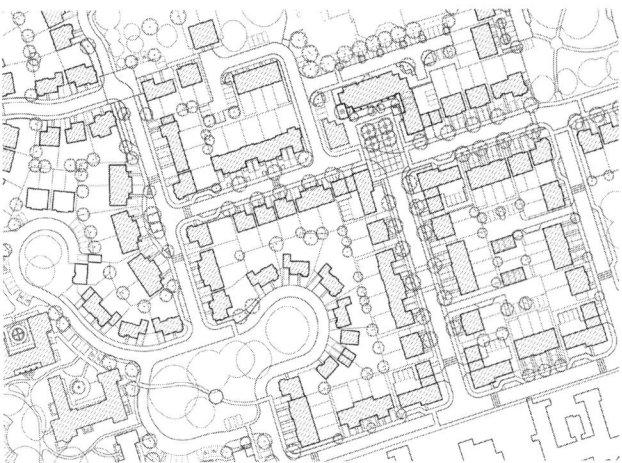

21.3 *Housing layout in a suburban location including conversion of existing buildings at an overall density of 30 Dw/Ha (150 HR/Ha). Parking ratio 1.7 spaces per unit*

20 per cent. Some authorities at present allow considerable relaxation of their requirements for social housing, on the basis of lower than average recorded car ownership. There is also a movement towards 'car free' developments, for some sites that are particularly well served by public transport.

2.3 The Homes and Communities Agency: Design and Quality Standards

The Design and Quality Standards apply to all new-build, general-needs, non-specialised, affordable and intermediate housing where the HCA is providing an element of grant funding, either facilitating or providing free or discounted land value or facilitating or funding major infrastructure investment as part of a regeneration project. Within the London area however, the HCA operates as regulator only. Responsibility for housing and regeneration activity in London lies with the Greater London Authority.

21.2 *Medium density housing layout of two and three storey houses and flats in a typical urban location with open car-parking area. Density 53 Dw/Ha (240 HR/Ha). Parking ratio 1.4 spaces per unit*

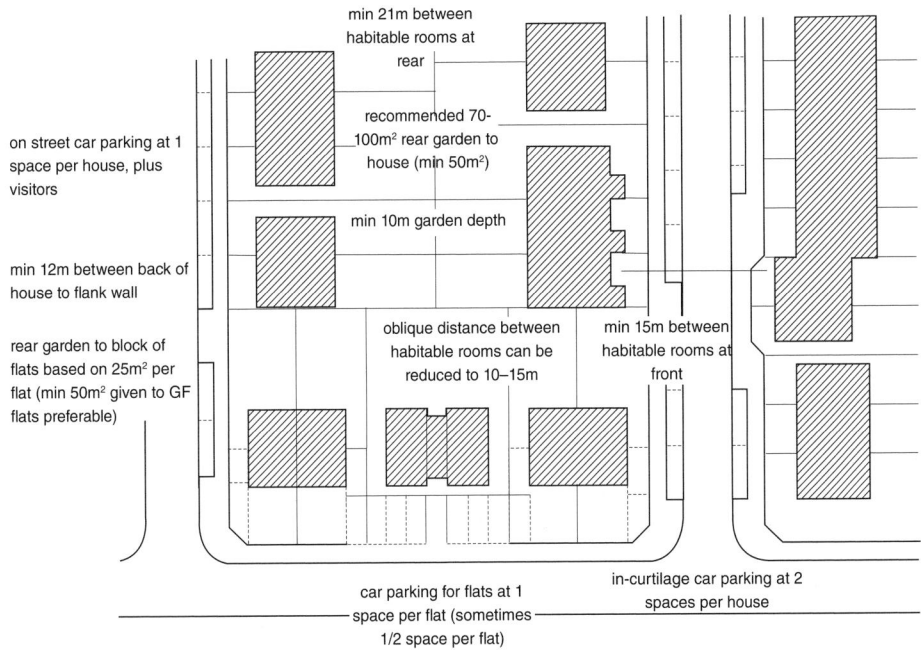

min 21m between habitable rooms at rear

recommended 70–100m² rear garden to house (min 50m²)

on street car parking at 1 space per house, plus visitors

min 10m garden depth

min 12m between back of house to flank wall

rear garden to block of flats based on 25m² per flat (min 50m² given to GF flats preferable)

oblique distance between habitable rooms can be reduced to 10–15m

min 15m between habitable rooms at front

car parking for flats at 1 space per flat (sometimes 1/2 space per flat)

in-curtilage car parking at 2 spaces per house

21.4 *Typical planning dimensions standards*

Table V　Housing Corporation requirements for furniture

Living space	1p	2p	3p	4p	5p	6p	7p	+
arm chair 850x850 – combination to equal one seat/person	2	2	3	1	2	3	4	+1
settee – 2 seat 850x1300 (optional; as above)								
settee – 3 seat 850x1850 (optional; as above)				1	1	1	1	
TV 450x600	1	1	1	1	1	1	1	1
coffee table 500x1050 or 750 diameter	1	1	1	1	1	1	1	1
occasional table (450x450)					1	1	1	1
storage units 500x1000 – and incrementally larger	1000	1000	1000	1500	2000	2000	2000	+
space for visitor chair 450x450	2	2	2	2	2	2	2	2
Dining space	**1p**	**2p**	**3p**	**4p**	**5p**	**6p**	**7p**	**+**
dining chair 450x450	2	2	3	4	5	6	7	8
dining table 800x800 – and incrementally larger	800	800	1000	1200	1350	1500	1650	+
sideboard 450x1000 (+ larger) (but not in dining/kitchen)	1000	1000	1000	1200	1500	1500	1500	+
Bedrooms	**1p**	**2p**	**3p**	**4p**	**5p**	**6p**	**7p**	**+**
Double bedroom	**n/a**							
double bed 2000x1500 or 2 singles 2000x900		1	1	1	1	1	1	1
bedside table 400x400		2	2	2	2	2	2	2
chest of drawers 450x750		1	1	1	1	1	1	1
table 500x1050, and chair/stool		1	1	1	1	1	1	1
double wardrobe 600x1200 – could be built in		1	1	1	1	1	1	1
occasional cot space 600x1200 for family dwelling				1	1	1	1	1
Twin bedroom	**n/a**							
single bed 2000x900		2	2	2	2	2	2	2
bedside table 400x400		2	2	2	2	2	2	2
chest of drawers 450 x750		1	1	1	1	1	1	1
table 500x1050, and chair/stool		1	1	1	1	1	1	1
double wardrobe 600x1200 (or two singles) could be built in		1	1	1	1	1	1	1
Single bedroom								
single bed 2000x900	1	1	1	1	1	1	1	1
bedside table 400x400	1	1	1	1	1	1	1	2+

Table V　(continued)

Living space	1p	2p	3p	4p	5p	6p	7p	+
chest of drawers 450x750	1	1	1	1	1	1	1	2+
table 500x1050 and chair/stool	1	1	1	1	1	1	1	2+
single wardrobe 600x600 – could be built in	1	1	1	1	1	1	1	2+
Kitchen	**1p**	**2p**	**3p**	**4p**	**5p**	**6p**	**7p**	**+**
1 sink top and drainer 600x1000	1000	1000	1000	1000	1000	1000	1000	1000
2 cooker space 600x600	600	600	600	600	600	600	600	600
3 washing machine position / worktop 600x630	630	630	630	630	630	630	630	630
4 other base units 600x length	1200	1200	1600	1600	1600	2700	2700	+
5 ancillary equipment space 600x length -					600	600	1200	1200
6 fridge/freezer space 600x600 (space above not in VOL)	600	600	600	600	600	600	600	600
7 broom cupboard 600x600x1950. (Note this may be counted towards the 'tall storage' requirement)	600	600	600	600	600	600	600	600
8 tray space 600x150	Inc.	Inc.	Inc.	Inc.	Inc.	Inc.	Inc.	Inc.
9 recycle bins space	300	300	600	600	600	600	600	600
10 length of fitments 1-9	4930	4930	5630	5630	6230	7330	7930	+
11 VOL- min capacity (cu m.) (MUST include drawers)	1.3	1.5	2	2.1	2.2	2.4	2.6	+

Any wall units provided should be 300 deep and 450 above base units.

Note: Item 3,5,6,7,9 may be in adjacent rooms to the kitchen.

Bathroom	**1p**	**2p**	**3p**	**4p**	**5p**	**6p**	**7p**	**+**
WC + cistern 500x700	1	1	1	1	2	2	2	2
Bath 700x1700	1	1	1	1	1	1	1	1
Wash hand basin 600x400 – 2nd one can be 250x350	1	1	1	1	2	2	2	2
shower tray 750x750 optional								

*All Sizes in mm

NB: The HQIs make use of material created for the Standards and Quality project by the NHF with the Joseph Rowntree Foundation (1998). This document includes illustrations of spaces required to access the furniture and to perform activities typical to each room.

For private-sale or open-market homes, the core standards would apply in any situation where a scheme receives HCA support through free or discounted land and/or through facilitating or funding major infrastructure investment.

The standards are accompanied by the Housing Quality Indicators (version 4 April 2008), inherited from the Housing Corporation which, whilst they do not lay down space standards for individual rooms, do include a schedule of furniture requirements which impinge on room sizes. See Table V.

2.4 National House Building Council (NHBC)
The National House Building Council publishes a comprehensive set of technical and performance standards for private house

Table VI NHBC Key design requirements

Item	Requirement
Roof access	520 mm min dimension in any direction
	Plus large enough for removal of any services or fittings
	Not to be sited directly over stairs or other hazard
Kitchen / utility layout	1 m² circulation space in front of fittings and appliances
Storage	General storage and clothes storage required and where no central heating, an airing cupboard
Airing cupboard	Where provided must have:
	Min 0.5 m² shelf space
	Min 300 mm between shelves
	No shelf over 1.5 m above floor

builders, the current edition being NHBC Standards 2014. These must be followed if seeking a warranty. Other warranty providers also impose similar standards. The standards concern construction and performance.

The NHBC does not set space standards, but requires that purchasers are provided with floor plans showing that bedrooms can accommodate bed or beds without obstructing the door swing. Other free-standing furniture such as wardrobes, chests of drawers etc. may be shown at the builder's discretion. The key design requirements are noted in Table VI.

2.5 Scotland
Space standards, based on the New Scottish Housing Handbook, Bulletin 1: Metric Space Standards document, were removed from Scottish Building Regulations in 1987. The Building Standards Technical Handbook gives guidance on the design of dwellings, including some spatial requirements, but does not give minimum dwelling or room areas.

The Scottish Housing Quality Standard (SHQS) was introduced in 2004 and is the Scottish Government's principal measure of housing quality in Scotland. The SHQS is a set of five broad housing criteria which must all be met if the property is to pass SHQS. These criteria in turn consist of 55 elements and nine sub-elements against which properties need to be measured. The purpose is to provide a 'floor' below which a property should ideally not fall. In the case of the social housing sector (local authority landlords and Registered Social Landlords), Scottish Government has set a policy target for those landlords to bring their stock up to every element of the standard (where applicable) by April 2015. Private sector landlords and owner-occupied households in Scotland are not subject to the April 2015 policy target either but each property can still be assessed against SHQS if required.

2.6 Wales
The Welsh Assembly published the Development Quality Requirements in 2005 which sets out the standards that HAs and RPs in Wales must meet. They apply to all funded or part-funded housing, both new build and existing. In 2008 the Assembly issued revised guidance for social landlords on the implementation of the standards.

2.7 Northern Ireland
In Northern Ireland the Department for Social Development is responsible for the Housing Association Development Guide Design Standards which apply to all funded or part-funded new build housing.

2.8 Greater London Authority; London Plan
The interim edition of the Mayor's London Housing Design Guide (LHDG) was published in 2010 and sets out the Mayor of London's aspirations for the design of all new housing in the capital. It is expected that a final version of the guide will follow in due course.

The guide promotes better neighbourhoods, high environmental standards, better accessibility and better design and includes new minimum standards for the amount of floor space and private outdoor space, as well as guidance on natural light and ceiling heights. The Supplementary Planning Guidance (SPG) for Housing develops and refines the standards set out in LHDG, setting out how the policies of the 2011 London Plan can be implemented, and applies these to all tenures of housing development. The standards are the most comprehensive that apply to housing at the present time and as such are summarised in Table VII.

2.9 Other statutory controls
Underground rooms regulations, published by some Local Planning Authorities under the Housing Acts, cover lighting and ventilation of basement habitable rooms.

3 DESIGN DATA
There are several other important standards which include dimensional and spatial requirements for dwellings. These are not covered by statutory control but are often required.

3.1 Lifetime Homes
The concept of 'Lifetime Homes' was initially published and promoted by the Joseph Rowntree Foundation (JRF) in the early 1990s, and is now administered by Habinteg Housing Association. The idea is to construct dwellings that can be more easily adapted to cope with residents' future disabilities, should these arise. Such disabilities could be either temporary, such as resulting from an accidental injury, or permanent, from accident or illness. The recommendations are based on 5 principles: inclusivity, accessibility, adaptability, sustainability and good value. They take the form of 16 points covering the planning and construction of new dwellings. These 16 points are listed in Table VIII. The standards for Lifetime Homes are not mandatory, but they relate to the requirements now in Approved Document M of the Building Regulations, and in effect extend their scope, towards the same ends of improving accessibility. HAs and RPs have widely adopted Lifetime Homes as part of their design briefs, and many local authority planning departments now also require them, at least for a proportion of new dwellings.

3.2 Space standards for housing in relation to people with disabilities and wheelchair housing
People who use wheelchairs are as varied in their housing needs as the rest of the population. However, very little existing housing, or new conversions, are suitable for people permanently confined to wheelchairs (estimated to be about 2–3 per cent of all people with disabilities). In order to redress this imbalance and give people with disabilities a choice of housing of different types and tenures and to enable more people to remain in their homes if they become disabled, a proportion of new build, general purpose housing needs to be built to be suitable for adaption for wheelchair occupants. It generally needs to be on one level and have above-average space standards in order to allow for full wheelchair manoeuvre throughout.

When planning dwellings for regular occupation by users of wheelchairs or walking frames, it might be supposed that recommended room areas would need to be augmented. This is not necessarily always the case. Much more important are linear dimensions across circulation areas and between fixed appliances or obstructions. For this reason the planning of kitchens and bathrooms is especially important.

The Wheelchair Housing Design Guide (second edition), produced by Habinteg and Stephen Thorpe is generally viewed as the definitive guide to Wheelchair Housing. However, although this document is currently the essential reference document for the design of wheelchair housing for HCA-funded schemes, it is not universally applied.

Table VII   London Plan Housing SPG; Summary of the Quality and Design Standards

Design Standards	
1.0	Shaping Good Places
1.1	**Defining Places**
1.1.1	Development proposals should demonstrate:-

- how the design responds to its physical context, including the character and legibility of the area and the local pattern of building, public space, landscape and topography
- how the scheme relates to the identified character of the place and to the local vision and strategy or how bolder change is justified in relation to a coherent set of ideas for the place expressed in the local vision and strategy or agreed locally

1.1.2   Development proposals should demonstrate:-

- how the scheme complements the local network of public spaces, including how it integrates with existing streets and paths
- how public spaces and pedestrian routes are designed to be overlooked and safe, and extensive blank elevations onto the public realm at ground floor have been avoided
- for larger developments, how any new public spaces including streets and paths are designed on the basis of an understanding of the planned role and character of these spaces within the local movement network, and how new spaces relate to the local vision and strategy for the area

1.2   Outdoor Spaces

1.2.1   Development proposals should demonstrate that they comply with the borough's open space strategies, ensuring that an audit of surrounding open space is undertaken and that, where appropriate, opportunities to help address a deficiency in provision by providing new public open spaces are taken forward in the design process

1.2.2   For developments with a potential occupancy of ten children or more, development proposals should make appropriate play provision in accordance with the LP SPG, Providing for Children and Young People's Play and Informal Recreation

1.2.3   Where communal open space is provided, development proposals should demonstrate that the space:-

- is overlooked by surrounding development
- is accessible to wheelchair users and other disabled people
- is designed to take advantage of direct sunlight
- has suitable management arrangements in place

2.0   Housing for a Diverse City

2.1   Appropriate density

2.1.1   Development proposals should demonstrate how the density of residential accommodation satisfies LP policy relating to public transport accessibility levels (PTALs)* and the accessibility of local amenities and services, and is appropriate to the location in London

2.2   Residential mix

2.2.1   Development proposals should demonstrate how the mix of dwelling types and sizes and the mix of tenures meet strategic and local borough targets and are appropriate to the location in London

3.0   From Street to Front Door

3.1   Entrance and approach

3.1.1   All main entrances to houses, ground floor flats and communal entrance lobbies should be visible from the public realm and clearly identified

3.1.2   The distance from the accessible car parking space of requirement 3.3.4 to the home or to the relevant block entrance or lift core should be kept to a minimum and should be level or gently sloping

3.1.3   The approach to all entrances should preferably be level or gently sloping

3.1.4   All entrances should be illuminated and have level access over the threshold. Entrance doors should have 300mm of clear space to the pull side, and clear minimum opening widths of 800mm or 825mm depending on the direction and width of approach. Main entrances should have weather protection and a level external landing

3.2   Shared circulation within buildings

3.2.1   The number of dwellings accessed from a single core should not exceed eight per floor, subject to dwelling size mix

3.2.2   An access core serving 4 or more dwellings should provide an access control system with entry phones in all dwellings linked to a main front door with electronic lock release. Unless a 24 hour concierge is provided, additional security measures including audio-visual verification to the access control system should be provided where any of the following apply:-

- more than 25 dwellings are served by one core
- the potential occupancy of the dwellings served by one core exceeds 100 bed spaces
- more than 8 dwellings are provided per floor

3.2.3   Where dwellings are accessed via an internal corridor, the corridor should receive natural light and adequate ventilation

3.2.4   The minimum width for all paths, corridors and decks for communal circulation should be 1200mm. The preferred minimum width is 1500mm, and is considered particularly important where corridors are 'double-loaded' and serve dwellings on each side, and where wheelchair accessible dwellings are provided

Table VII   (continued)

Design Standards	
3.2.6	All dwellings entered at the fourth floor (fifth storey) and above should be served by at least one wheelchair accessible lift, and it is desirable that dwellings entered at the third floor (fourth storey) are served by at least one such lift. All dwellings entered at the seventh floor (eighth storey) and above should be served by at least two lifts
3.2.7	Every designated wheelchair accessible dwelling above the ground floor should be served by at least one wheelchair accessible lift. It is desirable that every wheelchair accessible dwelling is served by more than one lift
3.2.8	Principal access stairs should provide easy access regardless of whether a lift is provided. Where homes are reached by a lift, it should be fully wheelchair accessible

3.3   Car parking

3.3.1   Standard 3.3.1 (and Policy 6.13) – All developments should conform to LP policy on car parking provision (see Annex 2.3 of this SPG for guidance on implementation of relevant policy including LP Policy 6.13 and associated standards below). In areas of good public transport accessibility and/or town centres the aim should be to provide no more than one space per dwelling. Elsewhere parking provision should be broadly as follows, depending on location as indicated in Annex 2.4

- 4+ bedroom dwellings: 1.5 – 2 spaces per dwelling
- 3 bedroom dwellings: 1 – 1.5 spaces per dwelling
- 1 – 2 bedroom dwellings: Less than 1 per dwelling

3.3.2   Each designated wheelchair accessible dwelling should have a car parking space 2400mm wide with a clear access way to one side of 1200mm

3.3.3   Careful consideration should be given to the siting and organisation of car parking within an overall design for open space so that car parking does not negatively affect the use and appearance of open spaces

3.3.4   Where car parking is within the dwelling plot, at least one car parking space should be capable of enlargement to a width of 3300mm. Where parking is provided in communal bays, at least one space with a width of 3300mm should be provided per block entrance or access core in addition to spaces designated for wheelchair user dwellings

3.4   Cycle storage

3.4.1   All developments should provide dedicated storage space for cycles at the following levels:

- 1 per 1 or 2 bedroom dwelling
- 2 per 3 or more bedroom dwelling

3.4.2   Individual or communal cycle storage outside the home should be secure, sheltered and adequately lit, with convenient access to the street. Where cycle storage is provided within the home, it should be in addition to the minimum GIA and minimum storage and circulation space requirements. Cycle storage in habitable rooms or on balconies is considered unacceptable

3.5   Refuse, post and deliveries

3.5.1   Communal refuse and recycling containers, communal bin enclosures and refuse stores should be accessible to all residents including children and wheelchair users, and located on a hard, level surface. The location should satisfy local requirements for waste collection and should achieve full credits under the Code for Sustainable Homes Technical Guide. Refuse stores within buildings should be located to limit the nuisance caused by noise and smells and provided with means for cleaning

3.5.2   Storage facilities for waste and recycling containers should be provided in accordance with the Code for Sustainable Homes Technical Guide and local authority requirements

4.0   Dwelling Space Standards

4.1   Internal floor area

4.1.1   All developments should meet the following minimum space standards:-

	Dwelling type (bedroom/persons)	Essential GIA (sq.m)
Single storey dwelling	1p	37
	1b2p	50
	2b3p	61
	2b4p	70
	3b4p	74
	3b5p	86
	3b6p	95
	4b5p	90
	4b6p	99
Two storey dwellings	2b4p	83
	3b5p	96
	4b5p	100
	4b6p	107
Three storey dwellings	3b5p	102
	4b5p	106
	4b6p	113

For dwellings designed for more than 6 people, at least 10sq.m gross internal area should be added for each additional person.

(continued)

Table VII (continued)

Design Standards	
4.1.2	Dwelling plans should demonstrate that dwellings will accommodate the furniture, access and activity space requirements relating to the declared level of occupancy (**Refer to Table 3 – HCA HQI standards**)
4.2	**Flexibility and adaptability**
4.2.1	Dwelling plans should demonstrate that dwelling types provide flexibility by showing that at least one bedroom is capable of being used and furnished as either a double or a twin room according to occupiers' preferences
4.3	**Circulation in the home**
4.3.1	The minimum width of hallways and other circulation spaces inside the home should be 900mm. This may reduce to 750mm at 'pinch points' e.g. next to radiators, where doorway widths meet the following specification:

Minimum clear opening width of doorway (mm)	Minimum width of hallway where door is in side wall (mm)
750	1200
775	1050
900	900

Where a hallway is at least 900mm wide and the approach to the door is head-on, a minimum clear opening door width of 750mm should be provided

4.3.2	The design of dwellings of more than one storey should incorporate potential for a stair lift to be installed and a suitable identified space for a through-the-floor lift from the entrance level to a storey containing a main bedroom and an accessible bathroom
4.4	**Living/dining/kitchen**
4.4.4	There should be space for turning a wheelchair in dining areas and living rooms and basic circulation space for wheelchairs elsewhere
4.4.5	A living room, living space or kitchen dining room should be at entrance level
4.4.6	Windows in the principal living space should be no higher than 800mm above finished floor level (+/- 50mm) to allow people to see out while seated. At least one opening window should be easy to approach and operate by people with restricted movement and reach
4.5	**Bedrooms**
4.5.3	In homes of two or more storeys with no permanent bedroom at entrance level, there should be space on the entrance level that could be used as a convenient temporary bed space
4.5.4	Building structure above a main bedroom and an accessible bathroom should be capable of supporting a ceiling hoist and the design should allow for a reasonable route between this bedroom and bathroom
4.6	**Bathrooms and WCs**
4.6.2	Where there is no accessible bathroom at entrance level, a wheelchair accessible WC with potential for a shower to be installed should be provided at entrance level
4.6.3	An accessible bathroom should be provided in every dwelling on the same storey as a main bedroom
4.6.4	Walls in bathrooms and WCs should be capable of taking adaptations such as handrails
4.7	**Storage and utility**
4.7.1	• In dwellings supported by the LDA or receiving public subsidy, built-in general internal storage space free of hot water cylinders and other obstructions, with a minimum internal height of 2m and a minimum area of 1.5 sq m should be provided for 1 and 2 person dwellings, in addition to storage provided by furniture in habitable rooms. For each additional occupant an additional 0.5 sq m of storage space is required
	• Private sector dwellings should ensure this minimum area (1.5 sq m) either within the dwelling itself or elsewhere within its curtilage provided minimum internal provision includes storage space free of hot water cylinders and other obstructions with a minimum internal height of 2m and a minimum area of 0.8 sq m for 1 and 2 person dwellings, in addition to storage provided by furniture in habitable rooms. For each additional occupant an additional 0.5 sq m of storage space is required
4.8	**Study and work**
4.8.1	Dwelling plans should demonstrate that all homes are provided with adequate space and services to be able to work from home. The Code for Sustainable Homes guidance on working from home is recommended as a reference

Table VII (continued)

Design Standards	
4.8.2	Service controls should be within a height band of 450mm to 1200mm from the floor and at least 300mm away from any internal room corner
4.9	**Wheelchair user dwellings**
4.9.1	Ten percent of new housing should be designed to be wheelchair accessible or easily adaptable for residents who are wheelchair users
4.10	**Private open space**
4.10.1	A minimum of 5 sq m of private outdoor space should be provided for 1-2 person dwellings and an extra 1 sq m should be provided for each additional occupant
4.10.2	Private outdoor spaces should have level access from the home
4.10.3	The minimum depth and width of all balconies and other private external spaces should be 1500mm
5.0	**Home as a place of retreat**
5.1	**Privacy**
5.1.1	Design proposals should demonstrate how habitable rooms within each dwelling are provided with an adequate level of privacy in relation to neighbouring property, the street and other public spaces
5.2	**Dual aspect**
5.2.1	Developments should avoid single aspect dwellings that are north facing, exposed to noise levels above which significant adverse impacts on health and quality of life occur, or contain three or more bedrooms
5.3	**Noise**
5.3.1	The layout of adjacent dwellings and the location of lifts and circulation spaces should seek to limit the transmission of noise to sound sensitive rooms within dwellings
5.4	**Floor to ceiling heights**
5.4.1	The minimum floor to ceiling height in habitable rooms should be 2.5m between finished floor level and finished ceiling level
5.6	**Air quality**
5.6.1	Minimise increased exposure to existing poor air quality and make provision to address local problems of air quality. Be at least 'air quality neutral' and not lead to further deterioration of existing poor air quality
6.0	**Climate change mitigation and adaptation**
6.1	**Environmental performance**
6.1.2	All homes should satisfy LP policy on sustainable design and construction and make the fullest contribution to the mitigation of and adaptation to climate change
6.2	**Energy and CO$_2$**
6.2.1	Development proposals should be designed in accordance with the LP energy hierarchy, and should meet the following minimum targets for carbon dioxide emissions reduction.

Year	Improvement on 2010 Building Regulations
2010 – 2013	25 per cent
2013 – 2016	40 per cent
2016 – 2031	Zero carbon

6.3	**Overheating**
6.3.1	Development proposals should demonstrate how the design of dwellings will avoid overheating during summer months without reliance on energy intensive mechanical cooling systems
6.4	**Water**
6.4.1	New dwellings should be designed to ensure that a maximum of 105 litres of water is used per person per day
6.4.2	Where development is permitted in an area at risk of flooding, it should incorporate flood resilient design in accordance with PPS25
6.4.3	New development should incorporate Sustainable Urban Drainage Systems and green roofs where practical with the aim of achieving a greenfield run-off rate, increasing bio-diversity and improving water quality. Surface water run-off is to be managed as close to source as possible
6.5	**Materials**
6.5.2	All new residential development should meet the requirements of the Code Level 4 with regard to using materials with lower environmental impacts over their lifecycle
6.6	**Ecology**
6.6.1	The design and layout of new residential development should avoid areas of ecological value and seek to enhance the ecological capital of the area in accordance with GLA best practice guidance on biodiversity and nature conservation

*Public transport accessibility levels (PTALs) are set out in The London Plan; Map 2A.3 for all London Boroughs and give a range of suitable densities in habitable rooms per hectare.

A much-distilled summary of some of the main requirements is given in Table IX. These recommendations will tend to lead to increases in the floor areas of kitchens and bathrooms, and widths of circulation spaces.

3.3 British Standard 9266:2013 Design of accessible and adaptable general needs housing

Whilst many British Standards have elements that can be applied to housing design, BS9266:2013 is a code of practice which specifically

Table VIII Lifetime Home standards (Latest edition published by Habinteg Housing Association in 2010).

1 Parking (width or widening capability)

1a 'On plot' (non-communal) parking
Where a dwelling has car parking within its individual plot (or title) boundary, at least one parking space length should be capable of enlargement to achieve a minimum width of 3300mm.

1b Communal or shared parking
Where parking is provided by communal or shared bays, spaces with a width of 3300mm, in accordance with the specification below, should be provided

2 Approach to dwelling from parking
The distance from the car parking space of Criterion 1 to the dwelling entrance (or relevant block entrance or lift core), should be kept to a minimum and be level or gently sloping. The distance from visitors' parking to relevant entrances should be as short as practicable and be level or gently sloping.

3 Approach to all entrances
The approach to all entrances should preferably be level or gently sloping, and in accordance with the specification noted.

4 Entrances
All entrances should:-
- Be illuminated
- Have level access over the threshold
- Have effective clear opening widths and nibs as specified

In addition, main entrances should also:-
- Have adequate weather protection
- a level external landing.

5 Communal stairs and lifts

5a Communal stairs
Principal access stairs should provide easy access in accordance with the specification below, regardless of whether or not a lift is provided.

5b Communal lifts
Where a dwelling is reached by a lift, it should be fully accessible in accordance with the specification noted.

6 Internal doorways and hallways
Movement in hallways and through doorways should be as convenient to the widest range of people, including those using mobility aids or wheelchairs, and those moving furniture or other objects. As a general principle, narrower hallways and landings will need wider doorways in their side walls. The width of doorways and hallways should conform to the specification noted.

7 Circulation space
There should be space for turning a wheelchair in dining areas and living rooms and basic circulation space for wheelchair users elsewhere.

8 Entrance level living space
A living room/living space should be provided on the entrance level of every dwelling.

9 Potential for entrance level bed-space
In dwellings with two or more storeys, with no permanent bedroom on the entrance level, there should be space on the entrance level of a dwelling, the entrance level that could be used as a convenient temporary bed-space.

10 Entrance level WC and shower drainage
Where an accessible bathroom, in accordance with Criterion 14, is not provided on the entrance level of a dwelling, the entrance level should have an accessible WC compartment, with potential for a shower to be installed.

11 WC and bathroom walls
Walls in all bathrooms and WC compartments should be capable of firm fixing and support for adaptations such as grab rails.

12 Stairs and potential through-floor lift in dwellings
The design within a dwelling of two or more storeys should incorporate:-
- Potential for stair lift installation
- A suitable identified space for a through-the-floor lift from the entrance level to a storey containing a main bedroom and a bathroom satisfying Criterion 14.

13 Potential for future fitting of hoists and bedroom/bathroom relationship
Structure above a main bedroom and bathroom ceilings should be capable of supporting ceiling hoists and the design should provide a reasonable route between this bedroom and the bathroom.

14 Bathrooms
An accessible bathroom, providing ease of access in accordance with the specification noted, should be provided in every dwelling on the same storey as a main bedroom.

15 Glazing and window handle heights
Windows in the principal living space (typically the living room), should allow people to see out when seated. In addition, at least one opening light in each habitable room should be approachable and usable by a wide range of people – including those with restricted movement and reach.

16 Location of service controls
Service controls should be within a height band of 450 mm to 1200mm from the floor and at least 300mm away from any internal room corner.

Table IX Key requirements for wheelchair housing (from the Wheelchair Housing Design Guide)

Using outdoor spaces	Approaching the home	Entering and leaving; dealing with callers	Negotiating the secondary door	Moving around inside; storing things	Moving between levels within the dwelling	Using living spaces	Using the kitchen	Using the bathroom
Footpaths require a minimum width of 1200 mm. Gates to private gardens should have a clear opening width of 850 mm. Gardens should provide: accessible paving outside external door, accessible clothes-drying facilities, and accessible route from external door, external storage and external gate, scope for accessible planting.	Provide a covered parking space (min. 3600 x 5400 mm) for every ground-floor level wheelchair user dwelling. Where a garage is provided it should be a minimum of 4200 x 5400 mm. Provide a level entrance landing 1500 x 1500 mm min. with a canopy 1200 mm x 1500 mm. Where wheelchair dwellings are above the ground floor, a lift should be provided. Negotiating the entrance door Provide effective clear width of at least 800 mm. Provide space beside leading edge of door, 200 mm min. for a door opening away from the wheelchair user, 300 mm min. for a door opening towards them, extending 1800 mm from face of door.	Provide a transfer space (1100 x 1700 mm) within the house to manoeuvre wheelchair to transfer to a second chair and to store the first, clear of circulation routes and the required approach to furniture and doors. Provide a 1500 x 1800 mm turning space to manoeuvre and turn. Where there is an entrance lobby incorporated or provision made for added inner door, ensure adequate space to manoeuvre between doors.	Provide nominally level landing (1500 x 1500 mm with 1200 mm clear of door swing. Provide effective clear width of 800 mm to single or main door leaf. Ensure space to approach, manoeuvre and pass through door on line.	Ensure that passage widths or approaches where no turning or door approach is required are no less than 900 mm clear of all obstructions. Ensure space beside latch edge of door, min 200 mm on push side and min. 300 mm on pull side. Ensure that passage widths or approaches to turn through 90° are no less than 1200 mm. Ensure that passage widths or approaches to turn through 180° are no less than 1500 mm. Ensure at right angles that passage width clear of all obstructions for the extent of the turn is no less than 1200 mm width in one direction and 900 mm in the other, or 900 mm in each direction in combination with angle splayed by 300 mm. Ensure 775 mm min. effective clear door width. Increase where approach is at an angle. Provide space to turn between doors at an angle to each other, 400 mm clear to each door from angle. Ensure that depth and width of storage space, in combination with any shelving layout, provides optimum access to space and to stored items.	Provide lift for independent use by a wheelchair user which connects floors and is accessed off circulation spaces at each floor level with adequate circulation space at each level to operate it.	Provide space for furniture and for wheelchair user to approach it, circulate, transfer to seating, and approach and operate doors, windows, equipment and controls.	Lay out the kitchen to provide a practical working kitchen for a wheelchair user. Ensure clear manoeuvring space not less than 1800 x 1500 mm. Ensure wherever practicable, that windows are positioned for ease of control and cleaning. Provide an appropriate length of 600 mm deep worktop, suitable for a wheelchair user. Provide integral shallow sink and drainer to maximise height adjustability, suitable for wheelchair user. Provide storage appropriate to the size of dwelling, the major proportion of which is in a position and format usable from a wheelchair. Provide hob and built-in oven. The hob should have a knee space below and the oven should be at an accessible height, adjustable to suit the user. Provide 3 spaces (4 in larger dwellings) in addition to hob and oven for appliances/white goods. Provide suitable internal refuse arrangements, manageable from a wheelchair.	In all dwellings provide fully accessible bathroom with WC, basin, and installed level access shower (1000x1000 mm min.) with provision for bath in place of shower. Ensure provision for direct access from main bedroom into bathroom. In dwellings of 4 or more persons, provide fully accessible second WC with basin. Ensure independent approach/ transfer to and use of all fittings, including manoeuvring space clear of fittings and door swing if inward opening. 450 mm transfer space required at end of bath, where provided.

Using bedrooms
Provide bedroom layouts to ensure access to both sides of beds in double bedrooms and outer sides of beds in single bedrooms, access to other furniture and to window.

Operating windows
Ensure that wheelchair user can approach window. Ensure that glazing line to windows in living, dining and bedrooms is no higher than 800 mm.

Table X BS9266: summary of key requirements

Externally

For blocks of flats or individual houses without on-plot parking one designated accessible parking bay should be provided in each parking location and/or lift core

Designated accessible parking bays should be 3600 mm x 6600 mm for parallel parking and 3600 mm x 6000 mm for perpendicular and echelon parking facilities

Setting-down points should be provided on firm and level ground and no more than 50m from an individual house or the communal entrance of a block of flats

Step-free access is required to the entrances of individual dwellings or blocks of flats from the street, parking spaces and setting-down points (an allowance is made on steeply sloping sites)

Steps should be provided in addition to any ramp where there is a level change of 300 mm or greater. The width of the flight should be a minimum of 1.2m when measured between walls, balustrades, etc. and a minimum of 1.0m between handrails. Handrails should be provided on both sides, be continuous around landings and provide a 300 mm run past

Internally

In blocks of flats with two floors in addition to the entrance level (i.e. three storeys), at least one passenger lift or one enclosed vertical lifting platform should be installed at each service core. Blocks of flats with three or more floors in addition to the entrance level (i.e. four or more storeys) should be served by at least one passenger lift at each service core. This includes floors with car parking and/or other communal facilities

Common steps and stairs should be designed to the same standard as external steps (see above)

On private stairs, the rise of each step should be between 150 mm and 200 mm, and the going of each step should be between 250 mm and 320 mm

In blocks of flats the effective clear width of entrance doors, and associated lobby and communal hallway doors, should be at least 1000 mm

A clear level space of at least 1500 mm x 1500 mm should be available in front of each individual flat entrance door, to enable a wheelchair user to turn

Internal circulation spaces should be not less than 900 mm wide × 900 mm deep, clear of door swings and other obstructions. There should be a space of not less than 900 mm deep clear of the front door swing

Provide a 300 mm clear space to the side of the leading edge of a swing door (on the opening side) for all rooms within an individual house or flat

Provide an accessible WC and washbasin (not a hand rinse basin)

Provide a manoeuvring space of 1500 mm diameter internally, adjacent to a balcony and in at least one bedroom

gives advice on the design of accessible and adaptable general needs housing. It is concerned largely with access to, within and use of, residential buildings covering both new build and refurbishment of general needs housing both in the form of flats and houses. Although not mandatory in its application, many housing providers require compliance with relevant British Standards as part of their brief. Table X details those clauses which may have the greatest impact on housing design and layouts as they are over and above other housing standards.

3.4 Code for Sustainable Homes

The Code for Sustainable Homes (the Code) is the national standard for the sustainable design and construction of all new homes, private or funded. The Code aims to reduce our carbon emissions and create homes that are more sustainable. It applies in England, Wales and Northern Ireland. It is entirely voluntary, and is intended to help promote higher standards of sustainable design above current Building Regulations.

The Code measures the sustainability of new homes against nine categories of sustainable design, rating the 'whole home' as a complete package. It covers energy/CO_2, water, materials, surface water runoff (flooding and flood prevention), waste, pollution, health and well-being, management and ecology. The Code uses a one to six star rating system to communicate the overall sustainability performance of a new home against these nine categories. The Code sets minimum standards for energy and water use at each level and, within England, replaces the EcoHomes scheme, developed by the Building Research Establishment (BRE).

The Code is not mandatory, nor is it a set of regulations, and designers should not confuse it with Zero Carbon policy. The only circumstances where the Code can be required are:

- where local authorities stipulate a requirement in their local plans;
- where affordable housing is funded by the HCA, which currently requires homes to be built to Code Level 4;
- where housing is funded by the GLA in London, which also requires homes to be built to Code Level 4.

The Level 3 energy standard was incorporated in the Building Regulations but removed in the revision to Approved Document L.

Clients may have a level set in their employer's requirements and a Code for Sustainable Homes pre-assessment carried out by a registered assessor will be required for most planning applications.

3.5 Secured by Design

Secured by Design (SBD) is owned by the Association of Chief Police Officers (ACPO) and is supported by the Home Office and Department of Communities and Local Government (DCLG). The publication is the source document for achieving a Secured by Design certification/award. It addresses the community safety and security requirements for most types of housing development including individual houses, housing estates and low- and high-rise apartment blocks.

The design and layout and physical security sections can be applied to both new and refurbished homes, regardless of their existing or future tenure. Additional information for sheltered housing projects is available from the SBD website (www.secured-bydesign.com).

Secured by Design is not a mandatory standard but should be applied as good practice and may be a specific client requirement. Compliance with the SBD scheme criteria can be a major indication that a scheme proposal has adequately addressed the crime prevention component required to be included in a Design and Access Statement (DAS).

The Code for Sustainable Homes awards points to developments that have met the requirements of Secured by Design – New Homes, Section 02; this section covers Physical Security (Building Control & Code for Sustainable Homes issues).

3.6 Building for Life

The latest version of Building for Life was published in 2012. It is an industry standard, endorsed by the government, for well-designed homes and neighbourhoods, based on the National Planning Policy Framework and is intended to reflect the vision that new housing developments should be attractive, functional and sustainable.

BfL12 consists of 12 questions which are designed to help structure discussions between local communities, the local planning authority and the development team. The 12 questions should be used at all stages of the development process. The performance of any scheme measured against the new criteria will be determined using a traffic light system of green, amber and red. As many 'green' lights as possible should be achieved, 'amber' lights should be minimised and 'red' lights avoided. Any 'ambers' and 'reds' should be identified early on in the process so that a suitable design solution can be found where possible. The overall assessment of a scheme will be reached by mutual agreement between the planning authority and the developer.

BfL12 is not mandatory but the partners expect that local planning authorities will adopt the guidance to help them assess the quality of proposed and completed developments and use it as a point of reference in the preparation of local design policies.

BfL12 is applicable for England only, however it may be requested by some local authorities in Wales. The HCA maintains a requirement for evidence of a BfL score in its 2011–2015 funding programme and the GLA and HCA London still encourage its use.

Regardless of whether it is a scheme requirement or not, Building for Life is a useful tool, which can be used to help

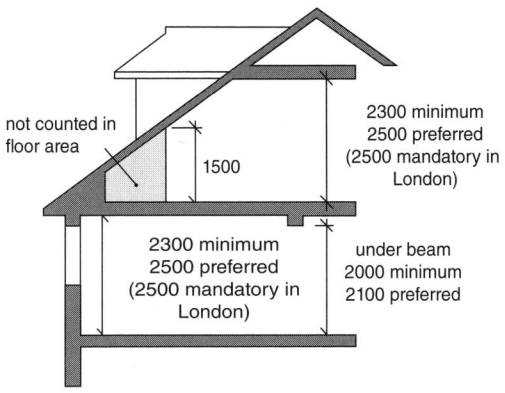

21.5 *Ceiling heights and rooms in the roof, (for guidance only – no longer covered by Building Regulations)*

demonstrate how a residential development provides a high quality external living environment.

3.7 Ceiling heights
These have not been covered by Building Regulations since 1985. Despite this, the old standard of 2.3 m should still be considered the minimum reasonable ceiling height for domestic buildings and 2.4 m is preferable. For funded housing the HQIs suggested that 2.5 m or more is provided but this is not mandatory. The London Housing SPG requires a minimum of 2.5 m to all dwellings.

For rooms in the roof, floor areas are calculated to include only those parts where the ceiling height exceeds 1.5 m (Figure 21.5).

3.8 Staircase widths
These have not been included in Approved Document K of the Building Regulations since 1992. For means of escape purposes, widths of staircases to blocks of flats are covered in Approved Document B; but this does not cover the majority of single-family houses. The movement of furniture should be considered, and 800 mm should be the minimum reasonable clear stair width in domestic buildings.

Some HAs and RPs may, in their design brief, require the facility for the future installation of a stair lift. To comply practically and economically, a straight flight staircase width of 900 mm is preferable although it is possible (at additional cost) to install a stair lift to stairs with winders. See also Section 6.4 regarding alternating tread staircases which are permitted for access to one bedroom in a loft conversion.

3.9 Kitchen units
Fitted kitchen units are very standardised. Despite evidence that for the majority of able-bodied people worktops at 950 mm and sink tops at 975 mm are the most comfortable, most manufacturers provide base units that are 870–880 mm to the underside of the worktop.

For older people and the less mobile, use of a lower worktop, at 800–850 mm, can sometimes be appropriate. However, providing lower worktops generally at this height is not recommended as 'white goods' will rarely fit underneath. It is possible to provide adjustable height worktops in certain areas, around the hob for example, which, in conjunction with standard height worktops elsewhere, might provide the best solution.

4 SINGLE-FAMILY HOUSES
4.1 General
There is now a broad consensus that families with children should be housed at ground level in single-family houses, or in ground-floor flats or ground and first-floor maisonettes with direct entrances. It is not just that children need private gardens. Equally,

if not more importantly, the shared entrances, staircases and corridors in blocks of flats, and the external spaces around them, have proved to be largely incompatible with family life. This is especially true in the public sector, where the resources to overcome the management and maintenance problems of communal areas are very limited.

4.2 Orientation and gardens
The relationship between the single-family dwelling and the adjacent public domain (i.e. the highway, the street, court, or much less satisfactorily the footpath) should be as clear and simple as possible. A private, front garden, with front gate and front path leading to the front door, and with minimum length of 2 to 3 m has proven benefits as defensible space. This is not to say that successful houses cannot be built without a front garden or with the front door opening directly, or via an inset porch, from the public pavement. There are many thousands of quite satisfactory houses planned like this in the Victorian inner cities; but in these cases the pavement is clearly part of the publicly maintained highway. When there is an intervening 'confused' space that is neither public nor private but needs to be communally managed, this is rarely satisfactory, and often leads to tangible neglect. Similarly, rear gardens benefit from simplicity and clarity of relationship to the house and of enclosure. Communal space is best kept either to a minimum or omitted altogether. Such is the concern about security that opinion is generally against any provision of rear access, especially from unsupervised rear pathways, even when these are of practical convenience, such as in uninterrupted terraces.

Orientation of the dwelling for best sunlight should not normally take precedence over achieving simple, clear relationships of private and public domains. However, within the dwelling it should normally be possible to arrange for one of the two day rooms (living room or dining kitchen) to get direct sunlight for a large part of the day. It is preferable for one of these rooms to face the front permitting supervision of the street, and for the other to face the rear giving direct garden access. Another factor is the potential for passive solar gain in the winter through the simple expedient of larger double-glazed windows on the southern elevation.

4.3 Height
Although the majority of family houses are of two storeys, three storeys can be appropriate in urban areas. The expense of building taller is usually more than compensated for by savings in foundations and roofs, making this an economical type. Four-storey houses, however, although possible, are difficult to plan, because of the need for an alternative escape route from the upper floors (Building Regulations Approved Document B1). Mutual escape is normally provided between adjacent houses via adjoining balconies; but this leads to potential security risks. However the provision of sprinkler coverage can eliminate the need for an alternative escape route.

4.4 Frontage widths
Because of the costs of providing roads and services infrastructure, there is often pressure to build narrow-frontage houses – especially in urban areas. Anything less than 4.8 m internal width can be considered narrow frontage. Although reasonably satisfactory houses have been built with frontages of 4.0 m, the stresses on internal planning start to build up below approximately 4.5 m. A reasonable minimum could be taken to be 4.3 m frontage. Below this width, rear gardens also become apologetic.

Taking 4.8 m as the normal terrace house frontage, Figure 21.6 shows a two-bedroom, four-person, two-storey house; Figure 21.7 a three-bedroom, five-person, two-and-a-half storey house; Figure 21.8 shows a four-bedroom, seven-person, two-and-a-half storey house.

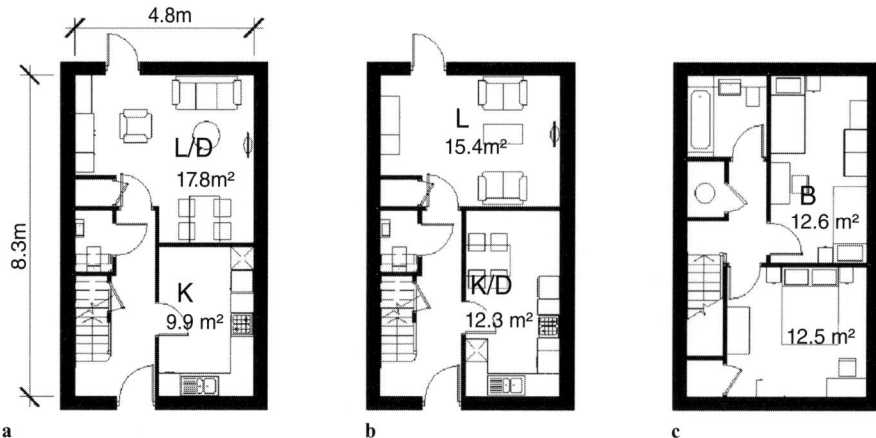

21.6 *A two-bedroom, four person, two storey terrace house of 79.5m². Architects: PRP Architects. a Ground floor plan with living/dining room; b Alternative ground floor with kitchen/dining room; c First floor*

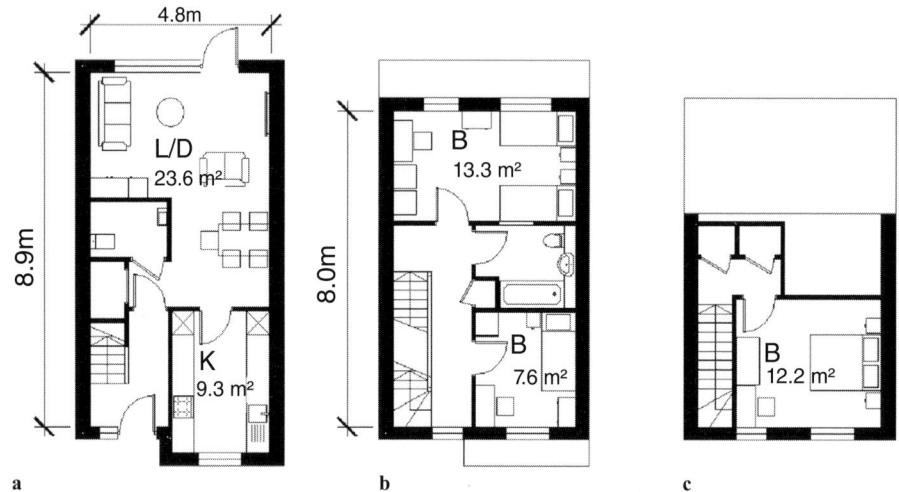

21.7 *A three-bedroom, five person, two and a half storey terrace house of 102.0m². Architects: PRP Architects. a Ground floor; b First floor; c Second floor*

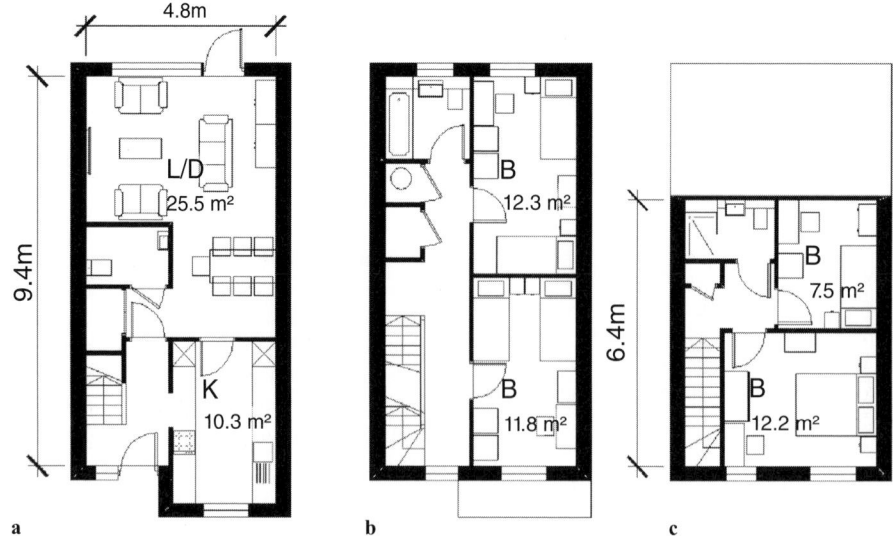

21.8 *A four-bedroom, seven person, two and a half storey terrace house of 123.5m². Architects: PRP Architects. a Ground floor; b First floor; c Second floor*

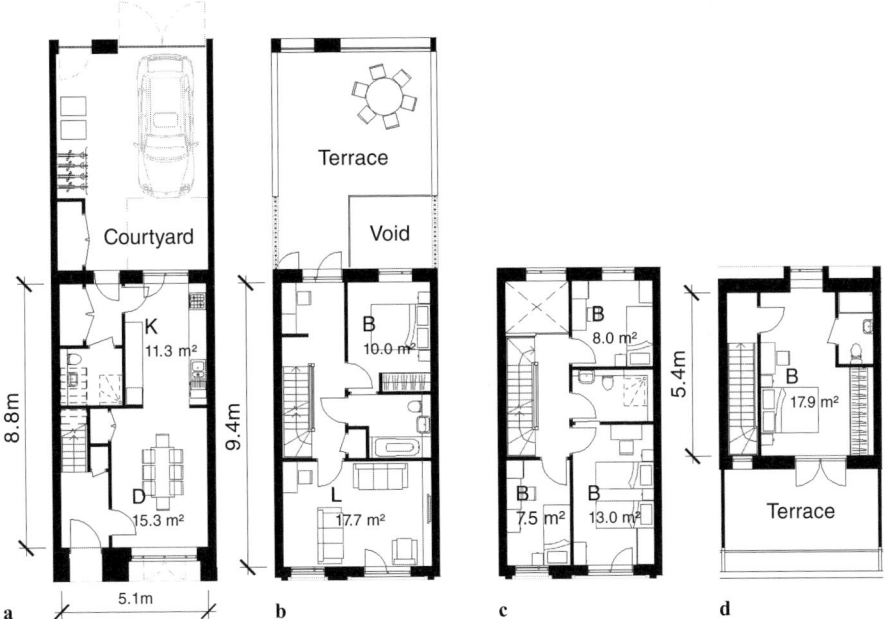

21.9 *A five-bedroom, seven person, four storey terrace house of 167.0m². Architects: PRP Architects. a Ground floor; b First floor; c Second floor; d Third floor. Provided courtesy of CM LLP*

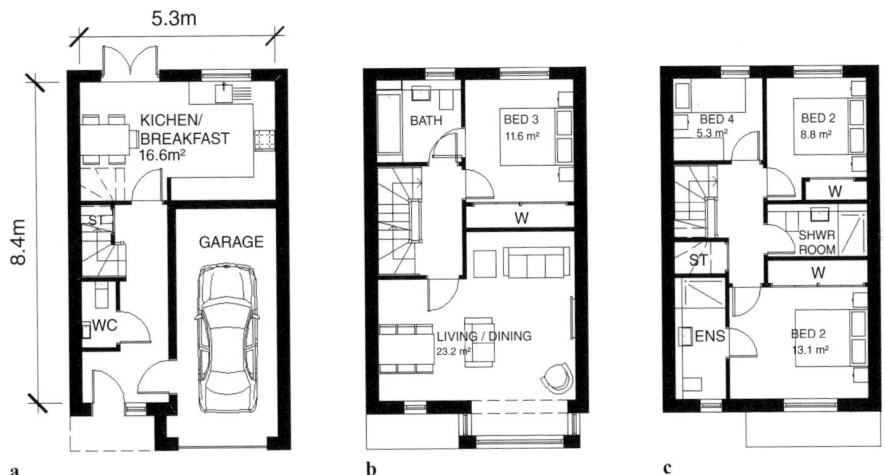

21.10 *A four-bedroom, three storey terrace house of 121.5m² (for Private sale). Architects: PRP Architects. a Ground floor; b First floor; c Second floor*

21.11 *A three-bedroom, five person, two storey terrace house of 90.5m². Architects: PRP Architects. a Ground floor with living room at the front of the dwelling, overlooking the street; b Ground floor with living room at the rear of the dwelling, overlooking the garden; c First floor to meet private for sale requirements; d First floor to meet affordable housing requirements*

Table XI General storage (from the HCA's Design and Quality Standards)

minimum shelf areas per person (m²)	1p	2p	3p	4p	5p	6p	7p	8p+
	1.5	1.5	2.25	3.0	3.75	4.25	5.25	+0.75

4.5 Internal planning

Opinions continue to differ over the relative positions of living room and kitchen. It is, however, rarely satisfactory for the only access to the rear garden to be via the living room (in fact Parker Morris ruled this out). In narrow-frontage houses where the living room needs to occupy most of the full width of the front of the house, the dining kitchen will therefore tend to be at the rear, where it can provide a route to the garden. In three or four storey houses this sometimes works well in combination with a front living room at first-floor level as in Figures 21.9 and 21.10. Rooms can then be full width, and offer good outlook and supervision both to the front and rear, as well as benefiting from sunlight with almost any orientation.

Figure 21.9 shows a medium frontage plan with a through dining/kitchen and first floor living room. This house is designed to London Housing Design Guide standards with good storage provisions. Figures 21.6 and 21.11 show a wider plan which gives greater flexibility. It allows the living room to be at the front or rear of the dwelling depending on its orientation. In this instance it is also possible to provide a first floor layout to suit the private for sale market (with an extra en-suite) or the affordable market.

4.6 Living/dining versus kitchen/diner

Certain types, such as Figure 21.6, have the great advantage of offering alternative ground-floor plans with the dining space in either the living room or the kitchen; also the possibility of opening the two spaces into one. Use of the kitchen/diner is generally preferable and suits current lifestyles better as it offers two reception rooms allowing greater flexibility for active family life. This arrangement also ensures that one reception room will receive sunlight for much of the day.

4.7 The main bathroom

This should preferably be located on the floor with the most bedrooms. In three-storey houses this might be the first or the second floor. A ground-floor WC is now a requirement in all family houses, however small (Building Regulations Approved Document Part M). Although there is no longer a legal prohibition of WCs opening directly from kitchens, this arrangement is not normally either popular or advised. An exception might sometimes be a utility room containing a WC and forming the route to the garden. WCs must always have a handbasin (Building Regulation Approved Document Part G).

In larger family houses with four or more bedrooms, a second bathroom, or shower room, is recommended. This can be useful in three-storey houses, as it can mean having a WC on each floor. One bathroom or shower room can be en-suite with the main bedroom; however, this has not normally been considered to be appropriate in social housing.

In private sector housing it is normal to provide one family bathroom plus en-suite shower rooms to the master bedroom and any further double bedroom. Thus in a four bed, seven person house, there would normally be a family bathroom and two en-suite shower rooms.

4.8 Storage

Where Parker Morris scored highly was in specifying good standards for storage. This proved popular, with people becoming more acquisitive all the time and this is still the case. PM specified that a large part of the general storage space should be at ground level, accessible from circulation areas rather than from rooms. It was not intended that the loft space should count, as this is not normally conveniently accessible (though a good-quality loft ladder will make it more so) and trussed rafter construction makes the space much less usable. However boarding to at least part of the loft will create valuable extra storage space.

In addition to general storage space, Parker Morris also stipulated space for hanging outdoor clothes in the entrance hall, a space for a pram (1400 × 700) in houses for three persons or more, and a linen cupboard, all of which remain good practice today.

Bedroom cupboards such as built-in wardrobes were not stipulated. These can be valuable especially for low-income families. However, they need to be carefully planned in order to prevent them making the bedrooms less furnishable.

The Design and Quality Standards reiterated the need for good storage, although the requirements are not as generous, as shown in Table XI.

A minimum of 0.4 m² of the general storage should be located within an airing cupboard.

In addition to the general storage noted in Table XI, 0.5 m² tall storage is required per dwelling. Externally, for units with 1–4 bed spaces, storage should be equal to or greater than 2.2 m². For units with greater than 4 bed spaces, storage should be equal to or greater than 3.0 m². Where a garage is provided the external storage requirement may be deemed satisfied.

4.9 Stair configuration

Although the Building Regulations do not rule out winders provided that certain minimum dimensions are met, winders are

Terrace house (shown as 5.1m internal width)

Enclosed hard standing for bins with robust paving

Line of building over

Soft planting strip behind fence, wall or railings

Covered cycle storage

Screening

Gate with latch

21.12 *Front garden of a terraced house showing refuse and cycle storage*

intrinsically less easily negotiated and more hazardous, especially for young children and older people. It is important that large wardrobes and other furniture can be taken up and down the stairs. This needs to be carefully planned for, especially in three-storey houses, where the soffit of the upper flight can restrict the head height over the lower flight, and winders make the problems worse.

Some HAs and RPs do not accept staircases with winders. This can be for reasons of safety, economy and to allow for the easy future installation of stair lifts (as noted in Table VIII).

4.10 External design
Refuse storage space is almost always needed at the front of the house, Figure 21.12. The location for the dustbins or 'wheelie-bin' needs to be clearly identified, for example, by partial enclosure or change of paving surface. It needs to be close to the highway, the front gate and path, and not too far from the front or kitchen door. It should not be where smells would cause a problem, such as immediately under the window of a habitable room. It should always be copiously ventilated, and from this point of view the best form of enclosure is none at all.

Refuse storage requirements can vary from borough to borough. Many now require two 'wheelie-bins', one for general waste and one for recycling. Many also offer an option to have one specifically for garden waste. Designers must check local requirements to ensure refuse storage is properly integrated into the design at an early stage in the process.

Changes are imminent. In 2013 the government announced it will publish guidance on suitable provision for proper waste storage in new homes to tackle 'bin blight' of bins dominating residential streets and contributing to increased odour and roadside litter. This could include covert storage units for residents' bins, or simply ensuring that there is space for bins to be stored in backyards so that they are taken out only when necessary, on bin-collection day.

In addition to this, a ruling, from the European Union, which will take effect from 2015, states that all paper, metal, glass and plastic rubbish will have to be collected separately, which could lead to an increase in the number of containers of these different types of waste.

Meter positions can sometimes be integrated with that of bins, so that one can partially mask the other. This is more the case now that the service companies require external or externally readable meters.

The function of a front garden enclosure is different from that of the rear garden, and this should be reflected in the design, Figure 21.12.

Front fences, railings or walls should allow easy visual surveillance, both ways. A height of between 800 mm and 1300 mm is usually appropriate, and it is useful if the enclosure can be seen through below this level, but does not let dogs through. Thus railings and paling fences score over walls. Front gates should be of roughly the same height. A closed gate effectively excludes dogs and makes a defensible space feel rather more so; but gates, gate posts and catches need to be sturdy and carefully designed.

Enclosure of rear gardens is simpler. An impermeable wall or fence of approximately 1.8 m height is normally recommended at the far end. The side (party fence) enclosures can be reduced to approximately 1.2 m. Most people seem to welcome some garden-to-garden contact with their neighbours, though not immediately next to the house, where a greater height is preferred. If gates are provided in rear garden walls or fences, these should be full height (at least 1.8 m) and lockable with security-grade dead locks. The security of rear fences and garden walls can be improved where these are located against public or communal spaces, by the addition of timber trellis on top; between 450 mm and 600 mm in extra height.

5 PURPOSE-BUILT FLATS

5.1 General
A block of flats nearly always involves shared entrances, stairs, landings, balconies or lobbies, and often one or more lifts. These features tend to make flats undesirable for families with children. In many developments, one would expect the majority of flats to be two-bedroom, with a lesser number of one-bedroom and three bedroom flats.

Common areas and facilities become exponentially more difficult to manage with increasing numbers of flats in the block. Small blocks of four or six flats are easier to manage than those where the numbers get into double figures. Shared systems such as entry phones rely upon responsible behaviour. This is more achievable with a small number of households who know each other. The LHDG has a requirement for a maximum of eight dwellings served off a single stair core and this can be considered good practice. There is also the need to consider the provision of ventilation and natural daylighting to common areas.

5.2 Height of blocks
Parker Morris stipulated the maximum walk-up to a flat front door to be two storeys. Although the Homes & Communities Agency no longer rules out four-storey blocks without lifts, these are on the limit of acceptability. For five storeys and above, a lift is essential although surprisingly, Approved Document M of the Building Regulations does not make the provision of lifts a legal requirement.

5.3 Common stairs, corridors and balconies
Common corridors and lobbies are generally required to be smoke vented in order to prevent smoke and the products of fire in a flat from reaching the fire protected common escape stair. This can be achieved by natural smoke venting to external air via an AOV (automatic opening ventilator) or an internal smoke shaft. Alternatively, a mechanical smoke exhaust or pressure differential system can be utilised. Dry risers and possibly fire-fighting lifts, staircases and lobbies may be required in certain arrangements depending on building heights and floor areas.

Common corridor lengths are normally determined by the limitations of travel distance allowed for means of escape. These are 7.5 m where a single direction of escape exists or 30 m if alternatives routes are available. The provision of designed smoke control systems can allow for extended travel distances. Also the provision of sprinkler coverage within the flats enables the travel distance to be doubled.

In small single stair buildings (with no more than four storeys and no floor level over 11 m above ground) some allowances are made. If there are only two flats per storey these can open directly into the stair core as long as the flats have internal fire protected hallways. Also, if the travel distance in a common lobby or corridor does not exceed 4.5 m then the lobby/corridor is not required to be smoke vented.

Designers should also be aware of the potential problem of common areas over-heating if not adequately ventilated. BS 5925:1991 recommends that a free area of 1/50th of the floor area is provided for adequate ventilation.

5.4 Internal flat layouts (from a fire perspective)
For fire safety purposes any flat that has an internal travel distance of over 9 m from the entrance door to any point of accommodation must be provided with a cellular layout around an internal fire protected hallway that in itself must not exceed 9 m length. Open plan layouts are therefore limited to small flats; however in larger flats the provision of sprinklers does enable open plan layouts. Duplexes require alternative escape routes from the non-entrance levels unless either a sprinkler system is installed or an internal fire protected hall, landing and stairway is formed and a LD2 automatic fire detection system is installed.

5.5 Stacking of similar rooms
All party floors have to provide sound insulation; but the levels of insulation that are mandatory cannot prevent all noise nuisance, and it is best if similar rooms are stacked one above the other. The worst combination is for a living room directly above another flat's bedroom.

5.6 Configuration of rooms around the common stairs
The minimum levels of sound insulation specified in the Building Regulations between all habitable rooms in flats and the common parts of the block are less than fully satisfactory and the adoption

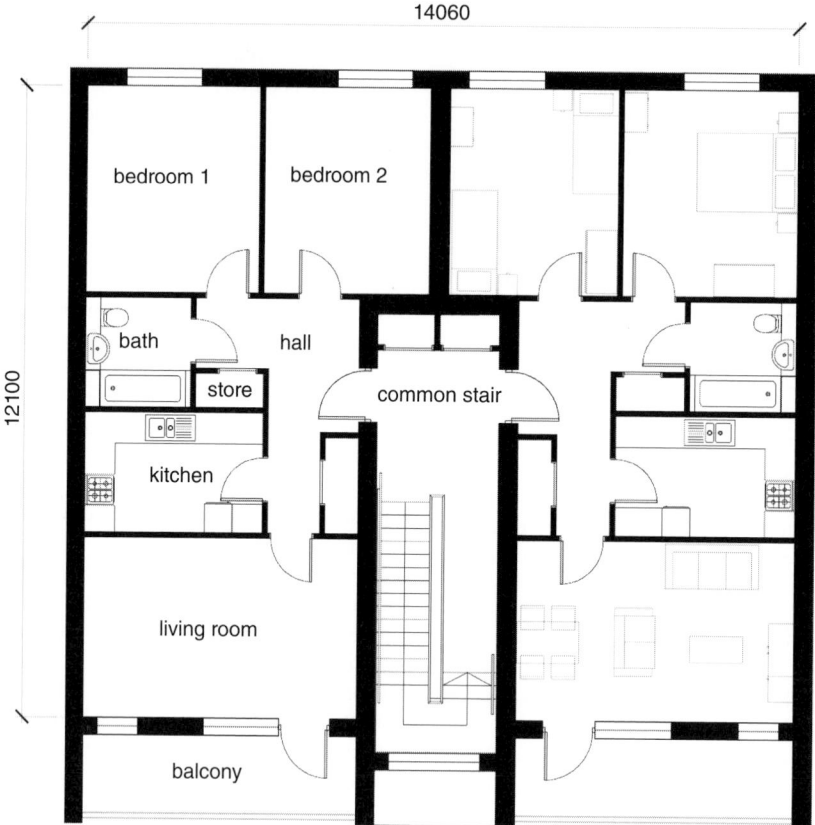

21.13 *Block of two-bedroom, four-person flats, bedrooms located away from stairs. Each flat is 72 m². Lobbies between stairs and flats are required in larger blocks*

of higher performance standards is always preferable. It is desirable therefore to situate bedrooms away from the common stairs, Figure 21.13; and particularly, well away from any lift shaft.

It is usually preferable to plan day rooms at the front and bedrooms at the quieter rear, perhaps alongside the kitchen. There are however, many examples of small blocks of flats with bedrooms at the front alongside the stairs, and living rooms at the rear. This plan form combines the worst exposure of the bedrooms to noise nuisance from the common stairs with the least satisfactory orientation of day and night rooms.

5.7 Balcony access

Balcony or deck access was largely discredited by the social failures of much of the deck-access, medium rise, LA housing built in the 1960s and 1970s. However, some of the smaller, self-contained balcony access flat blocks built between the wars have proved quite satisfactory in long-term use. Balcony or deck access can avoid the squalor associated with wholly internal common circulation areas and provide cross-ventilation (an advantage in avoiding over-heating) but they can also enable the planning of large extended blocks, with too many flats using a single entrance and stair. This should be resisted.

A problem with balcony access flats is the dual aspect; some windows are directly onto the balcony. These are not popular, owing to lack of privacy and the security risks. Kitchens and bathrooms tend to be placed on the balcony side, but residents dislike strangers passing close to their kitchen sinks. There is also the potential for means of escape to be restricted (compromised) in the event of smoke from fire escaping out of flat windows.

However, with careful design and a reasonable limit on the number of flats served by them, balcony or deck access has become acceptable more recently.

5.8 Lifts

In blocks of flats these should always be capable of taking a wheelchair, preferably an eight-person lift as defined by BS 5655. Approved Document M of the Building Regulation does however allow rather smaller lift car dimensions, equating to a five-person lift. A thirteen-person lift should also be capable of taking a horizontal stretcher. Lifts in medium-rise flat blocks have become rather easier to plan, using hydraulic lifts with pump rooms at or near the base, as opposed to electric lifts with motor rooms at the top. Hydraulic pump rooms can be very compact and flexibly positioned. In blocks of flats with a floor level higher than 18 m above entrance level a firefighter's lift must be provided.

5.9 Refuse

This is always a challenge with flats. Traditionally, public-sector housing has used chutes. These cause a noise nuisance and tend to get blocked, and the inlet points can become particularly unsavoury. Additionally, the chambers at the base of the chutes, with paladins or skips, collect overflowing rubbish, vermin, and general mess and squalor. If blocks of flats can be kept small (up to six or eight flats) then it is quite possible to provide a discreet but easily accessible area containing a separate rubbish bin for each flat, clearly and individually marked, Figure 21.14.

For large or tall blocks, Building Regulations have an implied recommendation for refuse chutes. In actuality they are hardly ever provided nowadays and even very tall blocks rely on ground level refuse storage chambers and residents using vertical transportation for disposal from flats. If they are provided, the base area needs to be carefully designed, with robust and easily cleaned surfaces, good access for cleaning and copious ventilation.

Building Regulations also contain guidance on the maximum distance that residents should be required to carry waste to the

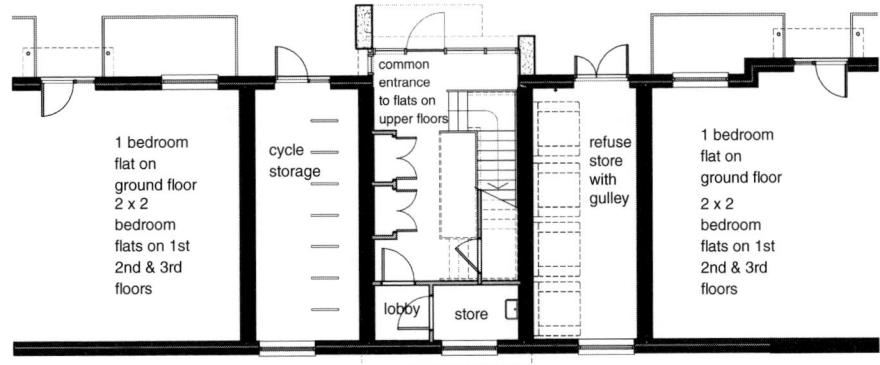

21.14 *External planning for typical three-storey block of flats showing refuse storage*

storage point (no more than 30 m). Waste collection vehicles should be able to get within 25 m of that point. Maximum reversing distances for vehicles will also have to be considered and this will have an impact on the building and road layouts.

5.10 Incoming utilities: meters and services ducts

The provision of sufficient space for meters and services to the apartment block is paramount when planning the floor layouts, particularly around the common access stairs, lobbies and corridors. It is usual to provide vertical risers to house all incoming services, such as electricity, gas, telecommunications, phone/video entry, cable TV, data cabling, etc. These should be accessible for both installation of these services and their ongoing maintenance. Access into these service risers is often via fire doors opening onto the ventilated lobbies as discussed above.

It is advisable to obtain advice and guidance from the relevant national and local service providers, particularly regarding location of meters and routing of their services. Gas routing needs special consideration as all spaces containing a gas pipe, meter, valve etc. need to be vented to prevent the building up of undetectable gas, which could lead to explosion.

Also, there may be a requirement for meters rooms to be designed into the ground floor or at basement level, to facilitate easy meter reading by the providing authority. Routing from these meters rooms and the vertical risers will need careful consideration to avoid the risk of clashes with structure or compromising fire integrity.

Horizontal routing of these services from the vertical service shafts into the apartments should also be considered at an early stage. Access for ongoing maintenance will be a consideration when choosing finishes to ceilings and floors.

5.11 External areas

Unless there is a very competent management regime, shared external areas should be either minimised or avoided. Clearly the latter is not entirely possible, as access is needed to the common front door. The route to this entrance should be as simple as possible: broad and short. Areas to the sides of this access can be given to the ground floor flats as front gardens; and these will be much more successful if these flats have separate front doors independent of the common entrance. Similarly, the best use for the ground behind the block is normally as rear gardens for the ground floor flats.

Communal gardens sound good but rarely work, unless there is an exemplary system of management by residents' association or landlord. External space for upper floor flats is often provided by private balconies. The enclosure of front and rear gardens to ground floor flats should be similar to that for single family houses (see Section 4.10). The shared approach to the main entrance door should be treated rather differently. If there is no unallocated garden space there will be no fencing except on either side of this approach.

If there is any soft landscaping along the shared approach route, it needs to be carefully planned to withstand limited care. If flanked by well cared for private gardens, then the common approach path is best left as good quality hard landscaping and paving.

6 HOUSE CONVERSIONS

6.1 General

The conversion of large houses into self-contained flats in the 1970s and 1980s used to be the stock-in-trade of inner city housing associations, as well as private developers. There has been a falling off of this type of rehabilitation project, partly because of a gradual shift in demand, but also because HAs have turned more towards new build schemes since the Housing Act 1988.

6.2 Planning

Splitting up a single-family house involves creating at least one new dwelling, and thereby constitutes 'development' under the Planning Acts. Unlike extending a single-family house by an allowed percentage of its volume, this is not 'permitted development'. Therefore house conversions require planning permission which allows planning authorities to control this type of development if they feel that it is eroding the balance of single-family houses in the district.

Houses that are statutorily listed have more onerous constraints and require Listed Building Consent for any demolition (however small). Certain restraints also apply to all properties within Conservation Areas, possibly depending on what Article 4 directions have been approved. Conservation Area approval is no longer required for a small amount of demolition, such as of an outhouse; but a proposal of this nature might well lead to a spot-listing, when a Listed Building Consent would then be required. In many of these cases, the planning authority and/or English Heritage may then get very involved in detailed design and aesthetics.

This introduces the first discipline when dealing with an existing house, which is to respect its existing qualities and character. A natural conversion should aim to keep well-proportioned rooms intact wherever possible. This commonly means at least the main front rooms at ground and first floor levels. Avoid boxed-in lobbies in the corners of previously good rooms. These disrupt original decorative elements such as cornices and picture rails, and also make the rooms more difficult to furnish. Another implicit aspect of natural conversions is the aim to keep similar rooms stacked over each other. Day rooms of one flat should not be planned over bedrooms of another flat and bathrooms and kitchens are best stacked, thereby simplifying drainage and plumbing.

The same considerations about accommodation for families with children apply as for new-build. Family dwellings should be at ground and/or basement level, or at least have direct street entry and garden access. This will usually mean only one large unit in the conversion of a house, with one or more smaller units over it. In a wish to reduce the common areas, many conversions have been built the 'wrong way up' with a large unit over a one-bedroom flat at ground-floor level. This is unsatisfactory, especially in social housing. Family life is noisy, and does not fit well over single people or couples.

However it should be the aim to abolish or minimise common areas and stairs wherever possible, as these often cause continuing management problems. New external stairs may be added in some cases to achieve the objective of a separate direct entrance for each dwelling.

6.3 Building Regulations

Creating new dwellings constitutes building work and is controlled by the Building Regulations. Most of the same parts (see Table III) apply to conversions as to new build. The main exception is Approved Document L. In recognition of the fact that it may not be reasonably possible to add thermal insulation to all elements of the existing fabric to the standards required for new buildings, conversions must meet the requirements of AD L1B which applies only to existing buildings.

Some elements such as top floor ceilings, though, are quite simple to insulate, and could be upgraded to a higher level than required for new build to compensate for not insulating the walls. Thermal insulation can also often be added to the walls of rear extensions, where there is a greater proportion of exposed wall surface to floor area, and decorative features, which would be lost, are absent. The replanning of rear parts of the house to provide new service rooms may also give opportunities to add insulating linings. Also worth considering (subject to planning restrictions) is external insulation, as this can theoretically give a better thermal performance and reduces cold bridging. Approved Document B1 (Means of Escape) and E (Resistance to the Passage of Sound) apply to conversions as for new-build, and can impose significant requirements.

6.4 Loft conversions

If habitable rooms are converted out of loft space, the resulting floor area is measured over those parts that are more than 1.5 m high. A two-storey house is covered by Approved Document B1 of the Building Regulations only for escape from upper floor windows. However, when its loft is converted, extra requirements of Approved Document B1 come into force.

Under Approved Document K, alternating tread stairs are specifically allowed up to single rooms and bathrooms in a loft. Despite this, there are considerable reservations about the safety of alternating tread stairs, and they are not recommended, especially in social housing. A reasonable width for a staircase leading to a single habitable room in a loft is 800 mm, with a minimum of 700 mm.

6.5 External areas

Similar considerations apply as to purpose-built flats. The best answer is often the simplest – to give both front and rear gardens to the lowest dwelling, which is likely to be the largest. Balconies to upper-floor units are less likely to be feasible than with new build, unless a low rear extension provides an opportunity for a roof terrace. Some planning authorities discourage these as prejudicing the privacy of neighbouring gardens. In cases of detached, semidetached and end-of-terrace properties with easy access to the rear, plots for the upper flats can be provided by dividing the rear garden. There are also examples where first floor flats have been given access by means of external stairs. There is however evidence that small, subdivided rear gardens can lead to neglect, because residents feel less well 'connected' to them.

6.6 Change of use: offices to residential

In a drive to increase the delivery of new homes the government has relaxed the planning policy for conversion of office buildings into residential dwellings. However the relevant standards set out above need to be met which can be difficult within an existing structure.

7 ACCOMMODATION FOR SINGLE PEOPLE

7.1 General

In the past, a distinction was drawn between the space requirement for *middle-aged permanent residents and for young mobile workers*. This led to a recommendation for small (25 m²) bedsitting room flats for the latter category – sometimes referred to as 'studio apartments' or 'micro-flats'. The trouble is that young, mobile tenants turn into middle-aged, permanent ones quicker than housing

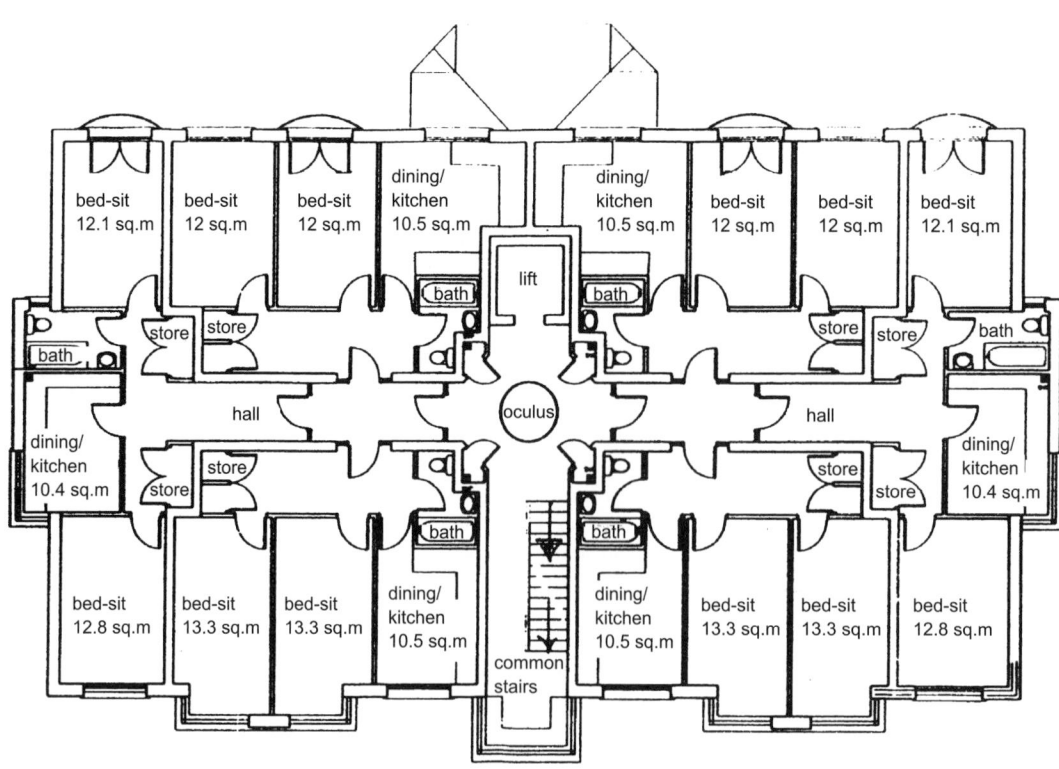

21.15 *First floor of a block containing six flats of 51m², each with two bedsitting rooms for single people sharing (see Figures 21.16 and 21.17 for other floors of this block)*

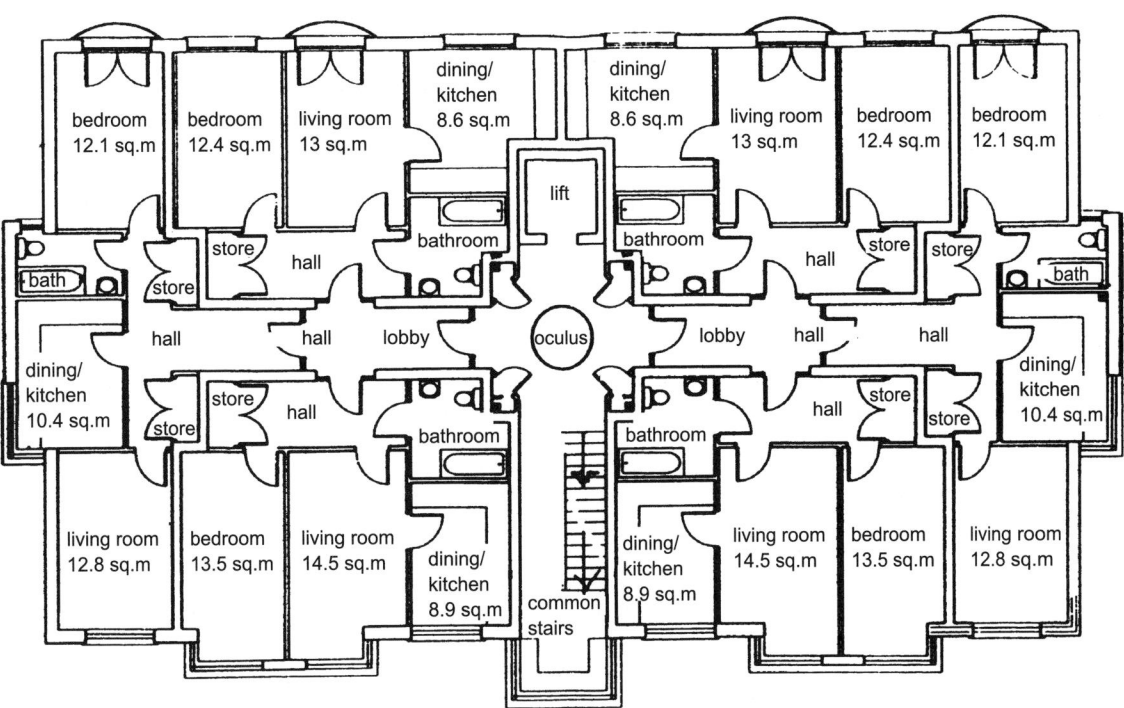

21.16 *Second floor of same block as Figure 21.15 with six one-bedroom category I sheltered flats of 51 m². The third floor is similar*

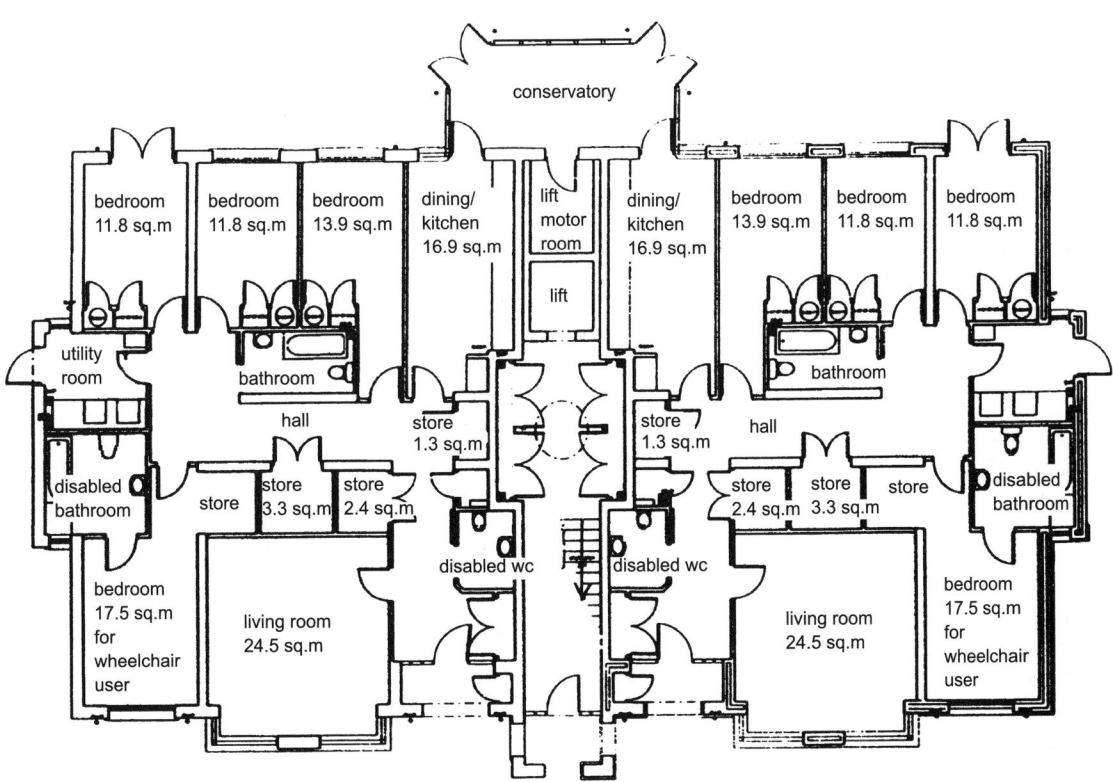

21.17 *Ground floor of same block as Figures 21.15 and 21.16 containing two flats each of 165 m² with four bedrooms, one of which is for a wheelchair user*

managers can respond. This has resulted in a great degree of dissatisfaction with bedsit flats for single people.

The four principal types of accommodation provided for single people are:

- Self-contained one-bedroom flats, for which the HQIs recommend an area of 30–35 m². For furniture requirements see Table V.

- *Cluster flats* providing a number of bedsitting rooms, with shared dining kitchens, living rooms and sanitary facilities, Figures 21.15–21.17, and including Foyers (see 7.4).
- That which is suitable for students, nurses, etc. (see Chapter 23; Student housing and housing for young people).
- Sheltered housing for older single people (see Chapter 22; Homes for older people).

Table XII Housing for single people from DB29

Numbers of single people sharing	1	2	3	4	Each additional person
Minimum areas (including storage) in:					
single-storey houses	33 m²	48.5 m²	65 m²	85 m²	20m²
houses more than 1 storey				90 m²	
flats	32.5 m²	47.5 m²	65 m²	85 m²	20m²
maisonettes				90 m²	
Personal storage					
including shelves or drawers	3 m³	6 m²	9 m²	12 m³	3m³
with area not less than:	2 m²	4 m²	6 m²	8 m²	2 m²
Dwelling storage					
including shelves or drawers	0.5 m³	0.5 m³	0.5 m³	0.5 m³	
with area not less than:	0.8m²	0.8 m²	0.8 m²	0.8 m²	
Kitchen storage					
Including shelves or drawers	1.4 m³	2.1 m³	2.8 m³	3.5 m³	0.7 m³
with area not less than:	5 m³	7 m²	9 m²	11 m²	2 m²
Electric socket outlets	9	12	15	18	3
Bath or shower	1	1	1	1	
Washbasin	1	1	1	2	
WC separate	1*	1*	1	2*	

*one may be in the bathroom.

7.2 Cluster flats

Because of the space needed for the individual bedsitting rooms, the floor areas for cluster flats should be rather greater than for the equivalent size of a general needs household, for three-person units and larger.

Storage space is particularly important for single persons sharing a dwelling. Still relevant as the definitive standard is DB29, published by the DOE (1974) which laid down minimum storage spaces, distinguishing between that for individuals and that for the dwelling as a whole (see Table XII). A minimum bedsitting room is 12 m², the recommended size for a medium to long-stay resident is 15 m², and a washbasin should be provided in each.

7.3 Common rooms

Where these are provided, the areas should be at least 20 m² for the first 25 persons plus 0.4 m² for each additional person. However, it is now less usual to provide common rooms, as schemes tend to consist of self-contained flats, either for one-person households, or of clusters, who share integral day rooms. Foyers are one exception that should be noted.

7.4 Foyers

A concept introduced from France in the early 1990s is the *foyer*, consisting of a complex containing accommodation for young single people either in one-person flats or more usually a number of cluster flats, or a mixture of the two types. It can also include substantial training facilities and other provision such as cafeterias, laundries and common rooms. To make it economically feasible, a foyer needs to house about 100 young people. Although successful in France, it has proved difficult to deliver as a viable model in the UK.

8 ESTATE REGENERATION

8.1 General

Local authorities have recently built little new housing, but they still own an enormous stock of existing estates built over the last hundred years. Many of these are now decrepit and out of date. Significant funds and initiatives are therefore being directed towards the special problems of these estates (see case study,

9).These initiatives have included government-financed Estate Action Programmes, City Challenge projects, Housing Action Trusts, Estate Renewal Challenge Funding, Single Regeneration Budgets and New Deal for Communities Initiatives. Funding via the HCA for stock transfers to housing associations has also been available, although the process is complex and costly and subject to a majority vote by residents so the outcome is uncertain.

8.2 Challenges

Many flat blocks built before the First World War are characterised by too small floor areas, outdated internal planning with inadequate kitchens and bathrooms, and unsatisfactory means of escape. The building services are probably obsolete, and central heating and thermal insulation absent. Some of these blocks, however, possess considerable architectural character, and have stable and supportive communities of residents.

Blocks built between the wars may also be lacking in modern services, heating and insulation but can be better planned internally and well-built structurally. Kitchens are still usually too small for modern requirements although otherwise floor areas increased. External planning was simple, but with more communal space than is now desirable. Blocks from this period represent a vast investment in housing stock, with enormous potential for improvement into good-quality modern housing.

Since the Second World War, social housing has suffered from too many well-intentioned attempts to rethink design and planning from scratch. Consequently the last 50 years have seen widely differing forms of housing, many of which have proved dramatically unsuccessful. High-rise blocks of flats are only the most prominent and publicised of mistakes. Some of the medium-rise (five or six storey) deck access estates have proved even less satisfactory.

Dwellings in these large usually inner-city estates generally complied with the good internal standards of Parker Morris. The problem is the external estate design that is often hated and feared by the residents, which fails to provide private and public open spaces appropriate for families with children.

8.3 Consultation

Estate modernisation presents many varied, peculiar and acute problems. First, an investigation to establish what the problems really are has to be carried out. These are rarely simple, and may vary widely from estate to estate. The people who understand the problems best are the residents, but they may need help to articulate them. Careful approaches and techniques under the general description of community architecture should be adopted to identify and address the tenants' concerns.

Architectural teams usually move onto the estate to conduct surveys, set up design surgeries, hold open meetings and distribute newsletters to reach their social clients.

8.4 Proposals

After this consultation, designs and proposals can be worked up in close collaboration with the residents. The works needed to improve estates will be different in each case; but may include some or all of the following:

- Moving family units down to ground level, perhaps by combining flats on ground and/or first floors into larger flats or maisonettes, and subdividing large flats on upper floors into small ones.
- Using unwanted external space to provide private gardens for the ground-floor units, with separate direct access from the public highway or estate road.
- Remodelling the flat interiors, giving larger dining/kitchens and better bathrooms.
- High-rise blocks that cannot be split up or effectively use entry phones can be provided with *concierge* systems; using

a combination of electronic and human portering to provide 24-hour security.

- Improving refuse arrangements, aiming to disperse rather than concentrate collection points.
- Improving the fabric; adding thermal and sound insulation; adding pitched roofs on top of flat roofs; replacing windows with double glazing and controllable trickle ventilation.
- Renewing the mechanical and electrical services; adding central heating; improving ventilation by putting extract fans into kitchens and bathrooms. Where there is district heating with a central boiler house and a history of problems, replacing with unit systems in each dwelling. Consider heat-retrieval systems.
- Consider converting some blocks to integrated sheltered housing. In these cases, entrances and gardens must be clearly distinguished and separated.
- Communal external spaces to be reduced to either a minimum or abolished.
- If all family flats and maisonettes have their own private gardens, there is an argument that communal children's play space within the estate may be unnecessary. If not, it must be carefully sited as it may cause nuisance to neighbouring dwellings. Play space in local parks is preferable if they are nearby; or situated in clearly public spaces such as the squares that might feature in some large estates. A lack of security is often perceived; ideally, family accommodation without sufficient, private, open space should be avoided.
- Estate roads, car parking and emergency vehicle access often need to be replanned. Parking within the curtilage may be possible if the front gardens are deep enough; otherwise provide small parking bays in clear view of the dwellings they serve. Basement parking and car courts at the rear of blocks are best avoided because of the security risks they pose.
- Replan pedestrian routes in order to eliminate unnecessary footpaths and to maximise natural supervision from the dwellings of all routes.
- Adding lifts if over three storeys high.
- Consider enclosing open balconies and staircases, and splitting up long balcony access buildings into smaller more manageable blocks, preferably with no more than 10 or 12 flats in each.
- Adding entry phones to privatise staircases.

9 CASE STUDY – PORTOBELLO SQUARE, KENSINGTON, PRP ARCHITECTS LLP

9.1 Introduction

The regeneration of a failing housing estate provided the catalyst for the Portobello Square development in North Kensington, London. The site is at the northern end of Portobello Road, which is famous for its diverse and eclectic street market. But the historic connection between Portobello Road and Ladbroke Grove was severed when the Wornington Green Estate was built during the 1960s and 1970s, disconnecting the estate from its immediate context and destroying the Victorian street pattern, Figure 21.18.

9.2 Site

The triangular 5.5 ha site is bounded by the main Paddington/ West Country railway line to the north, Portobello Road and Golborne Road and represents one of the largest regeneration programmes in the Royal Borough of Kensington & Chelsea in recent years. Wornington Green Estate comprised 538 flats and houses predominantly in the form of deck-access, interconnected H-blocks set out around courtyards. The block form is alien to the historic grain of the area and poor construction methods have accelerated the decline of the estate, which suffered from damp and condensation associated with cold-bridging and poor insulation.

The application boundary included a number of assets owned by the Royal Borough of Kensington & Chelsea: Athlone Gardens – a public park extending to almost 1 acre, a sunken ball court, a community centre and 20 lock-ups used by market traders. These assets were to be re-provided in the redevelopment.

9.3 Aims

The key design objectives for the development were to reintegrate the site with its immediate neighbourhood context in the form of street-accessed properties, to re-provide the poorly-located open space as a 'Green Flag' park at the heart of the development and to provide new high quality housing employing a range of different typologies drawn from traditional Kensington residential precedents.

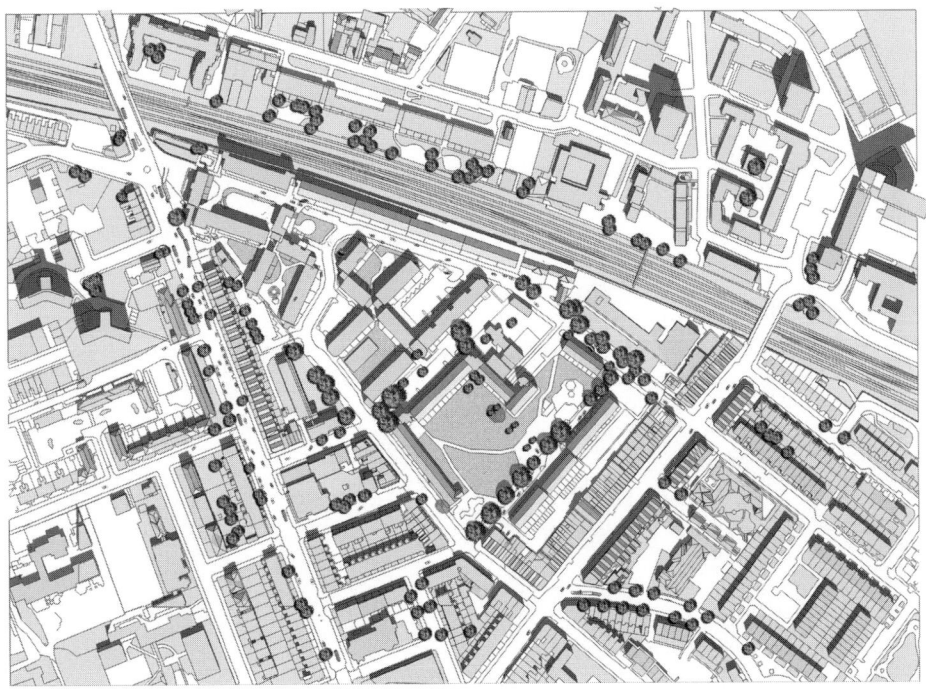

21.18 *Existing site*

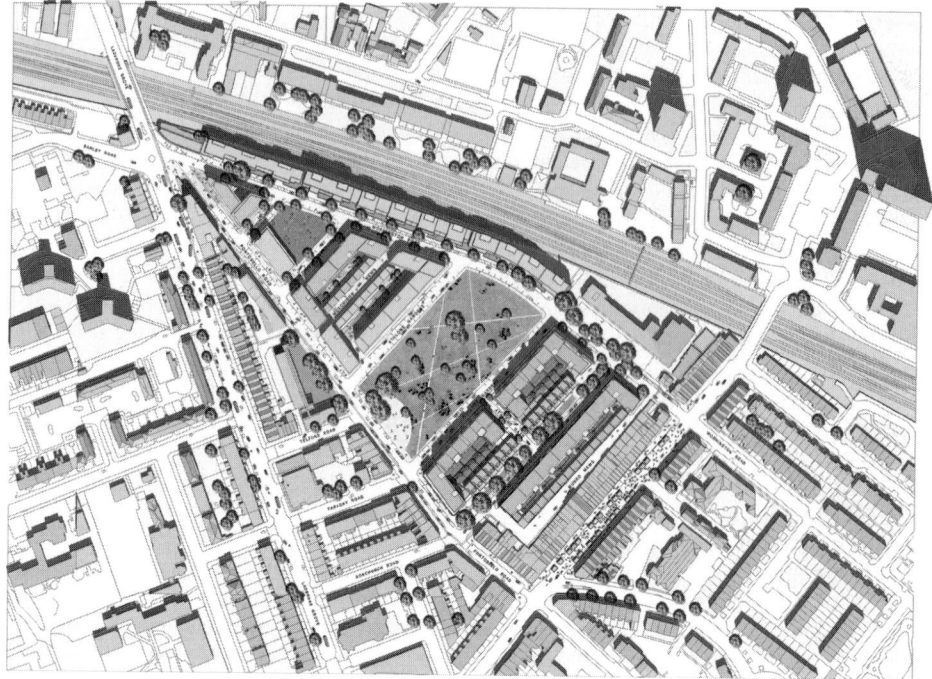

21.19 *Regeneration plan*

21.20 *Cross section*

21.21 *Mews houses*

21.22 *Mansion blocks*

21.23 *Terrace*

9.4 Options

The design brief was set out through a Supplementary Planning Document (SPD) written by the local authority, following an initial capacity study by PRP. This capacity study identified options for refurbishment, partial redevelopment and full redevelopment which were presented to residents, officers and other stakeholders at public consultation. A majority support for redevelopment led to the development of the consented masterplan through continued consultation with all relevant parties. The affordable housing mix was largely determined by the re-provision of existing homes against a housing-need survey carried out for the residents. Permission was granted for up to 1000 new homes with the outline masterplan showing circa 920, of which 58 per cent were social rent. This provided a density of 134 dwellings (or 404 habitable rooms) per hectare.

9.5 Design

The masterplan, Figure 21.19, reinstates a number of the historic road positions in order to mend the urban fabric, reconnecting Portobello Road and Wornington Road to Ladbroke Grove. A new park, in the tradition of a London garden square, is located at the heart of the development. The community centre is re-provided on its own site on Portobello Road ensuring an active hub for community activity and flexibility of this land parcel for the future.

Mixed-uses at street level include new shopping and community facilities along the new extension to Portobello Road. These reinforce the existing retail facilities in the area and the junction with Ladbroke Grove and provide a new focal point for the community with pubs and restaurants at the northern end of Portobello Road.

A range of building heights from 3 to 9 storeys accommodates a variety of dwelling types, Figure 21.20. Dwellings are tenure 'blind' from the outside to provide quality throughout the development. Building typologies draw on contemporary interpretations of the mews houses, Figure 21.21, mansion blocks, Figure 21.22, town houses and terraces, Figure 21.23 of the adjacent conservation area London vernacular. Terraces are simple and well ordered in terms of form, fenestration and detailing. Particular features are generous fenestration and recessed balconies that provide accessible amenity areas for the residents. Traditional materials in the public realm and traditional relationships between streets and buildings ensure a feel that will be consistent with the rest of the Borough.

A wide variety of affordable dwelling types are provided to meet existing tenant needs including 1, 2, 3 and 4 bedroom apartments, 4 bedroom mews houses and 3 and 4 bedroom duplexes. The latter have their own front doors to the street, with bedrooms at basement level, reflecting the traditional arrangement of many Victorian streets. The private dwelling types include 1, 2 and 3 bedroom apartments, 3 bedroom mews houses, 3 and 4 bedroom duplexes and four storey townhouses. The latter typology is specifically intended to maximise profit from private sale to cross-fund the redevelopment. The first phase is supported by significant HCA grant-funding but the remainder of the development will be self-funding through the private sale receipts.

The first phase complies with Parker Morris standards, as required by the design brief. Subsequent phases were designed to comply with the London Housing Design Guide or relevant standard. A high quality of design, finish and materials was achieved to maximise the benefit of private sale which helped to subsidise the redevelopment.

A range of energy efficiency and sustainability measures were incorporated into the development to achieve a Code for Sustainable Homes Level 4 rating. This includes Combined Heat & Power, brown roofs, photo-voltaic panels on all buildings apart from the houses and run-off water storage and attenuation below ground.

Construction commenced in 2011 with Phase 1 completion in 2016, and overall completion in 2020. The design represents part of an emerging new London vernacular through a number of important large-scale housing developments in the capital, and also a new benchmark in the approach to the regeneration of poor quality high density housing estates.

10 REFERENCES

Access Committee for England, *Building Homes for Successive Generations: Criteria for Accessible General Housing*, Access Committee for England, 1992

Association of Chief Police Officers (ACPO), Secured By Design (SBD), *New Homes*, ACPO, 2010

David Birkbeck and Stefan Kruczkowski, Paul Collins and Brian Quinn (eds.) *The Sign of a Good Place to Live: Building for Life 12*, Building for Life Partnership, 2012

British Standards Institution (B.S.I.). BS 9991:2011. *Fire Safety in the Design, Management and Use of Residential Buildings – Code of Practice, 2011*

British Standards Institution (B.S.I.). BS 9266:2013. *Design of Accessible and Adaptable General Needs Housing – Code of Practice, 2013*

Matthew Carmona, Nick Gallent, and Reetuparna Sarkar, *Space Standards: the Benefits*, University College, 2010

Code for Sustainable Homes: Technical Guide, Department for Communities and Local Government (DCLG), 2010

Alice Coleman, *Utopia on Trial: Vision and Reality in Planned Housing*, Shipman, 1990

Department for Communities and Local Government, (DCLG) *Building and Buildings, England and Wales, The Building Regulations 2010*. Statutory Instruments 2010 No. 2214, The Stationery Office, 2010

Department for Communities and Local Government *The Code for Sustainable Homes: Setting the Standard in Sustainability for New Homes*, DCLG, 2008

Department of the Environment, *Homes for Today and Tomorrow*, HMSO (known as The Parker-Morris report), 1961

Department for Transport, Local Government and the Regions (DTLR) and Commission for Architecture and the Built Environment (CABE), *Better places to live: by design: a companion guide to PPG3*, Thomas Telford. 2001

Department for Transport (DfT) and the Department for Communities and Local Government (DCLG), WSP et al. *Manual for Streets*, Thomas Telford, 2007

Department of the Environment, Transport and the Regions (DETR) and Commission for Architecture and the Built Environment (CABE), *By Design: Urban Design in the Planning System: Towards Better Practice*, DETR, 2000

Andrew Drury, *Standards and quality in development: a Good Practice Guide*. 2nd edition, National Housing Federation, 2008

Selwyn Goldsmith, *Designing for the disabled*, 3rd edition, RIBA Publications, 1976, Reprinted with Sections 90 and 94 up-dated, 1984

Selwyn Goldsmith, *Designing for the disabled: the new paradigm*. Architectural Press, 1997

Selwyn Goldsmith, with PRP Architects, *Universal design: a manual of practical guidance for architects*, Architectural Press, 2000

Chris Goodman, *Habinteg Housing Association Design Guide*, Habinteg Housing Association, 2003

Chris Goodman, *Lifetime Homes Design Guide*, IHS BRE Press for Habinteg Housing Association, 2011

Greater London Authority (GLA), *The London Plan: Spatial Development Strategy for Greater London*. GLA, 2011

Greater London Authority (GLA), *Housing: Supplementary Planning Guidance*, GLA, 2012

Greater London Authority (GLA), (October 2013) *The London Plan: spatial development strategy for greater London. Revised early minor alterations (REMA). Consistency with the National Planning Policy Framework*. London: GLA. (Replaces the Planning Policy Guidance Notes and Statements issues since 1991)

Habinteg Housing Association Lifetime Homes Standard. Habinteg Housing Association, 2010

Housing Corporation, *Design and Quality Standards*, Housing Corporation, April 2007

Housing Corporation, *Design and Quality Strategy*, Housing Corporation, April 2007

London Development Agency, *London Housing Design Guide: interim edition*, LDA, 2010

Manchester City Council, *Guide to Development in Manchester: Supplementary Planning Document and Planning Guidance*, Manchester City Council, 2007

Kevin McGeough (ed.) *Car Parking: What Works Where*, English Partnerships, 2006

National Affordable Homes Agency, *721 Housing Quality Indicators (HQI), Version 4*, Housing Corporation, 2008

National House-Building Council (NHBC), *NHBC Standards*, NHBC, 2013

Oscar Newman, *Defensible Space: People and Design in the Violent City*, Architectural Press, 1973

Northern Ireland Department For Social Development *Housing Association Development Guide Design Standards*.

Julia Park et al., *Non-Mainstream Housing Design Guidance: literature review*, Homes and Communities Agency, 2012

Parliament, *Housing Act*, Chapter 34. HMSO, 2004

PRP Architects, *Place and Home: the Search for Better Housing*, Black Dog Publishing. 2007

Scottish Government, Scottish Housing Quality Standard, 2004

South East London Housing Partnership (SELHP) *Wheelchair Homes Design Guidelines*, SELHP, 2011

Stephen Thorpe, and Habinteg Housing Association, *Wheelchair Housing Design Guide*. 2nd edition, BRE Press, 2006

Urban Task Force, *Towards an Urban Renaissance*, E & FN Spon, 1999

Urban Task Force, *Towards a Strong Urban Renaissance*. Urban Task Force, 2005

Welsh Government, The Welsh Housing Quality Standard: Revised Guidance for Social Landlords, 2008

Alan Young and Phil Jones (eds.) *Manual for Streets 2*, Chartered Institution of Highways and Transportation, 2010

22 Homes for older people

Ian Smith (updated by David Littlefield)

CI/SfB 44

Before his retirement Ian Smith was a partner in Hubbard Ford and Partners

KEY POINTS:
- *Because of other available accommodation, the people needing care are increasingly infirm*
- *There is a need for activities for residents other than watching TV*

Contents

1 Main elements of the plan
2 Relationship between elements of the plan
3 Planning allowances
4 Planning examples
5 Room data and space requirements
6 Building equipment and fittings
7 Furniture
8 Bibliography

1 MAIN ELEMENTS OF THE PLAN

1.1 Introduction

The design of homes for old people should create a homely, comfortable and friendly atmosphere. The importance of avoiding an institutional character is stressed in most design guides and instructions to architects.

1.2 Scope

This chapter deals with the design of homes in which the residents are in need of special care and attention. The special facilities provided may vary, depending on the degree of infirmity and mobility of the residents, but the basic relationship between the main elements of the plan are common to all homes for old people. Latterly, the concept of very sheltered housing (VSH) has been developed which can provide tenants with a home for life, offering them a choice of different levels of care and support which changes according to need. This removes the need for residents to move to other forms of supported housing. Independence is encouraged; residents can develop a sense of ownership over where they live and can be as self-sufficient as they choose.

1.3 Elements of VSH

A VSH development will likely include the following elements:

- independent self-contained flats designed to wheelchair-user standards. Flats would contain fully fitted kitchens, a shower room, bedroom and lounge;
- main catering kitchen and dining room providing at least one hot meal each day;
- communal lounge, often linked to the dining room;
- lift access to all floors;
- assisted bathrooms, usually one per floor;
- communal laundry;
- wheelchair/scooter recharging store;
- guest accommodation;
- non-resident building manager;
- separate care team based on site offering 24-h care. Facilities for staff and carers to include office, rest, meeting, changing and sleepover accommodation;
- extra community services, such as hairdressing, chiropody, shop, etc.

Design elements of a VSH development would include:

- full wheelchair standards;
- adequate passing points in circulation areas for wheelchairs and scooters;
- removal of obstructions such as fire compartment doors, which can be held open on magnetic pads;
- free swing door closers to residents' front doors and other doors regularly used by residents;
- centrally located lift and communal facilities to enable unobtrusive care delivery and minimise walking distances and possible feelings of isolation;
- centrally located staff facilities away from residential areas;
- clear separation between areas for residents, staff and visitors;
- good natural and artificial lighting particularly on circulation routes;
- good visual access throughout;
- carefully considered use of tone, colour and tactile materials to assist residents who are partially sighted or disorientated;
- interesting corridors, ideally naturally lit from windows or rooflights. Avoidance of long, dull vistas;
- handrails along both sides of circulation routes that are appropriately scored, and snag-free, to assist way-finding for those with visual impairments;
- appropriate ironmongery, taps, etc. for older people with limited dexterity;
- protected, sunny, sheltered outdoor spaces with design features appropriate for residents.

2 RELATIONSHIP BETWEEN ELEMENTS OF THE PLAN

2.1 Relationship structures

Figure 22.1 shows how the main areas of the building are interrelated. The aim should be to encourage social contact, but at the

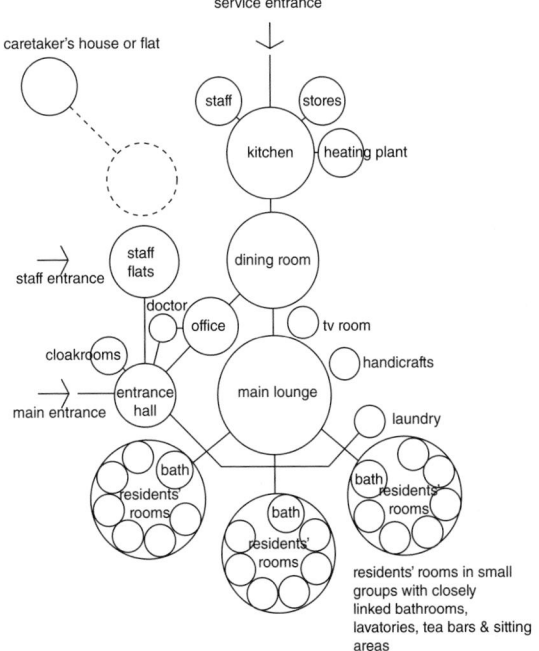

22.1 *Relationships between elements of the plan*

same time to preserve individual privacy. The residents' rooms are often grouped round a small sitting room and services area containing a bathroom and lavatories. Circulation routes to the communal lounges and dining room should be as short as possible, although routes through the residents' groups should be avoided. Communal areas may either be centralised or divided between the residential groups, but most homes have a main dining room, which should be close to a sitting area. The administrative offices should be close to the entrance hall, and, if possible, within easy reach of the kitchen. Staff accommodation should be provided in self-contained flats with separate outside entrances.

2.2 Lighting and materials

Internally, developments should seek to create an uplifting experience that is welcoming, non-institutional and friendly for both residents and visitors. Particular attention must be paid to the building's entrance. Careful lighting, colour schemes and use of materials can help create a special environment, although they should remain domestic in character and specified with consideration for the sensory impairments suffered by older people.

2.3 Circulation planning

The general arrangement of circulation spaces in a VSH scheme should be clear and 'rational' to assist people who are suffering from dementia or memory loss. Complicated planning of circulation routes must be avoided: they will confuse and disorientate. Breaking down the building into identifiable clusters and the provision of visual clues (through pictures and graphics) and signage will greatly assist easy way-finding. Careful planning can reduce the length of corridors, thus reducing the travel distances and minimising an institutional feel. Corridors should have contact with the outside at some points along their length to help people orientate themselves within the overall building and to provide some natural daylight. Windows in the end wall of corridors are not ideal as they create glare, making the corridor appear dark in contrast. A window in the sidewall, near the end of the corridor, will still provide daylight and ventilation while avoiding the glare problem.

3 PLANNING ALLOWANCES

Typical accommodation allowances are given in Table I.

Table I Planning allowances

Accommodation and facilities		
Residents	Single bedsitting rooms	9.6–12m²
	including private WC	15.3 m²
	Double bedsitting rooms	14.8m²–16m³
	Bathrooms and lavatories	8.8 m²
	Sitting areas and tea bars Stores	
Communal rooms	Entrance hall and visitors' cloakroom	
	Lounges	2.3 m² per person
	Dining room	1.5 m² per person
	Handicrafts or sewing room	15 m²
Kitchen	Larder and dry store	12.15 m²
	Food preparation and cooking	42.50 m²
	Washing up	15 m²
	Cloakroom and non-resident staff room	12 m²
Administration	Matron's office	11 m²
	Doctor's room	10 m²
	Visitors' room	10 m²
Ancillary rooms	Sluice rooms	6m²
	Laundries	20 m²
	Linen storage	8 m²
	Cleaners' stores	4 m²
	Box rooms	8 m²
	Boiler and plant room	25.30 m²
	Garden store and WC	10 m²
Staff accommodation		
Self-contained flat for matron		70 m²
Self-contained flat for assistant matron		60 m²
Two-staff bedsitting rooms		12 m²
Staff bathroom		
Staff kitchen		6m²
Two-staff garages		
Staff lounge		12 m²

Note: Room areas in typical 40-person home

4 PLANNING EXAMPLES

The plans of two typical homes are shown in Figures 22.2 and 22.3.

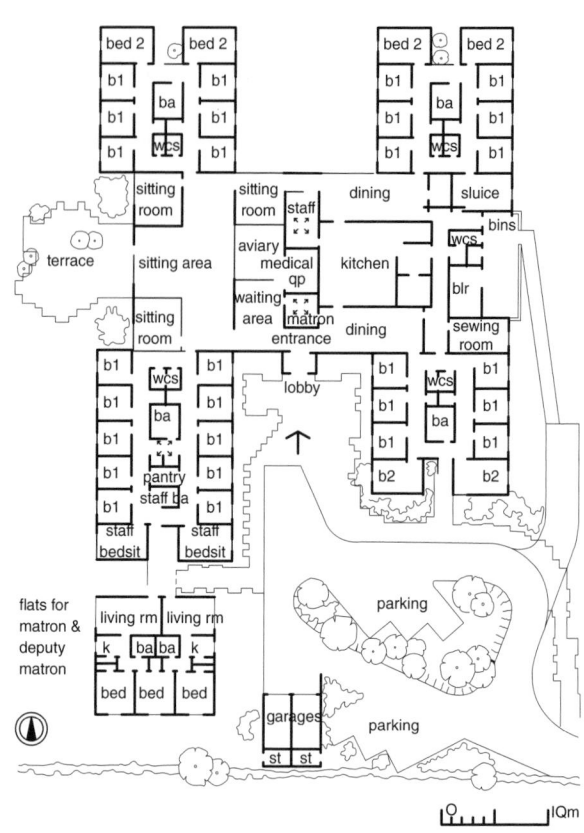

22.2 *Plan of Glebe House, Southbourne*

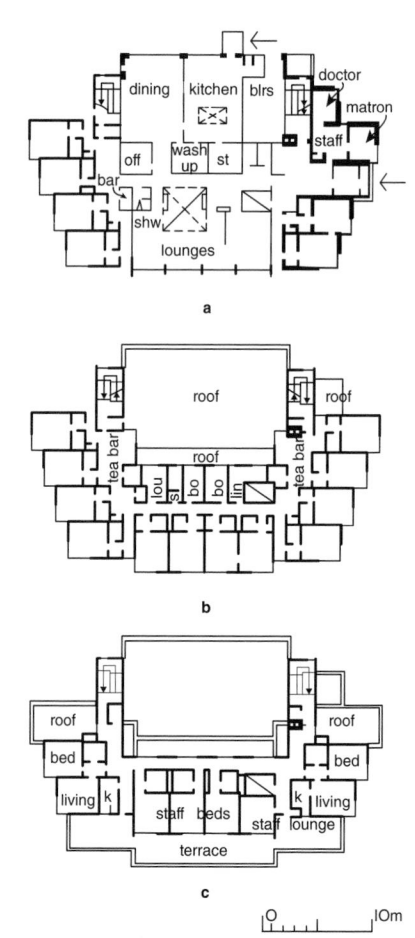

22.3 *Maidment Court, Dorset. a ground-floor plan. b plan of first and second floors. c third-floor plan*

5 ROOM DATA AND SPACE REQUIREMENTS

Typical layouts are given for single rooms (Figure 22.4) and double rooms (Figure 22.5). These layouts, from DHSS Building Note 2, with rooms of varying proportion, show ways of providing a flexible arrangement within clearly defined sleeping/sitting areas. With narrow rooms, corridor circulation is reduced to a minimum, but other types may well be suitable where a different overall plan form is chosen.

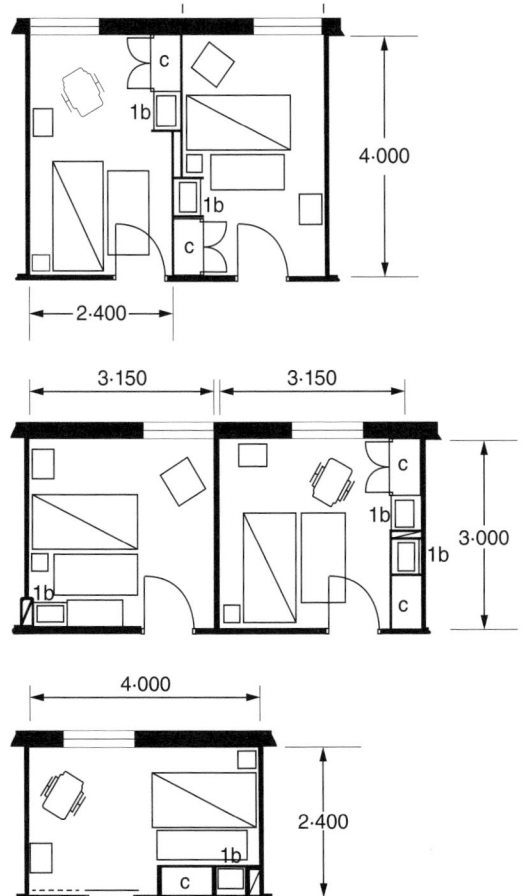

22.4 *Room data and space requirements for single rooms*

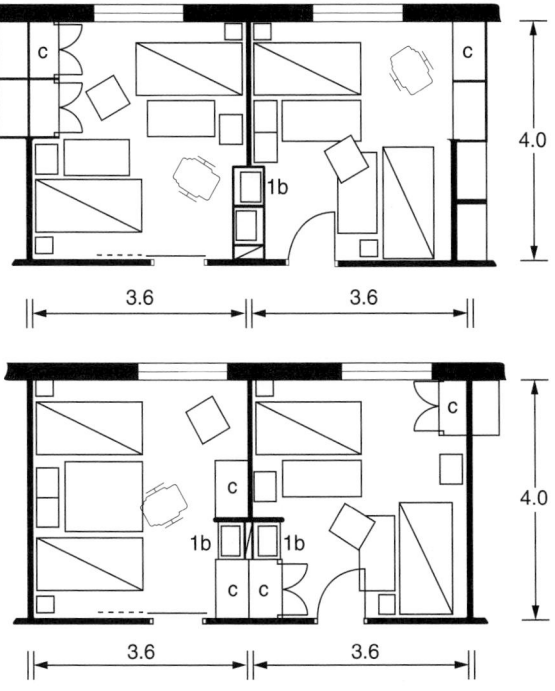

22.5 *Double room requirements*

6 BUILDING EQUIPMENT AND FITTINGS

6.1 Introduction

Some of the information below repeats material in previous chapters. It is also included here because of its importance for this building type.

6.2 Limitations

Elderly people should be encouraged to do as much as possible for themselves. To facilitate this, the design of the accommodation and appliances should take into account the limitations imposed by age.

6.3 Taps

Choose taps that can be manipulated by arthritic fingers. Surgeon's taps are not recommended, however, as in extreme cases ordinary taps can be modified to provide a similar facility. Within one building, it is sensible to maintain consistency as to the location of hot and cold, e.g. hot always on the right as is now provided in current standards. In addition, the taps should always be boldly colour-coded. It is hoped that in the near future a standard for additional tactile identification will be introduced.

6.4 Washhand basins and baths

Washhand basins should be fitted with their rims between 800 and 850 mm high. Bathrooms should be large enough for undressing and dressing, and for someone else to lend a hand. Low-sided baths are available, as the rim, which should be easy to grip (Figure 22.6), should not be higher than 380 mm from the floor. Alternatively, the bath may be set with the trap below floor level. It should have a bottom as flat as possible and should not be longer than 1.5 m; lying down is not encouraged. Grab handles and poles should be provided as in Figure 22.7 to help getting in and out. A seat at rim height is useful for sitting on to wash legs and feet. Bathroom and lavatory doors should open out, with locks operable from the outside in emergencies (Figure 22.8).

6.5 Showers

Some old people find showers more convenient to use than baths (Figure 22.9). If the floor of the compartment is of smooth non-slip material with a fall to a drain of 1:40, there is no need for a tray

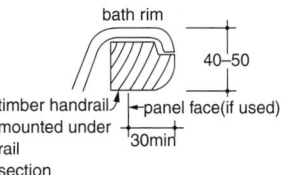

22.6 *Bath rim adapted for easy gripping*

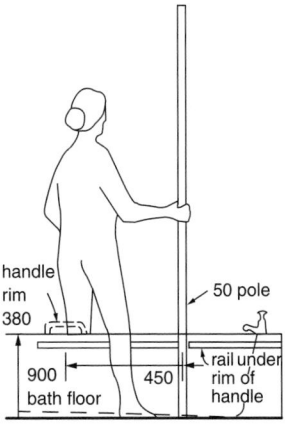

22.7 *Aids for getting in and out of the bath: pole, handle and rim. Maximum height of rim from floor 380 mm*

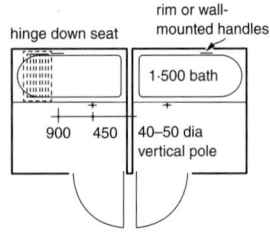

22.8 *Plan of bathrooms showing handing to suit people with disability of either right or left leg, and position of pole aid*

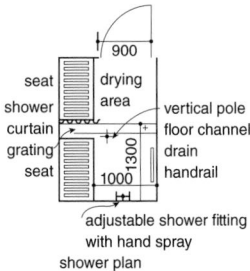

22.9 *Plan of shower room showing seats and aids*

with an upstand to be stepped over. The compartment should be well heated, with pegs for clothes on the dry side, divided from the wet with a shower curtain. The water supply should be automatically controlled to supply only between 35°C and 49°C. The shower head should be on the end of a flexible hose, with a variety of positions available for clipping it on. WCs should have a seat height of 380 mm, and handles provided as in Figure 22.10.

6.6 Cupboards
Shelves and cupboards should acknowledge the limitations of elderly people. The clothes cupboard rail should be mounted 1.5 m from the floor, and the cupboards should be at least 550 mm deep (Figures 22.11 and 22.12).

7 FURNITURE

7.1 Easy chairs
A variety of chair types should be provided in sitting and common rooms, to ensure maximum comfort for all the old people. Seats

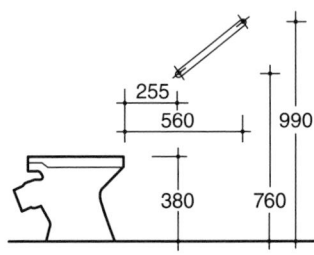

22.10 *Inclined rails mounted on walls of WC*

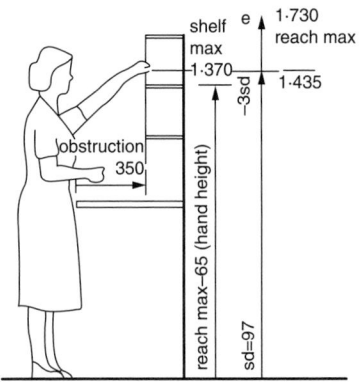

22.11 *Maximum reach over worktop*

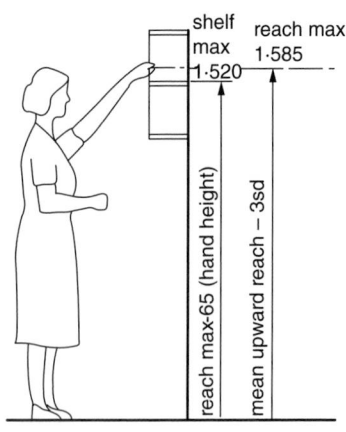

22.12 *Maximum reach to unobstructed wall-mounted cupboard*

should not be too low, as this makes the chair difficult to get out of; but if too high, the feet may end up off the floor. A height between 400 and 430 mm is about right, with footstools available for those with extra-short legs. A seat depth between 410 and 470 mm is ideal: any more and cushions become necessary. The back should be angled at 28° to the vertical, and high enough to support the head, for which an adjustable pad is useful. Armrests 230 mm above the seat at the front facilitate getting up, but if lower at the back, make sewing and knitting easier. There should be a gap under the seat to allow the heels to be drawn right back when rising. Generally, the padding should not be too soft and generous, as this can put strain on the tissues rather than allowing the bone structure to support the body.

7.2 Tables and dining chairs
Occasional tables in common rooms should not be lower than chair seat height. Dining tables should be 700 mm high and used with chairs having a seat height of 430 mm and a depth of 380 mm. There should be a gap for the thigh between the chair seat and the underside of the table top of at least 190 mm (Figure 22.13).

7.3 Worktops
Comfortable reach to worktops is shown in Figure 22.14.

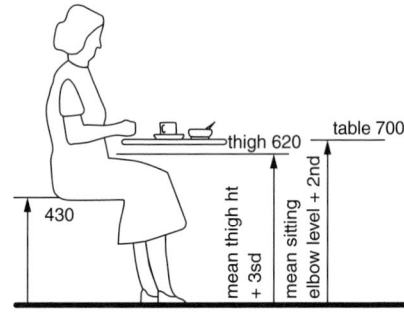

22.13 *Table and sitting worktop design, giving height and thigh clearance*

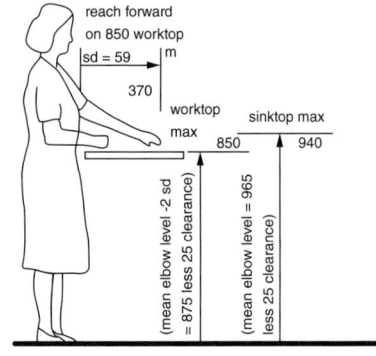

22.14 *Standing worktop design, giving height of working surface and reach forward to fittings (scale consistent with 3613)*

8 BIBLIOGRAPHY

Peter Barker, Jon Barrick and Rod Wilson. *Building Sight. A Handbook of building and interior design solutions to include the needs of visually impaired people*. RNIB, 1995.

Design Guide for the Development of New Build Accommodation for Older People. PRP Architects. The Abbeyfield Society, 2001.

Design Guide for Sheltered Schemes. *Improving the interior design of the entrance and shared areas*. Quattro Design. Bristol City Council Neighbourhood and Housing Services, September 2001.

David Littlefield, Growing old gracefully. *RIBA Journal*, July 2003.

Jeremy Melvin, Stephen Mullin, Peter Stewart. *Place & Home; the search for better housing. PRP Architects*. Black Dog Publishing, February 2007.

National Housing Federation. *Accommodating Diversity: Housing design in a multicultural society*. Penoyre & Presad Architects, 1988.

Sheila Peace and Caroline Holland (eds) *Inclusive housing in an ageing society: Innovative approaches*. The Policy Press, October 2001.

David Robson, Anne M. Nicholson, Neil Barker, *Homes for the third age: A design guide for extra care sheltered housing*, E & FN Spon, June 1998.

Scheme Development Standards. The Housing Corporation, August 2000.

Standards in Quality and Development. *A good practice guide*. National Housing Federation, June 1998.

S. Thorpe, *Wheelchair housing design guide*, Construction Research Communications Ltd, 1997.

Sien Winters (ed.) *Lifetime housing in Europe*, Katholieke Universiteit Leuven, 2001.

23 Student housing and housing for young people

Liz Pride

Liz Pride is an Architect and Director of MJP Architects LTD

Please note that plans used to illustrate this chapter are of built projects and that there may have been changes to standards and legislation since they were completed. They are therefore illustrative only.

KEY POINTS:
- *Student housing is normally designed to a budget that relates to the rent charged. There is an increasingly wide range of options to suit different preferences and budgets*
- *The availability, choice and quality of accommodation are factors students consider when choosing a university, and students are becoming more discerning as fees and charges increase*
- *Private companies, as well as universities, now develop and manage a significant proportion of student accommodation*
- *There is a trend towards larger schemes, including tower blocks, where designers should aim to avoid an impersonal, institutional feel*
- *Student housing that is also used for conference accommodation has additional requirements*

Contents
1 Introduction
2 Students
3 Types of accommodation
4 Building form
5 Standards and regulations
6 The study bedroom
7 Kitchen/dining rooms
8 Bathrooms
9 Other facilities
10 Conference use

1 INTRODUCTION

1.1 Scope
This chapter deals with the design of accommodation for students, but is also relevant to accommodation which is occupied for a limited period by other groups of independent, single people, such as 'spring-board' accommodation for young professionals. The term 'university' is used to refer to Higher Education Establishments (HEEs), Further Education Establishments (FEEs), colleges and other similar institutions.

1.2 Importance
In recent years legislative and economic change has had a significant effect on students and the provision of student accommodation. Recent government policy has led to a considerable expansion in student numbers while, at the time of writing, the impact of the sharp rise in student fees has yet to be discovered. However one effect is clear: students are becoming increasingly discerning and the availability, variety and quality of accommodation is an important factor when choosing a university. There is more competition between universities to attract good students and so the universities – and also some

private commercial providers of accommodation – are increasingly concerned with the 'student experience' that they offer. As costs increase, the views of parents on standards of accommodation are also becoming more important.

1.3 Ownership
Student accommodation is owned and managed in a variety of ways, which can have significant implications for design. Universities provide communal rented accommodation on or off campus, which they own and/or manage. In recent years there has been a significant growth in the number of private sector commercial operators building and managing accommodation, developments which are required to return a profit and to be a long-term financial asset. They usually accommodate large numbers of students – from 200 to 1,000 students or more. Private developments are often pre-let to a university and may be designed and managed in liaison with the university. A large proportion of students still live in individual shared houses or flats within the community, while others live at home.

1.4 Rents
The government does not fund student accommodation and schemes are normally self-funding through the rental income that is charged for the rooms. Project budgets are therefore determined by the level of rents that students can afford or are willing to pay, and this is directly reflected in the size of the study bedrooms and extent of other facilities provided in the scheme.

Where accommodation is provided by a university, there is a concern to keep rents to affordable levels, although their offer usually includes some choice of accommodation at different rents. The private market also offers a range of room types and rents, and there has been a marked increase in 'luxury' accommodation targeted at those who can afford high rents, including a high proportion of international students. To illustrate the wide range of accommodation available from universities and private commercial operators, rent levels in 2010 for a room in purpose-built accommodation with self catering varied between £50 and £285 per week.

1.5 Student experience
Issues relating to social sustainability and the 'student experience' are becoming increasingly critical, and are particularly challenging in the design of larger, potentially impersonal, schemes. Where accommodation is designed for a university, there will generally be a concern to make the students feel part of the university community. (This might be achieved by, for example, arranging buildings around a courtyard to provide a shared focus and identity for the residents, or by placing social spaces such as common rooms and kitchen/dining rooms where they are very visible.) Universities generally also have systems of pastoral care with wardens or senior students living among the students. With a private commercial provider, there is likely to be a different emphasis to the student experience, using the building design to promote a particular 'lifestyle' and branding.

1.6 Context

Consideration should be given to the relationship of the accommodation to the local community, particularly where it is located in a town rather than on campus. The design of the building and landscape can help to integrate the university and its students with the community, and it can also help to avoid potential conflict. Students can cause nuisance to neighbours, particularly where there are large areas of student accommodation within one neighbourhood (known as 'studentification'). Conversely there can be risks to the students for personal safety and theft of property.

1.7 Sustainability

Sustainability is an important issue for universities (as well as for many individual students) and the government, through the funding body HEFCE, has set demanding carbon reduction targets for university estates. Consideration should be given in the design of residences to reducing energy consumption and carbon emissions and the inclusion of renewable energy sources. Other issues include reducing water consumption, waste and recycling, sustainable urban drainage and sustainable transportation. Universities will usually set targets for BREEAM and possibly EPC ratings. Provision for future flexibility should be incorporated into the design where possible, as requirements and aspirations change – examples in recent years include the impact of computers and IT, the preference for en-suite bathrooms and improved standards for disabled access. Ultimately there may even be a need to adapt accommodation to new uses if the demand for student residences reduces.

1.8 Timing

Projects will generally be programmed to complete construction in late summer in time for occupation in a new academic year.

2 STUDENTS

2.1 Tenant range

Conventionally, students are perceived as young, single, mobile, adaptable and with little money to spend. While this is still largely true, there is also an increasing need to cater for a broader range of people from different cultural and economic backgrounds, and for students with different needs: students with disabilities, mature and married students and those with families. Postgraduate students are older and require a quieter and more 'adult' living environment. Many universities have a significant number of students from overseas, including 'international students' from outside the EU who pay higher fees and make a significant contribution to university income. Some students study part time, while many have to manage part time jobs to support themselves through university. There is an increasing demand for convenience and flexibility in the way that services, including accommodation, are provided to them.

2.2 Availability

Universities rarely have accommodation for all of their students, and priority is usually give to first year students and students from overseas who need more support to settle into the university community. Some accommodation is rented only during term time, and is used for conference and holiday lets out of term, while other accommodation is rented for the whole academic year.

2.3 Characteristics

The characteristics which differentiate student accommodation from other housing and from hotel accommodation, and which should be addressed in design, are:

- an appropriate environment in which to study as well as to live, socialise and sleep and a building in use 24 hours a day;
- creating a university community, with opportunities for informal academic and social interaction;

- privacy where people are living in close proximity and are sharing facilities – most students will not have the opportunity to choose their neighbours;
- design, including the selection of materials and fittings, must be appropriately robust for student use and easy to maintain – whole life costing is an important consideration;
- avoiding an unpleasant institutional character, which can easily arise where large numbers of identical study bedrooms are arranged to maximise efficiency;
- for many people student accommodation will be their first experience of living away from home. Well-designed student accommodation has the potential to broaden awareness of architectural design and environmental issues.

2.4 Priorities

The Times Higher Education's Student Experience polls reveal that students have the following concerns.

High importance:

- Availability of internet access in the study bedroom
- Availability of cooking facilities
- Security
- Journey time and closeness to the university
- Cost
- Local amenities and communal facilities.

Less important:

- Number of students in each flat
- Provision of en-suite bathroom
- ANUK accreditation (see Section 5.2)
- On site amenities
- Catering provided
- Car parking.

Other issues:

- Room size
- Noise
- Clean facilities.

3 TYPES OF ACCOMMODATION

3.1 The brief

When establishing the brief for accommodation, key items for discussion are:

- the 'style' of the accommodation: staircase, house, hall or flat?
- the number and mix of room types: single, shared and studio;
- the number of students sharing each kitchen;
- provision of en-suite bathrooms or shared bathrooms;
- provision of other facilities – common room, reception, gym, laundry etc.;
- the requirement for lift and wheelchair access – to all rooms?
- whether the facilities will be used for conferences out of term time.

3.2 Style of accommodation

The vast majority of student accommodation is based on provision of an individual study bedroom for each student, although universities and private providers are offering an increasing range of choice to suit different requirements and budgets, including study bedrooms shared by two students (for lower rents), 'studio' rooms with an en-suite bathroom and a kitchen area, or larger studio flats for one person or a couple. These larger units are particularly suited to postgraduates and mature students who are more independent. The studio model is also used for other young, single people outside the world of education – for example young professionals or key workers. A proportion of rooms should be designed for wheelchair users, with numbers agreed with the local authority.

In schemes with individual study bedrooms the 'style' of the accommodation is largely determined by the way that study bedrooms are grouped together to form a social unit, and the way that shared facilities (kitchens, common rooms etc.) are provided. A university may instill a sense of responsibility and independence by placing small groups of students in separate shared flats, or it may exercise a greater degree of supervision and pastoral care through a communal hall arrangement, where typically several hundred students are accommodated in rooms off shared corridors.

3.3 The number of students in each unit

Good social relationships are crucial to support students who are new to university and to reduce drop out rates. Students use computers a great deal, which can result in them spending too much time alone in their rooms. It is generally agreed that students form friendships more easily and are more likely to behave responsibly – reducing management and maintenance problems – if they are in small groups: typically 5 to 10 students sharing a self-contained flat or house. However, in small groups students who have not chosen to live together may not get on. Larger groups can provide a greater choice of friends, particularly when combined with a greater level of pastoral support from university staff: in a traditional 'hall', the social unit is the whole hall, creating a stronger sense of allegiance to the university itself.

3.4 The shared facilities in each unit

Kitchens: traditionally, central catering facilities were provided in larger halls of residence, with minimal facilities for cooking close to the study bedrooms. The intention was to encourage students to be a part of the wider university community, and many universities still offer accommodation with central catering included as part of the rent. However for reasons of economy, culture and convenience, most students prefer the freedom of catering for themselves or of eating out. As a consequence, in most new accommodation – whether in the form of halls, flats or houses – kitchen-dining rooms are provided for self-catering, each serving a group of study bedrooms and effectively defining the social groups. As noted above, some schemes include studio rooms, where each student has their own kitchen facilities.

Bathrooms: the majority of new study bedrooms are now provided with en-suite bathrooms, and where it is intended that the rooms will be used for conference accommodation out of term time, en-suite bathrooms are practically indispensable. In some schemes a single en-suite bathroom is shared by two study bedrooms. Schemes with en-suite bathrooms are not necessarily more expensive than those with shared bathrooms, particularly when washbasins are also provided in all of the study bedrooms as well. Costs will depend on the detailed arrangement of the plan and floor areas.

Other shared facilities: common rooms, laundries, reception, seminar rooms, staff/wardens' flats etc. will be provided where the student numbers are large enough to support them, where there is a demand associated with teaching or conference uses or, especially in the case of commercial providers, where the facilities are intended to attract a particular market. Facilities in commercial schemes can be extensive: for example a games room, gym, cinema or café.

4 BUILDING FORM

4.1 Study bedrooms

Study bedrooms form the basic building block of student accommodation and can be arranged in a number of ways. In each case the study bedrooms may have en-suite bathrooms or there may be shared bathrooms.

4.2 Staircase

In the traditional 'Oxbridge' model, buildings arranged around a quadrangle are divided into 'staircases' with a small number of study bedrooms at each level served by a single stair (Figure 23.1).

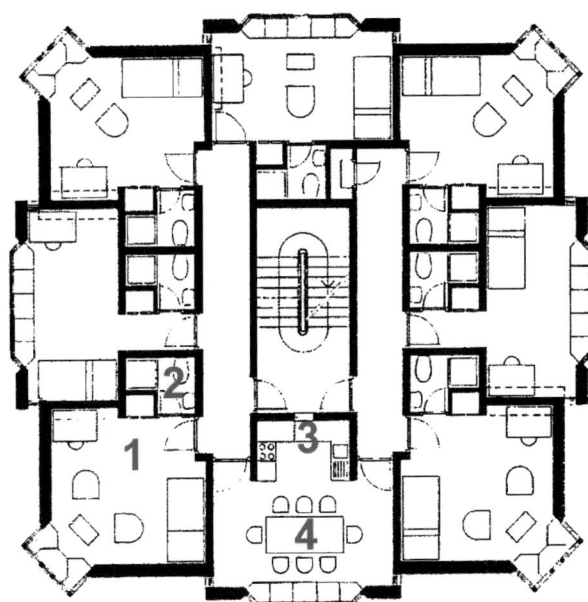

23.1 *Generic type: Student residence with a traditional college staircase arrangement, Jowett Walk, Balliol College, Oxford. Architects: MJP Architects. 1, study bedroom; 2, en-suite bathroom; 3, kitchen; 4, dining*

A kitchen may be provided on each floor or on one level, and is shared by the rooms on the staircase. A loose social group is defined by the staircase, but there is also a strong association with the wider college or university.

However, it is difficult to incorporate lift access economically, as separate lifts are required for each staircase. An arrangement where lifts are not provided and wheelchair access is restricted to the ground floor level may not be acceptable to the university and is unlikely to be appropriate where conference use is proposed.

4.3 House style

This replicates the popular model of a traditional private house shared by students (Figure 23.2). It is similar to the staircase model with a limited number of study bedrooms on several levels served by a single stair, and a shared kitchen/dining room at ground level. The house has its own front door so that the social group is well defined and there is a greater sense of independence. However the problems of incorporating lifts and disabled access are the same as for the staircase model.

4.4 Hall or corridor

Rooms are arranged off a corridor (Figures 23.3–23.5). Corridor schemes allow for large numbers of rooms to be served economically by lift, providing disabled access as well as easy access for conference guests, cleaning staff and students with luggage. The hall itself forms a single large social group, but smaller units are less easy to form. The corridors may be divided along their length to form groups of rooms with a shared kitchen, but this cannot provide the domestic character and scale of a shared flat or college staircase. In some schemes corridors are doubled up in order to form separate flats. Schemes which consist of studio rooms or studio flats are usually also arranged on corridors. Corridor access schemes tend to have a higher proportion of circulation area than staircase schemes. It is difficult to bring natural light and ventilation into double-loaded corridors, and their design requires careful handling to avoid monotony and a dull institutional character.

4.5 Flats

Rooms are grouped into self-contained flats with a number of study bedrooms (typically 5–8) and shared kitchen/dining room (Figures 23.6 and 23.7). This arrangement is very common and defines a self-contained social group with its own front door. Lift access can be arranged economically to serve groups of flats.

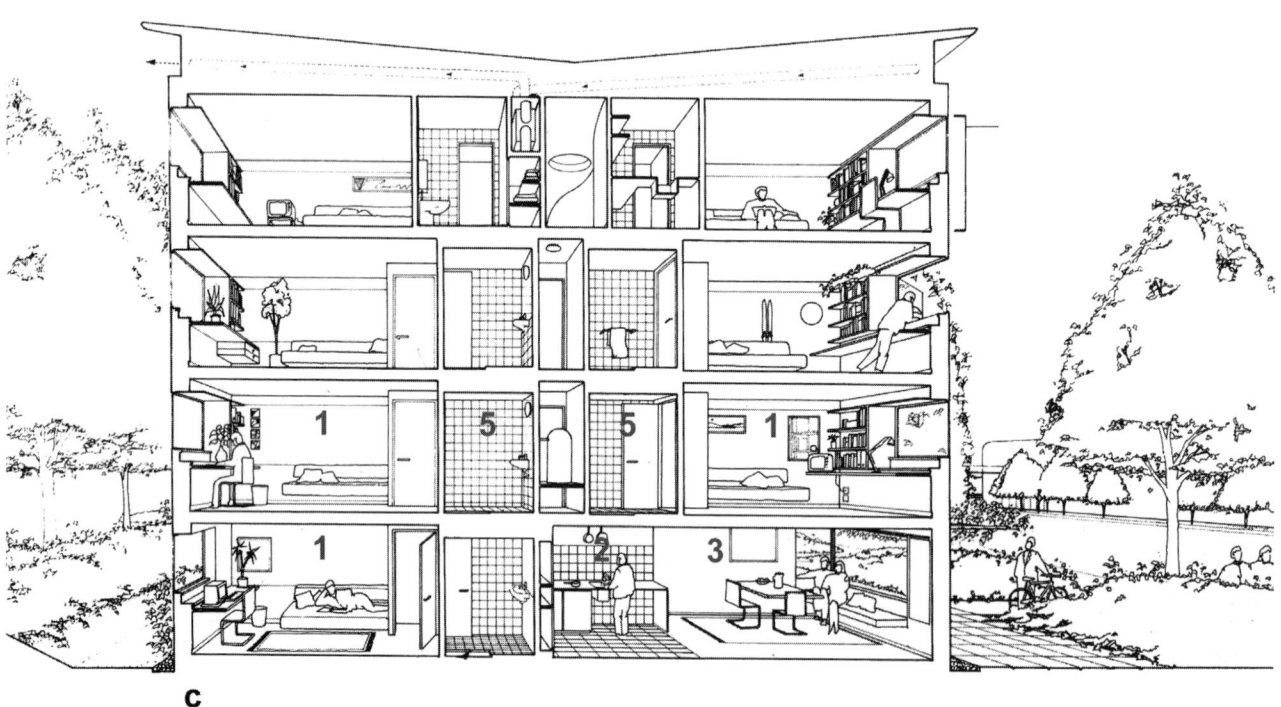

23.2 *Generic type: Terraced house plus self-contained flats. Constable Terrace, University of East Anglia. Architects: Rick Mather Architects. 1, study bedroom; 2, kitchen; 3, living/dining; 4, services/storage/cleaners; 5, shower/wc. a Ground floor plan, b First floor plan, c isometric sectional view*

4.6 General design factors

Depth of plan: student study bedrooms are usually small – typically $13m^2$ for a room with en-suite bathroom – and the space is more useable if the room is rectangular. Placing the en-suite bathroom at the back of the room in the centre of the building produces a deeper building plan, particularly with a double loaded corridor, and reduces the length of corridor. It is therefore generally the most cost-effective layout. Providing bathrooms as shared facilities (as opposed to en-suite) will impact on corridor length and escape distances.

Escape distances: the escape distance from the farthest study bedroom to the escape stair is a key factor in the arrangement of the plan. Arranging narrow study bedrooms in a row allows the number of rooms served by each escape stair to be maximised. However the width of the rooms must also be considered in relation

to use of the space and the need to maintain sufficient width for wheelchair access and manoeuvering.

Lifts: the requirement for inclusion and for access for wheelchair users to different parts of the building is discussed in Section 5.7. Provision of lift access to all floors and all study bedrooms will have implications for the arrangement of the plan, as it is normal to aim to limit the number of lifts in a scheme to reduce cost.

Modern Methods of Construction (MMC) and pre-fabrication: study bedrooms are repetitive units and, where large numbers are involved, they lend themselves to modern methods of construction such as tunnel form or off-site modular and volumetric construction, although care is required to ensure that this does not produce a dull, institutional character in the internal layout or elevations of the building. Pre-fabrication can be used for whole rooms or for separate elements such as en-suite bathroom pods. The system speeds

23.3 *Generic type: Student and key-worker housing with a corridor arrangement: Friendship House, London. Architects: MJP Architects. The corridor arrangement is wrapped around a courtyard to provide a focus for residents. 1, study bedroom; 2, study bedroom for disabled residents; 3, shared kitchen; 4, common room; 5, courtyard; 6, garden; 7, railway viaduct*

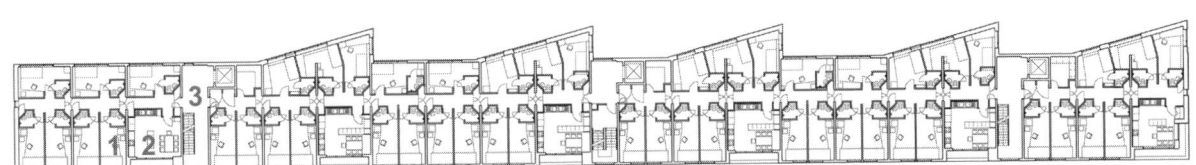

23.4 *Generic type: Student residence with a corridor arrangement: Pooley House, Queen Mary University of London. Architects: FCB studios. The long corridor is sub-divided to form flats. 1, study bedroom; 2, shared kitchen; 3, communal circulation area*

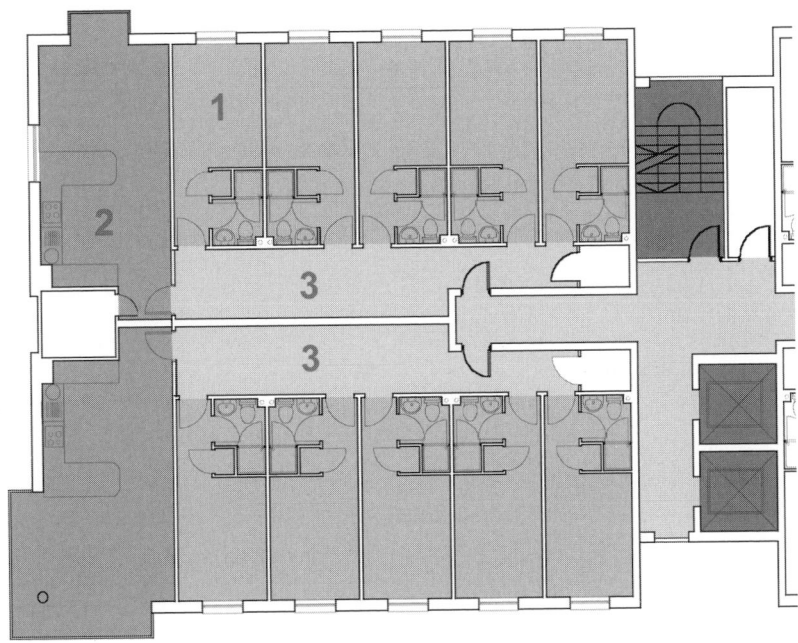

23.5 *Generic type: Student residence with twinned corridor arrangement to form separate flats: Purbeck House, University of Bournemouth. Architects: Architecture PLB. 1, study bedroom; 2, kitchen; 3, flat circulation*

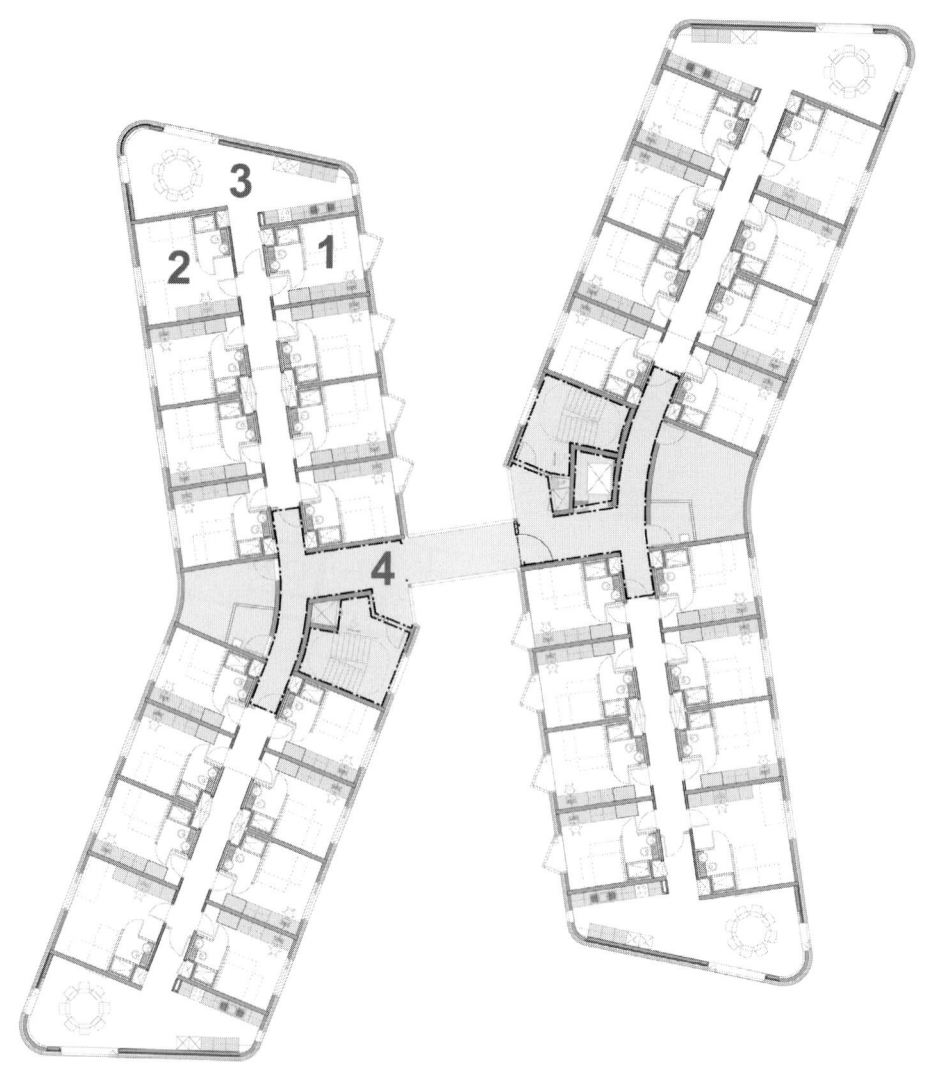

23.6 *Generic type: Student residence with flat arrangement: Bluebell Views Residences, University of Warwick. Architects: Page\Park Architects. The angled blocks help to define separate flats, while projecting windows reduce overlooking. 1, study bedroom; 2, twin study bedroom; 3, kitchen/dining room; 4, communal circulation area*

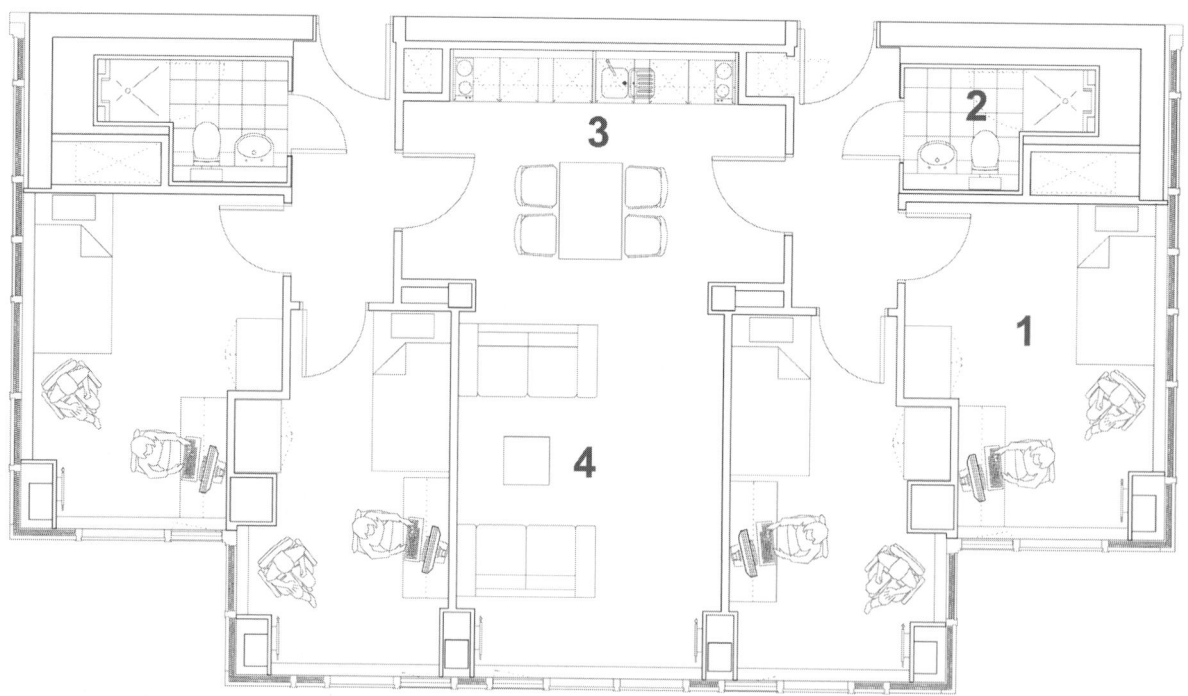

23.7 *Generic type: 4 bed cluster apartment: Nido Spitalfields. Architects: t p bennett. Private commercial developers have developed different flat types. 1, study bedroom; 2, shared bathroom; 3, shared kitchen; 4, living room*

up construction, reduces waste and allows complicated elements to be constructed to a high standard in factory conditions; however there is usually a capital cost premium to be balanced against any savings from the reduced construction programme. The decision to use modular construction needs to be taken at an early stage in the design process as there are implications for dimensions and interfaces with surrounding elements and for the procurement route.

5 STANDARDS AND REGULATIONS

This section gives guidance on key areas of legislation, but is not intended to be comprehensive. The standards and legislation referred to are current at March 2011. Designers should check that these have not been superseded. Illustrations are of completed projects and the standards that were current at the time they were built may have been superseded.

Designs should comply with all statutory requirements contained within Housing, Building, Planning, Disability Discrimination, Equal Opportunities, and other relevant legislation and standards.

5.1 Town and Country Planning Act 1990 and amendments – planning permission

Student accommodation falls into different use classes under the Town and Country Planning Act depending on size and whether it is provided by a university/college or by a private provider.

Developments by private providers

HOUSES IN MULTIPLE OCCUPATION – SMALL PROPERTIES
(3–6 OCCUPANTS)
In 2010 government legislation introduced a new use class – Class C4 houses in multiple occupation – which covers small shared houses or flats occupied by 3 to 6 tenants, who are not related to each other, and who share one or more basic amenities (such as a kitchen). Student accommodation which is managed by an educational establishment is excluded from Use Class C4.

Legislation allows local authorities to require a planning application for a change of use from a dwelling house to a house in multiple occupation, so that they can prevent a high concentration of rented houses in one area, a situation known as 'studentification' which can cause problems for the local community.

HOUSES IN MULTIPLE OCCUPATION – LARGER PROPERTIES
(OVER 6 OCCUPANTS)
Larger houses in multiple occupation with more than 6 tenants, are unclassified by the Use Classes Order and are described as 'sui generis' (of their own kind). Discussion with the planning authority will be required to clarify their requirements.

Developments by Higher Education Establishments
Student accommodation for residential colleges will generally fall into Use Class C2, 'Residential Institutions'.

5.2 The Housing Act 2004

Part 1: Housing conditions
Part 1 of the Housing Act relates to housing conditions and applies to every type of accommodation. It provides a system for assessing conditions – the Housing Health and Safety Rating System, HHSRS – and gives local authorities powers to tackle poor housing based on the severity of the health and safety hazards.

Part 2: Licensing of houses in multiple occupation (HMOs)

ACCOMMODATION MANAGED OR CONTROLLED BY PRIVATE
SECTOR PROVIDERS
Statutory controls on HMOs under the Housing Act can be confusing. The term HMO applies to a wide range of housing types, mainly in the private rented sector where standards have historically been low. In essence the Housing Act defines HMOs as accommodation occupied by more than one household and where households share one or more basic amenity (such as a kitchen).

Part 2 of the Housing Act regulates HMOs by providing for them to be licensed by the local authorities. Licensing is mandatory for larger HMOs (this includes those that are 3 stories or more, 5 or more people of 2 or more households) but can also be extended to smaller HMOs by the Local Authority.

ANUK/Unipol's *Code of Standards for Larger Residential Developments: for Student Accommodation Not Managed and Controlled by Educational Establishments, 2010* gives guidance for private sector providers of student accommodation and their tenants on similar lines to the codes that apply to HEEs described below.

ACCOMMODATION MANAGED OR CONTROLLED BY HIGHER
EDUCATION ESTABLISHMENTS
Student accommodation for people attending full time courses which is managed or controlled by an educational establishment can be 'excepted' from the definition of an HMO and from the licensing requirements of the Housing Act (except for Part 1, which still applies), provided the accommodation is designed and managed in accordance with an approved code of practice. The following codes were current in March 2011:

- *The Universities UK/Guild HE Code of Practice for the Management of Student Housing*, dated 17 August 2010;
- *ANUK/Unipol's Code of Standards for Larger Residential Developments for Student Accommodation Managed and Controlled by Educational Establishments*, dated 28 August 2008.

The codes deal with a range of physical standards and management practices and also address student welfare and the fair and reasonable treatment of student tenants, reflecting the special characteristics of student accommodation which encompasses more than the basic provision of facilities. The codes provide general guidance for the design of accommodation rather than detailed specifications, as the provision will vary between different projects and different locations. They include requirements for:

- furniture and storage;
- kitchen facilities – level of provision refers back to local authority requirements;
- toilet and personal washing facilities – level of provision refers back to local authority requirements;
- laundry facilities;
- mail deliveries;
- health and safety – gas and electric installations and appliances, fire safety, security;
- the environment – waste, recycling, energy, water supply, drainage, landscaping;
- windows and ventilation;
- lighting of communal areas;
- cleaning and maintenance;
- inclusion of accommodation for residential staff in larger schemes.

The ANUK/Unipol Code goes on to identify four key areas – student care, sustainability, security and community interface – where enhanced provision can achieve 'star' rating for a scheme. The codes are also appropriate for accommodation for other non-HEE students and young people, but additional legislation may apply, for example if accommodation is provided for students under 18 years of age in FE establishments.

5.3 Local authority requirements for HMOs

Different local authorities develop their own codes of practice for HMOs, which are generally more specific than the codes described above. The requirements may vary for different types of student accommodation – bedsits, studios, shared flats etc. – and there may be variation in the way they are applied, for example where there are requirements from other legislation, such as for listed buildings. The local authority's environmental department should be consulted at an early stage in the design. Typical requirements are as follows.

Space standards
- Minimum room areas for study bedrooms, for single and shared occupancy.
- Minimum room areas for kitchens, kitchen/dining rooms and living rooms.

HHSRS rating system (see above)
- Design requirements to avoid hazards – damp, cold, security, lighting, sanitation, water, falls, electricity, heating and cooking.

Personal washing facilities
- Ratio of baths/showers to number of occupants – typically a minimum of 1 bath or shower for 5 people.
- Washbasins to be provided with all toilets.
- Washbasins may be required within bedrooms in larger HMOs.
- Maximum distance of shared bathrooms from bedrooms – typically no more than 1 floor away.
- Design and layout of bathrooms, minimum dimensions of appliances, finishes, heating, lighting and ventilation

Toilet facilities
- Ratio of toilets to number of occupants – typically a minimum of 1 toilet for 5 people. Provided in a separate room to the bathroom if it serves more than 4 people.
- Maximum distance of shared toilets from bedrooms – typically no more than 1 floor away.
- Design and layout, finishes, heating, lighting and ventilation.

Facilities for storage, preparation and cooking of food
- Maximum distance of kitchen from bedrooms – typically no more than 1 floor away, but can be further in smaller buildings such as 'house' style accommodation.
- Provision of dining rooms and furniture.
- Design and layout of kitchens to allow safe use by several people at the same time. Finishes and minimum dimensions of appliances, heating, lighting and ventilation.
- Ratio of kitchen facilities to number of occupants – typically 1 set of facilities for 5 people comprising a sink and drainer, a food cupboard (500 mm wide base unit or 1000 mm wide wall unit), a fridge (130 litres), freezer space (60 litres), worktop (1000 mm min), 3 double power sockets in addition to those required for the appliances, a cooker with 4 burners, oven and grill. Additional facilities should be included where the kitchen is shared by larger numbers of people.

Fire safety and means of escape
- Requirement for fire doors, fire separation, lobbies, emergency lighting, fire fighting equipment and automatic fire detection systems.
- Internal layout of shared flats – escape from bedrooms must not be through a higher risk area such as a kitchen.

Management: The Management of Houses in Multiple Occupation (England) Regulations 2006
These regulations set out the responsibilities of both managers and occupiers. They include requirements for cleaning, maintenance and repairs, and provision of water supply, drainage, gas and electric supplies, means of escape, ventilation, recycling and waste management as well as safety protection to roofs, balconies and windows.

5.4 Fire safety
Each local authority has requirements prior to issuing a license for use of a building as a HMO. All must comply with The Management of Houses in Multiple Occupations (England) Regulations 2006.

As for other building types, the responsibility for safety lies with the 'responsible person', who is required to prepare a Fire Risk Assessment under the Fire Safety Order.

New build HMOs should be designed in accordance with the UK Building Regulations. Compliance can be achieved by following the guidance set out in the Approved Document B – Volume 2, Buildings Other than Dwellinghouses, which provides guidance on means of escape, external fire spread, internal fire spread and fire brigade access. It also provides guidance on fire safety systems required in buildings.

The Approved Document B helps define the number of occupants within the building and to design escape routes appropriately, with recommendations for the planning and protection of escape routes and separation between areas of higher fire load. It also sets out provisions for splitting larger buildings into smaller fire rated compartments. External fire spread from the building of fire origin to adjacent premises is addressed in Document B and provisions are made for the fire service to access the building externally and internally. Note that access for fire engines to different parts of the building can have significant implications for the site plan and form of the building, particularly on constricted sites.

An alternative approach to following the Approved Document B is to adopt a Fire Engineered solution where the fire safety for the building is tailored to the risk involved and the layout to achieve an equal level of life safety protection. The use of fire engineering is especially valuable when a change of use to an HMO is adopted, when it is often difficult to meet the recommendations of the Approved Document B. Means of escape in case of fire is also covered by the Housing Act and by the approved codes of practice that apply to educational establishments (see above).

False fire alarms can be a problem in student residences both for the fire services and for residents, particularly where full evacuation is required. In some areas the fire services will only answer an alarm call if the existence of the fire is confirmed. Fire systems should be designed to minimise accidental false alarms insofar as this is possible. The location of extinguishers, detectors and call points, the design of fire doors and glazing should be considered carefully to reduce the risk of misuse – e.g. extinguishers let off, fire doors wedged open – and to avoid an institutional feel.

5.5 Noise
The Building Regulations, Approved Document Part E (Resistance to Sound) applies to 'Rooms for Residential Purposes', and includes requirements for different parts of the construction. Noise is a major source of annoyance in student residences, because the uses of neighbouring study bedrooms rooms for leisure, study and sleep contain inherent conflict and students do not keep regular hours. Consider noise from both inside and outside the building: from kitchens and circulation areas, badly adjusted door closers, lifts, service ducts, telephones, etc. In planning the accommodation, it is important to separate potentially noisy areas from student bedrooms and to insulate each individual study bedroom to a high standard.

5.6 Ventilation
The Building Regulations, Approved Document Part F (Ventilation) apply to student accommodation.

Shared bathrooms and kitchens are used intensively. In student accommodation bathrooms are usually internal, so problems of condensation are common where ventilation is inadequate. Student rooms may be left unoccupied for long periods during the holidays, and adequate background ventilation is important.

5.7 Access and inclusion: BS8300, Disability Discrimination Act and Equality Act
Under the Equality Act 2010, universities must not discriminate against students in the provision of education, or access to any benefit, facility or service, by excluding them or by subjecting them to

any other detriment. From October 2010, the Equality Act largely replaces the Disability Discrimination Acts (DDA). The obligation to make adjustments for disabled students under the Equality Act 2010 remains and participation of the institutions and groups of disabled students at planning stages through construction is also important. BS 8300:2009+A1:2010 BS 8300 gives recommendations for the design of buildings and their approaches to meet the needs of disabled people including requirements for accessible rooms. It applies to university and college halls of residence.

The Building Regulations, Approved Document M (Access to and Use of Buildings) aims to ensure that buildings are accessible and useable by everyone, regardless of disability, age or gender, and without unnecessary separation or segregation. Universities place great importance on inclusion. It is likely that many more disabled students will be ambulant disabled or have visual or hearing impairments or learning disabilities, rather than be wheelchair users. Sleeping accommodation should aim to be convenient for all – a proportion should therefore be designed for independent use by wheelchair users, while standard rooms should have a degree of flexibility or adaptability to be suitable for people who do not use a wheelchair, but may have other difficulties, e.g. a visual impairment or limited dexterity. The Approved Document M puts provision for wheelchair accessible bedrooms at 1 for every 20 bedrooms (5 per cent). However BS 8300 suggests that for new buildings the percentage should be 15 per cent. The local authority are likely to have their own requirements based on local need, and early consultation is essential.

Accommodation for disabled people should be integrated with other student rooms, which suggests that they should be distributed throughout the residences at different floors. Wheelchair users should be able to reach and use all facilities – common rooms, kitchen, laundry etc. Socialising with other students is an important part of student life – and therefore protected through disability/equality legislation as a 'civil' right – so access to social areas, such as kitchen/dining rooms, is doubly important. These issues have implications for provision of lifts and consequently for the form of the accommodation (see section 4 above). Some universities will require disabled students and wheelchair users to be able to access all study bedrooms so that they can visit friends. Others provide study bedrooms for wheelchair users and the kitchen/dining room at ground floor level, but no lift access to other rooms (for example in 'house' style accommodation). This approach can be argued as acceptable, but it is still

likely to be interpreted on a case-by-case basis by each different local authority. Where residential accommodation is used for conferences and holiday letting, it becomes more like 'hotel' accommodation, and should therefore incorporate appropriate provisions, e.g. sizing of stairs, doors and the provision of lifts.

Access for wheelchair users increases the area required for circulation space, including the entrance to standard study bedrooms when there is provision for wheelchair users to visit other students: the effective clear width of doors to standard study bedrooms will need to be adequate to admit wheelchair users. Some students require a high level of assistance. Consideration should be given to the provision of an adjacent bedroom next to the accessible room, with a connecting door, for a 'companion'/personal assistant. Appropriate fittings and equipment will be required in shared facilities such as kitchen/dining rooms and laundries as well as in accessible rooms. A unisex wheelchair accessible WC should be provided for visitors.

6 THE STUDY BEDROOM

6.1 Functions
The study bedroom is the most important element in the design. It has to facilitate a range of functions in a small space – sleeping, studying, relaxing and socialising. It is the students' home while they are at university, and they should be able to impose their personality on it. The room should be designed to allow the furniture to be arranged in different layouts, to help avoid the institutional character that can easily arise with large numbers of repetitive rooms. It must feel private and secure and, ideally, have a reasonable view. It must have good light and ventilation which the student should be able to control. Good acoustic insulation from adjoining rooms, corridors and from the outside is very important. The room and furniture must be robust and easy to clean and maintain. Study bedroom types include rooms with or without en-suite bathrooms, and 'studio' rooms with en-suite bathroom and kitchen area. Rooms may be single or shared. The most common type is the single, en-suite study bedroom (Figure 23.8).

6.2 Room size and shape
A study bedroom for one person (without en-suite bathroom) can be as small as 8 m², but this is extremely tight and a more appropriate minimum area is 10 m². A small sized room with en-suite bathroom is typically 13m². To optimise the plan, study bedrooms

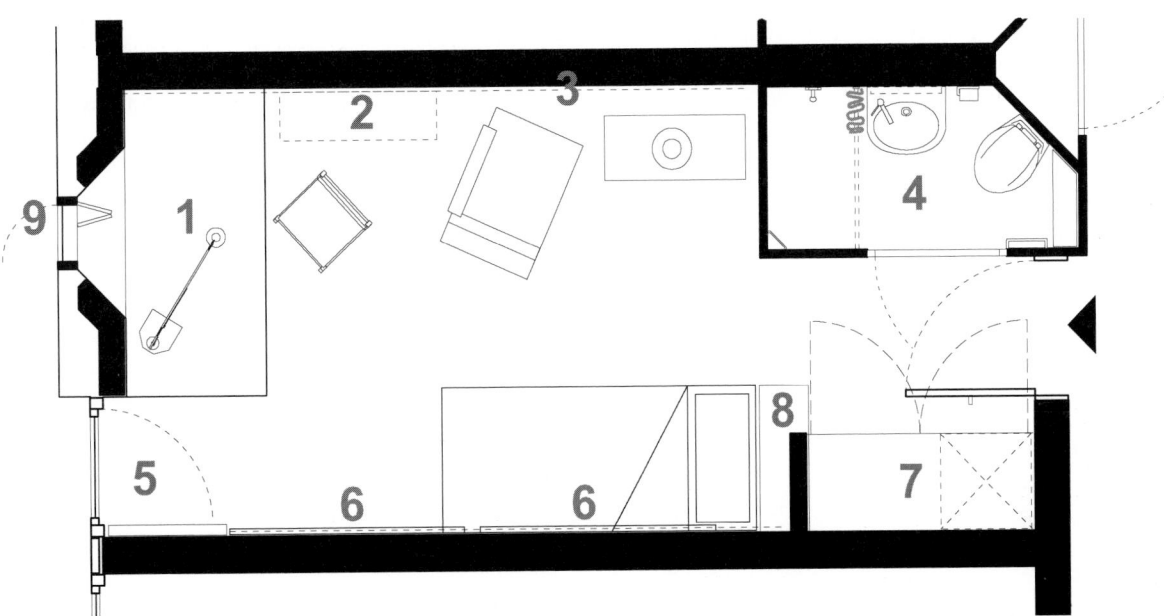

23.8 *Room with en-suite bathroom. St Hugh's College, Oxford. Architects: David Morley Architects. 1, desk; 2, movable shelf; 3, hanging rail; 4, bathroom pod; 5, full-height window; 6, movable pinboard; 7, wardrobe; 8, built-in bedhead shelf/storage; 9, window with shutter in splayed opening*

are usually rectangular with the en-suite bathroom at the rear of the room. Where there is wheelchair access to the room, the room width will need to be approximately 2.8 m to allow the wheelchair to pass the bathroom and turn within the room. Typical modest room sizes for other types of student room are:

- Study bedroom shared by two students with en-suite bathroom: 20 m²
- Studio room for one student with en-suite bathroom and kitchen area: 18 m²
- Studio flat for one student or a couple with en-suite bathroom and kitchenette: 30 m²

Carefully consider the proportions of the room – the furniture layout and the position of the door, window, built-in cupboards, sockets and fixed lighting to ensure that the room will accommodate different activities and moods. The larger the area, the easier this becomes, but even a small room should be designed to allow some variation in the arrangement of furniture. Features such as window seats, built-in shelves, alcoves, etc. can be also used to enhance character. Consider the height of the window and views when the student is sitting at the desk or on the bed. Where it is feasible to provide larger rooms – for example where students have a choice of rents – it is possible to design for greater flexibility and to 'zone' the different functions of the room (Figure 23.9).

6.3 Furniture and finishes
The careful design of built-in furniture and careful selection of loose furniture is essential to the function and appearance of small study bedrooms. Furniture and fittings should be robust, but not institutional in character. Built-in furniture can be used to enhance the character of the room. Typical provision is as follows:

- Bed: may have a storage drawer under. Usually doubles as a sofa, so consider providing a back rest along the wall. Wider beds (approx. 1350 mm) are provided in some schemes.
- Desk: should be as generous as possible to take a computer, books, files etc., with drawers large enough to take files. Incorporate hole for cable management. If the window cill is at, or slightly above, desk height it can be used as an extra shelf.
- Desk chair.
- Easy chair: if sufficient space.
- Shelving: often built-in. May be arranged to serve the function of a bed side table.
- Wardrobe: often built-in.
- Chest of drawers: can be used to extend the desk if it is same height and depth.
- Pinboard: generous provision to discourage use of walls. A small pin board on the outside of the room door is useful.
- Washbasin: a washbasin is often provided in study bedrooms when en-suite bathrooms are not provided, and should be separated from the main area of the room, by containing it within the wardrobe unit or behind a room divider.
- Mini-fridge: occasionally required.

6.4 En-suite bathrooms
En-suite bathrooms add approximately 2.8 m² to the study bedroom area and should be carefully planned to ensure that the small space functions well. They can be designed as a wet room with a floor drain, or incorporate a shower tray with a door. A wet room helps to optimise use of the space, but make it more difficult to keep the contents of the small space dry. The floor also takes time to dry. Bathrooms are often supplied as prefabricated pods, which allows the intricate work involved in the finishes and in waterproofing showers and floors to be carried out under factory conditions and avoids delays to other trades on-site.

6.5 Studio rooms
Studio rooms include an en-suite bathroom and a kitchen area (Figure 23.10). The kitchen area usually includes a small fridge,

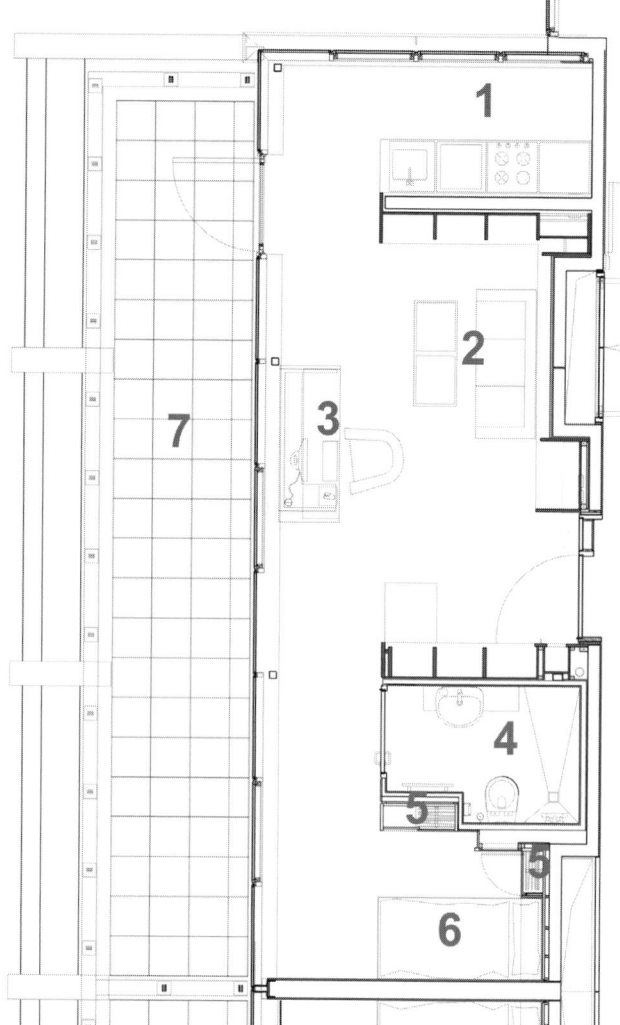

23.9 *Junior Research Fellows Suite. Kendrew Quadrangle, St John's College, Oxford. Architects: MJP Architects. The larger studio room is zoned. 1, kitchen; 2, living area; 3, desk; 4, shower room; 5, wardrobe; 6, bed; 7, terrace*

sink, cupboard, hob or microwave and cooker extract. Extraction to external space (rather than less efficient re-cycling of air) will require ducts to be incorporated into the plans. The kitchen should be designed so that it doesn't dominate the study bedroom. If the kitchen area is located on the escape route between the sleeping area and the room door, details should be agreed with the local authority. Additional fire provisions will be required.

6.6 Services
Students should be able to control their environment. Consideration should also be given to erratic patterns of occupation of study bed rooms and measures should be incorporated to reduce energy consumption, e.g. to ensure that lights are not left on when rooms are vacant (see also section 5). Access for maintenance and meter reading should be arranged from corridors to avoid the need for access to the student rooms.

- *Lighting:* good natural light is important. General artificial lighting should be supplemented by task lighting to serve desk and bed positions and should be switched so that it can be controlled from the bed and room door.
- *Internet and communications:* students require excellent internet access for study and social activities. TV provision is increasingly provided via the internet. Technology for internet access is constantly advancing, so that the most appropriate system should be agreed as each project is designed. Data cabling systems

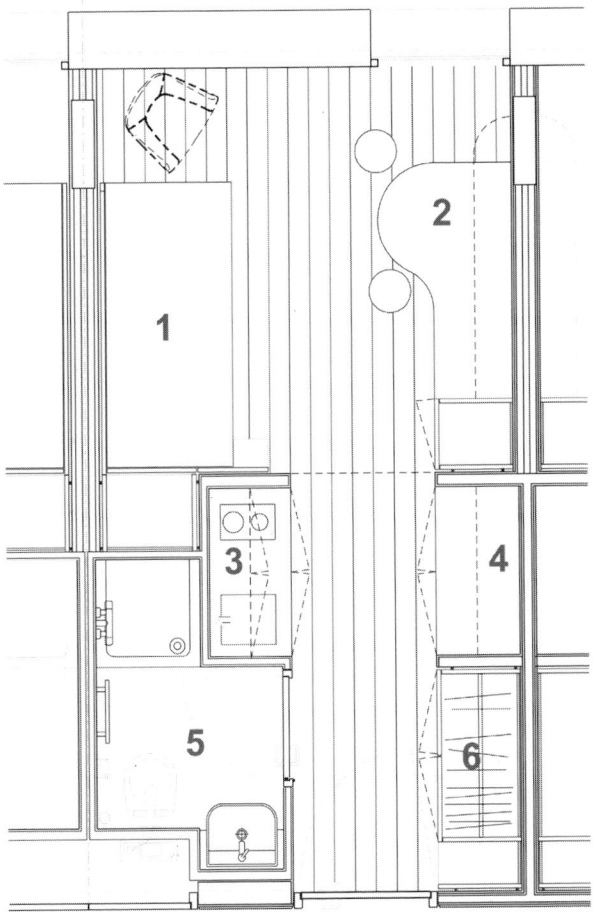

23.10a *Studio room with en-suite shower/WC/basin and kitchenette. 1, bed; 2, desk; 3, kitchenette; 4, kitchen storage; 5, shower room; 6, wardrobe.*

23.10b *Studio room with en-suite shower/WC/basin and kitchenette. Torquay Street, London. Architects: MJP Architects.*

perform better and are more secure than Wi-Fi, but Wi-Fi is significantly cheaper and gives students the flexibility to work where they choose. If trunking and sockets are provided, positions should be coordinated with furniture arrangements.

- Shared phones in common areas may be required for occasional or emergency use.
- *Heating and electricity:* systems and controls will be determined by the university or commercial provider's strategy for energy conservation and for charging, and also by the length of let (term time only, or all year). Background heating may be provided within the rent, with the facility to boost heat in each room.
- A minimum of four double sockets is appropriate for equipment, which may include computer/printer, phone charger, kettle, hair

drier, light fittings, etc. The location of sockets should be considered in relation to alternative furniture arrangements. Sometimes mini-circuit breakers are used to prevent use of larger electrical appliances.
- *Ventilation:* Natural ventilation should be provided with opening windows where possible, fitted with restrictors to prevent students from falling.
- *Recycling:* Bins for re-cycling may be required within the study bedroom.

6.7 Students with disabilities
Requirements for accessible rooms are addressed in BS 8300:2009+A1:2010. Wheelchair users require larger study bedrooms, with room for a wheelchair turning space between furniture and provision of an appropriate en-suite bathroom. The design of fittings and finishes should be suitable for access from a wheelchair. Study bedrooms may also require adaptations to meet the specific needs of individual disabled students, as these will vary depending on the particular nature of their disability. Consider:

- Design of room door and access into the room.
- Height of the desk (which may be adjustable) and space below for wheelchair to slide under.
- Access and use of cupboards and shelving.
- Design of ironmongery and controls for window opening, curtains and blinds.
- Position of electrical sockets and switches.
- Provision of telephone, emergency call point and fire alarm beacon.
- Provision of space to store the unused wheelchair without obstruction.
- Design of en-suite bathroom.
- Levels of lighting and choice of colours for people with visual impairments.
- Visual alarms or vibrating alarms for people with hearing impairments.

7 KITCHEN/DINING ROOMS
7.1 Role
In student accommodation, kitchen/dining rooms provide a key social focus for each group of students that they serve, with opportunities for casual encounters, friendship and support. This fosters a sense of ownership of the accommodation which in turn encourages responsible behaviour. One kitchen/dining room will typically serve 5–8 students, although in some universities they may serve 10 or more, particularly in 'house' type accommodation or in halls where the university also provides central catering facilities as an alternative.

Kitchen/dining rooms can be arranged to overlook common areas such as entrances, stairs and halls, providing further opportunities for interaction and a degree of security through informal supervision. They should be located to avoid noise and nuisance to study bedrooms. The dining areas should be designed to allow all the students in the unit to eat at the same time. Furniture should not be fixed to avoid creating an institutional character. Kitchen/dining rooms may be extended to incorporate a living area with sofas and a television. Provision of Wi-Fi will make dining and living areas more useful.

Kitchens will be heavily used and should allow several people to prepare food simultaneously. They must be designed to be functional, robust and easy to clean. As a guide, a length of work surface of approximately 3600 mm, including cooker and sink, will be sufficient for five people. Circulation space between units should be 1200 mm minimum. Where kitchens serve larger numbers of students, the provision of cookers, sinks, fridges and storage will need to be increased to meet statutory requirements (see item 5 above). Ideally a microwave oven should be provided as well as a conventional cooker. Cupboards should be provided for each student for storage of tins and dry goods. In some accommodation locks are provided on cupboards and even fridges to avoid food being stolen, while in others – particularly self-contained flats and houses – there are no locks, to promote a sense of mutual responsibility. At the other extreme, in some accommodation students are expected to keep cooking equipment and food in their rooms, but this is inconvenient, causes mess and undermines social interaction.

7.2 Services
Measures should be incorporated to reduce energy consumption (see Section 9.5):

- *Electric power:* provide sockets at worktop and at low level. Some universities monitor and charge for cookers separately to discourage wasteful use of energy. Cookers can be fitted with a time switch in case they are left on by mistake.
- *Lighting and mechanical extract:* Provide generous opening windows where possible (with restrictors) positioned to avoid nuisance from noise and smell to neighbouring study bedrooms.
- *Refuse and recycling:* position bins for easy cleaning and emptying. Separate recycling bins should be provided in line with university waste management strategies.

7.3 Inclusive access
Where the kitchen serves study bedrooms for wheelchair users, it should be designed with appropriate equipment and fittings and sufficient area to allow for wheelchairs to manoeuvre, including worktops with adjustable height and room for the wheelchair to slide below. Some duplication of equipment may be necessary.

8 BATHROOMS
8.1 Facilities
Bathrooms, showers and WCs are usually designed to the minimum practical area. Numbers of facilities should be in accordance with statutory requirements (see section 5). Shared WCs should be separate from bathrooms unless serving very few people. Where facilities are shared, additional washbasins are often provided in study bedrooms.

Facilities need to withstand rough use and simpler arrangements are potentially easier to construct, clean and maintain. Factory-assembled bathrooms 'pods' are often used to achieve a high standard of construction. Service ducts should be carefully detailed and located, with service access to en-suite bathrooms from corridors. Where bathrooms are not en-suite, consider proximity to study bedrooms and acoustic and visual privacy.

Provide good mechanical ventilation, especially in showers, with moisture-resistant light fittings. Towel rails, shelves and hooks in the shower area should be out of the way of the shower itself. Blocked or leaking showers are a common problem and even where a shower tray is used, the floor in a shower room should ideally drain to a floor gulley. Thermostatic balanced pressure mixers should be provided to showers to avoid risk of scalding. Flooring should be slip resistant.

9 OTHER FACILITIES
Provision will depend on the number of students living in the accommodation and on the availability of facilities nearby. They may include the following.

9.1 Reception and circulation areas
Entrances should be light and welcoming and avoid a mean or utilitarian character – the design should create an identity for the residences. In larger residences there may be a staffed reception or porter's lodge or office. In other schemes, provision may be required for a temporary reception to receive students at the start of term or conference guests in the holidays. In up-market commercial schemes, the design and 'branding' of the reception is important and a more generous area with seating will be required. A place for mailboxes may be required. Long narrow corridors without daylight or views should be avoided. Staircases are a place where chance meetings occur, and are an opportunity to design an attractive feature on circulation routes.

9.2 Laundry
A laundry serving groups of residents should be provided with washing and drying machines of a robust commercial type with emergency cut-off switch, plus a sink for hand-washing clothes, facilities for ironing and folding clothes and seats for waiting. Provide good lighting and ventilation and floor gullies to avoid flooding. Fittings and equipment should allow easy maintenance. Services such as electricity supply, hot water, etc. must be adequate for the level of use. Choose the location carefully – a laundry close to a common room can form part of a social hub, but laundries can be noisy, smelly and humid and should be arranged to avoid nuisance to study bedrooms or at the building's entrance.

9.3 Cleaners' storage
Where accommodation is in independent flats or houses, cleaning is generally the students' responsibility and a tall cupboard will be sufficient. Where the university arranges cleaning, provide central stores for the cleaners within a reasonable distance of the rooms. In larger schemes there should be a store on each floor. Provision may also be required for facilities for the cleaning and reception staff: WCs, lockers, staff room etc.

9.4 Other possible facilities
- Central common room/television room/party room: often poorly used if insufficient thought has been given to demand. Common rooms should be located so that activity is visible from main circulation routes to encourage use. Party rooms need to be located to reduce nuisance to study bedrooms. A kitchen area will be required for students to prepare food and drink.
- Seminar room/study area: central rooms with WiFi or data cabling can provide a place for group working and a sociable alternative to working in study bedrooms.
- Games room.
- Music practice room.
- In more luxurious schemes a gym, cinema, café or convenience store may be provided.
- Luggage store.
- Wardens/staff flats may be provided adjacent to or within the scheme, and may be studios or flats of various sizes, including family accommodation.
- Guest bedrooms.

9.5 External areas and parking
Well-designed landscaped areas around residences can provide places for socialising and informal working, particularly if Wi-Fi is available. Spaces for informal games – football, frisbee etc. – and for barbecues are popular.

The planning authority and the university will have policies for the provision of parking, and the allowance for student parking is usually very minimal, although spaces will be required for disabled parking, which should be close to entrances. To guard against theft and for personal safety, parking areas should be overlooked, well lit and relatively close to entrances. Each student arrives at the start of term with quantities of luggage and sufficient space should be provided near to entrances for unloading several vehicles simultaneously. Taxis are often used for nights out and there should be provision for taxi drop-off close to entrances. To encourage use of sustainable modes of transport, there should be well-designed foot paths and cycle routes and good provision of secure, covered cycle parking.

9.6 Energy consumption

There are many opportunities to reduce energy consumption in the detailed design of the accommodation and choice of controls, fittings and appliances, including:

- BMS systems, and a good understanding of how to use the building (heating, ventilation etc.) by staff and residents.
- Low energy light fittings.
- Presence detectors for kitchen and en-suite bathroom lights.
- Thermostatic radiator valves.
- Mini circuit breakers in study bedrooms.
- Heat recovery systems.
- Low flow rate taps and dual flush WCs.
- Sustainable urban drainage.
- Renewable energy sources.

9.7 Refuse and recycling collection

Develop a waste management strategy at an early stage and consult the waste collection services about their requirements for access. The size of any bin store will depend on the number of students, the requirements for re-cycling and the frequency of collection. Bins filled by staff may be cleaner and tidier than those used by students, but all are potentially untidy, smelly and attract vermin. Stores should be easy to access, clean and maintain. Locate to reduce nuisance to residents, and provide good ventilation.

9.8 Safety and security

The design should address potential risks of attack, vandalism and theft. Personal safety is a major issue in student housing and students often return home late at night. Theft is also a common problem, as students own computers and other valuable equipment, and it is difficult to prevent strangers entering residences by 'tailgating'. Windows to ground floor rooms are particularly vulnerable.

The building should be designed so that external areas – such as entrances, paths and car parks – and common areas within the building – such as staircases – are overlooked to provide informal supervision. Good external lighting is essential, with provision of safe walking routes. CCTV and alarm points may also be required in external areas.

Swipe card systems are often used for doors instead of keys, which are expensive to replace when lost. Where there are sufficient number of residents there may be a staffed reception. Where this is not possible entry phones may be provided, with handsets in each study bedroom. Provide spy holes in study bedroom doors.

The design should also avoid features that encourage anti-social or dangerous behaviour: skate-boarding and climbing are common problems.

10 CONFERENCE USE

10.1 Additional needs

Many universities use student residences for conferences or holiday lets during the vacations and this has implications for design:

- The Fire Risk Assessment should address the proposed conference use.
- Rooms with en-suite bathrooms will be preferred.
- A higher standard of fittings and finishes may be required.
- Central linen stores may be required with easy access to study bedrooms.
- A term-time store for equipment that is provided to conference guests, such as kettles.
- Lockable storage may be provided for students' possessions and a safe for conference guests.
- Reception area, seminar rooms or other facilities to support conference activities.

24 Industrial facilities

Jolyon Drury and Ian Brebner

The Jolyon Drury Consultancy advises on the design of production, distribution and storage systems and facilities. Ian Brebner is a partner of architecture practice Austin-Smith:Lord

KEY POINTS:
- *Constant change is endemic*
- *Increasing demand for small units and starter accommodation*

Contents

1 Introduction
2 Classification of production building types
3 Adaptability
4 Working methods
5 Machine sizes
6 Outline specification of a typical multi-strategy factory
7 Non-production accommodation
8 Bibliography

1 INTRODUCTION

1.1 Industrial facilities

An industrial facilty is a building enclosure and site within which goods are manufactured, assembled, stored or shipped/trans-shipped. Manufacturing processes continually develop, improve and evolve, but have generally been classified as either:

1 A transformation of elemental raw materials into a finished product or material that requires further manufacturing to become a finished product (commonly referred to as Heavy Industry). These are typified by traditional industries, such as steel manufacture, chemical manufacture, refining plants, etc.
2 An assembly process which integrates finished components into a finished product (commonly referred to as Light or Medium Industry). These are typified by automotive manufacturing, white goods manufacturing, electronics manufacturing, etc.

A third category of Technology manufacturing is rapidly evolving from the development of artificial/assisted intelligence, communications and biotechnology. The intellectual capital required to sustain this third category is a step change from the more traditional light and heavy industries that have previously predominated in the developed economies. Developed economies are changing their manufacturing base to this third category as a means of generating added value to sustain the increasing income aspiration of their workforce and maintaining their global trading position. This category demands greater integration of further education and research with the actual manufacturing activity. It is generally recognised that clustering together research and manufacturing facilities produces a catalytic effect where the total output (physical or intellectual) can exceed the sum of the parts – even though they may be separate enterprises. This has significant implications on the nature of the enclosure which accommodates these new industrial facilities.

1.2 History of industrial facilities

The history of industrial development has been one of the continual changes following improvements in production equipment, management and techniques. The key stages of the development of manufacturing which have influenced the design and nature of industrial building have been:

1 Craft-based manufacture, where individuals or small groups of individuals created the finished product from elemental raw materials. The buildings which facilitated this were in the main, relatively small-scale workshops, or indeed, individuals' dwellings. An industrial building typology was not generally identifiable.
2 Power-assisted manufacture, where production machines were powered rather than manually operated. Significantly, the use of power increased the capacity of the machine and allowed the subdivision of the production process, decreasing reliance on the skill of the individual. This, in turn, facilitated a greater concentration of manufacturing capacity in a single location. Early power systems relied on extended shaft drives with belt-driven power transfer to individual machines. Belt drives had a finite limit on their length and operated at right angles to the drive shaft. The buildings which accommodated these power systems were characterised by their distinctive long thin shape on multiple floors. The first distinctive industrial (factory) building typology had evolved, amongst the earliest examples being Cromford Mill at Belper in Derbyshire by Richard Arkwright, 1771.
3 The assembly line. The development of compact individual electrical, fluid- or air-driven 'engines' released the production machine from the constraint of being tied to a central power engine. These new machines had relatively unlimited capacity and power. Together, these factors allowed machines to be located to match the assembly sequence needed to produce the final product. The assembly evolved. The buildings which accommodated this new form of mass production were typified by being single storey, comparatively large with clear internal spans to provide the flexibility to reconfiguration of the assembly line to suit changes to the product in a more rapidly evolving marketplace. The industrial building typology evolved into large enclosures, single storey with large internal spans.

2 CLASSIFICATION OF PRODUCTION BUILDING TYPES

Factories can be broadly categorised as bespoke or generic.

2.1 Bespoke

These include:

- high-precision work in controlled conditions (Figures 24.1–24.3);
- highly tailored to a unique or very specialised process;
- primary manufacturing sites which double as headquarters or 'flagship' manufacturing sites.

Design will depend on circumstances, but will tend to approximate to laboratory or office type design conforming to Planning B1 classification.

2.2 Medium industries

The greatest need for careful and thoughtful design is in this field. These industries can be subdivided into:

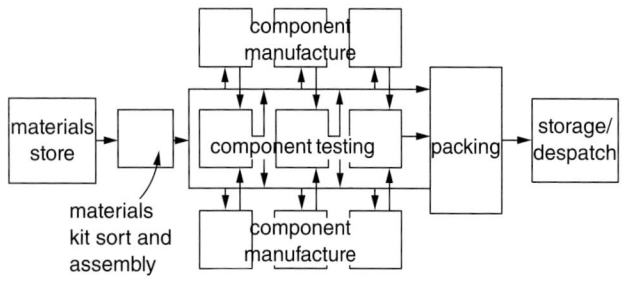

24.1 *Typical process flow diagram for light production and assembly such as small electronic components' manufacture, and similar high-technology processes. 'Kit sort' refers to the making up of kits of components for assemblers*

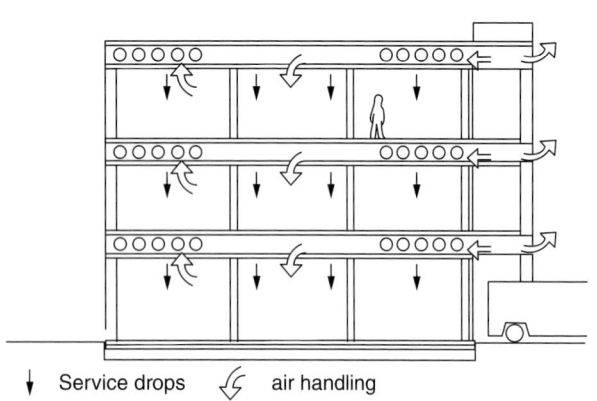

↓ Service drops   ⤺ air handling

24.2 *Section through typical factories for light, high-technology production; multi-storey construction, as new or conversion of existing building: could be flatted units*

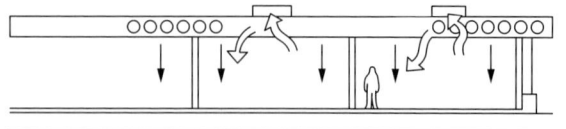

24.3 *Light production and assembly: single storey for small-scale and high-technology assembly. High degree of service freedom in roof zone*

- Light – medium small-scale engineering and assembly, clothing factories, paint shops, similar to Figure 24.4.
- General – medium batch production of components for other factories, medium-sized printing, Figures 24.5 and 24.6.
- Heavy – medium industries requiring intensive use of buildings and services as in mass production, Figures 24.7 and 24.8.

2.3 Heavy industries

Industries such as steel-making and shipbuilding require spaces (not necessarily enclosed) designed around the work or the mechanical plant (Figure 24.9). Traditionally, it is difficult to build adaptable structures (Figure 24.10), but modern handling techniques enable 'loose fit' buildings to be designed (Figure 24.11).

3 ADAPTABILITY

3.1 Design for change

An industrial facility is designed to either:

- 'institutional' standards, where the configuration of the building is geared to the requirements of the financial institutions who fund

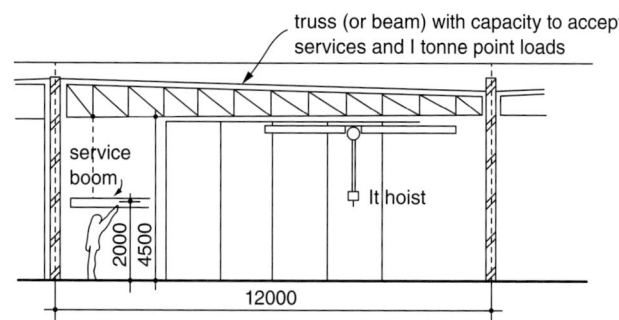

a *Section through unit*

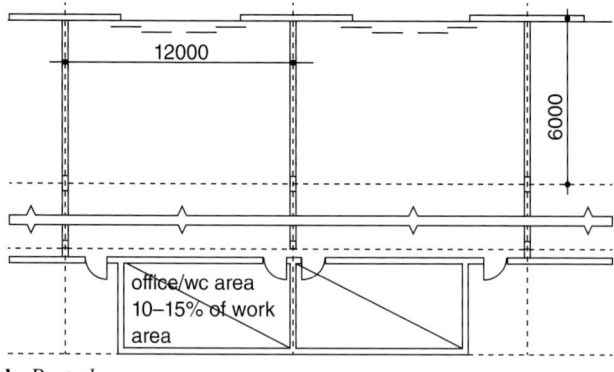

b *Part plan*

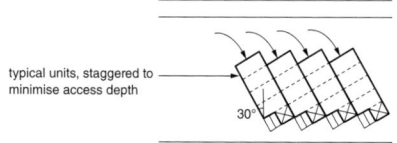

c *Units staggered in plan to reduce site depth required*

24.4 *Typical 'nursery' for light production and assembly, low technology, may be built speculatively*

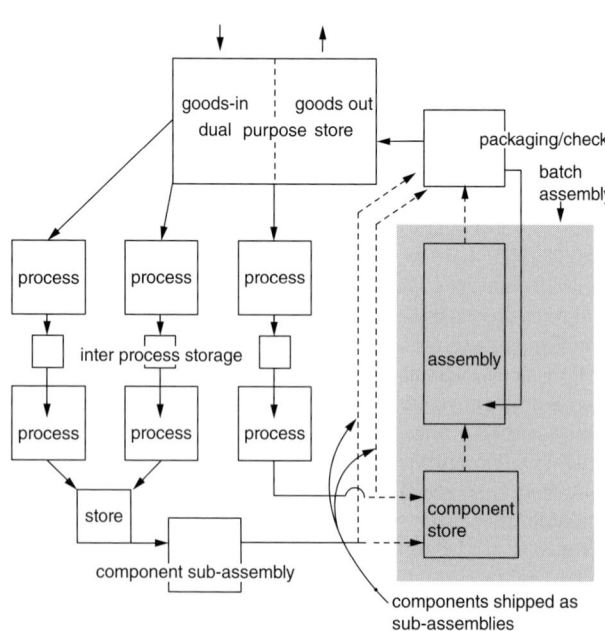

24.5 *Process flow diagram for batch production and assembly. Sometimes involves the assembly and shipping out of complete sub-assemblies, more commonly the production and dispatch of batches of discrete components*

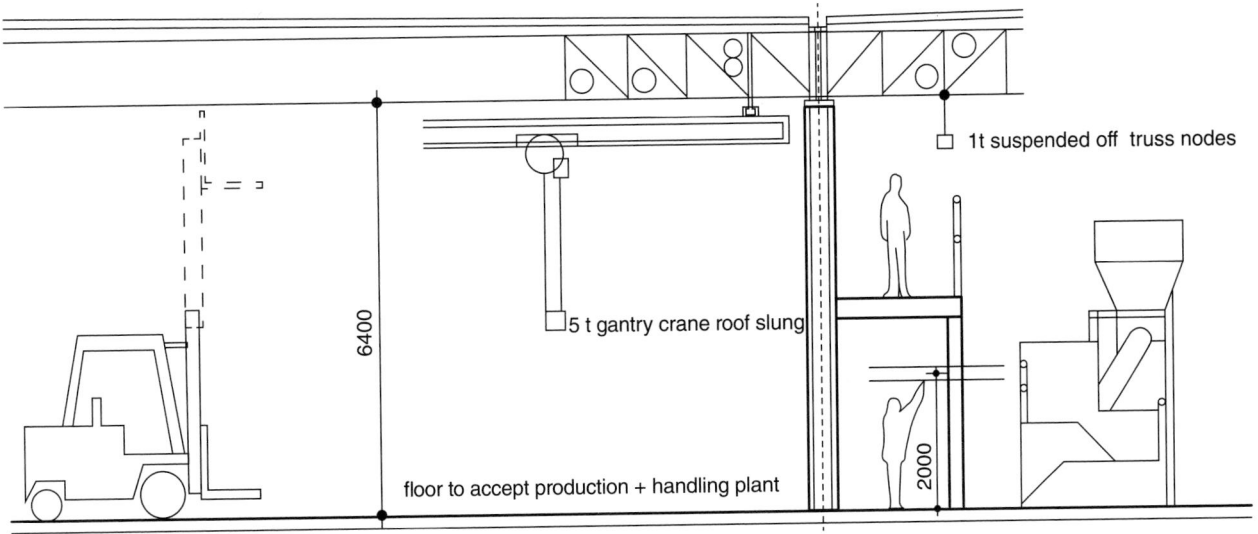

6400

1t suspended off truss nodes

5 t gantry crane roof slung

2000

floor to accept production + handling plant

24.6 *Section through typical purpose-built batch production building. The spans, typically 18 × 12 m and trussed roof construction are selected for cheap and rapid adaptation to a variety of uses. Floor loading 25 kN/m²*

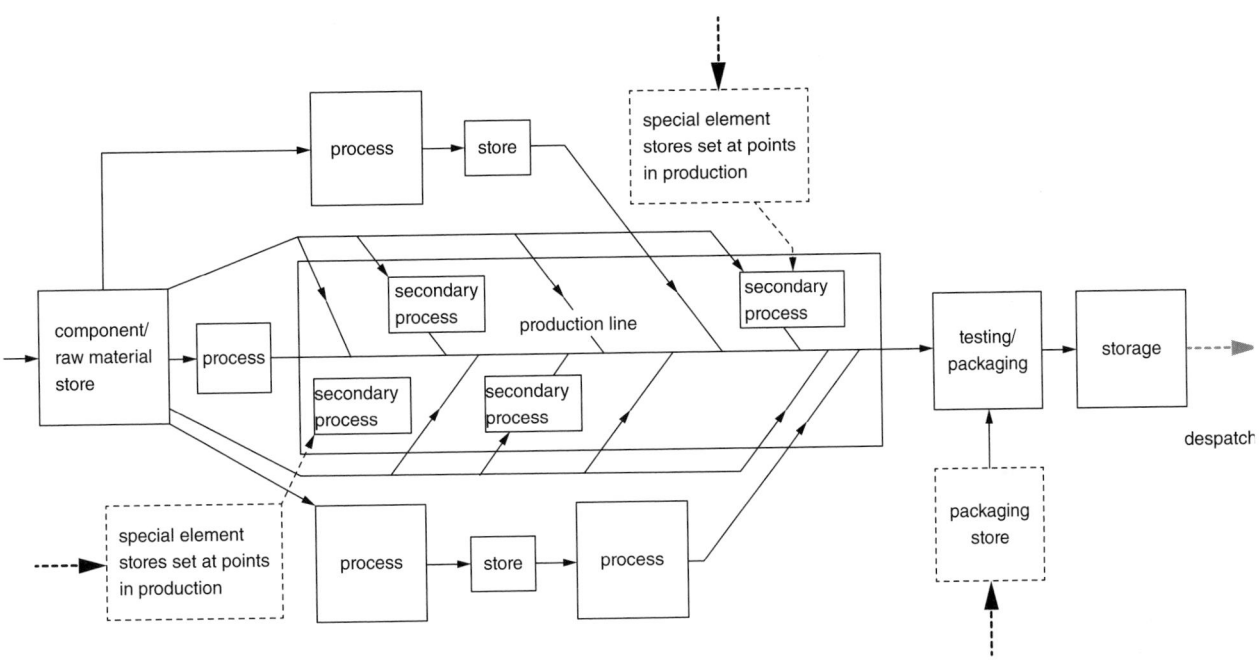

process — store

special element stores set at points in production

component/raw material store — process — secondary process — production line — secondary process — testing/packaging — storage — despatch

secondary process — secondary process

special element stores set at points in production — process — store — process

packaging store

24.7 *Process flow diagram for mass production and assembly. This applies to high-volume line assembly as in the motor industry, with some components being built into sub-assemblies before final assembly on the main line*

the development. These requirements manifest themselves in a very flexible building which can be adapted to other industrial process or distribution uses if the initial occupier vacates the building. Typically, the buildings are regular in shape (optimally around 2:1 to 3:1 ratio of length to width) with internal height related to the floor area (typically, 6 m clear to underside of structural obstructions for floor areas up to 2500 m² and up to 12 m clear to underside of structural obstructions for floor areas of 10,000 m² and above). Distribution facilities would normally start at a height of 12 m and rise to 18 m where automated 'picking' equipment is intended.

It is desirable to have the maximum clear internal spans. The most economic form of frame is the portal which can economically span up to 36 m and can be duplicated to increase the width of the building as required. The most economic primary grid spacing is between 6 and 7.2 m.

As proportion of the total floor area, the total of office and welfare accommodation will typically range from 10 per cent in total

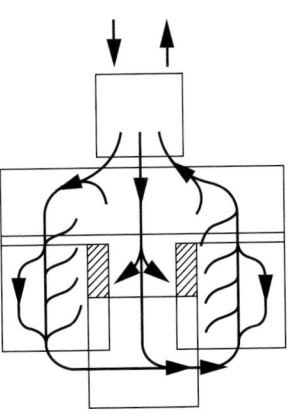

24.8 *Materials flow for mass production does not have to impose a predominantly linear building form. Group assembly 'cells' may feed onto a circulatory route, allowing personnel and services to be grouped into specifically equipped zones*

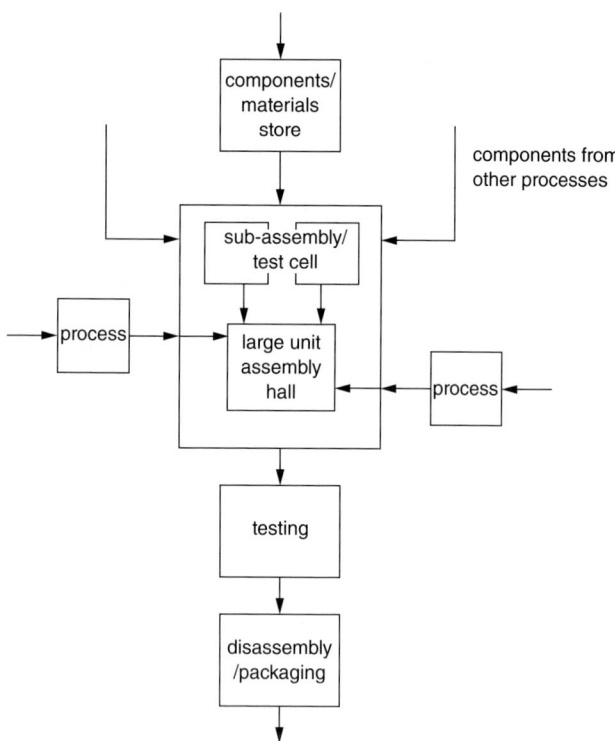

24.9 *Process flow diagram for typical heavy engineering. The workpiece is the centre to which sub-assemblies are routed. It is likely to be disassembled for shipment*

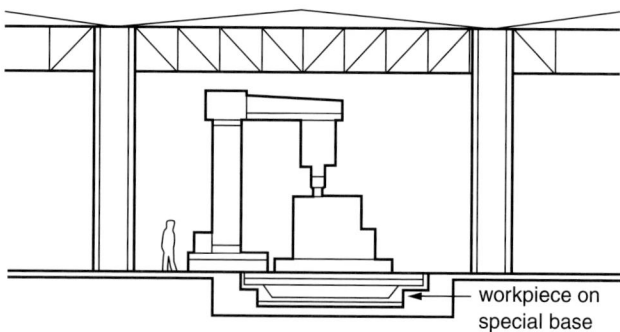

workpiece on special base

24.11c *Section and*

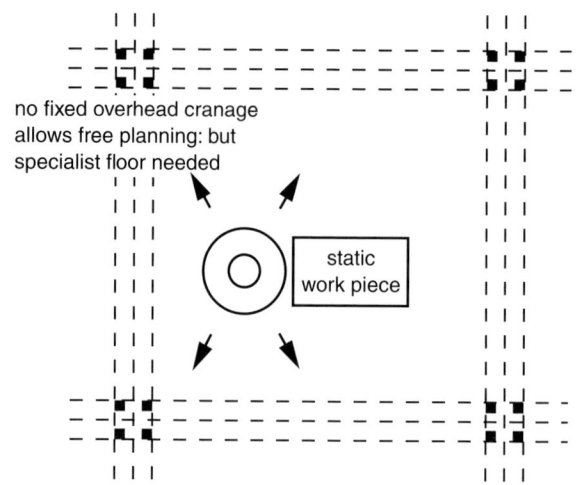

no fixed overhead cranage allows free planning: but specialist floor needed

static work piece

24.11d *Part plan of recently developed workshop where large workpieces remain static, being built up on special bases that are likely to be employed for transport and installation. Machine tools and components are brought to the workpiece, air-cushion techniques are widely used*

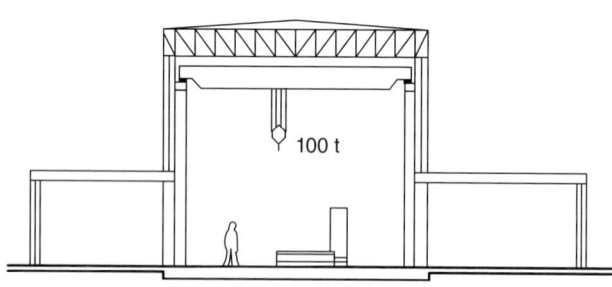

100 t

24.10a *Section and*

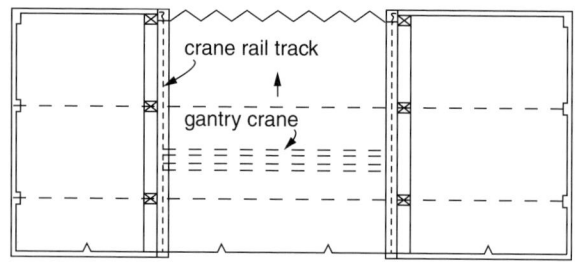

crane rail track

gantry crane

24.10b *Part plan of traditional type. Heavy-duty gantry cranes move the workpiece to the appropriate machine tools and assembly areas*

floor areas of 1000 m² to 5 per cent in total floor areas of 10 000 m² and more.

Recognising the needs of the occupier who is likely to require smaller floor areas, around 1000 m², the provision of dock levellers is much reduced in comparison with larger buildings of, say, 10 000 m², where as many as 6–8 may be desirable.

- Bespoke industrial facilities are usually required where the process is so unique that it is unable to fit within the simple flexible layout of the 'institutional' building, cannot be contained in a single building or does not require full enclosure. In these circumstances, the building enclosure effectively becomes part of the process. This will limit the future flexibility of the building, in the extreme, rendering it unusable for anything but its intended use. Bespoke buildings are usually associated with capital intensive processes where the process equipment is relatively immovable – in contrast to the type of process equipment that can be readily accommodated in the 'institutional' building. For the designer, a thorough understanding of the process requiring a bespoke solution can offer rich opportunity for expressive functional design.

The evolving technology industries tend to conform well to the 'institutional' building model which offers greater flexibility for change in the format and type of process. The extreme example is Biotech or Biopharma production processes which are organised as multiple production cells within a large uniform enclosure, each cell is capable of being stripped out and replaced with a completely different process without disruption to the remaining operating cells.

There is a reducing requirement for the bespoke industrial facility, at a practical level and resulting from the means of funding of modern industrial facilities.

Adaptability must allow:

- change of process to avoid obsolescence;
- change of process and product following change of ownership.

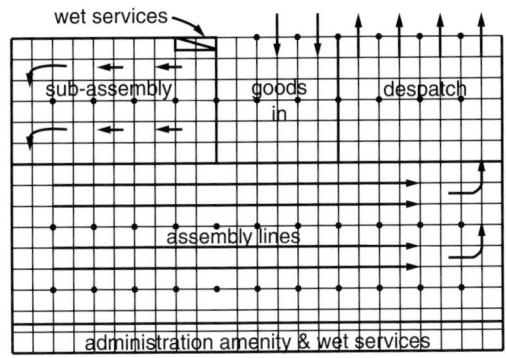

1 first stage factory   4 various options for office expansion
2 first stage office   5 car park
3 factory expansion   6 heavy vehicle area

24.12 *Small or medium-size factory development, with a free-standing office building. The uneven boundary increases the possibility of conflict when the factory and offices expand simultaneously, and restricts commensurate expansion of car parking*

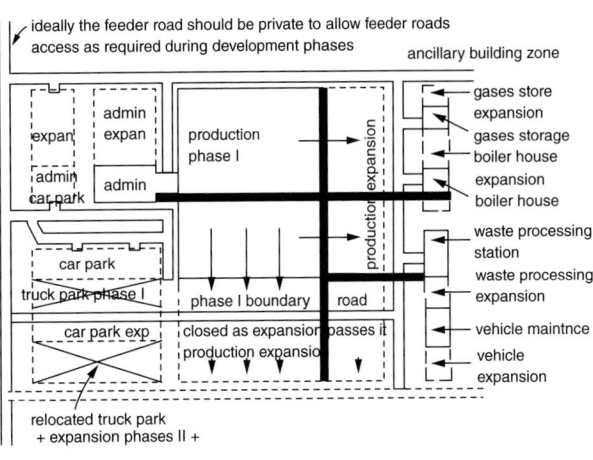

24.13 *A large plant with segregated development zones:*

- *The factory and associated car and truck parking. When the factory expands the truck park becomes the expanded car park and a new truck park is constructed adjacent to dispatch*
- *The administration block and associated car parking, separated from manufacturing by landscaping*
- *The ancillary area, incorporating individual growth provision for each element within the zone boundary.*

24.14 *Mass production buildings have to accept changes in production technology. This plan shows a conventional line assembly that may be adapted to the form in 24.15*

Changes will normally only be within the broad groupings of building types given in Section 2.2.

3.2 Design for extension
Apart from alterations within the envelope, there may also be requirements for extension; and the design should anticipate this (Figures 24.12 and 24.13).

4 WORKING METHODS
4.1 Alternative methods
The alternative methods of work organisation are:

- linear assembly
- team technology.

While the latter is a more recent introduction, there is no indication that it will completely supplant the former. Consequently, production buildings must be able to accommodate either or even both in different areas (Figures 24.14 and 24.15).

4.2 Linear assembly
In this method, machines are arranged along work-travel routes. At each station, components are added until the work has been completely assembled and finished. Supplies of components and materials are needed at each station; and waste must be removed.

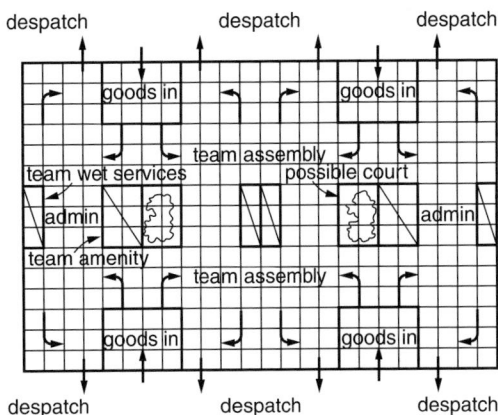

24.15 *The factory can change to team assembly due to new product. Note localisation of amenity and wet service areas to identify with teams. Chance of opening courts adjacent to amenity areas, though these may change position as production demands*

4.3 Team technology
This appears to restore to the labour force a feeling of responsibility and achievement. The machines are arranged in groups, and all or a substantial part of the work is assembled within the group. There is a need for storage of materials and components. The main planning requirements are for unrestrictive space and strong floors to enable the machines to be relocated at will, with adaptable overhead services systems. Storage and assembly spaces should be interchangeable.

5 MACHINE SIZES
The sizes of typical machines for light and medium duty industries are shown in Figures 24.16–24.21. The majority of machine tools do not exceed 7.5 kN/m² in loading on the floor.

6 OUTLINE SPECIFICATION OF A TYPICAL MULTI-STRATEGY FACTORY
Table I provides an outline specification of a typical multi-strategy factory.

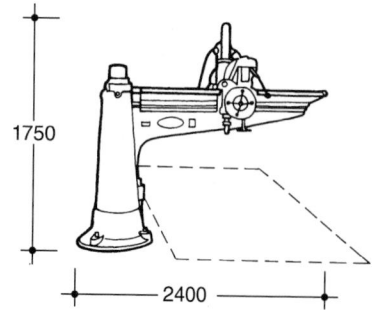

a *Plate drill*

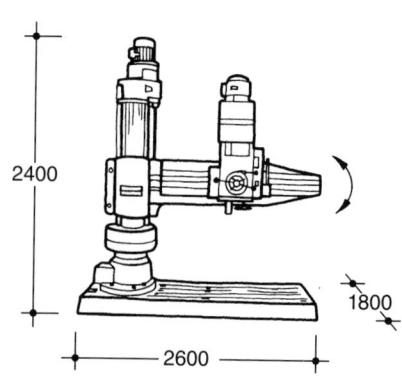

b *Radial drill*

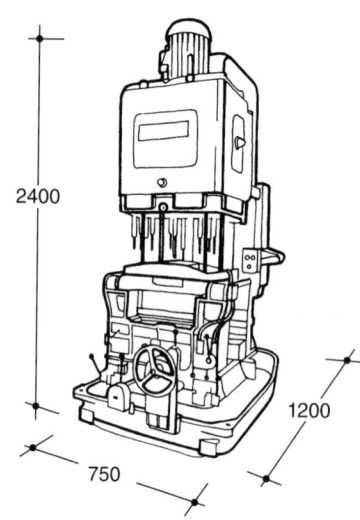

c *Adjustable multi-drill*

24.16 *Drilling machines*

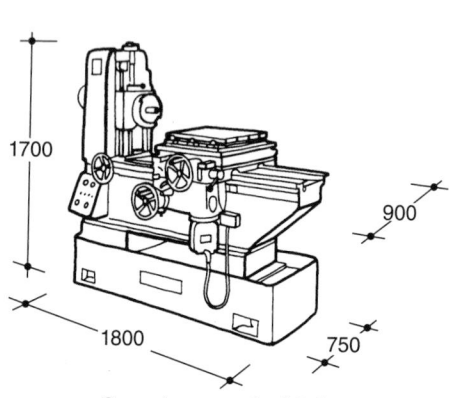

a *General purpose chuck lathe*

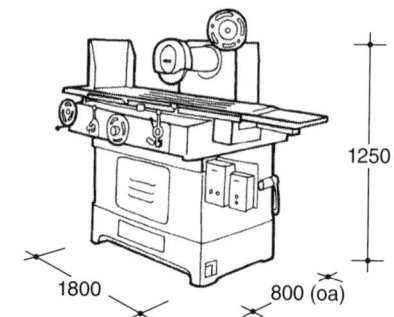

a *Surface grinder*

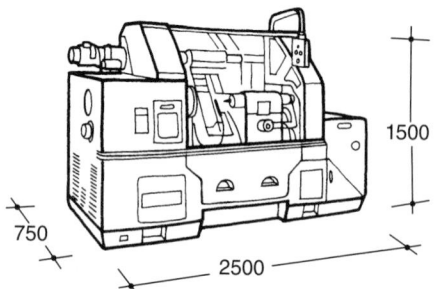

b *Hydraulic copying lathe*

24.17 *Lathes*

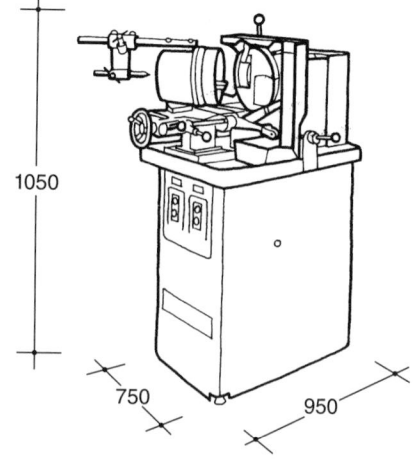

b *Twist drill grinding machine*

24.18 *Grinding machines*

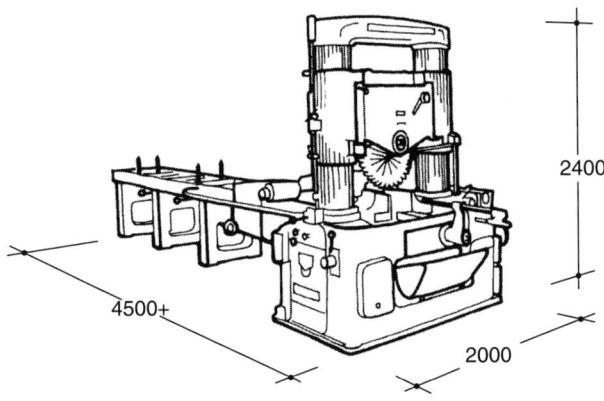

24.19 *Cold sawing machine*

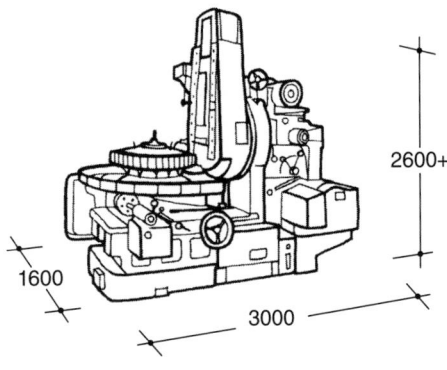

24.20 *Gear cutting machine*

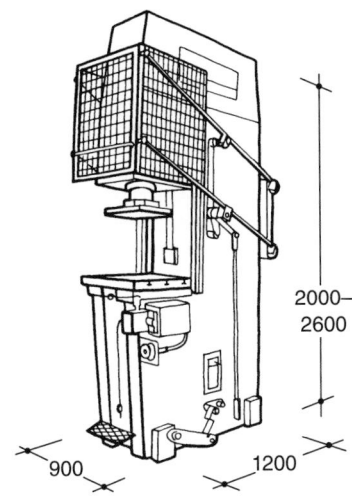

24.21 *Hydraulic pedal press*

7 NON-PRODUCTION ACCOMMODATION

7.1 Offices

There is a tendency for administrative and production space to be interchangeable. Two types of offices will be required in close conjunction with the production space:

- Foreman's desk space in sight and proximity of work supervised. This is formed from easily demountable components to allow for rapid relocation. Sometimes to avoid floor obstructions this accommodation is raised to mezzanine levels where visibility is improved.
- Executive offices for the local administrative staff, or the company headquarters where these are not elsewhere. This type of accommodation is designed in accordance with Section 16, Offices, Shops and Railway Premises Act 1963, and will depend on the numbers to be accommodated. As a rough guide, allow 10–15 per cent of the production floor area, or 5 m² per person.

Table I Outline specification of a typical multi-strategy factory

Scope		
Type of industries for which appropriate	Buildings of this type are suitable for most manufacturing functions, excluding 'light', 'heavy' and 'process' industries.	
Size of project	Total area of production space can vary widely. Average size of all projects is 2500 m², so most are smaller. This specification is suitable for projects from about 1000 m² upwards.	
Type of project	40% of industrial projects are adaptations and extensions of existing premises. This specification sets out the general requirements of those projects, or parts of projects, free from special restraints.	

Criterion	Performance specification	Design notes
Requirements of the process		
Adaptability	Should be designed for general-purpose use and not around a particular process. General-purpose characteristics should be maintained wherever possible, e.g. in stores and production warehousing as well as in production space itself.	Building positioned on site leaving maximum possible room for extension, preferably in two directions. Single-storey building designed as a large open space. Standardised, mainly dry construction, easily extended or modified. Framework able to carry a variety of alternative roof and wall claddings, services and handling equipment. Those external walls not on or near site boundaries designed for easy demolition.
Plan shape	Probably not critical except where linear flow processes employed. Rectangular form maximises usable area, facilitates extension.	Rectangular plan form with ratio of long to short sides between 1:1 (minimises internal travel distances where no particular traffic routes are dictated by process) and say, 3:1 (average 2:1).
Physical environment	Process requirements will not usually be critical: workplace environment and energy efficiency are very important.	See under 'Environmental requirements of labour force'. In general, the production process will not require special dust-free conditions, nor will it create a dusty or especially dirty atmosphere. If there are toxic or corrosive hazards within the general production space, these should be isolated by local compartmentation and extraction equipment. High standards of cleanliness (e.g. very exact avoidance of foreign matter) or hygiene (e.g. avoidance of bacterial contamination) for some high-technology factories.
Structural dimensions	Exact plan dimensions rarely critical, except where flow processes employed. Aim should be to optimise convenience for production layouts provided by open space, e.g. the convenience of stanchions for locating small equipment, switches, etc. balanced against the potential adaptability: freedom for service drops and the location of equipment against the cost of greater spans and the loss of overhead craneage.	Span 18 m; bay spacing 12 m or even 18 m (which would permit production line to be turned at right angles if needed). These are proven dimensions in the USA but are greater than those found in many British factory buildings and (excluding 18 m square bays) are unlikely to increase costs significantly over smaller spans.

(continued)

Table I (continued)

Criterion	Performance specification	Design notes
Structural loadings	Internal clear height probably most critical dimension, for once built can only be modified with difficulty. Height needed for high stacking, overhead equipment, possibly facility to install mezzanines (for works offices, lavatories, control gear, extension of production space, etc.), overhead conveyors, etc. Space for services needed above clear height level. Within economic restraints, design for heaviest likely loads.	Internal clear height minimum 6 m. Main vehicle entrance doors (ground level loading) 5 m. For intensive manufacture, high stacking, overhead hoists or mezzanine floors a minimum height of 7.5 m is recommended.
Provision for services	Facility to take any production service (water, steam, gas, electrical power, etc.) to any point within production area with minimum disturbance to building, and therefore production.	Ideally point loads of 36 kN, but 25 kN sufficient for general-purpose use for buildings less than 6 m high to eaves. For very dense storage, typically mini-load automated component stores, 30 kN/m² distributed loading. Production and building services carried in roof space above level indicated by 'clear height', with vertical droppers as required to machine positions. This eliminates overhead craneage, but allows monorail hoists and conveyors. Roof structure designed appropriately. Drainage used to be below floor level, although alternative more costly but flexible arrangements are preferable. A permanent grid of drainage runs beneath the floor (a minimum of, say, one run in the middle of each 18 m span) will minimise disturbance.
Provision for movement of materials and equipment	It should be possible for the production engineer to use the type of material-handling equipment best suited to the product and production methods. Use of fork-lift trucks or similar wheeled materials-handling equipment will be general; overhead conveyors may be used. Cranes more usual in engineering than other industries. Heaviest floor loading is likely to result from wheels of fork-lift trucks (36 kN) and point loads from stacked storage cages and from pallet racking.	Separate foundations will be provided for any special or heavy equipment, especially that which vibrates. Wherever possible, the upper surface of such foundations will be at or below finished floor level. Much equipment is now 'stuck-down' to the floor. Conventionally, an RC floor slab with integral granolithic finish is used, although deterioration of the floor finish is a common problem in industrial buildings. Durable floors can be obtained, but they require a suitable base, good workmanship and close supervision. Particular finishes may be needed to resist attack from acids or oils used in certain processes.
Support for production loads	There are two opposed points of view about supports for such production loads as conveyors, local hoists and other overhead equipment. One is that since production loads cannot be predetermined, they should not be allowed to bear on the building structure, and should be loads carried either on the plant or on a separate structure, as and when this becomes necessary. This can lead to substructures inhibiting floor area and future flexibility. Although initially more expensive the preferred alternative is to design the roof structure to carry a general minimum of local loads, and to provide the facility to suspend conveyors, etc. at will.	Design assumptions might be that bottom boom of trusses (assumed spaced at 3–3.6 m centres) carry uniformly distributed load of 8 kN/m run, and a point load of 10 kN on any panel point at, say, 3 m centres. Structural supports for heavier loads are then provided on an ad hoc basis by the production engineer.

Environmental requirements of the labour force

Criterion	Performance specification	Design notes
Visual environment	Practically all visual tasks will be met by illumination levels within the range of 200–750 lux; illumination in the middle of the range will be most common. Limiting values of glare index (as IES Code) are likely to be within 22–28. Colour schemes should be designed both to assist the distribution of light and to minimise fatigue. Natural light design levels: warehouse, packing, large assembly, heavy forging, casting, saw mills, Daylight Factor 2% (say 10–15% floor area) 300–500 lux: Bench and machine work, fine casting, motor repair, general office work, average general purpose lighting, Daylight Factor 4–5% (say 12–15% floor area) 500 lux: Drawing work, medium assembly, weaving, small typesetting, Daylight Factor 6% (say, 15–20% floor area) 500–750 lux: Small inspection and assembly, small bench and machine work, 1000 lux+Daylight Factor 10%.	Either daylight or 'windowless' design. If daylight design, 'north light' is a useful compromise between even light level and energy conservation. View windows in external walls. Fluorescent lighting installation arranged in regular pattern over whole production floor to give 300–500 lux consistent illumination level E_{min}/E_{max} must be at least 0.7 wired in three phases to reduce flicker, and in trunking for simple replacement. Point luminaires may be used in areas of higher headroom, or to provide a high and even intensity. Reflecting surfaces decorated with colours of high reflectivity (e.g. underside of roofs: Munsell value 9), but care that glare from surfaces does not disturb machine operators, e.g. fork-lift truck drivers. For 10% and over use PSALI (permanent supplementary artificial lighting installation). For a general purpose building and for resale the design level should not be below a Daylight Factor of 5%. The method of achieving this must be checked against insulation regulations.
Thermal environment	Optimum values of temperature, air movement, etc. will depend largely upon nature of work – whether, for example, it is sedentary or active. Main environmental problem will be to avoid uncomfortable heat in summer. Minimum temperatures: heavy work 10°, light work 13°C, sedentary 16°C.	For most light industry plant should be able to provide air temperature of 18–21°C. Mechanical ventilation, at least in factories of average or greater size. Air-change rate (fresh air supply) minimum 5 l/s/person
Acoustic environment	Production processes highly variable in noise output. Control by encapsulating machinery and by using interspersed storage stacks.	Thermal insulation material can give a measure of acoustic control, particularly in providing absorption.
Fire protection	Some industries are regarded as having 'abnormal' fire risk because of the process or materials used; building design will be affected by requirements for additional compartmentation. Generally, fire hazard is classed as 'moderate' to 'low'. The general requirement of fire safety, of a maximum division of the production area into self-contained fire-resisting compartments, is at variance with the general production need for open space, and should be carefully considered. The requirements of the occupiers' insurers may be more onerous than the requirements of Building Control. The most common standards to refer to are FM Global and LPCB – Loss Prevention Certification Board.	Fire division walls may be required to obtain acceptable insurance rate. Areas will depend on process, etc. 'Fire curtains' in roof space. Fire vents in roof surface of total area not less than 1% of floor area. Avoidance of combustible materials in sheeted claddings. Sprinklers are also being increasingly required by insurance companies, both over the process and in the roof depth to protect services.

Table I (continued)

Criterion	Performance specification	Design notes
Explosion hazard	Not normally considered critical, but can be accommodated with blow-out panels, or placing part of process outside the main building.	
Building economics	The cost of using a factory building is an important element in the long-term cost of manufacturing. Nevertheless, without adequate justification, few managements are prepared to pay more than the minimum to obtain their essential specification, one reason being that investment in plant, equipment, perhaps labour is likely to show a higher return than investment in buildings (see Sections 3.1 and 3.2).	A 'basic' specification: concrete floor slab; exposed structural framework and services; simple finishes, such as painted steelwork, untreated concrete, fairfaced brickwork; self-finished insulating materials forming roof lining.

7.2 Lavatories

For sanitary accommodation see Chapter 3. A first aid facility is normally provided in conjunction with this.

7.3 Canteens

Staff are not allowed to eat in dirty or dusty surroundings. If the process demands a clean environment the reverse may apply, and the importation of food into the working area may need to be discouraged. Canteens are therefore nearly always now provided. See Chapter 34 for details of design.

8 BIBLIOGRAPHY

Workplace (Health, Safety and Welfare) Regulations 1992 The Regulatory Reform (Fire Safety) Order 2005.

Building Regulations 2000 (Consolidated) and The Building (Approved Inspectors etc.) Regulations 2000 (Consolidated).

LPCB, Red Book, Volume 1: List of Approved Fire and Security Products and Services, Volume 2: Directory of Listed Companies, Construction Products, and Environmental Profiles & Assessments FM Global Guides, Data Sheets, Equipment Hazards, Fire Prevention and Control, Fire Fighting and Fire Service, Hot Work, Human Factors, Natural hazards, Property Loss Prevention Solutions, Property Protection.

Jit Factory Revolution: A Pictorial Guide to Factory Design of the Future, Hiroyuki Hirano, Productivity Press.

25 Industrial storage buildings

Jolyon Drury, updated with advice from Stephen George & partners

CI/SFB 284

The Jolyon Drury Consultancy advises on the design of production, distribution and storage systems and facilities.

KEY POINTS:
- *Modern warehouses need the height to use mechanical aids at maximum efficiency*
- *Scales have increased massively; a 'big shed' now is ten times the size of the largest building only 20 years ago*

Contents

1 Introduction
2 Identification of warehouse and storage types
3 Preliminary decisions
4 Height, area and type of handling system
5 Storage method
6 Disposition of the racking
7 Relationship of storage method, mechanical handling equipment and building height
8 Outline specification
9 Security
10 Handling equipment
11 Fire precautions
12 Bibliography

1 INTRODUCTION

Few industrial storage buildings are designed to make a profit (steel stockholders and cash and carry stores are exceptions); the majority perform the function of a valve or pipeline, limiting the supply of a product to suit demand, to stabilise prices and allow steady and economic manufacture within fluctuating market conditions. Industrial storage is therefore a service at a cost that must be minimised.

The payback period most frequently chosen for such a building is 25 years. During that time, it is likely that the storage method will need to change at least three times, and that the type of goods handled will change even more frequently. Flexibility for expansion and manner of use are therefore important design considerations.

Large distribution buildings are now even larger than they have ever been. Twenty-five years ago, a large industrial 'shed' contained approximately 100 000 ft^2 of space. Industrial storage buildings are now being constructed 10 times that size.

At the time of writing, industrial storage buildings cost approximately £32 per square foot to build (£336 per square metre). This price regime and changes to building regulations (Part L in particular) may well make the purchase and reinvention (through recladding, etc.) of an existing building unviable, i.e. it would be cost effective to construct a new building.

2 IDENTIFICATION OF WAREHOUSE AND STORAGE TYPES

The three main types are:

- Transit between manufacture and the market, Figure 25.1.
- Distribution: similar to a transit unit, but accepts a wide variety of goods from a number of manufacturers, sorts them into orders and distributes them to a number of outlets, Figure 25.2. A components warehouse for a factory performs a similar function.

- Repository: a warehouse used for stockholding, either as a service (e.g. a furniture repository) or within a company (e.g. a cold store), Figure 25.3.

3 PRELIMINARY DECISIONS

The initial decision about what type of building is required will involve a choice between these three types, dependent on the client organisation's needs. Such a study is generally undertaken in cooperation with a specialist consultant. Other factors to be considered at the pre-design stage are:

1 The orientation of the loading bays and the heavy vehicle marshalling areas. Future expansion must be taken into account.
2 The orientation of the goods sorting and load accumulation areas which must be related to the disposition of the storage area, i.e. block stacks or racking and loading bays.

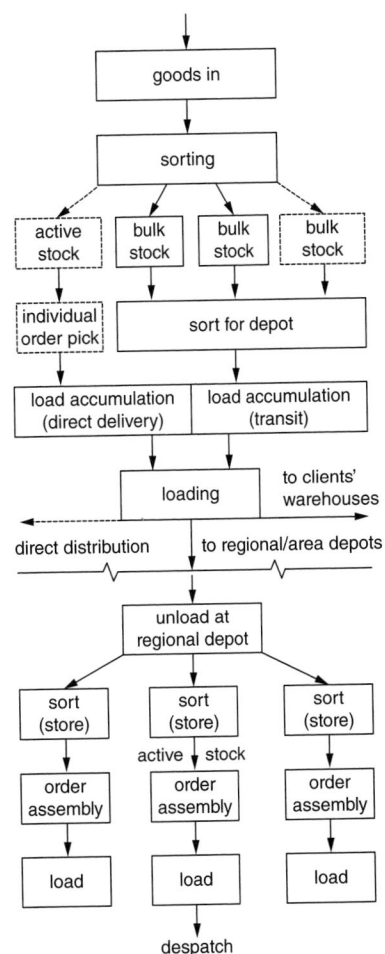

25.1 *Relationships in warehouse for transit between manufacturer and market*

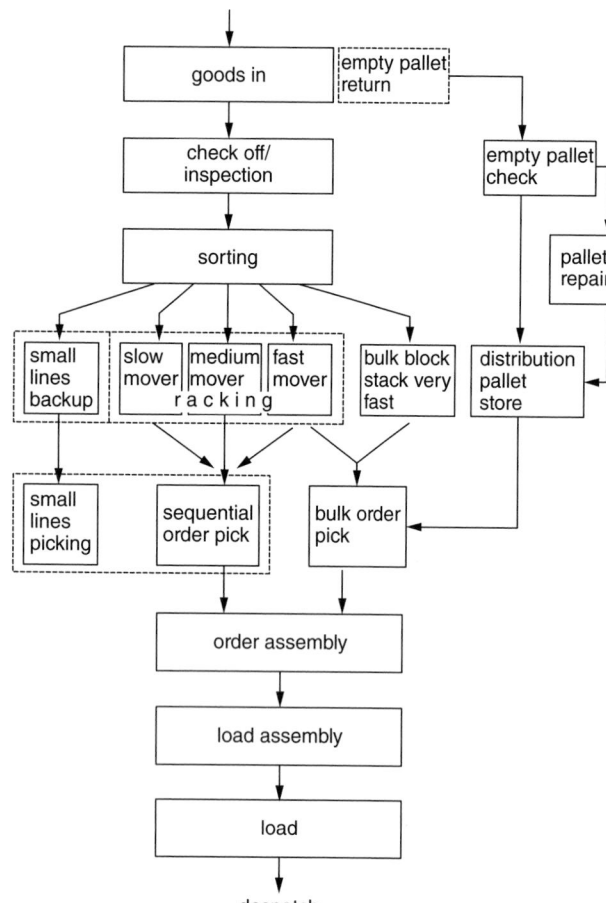

25.2 *Relationships in distribution warehouse*

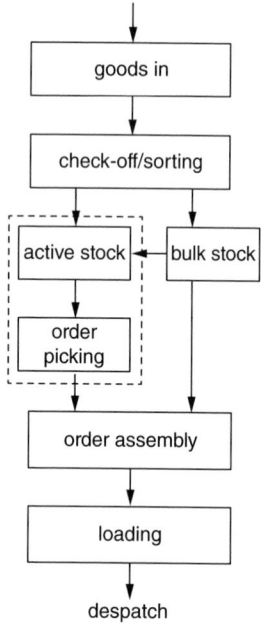

25.3 *Relationships in a stockholding warehouse. The bulk stock area is dominant*

3 Will the required bulk of the building be acceptable in terms of planning consent?
4 Are the existing roads suitable to meet increased demand?
5 Is there public transport for operatives?
6 Are there night operating restrictions which will entail special features to muffle night noise? Can this be catered for by any design measures/configurations?

4 HEIGHT, AREA AND TYPE OF HANDLING SYSTEM

The most economical way of gaining volume for storage is to use height – Table I; this affects the choice of the handling system to be employed. Typical structures are shown in Figure 25.4. Consider also:

- The type of unit load to be handled and the physical characteristic of the goods – crushability, durability, the type of unit loads that will be assembled after sorting (Table II).
- The speed of turnover. This will determine what storage method is the most efficient.
- The position of the construction and movement joints within a concrete floor. Generally, columns should be hidden within the racking, as should the floor joints. Access widths should suit the selected loading mechanisms and racking should not obscure exits. In a portal frame construction, columns are typically set at 32.2 m centres. A grid of 8.2 m can accommodate two dock levellers.

Table I Typical internal clear heights for storage areas

Minimum clear internal height* (m)	Type of storage
5–5.5	Minimum-cost low-rise block stacking warehouse. Suitable for light industrial factory use
7.5	Minimum for any industrial storage building combining racking and block stacking
9+	When narrow-aisle trucks are used
15–30	Fully automatic, computer-controlled warehouses and stacker cranes are to be used

*Clearance for structural members, sprinklers, lighting must be added to obtain overall height of buildings

Table II Classification of materials for handling and storage as unit loads

Description	Examples	Storage method
Materials not strong enough to withstand crushing – not suitable as integral unit load	Automobile components, made-up textiles, electrical appliance components, manufacturing chemists' sundries, light engineering products, glassware	On pallet in rack
Materials strong enough to withstand crushing – suitable for unit loads	Casks and drums, sawn and machined timber, sheet materials	On pallet, or self-palletised and block stowed
Irregular-shaped materials, strong in themselves suitably packed into unit loads	Goods in cases, creates or cartons	On post pallets and stacked, on pallets in rack or self palletised
Bagged materials which form a flat surface under load	Grain, powder and similar	On pallet and block stowed
Bagged materials which do not form a flat surface under load or will not take pressure	Forgings, moulded or machined parts, nuts and bolts	On pallet in rack
Large irregular loose materials	Moulded plastics; sheet metal pressings	On post pallets and stacked
Small irregular loose materials	Machined and moulded parts, pressings, forgings	In cage pallets and stacked
Materials hot from production process	Castings and forgings	On post pallets and stacked
Materials too long to be handled other than by side loader or boom	Steel sections, tubes, timber	Horizontally in tube or bar racks
Materials strong enough to withstand crushing but subject to damage	Partly machined automotive parts, painted finished materials, books	Steel box pallets with special partitions
Perishable goods	Frozen meat, vegetables, drink	Cartons, soft packs pallets, box pallets, etc.

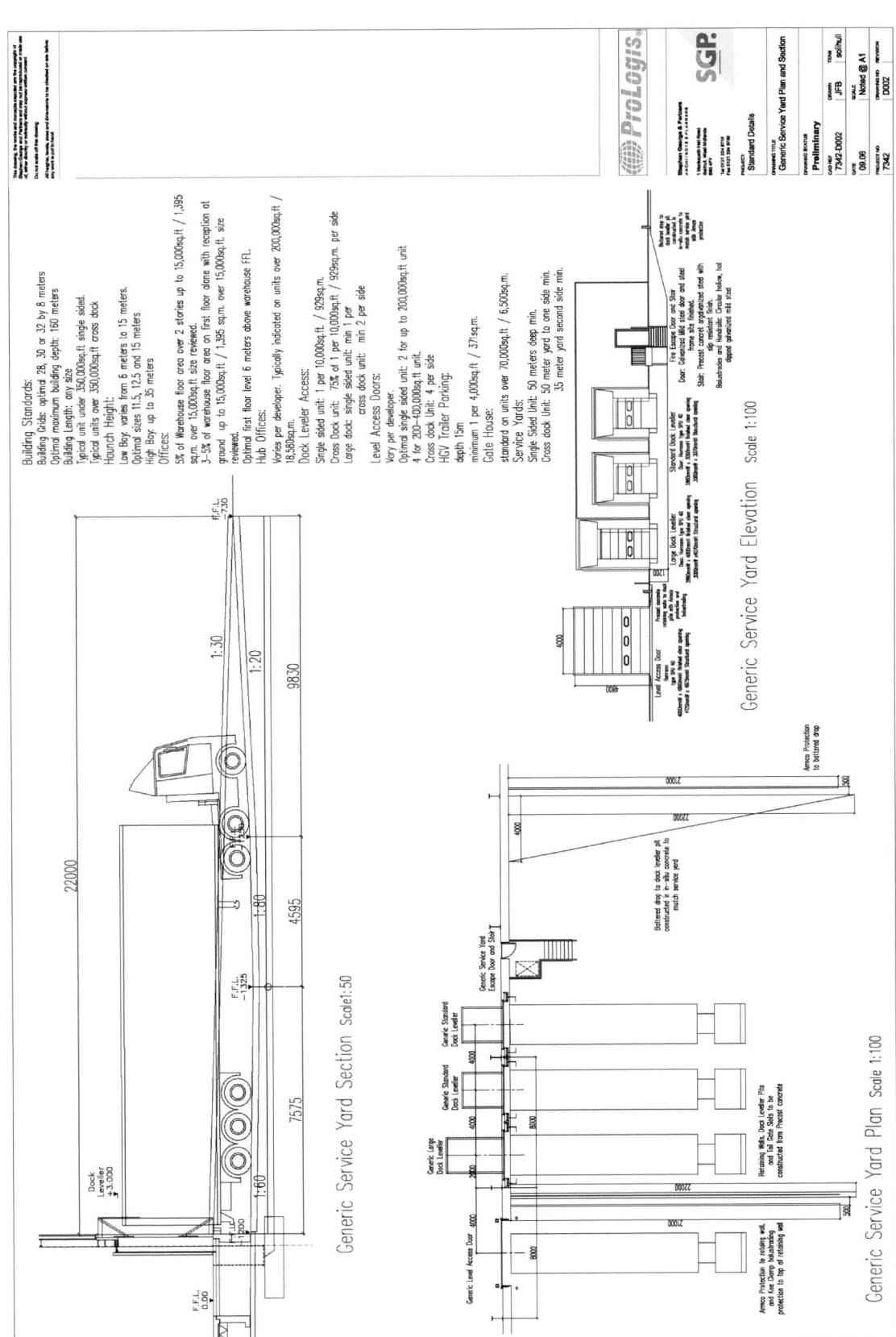

a Generic service yard section and elevation

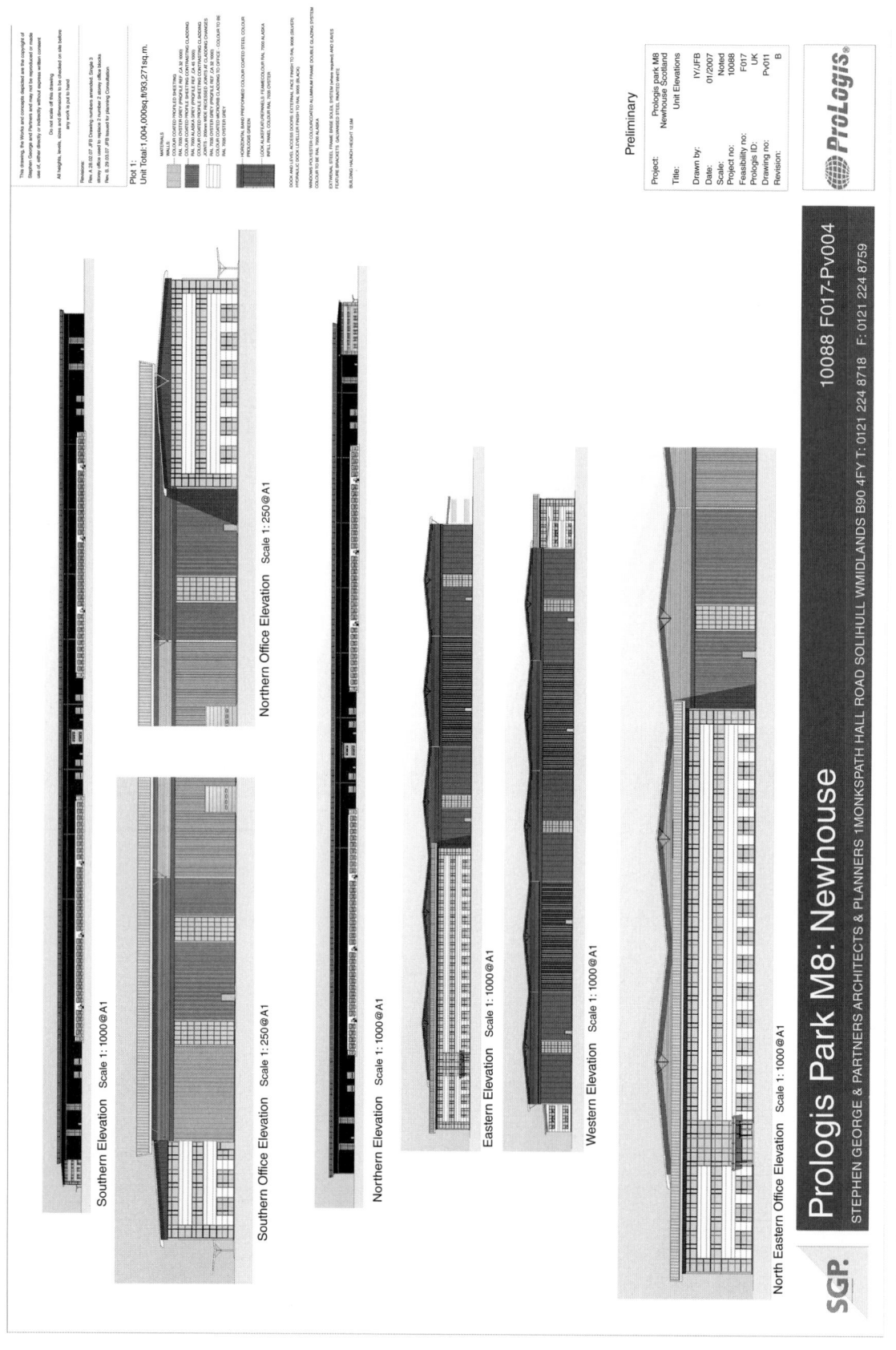

b *Modern 'big box' warehousing – 520 × 170 m industrial storage unit for ProLogis by Stephen George & Partners. The unit contains 78 loading bays on its northern and southern sides, with 5000 m² of office space*

25.4 *Examples of typical structures*

Table III Mechanical handling

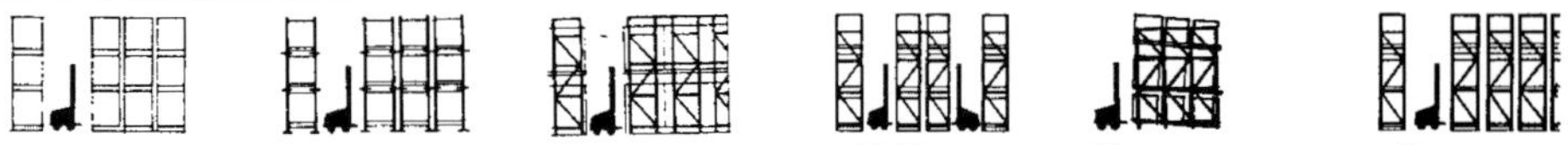

	Block stacking	Post pallets	Drive-in racking	Beam pallet racking	Gravity live storage	Powered mobile racking
Cubic space utilisation (%)	100	90	65	35–50	80	80
Effective use of installation capacity (%)	75	75	75	100	70	100
Accessibility of unit loads (%)	10	10	30	100	30	100
Order picking (%)	Poor	30	30	100	30	100
Speed of throughput	Fastest	Good	Poor	Good	Good	Quite good
Load crushing	Bad	Nil	Nil	Nil	Some	Nil
Stability of load	Poor	Fair	Good	Good	Fair	Good
Ease of relocation	Not applicable	Not applicable	Fair	Good	Difficult	Difficult
Speed of installation	Not applicable	Not applicable	Good	Fastest	Fair	Slowest
Rotation of stock	Poor	Poor	Poor	Good	Excellent	Good

Table IV Manual handling

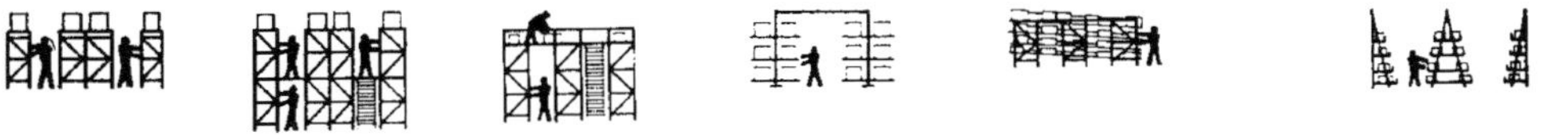

	Long-span Shelving	Tiered shelving	Raised storage area	Cantilever shelving	Lightweight live storage	Fir tree racking
Cubic space utilisation (%)	45	45	80	50	65	25
Effective use in installation capacity (%)	95	95	50	100	70	70
Accessibility of goods	Good	Good	Poor	Good	Excellent	Good
Ease of relocation	Good	Fair	Difficult	Fair	Very difficult	Best
Load range (kN/m²)	2–9.5	2–9.5	2.8–11	2–4.7	Up to 0.2 kN/m run of track	2.6–4.4 kN/arm
Speed of picking	Good	Fair	Poor	Good	Very good	Good
Speed of installation	Very good	Good	Fair	Fair	Slowest	Fastest
Rotation of stock	Very good	Good	Poor	Very good	Excellent	Very good

Table V Load mounting

Load mounting	Type of load								
	Heavy unstable load	Flat cards/ sheets	Sacked/ bagged loads	Small unit loads	Drums Reels Barrels	Coils	Casks	Bales	Textile Raw materials
Special cradle with/without pallet	•								
Standard pallet		•	•	•	•	•	•	•	
Flat board pallet + decking supports		•	•		•				
Direct mounting on timber panels		•	•	•		•	•	•	•
Drum supports					•				
Post pallets cage/bin			•	•		•	•		•
Coil supports					•	•			•
Skips/skeds							•		
With skids									

5 STORAGE METHOD

Storage methods (see Tables III–V) include:

1 Very fast throughput involving a limited number of products: block stacking, Figure 25.5, rather than racking. First in, first out, or first in, last out configuration, depending on the shelf life of the goods.
2 A wider variety of goods, but still with fast turnover: drive-in racking, Figure 25.6, or 'live' (roll-through) storage, Figure 25.7. Pallets are placed into racking up to four positions deep, with the pallets' edges resting on runners attached to the rack's uprights. First in, last out. Live racking involves inclined storage lanes. For heavy pallets and shock-sensitive goods, braking and separating equipment can be incorporated.
3 Pallet racking, Figures 25.8 and 25.9. For a wide variety of goods, the speed of throughput decreases. Pallet racking is the solution with a large variety of products, brands or pack sizes. Each pallet is normally allotted a unique position in the racking.

6 DISPOSITION OF THE RACKING

There are two common alternatives:

• The rack is oriented at 90° to the order assembly areas, with the fast turnover stock in the bays nearest to it or
• One complete racking face is oriented along one side of the order assembly area and reserved for very fast-moving stock.

7 RELATIONSHIP OF STORAGE METHOD, MECHANICAL HANDLING EQUIPMENT AND BUILDING HEIGHT

The effect of handling equipment on warehouse section is shown in Figures 25.10–25.13. These factors depend on site conditions:

1 For very constricted sites where a large volume of goods needs to be held high-bay, automated warehouses can prove the most economical solution. Such warehouses have been built up to 30 m high, the racking being used as the roof and wall cladding

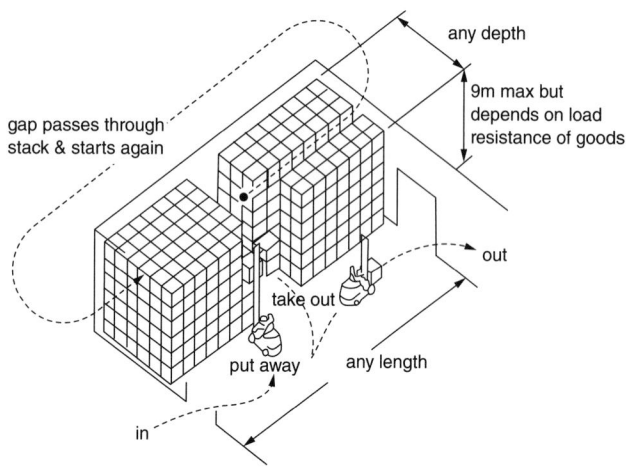

25.5 *Method of block stacking for stock rotation. Where cartons are being stacked on pallets, a height of three pallets is the normal maximum*

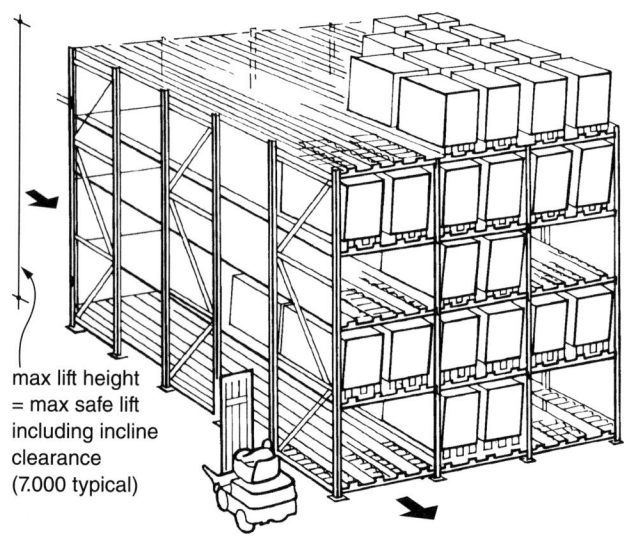

25.7 *Roll-through racking*

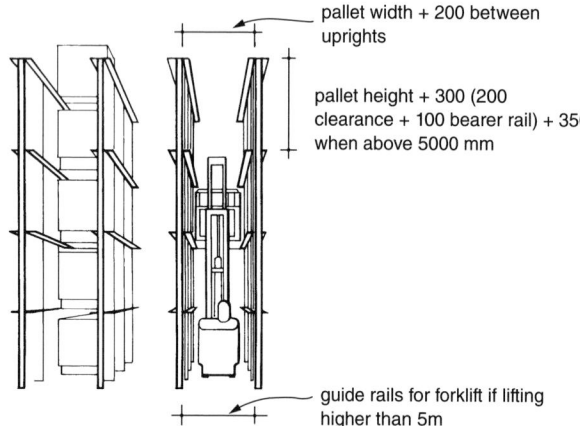

25.6 *Drive-in racking for fork-lift. A maximum depth of six pallets, with fluorescent lighting in the racking structure. Four-pallet depth is preferable*

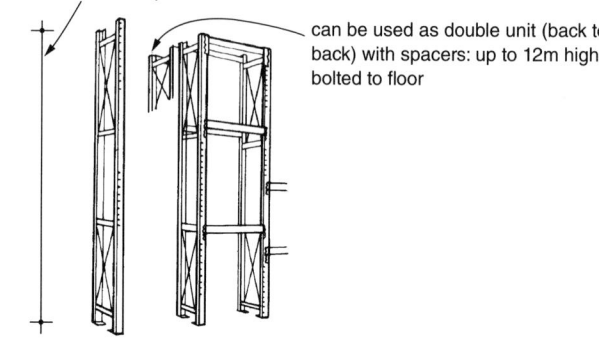

25.8 *Pallet racking*

supporting structure. Handling machines run on fixed tracks, Figures 25.13 and 25.14.

2 For medium- and large-scale installations where full automation is not justified, storage areas up to 12m high allow free-standing racking (bolted to the floor) with aisle widths marginally wider than the largest pallet, Figure 25.15. 'Narrow-aisle trucks' used in this type of plant are free path machines based on fork-lift technology, Figure 25.16.

3 Where the cost of high-bay stacking and high-lift machinery is not justified, fork-lifts and reach trucks are used, Figure 25.17. Reach trucks are suitable for conventional pallet weights (1–1.5 tonnes) over flat floors. They can lift to 9 m and operate in aisles of about 2.8 m. A fork-lift truck can carry heavier loads but requires aisles of 3.2–4 m width, Figure 25.18. Heavier trucks are required to lift greater heights and tend to require a greater aisle width.

4 Mobile racking where pallet racking is mounted on mobile bases and rests face to face may be suitable where storage is to be installed in an existing structure or where the site is limited in area and the turnover of products comparatively low. It is costly to install and the floor slab has to accept double the normal distributed load.

8 OUTLINE SPECIFICATION

8.1 Storage area

Pitched roofs, though strong on first cost, waste storage volume and run the risk of being damaged by handling equipment: Three factors favour the flat or low pitch roof type:

- The column pitch can be wide, Figures 25.17 and 25.18.
- They are more adaptable to a change of use or changes dictated by new processes.
- They are more suitable for the installation of services such as cooled air.

8.2 Order picking and assembly

Space demanded will vary with the type of business involved and the method of order assembly, in turn generated by the method of despatch and transport. For instance, a brewery warehouse may despatch whole pallet loads, Figure 25.7, but a pharmaceutical warehouse may handle and assemble a very large number of small items. Therefore, it may require a large area for order assembly, Figures 25.19–25.21.

8.3 Loading bay and load accumulation area

The loading bay is the critical link between the storage and distribution system, Figure 25.22. It usually combines inward and despatch movements. It must provide sufficient space for:

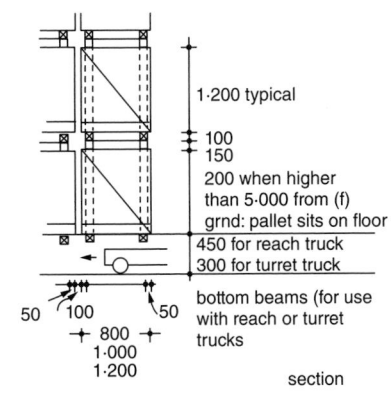

1·200 typical

100
150

200 when higher
than 5·000 from (f)
grnd: pallet sits on floor

450 for reach truck
300 for turret truck

bottom beams (for use
with reach or turret
trucks

50   100   50
800
1·000
1·200

section

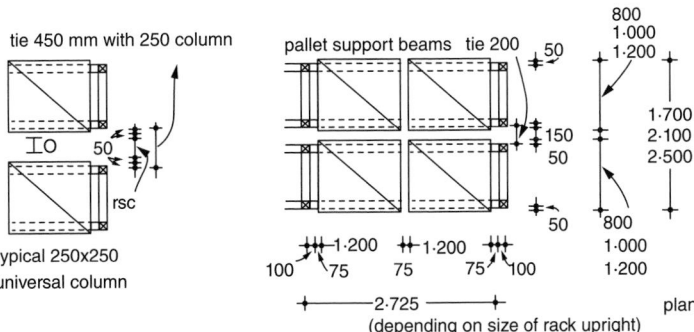

tie 450 mm with 250 column

50

rsc

typical 250x250
universal column

pallet support beams   tie 200   50

150
50

50

100   75   75   100

1·200   1·200

2·725
(depending on size of rack upright)

800
1·000
1·200

1·700
2·100
2·500

800
1·000
1·200

plan

25.9 *Construction of pallet racking*

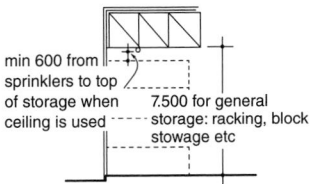

min 600 from
sprinklers to top
of storage when
ceiling is used

7.500 for general
storage: racking, block
stowage etc

25.10 *Section through small warehouse for fork-lift operation*

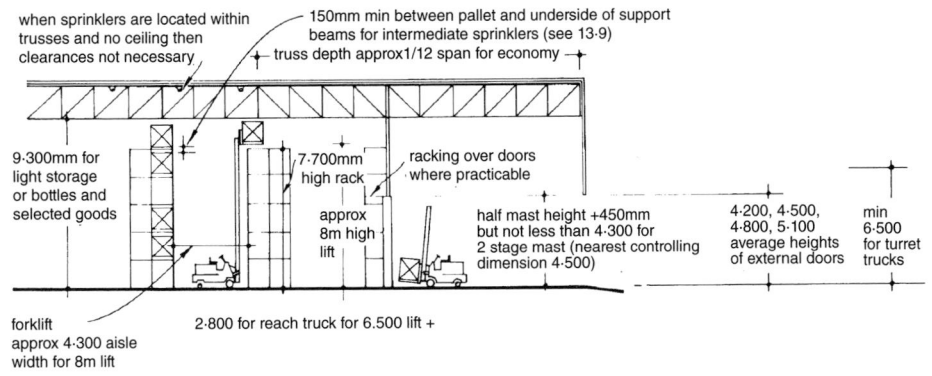

when sprinklers are located within
trusses and no ceiling then
clearances not necessary

150mm min between pallet and underside of support
beams for intermediate sprinklers (see 13·9)

truss depth approx1/12 span for economy

9·300mm for
light storage
or bottles and
selected goods

7·700mm
high rack

approx
8m high
lift

racking over doors
where practicable

half mast height +450mm
but not less than 4·300 for
2 stage mast (nearest controlling
dimension 4·500)

4·200, 4·500,
4·800, 5·100
average heights
of external doors

min
6·500
for turret
trucks

forklift
approx 4·300 aisle
width for 8m lift

2·800 for reach truck for 6.500 lift +

25.11 *Section through large warehouse for fork-lift or reach truck operation*

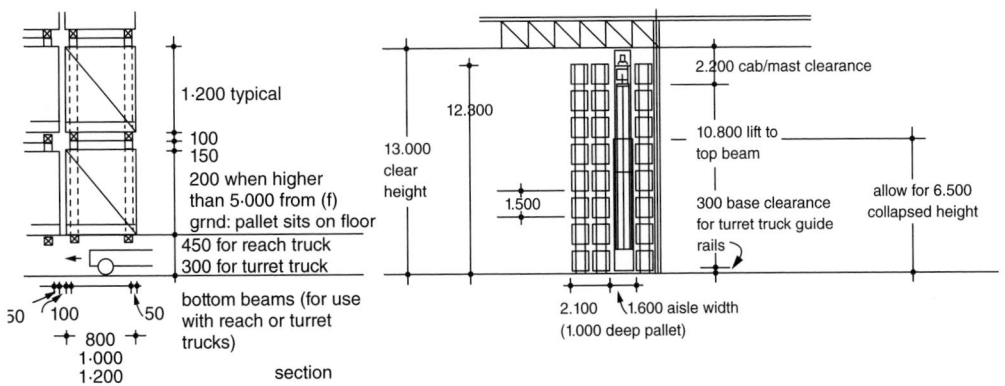

1·200 typical

100
150

200 when higher
than 5·000 from (f)
grnd: pallet sits on floor

450 for reach truck
300 for turret truck

50   100   50
800
1·000
1·200

bottom beams (for use
with reach or turret
trucks)

section

13.000
clear
height

12.300

1.500

2.100   1.600 aisle width
(1.000 deep pallet)

2.200 cab/mast clearance

10.800 lift to
top beam

300 base clearance
for turret truck guide
rails

allow for 6.500
collapsed height

25.12 *Section through warehouse for narrow aisle truck operation. Floor tolerance ±3 mm in 3 m run*

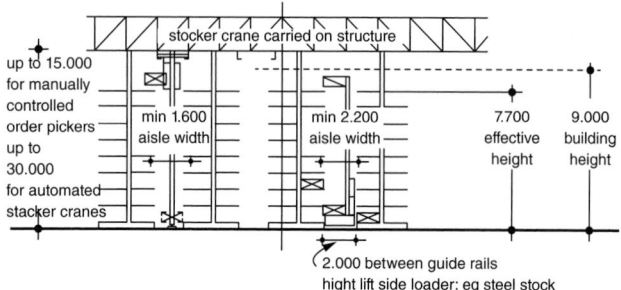

25.13 *Section through warehouse for stacker crane handling (left) and steel stockholding with side loader (right)*

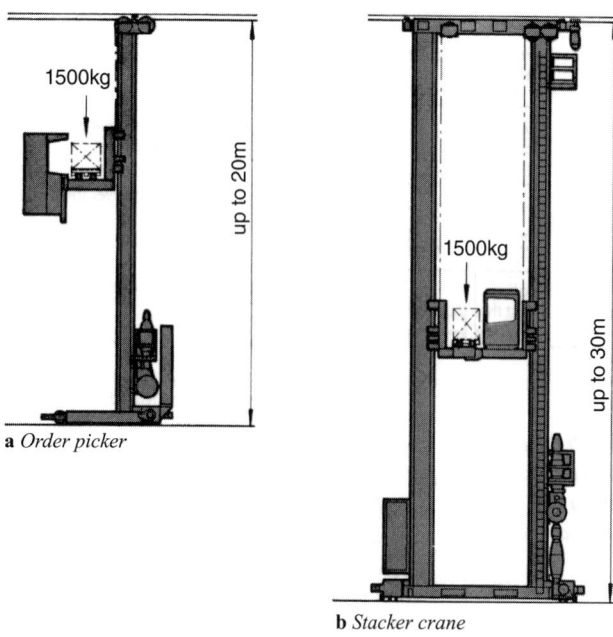

a *Order picker*

b *Stacker crane*

25.14 *Dimensions of: a order picker and b stacker crane*

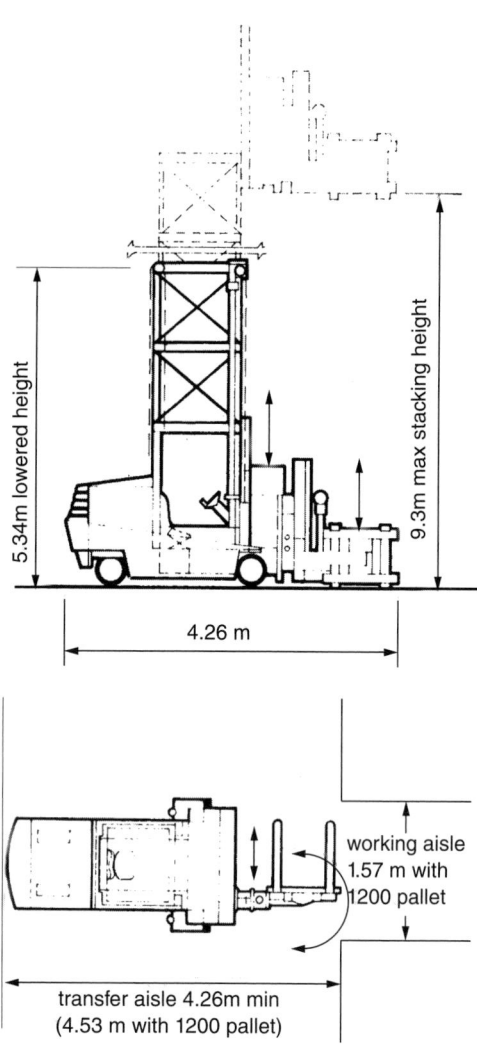

25.15 *Free path stacker/order picker with elevating cab, fixed mast and rotating fork. The four-post mast gives extra stability. Out of the aisle can also be used as a fork-lift truck. The free lift on the fork carriage also allows differential movement between the pallet and the picking platform. Minimum building height 2.2 m above top lifting level*

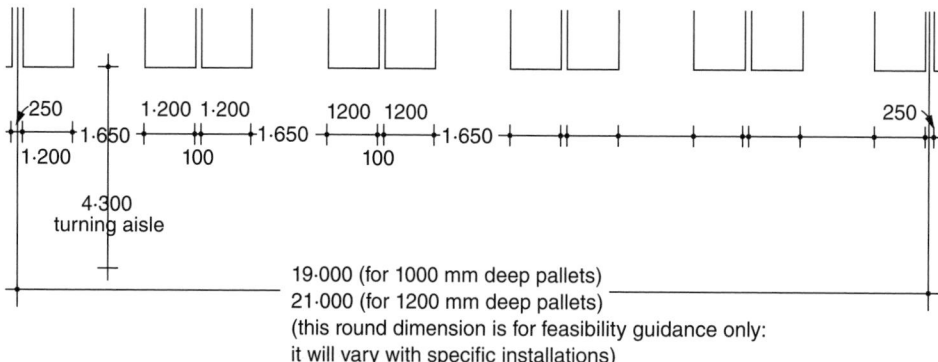

25.16 *Relationship to structure of narrow-aisle truck aisles*

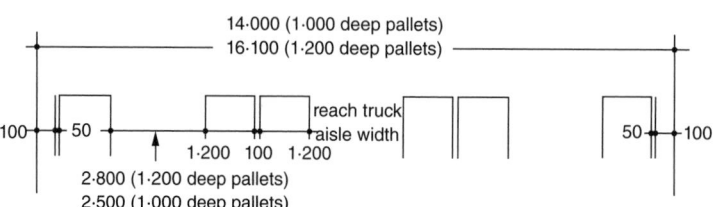

25.17 *Relationship to structure of reach truck aisles*

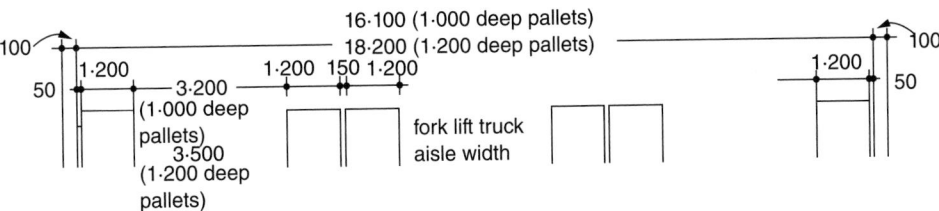

25.18 *Relationship to structure of fork-lift truck aisles. Note: 16100 mm span is common to fork-lift and reach truck requirements*

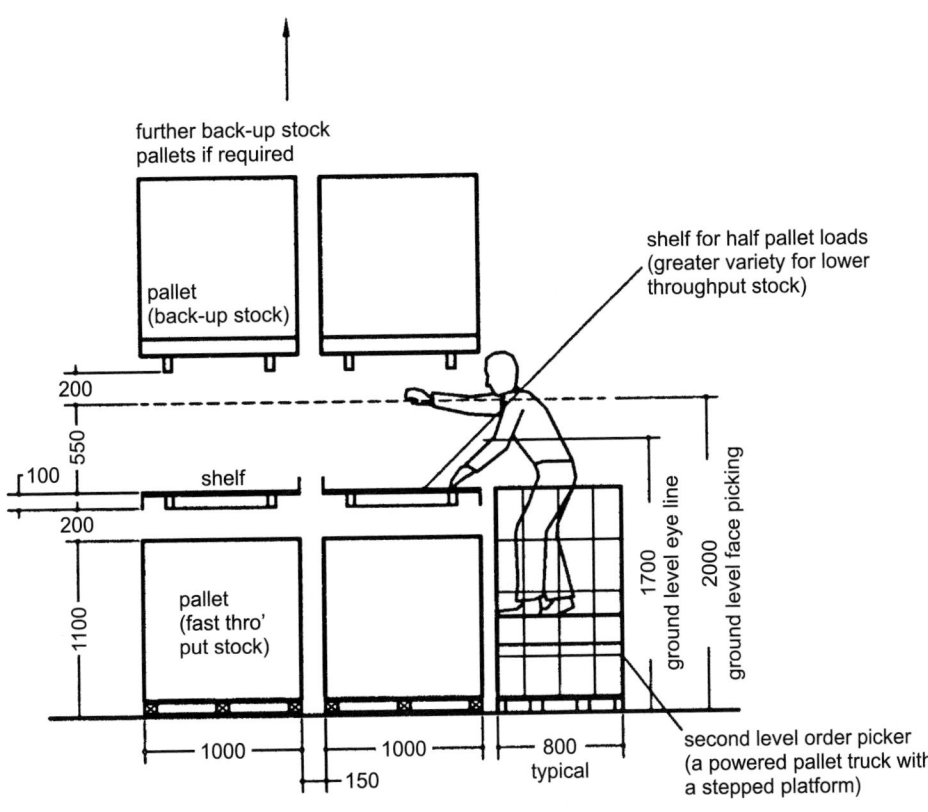

25.19 *Second level order picking, typically used for food distribution and supermarket replenishment. The operative fills a roll pallet or cage from the pallet on the floor and the shelf above it*

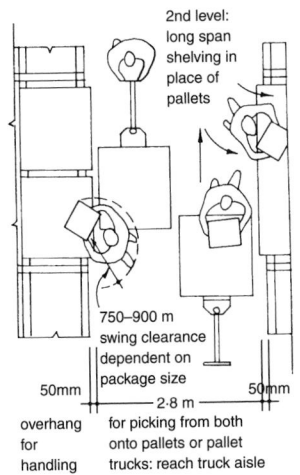

25.20 *Reach truck aisle for second-level order picking*

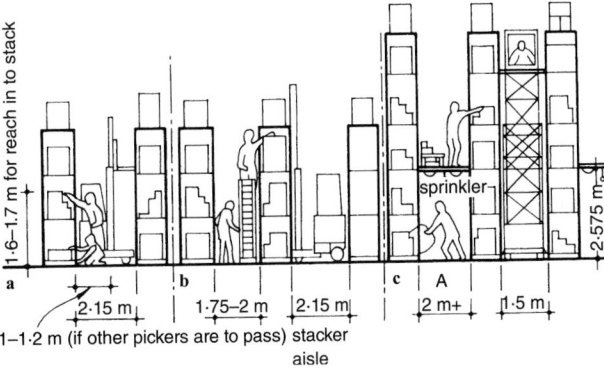

25.21 *Stacker aisles for order picking: a Pulling from lower levels – replenished by stacker truck (Figure 25.25) b Alternating pick-up and replenishment aisles c Multi-level alternative aisles, replenished by narrow aisle truck*

- incoming goods to be checked off;
- empty unit load devices to be removed;
- despatch loads to be accumulated

A full vehicle length (12m) should be allowed as the zone behind the loading dock.

8.4 Office and amenity areas

Large warehouses can employ more than 100 order-picking staff (mainly female) each shift. Extensive washing and changing facilities will be required, also space for operatives to rest and smoke outside the storage area. See BS 6465-1:2006 (which supercedes BS 6465-1:1994) for full details of sanitary installations.

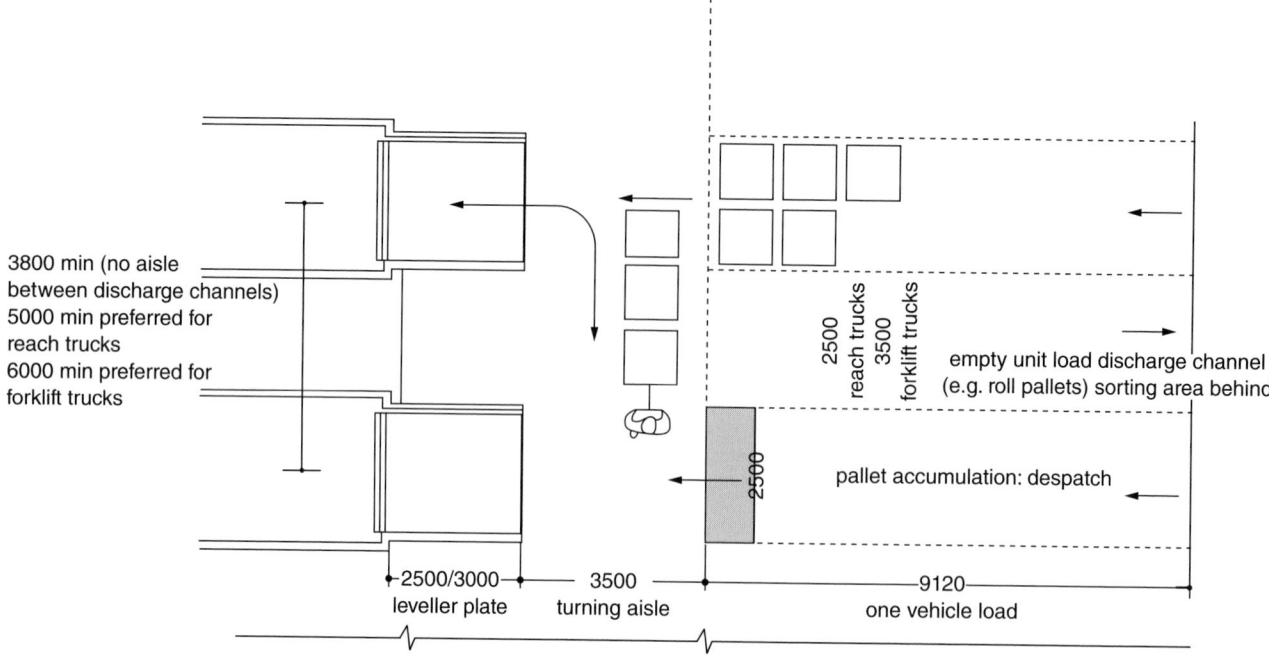

3800 min (no aisle
between discharge channels)
5000 min preferred for
reach trucks
6000 min preferred for
forklift trucks

2500
reach trucks
3500
forklift trucks

2500

empty unit load discharge channel
(e.g. roll pallets) sorting area behind

pallet accumulation: despatch

2500/3000
leveller plate

3500
turning aisle

9120
one vehicle load

a *Where available*

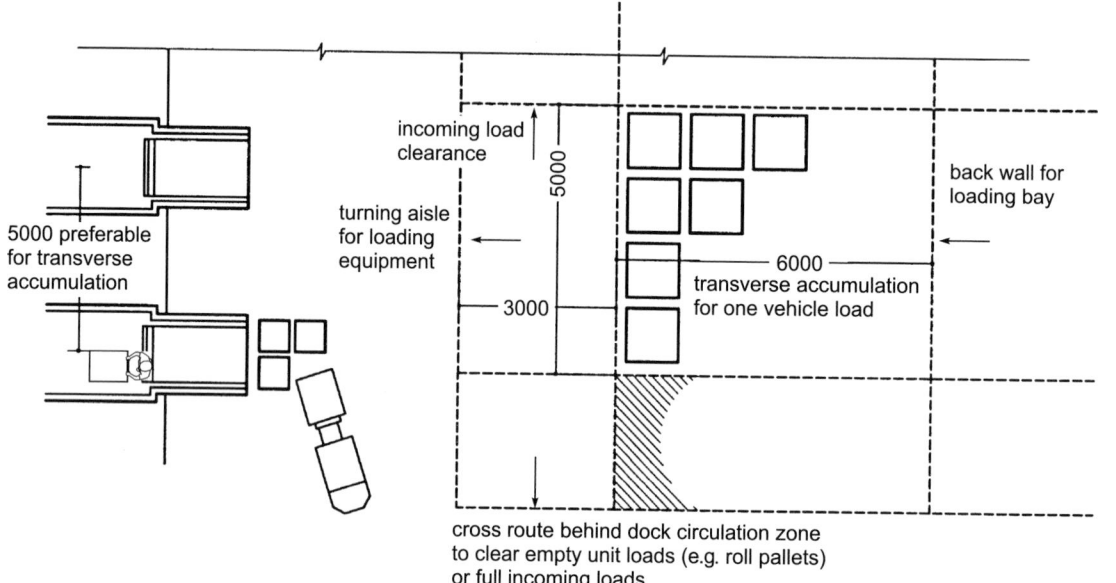

incoming load
clearance

5000

back wall for
loading bay

5000 preferable
for transverse
accumulation

turning aisle
for loading
equipment

3000

6000
transverse accumulation
for one vehicle load

cross route behind dock circulation zone
to clear empty unit loads (e.g. roll pallets)
or full incoming loads

b *Where depth is limited*

25.22 *Combined arrival/despatch loading bays*

Clients and developers generally prefer the office element of a distribution building to face the main entrance to the site, leaving loading/unloading at the rear. If this means offices facing south (taking advantage of sunshine) it may mean fixing brise soleil to the facade.

8.5 Equipment maintenance areas

Most mechanical handling equipment for internal use is battery-powered electric. The batteries need charging at night or after shifts of about 12 h. Requirements for maintenance areas are:

- a distilled water supply;
- tonne hoisting tackle for removing batteries;
- fume extraction;
- acid-resistant floor.

Major services and repairs tend to be done off site.

9 SECURITY

Warehouses are, by definition, prone to theft. Most thefts are carried out during working hours. This can be minimised by ensuring that:

- There is no direct access from loading bays to the warehouse, especially through the order-picking zone, without supervision.
- Access from office accommodation to the warehouse should be visible from the office area.
- The changing rooms, showers (necessary in cold stores) and WCs should not have direct access from the warehouse, and equally, should not be accessible from outside. Visiting drivers should have segregated WC facilities.
- If small, valuable goods are involved, a search room may be required.
- Operatives' parking should be well separated from heavy vehicles' parking and away from the loading area.

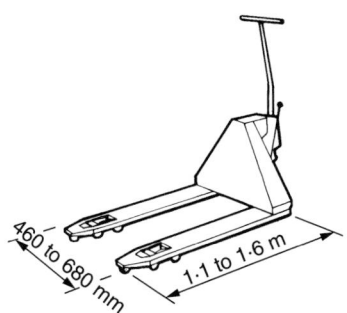

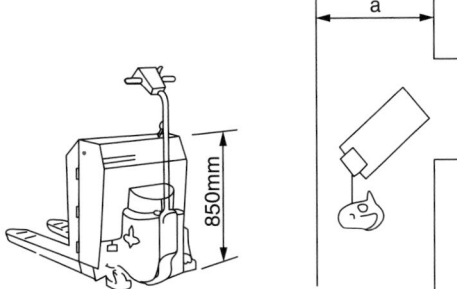

25.23 *Manual pallet truck. For use inside the warehouse building up orders, loading vehicles on raised docks or with tail-lifts, general pallet handling. Increasingly used in retail premises for handling bulk goods. Capacity up to 1500 kg generally and for short-distance travel (operatives soon tire when pushing heavy loads any distance). Forklengths available 0.8–1.6 m, widths from 460 to 680 mm. Heights: lowered 83 mm, raised 203 mm. Pallet width should be 150 mm overfork (typical length is 1.06 m for a 1.2 m pallet). Where gangways are narrow and stability is important, a heavy truck should be used with maximum width between forks. This device will turn in its own length but needs additional clearance for overhangs. Normally, it requires level floors to operate satisfactorily, but large wheels in nylon or with solid rubber tyres plus articulating axles are available for use in older buildings; although instability may occur. Steel wheels are available but are less popular. Where loading ramps are used, pallet trucks with brakes should be used. Adaptors are available for use as a stillage truck*

25.24 *Powered pallet truck. For internal transfer, loading vehicles on docks, order build-up, transporting roll pallets to load assembly position. For use with all types of pallet and cages. Capacity 1800–3000 kg, forklengths 0.75–1.8 m, speeds up to 3.6 km/h running light, widths up to 850 mm, usually 760 mm. Long forks available to carry three roll pallets at once. Special forks for drums and paper rolls. Will turn in its own length but needs additional clearance for overhangs. Some have 200° turn on the single power steering wheel. Aisle width depends on forklength:*

a *(90° stacking aisle) = 1840 mm (truck + 1 m pallet)*
b *(intersecting aisle) = 1570 mm*

Turning circle 1.78 m radius with 960 mm long forks. This device requires level floors and a three-phase charging point. It can manage ramps up to 10%. Some larger-capacity units can also be ridden on, and can tow non-powered pallet trucks if long distances are involved

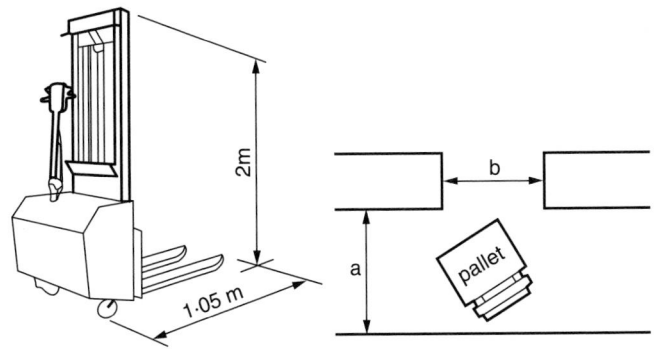

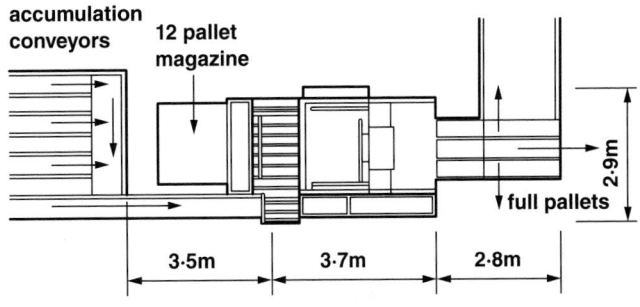

25.27 *Plan of typical palletising machine. Top right is buffer track required for slower shrink wrapper*

25.25 *Power travel and lift pedestrian-controlled stacker truck. When travelling the pallet rests on the stacker frame which has travel wheels. Power lifting is independent of the travel frame, and is directly into the rack. Only suitable for short travel distances. Lifting range up to 3.6 m. Can be supplied with attachments. Capacity up to 1500 kg at 600 mm centres, straddle width 0.86–1.3 m, travel speed up to 4.8 km/h laden. Will turn with full load on 2.1 m aisle*

10 HANDLING EQUIPMENT

Goods handling systems are now highly specialised and only their general layout falls into the architectural remit. Computerised and robotic handling systems, controlled from a central database, can represent half the build cost.

Some typical handling equipment is shown in Figures 25.23–25.27.

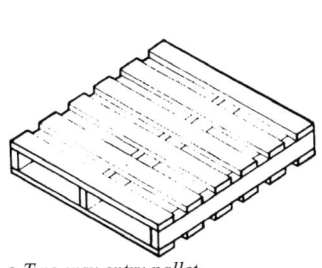

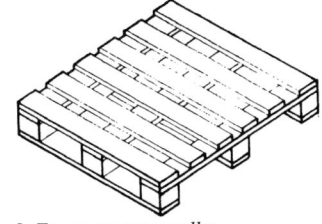
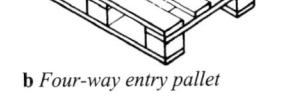

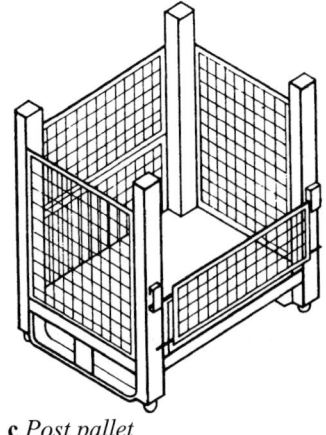

a *Two-way entry pallet*   **b** *Four-way entry pallet*   **c** *Post pallet*

25.26 *Types of pallet*

11 FIRE PRECAUTIONS

It is worth remembering that the goods stored within a building may be worth more than the building itself. Therefore, it may be worth considering the protection of the goods rather than the building – indeed, this may be a crucial part of the operator's business plan. Compartmentalisation and the judicious arrangement of sprinklers may need to be considered.

Table 12 of Approved Document B (Fire Safety), which came into effect April 2007, provides details about compartment sizes. If a building is fitted with sprinklers throughout, there is no need to compartmentalise; if a decision has been taken to dispense with sprinklers, then buildings must be compartmentalised. Each compartment must be no larger than 20 000 cubic metres and no higher than 18 m. In high bay buildings (up to 35 m), automatic sprinkler systems must be installed. Note: the more sophisticated and more sequential the sprinkler system, the less potential water damage.

12 BIBLIOGRAPHY

Jolyon Drury and Peter Falconer, *Buildings for Industrial Storage and Distribution*, Elsevier 2003 (2nd edition)

Jürgen Adam, Katharina Hausmann, *Frank Jüttner, Industrial Buildings: A Design Manual.* Birkhäuser, 2004

Approved Document B – Volume 2 – Buildings other than dwellinghouses (2006 Edition). Obtainable as a downloadable PDF from www.planningportal.gov.uk

Approved Document L2A: Conservation of fuel and power (New buildings other than dwellings) (2006 edition). Obtainable as a downloadable PDF from www.planningportal.gov.uk

26 Laboratories

Catherine Nikolaou and Neville Surti

Catherine Nikolaou and Neville Surti are both associates at Sheppard Robson Architects specialising in the design of laboratory facilities

KEY POINTS:
- *A modern laboratory should provide a stable environment for the production and replication of scientific data as well as adding value by considering flexibility and interaction via good space utilisation and planning*
- *Working collaboratively with key stakeholders in the production of a robust set of requirements for each space ensures a proper understanding of the activities undertaken and therefore the reduction of risks and hazards through design*

Contents

1 Introduction
2 Laboratory layout guidance
3 Space organisation
4 Environment
5 Case studies
6 Bibliography

1 INTRODUCTION

1.1 Definition

A laboratory is a facility which provides controlled conditions in which scientific methods including research, development and analysis may be performed and/or taught.

1.2 Scope

There is great diversity amongst laboratories; however, many commonalities are found in their architecture and engineering. This section of the handbook provides an indication of the basic requirements specific to a broadly representative range of laboratory facilities (the scope is far too extensive to cover in any detail in this document). The information provided relates primarily to bench-scale laboratories, focusing mainly on the commonalities and provides guidance for their planning and design. The figures presented are based on average requirements. Specific needs, ascertained through detailed briefing with the client, may vary these figures.

Whilst this section provides information on the design of new facilities, the broad principles can also be applied to renovation/refurbishment projects. In these instances, compromises may need to be made due to space restraints and operational procedures may have to be put in place to compensate.

1.3 Laboratory types and sectors

In this handbook, laboratories are grouped into two main types, wet and dry, all of which incorporate various scientific disciplines and work processes.

Wet laboratories: utilise, test and analyse chemicals, drugs or other material/biological matter. They typically require piped services (including water, specialised utilities) and ventilation, e.g. chemical science, biomedical laboratories.

Dry laboratories: contain dry stored materials, electronics and/or large instruments. They typically require some piped services, accurate temperature and humidity control, dust control and clean power, e.g. analytical, engineering laboratories.

Teaching laboratories may be wet or dry laboratories or a combination of both but they differ in that they *teach* scientific method.

They can be found in primary, secondary schools and higher education.

1.4 Sectors

Laboratories can be found in private, public or academic sectors.

Private laboratories: focus on research, development and analysis but are usually driven by the need to enhance the operation's profit potential

Public laboratories: focus on research, development and analysis specifically in the public's interest. They are in many respects similar to those of the private sector.

Academic laboratories (excluding schools): focus on teaching laboratory methods and include laboratories that engage in generating research within an academic institution. They may be privately or publicly funded. School laboratories focus on teaching science as set out in their curriculum and include laboratories that engage with other subjects such as design, technology and food studies.

Laboratories (excluding schools) are typically part of a facility which may include various space types such as:

- Reception/lobby
- Office/write-up
- Auditorium/conference/seminar/meeting
- Social/interaction
- General storage
- Library
- Food service
- Child care
- Clinic/health unit
- Physical fitness (exercise room)
- Joint use retail
- Loading dock
- Parking.

In the past, private sector facilities were more expensive and larger than government or academic facilities as commercial concerns need to produce a constant flow of discoveries that can be taken to market. Consequently, more 'incentives' were provided in the form of state of the art facilities to retain and attract talent. This model has been recently adopted by many academic institutions and smaller research organisations as a result of increasing competition within the industry leading to an improvement in the quality of their facilities as well.

1.5 Environmental conditions

A detailed assessment should be made with the stakeholders and the relevant regulatory authorities to define the environmental conditions and operational practices required for the facility as part of the briefing process and before the design starts, as this will impact on the specification of the laboratory's physical and servicing requirements and its operational costs.

The final form of the facility will also be dictated by the individual site constraints and opportunities for each project and the varied preferences and detailed needs of the stakeholders which are also defined as part of the briefing process.

1.6 Containment

In some laboratories, conditions are no more dangerous than in any other room. In many, however, hazards may be present that need to be contained and/or controlled including (but not limited to):

- Biological/infectious agents (to humans and/or animals)
- Genetically modified organisms
- Poisons/chemicals
- Flammable substances
- Explosives
- Radioactive material
- Magnetic interference
- Moving machinery
- Extreme temperatures
- High voltage

In accordance with legislative requirements, these hazards must be identified and countermeasures or mitigation strategies specific for each facility determined/implemented. Reference should be made to the legislative guidance, approved codes of practice and regulations produced by the law and relevant advisory bodies. Refer to Bibliography.

1.7 Cleanrooms

A laboratory may be designed as a cleanroom facility. A cleanroom is defined as a room in which the concentration of airborne particles is controlled; which is constructed and used in a manner to minimise the introduction, generation and retention of particles inside the room; and in which other relevant parameters such as temperature, humidity and pressure are controlled as necessary. Cleanroom conditions are typically required, for example, in micro and nanoelectronic research.

The grades of cleanroom are defined by the global ISO classification system, EN ISO 14644-1 which classifies ranges from ISO 9 (least clean) to ISO 1 (cleanest). Table I shows how it compares to other international standards in the ranges ISO 3 to ISO 8. Refer to EN ISO 14644-4 for guidance on the design, construction and start-up of cleanrooms.

Table I Comparison of the global ISO cleanroom classification system, EN ISO 14644-1, with other international standards

Standard and Date Published		Classifications					
	ISO 3	ISO 4	ISO 5	ISO 6	ISO 7	ISO 8	
EN ISO 14644-1 (1999)	ISO 3	ISO 4	ISO 5	ISO 6	ISO 7	ISO 8	
US Federal Standard 209D (1988)	1	10	100	1,000	10,000	100,000	
US Federal Standard 209E (1992)	M1.5	M2.5	M3.5	M4.5	M5.5	M6.5	
*EU GMP (1998)	–	–	A/B	–	C	D	

*Good Manufacturing Practice (GMP) is a set of regulations, codes, and guidelines for the manufacture of drugs, medical devices, diagnostic products, foods products and Active Pharmaceutical Ingredients (APIs). 'The Orange Book' (refer to Bibliography) covers most aspects of GMP.

Laboratories may be designed as both cleanroom and containment facilities. For example, some products require a containment level Category 2 to protect the operator and a cleanroom environment of ISO Class 5 to 8 to protect the product. Refer to bibliography for further reference on the design, construction and start-up of combined cleanroom and containment facilities.

2 LABORATORY LAYOUT GUIDANCE

2.1 Key points

The planning and design of modern laboratory facilities should be based on a combination of current best practice and predictions together with recognition of the future needs for flexibility.

Safe and secure: Safety must always be the first concern in laboratory design and what the law requires is to look at what the risks are and to take measures, so far as is reasonably practicable, to tackle them. Securing a facility from unauthorised access is also of critical importance to prevent theft, misuse or, for facilities handling infectious agents, the release of pathogens.

Statistically reproducible data: One of the most fundamental requirements of successful scientific research is to provide statistically reproducible data. The ability to achieve this relies not only on the availability of high quality reproducible material but also on the quality and appropriateness of the controlled physical environment.

Responsive to change: The need for change will result from the continuing and rapid developments in technology/equipment, evolving working methods and procedures and increasingly stringent regulations. It should therefore be a fundamental principle that the basic design of a laboratory allows sufficient flexibility for future changes to be accommodated without the need for major and often costly alterations and with minimum disruption to operations.

Interaction and collaboration: Scientific interaction and collaboration often leads to new inventions, new cures and faster progress. As a result, equipping laboratory facilities with spaces that encourage interaction and collaboration generally enhances the occupant's ability to succeed.

Recruit and retain staff: Because of increasing competition in the scientific field, more effort and money is often invested to recruit and retain the best talent by creating high quality facilities that include attractive environments, state-of-the-art laboratories, extensive amenities and the latest in computer technology. These facilities serve to support employees and enhance user satisfaction, efficiencies and productivity.

Sustainability: Laboratories are typically energy-demanding because of their requirements as highly serviced spaces. In addition, they may have intensive ventilation requirements and must meet health and safety codes which add to energy use. There are however significant opportunities for improving efficiencies while still meeting or exceeding operational and health and safety requirements. The basic objectives are to reduce consumption of non-renewable resources, minimise waste, and create healthy, productive environments. If deemed important, a suitable strategy should be agreed between stakeholders and the design team. Labs 21 (in USA and UK) and Lab 2020 (in Europe) are examples of organisations that provide useful information on sustainability in laboratories.

2.2 Laboratory planning modules

A starting point for the planning and design of many laboratory facilities is the planning module which accommodates basic planning requirements. It should provide adequate space for partitions, benches, floor standing equipment and extract devices and aisles which minimise circulation conflicts/safety hazards. The laboratory module should also be fully coordinated with the architectural and building engineering systems.

The width of a typical laboratory planning module is defined in Table II.

Table II Factors defining the width of a typical laboratory module

Planning requirement	Width (mm)
2 × half wall thickness between module (50mm)	100
2 × clear bench depths (600mm or 900mm)	1200–1800
2 × service spines above bench (200mm)	400
minimum space between benches	1500*
Total module width	**3200–3800 **

*This is the recommended minimum distance which will accommodate the required distance between a bench and a fume cupboard and also requirements for DDA compliance.

**The minimum and maximum figures are largely dependent on equipment requirements. A 3300 mm minimum module width is recommended for most generic laboratory facilities to ensure that a bench and a fume cupboard (nominal 900mm) can be accommodated on either wall.

The length of the module will depend on the unit size of the chosen laboratory furniture, requirements for freestanding equipment and the number of persons that will occupy the space (Figure 26.1); however further flexibility can be achieved by designing a laboratory module that works in both directions. This allows laboratory benches and equipment to be organised in either direction, Figure 26.2a. This concept is more flexible than the basic laboratory module concept but may require a larger building.

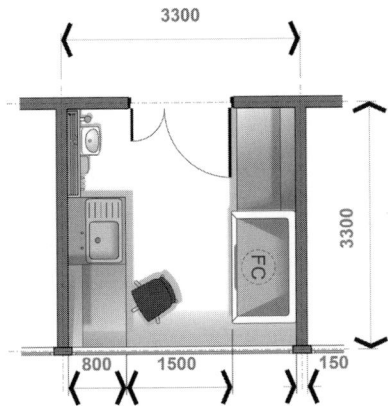

26.1 *The basic planning module. A two-directional laboratory planning module offers maximum flexibility*

2.3 Combining modules
In addition to accommodating the basic and functional spatial requirements, modularity maximises efficiency and the potential for flexibility/adaptability. As modifications are required because of changes in laboratory use, instrumentation or departmental organisation, partitions can be relocated and laboratory units expanded or contracted into larger or smaller units without requiring significant reconstruction of structural or mechanical building elements (Figures 26.2a, 26.2b, 26.2c).

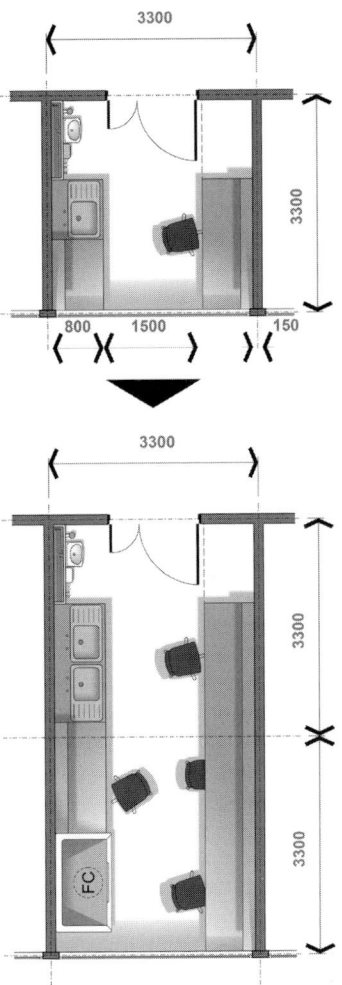

26.2a *The planning module needs to accommodate basic planning requirements for partitions, laboratory benches, equipment, extract devices and circulation in addition to laboratory personnel*

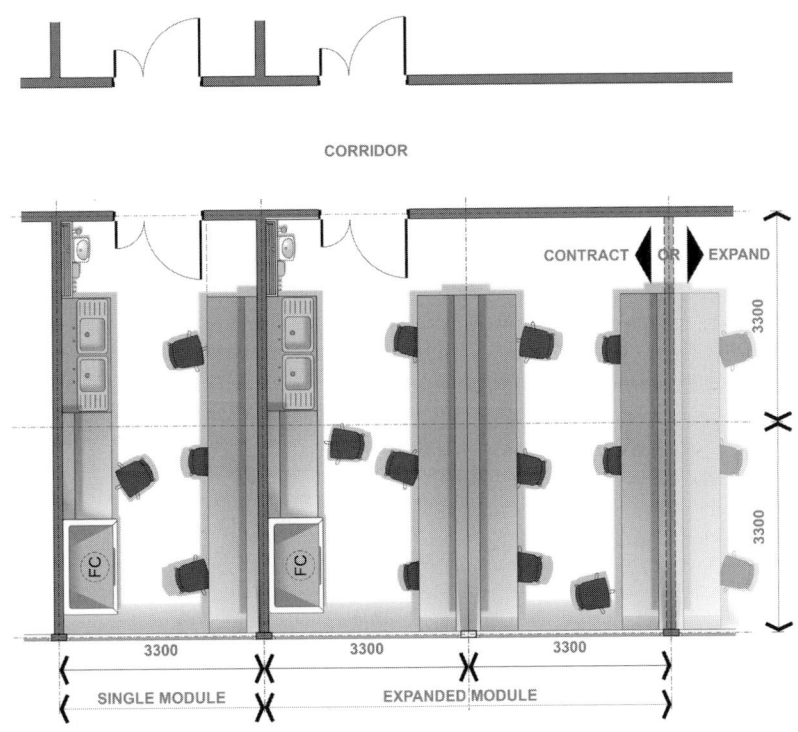

26.2b *Utilising the concept of modularity in laboratory planning to create efficient, flexible and adaptable spaces that can be expanded and contracted to meet changing requirements*

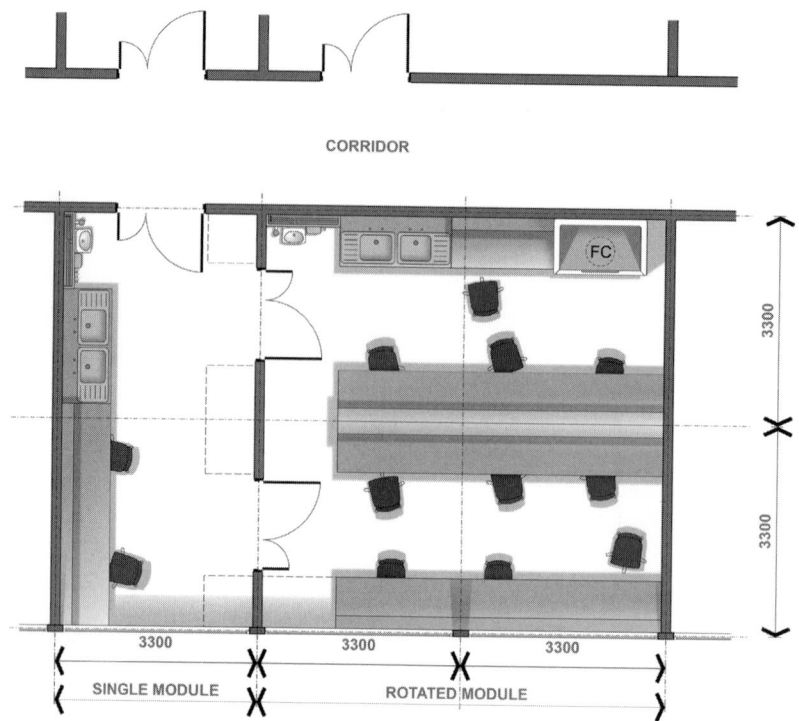

CORRIDOR

3300

3300

3300

3300

3300

3300

SINGLE MODULE   ROTATED MODULE

26.2c *A laboratory module that works in both directions allows laboratory benches and equipment to be organised in either direction*

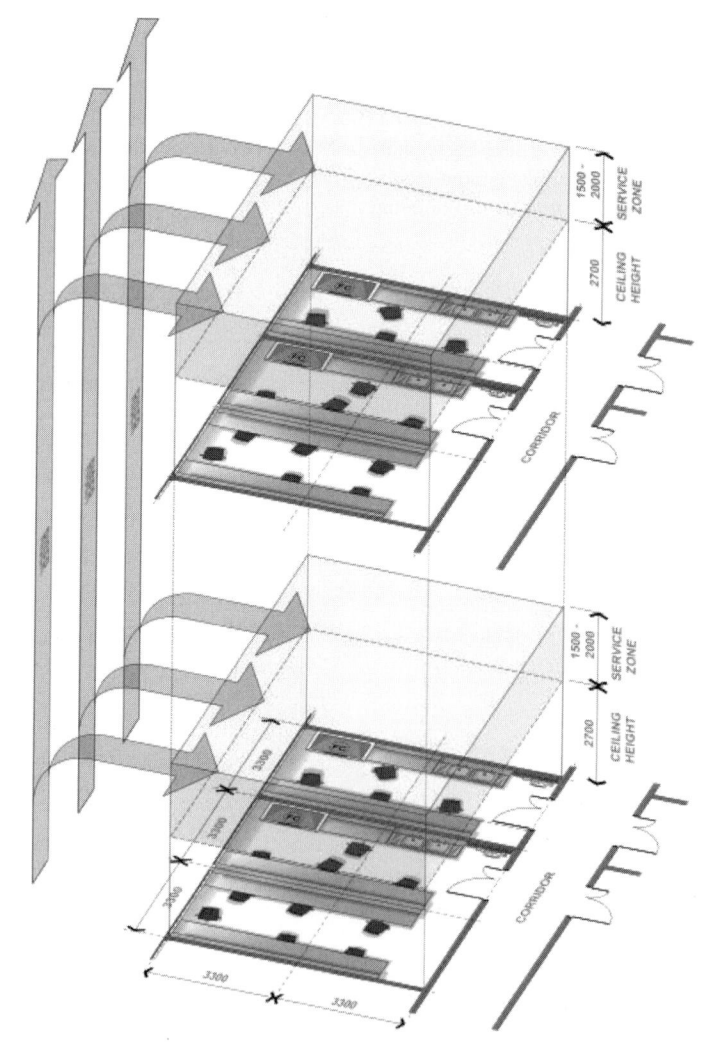

26.3 *Three-dimensional laboratory planning module*

Three-dimensional laboratory module: To create a three-dimensional laboratory module a basic or two-directional module must be defined, all vertical risers including fire stairs, lifts, restrooms and utilities shafts must be fully coordinated (for example, vertically stacked) and the mechanical, electrical and plumbing systems must be coordinated in the ceiling to work with the corridor/circulation arrangements, Figure 26.3. This concept provides the greatest flexibility.

2.4 Structure

Key design issues to consider in evaluating a structural system include:

- ability to coordinate the structure with the laboratory planning modules;
- slab thickness and effective floor to floor height;
- ability to create penetrations for laboratory services in the initial design as well as over the life of the building;
- potential for vertical or horizontal expansion;
- superimposed loads;
- vibration criteria;
- cost.

2.5 Structural grid

The basic laboratory planning module forms a 'template' for the building's structural grid. In most cases the structural grid width equals 2 basic laboratory modules. The structural grid length is determined by not only the basic planning requirements but also the cost effectiveness and functional requirements of the structural system (Figure 26.4).

Ideally, any columns placed on grid should either be incorporated into the design (for example within cores and built out walls or to the perimeter of the laboratory zone) to provide an obstruction free work zone. In addition to columns, all fixed elements of structure, for example floor slabs, braced bays, shear walls, service shafts, lift shafts and staircases, should be planned to minimise constraints on the extension and reconfiguration of the layout (Figures 26.4 and 26.5).

2.6 Floor to floor height

Actual floor to floor heights will need to be determined through thorough discussion with the stakeholders and the needs of the equipment and building services to be incorporated within the space. The issue of flexibility will also need to be reviewed and heights proposed to maximise the future use of the space (Table III, Figure 26.3).

In cases where floor to floors are more restrictive such as refurbishment works in existing buildings and where safety requirements do not require a cleanable suspended ceiling, exposed soffit fixed services could be considered.

Note, however, that the dimensions tabled may be inadequate for specialist equipment (for example cyclotron, MRI, PET/CT Scanners etc.). This requires individual consideration.

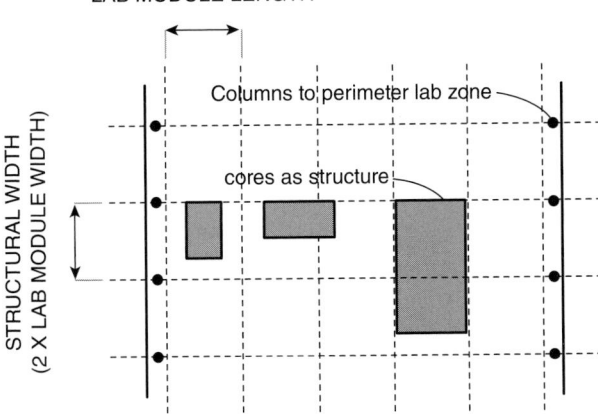

26.4 *The building's structural grid derived from the laboratory planning module, the cost effectiveness and the functional requirements of the structural system. For maximum flexibility, columns should be integrated or placed outside the grid*

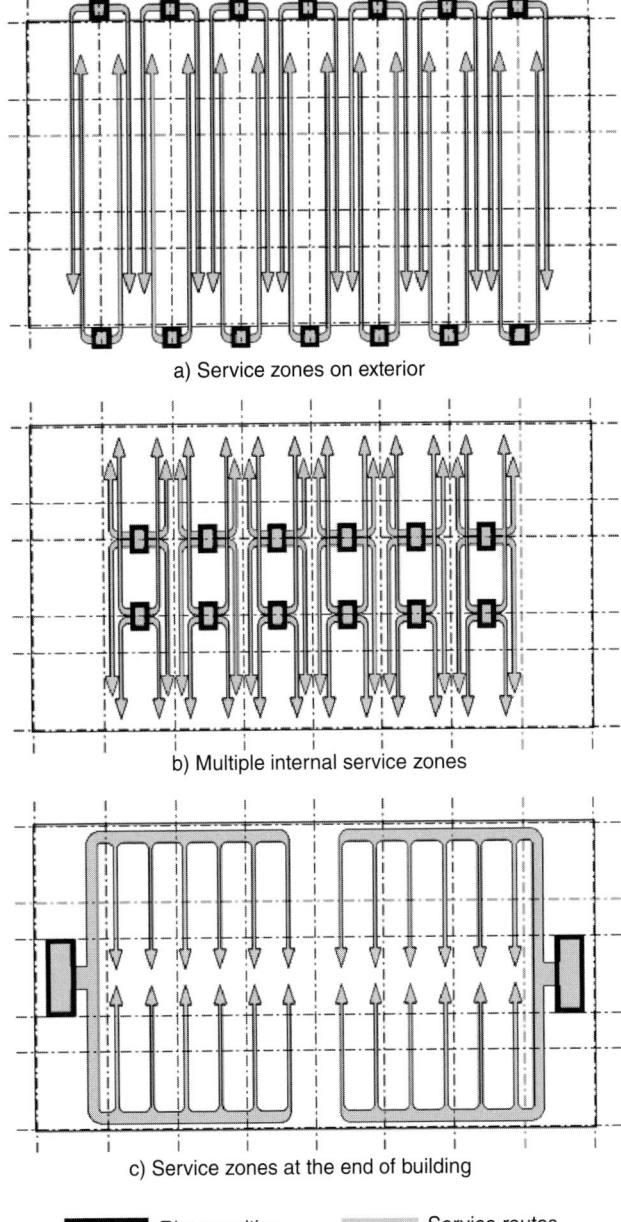

26.5 *Maximising flexibility through the rational placement of fixed elements such as risers*

Table III Effective floor to floor height, minimum and maximum recommended figures

	Height (m)
Minimum ceiling height in laboratories	2.7*
Minimum ceiling void	1.0**
Preferred ceiling void	1.5–2.0**
Slab thickness (nominal allowance)	0.3
Floor to floor height	**4.0–5.0**

*To allow clearance height for extract cabinets.

**To allow adequate depth for the installation of building services. Consider exposed mechanical, electrical and piped systems for easy maintenance access from the laboratory.

Superimposed loads: Structures must be designed in accordance with the appropriate British Standards which will depend on the structural material adopted for the structure. For generic/bench-scale laboratories including equipment and corridors subject to loads greater than from crowds, such as wheeled vehicles, trolleys and similar, design for:

5.0 kN/m² + 1 kN/m² for lightweight partitions

Heavy engineering equipment and rigs such as cyclotron, NMR, electron microscopes etc., are most economically located on ground floors and require individual and separate consideration.

2.7 Vibration

The structural frame system should take into account vibration throughout the laboratory areas where sensitive equipment, balances and microscopes are being utilised. The principal sources of vibration that need to be considered are shown in Table IV.

Note that noise induced vibration is an issue of acoustics requiring specialist input (refer to bibliography). This section deals primarily with human and equipment/plant induced vibrations in more detail.

Vibrations can either be controlled directly through the design of the structure, independently by the use of isolation bearings or damping materials, or a combination of the two. The aim should be to design an economic structure with an appropriate level of vibration response.

Basic techniques that should be utilised where possible to control vibration are listed in Table V.

The accurate selection of vibration criteria and prediction of vibration levels is important in laboratory design because construction costs increase as designed floor vibration levels decrease. Confirmation is also critical as it will significantly impact on slab thickness and weight with consequences to all other aspects of the structure (column sizes, transfer beams, foundations etc.).

Vibration criteria can be determined based on published vibration limits, manufacturer-provided criteria, and subjective tests of vibration-sensitive equipment.

ASHRAE and BBN: The ASHRAE studied the effects of vibration generated by HVAC equipment in buildings and defined criteria widely adopted through the industry. Similarly the BBN developed the VC curves.

Response factors: Vibration levels are referred to in terms of Response Factors (R) where human perception is the primary concern. The R is simply a multiplier on the level of vibration at the average threshold of human perception. Therefore R1 represents

Table IV Sources of vibration

Source	Description
Human induced	occupant activity
Ambient	external sources, surrounding infrastructure e.g. roads, railways
Plant	building services plant
Machinery	laboratory equipment e.g. centrifuges
Airborne	Noise

Table V Basic vibration control techniques

Vibration control	Technique
Building location	Away from traffic, vibration sources
Room location and floor features	Slab-on-grade/stiff floor/isolated floor
Equipment location	Away from centre of bay, motorised equipment
High rigidity and low weight tables/benches	Top honeycomb structures
Direct isolation of equipment	Rubber mounts/air springs/isolators
Active vibration isolation	Piezoelectric/electrodynamic actuators

the magnitude of vibration just perceptible by a human, R2 is twice that and so on.

Root Mean Square Velocity (RMS): In addition to human perception of vibration, in research spaces the vibration response needs to be limited for sensitive equipment such as microscopes, which often drives the design. Equipment manufacturers typically specify vibration limits in terms of RMS velocity (root mean square velocity) as measured in one-third octave bands of frequency over the frequency range of 8 to 100 Hz. This is a measure of average amplitude over a certain period.

Table VI compares both ASHRAE and BBN as well as Response Factors (R). The ISO criteria for human exposure are also shown. Criterion VC-A to VC-E are applicable to laboratory facilities.

Whilst it is a requirement to provide a high level of flexibility, it is normally accepted that to design all parts of the building such that extremely sensitive research equipment can be placed anywhere without further local isolation is not practical. Therefore, a vibration design criterion and design strategy must be adopted that will satisfy the majority of needs, whilst accepting that local isolation devices will be used where a particular item of equipment has more stringent requirements. An economic solution with a defined level of flexibility (agreed with the laboratory user) may be to categorise the vibration response of different areas of the floor using response curves. For example, a maximum rms velocity of 50 micrometers per second may be set as the target at the centre of floor panels. At points close to the columns the criterion would increase to 25 micrometres per second thus allowing more sensitive equipment to be located at the perimeter or column locations.

2.8 Building services

Typically, more than 35–50 per cent of the construction cost of a laboratory building can be attributed to the building services systems (mechanical, electrical and process). Close coordination of these systems is necessary to ensure a flexible, economic and successfully operating facility.

Three common strategies for servicing laboratories are as follows though needs may dictate a combination of any of them:

- Embedded Service Risers
- Sidestitial Service Zone
- Interstitial Floor Service Zone

Embedded service risers: Vertical service risers are located within the building floor plate as required (Figure 26.6). Whilst this option offers the most economical solution, it is also the least flexible with respect to floor planning (Table VII).

Sidestitial service zone: A vertical continuous service zone is located within the length of the laboratory area (Figure 26.7). This option offers good flexibility and maintenance access and is potentially best suited to sites with unsuitable/undesirable views to one side (Table VIII).

Interstitial floor service zone: A complete service floor zone is located either above or between laboratory floors (Figure 26.8). This is potentially the most expensive of the options however it

Table VI Design criteria for sensitive instrumentation and equipment not otherwise vibration-isolated

Criterion Curve	Max. Velocity Level V_{RMS} (µm/s)	Velocity Level (dB) Ref: 0.025µm/s	*Detail Size (µm)	Description of Use
Workshop (ISO2631& BS6472) R=8 ASHRAE J	800	90	N/A	Distinctly feelable vibration. Appropriate to workshops and non-sensitive areas.
Office (ISO2631& BS6472) R=4 ASHRAE I	400	84	N/A	Feelable vibration. Appropriate to offices and non-sensitive areas.
Residential Day (ISO2631& BS6472) R=2 ASHRAE H	200	78	75	Barely feelable vibration. Appropriate to sleep areas in most instances. Probably adequate for computer equipment, probe test equipment and low-power to 20× microscopes.
OP. Theatre (ISO2631& BS6472) R=1 ASHRAE F	100	72	25	Vibration not feelable. Suitable for sensitive sleep areas. Suitable in most instances for microscopes to 100X and for other equipment of low sensitivity.
VC-A (BBN-A or ASHRAE E) R=0.5	50	66	8	Adequate in most instances for optical microscopes to 400X, microbalances, optical balances, proximity and projection aligners etc.
VC-B (BBN-B or ASHRAE D) R=0.25	25	60	3	An appropriate standard for optical microscopes to 1000X, inspection and lithography equipment (including steppers) to 3 micron line widths.
VC-C (BBN-C or ASHRAE C) R=0.125	12.5	54	1	A good standard for most lithography and inspection equipment to 1 micron detail size.
VC-D (BBN-D or ASHRAE B) R=0.0625	6	48	0.3	Suitable in most instances for the most demanding equipment including electron microscopes (TEMs and SEMs) and E-Beam systems, operating to the limits of capability.
VC-E (BBN-E or ASHRAE A) R=0.03125	3	42	0.1	A difficult criterion to achieve in most instances. Assumed to be adequate for the most demanding of sensitive systems including long path, laser-based, small target systems and other systems requiring extraordinary dynamic stability.

*The detail size refers to the line widths for microelectronics fabrication, the particle (cell) size for medical and pharmaceutical research, etc. The values given take into account the observation that the vibration requirements of many items depend upon the detail size of the process.

offers the greatest flexibility and excellent access for maintenance with minimum disruption to the laboratory functions (Table IX).

3 SPACE ORGANISATION

3.1 Definitions

The following definitions apply for the purpose of measurement within research laboratories.

Laboratory worker: A user who is allocated a bench space within the primary laboratory space.

Researcher: A user who is directly involved in scientific work, including staff that may not have an allocated bench space within the primary laboratory space (e.g. staff working predominantly on computer applications or senior staff who may work principally from an office space).

Net Useable Area (NUA): The Net Useable Area (NUA) is the sum of Primary, Secondary and Tertiary space. In laboratories and large open plan spaces (e.g. multi-occupancy offices or grouped write-up spaces) the measurement of secondary circulation spaces as contributing to Net Usable Area or to Balance Area may depend upon the configuration of the spaces and the extent to which circulation space may be considered to contribute to the use of the space, other than exclusively for access and circulation. Schedules and drawings will clearly need to identify which areas have been measured as part of the Balance Area.

NUA = Primary space + Secondary space + Tertiary space

Gross Internal Area (GIA): The Gross Internal Area (GIA) is the sum of Net Usable Area (NUA) and Balance space. The GIA does not include plant areas. The area required for plant rooms is particularly difficult to define at the early stages of design as, depending

Table VII Pros and cons of embedded service risers within the building floor plate

Pros	Cons
Potentially unrestricted views out	Restricted flexibility
Short horizontal service runs within ceiling void	Changes could disrupt adjacent spaces
Least space required out of floor plate	Maintenance access within "clean" environment
Low cost impact	

Table VIII Pros and cons of a sidestitial service zone

Pros	Cons
Good flexibility especially if services are modular	Restricted views on one side
Short horizontal service runs within ceiling void	Medium cost impact
Maintenance access outside "clean" environment	Dedicated zone required out of floor plate

Table IX Pros and cons of an interstitial floor service zone

Pros	Cons
No restrictions to views out	High cost impact
Total flexibility for laboratories above or below	Increased building height
Maintenance access outside "clean" environment	
Limited horizontal service runs within ceiling void	

on requirements, this could be anything between 25–100 per cent of the laboratory floor area. Therefore comparative data is more useful if plant rooms are excluded from Balance & GIA.

GIA = NUA + Balance space

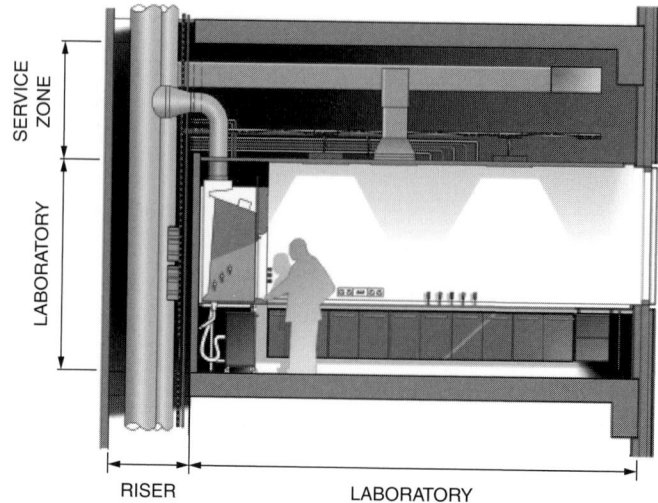

26.6 *Embedded service risers within the building floor plate*

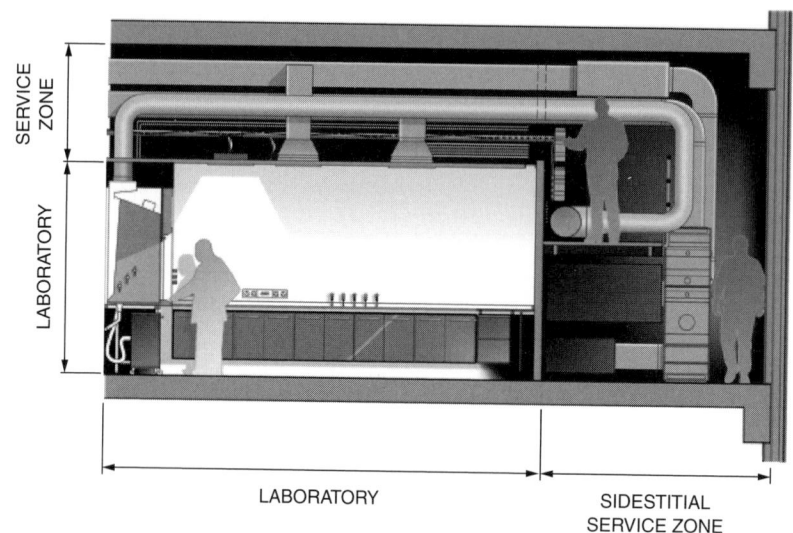

26.7 *Sidestitial service zone*

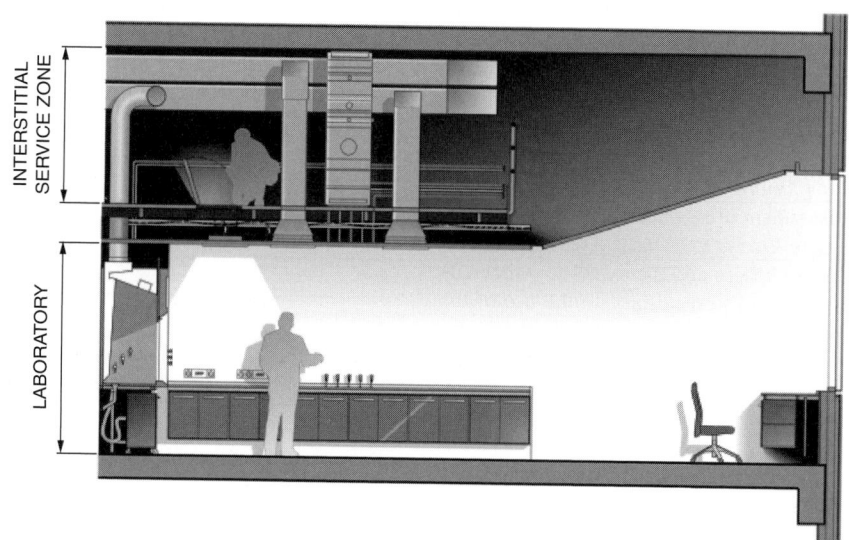

26.8 *Interstitial floor service zone*

3.2 Space designation (academic teaching)

In primary schools, science is regarded as one of the specialist practical activities in the curriculum and generally utilises a space that could also be used to teach design and technology (including food) and art. This space can either be a stand-alone discrete room or an open bay within a standard classroom. The base requirements for these spaces are a sink, washable floor and furniture for 'wet' practical activities.

In secondary schools, laboratories are generally located as suites. In addition to the laboratories, non-teaching support spaces are required such as preparation and storage areas. These areas would also provide a departmental staff base with space for the secure storage of pupil's records and other paperwork. Other associated teaching spaces for post-16-year-old students could include spaces such as a small science project room, green house or microbiology room. The Department for Children, School and Families (DCSF) has commenced various measures to improve the teaching of Science, Technology, Engineering and Mathematics (STEM) at all levels in line with comprehensive vision for UK science and innovation as set out in the government's Science and Innovation Investment Framework 2004–2014. One of the consequences of this could be that science teaching rooms become more flexible to allow the merging of computer design activities alongside the science curriculum.

In higher education, the traditional distinction between teaching and research laboratories has become less important and an increasing number of institutions are integrating these areas. There are several reasons for creating 'homogenous' laboratory facilities:

- Students at all levels are introduced to current techniques.
- Interaction is encouraged between faculty, graduate students and undergraduates.
- A standard serviced laboratory module accommodates change readily.
- Common and specialised equipment may be shared reducing project costs.
- Common facilities can share support spaces and specialty rooms.
- Greater utilisation of space and equipment enhances project cost justification.
- Teaching laboratories can be used for faculty research during semester breaks.

For these reasons, the standards applicable to academic research laboratories are also applicable to higher education.

3.3 Space designation (wet and dry research laboratories)

For the purpose of organisation, the different spaces in a laboratory facility are designated as primary, secondary, tertiary and balance spaces.

Primary space: Primary space is the area in which researchers perform their tasks. It is divided into primary laboratory space and primary office/write-up space, each with different accommodation and service requirements.

Primary laboratory space will normally include:

- Designated bench space for laboratory workers, including those who also have the use of an office/write-up space equipped with appropriate services and local storage.
- Additional workstations associated with a piece of equipment or an experimental procedure, which are not the principal work location of a particular person, but may be used by one or more persons from time to time including PC and other IT terminals, fume cupboards, extract cabinets and laminar flow cabinets.
- Shared storage for laboratory equipment and materials.
- Shared general facilities including display and notice boards, telecoms, dispensers.
- Facilities for waste disposal.
- Services as applicable to the laboratory type.

Primary office/write-up space will normally include:

- write-up areas for researchers/laboratory workers;
- offices for senior researchers/laboratory workers;
- services as applicable to the space type (similar to a standard office environment).

Secondary space: Secondary spaces (sometimes referred to as 'ancillary areas' or 'slave spaces') include all areas which accommodate functions directly related to the operations carried out in the primary space.

Secondary space will normally include:

- Facilities such as equipment rooms, instrument rooms and preparation rooms, which may not have special accommodation or service requirements, but which are better separated from the primary laboratories to increase utilisation through shared use.
- Highly specialised laboratory facilities such as containment suites, fermentation suites and decontamination suites whose accommodation needs are very different from primary laboratory spaces.
- Services as applicable to the laboratory type.

Tertiary space: Tertiary spaces are those whose functions, in addition to the primary and secondary spaces, support the goals and aspirations of the facility such as conference/meeting rooms, interaction spaces, general storage etc.

Balance space: Balance space will normally include cleaner's rooms, circulation spaces, lavatories, service risers and other circulation/support areas which are not defined as primary, secondary or tertiary space.

3.4 Assembly

Primary, secondary and tertiary space functional adjacencies: Zoning the building between laboratory and non-laboratory spaces will reduce costs because of the differing environmental requirements. For example, the ventilation of laboratories may require 100 per cent outside air while non-laboratory spaces can be designed with re-circulated air or naturally ventilated, similar to an office building.

Primary laboratory space is typically designed as modules to suit the briefed team sizes and their requirements with secondary laboratory spaces in close proximity to the primary space for ease of access. As the secondary spaces will be shared by the laboratory teams a separation zone or corridor should be included between the two to ensure no interference to the on-going research in the primary areas.

Primary office functions should be physically separated from the laboratory functions in accordance with Workplace Health and Safety guidelines. This ensures that laboratory activities are contained to areas where appropriate finishes, containment and air handling can be provided.

Primary write-up functions may be incorporated into the primary laboratory space subject to risk assessment in accordance with Workplace Health and Safety guidelines. Considerations for adjacencies between the office/write-up and laboratory space include:

- Visibility/safety: if processes are occurring in the laboratory that require viewing from a write-up space then laboratories and write-up should be directly adjacent to each other with good visibility between.
- Convenience: if the user is writing up an experiment and conducting an experiment simultaneously then direct adjacency is desirable.
- User preference: if neither of the above applies, then this is a matter of user preference.

Tertiary spaces do not always need to be close to the primary and secondary areas. Their location is a matter of preference and is determined through discussion with the stakeholders.

Refer to Section 4 with respect to two case studies which illustrate different ways of assembling primary, secondary and tertiary spaces for a biomedical facility. Data provided for each indicates the ratio of the areas relative to the gross floor plate as well as primary/secondary/tertiary split.

3.5 Layout considerations

- Views/wall space: do the stakeholders want a view from their laboratories to the exterior or will the laboratories be located on the interior with wall space used for laboratory benches and equipment?
- Light sensitivity: some scientific methods do not require or cannot be exposed to natural light. Special instruments and equipment such as nuclear magnetic resonance (NMR) apparatus, electron microscopes, and lasers cannot function properly in natural light. These are typically located in the interior of the building.
- Shape of space: regular and rectangular shapes are generally the most efficient for laboratories although in some instances the shape of a space can be dictated by the size of a specialist piece of equipment, such as a robotics rig. Irregularities on the perimeter of a space will reduce the overall effective area.
- Open/cellular laboratories: in open plan laboratories, partitions should be used only where required for environmental, privacy or security reasons. This allows researchers to share not only the space itself but also the equipment, bench space and support staff. This format facilitates communication between scientists and makes the laboratory more easily adaptable for future needs.
- Interaction/collaboration: are the different spaces within the laboratory facility arranged so that the potential for formal and unplanned interaction is maximised? This is seen as key to promoting innovation amongst scientists.

Table X shows the relative areas for primary, secondary and tertiary spaces in a laboratory facility.

3.6 Areas/workspace in schools

Primary school (combined food/science/design and technology room): In primary schools shared practical spaces are provided where activities such as science, food and design and technology are taught. These specialist spaces would normally be provided with a sink, washable floor area and resources for simple 'wet' practical activities. For an example of a room layout see Figure

Table X Table of relative areas for primary, secondary and tertiary spaces in a laboratory facility

Laboratory space type	% of Gross
Primary laboratory space	18–23
Primary office/write-up spaces	14–18
Total primary space	32–36
Secondary space	16–23
Total primary plus secondary space	50–59*
Tertiary space	9–18
Total net useable space	**65–70**
Gross internal area (excluding plant rooms)	100

*The ratio of secondary to primary space is in the range 40–70%. It will depend, among other things, on the disposition of equipment between laboratory space and special instrument rooms.

Table XI Space standards for primary education laboratories

School size: Number of places	Group size (maximum number)	Average room size (m²)	Number of rooms (minimum)
Less than 180 infants	8	24	1
Up to 120 juniors	8	24	1
121–360 juniors	8	38	2

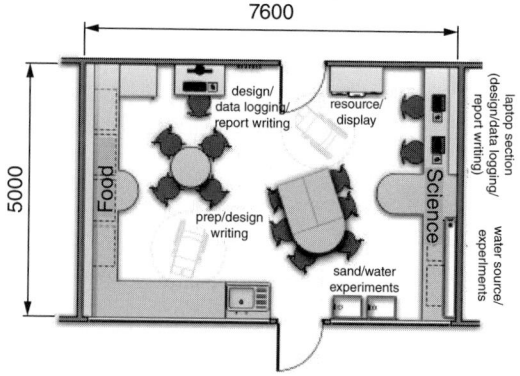

a *Primary school laboratory suite for science and food activities (38m²)*

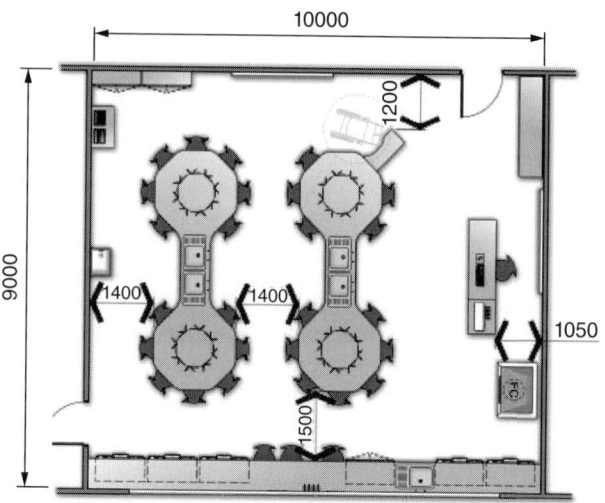

b *Secondary school laboratory suite (90m²) -lsland octagon option*

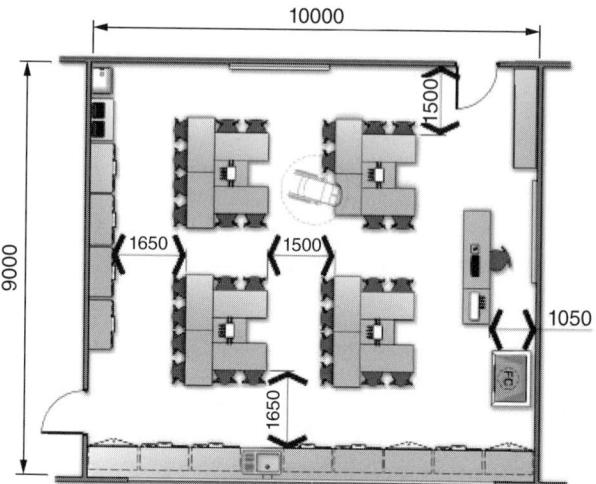

c *Secondary school laboratory suite (90m²) -8 person bollard/service column option*

26.9 *Typical layouts for academic (teaching) facilities (a) primary school; (b&c) secondary school laboratory suites*

26.9a. Space standards shown in Table XI are based on Building Bulletin 99 (2nd Edition): Briefing Framework for Primary School Projects, DFES (BB 99, refer to Bibliography).

Secondary school (science laboratory): In secondary schools the preferred layout is for laboratories to be planned as suites or clusters that are flexible enough to allow for group and individual teaching. These spaces should integrate latest IT technologies to incorporate the teaching of design and engineering as well as durable finishes to allow for the teaching of 'wet' science. For an example of a room

Table XII Space standards for secondary school laboratories

Secondary School 11–16 years old with no curricula emphasis
Space standards based on BB 98

School size: Number of places range in brackets	Group size (maximum number)	Average room size (m²)	Number of rooms (minimum)
600 (577–642)	30	90	5
900 (850–945)	30	90	7
1200 (1125–1251)	30	90	9
1500 (1399–1555)	30	90	11

In addition to the above each room will require a 13 m² combined science preparation room/chemical store space.

Secondary post-16 years old, i.e. sixth form with no curricula emphasis
Space standards based on BB 98

Form size: Number of places	Group size (maximum number)	Average room size (m²)	Number of rooms (minimum)
100	30	90	1
250	30	90	2

In addition to the above a single room will require 23 m² and two rooms will require 36 m² of combined science preparation room/ chemical store space.

Example of secondary school 11–16 years old with science, design and technology curricula emphasis

School size: Number of places	Group size (maximum number)	Average room size (m²)	Number of rooms (minimum)
834–927	30	90	8

In addition to the above each room will require a 13 m² combined science preparation room/chemical store space.

Example of secondary post-16 years old, i.e. sixth form (with science, design and technology, music performing arts curricula emphasis)

Space standards based on BB 98

Space standards for secondary education laboratories

Form size: Number of places	Group size (maximum number)	Average room size (m²)	Number of rooms (minimum)
137–361	30	90	3

Table XIII Table of average areas per person (academic, government sectors)

	Area/Person (m²)
Net primary laboratory area/laboratory worker	6–10*
Net total primary space/researcher	10–16
Net primary plus secondary space/researcher	15–25
Gross internal area (excluding plant rooms)/person	20–30

*Add 2–3 m² when a writing place is included in the laboratory area.

Table XIV Table of average areas per person (example of guidelines adopted by a large UK private pharmaceutical company)

	Area/Person (m²)
Net primary laboratory area/laboratory worker	10–11
Net total primary space/researcher	14–17
Net primary plus secondary space/researcher	18–24
Gross internal area (excluding plant rooms)/person	23–34

Table XV Recommended aisle distances in laboratories

Minimum distance	Width (mm)
Between front of bench or work station and a facing wall, other furniture or equipment or pedestrian route (with one person at bench)	1000*– 1400*
Between benches, furniture or equipment without work spaces either side allowing passage of one person at a time	1000*
Between two people back to back but no need for a third person to pass between front of facing benches, work stations or equipment where people work allowing one of the people to pass behind the other	1400*
Between two people back to back where space is required for a third person to pass between front of facing benches, work stations or equipment where people work allowing a third person to pass behind the others	1450*–1650 (1800 exceptionally)

*1200 mm is required for DDA compliance and 1500 mm (subject to risk assessment) when opposite a fume cupboard or microbiological safety cabinet.

reflects the complexity of uses in laboratory environments (e.g. US laboratories can range from 22.7–41.1m²/person, net primary plus secondary space/researcher). The areas provided in Table XIV are the guidelines adopted by a large UK private pharmaceutical company.

3.8 Circulation

General

- Corridors, stairs, lifts, ramps, holding and other balance areas must allow ease of movement of people, materials, waste and equipment in respect of access routes dimensions, configuration and doors.
- Circulation should provide safe pedestrian egress from each individual laboratory and laboratory support space through an uncomplicated path of egress to the building exterior at grade.
- Separation of workspace and circulation reduces the likelihood of accidents and eases the problem of escape from hazards.
- The circulation system should accommodate the preferred adjacencies identified for the relationships between primary, secondary and tertiary laboratory spaces.

Adjacencies with corridors can be organised with a single, two (racetrack) or a three-corridor scheme. There are a number of variations to organise each type (Figures 26.10, 26.11 and 26.12).

Distance between aisles
Recommended clear distances between aisles in laboratories is indicated in Table XV and illustrated in Figure 26.13.

Aisles and corridor widths
Recommended clear distances between aisles and corridors in laboratories is indicated in Table XVI and illustrated in Figure 26.14.

layout see 26.9b and 26.9c. Space standards in Table XII are based on Building Bulletin 98: Briefing Framework for Secondary School Projects, DFES (BB 98, refer to Bibliography).

In addition to the standards shown in Table XII each laboratory will require a 13 m² combined science preparation room/chemical store space.

3.7 Academic (research), government, private/corporate
Laboratory allocation may be driven by space per researcher (e.g. biology and chemistry laboratories) or by equipment needs (e.g. analytical and engineering laboratories) leading to greater variances between facilities. In this handbook, the areas provided are based on space per researcher. Equipment driven laboratories require individual consideration with the stakeholders on a project basis. Table XIII provides recommended average areas for laboratory workers/researchers in the academic (research) and government sectors.

Note: Whilst, for example, a biologist needs far less fume cupboard space than say a chemist, there is a significantly greater need for ancillary equipment such as refrigerators, incubators, centrifuges and environmental rooms. The overall space requirements balance, for the purpose of flexibility, should be generic.

Private/corporate sectors often have their own standards for space organisation. They typically use benchmarking to estimate the amount of space and benching to be provided to each researcher. Benchmarking can be an unreliable process in part because it is difficult to acquire solid, relevant data. There is a very wide range between the minimum and maximum for commercial data which

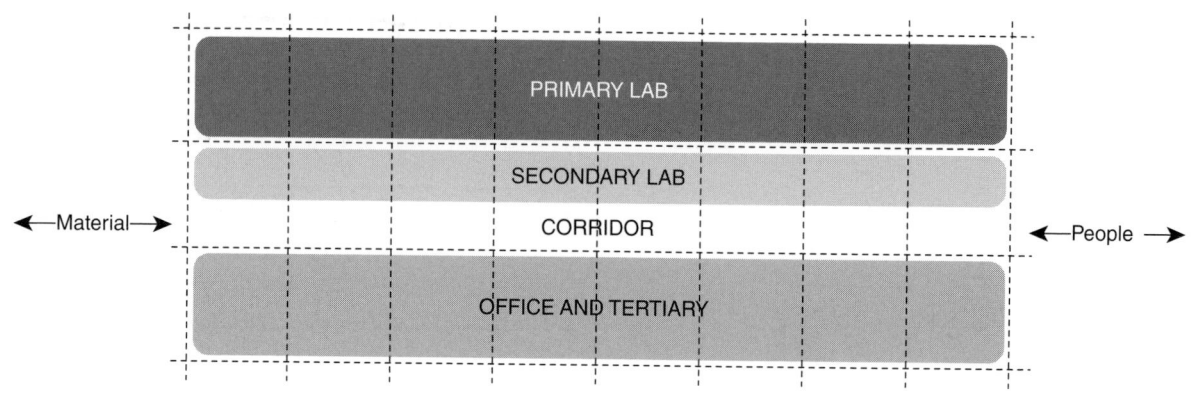

26.10 *Plan layout illustrating a single-corridor arrangement. This layout is efficient however the single circulation route may result in material/people flow cross-over and conflict*

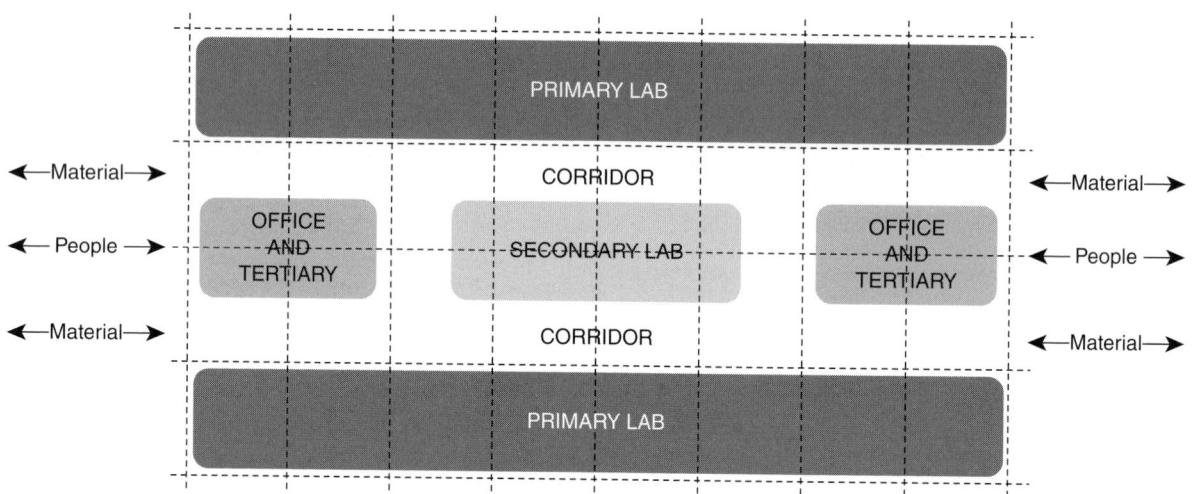

26.11 *Plan layout illustrating two-corridor (racetrack) arrangement. This layout effectively separates people and material circulation within the facility*

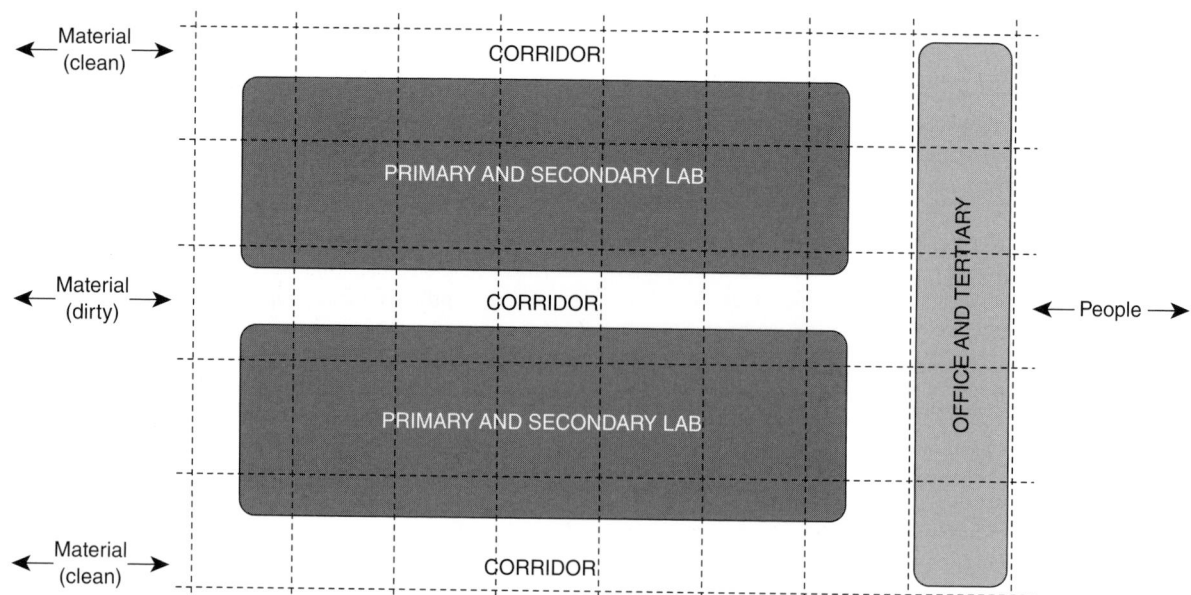

26.12 *Plan layout illustrating three-corridor arrangement. This layout provides the greatest opportunity for optimising circulation within the facility however it is also potentially the most inefficient with respect to area*

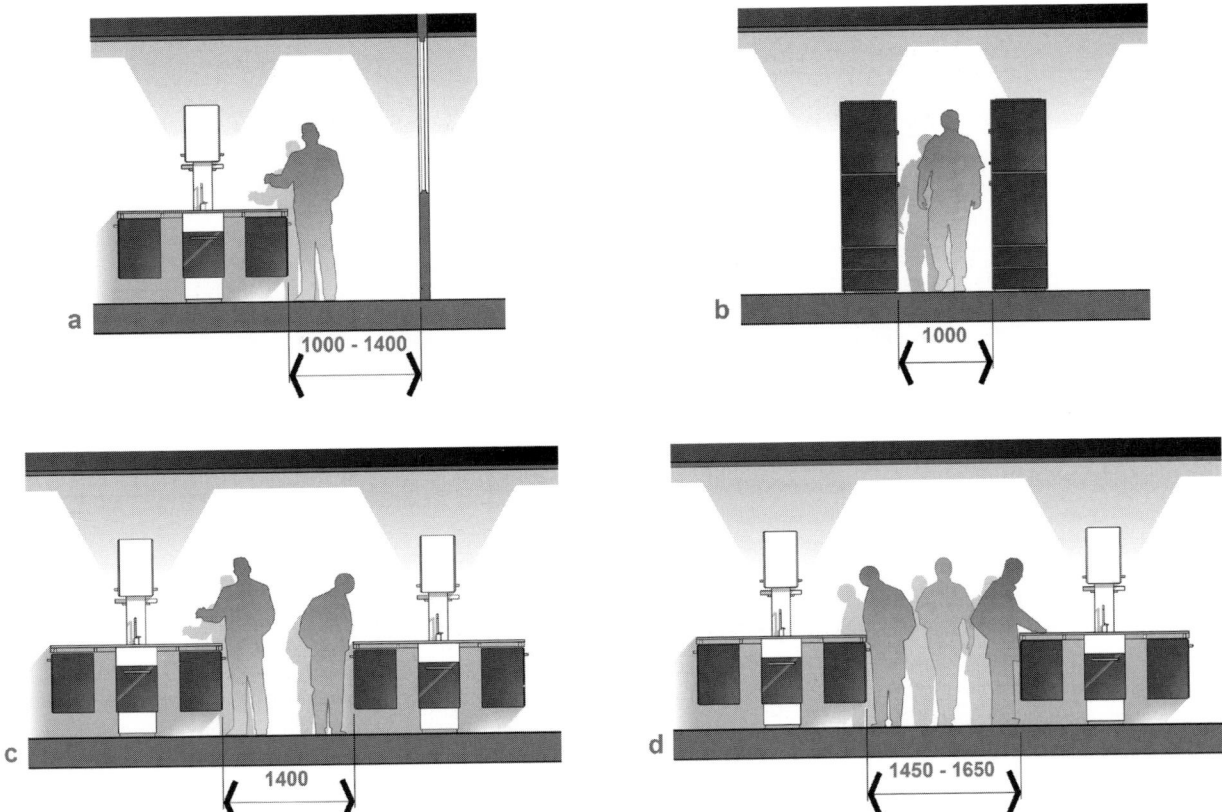

26.13 *Aisle distances (a) bench and wall/equipment, single throughway; (b) bench and/or equipment, no workstations, single throughway; (c) two workers back to back, single throughway; (d) two workers back to back, multiple throughways*

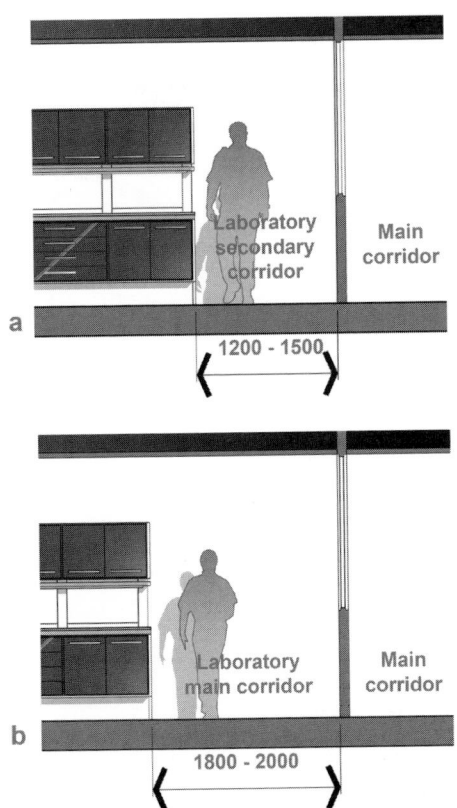

Table XVI Aisle and corridor widths

	Width (mm)
Aisles running along the ends of benches providing circulation within a laboratory	1200–1500*
Similar aisles, where there is no separate corridor for general circulation outside the laboratory	1800–2000*
General circulation corridors	1500–2000**

*Allowance must be made when the aisle may be partially obstructed, for example by staff using bench-end sinks, by doors opening into the aisle, by equipment and by fume cupboards and microbiological safety cabinets.
**Where possible and particularly when corridors are relatively long, a width of 1800–2000 mm is preferable, for both functional and aesthetic reasons.

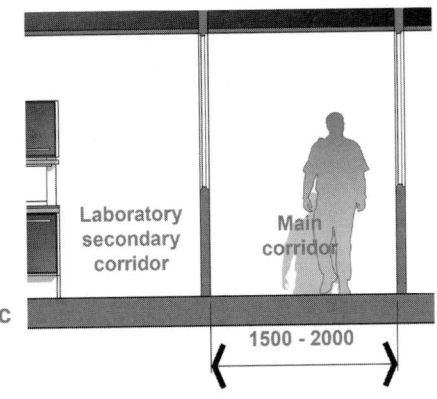

26.14 *Aisle and corridor widths (a) at the ends of benches, additional means of circulation within the laboratory; (b) at the ends of corridors, single means of circulation within the laboratory; (c) general circulation*

Doors
Table XVII indicates the minimum width dimension (clear opening) recommended for at least one door into laboratories and equipment rooms to accommodate the periodic movement of equipment.

This can be accomplished using an opening with a 900 mm active leaf and a 300 mm inactive leaf. Future equipment should be anticipated and equipment lists reviewed to verify that individual pieces of equipment can be transported and manoeuvred between spaces.

Table XVII Door width requirements (minimum)

	Leafs (no.)	Leaf width (mm)
At least one doors into laboratories and equipment rooms	1.5 leafs	1200

3.9 Escape

Under the Building Regulations 2000 Approved Document B (AD:B) Volume 2 (2006 Edition), laboratories are considered under the same purpose group as an office whereby the maximum travel distance where travel is possible in more than one direction is 45 m while if in one direction only it is 18m. In the past, the Building Regulations stipulated a variation to this of 18m travel distances where travel is possible in more than one direction while 9 m if in one direction only for laboratories with open heat sources (e.g. bunsen burners) defining them as 'Places of Special Fire Hazard'. This is no longer included in the latest amendment (2006) as all fire safety in work places is covered by Regulatory Reform (Fire Safety) Order 2005 where the onus now is for a 'responsible person' to arrange for a risk assessment for fire safety to be undertaken, Figure 26.15. Additionally, BS 9999:2008 – *Code of practice for fire safety in the design, management and use of buildings* offers alternative design solutions for fire escape provisions. Guidance is given on how the prescriptive requirements of AD:B can be relaxed using fire engineering principles.

Where a piece of equipment in a laboratory, which could be the source of a health hazard (such as a fume cupboard exploding), is located within an escape route it is recommended that an alternative route be allowed for in the design. In addition to this, if gas cylinders are required within a laboratory they should be securely fixed in a position away from any escape route or final exit (Figure 26.16).

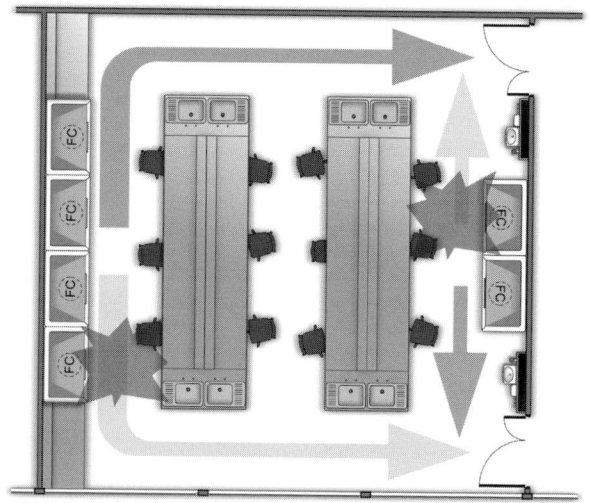

26.16 *Alternative means of escape where potential sources of hazard/s exist*

3.10 Lifts

The service lift also often doubles up as access to the plant room for items of plant. Engineers will typically ask for a lift with the capacity to take a 2 m cube (minimum) to allow items of air handling equipment to be dismantled and taken down in the lift and this would generally be a suitable size to accommodate most large equipment in a laboratory, for example, a –80° freezer or an item of furniture. Specific requirements should be confirmed with the stakeholder.

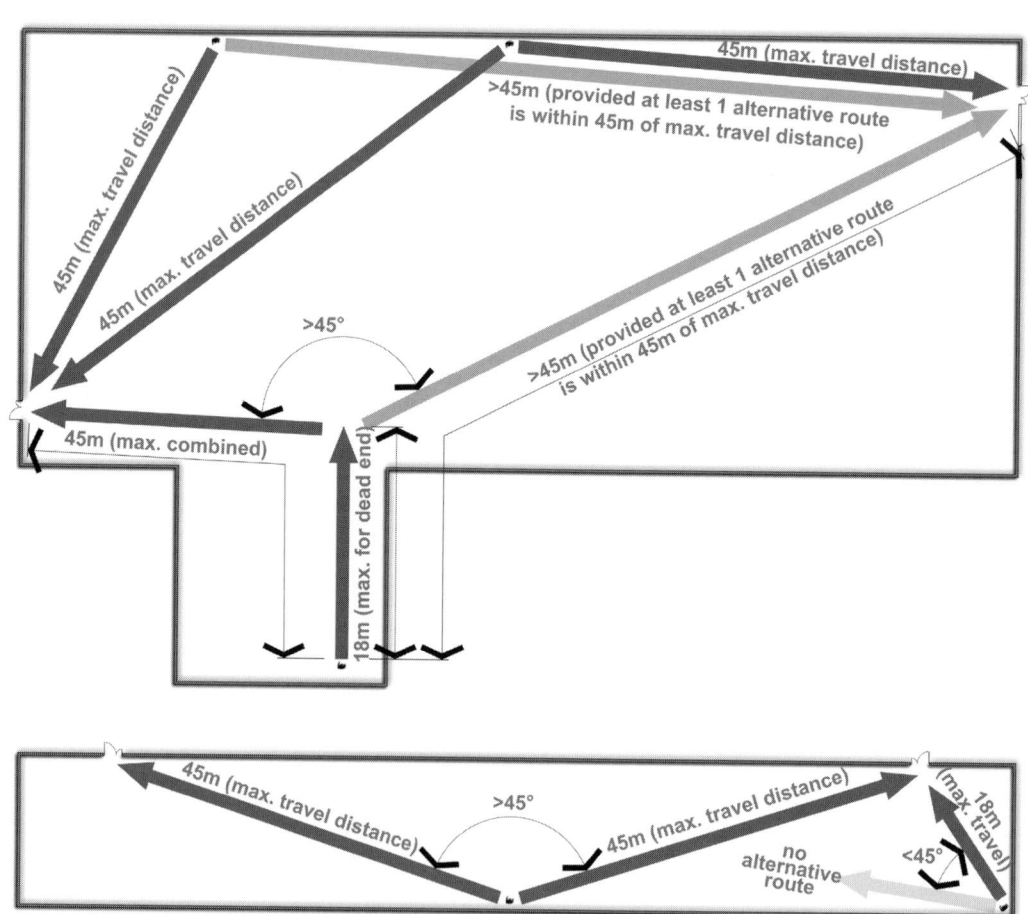

26.15 *Means of escape in a laboratory*

Table XVIII Recommended student laboratory benching dimensions for primary schools

	Dimension (mm)
Length of bench per student	600
Clear bench depth for normal requirements	500–750
Bench height seated	600–650
Bench height standing/seated on laboratory stool	650–725

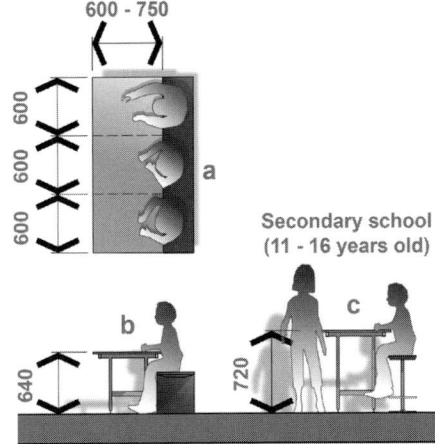

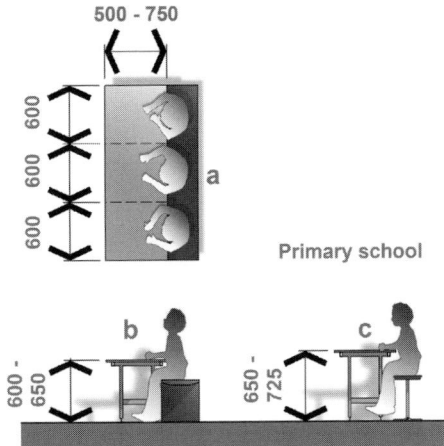

26.17 *Recommended student laboratory benching dimensions for primary schools (a) plan of bench; (b) seated; (c) standing/seated on laboratory stool*

26.18 *Recommended student laboratory benching dimensions for secondary schools (a) plan of bench; (b) seated; (c) standing/ seated on laboratory stool*

3.11 Furniture: general concepts

Laboratories should be designed to allow relocation of furniture within the limits of the modular configuration. Particular reference is made to the selection of laboratory benching and storage systems and the distribution of services systems. Performance criteria to consider when selecting laboratory benching include:

Modularity
- Modular lengths (typically in increments of 1000 mm for UK furniture manufacturers and 600, 900 or 1200 mm for other European manufacturers), depths and heights.
- Pre-installation services.
- Prefabrication of furniture.
- Provision of interchangeable components and accessories.

Flexibility
- Flexible and adaptable system that can be readily moved, repositioned with little or no impact on the building structure and finishes and with minimum disruption to the end user.

Table XIX Recommended student laboratory benching dimensions for secondary schools (a) plan of bench; (b) seated; (c) standing/seated on laboratory stool

	Dimension (mm)		
	Secondary (11–16 years)	Secondary (post-16 years)	DDA
Length of bench per student	600	600–1200	1200
Clear bench depth for normal requirements	600–750	600–750	600–750
Bench height seated	640	720	850
Bench height standing/ seated on lab stool	850	900	
Bench height adjustable	700–1050*	700–1050*	700–1050*

* Recommended height adjustability range where necessary.

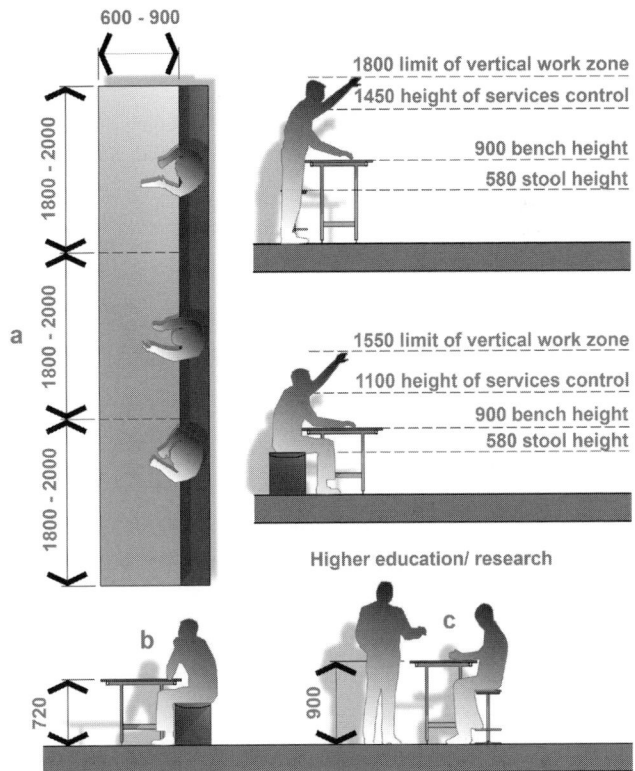

26.19 *Recommended laboratory benching dimensions (length, depth and height) for higher education/research. (a) plan of bench; (b) seated; (c) standing/seated on laboratory stool*

- Height adjustable bench and laboratory chair is recommended where possible (subject to budget and requirements for vibration control and cleanliness).
- Services distribution independent from the laboratory furniture with service pick-up points from ceiling, walls or pods.
- Under bench and overhead storage systems independent of laboratory furniture, movable and readily relocatable.
- Vibration (where sensitive microscopes are used, anti-vibration tables should be considered).

Maintenance
- Ease of cleaning and maintenance and ease of access for service and maintenance purposes.
- Robustness

Table XX Recommended laboratory benching dimensions for higher education/research

	Dimension (mm)
Length of bench per researcher	1800–2000 (2400 exceptionally)*
Clear bench depth for normal requirements	600–900**
Bench height seated	720***
Bench height standing/seated on laboratory stool	900****
Bench height adjustable	700–1050*****
Height of services control (sitting/standing)	1100/1450
Limit of vertical work zone (sitting/standing)	1550/1800

*Suitable length will depend upon the amount of bench-mounted equipment. 2000 mm is a good starting point. Exceptional cases include benchmark allowances made in private/corporate sectors.

**Certain operations and pieces of equipment may require a greater bench depth. These need to be identified early in the briefing process and are generally accommodated on double depth peninsular benches. 750 mm is a good median figure.

***Increases to 850 mm for DDA compliance.

****Care should be taken to co-ordinate the bench height with under bench equipment such as refrigerators and freezers as these vary in height.

*****Accommodates DDA requirements and is recommended where possible (subject to budget and requirements for vibration control and cleanliness).

Disabilities Discrimination Act (DDA) Requirements
- Provide height adjustable furniture where possible to accommodate various equipment and DDA requirements.
- Provide at least one DDA compliant workstation/write-up area for each laboratory unit and in accordance with stakeholder requirements.

Finishes
- Work surfaces should in general be impervious and readily cleanable and where required chemically resistant. Commonly used materials are laminate faced boards, stainless steel faced boards, solid timber sheets, laminated timber sheets, solid laminate sheets, solid epoxy resin sheets, solid phenolic resin sheets and acrylic polymer sheets. The most appropriate of these will depend on the materials and chemicals being used and cost parameters for the each laboratory bench.

Bench length, depth and height (primary schools)
As science is undertaken in a multi-functioning area around clusters of tables, perimeter benching or a combination of the two and limited to groups of 8 children the only critical dimension in planning such a space is to ensure wheelchair access to key facilities within it (Table XVIII and Figure 26.17).

3.12 Storage

General concepts
- Centrally located storage rather than local is preferred (for ease of maintenance, avoiding duplication, diversity and more intense use of equipment).
- Storage depth and height dimensions should be based on convenient reach.
- Modular (based on industry standard sizes where possible).
- Movable/adjustable.
- Robust.

Convenient reach
Comfortable reach into a 300–500 mm deep cupboard above floor level is as follows (Table XXI and Figure 26.20).

Cupboard depth and height
The depth of storage cupboards should be from 300–500 mm for ease of access and fit with bench top and rail, Figure 26.21. The maximum height and lowest level of storage which is frequently used should be based on convenient reach. Extreme high and low zones tend to be used for dead storage (Table XXII and Figure 26.22)

Table XXI Convenient reach dimensions for ages 7–18+ and DDA compliance

Age	Convenient Reach (mm)
7 years	1100
9 years	1170
10 years	1260
11 years	1300
12 years	1375
17 years	1640
18 years +	1675
DDA reach height	1160

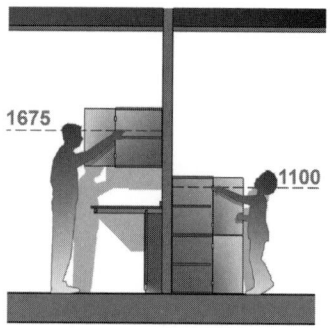

26.20 *Convenient reach dimensions for ages 7–18+ and DDA requirements*

26.21 *Storage depths based on convenient reach*

Table XXII Recommended storage heights based on convenient reach

	Dimension (mm)
Light objects infrequently used	1700–2200
Light objects frequently used	1100–1700
Heavy & light objects frequently used	800–1100
Heavy objects infrequently used	600–800
DDA control height	1200 max – 380 min

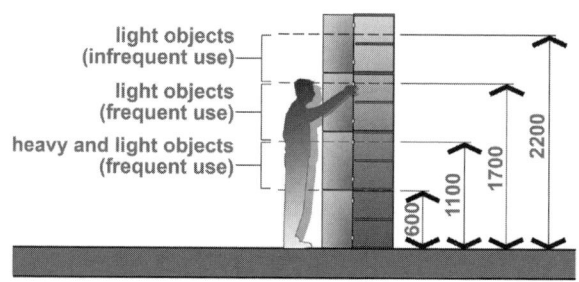

26.22 *Recommended storage heights based on convenient reach*

Underbench storage
Underbench storage is generally provided in three ways namely mobile (on castors or glides), suspended units (supported above the floor off furniture frame) and plinth mounted (floor standing), Figure 26.23. The location and number of these need to meet functional requirements allowing sufficient gaps where anyone will be working seated. Movable units (i.e. mobile or suspended) are recommended where cleaning around, ease of maintenance and

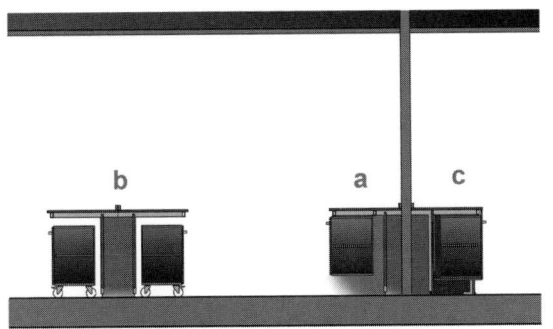

26.23 *Underbench storage options (a) suspended; (b) on castors or glides; (c) plinth mounted*

relocating of storage units in areas are seen as important. In an ideal situation space occupied by underbench units should not exceed 50 per cent of the underbench space.

Gas cylinder storage
The mechanical engineering consultant will be primarily responsible for defining gas cylinder storage requirements, however, the following should be considered:

- Local standards and regulations (refer to Bibliography).
- The types of gas required and whether they are to be temporarily stored for later transportation or permanently stored for piping to their locations.
- Gas store proximities, cylinder separation for different gas types, explosion proofing/venting/fire rating, accessibility for delivery lorry to refill dewar/s.
- Pipework distribution routes, venting, proximity to electrical services.
- Leak detection and alert systems including links to fire alarm/ building management system (BMS)/shut off at manifold and laboratory.
- Electrical equipment in store and laboratory.
- Ventilation equipment in laboratory.
- Gas supplier to the facility.
- Facility representative responsible for the above.

Liquid nitrogen storage
If the fill point is located internally, continuous ventilation and an oxygen level detection system linked to the BMS will be required. Ideally, store externally, located against a fire rated external wall. This requires no specialist venting. The only requirement for an external fill point would be a secured lightweight lean-to-roof arrangement, to protect it from the elements. In areas where liquid nitrogen is being transferred between containers, care should be taken in the selection of floor and wall finishes as contact with liquid nitrogen can lead to their rapid deterioration due to thermal shock.

3.13 Equipment

General concepts
Space allocation is dependent on individual requirements which are subject to change. Utilise removable or relocatable equipment in preference to purpose-built fixed facilities where possible. Ideally, laboratory benching should be removable to allow floor standing equipment to be incorporated as required during the life of the laboratory.

General equipment
General/standard floor standing equipment may include items noted below (indicative sizes are shown). Confirmation with manufacturers is necessary as individual sizes vary considerably depending on capacity and make.

- Underbench fridge/freezer   600w × 600d × 650–875h
- Tall/floor standing fridge/   600–750w × 600–750d ×
- freezer   1800h
- −50° to −80° freezer   1130w × 875d × 1990h
- Centrifuge   900–1200w × 900d × 950h
- Oven   1000w × 1000d × 800h

(Note: large storage freezers, typically −80°C, should be located within designated freezer rooms which will provide sufficient noise attenuation and local cooling also reducing energy usage.)

Special equipment
Special equipment may include:

- NMR
- X-ray and other imaging equipment
- IT equipment
- Balances and other measuring equipment
- Mass spectrometers
- Autoclaves.

Room dimensions, structural loading, rigidity and resonance, environmental conditions, wave and particle shielding and services connections for special equipment require individual consideration and therefore should be dealt with on a case-by-case basis and must take full account of manufacturer's and health and safety requirements. Where equipment that is affected by magnetic fields is being considered, care should be taken to check their proximity to moving metal objects such as lifts.

Local exhaust ventilation (LEVs)
A LEV is a ventilation system that takes dusts, mists, gases, vapour or fumes out of the air so that they can't be breathed in. The Control of Substances Hazardous to Health Regulations require prevention or adequate control of exposure to hazardous substances. Where the risk assessment determines that local exhaust ventilation is required as part of the control measures employed, the LEV must be suitably selected, used, tested and maintained and appropriate records kept. An LEV may be tiny and built into a hand-held tool or it may be large enough to walk into, such as a fume cupboard (described in more detail in this section).

Fume cupboards (FCs)
BS EN 14175 Parts 1 to 6 represents the most recent fume cupboard standard and partially supersedes some parts of the previous standard, BS 7258. BS EN 14175 applies to types of fume cupboard not previously covered by BS 7258, such as walk-ins, VAV, horizontal sashes and low cill cabinets. It is more of a product standard and is relatively weak with reference to installation requirements. BS EN 14175 puts greater onus on individual testing by manufacturers to justify the performance of their cupboard. It is hoped that as more tests are published greater guidance will become available on locating them. Until this is forthcoming, reference should continue to be made to elements of BS 7258.

All FC setting out should give optimum protection to the user working with chemicals/aerosols. Single person fume cupboards are generally 1500–1800 mm long. Larger standard units, generally for two persons, are up to 2400 mm long. They should be positioned to avoid disturbances to the cupboard and its operator (Figures 26.24 and 26.25). Disturbances include people walking parallel to it, open windows, air supply registers or laboratory equipment that creates air movement such as, for example, vacuum pumps and centrifuges. They should be located away from high traffic areas, doors and air supply/ exhaust grilles that may interrupt airflow patterns. There should be an alternative means of escape in the event of an explosion/fire.

The use of re-circulating fume cupboards (non-ducted) can greatly reduce energy consumption although the cupboard usage may be limited. Before selecting a re-circulating fume cupboard a

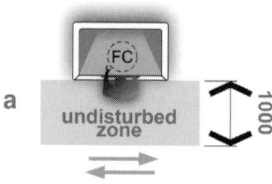

Separation of undisturbed
zones from traffic routes

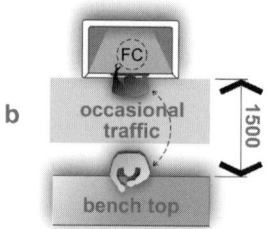

Spacing where operator uses
fume cupboard and bench
top or where occasional
traffic only is anticipated

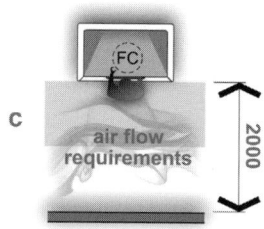

Spacing determined by
air-flow requirements – wall
in front of fume cupboard

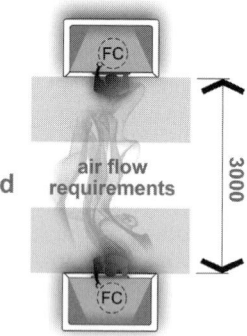

Spacing determined by
air-flow requirements – fume
cupboards on both sides

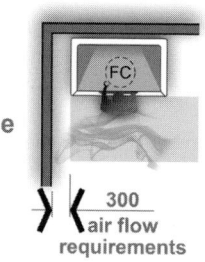

Spacing determined by
air-flow requirements –
corner condition

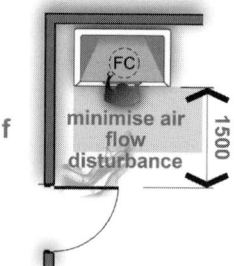

Spacings that avoid undue
disturbance of air flow – door
in front of fume cupboard

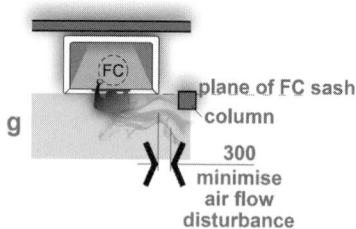

Spacings that avoid undue
disturbance of air flow – column
face in front of plane of sash

Spacings that avoid undue
disturbance of air flow – column
face in line with plane of sash

Spacings that avoid undue
disturbance of air flow – door on
either side of fume cupboard

26.24 *Fume cupboard minimum distances for avoiding disturbances to the fume cupboard and its operator (as stipulated in BS7258)*

review of the chemicals being used within needs to be undertaken to ensure its filter is able to maintain a safe working environment. Refer to BS 7989 specification for re-circulatory filtration fume cupboards. Though the standard is distinct from BS 7258, it is similar in structure and cross-references BS 7258.

Re-circulating and re-locatable FCs with flexible ducting and variable extract are recommended for maximising flexibility and minimising energy consumption. The number of fume cupboards required should be confirmed with stakeholders.

Microbiological safety cabinets (MSCs)
All MSC setting out should comply with BS 5726 and EN 12469 to give optimum protection to the user working with biological agents up to Hazard Group 4. Single person safety cabinets are generally 1300–1800 mm long. Larger standard units, generally for two persons, are up to 2400 mm long.

They should be positioned to avoid disturbances to the cupboard and its operator (Figures 26.26 and 26.27). Disturbances include people walking parallel to it, open windows, air supply registers or

laboratory equipment that creates air movement such as, for example, vacuum pumps and centrifuges. They should be located away from high traffic areas, doors and air supply/exhaust grilles that may interrupt airflow patterns.

All MSCs are designed to comply with one of the three classifications defined in BS EN 12469:

• A Class I safety cabinet provides a wide performance envelope for the user from aerosol hazards and other particulate within the cabinets work area. All extract air is exhausted through HEPA (high efficient particulate air) filtration generally to atmosphere. Re-circulating MSCs are also available though the usage of these is dependent on the work being undertaken within them.
• A Class II safety cabinet, unlike the Class I safety cabinet, provides protection to both the user and the material within the cabinet's working area. Protection for the user is provided by means of an advanced inflow air curtain whilst the sample material in the cabinet is protected from the dirty laboratory environment by a constant stream of HEPA filtered air.

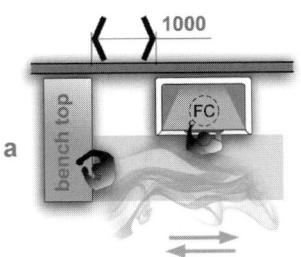

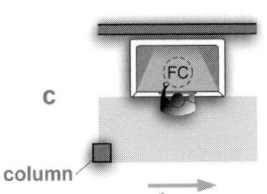

a Projecting bench will help to keep traffic clear of undisturbed zone. Work at bench will have little effect on air flow if sufficient distance between fume cupboard and projecting bench is allowed

b Work at projecting bench will cause disturbance to air flow

c Columns can assist the definitions of traffic routes

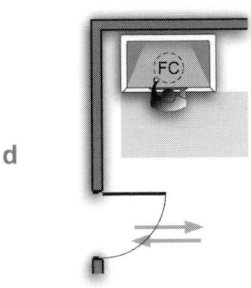

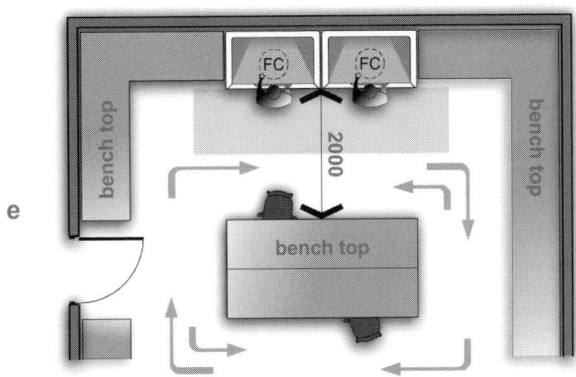

d Projecting walls and the positioning of doors can be effective in defining traffic routes

e Too much movement in front of fume cupboards should be avoided by providing more than the minimum distance between faces of the fume cupboards and bench tops

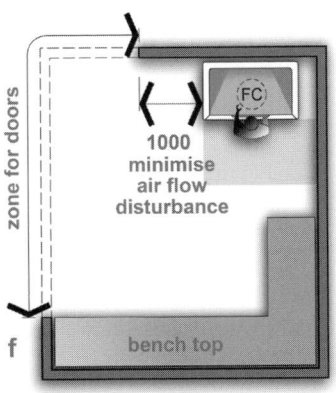

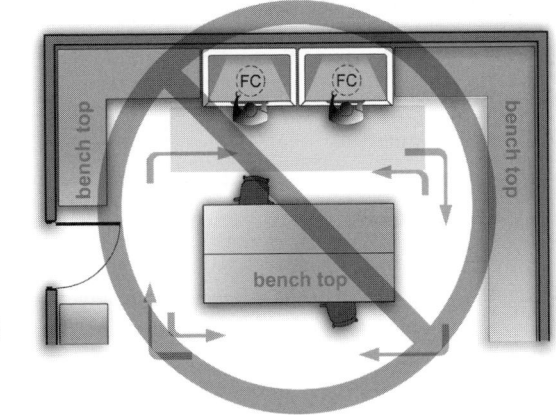

f In small laboratory, the fume cupboards should be clear of personnel entering through doors

g Too much movement in front of fume cupboards will cause disturbance to air flow

26.25 *Fume cupboard planning arrangements for avoiding disturbances to the fume cupboard and its operator and from other personnel (as stipulated in BS7258)*

- A Class III safety cabinet, like the Class II safety cabinet, provides protection for both the user and product but with a higher degree of protection than a Class II cabinet. For the user this is achieved by means of an additional barrier such as working through gloves or gauntlets and protection to the material within the cabinet by means of the filtered supply air operating at a negative pressure to the surrounding environment and with the exhaust air being vented through a HEPA filter to atmosphere. A Class III microbiological safety cabinet is a highly specialised product designed for the most hazardous work, typically carried out in a Containment Level 3 or 4 facility.

Some manufacturers also produce a hybrid Class I/III cabinet but this is not described within the British Standard. The hybrid, as the name suggests, can be used as either a Class I or a Class III cabinet by the use of a removable port that attaches to the front aperture. However the construction and testing of these cabinets is such that when used in Class III mode it is not equivalent to the specification of a standard Class III cabinet and should always be checked.

Both BS EN 12469 and the Advisory Committee for Dangerous Pathogens (ACDP) recommend that natural gas should not be used with the cabinet (as this will have an impact on the cabinet's airflow, the down flow filter integrity and could possibly prove to be a

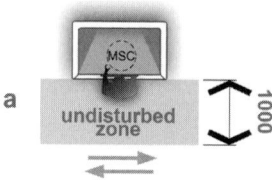

Separation of undisturbed zones from traffic routes

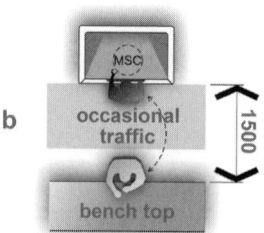

Spacing where operator uses microbiological safety cabinet and bench top or where occasional traffic only is anticipated

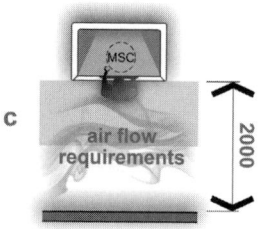

Spacing determined by air-flow requirements – wall in front of microbiological safety cabinet

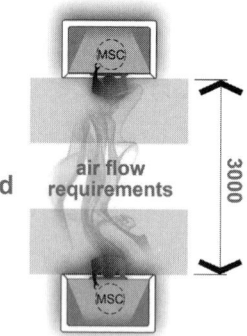

Spacing determined by air-flow requirements – microbiological safety cabinets on both sides

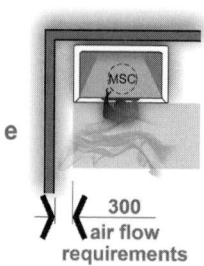

Spacing determined by air-flow requirements – corner condition

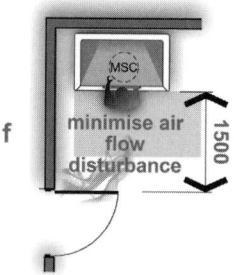

Spacings that avoid undue disturbance of air flow – door in front of microbiological safety cabinet

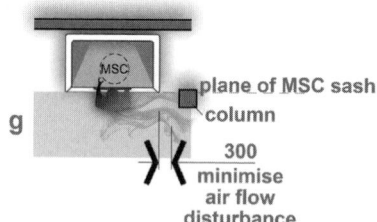

Spacings that avoid undue disturbance of air flow – column face in front of plane of sash

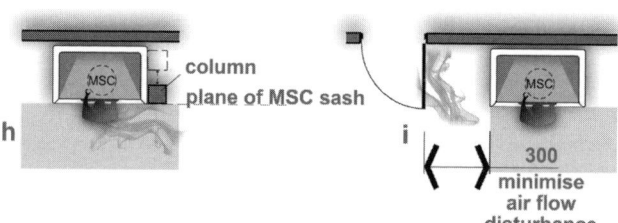

Spacings that avoid undue disturbance of air flow – column face in line with plane of sash

Spacings that avoid undue disturbance of air flow – door on either side of microbiological safety cabinet

26.26 *Microbiological safety cabinet minimum distances for avoiding disturbances to the cabinet and its operator*

fire hazard – several cabinets have been set alight this way), as such this should not be offered as a standard fixture on the Class II MSC. If, after a risk assessment, it is deemed necessary to have natural gas then a special gas solenoid type tap together with a low profile, foot operated ignition type burner should be used. The number of cabinets required should be confirmed with stakeholders.

3.14 Finishes and fittings

Finishes
Finishes should be suitable to the relevant usage, containment level and cleanroom classification for the laboratory. For general wet chemical and biological laboratories and darkrooms, a solvent resistant, slip resistant and coved vinyl or rubber flooring using sheet goods rather than tile is recommended. Walls and ceilings should be robust and cleanable. Generally a fully accessible suspended ceiling installation (where containment/cleanroom classifications do not require it to be fully sealed) will allow full access to above ceiling services infrastructure and allow some acoustic

treatment to the space though in some spaces no ceiling at all can be more appropriate. Refer to bibliography for further references on finishes specification.

Handwashing sinks
Handwashing sinks are typically required for each laboratory and should be located near the point of exit from the laboratory or in the anteroom. Handwashing sinks for particularly hazardous chemicals or biological agents may need elbow (for Containment Level 2 areas) or electronic sensor controls (for Containment Level 3 areas).

Emergency eyewash and safety shower facilities (EE/SS)
Laboratories using hazardous materials must have an eyewash and safety shower ideally located in the corridor, close to and highly visible from the laboratory exits and within nominal 10 seconds travel time from the chemical use areas or current Workplace Health and Safety Requirements (whichever is most stringent). Eyewashes and safety showers should preferably have plumbed drains, they should

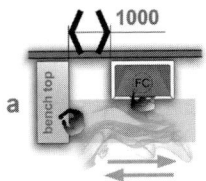
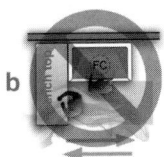
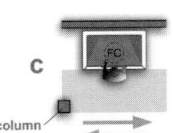

a Projecting bench will help to keep traffic clear of undisturbed zone. Work at bench will have little effect on air flow if sufficient distance between cupboard and projecting bench is allowed

b Work at projecting bench will cause disturbance to air flow

c Columns can assist the definitions of traffic routes

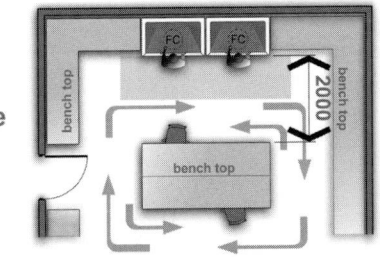

d Projecting walls and the positioning of doors can be effective in defining traffic routes

e Too much movement in front of fume cupboards should be avoided by providing more than the minimum distance between faces of fume cupboards and bench tops

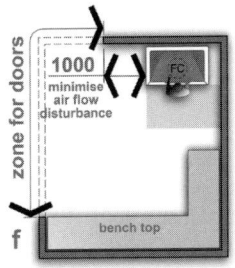
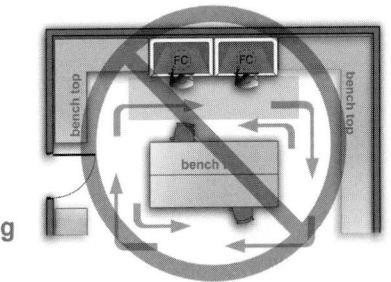

f In small laboratory, the fume cupboard should be clear of personnel entering through doors

g Too much movement in front of fume cupboards will cause disturbance to air flow

26.27 *Microbiological safety cabinet planning arrangements for avoiding disturbances to the cabinet and its operator and from other personnel*

be conspicuously labelled and flooring under safety showers should be slip-resistant. Safety showers may have privacy curtains, particularly in large laboratories or teaching laboratories.

3.15 Services requirements

General

Systems must deliver laboratory services suitable for the accurate and reliable conduct of research procedures, conforming to relevant standards and codes of practice and satisfying specific criteria, in respect of parameters, including:

- composition;
- purity;
- stability and reliability (e.g. temperature, pressure, uninterruptible power supply (UPS), flow rate);
- control of delivery.

A well-controlled system will provide flexibility and minimise the operational cost of the building. Considerations should include:

- Expansion space allowed in the utility corridors, ceilings and vertical chases for future heating, ventilation and air conditioning (HVAC), plumbing and electric needs.
- Easy connects/disconnects at walls and ceilings to allow for fast and affordable hook up of equipment.
- Modular distribution.

3.16 Power

Three types of power are generally used for most laboratory projects. Requirements should be confirmed with stakeholders during the briefing phase.

Normal Power: Circuits are connected to the utility supply only, without any backup system. Loads that are typically on normal power include some HVAC equipment, general lighting and most laboratory equipment.

Standby Power: Depending on the size or height of the building, standby power, which is created with generators, may be required for life safety systems (e.g. smoke control systems, sprinkler pumps, fireman's lift, car park extract etc.). Standby power may also be necessary from a business continuity/loss of product point of view in the event of a normal power cut-off (e.g. power to plant servicing critical temperature rooms, maintaining pressure to containment or clean room applications, power to sump and sewage pumps, extract systems for radioactive areas, etc.).

Uninterruptible Power Supply (UPS): UPS is required to condition and maintain uninterrupted power to critical loads for data recording, certain computers and micro-processor controlled equipment and selected bench outlets where long running experiments may be connected. The UPS can be either a central unit or a portable system pending extent of requirement, cost and space constraints. UPS systems are very expensive and therefore careful consideration is necessary when defining their rating.

Load: Connected electrical loads are anticipated loads estimated during the briefing phase. The loads provided in Table XXIII are

Table XXIII Connected electrical loads (indicative)

	Load (W/m²)
Laboratories	325
Equipment and Instrument Rooms	650
Shared Support Rooms	430
Glassware Washing/Autoclave Rooms	540

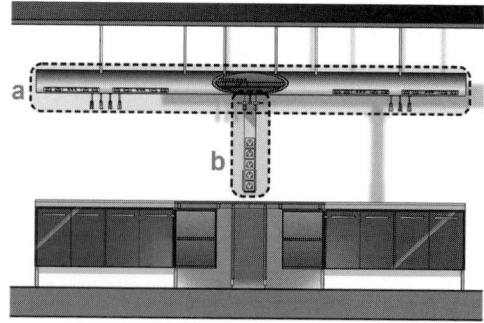

26.28 *Overhead fixed services distribution (a) service wing; (b) service column*

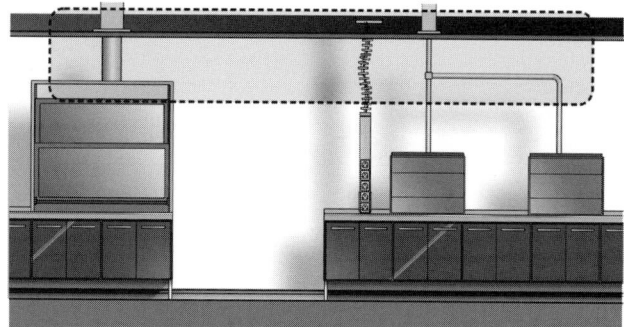

26.29 *Overhead flexible services distribution*

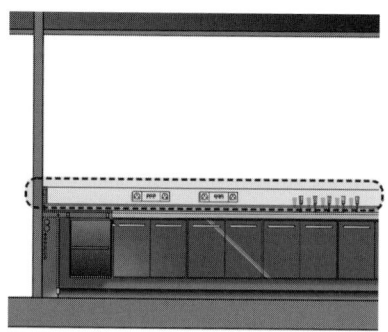

26.30 *Perimeter services distribution through walls and trunking*

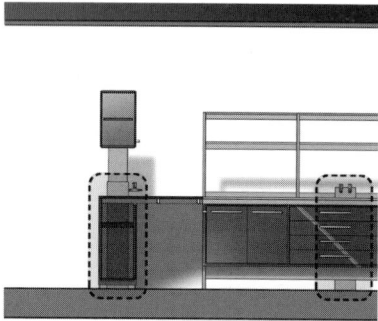

26.31 *Distribution of services through floor mounted bollards*

indicative to assist with preliminary sizing of a generic bench scale laboratory building.

3.17 Services distribution
The method of distributing services to furniture and equipment has a major influence on the flexibility of layout possible during the laboratory's total life. There are three main methods of distributing services (power, data, gas, water) to laboratory benching and equipment. This allows furniture to be arranged in peninsular/perimeter and/or island configurations (Figures 26.28–26.31).

* overhead (fixed services);
* overhead (flexible services);
* perimeter (on walls);
* under floor.

Where services are integral to the furniture, equipment and partitions, any major change in layout will involve adaptation or extension of the service runs. If, however, the distribution of services within the laboratory can be separated and flexible connections made to loose services units, layouts can be adjusted directly by stakeholders to meet new requirements.

The greatest flexibility can be achieved by providing flexible services delivery to point of use from movable ceiling pods and bench mounted masts connected to a ceiling services infrastructure via flexible hose connections and flying electrical leads (Figure 26.29). This is achieved through the use of fully relocatable services integrated with the ceiling and laboratory furniture and equipment.

This approach requires full design co-ordination and consultation with the mechanical, electrical and piping engineers.

Power and data services outlets: Utilise accessible trunking that can readily accommodate the future addition and subtraction of outlets as required. Extension leads should be avoided for health and safety reasons.

Socket outlets should not be placed immediately adjacent to sinks where splashing could present a risk (refer to BS7 671).

The number of outlets required should be confirmed with stakeholders and the services engineers. An indicative guide (typically maximum) for generically designed laboratories is as follows:

* Double power at 450 mm centres/bench and equipment run
* Double data at 900 mm centres/bench and equipment run

Cleaner's sockets should be provided and clearly identified to avoid cleaner's equipment interfering with active experiments/laboratory equipment.

Piped services: Laboratory piped services should be delivered to each laboratory on a modular basis (even though all services may not be initially required in all of the laboratories) for flexibility and to minimise remodel and retrofit costs as laboratory use changes. Each laboratory unit should have separate shut-off valves located in a consistent, accessible manner for repairs or emergency shut-off without affecting other laboratories. Except for waste and vent systems, distribution systems are recommended to be looped.

Initially the frequency and quality requirements should be assessed. Where demand is intermittent or a particular quality is required, localised sources may be provided.

Basic requirements include:

* Potable Water, Hot and Cold (HW, CW)
* Industrial Water, Hot and Cold (IHW, ICW)

Optional (as required):

* Deionised Water (DI)
* Purified Water (PW)

Table XXIV Basic laboratory piped services requirements (indicative – subject to confirmation with stakeholders)

Service	Outlets/Module
CW (for emergency eyewash and safety shower facilities)	1
IHW	1
ICW	2

- Laboratory Air (Air)
- Natural Gas (NG)
- Vacuum (VAC)
- Compressed Air (CA)
- Steam

Specialty gases (as required):

- Should be provided by local cylinders

Table XXIV provides guidance for basic requirements (to be determined with the engineer and stakeholders).

4 ENVIRONMENT

4.1 General

The typical laboratory uses far more energy and water per square metre than the typical office building due to intensive ventilation requirements and other health and safety concerns. Therefore, designers should strive to create sustainable, high performance, and low-energy laboratories that will minimise overall environmental impacts and optimise whole building efficiency on a life-cycle basis.

Systems must however maintain background environments suitable for the accurate and reliable conduct of research procedures satisfying criteria for each accommodation type, in respect of:

- temperature;
- relative humidity;
- ventilation rates (air change rate, heat loads, equipment extract);
- room pressurisation;
- control and variation of environmental parameters.

4.2 Design criteria

Temperature

The recommended temperature values listed in Table XXV for laboratory and laboratory support spaces are generally acceptable; however individual requirements should be confirmed with stakeholders. Natural ventilation and higher or lower values may be specified depending on laboratory containment/cleanroom classification, type of activity, equipment and personnel clothing.

Relative humidity (RH)

Requirements should be confirmed with stakeholders. Humidity lower than 30 per cent can cause electrostatic effects and relative humidity above 50 per cent can augment oxidation and corrosion. Relative humidity is more difficult to regulate than temperature. Reducing the relative humidity as low as 40 per cent is possible with standard cooling methods. Dehumidification below this level requires expensive desiccating equipment. Fluctuation ranges below +/–2 per cent are difficult to achieve and maintain and are very expensive.

Ventilation rates

Air Change Rate: Typical air changes per hour (ac/hr) for laboratory and laboratory support spaces are 6–10 ac/hr depending on the use and individual requirements.

Heat Loads: Heat loads from laboratory equipment for each space are calculated during the design stage for each project. The specific laboratory heat loads shown in Table XXVI are based on

Table XXV Indoor design conditions (temperature) for laboratory and laboratory support spaces

Space	Typical Summer Room Temperature °C	Typical Winter Room Temperature °C
Laboratory	24 max (22 +/–2 °C)	20 min (22 +/–2 °C)
Laboratory Support	24 max (22 +/–2 °C)	20 min (22 +/–2 °C)
Specialist areas	(to user specification requirements)	

Table XXVI Preliminary heat gain from laboratory equipment (indicative loads)

Space	Load (W/m)
Research Laboratory (wet, microbiological/clinical)	75
Research Laboratory (dry)	65
Laboratory Support (Equipment Rooms)	175
Laboratory Support (Instrument Rooms)	100

Table XXVII Preliminary extract requirements from equipment (indicative)

Extract Type	Extract Air Flow (m³/sec)
Fume Cupboard	0.30–0.50
MSC	0.15
Equipment Vent	0.02–0.04
Snorkel	0.07–0.1

anticipated loads for generic research scale laboratories and are provided to assist with the preliminary sizing of the building systems.

Equipment Extract Rates: Schedules should be developed for each space during briefing for each project. The extract schedule (Table XXVII) is provided to assist with the preliminary sizing of the building systems.

Room pressurisation: For environments requiring containment, relative pressure to surroundings is typically negative, principally for the containment of hazards and smells. For cleanroom environments, relative pressure to surroundings is typically positive, principally for the control of dust/particles into the room.

Lighting design: Lighting levels should not be less than CIBSE recommendations. The illumination levels recommended for general laboratories (performance of visual tasks of medium contrast or small size) are 350 lux generally, 500 lux on the working plane. Consider local task lighting to reduce overall illumination levels. Good to high colour rendering should be considered in laboratory areas. Emergency lighting needs to comply with BS6651.

Acoustics: The recommendation for background noise levels in general laboratories is NR 45. Noise control methods include the use of acoustically lined enclosures and reduced sound level operating equipment. Silencers may be used in air distribution systems within the materials and constraints available. Duct liners should be avoided.

Control and variation of environmental parameters: Where economically viable and without compromising the functionality of the research environment, stakeholders should be allowed limited control over their immediate environment including temperature and lighting. Consider natural ventilation to the offices and any atria/light-wells.

5 CASE STUDIES

5.1 Scottish Centre for Regenerative Medicine, University of Edinburgh

Client:	University of Edinburgh
Location:	Little France campus, Edinburgh
Team:	Architect: Sheppard Robson
	Engineers: Buro Happold
	Cost Consultant: Summers Inman
	Contractor, Miller Construction Ltd
Start:	2006
Finish:	2011

Research: The Scottish Centre for Regenerative Medicine will provide a unique environment, developing new treatments for human diseases affecting the nervous system, liver and other organs. It is the first large-scale purpose built facility of its kind in the UK.

26.32 *The Scottish Centre for Regenerative Medicine*

Assembly: The internal form mimics the 'pebble in a pond' effect; smaller, darker spaces such as the cell culture rooms, are positioned in the centre of the building. Laboratory spaces are positioned in the middle and write up spaces are located next to the outer walls, allowing opportunity for natural ventilation and lighting. The lower floor of research space consists of spaces requiring specialist clean environments while the upper floor provides a more generic and flexible laboratory environment. Sandwiched between them is an interstitial plant space which services both the laboratory floors.

Facilities within the building include:

- ACDP CL2 Research Laboratories
- ACDP CL2 Specialist Laboratories
- Translational Unit cGMP Grade A-D (Class 100 – 100,000) Cleanroom Suite and cGMP Grade B (Class 100) Radioisotope Cleanroom Suite
- Offices and Support (Meeting, Breakout, Tea-points)
- Administration and Stores

Furniture and fittings: The furniture within the laboratories consists of wall assemblies of fixed or movable tables and peninsulas consisting of movable tables around a fixed sink unit. All worktops are made of solid laminate panels with sealed joints. All underbench storage is mobile, which in places is supplemented by wall mounted cupboards or open height adjustable shelving. Services to wall benching are provided via wall mounted dado trunking while the peninsular areas have a floor standing fixed spine with a service dropper from the suspended ceiling set out to the laboratory planning modules. In specialist areas where holes in walls are not accepted the floor mounted frames are extended above the worktop to accommodate overhead storage. Each space has a handwash station incorporating eye wash unit, soap dispensers and paper towel dispenser.

Table XXVIII shows the building data summary for this project.

Sustainability: This is one of the UK's first laboratory buildings to have received a BREEAM Excellent certificate. The building employs a number of sustainable features, including ground source heat pumps, rainwater harvesting and chilled beams in order to reduce energy usage and to help achieve the targeted excellent

Table XXVIII Building data summary

Description	Type	Wet and Dry
	Sector	Public
	Environment	ACDP CL 2. Clean room Class A/B & D
Planning	Basic Module width	3.4m
Structure	Structural Grid	6.8m × 6.8m
	Floor to Floor	4.4m–5.0m
	Floor Load Design	5kN/m²
	Vibration Design (Response Factor)	R=1
Services	Riser Zoning Strategy	Interstitial floor
Area m²/ Researcher	Net/Gross Primary/ Secondary/Tertiary Net Primary Secondary	4843m²/6500m² (74.5%) 2085m²/2260m²/ 498m² (43%/47%/10%) 13.9m² + 15.1m²
Circulation	Type	Racetrack
	Bench/Equipment	Floor standing benching with mobile or fixed underbench storage units
	Distance Bench/Wall	n/a
	Distance Back to Back	1.8m
	Widths Bench Aisle	1.9m
	Width Main	2.4m
Laboratory Finishes	Floors	Epoxy Resin and non-slip vinyl and rubber sheeting
	Walls	Cleanable paint and pre-finished metal faced panels
	Ceiling	Cleanable paint and pre-finished perforated and solid metal tiles
Environment	Temperature (Summer) max	22°C+/–2°
	Temperature (Winter) min	19°C+/–2°
	Relative Humidity (RH)	50%+/–15%
	Ventilation Rates (Air Changes per Hour)	6–10 AC/Hr in general labs, 30 AC/Hr in specialist "clean" spaces.
	Room Pressurisation	Varies in steps between -10Pa to 50Pa
	Lighting (average levels)	500 lux at working surface
	Acoustics	40NR
	Control	BMS for all areas with BEMS to part
	CO₂ Emission Savings	18% reduction target

Table XXIX Building data summary

Description	Type	Wet
	Sector	Academic
	Environment	ACDP CL 2 & 3.
Planning	Basic Module width	3.3m
Structure	Structural Grid	9.9m × 10.5m
	Floor to Floor	4.7m
	Floor Load Design	5kN/m²
	Vibration Design (Response Factor)	R=4
Services	Riser Zoning Strategy	Sidestitial floor
Area	Net/Gross Primary/Secondary/Tertiary	4383m²/6760m² (64.8%) 3300m²/816m²/267m² (75%/19%/6%)
M²/ Researcher	Net Primary Secondary	13.6m² + 3.1m²
Circulation	Type	Racetrack
	Bench/Equipment	Floor standing benching with mobile or fixed underbench storage units
	Distance Bench/Wall	2.0m
	Distance Back to Back	1.8m
	Widths Bench Aisle	1.8m
	Width Main	2.1m
Laboratory Finishes	Floors	Epoxy Resin and non slip vinyl sheeting
	Walls	Cleanable or elastomeric paint and pre-finished metal faced panels
	Ceiling	Cleanable or elastomeric paint and pre-finished perforated and solid metal tiles
Environment	Temperature (Summer) max	24°C+/–1°
	Temperature (Winter) min	21°C+/–1°
	Relative Humidity (RH)	50%+/–20%
	Ventilation Rates (Air Changes per Hour)	6–10 AC/Hr in general labs, 14–20 AC/Hr in specialist "clean" spaces.
	Room Pressurisation	Varies in steps of 15 Pa between –45Pa to 0Pa
	Lighting (average level)	500 lux at working surface
	Acoustics	55NR
	Control	BMS for all areas
	CO₂ Emission Savings	13% reduction target

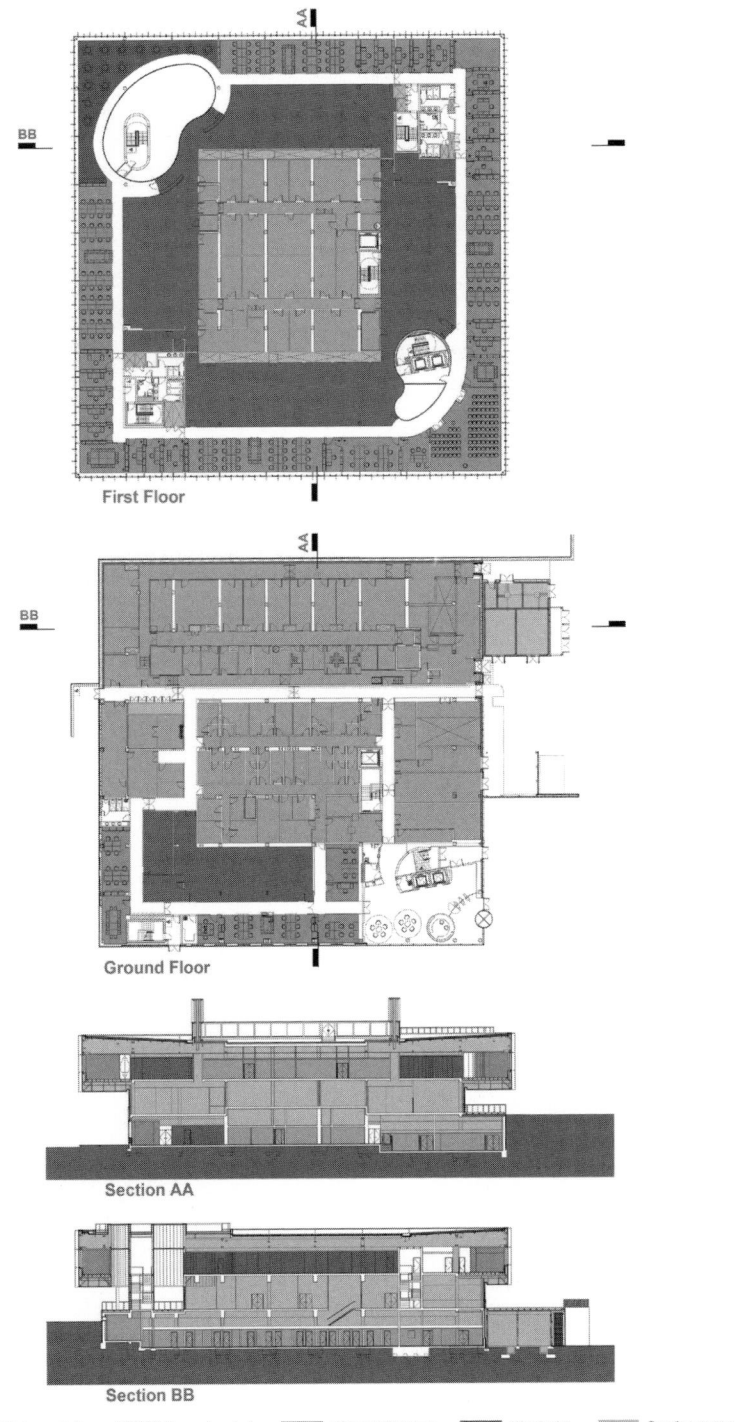

First Floor

Ground Floor

Section AA

Section BB

Primary Lab　　Secondary Lab　　Offices/ Write up　　Break-out　　Service zones

26.33 *Floor plans and sections indicating adjacencies of key spaces*

BREEAM rating. To achieve the buildings target emissions rating (TER) target of 18 per cent, an approximate 60 per cent on site renewable contribution is required.

5.2 Centre for Tropical and Infectious Diseases

Client:　　　　Liverpool School of Tropical Medicine
Location:　　　Pembroke Place, Liverpool
Team:　　　　Architect: Sheppard Robson
　　　　　　　Services Engineers: Hayden Young
　　　　　　　Structural Engineer: Arup
　　　　　　　Cost Consultant: Gleeds
　　　　　　　Contractor: Shepherd Construction
Start:　　　　2002
Finish:　　　　2007

Research: The Centre for Tropical and Infectious Diseases (CTID), for the Liverpool School of Tropical Medicine (LSTM), is the UK's leading specialist research centre for microbial diseases undertaking ground breaking research on malaria vector control.

Assembly: The Centre has been given a contemporary design with the laboratories in the middle of the floor plate and write up spaces and offices around the perimeter. The new facility provides 7,000 m² of laboratory, write up and office space set over four floors. The laboratories have fully glazed perimeters that allow daylight to penetrate to the core of the building. The circulation around the building is in a 'race track' form, increasing links between staff and visitors, maximising the opportunities for interaction and collaboration. The building's footprint follows the

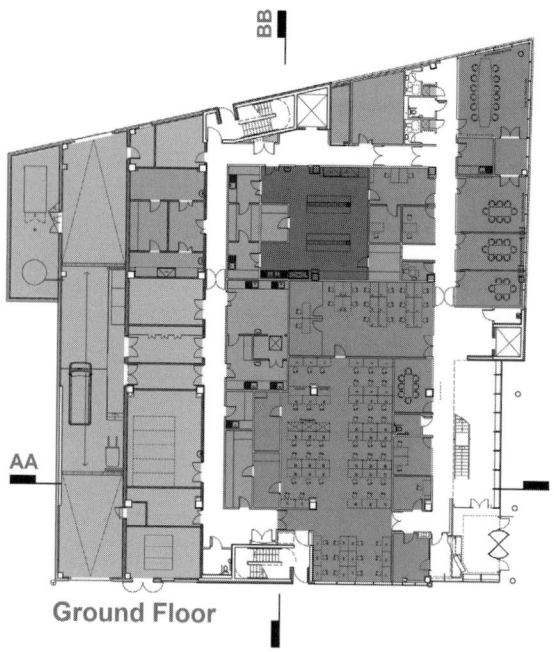

Ground Floor

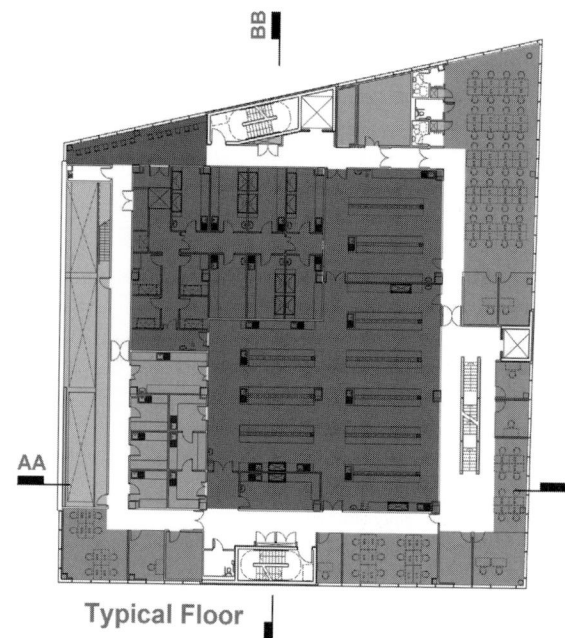

Typical Floor

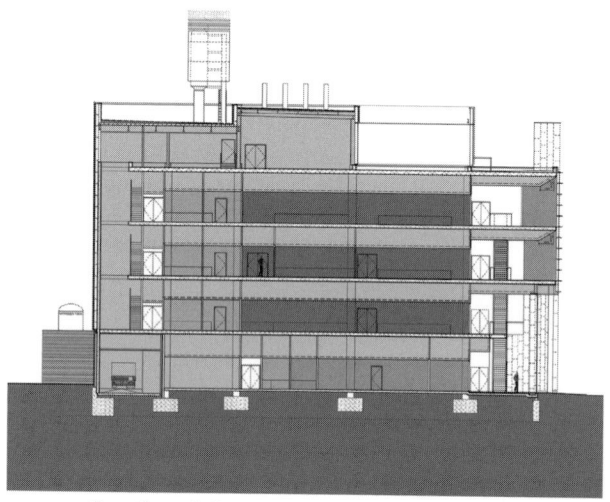

Section AA

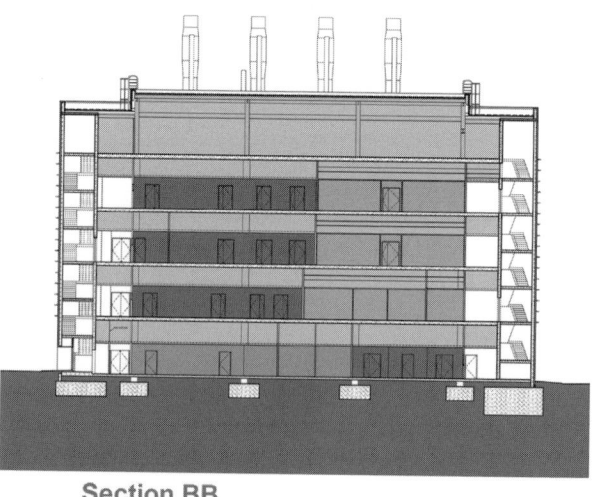

Section BB

■ Primary Lab   ■ Secondary Lab   ■ Offices/ Write up   ■ Break-out   ■ Service zones

26.33 *Floor plans and sections indicating adjacencies of key spaces (contd.)*

shape of the site in response to the brief to maximise the area of the building resulting in an 'oblong' shape. The laboratories are contained within a regular rectangular zone based on a standard laboratory module to maximise efficiency, with freer spaces such as meeting rooms, teapoints and support spaces, which can fit into the irregular corners of the building. A walk-in sidestitial service zone is located at the rear of the site adjacent to highly serviced laboratories.

Facilities within the building include:

- ACDP CL3/SAPO 2 Insectuary
- ACDP CL3 Specialist Research Suite
- ACDP CL2 Research Laboratories

- Offices and Support (Meeting, Breakout, Tea-points)
- Administration and Stores.

Furniture and fittings: The furniture within the smaller laboratories consists of wall assemblies of fixed workstops with fixed under-bench storage, while in the larger laboratories it consists of fixed workstops with mobile underbench storage along the perimeter walls and islands consisting of modular spines with 2-tiers of reagent shelves and ceiling mounted services columns with movable tables abutting each spine. Services to wall benching are provided via wall mounted dado trunking. All worktops are made of solid laminate panels with sealed joints.

Table XXIX shows the building data summary for this project.

Table XXX Legislation and standards

TITLE	AUTHOR/PUBLISHER	BRIEF SUMMARY
Bench and Equipment		
BS EN 285:1997 Sterilization. Steam sterilizers. Large sterilizers	British Standards Institution (BSI)	Provides guidance on specification requirements and the relevant tests for large steam sterilizers
BS 2646-2:1990 Autoclaves for sterilization in laboratories	British Standards Institution (BSI)	Provides guidance on basic setting and associated services for autoclaves
BS 3202-2:1991 Laboratory furniture and fittings. Specification for performance	British Standards Institution (BSI)	Provides guidance on specification & testing procedures for different grades of laboratory furniture
BS 3202-3:1991 Laboratory furniture and fittings. Recommendation for design	British Standards Institution (BSI)	Provides guidance on space and dimensional information for different types of laboratory furniture
BS 3970-1:1990 Sterilizing and disinfecting equipment for medical products	British Standards Institution (BSI)	Provides guidance on specification requirements and the relevant tests for sterilizers and steam sterilizers
BS 5726:2005 Microbiological safety cabinets	British Standards Institution (BSI)	Provides guidance on siting and use of cabinets
BS 7258-2:1994 Laboratory fume cupboards	British Standards Institution (BSI)	Provides guidance on siting and use of cabinets
BS EN 12347:1998 Biotechnology. Performance criteria for steam sterilizers and autoclaves	British Standards Institution (BSI)	Provides guidance on specification requirements and the relevant tests for sterilizers and autoclaves
BS EN 12469: 2000 Biotechnology. Performance criteria for microbiological safety cabinets	British Standards Institution (BSI)	Provides the minimum performance criteria for safety cabinets, test procedures for microbiological safety cabinets
BS EN 13150:2001 Work benches for laboratories	British Standards Institution (BSI)	Specifies safety requirements, test methods and recommendations on sizes
BS EN 14056:2003 Laboratory furniture – Recommendations for design and installation	British Standards Institution (BSI)	Provides basic information on furniture types and services provision
BS EN 14175 Parts 1–6: Fume cupboards.	British Standards Institution (BSI)	This standard was introduced to cover fume cupboards of the filtration type that were not covered by BS
BS EN ISO 15883-3:2006 Washer disinfectors Washer-disinfectors. Requirements and tests for washer-disinfectors employing thermal disinfection for human waste containers	British Standards Institution (BSI)	Provides guidance on basic setting and associated services for washer disinfectors
Services: electrical		
BS EN 61010-1 2001 safety requirements for electrical equipment for measurement, control and laboratory use	British Standards Institution (BSI)	Provides guidance on electrical equipment in laboratories
Energy efficiency in buildings. 2nd edition. (Including corrigenda 2004)	The Chartered Institution of Building Services Engineers (CIBSE)	Provides information on both the energy requirements committed by the design and the energy costs in use
Electricity at work regulations 1989. Statutory Instrument SI 1989/635	Legislation UK	
BS 7671:2001, Requirements for electrical installations.	The Institution of Electrical Engineers	Provides legal requirements for electrical works and their isolation
IEE Wiring Regulations. Sixteenth edition		All electrical wiring works must follow the Wiring Regulations to ensure a safe and efficient electrical installation
Services: gas		
Safety in the installation and use of gas systems and appliances: Gas safety (Installation and Use) Regulations 1998. 2nd edition	Health & Safety Executive (HSE)	Provides guidance on the safe installation, maintenance & use of gas
IGEM Technical Publications	Institute of Gas Engineers & Managers (IGEM)	Provides a variety of technical advice information
Industrial gas cylinder manifolds and distribution pipework/ pipelines (excluding acetylene) Code of Practice CP4: Revision3: 2005	British Compressed Gases Association (BCGA)	Provides guidance on the minimum safety standards for the design, installation, operation, and maintenance of industrial gas supply manifolds and associated narrow pipework
Code of Practice for the Storage of Medical, Pathology and Industrial Gas Cylinders.	Department of Health (DH)	Provides advice on design, installation and testing of gas systems
Safety of pressure systems. Pressure systems safety regulations 2000. ACOP (SI 2000 No 128)	Health & Safety Executive (HSE)	Provides guidance on pressure systems including gas cylinders
Guidance Notes for Siting Gas Manifolds	BOC Gases	Provides general guidance on the siting of gas manifolds and storage of cylinders
Guidance Note GN2: Guidance for the Storage of Transportable Gas Cylinders for Industrial Use	British Compressed Gases Association BCGA)	Provides basic design information on storage compounds and proximity of different types of cylinders
Guidance Note GN2: The Safe Use of Individual Portable or Mobile Cylinder Gas Supply Equipment	British Compressed Gases Association BCGA)	Provides guidance on the safe use of individual cylinder gas supplies provided from a single cylinder regulator
Guidance Note GN11: The management of risks associated with reduced oxygen atmosphere	British Compressed Gases Association BCGA)	Provides information on the risks of utilising gases which when accumulated can become hazardous
HSG71 Chemical warehousing–The storage of packaged dangerous substances.	Health & Safety Executive (HSE)	Provides guidance on the hazards associated with the storage of packaged dangerous substances includes safety; fire, emergency aspects
The safe use of gas cylinders	Health & Safety Executive (HSE)	Provides simple advice on eliminating or reducing risks
Dangerous Substances and Explosive Atmospheres Regulations 2002	Health & Safety Executive (HSE)	Require employers and the self-employed to carry out a risk assessment of work activities involving dangerous substances
Services: water		
Water supply (water quality) regulations 2001 SI 3911	Legislation UK	Provides legal standards for water to be used within a building
Plumbing engineering services design guide. 2002 edition. Part 2 – Hot and cold water supplies	Institute of Plumbing	Provides information and guidance on current technologies and practices
The Water Supply (Water Fittings) Regulations 1999	Office of Government Commerce (OGC)	These Regulations replace the water bylaws in England and Wales only
L8 Legionnaires' disease: The control of Legionella bacteria in water systems. Approved Code of Practice and guidance.	Department of Health (DH) Health & Safety Executive (HSE)	Provides the approved code of practice for preventing or controlling the risk from exposure to Legionella bacteria
TM13 Minimising the risk of Legionnaire's disease	The Chartered Institution of Building Services Engineers (CIBSE)	Provides advice on the design necessary to minimise the risk of infection from Legionella bacteria
Services: Environment/ventilation/energy		
BS 5720:1979 Code of practice for mechanical ventilation and air conditioning in buildings	British Standards Institution (BSI)	This standard has been withdrawn as the code of practice as it is now out of date, but still referred in the Building Regulations
Guide A Environmental Design	The Chartered Institution of Building Services Engineers (CIBSE)	Provides information on the design of low energy sustainable buildings.

(continued)

Table XXX (continued)

TITLE	AUTHOR/PUBLISHER	BRIEF SUMMARY
TM32 Guidance on the use of the carbon emissions calculation method	The Chartered Institution of Building Services Engineers (CIBSE)	Provides the basis of a procedure for applying the carbon emissions calculation method (CECM).
The Enhanced Capital Allowance Scheme	Carbon Trust	Provides guidance & forms for making an ECA claim; depends on the purchase energy-saving equipment
Conservation of fuel and power in new buildings other than dwellings (2006 edition) Building Regulations 2000: Approved Documents L2A or L2B	Office of the Deputy Prime Minister (OPDM)	Provides building control advice for England and Wales on environmental & energy issues
Best Practice Guide: Chilled Beams in Laboratories:	Laboratories for the 21st Century (Labs21)	Provides advice on effective design, construction and operation of chilled beams in laboratories
Best Practice Guide: Optimising Laboratory Ventilation Rates	Laboratories for the 21st Century (Labs21)	Provides advice on how to reduce energy requirements by optimising ventilation airflow
ASHRAE Handbook – HVAC Applications: Chapter 14 Laboratories, 2008	American Society of Heating, Refrigeration and Air Conditioning Engineers (ASHRAE)	Provides information on HVAC applications in laboratories
Health and safety		
The Health and Safety at Work etc. Act 1974	Primary Legislation UK	Sets out guidance, approved codes of practice and legislation with respect to occupational health and safety at work
Animal Health Act 1981	Primary Legislation UK	Aim to control the spread of diseases and to eventually eradicate them. This is done by controlling the movements of animals and isolating areas where disease is confirmed. Animal welfare is also controlled by the Act
The Control of Substances Hazardous to Health (COSHH) Regulations 2002	Secondary Legislation UK	Requirements for employers to assess the risks from hazardous subtances and take appropriate precautions
The United Kingdom Good Laboratory Practice Monitoring Authority. Guide to UK GLP Regulations 1999	Legislation UK	Sets out the organisational processes and conditions under which certain laboratory studies are undertaken
Various Guidance and advice notes	Health & Safety Executive (HSE)	HSE provide numerous useful guidance sheets which are relevant to different types of laboratories such as in sections on Biotechnology, Dangerous Pathogens, Health & Safety Regulations, Nanotechnology
The Workplace (Health Safety and Welfare) Regulations 1992	Legislation UK	Sets out legislation with respect to most workplaces
Microbiological protection		
BS EN 12128:1998 Biotechnology. Laboratories for research, development and analysis. Containment levels of microbiology laboratories, areas of risk, localities and physical safety requirements	British Standards Institution (BSI)	Specifies minimum physical requirements for the four levels of containment for biological safety in laboratories
BS EN 12738: 1999 Biotechnology. Laboratories for research, development and analysis. Guidance for containment of animals inoculated with micro organisms in experiments	British Standards Institution (BSI)	Specifies minimum physical requirements for the four levels of containment for biological safety in laboratories
BS EN 12740:1999 Biotechnology. Laboratories for research, development and analysis. Guidance for handling, inactivating and testing of waste	British Standards Institution (BSI)	Provides information on different types of waste produced by different containment level laboratories and methods for their disposal
BS EN 12741:1999 Biotechnology. Laboratories for research, development and analysis	British Standards Institution (BSI)	Provides information on basic protocols within different hazard level laboratories
BS EN 13441:2002 Biotechnology. Laboratories for research, development and analysis. Guidance on containment of genetically modified plants	British Standards Institution (BSI)	Provides information on safety measures in laboratories where plant biotechnology and genetic work is being undertaken
Advisory Committee on Dangerous Pathogens (ADCP) The management, design and operation of microbiological containment laboratories 2001	Health & Safety Executive (HSE)	Provides guidance on the management and operation of Containment Level 2 and 3 microbiological labs
The Genetically Modified Organisms (Contained Use) (Amendment) Regulations 2005	Legislation UK	Specifies minimum physical requirements for the four levels of containment for GM work in laboratories
CR 12739:1998 – Biotechnology. Laboratories for research, development and analysis. Guidance on the selection of equipment needed for biotechnology laboratories according to the degree of hazard	British Standards Institution (BSI)	Provides guidance on selecting safety measures and laboratory equipment to provide protection in differing bio-hazard areas
NHS Estates Health Building Note 15, Accommodation for Pathology Services.	Department of Health (DH)	Provides guidance on facilities for pathology services provided within acute general hospitals
Radiological protection		
HBN 6 Vol. 3 2002 Accommodation for magnetic resonance imaging	Department of Health (DH)	Provides design and specification information for MRI areas
BS 4094–1: 1966 Recommendation for data on shielding from ionizing radiation. Shielding from gamma radiation	British Standards Institution (BSI)	Provides information on legislation, regulations, guidance and other standards
HBN 6 Vol. 1 2002 Facilities for Diagnostic Imaging and Interventional Radiology, HBN 6 2002	Department of Health (DH)	Provides design and specification information for imaging & associated areas
Working with ionising radiation Ionising Radiations regulations 1999 Approved Code of Practice and guidance	Health and safety Executive (HSE)	Provides is guidance on safe working practices when in exposed to radiation arising from work with man-made or natural radiation
Fire protection		
Conservation of fuel and power in new buildings other than dwellings (2007 edition) Building Regulations 2000: Approved Documents B Vol. 2	Communities & Local Government	Provides building control advice for England and Wales on fire issues
BS 9999:2008 Code of practice for fire safety in the design, management and use of buildings	British Standards Institution (BSI)	Provides information on types of premises and relevant codes of practice, access and facilities for fire-fighting and covers vehicle access, water supply, control systems, heat and smoke control and electrical services, on measures that enable disabled people to be assisted to safety in the event of a fire, fire protection of services and fire safety systems

Table XXX (continued)

TITLE	AUTHOR/PUBLISHER	BRIEF SUMMARY
Building Bulletin 100: Design for Fire Safety in Schools 2007	Department for Education & Skills (DFES)	Provides information on fire safety in schools
Cleanrooms		
BS EN 14644-1: 1999 Cleanrooms and associated controlled environments. Classification of air cleanliness	British Standards Institution (BSI)	Provides guidance on definitions and classifications of clean rooms
BS EN 14644-4: 1999 Cleanrooms and associated controlled environments. Classification of air cleanliness	British Standards Institution (BSI)	Provides guidance on design and servicing of clean rooms
Rules and Guidance for Pharmaceutical Manufacturers and Distributors 2007 – the 'Orange Guide'	Medicines and Healthcare products Regulatory Agency (MHRA)	Covers most aspects of Good Manufacturing Practice (GMP)
Schools		
Building Bulletin 80: Science accommodation in Secondary School – Rev 2004	Department for Education & Skills (DFES)	Provides design information on laboratories in secondary schools
Building Bulletin 88: Fume cupboards in Schools	Department for Education & Employment	Provides design information on fume cupboards in secondary schools
Building Bulletin 98: Briefing Framework for Secondary School Projects	Department for Education & Skills (DFES)	Provides general spatial for secondary schools
Building Bulletin 99: Briefing Framework for Primary School Projects	Department for Education & Skills (DFES)	Provides general spatial for primary schools
Project Faraday Vol. 1 & 2 2008	Department for Education & Skills (DFES)	Examples of sciences facilities in schools
Science Labs for the twenty first Century	Department for Education & Skills (DFES)	Provides design and planning information on laboratories in schools
Designing & Planning Laboratories Guide G14-2009	Consortium of Local Education Authorities for the Provision of Science Services, (CLEAPPS)	Provides design and planning information on laboratories in secondary schools
The Good Lab – Concise Guide 2009	Andy Piggott	Provides design, planning and fittings information on laboratories in secondary schools
School Science Laboratories Design for the 21st Century, 2006	National Science Learning Centre (NSLC) North Eastern Education & Library Board (NEELB)	Provides design, planning & fittings information on laboratories in secondary schools
Laboratory Design for Health and Safely, Chapter 6, Topics in Safely, 3rd edition, 2001	The Association for Science Education (ASE)	Provides advice on school health and safety issues
Vibration		
Design of Floors for Vibration: A New Approach, SCI Publication 354, 2009	Steel Construction Institute (SCI)	Provides guidance on forms of construction and their response to vibration
Design Guide on the Vibration of Floors. SCI Publication 076, 1989	Steel Construction Institute (SCI)	Provides guidance for the design of floors in steel framed buildings against vibration
BS 6472-1:2008 Guide to Evaluation of Human Exposure to Vibration in Buildings (1Hz to 80Hz)	British Standards Institution (BSI)	Provides guidance on predicting human response to vibration in buildings
A Design Guide for Footfall Induced Vibration of Structures: CCIP-016, 2006	Willford, MR., and Young, P. The Concrete Centre	Provides advice on designing for footfall vibration with worked examples
Design of Stiff, Low-Vibration Floor Structures, 1991	Amick H., Hardash S., Gillet P. and Reaverley R. International Society for Optical Engineering (SPIE) Vol 1619	Conference paper on design of floors supporting vibration sensitive equipment.
ASHRAE Handbook – HVAC Applications: Chapter 47 Sound and Vibration Control, 2008	American Society of Heating, Refrigeration and Air Conditioning Engineers (ASHRAE)	Provides guidance on controlling sound transmission and vibration from many procedures with examples.
Other		
The BRE Green Guide to Specification	British Research Establishment	Provides guidance on the relative environmental impacts of elemental specifications
BCO Guide 2005 – Best Practice in the Specification of Offices	British Council for Offices (BCO)	Provides advice on future design and construction of office buildings, including sustainability, business performance and cost and value
The Disability Discrimination Act 1995 (DDA)	Legislation UK	Legislation concerning disabled requirements

Sustainability: The client prescribed from the beginning that the achievement of a BREEAM 'Very Good' rating was required to satisfy their project funding criteria from the Bill and Melinda Gates Foundation. The building employs a number of sustainable features, including specification of pre-fabricated and modular construction components that result in less waste on site, low energy lighting with controls (with presences detection/daylight linking/BMS automation) and heat recovery from the exhaust ventilation system.

6 BIBLIOGRAPHY

6.1 Legislation and standards

Any design shall be formulated acknowledging as relevant all design and codes, regulations, standards and statutory requirements. The examples listed in Table XXX should not be regarded either as prescriptive or inclusive. These generally state minimum requirements though there is nothing to prevent a designer from exceeding the applicable requirement especially once a risk assessment has been undertaken by the stakeholder on the space's operational requirements.

6.2 Websites

Table XXXI lists some useful websites.

6.3 Acknowledgements

Particular thanks are due to the late Gordon Kirtley for his pioneering work on the Wellcome Trust's 'Guidance on space standards, layout and specification for biomedical buildings'.

Sincere thanks are also due to Andrew Bowles for his support, to Patrick Ng and Robin Base, for producing the graphics and Anna Stamp, Daniel Bennett, Luke Thurman and Pedro Santos for their assistance with the case studies.

Table XXXI Websites

SITE ADDRESS	ORGANISATION	BRIEF SUMMARY
www.hse.gov.uk	Health & Safety Executive (HSE)	Provide numerous useful guidance sheets which are relevant to laboratory working environmental and safety requirements for UK.
www.cibse.org	The Chartered Institution of Building Services Engineers (CIBSE)	Provides numerous publications relevant to various service disciplines and environmental requirements for UK.
www.dh.gov.uk/	Department of Health (DH)	Provides statistical reports, surveys, press releases, circulars and legislation with respect to health care facilities in UK.
www.wbdg.org	Whole Building Design Guide (WBDG)	Provide information on various laboratory types based mainly on US projects.
www.dfes.gov.uk	Department for Education & Skills (DFES)	Provides information of school planning and spatial requirements in UK.
www.cleapss.org.uk	Education Authorities for the Provision of Science Services. (CLEAPPS)	Provides an advisory service for subscribers, supporting practical science and technology in schools in UK.
www.ase.org.uk	The Association for Science Education (ASE)	Provides information produced by teachers helping teachers that teach science.
www.phac-aspc.gc.ca	Health Canada	Provides considerable data on microbiological labs produced by Government of Canada.
www.bco.org.uk	British Council for Offices (BCO)	Provides research data on best practice in all aspects of the office sector in UK.
www.carbontrust.co.uk	Carbon Trust	Provides information on grants and technologies funded by UK Government to help promote low carbon technologies.
www.bcga.co.uk	British Compressed Gases Association BCGA)	Provides information on gases supplied to manufacturing industry, laboratories, and the medical sector for UK.
www.igem.org.uk	Institute of Gas Engineers & Managers (IGEM)	Provides a variety of technical advice information.
www.bsistandards.co.uk	British Standards Institution (BSI)	Provides opportunity to purchase UK and European standards.
www.labs21.org.uk	Labs21 UK	Established by the Higher Education Environmental Performance Improvement (HEEPI) project to support more sustainable design and operation of laboratories in Britain. It draws, with permission, on the experience and materials of the Labs21 initiative in the USA.
www.labs2lcentury.gov	Labs21	Labs 21 is a voluntary partnership program dedicated to improving the environmental performance of U.S. laboratories.
www.lab2020.com	Lab 2020	Lab2020 is a study based in Germany looking at sustainable environments for pharmaceutical and biotechnological laboratories exchanging the experience of manufacturers, designers and users.

27 Libraries

Brian Edwards with Ayub Khan

Brian Edwards is Emeritus Professor of Architecture at Edinburgh College of Art, Edinburgh University where he was director of the Graduate Research School before retirement. He trained as an architect, has a PhD from Glasgow University and is the author of 'Libraries and Learning Resource Centres', published by Architectural Press in 2002 and revised in 2009.

Ayub Khan BA (Hons) FCLIP is Head of Libraries – Strategy at Warwickshire County Council. He was previously Principal Project Officer (Library of Birmingham) where he worked on plans for the new city centre library in Birmingham.

KEY POINTS:
- *The community role of public libraries is changing rapidly*
- *Information is delivered in all kinds of media, not just books*
- *Libraries are social anchors and knowledge gateways*
- *Libraries are getting bigger and embracing more functions*
- *The university library is leading design and management changes*

Contents
1 Introduction
2 Community role of libraries
3 Library design
4 Room layout, furniture and shelving
5 Space standards
6 Environmental considerations
7 Financing and resources
8 Case study
9 Bibliography

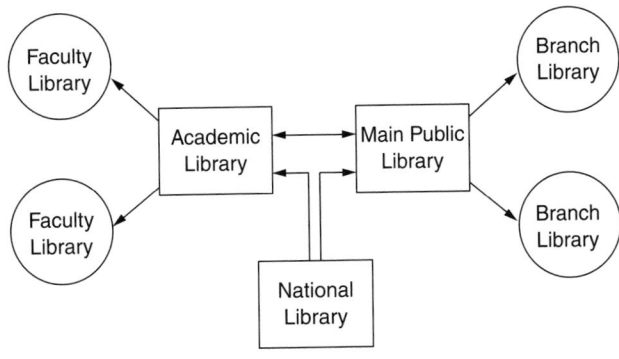

27.1 *Ideal pattern of public library*

Table II Main factors leading to change in design of library buildings

- New information technology and new forms of electronic data exchange
- Greater social, community and educational role for public libraries
- Expansion in types and diversity of education, including life-long learning, has undermined the exclusivity of public libraries
- Impact of mass culture and new social media
- Impact of environmental sustainability on the design of libraries

1 INTRODUCTION

1.1 Changing role of the library

The evolving role of the library has created a set of new and complex challenges for those delivering library buildings and services. The libraries of the twenty-first century are no longer simply familiar repositories for books with space for reading and lending. They have changed and expanded, been rethought and redesigned. Libraries now provide an increasingly wide range of services, using a multitude of media, and reach a more diverse audience than ever before; see Table I and Figure 27.1.

As libraries broaden their social and educational role to become 'ideas stores' and 'knowledge gateways', there is pressure to increase the extent of non-library accommodation within their walls. The problem for the architect is how to bring the library and non-library functions into a coherent whole (see Table II).

One trend is towards social or public functions rather than merely library ones on the ground floor. Such public functions may include cafes, bookshops, exhibition areas, meeting rooms, community and welfare offices. The library then rises from this welcoming community base. Many academic libraries follow a similar model with student, welfare and registry facilities linked to printing, binding, bookshops and cafes on the entrance level with the main library spaces above. With such plans, noise abatement may be required and careful zoning to ensure security of the collection.

Some argue that libraries of the future will be without books. Such buildings will be knowledge markets, open to all without security barriers, and freely engaged in social exchanges of various kinds from learning to networking, using ever advancing IT to expand human knowledge and creative potential. Recent examples include the bookless public library at San Antonio, Texas and the paperless academic library at the School of Engineering, Stanford University. However, books are likely to remain in most libraries but take an increasingly back seat in this fast evolving building type. Surviving books are likely to have sentimental or archival interest rather than be the first point of contact for readers.

1.2 Revival of the library

After years of relative neglect as a building type, the public library enjoyed a renaissance towards the end of the twentieth century. This was partly the result of new information technologies challenging the supremacy of the book and other forms of paper based media. The IT revolution highlighted the important social,

Table I Library types

Main types of library	Key features
National Library	• National collections of books, journals, maps etc. • Research focused • Conservation element • Specialist readership
Public Library	• Collections of books and CDs primarily for loan • Place to meet and exchange • Wide range of material of local interest • Community base for local people • Integration with other 'cultural' or civic buildings
Academic Library	• Support for teaching, learning and research • Place where new knowledge is generated and exchanged • Large specialist and research collections • Separate IT and multi-media areas • 24 hour access
Professional and Special Libraries	• Specialist collection of books and professional journals • Often contains rare or fragile non-paper material • Limited public access • Conservation element

educational and cultural role of library buildings, particularly to the life and welfare of cities. CABE in particular was instrumental in pushing forward a vision for more inclusive and dynamic public libraries. Under pressure from CABE and in response to wider social changes in Britain's cities, interesting new solutions to the architecture of the public library appeared in London's Watney Market, Whitechapel and Peckham as well as at Worcester, Norwich, Brighton and more recently in Birmingham, where Mecanoo's new public library opened in 2013 (see Section 8 Case Study). Although the pace of change has slowed under economic pressures in much of Europe, the USA, China and Canada are building a clutch of interesting new libraries that integrate media and promote cultural solidarity.

The university library too has undergone considerable change as the emphasis shifts from libraries as storehouses of knowledge to places where new knowledge is generated and existing knowledge (whether digital or paper) is openly shared in teaching, learning and research. Examples of a fresh approach to the design of academic libraries are found at the Saltire Centre, Glasgow Caledonia University, designed by BDP, new libraries at the Open University by Swanke Hayden Connell Architects, Leicester University by Associated Architects and at Aberdeen University by Schmidt Hammer Lassen. Many extensions to existing university libraries as at Liverpool, East Anglia and Portsmouth Universities provide space for IT and new forms of media to augment older book-based provision. These areas, known sometimes as 'Learning Commons', reflect the change in pedagogy from lecture-based teaching to student-focused open learning based on course work rather than examination. Useful examples can be sourced on the SCONUL journal *Focus* and the *Designing Libraries* website.

Outside the UK there has also been new thinking on the design and civic purpose of library buildings with OMA's public library in Seattle, the Snøhetta designed library in Alexandria, Egypt and that by Patkau Architects in Montreal being notable examples. Across Europe there has also been much new building of university libraries to meet the expansion in higher education including the Free University Berlin by Foster & Partners and Brandenburg Technical University by Herzog and de Meuron. The libraries of universities in particular have had to adjust to new pedagogic practices as well as a revolution in the form and use of knowledge.

1.3 A place to meet

Today the library, whether public or academic, is a place to meet, discover, learn and exchange information within welcoming, light and airy surroundings, Figures 27.2, 27.3. Libraries come in many shapes and forms. Generally, there are four main types but within each there is much variability. One trend is towards bigger libraries whether faculty or community based. Large scale provides the basis for better integration of book and digital media, of providing a wider range of support services (computer training, language skills, networking skills) as well as more extensive non-reader facilities (café, exhibition areas, shop).

It is important that libraries are well designed from a civic point of view, providing an architectural response which is welcoming, inclusive and offers a range of services able to attract young people as well as old, locals and new residents, whether IT literate or not. Today's libraries therefore need to provide a variety of different types of space to serve these different users. Although small libraries are good at community engagement, large ones are increasingly favoured since they serve the needs of readers, business and education on a regional basis.

2 COMMUNITY ROLE OF LIBRARIES

2.1 New functions for libraries

The revival of interest in the library as a building type has three main roots. First, new media technologies, particularly IT-based knowledge packages and new ways of communicating (Facebook and Twitter) have led government and university clients to reassess the role and design of libraries in a digital age. Second, the resurgence of interest in other cultural building types – notably the museum and art gallery – encouraged many public clients and their architects to see libraries as buildings to visit in their own right rather than merely providing access to books, journals and IT services. Third, the expansion of universities worldwide led to a re-assessment of the role of the academic library in teaching, learning and research, and this in turn influenced the design of public libraries.

As a result of these changes libraries have become inclusive and inviting buildings where their transparency acts as a lighthouse of knowledge in many towns and on many campuses. Once inside

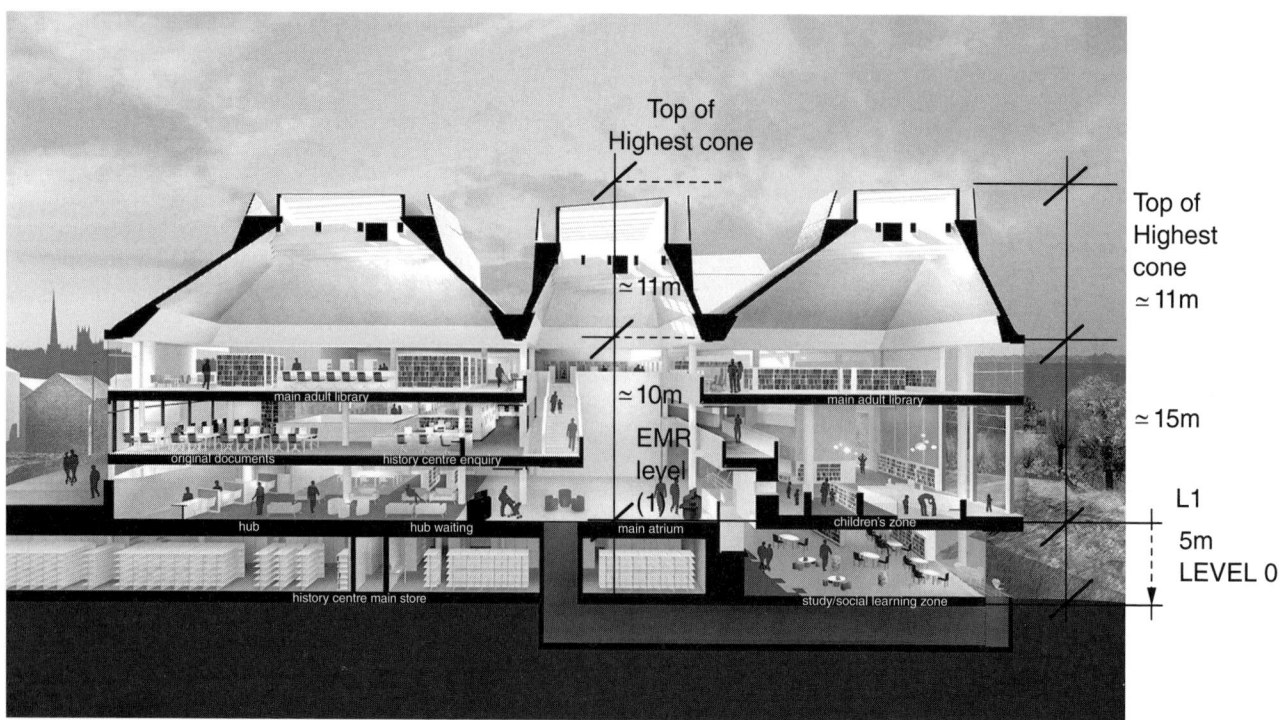

27.2 *Section of The Hive public library in Worcester, designed by Feilden Clegg Bradley Studios*

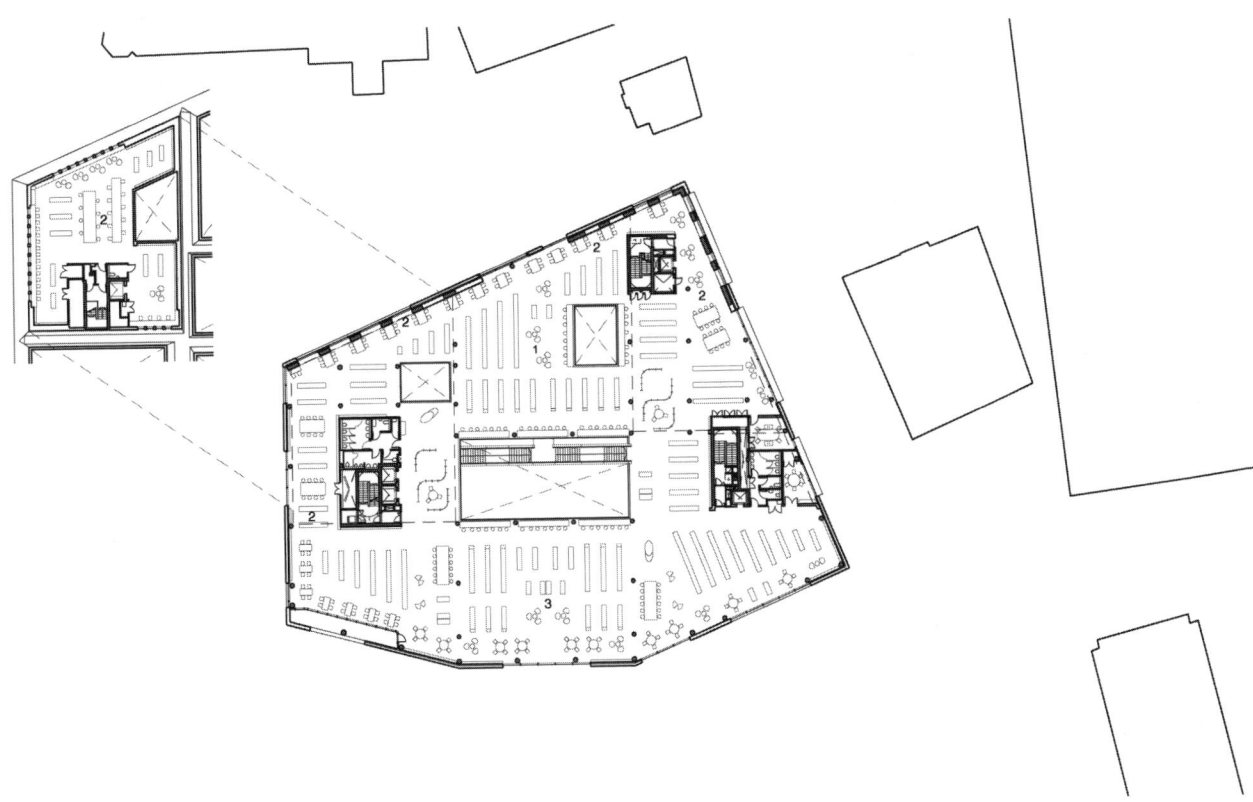

27.3 *Level 3 plan of The Hive public library in Worcester, designed by Feilden Clegg Bradley Studios*
Key: 1 Library/study, 2 Quiet study, 3 Social learning

these new libraries, the spaces are animated by the sound of knowledge use, knowledge sharing and social discourse. However, not all is noisy: new libraries have had to zone their spaces to meet different types of knowledge use and to serve the needs of different users.

The twenty-first-century library is typically a building with exciting external public spaces, interesting architectural forms and a more 'market place' interior quality. Attention is paid to urban design as well as building design, to the creation of reading rooms which invite contemplation, reflection and exchange across media types and between readers, and to the provision of exhibition, café and bookshop areas. Libraries have changed from being mainly depositories of books, newspapers and journals to being multi-media knowledge centres playing an active role in the modern digital age. Today the typical library (see Tables III and IV) is an interactive network of spaces which encompass books for loan, journals (many of which are electronic), CDs, videos, internet

sources and special study collections. Increasingly the network contains links to the home and educational centres, thereby supporting learning and reinforcing the role of schools, colleges and universities in the community. This expanded role has been accompanied by a change in design values, the job description of librarians and a broadening of the brief of a typical library.

Rather than lead to the obsolescence of the library, new technology has liberated the library from increasingly unpopular stereotypical forms, and altered the fundamental assumptions behind their design. One such is the requirement for silence in all but designated areas. The strategy today is to encourage the sharing of knowledge and to welcome the use of the spoken word either between individuals or in groups. Since the library is often used for teaching and learning within the community, silence is expected only in private study areas. Elsewhere the pleasure of discovery and exchange is welcomed (see Figure 27.4). Restricting silence to special areas allows the remainder to become a place for sharing ideas and jointly pursuing knowledge.

2.2 Integration of book and digital media
Although books remain vital to the library, the first point of contact is usually the catalogue screen or digitised media messaging. The

Table III Contemporary role of the public library

- Buildings which help cement together a community
- Buildings which are meeting places
- IT learning and support centre
- Complements art gallery and museum
- Access point to council services
- Life-long learning and literacy centre

Table IV CABE's summary of public library trends

- Each library will develop its own bespoke range of services
- Libraries will develop in partnership with other services
- Adaptability is a key factor in layout and design
- Reader development, communication and literacy skill are central library services
- Libraries will become communication centres for mobile populations
- Long stay use of libraries for study requires friendly and efficient support facilities
- Electronic links between homes and libraries will increase
- Children's services will grow in importance
- Virtual library services will be provided 24 hours a day
- Librarians will change their role from custodians of culture to knowledge navigators

Adapted from *Better Public Libraries*, CABE 2003 pp. 7–8.

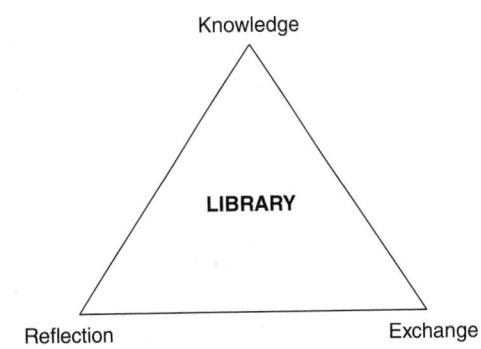

27.4 *Key relationships in the library (Brian Edwards)*

interaction between digital knowledge and the printed word is a dynamic one requiring space characteristics different from that of the traditional library. Many modern libraries place the computer screen at the front door allowing the reader to pass through knowledge layers as they navigate the library. The role of library staff is to aid navigation through types and modes of knowledge rather than exercise security or sit behind glass screens. Today's librarians are data networkers and media and subject navigators with direct contact with readers at the front desk and at various points within the library. In directing readers to the diversity of new material, there is a great deal of interaction, both verbal and digital, which inevitably affects the interior layout and character of the library.

Another significant shift over the past two decades has been the increasing role of libraries in life-long learning, in providing community information, and in supporting the needs of the elderly particularly in the area of IT provision and training. By 2020, nearly half of Europeans will be over 65 years old and here the library has particularly important services to provide. This has ramifications for the design and layout of library buildings, the level of lighting and provision of facilities from workstations to toilets and disabled access.

For people who do not possess English as their first language, or for individuals who are newly arrived in an area, the library is often the first point of community contact. Hence, the qualities and values expressed through architectural design leave a lasting impression. For these reasons the library today is seen as a gateway to learning and a shop window to new knowledge and community services. The latter leads to some public libraries taking on the role of citizens advice bureaus with librarians quasi social workers.

3 LIBRARY DESIGN

The design of library buildings should be addressed at three levels:

- Urban design
- Building design
- Interior design.

Each has specific requirements which involve dialogue with user and interest groups, and each level has its own exacting demands which cannot be overlooked (see Table V). Library design is more than an exercise in architectural form making in spite of the growing interest in typological reinvention.

Table V Planning

Principal site planning considerations	Issues to consider
Civic presence	• Relationship to other public buildings
	• Visible presence
Public access	• Access to public transport
	• Disabled access
Service access	• Access to road system
	• Delivery and storage areas
Urban design	• External public gathering space
	• Safe, secure and legible routes

3.1 Urban design

It is vital that libraries are buildings that the community can be proud of and want to use. The design should be open, inviting and transparent. There should be a sense of 'library-ness' in the design of the building as a whole, its main spaces and more intimate study rooms. This may be translated differently between a major public library and an academic one but the building should still communicate its essentials as a library: a place where society's knowledge is stored and made available free of charge.

The trend away from branch libraries and separate faculty libraries means the library is assuming ever greater importance as a prime civic building as it becomes a centralised facility. The public library therefore needs to be well connected to civic life and the academic library located at the centre of the college or university. Good access to pedestrian flows and public transport is essential, as

is the ability to service libraries with their ever evolving collections and needs.

Hence, there will normally be a public front and a service rear or undercroft. However, the public entrance is not normally the library door but a gathering space immediately outside it.

Libraries should turn outdoor spaces into assets that support meeting, exchanging ideas, reading outdoors or simply sitting in attractive surroundings. These should be designed with the characteristics of a public square with attention to landscape design, public comfort (i.e. seats) and community or personal safety. The library 'square' is where users will meet, escape from the confines of the library to reflect on the material, or take short breaks to eat sandwiches or visit local cafes and other cultural facilities. Aristotle defined the city as 'a collection of buildings where men live a common life for a noble end' and nowhere is this more evident than in the public library.

The external library space should be free of cars although public modes of transport can (and often should) pass nearby. There also needs to be provision for disabled access and facilities for the storage of bicycles. Hence, a level access is preferable and ramps essential where changes of level are inevitable. The public space alongside the library entrance provides an opportunity to make a statement of the building and this in turn can help signal the significance of the library. It also provides the chance to incorporate sculpture or other forms of public art into the city – some of which may contain text references to the library collection.

With university libraries the building needs to be centrally placed on the campus and located where 24 hour surveillance is possible. There is often a linear plaza at the centre of campus where other academic institutions are located such as senate house, refectory, gymnasium and registry. This provides an opportunity for the formation of a student-centred academic mall which ties together the key shared facilities with links to the separate faculty buildings further afield. Hence, one role of the academic library is to define the centre of the campus both spatially and in terms of building hierarchy.

The flows from the external public space to the main building entrance are more clearly defined if attention is paid to urban design at the briefing stage. The choice of site often dictates external relationships. Proximity to public transport and existing pedestrian or cycle flows is imperative. There are parallel flows too which need to be considered such as the delivery of books, newspapers, furniture and access for staff. The service entrance needs to have good road access and a limited amount of delivery and parking space. Increasingly, information is electronically delivered using wire or wireless technology and this eases the demand upon physical service areas. However, delivery and storage of the library material is a major consideration at the site planning level.

3.2 The design of the library

Libraries are used for long periods of time. Therefore if the public library is to serve society and the university library its students and teaching staff, then great attention is needed to interior design, furnishings and fittings of both study and more public spaces (see Table VI).

It is important that the brief for a new library mentions the values the building should entail (see Table VII). Briefs are more than flow diagrams and floor area charts. A good brief contains higher ambition, thereby ensuring the building meets society's aspirations for libraries. There needs to be a clear diagram for the library in

Table VI Design

Key design characteristics of libraries
Visible, recognisable and legible as a type
Adaptable to new information technology and physically extendable
Comfortable and disabled friendly
Inviting, safe and secure for users
Protection and security of the collection

plan and cross section. Clarity in plan allows the user to comprehend the logic of the layout with the main features (such as reading rooms and IT suits) in obvious locations. Creating a clear diagram is a challenge too in section and here the library needs to have a coherent strategy for daylight, ventilation and acoustics.

The external square or set back public space leads the library visitor immediately to the entrance doors. These need to be inviting, wide and transparent, and arranged so that the interior can be viewed immediately upon arrival. It should also be possible to see the major library spaces from the outside, thereby providing links to the life of the city (see Figure 27.5). Too frequently in the past the demands for security interrupted the physical and visible flows between the inside and outside worlds.

In large libraries it is often possible to form an outer foyer before the user reaches the library proper. Here there may be lockers, information boards relating to community activities, a café and sandwich bar and meeting rooms. This transition space between the inner and outer worlds requires particular attention in order to avoid disruption to the library. Once inside the library the user should be able to comprehend the key spaces and principal routes.

3.3 Library desk
The library desk and control barrier provides an essential element in the working of the library. It is the main point of contact between users and library staff and the spoken work is essential to aid navigation through the collection. The library control desk should not form an impervious wall but provide an inviting permeable barrier through which visitors pass. The trend towards self-service check in and out of books and other material frees up the librarians to become 'floor walkers' aiding readers in their search for information. The control or self-service point where books are checked in and out should remain part of the entrance experience rather than the dominant element for the visitor. Increasingly, the next point of contact is with the computerised catalogue or the IT support area which is usually nearby. To counter the dominance of digital information systems in some libraries (which can deter the elderly) there is often a magazine or newspaper area nearby.

3.4 Arrangement strategy
There are two main strategies for arranging the book collection. The first is to stack the books near the centre of the library arranging reading tables around the edge where there is good access to natural light and external views. The second is to place the books around the perimeter with a large central reading room often lit

from above. The latter provides the opportunity to create an interior volume where readers can move between paper and electronic media. The integration of modes of knowledge and types of media is often difficult in practice because of the specific requirements of computers and the nature of some paper-based collections such as old newspapers or photographs. So in spite of the ideal of integration, there are often special study areas dedicated to types of media or study material.

3.5 Flexibility
Since the storage and use of knowledge is changing rapidly, libraries need to retain a high level of flexibility. The ability of the building to change over time without compromising the key attributes of what constitutes architecturally a 'library' is an important consideration at the design stage. Libraries are recognisable buildings where spaces like the reading room help to define the type. To provide flexibility at the price of character risks removing the important civic dimension. However, libraries need to be able to adapt to changing information technologies and their evolving cultural or social role if they are to achieve their full relevance in the twenty-first century.

3.6 Circulation
Circulation, which may account for 10–20% of floor areas, is used for access and for socialising. Such areas should contain seats and niches off the flow to encourage informal exchanges. Major staircases should also be designed as processional spaces where the scope and fluidity of knowledge is experienced architecturally.

3.7 Zoning
Zoning the interior of the library into distinctive areas (Figure 27.6) rather than separate rooms is the policy generally adopted in all but national libraries (Figure 27.7). Integration is the norm within the constraints imposed by noise, PC screen conditions and reader comfort.

Table VII Key factors to consider in interior design

Technical
Are the floor loadings adequate for the collection?
Is the wiring and wireless layout suitable for future IT needs?
Are the environmental conditions acceptable for the planned use?
Is the building energy efficient?
Is the collection secure from fire or theft?
Aesthetic
Is the building welcoming as well as functional?
Are the routes and major spaces legible to the user?
Is there space for reflection?
Do readers have good access to daylight and views?

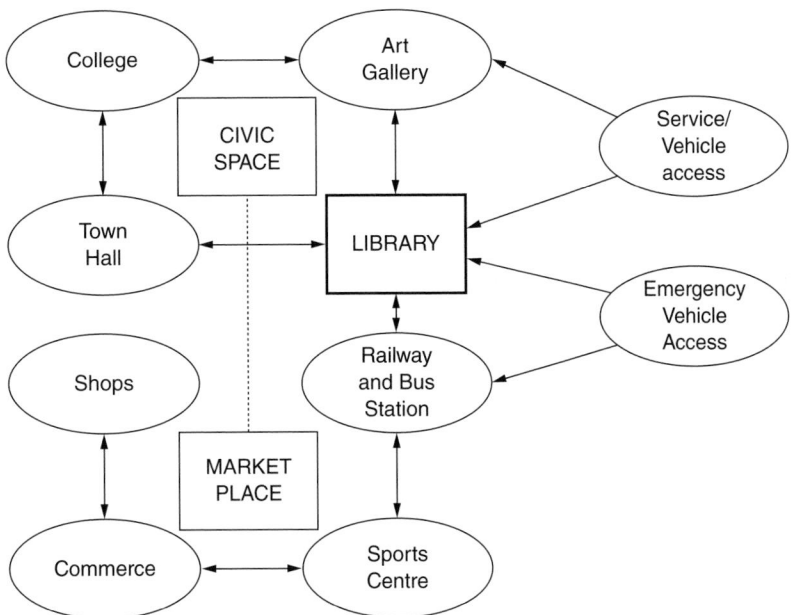

27.5 *Conceptual diagram of the relationship of library to other civic functions (Brian Edwards)*

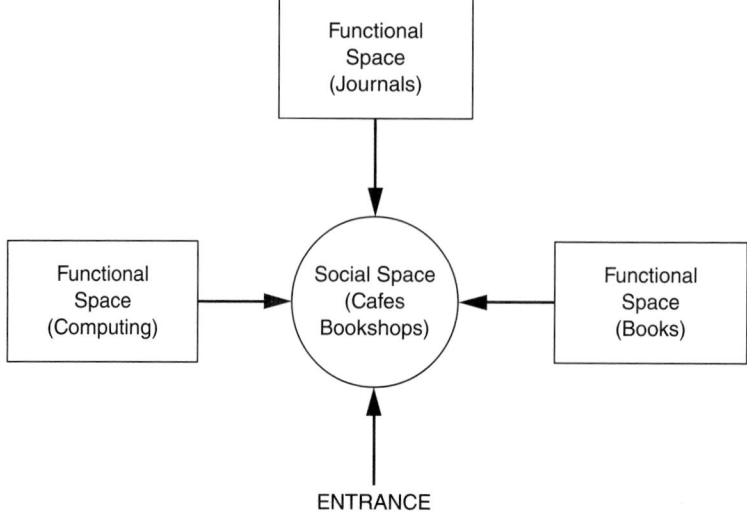

27.6 *Relationship between the functional and social zones in the library (Brian Edwards)*

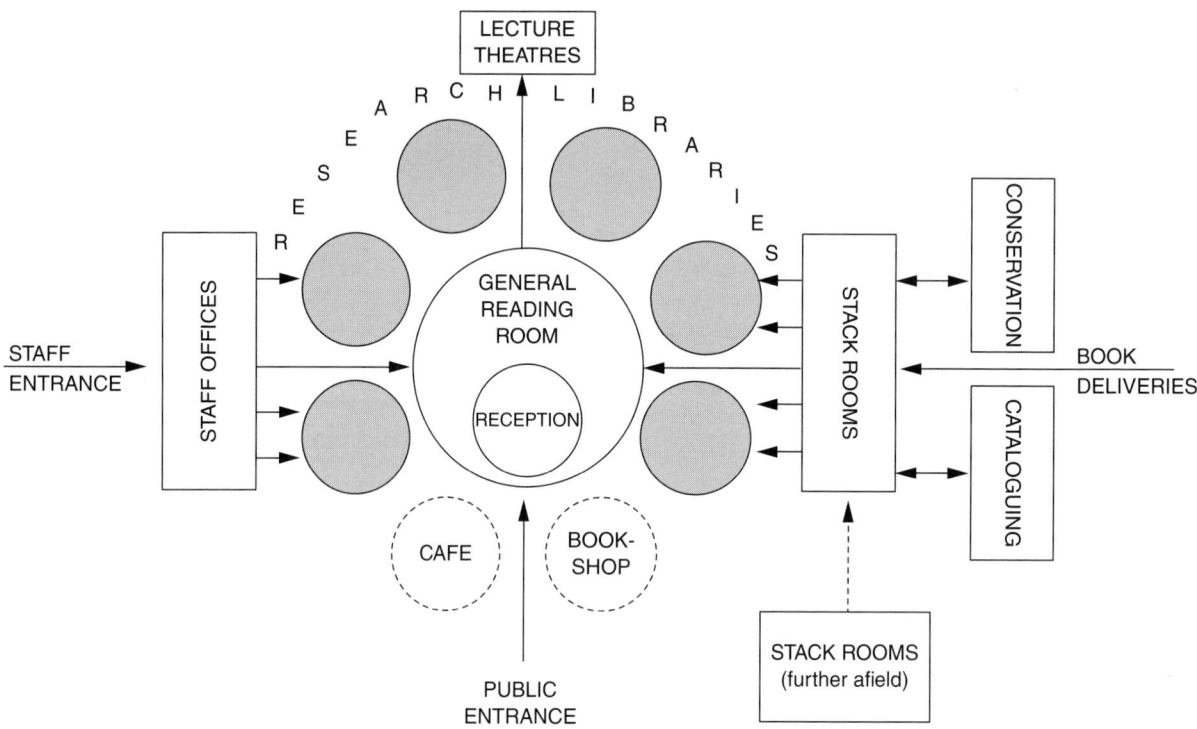

27.7 *Diagrammatic layout of a national library (Brian Edwards)*

These separate zones may be distinctive functional areas but they are generally linked by wide connecting spaces. Zoning allows one area to adopt a different policy on noise or security than another, permits internal change without disruption to the whole and allows different users to employ the library resources in different ways. A varied interior culture is preferable to one where there is a corporate standardisation across the whole building. Such variety can be engineered or left to grow as the nature of users and the collection changes (see Table VIII). At Peckham Library for example, there are three pods within the main book areas designed specifically to house the special collections. Each is specific to the collection and tailored to the tastes of potential users.

Increasingly paper and electronic sources are physically integrated on the reader's desk but there is usually a zone or room for computer users; a separate area for those referring to journals or newspapers; a defined floor area for the library book stacks; a separate space for reading desks and perhaps special study carrels.

Table VIII Typical services provided within a public or academic library

- Access to and loan of books
- Access to journals and newspapers
- Use of workstations
- Access to the Internet
- Electronic access to research journals
- Guidance to sources of information
- Community learning and visitor support
- Café and refreshment area

3.8 Access

Libraries require a great deal of service access for the delivery of books and study material, and for the removal of waste. However, the prime access consideration relates to users, both able and disabled. Wheelchair provision is essential in all areas of the library except in compact storage zones. Wheelchair users need to be able to reverse at the end of bookstacks and to rise unimpeded between floors. Security barriers should also be wide enough for wheelchair access. Disabled access in libraries is relatively straightforward. However, problems can occur around cafes and bookshops where wheelchair access for library users may become obstructed.

4 ROOM LAYOUT, FURNITURE AND SHELVING

4.1 Book stacks

Most libraries are sub-divided by book stacks which provide the basis for zoning areas into functional parts (see Table IX). The stacks provide also acoustic protection, have important environmental qualities (they provide thermal mass) and help define routes through the library. The position and type of shelving is essential to the smooth operation of a library and needs to be located carefully in relation to the fixed parts such as columns, lifts, stairs, walls and doors. The book stacks also dictate the layout of seating, tables and the position of workstations.

Table IX Book stacks

Layout of book stacks	Secondary issues
Position book stacks to define routes through library	Ensure safety exits are visible
Use book stacks as acoustic barriers	Consider acoustic and thermal properties of book stacks
Compress stacks to create reader areas at perimeter of building	Provide adequate space for safe and disabled use in dense stack areas
Provide light sensors in deep stack areas	In large libraries lighting is the major energy user hence use LED and other energy saving technologies
Ensure floor loadings are adequate for dense book stacks	Changing stack layout can be constrained by structural limitations

Normally, book stacks are centrally located with reading spaces around the edge of the building or around the perimeter of atria spaces (Figures 27.8, 27.9). However, main libraries have large and distinctive reading rooms. Such spaces may be on upper floors or overlooking external spaces and will in all probability be used by readers surfing book, journal and internet sources. Reading rooms are usually different to IT areas but there may be physical overlap.

4.2 IT provision and digital media

Growth in IT provision is sometimes at the cost of areas for book storage. As a result shelving is often closely spaced and increasingly aspects of the book collection are stored elsewhere. Growing use of libraries is sometimes at the expense of space standards, both in seating area and library shelving. Designers need to consider both the needs of readers and of staff who have the task of servicing the collection. Although books are generally decreasing in size, art books are getting larger, and whereas PCs are also shrinking with growing use of laptops and tablets, the number of readers who arrive armed with the latest digital technology is increasing rapidly. Hence, layouts and service points need to accommodate these changes.

Academic libraries provide much more computer space than public libraries (Figure 27.10). In some university libraries, the areas given over to IT-based learning resource centres can exceed that of book and journal storage. The use and loan of CDs, the development of a learning rather than a teaching culture has led also to the academic library being extensively employed in group teaching. Rooms are set aside for seminars within the library itself, and often the Internet provides the main resources on which students draw. As a result the nature of the interior spaces changes into a hybrid between the traditional library reading room and something more akin to a market trading floor (Figures 27.11, 27.12). The use of the library for seminar type teaching also puts pressure on the lifts, stairs and corridors at the end of timetabled teaching and this can disrupt private study areas.

Table layout is an important consideration since the distribution of reader spaces can influence the configuration of columns and interior walls (see Table X). The layout of tables and shelves is

Table X Furniture

Layout and design of library furniture	Secondary issues
Provide visible staff desks on each floor to guide readers	Library staff should be visible to aid readers
Provide reader tables in areas well served by natural light	Place tables at edge of library or in internal atria spaces
Divide large reader tables into personal study areas	Provide separate power points along length of table
Ensure mix of table sizes and layouts to suit nature of collection	Atlases and newspapers require different table designs
Ensure tables are connected to IT systems	Encourage mixture of media usage at study tables

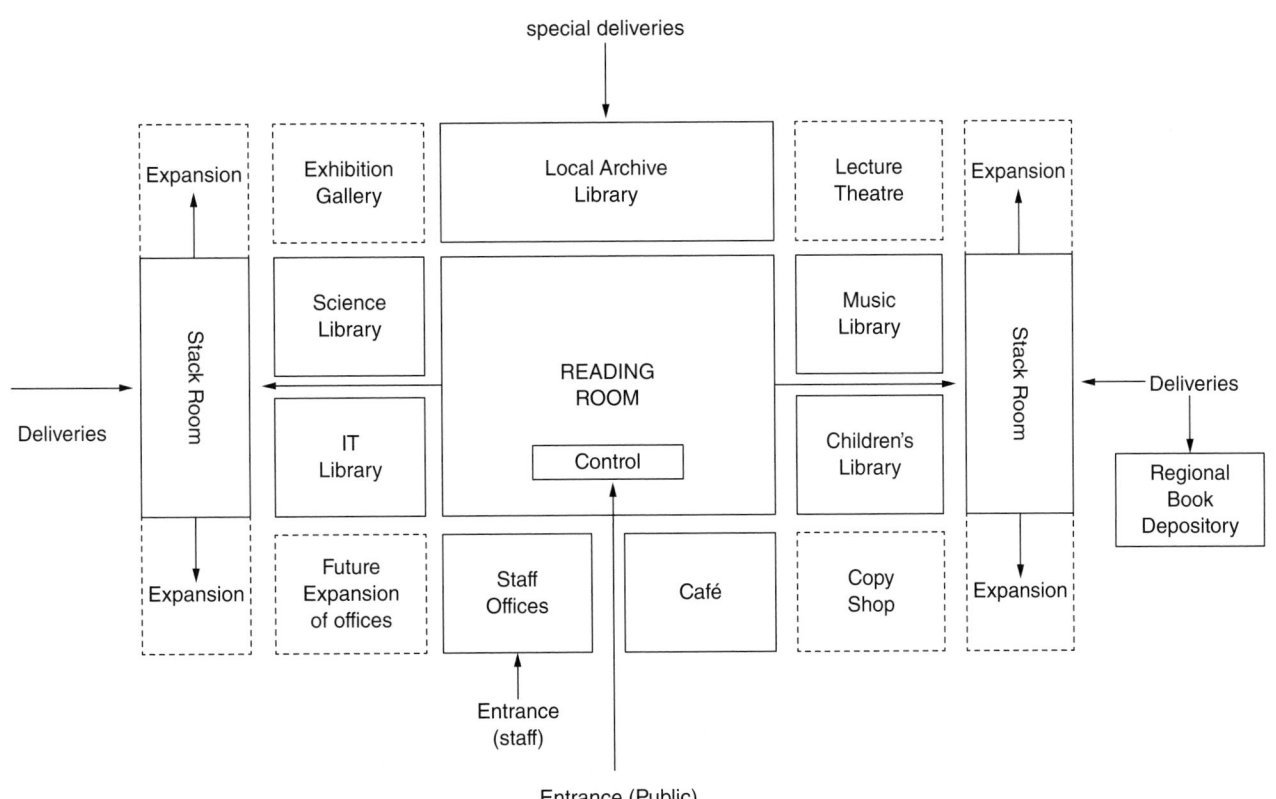

27.8 *Diagrammatic layout of a central public library (Brian Edwards)*

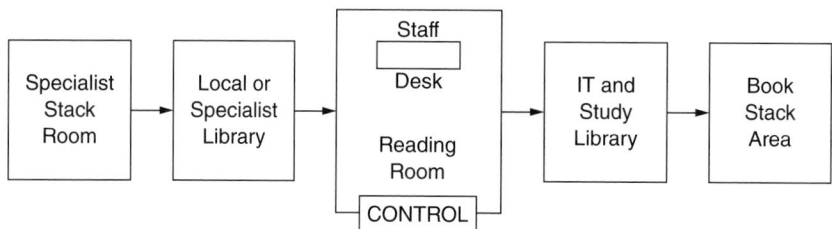

27.9 *Diagrammatic layout of a branch library (Brian Edwards)*

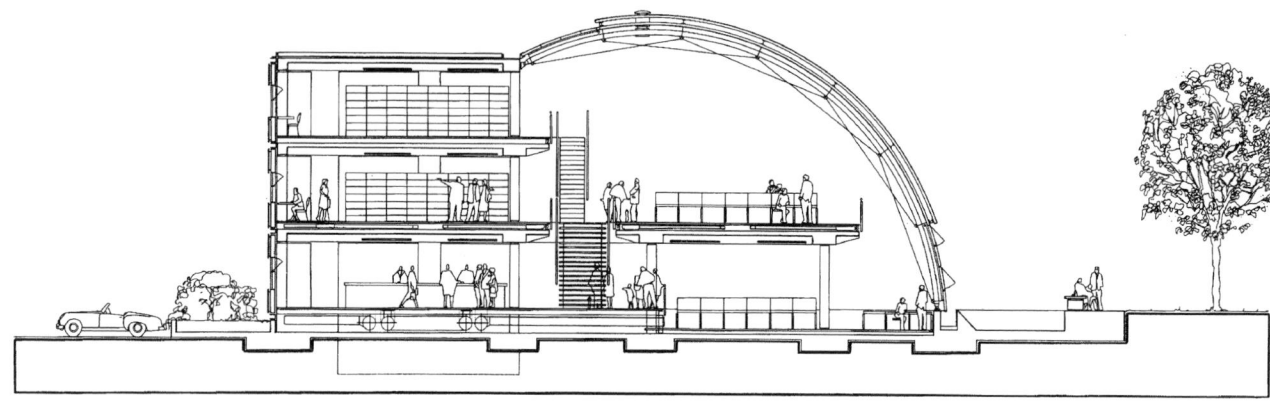

27.10 *Traditional library structure (left) and computer and discussion space (right) are combined effectively in the Learning Resource Centre at Thames Valley University (Richard Rogers Partnership)*

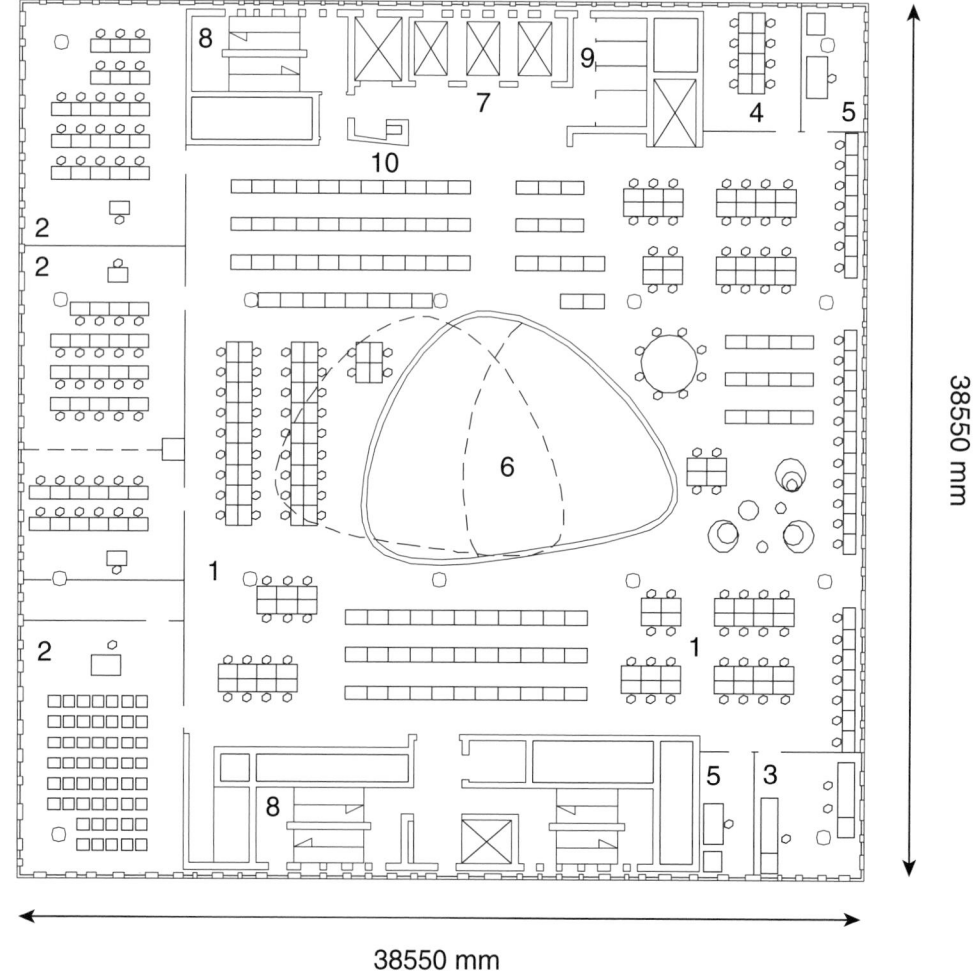

27.11a *Plans of Aberdeen University Library designed by Schmidt Hammer Lassen*

Level 2
1 Study space, 2 Seminar room, 3 Work room. 4 Group study space. 5 Office. 6 Atrium, 7 Lifts, 8 Stairs, 9 Toilets, 10 Information

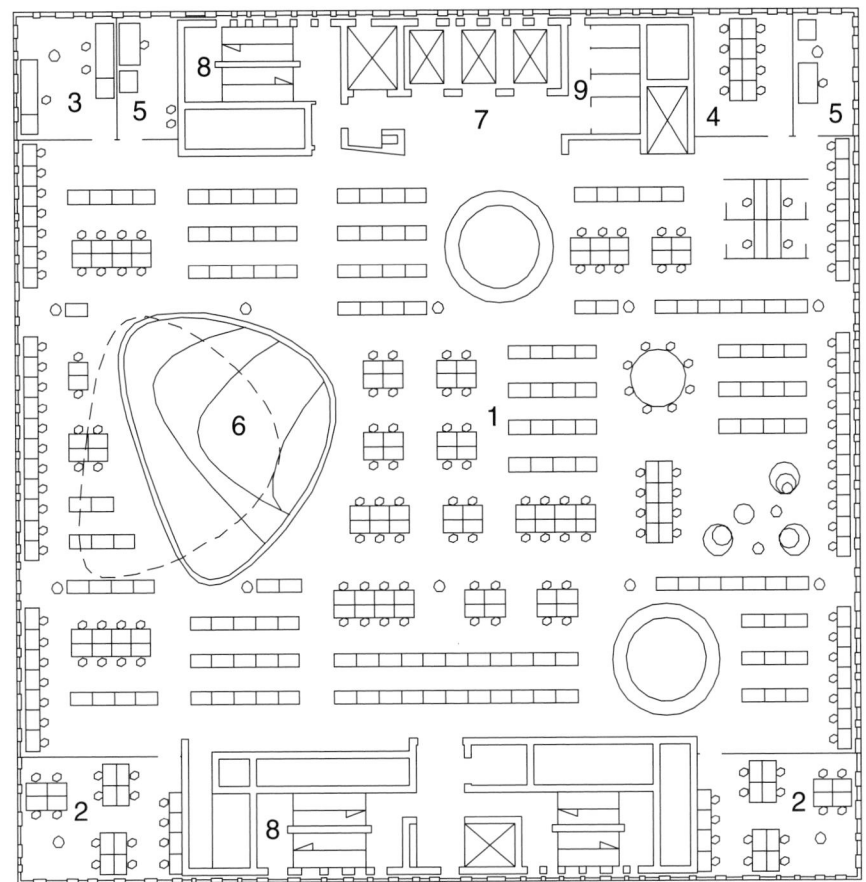

27.11b *Level 6*

1 General Library, 2 Quiet area, 3 Work room, 4 Group study space, 5 Office, 6 Atrium, 7 Lifts, 8 Stairs, 9 Toilets

largely dependent upon the type of library in question. Libraries with large book collections increasingly store less frequently used material in basement areas or in other locations. Here compact rolling book stacks can be employed, thereby saving on space and cost. Basement storage is useful because the high loadings can be more readily accommodated than on upper floors and the reader is not kept waiting too long for the material to be accessed. Reader tables, rather than individual study desks, are the norm and these are usually placed near the perimeter of the library or in special reader rooms. Tables usually have the facility to use a laptop and often

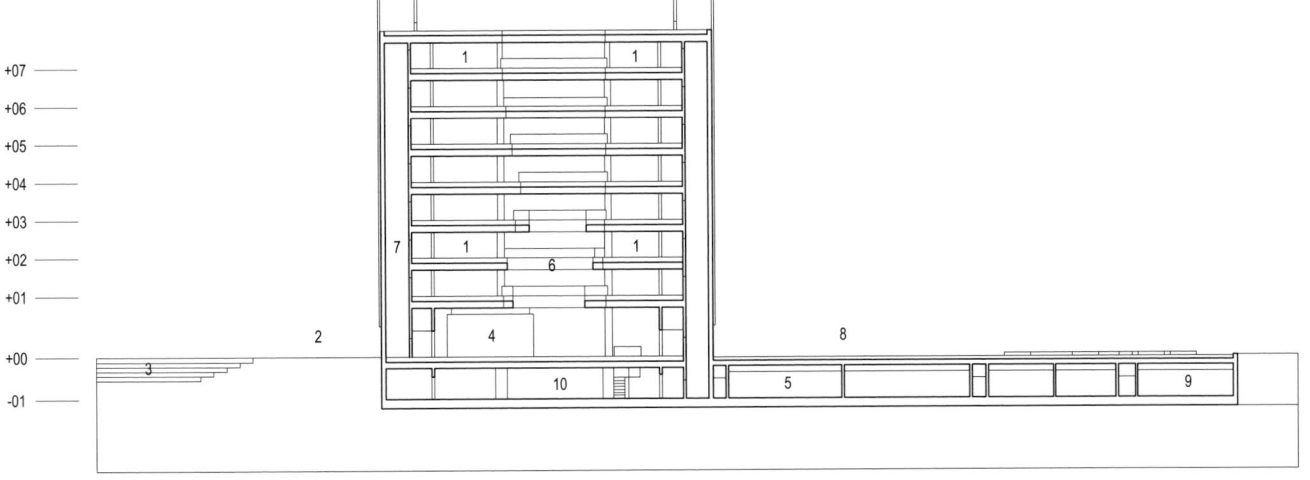

27.12 *Section of Aberdeen University Library designed by Schmidt Hammer Lassen*

Key: 1 Library, 2 Library garden, 3 Amphitheatre, 4 Exhibition area, 5 Archive, 6 Atrium, 7 Lifts, 8 Secret garden, 9 Conservation suite, 10 Reading room

there is a desk lamp and small storage area provided per reader space on a shared table of perhaps 8 seating positions.

An area needs to be set aside also for special library use such as employing large atlases or maps, broadsheet newspapers and archival material. There may be security issues to consider as well as furniture needs such as large tables. Often there is the need to make copies and this can pose a noise and environmental problem. In public libraries there is often a sharing of tables for a variety of purposes but in academic and professional libraries, study areas are set aside for specific purposes, Figures 27.13, 27.14, 27.15.

Dedicated areas for the use of electronic media are increasingly provided in libraries of all types. Although the integration of digital and paper-based systems is the ideal, often the constraints of security, noise and readership needs lead to the zoning of an area for the prime use of CDs and other forms of electronic media. In many academic libraries a dedicated learning resources centre is provided catering specifically for computer use often with associated mixed-media, printing and teaching spaces. These areas require provision not unlike that in many business premises. Hence, the design breaks the mould

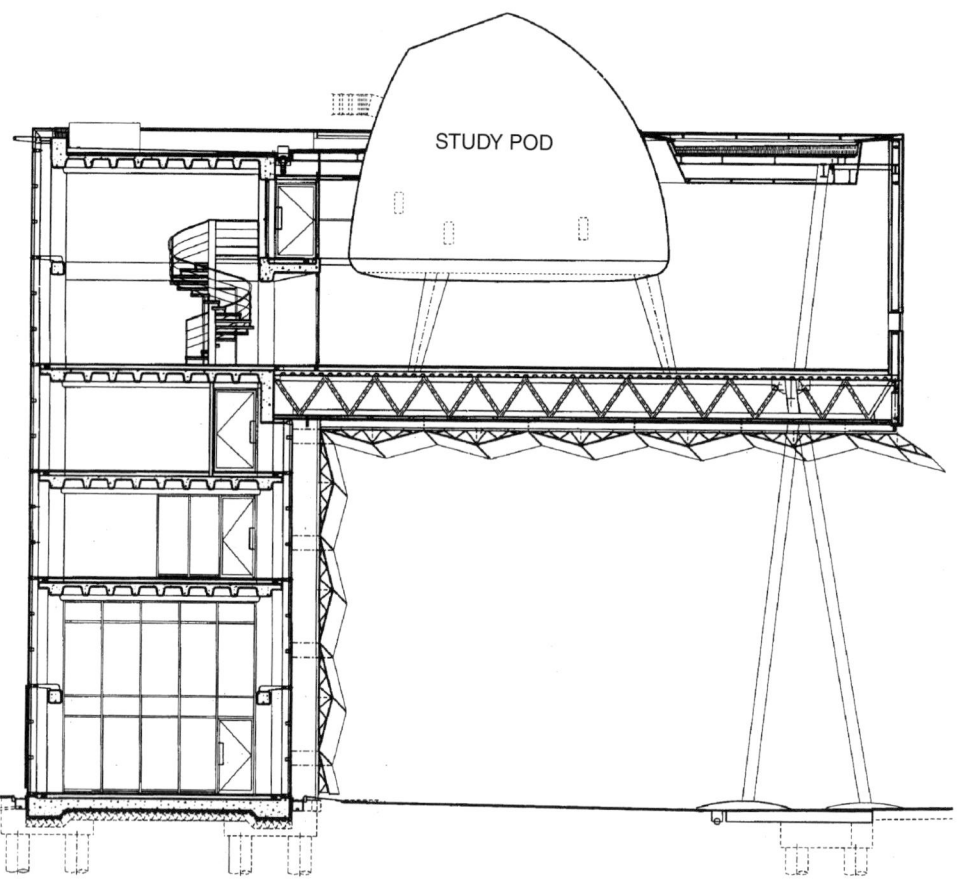

27.13 *Section through Peckham Public Library designed by Alsop and Störmer*

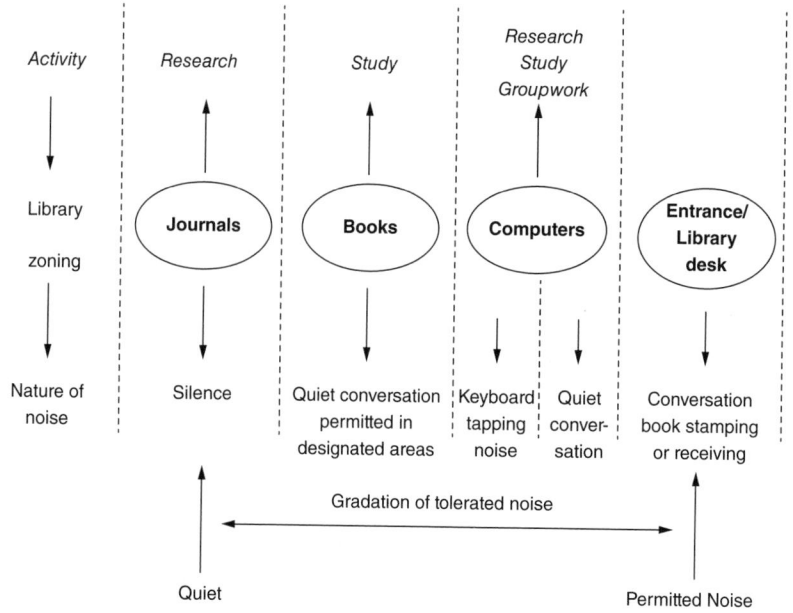

27.14 *Noise zoning in a typical academic library (Brian Edwards)*

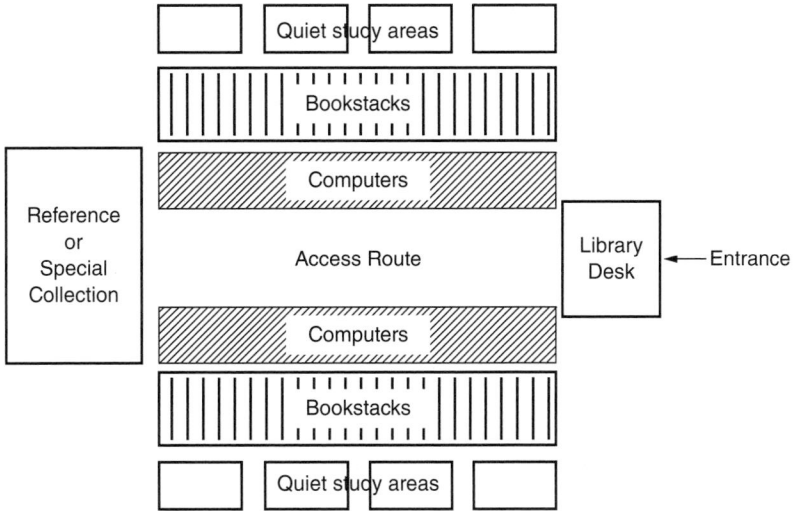

27.15 *Noise planning in a typical academic library (Brian Edwards)*

of the traditional library in the type of lighting, wiring layout and acoustic provision. As result there is often a library and IT learning centre side by side either as two joined buildings under the same envelope (Thames Valley University, Figure 27.10) or two separate but adjacent buildings (University of Sunderland). In public libraries where the level of IT provision is lower, the two activities are normally integrated.

5 SPACE STANDARDS

5.1 Space types

There are no international standards for space in relation to public libraries, as the range of groups served is deemed to be too variable (IFLA, 2001). However, schools and academic libraries have recommended space allowances related to the numbers of students.

Normally seven types of space need to be provided in a new library building:

- *Collection space* – to take account of books (open access and closed), periodicals (display and back issues) and non-print resources. Digital resources may need some space allocation.
- *Electronic workstation space* – for staff use, public use in the main areas as well as in meeting room areas. A public access catalogue used from a seated position requires 4 m^2.
- *User seating space* – at tables or alone. Plan for 5 seats per 1000 users. Table seating requires 2.5 m^2 per reader, a study carrel, and lounge chairs 3–4 m^2. A useful average is 3 m^2 per seated reader.
- *Staff work space* – including areas in the public part of the library and separate work room facilities. Fifteen square meters per staff work area (e.g. issue counter, help desk) is a good planning guide.
- *Meeting space* – including conference space, a lecture theatre or a room for children's activities. Space would also need to be allocated to other functions like cafes with storage space for equipment.
- *Special use space* – e.g. a local history room, job centre, tourist information centre or special collection with appropriate facilities for users to access the material.
- *Non-assignable space* – including toilets, stairs, lifts, corridors and space required for heating or other systems on which the library depends. In general, non-assignable space accounts for between 20 and 25% of the gross floor area of a typical library.

5.2 Usage data

Current library data should be taken into account in the specification for a new library relating to:

- opening hours (all or part of the library including out-of-hours);
- peak usage times;
- usage broken down by hours;
- days of the week library open;
- times of the year (particularly for university/college libraries);
- number of users (preferably separate figures for each part of the library);
- associated activities, e.g. meeting rooms, exhibition area(s);
- facilities, e.g. toilets, vending area, café;
- staff services to users – how many staff will be on duty/service points, security points;
- staff facilities, e.g. workroom, offices, post room, services, storage.

5.3 Public libraries

There are no absolute standards on the amount of public library space per capita. The 2001 International Federation of Library Associations guidelines state (p. 43) that:

> The amount of floor space required by a public library depends on such factors as the unique needs of the individual community, the functions of the library, the level of resources available, the size of the collection, the space available and the proximity of other libraries

and they go on to say that because these elements vary so much, 'it is not possible to propose a universal standard on the space required for a public library'.

Although dated, the publication 'The Public Library Service: IFLA/UNESCO Guidelines for Development' includes (in Appendix 4) a set of guidelines produced for Ontario Public libraries in 1997, which states that, for a community under 100 000, the appropriate amount of floor space for public libraries is 56 m^2 per 1000 capita. This set of guidelines goes on to prescribe:

- Collection space: 110 volumes/m^2
- User space: five user spaces per 1000 capita, user space = 2.8 m^2
- Staff space: 16.3 m^2 per member of staff (assuming 1 member of staff per 2000 population)
- Multi-purpose rooms: depends on community service and programme objectives
- Non-assignable space (staircases, toilets, etc.): 20% of net space (=space taken by first four categories).

In 2001, the DCMS consulted on a net figure of 23 m^2 of new library space per 1000 population as a potential public library standard. Analysis shows that figures currently in use for planning purposes are around 30 m² per 1000 population range. There has been a tendency for the figure to rise through time, not least because libraries are acquiring more functions, often at the behest of central government.

5.4 Academic and college libraries

CILIP's Guidelines for colleges recommend the following:

- 1 library study seat per 10 full-time students in further education
- 1 library study seat per 6 full-time students in higher education:
- 2.5 m² per student workspace in resource-based learning-rooms or learning resource centres
  - between 2.5 m² and 4 m² per student workspace in higher education
  - reader modules minimum 900 mm × 600 mm
  - ICT/ILT spaces minimum 1200 mm × 800 mm
  - circulation space (gangways) of 1200 mm minimum (1800 mm preferred); access to desk or workstation requires 1000 mm minimum; private space for user 600 mm outward from desk. However disabled space needs may exceed these figures.

6 ENVIRONMENTAL CONSIDERATIONS

6.1 Natural light and ventilation

Libraries are big consumers of environmental resources. The bulk of energy consumed is normally in artificial lighting. Hence, the design strategy should seek to maximise daylight and to use the incidental gains from electric lighting for supplementary heating. This assumes integration between lighting, heating and ventilation with mixed mode technologies, heat recovery and judicious use of renewable energy (see Table XI).

One trend is towards the use of atria to create internal lighting conditions which reduce the demand for artificial sources. Noise transmission and fire risk will, however, need to be considered in atria-based layouts.

Natural light and ventilation are preferable, especially in the reader areas, but security and plan depth can make this difficult to achieve. As a result most libraries employ a mixed-mode

Table XI Environmental considerations

Restrict plan depth to 15 metres for maximum daylight penetration
Create internal atria in large depth libraries
Provide solar shading and internal blinds on large south and west facing glazing areas
Use external light shelves to increase daylight penetration
Place reader tables in well-lit areas
Avoid air-conditioning except in 'hot spots'
Employ mixed-mode ventilation systems
Maximise natural ventilation in public areas

ventilation system which incorporates a hybrid of natural and mechanical systems, often employing atria spaces and sometimes double façades. Since libraries use a great deal of artificial lighting, solar heat gain can be a problem especially where large areas of glazing are provided on south facing elevations, leading to glare, discomfort and excess temperatures. It is better to avoid a southern orientation; ideally reading rooms should face north to avoid these problems. But where unavoidable, solar screening using internal and external blinds, or fixed solar shading or special glass may be required (Figure 27.16). However, the use of solid facades to exclude adverse external conditions is not advisable if the library is to assume a level of social engagement. It is façade transparency which often identifies the library as a key building in the city or on campus (Figures 27.17, 27.18).

In many ways the book collection itself stabilises internal temperatures using thermal mass. The position of bookstacks also helps too with acoustic zoning. Often exposed concrete construction is used to reduce temperature fluctuations using the thermal capacity of construction sometimes linked to chilled beams. Here it is worthwhile considering both the mass of the library collection and that of its structure together. However users, their equipment and lighting can stress temperature expectations leading to reader fatigue.

6.2 Artificial lighting

As a matter of course low energy light fittings and sensors should be fitted in all areas. The use of task lighting can result in lowering general light levels but with a growing elderly population, reducing overall light levels can result in accidents and poor user

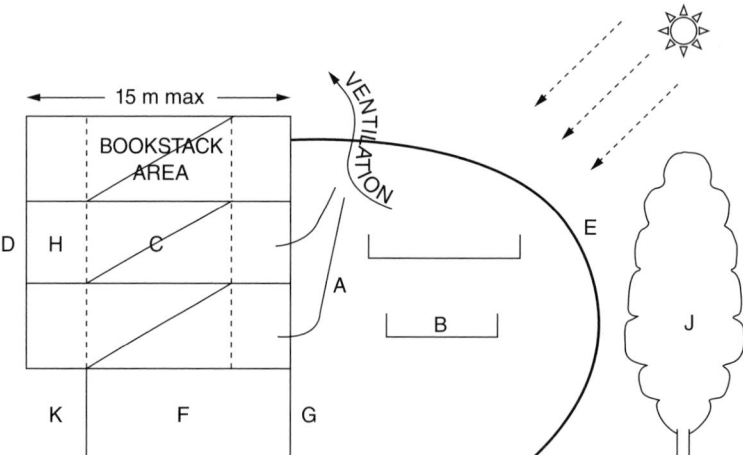

A - Open Plan Learning Resource Centre
B - Banks of computers on decks
C - Library floors, bookstacks in centre
D - Fully glazed north façade
E - Solar protected south façade, freely ventilated at top
F - Café, exhibition area
G - Entrance into library at central point
H - Reader carrels at building periphery
J - Planted shade on south side
K - Sheltered routes to library

27.16 *Diagrammatic section of a modern university library (Brian Edwards)*

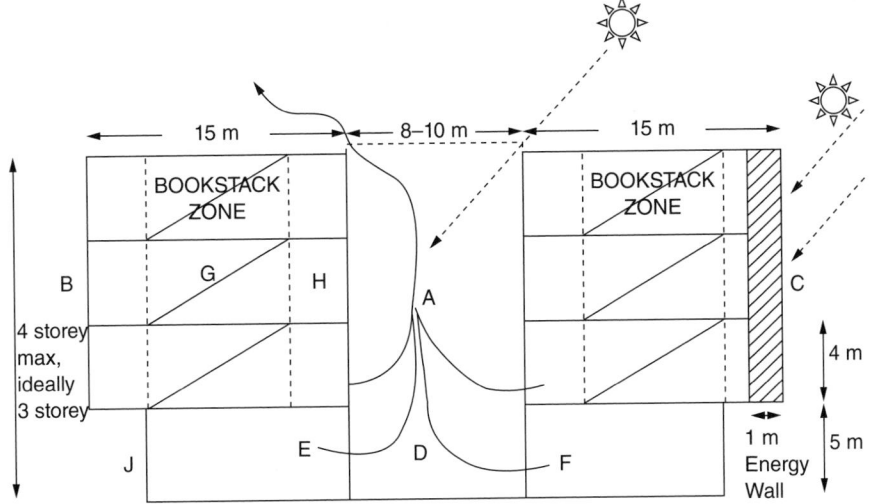

A - Atrium in centre for stairs and lifts.
       Direct sunlight and natural ventilation.
       Acoustic ceiling and walls.
B - Fully glazed north façade.
       Reader desks against periphery
C - Solar protected south façade.
       Shaded reader desks against periphery.
D - Well identified, sheltered entrance.
       Disabled friendly, pram and bicycle storage.
E - Café and exhibition space.
F - IT Resource Centre.
G - Library floors, bookstack in centre for thermal capacity.
H - Computer terminals in bays around atrium.
J - Sheltered routes to library

27.17 *Template for design of public library (Brian Edwards)*

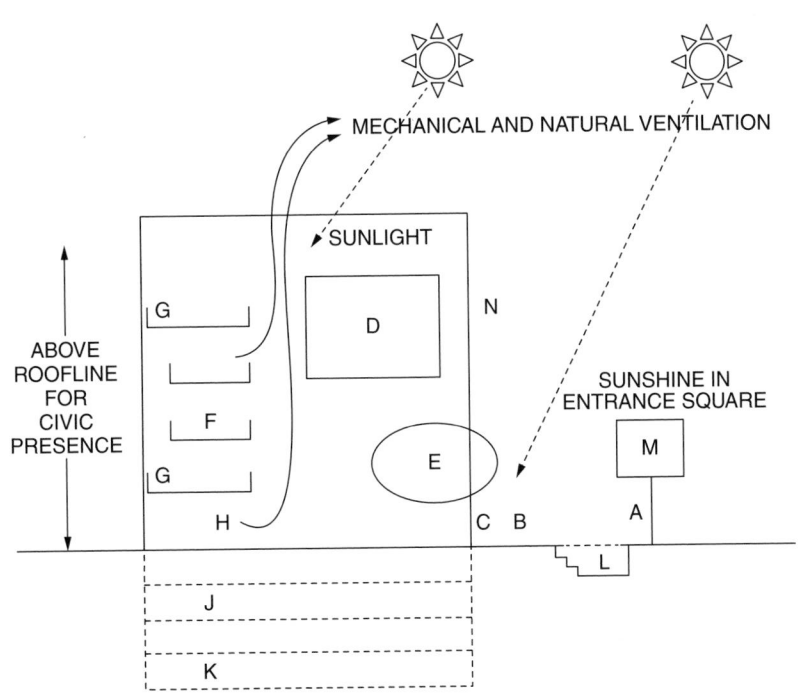

A - civic presence on street.
B - gathering square.
C - spacious entrance with exhibition space.
D - special collections readily identified.
E - auditorium near entrance.
F - library floors by subject.
G - reader spaces against permeter.

H - computer catalogue access and toilets.
J - conservation.
K - storage of collection.
L - amphitheatre for external performance.
M - conference.
N - energy conscious facade.

27.18 *Template for design of national library (Brian Edwards)*

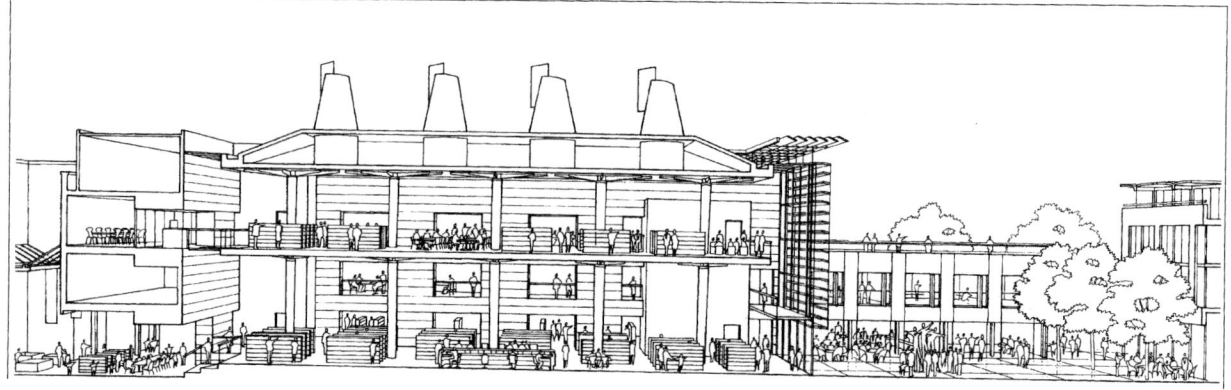

27.19 *Brighton Public Library is designed with both study and environmental concerns in mind (Bennetts Associates)*

satisfaction. Light reflection on computer screens is also a consideration and generally results in PCs being in more central areas.

In order to maximise natural light and ventilation, the plan depth should not exceed 15 meters. However, this is difficult to achieve in all but the smallest of libraries, and hence artificial conditions are provided in most areas. Since most libraries are constructed in urban centres, the main environmental factors are normally glare, solar gain, external air quality and noise pollution (Figure 27.19). Hence a great deal of attention should be directed to site choice and layout, the design of external facades and the internal zoning of the building using light wells and mini atria (as at the new Birmingham City Library).

As a general rule readers like to work in natural light. This normally results in the perimeter placing of reader tables. Some seating areas can also be provided in inner sunlit spaces, particularly where magazines and newspapers are read. The creation of relaxation areas as distinct from study areas should take into account the different environmental conditions which may exist. Readers like views and hence study spaces or carrels generally occupy the library perimeter with major reading rooms placed on upper floors. Views of the city and of nature are usually preferred.

7 FINANCING AND RESOURCES

7.1 Hard times and the centralising of facilities

The enthusiasm that accompanies the planning of a new library can induce an artificial atmosphere of plenty even amid harsh financial constraints, and architects need to remember that libraries, especially branch ones, can experience difficult times. While many cities such as Birmingham and the larger London boroughs are building large new facilities to catch the public eye and often employing architects of note, branch libraries are being starved of funding and community groups are increasingly helping to staff and maintain them under the present UK government's localism initiative. There may be staffing cuts, cuts in book fund or the need to cancel journal subscriptions.

7.2 Operating budgets

The problem in many new library projects is that the construction budget is not always reflected in the library's operating budget. When the new library opens its doors, the public will flock in to enjoy its many attractions, but if there is an inadequate budget to support new or expanded services, this can lead to difficulties. In a recent example, a new central library was planned with staffing based on a projected 5000 visitors a day. However, the day after opening, the number jumped to 9000. Moving the existing collection also requires many additional staff hours, as does the setting up and configuring of the large amount of state-of-the-art equipment.

7.3 Efficient staffing

Library staff numbers are generally reducing, while new electronic resources take an ever larger proportion of the budget. It is important to design a library that can be staffed safely and efficiently by the smallest possible number of people. For example, book stacks and work areas need to be arranged so that staff can use their time efficiently and flexibly. Generally, equipment needs to be centralised so that the building can be adequately operated and staff desks located so that one librarian can provide surveillance over a large physical area. A well-designed library of today is usually able to achieve lower staffing levels than a poorly designed library from the 1970s or 1980s allowing staff to be the readers' subject navigators.

8 CASE STUDY – BIRMINGHAM LIBRARY

Introduction

Redevelopment of Birmingham's central library, the largest public library in Britain, stemmed from a desire to build a new urban landmark as part of wider transformations of the city centre. The new library, designed by Dutch practice Mecanoo, replaces a modernist library built in 1974 to designs by the John Madin Partnership and addresses both urban design and library design in a fresh way which is as much about people as it is about books. It is one of a generation of super libraries found increasingly in the world's major cities where the book remains a prominent part of the library experience.

Urban design

The new Birmingham library stands in Centenary Square sandwiched between two distinguished neighbours – the Birmingham Repertory Theatre and the Art Deco Baskerville House. Mecanoo restructured the square and sought to revitalise it as a largely pedestrian experience, providing a place to meet before entering the library and somewhere to read or think within the hectic city. It also provides internal links to the theatre and an underground gateway to the library.

Entrance

The 35,000 sq metre library is approached beneath a large canopy which projects into the square (Figures 27.20, 27.21). Above this stands the double height reading room with external balcony which provides users with views into the square and beyond to the city.

Layout

The ten storey library houses a children's library and book store in the basement. On the ground floor (Figure 27.22), a lofty entrance foyer with café and exhibition area leads via escalators to eight floors of reading rooms, multi-media areas, IT study and archive spaces. On the roof within a gold coloured rotunda stands the reconstructed Shakespeare Memorial Room rescued from the original Birmingham public library built in 1874. It contains one of the largest Shakespeare collections in the UK.

Although books are found on all levels, three floors of the library contain book stacks housed in dense mobile storage systems

27.20 *Section of Birmingham Library with new public square to the left*

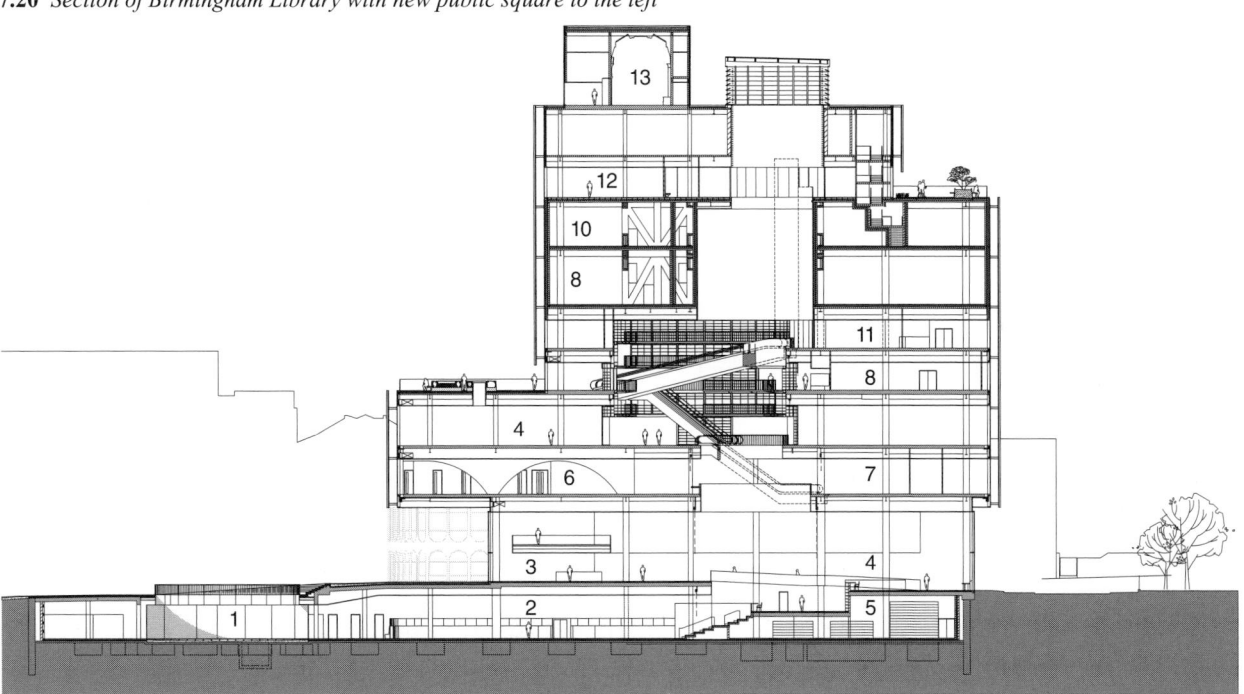

27.21 *Section of Birmingham showing library accommodation*

Key: 1 Music zone, 2 Children's library, 3 Foyer, 4 Readers' services, 5 Storage, 6 Meeting room, 7 Business & training, 8 Gallery, 9 Heritage, 10 Archive, 11 Archive & heritage open research, 12 Staff offices, 13 Shakespeare Memorial Room

or double height stack rooms. This compaction allows space to be provided for readers in well-lit areas around the library perimeter or close to atria. Here, IT and traditional reading tables are integrated although there are also separate multi-media and quiet study rooms. The main book collection is housed on open shelves which radiate out from the main atria giving readers views to the outside world.

Different spaces are designed according to the nature of the collection or the demands of the media employed (Figure 27.23). Rooms and study areas are therefore distinctive rather than standardised with archive, music and heritage collections having their

own special spaces fashioned by conservation demands or the character of the collection (Figure 27.24).

Circulation
Circulation is mainly via escalators and atria recalling the ambience of a department store. The circular atria are lined with books or murals and their distinctive character helps users navigate through this large library.

The atria also provide natural light and solar assisted ventilation within the deep planned areas. Light from above filtering into atria creates uplift physically (for air movement) and psychologically

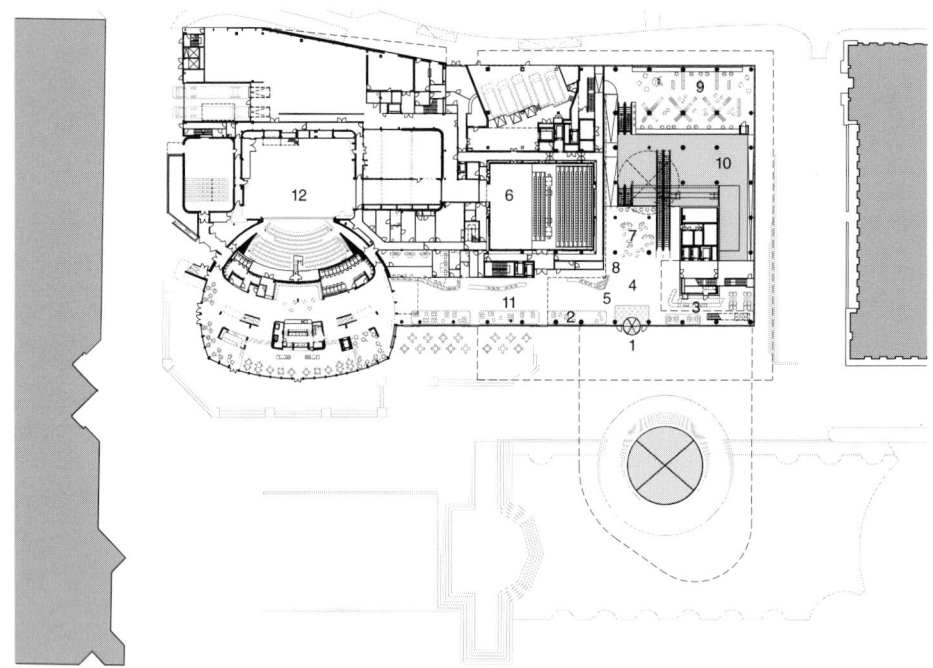

27.22 *Ground floor plan: Book Browse*

Key: 1 Entrance, 2 Retail, 3 Library café, 4 Foyer, 5 Information point/reception, 6 Studio theatre, 7 Spotlight, 8 Meeting point, 9 Upper lending terrace, 10 Lower lending terrace, 11 Seating area, 12 Repertory theatre

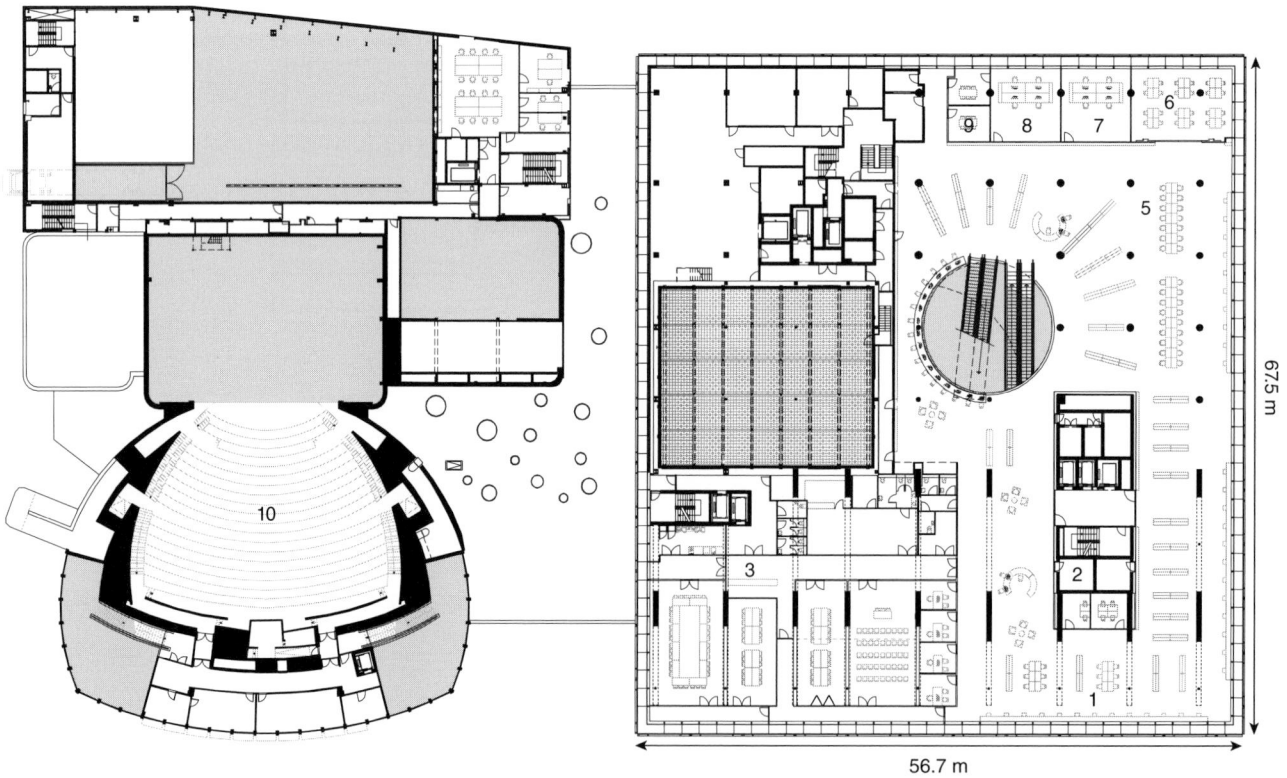

27.23 *Level 1 floor – Business, Learning & Health*

Key: 1 Supported learning, 2 Staff area, 3 Library meeting rooms, 4 Interview rooms, 5 Group study area, 6 Innovation hub, 7 Business incubation, 8 Training suite, 9 Recording studio, 10 Theatre

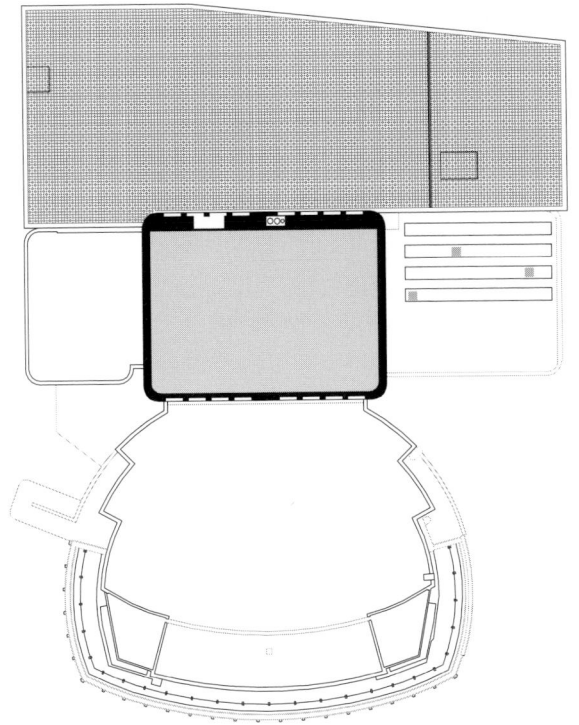
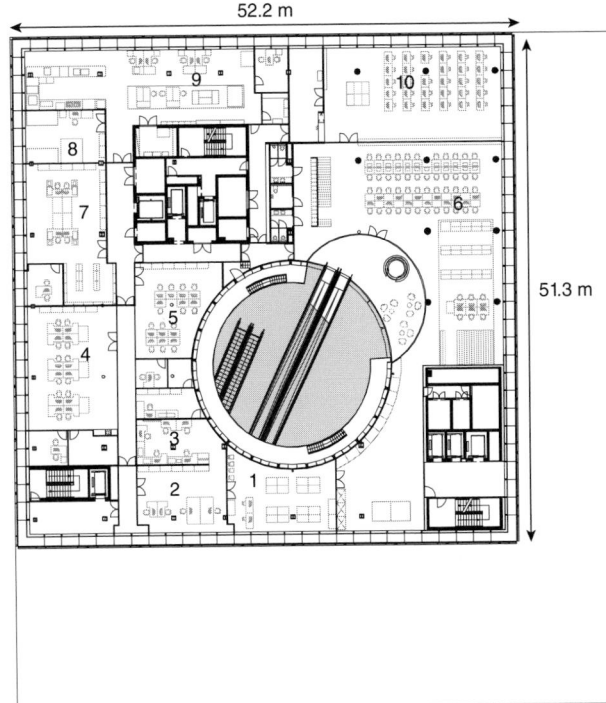

27.24 *Level 4 – Archives & Heritage/Search Area*

Key: 1 Learning space, 2 Outreach room, 3 Digital room, 4 Cataloging room, 5 Staff area, 6 Open search area, 7 Photograph office & cataloging room, 8 Box making machine room, 9 Conservation lab, 10 Supervised search area

(for the spirit). Fatigue is further relieved by generous provision of escalators and lifts which are placed to entice you into the building.

Routes are designed to make connections between digital and paper based media, and between open and enclosed spaces.

Facade design
The facades are unified by the application of an external metal grille of matt and silver circular bands. Where the inner facade is fully glazed, these act as solar shades and daylight filters to reduce heat gain and glare inside. Where the walls are solid, they provide a filigree pattern of shadows giving interest and depth to the facades. As a unifying motif this controversial circular decoration alludes to the industrial heritage of the city of Birmingham.

Energy
As with all libraries, the main users of energy are lighting and cooling. Birmingham Library is rated BREEAM Excellent and incorporates ground-sourced water from deep aquifers which provides chilling of the building structure as well as grey water systems. On the basement floor where the children's library is located, the mass of the soil provides acoustic buffering and thermal stabilisation.

The building has a mixed mode and natural ventilation strategy with the facade allowing fresh air intake and outflow.

9 BIBLIOGRAPHY/RESOURCES

Brian Edwards, *Libraries and Learning Resource Centres,* Architectural Press, 2009

CABE *Building Better Libraries,* 2003

CILIP, *The Primary School Library: Guidelines* (revised edn), 2002

Connecticut State Library, *Library Space Planning Guide,* 2002

Designing Libraries www.designinglibraries.org.uk

Andrew Eynon, (ed.) *Guidelines for Colleges: Recommendations for Learning Resources,* Colleges of Further & Higher Education Group of CILIP, Facet Publishing, 2005

IFLA, *The Public Library Service: IFLA/UNESCO Guidelines for Development,* 2001

Santi Romero, *Library Architecture: Recommendations for a comprehensive research project,* COAC, 2011

Ken Worpole, *Contemporary Library Architecture: A Planning and Design Guide,* Routledge, 2013

28 Masterplanning and landscaping

David Simister with Guy Walters and contributions by Sarah Burgess, Hugh Barton and Marcus Grant

David Simister is creative director of Aedas. Guy Walters is a landscape architect at, Aedas. Sarah Burgess, Hugh Barton and Marcus Grant teach at the University of the West of England

KEY POINTS:

- *A masterplan will describe a vision for the development of a large site in words and drawings*
- *A masterplan can be defined as a type of planning brief outlining the preferred usage of land and the overall approach to layout, with detailed guidance for subsequent planning applications*
- *A well-conceived masterplan will include proposals drawn in three dimensions, taking into consideration massing and scale and the location and role of open space*
- *A masterplan will contain a strategic framework – a statement of aims for physical regeneration over a large area of land extending beyond the spatial masterplan*

Contents

1 Introduction
2 Philosophy
3 Site analysis
4 Methodology
5 The strategic framework
6 The spatial masterplan
7 Implementation plan
8 Digital masterplanning
9 Coherence, variety and uniformity
10 Urban design analysis
11 Infrastructure and connectivity
12 The anatomy of the site: highways, servicing and car parking
13 Site planning and landscape design
14 Open space
15 The geometry of site planning
16 Plot testing
17 The built heritage
18 The importance of detail: delivering design quality
19 Some alarm bells
20 Conclusions: evaluating a masterplan design
21 Masterplanning for healthy communities
22 References
23 Appendix: Key documents and case studies

1 INTRODUCTION

A masterplan will describe a vision for the development of a large site in words and drawings whether for mixed-use, commercial, educational, industrial, cultural, and residential or landscape, and will be a blueprint for place-making.

A masterplan should address the following parameters:

- Planning and Development policies
- Uses
- Functional efficiency
- Form, building density and massing
- Public open space, private and semi-private space
- Commercial viability
- Topography and soils
- Landscape, landmarks and vistas/focal points, visibility
- Climate, micro climates, and aspect
- Environmental harmony, wildlife and ecology
- Sustainability, energy and resource efficiency
- Transport and movement in all forms,
- Site and plot drainage including sustainable urban drainage systems
- Security
- Phasing
- Materials.

The site could cover a region, district, zone or plot but would always look beyond its own border to consider adjoining land to either suggest influence or inform its own outputs.

Masterplan has become an often misused term to illustrate the mechanism for design and delivery of large projects over extended time periods. Planning departments, developers and their consultant teams have come to rely on masterplans for consultation with landowners and local people and this concept is reinforced by government studies through the Urban Task Force, The Landscape Institute, CABE and Homes and Communities Agency and has become enshrined in the statutory planning system.

The Planning Portal (http://www.planningportal.gov.uk/) defines 'masterplan' to be a type of planning brief outlining the preferred usage of land and the overall approach to the layout of a developer and to provide detailed guidance for subsequent planning applications. Planning Policy Statements (PPS) govern planning policy. Planning Policy Guidance Notes (PPGs) and their replacements Planning Policy Statements (PPSs) are prepared by the government after public consultation to explain statutory

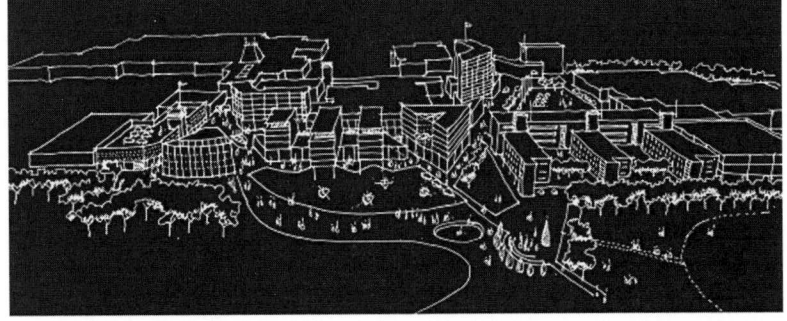

28.1 *Telford town plan extension, Aedas Architects*

provisions and provide guidance to local authorities and others on planning policy and the operation of the planning system. They also explain the relationship between planning policies and other policies which have an important bearing on issues of development and land use. Local authorities must take their contents into account in preparing their development plan documents. The guidance may also be relevant to decisions on individual planning applications and appeals.

Some of the key themes emerging from the Review of PPGs and replacement with PPSs are:

- Enhancing the quality of the local environment – distinctive local character and sense of place (PPS1 – 'Delivering Sustainable Development' and its supplements: 'Planning and Climate Change' and 'Eco Towns')
- Reducing the need to travel by promoting local facilities clustered around public transport nodes; designing streets for pedestrians and cyclists (PPG13 – 'Transport')
- Making best use of existing resources of urban land and buildings and thus regenerating decaying localities. Reducing the stimulus to car use by rationing parking in housing and commercial/institutional developments (PPS3 – 'Housing')
- Reviving rural market towns, by encouraging more local service provision and diversification of local economies (PPS7 – 'Sustainable Development in Rural Areas')
- Reducing waste during construction and use (PPS10 – 'Planning for sustainable waste management')
- Key ingredients of local spatial plans and the key government policies on how they should be prepared (PPS 12 – 'Local Spatial Planning')
- Consideration of the effect of development on areas susceptible to flooding (PPS25 – 'Development and Flood Risk')

The Countryside Agency and English Nature have produced a Character of England Map (1996) which identifies the unique character of an area in terms of landscape character, sense of place, local distinctiveness, characteristic wildlife and natural features which can all influence both large and small scale design and masterplanning and should be a starting point for understanding the context of a site.

Masterplans vary in their portrayal of architectural and urban design vision. Place making and high quality environment requires the masterplan to promote high standards in landscape and architecture even if not proscriptive about other aspects. Images will be used to capture special aspects of development through wide angle aerial or ground level views. Specialist software can be used, from simple block modeling to elaborate photo-realistic renders but equally effective is free-hand drawing.

The Rio Earth Summit of 1992 sets out three particular principles relevant to developments within the landscape:

- The promotion of environmental protection as an integral part of the development process, in order to achieve sustainable development.
- The participation at the relevant level of all concerned citizens in handling environmental issues with appropriate access to information.
- The need for Environmental Impact Assessment on developments that are likely to have adverse effects on the environment.

CABE guidance suggests the masterplanner's task is to determine the appropriate level of prescription and standard-setting, while also providing for flexibility in the face of an unpredictable future, bearing in mind that:

- Development is likely to occur in a number of phases and may not take place continuously.
- Individual buildings or groups of buildings may be developed by different architects and/or developers.

- The masterplan may only be implemented in part.
- Requirements and economic conditions may change during the course of its implementation.

A well-conceived masterplan will include proposals drawn in three dimensions, not necessarily in detail, but taking into consideration massing and scale and the location and role of open space. These drawings will be read in conjunction with the written part of a masterplan, which will deal with the following:

- What is the masterplan trying to achieve and what are its aims and objectives?
- What is the masterplan trying to define or to pin down, and in what respects are matters being left open?
- What is the policy context for the masterplan, and what is the need for aspects of the masterplan to be adopted as policy, for example through supplementary planning guidance or design briefs?
- Who are the key partners in the development and what are their respective roles: regeneration agencies, the local planning authority, developers, funders, designers, the community, and tenants, transport providers, etc.?
- What is the delivery strategy for the masterplan, for example phasing and funding?
- What is the mechanism for assessing detailed proposals as they come forward, against the masterplan?
- What is the mechanism for changing the masterplan if circumstances change?

It is likely that a masterplan will address the issues of land use, but that is not its principal purpose. Mixed-use neighbourhoods are now a primary aim of government planning policy, and close control of different uses is no longer given the priority it once had. While it will always be important to identify 'bad neighbour' uses, and potential conflicts, it is more important to try to create places of lasting quality which can accommodate changes to their patterns of use over time. Places of enduring quality can usually accommodate significant changes of use.

2 PHILOSOPHY

Various pillars underpin the philosophy and approach to master planning projects:

- *Context.* The character and setting of the area within which a masterplan will sit, including natural and human history; forms of settlements, buildings and spaces.
- *Integration.* Connection and overlap with surrounding areas, infrastructure, transport, movement, and social infrastructure.
- *Functional efficiency.* Creating individual elements which work together as part of an efficient whole.
- *Environmental harmony.* Creating a masterplan which is energy efficient and ecologically sensitive in both its construction and use.
- *Urban design.* Buildings and public realm.
- *Commercial viability.* Ensuring that the development responds to the realities of development mix and delivery within its local context.
- *Health and activity.* Working, living and leisure providing a place which can encourage healthy living and an active lifestyle. Combating heart disease, respiratory problems and mental illness, for example relies on factors such as healthy exercise, air quality, fresh food and local social networks, all of which are influenced by the physical nature of localities.
- *Creating a sense of place.* Creating a responsive environment which is recognisably distinct but simultaneously strengthens local identity.
- *Understanding the context.* The Urban Design Compendium sets out a number of benefits of understanding the full context of the scheme in order to understand the position of the development and how to position the development taking into account the following priorities:

o *Strengthening local communities.* To help ensure that proposed development reinforces, rather than undermines local communities and assists successful project delivery.

o *Creating places of distinction.* Drawing inspiration from a neighbourhood's indigenous character strengthens local identity. Context-less design leads to 'anywhere places'.

o *Harnessing intrinsic site assets and resources.* Harnessing intrinsic resources of the site – the existing development forms, soils and geology, drainage, landscape, solar and wind energy – to create a more sustainable development.

o *Integrating with surroundings.* Achieving careful integration with the landscape or surrounding built environment, using the right materials, forms and landscape elements for the locality; respecting footpaths, street and road linkages and relating to existing urban structures.

o *Ensuring feasibility.* To ensure economic viability and deliverability.

o *Providing vision.* A vision focuses community aspirations, sells a scheme to a developer and provides a long term aim for project participants. It embodies a strategy for the future that everyone can sign up to and work towards over a period of time.

3 SITE ANALYSIS

Before diving in to a design it is important to ensure that the design team have a deep understanding of the site and its characteristics. The following information should be compiled early on in the process and be made available to the whole design team.

- *Climate and microclimate.* Monthly and annual rainfall, wind direction and strength (wind rose), average temperatures, dates of first and last frosts; drainage of cold air across sites; frost pockets; shelter; shadow projections.
- *Geology and soils.* Solid and drift geology; trial holes positions and sections (ee BS ISO 25177-2008 *Soil quality – Field Soil Description* and BS 5930: *1999 Code of Practice for Site Investigations.* Check nature of the soil be it natural or made up.)
- *Hydrology and drainage.* Water courses; water bodies, direction of flow of surface water, land drain systems, flood plains and temporary flooding, access to existing drainage infrastructure, soil porosity for sustainable urban drainage systems.
- *Landscape value.* The Countryside Agency's and English Nature's joint Character of England Map (1996) illustrates the natural and cultural characteristics of the English Countryside based on biodiversity and landscape. (See the Landscape Institute's Guidelines for Landscape and Visual Assessment, 2013.)
- *Vegetation.* Trees and important shrubs, Tree Preservation Orders, existing tree and hedge lines, covenants and existing ground vegetation. (Survey guidelines in BS5837:2005 *Trees* in relation to construction.)
- *Biodiversity and habitats.* Aspirations of Local Biodiversity Action Plan. Types of habitat; associated flora and fauna. Ancient Woodlands, local and national nature reserves. Sites of Special Scientific Interest (See www.magic.gov.uk the UK government's web-base interactive environmental map service for England and Wales.)
- *Land use.* Current and proposed land uses in relation to neighbouring areas. Agricultural land classification.
- *User survey.* Social, demographic and economic factors of the proposed site in relation to neighbouring areas.
- *Structures, roads and services.* Existing buildings roads, car parks, hard standings, footpaths, paved areas, walls, fences, gates; foul and surface water drains; manholes (invert and cover levels); gas, water, electricity, telephone and TV services (overhead and underground); pipelines; notes on materials, including those suitable for re-use; underground workings.
- *Archaeological and local history data.* Information on site previous uses, scheduled buildings and ancient monuments, adjacent designed landscapes or listed buildings which may be affected by change in their setting.

- *Access and communication.* Existing pedestrian and vehicular routes to public roads, footpaths, rights of way, bridle paths, bus stops, railway stations, shops, schools and areas of employment.
- *Pollution factors.* Constraints on or off site that can affect future uses, e.g. noise or chemical pollution of air or soils.
- *Legal and planning aspects.* Land ownership; boundary ownership; rights of access, light etc.; easements and way-leaves; Structure Plan designation; road improvement lines; Areas of Outstanding Natural Beauty; requirement for an Environmental Impact Assessment.
- *Zones of influence.* Views in and out of the site and likely receptor areas to be affected by the development.

Blending the traditional techniques of analysis, drawing and measurement with a number of computer tools, some specifically developed by R&D professionals and as part of a suite of tools, it is possible to view drawn information compiled into a single framework enabling multiple layers of data, analysis and proposals to be read in conjunction with one another. Such tools assist clients, stakeholders, members of the public and consultants to engage with the project in an open and transparent manner.

Master planners enjoy a close working relationship with other consultants who bring depth and understanding to the work particularly around the subject of sustainability. Often R&D teams consist of a number of sustainability experts who always ensure that work carried out by others is fully integrated within the proposals. Beyond the core activities there are additional services that the masterplanner assists or becomes involved with, such as stakeholder consultations and design charettes.

Stakeholder consultations and design charettes support design development and the Urban Task Force in Towards an Urban Renaissance (1999) stated that a successful masterplan must be:

- *Visionary.* It should raise aspirations and provide a vehicle for consensus building and implementation.
- *Deliverable.* It should take into account likely implementation and delivery routes
- *Integrated.* Fully integrated into the land use planning system, while allowing new uses and market opportunities to exploit the full development potential of a site.
- *Flexible.* Providing the basis for negotiation and dispute resolution
- *Participatory.* The result of a participatory process, providing all the stakeholders with the means of expressing their needs and priorities.

4 METHODOLOGY

Each project is unique but the key stages of work are outlined below. These may happen sequentially but there is often a degree of overlap between them.

Opportunity and constraints mapping will show the significant results of the site analysis and will often set the framework within which the development will eventually be placed. This should identify key site-based drivers to the scheme (physical, planning, climatic, socio-economic).

4.1 Visioning, principles and objectives
- Framework analysis based on matching the key performance indicators to the constraints/site analysis.
- Landscape structure plan identifying key structural landscape elements of the plan and how they relate to the wider landscape.
- Bring together the strategic framework to structure the proposal.
- Develop the spatial masterplan: parameter drawings and design codes (including character areas) for reserved matters.
- Implementation plan: deliverability, phasing and flexibility.
- There are three key outputs from the masterplanning process outlined above – the strategic framework, the spatial masterplan and the implementation plan.

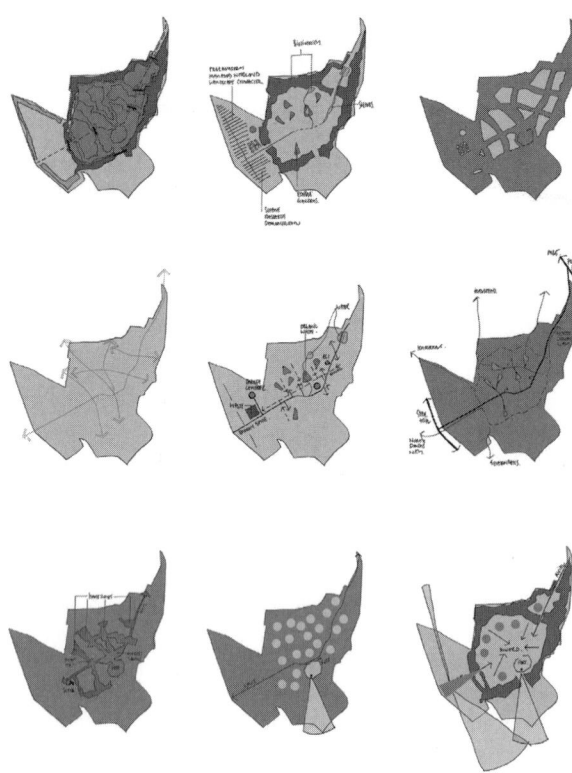

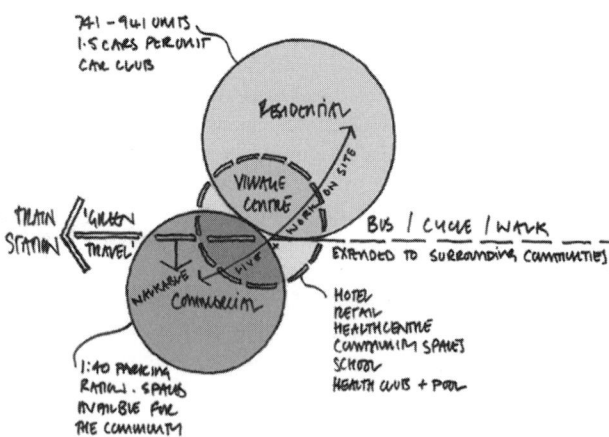

28.3 *Fort Halstead Masterplan, Sevenoaks, connectivity, Aedas Architects*

28.2 *Fort Halstead Masterplan, Sevenoaks, Aedas Architects reforestation, working landscape, building cells, permeability, energy/water/waste, connectivity*

5 THE STRATEGIC FRAMEWORK

This contains a statement of aims and objectives for physical regeneration over a large area of land and may consider a much wider area than the spatial masterplan. It is based on analysis of the baseline data and is a key output functioning as the brief for the spatial masterplan. It also incorporates early ideas about how to deliver the proposed developments.

6 THE SPATIAL MASTERPLAN

This develops the broad vision into three-dimensional proposals. It consists of plans, visuals and written documentation. A spatial masterplan is a sophisticated model which shows how streets, squares and open spaces of a neighbourhood are to be connected, defines the height, bulk and massing of buildings, sets out suggested relationships between buildings and public spaces, determines the activities and uses which will take place in the area, identifies the movement patterns for people on foot, or by bicycle, car or public transport, as well as looking at the needs of service and refuse vehicles, sets out the basis for the provision of utilities and other infrastructural elements, relates the physical form of the site to social, economic and cultural contexts and takes account of the needs of people living and working in the area, and shows ways in which new neighbourhoods can be integrated into existing ones.

7 IMPLEMENTATION PLAN

This is the strategy for how to turn the vision and plans into reality. The masterplan is not complete without considering and testing how the proposals will be implemented. Implementation will require a written statement addressing cost, programme and other issues. Even if actual work on site is not imminent, these issues must be considered early on.

8 DIGITAL MASTERPLANNING

This allows investors, public and private planners, architects and urban designers to generate and evaluate scenarios for accessibility, transport, visual integration, mixed-use developments, massing etc.

28.4 *Fort Halstead Masterplan, Sevenoaks, access levels, Aedas Architects*

8.1 Access levels

Access levels are calculated on the basis of walking times to/from access points. Pedestrian walking times are assumed to be shortest routes. Optimisation of the pedestrian network can be approximated by setting values for a distance within which the program searches for new path connections that would shorten the access time by a set value.

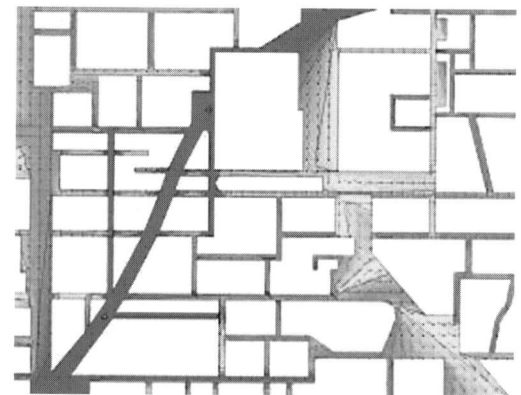

28.5 *Fort Halstead Masterplan, Sevenoaks, catchment areas, Aedas Architects*

8.2 Catchment areas

Catchment areas indicate the plots and spaces that use a given access point – i.e. public transport node. CDR calculates them not on manual straight radii but on 'actual' reachable distances.

28.6 *Fort Halstead Masterplan, Sevenoaks, desire lines, Aedas Architects*

8.3 Desire lines (movement and circulation)

CDR provides interactive tools to generate networks of desire lines through a site generally or to specific points. Desire lines can be based on shortest metric distances and/or simplest access routes (least turns). While local residents would use shortest metric routes, visitors and tourists are more likely to use simplest access routes.

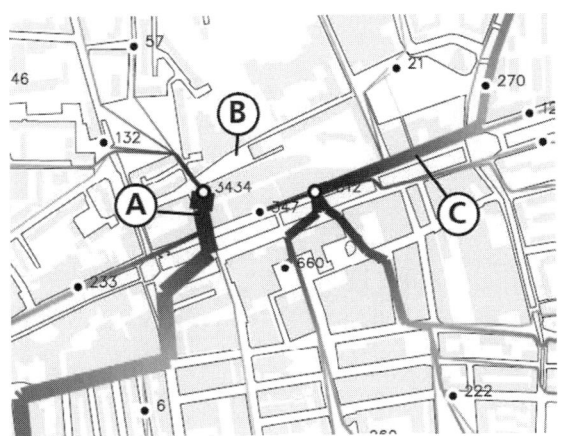

28.7 *Fort Halstead Masterplan, Sevenoaks, footfall approximation, Aedas Architects*

8.4 Footfall approximation

Desire lines and routes can be weighted by the number of people departing from surveyed locations. The resulting mapping indicates the loading of calculated routes showing the approximate footfall on routes. Footfall measurement can also help to identify types of routes into smaller and private to larger and public routes.

8.5 Movement/circulation

To find primary and secondary circulation and movement networks within a masterplan, a two step process generates the most 'sustainable' road network connecting activity locations on the basis of most direct and therefore shortest metric distance. Locations are set by the designer and can be site-internal and external. The resulting network of circulation defines the block outlines for massing development.

8.6 Way-finding and signage (visual integration)

From the desire line and footfall calculations, CDR combines the two measurements to load frequencies of visual instances along

28.8 *Fort Halstead Masterplan, Sevenoaks, movement and circulation, Aedas Architects*

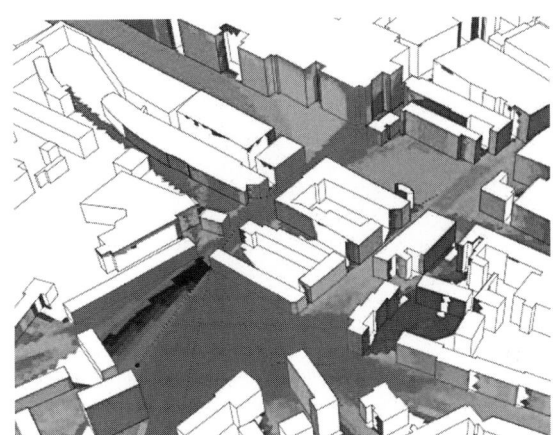

28.9 *Fort Halstead Masterplan, Sevenoaks, way-finding and signage, Aedas Architects*

the desire lines. The visual sampling in 3D provides evidence for elements in an urban and architectural context that are well visible during a journey and therefore become significant during way-finding. Elevations and locations that are well visible increase in rental/retail importance and serve as orientation support. Iconic buildings should have high values of visibility.

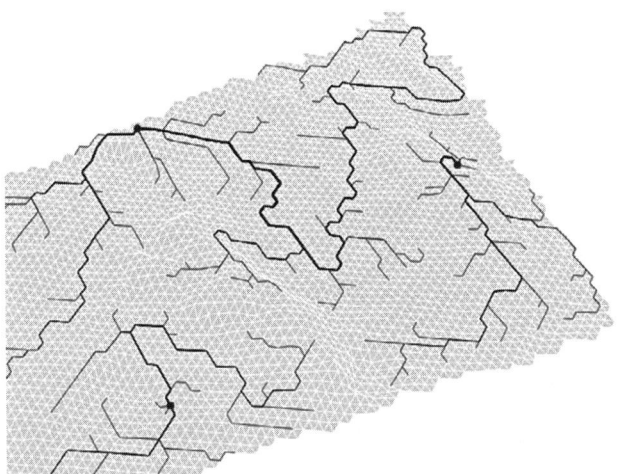

28.10 *Fort Halstead Masterplan, Sevenoaks, slope/height dependent access, Aedas Architects*

8.7 Slope/height dependent access

Design and access requires equal access opportunities for all demographic sections. CDR developed two tools that calculate access levels when topography or vertical circulation is taken into account. Especially for hot climates, a slope-dependent routing analysis helps to identify 'physically non-demanding' routes.

28.11 *Fort Halstead Masterplan, Sevenoaks, visual massing envelopes/landscaping, Aedas Architects*

8.8 Visual massing envelopes/landscaping

The visual disturbance of massing – single building or masterplan – can be calculated by an application that takes the terrain, building footprints and viewpoints on the terrain into account. The resulting massing indicates the extruded footprints that do not interfere with the selected viewpoints. Landscaping options can be analysed by visual performance.

28.12 *Fort Halstead Masterplan, Sevenoaks, land-use/mix, Aedas Architects*

8.9 Land-use/mix

Tolerances in area schedules for mixed-use development can be evaluated by building automated scenarios for land-use allocations, density and mix. All three aspects are computed simultaneously on the basis of constraint specifications including:

- land-use relations
- site conditions
- accessibility levels.

Densities per land-use are fixed at maxima and minima but the tool indicates the ideal quantities at all locations in relation to all other land-uses and accessibility values.

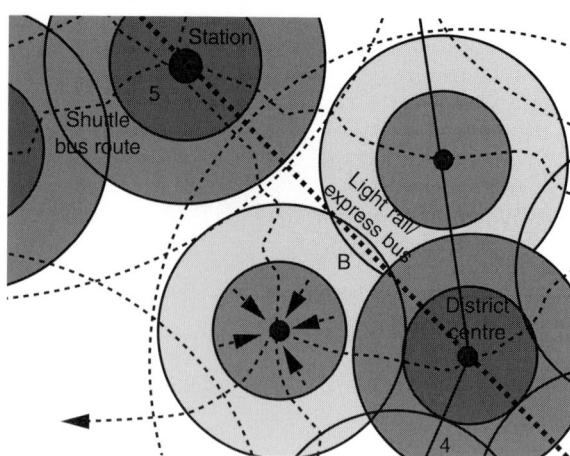

28.13 *Fort Halstead Masterplan, Sevenoaks, service provision modelling, Aedas Architects*

8.10 Service provision modelling

The land-use and mix simulation can absorb any number and type of land-use. Communal services such as schools or hospitals can be automatically suggested by the application on the basis of the density resulting from the development brief. The resulting quantities of required services will be fed-back into the development brief and urban codes.

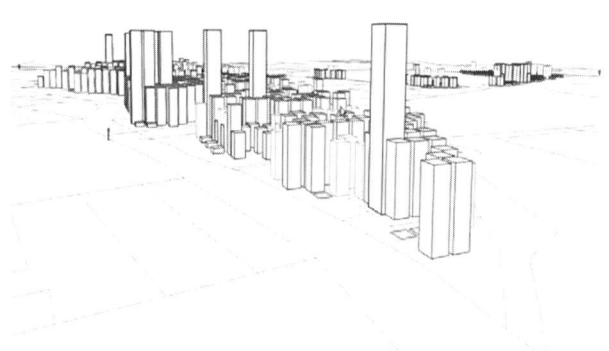

28.14 *Fort Halstead Masterplan, Sevenoaks, density indication, Aedas Architects*

8.11 Density indication

The scale and density of building mass on all plots can be indicated by a special visualisation function in the mixed-use application. The density indication visualises a relative height for each land-use to other neighbouring plots within given minimum and maximum height constraints. The indicative heights therefore integrate all other calculations on accessibility and land-use relations and generate autonomous neighbourhood scales.

8.12 Plot subdivisions/massing arrangement

For complex configurations of plot subdivision and plot massing arrangement, two design applications have been developed by the CDR that build scenarios for plot arrangements and plot/apartment arrangements. The plot/apartment arrangement applications can integrate daylight access calculations to generate optimised massing configurations for passive design.

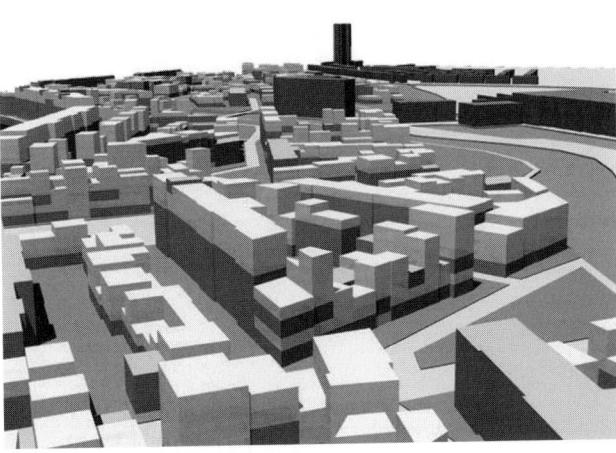

28.15 *Fort Halstead Masterplan, Sevenoaks, plot subdivision/ massing, Aedas Architects*

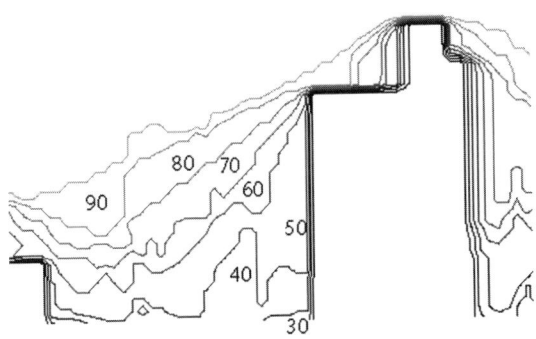

28.16 *Fort Halstead Masterplan, Sevenoaks, solar shading analysis, Aedas Architects*

8.13 Solar-shading analysis
To comply with daylight access regulations, a shading-envelope can be calculated that indicates the maximum massing achievable without overshadowing neighbouring plots and habitable rooms. All parameters are adjustable to duration of direct sunlight or amount of shading.

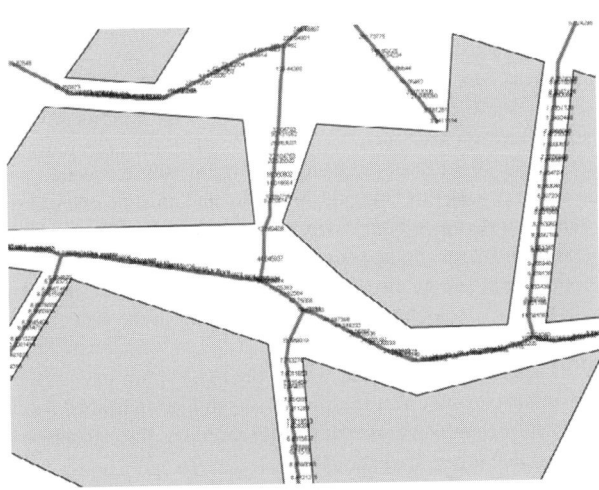

28.17 *Fort Halstead Masterplan, Sevenoaks, public realm appropriation, Aedas Architects*

8.14 Public realm appropriation
Maintenance of public and semi-public spaces depends on the sense of propriety and participation of individuals in society. This sense depends on clear definition of spaces through traffic regulation, urban furniture, landscaping and the shape of the built environment. Aedas R&D has developed an application that visualises the boundary between public and private spaces based on block outlines. The methods will help to establish what parts of public and open spaces 'belong' to which property.

8.15 Active frontages
Safety and crime levels within an urban context can be related to the level of activity and supervision within public realm. Activity measured by quantities of windows and doors bordering and overlooking public spaces can be evaluated and disclose the levels of 'activity' for distinct areas. Activity levels help to determine land-uses and surveillance installations, as well as potential pedestrian movement patterns.

8.16 Site loading scenarios
Development areas can be evaluated by visualising the diagram of density within an approximation of block outlines. Development areas for land-uses, maximum building heights and the block outlines need to be set by the designer. The block outlines can also be generated by a complementary application that produces a road network with maximum connectivity of roads and preset block size ratios.

28.18 *Fort Halstead Masterplan, Sevenoaks, scheme drawing, Aedas Architects*

Check lists are useful to assess the ingredients of a successful masterplan and CABE suggest these should include:

- A client committed to quality.
- A local authority committed to quality.

- Identifying what skills are required in the consultant team, and appointing a team with those skills in a timely manner.
- Getting the process right from the beginning, including the setting of realistic programmes and budgets, and the securing of funding to meet that budget.
- The right balance of design skills in the design team – urban design, architecture, landscape design, transport planning and others.
- A project structure with strong client leadership that encourages collaboration rather than competition between members of the design team.
- A collaborative relationship between local authority and applicant, involving mutual trust and understanding – and give and take.
- Early consultation of stakeholders, including community interests.
- Flexibility by local authority in relation to operation of statutory planning system.
- Recognition by all involved that the right degree of 'control' contributes to quality of place and therefore, to commercial success and liveability, rather than hampering would-be investors and developers.
- Genuine mixed use, rather than lip service to the concept.
- A commitment on behalf of local authority and landowner to seeing the vision through to completion.

9 COHERENCE, VARIETY AND UNIFORMITY

- Variety of uses.
- Planning geometries.
- Building typologies and building forms.
- Building height and massing.
- Architectural style, patterns of fenestration etc.
- Building and landscaping materials and colours.
- Consistency of public realm treatment, and hard and soft landscape design.
- Legibility of layout, are different routes and their nodes differentiated from one another by designing differing qualities of spatial enclosure.

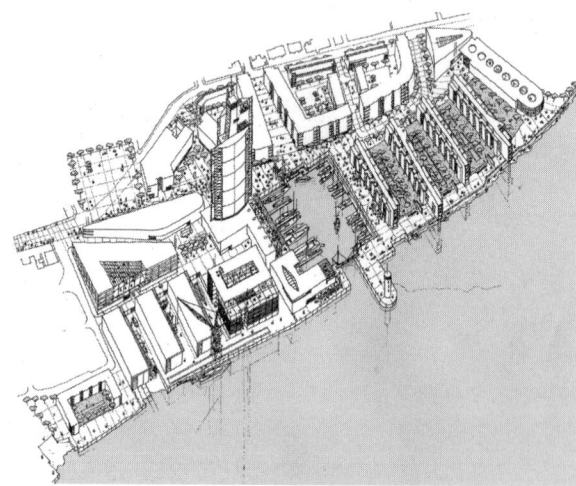

28.19 *Vosper site, Woolston, Southampton for SEEDA, Roger Stephenson Architects*

10 URBAN DESIGN ANALYSIS

- The nature, including surroundings, of a site.
- Connections and desire lines between site and surroundings, and the pattern of movement of pedestrians and vehicles.
- The existing patterns of built form on the site and around it, including heritage issues.

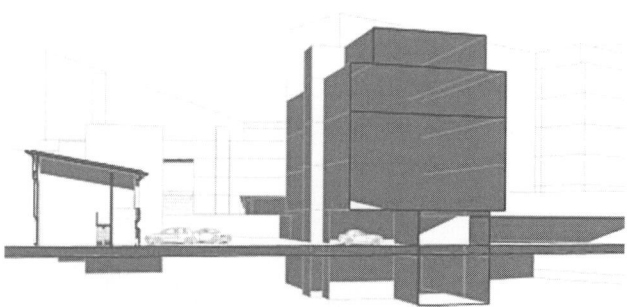

28.20 *Holbeck Village, Leeds, parking strategy, Aedas Architects*

- The site's topography, soil availability, its hard and soft landscape and its wildlife habitats and ecology.

11 INFRASTRUCTURE AND CONNECTIVITY

- Permeability: will the site be well connected, for pedestrian and vehicle movement in all directions?
- Are the desire lines and connections that have been brought out in the analysis addressed in the proposals?
- Are difficult infrastructure issues tackled, or have they been ducked?
- Will the 'site boundary' melt away, or will it remain as an actual or implied barrier?

12 THE ANATOMY OF THE SITE: HIGHWAYS, SERVICING AND CAR PARKING

- Is thinking about vehicle movement and highways design integrated with landscape design?
- Is the proposal honest about the impact of likely volumes of traffic?
- Does the design for traffic prioritise the needs of pedestrians over those of drivers?
- Has car parking been designed into the project from an early stage?

13 SITE PLANNING AND LANDSCAPE DESIGN

- Has an attitude to landscape design informed the development of the design from the beginning?
- Is there a good balance between the form of buildings and the form of open space?
- Robustness: have the buildings and open spaces been designed suitable for the widest range of likely activities and future uses?
- Visual appropriateness: has a vocabulary of contextual and visual clues been found to communicate levels of choice already designed into the plan?
- Richness: does the design increase choice for users through design for the senses with variety in visual stimuli, motion, smell, hearing and touch?
- Personalisation: does the design allow for future users to personalise places, this being the only way that most people can put their own stamp on their environment?
- Has the masterplanning been a holistic process, which reinforces commercial and public objectives whilst delivering resilience in the face of a changing climate and assisting in the reduction of greenhouse gas emissions?
- Will a lack of green areas within the masterplan intensify the urban heat island effect leading to risks to human health?
- Will the masterplan exacerbate water shortages through a lack of sustainable urban drainage systems?
- Is the masterplan likely to increase the biodiversity of the area?
- Is the proposed landscape scheme multifunctional by providing the ability to provide food, energy, water storage and flood

mitigation as well as providing a valuable resource for biodiversity and promoting health and well-being?

- Does the landscape response incorporate a range of, inter-linked and mutually reinforcing, mitigation and adaptation principles which can provide wider socio-economic and environmental benefits?
- Has the process provided a holistic approach to the protection, conservation and enhancement of urban and rural landscapes which will take into account current and future environmental, social and economic conditions?
- Does the design fully integrate building and site planning into the landscape planning process, taking into account landscape characteristics such as topography, vegetation and microclimate and help to maximise the benefits of shelter from intense wind and sun while seeking to incorporate maximum solar energy and water heating benefits?
- Has the layout provided for attractive opportunities for local outdoor leisure which will contribute to improving public health, well being and community engagement?
- Can the plan integrate and maximise local food production in the landscape, thereby reducing 'food miles' and promote more localised self-sufficiency?
- Has the plan included the creation of urban carbon sinks via the provision of green spaces which remove carbon from the atmosphere?
- Can the plan include for the installation of green roofs and green walls, thereby improving the thermal efficiency of buildings and reducing the use of conventional heating and cooling systems, whilst also alleviating flood risk?
- Could the open space be used for ground source heating and cooling?
- Has the choice of materials been considered on a local and sustainable basis?
- Can effective adaptation to climate change be facilitated by green infrastructure approaches to planning and design? Green spaces and corridors help to cool our urban environments, improve air quality and ameliorate surface run-off. A green infrastructure planning approach will reduce flood risk, protect building integrity and improve human health and comfort in the face of more intense rainfall and higher temperatures. Well-connected green infrastructure also provides wildlife corridors for species migration in the face of climate change as well as wider benefits for recreation, community development, biodiversity, food provision and place shaping.
- Can sustainable urban drainage systems (SUDs) reduce the negative impacts of development on surface water drainage? SUDS can minimise the risk of flooding and pollution via attenuation and storage with additional benefits including improvements to local environmental quality, the creation of habitats for biodiversity and general improvement to the quality of life for local communities.
- Does the landscape plan incorporate a robust green infrastructure with a network of spaces and natural elements that are currently present in and interconnect our landscapes?
- Will the proposed scheme recognise the important and multi-functional role green infrastructure has to play in providing benefits for the economy, biodiversity, wider communities and individuals?

14 OPEN SPACE

What is the space for?

- Could it accommodate a variety of uses?
- Does it require to accommodate community sports facilities?
- Does its location make sense in relation to its use – is it meant to be a focal point or a quiet, out of the way place?
- How big should it be?

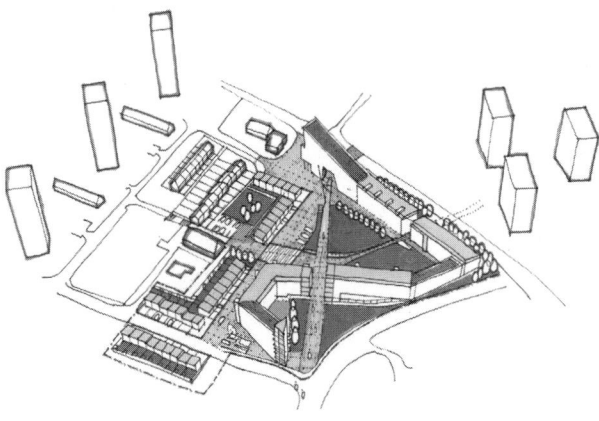

28.21 *Holbeck Village, Leeds, site planning and landscape, Aedas Architects*

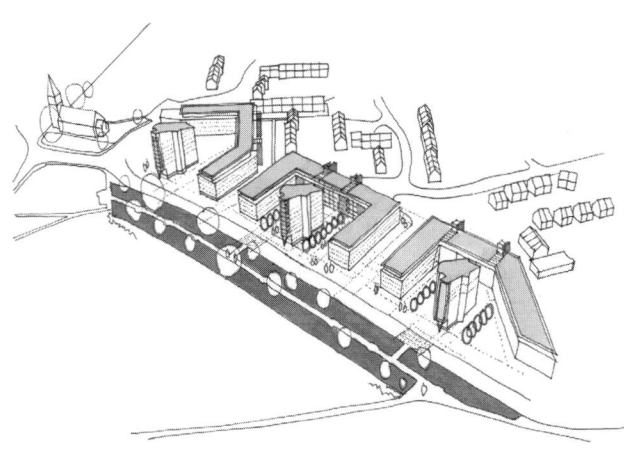

28.22 *Holbeck Village, Leeds, open space, Aedas Architects*

- Who will use it and at what hours of the day?
- Is it as safe as possible for everyone who will use it?
- Who will own and maintain it, and how will maintenance be paid for?

15 THE GEOMETRY OF SITE PLANNING

- Is the site planning informed by a clear attitude to geometry?
- Does the geometry contribute to the legibility of the site?
- Do the results make sense in terms of the blocks and building plots that result?

16 PLOT TESTING

- Does the plot make sense in relation to likely sizes, shapes and uses of buildings?
- In cases where there is not yet a developer or developers, will the blocks, plots and buildings implied by the master plan correspond to what developers will want to build?

17 THE BUILT HERITAGE

Does the site analysis demonstrate an understanding of the site's history?

- Has that understanding informed the design?
- Are the elements of built heritage given an appropriate status in order of the project?
- Is the built heritage treated as an asset rather than a liability?

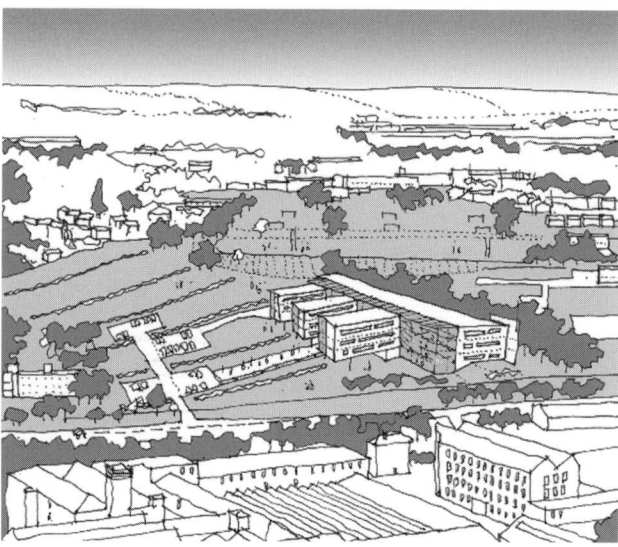

28.23 *Holy Trinity school, Halifax, Aedas Architects*

18 THE IMPORTANCE OF DETAIL: DELIVERING DESIGN QUALITY
- Does the masterplan set out a vision for the architecture of the buildings and the design of the landscape between them? Does it set quality standards?
- Will the process by which the master plan will be implemented address the question of how quality standards will be delivered?

19 SOME ALARM BELLS
- Unresolved conflicts within the client organisation.
- Lack of common ground between local authority and developer.
- Lack of clarity about the purpose of the masterplan.
- Lack of clarity about what the masterplan is intended to define.
- Lack of clarity about the status of 'indicative' illustrations of what buildings or places will look like.
- Failure to tackle existing infrastructure difficulties.
- Failure to recognise the importance of landscape design.
- Failure to deal with highways and parking issues as part of landscape design.
- Failure to make connections and 'think outside the red line'.
- Failure to acknowledge importance of design quality.
- Failure to put in place mechanisms to secure the quality of architecture, landscape design, details and materials.

20 CONCLUSIONS: EVALUATING A MASTER-PLAN DESIGN
- Does it reconcile, in terms of its site planning, economic goals and other public aspirations such as place-making?
- Does it propose an urban structure that connects well with its surroundings (in all directions)? Is it easy to explain and use, and is it robust for future cycles of redevelopment?
- Does it integrate with its surroundings so that the area to be developed and surrounding areas each benefit by presence of the other?
- Does it allow phased implementation? Will it work if only executed in part?
- Can landscape structure planting be achieved for the whole site at the outset in order to provide more mature landscapes for future phases of development?
- Is it flexible and open-ended, and so able to respond to changes in demand?
- Is it likely to achieve a sense of place and a distinct local identity?
- Does the master plan contain an overarching vision? If there is one, is it appropriate and relevant to the aims and objectives? If there isn't, is the lack of vision a problem?

- Does the design address the quality of the public realm and landscaping?
- In its proposals for urban blocks, building plots and buildings, does it provide opportunities to achieve good architecture and public places?

21 MASTERPLANNING FOR HEALTHY COMMUNITIES
Sarah Burgess, Senior Lecturer, UWE; Prof Hugh Barton, Director WHO Collaborating Centre for Healthy Cities and Urban Policy, UWE; Marcus Grant, Deputy Director WHO Collaborating; Centre for Healthy Cities and Urban Policy, UWE

21.1 Health
The World Health Organisation defines health as 'a state of complete physical, mental and social well-being and not merely the absence of disease or infirmity' (World Health Organisation, 1946). Health therefore is more than just the provision of health services and health care, it is about quality of life. The built environment has an important role in ensuring people have the opportunity to achieve this state of well-being, facilitating or prohibiting healthy lifestyle choices.

21.2 Health and the built environment
The issue of health and planning is not a new concept. The necessity to plan our towns and cities was borne out of the need to address health issues in the nineteenth century. In today's society however, many of our urban environments are having a detrimental effect on our health and well-being as shown in Figure 28.24.

There is a growing body of research on the relationship between the built environment and health with strong evidence that the urban environment has a significant influence over the wider determinants of health.

21.3 Considering health impacts
To ensure that new developments facilitate healthy choices and lifestyles, rather than restricting them, health impacts need to be considered throughout the masterplanning process, right from the concept development, including defining the brief, through to implementation and management. By considering health in the design of new neighbourhoods and development, the physical environment can help in tackling health inequalities and obesity issues, and supporting healthy ageing, active lifestyles and community cohesion. Other agendas such as climate change, facilitating adaptation and mitigation can also be met, leading to the design and implementation of cost effective interventions.

21.4 Creating healthier places – an integrated approach
There are a multiple of influences that affect a person's health and well-being. It is therefore fundamental that an integrated and collaborative approach to the planning, design, implementation and management of a development is undertaken to ensure that problems are understood and effective solutions can be promoted. This requires leadership, co-operation, creativity, a long-term view and commitment as well as an understanding of the local context and strategic direction for the wider area.

Figure 28.25 illustrates a seven stage process for undertaking a major development, to ensure that all stakeholders have a common vision and shared ownership of the project. Beginning with 'taking the initiative' and working around the circle to 'learning lessons', this needs to be undertaken collaboratively with the local community, the local authority and other stakeholders.

21.5 The health map
Adapted specifically for built environment professionals, the health map as shown in Figure 28.26 is a useful tool to better understand the relationship between health and well-being and the built environment. It strategically locates people at the centre of the diagram, who are surrounded by layers of social, physical, economic and

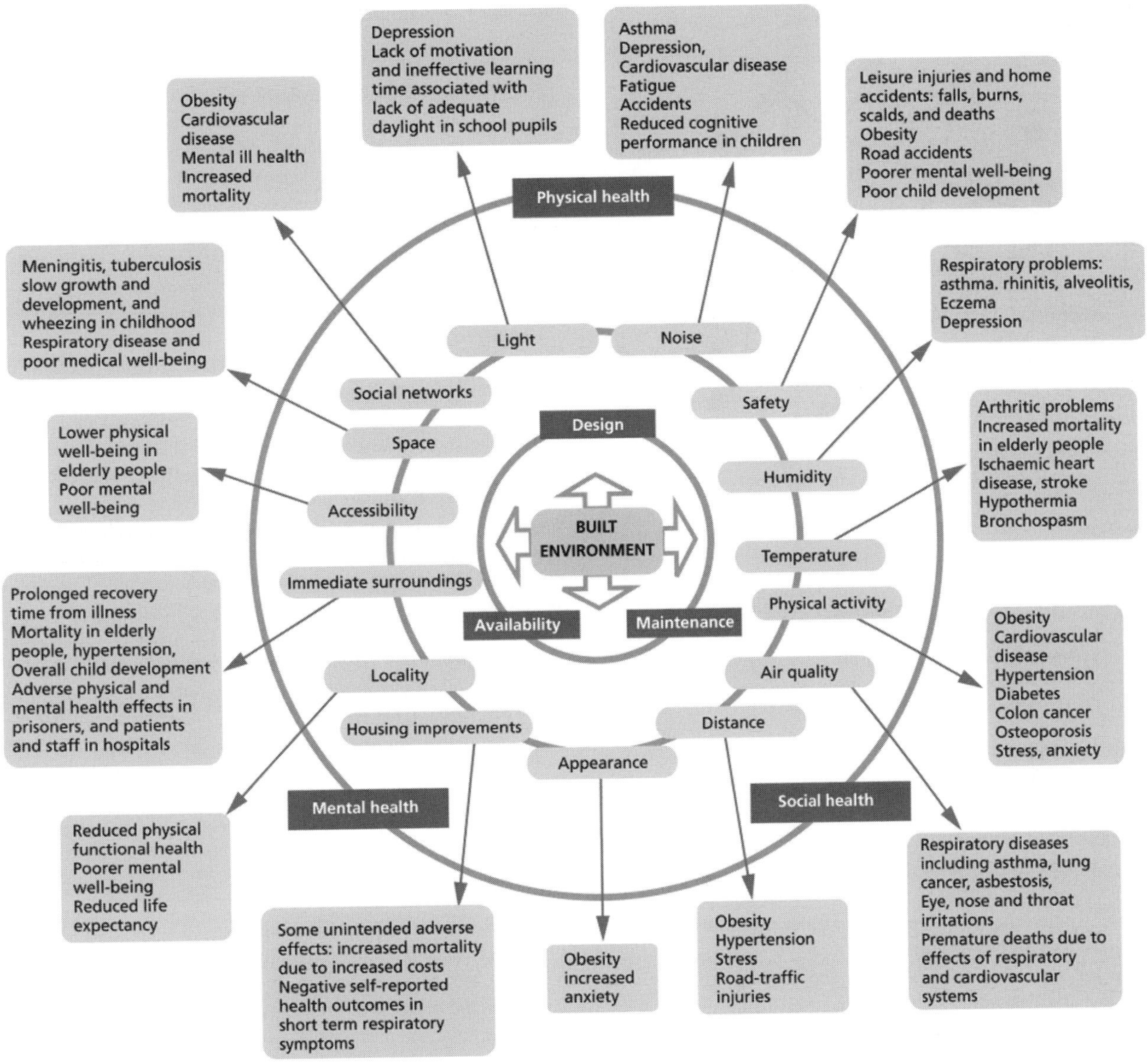

Obesity
Cardiovascular disease
Mental ill health
Increased mortality
Depression
Lack of motivation and ineffective learning time associated with lack of adequate daylight in school pupils
Asthma
Depression,
Cardiovascular disease
Fatigue
Accidents
Reduced cognitive performance in children
Leisure injuries and home accidents: falls, burns, scalds, and deaths
Obesity
Road accidents
Poorer mental well-being
Poor child development
Meningitis, tuberculosis slow growth and development, and wheezing in childhood
Respiratory disease and poor medical well-being
Respiratory problems: asthma. rhinitis, alveolitis,
Eczema
Depression
Physical health
Light
Noise
Social networks
Safety
Space
Design
Lower physical well-being in elderly people
Poor mental well-being
Humidity
Arthritic problems
Increased mortality in elderly people
Ischaemic heart disease, stroke
Hypothermia
Bronchospasm
Accessibility
BUILT ENVIRONMENT
Temperature
Immediate surroundings
Physical activity
Prolonged recovery time from illness
Mortality in elderly people, hypertension,
Overall child development
Adverse physical and mental health effects in prisoners, and patients and staff in hospitals
Availability
Maintenance
Obesity
Cardiovascular disease
Hypertension
Diabetes
Colon cancer
Osteoporosis
Stress, anxiety
Locality
Air quality
Housing improvements
Distance
Appearance
Mental health
Social health
Reduced physical functional health
Poorer mental well-being
Reduced life expectancy
Respiratory diseases including asthma, lung cancer, asbestosis,
Eye, nose and throat irritations
Premature deaths due to effects of respiratory and cardiovascular systems
Some unintended adverse effects: increased mortality due to increased costs
Negative self-reported health outcomes in short term respiratory symptoms
Obesity
increased anxiety
Obesity
Hypertension
Stress
Road-traffic injuries

28.24 *The detrimental effect of urban environments*

defining shared vision
taking the initiative
learning lessons
understanding the locality
taking action
developing ideas
agreeing a programme

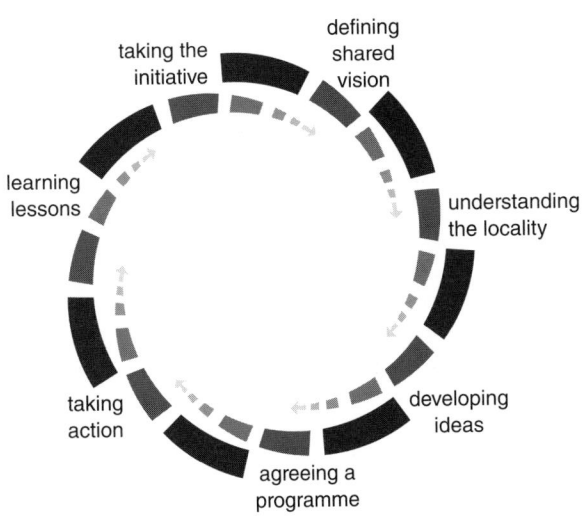

28.25 *Understanding a major development*

GLOBAL ECOSYSTEM
NATURAL ENVIRONMENT
BUILT ENVIRONMENT
ACTIVITIES
LOCAL ECONOMY
COMMUNITY
LIFESTYLE
PEOPLE
Climate stability
Biodiversity
Natural habitats
Buildings, Places
Working, Shopping, Moving
Wealth creation
Social capital
Diet, Physical activity
Work-life balance
Social networks
Resilient markets
Living, Playing, Learning
Streets, Routes
Air, Water, Land
Age, sex & hereditary factors
macro-economy, politics, culture, global forces
other neighbourhoods
other regions
The determinants of health and well-being in our neighbourhoods
The health map: Barton and Grant 2006 developed from a concept by Dahlgren and Whitehead 1991

environmental factors that all influence a person's health and well-being. Based on an ecosystem approach, the health map places all of these layers within the global context, which sets environmental limits on growth. The influence of each of the layers works in both

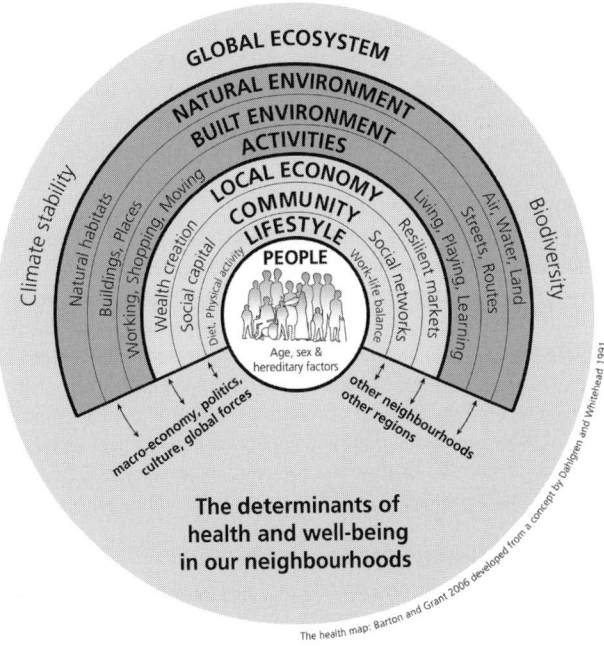

28.26 *Health map*

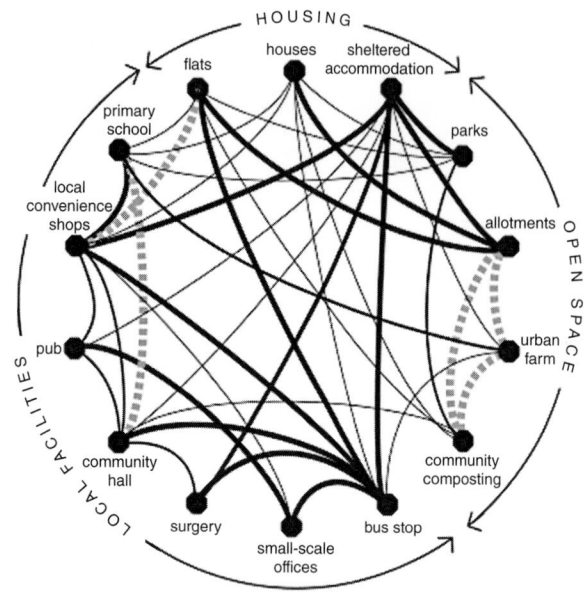

CONNECTIVITY BETWEEN LOCAL ACTIVITIES

▪▪▪   potential dual use combined use of space
▬▬▬   important 200 metres close pedestrian connections
——   important 400 metres connections
— —   other desirable 400 metres connections

28.27 *Connectivity between different land uses*

directions, with implications and impacts on other layers as well as people in the centre of the diagram.

21.6 Key principles of creating a healthier and more sustainable built environment

There are some key principles that should be considered when planning and designing for health and well-being. These are set out below.

21.7 Appropriate location

Providing access to employment, key services and facilities is fundamental to supporting healthy lifestyles and well-being. If the location of new development is inappropriate, where it is not integrated with existing areas, communities may not have access to local shops and services and also have limited transport options other than the private car. It is therefore critical that the site of new development should be in a location where it can integrate into existing public transport and cycle networks and provide residents with access to existing centres, jobs, services and facilities.

21.8 Mixed use environments

Mixed use environments encourage walking and cycling, offer opportunities for social interaction and can provide greater access to open space, recreation opportunities and fresh food. Shops, services and facilities should be located close to public transport stops and walking and cycling routes in locations that have sufficient foot-fall and catchment to ensure viability, clustered where possible to encourage shared use of facilities and pooling of resources, and at a level appropriate to their nature and scale. This will encourage active travel and social networks. Figure 28.27 illustrates connectivity between different land uses and recommended distances to encourage walking and cycling.

21.9 Graded density of people and land uses

The density of people and activity (not just housing density) should be higher around public transport nodes and core use areas (such as local centres and high streets) and lower near open countryside, major roads or open space wedges. This will increase land

efficiency, giving greater opportunity for the provision of public realm and open spaces and will increase the viability of local shops, services and public transport. This will contribute to maintaining people's independence and well-being.

> ★ *A fair average net density is 50 dwellings per hectare (approximately 100–120 people per hectare)*
> ★ *For dwellings located above ground floor, generous balconies or roof terraces should be provided*
> ★ *Land needed for other uses to support the community should be factored into gross density calculations*

21.10 Streets for people

Street networks should be permeable and promote walking and cycling to reduce reliance on private vehicle use. Streets are the longest lasting components of the built environment and they define the size of development plots, the character of the public realm, the movement opportunities, accessibility and connectivity in an area. It is therefore fundamental that they are designed to maximise opportunities for walking and cycling, and provide spaces for people to meet and interact in a pleasant and safe environment. This will assist in encouraging active travel as well as developing social capital and community cohesion.

> ★ *For pedestrian permeability, as a general rule, the maximum block size should be 100 m × 200 m*
> ★ *The Manual for Streets (DfT, 2007) promotes priority for the pedestrian and cyclist, slow traffic speeds, restricted sight lines, connectivity, multi-use streets and safety at junctions for pedestrians*
> ★ *Every dwelling should be within 400 m of a bus stop and the cycling network should be planned from the outset with a close grid of safe routes*

21.11 Interlinked green networks

Green networks should be carefully planned as an integral part of a place. Consideration about the location of green space and green corridors, the function of green space, how it is integrated into the neighbourhood and the management implications needs to be given at the start of the planning and design process. Green space provides the opportunity for healthy recreational activity and delight in nature. It can reduce stress, improve mental wellbeing, filter pollutants, increase biodiversity as well as provide a place for recreation and social interaction. It can also provide important movement corridors for people and wildlife and can also be used for composting and local food growing. Green space also plays an important role in carbon capture, climate mitigation and climate adaptation.

> ★ *Need to form partnerships to positively locate, design and manage green networks*
> ★ *The green network includes multi-functional greenspace areas which have different functions and may include designed, natural and semi-natural spaces, as well as allotments, fields, gardens and parks*
> ★ *Natural features such as steep slopes, watercourses, hedgerows, hill crests should be integrated into the green-space network*

This material has been derived from the publication Shaping Neighbourhoods *by Hugh Barton, Marcus Grant and Richard Guise (2010).*

22 REFERENCES

Urban Design Compendium, English Partnerships/Housing Corporation 2000
Creating Successful Masterplans, CABE 2004
Towards an Urban Renaissance, DETR 1999
The Value of Urban Design, CABE and DETR 2001

Grey to Green, CABE 2009

The Implications of Housing Type/Size, Mix and Density for the Affordability and Viability of New Housing Supply, National Housing and Planning Advice Unit 2010

Guidelines for Landscape and Visual Impact Assessment, Landscape Institute, 2013

Manual for Streets, DfT 2007

PLACEmaking, RUDI Ltd Resource for Urban Design Information with Academy of Urbanism 2008

Building Sustainable Transport into New Developments, DfT 2008

Capitalising on the Inherited Landscape, English Heritage/HCA 2009

Understanding Place: Historic Characterisation – guidance for planning and development, English Heritage 2009

Civic Realism, Rowe 1997

Gordon Cullen – Visions of Urban Design, David Gosling Academy Editions 1996

Hammarby Sjöstad – a unique environmental project in Stockholm, GlashusEtt 2007

Barton, H., Grant, M. and Guise, R. (2010) *Shaping Neighbourhoods,* 2nd edition, Routledge

Barton, H. (2009) 'Land use planning and health and wellbeing', *Land Use Policy*, Vol. 26 (Supplement 1), September, pp. 115–123.

Department for Transport (2007) *Manual for Streets*, Thomas Telford Publishing

National Heart Forum (2007) *Building Health: Creating and Enhancing Places for Healthy, Active Lives*, National Heart Forum

Barton, H. and Grant, M. (2006) A health map for the local human habitat. The Journal for the Royal Society for the Promotion of Health, 126 (6). pp. 252-253. ISSN 1466-4240 developed from the model by Dahlgren and Whitehead, 1991.

Dahlgren, G., Whitehead, M. (1991). "The main determinants of health" model, version accessible in: Dahlgren, G. and Whitehead, M. (2007) European strategies for tackling social inequities in health: Levelling up Part 2. Copenhagen: WHO Regional Office for Europe http://www.euro.who.int/__data/assets/pdf_file/0018/103824/E89384.pdf

23 APPENDIX: KEY DOCUMENTS AND CASE STUDIES

Key documents

PPG and PPS
Planning Policy Guidance and Statements

PPS1 Delivering Sustainable Development
PPS1 sets out the Government's overarching planning policies on the delivery of sustainable development through the planning system.

PPG2 Green Belts
This PPG outlines the history and extent of Green Belts and explains their purposes. It describes how Green Belts are designated and their land safeguarded. Green Belt land-use objectives are outlined and the presumption against inappropriate development is set out.

PPS3 Housing
Planning Policy Statement 3: Housing (PPS3) underpins the delivery of the government's strategic housing policy objectives and its goal to ensure that everyone has the opportunity to live in a decent home, which they can afford in a community where they want to live.

PPS4 Planning for Sustainable Economic Growth
Planning Policy Statement 4 (PPS4) sets out the government's comprehensive policy framework for planning for sustainable economic development in urban and rural areas.

PPS5 Planning for the Historic Environment
This document sets out planning policies on the conservation of the historic environment. The development plan making policies in this PPS must be taken into account by regional planning bodies in the preparation of revisions to Regional Spatial Strategies, by the Mayor of London in relation to the spatial development strategy for London, and by local planning authorities in the preparation of local development documents.

PPS7 Sustainable Development in Rural Areas
It sets out the government's planning policies for rural areas, which local authorities should have regard to when preparing local development documents and when taking planning decisions.

PPG8 Telecommunications
This PPG gives guidance on planning for telecommunications development, including radio masts and towers, antennas of all kinds, radio equipment housing, public call boxes, cabinets, polls and overhead wires.

PPS9 Biodiversity and Geological Conservation
PPS9 sets out planning policies on protection of biodiversity and geological conservation through the planning system. These policies complement, but do not replace or override, other national planning policies and should be read in conjunction with other relevant statements of national planning policy.

PPS10 Waste Management
This Planning Policy Statement forms part of the national waste management plan for the UK.

PPS12 Local Spatial Planning
This revised PPS12 puts in place the national policy framework for creating local development frameworks and concentrates on the key policy framework.

PPG13 Transport
This PPG's objectives are to integrate planning and transport at the national, regional, strategic and local level and to promote more sustainable transport choices both for carrying people and for moving freight.

PPG14 Development on Unstable Land
This PPG explains briefly the effects of land instability on development and land use. The responsibilities of the various parties to development are considered and the need for instability to be taken into account in the planning process is emphasised.

PPG17 Sport and Recreation
This PPG describes the role of the planning system in assessing opportunities and needs for sport and recreation provision and safeguarding open space which has recreational value.

PPG18 Enforcing Planning Control
This PPG introduces new and improved enforcement powers given to local planning authorities (LPAs) by the Planning and Compensation Act 1991. The note outlines the general approach to enforcement, including the primary responsibility of LPAs in the matter and the decisive issue of whether a breach of planning control would unacceptably affect public amenity or the existing use of land and buildings meriting protection in the public interest.

PPG19 Outdoor Advertisement Control
This PPG explains that the main purpose of the advertisement control system is to help those involved in outdoor advertising to contribute positively to the appearance of an attractive environment in cities, towns and the countryside.

PPS22 Renewable Energy
It sets out the government's planning policies for renewable energy, which planning authorities should have regard to when preparing local development documents and when taking planning decisions.

PPS23 Planning and Pollution Control
The policies in this statement and the advice in the accompanying Annexes (Annex 1: Pollution Control, Air and Water Quality and Annex 2: Development on Land Affected by Contamination) should be taken into account by Regional Planning Bodies (RPBs) and Local Planning Authorities (LPAs) in preparing Regional Spatial Strategies (RSSs) and Local Development Documents (LDDs) – referred to in this Statement as 'development plans'.

PPG24 Planning and Noise
This PPG guides local authorities in England on the use of their planning powers to minimise the adverse impact of noise. It outlines the considerations to be taken into account in determining planning applications both for noise-sensitive developments and for those activities which generate noise.

PPS25 Development and Flood Risk
Planning Policy Statement 25 (PPS25) sets out government policy on development and flood risk.

Minerals policy statements and minerals planning guidance for England
Minerals planning guidance notes (MPGs) and their replacements, minerals policy statements (MPSs), set out the government's policy on minerals and planning issues and provide advice and guidance to local authorities and the minerals industry on policies and the operation of the planning system with regard to minerals.

Marine Minerals Guidance
Marine Minerals Guidance Notes (MMGs) set out the government's policies and procedures on the extraction of minerals by dredging from the seabed in English marine waters.

Good Practice Guides
Good practice guidance is issued by 'Communities and Local Government' to augment policy and advise on the best way of achieving certain technical outcomes.

Case study: Hammarby Sjöstad – a unique environmental project in Stockholm
The water has inspired the name of the entire project – the town around the lake Hammarby Sjö. The first drawings of what would become Hammarby Sjöstad were pencilled in back in 1990. The idea was to showcase a unique opportunity – expanding the inner city with a focus on the water, while converting an old industrial and harbour area into a modern neighbourhood. Once fully built, Hammarby Sjöstad will have 11,000 residential units for just over 25,000 people and a total of about 35,000 people will live and work in the area. Hammarby Sjöstad will be fully built by 2015. Around 1200 homes per year are being constructed by three appointed developers who are responsible for their proportion of infrastructure costs borne by Stockholm Council at the outset of the project. The site had been acquired by the City as part of its bid for the Olympic Games 2004 and this ownership facilitated comprehensive planned development.

Architecture and urban design
Hammarby Sjöstad is Stockholm's biggest urban development project for many years. The area's location as a natural continuation of Stockholm's inner city has helped shape the infrastructure, planning and design of the buildings. This expansion has involved extensive reconstructions of the infrastructure, with traffic barriers

removed and the old industrial and terminal areas phased out, concentrated or given a new purpose.

The next phases
The areas around Sickla Udde, Sickla Kaj and Sickla Kanal are now fully developed. The next phases involve Hammarby Gård (1,000 apartments), Redaren and Sjöfarten (500 apartments), Lugnet (650 apartments), Henriksdalshamnen (850 apartments) and Sjöstadsporten (260 apartments with 15 000 m^2 office space and 15 250 m^2 hotel space). All of these areas offer a range of zoning types. The expansion of Hammarby Sjöstad coincides with the development of the area's municipal and commercial services, and with increased investment in public transport.

The history of Hammarby Sjö
In the 1800s, Sickla was a popular destination for excursions by the inhabitants of the Södermalm district of southern Stockholm, and was popularly known as 'Eastern Söder's Pearl'. The area was partially destroyed when the Hammarbyleden highway was built, and the seabed of the Lugnet bay area was filled in with excavated soil, rocks and refuse as part of the planned port area. The plans, however, came to nothing and the land was made available for storage depots and industrial use. But no single company or industry established itself in the area: instead, a shantytown began to grow up, and the area eventually became a small-scale industrial area. Constant threats of demolition meant the buildings in the area were of a temporary nature, largely consisting of a range of corrugated steel shacks. The shantytown lasted until 1998, when it was demolished to make way for Hammarby Sjöstad.

Soil decontamination
The shantytown left numerous environmental 'nasties' in the soil, so to ensure that no one is exposed to any risks in conjunction with service work in the future, e.g. repair work on pipes, or tree planting, the City of Stockholm Environment & Health Administration is monitoring the soil decontamination work throughout Hammarby Sjöstad, ensuring that the requisite standards are met to avoid harming either the environment or people's health. On Sickla Udde alone, the earth excavated contained 130 tonnes of oils and grease, and 180 tonnes of heavy metals.

ENVIRONMENTAL GOALS FOR LAND USAGE IN HAMMARBY SJÖSTAD

- Open space standard: There shall be at least 15 m^2 of courtyard space and a total of 25–30 m^2 of courtyard space and park area within 300 m of every apartment (equiv. 100 m^2 BTA).
- At least 15 per cent of the courtyard space shall be sunlit for at least 4–5 hours at the spring and autumn equinoxes.
- Development of undeveloped green public spaces shall be compensated for in the form of biotopes that benefit the biological diversity in the immediate area.
- Natural areas of particular value shall be protected from development.

Twice as eco-friendly
Right from the start, the city has imposed strict environmental requirements on buildings, technical installations and the traffic environment. The goal of the entire environmental programme is to halve the total environmental impact in comparison with an area built in the early 1990s. Another way of putting it is that the buildings in Hammarby Sjöstad will be twice as eco-friendly as a normal building. The architecture is modern, with the focus on sustainable materials such as glass, wood, steel and stone, and the ground was thoroughly decontaminated before building work began. Adapting the area to an environmentally friendly one has also entailed a heavy investment in green public spaces, with maintenance plans for the oak forest, a reed park with wooden jetties, a

broad avenue, and several large parks. Attractive forms of public transport are also offered, such as light rail link, boat traffic and access to a carpool.

THE CITY OF STOCKHOLM'S ENVIRONMENTAL GOALS FOR HAMMARBY SJÖSTAD

Land usage: sanitary redevelopment, reuse and transformation of old brownfield sites into attractive residential areas with beautiful parks and green public spaces.

Transportation: fast, attractive public transport, combined with carpool and beautiful cycle paths, in order to reduce private car usage.

Building materials: healthy, dry and environmentally sound.

Energy: renewable fuels, biogas products and reuse of waste heat coupled with efficient energy consumption in buildings.

Water and sewage: as clean and efficient as possible – both input and output – with the aid of new technology for water saving and sewage treatment.

Waste: thoroughly sorted in practical systems, with material and energy recycling maximised wherever possible.

An avenue linking the city district's new green public spaces and forming green corridors runs all the way through the southern part of Hammarby Sjöstad. The parks to the south of Hammarby Sjö are all linked to the major green public spaces of the Nacka nature reserve and Årsta forest, and form green wedges into the heart of Hammarby Sjöstad. The Nacka nature reserve is linked to the town area by means of ecoducts – planted viaducts – over the Södra Länken highway. New parks in northern Hammarby Sjöstad have been linked up with the Vitaberg park and the Stora Blecktorn park. Existing vegetation has been saved. The natural environment along the shores of Sickla Udde has been recreated using new trees and reed beds. The oak forest on Sickla Udde has been thinned and the living oaks and dead trees that have been left in place together form attractive environments for many species of insect and bird. The parks are intended to be attractive environments and serve as footpaths for people, but are also intended to serve as dispersal corridors and living environments for animals and plants.

Transportation imposes a heavy environmental burden in a densely built-up city district which is why Sjöstaden offers energy saving and attractive alternatives to private car usage. The aim was for 80 per cent of residents' and workers' journeys to be by public transport, on foot or by bicycle by the year 2010.

ENVIRONMENTAL GOALS FOR TRANSPORTATION IN HAMMARBY SJÖSTAD

- 80 per cent of residents' and workers' journeys shall be by public transport, on foot or by bicycle by the year 2010.
- At least 15 per cent of the households in Hammarby Sjöstad shall be signed up to the carpool by 2010.
- At least 5 per cent of the area's workplaces shall be signed up to carpools by 2010.
- 100 per cent of heavy transportation shall be by vehicles that meet current environmental zone requirements.

Light rail link
Substantial investments have been made in public transport in the area, both in the form of the new light rail link 'Tvärbanan' and bus traffic. Public transport has a central route running through Sjöstaden, with four stops along the avenue that connects one side of the city district to the other.

Ferry
Sjöstaden has ferry links. The ferry, which traffics Hammarby Sjö between the southern and northern sides of Sjöstaden, is run by the City of Stockholm and is free to use. The ferry runs 365 days of the year from early in the morning until late at night.

Carpool
A carpool open to both residents and those working here has been launched in the area. Around 10 per cent of households have joined the carpool to date, and there are 25–35 carpool cars parked in the area, with the number varying according to demand. Around 75 per cent of the cars are bifuel cars. The aim was for at least 15 per cent of households and at least 5 per cent of the Hammarby Sjöstad workplaces to be signed up to the carpool by 2010.

Environmental consideration across the board
Environmental consideration is the key for all of the materials used. This applies both to the visible materials used in the facades and on the ground as well as to the materials used in the internal parts of the buildings – their shells, installations and equipment. The guiding principle throughout has been to use tried and tested, sustainable materials and eco-certified products, and to avoid any use of chemical products or construction materials that contain hazardous substances. Rainwater must not be contaminated with metals or oils en route to Hammarby Sjö, which is why facade or roofing materials that could release heavy metals or other hazardous substances have been avoided, and why eco-friendly oil has been used for the footpaths along Sickla Canal and stainless steel has been used for the cycle bridge.

Eco-inspections
Everyone who builds in Hammarby Sjöstad must check and declare their chemical products and construction materials before work on their project begins, and eco-inspections are conducted regularly throughout the construction process.

ENVIRONMENTAL GOALS FOR CONSTRUCTION MATERIALS IN HAMMARBY SJÖSTAD

- Routines shall be drawn up for choosing the best materials from resource-related, environmental and health protection viewpoints, before the planning work begins.
- Pressure-treated timber may not be used.
- Copper may not be used as ducting material in horizontal or vertical piping trunks in the tap water system, either indoors or out. This does not apply to wet rooms and their connections within the apartment.
- Galvanised materials in the external environment shall be surface-treated.
- Use of newly extracted gravel and sand shall be minimised.
- Recycled materials shall be used wherever it is indicated for environmental and health reasons, provided that it is technically and economically feasible.

One of the goals of Hammarby Sjöstad is for the district to be a healthy place for people to live, a place that stimulates the body and soul, and hence a place that offers opportunities for exercise, sports and culture.

Exercise and sports
Sjöstaden has a number of exercise and sports facilities, such as Hammarbybacken, a slalom ski slope with amazing views. The sports facility at Hammarbyhöjden, near the southern side of Hammarbybacken is an important asset, not least for school and youth sports activities. The foot of the slope is also home to the valuable Nacka nature reserve. A sports hall with a large exercise facility has been built in Sjöstaden, and this positive feature is echoed in the annual Sjöstad Games held on Sweden's National Day under the administration of Hammarby IF sports association. Sjöstaden has numerous footpaths and cycle paths alongside the canals, as well as many attractive paths for strolling through a variety of green public spaces in the district. There are also cycle paths along Sjöstaden's main through-road.

Culture

A variety of different types of cultural activity are also important in terms of overall health. Cultural outlets in Hammarby Sjöstad include not only the Fryshuset social and cultural centre, but Kulturama, which offers tuition in a wide range of Arts for students of all ages, along with a library, not forgetting the cultural centre that will be opening soon.

Integrated planning with an eco-focus

The real key to the district's success is the integrated masterplanning work that was carried out before the area was developed. All of the various authorities and administrations that normally get involved in the various stages of the process sat down and drew up the plan for the new conceptual approach that would result in Hammarby Sjöstad. The integrated planning work carried out from the start was – and still is – unique. And the results were – and will continue to be – visible in Hammarby Sjöstad. The goal was to create a residential environment based on sustainable resource usage, where energy consumption and waste production are minimised, and resource saving and recycling are simultaneously maximised. Sjöstaden is home to exciting new technical solutions for energy supply and energy usage, a pilot sewage treatment plant facility where new technology will be tested, and a practical automated waste disposal system for waste management. One tried and tested example of integration solutions comes in the form of the heat extracted from the treated wastewater, which is used to produce district heating and, from the waste product of this process, district cooling.

Masterplanning guidance

Planning documents contain detailed spatial, landscape, height, fenestration, apartment size, balcony area, material and colour requirements to be followed by the developer teams for each area.

The Hammarby model – a unique eco-cycle

The integrated environmental solutions can be followed through an eco-cycle that has become known as the Hammarby model. The eco-cycle handles energy, waste, water and sewage for housing, offices and other commercial activities in Hammarby Sjöstad. The eco-cycle is also designed to act as a role model for the development of equivalent technological systems in big cities. The Hammarby model, along with explanatory texts, and the various sections of the cycle – namely energy, water and sewage, and waste – are presented on the following pages.

Sustainable and renewable energy

The City of Stockholm has always been well ahead of its time when it comes to finding new and renewable energy sources to make the city a better place to live in. For several decades now, Stockholm has been shifting over to using district heating to heat buildings. Hammarby Sjöstad has brought things one step further through the installation of various kinds of energy supply. New technology is being used as part of exciting development projects in Hammarby Sjöstad, e.g. as fuel cells, solar cells, and solar panels. The purpose is partly to test the new technology and partly to demonstrate methods of building a sustainable city. When the construction work on Hammarby Sjöstad is completed, the area's residents will produce half of all the energy they need. They will do this by utilising the energy present in treated wastewater and the energy to be found in the sorted-at-source combustible waste.

THE CITY OF STOCKHOLM'S ENVIRONMENTAL GOALS FOR ENERGY IN HAMMARBY SJÖSTAD

The goals relate to the sum of all the energy bought to heat the buildings and operate them each year. Household electricity is not included.

- District heating connection with exhaust air systems: 100, of which 20 kWh electricity/m^2 UFA
- District heating connection with heat extraction systems: 80, of which 25 kWh electricity/m^2 UFA
- The entire heating supply shall be based on waste energy or renewable energy sources.
- Electricity shall be 'Good Environmental Choice'-labelled, or equivalent.

Eco-friendly energy, district heating and district cooling

DISTRICT HEATING

The Högdalen combined heat and power plant uses sorted, combustible waste as an energy source (fuel) to produce electricity and district heating. Renewable energy sources are used wherever possible in order to spare the environment. Another example of sustainable heat supply is the Hammarby heat plant which extracts waste heat from the treated wastewater from the Henriksdal wastewater treatment plant.

DISTRICT COOLING

Stockholm's focus on centralised production of district heating and district cooling makes the city a world leader in this field. District cooling in Stockholm has developed over a decade into the world's largest system of its kind. From the cooled and treated wastewater that leaves the Hammarby plant's heat pumps, heat is exchanged into cooling in the water that circulates in the district cooling network in Hammarby Sjöstad. Cooling is, in other words, purely and simply a waste product from the production of district heating.

The sun provides energy and heats water

A variety of different kinds of energy supply are being tried out in Sjöstaden. Hammarby Sjöstad has several solar cell installations which capture the energy of the sun's light and convert into electrical power. Solar cells have been installed on several facades and roofs in Sjöstaden. The more effective the solar cells and the bigger the area they cover, the more effective the installation is. To date, solar cells have mainly taken the form of test projects from an energy viewpoint in urban environments. Two of the buildings on Sickla Kanalgata, for example, have been fitted with solar cells that are contributing to the buildings' energy supply by providing the energy needed for their public areas. Solar panels have also been fitted to the roof of one of Sjöstaden's larger apartment blocks.

Solar cells

Solar cells capture the sun's luminous energy and convert it into electrical power. The energy from a 1 m^2 solar cell module provides approximately 100 kWh/year, which corresponds to the domestic electricity requirement for 3 m^2 residential floor space.

Solar panels

On the roof of the Viken block, 390 m^2 of south-facing solar panels have been installed. These panels capture the warm rays of the sun and use them to heat the building's hot water supply. The solar panels produce half of the energy required to meet the building's annual hot water requirement.

Less water and cleaner sewage

Water consumption shall be reduced to streets with more than 8,000 vehicles per day shall be treated. One of Hammarby Sjöstad's goals is to reduce water consumption by 50 per cent: 200 litres/person/day is normally used in Stockholm, but the real aim is to reduce this figure to 100 litres/person/day. Thanks to eco-friendly installations (energy class A washing machines and dishwashers, low flush toilets and air mixer taps), consumption levels are currently approximately 150 litres/person/day. It is even more important to reduce the amount of heavy metals and non-biodegradable chemicals present in wastewater, because this will result in fewer contaminants being dispersed into the Stockholm archipelago via the treated wastewater, and will also give a better residual product, known as sludge, which can be reused on agricultural land. The strategy to systematically work with customers and society to reduce the amount of chemicals flushed into the wastewater system is called the Upstream approach. The Upstream approach is now endorsed by many wastewater companies throughout Europe as being part of their core business. By monitoring the wastewater, one can see whether campaigns in this area have any effect on the quality of the wastewater. In the spring of 2005, for example, a campaign to reduce the use of the bactericide Triclosan was conducted. Triclosan is an environmentally hazardous substance present in certain toothpastes and which there is no need whatsoever for ordinary consumers to use. Analyses of the wastewater before and after the campaign show that the amounts of Triclosan present had fallen.

THE CITY OF STOCKHOLM'S ENVIRONMENTAL GOALS FOR WATER AND SEWAGE IN HAMMARBY SJÖSTAD

- 95 per cent of the phosphorus in wastewater shall be reusable on agricultural land.
- The quantity of heavy metals and other environmentally harmful substances shall be 50 per cent lower in the wastewater from the area than in the wastewater from the rest of Stockholm.
- Lifecycle analyses (LCA) shall be carried out to determine the suitability, from an energy and emissions viewpoint, of returning nitrogen to agricultural land and of utilising the chemical energy present in the wastewater.
- Drainage water shall be connected to the storm water network and not to the wastewater network.
- Storm water shall primarily be treated locally.
- The nitrogen content of the purified wastewater shall not exceed 6 mg/litre and the phosphorus content shall not exceed 0.15 mg/litre.
- Storm water from streets with more than 8,000 vehicles per day shall be treated.

Sjöstadsverket – our own wastewater treatment plant with cutting edge technology evaluated in different processes

A new test wastewater treatment plant, Sjöstadsverket, has been built to evaluate new technology in the field of wastewater treatment. The first stage of Sjöstadsverket has four separate treatment lines for wastewater from the equivalent of 600 people in Hammarby Sjöstad. The various lines are being evaluated and a basis for decision-making for stage two – which may possibly see a water treatment plant built for the whole of Hammarby Sjöstad – will also be generated. The treatment lines under evaluation contain chemical, physical and biological processes that are run as efficiently as possible. The goal is both to treat the wastewater and to recycle resources from the wastewater with as little input of external resources, such as electrical energy and chemicals, as possible.

Cleaner biosolids and nutrient recycling

The buildings and infrastructure in Hammarby Sjöstad have been planned and built with great care when it comes to the choice of construction and building materials, and the processing of wastewater and refuse, for example. By avoiding the use of certain metals and plastics in the buildings, by ensuring that rainwater and snowmelt are treated and drained separately, and by providing residents with information, e.g. the importance of eco-labelled household chemicals, it can be ensured that households' wastewater is relatively clean. The wastewater that goes to the local wastewater treatment plant comes solely from housing in the area, and does not come from storm water and industries. This means that right from the start, the wastewater contains a minimum of contaminants, which makes it easier to treat and for the nutrients it contains to be reclaimed and, hopefully, be reusable on agricultural land. The environmental goal is for 95 per cent of the phosphorus to be separated out and recycled for agricultural use, and for the level of heavy metals and other hazardous substances to be reduced by 50 per cent. The treated sewage has to meet exceptionally high standards.

Biogas and biosolids extracted

Biogas is extracted from the digestion of sewage sludge. At the wastewater treatment plant, organic material is separated out from the wastewater in the form of sludge. The sludge is carried to large digestion tanks, where it is digested. Biogas, which is the most environmentally friendly form of fuel currently available, is produced during the digestion process. The biogas produced is primarily used as vehicle fuel, e.g. in inner city buses, garbage trucks and taxis. Biogas is also used in approximately 1,000 gas stoves in Hammarby Sjöstad. Once the digestion process is completed, the sludge – the biosolid – can be used as a fertiliser since it is nutritionally rich with a high phosphorus content. Stockholm Water sends biosolids to northern Sweden, where they are used as filling material in mines that have been closed down.

Architectonic storm water solutions

All storm water, rainwater and snowmelt is treated locally in a variety of ways, and the system is referred to collectively as LOD (the Swedish acronym for 'local storm water treatment'). Storm water from developed areas is infiltrated into the ground or drained to Sickla Canal, Hammarby Canal or Danvik Canal. A storm water canal runs through the park Sjöstadsparterren (the Sjöstaden parterre). The water runs from the surrounding buildings and courtyards via numerous small gutters and is then carried on to Hammarby Sjö through a water ladder designed by the artist, Dag Birkeland.

Green roofs

The green roofs seen on some of the buildings in Sjöstaden are another link in the local storm water treatment (LOD) chain. Their task is to collect the rainwater, delay it and evaporate it. At the same time, the small, dense sedum plants form living green areas in the cityscape.

Rainwater from the streets is treated locally

Rainwater and snowmelt from the streets is collected and treated in a variety of different ways in Sjöstaden. The most common way involves draining the water into special basins, and Sjöstaden has two closed settling tanks. The water is allowed to remain in the tanks for several hours, to allow the contaminants to sink to the bottom (settling), and is then drained out into the canals. Mårtensdal has an open storm water basin where the surface of the water can be seen. Here, the soil and plants in the area can handle the contaminants from dirty water when it sinks down into the ground water.

Waste must be reduced and recycled

These days waste is no longer just waste. It is a resource that is being utilised more and more. New things are being produced from recycled materials, allowing more economical use of nature's resources. A lot of things improve when everyone separates their waste, and if the waste is to be handled properly, everyone must do their bit. When you separate waste, you help ensure that hazardous substances are not incinerated along with the rest of the refuse bags. Extraction of virgin raw materials is reduced, when the recycled materials can be used instead. This makes waste into a resource that can be used for materials recycling and energy recovery. Quantities of domestic waste are reduced, and the refuse collection personnel's working environment improves.

THE CITY OF STOCKHOLM'S ENVIRONMENTAL GOALS FOR WASTE IN HAMMARBY SJÖSTAD

Energy shall be extracted from 99 per cent by weight of all domestic waste from which energy can be recovered by 2010. Reuse or recycling shall, however, be prioritised.

- The amount of domestic waste generated shall be reduced by at least 15 per cent by weight between 2005 and 2010.
- The amount of domestic bulky waste disposed of in landfill sites shall be reduced by 10 per cent by weight between 2005 and 2010.
- The amount of hazardous waste generated shall be reduced by 50 per cent by weight between 2005 and 2010.
- Residents shall be given the opportunity to separate their waste at source into the following fractions:

  o Materials with a producer responsibility, within the building
  o Separated food waste and 'refuse bags', within the building
  o Bulky waste, within the building
  o Hazardous waste, in the local area

- By 2010, 80 per cent of food waste by weight shall be handed in for biological treatment which utilises its component nutrients for plant cultivation and also utilises its energy content.
- A maximum of 60 per cent (vehicle km) of waste transports and transportation of recycled materials within the area shall involve the use of heavy vehicles, in comparison with the amount transported using conventional waste management transportation.
- A maximum of 10 per cent by weight of the total waste generated during the construction phase shall comprise waste that is disposed of in landfill sites.

Waste is separated at source and recycled or used to produce heating and electricity

THREE-LEVEL WASTE MANAGEMENT

In Hammarby Sjöstad, there are three different levels of waste management: building-based, block-based, and area-based: building-based separating at source. The heaviest and bulkiest waste is separated into fractions and deposited in different refuse chutes in or adjacent to the buildings.

- Combustible waste. Things made of plastic, paper and other forms of non-packaging are placed in ordinary plastic bags.
- Food waste. Food product waste is placed in bags made of corn starch which, unlike plastic bags, are biodegradable.
- Newspapers, catalogues, paper, etc. left loose, not packed.

BLOCK-BASED RECYCLING ROOMS

The types of waste that do not belong in the building-based refuse chutes can be left in block-based recycling rooms:

- Glass, paper, plastic and metal packaging.
- Bulky waste, e.g. old furniture.
- Electrical and electronic waste. Items that require an electric socket or batteries to function, as well as light bulbs, fluorescent tubes and low-energy light bulbs.
- Some of the recycling rooms also have containers for textiles.

AREA-BASED HAZARDOUS WASTE COLLECTION POINT

Waste that constitutes a danger to people and the environment, such as paint, varnish and glue residues, nail polish, solvents or cleaning agents, batteries and chemicals must never be placed in domestic waste or poured down the drain. It must be separated out and handed in at the hazardous waste collection point in GlashusEtt, the area's environmental information centre.

WHERE DOES THE WASTE GO?

- Combustible waste is transported to the Högdalenverket plant in southern Stockholm where it is incinerated and recycled as heating and electricity.
- Food waste is transported to Sofielund in Huddinge where it is composted and turned into soil. The ultimate aim is for food waste to be converted into biogas and bio-fertilisers.
- Newspapers are delivered to paper recycling companies and then sent on to paper mills where they are turned into new paper.
- Packaging. Paper, metal, glass and plastic packaging is recycled as new packaging or as other products.
- Bulky waste. Metal is recycled, combustible bulky waste is incinerated and recycled as heating and electricity. Non-combustible waste is disposed of in landfill sites.
- Electrical and electronic waste is disassembled and the materials are recycled. Leftover material is disposed of in landfill sites.

The automated waste disposal system reduces transport in the area

MOBILE AUTOMATED WASTE DISPOSAL SYSTEM

The waste collected in the mobile automated waste disposal system ends up in underground tanks that are emptied by a refuse collection vehicle equipped with a vacuum suction system. There are separated tanks for each fraction: combustible domestic waste and food waste. The refuse collection vehicle stops at docking points where several buildings' waste tanks are emptied simultaneously, but only one fraction at a time per collection round.

STATIONARY AUTOMATED WASTE DISPOSAL SYSTEM

All refuse chutes are linked by underground pipes to a central collection station to which they are carried by vacuum suction. The collection station houses an advanced control system that sends the various fractions to the right container. There is a large container for each fraction: combustible domestic waste, food waste and newspapers. The systems reduce transport in the area, which means the air is kept cleaner than when traditional refuse collection techniques are employed. In addition, the work environment for the refuse collection workers is improved when heavy lifting is avoided and there is a noticeable improvement in children's safety.

GlashusEtt is the area's environmental information centre

ENVIRONMENTAL INFORMATION CENTRE

The design and content of GlashusEtt make it the natural focal point for information on environmental issues in Hammarby Sjöstad. This knowledge centre also provides Stockholm with a natural hub for demonstrating the links between modern technology and a better environment in an atmosphere of harmony with exciting new architecture. The centre is also responsible for its own website – www.hammarbysjostad.se.

EXHIBITIONS – STUDY VISITS

The environmental information centre is tasked with spreading knowledge through study visits, exhibitions and demonstrations of the Hammarby Model and new eco-friendly technology. National and international visitors come to Sjöstaden to see not only how the City of Stockholm has planned the new city district, but also how an eco-minded approach has characterised the entire Sjöstaden planning process that went into making it the sustainable city.

CONFERENCE ROOMS

GlashusEtt's conference rooms are used, in part, to receive visitors, but they also function as a meeting place for discussions and conversations about the sustainable city. GlashusEtt is also used as a teaching centre for a variety of different courses on environmental and urban planning, public meetings, politicians' meetings and customer meetings.

EXPORTING ENVIRONMENTAL TECHNOLOGY

GlashusEtt also plays a very important role in exporting environmental technology. A very close cooperation is taking place with a range of authorities tasked with promoting environmental exports, such as Stockholm Business Region, the Swedish Ministry for Foreign Affairs, and the Swedish Trade Council. In just a short period of time, Hammarby Sjöstad has become one of the world's most high profile examples of sustainable urban development and is mentioned in specialist publications worldwide. Sjöstaden is visited by over 10,000 industry representatives and decision makers every year. Significant urban projects in Toronto, London, Paris and several cities in China have been influenced by the expertise and technology that forms the basis for its success.

Hammarby Sjöstad's own eco-cycle
ENERGY
- Combustible waste is converted into district heating and electricity.
- Biofuel from nature is converted into district heating and electricity.
- Heat from treated wastewater is converted into district heating and district cooling.
- Solar cells convert solar energy into electricity.

- Solar panels utilise solar energy to heat water.
- Electricity must be a 'Good Environmental Choice' product, or equivalent.

WATER AND SEWAGE
- Water consumption is reduced through the use of eco-friendly installations, low flush toilets and air mixer taps.
- A pilot wastewater treatment plant has been built specifically for the area in order to evaluate new sewage treatment techniques.
- Digestion is used to extract biogas from the sewage sludge.
- The digested biosolids can be used for fertilisation.
- Rainwater from yards and roofs is drained into Hammarby Sjö, rather than into the wastewater treatment plant.
- Rainwater from streets is treated locally using settling basins and then drained into Hammarby Sjö, rather than being drained into the wastewater treatment plant.

WASTE
- An automated waste disposal system with various deposit chutes, a blockbased system of recycling rooms and an area-based environmental station system help the residents sort their waste.
- Organic waste is converted/digested into biosolids and used as fertiliser.
- Combustible waste is converted into district heating and electricity.
- All recyclable material is sent for recycling: newspapers, glass, cardboard, metal, etc.
- Hazardous waste is incinerated or recycled.

29 Museums, art galleries and temporary exhibition spaces

Geoffrey Matthews, with additional information (case study) by Pamela Buxton

CI/Sfb:75

Geoffrey Matthews is a museum consultant. Pamela Buxton is editor of the fifth edition of the Metric Handbook

KEY POINTS:
- *Flexibility and potential for expansion is a priority*
- *Design must enhance visitor orientation*
- *Digital media brings new challenges and opportunities*

Contents

1 Introduction
2 Area data
3 General planning
4 Exhibition and collection storage spaces
5 Interpretation, communication and display
6 Environment and conservation
7 Security and services
8 Case study
9 Bibliography

1 INTRODUCTION

1.1 Scope

Museums are defined by the Museums Association in the UK as institutions that collect, safeguard and make accessible artefacts and specimens, which they hold in trust for society. They enable people to explore these collections for inspiration, learning and enjoyment.

The design of museums, art galleries and the temporary exhibition spaces associated with similar organisations involves the housing of a wide range of functions broadly indicated in the common definitions of a museum. Museums, however, vary considerably in size, organisation and purpose. It is important therefore to consider the particular context and features that characterise a museum in the process of developing concepts.

1.2 Collections

Collections in national museums are very large and varied in material and generally of international importance. The National Maritime Museum in Greenwich, for example, houses collections of machinery, boats, costumes, medals, ship models, paintings, silver, weapons and scientific instruments, among many other types of material. Such museums are staffed by a wide range of highly qualified experts in collection management, research, conservation, public relations and marketing.

In some local and private museums collections are small, specific in material content and of specialist or local interest. Many such museums have only one qualified curator to oversee management of the collections and public services, and many of the specialist functions may be provided by outside bodies such as the Area Museum Councils. Figure 29.1 shows a typology of museums based on subject/museological approach, collection characterisation and type of institution.

2 AREA DATA

2.1 Design guidelines

There is no convenient formula for determining the areas to be devoted to the different functions. The client's intentions in respect

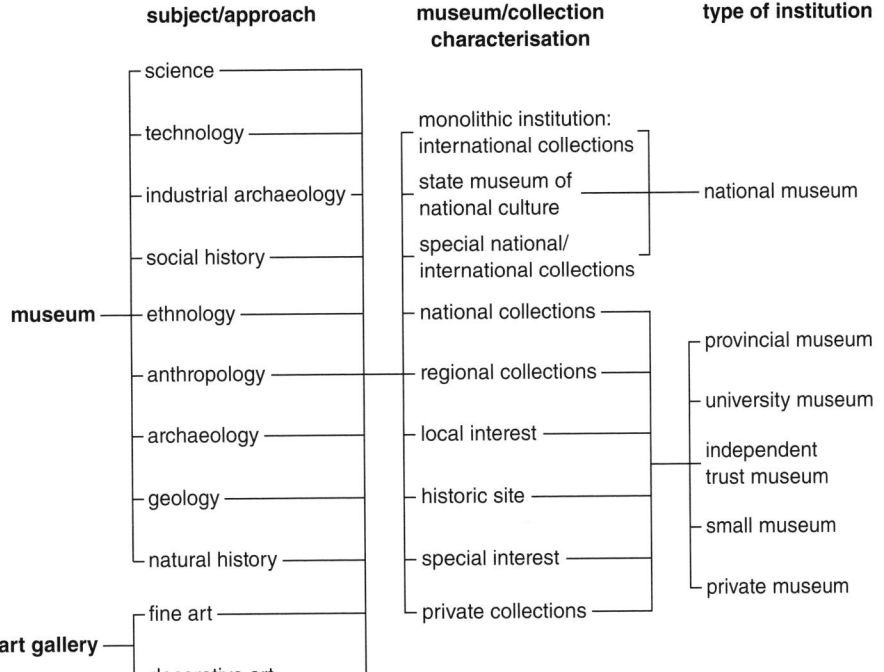

29.1 *A museum typology based on: museological approach/interpretive discipline; collection characterisation; and institution characterisation*

of public access to collections, information and staff, and of commitment to research and conservation will provide an initial guide and most major museums, for example the Victoria and Albert Museum, will have their own design guidelines.

2.2 Storage

Some museums may have only a small proportion of the permanent collections on public exhibition at any one time, the bulk remaining in storage and accessible for research and conservation purposes only. Well-serviced temporary exhibition space may be a priority in such cases. Other museums may have smaller collections attractive enough to the visiting public to warrant the development of sophisticated exhibitions with a designed life of several years. In such cases storage space may be needed primarily for the expansion of the collections, and considerable effort may be made to develop educational programmes.

3 GENERAL PLANNING

3.1 Organisation

The relationships between functions are common to all museums and art galleries. The flow diagram in Figure 29.2 shows collection item movements in the operation of collection services, but note that not every operation necessarily requires a separate space, and some services may be provided by outside agencies. As far as possible, collection movement and public circulation should be kept separate. Figure 29.3 shows one approach to zoning and expansion based on this principle. Figure 29.4 shows a possible layout for a small museum in which interpretive exhibitions and educational programmes are central to its operation. Where a museum is to be developed around a large-scale permanent installation this should be integrated into the interpretive

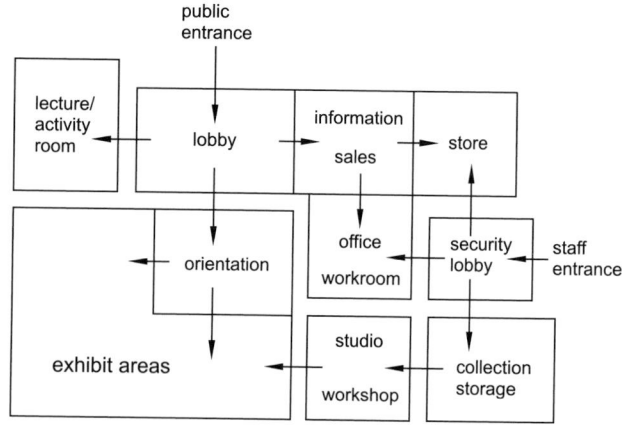

29.4 *A possible layout diagram for a small museum*

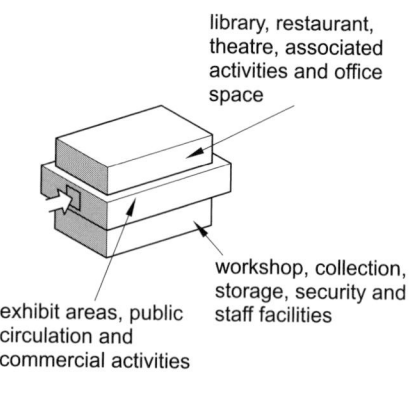

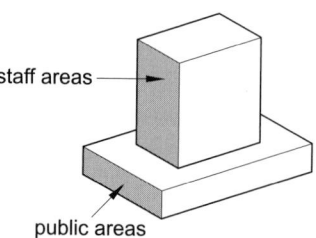

29.5 *Two basic massing concepts that allow public areas to be organised on one level*

scheme at an early stage. Examples are Jorvik Viking Centre's archaeological site and the National Railway Museum's turntables.

3.2 Flexibility

Museums are long-term developments: concepts for layout and massing should therefore be capable of expansion in all areas and a degree of internal rearrangement, particularly in work and ancillary areas. Figure 29.5 shows possible massing concepts and Figure 29.6 illustrates the three methods of expansion.

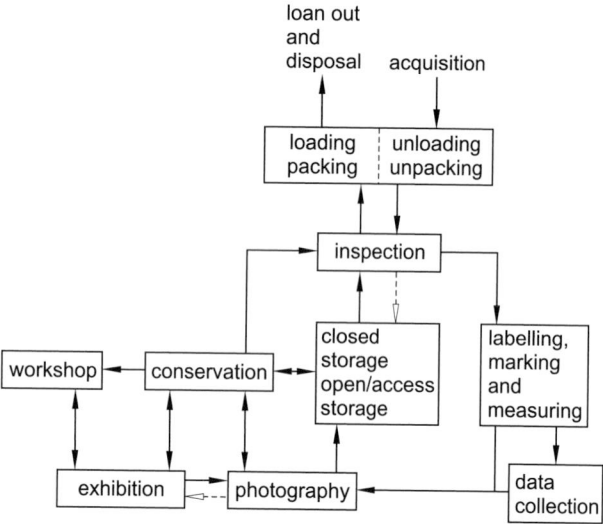

29.2 *Flow diagram of collection item movements in the operation of collection services: exhibitions, conservation and collections management*

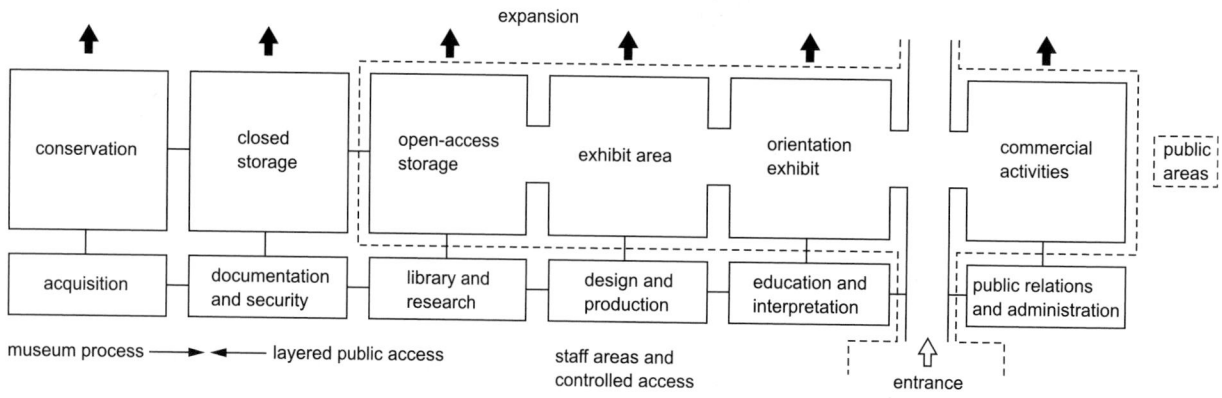

29.3 *A layout concept showing a clear relationship between museum functions and an approach to zoning and expansion*

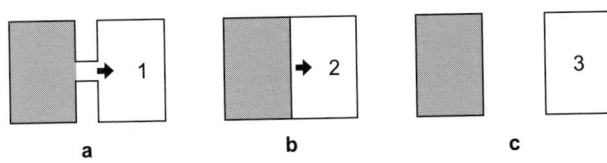

29.6 *Three modes of expansion: a Block addition; b Extension; c New building*

4 EXHIBITION AND COLLECTION STORAGE SPACES

4.1 Layout

The layout of public areas in a museum, Figure 29.7, may be based on a simple concept of free circulation around a single open-plan exhibition space, Figure 29.7a, or on more complex concepts related to generic interpretive structures. It is important to consider the nature of the narratives appropriate to the museum's objects of interest. The storyline of an exhibition may be translated into:

- a *linear* arrangement of spaces with beginning, middle and end, Figure 29.7c;
- a *loop* where the essentially linear storyline leads naturally back to the beginning, Figure 29.7d;
- an arrangement of *core and satellites* where each theme or detailed treatment of a subject leads back to a central introductory or orientational area, Figure 29.7b;
- a more *complex* scheme combining linear, loop and core-satellite arrangement of spaces which is specifically structured to account for more or less stable relationships between collections and interpretive themes, Figure 29.7e; or
- a *labyrinthine* arrangement where the relationships between areas can be varied from exhibition to exhibition by managing the public circulation, Figure 29.7f.

4.2 Orientation

In any arrangement of exhibition spaces considers the problem of orientation; at the entrance to the museum and at key decision points in the museum, information and visible clues should be provided to enable the visitor to grasp the organisation of the collections, the interpretive scheme and the public services offered by the museum. The aim of orientation is not only easy understanding of the building layout but more crucially to facilitate access to collections, information and museum services.

4.3 Storage

Many museums carefully control access to all collection storage spaces. However, it is increasingly worth considering the provision of open-access storage areas particularly for collection study. The former requires that storage areas are made secure and that visitors are closely supervised. Open access, on the other hand, requires that secure forms of storage equipment and furniture are arranged in very compact layouts. Figure 29.8 shows a typical layout for a storage area fitted out with ranks of secure display cases. Figure 29.9 shows a secure storage area with open-floor storage for larger collection items.

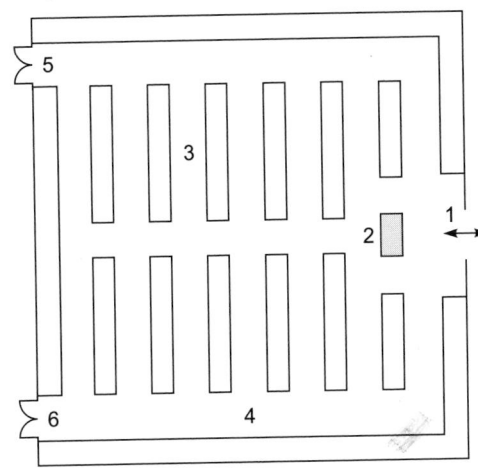

29.8 *Method of layout in open-access storage areas*

1 *Entrance from main exhibit areas*
2 *Orientation point*
3 *Ranks of cases glazed on all sides*
4 *Full-height wall cases*
5 *Fire exit*
6 *Controlled access to staff areas and secure storage*

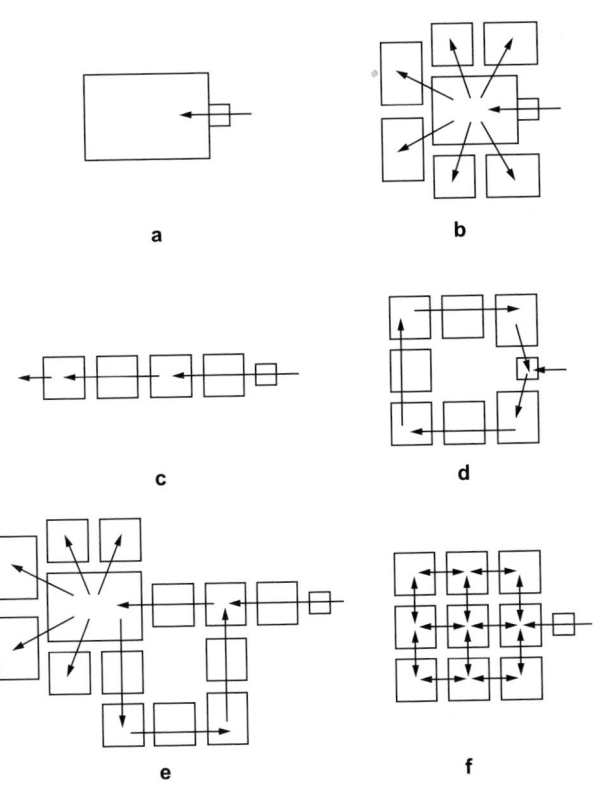

29.7 *Generic plans for exhibit and open-access storage areas: a Open plan; b Core + satellites; c Linear procession; d Loop; e Complex; f Labyrinth*

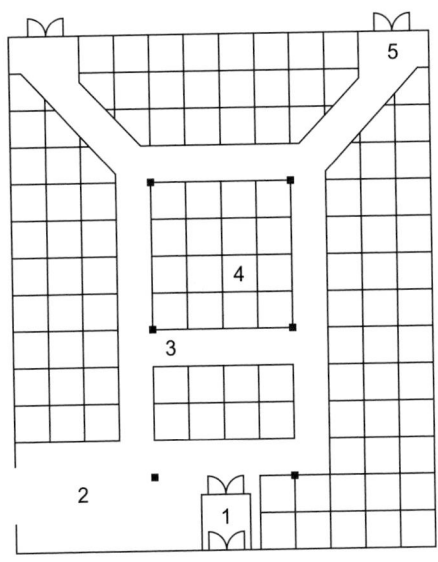

29.9 *Grid system for open-floor secure storage area*

1 *Controlled entrance lobby*
2 *Inspection area*
3 *Clear aisles*
4 *Grid marked on floor, e.g. 1.5 m squares lettered in one direction, numbered in the other*
5 *Fire exit*

5 INTERPRETATION, COMMUNICATION AND DISPLAY

5.1 Strategy

The communications strategy of the museum should be determined at an early stage. The relative importance and coordination of exhibition, education, publication, live interpretation and other forms of direct communication with the public are the essential factors that will determine the interface between staff and public. It is not sufficient to consider only the relationship between visitor and displayed collections; a wide variety of media are now used in museum exhibitions to enrich interpretation and facilitate communication with the visiting public – graphic display, audio-visual, theatre, video, computer graphics, digital media, animatronics, tableau and reconstruction, and working environments. Once beyond the stage of producing a general scheme it is important to consult an exhibition designer and a museum consultant to explore the matrix of interactions between people, information and collections that must be accommodated.

A wide range of academic expertise may be brought to bear in the interpretation of collections for exhibition purposes. Within the framework that the initial consultations provide, informed decisions may be made regarding the interpretive process and techniques, and the choice of media and types of exhibit to be employed. Figure 29.10 shows a broad typology of exhibit and media installations, and Figure 29.11 indicates the physical elements associated with exhibits. A design for a temporary exhibition at the Museum of London is shown in Figure 29.12. Reference should be made to the anthropometric data in Chapter 2 in determining coordinating dimensions; for example, the range of eye levels represented in the visiting population.

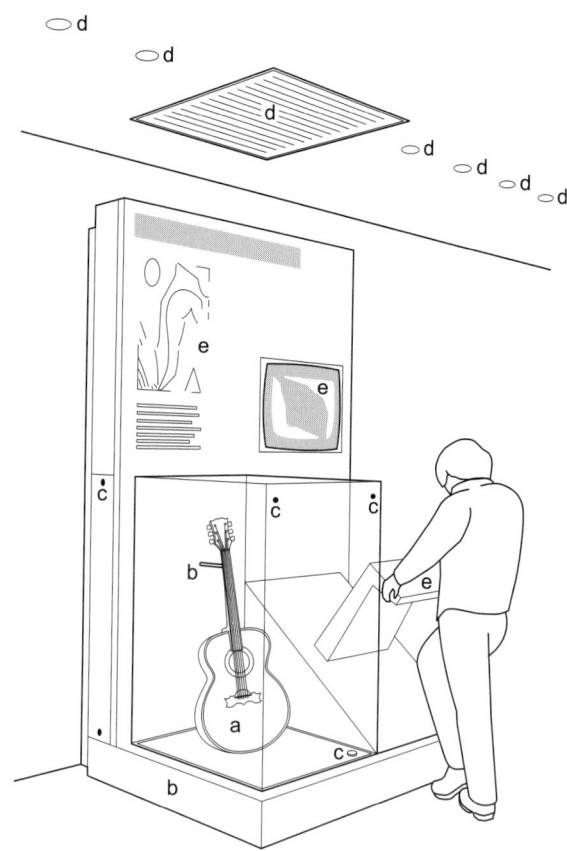

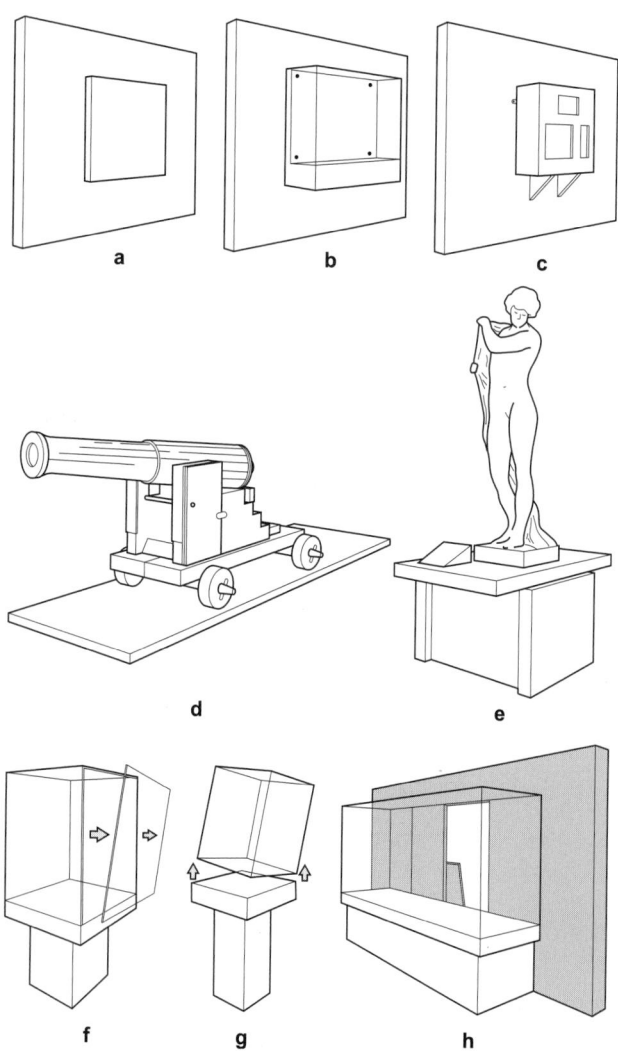

29.10 *Exhibits may be of four basic types: a, b, c Hanging or wall mounted; d, e Free-standing and open exhibits; f, g, h Contained exhibits and display cases*

29.11 *Each of exhibit types in 29.10 may have any combination of the following elements: a Item or items from the collection; b Fixing mount, support or plinth; c Preservation: protection of vulnerable or removable parts, lock, alarm, barrier, glazing, thermo-hygrometer (contained exhibits may have buffering material against changes in relative humidity); d Lighting; e Interpretive material: label, graphic information, sound, audio-visual, kinetic device, interactive device*

6 ENVIRONMENT AND CONSERVATION

6.1 Relative humidity and temperature

Special consideration must be given to proper control of relative humidity, temperature and air pollution in all collection areas of a museum or art gallery. This includes: exhibition areas; collection storage; and conservation, display and photographic work areas. Passive, low-tech approaches may be considered where climate and the inertia of the building allow. Full air conditioning may be required to cope with climatic extremes, even in this case the building envelope should provide a sufficient buffering effect to prevent sudden changes in relative humidity during periods of repair or maintenance. Figure 29.13 shows suitable conditions in museums, while Table I gives the ranges of museum interior temperature and relative humidity recommended in various climatic zones.

6.2 Air pollution

Information about local air quality should be sought and used to decide on the appropriate approach to control. If air filtration is necessary it should not be of the electrostatic type, as malfunction can result in the generation of highly damaging ozone levels.

6.3 Light and lighting

Museum lighting is a complex subject. It is important, particularly in art museums, to determine a clear policy on the approach to natural and artificial lighting. Direct sunlight should not fall on any collection item and UV radiation must be effectively eliminated from all light reaching a collection item: at the higher energy end of the spectrum light is very effective in initiating chemical change in vulnerable materials. The maximum light dosage recommended for different categories of collection item is summarised in

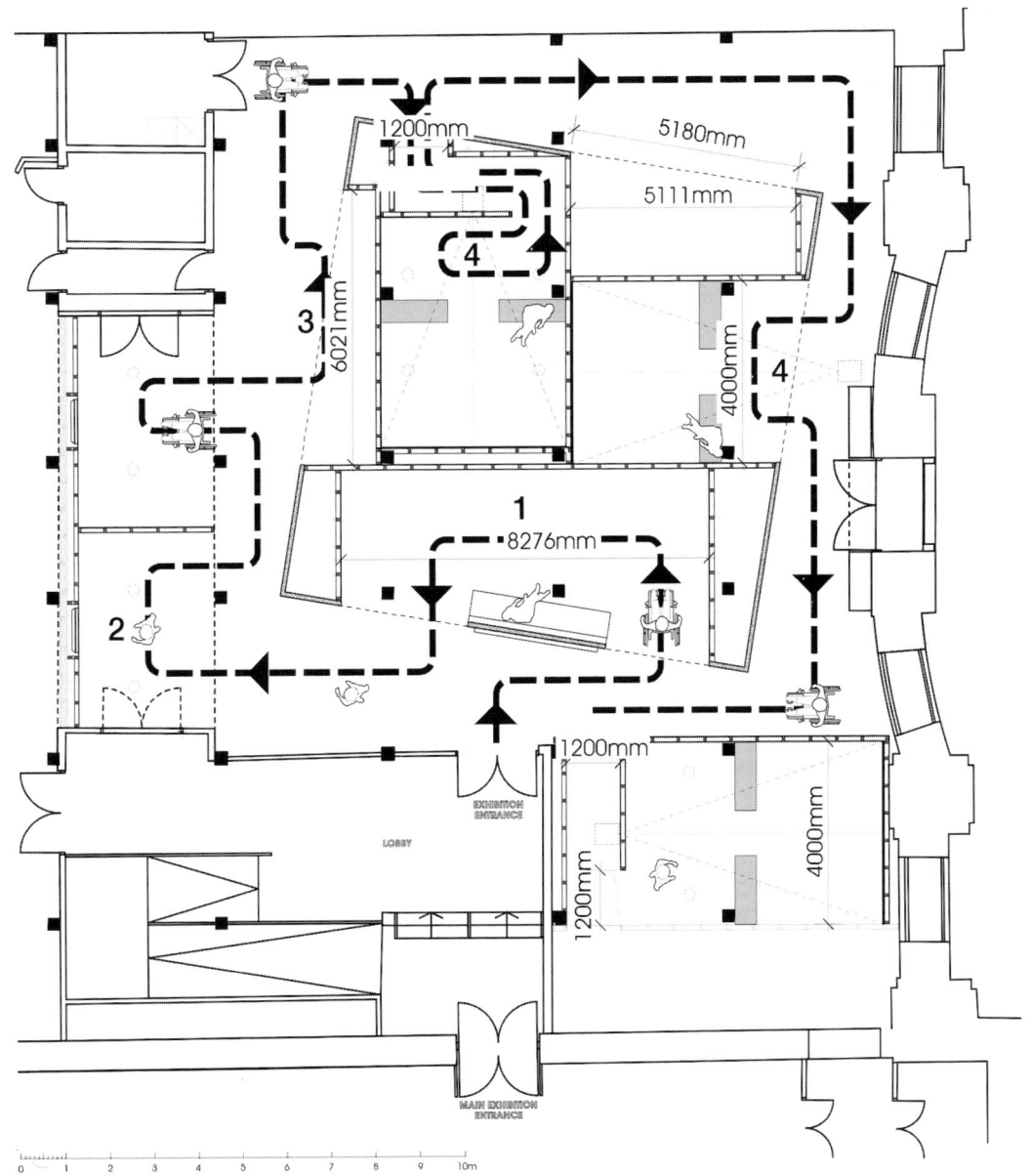

29.12 *Layout for the Estuary temporary exhibition at the Museum of London Docklands, designed by Urban Salon. Key 1, Open space for fine art exhibits; 2, Enclosed space for screen based video artists; 3, Long open flat surfacing for a series of flat works; 4, Staggered entrance for minimal light and sound spill for projection artists*

Table I Recommended temperatures and relative humidities in various climatic zones

Climate	Temp (°C)	RH (%)	Notes
Humid tropics	20–22	65	Acceptable for mixed collections. However, RH too high for iron and chloride-containing bronzes. Air circulation very important
Temperate coastal and other non-arid regions	20–22	55	Widely recommended for paintings, furniture, and wooden sculpture in Europe, satisfactory for mixed collections. May cause condensation and frosting difficulties in old buildings, especially inland Europe and northern North America
Temperate inland regions	20–22	45–50	A compromise for mixed collections and where condensation may be a problem. May be best level for textiles and paper exposed to light
Arid regions	20–22	40–45	Acceptable for display of local material. Ideal for metal-only collections

Table II Recommended maximum light dosages

Type of collection	Dosage (kilolux-h)	Notes
Objects specially sensitive to light, e.g. textiles, costumes, watercolours, tapestries, prints and drawings, manuscripts, miniatures, paintings in distemper media, wallpapers, gouache, dyed leather. Most natural history items, including botanical specimens, fur and feathers	200	Usually only possible to achieve with artificial lighting
Oil and tempera paintings, undyed leather, horn, bone and ivory, oriental lacquer	650	If a daylight component is used great reduction of UV is necessary
Objects insensitive to light, e.g. metal, stone, glass, ceramics, jewellery, enamel, and objects in which colour change is not of high importance	950	Higher dosage is possible but usually unnecessary

Table II. These dosages are normally achieved by limiting the level of illumination on collection items during visiting hours to 50 lux per annum on the most sensitive material such as paper, textile,

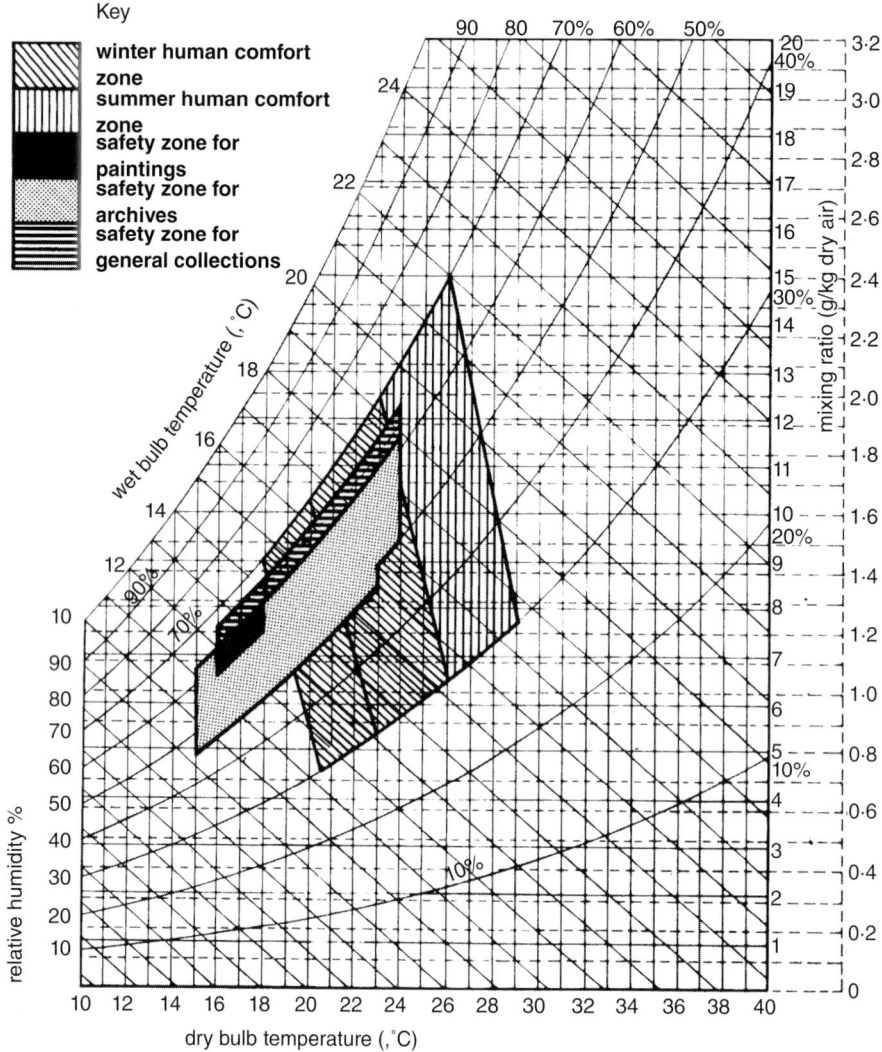

Key

/// winter human comfort zone
||| summer human comfort zone
■■■ safety zone for paintings
▓▓▓ safety zone for archives
≡≡≡ safety zone for general collections

29.13 *Psychrometric chart showing safety and comfort zones for museums, art galleries and archives wheelchair viewers. Digital captions and audio points are 700 mm off finished floor level.*

watercolour and 200 lux on other sensitive materials such as wood, leather, and oil paint.

The eye has a limited ability to adapt to changes in brightness, and as the visitor moves through the museum sudden changes in lighting levels and extreme contrasts of brightness in the field of view should be avoided. However, a reasonable range of contrast should be maintained in conditions of low illumination to prevent a dull effect and possible problems of visual accommodation.

6.4 Acoustics and zoning

The transport of sound through structure should be controlled. Functional zones should be provided with surface or sub-surface materials that dampen impact sounds and isolating cavities to interrupt the structural transmission of sound. Noise levels should be controlled within zones by appropriate choices of material finishes on floors, walls and ceilings, and the shaping of interior spaces to prevent flutter and unwanted amplifying effects. To generalise and simplify, the penetration of low-frequency sound is lessened by structural mass, of middle frequencies by diffusing and absorbing surfaces, and of high-frequency sound by the elimination of small-scale air gaps in doors, windows and partition walls.

7 SECURITY AND SERVICES

7.1 Security

Many security problems can be avoided by keeping the number of access points to the site and to the building to a minimum. The ideal

is one public entrance monitored by information staff and/or attendants, and one staff entrance controlled by the security staff responsible for key control and the checking of deliveries and outside contractors. Security staffing is also considerably more effective and economic if all exhibition and open storage areas are on one level.

7.2 Secure areas

The health and safety of the public and the staff and collection security are the prime considerations in determining the zoning of the museum into secure areas. During open hours it may be sufficient to separate public and staff areas. When the museum is closed to the public it is normal to secure more specific zones, for example:

1 Entrance, orientation/information, shop, café and toilets/cloakrooms.
2 Temporary and permanent exhibitions – in larger museums subdivided into several secure exhibit areas.
3 Educational facilities, lecture theatre, study collections.
4 Offices: administration, curatorial, conservation, design, etc.
5 Conservation workshops, laboratories, photographic facilities.
6 Collection storage, security staff areas, collection packing and inspection areas.
7 Exhibition and maintenance workshops.

7.3 Services

For general guidance see appropriate chapters in this book. In addition, special consideration should be given to minimising the risk to the collections when locating service installations and routing service ducts. For example, water and waste pipes should not be routed near collection storage and exhibition areas.

Risk management is also greatly enhanced if a separate heating/air conditioning system or independent control system is provided in collection areas.

8 CASE STUDY

Project: The Dr Susan Weber Furniture Gallery, Victoria and Albert Museum, South Kensington, London

Design: Nord Architecture

8.1 Introduction

The Victoria and Albert Museum commissioned Nord Architecture to design a 720sq m permanent gallery for furniture and fabrication techniques. Completed in 2012 with a budget of £1.4 million, the Dr Susan Weber Gallery shows more than 250 objects from the past 500 years.

8.2 Site

The site was a 72 m x 10 m gallery within the Grade I listed Aston Webb interior. The listing meant that all work had to be fully reversible, and required planning and listed building consent for the introduction of new air handling plant. Internally, the original interior cabinetry had to be removed and stored off site.

8.3 Challenges

The biggest challenge was creating a display solution that would allow so many diverse exhibits to sit well together. Another issue was the gallery plan. Since the gallery can be entered at either end, the content needed to legible in both directions. Also, the narrow shape of the plan meant that careful consideration of visitor flow was required while at the same time maintaining ample viewing distances from the objects. Because of the length and linear nature of the gallery, it was important to provide a varied rhythm of experience in order to retain interest.

Exacting conservation strategies were also required to respond to light sensitive content, with a maximum average annual daylight exposure of 50–70 lux stipulated. For a top lit gallery on a north-south axis, this implied extensive solar shading.

8.4 Design solution

The arrangement of objects was given a tripartite hierarchy to aid legibility. A chronological display created a spine to the exhibition along the centre of the gallery, Figure 29.14. Around the perimeter

29.15 *Completed gallery, with display portals down either side*

walls, objects were divided into sections, each addressing a distinct manufacturing technique, Figure 29.15.

To provide buffering between each display and variety within the linear display, a series of framed openings or portals each measuring 1800 mm x 3650 mm, was inserted along the length of the gallery, each focusing on an individual furniture maker. The portals followed the height, width and thickness of the existing black marble door architraves at either end of the gallery. This allowed them to be read as a perceptual 'doorway' inviting the visitor to enter the world of the maker, Figure 29.16.

A monochrome colour scheme created a holistic backdrop to the multitude of timber objects and materials. Ebonised oak strip was used throughout to form the plinths, portals and frieze. To contrast with this, white Corian linings were used for display space, cabinet linings and plinth tops.

Displays were kept to 350 mm off finished floor level to provide a suitable height for wheelchair viewers. Digital captions and audio points are 700 mm off finished floor level.

8.5 Interpretation

Each technique display was given a dedicated interpretive ledge to introduce the visitor to the process behind the technique. Films/touch objects/samples/illustrations and historical precedents were collated in groups to impart better understanding of the technique from the perspective of the maker. To limit captioning, digital touch labels were introduced within bespoke housings – the first digital labels at the museum.

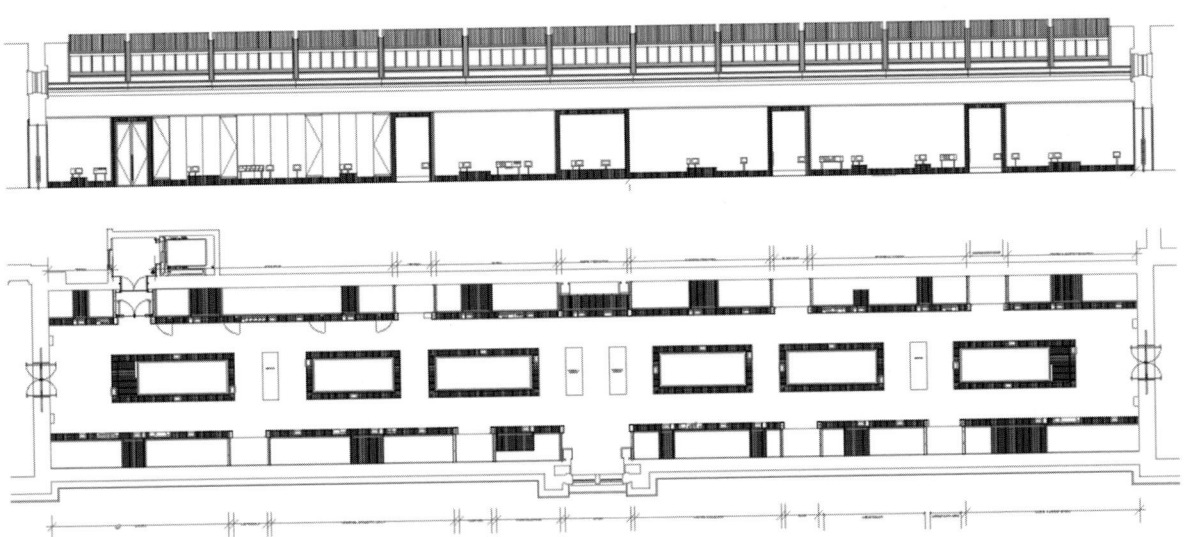

29.14 *Section (top) and plan, showing perimeter wall displays and central plinths*

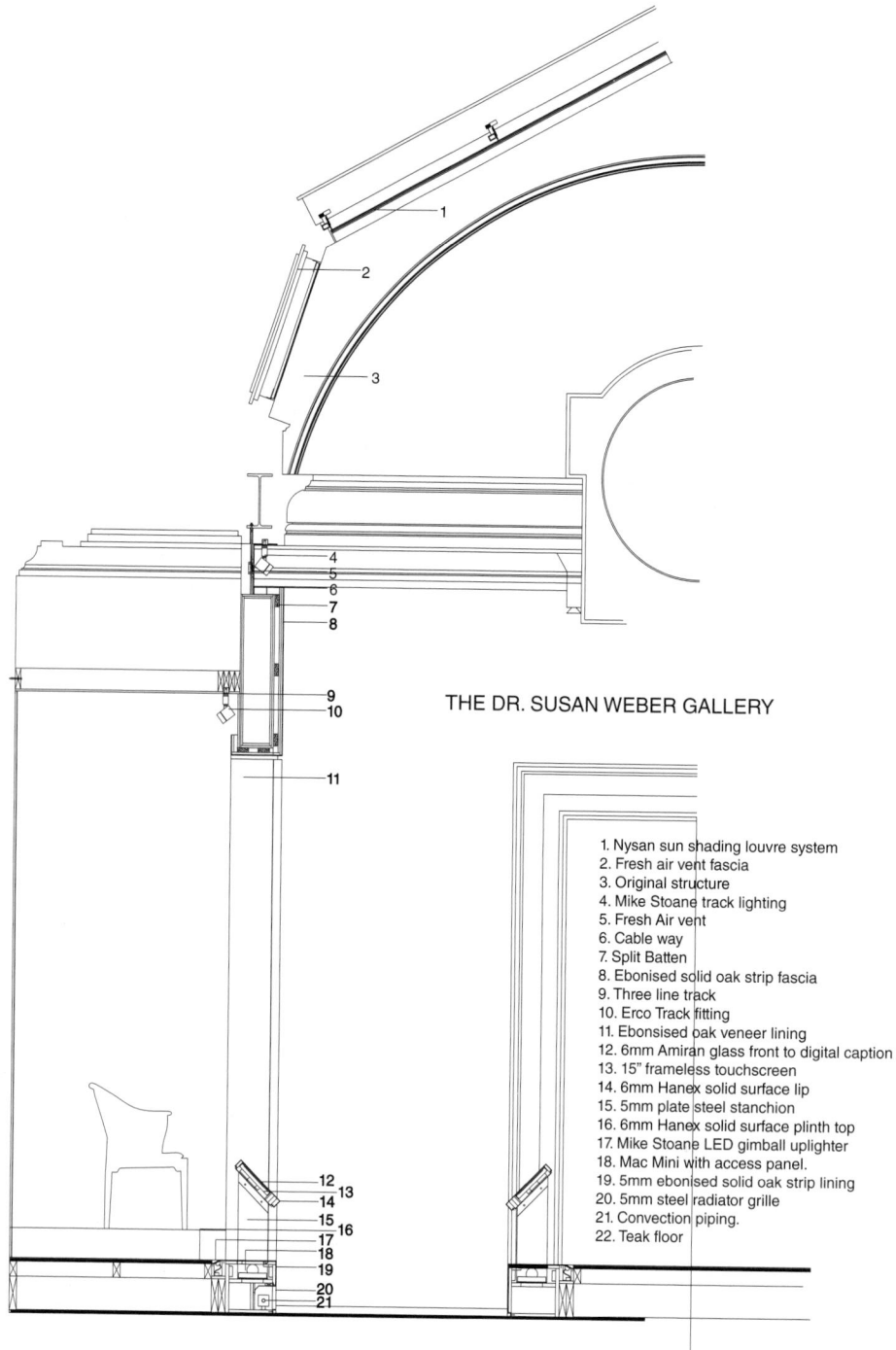

THE DR. SUSAN WEBER GALLERY

1. Nysan sun shading louvre system
2. Fresh air vent fascia
3. Original structure
4. Mike Stoane track lighting
5. Fresh Air vent
6. Cable way
7. Split Batten
8. Ebonised solid oak strip fascia
9. Three line track
10. Erco Track fitting
11. Ebonised oak veneer lining
12. 6mm Amiran glass front to digital caption
13. 15" frameless touchscreen
14. 6mm Hanex solid surface lip
15. 5mm plate steel stanchion
16. 6mm Hanex solid surface plinth top
17. Mike Stoane LED gimball uplighter
18. Mac Mini with access panel.
19. 5mm ebonised solid oak strip lining
20. 5mm steel radiator grille
21. Convection piping.
22. Teak floor

29.16 *Detail of display portal*

Each portal incorporated an audio point with a selection of recordings from architects and designers describing the maker's relevance today. At the centre of the gallery, two interactive workbenches allow visitors to explore materials and their production processes.

9 BIBLIOGRAPHY

Aurelia Bertron, Urich Schwarz and Claudia Frey, *Designing Exhibitions: A Compendium for Architects, Designers and Museum Professionals*, Birkhauser Verlag, 2012.

Adrian Cave, *Making Existing Buildings Accessible: Museums & Art Galleries*, RIBA Publishing, 2007.

Christopher Cuttle, *Light for Art's Sake: Lighting for Artworks and Museum Displays*, Elsevier, 2007.

Konzept Museums, Detail Magazine 9/2006.

Gail Dexter Lord and Barry Lord (eds) *Manual of Museum Planning*, 2nd edition, Altamira Press, 2000.

Suzanne Macleod, *Re-Shaping Museum Space: Architecture, Design, Exhibitions*, 2005.

RNIB, *See it Right, 2006.*

Mike Sixsmith, *Designing Galleries: The Complete Guide to Developing and Designing Spaces and Services for Temporary Exhibitions*, Arts Council of England, 2001.

30 Offices

Frank Duffy with Jack Pringle, Angela Mullarkey and Richard Finnemore of Pringle Brandon Perkins+Will

CI/SfB: 32

Frank Duffy was a founder of DEGW, a leading workplace design practice.
Pringle Brandon Perkins+Will is a global design firm with a specialism in corporate interiors

KEY POINTS:

- *Rapidly developing and widening range of types of office accommodation*
- *Office work can be accommodated in many ways, both physical and electronic, and at many scales and locations*
- *Improvements in information technology are continuing to have a huge impact on the workplace*
- *Twentieth century workplace conventions in the use of space and time are obsolete*
- *The office can no longer be considered as an autonomous building type but must take maximum advantage of location, adjacencies, and access to complementary functions and communications*
- *No single process of linking office supply and demand can be assumed to be dominant*

Contents

1 Introduction
2 Matching supply and demand
3 Standard method of building measurement
4 The time-based nature of the office environment
5 The office shell
6 Building services
7 Scenery and setting options
8 Trading floors
9 Conclusion
10 Bibliography

1 INTRODUCTION

1.1 The historical office

The office emerged as a distinct building type in the latter half of the nineteenth century. Previously, what would now be classed as office functions, especially those that were an adjunct to government, had often been accommodated literally in palaces such as the Uffizi in Florence. Somerset House in London, partly built to accommodate the Admiralty, followed a similar model. In the private sector, lawyers had worked for centuries in the quasi-collegiate environment of the Inns of Court. Sir John Soane's Bank of England is an early example of a very large, purpose built office complex of a very specific kind. By contrast, much early office work was peripatetic. Early members of the Corporation of Lloyds, the pioneer of the insurance market, conducted much of their business in adjacent, publicly accessible coffee houses, the Starbucks of their day.

1.2 The office building type

When the office building emerged as an independent building type in the United States in the latter part of the nineteenth century, it was distinctive physically in terms of large floor plates and increasingly high rise structures, but also in the very specific ways in which such purpose-designed office buildings were financed, designed, constructed and operated. For the first time, large floor plates were required to accommodate a rising number of clerical workers, equipped with the increasingly sophisticated technology of the typewriter and the telegraph followed quite quickly by the telephone and the copier.

The complementary roles of both office developer and facilities manager first emerged here along with a series of divisions of labour between the roles of architects, mechanical and electrical engineers, space planners and facilities managers, defined by how long each layer of designed artefacts was intended to last.

North American offices continued to become ever larger and more sophisticated, both architecturally and technologically, during the first half of the twentieth century, as is evident in many magnificent, very often high rise structures, designed by such architects as Frank Lloyd Wright, Mies van der Rohe, Philip Johnson and SOM. Meanwhile, British office buildings remained until the early 1980s a provincial variant of US practice, smaller, less efficient in construction and plan form, less well serviced, and more influenced by developers, letting agents and external planning considerations than by the internal operational requirements of occupiers.

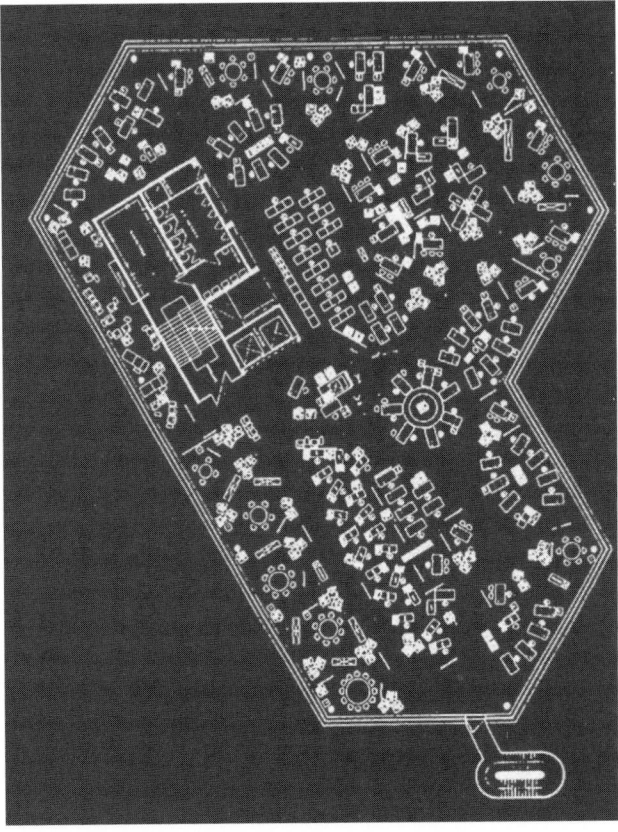

30.1 *Burolandschaft (office landscaping) at Ninoflax, Germany*

1.3 European office innovation

Two very different and original office design concepts developed in Northern Europe in the 1960s and 1970s:

- *Burolandschaft* (office landscaping) – introduced by the *Organisationteam Schnelle* in the early 1960s in Germany, Figure 30.1. This was largely based on studies of internal patterns of communication within organisations. User data led to free-flowing, open plan arrangements of workstations and meeting areas. One external corollary was a deliberately non-orthogonal architecture. Such developments were fuelled both by the presence of more independently owned businesses in Germany compared to the US, who were in a position to develop their own office buildings, and by the power of Workers' Councils with the constitutional right to be consulted on changes in working conditions. Consequently it became customary from the 1960s onwards, not just in Germany but also in Holland and Scandinavia, for office buildings to be purpose-designed from the inside out. Not only were many of the resulting buildings striking in architectural terms but internally they became spatially generous, often carpeted (rare until the 1970s in both the UK and USA) and much more domestic in feeling than corporate. Plants and colour were important interior features as were informal rest areas, called *Pausenraumen*, for refreshment, relaxation or informal, extempore conversations with colleagues.

- Office as city – A similar divergence from the top down culture of the corporate office was experienced in Holland and Scandinavia in the 1970s and 1980s. A key project in Holland was Herman Hertzberger's office for Centraal Beheer, an independent insurance company in Apeldoorn. This was conceived as a microcosm of an Italian hill town with strong internal as well as external architectural features – mini atria, columns and low walls – intersected and held together by internal streets. This created a network of small, semi-enclosed, interlocking places that the 'inhabitants' were encouraged to appropriate

in their own way in order to make the office as homelike and personal as possible. This created a radically different, user sensitive, and to many workers, a highly attractive office culture. Niels Torp's celebrated headquarters buildings for the airline SAS on the outskirts of Stockholm, Figure 30.2 and for British Airways near Heathrow were also conceived as little cities, with office pavilions on either side of an attractive, top-lit, internal 'street'. Many similar offices were erected in Scandinavia, Holland and Germany, but far fewer in the United Kingdom and the rest of Europe.

1.4 The global office

In London in the late 1970s and early 1980s, developers such as Stuart Lipton and Godfrey Bradman realised that an entirely new class of office building would be necessary to accommodate globalising organisations, particularly in the Financial Services sector. Such accommodation would allow occupiers to take maximum advantage of London's location in an intermediate time zone that permits overlapping daily communications with both Asia and North America. This led to the initial, immediate success of Canary Wharf and Broadgate and, cumulatively over the last three decades, the economy of the City of London and the capital as a whole, Figure 30.3.

Table I summarises the planning and design criteria for these different generations and locations of office buildings.

1.5 Facilities management

Facilities management (FM) is a North American concept and was an essential factor in the development of the office in the last century. FM skills may be considered as the software that enables the efficient and effective management and use of office space over time. Facilities managers tend to be undervalued, or at best taken for granted, partly because of the perceived difficulty of measuring their positive impact on business performance. However this is changing with the development of more scientifically conducted case studies.

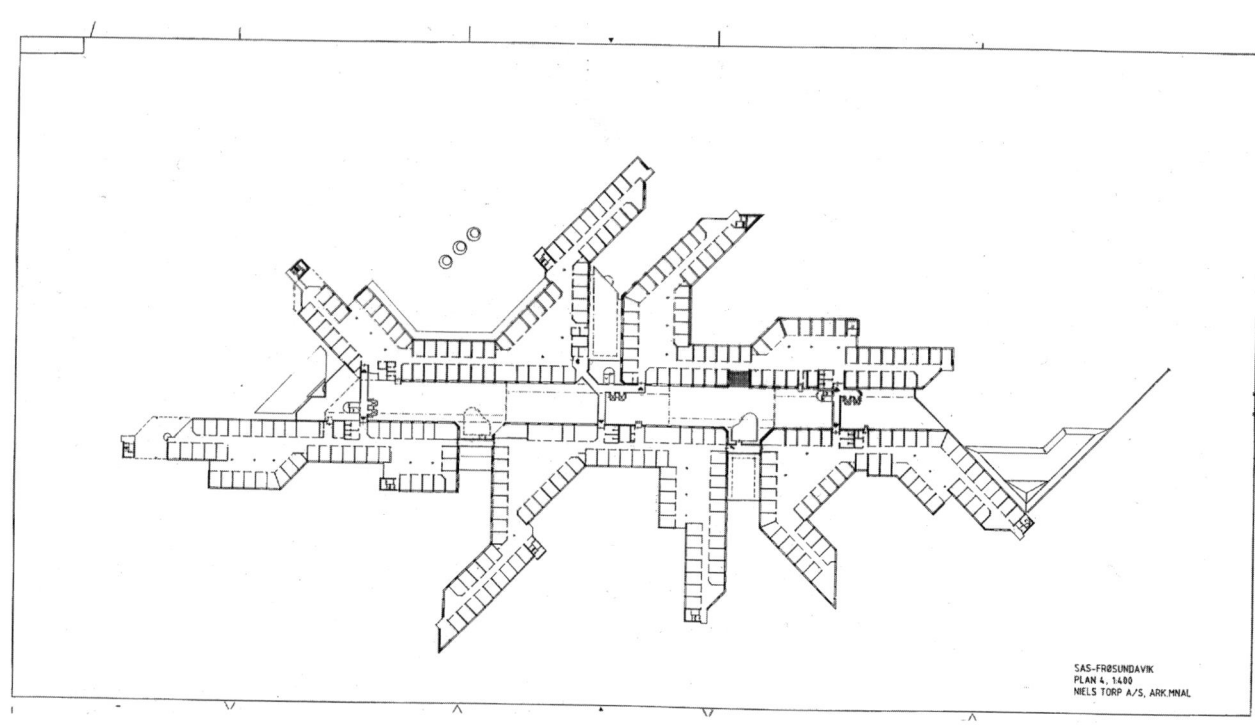

30.2 *Niels Torp's SAS headquarters in Stockholm, arranged office pavilions around an internal 'street'*

Table I Planning and design criteria for different types of office building

	US corporate high-rise, 1930s (Charles Center, Baltimore, US)	US corporate high-rise, 1950s (525 William Penn Place, Pittsburgh, US)	Office Landscaping, 1960s (Ninoflax, Germany)	UK financial services, 1980s (Broadgate, London, UK)	Scandinavian social democratic, 1980s (SAS, Stockholm, Sweden)	City as office, 21st century (Any city)
No. of storeys	25	41	5	8	5	N/A
Typical floor area (m²)	3000	1000	2000	3000	multiples of 200	N/A
Typical office depth (m)	20	20	30m	20	10	N/A
Furthest distance from perimeter (m)	18	18	15	18	5	N/A
Efficiency: net to gross	90%	85%	95%	85%	70%	N/A
Maximum cellularisation (% of usable)	50%	50%	5%	40%	80%	N/A
Type of core	Concentrated: central	Concentrated: central	Offset	Dispersed	Dispersed (street)	Urban fabric
Type of HVAC service	100% HVAC artificial Multiple users	100% HVAC artificial Multiple users	100% HVAC artificial Single user	Floor by floor Several users	Minimal HVAC High user control	Multiple systems High user control

1.6 Information technology

By contrast, the impact of information technology on business performance is dominant and is now highly visible in practically every sector of the economy. IT mobility has revolutionised how we work, leading to a wide variety of work settings rather than just the individual desk.

2 MATCHING SUPPLY AND DEMAND

2.1 Office type variety

The idea that there should be a single, definitive model for all office buildings, let alone for office interiors, is demonstrably outdated. The current different types can be summarised as:

- High quality, architect-designed corporate office space with many amenities to attract young talent for sophisticated global hi-tech organisations such as Apple, Google and Microsoft.
- Speculative, capable of utilisation in a mix of cellular/open plan workspace.
- Alternative, individualised and often highly informal workplace cultures, for entrepreneurial, technology-led enterprises such as those at the so-called 'Silicon Roundabout' around London's Old Street. These often re-utilise existing buildings. New build developments include the White Collar Factory, Figure 30.4.
- Shared/hotelling workspaces – where space and services can be hired within a communitarian atmosphere, often by start up businesses, for the day, the week or the month. Examples include The Hub at New Zealand House in London, Figure 30.5.
- Home/mobile.

The exploratory process of creating new kinds of workplace is by no means over as increasingly powerful technologies continue to be developed and different cultural and organisational stimuli present themselves.

2.2 Supply chain

Modes of delivery and space management are also changing beyond the conventional Anglo Saxon real estate supply chain. This starts with investors' money, leads on to the developer and is passed on to real estate brokers and then lawyers before it is given over to teams of architects, engineers and cost consultants. They in turn hand the project on to project managers and the construction industry after which corporate real estate, facilities managers, IT and human resources take over. Eventually, projects are handed over to users who, in the past, have been barely consulted. At its worst, this supply chain is uni-directional, unstoppable, mono-functional and, above all characterised by minimal, even zero, feedback.

2.3 Demand and supply

Figure 30.6 shows how demand and supply should be connected operationally. What is important here is the emphasis on feedback and the reconciliation of user demands (expressed through space and furniture standards, filing and information strategies, requirements for ancillary and support as well as design guidelines) with supply side features such as space planning and structural grids, depth of space, configuration and size of floors and number of storeys.

2.4 Improving user satisfaction, health and comfort

A good workplace building may be defined as one that satisfies through time both end user and organisational needs at reasonable cost, without unnecessary effort and within which, above all, occupants are happy to work. To achieve these goals three key features are required:

- *Adaptability* – to meet an open-ended range of spatial and servicing requirements. In addition to shell and core standards of provision, offices could, for the benefit of occupants, accommodate a wide range of choice in internal environmental services, such as natural ventilation and control of up-lighters.
- *Contact with the outside world* – many people like being adjacent to operable windows with clear glass. In Scandinavia and Germany this is having a major influence on office building design often resulting in office spaces arranged around a core or 'street' of common facilities.
- *Healthier and more stimulating internal environments* – many people find natural ventilation more acceptable than mechanical systems especially if they are able to control airflow and temperature, and benefit from a healthier and more stimulating environment.

3 STANDARD METHOD OF BUILDING MEASUREMENT

3.1 Common terms

The following terms, Figure 30.7, are often used to specify floor area requirements (see BCO Guide to Specification):

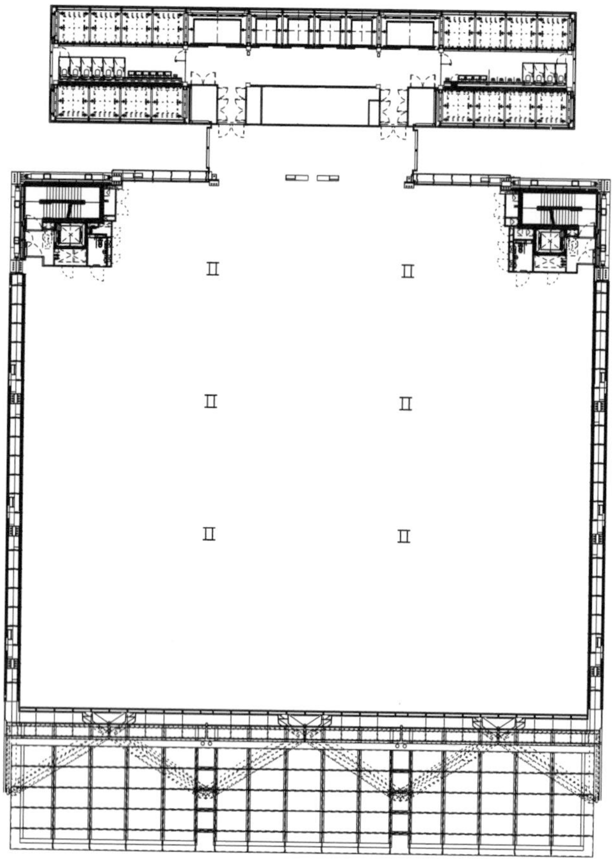

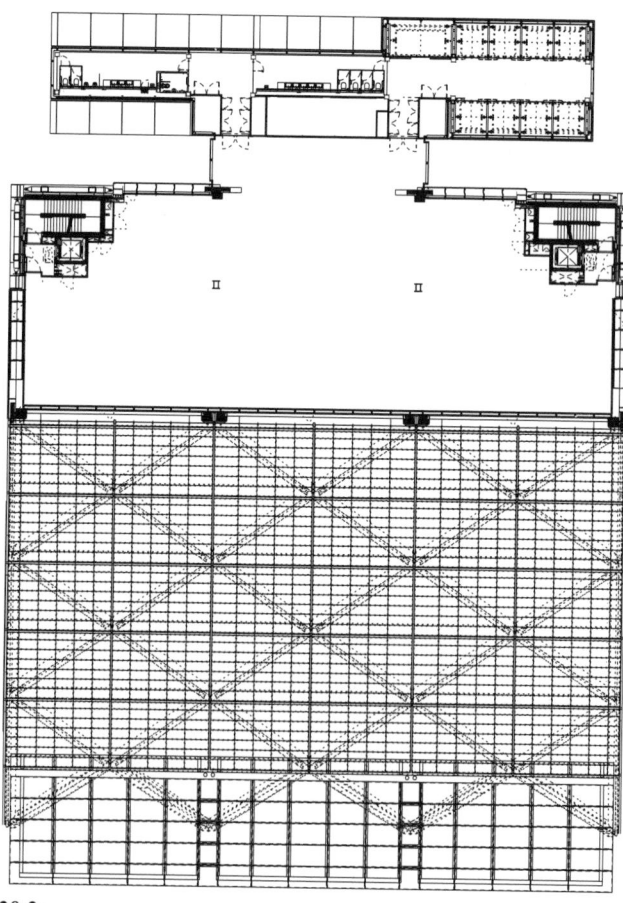

30.3a

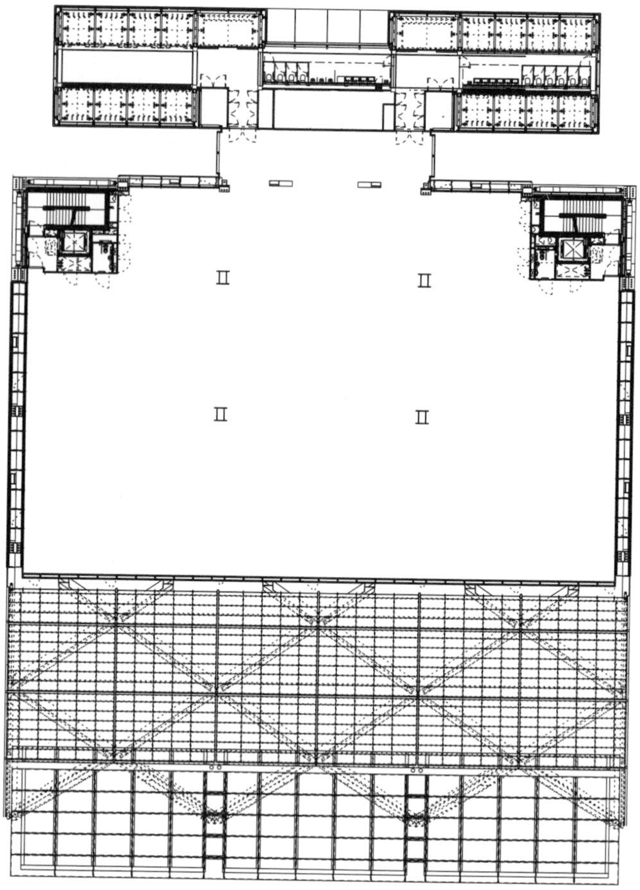

30.3b

30.3c

30.3a-c *Varying floor plans at the 50-storey Leadenhall Building designed by Rogers Stirk Harbour + Partners in the City of London for British Land Company plc/Oxford Properties. Key: a Floor 6, b Floor 22, c Floor 40*

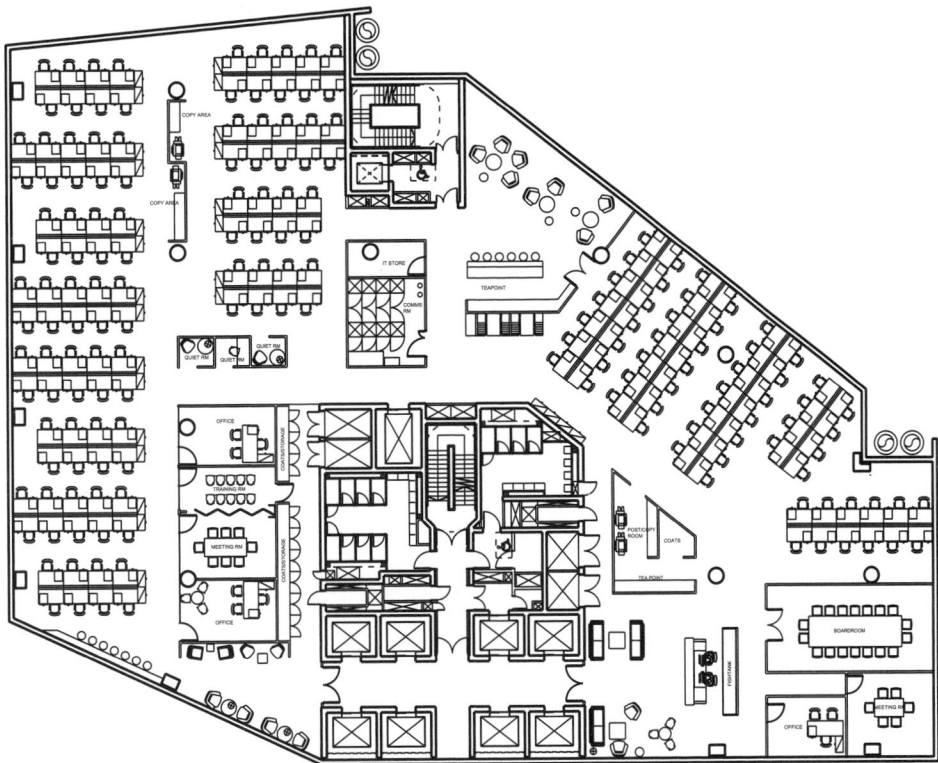

30.4a

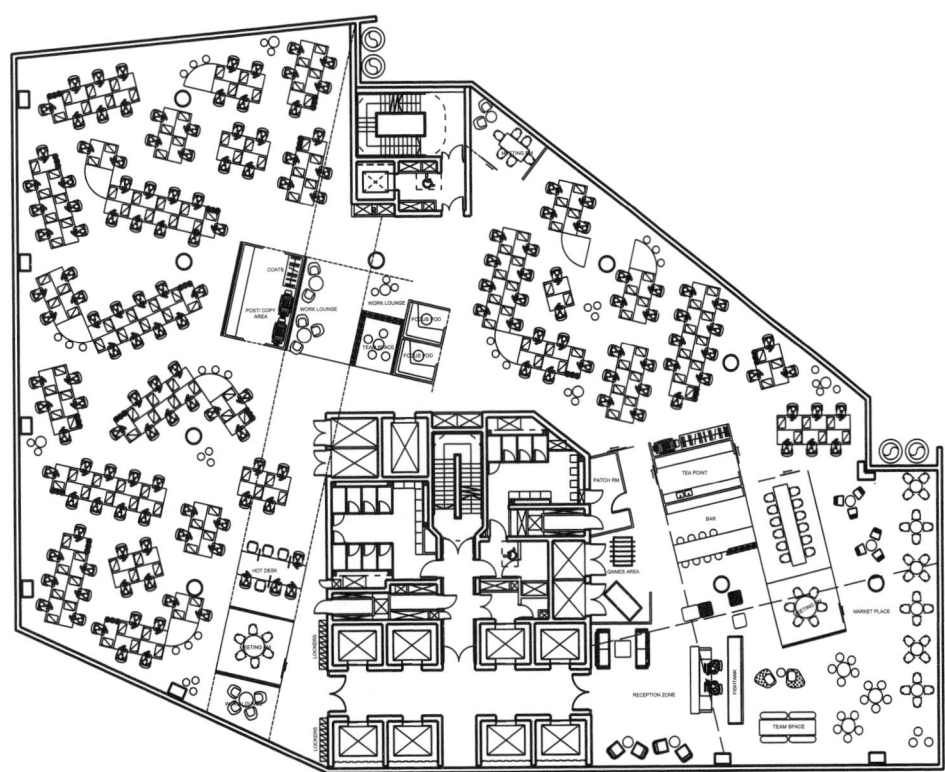

30.4b *The White Collar Factory at London's Old Street, designed by Allford Hall Monaghan Morris. a & b show alternative layout options for the eighth floor*

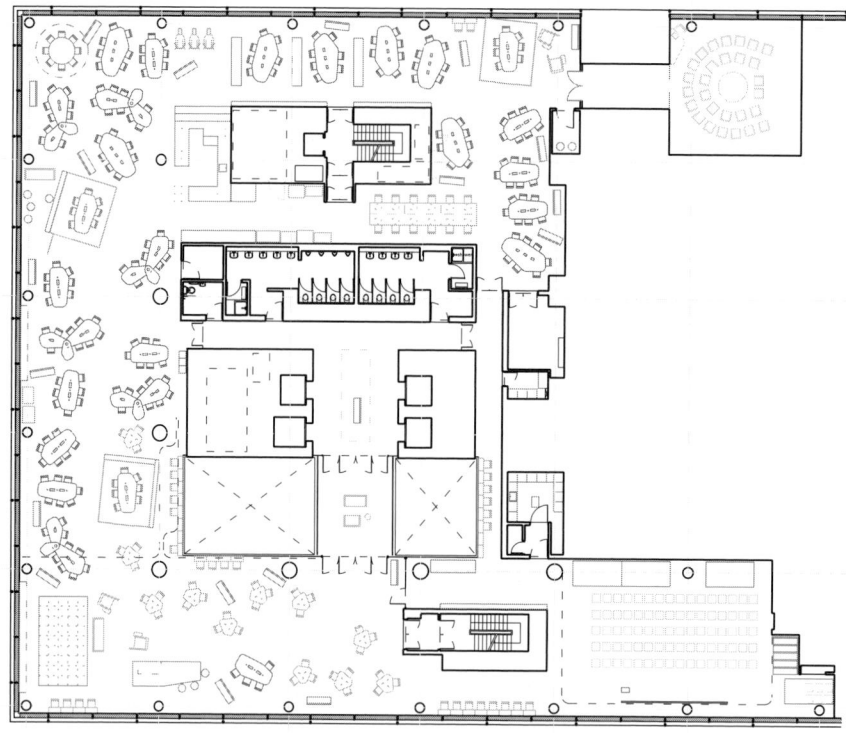

30.5 *The Hub, at New Zealand House in central London, is an example of a shared workspace increasingly popular with start-up companies buying a service rather than space.*

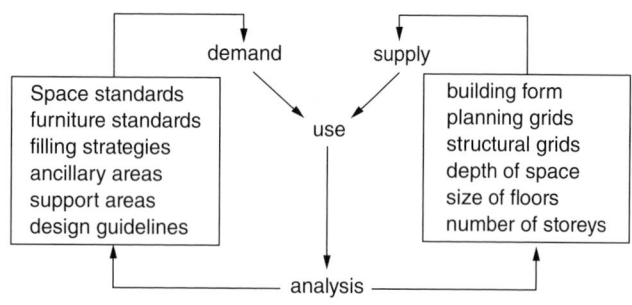

30.6 *Reconciling demand and supply*

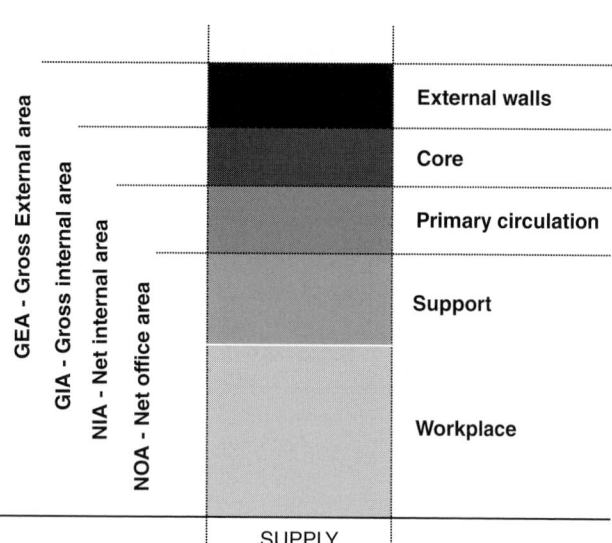

30.7 *Standard method of measurement*

• *Gross External Area (GEA):* the floor area contained within the building measured to the external face of the external walls.
• *Gross Internal Area (GIA):* the floor area contained within the building measured to the internal face of the external walls.

In both the above gross measures, features such as atria are calculated at the filled floor level – clear voids are not included in the total area. However, enclosed plant rooms are included in all gross measures.

Net Internal Area (NIA): GIA less floor areas taken up by;

• Common lobbies and foyers.
• Enclosed plant on roofs.
• Stairs and escalators.
• Mechanical and electrical services plant areas.
• Lifts.
• Internal structure such as columns.
• Toilet areas.
• Functions within the core enclosure.
• Ducts and risers.
• Car parking is included in gross area.

An additional term sometimes encountered is *Net Office Area (NOA).* This is NIA less main corridors and other primary circulation, i.e. the routes required to maintain life safety in emergencies. Secondary circulation to provide access to workstations off main corridors is included in NOA.

GIA and GEA are incorporated into the new International Property Measurement Standard, drawn up by The Royal Institution of Chartered Surveyors (RICS) and other global organisations.

3.2 The space budget

From the user's perspective, the components of a space budget are:

- *Workspace:* area given over to individual and shared workstations, work settings and occupants' immediate requirements such as personal filing – although more and more of this is now accessible electronically.
- *Ancillary space:* area given over to functions that are managed by and support departments or working group, including local meeting places, project rooms, storage areas, shared equipment, refreshment and copy areas. Such shared resources are increasing as a proportion of occupied space.
- *Support space:* area given over to functions that are centrally managed and support the whole organisation or building, including mail, reprographics, network rooms, switchboard rooms, library, conference, central meeting etc. Such areas may be located on separate floors or otherwise distant from individual departments or groups.

Office buildings in use are rarely, if ever, 100 per cent efficient for two prime reasons:

- Building configuration, grids and obstructions.
- The operational imperative of maintaining departmental integrity.

Consequently, in the calculation of space requirements a 'Fit Factor' – say 5 per cent or even 10 per cent depending on the configuration of the space to be occupied – should be added to the schedule of accommodation required, Figure 30.8.

Meanwhile more mobile ways of working and increasingly shared spatial resources are having a profound effect on such calculations of space requirements.

4 THE TIME BASED NATURE OF THE OFFICE ENVIRONMENT

4.1 Timescales
Buildings are relatively permanent entities unlike organisations within which activities and routines are continually changing. To allow for maximum flexibility, it is helpful to distinguish four

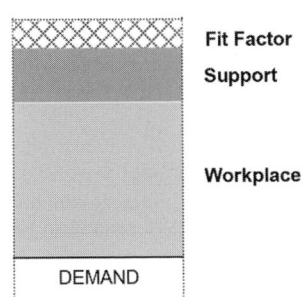

30.8 *The space budget represents the organisation's requirement for Net Useable Area*

different timescales, Figure 30.9, related to building briefing and design:

- The building shell – the structure and enclosure of the building which conventionally lasts perhaps 60 years. Within the same period operational functions are certain to change many times over. The ability of a shell to accommodate change is a function of depth of space, location of cores, floor-to-floor height to provide capacity to accommodate services as well as the configuration of the floor plate.
- Building services – the heating, ventilation and cabling infrastructure of a building, which usually has a life span of 15 years – or even less as technology becomes obsolescent and equipment has to be replaced.
- Scenery – the fitting out components of a building such as ceilings, lighting, finishes, which are used to adapt a building to tenants' (or departmental) changing requirements. Typically, the life span of an office fit-out is between 5 and 7 years.
- Settings – the increasingly important day-to-day re-arrangement of furniture and equipment, to meet ever-changing needs.

These terms, which are now in common use, have been coined because they relate office design to scenography, i.e. to the time-based rearrangement of settings behind the proscenium arch during theatrical performances.

4.2 Office mobility
Paper-based office work was relatively slow moving and often static. Storage and retrieval of non-electronic documents were important as was the provision of meeting places for customers, suppliers and consultants as well as for the organisation's own staff. However, information technology has changed the pace, the timetable and the location of office work.

The most striking impact is that office workers have become much more mobile both within and away from the office. Hourly measurements of the actual occupancy of individual workstations over the working day in many different kinds of business have shown that this rarely rises above 40 per cent at peak times and, in many cases over the day as a whole, much less, Figure 30.10. Evidence of office workers being present but not at their workplace – for example, a coat left over a chair – may appear to add another 10 or 20 per cent, to occupancy levels but it is safe to say that most workplaces and offices are mostly empty for at least half of the working day. Similarly, while meeting rooms are often fully booked, even more frequently they are observed to be empty.

4.3 An office revolution
The space planning and urbanistic implications of such demographic findings are profound. If information technology is making it possible for an increasing proportion of staff to work at least

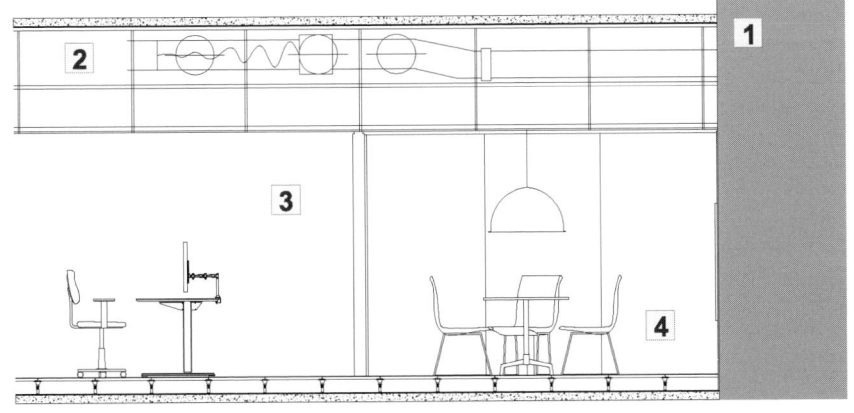

BUILDING SHELL
Expected life 60 years

BUILDING SERVICES
Expected life 15 years

SCENERY
Replaced after 7 years

SETTINGS
Changing from day to day

30.9 *Different building timescales*

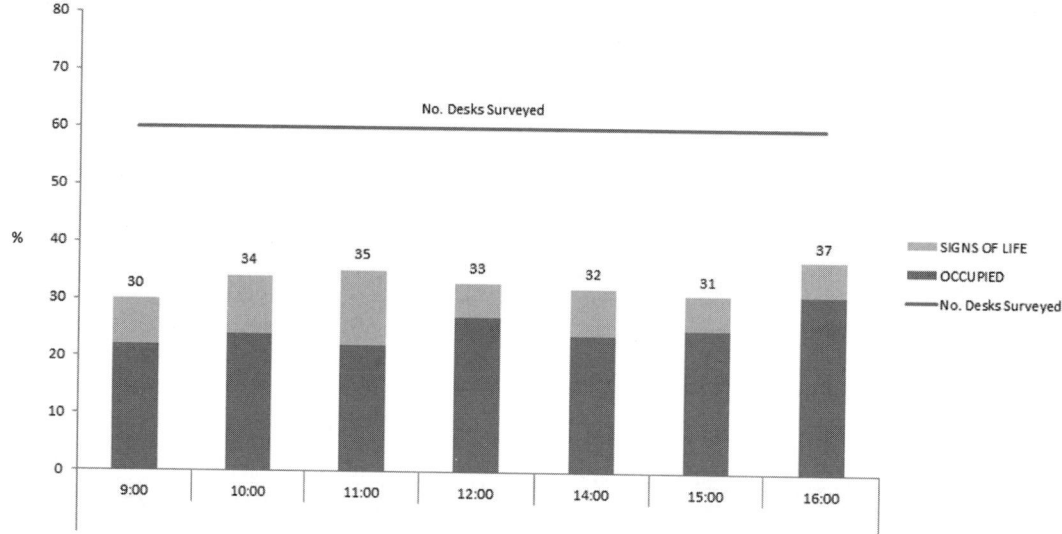

30.10 *Time utilization surveys show that actual desk occupancy is less than might be expected*

some of the time away from the office, not necessarily incidentally at home, the residual role of office accommodation is likely to be as social and communications centres within and between businesses. Such offices are likely to be occupied in very different ways over very different timescales.

These trends have important urbanistic implications. If offices are indeed half empty most of time, as seems to be already the case in many instances, the same cannot be said of cities. Like many other cities worldwide, city centres such as Manhattan or Central London have become more vibrant than ever before and over longer timescales – the opposite of what has been observed inside office buildings. Attention must be given to the programming and design of an urban fabric that would foster a business and intellectual community that operates for much of the time between, as well as within, distinct office organisations and buildings.

5 THE OFFICE SHELL

5.1 Needs

Building owners and facilities managers usually prioritise the following specification requirements:

- The ability to accommodate change and minimise operating costs.
- Freedom to address users' expectations for environmentally friendly working conditions.
- Local environmental control.
- Ease of maintenance.
- The opportunity to allow users to participate in design decisions.

5.2 Dimensions

The dimensions recommended in this section are based on those recommended by the BCO, and on what many facilities managers believe to be good practice. However, in some circumstances, such as inner city sites, different approaches may be appropriate to comply with planning restrictions or to ensure financial viability.

5.3 Floor depth

This determines the quality and dimensions of space to be provided at every level. Aspect, natural ventilation and lighting, zoning of activities and of support spaces should all be considered. Building depths are usually measured as either 'glass to core' or 'glass to glass':

- A glass to core dimension of 9–12m allows room for cellular office space or open plan plus circulation and storage.
- A glass to glass dimension of 13.5–18m allows two or three zones of office, circulation and support space.

5.4 Storey height

Related to floor depth and floor plate dimensions, storey height (floor to floor height) has a major impact on air conditioning, cable distribution, occupants' ability to have access to natural ventilation and daylight, as well as on visual comfort:

- Floor to floor heights of 4–4.5m provide more flexibility as well as visual comfort. However, a typical height of 2.75m from finished floor level to underside of ceiling is still considered good practice.

Floor depth and storey height are interrelated and, assuming glass-to-glass depths of 13.5–18m, should be thought of together. For example, narrower buildings do not require such generous storey heights because of the different servicing strategies that they use.

5.5 Floor sizes and configurations

These affect circulation and internal communication. Smaller floors are less efficient in terms of the ratio between the area of cores and usable floor space. They can also lead to splitting larger departments over several floors. Very large floor plates can create extended circulation and longer distances between departments:

- Large floor plates of 2500m² and over tend to be favoured by larger organisations. However dealing rooms can be much bigger.
- Landlord efficiency (the ratio between Net Internal Area and Gross Internal Area) should be 84–87 per cent in mid to high rise or 90 per cent in low rise buildings.
- Tenant efficiency, expressed as the ratio between Usable Area and Net Internal Area, should be 85 per cent or above, Figure 30.11.

5.6 Floor loading

This determines the amount of equipment and storage that can be placed in the work area while preserving the overall stability of the structure. The tendency in the UK and certain other parts of Europe

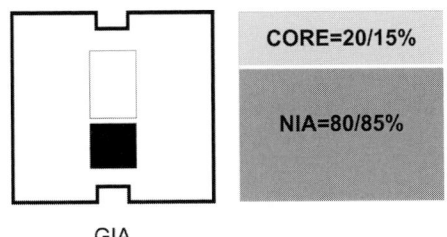

30.11 *Tenant efficiency*

has been to over-specify floor loadings, thus adding significantly to construction costs:

- The BCO recommends 2.5 kN/m², with hardened areas for extra weight of up to 7 kN/m², but says that institutions demand ranges of 3 to 4kN/m².

5.7 Planning and partition grids

Planning grids determine the size of enclosed offices and other enclosures as well as providing an overall modular discipline for many other design decisions that help determine the ongoing efficiency of space use, even in what may have been originally intended to be completely open offices:

- A 1.35 m grid allows 2.7 m wide minimum office enclosures (relatively rare in the UK).
- A 1.5 m grid allows 3 m wide offices that are much more common and have the additional advantage of relating well to 600 mm building components. This grid is much used in office planning in the UK.
- Structural grids should relate to space planning grids as well as to wider economic, engineering and environmental factors. It is not necessarily the case that fewer columns are always better. However, decisions about structural grids should always be tested during the design process against a wide range of typical patterns of enclosure and desk layouts.

5.8 Building skin

The role of office building skins is shifting from being designed solely as barriers to the external environment to becoming an integral part of overall servicing and environmental strategies.

Natural ventilation controlled by end users has long been popular in Northern Europe (see Section 6) – and is likely to become a more common feature of British offices particularly away from city centres. The provision of cross ventilation can be a critically important determinant of office building depth.

5.9 Communications infrastructure

We live in the information age. Hence local and wide-area communications have become an increasingly important factor at every level of office design. Office building shells and services should be designed to accommodate them. Particularly significant are the provision of main entry points for external communications and ensuring that the size and location of vertical risers are adequate:

- Risers for voice data and other services should not take up less than 2 per cent of Gross Floor Area (GFA) and the capacity should be provided to knock through easily at least another 2 per cent should the need arise.
- Cores containing risers should be widely distributed to avoid cable bottlenecks.

- Cores should be accessible from common parts and primary circulation routes in order to provide options for multi-tenancy.
- Communications rooms serving the entire building or major tenants measuring 2 x 2 m for each 500 m² of GFA should be adequate and located at a distance suitable for the adopted data/communication system.
- There should be space for dual-service entries into the building.
- Provision should be made on the roof, or nearby, for satellite or microwave dishes with good sight lines.
- Provision of alternative access to power supplies and communications. Security and continuity of access is a critically important consideration given that office organisations of all kinds are now more or less totally dependent upon electronic networks communication system.

5.10 Access for goods and materials

Ease of access for the entry of goods must be at least as good as access for people to avoid conflicts and bottlenecks. A clear strategy for entry supported by appropriate signage should keep people and goods separate. Typical materials regularly delivered are:

- loading bays
- goods lifts
- refuse and recycling
- stationery and office supplies
- office equipment, machinery and furniture
- food and supplies to dining areas, vending machines etc.
- post and couriers
- building maintenance supplies and equipment.

5.11 Building shell considerations

These are summarised in Table II.

Table II Building shell considerations

Depth of building	Flexibility of layout options
	• Amount of cellularisation
	• Need for mechanical ventilation/A/C
	• Spatial efficiency
Location of cores	• Ease of subletting
	• Security
	• Spatial efficiency
Floor-to-floor heights	• Method of cable distribution
	• Type of servicing
Floor size and shape	• Spatial efficiency
	• Planning flexibility
	• Size of working groups
Perimeter detail and grids	• Flexibility of subdivision
	• Efficiency of space use
	• Solar gain, heat loss, condensation
Construction	• Base of adaptation
	• Space for services
	• Image

5.12 Sectional considerations

Following Northern European practice, internal atria, small or large, linking several floors via prominent staircases, are becoming increasingly common. The purpose of such atria is to enhance the potential for interdepartmental movement and interaction. In some cases building in the possibility of creating such three-dimensional access is provided in the design even of the structure of speculative office buildings. However, real estate efficiency has to be balanced against potential longer-term operational advantages.

6 BUILDING SERVICES

6.1 Natural ventilation or air conditioning?

There is usually a straight choice between natural ventilation and full air conditioning for both speculative and purpose-built offices. In the UK many organisations choose the latter, although the consequences can be twice the building services energy costs and dearer building maintenance and management. Not all these costs are directly related to the air conditioning system but to the characteristics of the types of buildings that are air conditioned. Apart from improved comfort (not always realised), reasons for choosing air conditioning include:

- Prestige.
- Standard requirements, particularly for multinationals.
- Deeper plans, partly for alleged organisational needs and partly to maximise usable area.
- Flexibility to accommodate changing requirements – seldom achieved except at high cost.
- Higher rents giving a better rate of return.
- Poor external environments, particularly traffic noise.

6.2 New trends

Trends in office design have moved away from climate responsive forms, designed as coarse climate modifiers, towards climate rejecting, sealed designs within which the internal environment is created largely, and often entirely, artificially. This design strategy is now being questioned. Pointers for the future include:

- More powerful and reliable electronic communications systems and networks are raising questions about the long term operational value of large, deep, environmentally controlled buildings and spaces. Not least because patterns of occupancy are changing because of more mobile ways of working.
- Many occupants are expecting environments that are more natural, providing greater outside awareness, more daylight, natural ventilation and better individual control. These environments can be supported where appropriate by supplementary mechanical and electrical systems that are available on demand, including opening windows and solar controls linked to computerised building management systems. Such systems monitor the opening of windows so that heating, ventilation and air conditioning systems can be reconfigured as required.
- In difficult conditions, especially in the inner city, it may not be possible to have opening windows, but some form of solar protection should always be incorporated to minimise cooling loads.
- New materials, systems and design techniques permit closer integration of natural and mechanical systems with intelligent user-responsive controls that allow buildings which are not fully air conditioned to provide greater environmental control than ever before.
- Concern for the global environment implies greater energy efficiency through natural ventilation, light and solar heat rather than conventional mechanical and electrical systems.
- Energy consumption by desktop IT equipment is falling, reducing cooling loads in the general office though not necessarily in equipment rooms.

7 SCENERY AND SETTING OPTIONS

7.1 Layouts

Layouts must balance the desire for cellularisation (common in Germany and Scandinavian offices) against the need to keep costs down and to add value with strongly interactive work patterns in open-plan settings. Open areas should be designed and managed to allow quiet and reflective work, and the flexible use of space at different times. Using IT to allow mobile working within the office makes possible entirely new ways of planning space.

Layouts should:

- Maximise both communication and the need for quiet and reflection.
- Accommodate team and project work and also provide space for confidential and individual work.
- Provide access to daylight, aspect, and ventilation.

7.2 Typologies

Three typical office typologies and their densities are shown here: highly cellular, Figure 30.12, 90/10 open plan/cellular, Figure 30.13, and open plan, Figure 30.14. In Figure 30.14, desk provision is at 1:1, although many organisations now provide fewer desks than headcount and operate desk-sharing strategies in order to match true levels of occupation.

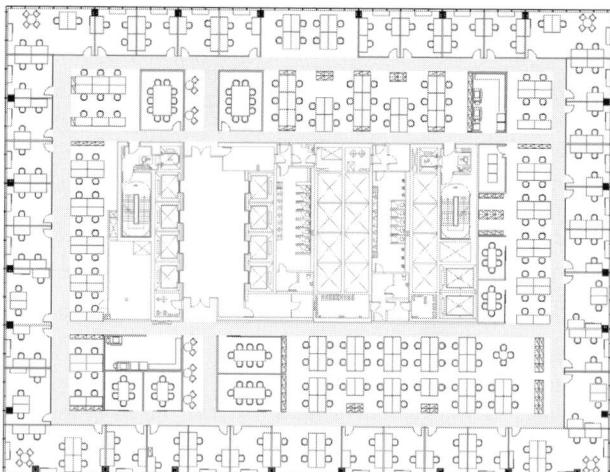

30.12 *Highly cellular layout with 253 desks. NIA 9.7 m² per desk*

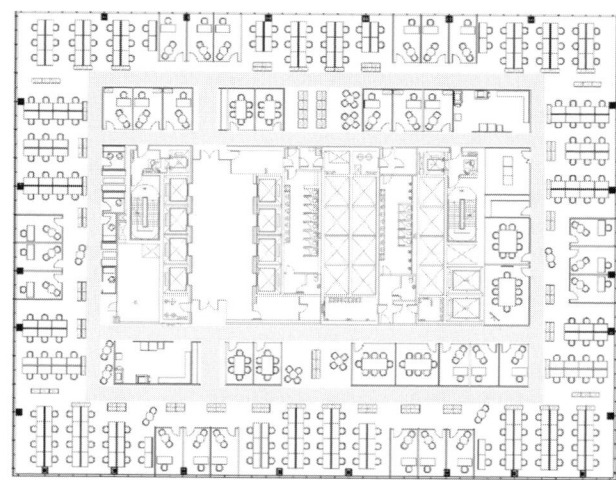

30.13 *90/10 open plan/cellular layout with 237 desks. NIA 10.3 m² per desk*

30.14 *Open plan layout with 233 desks + 68 other settings. NIA 10.5 m² per desk/8.1 per person*

7.3 Meeting rooms and collaborative spaces

These are key areas in any organisation. As well as formal meeting areas, Figure 30.15, and informal meeting areas, Figure 30.16, breakout areas are increasingly important, and may include sofas, banquettes, beanbags as well as traditional seating.

7.4 Individual settings

Many offices incorporate a variety of workplace settings for staff and visitors aside from the traditional desk such as bench seating, Figure 30.17, focus rooms, Figure 30.18, and touchdown areas, Figure 30.19a & b.

7.5 Space and circulation

Figures 30.20a, b, c, show typical distances and requirements for accessing storage cabinets. Copy areas are shown in Figure 30.21a & b.

7.6 Servicing strategy

Power and communication services can be taken to each workstation and meeting place in either:

- Raised floors, Figure 30.22.
- Perimeter ducting connected to cable management systems within furniture and screens, Figure 30.23.

Raised floors are popular with UK developers, which is surprising as it is the most expensive method. Unless an unacceptably low ceiling is provided, it means that the floor-to-floor height is increased by the depth of the raised floor. Power and telecommunication outlets are in sunken boxes accessed through flaps with slots for the flexes. These boxes have a capacity limited by their size, and usually only have room for three power sockets and a double telephone socket. It is not that easy or cheap to provide more boxes, or to move the ones that are there, so that furniture and screen arrangements tend to be fixed in relation to them. Sometimes boxes find themselves within major traffic routes, where they can cause a hazard.

Perimeter ducting is a system particularly suitable for smaller naturally ventilated offices without suspended ceilings. However, it does make moving the furniture and screens difficult, and can inhibit easy movement between workspaces.

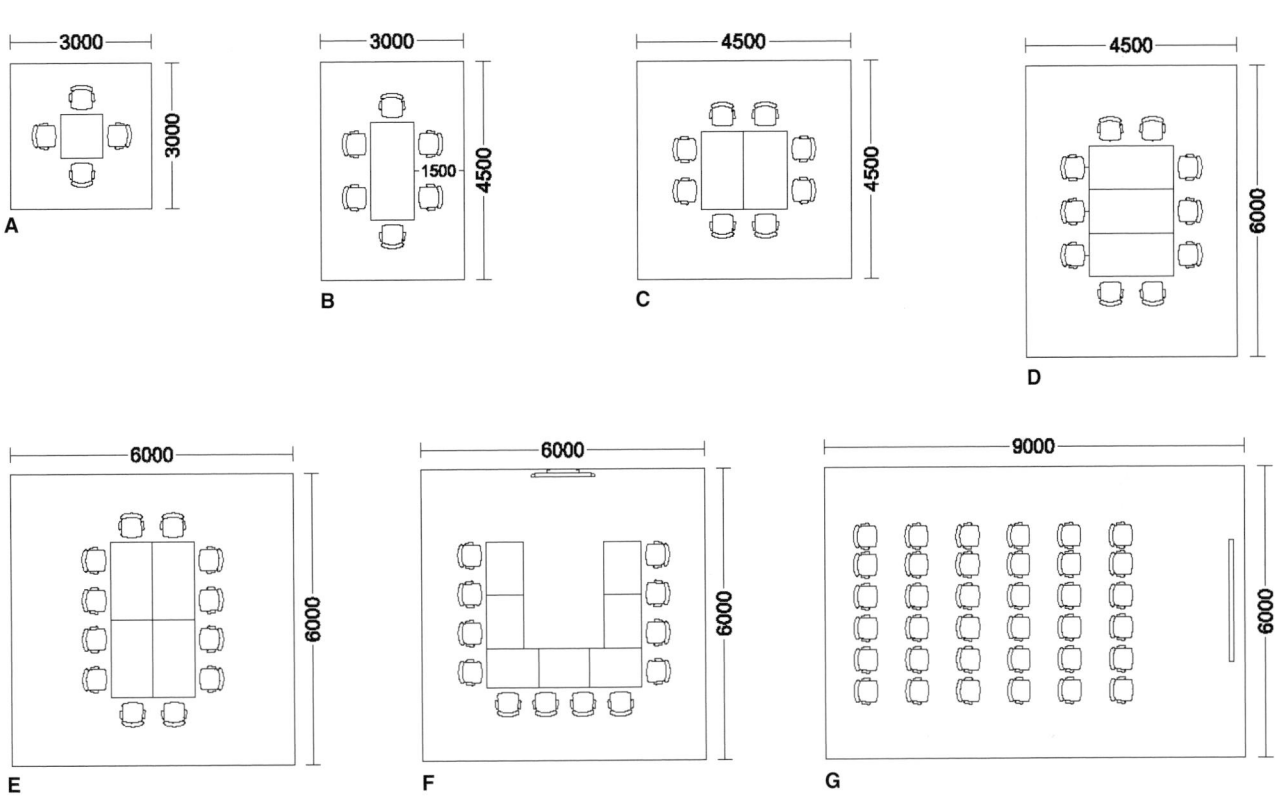

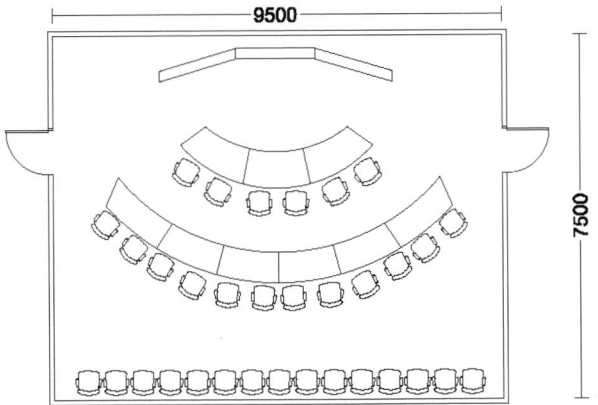

30.15 *Formal meeting rooms and spaces of varying sizes. A 4 seat; B 6 seat; C 8 seat; D 10 seat; E 12 seat presentation space; F 12 seat presentation space; G 36 seat presentation space. H Teleconference room. All dimensions in mm.*

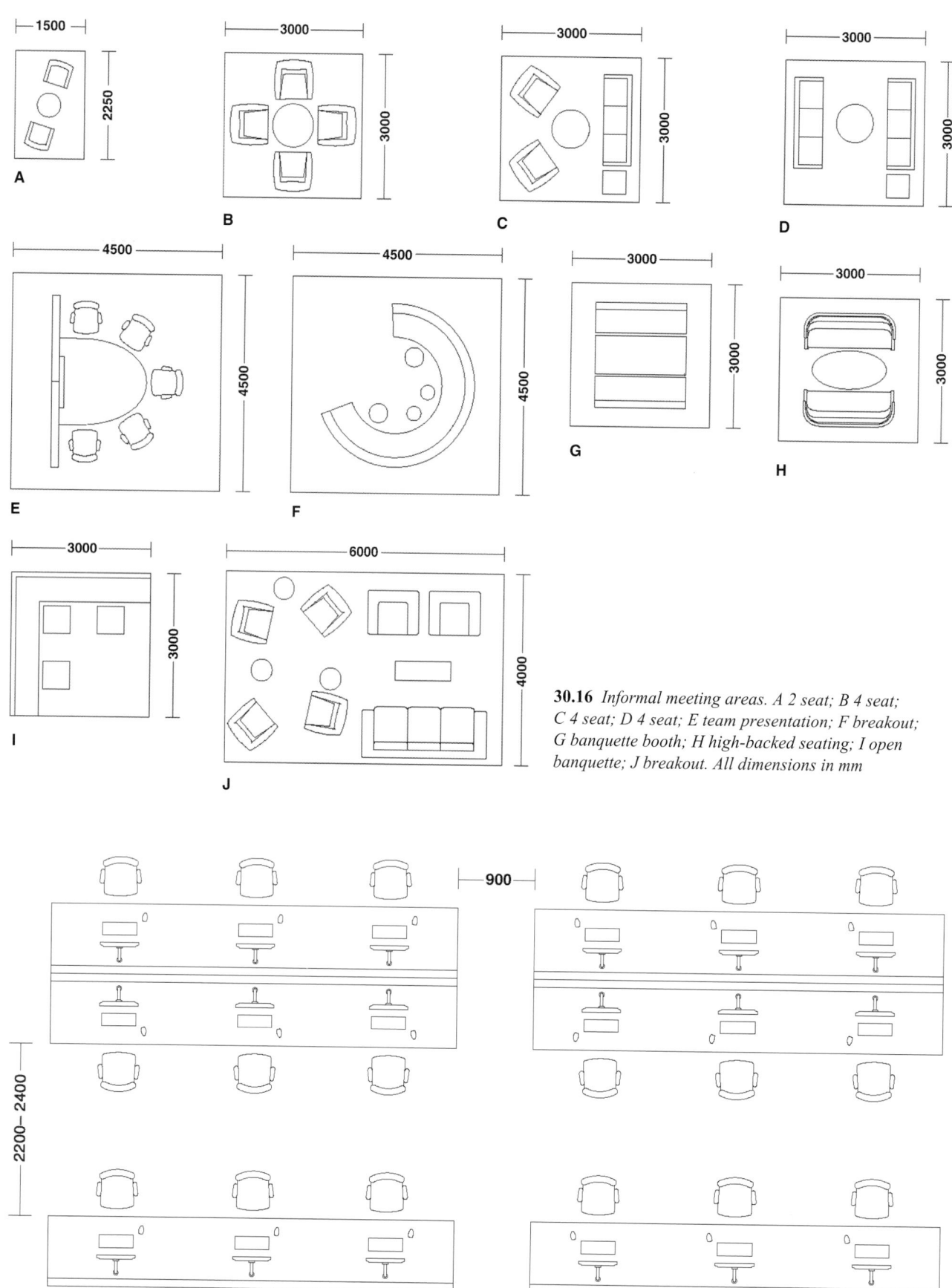

30.16 *Informal meeting areas. A 2 seat; B 4 seat; C 4 seat; D 4 seat; E team presentation; F breakout; G banquette booth; H high-backed seating; I open banquette; J breakout. All dimensions in mm*

30.17 *Bench seating*

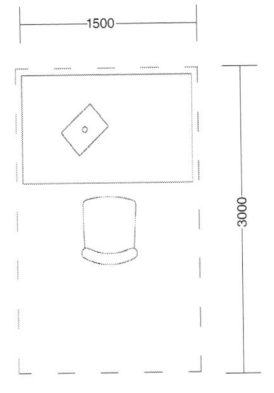

30.18 *Focus room*

30.19a *4 seat*

30.19b *8 seat*

30.19 *Touchdown areas*

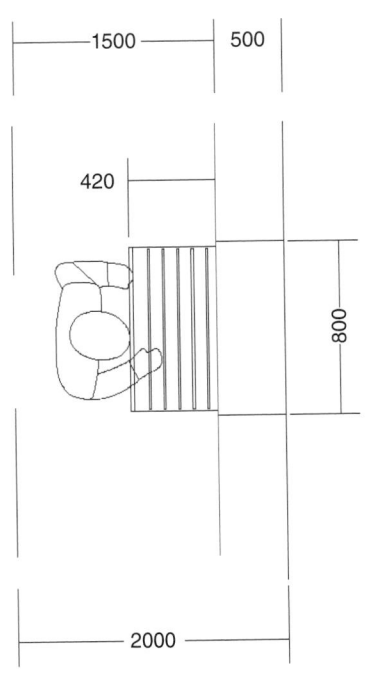

30.20a *Space requirement for lateral filing unit*

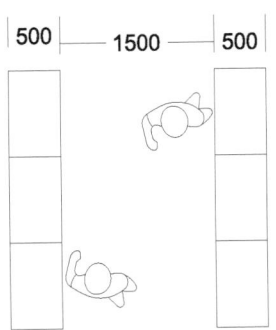

30.20b *Circulation required for lateral filing*

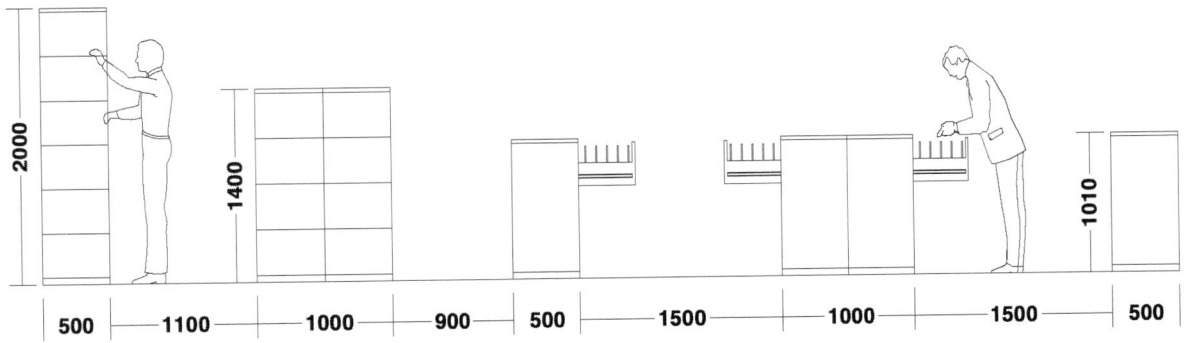

30.20c *Circulation and access to filing*

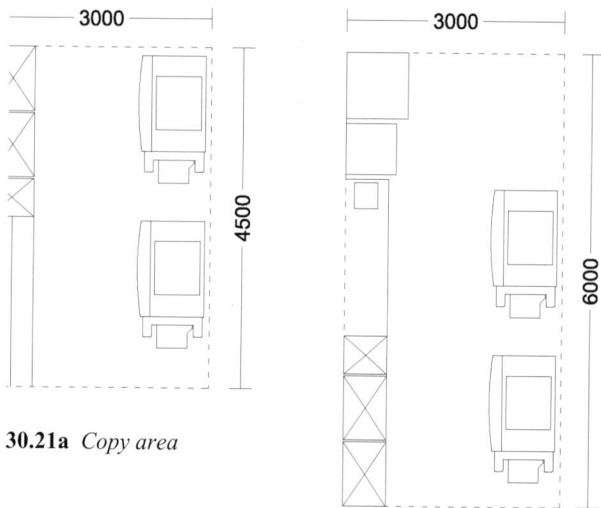

30.21a *Copy area*

30.21b *Copy and vending area*

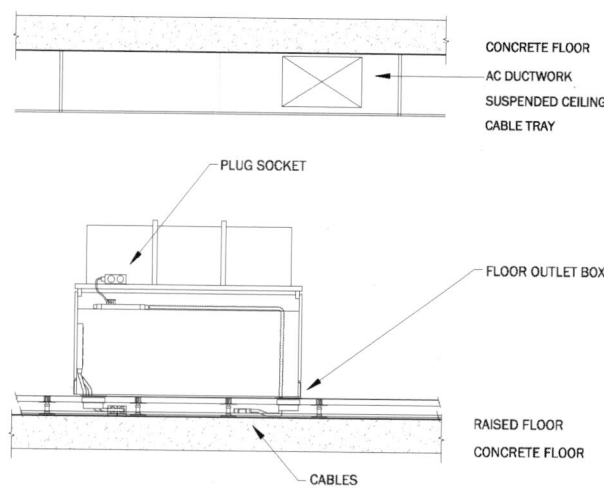

30.22 *Raised floor services strategy*

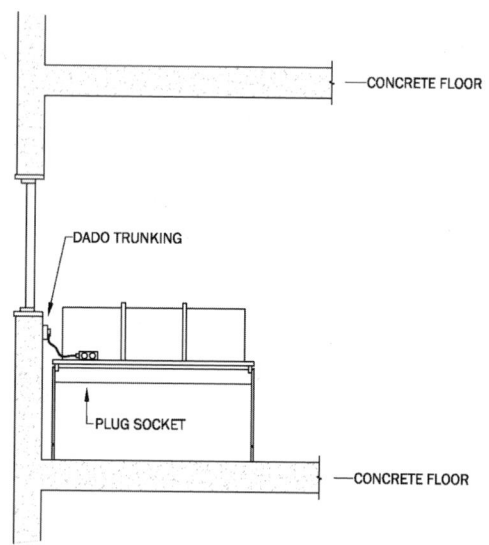

30.23 *Perimeter ducting services strategy*

Two other methods have been used in the past, but are no longer recommended. Ducts in the thickness of the floor screed require service outlets above floor level; and these can only be adjacent to the duct positions. These totally control the placing of furniture and pedestrian routes. An even worse system is to have the cables in the suspended ceiling below the floor in question. This means that when changes have to be made, construction work has to be done on a different floor, which may be occupied by a totally different organisation.

8 TRADING FLOORS

8.1 Organisation

The model for trading floors in recent years has been regimented rows of desks, Figure 30.24, to condense the greatest number of traders in close proximity, primarily to promote face-to-face communication and facilitate the integration of technology.

8.2 Desk design

The desk footprint is affected by three factors:

- Ergonomics/BS standards
- Accommodating technology and equipment.
- Heat management.

Ergonomics/BS standards
Refer to BS EN 527-1 for legroom, distance to screen and desktop space. This dictates a desktop of a minimum 800 mm deep, i.e. consistent with contemporary desk standards.

Screens and equipment
Desk design is driven by the number of screens, the preferred processing strategy (CPUs at desk or remote blade), and the requirement to incorporate a dealerboard:

- The on-floor cooling demand can be reduced by implementing remote processing which removes the primary heat source from

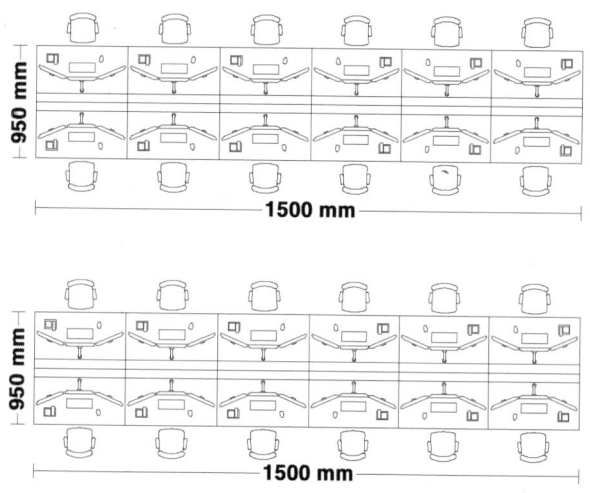

30.24 *Trading floor desks*

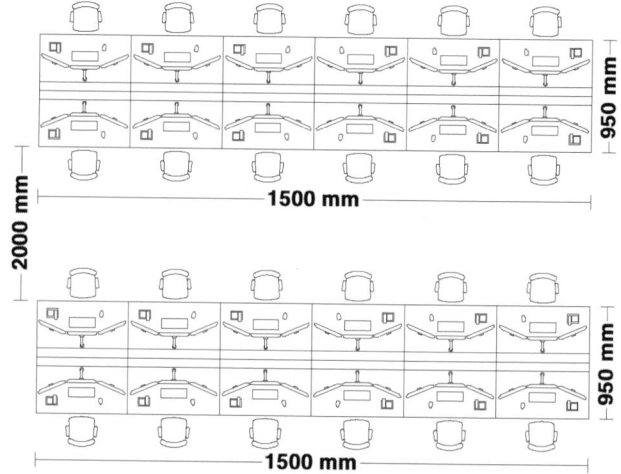

the desk to a central location where it can be more effectively managed.

- CPUs accommodated within the void beneath the desk remains the preferred processing solution, resulting in a 600 mm deep zone central to the desks to house standard PCs.
- Significantly, there has recently been a reduction in the number of screens required. There has been a shift from using multiple flat screen monitors sometimes stacked in a cockpit form to the introduction of only requiring 2 large format display screens therefore reducing the necessary width of the desk module. This has been made possible by improvements in HD providing accurate representation of on-screen market data.
- On-screen 'soft' dealer boards are now available on most trading platforms negating the requirement for a sizeable piece of kit on the desktop.
- Remote or cloud processing, particularly across wireless networks, is unlikely to have a significant impact on trading floor design due to the latency, (i.e. the fraction-of-a-second delays) experienced.

Heat management

Trading floors inherently generate a large amount of heat due to the amount of screens and processing equipment. Building services will require augmenting to manage this excess. There are primarily three solutions of conventional speculative office buildings:

- Floor plenum – pumping cool air through the raised floor void to cool equipment within the desk void via outlets below the desks, Figure 30.25. This requires a sealed base to the desk and a minimum raised floor void of 300 mm.
- Overhead (Fan Coil Unit and/or chilled beams) – less efficient than other solutions when used in isolation, Figure 30.27. Performance can be improved by incorporating a 'chimney' to the spine of the desks to duct heated air away from the equipment housed in the desk to high level where it can mix with the cooler air.
- Cool desks Figure 30.26 – effectively housing a FCU within the central spine to the desk to circulate cool air around the CPUs/ screens and deal with the heat at source. This is an efficient way to supplement existing building systems and means that standard speculative office buildings can be utilised for a trading operation since no increased floor void is required and there are reduced Category A enhancements at high level.

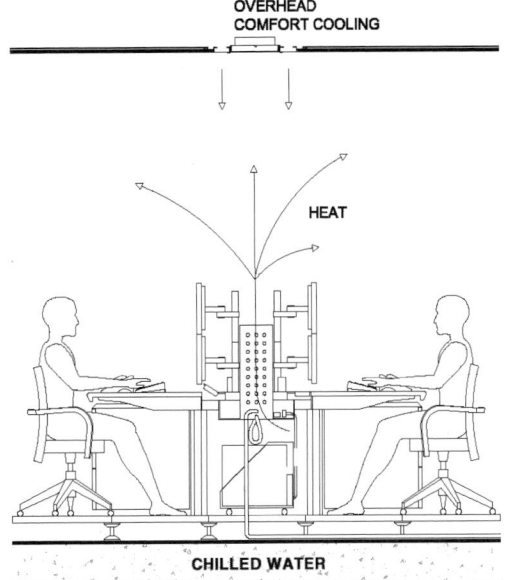

30.26 *In desk cooling*

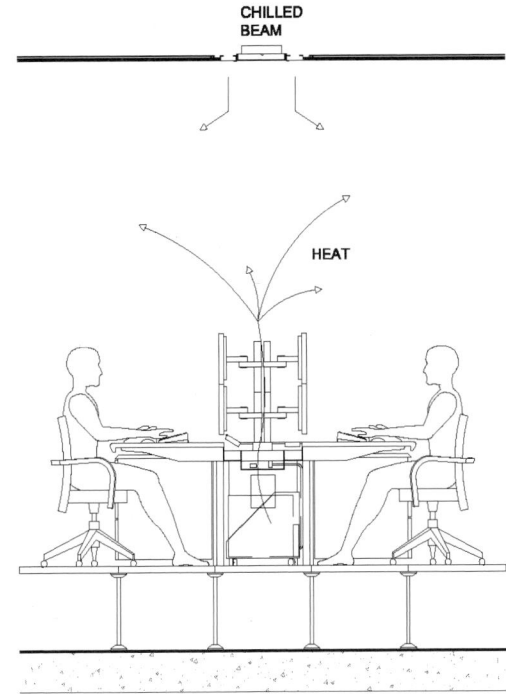

30.27 *Overhead chilled beam*

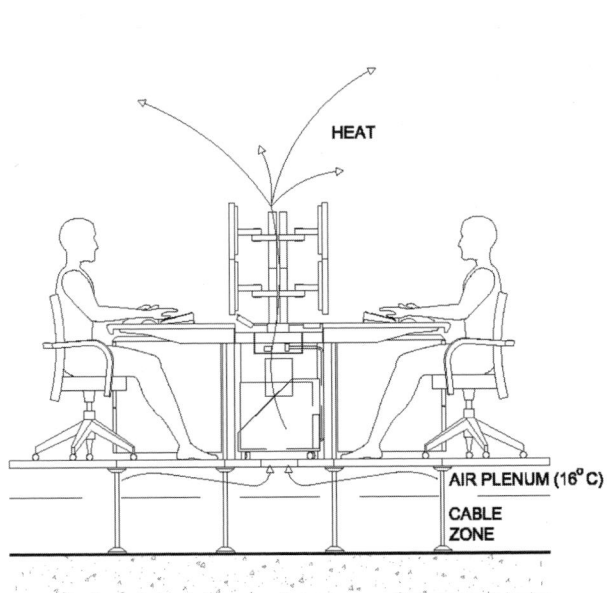

30.25 *Floor plenum*

8.3 Future

Emergence of automated trading and a consequent need for technical developers to be embedded within trading teams has seen a shift from endless rows to more organic layouts, thereby promoting team organisation and interaction. Standardisation of desks, hardware and software also allows greater mobility of users, which is essential for project focused, team-based work.

Another consequence of the multi-function trading floor is the requirement for alternative, collaborative spaces around the periphery of the trading floor to support the interactive functions. This space was traditionally occupied by managers in offices, but these are increasingly likely to want to sit within their teams. There may be a requirement for a large flexible meeting room close by, or a broadcast facility, to allow the 'morning call' briefing session to be streamed live to traders' desktops.

9 CONCLUSION – WORK AND THE CITY

Two apparently but not necessarily contradictory meta-trends need to be addressed, not just by architects, but by corporate clients as well as developers and their agents:

- The rising expectations of office workers, especially younger people, not just for higher standards of office accommodation but for more control of their use of time, workplaces and work styles, all of which are having a big impact on office design.
- Many clients and more importantly office workers are addressing the emerging reality that – with the emergence of new modes of working and new timetables made possible by ubiquitous information technology – it is no longer necessary to go to work in order to work.

Such changes raise fundamental questions not just about the nature and purpose of office buildings but about what kinds of urban development are likely to be appropriate to accommodate the knowledge economy.

As the twenty-first century progresses, conventional office developments and office buildings – mono-functional and based on strict timetables – are likely to be replaced by more permeable, responsive and mixed urban structures operating over very different timetables. What is already clear is that the city is far from obsolete – in fact very much the opposite.

10 BIBLIOGRAPHY

BCO Guide to Specification, British Council for Offices, 2014

Building Information Modelling for Commercial Office Buildings, British Council for Offices, 2013

Frank Duffy, *Work and the City (Edge Futures)*, Black Dog Publishing, 2008

Richard Hyde, *Sustainable Retrofitting of Commercial Buildings*, Routledge 2012

International Property Measuring Standard (IPMS) www.ipmsc.org

Anthony Speight, *The Architects' Legal Handbook, 9th ed.* Butterworth Architecture, 2010

Jeremy Myerson, Philip Ross *Space to Work: New Office Design*, Laurence King 2006

Nikil Saval, *Cubed: A Secret History of the Workplace*, Doubleday, 2014.

Juriaan Van Meel, Yuri Martens, Hermen Jan van Ree *Planning Office Spaces: A Practical Guide for Managers and Designers*, Laurence King, 2010

31 Payment and counselling offices

Richard Napier

Richard Napier is an Associate at Aedas Architects Ltd

KEY POINTS:
- *These are all facilities where security is a major consideration*

Contents
1 Introduction
2 General layout and design
3 Key components
4 Procurement

1 INTRODUCTION

1.1 General
This chapter covers retail banking premises, post offices, ticket desks and government services outlets which are generally characterised by: the need for security of staff, premises and public due to potential criminal activity where money is stored in quantity and exchanged or received over counters; where customers require privacy and discrete interaction with service providers; or where information which is exchanged is either sensitive or secure.

Due to the nature of design procurement for these types of buildings, this chapter provides a brief first point of reference for a designer who requires general guidance. It does not include details of functional space planning or fixtures and fittings, as that level of detail is now commonly provided by the individual organisations in their particular design manuals and brand templates.

1.2 Types
The building types and facilities included here are:

- banks
- building societies
- post offices
- foreign currency outlets
- ticket desks
- government services outlets
- ATMs and ATM lobbies
- interview spaces.

Common factors of all these facilities are the particular need for security for both staff and public, the requirement for surveillance and protection of the premises, and the balancing of those needs with the provision of accessible counter services and interview facilities.

1.3 Customer experience
What distinguishes these facilities today is the concept of customer-focused services, where the buildings are not designed to suit the internal operations of the organisations but to enable a more welcoming aspect and customer experience for the users. The need for additional security and application of technology have affected all these facilities; but as part of the modern high street retail offer, responses to lifestyle trends and the development of accessible government services, the open shopfronts of these buildings and the customer-friendly services and facilities they provide are key aspects in their design.

1.4 Banks
The way banks now do business and provide for customers' needs is referred to as Retail Banking, making them essentially more like shops than traditional banks. There is now less variation in the types of bank branch as they move towards providing a more uniform set of customer facilities and services. Branches now are likely to contain more ATMs than cashiers, and technological developments such as internet banking and the universal availability of ATMs in retail areas contribute to less dependency on tellers within banks for ordinary customer cash transactions.

The selling of additional products and services and the provision of more customer support services such as internet banking desks, rather than just over-the-counter money transfers, are a more dominant feature of bank branches today. Also, several main banks have merged in recent years, resulting in less competition, less variety of banks on the high street, and the development of new customer service concepts.

Because each bank organisation has its own corporate brand design manual, the figures below are indicative of the *principles* of current trends in bank branch layout.

1.5 Building societies
Building societies have become more like banks, if not actually taken over by mainstream banks. Consequently, they are following similar trends in branch design in terms of more welcoming layouts for their branches incorporating the same key components of reception desk, open-desk cashiers and open-plan customer meeting rooms. Many still retain the same requirement for secure screened cashiers, but they follow banking trends in provision of more ATMs.

1.6 Post offices
Post offices traditionally provided only counter services related to Royal Mail postal and ancillary business, but now provide a full range of financial services in order to compete with banks and insurance companies. Main city centre post offices now have a customer reception facility, automated ticket queuing operation, open counters, chip and pin cash dispensing, and premises generally provide a wider provision of stationery retail. Most main branches also provide foreign currency exchange.

There are an increasing number of sub-post offices which are operated as franchises within local shops, newsagents and supermarkets, and for security reasons those branches maintain the tradition of secure screened counters, albeit providing the same full range of postal and financial services as main city centre offices. As with banks, the detailed layout and facilities provided for the variety of post office sizes and locations will be specified within a design manual.

1.7 Foreign currency and money transfer outlets
Foreign currency outlets are now provided within a wide variety of locations and premises. These include international transport terminals (see Chapter 41), department stores and specialist retailers (see Chapter 35) as well as, of course, being a service provided within post offices. These facilities are basically secure screened cash exchange counters.

1.8 Ticket desks

Ticket desks in public facilities such as transport, sport and entertainment venues will often operate and be designed in a similar fashion to payment counters within banks. Such facilities would include:

- rail, bus and ferry terminals
- cinema, theatre and concert box offices
- events ticketing agencies
- public sports centres
- stadia and outdoor sports venues
- tourism attractions
- museums, art galleries and exhibitions.

As with banks, there will be a requirement in these buildings for ticket desk counters to provide secure ticket selling through protective screens or semi-secure open counters.

1.9 Government services outlets

The following additional types of similar facilities where interview and cash exchange are an essential function are:

- local government payment offices (Council Tax and Housing rent payment offices, etc.)
- DWP Jobcentre Plus offices
- DVLA offices
- HM Revenue and Customs offices
- regional Passport Offices
- Citizens Advice Bureau offices.

All of the above are likely to be included in many of the types of public buildings covered by Chapter 16 (Civic Buildings), but their designs are characterised by consisting of dedicated public counter services for either payment transactions, customer relations services or for the inclusion of customer interview and counselling rooms. They require similar levels of public access, security and counselling privacy as are provided in banks.

2 GENERAL LAYOUT AND DESIGN

2.1 Banks

High street banks now are more like shops, following a high street retail concept. Whereas in previous decades banks principally comprised a relatively small banking hall fronting a secure line of screened tellers and vast back-of-house office areas, the trend now is for a much more spacious public area with reception desk and waiting area, open-desk cashiers dispensing limited amounts of cash, together with open-plan meeting rooms, and less need for administrative offices. Larger branches will still have secure cashier screens, particularly for business banking, but these will be arranged to one side or to the rear of the public zone.

Figure 31.1 shows the relationship and zoning for a retail bank; Figure 31.2 illustrates a typical current retail bank concept layout. Large shopfront windows aggressively sell their products and services, and spacious interiors give more floor space over to customer services and convenience. The shopfront contains a wide display of the bank's products and services, as well as a clear view of the public area, together with ATMs on the street. Some city centre banks still have a separate 24-hour lobby for ATMs; this is shown in Figure 31.10. However, the preferred arrangement in current retail banking is to combine a number of external ATMs on the street with a number of internal ATMs within the main public area. This reduces the security risks associates with late-night open lobbies.

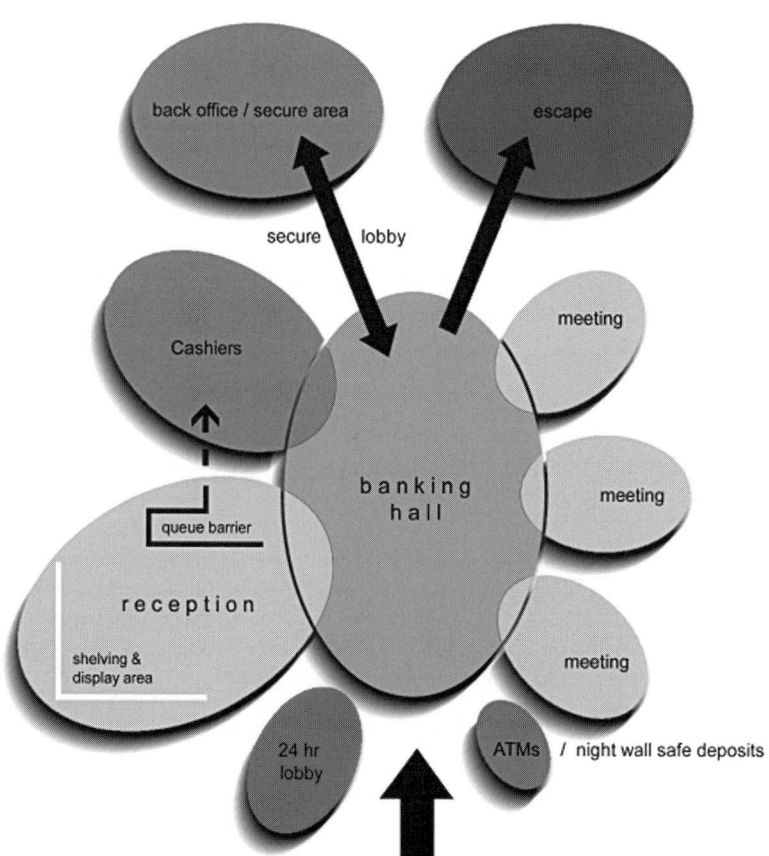

31.1 *Relationship and zoning diagram for a retail bank*

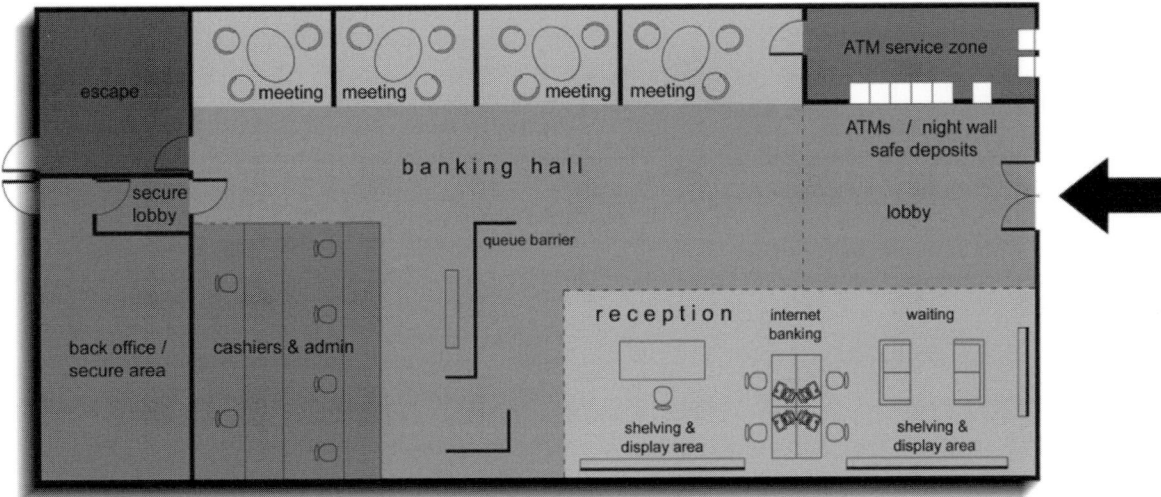

31.2 *Retail bank concept layout*

The main public banking area (about 70 per cent of the floor area) consists of:

- reception desk, which acts as a focal point for customers, in a prominent location in the centre of the main public area;
- waiting area with comfortable lounge seating;
- ATMs and cash/cheque deposit machine (some banks now include automatic pay-in machines accepting coins and cheques);
- internet banking terminals;
- open cashier counters and/or desks, which dispense limited amounts of cash, with space for queuing;
- customer interview/meeting spaces;
- enclosed customer meeting rooms.

Secure back-office area consisting of:

- secure screened cashiers, with space for queuing;
- ATM and deposit machine room;
- admin area with strong room for safes, for storage and handling of cash;
- staff room and toilets.

Architects and designers today are not required to provide an original design for a bank, but are expected to use their professional skills to integrate a set of standard designed components from a corporate brand manual into a site-specific project.

2.2 Building societies
The design of building societies now reflects that of mainstream banks. Smaller branches are still arranged with secure screened tellers, although the main public areas are much more customer focused in line with bank design trends, incorporating reception desk, comfortable waiting area and open-plan customer meeting spaces. Figure 31.3 illustrates a typical current building society layout.

2.3 Post offices
The relationship and zoning for a typical main post office is shown in Figure 31.4. There will be a requirement for a strong room for storage and handling of cash, and for staff facilities, as with banks. Also as with banks and building societies, the post offices will be designed in detail in accordance with a corporate design manual to suit a variety of locations and sizes from a main city centre location

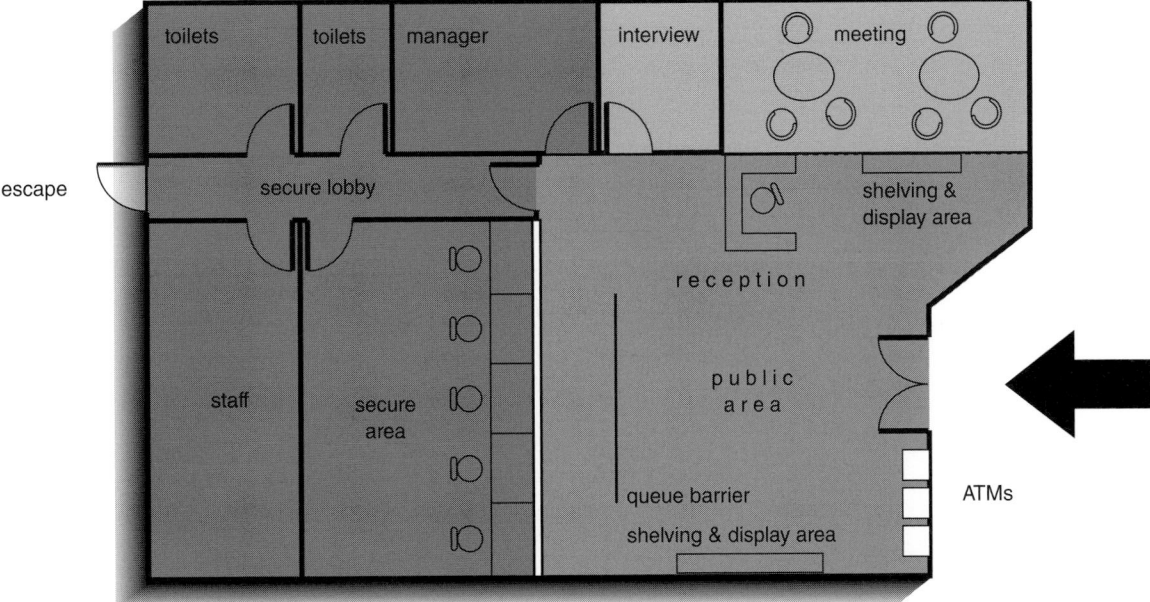

31.3 *Typical building society layout*

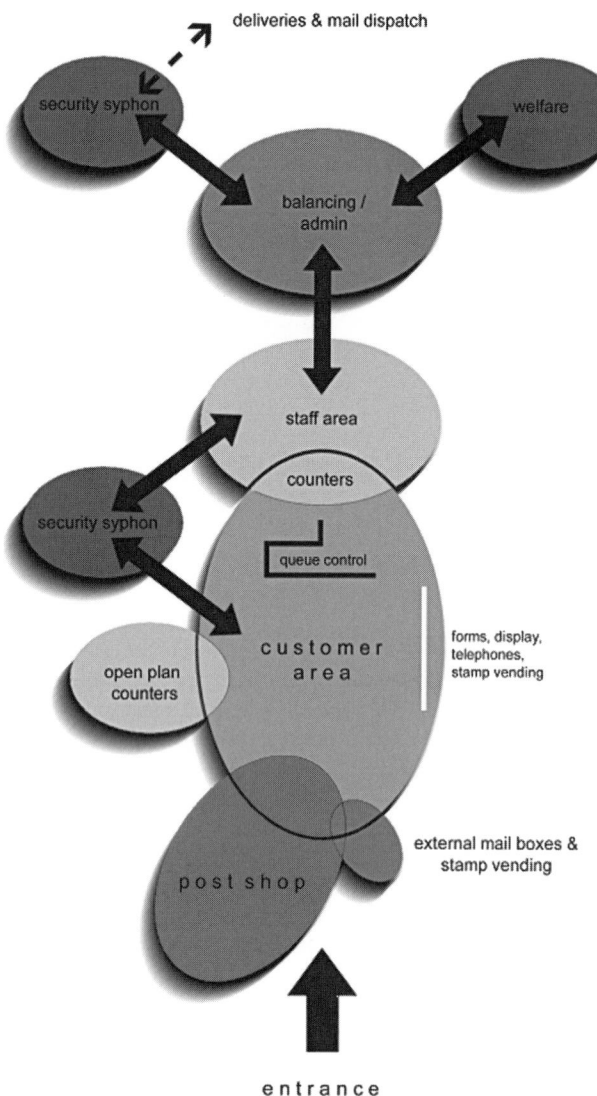

deliveries & mail dispatch

security syphon

welfare

balancing / admin

staff area

counters

security syphon

queue control

customer area

forms, display, telephones, stamp vending

open plan counters

external mail boxes & stamp vending

post shop

entrance

31.4 *Relationship and zoning diagram for a post office*

to a local sub-post office operated by private enterprises as a franchise within a retail store.

Figure 31.5 shows the layout of a typical main post office which includes a sorting office and parcel-collect facility. The main public area of a city centre post office now includes a substantial stationery retail zone, and for the counter services there will be an electronic queuing system attended by a member of staff. The main counters will be open-style with chip and pin cash dispensing facilities, and a separate foreign currency outlet will be provided by means of a secure screen cashier as elsewhere. In sub-offices the counters will be behind secure screens.

2.4 Foreign currency outlets

Chapter 35 (Retail shops and stores) and Chapter 41 (Transport terminals and interchanges) make reference to individual retail components that are likely to be included with retail complexes. Payment counters within larger retail or transport facilities will include foreign exchange outlets. These are essentially secure screened cashier counters, designed in a similar way to those within banks. Figure 31.6 illustrates a typical layout.

2.5 Ticket desks

Travel centres such as rail and bus stations which provide booking services and issue tickets also require a similar kind of secure counter to those within banks. Matters concerning circulation, ticketing and retail are described in Chapter 41 (Transport terminals and interchanges), but the design of the counter component is covered in Section 3.3.

2.6 Government services outlets

Local authority council and other government or public offices which incorporate payment and counselling facilities include: Council Tax payment offices, local authority housing rent offices, DWP Jobcentre Plus offices, DVLA offices, HM Revenue & Customs offices, Regional Passport Offices and Citizens Advice Bureau offices. These buildings require a number of functions similar to those found within banks such as open-plan or enclosed customer interview rooms and payment counters. Design aspects of those elements are described in Sections 3.3 and 3.4.

2.7 DWP Jobcentre Plus offices

As a type of government service outlet, the Jobcentre Plus, which is the Department of Work and Pensions' principal service for job-seekers, has been transformed in recent years to provide a more twenty-first-century high quality experience for users with modern, customer-focused services and facilities. Although its new system asks individuals to initially call a Jobcentre Plus call centre to register personal details, customers are then asked to attend an interview at their local Jobcentre Plus outlet. Its main function and attraction is its interactive computer system which can be accessed

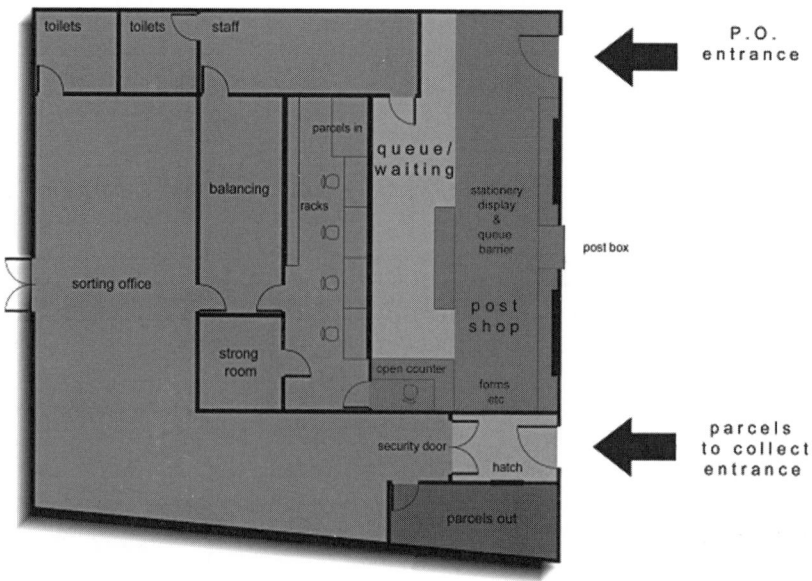

toilets

toilets

staff

parcels in

queue/ waiting

P.O. entrance

balancing

racks

stationery display & queue barrier

post box

sorting office

post shop

strong room

open counter

forms etc

security door

hatch

parcels to collect entrance

parcels out

31.5 *Post office layout with a sorting office and a parcel-collect facility*

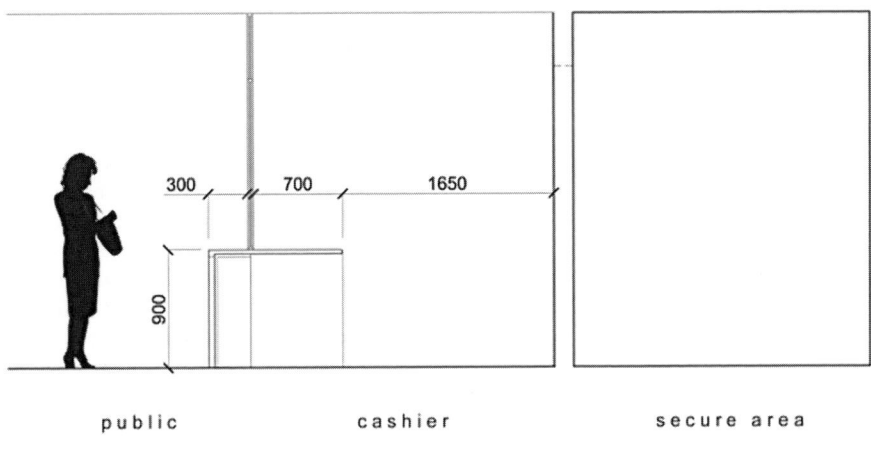

Section

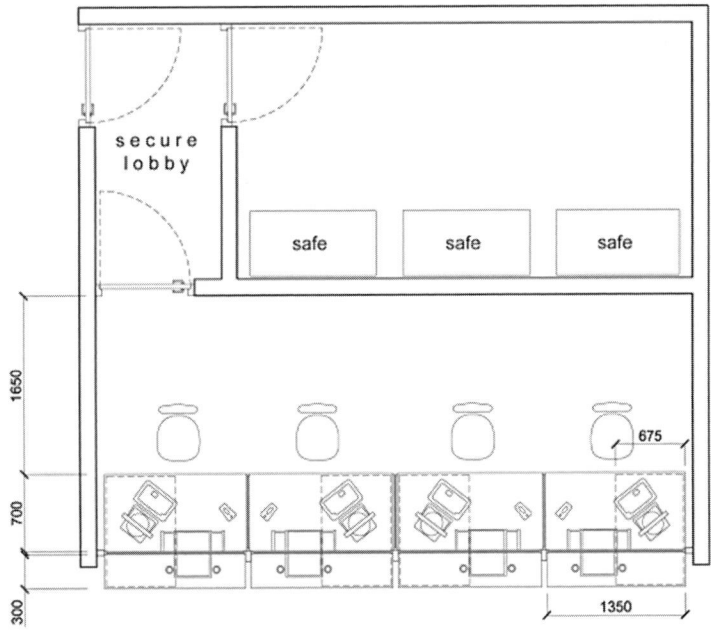

Plan

31.6 *Typical foreign currency outlet layout*

by customers using touch-screen computer terminals, together with the more customer friendly interview room facilities and services.

Figure 31.7 illustrates the zoning plan for a Jobcentre Plus office; Figure 31.8 illustrates a typical layout. In addition to accessible jobseeker terminals, the main customer reception area has a waiting area for interview services. This type of facility has a long history of having the potential for attracting aggressive customers, but with improvements in benefit distribution systems and jobseeker customer care, the Jobcentre Plus building is frequented by genuine customers making use of an essential service. However, security of staff and premises, customer privacy and discretion, and quality of service are still all key aspects of design for this building type.

3 KEY COMPONENTS

3.1 Automatic Teller Machines (ATMs)

ATMs are a universal item on the high street, not only being a staple component within the exterior shopfront and interior of banks and building societies, but also being widely available within other public zones such as retail areas, entertainment complexes and transport terminals. Figure 31.9 shows the setting out requirements for an ATM. Within banks, it will be usual for several ATMs to be grouped

together either on an external wall, on an internal wall in the main banking hall, or within a separate 24 hour lobby accessible from the street which has been a common element in city centre banks. The latter is described below, but the current trend in retail banking now is to omit any 24 hour lobby as this reduces the security risks and maintenance costs associated with late-night open lobbies.

ATMs require to be serviced from the rear for filling with cash or for maintenance via a secure room accessible either from within the bank's interior secure zone or from a lockable door. The latter is the case for all general ATMs located in retail or public areas. Level access is required to ATMs for people in wheelchairs, and where more than one ATM is provided at least one will be at a lower accessible level.

3.2 24 hour lobbies

A typical arrangement for 24 hour lobbies for ATMs provided by banks is shown in Figure 31.10. These will be directly accessible from the street, open during the day and accessible out of hours using a bank card. Although building societies are becoming more like banks, it is unlikely that they will follow the banking trend of recent years to provide 24 hour lobbies for ATMs due to the obvious risks.

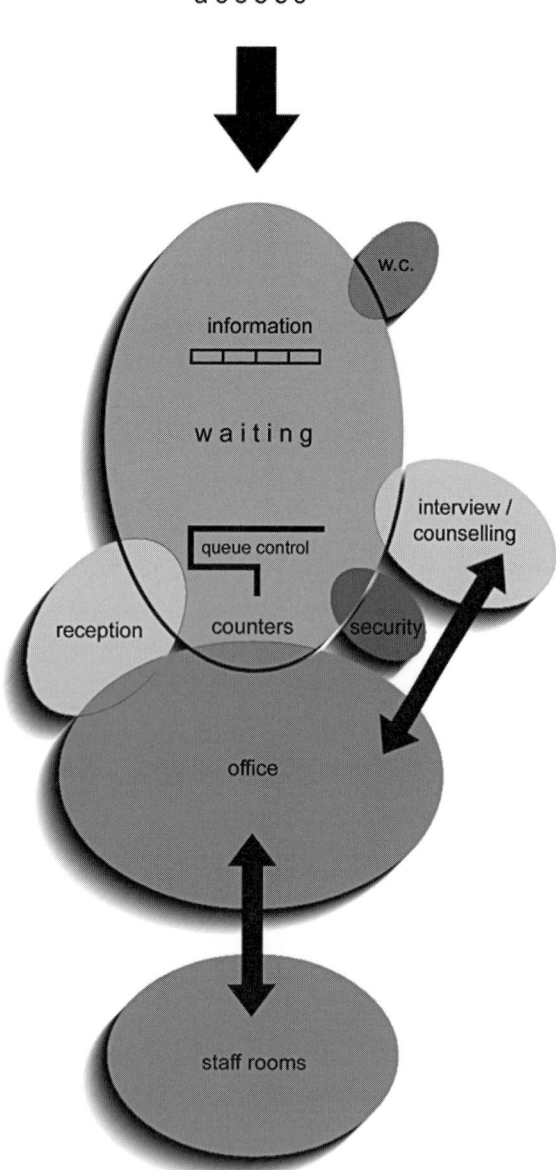

access

w.c.

information

waiting

interview /
counselling

queue control

reception   counters   security

office

staff rooms

31.7 *Relationship and zoning diagram for a Jobcentre Plus office*

3.3 Counters

Figures 31.11 and 31.12 illustrate traditional forms of secure screened counters; Figure 31.13 shows an example of an open bank cashier desk for use in current retail banking. Payment counters which require secure screening for safety and security purposes will be fitted with bulletproof glass. Microphone and speaker systems allow for communication through enclosed glass screens, and a pass-through slot or tray is provided at counter level. For people in wheelchairs, at least one counter will be at a lower accessible level.

Where there is little fear of firearms risk, but where the possibility still exists for physical assault, i.e. in many government services outlets, counters can be designed to be higher or deeper than normal, making it difficult for the customer to reach over to the staff behind.

3.4 Interview and counselling spaces

The majority of these building types provide customer interview facilities. These range from simple desks in open public areas, to open-plan interview spaces directly off a public space, to fully enclosed interview rooms. Banks and building societies tend to provide all three versions; post offices tend not to include any, apart from main city centre offices which are able to provide additional staff to advise on financial products; government services outlets usually require enclosed interview rooms, where there is commonly a need for privacy and customer sensitivity. All arrangements contain the same basic requirement of a desk or table with staff and customer seating, and these are illustrated in Figure 31.14.

3.5 Fixtures and fittings

Fittings in these buildings will be bespoke items provided by furniture manufacture specialists to corporate brand designs and specifications. Furniture design will therefore not usually be within the scope of the architect's work, and so this chapter does not cover the detailed content and functional requirements of fixtures and fittings. The organisations who procure these buildings will have their own design manuals of standard designs or proprietary specifications for fittings and equipment. However, there are key components such as counters and public accessibility issues which are required to comply with relevant legislation, and which therefore require careful dimensional location considerations.

4 PROCUREMENT

Gone are the days when an architect will be commissioned by a bank to design a bank branch. Banking corporations will each have their own in-house property divisions who will have separately commissioned brand design manuals for branch concept designs and details, for use

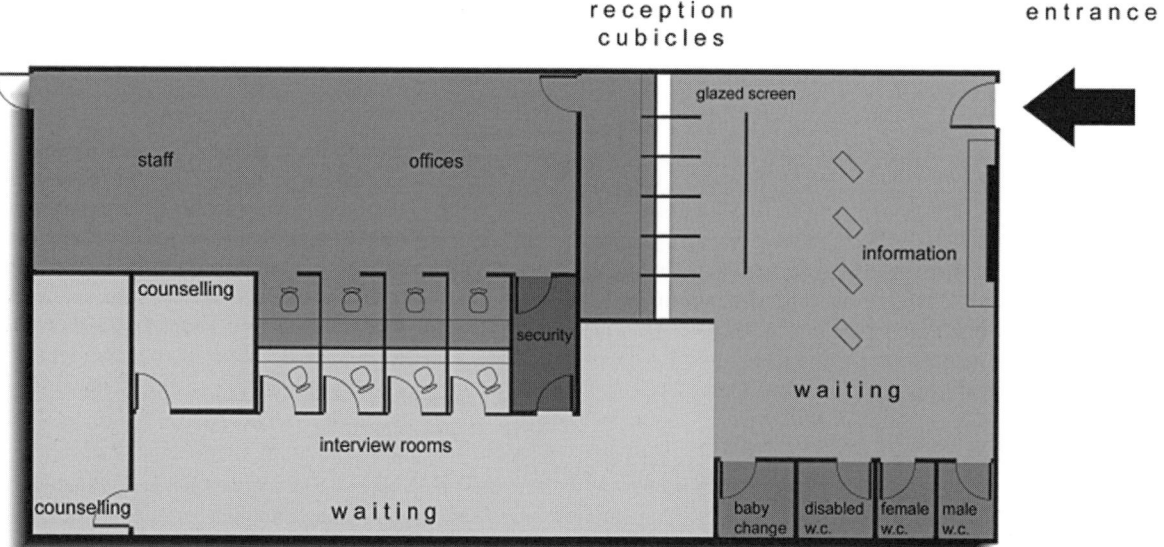

reception
cubicles

entrance

glazed screen

staff   offices

information

counselling

security

waiting

interview rooms

counselling   waiting

baby change w.c.   disabled w.c.   female w.c.   male w.c.

31.8 *A Jobcentre Plus office*

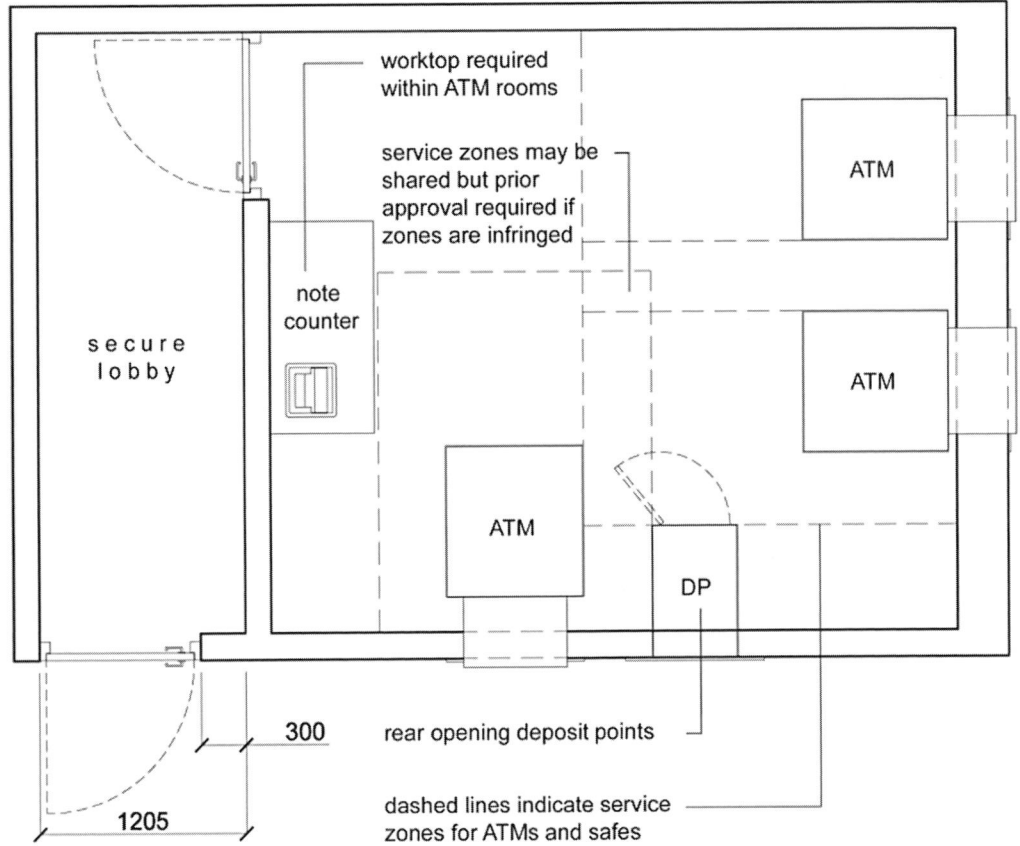

worktop required
within ATM rooms

service zones may be
shared but prior
approval required if
zones are infringed

note
counter

secure
lobby

ATM

ATM

ATM

DP

300   rear opening deposit points

1205

dashed lines indicate service
zones for ATMs and safes

a) Plan of ATM room in a bank

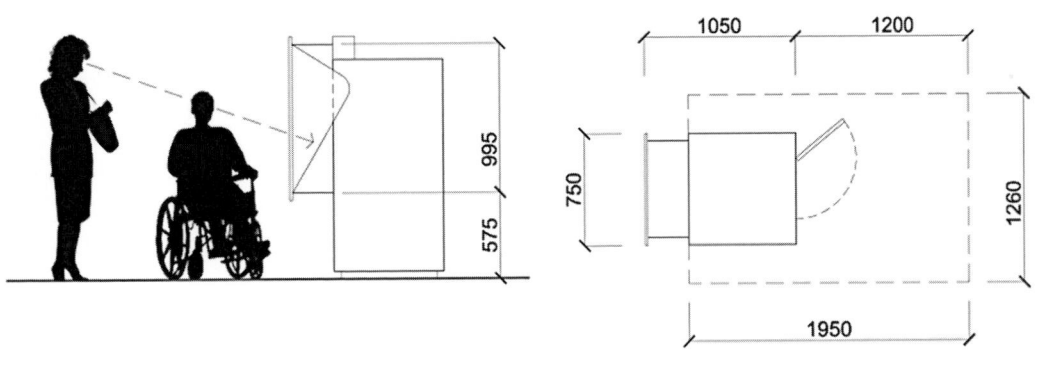

b) ATM setting out

31.9 *ATM setting out*

by architects and designers to be applied to any design project involving the fitting out of an existing bank interior as a refurbishment or the fitting out of a new build retail unit. The brand concept manual will comprise standard bank branch layouts to suit differing locations, and detailed designs for all necessary interior components down to signage and items of furniture and office equipment: all designed by others as a menu of components to be applied by specific project designers.

Design teams are likely to be appointed by specialist fit-out contractors who will be appointed through a design and build framework to project manage the design and construction works for the procurement of a number of projects; for that purpose a specific design manual brief will be supplied. Architects' and designers' scope of work will therefore be to apply the standard designs to a specific site and obtain

the necessary statutory approvals for its execution. Similarly, building societies, post offices and specialist outlets such as foreign exchange counters will be procured to specialist fit-out contractors who will employ design consultants to apply standard designs to specific sites.

For government services outlets, design and construction projects will be procured through official government contract procurement portals such as OJEU notices and/or OGC Buying Solutions methods. Local authority and government departments will, via such public procurement methods, either appoint single consultants or contractors to individual projects, or through framework agreements appoint a number of suppliers of design and/or construction services to procure a variety of larger and wider strategic projects within any specific geographical local authority area or national project scope.

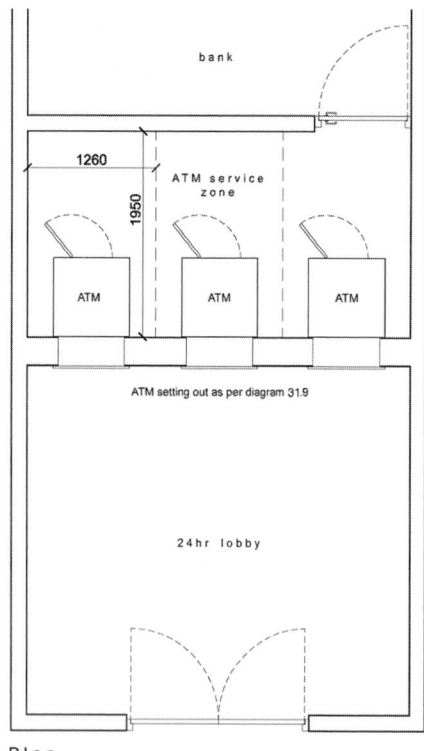

31.10 *ATM 24 hour lobby layout*

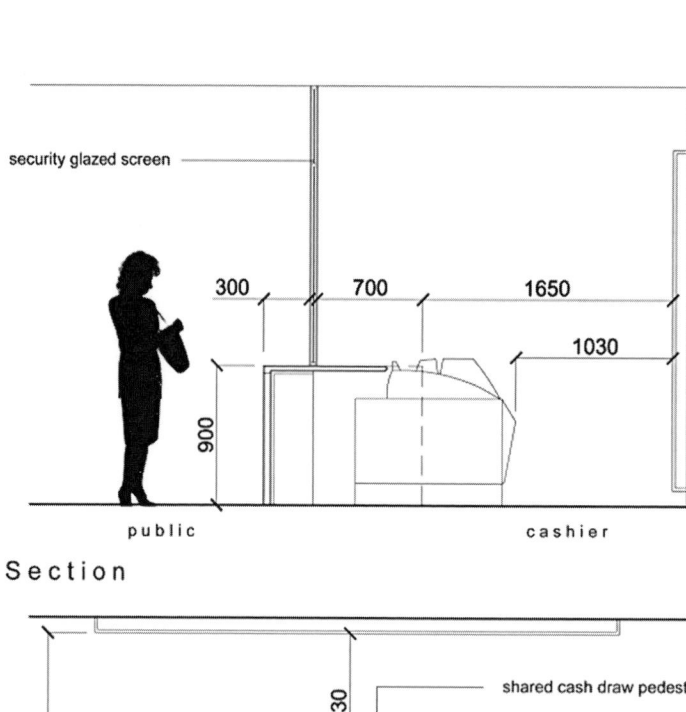

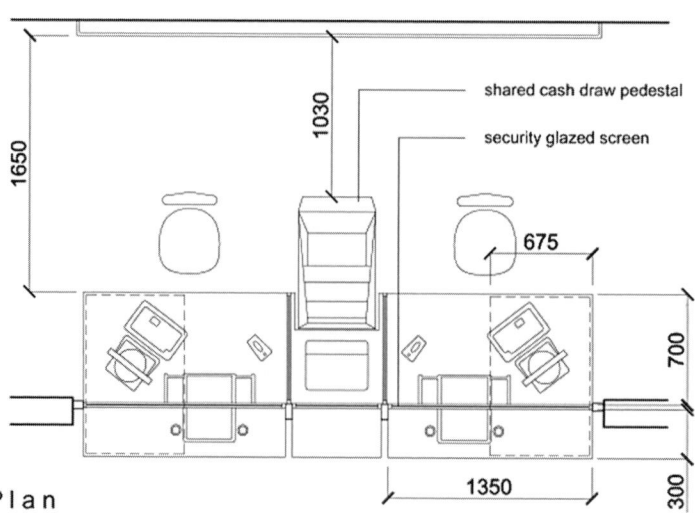

31.11 *Secure screened counter*

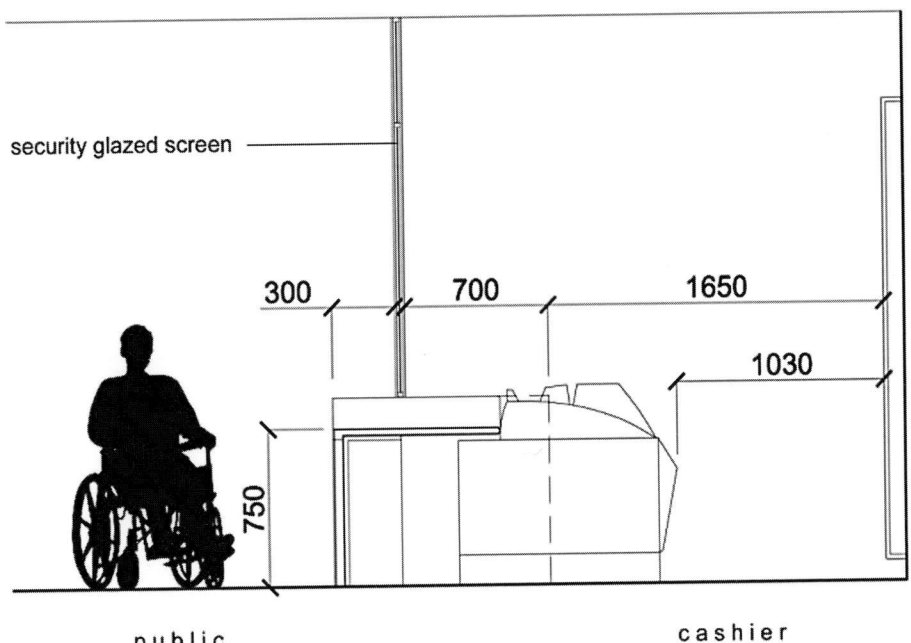

security glazed screen

300   700   1650

1030

750

public   cashier

31.12 *Secure screened counter at lower accessible level*

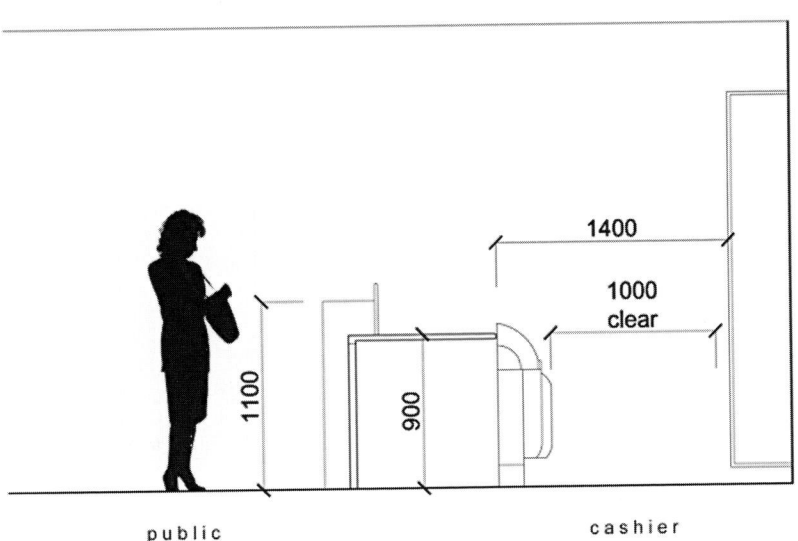

1400

1000 clear

1100

900

public   cashier

Section

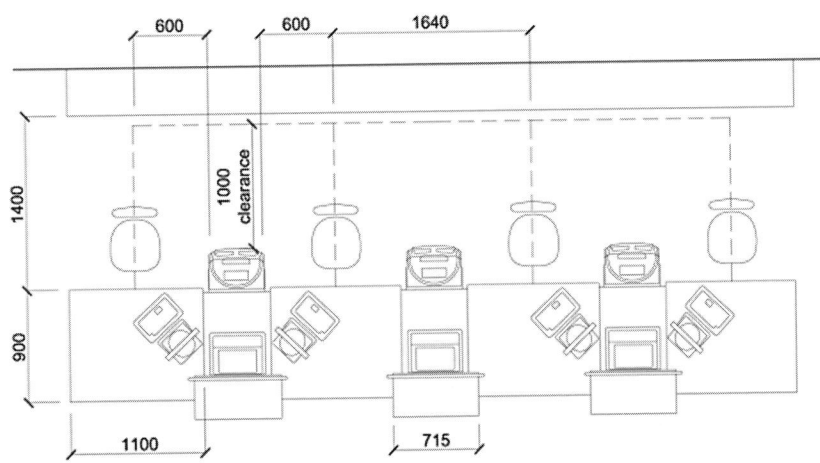

600   600   1640

1400

1000 clearance

900

1100   715

Plan

31.13 *Open bank cashier desk*

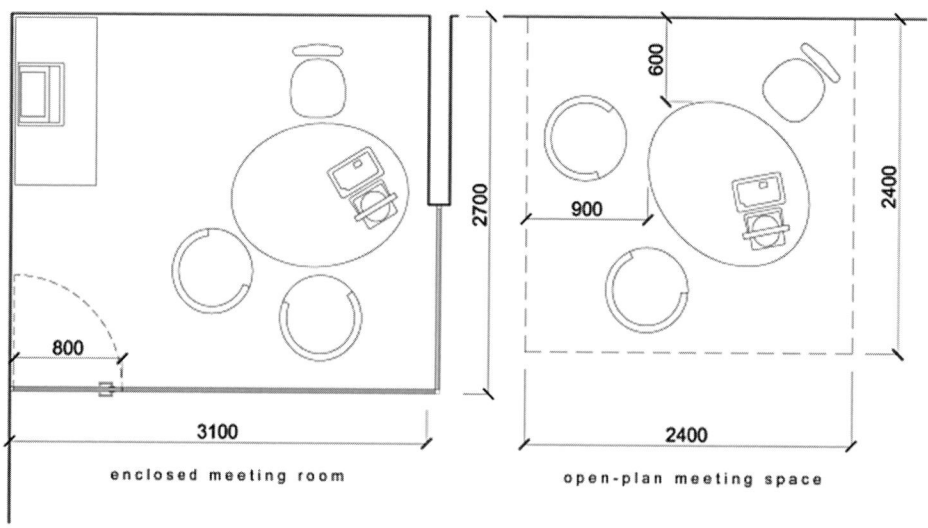

enclosed meeting room   open-plan meeting space

31.14 *Customer interview space*

32 Places of worship

Leslie Fairweather, Ian Brewerton, Atba Al-Samarraie, David Adler and Derek Kemp

CI/Sfb: 6

The section on Church of England buildings was revised by Maurice Walton in 2011

KEY POINTS:

- *Architects engaged with religious buildings and places of worship will inevitably be concerned with tradition and ritual to a greater extent than with buildings of other types*
- *Often, within churches or other Christian buildings, new architectural interventions concern the addition of secular/community spaces which allow the parish to extend its social reach and perhaps generate funds*

Contents

1 Introduction

Part A Guide to Christian denominations

2 Church of England
3 Roman Catholic Church
4 United Reformed Church
5 The Salvation Army
6 Methodist Church
7 Baptist Church and Baptistries
8 Society of Friends
9 Pastoral centres

Part B Design data

10 Altar or communion table
11 Sanctuary furniture and pulpit
12 Font
13 Reservation of the sacrament
14 General arrangements
15 Vestries and sacristies
16 Confessional
17 Organ and choir

Part C Non-Christian places of worship

18 Synagogues
19 Mosques
20 Hindu temple
21 Sikh gurdwara

Part D Additional information

22 Crematoria
23 Bibliography

1 INTRODUCTION

1.1 Scope

This chapter will cover churches and places of worship for various Christian denominations, synagogues, mosques and Hindu temples. Places of local worship only are dealt with, not larger buildings like cathedrals or those with social spaces, which are not significantly different from social spaces in secular buildings, and for which Chapter 17 (Community centres) provides further advice.

1.2 History and tradition

In the architecture of places of worship for the more established denominations the architect is bound to be more concerned with tradition than in other fields. Users are more conscious of history (and more sensitive about it) than most other clients: they will not allow an architect to ignore established precedents and will expect a full understanding of them. However many of the new 'Community Churches' expect to see a different approach more akin to performance architecture than established precedents. These new movements have also had a major impact upon the more established denominations and have resulted in a movement away from one-man ministry to more participation by members of the congregation. Large free-span structures are required to accommodate large congregation numbers, seating capacities of 500–1000 are not uncommon for which the conversion of redundant retail warehousing and similar structures are ideal.

Exact details of the forms of worship and building procedures should be discussed with the individual clients, and the architectural implications thoroughly understood. A fairly detailed general guide to the history, procedures and forms of worship (with architectural implications) of the Church of England, the Roman Catholic Church, the Presbyterian Church, the Salvation Army, the Methodist Church and the Society of Friends, is given in Church buildings, originally published as a series in The Architects' Journal and later in book form (now out of print).

1.3 Local ecumenical projects

Some protestant churches, particularly Methodist and United Reformed Church, are now uniting to form Local Ecumenical Projects (LEPs), both as a visible expression of church unity and in recognition of declining numbers and reducing resources. In these, the uniting congregations may either continue to worship separately in shared premises, or may unite to form a single congregation recognising the practices of each of the participant denominations. The building may be either that belonging to one of the congregations or (rarely) purpose built.

1.4 Additional factors

Such projects are set up under the Sharing of Churches Act which imposes some legal requirements in addition to the particular requirements of the participants. This may be relevant to designers, as the investment of capital in buildings is one of the areas dealt with in the Act. For every LEP there will (or should) be a formal 'Sharing Agreement' which sets out its terms. Architects involved in LEPs should take considerable time and care in formulating the brief, as there are often natural tensions within such a project.

Part A Guide to Christian denominations

2 CHURCH OF ENGLAND

2.1 The buildings, and how they are used for worship

After the Reformation the Church of England inherited many medieval, mostly Gothic, buildings, strongly directional in their east–west orientation and with the main action remote from the congregation. The people therefore had lost the sense that they were engaged with the clergy in a common action and tended to become spectators with an individualistic rather than a corporate response to the liturgy. The church has now moved into a period of experiment with a fuller expression of the corporate nature of worship and the equal importance of the Word (which must be heard) and of Sacrament within a building which remains true to the Anglican sense of proportion.

2.2 Altar (or table), priest and people

The influences of the Reformation and later the Oxford Movement have produced variations to the layout of the sanctuary. The Book of Common Prayer (BCP 1662) assumes the table, or altar, to be against the east wall with the priest standing at the north end, Figure 32.1.

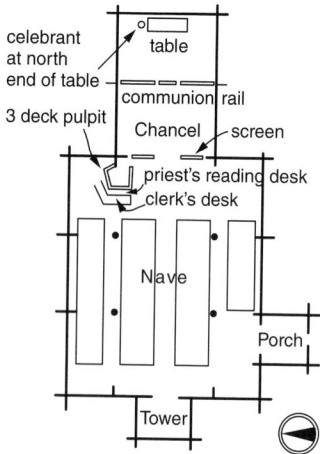

32.1 *Communion table is placed against east wall, priest stands at north end*

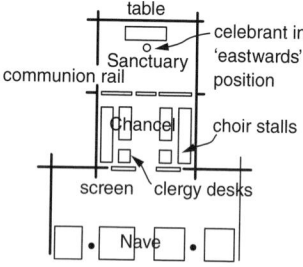

32.2 *Eastward position: priest faces altar with his back to the congregation*

In many churches this has been superseded by the priest facing east, Figure 32.2.

This was thought to be contrary to the spirit of the Anglican liturgy. Altars were moved west with the priest facing the people across the altar, Figure 32.3.

More recently there are churches which bring the people even closer to the celebration by positioning the altar in the centre of a square or circular building, with seating on three sides. Figure 32.4 shows the plan of the Church of St Paul at Bow Common in London (1960 Architect: Robert Maquire and Keith Murray).

2.3 The main services

There are several types of service:

- All Age Services
- the Eucharist
- the offices of matins and evensong
- Baptism
- Confirmation
- the solemnisation of matrimony
- Burial of the dead.

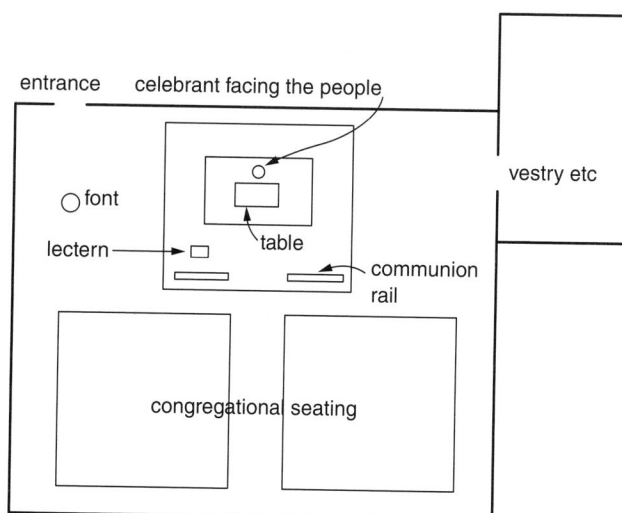

32.3 *One of the many variations of plan where the priest faces the congregation across the altar. The seating may extend around three sides of the altar*

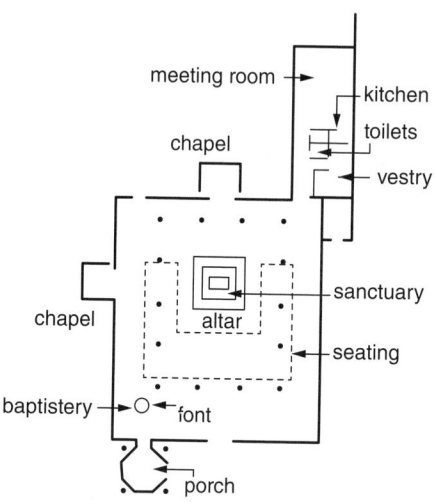

32.4 *Bow Common*

2.4 Church design

Apart from the altar, the general principles of layout and design are the same as for the Roman Catholic and Methodist Churches. These are described in Sections 3, 4 and 6. These sections also give appropriate space requirements for aisle widths, pew sizes and areas within the sanctuary.

2.5 Alterations and extensions to existing churches

Although some new churches are being built the majority of works are for the provision of community facilities, meeting rooms, toilets and kitchens. In listed buildings any proposals are judged with great scrutiny by the DAC and English Heritage. Recent decisions suggest that proposals that are reversible and do not encroach on the existing structure are favoured. The following examples illustrate different approaches.

Church of St Andrew, Farnham (Architect Ptolemy Dean Architects Ltd., see Figure 32.5)

Advantage is taken of the large floor space to create a glass and timber two storey pavilion structure at the west end of the nave and the two aisles taking no support from the existing fabric. The pavilion encloses meeting rooms and a kitchen with a viewing and meeting gallery over. The altar is in a centre position with seating on all four sides.

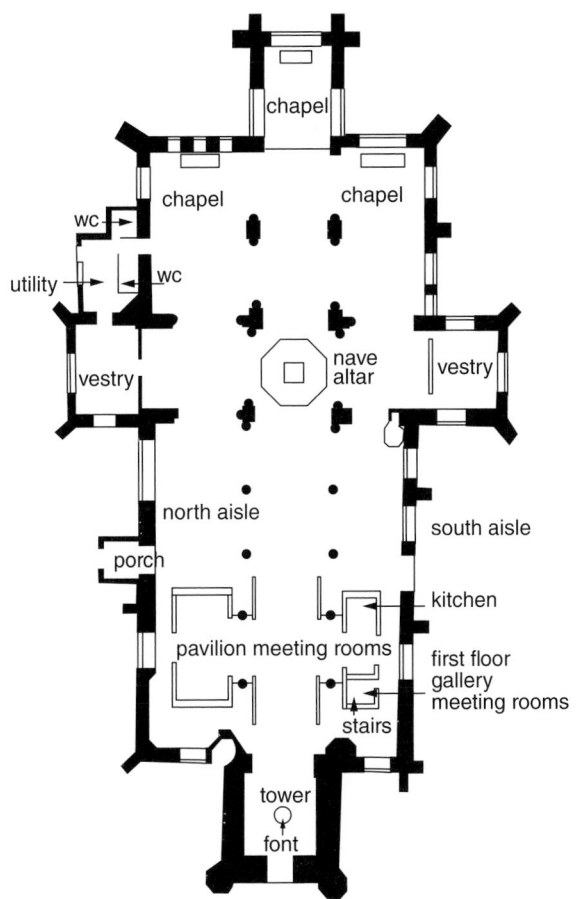

32.5 *Plan of Farnham*

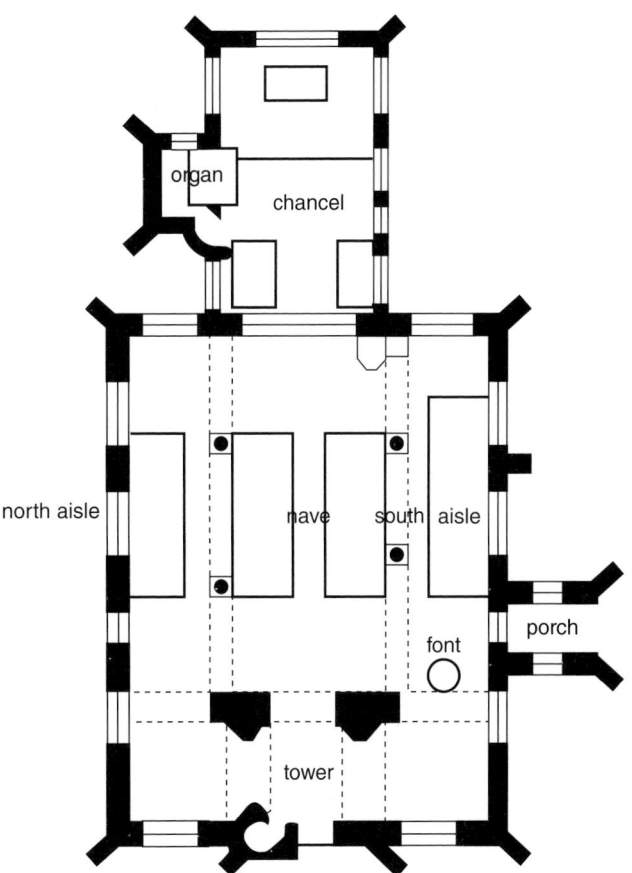

32.6 *Church of All Saints Flore, original plan*

Church of All Saints Flore, (2001, Architect: Stimpson Walton Bond, see Figures 32.6 and 32.7)
A mediaeval church with a Georgian flat ceiling. Walls are plain with cornice and panelled dado. The two aisles flank the west tower. The full width of the west end is separated from the aisles by full height walls, and the mediaeval tower arch glazed creating a meeting space, toilet, kitchen and vestry.

2.6 Obtaining a faculty

There are several considerations to bear in mind when securing a faculty for church building work:

- New, extensions and repair works are subject to faculty, an approvals procedure dating back several centuries.
- It was consolidated in 1993 by the *Care of Churches and Ecclesiastical Jurisdiction Measure Code of Practice* granting exemption from Listed Building Consent for work to Grade I and II* listed church buildings.
- The Measure is administered in each Diocese by a Diocesan Advisory Committee (DAC).
- The process is often initiated by a site visit with the PCC and the Architect followed by preliminary and detailed submissions to the DAC.
- If there are no objections the DAC informs the Parish and the Chancellor of the Diocese to whom the Parish submits a formal request for a Faculty. The Chancellor is a judge or a QC.
- Exemption is only from Listed Building Consent. External alterations may be subject to Planning Approval from the local Planning Authority.
- Either the DAC or the Chancellor may refer the proposals to an appropriate conservation body such as English Heritage whose observations may or may not be accepted by the DAC or the Chancellor.
- Other major Christian denominations have their own similar exemption procedures.

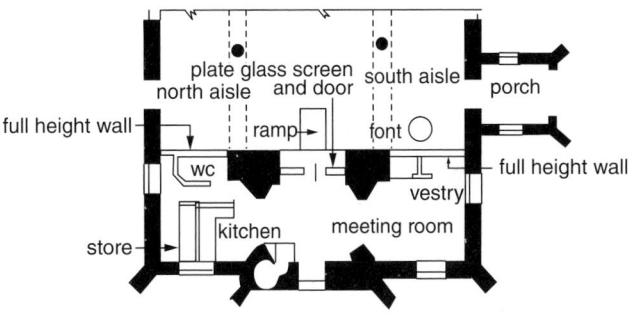

32.7 *Church of All Saints Flore, plan after conversion*

3 ROMAN CATHOLIC CHURCH

3.1 Worship as a corporate act

The term 'Roman Catholic' (or to members simply 'Catholic') denotes the Christian community which has continuously accepted the authority of the Pope. The chief problem of a community which is building a Catholic church is that, though its building must suit the liturgy as it now is, community and architect must also make some estimate of what the total ultimate change in form of services is likely to be.

The corporate nature of Catholic worship is again now being stressed. Catholic churchgoing has for centuries been highly individualistic. The congregation should participate in the liturgical action and not merely watch it. Baptism is being restored as the corporate act of the local assembly: but it is still conducted as a private ceremony held at a time to suit the parents and which only they and their friends attend. The architect must make corporate baptism possible in a church, even though it may not be practised for some time.

The existence of societies within the parish is always important in its social life and the architect should find out which they are, what they do, and whether they are to be accommodated in any way.

3.2 The main services

The six main services of the Catholic church are:

- Mass
- the Easter liturgy (Holy Week ceremonies)
- Baptism
- Marriage
- Burial of the dead
- Devotions.

Other liturgical activities include: blessing, dedication, consecration, confirmation, ordination.

3.3 Church design

Apart from the altar, the general principles of layout and design are the same as for the Church of England. These are shown, with separate altar details, in Part B.

4 UNITED REFORMED CHURCH

4.1 Origins and buildings

This was established by the merger of the Presbyterian Church of England and the Congregational Church of England, followed by most of the Scottish Congregationalists. It also merged with the Churches of Christ a few years ago. A number of English Congregational Churches did not join the United Reformed Church (URC) and continue as the Congregational Union.

4.2 Presbyterian

The Presbyterian Church of Scotland (PCS) remains separate; it claims to be a continuation of the Celtic church.

During the reformation one of the leaders, John Knox, became greatly influenced by the Swiss John Calvin and it was basically his system of church government and structure, as well as much of his theology, which he brought into the church. This system of church government by courts, basically government by the members of the church congregation, is known as 'presbyterian', as opposed to 'episcopalian' which is government by an appointed hierarchy.

4.3 Ways of worship

The Reformation established the doctrine of 'the priesthood of all believers': it was not necessary for any human being to come between God and a worshipper, and the only mediator accepted was Jesus Christ. There is therefore no good theological reason for a chancel in its literal sense of a 'railed-off area' in a URC or Presbyterian church.

All take part in the full worship and sacramental act. The sanctuary or chancel area is therefore now simply where the central act takes place, but the congregation are essentially participants in that act and the nearer they are to it the better. There is now a fairly general departure from the earlier rectangular form of church in favour of a more open form where the sense of gathering the people round the Word and sacrament, as represented by the pulpit and communion table, can be expressed.

Present thinking seeks to emphasise the close links between the worship room and the rooms for secular purposes, so that there may not be a complete divorce between the weekday and Sunday activities of the congregation. The economic situation may well lead to multi-purpose buildings where only a portion is kept entirely for worship, while the rest is used for other purposes, with the use of partitions and screens.

4.4 The main services

There is a wide variety of practices within the URC (reflecting Presbyterian, Congregational and Churches of Christ practices), and local churches can adopt their own practices. The types of services normally held are:

- normal morning public worship
- evening worship, which increasingly is taking a variety of forms, or may be largely a repetition of the morning service
- as above with addition of one or other of the sacraments, holy communion or baptism
- as above, with ordination of elders or admission of new communicants
- marriages.

Funeral services are infrequent.

Following the merger with the Churches of Christ, the URC now recognises and practises both that denomination's adult baptism by immersion (for which a baptistry is required, see Section 7) and infant baptism using a font.

4.5 Minister

The ordinary conduct of worship is left almost entirely to the minister who may choose to remain in the pulpit for the whole service or may take part of the service from a prayer desk or a lectern, or from behind the table, using the pulpit only for preaching. The minister may move from the pulpit to the communion table to receive the offering, and will certainly do so to administer the sacrament. The font will of course be used for administering baptism, and the front of the sanctuary steps for admission of new communicants or for ordination of elders.

4.6 Church design

The elders in the URC (and the members of the Kirk Session in the PCS) normally sit among the congregation. While there is great variety in the way services are conducted, most of the speaking is normally done by the minister. The congregation sit for prayers and do not kneel in the pews. The pews are seen as an extension of the communion table, so the congregation is, in effect, sitting around the table. Worshippers remain in their seats throughout the services, the elements of communion being passed around by the elders.

Baptism must take place in the face of the congregation and the font or baptistry should therefore be visible to all. The font should be in advance of, and probably to one side of, the communion table and at a slightly lower level. It can be movable but should have a permanent site in the sanctuary. It need *not* be at the entrance to the church. There are no special design requirements for Christmas or Easter services.

A central aisle is desirable for marriage ceremonies.

The choir should be visible to the congregation but should not be in the sanctuary.

There is little social activity connected with worship but ancillary accommodation for social and educational purposes may be needed outside the hours of service.

Many aspects of design are similar to those for the Church of England. The main differences are listed below:

- The communion table is a table and not an altar. It is usually rectangular but other shapes are not precluded. Basic sizes are given in Section 10.
- A large lectern is not essential but where provided should be to the sizes shown in Section 11. Sometimes pulpit and lectern are designed in one piece with upper and lower levels.
- Pulpit may be centrally in front or to one side of the table or, more rarely, behind the table. It should not be more elevated than is required for the congregation to see the preacher. General design is as shown in Section 11.
- A chair for the minister is provided centrally behind the communion table with often at least one additional chair on each side for elders. Alternatively seats for elders may be provided against the back wall of the sanctuary.

- A meeting room should be provided in addition to a vestry. This is where the elders (or the Kirk Session in the PCS) meet before services and where communion is prepared.

5 THE SALVATION ARMY

5.1 Origins

The Salvation Army arose from evangelical meetings conducted in east London during 1865 by the Reverend William Booth, a minister of the Methodist New Connection. Booth decided to take the church to the people. His services were held in the open air, in tents and in theatres: later he built barracks and citadels in which his converts could hold their meetings. His services were sensational: he used brass bands playing secular tunes to accompany hymns; converts (soldiers) wore uniform. He became a 'general' and directed the organisation in quasi-military style. Men and women had equal rights in office. Booth regarded social work, care of the poor and rehabilitation of the outcast as an essential part of his Christian mission.

The Christian mission, as it was first called, grew beyond all expectations and in 1878 became known as the Salvation Army. In its belief, it is orthodox, evangelical and prophetic. The corps assembles for worship in a hall – a multi-purpose building sometimes called a citadel, temple or barracks. Sometimes within the complex there are two halls, for senior and junior soldiers respectively. Religious services and social activities may be conducted in either or both halls.

5.2 Ceremonies

Ceremonies may be divided into two types:

- Ordinary services held on Sunday – morning, afternoon, and evening
- Ceremonies applicable to marriages, funerals, memorial services, covenants, swearing-in of soldiers and presentation of colours (these may be embodied within one of the ordinary meetings).

The architectural implications are shown in Figures 32.8 to 32.13.

5.3 Design of the assembly hall

There will be no communion service and visually there will be no elevation or placing of the sacred elements in a part of the building. The font, lectern, pulpit, communion table and altar are not essential to the Salvation Army form of worship. In every Salvation Army hall there is a place for the mercy seat, Figure 32.14. This is a simple wooden form, usually placed at the front of the platform in front of the congregation, and is a place where Christian and non-Christian penitents may kneel at any time.

Platform

The platform will be required to accommodate, at various times, officers taking a leading part in the services; the band (possibly a visiting one which may be larger than that designed for); the songster brigade or a visiting choir.

The size of the platform will depend on local conditions and requirements but approximately 0.5 to 0.6 m² per person (seated in rows) should be allowed. The platform should not be less than about 4–5 m depth, but will normally be more. Its height above the hall floor should not normally be less than 760 mm or more than 1100 mm but sight-lines must be considered in relation to a level floor both on the platform and in the hall.

If there is a gallery there must be a view of the mercy seat from every seat. Movable seats, not fixed pews, are always used both on the platform and in the hall: flexibility is important.

Hall

As a first estimate for the overall area of the hall, allow 0.56 m² for each person to be accommodated. Aisles should not be less than 1.35 m wide. The space between the front edge of the mercy seat and the front face of the congregational seating should not be less

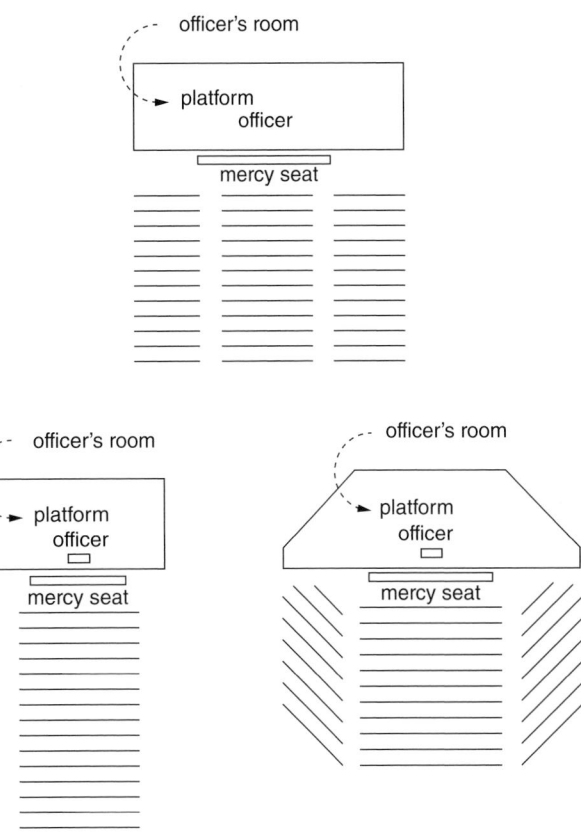

32.8 *Salvation Army: possible basic arrangements. Note that access from officers' room to platform may be on either a side or rear wall*

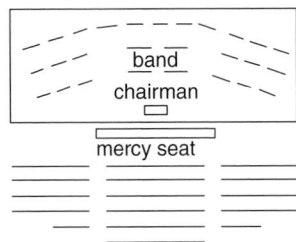

32.9 *Praise meeting or festival*

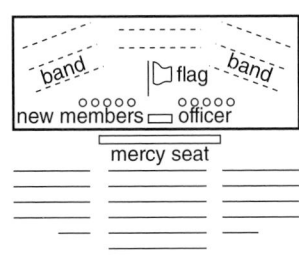

32.10 *Swearing-in ceremony*

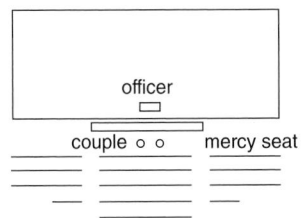

32.11 *Wedding*

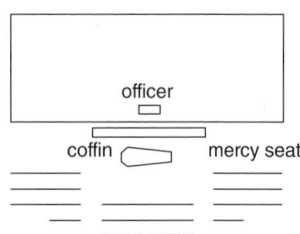

32.12 *Funeral*

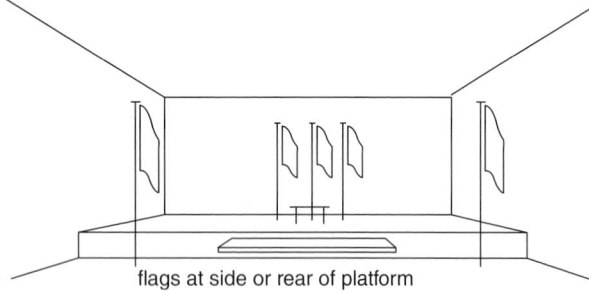

flags at side or rear of platform

32.13 *Presentation of colours*

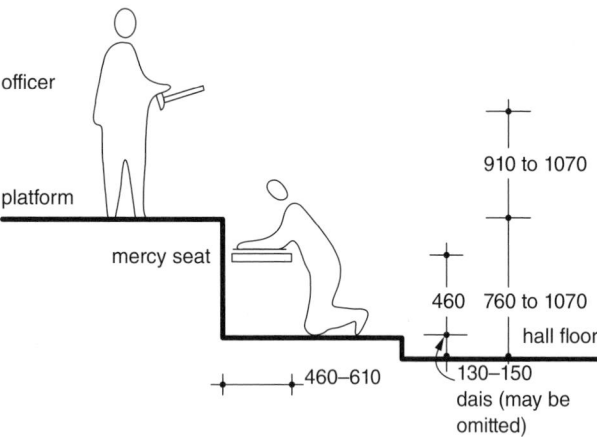

32.14 *Mercy seat*

than 1.5 m. A wide rectangle, polygon or square will be a more satisfactory shape than a long narrow rectangle.

The requirements will be for a reasonable standard of acoustics for speech, choral singing and brass band playing. There should be a reasonable level of natural lighting and a reasonable standard of artificial illumination, both on the platform and in the body of the hall. The ventilation in most cases should be natural.

Officers' room
The officers' room (vestry) is used as a meeting-place by leaders or chairmen of meetings and officers of the Census Board who will assemble in the room before taking their place on the platform. The room should accommodate between two and ten persons. Corps records will be kept in this room. Lavatory accommodation will be required, normally one unit for each sex.

Cloakrooms
Lavatory accommodation should be provided for both sexes near or adjacent to the entrance vestibules of the senior or junior halls. This will be required for women in the songster room and for men in the band room.

Storage
Storage will be required in a band room for brass band instruments, music stands and music. The room will also be used for assembly, briefing and cloakroom. Minimum area shown will usually be 23–28 m^2. Instruments are stored in individual lockers to suit sizes of instruments with a small store for reserve instruments and cupboard with shelves for music.

Storage will be required in a songster room for a wind-type portable organ or electric portable organ with amplifier, and music. The room will also be used for assembly, briefing and cloakroom for the women members who would number about 20 to 30 in an average-sized brigade: 18.5 m^2 would be a minimum area.

Where there are junior and senior corps activities, there may be a junior band and singing company (junior choir). Storage will be required for brass band instruments for this junior band and for music for the singing company.

Where there is a separate junior hall, storage compartments will be contained in that hall. Other social and club activities may also require storage.

6 METHODIST CHURCH

6.1 Origins
The Methodist Church grew out of the Church of England during the eighteenth century and was founded by John and Charles Wesley. A distinct feature of the new movement was the introduction of lay preachers or, as they came to be known, local preachers. The strong emphasis on evangelical preaching is rooted in the Methodist tradition: 'Methodism is nothing if it is not evangelical.'

The church or chapel is normally reserved for worship alone, although meetings, lectures and musical recitals of a specifically religious character may also take place there. A multi-purpose hall, with a sanctuary that can be screened or curtained off, may also be used for public worship during the early stages of the development of a local congregation. There may be other units within the complex such as classrooms, club rooms and assembly halls, both for religious and secular purposes.

6.2 Ceremonies and buildings
The kind of church required today will seat between 100 and 300 people. The influence of the liturgical movement is shown in certain specific ways, and particularly in a new emphasis on the place of the sacraments in the life of the church, and in the increasing use of set prayers and liturgical forms of service. The altar, therefore, is seen again as the Lord's table, used for the family. The font is no longer viewed as making possible a semi-magical act. It is the place at which and the means by which the person baptised, whether child or adult, is sacramentally incorporated into the body of Christ. This rediscovery of the laity, the Lord's table and the font has to be considered in designing a church, for in the end it is the function of the church which is of supreme importance.

These theological rediscoveries will affect the building of a Methodist church:

- in relation to the shape of the church
- in the arrangement of the sanctuary
- in the siting of the choir.

There are normally two services on Sunday, one in the morning and one in the evening. These are conducted by a minister or local preacher from the pulpit, though the earlier part of the service may be conducted from a lectern, the pulpit being used only for the sermon.

Holy Communion is normally celebrated once a month. In order to emphasise the theological statement that the ministry of the Word is of equal importance to the ministry of the Sacrament, pulpit and communion table may be placed close to each other. The minister dispenses the bread and the wine (the latter in small individual glasses) to each of those who have come forward from the congregation to kneel at the communion rail. A small trough or perforated shelf should be fitted to the inside of the communion rail, about 50 mm or 65 mm deep and slightly lower than the top of the rail, where communicants may place the empty wine glasses. See also Section 9, for dimensions of communion rails.

All other main services are similar to Church of England practice and the architectural requirements are the same, although a credence table is not required near the communion table. Specific guidance is contained in *The Methodist Church builders' decalogue* (from the Methodist Property Division, Central Buildings, Oldham Street, Manchester MI IJQ).

7 BAPTIST CHURCH AND BAPTISTRIES

7.1 Introduction
The chief difference in this denomination is the practice of deferring baptism to the age at which the person is able to make his or her own choices, normally 13 or older. This practice (often referred to as 'Believer's Baptism') is shared by other churches such as some of the URC and many independent churches.

The adult, known as 'candidate', is baptised through total immersion in public ceremony in the context of a service of worship. This requires the church to have a baptistry appropriate for such use, Figure 32.15.

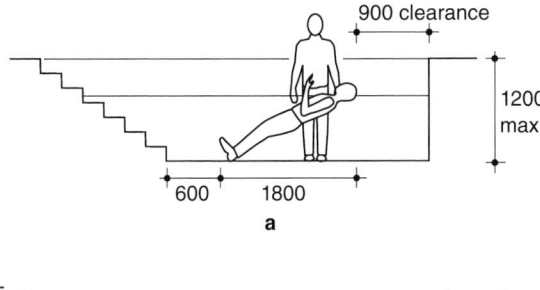

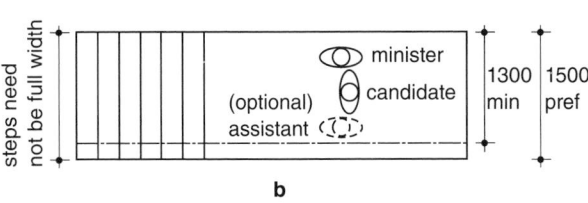

32.15 *Baptistry pool for adult baptism as used in Baptist, some URC churches and a number of others: a section, b plan*

7.2 Baptism ceremony
The minister will enter the baptistry first, followed by the candidate. If more than one candidate is to be baptised they will be dealt with one at a time. The minister may speak briefly, and the candidate may also make a personal statement (or may have done so earlier in the service). It follows that that minister and candidate should be visible while standing in the baptistry, ideally from the shoulders up. If only the head is visible the effect can become somewhat incongruous. The candidate turns to face the steps (unless there are steps at both ends of the baptistry) for the practical reason that they will be unable to see clearly when leaving the baptistry, due to water in their eyes. The minister faces the congregation.

The minister then supports the candidate by the shoulders, pronounces a blessing, lowers the candidate backwards into the water, submerging them completely, and immediately raises them again. The candidate leaves the baptistry, usually supported or guided by the minister and/or other assistants, to ensure they do not trip or slip.

On occasions, and particularly if either minister is small in stature (and ministers in the denominations practising adult baptism include women) or the candidate is large in stature, the minister may be assisted by another member of the congregation. Exceptionally, if the candidate is infirm, they may kneel.

7.3 Key dimensions
Width, absolute minimum 1300 mm, but this is known from experience to be inadequate when an assistant is present, and 1500 mm

to 1600 mm is better. The steps need not be the full width of the baptistry;

Length, about 3300 mm, determined by the tallest likely candidate (95th percentile) plus space to move and clearance at the 'head' end of the baptistry;

Depth (surrounding floor level to floor of baptistry), 1200 mm or a little less, determined by the shoulder height of minister and candidates (5th percentile);

Steps, suggested rise going and step profile to Part 'M' of the Building Regulations;

Figure 32.15 shows a rectangular plan, but other arrangements meeting the functional requirements are acceptable. The views of the local congregation should be sought.

7.4 Other functional requirements
The baptistry may be located either on a dais or in the body of the church; it is normally covered by a removable floor when not in use. In either case sightlines should be considered. If in the body of the church, consideration should be given to temporary edge protection when open to avoid accidents.

The removable floor sections should be as light and manoeuvrable as practicable. These will normally have to be moved by one or two of the congregation who may well be elderly or un-athletic, and the design of the floor sections should allow for this.

Floor surfaces. The baptistry base and the steps should have a non-slip finish. Adjacent floor surfaces may need protection.

Water supply needs to be available to fill the baptistry in a reasonable time (less than one hour), and drainage is needed to empty it in about half an hour. The floor of the baptistry should fall gently towards the outlet.

The drainage system should not be embedded or inaccessible. With infrequent use, water traps on the drainage line will tend to dry out. Any leak in the drainage system or the baptistry will be discovered at the most inconvenient moment. Suppliers should be asked to confirm that their specifications allow for long-term dry conditions with occasional use filled. The design life of the complete baptistry installation should equal the design life of the building without any significant maintenance.

Water heating. It is normal to temper the water temperature; the water need not be warm, but should not make the candidates gasp on entry! It is probably inefficient to design the main heating and hot water system to supply such a large volume of slightly warmed water. Portable electric immersion heaters have been used, but all fittings will need to be to an appropriate IP rating.

Changing spaces are required for candidates and minister, separate for opposite sexes, and possibly for the minister. They should be close to the room containing the baptistry, and normally in multi-purpose rooms, but consideration should be given to privacy.

8 SOCIETY OF FRIENDS

8.1 Origins
The Society of Friends (Quakers) originated through the experiences and preaching of George Fox (1624–1691). Early Quakers reacted strongly against the current religious practices and liturgy of the established church. All through their history, Quakers have been concerned with a sense of duty to the community.

Because Friends believe that God can communicate with man direct, they do not partake of the outward sacraments. They have no separated priesthood, they do not require their members to subscribe to a creed, and their worship does not make use of a liturgy. They are, however, in broad agreement with the main emphases of Christian belief, and would claim to be both orthodox and evangelical.

8.2 Ceremonies and buildings
In a meeting for worship, Friends gather in silence as a congregation of seeking souls, and 'wait upon the Spirit'. No one directs the worship. Out of the 'gathered' silence of united worship, one or

another may be led to engage in vocal ministry or in prayer or to read from the scriptures. There is no music or hymn singing.

The building must be designed to help the quiet worship and the vocal ministry of the participants. There is no observance of the Lord's supper or orthodox communion service; no baptism or initiation ceremonies involving ritual. There will therefore be no need for font, lectern, pulpit or altar.

Sizes of meeting halls vary, but they will mostly be designed to accommodate fifty Friends or fewer. A square, rectangular or polygonal room may meet the requirements. It is likely that seating will be required in a square or a circle. Meetings may prefer fixed or movable, tiered or level seating.

There is no need for a table in the meeting room, though there normally is one to act as a focal point. The position is not usually literally at the centre of the room; the seating will be arranged in the way felt by the group concerned to be most conducive to a good meeting for worship, and the table, if placed anywhere, will be fitted in with the general arrangement of the room. Its main use is for business meetings.

Society of Friends meeting halls when not required for worship are often used by other denominations, or for secular purposes of an appropriate nature. Other accommodation might include a multi-purpose hall, library, small kitchen foyer and cloakrooms and a caretaker's flat.

9 PASTORAL CENTRES

9.1 Form and function

Pastoral centres are alternatives to conventional church buildings and are increasingly being considered where there is to be a large new population with non-existent or inadequate ministry and buildings.

A pastoral centre could take many forms – basically it would be a small building or suite of rooms with facilities for consultation, meetings, refreshments and occasional worship. It could be a modified house, a transportable structure or a specifically designed community building: it could even be a converted shop or a caravan. Its purposes would be to shelter a Christian 'presence', comparable to a doctor's surgery or a citizen's advice bureau: ministers would be present for counselling and office work at advertised hours. Small meetings could be held and modest hospitality offered. It could be used for acts of worship though it would be linked to a major worship centre elsewhere. It should be sited in the local centre and could be integrated into a complex of amenity buildings or a shopping centre. If resources were available, and if the population distribution were suitable, two pastoral centres might be provided in a neighbourhood of 6000 to 10,000 people.

Part B Design Data

10 ALTAR OR COMMUNION TABLE

10.1 Symbolism

The altar symbolises three things:

- the body of Christ
- the altar of sacrifice
- the table of the last supper.

10.2 Canon law

A Church of England altar may be of wood, stone or other suitable material and may be movable. It should be covered with silk or other 'decent stuff' during divine services and with a fair white linen cloth at holy communion. A Roman Catholic altar must be of natural (not reconstructed) stone with the top member (the mensa) in one piece and containing the relics of two canonised martyrs or saints. However, this requirement may be fulfilled by a small portable altar which is in effect an altar stone often about 300 mm square (or less) and 50 mm deep containing a sealed cavity (the sepulchre) for the relics. The altar may be fixed (stone cemented to the structure) or unfixed (timber with inset portable stone altar as described

above). Only a fixed altar may be consecrated. Alternatively, relics may be sunk into floor below altar.

10.3 Position

The altar must be related to congregational seating in such a way that what is done at it is, and is seen to be, a corporate action of the whole assembly. Altars are being brought further forward in the sanctuary and with congregations grouped around, there is less need for the altar to stand so high as in the past, especially when the priest faces the congregation across the altar.

10.4 Size

For liturgical reasons, altars can be less long but possibly slightly deeper than in the past. Average sizes are shown in Figure 32.16 and anthropometric data in Figure 32.17.

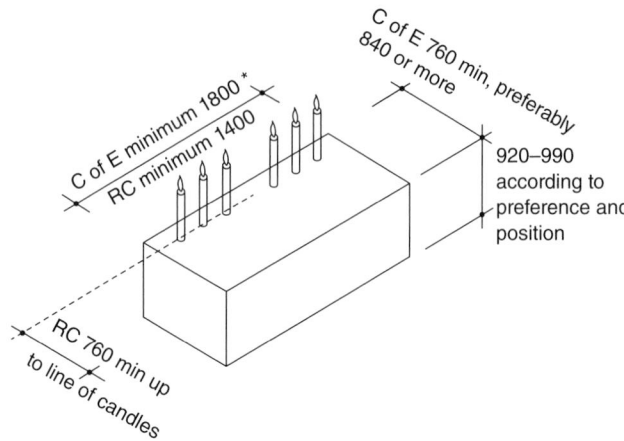

32.16 *Average size of altars. The exact proportions will depend on its position, and whether the priest is facing the congregation or has his back to them. Note that the tabernacle containing the reserved sacrament is not now normally placed on the altar (see section 13)*

10.5 Supports and coverings

Methods of supporting the mensa are shown in Figure 32.18. With the altar now normally nearer the congregation, the question of clothing the altar may need to be rethought. A traditional Church of England altar covering is shown in Figure 32.19.

10.6 Footspace

The platform or base on which the altar rests must be large enough for the number of priests expected to stand around while celebrating the Eucharist. It may be raised one or two steps above the level of the congregation, but in general the altar should be kept as low as possible to avoid any sense of separation between it and the people. Possible dimensions are shown in Figure 32.20.

10.7 Cross and candles

The exact requirements must be discussed with the priest. Candles and cross should not form a barrier between priest and people. Some possibilities for the cross are shown in Figures 32.21 and 32.22; and for the candles in Figure 32.23.

10.8 Communion table

A communion table with table lectern as used in Presbyterian churches is shown in Figure 32.24.

11 SANCTUARY FURNITURE AND PULPIT

11.1 Lectern

This should be in or near the sanctuary but sufficiently apart from the altar to constitute a separate focus, and conveniently sited to be accessible to the congregation to read from, Figure 32.25. Occasionally two lecterns may be asked for, one each side. The lectern must be in

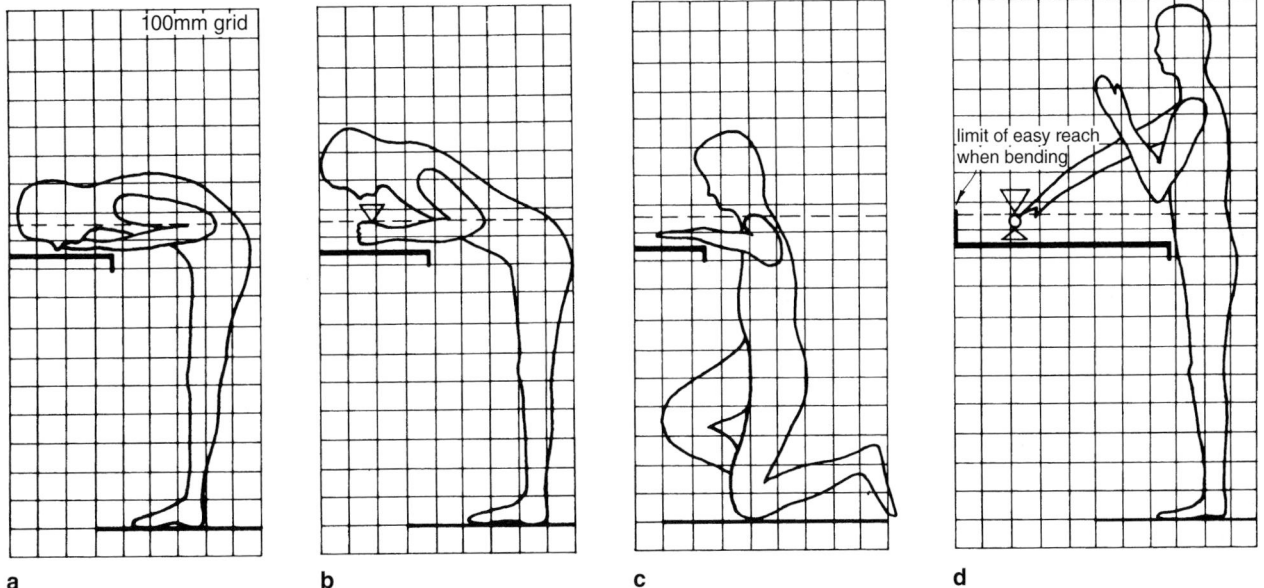

32.17 *Critical actions of priest when standing at the altar. The horizontal dotted lines represents the eye level of the average adult member of the congregation when kneeling. This should preferably not be less than 75 mm above the top of the altar, emphasising the importance of keeping that low. This represents some sacrifice to the priest, since actions a and b are easier if the top is at the traditional height of just over 1 m. a Kissing the surface of the altar. b Saying the words of consecration. c Genuflecting. This position emphasises the value of recessing the altar supports at least on the priest's side, to prevent him bumping his knee. d Reaching forward when standing upright, illustrating the extent of reach*

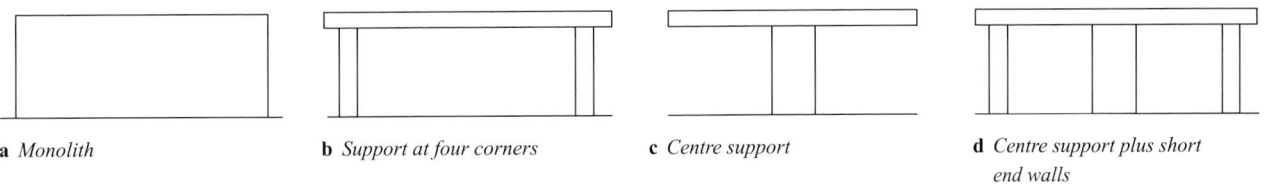

a *Monolith*　　**b** *Support at four corners*　　**c** *Centre support*　　**d** *Centre support plus short end walls*

32.18 *Supporting the mensa (altar top). Note that RC altars should not oversail their supports by more than 150 mm, so that the bishop can pass his thumb over the joints at the Consecration*

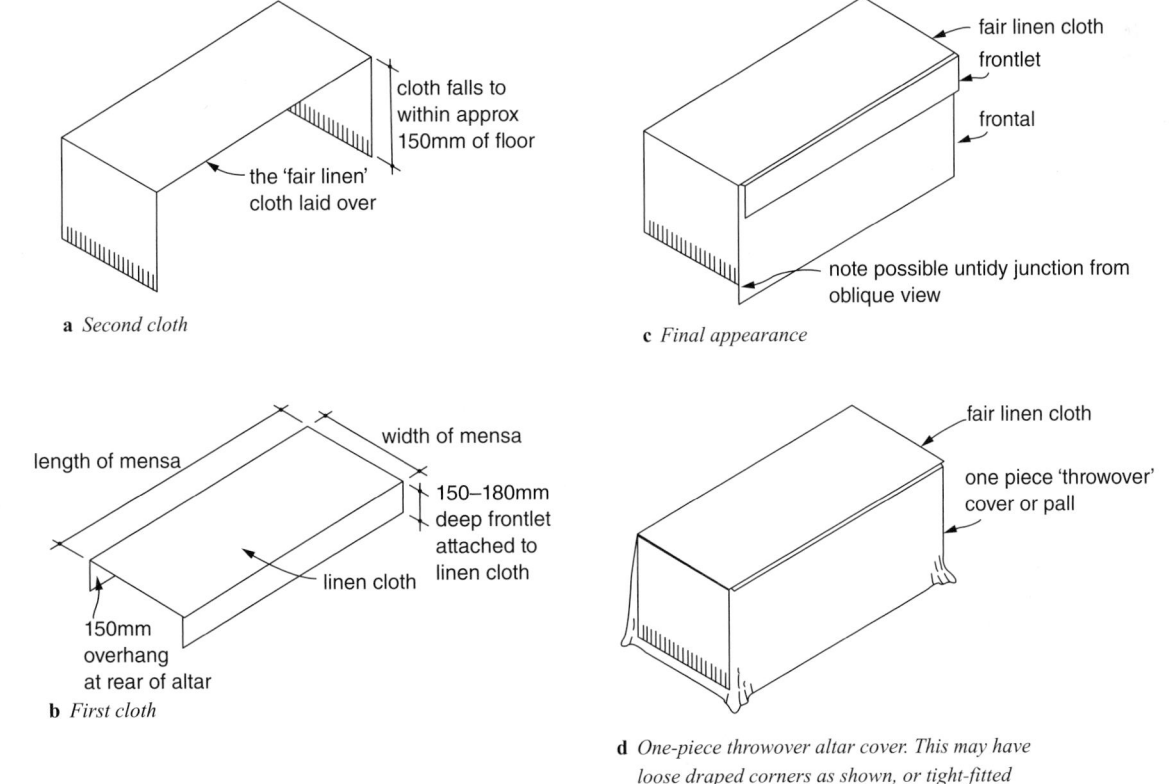

32.19 *Clothing the altar*

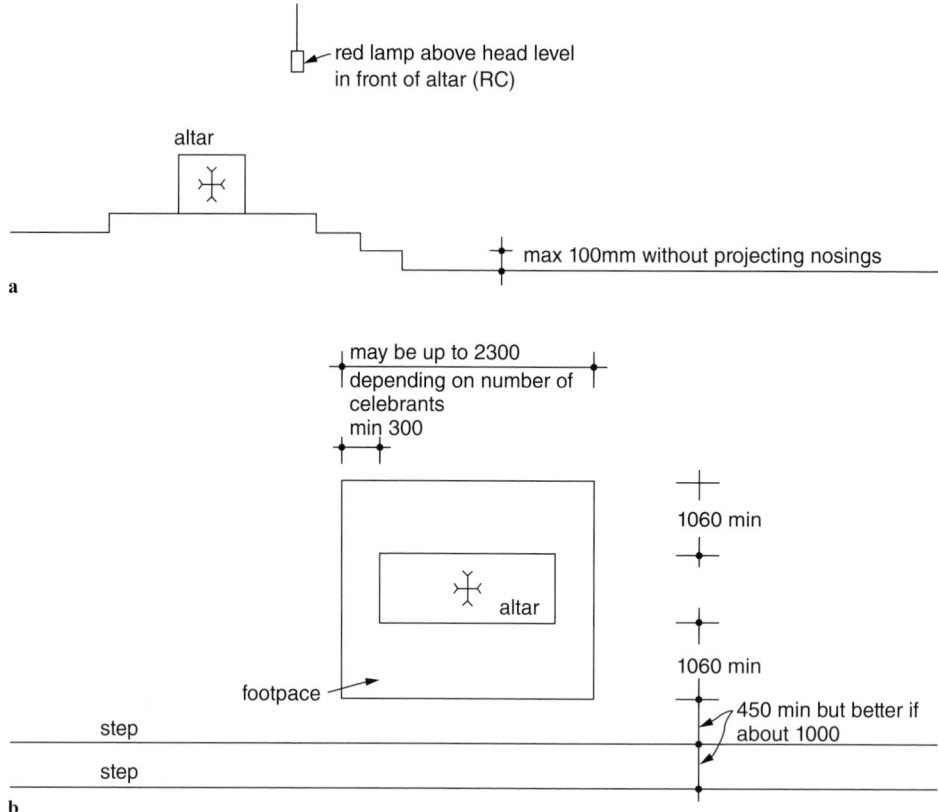

32.20 *Space around the altar. Keep altar as low as possible, usual maximum three steps. Position of the altar can also be defined by use of a canopy, structure, lighting, floor patterns, etc. a Section. b Plan*

32.21 *The cross behind the altar at a height where it will not be obscured by the priest. Crosses are not usually placed on the altar in 'facing the people' churches*

32.22 *The cross forward of the altar to one side or suspended above*

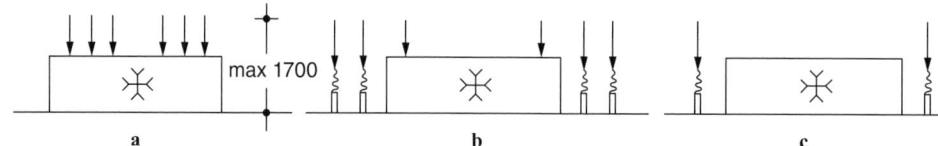

32.23 *Arrangement of candles. a, b Six candles. c Two candles only. Candles may also be placed on a step lower than the altar to reduce height and obstruction to view*

a position where everybody can see the reader's face including those within the sanctuary. It may be fixed or movable, and it may also serve as a pulpit. Dimensions are shown in Figure 32.26.

11.2 Altar rail

A rail may be dispensed with in some churches, but most will still provide lengths of rail for kneeling to receive communion. It need not be continuous, but must be rigid and firm. Minimum dimensions are given in Figures 32.27 and 32.28.

11.3 Credence table

This serves as a sort of sideboard for water and wine, but check if anything else is to be placed on it (e.g. offertory money, service books, etc.) in which case a shelf below the table may be needed. It should be to the right of the celebrant within the sanctuary but not where it might cause a visual obstruction. It could be a shelf instead of a freestanding table. Dimensions will vary from about 610 × 760 mm to 1200 × 460 mm, with a minimum height of 820 mm.

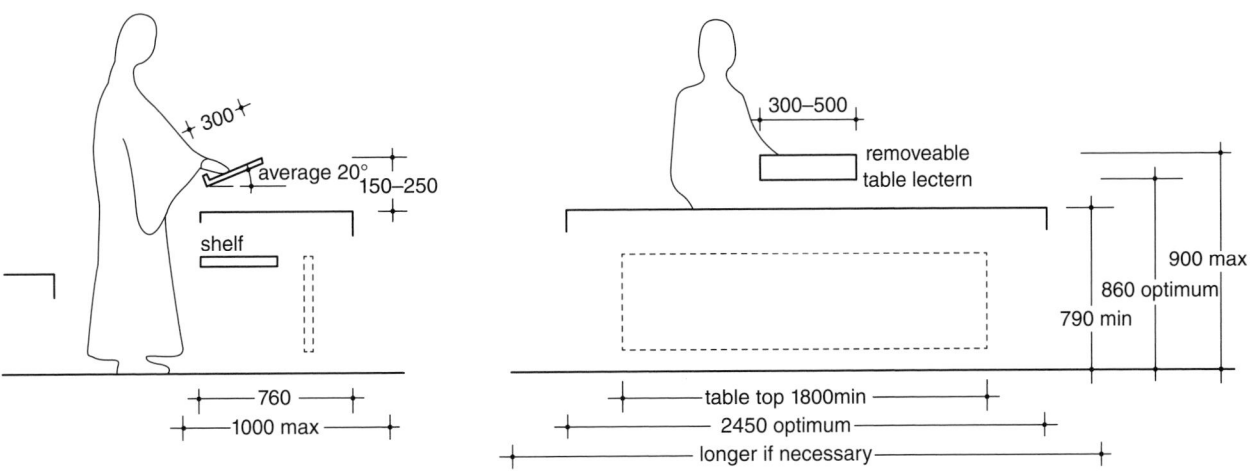

32.24 *Communion table with table lectern for use in Presbyterian churches instead of the altars described above*

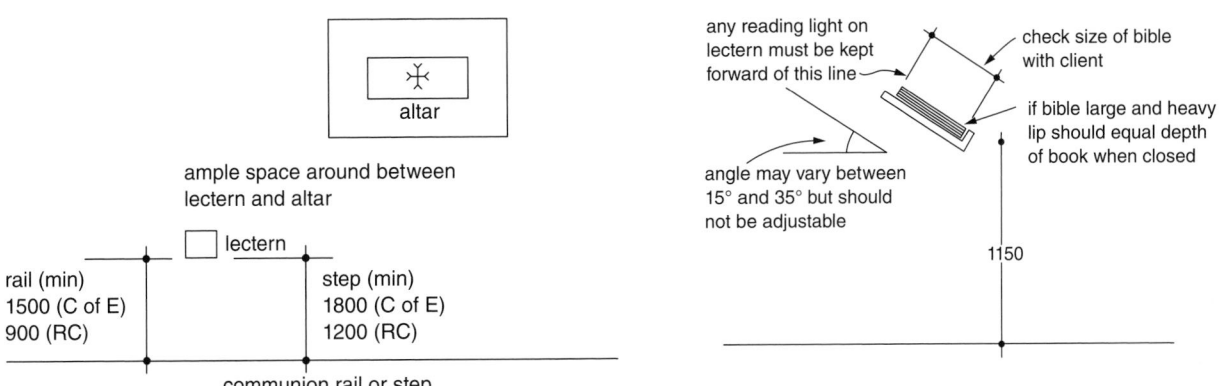

32.25 *Minimum dimensions around lectern depending on whether communion rail or only a communion step is provided*

32.26 *Minimum requirements for lectern*

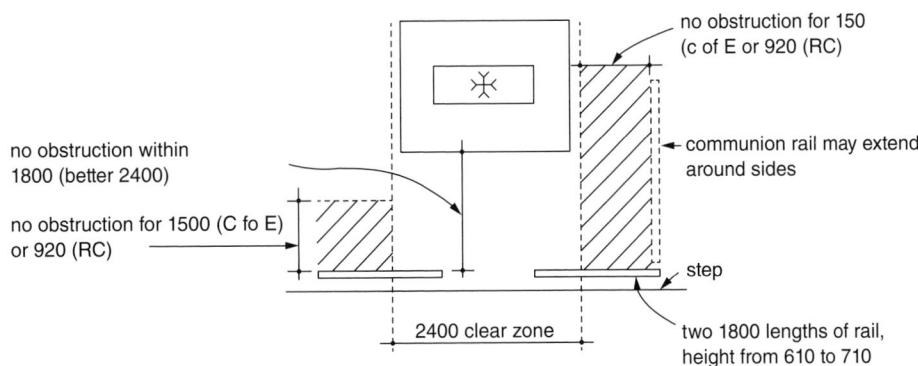

32.27 *Clear space requirements around communion rail*

11.4 Seating for officiants

These will vary considerably and requirements must be established with the local community. Ceremonial seats for priests. In Roman Catholic churches the 'president's seat' will be on the centre line behind the altar, raised up on one or two steps, Figure 32.29. The seat, which is used by the priest, must not look like a bishop's throne and will usually not have a back to it. The bishop's throne is portable, and placed in front of the altar whenever he visits the church. In Church of England churches it is often better to have the ceremonial seat (which is used by the bishop) at the side of the sanctuary facing the altar.

Incidental seating should be kept to a minimum. It will be needed for additional priests, servers, and lay people on special occasions. It will usually be in the form of benches at the side of the sanctuary.

Stalls will be needed (especially in Church of England churches) for priests at matins and evensong at the side of the sanctuary. Dimensions are similar to those for congregational seating (see Section 14) except that as priests are vested they will need more room to move in and out. Surface for resting a book should be deeper (say, 300 mm) and almost horizontal – not sloping – with a shelf below.

11.5 Pulpit

This should be sited outside but close to the sanctuary. No particular location is now insisted on apart from functional reasons of good sight and sound. Minimum internal area is about 1–2 m². Access should desirably be from the side (if from back, fit a door).

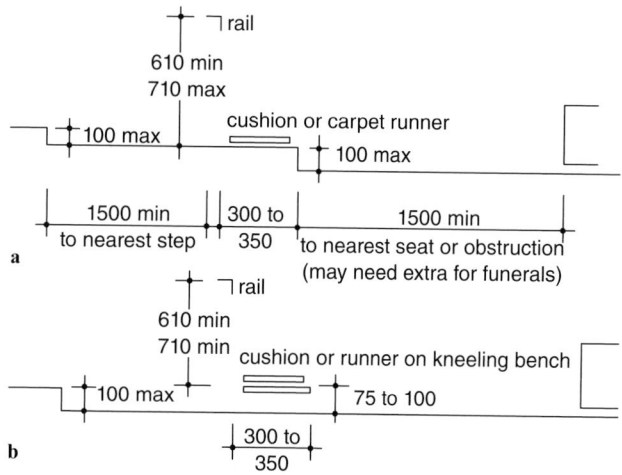

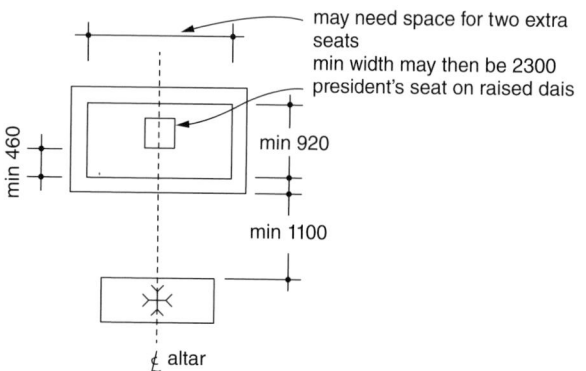

32.28 *Dimensions for altar rail (i.e. outside central zone of sanctuary). In a new Roman Catholic church there is unlikely to be a second step in the sanctuary, and the minimum unobstructed distance on the sanctuary side of the rail is 920mm. It is also normal for the whole of the sanctuary to be one step above the nave, but too many steps should be avoided. a With stepped floor. b With flat floor*

32.29 *Dimensions around the President's seat*

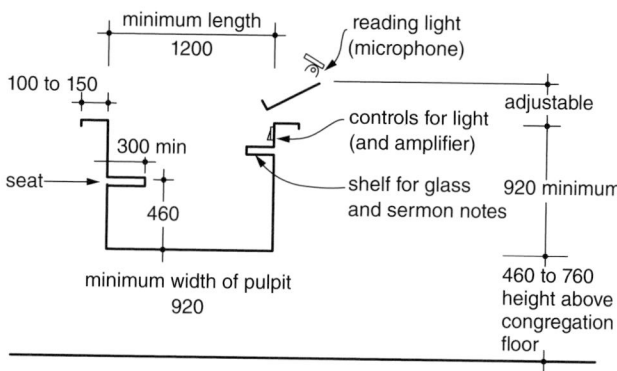

32.30 *Pulpit dimensions*

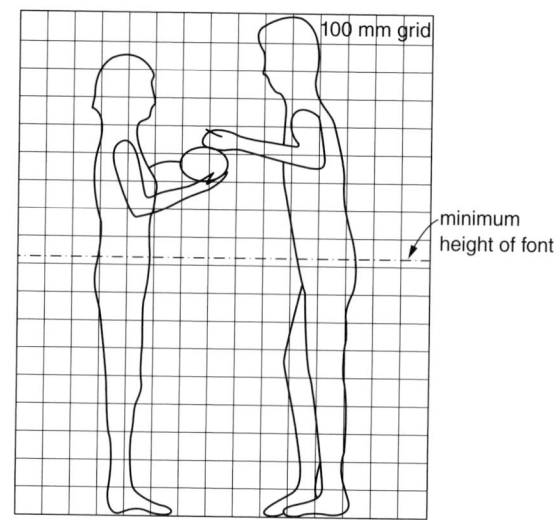

32.31 *Anthropometric diagram showing the critical action at the font*

Other details are shown in Figure 32.30. A Presbyterian pulpit may be behind the altar or at either side.

12 FONT

12.1 Description

In Roman Catholic churches movable fonts are not permitted and they are not generally approved of in the Anglican communion. They can be used in Presbyterian and Methodist churches. In Church of England churches fresh water is used for each baptism drained to a separate soakaway. In Roman Catholic churches water is blessed once a year and the baptismal water is stored in the font which has two compartments.

12.2 Dimensions and shape

Anthropometric requirements are shown in Figure 32.31. Shape is governed by the needs of the priest (space for service book and other small objects); the comfort of the priest in holding the baby; and the safety of the baby (the priest should not have to lean too far over).

12.3 Position of font

Various alternative positions are shown in Figure 32.32. The font must be approached from the church (congregation) side but be divided from it in some way (e.g. by difference in floor or ceiling levels). It must be in a prominent position and be seen by the congregation when seated, or space provided for most of the congregation to stand around. It should be a separate focus from the altar and therefore possibly not in the sanctuary.

13 RESERVATION OF THE SACRAMENT

13.1 Siting

The reserved sacrament in Roman Catholic churches (the consecrated bread of the Eucharist) is not now normally kept in a tabernacle on the altar. It is normally kept:

- in a separate chapel outside the sanctuary
- in a position which is architecturally important
- where its location will be easily recognised by the congregation.

The requirements are complex and the practice of the local church community must be established and agreed with the Diocesan Advisory Committee. Figures 32.33 and 32.34 show height limitations.

The reserved sacrament is occasionally found also in the Church of England, but is more rare and many methods of reservation are practised. For more explanation see the AJ information sheet 1529 contained in Church buildings.

14 GENERAL ARRANGEMENTS

14.1 Entrance requirements

There are several considerations for designing entrances:

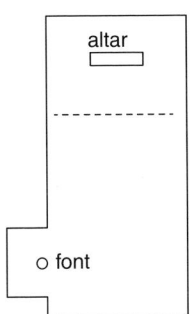

a *In separate baptistery.
Acceptable if only baptism
proper is performed here
with the rest of the service
is in the main body of the church*

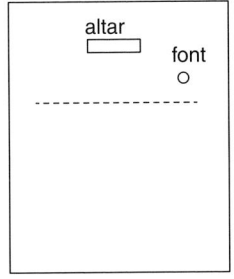

b *Font in sanctuary. It may
compete with altar, or be
made insignificant by it.
But in a Presbyterian church,
the font is often in this position
although lower than the table
and possibly on a side extension
of the lowest sanctuary step*

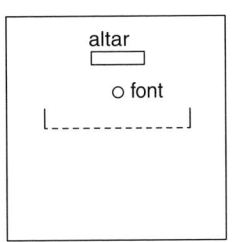

c *As for b, but the font is
also an obstruction to sight*

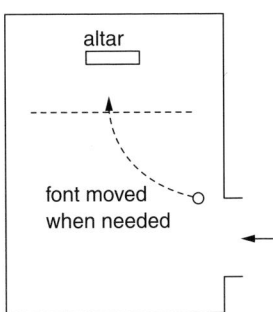

d *Care is needed with a moveable
font to retain the dignity of one
of the church's great sacraments*

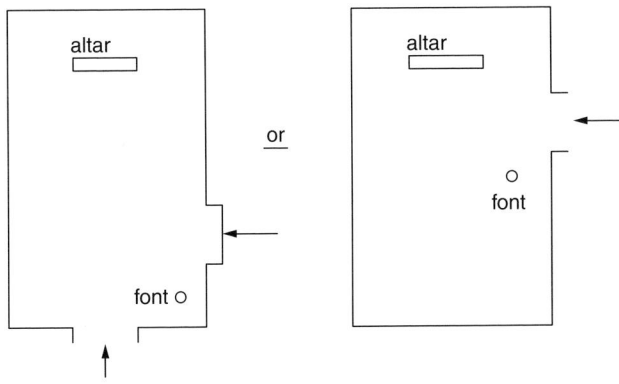

e *and* f *When font is placed near the entrance it is important to have the entrance
near the font and not the font near the entrance! This may mean that the main
entrance is in front of the people's seats and not behind*

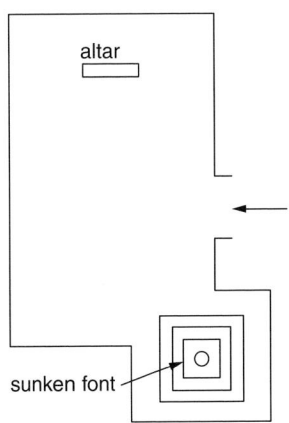

g *The font is sunk into a 'dry pool'
with a 'drowning' symbolism*

32.32 *Variations on font positioning*

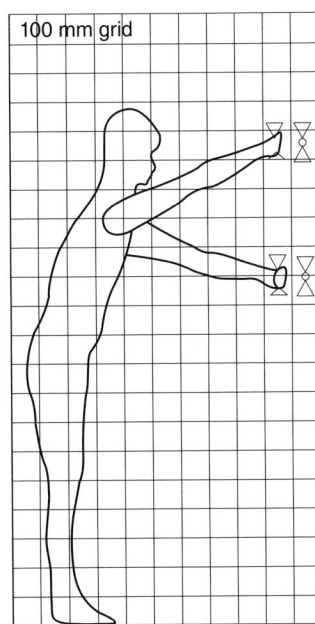

32.33 *Removing ciborium from tabernacle and putting on lower shelf*

- Provide wind lobbies outside entrance doors.
- Minimum clear door width (for processions and funerals) should be 1.7 m (1.1 m in a small church); minimum clear height (for processional cross) 2.3 m, otherwise 2.05 m is sufficient.
- Provide proper access for disabled people (see Designing for the disabled).
- Provide secondary exit door, especially for weddings.
- Provide gathering spaces inside and outside the church as part of the normal exit route where people can naturally gather to talk.
- Where needed (especially in RC churches) place a holy water stoup on the entrance side of each doorway leading into the church. Rims should be 710 to 760 mm above the floor.
- Provide considerable space for notices of all types in a conspicuous position.
- Allow space, where required, for one or two small credence tables just inside the entrance.
- Provide facilities for selling of publications, etc.
- Where possible provide access from the entrance area to the WC and to the sacristy or vestry.
- As a general rule try to keep the purely *secular* activities more in view when the congregation is *leaving* than when entering for a service.

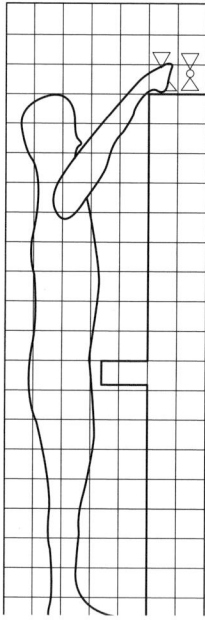

32.34 *Maximum height to give view of back of tabernacle*

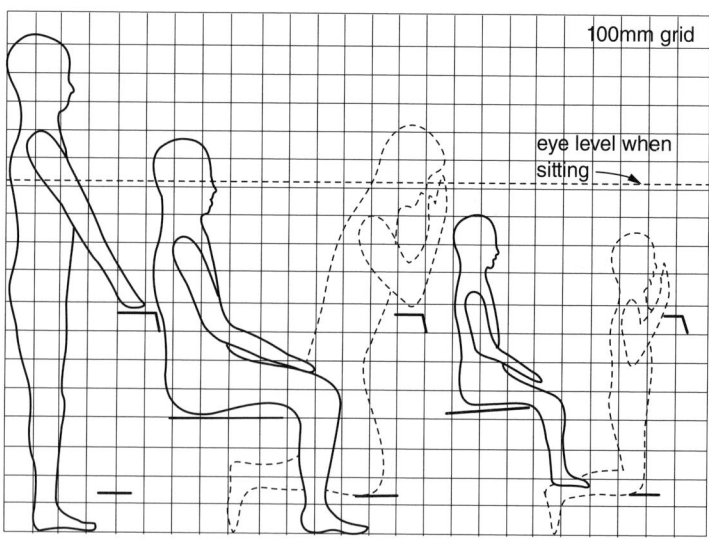

32.35 *Critical dimensions for seating. Black lines indicate one particular solution found very satisfactory in practice. The dotted line indicates 'eye' level when sitting, and concerns the relationship with the altar top*

14.2 Arrangement of seating

The congregation should be continuous with the minister with no strong dividing line between them. Equally, the congregation must be united with one another and all must have good access to circulation and to the sanctuary. Seats facing each other around an altar should not be closer than about 6 m, and nobody should look sideways on to anybody else closer than 1.5 to 3.0 m.

14.3 Spacing and dimensioning of seats

Anthropometric details are given in Figure 32.35. Note also:

- Minimum dimension of seat plus kneeling space front and back is 920 mm. Where congregations do not kneel (e.g. Methodists, Presbyterians), the dimension can be reduced to 760 mm.
- Leave a space of about 280 mm between front edge of seat and back edge of kneeler.

- Allow minimum width of 510 mm per person.
- Maximum length of row is 10 persons (5.1 m) with access from both ends, or 6 persons (3.06 m) with access from one end.
- The ledge for hymn books should be about 150 mm wide (300 mm for the choir).

14.4 Circulation

Basic dimensions are shown in Figure 32.36. Space must be allowed for invalid chairs during the service where the occupant can participate but not block circulation.

14.5 Sound reinforcement

Many churches now use systems of sound amplification of speech, singing and instrumental music. This is particularly important in connection with 'loop' systems for people who are hard of hearing. This is not of course confined to Christian buildings; it applies equally to other religious buildings (e.g. see Section 18.3).

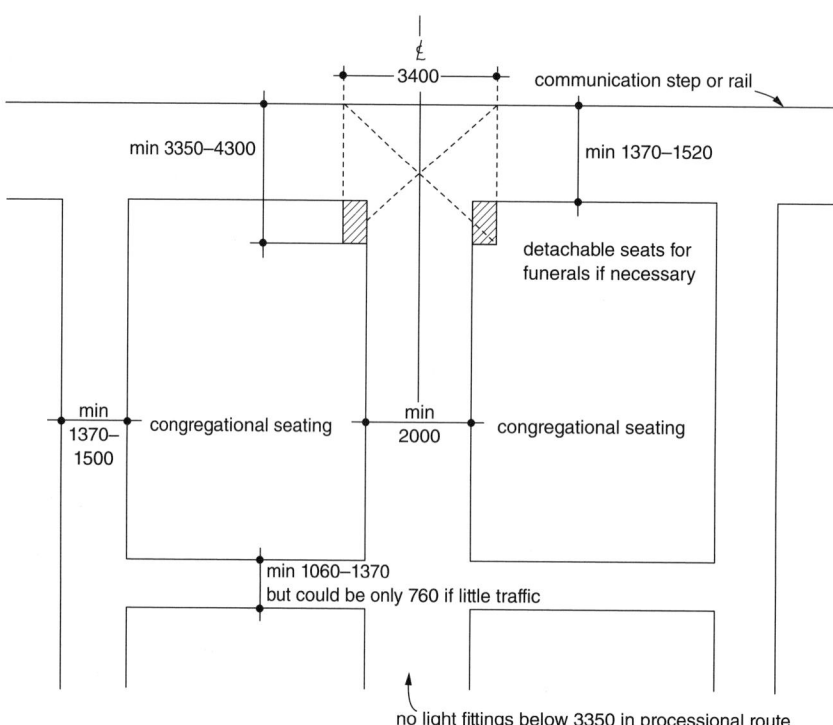

32.36 *Aisle widths. Size and pattern will depend on overall plan and liturgical considerations. Seating may be fan shaped or in blocks around the sanctuary*

Further, the increasing use of miniature and lapel microphones with radio transmitter/receivers linked to such a system enables the person leading the worship to move around when speaking. He or she is no longer tied to the pulpit and lectern. These traditional locations were determined largely by audibility and visibility requirements and the changed circumstances are now affecting their design and location; indeed there is some question whether they are needed at all. This can greatly increase the flexibility available, particularly where the worship function shares in a multi-use space.

15 VESTRIES AND SACRISTIES

15.1 Accommodation
Accommodation requirements will vary considerably. The most lavish could include:

- Priest's sacristy (sometimes called priest's vestry)
- Server's vestry
- Choir vestry and practice/committee room
- Women's choir vestry
- Churchwardens'/interview room
- Cleaners' room ⎫ sometimes placed together
- Flower arrangers' room ⎭ and called working sacristy
- Priest's WC
- Men's and women's WCs
- General storage
- Small kitchen.

15.2 Planning relationships
The tradition of the vestry/sacristy complex opening directly onto the sanctuary has disadvantages: it emphasises the separation of priest from the congregation and makes sharing of toilet facilities difficult. The vestry could be near the entrance (but ensure security) so that priest and procession go through the congregation to their place in the sanctuary. Since children often participate in adult worship for only part of its duration, movement between the main worship space and ancillary rooms should be considered.

There should be a lobby with double doors between the choir vestry and the worship room, and a space out of sight of the congregation for processions to form up. A door direct to the outside is essential as priests and choir should not have to go through the worship room to reach their vestries.

15.3 Detailed design
There is a very wide range of objects and vestments to be stored and the precise requirements must be ascertained. A vestment storage cupboard is shown in Figure 32.37. Doorways should be 1700 mm wide × 2300 mm high.

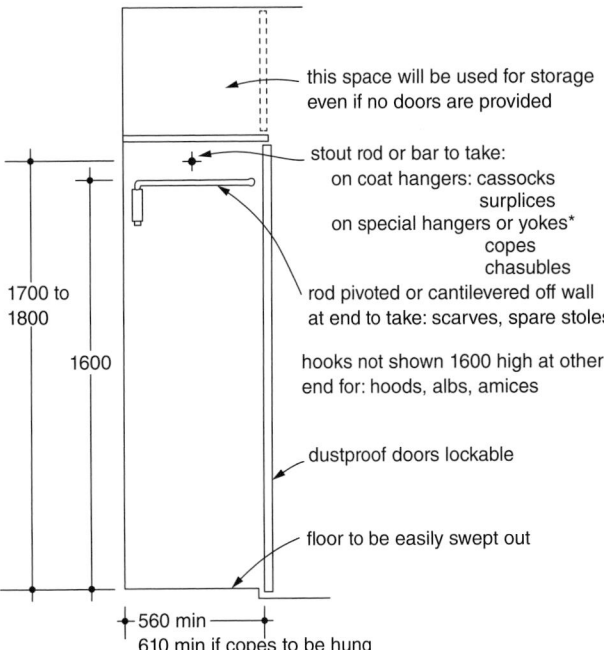

this space will be used for storage even if no doors are provided

stout rod or bar to take:
on coat hangers: cassocks
surplices
on special hangers or yokes*
copes
chasubles
rod pivoted or cantilevered off wall at end to take: scarves, spare stoles

hooks not shown 1600 high at other end for: hoods, albs, amices

dustproof doors lockable

floor to be easily swept out

560 min
610 min if copes to be hung

32.37 *Section through vestment cupboard*
Notes:
*These to be fitted with 'trouser bar' under to take stole and maniple of each set of vestments
†Choir vestry: part of bar at 1320 if there are children in the choir

16 CONFESSIONAL

16.1 Design requirements
Priest and penitent must be able to hear what each other has to say without being overheard by others. The bishop's requirements must be established, and the psychological expectations of the parish.

Either priest and penitent may be enclosed in an acoustically isolated box or, more desirably, they may be visible but placed far enough away from other people to make a physical acoustic barrier unnecessary. Basic dimensions are shown in Figure 32.38.

17 ORGAN AND CHOIR

17.1 Music in church
Use of music in worship can be a highly emotive subject with the type of organ and the placing of the choir two of the most difficult problems. For new churches organs based on the 'werk prinzip' (sometimes called 'neo-classic') should be considered rather than the more traditional Victorian organs with high wind pressures and powerful but muffled tone. The organ builder should be brought in at an early stage of the discussions.

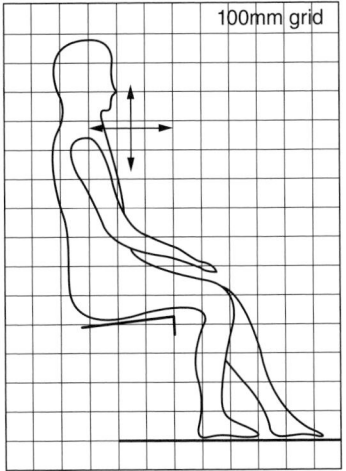

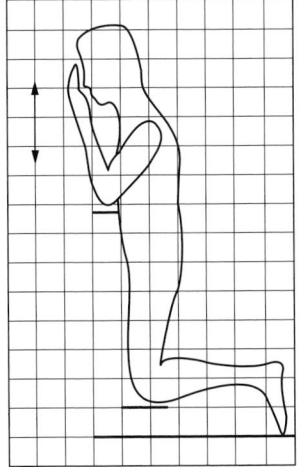

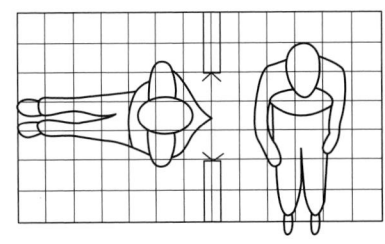

a *Relationship of grille to seated priest*   **b** *and* **c** *Kneeling penitents showing positioning of grille where it will serve both adult and child*   **d** *Plan view of priest and penitent*

32.38 *Anthropometric study of confessional*

17.2 Relationship of musical elements

A few basic principles must be observed:

- The player must be with his or her instrument (i.e. the organ console must be near the pipes), Figure 32.39.
- The choir should be as near as possible to the organ, Figure 32.40.
- Ministers should not be separated from either people or organ, Figure 32.41.
- People should not be placed between the choir and ranks of pipes, Figures 32.40 and 32.41.
- The organ must be in the main volume of the building and raised above the floor so that the pipes are above the heads of the listeners.

32.39 *Bad organ arrangement. Key: o organ, c organ console, p people, ch choir, m minister, a altar*

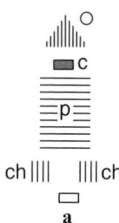

32.40 *Bad position of choir and people, key as for Figure 32.35*

32.41 *Bad position of choir, minister and people, key as for Figure 32.35*

Different possible locations of choir, organ and congregation are shown in Figure 32.42.

Part C Non-Christian places of worship

18 SYNAGOGUES

18.1 History

The original churches evolved from the synagogues set up to supplement and eventually to supplant the Holy Temple in Jerusalem. It is therefore not surprising that they have many elements in common.

There are two main strands of Judaism: orthodox and progressive. As far as the design of the synagogue is concerned the only difference between them is that in the orthodox tradition men and women are rigidly segregated, and women take no direct part in the service.

18.2 The sanctuary

Holy Ark

The principal architectural feature of the synagogue is the *Aron Kodesh* or Holy Ark, Figure 32.43 which contains the Scrolls of the Law. These scrolls, Figure 32.44, are hand written on a very long strip of parchment, and are the first five books of the Old Testament, called the *Torah*. Each end of the parchment is fixed to a stave, and the parchment is rolled around the staves. Because the portion to be read is not immediately accessible, as in a conventional book, it is usual to have several scrolls in the Ark, so that the correct place is not having to be found during the service.

Scrolls, when not being read from, are bound, covered with a mantle and usually adorned with a silver shield, a pointer and *rimonim*. The latter are detachable silver finials, often decorated with small bells, for the top ends of the staves on which the parchment is rolled. The Ark itself is raised and approached up steps from the floor of the synagogue. It should preferably, but not necessarily, be on the eastern wall of the synagogue. It has both doors and a curtain. It should be able to accommodate at least four scrolls, and may well be large enough for many more. It needs internal lighting, *not* operated by a door switch.

Traditionally the Ark is decorated with particular Hebrew texts, by representations of the Tablets of the Ten Commandments, and often by heraldic beasts.

Bima

The service is conducted from a reading desk raised above the floor of the synagogue. Traditionally this should be in the centre of the space, as in the plan of a synagogue in Figure 32.45; but some

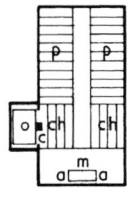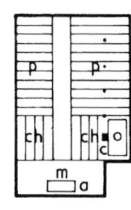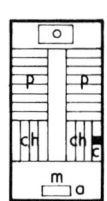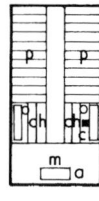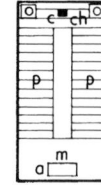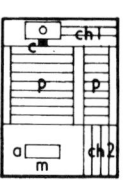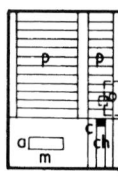

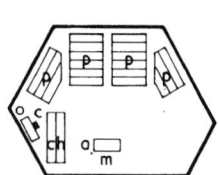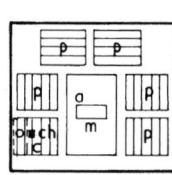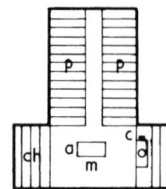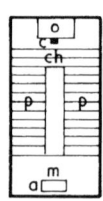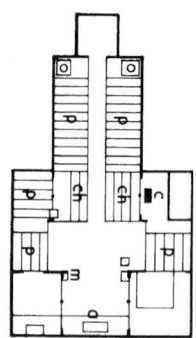

32.42 *Good relationships of organ, choir, congregation and minister/priest. Key as for Figure 32.35*

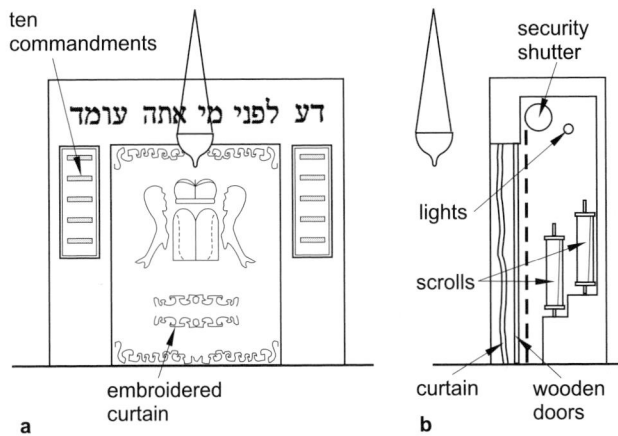

32.43 *Holy Ark. a Elevation, inscription means 'Know before whom you stand', b Section*

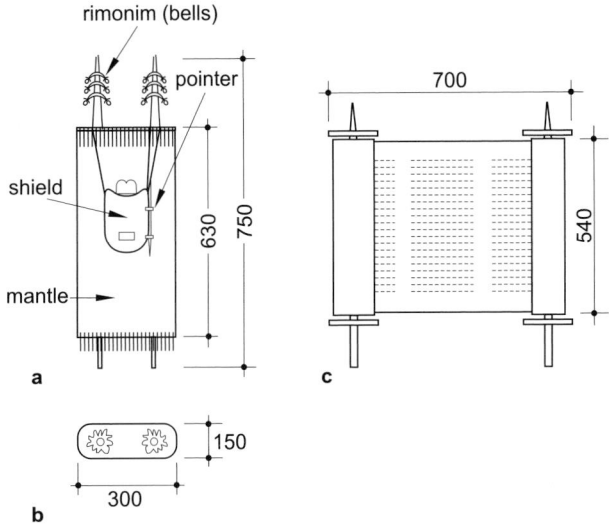

32.44 *Torah scroll, a Elevation, b Plan. c Scroll when open, on reading desk or when elevated*

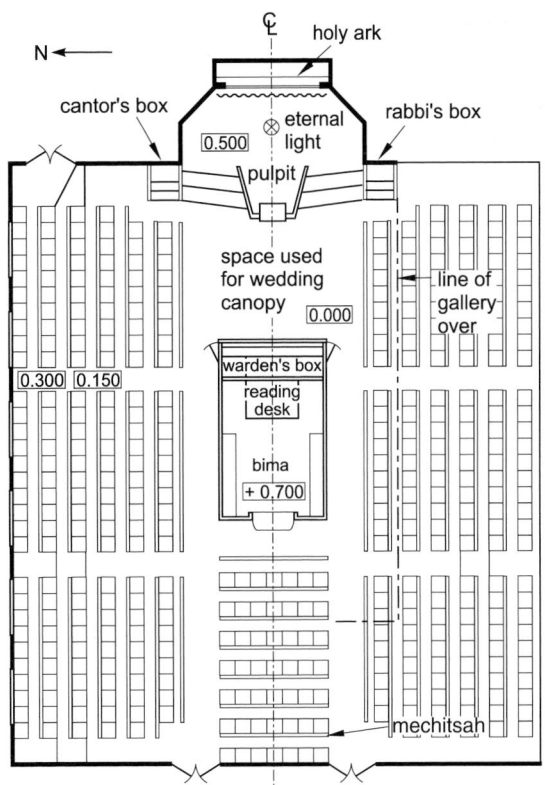

32.45 *Plan of synagogue with central Bima. This would seat 396 men downstairs, 7 women downstairs and 275 women in the gallery*

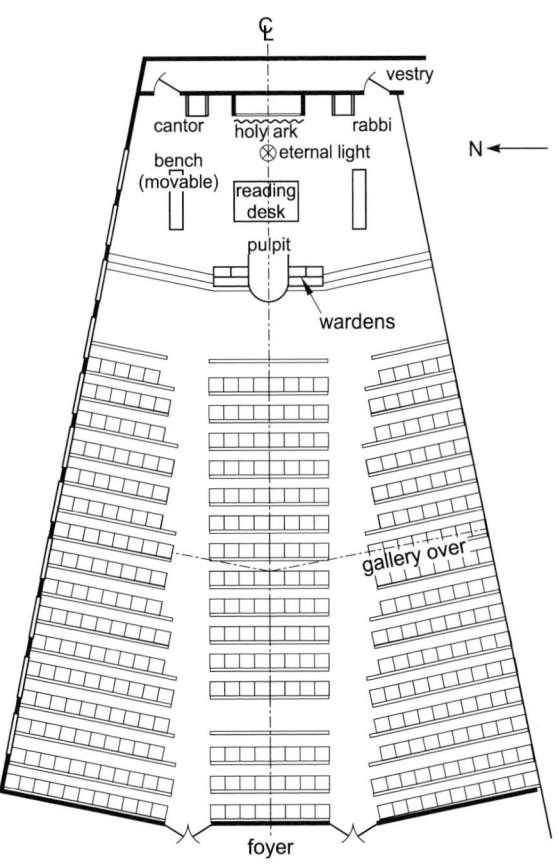

32.46 *Plan of synagogue with Bima before the Holy Ark, seating 376 downstairs and 234 upstairs. For weddings the reading desk and benches are moved aside to accommodate the canopy on the Bima*

synagogues have been designed with the Bima integrated with the Holy Ark, Figure 32.46. There is a custom that the Bima should be three steps above the floor.

The Bima contains a reading desk large enough to hold an open Scroll, with at least five people around three sides of it. The Bima should also be able to accommodate two people holding unused scrolls, with sufficient space for dressing them (separately). Facilities are provided for scroll vestments to be kept while that scroll is being read, including pairs of 'spikes' for the rimonim.

Pulpit
A pulpit is provided for the minister or rabbi from which to deliver a sermon. It is usually placed on the longitudinal axis of the synagogue immediately in front of the Holy Ark, and is not raised above the Ark's level. It does not have a door.

Congregational seating
The congregational seating surrounds the Bima. Since services can be very long (on *Yom Kippur* they take the whole day), the seats have to be comfortable. It is common for them to have lockable boxes beneath, as on the Sabbath orthodox people do not carry their prayer books, prayer shawls, etc. In larger synagogues the seating is banked to enable a good view for all.

The reading of the scroll is followed by the congregation from Hebrew bibles which are quite large. Each seat, therefore, needs a bookrest, Figure 32.47. However, some prayers have to be said

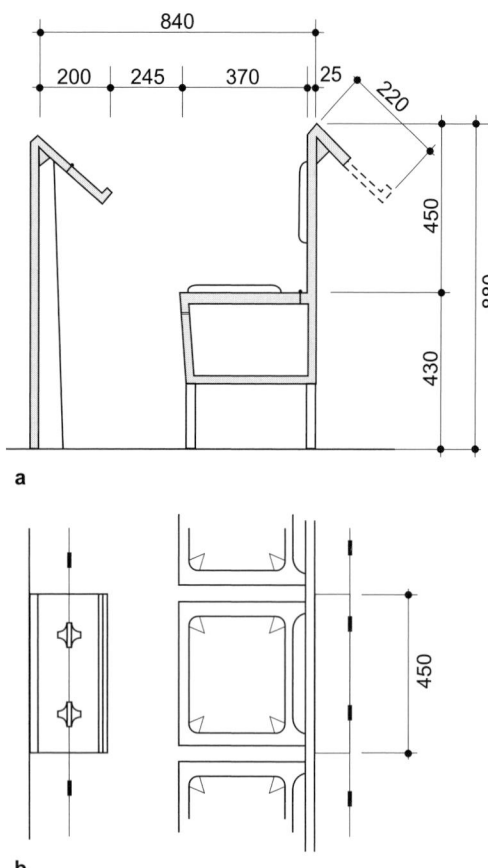

32.47 *Seat and bookrest. a Section. The bookrest folds up to make more clearance. The seat lifts to reveal a locker for prayer book, bible and prayer shawl. b Plan*

facing the Holy Ark; this means turning sideways in many seats. It is normal for the bookrests to be hinged to increase the clearance. Prayers are said either standing or sitting. Congregants *never* kneel in a synagogue.

Most larger synagogues have galleries and in orthodox synagogues the women sit here. Since the use of a lift is forbidden on the Sabbath and Holydays, they are not usually provided in orthodox synagogues. Women unable to climb stairs are accommodated in a section of the downstairs behind a curtain (*mechitsah*).

Processions
These are a feature of synagogue services. At services where readings are given from the Torah, the scroll or scrolls are taken from the Holy Ark and processed to the Bima before the reading, and processed back afterwards. On the Feast of Tabernacles most of the men will process behind the scrolls carrying palm branches and citrons. On the Rejoicing of the Law, all the scrolls that the congregation owns will be processed around the synagogue many times. The aisles must be wide enough for these processions.

Other features
- A *Ner Tamid*, eternal light, hangs before the Holy Ark.
- The rabbi or minister has a 'box' normally placed to one side of the Ark, with a seat facing the congregation.
- The chazan, or cantor, has a matching box on the other side of the Ark.
- The wardens have a box usually placed just forward of the Bima facing the Ark. It should have room for four wardens.
- Where there is a choir it may be accommodated in a normal seating area, or in a special place such as above the Holy Ark.
- Storage near the entrance should be provided for prayer books, bibles and prayer shawls.

- A display board similar to a hymn board is provided for service details.
- Progressive congregations need an organ. Some orthodox synagogues have a limited musical facility for weddings.
- For weddings, a *chupah* (canopy) is erected on the Bima if there is room, or forward of it on the floor of the synagogue. The couple and the rabbi are accommodated under the chupah, with as many others of the family and witnesses as there is room for.
- Funerals only take place in synagogues on rare, very special occasions. A special prayer hall, Figure 32.48, is provided at Jewish cemeteries. This is a covered open space with a few benches around the walls for infirm people. The floor is at ground level: the coffin is not carried by bearers but pushed on a wheeled cart. There are doors at both ends to signify the progress of man from birth to death. A small detached building on one side with open windows is provided for *cohanim* who are not permitted to enter any building containing a corpse.
- Purification using water, analogous to Christian baptism, takes place by total immersion not in a synagogue but in a separate facility called a *mikvah*. The design of this can be similar to a hydrotherapy pool. Such purification is not for infants, but is used by the orthodox at adult conversions, on certain occasions by women and by some men on a weekly basis.

18.3 Building services

Lighting
Lighting levels should be high as many services take place after dark. It is traditional for all available sources to be used even in daylight. Some may be symbolic, such as a *menorah* near the Holy Ark.

Heating
As services can be long, an efficient heating system is essential. Commonly this comprises hot water radiators; radiant sources such as used in churches are not popular.

Ventilation
This must be efficient as on occasion the synagogue will be packed. Control should preferably be automatic. It should not produce draughts or noise.

Speech reinforcement
This may be required in progressive synagogues, but is not permitted by the orthodox on Sabbaths and Holydays. However, nearly all synagogues are now allowed to use 'loop' systems for deaf people,

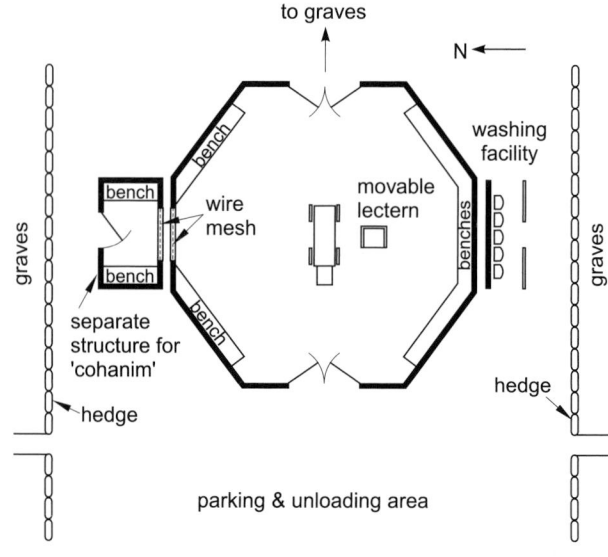

32.48 *Plan of cemetery prayer hall*

and this will require microphones to be placed very discreetly on the Bima, pulpit and the Holy Ark controlled automatically.

Large Orthodox synagogues need to be carefully designed for excellent acoustics in view of the lack of any reinforcement system. Even so, this implies a maximum capacity of about 1500.

18.4 Outside the sanctuary

Since services are long, synagogues need adequate cloakroom and lavatory accommodation. A vestry for the rabbi and chazan is often provided at the Ark end of the building with a direct entrance into the sanctuary close to the rabbi's box.

There is a foyer between the street entrance and the sanctuary and there are stairs from this to the ladies' gallery. The foyer should have notice boards to publicise the many activities in conjunction with the congregation. There may also be one or more built-in charity boxes (used only on weekdays). Immediately outside there will be a board giving the times of services, etc.

Most synagogues have additional halls, classrooms for religion school, kitchens, etc. Orthodox synagogues provide no car parking, as driving on the Sabbath and Holidays is forbidden. However, a very few parking spaces may be provided where land is available for the minister and for weekday use.

18.5 Holydays

The High Holydays occur around September and congregations are much larger than on a normal Sabbath. Some buildings are designed to open up hall and classroom areas to the main sanctuary at this time; alternatively, one or more additional services are provided in detached halls. As Orthodox synagogues use no electrical speech reinforcement, additional services are separately conducted. This usually involves using a mobile Holy Ark with the reading desk on the floors of the hall used; thus special provision in the building design for these occasions need not be made.

19 MOSQUES

19.1 Elements

Muslims actually need no special place to pray – praying can and does take place in the street. Where a purpose-built mosque is provided, it should comprise and conform to particular rules.

Every mosque has four basic elements, Figure 32.49. These are the *Mihrab, Bab Al-Sadir*, dome and minaret. Both the dome and minaret have a symbolic rather than a utilitarian function in contemporary mosque design. (Terms in *italics* are listed in the Glossary section 19.10.)

19.2 The Mihrab

The Mihrab, Figure 32.50, is indispensable, as it indicates the direction to the *Kaaba* in Mecca, Saudi Arabia. The direction to Kaaba is also known as *Qibla*. In symbolic terms, it is the most important element of the modern mosque.

It is essential that this direction is accurately established. The Ordnance Survey office on application can give the precise bearing and distance to Mecca, Saudi Arabia from anywhere in the

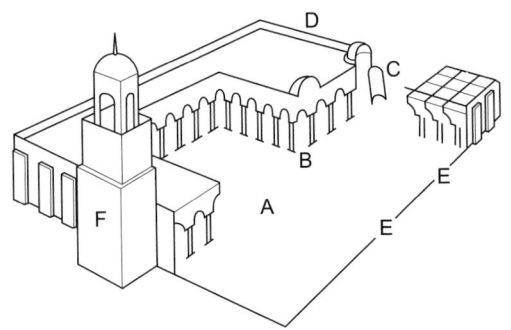

32.49 *Main features of a mosque. Key: A Fountain, B Worship hall, C Mihrab, D Qibla wall, E Entrances, F Minaret*

32.50 *Mihrab*

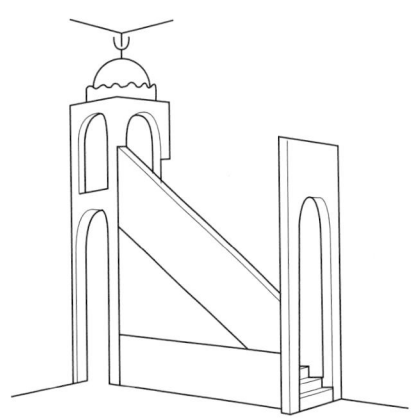

32.51 *Minbar*

UK. Generally it is in a south-easterly direction with a bearing of approximately 118° from the north.

The Mihrab is where the Imam leads the congregation for prayer and also houses the *Minbar*, Figure 32.51, a pulpit from which the *Imam* will address the congregation, particularly on Friday. The Minbar might be a low platform, or be at the head of a flight of stairs.

19.3 Bab Al-Sadir

Bab Al-Sadir is the grand entrance. In Arabic, 'Bab' means a gate or door and Al-Sadir means the frontal. Traditionally it symbolises the importance of the mosque in the life of the community:

19.4 The dome

The dome is generally centrally located over the main prayer hall and there may be more than one dome to a mosque. It is first and foremost a landmark, indicating the importance of the mosque to the life of the community. In addition, it has two practical functions; one is to echo the words of the Imam inside the mosque and the other is to cool the hot air when it rises upwards and draws in cooler air from outside. Modern technology compensates for the two functions above.

19.5 The minaret

The minaret is used to call the faithful to prayer. It is usually in the form of a circular, octagonal or square tower which projects above the mosque with at least one balcony along its length. It is possible to provide more than one minaret in a mosque and more than one balcony for each minaret.

Traditionally the minaret has an internal staircase leading up to the uppermost balcony, but these days it usually only carries a speaker system so that the Muezzin stays at ground level (sometimes a recording is used).

19.6 Prayers

Prayers are said standing, kneeling and prostrate. There are therefore no seats, but the prayer hall is carpeted and the carpet is marked with imprinted prayer mats pointing to Qibla. Allow at least 0.75 m² per person for praying.

No shoes are allowed past the main entrance, and there are places to leave them, usually in racks, to one or both sides of the entrance.

19.7 Other essentials

Other essentials to be provided are the *Wuzu, Wudu* or ablution area, the *Janaza* or morgue, and *Kutub Khana* or library.

19.8 Ablution area

The ablution area, Figure 32.52, is where the faithful wash their hands, elbows, faces, behind the ears and their feet in preparation for praying. This is performed under running water. The ablution area also houses the toilets and showers. The number of ablution seats, toilets and showers is governed by the size of the prayer hall.

19.9 Design

Mosque design must conform to particular detail rules, some of which are:

- Male and female entrance/exit, prayer hall and ablution areas must be separate.
- Toilets should be in compartments not cubicles: i.e. must be of solid wall construction not thin partitions or gaps at floor level.
- Their orientation is of paramount importance. Compartments must not face or back in the direction of Mecca.
- No other habitable enclosure or space should be behind the Mihrab within the confines of the site.
- Toilets may not be situated under or over the prayer hall, and no drainage pipes whatsoever should pass under or over it.

It is important for the fulfilling of the client brief that the designer combine the four elements in proportion to each other. Figure 32.53 shows plans of the two levels of a typical mosque.

19.10 Glossary

Bab Al-Sadir	main or grand entrance/gate
Imam	the holy man/preacher/leader of the prayer
Jami or Jame	Friday or congregational mosque
Janaza	Morgue
Kaaba	the holy shrine in Mecca
Kutub Khana	Library
Madrasa	School
Masjid	Mosque
Mihrab	a niche in the Qibla wall indicating the direction to Kaaba
Minor or Minara	Minaret
Minbar	pulpit or seat used by the Imam for Friday speech
Muezzin	person calling faithful for prayer
Qibla or Kibla	the direction of prayer oriented towards Kaaba in Mecca
Wuzu or Wudu	ablution

20 HINDU TEMPLE

20.1 Design

There are three main sections to a Hindu temple, Figure 32.54:

- The *garbagriha* or shrine room
- The *mandapa* or pillared hall
- The *ardhamandapa* or porch.

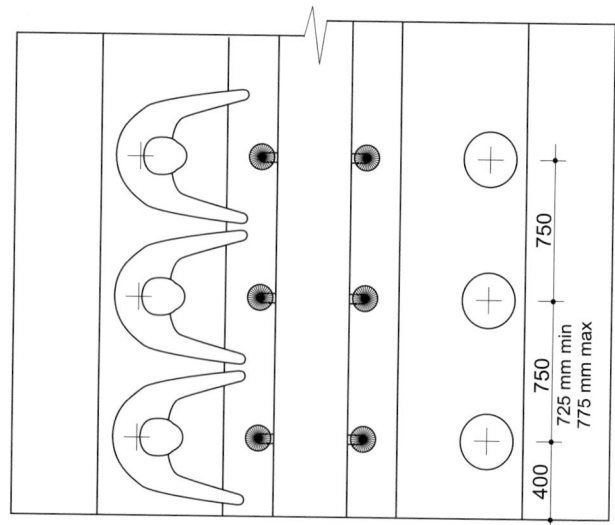

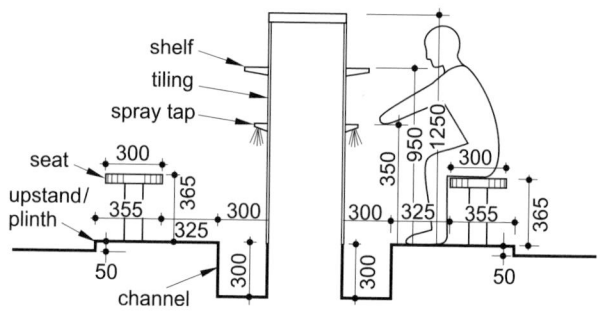

32.52 *Plan and section of ablution area*

20.2 The garbagriha

This contains the object representing the deity, usually a statue. It may be covered by a canopy, or the roof of the garbagriha itself may be in the form of a pyramid. There should be an ambulatory called the *pradakshina* between the statue and the outer wall.

20.3 The mandapa

This is the central hall where the worshippers assemble. They approach the garbagriha through the *antarala* which steps up. Prayers are said here, seated upon the floor. A portable fire altar is brought into the room at the time of worship. Some of the worshippers play musical instruments, others assist the priest.

20.4 The ardhamandapa

This is traditionally orientated towards the rising sun, and also is raised above the ground by steps.

21 SIKH GURDWARA

21.1 Design

The gurdwara, Figure 32.55, consists of a single large room with the takht platform at the end furthest from the entrance. There are no special requirements for orientation. On the takht stands the *palki*, a canopy over the *Guru Granth Sahib* which is the focal point of the gurdwara. The Guru Granth Sahib is the Sikh scripture, and is kept on the *Manji Sahib*, a low reading desk. The palki is free of the wall behind to permit circumambulation.

21.2 Services

Worshippers enter the gurdwara at random times, go directly to the takht and prostrate themselves before the Guru Granth Sahib. They leave offerings of money or of kind on the takht in front of it. They then sit on the floor, men on one side and women on the other, leaving the

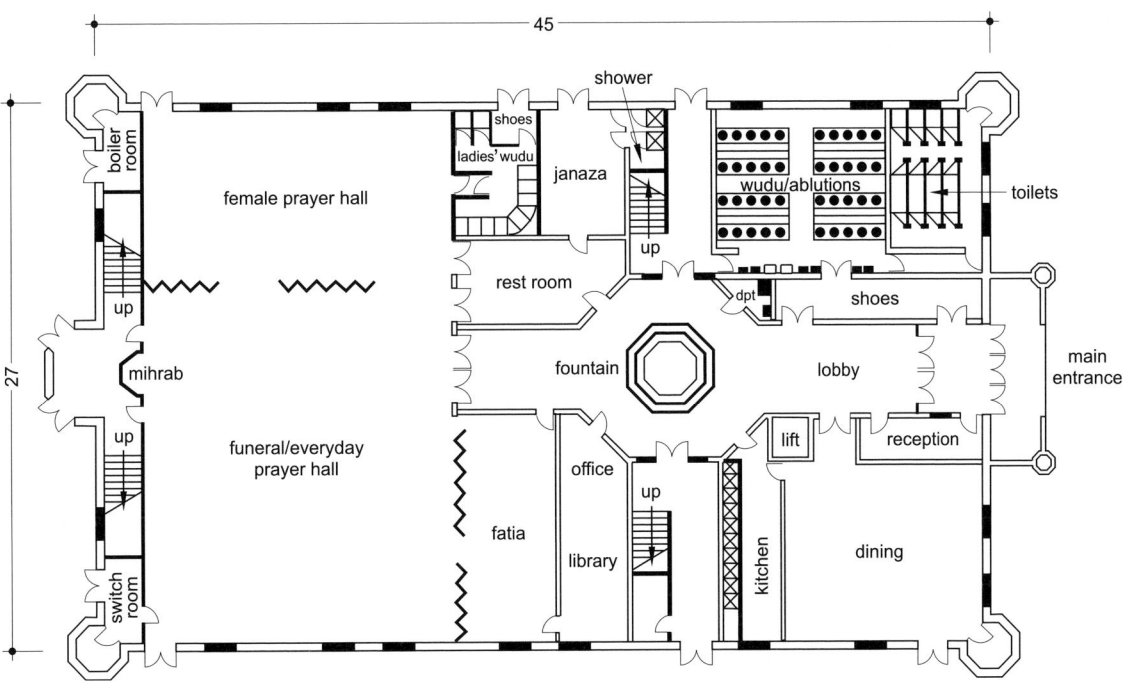

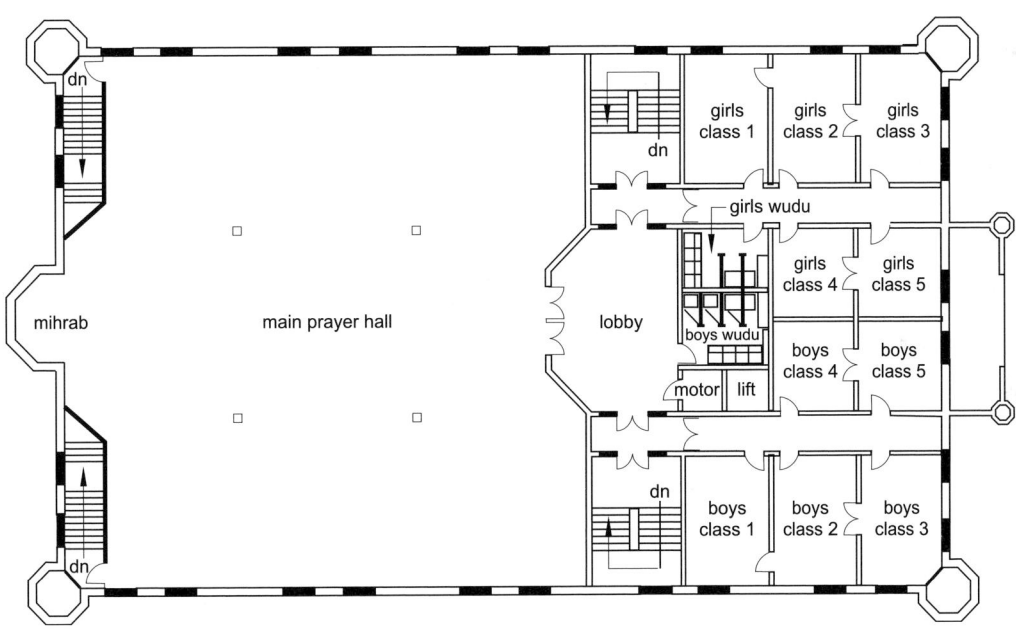

32.53 *Plan of a mosque, ground and first floor*

central aisle for later comers. During the service, verses are read from the Guru Granth Sahib; hymns are sung, music is played by the *ragis*, musicians seated on the takht. The distinguishing feature of a gurdwara externally is the Sikh flag. A tall flagpole is therefore necessary.

Part D Additional Information

22 CREMATORIA

22.1 Introduction
More people are cremated than buried now due mainly to the scarcity of land for cemeteries and the consequent high cost of grave space. However, some religions such as strict Catholicism and orthodox Judaism do not permit cremation.

In most cases of cremation a ceremony precedes the disposal. This may be religious or it may be a purely secular occasion. After the body has been cremated (which may not be immediately after the ceremony) the ashes may be:

- deposited in a columbarium associated with the crematorium;
- scattered in a Garden of Remembrance also at the crematorium;
- taken away for deposition or disposal elsewhere.

Crematoria may be municipal or commercial. In the former case they are usually situated in or next to a municipal cemetery. Columbaria and Gardens of Remembrance can be provided on the cemetery land. Private crematoria will also provide these facilities, as they can be financially rewarding. The designer must establish a clear brief from a client in these respects.

22.2 Siting
The crematory (i.e. where the furnaces are housed) should not be sited near existing buildings because the effluent from the flue can be unpleasant under certain climatic conditions. The statutory situation requires that crematoria may not be sited closer than 183 m (92 m in inner London) to domestic property. Ideally, crematoria

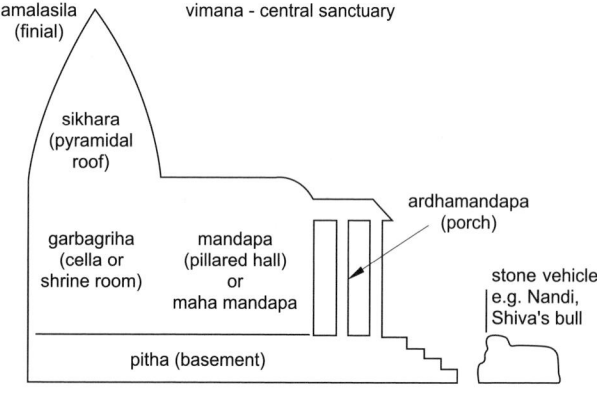

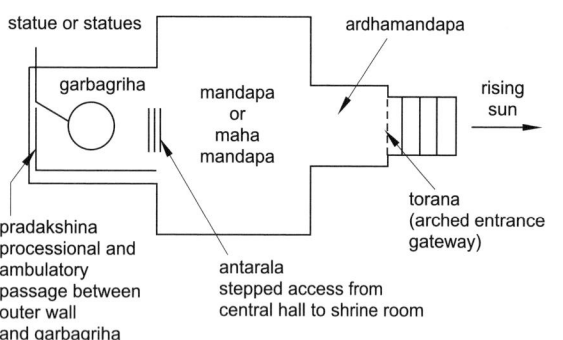

32.54 *Hindu temple, longitudinal section and plan*

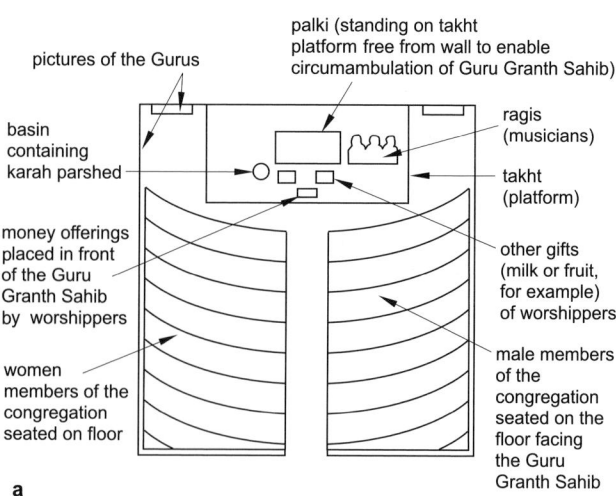

a

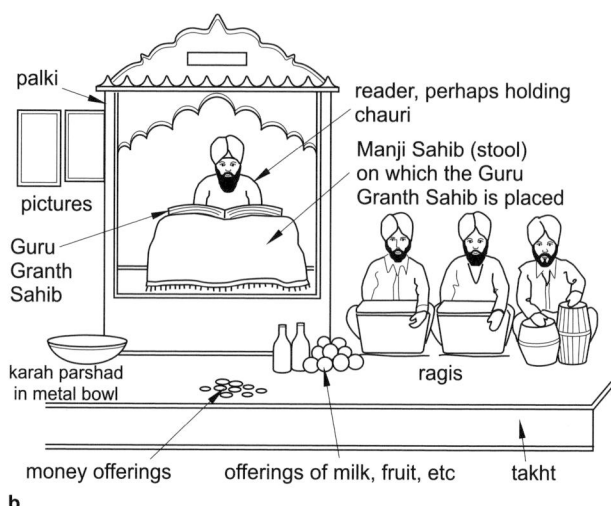

b

32.55 *Sikh Gurdwara. a Plan. There is no standard shape but the Guru Granth Sahib must be the focus of attention always visible from all points of the room. The aisle is left free for worshippers to pay their respects to the Guru Granth Sahib before sitting in the congregation. Sometimes separate entrances are required for men and women. b Elevation of the Takht*

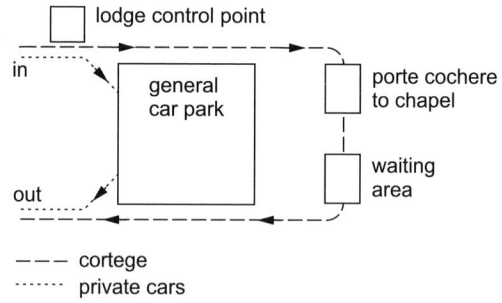

32.56 *Crematorium vehicular flow diagram*

should be located in quiet surroundings, with as much natural landscape as possible.

A minimum site of 1 hectare is required for the crematorium buildings themselves. Further space requirements will depend on whether a Garden of Remembrance is required, when a further hectare at least will be necessary, and more if commercial aspects are to be developed to the full. These areas include the space needed for traffic circulation, parking, a modest amount of room around the building, and the crematorium itself.

Vehicular access to the site should be simple and dignified and free from traffic hazards. The entrance should preferably not be immediately off a principal traffic route. If this is unavoidable, then it should be off a roundabout or where there is space in the central reservation of a dual carriageway for the hearse and mourners' cars to wait in a dignified manner.

22.3 On-site circulation

Clear routes should be provided within the site for vehicular and pedestrian traffic, Figure 32.56. Only the hearse, principal mourners' and disabled people's vehicles should be allowed beyond the car parking area. These vehicles should arrive at the building under a porte-cochère. The coffin will be transferred to the chapel and then the hearse and other vehicles routed to a waiting area, ready to pick up the principal mourners after the service. One or two parking bays should be provided close to the chapel for disabled people. All other mourners should park their cars in a car park away from the main building.

The entrances to and exits from the building should be located as far as possible from the furnace room so that mourners are not aware of the mechanics of disposal. The pedestrian traffic flow should follow that of the coffin into the chapel. Mourners arriving at the chapel should not meet mourners leaving the previous service. After the service, the people walk from the chapel to a covered way, where floral tributes are displayed, through to the chapel of remembrance (if provided) and then back to the car park via the garden.

22.4 Chapels

Chapels should take into account Christian, non-Christian and secular usage – perhaps separate chapels for Christian and other users; or if the same space is used for all, a system of easily changed symbols installed. Where more than one chapel is provided, one may be small (20 seats) and the other larger (110 seats). Organs are rarely used, but good facilities for playing recorded music are essential.

The chapel should be designed to reduce emotional disturbance caused by the proceedings, Figure 32.57. The event can be 'softened' in a number of ways. For example, windows can be provided at a number of levels to enable the mourners to look through the

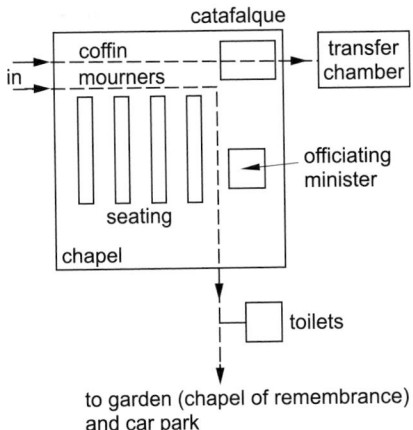

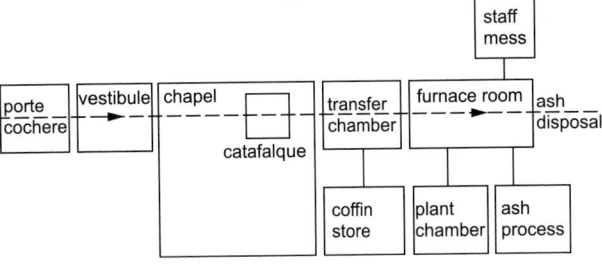

32.58 *Coffin circulation pattern*

32.57 *Chapel arrangement*

chapel into a restful and attractive external landscape; the designer should avoid a totally introspective environment. Again, the catafalque can be offset from a central position so that the mourners tend to concentrate on the minister conducting the service and not solely on the presence of the coffin.

22.5 Toilets
Many people become emotionally disturbed either before or during the service. The toilets should be easily accessible before the service, immediately after the service and at the point where relatives disperse after the ceremony. At least three groups of toilet facilities are required.

22.6 Coffin circulation
A diagram of the coffin circulation is given in Figure 32.58.

22.7 The furnace room
The finishes in the furnace room should be impervious and easily maintained. Blow-back on ignition may occur occasionally, and soot deposits can accumulate on walls and ceiling.

22.8 Ancillary accommodation
All or some of the following will be required depending on circumstances:

- administrative suite
- manager's office
- waiting rooms
- resting place with catafalque
- vestry for clergy
- flower room
- transfer chamber and coffin storage
- viewing room
- furnace operator's room and storage
- attendant's room
- public toilets
- gardener's store and porter's lodge.

The site plan of a recently constructed crematorium complex is shown in Figure 32.59. Plans of the main building are given in Figure 32.60.

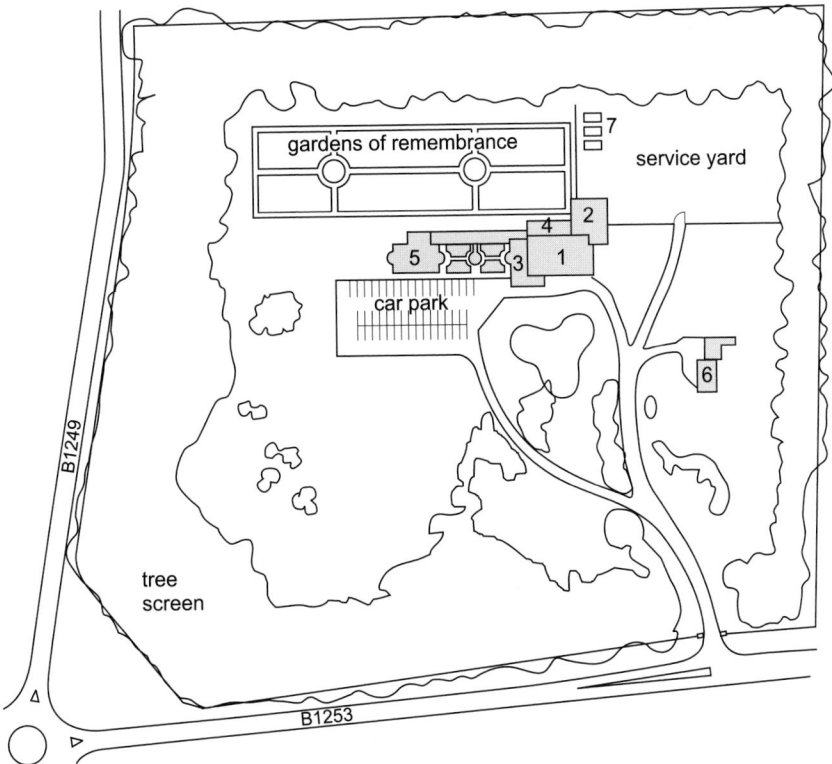

32.59 *Site plan of East Riding Crematorium Architect: R Peter Belt DiplArch RIBA. Key: 1 chapel, 2 cremators, 3 porte-cochère, 4 floral gallery, 5 hospitality suite, 6 superintendent's house, 7 gas tanks*

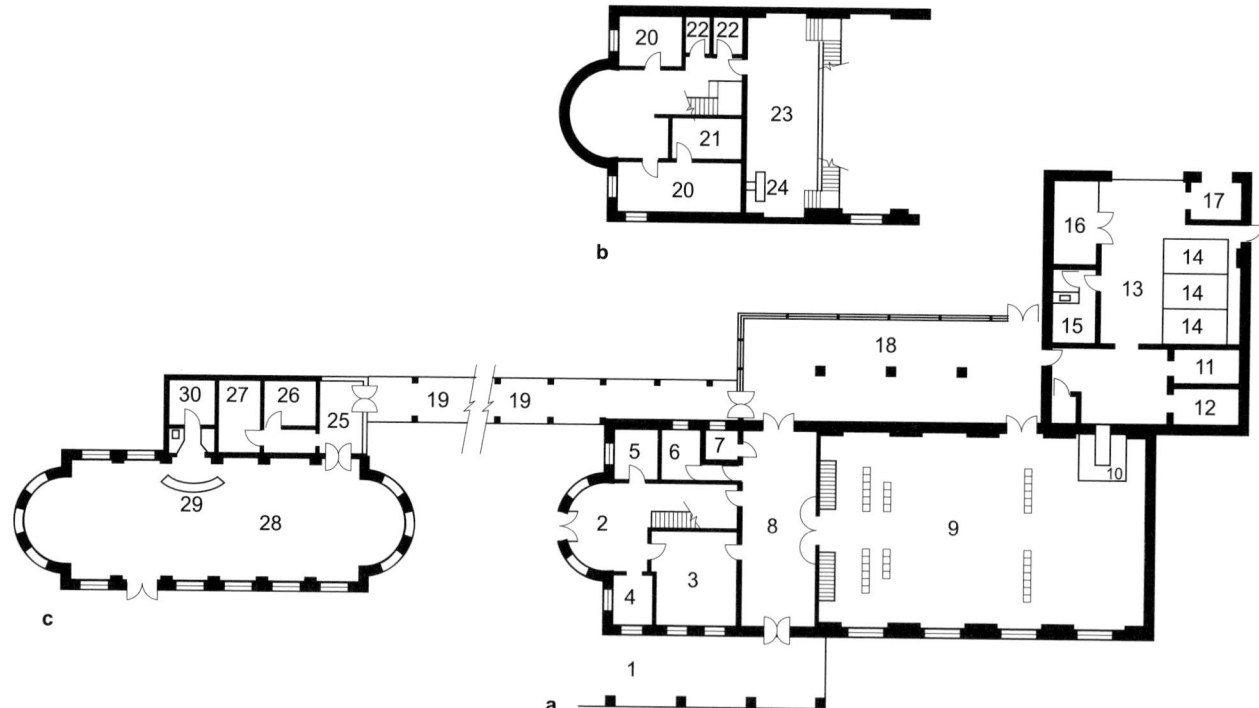

32.60 *East Riding Crematorium: plans of main building complex Architect: R Peter Belt DiplArch RIBA. Key: 1 porte-cochère, 2 entrance hall, 3 waiting room, 4 vestry, 5 enquiries, 6 men's toilets, 7 ladies' and disabled people's toilet, 8 foyer, 9 chapel, 10 canopy over catafalque, 11 flower store, 12 cold store, 13 cremation room, 14 cremators, 15 staff, 16 workshop, 17 fan room, 18 floral gallery, 19 covered walkway, 20 office, 21 records, 22 toilets, 23 gallery, 24 organ, 25 hospitality porch, 26 men's toilet, 27 women's toilet, 28 reception room, 29 servery, 30 store, a Ground floor of main area. b First floor. c Hospitality suite*

23 Bibliography

Frishman, Martin and Hasan Uddin Khan (eds), *The Mosque: History, Architectural Development and Regional Diversity*, Thames & Hudson, 2002

Heathcote, Edwin and Laura Moffatt, *Contemporary Church Architecture*, John Wiley & Sons, 2007

Heathcote, Edwin and Iona Spens, *Church Builders*, Academy, 1997

Kieckhefer, Richard, *Theology in Stone; Church Architecture from Byzantium to Berkeley*. Oxford University Press, 2004

Krinsky, Carol Herselle, *Synagogues of Europe: Architecture, History, Meaning*, Dover Publications, 1996

Kuban, D. *Muslim Religious Architecture: The Mosque and Its Early Development v. 1 (Iconography of Religions)*, Brill, 1974

Martin, Christopher, *A Glimpse of Heaven: Catholic Churches of England and Wales*, English Heritage, 2006

Meek, HA. *The Synagogue*, Phaidon Press, 2003

Norman, Edward, *The House of God*, Thames & Hudson, 2005

Places of Worship, Phaidon Press, 1999

Roberts, Nicholas, *Building Type Basics for Places of Worship*, Wiley, 2004

Stock, Wolfgang Jean, *Architectural Guide: Christian Sacred Buildings*, Prestel, 2004

Stock, Wolfgang Jean, *European Church Architecture, 1950–2000*, Prestel, 2003

33 Primary health care

Geoffrey Purves

Geoffrey Purves is a consultant chartered architect and has designed many primary care facilities whilst in practice. His PhD researched the design of primary health care buildings and he has published Healthy Living Centres *(2002) and* Primary Care Centres: A Guide to Healthcare Design *(2009).*

KEY POINTS:

- *The focus of health design is beginning to shift from an obsession with cost and functionality to one of quality, potential flexibility of use and whole life costs*
- *Primary health buildings closely reflect policy and guidance – as guidance changes, so do the buildings*
- *Patient choice will increasingly become a factor which drives the design of, and provision within, primary health buildings*

Contents

1 Executive summary
2 International background
3 A short history
4 Current position
5 Political framework and government policy
6 Approach to briefing and design
7 Key relationships
8 Engineering and IT services
9 Art in health
10 Holistic care
11 Conclusion
12 Case studies
13 References

1 EXECUTIVE SUMMARY

Primary care premises are generally complex small-scale buildings (when compared to hospitals) with many functional requirements to accommodate. They tend to be busy places with many people entering and leaving the building during the course of the day including patients, doctors, nurses and other service personnel. So it is understandable that the NHS has focused on issues of functionality and cost to evaluate the design of this building type. However, in the last few years there has been a fundamental shift in this approach and there is now much greater emphasis placed on the evaluation of the quality of design. Hence, this section attempts to set out that the ethos of the place is of paramount importance and the organisation of spaces within the building should flow from this overarching principle. The new wave of publications from the Department of Health recognise the importance of creating a high-quality working environment. These notes seek to guide the designer to establish qualitative factors through discussion with the users of the building and then refer to the detailed guidance on the ergonomic requirements for ensuring that room data sheets accommodate the functional requirements of a room. Current thinking is to assume that the use of rooms may change over time and, therefore, flexibility for change is also important.

Current design guidance issued by the Department of Health sets out some basic guidelines.

1.1 Robust planning

Ensure that robust strategic planning and rigorous capacity planning determine the service vision for the scheme. Demonstrate their impact on the investment decision for the physical improvements.

1.2 Forward-looking service delivery

Define organisational improvements and forward-looking service delivery plans and consider the change process involved to bring these about. Consider the impact of working practices on the functional requirements for physical space. Allow sufficient time to develop organisational changes alongside the building development programme.

1.3 Design quality

Establish design ethos. Improve design briefing by setting out quality requirements for the design of the built environment: make the design vision explicit particularly in relation to the patient experience. Encourage an integrated approach to design encompassing site planning, spatial arrangements, interior, landscape, and art.

1.4 Flexibility for the future

Devise planning and design strategies that cater for changes in service delivery over time. Seek further guidance to establish an optimal range of generic room sizes to enable greater utilisation of rooms. More detailed understanding of design approaches that facilitate flexibility will need to be developed.

1.5 Healthy neighbourhoods

Improve site planning to ensure convenient access, making the approach to the building visible and welcoming. Develop the potential for the buildings to contribute to the making of healthy neighbourhoods by considering the attractiveness of the adjoining built environment and open spaces to encourage, for example, cycle and pedestrian use.

1.6 Holistic care

Consider the sense of well-being and how personal and social factors influence our physical health. Be aware of the interaction between health and social policies in a locality and how their integration can contribute to happy personal lifestyles.

1.7 Sustainable investment

Define the requirements for sustainable investment and ensure these are fully appreciated at the start of the project. The shape and form of the building and the orientation on the site have a significant impact on sustainable performance. A social, environmental and economic approach to sustainability needs to be considered together for best results.

1.8 Training and support

Establish support for the project team on design quality throughout the project; for example, appoint client design advisors and design champions. Undertake design reviews during development as a quality check for commissioners. Develop training for project and design teams to help identify key issues, share good practice and understand how to make a step change in design quality for primary and community buildings.

2 INTERNATIONAL BACKGROUND

As we move into the second decade of the twenty-first century primary health care is increasingly viewed as an international issue with government policies in many countries, including the UK, being affected by the influences and effects of health programmes around the world. This is reflected in the design of primary care buildings in the UK, which are becoming based more on a philosophical approach with greater fluidity, flexibility of use and changing treatment practices compared to the ergonomic space standards which were advocated as the framework for good design in the 1980s and 1990s.

Primary Health Care, usually abbreviated as PHC and based on practical, scientifically sound and socially acceptable methods and technology, was ratified at an international conference held in Alma-Ata, USSR (6–12 September 1978). It was jointly sponsored by the World Health Organisation and the United Nations Children's Fund where it was declared that a state of complete physical, mental and social wellbeing, not merely the absence of disease or infirmity, was a fundamental human right. The aspiration was that by the year 2000 all peoples of the world would enjoy a level of health that permitted them to lead a socially and economically productive life.

Architects, therefore, should review not only the recent health care buildings constructed in the UK, but also look at the policies and influences that have shaped buildings in both developed and developing countries throughout the world.

3 A SHORT HISTORY

Historically, there has been a long tradition of a strong relationship between patient and doctor. The Dawson report (1920) advocated primary care policies based on local services by the GP. At the same time political and social pressures led to the formation of the welfare state and the creation of the NHS (1948). The Royal College of General Practitioners was not formed until 1952. GPs at that time (mid-twentieth century) did not have an influential position in the medical hierarchy. This developed into a pattern of control in the NHS which focused on ever more ambitious plans for large, technologically advanced hospitals during the second half of the twentieth century. In turn, this culminated in the failure to deliver services on time and within budget giving rise to wide-ranging reviews on the structure of the NHS.

Due to financial pressures and social changes giving more power to individuals as consumers the NHS had to change to reflect these realities. Hence, private capital has been introduced and health policies have been focused on providing patient focused care. Services are now examined in relation to convenience and the ability for medical care to be provided in the community. Community hospitals are being built reflecting considerable similarity to cottage hospitals many of which were closed with great speed in the 1980s.

Ambulance services are also being redeployed on community needs and increasingly being linked to medical facilities (GP practices and community hospitals particularly in rural areas) once again reflecting similarity to the recommendations of the Dawson Report of 1920. The advantages of a primary led health service are also reinforced by the successful policies found in developing countries. As young doctors have the means to work throughout the world often taking a 'gap' year before or after their medical training they see the successful results of primary health care services operating in poor countries.

The changing pattern of health care is beginning to re-establish the importance of the relationship between doctor and patient. Patient focused care returns power and influence to the individual who is able to exercise greater control over the medical interventions advocated for their body. The government is addressing the challenge of providing a consistent and high quality of technical competence, but in a manner which responds and reflects the needs and aspirations of the patient rather than the convenience of the medical and administrative staff of the NHS. The architectural design quality of new buildings is therefore of greater importance today than it has been for nearly a century. The therapeutic benefits of good design are now recognised.

3.1 Functionality and cost

The NHS Estates' procurement policy has been based until recently on the Capital Investment Manual which required a business case approach to justify new investment. This led to a position where design quality was understood to be represented by functionality. Design quality was assessed by its functional suitability. That methodology was enshrined in their Estate Code document which set out a five-facet analysis process:

- Space utilisation
- Functional suitability
- Energy efficiency
- Statutory standards (compliance)
- Physical condition.

These factors were used as a basis for design quality evaluation. With this background an assessment of design quality does not include qualitative issues, or an assessment of the desired ethos of a building. The criteria set out in the analysis process did not include emotional responses such as 'pleasantness' or 'calmness' or indeed any suggestion of 'therapeutic value'. However, the problem remains that even if appropriate categories of patient satisfaction were included there would be difficulties in measuring or placing values on these factors. Design quality had to be based on quantifiable data.

3.2 Development of hospice design

A comparison with NHS policies for GP surgeries can be made with the procurement of hospices. The concept of holistic healing had been lost in the development of technical medicine in the twentieth century. A holistic approach to health care was much more central to the care of those who were ill in earlier civilisations.

3.3 Development of the NHS

Until the last few years, the government's approach to financing health care facilities, in line with all government spending, has been based largely on negotiating lowest cost tenders within annual spending budgets. This tended to downgrade the consideration of 'whole-life' costs, and it is only recently that the Treasury has begun to promote 'best value' as the basis for selecting successful bidders for government contracts.

Inevitably, this led to an approach within the NHS to concentrate on setting targets for different sizes of GP surgeries and offering guidance on the space standards that would be acceptable. This created a cultural background to the provision of buildings encapsulated within the framework of the 'Red Book'. This document has now been superseded by the Statement of Financial Entitlement (SFE) with details available on the NHS website (www.gov.uk/government/publications/gms-statement-of-financial-entitlements).

Standards were set for accommodation, maximum allowances were set down for professional fees and cost limits were established. These principles were developed over many years resulting in a well-established set of procedures with which doctors needed to comply to improve or redevelop their premises. The environmental quality of these buildings was given scant attention. The philosophy regarding design was essentially that the administrators of NHS funds would establish a framework of requirements and set cost limits in the belief that this would leave designers free to interpret the built form in an imaginative way.

Because of the relatively short timescale between inception and completion for primary health care buildings, and the personal rapport between doctors and architects, many successful small surgeries have been completed over the last decade. There could have been more encouragement from NHS Estates to the doctors under their contract to build facilities that were more flexible, more responsive to their patients' requirements and more likely to offer better value to the community.

Functionality has been a key test of previous appraisal systems, a process devised by the administrators or service providers with negligible attempts to ask patients what they wanted. Functionality was seen as a measure of how efficient the building was for staff and doctors to process the patient. The emotional wellbeing of a patient was secondary to issues such as special and ergonomic requirements.

The new NHS Plan recognises the importance of putting patients first, and opportunities lie ahead as new approaches to satisfying consumer demands begin to be developed and implemented. Thus, the effects of supply and demand and qualitative factors will emerge as patients begin to exercise their freedom to make choices (about the location of their treatment for health matters) in a market economy.

4 CURRENT POSITION

The government is looking to make changes in two areas of the health sector.

1 Several initiatives have been launched to give patients more responsibility for their own well-being.
2 Contractual arrangements are being explored between the government and private providers, giving rise to a greater number of private health care services.

There are also changes taking place in the contractual arrangements between GPs and the government. The introduction of new providers (specialist companies) is beginning to create market forces within which competition will emerge between service providers.

As alternative procurement routes are evolving for primary health care buildings both in the public and private sectors the architectural responses are becoming more imaginative. Consumers are also becoming more selective in recognising the role that quality can play in providing health care facilities.

These changes have also led to the development of a number of evaluation techniques to assess and grade the quality of health care buildings, such as Advice, AEDET, KPIs and NEAT. The earlier NHS approach to the procurement of primary care buildings was based on the Red Book. The recent changes have seen a move to give greater consideration to design quality and these evaluation techniques attempt to structure qualitative assessments as part of the appraisal system for seeking approval.

The architectural profession has become more engaged with the design of health buildings, including primary care facilities, by developing evaluation techniques. These are tools which allow evidence-based design to be articulated with conviction. Today the argument that good design is beneficial, not only for patients but the whole community, has largely been accepted and the debate has moved on to the political arena. The architectural process is now better understood and better followed than in the past and the product is under closer scrutiny. The profession has good tools (e.g. computer software) and is more confident in asserting its intellectual property rights as a designer of high-quality architecture.

The architectural profession is also influencing the political climate and the importance of the brief is now better recognised than 20 years ago. In particular, the ethos of a building is understood to be an important component in a brief, a development that has been led by the hospice movement and the design of some very successful specialist buildings such as the Maggie Centres. It is a period of growing independence of patients who are beginning to demand higher standards from their GPs reflecting service provisions offered by other business sectors.

4.1 Architectural context

New design philosophy emerging
There has been a significant shift in government policy which now recognises the importance of good design in the development of new GP surgeries. The Red Book set the standards for the *modus operandi* of GP practice in the UK for many years. It represented the outcome from a long period of development, periodic reviews and updating of data. It typifies the outcome of a bureaucratic approach in a very large organisation. The rules, costs limits and schedules of permitted accommodation were very prescriptive. Although the official briefing methodology offered little encouragement for good design a wide range of innovative GP surgeries has been built over the last decade. This framework of controls is now rapidly breaking down as new forms of procurement expand and develop in the joint public private partnerships that the government is encouraging.

A different approach to building design is being advocated for the next wave of primary care buildings. They will be buildings that are flexible and can incorporate the demands of a knowledge based economy, respond to the rapidly changing demands for information technology, and different working methods which will develop from faster communications between doctor, patient and specialist testing facilities (e.g. x-rays, consultant reports). Government procurement methods are seeking to enable future buildings to be flexible shells within which highly serviced workstations can be developed and changed over short periods of time. For example, a doctor's consulting room may have entirely different requirements in five years time than it does today – although it is likely to remain the fundamentally important space within which patient and doctor exchange information.

4.2 Finance

Life cycle costs and 'best value' – the government's approach
Until recently the tradition has been to award contracts predominantly on a lowest cost basis. The Treasury has now changed its policy and the interest in design quality is also manifesting itself in a reassessment of whole life costs. This approach is encapsulated under the umbrella of 'best value'. All government departments and local authorities are taking a broader look at 'best value' issues and this is providing an opportunity to develop new thinking about a whole range of tangible and intangible aspects of a building during its overall life span. At the simplest level, building material manufacturers are able to demonstrate 'best value' for their products not only as the result of initial costs but also taking into account maintenance schedules and renewal timescales. With design issues the growing recognition of user reactions and user satisfaction levels is beginning to influence the decision making process.

There is a growing group of specialist companies forming partnerships with GPs to finance new primary health care facilities. Their success rate in putting together viable procurement packages is being helped because of the changes in attitude by District Valuers. District Valuers are moving towards the creation of a special class of valuation for medical facilities, whereas previously they were seriously disadvantaged by being included with residential or local commercial values. These high valuations that are being rentalised as surgeries are enabling contracts to be written for minimum of 25 year lease periods guaranteed by local health authorities under the terms of existing procedures.

5 POLITICAL FRAMEWORK AND GOVERNMENT POLICY

Government policy regarding the design quality of health buildings has changed significantly since 2000. Procurement routes are changing. Primary health care facilities are becoming larger multifunctional buildings offering integrated health and care services. A variety of agencies and professional skills will work in them serving the local community. Private finance will be provided by specialist developers and local initiatives will ensure greater control of matching requirements with services.

This will have the benefit of allowing the new community facilities to include a wider range of services such as pharmacies,

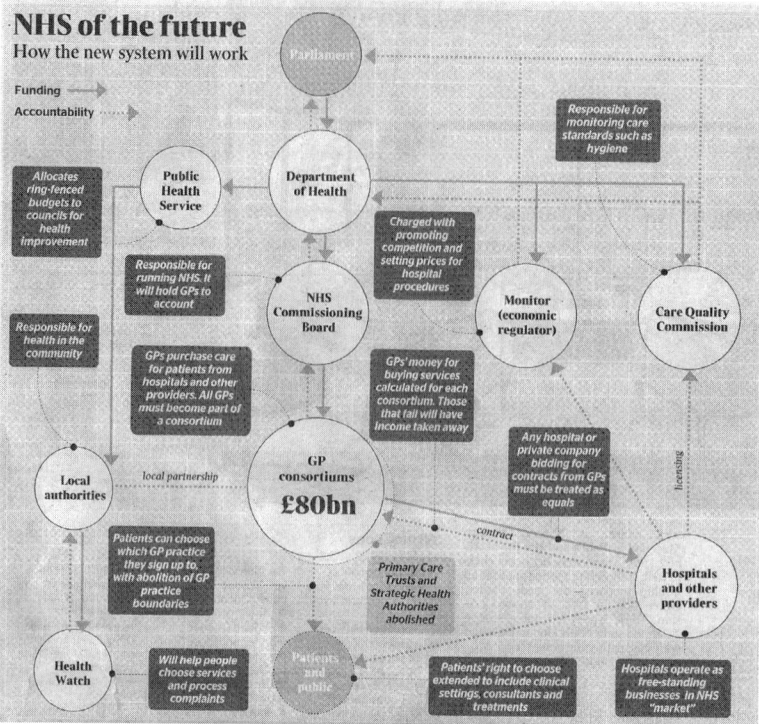

33.1 *Extract from The Times dated 20 January 2011*

dentists, physiotherapists and alternative or complementary medical practitioners all working under one roof, linked often to paramedic and ambulance services. As health and care services become more integrated the new community buildings will grow in size and become multifunctional.

The Darzi Report (2008) was a review of the progress made in the NHS since the publication of the NHS Plan. His recommendations suggest more private providers of healthcare in the primary care sector, and this will require more flexible approaches to the contractual terms of appointment for GPs. David Cameron said on 10 October 2006 that 'he would give doctors more power, patients more choice and health providers more competition'. Now in power the new coalition government is setting about to make significant changes to the structure of the NHS including the abolition of all PCTs (Primary Care Trusts) and SHAs (Strategic Health Authorities).

This radical new model of the NHS, set out in the Health and Social Care Bill, maintains a universal health service, free at the point of delivery which allows the market to increase efficiency. Competition is being introduced to healthcare provision which should drive up standards and lower prices. This is moving from a managed system of healthcare to something more like a regulated market but with GPs in a much more dominant role than they have occupied since the formation of the NHS over 60 years ago. Primary care trusts and strategic health authorities are to be abolished. The Bill signals a significant decrease in the dominance of state-provided healthcare. These changes are illustrated in Figure 33.1.

These radical changes to the management and finance of the NHS with a major swing to the control of health care programmes by patients and their GPs do not undermine the on-going awareness that design quality remains very important. Evidence based design and the evidence base of interventions are both seen as targets for defining and measuring preventative health budgets.

Politically, the government recognises the importance of greater patient participation in the management of each individual's health care. It is moving towards better prevention and early intervention for improved health, independence and well-being. Research undertaken by the Department of Health indicates that people want to take more control of their own health and well-being but wanted

more support to do this. This has led to the concept of NHS 'life check' which will be a two-part service – a self assessment followed by personalised advice and support for those shown to be at risk and is aimed at helping people to assess the risk of ill health created by their own lifestyles. Initially, NHS life checks are being developed for use at three key life stages – the first year of life, adolescence and mid-life (age 50–60). Piloting of these programmes is underway across the country.

Research has also indicated that millions of people suffer from mild to moderate mental health problems, and treating them takes up about a third of GPs' time. There is also a plan to pilot the use of individual budgets. The intention is that this will increase individual control over the services received. Individual budgets will build on some of the features of direct payments by increasing people's choice and control over the way they are supported. As well as social care funding, it will bring together different resource streams but an individual might receive, for example access to work and independent living funds, and allocate a single transparent sum to them.

Following the white paper 'Our Health, Our Care, Our Say: A New Direction for Community Services', published in January 2006 the government published a further document 'Our Health, Our Care, Our Say: Investing in the future of community hospitals and services' in July 2006. It announced that the Department of Health would invest £750 million of capital funding over the next five years in a new generation of community hospitals and services. They would:

- be locally led;
- provide high quality services;
- re-design patient pathways;
- anticipate future needs as the population changes;
- adopt new technologies;
- plan across primary and secondary care;
- be affordable for the whole health economy;
- promote integrated service solutions;
- engage and harness the potential of staff;
- enable the transition of staff;
- engage the public, the whole health and social care system and be innovative.

The government wants the people to have a real choice of the GP surgery they register with. The right of patients to choose one surgery over another will help to ensure that those surgeries are open at times that are suitable for them. The government argues that if patient choice and PBC (practice based commissioning) evolves then health services will develop that are safe, high quality and closer to home in the community. The aim is to meet people's aspiration for independence and greater control over their lives and to make services flexible and responsive to individual needs. This will enable people to be more in control of their health care and place greater emphasis on the prevention of illness.

Four main goals are identified:

1 Better prevention services with earlier intervention. The government response to this aspiration is the introduction of the new NHS life checks for people to assess their life style risks and to take the right steps to make healthier choices. The aim is for this to be a personalised service in two parts.

 a The assessment tool will be available either on line as a part of health direct online or downloaded locally in hard copy.

 b Specific health and social care advice and support for those who need it will be available.

2 More choice and a louder voice. Patients will be given a guarantee of registration onto a GP practice list in their locality. To help them to make this choice it will be easier for people to get the information they need to choose a practice and understand what services are available in their area.

3 Do more on tackling inequalities and improving access to community services. There will be a clear focus on those with ongoing needs and the quality and quantity of primary care will be increased in under served, deprived areas. People with particular needs will be targeted including young people, mothers, ethnic minorities, people with disabilities, people at the end of their lives, offenders and other special groups.

4 More support for people with long-term needs. The intention is to improve communications between health care and social care services.

These changes are inextricably moving the original philosophical arguments set out for the NHS in 1948 towards a consumer driven service with an increasing element of private finance introduced to the provision of services. It would give GPs more responsibility for local health budgets, and it seeks to re-orientate our health and social care services to focus together on prevention and health promotion. It is anticipated that more care will be undertaken outside hospitals and in the home. Work is also underway on commissioning social care services in conjunction with medical services. Health and well-being are essential planks of this shift in policy.

General practitioners enjoy special status within the NHS, being the most public face of health care because they have most contact with the public. Just about everyone has at some time had reason to 'see their doctor'. People are more likely to know the name of their doctor than that of any other public servant. But though GPs are paid out of the public purse, few of us think of them as public sector workers. They run their practices very much as private businesses – as independent contractors and for profit, and have done since 1948. In England, private firms provide hospital services for the NHS and privately run diagnostic and treatment centres for NHS patients have cut waiting lists considerably. It seems a natural progression for this kind of investment to find its way into general practice and so help bring health care to the doorstep.

6 APPROACH TO BRIEFING AND DESIGN

Design quality is now recognised as being very important and the approach to designing health buildings is focused on achieving flexibility and a sense of place rather than the previous approach of functionality and cost. Any briefing process is complex and ultimately depends on the clarity and vision of the client to identify the ethos of the project. Of course, a successful building also requires a good architect who is able to interpret this mission statement, and balance the inevitably conflicting requirements to create an architectural solution that adds to its urban context and provides (in the case of primary health care buildings) a healing environment.

In the UK there were political moves for money to follow the patient and to create an internal market in the NHS. These attempts to adjust the original philosophical concepts of the NHS were driven by an increasingly urgent need to address the rising costs of health care. An examination of government publications demonstrates the moves towards patient-focused care with the intention of raising the importance of primary care and community-based services.

Functionality and cost were seen to be best managed by high-level project management teams and option appraisal techniques to select the most appropriate design solutions. Although there was an increased recognition of the importance of primary care facilities, there continued to be a shortage of expectations of design quality in both hospitals and primary care facilities. The design of hospices, however, began to demonstrate an alternative way of providing high-quality health care facilities. The provision of hospices usually started with a clear expectation of the desired ethos and funding was often from charitable sources. There was therefore a complete reversal of priorities in the briefing process for hospices which was in sharp contrast with the conventional understanding of NHS design. Design quality expectations were high, the spiritual needs of patients were paramount and the focus of the building was firmly centred on individual patients.

Other factors began to emerge during this period, as experiments introducing art into health buildings were undertaken and architectural research programmes began to demonstrate that there were therapeutic benefits from well-designed environments. Increasingly, international comparisons became easier as young doctors travelled more widely.

6.1 Personal choice – care in the community

The government realised that people wanted their local services to:

- Understand how they live and support them to lead healthier lives.
- Help them to live independently if they have ongoing health or social care needs.
- Be easy to get to and convenient to use.
- Be nearer to where they live, or easily available in the areas they work.

 The government also aims to:

- Change the way services are provided in communities and make them as flexible as possible.
- Provide a more personal service tailored to the specific health or social care needs of individuals.
- Give patients and service users more control over the treatment they receive.
- Work with health and social care professionals and services to get the most appropriate treatment or care for their needs.

The government recognised that patients and service users should have more say in the services they needed and how they should be provided. Consequently, the government began to understand that it would be necessary for public, private, voluntary and charitable organisations to work together and in partnership to put the interests of the public first.

These political pressures, and the results of the consultation exercise, highlighted the need to adopt flexibility in the way health projects are provided, so that consumer choice is widened, but at the same time patients are invited to take greater personal responsibility for making decisions about their health care.

Architecturally, this reassessment of how health services should develop over the next five years has resulted in a range of solutions for providing primary care health facilities. The mixture of public and private finance has generated a range of buildings including community hospitals, walk-in centres and community health centres, including GP surgeries, each responding to the unique requirements of a particular locality.

These moves towards greater flexibility, with a range of financial models, have also produced some regional variations and initiatives within the UK. Trends are also emerging between the needs of urban and rural sites. In England the LIFT programme, despite being subject to considerable delays in obtaining approval for many of the schemes being designed, is resulting in an interesting range of buildings, usually in urban areas.

In rural areas, PCTs are favouring the community hospital approach and it is apparent that there is a close similarity between their buildings and the cottage hospitals which formed the backbone of rural health services in the 1970s and 1980s. It is also this building type which has such close similarities to that which was envisaged within the structure for health services set out by Lord Dawson in his report of 1920. It is interesting that the review of emergency services has recognised the advantages to be found from placing trained paramedics in community hospitals in rural areas.

Therefore, we are in a much more receptive culture to accept and understand the therapeutic benefits that can arise from well-designed primary care buildings. New design performance indicators are being developed to include a 'delight factor'.

- Functionality
  o Does the building perform its purpose?
  o What is a building's productivity?

- Whole life costing
  o Sustainability
  o In use costs/adaptability

- Delightfulness
  o Is it a focal point in the community?
  o What do passers-by think?
  o Effect on the mind and the senses

These issues are not just about measuring the performance of buildings but about raising public awareness of the quality and delight that can be enjoyed from well-designed environments.

6.2 Evolution of concepts

Evidence based design
The changing pattern of the approach to health has evolved through phases of holistic care, followed by more technical solutions. More recently (over the last decade) there is emerging a greater awareness of the importance of well-designed buildings and justification for this approach is being directed through 'evidence based design' (EBD). The most widely cited and quoted researcher internationally in the area of evidence based healthcare design is Roger Ulrich, Professor of Architecture at Texas A&M University. In 2005 he worked for a year in the UK for the NHS.

In the UK MARU (Medical Architecture Research Unit) has been a leader of research into the design of health care environments and has produced a wide range of documents and publications.

6.3 Future plans

Community based health/holistic approach (echoes of Finsbury and Peckham experiment)
It is interesting to compare the latest government proposals for the provision of primary health care buildings with the Peckham

Experiment and Finsbury Health Centre models of the 1930s. There is a return to providing primary health care facilities at a community level (80–90 per cent of all health care is provided by GPs outside of hospitals) through the programme of Health Living Centres and other initiatives which developed new procurement policies such as the PFI programme, Procure 21 and LIFT.

Better informed patients/consumerism
Patients are better informed today than when the NHS was introduced over 50 years ago. Consumerism will influence the attitude of patients who are used to high levels of customer care in other sectors of the economy. The influence of supply and demand in the market economy will inevitably challenge the providers of buildings to meet the new requirements.

Issues identified as being important include:

- fitness for purpose
- build quality
- sustainability
- adaptability
- safety
- efficiency
- appreciation of context
- an aesthetic impact that contributes to civic life.

CABE summarises good design as being a mix of the following attributes:

- functionality
- build quality
- efficiency and sustainability
- designing in context
- aesthetic quality.

CABE (The Commission for Architecture and the Built Environment) replaced the Royal Fine Art Commission and is now due to be wound up itself under cost savings by the coalition government. It played an important role in raising design standards particularly in the health sector.

Changing procurement systems
GP surgeries are too small to justify the competitive pre-contract procedures that potential development partners face under PFI procedures. The government policies for their Procure 21 method of procurement seem to be stalling, with considerable delays and increasing resistance from the contractors who have subscribed to the framework agreement. However there is a growing group of specialist companies forming partnerships with GPs to finance new primary health care facilities.

Primary health care buildings have been constrained by a set of procedures contained within the 'Red Book' which is now outdated. There have been enlightened solutions in recent years, by architects who have enjoyed a sustained period of work in this sector but imaginative solutions have been inhibited by the cost limits and tests of functionality. It was encouraging, therefore, that the government launched a new organisation, NHS LIFT (Local Improvement Finance Trust).

Many of the new facilities will also combine other services such as retail outlets, an optician's shop, pharmacy or other related services. Similarly, the intention is to bring primary care and social services together to improve communications, co-ordination of needs, thereby achieving a one-stop service for health, social services and housing. The NHS Plan is moving in the right direction. The new financial proposals through LIFT have introduced private finance and increased the flexibility of procuring new primary health care facilities.

We can anticipate that there will be fewer partnerships. Younger doctors, in common with many other professions, are increasingly reluctant to take on the financial responsibilities of a partnership in an economy that has seen sustained and steady growth with security of employment prospects. Financial success and security can often be achieved without taking on commercial risks. The historical advantages of partnership are increasingly being overtaken by new structures for professional services.

Therefore, we can see a major shift towards greater concern for design quality as more sophisticated measuring systems are introduced to evaluate 'value for money'. Much more research is required to develop accurate appraisals of whole life costs. From an environmental stance, all five senses of the human body should be considered.

1 Touch
2 Smell
3 Sight
4 Hearing
5 Taste

Procurement routes are changing. Primary health care facilities are becoming larger multi-functional 'Healthy Living Centres' offering integrated health and care services. A variety of agencies and professional skills will work in buildings serving the local community. Private finance will be provided by specialist developers and local initiatives will ensure greater control of matching requirements with services. This will have the benefit of allowing the new community facilities to include a wider range of services such as pharmacies, dentists, physiotherapists and alternative or complementary medical practitioners to all work under one roof.

Society has become more aware of the importance of a sustainable, environmentally friendly environment and is developing an understanding for designs which embrace the quality of life factors – the joy and delight that architecture can add to the fabric of society. This highlights the need to fundamentally shift priorities in the current briefing process. The ethos of the organisation must be the springboard for the development of the brief.

Procurement routes are therefore changing, and developing to reflect these requirements:

- Criticism of the PFI route – architects have felt their influence constrained by often being expected to work speculatively, or at peppercorn rates, during the competitive bidding stages of appointment often taking many months, (if not years) to reach a conclusion, and feel subservient to the main contractor after their novation in a winning team and sometimes losing authority over their own designs.
- Procure 21 – the NHS Estates proposals for meeting government expectations for repeat business to a selected list of approved large contractors but subject to much criticism by medium sized architects and contractors.
- The LIFT scheme promised to meet many of the difficulties inherent in the other procurement routes particularly for primary health care facilities.

6.4 LIFTS (Local Improvement Finance Trust)
The launch of LIFT (Local Improvement Finance Trust) was an initiative to stimulate the funding and operation of future primary health care facilities. The NHS Plan included proposals for LIFT designed to introduce private finance in a structure which devolves responsibility down to smaller building blocks at a regional and local level. This company has a board of advisers and oversees the allocation of funds to regionally organised LIFT companies. These in turn will attract further finance from local authorities, housing associations and primary care trusts and would operate with local boards.

The regional LIFT companies seek to enter into joint venture agreements with local developers to provide new local primary care facilities. Hence, the initial government funding was designed

to lever in a substantial proportion of private finance. A concern was whether the local companies would be of sufficient size to provide competencies in the key areas of:

- strategy
- construction
- FM and health services.

It might be anticipated that all these skills may be difficult to find within one company which would be of a size commensurate with the scale of project envisaged at a local level.

6.5 Local responsiveness and flexibility
To provide high quality local primary care facilities requires flexibility, and a local responsiveness to the needs and requirements that are particular to a community. It can be argued that the provision of the physical building should be separated from the provision of health services and the attendant facilities management needs during the life of a lease. Other sectors of the building industry and property market make clearer distinctions between the provision of the buildings and the operation of the services within them. As discussed elsewhere the office market has clearer structures which govern the way buildings are commissioned and occupied. Although some building owners occupy their own building, a much more sophisticated briefing process has evolved in recent years to enable a greater understanding of flexibility, efficiency and satisfaction by the people who use the spaces. The development of similarly comprehensive briefing documents should be a pre-requisite for all new primary health buildings.

Site acquisition is likely to be a critical factor, and location is a crucial component in the success of a primary health care building. It seems essential, therefore, to ensure that this imaginative initiative is fully explored at a local level, to ensure that the mechanisms are in place to provide the flexibility and responsiveness which will be required for its success. Medium sized developers, consultants and construction firms will need to work together so that collectively the competencies required are provided. This fundamentally different approach to PFI will encourage a 'bottom up' rather than a 'top down' approach to new solutions.

There are those who argue for repetition, and standardisation in the provision of primary health care facilities leading to ideas of the same building being reproduced on many sites. Perhaps there will be components of a building which could be standardised but health care needs to accommodate the social values that can flow from flexible and humane spaces.

6.6 Anticipating the future
The information age has given us the ability to share knowledge globally. There has been a new awakening of moral attitudes and responsibilities arising out of the Human Rights Act which is giving a greater sense of respect for the individual person. This is reflected in health care which is once again becoming focused on the patient as an individual. We should be encouraged by the opportunities now being presented to capture the ethos coming out of thoughtful building briefs.

Everyone involved in the provision of primary health care is increasingly aware that the individual must be the centre of their own health care, or well-being. There seems to be a universal acceptance that this policy can apply in both rich and poor economies. Health for All really is a policy for primary medical care which has no opponents, and crosses political boundaries.

The training of doctors is becoming more broadly based. Many university departments are now recognising that a scientific and technology based approach for medical education does not give a sufficiently well-rounded training for the doctors of the next generation. Humanities are being introduced to the curriculum of medical schools which reflect the recognition that doctors need to treat patients in a more holistic manner.

The government is moving its position on health care policy with a new understanding of the importance of patients' needs. The requirements for health care are being assessed from the perspective of patients and there is recognition that the social agenda for health care needs to become more inclusive. Inevitably, this will lead to greater complexity in the organisation of services, and the crossing of boundaries between traditional concepts of health care, social services such as housing and the treatment of mental health issues. One is led down the path of recognising the importance of the built environment to provide a humane place in which to live a healthy life.

6.7 Trends

The research brings together a range of solutions from which it is possible to distil a series of common strands in the design approach.

1 Policies around the world are concentrating on improving health care services at a primary level.
2 There is universal attention to patient centred care irrespective of the size of the building, or wealth of the country, in which it is located.
3 Architecture and medicine are talking to each other. The quality of the humane healing environment is seen as a positive benefit.
4 Our well-being is reflected in the environmental quality of our new health buildings: smaller, community based flexible spaces, easily accessible and welcoming. They are designed for the benefit of the patient rather than the provider of medical services.
5 There is a high incidence of curved shapes in the design of small health buildings. The building form envelopes the user, provides comfort and is reassuring. It is non-threatening, and not confrontational. By a combination of form, light and colour, buildings around the world straddle cultural differences with an architectural language which individuals can recognise whatever their mother tongue.

6.8 Objectives of a brief

Doctors and architects need to work more closely together. Through the development of briefing documents, we should be optimistic about the opportunities that will arise for primary health care buildings in the future. They will provide the physical framework within which the complex social interaction of the community can engage with the medical profession. There is agreement that many of the better examples of good design for health buildings have been built in the primary care sector.

1 The brief should be the central and fundamental cornerstone for the provision of future health care buildings. It should set down the ethos and culture for the health care environment. Many of these over-arching objectives will be common to the design of a doctor's surgery anywhere in the world.
2 There are both strategic and practical levels of planning. It is at the practical level where there may be more substantial differences in the briefing document between one country and another.
3 The brief should set down the design aspirations. It will set out the 'wish list' and establish the sense of wonder which excites the spirit when good architecture is encountered.
4 The brief must bring together current ideas and anticipate future trends.
5 It must also capture the sense of change which is sweeping through the primary health care design field not just in the UK, and the USA, but in many parts of the world.
6 In another decade we are likely to find much broader acceptance of alternative therapies. In the West, we have only recently begun to understand and accept the contribution that alternative health remedies can bring. How much more there must be to learn about traditional Chinese medicine, for example, and environments such as the Glasgow Homoeopathic Hospital may well be the forerunner of many other buildings in the future seeking

to combine traditional medicine, alternative therapies and a high quality of environmental design.
7 More sophisticated linkages are likely to emerge. Key words and phrases to consider when writing a brief are shown in Table I.

Table I Brief writing – key words and phrases

Key words: networking concepts	
• Government policy	• Finance and funding
• Community facilities	• Flexibility
• Education (training)	• Communications
• Sustainability	• Location (accessibility)
• Knowledge (transfer of skills)	• Transport policy
• Value for money	• Patient needs

An examination of these issues will assist in establishing the strategic framework for the design of a new primary health facility. It may be helpful to prepare checklists on these points as an aide mémoire during discussions with key members of the client and design team. This will give focus and direction to the establishment of both the strategic and practical aspects of the brief.

6.9 Design quality

Our modern understanding of a primary health centre was set out in the Dawson Report (1920) as 'An institution equipped for services of curative and preventive medicine to be conducted by general practitioners of that district, in conjunction with an efficient nursing service and with the aid of visiting consultants and specialists'. It remains a valid definition today.

A framework of issues for doctors and architects to discuss together when developing a brief for a healthy living centre is shown in Table II.

Table II Writing a brief – matrix of factors to consider

Issue		Architecture	Medicine
1	Functionality	space standards, initial cost effectiveness, data sheets	flexibility, meeting future working patterns
1	Multi–agency	planning flexibility, long life, loose fit	choice of agencies, services to be offered
1	Accessibility/ convenience	transport linkages, pedestrian routes, parking, disabled access	patient adjacency, alternative locations
1/2	Exemplar design models	environmental performance standards	good practice models, standard room plans
1/3	Site/location/ land acquisition	urban context, planning constraints, value for money	convenience, visibility of building, availability
2	Brief – the ethos of the building	architectural language, style, patient comfort, therapeutic benefits	personal rapport with patients, relationships, working environment, sense of well being
2	Community	quality of the place, welcoming, comfortable	friendliness, reassurance, accessible
3	Finance – procurement method, costs	contractual arrangements, PFI, LIFT, design criteria, project management, programming	PCGs/PCT's ability to influence funding, budgets, access to finance
3	Sustainability	energy consumption, life cycle costs	recycle facilities, medical efficiency
3	Standardisation	standard components within unique design, choice of materials	routine procedures, clinic requirements, compatibility with other surgery operating systems

Key
1 Physical
2 Emotional
3 Financial

6.10 Recurring themes
The following list sets out a number of key issues:

- Emphasis on quality of architectural design – importance of high quality environmental factors.
- Emphasis on the patient as an individual.
- Patient focused care as a local level of primary care being the hub of patient treatment rather than the start of a linear process of passing through various levels of specialisation.
- Building flexibility – design for change, openness, accessibility.
- Buildings have not played a key role in health policy, but need to in future.
- There has been insufficient recognition of the importance of environmental quality, and the effect that this can have on health care.
- Architects need to take up the opportunity to build on the new interest by doctors to embrace health and humanities.
- It is people that regenerate places, not places that regenerate people. Overreliance on economic, social and physical modelling techniques and statistical analysis at the expense of visual stimulus, undervalues the importance of architecture.
- Visual stimulus is a key ingredient of the built environment. The delight of architecture should not be squeezed out of the built environment by analytical methodologies.
- Give status to the product as well as the process (think of design as well as construction).
- Put architecture back into health.
- The patient must come first.

6.11 A framework for the brief – the ethos
Right at the beginning of the document there should be a section which encourages the design team to set out the quality aspirations expected from the building. It needs to encourage future users of the building to think about what the ethos of the building should be; to set out what the building users want out of the building; and what are the intangible values that the designers aim to achieve. For example, should the building be:

- friendly
- efficient
- welcoming
- relaxing
- comfortable
- warm
- pleasant
- accessible?

The brief should seek to encourage the achievement of high design standards through the eyes of the patient – the tests of functionality and cost should be a secondary, albeit essential, requirement of the procurement process for any new primary health care building.

Huge potential benefits are coming out of these changing philosophies in primary health care buildings which will influence the quality and procurement methodology for our health buildings at the specialised end of health care.

6.12 Strategic components of a brief
Having established a framework of ideas or ethos, and understanding the context and networking requirements for a particular building in a specific location, the strategic components of a brief can be more precisely laid down, as shown in Table III.

After the ethos of the project has been defined, and the strategic objectives have been agreed, the practical issues of functionality and cost can be explored. What this research has revealed is the benefits that would arise if a new data based handbook for primary health care facilities was available, but written through the eyes of the patient rather than from the perspective of the health service provider. Thus, new standards could be quantified and dimensioned for:

- patient control of their environment in treatment rooms, waiting rooms and other spaces;
- design of furnishings, fixtures and fittings;
- flexibility in the layout of equipment within a space;
- flexibility of use of a space;
- environmental design standards and performance specifications;
- compliance with access for the disabled;
- transportation links (on foot, cycle, car, or public transport);
- functionality;
- landscaping;
- building materials;
- cost limits.

7 KEY RELATIONSHIPS
The design of primary health care buildings has changed radically over the last few years and design quality is now seen as a very important aspect of the procurement process. This has been reflected in the recent Department of Health (DH) publications and essential reading for any architect working on a new primary care building is 'Primary and Community Care – Health Building Note 11–01: Facilities for primary and community care services'. This document, which is part of a suite of Health Building Notes, sets out an approach to designing new facilities which recognises the need for flexibility, changing relationships and how to set out firming up a brief that will result in user-friendly environments. The document does not provide detailed design guidance on specific rooms and spaces and refers to the need for planning and design teams to refer to the following publications for guidance on generic rooms and spaces.

- Health Building Note 00–02 – 'sanitary spaces'
- Health Building Note 00–03 – 'clinical and clinical support spaces'
- Health Building Note 00–04 – 'circulation and communication spaces'

This section follows this lead and does not attempt to set out generic ergonomical room data sheet type details which underpinned the design approach for primary health buildings when the main assessment criteria were functionality and cost. Rather, designers and architects working on new buildings for the future need to establish the ethos of the client and develop solutions that embrace that philosophy. Obviously, it is necessary to ensure that the practical space standards are met but this should flow through the evolution of the brief.

Health Building Note (HBN) 11–01 sets out best practice guidance on the selection and zoning of facilities for delivering primary

Table III Practical components of a brief

– The Vision	– how will the experience of visitors, patients and staff be enhanced by the building?
	– how will the design quality add to the expectation of excellence?
	– how will a high quality environment be achieved?
	– will it be patient focused?
– The Process	– select an appropriate procurement method to ensure that design quality isn't stifled.
– Urban Design	– will the building contribute to the sense of place?
	– will transport linkages work?
– Benchmarking	– is the building going to add to the level of competencies prevailing in the vicinity?
– Value for Money	– will it represent 'best value'?
– Patient Centred	– will the brief encourage good environmental design and achieve therapeutic benefits for patients and all other users of the building?
	– is it patient centred?

and community care services. The guidance is applicable to the following building types:

- GP premises
- Health centres
- Primary care centres
- Resource centres
- Urgent care centres (including walk-in centres and minor injuries units)
- Community hospitals (also known as intermediate care hospitals).

It describes the following:

- The range of services that may be delivered from primary and community care buildings.
- The types of space needed to deliver these services (many of which are generic).
- The way to quantify these spaces for briefing purposes.
- The way spaces can be organised into zones to create efficient, flexible, user-friendly environments.

This guide has been written with the provision of new-build facilities in mind. The principles described apply equally to the refurbishment and extension of existing buildings.

The document sets out the following.

Strategic design issues:

- Design quality
- Quality of place
- Art and integrated design
- Sustainability
- NHS identity.

Functional design issues:

- Accessibility
- Infection control
- Wayfinding
- Security
- Emergency preparedness.

As already mentioned the shift in design approach is towards flexibility and adaptability. HBN 11–01 sets out a list of criteria and offers an approach to the use of space which is multi-functional and time-managed.

Strategies include maximising flexibility and adaptability:

- Use generic patient/client contact spaces.
- Limit the number of specialist spaces.
- Standardise room sizes and position of built-in equipment.
- Consider future engineering service requirements at the outset.
- Consider flexible and adaptable forms of construction.
- Develop a modular approach to planning and construction.
- Provide space for future expansion, if relevant.

Most primary and community care services involve one or more of the following activities:

- Counselling
- Consultation
- Examination
- Diagnosis
- Treatment
- Physical therapy.

These activities may occur on a planned basis (for example specialist outreach consulting), unplanned basis (for example urgent

care or walk-in services) or a combination of the two (for example GP consultation). This affects the way services are managed rather than the facilities required.

Most activities involve a practitioner and an individual patient/client, although certain forms of physical therapy and counselling may take place in groups. Most activities can be delivered from the following generic patient/client contact spaces:

- Interview room
- Consulting/examination room
- Treatment room (that is, with mechanical ventilation)
- Examination/physical therapy room
- Group room.

Generic patient/client contact spaces should be shared on a time-tabled basis to maximise their use unless required on a dedicated basis for full-time use. Treatment activity requires special consideration. Treatments given in primary and community care settings fall under a number of categories, and can occur in different room types.

Non-invasive and minimally invasive treatments may take place in consulting/examination room, treatment room or examination/physical therapy room, depending on space requirements. (A noninvasive procedure is one that does not break the skin, for example changing a dressing. A minimally invasive procedure is one that breaks or punctures the skin, for example injections and taking blood.)

An invasive procedure is one that cuts the superficial layers of the skin, for example removal of moles, warts or corns, biopsies or any endoscopic procedure accessing any body orifice. A local anaesthetic or sedation may be required with an invasive procedure. Most invasive procedures and certain procedures using rigid endoscopes can take place in a generic treatment room. In addition, procedures that generate heat (for example ultrasound) and/or unpleasant odours (for example tissue viability clinic) should only take place in a treatment room (that is, with mechanical ventilation). Some invasive procedures may require all-round couch access, including access to the head of the couch.

7.1 Standardise room sizes and position of built-in equipment

Room sizes and dimensions should be standardised wherever possible. This may mean sizing up to some extent, but results in rooms that can be adapted (for alternative use) more easily. Experience and ergonomic analysis suggests the following room sizes provide a good fit for most generic rooms in primary and community care buildings:

- 8 m^2
- 12 m^2
- 16 m^2
- 32 m^2

The ability to standardise the position of built-in equipment (for example clinical wash-hand basin) will further enhance adaptability. This idea is shown in Figure 33.2.

The 16 m^2 consulting/examination room in Health Building Note 00–03 shows access to three sides of the couch. This is not generally required in primary and community care settings, where the couch can be aligned against one wall, leaving additional space for patients, escorts and mobile equipment. The couch should be correctly handed, however, and the clinical wash-hand basin should remain within the cubicle area – see Figure 33.3.

The 12 m^2 consulting/examination room with single-sided couch access identified in Health Building Note 00–03 is not recommended for use in primary and community care buildings as it offers less space for equipment and patients/escorts than the 16m^2 room.

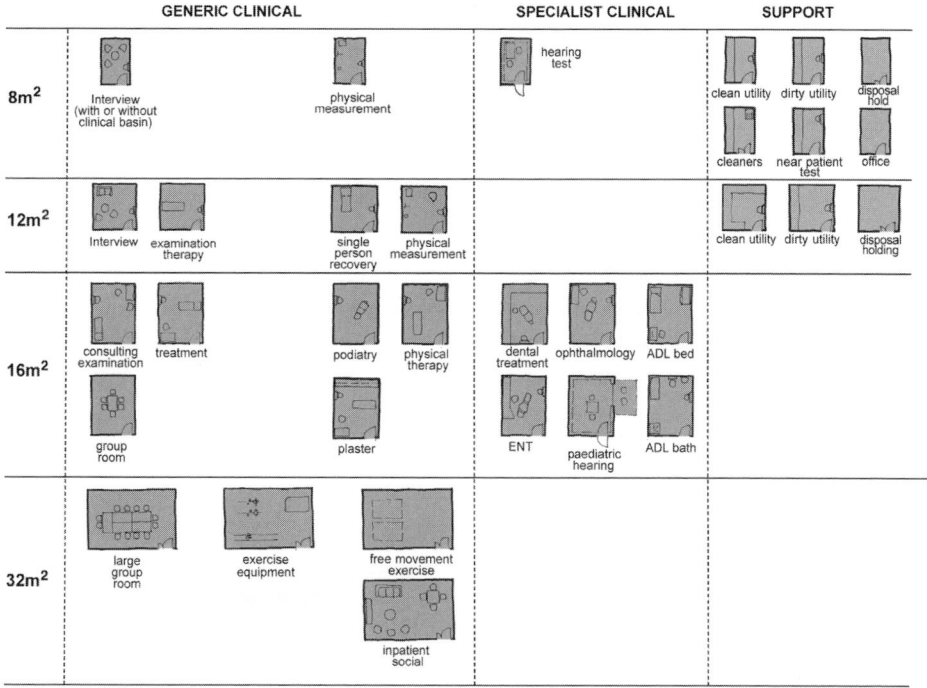

33.2 *Modular sizing concept*

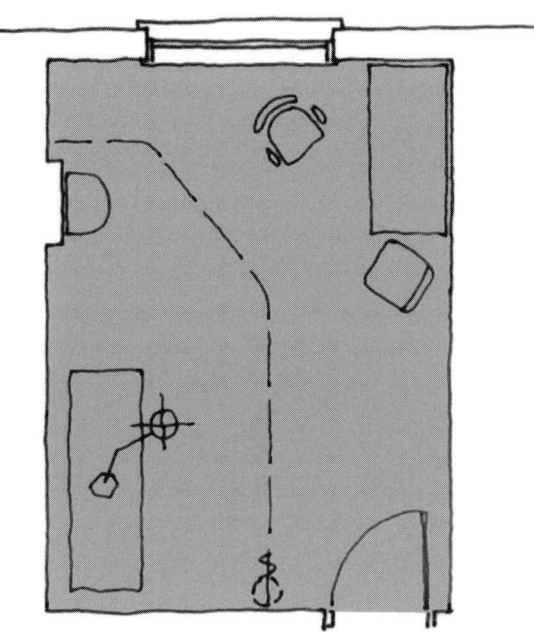

33.3 *Alternative layout for 16 sq m consulting/examination room with couch against wall*

7.2 Consider future engineering service requirements at the outset

At the beginning of the design process consideration should be given to which room functions are likely to change over time and the impact this will have on engineering service requirements. Two broad approaches are possible:

- Install sufficient engineering services at the outset to accommodate future uses of the room.
- Provide adequate infrastructure capacity, plant room and containment space to upgrade engineering services at a later date.

Decisions over which approach to employ will be influenced by the ability to predict future changes in use, economic constraints, and the need to satisfy any emergency preparedness provisions, which may require rapid conversion from one room type to another.

Where it is decided to install engineering services at the outset to accommodate future use, controls can be used to set ventilation, temperature control and lighting systems at the appropriate levels.

7.3 Consider flexible and adaptable forms of construction

To ensure day-to-day flexibility, consider the use of:

- Acoustically treated folding partition walls between adjoining group rooms, allowing rooms to be opened up to create larger spaces.
- Changeable signage, allowing room names and routes to be easily modified for individual sessions.
- Mobile, rather than fixed, equipment and furniture.
- Wireless and/or internet protocol technology, where appropriate.
- Standard data outlets (for example RJ45) and common structured wiring infrastructure to create a network for telephones, data and video.

To ensure that buildings are adaptable in the longer term, consider the following:

- The use of framed construction allowing partition walls to be altered.
- The installation of suitable surface fixed trunking to allow engineering services outlets to be added or altered, particularly where large numbers and types of outlet are concentrated on a small space. This is subject to infection control requirements being met.
- The use of structured wiring for IT and communication systems and modular wiring systems for lighting and small power.
- Provision of adequate spare plant and service access space, including ceiling void depths and service access space, including ceiling void depths and service risers, to have sufficient capacity to accommodate anticipated future M&E expansion and equipment replacement.
- Developing a modular approach to planning and construction.

Adopting a limited number of room sizes can lead to building layouts that use economic structural spans, stack efficiently and allow for nature cross-ventilation.

This approach to planning assumes three broad categories of the use of space:

- Public spaces
- Primary and community care spaces
- Staff areas.

Diagrammatically they are represented in Figure 33.4.

For those embarking on the design of a new primary care or community building more specific guidance is set out in HBN 11–01 and is recommended as essential reading.

8 ENGINEERING AND IT SERVICES

This is a rapidly changing area of design. Technology is evolving and the preferred methodologies for any particular site should be carefully checked with the client and appropriate public approval bodies.

The following list is an aide-memoire of topics for the designer to consider:

- Life expectancy of plant and equipment
- Metering
- Control of infection
- Space requirement for engineering services
- Piped medical gases
- Heating systems
- Ventilation and cooling
- Hot and cold water systems
- Acoustics
- Fire safety and alarm systems
- Lighting systems (internal, external and emergency)

- Call systems (patient/staff and emergency)
- Safety and security
- CCTV
- Car parking and control systems
- Door access control systems
- IT and telephone wiring (or wi-fi) systems
- Entertainment systems
- Document/data transport systems
- Controlled drugs storage
- Sustainability and energy efficiency
- Management and operational control of services.

The objective of the designer should be to offer the client flexibility and provoke dialogue with the users of the building to ensure imaginative solutions are considered.

9 ART IN HEALTH

The importance and influence of art, music, food and architecture have all re-emerged as significant factors in designing primary health care buildings. Designers should look at the importance of recognising that a sense of well-being includes healing the soul as well as mending the body. Broadly understood as holistic care, architects should discuss with clients, doctors, patients and other users of primary care buildings aspects of these ideas to incorporate them into the design of new projects. The briefing process for new buildings should focus on the patient and learn from the successes of good design developed in the hospice sector.

The concept of art in health buildings is at the heart of 'value for money evaluations' and applies equally in the primary care sector as well as in hospitals. Healing is a more embracing concept; it involves our minds and our feelings and our spirits as well as our bodies. It is, therefore, perfectly natural to go along with Handel's view and accept that music can heal our sadness.

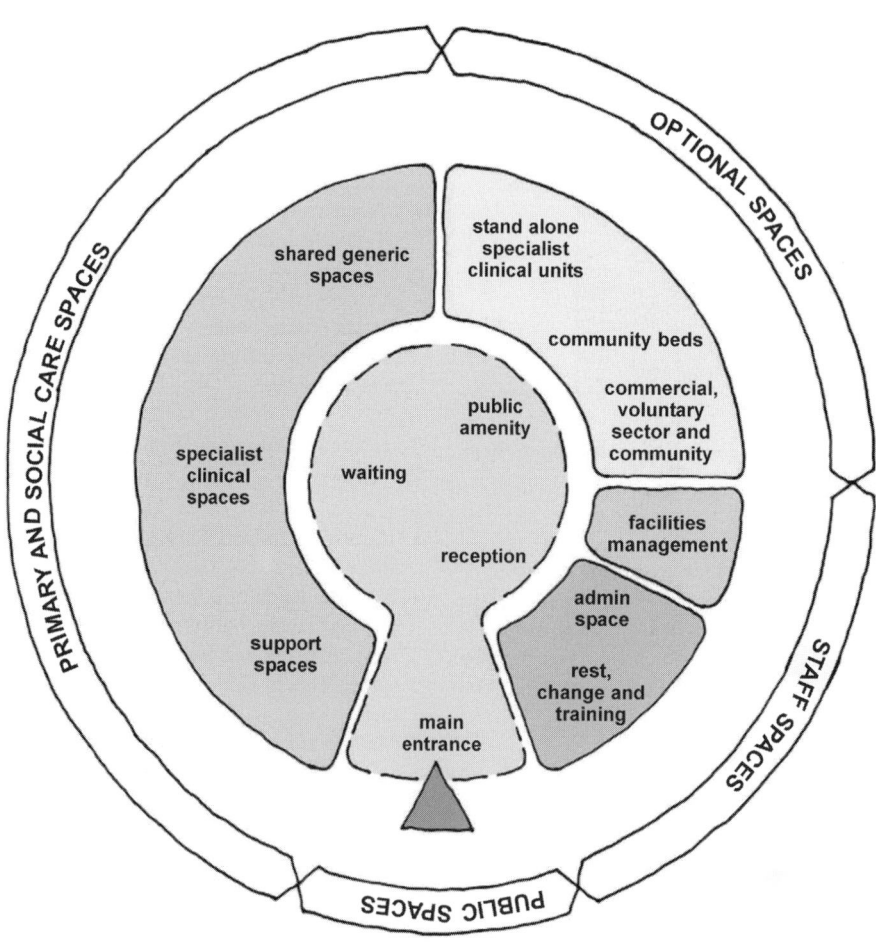

33.4 *Zoning concept diagram*

10 HOLISTIC CARE

As the focus for health care in the UK is shifting towards the primary care sector it is interesting to reflect briefly on historical attitudes towards treatment of those who are ill. In early civilisations (e.g. Egyptian and Roman) holistic care was a central part of caring for the sick. The development of hospitals began out of a wish to offer hospitality to those in need. In those early times, up until the renaissance, almost everything done for the sick in Western Europe was provided by the Church. However, with the development of scientific medicine much of this pastoral care was gradually taken out of the Church's hands and during the past two centuries the medical profession has become secularised. The development of the medical profession, in a technological sense, has developed with the creation of the Royal Colleges and the establishment of specialised qualifications. Unfortunately this led, until recently, to an attitude of mind that saw death as a failure of medical treatment.

The World Health Organisation has reported that the single most important factor for health in a hospital is the atmosphere. If this is true then the spirit in which the medicine is practised is important. However, with government policy rapidly changing the focus of attention onto patient centred care based in the community we know that the vast majority (75 per cent or more) of the health budget of the NHS is spent in the primary care sector. This would suggest that there is an urgent need to address the provision of holistic care services within the primary care sector including:

- provide appropriate spiritual and religious care to patients, staff and other users;
- provide pastoral care;
- provide regular opportunity for religious expression;
- identify and assess the needs for chaplaincy/spiritual care;
- support multi-faith working which respects and supports faiths identified.

Re-examine the role of holistic care in the primary health sector. Many GPs already have links with alternative medical treatment offering guidance on complementary medicine and alternative therapies. Should community-based GP surgeries have more direct links with chaplains or representatives of other faith groups? Should GP surgeries be encouraged to develop formal links with faith groups in their locality? Perhaps primary care buildings should reflect these issues of well-being in their design, and provide spaces for contemplation or rest. This is part of the development of an environment for healing. There is an immense shift from assessing the value of what is being done by many medical and nursing staff as a sense of vocation to assessing it in terms of cost effectiveness. Do staff need to rediscover the sense of vocation where they have to help in healing and not just regard themselves as 'service providers'? The use of language is important. A balance has to be struck between the book keeping elements of running a GP surgery and offering compassion for suffering people.

11 CONCLUSION

The primary health care sector in the UK is experiencing great change, and is also carrying a great deal more responsibility for the well-being of patients. Indeed, we are seeing government policy for health care move beyond the limitations of previous administrations to embrace wider issues such as the environmental conditions in socially deprived areas. More positively, connections are being made between the quality of the built environment and the physical well-being of patients living in a particular locality. Social policies and health policies are being recognised as interdependent.

12 CASE STUDIES

Case study 12.1
Project: The Heart of Hounslow Health Centre, Hounslow, London
Completion Date: 2007
Architect: Penoyre & Prasad
Developer name: Building Better Health
Main Contractor name: Willmott Dixon Construction
Quantity Surveyor name: Davis Langdon LLP
Services Engineer name: Whitby Bird
Structural Engineer name: Price & Myers LLP

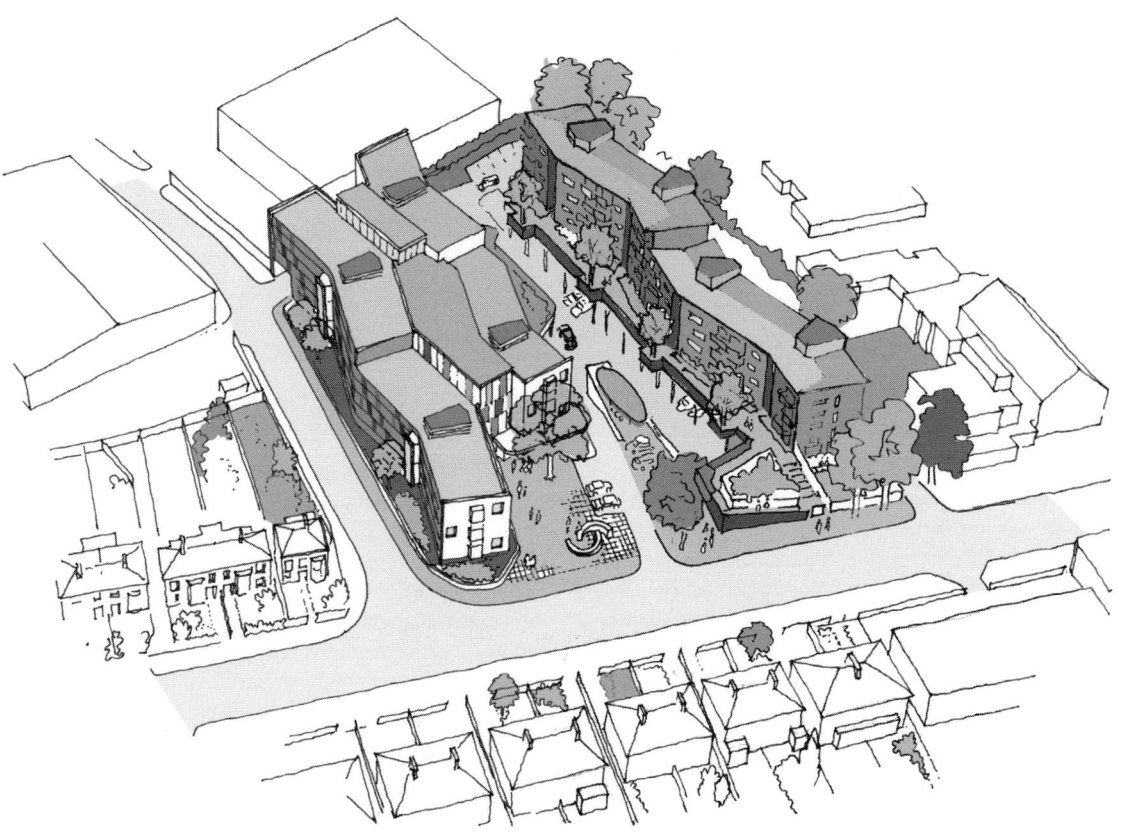

33.5 *The Heart of Hounslow Health Centre, London. Aerial sketch view showing health centre and key worker housing next door*

33.6 *The Heart of Hounslow Health Centre, London. The entrance and atrium maximise use of natural light to create an uplifting environment (photo by: Nick Kane)*

33.7 *The Heart of Hounslow Health Centre, London. View of atrium with waiting area in foreground (photo by: Nick Kane)*

33.8 *The Heart of Hounslow Health Centre, London. View of Main Entrance (photo by: Steve Townsend)*

33.9 *The Heart of Hounslow Health Centre, London. View of West Elevation (photo by: Dennis Gilbert)*

The Heart of Hounslow Centre for Health is now one of the largest Primary Care Centres in the UK. This centre was built in pursuit of new ambition for primary care in the NHS whereby a large range of services is gathered together in one place better to serve patients, develop staff capacities and provide 'joined up' delivery. This ambition needed to be expressed in the civic qualities of the architecture. The building was procured through a Public Private Partnership, which means that possible future uses of the building need to be considered in the design. Together with the constantly changing nature of health services that makes a compelling case for adaptive design.

The Heart of Hounslow Centre for Health currently accommodates some 14 separate departments and services. These are arranged on each floor to suit the optimum relationships. Heart of Hounslow hosts four GP practices, a range of clinical services, physiotherapy, podiatry, dentistry and speech and language services, social care outreach services, special facilities for children, adolescents and people with learning disabilities and health information/cafe. Almost half of the accommodation is workspace for domiciliary staff. All these functions are organised around a five storey high atrium with bridges and galleries that allows the parts of the building to be pointed out from the reception desk.

The concrete structure of the building is organised on a simple repetitive module that allows areas to be set up as open plan offices or as cellular clinical rooms with non-structural internal

33.10 *The Heart of Hounslow Health Centre, London. Wayfinding is clearly legible from the atrium and waiting area (photo by: Nick Kane)*

partitions. Externally windows alternating with coloured aluminium panels form horizontal bands. If necessary the window and panel position can be changed to follow internal reconfiguration; but they are positioned in such a way that partition positions can be extensively altered and still permit day lit internal rooms. The services strategy, with its ducted air heating and comfort cooling, supports this adaptability with the main distribution in a central spine following the corridor zone.

The atrium is painted white so that the coloured glass in clerestory windows and the entrance screens cast ever-changing patterns on its internal surfaces. The staff 'club' is located on the top floor with panoramic views over London.

Case study 12.2
Project Name: Loxford Polyclinic
Project Location: South Ilford, United Kingdom
Architect: Devereux Architects
Completion Date: 2009
Client: Loxford Complex Limited for Redbridge Primary Care Trust

London's first purpose built Polyclinic was recently opened by Lord Darzi in South Ilford, East London and is one of up to 150 to be opened as part of the Under Secretary for Health's 2008 vision for Primary Care in the NHS.

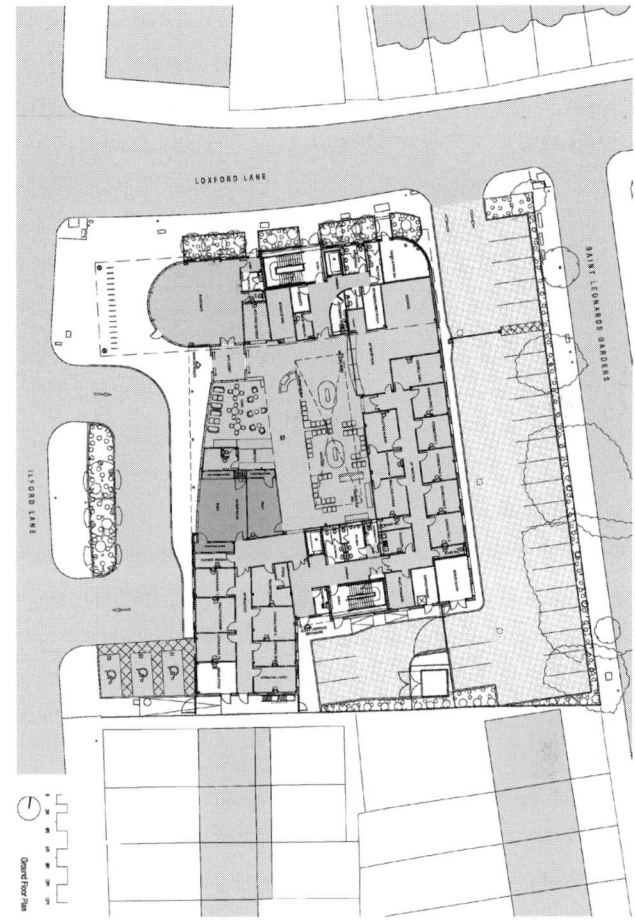

33.12 *Loxford Polyclinic, Essex Plan*

33.11 *Loxford Polyclinic, Essex Front Elevation (photo by: Ed Hill)*

33.13 *Loxford Polyclinic, Essex. Reception, waiting and Café (photo by: Ed Hill)*

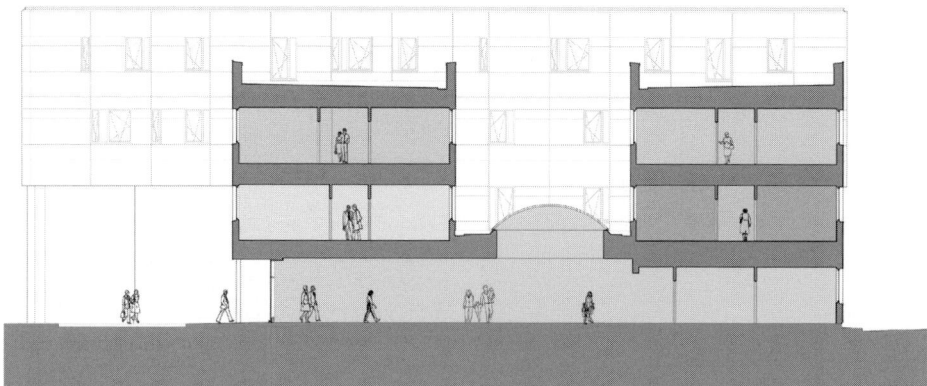

33.14 *Loxford Polyclinic, Essex. Section*

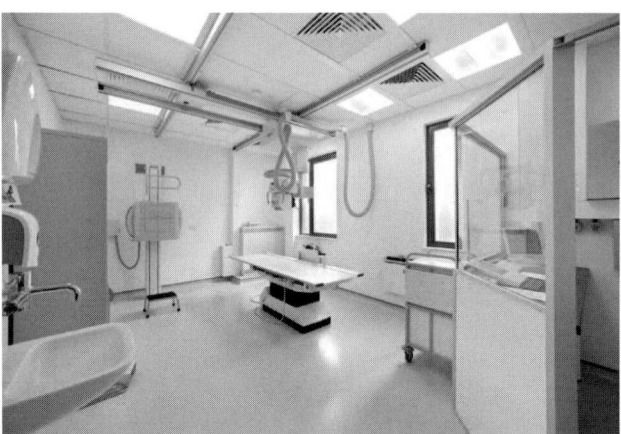

33.15 *Loxford Polyclinic, Essex. X-ray suite (photo by Ed Hill)*

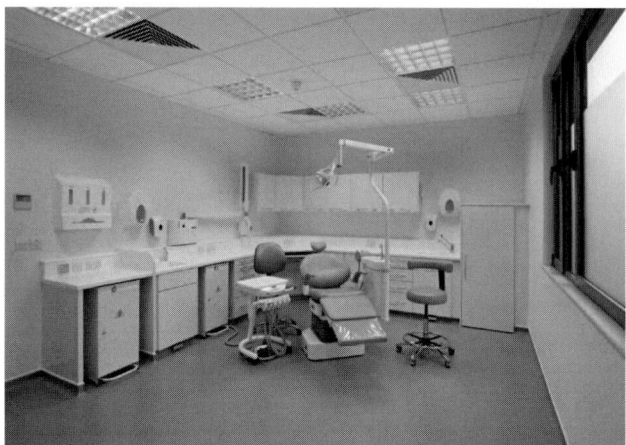

33.16 *Loxford Polyclinic, Essex. Dental surgery (photo by Ed Hill)*

Strategy

The Polyclinic sits at the centre of Redbridge PCT's new Loxford 'Polysystem': a new way of joining up health services and providing easier access to healthcare. The clinic is a Hub providing links with local Spoke facilities, i.e. GP surgeries, primary and other voluntary care services.

Innovation

The new 4 storey clinic will serve up to 50,000 local people and will offer early and late appointments 7 days a week for a comprehensive range of services traditionally provided only in hospitals. In addition to GP surgeries, new services include: minor ops, x-ray and ultrasound, ENT/audiology, phlebotomy, dentistry, podiatry, ophthalmology, rheumatology and gynaecology. To encourage healthy lifestyles there is a well-being clinic and a cardiology/physiotherapy unit complete with gym. Patients can pop in without appointment and use the Self Testing Facility for blood pressure and BMI, book into the flexible group rooms for health related activities or just relax in the community café. Complementing the Polyclinic services the '100 hour' pharmacy offers consulting facilities.

Place making

Located on a busy road within a dense residential district the building is now a contemporary landmark within the Ilford community and is easily reached on foot or by bus. On entering the building everyone is met by a 'meet and greet' point within a bright and spacious toplit waiting 'lounge' which is open plan with the café. The main reception desk provides all of the services in the building with a single control point for appointments and information. The waiting area is a designated Public Art space and the community are encouraged to contribute or just come in and view the displays.

The GP services and blood testing areas surround the waiting space on the ground floor. Above this are two further storeys of clinical services arranged around the central lightwell. Staff are well provided for with a suite of administration, changing and relaxation spaces on the third floor including a large lounge space with views over Ilford.

Adaptability

The lightweight form of panelled construction allows partition layouts to be adapted and moved flexibly to suit changing clinical requirements. Clinical spaces are standardised so that consulting and treatment rooms are interchangeable. GPs will use a 'Hotdesk' system where notes are written up in a separate suite of non-clinical rooms which will free up valuable consulting space.

Sustainability

The Polyclinic achieved a NEAT 'Excellent' rating through simple passive and active strategies:

- Located on a brownfield site easily reached by public transport.
- Building shape which provides natural light and ventilation to almost every single room including many wcs.
- Lightweight offsite construction system avoiding site waste.
- Waterless urinals and low flush systems.
- PIR sensors to switch off lights automatically.
- Underfloor heating for efficient distribution of energy.

Case study 12.3
Project name: Houghton le Spring Primary Care Centre, Tyne & Wear
Architect: P+HS Architects
Size: 7,500 m²
Client: Sunderland Teaching Primary Care Trust
Main Contractor: Willmott Dixon
M&E Engineers: Cundall Johnston & Partners LLP
Engineers: Breathing Buildings
Building Services Contractors: LJJ Contractors Limited

33.19 *Primary Care Centre, Houghton le Spring. Internal: the atrium allows light to flood into the central parts of the building*

33.17 *Primary Care Centre, Houghton le Spring. Entrance: the inviting entrance also has a civic presence*

33.20 *Primary Care Centre, Houghton le Spring. Model: the building in context with sports, leisure and wellness facilities also located on the site*

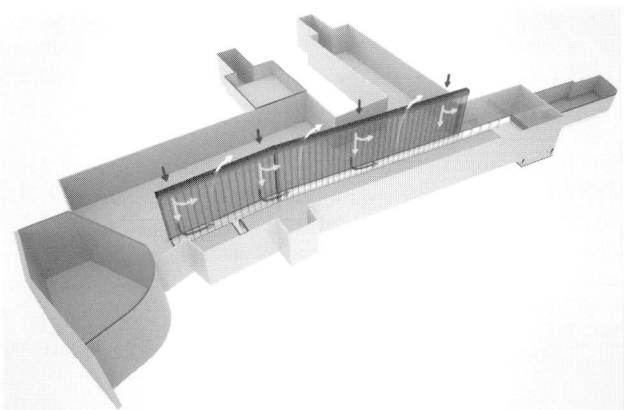

33.18 *Primary Care Centre, Houghton le Spring. Thermal wall image: the building is naturally ventilated using a thermal wall which is based on the principles of thermal mass and the stack effect*

'Raising the bar in sustainable design for Healthcare Buildings'.

A new primary care centre under construction at Houghton le Spring, Tyne and Wear, has achieved a BREEAM 'Outstanding' at design stage; the first healthcare building in the UK to achieve this. The new 7,500 m² centre incorporates an existing sports and leisure facility, with the new build element dramatically extending the original to three times its size, and bringing together healthcare, sports, leisure and wellness facilities on one site.

Main contractors Wilmott Dixon and P+HS Architects are working with Sunderland Teaching Primary Care Trust and Sunderland City Council to develop the £18m scheme. The project has been designed in collaboration with both CABE and Cambridge University's 'Breathing Buildings' consultants to ensure exemplary design quality and a highly sustainable solution. The project was procured under a local authority SCAPE framework contract.

Healthcare facilities in the new two storey centre will include a minor injuries walk-in centre, diagnostics facilities including x-ray and ultrasound, planned care clinical accommodation, a 24 bed rehabilitation unit and supporting accommodation, a community café and meeting rooms.

Alongside but integral to the healthcare centre will be new and refurbished sports and leisure facilities with accommodation for wellness classes, and physiotherapy facilities. Aiming for the highest BREEAM rating of 'outstanding', the development incorporates sustainable technologies to reduce the carbon load as far as possible. The building's orientation has been purposely designed to minimise excessive solar gain in summer, but to maximise sunlight during the winter months and exposed glazing is protected by solar shading.

The building is largely naturally ventilated using an innovative system designed by Breathing Buildings. Based on the principles of thermal mass and the stack effect, tempered air is delivered from an underground plenum via 49 chimneys to ventilate and condition the interior of the building. Ground source heat pumps are used to provide space heating which required 104 bore holes to be drilled on the site. Rain water harvesting is used to reduce water consumption and a sedum roof will not only encourage biodiversity but also attenuate rain overflow reducing the drainage load. Solar thermal panels are installed to provide preheated domestic hot water for the building and renewable energy sources, such as, a vertical axis wind turbine and 350 m² photovoltaic panels further contribute to the facility's energy requirements to reducing the building's carbon footprint.

The two principal elements of the scheme, the primary care centre and the leisure/sports facilities, are positioned either side of the main entrances. Because of the sloping site, the sports centre entrance is one floor level above that of the primary care centre, which requires two entrances to be linked by a main stairway within the two storey atrium. This atrium allows light to flood into the central parts of the building where the main reception points are located together with the café, self help area and principal reception lounges. A 24 bed rehabilitation ward is located on the first floor level to provide privacy for patients and visitors. All bedrooms are single, en-suite and have glazed doors opening onto Juliet balconies. The new building is structured around a steel frame with external elevations in a combination of natural stone, render and Trespa panelling. External works involve extensive landscaping and the creation of a new multi use games area as well as the refurbishment of an existing crown green bowling facility and relocation of the existing skate park.

There are 163 car parking spaces, including car sharing bays and electric car charging points, included in the scheme, as well as secure cycle storage. In addition, a public transport drop off area is being created to ensure easy bus access right to the door of the new facility.

Case study 12.4
Project: Blaydon Leisure and Primary Care Centre, Tyne and Wear
Architect: P + HS Architects
Size: 4,000 m² (Primary Care Element)
Client: Gateshead Primary Care Trust
Main Contractor: Willmott Dixon
M&E Engineers: Cundall
Structural Engineer: Cundall
Building Services Contractors: LJJ Contractors Ltd

A combined Primary Care and Leisure Complex set to benefit the community, Blaydon Primary Care and Leisure Centre has been developed by NHS South of Tyne and Gateshead Borough Council. It was constructed by Willmott Dixon using the SCAPE Framework and completed in less than 15 months. The council developed Leisure Centre, includes a state of the art gym and 25 metre swimming pool together with 12 metre learner pool. There are also additional changing facilities for users of the existing athletics track and games pitches on the site.

33.21 *Blaydon Leisure and Primary Care Centre, Tyne and Wear. Atrium: a two-storey central atrium, bathed in natural light, incorporates work from local artists (photo by Doug Jackson)*

The whole development aims to promote health and well being; and as part of this, the facility is designed to encompass views out over the adjacent conservation area, designated as an area of outstanding natural beauty.

The Primary Care Centre, developed by NHS South of Tyne and Wear, includes community services for physiotherapy, weight management, sexual health, dentistry, podiatry and breast screening as well as access to health information. GP services and minor injuries are due to relocate to the new centre from an existing nearby clinic.

The Centre is bathed in natural light from a two-storey central atrium, and the incorporation of work from local artists adds to the vision of a healing environment. P+HS Architects, who designed this health facility, are well known for their work in this field, having completed numerous health projects where art and colour are an integral part of the design.

Blaydon Leisure and Primary Care Centre is one of the UK's first combined leisure and health facilities, connected centrally by a communal atrium which was designed alongside local artists, the feel of this building is one of quality, with an appreciation for its semi rural setting. The leisure centre incorporates a 25 m, 6 lane swimming pool, learner pool, large gymnasium, multi-function studio, wet changing village, dry change, outdoor changing for community use, reception area and staff accommodation.

The Primary Care Centre takes into consideration the latest 'Health Technical Memorandums' and 'Health Building Notes'

33.22 *Blaydon Leisure and Primary Care Centre, Tyne and Wear. Rear elevation – the elevation incorporates brise soleil, tinted glass and locally quarried natural stone (photo by Doug Jackson)*

33.23 *Blaydon Leisure and Primary Care Centre, Tyne and Wear. Waiting area – generous waiting areas overlook thoughtful landscaping (photo by Doug Jackson)*

with innovation throughout. The facility incorporates a walk-in minor injury and illness unit, GP practice, podiatry, contraceptive and sexual health centre, primary care mental health service for people suffering common mental health problems, community physiotherapy, CATS service, X-ray services, speech and language therapy, community dental service, breast screening, audiology service, abdominal aortic aneurism (AAA) screening, healthy lifestyle services touch screen kiosk with access to health information, MRI 'plug in' facility and Japanese garden.

The aspiration for a highly sustainable project took precedence for both clients and Willmott Dixon right from the outset. Monthly review meetings were held between the BREEAM coordinator, Willmott Dixon and both clients to ensure that the correct decisions were made not just based on cost but on functionality and sustainability. BREEAM ratings of 'Very Good' for the Leisure Centre and 'Excellent' for the Primary Care Centre were achieved by continuously scrutinising design mindful of end user aspirations.

Sustainable features included glulaminated beams, rainwater harvesting to flush the WCs, biomass boilers and CHP which resulted in annual CO_2 emissions being reduced by 29,000 kg. 94 per cent of waste was diverted from landfill due to an on site two tier waste segregation system. Tinted glass and brise soleil to prevent thermal gain were installed. In addition to this, the M&E services have been designed to include leak detection on mains incoming services, auto-shut off to water supplies in public toilets, infra-red activation of light fittings, enhanced metering strategy to monitor mains services usage

The main external wall finish – a natural stone was quarried from a local quarry thus reduced carbon emissions from delivery vehicles by 25 per cent when comparing it to a material sourced outside the area. Local spend was a keen area of focus for the project team. Mindful of this, the site team managed to allocate 77 per cent of the contract value to businesses based within a 40 mile radius of the site. Sustainable operations were at the heart of the project with incentives given to site operatives who brought an environmentally positive aspect to the project such as car sharing and achievement of waste diverted from landfill targets.

Note: P+HS designed the Primary care element of the scheme. The leisure centre was designed by another firm of architects and the two schemes join at the central atrium.

13 REFERENCES

Anon. (2011) *Sickness in Health, Financial Times,* Wed 19 January 2011, p. 10.

CABE (2006) *Designed with Care: Design and Neighbourhood Healthcare Buildings,* Commission for Architecture and the Built Environment.

Department of Health (2006) *Our Health, Our Care, Our Say: New Direction for Community Services – A Brief Guide.* Department of Health Publications, www.dh.gov.uk/publications.

Department of Health (2007) *NHS Next Stage Review (Darzi Report) – Interim Report,* Department of Health Publications.

Department of Health (2009) *Primary and Community Care Health Building Note 11–01: Facilities for Primary and Community Care Services.* Estates and Facilities Division of the Department of Health.

(Details have been prepared based on information available at the time of publication. Any discrepancies or changes should not be interpreted as an attempt to provide false or misleading information but simply give due recognition for registered products and services.)

Francis, S. (2006) Healthcare Design Development in UK. *Design and Health IV – Future Trends in Healthcare Design,* International Academy for Design and Health, pp. 69–79.

Lister, S. (2011) Private sector waiting in wings as GPs take charge of £80 bn budget, *The Times,* 20 January, p. 8.

Loppert, S. (1999) 'The Art of the Possible'. *The Arts in Health Care: Learning from Experience,* eds. D. Haldane and S. Loppert, The King's Fund.

NHS Estates (2002) *Improving the Patient Experience: The Art of Good Health: Using Visual Arts in Health Care,* HMSO.

NHS Estates (2004) *Enhancing the Healing Environment: A Guide for NHS Trusts,* The King's Fund.

Purves, A. G. (2008) Unpublished PhD thesis, 'Design of Primary Health Care Buildings'.

Purves, A. G. (2009) *Primary Care Centres: A Guide to Health Care Design* London: Elsevier Limited. www.elsevier.com.

Royal College of General Practitioners (RCGP) *History of the College.* Available at: http://www.rcgp.org.uk/about_us/history_heritage__archives. aspx (accessed 16 February 2011).

Weaver, M. (2000) Delight Detector, *Building Design,* 24 November, 1.

World Health Organisation (1978) *Alma-Ata, 1978: Primary Health Care, 'Health for All' series, No. 1,* World Health Organisation.

34 Restaurants and foodservice facilities

Fred Lawson

Fred Lawson is a Visiting Professor at the University of Bournemouth, an international consultant on hotel and foodservice planning and the author of a number of books (published by the Architectural Press/Elsevier) in this field

KEY POINTS:
- *Services must satisfy customer demands and operating criteria*
- *A highly competitive sector at all levels of expenditure*
- *Labour intensive requiring efficient planning*
- *New concepts continuously being introduced*
- *Design life cycles are often short*

Contents

1 Introduction
2 Basic planning
3 Public areas
4 Food production areas
5 Restaurants
6 Cafeterias and food halls
7 Fast-food outlets and take-aways
8 Public houses
9 Hotels and resorts
10 Bibliography

1 INTRODUCTION

1.1 Profile

Restaurants and other facilities providing food and drink for consumption on the premises are labour intensive services which invariably operate in a highly competitive environment. These cover both *commercial businesses* aiming to attract the public and achieve profits from the investment and *semi- or non-commercial services* provided in institutions, places of employment and elsewhere. The latter need to meet specific requirements, including set cost limits, and are often operated by *catering contractors*. In all cases, the efficiency of every part of the operation needs to be maximised and this calls for careful planning and organisation.

Customer choice will vary with individual circumstances such as the location, time available, spending power, experience and particular requirements. The characteristics of potential market demands can be classified and quantified and this is used in market research to identify suitable locations and facilities.

The role of design in foodservice premises is to:

- attract identified markets of customers and communicate a suitable image (merchandising);
- create a comprehensive style and quality of ambience appropriate to customer expectations;
- plan the layout, equipment, technical installations and operating systems as integral parts of the overall concept;
- ensure the facility can meet the objectives, costs and other criteria set by the operator.

The design must reflect the basic concept, including range of menu and food preparation involved, style of service and staffing requirements, space allocation, desired atmosphere and other factors which influence customer choice.

1.2 Product development

Consumer requirements evolve with a desire for change, new styles of fashion and wider experiences of meals abroad. New concepts in food and beverage service operations are constantly being introduced and those which can be shown to be successful are invariably developed as specific product brands. Branding enables the same formula to be adapted to other sites as a chain of company owned, leased or franchised units with further advantages in marketing, customer confidence in quality and value, economies of scale and profitability. The development of new products also reflects socio-economic changes in an area, trends and influences on consumers such as promotion and health concerns (Tables I and II).

Table I Trends in foodservices

Influences	Effects
Markets (socio-economic changes): Changes in habits, Social acceptance, Multiple incomes, Single households, Demographic shifts	convenience, informality, increase in demand, take-away food, mature designs
Product supply (promotion, efficiency): Franchising Multiple outlets Promotion	systemisation standardisation branding
Consumer choice (education, experience): Healthy eating, Personal selection, Variety, wider interest	lighter meals, self-service, ethnic foods

Table II Product development

Trends in products reflecting market preferences	
Self choice:	food displays, food halls, multiple choice counters, buffets, self-help starter and salad bars, assisted service, carveries, trolleys
Variety:	displayed cooking, showmanship, 'ethnic' options, featured designs, pub meals, bistros, dining clubs, themed experiences, memorabilia eat in, take-away, home delivery
Reassurance:	attention to hygiene, cleanliness, environmental responsibilities, 'healthy' menu options, information, value for money, inclusive prices, confidence in standards, branding

1.3 Types of facility

Eating and drinking establishments fall into a number of broad categories:

- Commercial restaurants with self-service and waiter service operations, possibly licensed for sale of alcohol. Includes cafes and snack bars.
- Take-aways; fast-food outlets with or without customer seating space, supplying prepared food for consumption off the premises.
- Hotels and resorts: depending on standards, offering one or more restaurants, room service, banquets, bars, lounge services.
- Public houses, clubs: alcohol sales with or without food service.
- Semi- or non-commercial operations providing meals as a service in educational and institutional establishments and for employees in places of work.

Differences between these operations lie in:

- variety of food offered;
- method of service;
- space and facilities available to the customer;
- amount of food processed on site;
- emphasis on the sale of alcoholic drinks;
- décor and degree of sophistication;
- price level.

Boundaries between these factors can be blurred and the whole field is constantly changing.

1.4 Location
Location will determine the success or failure of a facility. Commercial food service establishments must be located where people need to obtain meals and refreshments such as:

- city and town centres;
- resorts and visitor attractions;
- at stopping places along main highways;
- airports, main railway stations;
- shopping centres.

These are best served by different types of outlets appropriate for the main markets involved. For instance, chain fast-food outlets are sited in busy high streets within city and town centres to attract a large demand from passers-by (*'footfall'*). Up-market restaurants are usually in less prominent locations, in or near good hotels, prime commercial districts and high class residential areas. Food services are also provided to complement existing business as in pubs and places which attract visitors.

A balance has to be found between:

- the availability of customers;
- cost of location and investment;
- operational considerations such as space, customer parking, goods access.

Major locations such as an airport or motor service station usually provide a selection of outlets allowing customer choice in types of meals, prices and time available (Figure 34.1). In city and town centres there will usually be a range of different restaurants: fast-food, bistros, ethnic, themed, food-speciality and high spend restaurants, as well as pubs, wine bars, cafes and snack bars.

Visibility is critical for casual trade and restaurants tend to be clustered in and around popular places, tourist attractions, squares and nearby side streets. Those sited in basements or on upper floors are at a disadvantage without specific promotion, attractive, easy access and designed facilities for transporting food deliveries and for the disabled.

1.5 Institutional foodservices
Foodservices provided in institutions and places of work generally fall into two categories:

- Centrally grouped: main cafeteria, refectories and/or restaurants sited conveniently for most of the people involved. The location often provides a refreshing contrast to the workplace environment and is adjacent to the food preparation facilities.
- Dispersed: remote service of food to individual stations such as in hospitals, some institutions and remote work sites.

In most cases these catering services are operated by contractors specialising in this field.

This also applies in other main locations such as airports, motorway service stations and shopping centres.

1.6 External considerations
Separate vehicular access and parking is essential for delivery of food and other supplies together with suitable provision for hygienic storage and collection of waste. In large premises, a staff entrance may also be required. Outside city centres well served by taxis and public transport, customer car parking is essential, particularly for evening dining and functions. Hotels need to make extra provision for this non-residential use. In restricted urban sites, nearby public car-parking is an advantage.

Key

Servery
1 Tray stand
2 Ambient display units
3 Hot food display
4 Cold display
5 Hot beverages
6 Cashiers (2)
7 Auxilliary cash positions
8 Cups, cutlery, condiments
9 Clearing trolley

Preparation and cooking
10 Refrigerated storage
11 Food preparation
12 Main cooking area
13 Call-order cooking
14 Racking and trolley park
15 Dishwash

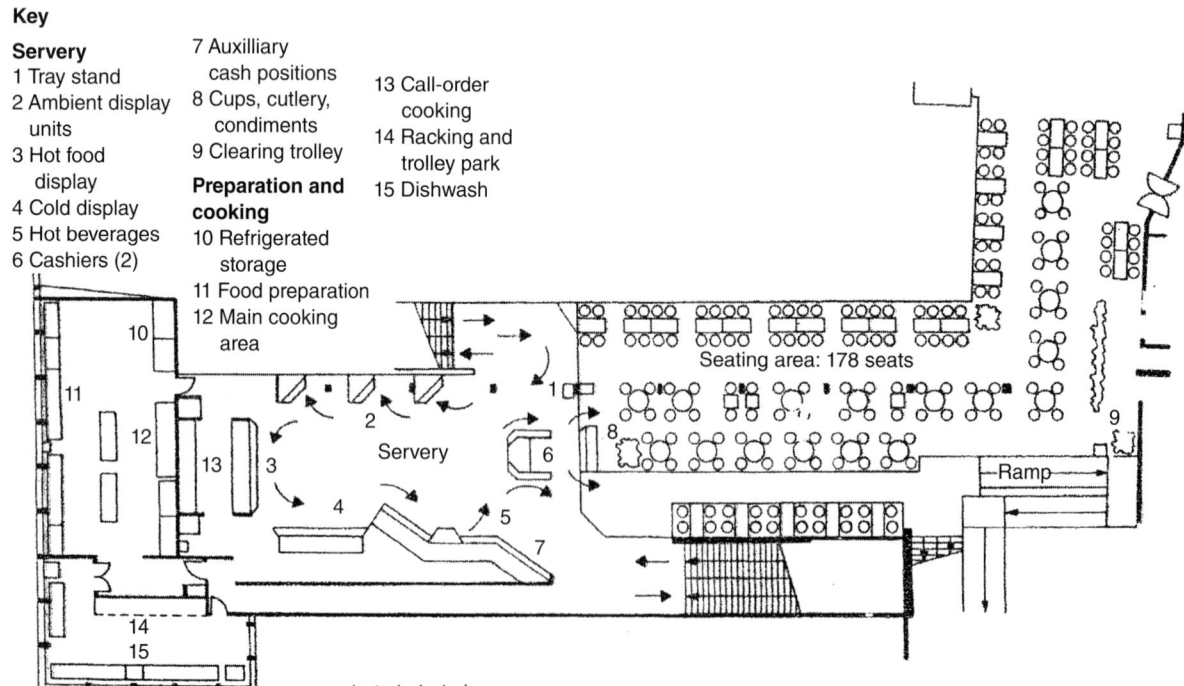

34.1 *Foodservice facilities at Prestwick Airport, UK. Located on a balcony above the concourse, the new self-service restaurant was designed to attract attention and provide an interesting range of local food specialities. Emphasis has been put on prominent signage and staircase design, as well as in menu graphics. Catering consultants: Tricon Foodservice Consultants Ltd. Client: British Airports Authority*

External appearance is important for self-advertising and communicating information, with views of the interior, display of menus and prices and, for evening dining, flood-lighting. The customer entrance must be clearly defined, distinctive and easy to use including provisions for people with disabilities. To attract passing customers, popular restaurants and cafes in large shopping centres, hotels, and airports may be seated within public concourses and atrium areas (Figure 34.1).

2 BASIC PLANNING

2.1 Foodservice operations

All foodservice operations involve three overlapping processes: production, service and customer areas (Figure 34.2). Each area will have specific requirements which will vary depending on the nature and scale of the operation.

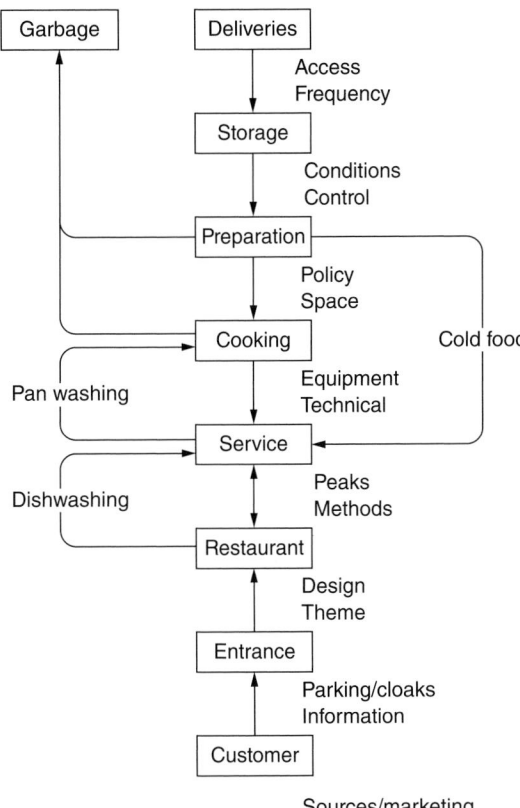

34.2 *Food service planning*

Production
- Delivery and checking of food supplies, beverages and other items.
- Storage: separate for vegetables/fruit, dry goods, chilled and frozen foods.
- Preparation: using fresh ingredients, partially or fully prepared foods.
- Cooking: with large scale centrally grouped or back-bar equipment.
- Assembly of meals to order, ready for service or refrigeration/ freezing.
- Dish-washing of utensils and tableware and disposal of solid waste.

Service of meals, designed around self-service or table service:
Self-service using display counters accessible to the customers.

- Waiter/waitress service collected from a servery and taken to the tables.
- Collection of soiled dishes and return to the kitchen.
- Side tables and storage: for table items, condiments, equipment, furniture.

Customer facilities
- Location: surroundings, character, site restrictions, parking.
- Entrance with cloakroom, toilets, reception services and bar if required.
- Seating areas: interior design to reflect concept and customer profiles.
- Billing and payment facilities.

2.2 Central food production

Large scale foodservice operations usually involve two stages of production: Bulk preparation and prime cooking followed by rapid chilling or freezing of the foods for later end-cooking (regeneration) when required near the place of service. *Cook-freeze* systems provide rapid cooling down to $-20°$ C for frozen storage (typical up to 1 month) whilst *cook-chill* equipment rapidly reduces food temperature to $1-3°$ C for refrigeration storage up to a maximum of 3–5 days. Chilling is commonly used in hotels and institutions for pre-preparation of meals on site to improve efficiency and hygiene.

Fast-food outlets use highly developed systems with specialised end-cooking equipment designed to provide rapid delivery of a limited menu of meals to order. Central cook-freeze systems are also used to supply prepared convenience foods to restaurants, airlines and other offsite catering arrangements. Cook-chill systems are more suitable for short time holding of meals prepared in advance of use, as in banquets and functions (Figure 34.3).

2.3 Legislation

Food service establishments are subject to Town and Country Planning and Building Regulations, disability discrimination, health and safety, food standards and hygiene requirements.

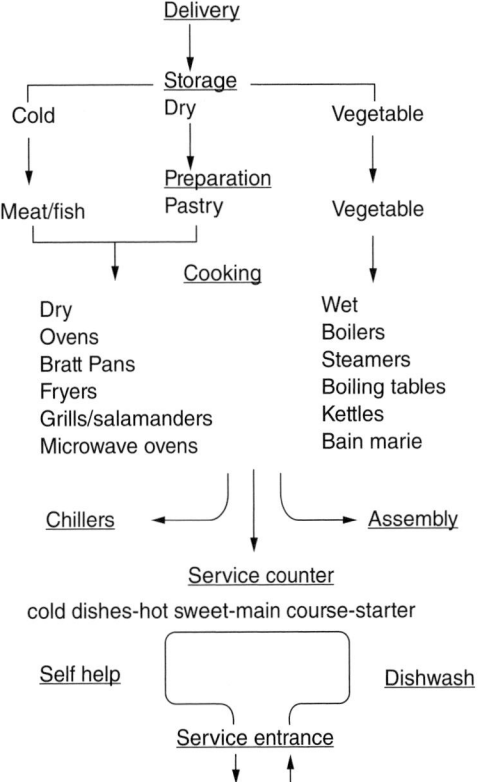

34.3 *Large-scale production*

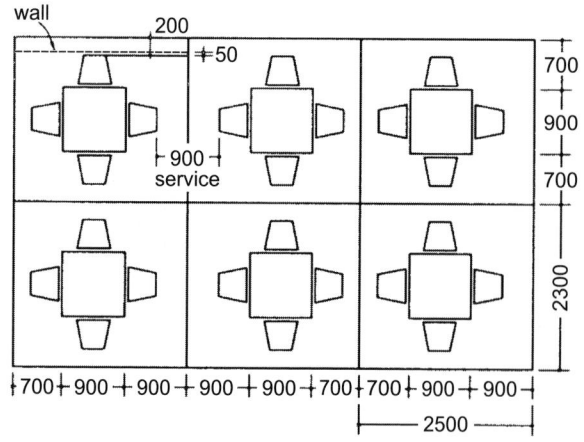

a *Square tables, square layout, local density 1.4 (in m² per diner)*

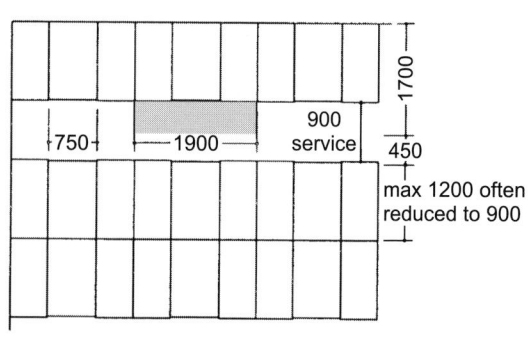

d *Banquette seating in booths, density 0.8*

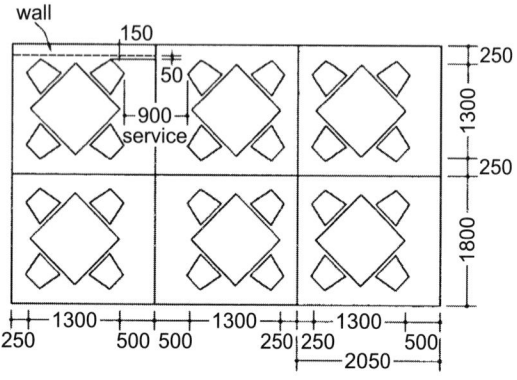

b *Square tables, diagonal layout, local density 0.92*

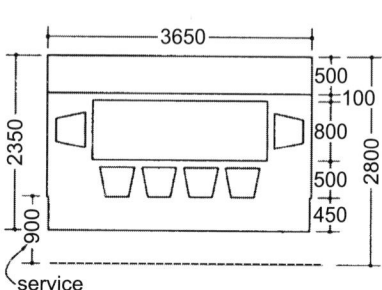

e *Large booth in recess, density 0.86 for 10 people, or 1.1 if only two people sit on bench seat*

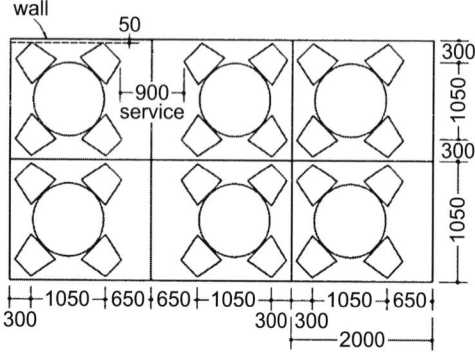

c *Circular tables, diagonal layout, density 0.82*

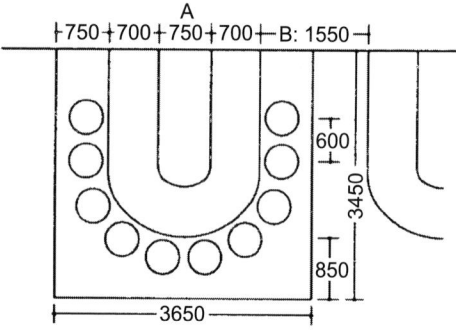

f *Counter service, density 1.26. (Dimensions A and B are increased where more than one waiter is employed)*

34.4 *Layouts for restaurant tables*

Premises selling alcoholic drink must also be licensed. In the work areas safeguards must be taken to reduce risks of accidents (e.g.: burns, scalds, cuts, falls, exposed machinery, electric shock and fires). Instruction and first aid facilities must be provided. Hygiene requirements include training in food handling and the provision of suitable clothing and hand-washing facilities. Specific fire and smoke protection requirements apply.

3 PUBLIC AREAS

3.1 Concept
Restaurant design is developed around the concept of the operation. This will take account of the intended market, the clients' objectives and proposals, the location and type of premises, structural changes involved and cost targets. Brand led designs, including

franchised and licensed outlets, are usually limited in scope but may be adapted to the type of building available.

The concept and operating strategies are invariably decided by the clients. Details of design may be set for brand consistency and customer assurance in chain operations. This applies particularly to middle and popular market requirements, including fast-food operations. However, entrepreneurs are also aware of social trends and changes in consumer requirements and new innovative design concepts are constantly being introduced.

3.2 Marketing criteria
Customer choice is influenced by price and expectations which vary depending on the occasion. Factors such as convenience, value and social atmosphere may be paramount. For others the sophistication,

menu choice and style of service may by important. Markets can be classified according to socio-economic categories which broadly indicate spending power and types of services required. Market studies also assess competition, changes in the area and optimum locations.

3.3 Design criteria

Interior design has to satisfy a number of requirements, both functional and aesthetic. It has to reassure confidence in standards, stimulate appropriate emotive responses, interest and visual appeal, and provide conditions which create the desired social atmosphere.
Considerations include:

- *Function*: operation, efficiency, order, hygiene, durability, maintenance.
- *Ambience*: luxurious, sophisticated, exotic, homely, romantic, lively.
- *Characterisation*: operating style, theme, food specialisation, features.
- *Seating plans*: room proportions, horizons of interest, windows, perimeters.
- *Perception:* attention to detail, consistency, linkage of areas, personalisation.

3.4 Coverage

A comprehensive design scheme covers:

- interior finishes, fittings and equipment, decoration;
- theme design, furniture, furnishings and features;
- tableware, linen, table appointments and uniforms;
- display counters, service equipment, circulation plans;
- lighting, airconditioning and technical installations;
- motif, graphics, menu and drinks folders;
- desks, registers and monitoring equipment.

Shop-fitting frontage, entrance, cloakroom and ancillary bars are normally included. Kitchen equipment including their technical plant, services installation and utensils may be treated as a separate contract but must be planned as part of the whole project. Client requirements for accounting and management systems and equipment must also be incorporated.

3.5 Seating plans

For meals consumed on the premises, maximum numbers of customers are dictated by numbers of seats (covers), mealtimes served and seat turnover. Customer densities (in m² per diner) depend on the room dimensions, method of service, table and chair sizes, seat groupings and layout within the room (Figures 34.4, 34.5, 34.6; Table III).

- Functions, banquets and conference groups require adaptable stackable furniture (Figure 34.7–34.10).
- Self-service requires wide aisles leading to and from the counter(s), orderly lines with increased space between tables (Figure 34.5). Waiter service layouts can be more flexible but service and customer circulations must not conflict.
- Table and chair sizes increase with sophistication and length of meal. Popular restaurants mostly provide tables for 4 which may be fixed or loose, square or round, in open or booth type layouts depending on style of operation. High-spend restaurants provide a higher ratio of tables for 2, often allowing grouping together for parties of 4, 6 or more as required. Employee and institutional arrangements use rows of tables to increase density which may also be removable for alternative use of the area.
- Layouts are influenced by windows and views. Individual seating areas may be separated by levels and partitions to extend choice (personalised areas, perimeter seating) and interest (features).
- Large hotels and resorts provide a choice of restaurants and facilities offering different menus, sophistication and prices (Figure 34.11).

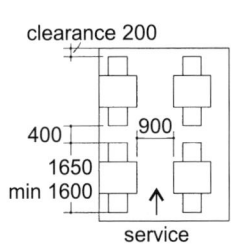
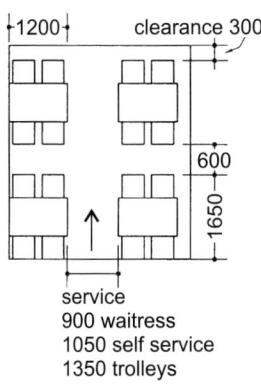
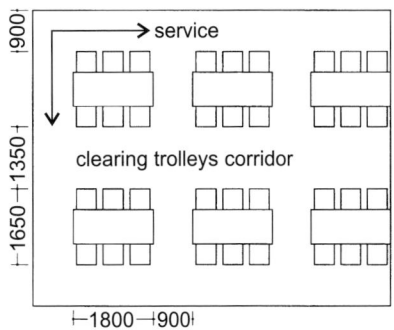
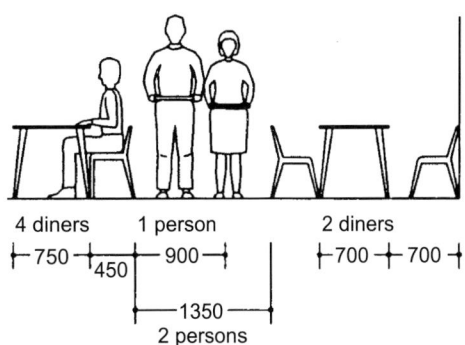

34.5 *Minimum space between tables to allow for seating, access and circulation*

Table III Space allowances

Type of restaurant or service Example	Area per seat (m²)	Service add (m²)
Fine dining Traditional 80 seats	2.0–2.4	table service
Food speciality or ethnic High standard 80 seats	1.6–1.8	table service
Mid-market restaurant Limited menu 100 seats	1.5–1.7	counter 0.2
Cafeteria 140 seats Single line counter	1.4–1.5	servery 0.4
Popular chain restaurant Limited menu 100 seats	1.2–1.4	table service
Fast-food/takeaway Set menu range 50 seats	0.8–1.0	counter 0.6
Pub bar (25% seating) Including counter	0.6–0.9	
Bar lounge (50% seating) Including counter	1.1–1.4	
Banquet hall dining area 200 seats	0.9–1.2	pantry 0.2
Employee cafeteria 200 seats	1.1–1.2	servery 0.2
Primary school Counter/family service	0.75–0.85	
Secondary school Including counter	0.9	
College refectory	1.1–1.2	servery 0.2

Note: Depends on rooms dimensions, circulations and type of furniture.

3.6 Furniture and table top design

Restaurant furniture must be strong, durable and resistant to soiling. Depending on the type of operation this includes:

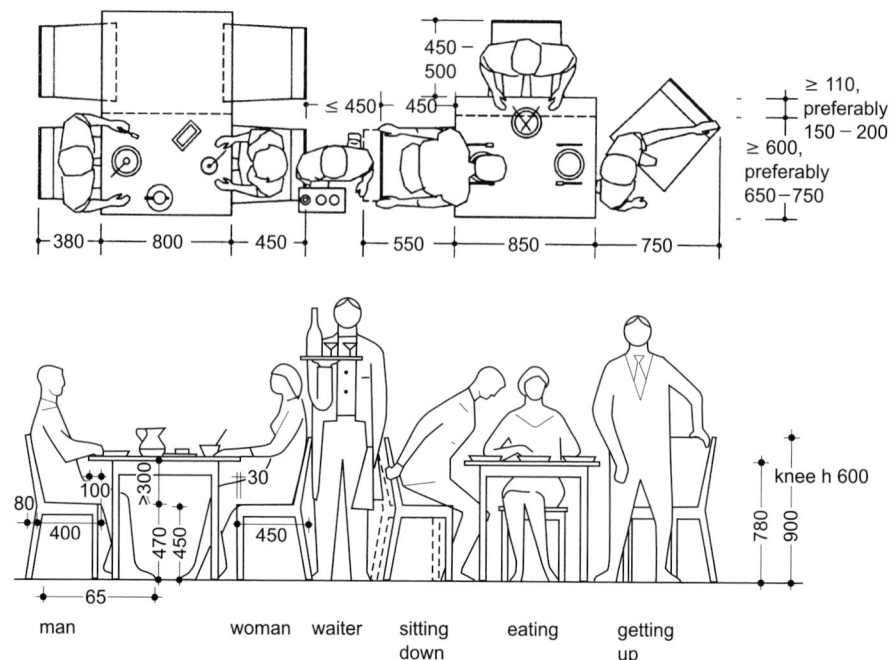

34.6 *Restaurant critical dimensions*

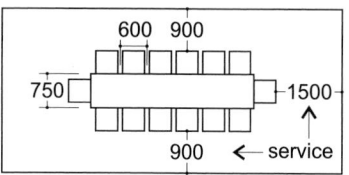

34.7 *Small formal dinner arrangement*

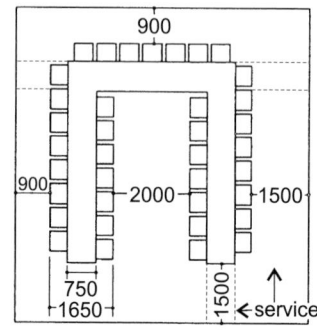

34.8 *Banquet layout. The U arrangement can be extended in both directions to the limits of the banqueting room*

- Fitted counters and bars. Fixed bar/counter stools. Fixed tables, usually pedestal or cantilevered for leg clearance, with loose chairs or fixed booth-type seating (Figures 34.12, 34.13).
- Movable tables with loose chairs or fixed banquette seating.
- Stackable tables and chairs with carrier systems. Tables with extension brackets or alternative tops (square/round). With level access to storage area.
- Side tables and designed trolleys for food presentation and service at the table.
- Reception and cash desks with terminals, screens, cash registers and other equipment.

Table top design must be compatible with the overall concept and style of operation. It will range from high class sophistication requiring

number of seats		table size: drinking mm	table size: eating mm
1		450 to 600	600 to 700
2		600 square	750 square
4		750 square	900 × 950
		–	1500 × 750
6		–	1400 × 950
		–	1700 × 750
8		–	1750 × 900
		–	2300 × 750

34.9 *Recommended rectangular table sizes relating to place numbers*

number of seats	table size: drinking mm	table size: eating mm
1	450 to 600	750
2	600	850
4	900	1050
6	1150	1200
8	1400	1500

34.10 *Recommended circular table sizes for various place numbers*

quality linen, china, glassware and silverware to stylised easy clean laminated surfaces with durable ware and stainless steel utensils.

3.7 Steps in interior design

- Brief, terms of reference: scope, aims, guidance, requirements, programme.
- Sketches, proposals: design concept, visual ideas, preliminary estimates.
- Schematic drawings: perspectives, images, key features.
- Sample board: selected materials, finishes.
- Detailed drawings: scaled drawings for construction and installations.
- Specifications: requirements, quality, quantities.
- Suppliers: sources costs, discounts, replacements.
- Contracts: conditions, coverage of work, critical dates.

3.8 Maintenance and life-cycle planning

Food and beverage service areas are subject to intensive use, breakage, spillage and damage requiring daily cleaning and frequent replacement or substitution. Carpets and finishes are selected to camouflage scratching or staining. Furniture and equipment must be durable and retain good appearance over the planned life-time of use.

Flexibility may be required to adapt to variable needs such as table groupings and re-arrangements or changes in service style from daytime to evening dining or for entertainment. This will call for furniture stacking and equipment storage facilities

The life cycle of a restaurant will be affected by many factors such as changes in the surroundings, fashion and meal preferences; increasing competition; decline in standards and obsolescence. Kitchen equipment is usually planned for 7 years usage but furniture and furnishings may need replacement in 5 years. In planning major refurbishments it

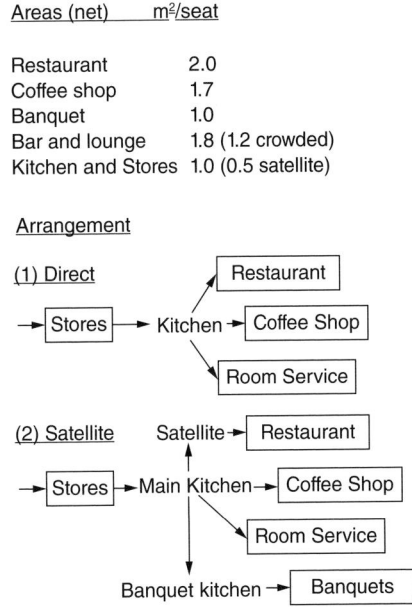

Areas (net)   m²/seat

Restaurant	2.0
Coffee shop	1.7
Banquet	1.0
Bar and lounge	1.8 (1.2 crowded)
Kitchen and Stores	1.0 (0.5 satellite)

Arrangement

34.11 *Food and beverage services in large hotels*

is opportune to revise the original concept and introduce changes in menu, design and style to meet new market opportunities.

4 FOOD PRODUCTION AREAS

4.1 Size and type

The size of the kitchen depends on the number of seats (covers) served at the peak period of demand – lunch or evening. It will also vary with the type of the menu and the extent to which food is prepared in advance. With a fixed menu, equipment and labour can be rationalised and ready-prepared food enables the kitchen to concentrate on finishing the meals to order. Conventional kitchens providing a varying (usually cyclical) range of menu choice are required in institutions and employee catering. They are also required in high class restaurants and hotels and have a size ratio of 0.3 to 0.5:1 in relation to the size of the dining area. Convenience food is prepared in advance in bulk in central kitchens and chilled or frozen for distribution and storage prior to use (see Section 2.1). This allows economies of scale, larger, purpose designed equipment and factory type processing. Finishing kitchens can be reduced in size and equipment with a size ratio of 0.1 to 0.3: 1 in relation to the size of storage and dishwashing.

Examples of kitchen areas are indicated in Table IV. Space requirements in large kitchens show the economies of scale by centralisation (Figure 34.14). In large hotels, a central food production and dishwashing area may be located to serve a number of alternative restaurants directly or by circulation to more remote outlets such as in room service and banquet serveries.

4.2 Goods access

For sizes of vehicles see Chapter 39. Typical delivery arrangements are:

- dry goods: weekly or fortnightly;
- frozen goods: weekly;
- vegetables and fresh fruit: twice weekly;
- perishable foods: daily;
- refuse and waste removal: depends on size and contract: weekly.

Large premises use bulk refuse containers (0.57 m²–0.85 m²) together with separate bottle, broken glass, metal compaction and packaging storage areas. Food waste must be sited in a refrigerated

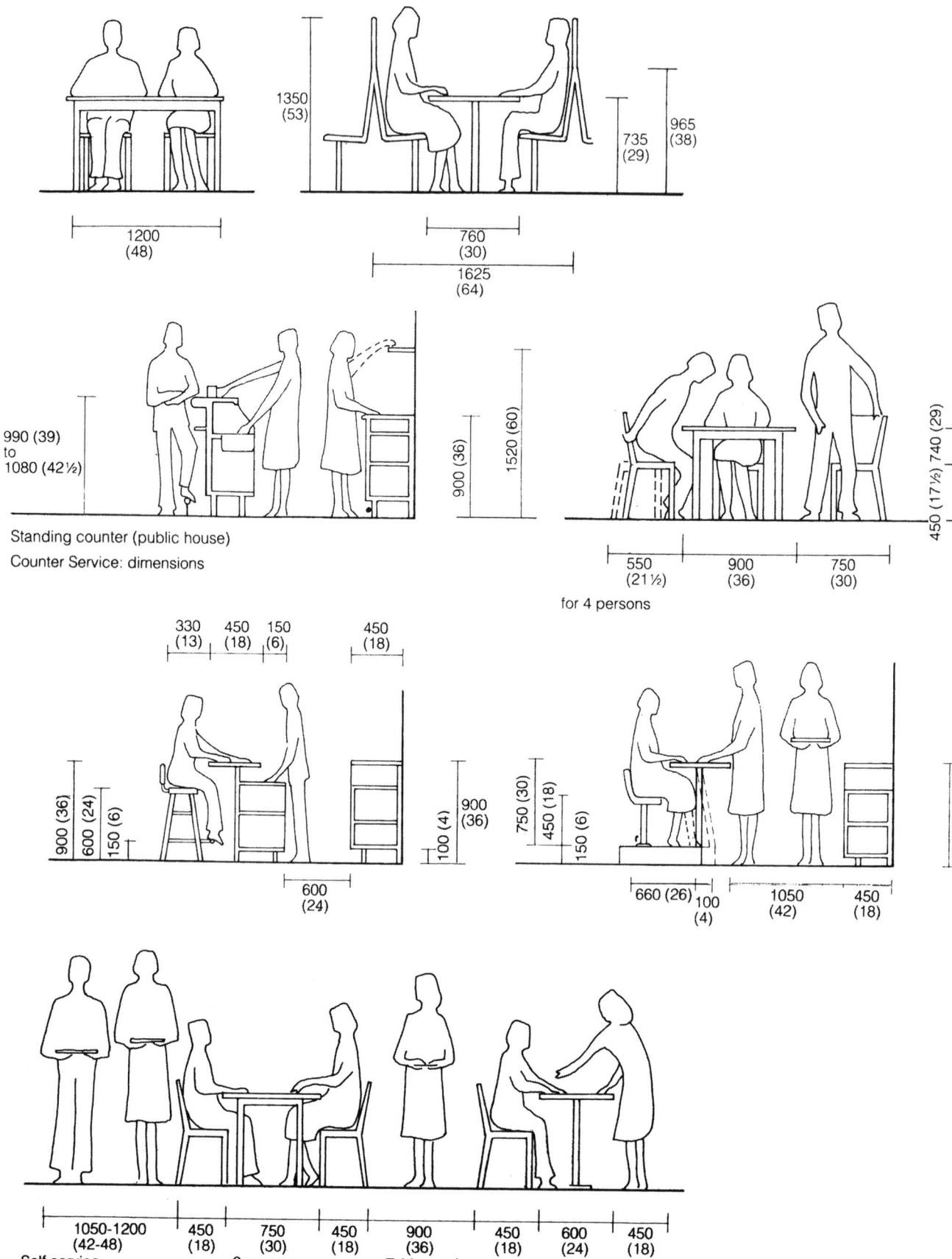

34.12 *Typical counter and table service dimensions*

area (3–5° C) with suitable screening, vermin exclusion, washing facilities and drainage.

4.3 Storage areas
Storage depends on throughput and frequency of deliveries. Cold stores are grouped together and preferably entered through chilled holding areas to save energy. Floor slabs may need to be recessed to allow level wheeled entry to the store. Vegetable stores have direct access to their preparation area.

Purpose designed moveable racks are used in food stores. Racks and shelves should allow about 50 mm between and above packages for easy access. The top shelf should not be higher than 1800 mm and

Counter seating

mm (in.)

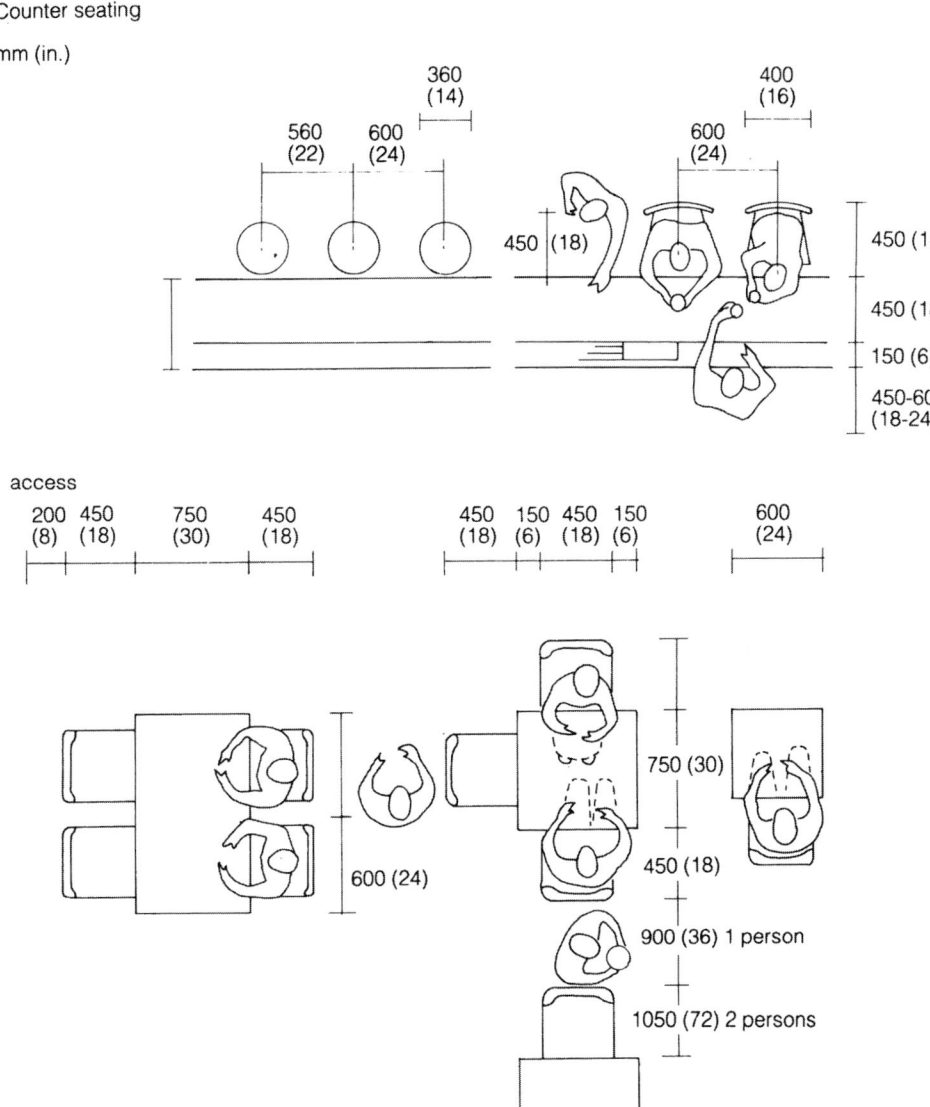

34.13 *Dimensions for various tables and local seating densities*

the lowest at least 200 mm above floor (Figure 34.15). Shelves for heavy and frequently used items are best between 700 and 1500 mm high. Space may be required for containers awaiting return to suppliers.

4.4 Preparation areas
Kitchen areas and layout are determined by:

- the sizes of equipment and benches;
- space for working access and circulation.

Some typical dimensions are:

- Work top and sink rim height 870–900 mm.
- Wall bench width 600–750 mm.
- Island bench or table width 900–1050 mm.
- Length of work area with convenient reach 1200–1800 mm.

Four main areas are required for conventional food preparation:

- fresh vegetables, salads and fruit;
- meat and fish;
- pastry;
- general including assembly of cold foods.

Table IV Typical food production areas per restaurant seat

Type of restaurant Example	Kitchen area (m² per seat)	Type of food prepared
Fine dining 80 seats	0.9	choice menu, fresh food cooked to order
Speciality food/ethnic 80 seats	0.7	a la carte menu, cooked to order
Midmarket restaurant themed 100 seats	0.6	limited menu part convenience food
Cafeteria 140 seats	0.4	cooked and cold choices part convenience food
Popular restaurant 100 seats	0.4	standard menu convenience food
Fast-food/take-away 50 seats	0.8–1.0	system production high volume sales

Note: Preparation, cooking and dishwashing take up about 50% of the total kitchen areas. Storage, service and staff facilities the remainder.

Specialised operations may require separate bakery and cake decoration areas. Preparation areas may be segregated in separate rooms, by low walls 1200 mm high between the areas and main kitchen or the grouping of benches and fittings in specific areas around the sides (Figure 34.16). Cross-contamination of food must be avoided and adequate work space with separate sinks provided in each area as well as for pan washing.

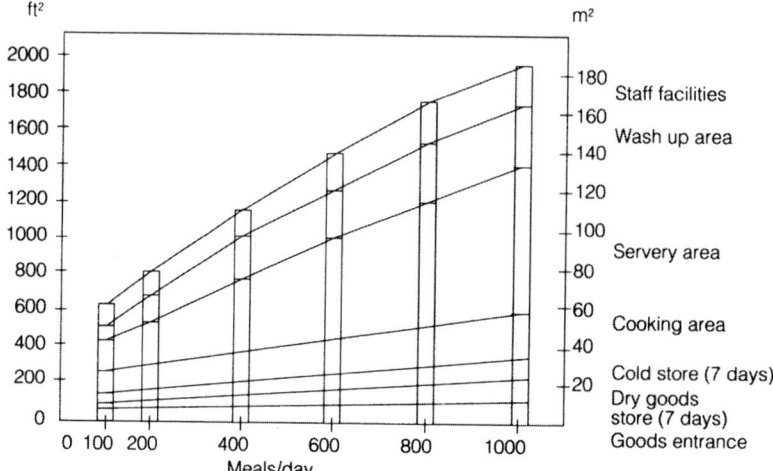

34.14 *Kitchen space requirements for various functions*

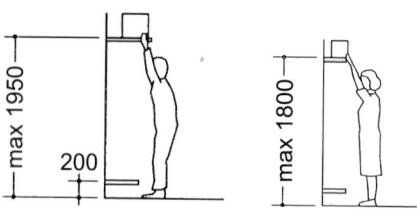

a *Limits for maximum reach for men and women*

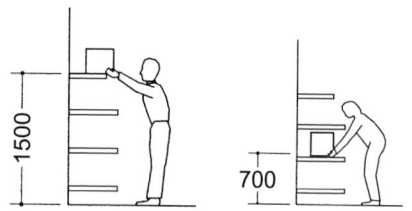

b *Convenient reach for heavy or frequently used items*

34.15 *Heights for storage shelving*

4.5 Cooking equipment

About 30 per cent of the kitchen floor is occupied by equipment, 10–20 per cent by benches and trolleys and 50 per cent for circulation and access. Crowded space can lead to obstruction and accidents but excess space adds to circulation cleaning, energy and maintenance costs (Figure 34.17).

Details of typical modern equipment are given in Table V. Size and duty is related to output and most ovens are designed to receive gastronorm sizes of dishes and trays. Some items are shown (Figure 34.18). Combination ovens incorporate both steam and hot air convection modes. Other accelerated cooking includes microwave power with hot air convection. Vitreoceramic induction hobs may be used instead of open burners.

A typical kitchen layout is shown in Figure 34.19 with elevations in Figure 34.20.

Back-bar equipment fitted along a wall behind the serving counter is common in small kitchens and for finishing meals enabling savings in engineering services, space and labour. Island grouping in the centre is better in larger units giving easier access from all areas, cleaning and maintenance. Engineering services, including fume extraction and floor drainage, are concentrated and perimeter sites can be used for refrigerators, storage, preparation areas and service counters. The minimum aisle width is 1050 mm but may

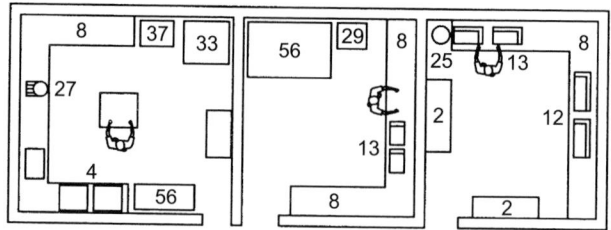

a *Separate rooms*

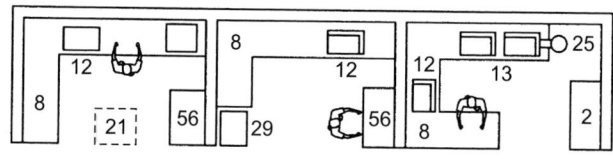

b *Bays*

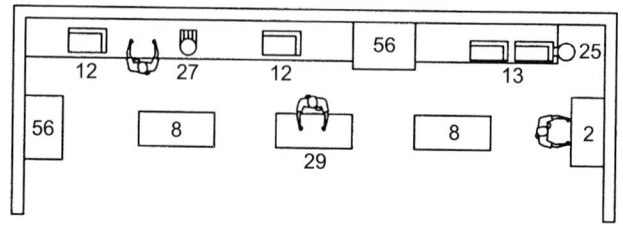

c *Open plan kitchen*

34.16 *Alternative preparation area arrangements (see Figure 34.31 for key to numbers)*

need to be increased to 1500 mm to allow for cooker door swings or if trolleys are used.

4.6 Dishwashing

Dishwashing is expensive in terms of space, equipment, labour and energy costs. Disposables may be used in fast-food and transport catering but give a poor image and problems in disposal. Methods of collection for used dishes include self-removal with trays, trolleys or waiter removal. This must be decided at the initial planning stage. Trolleys will require straight aisles with minimum 1050 mm width and screened trolley parks.

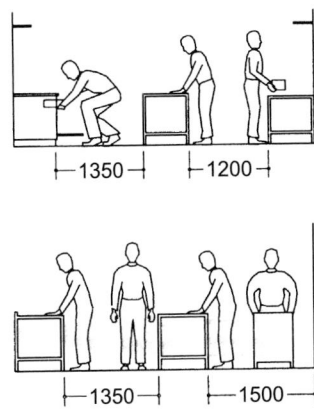

Manual dishwashing in a double sink is inefficient and unhygienic for public foodservices. Spray machines may be intermittent or continuous through-flow and designed for corner (small kitchens) or in line position (Figure 34.21). Water softening is often used and modern machines incorporate energy and water saving devices. Space is required for depositing soiled dishes, scraping/spraying and loading as well as separate unloading sections. Trolley spaces should be allowed for return of clean dishes and utensils to the servery. Typical sizes for table ware are given in Table VI and allowances for dishwashing spaces are show in Table VII.

34.17 *Minimum space between equipment for working and circulation*

4.7 Serveries
Arrangements for plating and serving food depend on the type and scale of operation. In each case, circulation routes must be planned. Counters are designed to avoid risk of accidents, spillages and contamination, keep food hot, cool or chilled and retain an attractive hygienic presentation of the foods on offer.

Table V Kitchen equipment

Type	Main features	Typical size and rating	
Ovens	Transfer heat to food within an enclosure. May use hot air (circulated by natural or fan-assisted convection), infrared or microwave emission	(s) –small units (m) – medium duty (h) – heavy duty	
General-purpose	Using hot air for baking, roasting or reheating. May be raised on stand or in tiers. Preloaded mobile racks used for speed and convenience. Working capacities: Trayed dishes 65–75 kg/m³ (4–5 lb/ft³) Poultry, meats 110–130 kg/m³ (7–8 lb/ft³)		
Oven range	Ovens combined with boiling hob top. Oven capacity based on shelf area 0.015m² (24in.2) per meal	(s) 801. (m) 160 1. (h) 200 1.	11kW 14kW 16kW
Forced convection oven	Hot air circulated at high velocities up to 4.5 m/s (900ft/min) with directional flows to provide rapid heating, larger batch loadings, even temperatures. Normal cooking cycle: frozen food 25–35 min Combination (Combi) ovens incorporate both hot-air and steam convection modes. Accelerated cooking ovens include hot-air convection and microwave.	(s) 50 1. (m) 110 1. (m) 200 1. (h) 300 1.	2.6 kW 6kW 9.3 kW 13.3kW
Pastry oven	Tiered shallow ovens to give uniform heating for baking, pastry, pizza, etc. Capacity based on area: 0.004² (6 in.²) per meal		
Roasting cabinet Rotary or reel ovens	Special cabinets for roasting meat, or mechanised spit roasting (poultry, joints, kebabs)		
Low-temperature ovens	Specialised equipment for large-scale bakeries and continuous-cooking ovens For slow cooking of meat, etc. at 107° C (225° F) to reduce moisture loss. Specialist applications		
Microwave ovens	High-frequency (2450 MHz) alternating electromagnetic waves used to generate heat in dipolar molecules of food and water. Energy conversion factor high. Typical cooking cycle: 45–60 s (reducing with quantity)	(s) 20 1. (m) 28 1. (h) 28 1.	0.G kW 1.3 kW 2kW
Infrared ovens	Interspaced rows of heating elements in quartz tubes emitting mainly radiant heat in waveband 1.5–5.0 mm. Mainly used for reheating frozen food. Heating cycle 20–25 min		
Steam ovens Pressure steamers	Free steam at or near atmospheric pressure: 3.5kN/m² (1/21 b/in.²) Used for large-scale catering Pressure steam up to 103kN/m²(15 lb/in.²) using jets for rapid heating of frozen food. May have option of free-vented steam	(m) 200 1. (m)	9kW 120kW
Boiling and frying	May use loose pans and containers placed on or over external heat (gas burner, electric element, heated plate) Larger units incorporate heaters as part of design (with thermostatic control)	(s) 2 ring (m) Solid	3.6 kW 11kW

(continued)

Table V (Continued)

Type	Main features	Typical size and rating	
Boiling tables	Usually provide four or six open burners or solid tops with tapered heat. Used as supplement or alternative to oven range	(s) 1 ring (m) 2 ring	3.6 kW 7kW
Halogen elements	Alternative to gas burners and electric radiant rings. Used in hobs to provide instantly adjustable heat output		
Induction heaters	Electromagnetic alternating currents of 25 kHz directed through ceramic hob. Used to induce eddying currents in steel pans producing indirect heating for boiling or frying		
Boiling pans and kettles	Containers heated directly or indirectly (preferred) Emptied by tap or by tilting over drain Output 451 pan root vegetables – 100–150 meals Soup- 150–200 meals	(h) 4 ring (m) 45 1. (m) 90 1. (h) 135 1.	14kW 7kW 11.5kW 14.5 k W
Bratt pans	Shallow tilting frying pans which are also used for stewing and braising. 150–350 mm (6–10 in.) deep. Mounted on trunnions for emptying	(m) 0.28 m² (h) 0.44 m²	6.4 kW 12kW
Deep-fat fryers	Food immersed in heated oil. Frying temperatures typically 160–190° C (320–375° F) Fume extraction required Cooking cycles: typically 6–7 min	(s) 5 1. (m) 7 1. (m) 16 1. (h) 20 1.	3kW 5.8 kW l0kW 20 kW
Pressure fat fryers	Fryer fitted with sealed lid. Operated at 63 kN/m² (9 lb/in.²), combining frying with pressure steaming of moisture Output: 80–90 portions/h		
Griddles	Shallow frying using surface contact with heated plate. Temperatures. 170–220° C (340–430° F)	(s) 0.17m² (m) 0.4m²	4kW 7.5kW
Grilling	Food exposed to elements emitting high-intensity radiation in wave band 0.7–2.2 mm(s)0.1 m	(s) 0.1m² (m) 0.25m² (h) 0.27m²	3kW 5.7kW 7.5kW
Salamanders, broilers	Top heating over food on grating or branding plates	(s) 28 1./h	2.8kW
Grills, chargrills, charbroilers	Bottom heating using red-hot tiles, plates or charcoal. Fume extraction required. May be featured in display cooking	(m) 48 1./h (h) 68 1./h	5.3kW 7.5kW
Water boilers, beverage-making equipment	Includes boilers operated by steam pressure or expansion of water May be installed in kitchen, in vending units, under service counter or as cafe sets. Capacity: Per litre 4–5 cups Per gallon 18–20 cups	(s) 2 units (m) 4/6 units	0.5kW 2kW
Holding units	Used to keep food hot or cold until served. Mainly incorporated into service counters		
Bains-marie	Heated well fitted with loose containers (standardised sizes). May be dry or water filled. Thermostatically controlled at about 74° C (165° F)		
Chilled shelves, wells and plates	For cold storage and display of salads, dairy products and prepared sweets. Usually incorporates under-counter refrigerator. Temperature about 3.5° C (37–41° F)		
Hot cupboards	Heated cabinets to keep plates and food warm prior to service. May be under-counter units. pass-through cabinets or mobile. Temperature kept at 76–88° C (170–190° F). Capacity: Standard 1,200mm (4 ft) counter unit holds about 300 plates	(m) 1.2m wide (m) 1.8m wide	3kW 4.5kW

Waiter/waitress service

Service counter sited within the production area with hot, cold and refrigerated sections, shelves for plates and dishes and adjacent pantry area for supplementary serving items. Provided with a lobby which must be noise and glare screened from the dining area and have separate in-out doors, opening in direction of flow. May be supplemented by:

- sideboard(s) within dining area;
- side table or trolley circulation, including flambé preparation/ service at the table;
- featured display cooking section for special dishes;
- family service or self selection from dishes brought to the table.

Self-service

Serving counter arranged for self selection of meal items with planned circulations for customers and food replacement (Figure 34.22). Display counters arranged in sequence of meal choice. Variations include:

- cafeteria style service for high throughput and sales promotion;
- food hall and food court service with alternative counters and a common seating area;
- temporary or installed buffet presentations, including assisted service at the counter;
- snack and/or beverage vending machines with or without seating areas.

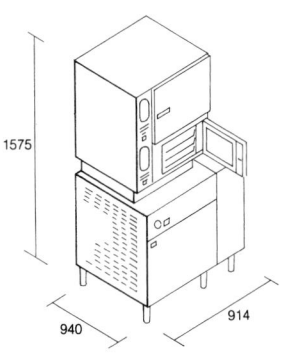

a *Convection steamer*
with two compartments

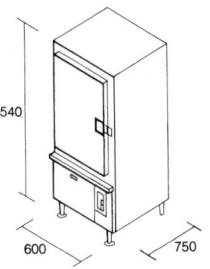

b *Atmospheric steaming oven*
with steam generator in base

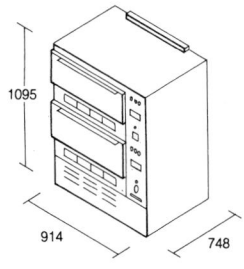

c *Tiered convection ovens,*
each 65 l rated 8.8kW

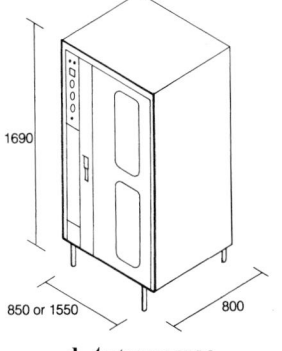

d *Autoreverse*
convection oven

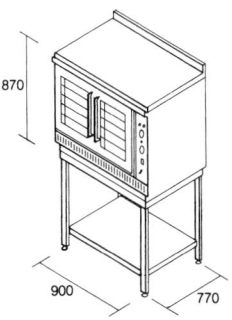

e *Forced convection oven*
on stand, 145 l, 9.2kW

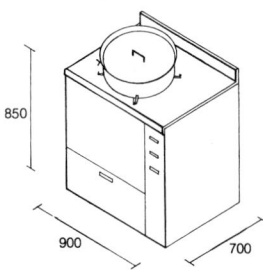

f *Dual-purpose boiling pan, 90 l*
Direct fired or steam jacketed

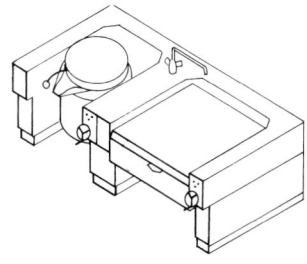

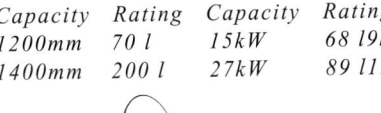

g *Tilting kettle and braising pan console:*

Unit width	Kettle		Bratt pan	
Capacity	*Rating*	*Capacity*		*Rating*
1200mm	*70 l*	*15kW*	*68 l*	*9kW*
1400mm	*200 l*	*27kW*	*89 l*	*12kW*

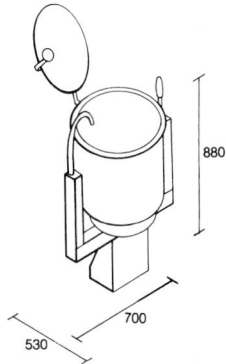

h *Tilting kettle with swivel cold*
water feed, 40 l capacity,
electric or steam heated

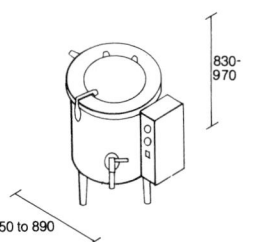

i *Vacuum boiling pan with*
electric or steam heated jacket,
20, 90 or 135 l

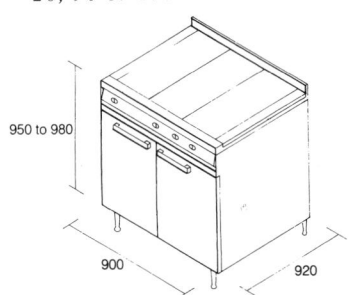

j *Heavy-duty oven range, 200 l,*
18kW (electric), hob with three
solid hotplates or griddle plate

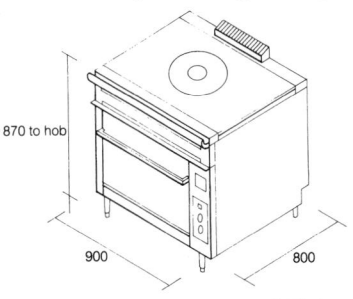

k *Heavy-duty oven range, 150 l,*
16.5kW, with drop-down door
and solid hob top with tapered heat

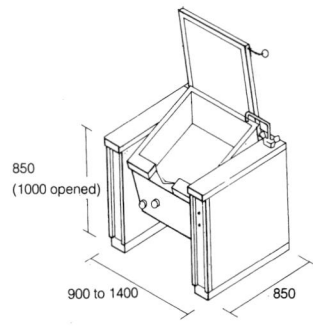

l *Bran or braising pan with*
pillar support:

Capacity	Width	Rating
40 l	*900mm*	*6.4kW*
80	*1200*	*11.8*
100	*1400*	*14.8*

34.18 *Kitchen equipment (continued over)*

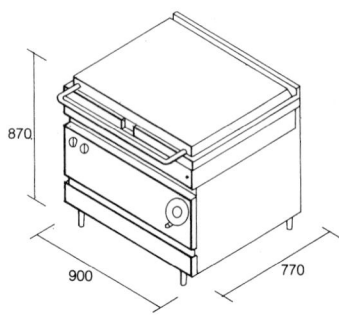

m　*Tilting Bratt pan with operating wheel and trunion*

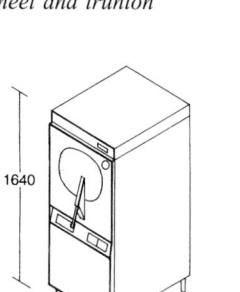

n　*High-pressure steamer on stand, 12 kW rating*

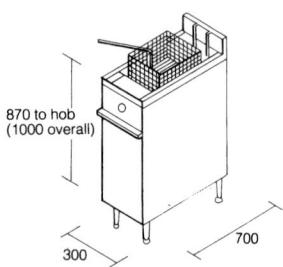

o　*Deep fryer with one basket of 16 l oil capacity, 9 kW. Output 22.7 kg chips per hour*

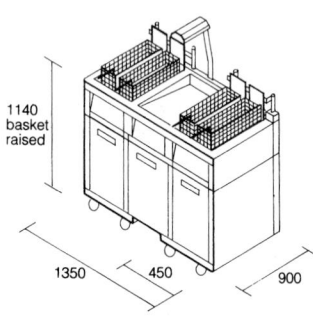

p　*Combination of fast-food fryer with dual deep fryers and central chip dump. Each fryer 21.5 kW. Automatic basket lifting, integral oil filtration*

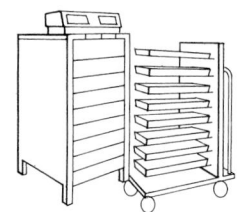

q　*Infrared (regethermic) oven system, 4.7–5.0 kW*

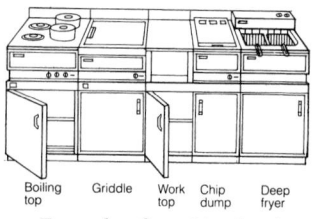

Boiling top　Griddle　Work top　Chip dump　Deep fryer

r　*Example of combined units with under-counter cupboards*

s　*Bulk loading system with mobile transporter*

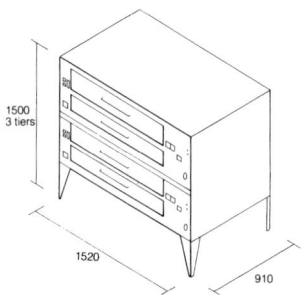

t　*Tiered pastry or pizza oven*

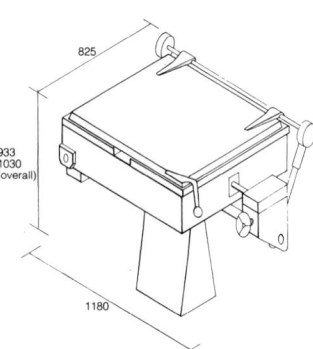

u　*Tilting bratt pan*

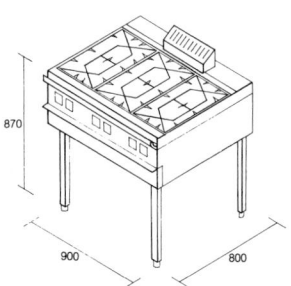

v　*Heavy-duty boiling table with open gas burners*

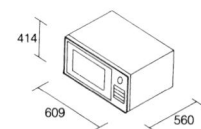

w　*Microwave oven, 2.6 kW supply, 1300 W output rings, 8 kW rating*

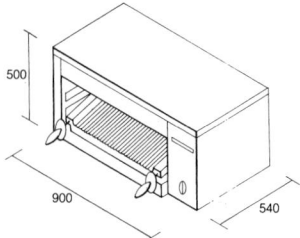

x　*Salamander grill, wall or stand mounted, 7.5 kW rating*

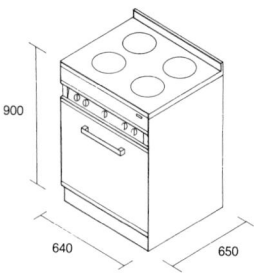

y　*Medium-duty oven range, 84 l with four radiant rings, 8 kW rating*

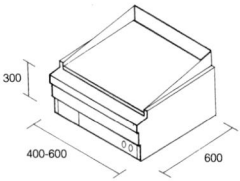

z　*Griddle, counter or stand mounted, 8 kW rating*

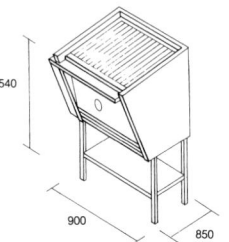

aa　*Underfired grill, 37 kW*

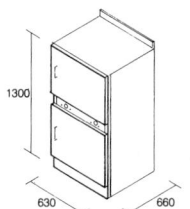

ab　*Two-tier general purpose oven each 80 l capacity*

34.18　*(continued)*

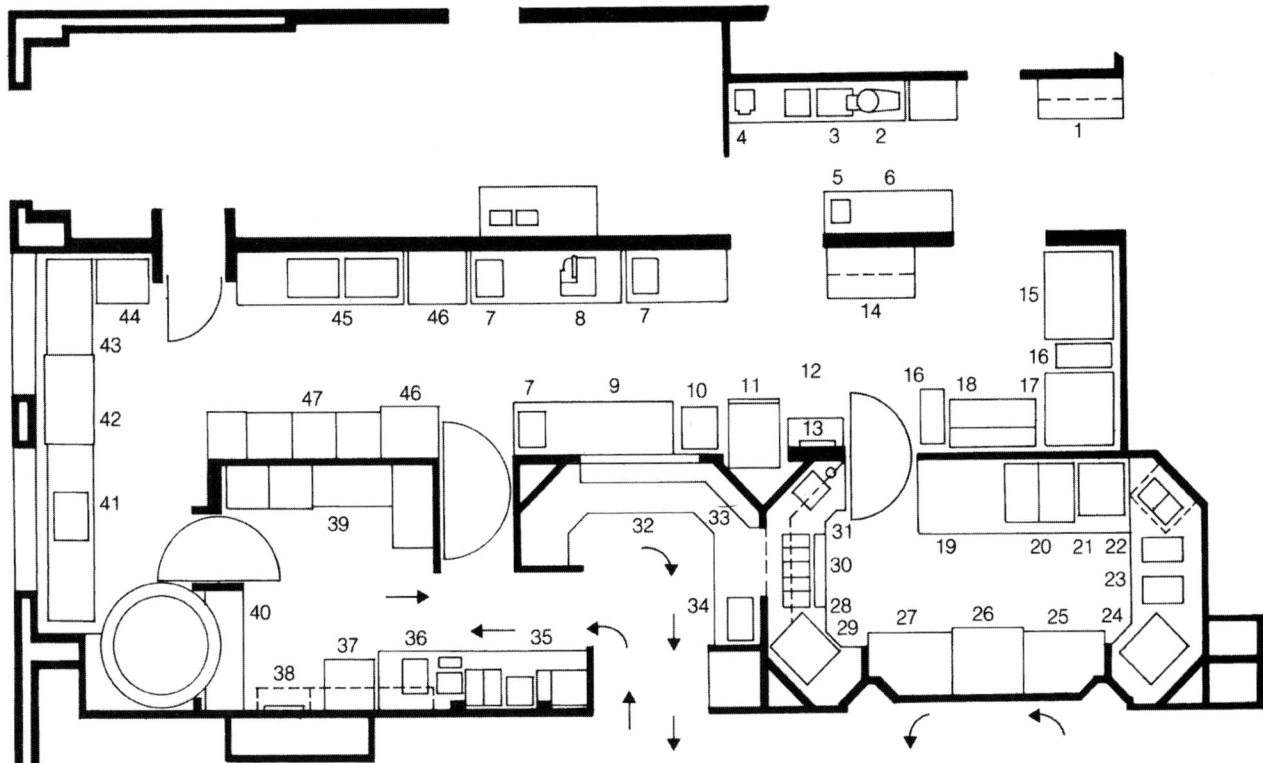

34.19 *Kitchens of Post House Hotel, Sevenoaks. Development: Trust House Forte Ltd. Plans prepared by Stangard Ltd (see key in 34.31)*

Central service
Distribution of centrally prepared dishes as hot, chilled or frozen foods to other locations for service. Central production calls for a fully integrated system, with standardised containers, equipment, transport and controls. Examples include:

- commissary systems to supply meals to finishing kitchens and in transit;
- hospital systems to distribute meals to wards and individual patients;
- banqueting systems to prepare meals in advance of functions;
- central production of convenience foods for catering and restaurant outlets.

4.8 Facilities for staff
Employee ratios vary widely with the type of establishment and demand. The ratio of total employees to meals served over the peak period is about one employee to 8 meals served for full-menu, table service restaurants, 20 meals in limited menu table service and institutions, and 33 or more in fast-food outlets. Changing rooms, lockers and sanitary facilities are required for total full and part-time employees.

5 RESTAURANTS

5.1 Investment
Commercial restaurants are affected by location, image, association and publicity. Location is critical in dictating the catchment area and potential market which may be based on local or transient customers. The image and association helps to create demand. However, sustained success depends on the customers' valuation of the meal experience.

Commercial restaurants are notoriously subject to fashion. They tend to have a short life, not often more than eight years, and both the types of food served and facilities may need to be frequently changed. Investment has to be recovered within the planned life cycle period, requiring careful control of finance and operation.

Full-service high class restaurants are only 5 per cent of establishments. The mid-market range includes steak and seafood restaurants, grilles, brasseries and most ethnic restaurants. Commercial restaurants usually offer table service but self-service (see Section 6.1) from attractive counter displays is common in departmental stores and some of the larger mid-market restaurants for convenience and sales promotion.

5.2 Ethnic restaurants
In Britain the increase of ethnic restaurants – particularly Chinese and Indian/Pakistani – has displaced many of the traditional establishments. Ethnic restaurants are the main choice for evening dining. Design is often symbolic rather than authentic and it is essential to research the types of foods, spices, traditional preparation and cooking methods represented. Specialist cooking equipment is often required to supplement the standard range normally used and in international hotels separate Western, Oriental and other types of finishing kitchens are required to serve the variety of restaurants provided (Figure 34.23).

Ethnic restaurants cover a wide range of quality and sophistication. The range of food choice is ever increasing with travel, holidays abroad and migration. Chinese food divides into four regions: Canton, Peking, Szechuan and Shanghai. The kitchens need to provide the extensive menus which can be up to 300 items. 'Indian' food is strongly spiced and much of it can be cooked by standard equipment although special ovens may also be used. Japanese food is subtle: preparation and service are seen as an art form and used as part of the presentation. Scandinavian food usually requires a counter display of smoked food, fish and cold meats. Greek restaurants are often designed as peasant-style tavernas and this approach is common in Turkish, Mexican, Spanish, Thai and other popular ethnic restaurants. These traditionally use family service with a series of communal food dishes brought to the table. Italian food is more universal ranging from themed trattorie to specialised pizza chain outlets with purpose designed ovens and preparation areas (Figure 34.24).

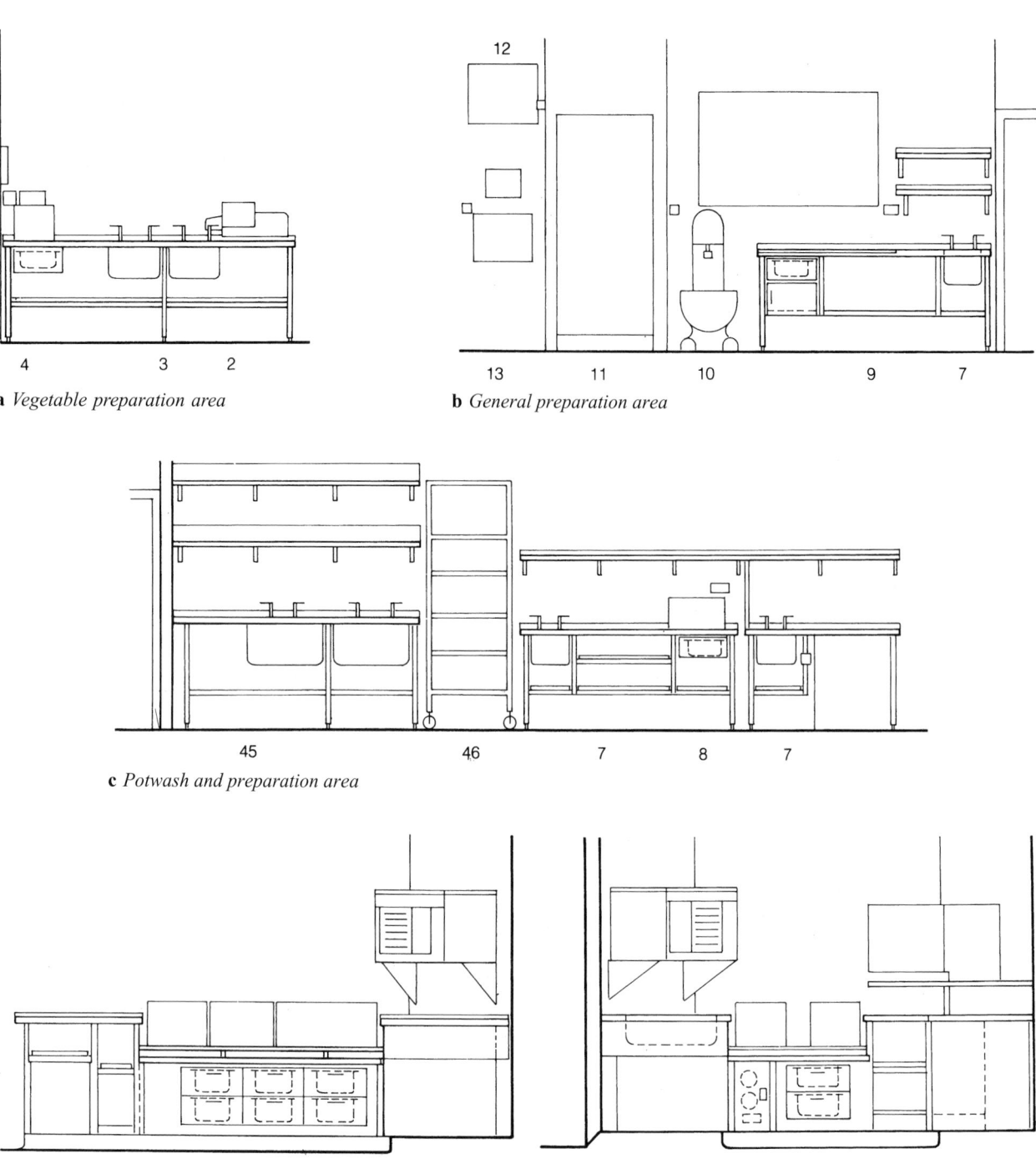

a *Vegetable preparation area*

b *General preparation area*

c *Potwash and preparation area*

d *Display kitchen, finishing area and servery*

e *Display kitchen, finishing area and servery*

34.20 *Elevations of installed kitchen equipment (continued opposite)*

5.3 Cafes, coffee bars and snack bars

Typically, these have limited space and seating. The menu range of food offered is short and simply produced, normally operated with counter service and back-bar equipment. Beverages are an important product, particularly in the more specialised coffee bar chains. Cafes tend to emphasise a domestic character and are often located in shopping and visitor areas. Snack bars and sandwich bars have very restricted seating areas and primarily cater for local workers and others requiring snack meals or take-away food prepared to order. Compact table or booth areas and/or counter seating are used. Chains of specialist coffee bars have expanded into almost every town using standard designs and equipment which offer a quick service of selected coffee beverages and pastries in comfortable surroundings.

6 CAFETERIAS AND FOOD HALLS

6.1 Cafeterias

Self-service is mainly used in employee, educational and institutional catering, airports, motorway service stations and other locations which serve large numbers of people at peak meal times or in which time for meals is limited.

   Characteristics:

- Scale of operation: usually large numbers of meals served allowing economies of scale in production.
- Concentrated demand: a short service period or limited time available for a meal demands a high rate of service with minimum delay. Above 600 meals per day, free-flow and multi-counter service is practical and the counters are often grouped in a food hall separate from the seating areas.

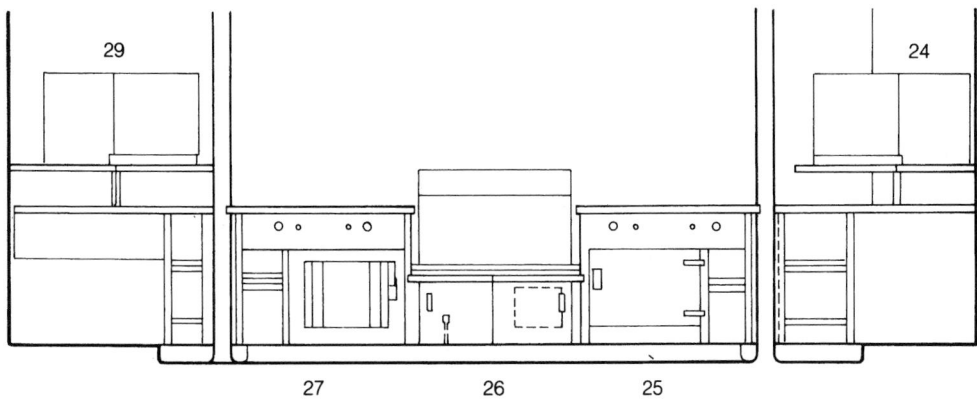

f *Display kitchen, finishing area*

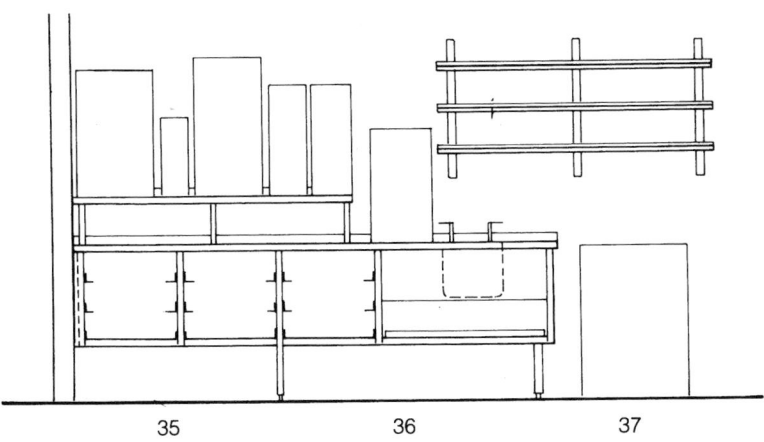

g *Beverage counter*

34.20 *(continued)*

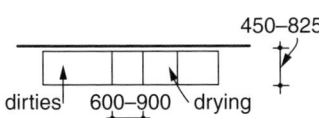

a *Small spray-type dishwasher*

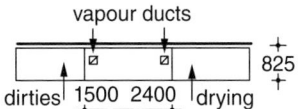

b *Medium-size automatic conveyor dishwasher*

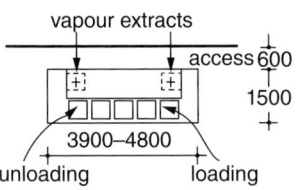

c *Rotary conveyor-type dishwasher*

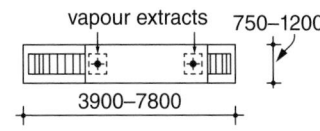

d *Large 'flight'-type dishwashing machine with continuous escalator type conveyor*

34.21 *Alternative layouts for wash-up areas, with equipment dimensions*

- Space: counters add 0.2–0.3 m² to area per seat in the dining room
- The average rate of customer flow through a single counter is 6–9 persons per minute, dictated mainly by the speed of beverage service, cash payments and variety of menu choice.
- By-pass arrangements, duplication of the counter and cash point can increase the flow to 14–16 persons per minute. Beverage service may be in a separate area.
- Larger numbers require multi-counters choices, each serving particular types of meals and these may be arranged in a food hall separate from the seating areas.

- The layout must allow for direct access to the production area for easy food replacement.
- Menus: balanced to meet nutritional standards. The extent of choice will determine counter layout and length.
- Counter sections are heated or refrigerated and fitted out for food holding and display. Critical features are the design of tray slides, easy access to the food items with protection from contamination.
- Cash-out desks are sited at or near the end of the service lines, duplicated where necessary and fitted with tray slide waiting areas. Cutlery, condiment, etc. stands must be sited to avoid congestion.

Table VI Range and sizes of tableware in general use

Type	Range	Size (rounded)
Pots	Tea	430, 570, 850, 1140 ml
(related to cups and pint sizes)		
Jugs	Coffee, hot milk/water	280, 570, 850, 1140 ml
	Cream	30, 40, 70 ml
	Milk	140, 280, 430 ml
Cups	Tea	170, 200, 230 ml
	Coffee (demitasse)	110 ml
Saucers	Size related to cups but should be interchangeable	
Plates	Side	165, 180 mm
	Dessert	190, 205 mm
	Fish/dessert	215, 230 mm
	Meat	240, 255 mm
	Oval meat	240, 255 mm*
Bowls	Cereal/fruit	155, 165 mm
	Sugar	90 mm
	Soup	215, 230 mm

*Usually maximum size for a dishwashing machine.

Table VII Allowances for dishwashing spaces (intermittent use)

Area/activity	Space (mm)
Collection area for unsorted tableware prior to sorting and scraping	600 length per 10 meals* Minimum 900 Maximum 2400
Stacking area for tableware sorted and stacked for manual washing	300 length per 10 meals† Minimum 900 Maximum 3600
Loading onto racks for machine washing	Depends on rack/basket size Minimum 1000
Draining and drying in racks or baskets after washing and sterilising	Minimum 1200 – Conveyor or spray-type machines up to 3600
Unloading baskets and racks for clean crockery awaiting removal	100 length per 10 meals Minimum 600 Maximum 2400
Spray-type machines with mechanised conveyor systems	Space occupied by machine conveyor system
Rotary conveyor type (600–1000 meals/h)	Width Length 1500 3900–4800
Flight-type escalator conveyor (over 1000 meals/h)	750–1200 3900–7900

*Based on self-clearance. Smaller areas suitable where part stacking is provided.
†Assumes some accumulation of dishes before washing up. The lengths relate to tabling 750 mm wide.

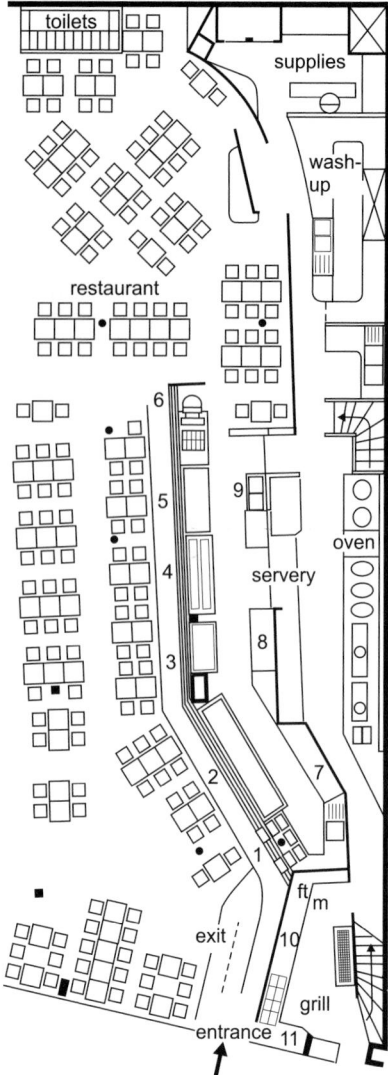

34.22 *Self-service restaurant in Paris. Architect: Prunier*

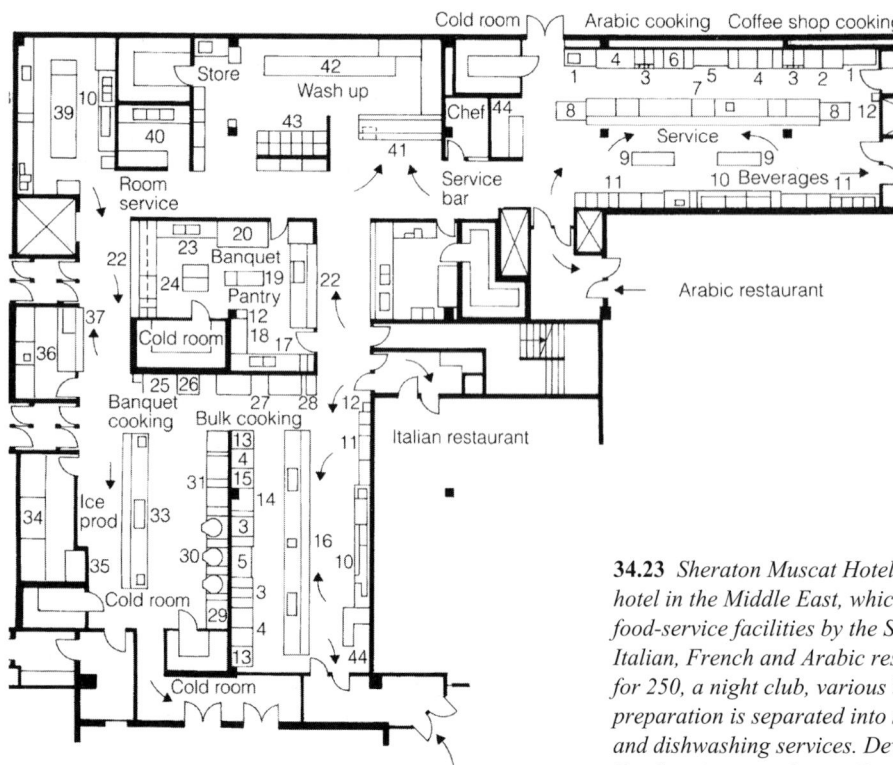

34.23 *Sheraton Muscat Hotel. This is a recently built 350-room hotel in the Middle East, which illustrates the careful planning of food-service facilities by the Sheraton Group. It offers a choice of Italian, French and Arabic restaurants in addition to banqueting for 250, a night club, various bars and room service. Food preparation is separated into specialised areas with common storage and dishwashing services. Development: Sheraton Corporation Foodservice consultants: David Humble Associates*

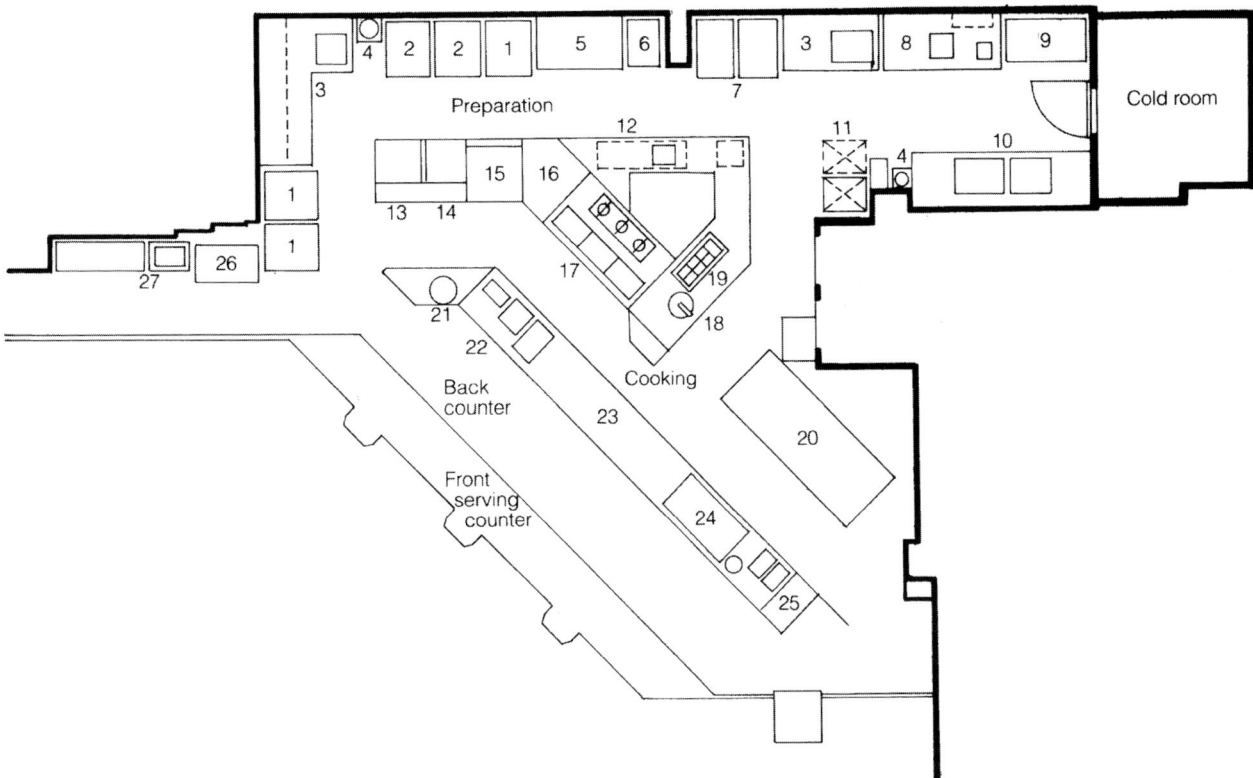

34.24 *Seasons pizzeria, London*

Self-service arrangements require seating areas to be arranged in regular order with wide aisles, particularly in the circulation to and from the serving counters. Self-clearance or/and trolleys may be used. Furniture must be durable, easily cleaned and retain good appearance. Counter arrangements are shown in Figures 34.25, 34.26 and 34.27 indicate equipment requirements although these will depend on the type and range of menu. To minimise food handling, counters are designed to receive standard gastro-norm containers (Figure 34.28). An example of a mid-sized employee cafeteria is shown in Figure 34.29 and a large hospital arrangement in Figure 34.30 with the standard key for three kitchens in Figure 34.31. A large scale, multi-choice layout is illustrated in Figure 34.32 and a large employee service in Figure 34.33.

7 FAST-FOOD OUTLETS AND TAKE-AWAYS

7.1 Fast-food systems

Fast-food has been a rapidly growing sector accounting for about one-third of the market for meals outside the home. Outlets mainly concentrate on a limited range of popular products such as hamburgers, chicken, pizza. Food is highly standardised and operations are designed around systems which enable tight control over production and costs to ensure fixed competitive prices. Most outlets are chain operated.

Investment costs are high with sophisticated equipment designed for high volume output with low skill operatives. Locations are critical and prime high street sites having large pavement flows are preferred for major franchised units. The average size of large counter and table service outlets ranges from 320–460 m². Operations often extend over 15 hour day, 7 day week to finance high investment and operating costs.

7.2 Operation

Most fast-food operators aim for a maximum door time (entering to leaving) of 3.5 minutes, 2.5 minutes queueing and 1 minute serving. Counters are designed for rapid ordering and service with multiple stations. Production processes use automated equipment with control over cooking and holding time, portions and additions (Figure 34.33).

Food is delivered to outlets ready prepared, portioned and frozen or chilled. The entire procedure is tightly controlled and unsold hot food kept only a fixed period then discarded. Employees have specific roles as till operators, backers and crew. Disposable containers are used for all food and beverage items and suitably designed waste receptacles and cleaning services must be provided in store and the vicinity.

Depending on the type of outlet, most fast-food stores also provide table and counter seating areas for meals on trays. These are grouped clear from the take-away routes and may be on upper or lower floors. Seating areas are designed for a high turnover, with self-service and self-clearance. Arrangements include fixed tables and seats, loose seats and wall counter seating. High standards of hygiene, cleaning and maintenance are important in system design. Trends are towards health conscious eating with emphasis on lower fat, salt and sugar products and additional choice of salads, vegetarian, fresh fruit, yoghurt and real juices.

7.3 Food courts

Food courts are provided to offer a wider range of choice with a number of food outlets serving alternative products grouped around a common seating area. They may be provided in shopping centres, airports, universities and other places where the demand is high. Serving counters are backed by end-cooking, preparation and storage areas supplied from a service corridor (Figure 34.34).

7.4 Other foodservice outlets

Food and refreshment services are required by motorists, coaches and truck drivers. These are mainly grouped with filling stations, lodges and other services at convenient stopping places along main routes, near major junctions and within scenic tourist attractions (Figure 34.34).

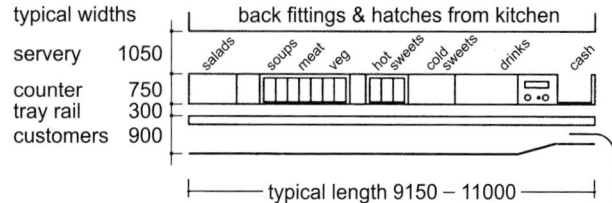

a *Single-line counter, 60–90 customers per min*

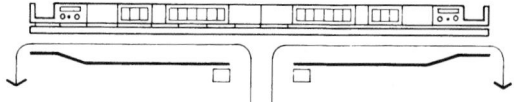

b *Divergent flow*

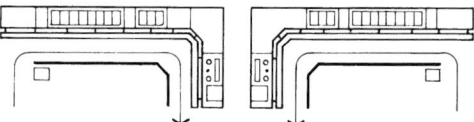

c *Convergent flow*

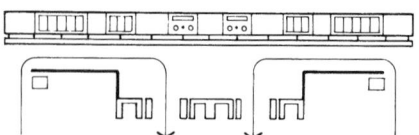

d *Multiple outlets*

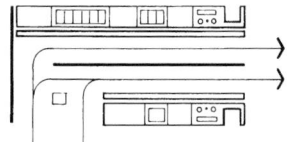

e *Parallel flow*

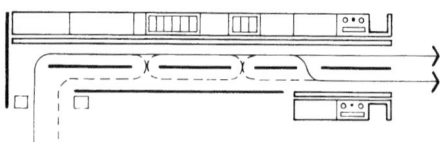

f *Bypassing*

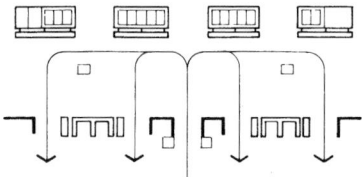

g *Free flow with counters in line*

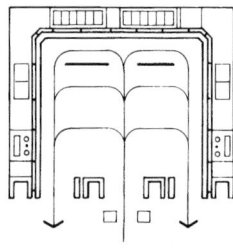

h *Free flow with counters in perimeter*

34.25 *Alternative arrangements for self-service counters*

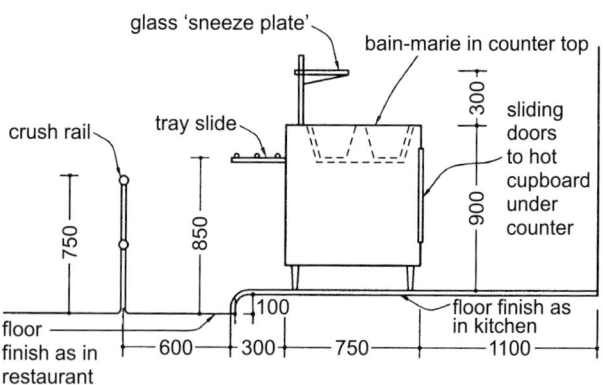

a *Section through counter for hot food*

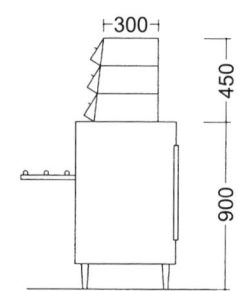

b *Section through cold-food counter*

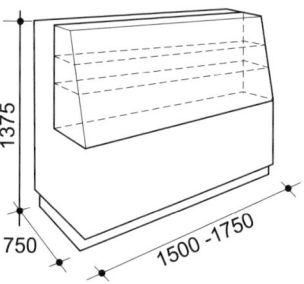

c *Refrigerated showcase*

34.26 *Servery equipment*

Snack bars, most delicatessens and food shops offer food ready for consumption off the premises. This may range from products freshly prepared, baked or cooked to order, including fish and chips, pizza, pies and pastries to pre-packed sandwiches and vended beverages. Some include limited table and counter seating areas. Many popular and ethnic restaurants also offer a take-away facility, some with home delivery.

8 PUBLIC HOUSES

8.1 Licensing

The requirements of public houses and wine bars are different from other food-service outlets in that alcohol sales are the dominant rather than a subsidiary activity. Licenses to sell alcoholic liquor are granted only if the applicant and premises are suitable for the purpose. Safety, means of escape, sanitary facilities and separation of bars from other areas must be approved before a license is granted as well as approval of any structural alterations before renewal. Few new public houses are built. The majority of works are alterations to update the facilities and provide food services.

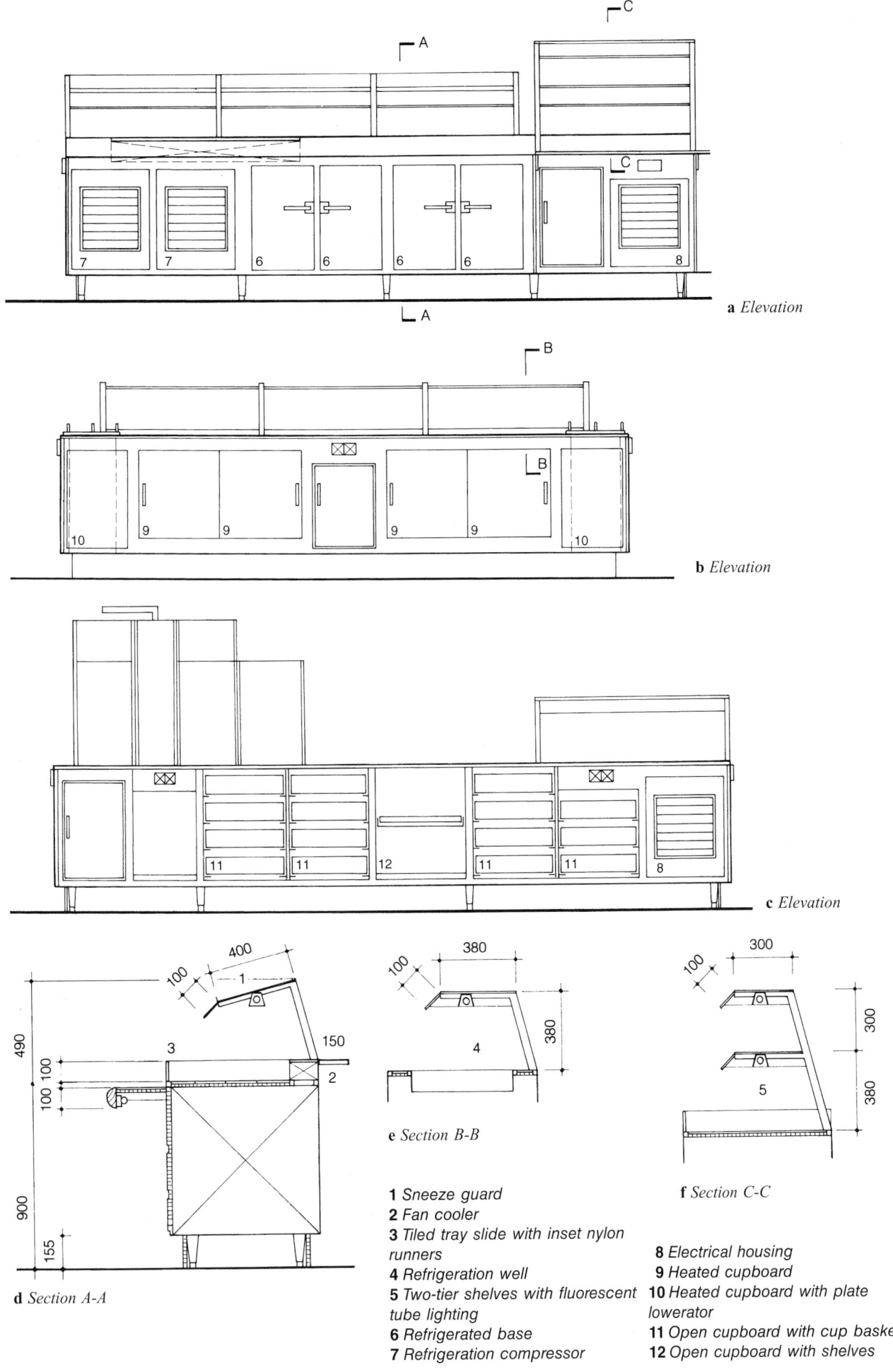

a *Elevation*

b *Elevation*

c *Elevation*

d *Section A-A*

e *Section B-B*

f *Section C-C*

1 Sneeze guard
2 Fan cooler
3 Tiled tray slide with inset nylon runners
4 Refrigeration well
5 Two-tier shelves with fluorescent tube lighting
6 Refrigerated base
7 Refrigeration compressor

8 Electrical housing
9 Heated cupboard
10 Heated cupboard with plate lowerator
11 Open cupboard with cup basket
12 Open cupboard with shelves

34.27 *Self-service counter*

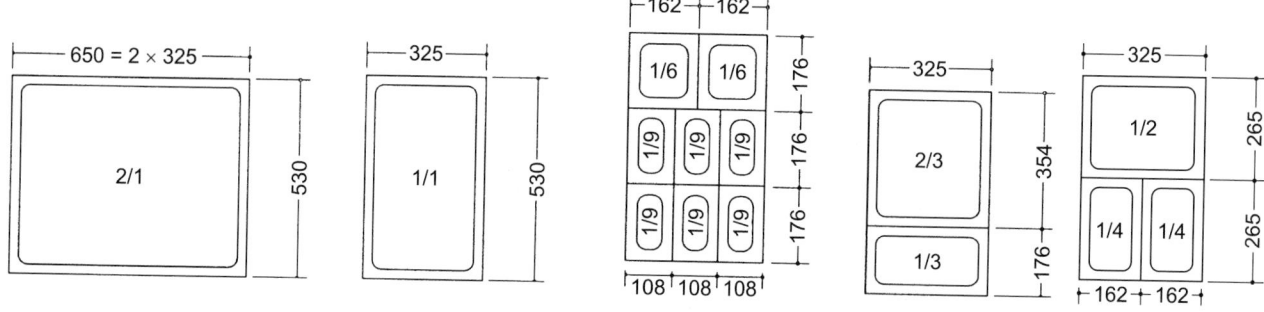

34.28 *Module sizes for gastronorm containers*

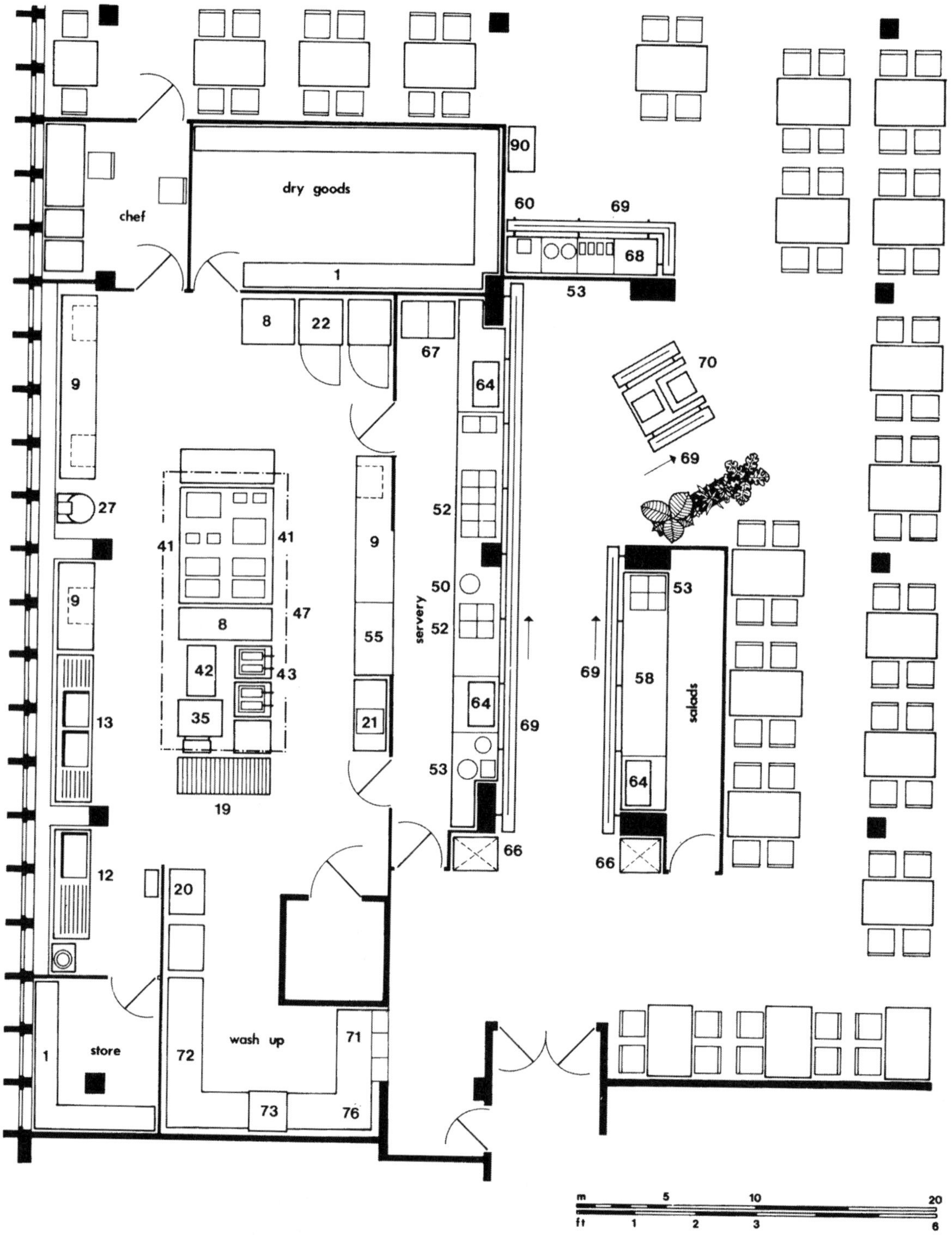

34.29 *A self-service restaurant to serve 350 diners over a 1 hour 30 minutes period. The island salad bar is designed to divide the flow and increase the speed of service. Standard key, Figure 34.31*

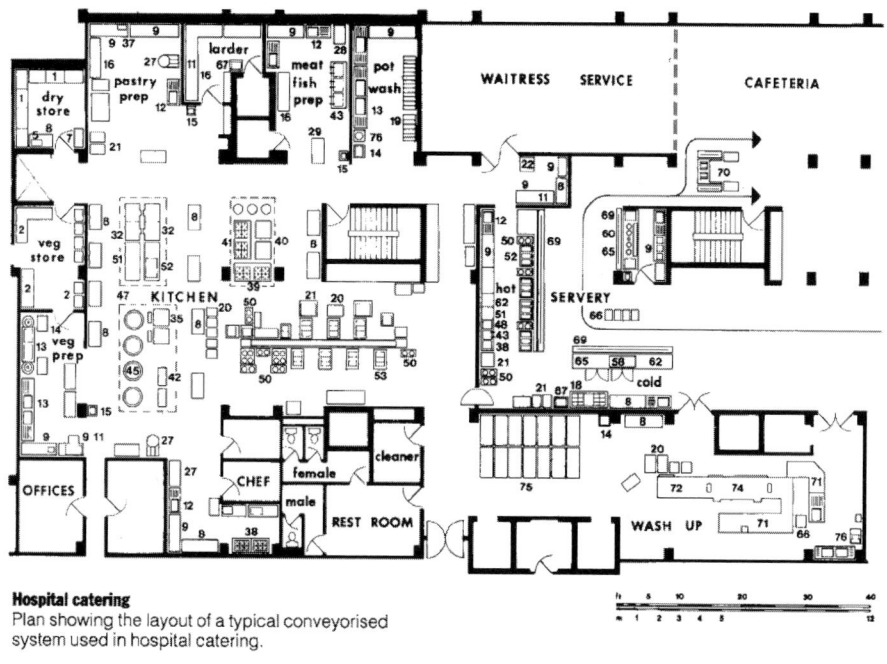

Hospital catering
Plan showing the layout of a typical conveyorised
system used in hospital catering.

(see general key)

34.30 *Plan showing the layout of a typical conveyorised system used in hospital catering*

Storage areas	**Cooking area**	62 *Counter unit – unheated*
1 *Shelving*	34 *Forced-air convection oven*	63 *Counter unit with infrared lamps above*
2 *Vegetable racks*	35 *Steaming oven/pressure steamer*	64 *Counter display cabinet*
3 *Vegetable bins*	36 *Microwave oven*	65 *Compressor or boiler under counter*
4 *Storage bins*	38 *Boiling top with oven top*	66 *Tray stand*
	39 *Boiling top with solid top*	67 *Ice cream conservator*
	41 *Oven range with boiling top*	68 *Cutlery stand*
Preparation areas	42 *Griller or salamander*	69 *Tray rail*
8 *Worktable or bench*	43 *Deep fat fryer*	70 *Cashier's desk*
9 *Workbench with cupboards/drawers*	46 *Open-well bain-marie*	
12 *Single sink with drainer*	47 *Extraction hood over equipment*	
13 *Double sink unit*		**Wash-up area**
14 *Mobile sink*		71 *Receiving table for soiled dishes*
15 *Wash-hand basin (with dryer)*	**Serving area**	72 *Stacking table for clean dishes*
16 *Marble-topped bench*	50 *Plate lowerator or dispenser*	73 *Dishwashing machine – semi-automatic*
19 *Pot rack*	52 *Hot cupboard with bain-marie top*	76 *Waste-disposal unit or scraping point*
20 *Trolley*	53 *Bench type bain-marie unit*	
21 *Mobile trays*	54 *Pass-through unit – heated*	
22 *Refrigerator*	55 *Pass-through unit – cold*	**Dining areas**
25 *Potato peeler*	56 *Refrigerator under-cupboard/drawer*	90 *Beverage vending unit*
26 *Chipping machine*	57 *Refrigerated cupboard with doleplate*	91 *Food vending unit*
27 *Mixing machine*	58 *Refrigerated display cabinet*	92 *Waiter/waitress serving station*
28 *Slicing machine/vegetable mill*	59 *Milk dispenser*	
29 *Chopping block*		

34.31 *Standard key for three kitchen examples*

8.2 Separation

Pubs require two separate parts:

- public areas: bars, lounges, dining areas, toilets and circulation used by customers;
- private areas: serveries, storage (cellars), kitchen and accommodation used by staff.

Most pubs traditionally offer a choice of public bar and lounge areas. Drink storage areas must be easily accessible to each bar servery. Access to the kitchen is required for taking food orders from the counter and serving food directly to the dining area.

The main pub entrance and secondary entrances from car parks are usually through lobbies to control temperature and airconditioning. Facilities must provide suitably located toilets of adequate size, separated for men, women and disabled and entered through a screened, ventilated lobby. Relationships between areas are illustrated (Figure 34.35) in a modernised town pub.

8.3 Pub meals

Most pubs offer meals to boost their sales by attracting a wider clientele and increased use of existing facilities and staff.

Usually a separate room or area of the lounge is used for food service with access (directly or via food hoist) to the kitchen. In country inns, glass-house extensions are common to extend the space into a garden environment. Most menus are standardised around popular choices with daily special additions to add variety – often with blackboard listings. Much of the food is bought in ready prepared. Kitchens are typically fitted with backbar equipment (e.g. microwave oven, grill, griddle, convection oven, boiling hob), together with preparation worktops, sinks, dishwasher, under-bench cupboards and refrigerators including chilled salad and food counters. An example of a pub conversion is shown (Figure 34.36).

8.4 Drink storage and bars

Traditional drink storage is in naturally cool cellars with CO_2 pressure or pumps to transfer ale and other brewed drinks from metal kegs or barrels to ground floor bars. Access to adjacent truck bays must be provided for deliveries (Figures 34.37, 34.38, 34.39, 34.40). Temperature control is critical and cooling may be required for the 'cellar' (including secure wine stores) and may be installed in the pipeline to dispense cold beer and other beverages. Pipelines are contained in ducts, usually insulated and may supply more than

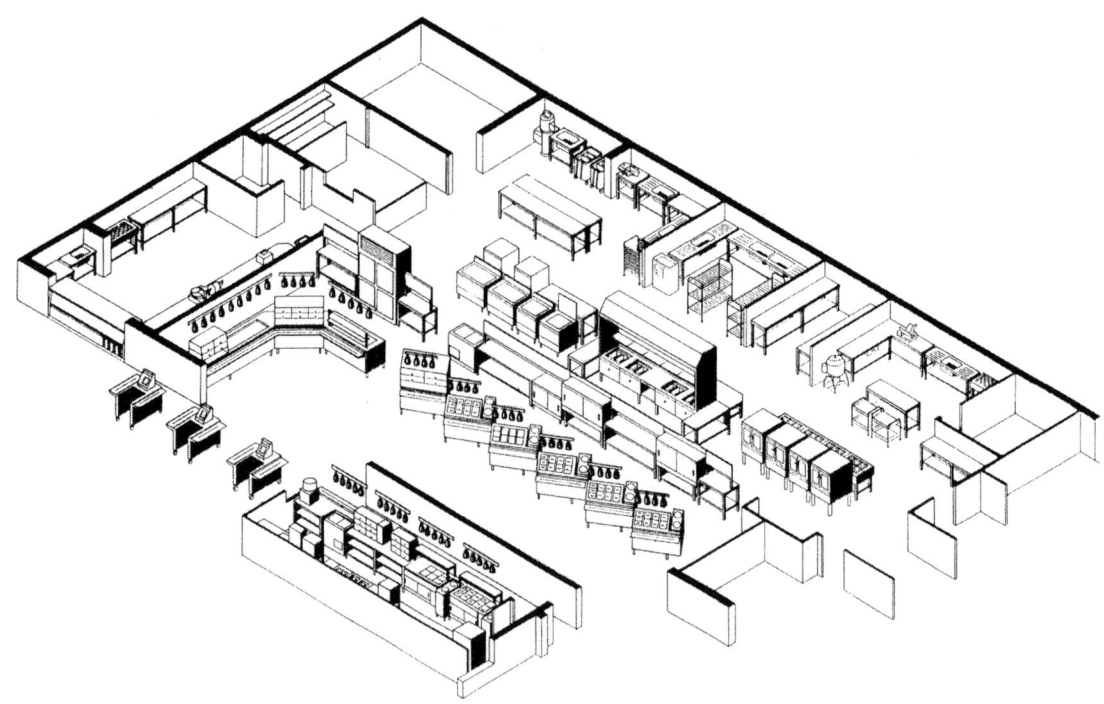

34.32 *Example of large-scale catering using multi-choice counters*

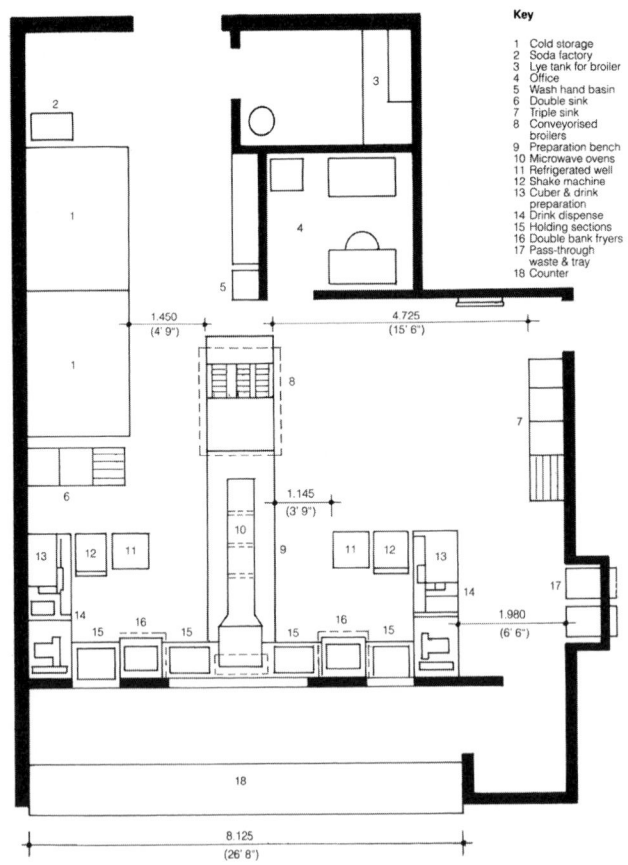

Key

1 Cold storage
2 Soda factory
3 Lye tank for broiler
4 Office
5 Wash hand basin
6 Double sink
7 Triple sink
8 Conveyorised broilers
9 Preparation bench
10 Microwave ovens
11 Refrigerated well
12 Shake machine
13 Cuber & drink preparation
14 Drink dispense
15 Holding sections
16 Double bank fryers
17 Pass-through waste & tray
18 Counter

34.33 *Fast-food outlet*

one floor level (Figure 34.41). Hoists can be used to transport cases of drinks.

Drink serveries are usually centrally located to serve more than one room and provide a bar counter, and back bar fitting with work space between having access to the bar store. Counter lengths vary but the height and width are standard. A worktop with inset sink is provided below the counter top and dispense points. The backbar is designed as a decorative feature and includes a sideboard with cooled shelves, a display for spirits ('optics'), wine and glasses, cash register, cooler and glass washing machine (Figures 34.42, 34.43).

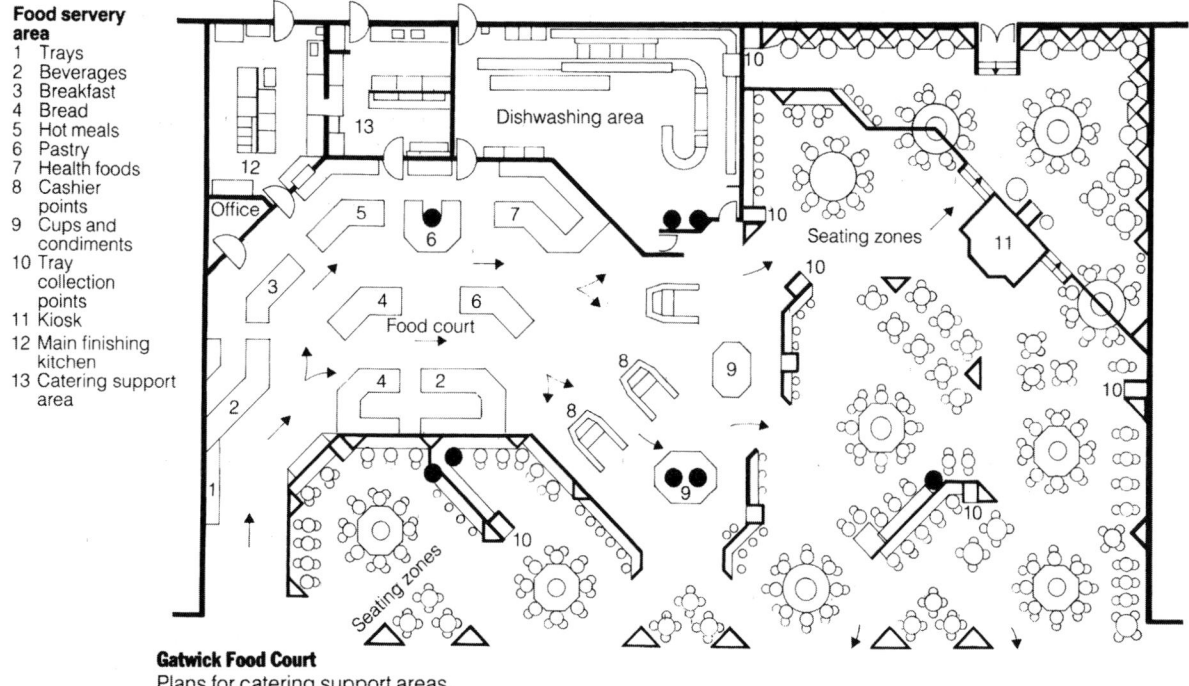

Food servery area

1 Trays
2 Beverages
3 Breakfast
4 Bread
5 Hot meals
6 Pastry
7 Health foods
8 Cashier points
9 Cups and condiments
10 Tray collection points
11 Kiosk
12 Main finishing kitchen
13 Catering support area

Gatwick Food Court
Plans for catering support areas.

Catering consultants: Tricon Foodservice Consultants Ltd

34.34 *Gatwick food court*

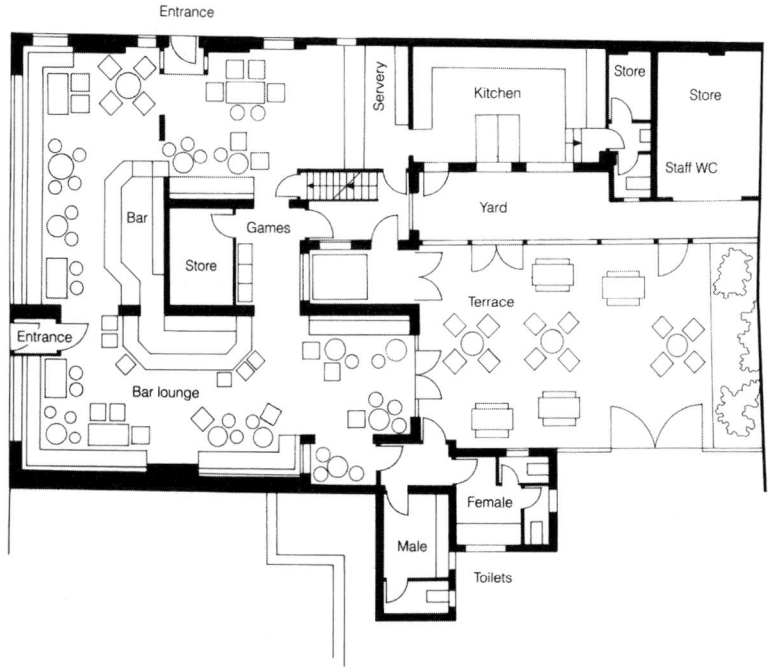

34.35 *Example of a modernised town pub*

An alternative choice of bars is often provided and one may be adapted for food service. A high proportion of drinkers stand at the bar and stools may be fitted or loose. Traditional pub tables are heavy, with cast iron base or wood frame, and used with peninsular seating and stools.

Depending on trade, drinking bars often provide a large screen television for sports interests and areas may be set aside for darts, pool, game machine(s) and a piano (Figure 34.44). Located mainly in city commercial districts, wine bars are more upmarket and often offer a bistro-type food outlet. Cocktail bars are sophisticated in

design and service style, usually associated with high class dining facilities, hotels and clubs.

8.5 Clubs

Clubs tend to specialise in late entertainment together with sales of beverages. Food may be served as in night clubs. In each case the design is specific to create the desired atmosphere and mode of operation. Entertainers require changing rooms with direct access to the stage. Sophisticated lighting, projection and sound systems with programmed control equipment are required as well

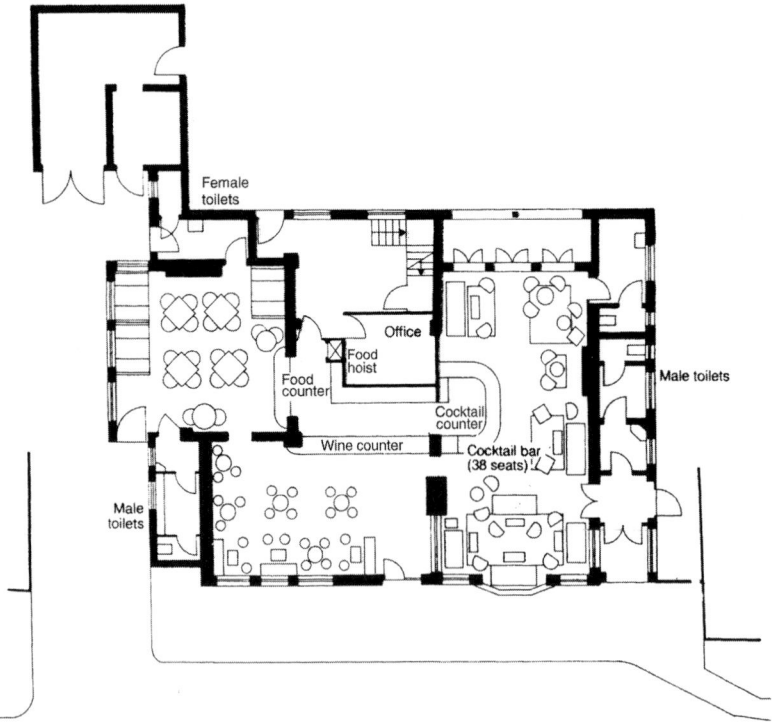

34.36 *Example of first-floor conversion of public house to provide an upmarket bistro-diner and cocktail bar. Lee Associates Ltd*

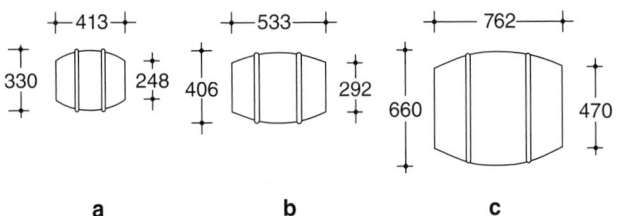

34.38 *Traditional sizes of metal barrels or kegs*

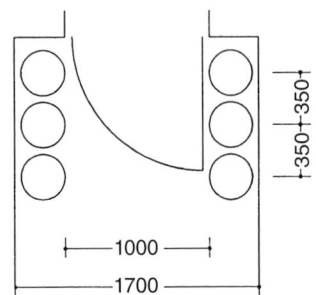

34.40 *Keg storage*

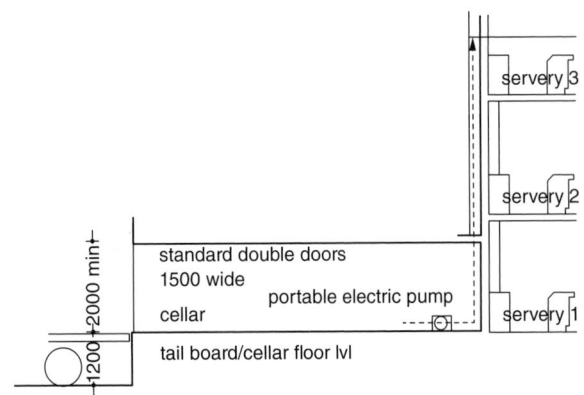

34.41 *Beer supplied through several storeys from ground-level cellar. A standard electric cellar pump will raise beer up to 9 m*

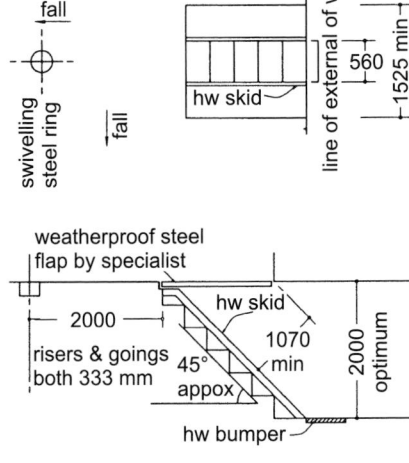

34.37 *Cellar flap and barrel chute for below ground storage of metal barrels or kegs*

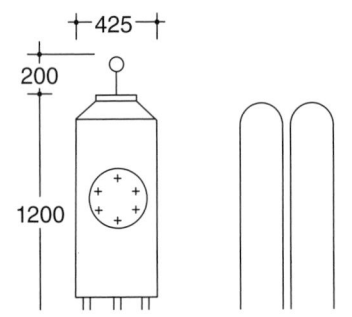

34.39 *Bulk storage in typical CO_2 canisters. Larger canisters also exist*

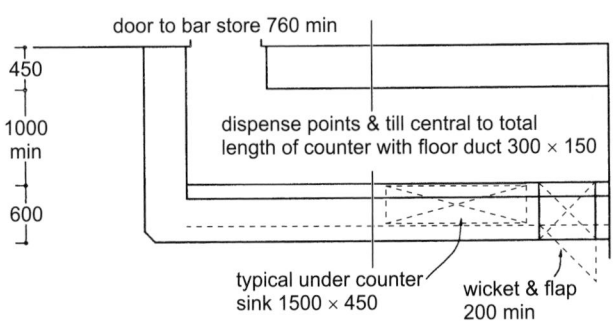

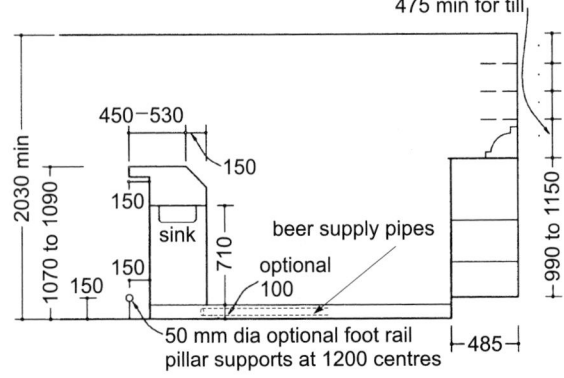

34.42 *Plan and section of a bar servery. Dispense points for various brands of drinks are usually sited at 225 mm centres along the counter top*

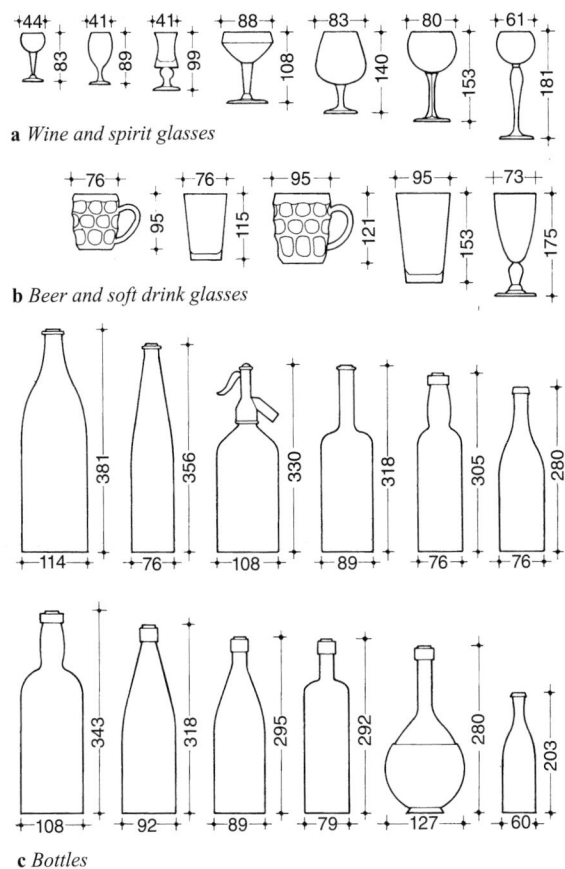

a *Wine and spirit glasses*

b *Beer and soft drink glasses*

c *Bottles*

34.43 *Sizes of pub glassware:*

a *Wine and spirit glasses*
b *Beer and soft drink glasses*
c *Bottles*

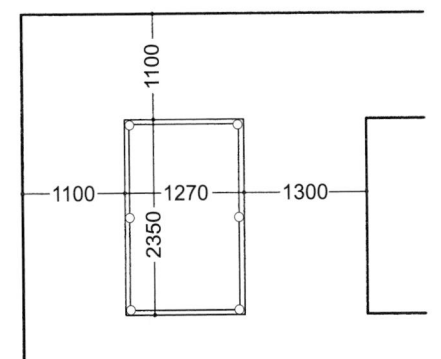

34.44 *Smallest size of pool table with cue space (for short cues) now common*

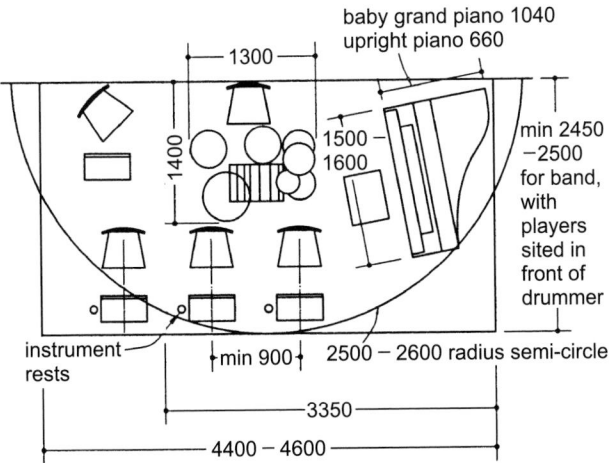

baby grand piano 1040
upright piano 660

min 2450
–2500
for band,
with
players
sited in
front of
drummer

instrument rests

min 900

2500 – 2600 radius semi-circle

3350

4400 – 4600

34.45 *A band platform. Club entertainers use own equipment*

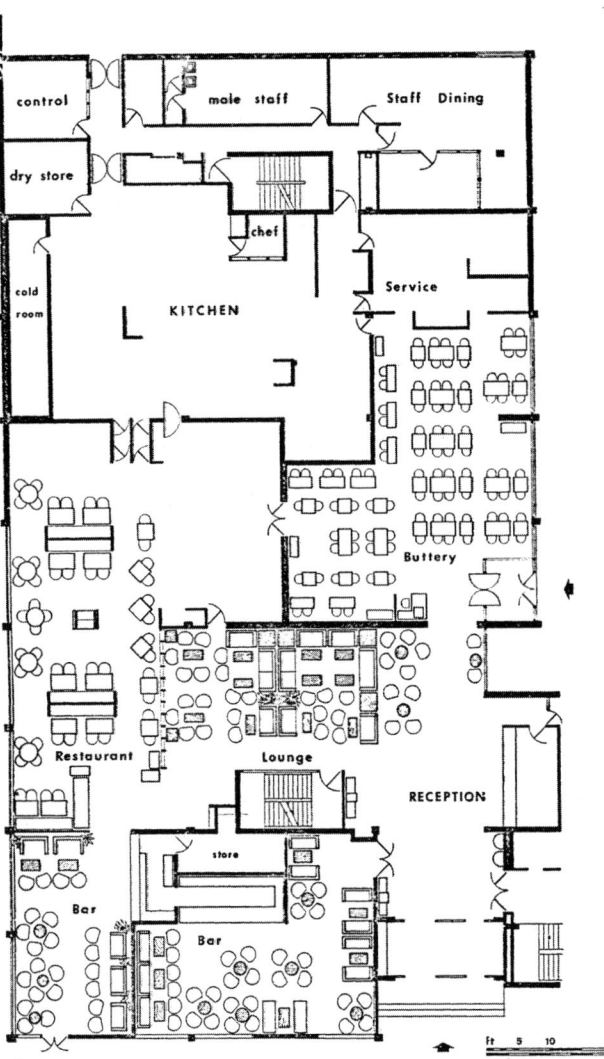

34.46 *Variety of food and beverage outlets in a hotel*

as discotheque music centres. A traditional band stand is illustrated (Figure 34.45).

9 HOTELS AND RESORTS

9.1 Hotels and cruise ships

Hotels are graded according to the quality of accommodation, price and range of services offering to guests. The extent of restaurant provision will also depend on the location and number of rooms. Typical space allowances are shown. Food production arrangements are rationalised to enable the main kitchen to supply several outlets directly or via satellite kitchens (Figure 34.11). An example of food production in a large international hotel is shown in Figure 34.23.

A high grade city centre hotel with more than 200 rooms will usually provide at least two restaurants offering choice between fine dining and coffee shop style operation – this also serves the peak breakfast demand (Figure 34.46). Resident demand for midday meals is often limited and a speciality restaurant may be featured to attract outside market interest. A hotel of this standard will also provide room service of meals, banquets for group meetings and events and meals for staff. Separate lobby, lounge, bar and restaurants may be designed to allow spatial continuity (Figure 34.47).

Resort hotels of high grade also offer guests and visitors a choice of restaurants and bars, including poolside bars. Bar and dining areas are commonly grouped together to serve evening entertainment. In mid-grade establishments, restaurant and bar provision is

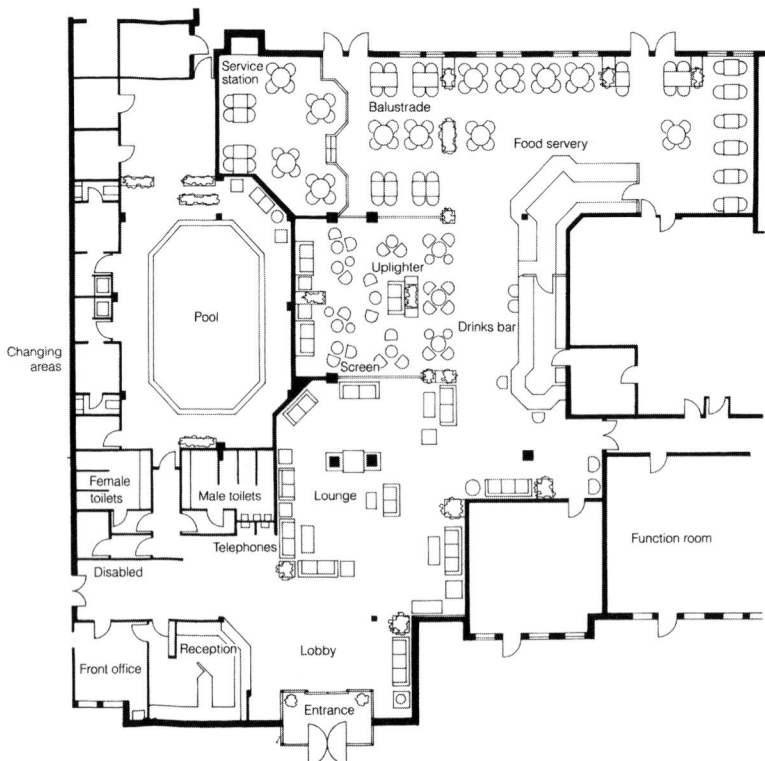

34.47 *Ladbroke Hotel. The restaurant (90 seats) is operated with a carvery buffet counter and table service of starters and sweets. The drinks bar allows dual purpose use of the lounge with areas separated by changes in floor level, balustrades and screens*

rationalised and budget accommodation may use external restaurants in the vicinity. Food production is generally centralised.

Cruise ships are broadly similar to high grade hotels and need to provide a variety of foodservice outlets and bars to accommodate the number of passengers and crew involved. These services are often an important part of cruise attraction and are linked to entertainment and other facilities. Menu planning is complex to take account of dietary requirements, choice, variety of outlets, supply provisions and hygiene standards. Extensive storage and preparation facilities are involved with added fresh foods at pre-arranged supply ports.

9.2 Resorts and attractions

Self-contained holiday centres and villages offer food service options, ranging from all-inclusive to self-catering facilities. In a large complex, a variety of themed restaurants, cafes, bars and other outlets is provided, often operated independently under license. Large visitor attractions usually need to provide cafes and restaurants as part of the facilities. These are invariably operated by catering contractors who supply the food partially or fully prepared to rationalise kitchen and staff requirements.

10 BIBLIOGRAPHY

Fred Lawson, *Restaurants, Clubs and Bars: Planning, Design and Investment*, 2nd Edn 1994, Architectural Press.

Fred Lawson, *Hotel Planning, Design and Refurbishment*, 1995, Architectural Press.

Walter A. Rutes, Richard H. Penner, Laurence Adams, *Hotel Design – Planning & Development*, 2001, Architectural Press

Bernard Davis & Sally Stone, *Food & Beverage Management*, 4th Edn, 2007 Butterworth Heinemann

Peter Coleman, *Shopping Environments: Evolution, Planning and Design*, 2006, Architectural Press

Fred Lawson, 'Restaurants and Catering Facilities', in Quentin Pickard (Ed), *The Architects Handbook*, 2002, Blackwell Science Ltd, pp. 322–334

Magazines

Hotels, Reed Business Information, Oak Brook, IL, USA

Catering Update, Reed Business Information, Sutton, UK

Restaurants and Institutions, Cahners Business Information, Des Plaines, IL, USA

Leisure Management, Leisure Media Co Ltd, Hitchin, UK

35 Retail shops and stores

Fred Lawson

CI/Sfb(1976): 34

Fred Lawson is a Visiting Professor at the Department of Service Industries, University of Bournemouth. He is also an international consultant and author of several books on planning and design

KEY POINTS:

- *Retail trading is affected by marketing, competition, polarisation, and store locations*
- *Market research of customers and focus groups is highly developed*
- *New concepts, innovations and efficiencies in operation are continuously being introduced*

Contents

1 Introduction
2 Terminology
3 Markets
4 Shops and stores
5 Small shops
6 Department stores
7 Variety stores
8 Supermarkets
9 Hypermarkets and superstores
10 Shopping centres
11 Retail parks
12 Regional centres
13 Bibliography

1 INTRODUCTION

1.1 General

Retail outlets consist of buildings or rooms where goods or services are sold to the public. They include shop and store premises and also concessionary space.

1.2 Scale and polarisation of business

A total of 33.7 per cent of consumers' overall expenditure in Great Britain in 2004 was spent in retail outlets. This proportion has progressively reduced from 37.5 per cent in 1995, showing the benefits of scale and sourcing made possible by polarisation of retail business into large groups serving particular segments of the consumer market. In 2004 the total turnover in predominantly food stores was over £112 billion and in non-food stores £128 billion.

Polarisation of retail business has also had a dramatic impact on shop numbers and the retail landscape. In 2006, 6452 multiple grocers with 10 or more stores commanded over 70 per cent of the total grocery turnover. This compares with 67 590 individual and other small grocery outlets that together achieved less than 30 per cent. A similar concentration of business has occurred in non-food retailing with some 90 000 stores belonging to multiples now dominating this sector. With corporate finance to pay increasing rents and building conversions to represent the brands, the character of High Street shops has lost much of the variety of individual tenancies.

1.3 Changes in space and location

Total shop floor space has grown with the penetration of chain stores into further market catchment areas as well as to extend individual store space for more product lines, customer choice and self-service checkouts. In 1992, following extensive development of shopping centres, retail warehouse parks and standalone superstores in the 1980s, total shop floor space had risen to 93 million m². By 2004 this total was estimated to be over 100 million m², much of the increase arising from large-scale regional shopping centres and brownfield redevelopments.

2 TERMINOLOGY

2.1 Shopping activities

Shopping activities vary with different needs and may be described as essential, convenience, comparison, purposive (specific), leisure or remote (mail order, teleshopping, internet retailers).

2.2 Selling methods

Personal service: individual service, usually over counters or desks by staff in attendance. (Examples: high-value goods, technical equipment, specialist boutiques and salons, delicatessen shops, financial and travel agency services.)

Self-selection: by customers who handle, compare and select goods prior to taking them to cash points for payment and wrapping. (Examples: department stores, variety stores.)

Self-service: of prepackaged groceries and durables collected in baskets or trolleys and taken to checkout points for cashing and packing. (Examples: supermarkets, superstores, discount stores.)

Assisted service: self-selection by customers combined with despatch of similar goods from stockroom to collection point or home delivery. (Examples: hypermarket, warehouse stores, furniture stores.)

2.3 Stock

Forward or displayed stock: held in sales area.

Support or reserve stock: in stockrooms ready for replenishing sales. The method of replacing displayed stock is a critical consideration in planning and organisation.

Amounts of stock in reserve are related to the stock-turn (average time held prior to sale), weekly turnover, delivery frequency and stock control. Electronic point of sale (EPOS) monitoring is used to predict sales patterns, reduce reserve stock and coordinate distribution and manufacture.

2.4 Areas

Gross leasable area (GLA): total enclosed floor area occupied by a retailer. This is the total rented space and includes stockrooms, staff facilities, staircases, preparation and support areas. It is usually measured to outside of external walls and centre line between premises.

Net sales area (NSA): internal floor space of a retail unit used for selling and displaying goods and services. It includes areas accessible to the public, e.g. counter space, checkout space and window and display space. Net areas are used to calculate the density of trading turnover (sales per m² or ft²).

The ratio of sales to ancillary space ranges from about 45:55 in small shops and departmental stores to 60:40 in supermarkets.

2.5 Rents

Rents are based on gross floor area measured in ft² or m² (1 ft² = 0.0929 m²). Three main types of rental agreement are used:

Guaranteed rent: with minimum annual rent guaranteed by the tenant irrespective of sales.

Percentage rent: based on a stated percentage of the gross sales of the tenant.

Turnover lease: the rent being related to the actual gross turnover achieved by the tenant, based on the total trading receipts less stated allowable deductions.

Rents are normally subject to review every four or five years.

Leases usually include the right to assign after an initial period (five years) and may provide a landlord's option to buy back. Premiums may be charged when leases are sold for premises in good trading positions with favourable lease and rent review conditions.

2.6 Retail operations

Independent: Shops and stores operated by individual or sole trader with less than ten branches (usually one or two). May be affiliated to a collective marketing and purchasing association.

Multiple: Mainly joint stock companies, with ten or more branches operated as a chain of shops and stores including large space users. Goods may include own-branded products.

Cooperative societies: Development has polarised into large supermarkets/superstores and small convenience shops serving local communities. Goods may be sourced through the Cooperative Wholesale Society or competitive suppliers.

Concessions: Granted rights to use land or premises to carry on a business – which may involve selling or promotion. The agreement may be based on rent, fees or profit sharing. (Examples are department stores, concourses in shopping centres and catering operations.)

Franchises: Contractual relationships between two parties for the distribution of goods and services in which the franchisee sells a product designed, supplied and controlled by and with the support of the franchisor. (In the UK franchising has been mainly used in fast-food brands, launderettes, car maintenance, bridal wear and some electrical trading.)

3 MARKETS

3.1 General

A market is a public area, open or covered, provided with stalls, where traders may sell their wares on recognised market days subject to payment of a statutory charge. This franchise confers sole and exclusive market rights over a distance of 10.73 km.

Markets make up less than 1 per cent of total retail sales in the UK, but attract potential customers to the town area. The character of markets relies on variety, mix of traders, simplicity and liveliness.

3.2 Open markets

Markets may be set up in streets, squares and open spaces, Figure 35.1. Stands comprise erected stalls and fitted-out vans and trailers set out in line along kerbs or back to back between aisles. Key considerations are:

- vehicle parking and loading (near stalls);
- traffic control;
- garbage storage and collection;
- washing facilities;
- protection of exposed food.

3.3 Covered markets

Permanent market stalls are sited in town centres and fringe areas (associated with auction rooms). New projects include craft markets (permanent or temporary) combined with workshops or forming part of shopping centres. Redevelopment of existing market halls often involves linkages with shopping centres and car parks.

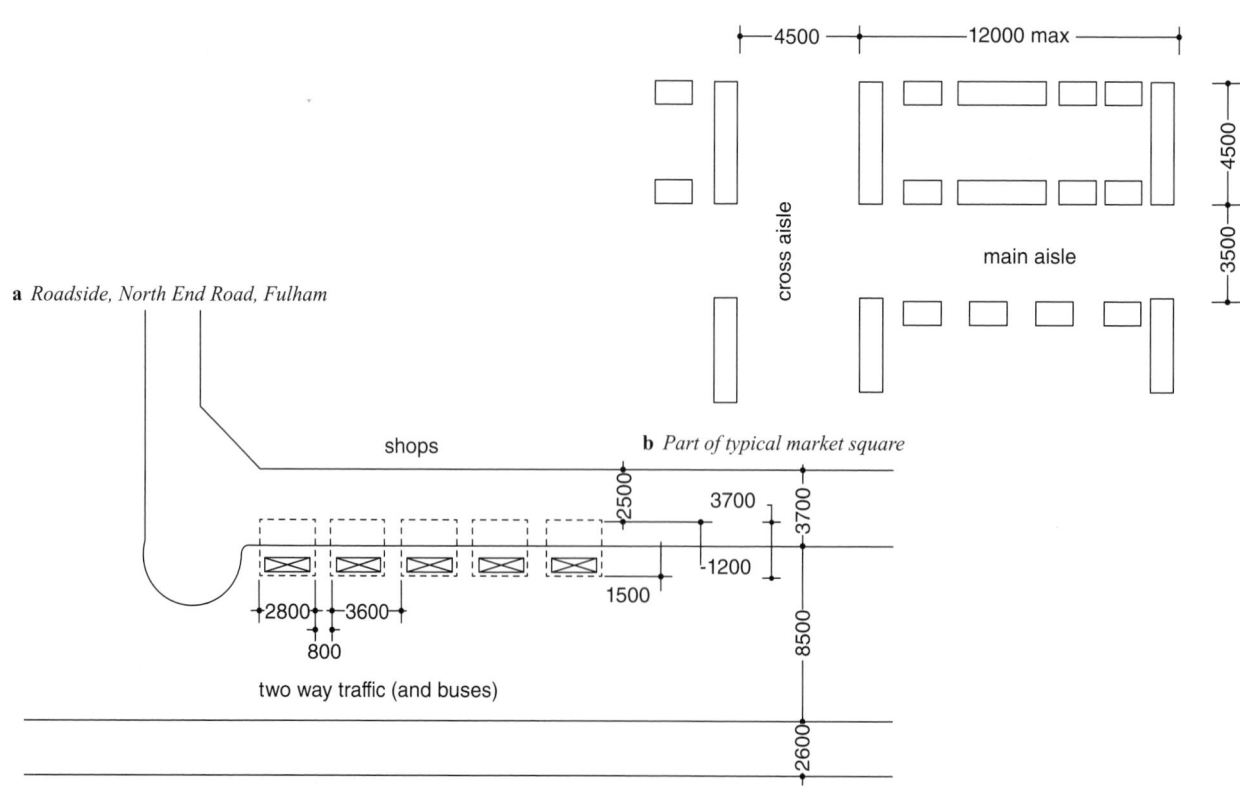

a *Roadside, North End Road, Fulham*

b *Part of typical market square*

35.1 *Markets*

3.4 Planning

Halls are usually designed to give a large-span open space having natural roof lighting, good ventilation and service connections. One-floor trading is preferred. Any upper floor is usually limited to a perimeter balcony served by escalators, stairs, goods and disabled lifts. Perimeter stalls and other grouped layouts have service corridors. Fish, meat and food stalls are sited in zoned areas with more sophisticated ventilation, drainage and services.

Key considerations: Access and linkage to car parks, shopping areas, goods delivery and parking bays. Mix of traders. Risk of fire (incombustible materials, fire-resistant construction smoke evacuation) and means of escape.

4 SHOPS AND STORES

4.1 Locations

Main locations for retail development in the UK are:

- *High street*: inner cities and towns, including backland development of shopping centres, shopping malls and street frontages.
- *Urban fringes*: industrial wasteland, redevelopment areas (superstores, retail parks, discount stores).
- *Out-of-town*: near motorway/main road junctions, easy access to large population catchment (retail complexes, regional centres, discount warehouses).
- *Neighbourhood*: association with estate development, filling stations (convenience shops), nurseries (garden centres), tourist attractions (souvenir shops, cafes).

Out-of-town retail developments generally allow much lower rents, easier access and parking, economical purpose-built 'shed' designs with flexible large-span spaces. Retail parks and complexes also generate mutual benefit from association of stores and services. Planning guidelines in the UK have stiffened resistance to development on greenfield sites with policies directed towards town-centre shopping and sensitive integration of new frontages.

Key factors affecting location:

- *Trading Zone*: Population, demographics, socio-economic profiles.
- *Accessibility*: Journey times, footfalls, transport systems, parking.
- *Attractions*: Range of goods and services, associated benefits.
- *Deterrents*: Travel costs, development, lease conditions and cost.
- *Economic*: Market maturity, trade saturation, economic trends.

For store planning and location these factors are often expressed in comprehensive shopping models. Customer parking and goods supply arrangements requirements also require detailed analysis.

4.2 Range of shops and stores

Retail outlets can be broadly divided into small shops (less than 280 m² sales area) and large space users. The latter include supermarkets and stores which may specialise in food or non-food lines or sell a wide variety of products (composite shops, variety shops, departmental stores).

Distinctions between stores tend to become blurred with:

- *Retail polarisation*: trends towards both larger (one-stop shopping) and smaller retailers (speciality and convenience shops, financial, etc. services, franchised units, workshop-craft outlets).
- *Competition*: innovation, market penetration and development of new merchandise and selling methods, creaming of popular lines.
- *Acquisition*: merger of competing outlets, focusing of business and market positioning of company products, rationalisation of lines of goods and resources.

- *Image and service improvement*: extension of added value and high-profit value lines. Improved customer services and design environment.

4.3 Planning guidelines

Table I gives guidelines on planning shop space.

Table I Shop space

Structural models	Width (m)	Notes
Small shops	5.3 to 6.0	Mostly 5.4 m
Large-space users	7.3 to 9.2	Depending on beam depth.
		Single-storey buildings – larger spans
Clear ceiling	*Height(m)*	*To underside of beams*
Small shops	3.3 to 3.8	Sales area
	3.2 to 3.6	Non-sales area
Large-space users	3.6 minimum	With floor: floor spacing 4 to 5 m
Typical floor loading	kN/m^2	
Shop sales area	5	
Shop storage	10	Increase in loading docks
Car parking	*Car spaces per 100 m² gross retail area*	
Supermarkets, Superstores	10–12	
Shopping centres	4–5	
Goods and service docks	*m*	*Notes*
Typical provision for large-space user		
Two 15 m articulated lorries: width	10.7	Allowing 1.5 m each side
Minimum clearance height	4.7	Approach road – 5.00 m
Design load for service yard	20 kN/m²	
(See also Chapter 3.)		

Deliveries may be controlled or random. Provision must be made for manoeuvring space and waiting bays, for separate refuse storage with compaction equipment, refrigerated garbage and collection skips.

Staff facilities (general guide only)
Staff numbers: net sales areas, 1:50 m² to 1:80 m²

Additions to the net sales area	Net areas	Gross areas
Staff facilities	10–15 per cent	25–30 per cent
Offices	5–8 per cent	

Staff facilities include: restaurant with kitchen and servery, coffee and recreation rooms, changing areas, toilets, personnel and training and reception/control area.

4.4 Shop fittings

Shop fittings may be individual bespoke designs, fabricated or modular units. While the range and style vary widely, fittings must satisfy functional needs (including ergonomics) and be compatible with the design, versatile, durable, stable and safe in use.

Display units can be broadly divided into wall-anchored fittings and free-standing units, the latter being designed for perimeter or central locations.

Figures 35.2 and 35.3 are examples of mobile display units, while Figures 35.4 to 35.6 show units suitable for supermarkets.

Examples include:

- wall systems (slotted panels, frames, suspensions)
- fitted furniture (cupboards, wardrobes, trays)
- free-standing racks and garment rails
- gondolas and island displays
- cases (counters, showcases, wall cases)
- cabinets (front or top access)
- shelving systems (modular, adjustable)
- forms, mannequins, displays (counter or free-standing)
- bins, tables, risers
- counters (cash and wrap, checkout, service).

Construction materials include hardwoods, laminates (lipped) acrylics, toughened glass, polycarbonate, UPVC, chrome-plated and stainless steel, anodised aluminium.

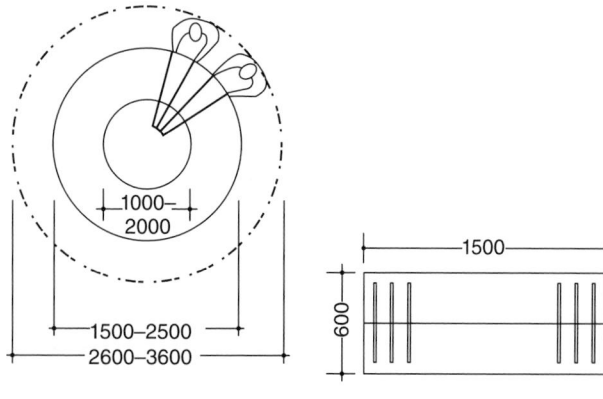

35.2 *Storage and display racks for clothing shops*

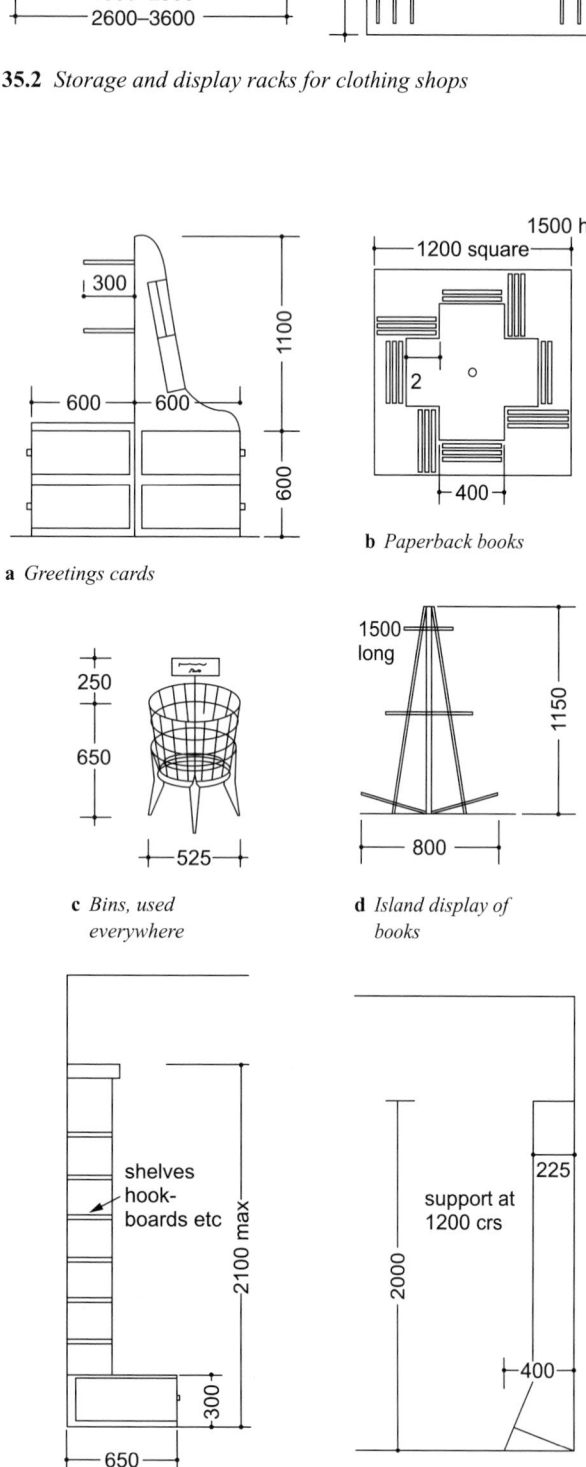

a *Greetings cards*

b *Paperback books*

c *Bins, used everywhere*

d *Island display of books*

e *Wall units for stationery and books*

f *Wall units for books*

35.3 *Storage and display fittings for stationery and bookshops*

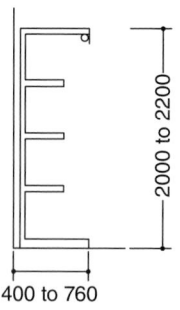

35.4 *Section through supermarket wall shelving*

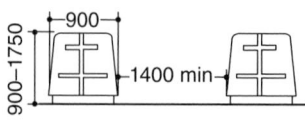

35.5 *Section through supermarket shelving*

4.5 Lighting

Table II gives guidance for lighting.

Table II Lighting levels

Lighting	Standard service illuminances	
	(lux)	Notes
Conventional shops	500	Concentrated over displays
Supermarkets	500	Usually increased to 700–800 lux with three levels of control: 100 per cent – sales, 50 per cent – stacking, 30 per cent – security
Covered shopping centres	100–200	Malls, arcades, precincts
Lifts, main circulation	150	
Staffrooms	150	
External covered ways	30	

Luminaires include low-voltage units (displays), colour-balanced fluorescent (sales areas), metal halide (high intensities).

4.6 Temperature

Table III gives recommended temperatures and ventilation for different sizes and types of shop.

Table IV gives temperatures for various food cabinets.

Table III Temperatures: design conditions

	Temperature (°C)	Air infiltration (Changes/hour)	Ventilation allowance (W/m³°C)
Small shops	18	1	0.33
Large shops	18	½	0.17
Department stores	18	¼	0.08
Fitting rooms	21	1½	0.50
Store rooms	15	½	0.17

Table IV Food cabinets

Display of food	Cabinets (°C)
Fresh products (chilled)	+8
Dairy products, cooked meats	+3
Fresh meats, poultry, fish	0
Frozen foods	–18
(subject to EU regulations)	

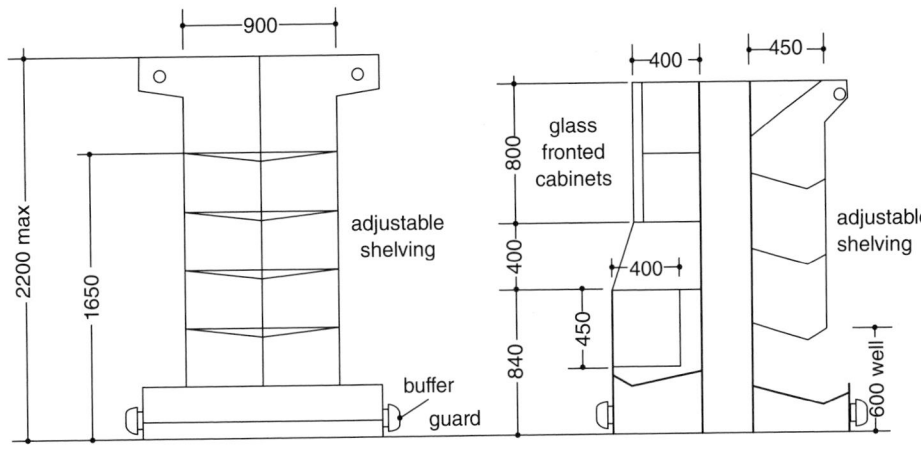

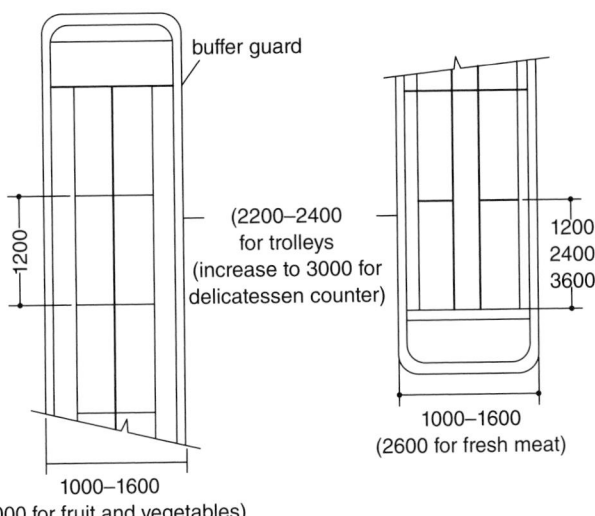

35.6 *Plan and section through supermarket display cabinets*

4.7 Air conditioning
The recommended outdoor supply rate for air conditioning spaces is 8 per person with a minimum of 5 per person, 3 per m² of floor area. In large stores, occupancies are on average 1 person per 5–6 m² and 1 person per 1.8 m² for peak areas.

Air conditioning is usually designed for 18–21°C at 50 per cent ± 5 per cent RH (below-risk of static) pressurised to + 5 per cent actual air volumes.

4.8 Energy management
Most multiple and large stores use energy management systems with remote station monitoring. Waste heat is recovered from refrigeration for hot water supplies and cool air recycled from refrigerated display areas. Refrigerants are changing to hcfcs (non-ozone reactive) with leakage-detection systems.

5 SMALL SHOPS

5.1 General
These are shops having a sales area less than 280 m² and not more than three stores, one of which may be a basement. Shops employing fewer than 20 people or 10 above the ground floor do not normally require a fire certificate.

5.2 Location
Convenience shops need to be near populated areas or stopping places (filling stations, airports, railway stations).

Speciality shops are best grouped with other shops and large space users to increase market exposure or in speciality areas associated with tourist attractions, etc.

Financial, etc. services: shop units usually combined with offices and ancillary rooms above.

5.3 Planning
Typical small shop plans are shown in Table V.

5.4 Servicing arrangements
Stock replenishment and waste removal is usually through a rear service road but in a shopping complex this may be accessed through a service corridor and goods lift. Some pedestrianised precincts allow vehicle access to front of shops outside restricted hours.

5.5 Design
The design of the shop frontage, graphics and window display is a major consideration. Multiple and franchised outlets usually reflect a uniform brand image. In environmentally sensitive areas, the scale and character of existing facades may need to be retained.

Interior layouts, fittings and design features depend on the nature and volume of goods sold.

Table V Small shop plans

	Typical	Minimum
Width of frontage	5.4 to 6.0 m	4.0 m
Depth	18.0 to 36.0 m	12.0 m
Height (depending on services)		3.0 m
Sales:ancillary areas	50:50	45:55
Staff facilities		1 wc plus 1 washbasin for each sex (minimum)
		Changing area with individual lockers Restroom
		with small food-preparation area
Office		Files, safe, desk, terminals

Rental charges are mainly determined by location and width of frontage. The width:overall depth ratio is typically 1:4 or 5, the lower value rear areas being used for goods storage, processing and staff facilities.

6 DEPARTMENT STORES

6.1 General
Department stores are large complex shops, invariably extending over several floor levels, selling a wide variety of goods, particularly clothes. Sales areas are grouped into departments corresponding to different categories of shops but are flexible in size and position. Departments may be operated directly by the store or let to other traders and franchisees.

Main high street stores usually have more than 20 000 m² sales areas but 'Junior' department stores in new shopping centres are less than 10 000 m² over two floors. Sales:gross area ratios are relatively low, 45:55.

6.2 Planning
A frontage to more than one street or mall is preferred for extended window displays, customer entrances and emergency exits. Separate staff entrances and goods delivery and despatch areas (with customer collection bay) are essential.

Internal areas must be planned for maximum clear space to allow for changes in seasonal sales and tenancy arrangements. Exceptions are food areas (food halls, food-preparation kitchens) which require permanently fitted equipment and special services.

6.3 Fire requirements
Compartmentation: most regulations permit up to 2000 m² and 7000 m³ or twice this size (4000 m²) with automatic sprinkler system.

Smoke evacuation: reservoir space with exhaust ventilation and controlled airflows.

Construction: fire-resisting structures and limitations on surface flame spread of lining materials.

Isolation: sprinklers, water curtains and physical separation of escalators, lift shafts and voids.

Means of escape: travel distances to protected staircases and adequate exits to street.

6.4 Locations
Locations for departments are rationalised by floor levels of related goods but influenced by turnover values and unit selling times. The ground floor is used for quick sales or small items to attract customer interest.

Restaurants, toilets and customer services are usually accessed through selling areas.

Subsidiary accommodation is needed to service departments on each floor but main stock rooms, staff facilities and administration are located in lower-value areas (rear, basement or upper floor).

Escalators and lifts are usually centrally positioned to create a focus and draw customers through departments.

6.5 Trends
Department stores have relatively high staffing and operating costs. Life-cycle renovation may be used to remodel, divide and/or extend stores as shopping centres and shops within shops. Developments include Junior Departmental stores, Anchor stores in regional centres and airports. Flagship store designs stress customer focused ambience, distinctive lines, quality branded merchandise and range of customer services.

7 VARIETY STORES

7.1 General
These are large-space users selling a wide range of non-food goods, mainly by self-selection in an open sales area. In some stores part of the area is used for self-service food sales. Includes independent and multiple chain stores (Marks & Spencer, John Lewis etc.).

7.2 Size and location
Sales areas range from 500 to 15 000 m², most major stores being between 10 000 and 15 000 m² with sales:ancillary area ratios of 50:50.

Locations
- Prime high streets: serving sizeable catchment populations.
- Shopping centres: multi-level links to upper and lower floors.
- Regional shopping complexes and retail parks (space allowing introduction of wider ranges of goods).

Major stores require catchments of 80 000 to 100 000.

7.3 Planning
A rectangular plan with one-level trading is preferred with frontages on the high street and shopping mall. Sales floors in large stores are on two levels (sometimes three) with food areas having access to parking or collection points. Escalators, stairs and lifts for the disabled and goods distribution are kept to the perimeter to allow uninterrupted space for display and circulation planning.

7.4 Layout
Main aisles with distinctive flooring lead from entrances to assemblies of display fittings and cash and wrap points positioned for visibility and convenient access.

Displays include both perimeter and island fittings with related goods grouped together for easy location and comparison. Stores selling clothes and fashion goods must provide changing rooms and multiple mirror points. The self-service areas for food goods are planned on supermarket lines.

7.5 Facilities
Some stores provide a cafe or restaurant for customer use usually located on the upper floor to promote other impulse buying. Toilets and other customer services are in this vicinity.

Ancillary areas for staff and reserve stock are at the rear or on a higher floor, with separate staff entrance, reception and control leading to changing and associated facilities.

8 SUPERMARKETS

8.1 General
Supermarkets sell food and regular domestic necessities on self-service lines. The sales areas of large-space users range from 1000 to 2500 m² although many small grocers also use self-service.

8.2 Planning
Sales are invariably on one floor, planned to allow trolley circulation from car park through the store. Where required, upper floors are limited to non-food goods. A simple rectangular plan is preferred with 30 to 60 m frontage. (Minimum frontage (18 m) may require double-banked checkouts.)

The position and layout of the checkout points govern entrance, exit and circulation plans. Sales areas have large unobstructed spaces with structural grids of 9.0 m or more (to suit stand spacing) and 3.66 m clear ceiling heights. Supermarkets and store chains have their own evolving standards for aisle widths, till layouts, loading docks, etc.

8.3 Layout
A standard arrangement of parallel shelf racks and cabinets on each side of circulation aisles is invariably adopted. The main aisles are 2.2 to 2.5 m wide increasing to 2.8 to 3.2 m in front of delicatessen counters and fresh/frozen meat cabinets. 3.0m across aisles are

provided at the end of turns and a clear area 2.2 to 3.0m deep on each side of the checkout line.

Displays are grouped into food, non-food and off-licence sections. Delicatessen, bakery and perishables prepared on the premises need to be adjacent to the preparation areas, with easy access to stores (refrigerated).

As a rule, refrigerated display cabinets are grouped together to facilitate service connections and airflow recovery.

Demand goods (vegetables, fruit) are usually placed near the entrance to initiate buying and promotional items displayed in bins and in racks at the end of rows and checkout stations.

Space has to be allocated for customers to collect and restore baskets and trolleys, Figures 35.7 and 35.8. Where virtually all customers arrive by car, trolley parks are normally situated within the car parking area, often in lightly covered kiosks; and few (if any) baskets are provided. In urban areas, substantial areas within the store curtilage have to be provided, and many customers will use baskets.

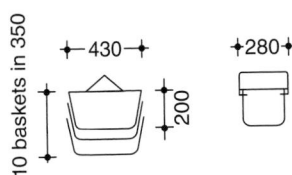

35.7 *Supermarket baskets*

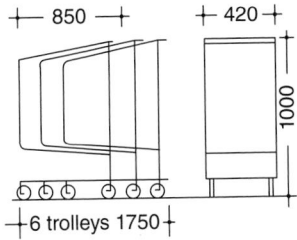

35.8 *Supermarket trolleys*

In self-service shops, supermarkets and hypermarkets the customer pays for his or her purchases at a checkout. These vary greatly in design, depending on the type and quantities of merchandise, and the policies of the company concerned. Some contain automatic price-checking equipment and semi-automatic packing arrangements. Figure 35.9 shows a fairly standard basic design.

Separate shop units (newsagents, florist, chemist, cafe) may be sited independently of the checkout and direct access is required to public toilets, public telephones and management offices.

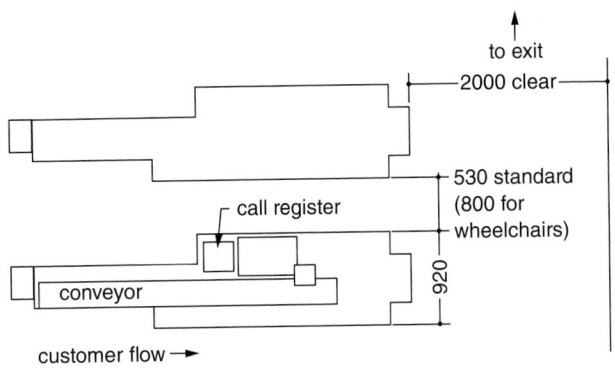

35.9 *Typical check-out*

8.4 Trends

The intensity of sales/m^2 is a critical consideration with trends towards increase of high added value (own-preparation bakery, butchery) and profit margins (delicatessen, wines, plant sales, made-up goods).

Technical equipment includes barcode scanning, EPOS monitoring and stock control, and the introduction of liquid display shelf edge/labelling, robot packing and self-checkout facilities.

With opposition to out-of-town location, some multiples are developing convenience stores in town centres selling a limited range of goods.

9 HYPERMARKETS AND SUPERSTORES

9.1 Hypermarkets

These are very large stores on supermarket lines but with at least 2500 m^2 sales floor such as Tesco Extra.

Compared with supermarkets the range of non-food lines is extended up to 50 per cent of the area. Hypermarkets tend to be built on derelict industrial land and urban fringes within large catchments, Figure 35.10.

Superstores are similar but tend to be larger with 5000–10000 m^2 of selling space. Located out of town, they occupy large sites, with extensive parking, a petrol-filling station and an associated square or arcade of small shops, Figure 35.11. The overall development often combines out-of-town shopping with community facilities such as a village hall, public house, sports ground or/and leisure centre.

Discount stores and warehouse clubs concentrate on lower costs by limiting the range of goods (e.g. 650 compared to a supermarket's 3500 brand lines) and using simpler warehouse-style buildings and fittings.

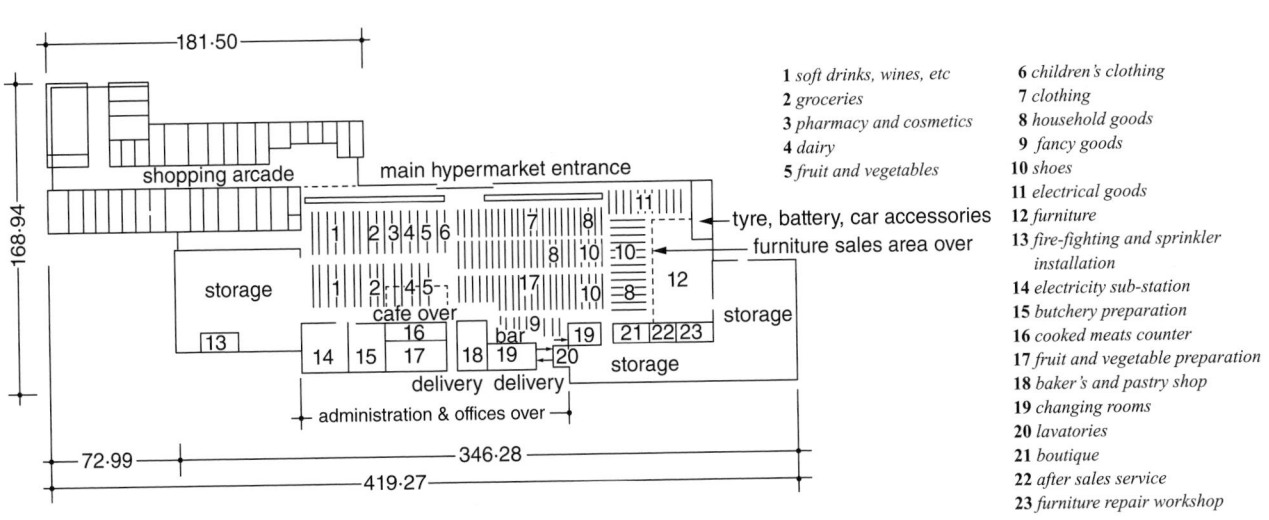

35.10 *General layout of a major hypermarket*

1 *soft drinks, wines, etc*
2 *groceries*
3 *pharmacy and cosmetics*
4 *dairy*
5 *fruit and vegetables*
6 *children's clothing*
7 *clothing*
8 *household goods*
9 *fancy goods*
10 *shoes*
11 *electrical goods*
12 *furniture*
13 *fire-fighting and sprinkler installation*
14 *electricity sub-station*
15 *butchery preparation*
16 *cooked meats counter*
17 *fruit and vegetable preparation*
18 *baker's and pastry shop*
19 *changing rooms*
20 *lavatories*
21 *boutique*
22 *after sales service*
23 *furniture repair workshop*

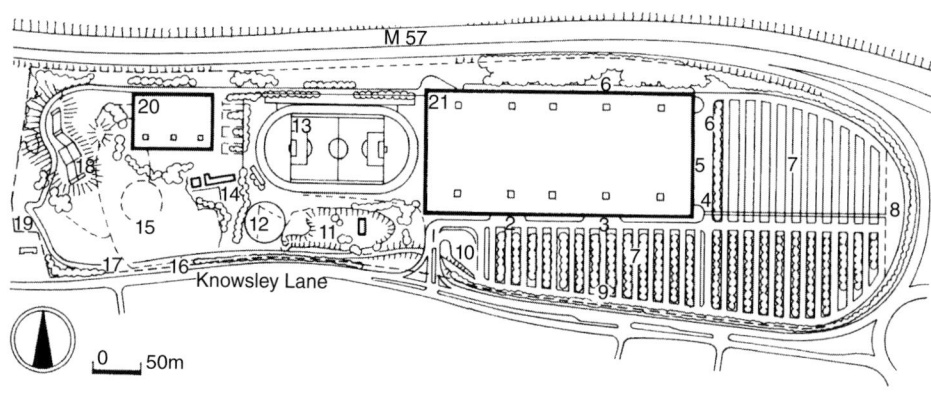

1 *site entrance*
2 *bus*
3 *taxi*
4 *service road*
5 *service bay*
6 *staff car park*
7 *car parking*
8 *coach parking*
9 *perimeter exit road*
10 *petrol service station*
11 *adventure playground*
12 *open play space*
13 *sports pitches and athletic track*
14 *horticultural centre*
15 *riding school field*
16 *bridle path*
17 *cycle training and racing track*
18 *dry ski and toboggan slopes*
19 *site boundary*
20 *riding school*
21 *pavilion containing superstore,
    leisure pool, sports hall,
    restaurants, library, cinema,
    exhibition gallery, etc.*

35.11 *Superstore at Knowsley, Lancashire: site plan Architects: Foster Associates*

9.2 Planning

Large stores are basically constructed as large rectangular boxes having large-span clearances to allow mainly one-level trading. If required, upper storeys are confined to part of the building and used for non-food sales, and ancillary services. The sales:ancillary ratio is high 60:40, with maximum goods on display and highly mechanised stock replenishment.

Compared with supermarkets, the stores use larger trolleys, wider and level circulation routes and easier transfer to car park areas (some with prepacking and mechanised conveyors).

10 SHOPPING CENTRES

10.1 Types

These are planned as a shopping complex under one central management which has a high degree of overall control, leasing units to individual retailers.

Shopping centres may be:

- *Open, in terraces*, squares, piazzas or village-style groupings.
- *Partially covered*, with canopies over frontages (3.6 m high for clearance) or setbacks creating arcades.
- *Fully covered*, single-level or multi-level shopping malls, converted warehouses, etc.

10.2 Locations

New centres:

- in new towns and expanding residential areas;
- out-of-town regional shopping centres.

Integrated centre:

- in existing high street areas;
- open up backland for commercial use;
- provide linkages with other developments, carparks, etc.;
- extend pedestrianised areas.

10.3 Planning

Centres should, where practicable, follow existing street patterns and be sensitively integrated into the existing street architecture.

Commercial and operational considerations

- Number, size and locations of large space users and other attractions (magnets) which will increase pedestrian flows.

- Distribution, number and size of small shop units, numbers of shopping levels.
- Servicing needs and access for goods vehicles.
- Entrances and links with parking, public transport and other shopping areas.
- Focuses and features to provide an identity and sense of place.
- Environmental control in the mall and individual shops.
- Fire regulations, safety and security requirements.

10.4 Plan forms

Shopping units are mainly one or two levels. Upper levels are usually required to join multi-storey variety and department stores and form galleries around a central square or atrium. Gross leasable areas vary, many infilling centres fall within 25 000 and 50 000 m² GLA providing 40 to 100 units. New regional centres may provide up to 100 000 m² GLA with 40 per cent allocated to large space users (magnets).

Magnets are sited near the ends of malls and branches to attract flows of shoppers past individual shops and have an effective range of 90 to 120 m. It is not practical to extend a mall more than 350 m and large developments call for more than one level with concentrated plan forms. L (Figure 35.12), T (Figure 35.13), C and Square plans are common but out-of-town centres may use cruciform (Figure 35.14), pinwheel (Figure 35.15) and figure-of-eight (Figure 35.16) layouts extending out from a central concourse. A common variant in new UK centres is the loop or racetrack such as at the Westfield, London.

10.5 Details

In the UK mall widths have progressively increased from 5.4 m to in excess of 8 m. The average French centre uses a 16 m mall while North American malls vary from 12 to 27 m. Galleries around central courts are often 4 m wide. The preferred frontage for small shops is 5.4 m to 7.3 m with a depth of 13 m to 39 m but smaller units (1.8 × 3.6m) are often required for service outlets and specialised trades. The centres of wide malls are often populated by retail merchandising units (RMUs) typically up to 2 m wide. 2500 mm is the minimum shop front height. The optimum floor to floor level of a new build is generally 6 m. Airconditioning arangements are commonly provided by a vertically mounted grill running above the shop fronts.

Glazed frontages are necessary when the mall remains open to the public at night but otherwise Continental (fully or partly open) frontages are more convenient with latticework shutters or fire barriers (if required) to secure the shop at night. The centres of wide malls are often populated by retail merchandising units

35.12 *L-shaped plan: Arndale Centre, Luton*

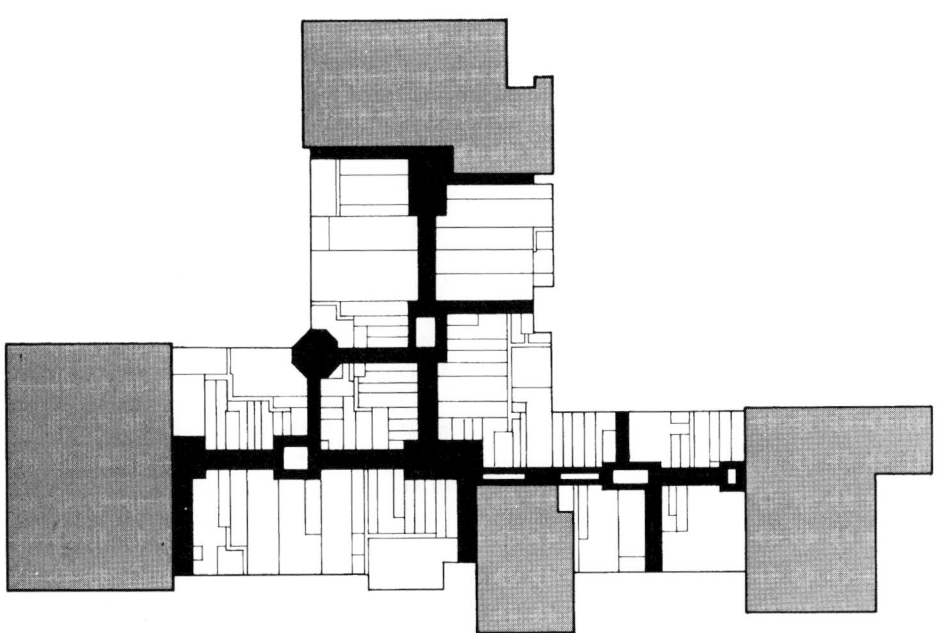

35.13 *T-shaped plan: Willowbrook Mall, New Jersey*

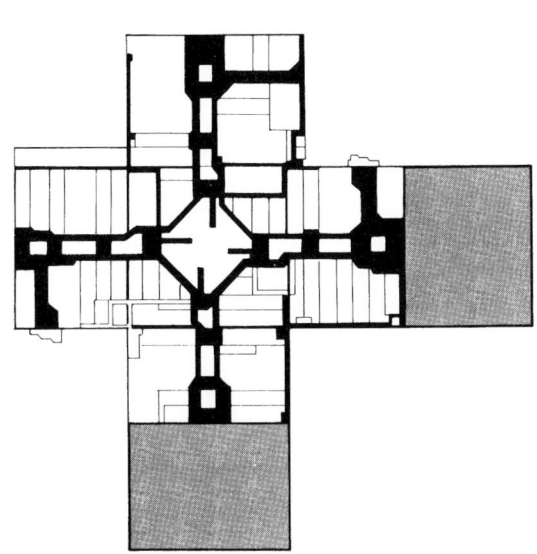

35.14 *Cruciform plan: La Puente, California*

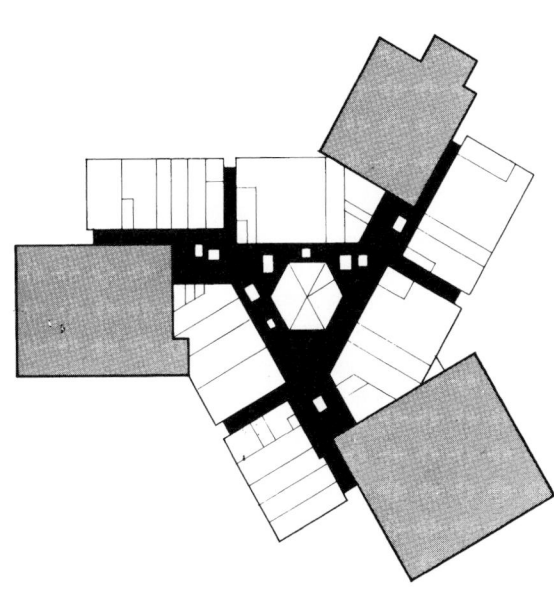

35.15 *Pinwheel plan: Randhurst, Illinois*

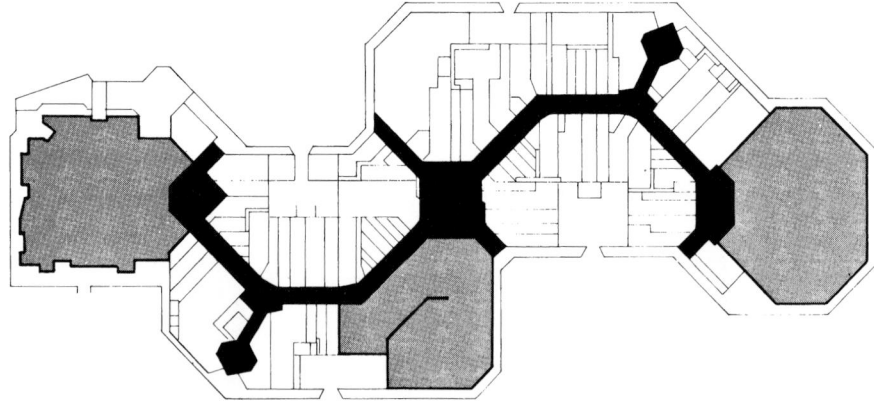

35.16 *Figure-of-eight plan: Sherway gardens, Toronto*

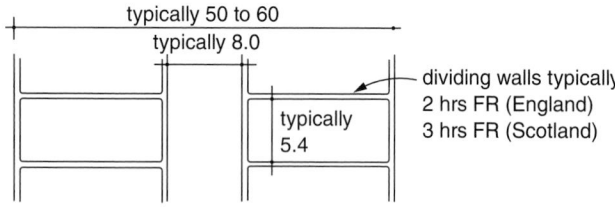

35.17 *Plan of a mall showing fire separation between shop units*

(RMUs) typically up to 2 m wide (2500 mm is minimum shopfront height).

10.6 Food courts and focuses
Large atria and glazed courtyards provide activity spaces which are often landscaped and used as revenue-generating open restaurants or food courts. Features such as water fountains, kiosks, planted containers and children's play centres also create focuses for interest and direction.

10.7 Fire precautions
The design of shopping centres does not conform with conventional compartmentation arrangements and specific requirements will be stipulated by each fire authority.

Fire control
Fire separation walls are required between shops in different tenancies, Figure 35.17. Malls must be of non-combustible construction, with incidental combustible material controlled, and have an automatic sprinkler system installed.

Specific requirements apply to adjoining or facing frontages of large space users (more than 2000 m²).

Smoke control
Smoke reservoirs, Figure 35.18, are created by downstand beams on fascias at shop frontages and intervals along the mall. Smoke detectors activate exhaust fans in the reservoirs and lower fresh air supply fans to ensure clear escape routes. Further smoke ventilation and smoke control facilities are shown in Figures 35.19 to 35.20.

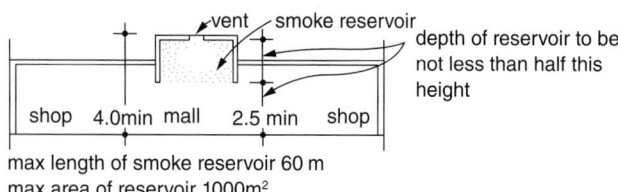

35.18 *Section showing smoke reservoir*

Escape routes
Maximum occupancy levels are estimated on the basis of:

- Shops, showrooms, supplementary areas – 7.0 m²/person
- Supermarkets, department sales floors – 2.0 m²/person

No more than 50 per cent of occupants should be assumed to escape through the rear of a shop, the rest using the mall. Escape routes from the mall must be provided at intervals with exits to open streets directly or via separated structures.

Controls
Automatic fire alarm and indication systems must be installed.

Access
Requirements of the fire authority for appliance access into the mall must be adopted together with positions for hydrants, hoses and extinguishers.

10.8 Circulations
Vertical circulation between storeys requires escalators, featured lifts and stairs designed to stimulate interest. These are usually located in a spacious central concourse or atrium, at junctions or corners and within the large space users.

Servicing shops
Vehicular access is required to loading docks and waiting bays directly accessible to each of the larger stores, with service roads, goods lifts and tunnels extending to the rear of shops. Service entry is usually at basement and street level but may be at an upper level on sloping sites.

10.9 Engineering services
The landlord is normally responsible for installing mains and providing the communal services of the mall including comfort cooling and heating or air-conditioning, lighting, cleaning, fire control and security systems. As a rule, individual tenants install their own services and equipment subject to agreement. Food-preparation areas, public toilets and plant areas require the installation of specific ventilation, drainage and electrical services.

Sections through a typical centre showing the complexity of structure and servicing are illustrated in Figures 35.19 to 35.21.

10.10 Other facilities
Public toilets including facilities for the disabled are installed and maintained by the landlord. Access to a public car park is often a primary consideration in letting units.

10.11 Town-centre shopping centres
Some examples of town-centre shopping centres are shown in Figures 35.22 and 35.23.

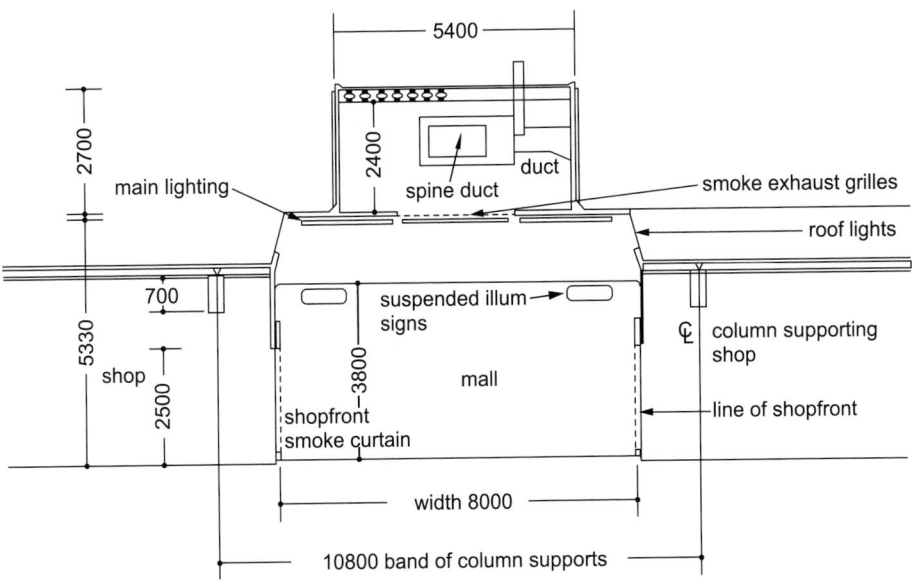

35.19 *Detail cross-section through a shopping mall*

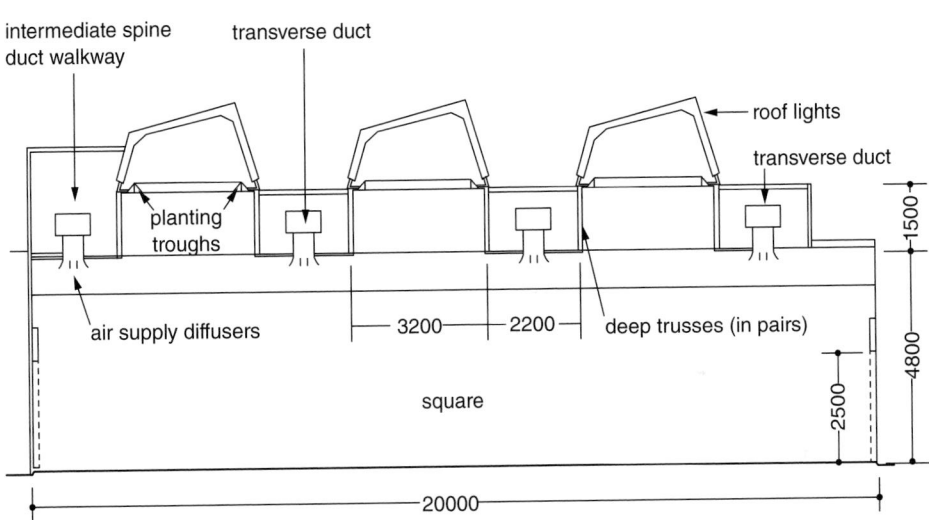

35.20 *Detail cross-section through central square. Note: 2500 mm is the minimum shopfront height. The optimum floor to floor level of a new build is generally 6m*

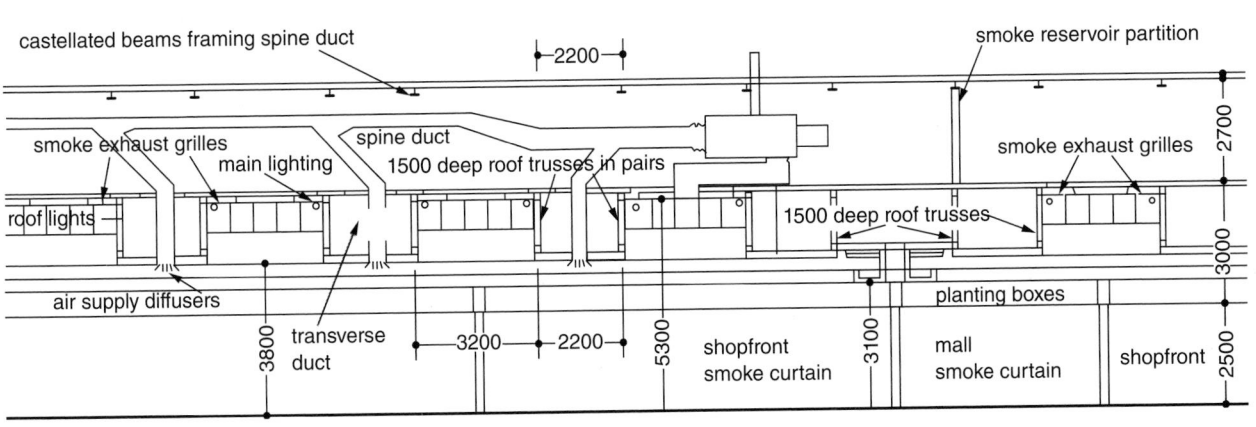

35.21 *Detail longitudinal section along mall. Note: Another, more common, arrangement is a vertically mounted grill running above the shopfronts*

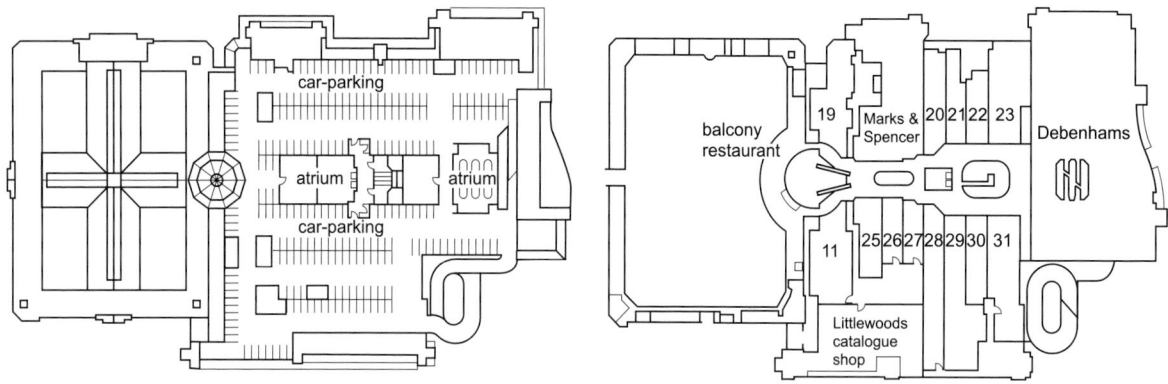

a *First-floor level*   **b** *Upper ground-floor level*

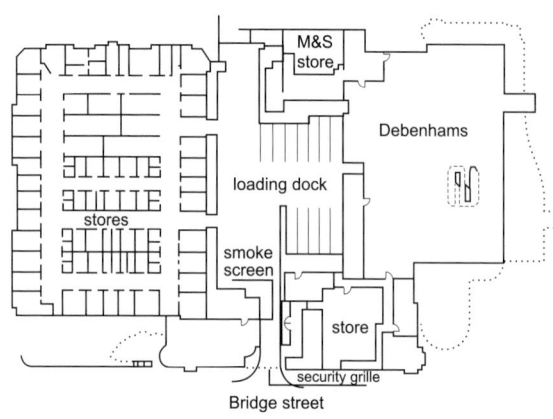

c *Ground-floor level*

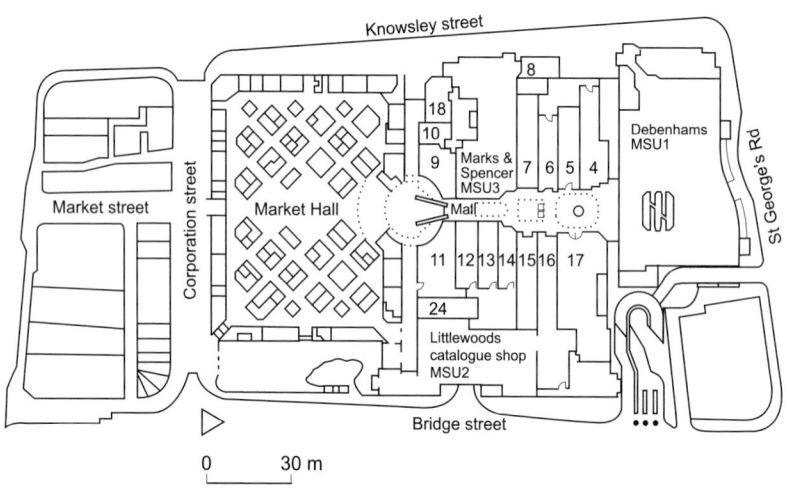

d *Lower ground-floor level*

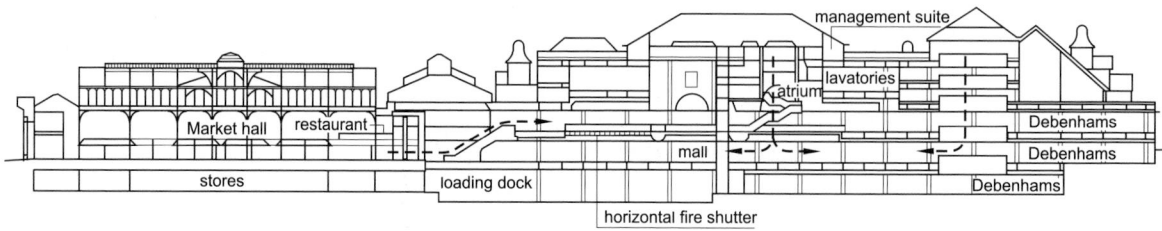

e *Section south–north*

35.22 *Bolton Market Place: a shopping centre on two levels linked to the refurbished existing Market Hall. Deliveries and storage are in the basement, and car parking on three upper floors. Total area is 49796 m² Architects: Chapman Taylor & Partners*

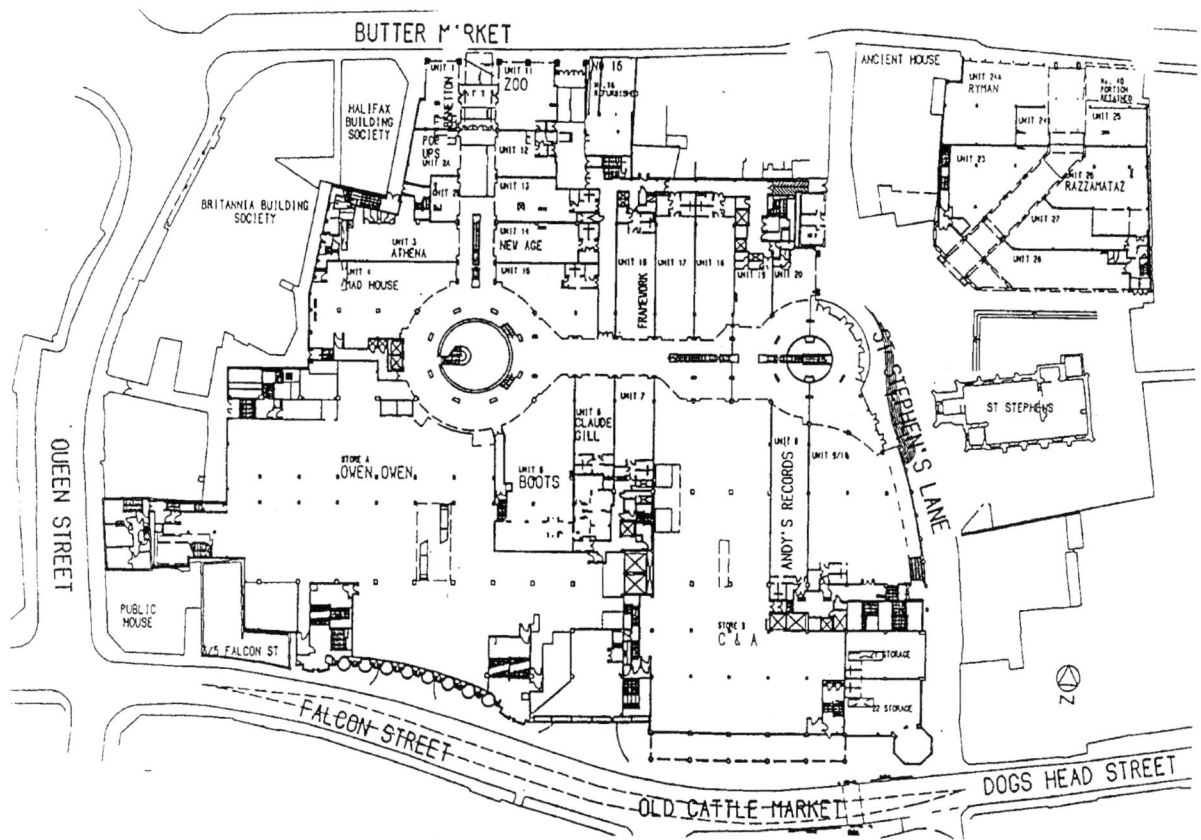

35.23 *Buttermarket, Ipswich. Development of a shopping centre in a sensitive historic area, incorporating a church restored as an amenity area, and two level basement parking. Completed in 1992 with 49 units. Built area 25083 m², cost £37 million Ground-floor plan Architects: Building Design Partnership*

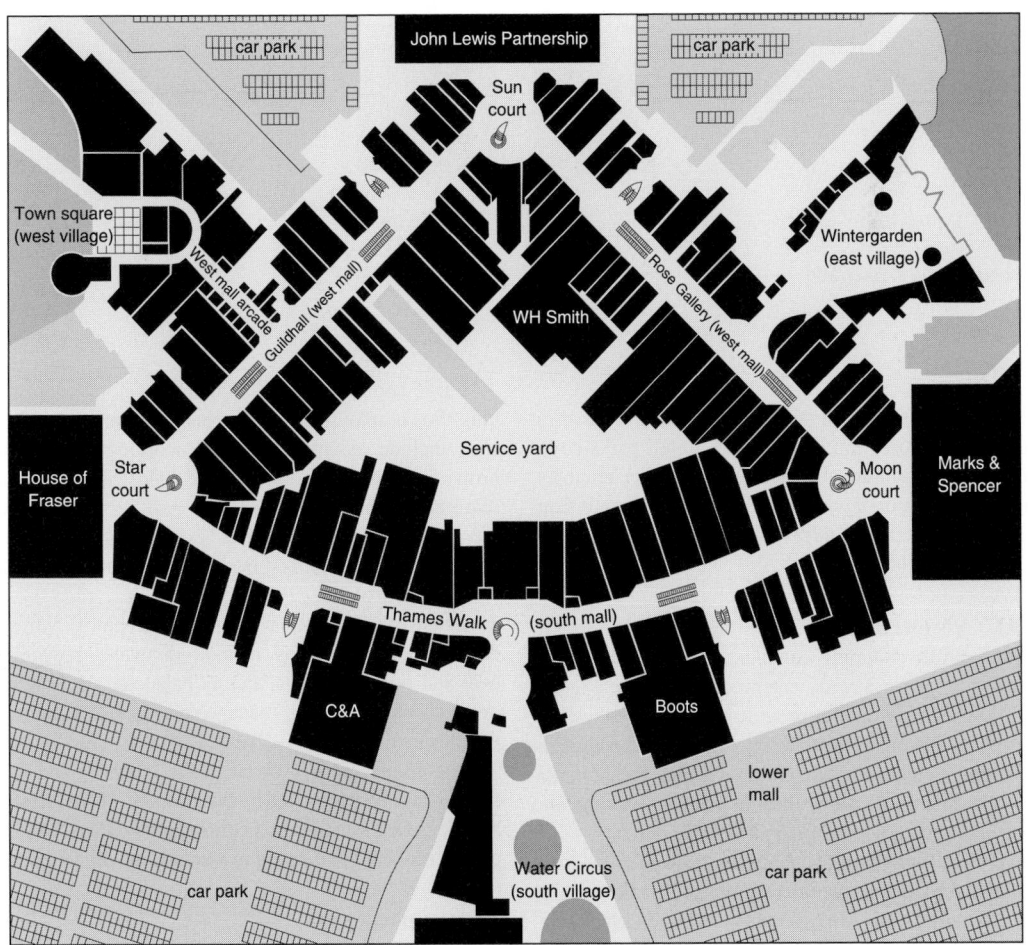

35.24 *Bluewater Park near Dartford, Kent. Europe's biggest retail centre to date. Architects: Eric Kuhne and Benoy*

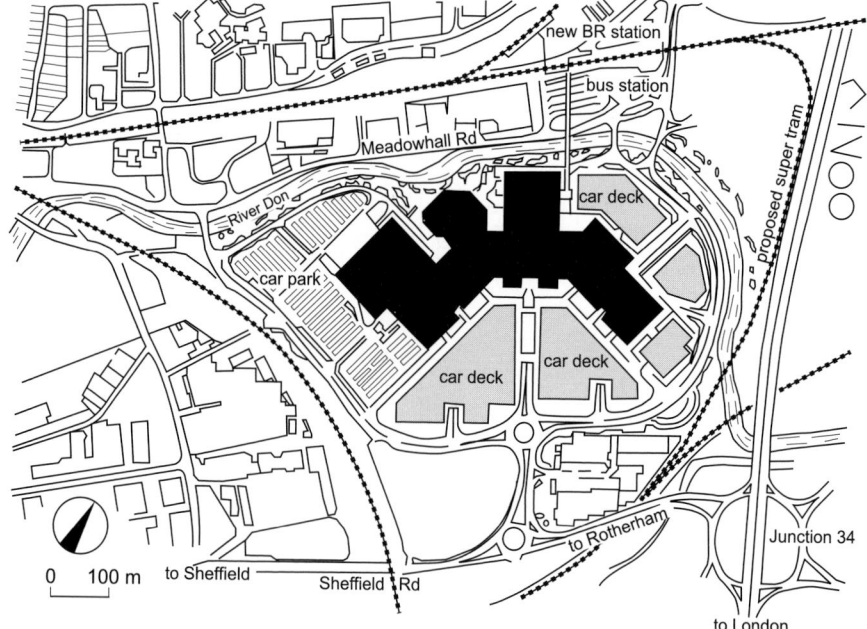

a *Site plan of the regional shopping centre*

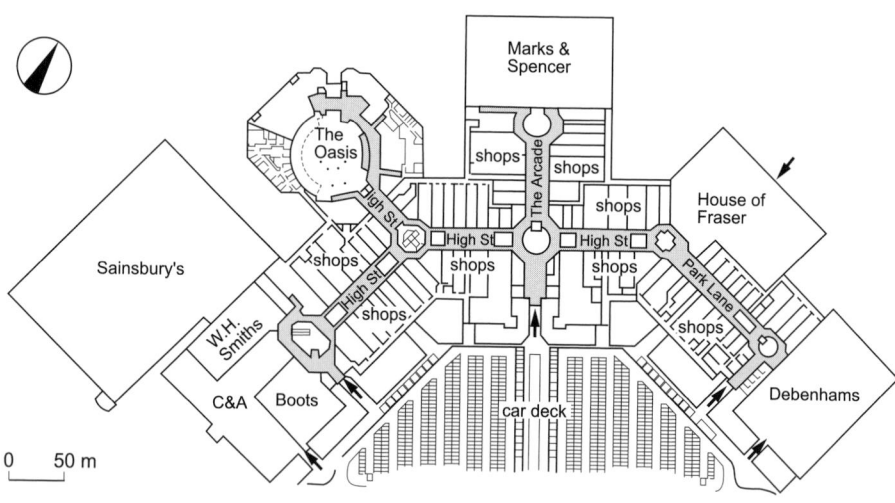

b *First-floor level of the dome's shopping mall with shops on two levels*

35.25 *Meadowhall Centre, Sheffield*

11 RETAIL PARKS

These are centres of at least 4500 m² sited outside a town consisting of at least three single-storey units of 900 m². Retail parks cover non-food goods (DIY, furniture, furnishings, consumer durables, etc.). Buildings are generally of warehouse design and benefit from the combined attraction, shared infrastructure, parking and extra facilities (cafe/fast food outlets).

12 REGIONAL CENTRES

These are large multiple shopping complexes located near major highway junctions to serve a wide catchment area (see Figures 35.24 and 35.25). The larger centres provide both leisure and shopping attractions to extend market and family interest. Depending on scale, the amenities include crèches, children's play areas, multicinemas, live entertainment, fitness/health centres, waiting and lounge meeting areas and a wide choice of catering outlets.

In 2011 there were 19 regional shopping centres with a floor area exceeding 100 m² in the UK together offering almost 3.9 million m² of retail space. The largest are the Metrocentre, Gateshead (194,000 m² including retail park), Bluewater, Dartford (155,700 m²) Westfield, Dudley (154,002 m²) and Westfield, London (139,000 m²).

Large comprehensive shopping developments provide a stimulus for employment and urban regeneration. Redevelopment sites include exhausted mineral workings landscaped as lakes, brownfield sites and discontinued industrial wasteland. The areas required for buildings, customer parking and goods distribution are extensive. Access, traffic movements and circulations must be modelled and planned in detail including means of escape and security control.

Extensive demands are made on technical infrastructures and conservation provisions include rainwater recycling, combined heat and power systems, energy balancing, airflow control, fabric insulation and shading, management control systems and planned maintenance.

The arrangement of shops, malls and halls and vertical circulations is largely determined by the locations of anchor stores and food-service outlets which attract customer movements. Staff facilities and central services are planned in association with tenant requirements.

13 BIBLIOGRAPHY

S. Appelby (ed.), *Shop Spec. Shopfitting Specification International*, Purple Media, 2006

N. Beddington, *Shopping Centres*, Butterworth Architecture, 1991

British Council of Shopping Centres, *A Briefing Guide for Shopping Centre Development*, BCSC, 2000

P. Bernman and J. Evans, *Retail Management – A Strategic Approach*, 10th Edn, Harlow, Pearson Prentice Hall, 2006

Chapman Taylor Partners, 'Trading architecture: The Bolton Market Place', *Architects' Journal*, 19 April 1989

P. Coleman, *Shopping Environments: Evolution, Planning and Design*, Architectural Press, 2006

Cox and Britain, *Retail Management*, MacDonald and Evans, 1993

A.C. Nielsen, *Retail Pocket Book 2006*, World Advertising Research Center, 2006

Q. Pickard (ed.), 'Shops and Retail', *The Architects Handbook*, Blackwell Science, 2002

J. Prior, *Sustainable Retail Premises, An Environmental Guide to Design, Refurbishment and Management of Retail Premises*, BRE Publications, 1999

36 Schools

Anthony Langan

Anthony Langan is sector lead for education at AHR Architects (formerly Aedas)

KEY POINTS:

- *This chapter brings together good practice and recent standards, but the Department for Education should be consulted for the very latest standards and guidelines*
- *The design of schools is a highly political, and constantly evolving, field of study*
- *The current emphasis is on efficient, compact forms that are easy to extend*
- *Schools should be designed as low-carbon environments with high quality natural lighting and should be naturally ventilated in all but the most exceptional circumstances*

Contents

1 Introduction
2 School types
3 Key design information and design standards
4 Environmental design, sustainability and low carbon design
5 School furniture and ergonomics
6 Security and fire safety
7 Early Years school design
8 Primary schools
9 Secondary schools
10 SEN provision
11 References

1 INTRODUCTION

This chapter specifically relates to the design of schools in England and Wales at the time of writing. In other parts of the UK, design standards and education delivery varies.

1.1 Sector changes

Over the past decade, school design development has increased significantly as development of curriculum and education delivery methods along with major programmes of school renewal, have driven the education design debate.

Education is at the fulcrum of social and economic renewal. Transforming education delivery and engaging students in new ways of learning is seen as the key to raising education standards and preparing young people to meet future challenges. Curriculum delivery has changed to develop a wider engagement in education, and greater emphasis is given to vocational subjects and student subject choice.

There have been several key recent changes. The DfE (Department for Education) is currently promoting capital programmes to deliver the development of new academies under the stewardship of Local Education Authorities in partnership with Academy sponsors. There is also the development of Free Schools offering alternative models to LEA provision, and the introduction of the Primary Capital programme for the redevelopment of Primary Schools to meet the demographic growth demand.

1.2 National Curriculum

The National Curriculum defines the core entitlement of pupils at all stages of their education. It is monitored by the Qualifications and Curriculum Authority (QCA).

The National Curriculum applies to pupils of compulsory school age in community and foundation schools, including community special schools and foundation special schools, and voluntary aided and voluntary controlled schools. It sets out a series of statutory requirements and is organised on the basis of four key stages:

1 Key Stage 1: Ages 5–7 (Years 1–2).
2 Key Stage 2: Ages 7–11 (Years 3–6).
3 Key Stage 3: Ages 11–14 (Years 7–9).
4 Key Stage 4: Ages 14–16 (Years 10–11).

Developed in a series of Key Stages, the Primary Curriculum KS1 and 2 is based upon a wide breadth of learning as well as developing key skills in literacy, numeracy and ICT. At these early stages of a child's development, emphasis is placed on social and emotional development along with key personal and thinking skills, while engaging children in learning through play and activity-based learning.

The Secondary Curriculum seeks to provide a cohesive structure for learning from the ages 11–19 years (KS3 and 4). These build on the experiences of children in primary school to help students achieve high standards and develop personal, learning and thinking skills (PLTS). More recently, the government has introduced the concept of the English Baccalaureate. This is a grouping of subject areas rather than a formal qualification in its own right.

1.3 Role of Ofsted

Ofsted is the Office for Standards in Education, Children's Services and Skills. Ofsted was set up under the Education and Inspections Act by the government to regulate and inspect and to help achieve excellence in the care of children and young people. As part of its role, Ofsted inspects schools and produces reports into its findings using a set framework of criteria on a range of subjects from the safety of the environment that the school provides to the quality of teaching and learning in individual lessons. Parents will often use the Ofsted reports when choosing a school for their child. See www.ofsted.gov.uk.

2 SCHOOL TYPES

Formal education is compulsory between the ages of 5 and 16 years. Typology of schools has increased in recent years with the introduction of Academies and Free Schools. The main different types are now as follows:

- State maintained. These are funded by the DfE through taxation at national and local level, often with contributions from local diocese and archdiocese organisations. Most maintained schools are comprehensive or non-selective of students. However there is a tradition of religious influence in schools through the Voluntary Controlled or Voluntary Aided system. These schools can develop an admissions policy which allows them to select a proportion of students. Students are also usually drawn from a much wider catchment than LEA schools. Some authorities still operate a grammar school selective system of selection at the age of 11. Some operate a middle school system where the upper years of primary school and the lower years of primary school are combined.

- Academies, where LEAs work with sponsors to organise a school. Sponsors are often from faith or commercial backgrounds and can influence the ethos of the school and curriculum that is delivered, Figure 36.1. Existing schools can also 'opt out' of local authority control to become Academies. Academies are allowed to select a small proportion of students based upon their specialism.
- Free schools, set up by groups interested in the promotion of education outside the control of local education authorities.
- Privately funded schools run by their owners or charitable foundations.

Many Academy and grant maintained schools adopt a specialism – a subject in which they excel. Schools must present evidence and apply to the DfE for specialist status from the number of subject areas approved by the department. See also the Specialist Schools and Academies Trust.

All through schools, which take students from early years to the age of 19, have increased in number recently and the exemplar design study by the DfE shows an example of how these may be organised.

36.1 *Oasis Academy, Enfield, a specialist maths, ICT and music school with a Christian ethos designed by John McAslan + Partners. (Photograph: Hufton + Crow)*

3 KEY DESIGN INFORMATION AND DESIGN STANDARDS

3.1 School design standards
There is a significant amount of design guidance, both formal and informal, and also best practice documents available for the design of schools.

3.2 Legislation
The legislative framework is based upon the School Premises Regulations 2012 and the adoption of the Building Regulations. The legislative aspects also apply to independent schools (see DfE website).

Often DfE non-statutory Building Bulletin publications are referred to in the approved documents.

3.3 Guidance
The DfE has published a significant number of Building Bulletins and best practice guidance in the form of design notes. This guidance includes:

- Baseline Designs introduced in 2012 (see Section 3.4).
- Area guidance briefing framework BB103 for secondary and primary schools.
- Inspirational designs for schools such as the Schools for the Future Exemplar Designs for Schools, 2003.
- Very detailed standards such as Environmental Design and Ventilation (BB87 and 101) and Acoustic Design in schools (BB93).

3.4 Baseline Designs
The Baseline Designs are a series of primary and secondary school designs developed by the Education Funding Agency (EFA) in 2012. The designs demonstrate how the standard output specification developed for the Private Finance 2 (PF2) procured schools can be met. This specification is also being adopted for other schools currently being procured by the EFA to ensure consistency across the new estate.

The Baseline Designs have been developed to Stage 2 of the RIBA Plan of Work. One of the key drivers of the designs is standardisation – in conceptual approach, detail design and specification. This is seen by the EFA as a way of reducing design and construction costs and also of producing an equality of provision across all schools countrywide.

The designs meet a standard curriculum in England and Wales, but provide flexibility in order to react to other organisations. The EFA have undertaken consultations with other user groups to help ensure that the designs meet the needs of certain types of extracurricular provision.

Key features of the designs are:

- Simple organisational concepts, such as finger schemes, Figure 36.2, where linear classroom wings emanate from a core of common spaces, halls, dining, administration etc. and a 'superblock' concept, Figure 36.3, that places the core large spaces at the centre of the building and then wraps classroom spaces around,
- A plan organisation that provides for suites of subject-driven teaching accommodation. Emphasis is placed on how these suites are organised so that this may be repeated across multiple projects.
- Area standards that are different from the BB98 and 99 guidance notes with strict emphasis placed on the provision of teaching accommodation over non-teaching.
- For secondary schools, the overall area formula is: 1050 m² (+ 350 m² if there is a sixth form) + 6.3 m²/pupil place for 11- to 16-year-olds + 7 m²/pupil place for post-16s.
- For primary schools the overall area formula is: 350 m² + 4.1 m²/pupil place.
- Environmental strategies that have been worked up in some detail to ensure that the designs will conform to the environmental standards of the output specification but also provide longer term flexibility by providing robust and flexible environmental concepts that will stand up to the building footprint being adapted internally.
- Environmental strategies for teaching spaces that are designed to mitigate summertime maximum temperatures, reduce CO_2 levels and provide adequate natural daylight. Daylight is measured against how the design utilises available daylight, how even the spread of the daylight provided is and whether it is glare free. This approach has necessitated that the majority of classroom spaces are lit also from the back or corridor face of the room by clerestory glazing and top lighting to the corridor spaces.

3.5 Design Quality Indicators (DQI)
In 2005 the DCFS published a methodology of evaluating school design for LEAs and schools, known as DQI for Schools. This is a framework of design criteria which is tailored by the individuals involved in the project. This tool allows LEAs to represent their needs more succinctly to the designers involved in the project. See www.dqi.org.uk.

3.6 Commission for Architecture and the Built Environment

The Commission for Architecture and the Built Environment (CABE) – now part of the Design Council – has developed a framework of design support for local authorities involved in the development of school buildings. In 2008, minimum design standards developed by CABE were adopted by the government for school projects and are still a useful guide to successful school design.

CABE's 10 criteria for successful school design are:

- Identity and context: making a school the students and community can be proud of.
- Site plan: making the best use of the site.
- School grounds: making assets of the outdoor spaces.
- Organisation: creating a clear diagram for the buildings.
- Buildings: making form, massing and appearance work together.
- Interiors: creating excellent spaces for learning and teaching.
- Resources: deploying convincing environmental strategies.
- Feeling safe: creating a secure and welcoming place.

- Long life, loose fit: creating a school that can adapt and evolve in the future.
- Successful whole: making a design that works in the round.

3.7 Design Share

International design websites such as the site Design Share help to promote an understanding of design standards and methodologies utilised in other parts of the world. The incorporation of international best practice into school design in the UK is becoming increasingly prevalent. Many authorities undertake international design study tours in the preparation for major projects, particularly to Scandinavia and Europe.

4 ENVIRONMENTAL DESIGN, SUSTAINABILITY AND LOW CARBON DESIGN

4.1 Background

In 2007 the government commissioned a report into the carbon emissions of schools by the Sustainable Development Commission. This developed a baseline target of a reduction of around 60 per

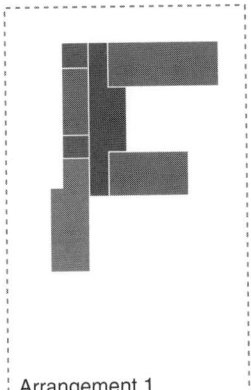

Arrangement 1

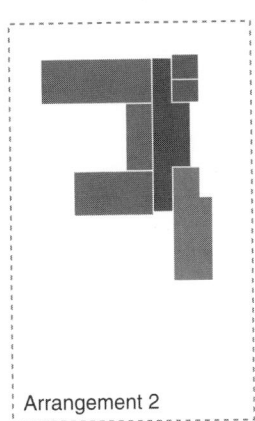

Arrangement 2

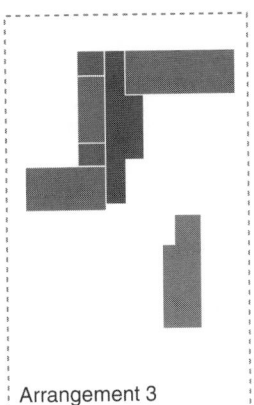

Arrangement 3

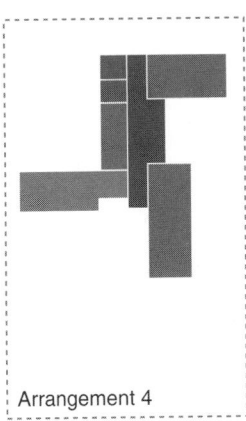

Arrangement 4

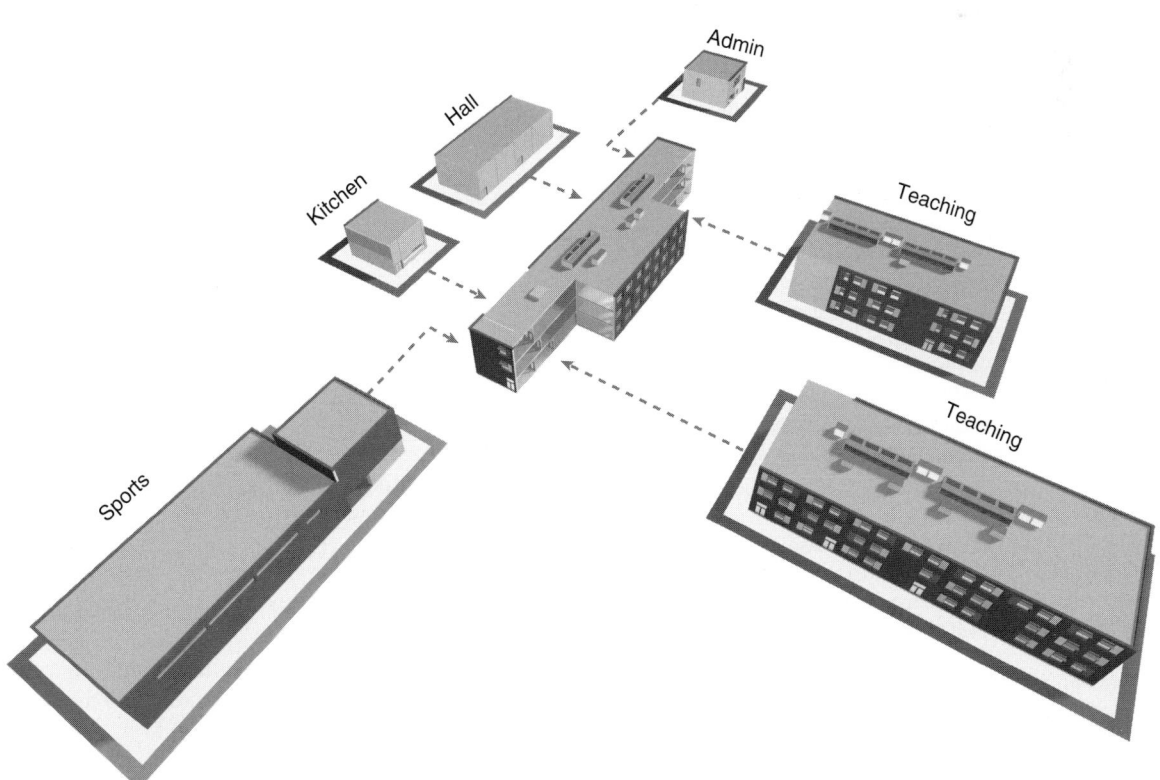

36.2 *Education Funding Agency Baseline Design for a 1200-place secondary school designed as a 'finger block' kit of parts (Type 1)*

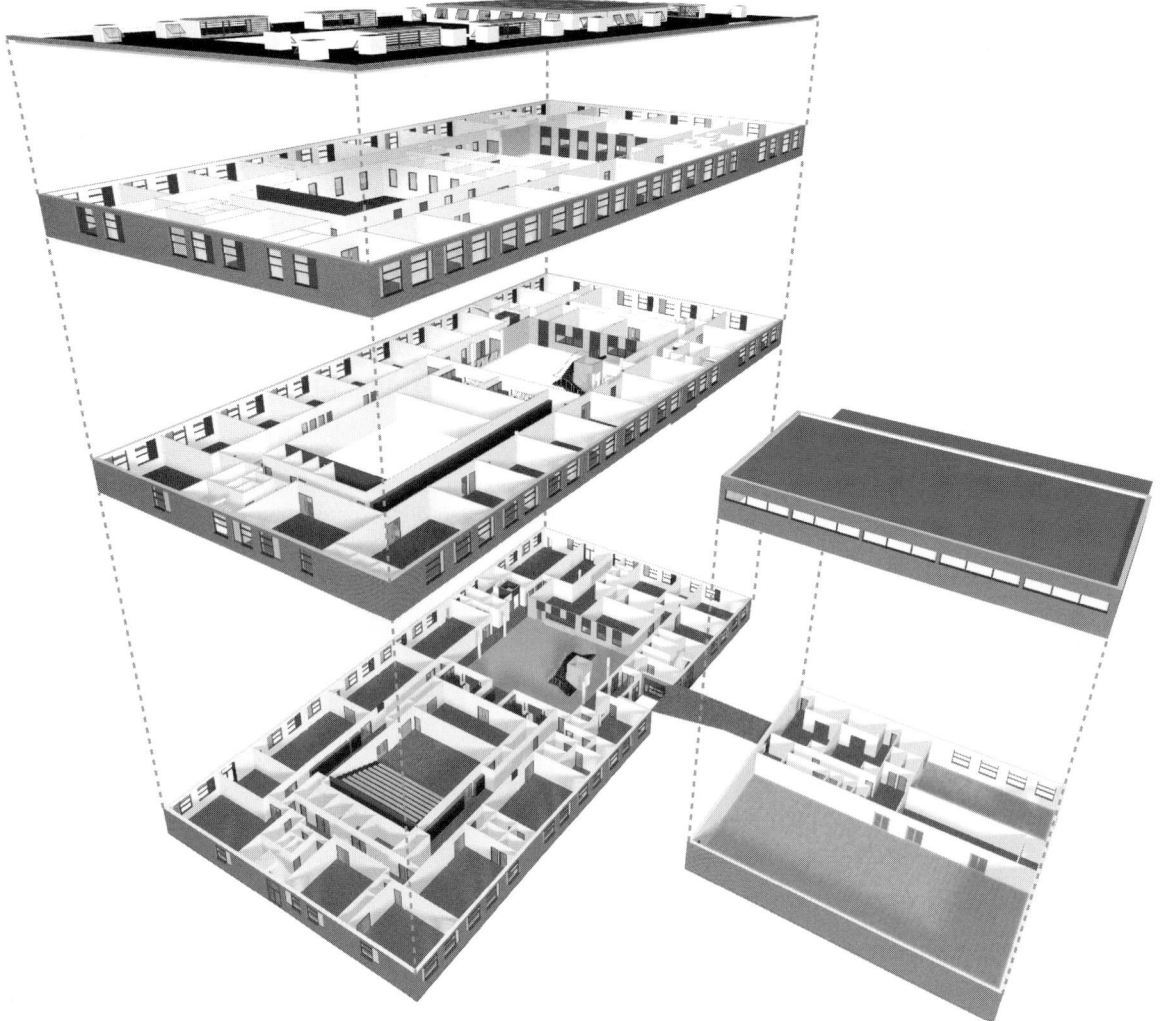

36.3 *Education Funding Agency Baseline Design for a 1200-place secondary school designed superblock (Type 2)*

cent based upon the 2002 Building Regulations. Development of the building regulations subsequently has incorporated a sizable proportion of these targets.

The DCFS developed the 'Carbon Calculator' as a design tool. This sets out the environmental and carbon reduction standards to be achieved in the design of school buildings and also provides a series of methods and energy efficiency measures for achieving the required targets. These include reviewing the fabric and form of the proposed building, including the U values, along with its orientation to maximise the passive measures in reducing energy consumption.

The guidance also describes the various technologies that can be adopted to reduce the carbon emissions in schools. According to the Sustainable Development Commission, almost 40 per cent of the carbon is spent in maintaining the environment of the school.

4.2 Ventilation

The guidance for the carbon calculator also confirms that air-conditioning is not within standard school construction costs and that in all but the most exceptional circumstances, natural ventilation of some form should be adopted to optimise both capital and recurrent costs.

Refer also to BB 101 'Ventilation of School Buildings' and the complementary calculation tools, 'Classcool and Classvent'. BB101 introduces ventilation performance standards and also criteria for the prevention of summertime overheating and classroom carbon dioxide levels. The maintenance of a suitable classroom environment, within suitable temperatures and carbon dioxide levels, is seen as key to maintaining concentration in students.

Potential natural ventilation strategies include:

- Night time cooling via exposed thermal mass. The UK has cooler summer temperatures at night. These may be exploited using thermal mass or thermal inertia, thereby smoothing daily temperature swings. By exposing heavy building fabric in the ceiling it absorbs heat during the day then cools during the night when exposed to cool night time air.
- Earth tubes. These are concrete or clay pipes in the ground through which the supply air is passed. They are able to supply pre-warmed air in the winter and cooled air in the summer as the ground itself does not vary much in temperature over the seasons. They still have an energy requirement for fans.
- Borehole cooling. If a school has access to ground water at a suitable depth and extract licences are granted, cool water at 12–15°C can be pumped though the pipes of an underfloor heating and cooling system to cool the rooms in the summer.
- Mixed mode cooling. A building designed to limit solar gain and equipment gains may only overheat for a small percentage of the time. If a reduced size of cooling system is provided for extreme conditions only, and natural ventilation is used for most of the time, it is termed mixed mode.

4.3 Day lighting

Natural day lighting is seen as the primary light source in school design and depends on the proportions of the room, amount and position of glazing, reflectivity of surfaces, and whereabouts in the room it is being measured. The Baseline Designs give some simple practical guidance to achieve good day lighting.

The use of daylight as the main means of lighting is also recommended in BB87. Sometimes site constraints such as adjacent buildings or trees will mean electric lighting will be the main source, but the designer should strive to avoid this. Daylight provides a less stressful environment for pupils and teachers, and saves energy.

Uniformity or Daylight Autonomy is equally important. If a classroom was illuminated perfectly evenly throughout, then it would have a uniformity of one. The importance of uniformity in day lighting can be illustrated by the fact that lights can often be found on in classrooms even though average daylight is good. Again, the Baseline Designs show principles of good day lighting; providing daylight from two sides of the room significantly enhances uniformity.

As far as space planning is concerned, natural lighting and natural ventilation are in sympathy. The maximum depths of spaces for natural ventilation are comparable to the maximum depths for effective day lighting.

4.4 ICT

The exponential use of technology in the classroom places significant burden on the environmental design of individual spaces. However, as technology develops both PCs and laptop computers are becoming more energy efficient and therefore placing less burden per unit on the environmental conditions. This is denoted through the Energy Star standards on the units.

There are also a number of strategies for reducing the processing power of the computer itself, known as 'Thin Client'. Here, the processing is undertaken by a remote server rather than the individual computer, thus reducing the energy and heat load in the individual space. For details, refer to guidance by the government's ICT advisors BECTA.

4.5 Energy sources

Development of low carbon energy solutions is central to lowering the carbon footprint of the nation's schools and a number of technical solutions have been adopted over the past few years. The adoption of any one or combination of these measures needs careful consideration by the design team and client as they incur considerable capital cost and also recurrent cost over the life of the school.

The main options are:

- Biomass. This refers to an energy source derived from organic matter, including wood from forests, waste wood sources and factory waste. Over the past few years a number of local authorities have developed supply chain networks to ensure continuity of supply as more schools adopt this technology.

    Ideally, biomass should be used close to its source of supply to minimise the environmental impact of transportation. Chips require significant storage space below or above ground prior to being burned. Pellets are denser than chips and have greater calorific value but are more expensive.

    Biomass can potentially meet all of a school's heating needs, although it is usual to have some gas back up. It typically reduces carbon emissions by 20–30%, being 1/8th of the emissions of gas and 1/16th of that of electric heating.

- Combined heat and power (CHP). This is the production of electricity and useful heat in a single process. It can be up to 80% efficient, albeit the overall efficiency of the system depends on the ability to use the heat available. This is usually dependent on a constant heat requirement of, for instance, a swimming pool or possibly matching load to surrounding housing, where the school uses heat during the day and the excess heat is distributed later to local housing via a district heating system. Excess electricity can be put back into the national grid.

- Ground source heat pumps (GSHP). These use the constant temperature of the ground to provide heating or possibly cooling, which is extracted through boreholes or loops under the ground. It then produces heat in the school through underfloor heating systems. These systems are not carbon zero as they use electricity in their operation, but have a coefficient of production of usually 3 or 4 to 1, thus for every 1kw that is used, 3 or 4kws are produced in heat.

- Photovoltaic cells (PV). These convert energy from the sun into electricity through semiconductor cells. They are often applied to facades or roofs of buildings. However they are expensive and have a simple payback period of circa 70 years.

- Solar thermal. Solar hot water systems use energy from the sun to heat hot water. Fluid is heated in the panels and then water in a cistern is heated through a simple heat exchanger. There are two types of systems: flat plate and evacuated tube systems. Solar thermal hot water can work in the less clement months of the year to pre-heat water that is boosted by an alternative system.

- Wind generation. Wind turbines are one of the most cost effective renewable energy options with a simple pay back period of around 25 years. Modern free standing turbines of 6–20kw are suitable for suburban areas, subject to consultation with local planning authorities and their use is becoming more accepted.

5 SCHOOL FURNITURE AND ERGONOMICS

5.1 Suitability

Students come in all shapes and sizes and the furniture that is provided for them must respond to this. The provision of inappropriately sized furniture can lead to problems with posture in later life and can also affect the ability of the individual student to concentrate on the task in hand, reducing their ability to learn effectively.

Over the past decade, the market for the provision of furniture to schools has increased, as have the design solutions that the companies involved now provide. Often project teams will have a consultant who will take the lead on the selection and design of the Fixed Furniture and Equipment (FFE) to be installed. In major projects it is the FFE designer's responsibility to ensure that the selection of FFE meets the relevant British and European standards (BS EN 1729 part 1 and 2 of 2007) and also to ensure the furniture has a suitable life span and durability. The FFE designer will consult with the client team, educationalist and architect to ensure that the FFE to be provided is fully coordinated with, and flexible enough to respond to, the various learning styles to be adopted.

Key design considerations for the architect include ensuring:

- That the FFE provided is suitably flexible to adapt with the building to the likely pedagogical styles.
- That the FFE should also be suitably flexible to accommodate the physical needs of individual students and adapt to their size and shape if required, and also be suitable to accommodate less able students.
- That the selection of FFE is in concert with the proposed concept for flexibility and adaptability within the building layout and structure and services, so that the FFE used does not inhibit future flexibility.

5.2 Flexibility of FFE layouts

The ability for spaces to flex on a daily basis is a key design driver in education design and is essential to the delivery of education in varied modes to meet the learning styles of students, Figure 36.4. Therefore the ability for spaces to be able to encompass more activities is very important. Often, general teaching spaces may need to be adapted from time to time to provide light practical work space. This can easily be done through FFE but can be enhanced by simply providing a single sink. Specialist spaces such as science need to maintain flexibility and the trend is therefore for services such

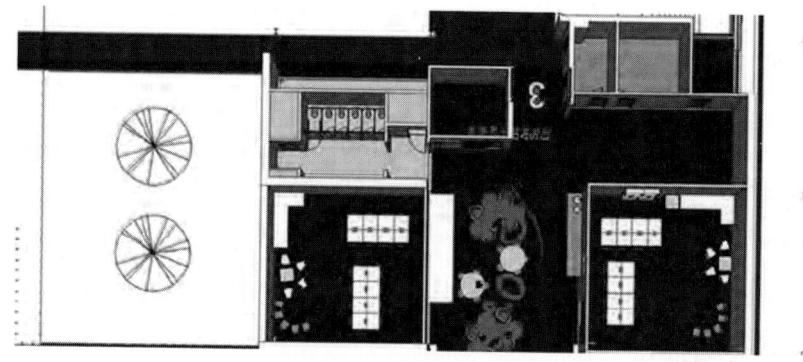

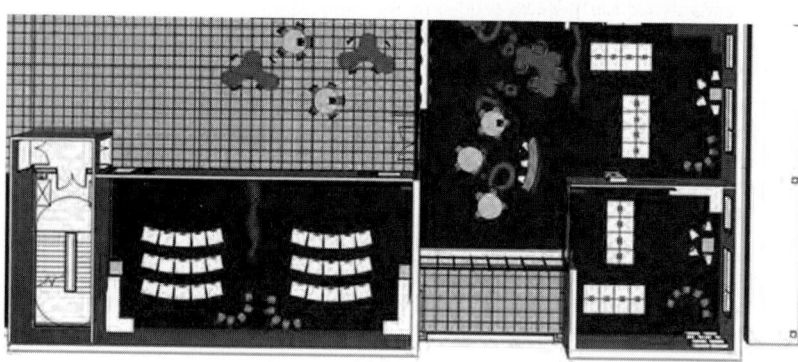

36.4 *Flexible FFE layouts by AHR Architects*

as hardwire ICT and water, gas, electrical supplies to be provided to the perimeter of the spaces, leaving the centre of the room unencumbered to increase flexibility.

6 SECURITY AND FIRE SAFETY

The design of a safe environment for students, staff and the wider community is a paramount concern in the design of any school. Ofsted pays particular attention to a school's ability to provide a safe environment for students, particularly from the viewpoint of deterring intruders. Simple yet effective measures involving single entrance points and secure perimeters should be incorporated into each school design.

The local planning authorities will expect that the local Police Architectural Design Liaison Officer has been consulted in the development of the design and that the principles of Secured by Design have been incorporated into the design of the new facilities. Secured by Design's 2010 Schools Guidance provides a range of advice on the design of site strategies, the security of the shell of the building, internal layout and design through to the management of the facilities.

School insurers such as Zurich Municipal produce their own design guidance for architects. Often local authorities are keen to ensure this guidance is followed to ensure the building will be insurable.

Published by the DFE, BB100 provides design guidance on design for fire safety in schools. Design against the risk of fire in schools is regulated under the Building Regulations and BB100 demonstrates design principles for meeting the standards set in the Building Regulations Approved Documents. The Baseline Designs have developed a fire strategy that has been informed by the BS 9999 Code of practice for fire safety in the design, management and use of buildings, and is based on the risk profile of the building's occupants.

The fire strategy provides for flexibility in the spatial arrangements and internal layouts. A life safety sprinkler system has been included in the secondary school. The simpler primary school design does not require a system for life safety.

Larger projects have become increasingly sophisticated in their design over the last decade, for instance many schools incorporate atria spaces. Therefore the design for fire prevention often involves fire engineering design. This is undertaken by a Fire Engineer to ensure that the design meets the design standards of the Approved Documents. The role of the architect is to agree the fire strategy with the client and design team and to see that the strategy works with the overall design concept for the new facilities.

7 EARLY YEARS SCHOOL DESIGN

7.1 Provision

Early Years Foundation Stage (EYFS) education serves children to the age of 5 including the reception class of compulsory education. In terms of compulsory education, a child must start school at the beginning of the next school term following their fifth birthday and would at this time enter reception class. However most children start earlier than this at a nursery class as provision has been expanded to provide a part time place for all 3 and 4 year olds.

To help meet this commitment, many other forms of early years provision has been developed including Sure Start Children's Centres, which are often but not always attached to primary schools.

All registered providers of Early Years care are required to use the EYFS statutory framework. The framework is set around a number of key themes: the development of a unique child; the ability for the child to develop positive relationships with others; the creation of an environment which supports the role of learning; and the recognition that children learn in different ways and at different rates.

Schools often provide an extended schools provision for students from the age of 4 to 14 providing childcare, breakfast and homework clubs for pupils to allow parents flexibility in their work arrangements and bring community services into schools. (See the DfE publication *Designing Schools for Extended Services 2006*).

7.2 Design principles

The design of the environment should respond to these EYFS framework issues and the architect should be aware of the ways in which early years pupils learn. CABE in association with the DfE has produced a design guide on Sure Start Centres, the principles of which are applicable to all environments for early years learning.

Some of the key design principles for Early Years design are:

- Development of a rich and varied space to encourage all learning styles and independence.
- Natural light and ventilation.
- Sense of scale that relates to the individual.
- Creation of an indoor/outdoor environment with instant accessibility to both.
- Innovative and challenging landscape.
- Involvement of the whole community in a building that is welcoming and friendly.

7.3 Area standards

Area standards for Early Years provision are set out in the EYFS statutory framework and give statutory requirements for various ages of children (see also BB103):

- 0–2 years 3.5m² per child.
- 2–3 years 2.5m² per child.
- 3–5 years 2.3m² per child.

As a guide, 9m² per pupil should be provided for outdoor areas. These should provide a diverse, fun and challenging environment in which children can learn and grow. Directly outside of learning spaces, a covered area should be provided where learning can be taken outside in inclement weather. This can, through use of shutters, also act as a large storage area for play equipment out of hours. Storage is a key requirement both externally and internally since equipment and toys are often bulky.

7.4 Other design considerations

There are several other design considerations:

- WCs and hand basins should be provided at a ratio of 1 for every 10 children over the age of 2.
- Provision of a relaxation and sleep area for children who wish to rest.
- Provision of a kitchen to provide healthy meals and snacks.
- Facilities for the preparation of babies' feeds.
- Suitable hygienic changing facilities.
- Staff welfare facilities.
- Suitable office space for the secure keeping of records and meetings with parents.

8 PRIMARY SCHOOLS (INCLUDING INFANT, JUNIOR AND FIRST SCHOOLS)

8.1 Background

Many primary schools incorporate nurseries and many share sites with Sure Start Centres, to provide a full EYFS provision. The first

ADS Code	Zone	Area Data Sheet (ADS) name and description	Size used in SoA tool
PRI03	D	**Nursery playroom:** For a range of FF&E layout options and activities for 3 to 4 year olds	55m² for 26
PRI13	D	**Reception classroom:** For a range of FF&E layout options and activities for reception pupils	62m² for 30
PRI23	D	**Infant classroom (extensive):** For a full range of FF&E layout options and activities for Key Stage 1 pupils	62m² for 30
PRI33	C	**Junior classroom:** For a range of FF&E layout options and activities for Key Stage 2 pupils	55m² for 30
PRI22	B	**Classbase with sink:** For limited primary activities including water-based, typically for infant (Key Stage 1), with easy access to a shared teaching area without sink	50m² for 30
PRI26	C	**Shared teaching without sink:** Open plan teaching area shared by adjacent classbases with sinks to enhance the range of activities, typically infant (Key Stage 1)	varies
PRI32	B	**Classbase without sink:** For limited primary activities, typically for junior (Key Stage 2), with easy access to a shared teaching area with sink	50m² for 30
PRI36	C	**Shared teaching with sink:** Open plan teaching area shared by adjacent classbases without sinks to enhance the range of activities, typically junior (Key Stage 2)	varies
PRA01	D	**ICT rich practical room** Classroom used for fixed ICT devices for all workplaces with limited layout options	62m² for 30
PRA11	D	**Food bay/ practical resources:** For primary food preparation with a small group and pupil access to practical resources	13m² for 4
PRA12	D	**Food/ science/ DT area:** Specialist space for primary food preparation, science, art and Design Technology activities	34m² for 15 62m² for 30
RES00	B	**Large group room:** Room for assistance with individuals and groups	27m² for 15

36.5 *Key area formulae from Building Bulletin 103*

year of statutory school provision is the reception class. This takes children from 4 to 5 years of age.

Primary schools deliver Key Stages 1 & 2 of the National Curriculum as set out by the Qualifications and Curriculum Agency (QCA).

Primary schools are usually organised in Forms of Entry (FE) e.g. 1FE, 2FE, 3FE with notionally circa 30 children per class. Therefore a 1FE school would have a capacity of circa 210 children and so on.

8.2 Design guidance

Guidance including sample schedules of accommodation can be found in BB103. This superseded BB99, which still proves useful for adjacencies and school organisation. A primary school designed to these standards is shown in Figure 36.6.

According to the Baseline Designs developed by the Education Funding Agency (see Section 3.4) the overall area formula for primary schools should be: $350m^2 + 4.1m^2$/pupil place. Examples of designs for 2FE schools of different sizes are shown in Figures 36.7 and 36.8. All Baseline Designs and BB103 are shown on the DfE website www.gov.uk/government/organisations/department-for-education.

8.3 Key Stage 1 & 2 curriculum organisation

At Key Stages 1 & 2, the statutory subjects that all pupils must study are art and design, design and technology, English, geography, history, information and communication technology, mathematics, music, physical education and science. Religious education must also be provided at Key Stages 1 & 2.

Children are organised in classes of approximately 30 and are sedentary in that the majority of activities are undertaken in the classroom. Therefore the classroom should provide a varied environment, particularly in the early years organisations/department-for-education in the upper years of KS2; the teaching and learning experience becomes more formal and the learning setting responds to this.

Classrooms should have direct access to external areas to take teaching and learning outside. This needs to be an immediate

1.	Main Entrance
2.	Heart Space
3.	Administration Office & Staff
4.	Nursery
5.	WC Pod
6.	Reception Classrooms
7.	Classroom
8.	External Courtyard
9.	Small Hall
10.	Main Hall
11.	Changing
12.	Kitchen

Ground Floor Plan
Hylands Primary School

36.6a *Hylands Primary School in Hornchurch, Essex was designed by Walters and Cohen for the London Borough of Havering and conforms to BB99. This ground floor plan shows classrooms and hall on the perimetre with a central courtyard and inner 'heart' space*

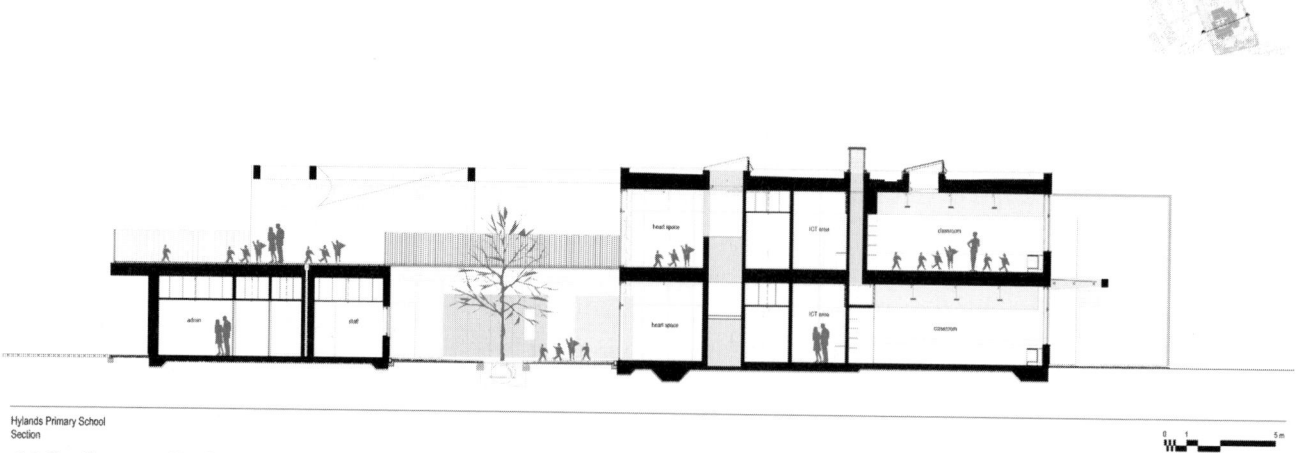

Hylands Primary School
Section

0 1   5m

36.6b *Section of Hylands Primary School, designed by Walters and Cohen, showing the central courtyard.*

relationship to give the greatest opportunity to enhance the learning experience.

Specialist activities, such as music, drama and PE, usually take place in the school hall or in the case of music, small support spaces. Occasionally schools will increase the amount of specialist space by enhancing a classroom in KS2 to undertake light practical work in science and technology for the older students.

8.4 ICT

ICT plays an ever-increasing part in the delivery of learning. In primary schools, significant ICT provision is usually confined to an

ICT suite or room, often located adjacent to or within the library or Learning Resource Centre area. However, each classroom from the Early Years onward will contain up to approximately three computers for use during the various class settings utilised throughout the day.

8.5 Site organisation

Since primary schools serve a very close catchment area, it is likely that a significant proportion of the children will walk to school. There are a number of initiatives to encourage this and many authorities encourage 'walking buses' by providing equipment such as highly visual jackets, for parents to organise themselves.

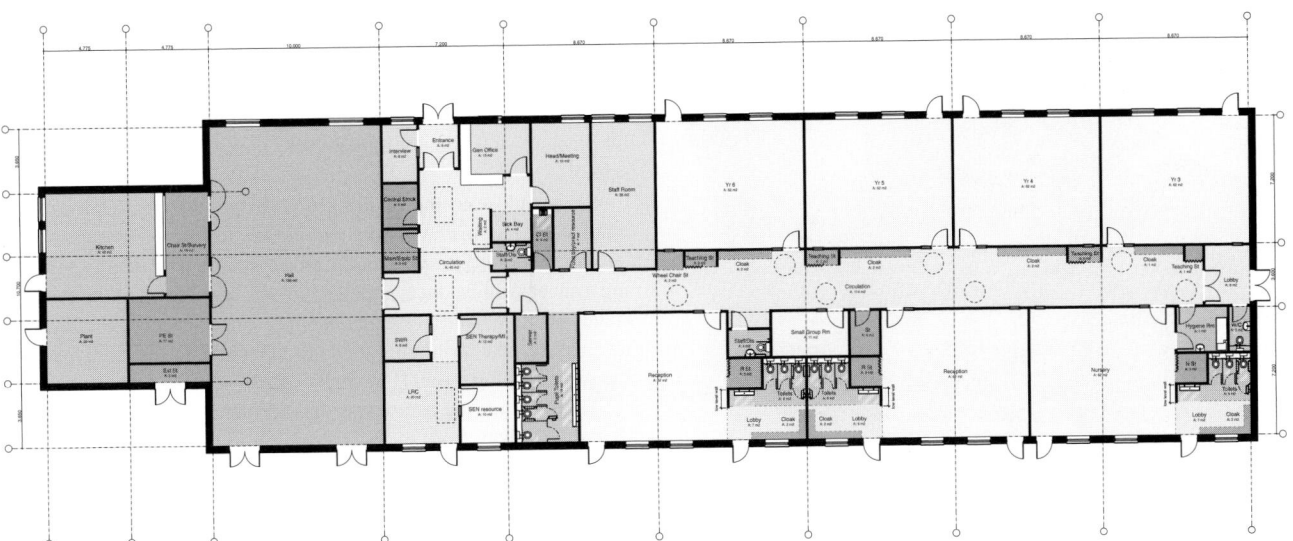

36.7 *Education Funding Agency Baseline Design for a 2FE, 180-place primary school*

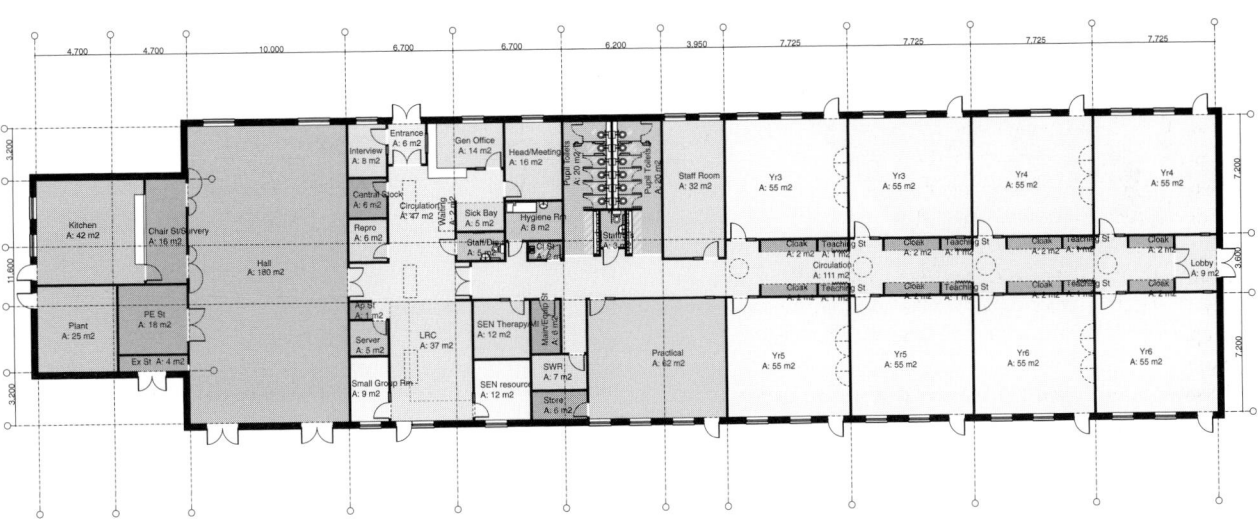

36.8 *Education Funding Agency Baseline Design for a 2FE, 240-place junior school*

Therefore in all schools, design to separate vehicular traffic and pedestrians will be a key concern of planning and highways authorities when assessing the scheme. This is particularly important at times of access and egress when the site is very busy. However car drop off and pick up by parents in many instances is inevitable, and the design needs to manage this well to avoid congestion, providing turning and waiting areas. There will also be the need to accommodate bus use either for occasional trips or in more rural circumstances the drop off and pick up of students from outlying areas.

Provision of staff parking is usually restricted by local planning regulations and must be considered as part of an overall transport policy by the school and the LEA together in a 'Green Travel Plan'. Many schools have adopted the Eco School standard which aims to make children and their parents aware of the carbon footprint of the schools and their own personal activities including how they get to school.

Security of the site is also a key consideration and the building form and site organisation should create clear areas of public and private domain to ensure the security of the children and teachers.

Often children will access the school through their individual classrooms via the playground. This needs to be a managed progression from the public areas of the site.

8.6 Community use

Community use of school buildings is increasing, with buildings seen as a resource for the whole community. This can range from:

- Use of the school for breakfast and after school clubs.
- Community drop-in facilities for the local authority to give advice, community policing or even community health services.
- Community library facilities which are shared by the school.
- Often community support facilities will be linked to a Sure Start Children's Centre.

8.7 Building form

Over the past few decades primary schools have usually been single storey buildings, which have related to a particular context and construction methodology. In recent years however several notable projects have challenged this conception as site areas have become more constrained and resources more scarce. Hampton Gurney School in London by BDP and St Johns School in Blackpool by AHR Architects (Figure 36.9) are examples of this, and maintain the crucial relationships between indoor and outdoor spaces through the provision of play decks.

8.8 Organisation

There are several core spaces common to all schools:

- Reception. This is the arrival point for parents and visitors during the day. The space should be bright and welcoming and give a view of school activity to demonstrate that the building is a place of learning. It should also be able to display the work of the school. Around the reception will be administration spaces, often

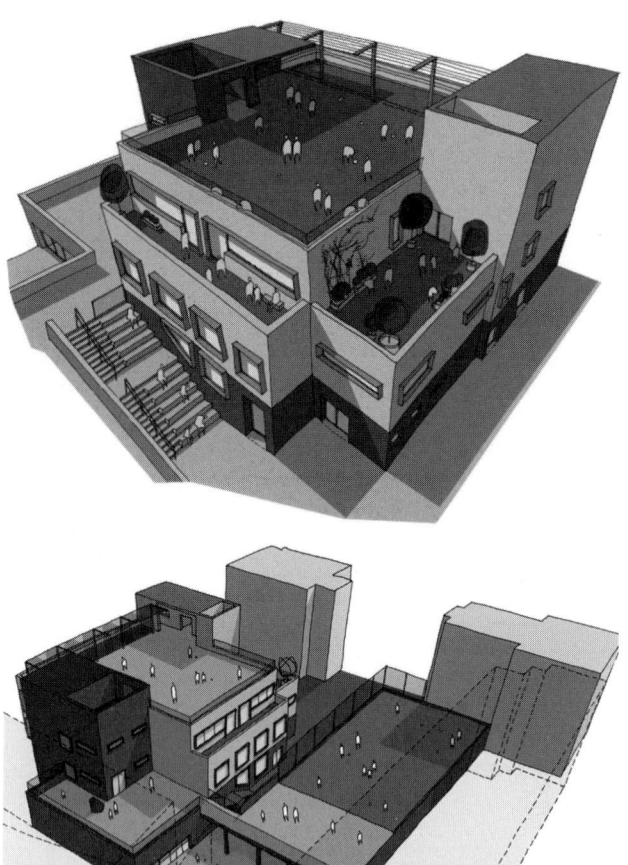

as educationalists strive to create a diverse number of learning settings. This is to ensure that children are able to learn according to their individual needs.

BB103 shows the overall areas to be provided, but environmental diversity is critically important to the creation of a successful school.

Spaces close to the building need to provide shelter from the wind and cover from the rain, particularly for the earliest years.

Orientation of teaching and learning spaces is critical in achieving a successful balance, and this must be considered at the earliest stages of site planning. Provision of protected spaces will allow the teachers to take children outside to demonstrate the principles of the subject being learnt (Figure 36.10).

There should be a progression and hierarchy in the spaces as they move away from the building form to give harder play areas and also spaces that allow children to read and socialise. Hard areas usually double as court spaces for outdoor PE. Playing fields are usually positioned furthest away from the building but with direct access from hard areas to give a natural progression in the warmer months of the years and an open feel to the site's periphery.

36.9 *St Johns' CE Primary school by AHR Architects*

including the office of the head, and a parent or visitor room for meetings with parents, or use by peripatetic health visitors and others.

- The Hall. This will be used for numerous activities including PE, Music, Drama, assemblies, social events and dining. Most children will stay in school for school dinners or will eat their packed lunch in the hall so the kitchen needs to be adjacent but also have safe access and egress for deliveries.
- Classrooms. These spaces must provide a varied environment, and be supported by flexible spaces between classes for breakout or the withdrawal of students for personalised tuition. Storage is also critical to the successful operation of a school to store both resources and work in progress.
- Toilets. These should be provided at a minimum standard of 1 for every 20 children, often at a rate of 2 per class. It is often associated with cloakrooms en route to the play areas, and provides a wet lobby area. Often schools operate an indoor shoe policy where children change shoes on entering. Separate sex WCs need to be provided for children over the age of 8. Disabled WCs should be provided for staff and children and many authorities do not allow these to be doubled up.
- Staff facilities. These should provide a relaxing environment, but equally often provide a small work area for preparation of lesson material. Staff WCs are positioned close by. The Deputy Head's room often doubles as a visitors' interview room.
- Caretaker's facilities. These include storage and maintenance equipment, usually with easy access to the service areas of the school.

8.9 Landscape and recreation

The relationship between indoor and outdoor spaces has become increasingly important to the education environment in recent years

36.10 *Outdoor Classroom by BDP from Exemplar Designs for Schools by DfE*

9 SECONDARY SCHOOLS

9.1 Background

Students move to secondary school at the age of 11 and study the secondary national curriculum through KS3 and 4 to the age of 16. Full details of the secondary national curriculum can be obtained from the Qualifications and Curriculum Authority website. The studies are directed towards formal qualifications obtained at the age of 16. From secondary education, many students stay on in education, either by attending a sixth form in the school or another school or by moving to local FE colleges which provide a range of vocational and academic courses as a stepping stone to university, further training or employment.

Secondary schools take many forms. The majority are comprehensive schools in that they do not choose their student intake on academic ability. However specialist schools and academies can apply some methods of selection based upon the specialism of the particular school.

9.2 Size and structure

Schools vary greatly in size, from the smallest secondary at 450 pupils to the largest at over 2000. However there has been a move in recent years to have a minimum size of 750 students and a maximum at 1500 students, rising to circa 1800 if the school includes a sixth form. The optimum sizes and the most common in recent school design are 900, 1050, 1200 and 1500 students.

The larger the school, the greater the need to break the size of the school down into manageable pastoral groups where students and staff can relate to each other in a positive way. Schools are responsible for the wellbeing of the whole student, not just academic achievement, and pastoral management of students is a crucial issue. Therefore, the creation of pastoral groups around houses or year groups is common in schools. House groups involve a vertical structure, which brings a number of students from each year group together into a house. The advantages of this are that the older students help to peer mentor younger students. A negative may be that the group are likely only to be together for pastoral times in the timetable.

Alternatively, pastoral groups may be based on year or half year groups. This does not have the positives of bringing together older and younger students, but other than for streaming of certain subjects, the students will spend the majority of time together.

Year 7, the first year in secondary school, is often separated out from the other years. This is to avoid any dip in performance during the Year 7 transition between primary and secondary schools. Often Year 7 will have separate social and play areas and will gradually integrate themselves into the wider social life of the school.

9.3 Guidance

Details of standard schedules of accommodation can be found in BB103 Area Guidelines for Mainstream Schools which replaces BB98 by the DFE, Figure 36.11.

According to the Baseline Designs developed by the Education Funding Agency (Section 3.4), the overall area formula for secondary schools should be: $1050m^2$ (+ $350m^2$ if there is a sixth form) + $6.3m^2$/pupil place for 11- to 16-year-olds + $7m^2$/pupil place for post-16s. Baseline Designs are shown in full on the DfE website. A design for an 1850-pupil secondary school is shown as Figure 36.12

9.4 Educational organisation

Traditionally schools have followed a subject based curriculum organisation, bringing together all general teaching spaces which would cater for subjects such as English, maths and humanities, and separating out specialist spaces for science and technology. Spaces for ICT would traditionally be located as a central resource and music and drama space with the hall for performances and also as a potential community facility. Sports would also be located with proximity to playing fields and MUGA (Multi Use Games Area) spaces, but also close to car parking for ease of community use.

This organisation is still relevant and with good design can be made into a very flexible, educationally driven solution. However education theory and practice often moves architects to consider other ways of organising schools.

At one end of the spectrum is the 'schools within schools' model, which brings a series of spaces together to cater for the needs of a particular cohort, of, say 150 students. They would be provided with the majority of facilities required to enable the group to remain in this area for the majority of the time, only moving away to access very specialist facilities or to participate in sports. Typically, the group would have a series of general classrooms,

ADS Code	Zone	Area Data Sheet (ADS) name and description	Size used in SoA tool
CLA02	C	**Seminar room:** For smaller 14-19 groups with a range of FF&E layout options and activities	41m² for 30
CLA12	C	**General classroom:** For a range of FF&E layout options and activities	55m² for 30
CLA13	D	**Extensive classroom:** Suitable for all classroom FF&E layout options and activities	62m² for 30
CLA32	D	**ICT-rich classroom:** With fixed ICT devices for all workplaces and a range of FF&E layout options	62m² for 30
CLA35	D	**ICT-rich learning area:** Semi-open plan area with fixed ICT devices for all workplaces and range of FF&E layout options	62m² for 30
CLA41	D	**ICT/business studies room:** Classroom with fixed ICT devices for half of the workplaces with business environment	62m² for 30
DAT02	F	**General art room:** For a range of FF&E layout options and activities suitable for general 2D art	83m² for 30
DAT03	G	**3D art room:** for general and 3D art including clay work	97m² for 30
DAT05	G	**3D art room (textiles):** For general artwork and printing techniques and 3D art	104m² for 32
DAT12	H	**Hair and beauty salon:** for hair styling and beauty therapy	69m² for 16
DAT22	G	**Graphic products:** For graphics and light, small scale product design	83m² for 25
DAT25	G	**Constructional textiles:** For working with textiles	83m² for 25
DAT28	G	**Electronics and control systems:** For electronics, pneumatics and light, small scale product design	83m² for 25
DAT32	F	**Food studio:** for demonstrations of food preparation	69m² for 24
DAT35	H	**Food room:** For non-vocational practical cookery activities by pupils in pairs	104m² for 24 if 1 space, 97m² if 2
DAT43	H	**Resistant materials workshop:** for working with resistant materials and electronics	104m² for 24 if 1 space, 97m² if 2
DAT46	I	**RM workshop with heat bay:** For working with a range of resistant materials, including wood, metal and plastics	111m² for 24
DAT49	J	**Construction workshop:** workshop for vocational construction courses	97m² for 16
PER01	D	**Music classroom:** for performance, composing and theory	62m² for 30
PER02	E	**Extensive music classroom:** for performance, composing and theory, with option of keyboards for all pupils	69m² for 30
PER04	F	**Music recital/drama studio:** studio space for drama and large music recital room combined	83m² for 30
PER05	F	**Drama studio:** studio space for drama	90m² for 30
SCI02	E	**Science studio:** For demonstration and light experiments	69m² for 30
SCI05	F	**General science laboratory:** For demonstration and a wide range of 'hands on' experiments	83m² for 30
SCI11	F	**Specialist science laboratory:** For demonstration for all types of experiments, up to A-level	90m² for 30

36.11 *Key area formulae from BB103 by DfE*

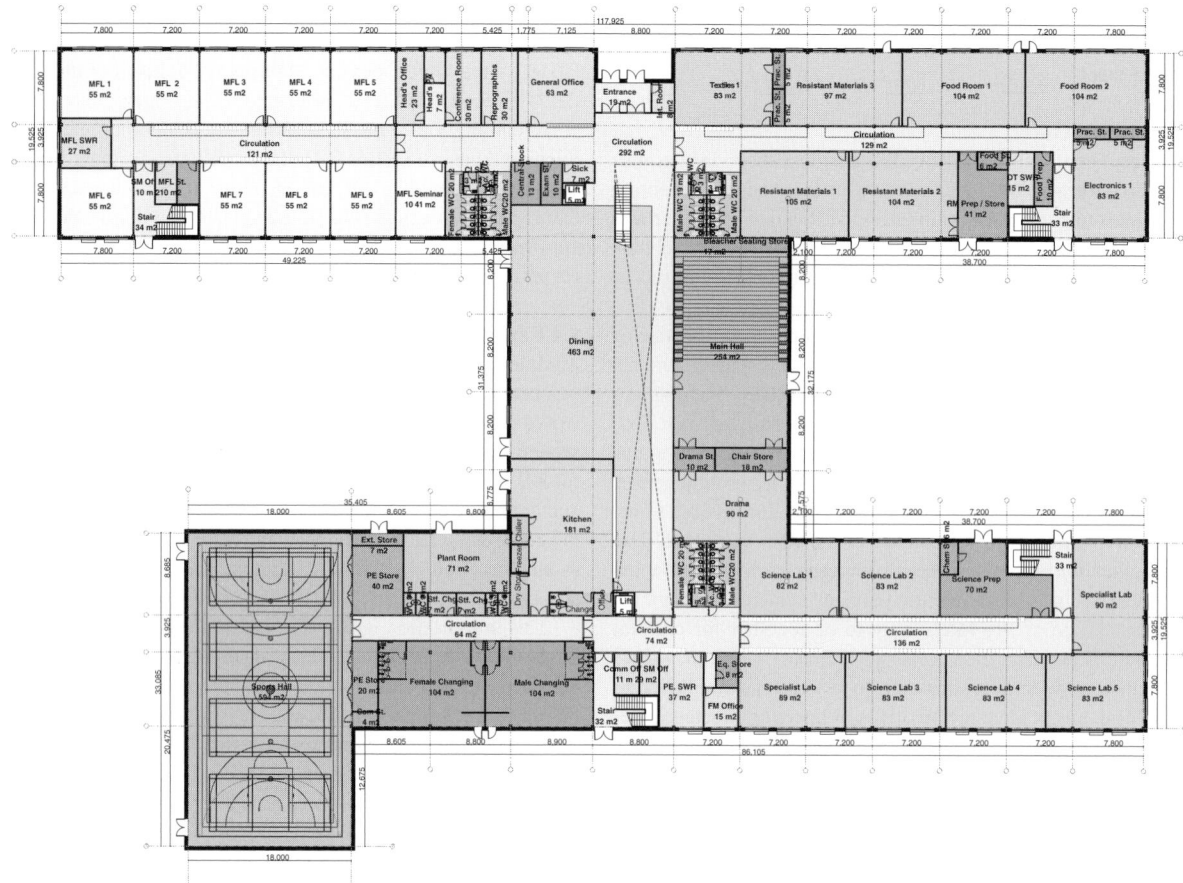

36.12 *Education Funding Agency Baseline Design (ground floor) for an 1850-pupil Type 1 secondary school*

breakout facilities and small group rooms, and also a number of specialist facilities to provide technology and science facilities. The group would have direct access to a varied landscape. Dining could be communal or taken in the breakout space of the school dependent upon the philosophy.

This model brings together the positive mentor relationships between a small group of students and staff who would essentially deliver all teaching and learning to the group all of the time. The model is particularly adaptable to project-based learning where cross subject teaching is implemented. Often the school would be designed so that each school could be adjusted to create larger or smaller groups as the circumstances dictated.

A similar but less radical model is the creation of *'home base'* spaces within a school, with group teaching spaces around them. These can be designed to accommodate a year or house group rather than necessarily being purely subject based. Specialist spaces can be positioned remotely from the home base for efficiency of use. Again, the organisation principle is that the student would spend the majority of time relating directly to the group in cross-subject teaching relating directly to a smaller number of teachers and mentors.

9.5 Site organisation

The key principles of organising a school site are to:

- Create a positive public domain, which welcomes the community onto the site.
- Create distinct public and private domains that create a safe working environment for all.
- Create a clear separation of vehicular traffic and pedestrians and organisation of drop off and pick up.
- Create a diverse landscape that enhances the curriculum.
- Optimise the orientation of buildings and indoor and outdoor space to make the most of the climatic conditions and help create a sustainable solution. This needs to be considered in the earliest stages of design.

Schools are major buildings in their local communities. New school buildings create a sense of local pride and the architecture and design should respond positively to these issues. Creating a positive public domain is critical to the way in which the school announces itself to its local community and many school designs incorporate plaza type spaces for the community to inhabit. Car parking and accessibility for bus drop off and pick up is a major logistical issue on any school site, and must be designed logically and to enhance safely.

9.6 Landscape and recreation areas

BB103 Annex B provides guidance on the provision of the net site area and playing field provision. Often the planning authorities will ask for the views of Sport England to be considered during the planning process. Provision includes:

- Sports pitches.
- Games courts (MUGA).
- Soft informal and social areas.
- Hard informal and social areas.
- Habitat areas.

The diversity of the landscape and the learning environment that it provides is key to creating a successful school environment. The Faraday Project, a research project into the teaching of science by the DfE, places a significant importance on the development of a creative landscape for learning.

The development of successful social spaces is also critical to the development of social skills in young people and the relationship between dining and external areas as overspill space is an important consideration.

On more confined sites, the creative development of sports facilities, including mountain bike tracks and trim trails, are often incorporated to encourage the maximum use of sporting facilities and also encourage students who dislike team sports to become active. All weather facilities allow much more intensive use and synthetic pitches can be a significant community resource, particularly when used with floodlighting, and so can be counted as double in the space provision in BB98.

9.7 Community use

Secondary schools are seen as major community resources and as such are often open for many more hours beyond the school day for:

- Serving the extended schools agenda and also encouraging students to remain in school to undertake homework, use ICT facilities or participate in group activities.
- Accommodating other local authority services, community police, and health facilities.
- Crèche services for students and the wider community.
- Significant community facilities such as libraries with associated cafe. It may be part of the ethos of the school to allow the community to access such facilities during the school day. Clear lines of security and separation are needed to ensure that this is done elegantly.

The design of a new school should be zoned in both security and environmental terms to accommodate community use. A clear and simple zoning strategy will allow the building to be operated out of hours at minimal cost by minimising attendance and heating and lighting use.

9.8 Reception and social spaces

It is common practice provide a single point of entry for all users of the building, students, staff and visitors alike. Therefore a key requirement is to be able to receive high volumes of people efficiently and effectively while providing a pleasant environment that will engage visitors in the work and ethos of the school. This involves detailed design of reception spaces, and the ability for the reception to have a direct connection with other parts of the school.

Administration facilities are positioned adjacent to the reception. These are an extensive facility dealing with school finances and the administration of student records etc.

Social spaces for students are important. They can act as break out spaces for teaching and learning when not in use, but also help to give the students a sense of ownership, as well as providing space where lockers, if required, can be easily accessed. Often these are provided for each year group. They can also form home base spaces for student groups.

9.9 General teaching spaces

BB103 provides sizes of teaching spaces and associated storage based upon the group sizes. General teaching spaces need to provide a flexible environment and are often grouped in curriculum areas. Furniture needs to be flexible and easily moved and stored to enable the room to accommodate various teaching and learning settings. These settings may need to be changed quickly.

All services will be to the periphery of the room. These will consist of power and data facilities. ICT will often be wireless and connected through lap top computers as non-specialist activities use less memory.

Within each group of general classrooms it is useful to have a flexible dividing screen between two rooms to provide a larger space for activities, lectures or small examinations. Flexible screens are expensive and are compromised in terms of acoustics, however when used judiciously they can add great flexibility to a working environment.

9.10 Science

The development of science teaching environments has been greatly influenced by the Project Faraday publication by the DfE, Figure 36.13. This is an exemplar study into the range of spaces required to deliver the teaching of science in the new century. Many of the studies suggest a mix of spaces, moving away from purely using the traditional science laboratory to the development of science studio spaces. These spaces are usually central to a suite of laboratories but are lightly serviced spaces that can flex to become a large demonstration space for experiments, a space where results are collated using ICT, or a flexible breakout space from the surrounding laboratories. Preparation facilities are often centralised in the department to provide a facility for the preparation of materials for lessons and the storage of equipment.

Laboratories are also now more lightly serviced and flexible, with servicing, water, gas and electricity, to the periphery of the room. This gives flexibility to the centre of the space. Rooms within the department are often more open with the use of glazed screens creating visual links between spaces and creating a more professional world of work environment.

Science is also taken out of the classroom into the whole school site using the built and natural environment as the backdrop for the exploration of science, creating, for example, living recycling systems.

9.11 Technology

Technology is the subject that most naturally replicates the world of industry, and incorporates subjects that design an object or product, then creates the product and markets it through graphics and media. Technology studies are also expanding to include vocational subjects such as land-based studies, food and catering and construction as part of the expanding 14–19 agenda.

A typical technology department will have a series of specialist spaces in enclosed areas around a central space that will be ICT based, possibly a design subject. The whole department will often be open with glazed screens between rooms. Often spaces of a similar type, for instance resistant materials, will be joined to give an open studio feel. This also ensures access to equipment so that expensive machinery is not doubled up.

Guidance on areas for each subject area is given in BB98, Figure 36.11, the spaces are much larger than general teaching spaces, usually between 90 and 130 m² depending on the subject. The storage and preparation facilities for the materials, equipment and tools associated with these areas are also large. In addition, secure storage for students' work is essential – both work in progress and completed work awaiting final assessment.

ICT is usually hard-wired fixed machines which can use high memory capacity for design and graphics programmes. This usually increases the cooling load on the spaces.

9.12 Art and design

Often associated with technology, these spaces can create an open studio feel. When possible, spaces should be higher than standard floor-to-floor height. This can help the display and storage of work. 2D art rooms can often be used with textiles, whilst 3D art rooms are often self-contained. Ceramics is dusty and the need to provide a separate kiln space often precludes pairing ceramics with other art subjects.

9.13 LRC (Learning Resource Centre)

With the increasing use of ICT throughout schools, the LRC is no longer the hub of technology and the trend is for the spaces to revert to the written form. Often a LRC will have a series of areas from informal lounge area to formal teaching area that can be used for lessons when needed. Community use of these spaces for internet access is high and some schools encourage this during the school day and provide refreshment facilities. In these circumstances, the operation and security arrangements need to be very carefully considered.

The environment should be bright and stimulating and given the high degree of community access, schools often display the work of the students and their outreach work to the community.

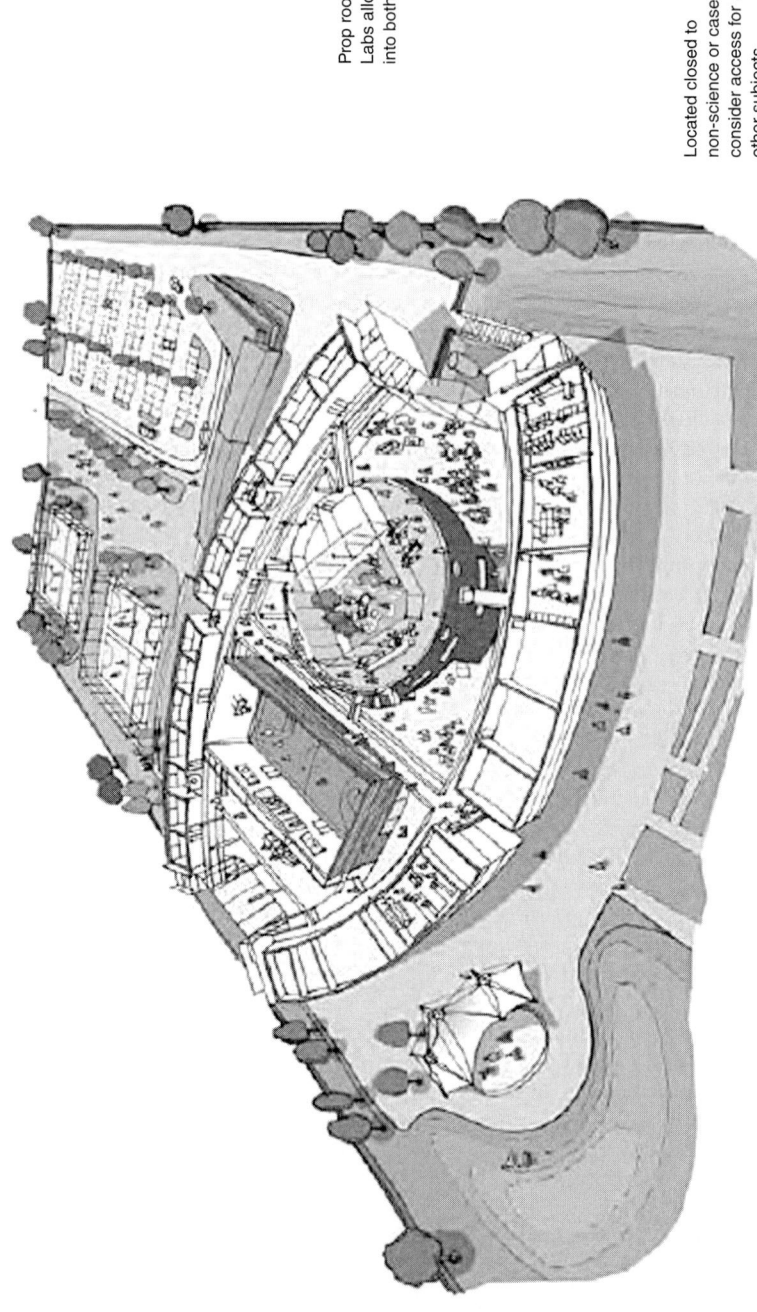

Started central area, a key part of triple E project. based learning

Vertical connection with D&T exhibition space provides opportunity for long-term susparetion exhibit.

Super Lab

Prop rom and start area —possibility of combining the two

Prop room between the two Labs allows for easy access into both

Shorter travel distance, direct acrosses closer sight lines

Located closed to non-science or cases consider access for other subjects

Folding wall between will slow for these to be opened up into one space

Possible giant suspected projection section suspected from coding

Focus of the space

Concept plan showing key features of the design

This 3D cut-away shows East Barnet's science accommodation to the right.
Image credit: Building Design Partnership

36.13 *Project Faraday design by DEGW and BDP*

9.14 Music and drama

Often grouped together, the larger dance spaces may also double up as activity studios with the sports department. Music other than group performances in the hall or other small performance spaces takes place in smaller group or ensemble rooms, with one or two larger rooms for teaching. The acoustic qualities of these spaces are a key consideration, as is the provision of secure storage since instruments are often large and expensive. Storage is often used as an acoustic buffer between spaces.

Dance spaces need extra height and the use of sprung flooring with a series of curtains and mirrors. Drama spaces often benefit from extra height for lighting for rehearsals. Neither space is elaborate.

9.15 Hall spaces

Hall spaces need to be flexible and offer themselves to as many uses as possible such as performances, parents' evenings and assemblies (but not of the whole school as the space is seldom big enough). As sports halls are often used for examinations they need to have some acoustic isolation, although the trend is away from this as examination pressure can often be taken up in other ways.

9.16 Dining

Dining is often seen as a social experience that is part of the development of the whole child. Staff are also encouraged to use the facilities to help create positive relationships. Therefore dining periods are being extended to make the experience more pleasurable and more detail is being placed on the design and operation of the facilities, particularly the installation of FFE and the provision of outdoor dining.

Often dining is divided into several offers ranging from a full service incorporating hot meals, salads and jacket potatoes, to a sandwich take away often located away from the main dining areas.

Kitchens are designed by specialist catering designers in order to ensure that hygiene regulations are met and also that the throughput of pupils to be served in the time allowed is met. The architect should see that the kitchen design is coordinated into the design concept for dining.

9.17 Staff facilities

A welfare room with associated toilets is provided for staff. This will vary in size and capacity dependent upon the ethos of the school and the function that is to be met. WCs should also be provided at strategic locations throughout the school, within regulation distances. Staff should not share WCs with students. Staff offices and workspaces should be located strategically throughout the school in order to maximise passive supervision.

10 SPECIAL EDUCATIONAL NEEDS PROVISION

10.1 Strategy

The government's strategy for students with Special Educational Needs (SEN) is set out in the DfE document *Removing Barriers to Education*. This sets out the policy framework for local authorities and schools to follow and is aimed at assessing the needs of pupils quickly and developing a personalised plan for learning. This can be set within mainstream or more traditional special school settings dependent upon the abilities of the pupil.

Following on from this document there has been a move toward accommodating pupils with fewer difficulties in mainstream schools and also to co-locating special needs provision with mainstream. This is either on the same campus or within the same building and creates a design challenge to integrate students while protecting the most vulnerable.

The landscape of special needs provision has changed significantly in recent years and the design guidance has been updated in the form of Building Bulletin 102: Designing for Pupils with Special Educational Needs. This replaced Building Bulletins 77, 91 and 94.

10.2 Provision within mainstream schools

Accessibility legislation in recent new build schools ensures a certain level of accessibility for students with mobility, sight and hearing issues. However, to accommodate pupils with more complex issues, schools may have to be adapted to the particular needs of an individual student.

Often schools will encompass a unit to address particular issues, for instance autism, or hearing or sight impairment. These are located within the school but the design of the learning environment will be tailored to the special need that the space addresses. This has become increasingly common as authorities seek to accommodate students with less complex needs in mainstream education. This is to ensure the entitlement of the individual pupil to a full and fulfilling education.

10.3 Special school provision

The move toward personalisation of education and the emphasis on the uniqueness of the individual has removed a significant amount of generic terminology in special school design. No longer are schools for Moderate Learning Difficulties (MLD) or Profound and Multiple Learning Difficulties (PMLD) students, schools must have the ability to react to the needs of all students. Often schools will accommodate students with completely varying ranges of abilities across the whole spectrum of special needs. BB102, Figure 36.14, neatly summarises within Annex F the key definitions and issues relating to the various difficulties that pupils may have. Schools may also be of all-through age ranges.

10.4 Areas and space

BB102 provides a series of schedules and design examples for the provision of special school facilities. These provide areas per pupil ranging between 40 and 45 m² per pupil – significantly higher than mainstream schools. A classroom of 65 m² usually accommodates 8 to 10 pupils dependent upon their abilities and age. Schools will have a mix of general teaching and specialist spaces; specialist spaces for art, food technology and ICT are most common.

Particular areas to consider when designing for SEN include:

- A significant area for the equipment to support the pupils in the teaching space and to create a series of learning environments within the room.
- A direct and level link to a covered and secure outdoor space is essential. Often schemes are centred around an external court with raised beds and sensory gardens.
- Significant areas should be given to non-teaching space, for instance large hygiene facilities adjacent to general classrooms often with hoists to assist the less able students.
- Large areas for the storage of equipment. Often pupils will have more than one wheelchair and will change from one to another on entering the building.
- Medical facilities for visiting peripatetic clinicians.
- Hydrotherapy pool for physiotherapy with associated changing facilities.
- A sensory environment with soft furnishings, lighting equipment and music.
- A central hall that is easily accessible. This is important because it is common practice for pupils to gather morning and evening for arrival and departure via mini buses and taxis. The hall is often multi use for sport and dining dependent upon the size of the school.
- External spaces need to be secured and sheltered from the elements and have a variety of surfaces. Planting is often raised in order for pupils to be able to access the plants.

Children's need	Typical support	Design issues	Space needed in classroom for…
Cognition and learning			
Specific learning difficulty SpLD	3D learning aids; occupational and/or physiotherapy; learning, behaviour/speech & language (SpLg) support	Good acoustics for SpLg therapy; storage for learning aids; SEN resource base	Learning aids, ICT; practical work; flexible layouts for movement work; appropriate positioning of child in class
Moderate learning difficulty MLD	SpLg therapy; learning & behaviour support; social skills training	Good visibility for supervision; good acoustics for SpLg; H&S risk assessments; storage for resource and learning aids; SEN resource & specialist bases	Learning aids, ICT; practical work; flexible use of FF&E; appropriate positioning of child in class
Severe learning difficulty SLD	3D learning aids; multi-sensory work; adapted ICT; social skills & independence training; SpLg therapy; learning & behaviour support; physio-, occupational & hydrotherapy	Good visibility for supervision; wayfinding to aid independence; good acoustics for SpLg therapy; specialist SEN support; H&S risk assessments; storage & use of mobility/learning aids	Multi-sensory and practical activities; learning aids, ICT; flexible use of FF&E; movement and circulation (some mobility aids); additional support staff
Profound & multiple learning difficulty PMLD	3D learning aids; multi-sensory work; sensory impairment support; SpLg therapy; occupational, physio- and/or hydrotherapy; medical & personal care; soft play	As SLD but more space for greater support, storage and concentration of needs; higher accessibility standards; intensive use of mobility aids & hoists; H&S risk assessments: manual handling, infection control; storage and use of mobility & learning aids	Multi-sensory, practical & therapy work; adapted ICT & access technology; additional staff; flexible use of FF&E; movement and circulation (bulky mobility aids)
Behaviour, emotional and social development			
Behaviour, emotional and social difficulty BESD	Behavioural, cognitive, social skills support; learning mentors; social workers, educational psychologists, mental health service (CAMHS)	Good sightlines, balance between privacy and ease of overseeing children; secure storage; robust materials, tamper proof FF&E & concealed services; H&S risk assessments; large spaces for social and outdoor activities	Avoiding distraction and conflict; varying layout (e.g. separated or grouped tables); supervision; developing social skills; quiet/informal corner
Communication and interaction			
Speech, language & communication needs SLCN	Social skills support; learning & communication aids, synthetic speech production equipment, assistive technology; SpLg therapy; learning and behaviour support	Easily understood whole school layout with clear signage; good lighting, room acoustics and sound insulation; sound-field systems, extra ICT and associated services	Position of child in class; use of signs, symbols, communication aids and synthetic speech production equipment; SpLg therapy
Autistic spectrum disorder ASD	Learning & behaviour support; social skills programmes in class and by withdrawal; specialist ASD teaching approaches; specialist ASD resource base	Simple layout: calm, ordered, low stimulus spaces, no confusing large spaces; indirect lighting, no glare, subdued colours; good acoustics, avoiding sudden/background noise; robust materials, tamper-proof elements and concealed services; possibly H&S risk assessments; safe indoor and outdoor places for withdrawal and to calm down	Varying approaches; structured activities using ICT and FF&E; position of child in class; screened workstations; safe quiet place to calm down
Sensory and/or physical			
Hearing impairment HI	Use of CCTV; HI teaching strategies; oral signing; HI learning & communication support; SpLg therapy & social skills training; audiology & HI assessment	Avoid distraction: low sensory stimulus & subdued colours; good quality low glare lighting, avoiding shadows & silhouetting; good quality acoustics, low background noise; visual alarms, sound-field systems, hearing loops; storage & maintenance of technical aids	Signing, communication worker; U-shaped or other layout for good visibility; visual aids/ICT/TV/CCTV; radio aids
Visual impairment VI	VI specialist aids e.g. tactile and visual aids, Braille, CCTV viewers, ICT text magnification, speech & sound output; VI support by mobility training officer	Good quality ambient & task lighting & controls; visual contrast, cues, symbols, tactile trails & maps; good acoustics, low background noise, speech & audio aids; sounder alarms, H&S warnings; VI resource room; storage and maintenance of technical aids	Clear, safe uncluttered layout; specialist (e.g. tactile and visual) aids; adapted ICT
Multi-sensory impairment MSI	Visual, tactile, mobility, communication aids and multi-sensory work; varied support as needed; MSI assessment, 1-1 learning and behaviour work; soft play room	As for HI and VI: clear, simple layout for sensory wayfinding with visual, audio & tactile cues; good quality non-glare lighting; good quality room acoustics, no background noise; greater use of mobility aids, hoists & hydrotherapy (see PD); large store	Individual or small groups, with HI, VI, MSI workers; practical learning aids; multi-sensory work; adapted ICT & access technology; flexible use of FF&E
Physical disability PD	Learning and mobility aids, scribe, adapted ICT, communication aids, assistive technology; use of hoists, mobility aids; occupational, physio- & hydrotherapy; personal carers, nurse, medical and/or health care support	Higher accessibility standards; much bulky mobility equipment (independent or assisted use), equipment store, storage bays off corridors; H&S risk assessments; manual handling; shallow pitch stairs, rest places; hygiene & infection control; assisted emergency escape, evacuation lifts & safe refuges: space for rest & respite; large equipment storage spaces	Learning & communication aids, adapted ICT, assistive technology; scribe, assistant, carers, occupational therapist; specialist adjustable height FF&E; equipment storage; movement & circulation (some bulky mobility aids)

36.14 *Annex F BB102 by DfE*

10.5 Schools for students with behavioural, emotional and social difficulties

Behavioural, emotional and social difficulties (BESD) pupils often follow a curriculum the same or near to that of mainstream schools, albeit with a vocational emphasis. The emphasis is on re-engagement of the student with education and behavioural modification. The buildings and external environment are often secure to ensure that the pupils stay in place. The subjects taught will include, for instance, car maintenance at the upper years and are aimed at the need to provide the pupils with a transferable skill. Subjects such as this are also used to engage the pupils with education.

Buildings are often arranged around a court. Internal spaces are usually smaller than mainstream schools and accommodate fewer pupils. A series of chill out spaces are provided to give space to the individual as and when required. Sport and outdoor activity will often play a big part in the curriculum, through the provision of 5-a-side courts and indoor sports facilities.

Pupils often arrive alone or in small groups by taxi or mini bus. Drop off facilities very close to the secure main entrance are essential.

11 REFERENCES

The DfE publish a significant number of design guidance documents, which are available from The Stationery Office (TSO), formerly HMSO.

11.1 DfE regulatory guidance

School Premises (England) Regulations 2012
Assessing the Net Capacity of Schools DfES, 2001

11.2 DfE Building Bulletins

BB103 – Area Guidelines for Mainstream Schools
BB102 – Designing for Disabled Children and Children with Special Educational Needs
BB101 – Ventilation of School Buildings
BB100 – Design for Fire Safety in Schools
BB99 – Briefing Framework for Primary School Projects
BB98 – Briefing Framework for Secondary School Projects
BB96 – Meeting the Educational Needs of Children and Young People in Hospital
BB94 – Inclusive School Design
BB93 – Acoustic Design of Schools
BB92 – Modern Foreign Languages Accommodation: A Design Guide
BB91 – Access for Disabled People to School Buildings: Management and Design Guide
BB90 – Lighting Design for Schools
BB89 – Art Accommodation in Secondary Schools
BB88 – Fume Cupboards in Schools
BB87 – Guidelines for Environmental Design
BB86 – Music Accommodation in Secondary Schools
BB85 – School Grounds: A Guide to Good Practice
BB84 – School Boarding Accommodation: A Design Guide
BB83 – Schools' Environmental Assessment Method (SEAM)
BB82 – Area Guidelines for Schools – revised 2002
BB81 – Design and Technology Accommodation in Schools: A Design Guide
BB80 – Science Accommodation in Secondary Schools: A Design Guide
BB79 – Passive Solar Schools: A Design Guide
BB78 – Security Lighting Crime Prevention on Schools Series
BB77 – Designing for Pupils with Special Educational Needs: Special Schools
BB76 – Maintenance of Electrical Services Maintenance and Renewal in Educational Buildings Series

BB75 – Closed Circuit TV Surveillance Systems in Educational Buildings Crime Prevention in Schools Series
BB73 – A Guide to Energy Efficient Refurbishment Maintenance and Renewal in Educational Buildings Series
BB72 – Educational Design Initiatives in City Technology Colleges
BB71 – The Outdoor Classroom Second Edition
BB70 – Maintenance of Mechanical Services Maintenance and Renewal in Educational Buildings Series
BB69 – Crime Prevention in Schools: Specification, Installation and Maintenance of Intruder Alarm Systems
BB67 – Crime Prevention in Schools: Practical Guidance
BB95 – Schools for the Future: Designs for Learning Communities, DCFS, 2002

11.3 Other publications

Asset Management Plans Guidance, DCSF
Better Buildings, Better Design, Better Education, DCSF, 2007
Building for Sure Start: A Design Guide, Department for Education, 2005.
Bursars' Guide to Sustainable School Operation, DFES, 2006
City Academies2, DCSF
City Learning Centres: design guide, DfEE, 2000
Classrooms of the Future, DCSF, 2003
Client Guide to Developing School Buildings, RIBA Policy & International Relations, 2007
Community Use of School Facilities Guidance, Sport England, updated 2009
Design of sustainable schools – Case Studies, DfES, 2006
Designing schools for extended services, DCSF, 2006
Designing Space for Sports and Arts, DfEE/Sport England, 2000
Designing School Grounds, Schools for the Future, DfES, 2006
Exemplar Designs: concepts and ideas, DCSF, 2004
Energy and water management: A guide for schools, DfES, 2002
Equalities impact assessment: building schools for the future, DfE, 2012
Every Child Matters, DfE, 2003
Inspirational Design for Kitchen & Dining Spaces, DCSF, 2007
How to Combat Arson in Schools, Arson Preventions Bureau, 2004
Inspirational Design for PE & Sport Spaces Department for Education, DFES, 2005
Managing Schools Facilities guides (www.education.gov.uk)
Primary ideas: projects to enhance primary school environments, Department for Education and Skills, 2006
Project Faraday – Exemplar designs for science, DCSF, 2007
Sustainable Water Management in Schools, CIRIA, 2006
Standard Specification, Layouts and Dimensions Guidance, DCSF, 2007/8
Transforming Schools: an inspirational guide to remodelling secondary schools, DCSF, 2004
21st Century Schools Learning Environments, OECD, 2006
Year of Action – Top Ten Tips for Saving energy and water and reducing waste in schools, DfE, 2012

11.4 Useful websites

BECTA www.becta.org.uk
BREEAM www.breeam.org
CABE www.designcouncil.org.uk/our-work/cabe
Department for Education www.education.gov.uk
Design Share www.designshare.com
Design Quality Indicators www.dqi.org.uk
Ofsted www.ofsted.gov.uk
Qualifications and Curriculum Authority (QCA) www.qca.org.uk
Specialist Schools and Academies Trust www.ssatuk.co.uk

37 Security and counter-terrorism

Mark Whyte and Chris Johnson

Director, Security Consulting and Explosion Effects, TPS
Managing Principal, Gensler

KEY POINTS:

- *In the contemporary society, with an increasingly crowded urban environment, 'resilience' is the critical term: resilient not just against natural hazards but against all forms of criminality, terrorist attacks and the deadly threats*
- *The level of security provision should be such that would-be attackers – criminal, terrorist or simply anti-social – are dissuaded from targeting the completed scheme. Bluntly, their activities are either halted or displaced to an alternative, less well-protected site*

Contents

1 Introduction
2 Security design principles
3 Designing a system
4 Counter terrorism concepts and standards
5 References
6 Sources of advice
7 Appendix 1 Security risk register example
8 Appendix 2 Physical security concepts and standards

1 INTRODUCTION

Security has not traditionally been at the forefront of concerns when architects, planners and designers consider the central requirements of a new-build project. Aesthetics, accessibility, functionality and cost will trump security in most cases, save perhaps for specific high profile, military or secure facility projects. However, it is increasingly recognised that designers have a responsibility to consider security requirements. In the contemporary risk society, with an increasingly crowded urban environment, 'resilience' is perhaps the critical term: resilient not just against natural geo- and hydro-meteorological hazards (such as earthquakes and floods), but against all forms of criminality, terrorist attacks and the deadly threat of a VBIED (vehicle-borne improvised explosive device) detonation or CBRN (chemical, biological, radiological or nuclear) attack. This chapter covers the incorporation of security measures into projects to help address such threats and risks.

1.1 Definitions

For purposes of clarity and to ensure a common understanding some common security terms are explained

- Security: can be used to describe either:

  o The condition where our people, assets and interests are protected from harm or loss from criminality and terrorism.

or

  o The identification of threats and risks from criminality and terrorism and the measures taken to mitigate them.

- Physical security: these are hard measures put in place to help deliver security. It can include electronic systems (CCTV, access control, intruder detection) fences, gates, door sets, glazing systems, barriers and bollards.

- Counter terrorism measures: physical measures taken to eliminate or limit the impact of a terrorist incident on buildings and their occupants and on infrastructure.
- Hostile vehicle mitigation: the deployment of appropriately rated and designed barriers, blockers and bollards to constrain or prevent the movement of vehicles being used for terrorist or criminal purposes,
- Threat: threats are potential events or activities that have the potential to cause harm or loss and can be expressed as Threat = Capability × Intent.
- Risk: risk is a way of expressing the potential for a threat to cause loss or harm expressed in terms of probability and impact. This can be shown as Risk = Probability (of an occurrence) × Impact (of an event or threat).
- Risk treatment: these are the measures taken to reduce the impact and probability of an event and can include avoidance, transfer, mitigation or acceptance.
- Residual risk: this is the level of risk remaining once mitigation measures have been applied.

2 SECURITY DESIGN PRINCIPLES

In designing security measures for a project, the following principles should be considered:

- Deterrence
- Detection
- Delay
- Response
- Pursuit
- Reassurance

2.1 Deterrence

The level of security provision should be such that would-be attackers – criminal, terrorist or simply anti-social – are dissuaded from targeting the completed scheme. Bluntly, their activities are either halted or displaced to an alternative, less well-protected site. Deterrence can be achieved by measures that may include:

- Adherence to concepts such as 'defensible space' and security through environmental design.
- Visible security features including perimeter fences, CCTV and lighting. For those who have been granted legitimate access to a location, physical measures such as security turnstiles, internal CCTV and intruder detection will provide a strong visual deterrent. A determined attacker carrying out a hostile reconnaissance will identify these measures as well as less overt ones such as fence line Perimeter Intrusion Detection System (PIDS) and infra red lighting on fully functional Pan Tilt Zoom (PTZ) CCTV.
- The provision of vehicle access control measures.
- The deployment of a well trained and motivated guard force.
- Internal CCTV coverage within reception areas and loading docks.

2.2 Detection

Should someone wish to target a particular site, there should be a high probability that they will be detected. This may be during a reconnaissance/planning stage by a determined criminal, or while in the process of committing a crime. Detection can be achieved through measures that include:

- A PIDS system on a perimeter fence that will detect cutting and climbing attacks.
- CCTV linked to PIDS to provide verification of the cause of an alarm.
- Fully functional PTZ cameras with a day and night capability to track attackers attempting to breach a fence line or building envelope.
- Detection system on external doors, access hatches and glazed services
- CCTV slaved to detection to provide verification of the cause of an alarm on any of these detectors.
- Access control and intruder detection on designated doors and rooms within buildings.
- Facilities for the screening of visitors.

2.3 Delay

Measures should be in place that are sufficient to slow an attacker down and to prevent an attack succeeding prior to a response being mounted by the security personnel or police. It therefore follows that speed of response must be linked to the delay that can be imposed through the use, for example, of appropriate external door and window sets.

2.4 Response

There must be a capability to respond to incidents or potential incidents rapidly. This may be by security or FM personnel or by the police, and can be achieved through:

- well-understood internal reporting systems for staff;
- local security control rooms;
- automatic response generated from remote monitoring centres.

2.5 Pursuit

In the event of incident in or around a site, sufficient information must be retrievable from electronic systems and manned security personnel to support investigation and, if required, prosecution. This is achieved through:

- the deployment of CCTV cameras specified to achieve 10%, 25%, 50% and 100% screen heights (images of subjects) matched to their location and role;
- the permanent recording and archiving of CCTV images;
- the recording and archiving of access control and intruder detection systems event records;
- the recording of reports by security and other personnel

2.6 Reassurance

Security provision must provide building occupants and visitors with the confidence that they are properly protected without creating an oppressive feel and should also instil confidence in all stakeholders. Measures can include:

- appropriate lighting levels and clear lines of site;
- the use of high reliability access control systems and other security devices with high availability and minimum false alarms;
- deployment of security hardware such as turnstiles and car park access control systems;
- procedures at staff and visitors access points that are efficient and professionally executed.

3 DESIGNING A SYSTEM

3.1 Integration

Security must be considered as a whole to achieve the vision and objectives of a given scheme. Integrated technical, physical and procedural measures, within the context of a threat and risk assessment, should be applied. No one item should be considered in isolation. The physical performance of a fence for example is considered in the context of the threat and risk; the capability of detection and surveillance systems; the ability of security guards to respond; and the policies and procedures that will hold the elements together.

3.2 Security planning

Security requirements should be considered as early as possible within the design process. The earlier it is considered, the more economic and operationally effective the solution. A suggested design process flow chart is shown in Figure 37.1.

3.3 Physical and technical security

The following security measures fall into the category of physical provision. Professional advice should be sought regarding the application and design of such measures which are covered by a myriad of standards and which are discussed in more detail later.

- fences;
- perimeter intruder detection and surveillance;
- electronic access control;
- turnstiles;
- door and window sets;
- internal detection and surveillance;
- fixed and fully functional pan-tilt-zoom cameras;
- fixed cameras viewing points of entry.

The application of these measures will help deliver the following.

3.4 Surveillance and detection

A surveillance and detection plan should be considered for any scheme and will involve the deployment of technology alongside the concepts of natural surveillance and manned security. Surveillance can provide advance warning of an incident; support the management of an ongoing incident; provide a deterrent and

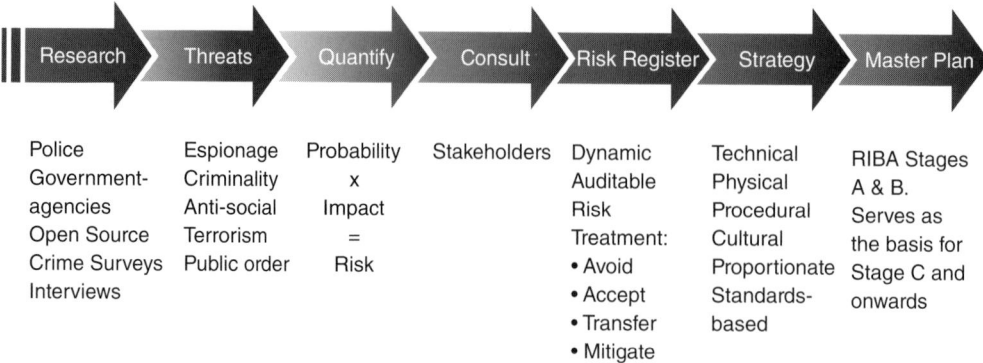

Research	Threats	Quantify	Consult	Risk Register	Strategy	Master Plan
Police	Espionage	Probability	Stakeholders	Dynamic	Technical	RIBA Stages
Government-	Criminality	x		Auditable	Physical	A & B.
agencies	Anti-social			Risk	Procedural	Serves as
Open Source	Terrorism	Impact		Treatment:	Cultural	the basis for
Crime Surveys	Public order	=		• Avoid	Proportionate	Stage C and
Interviews		Risk		• Accept	Standards-	onwards
				• Transfer	based	
				• Mitigate		

37.1 *An incremental approach to security design*

support investigations. Importantly, CCTV can also be used to provide verification of detection system alarms.

3.5 Secure sites/building envelope

The integrity of buildings should be capable of being maintained 24 hours per day and can be achieved through measures that include:

- Robust construction.
- Electronic and physical access control arrangements.
- The surveillance of the building envelope by CCTV linked to detection technologies.
- The positioning of intruder detection on exterior doors and glazing.

3.6 Maintaining internal integrity of buildings

Ensuring that security threats can be kept outside of the building envelope, or within reception zones, is an important principle. The integrity of buildings can be maintained through the screening of visitors at reception areas, electronic access control systems or other local access control arrangements. It can be useful to consider a scheme in terms of security zones, each with their own security levels and standards. Typically zones would be:

- public areas such as building approaches and car parks;
- reception areas;
- operations areas where business is carried out;
- security areas such as data centres.

3.7 Procedural security

General

Technology and physical measures alone will not provide the levels of security required and there will always be a procedural and human element that will tie these measures together. Procedural security is also among the most visible of the elements of security provision and can be stepped up and down very quickly to respond to changing threats.

Scalability

Macro and micro security threat levels can rise and fall and the security posture within a location may need to be capable of being raised and lowered accordingly. Changing security postures can also act as a deterrent by creating uncertainty in the minds of would be aggressors and can serve to keep security personnel focused and motivated.

3.8 Manned security

For certain sites and office locations manned security provision may be appropriate. Manned security can provide a uniformed, visual presence at designated points as a deterrent to criminality and terrorism and to provide reassurance to staff. Typical roles include:

- Operation of security control rooms, surveillance and detection equipment.
- Supervision and control of access control gate lines.
- Patrol of designated areas to detect and deter criminal activity and to provide reassurance.
- Reaction capability to respond to emergencies.

The relationships between the elements of an integrated security system are illustrated in Figure 37.2.

3.9 Standards and compliance

All technical, physical and procedural security should be designed and operated in accordance with the appropriate legislation, regulation and standards (e.g. Data Protection Act (1998), ISO, BS/EN). Where clients such as the MoD or insurers impose particular requirements, these must also be met. There is a wealth of freely

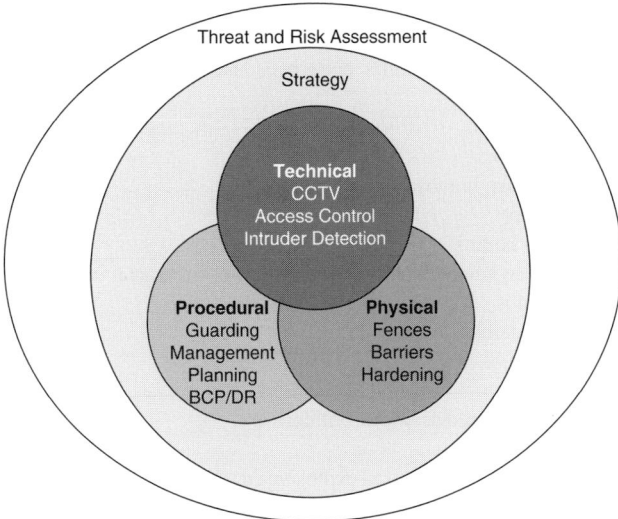

37.2 *Elements of an integrated security system*

available information on security planning, standards, tested products and their application which include:

- Home Office Protecting Crowded Places Suite of Documents (2010)
  - Crowded Places: The Planning System and Counter-Terrorism
  - Protecting Crowded Places; Design and Technical Issues

- National Counter Terrorism Security Office Suite of Guidance Documents
- Secured by Design guides
- Private sector physical security standards:
  - Loss Prevention Certification Board (LPC) List of Approved Fire and Security Products and Services – The 'Red Book'

- Public Sector Standards:
  - Security Equipment Approvals Panel (SEAP) Catalogue of Security Equipment

- BS/EN and ISO

Applicable standards are covered in Appendix 2.

4 COUNTER TERRORISM CONCEPTS AND STANDARDS

Terrorism is the systematic use of terror especially as a means of coercion. An abiding characteristic is the indiscriminate use of violence against non-combatants for the purpose of gaining publicity for a group, cause or individual. The groups and individuals that practise terrorism in any one region will vary over time. Different groups and individuals will have different capabilities and resources, different objectives and different practices, and those of any one group and individual will develop over time. Although risk assessments at any one time can and should be based on current knowledge, a longer term view should also be taken into account when assessing the desirable levels of protection against terrorism for a new building.

The objective of counter-terrorism measures in buildings is to limit damage to the building fabric and injury to the occupants when an explosive device is detonated, and to limit the effectiveness of other forms of terrorist attack on the building and its occupants. They can serve either to reduce the probability of a successful attack or to reduce the consequences of an attack.

4.1 Types of attack and levels of protection

The major terrorist activity that impacts on the built environment is the use of improvised explosives devices (IED) in or near buildings that will cause damage to buildings and injury, possibly fatal injury, to occupants of the buildings and their surroundings.

A wide range of IEDs have been used by terrorists. These include:

- lorry bombs
- van or truck bombs
- car bombs
- suitcase bombs
- pedestrian suicide bombs as waistcoats or rucksacks
- fire bombs
- parcel bombs
- letter bombs.

These show three basic forms of delivery:

- vehicle borne improvised explosives devices (VBIED);
- carried into place, generally inside a building, by a terrorist;
- through third party delivery services such as mail and courier services.

The counter terrorist measures appropriate to reduce the hazard from these different forms of delivery are generally different, and combinations of measures are generally required to protect against all IED threats.

At different locations and different times the relative risk of the different forms of attack will vary, depending on the capability of the currently active terrorist organisations. In locations such as the UK where bulk explosives materials are not easily obtained and access to key ingredients in bulk quantities is controlled, terrorist organisations require high logistical expertise to create large VBIEDs. This is not so critical in locations where explosive materials are readily available.

Subject to these relative risks, VBIEDs present the largest terrorist hazard to buildings and their occupants, as they are capable of causing extensive damage and risk to occupants across whole buildings and multiple buildings, and are capable of causing major damage and extreme risk to a building in close proximity. Counter terrorist measures to mitigate the consequences of VBIEDS may include:

- Hostile vehicle mitigation including barrier systems to keep vehicle bombs at a distance from the building.
- Location of delivery bays and visitor car parks to keep uncontrolled vehicles as far as possible from the building, and particularly out of basements.
- Access control, moving blockers and search facilities for vehicles allowed to approach or enter.
- Avoidance of features in the building at exposed positions that will enhance the blast loading from an explosion, e.g. re-entrant corners.
- Avoidance of features in the building at exposed positions that will reduce the strength, e.g. transfer structures at first floor with widely spaced ground floor columns.
- Enhancement of the building structure, particularly at ground and first floor level, to limit structural damage and prevent disproportionate or progressive structural collapse.
- Choice of facade design to reduce glazing area on exposed facades.
- Enhancement of glazed facades to reduce the risk of hazardous glazing fragments in the building, and to reduce any blast pressures entering the building.
- Choice of layout within the building to place low occupancy spaces at the exposed perimeter as a buffer area to the high occupancy spaces.
- Preparation of shelter areas within the building into which occupants can be evacuated in the event of a warning of immanent threat, in conjunction with suitable means of warning.

Smaller IEDs need to be closer to the building to cause a similar level of damage and hazard, and the damage will be more localised. Terrorists may try to detonate the IEDs inside the building, so visitor access control becomes critical. Counter terrorist measures to mitigate the consequences of carried or worn IEDs may include:

- Staff entrance separate from visitor entrance with pass and PIN entry control to reduce numbers at risk from visitors.
- Visitor reception and inspection in a dedicated satellite block separate from, but linked to, the main building.
- Baggage and visitor search and scan facilities on entry.
- Multiple search and entry lanes with protection between to reduce numbers at risk.
- Design of satellite block to vent internal package explosion.
- Security guards and suitable procedures and training.
- Blast and fragment protection to guard and reception positions when not directly interacting with visitors.
- Pedestrian access with external approach channelled perpendicular to facades rather than against the facades.
- Avoid locations where packages can be concealed close to or against the ground floor facade.
- Avoid deep and/or flat external windowsills at ground floor level where packages can be left placed against glazing.

Parcel or letter bombs may be delivered by innocent postmen or couriers mixed up with innocent deliveries. Bulk scanning of mail and other deliveries and inspection of deliveries too large for the scanner is required if such devices are to be excluded from the building. Counter terrorist measures to mitigate the consequences of delivered devices may include:

- Mail and delivery scanner located in the building.
- Scanner room on an external or courtyard face to vent internal blast outwards.
- Blast resistant container provided for suspect packages.
- Low occupancy buffer areas in rooms around the scanner room.
- Enhanced floor, walls, ceiling and door of the scanner room to avoid venting into the building.
- Mail and delivery scanning in a remote facility. This facility could serve more than one building. All deliveries to be made to the facility, and items to be transferred to the building after scanning in controlled vehicles only.

Other common forms of attack include the use of IEDs against public transport such as planes, trains and buses or against private motor vehicles and the use of firearms or other weapons against people, whether in the street, in vehicles or in buildings. These may affect buildings as collateral damage, even though they were not targeted at the building or its occupants. In general these are likely to be of less significance to the building design than a deliberate attack on the building, except for buildings that form part of the transport system such as airport terminals and railway stations. However, transportation threats may set a lower threshold for otherwise low risk buildings. For example, in the light of the London attacks in July 2007 it may be desirable to consider a pedestrian suicide bomb in the street as the minimum threat to be considered for any building on a bus route.

Less common but not unknown are chemical, biological, radiological or nuclear (CBRN) terrorist attacks. These are attacks on people using a vector carried usually in the air, but possibly also in the water supply. The building fabric will not be directly affected, but if the ventilation or water system has been used as a means of dispersion or distribution the contamination of the building may be a major problem.

Military level CBRN protection uses special charcoal filters for incoming air and positive pressurisation, or complete closedown with oxygen supply and carbon dioxide scrubbers. Entry and exit is very restricted requiring airlock and decontamination facilities and special clothing.

This is very expensive and disruptive, and is limited to a few specialist buildings. For most buildings in the public or private sector, full CBRN protection is not warranted. However, some precautions in the design of ventilation systems can reduce the vulnerability of a building without ensuring complete protection. These may include:

- Separate ventilation system for visitor reception.
- Separate ventilation system for mail scanner room.
- Dual air intakes at high and low level that can be closed from the security control room depending on CBRN attack vector – aircraft or ground released.
- Ventilation mode to pressurise building by increasing input fan and recirculation and reducing exhaust fan – to be implemented from security control room.

The alternative choices, combinations and levels of counter terrorist measures considered suitable for any particular building will depend on the risk assessment, the dual purpose measures that will be implemented anyway for other reasons, the available budget and the acceptability of the residual risks. It is not expected that all terrorist risks can be eliminated, but by prioritising the appropriate protective measures the overall residual risks can be minimised.

Many protective measures will have little or no financial cost if they are incorporated from the start in the site masterplan and the building layout, but would be very expensive to implement at a later stage, either as a change in construction or a retrofit. Some active measures such as body and baggage search can be adjusted to match the current threat level, but only if provision for them has been made in the design, in the form of space and power supplies at the appropriate location in the visitor reception.

Early consideration of counter terrorism needs and the constraints that they may impose on other aspects of design is desirable to produce a building with an appropriate and flexible level of protection.

4.2 Blast loading on structures and facades

Blast waves are shock waves in air initially travelling away from the source, and are caused by a sudden release of energy, for example by the detonation of a chemical explosive. The blast wave takes the form of an abrupt rise from atmospheric pressure to a peak pressure, and then a rapid but gradual reduction in pressure back to atmospheric pressure (the positive phase), followed by a longer period of reduced pressure that eventually returns to atmospheric pressure (the negative phase). The positive and negative impulses are the areas under the overpressure-time curve over the positive and negative phases respectively.

The parameters of a blast wave depend on the quantity of blast energy, that is the mass of explosives, and the distance from the source. The parameters can be related to a unit charge using a scaling factor equal to the cube root of the explosives weight, and evaluated for a given scaled range, that is the range divided by the scaling factor. For example, a charge eight times as big at twice the range will produce the same peak pressure over twice the time and hence produce twice the impulse.

Different explosives materials release different energy, and so will produce different blast levels. These are often related to trinitrotoluene (TNT) as a 'standard' explosive. Many military explosives are more powerful than TNT, but many home made explosives (HME) used in IEDs are sensitive to variations in manufacture, and can vary from failure to detonate at all to power greater than TNT. In many cases a TNT equivalent of IEDs has been assessed from the extent of damage caused.

As a shock wave expands from a detonation it interacts with obstructions, reflecting off exposed faces and refracting around corners to load non-exposed faces. A blast wave moving parallel to a face is not modified, but exerts a transient load equal to the pressure history on the face. Reflection of a blast wave from near perpendicular faces amplifies the pressures in the air against the face, and hence the loading on the face. For intense shocks the positive pressures can be amplified by reflection factors up to 8, but for weak shocks the reflection factor will be just over 2, and the reflection factor of the negative phase will be less than 2.

For simple geometries of an air burst with no interaction before reaching the building, or a ground burst with interaction only with the ground, blast parameters can be interpolated by experienced blast engineers from accumulated blast trial data, using charts or simple computer programs. More complex streetscapes may include multiple and oblique reflections, refraction and clearing of reflected waves. Blast loading can be calculated numerically by an analyst modelling blast wave propagation in three dimensional models using Hydrocode or advanced Computational Fluid Dynamics (CFD) software.

For counter terrorist design, IED threats are commonly identified as a TNT equivalent charge size at a given stand-off range. However a common alternative approach is to specify a peak positive pressure and impulse. For a simple geometry, including for blast trials of cladding, these will have a one-to-one correspondence with a ground burst charge size and stand-off range from a building. For analysis the blast loadings are often simplified to a triangular pressure-time distribution and the negative phase ignored, although this may be conservative for some types of analysis and cannot assess rebound reactions.

For high risk buildings that are likely to be a direct target, a security risk analysis should identify specific locations where different charges might be placed taking account of different security measures such as access control and hostile vehicle mitigation, and the building structure and facade can then be designed to provide an appropriate level of protection from these site specific blast threats. For lower risk buildings where the probability of direct attack is small, some risks such as a lorry VBIED may not be designed against at the closest approach. Instead, design may be based on a generic threat level, say a car VBIED at 30m, and the possibility of a larger charge at this range or this charge at a closer range can be accepted as a residual risk.

The blast tests specified in BS EN ISO 16933 for arena blast testing of glass are increasingly being specified as generic threat levels, such as EXV25, with a peak pressure of 80 kPa and an impulse of 380 kPa.ms. This allows products that have been successfully tested to that level already to be offered for inclusion in the building without further blast testing.

Typical reflected blast loading on large facades from ground bursts that might be specified for design of blast resistant facades are given in Table I.

Threats would have to be significantly closer for these charges to be likely to cause failures of modern framed structures. Table II

Table I Typical blast threats requiring enhanced facade glazing

Threat	Charge size	Stand-off range	Scaled range	Peak positive pressure	Positive impulse
	kg TNT	m	m.kg$^{-1/3}$	kPa	kPa.ms
Lorry VBIED	1000	100	10	31.5	593
Car VBIED	100	25	5.39	87.1	537
Suitcase IED	25	10	3.42	236	564
Package IED	5	5	2.92	354	486

Table II Typical blast threats at the threshold of damage to conventional framed structures

Threat	Charge size	Stand-off range	Scaled range	Peak positive pressure	Positive impulse
	kg TNT	m	m.kg$^{-1/3}$	kPa	kPa.ms
Lorry VBIED	1000	40	4	162	1612
Car VBIED	100	10	2.15	846	1543
Suitcase IED	25	4	1.37	3334	1713
Package IED	5	1.5	0.88	11480	1808

shows the order of threats likely to cause limited damage to modern structural frames not designed for blast resistance. Significant damage could be expected in non-framed buildings subject to this level of loading.

Blast loading can be taken to fall into three types:

- Relatively small charges close in have total loading times much shorter than the response times of the target structures and facades. These loadings are called impulsive, and the degree of damage is likely to be related to the net impulse. For small scaled ranges the negative phase impulse will be substantially smaller than the positive phase impulse, and the net impulse will be a substantial proportion of the positive impulse. However, a larger charge at the same scaled range will cause the same degree of damage over a larger area which will cause a greater extent of damage.
- Very large charges at long ranges with positive phases much longer than the response time produce quasi-static loading where the damage is controlled by the peak pressure. However, this is more typical of petrochemical or distant nuclear explosions than IEDs.
- Between these extreme cases are dynamic loadings where both the impulse and the peak pressure will influence the response and a dynamic analysis is required to determine the response. The negative loading may have a significant effect.

In addition to the shock wave, a chemical explosion will produce an increase in air pressure due to the conversion of the explosives to gas and the heating of the air by the total energy of combustion, which is normally the combined energy of the shock wave and the afterburn that produces a fireball. In the open this residual gas pressure dissipates rapidly and does not increase the loading on structures. However, if the explosion is confined, the residual gas pressure will vent slowly and will produce a quasi-static loading on the confining surfaces in addition to the blast loading, which in itself will be amplified by multiple reflections. Even with moderate opening areas to vent the gas the gas impulse may overcome the negative phase of the blast and produce a positive impulse several times the enhanced blast impulse. Open venting area equal to one full side of a cubic volume, that is, $Volume^{2/3}$ is required for the gas pressure to dissipate as fast as the blast.

This gas pressure, combined with the multiple blast reflections, can result in much increased structural damage from a charge that explodes internally compared to the same charge outside the building. This is the reason that uncontrolled vehicle entry into basements for parking or delivery should be avoided, and why visitor entry control and delivery scanners should be external, or on an external face to allow rapid venting.

Design of a panel to resist external blast loading and yet to vent rapidly after an internal explosion is a careful balance using lightweight materials, and such a panel is likely to be substantially different from the normal building facade. Incorporating visitor entry or scanner rooms into the main structure will often require structural strengthening and compromises of appearance to maintain safety.

4.3 Structural robustness and disproportionate collapse

Large charges close to a conventional building will overwhelm the closest facades, generally on the lowest floor or two, and will cause local damage to the structure, most commonly to one or more ground floor columns at the perimeter. The structural design of the building will determine whether the immediate blast damage is the total damage, or whether the loss of structural support will cause further structural failures in the building, resulting in a progressive collapse of part or all of the building that may be completely disproportionate to the original blast damage.

Even large VBIEDS close outside modern multi-storey framed buildings will not normally cause immediate collapse due to blast

loading. The loads are of very short duration and arrival times are staggered up the building. The mass of multiple floors is very large and will result in very limited overall response, often smaller than the sway expected in high rise buildings from a 3 second gust wind loading. In general, bracing systems for substantial buildings do not need to be considered for blast, and even in lightweight buildings with steel bracing the requirements are normally for stronger fixings rather than increased member strength. The large mass of the soil around foundations results in negligible blast response at ground level, and the effect of blast on foundations can be ignored provided the fixings of directly loaded members such as perimeter columns are adequate.

In extreme cases an internal detonation can demolish a substantial building, as was the case for the US Marine Barracks in Beirut in October 1983, where a 5.4 tonne TNT equivalent VBIED entered the building before detonating, causing complete collapse and 241 fatalities. However, this can best be prevented by Hostile Vehicle Mitigation to keep vehicles at a distance, designing out basement delivery bays and car parks close to loadbearing structure and entry control and inspection of vehicles that are allowed past the perimeter. Structural design to resist a major internal explosion is not likely to be an economic solution.

Disproportionate collapse of all or part of a building risks a major increase in fatalities and serious injuries, above those caused directly by the blast, and so is unacceptable. There are three main routes to avoid progressive collapse, often applied in combination:

- Prevent local failure of the structure, for example by increasing standoff from explosions or designing the ground floor columns to resist the blast loading without failure (although not necessarily without damage).
- Provide alternative load paths in the structure that can support the upper structure even if one or several adjacent ground floor columns are removed by analysing the structure with columns removed.
- Use prescriptive rules in structural Codes of Practice that are intended to provide alternative load paths in a damaged structure, that is, tying rules.

The robustness of a building is its insensitivity to local failure, which is provided by the second and third routes above. The standards for robustness in British buildings were set following the collapse of a full height corner of the 22-storey Ronan Point in May 1968 following a domestic gas explosion on the eighteenth floor, with four fatalities. These standards are incorporated into UK Building Regulations, and means of satisfying these standards have been incorporated into structural Codes of Practice. They are aimed at general robustness rather than specifically at bomb blast loading. Similar rules have been adopted in many other countries.

Loadbearing masonry buildings without vertical ties are inherently less robust because breach of the weakest parts of the facade (i.e. doors and windows) and blast entry causes uplift of the floors and roof, which removes lateral support to the loadbearing walls, allowing them to displace so that they cannot support the floors and roof against gravity afterwards. This is illustrated by the complete collapse of St Ethelbura's church 70 m from a 1 tonne bomb in Bishopsgate, London in April 1993, while framed buildings nearer to the detonation remained standing, even with column damage, and were reparable. Loadbearing masonry construction should be avoided for high risk buildings.

Because attack by VBIEDs will normally only occur at street level, some additional measures can be applied to enhance robustness of framed buildings under bomb blast loading. These are:

- Design the first floor slab and beams for reversal of gravity floor loading due to blast entering the ground floor and lifting the floor.
- Provide enhanced shear reinforcement at closer centres in perimeter ground floor columns to make the columns more ductile and less likely to fail catastrophically by shear.

- Provide main bracing systems for the building distributed in plan so that only part of the bracing system in any direction can be damaged by close proximity to a VBIED.

With the exception of increasing the standoff, most of this is the work of the structural engineer or a specialist blast engineer. However, these requirements should inform the architect's design, which should not work against them. For example, the use of a transfer structure at first floor level and fewer ground floor columns in the Alfred Murrah Building in Oklahoma reduced the alternative load paths, without the remaining columns being capable to resist blast loading. Failure of two or three adjacent ground floor columns on one face of the building under bomb blast in April 1995 resulted in a substantial part of the building collapsing with 168 fatalities.

4.4 Blast resistance of facades

The primary concern for blast resistance of facades is to prevent fragments of glass entering the building and injuring people. Monolithic annealed window glass is the weakest part of any building facade, breaks easily into jagged fragments and is ubiquitous in the built environment. As a result, glass fragments are the greatest source of injury in a blast in a built-up area. Glazing injuries can occur for hundreds of metres around a VBIED explosion, while other incidents may cause structural damage and direct blast injuries occur only within tens of metres of the explosion.

There are two possible solutions to the risk of glass fragments caused by blast. The first is to design the glazing not to break. However, for IED explosions this can result in very thick glazing that causes very high reaction forces on the window frame, which requires very strong structural supports back to the building frame. This may result in uneconomic facades that are not a realistic option for most buildings. This approach is normally required for quasi-static blast loads such as petrochemical explosions, but the low peak pressures make this design economic.

In-plane reactions from uncracked glass are small, so gasket, silicone and glazing tape bonding are all suitable, but the inwards and rebound reactions are very high, so the frames have to be very strong. One way spanning glass is less stiff and deflects further before cracking, and so may be beneficial for an uncracked design.

Bolted laminated glass systems have little strength at the concentrated supports after cracking, so bolted systems should be designed to remain uncracked under blast loading. However, bolted glazing systems will be substantially weaker than edge supported glazing, and are generally not recommended for blast resistant glazing.

The alternative solution is to design glazing that retains the glass fragments after the glass cracks. For new construction, this can best be provided by using a PVB laminated glass inner leaf in the glazing system, adequately anchored to the frame. Under blast-loading the inner leaf cracks and the PVB interlayer stretches, adsorbing energy and catching the fragments of the outer leaf if double glazing is used. This results in a lower reaction over a longer period that is easier for the frame and supports to resist, together with an in-plane reaction that tries to pull the glazing from the frame, so anchorage of the glazing into the frame is important to generate the full resistance of the laminated glass.

A similar behaviour is possible with application of anti-shatter film on the inside of existing glazing, but the limited possibilities for anchorage of the film and the limited strength of frames not designed to resist the reactions tends to limit the performance to the lower levels of blast protection. Unanchored anti-shatter film has frequently been applied to existing glazing and affords a limited enhancement in protection, mostly by bringing the velocity of glass fragments down to the mean velocity and reducing the exposure of sharp points and edges. The acrylic adhesives are degraded by ultra-violet light, so modern anti-shatter film has a useful life of about 10 to 15 years depending on exposure.

The outer leaf of a double glazed unit can be annealed, heat strengthened or toughened glass. The choice may have some effect on blast resistance, but will not be critical provided the inner leaf is laminated, as debris from a failed outer leaf can ride on the inner leaf and be expelled when the inner leaf rebounds. The choice of glass type is likely to be driven by other considerations like impact resistance, thermal shock or security against intrusion. Laminated glass can also be used in the outer leaf, but the performance of the PVB interlayers against blast may be reduced by high temperatures in the outer leaf, particularly if the glazing included thermal coatings.

Blast resistance is not fully standardised, so design threats tend to be site or client specific. Minimum standard threat levels for low risk UK government buildings are covered by recipe designs, with 6 mm toughened outer glazing and 6.8 mm thick laminated glass in conventionally designed metal frames. For more severe blast levels, blast testing or dynamic analysis informed by blast testing is the norm, using laminated glass with at least a 1.5 mm thick PVB interlayer and solid gaskets at least 30 mm deep or structural silicone at least 20 mm deep to anchor the glass in the frame. Fragility curves for a range of glass construction have been created by the Home Office for panes supported along all four edges. Derived from extensive testing, these are based on only two sizes of window pane, but provide an initial idea of performance. Glass is expected to crack, but the vast majority of fragments are expected to remain bonded to the interlayer. The interlayer will stretch as it deflects, adsorbing energy and slowing the response. Laminated glass has been demonstrated to deflect up to 32 per cent of the shorter span under blast loading without failure.

Gasket systems hold cracked laminated glass in position by framing and/or cover plates on both faces while a compression ring forms in the cracked glass to resist the tension in the PVB interlayer. This is only possible with support on all four edges of a glass pane. For windows of about 2 m^2 in size and aspect ratios up to about 1.5, blast tests have shown that stiff gaskets 30 mm deep will always provide adequate support and some systems with 25 mm deep gaskets may also be adequate. However, deeper gaskets and frame bites may be required for larger panes or higher aspect ratios. Gasket support of cracked glass is not amenable to calculation, and so needs to be demonstrated by blast testing.

Some structural silicones have been subjected to high strain rate laboratory testing that allows the strength of silicone anchorages to be calculated. Suitable silicone depths start from about 20 mm. Silicone supports are not sensitive to the size or aspect ratio of the glass, but are sensitive to the total thickness of PVB in the glazing make-up. Silicone can be used to provide single sided support against blast loading, but the silicone will also have to be designed for long-term support of the glass weight.

Blast trials of silicone attached curtain walling underpin the design approach, but new tests are not necessarily required for different cases.

Structural silicone can be used to support cracked one-way spanning laminated glass against blast loading on two opposite edges. However, slender glass plies must be avoided as they can cause failure of the silicone before the last ply cracks. Some modern glazing tapes at 25 mm width have been successfully tested to support glazing against moderate blast levels, but this is still under development and designs will currently need to be verified by testing.

For single windows piercing a stronger facade (e.g. masonry), frame enhancement only requires an increased bite to anchor the glazing and adequate fixings to resist the reaction and the in-plane tension in the PVB interlayer. For multi-panel windows or curtain walling, the transoms and mullions that span between supports will also require either to be designed dynamically for reaction from the glazing or proven by blast trials, but plastic deformation is permitted. Loadbearing structural supports of multi-bay glazing, such as columns that support the facade and roof, may also require to be designed dynamically for glazing reaction or blast loading, but should remain elastic.

Multi-bay glazing may be supported by a non-loadbearing secondary structure back to the main structure. When this works purely in bending it can be designed by dynamic analysis and allowed to undergo plastic yielding. However, some structures are designed to work as a truss with axially loaded members, or as a mixed system with both axial and bending forces on the members. These must be designed to remain elastic under the blast loading, and buckling of compressive members will need to be considered. Static buckling capacity limits are conservative but can be applied to linear dynamic analysis. Dynamic buckling assessment will require a nonlinear transient analysis which is very onerous. Specialist blast design advice should be sought as early as possible.

Where vulnerable supports such as glass fins or external fins prone to lateral-torsional buckling are used to support blast resistant glazing against normal loading, it may be necessary to incorporate secondary support systems such as cables to provide an alternative support path under blast loading. These in turn may impose large concentrated reactions on the building structure locally. Specialist blast design advice should be sought as early as possible.

Blast glazing design and materials are still developing rapidly, and various alternative solutions such as polycarbonate or glass clad polycarbonate glazing, ionoplast interlayers and cast plastic glazing materials are at different levels of development, experience and acceptability. Most of these are significantly more expensive than PVB laminated glass, and have additional issues such as deeper bites or larger reaction forces that need to be resolved. Specialist blast design advice should be sought before any of these alternatives are proposed.

Masonry facades are less vulnerable to blast than most glazing, but tend to resist blast primarily by inertia rather than strength. For a pressure high enough to crack the masonry, increasing impulse levels will cause more damage up to the collapse threshold. Injury can be caused by falling masonry debris even at low velocities. Some indicative capacities at the threshold of failure for brickwork or dense concrete blockwork are shown in Table III for well-supported storey height masonry panels. There will be significant variation around these values for panel sizes, support conditions and window openings. Lightweight blockwork will be more vulnerable.

Table III Indicative blast capacities of brickwork and dense blockwork

Masonry thickness Mm	Threshold pressure kPa	Collapse impulse kPa.ms
112	55	620
225 or 280 cavity wall	110	1240
340	165	1860

Facades of precast concrete cladding or structural reinforced concrete walls behind architectural cladding can be designed to resist substantially greater blast loading on a case-by-case basis, and should be the preferred choices where close-in VBIEDs are an expected threat, such as at vehicle entry control facilities. These facades can also offer substantial resistance to entrance of primary fragments from the device and secondary fragments of the delivery vehicle.

4.5 Blast testing of glazing

Blast testing of glazing systems is common, using either an explosives charge in front of a glazing unit (arena testing) or a focused shock wave created in a shock tube either by a small quantity of explosives or by compressed air and a bursting membrane. The standards on Arena and Shock tube testing, ISO 16933 and ISO 16934 strictly speaking cover testing of standard sized glazing in a frame of standard detail. In practice, the pressure and impulse combinations from these standards are also applied to systems of various sizes made with proprietary systems, and the fragment hazard. Threats in arena tests that represent VBIEDS are given in Table IV, while threats that represent package bombs are given in Table V. Comparable but not identical sets of tests apply to shock tube tests.

Table IV Arena blast test classification representing VBIEDs

Classification code	Mean airblast pressure kPa	Mean positive phase impulse kPa.ms	Approximate Equivalent TNT charge for a large facade	
			Charge size kg	Stand-off m
EXV45	30	180	30	32
EXV33	50	250	30	23
EXV25	80	380	40	19
EXV19	140	600	64	17
EXV15	250	850	80	14.4
EXV12	450	1200	100	12.4
EXV10	800	1600	125	11

Table V Arena blast test classification representing package IEDs

Classification code	Mean airblast pressure kPa	Mean positive phase impulse kPa.ms	Nominal TNT charge for a 2.4m × 2.4m cubicle			Nominal equivalent TNT charge for a large facade	
			Charge size kg	Charge level m	Stand-off m	Charge size kg	Stand-off m
SB1	70	150	3	0.5	9	3.25	9.0
SB2	110	200	3	0.5	7	3.5	7.26
SB3	250	300	3	0.5	5	3.5	5.07
SB4	800	500	3	0.5	3	3.7	3.4
SB5	700	700	12	0.8	5.5	12	5.26
SB6	1600	1000	12	0.8	4	12.6	4.06
SB7	2800	1500	20	0.8	4	21.0	4.0

These arena tests are designed to be conducted using charges of no more than 100 kg TNT equivalent so that they can be conducted at any trial site licensed for that quantity of explosives. The number in the classification code represents the approximate stand-off in metres for a 100 kg TNT charge to produce the listed loading on a standard test sample mounted on the front of a 3 m × 3 m testing cubicle.

The reduction in impulse due to clearing around the edges of the support structure is taken into account in these values, so the same pressure/impulse combination would be produced by a different sized charge at a different range in front of a large facade with no clearing. However the loading at short range is impulsive so the damage is representative of that produced by a similar impulse but lower pressure produced by a larger charge at greater range.

The EXV 45 test was included to assess non-anchored anti-shatter film, and is not normally used to assess laminated glazing.

Because the package bombs will be at close range to smaller parts of a building facade, the fragment threat applies to smaller numbers of people and they therefore represent lower risks. It is rarely economically justified to undertake both VBIED and package IED testing for the same facade.

Shock tubes can produce an approximately triangular pressure-time history closely resembling the positive phase of a blast wave, but cannot produce a significant negative blast wave. They are therefore suitable either for impulsive short duration tests where the shock tube impulse can be compared to the net impulse from a charge at a low scale range, or long duration loading approaching quasi-static, where the peak response will occur before the end of the positive phase. They are least suited for the intermediate dynamic blast tests where the timing of the negative phase in a real blast will have a significant effect on the results.

Shock tubes generate a focused shock wave over a limited aperture. The equipment is more complex than for arena tests but requires less space. The number of shock tubes capable of emulating IED and VBIED blast over an aperture large enough to accommodate whole windows is small world wide, and there are currently none in the UK. The largest apertures are currently 3 m × 3 m, which cannot test full storey height glazing units.

In contrast, there are support structures available for arena tests that can support storey high curtain wall units or multi-bay test

Table VI Fragment hazard ratings from blast trials

Hazard rating	Hazard rating description	Definition
A	No break	No fracture or visible damage
B	No hazard	The glazing fractures but the inner leaf is fully retained in the frame with no breach or material loss from the interior surface
C	Minimal hazard	The glazing fractures but the inner leaf shall be substantially retained with total length of tears and edge pullout less than 50 % of the glazing perimeter (or more if firmly anchored and designed to pull out), plus • No more than 3 perforations in the witness panel • Sum total united dimensions of fragments between 1m and 3 m from glazing no greater than 250 mm • Glass dust and slivers with sum total dimensions less than 25mm are not counted as fragments
D	Very low hazard	The glazing fractures and significant parts are located no more than 1 m behind the glazing line, plus fragments as for rating C
E	Low hazard	The glazing fractures and fragments or the whole of the glazing fall beyond 1 m and up to 3 m behind the glazing line and not more than 0.5m above the floor at the witness panel, plus • No more than 10 perforations in the witness panel above 0.5 m • None of the perforations penetrate more than 12 mm.
F	High hazard	• more than 10 perforations in the witness panel above 0.5 m • One or more perforations more than 12 mm deep

facades up to about 10m high and 20+m long. Damage is assessed in terms of fragment positions inside the testing cubicle with a Styrofoam witness panel to intercept fragments 3m behind the glazing, as listed in Table VI.

BS EN 13123:2004 and the DIN standard from which it was derived have effectively been superseded by the ISO standards, but some existing test results may be based on it. The tests EXR1 to EXR5 closely resemble tests SB3 to SB7, but the hazard rating approach is different.

The ASTM F 1642 test specification is based on a late draft of the ISOs and contains effectively the same tests, but requires three tests for a certificate and has small but significant differences in the definitions of the hazard ratings. Some tests may also be aimed at meeting the US GSA blast standards. For these, the pressure-impulse combinations are different and may require a larger charge, but the hazard rating is similar in principal but different in definition and nomenclature.

Most common are Arena tests to the EXV test standards that are representative of 100 kg TNT charges at stand-off ranges between 45 m and 10 m from the sample. If the required level of protection for a building is specified, such as to meet EXV25(E), then manufacturers can provide reports on systems that achieved this performance in test, can test their systems to this standard or can provide dynamic analyses to demonstrate that their proposed systems should meet this performance.

The performance of a glazing system will depend on the size and proportions of the panes, so test results need to be for samples of a similar size. Test results for isolated windows are fairly common, and for panels with a mixture of opening lights or doors and fixed lights are available, but test results for storey height curtain wall panels are much rarer, as the test samples become more expensive to manufacture and support.

Tests for multi-storey, multi-bay facades have been conducted for a few facade designs. These are very expensive and primarily

evaluate the supporting structure rather than the glazing units. For most facades the supporting structure can be evaluated by analysis so these tests are normally only considered for unusual supporting systems.

4.6 Bomb shelter areas and buffer zones

It is usually impractical to design a building to provide complete protection from all feasible terrorist blast threats, so most buildings leave a residual risk for occupants from the whole range of terrorist attacks. However, not all parts of a building will be equally vulnerable.

In the event of a warning of an imminent attack, the overall risk of injury and fatality can be minimised if the occupants of the building are temporarily moved to the least vulnerable parts of the building. This inwards evacuation of a building in the event of a bomb warning is more appropriate in the first instance than an outwards evacuation of a building which could take people into greater danger, particularly when the location of the bomb is still unknown.

Locations in a building identified or created as areas of low vulnerability are referred to as bomb shelter areas or protected spaces. In offices and similar buildings it is recommended that sufficient shelter areas are identified or created to accommodate all the building occupants temporarily and an inwards evacuation strategy be developed and practised, comparable to the fire evacuation strategy.

UK government recommendations for shelter areas include:

- 0.6 m² of floor area per person expected to use that shelter, but greater preferred.
- Ideally at least one per floor, but with maximum 90 m travel distance from any point.
- Reasonable access to toilet facilities (toilets can be part of the shelter area).
- Reasonable access to normal escape routes.
- Shelter areas can include staircases at 1.0 m² per person, but some unobstructed staircases desirable.
- Provision of adequate ventilation, perhaps by activation of smoke extract ventilation for shelter areas in enclosed spaces.
- PA from control room (also to shelter area standard) and telephone feedback.
- Located in the most robust parts of the building, ideally within solid internal walls or blast enhanced partitions.
- Remote from:
  o Extensive glazed elevations
  o External doors
  o Underground car parks
  o Gas and fuel lines and bulk storage
  o Areas prone to progressive collapse
  o Top floors under weak roof construction
  o Areas exposed to high blast and direct fragment hazard

- Ideally shelter areas should provide protection levels of:
  o Internal pressures less than 35 kPa (eardrum rupture threshold)
  o Doors to withstand a blast impulse of 450 kPa.ms
  o Glazing fragment hazard less than High Hazard
  o Shielded against perforation by primary fragments of the bomb and secondary fragments from the vehicle
  o No structural collapse and protected from falling debris

In many cases, areas that cannot offer the full specification will still afford substantial protection and are often termed deficient shelter areas. For example, in open plan offices the enclosed areas of toilets, staircases, lift lobbies and kitchens will often not offer enough area behind walls or partitions that resist fragments.

However, with a deep floor plate, the core open plan area can be substantially protected from fragments from an explosion on the ground. The fragments penetrate at a rising angle, and fast fragments hit the ceiling, while slow fragments fall back to the floor before penetrating deeply. Similarly, for buildings with road access only at the front, open plan area behind the core but remote from the rear glazing may also be protected from fragments, even on the ground floor.

These areas may provide adequate shelter areas even though not enclosed. Glass walled meeting rooms in such locations may also be adequate provided the glazing is either laminated or toughened and fitted with anti-shatter film. Shelter areas are only of use if a suitable warning will be received and acted upon in the event of an immediate bomb risk. A number of police forces offer a warning service by automated messaging services to subscribing building managers. Procedures then need to be in place to call for an inwards evacuation when a valid warning is received.

In the 1980s and 1990s many bomb attacks were aimed at damage and disruption rather than fatalities, and bomb warnings by the terrorists were common. Now that the risk of suicide VBIEDs without warning is significant, police would need to have warnings from their intelligence sources that a bomb was in play and have a good idea of its target to call a warning in the vicinity. In these circumstances the benefits of shelter areas are reduced.

An alternative approach for high risk buildings is to provide buffer zones on the vulnerable periphery of the building, effectively turning most of the building into a large protected space. A wall or secure partition at the back of the buffer zone can provide additional blast protection and protection from bomb fragments and high hazard glass fragments if the main facade is overloaded.

Depending on the circumstances, the buffer zone may be unused dead space, sacrificed to give enhanced protection, could be used as unoccupied window display space, or could be filled with low occupancy spaces such as toilets, storerooms, plant rooms and service risers. These will provide both an increased stand-off of the occupied spaces from the charge, and space behind the visible facade to provide additional lines of protection to attenuate close-in blast affects, for example from a VBIED in the street immediately outside. This concept may have significant benefits in refurbishing existing buildings to enhance resistance to attack.

For high threat environments this concept can also be used to plan new inherently protected buildings. One example would be inwards facing courtyard buildings, with a shallow layer of low occupancy rooms around the outside perimeter and a circulation corridor between these and the main occupied spaces around the courtyard. The external facade would require only moderate glazing area, giving a less vulnerable facade, and the two corridor wall lines could be used to provide additional protection around the occupied space. The courtyard facades would be loaded only by indirect blast refracting over the building, and could be extensively clad with blast resistant glazing.

5 REFERENCES

The definition of terrorism, C.L. Ruby, *Analyses of Social Issues and Public Policy*, 2002, pp 9–14.

BS EN ISO 16933:2007 Glass in buildings – Explosion resistant security glazing – Test and classification for arena air blast loading.

BS EN ISO 16934:2007 Glass in buildings – Explosion resistant security glazing – Test and classification by shock tube loading.

RIBA guidance on designing for counter-terrorism. RIBA, London 2010.

6 SOURCES OF ADVICE

The Centre for Protection of National Infrastructure (CPNI) is a UK government authority which provides protective security advice to businesses and organisations across the national infrastructure. Their advice aims to reduce the vulnerability of the national infrastructure and crowded places to terrorism and other threats (www.cpni.gov.uk).

The National Counter Terrorism Security Office (NaCTSO) is a police unit co-located with CPNI. It trains Police CTSAs and the Argus Professional initiative to raise awareness of designing in counter-terrorism measures at the design stage. Its website includes general sector related guidance (http://www.nactso.gov.uk).

Police Counter Terrorist Security Advisors (CTSA) identify and assess local critical sites within their force area that might be vulnerable to terrorist attack; then devise and develop appropriate protective security plans to minimise impact on that site and the surrounding community. Architectural Liaison Officers (ALO) or Crime Prevention Design Advisors (CPDA) provide advice on crime prevention through the built environment to planners, developers, designers, builders, landlords and estate and facility managers. They will refer you to a CTSA if necessary. They can be contacted via your local police force websites or through www.securedbydesign.com.

The Register of Security Engineers and Specialists (RSES) is sponsored by CPNI and maintained by the Institution of Civil Engineers. The register lists experts who are able to provide a range of advice from initial risk assessment, potential design considerations and solutions, to design detailing and testing in the fields of security and counter-terrorism. The register can provide contacts in consultants that employ these experts (www.ice.org.uk).

7 APPENDIX 1

Security risk register example

RISK REF	ASSET	SITE	THREAT	PROBABILITY	IMPACT				RISK	MITIGATION MEASURES			RESIDUAL RISK (following application of E, D or AM mitigation measures)			RISK OWNER
					DENIAL OF SERVICE	LOSS OF REPUTATION	LOSS OF LIFE	FINANCIAL LOSS		ESSENTIAL	DESIRABLE	ADDITIONAL MEASURES	ESSENTIAL	DESIRABLE	ADDITIONAL MEASURES	
GEN1			TERRORISM - ALL	LIKELY	MAJOR	MAJOR	MAJOR	MAJOR	H	HVMM Security Doors, Turnstiles, Locks EACS, IDS, Guards, Postal Scanners, Hand Searches CCTV, Policies, Training	Hand Held FX Search Equipment, ArchwayFX Detection Equipment	Video Verification on ACS, Crime/Security Analyst, Integrated C1 facility	M	M-L	L	
GEN2			PEOPLE CRIME	POSSIBLE	SIGNIFICANT	SIGNIFICANT	SIGNIFICANT	MINOR	M	Security Doors, Turnstiles, Locks EACS, IDS, Guards, Hand Searches CCTV, Policies, Training	Staff Lockers, cashless vending, staff & contractor vetting	Crime/Security Analyst, Lone Worker Protection Integrated C1 facility	L	MIN	MIN	
GEN3			PROPERTY CRIME	Likely	SIGNIFICANT	MINOR	MINOR	MINOR	M	Security Doors, Turnstiles, Locks EACS, IDS, Guards, Hand Searches CCTV, Policies, Training	Property Marking (DNA Tags) Register	Smartwater, SmokeCloak, RFID Tagging Integrated C1 facility	L	MIN	MIN	
GEN4			ENVIRONMENT	POSSIBLE	SIGNIFICANT	MINOR	MINOR	MINOR	M	CCTV, Policies, Training, Continuity & resillience co-ord & plans		Integrated C1 facility	L	MIN	MIN	
GEN5			SINGLE ISSUE	POSSIBLE	SIGNIFICANT	SIGNIFICANT	SIGNIFICANT	SIGNIFICANT	M	Security Doors, Turnstiles, Locks EACS, IDS, Guards, Hand Searches CCTV, Policies, Training	Intelligence/Screening, Staff & Contractor vetting	Crime/Security Analyst Integrated C1 facility	L	MIN	MIN	
GEN6			CBRN	UNLIKELY	MAJOR	MAJOR	MAJOR	MAJOR	M	Security Doors, Turnstiles, Locks EACS, IDS, Guards, Hand Searches CCTV, Policies, Training	Air Filtration	Air Sampling/Detection Integrated C1 facility	M-L	L	MIN	
GEN7	London Head Office	Canary Wharf	DISORDER	POSSIBLE	SIGNIFICANT	MINOR	MINOR	MINOR	M	Security Doors, Turnstiles, Locks EACS, IDS, Guards, Hand Searches CCTV, Policies, Training	Intelligence & Co-ordination	Crime/Security Analyst Integrated C1 facility	L	MIN	MIN	

8 APPENDIX 2

Physical security concepts and standards

Fences and Walls	Fencing may be used either round a property boundary, or to enclose specific buildings/areas within a larger site. The function of fencing falls into two general categories – (a) demarcation of property boundary only OR (b) Security fencing which provides levels of delay against forced entry/ intrusion. Note walls should be regarded as equivalent to fencing, and should specified in terms of height and anti-climb requirements.	Define whether the fence is required to demarcate site boundary OR meet a rated security standard. Where security fencing is proposed consider anti-climb and anti-burrowing solutions. Where anti-climb is applied minimum height requirements apply Planning Consent is a key constraint particularly when in close proximity to residential areas.	BS1722 – All Parts: Note security type fences are listed as below Part 10: Anti-Intruder fences from Chain Link and Welded Mesh Part 12: Steel Palisade Fences Part 14: Open Mesh Steel panel fences Part 17: Power fencing (superseding PAS47) Where fencing requirements are for installations that may be inspected by Government agencies, appropriate test standards and delay times should be specified. Refer to any 'Secured By Design' design guidance if applying to the client property
Doorsets	Doorsets can be specified to provide security protection against – • Physical/manual attack • Ballistics • Blast Define the requirements for each of the above security criteria, to achieve an attack time equivalent to walls and glazing for the structure. Security ratings for doorsets should apply where required to passive leaves and overpanels/sidepanels.	Consider DDA requirements e.g. Vision Panels/ Automation while ensuring Security rating is not reduced Consider emergency exit/panic exit requirements based on area occupancy. For any oversized doorsets (particularly loading bays etc.) LPCB ratings will be based on systems tested to a maximum size so note that oversized doorsets may not achieve accreditation.	PAS23-1:1999 PAS24-1:1999 LPCB standards — LPS1175 Security Rating (SR as appropriate) BS EN1125: 2008 Panic BS EN179: 2008 Emergency BS EN1522:1998 Ballistic Testing Where manual attack requirements for doorsets are for installations that may be inspected by Government agencies, appropriate test standards and delay times should be specified. Refer to any 'Secured By Design' design guidance if applying to the client property
Window sets		
CCTV	Closed Circuit Television (CCTV) can be utilised to provide surveillance and recording of areas of a client property. CCTV can provide a number of different functions dependent upon client requirement including the following: • Surveillance live monitoring of all images • Surveillance and recording (for post incident purposes) • Event triggered displays using CCTV to provide images of areas where intrusion is detected.	Define the function and therefore required image size and resolution **for each individual camera** based on the functional requirement i.e.: • Identification 100%R • Recognition 50%R • Observation 25%R • Detection 10%R • Monitoring 5%R Define the period for which images should be retained. Assess and define preference for IP based or analogue CCTV solutions (specifically considering impact on LAN bandwidth and resilience) Define early in the design process whether site lighting will be used for CCTV purposes, so that general lighting design allows for CCTV requirements. Alternatively specify suitable illumination to support CCTV, and compatible cameras. Establish all data protection requirements applying to CCTV in the environment. Confirm the system function with the client's data controller	BS EN50132:2001 All Parts Data Protection Act 1998 (DPA) Data Protection Act Code of Practice 2008 (issued by ICO) Refer to any 'Secured by Design' design guidance if applying to the client property

Access Control

Intruder Detection (IDS)	Intruder Detection Systems (IDS) can be used to provide detection and reporting of intruders either to off-site monitoring agencies OR to local security personnel on site. IDS can provide detection and verification of intrusions either as a stand-alone system; operating in conjunction with CCTV to provide a 'visual confirmation' solution; or as part of a site wide fully integrated solution.	Confirm whether the IDS is required to initiate Police attendance. Confirm the grading of system required, i.e.1–4 dependent on the nature of the property and assets. Where buildings require Listed Building Consent, full installation details including equipment types, method of installation, disturbance to building fabric, and any enabling works (cable routes etc.) should all be defined at design stage.	BS EN50131:2006 — All Parts PD6662:2004 DD243:2004 Where IDS forms part of an integrated system confirm any equipment proposed supports serial connectivity, and protocol interfaces/drivers to the Security Management System (SMS). Refer to any 'Secured by Design' design guidance if applying to the client property

Perimeter detection

Search and scanning equipment	Search and scanning equipment is used to assist in the detection of weapons, explosives or chemical, biological or radiological material. Such material could be concealed on the person, in bags or sent via the mail or courier systems. Search and detection options are: A visual search Hand held search 'wands' Passage through metal detecting arch X ray of packages and cases Body scanning Explosive scanning CBR scanning Vehicle and Truck Scanning	Search and scanning will normally occur in reception areas, shipping and receiving areas or in designated mail/scanner rooms. Specialist advice should be sought on current technologies and equipment capabilities When designing such areas, considerations are: • The size of the search equipment. • Whether it is to be permanent, temporary or occasional • Visual screening of personnel search areas • Requirements for blast enhanced mail scanning rooms • Containment, particularly where temporary equipment may be required in foyer and reception areas.	PAS 97:2009 A Specification for Mail Screening and Security. Major Manufacturers: Smiths Detection www.smithsdetection.com Rapiscan www.rapiscansystems.com

Security control centres

38 Sports facilities: indoor and outdoor

Philip Johnson and Tom Jones

Philip Johnson and Tom Jones are architects at Populous

KEY POINTS:

- *All sports are conducted on a field of play, whether that is a pitch, track, course, pool, field or court. The governing body for each sport will generally define dimensional requirements*
- *Within certain dimensional ranges, a number of surfaces are capable of accommodating a number of sports*
- *When planning indoor facilities, the designer must take into account the height of the performance space required for each sport. Some vary according to the standard of competition so governing bodies should be consulted*
- *When designing sightlines, the designer must determine what is required to be seen. This could be the touchlines of a pitch, the likely height of a rugby ball kicked high into the air, or the referee sat high on a chair. It should also be remembered that it may be impossible to see the entire course*

Contents

1 Executive summary
2 General introduction
3 Field of play
4 Viewing structures
5 Sports equipment
6 Support facilities for competitors and officials
7 Support facilities for spectators
8 Facilities for the media
9 Support accommodation for facility management
10 Examples of sports facilities for various sports
11 Bibliography
12 Case study

1 EXECUTIVE SUMMARY

Sports facilities take many forms but this chapter provides guidance for their technical design whether they are used for competition, training or recreation. The guidance is set out starting with the key dimensional data of the field of play for each sport, followed by principles to be applied to the design of viewing structures, and lastly the accommodation for the various users of the facility. A comprehensive reference bibliography is included at the end of the chapter as this field of design is technically complex; but because it evolves from year to year, designers should consult the guidance from the governing body of each sport, and other regulatory and guidance frameworks.

2 GENERAL INTRODUCTION

2.1 Indoor and outdoor facilities

Design information related to sports facilities is documented here in a single chapter irrespective of whether the sport is conducted inside or outside. The authors have concluded that the many factors that influence the design of a sports facility are relevant whether the sport is conducted inside or outside. That is not to say that the conditions are identical and of course the design of appropriate finishes and the design of mechanical and electrical services must be carefully considered to ensure the facility is fit for purpose. Roofs do however play a key role in the design of sports facilities and they are discussed in Section 4.9.

2.2 Scale

Sports facilities come in many different shapes and sizes, from a sandpit in a park where a casual game of petanque is played, through a small community tennis club, a local authority sports centre, school or university facilities, regional racecourse, football league stadium, to a national stadium or even an international 'sports city'. The design of these facilities clearly changes in scope and complexity but this chapter should provide the basis for the core facilities that relate to most if not all.

2.3 Sporting places

The places where sport can occur are virtually limitless. Competitions take place upon the ocean waves, alpine pass roads, and the tarmac of city centres; on turf and dirt as well as the prepared surfaces of a tennis court or bowling green. Some of these places are not designed at all, except to locate key points along a route, and some require meticulous design work. The chapter provides the dimensional considerations for the sports that require the intervention of a designer.

3 FIELD OF PLAY

3.1 Definition

This section introduces the concept that all sports are conducted on a field of play, whether that is a pitch, track, course, pool, field or court. The governing body for each sport will generally define the dimensional requirements for this, which may vary depending on the level of competition. Dimensions for the field of play for most sports can be grouped into categories.

3.2 Pitch/park/ground

The first category illustrated here, Figures 38.1–38.10, are sports that are conducted on a level surface that would have been originally turfed, but at the professional level, the surfaces are becoming increasingly sophisticated. They are all team sports and can be played in a local park or in an international stadium. They are most commonly played outdoors although indoor facilities exist for some.

3.3 Track

The second category of sports is conducted on a track, sometimes in individual competition and sometimes as team events, Figures 38.11–38.15. The dimensions of the tracks for athletics and track cycling are standardised to a degree although some degree of variation is permitted, whereas the tracks for BMX racing and motorsport are all different.

3.4 Court

Sports that are played on courts of various different configurations can be played both indoors or outdoors and often on a number of different surfaces, Figures 38.16–38.23.

3.5 Pool

Pool-based sports are obviously conducted in standard length swimming pools, although their widths do vary, Figures 38.24–38.28. The pools are increasingly more sophisticated with moving floors to increase their usability by participants of varying competence.

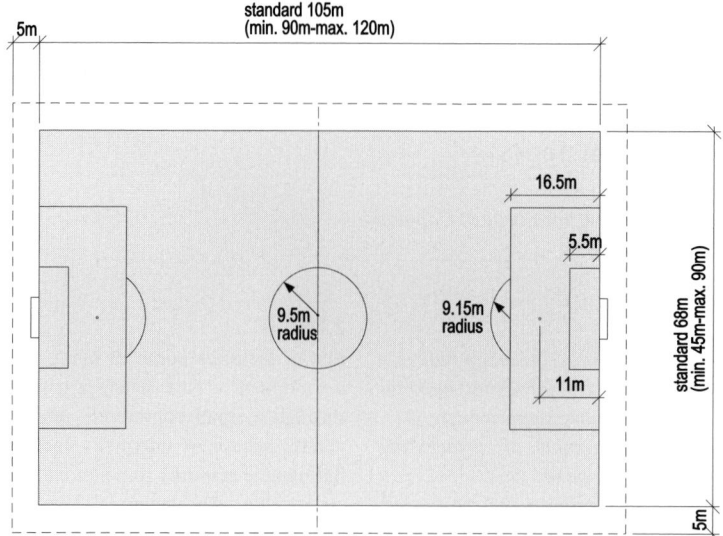

38.1 *Football (soccer) pitch layout*

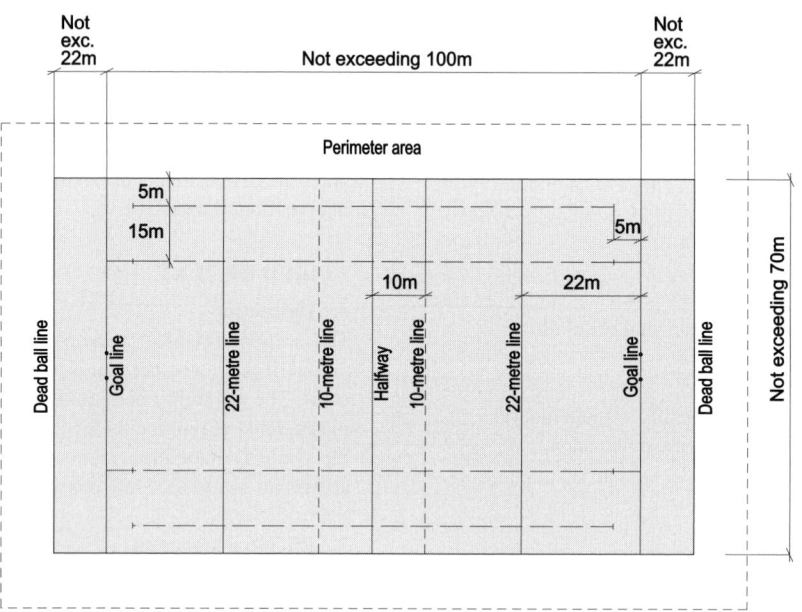

38.2 *Rugby union, rugby league pitch layout*

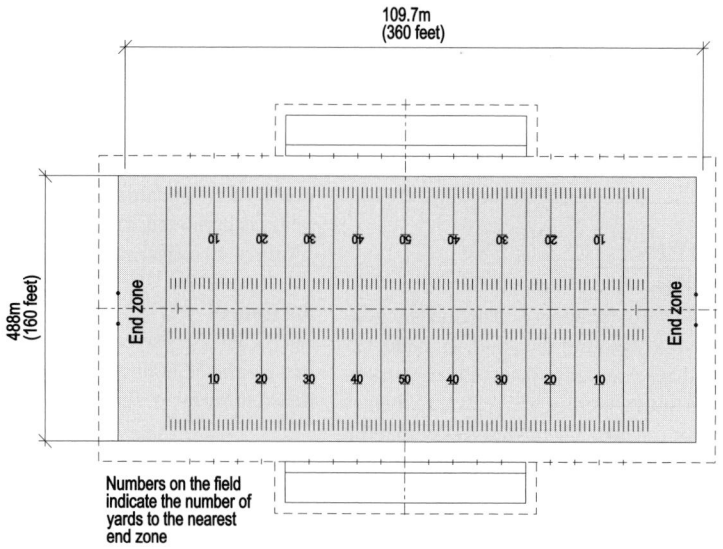

38.3 *American football pitch layout*

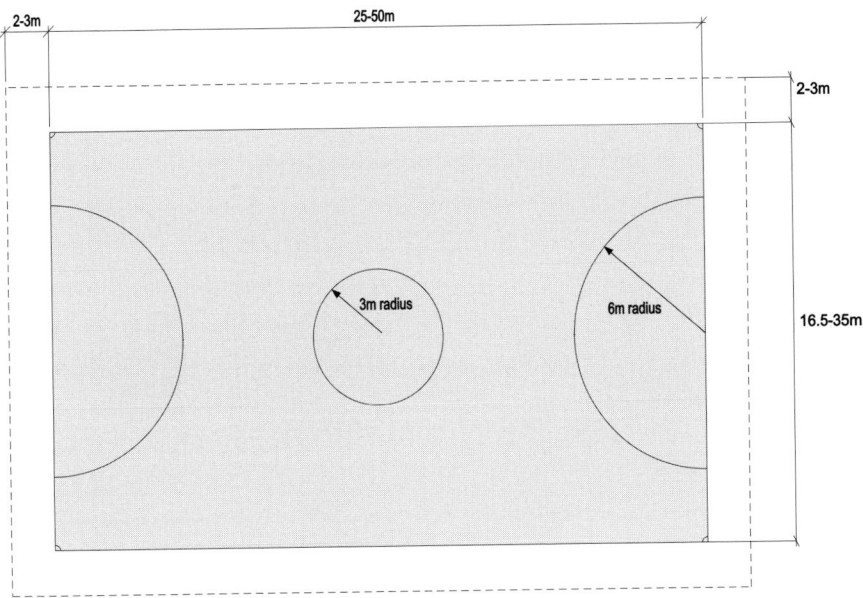

38.4 *Five-a-side football pitch layout*

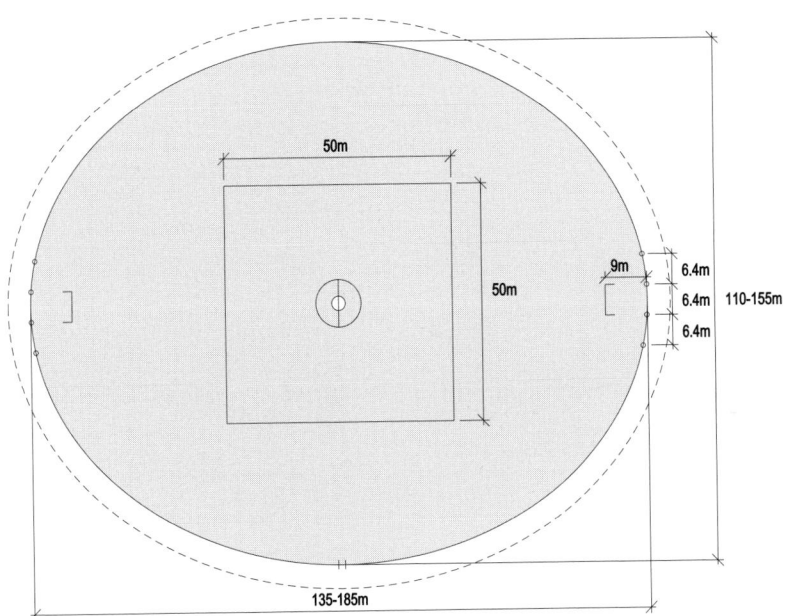

38.5 *Australian football pitch layout*

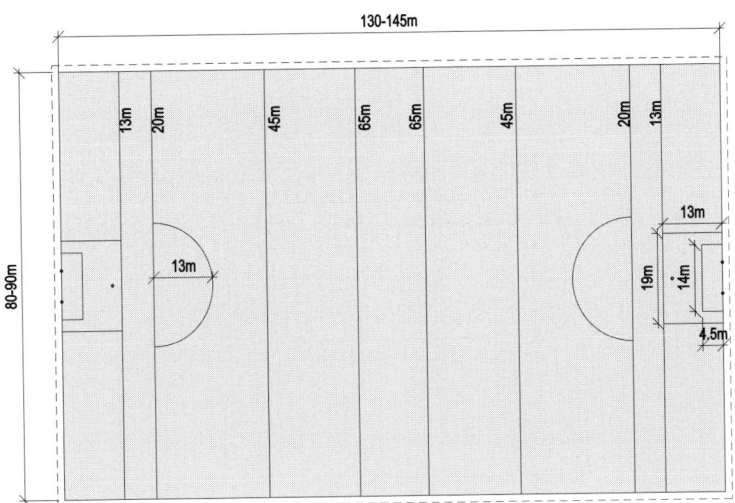

38.6 *Gaelic football pitch layout*

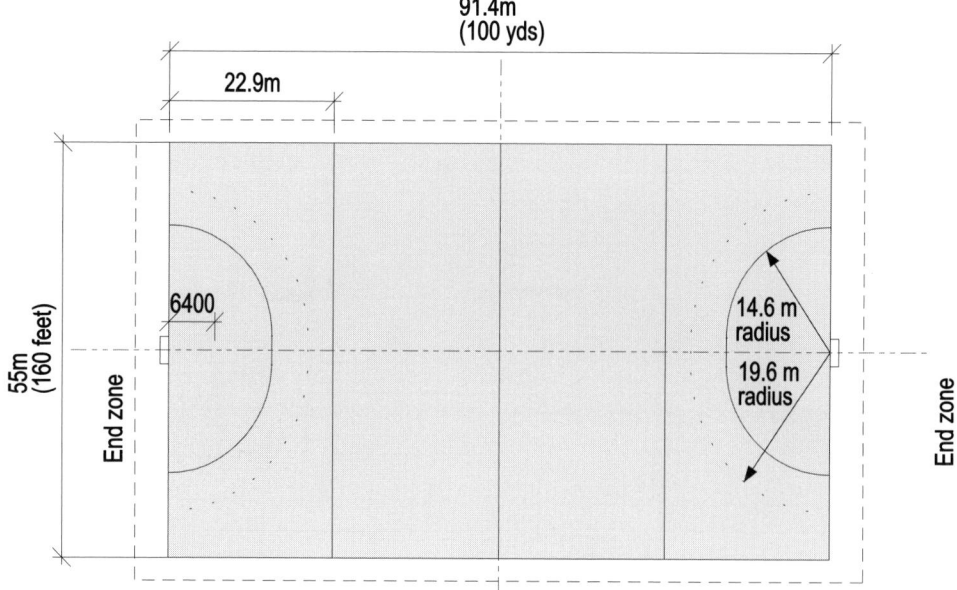

38.7 *Field hockey pitch layout*

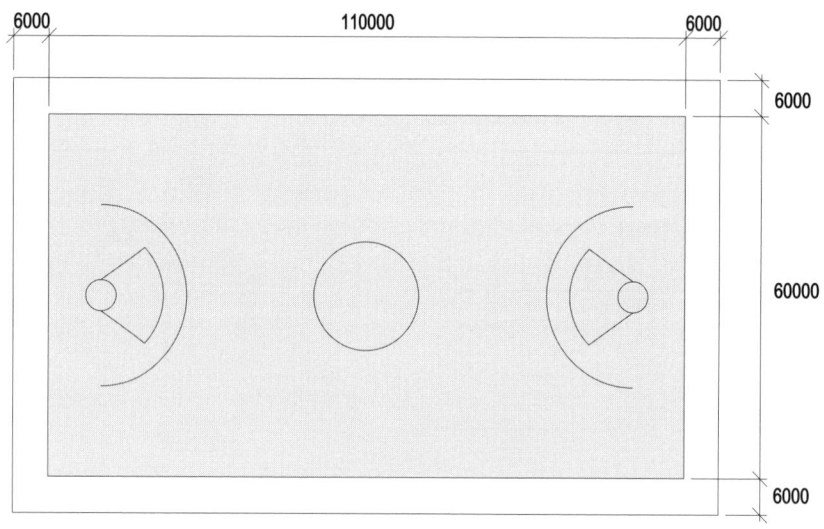

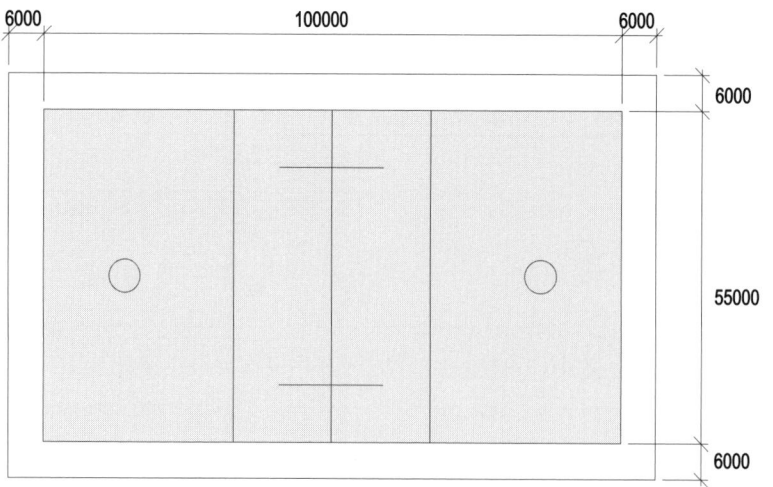

38.8 *Lacrosse (women's and men's) pitch layout*

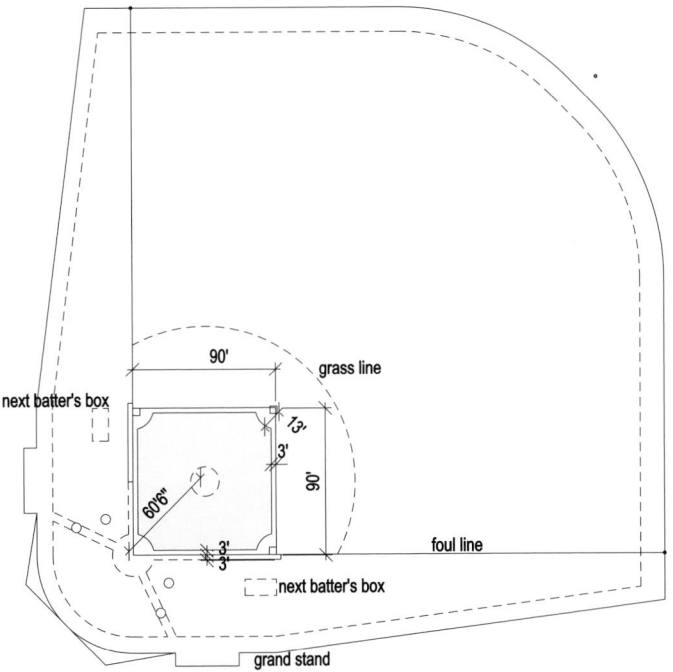

38.9 *Baseball pitch layout*

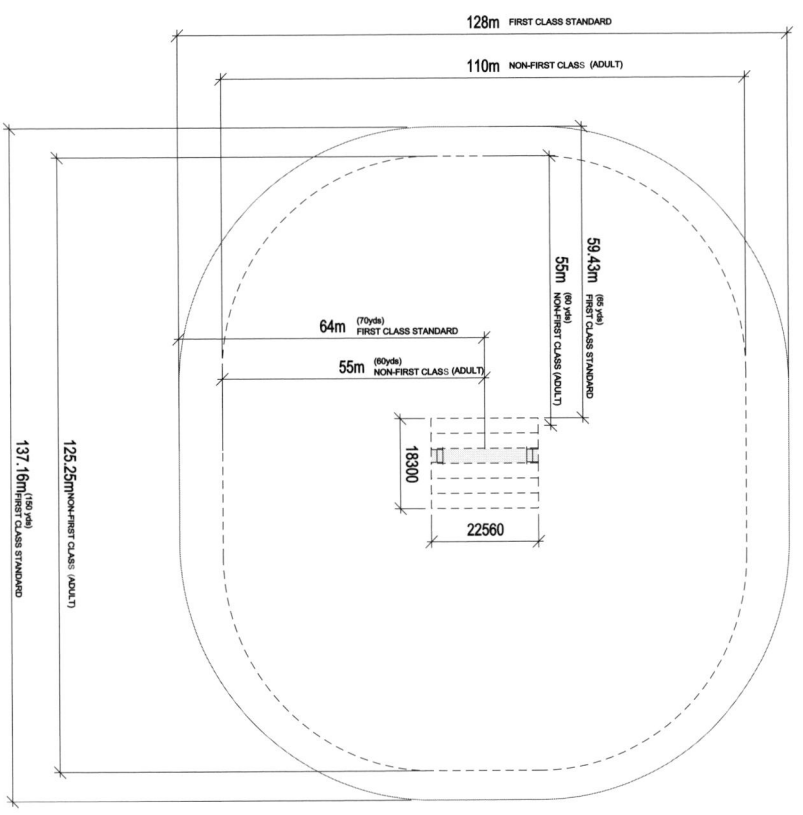

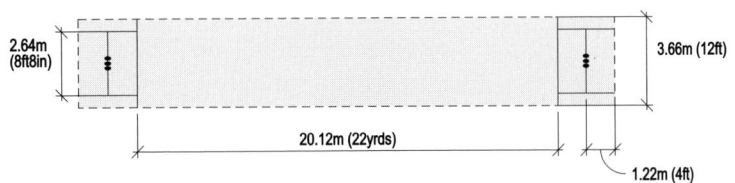

38.10 *Cricket pitch layout*

Finish line   Start line &
Pursuit Finish line

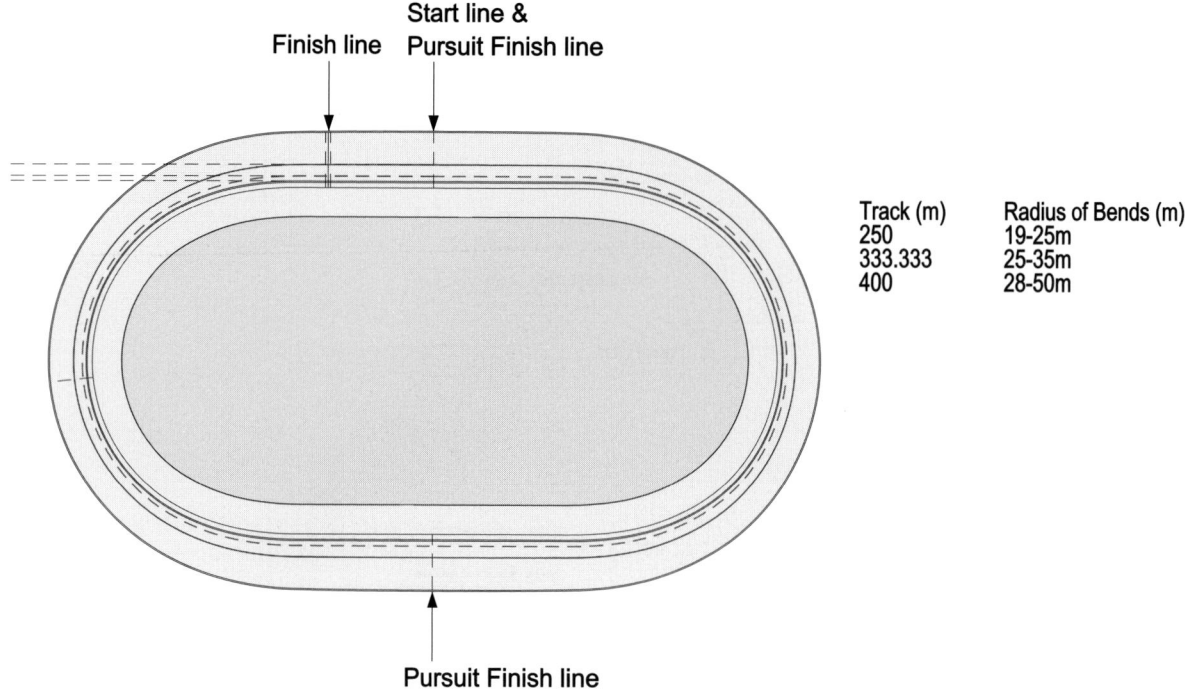

Track (m)	Radius of Bends (m)
250	19-25m
333.333	25-35m
400	28-50m

Pursuit Finish line

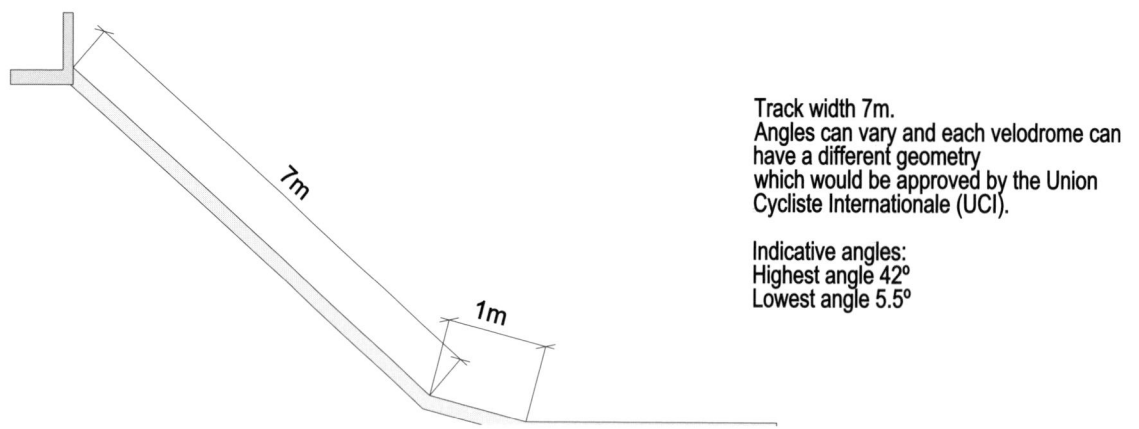

7m

1m

Track width 7m.
Angles can vary and each velodrome can
have a different geometry
which would be approved by the Union
Cycliste Internationale (UCI).

Indicative angles:
Highest angle 42°
Lowest angle 5.5°

38.11 *Cycling track*

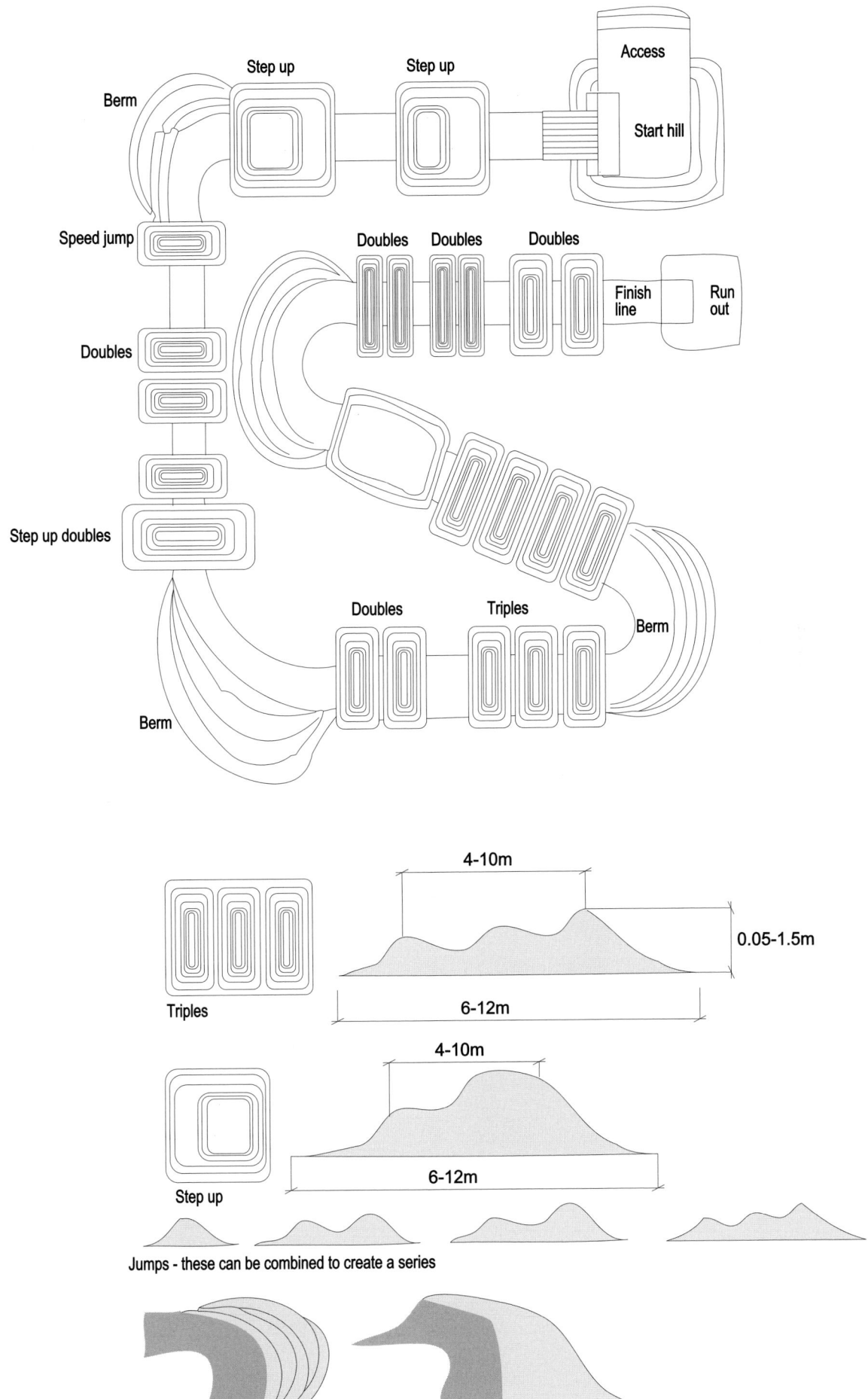

38.12 *BMX track*

160m
35m
80m
35m
4.88m
6
3
1
5
2
80m
3
4
73.2m
3m
10m
100m
130m
1 Shot put facility
2 Javelin runway
3 Discus/hammer throw facility
4 Pole vault landing areas
5 High jump runway
6 Long jump/triple jump pit

38.13 *Outdoor athletics track*

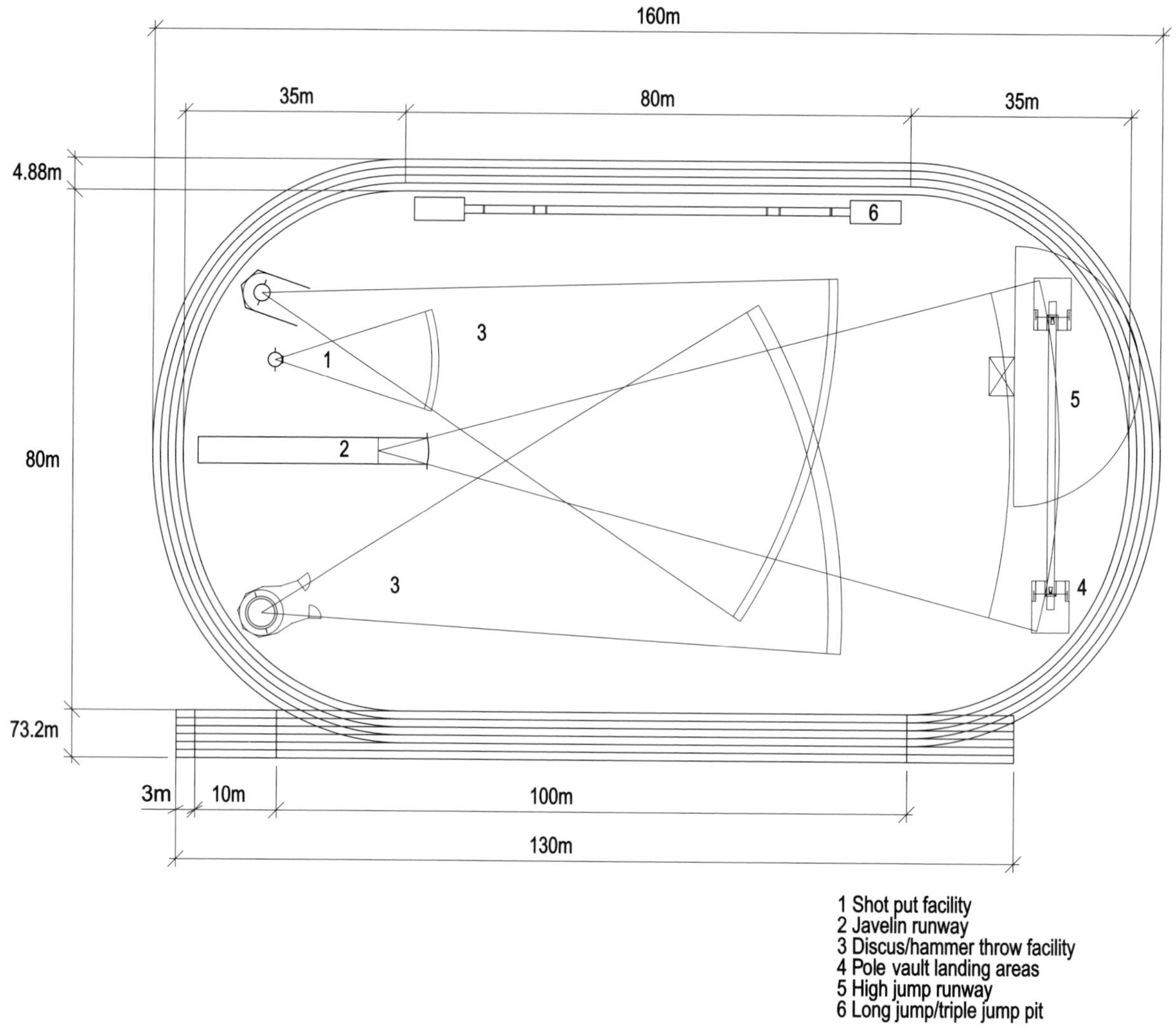

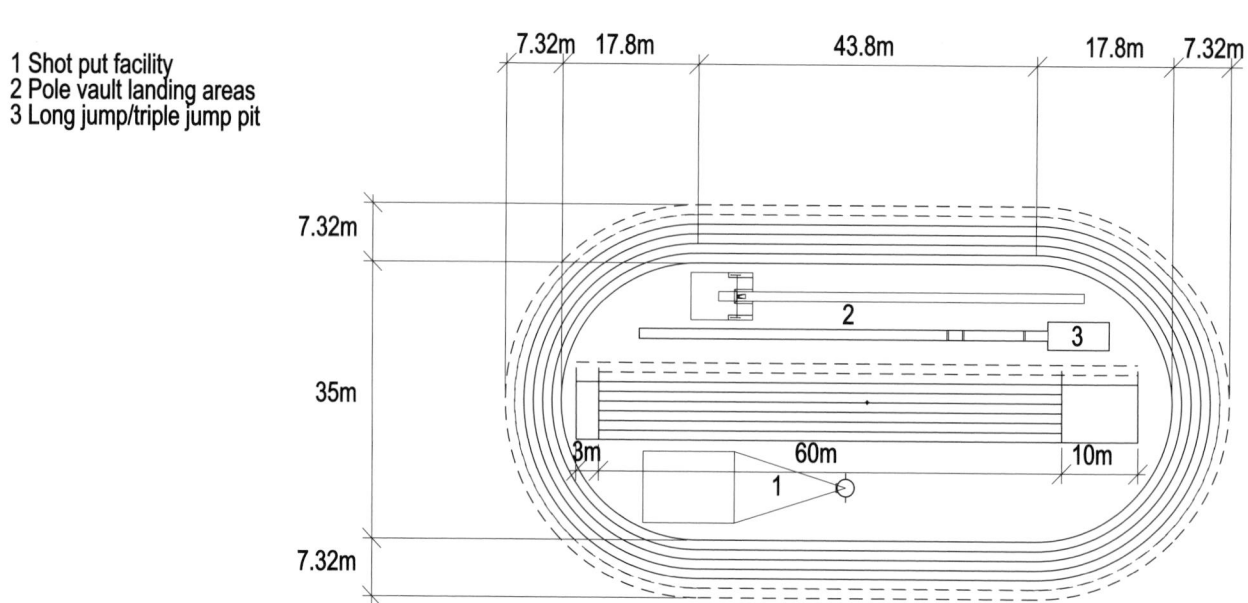

1 Shot put facility
2 Pole vault landing areas
3 Long jump/triple jump pit
7.32m
17.8m
43.8m
17.8m
7.32m
7.32m
2
3
35m
3m
60m
10m
1
7.32m

38.14 *Indoor athletics track*

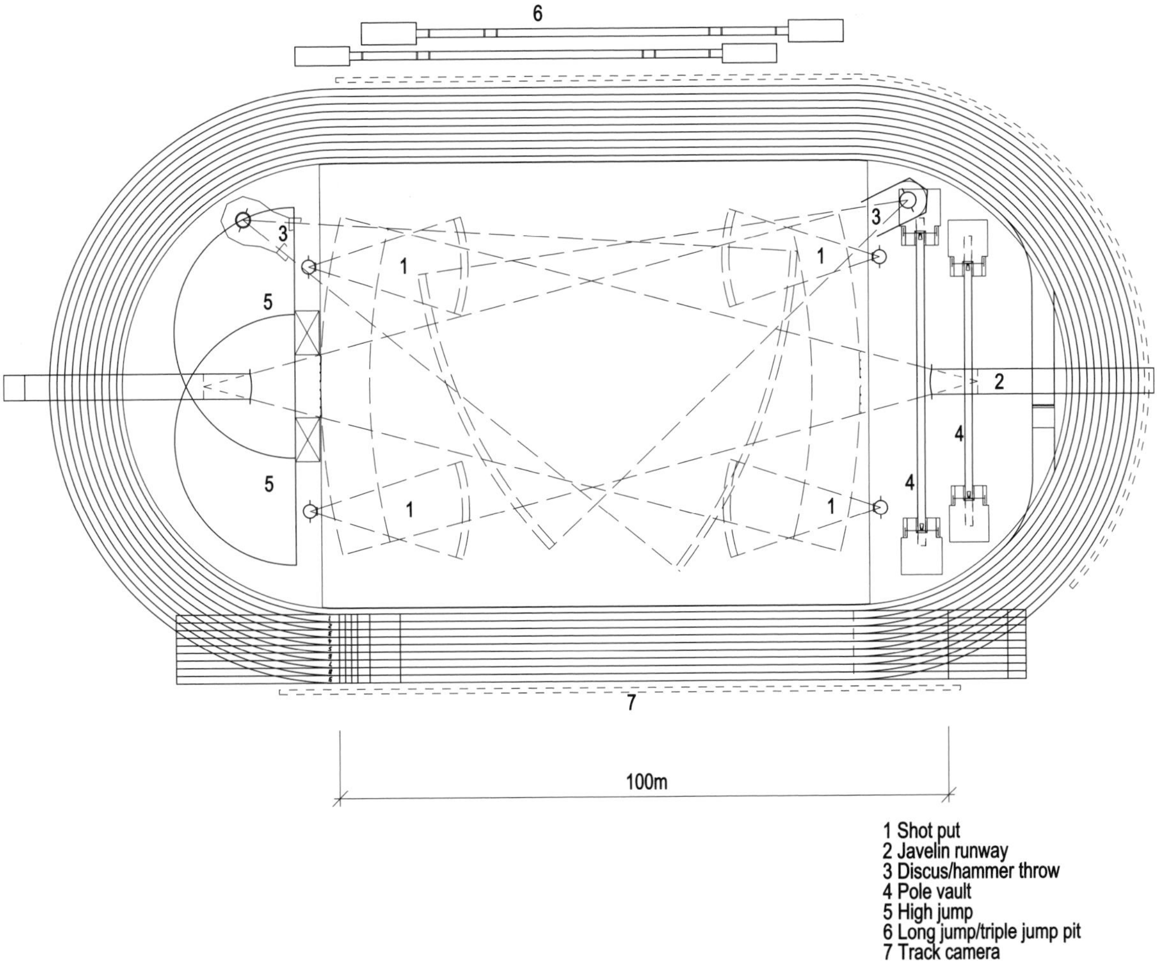

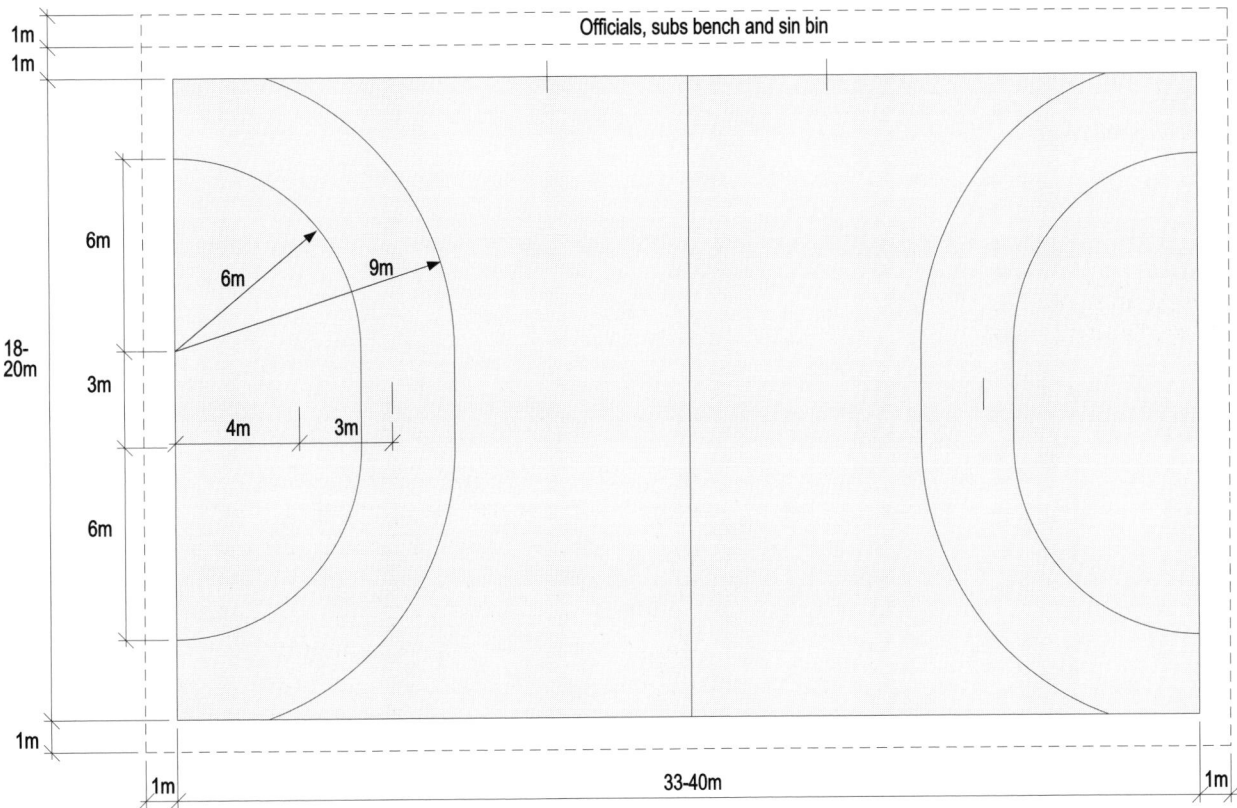

6
3
3
1
1
1
1
5
5
2
4
4
7
100m
1 Shot put
2 Javelin runway
3 Discus/hammer throw
4 Pole vault
5 High jump
6 Long jump/triple jump pit
7 Track camera

38.15 *Olympic athletics track*

Officials, subs bench and sin bin
1m
1m
18-20m
1m
6m
3m
6m
6m
9m
4m
3m
1m
33-40m
1m

38.16 *Handball court*

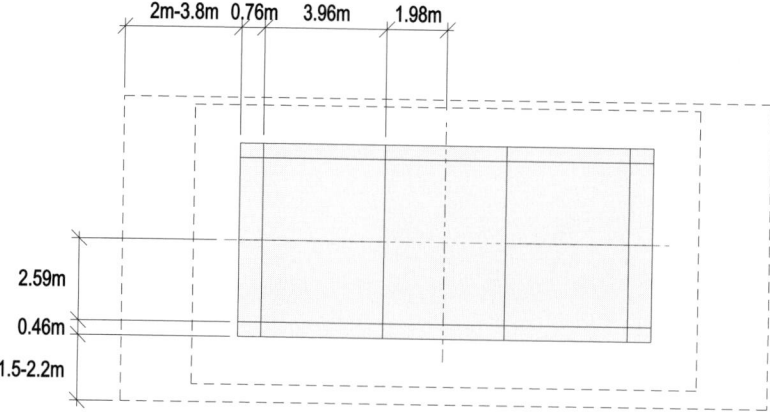

38.17 *Badminton court*

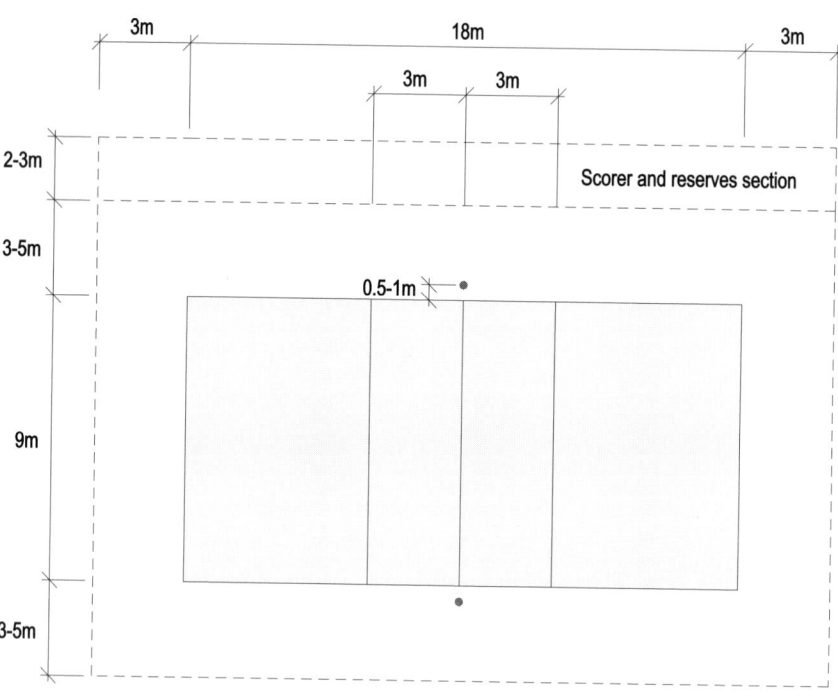

Scorer and reserves section

38.18 *Volleyball court*

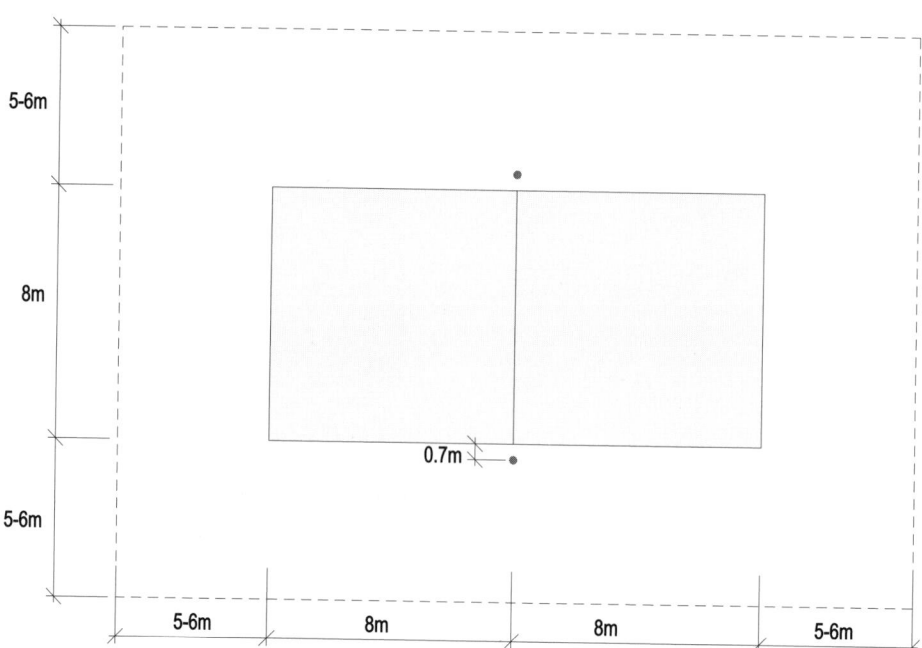

38.19 *Beach volleyball court*

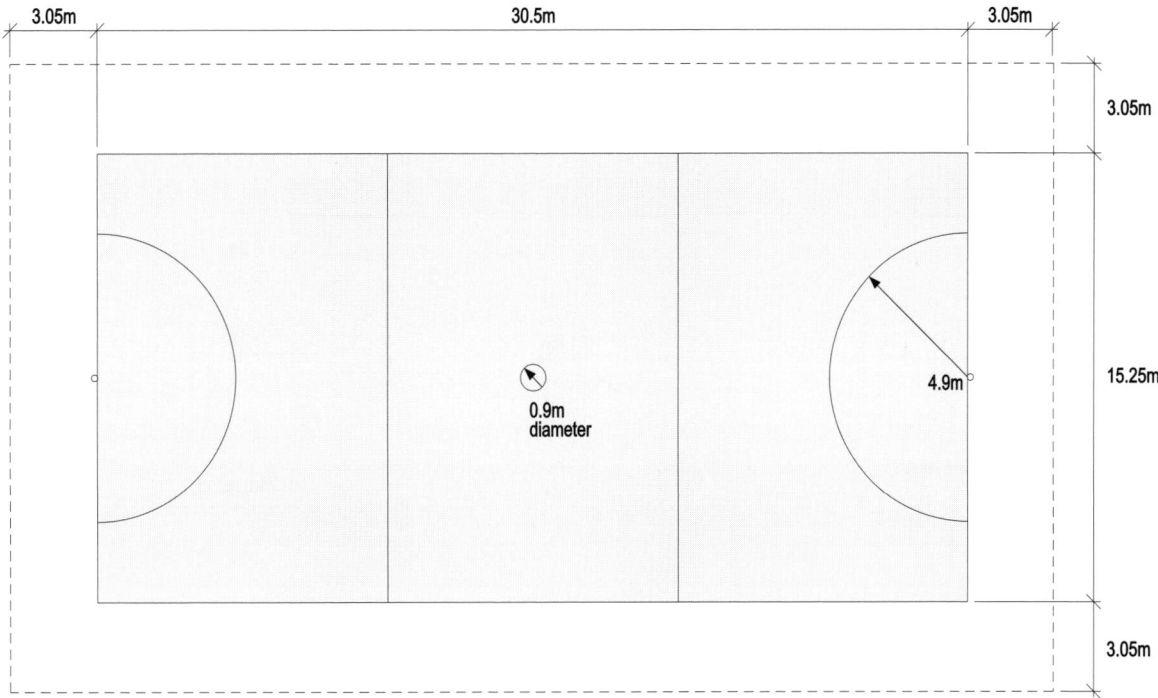

38.20 *Netball court*

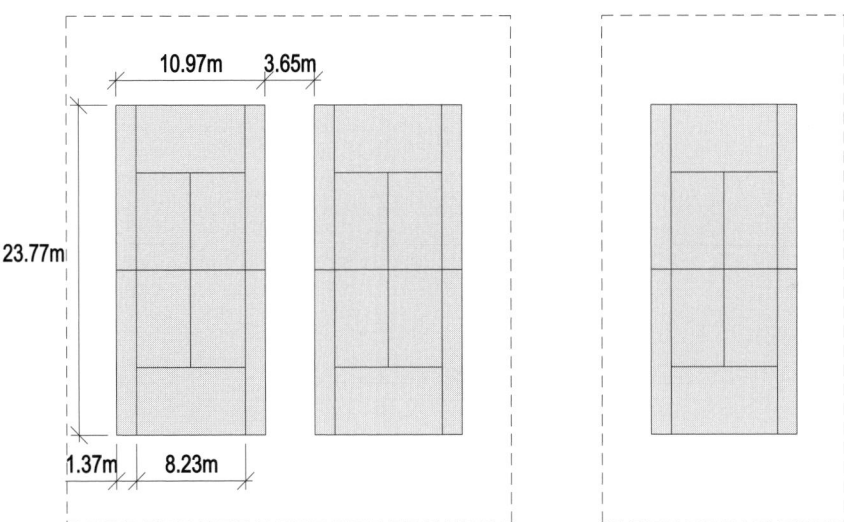

38.21 *Lawn tennis court*

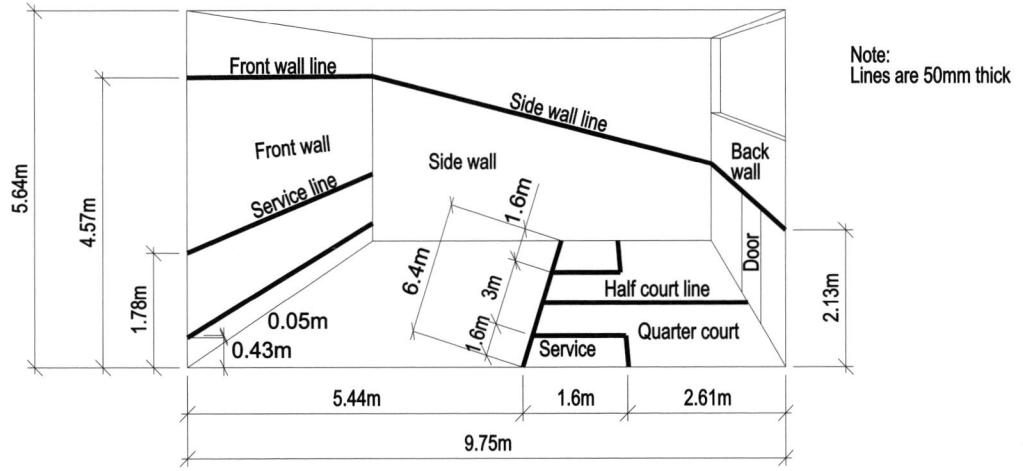

38.22 *Squash court*

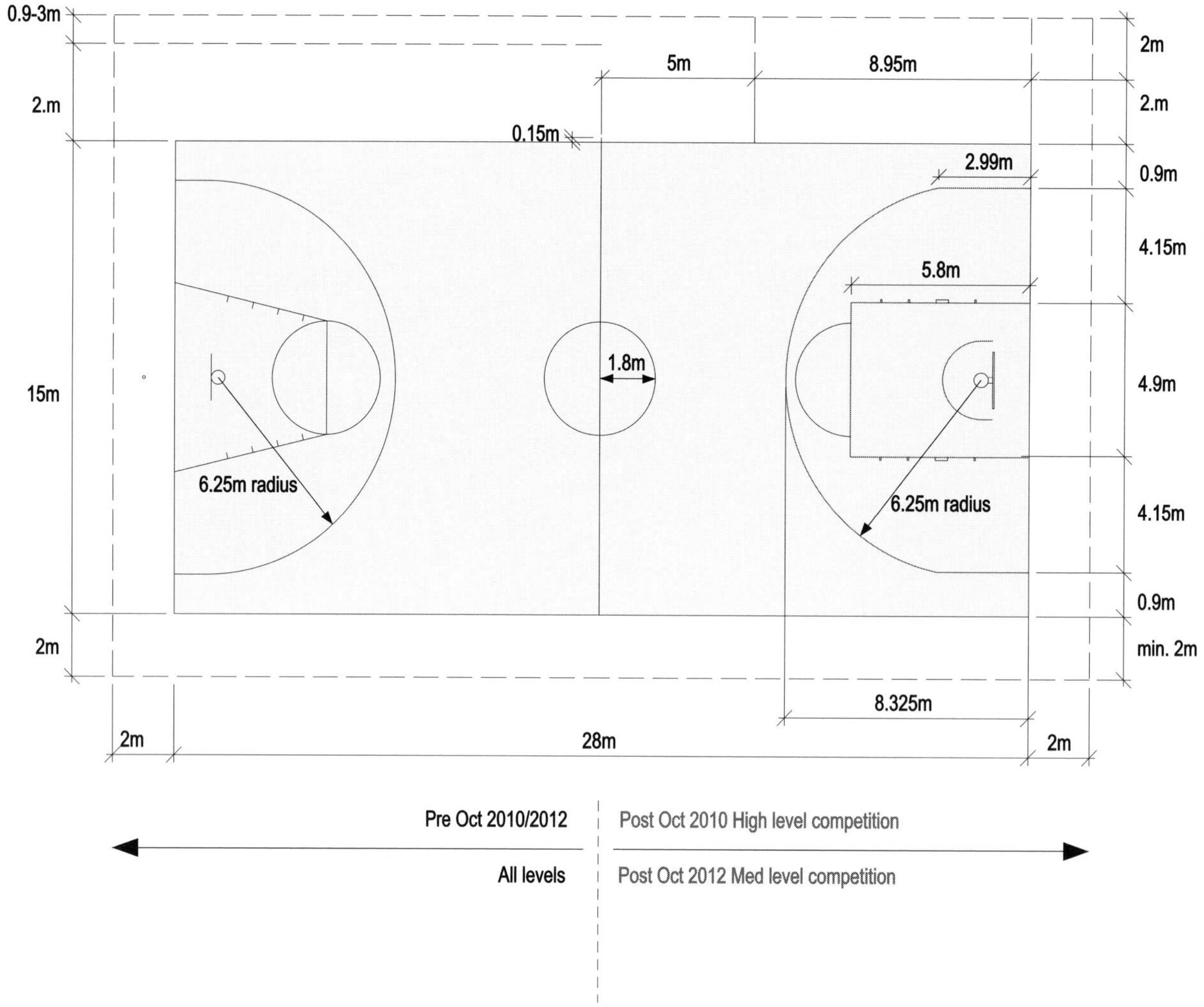

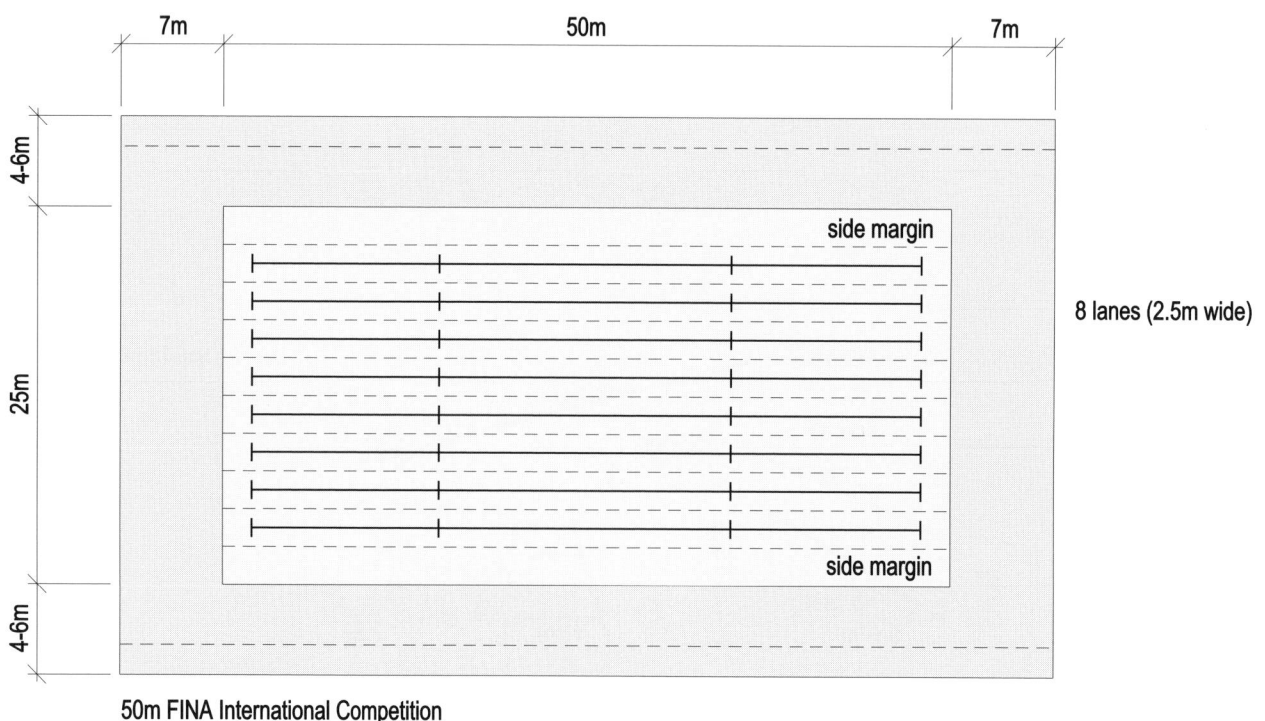

38.23 *Basketball court*

38.24 *Swimming pool*

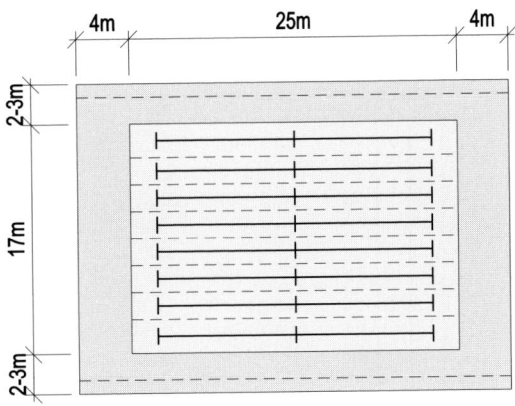

25m Competition
Depth: 1m-1.8m

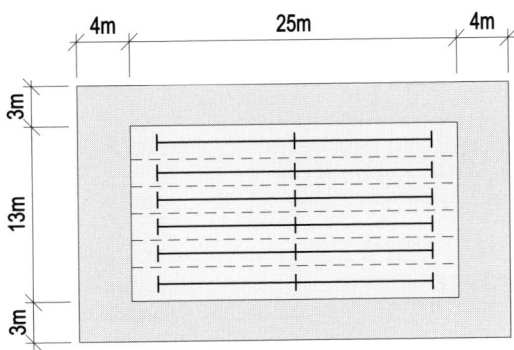

25m Community Pool
Depth: 0.9m-1.25m, Preferred Depth: 1-2m

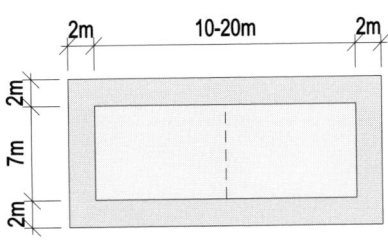

Learner Pool
Depth 0.6-0.9m

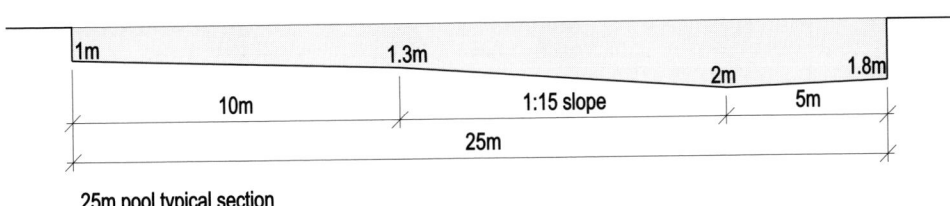

25m pool typical section

Learner Pool typical cross section

38.25 *Swimming pool*

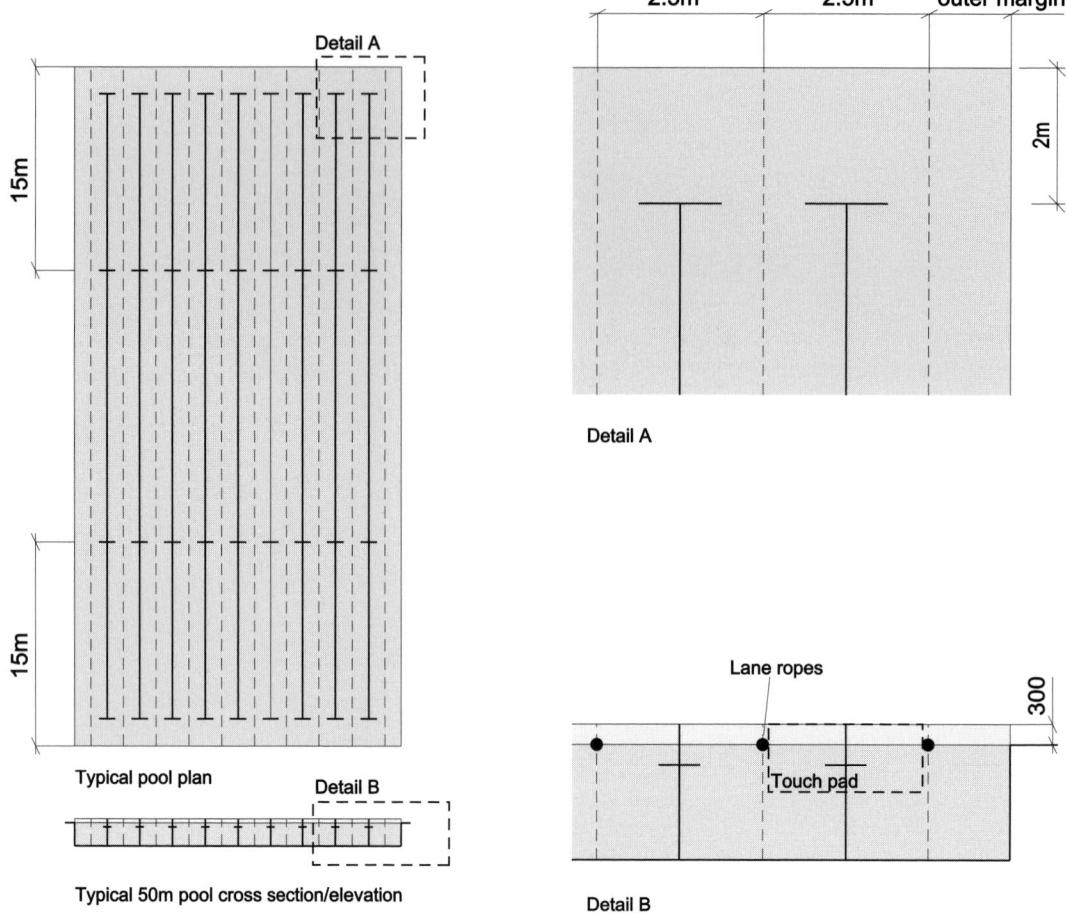

38.26 *Swimming pool*

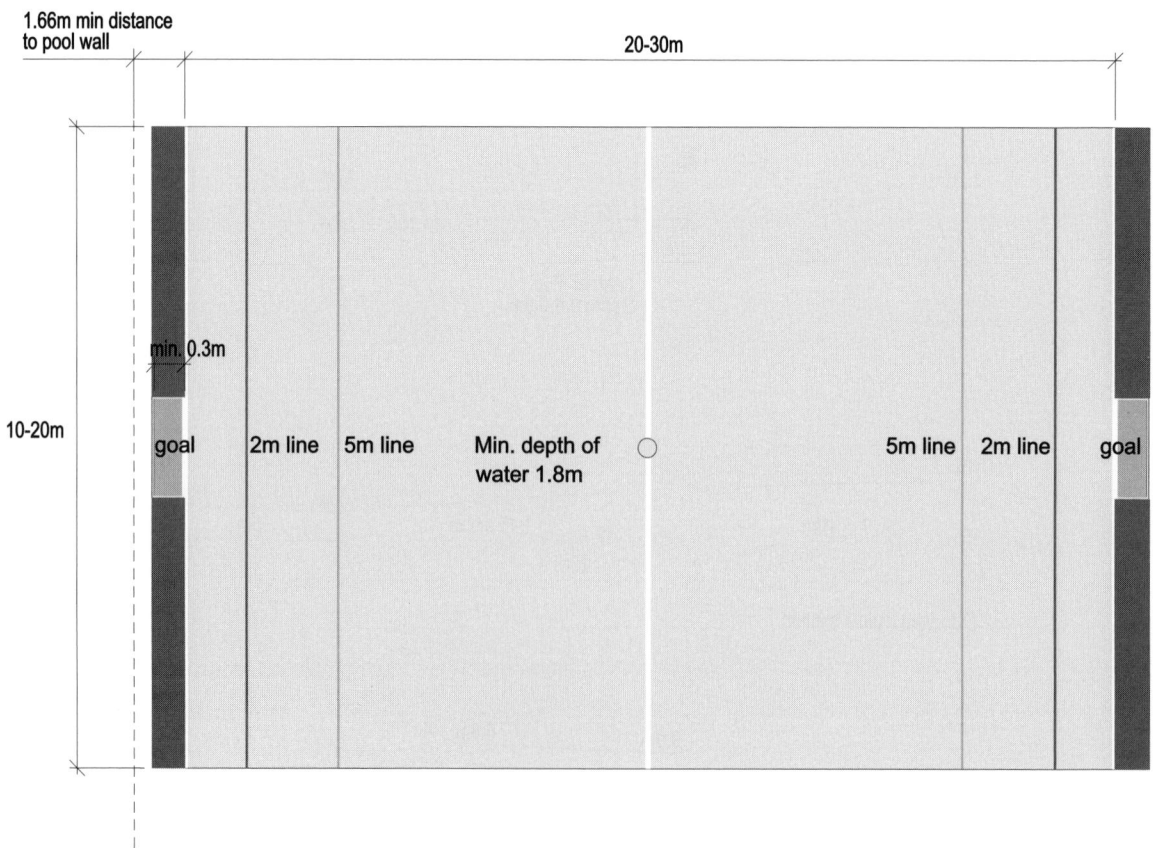

38.27 *Water polo pool*

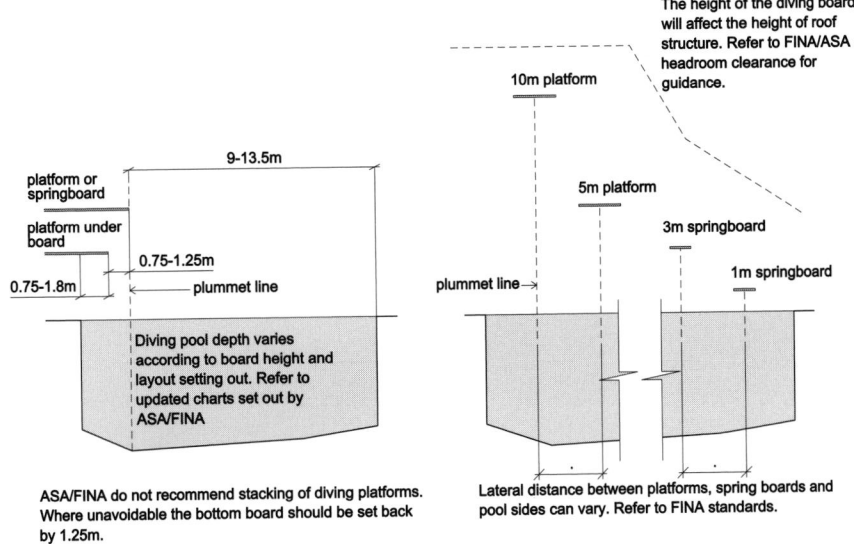

38.28 *Diving pool*

3.6 Course

Courses for the sports in this category are rarely the same; in fact their difference is part of their appeal, Figures 38.29–38.30.

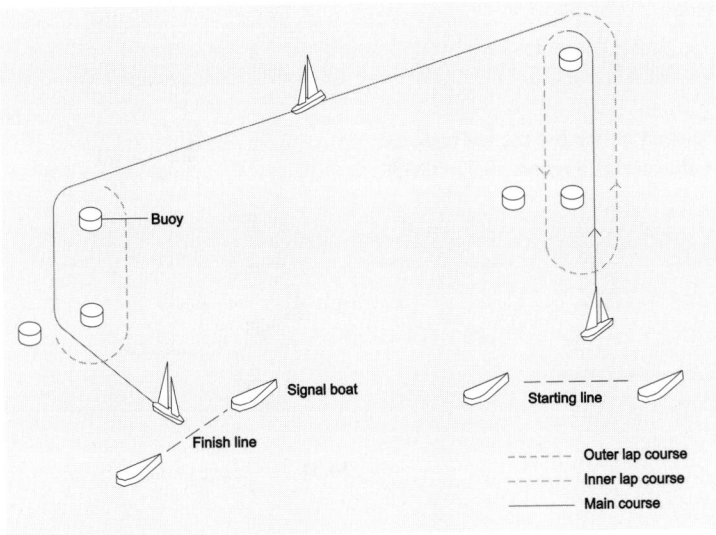

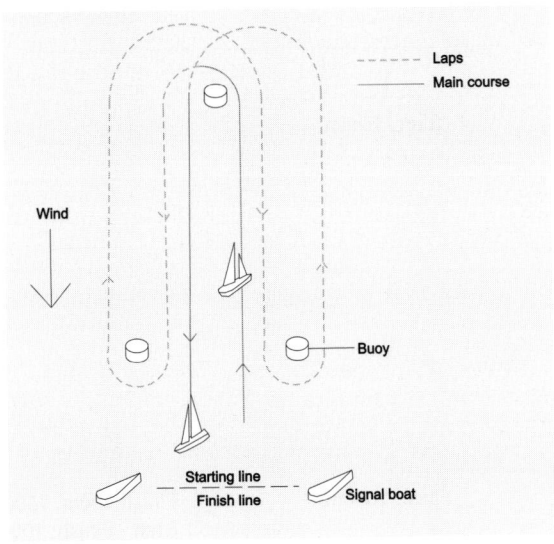

38.29 *Sailing courses*

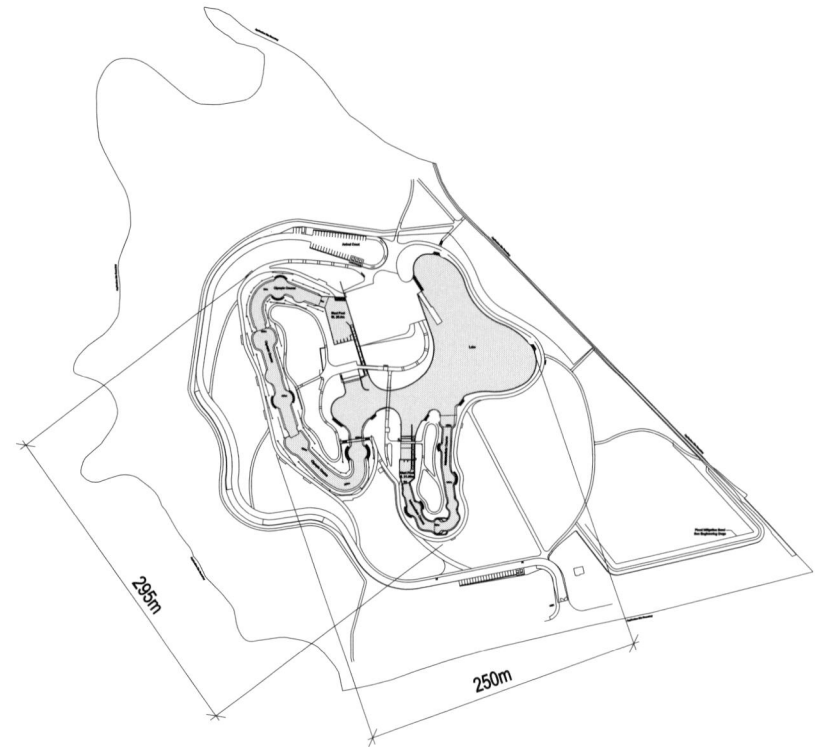

38.30 *White water kayaking course*

3.7 Rink

The following sports are each played on ice but the ice pads are required to be of quite different dimensions, Figures 38.31–38.33.

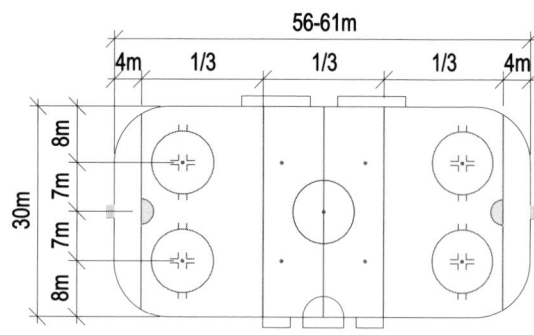

38.31 *Ice hockey rink*

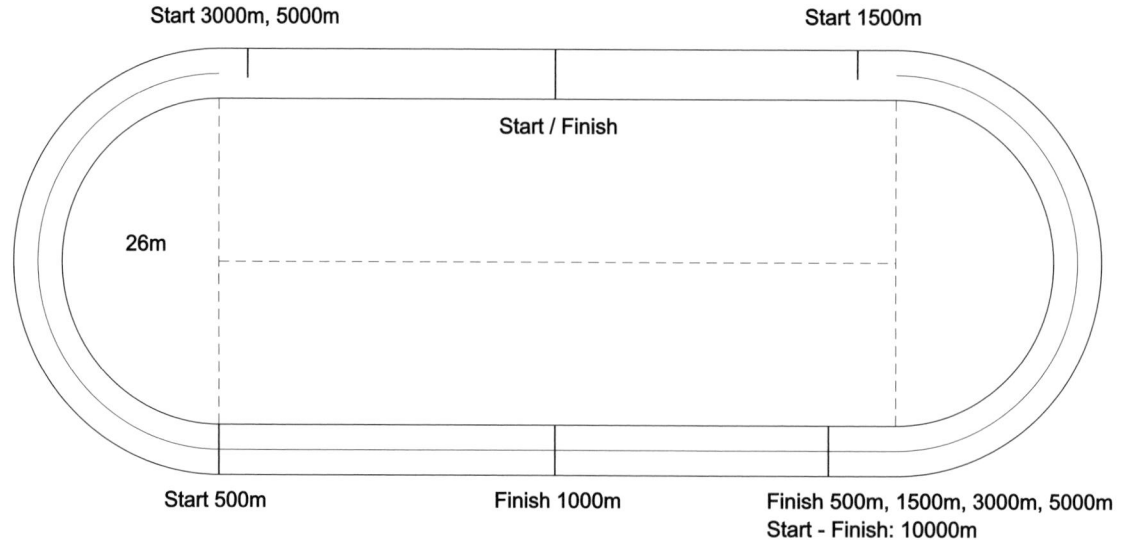

38.32 *Speed skating (long course)*

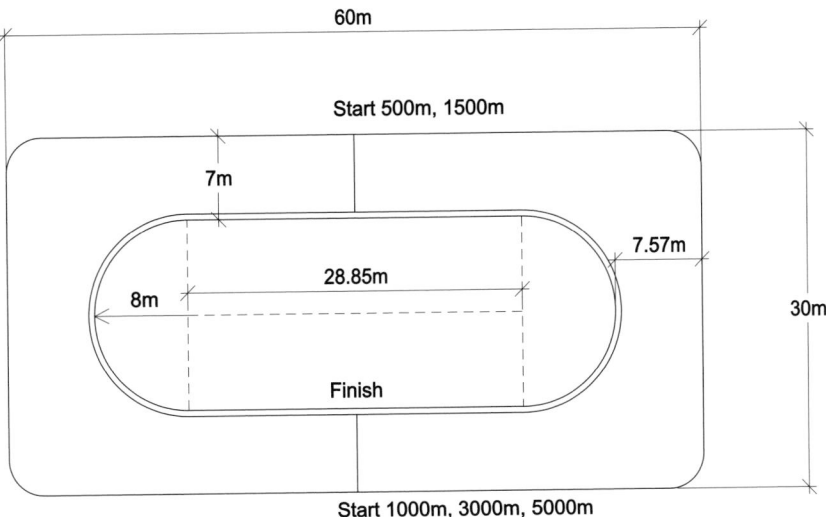

38.33 *Speed skating (short course)*

3.8 Other sports

The remaining sports illustrated in this chapter do not so easily fall
into categories. Some require a ring, some a mat, others a range,
green, lawn or table, Figures 38.34–38.45.

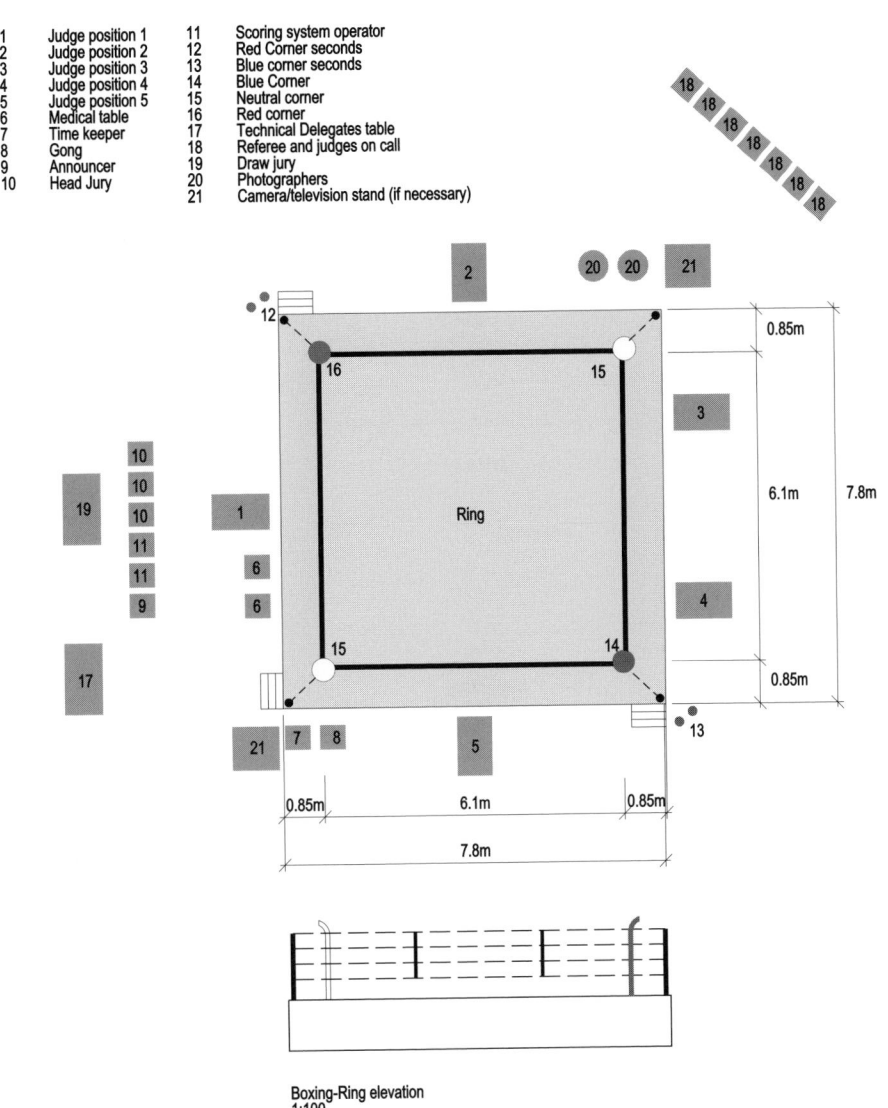

1	Judge position 1	11	Scoring system operator
2	Judge position 2	12	Red Corner seconds
3	Judge position 3	13	Blue corner seconds
4	Judge position 4	14	Blue Corner
5	Judge position 5	15	Neutral corner
6	Medical table	16	Red corner
7	Time keeper	17	Technical Delegates table
8	Gong	18	Referee and judges on call
9	Announcer	19	Draw jury
10	Head Jury	20	Photographers
		21	Camera/television stand (if necessary)

Boxing-Ring elevation
1:100

38.34 *Boxing*

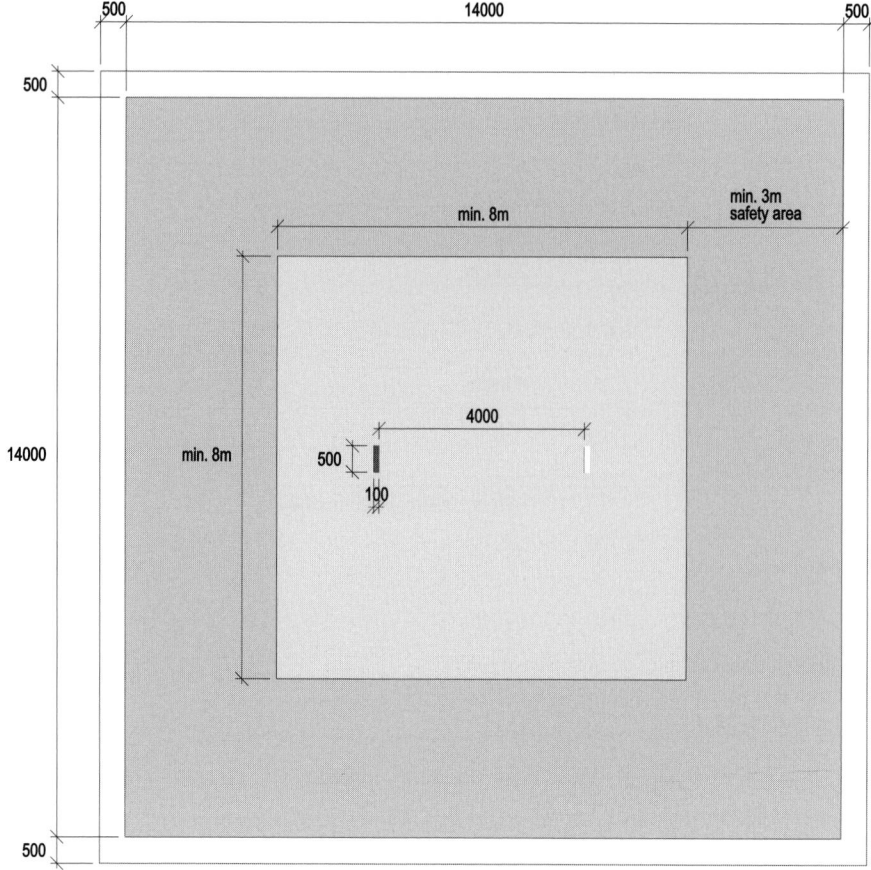

38.35 *Judo*

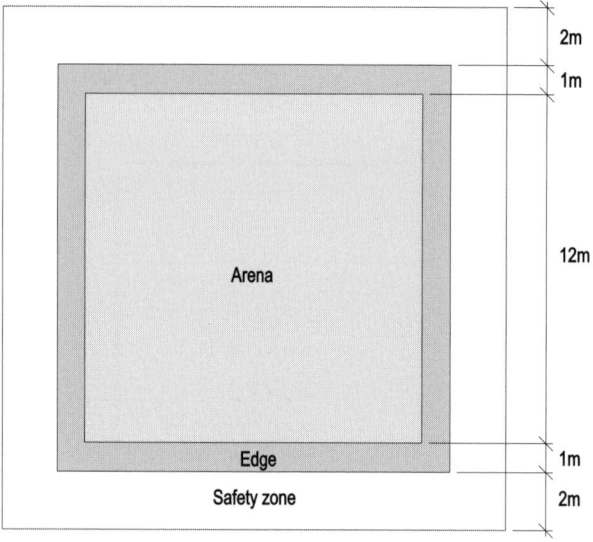

38.36 *Gymnastics (men and women)*

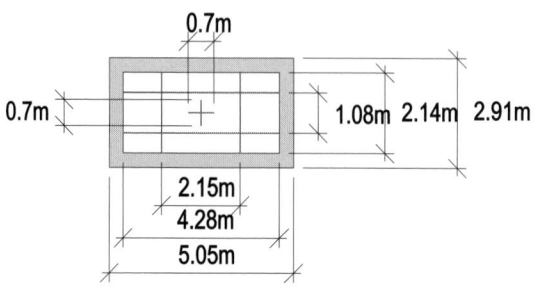

38.37 *Trampoline*

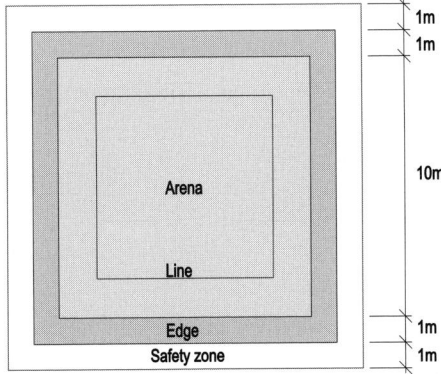

38.38 *Acrobatic gymnastics*

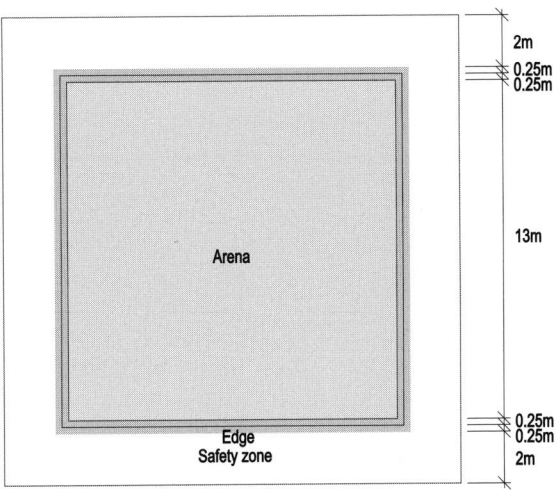

38.39 *Rhythmic gymnastics*

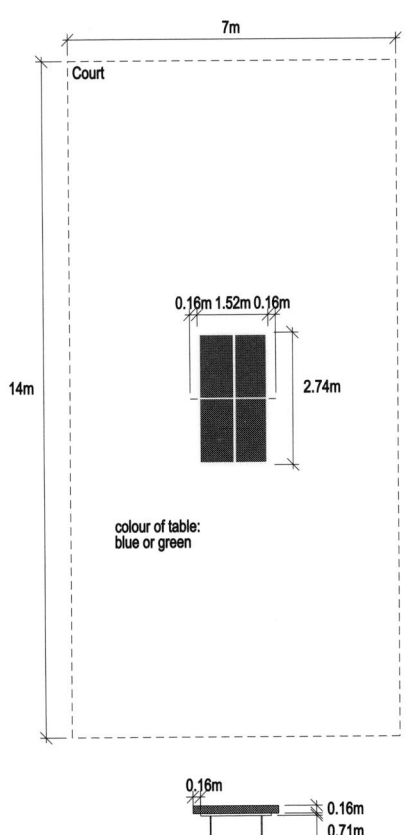

38.40 *Table tennis*

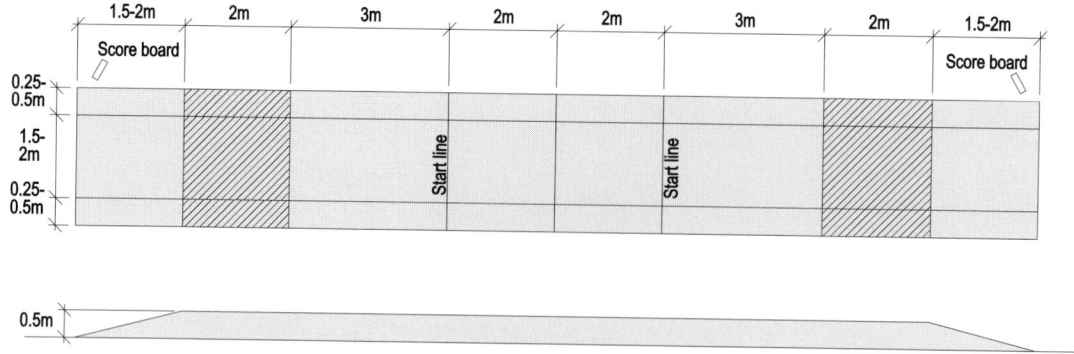

38.41 *Fencing*

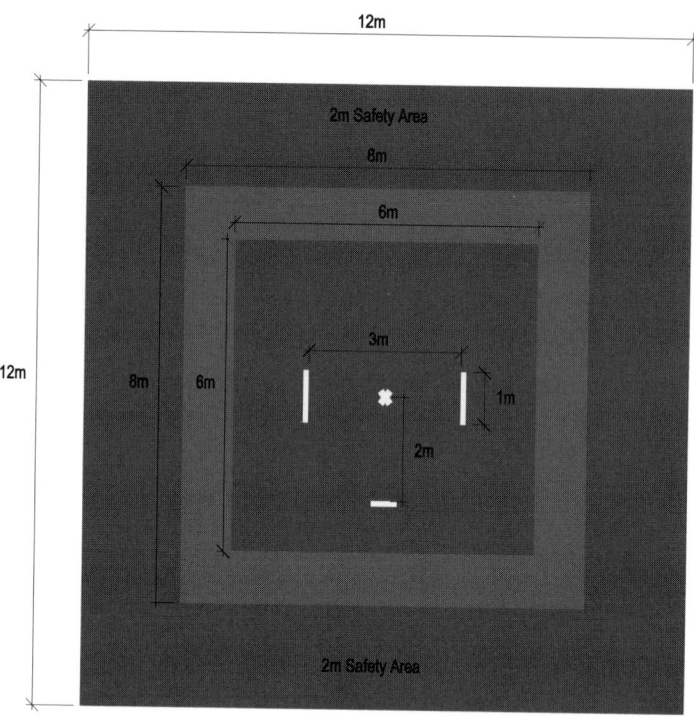

38.42 *Karate*

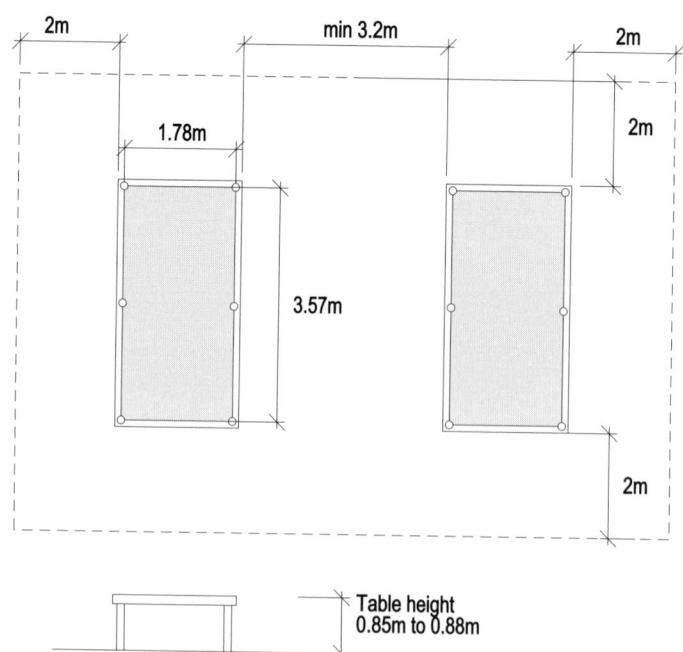

38.43 *Snooker*

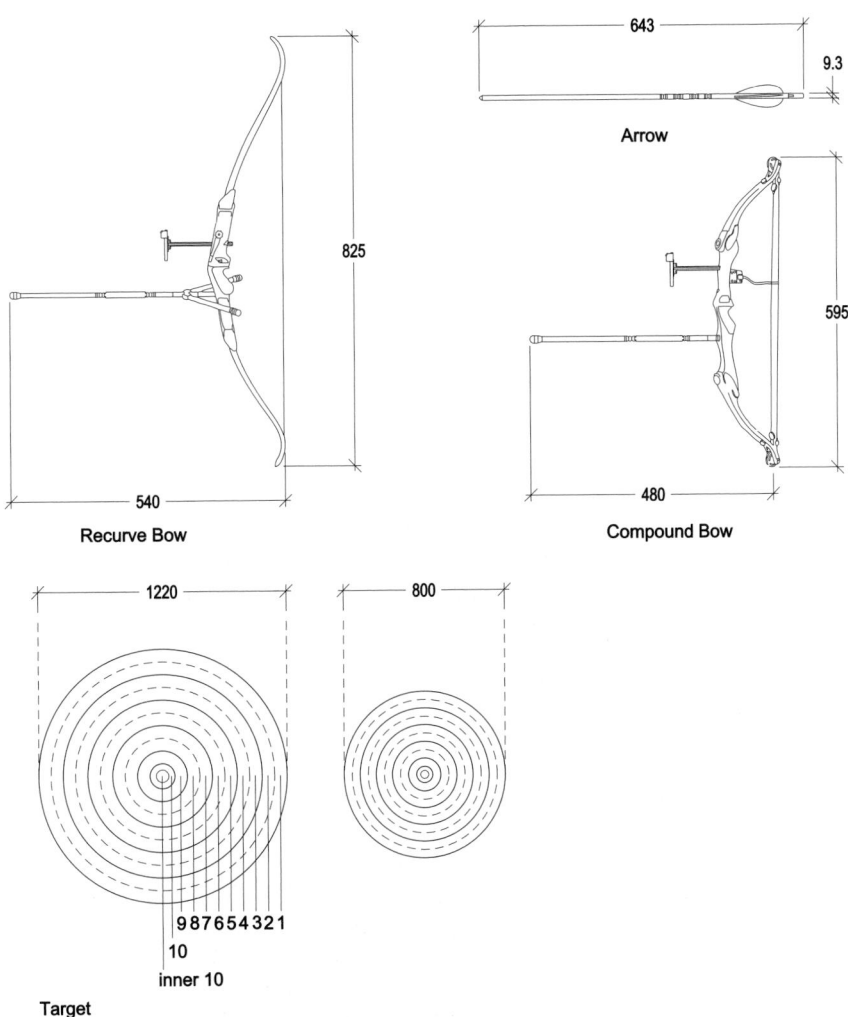

38.44 *Archery*

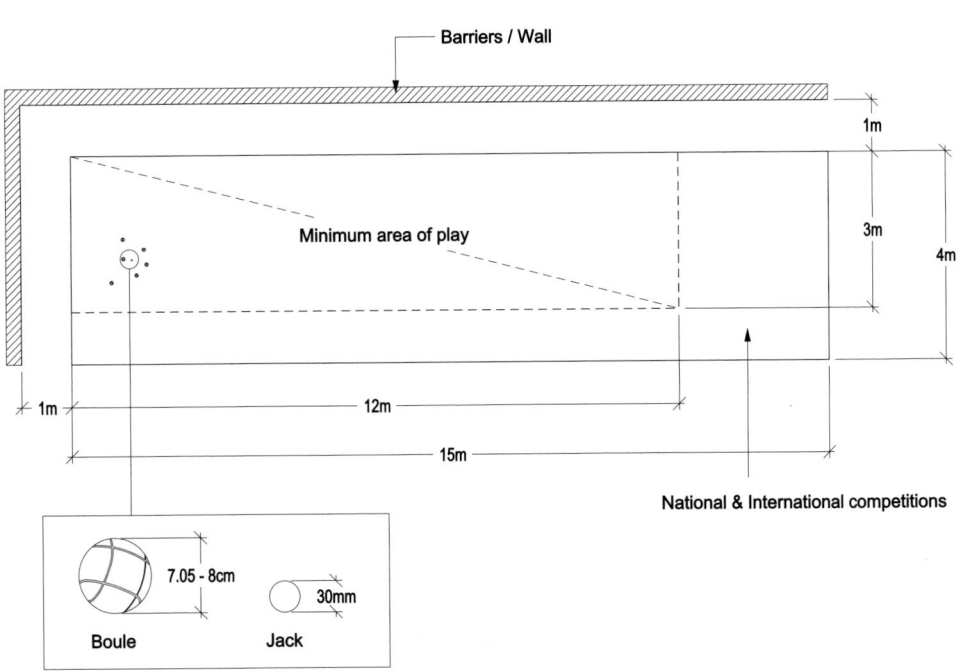

38.45 *Petanque*

3.9 Compatibility

Within certain dimensional ranges, a number of surfaces are capable of accommodating a number of these sports, subject to changes to markings. Some surfaces can display the markings of more than one sport subject to appropriately coloured markings being used to clearly distinguish one from another. It is quite common for the multi-sports hall of a school or local authority sports centre to be marked out to accommodate tennis, five-a-side football, basketball, netball, volleyball and badminton, Figure 38.46.

One of the great advantages of a modern indoor arena such as the O2 Arena in London is their flexibility to accommodate a number of different events, Figure 38.47. It is possible to design the field of play to be transformable between ice hockey, basketball, netball, tennis, boxing, badminton, gymnastics, or even dressage.

International stadia are increasingly being designed to accommodate a number of sports that can attract large crowds, including football (soccer, American football and Australian football), rugby (both codes), athletics and cricket, Figure 38.48. The

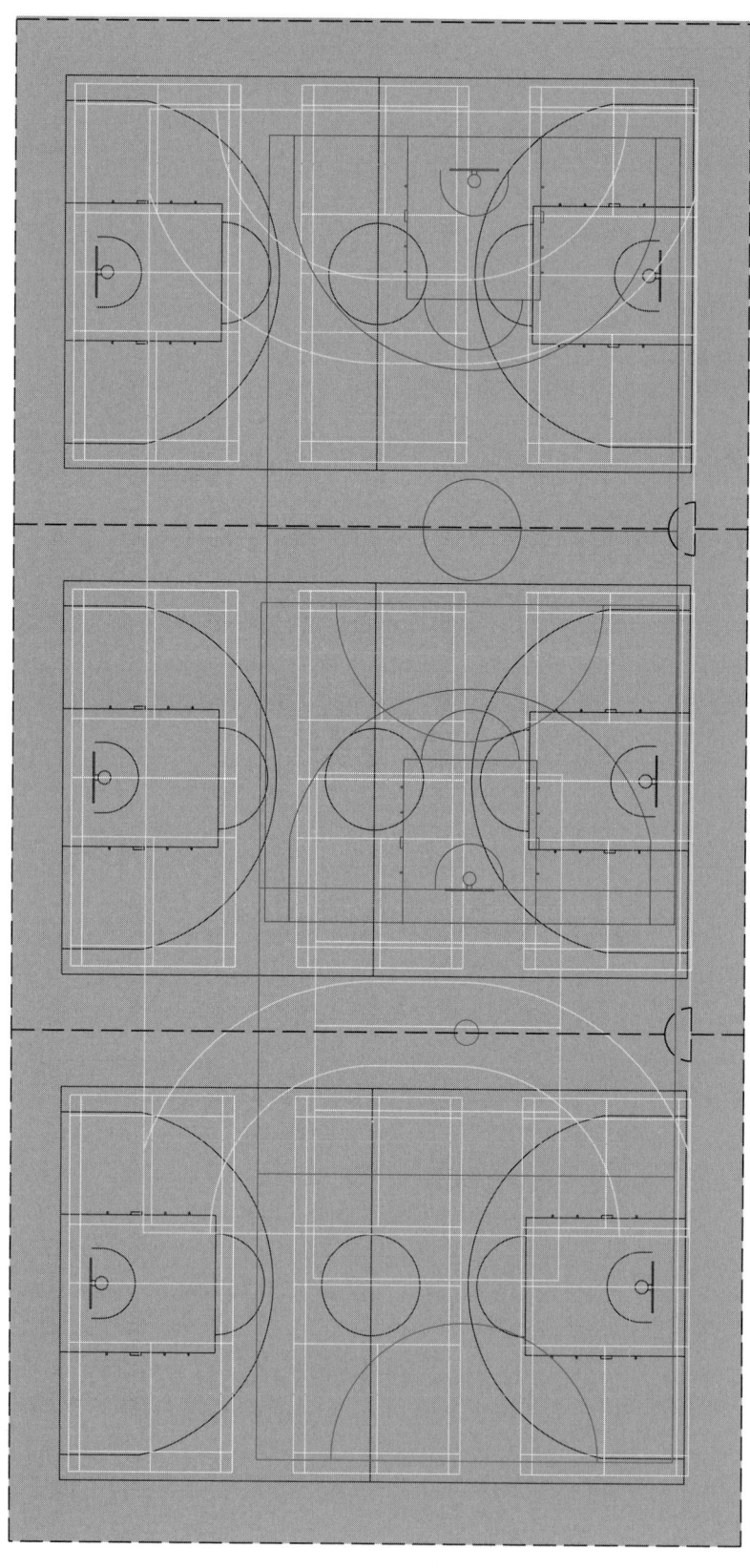

YELLOW - HANDBALL
(40,00X20,00 metre)
BLACK - FULL SIZE BASKETBALL COURT
(28,00x15,00 metre)
DARK BLUE - BASKETBALL COURT FOR
TRAINING PURPOSES
(23,00x14,00 metre)
WHITE - BADMINTON
(13,40x6,10 metre)
LIGHT BLUE - VOLLEYBALL
(18,00x9,00 metre)
GREEN - VOLLEYBALL
(18,00x9,00 metre)
RED - NETBALL
(30,50x15,25 metre)

38.46 *Multi-sport hall markings*

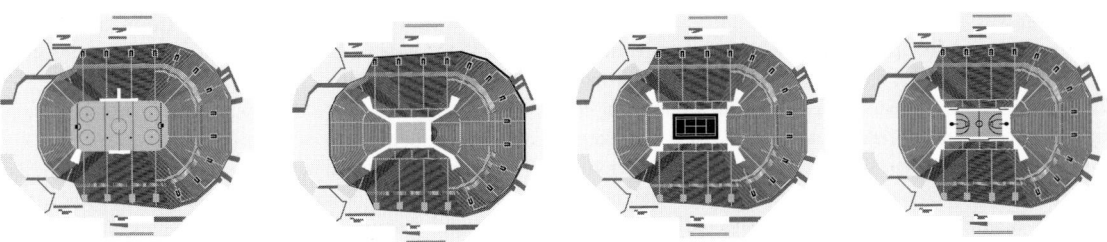

38.47 *O2 Arena field of play configurations*

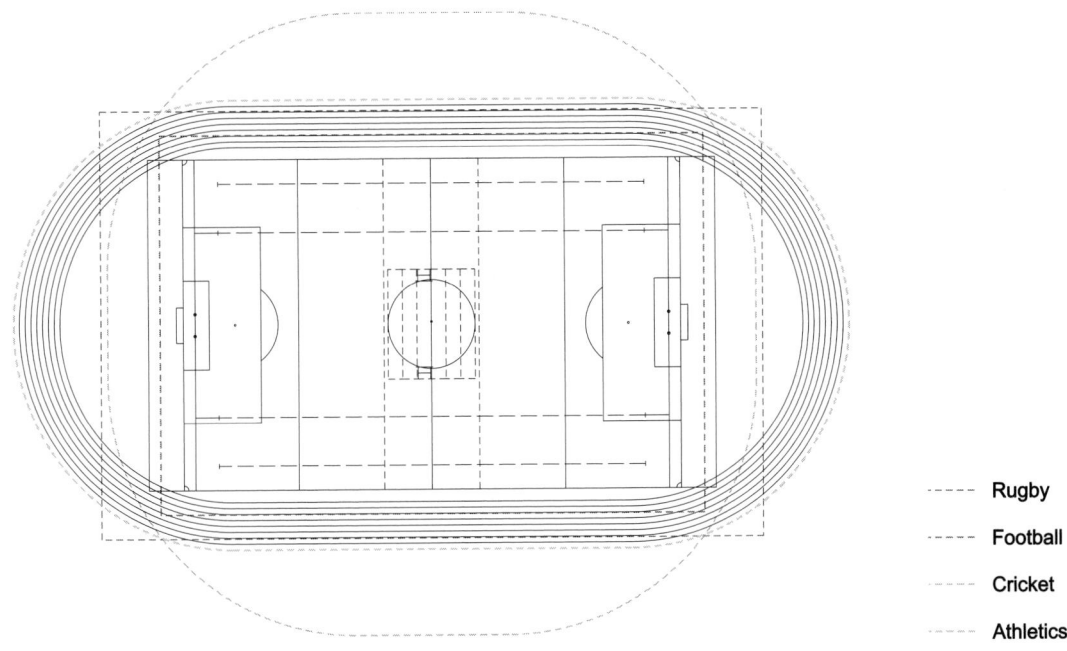

- - - - Rugby

- - - - Football

- - - - Cricket

- - - - Athletics

38.48 *Diagram showing rugby, football, cricket and athletics overlaid*

transformation of the field of play can take many forms and is discussed in Section 4.8.

3.10 Playing surface
Sports are played on a vast array of different surfaces from simple sand, for beach volleyball and petanque, through turf of varying complexity to quite sophisticated sprung timber floors for indoor courts.

Natural turf
Considerable research has been conducted into sports turf, in order to provide the appropriate specification for the intended purpose. This includes the species of grass, the growing medium build-up, flexible reinforcement to aid longevity but protect players, irrigation systems and under-pitch heating to maintain appropriate playing conditions around the calendar. Consideration also needs to be given to the health of the grass which requires, for good sustainable growth both wind and natural light, sometimes supported by artificial means. Reseeded every year, rye grass courts are still used in the UK and some other parts of the world for tennis, notably for the Queens and Wimbledon tournaments. Grass courts are generally the fastest type of court surface with the least bounce which has historically favoured the serve and volley style of play.

Artificial grass
All weather pitches laid with artificial grass, made from synthetic, often polyethylene, fibres made to look like natural grass are becoming increasingly common in order to reduce the maintenance required for natural turf and guarantee playability throughout the year. Most pitch-based sports can be played on artificial grass,

including football although some tournaments prevent their use. Artificial grass surfaces provide a consistency and flatness which is particularly suitable for field hockey and for cricket nets, and of course because neither sunlight nor irrigation is required, are especially suitable indoors.

Rubberised surfaces
The fastest athletics tracks have a natural or synthetic rubber surface, which can be applied in long strips or as a homogenous surface on top of a tarmac sub-base. This gives a sprung feel which is supportive to the athletes' efforts and less damaging to their bodies. Similar surfaces can be applied to sports halls and the like and are suitable for a range of pitch and court sports.

Timber floors
Indoor halls are often fitted out with a timber playing surface, sprung to protect the participants, making them suitable for a range of sports such as gymnastics, tennis, netball, squash, badminton etc. They are typically constructed on a screeded sub-floor using 22 mm solid timber board nailed or clipped to a batten system laid on a resilient underlay. Timber species include beech, maple and ash.

Although velodrome tracks have historically been constructed from a variety of materials including concrete and cinder, modern indoor velodrome tracks are usually constructed from pine. The track at the velodrome in the Olympic Park in London was constructed using Siberian pine, because the trees are known for being straight and tall making them suitable for the lengths of timber required to shape the track; and the extreme Siberian climate also means the timber is very stable and will not shrink or contract in the environmental conditions of the velodrome.

Other tennis surfaces

There are four surfaces used for professional tennis competitions: grass courts (discussed above), clay courts, hard courts and carpet courts. Clay courts are made from crushed shale, stone or brick, can be either red or green and are common in Europe and South America. Red clay, slower than the green, is used for the French Open at Roland Garros. Clay surfaces tend to be slower than others resulting in less dominance of the server during the game. Hard courts can be acrylic or synthetic with a painted surface containing sand. They are generally between grass and clay in terms of speed and bounce. Hard courts are used for the Australian Open in Melbourne and US Open at Flushing Meadows, and are common throughout the world. Short artificial grass weighed down with sand is a removable carpet court and is common in Asia. Indoor courts are normally hard courts although when tennis is played in a multi-event arena, a rubberised carpet is laid on the arena floor.

At lower levels of the game, tarmac surfaces are cheaper low maintenance substitutes.

3.11 Field of play orientation

There are general 'rules of thumb' and sometimes regulations for the orientation of outdoor pitches, particularly those that are designed for spectators and television coverage, Figure 38.49. Generally for temperate climate situations, locating the long axis of the pitch in a north-south orientation is preferred with a 15 degree tolerance either side. This is to ensure that neither team is looking into a low westerly sun in the afternoon/evening. Spectators will therefore naturally gravitate to the west side of the pitch as they too will not be looking into the sun. The prevailing wind direction can

also be a factor in orientation. There are of course always exceptions to the rule including famously Wembley Stadium which is orientated East–West.

3.12 Pitch technology

The most sophisticated natural turf pitches built for professional play will often employ a range of technology in order to maximise the quality and usability of the pitch; they can include built in irrigation systems with pop-up sprinklers or pitch-side canons, and heating and systems embedded in the sub-base which can be electrical, water or air based. The system beneath the pitch at the Cardiff Millennium Stadium employs a series of large ducts which can be used to heat, drain and ventilate the root zone. Where the field of play needs to be changed to suit different sports or activities, it is becoming increasingly common for pitches to be laid in pallets that can be slotted together by forklift truck and then removed when required. This allows a turn-around time of approximately 2 days. A few stadia around the world have even been constructed where the entire pitch can be slid out of a letterbox opening at one end of the stadium; this can be a swift process and allows for the grass to be grown and maintained in an open air environment and then deployed inside the stadium where the environment is not as conducive to long term grass growth.

3.13 Floodlighting

If the sport is to be played outside at night then clearly floodlights will be required so that the participants can play and train in safety, Figure 38.50. If the facility is designed to accommodate spectators then care needs to be taken to ensure that glare from the floodlights is avoided. At major events where television cameras will

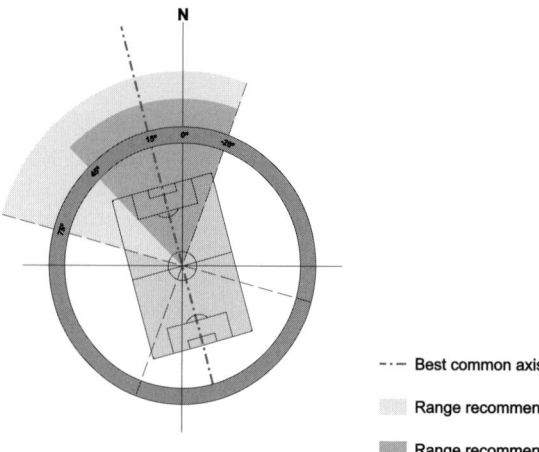

--·— Best common axis of orientation for many sports

Range recommended for football & rugby

Range recommended for track and field pitch sports

38.49 *Field of play orientation*

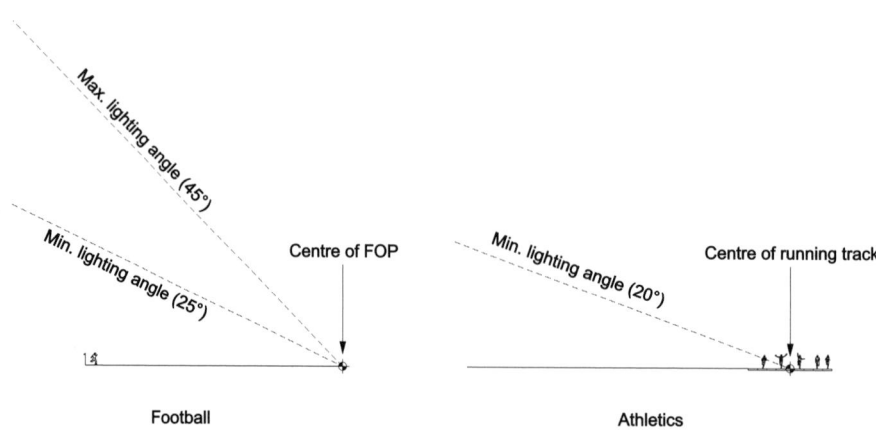

38.50 *Diagram showing lighting distribution onto stadium field of play*

be present, the light levels on the field of play need to be suitable for broadcast requirements. Whilst fixed floodlights are most common, either as part of the roof design or at the top of dedicated towers, a number of facilities including Lords Cricket Ground have erected retractable lighting towers so that their visual impact on the city skyline is reduced on non-event days, Figure 38.51. The height of the lights will depend on the illumination levels required on the field of play and the angle of the projected light.

3.14 Head/clearance height

When planning the design of indoor facilities, the designer must take into account the height of the performance space required for each sport. Some vary according to the standard of competition so governing bodies should be consulted, however Figures 38.52–38.54 show recommended minimum heights for club, county, regional and national level competition.

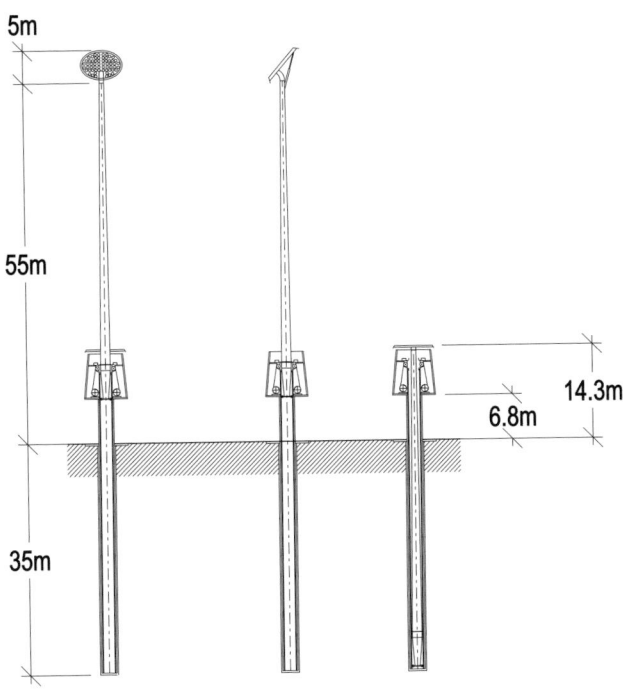

38.51 *Diagram of retractable floodlights*

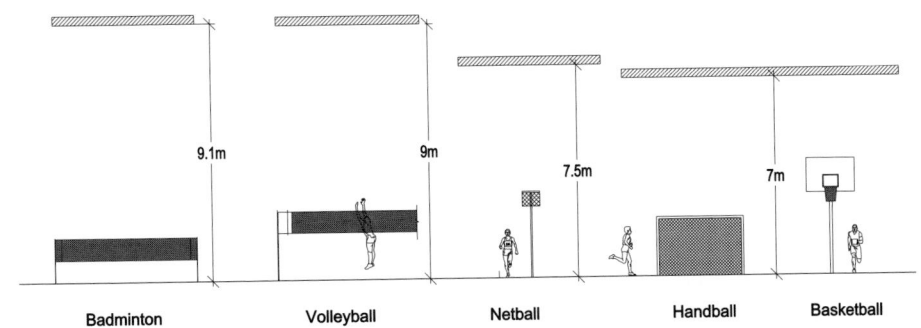

38.52 *Diagram for vertical clearances for different sports (badminton, volleyball, netball, handball, basketball)*

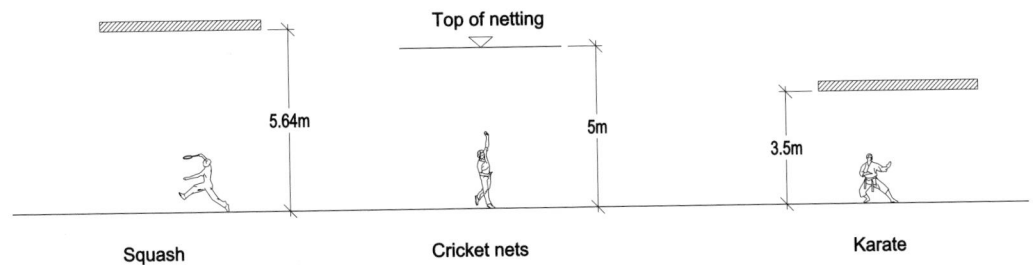

38.53 *Diagram for vertical clearances for different sports (squash, cricket, karate)*

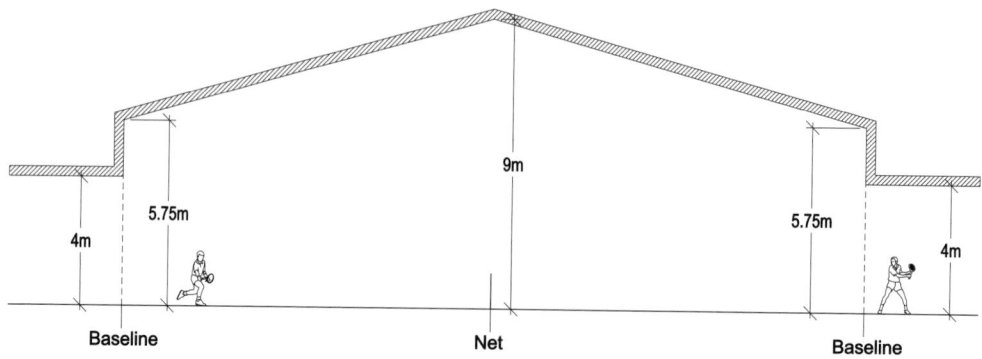

38.54 *Diagram for vertical clearances for indoor tennis*

4 VIEWING STRUCTURES

4.1 Introduction

This section relates to the requirements for spectator viewing structures should these be required to observe the action on the field of play. Clearly a school playing field may have some spectators attending a match and they may simply stand at the touchline, but once the numbers of spectators reaches 2 or 3 rows of people, then viewing of the action becomes more difficult and so tier structures will be required, Figure 38.55. For example a road stage of a large cycle race such as the Tour de France will often attract thousands of spectators along the route but because the route is so long, viewing structures are only required at the finish.

The design of viewing structures can have a significant effect on the atmosphere enjoyed by the spectators and indeed the participants. This is where the art and science of design are indivisible. For any given seating capacity, the spectators can be accommodated in a number of ways, related to the overall footprint and height, resulting in quite different experiences for all.

4.2 Viewing standards and sightlines

The first step when designing sightlines is to determine what is required to be seen. This could be the touchlines of a pitch, the likely height of a rugby ball kicked high into the air, video screen and scoreboards, the pitch-side dug out so a manager's reaction can be seen, or the referee sat high on their chair at a tennis match. It should also be remembered that it may be impossible to see the entire course for some sports such as motor-racing or horse racing depending on the terrain of the course.

Once the sightline target line or point is established, then the rows of spectators can be laid out. Consideration should be given to whether the spectators will be standing or seated, or sometimes in combination, to view the event. The specific rake of the terracing is established by determining the distance of the first row of spectators from the target line and the c-value. The c-value is a dimension measured in millimetres between the sightlines of spectators in adjoining rows, perpendicular to the target, as shown in Figures 38.56 and 38.57. This is typically between c. 60 and c.

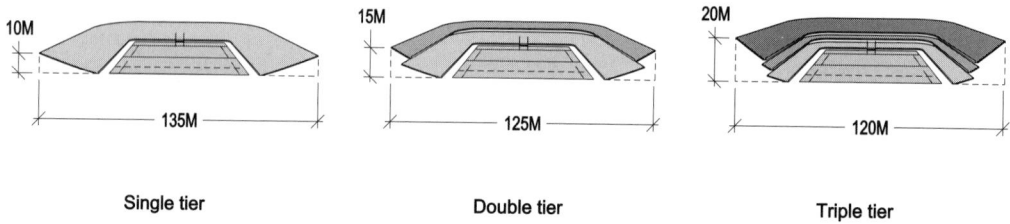

Single tier   Double tier   Triple tier

38.55 *Diagrams showing how spectators can be accommodated in different configurations*

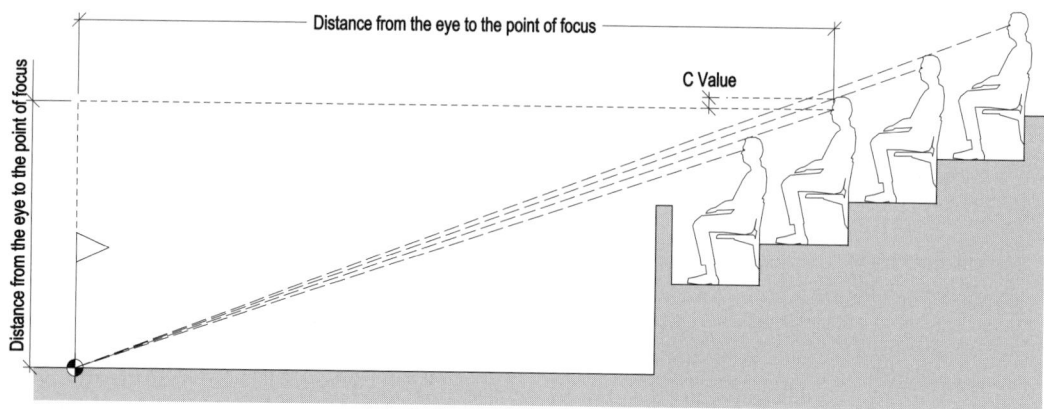

38.56 *Diagram showing definition of c-values*

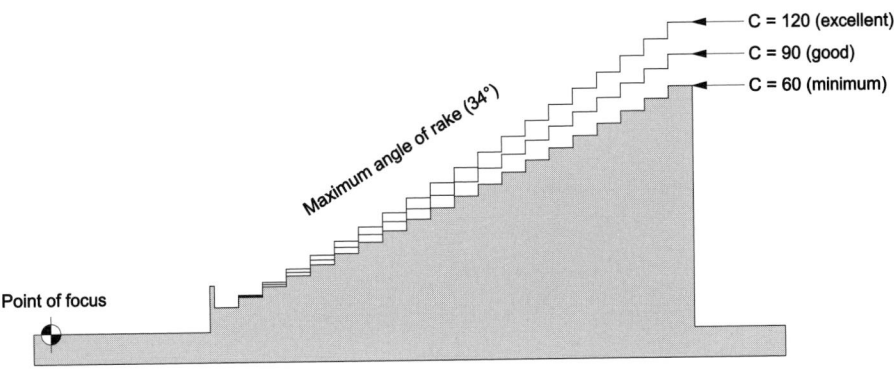

38.57 Diagram showing effect of different c-values

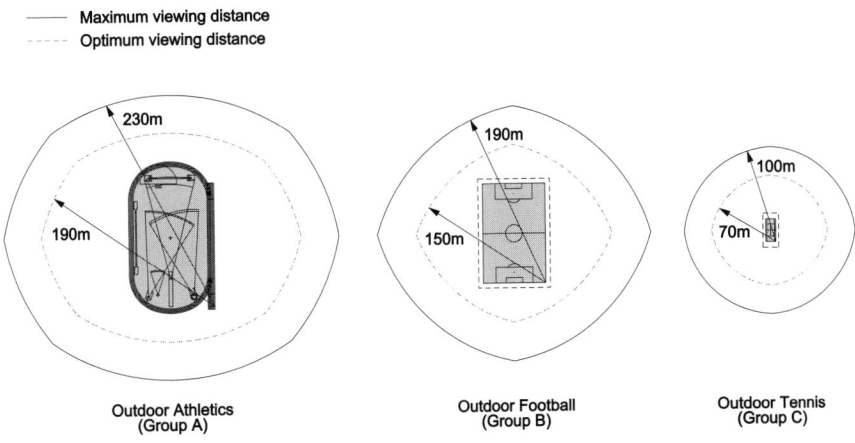

38.58 Diagram showing maximum viewing distances for 3 sports

120 with the higher numbers offering superior views. The mathematics calculation results in a parabolic curve for the profile of the tier, but an important consideration is that the maximum allowable rake of a tier is 34 degrees. The technical dimensions of sightlines however are only one part of perception of quality of view, and other factors are relevant. Some spectators prefer to be close to the action and will sacrifice the birds-eye view effect that a higher viewpoint would offer, and the reverse is also true. At sports such as horse racing and motor-racing, the view may need to be more panoramic where diagonal views are arguably just as important as views directly to the track in front. The speed of movement of the action is also a relevant factor.

4.3 Viewing distance
The size of the viewing area is determined by a number of factors, including client aspiration, the business plan, site constraints and essential activities on the field of play perimeter, but also by the relevant recommended maximum viewing distance for each sport. For a ball sport, the smaller the ball and the faster it moves, the harder it is to see and therefore the closer the spectator needs to be. Conversely a larger ball moving more slowly can be seen from a greater distance. This means that the maximum viewing distance for tennis would be considerably smaller than that for football, Figure 38.58.

There are of course exceptions to this rule, such as golf or cricket where spectators aren't really expected to be able to follow the ball in flight, but simply observe the reactions of the relevant sportsmen and women.

4.4 Seating and standing provision.
Some spectators will prefer to stand and others to sit, Figure 38.59. This may depend on the tradition of the sport, the level of

excitement, the duration of the event and governing body regulations. Football grounds to the UK are required to be all-seated, whereas there is more flexibility for other sports. The sightlines will clearly be different for each so care should be taken to ensure that views are not impeded should standing spectator positions be located in front of seated spectators.

4.5 Seats
Seating can take many forms depending on the type of event and nature of the tier to which they are fixed, Figure 38.60. Simple bleacher benches without backs are common in the USA typically for High School or University facilities but less so in the UK. Plastic tractor seats, without backs, which are fixed down to the terraces are common in continental Europe but again less so in the UK. Whilst fixed seats with backs are occasionally also used, the most common form is for a tip-up seat, which permits the greatest area for circulation when the spectators are on the move. Advances in the design of the seats, using polypropylene injection moulding, have significantly improved the comfort of spectators with padding increasingly used and upholstered seats in VIP areas. The addition of UV-stable additives into the plastic can reduce the faded appearance common at older exterior stands. The recommended minimum spacing of seats is 500 mm with a maximum number of 28 seats between gangways or aisles, Figures 38.61 and 38.62.

4.6 Access to and egress from seating
When large numbers of people are gathered together, the dynamics of crowd movement needs to be carefully considered in order to ensure the safety of everybody involved. The Guide to Safety at Sports Grounds (the Green Guide) exists to assist designers and inspectors of sports facilities and should be used as a primary reference document.

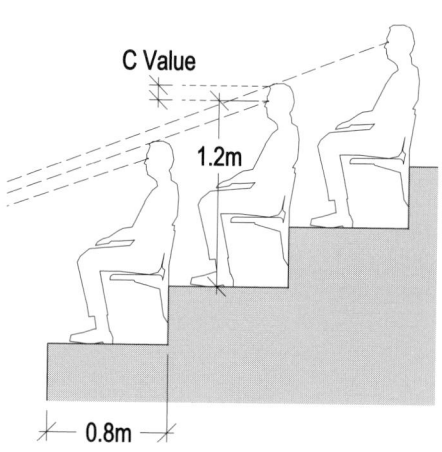

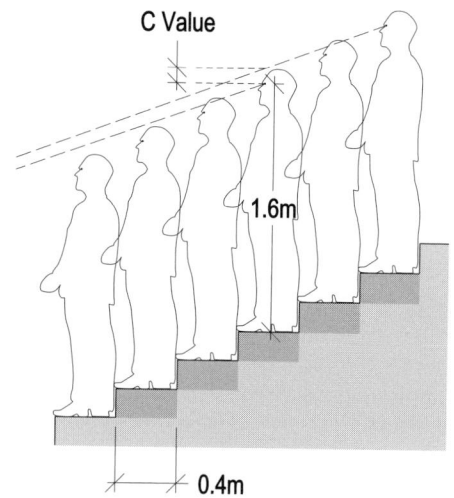

38.59 *Diagrams showing c-value calculations*

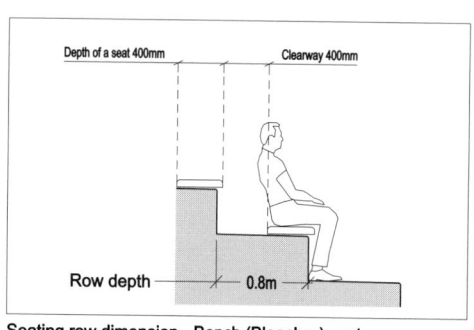

Seating row dimension - Bench (Bleacher) seat

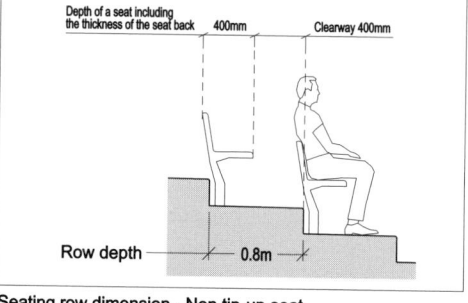

Seating row dimension - Non tip-up seat

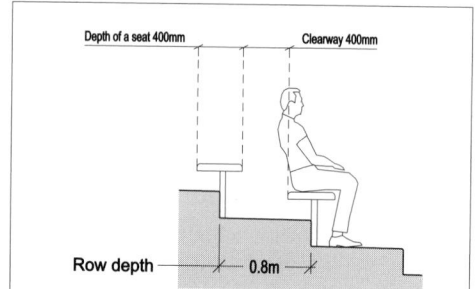

Seating row dimension - Bench (Bleacher) seat

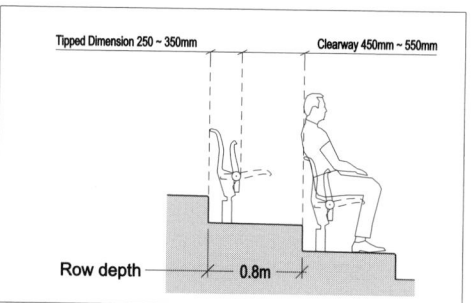

Seating row dimension - Tip-up seat

38.60 *Diagrams showing different seat types*

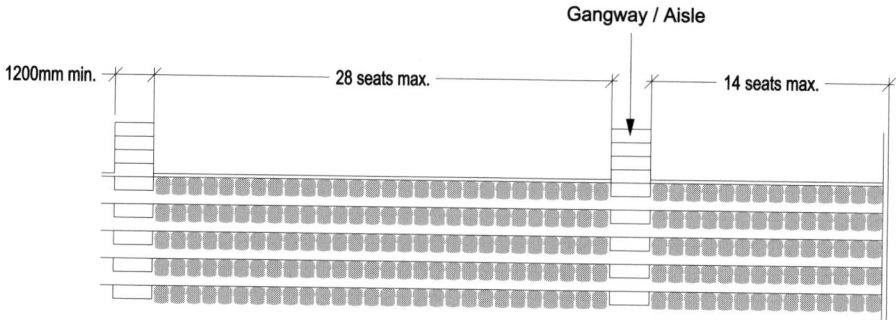

38.61 *Diagram showing maximum number of seats in a row*

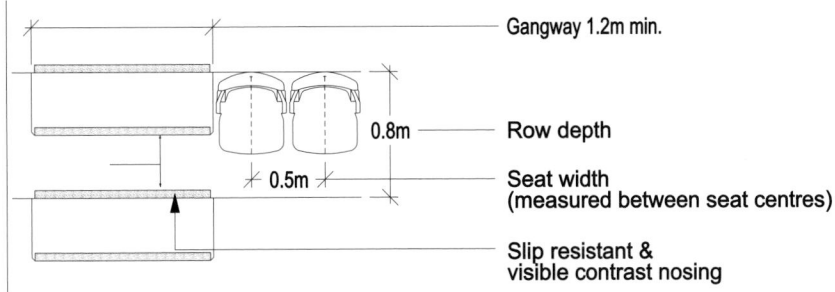

38.62 Diagram showing seats spacing

At the earliest stage of planning a sports facility, the crowd movements of spectators, be that from local transport links, car parks or a combination of the two, need to be understood in order to ensure that the areas outside the facility are correctly sized to accommodate them. This logic flows through to the number of turnstiles or other ticket checking measures required, as the UK venue licensing laws require that an accurate record of spectators attending events is maintained.

The space inside that ticket check zone is often termed the concourse and there are minimum sizes recommended for this area depending on the event. From here, access is gained into the viewing structures, terraces or auditorium by means of aisles or gangways – apertures formed in the seating tier. The minimum width for these access ways is 1200 mm but the actual size should be calculated in relation to the number of people using the route, the rate at which they flow through along it and the length of time they need to do it in. The Green Guide advises rate of passage such that 82 spectators can reasonably exit per minute for every metre width on a level surface. Clearly the larger the venue, the more complex the calculation will be. The guide also recommends that no seat should be further than 30 m from a point of exit, Figure 38.63. Once inside the seated viewing area, the minimum distance between adjacent rows of tiered seating is 800 mm, with increased row depths recommended when larger upholstered seats are used. The aisle, row and seat numbers all need to be clearly identified.

4.7 Disability Discrimination Act, 2005

In order to comply with the DDA, the viewing areas of a venue need to take into account the needs of disabled people in order to be inclusive. This equally applied to wheelchair users, ambulant disabled people and people with other disabilities. Particular care should be taken in the design of viewing structures to ensure that the view from a wheelchair position is not obscured by a spectator standing in the row in front, Figures 38.64, 38.65. Wheelchair positions, with adjacent companion positions, would be expected to be distributed in a number of locations throughout the viewing areas to offer the similar level of choice as for other spectators. The minimum recommended number of wheelchair viewing positions and other accessible seating types is defined in the Football Licensing Authority (FLA) document, 'Accessible Stadia'.

4.8 Stand design

The construction of the viewing tiers can take many forms, depending on the nature of the event or events, Figure 38.66. For one-off or annual temporary events such as the London 2012 Olympics Beach Volleyball event at Horseguards' Parade in London or Henley Regatta or where supplementary seating is required for large events such as Royal Ascot or the British Grand Prix at Silverstone, it is common for these tiers to be provided in a temporary form based on a scaffold system. For permanent tiers, the construction favoured is usually insitu concrete or bespoke precast concrete planks spanning between raker beams. The use of timber for these structures is now rare due to fire risk concerns. Steel sandwich plates with an inert core to deaden the sound are also beginning to be used as an alternative to concrete. In some major stadia around the world, the tiers have been designed to move, so that they can be reconfigured for events with different requirements. For example the stadium built for the Olympic Games in Sydney included a retractable lower tier so that it can be transformed between Australian Rules Football and Rugby pitch configurations.

All types of tier need to be designed to accommodate the fixing and the considerable loads applied to safety barriers, and care needs to be taken in the design of these barriers to limit as much as possible any obstructions to viewing, Figure 38.67.

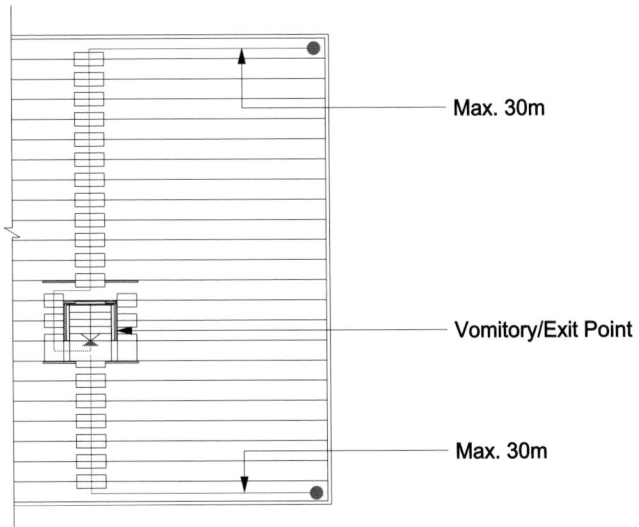

38.63 Diagram showing the 30 m rule

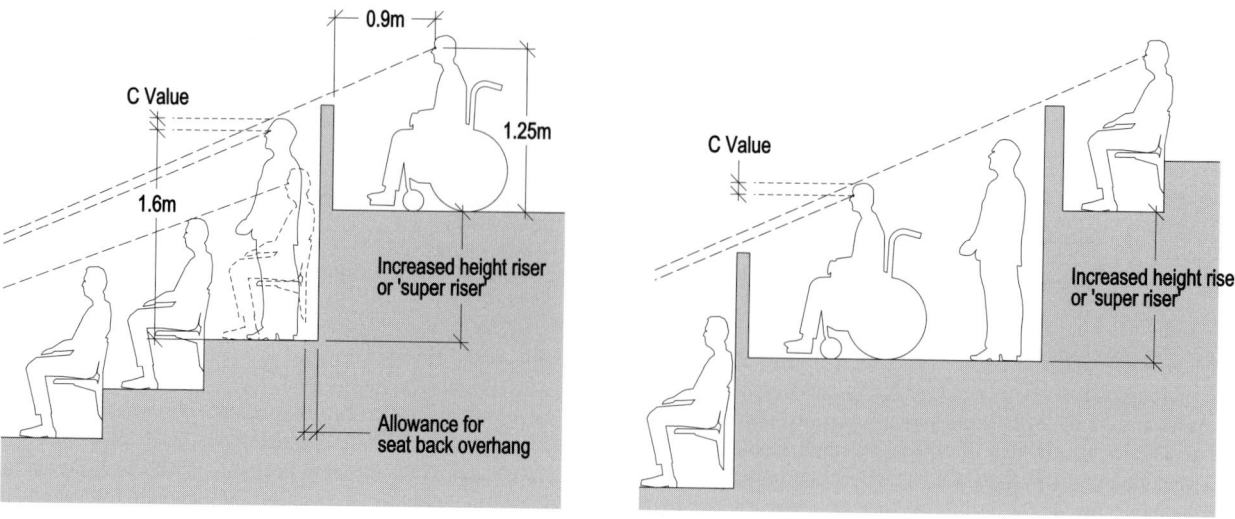

38.64 and 38.65 *Diagrams showing wheelchair viewing relative to other viewing*

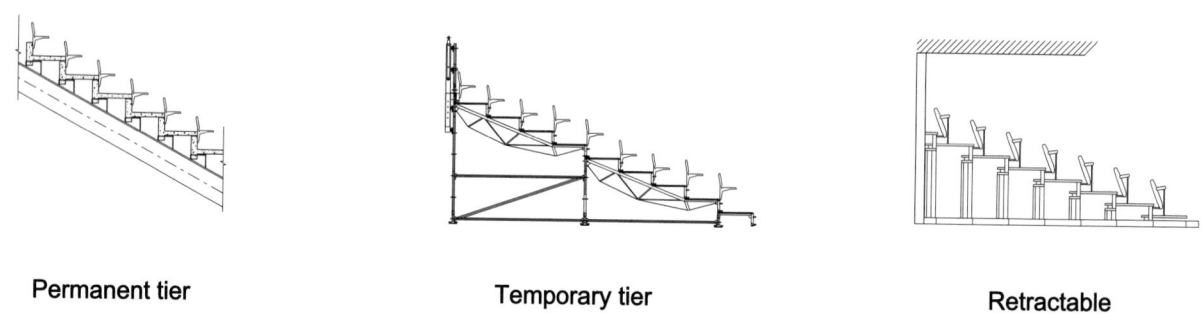

Permanent tier   Temporary tier   Retractable

38.66 *Diagram showing different kinds of stand*

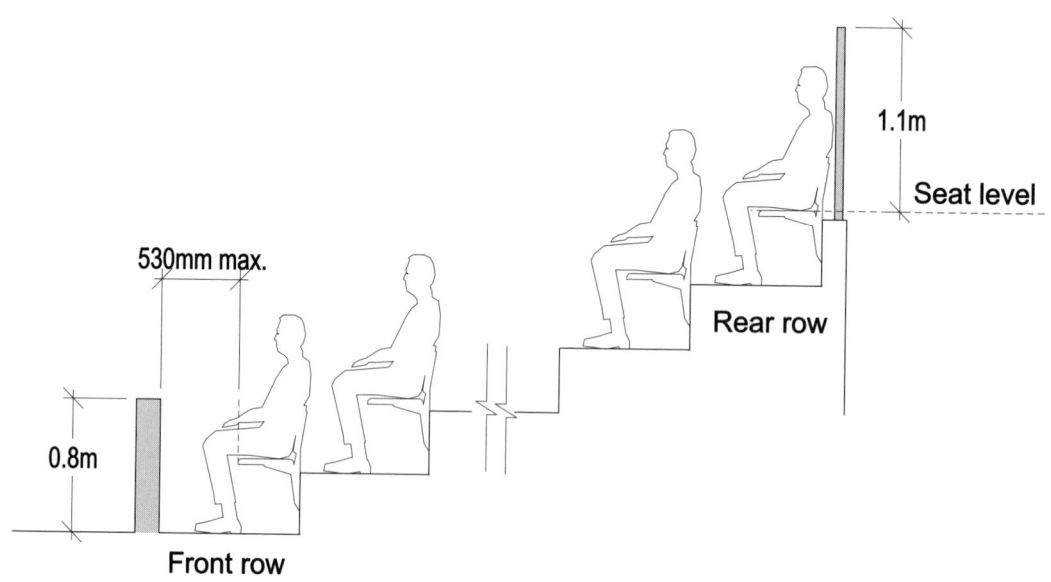

38.67 *Diagram showing barrier design*

4.9 Roofs

The degree to which shade and/or shelter will be required over the spectators will depend on a number of factors including national climate, local conditions including prevailing wind strength and direction, client aspirations and any relevant governing body regulations, including viewing to high balls and other projectiles, Figure 38.68. For example: at the highest club level of both football and rugby, a roof over all spectators is recommended. Roofs can be erected as temporary structures, although their support columns will often obstruct views, which is obviously not desirable. In UK stadia it is common for a permanent canopy to be provided over the spectators, but not over the field of play. Larger international stadia, such as the Millennium Stadium in Cardiff, are being increasingly designed with retractable roofs to afford them the flexibility to accommodate a number of different kinds of events. Modern international arenas such as the O2 arena in London have fixed roofs that cover both the spectators and the field of play.

The roofs of larger sports facilities often involve large span structures, for which reinforced concrete, timber glulam and steel cable or trussed designs have all been employed. Roof coverings tend to be steel or aluminium-profiled sheet, polycarbonate or tensile fabrics like PTFE/glass or PVC/polyester. The larger the span, the more the efficiency of lightweight designs is required. At the scale of the stadium or arena, the roof is often the defining element of the architectural design.

4.10 Video screens and scoreboards

Central to the modern spectator experience is information. Scores, statistics and replays bombard the viewer on television and the spectator at a live event is increasingly demanding a similar experience, Figure 38.69. Advances in LED and other technologies have allowed significant improvements over older dot-matrix scoreboards and typical cricket scoring devices. The size of the information displayed needs to relate to the distance from which it is viewed to ensure that it is readable. For examples, at athletics, the height of the characters of the display should be between 3 and 5 per cent of the distance to the furthest spectator. The number, size and position of screens should not impede the view of the action on the field of play.

5 SPORTS EQUIPMENT

This section includes dimensional data for sports equipment typically incorporated into the planning of sports facilities, whether they are for training or competition.

5.1 Gymnasium equipment

This may include the following:

- Rowing machines
- Spin bikes
- Weights machines
- Treadmills, Figure 38.70.

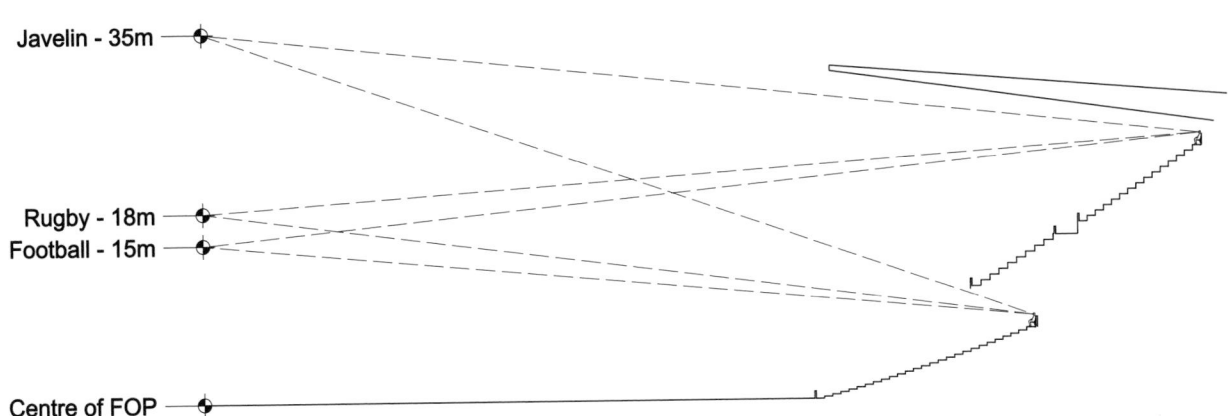

38.68 *Diagram showing high-ball viewing for football, rugby and javelin*

38.69a *Video screen between stands at a stadium*

38.69b *Video screens incorporated amongst the stadium seating*

5.2 Pitch sport equipment
Figures 38.71–38.80 show dimensions for pitch sport equipment.

5.3 Track sports equipment
Figures 38.81–38.86 show dimensions for track sport equipment.

5.4 Pool equipment
Figure 38.87 shows dimensions for diving boards.

5.5 Court sport equipment
Figures 38.88–38.92 show dimensions for courts sport equipment.

5.6 Water sport equipment
Figures 38.93 and 38.94 show dimensions for water sport equipment.

5.7 Other sport equipment
Figure 38.95 shows dimensions for gymnasium equipment.

6 SUPPORT FACILITIES FOR COMPETITORS AND OFFICIALS

6.1 Introduction
The size and range of accommodation for participants and officials will vary depending on the level of competition. These facilities will typically include changing rooms, toilets and showers, gymnasia, strength and conditioning areas, warm-up areas, sometimes supplemented by medical and drug testing facilities for professional sports and areas for information and results. The accessibility of

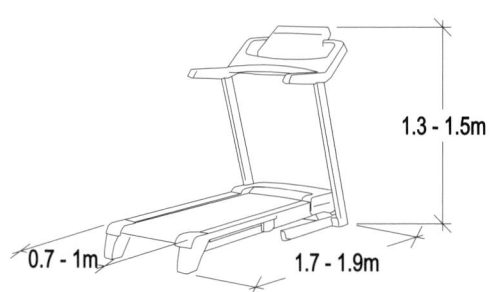

38.70 *Treadmill*

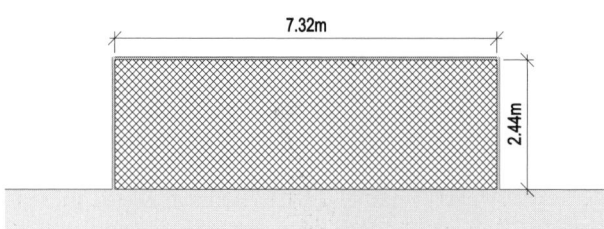

38.71 *Football (soccer) goalposts*

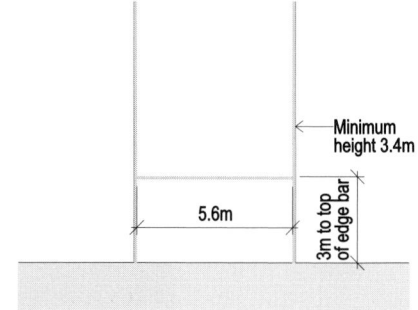

38.72 *Rugby posts*

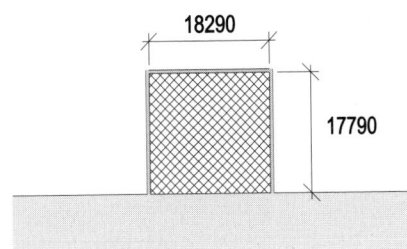

38.77 *Lacrosse*

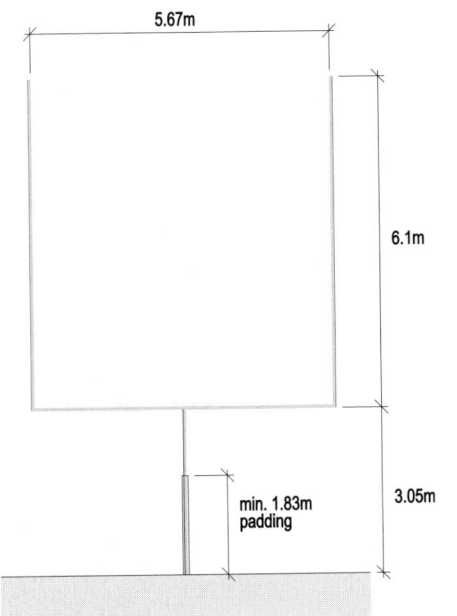

38.73 *American football posts*

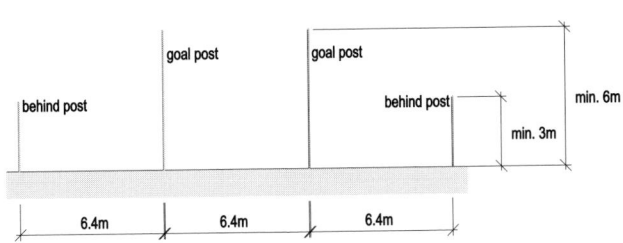

38.74 *Australian rules posts*

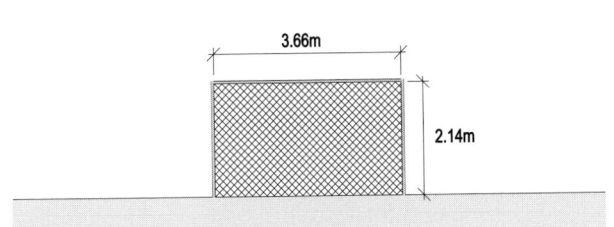

38.75 *Hockey goal*

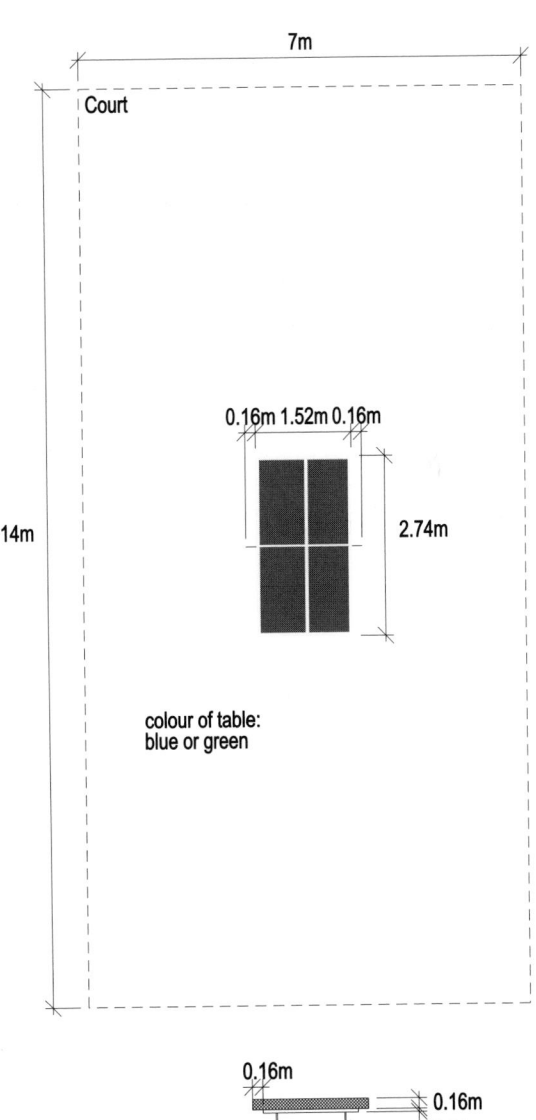

38.78 *Table tennis*

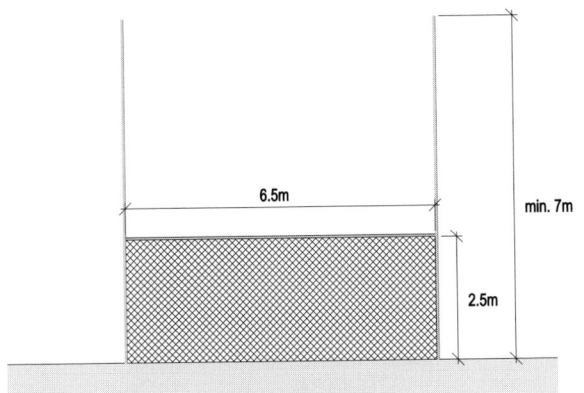

38.76 *Gaelic football*

these facilities must also be considered. The degree to which these facilities can be and are shared by the general public varies from sport to sport as well as by the level of competition.

6.2 Competitors and other participants

Most sports' buildings will require changing facilities for competitors, appropriate to the nature of events being held at the venue. The amount and type of accommodation varies depending on the type and scale of the event. For school, university and club level sport or for where competitors are not divided into teams, a changing room with toilet and shower facilities for each gender may be all that is required. For team sports, separate changing rooms are

Goal Posts:
Recommended size between 3.66m wide by 1.83m high.
Indoor with restricted height: 4.88m wide by 1.22m high (seniors) or 3.66m/2.44m wide by 1.22m high (juniors)

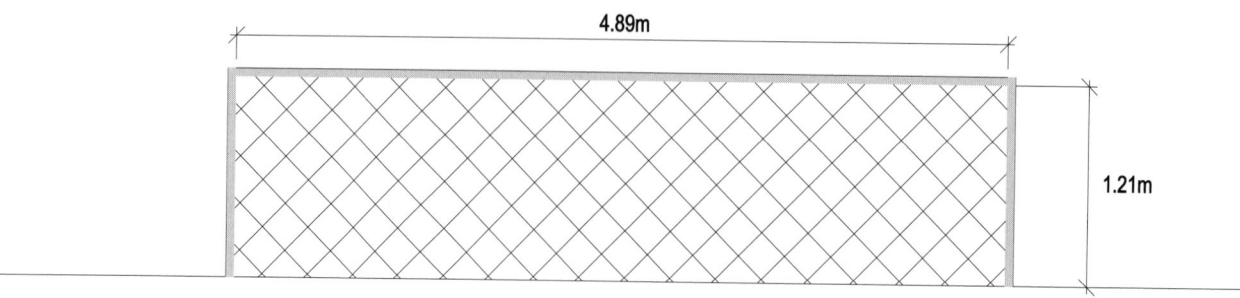

38.79 *5-a-side football*

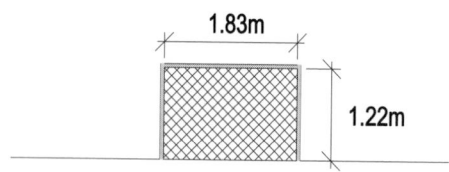

38.80 *Ice hockey*

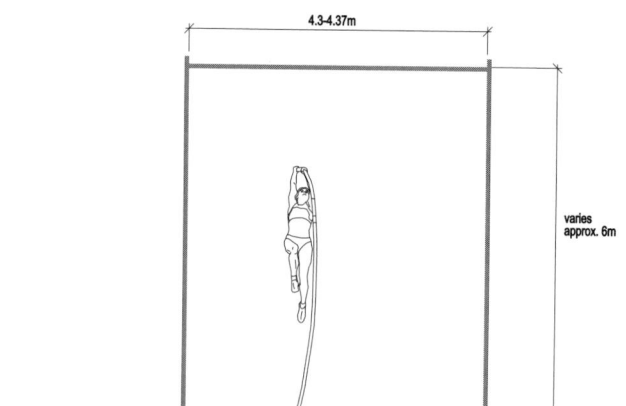

38.81 *Pole vault*

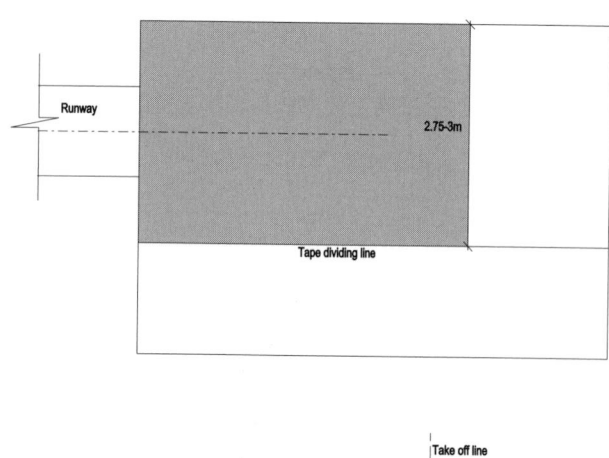

38.82 *Long jump*

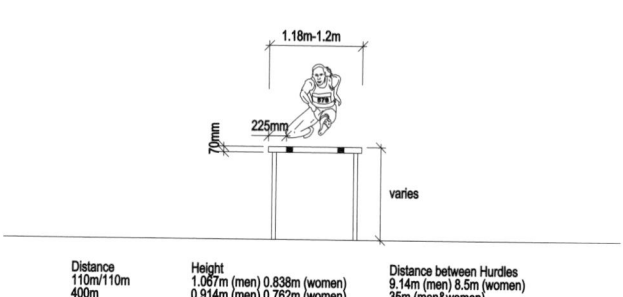

Distance	Height	Distance between Hurdles
110m/110m	1.067m (men) 0.838m (women)	9.14m (men) 8.5m (women)
400m	0.914m (men) 0.762m (women)	35m (men&women)

38.83 *Hurdles*

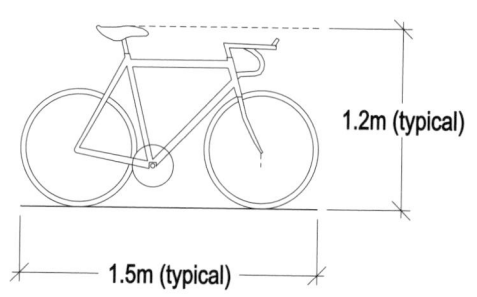

38.84 *Racing bike*

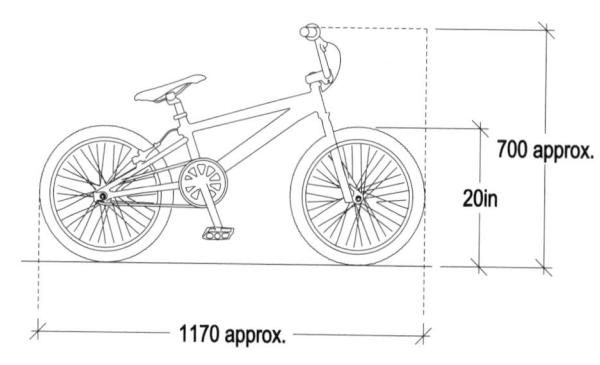

38.85 *BMX bike*

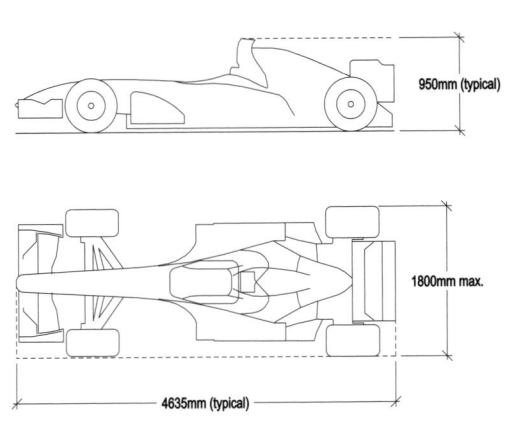

38.86 *Formula 1 car*

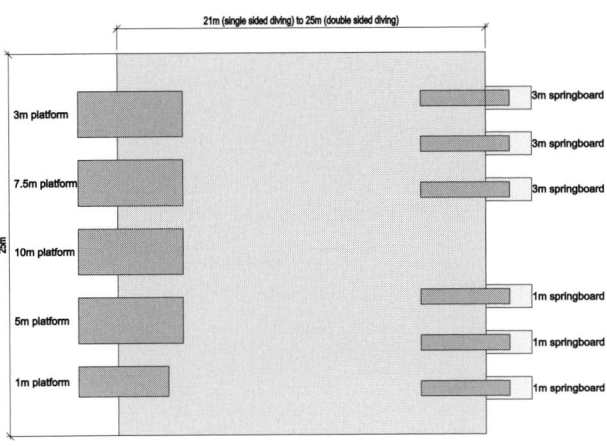

38.87 *Diving boards*

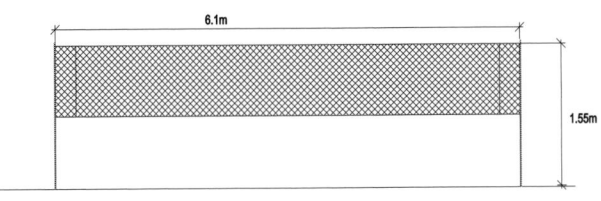

38.88 *Badminton net*

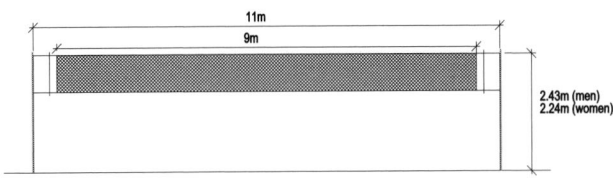

38.89 *Volleyball net*

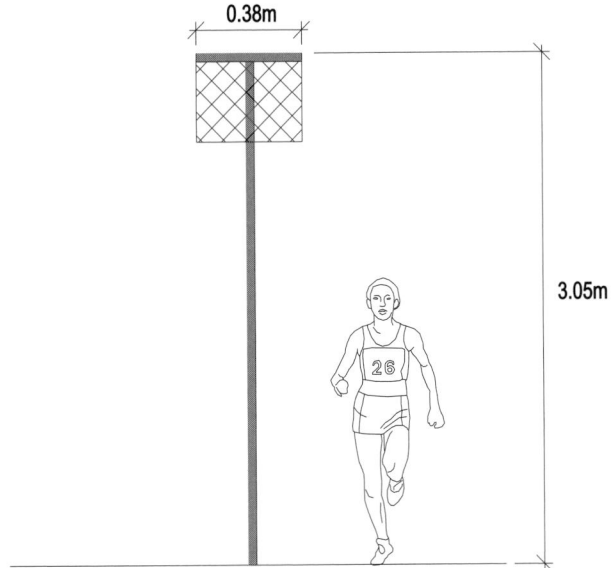

38.90 *Netball hoop*

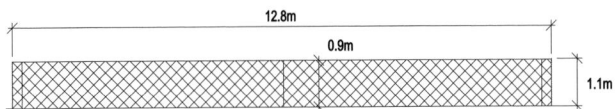

38.91 *Tennis net*

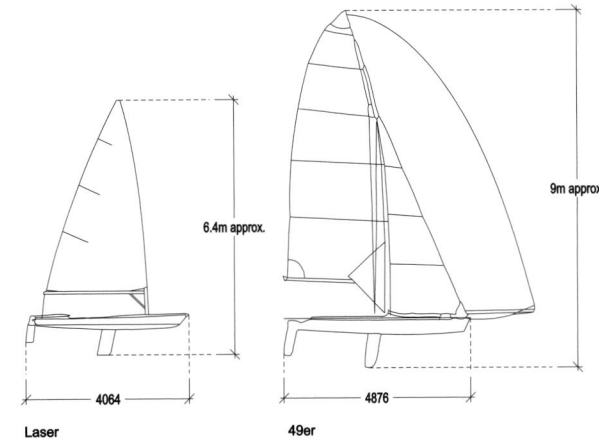

38.93 *Sailing dinghies (49er, Laser)*

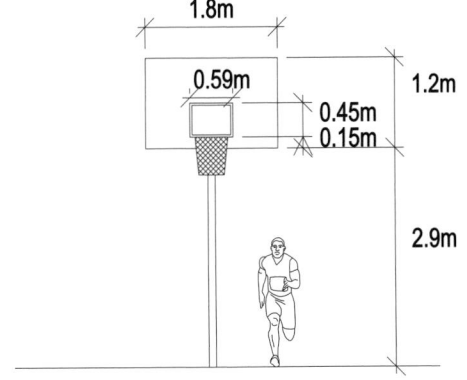

38.92 *Basketball hoop*

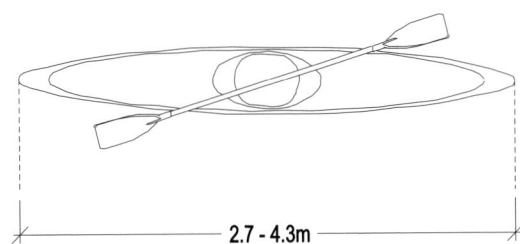

38.94 *Kayak*

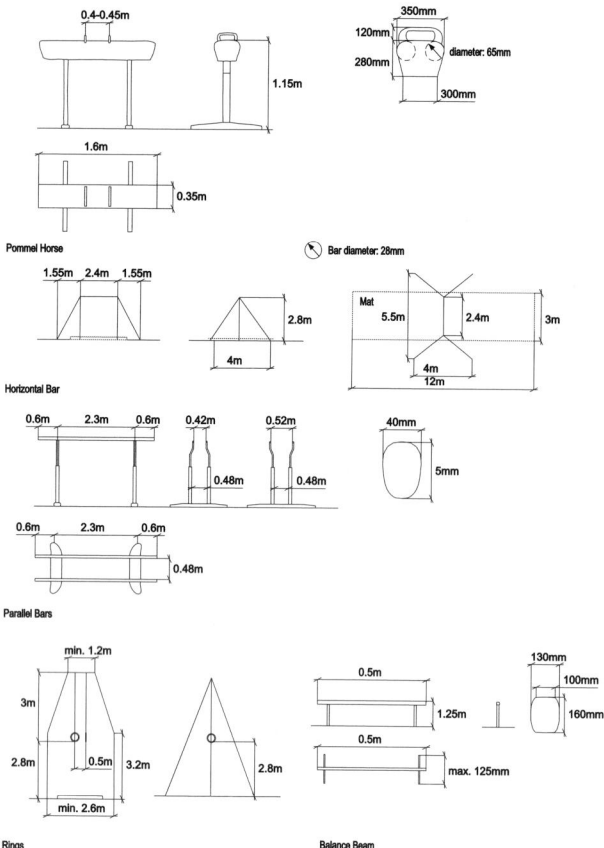

38.95 *Gymnastics equipment: vaulting horse, balance bar, parallel bars, rings*

usually required for each team as the rooms will be used for team briefing. If there is a 'home team', then most of the accommodation is concentrated on their requirements; however consideration should be given for multi-purpose use. In larger stadia the use of four changing rooms can provide flexibility in catering for a range of team sizes and additional participants such as ball boys and girls, mascots, marching bands and other entertainers.

Corridors used by competitors should be generously sized, preferably to a minimum of 1800 mm clear width. Consideration should be given to the requirements of wheelchair competitors for the intended sports, as competition chairs can have very a wide or long wheelbase. This will inform the requirements for corridor widths and turning spaces and doors, where competitors are likely to be using their competition chairs within the building.

Changing rooms should be laid out to suit the requirements of the intended sport, and should allow for a minimum of 1.6 m² per person. Generally team-based pitch sports require open layouts with a peripheral array of changing stations and lockers for competitors, which allows the team coach or manager to see and address all the occupants. Each changing room should contain locker facilities, bench seating and garment hanging space for each individual competitor, including substitutes. For elite sports facilities each changing position should be at least 750 mm wide, on the assumption that all changing positions will be occupied by the team during key periods. For community sports facilities each changing space of bench seat should be provided at a minimum width of 500 mm.

Elite sports changing rooms, Figure 38.96, will also require space for TV monitors and tactics boards, small refrigerators for refreshments storage, telephone and adjacent space for massage and physiotherapy beds. Integrated coaches' office and changing rooms may also be required. Multiple event and individual event venues such as athletics may have changing rooms divided into zones by free-standing banks of lockers and bench seating. Public access sports buildings should also contain family changing cubicle

facilities within the changing rooms. For larger family groups, cubicles measuring 2 m × 2 m are also suitable as accessible changing groups. All changing rooms should include accessible changing facilities.

Sanitary facilities, including WCs, urinals, hand basins, hand drying fixtures and showers should be designed to meet local building regulations. For elite competition venues, main changing rooms should be provided with dedicated sanitary facilities, accessed from within the changing facility. The toilet fixture numbers should be based on the likely peak occupancy of each changing room and the sport code recommendations. Publically accessible venues should have toilet facilities located adjacent to the changing room entrances, but accessed from common circulation areas. The toilet fixture numbers should be based on the likely total building occupancy. As a minimum, at least one unisex accessible toilet facility should be provided for participants' use adjacent to other toilet provisions. In larger facilities, accessible sanitary facilities should be included in gender specific toilet facilities, in addition to the unisex facilities.

Elite competition venue main changing rooms should be provided with shower facilities in accordance with sport code recommendations, and generally at not less than 1 shower per 2.3 changing positions. Publically accessible venue changing rooms should have shower facilities provided at not less than 1 shower per 10 changing positions and preferably 1 shower per 6 changing positions, and include some showers with cubicle enclosures. Dependent on layout drying areas between showers and main changing areas may be required.

6.3 Officials

Each sports event requires officials, judges, umpires, linesmen or referees, who normally require separate changing and toilet accommodation. Their changing facilities should be close to but ideally separate from the competitors' facilities and in good proximity to the field of play, but must be inaccessible to the public or the media. The accommodation should be sized for the appropriate number of officials, allowing 2.5 m² per person including associated lockers, toilets and showers in accordance with the sports code recommendations.

The nature of sport requires different event-specific facilities for officials: these might vary from a race committee room or boat for a sailing race, a timing and scoring room at an athletics track or a velodrome, or space for a third umpire and scorers at a cricket ground. In most instances a view of the field of play is essential and increasingly technological links will also be required. Internally, a seat and desk with clear sight of the playing area is a recommended minimum. Other facilities may also be required for operating the event. These could include an appeals room for up to ten people, a competition management room and also a place for processing results, and other sport-specific areas such as a weighing room at a racecourse, Figure 38.97.

6.4 Team management

If a sports building houses a home team, then it is likely that a suite of team management spaces will be required, preferably in close proximity to the main changing rooms. These facilities should not be confused with venue management facilities described in Section 9. The spaces could include: a designated reception area with general support office and secretariat, team manager and assistant managers' offices, and meeting rooms (which could be shared with other administrative activities).

Other subsidiary activities of team management and participant management that also require space may include uniform and kit storage, laundry and drying rooms, boot and shoe stores, equipment storage, and equipment repair and maintenance facilities such as tennis racquet stringing services.

6.5 Warm-up

Many sports require a space for the competitors to warm up, prior to engaging in their sport. This could be a simple space to stretch,

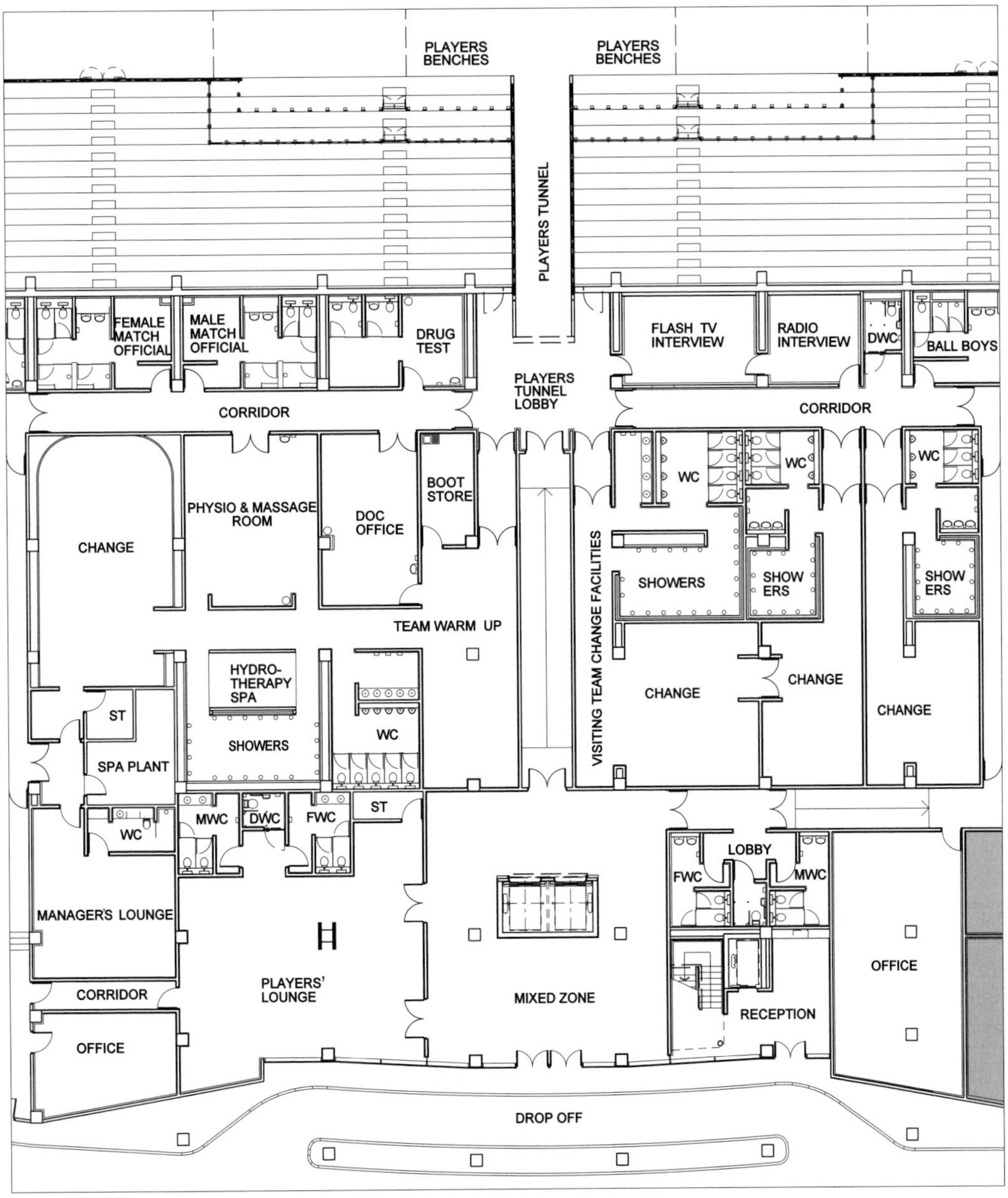

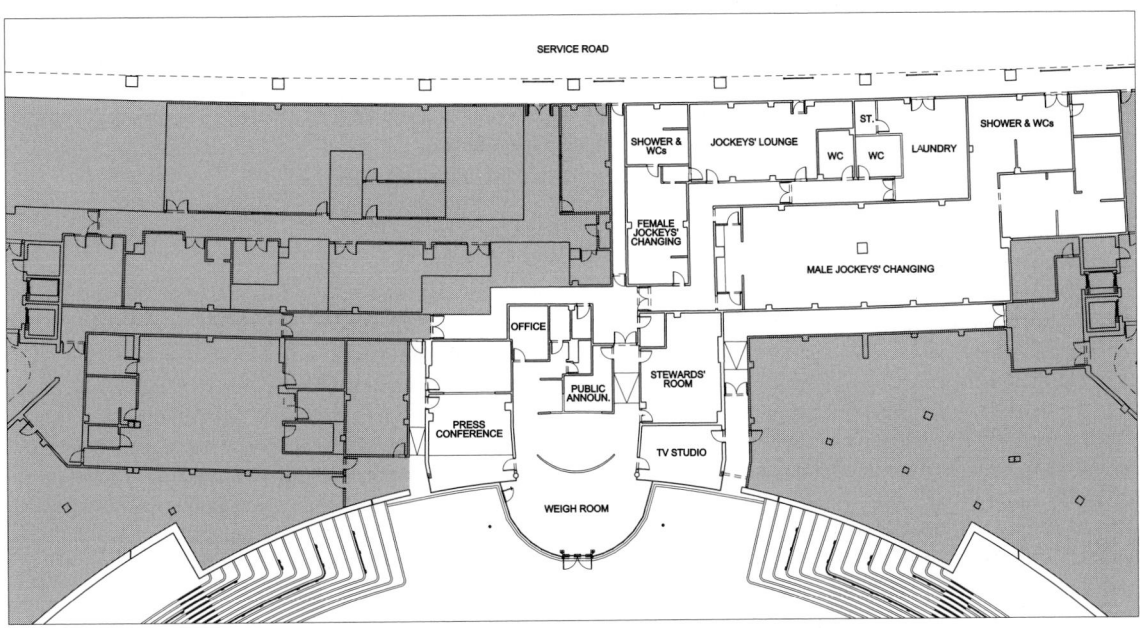

38.96 *Plan of Premier League football stadium players' facilities*

38.97 *Plan of racecourse weighing room complex*

usually part of the changing room, dedicated areas adjacent to changing rooms, an indoor 60 m warm-up track for athletics, or even a completely separate warm-up track and field for major athletics events. If a separate warm-up area is provided, then a dedicated connection will be required to link the warm-up area to the field of play.

6.6 Marshalling area/players' tunnel

Many sports require the competitors to be gathered into their teams, heats or event groups prior to entering the field of play. For example, athletics meets will have a final call room where athletes are checked for event schedule, compliant kit and correctly displayed identity numbers before being escorted with their event group onto the field of play. For pitch sports, competing teams will be assembled in a designated players' tunnel to run out in formation onto the field of play as part of the event spectacle. Competitor tunnels and field of play entrances may also be used for the movement of event entertainers, essential field of play equipment and officials as required during the event.

6.7 Medical facilities

Medical support facilities should be designed in accordance with local safety and licensing requirements, and sports codes recommendations. In major competition venues, the medical room is generally located in close proximity to the main changing rooms, with designated step-free access routes suitable for stretcher transport from the field of play and to a nearby ambulance parking bay. Ideally the routes from the field of play and to the ambulance point should be away from media areas.

This medical room is likely to be staffed by a doctor and other medical staff during the event, and should have more than one stretcher bed or treatment table position separated by mobile screens, and space for competitors to sit awaiting treatment. In large venues, a suite of rooms may be provided, including reception and waiting area, a small staff office, stretcher treatment and ambulant minor injury treatment areas and shower facilities. Medical rooms should be provided with at least one accessible WC cubicle, and separate hand washing facilities, secure medical supplies storage cabinets and space for treatment and diagnostic equipment. For very large events, more than one medical room may be required.

For publically accessible sports buildings, such as sports halls, a first aid room will be required. This room will be sized to suit the venue activities and management strategy, and may range from a dual purpose office or staff room to a dedicated facility. As a minimum, a shared room should contain hand washing facilities, a drinking water supply, a secure first aid cabinet, a clear space of 2.0 m x 1.6 m and door width suitable for stretcher access, and an adjacent accessible WC compartment.

A dedicated first aid room should be large enough for a treatment trolley bed in addition to the above facilities. Large sports facilities may have dedicated doctor's rooms or consultation rooms as part of more extensive sports medicine or therapy facilities. These may also include dedicated x-ray or ultrasound diagnostic rooms, specialist physiotherapy and other treatment spaces.

6.8 Doping control facilities

Major competition venues will require a facility which can be used for doping control activities, where competitors are tested. This does not have to be a dedicated facility, if appropriately equipped spaces can be provided for the duration of the event, although they must be in a discrete location in close proximity to the competitors' changing rooms.

The size of facility will depend on the event and numbers of competitors to be tested; however the suite of facilities will generally include a reception/waiting area with seating for competitors and chaperones, with a drinking water supply; a working or testing room with a desk and chairs and a secure samples refrigerator, with dedicated access to a WC cubicle with hand-washing facilities.

Some sports codes also recommend shower facilities. Doping control testing may also occur at smaller venues and outside of events. A dedicated large first aid room may also be used for this occasional purpose, provided it meets the minimum criteria set out above.

6.9 Lounge/recreational space

A lounge or recreational space is desirable for participants to use after their activity and in smaller facilities can take the form of a club room. This consists of an open lounge often equipped with a bar and sometimes adjacent catering facilities. In most professional sports this space will be segregated from the public, but in other sports facilities this will be a communal space to gather after an event.

Some sports, such as cricket, take place over a long period of time and therefore require catering facilities. This would include a kitchen, server, catering storage and space for the participants to eat. For amateur sports this space would double-up as the recreational space. In facilities open to the public, such as an indoor training centre, a café or cafeteria is usually available, where participants and visitors alike would share the area.

6.10 Access and inclusion

Designers should refer to Football Licensing Authority (FLA) 'Accessible Stadia', BS 8300 and Approved Document M of the UK Building Regulations, in order to address the Disability Discrimination Act 2005 (DDA) and Equality Act 2010 in relation to the built environment. These documents cover the requirements for accessible and inclusive design including but not limited to the design of parking, corridors, vertical circulation, doors, toilets and washing facilities, ensuring the needs of all participants and officials are met.

6.11 Parking/drop off/storage

Consideration should be given to how participants may arrive at the venue. Some will arrive on foot carrying kit bags, some in cars requiring car parking, and some may arrive on a team bus. Parking will be required close to the changing facilities, including a drop-off point for team buses. Sports that require personal equipment such as sailing, rowing, kayaking, triathlon will need space for parking trailers and for storing the equipment. Watersports will also need launching facilities at the water's edge.

6.12 Gymnasium/fitness centre

Used for training rather than competition, a gymnasium or fitness centre will provide a range of equipment and spaces and can include the following:

- Open-plan studio with fitness training equipment and free weights
- Separate studios for dance, aerobics and other specific work-out classes
- Swimming pool
- Hydrotherapy
- Sauna
- Steam room.

7 SUPPORT FACILITIES FOR SPECTATORS

7.1 Introduction

The size and range of facilities for spectators will vary depending on the level of competition. As a minimum, toilets will be a requirement of the venue licence, with catering facilities such as cafes, bars, and restaurants often provided. Ticketed events obviously require accommodation for ticketing and larger venues often contain private boxes/suites and lounges for hospitality, retail and merchandising, medical facilities and information.

7.2 External circulation/approach to venue

The approach to a venue needs to provide clear and safe access for all spectators. This will require the use of wayfinding signage, PA/VA systems and external lighting. Where large crowd numbers are expected to attend an event, crowd management barriers may also be required to control the flow of people.

7.3 Ticketing and security

All spectators attending a ticketed event will need to pass through a ticket control point, Figure 38.98. This can be a simple manual ticket check, digital ticket scan or via a turnstile, depending on whether the venue licence requires an accurate count of the number of people attending as is usually the case at a large UK event. Turnstiles can be half-height, offering little in the way of a secure perimeter but a more user-friendly experience, or full-height acting as a perimeter fence also. They should be provided on the basis of one per 500 to 750 spectators. If spectators do not have a ticket when they arrive at the venue then they will need to pick one up from the ticket office. This usually consists of a counter with an in-built tray that enables the exchange of money for tickets. The counter should have one lowered section at 760 mm for wheelchair users. For larger events, spectators will often be required to pass through either random or mandatory security searches with magnetic detectors for both spectators and their bags.

7.4 Sanitary provision

The quantity and gender ratio of toilet provision will vary in accordance with the type of sports venue and event and should be addressed with the local licensing authorities. General guidance advises that the gender split of toilet fixtures should be based on 50% female: 50% male provision, see Table I. However, it is accepted that for many sports facilities, the gender ratio should be based on the normal (or expected) number of male/female spectators. This may alter the ratio significantly, for example to 30% female:70% male for some pitch sports.

Also, for multi-purpose venues, where significant swings in the audience gender balance can be expected, a level of flexible provision or over-provision should be considered where the number of spectators is increased above 100% for the purpose of the calculation, up to 120%. For competition venues, reference should be made to BS 6465:2009 for initial guidance, particularly Section 6.8 and Table 7 – 'Minimum provision of sanitary appliances for assembly buildings where most toilet use is during intervals' for pitch sport and similar short duration events.

7.5 Food, drink and other spectator services

The range of food and drink on offer to spectators will depend on the length and type of the event and the aspirations and business plan of the venue owner or operator. At the very least, all spectators should be provided with a water supply. Visitors to a club level

Table I Sanitary provision

	Urinals	WCs	Wash basins
Male	2 for every 50 males, plus 1 for every additional 50 males or part thereof	2 for up to 250 males, plus 1 for every other 250 males or part thereof	1 per WC and in addition 1 per 5 urinals or part thereof
Female		2 for up to 20 females or part thereof up to 500 females; and 1 per 25 females or part thereof over 500 females	1, plus 1 per 2 WCs or part thereof

competition might expect vending machines or a cafe or server providing basic food. At larger facilities, spectators will often expect to be able to access a range of food and beverage outlets during their time at an event, provided either on a temporary or permanent basis. Temporarily provided concessions typically take the form of road trailers with fold-down counters serving a range of fast food, and both alcoholic and soft drinks, and so need sufficient space for delivery, set up and collection. Permanent concessions can be provided either in a single booth or in a range of dedicated booths. A typical concession will consist of a preparation area with serving position and counter. A standard module for 2 serving points is 2.6 m and each length of counter should have one lowered section at 760 mm for wheelchair users. Queuing lines or rails may be required in larger facilities to control the approaches to concessions and prevent crowd circulation problems.

It is also typical at larger events to include areas where information can be provided to spectators, both to assist wayfinding around the venue, but also a results service related to the competition schedule. Some buildings, especially racecourses, will require a range of betting facilities, in the form of Tote booths or betting shops. First aid facilities will need to be distributed throughout spectator areas, with access to a central area for more serious injuries.

7.6 Hospitality

Larger sports buildings will incorporate a range of hospitality lounges and restaurants within their premises as required by their business plan. These don't have to be but can be of higher value if arranged to afford a view of the field of play. The following categories are typical:

- Club Lounge – where spectators have access to food and drink in an open lounge and a seat within the seating bowl.
- Box/Suite – spectators have access to food and drink in a private room and dedicated seats immediately in front of the Box/Suite.

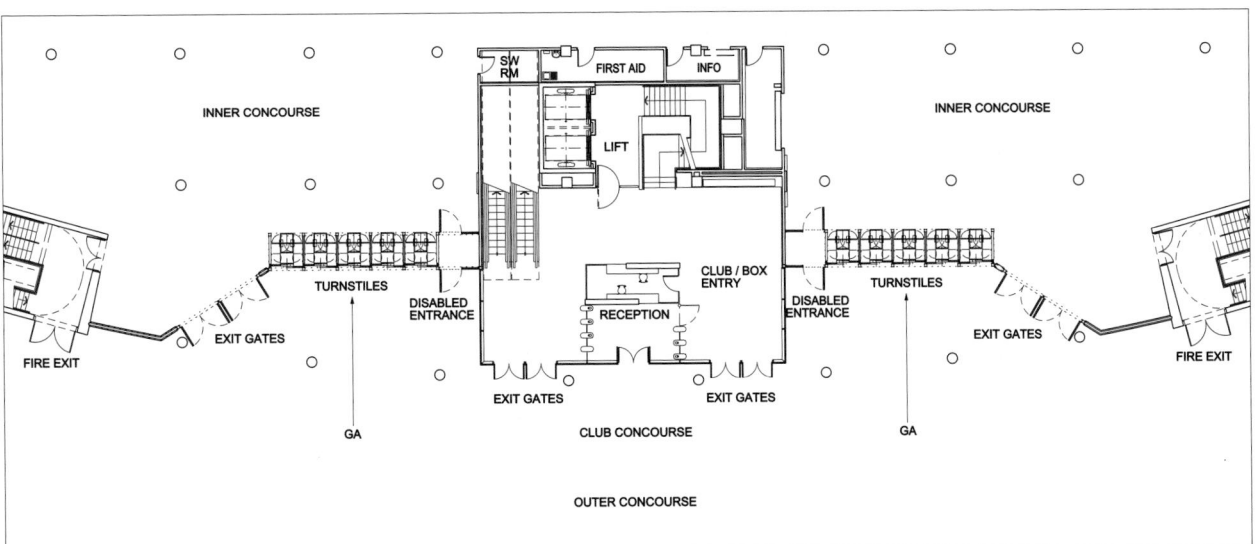

38.98 *Plan of Premier League football stadium spectator entry*

- Premium Club – where spectators have access to food and drink in a small, exclusive lounge and dedicated seats in front of the Club.
- Owners/Directors/Royal Box – where VVIPs have access to food and drink in a small, exclusive lounge and dedicated seats in front of the Box.

7.7 TV screens

In addition to information points, TV screens and monitors are often helpful in relaying information or footage of an event to spectators. These need to be mounted at a suitable height to maintain visibility within crowded areas.

7.8 Retail

Retail spaces enable spectators and other visitors to purchase sports-related equipment or merchandise related to a sports team or activity, Figure 38.99. These can range in size from a display at the reception desk of a community sports facility, to a dedicated megastore at larger sports buildings. The layout of the retail spaces will depend on the range of merchandise on offer, but can include rails and wall displays. Shirt printing is a popular offer in some sports buildings and may require queuing rails. Payment is usually processed at tills or counters set out at the exit point of the retail space.

7.9 Museum/visitor attraction/tours

Some sports grounds can attain national or regional tourist significance and will incorporate a museum or visitor attraction that can be open during non-event days. These are often linked to tours of the sports building, which inevitably finish their journey in the retail space.

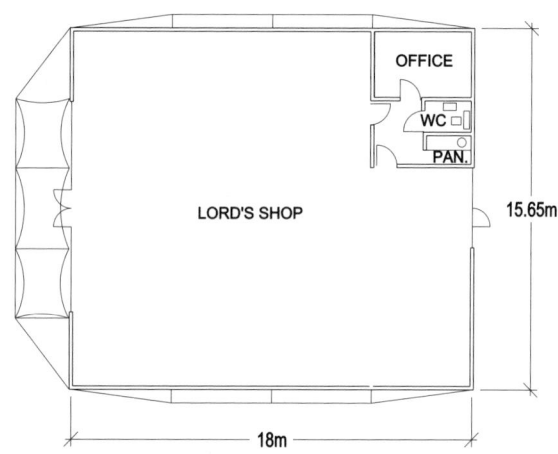

38.99 *Plan of Lord's cricket ground shop*

7.10 Access and inclusion

Designers should refer to Football Licensing Authority (FLA) 'Accessible Stadia', BS 8300 and Approved Document M of the UK Building Regulations, in order to address the Disability Discrimination Act 2005 (DDA) and Equality Act 2010 in relation to the built environment. These documents cover the requirements for accessible and inclusive design including but not limited to the design of parking, corridors, vertical circulation, doors, toilets and washing facilities, ensuring the needs of all spectators are met.

8 FACILITIES FOR THE MEDIA

8.1 Introduction

For events at which the media is in attendance, the needs of broadcast (radio and TV), written press and photographers need to be taken into account in the planning of the venue. The size and range of facilities will vary depending on the level of competition, and may need to include press workrooms, a press conference suite and outside broadcast.

8.2 Dedicated routes

The media are often provided with a separate entrance point to sports buildings. This entrance will usually have a reception desk, which is used to undertake accreditation, prior to the media entering the building.

8.3 Specific media requirements

There are a wide range of media and each type has their own requirements, as follows:

- Written press: this group requires access to the seating structures, and ideally a desk there at which to work, Figure 38.100. Larger facilities typically have a press workroom in addition where copy can be completed and uploaded to editors, Figure 38.101.
- Photographers: this group requires access to the perimeter of the field of play of a pitch sport, with moats sometimes provided around the edge of a field of play to enable photographers to work during an event, without restricting the view of spectators. At some course sports such as road cycling, photographers would travel in media cars in order to photograph en route.
- Broadcast media (radio and television): this group is the most difficult to accommodate since the technology advances so rapidly and different broadcasters have different requirements. Radio broadcasters will typically want to relay commentary from the event either from within the seating area or from a room with a view of the field of play, and sometimes an opening window so the sound of the crowd can be heard in the background. They may also want to conduct pitch-side or 'flash' interviews prior to and after the event. Television broadcasters require a number of television camera positions within the viewing structures, which need to be carefully designed in order to limit obstructions to spectator sightlines. These are typically 4 m². Television studios from where the event can be presented can be incorporated either as a permanent facility or as part of the temporary event overlay, but an elevated view of the field of play is usually required.

8.4 Press workroom

This room is essentially an office with an extensive array of tables and chairs to provide individual working spaces for the media and will generally require full IT network capacity for instantaneous data transfer. A central location for the distribution of notices, results and general information to the media will also be required, together with a lounge serving food and drink.

8.5 Press conference room – including translation booth

In some larger sports buildings a press conference room will be required to facilitate interaction between participants in an event and the media. This would typically be a dais for the participants and seating, sometimes raked, for the media, Figure 38.102. For

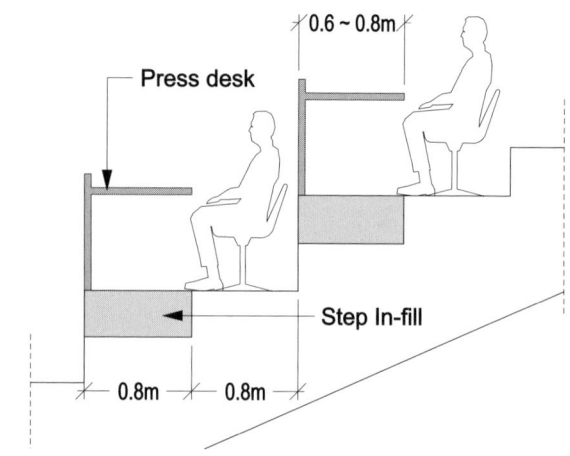

38.100 *Conversion to press seat*

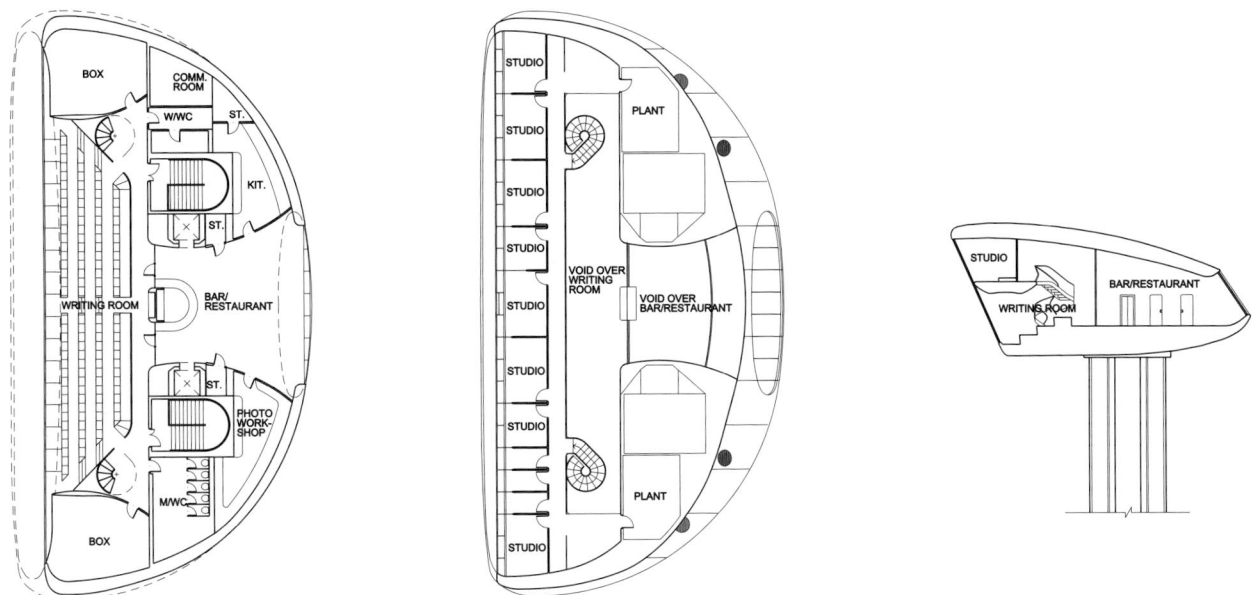

38.101 *Plan and section of Lord's cricket ground media centre*

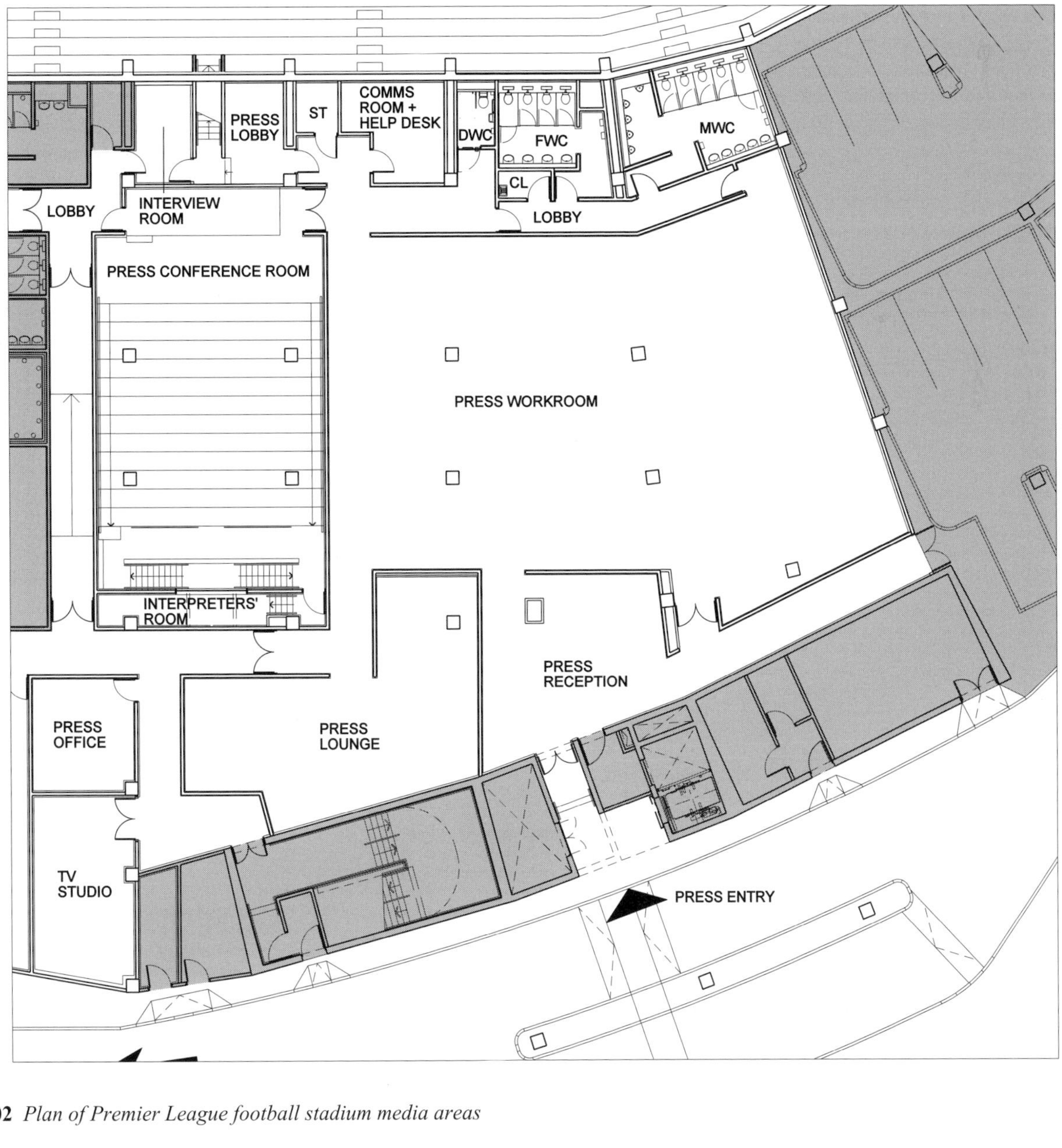

38.102 *Plan of Premier League football stadium media areas*

international events, translation facilities may also be required and this can be provided with enclosed translation booths at the rear of the conference room.

8.6 Mixed zone

For some events, such as a major athletic or football event, a mixed zone is provided for participants and the media to interact. This is a controlled environment that has access from both the participants' changing rooms and the media workroom. A designated space is usually allocated for this purpose.

8.7 Outside broadcast

Broadcasters will also require an outside broadcast area, which will need to be sufficiently large to accommodate the trucks and vehicles that are required. This area will also need to have the ability to connect satellite uplinks, for the instant transmission of sporting action being broadcast from the event. This space is often provided in a separate compound, but can also be built into larger sports buildings.

9 SUPPORT ACCOMMODATION FOR FACILITY MANAGEMENT

9.1 Introduction

Sports buildings need to be managed as do the competition events they contain. Apart from the smallest clubhouse-type buildings, most facilities would typically include offices, with larger buildings including control rooms overlooking the field of play for the safety and security of spectators, for the control of video screens and scoreboards and for competition management. Other back of house areas may be required for equipment stores, catering facilities, storage of catering and other consumables, plant and waste management.

9.2 Reception

A reception desk, located within view of the main entrance of the building, is required where visitors are expected. Larger sports

buildings may have a separate service entrance, usually associated with the movement of vehicles in and out of the building, with the reception acting as a security point.

9.3 Venue management offices

In larger sports buildings, and where the operating management is located at the venue, there should be offices for the director (20 m²), secretariat (12 m²), other staff members (12 m² per person), public relations and marketing (12 m² per person) and event organisation (12 m² per person). In smaller sports buildings some of these rooms and functions can be combined for efficiency. A boardroom may also be required for meetings and the display of trophies and other associated memorabilia. This room would typically be between 30 m² and 50 m².

9.4 Venue control room

A venue control room, often linked to an adjacent security control room (in larger facilities), is required to enable management of the sports competition and also the operation of the sports building, Figures 38.103 and 38.104. This should have a clear sight of the field of play and may require a specific position, depending on the requirements of the particular sport. Should CCTV be required at the venue, then the screens and recording equipment would be located in this room.

9.5 Scoreboards and video screens

Most sports buildings will require a scoreboard for the display of competition results and this should to be located in a position where both participants and spectators can view them clearly. In smaller buildings the scoreboard may be operated manually, but in larger buildings the scoreboard is likely to be electronic and controlled from either the venue control room or timing and scoring control room depending on whether these functions are separate. Spectators increasingly expect to see live action relayed onto large screens, or at the very least replays of key action, so large format LED screens play an important role in the design of this building type. The screen

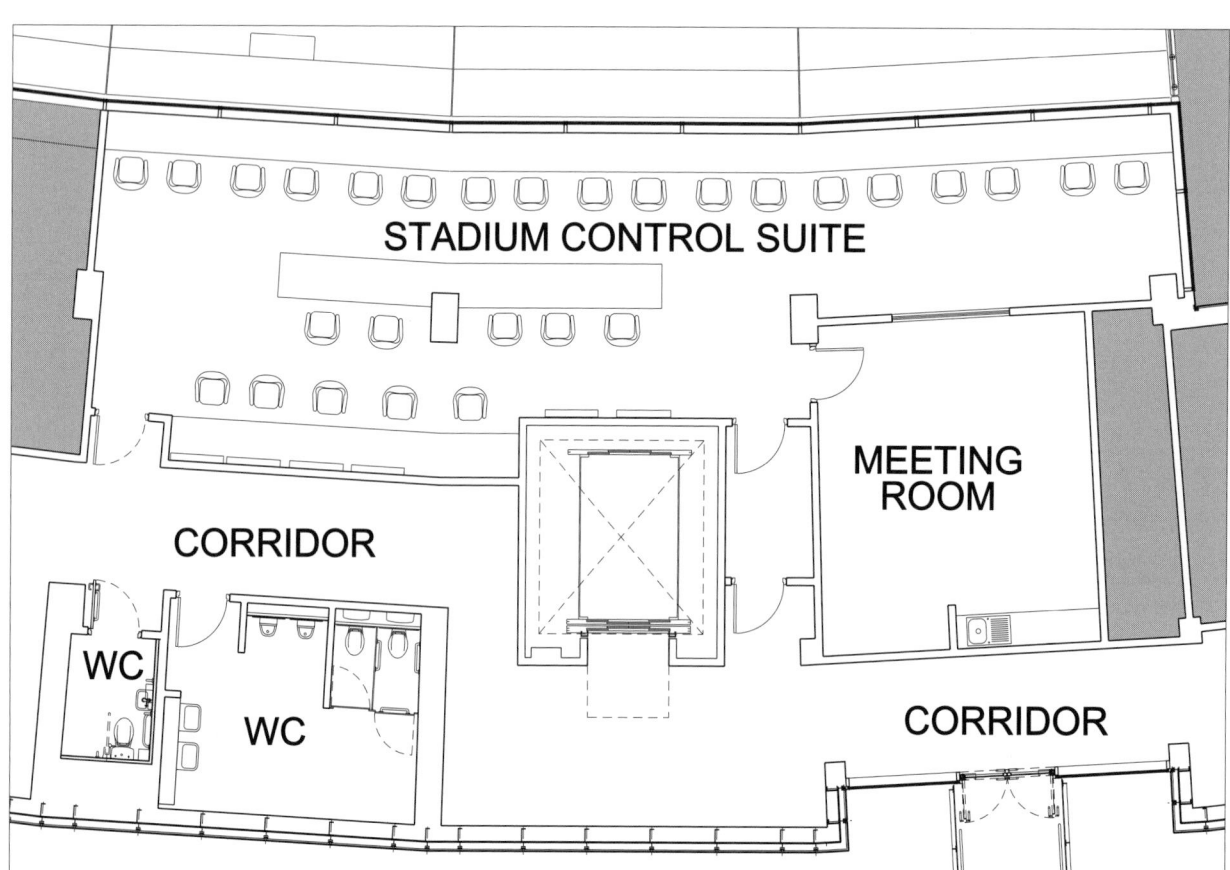

38.103 *Stadium control suite – example 1*

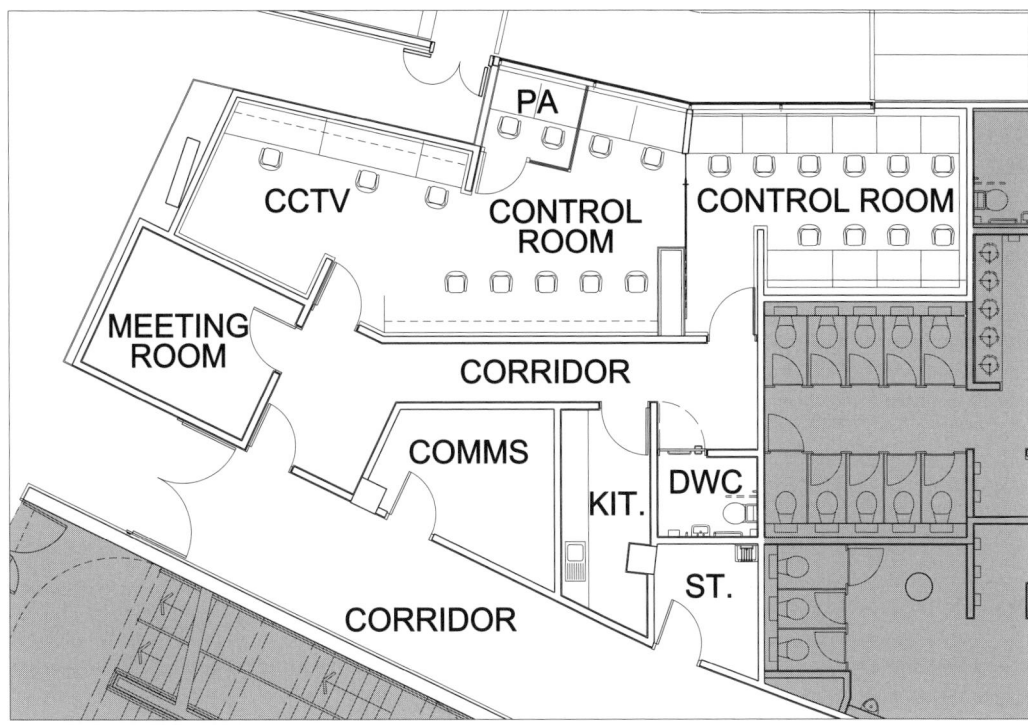

38.104 *Stadium control suite – example 2*

size and location will depend on the size of the building and the type of event, but like scoreboards, needs to be located in a position where the majority of spectators can view it without glare.

9.6 Staff accreditation
Staff entering a sports building will need to be registered and accredited upon arrival. This usually requires a reception area and desk for this purpose. For larger sports events the permanent staff can be supplemented by a large number of temporary staff and the accreditation area will need to be sized accordingly.

9.7 Staff change
The staff change area should provide a staff cloakroom, where staff can change and leave their clothing in lockers, as well as storage for uniforms and a small refreshment area.

9.8 Briefing room
A briefing room should be provided for issuing instructions to staff about the operation of an event. The room should be based on 1.5 m^2 per person.

9.9 Catering
Most sports buildings will require some form of kitchen, although off-site kitchens may sometimes be used to provide catering facilities. The main kitchen will require spaces for storage, preparation, delivery and clean-up. Bar stores may also be required for buildings serving alcohol. Larger buildings may employ a series of satellite kitchens that provide warm-up and distribution facilities closer to hospitality spaces located throughout the building.

9.10 Police/security
Some sports buildings and events will require a police presence, as part of the operational strategy for those events. The number of police and range of facilities will vary, depending on the type of event and licensing requirements. Some individual events may require a very small police presence, while others may require hundreds of police officers, in addition to the security staff employed by the building itself. The larger stadia may require detention rooms with two cells and associated toilets, mass arrest facilities for up to 60 spectators, a waiting and information room and refreshment rooms.

9.11 IT comms rooms
A dedicated IT comms room is likely to be required in all but a small clubhouse, with a controlled environment to protect the IT equipment. Larger facilities may require a number of IT comms rooms, which should be located throughout the building.

9.12 Equipment stores
Each sport will have a different requirement for the size and extent of equipment stores, ranging from simple sports equipment to large boats. The stores should be sized to accommodate storage racks for the equipment and may also need to include set-up space and workshops for maintaining and repairing equipment.

9.13 Groundskeeping
An area will be required by the groundskeeping staff to store and maintain the equipment required to manage the field of play. This may include vehicles, field equipment, tools, covers and pitch lighting, as well as a wash-down facility. Playing fields may also require irrigation tanks as part of the pitch maintenance strategy, which can take up a significant amount of space.

9.14 Waste management
The amount of waste generated at a modern venue can be considerable, despite recent trends for more sustainable packaging used in the food and beverage outlets. At a multi-level stadium, waste is generally collected on each tier of the seating bowl and then moved down to a central collection point in the service level for sorting, recycling and disposal. Larger facilities may require compactors to handle the level of waste generated in the building.

10 EXAMPLES OF SPORTS FACILITIES FOR VARIOUS SPORTS
As noted in the introduction to this chapter, sports facilities can come in many shapes and sizes, ranging from a simple recreation space, up to a complex, multi-functional building. The scales of facility can be categorised as follows.

10.1 Playing area
This sports facility simply comprises a playing area on which the sporting activity takes place, such as a football field marked out in

a park; lanes marked on rivers for canoeing; or the use of roads for marathons.

10.2 Playing area with clubhouse (training grounds)

This sports facility comprises a playing area and some accommodation that simply serves the needs of the participants, such as a cricket pavilion located adjacent to a cricket pitch; a boathouse placed next to a lake for rowing; or some changing rooms set alongside a rugby field.

10.3 Sport-specific venues

This sports facility comprises a specific playing area and a range of accommodation that will serve the needs of participants, spectators, media and facilities management for a specific sport. The shape of the playing area will often give a unique characteristic to the design of the sports facility, such as a grandstand running alongside the closing straight of a racecourse or motor-racing circuit; the V-shaped seating arrangement of a baseball park; or the undulating form of the seating bowl responding to the contours of the cycle track in a velodrome.

10.4 Multi-purpose venues (hosting concerts and events)

This sports facility comprises a playing area that can often be used for multiple events and provides a range of accommodation that will serve the needs of participants, spectators, media and facilities management for more than one type of sport or event. The shape of the playing area will often enable more than one sport to be undertaken within the facility, such as football and rugby in rectangular stadia; cricket and Australian football in oval stadia; multiple sports and events in an indoor arena; multi-sports in a sports hall or leisure centre; or a wide variety of water sports on an inland lake or sheltered harbour.

11 BIBLIOGRAPHY: (REFERENCES TO LEGISLATION AND REGULATIONS)

ADA and ABA: Accessibility Guidelines for Buildings and Facilities, 2006

Australian Football League: Laws of Australian Football, 2011

BS 6465 Part 1: Table 12 minimum provision of sanitary appliances for swimming pools, 2009

BS 8300: 2001 Design of buildings and their approaches to meet the needs of disabled people – code of practice: BSI, 2001

BS6465 Part 1: Minimum recommendations for cinemas, concert halls and similar buildings

BSEN 13200 – 1: Spectator Facilities, Layout Criteria for Spectator Viewing Area: BSI, 2003

CIBSE SLL Lighting Guide 4: Sport, Chartered Institute of Building Surveyors, 1990

Disability Discrimination Act 2005

Donald W Adie: Marinas, a Working Guide to their Development and Design, Architectural Press, 1975

ECB Facility Briefs and Guidance Notes for Indoor Sports Halls with Cricket Provision, TS3

FA, Guide to indoor and outdoor areas for small sided football, mini-soccer and futsal, 2005

Fédération Internationale de Gymnastique: Apparatus Norms, 2009

Federation Internationale De L'Automobile, Circuit Drawing Format, 2009

FIFA Football Stadiums Technical Recommendations and Requirements: Section 05, 2011

FIFA Guide to the artificial lighting of football pitches: FIFA, 2002 FIFA Technical Recommendations and requirements for the construction of New Stadia: Federation Internationale de Football Association, 2010

FITA Constitution and Rules, Indoor and Outdoor Archery Rules 2010

FIVB, Official Beach Volleyball Rules, 2009

Football Licensing Authority, DCMS: Guide to Safety at Sports Grounds, 2008, 5th Edition

Football Licensing Authority: Sports Grounds and Stadia Guide 1: Accessible Stadia

Football Licensing Authority: Sports Grounds and Stadia Guide 2: Concourses

Football Licensing Authority: Sports Grounds and Stadia Guide 3: Control Rooms

Football Stadia Advisory Design Council: Seating, Sightlines Conversions of Terracing Seat Types, 1991

Football Stadia Advisory Design Council: Stadium Roofs, 1992

FSADC: Seating, Sightlines, Conversion of Terracing, Seat Types: Football Advisory Design Council, 1991

FSIF/FLA: Accessible Stadia: Football Stadium Improvement Fund/Football Licensing Authority, 2005

Gaelic Football Association: Official Guide, 2010

IAAF Track and Field Facilities Manual, 2008

IBF, Official Baseball Rules, 2010

International Boxing Association: Technical and Competition Rules, 2010

International Hockey Federation: Guide to the Artificial Lighting of Hockey Pitches, 1997

International Judo Federation: Sports and Organization Rules, 2009

International Tennis Federation (ITF): Rules of Tennis, 2011

International Tennis Federation: Guide to the Artificial Lighting of Tennis Courts, 1991

IRB: Laws of the Game of Rugby Union, 2008

ISSF: Rules and Regulations, 2009

Geraint John and Helen Heard: Handbook of Sports and Recreational Building design, Volume 2, Indoor Sports: Architecture Press, 1995 Geraint John and Kit Campbell: Handbook of Sports and Recreational Building Design Volume 1 Outdoor Sports, 1993

Geraint John and Kit Campbell: Ice Rinks, Swimming Pools: Handbook of Sports and Recreational Design Volume 3, 1996

Geraint John, Rod Sheard and Ben Vickery: Stadia, A Design and Development Guide, Architectural Press, 2007

Planning Policy Guidance Note: Sport and Recreation: Department of Environment, 1991

R&A: Rules of golf and the rules of amateur status, 31st Edition, 2008–2011

Shields, Andrew, Wright, Michael: Arenas: A Planning, Design and Management Guide, London Sports Council, 1989

Sport England Design Guidance Note: Comparative Sizes of Sport Pitches & Courts, 2009

Sport England Design Guidance Note: Design Guide for Athletics, 2007–2012

Sport England Design Guidance Note: Design Guide for Badminton, 2005

Sport England Design Guidance Note: Design Guide for Cycling, 2003

Sport England Design Guidance Note: Design Guide for Fitness and exercise spaces Guidance Notes, 2008

Sport England Design Guidance Note: Design Guide for Indoor Sports, 2007

Sport England Design Guidance Note: Design Guide for Swimming Pools, 2008

Sport England Design Guidance Note: Pavilions and Clubhouses: Changing Rooms, 1999

Sport England Design Guidance Note: Sports Halls: Changing areas, 2011

Sport England Design Guidance Note: Sports Halls: Toilet Accommodation, 2011

Sports Council: Planning and Provision for Sport Selection Planning for Stadia, 1997

Sports Council: Toilet Facilities at Stadia, Planning Design and Types of Installation, 1993

The Event Safety Guide (Purple Guide), A guide to health, safety, and welfare at music and similar events, 2002

The Oxford Companion to Sports and Games: Oxford University Press, 1976

UEFA European Football Championship: Bid Requirements, 2012
UEFA Stadium Infrastructure Regulations, 2006
World Karate Federation: Competition Rules Kata & Kumite, 2009

12 CASE STUDY: RAVENSCRAIG REGIONAL SPORTS FACILITY (A SPORTSCOTLAND INITIATIVE)

Project information:

Client (Joint Venture):	North Lanarkshire Council
	Sportscotland
	Ravenscraig Ltd
	Motherwell College
Architect:	Populous
Structural Engineer:	Buro Happold
Services Engineer:	Buro Happold
Fire Engineers:	Fedra
Main Contractor:	Balfour Beatty
Location:	Ravenscraig, Motherwell, North Lanarkshire, Scotland
Gross Internal Floor Area:	18,300 m²

Outline brief

The brief for the project was developed with the client team in consultation with their stakeholders. Motherwell College's interest in the project related to their sports science course for which classroom and access to training facilities was required.

The brief was for a multi-sports facility with both indoor and outdoor facilities capable of being used for competitive sport and training at the full range of levels from school to elite. The facility should be capable of accommodating 5000 spectators. It is hoped that the facility would be one of the training bases for one of the large national teams for the 2014 Commonwealth games.

Response to brief

The architect's aim was to create as much mix between the different sports and different levels of sports as possible, so that all the building's users could learn from each other. A key part of the strategy was to establish visible links within the building. A central spine was created that connected the three halls, which contain: a full-size indoor football pitch, athletics and a multi-sport hall, Figures 38.105–38.111. This central spine has two levels: changing and toilet facilities at the lower level, and cafeteria, classrooms and offices at the upper level with views into the halls. In order to accommodate the potential capacity of 5,000 for a large event, the hall has fire exits and ventilation to cater for 5,000 users, on the assumption that additional services including sanitary accommodation will need to be brought to site for the event.

General description of the building and site

The building is situated on a former steel mill site. The architecture of the building reflects this industrial past with its profiled metal cladding and pared-down internal finishes. The tilted forms of the building derive from allowing north light into the large halls to eliminate glare for competitors. This results in a distinctive profile to the building that sits well in the landscape.

The facility fits into the approved masterplan for the new town, part of the area planning brief. The new town is yet to be built. The facility incorporates an outdoor full size all-weather artificial football pitch, and 6 five-a-side pitches. These are all artificial grass pitches due to the extended period of use throughout the year and the reduced maintenance costs when compared to natural turf. There is also an external 1km running track, well lit, and surfaced with tarmac, that loops around the complex. There are also 450 parking spaces, of which 8 are reserved for families and 22 for disabled drivers, with options for car pool spaces.

Sports and events

Football, track and field athletics, badminton, volleyball, basketball, handball and netball are all played at the facility. As well as the outdoor pitches, there is a full size indoor football pitch which is a third generation (3G) artificial pitch, achieving a FIFA 2 star rating. It is used by local professional teams for training. There is a hall for athletics, with a rubber sports floor, equipped with a 135 m running track, long jump pits and throwing cages. It is predominantly used for training but is also used for low level competition.

The multi-sports hall hosts badminton, volleyball, basketball, handball and netball competition events on a sprung timber floor and has a 9.2 m vertical clearance to accommodate national level badminton events, but not international ones.

Technology

There are scoreboards in each of the halls, with camera technology in the athletics hall used for timing and scoring during competition. There is a central public address system for the building, along with CCTV. The extensive natural lighting of the halls is supplemented by motion-controlled artificial lighting. The football and athletics halls are naturally ventilated. There is a combined heat and power plant supplying heating and hot water, supplemented by radiant heating in the athletics hall. The football hall is treated as a 'garage' space so is not heated but well insulated for acoustic reasons, so is protected from extremes of temperature. In the multipurpose hall, the air handling system is controllable to limit drafts so that the flight of the shuttlecock is unaffected. Entry into the hall is gained by draft lobbies for the same reason. A fire engineering approach was developed for the building which required sprinklers to be installed in the spine building with automatic smoke vents in the roof combined with smoke reservoirs calculated to coordinate with the required escape times. The football hall also has automatic smoke vents, which have been designed to cater for the possible use as an event building for 5,000 people.

Viewing structures

Retractable tiered seating systems are installed in both the football and multi-sport hall, providing 400 seats in the former and 750 seats in the latter. Wheelchair positions are included with companions in both locations. Informal viewing is also possible from the 1st floor viewing gallery.

Accommodation

Eight changing rooms with toilet facilities are provided for players and two for officials with direct access to each hall and to the external pitches, all with exemplary DDA access. They are located in close proximity to break-out areas where results of training can be analysed and athletes can relax. For the training of elite athletes there is a strength and conditioning area, equipped with benches and free weights. There is also a medical room for sports injuries as well as a drug testing area. For the general public there is a gymnasium equipped with the usual combination of cardio (stationary bikes, rowing machines, treadmills) and weights machines. There are also two dance/general exercise studios with sprung timber floors. Behind the reception desk is a small shop. At the upper level, accessed by stairs and lift is the cafeteria, located above reception with panoramic views, classrooms, building management room, and satellite offices for the regional sports bodies and the facility managers.

Construction

The building has a steel frame, internal concrete block walls with steel ring beam with 3.5 m height for impact resistance. The floor of the spine building is finished with quartz acrylic resin providing a robust but attractive finish. Externally, the roof and walls of the building are clad with an aluminium standing seam system. The finish of the ceilings in the halls is the galvanised liner trays for the cladding system, but in the multi-sport hall, the liner is powder

38.105 *1:1250 scale plan*

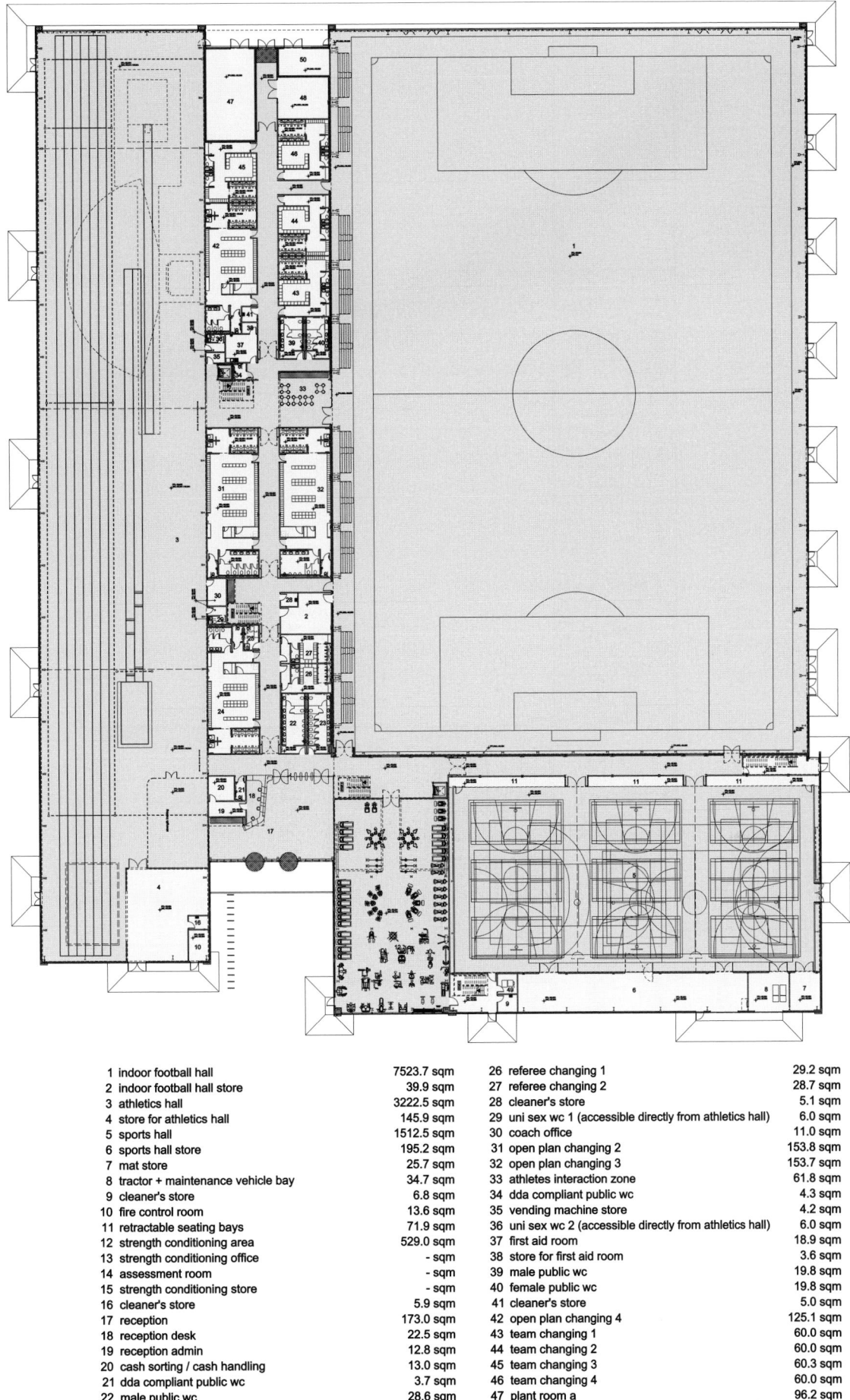

1 indoor football hall	7523.7 sqm	26 referee changing 1	29.2 sqm
2 indoor football hall store	39.9 sqm	27 referee changing 2	28.7 sqm
3 athletics hall	3222.5 sqm	28 cleaner's store	5.1 sqm
4 store for athletics hall	145.9 sqm	29 uni sex wc 1 (accessible directly from athletics hall)	6.0 sqm
5 sports hall	1512.5 sqm	30 coach office	11.0 sqm
6 sports hall store	195.2 sqm	31 open plan changing 2	153.8 sqm
7 mat store	25.7 sqm	32 open plan changing 3	153.7 sqm
8 tractor + maintenance vehicle bay	34.7 sqm	33 athletes interaction zone	61.8 sqm
9 cleaner's store	6.8 sqm	34 dda compliant public wc	4.3 sqm
10 fire control room	13.6 sqm	35 vending machine store	4.2 sqm
11 retractable seating bays	71.9 sqm	36 uni sex wc 2 (accessible directly from athletics hall)	6.0 sqm
12 strength conditioning area	529.0 sqm	37 first aid room	18.9 sqm
13 strength conditioning office	- sqm	38 store for first aid room	3.6 sqm
14 assessment room	- sqm	39 male public wc	19.8 sqm
15 strength conditioning store	- sqm	40 female public wc	19.8 sqm
16 cleaner's store	5.9 sqm	41 cleaner's store	5.0 sqm
17 reception	173.0 sqm	42 open plan changing 4	125.1 sqm
18 reception desk	22.5 sqm	43 team changing 1	60.0 sqm
19 reception admin	12.8 sqm	44 team changing 2	60.0 sqm
20 cash sorting / cash handling	13.0 sqm	45 team changing 3	60.3 sqm
21 dda compliant public wc	3.7 sqm	46 team changing 4	60.0 sqm
22 male public wc	28.6 sqm	47 plant room a	96.2 sqm
23 female public wc	27.8 sqm	48 plant room b	45.3 sqm
24 open plan changing 1	124.5 sqm	49 satellite comms room	6.9 sqm
25 assisted changing facility	8.0 sqm	50 plant room c	30.0 sqm

38.106 *1:500 scale floor plan 00 with legend*

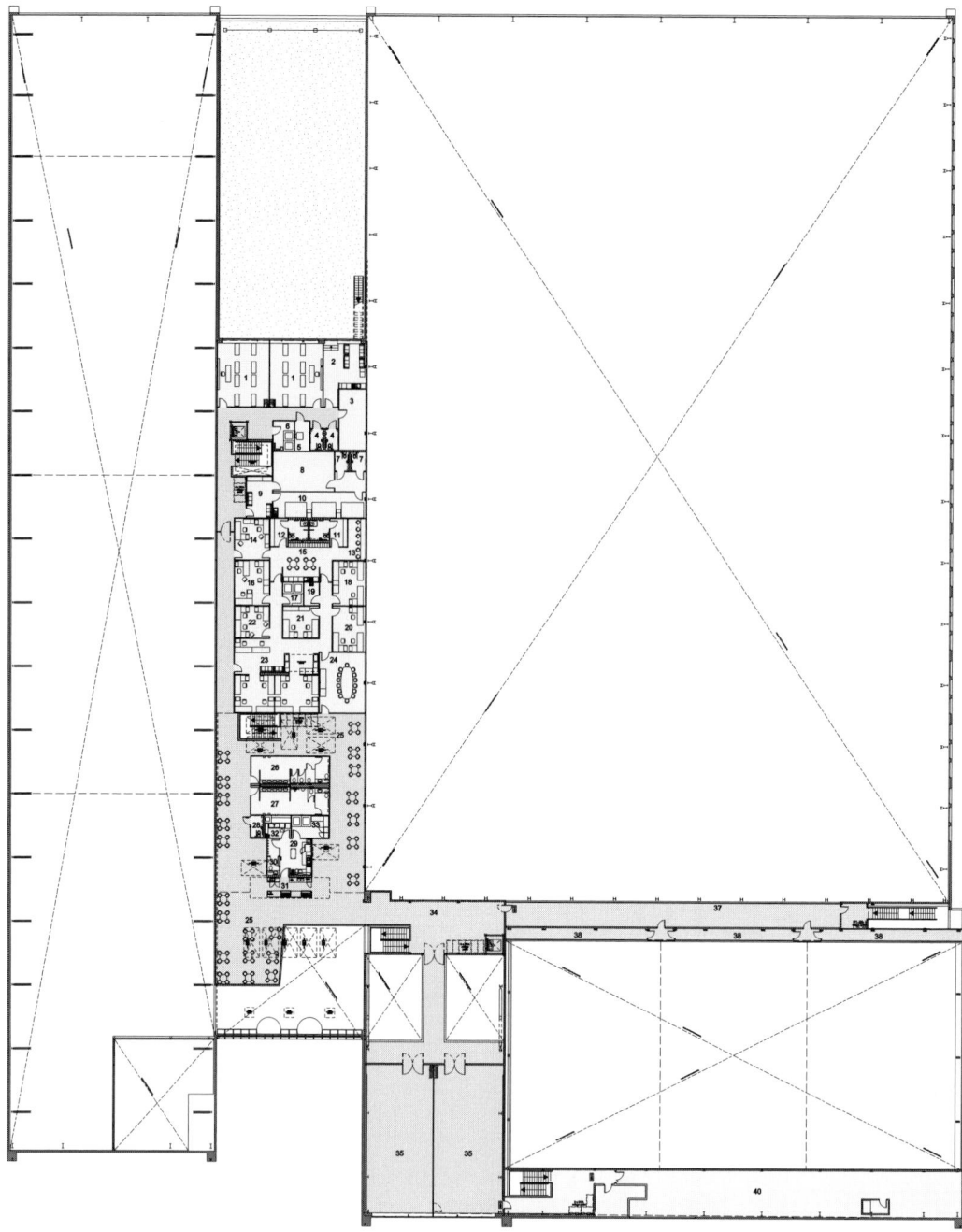

1 Motherwell College class rooms	100.4 sqm	21 operations managers office	17.0 sqm
2 Motherwell College staff area	33.1 sqm	22 North Lanarkshire⁴ football development office	17.1 sqm
3 Motherwell College storage space	24.2 sqm	23 reception / open plan office	81.3 sqm
4 Motherwell DDA compliant wc	8.0 sqm	24 meeting room	41.0 sqm
5 comms room	6.5 sqm	25 seating area cafe	368.6 sqm
6 riser cupboard	9.3 sqm	26 female public wc	31.6 sqm
7 medical area dda compliant wc	8.1 sqm	27 male public wc	31.6 sqm
8 medical area consultation office	35.3 sqm	28 DDA complaint public wc	3.9 sqm
9 medical area waiting area	16.2 sqm	29 kitchen	17.3 sqm
10 medical area treatment area	35.2 sqm	30 kitchen wc and cloakroom	5.5 sqm
11 male staff changing (incl. wc and shower)	13.3 sqm	31 servery	14.0 sqm
12 female staff changing (incl. wc and shower)	13.3 sqm	32 fresh food store	5.9 sqm
13 break out space	10.8 sqm	33 dry food store	9.0 sqm
14 maintenance and grounds office	21.9 sqm	34 gallary overlooking football hall	83.3 sqm
15 staff kitchen	14.4 sqm	35 dance studios/multi purpose room	269.1 sqm
16 Scottish Atheletics office	23.6 sqm	36 store for dance studios/multi purpose room	25.3 sqm
17 riser cupboard	6.9 sqm	37 gallary overlooking football fall (unheated)	114.4 sqm
18 Scottish Football Association office	21.8 sqm	38 gallary overlooking sports hall	64.7 sqm
19 cleaners store	5.0 sqm	40 plant room d	238.6 sqm
20 event managers' office	22.3 sqm		

38.107 *1:500 scale floor plan 01 with legend*

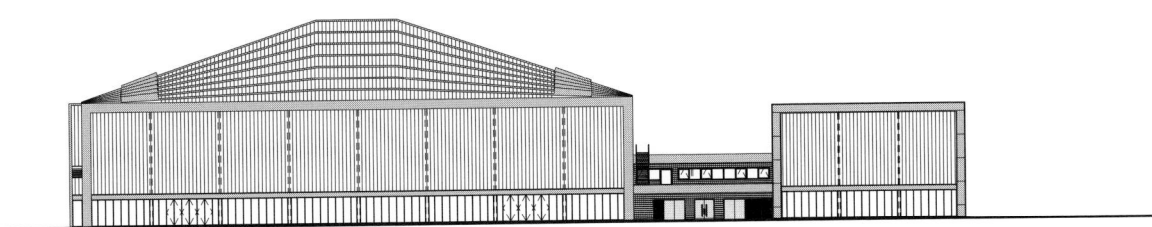

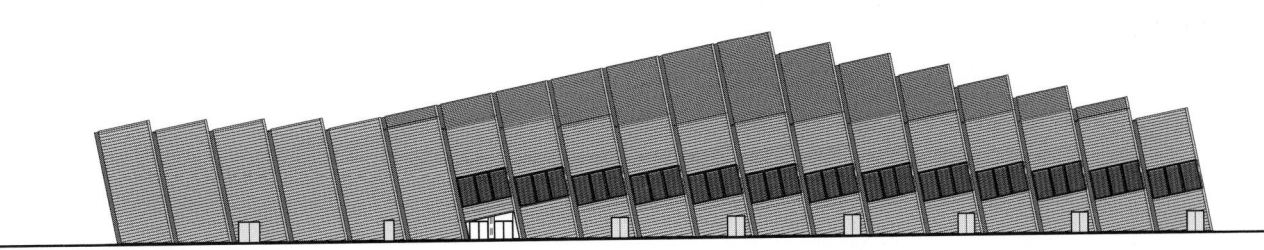

38.108 *Elevations*

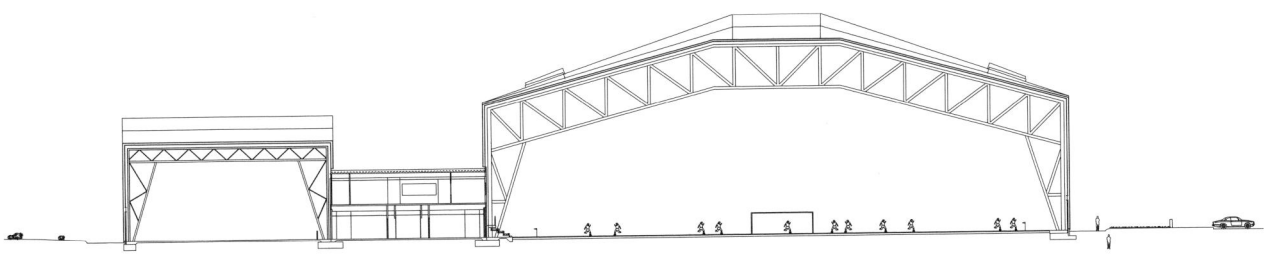

38.109 *Short section*

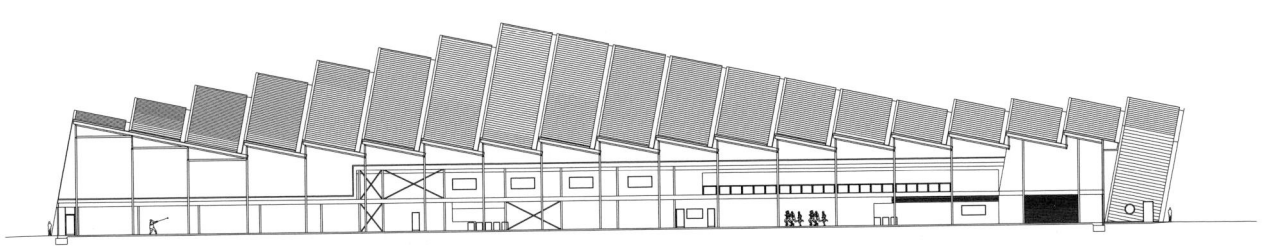

38.110 *Long section through athletics hall*

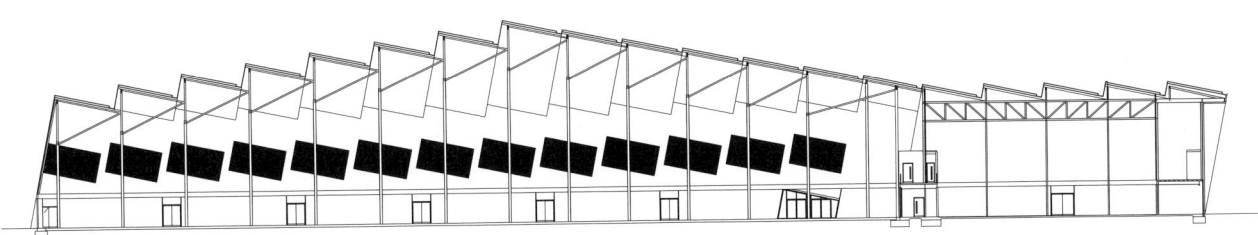

38.111 *Long section through football hall and sports hall*

coated a dark grey so that a shuttlecock is visible. The north lights are polycarbonate, but in the multi-sport hall they are translucent to further diffuse the light. Primary steelwork is painted yellow internally and on the door externally, which provides bright contrast to the industrial aesthetic of silver cladding that is reminiscent of the industrial heritage, Figures 38.112 and 38.113.

38.112 *Ravenscraig Regional Sports Facility. Architect: Populous. View into the internal football hall. (Photo: Andrew Lee)*

38.113 *Ravenscraig Regional Sports Facility. Indoor sports hall. (Photo: Andrew Lee)*

39 Streets and spaces for people and vehicles

Updated by Ben Hamilton-Baillie (introduction, shared space and place-making) and Sustrans (cycling routes and parking)

CI/SfB: 12

Ben Hamilton-Baillie is the founder of Hamilton-Baillie Associates, and is a specialist in street design, safety and traffic movement. Sustrans is a charity enabling people to travel more by foot, bike or public transport

KEY POINTS:

- *Policy is moving away from a blanket segregation of traffic and pedestrians towards integration*
- *Defining preferred vehicle speeds is critical*
- *Commercial vehicles are getting larger and heavier*
- *Promoting walking and bicycling is of growing importance*

Contents

1 Introduction
2 Vehicles
3 Roads in general
4 Road design details
5 Cycle routes and cycle parking
6 Parking
7 Loading and unloading
8 Shared space
9 Place-making
10 Case study
11 Bibliography

1 INTRODUCTION

1.1 Role

Streets are defined as the public roads and spaces between private buildings in cities, towns or villages. Streets make up the great majority of the public space of any community. Their design, management and maintenance are critical to the economic and social quality of the built environment.

Streets are complicated spaces. They serve a wide range of functions from providing access and the foreground to buildings, to accommodating drainage and service channels. The principle functions fall into two categories:

- Space for transport and movement – streets provide the corridors for pedestrian and bicycle movement, vehicular traffic and public transport in all its variations.
- Space for exchange and interaction – streets provide the public space for formal and informal encounters and transactions, including trade, information, political activities, festivals and events, and day-to-day social intercourse.

1.2 Policy

The need to balance these two main functions of streets lies at the core of design policy developments over much of the past century. The arrival of automobiles at the outset of the twentieth century, and their huge impact on the spatial patterns and form of the built environment, has generated significant challenges for architects, urban designers and engineers. Designing spaces for people whilst coping with the practical realities of vehicles continues to require experimentation and creativity.

Policy and best practice in this area is in transition. In 1963, the publication of *Traffic in Towns*, often referred to as the *Buchanan Report* after the chair of the advisory committee responsible, set out a number of key principles for addressing the pressure from motor traffic. This argued that the two functions of streets, their traffic role on the one hand and their civic and social role on the other, were fundamentally incompatible and advocated a policy of segregation of traffic from the pedestrian role.

Traffic in Towns' legacy is notable for the introduction of concepts such as pedestrian precincts, ring-roads and high-level pedestrian walkways, and also the underpasses, overbridges, signals, barriers and bollards associated with physical separation.

By the end of the 1970s, a reaction to the principles of segregation was evident across many European countries. In The Netherlands, pioneers such as Joost Váhl experimented with mixed use, low speed residential streets giving rise to the *woonerf*, later introduced into the UK as 'home zones.' Hans Monderman, a traffic engineer responsible for road safety in the north of The Netherlands, explored ways to combine behavioural psychology and engineering to extend informal unsegregated street design into busier intersections and town centres. The term 'shared space' was coined in 2003 to describe the emerging paradigm of fully integrated, mixed-use streets, in contrast to conventional segregation (see section 8).

The publication of the *Manual for Streets (1 and 2)*, covering England and Wales, in 2007 and 2011 reflected this critical shift in street design policy. The Scottish Executive published similar guidance with *Designing Streets*, and the Irish Government has followed suit with *Design Manual for Urban Roads and Streets* (2013). Research and guidance by CABE, English Heritage and the CIHT has helped articulate the implications of a policy of integration, rather than segregation, of traffic from the social fabric of towns and cities.

2 VEHICLES

2.1 Scope

This section deals with data on:

- Cycles.
- Motor-cycles and scooters.
- Automobiles: cars and small vans up to 2½ tonnes unladen weight.
- Commercial vehicles up to 10 tonnes unladen weight.
- Public Service Vehicles (PSVs): buses and coaches.
- 'Juggernauts', large commercial vehicles maximum 40t. This class includes those with draw-bar trailers.

2.2 Dimensions

The dimensions of some examples of each class are given in Figure 39.1. In any specific case, the manufacturer's data should be consulted.

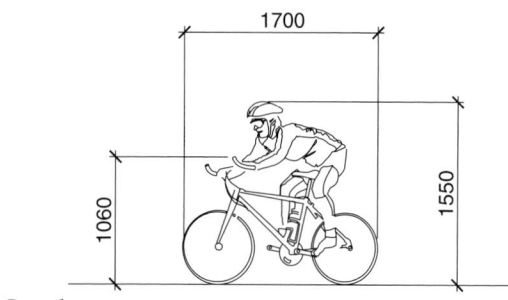

a *Bicycle*

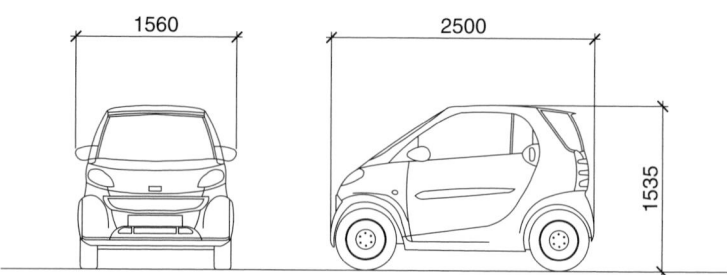

b *Motorcycle*

c *Small low emission two seater car*

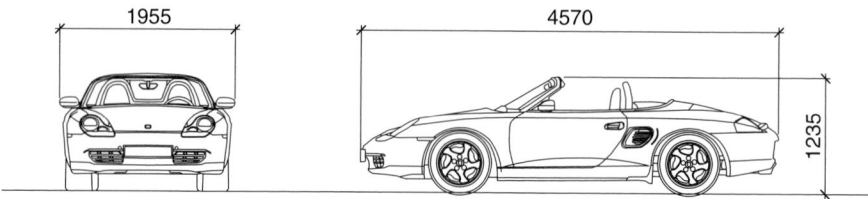

d *Small car*

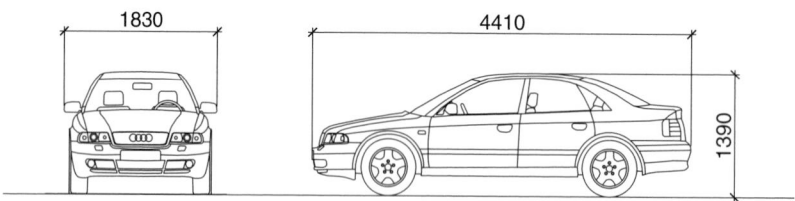

e *Sports car*

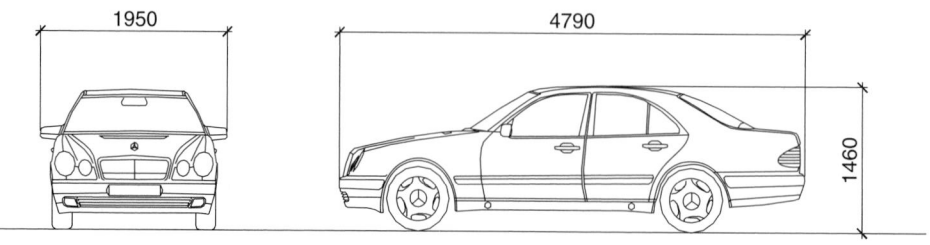

f *Family saloon car*

g *Luxury saloon car*

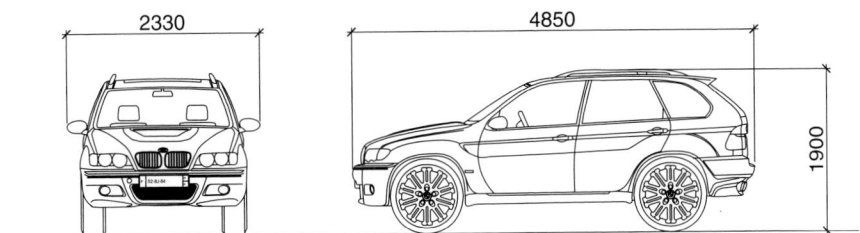

h *4 wheel drive car*

i *Ambulance*

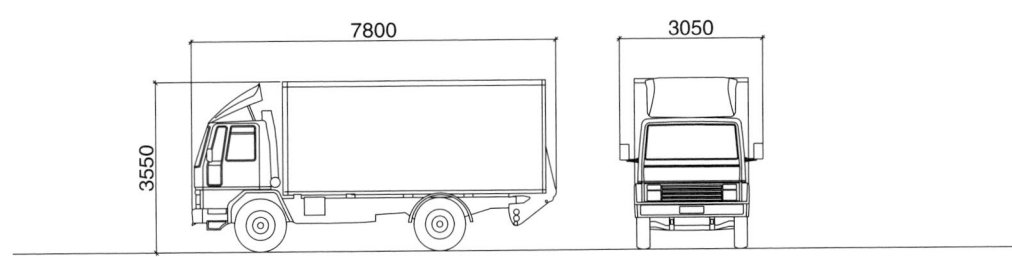

j *2 axle rigid-body lorry*

k *3 axle rigid-body lorry*

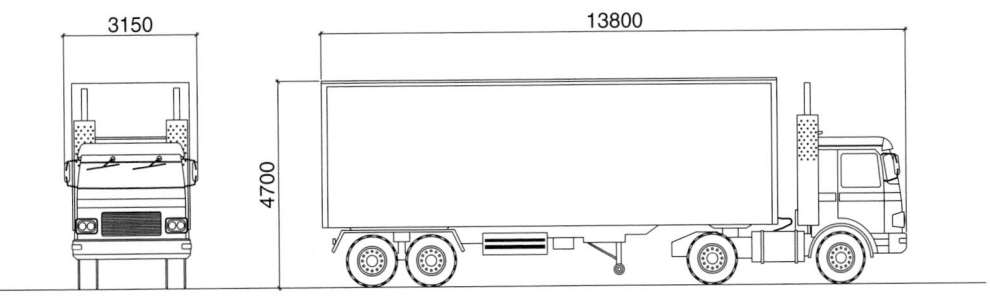

l *4 axle articulated lorry*

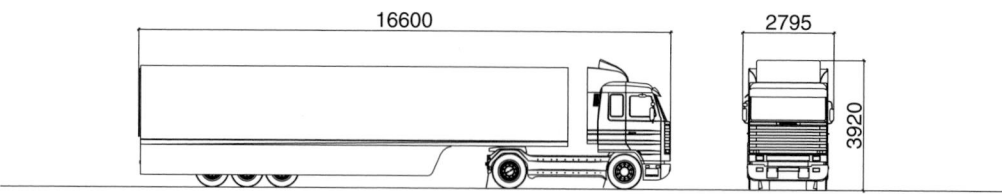

m *5 axle articulated lorry*

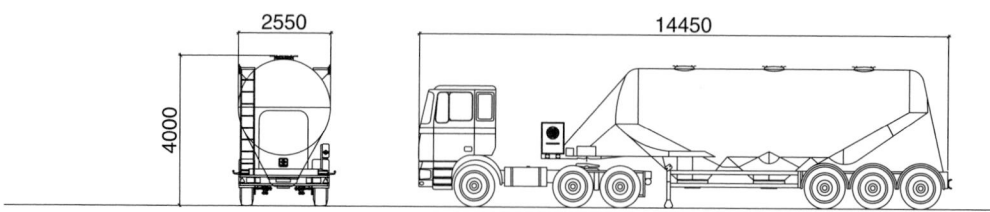

n *6 axle articulated tanker lorry*

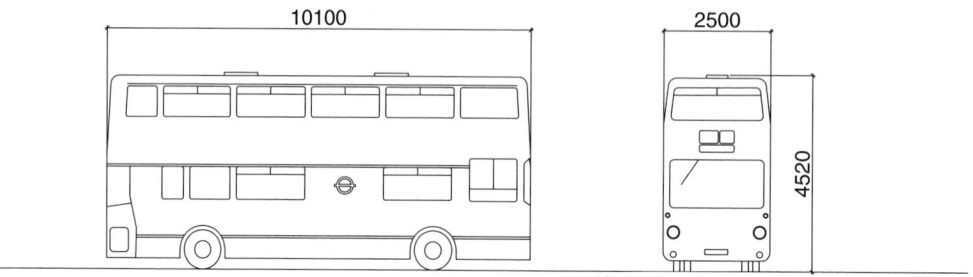

o *Double-decker bus*

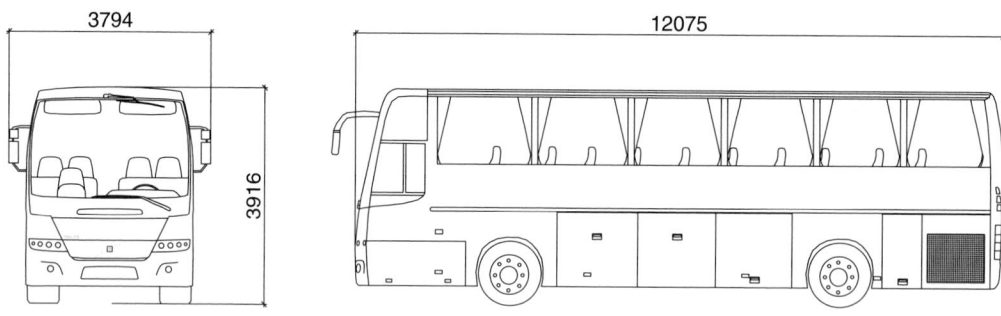

p *Passenger coach*

39.1 *Dimensions of typical road vehicles*

2.3 Unit construction

In the field of the larger commercial vehicles, unit construction is now almost universally employed. In this system a given chassis can be fitted with a variety of body shells for specific purposes and loads, mainly of standard dimensions. The body can be changed at will, permitting one body to be loaded while the chassis is on the road with another body delivering goods elsewhere.

A particular example is the standard container, which is used on lorries, ships, railways or even as a storage unit in the open, Figure 39.2. As this system was first developed in the USA, the standard dimensions are imperial, but the German railways developed a parallel version.

2.4 Turning circles

Apart from the physical dimensions, it is necessary to know the critical characteristics of the vehicle in motion, particularly when manoeuvring while parking or preparing to load. These characteristics are complicated, and usually the manufacturer will quote solely the diameter of the turning circle, either between kerbs or between walls.

Manoeuvring diagrams have been published for various vehicles for the following operations:

- Turning through 90°.
- Causing the vehicle to face in the opposite direction by means of a 360° turn in forward gear.

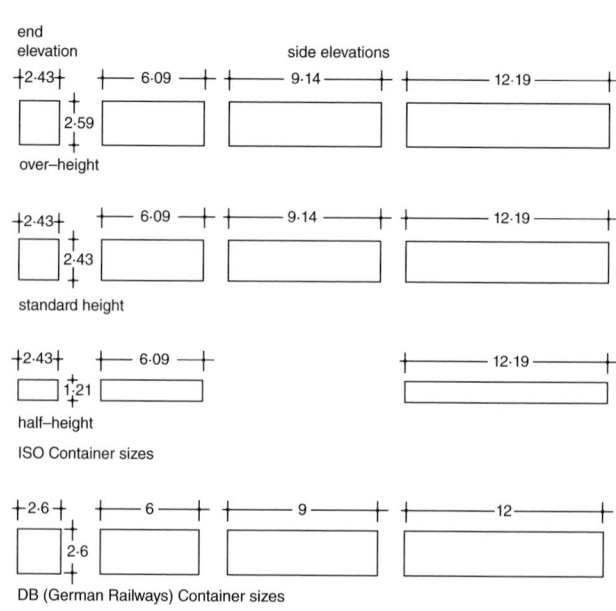

39.2 *Dimensions of standard containers*

- Ditto in reverse gear.
- Causing the vehicle to face in the opposite direction by means of both the forward and reverse gears (three-point turn), in T-form.

- Ditto in Y-form.
- Ditto in a forward side turn.
- Ditto in a reverse side turn.

Figure 39.3 shows the 90° turns for some of the common vehicles. The other diagrams will be needed for the design of turn-rounds in cul-de-sacs, etc. The use of the published turning circle sizes is not sufficient for the following additional factors:

- The distance required for the driver to turn the steering wheel from straight ahead to full lock depends on the speed, which for the purposes of Figure 39.3 is between 8 and 16 km/h.
- The radius of turn differs between a right-hand and a left-hand turn.
- The path traversed by the rear wheels is different from that by the front wheels. In a commercial vehicle travelling at slow speed, the rear wheels follow a smaller arc to the front wheels, the amount depending largely on the distance between the axles. The divergence between the arcs of the wheels on the same side of the vehicle is termed the 'cut in', and value of this determines the total track width of the turning vehicle, always greater than when on the straight.
- While few vehicles have a measurable side overhang of the body beyond the wheel track, many have considerable overhang at front and rear. This is important at the front: the extra width beyond the wheel tracks described by the body is known as 'cut-out'. Allowance should be made for front and rear overhang when designing turn-rounds, etc. by having no vertical obstructions within 1.2 m of the carriageway edge.

3 ROADS IN GENERAL

3.1 Introduction

This chapter will generally deal only with roads and facilities within development sites, such as industrial parks and housing estates. Public roads are not normally the concern of the architect, but Table I gives the recommended carriageway widths for most road types.

The broad hierarchy of roads is:

- motorways and trunk roads
- distributors (primary, district and local)
- access roads.

Definitions:

Carriageway: the area of road surface used by moving vehicles.

Carriageway width: the distance between the kerbs forming the carriageway edges.

Dual carriageway: a road with a central reservation, each separate carriageway carrying traffic in the reverse direction lane: a width

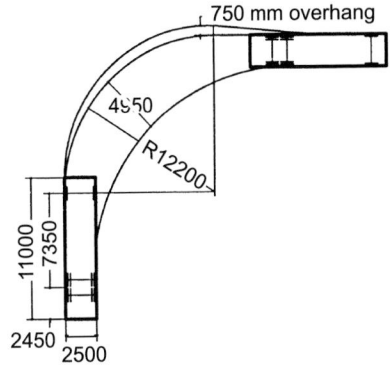

d *medium commercial vehicle*

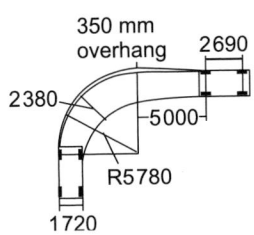

a *private car*

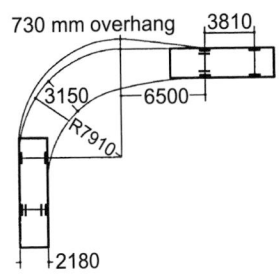

e *fire appliance*

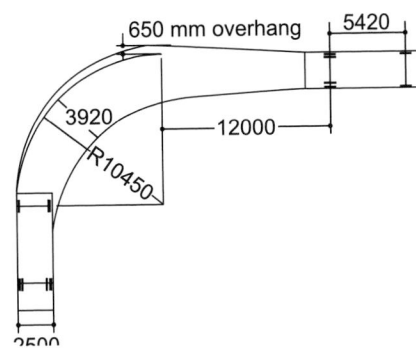

b *pantechnicon*

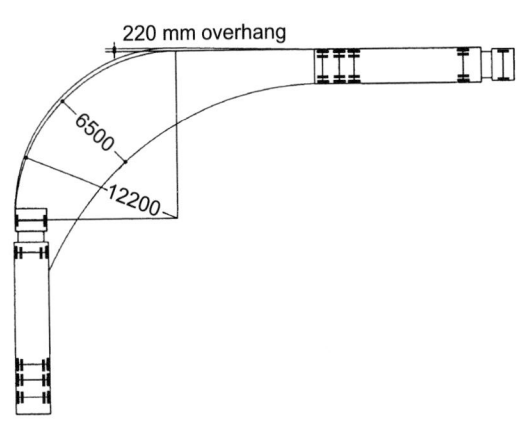

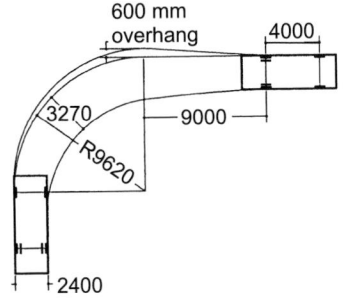

c *refuse collection vehicle*

f *largest commercial vehicles*

39.3 *Geometric characteristics of typical vehicles turning through 90°*

Table I Recommended carriageway widths

Road type	Recommended carriageway width (m) between kerbs or edge lines	
Primary distributor	One-way, four lanes	14.6
	Overall width for divided carriageway, two lanes each way with central refuges	14.6
	Two-way, four lanes total, no refuges	13.5
	One-way, three lanes	11
	Two-way, three lanes (recommended only for tidal flow)	9
District distributor	One-way, two lanes	7.3
	One-way, two lanes	7.3
	One-way, two lanes if the proportion of heavy commercial traffic is fairly low	6.75
	Two-way, two lanes	7.3
Local distributor and access road in industrial district	Two-way, two lanes	7.3
Local distributor and access road in commercial district	Two-way, two lanes	6.75
	Minimum two-way, two lane back service road used occasionally by heavy vehicles	5
Local distributor in residential district	Two-way, two lanes used by heavy vehicles minimum	6
Access road in residential district	see text and Figure 39.5	
	Where all vehicles are required to be able to pass each other	5.5
	Where a wide car can pass a pantechnicon	4.8
	Where two wide cars can pass each other, but a pantechnicon can only pass a cyclist	4.1
	Where a single track only is provided, as for a one-way system, or where passing places are used	
	for all vehicles	3
	for cars only (drives)	2.75
Rural roads	One-way, four lanes	14.6
	One-way, three lanes	11
	Two-way, three lanes	10
	One-way, two lanes	7.3
	Two-way, two lanes	7.3
	Motorway slip road	6
	Minimum for two-way, two lanes	5.5
	Minimum at junctions	4.5
	Single-track between passing places	3.5
	Overall at passing place	6

of carriageway capable of carrying a single line of vehicles, usually delineated with white-painted dashed lines on the carriageway surface.

Lane width: since the maximum vehicle width permitted is 2.5 m, and the minimum clearance between parallel vehicles at 30mph is 0.5 m, the minimum lane width is 3 m. However, vehicles travelling at speed require greater clearance and large vehicles need greater widths on curves, so faster roads have wider lanes

Cycle track or cycle path: a completely separated right-of-way primarily for the use of bicycles

Cycle lane: a portion of a roadway which has been designated by striping, signing, and pavement markings for preferential or exclusive use by cyclists

Shared roadway: a right-of-way designated by signs or permanent markings as a bicycle route, but which is also shared with pedestrians and motorists

Footway: an area of road devoted solely for the use of pedestrians, including those in wheelchairs or with prams, and running alongside the vehicular carriageway. In Britain the footway is also called the 'pavement', in the USA the 'sidewalk'.

Footpath: a facility for pedestrians not forming part of a road.

3.2 Roads in residential areas
This section focuses mainly on roads in residential areas and in housing estates. However, the principles are the same in industrial and business areas, only the details will differ.

Environmental areas
An 'environmental area' is surrounded by distributor roads from which access to the properties within is gained solely via the access

roads within it. The access road network is designed with the following in mind:

- Road access to within 25 m (or 15 m in certain cases) of each house.
- Road access to all private garages, whether within curtilages or in garage courts; and to all parking areas.
- Through traffic from one distributor road to another, or to another part of the same road (avoiding a traffic blockage) is either impossible, or severely discouraged.
- Necessary tradesmen, e.g. 'milk-rounds', calling at all or most properties in sequence, are not unreasonably diverted.
- In general, traffic is not allowed to proceed too fast, but visibility at all times is at least the stopping distance for the intended speed (not the legal) limit.

Figure 39.4 illustrates typical access road layouts.

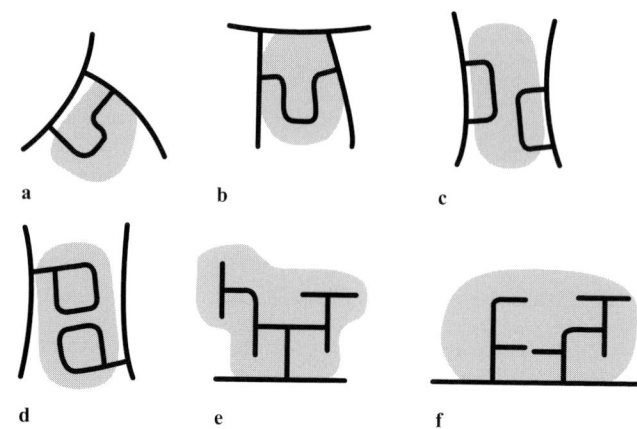

a   b   c

d   e   f

39.4 *a and b are through roads, so tortuous as to discourage through traffic; c and d are non-through systems, but avoid the need for hammer-head turnrounds; e is a cul-de-sac system, but will have substantial traffic at the entrance; f is to be preferred on this count, although both systems pose problems for permeability*

Types of access road
Access roads in residential areas are of three types:

- *Major access roads (or transitional)*. These are short lengths of road connecting a distributor road with the minor access road network, the latter at a T-junction. They are normally 6 m wide, have no direct access to property along their length and serve from 200 to 400 dwellings.
- *Minor access or collector roads*. These form the backbone of the network, will serve up to 200 dwellings and be 5.5 m wide with only one footway. Occasionally a single track 'car way' 2.75 m wide is used for access to about 50 dwellings, in conjunction with a separate footpath system.
- *Shared private drives, mews courts, garage courts and housing squares*. Generally these facilities serve up to 20 dwellings, and are designed for joint pedestrian/vehicle use with hard surfaces, no upstand kerbs and no footways. Access to them from the collector roads is marked by some device such as a short ramp or rough surface material, with the purpose of slowing down the traffic.

Designed controls
Conventionally roads were designed so that cars could be parked on both sides, and two cars could still pass. This encouraged use by vehicles trying to avoid congestion on main roads, with excessive speed and consequent nuisance and danger to the inhabitants. Figure 39.5 shows the characteristics of the various carriageway widths.

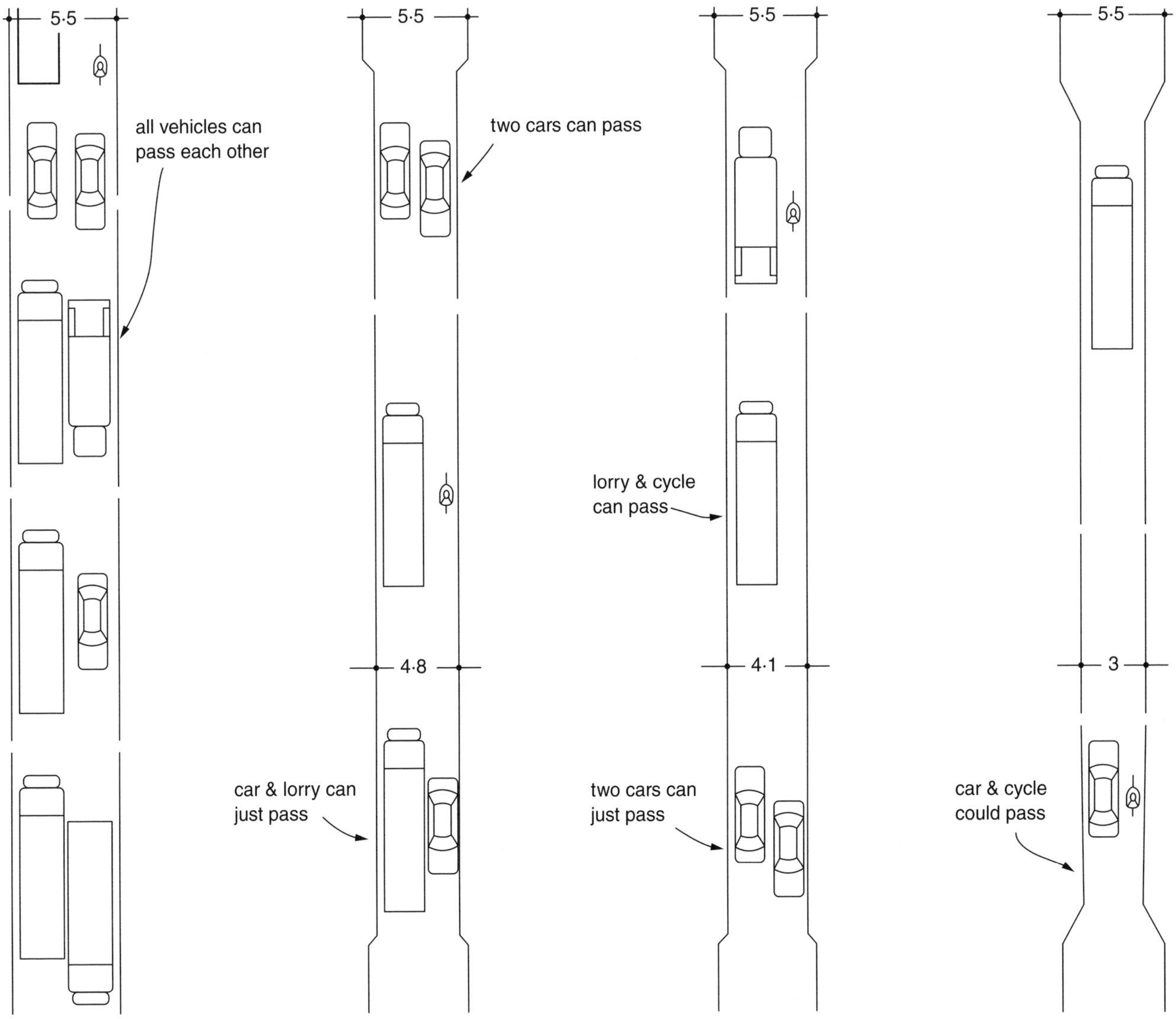

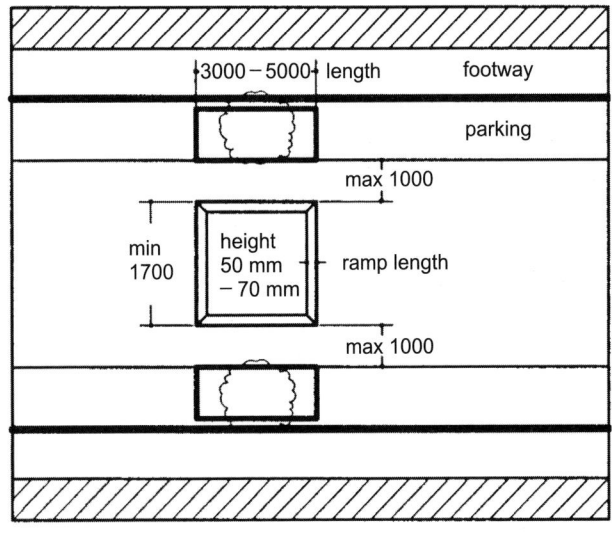

39.5 *Characteristics of various carriageway widths on two-way roads*

While legal penalties can apply to misuse of these roads, these require enforcement resources which are rarely available. It is therefore the designer's responsibility to build-in the discouragement required. Closures, narrowing and speed humps are now used in existing roads; but these have unwanted side-effects such as complications for ambulances, fire engines and even local buses. In new developments it should be possible to avoid these measures and still provide sufficient restraints.

Figures 39.6 to 39.8 show typical arrangements of humps. The slowing effect of various ramps is detailed in Figure 39.9. Figures 39.10 and 39.11 give the Department of Transport requirements for hump dimensions.

There are considerable disadvantages to the use of humps. Vehicles, such as delivery vans, that are continuously using roads with humps find that maintenance costs on tyres, wheels and suspensions are significantly increased. Buses and ambulances find that their passengers experience discomfort and even danger. An alternative slowing device to the hump is the 'chicane', examples of which are shown in Figure 39.12.

Once garages and visitors' parking spaces are provided, kerbside parking may be discouraged by minimising the width of the road carriageway. However, occasional access by large furniture vans (and, unfortunately, fire appliances) will be necessary; and regular visits by refuse collection vehicles have to be as trouble-free as possible. For example, local authorities dislike culs-de-sac with end turning areas permanently obstructed by parked cars, and may well insist on residents bringing their refuse to the entrance of the road.

39.6 *Cushion hump*

Refuse vehicles and delivery vans blocking narrow roads cause annoyance to other residents trying to pass; consider having at least two routes of access/egress for most parts of the area.

3.3 Roads in industrial parks
These must provide for use by the largest vehicles, but otherwise pose the same problems as roads in housing estates. Layout should

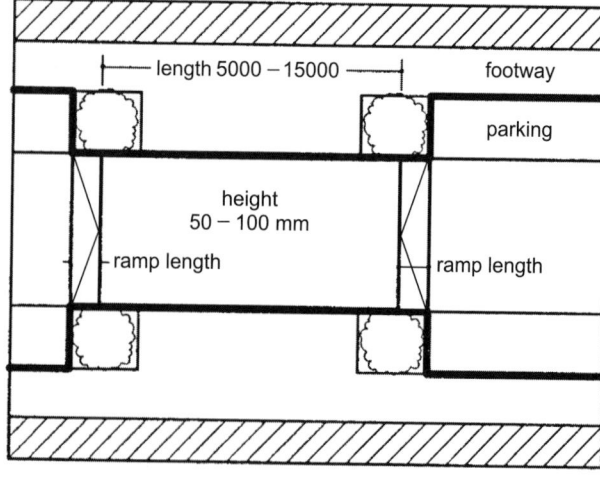

39.8 *Flat top hump used as a pedestrian crossing*

39.7 *Double cushion humps*

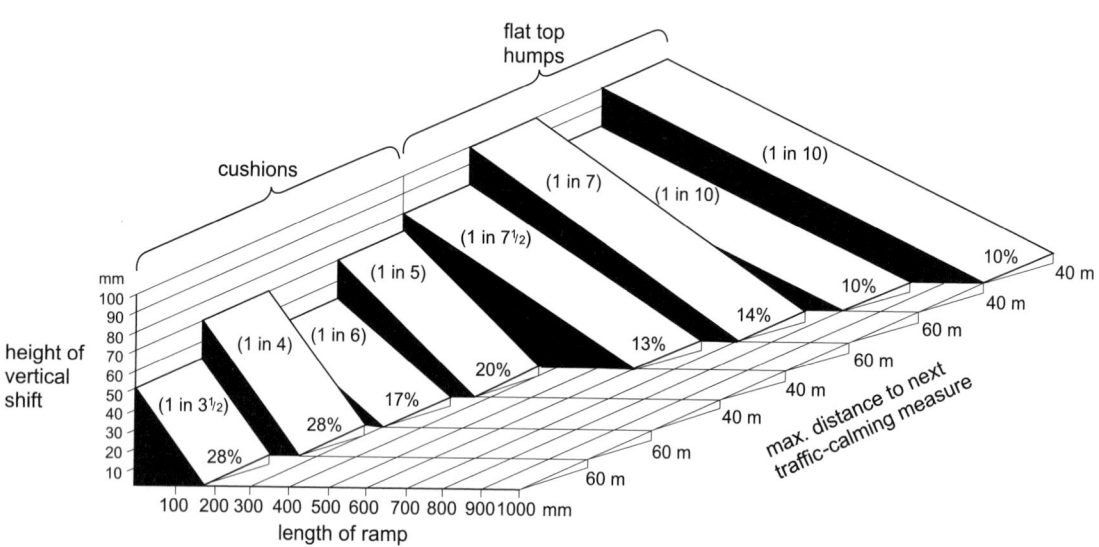

39.9 *Results of research into ramp dimensions for 85 percentile speed of 32 kph (20 mph)*

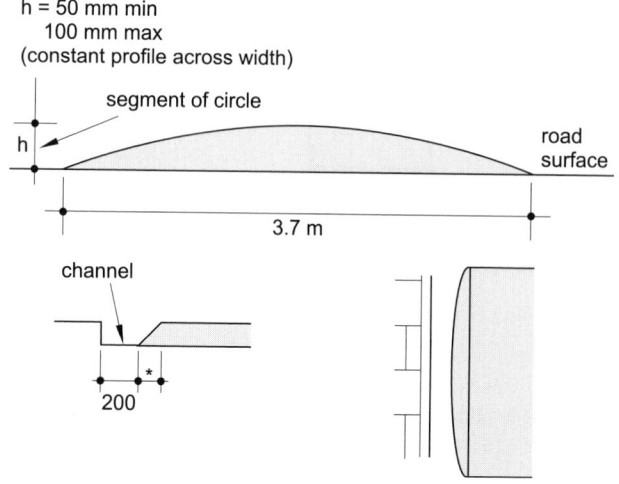

39.10 *Dimensions of round top road hump from the Highways (Road Hump) Regulations 1990*

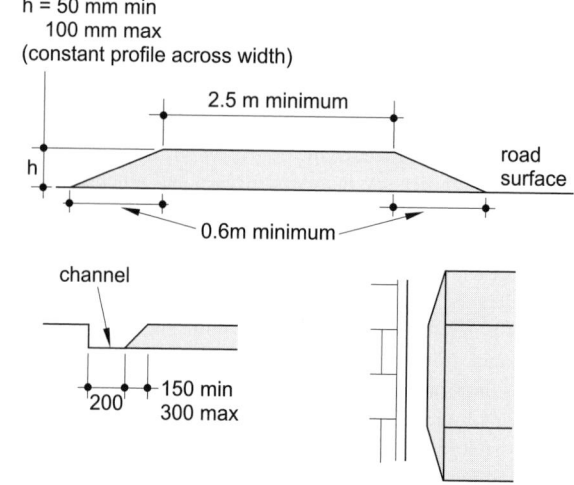

39.11 *Dimensions of flat-top hump from the same source*

discourage traffic using the roads as a cut-through, and should also ensure that the speed of the legitimate traffic is kept low. This is not a simple matter, as corner radii cannot be too sharp when heavy vehicles constitute a substantial proportion of the traffic.

4 ROAD DESIGN DETAILS

4.1 Visibility and stopping distance

It is an axiom of road design that the driver should be able to see a distance at least as far as the distance he or she needs to stop in. If the object seen is also a moving vehicle, the sight distance must allow both vehicles to stop before colliding.

Figure 39.13 gives the design stopping distances for speeds up to 110 km/h (approx 70 mph). These distances are about $2\frac{1}{4}$ times the stopping distances given in the Highway Code for vehicles with good brakes in ideal conditions. This is to allow for reduced brake performance, poor weather conditions and impaired visibility. When emerging from a side road onto a through road the driver must be able to see a vehicle on the through road a distance of that vehicle's stopping distance. When crossing a footway the driver should be able to see 2.4 m along it. Where small children are to be

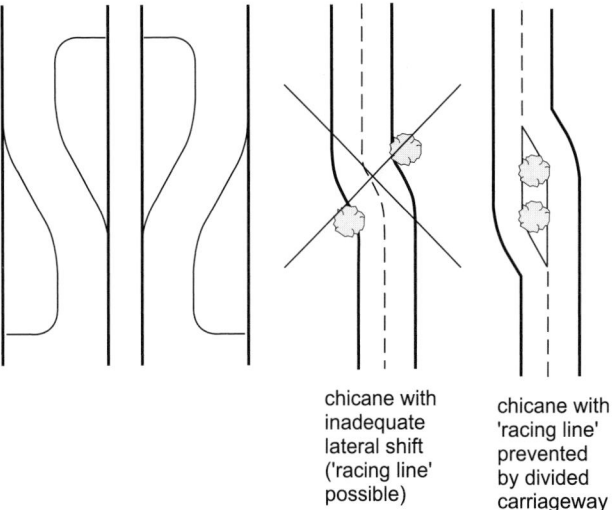

chicane with inadequate lateral shift ('racing line' possible)

chicane with 'racing line' prevented by divided carriageway

39.12 *Chicane types of traffic slowing device*

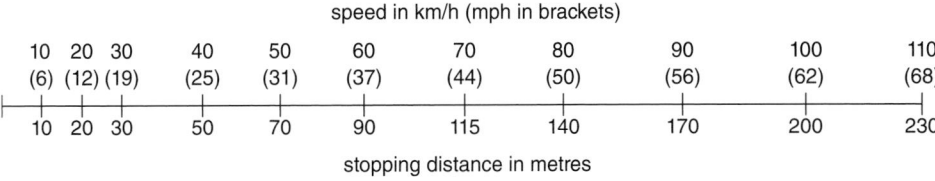

speed in km/h (mph in brackets)

10	20	30	40	50	60	70	80	90	100	110
(6)	(12)	(19)	(25)	(31)	(37)	(44)	(50)	(56)	(62)	(68)
10	20	30	50	70	90	115	140	170	200	230

stopping distance in metres

39.13 *Design stopping distances*

Table II Recommended standards in junction design

Junction type		Radius (m) R	Minimum junction spacing (m) adjacent	Opposite X		Sightlines(m) Y
Road A	Road B					
Local distributor	Any other road	10	80	40	5	60 in 30 mph zone 80 in 40 mph zone 100 in 50 mph zone
Minor access road	Major access road	6			2.4	40
Minor access road	Minor access road	6	25	8	2.4	40
Minor access road	entrance to mews or garage court	4.2	25	8	2.4	40
Single track road	entrance to mews or garage court	8 & 5 Offset	25	8		Junctions must be intervisible
Mews or garage court	entrance to mews or garage court	4.2			2.4	10

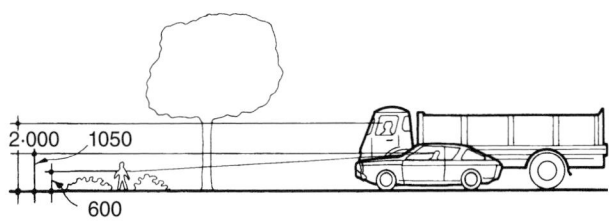

39.14 *Required heights for unobstructed visibility*

expected this visibility should be to within 600 mm of the ground; but where there are no small children (such as in industrial areas) 1050 mm will be sufficient. Figures 39.14 and 39.15 indicate the areas that must be free of obstruction, and Table II gives some recommended standards in residential areas.

4.2 Curves

As mentioned in Section 3.4, when a vehicle travels round a curve the road width it occupies is greater than the track width on the straight. Table III combined with Figure 39.16 indicates the magnitude of this – the width of carriageway should be increased on curves to compensate.

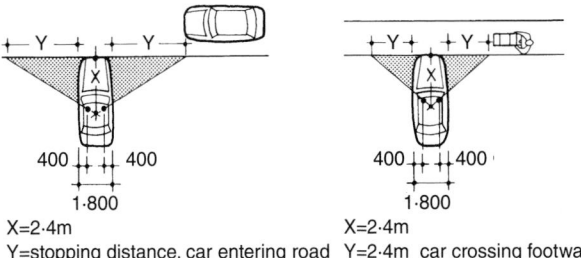

X=2·4m
Y=stopping distance. car entering road

X=2·4m
Y=2·4m car crossing footway

39.15 *Required distances for unobstructed visibility*

4.3 Corners

Since the internal radius of turn of a large commercial vehicle is about 8 m, it will be seen that a kerb radius of 10 m will be needed for such vehicles to maintain a constant distance from the kerb while turning the corner, also allowing some spare for the distance covered while turning the steering wheel. A kerb radius of 10 m in

Table III Outside turning radius of front axle (m)

Minimum radius			15		30		45		60		75–400		400+		
R	X	Y	X	Y	X	Y	X	Y	X	Y	X	Y	X	Y	
10.45	3.92	4.57	3.44	3.89	2.96	3.19	2.80	2.95	2.73	2.84	2.68	2.77	2.53	2.54	Pantechnicon
9.62	3.27	3.87	2.94	3.33	2.66	2.85	2.58	2.71	2.53	2.63	2.50	2.58	2.42	2.43	Refuse vehicle
7.91	3.15	3.88	2.67	3.06	2.42	2.61	2.34	2.47	2.30	2.40	2.27	2.35	2.19	2.20	Sightlines(m)
5.78	2.38	2.73	1.96	2.10	1.84	1.91	1.80	1.85	1.78	1.81	1.76	1.78	1.73	1.74	Private car

X = Maximum width of wheel path
Y = Maximum width of wheel path plus overhang

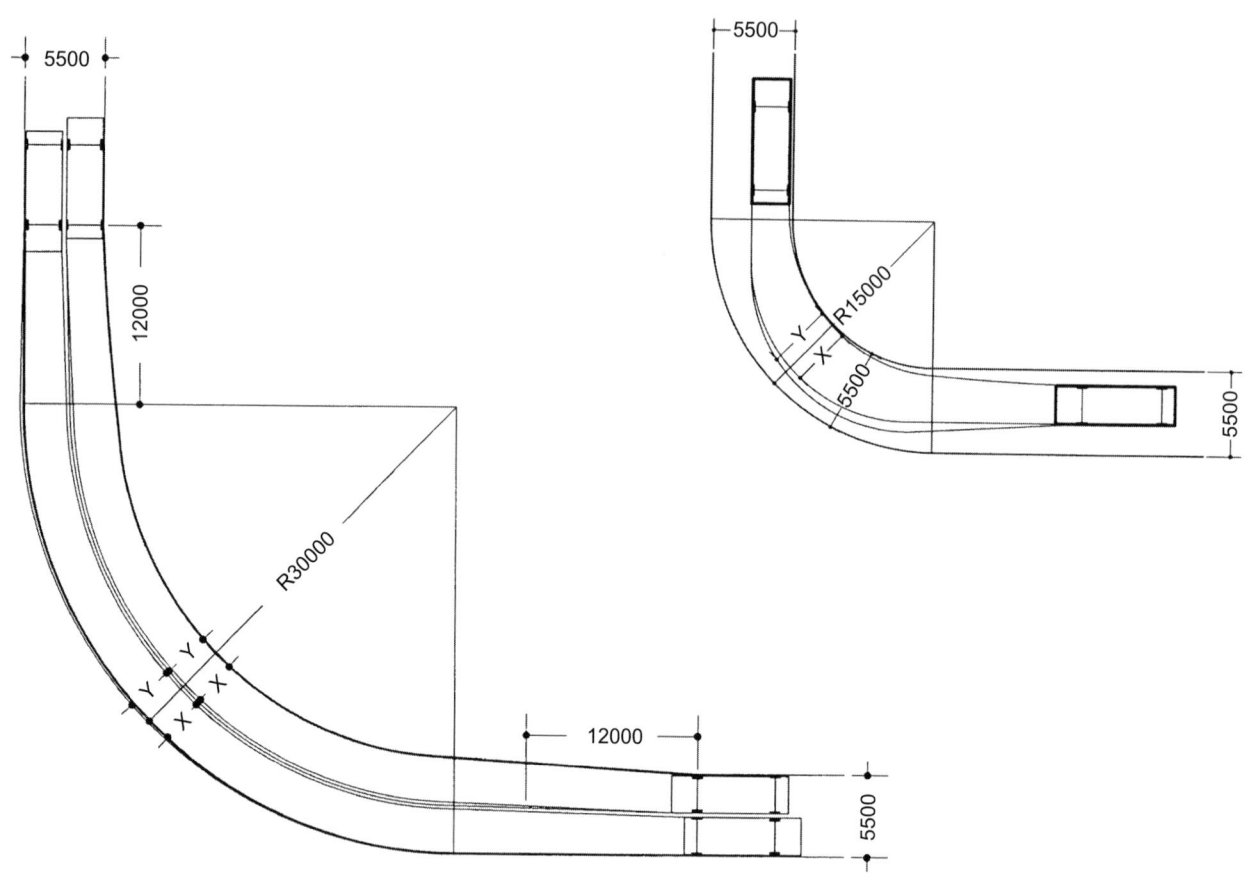

39.16 *Widening on bends; dimensions X and Y are given in Table III*

all cases would mean large areas of carriageway at junctions, and would be inappropriate in scale in many places, particularly in residential areas. Where traffic volumes are low there is no reason why the occasional large vehicle should not encroach on the opposite side of the road, provided that clear visibility is maintained so that vehicles affected by the manoeuvre can take avoiding action in time. Figure 39.17 illustrates the effects of using radii of 10, 6 and 4 m.

4.4 Turn-round areas

Where conventional arrangements are used in turn-round areas in mews courts and housing squares, the minimum standards in Figure 39.18 can be employed. Some local authorities require more generous minimum standards for their refuse collection and fire-fighting vehicles. In cases of doubt, use the specimen vehicle track diagrams in Figure 39.3.

4.5 Gradients

Acceptable gradients are hard to define. What would be quite normal in the Peak district would be considered horrendous in Lincolnshire. Consider the likelihood of snow and icy conditions in winter, when anything greater than about 12 per cent becomes impassable without snow tyres or chains. Most general-purpose roads are now constructed to 7 per cent or less. Ramps to lorry loading bays and car parking garages are limited to 10 per cent.

Some car parks in basements or multi-storey have gradients up to 15 per cent (and occasionally beyond). These steep gradients require vertical transition curves at each end to avoid damage to vehicles. Also, steep gradients either up or down should be avoided close to the back of pavement line or road edge, as it is difficult to see clearly, or to take preventative action if needed.

4.6 Verges

Where there is no footway, a soft verge of 1 m width should be provided for the accommodation of services (water, gas, electricity, communications, etc.) and to allow for vehicular overhang.

5 CYCLE ROUTES AND CYCLE PARKING

5.1 Scope and guidance

This section mainly applies to off-road cycle provision. Guidance on this, and the complexities of on-carriageway and junction cycling provision, is found in the Department of Transport's Local Transport Notes 2/08 and 1/12, and in Transport for London's London Cycling Design Standards.

5.2 Gradients

Cyclists will avoid steep gradients. Studies show that if gradients exceed 5 per cent there will be a sharp drop in the length of uphill

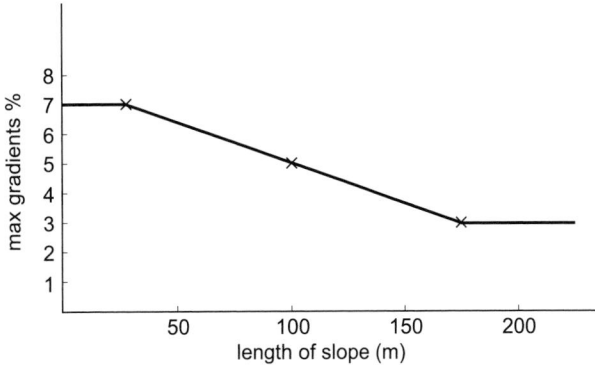

39.19 *Acceptable gradients for bikeways*

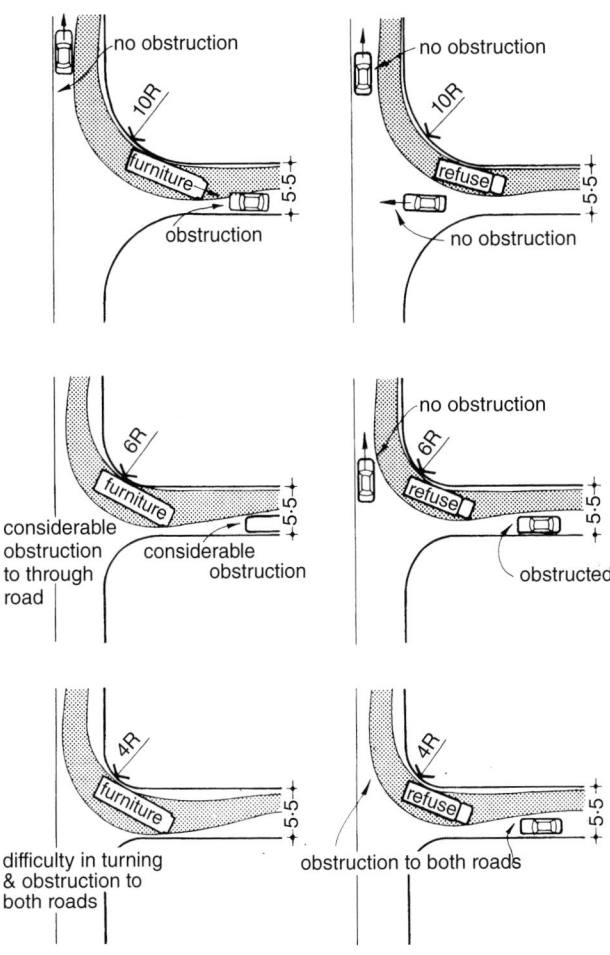

39.17 *Junction design; the effect of kerb radius on traffic flow at the T-junction of two 5.5 m wide roads*

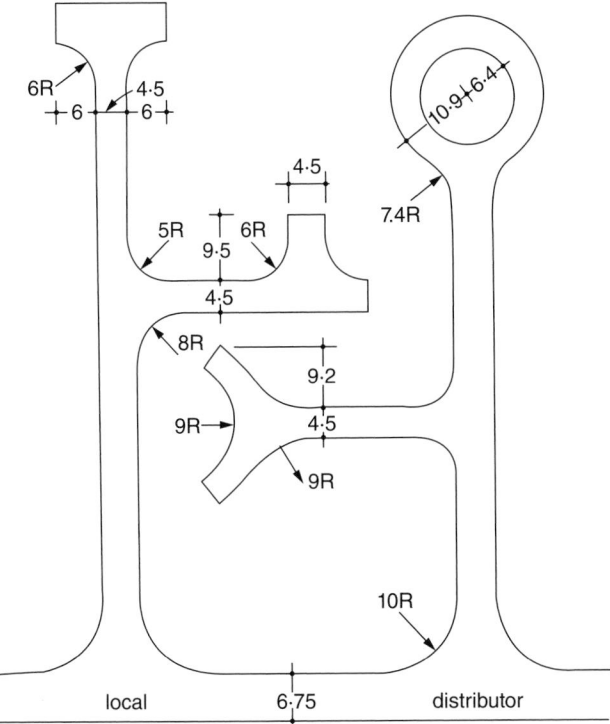

39.18 *Typical recommended dimensions for use in urban areas*

grade that cyclists will tolerate. Figure 39.19 illustrates commonly accepted maximum uphill grades based on length of grade; downhill gradients of 6.5 per cent are acceptable. Note that this does

not apply to ramps to subways and foot/cycle bridges where the maximum gradient should normally be 5 per cent.

5.3 Width

Factors to consider when determining widths for bikeways must include:

- the dimensions of the cyclist and the bicycle;
- manoeuvring space required for balancing;
- additional clearance required to avoid obstacles;
- gradient – where this is steep, additional width is helpful;
- whether on lightly used routes, a substandard width facility is better than none.

Local Transport Note 1/12 summarises minimum widths for off-road cycle tracks as below:

- unsegregated shared use: 3m preferred (effective);
- pedestrian path unbounded on at least one side: 1.5m (actual);
- pedestrian path bounded on both sides: 2m (actual);
- one-way cycle track: 2m preferred (effective);
- two-way cycle track: 3m preferred (effective).

Additional clearance is required when there are edge restraints to maintain effective widths:

- flush or near-flush surface: no additional width needed;
- kerb up to 150mm high: add 200;
- vertical feature from 150–600mm high: add 250;
- vertical feature above 600mm high: add 500.

In almost all cases two-way travel will occur on cycle paths regardless of design intentions; appropriate widths should be provided. Various paths are shown in Figures 39.20, 39.21 and 39.22,

39.20 *Single-track cycle path*

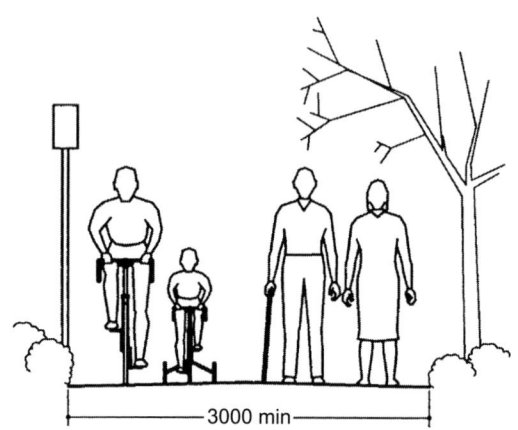

39.21 *Two-way bicycle path on separated right of way*

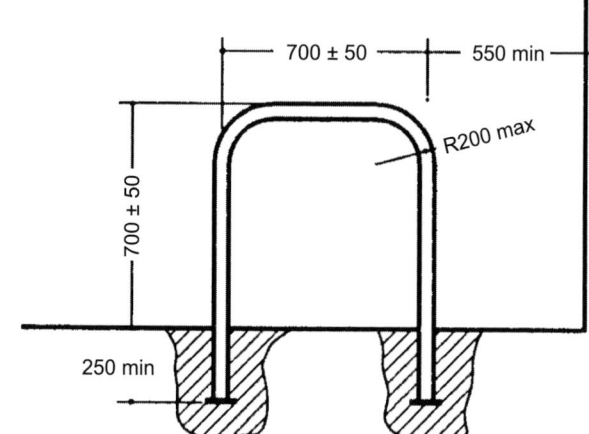

39.22 *Cycle path shared with pedestrians*

5.4 Surfacing

A separate bikeway should have a high quality smooth surface and have a thickness capable of supporting maintenance vehicles. Asphalt, concrete, gravel and stabilised earth are materials commonly used. Machine-laid surfaces are preferred for cycle tracks as it is often difficult to achieve a satisfactory surface that is comfortable for cyclists. Unbound surfaces are not recommended unless on very quiet routes.

5.5 Drainage

Surfaces should have a crossfall of between 1 and 2.5 per cent to provide positive drainage. Drainage grilles should have their slots at right angles to the cyclists' line of travel and be designed and located to minimise danger.

5.6 Cycle parking

This should be located as close to destinations as possible without interfering with pedestrian traffic; and where visual supervision, lighting and shelter from inclement weather can be achieved. It is essential to provide facilities for securely locking the bicycle frame and the front wheel to something immoveable. The favourite is the Sheffield stand, Figure 39.23, or in certain situations, wall bars, Figure 39.24. In extreme cases, lockers large enough to contain a bicycle can be provided. Figures 39.25 to 39.28 show arrangements where larger numbers of cycles are expected. See Section 6 for suggested scale of cycle parking provision.

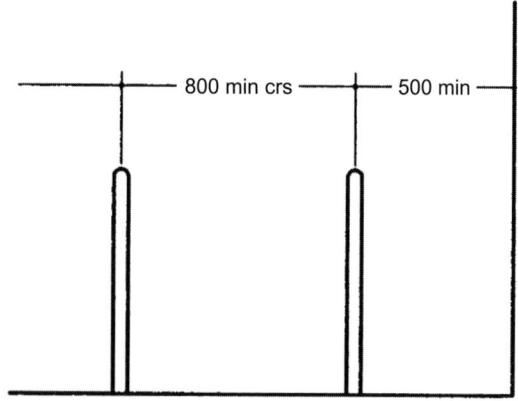

39.23 *Basic Sheffield parking stand*

6 PARKING

6.1 General

A clear parking policy for each area is an essential. Many facilities now provide little or no parking in order to discourage the use of private transport. This is only effective if it is clearly impossible to park on the adjacent roads, and if there is adequate public transport available. Consider also the needs of disabled people.

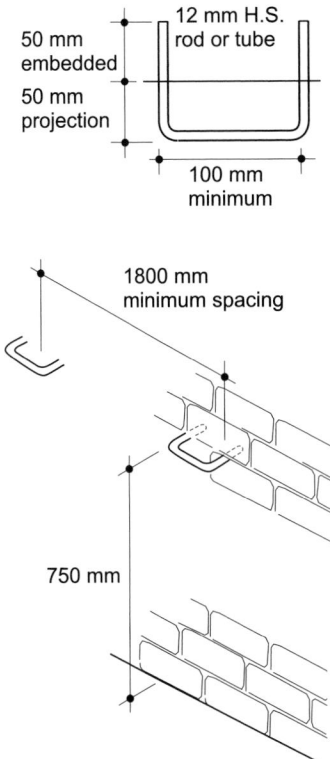

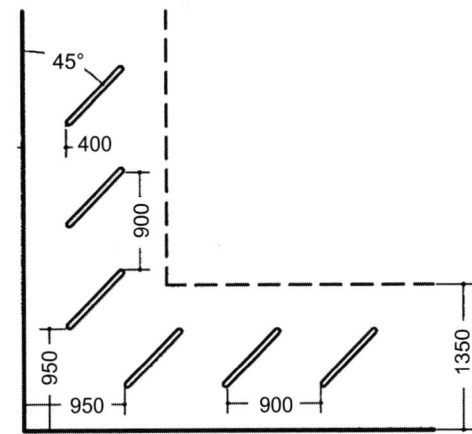

39.26 *An arrangement in an angle between two walls*

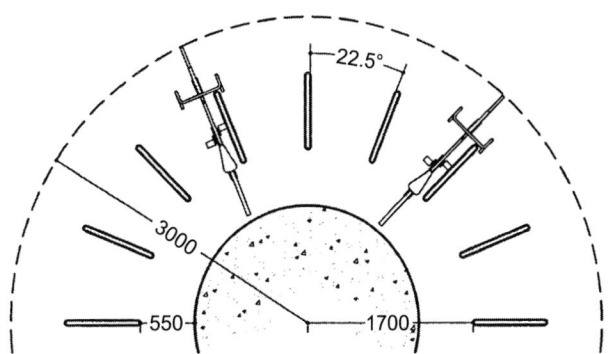

39.24 *Wall bar, suitable for small parking spaces where short-term parking is required*

39.27 *Circular array with a capacity for 32 cycles*

expected requirements. Some planning authorities now restrict parking provision for cars in order to give a measure of restraint to traffic.

Table IV also includes recommendations for the scale of bicycle parking. These are quite generous so as to encourage greater use of bicycles. However, account should be taken of the local conditions – in places where there are substantially more bicycles than average, greater provision should be made.

6.2 Domestic garages
The domestic garage is the basic provision for residential areas. This can be:

* within the envelope of the house or block of flats;
* a separate detached building;
* one of a number in a garage court.

Figures 39.29 to 39.35 show a number of typical arrangements.

6.3 Car parks
Once the scale of provision has been decided, the form will depend on the size and shape of the available area, and also on the type of vehicle expected. Figures 39.36 and 39.37 give examples of various arrangements, but again, these should be taken purely as a guide. This type of car park assumes that vehicles arrive and leave in a random fashion. In some situations, such as sporting events, a dense arrangement can be adopted which means that all vehicles have to leave approximately in the sequence in which they arrived.

Figure 39.38 shows various types of multi-storey garage. No dimensions are shown as these vary with the site. An additional type, not illustrated, incorporates a mechanical stacking system operated by attendants. In practice, this rarely shows any advantage over conventional types.

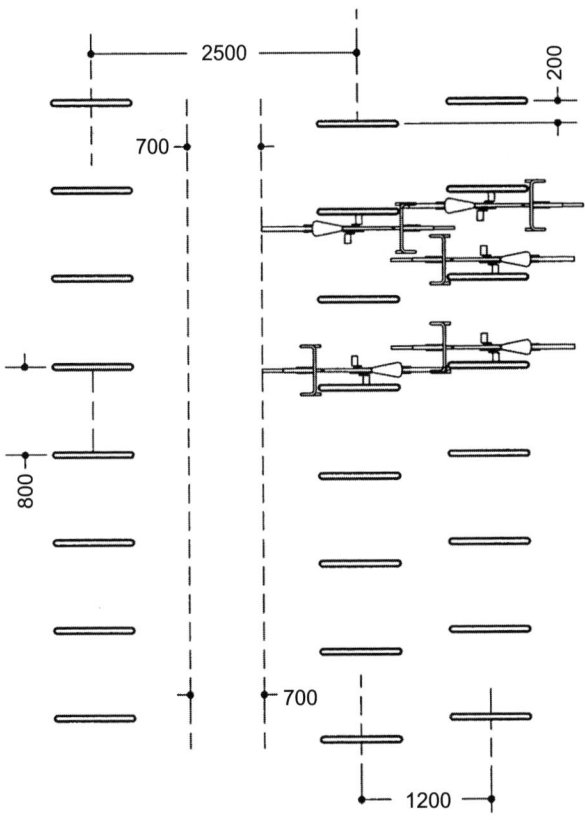

39.25 *It is important that arrays of Sheffield stands make best use of space. Attempts at closer spacing than shown will not succeed due to blocking of some positions by carelessly parked cycles*

There are no statutory requirements and few guidelines for the scale of parking provision. Table IV gives recommendations, but each specific case should be examined to determine

Table IV Parking and loading/unloading requirements

Type of building	Car parking provision	Loading/unloading provision		Cycle parking
Normal housing	Residents: one garage space for each occupancy, (preferably within the curtilage) Visitors: where houses are served directly from a road, driveways provide a minimum of one car space within curtilage of each Where visitors cannot park within curtilage, one off-street space per four dwellings	Refuse collection vehicle within 25 m of each disposal point (dustbin position). Some authorities require vehicle within 15 m. Where communal containers (paladins) are used, maximum distance 9 m Furniture removal vehicle as near as possible, not further than 25 m		
Minimum-cost housing	Space should be provided, if not laid out, to allow for one resident's or visitor's parking space per dwelling, provided public transport is available	As above		
Old people's housing	One garage space per two dwellings	As above		
Sheltered housing	Resident and non-resident staff: one car space per two members present at peak period Visitors: use empty staff places, but provide one additional place per five dwellings	As above, plus provisions for special passenger vehicle with tail lift, etc. Minimum provision for daily loading/unloading 50 m		
Shops	Staff: one car space (preferably in enclosed yard behind shop) for each 100 m² gross floor area or, if known, one space per managerial staff plus one for every four other staff	See diagrams of loading bays. General minima as follows: Gross floor space not exceeding: 500 m²	Minimum space required: 50 m²	1 per 200 m² with minimum of 4
	Customers: one space for each 25 m gross floor area. In superstores with gross floor area exceeding 2000m² allow one space per 10m². (Not appropriate when goods sold are obviously bulky, e.g. carpets, boats)	1000 2000 each additional 1000 m²	100 150 50 m²	
Banks	Staff: one space for each managerial or executive staff, plus one per four others Customers: one space per 10 m of net public floor space in banking hall	Minimum 25 m²		2
Officers	Staff: one space for each 25 m of gross floor area, or one space for each managerial and executive staff, plus one space per four others Visitors: 10% of staff parking provision	General minima: Gross floor space not exceeding: 100 m² 500 1000 each additional 1000 m²	Minimum space required: 50 m² 100 150 25 m²	1 per 200 m² with minimum of 4
Production buildings (factories)	Staff: one car space per 50 m of gross floor area Visitors: 10% of staff parking provision	See loading bay diagram. Provision to be commensurate with expected traffic General minima as follows: Gross floor space not exceeding: 100 m² 250	Minimum space required: 70 m² 140	1 per 500 m² with minimum of 4
Storage buildings (warehouses)	Staff: one space per 200 m² of gross floor space	500 1000 2000 each additional 1000 m²	170 200 300 50 m²	1 per 1000 m² with minimum of 4
Hotels, motels and public houses	Resident staff: one space per household Non-resident staff: one space for each three staff members employed at peak period	General minima as follows: Gross floor space not exceeding: 500 m²	Minimum space required: 140 m²	1 per 10 beds with minimum of 4
	Resident guests: one space per bedroom Bar customers: one space for each 4 m² of net public space in bars Occasional diners: no additional provision required If conferences are held in the hotel, space required should be assessed separately at one space for each five seats	1000 2000 each additional 1000 m²	170 200 25	
Restaurants and cafés	Resident staff: one space per household Non-resident staff: one space per three members employed at peak period	General minima as follows: Dining floor space not exceeding: 100 m²	Minimum space required: 50 m²	1 per 25 m² with minimum of 4
	Diners: one space for each two seats in dining area (For transport cafes, the space should be a lorry space of 45 m, and the arrangement should be such that vehicles can enter and leave without reversing)	250 500	75 100	
Licensed clubs	Resident staff: one space per household Non-resident staff: one space for each three members employed at peak period Performers: one space for each solo performer and/or group expected at peak Patrons: one space per two seats, or one space per 4 m² net public floor space	Minimum 50 m²		1 per 25 m² with minimum of 4
Dance halls and discotheques	Staff: one space per three members at peak period Performers: three spaces Patrons: one space per 10 m of net public floor space	Minimum 50 m²		1 per 25 m² with minimum of 4
Cinemas	Staff: one space per three members at peak period	Minimum 50 m²		1 per 100 seats with

Table IV (continued)

Type of building	Car parking provision	Loading/unloading provision		Cycle parking
	Patrons: one space per 5 seats	Space required within site by main entrance for two cars to pick up and set down patrons		minimum of 4
Theatres	Staff: one space per three members at peak period Patrons: one space per 10 m² of gross dressing room accommodation	Minimum 100 m² Space required within site by main entrance for two cars to pick up and set down patrons		1 per 100 seats with minimum of 4
Swimming baths	Patrons: one space for each three seats Staff: one space for every two members normally present Patrons: one space per 10 m pool area	Minimum 50 m²		1 per 4 staff
Sports facilities and playing fields	Staff: one space per three members normally present Players: one space for each two players able to use the facility simultaneously, provided public transport is reasonably close. Otherwise two spaces for each three players Spectators: provide only if more than three times the number of players	Minimum 50 m²		1 per 4 staff
Marains	Staff: one space per three members normally present Boat-users: two spaces for each three mooring-berths. (If other facilities are included, e.g. restaurant, shop etc., provide additional spaces at 50% normal provision for each additional facility)	Minimum 50 m²		1 per 4 staff
Community centres and assembly halls	Staff: one space for each three members normally present Patrons: one space for every five seats for which the building is licensed	Minimum 50 m²		1 per 4 staff
Places of worship	Worshippers: one space per ten seats in space for worship	Minimum 50 m² Space provided within site close to main entrance for two cars to set down and pick up worshippers		1 per 60 seats minimum 4
Museums and public art galleries	Staff: one space per two members normally on duty Visitors: one space per 30 m² of public display space	Minimum 50 m²		1 per 300 m² minimum 4
Public libraries	Staff: one space per three members normally on duty Borrowers: one space for each 500 adult ticket holders with a minimum of three spaces. If there are separate reference facilities, provide additional spaces at one for each ten seats	Minimum 50 m²		1 per 300 m minimum 4
Hospitals	Staff: one space for each doctor and surgeon, plus one space for each three others Outpatients and visitors: one space for each three beds	General minima as follows: Gross floor space not exceeding: 1000 m² 2000 4000 6000 every additional 200 m²	Minimum space required: 200 m² 300 400 500 100 m²	1 per 12 beds
Health centres, surgeries, clinics	Staff: one space per doctor etc. Patients: two spaces per consulting room	Sufficient for requirements specified, including if necessary space for special vehicle for non-ambulant patients	4	
Special schools, day-care centres and adult training centres	Attenders: in many cases these will be transported to the centre. For certain centres for the physically handicapped, allow one space for special or adapted self-drive vehicle per four attenders	Accommodation for special passenger vehicle Space provided within the site for cars and/or buses to set down and pick up	1 per 6 staff	
Nursery and primary schools	Staff: one space per two members normally present Visitors: two spaces Hard surface play area used for parking on open days etc.	Minimum 30m²	1 per 6 staff	
Secondary schools	Staff: one space per two members normally present Visitors: schools with up to 1000 pupils – four spaces, larger schools – eight spaces. Hard surface play area used for parking on occasion	Minimum 50 m² Space provided within site for school buses to set down and pick up	1 per 6 staff 1 per 3 students	
Sixth form colleges	Staff: one space per two members normally present Visitors: colleges with up to 1000 pupils – five spaces, larger schools – ten Hard surface play area used for parking on occasion	Minimum 50 m²	1 per 6 staff 1 per 3 students	
Further education colleges and retraining centres	Staff: one space for each member normally present Students and visitors: one space for each three students normally present	Minimum 50m²	1 per 6 staff 1 per 3 students	

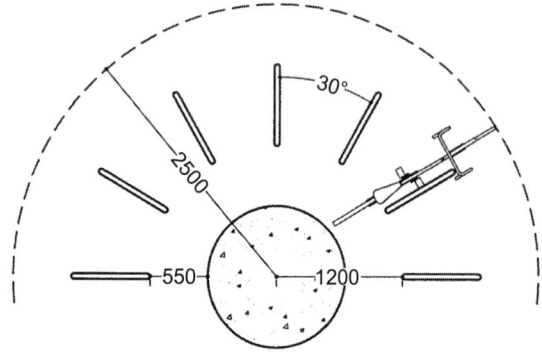

39.28 *Circular array with a capacity for 24 cycles*

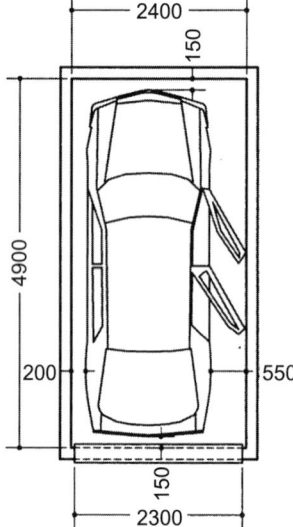

39.29 *A domestic garage of minimum dimensions*

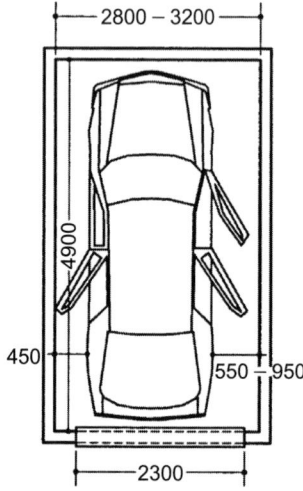

39.30 *A more generous garage permitting passenger access*

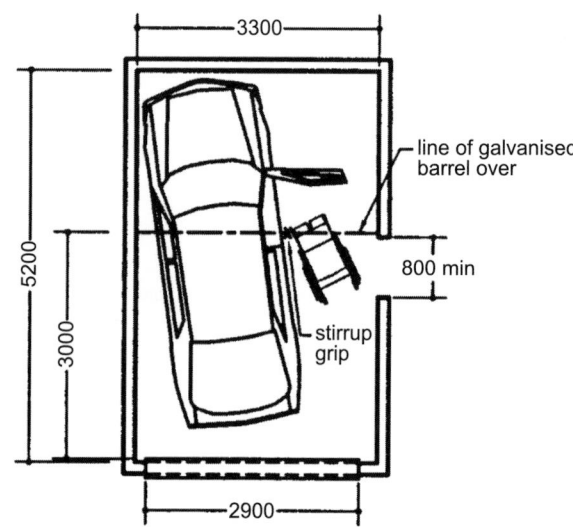

39.31 *Garage for a driver who is a wheelchair user (for an ambulant disabled driver, a width of 2.8 m is adequate)*

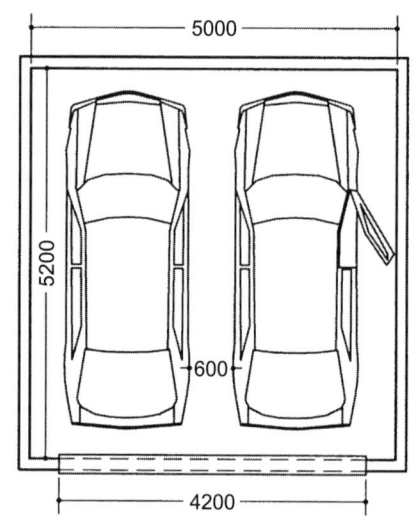

39.32 *A garage for two cars*

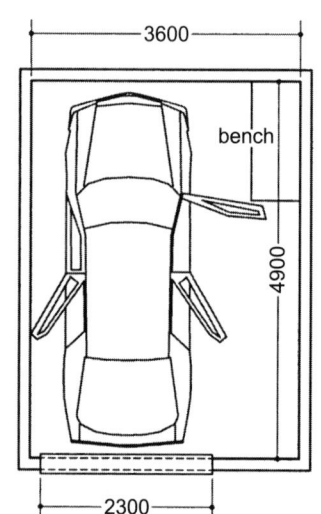

39.33 *A garage of minimum length but width sufficient for a workbench*

Wherever public or private parking facilities are provided, appropriate arrangements for disabled people, whether drivers or passengers, should be made. Disabled parking bays should be as close as possible to the place that the user needs to go, and preferably under visual supervision to discourage misuse by others. Bays should be at least 800 mm wider than standard, to permit manoeuvring of wheelchairs for transfer, and any kerbs should be ramped.

7 LOADING AND UNLOADING
Figures 39.39 to 39.44 show requirements for loading, unloading and parking large vehicles.

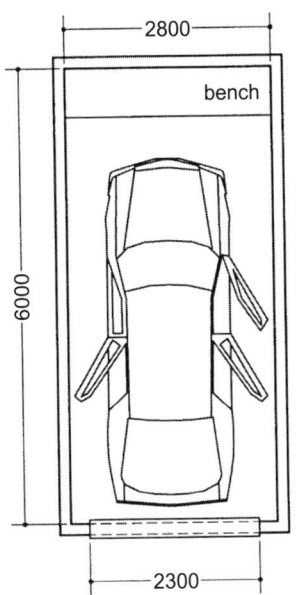

39.34 *A garage with a workbench at the end*

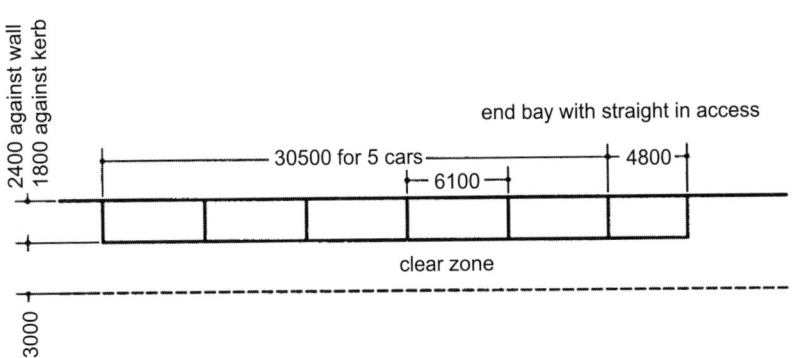

a *in-line parking 20.1 m² per car against kerb, 23.8 m² against wall*

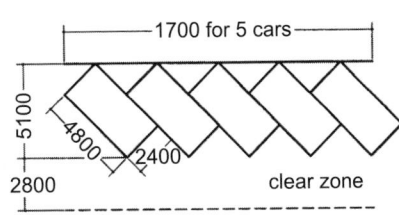

b *echelon parking at 45° (other angles can be used): 22.1 m² per car or 19.2 m² where interlocking in adjacent rows*

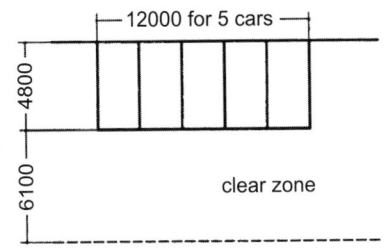

c *head-on parking, 18.8 m² per car*

39.36 *Basic parking dimensions. Standard European parking bay or stall 4.8 × 2.4, allow 24 m² per car, including half the clear zone but no access gangways*

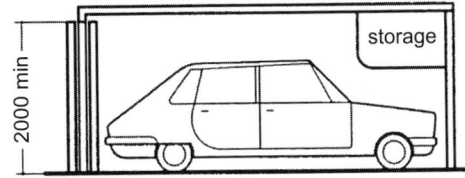

39.35 *Cross-section through a garage showing raised storage area*

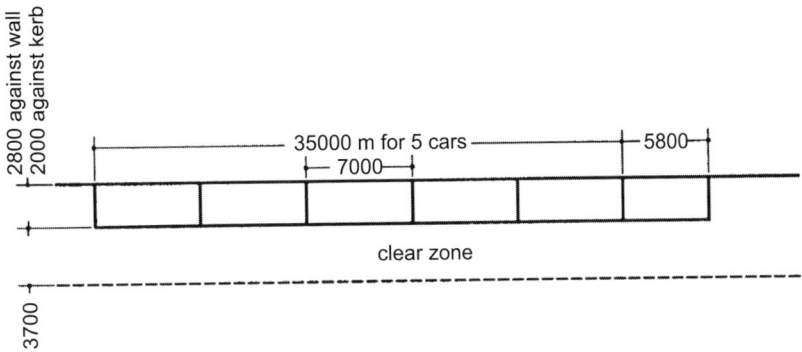

a *in-line parking 27.0 m² per car against kerb, 32.6 m²per car against wall*

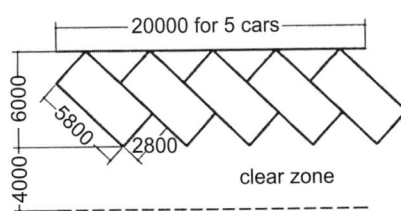

b *echelon parking at 45° (other angles can be used): 32.0 m² per car or 28.0 m² where interlocking in adjacent rows*

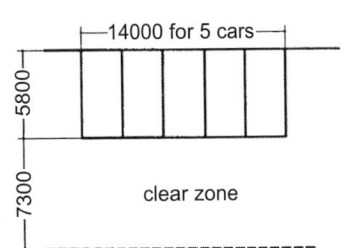

c *head-on parking, 26.5 m² per car*

39.37 *Basic parking dimensions. Large European parking or American bay or stall 5.8 × 2.8, allow 33 m² per car, including half the clear zone but no access gangways*

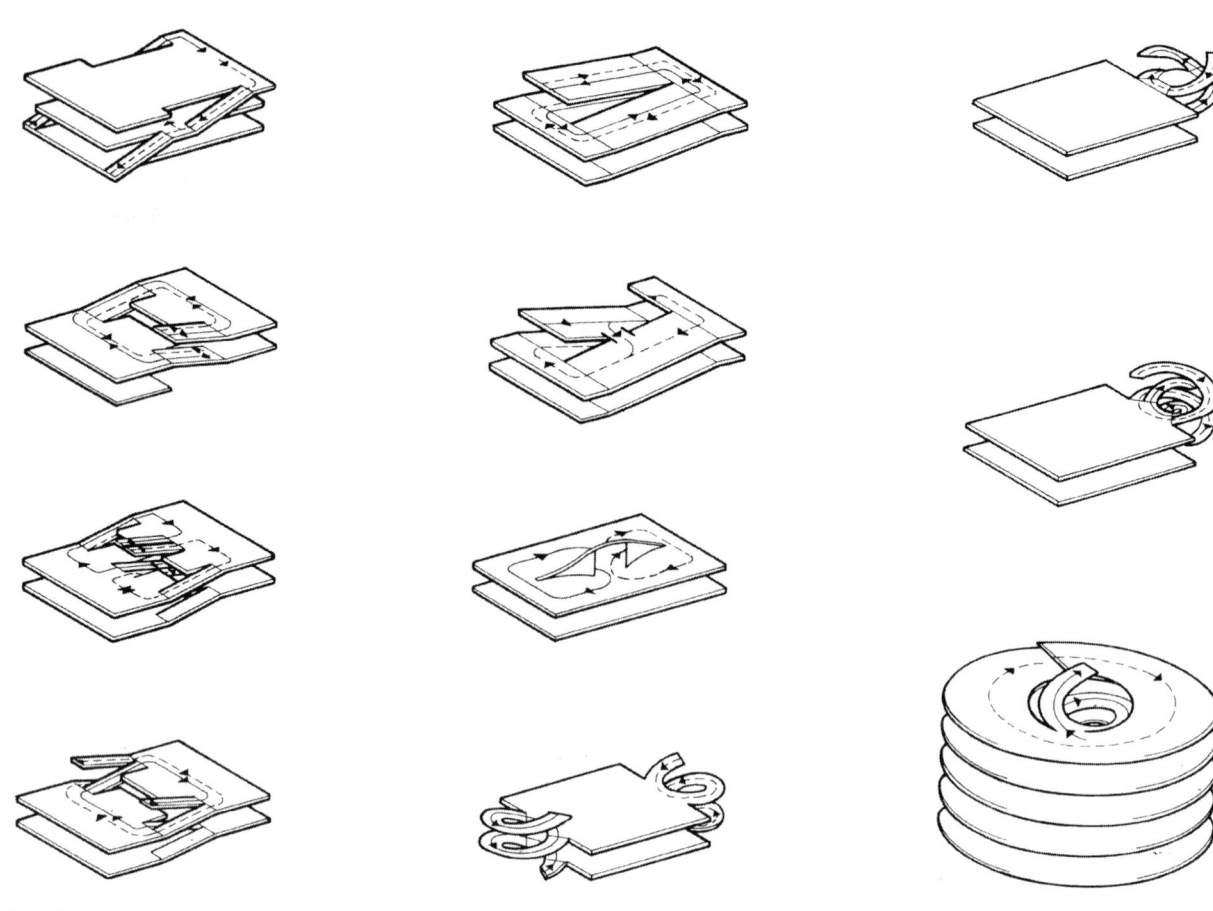

39.38 *Types of multi-storey car parks*

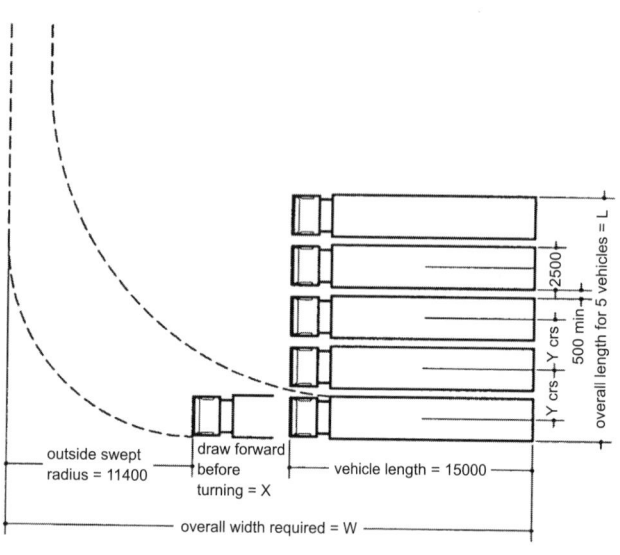

X draw forward	Y centres	W o/a width	L o/a length for 5	Area per vehicle (m²)
1	5.0	27.4	22.5	123
2	4.4	28.4	20.1	114
3	4.0	29.4	18.5	109
4	3.7	30.4	17.3	105
5	3.4	39.4	16.1	101
6	3.0	32.4	14.5	94

39.39 *Lorry parking and loading bays: diagonal (45°) for the largest vehicles*

X draw forward	Y centres	W o/a width	L o/a length for 5	Area per vehicle (m²)	
				gross	net*
4	4.8	18.4	39.5	145	113
5	4.5	19.1	37.8	144	111
6	4.2	19.8	36.1	144	108
7	3.9	20.5	34.4	141	105
8	3.6	21.2	32.7	139	101
9	3.4	21.9	39.6	138	100
10	3.2	22.6	30.5	138	98
11	3.1	23.4	29.9	140	99
12	3.0	24.1	29.3	141	99

*Excluding the empty triangles at each end.

39.40 *Lorry parking and loading bays: diagonal (45°) for the largest vehicles*

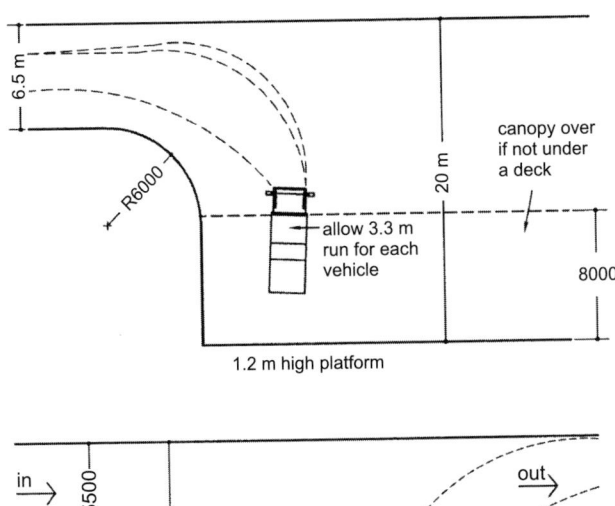

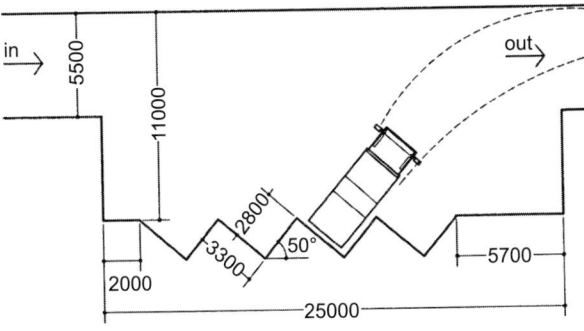

39.41 *Minimal loading docks appropriate for limited number of vehicles per day, extremely high land costs or other physical restraints*

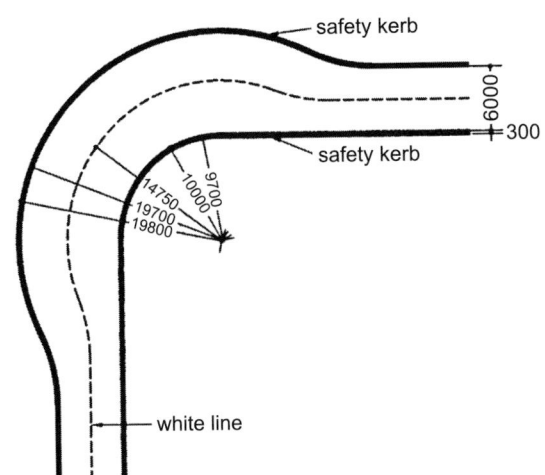

39.43 *Ramp on a sharp curve, such as access to a shopping centre loading dock. Maximum gradients 10 per cent on straight, 7 per cent on inner kerb*

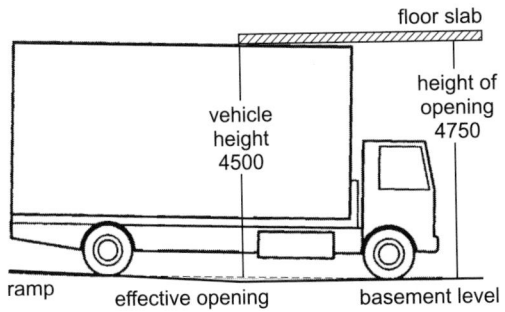

39.44 *Headroom criteria for covered loading docks*

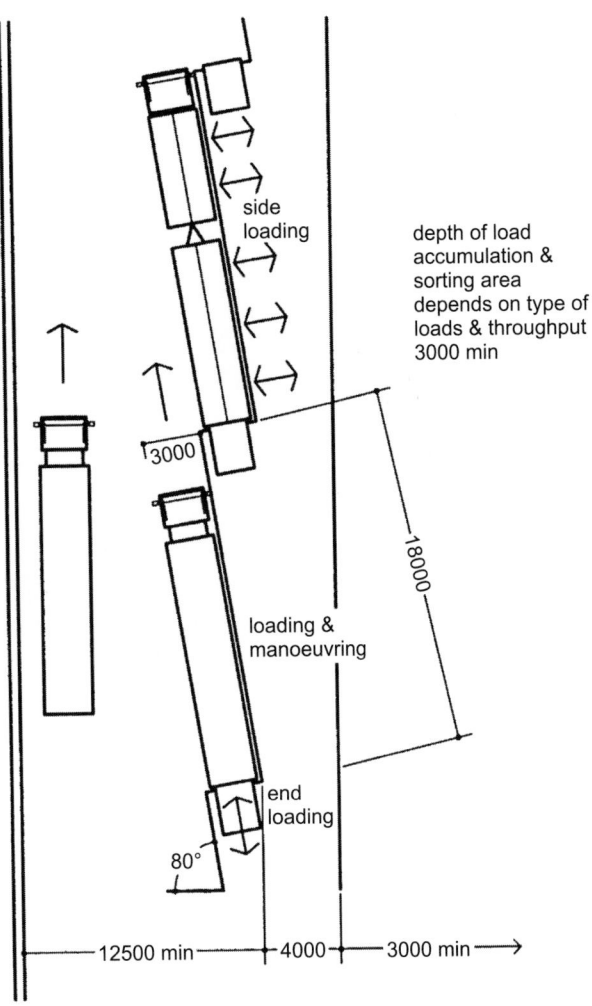

39.42 *Finger dock, where manoeuvring depth is limited and side loading is required as well as end loading. Very fast turnround times are possible although capacity is small*

8 SHARED SPACE

8.1 Principles

The emerging principles behind the concept of shared space for the design of streets and public spaces relies on a clear distinction between two worlds, that of the highway and of public space. Both demand fundamentally contrasting characteristics. On the one hand, the high-speed, single-purpose, regulated and standardised world of the highway, on the other, the low-speed, multi-purpose, contextual and socially defined qualities of the public realm. The contrasting characteristics can be summarised in Table V.

Behavioural psychologists have noted that drivers' speed and responses are largely determined by perceptions of time, and our expectations of progress. In the highway world, high-speeds are part of 'system time', based on anticipation of arrival at a destination at a particular time. By contrast, public space is governed by 'context time', where interest in people and surroundings triggers the brain to expect and demand low speeds to allow time for interpretation and localised responses.

Table V Characteristics of highway and public realm

The Highway	Public Realm
Single purpose	Multiple purposes
Regulated and controlled by the State	Governed by social protocols
High speed	Low speed
Segregated	Integrated
Predictable, consistent, certain	Unpredictable, intriguing, ambiguous
Standardised	Contextual
Interpreted through signs and markings	Multi-layered human communication

39.45 *Shared space at Exhibition Road in South Kensington, designed by Dixon Jones with Project Centre and Hamilton-Baillie Associates for the Royal Borough of Kensington & Chelsea*

Shared space is a term used to describe the shift towards the use of 'context time' to achieve the safe and efficient integration of vehicular traffic into the streets and spaces that constitute the public realm, Figure 39.45. In practice this requires a combination of design elements and an understanding of the spatial and dimensional implications of low-speed design. Key themes are set out in Sections 8.2–8.6.

8.2 Gateways or transition spaces

The interface between the two worlds of the highway and public space calls for careful treatment, for example at the entry point into a town or village. This requires clarity and consistency. The change of scale from high-speed to low-speed can be achieved through a combination of tighter dimensions, materials, lighting, planting and landscaping, public art and place-making. Consistency between highway measures and the town's architecture and morphology is essential. The transition, Figure 39.46, from highway to shared space requires road markings such as centre lines to end, and the introduction of lower-height, place-specific lighting in place of standard highway masts.

8.3 Visual narrowing

Driver speeds are largely determined by perceptions of carriageway widths. Reducing the apparent width of the vehicular carriageway is one element in creating the necessary low-speed environment for shared space. An edge strip installed parallel to the kerb, in a material close in tone, texture and colour to the footway, can

Market stalls in the street

informal parking

tree planting where practical

Bollards (used sparingly) reinforce speed reduction

End of road markings

Market Cross, or other feature, with seating contribute to reducing vehicle speed.

Paving & kerbs appropriate to the context & pedestrian usage

Change in road surface

APPROACHING THE CENTRE OF THE VILLAGE/TOWN

39.46 *Village transition (Hamilton-Baillie Associates)*

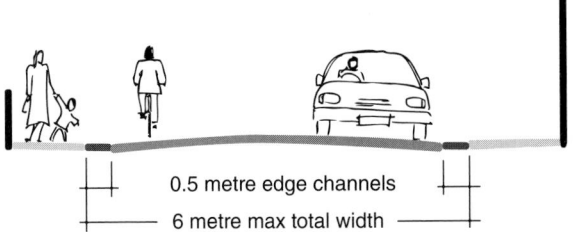

39.47 *Cross section showing narrowing of carriageway width perception (Hamilton-Baillie Associates)*

successfully reduce the perceived width of carriageway, Figure 39.47. For low speeds, a two-way carriageway of around 6 m can be reduced to an apparent width of 5 m with the inclusion of twin edge strips of 500 mm.

8.4 Edge friction

Vehicle speeds are also determined by the richness of information and activity in the driver's peripheral vision. Where high speeds are expected on highways such as motorways, the edge conditions are maintained as empty and blank as possible. By contrast, low speed environments can be created by enriching the carriageway edge with as much activity, variation and interest as possible. Vertical elements such as trees or lamp columns can combine with spill-out from shops or pavement activity to create edge friction.

8.5 Central medians

One method of increasing edge friction is to introduce a central strip to separate the opposing carriageways. Such a strip can be helpful in minimising the crossing distance and number of negotiations pedestrians have to undertake, allowing a street to be crossed in two phases. A median strip, Figure 39.48, can be of any

width, but it is often helpful to allow 2 m in order to accommodate transverse bicycle parking or tree planting. Lighting columns can be well placed on a median strip, providing a useful change in arrangements at the transition point.

8.6 Junction design

The move from segregated towards integrated traffic design allows for greater creativity in the design of intersections, which often lie at the heart of the community. All too often such spaces are dominated by traffic infrastructure. Junctions work more efficiently the lower the approach speed of vehicles, and the less interference is generated by pedestrian crossings. Lower design speeds remove the need for signal control, saving long-term capital and revenue costs for the local highway authority. Shared space junction design strategies include:

- Creating low approach speeds. This will often require the introduction of entry lobbies some 80–120 m distant from the main junction in order to establish appropriate driver expectations.
- Inclusion of a central feature, such as an obelisk, statue, fountain, tree or lamp around which traffic can circulate. Where the available space is limited, a simple roundel or geometrical pattern in the junction can be helpful.
- Avoiding the formality of a mini-roundabout. This helps maintain place qualities and increases driver awareness of fellow street users. The use of tracking software to establish the turning capabilities of large vehicles can be helpful, although lower speeds can allow much tighter dimensions than standard programs allow. A 25 m diameter circle is usually the minimum required to allow large HGVs to turn through 180°.
- For busy intersections, it is helpful to set pedestrian courtesy crossings back 5 m from the junction entry point, in order to allow a vehicle to be free to negotiate solely with other drivers on entering a junction. This set back has to be balanced with minimising any deviation in pedestrian desire lines.

39.48 *Median strip in the centre of Oxford*

9 PLACE-MAKING

9.1 Benefits

The art of place-making is key to successful urban design and planning and traffic management. Simple measures can help transform a featureless linear street into a rich sequence of places, punctuating and enriching the driver's understanding of context. The positioning of a tree, fountain or lamp in the centre of an intersection can help create a place, or merely the inclusion of a notional frame around a space using setts, blocks or contrasting paving. Special lighting and the disposition of street furniture are also valuable ingredients in place-making.

9.2 Streets and buildings

Conventional segregated highways bear no relationship to the buildings they serve or the activities such buildings generate. Integrated street design seeks to establish a close relationship between the context of a street's surroundings and the design of the street itself. Thus a street might vary its design and form in response to the presence of a school, a park, a pub, a church or a major building. Finding creative ways to establish such conversations is central to current good practice in street design.

9.3 Pedestrian movement

Good street design begins with establishing a clear picture of the likely pedestrian flow patterns, the 'desire lines', established by key pedestrian attractors. Research by Space Syntax and others has highlighted the need to avoid sharp changes in directions in order to provide the legibility and confidence pedestrians demand. Barriers such as guard-rails, high kerbs, bollards and highway clutter should be avoided wherever possible. Pedestrian crossings should be positioned where desire lines suggest pedestrians will wish to cross traffic. Most often this will not be orthogonal to the flow of traffic (as in conventional formal crossings), but is more likely to reflect the diagonal movements associated with pedestrian movement.

Lower speeds in shared space allow for greater use of 'courtesy crossings' – the use of paving material and lighting to highlight to drivers where people are likely to wish to cross. Keeping the width of carriageway where pedestrians cross to an absolute minimum (3 m per lane) is critical in minimising the disruption to traffic flows and encouraging easy pedestrian movement.

9.4 Designing for cyclists

A guide to good design and infrastructure for cyclists is provided in Section 5. Where speeds are sufficiently low to minimise the differential between motor traffic and cyclists, informal sharing of the carriageway becomes more feasible. The presence of cyclists is helpful in establishing the informal negotiations and mutual awareness central to shared space. Where one-way streets for motor traffic cannot be avoided, measures should be introduced to allow two-way flows for cyclists. Off road, traffic-free links and connections form a critical part in a comprehensive network for cyclists. Only where speeds or traffic volumes are over-dominant in a given street or space should separate lanes be marked out on carriageways or on shared-use footways, where widths should not be lower than 1.2 m.

9.5 Designing for people with disabilities

Current street design continues to seek creative means to allow and foster universal access to as much of the built environment as possible. Establishing low speeds is the most critical factor above all in achieving such universal access. The quality of experience and confidence of people with disabilities requires an environment that fosters an awareness and alertness of drivers towards individual circumstances. Elements such as courtesy crossings, supplemented tactile or physical measures to ease navigation and orientation, combined with a clear understanding of the importance of landmarks, sound, paving surfaces, lighting, sunlight and many other clues, can minimise the barriers facing those with disabilities.

9.6 Street furniture

Street furniture and planting can be central to successful place-making, and can help establish the overall design approach appropriate to the context. The arrangement, positioning and design of the benches, litter bins, lighting columns, bicycle parking and other items of street furniture are best considered as an integral part of the overall design, rather than left until last. Wherever possible, any necessary signing can be designed into the street furniture to minimise clutter.

10 CASE STUDY – POYNTON

10.1 Introduction

Poynton is a small market town between Stockport and Macclesfield in Cheshire. It is a crossroads settlement, centred around the intersection of the busy north-south London Road, with the east-west Chester Road. Park Lane, the town's main high street, runs eastwards from the main intersection of Fountain Place.

In 2007, the decline in economic activity had become critical for the future of the town, with over half of its high street shops standing vacant.

10.2 Traffic blight

This retail decline was partly associated with the poor quality of street design and layout in Park Lane. But the more significant factor was the bifurcation of the residential community caused by the heavy traffic and wide, impersonal carriageways of the signal-controlled junction at Fountain Place. As a result, one half of the town's residential area, including its railway station, was physically and psychologically divided from Park Lane. Heavy congestion and delays associated with the traffic signals had generated poor air quality, and traffic speeds were a concern. The magnificent parish church, designed by Alfred Waterhouse and very popular for local weddings, had an especially poor connection to the town.

10.3 New street design

Street design, and a radical approach to traffic management, were central to the master plan for the regeneration of Poynton designed by Hamilton-Baillie Associates and completed in 2012, Figure 39.49. This included a redesigned Park Lane premised on low-speed, continuous flow traffic. Visual widths of carriageways were reduced to 2.6 m, combined with an informal central median strip. The signal-controlled pedestrian crossing was removed, and a number of diagonal courtesy crossings were introduced. New lighting, street furniture and a coherent arrangement for shop fronts completed the design.

10.4 Fountain Place

The second phase of the £4 million project involved re-establishing a town centre and a sense of place at the Fountain Place junction, Figure 39.50. This was the first time that shared space principles had been applied to a major junction with such high volumes of traffic. Removal of the traffic signals and the introduction of low-speed, shared space arrangements allowed significantly greater space to be allocated for pedestrians, including a key space outside the church gate. All road markings, signs and signals were removed, and new gateways were created on each of the four approaches to the junction. Fountain Place was laid out as two interconnected circles in a granite block paving pattern, marked by informal roundels, to reinforce the sense of place, Figure 39.51.

39.49 *Hamilton-Baillie Associates' masterplan for Poynton, including a median strip and a new junction at Fountain Place to the left*

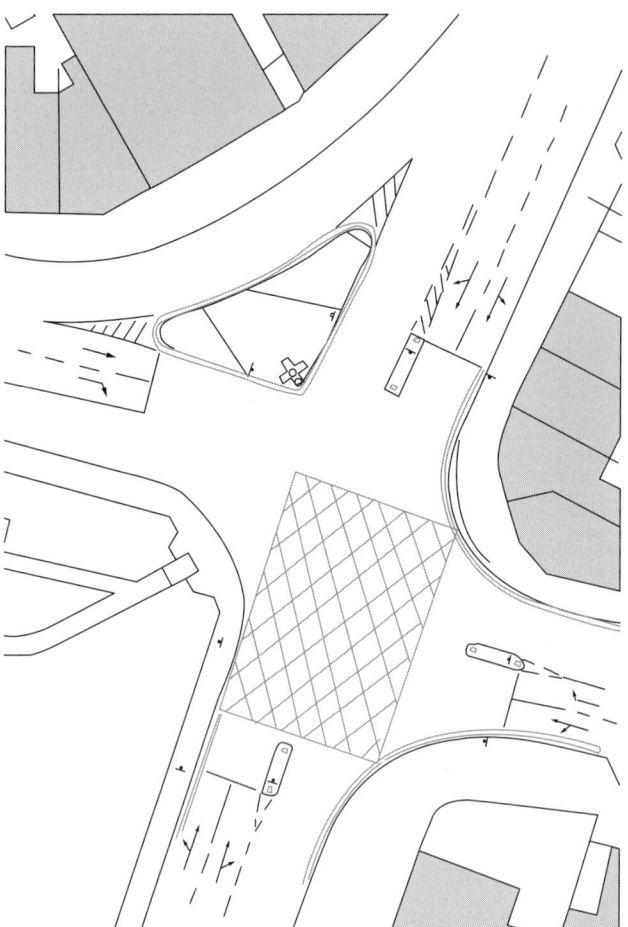

39.50 *Fountain Place's signal-controlled junction layout before its redesign*

39.52 *Fountain Place pictured after its redesign, with significantly less congestion*

39.51 *Fountain Place's new junction layout*

10.5 Impact

Within 10 months, all remaining vacant shops had been successfully let, and footfall has increased by around 80 per cent. Congestion levels fell more dramatically then expected, Figure 39.52, and journey times for vehicles passing through Poynton have reduced by 35–50 per cent. Road traffic accidents and injury rates, at the time of writing, showed a marked improvement on the signal-controlled arrangement.

11 BIBLIOGRAPHY

Baldwin & Baldwin (eds). The Motorway Achievement – Volume 1 Visualisation of the British Motorway System: Policy and Administration. Thomas Telford, 2004

Colin Buchanan, et al., *Traffic in Towns*, HMSO, 1963

CABE, *This Way to Better Streets*, 2007 www.designcouncil.org.uk

CIHT, *Streets and Transport in the Urban Environment*, 2014

Cambridge City Council, *Cycle parking guide for new residential development*, 2010

Construction Industry Council, *Integrated Transport and Land Use Planning*, 2002

Croney & Croney, *The design and performance of road pavements*. McGraw Hill, 1998 (3rd edition)

Department of Environment, Transport and the Regions, *The Highways (Road Humps) Regulations 1999*

Department for Transport, *Inclusive Mobility*, 2005

Department for Transport, *Local Transport Note 2/08 – Cycle Infrastructure Design*, 2008

Department for Transport, *Local Transport Note 1/12 – Shared Use Routes for Pedestrians and Cyclists*, 2012

Department for Transport, *Manual for Streets*, 2007

Department for Transport, *Manual for Streets 2*, 2011

Department for Transport, *Shared Space Local Advice Note 1/11* 2011

Department for Transport, Local Transport Note 1/08 -*Traffic design and Streetscape, 2008*

Dorset AONB, and Ben Hamilton-Baillie, *Traffic in Villages: A Toolkit for Communities*, 2011

English Heritage, *Streets for All*, 2006

D. Engwicht, *Mental Speed Bumps*, Enviropress, 2005

Jan Gehl, *Life between Buildings*, Danish Architectural Press, 2001

Jan Gehl, *Cities for People*, Island Press, 2010

Hill et al., *Car Park Designers' Handbook* (X401). Thomas Telford 2005

B. Hillier & J. Hanson. *The Social Logic of Space*. Cambridge University Press

Irish Government, Dept. Transport, Tourism & Sport, *Design Manual for Urban Roads and Streets*, 2013

Allan B Jacobs, *Great Streets*, MIT Press, 1995

Jha, MK et al. *Intelligent Road Design*. WIT Press, 2006

Lamm et al., *Highway Design and Traffic Safety Engineering Handbook*. McGraw Hill 2000

The Scottish Government, *Designing Streets*, 2010

Sustrans, *The National Cycle Network – Guidelines and Practical Details, 1996*

Transport for London, *London Cycling Design Standards*, www.tfl.gov.uk

H.G. Váhl & J Giskes, *Traffic calming through integrated urban planning*, Amarcande, 1988

Tom.Vanderbilt, *Traffic: Why We Drive the Way We Do*, Penguin, 2008

40 Studios for sound and vision

David Binns

CI/SfB 528

David Binns is the senior partner of Sandy Brown Associates, architects and acoustic consultants

KEY POINTS:
- *Avoidance of extraneous sound is essential*
- *Production staff need both full observation and easy access to the studio floor*

Contents
1 Introduction
2 Studio types
3 Planning
4 Services
5 Acoustics
6 Statutory requirements

1 INTRODUCTION

1.1 Scope
A TV studio is an area in which activities are performed specifically for observation. (Television cameras are also used outside studios for surveillance in stores, banks and so on.) A sound studio may be used for live broadcasts such as news bulletins, but is most likely to be required for making recordings.

1.2 Broadcasting studios
The greatest differences between studios will be in the ancillary areas rather than the studio *per se*. These differences reflect the nature and attitudes of the client: the BBC in the UK, for instance, is a public service organisation whereas the independent companies are not (although they must adhere to standards set by the Independent Broadcasting Authority).

1.3 Independent and educational studios
There are now many small independent studios, operating for private commercial use, for making programmes under contract and for making educational and instructional videos. Some are attached to higher-education institutions.

2 STUDIO TYPES

2.1 Sound studios
Small sound studios may be used for such purposes as local broadcasting and for recording advertisements and jingles for commercial radio. Figure 40.1 shows the scheme for such a facility. Where larger spaces are required, for example for recording orchestral music, studios primarily designed for TV might well now be used. The principles behind both sound and TV studios are similar, although sound studios are more likely to have direct vision windows.

2.2 Multi-purpose TV production studios
Previously, TV studios differentiated between music and drama. Now, all are multi-purpose largely due to economic pressures. They have accepted acoustically 'dead' conditions, reverberation or presence being added electronically. Greater use of zoom lenses in preference to camera tracking means microphones are located further from performers, necessitating low reverberation times and background noise levels. Camera tracking requires a floor laid to very precise tolerances (currently ±3 mm in 3 m). The floor

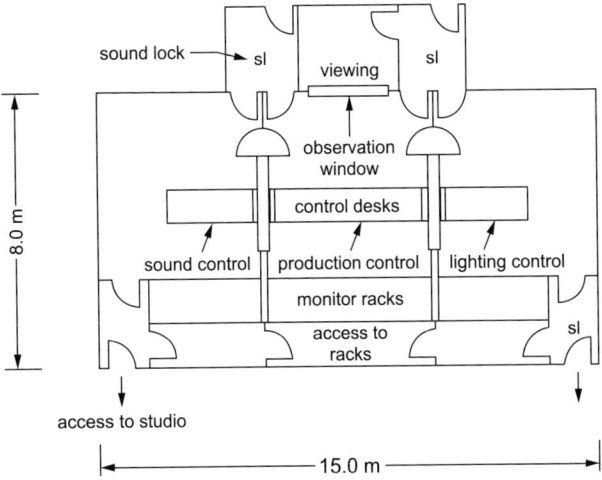

40.1 *Relationship diagram for sound recording studio suite*

is normally heavy duty linoleum sheet laid on an asphalt mastic screed; it requires a specialist floor laying contractor to achieve these fine tolerances.

Studio length-to-breadth ratio should be in the region of 1:1.5. The minimum practical floor area for a small commercial TV studio would be 60 m² with static cameras. TV station studios range between 200 and 400 m². The studio height is determined by the clear space required below the lighting grid (a function of the longest camera angle). The minimum height for a small studio is 4 m; in the larger studios 11 m to the grid with a clear height above of 2.5 m, making something over 13.5 m overall. In these studios an access gallery is required *at grid level approximately 4.5 m above studio floor level*. This is normally to avoid obstruction of access doors and observation window. Access to the galleries from studio floor level is mandatory and direct access to lighting grid level is desirable.

A cyclorama or backdrop cloth is suspended below lighting grid level. It should be at least 1.25 m away from the walls to allow a walkway around the studio and is on a sliding track with radiused corners to enable it to be stored.

2.3 Interview and announcers' studios
These studios range in size from 30 to 60 m² with a height of 4 to 6 m. Static cameras and a simple form of lighting grid combined with floor lighting stands are used.

2.4 Audience participation studios
Some productions require audience participation and fixed theatre-type seating on terraces is provided. In smaller studios this is demountable, so storage space has to be provided. Audiences place more stringent demands on the planning of a TV complex, as segregated access and emergency escape routes have to be provided (see Chapter 15, Auditoria).

3 PLANNING

3.1 Layout
A typical layout for a TV broadcasting studio complex is shown in Figure 40.2. Larger installations will have workshop facilities

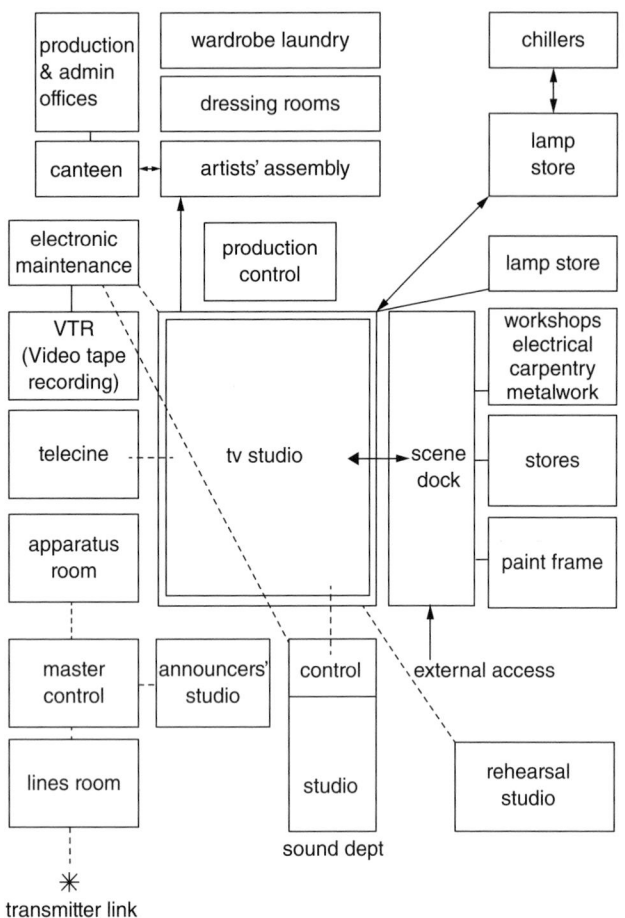

40.2 *TV studio complex; block planning diagram*

adjacent to the scene dock and if flats and backdrops are made on-site a paint frame will need to be the full height of the cyclorama curtain. Further details of such facilities will be found in Chapter 15.

Equipment areas
Ancillary equipment areas will include separate areas for VTR (video tape recording) and telecine (transference of filmed material to video). The machine operator should be able to hear sound track and cues above the noise of other machines in the room which are usually enclosed in open-fronted cubicles with heavily acoustically treated walls.

Master control room
Adjacent to these equipment areas will be the master control room, which is the last monitoring link in the video and audio chain before transmission. Here programme material, either recorded (VTR and telecine) or live from the studios, will be linked with continuity from the announcer's studio.

Dressing rooms
Artists' facilities adjoining the studio will include dressing rooms with associated wardrobe and laundry, rest and refreshment areas (see Chapter 15).

Rehearsal spaces
Separate rehearsal spaces are required as there is considerable pressure on studio floor time (much of which is used in setting and striking scenery, and setting up lighting and cameras for productions). These need not be the full studio size as several sets will occupy the studio floor and scenes are rehearsed individually, often in remote assembly halls.

Service spaces
In addition to the areas detailed in Figure 40.2, space will be required for a sub-station, emergency generator and tape stores.

The small commercial and education studios which do not broadcast will have simpler planning arrangements.

3.2 Control suites
TV control rooms do not now overlook the studio they monitor for the following reasons:

- The cyclorama track and studio scenery are likely to interfere with the producer's view; production decisions are made off monitor screens.
- The chroma of glass in the observation windows must be adjusted to confirm colours reproduced by TV monitors. This is done using an applied tinted finish which requires frequent replacement.
- Windowless production suites do not need to be elevated, hence production staff have direct access to the studio floor. A typical control suite layout of this type is shown in Figure 40.3.

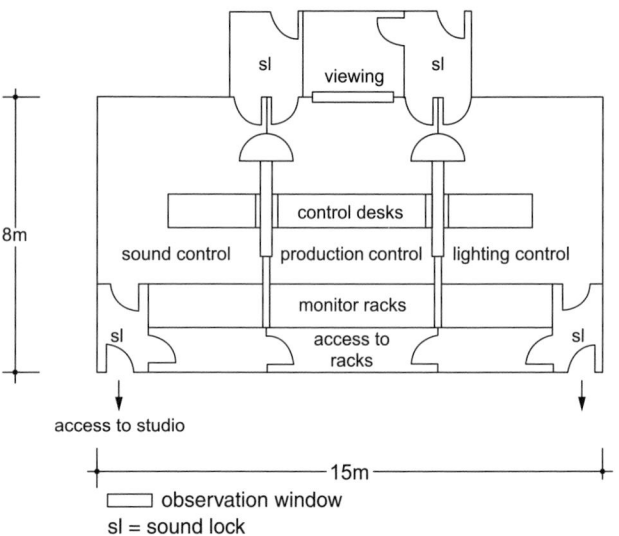

40.3 *Layout of a production control suite with no direct visual access to studio*

Minimum clear height in the control room, including a false ceiling for services, is 4 m.

Separate control areas for production, lighting, and sound are required with 25 dB insulation between each and visual contact via observation windows. A viewing area for visitors separate from that for production staff is desirable.

The disadvantage of such a layout is that the producer has no direct visual contact with the floor manager or performers.

4 SERVICES
4.1 Lighting
Television studio lighting is highly specialised. The large production studio will have a remotely operated lighting grid, whereas the small studio will have a simple pre-set system.

Lamp support systems
There are three basic types of lamp support systems:

- The most elaborate is a grid of 'railway' tracks covering the whole studio. On these tracks run carriers which have a telescopic arm holding the lamp. The arm is motor driven (either electrically or hydraulically) and lowers the lamp to studio floor level for setting and adjustment. Each lamp can be separately panned, tilted and dimmed remotely. An additional overhead rail at the perimeter of the grid will carry carts on to which the 'monopole telescopes' and lamps can be run off the grid to a lamp store. Where several studios exist this rail will interconnect them all via a central lamp store. The latest grids are equipped with an electronic memory to enable a whole production of lighting settings to be stored.

- A simpler form has lighting bars which can be raised or lowered electrically or manually fixed direct to the studio. The bars take several forms from the 'lazy scissors' principle to a simple bar on cables and pulleys.
- The third and simplest type is a fixed barrel grid. As in the second type no space is required above this grid for access as lamps are clamped direct to the bars and set from studio floor level.

Lighting to equipment and control areas needs to be carefully studied to avoid reflections and provide correct levels for viewing. Special fittings are often required.

4.2 Air conditioning
Air conditioning presents the designer with a number of unique problems: the large volume, the high heat loads generated by lamps, low background noise levels and the need to provide comfortable conditions in parts of the studio obscured in all but one plane by scenery. Low air speeds have to be used to achieve the noise levels. The most successful system has been the 'dump' system where cooled air is fed from a large plenum chamber above grid level and returns via natural convection of heat from the lamps to a similar exhaust plenum at an even higher level. Plant rooms, unless remote from the studios, require structural isolation to prevent vibration transmission (see Section 5.3); adequate space must be allowed for attenuation. Mechanical engineers are familiar with duct-borne noise problems, but do not normally investigate noise break-in through duct walls or the architectural acoustic problems. The architect should make certain that this forms part of the specialist consultant's brief.

4.3 Technical wiring
Extensive provision has to be made for power, audio and video wiring connecting the studio to control suites and equipment areas. Camera cables are approximately 50 mm in diameter and have a minimum bending radius of 0.5 m. Power wiring, which may include low-voltage power, has to be run in separate trunking from audio wiring to avoid interference. Trunking is often concealed within the acoustic finishes and all perforations of the studio enclosure have to be sealed airtight to avoid sound transmission.

4.4 Other services
Large production studios will require compressed air, gas, water (including drainage) and a smoke-detection system, in addition to electrical services.

5 ACOUSTICS
5.1 Identify standards
The standards to be achieved should be identified by the specialist consultant and agreed with the client at the outset. The two main sources are the BBC and the ISO (International Standards Organisation).

5.2 Airborne sound insulation
For every location a full one-third octave band, site noise level survey must be carried out to determine the design of the enclosing structures. Additionally, all internal transmission loss defined by frequency should be established and can be extended to provide the mechanical engineer with the requirements for in-duct crosstalk attenuation. For this it will be necessary to establish the maximum permissible noise levels from all sources in each room.

5.3 Vibration isolation
The noise and vibration levels of all mechanical plant should be studied and the architect must identify who should be responsible for defining maximum permissible levels and designing to achieve

them. Structure-borne sound transmission, particularly on the upper levels of framed buildings, may necessitate the 'floating' of plant rooms and noise-protected areas.

This involves isolating the walls, floor and roof from the surrounding structure. The walls are built off a secondary floor bearing on steel spring or rubber carpet mountings designed to a maximum natural frequency not exceeding 7 to 10 Hz. Footfall impact noise often requires floors to be carpeted with heavy underfelt or in extreme cases, the floating of studios.

5.4 Reverberation time
Figure 40.4 relates reverberation time to volume for television studios. Calculation will indicate the amount and type of absorption required. Details of a typical wide band modular absorber are shown in Figure 40.5. Approximately 200 mm should be added to the clear studio height and to each wall thickness to accommodate the acoustic treatment. Sound control rooms need to be similarly treated, with the other production control rooms and technical areas made as dead as possible.

5.5 Background noise levels
Maximum permissible background noise levels are shown in Figure 40.6. These should be related to the external ambient levels and to noise from air-conditioning plant. In certain situations where plant rooms are adjacent to noise-sensitive areas, maximum permissible noise levels at intake and extract louvres should be specified to limit this noise breaking back in through the external skin, particularly at windows.

5.6 Special details
Acoustic doors and sound lock
Typical details for an acoustic door and an observation window are shown in Figures 40.7 and 40.8. All noise-sensitive areas should be approached via a sound lock lobby consisting of acoustic doors, with either end of the lobby treated to be acoustically dead. The mean sound transmission loss of each door is 33 dB and sealing is effected by means of magnetic seals.

Scenery doors
The transfer of scenery into the studio requires an opening in the region of 5m high by 5m wide with a sound reduction index between 50 and 60 dB. This door will almost certainly be of steel construction. Hinged doors have been used but the forces required to ensure that the edge seals close airtight produce operational difficulties. A 'lift and slide' door is more satisfactory. An electric or hydraulic drive opens and closes the door while radius arms lower it inwards and downward to compress the edge seals all round. This type of door does not require an upstanding threshold as does the hinged door, and this is a considerable operational advantage.

6 STATUTORY REQUIREMENTS
Careful examination should be given at the planning stage to means of escape and fire resistance. Statutory requirements vary considerably

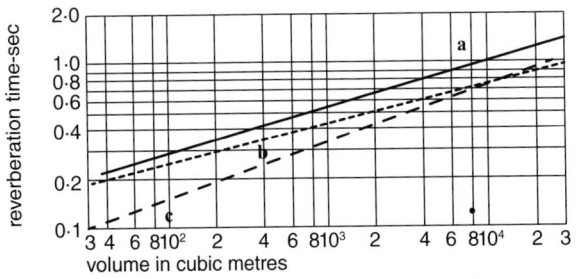

a *highest acceptable reverberation time*   b *optimum reverberation time*
c *lowest practicable reverberation time*

40.4 *Reverberation times for TV studio*

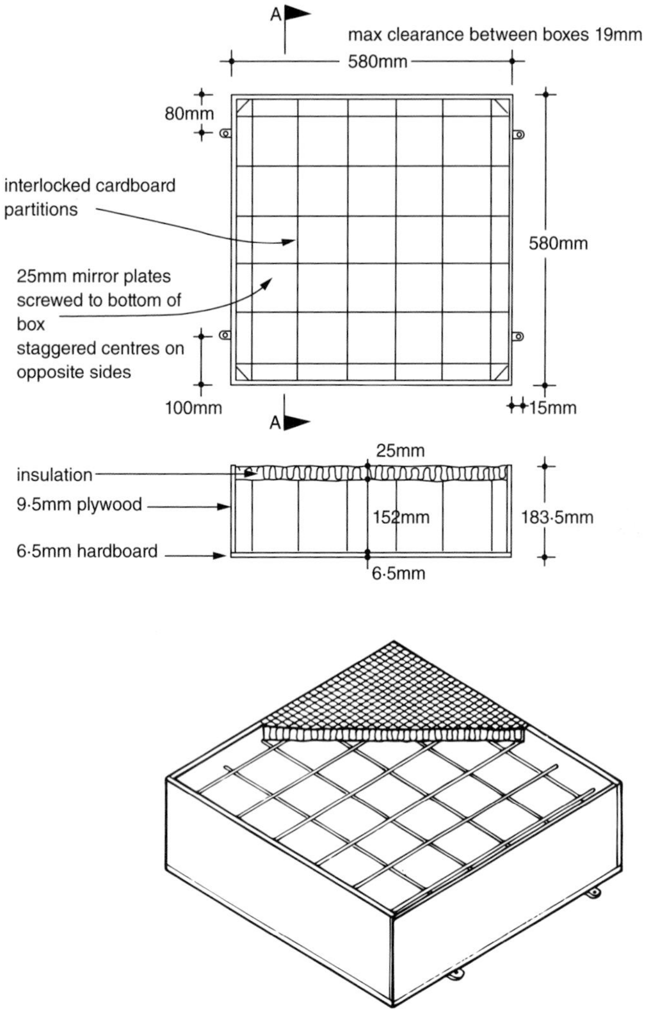

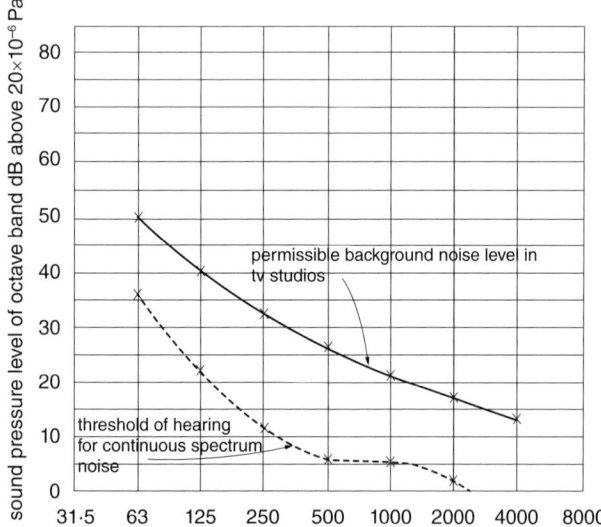

max clearance between boxes 19mm
580mm
80mm

interlocked cardboard partitions

25mm mirror plates screwed to bottom of box
staggered centres on opposite sides

580mm

100mm

15mm

insulation
9·5mm plywood
6·5mm hardboard

25mm
152mm
183·5mm
6·5mm

40.5 *Modular sound absorbing unit*

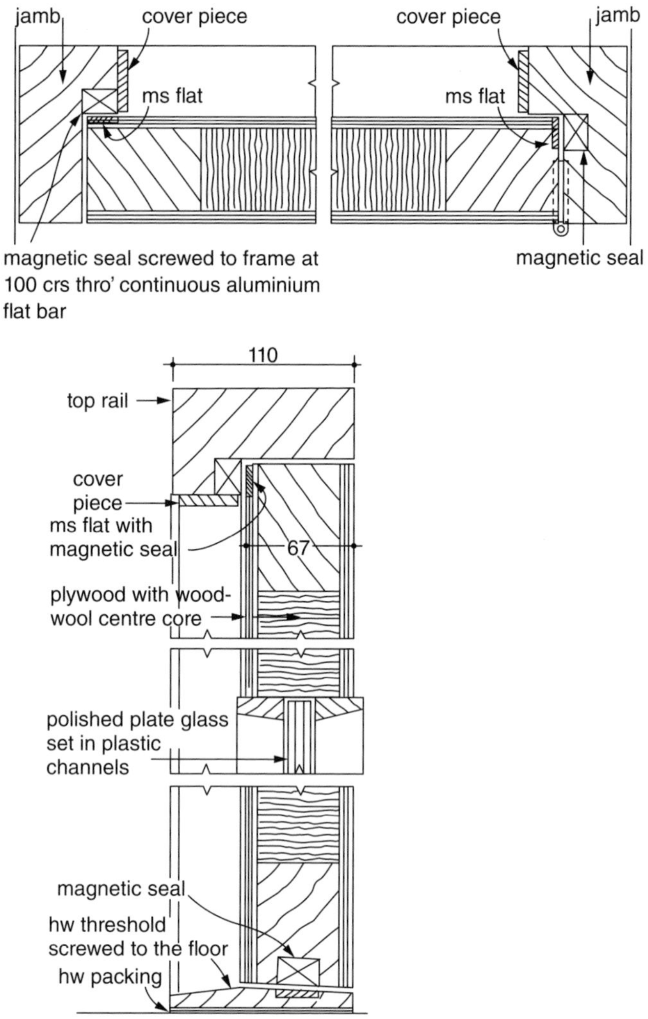

jamb   cover piece   cover piece   jamb

ms flat   ms flat

magnetic seal screwed to frame at 100 crs thro' continuous aluminium flat bar

magnetic seal

110

top rail

cover piece
ms flat with magnetic seal

plywood with wood-wool centre core

67

polished plate glass set in plastic channels

magnetic seal
hw threshold screwed to the floor
hw packing

40.7 *Acoustic door construction*

sound pressure level of octave band dB above 20×10⁻⁶ Pa

80
70
60
50
40
30
20
10
0

permissible background noise level in tv studios

threshold of hearing for continuous spectrum noise

31·5   63   125   250   500   1000   2000   4000   8000

40.6 *Background noise levels*

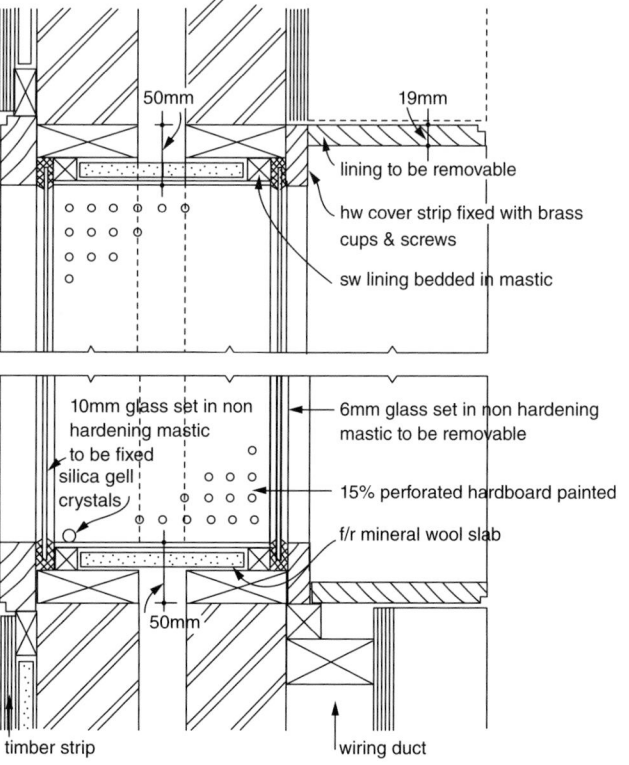

50mm   19mm

lining to be removable

hw cover strip fixed with brass cups & screws

sw lining bedded in mastic

10mm glass set in non hardening mastic to be fixed
silica gell crystals

6mm glass set in non hardening mastic to be removable

15% perforated hardboard painted

f/r mineral wool slab

50mm

timber strip   wiring duct

40.8 *Observation window*

in all parts of the world, but the most stringent are those operated in the UK where Class O flame spread may be required for all finishes and up to a four-hour fire separation for the studio walls. This necessitates double steel roller shutters on all perforations through walls. Smoke vents are sometimes required and these must be designed to match the sound insulation of the roof.

41 Transport terminals and interchanges

Airports updated by Andrew Perez with additional contributions by Richard Chapman. Railways by Declan McCafferty.
CI/SfB 114, 124, 144

Andrew Perez is a principal at Grimshaw Architects. Declan McCafferty is a partner at Grimshaw Architects. Richard Chapman is director of Airport Design Consult Ltd

KEY POINTS:

- *Airport terminals are now major public buildings with increasingly diverse functions*
- *Intermodality between all forms of transport is a critical consideration*
- *Moving large numbers of passengers safely, simply and efficiently are key components of a successful terminal and interchange design*

Contents

1 Introduction
2 Airports
3 The terminal building
4 Departures – landside
5 Departures – airside
6 Arrivals – airside
7 Arrivals – landside
8 Levels and volumes
9 Aircraft and apron requirements
10 The changing airport
11 Case study
12 Railway stations
13 Bus and coach stations
14 Trams and light rail
15 Bibliography

1 INTRODUCTION

Air travel is now available to many more people than ever before in its relative short history. As a result, airport terminals are now major public buildings and accommodate diverse functions from the social to the commercial as well as processing departing and arriving passengers. These buildings can be part-theatre, part-urban plaza, part-museum, part-shopping mall and part-leisure centre. Serving as gateways, both literally and figuratively, these buildings have become important emblems for nations as well as major transport processors. As their size, critical, social and commercial mass increase, airport terminals become ideal centres for major transport interchanges, capturing large movements of people, many of whom may not necessarily be travelling by air.

2 AIRPORTS

2.1 History

The airport terminal has been an established building type for only ninety years since London's first airport at Croydon, but many typologies have evolved. The rapid development of air travel has meant that buildings have swiftly become obsolete and needed either replacement or reconstruction.

A notable early example is the original terminal at Gatwick Airport, Figure 41.1 that offered passengers in 1936 a direct and sheltered route from railway to terminal and from terminal to aeroplane. It was therefore an early true transport interchange facility.

2.2 Airport terminal planning

There are two major influences on airport and terminal size:

- passenger demand;
- airline traffic scheduling.

2.3 Airport terminal capacity and size

Passengers per year and passengers per hour are the key factors in terminal design. Large peak concentrations will produce a high hourly demand in relation to the annual traffic. A substantial constant traffic level will produce a high annual rate in relation to the hourly demand.

Global air travel is growing on average by 5–6 per cent every year and estimates suggest that passenger numbers will continue to increase by 3–5 per cent annually for the foreseeable future.

Sophisticated mathematical models can be used to represent the flow of passengers. Where appropriate, standards are applied to various future times such as five and ten years ahead.

The term *standard busy rate* (SBR) is used in terminal design, and is the number of passengers predicted in the thirtieth busiest hour of scheduled use. This means that for 29 hours in the year the facilities will not match up to the requirement, but reasonable standards and economy are balanced.

Other factors to be considered are:

- *Aircraft movements*: number of arrivals and departures per hour, aircraft sizes, number of stands for each size or range of sizes, passenger load factors.
- *Baggage quantities*: number of pieces per passenger, by class of travel and traffic type.
- *Visitors*: number of accompanying visitors with departing and arriving passengers by class of traffic type.
- *Employees*: number and proportion for airport, airline, concessionaire, control authorities, etc. and proportion of males and females.
- *Landside transport*: number of passengers, visitors and employees arriving by private vehicles and by public transport (bus, coach, hire car, taxi, train, light rail, etc.).

A very simple rule of thumb for approximating terminal floor area is:

- For every one million passengers per annum (mppa) the terminal expects to process, multiply by this by 10,000 m².

So, a terminal planned to process some 30 mppa will be approximately 300,000 m² total gross floor area.

2.4 Type of traffic

There are three main types of traffic:

- *International*: involves customs and immigration procedures.
- *Domestic*: does not involve customs and immigration procedures so can be simpler buildings.
- *Combined international/domestic.*

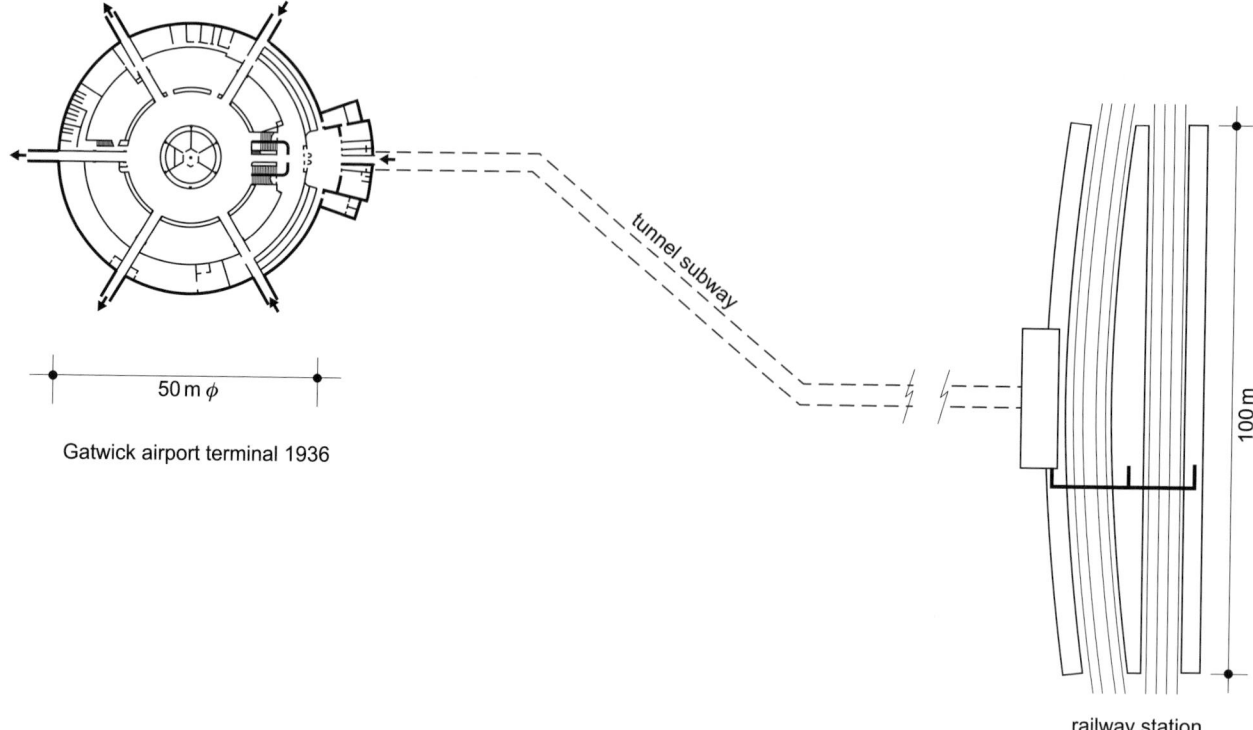

41.1 *Gatwick Airport Terminal, 1936*

2.5 Type of passenger

There are two main types of passenger:

- *Origin and Destination (O&D):* Fly to the terminal, which is the final destination.
- *Transfer:* Fly to the terminal which is not their final destination, connecting with another flight to travel onward to the final destination. This can be either international-to-international connections or domestic-to-international (or vice versa) connections.

2.6 Type of airport

There are two main types of airport:

- *Point to Point:* Airports with no transfer passengers i.e. passengers directly fly to this airport as their final destination.
- *Hub:* Airports with a percentage of passengers transferring to an onward flight to their final destination.

2.7 Passengers versus planes

Major airport terminals require large multi-runway airfields. The challenge for terminal buildings is to exist within these complex environments and remain accessible, functional and amenable for passengers and staff. Whereas an air traffic controller may judge the success of an airport in terms of short taxiing distances and the number of air traffic movements per hour, a passenger would use quite different criteria for measuring success. These are all focused on the terminal building itself such as general comfort, ease of use, legibility of wayfinding, and the range and variety of services offered. As designers we must remember that terminal buildings are designed for passengers first. The plane must not rule. However airfield configuration is a major influence on the positioning, footprint and configuration of the terminal buildings.

2.8 Position of the terminal building

Many if not most airfield configurations are pre-existing or re-configured as a legacy from earlier times. Key fixes for any airfield configuration are the length and alignment of the runway(s). These two factors, along with public vehicular access, will be major drivers in determining where exactly the terminal will or can be positioned within the airfield. Various examples are shown in Figure 41.2.

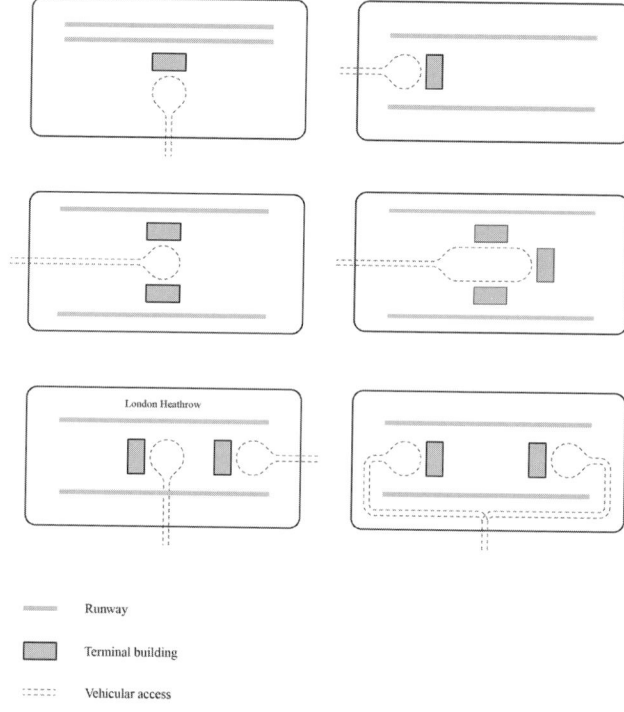

Runway

Terminal building

Vehicular access

41.2 *Examples of terminal building/airfield relationship*

2.9 Footprint of the terminal building

Emblematic shapes, evocative geometries, all seen from the air, do become indelible images representing particular airports. Easily identified, these can in themselves form part of the airport's, and indeed the city's identity. However, these forms are not a result of simple shape-making. Three key drivers forge the terminal building footprint:

- *the available site boundary.* This is the plot which the terminal building can occupy within the airfield without interfering with any aircraft movements on the ground.
- *the number of contact aircraft stands serving the terminal directly (rather than remotely via a coach).* This number of

required aircraft stands is represented in lineal metres and this figure is known as the stand frontage. The total stand frontage is therefore the building perimeter required to be made available for adjacent plane parking.

- *maximum walking distance within the terminal.* Set a reasonable maximum walking distance for passengers (IATA suggests 650 metres from the exit of security).

These three parameters will then inform the shape of the terminal footprint. There is also a fourth parameter – limits set by airfield operating parameters such as the obstacle limitation surface and runway approach slopes. This will not necessarily influence the terminal footprint but will set vertical height limits for the terminal. Figure 41.3 describes this process of 'shaping' the footprint.

2.10 Configuration of the terminal building

There are however several configuration types possible, both centralised or de-centralised, Figure 41.4. A centralised terminal, Figure 41.5, is where all the main processing functions are located in one zone. In a de-centralised terminal, these functions are distributed along the terminal building or even in separate buildings.

Key factors influencing configuration type may be:

- *Physical space*: space may not be available.
- *Airfield needs*: separating piers from processor may optimise air traffic movements, reducing taxiing distance.
- *Economic*: a large single terminal may be expensive to build but a network of smaller terminals may be more expensive to operate.
- *Flexibility*: the need for phasing and future expansion dependent on passenger forecasts.

Another factor to consider is size. A single terminal building processing in excess of 60mppa will need to be so large that it will be

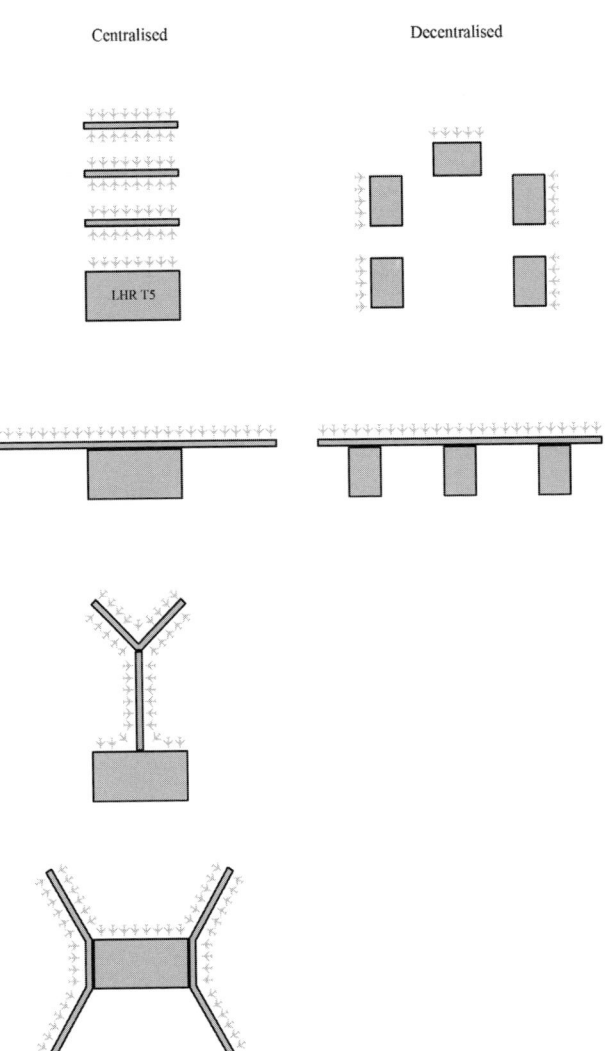

41.4 *Typical terminal building configuration*

at the limits of operating as a single terminal. The sheer scale of such a building will require passengers to walk very long distances. While this can be mitigated by the use of automated people movers (APM), this can add complexity to the passenger journey. Also, as airports find the need to expand in response to increased traffic numbers, it may be easier in terms of maintaining an uninterrupted operation to build smaller but more terminals.

This approach has the benefit, particularly for hub airports, of conveniently accommodating airlines and/or airline alliances in dedicated terminal buildings. This co-location of airlines of the same alliance simplifies passenger wayfinding and greatly assists with reducing transfer times, as most transfers tend to occur within alliances. However, multi-terminal hub airports like Heathrow face the challenge of moving transfer passengers from terminal to terminal, easily and quickly.

Efficient and speedy connection between terminals and the piers served by them is the key to the success of a hub airport, enabling transferring passengers to safely make their onward connecting flight, ideally in as short a time as possible. This Minimum Connect Time (MCT) is key. The shorter the guaranteed MCT, the greater the number and variety of connections with other flights that the passengers will be able to connect to, offering more choice to more destinations.

Finally, it is worth noting that there are three key stakeholders in the running of any airport:

- owner/operator
- airline(s)
- regulator.

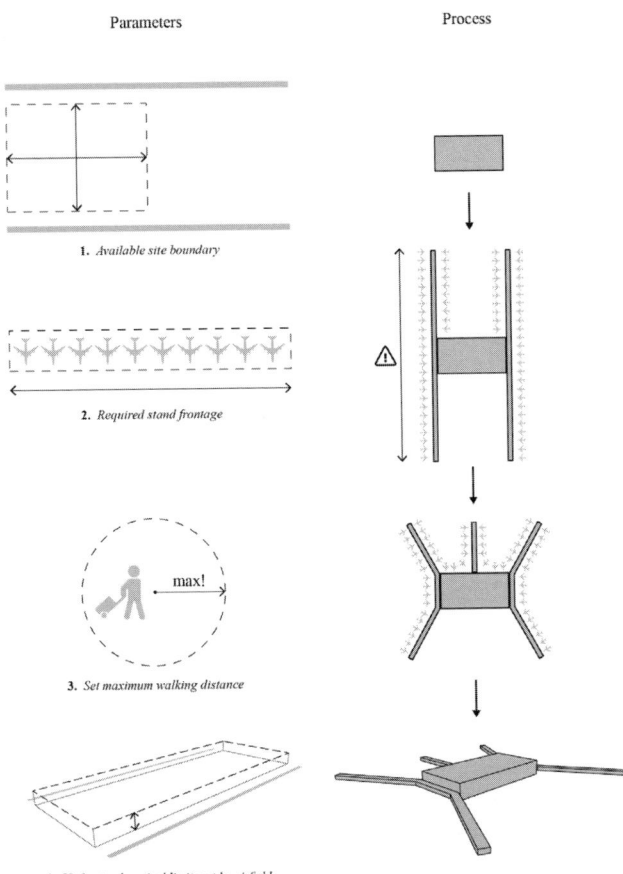

41.3 *Factors influencing the terminal building footprint*

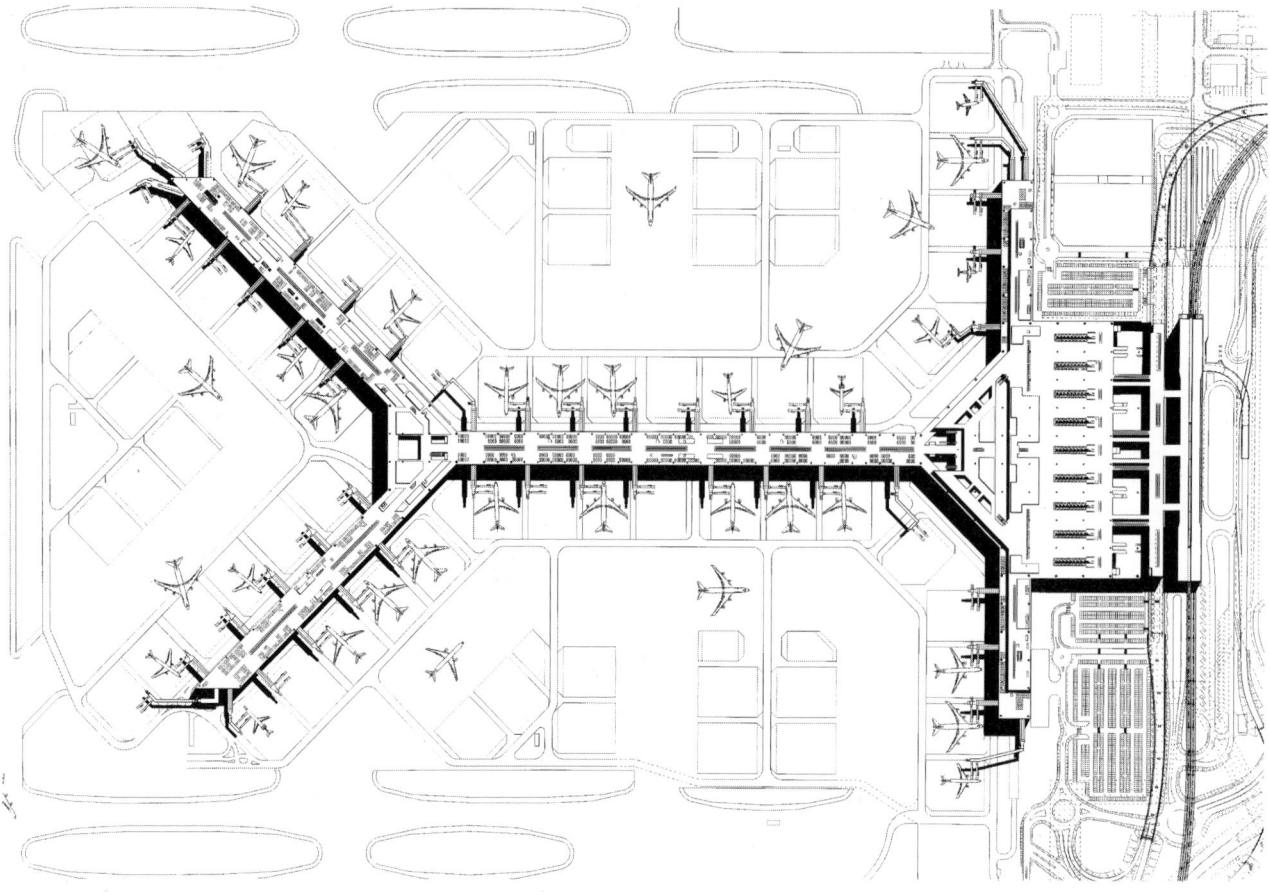

41.5 *Chek Lap Kok airport, Hong Kong (Foster + Partners)*

The relationship between these three may vary from country to country, and its nature and dynamic may also influence the optimum configuration of the terminal building(s).

3 TERMINALS

3.1 A processing machine
Terminal buildings are effectively machines processing two main movement flows; one for passengers, and one for their baggage. Both of these flows move in two opposing directions with departing and arriving (passengers) and outbound and inbound (baggage). In hub airports there is an additional 'cross' flow or re-directed flow, that being for transferring passengers and their baggage.

3.2 Passenger flows
Passenger flows are governed by a series of processes that are required for security and border control, Figures 41.6 and 41.7.

The processes dictate the sequence, direction and order of the flows, but each process also represents a space in which it takes place, and it is the series of these spaces that comprises the complete passenger journey through the terminal building, Figure 41.8.

The adequate sizing of these spaces is critical to accommodate the volume of the passenger numbers so that the flows keep moving and bottlenecks are avoided, and also to provide a degree of passenger experience and comfort.

The exact degree of passenger experience and comfort can vary dependent on the Level of Service (LoS) that is to be provided by a particular terminal.

IATA Airport Development Reference Manual identifies the following Levels of Service:

A Excellent level of service; condition of free flow; excellent level of comfort.
B High level of service; condition of stable flow; very few delays; high level of comfort.

C Good level of service; condition of stable flow; acceptable delays; good level of comfort.
D Adequate level of service; condition of unstable flow; acceptable delays for short periods of time; adequate level of comfort.
E Inadequate level of service; condition of unstable flow; unacceptable delays; inadequate level of comfort.
F Unacceptable level of service; condition of cross flows; system breakdown and unacceptable delays; unacceptable level of comfort.

These Levels of Service translate into space standards and are represented in the form of an area (m²) provided per person for the major terminal zones, such as check in, security, baggage reclaim, etc. The higher the LoS, the more space provided per passenger.

4 DEPARTURES – LANDSIDE

4.1 Departures vehicle drop-off forecourt (also known as kerbside)
Factors to consider:

• *Security*: consider a suitable vehicular bomb-blast stand-off distance for uncontrolled private vehicle traffic. Typically this is 30 m from the terminal façade to the first lane of traffic.
• *Commercial*: the whole forecourt or at least the private car section may be incorporated into the short-term or nearest car park. This will require motorists to pay for the privilege of parking close to the check-in area.
• *Baggage*: baggage trolleys should be available for passenger use. For heavy package tours traffic, with coaches setting down large pre-sorted amounts of baggage, a dedicated area and route to the baggage areas may be desirable.
• *Airline needs*: in large terminals shared by many airlines, signed sections of forecourt may be appropriate.

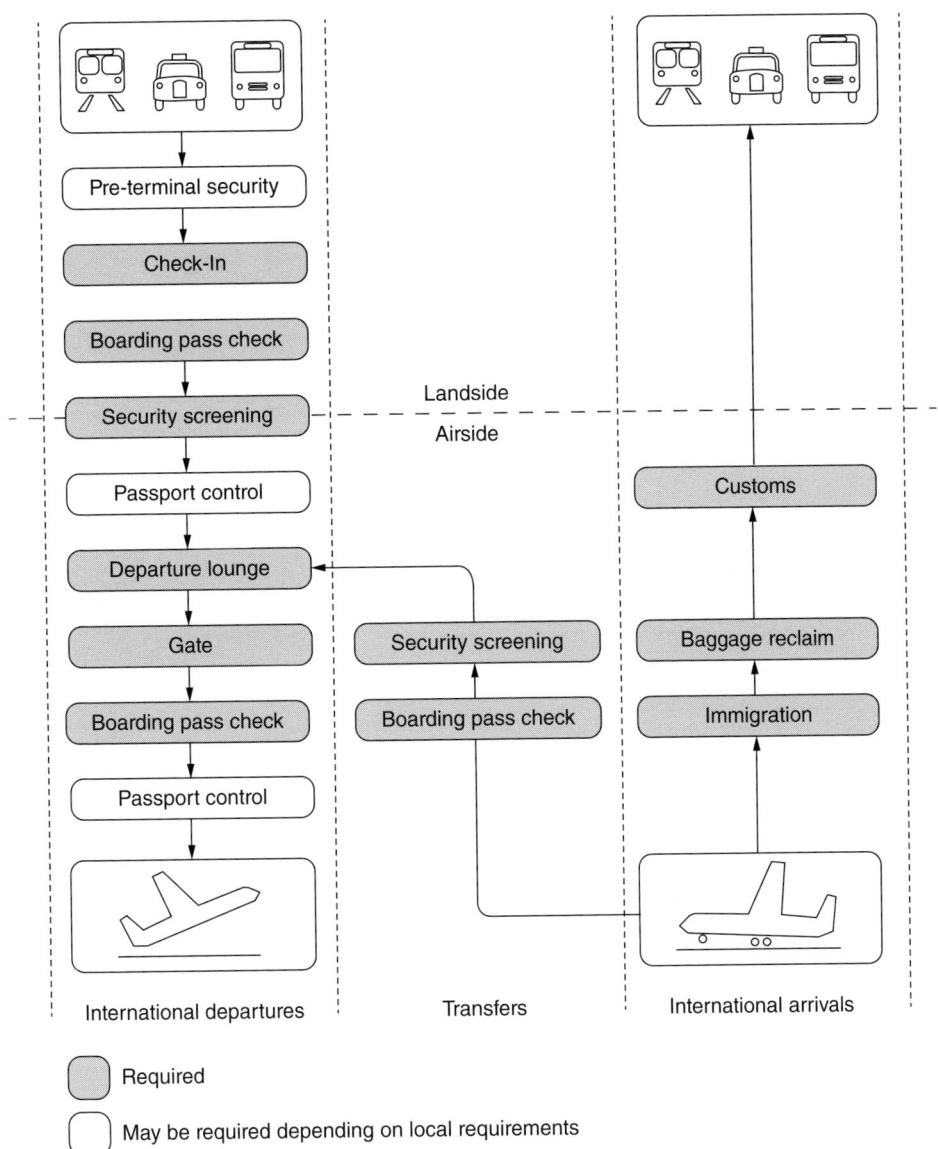

41.6 *International passenger process flow*

- *Predicted changes*: allow for predictable changes in traffic mix which may affect the modal split (the percentages of passengers arriving by car, bus, train).

Quantities to be assessed:

- *Hourly passenger flows*: in the case of a combined departures and arrivals forecourt a planned two-way rate will be relevant.
- *Estimated dwell time*: an average of 1.5 minutes may be allowed for cars and taxis.
- *Modal split*: Often influenced by local custom/preference.

Typical space calculation based on 2000 originating passengers/hour:

- Number of passengers/hour at kerbside for cars + taxis: 1000.
- Number of passengers per car or taxi: 1.7.
- Number of cars and taxis: 1000/1.7 = 588 per hour.
- Time spent at kerb by each vehicle: 1½ minutes.
- Number of cars and taxis at one time: 588/40 =16.
- Length of kerb per vehicle: 7 m + 10 per cent.
- Length of kerbside for cars and taxis: 105.6 m.
- Overall rule of thumb: 1.2 m of total kerbside (including public transport) per 10 passengers/hour.

Figure 41.9 describes a typical landside forecourt arrangement.

4.2 Departures concourse
Key factors to consider:

- *Security*: entry to the concourse is generally not controlled but can be via a pre-security check that requires all persons entering the terminal to be searched, both passengers and visitors alike. This is required in some countries, for example Russia, India and Turkey.
- *Commercial*: shopping and catering facilities will be appropriate here, together with bureau de change (international terminal only) and including food and beverage provision for persons not travelling but seeing passengers off.
- *Baggage*: all circulation areas should make allowance for baggage trolleys.
- *Government controls*: access to airside for staff.
- *Airline needs*: airlines require ticket sales desks and offices.
- *Information systems*: public display of information on flights and information desk. There may be an opportunity to provide flight information in the forecourt (if covered) which allows passengers to orientate themselves prior to entering the terminal.
- *Predictable situations*: provision may be needed for exceptional conditions occasioned by delayed flights, with additional seating and extra catering space. This is usually a large food and beverage outlet that is designated for this purpose should delays occur.

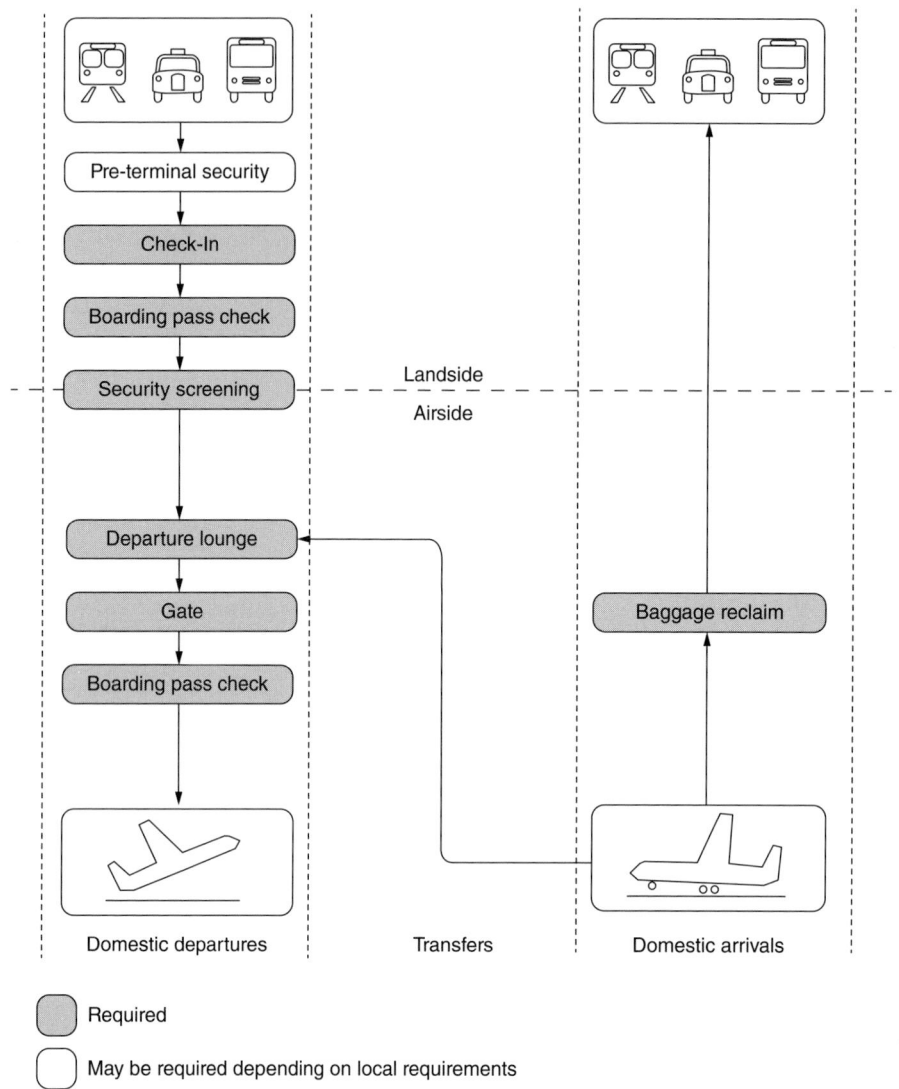

41.7 *Domestic passenger process flow*

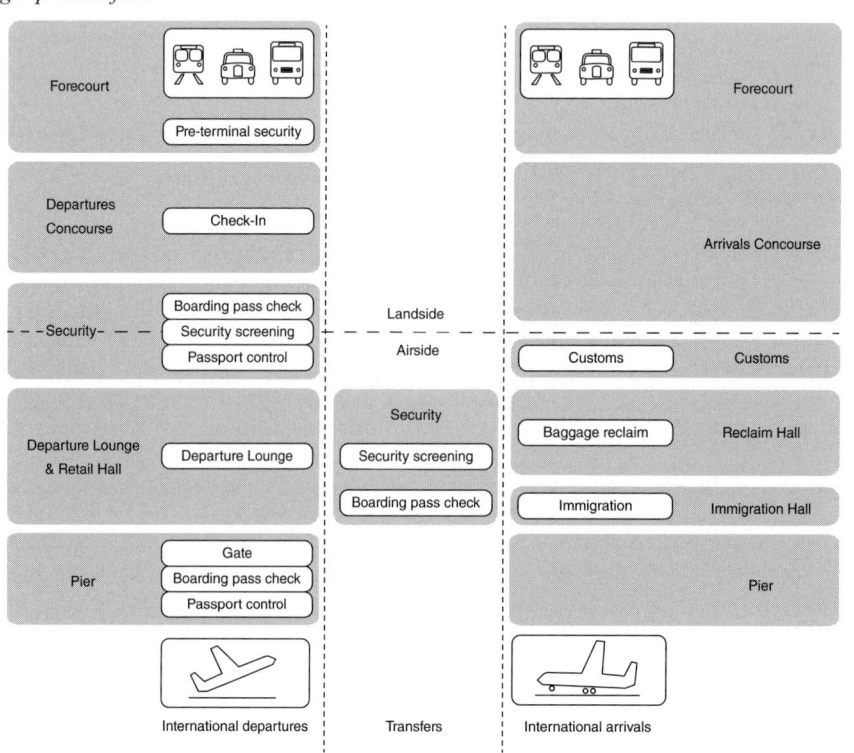

41.8 *Passenger process flow and associated spaces*

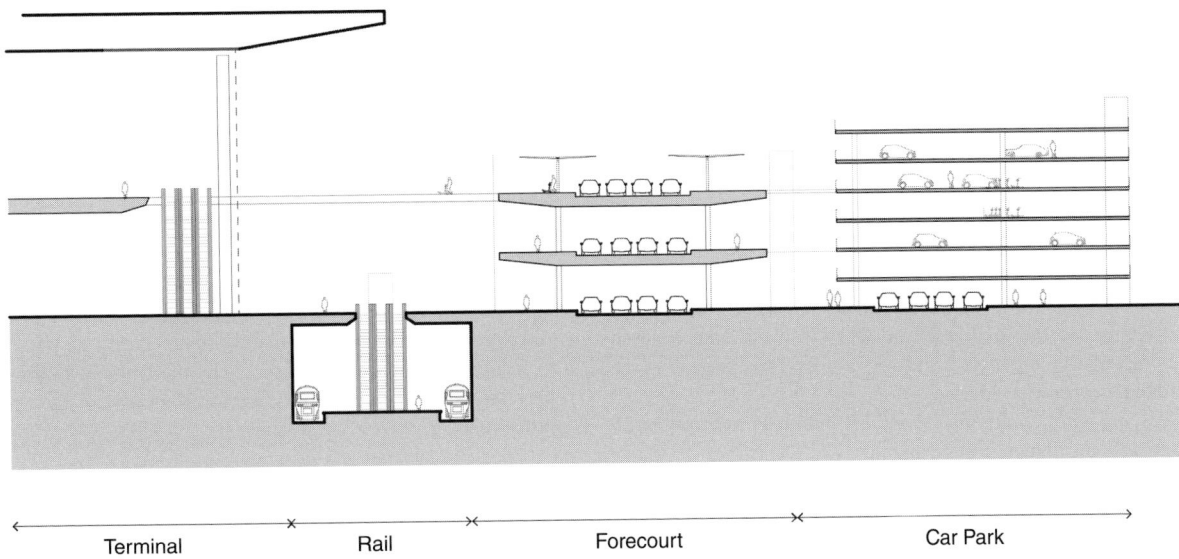

| Terminal | Rail | Forecourt | Car Park |

41.9 *Typical landside forecourt arrangement*

There are several quantity factors to be assessed:

- Hourly passenger flows: two-way flow will be relevant where there is to be a combined departures and arrivals area.
- Visitor ratio: a common ratio in the West would be 0.5 to 0.2 visitors per passenger (with even lower ratios for certain domestic traffic) but 2.5 to 6 or even higher in the East or Africa.
- Estimated dwell time: a common time would be 20 minutes.

Typical space calculations based on 2000 originating passengers/ hour are as follows:

- Number of people per hour: 3000 (0.5 visitors/passenger).
- Number at one time (peaking factor, say 50 per cent in 20 minutes): 1500.
- Space per person: 2.7 m^2 (LoS 'A'); 2.3 m^2 (IATA LoS 'B')
- Area required: 3450 m^2. Some area may be in shops and catering spaces.

4.3 Check-in

Traditionally, at check-in passengers showed their tickets, had seats allocated and if necessary had large items of baggage weighed (and possibly security screened) for registration and loading into the aircraft hold. However, in recent times the check-in process has undergone great change, with most passengers now checking in online from home. This means that many passengers arrive at the terminal having already checked-in and printed a boarding pass with a seat allocated.

Whereas previously passengers used a check-in counter or desk to do all of the above, the check-in concourse is now generally comprised of a three-part check-in desk option:

- self-service check-in kiosk
- self-bag drop
- traditional (full service) check-in desk.

See Figure 41.10 for the range of check-in options and typical check-in desk types.

Factors to consider:

- *Security:* if pre-security terminal checks are not required (see Section 4.2) then designers must be aware that the materials selected for use in check-in concourse may be subject to bomb-blast criteria.
- *Baggage:* one or more delivery points may be required for out-of-gauge (oversized) baggage.

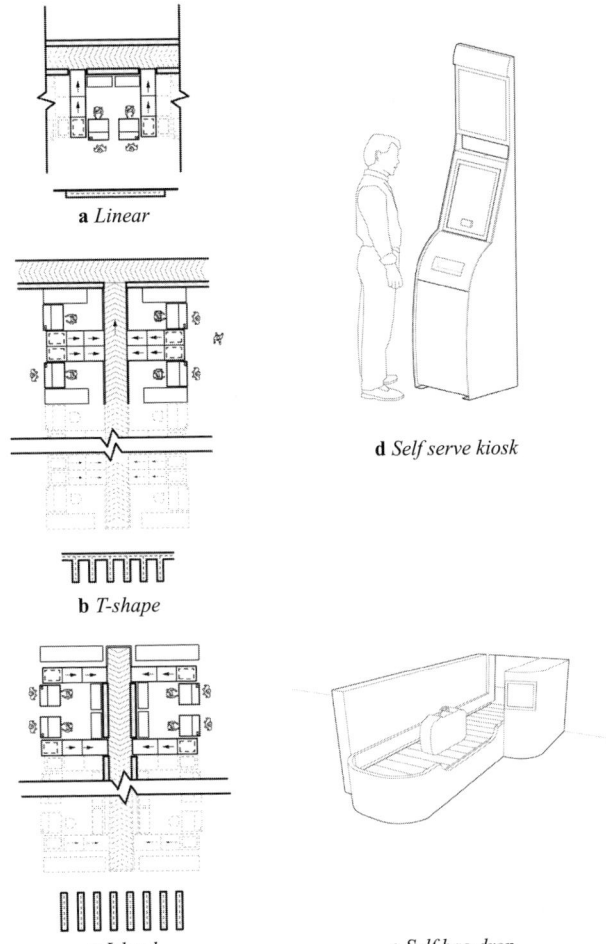

a *Linear*

b *T-shape*

c *Island*

d *Self serve kiosk*

e *Self bag drop*

41.10 *Check-in desk options*

- *Government controls*: a customs check facility immediately after bags are checked-in (prior to the bags entering the baggage system) may be required in some countries (e.g. South Korea). This check may require accommodation for customs officials to remove and inspect bags and interview passengers.
- *Airline needs*: offices for airlines and handling agents will be needed with close relationship with the check-in desks.
- *Information systems*: CUTE (common user terminal equipment) will make it possible to allocate desks to any airline at any time,

thereby reducing the number of desks needed. Otherwise the number of desks required is the sum total of those required by each handling agent.

- *Predicted changes*: following automated ticketing and issuing of boarding passes, self-bag-tagging is likely to be the next advance with systems currently in operation in Australia and Ireland, and being trialed in the UK.

There are several quantities to be assessed:

- *Hourly passenger flows*: if CUTE (common user terminal equipment) is in use the total hourly flow to all desks can be used to compute the number. Landside transfer passengers to be included.
- *Processing rate*: commonly about 1.5 minutes/passenger, with faster rates for domestic passengers.
- *Estimated dwell time*: this is dependent upon the number of staffed check-in desks for each flight, but all check-in layouts have to make provision for queuing. Assume a wait of 20 minutes is acceptable to passengers.

A typical space calculation based on 2000 originating passengers/hour with a central check-in is:

- *Number of passengers per hour*: 2000 excluding transfers and including gate check-in numbers.
- *Equivalent number/hour* (peak factor, say 50 per cent in 20 minutes): 3000.
- *Number of desks*: 3000/40 = 76.
- *Queue depth might* be 20 passengers at 0.8 m per person with check-in desks at approximately 2.0m centres.
- *Space per person* (with a high % of trolley use): 2.3m^2 (LoS 'A'); 1.9m^2 (LoS 'B'); 1.7m^2 (LoS 'C').
- *Space per person* (with few trolleys/average 2 bags): 1.8m^2 (LoS 'A'); 1.5m^2 (LoS 'B'); 1.3m^2 (LoS 'C').
- *Total queuing area*: 76 × 2.0 × 16 = 2432 m^2.

4.4 Security control
Factors to be considered:

- *Baggage*: hand baggage only at this point. Allow for sufficient space prior to the security comb for passengers to prepare for the liquid, pastes and gels 100mL compliance. In this area allow provision of plastic bags and counters for re-packing.
- *Government controls*: security control will be the responsibility either of the government or of the airport authority.
- *Airline needs*: some airlines conduct their own additional security checks; often this will be at the gate (e.g. American Airlines for flights to the USA).
- *Predictable changes*: ever-changing regulations in response to the terrorism threat levels make this process susceptible to frequent change. Automation is another area of change. An auto-gate boarding-pass check (similar to a metro turnstile that scans passenger boarding pass and permits entry into the security comb) is being trialed in various airports currently (e.g. Heathrow T5).

Full body scanning is also being introduced. This non-invasive scan occurs immediately upon passing through the metal-detector arch.
   Figure 41.11 shows a typical security lane layout.
   Quantities to be assessed

- *Hourly passenger flows*: for central security allow for transfer passengers.
- *Processing rate*: X-ray units handle 360 items per hour, with two X-ray units per metal detector archway.
- *Estimated dwell time*: this is not calculable, since a problem item or passenger can rapidly cause a queue to build up. The security

check should not unduly interrupt the flow of passengers. In reality staffing levels cannot totally eliminate queuing, and space for a long queue must be provided to avoid obstructing other functions.

Typical space calculation:

- Assume one item of baggage or hand baggage per passenger. One set of equipment consisting of a personnel metal detector and two X-ray units can handle 360 passengers per hour.
- 2000 passengers per hour, excluding transfers, require 6 sets.
- Allow sufficient space immediately after security for passengers to gather their bag, replace shoes, belts and items of clothing that may have been required to be removed as part of the security process.

5 DEPARTURES – AIRSIDE
5.1 Departures lounge
Here passengers wait, shop, eat, drink before moving sooner or later to their flight departure gate. This may mean walking to the gate, or to the people-mover leading to a satellite or the coach station serving remote stands. It may be possible to have an Integrated Departures Lounge (aka IDL) accommodating both international and domestic passengers. If local regulations do not permit this integration, then separate lounges must be provided for international and domestic passengers.
   Factors to be considered:

- *Security*: no further security checks will be needed where there is comprehensive centralised security at entry to the airside. Otherwise checks may be made at each gate or entry to a lounge.
- *Commercial*: there will be shopping and catering facilities here, particularly duty-free.
- *Airline needs*: airlines will have specific requirements at the gates. They often have CIP (commercially important passengers) lounges for first-class and business-class passengers.
- *Information systems*: full information on flight numbers, departure times, delays and gate numbers must be provided throughout, but especially at the entries. Take care with the positioning of these to avoid the creation of congestion spots, as passengers will congregate at these screens.

Quantities to be assessed:

- *Hourly passenger flows*: include landside and airside transfers.
- *Estimated dwell time*: commonly about 30 minutes.

Typical space calculation based on 2000 originating passengers/hour:

- *Passengers per hour*: 2000 excluding transfers.
- *Passengers at one time*: 1000.
- *Space per person*: 2.7m^2 (IATA LoS 'A'); 1.9m^2 (IATA LoS 'B'); 2.3m^2 (IATA LoS 'C').
- *Area required*: 2300 m^2. Some may be in shops and catering spaces.

A very simple rule of thumb for approximating retail floor area is:

- For every one million passenger per annum (mppa) the terminal expects to process, multiply by this by a range of 300 to 1,000 m^2.

So, a terminal planned to process some 30 mppa will should have approximately between 9,000 to 30,00 m^2 of retail space.

5.2 Gate holding areas
These should be able to hold 80 per cent of the number of passengers boarding the largest aircraft which can dock here:

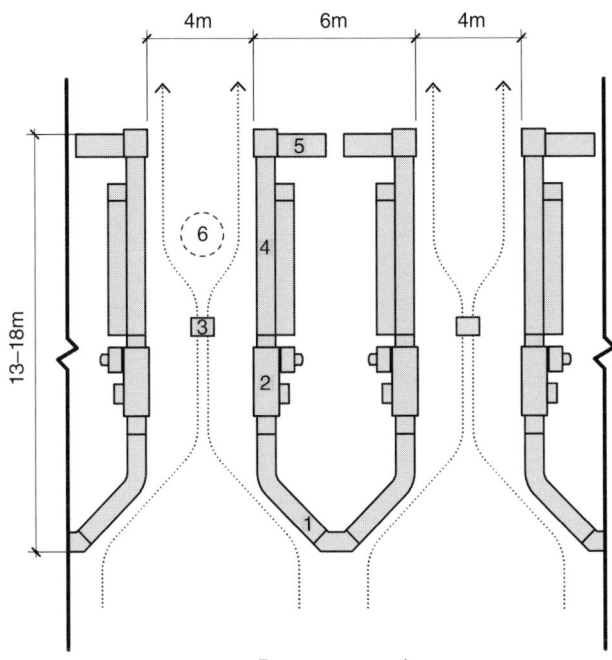

Passenger queuing

41.11 *Security lane Key: 1 Empty tray collection, 2 X-ray machine, 3 Metal detector, 4 Bag retrieval, 5 Bag Search, 6 Option for full body scan machine*

- *Space per person* (level of service A): 1.4 m^2.
- *Area for 400-seater aircraft*: 320 × 1.4 = 448 m^2.

6 ARRIVALS – AIRSIDE

6.1 Immigration check

Factors to be considered:

- *Security*: none.
- *Government controls*: national policy determines the allocation of separate channels for different passport holders. There may also be checks here for which offices (with viewing platforms), interview and detention rooms will be required.
- *Predictable changes*: changes to border controls within the European Union are an example of the effect of international policy making. The introduction of biometric 'chip' passports has enabled an automated immigration clearance system, not dissimilar to a turnstile system in some airports.
- *Other*: in certain countries (e.g. Gulf States), allow for provision of a visa counter prior to the immigration queue. This permits passengers to purchase their visa on landing.

Layout for a typical immigration desk is shown in Figure 41.12.
  Quantities to be assessed:

- *Hourly passenger flows*: include landside transfers.
- *Processing rate*: commonly 0.5min/passenger for departing, 1–1.5min for arriving.

Typical space calculation based on 2000 originating passengers/hour:

- Number of passengers per hour: 2000 excluding transfers.
- Number of desks required: 17 (departing); 50 (arriving).
- Area required: 2.4 m^2 including gangway per desk.

6.2 Baggage reclaim

Here passengers await and reclaim their luggage which has been unloaded from the aircraft while they have been through the terminal and passing through the immigration control.
  Factors to consider:

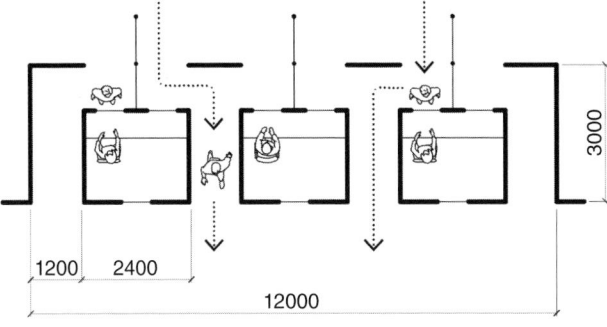

a *Frontal presentation*

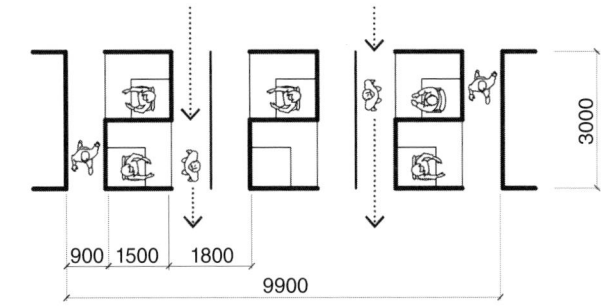

b *Side presentation*

41.12 *Typical immigration desk layouts showing a Frontal presentation b Side presentation*

- *Baggage*: some means of delivering outsized luggage to the passengers is required.
- *Information systems*: display the numbers of reclaim units against the arriving flight numbers, particularly where passengers enter the reclaim area.
- *Trolleys*: considerable space will be required for trolley magazines, ensuring all passengers have access to a trolley. Trolley re-circulation should also be considered.

Quantities to be assessed:

- *Hourly passenger flows*: passengers transferring on the landside need to reclaim their baggage.
- *Processing rate*: there are several ways of calculating throughput in baggage reclaim, but the one used here is from the *IATA Airport Terminals Reference Manual*. Reclaim devices should have a length of 30–40 m for narrow-bodied aircraft, 50–100 m for wide-bodied. Average occupancy times are 20 and 45 minutes respectively.
- *Estimated dwell time*: Commonly about 30 minutes.
- *Number of checked-in bags per passenger*: average 1.0, depending on whether the flight is long haul or short haul, although the flow calculation method used does not depend upon this factor.

Typical space calculation based on 2000 terminating passengers/hour.
  The important calculation is for the required number of reclaim units and the space round each for a flight load of passengers waiting:

- *Number of passengers per hour*: 2000 excluding transfers.
- *Number of passengers* per narrow-bodied aircraft at 80 per cent load factor: 120.
- *Number of passengers* per wide-bodied aircraft at 80 per cent load factor: 280.
- *Number of narrow-bodied devices*: 1000 ÷ (3 × 120) = 2.7, say 3.
- *Number of wide-bodied devices*: 1000 ÷ (1.33 × 280) = 2.7, say 3.
- *Space per person*: 2.0m^2 (IATA LoS 'B'); 1.7m^2 (IATA LoS 'C').
- *Waiting area for narrow-bodied device*: 240m^2 (IATA LoS 'B'); 204m^2 (IATA LoS 'C').

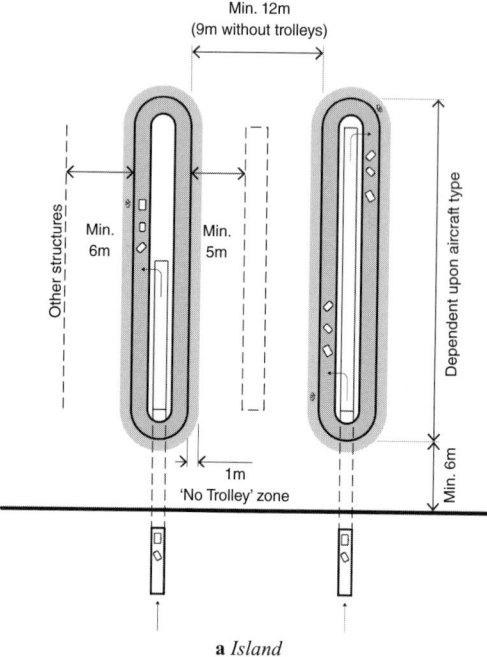

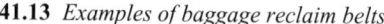

a *Island*

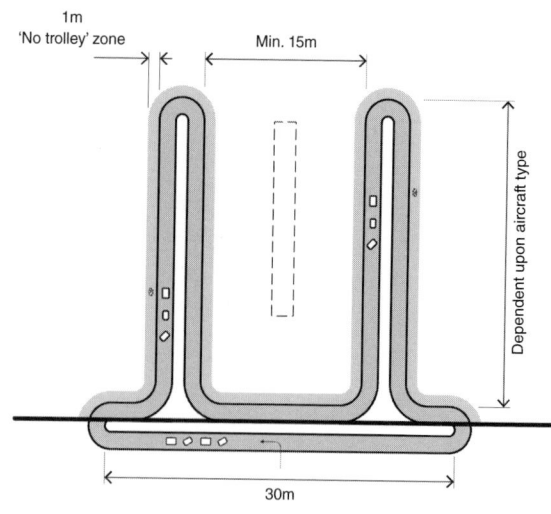

b *Through-the-wall*

41.13 *Examples of baggage reclaim belts*

- *Waiting area for wide-bodied device*: 560m² (IATA LoS 'B'); 476m² (IATA LoS 'C').
- *Total waiting area*: 2040–2400m² (excluding central waiting space at entry to baggage reclaim area).

The two main types of reclaim installations are the oval and racetrack, Figure 41.13.

6.3 Customs

Factors for consideration:

- *Security*: none specifically. Self-sorting of passengers is now the norm in the EU with passengers selecting one of 3 channels (red, green and blue – red for passengers with something to declare, green and blue being for passengers with nothing to declare, and depends on their originating flight – blue is from the EU, green is from destinations other than EU).
- *Government controls*: offices with viewing windows (one-way), interview and search rooms will be required.
- *Predictable changes*: non-intrusive scanning equipment (e.g. for explosives and/or drug detection) is being introduced in some parts of the world.

Quantities to be assessed:

- *Hourly passenger flows*: include landside transfers.
- *Processing rate*: allow 2 minutes per passenger searched.

Space calculation based on 2000 terminating passengers/hour:

- *Area required* if rule of thumb is 0.5 m² per passenger per hour: 1000 m².

7 ARRIVALS – LANDSIDE

7.1 Arrivals concourse

These are the factors to consider:

- *Security:* none.
- *Commercial*: shopping and catering facilities will be appropriate here, together with onward travel services such as hotel bookings, train tickets, rental car desks etc. Includes food and beverage provision for persons not travelling but meeting passengers and for taxi/private car drivers.
- *Baggage*: allow for trolley drop-off and sufficient circulation for trolley recirculation routes.

- *Government controls*: none
- *Airline needs*: provision of a landside CIP arrivals lounge.
- *Information systems*: public display of information on flights and information desk for meeters and greeters.
- *Predictable situations*: provision may be needed for exceptional conditions occasioned by delayed flights, with additional seating and extra catering space.

Quantity factors to be assessed:

- Hourly passenger flows: two-way flow will be relevant where there is to be a combined departures and arrivals area (e.g. Stansted Airport).
- Visitor ratio: a common ratio in the West would be 0.5 to 0.2 visitors per passenger (with even lower ratios for certain domestic traffic) and in the East or Africa 2.5 to 6 or even higher.
- Estimated dwell time: around 10 minutes for passengers and 30 minutes for meeters and greeters.

Typical space calculation based on 2000 terminating passengers/hour:

- Number of people per hour: 2500 (0.25 visitors/passenger).
- Number at one time (2000/6 + 3000/2): 583.
- Space per person: 2.7m² (IATA LoS 'A'); 2.3m² (IATA LoS 'B').
- Area required: 1340m² excluding retail and food and beverage spaces. These add 20 per cent to the concourse area, making a total of 1608m².

7.2 Arrivals vehicle pick-up forecourt (also known as kerbside)

These are the factors to consider:

- *Security*: consider a suitable vehicular bomb-blast stand-off distance for uncontrolled private vehicle traffic. Typically this is 30m from the terminal façade to the first lane of traffic.
- *Commercial*: the whole forecourt or at least the private car section may be incorporated into the short-term or nearest car park. This will require motorists to pay for the privilege of parking close to the check-in area.
- *Baggage*: drop-off areas for baggage trolleys should be available for passengers.
- *Airline needs*: often a dedicated pick-up area for CIP passengers is required.
- *Predicted changes*: increased premium services such as limousine pick-up and associated waiting lounges are a growing trend.

Quantities to be assessed:

- *Hourly passenger flows*: in the case of a combined departures and arrivals forecourt a planned two-way rate will be relevant.
- *Estimated dwell time*: an average of 1.5 minutes may be allowed for cars and taxis.

8 LEVELS AND VOLUMES
Smaller terminals may be able to accommodate these processes on one level, with departures and arrivals journeys segregated horizontally. However, depending on the number of mppa the terminal building is processing, the processes described in the previous sections may be split horizontally over various levels.

Care must be taken as level changes, whilst improving large volume passenger flows and better accommodating the mix of transfer and destination passengers, do introduce complexity for passenger wayfinding.

Multi-level terminals do reduce the distance that passengers need to travel and allow for better and more direct access to the aircraft door (typically 4m or more above ground level).

Another key consideration is how to 'stack' the different net passenger journeys; departures above arrivals or vice versa, Figure 41.14. Again, relationship to the aircraft door can be a key consideration.

Multi-level terminals also provide the opportunity to exploit the volume afforded by these tall, soaring spaces. Large double-height spaces within the terminal building provide drama, introduce light deep into the lower levels of the building and provide opportunities for a collective enjoyment of these cathedral-like spaces.

Care however should be taken to differentiate the volumetric quality of these spaces based on the process they accommodate, Figure 41.15. Large, soaring halls welcoming passengers at check-in provide real delight and the ideal fond farewell. Again, these large volumes airside, in the retail halls of the departures lounge, afford a generous environment.

However evidence suggests that in areas where security processes are involved, such as immigration, security control and customs, passengers respond better to a more controlled volume, enhancing the feeling that the process is controlled, robust and serious.

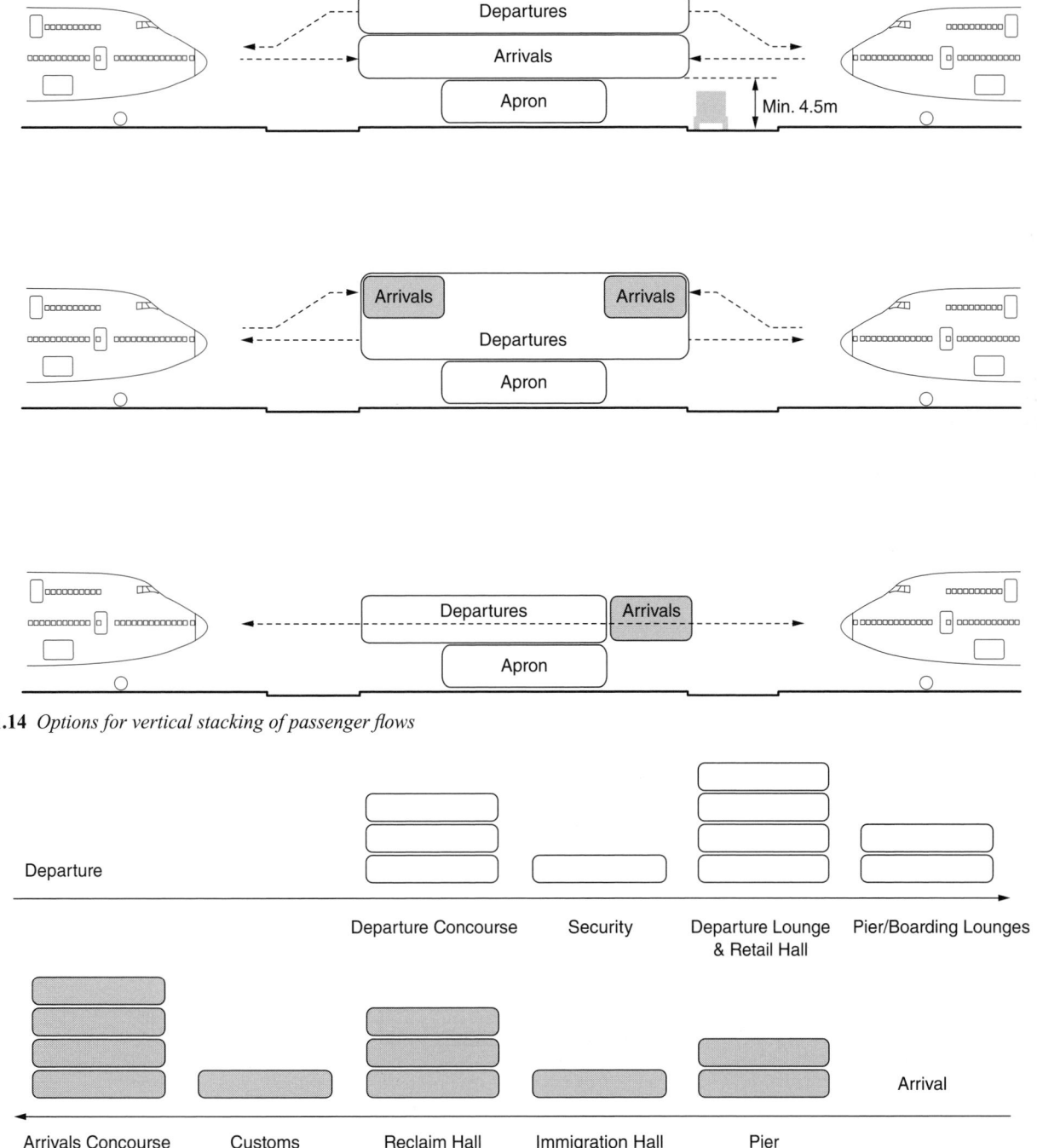

41.14 *Options for vertical stacking of passenger flows*

41.15 *Sectional arrangement of volumetric response to the passenger process*

9 AIRCRAFT AND APRON REQUIREMENTS

9.1 Baggage handling
Figure 41.16 shows a container (aka ULD or Unit Load Device) and trailer used to assemble baggage. These trailers are transported hitched to a tug (electric or diesel) and are combined as a 'tug & dolly' combination of one tug and one, two, three or four trailers (i.e. tug plus one, two, three or four). The manoeuvering of trains of these trailers determines the layout of baggage loading and unloading areas.

9.2 Loading bridges
Figure 41.17 shows three types of loading bridges, otherwise known as air bridges, air-jetties or jetways, which connect terminal to aircraft.

9.3 Apron servicing
Figure 41.18 shows apron servicing arrangements with all necessary vehicles clustered around a parked aircraft. They determine the space requirement. Alternatively, sub-apron hydrants and power can supply fuel by connection through the loading bridge.

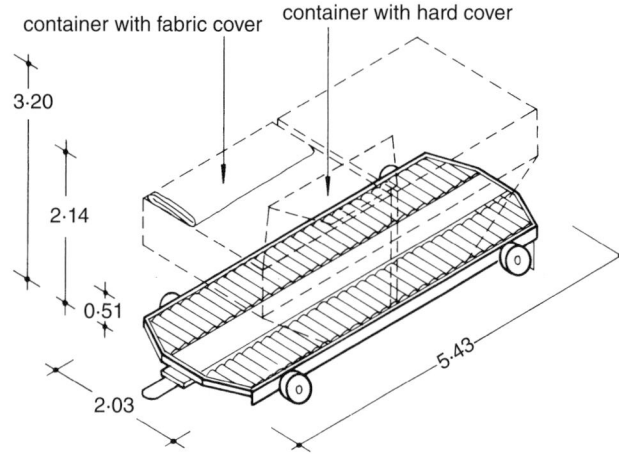

41.16 *Baggage handling transport: double container dolly*

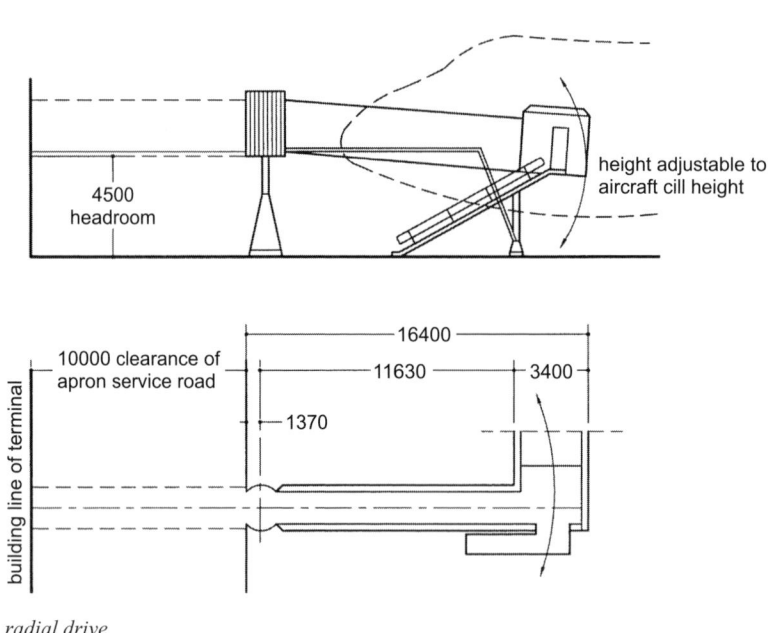

radial drive

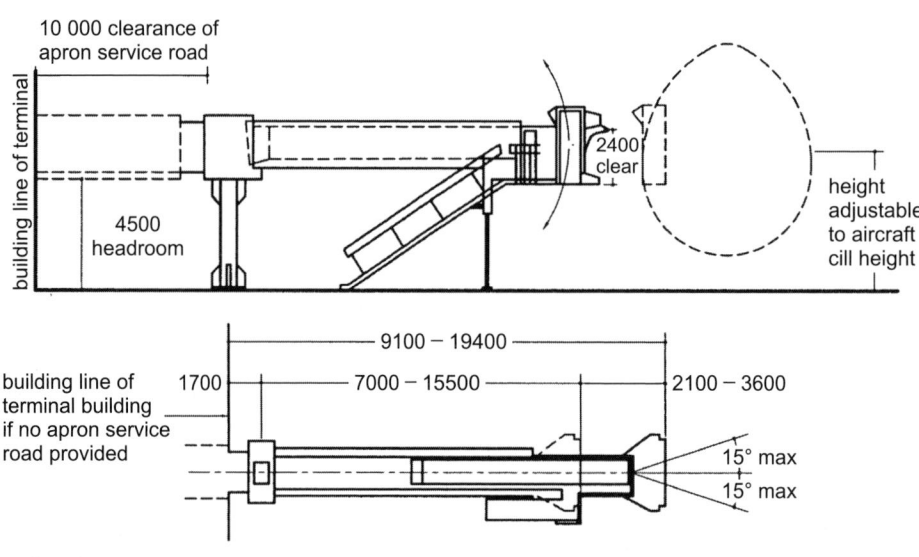

pedestal

41.17 *Loading bridge types: plans and elevations*

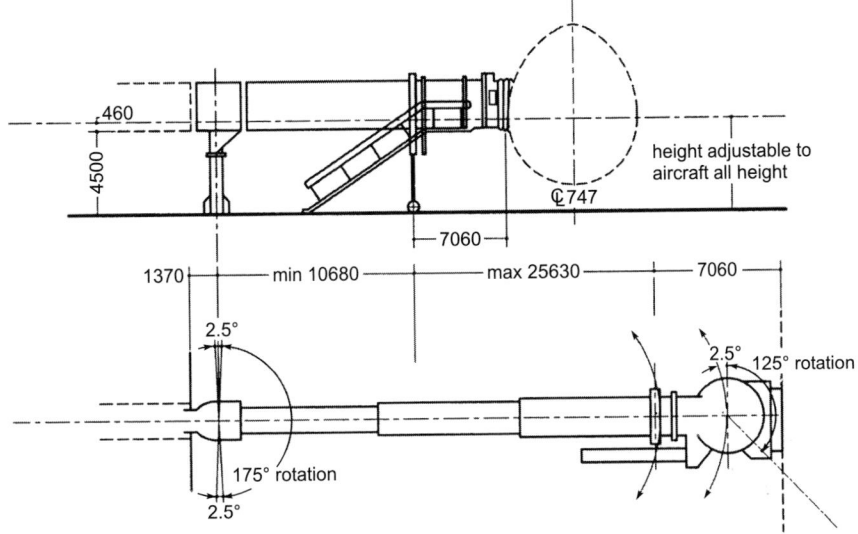

apron drive

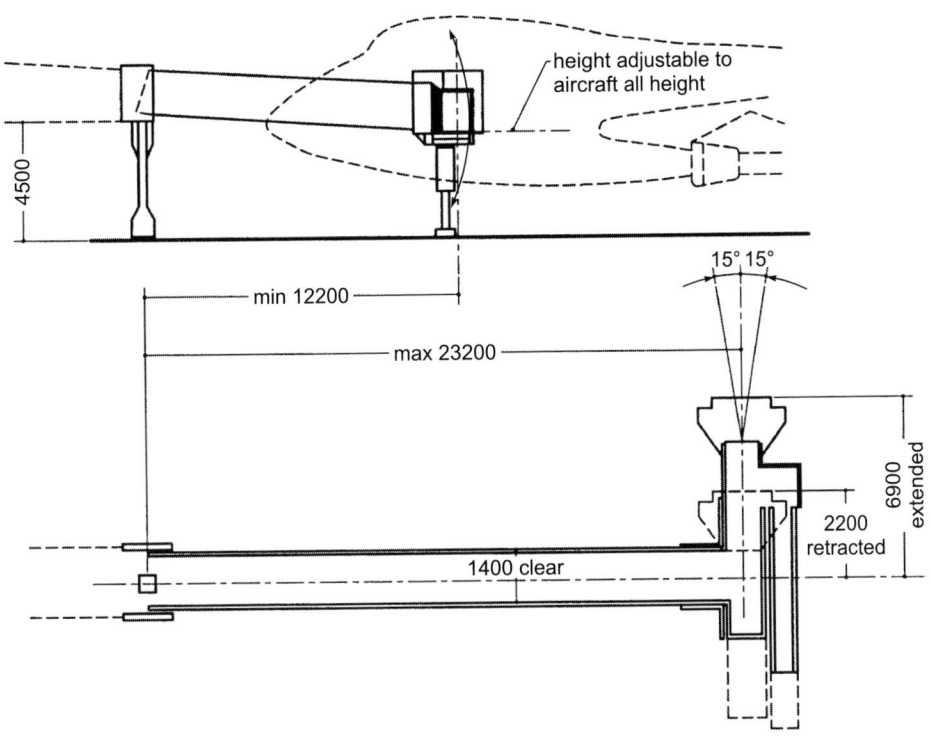

elevating

41.17a *Loading bridge types: plans and elevations (contd.)*

9.4 Apron accommodation

Office, workshop, store and staff facilities will be required adjacent to the apron. This accommodation is generally located at apron level as this level is usually not allocated to passenger processes, particularly in stacked terminals (see Figure 41.14).

10 THE CHANGING AIRPORT

10.1 Low cost terminals

Traditional multi-terminal airports are now planning low-cost terminals within their terminal mix, seeking to provide a complete range of passenger options from the one airport.

10.2 Airport as a total integrated transport hub

Airports are becoming a centre of gravity, attracting greater numbers of passengers from further afield, and in turn collecting and distributing these passengers both by air, rail, coach and car, internationally, nationally, regionally and locally. Airports are ideally placed to serve as major transport interchanges, serving heavy rail, metro, high speed rail and coach services, acting as an interconnected multi-modal transport hub.

10.3 Airport city

Airports have long been likened to small cities. Heathrow employs some 80,000 people on airport, and it is estimated some 250,000 others in related industries in close proximity to the airport. The very presence of the airport as an attractor makes land adjacent to it valuable. This has led to the advent of the 'airport city' with landside commercial and cultural developments supporting hotels, conference centres, and offices, all benefiting from their proximity to a busy hub airport. This proximity is convenient for business passengers who do not wish to have to travel into city centres for meetings, for passengers on longer transits and also for staff.

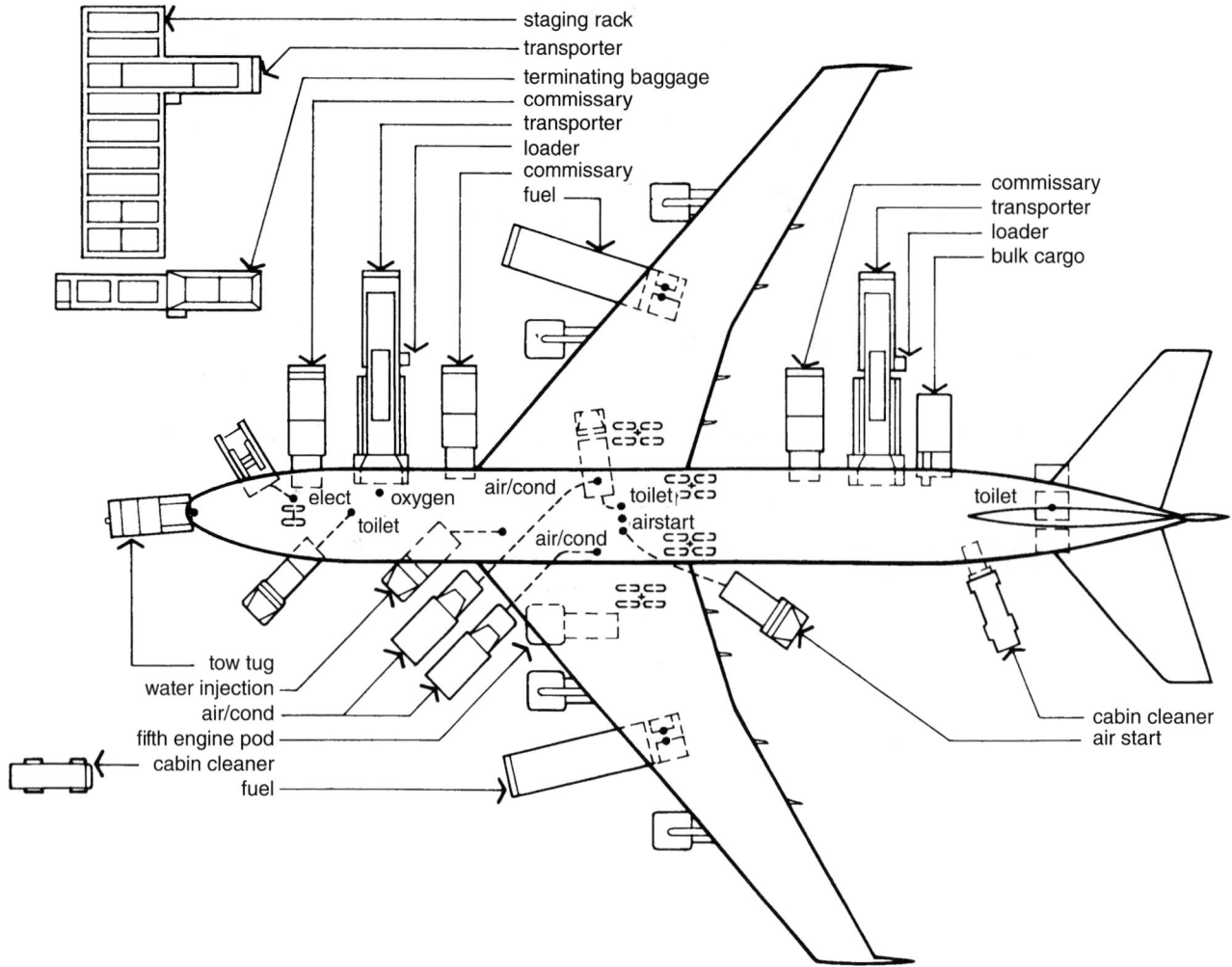

41.18 *Servicing arrangements for passenger model Boeing 747-100/200B + C. Under normal conditions external electric power, airstart and air conditioning are not required when the auxiliary power unit is used*

11 CASE STUDY
Pulkovo Airport terminal, St Petersburg, Russia
Architect: Grimshaw

11.1 Introduction
Grimshaw won an international competition to masterplan the expansion of Pulkovo Airport in 2007 as part of a team with Naco, Arup, Buro Happold and Chapman Taylor. The airport is conceived as the gateway to both St Petersburg and Russia and is an expansion of the existing 1950s airport to the south of the city. The first phase completed in 2013 with an annual capacity of 12 million travellers. A second phase will allow the airport to handle 17 million.

11.2 Masterplan
The new, second terminal at Pulkovo is part of the Airport City masterplan which centres on a new sculpture-lined boulevard. This forms the Airport Gateway and is designed to be reminiscent of St Petersburg's wide avenues. The boulevard terminates in a large square that fronts the 1950s old terminal to create a 'heritage quarter'. The new terminal is positioned adjacent to the existing building and can be viewed unobscured on approach from most directions, Figure 41.19. A series of new buildings, known as 'The Wedge', provides a service and business park to the airport.

11.3 Terminal brief
The brief was for a new terminal that responds to the rich cultural heritage of St Petersburg, the geographical location of the airport by the river Neva and the extreme climate of St Petersburg. This is

characterised by short, mild periods during the summer and long, harsh winters with heavy snowfalls.

11.4 Design solution
The airport is a single terminal of 110,000 sq m designed over 3 segregated levels, Figure 41.20a. Conceived as the first and last great public space of the city, the terminal's internal layout consists of separate zones connected by individual walkways to echo the external layout of islands and bridges that make up St Petersburg. The new terminal has 88 check-in counters, 110 passport control booths and 7 baggage belts. Restaurants, cafes, bars, duty free, and numerous shops take over 15,400 sq m of the internal space. Arrivals, Figure 41.20b is on the lower level, with departures, Figure 41.20c on the upper level.

The terminal is designed without the usual bias towards departing passengers. Grimshaw's design brings natural light down into the very lowest levels of the arrival spaces, via great skylights over the voids between departure islands above, Figure 41.21. This helps to provide an immediate orientation for the arriving passenger. The arrival areas are designed with exactly the same attention to detail as the departing areas, allowing for the same clarity of progression through the building.

11.5 Roof
The sweeping roof is created from a series of 18m bays, which effectively act as large hoppers, shallow enough not to encourage gathering snow, but deep enough to provide effective drainage. The drains are located directly above the roof's supportive columns to ensure that the greatest snow load is concentrated on the area of maximum structural support. The roof lights are positioned above the datum

41.19 *Pulkovo Airport site with new terminal (right)*

41.20a *Elevation*

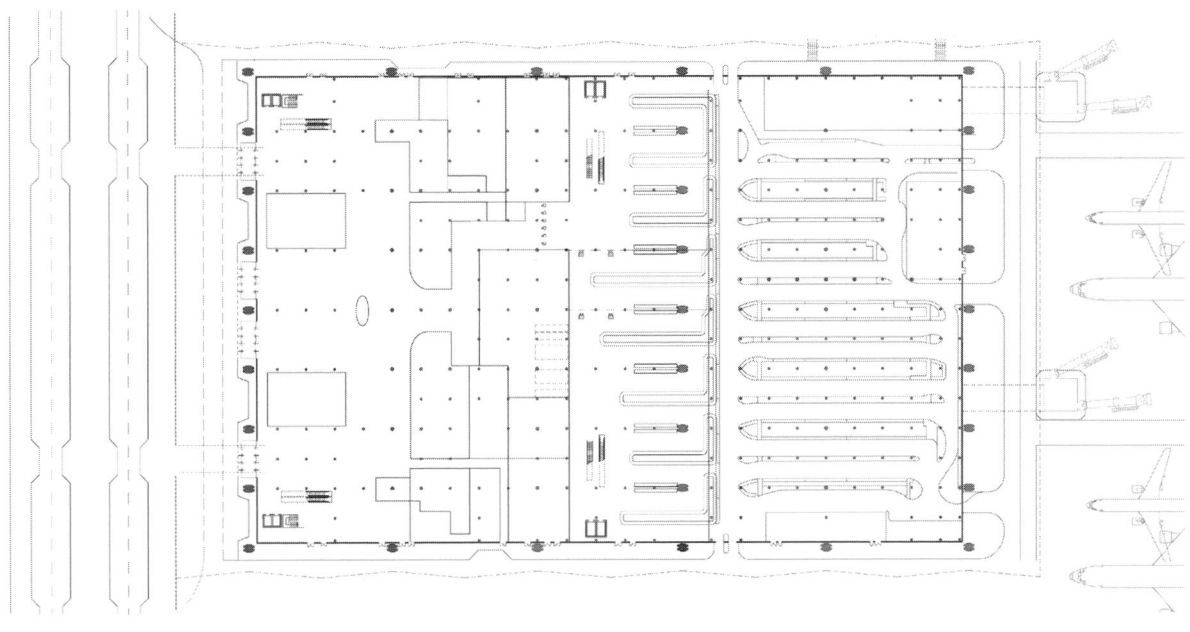

Arrivals

41.20b *Arrivals level plan*

41.20 *Pulkovo Airport elevation and plans*

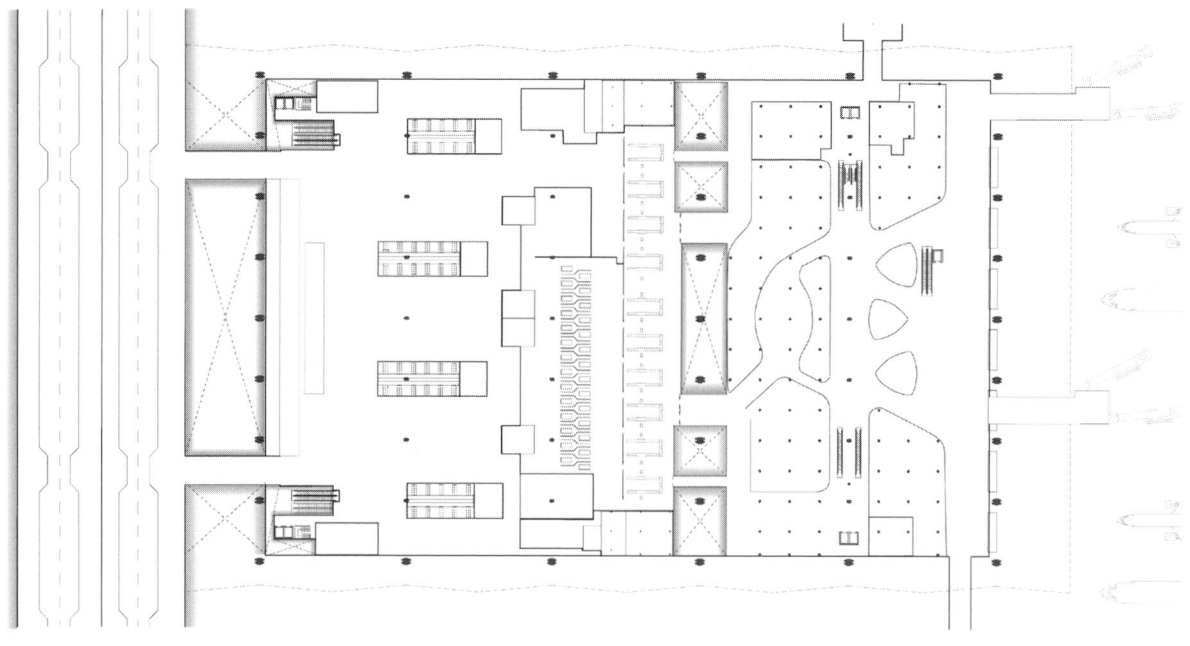

Departures

41.20c *Departures level plan*

41.20 *Pulkovo Airport elevation and plans*

41.21 *Pulkovo Airport interior*

line to give them the greatest protection from blanketing snow and to enable them to make optimal use of the low angle natural light.

It has a clear span over the landside and airside zones, creating column free, flexible rooms. This flowing structure unifies the new terminal and aids the intuitive direction of passengers throughout.

12 RAILWAY STATIONS

12.1 Introduction

This chapter provides guidance for the design of mainline railway stations only.

There has been a growth in railway station projects in the UK since the 1990s, driven by the increase in demand for rail travel and the ageing of much of Britain's rail infrastructure. Railway stations have complex contextual, constructional, urban design and user requirements and these need to be considered from concept design onwards. Most

railway projects also need to consider the civic, cultural, and community impact that a station redevelopment can have on its surroundings. For all railway proposals, designers will need to have a thorough understanding of passenger movement and station operation to ensure that an efficient and functional station layout is developed.

12.2 Operational types

Designers should consider what type of station they are designing as part of the preliminary design. One of the most important factors is how the station will operate, for example, is it a terminus station, a through station or a mixed terminating/through station? Each of these categories has different size and arrangement requirements.

Some operational characteristics are not defined entirely by whether or not services terminate at the station. Some stations, such as Birmingham New Street, have a majority of through platforms, but because of the capacity of the station and the size of the city they serve, operate in a similar way to terminus stations. Designers should use their judgement to determine which of the categories below best describes the particular station under consideration.

Terminus stations

Terminus stations are stations where all tracks stop and there are no through services.

- Almost always located in major urban centres at the end of a particular line.
- Tend to be larger than through stations.
- Concourse tends to be located at the end of the platforms and normally at the same level.
- Passengers tend to wait longer at terminus stations, and are normally encouraged to wait in the concourse rather than on the platforms.
- Normally have more retail facilities than through stations with few, if any, facilities provided on the platforms.
- Onward travel is often onto another type of public transport (bus, metro, taxi etc.).
- Normally accommodate more operational facilities than through stations, including offices for train operating companies; facilities for train servicing, staff accommodation, food preparation, etc.
- Few passengers interchange between platforms at terminus stations.
- Often important and distinctive buildings with a civic and historical importance beyond their transport function.

Through stations

At through stations none of the tracks terminate. Most stations in the UK are through stations, including most smaller suburban and rural stations.

- Normally located in smaller urban centres, in suburbs, or rural areas.
- Tend to be smaller than terminus stations, with less regular train services.
- Normally don't have defined concourse areas, but often have enlarged entrances or wider areas of platforms where retail, ticketing and other facilities are located.
- Passengers normally wait on the platforms.
- Onward travel by private car is proportionally more common than at terminus stations.
- Normally accommodate few, if any, operational facilities aside from those directly associated with the running of the station itself.
- Station entrances are normally located on one side of the station only, with bridge or subway links required to access some platforms.

Mixed-operation (terminus/through) stations

Many stations have a mixture of both terminating and through platforms. They are normally operated in a similar way to through stations, although this depends on the balance of services, the capacity of the station and the size of the town or city served:

- Rarely located in rural areas, but can be located in towns and major urban centres.
- Vary significantly in size, but tend to be larger than through stations.
- Concourse is generally located at platform level but not always. It is not uncommon for a concourse to be provided at the end of the terminating platforms with a bridge or subway link provided to access any platforms separated from the concourse.
- Most passengers wait on the platforms, although in some mixed stations passengers for terminating services are encouraged to wait in the concourse while passengers for through services tend to wait on the platforms. This is normally dependent on the service frequency and predictability of platform allocation.
- Normally have more retail facilities than through stations with few, if any, facilities provided on the platforms.
- Onward travel is often onto another type of public transport (bus, metro, taxi, etc.), but passengers often complete their journey by private car, particularly in stations outside urban centres.
- May need to accommodate many of the same operational facilities as terminating stations, depending on their location on the network and service pattern.
- Some have significant interchange movements within the station, particularly between through and terminating platforms.

12.3 Rail approach typology

In addition to the station typology, designers should also consider how the station relates to its context. One of the most important factors in determining this is whether the tracks and platforms are located below, level with or above street level.

It is customary for the track and platform layout to be determined first in the design process, often by specialist railway engineers. It is important that the constraints the track layout imposes on the remainder of the station design are considered carefully as part of preliminary feasibility studies as they will have significant impacts on how the station operates, passenger movement and how the station relates to the surrounding townscape.

Raised track (viaduct) station (Figure 41.22)

A raised viaduct allows pedestrians and traffic to move freely beneath without having to cross the tracks at grade.

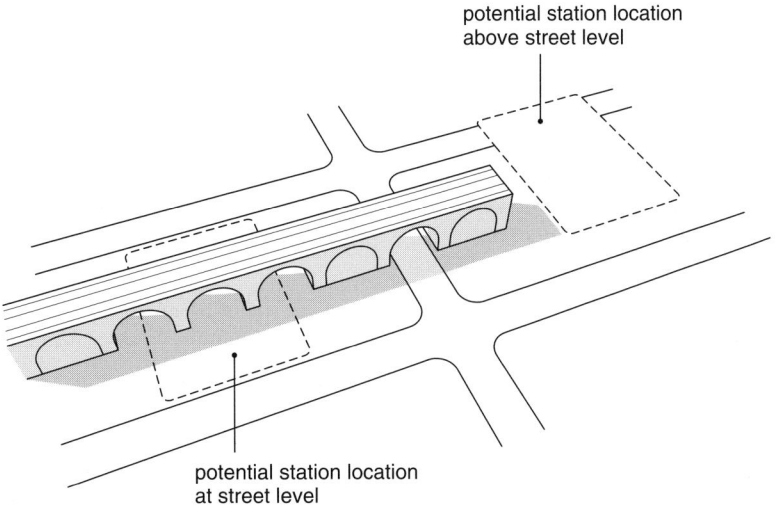

potential station location above street level

potential station location at street level

41.22 *Raised track (viaduct) illustrative diagram*

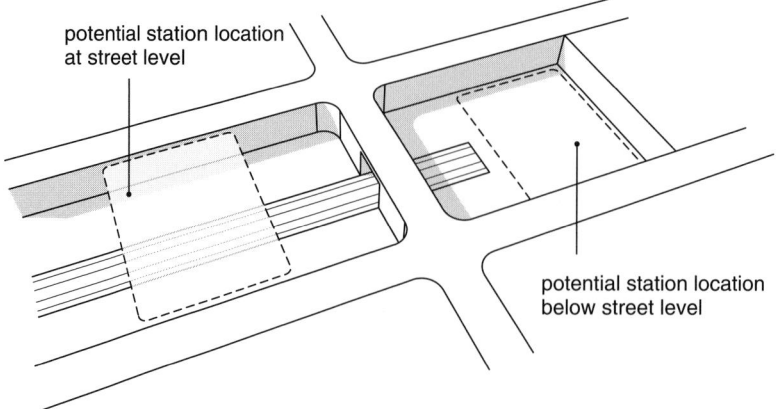

41.23 *Sunken track (cutting) illustrative diagram*

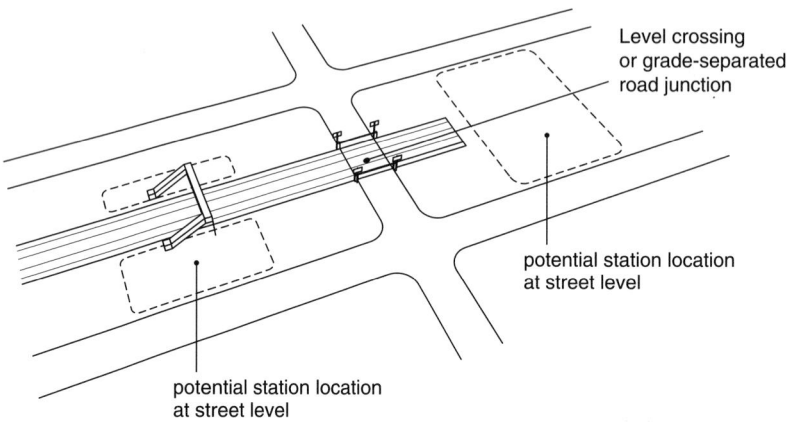

41.24 *At grade track illustrative diagram*

- More expensive to construct than accommodating tracks at grade but causes less severe severance to streets and less restriction on railway capacity.
- Viaduct is highly visible and can have a negative impact on the quality of the urban or rural environment.
- Can result in an adverse train noise impact on neighbouring buildings.
- Allows a station entrance to be located at street level below the tracks, or above street level at platform height which is less than ideal because the station normally has a poor relationship with the street.

Sunken track (cutting) station (Figure 41.23)
This allows pedestrians and traffic to move freely on bridges above without having to cross the tracks at grade.

- More expensive than accommodating tracks at grade, but causes significantly less severance to streets and less restriction on railway capacity.
- Can still cause severance, particularly in urban areas, but has significantly less visual impact than either a viaduct or an at-grade railway line.
- Mitigates impact of railway noise.
- Allows a station entrance to be located at street level above the tracks, or below street level at platform level (less than ideal because the station normally has a poor relationship with the street)

At-grade track (level) station (Figure 41.24)
Lengthy at-grade railway track approaches to stations should be avoided. Other than in exceptional circumstances, no new level crossings should be built.

- Cheaper to construct than accommodating tracks in a cutting or on a viaduct.
- Likely to result in unacceptable severance to roads and restrictions to railway capacity.
- Significant safety issues associated with level rail crossings across roads, which are considered unacceptable for new railway lines.
- Has no impact on railway noise.
- Station entrances will normally be located at platform level as this allows easy access to both trains and the surrounding streets. For a through station, a platform access bridge will be required to access some platforms.

12.4 Station arrangement
There are a number of factors common to the arrangement of all stations. Most have pay barriers, or gate lines, dividing the areas for passengers with tickets (paid side) from the public areas (unpaid side). Many smaller through stations do not have pay barriers, but their arrangement still separates entrance and ticketing areas (analogous to unpaid side) from platform areas (analogous to paid side).

Terminus station arrangement
Figure 41.25 shows an arrangement for the different zones in a terminus station.

Key:

A – The public space in front of a terminus station accommodates a number of important functional requirements for the station. It is normally the place where interchange between the station and other modes of surface transport occur. It allows a space for people to wait and meet, and to orientate themselves before

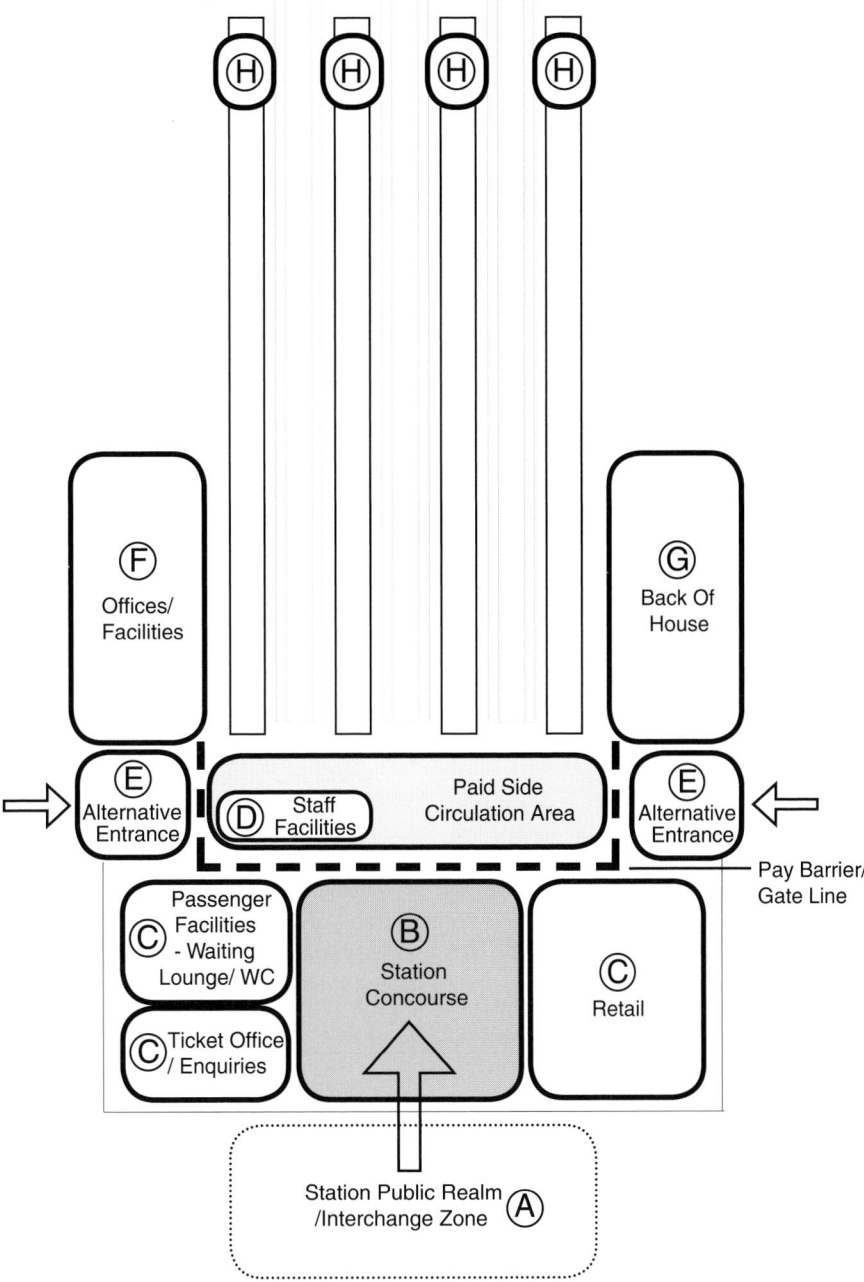

41.25 *Terminus station adjacency diagram*

making any onward journey. It also allows space for passengers to gather safely during an emergency situation or service disruption. It tends to be an important civic space for the town or city itself and designers should consider its urban-scale relationship to its surrounding context.

B – The station concourse normally accommodates information, ticketing and retail. For termini it tends to be a grand space, positioned at the end of platforms. It can also be located above or below the tracks depending on context and railway approach typology.

C – Typically, retail, ticket and enquiries offices, and other passenger facilities such as waiting lounge, toilets, left luggage, etc., are arranged around the concourse.

D – Facilities for staff may be required close to the gate line. This may just be a small secure room in which to rest between work periods, or a larger mess room with kitchen and toilets.

E – Most termini incorporate more than one entrance to the station, allowing easier movement and access to and from the surrounding streets.

F – Termini will normally require facilities for train, rail and freight operating companies. They may also require accommodation for organisations such as British Transport Police, maintenance

personnel, and food and beverage suppliers. Needs vary from station to station depending on the operational requirements, but will normally include office space, changing rooms, showers, toilets, mess rooms, etc.

G – Larger stations will also require large back-of-house areas for functions such as train servicing, retail servicing, waste management, food preparation, staff parking, plant, etc.

H – Platforms for terminus stations normally house few, if any, passenger facilities. Depending on how the station is operated, it may be necessary to locate accommodation for train dispatch staff or train drivers on the platforms.

12.4.2 Mixed-operation station arrangement

Figure 41.26 shows for the different zones in a mixed operation station.

Key

A – The public space in front of a mixed-operation station is similar in function to that of a terminus station. It doesn't always have the same civic importance as a terminus station's public realm, but designers should still consider its functional, urban and contextual requirements.

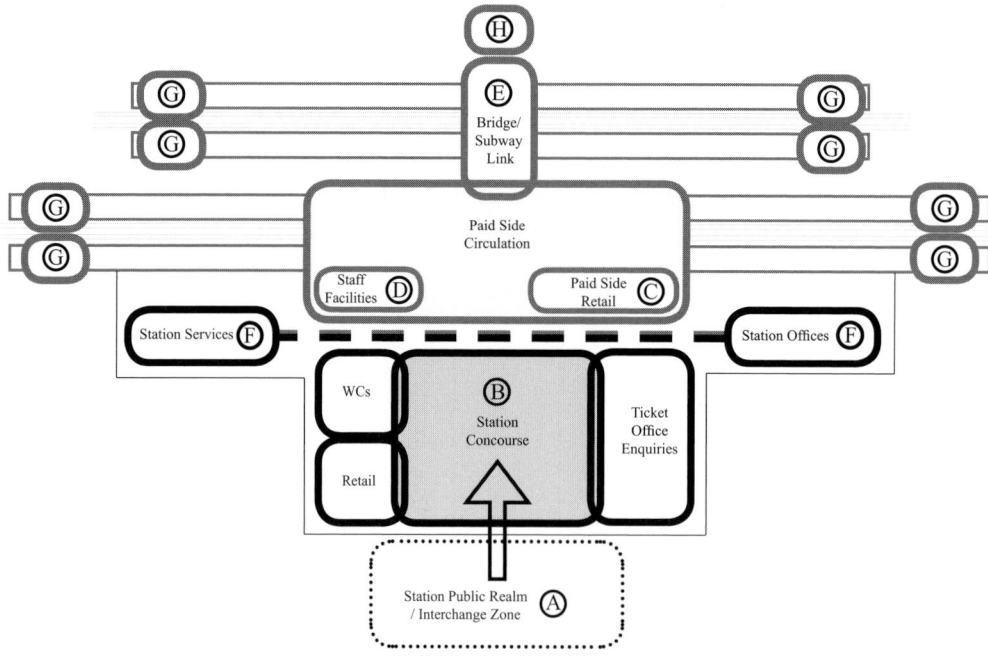

41.26 *Mixed-operation station adjacency diagram*

B – Although typically smaller in scale, the station concourse has the same function as that of a terminus station typically positioned alongside the platforms at the same level. It can also be located above or below the tracks depending on context and railway approach typology.

C – Mixed-operation stations may incorporate some paid-side or platform retail.

D – Facilities for staff may be required close to the gate line. This is likely to be a small, secure rest room.

E – To access the through platforms, mixed-operation stations are likely to require bridge or subway access, ideally located close to the gate line, away from congested areas. For new stations, lifts and stairs – as a minimum – will be required to accommodate the level change. If the change is greater than 4 or 5 m, escalators may also be required.

F – Mixed-operation stations will require some space for staff offices and station servicing, but these areas are likely to be much smaller than those provided at terminus stations.

G – Depending on how the station is operated, it may be necessary to locate accommodation for train dispatch staff or train drivers, as well as waiting areas for passengers, on the platforms.

H – Some stations will require an alternative entrance depending on the surrounding areas.

12.4.2 Through station arrangement
Figure 41.27 shows the different zones in a through station.

Key:

A – The public space in front of a through station is similar in function to that of a mixed-operation station.

B – Through stations may just have an enlarged entrance rather than a full concourse, typically positioned alongside the platforms at the same level. It can also be located above or below the tracks depending on context and railway approach typology.

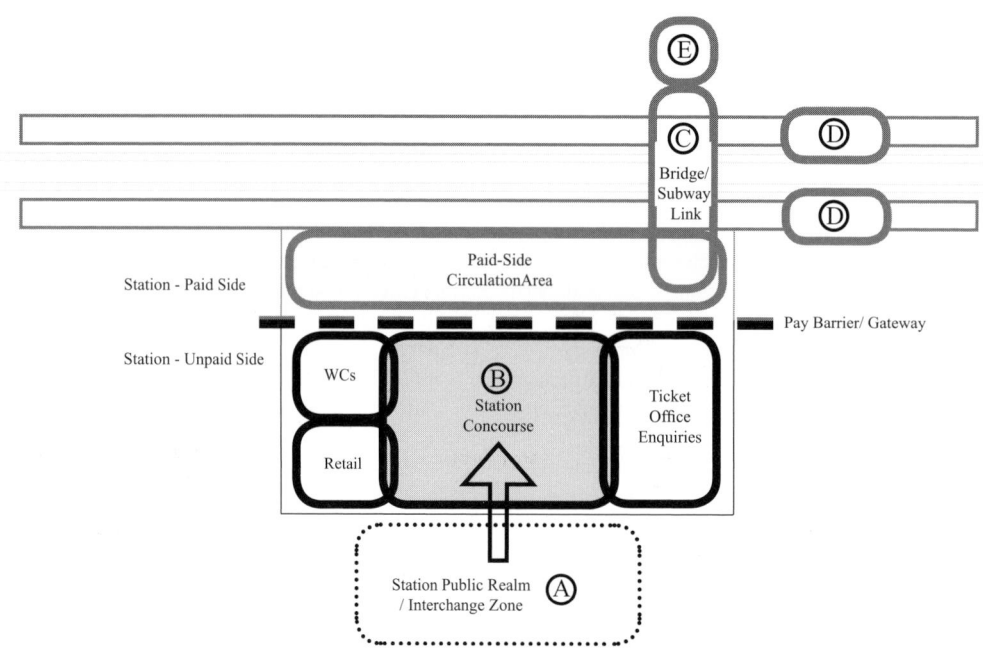

41.27 *Through station adjacency*

C – To access the platforms furthest from the station entrance, through stations will require bridge or subway access, ideally located close to the gate line, away from congested areas. For new stations, lifts and stairs – as a minimum – will be required to accommodate the level change.

D – At through stations the majority of passengers wait on the platforms, so sheltered waiting areas will be required.

E – Some stations will require an alternative entrance depending on the surrounding area.

12.5 Passenger movement

Station designs should be based on a thorough understanding of pedestrian movement requirements. The station brief should define the anticipated passenger numbers that the station will need to accommodate, as well as the level of service required. Figure 41.28 illustrates the basic Fruin Levels of Service. The Levels of Service will vary within a station, with more congested areas concentrated close to gate lines, entrances, and vertical circulation areas. Stations should normally aim to achieve a Fruin Level of Service C, but this is not a universal requirement. To prove the design will meet requirements, test using pedestrian flow software.

Figure 41.29 shows typical run-off zones associated with station components. When block-planning station accommodation, these zones should be kept clear of main pedestrian routes. The diagrams should be used as approximate guidelines only. They will need to be tested against a full pedestrian flow model to determine whether the dimensions indicated are appropriate for a particular station, The run-off zones are cumulative refer to Network Rail Station Capacity Assessment Guidance.

There are some general passenger-movement principles that can be applied when planning the majority of stations:

- Aim to minimise the number and height of level changes required to move between different parts of the station.
- Where up and down level changes are required along a single route, design the station to have breaks or level areas in between.
- Wherever possible, avoid cross-flows between different passenger movements as this is confusing and causes congestion.

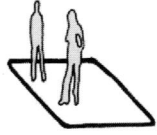
A *Free circulation*

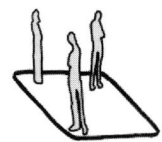
B *Uni-directional flow and free circulation. Reverse and cross-flows with only minor conflicts*

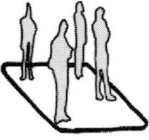
C *Slightly restricted circulation due to difficulty in passing others. Reverse and cross-flows with difficulty*

D *Restricted circulation for most pedestriants. Significant difficulty for reverse and cross-flows*

E *Restricted circulation for all pedestrians. Intermittent stoppages and serious difficulties for reverse and cross-flows*

F *Complete breakdown in traffic flow with many stoppages*

41.28 *Illustrative Fruin Levels of Service*

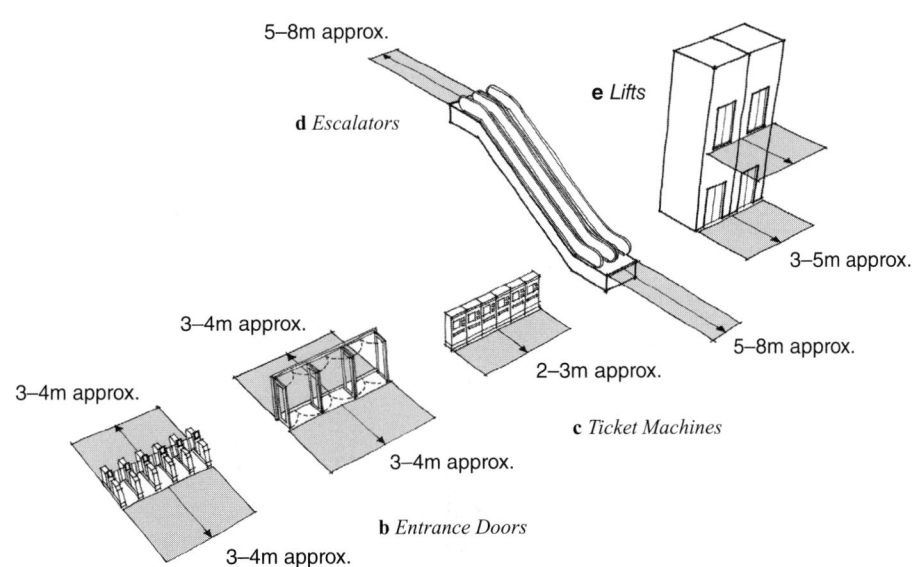

41.29 *Typical minimum run-off zones associated with station components*

- Aim to maintain visibility along primary routes from start to finish to promote intuitive wayfinding.
- Minimise changes of direction along primary routes, particularly 180° turns.
- Position bridges and vertical circulation to distribute passengers evenly along platforms, to minimise journey times and congestion.

12.6 Platform dimensions

Figure 41.30 shows some typical platform dimensions for a two-sided island platform. To determine accurate platform dimensions, designers will need to take account of the rail layout, the passenger movement requirements and the size of elements that need to be located on the platform. Designers will also need to consider the space required by the train when in motion, known as the kinematic envelope. Reference should also be made to *Accessible Train Station Design for Disabled People: a Code of Practice*.

Key

A – Zone to be kept clear of structure, furniture and other obstruction. Dimension depends on speed of trains. Refer to the Network Rail *Track Design Handbook NR/L2/TRK/2049*. As a rule, nothing requiring maintenance or access such as lights, speakers, cameras etc. should be positioned within the vertical zone 1.25m from the platform edge.

B – The central platform zone should be designed to accommodate passenger numbers as well as any platform structures and vertical circulation. Platforms often vary along their length and taper towards their ends to respond to track alignment. As a guide, island platforms tend to have a typical width of between 8 and 12 m.

C – This dimension should be calculated from the dimensions associated with the kinematic envelope of the relevant trains, with allowance made for passing clearances. Refer to the Network Rail *Track Design Handbook NR/L2/TRK/2049*.

D – Dimension between running edge of rails.

E – Dimension varies depending on the kinematic envelope of the relevant trains and the stepping distance required by different train designs. Refer to the Network Rail *Track Design Handbook NR/L2/TRK/2049*.

F – Height above rail for 25kV 50Hz electrification systems. Additional height may sometimes be required. Refer to the Network Rail *Track Design Handbook NR/L2/TRK/2049*.

G – Dimension from top of running rail to surface of platform. Refer to the DfT Accessible Train Station Design for Disabled People: A Code of Practice

H – Minimum clear height above platform. Any signage or lighting should be clear of this zone.

I – Additional height is required above the platform edges with overhead electrified lines. This dimension is for primary Inter-City routes. It may be possible to have tighter clearances on other routes, or where there is no overhead electrification. Refer to the Network Rail *Track Design Handbook NR/L2/TRK/2049*.

13 BUS AND COACH STATIONS

13.1 Location

A bus station is an area away from the general flow of road vehicles, which enables buses and coaches, to set down and pick up passengers in safety and comfort. The best locations are near shopping centres or other transport terminals.

Two particular trends have affected urban bus and coach operations:

- one-driver buses for economy;
- deregulation with new companies with new operating methods and equipment such as minibuses.

13.2 Vehicles

A variety of bus and coach types are now used, Figures 41.31 to 41.33. Turning dimensions are shown in Figures 41.34 to 41.36. A kerbside bus stop in a lay-by is shown in Figure 41.37. Overall length is $A + n B + C$, where n is the number of buses to be accommodated. So for one stop 44.6 m, two stops 56.8 m and three stops 69 m.

13.3 Factors affecting size of station

Apart from the physical site constraints, station size is governed by the following:

- *Number of bays to be incorporated* (the term bay is used in bus stations instead of bus stop), determined by the number of services operated from the station; and by how practical it is, related to the timetable, to use each bay for a number of service routes.
- *Vehicle approaches to the bays*. Three types of manoeuvre are used, Figure 41.38. The 'saw-tooth' is further explored in Figures 41.39 and 41.40.

The choice of manoeuvre will be influenced by the size and shape of the available site, the bus operators' present and anticipated

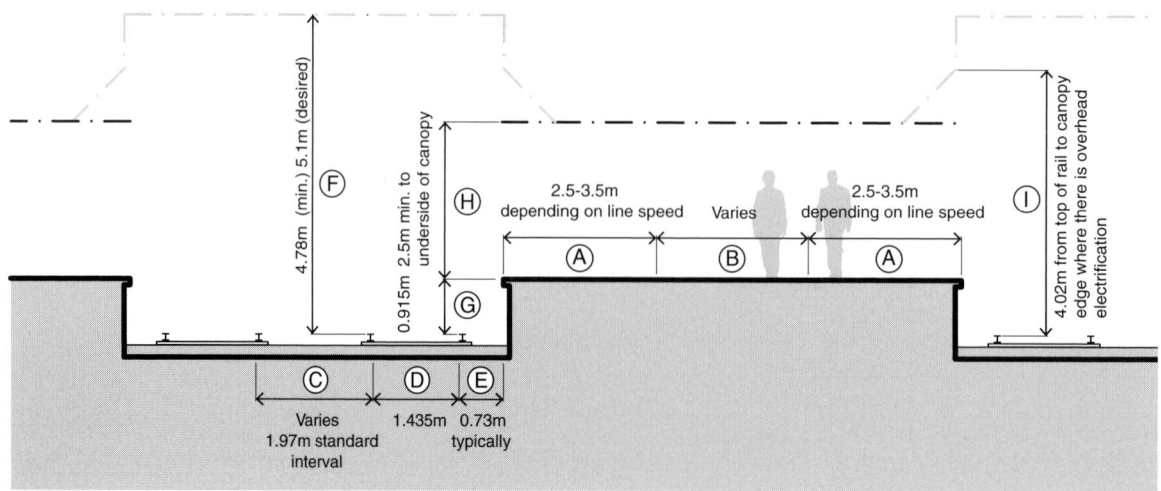

41.30 *Two-sided island platform section*

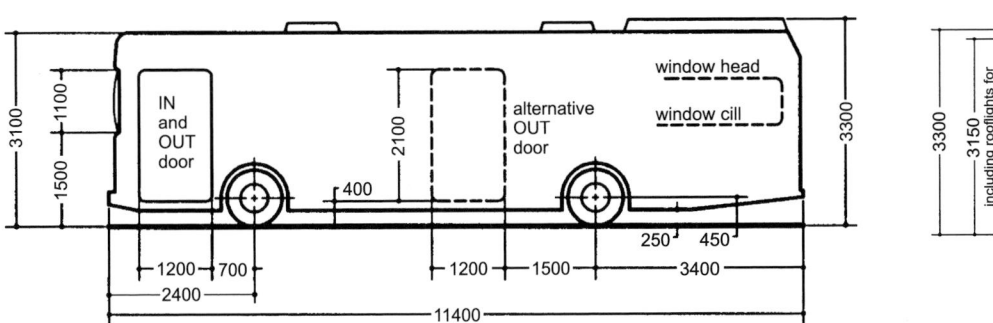
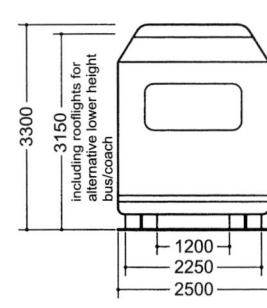

41.31 *Single-decker bus*

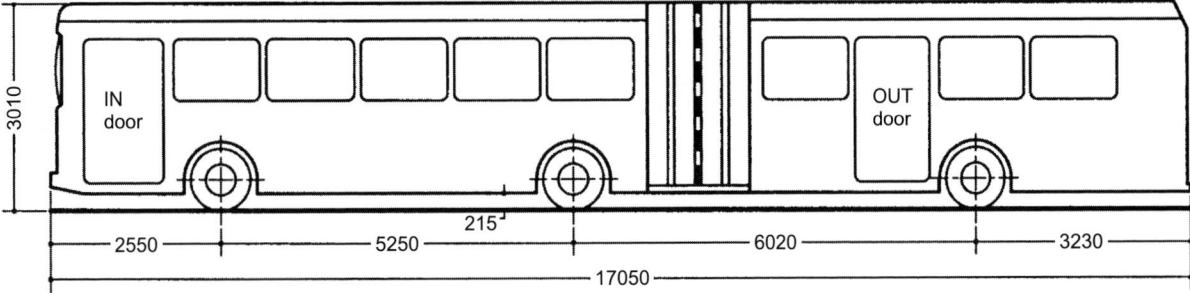

41.32 *Articulated bus*

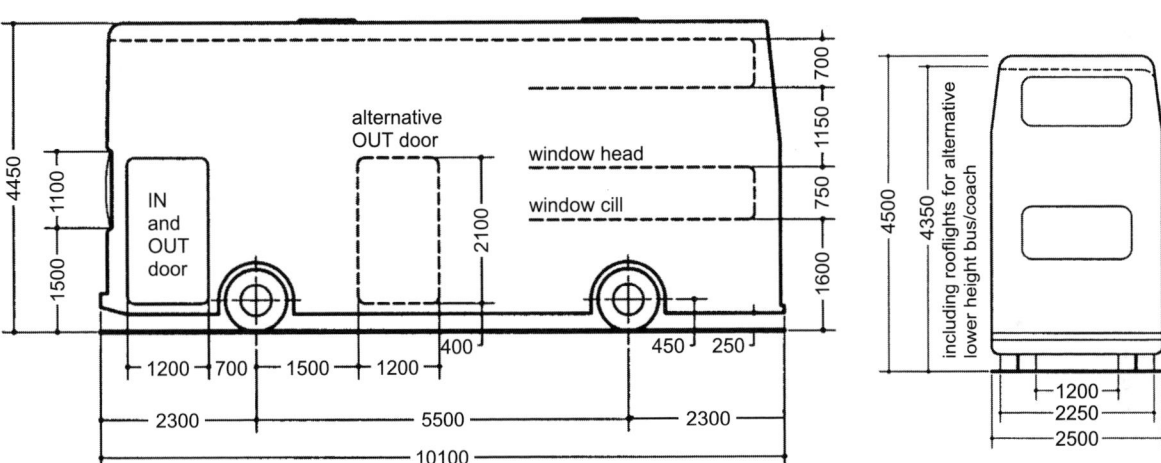

41.33 *Double-decker bus*

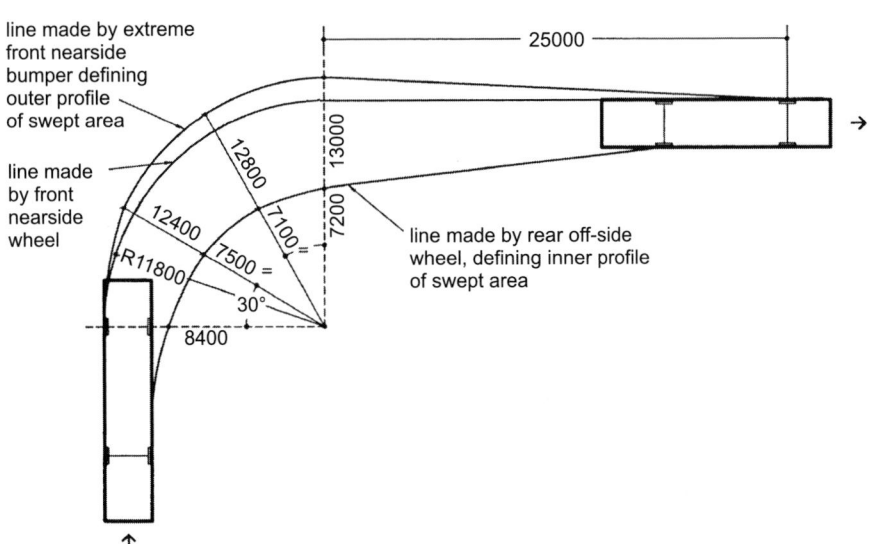

41.34 *Rigid 12 m vehicle turning through 90°*

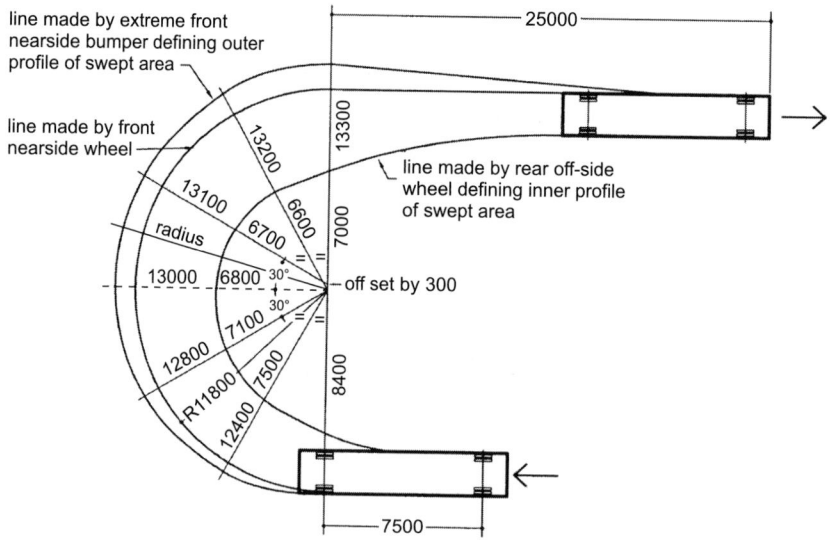

41.35 *Rigid 12 m vehicle turning through 180°*

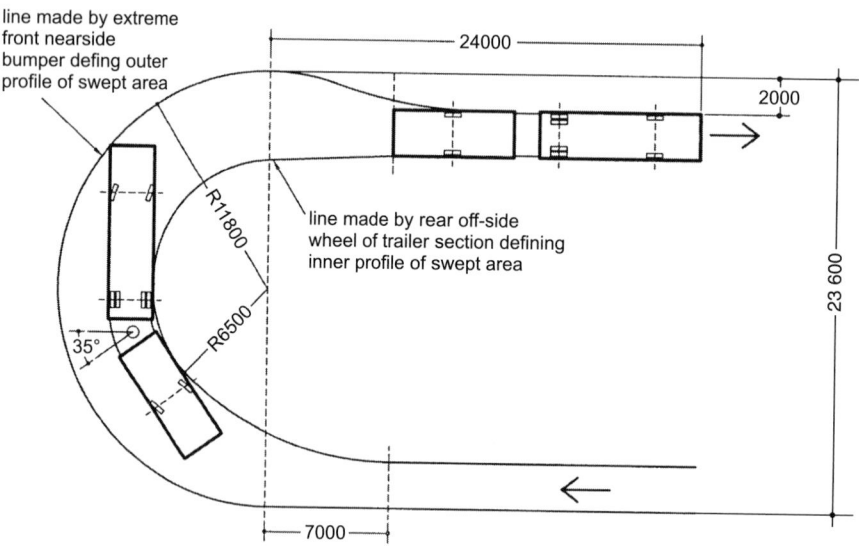

41.36 *17m articulated vehicle turning through 180°*

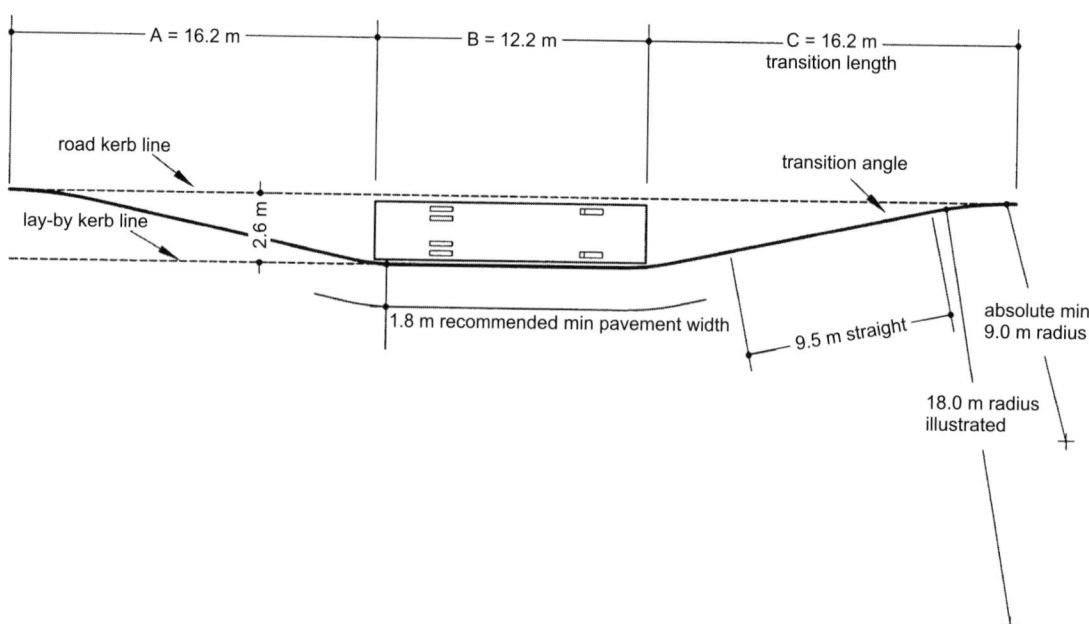

41.37 *A lay-by with one bus stop, assuming normal urban speed of approach. The transition length of 16.2 m is the minimum for a 12 m rigid vehicle. Three bus stops is the desirable maximum in a lay-by, the maximum comfortable distance for a passenger to walk*

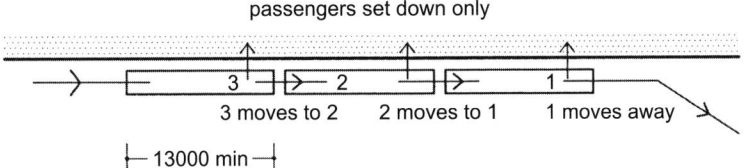

41.38a *Shunting, where a vehicle only sets down passengers on the concourse before moving off to park pick up more passengers. This avoids waiting to occupy a pre-determined bay, and reduces effective journey time*

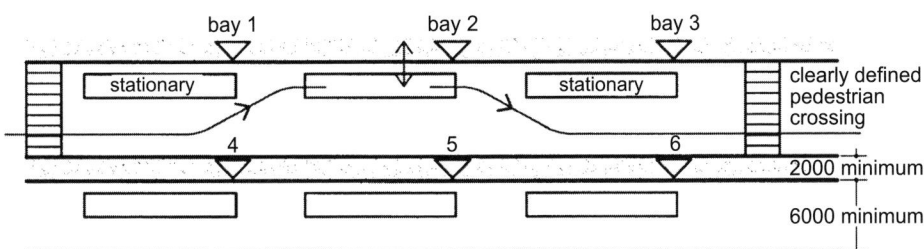

41.38b *Drive-through bays are fixed positions for setting down and/or collecting passengers. They are in a line, so a vehicle often has to approach its bay between two stationary vehicles. In practice it is often necessary to have isolated islands for additional bays, with the inevitable conflict between passenger and vehicle circulation*

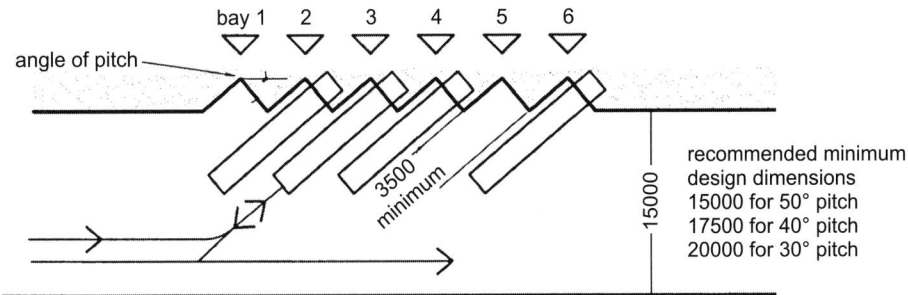

41.38c *'Saw-tooth' layouts have fixed bay positions for setting down and/or collecting passengers with the profile of the concourse made into an echelon or saw-tooth pattern. In theory the angle of pitch between the vehicle front and the axis of the concourse can be anything from 1° to 90°; in practice it lies between 20° and 50°. The vehicle arrives coming forward, and leaves in reverse, thus reducing the conflicts between vehicle and passenger circulation, but demands extra care in reversing*

41.38 *Vehicle manoeuvres used in approaching parking bays*

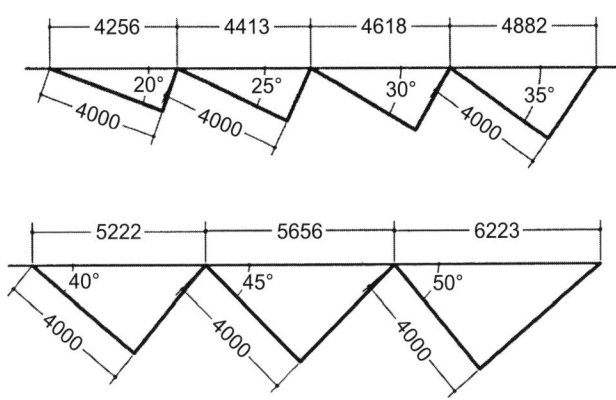

41.39 *As the angle of pitch in saw-tooth bays increases so does the distance between each bay*

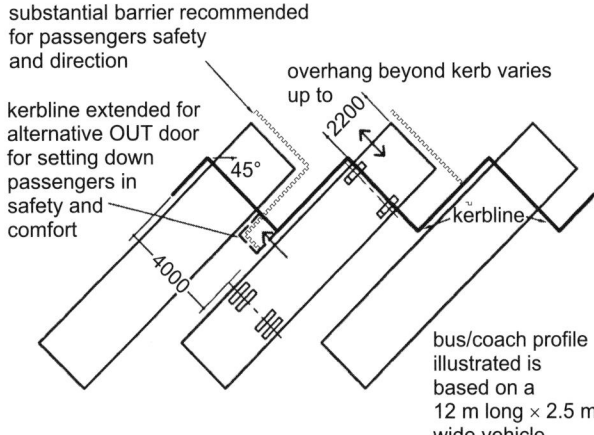

41.40 *Passenger safety and control are particularly important when detailing saw-tooth bays*

needs, and in particular the preference of their staff. Some will accept the saw-tooth arrangement while others prefer the drive-through.

The required area of the site is further increased by the need for lay-over. This is when vehicles are parked after setting down passengers, but which are not immediately required to collect more passengers. The layout for this should be as for parking, Figures 41.41

and 41.42, preferably so that no vehicle is boxed in or interferes with other bus movements.

Economy of space may be achieved, again dependent upon timetables, by using spare bays for lay-over purposes.

Facilities for passengers: these will depend entirely upon anticipated intensity of use and existing amenities. If, for example, there are already public toilets, a bus and coach information centre and

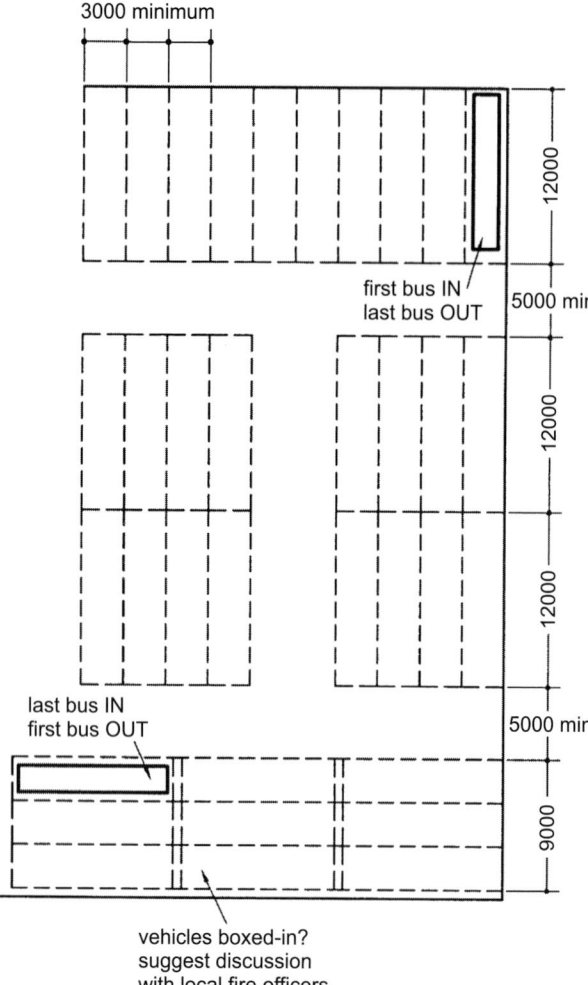

3000 minimum

12000

first bus IN
last bus OUT

5000 min

12000

12000

last bus IN
first bus OUT

5000 min

9000

vehicles boxed-in?
suggest discussion
with local fire officers

41.41 *Bus garaging layout for where the buses are parked in a pre-determined order to get the maximum number of buses in the available space, subject to the fire officer's limitations*

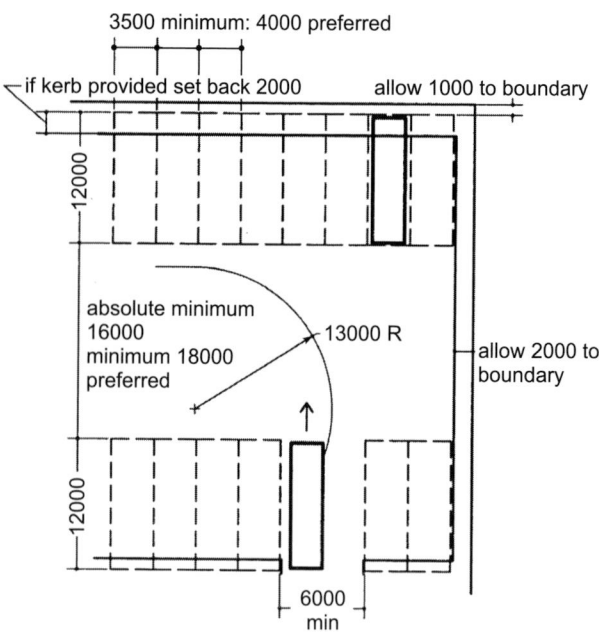

3500 minimum: 4000 preferred

if kerb provided set back 2000   allow 1000 to boundary

12000

12000

absolute minimum
16000
minimum 18000
preferred

13000 R

allow 2000 to
boundary

6000
min

41.42 *Coach park for random arrival and departure of vehicles. The larger bay size (4 m) is necessary if coach parties enter and leave the coaches in the park*

cafes nearby, then these will not be required on the station concourse. However, waiting room facilities may be required with someone on hand to give information and supervision. In more comprehensive schemes consider:

- waiting room
- buffet
- public toilets
- kiosks
- enquiry and booking
- left luggage
- lost property.

Facilities for staff: there are invariably inspectors who, as well as assisting passengers, are primarily concerned with organising the movements of vehicles, and supervising their drivers and conductors. If there is a depot near the station then staff facilities will be provided there. If not, canteen and toilets facilities will be needed for staff on the station site, so that during breaks and between shifts they do not need to get back to the depot until they return their vehicle for long-term parking. Should the depot be even more remote, all facilities should be provided at the station and only basic amenities at the depot. In addition to those listed above these include a recreation area, locker rooms and a facility

for paying in takings. This would be an office where drivers or conductors check, then hand over monies taken as fares, which in turn are checked and accounted for by clerical staff. Secure accommodation for any cash that cannot be immediately banked will be needed.

Facilities for vehicle maintenance: the inspection, repair and servicing of buses and coaches is an integral part of an operator's responsibility. Normally such work would be carried out at a local depot, with a repair workshop together with fuelling, washing and garaging facilities. The provision of any such facility within a station complex is unusual, but not unique. For a new town bus station or one where it will be difficult and time consuming to drive to and from the station and depot because of traffic congestion, it would be advantageous to provide at least a workshop.

13.3 Planning
Whatever facilities are to be provided on the station site, the final arrangement must be carefully planned, Figure 41.43.

13.4 Joint company use
If two or more bus and coach companies operate from the same station, this can mean that different types of vehicle manoeuvre are used on one site. Figure 41.44 is based on a proposal for a new station within a centre-town commercial development in the south-east of England, and illustrates this. The predominant company (which is a local one) favoured the saw-tooth layout, while the other preferred the drive-through arrangement. Full use has been made of a restricted site, and conflict between passenger and vehicular circulation has been minimised.

14 TRAMS AND LIGHT RAIL
There are a wide variety of these installations. Figure 41.45 shows a typical light railcar designed to facilitate use by wheelchair users.

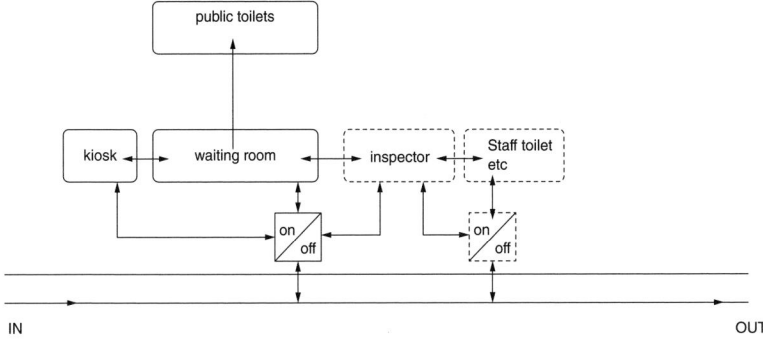

a *In a small town where all services run through*

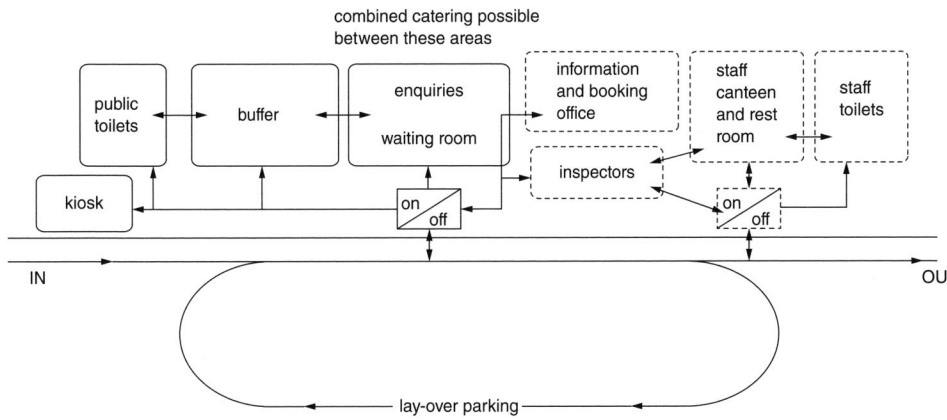

b *For a medium-sized town with both terminal and in transit services*

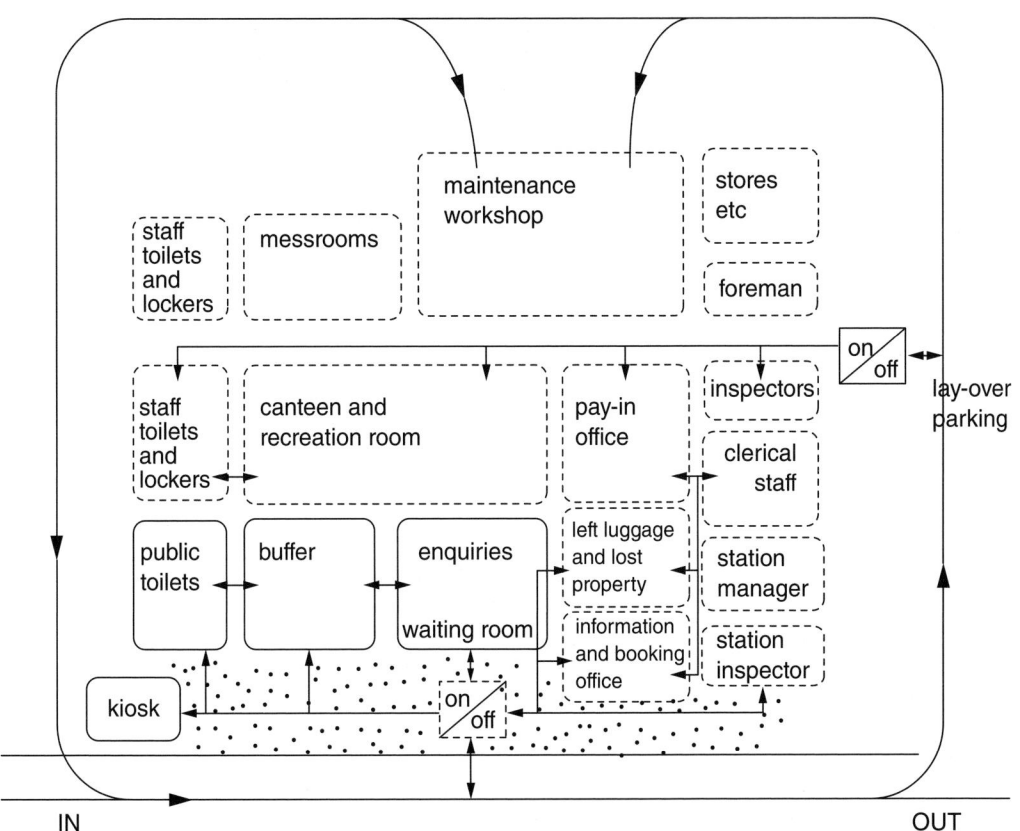

41.43 *Relationship diagram for different types of bus station*

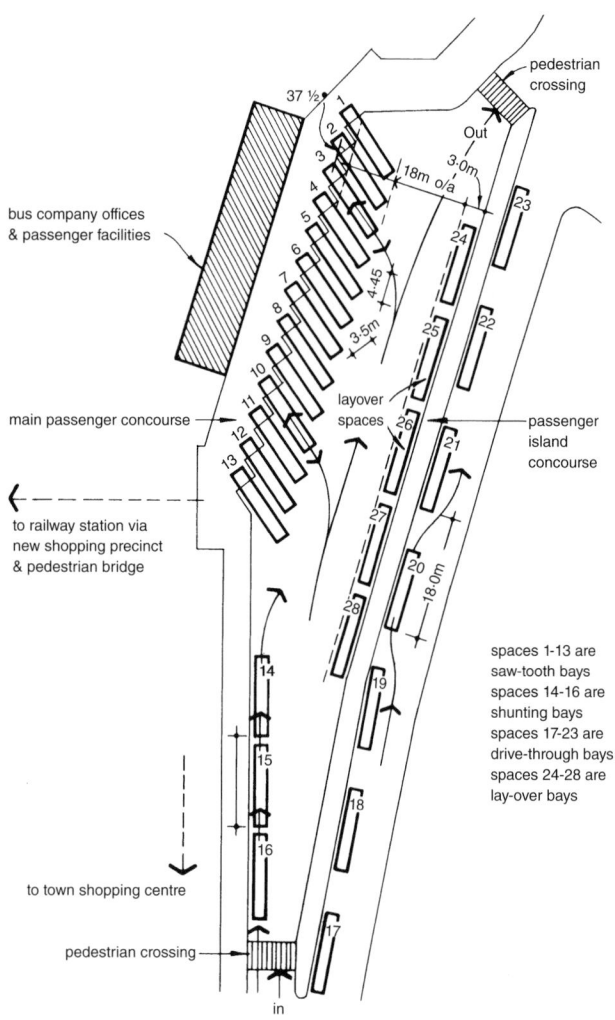

41.44 *Bus station accommodating two bus companies, each with different bay requirements*

spaces 1-13 are saw-tooth bays
spaces 14-16 are shunting bays
spaces 17-23 are drive-through bays
spaces 24-28 are lay-over bays

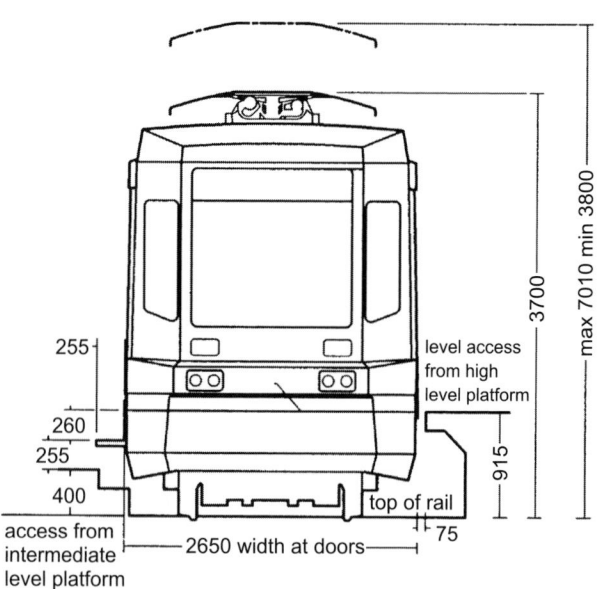

41.45 *Manchester Metrolink: a typical modern tramway system. Frontal view of a car, showing level access for wheelchairs from a high-level platform*

15 BIBLIOGRAPHY

Air

Norman Ashford, *Airport Operations,* McGraw-Hill Professional, 1984

Christopher Blow, *Airport Terminals,* Architecture Press, *1996*

Guilio de Carli, *New Airports,* 24 Ore Cultura, 2010

Brian Edwards, *The Modern Airport Terminal: New Approaches to Airport Architecture,* Taylor & Francis, 2005

Anne Graham, *Managing Airports*, 3rd Edition, Routledge, 2008

IATA Airport Development Reference Manual, 10th Edition, 2014

ICAO Publications (refer to catalogue) in particular *Design Manual ICAO 9157 for Aerodrome Design, Design Manual ICAO 9184 for Masterplanning*

Richard de Neufville, Amedeo Odoni, *Airport Systems: Planning, Design and Management*, McGraw-Hill Education, 2013

Hugh Pearman, *Airports – A Century of Architecture*, Laurence King Publishing, 2004

www.airports-worldwide.com

www.iata.org

www.icao.int

Rail

Department for Transport and Transport Scotland *Accessible train station design for disabled people: A code of practice,* 2011

Network Rail *Making Rail Accessible: a guide to our policies and pratices,* 2012

Network Rail *Station Capacity Assessment Guidance,* 2011

Network Rail *Track Design Handbook NR/L2/TRK/2049*

42 Tropical design

Patricia Tutt

CI/SfB: (H11)

Patricia Tutt is an architect, architectural photographer and editor who has spent half her life in central Africa. She co-edited an earlier edition of the Metric Handbook *and is now a lecturer at the Isle of Man College*

KEY POINTS:

- *Study existing buildings that work, and learn from them*
- *Apply normal good design and environmental practice, being sensitive to site, climate, culture and construction industry practices*
- *Review and revalidate all design assumptions*
- *Use local information and expertise*
- *Carry out a thorough desk study*
- *Anticipate extremes of climate change*

Contents

1 Introduction
2 Desk study – factors affecting design
3 Climate-responsive design: climate types
4 Environmental design strategies: passive design
5 Environmental control strategies: active measures
6 Structure, services and environmental design
7 Building science data
8 Bibliography, information sources and further reading

1 INTRODUCTION

1.1 'The Tropics'

'The tropics' are, technically, the low latitudes contained in the 'Torrid Zone' between the Tropics of Cancer and Capricorn, Figure 42.1, but the term is most typically applied to the world's hot, humid, equatorial coastal regions which have high rainfall, lush vegetation and, almost invariably, a colonial past. For our purposes here, however, the term can be applied to all climates in which the cooling load in buildings significantly exceeds the heating load, Figure 42.2. This extends into the hot dry areas, the composite climates in the centre of large continental land masses, and some areas tempered by warm seas or prevailing winds that are as far away from the equator as latitudes 45° north and south. This section provides an introductory design guide for architects undertaking work in unfamiliar environments and climates. All guidance must be substantiated by site-specific data.

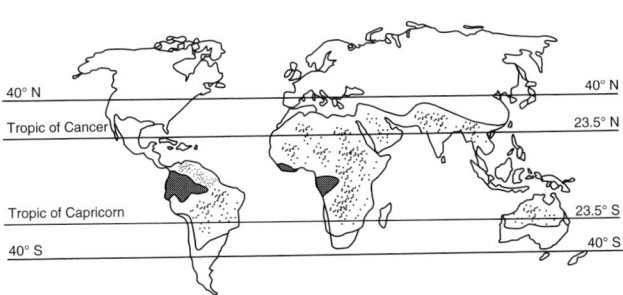

42.1 *The 'Torrid Zone' lies between the Tropics of Cancer and Capricorn. Toned areas have a mean annual temperature of 20°C or above; black areas have persistent overcast skies with less than 1600 h sunshine per annum*

1.2 Current agendas

Within the last 20 years, there has been a major shift in design agendas worldwide, with increasing awareness of global warming, climate change and the need for responsible, sustainable design. Environmental design has become an essential component of building design. There has been widespread high-tech adaptation of traditional third world technologies by architects working in temperate climates, Figure 42.3. There is increasing awareness of the limitations of globalisation when compared to the merits of regionalism. Increasing sophistication in building design has become apparent in many tropical countries, especially those around the Pacific Rim; and web-based documentation, communication and transfer of knowledge have revolutionised design methodologies in all climates, whilst research has revalidated many traditional tropical design technologies.

Many governments are dependent on external funding to enable them to execute major development programmes and government agendas may, therefore, be diverted or constrained by the policies of the donor agencies which may be single governments (USAID, CIDA), regional organisations (EC, ADB, AfDB), international agencies (UN, World Bank, WHO) or charities (Oxfam, Red Cross, Red Crescent). *(The acronyms stand for the United States Agency for International Development, Canadian International Development Agency, the European Community, Asian Development Bank, African Development Bank, the United Nations and the World Health Organisation.)*

1.3 Tropical design

Tropical design is no longer seen as a separate entity, but as good design that is attuned to specific variations in climate, construction industry structure, culture and socio-economic conditions, Figures 42.4 and 42.5. A high-tech, expensive building can disregard context and be built anywhere if funding is available; the harder task is to design a sensitive, sustainable, lower-tech, climate-responsive building that will serve its intended community well and need little maintenance. Ideally, this building should embody cultural memory without being a pastiche of the vernacular or colonial model, using valid older principles in ways that suit a modern, urban and, in many cases, industrial society. Whilst many third world clients understandably aspire to the twentieth century, high-tech Western model for their new buildings, it is the responsibility of their architect to ensure that they are aware of this twenty-first century shift in thinking towards sustainable models, and to understand the options available to them and the potential long-term consequences of their choice.

The purpose of this chapter is to provide prompts and checklists to enable the building designer working in an unfamiliar region to carry out a detailed desk study, having first identified those issues that require detailed research. Many of these prompts would be relevant in any climate, but the details given here highlight tropical contexts.

2 DESK STUDY – FACTORS AFFECTING DESIGN

2.1 General

Whenever a building is being designed for an unfamiliar environment, the architect must check and revalidate even the most basic

42.2 *Colonial bungalow, Zomba, Malawi, with clerestory windows, high ceilings and deep shaded verandas, including one for the car. Drawing by the Rev'd D Brian Roy, RIBA*

a   b

42.3 *Many of the traditional environmental strategies used throughout the Middle East have been co-opted into current mainstream architectural design. Portcullis House, the new offices for MPs alongside the Houses of Parliament, in London, updates the wind-catcher and wind-venting tower by incorporating heat recovery and mechanical back-up systems (Smith, 2001)*

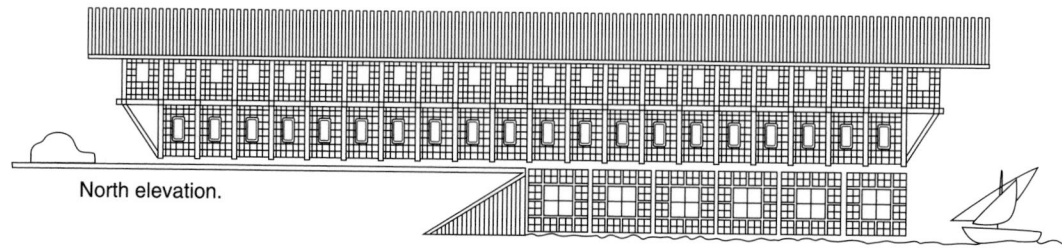

North elevation.

42.4 *The work of the Singhalese architect, Geoffrey Bawa, ranges between a restrained aesthetic using modern materials, and a sophisticated and heightened reinterpretation of the vernacular in private houses and tourist hotels, and, as can be seen in his exquisite drawings. Steel Corporation Offices, Oruwela, Sri Lanka, 1968 – set half in the large pool (steel production holding tank) and in reinforced concrete throughout, with precast perforated and windowed walls*

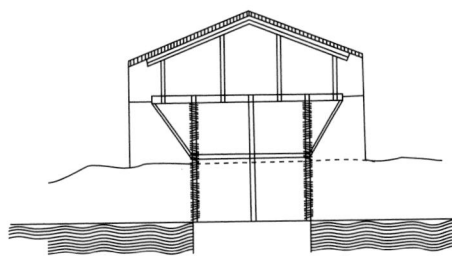

Transversal section.

42.5 *Bawa's Ena De Silva house, Colombo, 1962 – the courtyards for secure outdoor living are kept cool by through ventilation, deep overhangs and shade trees. All materials except a small amount of glass and some steel reinforcement are local. One of the large trees was brought onto the site by elephant; the other was already on site and influenced the design*

design assumption, as it might be invalid in the new context. This section highlights some areas where research may be necessary. Relevant building science data is given in Section 7.

2.2 Climate and microclimate

Confirm the climate type, Table I, and obtain as much site-specific data as possible, Tables II and III. Make sure you understand the terms used and are comparing like with like when evaluating data from differing sources. (Annual average temperature is the average of the mean monthly maximum and minimum temperatures. The average of the highest mean monthly maximum and lowest mean monthly minimum gives a close approximation.)

It is particularly important to ensure that data has not been distorted by periodic aberrations, especially if based on short-term records. A comparison of annual rainfall records will show if any cyclical pattern occurs. The great lakes of east Africa had a pattern of rising and falling over a 7-year cycle in the first half of the twentieth century – believed to be related not only to rainfall but also to activity in the Great Rift through which the lakes seem to be interlinked. The continuation of this pattern will have been distorted by deforestation, the change from subsistence to cash crop agricultural practices that have allowed extensive run-off of topsoil and fertiliser into the lakes, and the construction of dams, barrages and other features that alter natural hydrological cycles.

A lot of the current and historical weather data will be available on the internet, as will definitions of the terms used, but as weather bureaux are often located at airports, which tend to have distinctive microclimates, this data needs confirmation on site. Where rainfall is dependent on prevailing winds from one direction, a hillside site may be in the rain shadow and very much drier that the records suggest. On large projects, it may be advisable to establish a weather station on site to verify data and study microclimate. If climate change (see Section 2.3) accelerates as expected, more extreme weather will occur, causing catastrophes of increasing magnitude. In particular, extreme storms, wind, rainfall or drought may get worse as well as occurring more frequently. Building design and site selection need to take account of this.

Thermal comfort

Thermal comfort is dependent on temperature, humidity, radiation and air movement as well as type of activity, clothing and degree of acclimatisation. No two people will perceive and describe comfort equally. In a hot dry climate, perspiration evaporates quickly,

Table I Occurrence and characteristics of main climatic zones

Zone	Approximate latitude range	Natural vegetation	Typical cultivation	Climate	Problems	Requirements
Warm humid equatorial	7½°N–7½°S	Tropical rain forest	Banana, palm oil	Warm with high humidity and rainfall	Humidity prevents sweat evaporation; hot nights make sleep difficult; high rainfall and glare from overcast sky, sun on east and west facades	Air movement from fans or cross ventilation, low thermal capacity construction, sloping roofs and large overhangs, windows facing north and south
Tropical island	5–30°N 5–30°S	Rain forest	Sugar cane	Warm, humid but less cloud than warm humid zone	Similar to warm humid equatorial, but clear skies and bright sun more frequent	Similar to warm humid but with additional care in the design of shading the south facing windows in the northern hemisphere (vice versa in the southern)
Hot dry tropical	15–32°N 15–32°S	Desert, steppe	Palms, grazing (nomadic)	Hot and dry with high annual and daily variation of temperature	High diurnal range, very hot days in summer, cool winter days, low rainfall, very strong solar radiation and ground glare, sandy and dusty environment	High heat capacity construction, shading devices which allow solar heating in winter, small windows, flat roofs (often used for sleeping), small courtyards to give shade and protection
Maritime desert	15–30°N 15–30°S	Desert	Palms, grazing	Hot, humid with low rainfall	Similar to hot dry climates but with high humidity causing discomfort by preventing sweat evaporation	Similar to hot dry but air movement is desirable at times
Intermediate composite or monsoon	5–20°N 5–20°S	Monsoon forest, dry tropical forest or scrub, savannah	Paddy rice, sugar cane, millet	Warm humid and hot dry seasons often with cool season	Combines the problems of warm humid and hot dry climate	Compromise between the requirements of warm humid and hot dry climate or ideally (but more expensively) two buildings or parts of buildings for use at different times of the year
Equatorial upland	10°N–10°S	Broadleaf forest, mountain vegetation	Millet	Temperate to cool depending on altitude	Combine the problems of warm humid and hot dry climates with those of a temperate or cold climate for all or part of the year	Design to take advantage of solar radiation when cool or cold. Heating and additional insulation may be required
Tropical upland	10–30°N 10–30°S	Steppe, cedars	Wheat	Hot summers, cold winters	Ditto	Ditto
Mediterranean	32–45°N 32–45°S	Mediterranean scrub	Vines, olives, citrus fruits	Hot dry summers, cold wet winters	Summers have some of the problems of a hot dry climate while winters are cold and humid with moderate rainfall	Design with high thermal capacity, medium to small opening, and courtyards to give shade and protection

Table II Climatic data

Data required	Units	Relevance
Monthly mean maximum temperature	°C	thermal comfort analysis
Monthly mean minimum temperature	°C	
Monthly mean maximum humidity	%	
Monthly mean minimum humidity	%	
Monthly mean rainfall	mm	vegetation
Peak rainfall intensity and duration	mm/unit of time	storm damage
(Daily or hourly rainfall may be the only data available)	mm	rainwater drainage
Sunlight	hours	natural lighting
Cloud cover	oktas* or %	
Absolute maximum temperature	°C	thermal expansion
Absolute minimum temperature	°C	and effect on building materials
Frequency distribution of wind for different speeds and directions	% m/s	siting and orientation
Frequency of special phenomena, i.e. sandstorms, fog, hail, thunder	days per year	provision of special precautions

* 1 okta = 1 eighth of the sky.

Table III Action points for weather data collection

Historical data	• Check local weather bureaux, starting with the airport, making sure the data is relevant for the specific site. Even small countries can manifest several different climate types. Note changing patterns and periodic cycles that have recurred since record keeping began.
Now	• As a priority, collect weather data on site, as soon as the site is identified
Rainfall	• Establish the rainfall pattern – peaks, daily patterns (monsoon or 'main' rains often recur at the same time every day; some areas have a week or two of 'planting rains' a month or so before the main rains appear)
	• In areas with distinct seasonal variations, are there two (or more) 'rainy' seasons (as in Kenya)
	• Are the rains reliable or is there evidence of climate change?
	• Is there a known periodic cycle, such as El Niño?
	• Does the rain come from one direction and, if so, does this affect micro-climate on the site?
	• How heavy is the rainfall – does it drizzle for months or all come at once in a torrential cloudburst?
Other precipitation	• Is there a risk of hail or snow – not unknown in the tropics?
Storms, sandstorms, gales, hurricanes, tsunami, tornadoes, earthquakes, flash floods, landslides and other extreme weather events	• There are two aspects to these risks – how extreme are these events, and how often do they occur?
	• How often are two or more of these events inter-related or dependent on other, predictable or observable climatic events (tornadoes and changes in atmospheric pressure, earthquakes and tsunami, hurricanes and landslides)?
Sunlight and cloud cover	• Are there clear skies all year, or does the sky stay overcast during the rains for weeks on end?
	• How predictable is the cloud cover?
Relative humidity	• Records, seasonal variation
	• Is there a risk of mould growth in cupboards?
	• Does high humidity affect normal tasks or construction materials?
Temperature	• Yearly graph
	• Seasonal variations
	• Diurnal maximum and minimum

Table IV Thermal comfort limits (°C)

Monthly average relative humidity (RH)%	Annual average temperature					
	Over 20°C		15–20°C		Under 15°C	
	Day	Night	Day	Night	Day	Night
0–30	26–34	17–25	23–32	15–23	21–30	14–21
30–50	25–31	17–24	22–30	15–22	21–27	14–20
50–70	23–29	17–23	21–28	15–21	19–26	14–19
70–100	22–27	17–21	20–25	15–20	18–24	14–18

Table V Indicators of requirements for comfort for each month

Humid indicators		
H1	Air movement essential	mean monthly maximum temperature above the day comfort limits combined with humidity over 70% or humidity between 30 and 70% and a diurnal range of less than 10°C
H2	Air movement desirable	mean monthly maximum temperatures within the comfort limits combined with humidities over 70%
Arid indicators		
A1	Thermal storage required	diurnal range of temperatures over 10°C and humidity less than 70%
A2	Space required for outdoor sleeping	mean monthly minimum temperatures above the night comfort limits and humidity below 50%. Outdoor sleeping may also be indicated where maximum temperatures are above the day comfort limits and diurnal range is above 10°C with humidities less than 50%.
Cold indicators		
C1	Solar radiation desirable	mean monthly maximum temperatures below day comfort limits
C2	Additional heating required	mean monthly maximum temperature below 15°C

enabling rapid cooling of the body; humid conditions prevent this, leading to heat gain and discomfort. Table IV indicates the range of bulb temperatures that are likely to be perceived as comfortable at particular levels of relative humidity.

These thermal comfort limits assume that there has been no heat loss or gain due to ventilation or insolation. Comparing monthly mean maximum and minimum temperatures for known levels of relative humidity will indicate whether that particular month will have days and nights that are comfortable or uncomfortable due to either heat, cold or humidity, Table V.

Various formulae for relating these indicators to design solutions have been developed. The most successful of these are the 'Mahoney tables' developed for the UN by Carl Mahoney and reproduced in *Manual of Tropical Building and Housing: Part 1 – Climatic Design* Koenigsberger et al. (1974). This remains an important text.

Meteorological data

Geographers and meteorologists distinguish a wide range of climate types in hot and warm climates and disagree over what to call them, but:

• The wet climates can be broadly distinguished by intensity and pattern of rainfall, humidity and cloud cover,
• The dry climates by how dry they are, how cold they get in the cold season (for simplicity, referred to hereafter as 'winter') and whether what little rain they do get falls in summer or winter.
• The composite climates by the degree of seasonal fluctuation in all climatic indicators; and whether it gets really cold in winter.

All these variables are moderated by latitude, altitude, prevailing winds, and whether they are at the centre of large landmasses. They can be covered by short lists of three or four types, based on data critical to particular groups (farmers concerned about rain,

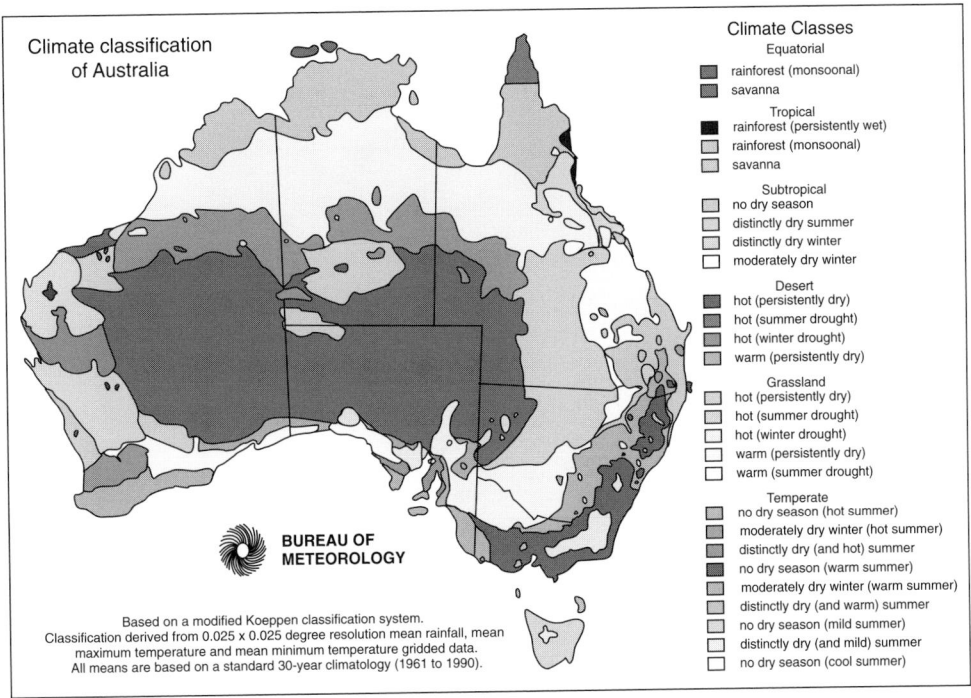

42.6 *Range of tropical and subtropical climates found in Australia*

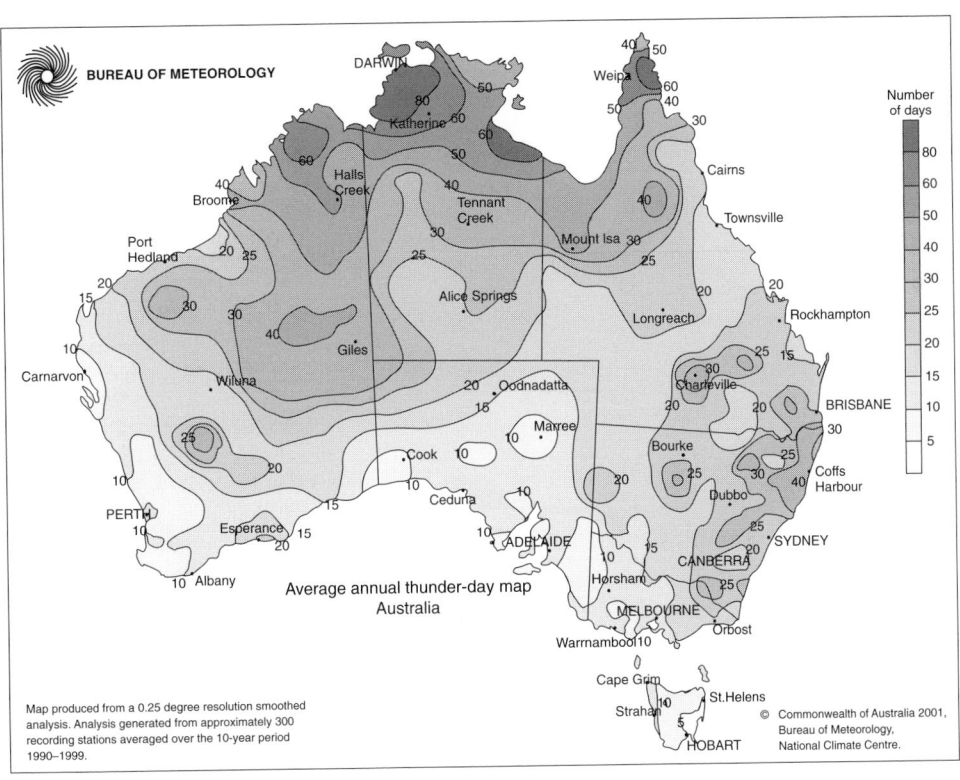

42.7 *Average annual thunder days in Australia*

tourists concerned about humidity and clear skies, skiers wanting snow) or broken down into a longer definitive list. The Bureau of Meteorology, Australia, produces a range of maps showing different criteria, Figures 42.6–42.9.

2.3 Climate change

Climate Change 2007, the Fourth Assessment Report (AR4) of the United Nations Intergovernmental Panel on Climate Change (IPCC), offers authoritative assessment of climate change implications for the tropics:

- low-lying island nations may be overcome by rising sea levels;
- future tropical cyclones (typhoons and hurricanes) are expected to become more intense, with larger peak wind speeds and more heavy precipitation, but the number of cyclone events may decrease overall;
- increase in drought in the centre of large continental land masses;
- increases in temperature;
- increasing unpredictabilty of weather patterns.

The report also anticipates 'substantial reduction in regional differences in per capita income' which will drive an expanding

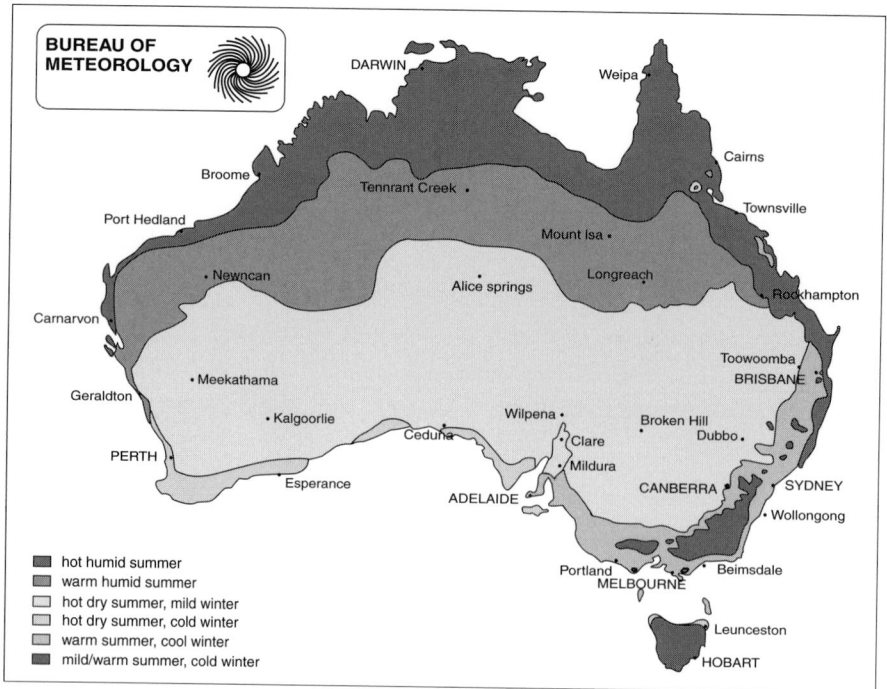

42.8 *Map based on temperature and humidity only*

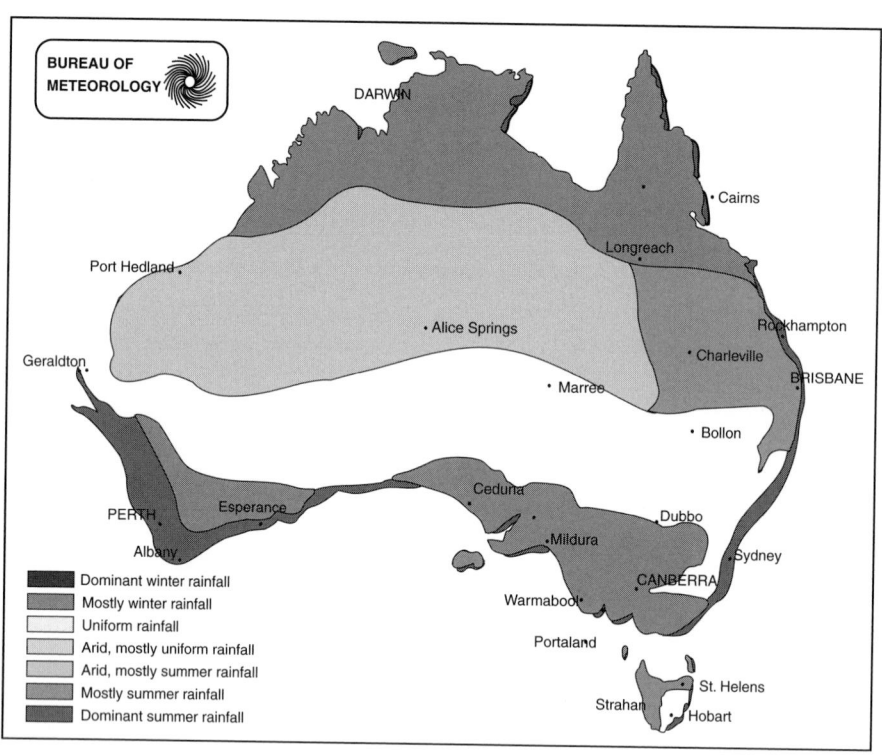

42.9 *Map based on rainfall only*

construction programme needing more resources and technological input.

2.4 Site selection

Sites and the detailed siting of individual buildings should primarily be chosen to maximise human comfort. Efficient performance of the building should follow from this.

Buildings should be sited:

- close to, and downwind of, large heat sinks such as forests, rivers or lakes, which lower temperature and screen the site from airborne dust and noise, Figure 42.10;
- remote from major traffic routes and those industries which generate heat, noise, pollution and smells, Figure 42.11;
- where they will be shaded by trees or other buildings during the hottest part of the day and/or the hottest times of the year;

- where they will take advantage of the prevailing breezes (wet and humid climates);
- where they will be screened from dust-laden winds and glare (hot arid climates);
- where they will not be subjected to solar dazzle from other buildings, Figure 42.12;
- where they will not maximise heat gain and glare reflected from bright external paving or adjacent buildings with pale reflective surfaces (high albedo – see Section 7.2).

2.5 Site characteristics

Altitude, aspect, insolation, gradient, prevailing wind, shelter, soil, geology, water table, vegetation, existing structures, archaeology and ecology may all be important. Traditional uses of the site, for grazing, footpaths or cultivation, may all need negotiation. Crops on a site may need to be reimbursed to their full value if destroyed, or allowed time to be harvested.

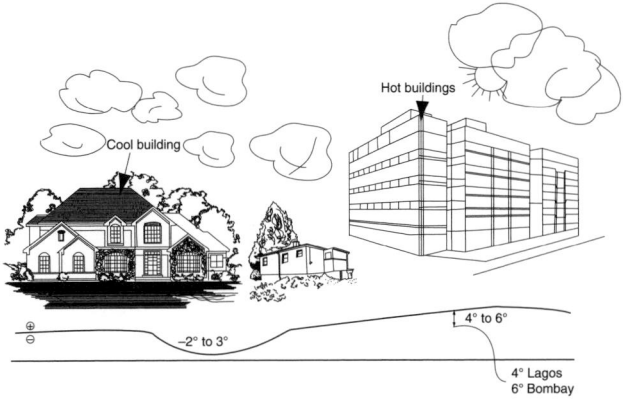

42.10 *Site buildings downwind of heat sinks*

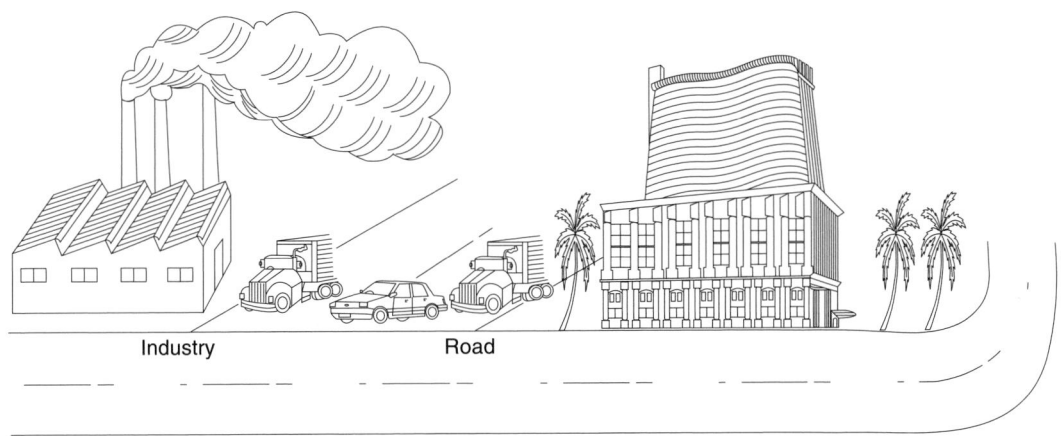

42.11 *Site buildings well away from busy roads and industry*

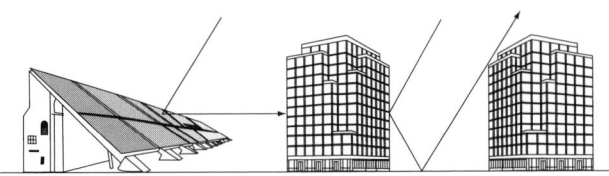

42.12 *Solar dazzle off sloping glazed facades is more likely to be reflected horizontally into adjacent buildings or into the eyes of approaching drivers. Similarly, it is an offence in some countries to use uncoated metal sheeting on roofs, as it can temporarily blind airline pilots*

Pollution
Pollution and smells from tanneries and other industries, saltpans, open storm drains and sewers, contaminated water supplies and aerobic sewage treatment works may present serious problems in countries without environmental legislation.

Environmental impact
Even small projects may affect water supply, soil stabilisation, fragile flora and fauna, and local inhabitants and their patterns of agriculture. An environmental impact assessment may be required and should always be considered.

2.6 Site investigations and geotechnics

Soils and geotechnics
The site may present unfamiliar soil and ground conditions and behaviours. In southern Africa, for example, there are no glacial soils, there is much more igneous rock than elsewhere and the weathering of the ancient landmass has produced a much higher percentage of residual soils. Most of these soils are non-saturated and many are either of expansive or collapsing types where smaller structures need to be lightweight and flexible rather than heavy and rigid. Larger structures may need piled foundations. The absence of ground frost frees foundation design from some of the constraints that operate in cold climates, but other factors, such as soil type and seasonal cycles of saturation and desiccation, may present other problems. In many areas, tropical soils are thin and vulnerable to rapid erosion once tree-cover is removed or the surface exposed or cultivated. Soil stabilisation may be necessary, using planting, geo-membranes or gabions. It is rare to be working in a country that has not been extensively mapped geologically, however, and knowledge and expertise should be available.

Water supply
It may be impossible to ensure an adequate water supply throughout the year in dry or seasonally dry climates. There may be aquifers that can be tapped using wind pumps, but if water has to be piped over long distances or brought in by tanker, a scheme may become uneconomic. Ground water must be thoroughly tested by government or independent analysts to ensure that it is potable and free from contamination. (The widespread arsenic poisoning in Bangladesh is the worst of many examples of unforeseen contamination. This disaster arose from well-intentioned international aid intended to improve health by stopping people drinking contaminated surface water. Four million tubewells were sunk – into contaminated ground.)

Water table and flooding
The water table may fluctuate seasonally or be altered by other constructional or civil engineering work in the vicinity. Flash flooding

may be a risk in any dried out riverbed or low-lying area and roads may become impassable very quickly. Take advice, have up-to-date weather information and be alert to distant thunder.

Earthquakes and hot springs

World seismic data and geothermal activity are well recorded by the British Geological Survey and the US Geological Survey. Their web-based information is excellent.

Burial sites

Traditional burial sites may be unearthed in unexpected places, especially where the population is nomadic and the written record recent. All graves and religious sites must be treated with respect and local advice heeded. Burial sites may be indicated by the presence of particular tree species, or some other environmental marker.

Archaeological finds

Archaeological finds should be reported to local museum authorities. It may be wise when excavating a virgin site to take advice as to what to be looking out for, as remains or other finds may take unfamiliar forms, ranging from dinosaur eggs, through gemstones to rock paintings.

2.7 Culture and religion

Cultural and religious criteria

Many questions must be asked if they are germane to building design:

- Is the society homogeneous or divided on ethnic, political, religious or economic lines?
- Are there minority demands which have to be met?
- Are there strict gender-based criteria?
- Are there strict taboos with regard to personal hygiene and the butchering and eating of meat?
- Are some castes isolated?
- Do holy days vary?
- Does the workplace have to make provision for specific religious or social practices?
- Will shrines be required?
- Is Feng Shui practised?

Historical factors

Colonial procedures can be very persistent in former colonies including the former and present members of the (British) Commonwealth and in Francophone Africa, and the former American, Portuguese, Dutch and German colonies. Government and legal processes, the police, the army and a wide variety of social practices will all reflect the past administrators to a greater or lesser degree – as will the past and, sometimes, the present architecture.

Social and ethical criteria

Limited literacy or the absence of a common language may necessitate a different approach to building signage. If labour is cheap, buildings may need to accommodate the proliferation of servants, messengers and other service personnel that this permits. In some countries, they will be provided with residential accommodation on-site and will be able to keep their extended families there – with implications for power, water and sanitation provision.

2.8 Politics and economics

Business practices

Are people taking a siesta at midday, when the sun is overhead, but working later in the afternoons, when glare from low sun and solar gain are most difficult to keep out of buildings? Do meetings and other interactions require special facilities? Are there regular group activities (Tai Chi, mid-morning coffee, emergency drills) that need special spaces?

Political factors

Political instability and conflicting political, ethnic, religious or tribal agendas may influence design and affect the buoyancy of the construction industry.

External aid and funding

International debt repayment agreements may skew local economies and suppress regeneration; purchases of military hardware from the more aggressive vendors in this field have been particularly bruising. In the recent past, newly independent countries received large amounts of unconditional project funding as donor governments sought to keep undesirable influences from the Communist bloc, Cuba or China out of vulnerable and potentially unstable areas. Much of this aid was designed to provide employment in the donor country (… you will use our architects, our materials, our equipment …) with little regard for local expertise, culture or long-term viability: funding provided vehicles, but not the means of servicing them; hospitals, but not the staff to run them.

More recently, the more enlightened donors have started to move out of providing buildings and into support for sustainable, self-help projects that are intended to support local industries and generate wealth. Things still go wrong however – the never-ending stream of cheap second-hand clothing that charities are sending into Africa has destroyed the textile industry in several countries and stripped thousands of self-employed tailors of custom.

2.9 Construction industry, job management and professional expertise

Labour skills and costs

International price guides are now available for most countries and provide a good guide as to good local materials, cost peculiarities, materials that are difficult to source, labour rates and other cost indicators. It is important for architects to be familiar with local skills and use them, rather than to impose imported techniques that they are familiar with but local craftsmen are not.

Transport, accessibility and infrastructure

Transport can present many unforeseen problems on construction projects: vehicle availability, spares, maintenance, drivers, insurance, risks, road safety, road conditions, bad weather, roadblocks (official and unofficial) and drivers using official vehicles as unofficial, uninsured taxis.

Access and travelling

Is the country easy to get into and out of? Are permits, interpreters, guides, cost of flights, taxis, trains, buses or car hire required? It is important to develop local contacts and networks, using embassies, professional bodies and other agencies.

Project management strategies

Will these be local, international, co-partnership; via phone, fax or online?

Planning applications

Planning and other statutory procedures may be Anglophone, Francophone … or Byzantine. Local guidance is essential. Professional accreditation may be instantly available or complex and lengthy to obtain.

Cost

Costs will be unfamiliar and cost advice from resident consultants will be essential.

2.10 Resources and technologies

Utilities and services

Incoming services may include water (potable and recycled 'grey water'), electricity, telecommunications (including satellite and data services) oil and gas. Availability, reliability, method of reticulation and system type all need to be determined. In many countries, the very low density of new urban development imposes great strain on current and future services reticulation. Outgoing services – sewerage (mains and septic tank), storm drains and refuse – may also require non-standard design solutions. In areas without supply, alternatives must be considered.

Construction industry resources
Availability and reliability of materials, tools, plant, water supplies, resources, labour, skills, crafts, expertise, organisational structures, technologies and reliability of utility supplies will all affect the construction process, as will seasonal or climate events that affect employment, restrict transport movement or materials production, or stop construction (groundwork may not be possible during the rainy season). Local craftsmen may be adept in special applications of trades such as plastering and rendering, which have been lost in much of Europe or the USA. Scaffolding might use bamboo – a material worth exploring for a wide range of applications.

Alternative power sources
Water (hydro and wave), wind or solar power may be feasible. Grid-connected building-integrated photovoltaics (BIPV) are becoming more efficient and better documented.

Sustainability
The terms may differ – sustainable, ecological, 'green' – but the principles remain.
  Good building design:

- should 'touch the earth lightly' by minimising use of nonrenewable fossil fuels in collecting, manufacturing, transporting or using building materials;
- should reduce the need for the power derived from these fossil fuels in heating, lighting, ventilation and cooking by using passive design strategies in buildings and
- lifestyle and working practices should reduce the need to consume excessive energy in transport, workplace, leisure or entertainment.
- In the longer view, this should affect urban planning, the nature of residential development, the reticulation of services and the policies of central governments.

Sustainable strategies to consider include:

- use local materials – but don't consume beyond the capacity to regenerate;
- make use of local waste products;
- use passive design;
- recycle energy;
- restrict water consumption.

Appropriate technology
It is dangerous to make assumptions about suitable solutions: two neighbouring countries may appear similar in terms of climate, environment and socio-political culture, but may have very different construction industries. One may have good labour, traditional brick-making skills, popular decorative traditions, and use steel extensively, whilst its neighbour has no masonry construction, but builds in cement block and reinforced concrete. One may welcome low-tech solutions; another might be insulted by them. Clay ovens, sisal-reinforced roofing sheets and modern pit-latrines may work wonderfully but are unlikely to satisfy people wanting to come up to speed in the modern world. Indeed, these solutions are most effective when offered to refugees from that modern world, who wish to experience the 'bush' for a week or two. A technology is only appropriate if people want it.

Transferable technologies
High-tech buildings in temperate climates now use design strategies that originated in the tropics (cooling towers, vented ridges, brises soleil). These sometimes perform less well than expected, as temperature variation is not sufficiently extreme to generate air movement, but when updated and reinterpreted in the tropics, they should work more efficiently. Conversely, temperate climate details (such as thermal insulation) can benefit tropical design, especially in composite climates at higher altitudes.

2.11 Environmental design

Environmental comfort within the building
Comfort depends on responding to climate specifics – humidity, seasonal variations that relate to altitude, prevailing winds and rainfall patterns, and the site and its environs. Do not forget that higher altitudes inland can get very cold overnight in the cold season – some areas have snow and frost; houses in the centres of large land masses and at altitudes over 1000 m often need room-heating fires in the sitting rooms and to take advantage of solar gain in winter. Effective passive solar design is an essential component of good design.

Environmental design around the building
Shading, restriction or enhancement of air movement, placement and type of landscaping, the use of water, reflectivity of surfaces, glare, screening against noise or dust and seasonal storm protection may all be important. Adjacent buildings may produce solar dazzle, block air movement or cast shade when it is most wanted. Public and private spaces, including car parking, may influence light levels, glare and general amenity.

Performance of the building envelope in the context of the local climate
Buildings may have to withstand torrential driving rain, lightning, cyclones, hurricanes, sandstorms, very high temperatures, extreme diurnal temperature variations with associated extremes of thermal movement, persistent high humidity, extended dry periods or salt-laden atmospheres, Figure 42.13. Structures that are elevated to catch the breeze will need additional structural measures to withstand high winds.

2.12 Flora, fauna and biohazards

Tropical diseases and infections
With climate change, global public health is declining as tropical diseases and their carriers spread into new areas where populations do not have natural immunities. The World Health Organisation offers current information on the following diseases on its website: Leishmaniasis, Onchocerciasis, Chaga's disease, Leprosy, Tuberculosis, Schistosomiasis (Bilharzia), Lymphatic filiariasis, Malaria, African trypanosomiasis (Sleeping sickness) and Dengue.

Snakes, spiders and flying insects
Find out whether the habitat offered by the site suits any venomous snakes and spiders. If it does, make personnel aware of the appropriate remedial treatment for bites. Be aware of any risks of diseases, including water-borne diseases and of diseases transmitted by insects. Any stagnant or still standing water may carry diseases or their mechanisms of transmission (such as bilharzia in Africa). Bees and wasps may be very aggressive and inclined to swarm in roof voids. Cockroaches can be difficult to eradicate.

Mosquitoes
Mosquitoes are endemic in the tropics, and several species are capable of transmitting a range of diseases (malaria is the most widespread) by transferring infected blood from one person they have bitten to the next. Recently, the increased incidence of

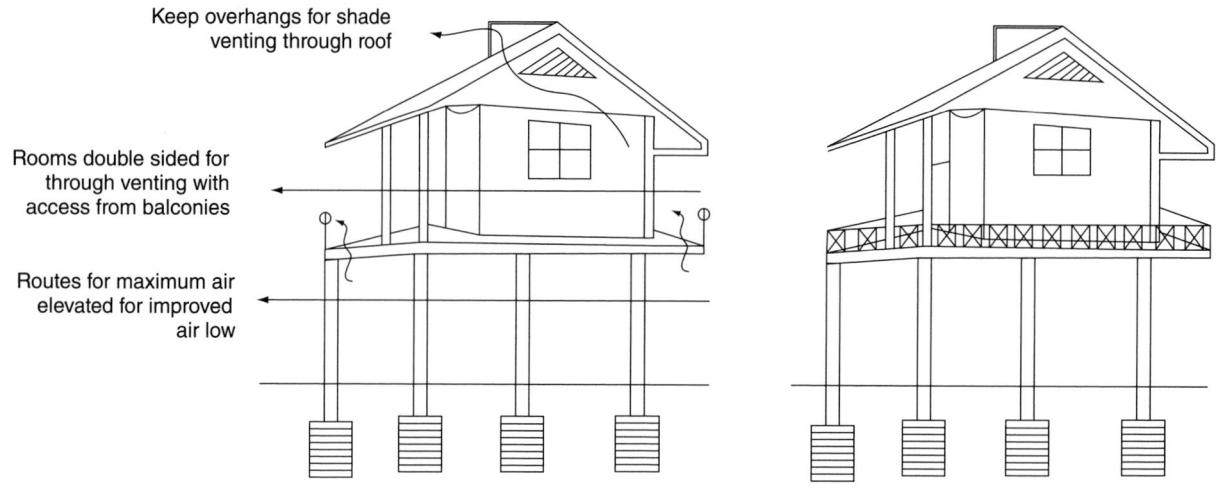

Keep overhangs for shade
venting through roof

Rooms double sided for
through venting with
access from balconies

Routes for maximum air
elevated for improved
air low

Structure strengthened & braced to resist extra
loading from elevated position in cyclonic condition

42.13 *Structures that are raised on platforms or pilotis may need strengthening to withstand strong winds*

the more extreme forms of malaria (Blackwater fever, cerebral malaria) has been accompanied by hardening resistance to the known treatments; so prophylactic medication regimes and technical solutions need greater vigilance. Government health departments, tropical disease hospitals (most countries with a colonial past or significant immigration from the tropics will have tropical expertise) and national airlines can advise on precautions. See Section 6.8 for guidance on design strategies to keep mosquitoes at bay.

Many tropical climates have cyclical patterns of temperature and rainfall variation, such as El Niño, that recur over a number of years. These cycles will affect the water table and extent of open water created and, when wet phases are linked to high temperatures, there will be epidemics of diseases linked to mosquitoes and other water-breeding insects. In Australia, outbreaks of Murray Valley encephalitis occur at the peaks in the Southern Oscillation Index, which coincides with El Niño years.

Larger mammals
In rural areas, wild animals can cause problems, as can free-ranging livestock. Hippos leave the water to go night-grazing, elephants strip bark from trees and feeding monkeys cause a lot of willful damage.

Wood-boring insects
Structural timber and timber furniture may be at risk of disfiguring borer attack.

Termites
The presence of termites, Figure 42.14, may only be apparent if they are of the type that constructs mounds or 'anthills'. Termites can penetrate small spaces and destroy constructional timbers very quickly. They will also destroy landscaping, stripping trees and shrubs of bark. Where they are prevalent, allowance should be made for the need to replace a percentage of all landscaping due to termite damage. Termites may affect the soil profile, leaving a distinctive line of stones at the lower limit of their activity.

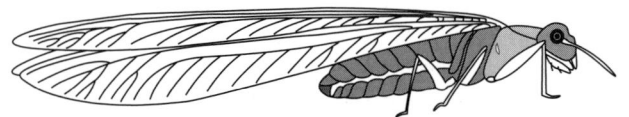

42.14 *Winged termite. Drawing copyright D G Mackean*

There are three main types of termites:

- *Dampwood termites* inhabit damp rotting logs or pockets of rot in dead or living trees. They obtain all the water they need from their habitat and do not need contact with the ground.
- *Drywood termites* are similar to wood-boring beetles found in temperate climates. They can fly into buildings or be introduced in previously infested timber. They can be deterred by the use of (expensive) naturally resistant timbers, by pre-treatment of timber with a wood preservative and by including physical barriers in the design, especially at roof level.
- *Subterranean termites* need to maintain contact with the ground and can survive in drier conditions than the drywood termites. They present the greatest risk to buildings. They can pass through fine cracks in slabs and mortar and construct mud galleries, linking their nest and a source of moisture underground with the cellulose food source within the building. Poorly ventilated, damp and dark spaces below floors and around the perimeter of the building will increase the risk of infestation. Landscaping can conceal activity, whilst disturbed soil or materials stored beneath the floor will facilitate it. Naturally resistant timber species are in short supply.

The options are to destroy the nest, and to use physical or chemical barriers. Low-pressure spraying of the ground with poison (usually the organophosphate chlorpyrifos or the pyrethroid bifenthrin) is generally considered the most effective treatment, but it must be continuous and not be compromised by later alterations or additions to the structure. In Australia, a fine-gauge stainless steel mesh is used as a barrier in any location, including below the floor slab. Smooth exposed faces of ground floor slabs (minimum 75 mm) assist detection and if constructed with sharp exposed corners, can deter termites, Figure 42.15.

Materials used in the floor slab and lower courses of walls, including hardcore, building sand, mortar and render, are also usually poisoned with a pitch-based sealing compound and effective sealing of all cracks, joints and holes is essential. Termite shields are also used, but can be bridged and will become corroded, needing replacement. Chemical use should be by licensed persons who can also destroy nests by blowing arsenic trioxide into the colony using a hand blower. Regular inspection is essential.

2.13 Other essential design data

Design philosophy and practice
Be sensitive to local and regional practices and procedures, without producing a pastiche of the vernacular tradition.

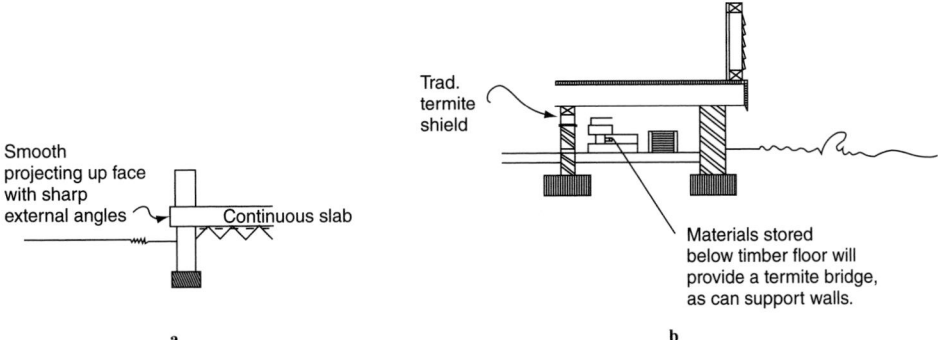

42.15 *Ground floor design can deter or encourage termites: a ground-bearing concrete floors; b suspended timber floor*

Anthropometrics and ergonomics
European anthropometrics data tends to be out of date (we have got taller and bigger); elsewhere, particular tribal and ethnic groups may have distinctly different characteristics, especially with regard to height and reach. If there is no data available, arrange for a local agency to obtain it, rather than trying to do it yourself – you might unwittingly cause offence.

Disabled access
Policies will vary, as will the numbers of disabled, especially in current and former war zones. Polio may also have left its mark.

Special factors in the design of the spaces around the building
National attitudes to land ownership, landscaping, public access, vehicular access and the use of public art can vary greatly. In some areas where there are no public facilities, indeterminate public spaces and open drains may be used as latrines.

Security
Abductions, muggings, desecrations or petty thefts may be problems that constrain design. Diplomats, and some nationals in particular, can feel extremely vulnerable and demand extreme measures, including 'safe rooms'. Burglar bars and other security measures may restrict means of escape in case of fire, boundaries may be marked by high walls topped with razor-wire enclosing a patrolled *cordon sanitaire*, and gates may be protected by armed guards.

Landscape design
Plant availability, local knowledge and expertise vary from country to country – look at the landscaping of public buildings to gauge attitudes and possibilities. There may be some protection of indigenous flora and restrictions on exotic (imported) species. Throughout most of the tropics, previous colonial administrators and later horticulturalist and landscape architects have imported species from all parts of the world. These can homogenise tropical landscaping and there is a move towards using indigenous species.

Irrigation may be a problem, in which case species that are drought-resistant must be used in dry or seasonally dry climates, where plantings needing irrigation should be restricted to designated 'watered' beds. Landscaping should support the environmental agenda of the building design – shade, air-flow, cooling, etc.; soft landscaping can harbour insects, snakes, and vermin and, as a consequence, some clients may insist there is no planting close to the building. Irrigation will cool the air but raise humidity.

Rainwater dispersal
In any climate where there are frequent heavy rains, it is inappropriate to fit the small gutters and down-pipes that are normally used in temperate climates. A short rainstorm may well cause a flash flood and the conventional solution in some countries is to discharge water from overhanging eaves into open dish drains which convey the water to large open storm drains which increase rapidly in width and depth as more inlets are added. It is imperative that these all drain effectively, without leaving standing water in which mosquitoes, bilharzia (*schistosomiasis*) and other diseases and bacteria can flourish. In public buildings and cities, where gutters normally will be used, they must be able to carry the heaviest rainfall or be able to overflow without causing damage or nuisance.

2.14 Desk study
It is essential that all these issues be investigated in a thorough desk study before detailed design work begins. Additionally, there will be an enormous range of built and documentary evidence, knowledge, expertise and experience within the country that can be invaluable in ensuring that an appropriate design solution is found. The architect who ignores this will compound the resentment of skilled local architects who have been overlooked when the commission to design the building was awarded. By including local expertise within the team, a whole range of subtle local factors may emerge, greatly enhancing the outcome.

3 CLIMATE-RESPONSIVE DESIGN: CLIMATE TYPES

3.1 Bioclimatic design
A careful evaluation of traditional and current aesthetic and technological local solutions will help to define the important design issues. In particular, if there is a highly evolved, almost iconic traditional building form, a detailed analysis of this form may prove particularly rewarding. Modern buildings and urban planning have usually derived from Western models and have not always been successful in resolving environmental problems or addressing social needs. The intention should be to reinterpret and add value to proven successful solutions, or to come up with different solutions that respond more effectively to changes in conditions or scale. A clear understanding of the issues and options is essential.

The international style of architecture seen around the world today is based on temperate-climate models and, like vernacular dry and arid climate architectures, it is enclosed, contained and defensive – based on solid geometry. Architecture in humid and composite climates, however, is often a fluid, unconstrained space under a canopy where people move in and out – through voids defined only by their upper surface. There is little physiological differentiation between being 'inside' and being 'outside' under a shady tree. In wall-less spaces, dramatic roof forms can make a much stronger statement.

In climates where much of daily life is conducted outside, it is common for buildings to take the form of a series of pavilions set in parkland and linked by covered walkways. In more congested sites, and where security is important, links between buildings may be semi-enclosed breeze-ways, walled with *brises-soleil* or some other form of defensive trelliswork.

Table VI Climate responsive design strategies – hot dry desert climates (Baghdad, Alice Springs, Phoenix)

Indicators	Measurements	Design response
Latitudes	Between 15° and 30°N and S	Establish sunpath data; use to determine position of windows and other features
Location – within continental land mass	Altitude	
High daytime temperatures (up to 50°C), and cold nights (clear skies permit re-radiation of daytime solar gain)	Monthly mean maximum and minimum temperatures	Deep shade and high thermal mass with time lag to release warmth during cold night
High diurnal range		Stone and tiled floors will stay cool if fully shaded Use sound and sight of water for psychological cooling during the day
Low humidity, dry air	Average monthly relative humidity (RH) (from monthly mean maximum and monthly mean minimum) 10–55%	Use water for evaporative cooling
Low rainfall (precipitation)	Annual rainfall (range 50–155 mm)	Flat roofs, no gutters Provide for cleaning dust off the building envelope, especially windows
Two seasons, one hot, one cooler or cold	Monthly mean maximum and minimum temperatures	Use reduced solar altitude in winter to capture and store solar energy in trombe walls and on high mass paved floors. Reduce shading to permit solar gain in structure. Stabilise temperature with ground storage of water or energy.
Deep blue sky; glare from horizon worsens at end of dry season as dust in the atmosphere creates a haze	Solar radiation, luminance (1700–2500 cd/m², haze up to 10 000 cd/m²)	Small windows placed at high level with view of deep blue sky (not facing into the sun's path) Use screens to cut glare (jail, mesh, masrabiya) with smaller apertures at lower levels to cut glare from horizon.
Air movement will contain dust and sand; whirlwinds will occur	Wind speed	Ventilation strategies depend on cooling and filtering air

Indicators	Measurements	Design response
Arid landscape with drought-tolerant species or desert conditions	Rainfall	Landscaping will depend on drought-resistant species or irrigation – but water use may be costly or restricted. Low humidity will affect growth.
Sandstorms	Wind speed	Defensive land-forming and building envelope with tight-fitting infill of openings (windows, doors, shutters, storm guards) Air vents and filters will require regular cleaning.

Variation – hot dry maritime desert climate (Kuwait, Karachi)

Temperature – not as hot but with less seasonal variation)		
Relative humidity	50–90%	A particularly uncomfortable climate – encourage air movement with overhead fans. Air-conditioning may be needed.
Cloud cover – there may be a thin haze, causing glare	Sunshine hours per annum	
Local breezes, off the sea during the day, from the land at night	Wind speed	Orient openings to take advantage of daytime breezes.
Salty atmosphere – risk of corrosion	Distance from sea	Specify appropriate materials

Design solutions

Individual buildings	Buildings are inward looking and defensive with thick walls and small high windows. Building mass should be efficient with as little of the envelope exposed to the sun as possible, especially on the west where the afternoon sun is the hottest. Internal courtyards are widely used, with the use of water for evaporative cooling and decorative screens to cut down glare. Roofs, walls, windows, terraces and courtyards can be shaded with canopies or secondary structures.
Urban development	Buildings are packed close together – in particular, east and west facing party walls should be protected from the sun. This reduces travel distances – to markets, shops and services. Adopt strategies that reduce physical effort. Narrow streets running north–south will receive least sun. Wind towers catch the breezes and cool the air, drawing it over water into shaded courtyards.
Landscaping	Create an artificial oasis by contouring land and planting shelterbelts with drought-resistant species. If irrigation is possible, other species may be grown. Soil may have to be imported. If so, it will need stabilising and protection or the wind will take it away. Use water for functional, decorative and psychological benefits. Shade paved areas to cut down glare.

Generically, designers recognise three main climatic types: hot dry, hot wet and composite (with seasonal variation). In reality, most locations will have some seasonal variation and overlap with other types. Tables VI–VIII summarise the main indicators and design responses.

3.2 Design in hot dry and arid climates

The hot dry climate building needs to be ventilated whilst keeping out sand and dust, have a slow thermal response – achieved by high mass outer walls and should have small windows at high level, to cut down glare and solar gain, Figure 42.16. Traditional solutions achieve high mass by using thick walls of stone, air-dried mud bricks or rammed earth (*pisé de terre*). The unfired clay usually has a protective render or coating that will withstand occasional rain, provided it is repaired from time to time. Regional variations using the same materials can be quite distinctive – adobe in New Mexico, barrel vaults as used by Hassan Fathy in Egypt or tower houses in Iran. The same unfired materials recur in composite climates, but are protected from heavier, more persistent rain by deep overhangs,

being placed on raised floor platforms and being repaired every year. In the dry tropics, there is a flat roof, often used for sleeping in the hottest weather. Any dense material may be used for the thick outer wall. Choice of material and wall thickness will depend on the desired time lag of the thermal response.

3.3 Design for hot wet and humid climates

The main requirements here are to maximise ventilation, shade and protection from rain, and to have a thin-skinned rapid thermal response building envelope, Figure 42.17. The maritime equatorial climate exhibits little variation over the year.

3.4 Design for composite climates

A composite climate has distinct seasonal variation. A decision needs to be made as to priorities in terms of climate-response, Figure 42.18. The seasonal variation in sunpath can be used to vary building response to the different climatic conditions, supplemented by movable elements, insulation and mechanical heating or cooling systems.

Table VII Climate responsive design strategies - warm humid equatorial climates

(Lagos, Dar-es-Salaam, Colombo, Singapore, Djakarta, Quito)

Indicators	Measurements	Design response
Latitudes	Between 15°N and 15°S	High solar altitude with small seasonal variation enables specific shading solutions to be accurately designed; principal elevations should face north and south
Typical mean maximum daytime temperature 27–32°C and mean minimum at night 21–27°C; low diurnal range	Monthly mean maximum and minimum temperatures	Temperatures exacerbated by humidity – use thin-skinned structures to speed cooling and ventilation
		Design should include covered and fly-screened verandas, etc.
High humidity all year, around 75% but may range from 50 to close to 100%	Average monthly relative humidity (RH)	High humidity may necessitate the use of air-conditioners at night
High rainfall which may get heavier for a few months	Annual rainfall (range 2000–5000 mm)	Pitched roofs with deep overhangs; no gutters or wide gutters.
		Verandas, colonnades and covered walkways will provide protection from the rain.
Rainfall will increase insect nuisance (mosquitoes, etc.)		Verandas should be fly-screened
		Eliminate stagnant standing water and take other precautionary measures.
Little seasonal variation, with perhaps some increase in rainfall, wind or storm conditions from time to time	Precipitation, monthly mean maximum and minimum temperatures	Little need for seasonal variation in design use
Overcast sky persists; cloud cover varies between 60 and 90%. Glare is intensified by reflection off cloud and can be intense. Cloud traps warm air, preventing night	Sky cover and sunlight hours. Luminance range between heavy and bright overcast skies 850–7000 cd/m² radiation to sky.	Fly-screens, *brises soleil* and other screening devices will cut down glare, as will deep overhangs and verandas.
There is little wind movement, but gusts are occasionally recorded	Wind speed	Elevate buildings to maximise air movement; use louvre windows for maximum ventilation; rooms must have through ventilation.

Table VII (continued)

Indicators	Measurements	Design response
Lush landscape with tropical forests, buttressed trees and vines. Impoverished laterite soils produce vegetables with little mineral content.	Rainfall, albedo	Landscaping will need to be controlled or will become overgrown. Waterlogged sites may need draining or planting with appropriate species.

Variation – warm humid island climate (Caribbean, Philippines, Hawaii)

Indicators	Measurements	Design response
Daytime mean maximum 29–32°C and mean minimum at night 18–24°C. Small diurnal and annual temperature ranges.	Monthly mean maximum and minimum temperatures	
Relative humidity	55%–almost 100%	Assist ventilation with design
High rainfall; storms may be heavy; sea spray may be a nuisance	Annual rainfall 1250–1800 mm	Roofs must be well constructed
Skies are clear or with broken cloud except during storms.	Clear sky luminance 1700–2500 cd/m²	
Trade winds are regular; cyclones may be severe	Wind speed	Design for high winds
Salty atmosphere – risk of corrosion	Distance from sea	Specify appropriate materials

Design solutions

Individual buildings	Roofs must be robust to withstand heavy rain, and usually have deep overhangs to shed the rain; thin-walled structures with rapid thermal response (cooling) and cross-ventilation (avoid back-to-back rooms and central corridors – circulation can be via perimeter verandas); habitable verandas, some fly-screened; main axis east–west; windows face north and south; use clerestory windows, vented ridges and wind towers to improve ventilation; shade trees should have high canopy but not block ventilation below the eaves; position structures to catch the breeze; anticipate damp and mould, insects and vermin.
Urban development	Buildings should be positioned to obtain maximum ventilation; line buildings with verandas, colonnades and covered walkways.
Landscaping	Dramatic landscaping is possible, but beware of wind rock in trees close to buildings.

Table VIII Climate responsive design strategies – composite or monsoon climates

(New Delhi, Kano)

Indicators	Measurements	Design response
In large continental landmasses, close to the Tropics (23.5°N and S)	Latitude, altitude	Distance from equator results in seasonal variation and compromises in design
High daytime temperatures (up to 50°C), and cold nights (clear skies permit re-radiation of daytime solar gain)	Maximum and minimum temperatures	Design for different lifestyle, adjusted to suit climate; ensure daytime shade, night-time heat retention
High diurnal range		
Dry season humidity 20–55%; wet season humidity 55–95%	Average monthly relative humidity (RH)	If high humidity is short-lived, prioritise longer-term conditions, and use mechanical fans, etc.
Seasonal rainfall (monsoon) can be heavy and prolonged – up to 38 mm/h	Annual rainfall (range 500 – 1300 mm)	Pitched roofs with overhangs
Two seasons –hot-dry and warm-humid (21–43°C); further from equator, third season – cool-dry (4–27°C).	Monthly mean maximum and minimum	Include adjustable building elements; different spaces to suit different conditions; create micro-climate
Diurnal range up to 22°C		
Sky overcast during rains, clear deep blue during dry season, becoming dust-laden and hazy towards end of dry season	Solar radiation, luminance, cloud cover, sunshine days	Placement of windows; screening of windows

Table VIII (continued)

Indicators	Measurements	Design response
Monsoon winds strong and may come from different direction than winds at other times of the year; winds carry dust in dry season		Variable features; shutters and screens
Landscape changes appearance seasonally – lush in rains, becoming parched in dry season	Rainfall	Use drought-resistant species or irrigation
Termites are common	Anthills, nests	Use barriers, poison, appropriate design measures; expect high wastage.

Variation – Tropical upland climate (Bogota, Nairobi)

Indicators	Measurements	Design response
Upland zones	Altitude 900–1200 m	
Distance from the equator increases seasonal variation	Latitude	Design will need to meet winter conditions, as well as summer.
Temperature reduces with altitude; diurnal range large, ground frost may occur	Weather data	Open fires, winter solar gain
Rainfall often heavy – up to 80 mm/h	Precipitation + 1000 mm	Pitched roofs, deep overhangs, storm drains
Heavy dew at night; radiation heat loss at night may cause radiation fog; hail; thunder and lightning	Weather data	Lightning protection, thermal insulation

Design solutions

Individual buildings	Design depends on winter temperatures, duration of high humidity and duration of rains.
Urban development	Colonnades and arcades provide shelter from rain.
Landscaping	Many species will tolerate these climates, but may need irrigation unless resistant to seasonal drought. Risk of frost needs to be determined Termite damage can be considerable

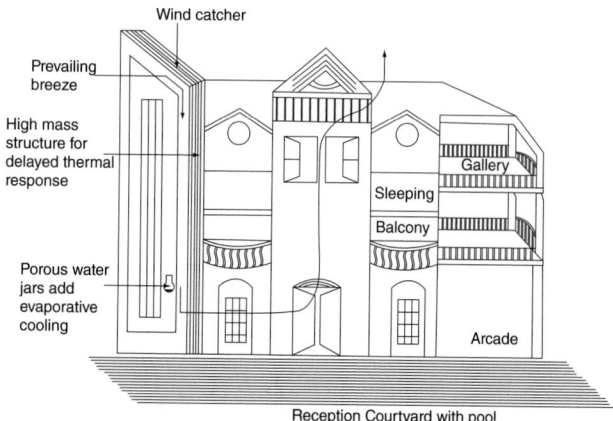

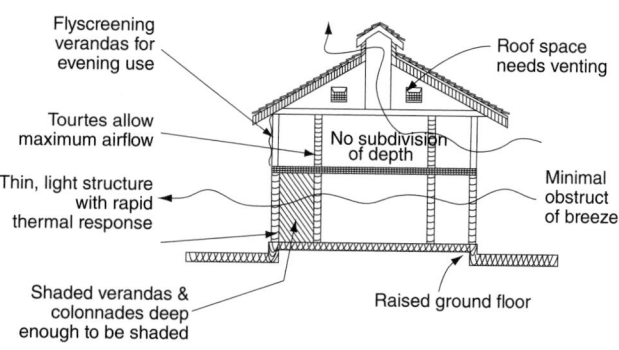

42.16 *The hot arid climate building is cool, shaded, and heat retaining. Its form prevents normal ventilation flows, so these must be induced by the use of wind-catching towers and wind vents, water placed strategically to provide evaporative cooling and the creation of temperature differentials within the central spaces to drive air movement*

42.17 *The hot humid climate building is airy, shaded and thin-skinned with a roof that can disperse torrential rain. All habitable rooms should have cross-ventilation*

4 ENVIRONMENTAL DESIGN STRATEGIES: PASSIVE DESIGN

4.1 General

There are two approaches to the provision of climate-responsive design – passive or active. Passive design is architect-driven and architectonic; it suits smaller, individual buildings, especially the one-off house; and it does not usually attract large research grants. Active design is the domain of the scientist and engineer: it is mathematical and appears more measurable; and it tends to attract government grants, the support of industry (there is a marketable product) and is used on prestige projects. In the 1980s, these two stances tended to polarise the specialists in this field, but today, there is more recognition that a mix of both is needed to get the best outcome. Design is becoming more integrated – and more pragmatic.

Passive design is the careful siting, orientation, design and detailing of buildings to ensure that maximum advantage is taken of aspect, sunlight, wind, contour and shelter to minimise dependency on fossil fuels and externally generated power, heat or artificial light, Figure 42.19. Passive solar design uses fixed elements

of the building fabric and its environs to manage solar radiation and optimise natural heating or cooling. The benefits of passive design are a more comfortable natural environment, reduced energy consumption, reduced costs, lower maintenance and long-term viability as a building which will meet future higher energy regulations and which will remain economic to run as fuel prices increase. This topic is covered extensively in academic websites worldwide. Many of these are illustrated with regional design solutions.

4.2 Shading

The best way to control solar radiation is to use external shading. This must be designed with a thorough understanding of sunpath data, obtained with the aid of sun path diagrams and a shadow angle protractor (Section 7.1). Shading of buildings, windows and internal courtyards can reduce the cooling load on buildings and alter ventilation, glare and daylight levels. It may affect views out of the building.

Passive shading, Figures 42.20, 42.21, may be achieved using:

- landscaping
- free-standing structures
- pergolas, porches, verandas and colonnades (Section 3.7)
- structural elements
- non-structural elements of the building envelope.

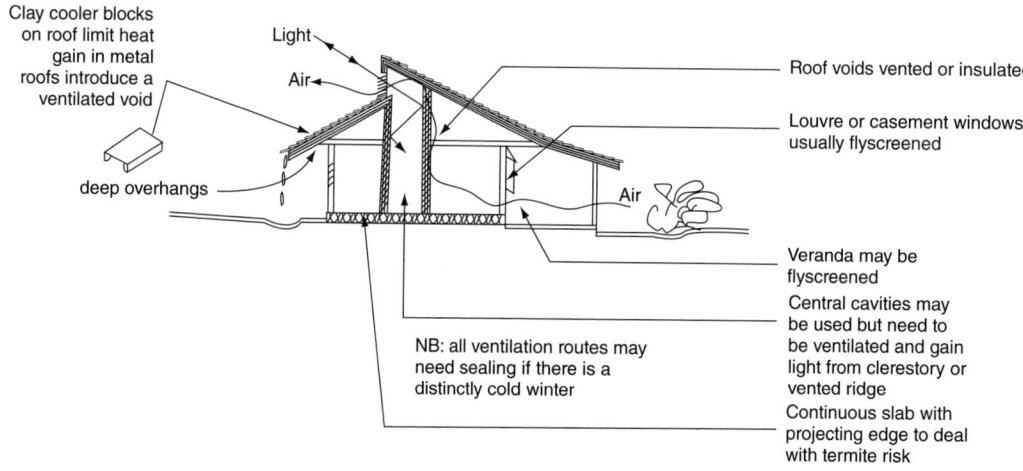

42.18 *The composite climate: different regions have different solutions depending on climate variables. This example is based on typical housing in Malawi at altitudes of 1000m. These houses are provided with an open fire in the sitting room. Cooler blocks are fired clay U-profile blocks loose-laid over profiled aluminium metal sheeting. They keep the worst of the solar radiation off the aluminium and create a ventilated space between the block and the roof-covering. Pitch is usually no more than 27.5°*

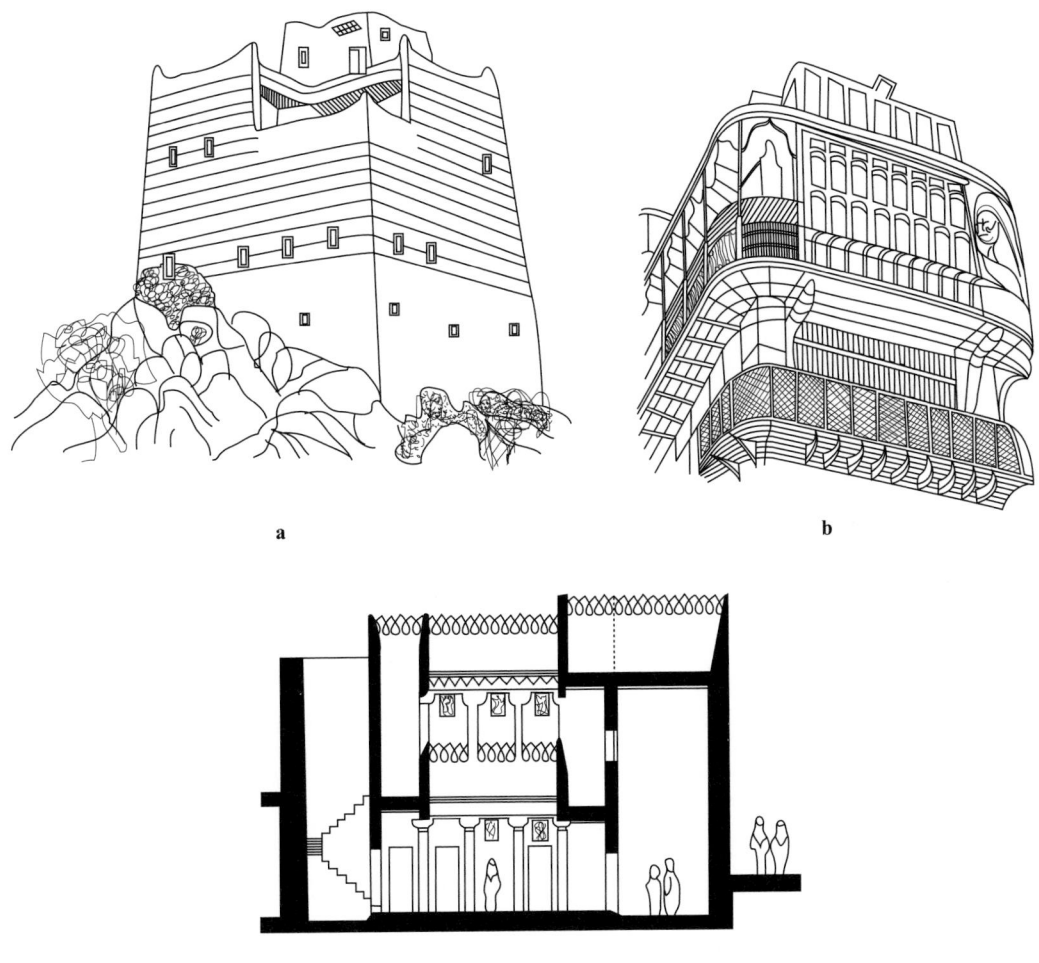

a   b

c

42.19 *Passive design in the hot arid tropics: a thick-walled defensive structures with small, high-level window apertures keep out heat, glare and dust; b traditional timber mashrabiÿa provide shaded and screened views into urban streets; c interiors are shaded and arcaded, with inner courtyards*

a *Landscaping*   **b** *Free-standing structures*   **c** *Porches, colonnades and pergolas*   **d** *Structural elements*   **e** *Non-structural elements*

42.20 *Passive shading options*

Passive shading elements, Figure 42.22, include:

- light shelves
- egg-crates
- screens (jail, mashrabiÿa, metal grillages, cascading planting on wire framing)
- overhangs
- fins.

Active shading, Figure 42.23, may be provided by:

- manually controlled awnings and blinds
- automatically controlled awnings and blinds
- shutters – which may be removable
- independent and temporary canopies.

A recent project at Valletta in Malta has a sealed glazed roof that opens in hotter weather, Figure 42.24.

4.3 Porches, pergolas, balconies, verandas and colonnades

Any shaded or covered space around the edges of buildings or around internal courtyards will act as a transitional space which, depending on its particular function, can be seen as an extension of habitable space or as a barrier or a bridge between public and private space. In all cases, this shaded space will moderate temperature, keeping the sun off the main structure and maintaining a more consistent temperature in the interior. This interior will be glare-free and relatively dark, unless lit by clerestory windows, a split ridge, light scoops or light pipes, Figure 42.25. (Light pipes are highly polished metal tubes that reflect light gathered via a

External devices to protect buildings from direct sunlight

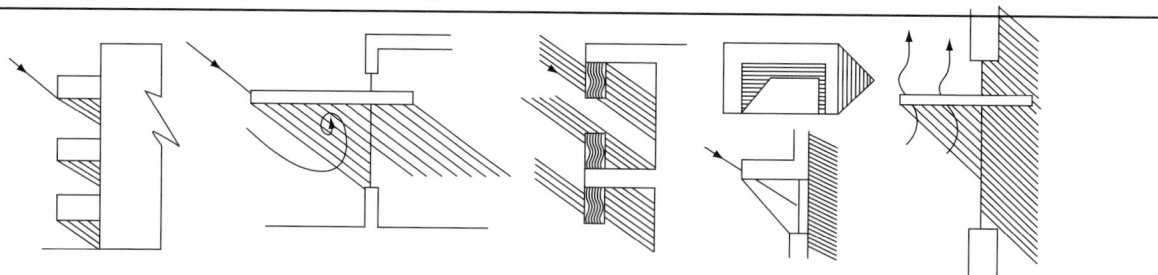

a External shading: *Balconies, light shelves, screening walls, window hoods, brises soleil, and other structural devices will provide shade, but should be designed not to trap heat.*

b Soft landscaping: *Trees may shade the roof, driveways, patios – the larger the better. Transpiration is evaporative cooling. All trees with foliage at high level permit low air movement.*

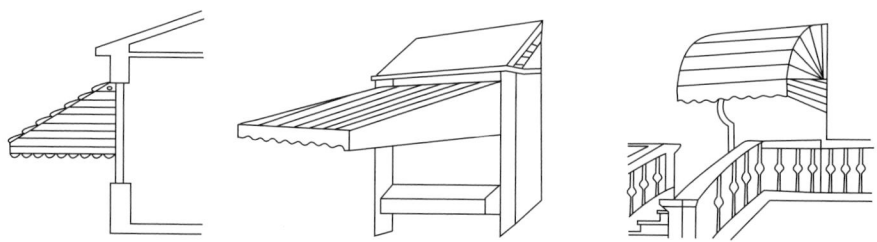

c Awnings: *Awnings are decorative, relatively cheap and adjustable. They block part of the view, can trap air and may suffer mechanical damage.*

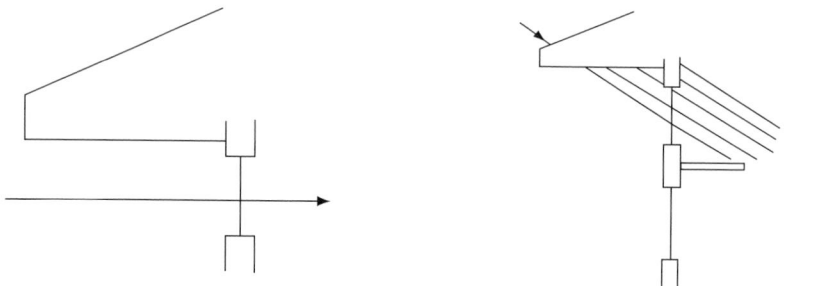

d Deep overhangs: *Overhangs do not provide relief for east and west-facing windows that face low sun. They will not shade the ground floor windows on a two-storey building.*

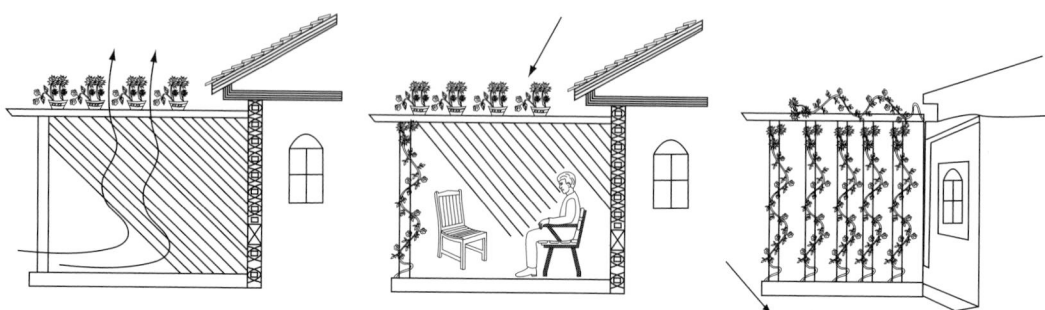

e Pergolas and trellises: *These permanent structures provide shade; climbing plants add evaporative cooling. If air conditioners and other electrical equipment are shaded, it improves their performance.*

42.21 *Passive shading devices (continued over)*

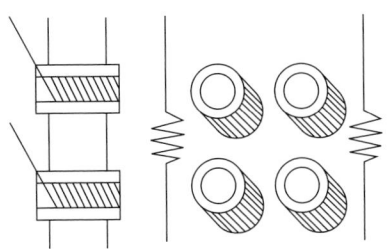 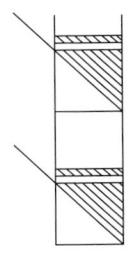 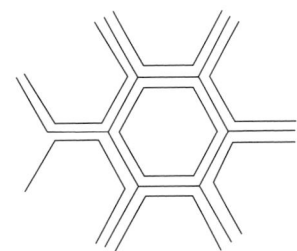

f Screen walling and 'egg crates': *Perforated screen walling can admit light and breezes whilst keeping out the sun and ensuring security.*

Devices at or within the window to protect from direct sunlight.

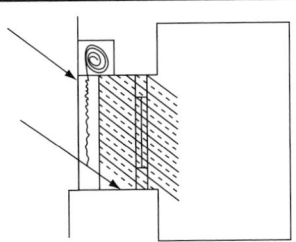 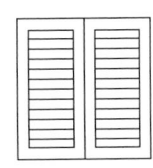 

g Louvres and shutters: *External louvres and shutters will be more effective than internal ones. Metal shutters will become very hot and radiate heat into the building. The louvres on American shutters can be adjusted to retain some view and admit light whilst completely blocking the sun.*

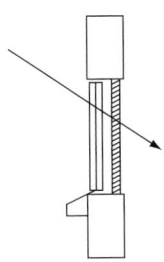 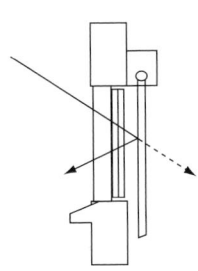

h Venetian blinds, etc: *Internal Venetian or roller blinds, or curtains (sheer or heavy drapes) should have a pale lining facing out to reflect heat back out of the window, fit tightly to prevent heat dispersing into the room, cover the whole window, and, for maximum effect, be made in a insulating material.*

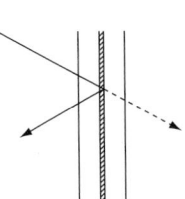

i Special glass: *A wide range of solar control glass is available, in grey, gold, green, blue and pink tints, usually applied as the filling in a laminated sandwich. Outlook will be affected by the colour of the tint and degree of light reduction.*

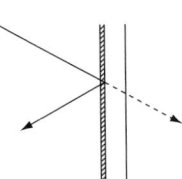

j Special films applied to the glass: *Plastic films containing gold and other minerals can be applied to achieve a wide range of effects. They are comparatively expensive and affect the outlook from the building.*

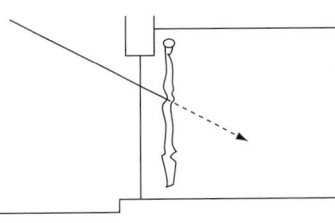

k *Curtains – sheers: Sheers will reduce glare, but will not significantly reduce solar gain.*

Devices to enhance light transmission (and reduce glare)

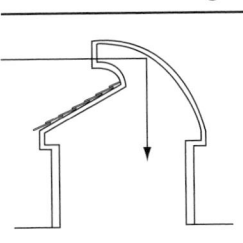 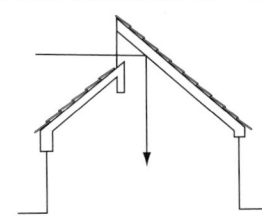

l *Light scoops*

m *Sunpipes*

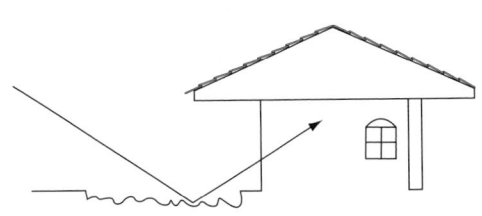

n *Water*

42.21 *Passive shading devices (contd.)*

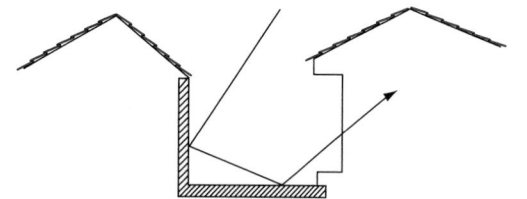

o *Bright external surfaces*

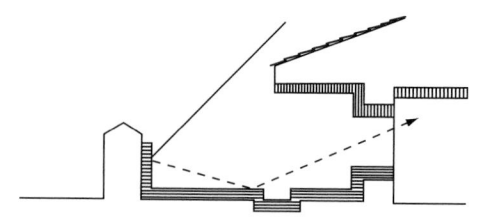

s *Colour – outside and in window frame and reveal*

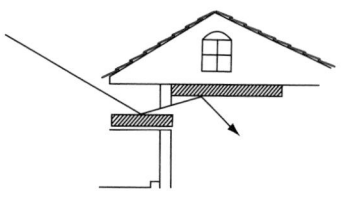

p *Reflectors*

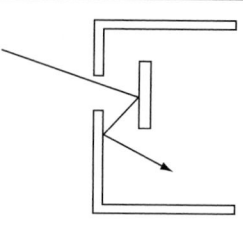

t *Light baffles*

White paint not used – take the 'bite' out of white by adding a touch of a dark colour.

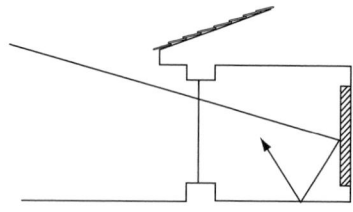

q *Mirrors*

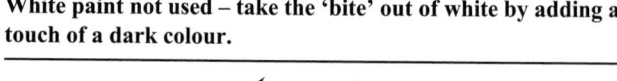
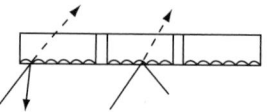

u *Light absorbing or deflecting glass or glass blocks*

Devices to reduce brightness and glare

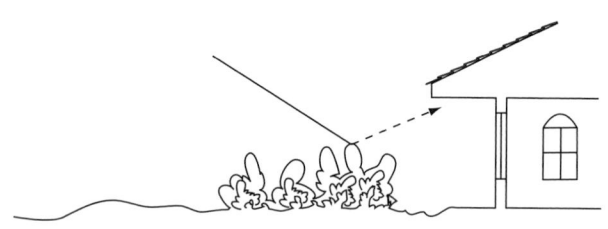

r *Planting*

v *Screen walling*

42.21 *Passive shading devices (contd.)*

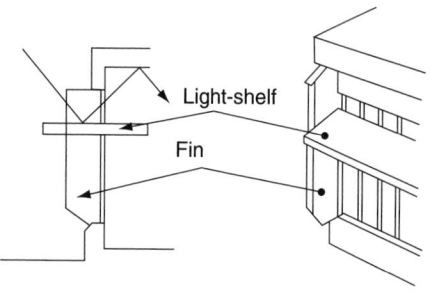

Light-shelf

Fin

Egg crates

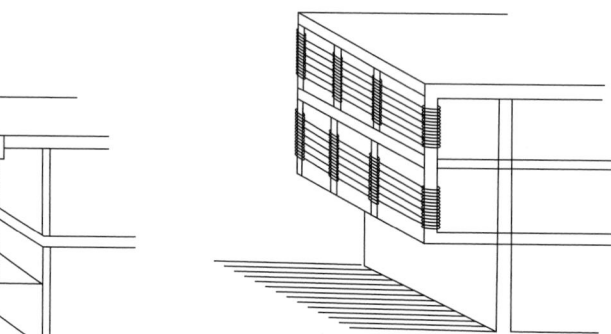

Metal grillage on screen

Planting trained on tensioned wires provides shade & allows air movement

42.22 *Passive shading at windows must be designed to suit the sun path:*

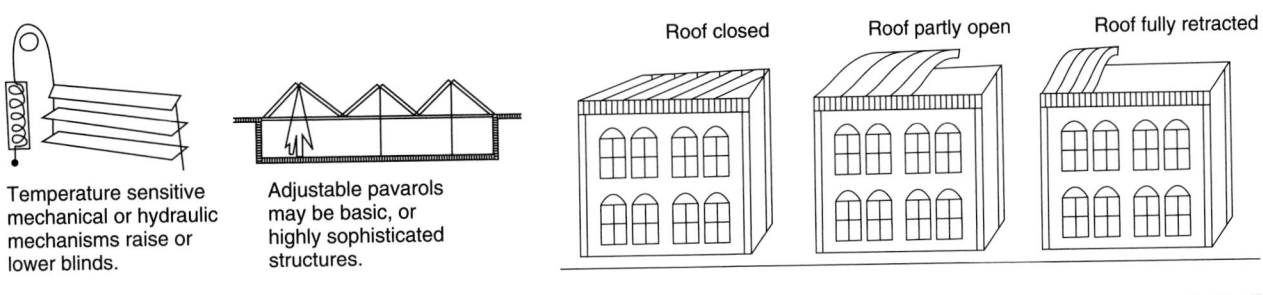

Temperature sensitive mechanical or hydraulic mechanisms raise or lower blinds.

Adjustable pavarols may be basic, or highly sophisticated structures.

Roof closed   Roof partly open   Roof fully retracted

42.23 *Active shading devices are movable or adjustable, using techniques ranging from simple manual actions to very sophisticated computer controlled mechanisms that respond to changes in temperature or light intensity*

42.24 *The Manoel theatre, Valletta, Malta by Architecture Project has a retractable sealed, glazed roof over an inner courtyard that folds back in hot weather*

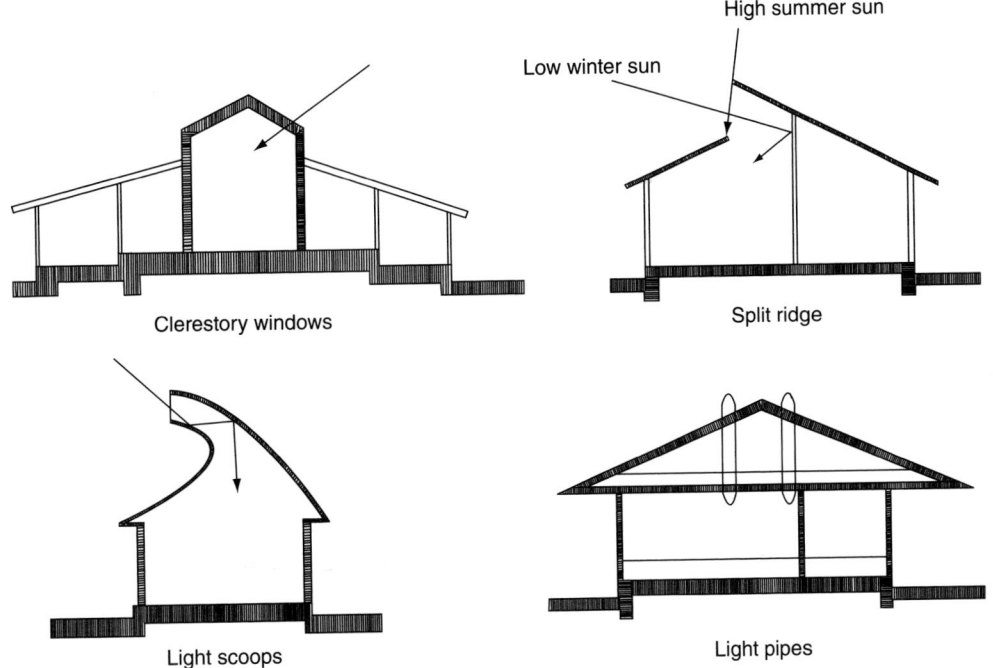

Clerestory windows

High summer sun
Low winter sun
Split ridge

Light scoops

Light pipes

42.25 *Light-gathering strategies for dark interiors, all of which can be vented: clerestory windows, split ridge, light scoops and light pipes*

Perspex dome at roof level and discharged via a similar inverted dome diffuser into a dark interior space, Figure 42.26. They are economical, efficient and effective.)

The dark interior may be gloomy in cold weather, except when low winter sun penetrates to the inner walls, but this darkness is psychologically cooling and pleasant, provided that it does not necessitate the use of artificial light during the day.

The effectiveness of these shade-giving spaces will depend on orientation, latitude, depth, prevailing breezes and width/height ratio, Figure 42.27. In all hot climates, verandas may become the main living spaces for most of the year, and any building design should recognise the social and environmental importance of these spaces. Except in balconies to individual bedrooms, the covered space should have sufficient depth to allow a group of people to sit around a small table (private houses) or to allow people to work or promenade in comfort (public colonnades). The depth of shade should be sufficient to enable the anticipated activity to be carried out in comfort, Figure 42.28.

The iconic colonial bungalow has a veranda on all four elevations, with each one being used at different times of the day or year, Figure 42.29. In all climates with a marked seasonal variation in temperature, the main shaded space should be on the elevation facing the equator so that when the sun is overhead in the hot season, it barely penetrates into the space, but in the cold season, when the sun is lower, it shines into the recess, providing warmth, Figure 42.30.

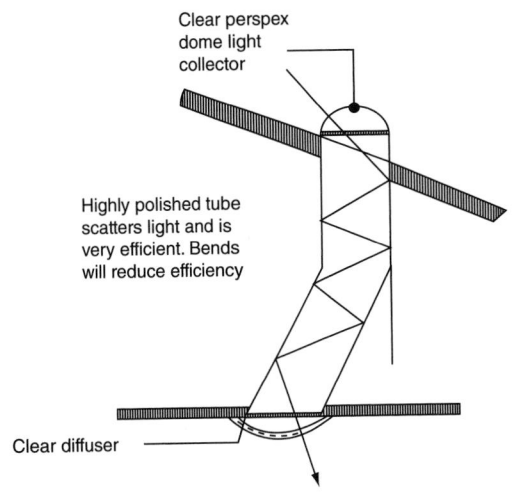

Clear perspex dome light collector

Highly polished tube scatters light and is very efficient. Bends will reduce efficiency

Clear diffuser

42.26 *The light pipe (which can also be enclosed in a vented duct with the clear domed toplight set within a louvred venting frame)*

In hot humid climates, conditions may be too unpleasant indoors, during both the day and the night. In the humid evening and night, flying insects are a particular nuisance, and one or more of the verandas will be fly-screened. This cuts down air

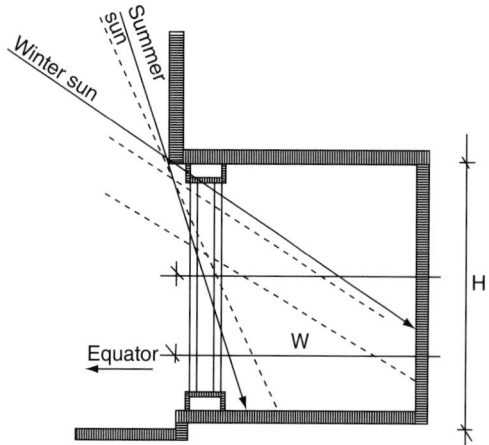

42.27 *The critical height/width ratio of a colonnade will depend on orientation, latitude and the particular use the space will be put to*

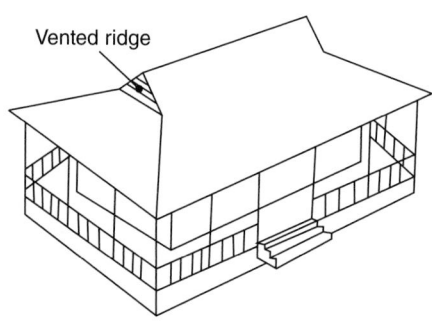

42.29 *The colonial bungalow with a veranda on all sides – the archetypical Australian farmhouse. Note the vented ridge, extending over the hip – a lesson learnt from the Indonesian lodge house*

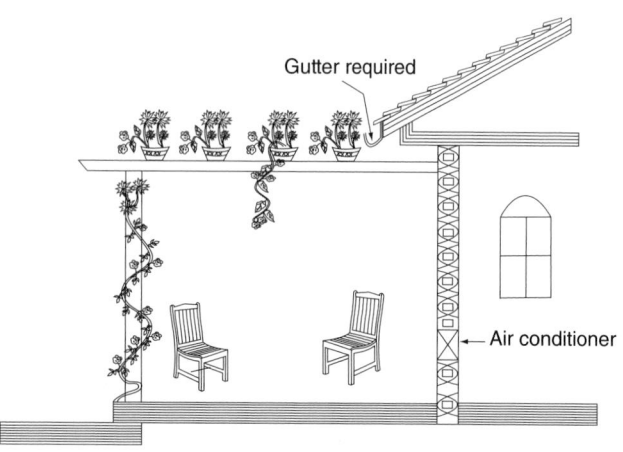

42.28 *Pergolas provide an attractive dappled shade. If used where they shade air conditioners, they will reduce intake temperatures and thereby reduce cooling load*

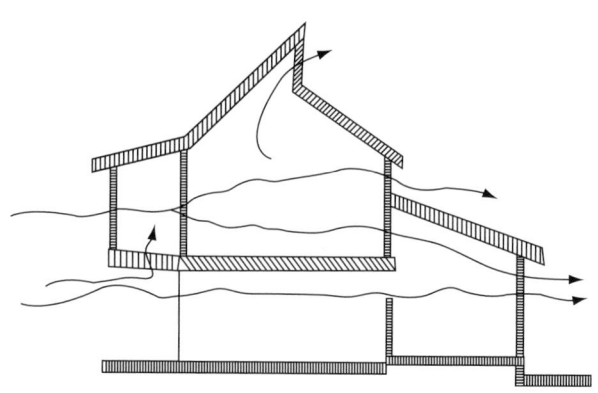

42.30 *In summer, the overhead sun is kept out of the veranda, but in winter, the sun is lower and warms the spaces under the roof on cold mornings and evenings*

movement but is essential. In two-storey houses, a secure screened upper veranda may be used for sleeping on the hottest nights, Figure 42.31. In these climates, it is common practice to raise the house, sleeping areas and verandas as high as possible above the ground, to catch the night breezes. On cooler days, the dappled shade under a pergola supporting a vine or other climbing plant may be more pleasant than deep shade.

Security will be a consideration in the design of most external spaces.

4.4 Courtyards, patios and atria
Courtyards or patios, Figure 42.32, are traditional features in most hot climates and serve several purposes:

- they defend the occupants from the busy, noisy, smelly street;
- they ensure privacy;
- they reduce built depth and should increase through-ventilation, Table IX.

Courtyards may be lined with verandas or colonnades (as was the monastic cloister). The surrounding walls and roof will cast shade

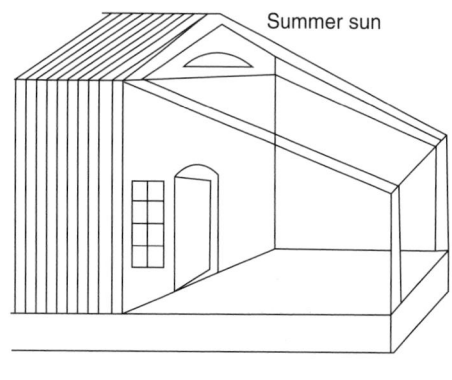
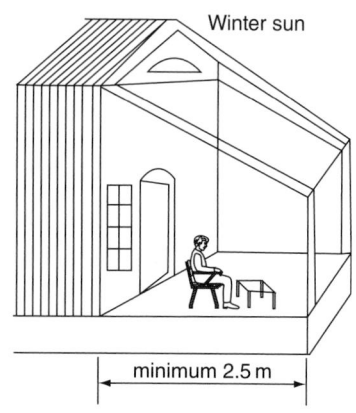

42.31 *In hot humid tropical conditions, ventilated sleeping verandas may be essential for a comfortable night*

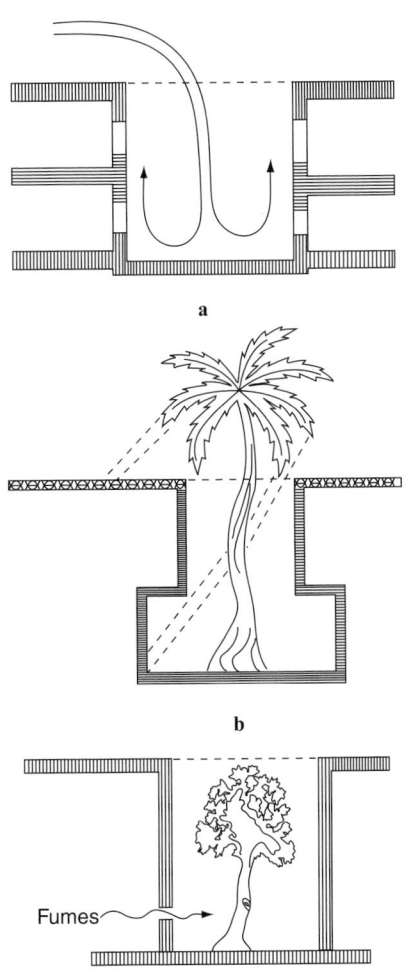

42.32 *In courtyards, a at night, cool night air sinks into the centre, whilst warmer air trapped in the courtyard rises around the perimeter, warming the rooms alongside; b tall trees with canopies above the yard will give effective shading whilst allowing air movement; c trees with their canopy below the courtyard roofline may trap air and fumes from appliances. Trees and retractable awnings can improve the performance of the courtyard*

Table IX Courtyards

Benefits	Deficits
Courtyards: – will increase privacy from the street – will reduce noise from street – will reduce building depth – should have increased air flow through rooms as a result of reduced depth – may cool the building at night by drawing in cool night air and accelerating dispersal of warm air – with trees will be shaded and the trees will transpire in the evening to accelerate cooling (deciduous trees will admit sun in winter) – can use water effectively to modify temperature – will effectively enlarge the habitable space, as they can be used for many social and working activities, and may have temporary or retractable coverings for weather protection, decorative effect or additional privacy.	Courtyards: – may reduce privacy for rooms facing one another across small courtyards – may make sound ricochet around the space – will increase footprint and cost – may trap air and restrict air movement – may accumulate pollutants dispersed into the courtyard – with deciduous trees will need clearing of leaf litter – will have an enlarged and more complex building footprint and the more complex design will incur extra costs – to be offset against the many gains.

into the courtyard from the east in the early morning and from the west in the early evening. The courtyard itself may be shaded by tall trees, awnings or retractable canopies.

The aspect ratio, Figure 42.33, of courtyards is critical to their effectiveness.

Where H = height and W = width

a low aspect ratio has $H/W < 0.3$
a medium aspect ratio has H/W between 0.3 and 1
a high aspect ratio has $H/W > 1$.

An atrium (a Roman open courtyard, but today the term usually means an inner courtyard roofed over with glass) may overheat in hot climates unless carefully designed. It will provide an attractive large space within a building that acts as a focus point and, like any lightwell, it will admit and reflect light into spaces that would otherwise have been dark. The fall-off in lighting levels will be quite rapid at lower levels, as the no-sky line is passed, Figure 42.34. It

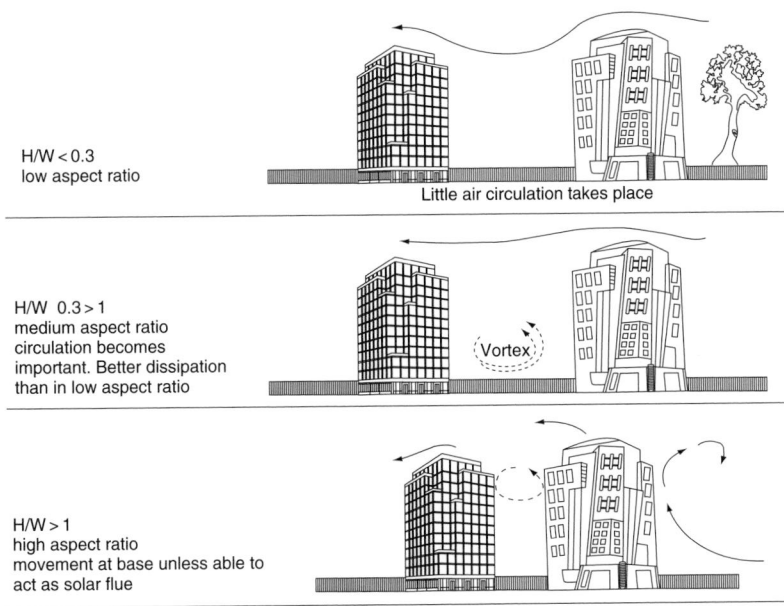

H/W < 0.3
low aspect ratio

Little air circulation takes place

H/W 0.3 > 1
medium aspect ratio
circulation becomes
important. Better dissipation
than in low aspect ratio

Vortex

H/W > 1
high aspect ratio
movement at base unless able to
act as solar flue

42.33 *Aspect ration of courtyards: a the low aspect ratio courtyard (H/W <0.3): access to external air is good, but there is little recirculation; b the medium aspect ratio courtyard (H/W 0.3–1): re-circulation becomes important; heat dissipation is better than in the low aspect ratio courtyard; c the high aspect ratio courtyard (H/W > 1): unless the courtyard acts as a solar flue, there will be turbulence at the top, but no air movement at the bottom*

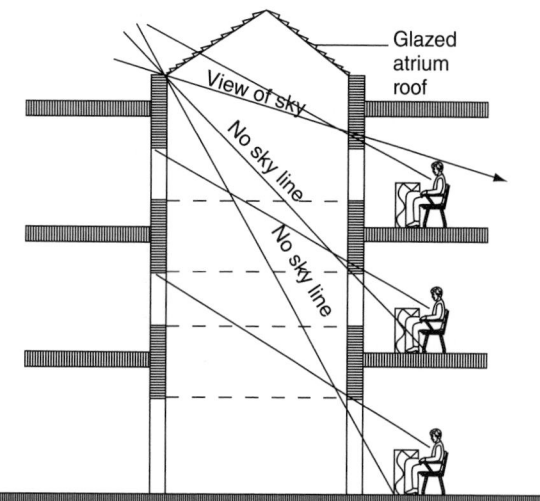

42.34 *The 'no-sky line' is the point at which the occupant is unable to see the sky: it is the point at which internal light levels drop off sharply*

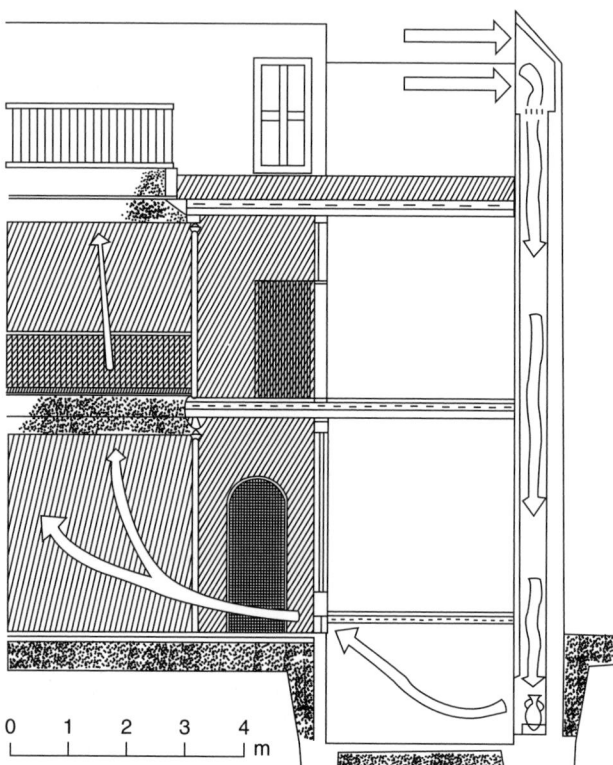

42.35 *A wind-catcher bringing fresh air into a basement. The air passes over the cool walls of the flue (shaded by neighbouring houses) and a porous jug containing water. Evaporative and contact cooling is effected*

has the potential to act as a solar flue if adequately ventilated (naturally or mechanically), drawing stale air out of the surrounding spaces. In climates with regular rainfall, atria can provide considerable amenity as meeting, eating and sheltering spaces. Their height means that landscaping can include tall trees. Glare and brightness can be reduced by using blinds below the glazing, or temporary tented canopies above it.

4.5 Wind towers, wind scoops and wind catchers

Wind towers are air extract or inlet flues, used to ventilate and cool buildings. The origin of these towers is in the arid tropical climate of the Middle East, where they are used to ventilate and cool the lowest floors of town houses. Houses in these climates are enclosed, with few external openings, to keep out sand and dust,

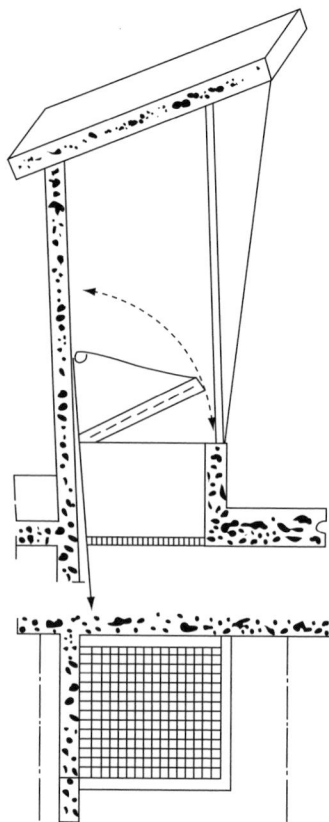

42.36 *The trap on the wind-catcher can be closed and screens can be fitted to filter dust and leaves*

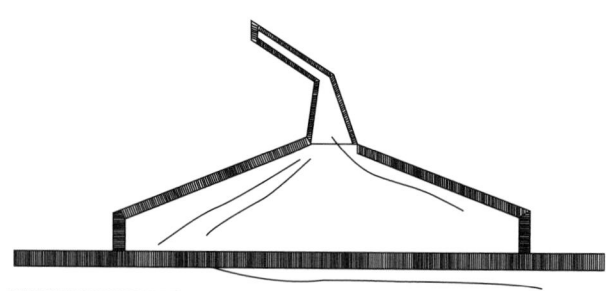

42.37 *The Bluewater Shopping Centre in Dartford, England uses giant revolving wind scoops, reminiscent of Kentish oast house*

as well as to minimise solar gain. They have a high thermal mass, which maintains some warmth in the cold winters.

The prevailing breeze is caught and funnelled down into the base of the house through a duct or flue in a party wall. This flue does not receive any solar radiation, so it remains cooler than the rest of the house during the day. Incoming air is cooled by conduction during its contact with the cool walls of the flue and relative humidity is increased when it passes over porous water jugs, Figure 42.35.

In Iraq, the cool breeze is discharged into a basement, used for the afternoon siesta. During the hottest months, the roof terrace is used for sleeping at night. The top of the wind-catcher is capped to keep rain out, and usually can be closed in winter, when it will have the reverse benefit of keeping the house warmer. Screens keep birds and insects out of the flue, Figure 42.36.

Urban wind towers

Air at street level in cities can be laden with toxic particulate matter and noxious gases. Air drawn from this environment will be polluted and will also introduce noise pollution. If we wish to use natural ventilation in city buildings, the cleanest air will be obtained from high level. Current UK government sponsored research focuses on the 'top-down' ventilation of urban buildings.

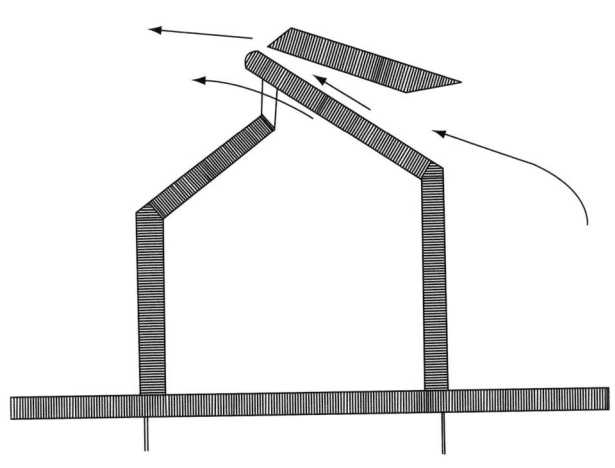

42.38 *Aerofoil shapes in conjunction with narrowing spaces act like aeroplane wings, creating pressure differentials that will draw air out of buildings*

42.39 *The Environmental Building at BRE, by Fielden Clegg Architects, is a demonstration/experimental building that makes use of solar flues*

In cities, the maze of streets, differing heights of buildings, levels of pollution, vortices, pressure differentials, etc. create local air movement patterns. Fixed wind-catchers can be ineffective in these situations, and scoops that can rotate with the wind become essential. The Bluewater development at Dartford, England uses large revolving scoops, Figure 42.37. Air inlets serving the flues may be windows, open courtyards, grilles, under-floor ducts (which can pre-cool the air) or wind scoops.

The use of wind towers reduces reliance on mechanical ventilation, chilling and air conditioning. Devices may also be used to accelerate air movement, and thereby improve ventilation, using aerofoils which catch the wind, Figure 42.38.

4.6 Solar flues
Solar flues are wind towers where air movement is achieved by heating the air in the tower or flue by intensifying solar radiation on the walls of the flue, as demonstrated by the Environmental Building at the BRE, Figure 42.39.

- the combination of the light-shelf and vertical fin will provide protection from lateral as well as overhead angles, but will trap hot air unless partially slatted to allow air movement;
- egg crates, or some other form of brises soleil can create a striking design which may also serve as a security screen, but keep horizontal elements away from eye level in habitable rooms as they can be visually disturbing;
- recent buildings in Europe have used metal screens suspended up to a metre away from the window. These can be visually striking and functionally effective. They may also have the effect of acting as a 'rainscreen';
- another recent development is the use of sophisticated tensioned wire 'rigging' which may be suspended over facades to provide a support for climbing plants. Plants may grow up from the ground or down from high level irrigated containers. They will provide an attractive dappled shade but will need maintenance.

4.7 Trombe walls
The Trombe wall is a thick dense wall within a building that receives and stores solar radiation (usually through the intensifying medium of glass) during daylight hours, and then radiates the heat into internal spaces during the evening. The wall is designed (material, thickness, location) to provide the desired time lag to provide the heat when it is most needed, Figure 42.40.

4.8 Site
Time and time again, in low and medium cost housing, the site layout is entrusted to a junior technician who has no concept of the

42.40 *The Trombe wall: storing heat at the times of the year when it is needed. The Trombe wall (like the stone floor, in this instance) acts as a heat store, with the hot sun passing through glass onto both surfaces. The dense mass of these materials retains the heat and, after a time lag, releases the stored warmth into the room during the cold night (Bruce Anderson – The Solar House Book)*

importance of orientation or aspect. A house carefully designed to have principle elevations facing north or south is swung through 90° and meticulously lined up parallel to the next house so that there will be no breeze – and discomfort and dissatisfaction are assured. Orientation (and design to suit that orientation) are paramount, even if this conflicts with the normal good advice to follow the contour and keep substructure costs down. Building across the contour provides an opportunity to use a split-level plan, with associated discontinuities in the roofline to admit light and allow air movement.

4.9 Landscaping
Trees and lush landscaping, together with lakes, fountains, pools and other open bodies of water, are visually attractive and will induce cooling. Strategic planting of trees and shrubs can shade

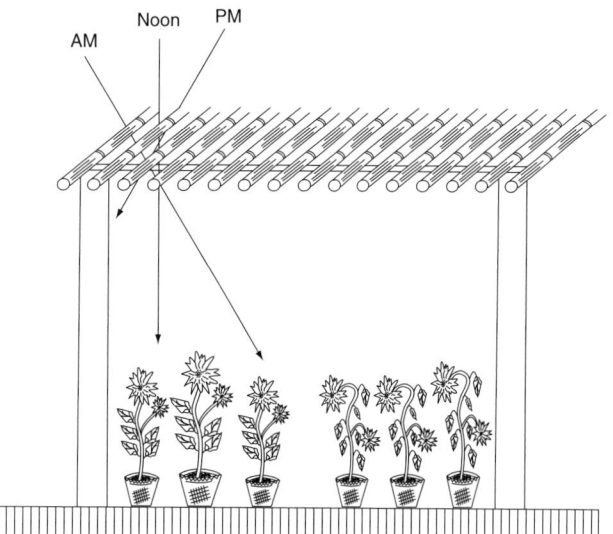

42.41 *The shade house, roofed and walled with an open-woven split bamboo mat. Many tropical plants used in landscaping are forest species used to lower levels of light: using a slatted baffle allows a continual hit-miss pattern of daylight to pass over the plant as the sun moves across the sky, ensuring that the plants get adequate light on all sides, whilst being tricked into accelerating growth by the on–off daylight*

buildings and lower temperature, reducing energy costs in mechanical cooling by up to 40 per cent. This is achieved directly, by shading, and indirectly, through evaporative cooling induced by transpiration.

Plants grow quickly in the tropics and schemes can be established very quickly, but may require the establishment of on-site nurseries. Nurseries consume a lot of water and will require the construction of shade houses, Figure 42.41. The use of any hard or soft landscaping implies a commitment to irrigate, maintain, restock and clear leaf litter and rubbish from these areas, and to employ staff who will carry out these tasks. If sites such as roundabouts and the central strip of dual carriageways are to be landscaped, these will need a water supply, unless the landscaping is intended to be long-term and self-sufficient.

In some countries, landscaping is highly valued, state-supported and recognised as providing valuable employment; in others it is politically frowned upon, being seen as diverting funding from schools, hospitals and other socially important programmes. In either scenario, there may be a thriving agricultural industry that may include the cultivation of exotic species for exporting to distant world markets.

Soft landscaping that uses or integrates indigenous species will help to contextualise planting schemes and encourage use by wildlife. Whereas the mono-specific planting that is currently fashionable in Europe will not.

Hard landscaping strategies should take advantage of local materials and resources (such as local stone and specialised schools of carving and sculpting) and provide facilities for local cultural practices and acceptable activities (such as pavement cafes, street theatre, public exercise sessions, street traders and curio sellers). Public and company space may be required for sports (basketball, bowling, chess, football …). Some of these may need to be shaded. Sitting areas may need to be in the shade, rather than the sun, and drinking fountains may be required. Many activities, including produce markets, can be accommodated under shade structures, which lend themselves to simple but dramatic structural forms, such as shells or tents. Pergolas and shade trees, whether used for shading people or vehicles, should use species that give good dappled or deeper shade, have a root system that stays below paved surfaces, and that do not drop leaves, flowers, pods or fruit that will cause nuisance or damage.

An indicative list of tree and shrub species used in landscaping schemes is given in Table X. Unless listed as drought-resistant, most species will require irrigation in climates with a marked dry season.

4.10 Urban centres and street layouts

Temperature in cities

All large urban areas are hotter than the surrounding rural areas: people, industry, machines, vehicles, buildings – all generate heat, pollution and gases including CO_2. In hot climates, it is particularly important to incorporate heat sinks (lakes, parks, woodland) that can lower air and ground temperature.

Urban streets

Narrow streets are cooler than wide boulevards, unless these are planted with large street trees, Figure 42.42.

On streets running north–south, the higher the height to width ratio (H/W ratio), the less time the sun has on the street surface and on facades facing the street, Figure 42.43. The street will be cool in the morning and evening.

On streets running east-west, latitude becomes more important than H/W ratio, Figure 42.44. On or near the equator, the sun will be overhead or rising and setting on the street alignment. As distance from the equator increases, there is greater likelihood that in the hot season most of the street surface and the elevation facing the equator will receive solar radiation all day, whilst in the cold season, narrower streets and one elevation may be in shade all day, with the elevation facing the equator only receiving significant solar radiation when the sun is above the roof level of the buildings on the other side of the street.

Vehicles

Vehicles parked in open sunlight will become unbearably hot and petrol will evaporate. Car parking that is not inside or under buildings must be shaded by freestanding canopies, shade trees or pergolas. Parking areas and street layouts may need to take account of specialised vehicles (bicycle-rickshaws, horse-drawn cabs,

Near the equator street runs E–W

Figure 42.42 *The width of the spaces between buildings (in addition to their orientation) and the placement of large trees are critical to the amount of direct insolation they will receive*

Table X Species used in tropical landscaping schemes

PLANT CHARACTERISTICS, REQUIREMENTS AND ORIGIN

SPECIES

Almost anything will grow in the tropics if it gets the right amount of water and humidity.

Plant species				Habitat criteria				Continent of origin						SPECIES		
Tree – Large, Medium or Small	Shrub – Large, Medium or Small	Climber	Herbaceous and other plants	Significant Flowers or foliage	Frost tolerant	Drought tolerant – Arid, Seasonal	Altitude tolerant – Low, Med, High	Africa	Asia and Pacific	Australasia	Mediterranean Europe	North America	South and Central America and West Indies	Species	Description	Suggestions
	M			O			H		✓					Acalypha wilkesiana (*Beefsteak plant, Jacob's coat*)	Medium sized shrubs with dramatic variegated foliage – predominantly green or brown with every leaf different – green/yellow/cream/pink/red/brown. Leaves are large and obovate or narrow and dissected.	They are dramatic and reliable. It is easy to over-use them.
			H			A S								Agave americana (*Century plant*)	Large rosette-forming succulent with a sharp spine on the leaf tips, and a spiny cream margin. The flower spikes are up to 8m tall.	Agave species are used in mass planting, as specimens and as impenetrable hedges (traditionally around prisons).
			H					✓					✓	Aloe sp.	Tall spikes of massed small bell-shaped flowers rising from rosettes of agave-like fleshy leaves with spiny margins.	
S				F		S			✓					Bauhinia purpurea (*Orchid tree*)	Elegant fragrant purple, pink or white flowers. Erect tree, some varieties are more lax and have softer less waxy flowers. Pods long, thin and some split and spiral explosively.	Attractive small street or garden tree with beautiful flowers. Lax varieties wider spreading. Pods are noisy when they explode open.
		C				S							✓	Bougainvillea glabra	Vigorous spiny scrambler smothered in distinctive magenta bracts. Cultivars include white, orange, pink, yellow of varying vigour.	Can be trained to form mounds, will scramble up trees and over walls. Can damage foundations and roofs if planted too close to houses and not controlled.
						S			✓					Brugmansia × candida [Datura] (*Moonflower*)	Reliable shrub with powerful scent and pendulous trumpet-shaped flowers, usually white or cream, but occasionally pink or peach. There are double forms. Narcotic.	
S														Caesalpinia pulcherrima (Pride of Barbados)		
S	M									✓				Callistemon sp. (Bottle brush)	Evergreen small trees or shrubs. Upright or weeping forms. Lanceolate leaves and red bottle brush flowers of varying sizes.	

(continued)

Table X (continued)

PLANT CHARACTERISTICS, REQUIREMENTS AND ORIGIN

SPECIES	Characteristics	Codes
Cassia spectabilis	Fast-growing tree with dense umbrella shaped canopy and large pinnate leaves. Large upright panicles of sweet-scented bright yellow flowers.	M; F; L, M ✓ — So fast growing and spectacular, it will occasionally collapse under its own weight. Stunning as a street tree, where the regularity of size and form is exceptional.
Casuarina equisetifolia	Delicate foliage resembling a pine tree with long needles. Tolerates waterlogged ground and salt atmosphere.	M; G; L, M ✓ — Often planted on beaches as windbreaks and to stabilise the ground.
Cestrum nocturnum (*Queen of the night*)	Unexceptional shrub with sprays of narrow off-white tubular flowers that open at night with a very powerful scent.	✓ — Often planted too close to bedrooms. The scent can be overwhelming at close range.
Coedaium variegatura Congea tomentosa	Like Acalypha, but more upright, with smaller, thicker and glossier leaves and preferring a hot humid climate. A scrambling shrub with sprays of downy white to pinky-lilac bracts.	G; ✓✓ — Attractive and reliable. Looks spectacular on trellises or climbing up trees. The colour is subtle. Sprays can be dried.
Delonix regia (*Flamboyant, flame tree*)	Elegant spreading tree with masses of bright red orchid-like flowers on leafless branches. Leaves are bi-pinnate, similar to the jacaranda, which it follows into flower. Wide range of climates and altitudes.	L; S; L, M, H ✓ — This stunning tree needs space to show off in and to be allowed to retain its carpet of fallen flowers. Surface roots prevent planting or development under the canopy.
Erythrina abyssinica	This large tree has distinctive red flowers and flat pods with decorative red seeds. Other Erythrina species are also used.	✓ — Occasionally used as a street tree, or in larger gardens.
Eucalyptus sp.	—	M; F; S ✓
Euphorbia leucocephala (*snow bush*)	Medium sized shrub which is covered with spectacular rosettes of white bracts.	Spectacular in massed planting. Usually cut back hard each year to create a rounded bush about 1.5–2 m high.
Hibiscus rosa-sinensis	Shrub or small tree with showy red flowers. White, yellow, orange and pink varieties available.	✓ — Widely planted in the tropics. Best in humid lower altitudes.
Jacaranda mimosafolia	Stunning pale blue-violet flowers in clusters on leafless canopy in late dry season; large, airy bi-pinnate leaves with tiny leaflets.	L; F; S; M, H ✓ — Widely used as a street tree and in gardens; gives light dappled shade; surface rooter; grown at sea level and at high altitude in composite climates

PLANT CHARACTERISTICS, REQUIREMENTS AND ORIGIN

B	A	SPECIES		Used for
	✓	Kalanchoe sp.	Large family of decorative flesh-leaved plants that put up a spike of bell-shaped flowers. Foliage is mostly grey, flowers mostly pink/orange.	Used for mass bedding without irrigation.
	✓	Melia azedarach (*Neem tree*)	Large fast-growing tree with attractive but not spectacular racemes of pale lilac flowers.	Widely used as a street tree with lightly dappled shade. Found in any country with Indian (Asian) residents.
	✓	Nerium oleander (Oleander)	Pretty fragrant flowers on a shrub with lanceolate leaves.	All parts of the plant are poisonous.
C	✓	Petrea volubilis	Evergreen climber with pendulous racemes of beautiful star shaped lilac-purple flowers.	Covers walls, trellises and fences. Colour like the Jacaranda, which flowers at the same time, but more intense.
L S F	✓	Poinsettia pucherrima	Large shrub with decorative bright red bracts. Many other species with a range of colours and forms. All are euphorbiacae – with latex sap.	Usually cut back hard after 'flowering'. Avoid contact with latex. Needs 12 h of darkness to produce bracts.
C	✓	Pyrostegia venusta	Vigorous evergreen climber with long flowering season. Clusters of bright orange tubular bell-shaped flowers.	Climbs tall trees, covers walls and looks spectacular as raised ground cover, trained over a wire framework.
	✓	Roystonea regia (Royal Palm)		
	✓	Russelia equisetiformis	Small tubular red flowers are set along the drooping rush-like stems.	Planted in raised beds, to allow it to droop.
s	✓	Solanum (*Potato tree*)		A decorative small tree.
	✓	Solanum jasminoides (*Potato creeper*)	Papery blue or white flowers on a shrubby climber to 5 m.	
C		Spathodea africana (African tulip tree)	This large tree has erect terminal racemes of orange-red flowers emerging from hairy liquid-filled buds.	Street or specimen tree.
L		Tecoma stans	Shrub with bright yellow bell-shaped flowers.	Widely used as a hedging plant. Withstands cutting well.
		Thunbergia grandiflora (*Heavenly blue*)	A large climber. The flowers have five lilac-blue petals around a yellow tube.	Climbs over walls, fences and verandas.

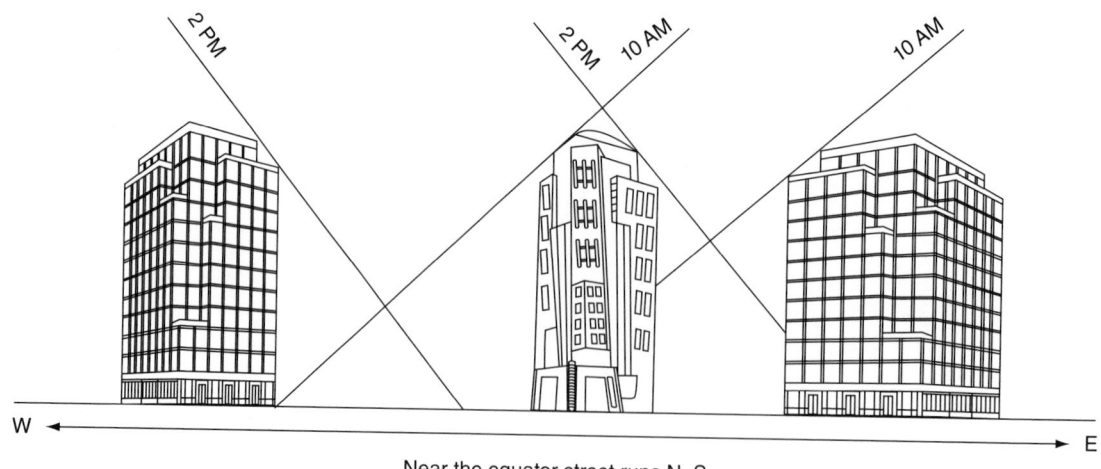

42.43 *When streets run north–south, a narrow street near to the equator will only receive direct sunlight for a relatively short time – the principle used in the North African trading street – the souk*

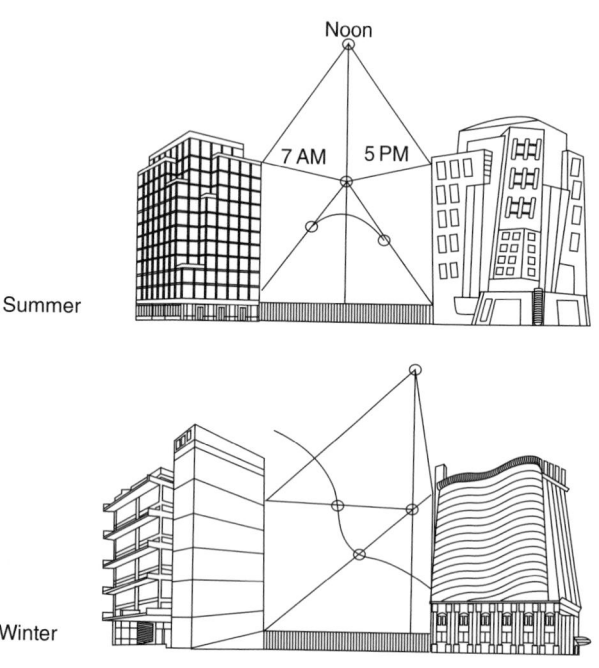

42.44 *When streets near the equator run east–west, the sun will be shining into the street all day unless blocked by structures across the street*

articulated buses) and differing percentages of pedestrians, public transport, car ownership or bicycle use in cities.

Litter

Some people generate more litter; some city administrations administer severe penalties for littering the streets (especially for dropping chewing gum or sugar cane waste).

5 ENVIRONMENTAL CONTROL STRATEGIES: ACTIVE MEASURES

5.1 Alternative energy

Energy supplies may be unreliable or non-existent on remote sites. Power may need to be supplied by a diesel generator, or some other means that capitalises on latent potential in or near the site, such as:

- *Biomass* – using crop and forestry wastes, slurries and rapid cropping trees and herbaceous plants which are dried, prepared and burnt, usually in a combination with gas, to produce energy.
- *Geothermal* – naturally occurring subterranean hot water and gas.
- *Biodiesel and biofuels* – ethanol may be a by-product of agroindustry (as in the conversion of sugar cane to granular sugar or cane spirit).
- *Solar power* – photovoltaics, water heating.
- *Water* – micro-hydro, estuarine and tidal mini turbines.
- *Wind* – free-standing wind pumps or building-integrated turbines, Figure 42.45.

42.45 *Wind turbines*

5.2 Photovoltaics

Grid-connected BIPV are flat solar cells fixed to parts of the building envelope in an array that faces into the sun. They generate direct current (DC) which must be converted into alternating current (AC) and, although expensive and offering poor efficiency at present, can bring cost savings by downloading power to the national grid during the day, thereby reducing the cost of upload from the grid at night. These savings depend on an equitable arrangement with the national generating company, and on associated passive measures that use the building envelope efficiently. All photovoltaic cells use silicone, in various forms, and are either black or blue in appearance. The electrified arrays are dangerous, and must be installed, maintained and supervised by electricians with specialist expertise.

Photovoltaic slates have recently become available in the UK that appear no different to regular natural slates and which are claimed to achieve savings of up to 25 per cent on domestic energy consumption.

5.3 Wind turbines

If these are attached to buildings, the design must accommodate the swing of the turbine blades and the additional structural loading from vibration. Risk of damage and injury from broken blades must be assessed.

Turbines may be 500 mm or 50 m in diameter. Siting is critical. The Danish Wind Industry Association website gives extensive design guidance (www.windpower.org/en).

5.4 Ventilation and air conditioning

The need for mechanical aids and the costs in running and maintaining them will be reduced by passive design strategies that offer improved ventilation, shading and temperature management. Wherever possible, design out the need for mechanical solutions. Designers are increasingly using wind towers and solar flues to drive ventilation.

Ceiling fans

Allow adequate headroom below the blades of the fan. Ceiling fans give a wide distribution of blown air. Since the diameter of the fan is large, the fan can have a relatively low speed, reducing noise.

Typical installation:

- ceiling height   3.0 m minimum
- minimum blade height above floor   2.5 m
- fan diameter   1.0 m

Wall and floor-mounted fans: Because the blades are set within a cage, these can give higher air speeds and a more concentrated air stream. They may be fixed or can oscillate.

Typical data:

- mounting height   1.5–2.0 m
- angle of oscillation   up to 60°
- 'reach' of blown air   3–4 m

Roof extract fans and passive stack vents: With light roof constructions, extract fans are used to remove hot air from the ceiling void and internal rooms. Internal air temperatures may be reduced by 3–5°C in climates where high solar radiation is combined with moderate air temperatures. The extract fan does not give perceptible air movement within the building.

Unit air conditioners: Room air conditioners are available with a cooling capacity in the range from 1.5 to 7 kW (Btus/h are commonly used to measure capacity as many manufacturers and designs originate in the USA). Specifications vary considerably and may include heaters and fan-only options, as well as chillers. They are usually accommodated in walls or under windows (often as afterthoughts). Unit air conditioners require external air for removing excess heat, a fresh air inlet and drainage for water removed from the air during cooling.

Split air conditioning units: Split air conditioning units have the following advantages over unit (or 'room') air conditioners:

- Minimal structural alterations if installed in an existing building or minimal requirements for new buildings: the two pipes connecting the condenser to the air handler will fit through a 100 mm hole.
- Greater security; important for banks, shops, etc.
- Reduced noise within the room, due to external position of condenser.
- Greater flexibility internally as air handler may be placed on internal wall or even ceiling.
- Improved external appearance as condenser may be placed on the roof, reducing problems of dripping condensate.

The disadvantage is:

- the condenser unit is unsightly and noisy and a space needs to be found for it: it may annoy the neighbours, rather than the room occupant.

6 STRUCTURE, SERVICES AND ENVIRONMENTAL DESIGN

6.1 Structural design

The structural form must be a viable economic choice and must facilitate the appropriate design response to climate. Hot arid climates suit dense masonry construction; hot humid climates suit a lightweight frame with a low mass ventilated infill. Composite climates require a mix – perhaps solid heat-storing floors with a lighter superstructure and adjustable shading. All structures must be able to withstand predicted climatic extremes that affect stability and structural integrity. There is less need for enclosure in all but the arid tropics and many structures will consist of a dramatic roof on exposed supports, with no permanent walls.

Concrete

Concrete is widely used in the tropics, where steel and other imported materials may be costly. Low-labour costs may have permitted the adventurous use of the plastic properties of concrete, in hypar, shell and other one-off forms (see the structures section). Use of concrete will depend on availability of cement and adequate water supplies. Taller buildings will need pumping capabilities. Hot climates may necessitate chilling of concrete (ice in tankers), the use of retarding agents and the shading and repeated wetting of poured concrete during the curing stage. Suitable formwork may be difficult to obtain.

Steel

Transportation costs may make steel structures uneconomic. Humid environments may necessitate special treatments. Steel doorframes and windows may be used in preference to timber, to reduce termite damage.

Timber

Timber should be from sustainable forests and must withstand termites, heat and desiccation or humidity, where applicable. Drying shrinkage and warping may be unacceptable. Seasoning may be required before timber can be used. The performance capabilities of each particular species must be known, especially for structural timbers. If large sections of structural timber are not available, glulam may be good alternatives (glulam – thin strips of timber built up in laminations to produce an attractive, consistent material with excellent structural properties). In some areas, profligate consumption of forest timber, in construction and as fuelwood, has left some forest species critically depleted. Converted timber, as plywood and other board products, may be available to locally established specifications.

Structural form

Design issues are highlighted in Table XI: Design of building elements.

Table XI Design of building elements

Element	Type	Advantages or purposes	Disadvantages or problems	Details
Structure	*Generally*	• Absence of freezing conditions • Regulatory controls may permit more imaginative solutions • Local expertise in alternative technologies may offer new design potential	• Climate extremes, including diurnal temperature range, wind and rainfall • Limited skills or technical knowledge in some places • Limited performance data on local materials (Are there local materials testing labs?) • Season restrictions on working (dust storm, monsoon, etc.)	• Check if in earthquake zone • Check windloading from cyclones, etc. • Obtain rainfall data for short-term loading on roofs, gutters, etc. • Consider sustainability of all aspects of design (embodied energy, consumption of non-renewable resources, environmental contamination and depletion, especially of water supplies)
	Loadbearing masonry	• Are bricks and stone local materials? • Is brickwork a local skill? • Is masonry part of the vernacular style? • Thermal mass • Able to accommodate small fillings and accommodate alterations	• Limited availability, quality and consistency of materials and accessories • Traditional clamp-firing may consume huge quantities of non renewable forest timber	• Check local practice • Is cavity wall construction used? • Establish strength and consistency of locally produced materials and materials testing regime
	Concrete frame and in-situ concrete work	• Is cement manufactured locally? • Is concrete construction a locally familiar technology? • Lower labour and formwork costs may facilitate one-off designs (hypars, etc.)	• Limited availability, quality and consistency of materials, plant and resources • Extreme care needed during curing	• Is/are formwork, reinforcement, mixing and transporting plant available? • Is there sufficient water for mixing, cooling, cleaning of plant?
	Steel frame	• Reusable material	• Limited availability, quality and consistency of materials and resources including skilled labour • Humidity	• What is the distance from foundry, workshop or supplier to site?
	Timber frame	• Timber produced locally? • From renewable forests?	• Resistance to humidity and termites • Effect of climate on lifespan	• Check windloading from cyclones, etc. • Strapping and bracing of timber elements
Floors	*Ground-supported floors*	• Use the delayed thermal flywheel effect of ground and/or floor mass to stabilise floor temperature and keep it cool (concrete, stone and ceramic floors always feel cooler and in some circumstances can be wetted to produce evaporative cooling – but this will increase humidity) • Reduce costs • Provide disabled access • Concrete floors are easy to clean – they are often waxed or polished in the tropics	• Seasonal flooding risk • Risk of rain splashback • Termites, vermin, snakes, etc. • Restricted structural option – concrete? • Suitability of ground conditions for foundation type • Risk of damp and mould growth • Concrete, stone and ceramic floors, if polished, can be very* slippery and cause accidents • Snakes may breed in poorly compacted hardcore under the slab	• Take precautions against termites and vermin penetrating the slab at junctions, changes of level, and points where the slab is penetrated by services or structure • The slab must be continuous (not split into bays separated by internal walls) • Keep termites out by poisoning soil (but avoid organophospates such as Aldrin or Dieldrin) or by using a special oversite steel mesh with a gauge too small for insects to penetrate (Australian solution) • Project slabs beyond foundations, with sharp external 90° angles which termites dislike • Floors with a high thermal mass should be kept shaded in hot weather, but can be allowed to absorb some solar radiation in the cold season to warm up the building (passive design).
	Suspended floors	• Keeps floor clear of seasonal flooding and splash-back from heavy rain • Keeps the floor away from termites and vermin • Use materials other than concrete, including open deck vented floors to improve air movement	• Floors should remain dry and free from damp • Security risk from below • Accessible soffit may be colonised by bats, snakes, etc. • Voids within the floor structure may be used by insects and small mammals (wasps, ants, etc.) • Termites may find timber and destroy it • In humid climates, damp and mould growth may accumulate unseen in sealed voids	• Low mass floors will maintain temperature closer to air temperature – an advantage in winter • All voids must be protected on the external faces by mesh strong enough to deter gnawing by rodents and of a gauge fine enough to keep out ants – except where bats, etc. are tolerated • Check timber floors (and structures) for fire risk from bush fires • Suspended floors may permit the introduction or seasonal use of vent stack/solar chimneys drawing cool air from shaded ground. • Leave underside of floor visible for inspection • Allow airflow and ventilation below the floor
	Raised access floors	• May be used to duct cooling air through a structure, or to recycle or remove heated air	• Do not contribute thermal mass • May be difficult to maintain • Insects and vermin may infest voids	• Failure of a raised access floor in an earthquake may critically affect escape from office buildings
	Intermediate floors and mezzanines	• Discontinuities in the building section, with mezzanine floors and variation in storey height, permit air movement	• Continuous floor slabs restrict vertical air movement • Structural continuity may be essential to maintain rigidity in earthquake zones	• Sound transmission • Spread of fire
	External floors, decks, platforms, balconies and terraces	• Can shade lower floors and walls • If in low mass materials (timber) and perforated, will reduce temperature and allow air movement	• May reflect light, glare and heat into buildings if light coloured and reflective, but if used as a light shelf, can shade windows whilst reflecting light off ceilings	• Outdoor living and sleeping in sun, shade or breeze should utilise roof spaces, courtyards, atria and the periphery of the building in a range of climate-responsive ways.
Ceilings	*Suspended ceilings*	• Ceiling may be used to deflect or reflect light • May contain heat or light sensors to adjust temperature, or the position of external or internal blinds	• Void may harbour insects and vermin – must be accessible • Void may trap hot air if poorly designed • Materials used for acoustic insulation in ceilings may be attractive to insects – avoid any containing cellulose	• Use wire or plastic mesh of appropriate gauge to keep out bats, birds, vermin whilst maintaining ventilation
	Exposed soffits; integrated ceilings	• Reduce costs	• Reduce options in servicing and air movement	

Element	Type	Advantages or purposes	Disadvantages or problems	Details
Wall features	*Flyscreens*	• Essential in food preparation, kitchen and sleeping areas where any flying insect is a nuisance • In mosquito infected areas, *all* rooms should be fly-screened.	• Impede air circulation	• Usually green or black plastic or coated wire gauze – must be robust • Fix with timber bead or metal cramp
	Shutters	• Personal security • Protection from severe weather • Adjustable (American) shutters cut down glare • Cut down extraneous noise	• Trap heat	• Consider fixing and maintenance
Cladding	*Rainscreen*	• Allows use of rough finish to structure concealed behind rainscreen • Can be used over pisé/adobe	• Voids can harbour vermin and conceal defects and deterioration	• Consider fixing and maintenance
Roof	*Pitched roof*	• Essential in wet climates • Void can be used to vent inner rooms	• Can trap heat if not vented • Voids can harbour vermin and conceal defects and deterioration	• Large overhangs in wet tropics • Roof pitch, valleys, etc. must cope with intense rainfall
	Flat roof	• Can be used as sleeping platform	• Difficult to weatherproof against rainstorms • Climate change may cause unpredictable weather	• Security is increasingly an issue
	Double roof including aerofoil roof	• This structure places an open ventilated space between the weather-protection of the upper roof and the shaded element of the inner and lower roof, which may serve as a sleeping platform in hot weather • The aerofoil uses two converging and aerodynamically designed profiles to accelerate air movement over the roof	• May be vulnerable to storm damage in severe weather • There may be loss of security or privacy • Extra height • Extra cost • Aerofoil may need extensive modelling and testing to prove	• See Le Corbusier's houses in India and more recent European buildings

6.2 Design in earthquake zones

Earthquakes may occur anywhere on the globe, but are more common in the hotter regions. In earthquake zones, it is generally accepted that choosing the right type of structure is more important than minor variations in detail. Failures occur due to inelasticity – and these failures are difficult to model, especially in complex structures. Chilean good practice provides a good model: provide reliable strength, structural continuity and redundancy. Always work with a structural engineer. Always consider the impact of siting and landscaping and potential damage from surrounding structures and trees.

When designing buildings in earthquake zones, the following points should be noted:

Structural form
Use:

• simple, compact structural forms with continuous lines of structural force and inbuilt redundancies;
• compact symmetrical plans with maximum resistance to torsional stresses;
• symmetry in loading, fenestration, stair placement, cladding patterns and infilling.

Avoid:

• complex forms with irregular and diverted lines of structural force – H, L, T, U, X and E plan forms are particularly vulnerable, as vibration may differ along each axis;
• discontinuities in form, mass, storey height, materials, setbacks, overhangs, or in infilling, which may create a 'soft storey' at any level and precipitate failure;
• breaks in columns and shear walls – failure to continue upper floor columns and shear walls through the ground floor (creating a 'soft storey') have contributed to loss of structural integrity or serious progressive collapses in earthquakes (and terrorist bombings);
• windows within 600 mm of external corners.

Structural detail
• Engineers may adopt a weak beam/strong column philosophy to allow beams to flex more than columns.
• Corner columns are more at risk: elevations may act as plates and twist corners.
• The continuity, linking and placement of reinforcement can be crucial.
• Floor slab-to-column connections must resist punching shear.
• Continuous bottom reinforcement through slabs and beams will act as catenaries and resist collapse.
• Partial restraint of columns by partial height infilling can expose the remaining unrestrained section of the column to excessive shear at the expense of flexural yield, leading to failure.

Damage and injury
• Some earthquake damage to the fabric will appear and must be accepted, but loss of structural integrity or collapse of inhabited buildings is never acceptable.
• All significant structural and non-structural elements (cladding, parapets, staircases, etc.) must be securely tied to the structural system.
• Protect escape routes from falling glass or cladding.

Non-structural elements
• Structural damage, gas explosions and fire can be caused by movement and failure of non-structural elements.
• Incoming gas services should have automatic safety shut off valves.
• Performance of structural elements can be compromised or altered by the action of non-structural elements.
• Injury and death can be caused by falling non-structural elements.
• Cost of repair of non-structural elements can render a building unviable.
• All large appliances, cylinders and tall furniture should be bolted or strapped in place and loose items such as crockery or books that could fall and cause injury should be stored at low level.

42.46 *Braced timber-framed structures are likely to fail at their weakest point – usually where they are un-braced in their supporting storey of extended timber piles*

Concrete structures
- Concrete fill and landscaping soil on top of concrete slabs have no cohesion, no benefit and may cause excessive loads which contribute to collapse.
- Concrete structures shaken by successive earthquakes may suffer unseen and cumulatively worsening damage.

Steel framed structures
Assumptions that welded steel frames will have sufficient ductility to perform well during tremors have not been borne out by recent events in Kobe and California. Beam-to-column connections have cracked due to construction, material and bonding failures. Standards and codes have been revised in these areas.

Timber framed buildings
It is essential to create rigidity by using shear walls (studs stiffened by rigid ply panels) and to maintain continuity through the structure. Cripple walls, especially as aboveground substructure, form a 'soft storey' and are a regular point of failure, Figure 42.46. Structures built on top of piers must be securely restrained. Masonry chimneys set into timber framed buildings may collapse and upper floors with structural panels in the floor around the chimney will reduce the risk of injury.

6.3 Power
Mains power supply may be unreliable or only available in larger urban areas; however, many tropical countries have modern reliable utilities. Standards for voltage vary. The design of the distribution system is as for temperate climates except that high soil temperatures may lead to a requirement for cable sizes to be larger to avoid overheating and cables might need protection against termites and other hungry fauna.

6.4 Solar heating
At its simplest, a solar heater is a coil of hosepipe drawing water from the mains water supply which is set into a flat framed box set at an angle, usually on a roof, that will enable it to absorb the maximum amount of sunlight. In the box, the hosepipe is laid on a reflective surface, and covered with a sheet of heat-absorbing glass, both of which are designed to heat up the water in the hosepipe as quickly as possible. The heated water is drawn off as needed using separate taps, or is stored once a predetermined temperature is reached. These water heaters are simple and effective, but do not raise water temperature significantly on cold or heavily overcast days, when hot water is most needed. They also need maintaining,

as the hose is subjected to extreme heat and has a relatively short life. Ready-made solar heaters use more sophisticated materials. The heated water is usually stored in a tank and drawn off as needed.

6.5 Water supply
Table XII gives standards that have been recommended by international organisations. However, the standards actually adopted must be related to local resources and conditions. In some countries, brackish water for irrigation is supplied by an independent system to conserve drinking water. Table XIII shows the large amounts of water required to maintain lawns and Western style gardens.

Where water supplies are erratic, scarce or costly, measures that reduce water consumption should be considered. These include using low-flush or dry toilets, showers in lieu of baths and the use of 'grey water'. Grey water is water that has already been used, in domestic washing, in chilling plant or in industry, and it is used to flush toilets and for uses other than drinking and cooking.

Design of a rainwater collection and storage system may be part of the building designer or services engineer's task. Water may be collected off expanses of sloping smooth surfaces, in seepage dams or in open tanks. Bacteria multiply at an astonishing rate in open water exposed to the sun.

Table XII Daily domestic water standards (litres per capita)

Distribution	Minimum (or reduced or temporary supply)	Normal	With wastage allowances
Standpipe for up to 100 persons	120	140	160
Single tap connections	120	160	180
Multiple tap connections	160	200	240
Multiple tap connections in areas of water shortage	100	150	–

Source: WHO, World Bank.

Table XIII Water supply for irrigation in hot dry climates

Type of vegetation	Water supply requirement	litres/hectare/day
Private gardens	Maximum	350 000
Private gardens	Average	225 000
Private gardens without grass		170 000
Irrigated vegetables	Average	80 000
Public parks		60–140 000
Tree plantations		2–7000

6.6 Sanitary installations and waste disposal

Sanitary appliances

Customary and religious practices vary. Some societies prefer the more ergonomically correct squat pan to the Western WC. Muslims wash in running water, so prefer the shower to the bath, and wash hand basins should have a mixer rather than separate hot and cold taps.

Foul sewerage

The capacity of piped systems will be related to the water supply standard. Where sewers are laid with low falls and where high soil temperatures exist, sewage may become septic and attack asbestos cement and cement pipes. Sewage disposal may be by pit latrine, aqua privy or septic tank in low-density development. Pit latrines require adequate space for replacements after the average life of five years, although this depends on soil conditions, etc. They should be stack vented. European toilets and septic tanks sized in accordance with Western data will not be able to cope with the bulky stools produced by a high-bulk cereal diet based on maize and similar cereals. Standard design data for septic tanks will be available. The length of tail drains depends on the soil type.

6.7 Storm and surface water drainage

Design rainfall intensities may not have been measured, making it difficult to calculate the size of gutters but indicative data could be collected on site. Tropical storms can have brief periods with rainfall intensities of 100 mm/h. Frequently, very heavy rain follows a long dry period during which drainage channels become blocked with sand and soil. In these zones, open or openable monsoon or storm drains are used to provide adequate capacity and ease of cleansing. Where piped systems are employed large sand traps are needed at each gully, and a minimum pipe size of 150 mm is necessary (200 mm is sometimes mandatory). Gradients should give a minimum self-cleansing velocity of 1 m/s. Roof gutters may not be provided at the eaves where torrential rains are experienced, as they cannot cope with the volume of water. Water discharges straight off the roof into open dish drains, or onto a wide concrete apron with a fall away from the building to prevent any splashback onto walls which may be single skin. Porches that redirect the water are needed at entrances. Mosquitoes would breed in shallow water lying in gutters with low falls. On larger buildings where gutters are provided, these may be in the form of heavy and costly concrete features, but large section gutters are becoming available in a range of materials, including aluminium and steel. Large gutters in GRP or other more flexible materials would need to tested for strength to withstand the full water load if not fully supported.

6.8 Controlling mosquitoes and other flying insects

Mosquitoes (and other insects, including moths) are attracted to bright lights, still air and water. Geckoes and chameleons eat them.

The normal means of deterring mosquitoes have been to:

- prevent insects from entering buildings at all times;
- attract insects away from buildings;
- protect the body at night, especially early evening – when mosquitoes are most prevalent;
- take measures to kill any insects that have entered buildings;
- increase air movement in and around buildings (mosquitoes like still air);
- eliminate breeding sites around buildings; and
- undertake mass spraying programmes over larger areas.

Design solutions include:

- fly-screening all windows and open doorways;
- using mosquito nets over beds;
- increasing air movement using fans, stack venting and wind funnelling devices;
- avoiding bright lights, especially in open sitting or dining areas;
- using exterior lighting to draw them away from occupied buildings;
- using electronic devices that use bright light or smell to attract and kill insects;
- eliminating all existing or potential areas of standing water where mosquitoes breed, which will include cutting back undergrowth and controlling landscaping.

Mosquito nets are essential, but they restrict ventilation. The net may be suspended from a timber or metal frame, like a lightweight four-poster, or from the ceiling on a frame or circular ring (a hospital net). The net should be long enough to tuck securely around and under the mattress.

The use of sprayed insecticides within buildings at night has traditionally included organo-phosphates and other cumulative poisons. Long-term use of these substances is harmful. All chemicals need to be treated with caution. In the tropics, spraying, on either the domestic or mass scale, may still be carried out using chemicals such as DDT, which are banned in the developed world.

Elimination of standing water is very important, and extends beyond the careful design of open gutters and drains to ensure that the fall is sufficient to take water away from inhabited areas. Some local authorities will have strictly enforced byelaws banning the planting of maize and other plants where the leaf forms a sheath around the stem, trapping water. Water used in landscaping should be agitated by fountains or the recycling mechanism and not allowed to become stagnant. Swimming pools and their overspill areas will need similar care, especially if not treating with the type of chemicals that keep insects at bay. Other breeding sites can include sedimentation ponds on sewage farms, agriculturally dammed fields (paddy fields) and the large lagoons that linger in low-lying areas after heavy rains or coastal storms.

7 BUILDING SCIENCE DATA

7.1 Sun path diagrams

The use of sunpath diagrams and shadow angle protractors is fully detailed in the texts listed in the Bibliography. When the sunpath diagrams for the northern hemisphere are used for the southern hemisphere, changes should be made to the time, month, azimuth, direction as shown in Table XIV. Shading coefficients are given in Table XV. Online sunpath calculation tools are available.

7.2 Albedo (also known as solar reflectance or ground reflectance)

Albedo is the percentage of solar radiation reflected from a surface, compared to the incoming (incident) solar radiation that the surface receives. The term signifies 'Whiteness' and therefore reflectance within the visible spectrum, but is usually taken to mean total short-wave energy. Albedo varies according to the colour, seasonal

Table XIV Changes for sunpath diagrams in southern latitudes

Time (solar time)		Date		Azimuth degree clockwise		Direction
North→South		North→South		North→South		North→South
4	20	28 Jan	30 July	0	180	
5	19	28 Feb	30 Aug	30	210	
6	18	21 Mar	23 Sept	60	240	North–South
7	17	15 April	15 Oct	90	270	
7	17	15 May	15 Nov	120	300	
11	13	22 June	22 Dec	150	330	East–West
12	12	30 July	28 Jan	180	360	
13	11	30 Aug	28 Feb	210	30	
13	11	23 Sept	21 Mar	240	60	South–North
17	7	15 Oct	15 April	270	90	
18	6	15 Nov	15 May	300	120	
19	5	22 Dec	22 June	330	150	West–East
20	4			360	180	

Table XV Shading coefficients: the quantity of solar radiation transmitted as a proportion of that transmitted through clear glass

Fenestration	Shading coefficient
Clear 6 mm glass	1.00
Glass with internal dark roller blind	0.70–0.80
Glass with internal dark Venetian blind	0.75
Glass with internal medium Venetian blind	0.55–0.65
Glass with internal white Venetian blind	0.45–0.55
Glass with external miniature louvres	0.50–0.10 (depends on angle of incidence)
Glass with dark canvas external awning	0.20–0.28
Glass with dense trees providing shade	0.20–0.30
Glass with movable louvres	0.10–0.20
Heat absorbing glasses	0.45–0.80

Table XVI Albedo of surfaces on and around buildings*

Category	Type	Albedo (%)
Soil	White sand	34–40
	Light clay	30–31
	Grey earth – dry	35–30
	Grey earth – moist	10–12
Natural vegetation and ground cover	Fresh snow	75–95
	Rock	12–15
	Tall grass	18–20
	Deciduous woodland	18
	Short grass – lawn	23–25
	Water – lakes, sea	3–10
Building materials	Weathered concrete	22
	Red cement tile	18
	White concrete tile – new	77
	Asphalt shingle – black	3.4
	Asphalt shingle – white	26
	Coated metal roofing – white	59
	Coated metal roof – slate blue	19
	Coated metal roof – various greens	8–24
	EPDM – grey	23
	Aluminium roofing – untreated	71

*Sources: Muneer (1997) [soil and vegetation] and Parker et al. of FSEC (2000) [building materials, except 'weathered concrete'].

variations in ground cover (snow, deciduous trees, crops) and, to a lesser extent, humidity of the surface covering. To avoid overheating, surfaces exposed to solar radiation will have low absorptivities and high emissivities (high albedo) and, to accumulate heat gains and act as heat stores, will have high absorptivities and low emissivities (low albedo). Table XVI gives the albedo for a range of surfaces.

For all materials:

$$\text{Reflectivity} = \frac{1 - \text{absorptivity}}{\text{(for radiation of a given wavelength)}}$$

Absorptivity = emissivity (for radiation of a given wavelength)

$$\text{Albedo} = \frac{\text{reflected solar radiation}}{\text{incident solar radiation}}$$

Pale surfaces reflect the greatest percentage of incident radiation, thereby reflecting the associated heat away from the surfaces of the building or paving. This may make glare and heat gain worse in the adjacent building. The impact of albedo on the heat island effect in cities is an area of current research in many centres. Trees, with a low albedo, will lower temperature through different mechanisms – including metabolism and transpiration; bright surfaces reduce temperature by reflection. In the city, surfaces tend to be dark and with a low albedo (brick, asphalt, slate) so they absorb and store heat that can not easily be radiated back into the sky due to the canyon effect of city streets. These raised temperatures accelerate decay of the urban fabric, exacerbate pollution and worsen ozone concentration. Smog in the atmosphere above cities traps the hot air beneath it. It would appear that tree-planting in cities has greater benefits than high albedo of surfaces, especially as we know that raising albedo outside the city, by stripping tree cover

and replacing it with cultivation, has the effect of lowering rainfall and increasing the risk of drought.

7.3 Sol air temperature

Sol air temperature is the temperature of the outside air that would give the same rate of heat transfer and the same distribution of temperature through a construction as the combined effects of solar radiation and air temperature. Sol air temperature will be higher than air temperature when a surface is subject to solar radiation:

$$\theta_{sa} = \frac{\alpha I +}{f_o} \theta_o$$

where

θ_{sa} = sol air temperature (°C)
α = absorptivity of surface to solar radiation
f_o = outside surface conductance (W/m²K)
I = intensity of solar radiation (W/m²)
θ_o = outside air temperature (°C).

The solar heat factor is the heat flow through the construction due to solar radiation, expressed as a proportion of the total solar radiation incident on the surface of the construction. When a building has large openings and is well ventilated to the exterior (as is often the case in the tropics), the solar heat factor is dependent on the U-value and absorptivity (the external surface conductance 'f_o' can be taken as a constant):

$$\frac{q}{I} = \frac{U\alpha}{f_o}$$

Surfaces will be hottest when wind velocities are low; therefore, external surface resistances for cold conditions should not be used. In hot conditions with low wind speeds, a recommended value for f_o is 20 W/(m²K). If the solar heat factor is expressed as a percentage then:

$$\frac{q}{I} = \frac{U\alpha}{20} \times 100 = 5U\alpha$$

U-values may be increased if absorptivities are proportionately reduced, while still maintaining a constant solar heat factor. Most reflective surfaces require regular maintenance to remain effective, so if maintenance or repainting of surfaces cannot be assured, U-values should be decreased to obtain realistic standards.

A solar heat factor of less than 4 per cent will ensure that ceiling temperatures will not be more than 5°C above air temperatures and will not add to discomfort.

The approximate absorptivity of solar radiation of paints can be calculated if the Munsell value is known (as it is for colours in the BS range of paints for building purposes). The 'value' of the colour is given by the number which appears after the 'hue' letter in the Munsell number. This should be substituted for V in the formula:

Absorptivity = 100 − <V(V−1)] (for solar radiation)
Example: Munsell number 6.25Y8.5/13 (Yellow)
V= 8.5, Absorptivity = 38% (at low temperatures most paints have an emissivity of 80–90%).

7.4 Solar radiation

The intensity of solar radiation on a surface depends on the altitude of the sun, the orientation of the surface in relation to the sun and the absorption of solar radiation by the atmosphere, pollution, cloud, etc., Figure 42.47.

Calculation: For vertical surfaces inclined at an angle θ to the azimuth (horizontal angle of sun on plan), the intensity of radiation on surface I will be:

$I_\theta = I_v \times \cos\theta$, where I_v is taken from Figure 42.47.

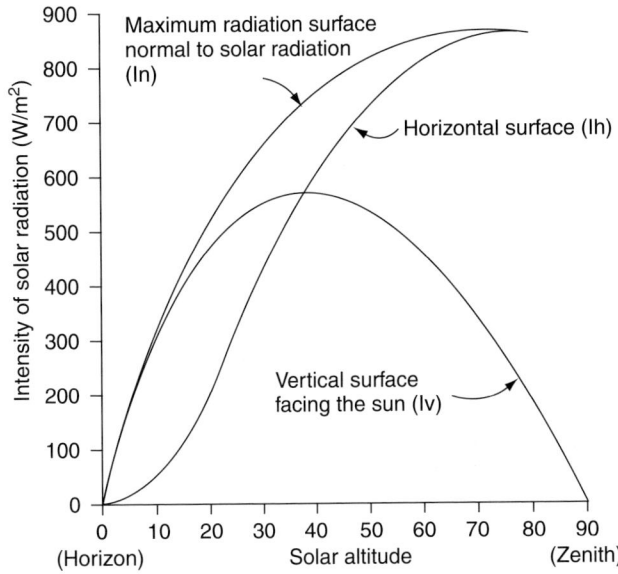

42.47 *Intensity of solar radiation*

Table XVII Increase in solar radiation with altitude

Height above sea level	Altitude of sun in degrees				
	20°	**30°**	**40°**	**60°**	**80°**
900	1.14	1.12	1.10	1.08	1.08
1500	1.26	1.20	1.17	1.15	1.15
3000	1.30	1.31	1.28	1.25	1.23

Table XVIII Effect of cloud and atmospheric pollution on radiation*

Very low humidities and clear skies	1.1 (increase)
High humidities and pollution 'clear sky'	0.9 (decrease)
Overcast sky	0.1–0.3 (decrease)

*Varies greatly with cloud and solar altitude

Table XIX Illumination from a design sky

Latitude (N or S)	Design sky illumination
0°	17 000 lux
10°	15 000 lux
20°	13 000 lux
30°	9 000 lux
40°	6 000 lux
50°	5 000 lux

The altitude and azimuth of the sun can be found from sunpath diagrams or online calculation tools. The radiation from Figure 42.47 should be multiplied by the values from Tables XVII and XVIII to give total radiation at the appropriate altitude and/or for appropriate atmospheric conditions.

7.5 Illumination from sun and sky in the tropics

Illumination at work surfaces
The illumination required at the work surface for a given task is the same regardless of latitude. However, since light is associated with heat (both physically and psychologically), there is a case in the tropics for adopting slightly lower lighting standards to achieve higher levels of thermal comfort. In some countries, the cost of achieving high lighting standards may also be a factor.

The illumination from the sky is greater in tropical and sub-tropical regions so that a lower daylight factor can be used to achieve the same illumination at the work surface. The illumination from an overcast sky varies with latitude, altitude, degree of cloudiness and pollution. A guide is given in Table XIX.

Table XX Sun, sky and ground brightness

Hot dry desert conditions	Sky (away from sun)	3 000 lux
	Sun	50 000 lux
	Ground (20% reflectivity)	11 000 lux
Warm humid equatorial conditions	Sky (overcast)	10 000 lux
	Ground (20% reflectivity)	2000 lux

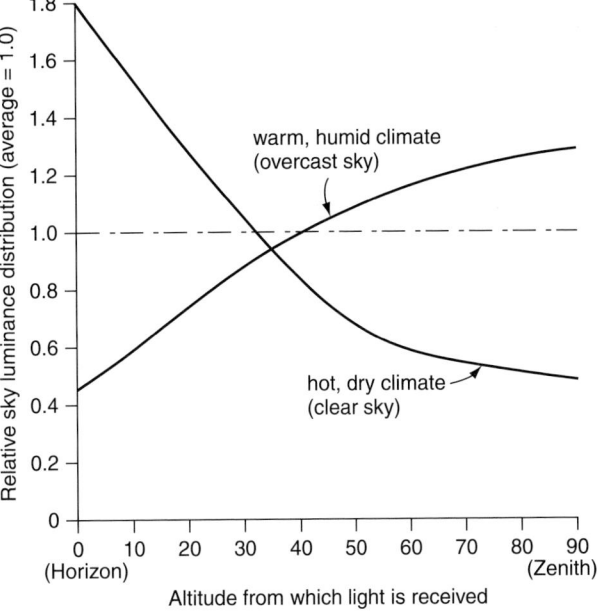

42.48 *Sky luminance distribution*

Position of windows – overcast skies
An overcast sky can be extremely bright and cause unacceptable glare from higher angular altitudes above 35°. Windows that offer a view below the 35° angle will increase comfort. In the warm humid equatorial regions, however, the luminance of the constant overcast sky may drop to 10 000 lux or below.

Position of windows – clear skies
Hot dry desert regions receive light mainly from direct sunlight and considerably less from the (usually) deep blue sky, so windows should allow a view of this high altitude deep blue sky rather than along the horizon, which can reflect glare from distant haze and the sunlit ground. The window must be protected from direct solar radiation, if facing into the sun's path.

Incidence of light
Table XX gives a very rough comparison of the relative amount of light from different sources. Figure 42.48 shows the relative sky luminance distribution in hot dry desert climates with a clear sky, and for warm humid climates with an overcast sky. (It is assumed that the warm, humid climate has a similar distribution to the CIE standard overcast sky.)

7.6 Glazing used in solar control
The best way to reduce solar radiation heat gain is to reduce window size (or provide external shading). Special solar control glass absorbs heat and this will cause thermal expansion, Table XXI. The high temperature of the glass may also cause physical discomfort. For comparison, a sheet of aluminium or an uninsulated concrete slab has been included in the table. Most special glasses will match these temperatures.

Body-tinted glass
Oxides are added to clear glass to change the colour and vary light and solar radiant heat transmission: iron oxide (green), cobalt oxide (grey and blue) and selenium oxide (bronze). Increased thickness darkens the colour and reduces light and heat transmission.

Table XXI Solar heat gains through glass*

Fenestration	Visible radiation transmitted %	Direct solar radiation transmitted %	Total solar radiation transmitted %	Index of increase of surface temp. above air temp (clear glass = 1)
Clear float glass	85	80	84	1
Glass with reflective polyester film	18	17	25	2
	33	31	39	2
Solar energy reflecting glass	42	47	52	2.5
	58	59	62	4
Surface modified heat absorbing glass	50	56	67	3
	50	48	62	4
Tinted solar control glass grey	42	45	62	4
	42	40	58	4
	24	22	47	4
	19	16	43	4.5
	76	52	66	4
green	74	45	61	4
	62	30	51	4
Clear glass with open weave curtain internally	40	70	82	1
Corrugated aluminium (new)	0	0	9	2
100 mm concrete	0	0	15	4

* Ranges of products are given. Consult manufacturers for specific data.
Sources: Manufacturers' data; heat gains through fenestration. F. J. Lotz and J. F. van Straaten, CSIR: R/Bov 223.

Coated and surface modified glasses
A film of microscopically thin metallic oxides is laid on the surface of clear or body-tinted glass and is usually protected or sealed within a sandwich of two or more layers of glass. Film performance is independent of glass thickness. Coated glasses receive their coating in a vacuum chamber; surface modified glasses are produced during the float process, using clear glass.

These coated and surface-modified glasses may modify:

- light transmission
- solar radiation properties
- thermal insulation characteristics (by modifying surface emissivities).

Glass blocks
Glass blocks are available with different surface finishes that can diffuse, reduce or deflect light transmission. The mortar joint reduces thermal performance when compared to double-glazing, but they can also serve structural or fire protection functions. Most manufacturers recommend that glass blocks be used in shaded locations as the blocks can overheat or, in some cases, act as prisms with consequent risk of fire.

7.7 Wind
The Beaufort wind scale was initially developed for use at sea. It does not indicate wind speed and is usually replaced today by wind speed, measured 10 m above ground, in knots. Table XXII provides a conversion chart.

Wind loading on buildings varies with height, as friction with the ground slows down the wind at lower levels. This wind gradient is complex, but may be calculated. The American (USA) Building Codes give gradients levels of 300 m for cities, 400 m for suburbs

Table XXII Beaufort scale: descriptors and equivalent speeds for use on land. Separate descriptors apply at sea

Force	Description	Miles/hour	Kilometre/hour	Knots	Specification on land
0	Calm	0–1	0–1.6	0–1	Smoke rises vertically
1	Light air movement	1–3	1.6–5	1–3	Direction shown by smoke but not wind vanes
2	Light breeze	4–7	6–11	4–6	Wind felt on face, leaves rustle
3	Gentle breeze	8–12	13–19	7–10	Wind extends light flags, leaves in constant motion
4	Moderate breeze	13–18	21–29	11–16	Raises dust and loose paper, small branches are moved, onset of mechanical discomfort
5	Fresh breeze	19–24	31–39	17–21	Small trees in leaf begin to sway, uncomfortable in urban areas
6	Strong breeze	25–31	40–50	22–27	Large branches in motion, telegraph wires whistle, umbrellas difficult to use
7	Near gale	32–38	31–61	28–33	Whole trees in motion, difficult to walk against wind
8	Gale	39–46	63–74	34–40	Breaks twigs off trees, generally slows down walking
9	Strong gale	47–54	76–87	41–47	Slight structural damage occurs, tiles and slates dislodged
10	Storm	55–63	89–101	48–55	Seldom experienced inland
11	Violent storm	64–72	103–121	56–63	Trees uprooted
12	Hurricane	73–83	122+	64–71	Rarely experienced, accompanied by widespread damage
13–17					Beaufort numbers from force 13 to force 17 were added in 1955 by the United States Weather Bureau in 1955 to accommodate the exceptional winds experienced during a hurricane.

and 500 m for flat open terrain. Structural engineers may use the power law wind speed profile given below:

$$v_z = v_g \cdot \left(\frac{z}{z_g} \right)^{\frac{1}{\alpha}}, 0 < z < z_g$$

where:

v_z = speed of the wind at height z

v_g = gradient wind at gradient height z_g

α = exponential coefficient

Effect of internal wind speeds in warm humid climates
We can measure the effect of air movement within buildings, Table XXIII.

Hurricanes, typhoons, tsunami and tornadoes
Terminology varies from region to region. In addition to generating abnormally high wind loads, hurricanes, typhoons and tornadoes also cause extreme pressure differentials. Structural detailing and the fixing of non-structural elements must withstand the forces

Table XXIII Effect of internal wind speed in warm humid climates

Windspeed M/minimum	Effect
0–15	Not noticeable, less than 1°C of apparent cooling to the body
15–30	Cooling just noticeable – effect equal to a drop of temperature of 1–2°C
30–60	Effective and pleasant cooling
60–100	Maximum windspeed for cooling without undesirable side effects
100–200	Too fast for desk work; papers start to blow around
+200	Too fast and uncomfortable for internal conditions

Table XXIV Effect of wind on sand

Windspeed M/minimum	Effect*
200	Sweeping sand. Visibility not impaired. Sand blown along the surface or up to 1 m above the ground.
300	Driving sand. Visibility impaired. Sand rises up to 2 m above the ground.
600	Sandstorm. Particles of sand remain suspended in the air.

*Depends on size of sand grain and on sand humidity.

Table XXV Time lag for homogeneous materials (in hours)

Materials		Thickness of material (mm)					
		25	50	100	150	200	300
Dense concrete	minimum	–	1.5	3.0	4.4	6.1	9.2
	maximum	–	1.1	2.5	3.8	4.9	7.6
Brick	minimum	–	–	2.3	–	5.5	8.5
	maximum	–	–	3.2	–	6.6	10
Wood	minimum	0.4	1.3	3.0	–	–	–
	maximum	0.5	1.7	3.5	–	–	–
Fibre insulating board	ave	0.27	0.77	2.7	5.0	–	–
Concrete with foamed slag aggregate	ave	–	–	3.25	–	8	–
Stone	ave	–	–	–	–	5.5	8.0
Stabilised soil	ave	–	–	2.4	4.0	5.2	8.1

Table XXVI Time lag for composite roof constructions

Construction		Time lag (hours)
(described from the external surface inwards)		
40 mm	Mineral wool	
100 mm	Concrete	11.8
100 mm	Concrete	3
40 mm	Mineral wool	(same as concrete alone)
14 mm	Cement plaster	
165 mm	Concrete	
14 mm	Cement plaster	3.8
14 mm	Cement plaster	
50 mm	Vermiculite concrete	
115 mm	Concrete	
14 mm	Cement plaster	13
Any finish		
25 mm	Expand polystyrene any structural concrete slab	over 8
Any finish		
75 mm	Lightweight concrete screed	
100 mm	Concrete slab	over 8
30 mm	Concrete tiles	
20 mm	Motor bed waterproof membrane	
60 mm	Screed	
240 mm	Hollow pot slab	
14 mm	Render	12

the actual internal conditions can only be calculated when the heat flow into rooms and onto all room surfaces is considered.

8 BIBLIOGRAPHY, INFORMATION SOURCES AND FURTHER READING

Regional Building Research Institutes
Governmental Agencies (such as the local Ministry of Works)
Professional bodies
Centres with expertise, including aid agencies
Regional Trade Associations using locally sourced or manufactured materials
National Archives

Websites

Website references were correct at the time of printing, but are tiresomely ephemeral. Check copyright notices and disclaimers before using material. Most aspects of tropical design are extremely well covered on the Internet.

Alternative energy including Photovoltaics
CIBSE TM25 – Dr Rosemary Rawlings & Mark Roper (2000)
Understanding building integrated photovoltaics, CIBSE
Studio E Architects (2000) BIPV Projects: photovoltaics in buildings, DTI New & Renewable Energy Programme, London
The Centre for Alternative Technology – www.cat.org.uk
The Energy Technology Support Unit (ETSU) – www.etsu.com
The International Solar Energy Society – www.ises.org

Climate
Givoni, B. ed. (1969) *Man, Climate and Architecture*, Elsevier, London
Koenigsberger, H., Ingersol, T. G., Mayhew, A. and Szokolay, S. V. (1974) *Manual of Tropical Building and Housing: Part 1 – Climatic Design*, Longman, Harlow
Couto Erminda da C. G., Zyngier, Nicole A. C., Gomes, Viviane R., Knoppers, Bastiaan A. and Landim de Souza, Marcelo F. DIN and DIP budgets for Maricá-Guarapina coastal lagoons, Rio de Janeiro State Bureau of Meteorology, Australia – www.bom.gov.au/lam/climate
US Department of Energy
www.worldclimate.com
www.weathersite.com
The Met Office – www.met-office.gov.uk
www.millennium-debate.org/climatechange.htm

caused by the negative and positive pressure generated in these storms. Most countries experiencing these climatic events have appropriate building regulations concerning fixing and bracing for roofs, windows and structural design loadings. The risk of lightning strikes must also be considered. Electrical storms can be frequent and dramatic.

Sandstorms
Table XXIV shows the effect of wind on sand movements. This may vary with building height, sometimes becoming more severe at greater heights. Tight closing of all openings is required to reduce nuisance from blown sand. Finishes may need to withstand scouring and abrasion. Complete protection is not usually practical.

7.8 Ventilation

Data on ventilation requirements and on mechanical ventilation is now widely available from CIBSE and other professional engineering institutions.

7.9 Lag

Time lag is the phase difference (delay) between external periodic variations in temperatures and the resulting internal temperature variations. The period of variations is 24 h and the lag is measured in hours. Table XXV gives time lag for homogeneous materials. For composite construction, the order in which different layers are placed can change the time lag considerably. If insulation is placed on the external surface of a dense material, the time lag is considerably increased. Table XXVI gives the time lag of a range of constructions. Although the time lag indicates when the thermal impact of outside temperature swings will affect the interior,

Design

Fathy, Hassan (1986) *Natural Energy and Vernacular Architecture: Principles and Examples with Reference to hot Arid Climates*, The University of Chicago Press, Chicago

Fry, Maxwell and Drew, Jane (1964) *Tropical Design*, Batsford Oliver, Paul ed. (1976) *Shelter in Africa*, Barrie and Jenkins Ltd

Hyde, Richard (2000) *Climate Responsive Design: a study of buildings in moderate and hot humid climates*, E & FN Spon

Konya, Allan (1980) *Design Primer for Hot Climates*, Architectural Press

Littlefair, P. J., et al. (2000) Environmental site layout planning: solar access, microclimate and passive cooling in urban areas, BRE

Tzonis, A., Lefaivre, L. and Stagno, B. eds. (2001) *Tropical Architecture: Critical Regionalism in the Age of Globalisation*, Wiley-Academy

Earthquakes

British Geological Survey – www.gsrg.nmh.ac.uk

US Geological Survey – www.earthquake.usgs.gov

National Earthquake Information Centre World Data Center for Seismology – www.neic.usgs.gov

Moehle, J. P. and Mahin, S. A. (1991) Observations on the behaviour of reinforced concrete buildings during earthquakes, American Concrete Institute publication SP-127, re-published by National Information Service for Earthquake Engineering – University of California, Berkeley – www.eerc.berkeley.edu/lessons/concretemm.html

The US Federal Emergency Management Agency (FEMA) has research on steel frame buildings – www.fema.gov

The American Plywood Association – APA Homeowner's guide to earthquake safeguards – www.mcvicker.com/twd/apa/eqguide/eqguid01.htm

Building Research Station Tropical building legislation: model building regulations for small buildings in earthquake and hurricane areas, 1966

Economics

Roberts, Peter (1995) *Environmentally sustainable business: a local and regional perspective*, London: Paul Chapman Publishing

Health

World Health Organisation – tropical diseases home page – www.who.int/tdr/

Hospital for Tropical Diseases, University College Hospital and Mortimer Market, London – www.uchl.org/services/htd/

Housing

NBRI Researchers (1987) Low Cost Housing, National Building Research Institute, Council for Scientific and Industrial Research, Pretoria, South Africa

Monographs

Taylor, Brian Brace (1995) *Geoffrey Bawa*, Thames and Hudson, London

Natural light (daylight, sunlight)

Online sunpath calculation tool – www.susdesign.com/sunangle/ – Read the disclaimers and shareware notices

Bartlett School of Graduate Studies (1998) Daylighting design in architecture: making the most of natural resources, BRESCU CIBSE LG10:1999 – Daylighting and Window Design, CIBSE

Lam, W. (1986) *Sunlight as Formgiver for Architecture*, Van Nostrand, New York

Littlefair, P. J. (1988) BRE IP 15/88: Average daylight factor: a simple basis for daylight design, Construction Research Communications, London

Muneer, T. (2000) *Solar Radiation and Daylight Models for the Energy-Efficient Design of Buildings*, Architectural Press, Oxford

Parker, D. S. et al. (2000) Laboratory testing of the Reflectance Properties of Roofing Materials, Florida Solar Energy Centre – http://www.fsec.ucf.edu/~bdac/pubs/CR670/CR670.html

Sharma, M. R. and Rao, K. R. Solar radiation protractors Central Building Research Institute. Rorkee, India. Equidistant projection 15°N–15°S; 15°N–35°N at 5 degree intervals (reproduced in Givoni Man, climate and architecture Elsevier 1969)

Solar charts and shadow angle protractor for daylight planning Catalogue no 374. Henry Hope & Sons. London. 1969. Stereographic projection 32°N–28°S at 4 degree intervals Richards, S. J. South African architectural record Vol 36 No 11. Stereographic projection 20°S–34°S at 2 degree intervals (reprinted by South African Council for Scientific and Industrial Research, Pretoria 1952)

AJ Handbook of Building Environment. Information Sheet-Sunlight 5, 30.10.68 pp. 1024–1035. Gnomic projection 040° (N or S) at 2 degree intervals

NB: All sunpath diagrams for the northern hemisphere can be used for the southern hemisphere by reversing the hours and months and rotating the azimuth scale by 180°.

Sustainable design

Edwards, Brian (2nd ed 1999) *Sustainable Architecture: European directives and Building design*, Architectural Press, Oxford

Smith, Peter F. (2001) *Architecture in a climate of change – a guide to sustainable design, Architectural Press*, Oxford

Termites

Australian Standard AS 3660-1993: Protection of buildings from Subterranean Termites – Prevention, Detection and treatment of Infestation, Standards Association of Australia

Ventilation

NatVent Consortium (1999) Natural ventilation for offices, BRESCU, BRE

43 Universities

Mike Hart and Rod McAllister

Mike Hart is an Education Design Consultant and Rod McAllister is a partner of Sheppard Robson Architects – both specialise in university design

KEY POINTS:

- *The UK higher education system is becoming increasingly diverse. This diversity is expressed in the use of space, particularly between teaching-led and research-led universities. Space will be subject increasingly to remodelling for new needs or to meet new standards. With imaginative design, space can be deployed flexibly to meet multiple uses*

- *Increasingly, more provision is being made for student-led and 'blended learning' (a mixture of face-to-face plus IT-mediated learning). This will demand more relatively small and adaptable spaces. IT developments are enabling more intensive use of space for teaching and learning*

Contents

1 Introduction
2 Layout guidance
3 Environment
4 Do's and don'ts
5 Briefing overview
6 Bibliography

1 INTRODUCTION

1.1 Definition

Universities are places of learning and research in a variety of subjects at the highest level and are often, therefore, described as being institutes within the Higher Education sector. Derived from the Latin *universitas magistrorum et scholarium*, which could be translated as a 'corporation of masters and scholars', the university was conceived as a place of academic freedom in contrast to specific training for crafts or trades in the medieval period. In time, universities were authorised to confer degrees and are now significant contributors to national and regional economies all over the world.

1.2 Scope

Modern universities vary hugely, having differing emphases on subjects and research. Their locations and student base are also diverse. This section of the handbook seeks to provide broad guidance for designers of new university facilities but this guidance could be extended to upgrading or extending existing buildings. The range of accommodation examined represents the typical core building stock of modern, Western universities. The figures provided represent average or recommended dimensions and values and would be subject to adjustment for more specific requirements.

1.3 Types

Urban universities

The traditional university model has been linked with city life in Europe since the Universities of Bologna and Paris were founded in 1088 and 1150 and later in Oxford (1167) and Cambridge (1209), Figure 43.1. The study of theology was central to university life and consequently these early institutes bore strong relation to monasteries in their arrangements being characterised by cloistered courtyards, chapels and refectories. Some would argue that Western universities may have been influenced by, or were based on, Islamic *Madrasha* schools in the ninth century Middle East as observed by crusaders.

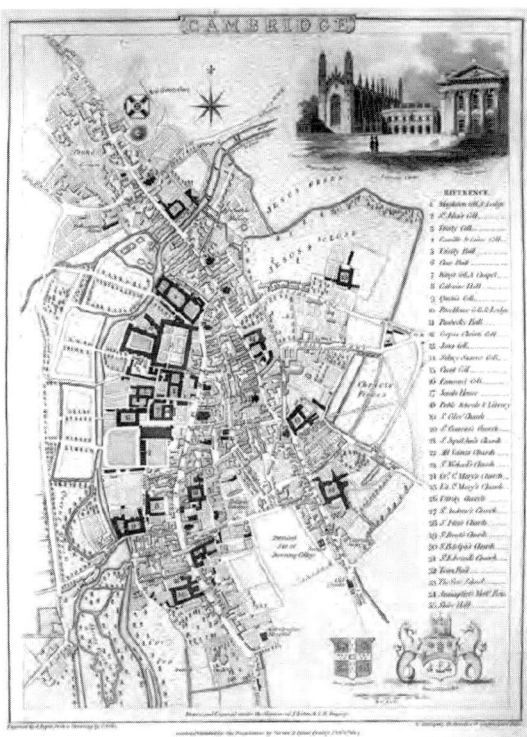

43.1 *Cambridge town plan: Cole and Roper map of Cambridge, 1804*

Collegiate universities

Many universities evolved into college-based institutes, the earliest include Paris, Oxford, Cambridge and, later, Durham. In this model, formal lectures, governance and administration are provided by the university and residential, dining, tutorial and pastoral functions are provided by member 'colleges' or 'houses'. The non-college accommodation is normally organised into 'schools', 'faculties' or departments and some ceremonial buildings. Consequently, the host cities, or city quarters, developed around these universities and their colleges over many centuries and are largely defined by their presence.

Scotland established four 'Ancient' universities between 1410 and 1582. In London, a number of large and almost independent colleges were founded from 1826 onwards, each acting as a quasi-university. Some of these specialised in subject areas such as science and engineering as in the case of Imperial College London. Their buildings tend to cluster in city-centre sites later referred to as 'campuses' after the College of New Jersey (later renamed Princeton University).

Subsequent urban universities

There followed an explosion in university creation in major cities across the UK and Ireland from 1828 to 1909. Whilst these were not necessarily based on the collegiate model, some included colleges and most became important parts in inner-city life, often creating distinctive academic city 'quarters'. Their physical composition

43.2 *Red brick university: University of Birmingham*

moved away from the monastic model, through classic palatial and towards Victorian civic grandeur, Figure 43.2.

From 1992, over seventy new universities were created from former polytechnics, 'university colleges' and higher education institutes. Most of these occupy urban groupings that were consolidated from disparate buildings to create urban campuses wherever possible. In this way, many new universities have more in common urbanistically with the 'Ancient Universities' than those of the Victorian and Edwardian eras.

Rural and suburban campus universities
Waves of university construction following the World Wars, driven by government policy aimed at social mobility, led to a proliferation of sylvan campuses across Britain. Their compositions were varied and experimental, often laid out in response to masterplans by individual architects.

Further education
Further education (FE) is post-compulsory education that is distinct from education offered in universities, and has grown significantly to become recognised as a separate sector. It provides education, from basic training to HND or Foundation Degree.

Institutions considered part of the FE sector include:

- general FE and tertiary colleges;
- sixth form colleges;
- specialist colleges (e.g. land-based colleges);
- adult education institutions.

Further education is seen as forming one part of a wider learning and skills sector, alongside workplace education and other types of non-school, non-university education and training.

It provides 14–19-year-old learners the opportunity to progress to HE and skilled employment. It provides adult learners access to basic skills, training for work and learning for personal development. FE planning and design guidelines and best practice are significantly different from HE and are therefore not included in this chapter.

1.4 Circulation
It is essential to develop attractive and novel concepts for main entrances, external/internal wayfinding, connectivity, and the external spaces and links between buildings. Developing ideas for making the campus more inviting by creating selective transparency into student active zones/spaces should also be exploited.

External
It is desirable to determine the nature and scope of all vehicle and pedestrian circulation routes within and around the campus to minimise conflict, including movement on/off the site that is significant to the effective operation of campus facilities in order to establish proper access and egress arrangements, compliance with DDA, aggregation of flows of traffic, people and materials, and control and security provisions.

Internal
It is also desirable to develop concepts for improving the flexibility and quality of the internal spaces, particularly the de-institutionalisation of circulation routes with creative impromptu interaction spaces for students and staff, together with attractive and conducive internal vertical and horizontal circulation to enhance social contact, e.g. atria, galleries, 'streets'.

1.5 Sustainability
This is a brief summary of the key design issues to consider when developing a 'sustainable' university building. These issues may not all be relevant to the particular building, site or budget. Please note that this is written for a temperate UK/West European climate and will not be suitable for other locations.

Form
There are many matters to consider when designing the university form:

- Use narrower, open plan floorplates (12–13.5 m) if maximum daylighting and natural cross-ventilation is desirable.
- Use the building form to enhance passive/low energy strategies. Consider the use of atria, solar chimneys, lightwells and wind stacks to assist stack ventilation and make use of heat reclaim.
- Atria should extend well beyond the roof level to prevent warm, stale air build-up affecting the occupants of the upper floors.
- A compact form with a low ratio of envelope:floor area will have much lower heat loss or heat gain.
- Consider high floor to ceiling dimensions to increase daylight penetration and to prevent warm, stale air build-up at occupant level.

Orientation
- Orientate along east/west axis with primary north and south elevations.
- Eliminate solar gain as far as possible. South aspect is easier to control using screens, louvres and blinds. Also consider ratios of glazed:opaque envelope and translucent insulation.
- East and west elevations get low angled sun, which can cause problems with glare. This is very difficult to control using standard louvres.
- Specialist spaces with predominantly opaque walls (e.g. stairs, lifts cores, toilets) should ideally be positioned on east and west facades to reduce issues of glare and solar gain.

Energy use
- Primary energy use is for heating (50%), ventilation and cooling (30%), and lighting (20%). Deep plan air-conditioned buildings will have a higher proportion of ventilation and cooling costs.
- Maximise the integration of passive strategies to minimise the use of active systems that use energy (e.g. wind/solar assisted ventilation).
- Use thermal mass (preferably exposed in ceilings or walls) to absorb heat during the day and purge it at night to provide comfort conditions in the morning. This also reduces temperature swings within the space.
- Use natural or mixed-mode ventilation in preference to full air conditioning. Displacement ventilation is preferable, as it requires lower energy use for the same cooling capacity.

However it also requires larger risers and underfloor voids. A strategy that uses the atrium space or double-skin cladding systems as a return air duct can increase net floor area.

- Optimise daylight whilst being aware of glare and solar gain. Consider narrow plan form, use of atria and lightwells, ceiling profile, high ceilings, prismatic glass and light-shelves.
- Recover waste heat for pre-heating winter supply air for heat exchanging with hot water supply.
- Ensure correct balance of insulation within the facades to minimise winter heat loss and reduce summer solar gain (south and west).
- Develop a low-energy artificial lighting strategy and integrate the system with the daylighting. Use low-energy light fittings and consider controls carefully (occupancy detection, daylight sensors etc.).
- Extract air through or close to light fittings to extend lamp life and reduce heat gains.
- A 'double-skin' wall may provide various energy-saving advantages using a combination of louvres, vents, reflectors, fans and controls to create an environment buffer that reacts to the changing external climate. Summer heat gains can be vented out before they reach the inner spaces (louvres are required between the two skins). In winter, this can also provide a thermal buffer. A 'double skin' to the east facade may be used to collect passive solar gain on winter mornings, which can be used to pre-heat ventilation air.
- Design the various facades in relation to their specific orientation. Each will require a different combination of glazed areas, opaque areas, types of glass, blinds, louvres and screens.
- The facade design should be carefully integrated with the design of the services in order to create an integrated building. Too often these systems work against each other, rather than together in harmony.
- Environmental systems do not need to be technologically complex. Often the most sustainable system is one that has minimum embodied energy, fixed components, reduced capital and life-cycle costs and minimum maintenance.
- Minimise internal heat gains through specification of low heat-emitting appliances and lighting.
- Ensure that the internal comfort criteria brief is realistic so that the services system is not over-designed for heat loads that may only occur during a few days of the year. This leads to inefficient operation when the plant is running at lower capacities.
- Ensure that the detail design maximises airtightness in cold weather as this is a major contributor to heat loss.
- Deciduous trees to the south will reduce summer heat gains whilst allowing for winter gains.
- Solar thermal systems can provide 40–60% of hot water requirements. They require roof or southerly orientation (within 30 degrees of south). The hot water can be used with an absorption heat pump to provide cooling through chilled beams/ceilings or underfloor systems (maximum output is available when the cooling is required most).

Water
- Maximise area of roof and landscaping for rainwater collection.
- Provide a storage tank within the landscape or basement for rainwater storage.

Health and wellbeing
- Provide user control of lighting, humidity, heating, and ventilation. This may be arranged by groups and linked to the telephone system and/or BMS.
- Provide openable windows where possible, as occupant control has psychological health and wellbeing benefits (if external noise is not a problem).
- Pay attention to landscaping and planting inside and out. This can be used to temper the environment through natural shading, cooling and humidifying. It has been shown that certain plants also improve air quality within a building.
- Create indoor and outdoor spaces that encourage interaction, social exchange and a sense of community.
- Integrate water and planting to improve air quality, natural humidity and improve occupants' sense of wellbeing.

2 LAYOUT GUIDANCE
The UK higher education system is becoming increasingly diverse. This increasing diversity is leading to diverging approaches to the use of space, particularly between teaching-led and research-led universities. Space will be subject increasingly to remodelling for new needs or to meet new standards. With imaginative design, space can be deployed flexibly to meet multiple uses.

'Learning space' is seen as one of these new needs, with more provision being made for student-led and 'blended learning' (a mixture of face-to-face plus IT-mediated learning). This will demand more relatively small and adaptable spaces. IT developments are enabling more intensive use of space for teaching and learning.

2.1 Key points
An educational building is an expensive long-term resource. The design of its individual spaces needs to be:

- Flexible: to accommodate both current and evolving pedagogies.
- Future-proofed: to enable space to be re-allocated and reconfigured.
- Bold: to look beyond tried and tested technologies and pedagogies.
- Creative: to energise and inspire learners and tutors.
- Supportive: to develop the potential of all learners.
- Enterprising: to make each space capable of supporting different purposes.

Learning space should be able to motivate learners and promote learning as an activity, support collaborative as well as formal practice, provide a personalised and inclusive environment, and be flexible in the face of changing needs. Technology plays a key role in achieving these aims.

2.2 General teaching and learning
General teaching spaces have been dominated by one type of design: tutor-focused, one-way facing and presentational, with seating arranged in either a U-shaped or in straight rows. Technologies have been added – interactive or conventional whiteboards mounted on the wall behind the main speaker, ceiling-mounted projectors with cabling to a laptop, a wireless network and/or wired computers – but these have rarely altered the dynamics of the design.

The formal lecture is still seen as an effective means of inducting students, delivering whole year (first year) courses and meeting increasing student numbers on popular courses. More creative design of lecture theatres is needed with better shaped layouts, better eye contact and easier to use technology to present material in a variety of formats. Many institutions are already using general teaching rooms more intensively by not only adopting timetabling regimes but also extending the teaching hours. The latter has access and catering implications to consider.

Formal teaching
The prevailing approach is moving towards active and collaborative learning, but the room design does not always reflect this. Effective dialogue is needed to establish what will be required from these spaces and what changes in approach are desirable. The design of most general teaching spaces will need to support both tutor-led and learner-led activities. These will include presentations, discussion, collaborative project work and information retrieval and sharing. These needs can be met in different ways, with separate rooms being allocated to different purposes in some models and, at the other end of the spectrum, teaching taking place in open-plan flexible 'learning studios'. Future technological and

pedagogic developments cannot always be anticipated but what is important is to ensure that design will accommodate change.

THE INTERACTIVE CLASSROOM

Replacing the standard combination of tutorials, lectures and workshops with learning sessions involving mini-lectures, videos, demonstrations and problem solving. Questioning and discussion replaces knowledge transfer as the main model of delivery. An electronic voting system to help students test their understanding of concepts in response to multiple choice questions, and collaborative discussion before and after voting. An integral pedagogic approach.

THE TEACHING CLUSTER

A centrally managed suite of rooms that includes interactive classrooms, seminar rooms and a teaching studio, providing a mix of peer instruction, problem-based learning and studio teaching. To gain maximum collaborative discussion, curved desks added in some rooms to increase interactivity.

CENTRALISED BOOKING

Centralised online booking systems are gaining ground in higher education as a means of increasing the effectiveness in managing space utilisation of general teaching space. Most institutes consider general teaching space as non-dedicated space, shared across faculties and even across the campus. This can present the need for more storage adjacent to support the variety of general teaching carried out. This presents location considerations, as these rooms will need to be central with convenient access to all users.

Some institutions have also adopted space charging as a measure against block booking of rooms.

TIMETABLED GENERAL TEACHING ROOMS

Centralised bookable (timetabled) general teaching rooms are generally:

- lecture theatres – large (250); medium (120); small (90)
- seminar rooms – large (60); small (30)
- IT rooms – various capacities used (30+).

TUTORIAL AND SMALL GROUP TEACHING SPACE

There is a trend, by some institutes, to remove tutorial space from within academic staff offices and provide conveniently located groups of bookable tutorial rooms that can also be used for other purposes – staff meetings, interviews, confidential work/discussion, private study, professional visitors, etc. In some institutes there is a move away from individual tutorials to small group tutorials (5–6 students). There is also a demand for bookable small group teaching rooms (10–15 students), in response to electives and short courses. These rooms can also be used for other purposes.

IDENTITY AND OWNERSHIP

The centralisation and timetabling of general teaching space means it has been designated non-dedicated accommodation, diminishing the identity and ownership of departmental accommodation. However, the identity and ownership of departments can be restored by the imaginative collocation of their specialist teaching and research space, staff, tutorial rooms, resource and support facilities to stimulate a sense of community.

Informal and social learning

Learning is a remarkable social process. It occurs not as a response to teaching, but as a result of a social network that fosters learning.

SOCIAL SPACES

Well-designed social spaces are likely to increase students' motivation and may even have an impact on their ability to learn. High quality space for informal learning will also enhance the profile of the institution. Social spaces could therefore be given a high priority in new designs. If catering facilities, common rooms, even circulation spaces ('learning streets'), are considered as social meeting and group learning environments, institutions could save on large-space provision and make a statement about their vision for learning as a pervasive and inclusive activity based on social interaction.

THE LEARNING STREET

'Learning streets' are emerging in designs. Alcoves are set into the sides of wide circulation spaces, where classroom activities can extend in informal group working, or learners can 'touchdown' to access work online before a class. They are wireless enabled, as is the entire building, in anticipation of more widespread use of mobile devices. Some alcoves have grouped arrangements of computers which learners can book online. Learning is visible and active.

THE LEARNING CAFE

The 'learning cafe' was originally an early experiment in the use of space to support problem-based learning and group work and has since become successful and developed even further. They are now running successfully in many institutions. The deliberate mix of refreshments, social activities and IT makes this a relaxing and friendly place where conversation and social interaction are seen as an essential part of learning. A variety of layout, furniture and IT access for group and individual work is made available together with a refreshment bar.

2.3 Specialist teaching and research

Specialist teaching and research spaces are:

- teaching spaces that by virtue of particular servicing, fit-out, or uses need to be dedicated to a particular function or school, but which could be accommodated in a standard structural shell; or
- teaching spaces that by virtue of particular dimensional, loading or servicing requirements cannot fit into a standard shell.

Libraries/learning centres

The concept of the learning centre is still evolving, usually blending with other previously distinct spaces to absorb more of their functions. Rethinking the learning centre has led to substantial new-build projects in universities, especially where the space is envisaged as the social and academic 'hub' of the campus. However, smaller scale learning centres are also appearing connected to teaching accommodation to form 'curricular clusters' or as a separate high-tech highly personalised learning environment or 'resource centre' managed by a department/school, in addition to the library.

More intensive use is being seen in longer library opening hours, with 24 hour opening during the working week becoming more common, especially where many students are part-time. Self-service machines have facilitated this trend. Learning space is also sometimes provided in the form of rooms with banks of PCs, printers, etc. available for general student use.

THE LEARNING CENTRE

The large central learning centre is now a multifunctional facility providing social spaces, student services and study support, book and laptop loan, access to IT, and different kinds of working environments, from comfortable seating for collaborative group work, to 'board rooms' for practice presentations. Elements of teaching may also take place within a learning centre environment. These varied purposes demand a clear vision for each area within the centre. Zones for different modes of learning are common strategies. Sound and visual clues, layout and style of furniture, and different technologies in different configurations can signal the different purposes of areas.

The following lists some of the types of zones anticipated:

- Social zone – fairly noisy; variety of tables and informal seating; laptops used via wireless; catering available.
- Group zone – reasonably quiet but busy; group work; with or without IT; circular tables; open and closed 'pods' with (inter-active) whiteboards.
- Study zone – quiet but not silent; individual work or 2–3; circular or rectangular tables; mixture of fixed IT workstations and spaces for laptops.
- Silent zone – silent individual study; physically enclosed.
- IT zone – busy space; high density IT provision; fixed workstations and printing.
- Touchdown zone – short tasks; standing spaces only; suitable for laptops, some fixed.

Will teaching benefit from migrating into learning centres? Maybe for some courses. However, bookable seminar rooms within centres can offer a compromise.

LIBRARY/LEARNING CENTRE SUPPORT FUNCTIONS
The following lists the types of space that will be needed for the library support functions:

- Library enquiry/information point – counter, desk, storage (satellite floor based enquiry desks);
- Library administration – offices, workrooms, storage;
- IT administration – offices, workrooms, storage;
- Open stack space – books, periodicals, DVDs, CDs;
- Compact shelving;
- Library support facilities – self issue/return, OPACs, printing/photocopying, collection bins;
- Careers section.

The following lists other support functions that can be within a learning centre:

- Learning advice centre – skills, language, academic writing;
- CCAV studio – pre/post production;
- Video conferencing;
- Staff resource area – prep online, video streaming;
- Archive reading room and collection;
- Student lockers.

Sciences, research and laboratories
TYPES OF LABORATORY
Research and laboratory space needs vary markedly between schools and departments, types of teaching or research being undertaken, and special equipment needs. There are a number of different types of 'primary' laboratories that exist on campus, including:

- Computer labs
- Wet labs
- Dry labs
- Studio or design-based labs
- Teaching labs
- Special large equipment labs

There are also a number of different 'secondary' labs and support spaces needed to support 'primary' labs, including:

- Temperature controlled rooms
- Specialist equipment rooms
- Special collection rooms
- Containment suites
- Prep rooms
- Chemical, radioactive, flammable and gas cylinder stores
- Write-up areas

SPACE PLANNING OF PRIMARY LABS
Comprehensive planning of new space should ensure flexibility, modularity and consistency in space allocation. While laboratory types vary markedly and can be so specialised to defy space-planning guidelines, there are some common themes to keep in mind in laboratory space planning. Some of these are as follows:

- Modularity – making laboratory design as modular and flexible as possible is key, particularly in terms of HVAC design, specialised systems and structural loading designs.
- Zoning – creating laboratory 'zones' which also enable flexibility and ease of operations is very important.

These themes will have different applications in laboratory design, depending upon the type of laboratory. Wet labs are very different to computer labs or teaching labs.

THE BASIC LABORATORY MODULE (MOST APPLICABLE TO WET LABS)
While laboratory needs vary widely between disciplines the principle is to configure laboratory space in as flexible and modular a way as possible because of the fact that teaching and research needs and methods change and evolve over time. Laboratory space is typically configured in standard modules, which become space denominators that are designed to meet a variety of teaching and research needs. These modules allow for flexibility in planning the following:

- mechanical, electrical and plumbing systems
- heating, cooling and ventilation systems
- special laboratory gases
- laboratory benching systems
- laboratory support spaces
- specialised functions
- partitions
- fume cupboards, etc.

Laboratory modules then become the building blocks for planning space. Aggregating a number of modules can create larger labs, and smaller labs are created by portions of modules. The planning module is repetitive and regular. The size, actual layout and zoning depends upon the specific laboratory function, teaching or research purpose, equipment required as well as the building floor plan. The relationship between laboratory and office zones or between laboratory and support zones will vary depending upon the type of teaching or research and laboratory need.

Refer to Chapter 26 for detailed laboratory planning and design guidelines.

TRENDS IN LABORATORY TEACHING
There is a consensus amongst students and academics that there is a need to make learning and teaching in the laboratory more challenging and engaging. Recently there have been novel laboratory exercises designed to enthuse and stimulate students through active learning. These innovative methods exploit computer-based approaches, encourage enquiry-based learning and many involve students in cutting edge research during undergraduate (UG) laboratory classes. Results of these exercises indicate there is a pressing need to re-think the traditional, didactic approach to laboratory teaching in HE. In particular to move away from 'spoon feeding' students during interminable, repetitive and boring practical classes that have highly predictable results.

ENQUIRY-BASED LEARNING WITH E-LEARNING IN SUPPORT
This is an approach where students use online learning that involves video clips, interactive simulations, virtual lectures or annotated digital slides to observe, understand and practice techniques before attending practical laboratory classes during which the material

is considered and then team based exercises are carried out that include student presentations and question/answer sessions.

COMPUTER MODELLING

There is a trend towards the replacement of laboratory work by computer modelling throughout science and technology. Space savings are achieved, however some laboratory space may still be required, and space is obviously needed for the computer work. An exception to this trend is in the progress of radically new science and technology. Currently an example of this is nanotechnology, which demands buildings or parts of them to be separate and purpose built to prevent external vibration as well as highly specialist equipment. Future radical scientific and technological developments may be so expensive that they will probably be concentrated at a small number of national or international centres.

Music

Music is studied at a department/school within a university faculty of performing arts, or at a specialist college, academy or conservatoire. There are many elements of accommodation that comprise a music department/school, and the guiding principles for locating the accommodation and planning the space. The spaces in a music department/school consist of a range of rooms of different sizes, with stringent acoustic requirements. Each department/school will individually decide how best to create and configure the range of spaces that will serve its current and future needs. There are a wide range of approaches to planning the accommodation reflecting different approaches and priorities. There are also many different ways to achieve a satisfactory outcome, so it is important that the briefing and design process is carefully detailed.

TYPES OF ACCOMMODATION

Music departments/schools include combinations of the following spaces:

- music classrooms (dedicated) – large learning and teaching spaces;
- practice rooms – solo, group, ensemble;
- music technology (digital) and keyboard rooms;
- instrument and other stores – department/school use, student use;
- music library and resource area – including music scores, CDs, DVDs;
- rehearsal studios;
- recital studios;
- recording/control studios;
- performance space (or shared use of a central university facility);
- small breakout spaces associated with music rooms;
- academic staff rooms and support.

ENVIRONMENTAL CONSIDERATIONS

Music spaces are for creating and listening to sound and therefore an appropriate acoustic environment is essential. Sound can travel through the building fabric or structure, even if it has a high specification. Doors, windows and vents are particularly difficult to insulate. In planning spaces it is essential to remember that:

- The aim is to enable people to hear music clearly, without distraction, and with suitable enhancement by the room acoustics.
- The two main acoustic concerns are sound quality and sound insulation.
- The main influences on the quality of musical sounds are room volume, room geometry and surface finishes.
- Successful sound separation between spaces depends on good planning, structure and construction detail.
- The location of the music department/school, relative to the rest of other department/schools (or neighbours), should be carefully considered.

SPACE PLANNING PRINCIPLES

Most music department/schools host a range of activities and events including performances outside the normal teaching day. All these activities will involve groups of people (students, staff, external musicians) arriving and leaving throughout the day. Therefore, the location of the department/school should make this as easy as possible, while maintaining security for the community. Important points to consider when planning space are:

- Acoustic issues – disturbance to and from neighbouring spaces, including external spaces.
- Ensuring music spaces are near to other facilities that will be used for musical activities.
- Creating easy access for the movement of musical instruments and equipment for performance in spaces outside the department/school.
- Locating the music department/school on or close to the main entrance.
- Providing a separate dedicated reception that can be used outside normal hours without compromising overall security.
- Allocating sufficient parking for the group sizes anticipated.

CRITICAL RELATIONSHIPS

When deciding how to arrange the layout of a music department/school, there are some critical relationships, or adjacencies, between dissimilar spaces – for example where percussion is practised. Percussion sounds are likely to cause the greatest potential disturbance to neighbours, because of the repetitive patterns and low frequencies, in particular drum practice groups. Buffering between dissimilar practice spaces can be achieved by relatively underused spaces, such as storerooms, corridors, resource centres. Some department/schools like to have group rooms directly accessed from classrooms for breakout activities. Recording/control studios are best placed adjacent to large group rooms, rehearsal, and recital and performance space. Windows in music spaces, if left open, are likely to cause a noise nuisance to neighbours. Therefore, window and ventilation strategies will need careful consideration.

Business schools

A business school can either be a school or department based within a university or an independent international graduate school and research institution.

UNIVERSITY-BASED BUSINESS SCHOOLS

Undergraduate (UG) teaching is usually undertaken in the university's centrally time-tabled general teaching accommodation – lecture theatres, seminar rooms and IT rooms. Depending on the university a dedicated UG workroom and lounge may be provided within the school.

Postgraduate (PG) teaching and research is usually undertaken in dedicated accommodation, and can comprise:

- lecture theatres (small) (stepped amphitheatre-style with continuous writing desks and fixed seating);
- seminar rooms (small);
- syndicate rooms (conference style);
- PGT group workspace (drop-in facility, with wireless connectivity);
- PGT PC lab (learning facility);
- PGR group workspace (cafe-style linked to syndicate rooms, with wireless connectivity);
- the school may also have dedicated PGR social space.

The MBA accommodation is usually planned as a dedicated suite of accommodation within the business school or department and comprises:

- reception, social/interaction/breakout space, refreshment bar/service;

- lecture theatres (small) (stepped amphitheatre-style with continuous writing desks in wide rows and mobile/revolving executive chairs);
- seminar rooms (small) (cafe-style with circular tables and mobile/revolving executive chairs, with wireless connectivity);
- syndicate rooms (mobile/revolving executive chairs around conference tables, with wireless connectivity).

A few schools may incorporate a dedicated Executive Training Suite offering custom training to professionals. The training suite may need to be easily accessible for evening customers and will probably comprise:

- reception, social/interaction/breakout space, refreshment bar/service;
- executive training room (small) (cafe-style circular tables with mobile/revolving executive chairs);
- reference/resource facilities.

A dedicated Bloomberg Suite is usually included in a business school to provide UG and PG students training in a simulated dealing room environment.

INDEPENDENT GRADUATE BUSINESS SCHOOLS

These institutions are pre-eminent global graduate business schools (e.g. Harvard, INSEAD, London Business School). They specialise in offering 'top-class' MBAs and executive education. They have complete operational independence and separate funding.

Depending on their vision, aims and objects they will each have different approaches and operational areas, e.g.:

- teaching – MBAs, EMBAs, MiFs, Executive Education (open and custom programmes), PhDs;
- research – faculty working on specialist research initiatives based on chosen subject areas;
- external relations – school brand/fundraising, alumni, communications, development, events;
- support departments – finance/accounts, information services, careers, facilities, human resources;
- outreach activities.

Comprehensive programmes of evening and day events will take place throughout the year, such as residential courses, conferences, corporate presentations, networking, ceremonies, distinguished speaker lectures, recruitment and alumni reunions. Most of these events will require good quality residential accommodation, conferencing, community networking and catering facilities.

The planning, design and range of accommodation and the quality of the physical space will be characterised by the spirit and ethos of the school, and the school's perceived international brand.

The range of accommodation for teaching MBAs will generally be similar to university-based schools except the quality and space standards will be higher. Similarly Executive Education accommodation will be of a higher quality and standard, more extensive and include a business centre, breakout and refreshment areas for delegates.

Additional facilities will include:

- conference centre – high quality large theatre/hall with cinema style seating, including reception/registration area, foyer/breakout space and hospitality service;
- large community networking space – at the centre of the school to encourage interaction/integration;
- a range of catering facilities – banqueting and hospitality (breakfast/lunch/dinner), restaurant with service, cafe, coffee bar/shop, and dispersed refreshment zones;
- teaching support – PC labs, library/resource centre and study spaces;
- student services/support facilities;
- alumni centre;
- offices – faculty, support, admin staff;
- school reception area – visitors, information, exhibition.

Environmental considerations for lecture/conference facilities:

- naturally lit and air-conditioned;
- programmable lighting and blackout;
- sound reinforcement, microphones and high quality acoustics;
- wireless network, video/filming facilities;
- interactive whiteboards, projection and LCD screens;
- control of environment from lecturer's desk/console.

Arts

Art is studied at a department or school within a university faculty of creative arts, or at a specialist art college. Art is a practical and creative discipline in which students learn through investigation, observation, analysis and experimentation. Students work in both two and three dimensions and at a range of scales.

TYPES OF ACCOMMODATION

Students select to specialise and develop techniques in a variety of media. These vary but may include the following studio or workshop spaces:

- drawing
- graphic design
- painting
- screen printing
- photography/moving image
- textiles/embroidery/fashion
- ceramics/glass
- jewellery
- sculpture
- digital media including desktop publishing, animation, multimedia.

Supplementary and storage spaces may include:

- resource areas
- dark rooms
- editing and production suites
- prep/cleaning areas
- screening room
- clay, damp and plaster stores
- kiln rooms
- wood, metal, stone, equipment stores
- media consumables store
- display/exhibition space
- students' work stores.

MAIN PLANNING CONSIDERATIONS

The location of the art department or school can effect the accommodation in a number of ways. Some of the main considerations are listed below:

- Quality and level of light – particularly important in art studios is orientation and floor level, which can effect the amount of daylight reaching the space.
- Ground floor location – direct access to sheltered outside areas for external work for messy or large scale projects.
- Views – from carefully placed windows can be a source of inspiration.
- Collocation – where overlaps in disciplines are likely plan relevant spaces close together to facilitate sharing of resources.
- Vehicle access – delivery of bulky or heavy materials needs to be considered.

OTHER PLANNING CONSIDERATIONS
Additional issues to consider include:

- As daylight is important for art studios, consider the depth of spaces where daylighting is only from side windows.
- Grouping of art spaces into suites allows more efficient use of materials and equipment and provides equal access to resource areas.
- A display area for students' work provides a learning stimulus as well as a welcoming approach to the department or school.
- Store rooms should be directly accessible from the studio spaces.
- Views into an art studio can provide an attractive 'shop window' to the department or school.

Suites of art spaces are sometimes designed as open plan areas, which can create a sense of light and space, and with less definition between spaces can also increase flexibility. However, noise transmission or dust can be a problem in open plan areas between dissimilar disciplines, as in the case of ceramics, etc. where dust is less easily contained. Also more open plan areas can reduce the wall surface area, which is useful for display and as a large scale work surface.

BUILDING SERVICES
It is advisable to produce wall elevations of each space showing the location of building services (electricity, gas, compressed air, water, etc.) and fixed equipment. This will help to make the best use of available surfaces, which is important where walls are used extensively for display and as vertical work surfaces. Overhead supplies for mobile equipment may be considered an alternative system where appropriate for certain disciplines.

ENVIRONMENTAL CONSIDERATIONS
Some of the main factors to be considered are:

- Daylight – maximise daylight but control glare and solar gain, where fine detail and colour rendering is important. Increase ceiling heights and maximise surface reflectance.
- Artificial light – An even spread of light without glare. Adopt recommended luminance levels and colour rendering of lamps.
- Acoustics – noise disturbance between dissimilar disciplines working in the same or adjacent spaces.
- Ventilation – extraction systems needed for specialist activities and equipment including removal of heat, noxious gases/fumes, dark room chemicals, dust, aerosols/airbrushes.

Creative environments for teaching and learning
An initiative between two universities looked into what extent learning designs could promote innovative ways of thinking. The aim was to create a 'Centre of Excellence in Teaching and Learning' (CETL) – an experimental new teaching and learning space, the 'Creativity Zone'. The concept was to blur the boundaries between disciplines, between formal and informal learning, and between learning and creative practice.

In the 'Creativity Zone' ingenious partitions, screens and items of furniture were fitted into the fabric of the space. Multiple projectors, wireless connectivity and location-aware technology was embedded. Any part of the space could be varied to offer a progression of opportunity for interaction – with objects and participants. In this space real-world practices could be simulated, creating a cross-disciplinary experience that brings individuals from different disciplines together in one collaborative exercise. This concept could be a prototype for re-thinking the way forward for effective learning and teaching in the future.

2.4 Incubators
An incubator is a term given to a facility that fosters and encourages entrepreneurship and minimises obstacles to new business formation and growth. It provides the opportunity for 'start-ups' and 'spin-offs'.

Start-ups and spin-offs
The incentive confronting an individual or group that discovers a significant invention is a choice between start-up and spin-off. 'Startup' is the term given to the choice that keeps the intellectual property rights (knowledge) of the invention, acquires start-up capital or 'seed' funding and forms a new company to develop the invention. 'Spin-off' is the term given to the choice that transfers the knowledge of the invention to an existing company to gain substantial benefit via compensation, profits or shares from development of the invention.

2.4.2 University incubators
University incubators aim to:

- create a bridge between education and the economy;
- accelerate technology transfer between the university and companies;
- sponsor 'spin-off' from academia and create 'start-ups'.

Originally incubators were located in abandoned or underused university buildings, but have since grown rapidly and developed into new high quality purpose built 'centres' affiliated to universities. These 'centres' will vary in the facilities provided reflecting and influenced by the research focus (science, technology, business) of the affiliated university. Many UK universities have new build 'centres' and their growth continues. Within these centres incubator units will be planned on a modular basis and can vary in size from 10 m² to 500 m², with a mix of office, science or technology-type units, together with all the supporting facilities and services.
   Types of accommodation will vary but may include:

- modular labs (200 m²) fitted out with write-up and wet lab areas;
- flexi-labs (500 m²) either wet lab, office, or combination;
- offices (10 to 200 m²) for SMEs;
- workshop facilities;
- meeting rooms, conferencing and exhibition space;
- reception and visitor areas;
- mailing, faxing and copying services;
- computer services, including secure internet connections;
- cleaning and security facilities;
- kitchen facilities, local catering;
- business support links – finance, legal, public funding, banking, accountancy, patent agents.

To protect the confidential and novel nature of the research and development work being undertaken 24/7 high-level access and security control to the building is important, with additional dedicated access and security control to each of the inner modular incubator units.

2.5 Support facilities
Student
The provision of student support facilities may be allocated on a university wide basis, site/campus basis or faculty basis. The content and location will primarily be determined by the university's estate strategy and secondly by faculty need regarding other student support facilities.
   The list of accommodation provided will vary. The following is a guide.

Student union

- Student union and association offices
- Club activities and social rooms
- Large multi-function events space

- Bar and cafe areas
- Storage (records, stationery, equipment).

Student services

- Student information centre (including reception and waiting area)
- Admissions and funding/finance
- Counselling, advice and guidance
- Careers and employment
- Student/learning support
- Heath services (outsourced), welfare and first aid
- Nursery
- Chaplaincy and multi-faith prayer rooms.

Other student support facilities

- UG student common room (including refreshments)
- UG student society office
- UG student group workroom
- UG student individual/quiet study room
- UG student computing labs
- PGT student study room
- PGT student computing lab
- PGR workrooms.

Similar functions, e.g. student union and student services, could be col-located to form a central focus for students on campus (a 'student cen-tre') providing security, noise and confidentially is not compromised.

Staff

The provision of staff support facilities may be allocated either on a site/campus basis or faculty basis. The content and location will primarily be determined by the university's estate strategy and sec-ondly by faculty need. The list of accommodation provided will vary. The following is a guide:

- staff common room (including refreshments)
- staff meeting and interview rooms
- storage (archives, records, stationery, equipment)
- staff print and post room
- porter's room
- computer systems manager's office
- technician's office/workspace/help desk
- faculty based staff resource centre
- faculty based externally funded research institute space (includ-ing reception).

Public

It is essential to develop attractive and novel concepts for main entrances and front of house facilities, not only for regular users but also to encourage visitors and the public to 'cross the threshold'.

The following accommodation is a guide:

- main reception desk area
- visitors waiting and collection area
- information and exhibition area (including displays of student output and future events)
- external affairs office (colleges/schools liaison)
- security control point
- security control office.

It is important that major facilities available to visitors or the public are easily accessible from the main entrance without compromising security or user movement.

Conference

Many universities desire conference facilities to showcase their profile and maintain external links by providing corporate and distinguished speaker events, presentations, symposia and confer-ences. Conference facilities are expensive facilities if underutilised. Therefore alternative uses for formal teaching of large and medium size cohort lecture groups ought to be considered.

The following accommodation is a guide:

- auditoria (300 seat and 150 seat)
- foyer/break-out/interaction/display space
- hospitality service room
- equipment/store room
- control room
- green room
- cloakrooms.

Catering

The provision of catering facilities may be allocated on a university wide basis or site/campus basis.

It will generally include a central facility supplemented by dis-persed satellite refreshment facilities located in various academic buildings. The content and location will be determined by the uni-versity's estate strategy and generally franchised to outside cater-ing specialists. Under this arrangement the university provides the built space with the catering specialist providing the supply and service of food/drinks, equipment and staff.

The list of accommodation provided will vary. The following is a guide for a central facility.

Informal and formal dining

- Food court – buffet style (including seating, servery, self-service islands and 'back of house facilities')
- Deli bar (including seating, servery, self-service gondolas and 'back of house' facilities)
- Coffee bar (including seating, servery, self-service dispensers and 'back of house facilities')
- Formal dining area (including seating area and finishing kitchen).

Main kitchen

- Prep, cooking and plating areas
- Wash-up area
- Utensils, cutlery and crockery stores
- Dry, cold and deep freeze stores.

Catering support

- Goods reception
- Catering office
- Staff toilets, changing and lockers
- Cleaner's store
- Bin storage area (external).

Retail

The provision of retail facilities may be allocated on a university wide basis or site/campus basis. The content and location will pri-marily be determined by the university's estate strategy and gener-ally franchised to outside retail outlets. Under this arrangement the university provides the built space with the retail outlets providing the supply and service of goods, equipment and staff. Retail facil-ities are usually collocated in the form of a 'Mall' on campus. The list of accommodation provided will vary depending on the level of local competition. The following is a guide:

- bookshop (including DVDs/CDs)
- university memorabilia /giftware
- banking (including ATMs)
- newsagency/refreshments/stationery ('one stop shop')
- post office (or incorporated in 'one stop shop')
- whole foods store

- travel agency
- pharmacy (or incorporated in 'one stop shop')
- hairdresser.

2.6 Residential

Student

University student accommodation is usually called 'Halls of Residence' (commonly 'Halls'), except at Oxbridge type universities where they are incorporated in each College's complex and known as 'Rooms'. A brief description of Halls of Residence is included in this chapter.

HALLS OF RESIDENCE

Most universities provide halls for a high proportion of first year students. Standards of accommodation can vary.

Older accommodation is based on institution-type halls – long ('run-through') corridors with individual study bedrooms off each side (some incorporate a washbasin/vanity unit) and shared bathrooms. Usually there was a choice between self-catered halls (which incorporated shared kitchen/dining space) and catered halls (using central dining facilities).

Later accommodation is based on self-contained flat-type halls – 8 to 10 individual study bedrooms each incorporating en-suites with shared kitchen/dining and soft seating spaces. A variation on the flat-type halls is now the preferred option.

A percentage of disabled study bedrooms complying with planning guidelines need to be provided. Kitchen/dining spaces need to comply with environmental health authority standards. Halls need to incorporate support accommodation – laundry (self-service), linen store, luggage store, cleaner's store and refuse store.

Some universities provide a degree of residential accommodation on campus for married students in the form of two person flats incorporated in halls.

Conference

Most universities operate a comprehensive programme of conferences or similar events during key vacation periods to create an income stream. Some of these events will require residential accommodation as part of the package offered. Good quality student accommodation that can be vacated will be set up and used for these purposes. Therefore, it is important that some accommodation is planned to a standard to facilitate 'conference' use.

Staff

Some universities will provide residential accommodation for particular members of staff. These may be 2 or 4 person flats for Wardens attached to halls, and visiting faculty or eminent personnel in hospitality suites.

Refer to Chapter 23 for detailed planning and design guidelines for residential accommodation.

2.7 Sport and recreation

Indoor facilities

Indoor sport and recreation facilities will include:

- sports hall – 8 court badminton hall with lines for badminton, basketball, volleyball, handball, netball and tennis, provision for segregating the hall with net partitions;
- fitness suite – comprising cardio-vascular and resistance stations, small reception and dedicated storage;
- aerobics studio – used for dance, yoga and pilates;
- martial arts room;
- swimming pool – 6 lane 25 m pool and seating area;
- squash courts – with seating area to one/two courts;
- staff office – permanent and part-time staff;
- indoor sports (dry) changing/showers/toilets – separate male/female, number of private cubicles and lockers;
- pool (wet) changing/showers/toilets – separate male and female, private cubicles and lockers;

- equipment store – to accommodate sports hall equipment;
- mat store – fire resistant room;
- kitchen – small with storage, work surface and sink;
- treatment room – treatment bench and desk, may double as first aid room;
- store room(s) for sports clubs;
- bar, lounge, catering – optional;
- cleaner's room – close to sports hall, sink and storage.

Outdoor facilities

Outdoor sport and recreation facilities will include:

- sports pitches – rugby, football, cricket, hockey;
- sports courts – 5-a-side football, hockey, netball, tennis (AWPs);
- outdoor sports changing/showers/toilets – separate male/female, including lockers;
- external referees' changing/showers/toilets – separate male/female, including lockers;
- equipment store – posts, nets, etc.

Other considerations

The following should be taken into account:

- operational and management aspects of the sports facilities will impact upon the use, planning and design of the facilities;
- other users – will it also include community, corporate memberships, clubs, etc.?
- graduations, examinations, exhibitions;
- car parking;
- compliance with Sport England/Northern Ireland/Scotland/Wales competition standards.

Refer to Chapter 38 for detailed planning and design guidelines for sports and recreation facilities

2.8 Administration

Academic offices

The provision of academic office accommodation is a sensitive topic probably in every institution. Individual academic offices in pre-1992 universities were provided on the assumption that they would be used for tutorial teaching of 2–4 students at a time. The academic office was therefore a complex environment: private study, semi-public teaching space, small staff meetings, and reception of professional visitors. However, tutorial groups are now often larger and academic offices are too small for teaching them.

INDIVIDUAL OR SHARED OFFICES

In many institutions, the need for all academic staff to have their own office is seen as an important aspect of academic life. However, it is often considered by management that offices are too large for one member of staff. Where remodelling or new building takes place individual academic offices may be replaced with shared offices. There then needs to be a conveniently located set of small rooms, which can be used for meetings and tutorials. This arrangement may be particularly appropriate when academic staff are out of their offices a great deal because of high class contact hours, visits to students on work placements, professional practice of various kinds, or specialist facility based research work. The acceptance of shared offices may be enhanced if good common room facilities are provided, such as a reception area with secretarial staff and other support service facilities.

A BALANCED APPROACH

A model of provision promoted by one institute and accepted by staff involved a compromise between individual and shared offices for full time staff: 25% of the offices were allocated for individual academic staff (Dean 20 m², HOD 15 m², other 10 m²) with the remaining 75% allocated to shared offices split equally between offices for 2 academic staff (16 m²) and offices for 4 academic staff (32 m²). The faculty could decide how to allocated their offices to academic staff. A set of small, bookable rooms were provided for tutorials, meetings, etc.

Open plan shared 'hot-desking' offices were provided for part-time staff (4 m²/50% of PT staff).

Administrative offices

Demand for administrative space (administration and central services) in HE has grown. This reflects the creation of essentially new functions such as quality assurance, marketing, central fundraising, and widening participation work, together with the provision of more sophisticated services in established areas such as finance, research administration and student support of various kinds. It is likely that there will be further growth in demand for administrative space, as students become more demanding users of services. Other services related to more market orientated HE organisations will also demand more space. A typical list of university administration and central departments includes:

- University management
- Finance
- Human resources
- Marketing
- Quality assurance
- Business development
- IT systems support
- Registry, admissions and exams
- Student and academic services
- Estates and facilities.

OPEN PLAN OFFICES

New buildings offer an opportunity to collocate administrative functions to improve efficiency, offer an enhanced service to academic staff and students and save space. Space savings can be achieved by arranging administrative departments or functions in suites of large open plan offices, which include small-embedded offices or 'pods' where privacy, confidentiality or breakout time is needed. Creatively and appropriately designed open plan offices can provide flexibility and a conducive and effective environment for team working, interaction and communication.

2.9 Operational requirements

The briefing process should not only capture the functional requirements of the project but also just as importantly include a statement of the institute's relevant operational requirements that will have an impact upon the planning and design of the project.

Checklists of operational requirements are listed below for discussion with the relevant departments of the institute.

Each should include a summary of the current arrangements and proposed future requirements.

Security
- Whole site
- Site entry
- Car parks
- Building facades
- Entry for staff, students, visitors and deliveries
- Reception desk
- Access points and circulation within building
- Control room

Waste and recycling
- Paper and packaging
- Glass
- Food and catering
- Manufacturing
- Solvents and oils
- Radioactive

Catering
- Status/type
- Franchised areas
- Sittings
- Seating area
- Other uses

Materials handling
- Loading bays
- Central stores
- Designated stores
- Handling modes
- Distribution

Post
- Post/sorting room
- Delivery arrangements

Maintenance and cleaning
- Site
- Building
- Equipment
- Central storage
- Local storage
- Changing/locker/showers
- Offices/labs/workshops

Archives
- Policy
- Holding areas
- Materials and methods of storage
- Retrieval

Communications
- Telephone
- Data
- IT
- Audio visual

Deliveries and storage
- Central/local
- Loading/unloading
- Types of storage

Staff welfare
- Medical
- First Aid
- Creche
- Fitness

Parking and commuting
- Staff
- Students
- Visitors

Environmental health and safety
- Low energy
- Natural ventilation
- Minimise pollutants
- Maximise daylight
- Green materials and construction

2.10 The virtual campus

Definition

The concept of a virtual campus refers to a specific format of distance education and online learning in which students, teaching staff and even university administrative and technical staff mainly 'meet' or communicate through technical links. A virtual campus can also refer to the online offerings of a university where course work is completed either partially or wholly online, often with assistance from a tutor, teacher or teaching assistant. Although the phrase 'virtual campus' is an important concept in education, there is no theoretical framework for it. There appears to be a lot of variables involved in the concept with different technologies involved. The general view is that it can involve both campus-based e-learning and distance e-learning.

e-University

In 2003 the e-university was launched as a single vehicle of UK universities' HE programmes over the internet. Following its launch it attracted just 900 students against a target of 5,600. In effect it failed and HEFCE decided to switch to support the development of e-learning in universities that provided coherent progress. Failure in part was due to an over-confident presumption about the scale of demand for wholly based e-learning.

Embedded e-learning

The failure of the e-university has impacted on e-learning and shown the importance of holding a narrowly skewed focus or definition of e-learning. A learner-centred approach not a technology-driven approach is now considered the way forward. This is known as 'embedded e-learning'.

Information communications technology

Technologies used in learning, such as interactive whiteboards, personal learning environments, wireless networks and mobile devices, plus the internet and high-quality digital learning resources, and the ability to access many of these from home and the workplace, are altering the experience and aspirations of learners.

MOBILE AND WIRELESS TECHNOLOGIES

Mobile and wireless technologies have increasingly widespread use in HE and the current trend is towards planning innovative methods in which to incorporate these technologies into e-learning. Key benefits in their use are seen as:

- portability and anytime, anyplace connectivity;
- flexibility and timeless access to e-learning resources;
- immediacy of communication;
- empowerment and engagement of learners;
- active learning experiences.

MOBILE AND WIRELESS LEARNING

'Mobile and wireless learning' is an adopted term for the broad concept involving many of the same technologies and facilities as e-learning, but with access via mobile devices or wireless networks rather than cable networks. Mobile and wireless devices have supported presentational, interactive and creative forms of learning, and when combined with e-learning, multi-media opportunities have resulted. Current best practice has been with the most well known technologies: USB storage devices, PDAs, laptops, tablet PCs, mobile phones and electronic voting. The reason for adoption of these is:

- wider availability
- ability to support a range of functions
- desktop functionality
- ease of use
- acceptance by learners
- potential to support pedagogical aims.

The easier the mobile device can become the property of the learner the more it is used. However, provision needs to be made for equipment booking, battery charging, induction and IT support systems.

ON-LINE EXAMS AND ASSESSMENTS

Technology is also being used for regulated online computer-assisted assessments and exams replacing paper-based methods at many universities. This is proving very successful with students. It will require supervised and controlled environments within the university in the form of dedicated secure rooms.

e-learning

As mentioned above, across the sector the general expectation is that e-learning at a distance will not wholly supplant face-to-face teaching in a significant way. However, campus-based e-learning will continue to develop and allow students to work more flexibly, on and off campus. At any one time students can work elsewhere on their projects, using their laptops or mobile devices linked to the campus wireless network.

DISTANCE LEARNING

Distance learning, sometimes called e-learning, is a teaching and learning system designed to be carried out remotely using electronic communication. It offers opportunities in situations where traditional education has difficulty in operating. It is more flexible in time and can be delivered anywhere. Popular technologies are CDs, MP3, webcasts, DVDs, video conferencing and internet. There is student-teacher interaction with feedback. The Open University, other universities and distance learning centres specialise in supplying distance learning courses, home study courses, online training and courses in a variety of subjects to gain nationally recognised qualifications.

DISTRIBUTED LEARNING

Distributed learning, also called IT-mediated instruction, is an instructional model that involves using various information technologies to help students learn. It encompasses technologies such as video or audio conferencing, satellite broadcasting and web-based multi-media formats. It can be implemented in various forms and scales, for example:

- Course enhancement – instructional technologies embedded in traditional classroom settings can be made available for students to consult before or after class sessions via the website making learning less dependent on time and location.
- Hybrid delivery – a web-based multi-media lecture made available to students to view online before attending a class session, and also made available for use in other courses multiplying their usefulness.
- Virtual classroom – 'any time, any place, at any pace' of learning. A course can be packaged on a CD-ROM, including prerequisite online lectures and the PowerPoint presentations coupled with audio for distance learners.

Other modes of learning
WORK-BASED LEARNING

Workplace-based learning is expected to increase although the expectation is that it will remain a minor aspect of HE activity. Some institutions are likely to become more involved in this work, particularly at foundation degree level and with tailor-made masters courses delivered on organisations' premises. There will be a saving on teaching space, but not support space.

PARTNERSHIPS

In some fields, notably creative arts, staff and students are becoming more itinerant, using cities' cultural infrastructures, and practitioner workplaces. Partnership arrangements of this kind are often involved and unlikely to lead to a saving on teaching space.

3 ENVIRONMENT

Environmental, economic and social issues form an integral part of the decision process in planning new educational facilities. Applying sustainable solutions where appropriate to education projects that reduce environmental impact is an important consideration. Some of the issues to be considered are:

- Zoning of space to minimise mechanical and cooling requirements.
- Creation of open plan, flexible and adaptable environments to reduce churn.
- Facades that significantly reduce incident solar gains, moderate external noise, provide opportunities for natural ventilation, and allow user control to provide satisfactory comfort conditions.
- Facade U-values that exceed building regulations.
- Material specifications that select recycled materials and products from sustainable sources.
- Robust materials requiring low maintenance.
- Low energy artificial lighting and controls, via presence detectors and daylight linking, to maximise the use of daylight and provide a visually comfortable space.
- Low energy cooling and mechanical ventilation systems, via displacement air systems, with heat recovery to reduce energy use.
- Low maintenance requirements during the operational life of systems.
- Introducing measures to reduce water use such as dual flush WCs, low pressure water systems and aerating taps.
- Rainwater recycling to reduce consumption of potable water.
- Integrating photovoltaic arrays to reduce energy consumption.
- Providing cycle and subsidised public transport networks to discourage private vehicle use and reduce carbon emissions.
- Using local suppliers and contractors to support local economy and minimise carbon emission.
- Using fuel cell powered site vehicles.

3.1 Space planning

The following are some key issues to consider when space planning new educational facilities:

- Adopt a modular planning system, clear and simple to use, with the ability to maximise the range of plan alternatives needed by the university that meet the objectives of functionality, cost effectiveness and adaptability. A modular system that offers practical and economic advantages during design, construction and the life of the building.
- Distinguish between those parts of the building designated to be fixed or unchanging – the structure, primary circulation, services cores; and those parts designated to be flexible or permit changes – usable teaching spaces, local servicing systems, internal partitions, flooring and ceiling systems.
- Consider non-cellular construction techniques, using large span framed structures, creating column free flexible space.
- Plan space in terms of broad categories of use, with provision not only suitable for its foreseen purpose but easily adaptable.
- Make fuller use of general purpose teaching space, by in addition to adopting appropriate ranges of room sizes, using partitions between rooms that can be moved without major disruption.
- Locate general teaching rooms in a common pool for timetabling and sharing between departments/schools.
- Locate accommodation used by large numbers of students at lower levels of the building, with less used and discreet areas located at upper levels.
- On a broader scale, plan boundaries between departmental areas to be adjustable without major adaptations, with accommodation not planned in rigidly separate categories, the differences and boundaries being flexible.

3.2 Design criteria

The following space norms and space standards exclude figures for pre-clinical and clinical medicine and dentistry.

Space norms

Space norms used to be published by the University Grants Committee (UGC) and the Polytechnics and Colleges Funding Council (PCFC). They were based on observations and assumptions about how students in different disciplines were taught – number of hours, type of teaching activity, staff/student ratio, and area per workplace. They were widely used by institutions and UK HE Funding Councils to inform the size of new building projects, but there have been no new or updated norms published for decades. Although there has been a shift away from them many institutes still use space norms or space weightings often with modifications.

UGC SPACE NORMS
UGC space norms were expressed as an 'allowance' of net usable area per FTE student for departmental academic areas. The allowance was made up of different types of space:

- general teaching space (excluding lecture theatres);
- academic offices and research labs;
- non-academic offices and stores;
- teaching and PG research labs;
- lab ancillaries.

There were also space norms for non-departmental academic areas expressed as an 'allowance' of net usable area per FTE student for:

- lecture theatres;
- library;
- administration (including maintenance);
- social, dining, health centres;
- sports facilities (building) – indoor and outdoor.

The norm varied according to academic discipline and was a guide to quantifying overall space requirements as a basis for project briefs. A recent survey carried out by the UK HE Space Management Group (SMG) suggests that while some HEIs do not want updated norms, others would welcome them. So in 2003/4 the SMG carried out a feasibility study in updating UGC norms taking into consideration the changes in academic delivery and decline in the amount of space need. The analysis found on average the HE sector is operating at 80% of UGC norms. The SMG updated UGC norms in Table I were published in 2006.

PCFC SPACE NORMS
The PCFC introduced a new system of space norms for PCFC institutions (Polytechnics and Colleges) in 1990 with reduced area

Table I SMG updated UGC space norms (net usable m²/FTE student)

Subject group	Academic staff: student ratio	UG	PGC	PGR	Allowance inc. for academic staff
Biological sciences	1:6.8	8.2	10.6	16.1	3.6
Psychology	1:14	6.0	7.8	15.0	1.9
Agric. & Forestry	1:7.7	7.8	10.2	15.7	3.2
Physical sciences	1:6.3	8.6	10.6	15.5	3.8
Mathematics	1:12.2	2.8	2.8	3.9	0.9
Computer sciences	1:15.1	5.3	7.6	8.4	1.3
Engineering & Technology	1:9.3	7.7	13.1	14.2	2.5
Architecture, building and planning	1:16	6.9	6.9	6.6	0.9
Geog. & Economics	1:12.6	4.4	5.5	5.7	0.9
Social studies	1:17.3	1.6	1.6	3.6	0.7
Business	1:22.2	2.1	2.1	3.5	0.5
Languages	1:14.6	2.4	2.4	3.8	0.8
Humanities	1:15.7	1.8	1.8	3.8	0.7
Archaeology	1:8.8	4.5	5.6	5.9	1.3
Art, design, music & drama	1:16.4	6.7	6.7	6.4	0.9
Education	1:19.1	3.5	3.5	3.4	0.6
Catering & hospitality management	1:21.4	5.8	8.1	13.6	1.1

allowances to reflect the practice at the time. These norms were around 15% less than previous DES methods of calculation. They included:

- specialist and non-specialist areas
- general teaching spaces
- libraries
- staff, administration
- sports and catering facilities.

There was no allowance for research space.

The SMG carried out a similar study in updating PCFC norms and found institutions were operating at 20.5% below the 1990 area allowances. The SMG updated PCFC norms in Table II were published in 2006.

Table II SMG updated PCFC space norms (net m²/FTE student)*

Programme area	
Engineering	11.9
Built Environment	7.6
Science	11.9
IT & Computing	8.7
Business	6.4
Health & Life Science	8
Humanities	6
Art & Design	11.1
Education	7.6

*Areas are net of circulation

Space standards

Space standards are area guidelines per (student or staff) workplace for the various types of activity or accommodation – general teaching, offices, laboratories, libraries, etc. They should be regarded as an overall check against functionality and will need adjustment in many situations to suit the specific needs of the activity carried out and the occupation levels. Both UGC and PCFC used a series of space standards for given activities or accommodation. These are listed in Table III.

However, most institutions have since adopted their own indicative space standards, which vary from the UGC/PCFC guidelines. Examples of these are listed in Table IV.

Area definitions

Five definitions of floor area are used in construction projects in HEIs, Figure 43.3:

- Gross external area (GEA)
- Gross internal area (GIA)
- Net internal area (NIA)
- Net usable area (NUA)
- Balance area.

It is imperative that any area stated is qualified by one of these definitions.

GEA – for planning applications: the area of the building measured externally at each floor level, including all spaces within the building, and perimeter wall thicknesses, external projections, loading bays and garages. It excludes open balconies, canopies and roof terraces.

GIA – for building costs estimation: the area of a building measured to the internal face of the perimeter walls at each floor level. It includes all spaces within the building, internal structure, walls and partitions, loading bays and garages. It excludes voids over atria.

NIA – equivalent of net lettable area: the area within a building that comprises usable areas (including built-in fixtures that occupy usable space) and primary horizontal circulation. It excludes common entrance halls, atria, landings and balconies, toilets, bathrooms, cleaners' rooms, plant spaces (rooms, ducts and stores),

Table III UGC and PCFC Space Standards (net usable m²/workplace)

Space types	UGC	PCFC
General Teaching		
Lecture theatres and lecture rooms		
Raked or flat with close seating in rows	1.0	1.0
Teaching rooms		
Flat with close seating with writing flaps in rows	1.2	
Teaching rooms		
Flat with informal seating	1.9	1.8
Tutorial rooms		1.8
Seminar rooms		
Flat with tables and chairs	2.3	2.3
Teaching rooms		
Flat with demonstration facilities		2.5
Teaching Laboratories (UG and PGT)		
Languages	2.8	
Geography, Archaeology	3.3	
Experimental Psychology	4.0	
Biological Sciences-general purposes	4.0	
Biochemistry & PG BS	5.0	
Physics	3.7	
Physics-final year and PG	7.5	
Chemistry	5.0	
Engineering	4.6	
Engineering-final year & PG	6.5	
Computer Studies	5.0	
Information Technology		2.8
Science (Biology, Chemistry)		3.6
Art and Design		4.0
Management and Business Studies – management suite		5.1
– work study		4.6
– accounting		2.8
Science and Technology (large scale)		5.6
Engineering		5.6
Mathematics		5.3
Research Laboratories		
Experimental Psychology, Biology, Physics, Chemistry		
– PG and research fellows	9.5	
– staff	11.0	
Engineering	11.0	
Computer Studies	6.8	
Offices		
Professors, including small group space	18.5	
Tutorial staff, including small group space	13.5	
Non-tutorial staff (e.g., researchers, secretaries)	7.0	
Work study space for PGR (range 2.3 to 4.0)	3.4	
Administrative staff		0.44/FTE
Academic staff		0.69/FTE
Non-Academic staff		0.3/FTE
Research staff		0.58/FTE
Libraries/learning		
Library	1.25/FTE	0.8/FTE
Addition for law students	0.8/FTE	
Reader seat	2.3	
Studies	4.0	
Library/resource centre		2.5
Terminal room		3.0
Open access – books	4.7/1k vols	
Open access – journals	9.4/1k vols	
Fixed closed access – books	4.0/1k vols	
Fixed closed access – journals	8.1/1k vols	
Rolling closed access – books	2.1/1k vol	
Rolling closed access – journals	4.1/1k vols	

Table IV Examples of indicative space standards used by institutions (net usable m²/workplace)

Space type	net usable m²/workplace
Management offices	20
Single offices	9
Other office space	7
Professors and Heads of Schools	20
Academic staff	15
Support staff	8
Non-academic staff	10
Standard computing area	3.5
Office space overall average	6–8
Office space per FTE	10
Offices	7
Laboratories	3

vertical circulation, internal structure (walls, columns, piers, etc.), loading bays and garages.

NUA – area available in rooms for people to use: the area within a building available for people to use. It excludes primary horizontal circulation in addition to all of the above.

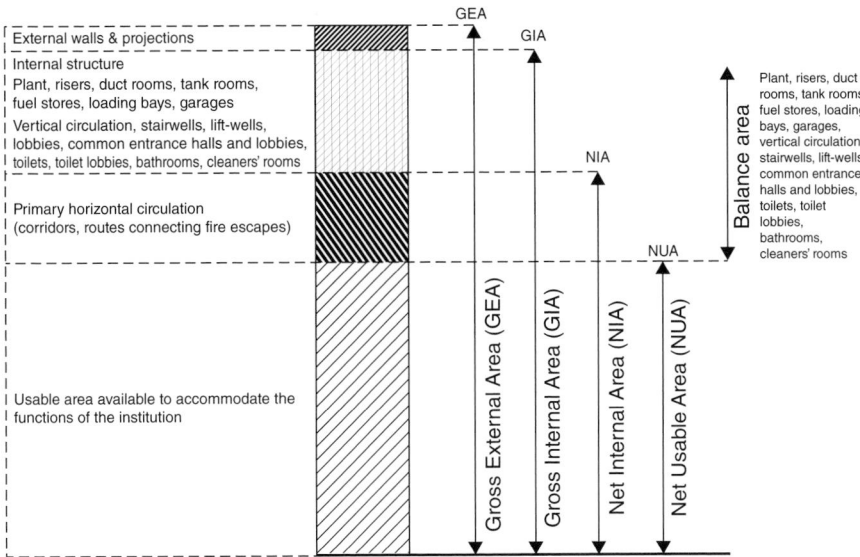

43.3 *Diagram illustrating area definitions: RICS Code of measuring practice (6th ed.)*

Balance area – area to enable the building to function: the floor area planned to enable the building to function. It includes primary horizontal and vertical circulation, entrance lobbies, atria, foyers, lifts, toilets, cloakrooms, cleaners' rooms and stores, plant spaces (rooms, ducts, stores), loading bays and garages, internal structure (wall, columns, piers, etc.).

Gross Floorspace (GIA) Area Breakdown
Guidance now recommends that new-build projects should target the following GIA floorspace area breakdown:

- Net Usable Area 70%
- Balance Area 30%
- Total (GIA) 100%

4 DO'S AND DON'TS

4.1 Do's
It is advisable to consider the following:

- *Culture and aspirations.* Interpret through discussion with the Client/User a clear perception of the qualitative needs derived from their ethos/vision that must be embraced by the project.
- *Needs analysis.* Review with the Client/User their academic and administrative operational and business needs and the impact/influence on the project.
- *Functional content.* Establish with the Client/User the complete range of academic, administrative and supporting functions to be accommodated.
- *Space requirements.* Discuss and agree with the Client/User the space standards and space provision to be applied to the various space types.
- *Organisational requirements.* Review with the Client/User the optimum organisational models to be applied to the accommodation to suit functional and operational needs.

4.2 Don'ts
It is advisable to consider the following:

- *General teaching accommodation.* Locate general teaching accommodation used by large numbers of students at higher levels of the building. Locate at the lowest levels to avoid congestion/disruption and excessive movement through the building.

Disperse and embed general teaching rooms in various faculties/departments. Group together in a 'common pool' to assist timetabling and ease of sharing between faculties/departments.

- *Modular planning.* Adopt a restrictive modular planning system. Adopt a flexible planning system that is able to maximise the range of plan alternatives needed by the university to meet functional objectives and future adaptability.
- *Space planning.* Plan space in a multitude of fixed categories of use. Distinguish between parts designated as fixed or unchanging and those parts designated to be flexible or to permit changes.
- *Construction techniques.* Adopt restrictive cellular construction techniques. Large span framed structures create a column free flexible planning space.

5 BRIEFING OVERVIEW

5.1 The client brief
In its broadest sense the client brief is a 'model' of the functional components of the client organisation, which are to be accommodated in the planning or design proposal.

It will comprise qualitative and quantitative descriptions of aspects of the client's objectives and requirements, which are salient to the development of a planning or design proposal.

Developing the brief
The development of this 'model' is an integral part of design. It has the following characteristics:

- The more comprehensive the guidance and the more certain the criteria, the greater is the probability that the planning or design solution will provide an appropriate and satisfactory framework for the client's function.
- Each stage of brief development must establish guidance and criteria, which are salient to the progress of the design to a higher level of certainty and detail.
- Brief development, like design itself, is an iterative process. A brief in some form must precede design, but the sequence of events and interaction between briefing and design must accommodate widely varying preferences, working methods and levels of expertise in different clients.

Briefing stages
In general, however, the development of the brief takes place in clearly defined stages, which establish approved guidance and criteria for corresponding planning and design stages. The stages generally are:

- Strategic brief: Strategic plan; master plan; feasibility study
- Concept brief: Concept design; preliminary design
- Scheme brief: Scheme design; final design
- Detail brief: Detail design; production information.

A preliminary version of the relevant stage brief should be approved before planning or design work is started on the corresponding design stage.

Scope and content of the brief
- The content and structure of the brief will vary according to the needs and customs of each client. Public bodies in particular have to follow guidelines and procedures prescribed by central government.
- The scope and level of the brief will also vary according to the client's business and the type of facility for which the brief is intended.

5.2 Briefing process summary
The briefing process is an iterative process necessitating the engagement of key 'client' personnel. A summary of the process is described below.

Steering group
- The 'client' brief and the schedule of requirements must reflect the strategic aims and objectives for the project.
- It is therefore recommended that key client representatives be nominated from both the 'user' and 'technical' groups selected from within the range of education stakeholders to form a 'Project Steering Group' under the direction of a 'Project Sponsor'.

Vision statement and background
- It is important and recommended that at the outset of the briefing process a high level meeting be held with selected senior representatives of the education institute.
- At this meeting the senior representatives should present an overview of its vision, aims and objectives, operational and delivery aspects for the project.
- A statement of need for the project should also be presented together with the release of relevant background briefing information and documents covering previous work undertaken and pertinent to the project so these can be studied.

Interview meetings
- Following the high level meeting a meeting should be held with the 'Project Sponsor' to agree the list of key personnel within the education institute to be interviewed as the first step in the process of collecting and developing the brief for the project.
- A suitable timetable for the interview meetings should be agreed.
- The key personnel to be interviewed should be asked to prepare and forward an outline statement covering a profile of the proposed requirements for discussion during the interview meetings.
- The interview meetings should be based on a structured format.

Questionnaire proforma
- Prior to the interview meetings the key personnel should be issued with a standard questionnaire proforma to complete and bring to the meetings for review and discussion during which further data will also be gathered.
- Following the meetings the data gathered should be developed as the basis for defining the preliminary space need, space relationships and space modelling options.
- At this early stage in the briefing process the questionnaire proforma should seek to obtain the essential data sufficient to inform preliminary space planning and design.

Visits and benchmarking
- During the interview process all the existing functional space relevant to the project within the institute should be visited to understand how the existing space is being used and to seek comments on the good and bad aspects of how the existing accommodation meets functional and operational requirements (Figure 43.4).
- Existing comparative projects should also be visited as part of a benchmarking exercise which should involve undertaking a quantitative and qualitative analysis of current standards and criteria that represent best practice in the HE sector.
- This should also include analysing HEFCE/DELNI/SFC/HEFCW published space planning and design guidelines.

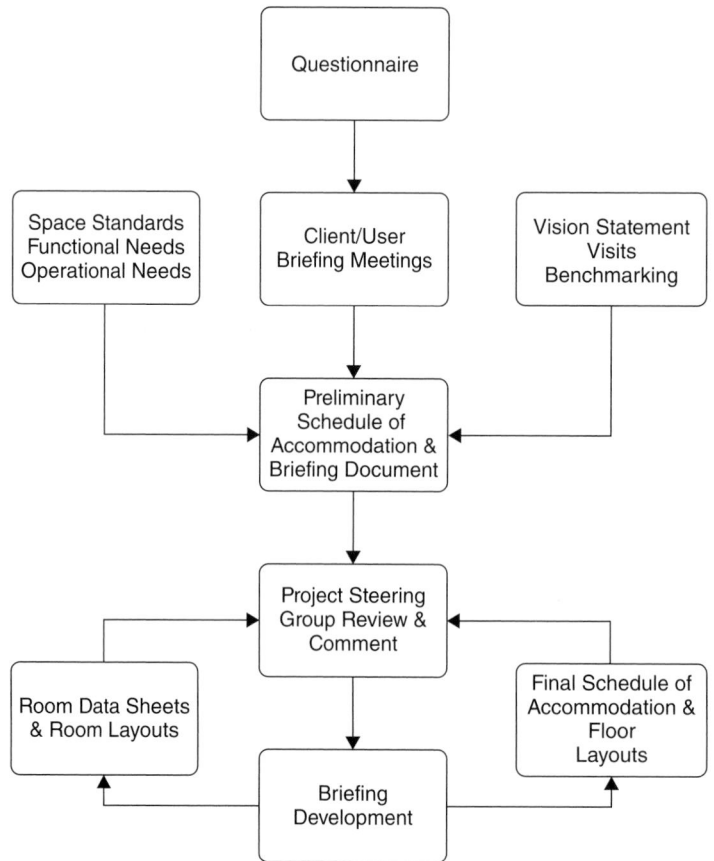

43.4 *Briefing Process Diagram*

Preliminary briefing document
- A complete record should be made of all the meetings held from the outset of the briefing process in the form of briefing notes, a vision statement, a description of functional and operational requirements, structure charts, population schedules, schedules of accommodation (assuming shared/non-shared facilities), preliminary activity space data, significant/desirable functional relationships and process flow diagrams.
- The above should be incorporated into a preliminary briefing document prepared for review and discussion with the 'Project Steering Group' for 'client' comment and approval.

Briefing development
- Following approval of the preliminary briefing document the planning and design process should develop concept options based on the preliminary brief for review with the 'Project Steering Group'.
- The concept options can then be tested against the preliminary brief as part of the process of determining the most appropriate design proposals for the project.
- The briefing process should continue in parallel as needed to obtain all the briefing criteria needed for the subsequent design development, with more detailed schedules of accommodation and detailed room data being incorporated within the development of subsequent briefing documentation for discussion with the 'Project Steering Group' and for client comment and approval.

6 BIBLIOGRAPHY

6.1 Legislation and standards

Designing Space for Effective learning
JISC Development Group, HEFCE
  A guide to 21st century learning space design.

Innovative Practice with e-Learning
JISC Development Group, HEFCE
  A good practice guide to embedding mobile and wireless technologies into everyday practice.

Design with distinction
CABE
  Studies the value of good building design in HE.

Learning Spaces
EDUCAUSE
  Focuses on how learner expectations influence learning spaces.

Effective learning and teaching in UK higher education
TLRP, Institute of Education
  Studies the effect of a more inclusive and connective approach to learning and the impact on space planning and layouts.

Space planning guidelines
Stanford University, USA
  Comparative example of guidelines and layouts for offices, classrooms, computer clusters, conference rooms, research and laboratory space.

Space planning guidelines
AAPPA.
  Benchmark basis to assess space requirements.

Case studies
UK Higher Education Space Management Group
  Investigates aspects of general and specific design topics through three different case studies.

Review of space norms
UK Higher Education Space Management Group
  Results of a study into providing updated space norms for HE.

Impact on space of future changes in higher education
UK Higher Education Space Management Group
  The future impact of changes in teaching methods, widening participation and research activity.

Promoting space efficiency in building design
UK Higher Education Space Management Group
  Identifies aspects of building design contributing most to optimum space efficiency in HE projects.

Space utilisation: practice, performance and guidelines
UK Higher Education Space Management Group
  Review of space use practice and performance, and scope for updating guidance.

Managing space: a review of English further education and HE overseas
UK Higher Education Space Management Group
  Assesses how LSC and overseas HE space guidance could add value to UK HE space guidance.

6.2 Web sites
www.hefce.ac.uk
www.delni.gov.uk
www.sfc.ac.uk
www.hefcw.ac.uk
www.smg.ac.uk
www.aude.ac.uk
www.architecture.com/UseAnArchitect/PublicBuildings/University ClientForum/HigherEducationDesignQualityForum.aspx
www.educause.edu/learningspaces
www.sconul.ac.uk
www.breeam.org/

Appendix A
The SI system

Table I Base units of the SI system

Quantity	Name of unit	Unit symbol
Length	metre	m
Mass	kilogram	kg
Time	second	s
Electric current	ampere	A
Thermodynamic temperature	kelvin*	K
Amount of substance	mole	mol
Luminous intensity	candela	cd
Supplementary units		
Plane angle	radian	rad
Solid angle	steradian	sr

Table II Derived SI units

Quantity	Name of unit	Symbol	Remarks
Frequency	hertz	Hz	$1\ Hz = s^{-1}$
Force	newton	N	$1\ N = 1\ kg.m/s^2$
Pressure	pascal	Pa	$1\ Pa = 1 N/m^2$
Stress			
Energy	joule	J	$1J = 1\ N.m$
Work			
Quantity of heat			
Power	watt	W	$1W = 1\ J/s$
Radiant flux			
Electric charge	coulomb	C	$1C = 1\ A.s$
Quantity of electricity			
Electric potential	volt	V	$1V = 1\ W/A$
Potential difference			
Tension			
Electromotive force			
Capacitance	farad	F	$1F = 1\ C/V$
Electrical resistance	ohm	Ω	$1\ \Omega = 1\ V/A$
Electrical conductance	siemens	S	$1\ S = 1\ S2^{-1}$
Magnetic flux	weber	Wb	$1\ Wb = 1\ V.s$
Magnetic flux density	tesla	T	$1\ T = 1\ Wb/m^2$
Inductance	henry	H	$1H = 1\ Wb/A$
Celsius temperature	degree Celsius	°C	$1\ °C = 1\ K$
Luminous flux	lumen	lm	$1\ lm = 1\ cdsr$
Illuminance	lux	lx	$1\ lx = 1\ lm/m^2$

Table III Multiples and submultiples of SI units

Power of 10	Prefix	Symbol
24	Yetta	Y
21	Zetta	Z
18	Exa	E
15	Peta	P
12	Tera	T
9	Giga	G
6	Mega	M
3	Kilo	k
2	hector	h
1	Deca	da
−1	Deci	d
−2	Centi	c
−3	Milli	m
−6	Micro	μ
−9	Nano	n
−12	Pico	p
−15	Femto	f
−18	Atto	a
−21	Zepto	z
−24	Yocto	y

Table IV Approved SI units, multiples and submultiples together with other units commonly in use

Based on BS 5555:1981 An asterisk indicates a unit outside the SI system currently recognised by the CIPM for a specific use

Item no in ISO 31:1992	Quantity	SI unit	Recommended multiples and sub-multiples	Other units which may be used	Remarks
1 Space and time					
1–1	Plane angle	rad (radian)	mrad µrad	degree (°) = p/180 rad minute (′) = (1/60)° second (″) = (1/60)′ grade (^{G}) = p/200 rad	Radians are principally used in purely mathematical situations. In practice, degrees and its subdivisions are normally used in the UK. The symbol °, ′ and ″ are exceptions in that there is no space between the value and the symbol. Decimal subdivisions of the degree are preferred to minutes and seconds; this facilitates the using of pocket calculators. On continental Europe, the grade (or its alternative name, the gon) is often used, always decimally subdivided.
1–2	Solid angle	sr (steradian)			
1–3	Length	m (metre)	km, cm, mm, mm, nm, pm, fm	*nautical mile 1 n mile = 1852 m exactly	The statute mile is currently intended to stay for the moment on road signs in the UK 1 mile = 1.609 344km exactly. On road signs the mile is confusingly abbreviated m, ml is preferred
1–4	Area	m^2	km^2, dm^2, cm^2, mm^2	*hectare (ha), *are (a) 1 ha = 10^4 m^2 1a=10^2m^2	The square foot is still used by commercial estate agents in the UK 1 sq ft = 0.092 290 304 m^2 exactly. The acre is also commonly found in the UK 1 acre = 0.404 685 6422 ha exactly
1–5	Volume	m^3	dm^3, cm^3, mm^3	* litre (l), *hl, *cl, *ml 1 hl = $10^{-1}m^3$ 1l=$10^{-3}m^3$ = $1dm^3$ 1cl = $10^{-5}m^3$ 1ml=$10^{-6}m^3$ = $1cm^3$	The abbreviations l and L may each be used for litre; the full name is often used to avoid confusion. The imperial pint (pt) has been approved for continuing use in the UK, but only for draught beer and for milk in bottles (not cartons!). 1 pt = 0.568 2451
1–6.1	Time	s (second)	ks, ms, ms, ns	minute (min) 1 min = 60s exactly hour (h) 1h = 60min exactly day (d) d = 24h exactly	Other units such as week, month and year (a) are in common use; definitions of month and year often need to be specified
1–8.1	Angular velocity	rad/s			
1–10.1	m/s	m/h kilometre per hour (km/h) 1 km/h = (1/3.6) m/s			1 *knot = 1.852 km/h exactly (no abbreviation approved) Miles per hour (mph) are continuing on UK road signs 1 mph = 1.609 344 km/h exactly
1–11.1	m/s^2				
2 Periodic and related phenomena					
2–3.1	Frequency	Hz (hertz)	THz, GHz, MHz, kHz		
2–3.2	Rotational frequency	s^{-1}		min^{-1}	revs per min (r/min) and revs per sec (r/s) are also used
2–4	Angular frequency	rad/s			
3 Mechanics					
3–1	Mass	kg (kilogram)	Mg, g, mg, mg	tonne (t) unified atomic mass unit (u)	1 t = 10 kg tonne in the UK also called metric ton 1 u approx = 1.660 540 x 10^{-27} kg
3–2	Volumic mass Density Mass density	kg/m^3	Mg/m^3 kg/dm^3, g/cm^3 (all the same)	t/m^3, kg/l (kg/litre), g/ml, g/l	
3–5	Lineic mass Linear density	kg/m	mg/m		1 tex = 10^{-6} kg/m = 1 g/km The tex is used for textile filaments
3–7	Moment of inertia	$kg.m^2$			
3–8	Momentum	kg.m/s			
3–9	Force	N (newton)	MN, kN, mN, µmUM		
3–11	Moment of momentum Angular momentum	$kg.m^2$			
3–12.1	Moment of force	N.m	MN.m, kN.m, mN.m, µN.m		Moment of force is often called simply moment or bending moment
3–15.1	Pressure	Pa (pascal) Pa	GPa, MPa, kPa, hPa, mPa, µPa	*bar = 100kPa exactly 1 mbar = 1 hPa bars are used only in fluid pressures	
3–15.2	Normal stress		GPa, MPa, kPa		1MPa = $1N/mm^2$
3–23	Dynamic viscosity	Pa.s	mPa.s		poise (P) 1cP = 1mPa.s The poise is only used in conjunction with CGS units
3–24	Kinematic viscosity	m^2/s	mm^2/s		stokes (St) 1 cSt = $1mm^2/s$ The stokes is used only in conjunction with CGS units
3–25	Surface tension	N/m	mN/m		
3–26.1	Energy	J (joule)	EJ, PJ, TJ, MJ, kJ, mJ	electronvolt (eV) 1 eV = (1.602 10 ± 0.000 07) × 10^{-19} J eV, MeV and GeV are used in accelerator technology	kilowatt-hour (kW.h) 1 kWh = 3.6 × 10^6 J = 3.6 MJ W.h, kW.h, MW.h, GW.h and TW.h are used in the electrical power industry
3–26.2	Work				
3–27	Power	W (watt)	GW, MW, kW, mW, µmUW		1W = 1J/s
4 Heat					
4–1	Thermodynamic temperature	K (kelvin)			

Item no in ISO 31:1992	Quantity	SI unit	Recommended multiples and sub-multiples	Other units which may be used	Remarks
4–2	Celsius temperature	°C (no space beween value and symbol)			1 °C = 1 K The temperature in °C is the temperature expressed in kelvins minus exactly 273.15 K
4–3.1	Linear expansion coefficient	K^{-1}			
4–6	Heat, quantity of heat	J	EJ, PJ, TJ, GJ, MJ, kJ, mJ		
4–7	Heat flow rate	W	kW		1 W = 1 J/s
4–9	Thermal conductivity	W/(m.k)			
4–10.1	Coefficient of heat transfer	W/(m.K)			
4–11	Thermal insulance	m.k/W			
4–15	Heat capacity	J/K	kJ/K		
4–16.1	Massic heat capacity (was specific)	J/(kg.K)	kJ/(kg.K)		
4–18	Entropy	J/K	kJ/K		
4–19	Massic entropy	J/(kg.K)	kJ/(kg.K)		
4–21.2	Massic thermodynamic energy (was specific energy)	J/kg	MJ/kg, kJ/kg		
5 Electricity and magnetism					
5–1	Electric current	A (ampere)	kA, mA, µA, nA, pA		
5–2	Electric charge, quantity of electricity	C (coulomb)	kC, µC, nC, pC		1 A.h = 3.6 kC
5–3	Volumic charge, charge density	C/m^3	C/mm^3 or GC/m^3, MC/m^3 or C/cm^3, kC/m^3, mC/m^3, $\mu C/m^3$		
5–4	Areic charge, surface density of charge	C/m^3	MC/m^2 or C/mm^2, C/cm^2, kC/m^2, mC/m^2, $\mu C/m^2$		
5–5	Electric field strength	V/m	MV/m, kV/m or V/mm, V/cm, mV/m, µV/m		
5–6.1	Electric potential	V (volt)	MV, kV, mV, V		
5–6.2	Potential difference tension				
5–6.3	Electromotive force				
5–7	Electrical flux density	C/m^2	C/cm^2, kC/m^2, mC/m^2, $\mu C/m^2$		
5–9	Capacitance	F (farad)	mF, µF, nF, pF		
5–33	Resistance to direct current	Ω (ohm)	GΩ, MΩ, kΩ, mΩ, µΩ		
5–34	Conductance of direct current	S (siemens)	kS, mS, µS		1 S = 1/Ω
5–36	Resistivity	S/m	GΩm, MΩm, kΩm, Ωcm, mΩm, µΩm, nΩm		µm = 10^{-2} Ωm (µmUmm²)/m = 10^{-6} Ωm = µmUΩm are also used
5–37	Conductivity		MS/m, kS/M		
5–38	Reluctance	H^{-1}			
5–39	Permeance	H (henry)			
5–49	Active power	W	TW, GW, MW, kW, mW, mW, nW		In electric power technology active power is expressed in watts, apparent power in volt amperes V.A and reactive power in vars (var)
5–52	Active energy	J	TJ, GJ, MJ, KJ		1 W.h = 3.6 kJ exactly TW.h, GW.h, MW.h, kW.h
6 Light					
6–3	Wavelength	m	µmUm, nm, pm	*ångstro¨m (Å)	1ÅR = $10r^{-10}$m= 10^{-4} µm Um= 10^{-1} nm
6–7	Radiant energy	J			
6–10	Radiant power energy flux	W			
6–13	Radiant intensity	W/sr			
6–15	Radiant exitance	w/m^2			
6–29	Luminous intensity	cd (candela)			
6–30	Luminous flux	lm (lumen)			
6–31	Quantity of light		lm.h	1 lm.h = 3600 lm.s exactly	
6–32	Luminance	cd/m^2			
6–33	Luminous exitance	lx (lux)			
6–35	Light exposure	lx.s			
6–36.1	Luminous efficacy	lm/W			
7 Acoustics					
7–1	Period, periodic time	s	ms, ms		
7–2	Frequency	Hz	MHz, kHz		
7–5	Wavelength	m	mm		
7–8	Volumic mass Mass density Density	kg/m^3			
7–9.1	Static pressure	Pa	nPa, µPa		
7–9.2	(Instantaneous) sound pressure				
7–11	(Instantaneous) sound particle velocity	m/s	mm/s		
7–13	(Instantaneous) volume flow rate	m^3/s			
7–14.1	Velocity of sound	m/s			

(continued)

Table IV (continued)

Item no in ISO 31:1992	Quantity	SI unit	Recommended multiples and sub-multiples	Other units which may be used	Remarks
7–16	Sound power	W			
7–17	Sound intensity	W/m^2	mW/m^2, mW/m^2, pW/m^3		
7–18	Acoustic impedance	Pa.s/m^3			
7–19	Mechanical impedance	N.s/m	Mechanical impedance		
7–20.1	Surface density of mechanical impedance	Pa.s/m			
7–21	Sound pressure level		bel (B), dB	1 dB = 10^{-1} B	
7–28	Sound reduction index		B, dB		
7–29	Equivalent absorption area of surface or object	m^2			
7–30	Reverberation time	s			

Appendix B
Conversion factors and tables

Table I Conversion factors

Bold type indicates exact conversions. Otherwise four or five significant figures are given.

Quantity	Conversion factors	
General purposes		
Length	1 mile	= 1.609 km
	1 chain	= **20.1168** m
	1 yard	= **0.9144** m
	1 foot	= **0.3048**m = **304.8** mm
	1 inch	= **25.4**mm = **2.54** cm
Area	1 square mile	= 2.590 km² = 259.0 ha
	1 hectare	= **10 000**m²
	1 acre	= 4 046.9 m² = 0.40469 ha
		= **4 840** yd²
	1 square yard	= 0.8361 m²
	1 square foot	= 0.09290 m² = 929.03 cm²
	1 square inch	= 645.2 mm² = 6.452 cm²
Volume	1 cubic yard	= 0.7646 m³
	1 litre	= 1dm³ = **1000**cm³
	1 m³	= **1 000** litres
	1 millilitre	= 1cm³ = **1000**mm
	1 cubic foot	= 0.02832 m³ = 28.32 litre
	1 petrograd standard	= 4.672 m³
	1 cubic inch	= 16 387 mm³ = 16.387 cm³
		= 16.387ml = 0.016387 litre
Capacity	1 UK gallon	= 4.546 litre
	1 UK quart	= 1.137 litre
	1 UK pint	= 0.5683
	1 UK fluid ounce	= 28.413 cm³
	1 US barrel (for petroleum)	= 159.0 litre
	1 US gallon	= 3.785 litre
	1 US liquid quart	= 0.9464 litre
	1 US dry quart	= 1.101 litre
	1 US liquid pint	= 0.4732 litre
	1 US dry pint	= 0.5506 litre
	1 US liquid ounce	= 29.574 cm³
Mass	1 UK ton	= 1.016 tonne = 1016.05 kg
	1 US (or short) ton	= 0.9072 tonne = 907.2 kg
	1 kip (1000 lb)	= 453.59 kg
	1 UK hundredweight	= 50.80 kg
	1 short (US) hundredweight	= 100lb = 45.36 kg
	1 pound	= 0.4536 kg
	1 ounce avoirdupois	= 28.35 g
	1 ounce troy	= 31.10 g
Mass per unit length	1 UK ton per mile	= 0.6313 kg/m = 0.6313 t/km
	1 lb per yard	= 0.4961 kg/m
	1 lb per foot	= 1.4882 kg/m
	1 lb per inch	= 17.86 kg/m
	1 oz per inch	= 1.1161 kg/m
Length per unit mass	1 yd per lb	= 2.016 m/kg
Mass per unit area	1 ton per square mile	= 392.3 kg/km² = 0.3923 g/m²
		= 3.923 kg/ha
	1 ton per acre	= 0.2511 kg/m²
	1 hundredweight per acre	= 0.01255 kg/m²
	1 lb per square foot	= 4.882 kg/m²
	1 lb per square inch	= 703.07 kg/m²
	1 oz per square yard	= 33.91 g/m²
	1 oz per square foot	= 305.15 g/m²
	1 kg/cm²	= 10t/m²
Mass density (mass per unit volume)	1 ton per cubic yard	= 1329 kg/m³ = 1.3289 t/m³
	1 lb per cubic yard	= 0.5933 kg/m³
	1 lb per cubic foot	= 16.02 kg/m³
	1 lb per cubic inch	= 27.68 g/cm³ = 27.68 t/m³

Table I (continued)

Quantity	Conversion factors	
Area coverage	× square yards per ton	$= \dfrac{1}{x} \times 1215 \text{kg/m}^2$
	× square yards per gallon	$= \dfrac{1}{x} \times 5.437 \text{ litre/m}^2$
Volume rate of flow	1 cubic feet per minute	= 0.4719 litre/s
		= 471.9 cm³/s
		= 0.0004719 m³/s
	1 cusec (cu ft per sec)	= 0.02832 m³/s ('cumec')
	1 cu ft per thousand acres	= 0.06997 litre/ha
		= 0.006997 m³/km²
		= 6997 cm³/km²
	1 cubic inch per second	= 16.39 ml/s
	1 gallon per year	= 4546 cm³/a* = 0.004546 ³/a
	1 gallon per day	= 4546 cm³/d
	1 litre/s	= **86.4** m³/d
	1 million gallons per day	= 0.05262 m³/s
	1 gallon per person per day	= 4.546 litre/(person day)
	1 gallon per sq yd per day	= 0.005437 m³/(m².d)
		= 0.000062928 mm/s
	1 gallon per cu yd per day	= 0.005946 m³/(m³.d)
	1 gallon per hour	= 4.5461 litre/h
	1 gallon per minute	= 0.07577 litre/s
	1 gallon per second	= 4.5461 litre/s
Fuel consumption	1 gallon per mile	= 2.825 litre/km
	1 mile per gallon	= 0.354 km/litre
	× miles per gallon	$= \dfrac{1}{x} \times 282.5 \text{ litre } 100 \text{ km}$
Velocity	1 mile per hour	= 1.609 km/h = **0.44704** m/s
	1 foot per minute	= **0.3048** m/min = 0.0051 m/s
	1 foot per second	= **0.3048** m/s
	1 inch per second	= **25.4** mm/s
	1 UK knot	= 0.5148 m/s = 1.853 km/h
		= 1.00064 international knot
Acceleration	1 foot per sec per sec	= **0.3048** m/s²
	1 mile per hr per sec	= **0.44704** m/s²
	1 g (standard gravity)	= **9.806 65**m/s²
Heating Temperature	× Fahrenheit	$= \dfrac{5}{9} \times (x - 32)$ ° Celsius
Temperature interval	1°F	= 0.5556 K = 0.5556°C
Energy (heat)	1 British thermal unit	= 1055J = 1.055 kJ
	1 Therm	= 105.5 MJ
	1 calorie	= **4.1868** J
	1 kilowatt–hour	= 3.6 MJ
	1 foot pound–force	= 1.356 J
	1 kilogram force–metre	= **9.806 65**J
Power (also heat flow rate)	1 J/s	= 1W
	1 Btu per hour	= 0.293 07W
	1 horsepower	= 745.70 W
	1 ft–lbf per second	= 1.356 W
	1 kgf–metre per second	= **9.806 65**W
	1 calorie per second	= **4.1868 W**
	1 kilocalorie per hour	= **1.163 W**
	1 metric horsepower	= 735.5 W
Density of heat flow rate	1 Btu per square foot hour	= 3.155 W/m²

Quantity	Conversion factors	
Thermal conductivity k value	1 Btu inch per square foot hour degree Fahrenheit	= 0.1442 W/(m.K)

Table I (continued)

Quantity	Conversion factors	
Thermal transmittance or coefficient of heat transfer or thermal conductance or *U* value	1 Btu per square foot hour degree Fahrenheit	= 5.678 W/(m²K)
Thermal resistivity 1/k value	1 sq ft hr °F per Btu inch	= 6.933 m.K/W
Thermal or specific heat capacity	1 Btu per lb °F	= 4.187 (kJ.K)
	1 Btu per cu ft °F	= 67.07 kJ/(m³.K)
Calorific value	1 Btu per pound	= 2.326 kJ/kg
	1 Btu per cubic foot	= 37.26 kJ/m³ = 37.26 J/litre
	1 Btu per gallon	= 232.1 J/litre
Refrigeration	1 ton	= 3517W
Lighting	1 foot–candle	= 10.76 1 ×
Illumination	1 lumen per sq ft	= 10.76 1 ×
Lumination	1 candela per square inch	1550 cd/m²
	1 candela per square foot	= 10.76 cd/m²
	1 apostilb	$= \dfrac{1}{\neq}$ cd/m = 0.3183 cd/m

Structural design (All tons are UK tons)

Force		
	1 pound–force	= 4.448 N
	1 kip–force	= 4.448 kN
	1 ton–force	= 9.964 kN
	1 kilogram–force	= 9.807 N
	1 kilopond	= 9.807 N

Table I (continued)

Quantity	Conversion factors	
Force per unit length	1 pound–force per foot	= 14.59 N/m
	1 pound–force per inch	= 175.1 kN/m = 175.1 N/mm
	1 ton–force per foot	= 32.69 kN/m
	1 kilogram–force per metre	= 9.807 N/m
	1 kilogram–force per centimetre	= 0.9807 kN/m
Force per unit area or	1 lbf per square foot	= 47.88 N/m² = 47.88 Pa
		= 0.04788 kN/m²
Stress or Pressure	1 lbf per square inch	= 6.895 kN/m² = 6.895 kPa
	1 tonf per square foot	= 107.3 kN/m² = 107.3 kPa
	1 tonf per square inch	= 15.44 MN/m² = 15.44 N/m²
		= 15.44 MPa
	1 kgf per square metre	= 9.807 N/m² = 9.807 Pa
	1 kgf per sq centimetre	= 98.07 kN/m² = 98.07 kPa
	1 bar	= **100** kN/m² = **100** kPa
	1 millibar	= **100** N/m² = **100**Pa
	1 standard atmosphere	= **101.325** kPa
	1 inch of mercury	= 3.386 kPa
	1 foot of water	= 2.989 kPa
		= 300 mbar approx
Bending moment of torque	1 pound–force foot	= 1.356 Nm
	1 pound–force inch	= 0.1130Nm = 113.0Nmm
	1 kip–force foot	= 1.356 kNm
	1 kip–force inch	= 0.1130 kNm = 113.0 Nm
	1 ton–force foot	= 3.037 kNm
	1 ton–force inch	= 0.2531 kNm = 253.1 Nm
	1 kilogram–force metre	= 9.807 Nm

* a (for annum) is the symbol for year.

Table II Inches and fractions of an inch to millimetres (¹/₁₆ in increments up to 11 ¹⁵/₁₆ in)

Inches	¹/₁₆	¹/₈	³/₁₆	¹/₄	⁵/₁₆	³/₈	⁷/₁₆	¹/₂	⁹/₁₆	⁵/₈	¹¹/₁₆	³/₄	¹³/₁₆	⁷/₈	¹⁵/₁₆
	Millimeters														
0	–	1.6	3.2	4.8	6.4	7.9	9.5	11.1	12.7	14.3	15.9	17.5	19.1	20.6	22.2	23.8
1	25.4	27.0	28.6	30.2	31.8	33.3	34.9	36.5	38.1	39.7	41.3	42.9	44.5	46.0	47.6	49.2
2	50.8	52.4	54.0	55.6	57.2	58.7	60.3	61.9	63.5	65.1	66.7	68.3	69.9	71.4	73.0	74.6
3	76.2	77.8	79.4	81.0	82.6	84.1	85.7	87.3	88.9	90.5	92.1	93.7	95.3	96.8	98.4	100.0
4	101.6	103.2	104.8	106.4	108.0	109.5	111.1	112.7	114.3	115.9	117.5	119.1	120.7	122.2	123.8	125.4
5	127.0	128.6	130.2	131.8	133.4	134.9	136.5	138.1	139.7	141.3	142.9	144.5	146.1	147.6	149.2	150.8
6	152.4	154.0	155.6	157.2	158.8	160.3	161.9	163.5	165.1	166.7	168.3	169.9	171.5	173.0	174.6	176.2
7	177.8	179.4	181.0	182.6	184.2	185.7	187.3	188.9	190.5	192.1	193.7	195.3	196.9	198.4	200.0	201.6
8	203.2	204.8	206.4	208.0	209.6	211.1	212.7	214.3	215.9	217.5	219.1	220.7	222.3	223.8	225.4	227.0
9	228.6	230.2	231.8	233.4	235.0	236.5	238.1	239.7	241.3	242.9	244.5	246.1	247.7	249.2	250.8	252.4
10	254.0	255.6	257.2	258.8	260.4	261.9	263.5	265.1	266.7	268.3	269.9	271.5	273.1	274.6	276.2	277.8
11	279.4	281.0	282.6	284.2	285.8	287.3	288.9	290.5	292.1	293.7	295.3	296.9	298.5	300.0	301.6	303.2

Table III   Feet to millimetres (up to 200 ft)

Feet	0	1	2	3	4	5	6	7	8	9
	Millimetres									
0	–	304.8	609.6	914.4	1219.2	1524.0	1828.8	2133.6	2438.4	2743.2
10	3048.0	3352.8	3657.6	3962.4	4267.2	4572.0	4876.8	5181.6	5486.4	5791.2
20	6096.0	6400.8	6705.6	7010.4	7315.2	7620.0	7924.8	8229.6	8534.4	8839.2
30	9144.0	9448.8	9753.6	10058.4	10363.2	10668.0	10972.8	11277.6	11582.4	11887.2
40	12192.0	12496.8	12801.6	13106.4	13411.2	13716.0	14020.8	14325.6	14630.4	14935.2
50	15240.0	15544.8	15849.6	16154.4	16459.2	16764.0	17068.8	17373.6	17678.4	17983.2
60	18288.0	18592.8	18897.6	19202.4	19507.2	19812.0	20116.8	20421.6	20726.4	21031.2
70	21336.0	21640.8	21945.6	22250.4	22555.2	22860.0	23164.8	23469.6	23774.4	24079.2
80	24384.0	24688.8	24993.6	25298.4	25603.2	25908.0	26212.8	26517.6	26822.4	27127.2
90	27432.0	27736.8	28041.6	28346.4	28651.2	28956.0	29260.8	29565.6	29870.4	30175.2
100	30480.0	30784.8	31089.6	31394.4	31699.2	32004.0	32308.8	32613.6	32918.4	33223.2
110	33528.0	33832.8	34137.6	34442.4	34747.2	35052.0	35356.8	35661.6	35966.4	36271.2
120	36576.0	36880.8	37185.6	37490.4	37785.2	38100.0	38404.8	38709.6	39014.4	39319.2
130	39624.0	39928.8	40233.6	40538.4	40843.2	41148.0	41452.8	41757.6	42062.4	42367.2
140	42672.0	42976.8	43281.6	43586.4	43891.2	44196.0	44500.8	44805.6	45110.4	45415.2
150	45720.0	46024.8	46329.6	46634.4	46939.2	47244.0	47548.8	47853.6	48158.4	48463.2
160	48768.0	49072.8	49377.6	49682.4	49987.2	50292.0	50596.8	50901.6	51206.4	51511.2
170	51816.0	52120.8	52425.6	52730.4	53035.2	53340.0	53644.8	53949.6	54254.4	54559.2
180	54864.0	55168.8	55473.6	55778.4	56083.2	56388.0	56692.8	56997.6	57302.4	57607.2
190	57912.0	58216.8	58521.6	58826.4	59131.2	59436.0	59740.8	60045.6	60350.4	60655.2
200	60960.0	–	–	–	–	–	–	–	–	–

Note: use Tables II and III together to obtain the metric equivalent of any dimension up to 200 ft. For example

56 ft 3¼ in: 56 ft = 17068.8
3¼ in =   95.3
TOTAL = 17164.1 mm = 17.164 m

Table IV   Miles (up to 100 miles) to kilometres (to two places of decimals) may also be used to convert mph to kph

Miles	0	1	2	3	4	5	6	7	8	9
	Kilometres									
0	–	1.61	3.22	4.83	6.44	8.05	9.66	11.27	12.87	14.48
10	16.09	17.70	19.31	20.92	22.53	24.14	25.75	27.36	28.97	30.58
20	32.19	33.80	35.41	37.01	38.62	40.23	41.84	43.45	45.06	46.67
30	48.28	49.89	51.50	53.11	54.72	56.33	57.94	59.55	61.16	62.76
40	64.37	65.98	67.59	69.20	70.81	72.42	74.03	75.64	77.25	78.86
50	80.47	82.08	83.69	85.30	86.90	88.51	90.12	91.73	93.34	94.95
60	96.56	98.17	99.78	101.39	103.00	104.61	106.22	107.83	109.44	111.05
70	112.65	114.26	115.87	117.48	119.09	120.70	122.31	123.92	125.53	127.14
80	128.75	130.36	131.97	133.58	135.19	136.79	138.40	140.01	141.62	143.23
90	144.84	146.45	148.06	149.67	151.28	152.89	154.50	156.11	57.72	159.33
100	160.93	–	–	–	–	–	–	–	–	–

Table V   Square inches (up to 100 sq in) to square millimetres (to one place of decimals)

Square inches	0	1	2	3	4	5	6	7	8	9
	Square millimetres (mm^2)									
0	–	645.2	1290.3	1935.5	2580.6	3225.8	3871.0	4516.1	5161.3	5806.4
10	6451.6	7096.8	7741.9	8387.1	9032.2	9677.4	10322.6	10967.7	11612.9	12258.0
20	12903.2	13548.4	14193.5	14838.7	15483.8	16129.0	16774.2	17419.3	18064.5	18709.6
30	19354.8	20000.0	20645.1	21290.3	21935.4	22580.6	23225.8	23870.9	24516.1	25161.2
40	25806.4	26451.6	27096.7	27741.9	28387.0	29032.2	29677.4	30322.5	30967.7	31612.8
50	32258.0	32903.2	33548.3	34193.5	34838.6	35483.8	36129.0	36774.1	37419.3	38064.4
60	38709.6	39354.8	39999.9	40645.1	41290.2	41935.4	42580.6	43225.7	43870.9	44516.0
70	45161.2	45806.4	46451.5	47096.7	47741.8	48387.0	49032.2	49677.3	50322.5	50967.6
80	51612.8	52258.0	52903.1	53548.3	54193.4	54838.6	55483.8	56128.9	56774.1	57419.2
90	58064.4	58709.6	59354.7	59999.9	60645.0	61290.2	61935.4	62580.5	63225.7	63870.8
100	64516.0	–	–	–	–	–	–	–	–	–

Table VI   Square feet (up to 500 ft²) to square metres (to two places of decimals)

	0	1	2	3	4	5	6	7	8	9
Square feet	**Square metres (m²)**									
0	–	0.09	0.19	0.28	0.37	0.46	0.56	0.65	0.74	0.84
10	0.93	1.02	1.11	1.21	1.30	1.39	1.49	1.58	1.67	1.77
20	1.86	1.95	2.04	2.14	2.23	2.32	2.42	2.51	2.60	2.69
30	2.79	2.88	2.97	3.07	3.16	3.25	3.34	3.44	3.53	3.62
40	3.72	3.81	3.90	3.99	4.09	4.18	4.27	4.37	4.46	4.55
50	4.65	4.74	4.83	4.92	5.02	5.11	5.20	5.30	5.39	5.48
60	5.57	5.67	5.76	5.85	5.95	6.04	6.13	6.22	6.32	6.41
70	6.50	6.60	6.69	6.78	6.87	6.97	7.06	7.15	7.25	7.34
80	7.43	7.53	7.62	7.71	7.80	7.90	7.99	8.08	8.18	8.27
90	8.36	8.45	8.55	8.64	8.73	8.83	8.92	9.01	9.10	9.20
100	9.29	9.38	9.48	9.57	9.66	9.75	9.85	9.94	10.03	10.13
110	10.22	10.31	10.41	10.50	10.59	10.68	10.78	10.87	10.96	11.06
120	11.15	11.24	11.33	11.43	11.52	11.61	11.71	11.80	11.89	11.98
130	12.08	12.17	12.26	12.36	12.45	12.54	12.63	12.73	12.82	12.91
140	13.01	13.10	13.19	13.29	13.38	13.47	13.56	13.66	13.75	13.84
150	13.94	14.03	14.12	14.21	14.31	14.40	14.49	14.59	14.68	14.77
160	14.86	14.96	15.05	15.14	15.24	15.33	15.42	15.51	15.61	15.70
170	15.79	15.89	15.98	16.07	16.17	16.26	16.35	16.44	16.54	16.63
180	16.72	16.82	16.91	17.00	17.09	17.19	17.28	17.37	17.47	17.56
190	17.65	17.74	17.84	17.93	18.02	18.12	18.21	18.30	18.39	18.49
200	18.58	18.67	18.77	18.86	18.95	19.05	19.14	19.23	19.32	19.42
210	19.51	19.60	19.70	19.79	19.88	19.97	20.07	20.16	20.25	20.35
220	20.44	20.53	20.62	20.72	20.81	20.90	21.00	21.09	21.18	21.27
230	21.37	21.46	21.55	21.65	21.74	21.83	21.93	22.02	22.11	22.20
240	22.30	22.39	22.48	22.58	22.67	22.76	22.85	22.95	23.04	23.13
250	23.23	23.32	23.41	23.50	23.60	23.69	23.78	23.88	23.97	24.06
260	24.15	24.25	24.34	24.43	24.53	24.62	24.71	24.81	24.90	24.99
270	25.08	25.18	25.27	25.36	25.46	25.55	25.64	25.73	25.83	25.92
280	26.01	26.11	26.20	26.29	26.38	26.48	26.57	26.66	26.76	26.85
290	26.94	27.03	27.13	27.22	27.31	27.41	27.50	27.59	27.69	27.78
300	27.87	27.96	28.06	28.15	28.24	28.34	28.43	28.52	28.61	28.71
310	28.80	28.89	28.99	29.08	29.17	29.26	29.36	29.45	29.54	29.64
320	29.73	29.82	29.91	30.01	30.10	30.19	30.29	30.38	30.47	30.57
330	30.66	30.75	30.84	30.94	31.03	31.12	31.22	31.31	31.40	31.49
340	31.59	31.68	31.77	31.87	31.96	32.05	32.14	32.24	32.33	32.42
350	32.52	32.61	32.70	32.79	32.89	32.98	33.07	33.17	33.26	33.35
360	33.45	33.54	33.63	33.72	33.82	33.91	34.00	34.10	34.19	34.28
370	34.37	34.47	34.56	34.65	34.75	34.84	34.93	35.02	35.12	35.21
380	35.30	35.40	35.49	35.58	35.67	35.77	35.86	35.95	36.05	36.14
390	36.23	36.33	36.42	36.51	36.60	36.70	36.79	36.88	36.98	37.07
400	37.16	37.25	37.35	37.44	37.53	37.63	37.72	37.81	37.90	38.00
410	38.09	38.18	38.28	38.37	38.46	38.55	38.65	38.74	38.83	38.93
420	39.02	39.11	39.21	39.30	39.39	39.48	39.58	39.67	39.76	39.86
430	39.95	40.04	40.13	40.23	40.32	40.41	40.51	40.60	40.69	40.78
440	40.88	40.97	41.06	41.16	41.25	41.34	41.43	41.53	41.62	41.71
450	41.81	41.90	41.99	42.09	42.18	42.27	42.36	42.46	42.55	42.64
460	42.74	42.83	42.92	43.01	43.11	43.20	43.29	43.39	43.48	43.57
470	43.66	43.76	43.85	43.94	44.04	44.13	44.22	44.31	44.41	44.50
480	44.59	44.69	44.78	44.87	44.97	45.06	45.15	45.24	45.34	45.43
490	45.52	45.62	45.71	45.80	45.89	45.99	46.08	46.17	46.27	46.36
500	46.45	–	–	–	–	–	–	–	–	–

Table VII   Cubic feet (up to 100 ft³) to cubic metres (to two places of decimals)

	0	1	2	3	4	5	6	7	8	9
Cubic feet	**Cubic metres (m³)**									
0	–	0.03	0.06	0.08	0.11	0.14	0.17	0.20	0.23	0.25
10	0.28	0.31	0.34	0.37	0.40	0.42	0.45	0.48	0.51	0.54
20	0.57	0.59	0.62	0.65	0.68	0.71	0.73	0.76	0.79	0.82
30	0.85	0.88	0.91	0.93	0.96	0.99	1.02	1.05	1.08	1.10
40	1.13	1.16	1.19	1.22	1.25	1.27	1.30	1.33	1.36	1.39
50	1.42	1.44	1.47	1.50	1.53	1.56	1.59	1.61	1.64	1.67
60	1.70	1.73	1.76	1.78	1.81	1.84	1.87	1.90	1.93	1.95
70	1.98	2.01	2.04	2.07	2.10	2.12	2.15	2.18	2.21	2.24
80	2.27	2.29	2.32	2.35	2.38	2.41	2.44	2.46	2.49	2.52
90	2.55	2.58	2.61	2.63	2.66	2.69	2.72	2.75	2.78	2.80
100	2.83	–	–	–	–	–	–	–	–	–

Table VIII Pounds (up to 500 lb) to kilograms (to two places of decimals)

Pounds	0	1	2	3	4	5	6	7	8	9
Pounds	Kilogrammes (kg)									
0	–	0.45	0.91	1.36	1.81	2.27	2.72	3.18	3.63	4.08
10	4.54	4.99	5.44	5.90	6.35	6.80	7.26	7.71	8.16	8.62
20	9.07	9.53	9.98	10.43	10.89	11.34	11.79	12.25	12.70	13.15
30	13.61	14.06	14.52	14.97	15.42	15.88	16.33	16.78	17.24	17.69
40	18.14	18.60	19.05	19.50	19.96	20.41	20.87	21.32	21.77	22.23
50	22.68	23.13	23.59	24.04	24.49	24.95	25.40	25.85	26.31	26.76
60	27.22	27.67	28.12	28.58	29.03	29.48	29.94	30.39	30.84	31.30
70	31.75	32.21	32.66	33.11	33.57	34.02	34.47	34.93	35.38	35.83
80	36.29	36.74	37.19	37.65	38.10	38.56	39.01	39.46	39.92	40.37
90	40.82	41.28	41.73	42.18	42.64	43.09	43.54	44.00	44.45	44.91
100	45.36	45.81	46.27	46.72	47.17	47.63	48.08	48.53	48.99	49.44
110	49.90	50.35	50.80	51.26	51.71	52.16	52.62	53.07	53.52	53.98
120	54.43	54.88	55.34	55.79	56.25	56.70	57.15	57.61	58.06	58.51
130	58.97	59.42	59.87	60.33	60.78	61.24	61.69	62.14	62.60	63.05
140	63.50	63.96	64.41	64.86	65.32	65.77	66.22	66.68	67.13	67.59
150	68.04	68.49	68.95	69.40	69.85	70.31	70.76	71.21	71.67	72.12
160	72.57	73.03	73.48	73.94	74.39	74.84	75.30	75.75	76.20	76.66
170	77.11	77.56	78.02	78.47	78.93	79.38	79.83	80.29	80.74	81.19
180	81.65	82.10	82.55	83.01	83.46	83.91	84.37	84.82	85.28	85.73
190	86.18	86.64	87.09	87.54	88.00	88.45	88.90	89.36	89.81	90.26
200	90.72	91.17	91.63	92.08	92.53	92.99	93.44	93.89	94.35	94.80
210	95.25	95.71	96.16	96.62	97.07	97.52	97.98	98.43	98.88	99.34
220	99.79	100.24	100.70	101.15	101.61	102.06	102.51	102.97	103.42	103.87
230	104.33	104.78	105.23	105.69	106.14	106.59	107.05	107.50	107.96	108.41
240	108.86	109.32	109.77	110.22	110.68	111.13	111.58	112.04	112.49	112.95
250	113.40	113.85	114.31	114.76	115.21	115.67	116.12	116.57	117.03	117.48
260	117.93	118.39	118.84	119.30	119.75	120.20	120.66	121.11	121.56	122.02
270	122.47	122.92	123.38	123.83	124.28	124.74	125.19	125.65	126.10	126.55
280	127.01	127.46	127.91	128.37	128.82	129.27	129.73	130.18	130.64	131.09
290	131.54	132.00	132.45	132.90	133.36	133.81	134.26	134.72	135.17	135.62
300	136.08	136.53	136.99	137.44	137.89	138.35	138.80	139.25	139.71	140.16
310	140.61	141.07	141.52	141.97	142.43	142.88	143.34	143.79	144.24	144.70
320	145.15	145.60	146.06	146.51	146.96	147.42	147.87	148.33	148.78	149.23
330	149.69	150.14	150.59	151.05	151.50	151.95	152.41	152.86	153.31	153.77
340	154.22	154.68	155.13	155.58	156.04	156.49	156.94	157.40	157.85	158.30
350	158.76	159.21	159.67	160.12	160.57	161.03	161.48	161.93	162.39	162.84
360	163.29	163.75	164.20	164.65	165.11	165.56	166.02	166.47	166.92	167.38
370	167.83	168.28	168.74	169.10	169.64	170.10	170.55	171.00	171.46	171.91
380	172.37	172.82	173.27	173.73	174.18	174.63	175.09	175.54	175.99	176.45
390	176.90	177.36	177.81	178.26	178.72	179.17	179.62	180.08	180.53	180.98
400	181.44	181.89	183.34	182.80	183.25	183.71	184.16	184.61	185.07	185.52
410	185.97	186.43	186.88	187.33	187.79	188.24	188.69	189.15	189.60	190.06
420	190.51	190.96	191.42	191.87	192.32	192.78	193.23	193.68	194.14	194.59
430	195.05	195.50	195.95	196.41	196.86	197.31	197.77	198.22	198.67	199.13
440	199.58	200.03	200.49	200.94	201.40	201.85	202.30	202.76	203.21	203.66
450	204.12	204.57	205.02	205.48	205.93	206.39	206.84	207.29	207.75	208.20
460	208.65	209.11	209.56	210.01	210.47	210.92	211.37	211.83	212.28	212.74
470	213.19	213.64	214.10	214.55	215.00	215.46	215.91	216.36	216.82	217.27
480	217.72	218.18	218.63	219.09	219.54	219.99	220.45	220.90	221.35	221.81
490	222.26	222.71	223.17	223.62	224.08	224.53	224.98	225.44	225.89	226.34
500	226.80	–	–	–	–	–	–	–	–	–

Table IX Pounds per cubic foot to kilogrammes per cubic metre (to one place of decimals)

Pounds per cubic foot	0	1	2	3	4	5	6	7	8	9
	Kilogrammes per cubic metre (kg/m^3)									
0	–	16.0	32.0	48.1	64.1	80.1	96.1	112.1	128.1	144.2
10	160.2	176.2	192.2	208.2	224.3	240.3	256.3	272.3	288.3	304.4
20	320.4	336.4	352.4	368.4	384.4	400.5	416.5	432.5	448.5	464.5
30	480.6	496.6	512.6	528.6	544.6	560.6	576.7	592.7	608.7	624.7
40	640.7	656.8	672.8	688.8	704.8	720.8	736.8	752.9	768.9	784.9
50	800.9	816.9	833.0	849.0	865.0	881.0	897.0	913.1	929.1	945.1
60	961.1	977.1	993.1	1009.2	1025.2	1041.2	1057.2	1073.2	1089.3	1105.3
70	1121.3	1137.3	1153.3	1169.4	1185.4	1201.4	1217.4	1233.4	1249.4	1265.5
80	1281.5	1297.5	1313.5	1329.5	1345.6	1361.6	1377.6	1393.6	1409.6	1425.6
90	1441.7	1457.7	1473.7	1489.7	1505.7	1521.8	1537.8	1553.8	1569.8	1585.8
100	1601.9	–	–	–	–	–	–	–	–	–

Table X UK gallons (up to 100 galls) to litres (to two places of decimals)

	0	1	2	3	4	5	6	7	8	9
UK gallons	**Litres**									
0	–	4.55	9.09	13.64	18.18	22.73	27.28	31.82	36.37	40.91
10	45.46	50.01	54.55	59.10	63.64	68.19	72.74	77.28	81.83	86.37
20	90.92	95.47	100.01	104.56	109.10	113.65	118.20	122.74	127.29	131.83
30	136.38	140.93	145.47	150.02	154.56	159.11	163.66	168.20	172.75	177.29
40	181.84	186.38	190.93	195.48	200.02	204.57	209.11	213.66	218.21	222.75
50	227.30	231.84	236.39	240.94	245.48	250.03	254.57	259.12	263.67	268.21
60	272.76	277.30	281.85	286.40	290.94	295.49	300.03	304.58	309.13	313.67
70	318.22	322.76	327.31	331.86	336.40	340.95	345.49	350.04	354.59	359.13
80	363.68	368.22	372.77	377.32	381.86	386.41	390.95	395.50	400.04	404.59
90	409.14	413.68	418.23	422.77	427.32	431.87	436.41	440.96	445.50	450.05
100	454.60	–	–	–	–	–	–	–	–	–

Table XI Acres (up to 1000 acres) to hectares (to two places of decimals)

	0	1	2	3	4	5	6	7	8	9
Acres	**Hectares**									
	–	0.40	0.81	1.21	1.62	2.02	2.43	2.83	3.24	3.64

	0	10	20	30	40	50	60	70	80	90
Acres	**Hectares**									
0	–	4.05	8.09	12.14	16.19	20.23	24.28	28.33	32.37	36.42
100	40.47	44.52	48.56	52.61	56.66	60.70	64.75	68.80	72.84	76.89
200	80.94	84.98	89.03	93.08	97.12	101.17	105.22	109.27	113.31	117.36
300	121.41	125.45	129.50	133.55	137.59	141.64	145.69	149.73	153.78	157.83
400	161.87	165.92	169.97	174.02	178.06	182.11	186.16	190.20	194.25	198.30
500	202.34	206.39	210.44	214.48	218.53	222.58	226.62	230.67	234.72	238.77
600	242.81	246.86	250.91	254.95	259.00	263.05	267.09	271.14	275.19	279.23
700	283.28	287.33	291.37	295.42	299.47	303.51	307.56	311.61	315.66	319.70
800	323.75	327.80	331.84	335.89	339.94	343.98	348.03	352.08	356.12	360.17
900	364.22	368.26	372.31	376.36	380.41	384.45	388.50	392.55	396.59	400.64
1000	404.69	–	–	–	–	–	–	–	–	–

Table XII Miles per hour (up to 100 mph) to metres per second (to two places of decimals)

	0	1	2	3	4	5	6	7	8	9
Miles per hour	**Metres per second**									
0	–	0.45	0.89	1.34	1.79	2.24	2.68	3.13	3.58	4.02
10	4.47	4.92	5.36	5.81	6.26	6.71	7.15	7.60	8.05	8.49
20	8.94	9.39	9.83	10.28	10.73	11.18	11.62	12.07	12.52	12.96
30	13.41	13.86	14.31	14.75	15.20	15.65	16.09	16.54	16.99	17.43
40	17.88	18.33	18.78	19.22	19.67	20.12	20.56	21.01	21.46	21.91
50	22.35	22.80	23.25	23.69	24.14	24.59	25.03	25.48	25.93	26.38
60	26.82	27.27	27.72	28.16	28.61	29.06	29.50	29.95	30.40	30.85
70	31.29	31.74	32.19	32.63	33.08	33.53	33.98	34.42	34.87	35.32
80	35.76	36.21	36.66	37.10	37.55	38.00	38.45	38.89	39.34	39.79
90	40.23	40.68	41.13	41.57	42.02	42.47	42.92	43.36	43.81	44.26
100	44.70	–	–	–	–	–	–	–	–	–

Table XIII Pressure and stress. Pounds–force per square inch to kilonewtons per square metre (to two places of decimals)

Ibf per sq In	0	1	2	3	4	5	6	7	8	9
	kN/m² or kPa									
0	–	6.90	13.79	20.68	27.58	34.48	41.37	48.26	55.16	62.06
10	68.95	75.84	82.74	89.64	96.53	103.42	110.32	117.22	124.11	131.00
20	137.90	144.80	151.69	158.58	165.48	172.38	179.27	186.16	193.06	199.96
30	206.85	213.64	220.64	227.54	234.43	241.32	248.22	255.12	262.01	268.90
40	275.80	282.70	289.59	296.48	303.38	310.28	317.17	324.06	330.96	337.86
50	344.75	351.64	358.54	365.44	372.33	379.22	386.12	393.02	399.91	406.80
60	413.70	420.60	427.49	434.38	441.28	448.18	455.07	461.96	468.86	475.76
70	482.65	489.54	496.44	503.34	510.23	517.12	524.02	530.92	537.81	544.70
80	551.60	558.50	565.39	572.28	579.18	586.08	592.97	599.86	606.76	613.66
90	620.55	627.44	634.34	641.24	648.13	655.02	661.92	668.82	675.71	682.60
100	689.50	–	–	–	–	–	–	–	–	–

Note: the same table will convert kipf per.sq in to MN/m² or MPa

Table XIV British thermal units per hour to watts

Btu per hr	0	1	2	3	4	5	6	7	8	9
	W									
0	–	0.29	0.59	0.88	1.17	1.47	1.76	2.05	2.34	2.64
10	2.93	3.22	3.52	3.81	4.10	4.40	4.69	4.98	5.28	5.57
20	5.86	6.16	6.45	6.74	7.03	7.33	7.62	7.91	8.21	8.50
30	8.79	9.09	9.38	9.67	9.97	10.26	10.55	10.84	11.14	11.43
40	11.72	12.02	12.31	12.60	12.90	13.19	13.48	13.78	14.07	14.36
50	14.66	14.95	15.24	15.53	15.83	16.12	16.41	16.71	17.00	17.29
60	17.59	17.88	18.17	18.47	18.76	19.05	19.34	19.64	19.93	20.22
70	20.52	20.81	21.10	21.40	21.69	21.98	22.28	22.57	22.86	23.15
80	23.45	23.74	24.03	24.33	24.62	24.91	25.21	25.50	25.79	26.09
90	26.38	26.67	26.97	27.26	27.55	27.84	28.14	28.43	28.72	29.02
100	29.31	–	–	–	–	–	–	–	–	–

Table XV *U* value: British thermal units per square foot per hour per degree Fahrenheit to watts per square metre per Kelvin

Btu per sq ft hr °F	0	0.01	0.02	0.03	0.04	0.05	0.06	0.07	0.08	0.09
	W/(m²K)									
0	–	0.057	0.114	0.170	0.227	0.284	0.341	0.397	0.454	0.511
0.1	0.568	0.624	0.681	0.738	0.795	0.852	0.908	0.965	1.022	1.079
0.2	1.136	1.192	1.249	1.306	1.363	1.420	1.476	1.533	1.590	1.647
0.3	1.703	1.760	1.817	1.874	1.931	1.987	2.044	2.101	2.158	2.214
0.4	2.271	2.328	2.385	2.442	2.498	2.555	2.612	2.669	2.725	2.782
0.5	2.839	2.896	2.953	3.009	3.066	3.123	3.180	3.236	3.293	3.350
0.6	3.407	3.464	3.520	3.577	3.634	3.691	3.747	3.804	3.861	3.918
0.7	3.975	4.031	4.088	4.145	4.202	4.258	4.315	4.372	4.429	4.486
0.8	4.542	4.599	4.656	4.713	4.770	4.826	4.883	4.940	4.997	5.053
0.9	5.110	5.167	5.224	5.281	5.337	5.394	5.451	5.508	5.564	5.621
1.0	5.678	–	–	–	–	–	–	–	–	–

Table XVI Feet and inches to metres and millimetres (to nearest millimetre)

Feet	Inches 0	1	2	3	4	5	6	7	8	9	10	11
	Metres and millimetres											
0	–	0.025	0.051	0.076	0.102	0.127	0.152	0.178	0.203	0.229	0.254	0.279
1	0.305	0.330	0.356	0.381	0.406	0.432	0.457	0.483	0.508	0.533	0.559	0.584
2	0.610	0.635	0.660	0.686	0.711	0.737	0.762	0.787	0.813	0.838	0.864	0.889
3	0.914	0.940	0.965	0.991	1.016	1.041	1.067	1.092	1.118	1.143	1.168	1.194
4	1.219	1.245	1.270	1.295	1.321	1.346	1.372	1.397	1.422	1.448	1.473	1.499
5	1.524	1.549	1.575	1.600	1.626	1.651	1.676	1.702	1.727	1.753	1.778	1.803
6	1.829	1.854	1.880	1.905	1.930	1.956	1.981	2.007	2.032	2.057	2.083	2.108
7	2.134	2.159	2.184	2.210	2.235	2.261	2.286	2.311	2.337	2.362	2.388	2.413
8	2.438	2.464	2.489	2.515	2.540	2.565	2.591	2.616	2.642	2.667	2.692	2.718
9	2.743	2.769	2.794	2.819	2.845	2.870	2.896	2.921	2.946	2.972	2.997	3.023
10	3.048	3.073	3.099	3.124	3.150	3.175	3.200	3.226	3.251	3.277	3.302	3.327
11	3.353	3.378	3.404	3.429	3.454	3.480	3.505	3.531	3.556	3.581	3.607	3.632
12	3.658	3.683	3.708	3.734	3.759	3.785	3.810	3.835	3.861	3.886	3.912	3.937
13	3.962	3.988	4.013	4.039	4.064	4.089	4.115	4.140	4.166	4.191	4.216	4.242
14	4.267	4.293	4.318	4.343	4.369	4.394	4.420	4.445	4.470	4.496	4.521	4.547
15	4.572	4.597	4.623	4.648	4.674	4.699	4.724	4.750	4.775	4.801	4.826	4.851
16	4.877	4.902	4.928	4.953	4.978	5.004	5.029	5.055	5.080	5.105	5.131	5.156
17	5.182	5.207	5.232	5.258	5.283	5.309	5.334	5.359	5.385	5.410	5.436	5.461
18	5.486	5.512	5.537	5.563	5.588	5.613	5.639	5.664	5.690	5.715	5.740	5.766
19	5.791	5.817	5.842	5.867	5.893	5.918	5.944	5.969	5.994	6.020	6.045	6.071
20	6.096	6.121	6.147	6.172	6.198	6.223	6.248	6.274	6.299	6.325	6.350	6.375
21	6.401	6.426	6.452	6.477	6.502	6.528	6.553	6.579	6.604	6.629	6.655	6.680
22	6.706	6.731	6.756	6.782	6.807	6.833	6.858	6.883	6.909	6.934	6.960	6.985
23	7.010	7.036	7.061	7.087	7.112	7.137	7.163	7.188	7.214	7.239	7.264	7.290
24	7.315	7.341	7.366	7.391	7.417	7.442	7.468	7.493	7.518	7.544	7.569	7.595
25	7.620	7.645	7.671	7.696	7.722	7.747	7.772	7.798	7.823	7.849	7.874	7.899
26	7.925	7.950	7.976	8.001	8.026	8.052	8.077	8.103	8.128	8.153	8.179	8.204
27	8.230	8.255	8.280	8.306	8.331	8.357	8.382	8.407	8.433	8.458	8.484	8.509
28	8.534	8.560	8.585	8.611	8.636	8.661	8.687	8.712	8.738	8.763	8.788	8.814
29	8.839	8.865	8.890	8.915	8.941	8.966	8.992	9.017	9.042	9.068	9.093	9.119
30	9.144	9.169	9.195	9.220	9.246	9.271	9.296	9.322	9.347	9.373	9.398	9.423
31	9.449	9.474	9.500	9.525	9.550	9.576	9.601	9.627	9.652	9.677	9.703	9.728
32	9.754	9.779	9.804	9.830	9.855	9.881	9.906	9.931	9.957	9.982	10.008	10.033
33	10.058	10.084	10.109	10.135	10.160	10.185	10.211	10.236	10.262	10.287	10.312	10.338
34	10.363	10.389	10.414	10.439	10.465	10.490	10.516	10.541	10.566	10.592	10.617	10.643
35	10.668	10.693	10.719	10.744	10.770	10.795	10.820	10.846	10.871	10.897	10.922	10.947
36	10.973	10.998	11.024	11.049	11.074	11.100	11.125	11.151	11.176	11.201	11.227	11.252
37	11.278	11.303	11.328	11.354	11.379	11.405	11.430	11.455	11.481	11.506	11.532	11.557
38	11.582	11.608	11.633	11.659	11.684	11.709	11.735	11.760	11.786	11.811	11.836	11.862
39	11.887	11.913	11.938	11.963	11.989	12.014	12.040	12.065	12.090	12.116	12.141	12.167
40	12.192	12.217	12.243	12.268	12.294	12.319	12.344	12.370	12.395	12.421	12.446	12.471
41	12.497	12.522	12.548	12.573	12.598	12.624	12.649	12.675	12.700	12.725	12.751	12.776
42	12.802	12.827	12.852	12.878	12.903	12.929	12.954	12.979	13.005	13.030	13.056	13.081
43	13.106	13.132	13.157	13.183	13.208	13.233	13.259	13.284	13.310	13.335	13.360	13.386
44	13.411	13.437	13.462	13.487	13.513	13.538	13.564	13.589	13.614	13.640	13.665	13.691
45	13.716	13.741	13.767	13.792	13.818	13.843	13.868	13.894	13.919	13.945	13.970	13.995
46	14.021	14.046	14.072	14.097	14.122	14.148	14.173	14.199	14.224	14.249	14.275	14.300
47	14.326	14.351	14.376	14.402	14.427	14.453	14.478	14.503	14.529	14.554	14.580	14.605
48	14.630	14.656	14.681	14.707	14.732	14.757	14.783	14.808	14.834	14.859	14.884	14.910
49	14.935	14.961	14.986	15.011	15.037	15.062	15.088	15.113	15.138	15.164	15.189	15.215
50	15.240	15.265	15.291	15.316	15.342	15.367	15.392	15.418	18.443	15.469	15.494	15.519
51	15.545	15.570	15.596	15.621	15.646	15.672	15.697	15.723	15.748	15.773	15.799	15.824
52	15.850	15.875	15.900	15.926	15.951	15.977	16.002	16.027	16.053	16.078	16.104	16.129
53	16.154	16.180	16.205	16.231	16.256	16.281	16.307	16.332	16.358	16.383	16.408	16.434
54	16.459	16.485	16.510	16.535	16.561	16.586	16.612	16.637	16.662	16.688	16.713	16.739
55	16.764	16.789	16.815	16.840	16.866	16.891	16.916	16.942	16.967	16.993	17.018	17.043
56	17.069	17.094	17.120	17.145	17.170	17.196	17.221	17.247	17.272	17.297	17.323	17.248
57	17.374	17.399	17.424	17.450	17.475	17.501	17.526	17.551	17.577	17.602	17.628	17.653
58	17.678	17.704	17.729	17.755	17.780	17.805	17.830	17.856	17.882	17.907	17.932	17.958
59	17.983	18.009	18.034	18.059	18.085	18.110	18.136	18.161	18.186	18.212	18.237	18.263
60	18.288	18.313	18.339	18.364	18.390	18.415	18.440	18.466	18.491	18.517	18.542	18.567
61	18.593	18.618	18.644	18.669	18.694	18.720	18.745	18.771	18.796	18.821	18.847	18.872
62	18.898	18.923	18.948	18.974	18.999	19.025	19.050	19.075	19.101	19.126	19.152	19.177
63	19.202	19.228	19.253	19.279	19.304	19.329	19.355	19.380	19.406	19.431	19.456	19.482
64	19.507	19.533	19.558	19.583	19.609	19.634	19.660	19.685	19.710	19.736	19.761	19.787
65	19.812	19.837	19.863	19.888	19.914	19.939	19.964	19.990	20.015	20.041	20.066	20.091
66	20.117	20.142	20.168	20.193	20.218	20.244	20.269	20.295	20.320	20.345	20.371	20.396
67	20.422	20.447	20.472	20.498	20.523	20.549	20.574	20.599	20.625	20.650	20.676	20.701
68	20.726	20.752	20.777	20.803	20.828	20.853	20.879	20.904	20.930	20.955	20.980	21.006
69	21.031	21.057	21.082	21.107	21.133	21.158	21.184	21.209	21.234	21.260	21.285	21.311

Index

2D CAD systems **1**:1
3D parametric object-based modelling systems **1**:1, **1**:5
3D projection systems **15**:36
5 Churchill Place, London **1**:11–13

Aberdeen University Library **27**:8, **27**:9
absorption coefficients **10**:2, **10**:3
absorptivity **8**:5, **8**:6, **42**:34
academic laboratories **26**:1, **26**:9, **26**:11, **26**:16, **26**:23–6
academic libraries **27**:1, **27**:2, **27**:4, **27**:7, **27**:8–9, **27**:10–11, **27**:12, **43**:5–6, **43**:14
academies **36**:2
access: auditoria **15**:9, **15**:10, **15**:19, **15**:23; churches **32**:12–13; crime prevention design **13**:2; entrance doors **3**:3; for firefighters **11**:4–5, **11**:6, **20**:5, **23**:8; fire stations **18**:2; and flooding **12**:9; hotels **20**:2; housing **21**:5; libraries **27**:6; for maintenance **2**:6–7; masterplanning **28**:4–5; offices **30**:9; ramps **3**:1, **21**:5; shopping centres **35**:10; slope-dependent **28**:5; sports facilities **38**:27, **38**:29, **38**:38–9; steps **3**:2–3, **21**:5; see also wheelchair access
access control systems **20**:5, **23**:13, **37**:2
accessible facilities: ATMs and ATM lobbies **31**:5, **31**:7; auditoria **15**:3, **15**:8, **15**:9, **15**:35, **15**:40; dimensions **4**:1–6; doors **3**:3; hotel guestrooms **20**:11; housing **21**:3, **21**:5, **21**:8, **21**:12, **21**:13, **21**:22; laboratories **26**:16; libraries **27**:6; lifts **3**:9, **3**:10; lobbies **3**:4; older people's housing **22**:1, **22**:3–4; payment counters **31**:6, **31**:9; ramps **3**:1, **21**:5; sanitary facilities **2**:7, **2**:8, **2**:9–11, **4**:6, **18**:9, **21**:5; shopping centres **35**:10; sports facilities **38**:29, **38**:30, **38**:36, **38**:38, **38**:39, **38**:40; steps **3**:2–3, **21**:5; street design **39**:22; student housing **23**:8–9, **23**:11, **23**:12; tropics **42**:11
access roads **39**:6–7
Accident & Emergency (A&E) facilities **19**:7–8, **19**:10
acoustic barriers **10**:4
acoustic doors **40**:3, **40**:4
acoustic lining systems **10**:9–10
acoustics: absorption coefficients **10**:2, **10**:3; auditoria **10**:16, **10**:17, **15**:2, **15**:4, **15**:12, **15**:35; broadcasting studios **40**:3, **40**:4; community centres **17**:3; courtrooms **16**:10; fundamentals **10**:1–3; laboratories **26**:23; museums **29**:6; music teaching **43**:6; performance spaces **10**:16, **10**:17; reducing sound transmission **10**:3–6; reverberation times **10**:2–3, **10**:15, **10**:16–17, **40**:3; synagogues **32**:19; see also sound insulation
active frontages **28**:7
active shading **42**:15, **42**:19
adaptability: foodservice facilities **34**:7; industrial buildings **24**:2–5, **24**:7; libraries **27**:5; museums **29**:2, **29**:3; offices **30**:3; primary health care buildings **33**:11–12, **33**:16; school furniture layouts **36**:5–6
adhesives **7**:25–6
AEDET hospital design **19**:3
aerofoils **42**:23
affordable housing **21**:2, **21**:13, **21**:26, **21**:27
aggregates **7**:9
agricultural buildings **14**:1–20; legislation **14**:20; livestock housing **14**:2, **14**:4–11, **14**:12, **14**:13; stables **14**:12, **14**:15, **14**:16–20; storage **14**:1, **14**:13–15
AHUs see air handling units (AHUs)
air change rates **8**:10, **26**:23

air conditioning see mechanical ventilation systems
air displacement systems **8**:29
airflow models **8**:33–4
air handling units (AHUs) **8**:28
air infiltration **8**:10, **8**:22–3
air leakage measurements **8**:35
air moisture content **8**:20–1; see also relative humidity (RH)
air pollution **29**:4
airports **41**:1–16; air infiltration rates **8**:10; apron requirements **41**:12–13, **41**:14; arrivals areas **41**:9–11; case study **41**:14–16; departures areas **41**:4–9; foodservice facilities **34**:2, **34**:19, **34**:25; levels and volumes **41**:11; security **41**:4, **41**:5, **41**:7, **41**:8, **41**:9; see also cafeterias
air source heat pumps **8**:31
air speed **8**:7–8, **8**:9
air temperature **8**:7, **8**:11–12
airtightness **8**:35
aisles: auditoria **15**:4, **15**:7, **15**:32–3; churches **32**:14; laboratories **26**:11–13; warehouses **25**:6, **25**:7–9
alarms, fire **11**:22, **15**:12, **23**:8
albedo **42**:33–4
alcohol gel dispensers **19**:7
alloys **7**:2, **7**:5, **7**:10–11
altar rails **32**:10, **32**:11, **32**:12
altars **32**:2, **32**:6, **32**:8–9
alternating stairs **3**:5, **3**:6
alternative energy see renewable energy
aluminium **7**:10–11; alloys **7**:5, **7**:10–11; fire resistance **11**:19; properties **6**:13; roofing **7**:12; structural **7**:10–11; windows **7**:26
ambulances **39**:3
ambulance services **33**:2
ambulance stations **18**:7–9
amenity areas: ambulance stations **18**:9; fire stations **18**:4, **18**:5
American football **38**:2, **38**:33
amphibious structures **12**:9
angles: aluminium **7**:11; steel **7**:4
animals: assistance dogs **2**:7, **4**:4, **15**:35; farm **14**:2, **14**:3, **14**:4–11, **14**:12, **14**:13; horses **14**:12, **14**:15, **14**:16–20; tropics **42**:10
annealed float glass **6**:6, **6**:13
anthropometrics **2**:1–5, **4**:2, **42**:11
anti-shatter film **37**:7
ANUK/Unipol Code of Standards **23**:7
archaeological finds **42**:8
archery **38**:21
arching **6**:21–2
Architectural Liaison Officers (ALOs) **36**:6, **37**:10
ardhamandapa **32**:20
arid climates **42**:3, **42**:4, **42**:12, **42**:15
Arndale Centre, Luton **35**:9
art, in health **33**:12
art galleries **8**:10, **29**:1–8, **39**:15
artificial grass **38**:23
art teaching **36**:13, **43**:7–8
Arum Hotel, Side, Turkey **20**:14
asbestos **11**:19
ASPECT hospital design **19**:3
assembly buildings: access stairs **3**:5; escape routes **11**:12; gender ratios **2**:7; parking **39**:15; permissible noise levels **10**:8; sanitary facilities **2**:8

assistance dogs 2:7, 4:4, 15:35
at-grade track (level) stations 41:18
athletics 38:8–9, 38:23, 38:27, 38:34
ATMs and ATM lobbies 31:1, 31:2, 31:3, 31:5–6, 31:7, 31:8
atria 42:21–2, 43:2
audience participation studios 40:1
audiovisual facilities 15:29–31
auditoria: acoustics 10:16, 10:17, 15:2, 15:4, 15:12, 15:35; concert
    halls 10:17, 15:23–5, 15:26; conference facilities 15:3, 15:25–
    31, 15:37, 43:9; design 15:3–12; formats 15:5–6, 15:13, 15:14,
    15:23, 15:24, 15:25–6, 15:37; legislation 15:40; multi-purpose
    15:36, 15:37; seating 15:1–3, 15:4, 15:5–6, 15:7, 15:11;
    sightlines 15:1, 15:4–8, 15:15, 15:24, 15:32, 15:34; studio
    theatres 15:23; support facilities 15:36–40; see also cinemas;
    theatres
aural impairments 15:3, 15:35, 15:40, 23:9
Australia 42:5, 42:6
Australian football 38:3, 38:33
automatic fire detectors 11:21–2
awnings 42:16
axial control 1:9

Bab Al-Sadir 32:19
baby changing facilities 2:11, 4:6, 17:4
badminton 38:10, 38:23, 38:25, 38:35
baggage handling, airports 41:4, 41:7, 41:8, 41:9–10, 41:12
balanced supply and extract systems 8:28
balconies: auditoria 15:4, 15:6, 15:9, 15:10; flats 21:18, 21:20,
    21:21; hotels 20:9; shading 42:16
balcony access flats 21:19
Balliol College, Oxford 23:3
banisters 3:7
banks 31:1, 31:2–3, 31:5–6, 31:7, 31:8–9, 39:14
banquet halls 20:13
baptisms 32:3, 32:4, 32:6
baptistries 32:7
barns 14:13, 14:14; see also agricultural buildings
barriers, wind 8:14–15
bars: aluminium 7:10; steel 7:1, 7:2, 7:3
baseball 38:5
Baseline Designs, schools 36:2, 36:3, 36:4, 36:8, 36:9, 36:11,
    36:12
basketball 38:12, 38:25, 38:35
bathrooms: accessible standards 21:12; hotel guestrooms 20:11;
    older people's housing 22:3–4; single-family houses 21:17;
    student housing 23:3, 23:4, 23:8, 23:10, 23:12; see also sanitary
    facilities
baths 2:10, 22:3–4
battery houses 14:11–12
beach volleyball 38:10
beams 6:6; increasing effective span 6:23; laminated 6:8, 6:11;
    loading 6:17–20; reinforced concrete 6:12; steel 6:14, 7:3,
    7:4–5; timber 6:8, 6:12
Beaufort wind scale 42:36
bedding planes 7:17
bedrooms: accessible standards 21:12; hospitals 19:2–3; hotels
    20:2–3, 20:4, 20:6–11; older people's housing 22:3; student
    housing 23:3, 23:4, 23:9–11
beds, hospital 19:9
bedsitting rooms 21:21–2, 21:23
behavioural, emotional and social difficulties (BESD) education
    36:17
benchmarking 43:16
bench marks 1:11
bending 6:5–6, 6:17
bending moments 6:6
bespoke industrial buildings 24:1, 24:2, 24:4
betting facilities 38:39

bicycles 38:34, 39:2; see also cycling
BIM see Building Information Modelling (BIM)
Bima, synagogues 32:16–17, 32:18
biodiversity 7:14, 28:3, 28:12
biofuels 42:28
biogas 28:17
biohazards 42:9–10
biomass 36:5, 42:28
Birmingham library 27:14–17
bitumen-based adhesives 7:26
bitumen roofing membranes 7:13–14
blast loading 37:5–7
blast resistance 18:12, 37:7–8
blast testing 37:8–9
Blaydon Leisure and Primary Care Centre, Tyne and Wear
    33:18–19
bleacher seating 15:11
blinds 8:19, 42:17
block stacking 25:5, 25:6
blockwork 7:9, 8:4, 8:16; low-density 8:17
Bloomberg Suites 43:7
blown insulation cavity fill 8:17
Bluewater shopping centre, Dartford 35:13, 42:22
BMX tracks 38:7
body-tinted glass 42:35, 42:36
boilers 8:26
Bolton Market Place 35:12
bomb attacks 37:3–10
bomb shelter areas 37:9–10
book stacks 27:7, 27:12
borehole cooling 36:4
boundaries, property 13:3, 21:18
boundary conditions 1:10
boundary layers 8:13, 8:14
bow-string truss 6:23
boxing 38:17
box offices 15:37, 15:38
bracing 6:20–1
brand value 5:1
BRE Environmental Assessment Method (BREEAM) 1:12, 27:19,
    33:17, 33:19
Brent Civic Centre 16:4–7
brickwork 7:8–9, 8:3, 8:4, 8:16, 11:19
bridges, auditoria 15:15, 15:19
briefing process, university design 43:11, 43:15–17
brightness 9:10
Brighton Public Library 27:14
broadcasting, sports facilities 38:40–2
broadcasting studios 10:13, 15:40, 40:1–4
buckling 6:5, 6:22–3
buffer zones 37:10
building energy models 8:33, 8:34
building envelopes: blast loading 37:5–6; blast resistance 37:7–8;
    blast testing 37:8–9; climate modification 8:1–2; fabric heat
    loss 8:26, 8:27; facade attenuation 10:4, 10:5; offices 30:9;
    security 37:3; thermal bridging 8:17–18, 8:20; thermal
    insulation 8:17, 8:18; tropics 42:9; U-values 8:15–17, 8:18–19,
    8:20, 8:32, 8:35, 42:34; see also facades
Building for Life 21:13–14
Building Information Modelling (BIM) 1:1, 1:5, 1:11–13
Building Regulations: accessible facilities 2:8, 23:9; agricultural
    buildings 14:20; doors 7:27; energy efficiency 7:14–15; escape
    routes 11:19, 26:15; fire resistance 11:2, 11:3; fire safety 11:22,
    36:6; house conversions 21:21; houses in multiple occupation
    (HMOs) 23:8; housing 21:2–3, 21:5; lighting 9:8–9; refuse
    storage 21:19–20; sound insulation 21:18; structural robustness
    37:6
building services see services

building societies **31**:1, **31**:3, **31**:6, **31**:7
burial sites **42**:8
Burolandschaft (office landscaping) **30**:1–2
buses and coaches **39**:4, **41**:23
business schools **43**:6–7
bus stations **8**:10, **41**:22–8
Buttermarket, Ipswich **35**:13
butt joints **7**:24

CABE *see* Commission for Architecture and the Built
    Environment (CABE)
CAD systems **1**:1
cafes **2**:8, **8**:10, **10**:8, **34**:16, **39**:14, **43**:4
cafeterias: food production areas **34**:9; self-service **34**:2,
    34:16–17, **34**:19, **34**:20, **34**:21–2, **34**:24; space allowances **34**:5;
    sports facilities **38**:38; *see also* catering facilities
calcium silicate boards **7**:22
calf housing **14**:7
Cambridge University **43**:1
canteens **24**:9; *see also* cafeterias; catering facilities
cantilever beams **6**:6, **6**:12, **6**:19–20
canyon effects **8**:14, **8**:15
capital allowances **5**:6
capital asset replacement **5**:6
Carbon Calculator **36**:4
carbon dioxide: emissions **8**:27; fire protection systems **11**:21;
    metabolic **8**:23
Cardiff Millennium Stadium **38**:24, **38**:30
car parking **39**:12–18; crime prevention design **13**:3, **13**:4;
    domestic garages **39**:13, **39**:16, **39**:17; housing **21**:5–6, **39**:13,
    39:14; multi-storey **39**:13, **39**:18; police stations **18**:12; schools
    36:9, **39**:15; shopping centres **35**:10; sports facilities **38**:38,
    39:15; student housing **23**:12; synagogues **32**:19; universities
    43:11
carpentry workshops **15**:39, **15**:40
carriageway widths **39**:5–6, **39**:7
cars **39**:2–3
casino hotels **20**:13
cast stone **7**:17, **7**:19
catchment areas **28**:4
catering facilities: air infiltration rates **8**:10; auditoria **15**:37–8;
    hospitals **34**:23; hotels **20**:12–13; industrial buildings **24**:9;
    law courts **16**:14; police stations **18**:12; schools **36**:15; sports
    facilities **38**:38, **38**:39, **38**:43; universities **43**:7, **43**:9, **43**:11; *see
    also* cafeterias; foodservice facilities
cattle housing **14**:2, **14**:4–7
CCTV **13**:4, **20**:5, **23**:13, **37**:1, **37**:2, **37**:12
ceilings: auditoria **15**:12; housing **21**:14; police custody suites
    18:13; stables **14**:19; tropical design **42**:30
cells, police stations **18**:12, **18**:13–14
cellular glass **7**:23
cellulose insulation **7**:24, **8**:4
cement **7**:9, **7**:21, **8**:3
cement-bonded particleboard **7**:7, **7**:8
cemetery prayer halls **32**:18
central heating systems **8**:25
centralised online booking systems, universities **43**:4
Centre for Protection of National Infrastructure (CPNI) **37**:10
Centre for Tropical and Infectious Diseases, Liverpool **26**:24,
    26:25–6, **26**:29
Centre of Excellence in Teaching and Learning (CETL) **43**:8
ceramic materials **7**:15–16
CET *see* corrected effective temperature (CET)
CFD *see* computational fluid dynamics (CFD) models
chairs *see* seating
change of use **21**:21
changing rooms: accessible **2**:9–10, **4**:6; baptistries **32**:7; sports
    facilities **38**:32–3, **38**:36, **38**:37

channels **6**:27; aluminium **7**:11; steel **7**:4
chapels: crematoria **32**:22–3; Methodist **32**:6–7
check-in areas, airports **41**:7–8
checklists, masterplanning **28**:7–10
Chek Lap Kok airport, Hong Kong **41**:4
chemical, biological, radiological or nuclear (CBRN) attacks
    37:4–5
chicanes **39**:7, **39**:9
child care facilities **17**:3
children: anthropometrics **2**:4, **4**:2; disabled **4**:2; hospital services
    19:13–14, **19**:17–18; sanitary facilities **2**:8, **2**:11, **4**:6, **17**:4; *see
    also* schools
chilled surface cooling systems **8**:30–1, **30**:15
chipboard *see* wood particleboard
choirs, church **32**:15–16
churches **8**:10, **10**:17, **32**:1–16
Church of All Saints Flore **32**:3
Church of England **32**:1–3, **32**:8, **32**:12
Church of St Andrew, Farnham **32**:2–3
Church of St Paul, Bow Common **32**:2
cinemas **15**:32–6; acoustics **10**:17, **15**:35; parking **39**:14–15;
    permissible noise levels **10**:8; sanitary facilities **2**:8; sound
    insulation **10**:9, **10**:13, **10**:15
circular hollow sections (CHS) **6**:26, **7**:3
circulation areas: accessible standards **21**:5; auditoria **15**:9;
    churches **32**:14; crematoria **32**:22; hotels **20**:2, **20**:3–4, **20**:5;
    laboratories **26**:11–13; learning streets **43**:4; libraries **27**:5,
    27:12, **27**:15, **27**:19; masterplanning **28**:5; museums **29**:2;
    offices **30**:13; older people's housing **22**:2; shopping centres
    35:10; sports facilities **38**:38–9; student housing **23**:12;
    universities **43**:2, **43**:4
civic buildings: law courts **16**:7–16; and libraries **27**:5;
    permissible noise levels **10**:8; reverberation times **10**:16; sound
    insulation **10**:9, **10**:13, **10**:15; town halls **16**:1–7
civic centres **16**:1–7
Civic Theatre, Helsinki **15**:16
civic value **5**:1
cladding: fire safety **11**:7, **11**:8; gaskets **7**:25; materials **7**:11–15;
    stone **7**:17, **7**:18; tropical design **42**:31
classrooms **36**:10, **36**:13; interactive **43**:4
clay tennis courts **38**:24
cleaning: community centres **17**:2; student housing **23**:12
cleanrooms, laboratories **26**:2, **26**:23
clearance **2**:2
clerestory windows **42**:15, **42**:19
climate **8**:11–15, **42**:3–5, **42**:6, **42**:11–14
climate change **8**:15, **42**:5–6; and flooding **12**:2–3
climate-responsive design **42**:11–14; active design **42**:28–9;
    passive design **8**:2, **8**:33, **9**:1–5, **42**:14–28
clothing **8**:7
cloud cover **8**:11
clubs **34**:25, **34**:27, **39**:14
cluster flats **21**:22, **21**:23
coaches and buses **39**:4, **41**:23
coach stations **8**:10, **41**:22–8
coanda effect **8**:29
coastal flooding **12**:2
coated glasses **42**:36
coated steels **7**:5
COBie: Construction Operations Building information exchange
    1:1
Code for Sustainable Homes (CforSH) **10**:10–11, **21**:13, **21**:27
coffee bars **34**:16, **43**:9; *see also* cafes
collections *see* museums
colleges **8**:10, **39**:15, **43**:2; *see also* universities
collegiate universities **43**:1
colonial bungalows **42**:2, **42**:19, **42**:20
columns **6**:5; masonry **6**:7; steel **6**:15, **7**:3; timber **6**:11

combined heat and power (CHP) **36**:5
Commission for Architecture and the Built Environment (CABE) **27**:2, **27**:3, **28**:1, **28**:2, **28**:7–8, **33**:6, **36**:3, **36**:6
committee rooms **16**:3
communal areas: flats **21**:18; gardens **21**:20; older people's housing **22**:1, **22**:2; sanitary facilities **2**:13; student housing **23**:3, **23**:8, **23**:11–12; *see also* circulation areas; public areas
communications systems: courtrooms **16**:10; fire stations **18**:1; hotels **20**:5–6; offices **30**:9; police stations **18**:10, **18**:11; student housing **23**:10–11
communion tables **32**:2, **32**:4, **32**:6, **32**:8, **32**:11
community centres **17**:1–4, **39**:15
Community Churches **32**:1
community facilities, schools **36**:9, **36**:13
community hospitals **19**:2, **33**:2, **33**:4, **33**:6, **33**:10
composite climates **42**:3, **42**:4, **42**:12, **42**:13
composite plastics **7**:20
compression stresses **6**:5, **6**:11–12, **6**:20–1
computational fluid dynamics (CFD) models **8**:34
computerised tomography (CT) **19**:9
computer modelling **43**:6
computer simulations **28**:4–8
computer workstations **2**:5
concept design **1**:3
concert halls **10**:17, **15**:23–5, **15**:26
concrete: aggregates **7**:9; blast resistance **37**:8; cement **7**:9; components **7**:10; cover to reinforcement **6**:13; density **8**:4; earthquake zones **42**:32; embodied energy **8**:3; fire resistance **11**:19; foamed **7**:22; lightweight aggregate **7**:22, **7**:23; low-density blocks **8**:17; mixes **7**:9–10; precast concrete panels **7**:10, **37**:8; tropics **42**:29, **42**:30; waterstop seals **7**:25; *see also* reinforced concrete
condensation **8**:6, **8**:19–22
condensing boilers **8**:26
conduction **8**:3–4, **11**:1
conference facilities: auditoria **15**:3, **15**:25–31, **15**:37, **43**:9; hotels **20**:13; student housing **23**:13; universities **43**:7, **43**:9, **43**:10
confessionals **32**:15
constant air volume (CAV) **8**:30
constant illuminance controls **9**:9
construction management **5**:2
container vehicles **39**:4
continuous beams **6**:6
Control of Substances Hazardous to Health Regulations **26**:17
control panels **15**:28
control rooms **15**:20–1, **15**:29–30, **38**:42–3, **40**:2
convection **8**:4, **11**:2
conversion tables **6**:2
cooking equipment **34**:10–12, **34**:13–14
cool desks **30**:15
cooling systems **8**:29, **8**:30–1, **8**:32; police stations **18**:12; schools **36**:4; trading floors **30**:15
cooperative societies **35**:2
copper roofing **7**:12, **7**:13
cork **7**:23
corners, road **39**:9–10, **39**:11
corrected effective temperature (CET) **8**:9
corridors **3**:4–5; accessible standards **21**:5; fire safety **11**:16–17, **11**:18, **20**:4; flats **21**:18; hotels **20**:3–4, **20**:11; laboratories **26**:11–13; older people's housing **22**:2; police custody suites **18**:12; sports facilities **38**:36; student housing **23**:3, **23**:7; widths **3**:4–5
cost limits **5**:3
cost planning **5**:1, **5**:3; rates **5**:5; stages **5**:4–6
costs: checking **5**:6; estimating **5**:3–6; industrial buildings **24**:9; industrial storage buildings **25**:1; libraries **27**:14; primary health care **33**:2, **33**:3; whole life **5**:6–7

council chambers **16**:2, **16**:3
counselling spaces, payment offices **31**:6
counters, payment offices **31**:6, **31**:8–9
counter terrorism **37**:1, **37**:3–10
Counter Terrorist Security Advisors (CTSA) **37**:10
counterweight systems, theatres **15**:17
Countryside Agency **28**:2, **28**:3
court buildings **16**:7–16
court sports **38**:1, **38**:9–12, **38**:23, **38**:24, **38**:25–6, **38**:35
courtyards **42**:20–1
CPTED *see* Crime Prevention Through Environmental Design (CPTED)
Creativity Zones **43**:8
credence tables **32**:10
crematoria **32**:21–4
cricket **38**:5, **38**:23, **38**:25
crime generators **13**:3
crime prevention design **13**:1–5, **21**:13; *see also* security
Crime Prevention Design Advisors (CPDAs) **13**:1, **13**:2, **13**:5, **37**:10
Crime Prevention Through Environmental Design (CPTED) **13**:1–5
crop storage **14**:13–15
cross-gangways, auditoria **15**:7
cross-laminated timber **7**:7
cross ventilation **8**:14, **8**:24, **30**:9
cruise ships **34**:28
crutches **4**:4
CT *see* computerised tomography (CT)
CUBE civic centre, Corby **16**:4
cubicles, cattle housing **14**:2, **14**:4
cul-de-sacs **13**:2
cultural factors **42**:8
cupboards: laboratories **26**:16; older people's housing **22**:4; student housing **23**:12
curtains **42**:17
curtain walling **7**:28
curves, road **39**:9–10
custody suites: law courts **16**:12–13; police stations **18**:12–15
customer services **16**:3–4
customs areas, airports **41**:10
cyanoacrylate adhesives **7**:26
cycle lanes/paths **39**:6, **39**:10–12
cycle parking **27**:4, **39**:12, **39**:13, **39**:16
cycles **38**:34, **39**:2
cycling **28**:12, **39**:22, **43**:13
cycling tracks **38**:6–7, **38**:23

damp-proofing **7**:22
dance studios **15**:38, **15**:39
Darent Valley Hospital, Dartford **19**:5
Darzi Report (2008) **33**:3
data projection facilities **15**:31
Dawson Report (1920) **33**:2, **33**:6, **33**:8
Daylight Autonomy **36**:5
daylighting *see* natural lighting
daylight linking controls **9**:9
dead loads **6**:2, **6**:17
Deal Ground site, Norfolk **12**:10–14
decimal marker **1**:2
deck access flats **21**:19
decking **6**:12
defensible space **13**:3–4
deflection **6**:1, **6**:6, **6**:12, **6**:17–18
delivery areas **34**:7, **35**:3, **35**:10, **39**:18–19, **43**:11
demand and supply **30**:3
demonstration benches **15**:28
densities, materials **6**:2, **8**:4, **8**:6

densities, planning **21**:4–5, **21**:6, **28**:12
density indication **28**:6
Department of Health **19**:1, **19**:3, **19**:6, **19**:19
department stores **35**:6
design and build contracts **5**:2
Design and Quality Standards (D&QS) **21**:2, **21**:6–7, **21**:17
design development **1**:3
design for change **24**:2–5
design for extension **24**:5
design heat loss **8**:26
design information standards **1**:1
Design Quality Indicators (DQI), schools **36**:2
Design Share website **36**:3
design stages **1**:3, **5**:3
desire lines **28**:5
desks **2**:5, **30**:14, **30**:15
detention suites **18**:12, **18**:15
deterrence **37**:1
dewpoint temperature **8**:20, **8**:22
diagnostic imaging facilities **19**:7, **19**:9–10, **19**:12, **19**:13, **19**:19
digital masterplanning **28**:4–8
digital media, libraries **27**:3–4, **27**:7, **27**:10–11
digital projection systems **15**:32
dimensional coordination (DC) **1**:7–10
dimensions: accessibility **4**:1–6; agricultural buildings **14**:4, **14**:6–11; anthropometrics **2**:1–5, **4**:2; auditorium seating **15**:1–2, **15**:4, **15**:7; baptistries **32**:7; car parking **39**:17; church seating **32**:14; corridors **3**:4–5; domestic garages **39**:16, **39**:17; doors **3**:3, **3**:4; equestrian design **14**:16–18, **14**:19; ergonomics **2**:5–7; fire appliances **11**:5, **11**:6, **18**:2–3; foodservice facilities **34**:4, **34**:5–11, **34**:13–14, **34**:17; hotel guestrooms **20**:7–9, **20**:11; industrial buildings **24**:7–8; industrial machines **24**:5, **24**:6–7; kitchens **34**:7, **34**:9–11, **34**:17; laboratories **26**:5–6; laboratory furniture **26**:15–16; mobility ranges **4**:5; offices **30**:8–9; older people's housing **22**:2, **22**:3; paper sizes **1**:10–11; primary health care buildings **33**:10–11; public houses **34**:26–7; pulpits **32**:11–12; pushchairs **4**:3; reach ranges **4**:4–5; shop fittings **35**:4, **35**:5; shopping centres **35**:8, **35**:11; shops **35**:3, **35**:5, **35**:6; sports equipment **38**:32, **38**:33, **38**:34–6; sports facilities **38**:2–21; steel **7**:1–5; vehicles **39**:1–5; warehouse handling equipment **25**:11; warehouses **25**:7–9; wheelchairs **4**:2–4, **4**:5
dining rooms **21**:17, **23**:11–12, **36**:15
Diocesan Advisory Committees (DACs) **32**:2, **32**:3
disabled people **4**:1, **4**:4; community centres **17**:3; escape routes **11**:18–19; street design **39**:22; see also accessible facilities; wheelchair access
discounting **5**:6, **5**:7
discount rates **5**:6, **5**:7
dishwashing, foodservice facilities **34**:10–11, **34**:17, **34**:18
displacement ventilation **43**:2–3
disproportionate collapse **37**:6
distance attenuation **10**:3–4
distance learning **43**:12
distributed learning **43**:12
district heating and cooling **28**:16
diving pools **38**:15, **38**:35
dogs, assistance **2**:7, **4**:4, **15**:35
domes, mosques **32**:19
domestic buildings see residential buildings
domestic space standards **2**:13
door entry systems **20**:5, **23**:13, **37**:2
doors: accessible **3**:3, **3**:4; acoustic **40**:3, **40**:4; entrance **3**:3; fire resistance **11**:20, **20**:4; laboratories **26**:13–14; lobbies **3**:4; materials **7**:27; police custody suites **18**:14; scenery **40**:3; security **37**:12; stables **14**:20
Door Set Energy Ratings (DSERs) **7**:27
doping control facilities **38**:38

drainage: baptistries **32**:7; cycle lanes/paths **39**:12; site analysis **28**:3; stables **14**:20; Sustainable Drainage Systems (SuDS) **7**:14, **12**:9–10, **12**:13, **12**:14
drama teaching **36**:15
drawings **1**:2–7; dimensional coordination **1**:9; graded components **1**:7; RIBA work stages **1**:3; scales **1**:2, **1**:3, **1**:6–7; symbols **1**:5–6; traditional types **1**:2, **1**:3–5
dressage arenas **14**:19
dressing rooms **15**:21–3, **40**:2
drive-in racking **25**:5, **25**:6
driving rain index **8**:12
drying-out **8**:21
dry laboratories **26**:1, **26**:9
dry powder installations **11**:21
dry proofing **12**:7, **12**:8
dual carriageways **39**:5–6
Dutch barns **14**:14
dwellings see residential buildings
DWP Jobcentre Plus offices **31**:4–5, **31**:6
dynamic loads **6**:2
dynamic wind pressure **8**:13–14

Early Years Foundation Stage (EYFS) education **36**:6–7
earthquakes **42**:8, **42**:31–2
earth tubes **36**:4
East Riding Crematorium **32**:23, **32**:24
Ecohomes **10**:10–11, **21**:13
Eco School standard **36**:9
education see schools; universities
Education Funding Agency (EFA) see Baseline Designs, schools
effluent production **14**:11, **14**:14
egg crates **42**:17, **42**:18
elastic sealants **7**:24–5
elastic zone **6**:5
elastomers **7**:20, **7**:21
elastoplastic sealants **7**:24
e-learning **43**:5–6, **43**:12
electrical installations **11**:2
electrical supply: accessible standards **21**:5; broadcasting studios **40**:3; laboratories **26**:21–2; police stations **18**:12; student housing **23**:11, **23**:12; tropics **42**:32
electric lighting see lighting
elemental cost planning **5**:3
embedded e-learning **43**:12
embedded service risers **26**:6, **26**:7, **26**:8
embodied energy **8**:2–3, **8**:33
emergency electrical supply **18**:12, **20**:4, **26**:21
emergency eyewash facilities **26**:20–1
emergency lighting **11**:17, **15**:35, **20**:4, **26**:23
emergency services: ambulance stations **18**:7–9; fire stations **8**:10, **18**:1–7; police stations **18**:9–15; see also Accident & Emergency (A&E) facilities
emissivity **8**:5, **8**:6, **42**:34
Ena De Silva house, Colombo **42**:3
encastré beams **6**:6
end-bearing piles **6**:16, **6**:17
energy **8**:2–3; building energy models **8**:33, **8**:34; embodied **8**:2–3, **8**:33; masterplanning **28**:16, **28**:19; reducing demand **8**:33; renewable **8**:33, **28**:16, **36**:5, **42**:28–9, **43**:13; schools **36**:5; seasonal energy use **8**:26, **8**:27; shops **35**:5; universities **43**:2–3
energy efficiency **7**:14–15; boilers **8**:26; design **8**:1–2; doors **7**:27; electric lighting **9**:8–9; heat-recovery systems **8**:25, **8**:28–9; hotels **20**:4; housing **21**:27; mechanical ventilation systems **8**:28; student housing **23**:13; windows **7**:26–7
Energy Star standards **36**:5
English Heritage **32**:2, **32**:3
English Nature **28**:2, **28**:3

entrances **3**:3; auditoria **15**:9, **15**:10, **15**:36–7; churches **32**:12–13; community centres **17**:3–4; hotels **20**:5, **20**:11; student housing **23**:12; town halls **16**:3; *see also* lobbies

entry control systems **20**:5, **23**:13, **37**:2

Environment Agency **12**:3, **12**:10

Environmental Building, BRE **42**:23

environmental conditions: climate **8**:1–2, **8**:11–15; condensation **8**:6, **8**:19–22; courtrooms **16**:10; industrial buildings **24**:8–9; laboratories **26**:1, **26**:23; libraries **27**:12–14, **27**:15, **27**:19; museums **29**:4–6; music teaching **43**:6; offices **30**:10; schools **36**:2; shops **35**:4–5; stables **14**:18, **14**:19; thermal comfort **8**:1, **8**:7–10, **42**:3–4; universities **43**:6, **43**:7, **43**:8, **43**:11

environmental design **42**:9; active design **42**:28–9; Crime Prevention Through Environmental Design (CPTED) **13**:1–5; masterplanning **28**:14–19; passive design **8**:2, **8**:33, **9**:1–5, **42**:14–28; schools **36**:3–5

Environmental Impact Assessments **28**:2, **42**:7

environmental site analysis **8**:15

environmental temperature **8**:27

epoxy resin adhesives **7**:26

Equality Act (2010) **23**:8–9

equestrian design **14**:12, **14**:15, **14**:16–20

equipment: foodservice kitchens **34**:10–12, **34**:13–14, **34**:16, **34**:17; industrial machines **24**:5, **24**:6–7, **24**:8; laboratories **26**:17–21, **26**:23; sports **38**:31–2, **38**:33, **38**:34–6, **38**:43; warehouses **25**:5–6, **25**:7–9, **25**:10, **25**:11

ergonomics **2**:5–7, **30**:14, **36**:5–6, **42**:11

escalators **3**:7–8

escape routes **11**:8–19; alternative routes **11**:13–14; auditoria **15**:8–9; community centres **17**:3; corridors and lobbies **11**:16–17, **11**:18, **20**:4; disabled people **11**:18–19; evacuation procedures **11**:14–15, **11**:16; flats **11**:9–12, **21**:18; hospitals **19**:7; hotels **20**:4; housing **21**:14; laboratories **26**:15; lighting **11**:17; maisonettes **11**:9, **11**:11–12; numbers required **11**:12–13; offices **11**:16; shopping centres **11**:13, **35**:10; shops **11**:16, **35**:6; statutory requirements **11**:22; student housing **23**:4, **23**:8; travel distances **11**:13–14, **11**:16, **11**:18, **15**:8, **19**:7, **21**:18, **26**:15; widths **11**:14

estate regeneration **21**:23–7

esteem value **5**:1

ethnic restaurants **34**:15

e-University **43**:12

evacuation procedures **11**:14–15, **11**:16, **19**:7

evaporation **8**:6

evidence based design (EBD) **33**:6

Executive Training Suites **43**:7

exercise yards, police stations **18**:13

exfoliated vermiculite **7**:23

Exhibition Road, South Kensington **39**:20

exhibition spaces *see* museums

expanded perlite **7**:23

expanded polystyrene (EPS) **7**:23, **8**:4

expanded PVC **7**:23

expansion: industrial buildings **24**:5; museums **29**:2, **29**:3

explosion hazards **24**:9; *see also* bomb attacks

extension, design for **24**:5

extensions, churches **32**:2–3

external areas, housing **21**:17, **21**:18, **21**:20, **21**:21

external shading **42**:16

external sheltered areas **8**:14–15

extinguishers, fire **11**:21, **15**:12, **23**:8

extruded polystyrene **7**:23

fabrics: structural **6**:6, **6**:15; tensile roof structures **7**:14

facades: attenuation **10**:4, **10**:5; blast loading **37**:5–6; blast resistance **37**:7–8; blast testing **37**:8–9; double-skin **43**:3; libraries **27**:12, **27**:19; and sustainability **43**:3, **43**:13; universities **43**:3, **43**:13; *see also* building envelopes

facial control **1**:9

facilities management (FM) **30**:2

factories *see* industrial buildings

Fanger's comfort equation **8**:9

fans **42**:29

farm animals **14**:2, **14**:3, **14**:4–11, **14**:12, **14**:13; *see also* horses

farm machinery **14**:3

farm shops **14**:20

farrowing houses **14**:10

fastenings, fire exits **11**:17–18

fast-food outlets **34**:1, **34**:2, **34**:5, **34**:19–20, **34**:24

fattening houses **14**:8, **14**:9

fencing **13**:3, **21**:18, **37**:12, **38**:20

FFR *see* flux fraction ratio (FFR)

fibreboards **7**:8, **8**:4, **11**:20

fillet joints **7**:24

film projection facilities **15**:31, **15**:32, **15**:33, **15**:36

filter strips **12**:9, **12**:10, **12**:13

finishes: community centres **17**:1–2; laboratories **26**:20; laboratory furniture **26**:16; paints **7**:26, **42**:34; plaster and boards **7**:21–2, **8**:4; tooled stone **7**:18

fire **11**:1–2

fire alarms **11**:22, **15**:12, **23**:8

fire appliances **11**:5, **11**:6, **18**:2–3

fire compartments **11**:2, **11**:4, **11**:9, **19**:7

fire detectors **11**:21–2

fire doors **11**:17–18, **11**:20, **20**:4

fire-engineering solutions **11**:8

firefighting shafts **11**:5, **11**:6

fire resistance **11**:2, **11**:3, **11**:19–21

fire safety **11**:1–23; appliances and installations **11**:21–2, **15**:12, **23**:8; auditoria **15**:12; broadcasting studios **40**:3–4; cladding **11**:7, **11**:8; department stores **35**:6; evacuation procedures **11**:14–15, **11**:16; exfoliated vermiculite **7**:23; fire doors **7**:27; flats **21**:18; glass **7**:15, **7**:16; hospitals **19**:6–7; hotels **20**:4, **20**:5; industrial buildings **24**:8; management **11**:19; plasterboard **7**:22; plastics **7**:20, **11**:20; precautions **11**:2; principles **11**:2–8; roof coverings **11**:8; schools **36**:6; shopping centres **35**:10; stables **14**:19; statutory requirements **11**:22–3; student housing **23**:8; unprotected areas **11**:6–7; warehouses **25**:12; *see also* escape routes

fire stations **8**:10, **18**:1–7

first aid rooms **38**:38

fitness centres **38**:38

fittings: hotel guestrooms **20**:11; laboratories **26**:20–1, **26**:24, **26**:26; older people's housing **22**:3–4; payment offices **31**:6; shops **35**:3–4, **35**:5; stables **14**:20; student housing **23**:10

five-a-side football **38**:3, **38**:34

fixed end beams **6**:6

Fixed Furniture and Equipment (FFE) **36**:5–6

fixings, stone cladding **7**:18

flanking sound transmission **10**:6

flats: air infiltration rates **8**:10; escape routes **11**:9–12, **21**:18; purpose-built **21**:18–20; student housing **23**:3, **23**:4, **23**:5, **23**:6

flexibility *see* adaptability

flipcharts **15**:29

floating structures **12**:9

flood-aware design **12**:1–14; case study **12**:10–14; planning for flood risk **12**:3–4, **12**:11; reducing flood risk **12**:4–10, **12**:11–12; Sustainable Drainage Systems (SuDS) **7**:14, **12**:9–10, **12**:13, **12**:14; understanding flood risk **12**:1–3, **12**:10–11

flooding **12**:1–3, **42**:7–8

floodlights **38**:24–5

Flood Risk Assessments (FRAs) **12**:3

flood voids **12**:13

flood zones **12**:3, **12**:10

floor areas: community centres **17**:3; hotels **20**:3; retail **35**:1; schools **36**:2, **36**:7, **36**:11, **36**:15; universities **43**:13–15

floor depths, offices **30**:8
floor loads **6**:4
floor plenum **30**:15
floors **8**:4; auditoria **15**:10; raised **30**:11, **30**:14; timber **6**:9, **6**:10, **6**:11; tropical design **42**:30; *see also* surfaces
floor tiles **7**:15, **7**:17
floor to floor heights: laboratories **26**:5–6; offices **30**:8
flux fraction ratio (FFR) **9**:8
fly screens **42**:19–20, **42**:31, **42**:33
flytowers **15**:15, **15**:16–17
foam installations **11**:21
follow spots **15**:20
fonts **32**:4, **32**:6, **32**:12, **32**:13
food cabinets, shops **35**:4
food courts **34**:19, **34**:25, **35**:10, **43**:9
foodservice facilities **34**:1–28; cafes **2**:8, **8**:10, **10**:8, **34**:16, **39**:14, **43**:4; fast-food outlets **34**:1, **34**:2, **34**:5, **34**:19–20, **34**:24; food courts **34**:19, **34**:25, **35**:10, **43**:9; food production areas **34**:3, **34**:7–15, **34**:16, **34**:17; hotels **20**:12–13, **34**:1, **34**:2, **34**:5, **34**:7, **34**:18, **34**:27–8; public areas **34**:3, **34**:4–7, **34**:8, **34**:9; *see also* cafeterias; catering facilities; restaurants
football **38**:2–3, **38**:23; competitors and officials areas **38**:37; equipment **38**:32, **38**:34; media areas **38**:41; spectator facilities **38**:39; viewing distances **38**:27
footfall measurement **28**:5
footpaths **39**:6
footways **39**:6
force **6**:2
foreign currency outlets **31**:1, **31**:4, **31**:5, **31**:7
fork-lift truck operations **25**:6–9, **25**:11
Formula 1 cars **38**:35
Fort Halstead Masterplan, Sevenoaks **28**:4–7
foundations **6**:15–17
found property stores **18**:9
foyers: auditoria **15**:37, **15**:38; single person accommodation **21**:23; synagogues **32**:19; *see also* entrances; lobbies
franchises **35**:2
free schools **36**:2
frequency distribution curve **2**:1–2
friction piles **6**:16–17
Friendship House, London **23**:5
frontage widths **21**:14
front gardens **13**:3, **21**:14, **21**:18
Fruin Levels of Service **41**:21
fume cupboards (FCs) **26**:17–18, **26**:19
function rooms **20**:13
furnace rooms **32**:23
furniture: churches **32**:8–11; foodservice facilities **34**:5–7; hotel guestrooms **20**:10, **20**:11; laboratories **26**:15–16, **26**:24, **26**:26; libraries **27**:7–10; older people's housing **22**:4; police custody suites **18**:14; schools **36**:5–6; space standards **21**:7; street **39**:22; student housing **23**:10; *see also* seating
further education (FE) colleges **43**:2

gabions **7**:19
Gaelic football **38**:3, **38**:33
galvanized steel **7**:5
gangways, auditoria **15**:4, **15**:7, **15**:32–3
gap-filling adhesives **7**:26
garages, domestic **39**:13, **39**:16, **39**:17
garbagriha **32**:20
gardens **13**:3, **21**:14, **21**:18, **21**:20, **21**:21
Gardens of Remembrance **32**:21, **32**:23
gas cylinder storage **26**:17
gaseous installations **11**:21
gaskets **7**:25
gates **13**:3, **21**:18
Gatwick Airport **34**:25, **41**:2

GEA *see* gross external area (GEA)
gender ratios **2**:7, **38**:39
General Practitioners **33**:2, **33**:3, **33**:4, **33**:5, **33**:6, **33**:13
geotechnics **42**:7
geothermal energy **42**:28
GIA *see* gross internal area (GIA)
GLA *see* gross leasable area (GLA)
glass and glazing **6**:13, **6**:15, **7**:14–15; blast resistance **37**:7–8; blast testing **37**:8–9; cellular **7**:23; curtain walling **7**:28; density **8**:4; design requirements **7**:15; embodied energy **8**:3; fire resistance **11**:20; gaskets **7**:25; G-values **8**:19; libraries **27**:12, **27**:19; properties **6**:6; radiation transmission **8**:5; solar control **42**:17, **42**:18, **42**:35–6; sound insulation **7**:15, **7**:16, **10**:4, **10**:5; systems **7**:16; thermal conductivity **8**:4; thermal design **8**:18–19, **8**:20; types **7**:15–16; U-values **8**:18–19
glass blocks **42**:18, **42**:36
glass-fibre reinforced cement **7**:21
glass-fibre reinforced gypsum **7**:21, **7**:22
glass-fibre reinforced plastics **6**:6, **7**:20–1
glass wool **7**:22–3, **8**:4, **8**:16
glazing *see* glass and glazing
Glebe House, Southbourne **22**:2
global warming **8**:15
globe temperature **8**:9
goods handling equipment **25**:5–6, **25**:7–9, **25**:10, **25**:11
government services outlets **31**:2, **31**:4–5, **31**:6, **31**:7–8
gradients: cycle lanes/paths **39**:10–11; ramps **3**:1; roads **39**:10
grain stores **14**:13, **14**:15
granite **7**:17–18
grants **5**:6
graphic techniques **1**:2
grass, sports facilities **38**:23
Greater London Authority **21**:8, **21**:9–10
greenhouse gas emissions **8**:5, **8**:27
green roofs **7**:14, **12**:9, **12**:13, **28**:17
green spaces **28**:12
Green Travel Plans **36**:9
grids **1**:7–8, **1**:9–10, **30**:9
gross external area (GEA) **30**:6, **43**:14, **43**:15
gross internal area (GIA) **26**:9, **30**:6, **43**:14, **43**:15
gross leasable area (GLA) **35**:1, **35**:8
ground cooling systems **8**:31, **36**:4
groundskeeping **38**:43
ground source heat pumps (GSHP) **8**:31, **8**:32, **36**:5
groundwater **12**:2, **36**:4, **42**:7
guarding, staircases **3**:7
guide dogs *see* assistance dogs
G-values, glazing **8**:19
gymnasium equipment **38**:31, **38**:32, **38**:36
gymnasiums **38**:38
gymnastics **38**:18–19, **38**:23, **38**:36
gypsum: glass-fibre reinforced **7**:21; plaster **7**:21, **7**:22

Habinteg Housing Association **21**:8, **21**:11
halls: community centres **17**:4; Salvation Army **32**:5–6; schools **36**:10, **36**:15; Society of Friends **32**:7–8
halls of residence **43**:10; *see also* student housing
Hammarby Sjöstad, Stockholm **28**:14–19
Hammersmith Town Hall **16**:2
handball **38**:9, **38**:25
hand drying facilities **2**:13
handrails: auditoria **15**:9–10, **15**:11; escalators **3**:8; ramps **3**:1; staircases and steps **3**:2–3, **3**:6, **3**:7, **4**:6
hand washing facilities **2**:8, **2**:12, **2**:13, **19**:7, **26**:20; *see also* washbasins
hazardous waste management **28**:18
hazards: laboratories **26**:2, **26**:17–20; trips **3**:3, **4**:5–6; *see also* fire safety

hazard warning surfaces **3**:3

headroom: escalators **3**:8; staircases **3**:6

health: masterplanning **28**:10–12; offices **8**:10, **30**:3; sick building syndrome **8**:10; universities **43**:3; *see also* hospitals; primary health care buildings

Health Building Notes (HBNs) **19**:19, **33**:9–10

health care buildings *see* hospitals; primary health care buildings

Health Technical Memoranda (HTMs) **19**:19

Healthy Living Centres **33**:6, **33**:7, **33**:8

hearing impairments **15**:3, **15**:35, **15**:40, **23**:9

heat detectors **11**:21, **15**:12

heat gains **8**:26–7, **8**:29, **26**:23; *see also* solar gain

heating **8**:25–7; auditoria **15**:2, **15**:12; baptistries **32**:7; boilers **8**:26; and condensation **8**:21; distribution systems **8**:25, **8**:26; Passive Haus **8**:32, **8**:33; police custody suites **18**:14; seasonal energy use **8**:26, **8**:27; solar water heating **28**:16, **36**:5, **42**:32, **43**:3; student housing **23**:11; synagogues **32**:18

heat loss **8**:23–4, **8**:26, **8**:27

heat-recovery systems **8**:25, **8**:28–9

heat transfer mechanisms **8**:3–7, **11**:1–2

heavy industries **24**:2, **24**:4

hedges **13**:3

heliodons **9**:4, **9**:5

HEPA (high efficient particulate air) filtration **26**:18, **26**:19

Hindu temples **32**:20, **32**:22

Hive public library, Worcester **27**:2, **27**:3

hockey **38**:4, **38**:23, **38**:33

Holbeck Village, Leeds **28**:8, **28**:9

holiday centres and villages **34**:28

holistic care **33**:1, **33**:13

hollow joins **7**:13

Holy Ark **32**:16, **32**:17, **32**:18, **32**:19

Holy Trinity school, Halifax **28**:10

'home base' model for schools **36**:12

Homes and Communities Agency (HCA) **21**:2, **21**:6–7, **28**:1

Hooke's Law **6**:5

horse boxes **14**:19

horses **14**:12, **14**:15, **14**:16–20

hose reels **11**:21

hospices **33**:2

hospitality suites, sports facilities **38**:39–40

hospitals **19**:1–19; Accident & Emergency (A&E) facilities **19**:7–8, **19**:10; air infiltration rates **8**:10; catering facilities **34**:23; children's services **19**:13–14, **19**:17–18; community **19**:2, **33**:2, **33**:4, **33**:6, **33**:10; department relationships **19**:5–6; design **19**:2–7; diagnostic imaging facilities **19**:7, **19**:9–10, **19**:12, **19**:13, **19**:19; hi-tech specialties **19**:19; infection control **7**:12, **19**:7, **19**:8–9, **19**:11; maternity services **19**:18–19; mental health services **19**:19; older people's services **19**:14, **19**:18; operating theatres **19**:8–9, **19**:11, **19**:15; outpatient facilities **19**:8, **19**:14–15, **19**:16, **19**:17, **19**:18, **19**:19; parking **39**:15; rehabilitation services **19**:16–17; sound insulation **10**:9, **10**:11, **10**:13, **10**:14, **10**:17; wards **19**:2–3, **19**:4, **19**:10–11, **19**:13–14, **19**:18–19; *see also* primary health care buildings

Hospital Streets **19**:7

hostile vehicle mitigation **37**:1, **37**:4, **37**:6

hot-desking offices **43**:11

hot dry climates **42**:3, **42**:4, **42**:12, **42**:15

hotels **20**:1–17; air infiltration rates **8**:10; case studies **20**:14–18; classification **20**:1; design considerations **20**:1–6; foodservice facilities **20**:12–13, **34**:1, **34**:2, **34**:5, **34**:7, **34**:18, **34**:27–8; guestrooms **20**:2–3, **20**:4, **20**:6–11; parking **39**:14; permissible noise levels **10**:8; public areas **20**:2, **20**:4–5, **20**:11–13; sanitary facilities **2**:8; sound insulation **10**:9, **20**:4

hot-melt adhesives **7**:26

hot springs **42**:8

hot water heating, solar **28**:16, **36**:5, **42**:32, **43**:3

hot wet climates **42**:3, **42**:4, **42**:12, **42**:13

Houghton le Spring Primary Care Centre, Tyne & Wear **33**:17–18

Hounslow Health Centre, London **33**:13–15

house conversions **21**:20–1

houses in multiple occupation (HMOs) **23**:7–8; *see also* student housing

housing: air infiltration rates **8**:10; estate regeneration **21**:23–7; house conversions **21**:20–1; for older people **21**:22, **22**:1–4, **39**:14; parking **21**:5–6, **39**:13, **39**:14; purpose-built flats **21**:18; single-family houses **21**:14–18; single person accommodation **21**:21–3; standards **21**:1–14; students and young people **23**:1–13, **43**:10; *see also* residential buildings

Housing Act (2004) **23**:7

Housing Quality Indicators (HQI) **21**:2, **21**:7

humid climates **42**:3, **42**:4, **42**:12, **42**:13

hybrid ventilation systems **8**:31–2

hydrant systems **11**:21

hydraulic systems: auditoria **15**:11, **15**:17; lifts **3**:9, **3**:10

hygiene: foodservice facilities **34**:9; hotels **20**:5; infection control **7**:12, **19**:7, **19**:8–9, **19**:11

Hylands Primary School, Hornchurch, Essex **36**:8

hypermarkets **35**:7–8

ice hockey **38**:16, **38**:34

ice rinks **38**:16–17

ICT *see* information technology

identity parade suites **18**:11–12

IFC *see* Industry Foundation Class (IFC)

illuminance **9**:10

immigration desks, airports **41**:9

imposed loads **6**:2

improvised explosives devices (IED) **37**:3–4, **37**:5, **37**:6–7, **37**:8, **37**:10

inclusive design **4**:1

incubators, university **43**:8

induction loop systems **15**:3, **15**:35, **15**:40, **32**:14, **32**:18–19

industrial buildings **24**:1–9; air infiltration rates **8**:10; parking **39**:14; permissible noise levels **10**:8; reverberation times **10**:16; storage buildings **8**:10, **25**:1–12, **39**:14

Industry Foundation Class (IFC) **1**:1

infection control **7**:12, **19**:7, **19**:8–9, **19**:11

information technology: hospitals **19**:1; libraries **27**:7, **27**:8, **27**:10–11; offices **30**:3; primary health care buildings **33**:12; schools **36**:5, **36**:8, **36**:13; sports facilities **38**:43; trading floors **30**:14–15; universities **43**:12

insects **42**:9–10, **42**:11, **42**:19–20, **42**:33

institutional foodservices *see* cafeterias; catering facilities

insulation: densities **8**:4; fire safety **11**:8; installation of **8**:18; thermal conductivity **7**:23, **8**:4, **8**:17; transparent insulation material (TIM) **8**:19, **8**:20; types **7**:22–4, **8**:17; U-values **8**:16

Integrated Project Delivery (IPD) **1**:1

Intensive Therapy Units (ITUs) **19**:7, **19**:9

interactive classrooms **43**:4

InterContinental Hotel, Westminster **20**:16–18

Intergovernmental Panel on Climate Change (IPCC) **42**:5

interior design: mental health services **19**:19; purpose-built flats **21**:18–19; reducing sound transmission **10**:5; single-family houses **21**:15–16, **21**:17–18

international aid **42**:8

internet access **23**:10–11

interstitial condensation **8**:22

interstitial floor service zones **26**:6–7, **26**:8

interview spaces, payment offices **31**:6, **31**:10

Intruder Detection Systems (IDS) **37**:13

intumescent coatings **11**:21

intumescent strips **11**:20

IPD *see* Integrated Project Delivery (IPD)

irrigation, sports pitches **38**:23, **38**:24

IT-mediated learning **43**:12

Jobcentre Plus offices **31**:4–5
joints **7**:24
joists: floor **6**:9, **6**:10, **6**:11; steel **6**:14, **7**:3
Joseph Rowntree Foundation (JRF) **21**:8
Judaism **32**:16–19
judo **38**:18
junctions, road **39**:9, **39**:11, **39**:21

karate **38**:20, **38**:25
kayaking **38**:16, **38**:35
kennels, cattle housing **14**:2, **14**:4
keratin **7**:21
kerbs **3**:1
key reference planes **1**:10
King Edward Memorial Hospital, Ealing **19**:12
kitchens: accessible standards **21**:12; community centres **17**:4;
    equipment **34**:10–12, **34**:13–14, **34**:16, **34**:17; foodservice
    facilities **34**:7, **34**:9–12, **34**:13–14, **34**:15, **34**:16, **34**:17; schools
    36:15; single-family houses **21**:17; space standards **2**:5–6;
    student housing **23**:3, **23**:8, **23**:10, **23**:11–12; work surface
    heights **2**:5–6, **21**:14, **22**:4, **34**:9

laboratories **26**:1–29; case studies **26**:23–6; environmental
    conditions **26**:1, **26**:23; equipment **26**:17–21, **26**:23; furniture
    26:15–16, **26**:24, **26**:26; planning modules **26**:2–5, **43**:5;
    schools **26**:1, **26**:9, **26**:10–11, **26**:15, **26**:16, **36**:13; services
    26:5, **26**:6–7, **26**:8, **26**:21–3; space organisation **26**:7, **26**:9–17;
    types and sectors **26**:1; universities **26**:1, **26**:9, **26**:11, **26**:16,
    26:23–6, **43**:5–6, **43**:14; vibration **26**:6, **26**:7, **26**:15
lacrosse **38**:4, **38**:33
Ladbroke Hotel **34**:28
Lady Mitchell Hall, Cambridge **15**:27
laminated beams **6**:8, **6**:11
laminated glass **6**:15, **7**:16, **37**:7
laminated timber **7**:7
laminated veneer lumber **7**:7
lamp efficacy **9**:8
landings **3**:1, **3**:2, **3**:6
landlord efficiency **30**:8
land remediation allowances **5**:6
landscape design **28**:8–9; tropics **42**:11, **42**:23–4, **42**:26–7
Landscape Institute **28**:1
land-use and mix simulation **28**:6
lap joints **7**:24
La Puente, California **35**:9
laser beam detectors **11**:22
laundries **18**:9, **23**:12
law courts **16**:7–16
layered glazing systems **8**:19
lead **7**:5, **7**:12–13
Leadenhall Building, London **30**:4
learning cafes **43**:4
learning centres **43**:4–5, **43**:14
Learning Resource Centre, Thames Valley University **27**:8
Learning Resource Centres (LRCs) **36**:13
learning streets **43**:4
lecterns **15**:27–8, **32**:4, **32**:8, **32**:10, **32**:11
lecture theatres **15**:25, **15**:27, **43**:3, **43**:4, **43**:6, **43**:7
legislation: agricultural buildings **14**:20; auditoria **15**:40;
    community centres **17**:3; foodservice facilities **34**:3–4;
    laboratories **26**:2, **26**:27–9; schools **36**:2; student housing
    23:7–9; *see also* Building Regulations
leisure facilities: hotels **20**:13; *see also* sports facilities
letter bombs **37**:4
level, changes in **4**:5–6
Levels of Service, airports **41**:4
libraries **16**:4, **27**:1–19; air infiltration rates **8**:10; case
    study **27**:14–17; community roles **27**:2–4; design **27**:4–6;

environmental conditions **27**:12–14, **27**:15, **27**:19; layouts
    27:7–11; parking **39**:15; space standards **27**:11–12, **43**:14;
    university **27**:1, **27**:2, **27**:4, **27**:7, **27**:8–9, **27**:10–11, **27**:12,
    43:4–5, **43**:14
library desks **27**:5
licensing **17**:3
LifE *see* Long-term Initiatives for Flood-risk Environments (LifE)
life cycle analysis (LCA) **5**:6
life cycle costs **5**:6, **8**:32, **33**:3
Lifetime Homes **21**:8, **21**:11
Lifetime Homes standard **2**:13
LIFT (Local Improvement Finance Trust) **33**:6, **33**:7
lifting platforms **3**:9
lifts **3**:9–12; firefighting **11**:5, **20**:5; flats **21**:5, **21**:19; laboratories
    26:15; lobbies **3**:11; service **20**:4; specifications **3**:12; student
    housing **23**:3, **23**:4
light baffles **42**:18
lighting: auditoria **15**:12, **15**:19–20, **15**:23, **15**:35; broadcasting
    studios **40**:2–3; controls **9**:9; courtrooms **16**:10; crime
    prevention design **13**:3, **13**:5; display **9**:10; emergency **11**:17,
    15:35, **20**:4, **26**:23; energy efficiency **9**:8–9; escape routes
    11:17; glazing **7**:15, **7**:16; glossary **9**:10–12; hotels **20**:4;
    industrial buildings **24**:8; laboratories **26**:23; libraries **27**:12–14,
    27:15; museums **29**:4, **29**:5–6; older people's housing **22**:2;
    police custody suites **18**:14; schools **36**:4–5; shops **35**:4; sizing
    installations **9**:9; sports floodlighting **38**:24–5; student housing
    23:10, **23**:12; synagogues **32**:18; universities **43**:3, **43**:8, **43**:13;
    and visual display terminals **9**:10; *see also* natural lighting
lighting control rooms **15**:20, **15**:30
light pipes **42**:15, **42**:17, **42**:19
light pollution **13**:5
light rail **41**:26, **41**:28
light scoops **42**:15, **42**:17, **42**:19
lightweight aggregate concrete **7**:22, **7**:23
lime **7**:21
limestones **7**:17, **7**:19
limit states **6**:1
linear assembly methods **24**:5
lintels **6**:6
liquid nitrogen storage **26**:17
Listed Building Consent **21**:20
listed buildings **32**:2, **32**:3
litter **42**:28
Liverpool School of Tropical Medicine (LSTM) **26**:24, **26**:25–6,
    26:29
livestock **14**:2, **14**:3, **14**:4–11, **14**:12, **14**:13; *see also* horses
loadbearing capacity **11**:19
loading bays **25**:6, **25**:9, **25**:10, **39**:18–19
loading bridges, airports **41**:12–13
load mounting **25**:5
loads **6**:1–3, **6**:4; on beams **6**:17–20; industrial buildings **24**:8;
    laboratories **26**:6; masonry elements **6**:7, **6**:8; offices **30**:8–9
lobbies **3**:4; ATM **31**:2, **31**:5–6, **31**:7, **31**:8; auditoria **15**:36–7,
    15:38; fire safety **11**:16–17, **11**:18; hotels **20**:11–12; lifts **3**:11;
    see also entrances; foyers
Local Ecumenical Projects (LEPs) **32**:1
local exhaust ventilation (LEV) **26**:17
lockers **18**:5, **18**:6, **18**:7, **18**:9
loft conversions **21**:21
London Housing Design Guide (LHDG) **21**:8, **21**:27
London Plan **21**:8, **21**:9–10
Long-term Initiatives for Flood-risk Environments (LifE) **12**:5
Lord's cricket ground **38**:40, **38**:41
lorries **39**:3–4, **39**:18–19
louvres **42**:17
low carbon design **8**:32–3, **36**:3–5
low-density concrete blocks **8**:17
low-emissivity glass **8**:19

Loxford Polyclinic, Essex **33**:15–16
LRCs *see* Learning Resource Centres (LRCs)
luminaires **9**:8–9, **35**:4
lump sum contracts **5**:2
Lyttleton Theatre, London **15**:16

magnetic resonance imaging (MRI) **19**:9, **19**:19
Maidment Court, Dorset **22**:2
mail scanning **37**:4
maintenance: access for **2**:6–7; and crime prevention design
    13:4; foodservice facilities **34**:7; universities **43**:11; warehouse
    equipment **25**:10
maisonettes, escape routes **11**:9, **11**:11–12
management, crime prevention design **13**:4
Manchester Metrolink **41**:28
mandapa **32**:20
manned security provision **37**:3
Manoel theatre, Malta **42**:19
manufacturing *see* industrial buildings
manure **14**:11, **14**:14
marble **7**:18
markets **35**:2–3
masonry **6**:7, **6**:8; blast resistance **37**:8; fire resistance **11**:19;
    properties **6**:6; structural robustness **37**:6; tropics **42**:30;
    U-values **8**:16
mass **6**:2–3; *see also* thermal mass
masterplanning **28**:1–12; case study **28**:14–19; checklists **28**:7–10;
    digital **28**:4–8; and health **28**:10–12; key documents **28**:13–14
mastic asphalt roofing **7**:14
matchbox sundials **9**:4–5
materials: bending **6**:5–6; densities **6**:2, **8**:4, **8**:6; emissivities/
    absorptivities **8**:5, **8**:6, **42**:34; fire resistance **11**:19–21; for
    fire stopping and cavity barriers **11**:21; masses **6**:3; moisture
    content **8**:21; older people's housing **22**:2; sound absorption
    10:2, **10**:3, **10**:6; storage and handling **25**:2; structural **6**:6–15;
    thermal capacity **8**:6–7; thermal conductivity **7**:23, **8**:3–4; time
    lag **42**:37; vapour resistance **8**:22; *see also individual materials*
maternity services **19**:18–19
matrix glazing systems **8**:19, **8**:20
MDF *see* medium density fibreboard (MDF)
Meadowhall Centre, Sheffield **35**:14
means of escape *see* escape routes
measurement **5**:3–6, **30**:3, **30**:6–7
mechanical smoke extraction systems **11**:4
mechanical ventilation systems **8**:23, **8**:27–30; air speed **8**:8;
    auditoria **15**:12; broadcasting studios **40**:3; CBRN attacks **37**:5;
    design **8**:2; fire safety **11**:18; heat-recovery systems **8**:25, **8**:28–
    9; museums **29**:4; police stations **18**:12; shops **35**:5; tropics
    42:29; universities **43**:13
mechanised passenger conveyor system **3**:8–9
media: broadcasting studios **10**:13, **15**:40, **40**:1–4; sports facilities
    38:40–2
median strips **39**:21, **39**:23
medical facilities: sports buildings **38**:38; *see also* hospitals;
    primary health care buildings
medium density fibreboard (MDF) **7**:8
medium industrials **24**:1–2, **24**:3
meeting halls, Society of Friends **32**:7–8
meeting rooms **15**:38, **16**:3, **17**:4; churches **32**:5; libraries **27**:11;
    offices **30**:11, **30**:12; payment offices **31**:6, **31**:10
mental health services **19**:19
mesh reinforcement **6**:11
metabolic carbon dioxide **8**:23
metabolic heat **8**:7
metals: alloys **7**:2, **7**:5, **7**:10–11; fencing **13**:3; roofing **7**:11–13;
    see also aluminium; steel
metalwork shops **15**:39
Methodist Church **32**:6–7

metric annotation **1**:1–2
microbiological safety cabinets (MSCs) **26**:18–20, **26**:21
middens **14**:20
Mihrab **32**:19
milking parlour systems **14**:2, **14**:5, **14**:6
minarets **32**:19
mineral wool **7**:22, **8**:4, **8**:16, **8**:17
mixed mode cooling **36**:4
mixed use environments **28**:12
mobile and wireless learning **43**:12
mobility ranges **4**:5
Modern Methods of Construction (MMC) **23**:4
modified wood **7**:8
modules, laboratories **26**:2–5, **43**:5
moisture: condensation **8**:6, **8**:19–22; evaporation **8**:6; *see also*
    relative humidity (RH)
Mold Community Hospital **19**:2
moment joints **6**:25
money transfer outlets **31**:1, **31**:4, **31**:5, **31**:7
monsoon climates **42**:3, **42**:4, **42**:12, **42**:13
mosques **32**:19–20, **32**:21
mosquitoes **42**:9–10, **42**:11, **42**:33
motorcycles **39**:2
mould growth **8**:20
movement **3**:1–12; access to buildings **3**:1–3; crime prevention
    design **13**:2; escalators **3**:7–8; moving walkways **3**:8–9; *see
    also* lifts; passenger movement
moving walkways **3**:8–9
MRI *see* magnetic resonance imaging (MRI)
multi-layer thermo-reflective materials **7**:24
multi-sports halls **38**:22
multi-storey car parks **39**:13, **39**:18
Munsell numbers **42**:34
Museum of London Docklands **29**:5
museums **8**:10, **29**:1–8, **38**:40, **39**:15
musicians **15**:17–18, **15**:22, **15**:24–5, **15**:26
music teaching **36**:15, **43**:6
Muslims **32**:19–20

National Affordable Housing Programme **21**:2
National Counter Terrorism Security Office (NaCTSO) **37**:10
National Curriculum **36**:1, **36**:8, **36**:10
National House Building Council (NHBC) **21**:7–8
national libraries **27**:1, **27**:6, **27**:13
National Planning Policy Framework (NPPF) **21**:4–6, **21**:13
natural lighting: daylight factors **9**:5–6; glazing **7**:15, **7**:16; industrial
    buildings **24**:8; libraries **27**:12, **27**:13, **27**:15; maintenance factors
    9:7, **9**:11; schools **36**:2, **36**:4–5; tropics **42**:35; uniformity in **36**:5;
    universities **43**:2, **43**:3, **43**:7, **43**:8, **43**:13; window design **9**:6–8
natural turf **38**:23
natural ventilation **8**:23; design **8**:24–5; fire safety **11**:4; hybrid
    systems **8**:31–2; libraries **27**:12, **27**:13, **27**:14, **27**:15; offices
    30:9–10; schools **36**:4; universities **43**:2–3
natural wood finishes **7**:26
NEAT hospital design **19**:3–4
neoprene **7**:20
netball **38**:11, **38**:23, **38**:25, **38**:35
net internal area (NIA) **30**:6, **43**:14, **43**:15
net office area (NOA) **30**:6
net sales area (NSA) **35**:1
net useable area (NUA) **26**:9, **43**:14, **43**:15
network models **8**:33–4
neutral axis **6**:5
Newport Law Court **16**:8
New Rules of Measurement (NRM) **5**:3–6
New Zealand House, London **30**:6
NHS *see* primary health care buildings
NHS Estates **33**:2

NHS LIFT (Local Improvement Finance Trust) 33:6, 33:7
NIA *see* net internal area (NIA)
night time cooling 36:4
NOA *see* net office area (NOA)
noise: broadcasting studios 40:3, 40:4; community centres
    17:3; external sources 10:3–5; hotels 20:4–5; industrial
    buildings 24:8; laboratories 26:6, 26:23; libraries 27:6, 27:10,
    27:11; museums 29:6; permissible levels 10:6–8; reducing
    transmission 10:3–6; stables 14:19; student housing 23:8;
    universities 43:6, 43:8; *see also* sound insulation
Noise Rating (NR) standards 10:6–7, 15:12, 20:4
non-condensing boilers 8:26
normal distribution curve 2:1–2
Northern Ireland, housing standards 21:8
North Somerset Courthouse 16:14–16
nosing 3:2, 4:6, 11:15
no-sky line 9:1, 9:6, 42:21–2
notation 1:2
NSA *see* net sales area (NSA)
NUA *see* net useable area (NUA)
nursery classes 36:6–7

O2 Arena, London 38:22, 38:23
Oasis Academy, Enfield 36:2
obesity 4:2
occupancy-linked lighting controls 9:9
office as city concept 30:2
offices 30:1–16; air infiltration rates 8:10; auditoria 15:38;
    conversion to residential 21:21; design 30:1–2, 30:3; dimensions
    30:8–9; ergonomics 2:5; escape routes 11:16; in industrial
    buildings 24:7, 25:9–10; layouts 30:10–14; life spans 30:7;
    parking 39:14; payment 31:1–10; permissible noise levels 10:8;
    reverberation times 10:16; services 30:7, 30:9–10, 30:11, 30:14;
    sick building syndrome 8:10; sound insulation 10:9, 10:13,
    10:15; space requirements 30:6–7; town halls 16:3; trading floors
    30:14–16; types 30:3; universities 43:10–11, 43:14
Ofsted 36:1, 36:6
older people 4:1–2; hospital services 19:14, 19:18; housing 21:22,
    22:1–4, 39:14
Olympic Games 38:9
one-bedroom flats 21:22
onion stores 14:15
on-line exams and assessments 43:12
online learning 43:5–6
open plan offices 43:11
open-stage auditoria 15:5, 15:13, 15:14, 15:18–19
Opera House, Essen 15:16
operating theatres 19:8–9, 19:11, 19:15
operational costs 5:6
operational value 5:1
option studies 5:6
orchestras 15:17–18, 15:22, 15:24–5, 15:26
order assembly, warehouses 25:6, 25:8, 25:9
order of cost estimate 5:3–4
Ordnance Survey maps 1:11
organs, church 32:15–16
orientation: housing 21:14, 42:23; and noise 10:4, 10:5, 17:3;
    sports facilities 38:24; universities 43:2
oriented strand board (OSB) 7:7, 7:8
outpatient facilities 19:8, 19:14–15, 19:16, 19:17, 19:18, 19:19
outside broadcasts 38:42
ovens 34:10, 34:11, 34:13, 34:14
overhangs 42:16
overhead projectors 15:29, 15:30
oxygen level detection systems 26:17

pad foundations 6:15
paints 7:26, 42:34

paint shops 15:39
pallet racking 25:5, 25:6, 25:7
pallets 25:11
pallet trucks 25:11
panic bolts 11:18
paper insulation 7:24, 8:4, 8:17
paper sizes 1:10–11
parallel flange channels (PFC) 6:27, 7:4
parcel bombs 37:4
pareto rule 5:5
Parker Morris standards 21:1, 21:2, 21:4, 21:17, 21:18, 21:27
parking *see* car parking; cycle parking
particleboards 7:7–8
passenger movement: airports 41:4, 41:5, 41:6, 41:7, 41:8, 41:9,
    41:10, 41:11; railway stations 41:21–2
passive design 8:2, 8:33, 9:1–5, 42:14–28
Passive Haus 8:32, 8:33
passive shading 42:14–15, 42:16–18
passive solar design 9:1–5
passive stack ventilation (PSV) 8:25
pastoral centres 32:8
Patients Charter 19:2
patios 42:20–1
pavements 39:6
paving flags 7:10
payment offices 31:1–10
Peckham Public Library 27:6, 27:10
pedestrian permeability 28:12
pedestrians 27:4, 28:12, 39:22
percentage people dissatisfied (PPD) 8:9
percentiles 2:2
pergolas 42:16, 42:20
perimeter ducting 26:22, 30:11, 30:14
Perimeter Intrusion Detection Systems (PIDSs) 37:1, 37:2
permeable paving 12:9
permissible stress design 6:1
personal space requirements 2:2
personal symptom index (PSI) 8:10
petanque 38:21
PFI programme 33:6, 33:7
pharmacy services 19:1, 19:8, 19:14–15
phased evacuation 11:14–15, 11:16
phenolic foam 7:23, 8:4
photographers, sports facilities 38:40
photovoltaics 28:16, 36:5, 42:29, 43:13
physiotherapy 19:16
piano stores 15:21
Picture Archiving and Communication Systems (PACS) 19:10
piers 6:5, 6:7
pig housing 14:8–10
pile foundations 6:15, 6:16–17
pin-jointed frames 6:5
pin joints 6:25
piston and cylinder principle 1:8
pitch sports: competitors and officials areas 38:36–8; equipment
    38:32, 38:33, 38:34; media areas 38:41; pitch layouts 38:1,
    38:2–5; playing surfaces 38:23; spectator facilities 38:39
pitch technology 38:24
place-making 39:22
places of worship 32:1–24; air infiltration rates 8:10; Christian
    churches and meeting halls 32:1–16; crematoria 32:21–4;
    Hindu temples 32:20, 32:22; mosques 32:19–20, 32:21; parking
    39:15; Sikh gurdwara 32:20–1, 32:22; synagogues 32:16–19
planning grids 1:9–10, 30:9
planning modules, laboratories 26:2–5, 43:5
planning permission 21:20
planning policy: crime prevention design 13:2; flood risk 12:3–4;
    house conversions 21:20

Planning Policy Guidance Notes (PPGs) **28**:1–2, **28**:13–14

Planning Policy Statements (PPSs) **28**:1–2, **28**:13–14

Planning Portal **28**:1

planting: crime prevention design **13**:3, **13**:4–5; tropics **42**:16, **42**:18, **42**:24, **42**:26–7

plaster **7**:21–2, **8**:4, **8**:16

plasterboard **7**:21–2, **8**:4, **11**:20

plastic films **7**:16, **42**:17

plastic pipe adhesives **7**:26

plastics **7**:19–20, **7**:21; fire safety **7**:20, **11**:20; glass-fibre reinforced **6**:6, **7**:20–1; rooflights **11**:8, **11**:9; sealants **7**:24

platforms: cinemas **15**:36; concert halls **15**:24, **15**:25; conference halls **15**:27–8, **15**:31; railway stations **41**:22

playing fields **36**:11, **38**:43–4, **39**:15

pluvial flooding **12**:2

plywood **7**:7

PMV *see* predicted mean vote (PMV)

point loads **6**:17

pole barns **14**:13

pole houses **18**:3, **18**:6

Police Counter Terrorist Security Advisors (CTSA) **37**:10

police stations **18**:9–15

political factors **42**:8

pollution **13**:5, **29**:4, **42**:7

pollution control **12**:9

polo fields **14**:19

polyethylene **7**:19, **7**:20, **7**:21

polyisocyanurate foam **7**:23

Polytechnics and Colleges Funding Council (PCFC) **43**:13–14

polyurethane foam **7**:23, **8**:16

polyvinyl chloride (PVC) **7**:19, **7**:20, **7**:21; expanded **7**:23

pool-based sports **38**:1, **38**:12–15, **38**:35

Portcullis House, London **42**:2

Portobello Square, Kensington **21**:24–7

Post House Hotel, Sevenoaks **34**:15

post offices **31**:1, **31**:3–4, **31**:6, **31**:7

potato storage **14**:14

poultry housing **14**:11, **14**:12, **14**:13

power supply *see* electrical supply

Poynton, Cheshire **39**:22–5

PPD *see* percentage people dissatisfied (PPD)

precast concrete panels **7**:10, **37**:8

predicted mean vote (PMV) **8**:9

pre-fabrication **23**:4, **23**:7

pregnant women **4**:2

Presbyterian Church of Scotland (PCS) **32**:4

presence detectors **9**:9

press rooms **15**:31, **38**:40–2

pressure: vapour **8**:22; wind **8**:13–14

pressure coefficients **8**:14

Prestwick Airport **34**:2

primary health care buildings **33**:1–13, **39**:15; case studies **33**:13–19

primary schools **36**:1, **36**:7–10, **39**:15

prisoners' vehicle docks **18**:11

private laboratories **26**:1, **26**:11

private schools **36**:2

problem analysis triangle **13**:1

procedural security **37**:3

procurement **5**:2–3; payment offices **31**:7–8; primary health care **33**:6–7

production information **1**:3

Project Faraday **36**:13, **36**:14

projection facilities **15**:29–31, **15**:32, **15**:33, **15**:36

proscenium stages **15**:5, **15**:6, **15**:13–15, **15**:37

PSI *see* personal symptom index (PSI)

PSV *see* passive stack ventilation (PSV)

public areas: bus and coach stations **41**:25–6; foodservice facilities **34**:3, **34**:4–7, **34**:8, **34**:9; hotels **20**:2, **20**:4–5, **20**:11–13; law courts **16**:13; museums **29**:2, **29**:3; police stations **18**:9; primary health care buildings **33**:12; town halls **16**:3–4; universities **43**:9

public houses **34**:1, **34**:5, **34**:20, **34**:23–7, **39**:14

public laboratories **26**:1, **26**:11

public libraries *see* libraries

public outdoor spaces **27**:4, **27**:5; green spaces **28**:12; *see also* streets/roads

public realm appropriation **28**:7

public transport: bus and coach stations **8**:10, **41**:22–8; and libraries **27**:4; masterplanning **28**:15; railway stations **8**:10, **41**:16–22; and universities **43**:13

Pulkovo Airport, St Petersburg, Russia **41**:14–16

pulpits **32**:4, **32**:6, **32**:11–12, **32**:17

pushchairs **3**:4, **4**:3

PVA adhesives **7**:25, **7**:26

PVB laminated glass **37**:7

PVC *see* polyvinyl chloride (PVC)

Quakers **32**:7–8

quartzite **7**:19

Queen Mary University of London **23**:5

racecourses **38**:37, **38**:39

racking **6**:20–1, **25**:5, **25**:6, **25**:7, **34**:8–9

radiant temperature **8**:7

radiation **8**:5, **11**:1

radiation detectors **11**:21

radiation protection **7**:16

rafters **6**:9, **6**:12

raft foundations **6**:15, **6**:16

railings **13**:3, **21**:18

railway stations **8**:10, **41**:16–22

rainfall **8**:12, **12**:2

rainwater collection **42**:32, **43**:3, **43**:13

raised buildings **42**:10

raised floors **30**:11, **30**:14

raised track (viaduct) stations **41**:17–18

ramps **3**:1, **4**:5–6, **15**:9, **21**:5

Randhurst, Illinois **35**:9

Rapid Diagnostic and Treatment Centres (RDTC) **19**:14

Ravenscraig Regional Sports Facility **38**:45–50

reach ranges **4**:4–5, **22**:4

reading rooms, libraries **27**:3, **27**:5, **27**:7, **27**:14

reception areas: schools **36**:9–10, **36**:13; town halls **16**:3

recording studios **10**:13, **15**:40, **40**:1–4

rectangular hollow sections (RHS) **6**:26, **7**:4

recycled paper insulation **8**:17

recycling facilities **23**:11, **23**:12, **23**:13, **28**:17–18, **43**:11

reference systems **1**:9

reflectance **9**:10, **9**:11

reflected radiation **8**:11, **8**:12

refrigeration **8**:31, **8**:32, **35**:5

refuse storage **21**:18, **21**:19–20, **23**:12, **23**:13, **34**:7–8

regeneration, housing estates **21**:23–7

Register of Security Engineers and Specialists (RSES) **37**:10

rehabilitation services **19**:16–17

rehearsal rooms **15**:38, **15**:39, **40**:2

reinforced bitumen roofing membranes **7**:13–14

reinforced concrete **6**:6, **6**:9–13; blast resistance **37**:8; concrete cover **6**:13; reinforcement **6**:11–12, **7**:5

relative humidity (RH) **8**:7, **8**:8, **8**:9; and condensation **8**:20, **8**:21; external **8**:12, **8**:13; laboratories **26**:23; museums **29**:4, **29**:5, **29**:6

religious buildings *see* places of worship

religious factors **42**:8

renewable energy **8**:33, **28**:16, **36**:5, **42**:28–9, **43**:13

rents **23**:1, **35**:2

reservation of the sacrament **32**:12, **32**:13, **32**:14

residential buildings: permissible noise levels 10:8; reverberation times 10:16; sound insulation 10:9, 10:10–11, 10:13, 10:17; *see also* flats; housing

resort hotels 20:1, 20:13, 20:14, 34:27–8

restaurants 34:1, 34:2, 34:15–16; air infiltration rates 8:10; food production areas 34:9; parking 39:14; permissible noise levels 10:8; sanitary facilities 2:8; seating plans 34:4, 34:5, 34:6; *see also* cafeterias; foodservice facilities

resultant temperature 8:9, 8:27

retail 35:1–14; air infiltration rates 8:10; markets 35:2–3; retail parks 35:3, 35:14; shopping centres 11:13, 34:2, 34:19, 35:4, 35:8–14; sports facilities 38:40; supermarkets 25:9, 35:4, 35:5, 35:6–8; universities 43:9–10; *see also* shops

reverberation times 10:2–3, 10:15, 10:16–17, 40:3

revolving doors 3:3

revolving stages 15:15

RIBA work stages 1:3

rigid board insulation 8:17

Rio Earth Summit 28:2

risk 37:1; fire 11:1; flooding 12:1, 12:3–4

risk management 5:2, 29:7

risk matrix 5:2

risk register 37:11

river flooding 12:1

Rivers Agency, Northern Ireland 12:3

roads *see* streets/roads

roll-through racking 25:5, 25:6

Roman Catholic Church 32:3–4, 32:8, 32:12

roofing materials 7:11–15, 8:4

roofing slates 7:18

roofing tiles 7:10, 7:15, 7:17, 8:4

rooflights, plastic 11:8, 11:9

roofs: coverings 11:8; fire safety 11:8; forces acting on 6:24–5; green 7:14, 12:9, 12:13, 28:17; sports facilities 38:30–1; structural timbers 6:8–9, 6:12; tropical design 42:31

roof trusses 6:8–9, 6:12, 6:25, 8:16

room pressurisation 26:23

room sizes: hotel guestrooms 20:7–9, 20:11; housing 21:2, 21:3–4; older people's housing 22:2, 22:3; primary health care buildings 33:10–11; student housing 23:8, 23:9–10; *see also* space standards

rostra 15:11

rubber 7:20

rugby 38:2, 38:23, 38:32

running dimensions 1:9

Sabine formula 10:2

sacristies 32:15

safety: community centres 17:2; glass 7:15, 7:16; hotels 20:5; laboratories 26:2, 26:17–20; lifts 3:9; steps 3:3; student housing 23:13; windows 7:26

safety curtains 15:15, 15:16

safety shower facilities 26:20–1

sailing 38:15, 38:35

St Francis Church, Westborough 17:2

St Hugh's College, Oxford 23:9

St James's Church, Finchampstead 17:2

St John's College, Oxford 23:10

St Johns School, Blackpool 36:9, 36:10

Salvation Army 32:5–6

sandstones 7:17, 7:19

sandstorms 42:37

sanitary facilities: accessible facilities 2:7, 2:8, 2:9–11, 4:6, 18:9, 21:5; ambulance stations 18:9; for children 2:8, 2:11, 4:6, 17:4; community centres 17:4; crematoria 32:23; hospitals 19:2, 19:4; hotel guestrooms 20:11; industrial buildings 24:9; mosques 32:20; numbers required 2:7, 2:8; older people's housing 22:3–4; police stations 18:9, 18:12; schools 2:7, 2:8, 36:7,

36:10, 36:15; shopping centres 35:10; single-family houses 21:17; space standards 2:7–13; sports facilities 38:36, 38:37, 38:39; student housing 23:8, 23:12; tropics 42:33; warehouses 25:9, 25:10

sanitary ware, materials 7:15, 7:17

SAS headquarters, Stockholm 30:2, 30:3

SBS *see* sick building syndrome (SBS)

scaffolding-type auditorium seating 15:11

scales 1:6–7; drawings 1:2, 1:3

scenery doors 40:3

scenery workshops 15:38–40

Scheme Development Standards (SDS) 21:2

schools 36:1–17; air infiltration rates 8:10; design standards 36:2–3; Early Years Foundation Stage 36:6–7; environmental design 36:3–5; fire safety 36:6; foodservice facilities 34:5; furniture 36:5–6; laboratories 26:1, 26:9, 26:10–11, 26:15, 26:16, 36:13; National Curriculum 36:1, 36:8, 36:10; outside areas 36:10, 36:12–13; parking 36:9, 39:15; permissible noise levels 10:7; primary schools 36:1, 36:7–10, 39:15; reverberation times 10:16; sanitary facilities 2:7, 2:8, 36:7, 36:10, 36:15; secondary schools 36:10–15, 39:15; security 36:6; sound insulation 10:9, 10:11, 10:12, 10:13, 10:17; Special Educational Needs 36:15–17; sports facilities 38:22; types 36:1–2

'schools within schools' model 36:11–12

science teaching 36:13, 36:14, 43:5–6

scoreboards 38:31, 38:32, 38:42–3

Scotland, housing standards 21:8

Scottish Centre for Regenerative Medicine, University of Edinburgh 26:23–5

Scottish Environment Protection Agency (SEPA) 12:3

Scottish Housing Quality Standard (SHQS) 21:8

screens: cinemas 15:35–6; conference facilities 15:30; sports facilities 38:31, 38:32, 38:40, 38:42–3; trading floors 30:14–15

screen walling 42:17, 42:18

sealants 7:24–5

search and scanning equipment 37:13

seasonal energy use 8:26, 8:27

Seasons pizzeria, London 34:19

seating: auditoria 15:1–3, 15:4, 15:5–6, 15:7, 15:11; churches and meeting halls 32:2, 32:5–6, 32:8, 32:11, 32:14; cinemas 15:32; council chambers 16:2, 16:3; foodservice facilities 34:4, 34:5–7, 34:8, 34:9; older people's housing 22:4; sports facilities 38:27, 38:28–9, 38:30; synagogues 32:17–18; *see also* chairs

secondary schools 36:10–15, 39:15

sections 6:26–7

Secured by Design (SBD) 13:1, 13:2, 13:5, 21:13

security 37:1–10; active frontages 28:7; airports 41:4, 41:5, 41:7, 41:8, 41:9; community centres 17:3; counter terrorism 37:1, 37:3–10; crime prevention design 13:1–5, 21:13; gardens 21:18; glass 7:15, 7:16; hardware 13:5; hotels 20:5; laboratories 26:2; museums 29:6; payment offices 31:2, 31:3, 31:6; risk register 37:11; schools 36:6; sports facilities 38:39, 38:43; standards 37:3, 37:12–13; student housing 23:13; surveillance 13:2–3, 21:18, 28:7, 37:2–3; tropics 42:11; universities 43:11; warehouses 25:10

self-cleaning glass 7:16

self-service foodservices: cafeterias 34:2, 34:16–17, 34:19, 34:20, 34:21–2, 34:24; serveries 34:12, 34:20, 34:21; space allowances 34:5

SEN *see* Special Educational Needs (SEN)

serveries 34:11, 34:12, 34:15, 34:20, 34:21

serviceability limit states 6:1

service lifts 20:4

services: access 2:6–7; broadcasting studios 40:2–3; distribution systems 8:25, 8:26, 26:22–3, 30:11, 30:14; fire safety 11:18; fire stations 18:4; flats 21:20; hotels 20:3, 20:6, 20:9, 20:13–14; industrial buildings 24:8; laboratories 26:5, 26:6–7, 26:8, 26:21–3; masterplanning 28:6; museums 29:6–7; offices 30:7,

30:9–10, 30:11, 30:14; primary health care buildings 33:11, 33:12; shopping centres 35:10, 35:11; site analysis 28:3; stables 14:20; student housing 23:10–11; synagogues 32:18–19; tropics 42:8–9, 42:32–3; universities 43:3, 43:8
sewage management 28:16–17, 28:19, 42:33
sewer flooding 12:2
shade houses 42:24
shading 8:19, 27:12, 27:19, 42:14–20, 43:2
shading coefficients 42:34
shared space 39:6, 39:19–21, 39:22, 39:24
Sharing of Churches Act 32:1
shear forces 6:6, 6:12
sheaves 3:9
sheep housing 14:7–8
sheep's wool 7:24
sheet metal roofing 7:11–13
sheltered areas, external 8:14–15
sheltered housing 21:22, 22:1–4, 39:14
shelving: foodservice facilities 34:8–9, 34:10; shops 35:3, 35:4
Sheraton Muscat Hotel 34:18
Sherway gardens, Toronto 35:10
shock tubes 37:8
shopping centres 11:13, 34:2, 34:19, 35:4, 35:8–14
shops 35:3–8; air infiltration rates 8:10; auditoria 15:38; department stores 35:6; escape routes 11:16, 35:6; farm 14:20; parking 39:14; small 35:5–6; sports facilities 38:40; supermarkets 25:9, 35:4, 35:5, 35:6–8; universities 43:9–10; see also retail
short-bored piles 6:16, 6:17
showers 2:10, 17:4, 22:3–4, 23:12
shutters 11:20, 42:17, 42:31
sick building syndrome (SBS) 8:10
sidestitial service zones 26:6, 26:7, 26:8
sightlines: auditoria 15:1, 15:4–8, 15:15, 15:24, 15:32, 15:34; sports facilities 38:26–7, 38:28, 38:30
signage: auditoria 15:38; escape routes 11:17; hotels 20:3; masterplanning 28:5
Sikh gurdwara 32:20–1, 32:22
silencers, laboratories 26:23
silicones, structural 37:7–8
silos 14:13
single-family houses 21:14–18
single person accommodation 21:21–3
single-ply roofing systems 7:14
site analysis 28:3, 42:7–8
site loading scenarios 28:7
site planning 28:8–9; and climate 8:11–15; hotels 20:1–2, 20:6; skylight and sunlight 9:1–3; tropics 42:6–8, 42:23
sitting dimensions 2:2–5
sitting work spaces 2:5
skating 38:16–17
skin-friction piles 6:16–17
skylight 9:1–3, 42:35
skylight indicators 9:2, 9:11
sky lobbies 3:11
slate 7:18
slatted yards 14:6
slide projectors 15:30–1
sliding doors 3:3
slope-dependent access 28:5
slurry storage 14:14
smoke 11:1, 11:2; control 11:8, 11:18, 21:18, 35:10, 35:11
smoke detectors 11:21, 15:12
smoke reservoirs 11:4, 35:6, 35:10, 35:11
snack bars 34:16
snooker 38:20
soakaways 12:9
soccer 38:2, 38:3

social housing 21:1–2
social value 5:1
Society of Friends 32:7–8
soil 6:15, 42:7
soil decontamination 28:14
sol-air temperature 8:12, 8:27, 42:34
solar control glass 42:17, 42:18, 42:35–6
solar dazzle 42:7
solar declinations 9:4
solar flues 42:23
solar gain 8:19, 8:26, 8:27, 8:29, 9:7, 36:4; housing 21:14; solar heat factors 42:34; through glass 42:36; universities 43:2, 43:3, 43:13
solar geometry 9:3
solar heat factors 42:34
solar power 28:16, 36:5, 42:28, 42:29, 43:13
solar radiation 8:5, 8:11, 9:1–5, 42:34–5
solar screening 8:19, 27:12, 27:19, 42:14–20, 43:2
solar-shading analysis 28:7
solar water heating 28:16, 36:5, 42:32, 43:3
sound see acoustics; noise
sound control rooms 15:20, 15:30
sound insulation 10:8–15; auditoria 15:12; broadcasting studios 40:3, 40:4; community centres 17:3; flats 21:18–19; glazing 7:15, 7:16, 10:4, 10:5; hotels 10:9, 20:4; plasterboard 7:22
sound studios 10:13, 15:40, 40:1–4
sound systems: induction loop systems 15:3, 15:35, 15:40, 32:14, 32:18–19; places of worship 32:14–15, 32:18–19
sound transmission 10:1–2; absorption coefficients 10:2, 10:3; external sources 10:3–5; and interior design 10:5; reducing 10:3–6; reverberation times 10:2–3, 10:15, 10:16–17, 40:3; through structure 10:5–6
space budget, offices 30:6–7
Space Management Group (SMG) 43:13, 43:14
space standards: domestic 2:13; ergonomics 2:5–7; furniture 21:7; housing 21:2, 21:3–4; kitchens 2:5–6; libraries 27:11–12, 43:14; older people's housing 22:2, 22:3; personal 2:2; sanitary facilities 2:7–13; schools 36:2, 36:7, 36:11, 36:15; student housing 23:8; universities 43:13–15; see also dimensions; room sizes
spandrel construction 7:28
Special Educational Needs (SEN) 36:15–17
special schools 36:15, 39:15
speech therapy 19:16
speed humps 39:7, 39:8
speed restriction design 39:6–7, 39:8, 39:9, 39:19–21
speed skating 38:16–17
split ridges 42:15, 42:19
sports facilities 38:1–50; air infiltration rates 8:10; case study 38:45–50; community centres 17:1, 17:4; competitors and officials areas 38:32–3, 38:36–8; equipment 38:31–2, 38:33, 38:34–6, 38:43; fields of play 38:1–25; floodlights 38:24–5; management areas 38:42–3; masterplanning 28:15; media areas 38:40–2; orientation 38:24; parking 38:38, 39:15; pitch technology 38:24; playing surfaces 38:23–4; scales of 38:43–4; schools 36:11, 36:12–13; sightlines 38:26–7, 38:28, 38:30; spectator facilities 38:38–40; universities 43:10; vertical clearances 38:25–6; viewing structures 38:26–31, 38:32
sprinkler systems 11:3–4, 11:21; auditoria 15:12; department stores 35:6; flats 21:18; hospitals 19:7; hotels 20:4, 20:5; industrial buildings 24:8; warehouses 25:12
square hollow sections (SHS) 6:26, 7:3
squash courts 38:11, 38:23, 38:25
stables 14:12, 14:15, 14:16–20
stack effect 8:24
staff facilities: bus and coach stations 41:26; schools 36:10, 36:15; universities 43:9
stages, auditoria 15:5, 15:6, 15:13–17, 15:18–19, 15:36
stainless steel 7:5, 7:12

staircases **3**:2–3, **3**:5–7, **4**:6; accessible standards **21**:5; auditoria
  15:9; design **11**:15–16; escape routes **11**:15–16; external **11**:16;
  flats **21**:18; guarding **3**:7; handrails **3**:2–3, **3**:6, **3**:7, **4**:6; hotels
  20:3–4, **20**:5; housing **21**:14; pitch **3**:2, **3**:5; single-family houses
  21:17–18; student housing **23**:3; widths **3**:5, **3**:7; *see also* steps
stairlifts **3**:9, **3**:10
stanchions **6**:5
standard busy rate (SBR) **41**:1
standard deviation (SD) **2**:2
Standard Method of Measurement (SMM) **5**:3, **30**:3, **30**:6–7
Standard Overcast Sky **9**:5
standards: housing **21**:1–14; laboratories **26**:27–9; security **37**:3,
  37:12–13; student housing **23**:7–9
standby power, laboratories **26**:21
standing dimensions **2**:2–5
standing work spaces **2**:5–6
state maintained schools **36**:1
static wind pressure **8**:13
steel **7**:1–5; bars **7**:1, **7**:2, **7**:3; coated **7**:5; dimensions
  7:1–5; earthquake zones **42**:32; embodied energy **8**:3; fire
  resistance **11**:19; hot-dip galvanized **7**:5; properties **6**:6, **6**:13;
  reinforcement **6**:11–12, **7**:5; roofing **7**:12; sheet **7**:1; stainless
  7:5, **7**:12; structural **6**:13, **6**:14–15, **7**:1–2, **7**:3–4; tropics **42**:29,
  42:30; U-values **8**:16; weather-resistant **7**:2, **7**:5; windows **7**:26
Steel Corporation Offices, Sri Lanka **42**:2
steering groups **43**:16, **43**:17
Stefan-Boltzmann law **8**:5
steps **3**:2–3, **4**:5, **4**:6, **21**:5; *see also* staircases
stick construction **7**:28
stiffness **10**:6
stone **7**:17–19
stopping distances **39**:9
storage **21**:12; agricultural **14**:1, **14**:13–15; ambulance stations
  18:9; auditoria **15**:21, **15**:39; community centres **17**:4;
  foodservice facilities **34**:8–9, **34**:10; laboratories **26**:16–17;
  museums **29**:2, **29**:3; older people's housing **22**:4; public
  houses **34**:23–4, **34**:26; Salvation Army halls **32**:5–6; single-
  family houses **21**:17; single person accommodation **21**:23;
  space standards **2**:6; sports facilities **38**:43; universities **43**:11;
  warehouses **8**:10, **25**:1–12, **39**:14
stores *see* shops
stormwater management **28**:17; Sustainable Drainage Systems
  (SuDS) **7**:14, **12**:9–10, **12**:13, **12**:14; tropics **42**:11, **42**:33
strain **6**:3, **6**:5
straw-covered yards **14**:6, **14**:7
street furniture **39**:22
streets/roads **28**:12, **39**:1–25; case study **39**:22–5; cycle lanes/
  paths **39**:6, **39**:10–12; design details **39**:9–10, **39**:11; place-
  making **39**:22; residential **39**:6–7; shared space **39**:6, **39**:19–21,
  39:22, **39**:24; speed restriction design **39**:6–7, **39**:8, **39**:9,
  39:19–21; tropics **42**:24, **42**:28; vehicles **39**:1–5; widths **39**:5–6,
  39:7; *see also* car parking
stress **6**:3, **6**:5, **6**:6
strip foundations **6**:15, **6**:16
structural grids **1**:9–10, **26**:5, **30**:9
structural sections **6**:26; aluminium **7**:10–11; steel **7**:1–2, **7**:3–4
structural silicones **37**:7–8
structure **6**:1–27; blast loading **37**:5–7; earthquake zones **42**:31–2;
  foundations **6**:15–17; laboratories **26**:5–6; materials **6**:6–15;
  offices **30**:7; robustness **37**:6–7; sound transmission **10**:5–6;
  theory **6**:1–6; thumb-nails **6**:17–27; tropical design **42**:29–32
struts **6**:5, **6**:21
student housing **23**:1–13, **43**:10
student support facilities **43**:8–9
student union buildings **43**:8–9
studio rooms, student housing **23**:10, **23**:11
studios: recording **10**:13, **15**:40, **40**:1–4; rehearsal **15**:38, **15**:39
studio theatres **15**:23

study bedrooms **23**:3, **23**:4, **23**:9–11
sunken track (cutting) stations **41**:18
sunlight **9**:1–5, **42**:35
sunlight availability indicators **9**:2, **9**:3, **9**:12
sun-on-ground indicators **9**:4, **9**:12
sunpath indicators **9**:4, **9**:12, **42**:33
sunpipes **42**:15, **42**:17, **42**:19
supermarkets **25**:9, **35**:4, **35**:5, **35**:6–8
superstores **35**:7–8
Supplementary Planning Documents (SPDs) **21**:4, **21**:26
supply chain **30**:3
Sure Start Children's Centres **36**:6, **36**:7
surface condensation **8**:20–2
surface-modified glasses **42**:36
surfaces: corridors **3**:4; lobbies **3**:4; ramps **3**:1; steps **3**:3
surface temperatures **8**:20
surgical facilities **19**:8–9, **19**:11, **19**:15
surveillance **13**:2–3, **21**:18, **28**:7, **37**:2–3, **37**:12
sustainability **12**:5, **28**:2; Code for Sustainable Homes (CforSH)
  10:10–11, **21**:13, **21**:27; and health **28**:10–12; housing **21**:27;
  laboratories **26**:2, **26**:24–5, **26**:29; libraries **27**:19; low carbon
  design **8**:32–3, **36**:3–5; masterplanning **28**:14–19; Passive Haus
  8:32, **8**:33; primary health care buildings **33**:1, **33**:16, **33**:17,
  33:19; renewable energy **8**:33, **28**:16, **36**:5, **42**:28–9, **43**:13;
  schools **36**:3–5; student housing **23**:2; tropics **42**:9; universities
  43:2–3, **43**:12–13; zero carbon buildings **8**:33
Sustainable Development Commission **36**:3–4
Sustainable Drainage Systems (SuDS) **7**:14, **12**:9–10, **12**:13,
  12:14
swales **12**:9, **12**:13
swimming pools **8**:10, **38**:12–14, **39**:15, **42**:33
switches, light **9**:9
synagogues **32**:16–19

tabernacles **32**:12, **32**:13, **32**:14
tables: auditoria **15**:3; communion **32**:2, **32**:4, **32**:6, **32**:8, **32**:11;
  credence **32**:10; foodservice facilities **34**:4, **34**:5–7, **34**:8, **34**:9;
  older people's housing **22**:4; panel **15**:28
table tennis **38**:19, **38**:33
tableware **34**:18
tack rooms **14**:18
take-aways **34**:1, **34**:2, **34**:5, **34**:19–20, **34**:24
tapered flange channels **7**:4
taps **22**:3
teaching laboratories **26**:1, **26**:9, **26**:10–11
team sports *see* pitch sports
team technology methods **24**:5
technical design **1**:3
technology: pitch **38**:24; tropics **42**:9; *see also* information
  technology
technology teaching **36**:13
television viewing facilities **15**:10, **15**:31
temperature: air **8**:7, **8**:11–12; corrected effective (CET) **8**:9;
  dewpoint **8**:20, **8**:22; environmental **8**:27; industrial buildings
  24:8; laboratories **26**:23; libraries **27**:12; museums **29**:4, **29**:5,
  29:6; radiant **8**:7; resultant **8**:9, **8**:27; shops **35**:4; sol-air **8**:12,
  8:27, **42**:34; stables **14**:18; surface **8**:20; thermal comfort **8**:1,
  8:7–10, **42**:3–4; urban centres **42**:24
temporary bench marks (TBMs) **1**:11
temporary exhibition spaces **29**:2, **29**:5
tenant efficiency **30**:8, **30**:9
tennis **38**:11, **38**:23, **38**:24, **38**:26, **38**:27, **38**:35
tensile fabric roof structures **7**:14
tensile stresses **6**:5, **6**:11–12, **6**:20–1
termites **42**:10
terraced houses **21**:15–16
terraces, hotels **20**:9, **20**:10
terracotta **7**:17

terrorism *see* counter terrorism
theatre-in the-round auditoria **15**:5, **15**:9, **15**:14, **15**:19, **15**:20
Theatre Royal, Plymouth **15**:17
theatres **15**:12–23; acoustics **10**:17; control rooms **15**:20–1;
   dressing rooms **15**:21–3; lighting **15**:19–20; parking **39**:15;
   permissible noise levels **10**:8; sanitary facilities **2**:8; stages
   15:13–17, **15**:18–19; studio **15**:23
thermal bridging **8**:17–18, **8**:20
thermal capacity **8**:6–7
thermal comfort **8**:1, **8**:7–10, **42**:3–4; *see also* temperature
thermal conductivity **7**:23, **8**:3–4, **8**:15, **8**:17
thermal design **8**:1–2; climate **8**:11–15; condensation **8**:19–22;
   glass and glazing **7**:15, **7**:16, **8**:18–19, **8**:20; low carbon design
   8:32–3, **36**:3–5; Passive Haus **8**:32, **8**:33; prediction and
   measurement techniques **8**:33–5; thermal bridging **8**:17–18,
   8:20; thermal insulation **8**:17, **8**:18; U-values **8**:15–17,
   8:18–19, **8**:20, **8**:32, **8**:35, **42**:34; ventilation **8**:22–5; zero
   carbon buildings **8**:33; *see also* heating; mechanical ventilation
   systems
thermal mass **8**:6–7; libraries **27**:12; schools **36**:4; trombe walls
   42:23; universities **43**:2
thermal resistance **8**:3, **8**:4, **8**:15
thermal response **8**:6–7
thermal transmittance **8**:17–18
thermographic surveys **8**:34–5
thermoplastics **7**:19, **7**:20, **7**:21, **11**:20
thermo-reflective insulation **7**:24
thermosetting plastics **7**:19–20, **7**:21, **11**:20
thousand marker **1**:2
ticket desks **31**:2, **31**:4
ticketing, sports facilities **38**:39
ties **6**:5, **6**:9, **6**:21, **6**:24–5
tile adhesives **7**:25
tiles **7**:10, **7**:15, **7**:17, **8**:4
TIM *see* transparent insulation material (TIM)
timber **7**:5–8; density **8**:4; earthquake zones **42**:32; embodied
   energy **8**:3; fire resistance **11**:19; hardwoods **7**:6; products
   7:6–8; properties **6**:6; softwoods **7**:6; strength classes **7**:5, **7**:6;
   structural **6**:7–9, **6**:10, **6**:11, **6**:12, **7**:5; thermal conductivity
   8:4; tropics **42**:29, **42**:30; use classes **7**:6, **7**:7; U-values **8**:16;
   windows **7**:26, **7**:27
timber frame **6**:8, **6**:11, **6**:12, **8**:16, **42**:30, **42**:32
time lag **42**:37
time switching **9**:9
tin **7**:5
titanium **7**:13
toilet facilities *see* sanitary facilities; WCs
tooled stone finishes **7**:18
Torah scrolls **32**:16, **32**:17
Total Cost Indicators (TCIs) **21**:2
total evacuation **11**:14, **11**:15
toughened glass **6**:13, **7**:16
tourist accommodation **20**:1; *see also* hotels
Town and Country Planning Act (1990) **14**:20, **23**:7
town halls **16**:1–7
track sports **38**:1, **38**:6–9, **38**:23, **38**:34–5
traction lifts **3**:9–11
trading floors **30**:14–16
training facilities, fire stations **18**:3–4, **18**:6–7
trampolines **38**:18
trams **41**:26, **41**:28
translators' booths **15**:28–9
transparent insulation material (TIM) **8**:19, **8**:20
transport *see* bicycles; public transport; vehicles
transport terminals and interchanges: bus and coach stations **8**:10,
   41:22–8; railway stations **8**:10, **41**:16–22; *see also* airports
Travelodge, Southwark **20**:14–16
treadmills **38**:32

trees **28**:3, **42**:16
trellises **42**:16
triangulation **6**:20–1
trip hazards **3**:3, **4**:5–6
trolleys, hospital **19**:9
trombe walls **42**:23
tropical design **42**:1–38; active design **42**:28–9; building science
   data **42**:33–7; climate types **42**:11–14; factors affecting
   42:1–11; passive design **42**:14–28; services **42**:32–3; structural
   42:29–32
tropical diseases **42**:9, **42**:11
turbines, wind **42**:29
turnbuckle locks **11**:18
turning circles **11**:5, **11**:6, **18**:2, **18**:11, **25**:11, **39**:4–5, **41**:23–4
turn-round areas **39**:10, **39**:11
turnstiles **38**:39
TV broadcasting, sports facilities **38**:40–2
TV production studios **40**:1–4; *see also* broadcasting studios
Tyrone Guthrie Theatre, Minneapolis **15**:18

ultraviolet detectors **11**:21
under-reamed piles **6**:17
uninterrupted power supply (UPS) **18**:12
Uninterruptible Power Supply (UPS) **26**:21
United Reformed Church (URC) **32**:4–5
unitised construction **7**:28
units **1**:1–2
universal beams **6**:26, **7**:3
universal bearing piles **7**:3
universal columns **6**:26, **7**:3
universal design **2**:1
universities **43**:1–17; briefing process **43**:11, **43**:15–17; circulation
   areas **43**:2, **43**:4; incubators **43**:8; laboratories **26**:1, **26**:9, **26**:11,
   26:16, **26**:23–6, **43**:5–6, **43**:14; libraries **27**:1, **27**:2, **27**:4, **27**:7,
   27:8–9, **27**:10–11, **27**:12, **43**:4–5, **43**:14; offices **43**:10–11,
   43:14; space standards **43**:13–15; sports facilities **43**:10;
   student housing **23**:1–13, **43**:10; support facilities **43**:8–10;
   sustainability **43**:2–3, **43**:12–13; teaching spaces **43**:3–8, **43**:14,
   43:15; types **43**:1–2; virtual campus **43**:11–12
University Grants Committee (UGC) **43**:13
University of Birmingham **43**:2
University of Bournemouth **23**:5
University of East Anglia **23**:4
University of Edinburgh **26**:23–5
University of Warwick **23**:6
upholstery **15**:2, **15**:3
UPS *see* Uninterruptible Power Supply (UPS)
urban design: libraries **27**:4, **27**:14; tropics **42**:24, **42**:28
Urban Task Force **28**:1, **28**:3
urban universities **43**:1–2
urinals **2**:8, **2**:13, **38**:39
U-values **8**:15–17, **8**:18–19, **8**:20, **8**:32, **8**:35, **42**:34

value **5**:1–2
value management **5**:2
vaporising liquid installations **11**:21
vapour pressure **8**:22
vapour resistance **8**:22
variable air volume (VAV) **8**:30
variety stores **35**:6
varnishes **7**:26
vehicle-borne improvised explosive devices (VBIEDs) **37**:4, **37**:5,
   37:6–7, **37**:8, **37**:10
vehicles **39**:1–5, **41**:23; *see also* fire appliances
vehicle workshops: ambulance stations **18**:8; bus and coach
   stations **41**:26; police stations **18**:11
velodromes **38**:6, **38**:23
vending machines **38**:39

vented ridges **42**:20

ventilation **8**:22–5; air change rates **8**:10, **26**:23; air infiltration **8**:10, **8**:22–3; auditoria **15**:2, **15**:12; and condensation **8**:21; courtrooms **16**:10; effectiveness and efficiency **8**:23; fire safety **11**:4, **20**:4; flats **21**:18; heat loss **8**:23–4, **8**:26, **8**:27; hybrid systems **8**:31–2; industrial buildings **24**:8; laboratories **26**:9, **26**:17, **26**:23; libraries **27**:12, **27**:13, **27**:14, **27**:15; models **8**:33–4; offices **30**:9–10; police custody suites **18**:14; schools **36**:4; shops **35**:4; student housing **23**:8, **23**:11, **23**:12; synagogues **32**:18; tropics **42**:29; universities **43**:2–3, **43**:8; wind effect **8**:14, **8**:24, **30**:9

verandas **42**:19, **42**:20

verges, road **39**:10

vertical sky component **9**:1, **9**:2

vertical support elements: masonry **6**:7, **6**:8; timber **6**:11

very sheltered housing (VSH) **22**:1–4

vestries **32**:15, **32**:19

veterinary boxes **14**:18

vibration: broadcasting studios **40**:3; laboratories **26**:6, **26**:7, **26**:15

victim examination suites, police stations **18**:9, **18**:10

Victoria and Albert Museum, London **29**:7–8

video projection facilities **15**:31

video screens, sports facilities **38**:31, **38**:32, **38**:40, **38**:42–3

viewing distances, sports facilities **38**:27

visibility, roads **39**:9

vision statements **43**:16, **43**:17

visual display terminals (VDTs) **9**:10, **30**:14–15

visual impairments **4**:4, **15**:35, **15**:40, **23**:9

visual massing envelopes **28**:6

visual narrowing **39**:20–1

volleyball **38**:10, **38**:25, **38**:35

vomitories, auditoria **15**:9, **15**:10

Vosper site, Southampton **28**:8

voting panels **15**:31

vulnerability to flooding **12**:4

wagon stages **15**:15

Wales, housing standards **21**:8

walking **4**:5, **27**:4, **28**:4, **28**:12, **36**:8–9, **39**:22

walkways, moving **3**:8–9

walls: crime prevention design **13**:3, **21**:18; fire safety **11**:7, **11**:8; masonry **6**:7; security **37**:12; stables **14**:19; stone **7**:19; thermal resistance **8**:4, **8**:15; timber panels **6**:11; U-values **8**:15–17

wall tiles **7**:15

wall to floor ratio **5**:3, **43**:2

wardrobe departments **15**:40

wards, hospital **19**:2–3, **19**:4, **19**:10–11, **19**:13–14, **19**:18–19

warehouses **8**:10, **25**:1–12, **39**:14

washbasins **2**:8, **2**:12, **2**:13; hospitals **19**:7; hotels **20**:11; older people's housing **22**:3; police custody suites **18**:12; sports facilities **38**:39; student housing **23**:3, **23**:8, **23**:10; *see also* hand washing facilities

washing facilities, mosques **32**:20

waste management **28**:17–18, **28**:19, **38**:43, **43**:11; *see also* refuse storage

wastewater treatment **28**:17

water drenchers **11**:21

water energy **42**:28

water management: masterplanning **28**:16–17, **28**:19; Sustainable Drainage Systems (SuDS) **7**:14, **12**:9–10, **12**:13, **12**:14; tropics **42**:11, **42**:33; universities **43**:3, **43**:13; *see also* flood-aware design

water polo **38**:14

Water Sensitive Urban Design (WSUD) **12**:10

water sports **38**:15–16, **38**:35

water spray projector systems **11**:21

waterstop seals **7**:25

water supply, tropics **42**:7, **42**:32

water vapour **8**:20

WCs **2**:8; accessible facilities **2**:8, **2**:9–11, **4**:6, **21**:5; for children **2**:8, **2**:11, **4**:6, **17**:4; compartments and cubicles **2**:11–12; police stations **18**:12; schools **36**:10, **36**:15; single-family houses **21**:17; sports facilities **38**:39; student housing **23**:8, **23**:12

weight **6**:2–3

welt joins **7**:13

West Yorkshire Playhouse, Leeds **15**:18, **15**:39

wet laboratories **26**:1, **26**:9, **43**:5

wet proofing **12**:7–9

wheelchair access **4**:1; ATMs and ATM lobbies **31**:5, **31**:7; auditoria **15**:8, **15**:9, **15**:35, **15**:40; dimensions **4**:2–4, **4**:5; doors **3**:3; housing **21**:3, **21**:8, **21**:12; libraries **27**:6; lifts **3**:9, **3**:10; lobbies **3**:4; older people's housing **22**:1; payment counters **31**:6, **31**:9; sanitary facilities **2**:7, **2**:9–11, **18**:9; sports facilities **38**:29, **38**:30, **38**:39; student housing **23**:9, **23**:11, **23**:12

Wheelchair Housing Design Guide **21**:8, **21**:12

wheelie-bins **21**:18

White Collar Factory, London **30**:5

whole life costs **5**:6–7

Wi-Fi **16**:4, **23**:11, **23**:12

wildlife **7**:14

Willowbrook Mall, New Jersey **35**:9

wind **8**:12–15, **42**:36–7

wind catchers **42**:22

wind effect ventilation **8**:14, **8**:24, **30**:9

wind energy **36**:5, **42**:28, **42**:29

Window Energy Ratings (WERs) **7**:26–7

windows: crime prevention design **13**:2–3; materials **7**:26–7; natural lighting **9**:6–8; police custody suites **18**:13; sound insulation **10**:4, **10**:5; stables **14**:20; U-values **8**:18–19; *see also* glass and glazing

wind roses **8**:13

wind towers **42**:22–3

wind tunnel modelling **8**:34

wired services, auditoria **15**:3

wood *see* timber

wood adhesives **7**:26

wood-boring insects **42**:10

wood-cored joins **7**:13

wood fibre insulation **7**:23

wood particleboard **7**:7, **7**:8

wood stains **7**:26

wood wool slabs **7**:22, **8**:4

working spaces **2**:5–7

workplace-based learning **43**:12

workshops: ambulance stations **18**:8; auditoria **15**:38–40; bus and coach stations **41**:26; police stations **18**:11

work surface heights **2**:5–6, **21**:14, **22**:4, **34**:9

writing boards **15**:29

writing surfaces, auditoria **15**:3

X-ray facilities **19**:7, **19**:9–10, **19**:12, **19**:13

X-ray plaster **7**:22

young people: housing **23**:1–13, **43**:10; *see also* children

Young's Modulus **6**:5

zero carbon buildings **8**:33

zinc **7**:5, **7**:13

zoning: banks **31**:2–3; government services outlets **31**:5, **31**:6; learning centres **43**:4–5; libraries **27**:5–6; museums **29**:2, **29**:6; primary health care buildings **33**:12

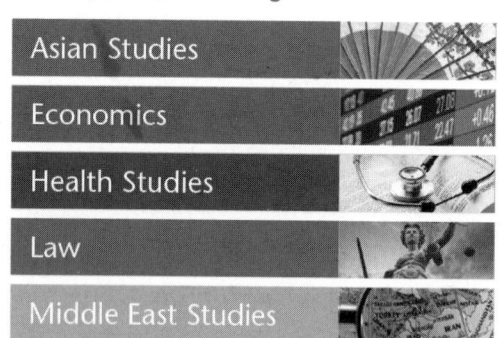